STREET ATLAS London

Contents

II **Key to map pages**

IV *Administrative and Postcode boundaries*

VI **Route planning**

X **Key to map symbols**

1 **Street maps**

228 **Keys to enlarged map pages and symbols**

229 **Enlarged street maps**

271 **Index**

380 **List of numbered locations**

391 *Hospitals*

392 *Shopping, theatres, cinemas*

394 *Central London buses*

396 *Local rail and London Underground*

398 *Places of interest*

First published 2000 by

George Philip Ltd, a division of
Octopus Publishing Group Ltd
2–4 Heron Quays
London E14 4JP

ISBN 0 540 07811 5 paperback
ISBN 0 540 07812 3 spiral

To the best of the Publishers' knowledge, the information in this atlas was correct at the time of going to press. No responsibility can be accepted for any errors or their consequences.

The representation in this atlas of a road, track or path is no evidence of the existence of a right of way.

The mapping between pages 1 and 270 inclusive in this atlas is derived from Ordnance Survey® OSCAR® and Land-Line® data and Landranger® mapping.

Ordnance Survey, OSCAR, Land-Line and Landranger are registered trade marks of Ordnance Survey, the national mapping agency of Great Britain.

Printed and bound in Spain by Cayfosa.

PHILIP'S

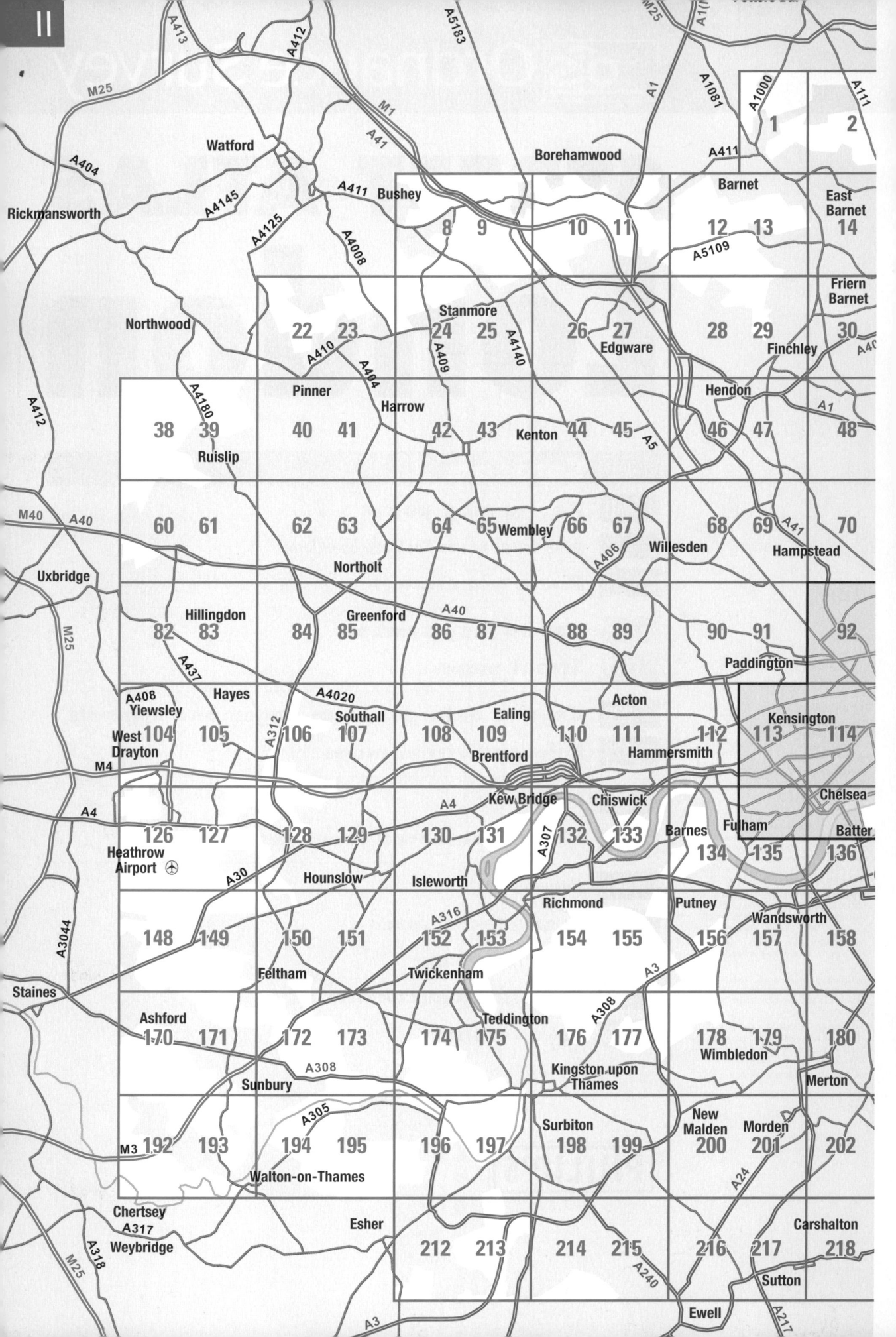
A413
A412
A5183
M25
A1
M25
A1000
A1081
A111
1
2
M1
A41
Watford
A404
Borehamwood
A411
Rickmansworth
A4145
A411
Bushey
Barnet
East
Barnet
A4125
A4008
8
9
10
11
12
13
14
A5109
Friern
Barnet
Northwood
Stanmore
22
23
24
25
26
27
28
29
30
A410
A409
A4140
Edgware
Finchley
A404
A4180
Pinner
Harrow
Hendon
A412
A1
38
39
40
41
42
43
Kenton
44
45
A5
46
47
48
Ruislip
M40
A40
60
61
62
63
64
65
Wembley
66
67
68
69
A41
70
Willesden
Hampstead
A406
Uxbridge
Northolt
Greenford
A40
Hillingdon
82
83
84
85
86
87
88
89
90
91
92
M25
A437
Paddington
A408
Yiewsley
Hayes
A4020
Acton
A312
Southall
Ealing
Kensington
West
Drayton
104
105
106
107
108
109
110
111
112
113
114
Brentford
Hammersmith
M4
Kew Bridge
Chiswick
Chelsea
A4
A4
126
127
128
129
130
131
A307
132
133
Barnes
Fulham
Batter
Heathrow
Airport
134
135
136
A30
Hounslow
Isleworth
Richmond
Putney
Wandsworth
A316
148
149
150
151
152
153
154
155
156
157
158
A3044
Feltham
Twickenham
A3
Staines
Ashford
Teddington
A308
170
171
172
173
174
175
176
177
178
179
180
Wimbledon
A308
Kingston upon
Thames
Merton
Sunbury
A305
New
Malden
Morden
Surbiton
M3
192
193
194
195
196
197
198
199
200
201
202
A24
Walton-on-Thames
Chertsey
Esher
Carshalton
A317
Weybridge
212
213
214
215
216
217
218
A318
M25
A240
Sutton
Ewell
A3
A217

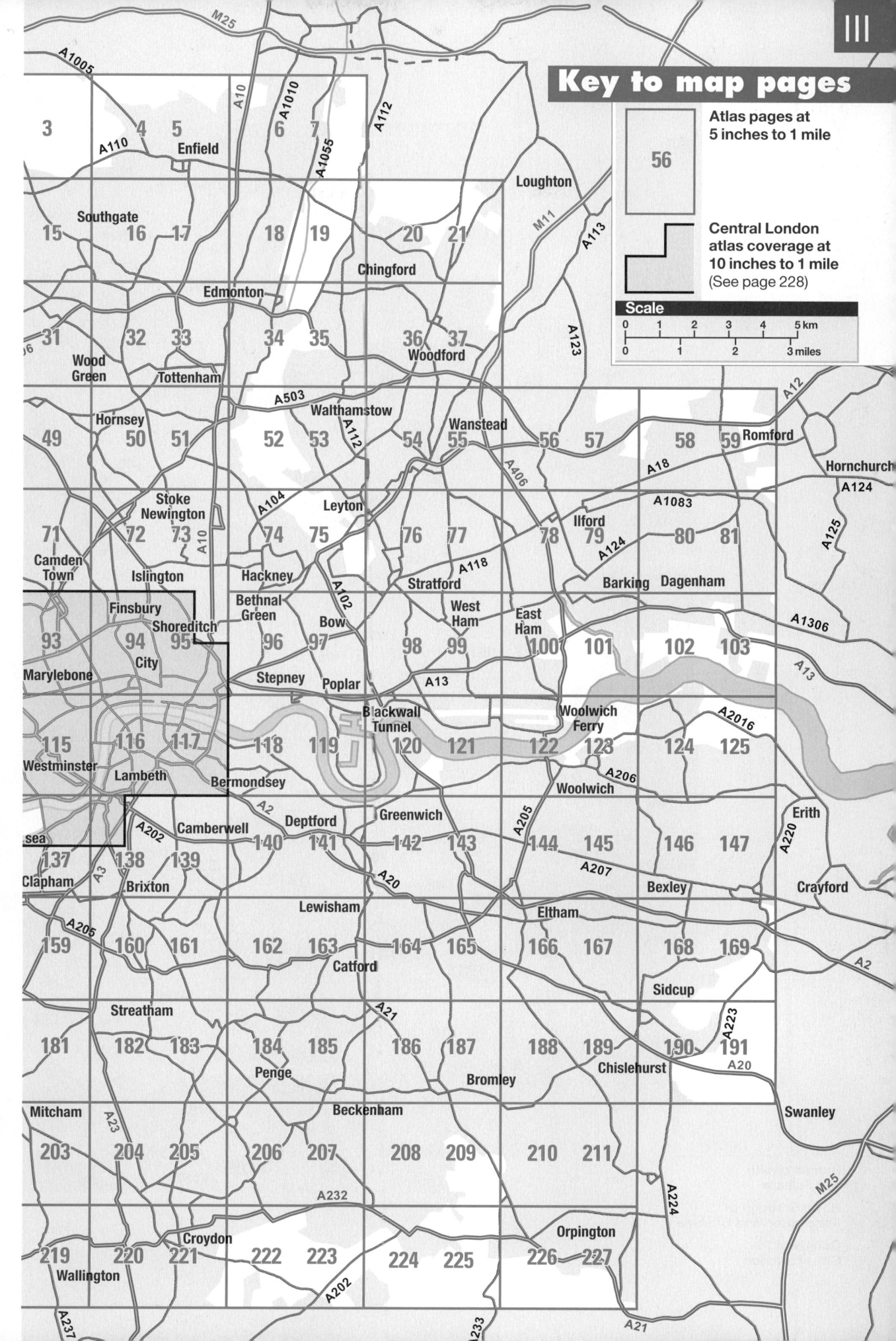

III

Key to map pages

Atlas pages at
5 inches to 1 mile

56

Central London
atlas coverage at
10 inches to 1 mile
(See page 228)

Scale

| 0 | 1 | 2 | 3 | 4 | 5 km |

| 0 | 1 | 2 | 3 miles |

3   4   5   Enfield

A1005
A110
A10
A1010
A1055
A112
M25
M11

15   Southgate   16   17   18   19   20   21   Loughton

A113
A123

Chingford

31   32   33   34   35   36   37   Woodford

Wood
Green   Tottenham
A503
A12

49   Hornsey   50   51   52   53   54   Wanstead   55   56   57   58   59   Romford

A104
A112
A406
A18
Hornchurch
A124

71   Stoke   72   73   74   Leyton   75   76   77   78   Ilford   79   80   81
Newington
A1083
A125
A10
A124

Camden
Town   Islington   Hackney   Stratford   Barking   Dagenham

93   Finsbury   94   95   96   97   98   99   East   100   101   102   103
Shoreditch   Bethnal   Bow   West   Ham
Green   Ham
City   Stepney   Poplar   A13   A1306
Marylebone   A102   A13

115   116   117   118   119   Blackwall   120   121   Woolwich   122   123   124   125
Tunnel   Ferry
Westminster   A2016
Lambeth   Bermondsey   Woolwich
...sea   A206
Camberwell   Deptford   Greenwich   Erith

137   138   139   140   141   142   143   144   145   146   147
A202   A2
A205   A220
Clapham   Brixton   A20   A207   Bexley   Crayford
A3

159   160   161   162   163   164   165   Lewisham   166   Eltham   167   168   169
A206
A2
Catford   Sidcup

181   182   183   184   185   186   187   188   189   190   191
Streatham   A21   Chislehurst
Penge   A223
Mitcham   Bromley   A20   Swanley
A23   Beckenham

203   204   205   206   207   208   209   210   211
A232   A224
M25

Croydon   Orpington

219   220   221   222   223   224   225   226   227
Wallington   A202
A237   A21

IV

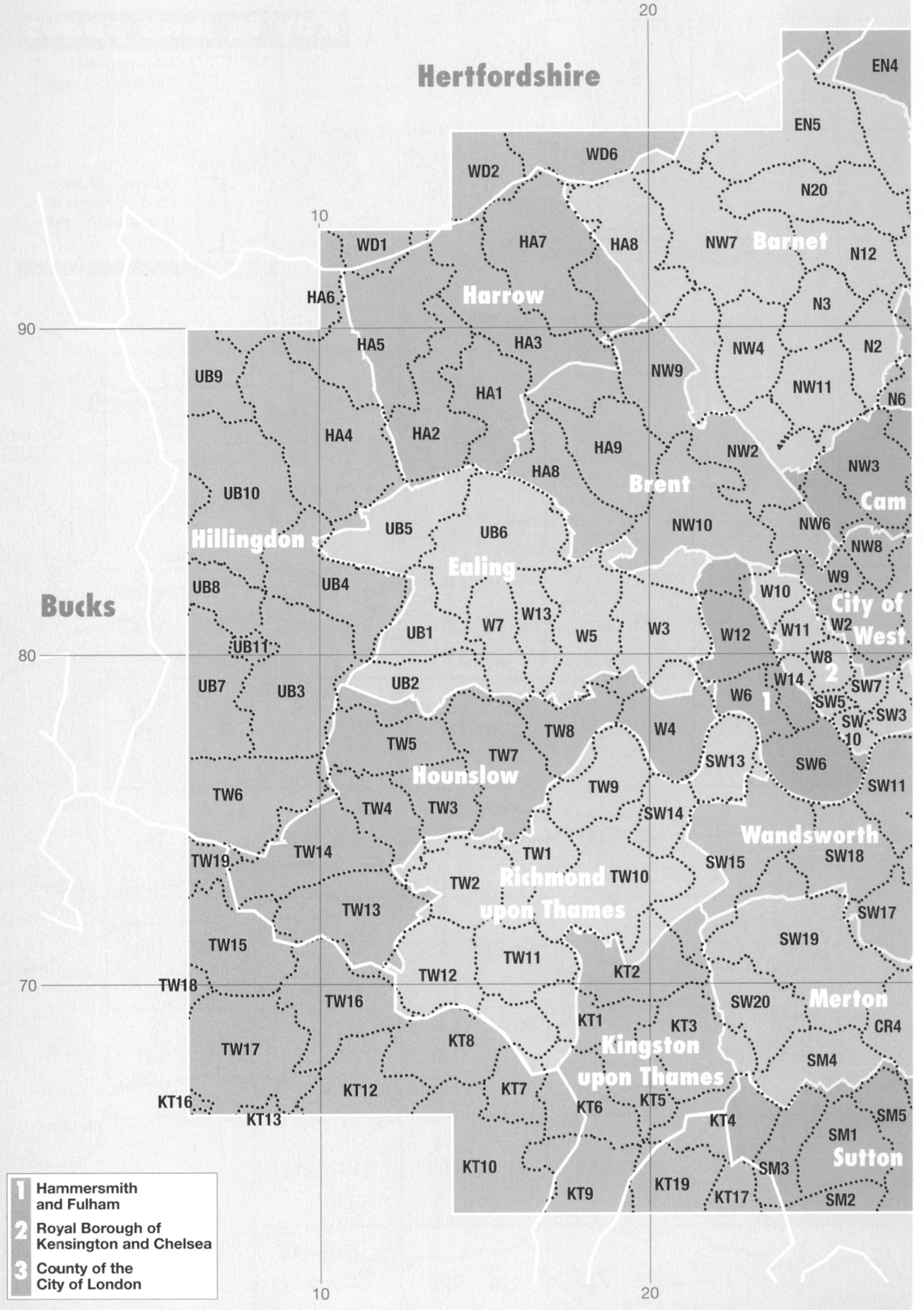

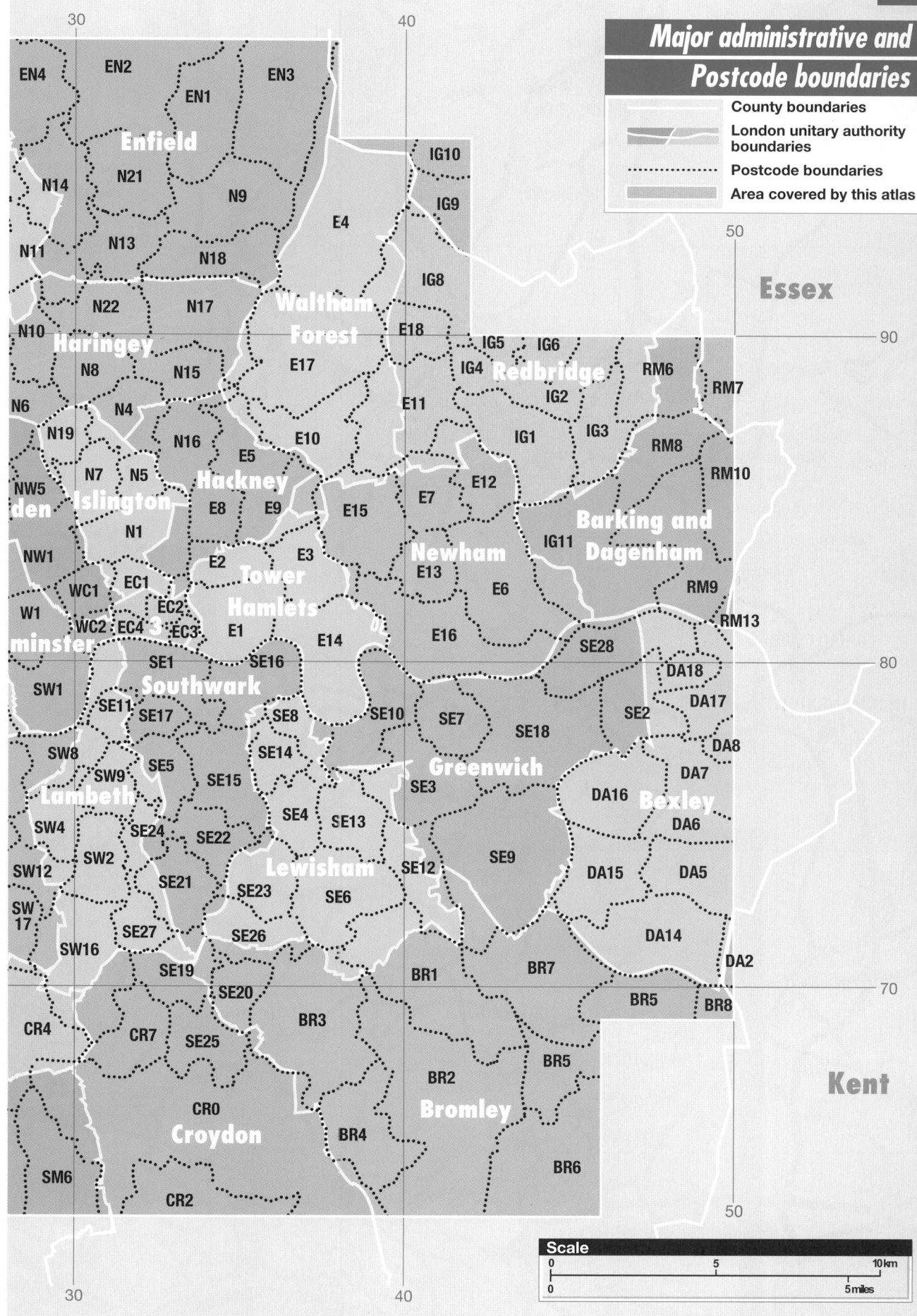

V

Major administrative and Postcode boundaries

County boundaries
London unitary authority boundaries
Postcode boundaries
Area covered by this atlas

Essex

Kent

Scale
0   5   10 km
0   5 miles

EN4   EN2   EN1   EN3

Enfield

N14   N21   N9

N11   N13   N18

N22   N17

N10   Haringey   Waltham Forest   E18

N8   N15   E17

N6   N4   E11

N19   N16   E10

N7   N5   Hackney   E5

NW5   Islington   E8   E9   E15   E7   E12

den   N1

NW1   E2   Tower   Newham

WC1   EC1   Hamlets   E13   E6

W1   EC2   E3

minster   WC2   EC4   EC3   E1   E14   E16

SW1   SE1   SE16   SE28

Southwark

SE11   SE17   SE8   SE10   SE7   SE18   SE2

SW8   SE14

SW9   SE5   SE15   Greenwich

Lambeth   SE4   SE13   SE3   SE9

SW4   SE24   SE22

SW12   SW2   SE21   Lewisham   SE12

SW17   SE23   SE6

SW16   SE27   SE26

SE19   BR1   BR7

CR4   SE20

CR7   SE25   BR3

SM6   CRO   Bromley

CR2   BR4   BR2   BR6

IG10   IG9   E4   IG8   IG5   IG6

Redbridge   IG4   IG2   RM6   RM7

IG1   IG3   RM8   RM10

Barking and Dagenham   IG11   RM9   RM13

DA18   DA17

DA8   DA7

DA16   Bexley   DA6

DA15   DA5

DA14   DA2

BR5   BR8

BR5

30   40   50   90   80   70   50

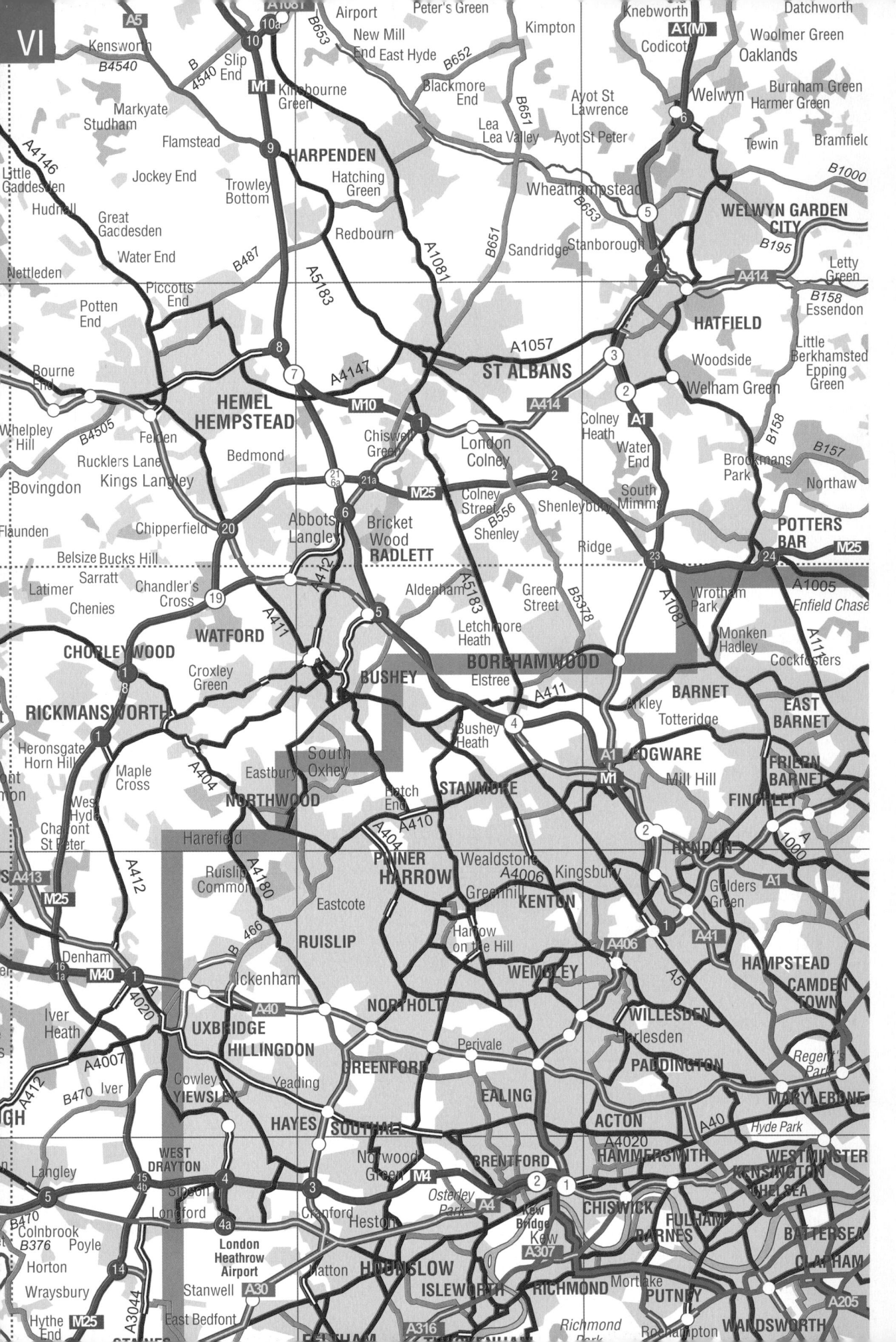
A5
Kensworth
B4540
B4540
Slip End
M1
10
10a
Airport
B653
Peter's Green
New Mill End
East Hyde
B652
Kimpton
Knebworth
A1(M)
Codicote
Datchworth
Woolmer Green
Oaklands
Kinsbourne Green
Blackmore End
Ayot St Lawrence
Welwyn
Burnham Green
Harmer Green
Markyate
Studham
Flamstead
9
HARPENDEN
B651
Lea Valley
Ayot St Peter
6
Tewin
Bramfield
A4146
Little Gaddesden
Jockey End
Trowley Bottom
Hatching Green
Wheathampstead
B1000
Hudnall
Great Gaddesden
Redbourn
B653
5
WELWYN GARDEN CITY
Water End
B487
A5183
A1081
B651
Sandridge
Stanborough
B195
Nettleden
4
Letty Green
Piccotts End
A414
B158
Potten End
Essendon
HATFIELD
8
A1057
3
Little Berkhamsted
Woodside
Epping Green
Bourne End
7
A4147
ST ALBANS
2
Welham Green
HEMEL HEMPSTEAD
M10
A414
A1
Colney Heath
Whelpley Hill
B4505
Felden
1
Chiswell Green
London Colney
Water End
B158
B157
Bedmond
Brookmans Park
Rucklers Lane
Bovingdon
Kings Langley
21
6a
21a
M25
2
Colney Street
Shenleybury
South Mimms
Northaw
Flaunden
Chipperfield
20
6
Abbots Langley
Bricket Wood
B556
Shenley
POTTERS BAR
RADLETT
Ridge
23
24
M25
Belsize
Bucks Hill
Sarratt
Latimer
Chenies
Chandler's Cross
19
A412
Aldenham
A5183
Green Street
B5378
A1005
Enfield Chase
Wrotham Park
A1081
5
WATFORD
A411
Letchmore Heath
Monken Hadley
A111
Cockfosters
CHORLEYWOOD
BOREHAMWOOD
1
8
Croxley Green
BUSHEY
Elstree
BARNET
RICKMANSWORTH
A411
Arkley
EAST BARNET
Totteridge
4
Bushey Heath
Heronsgate
Horn Hill
1
Maple Cross
A404
South Oxhey
Eastbury
A1
EDGWARE
FRIERN BARNET
M1
Mill Hill
NORTHWOOD
Hatch End
STANMORE
West Hyde
Chalfont St Peter
A404
A410
FINCHLEY
2
A1000
Harefield
PINNER
HARROW
Wealdstone
HENDON
A413
A412
Ruislip Common
A4180
A4006
Kingsbury
Golders Green
A1
M25
Greenhill
KENTON
Eastcote
1
A41
B466
RUISLIP
Harrow on the Hill
A406
Denham
16
1a
M40
1
A4020
Ickenham
WEMBLEY
HAMPSTEAD
CAMDEN TOWN
A5
NORTHOLT
A40
Iver Heath
UXBRIDGE
WILLESDEN
Harlesden
HILLINGDON
Perivale
Regent's Park
A4007
PADDINGTON
Cowley
Yeading
GREENFORD
A412
YIEWSLEY
EALING
MARYLEBONE
B470
Iver
HAYES
SOUTHALL
ACTON
A40
Hyde Park
WEST DRAYTON
A4020
HAMMERSMITH
WESTMINSTER
Norwood Green
BRENTFORD
KENSINGTON
Langley
15
4b
4
Sipson
3
M4
2
1
CHELSEA
5
Osterley Park
A4
CHISWICK
B470
Longford
4a
Cranford
Heston
Kew Bridge
FULHAM
Colnbrook
B376
Poyle
Kew
BARNES
BATTERSEA
London Heathrow Airport
A307
CLAPHAM
Horton
14
Hatton
HOUNSLOW
Wraysbury
Stanwell
A30
ISLEWORTH
RICHMOND
Mortlake
PUTNEY
A3044
A205
Hythe End
M25
East Bedfont
A316
Richmond Park
Roehampton
WANDSWORTH

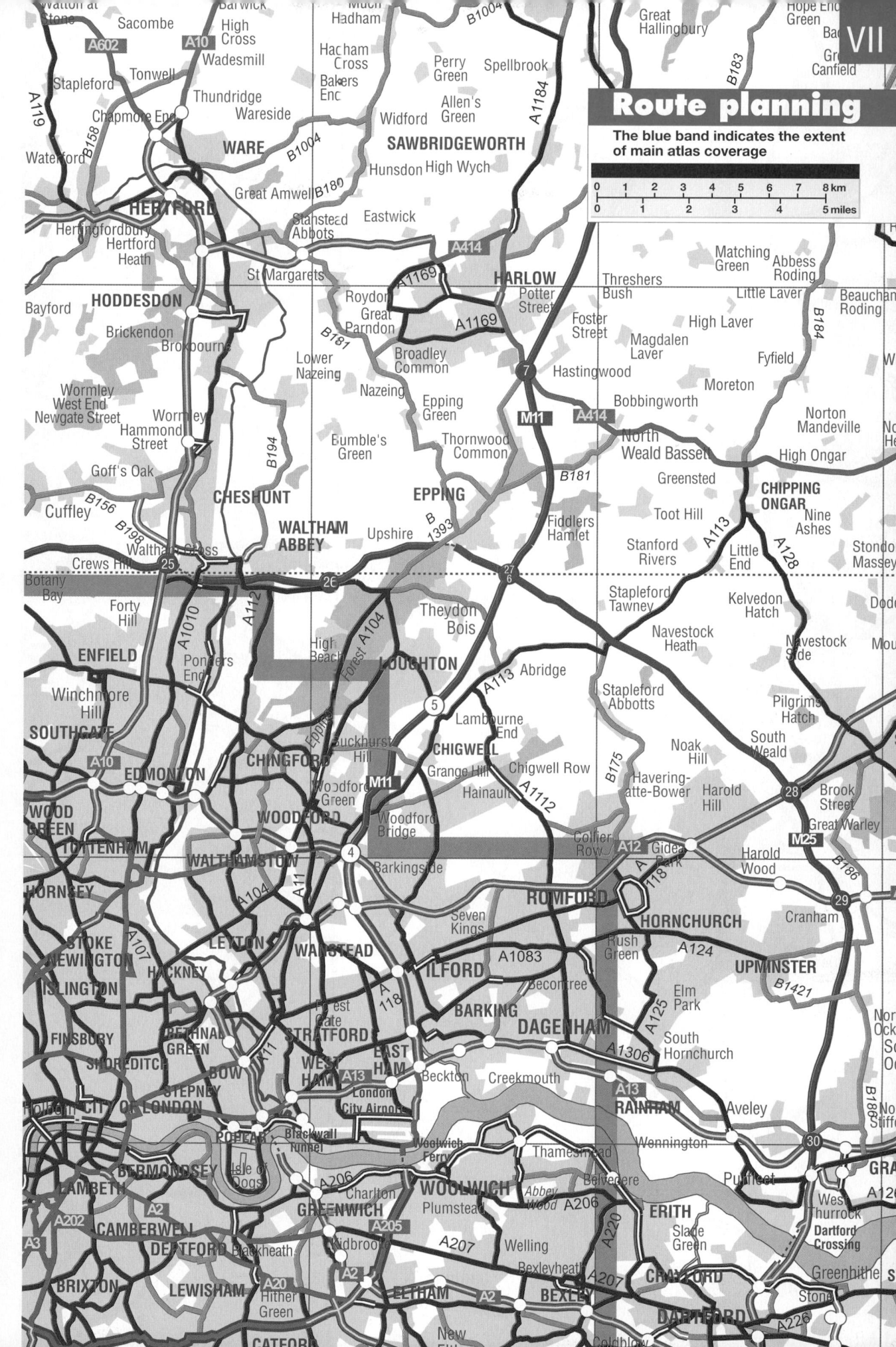

Route planning

The blue band indicates the extent of main atlas coverage

| 0 | 1 | 2 | 3 | 4 | 5 | 6 | 7 | 8 km |
| 0 | | 1 | | 2 | | 3 | | 4 | 5 miles |

VIII
Maple Cross
Eastbury
South Oxhey
Heath
EDGWARE
FRIERN BARNET
NORTHWOOD
Hatch End
STANMORE
Mill Hill
FINCHLEY
Chalfont St Peter
Harefield
A404
A410
M1
HENDON
A412
A4180
PINNER
HARROW
Wealdstone
A4006
Kingsbury
A1000
A413
Ruislip Common
Greenhill
KENTON
Golders Green
A1
M25
Eastcote
RUISLIP
Harrow on the Hill
A406
A41
B466
Denham
M40
Ickenham
WEMBLEY
HAMPSTEAD
A4020
A5
CAMDEN TOWN
Iver Heath
A40
NORTHOLT
WILLESDEN
UXBRIDGE
Harlesden
HILLINGDON
Perivale
PADDINGTON
A4007
GREENFORD
Regent's Park
Cowley
Iver
Yeading
EALING
B470
YIEWSLEY
MARYLEBONE
HAYES
SOUTHALL
ACTON
Hyde Park
WEST DRAYTON
Norwood Green
A4020
HAMMERSMITH
WESTMINSTER
Langley
BRENTFORD
KENSINGTON
M4
CHELSEA
Sipson
Osterley Park
Longford
Cranford
A4
Kew Bridge
CHISWICK
FULHAM
Colnbrook
Heston
Kew
BARNES
BATTERSEA
B376
Poyle
London Heathrow Airport
A307
CLAPHAM
Horton
HOUNSLOW
Hatton
Mortlake
Stanwell
A30
ISLEWORTH
RICHMOND
PUTNEY
Wraysbury
A205
A3044
East Bedfont
Richmond Park
Roehampton
WANDSWORTH
Hythe End
STAINES
FELTHAM
A316
TWICKENHAM
Wimbledon Park
Upper Tooting
A308
A3
Ham
A308
A30
A244
Hanworth
TEDDINGTON
WIMBLEDON
EGHAM
ASHFORD
KINGSTON UPON THAMES
A24
SUNBURY
B377
MERTON
A308
Bushy Park
Hampton
Laleham
MITCHAM
A320
East Molesey
Thorpe
Littleton
A3050
SURBITON
MORDEN
WALTON -ON- THAMES
Thames Ditton
NEW MALDEN
A217
M3
Lyne
Shepperton
B375
Long Ditton
Tolworth
A24
B386
CHERTSEY
A317
CARSHALTON
Worcester Park
ADDLESTONE
A244
ESHER
Hook
WEYBRIDGE
A240
Cheam
Ottershaw
B3121
Hersham
Chessington
A318
Esher Common
Claygate
EWELL
SUTTON
A319
B374
B365
Whiteley Village
A237
B385
Woodham
B280
A243
EPSOM
A245
A2022
A245
Byfleet
Cobham
Oxshot
Woodmansterne
B382
Pyrford
Stoke D'Abernon
A244
A245
BANSTEAD
B367
Wisley
A24
A240
B2219
Burgh Heath
WOKING
M25
Chipstead
Ashtead
Kingswood
Mayford
Ripley
Ockham
Tadworth
B2032
A23
A3
LEATHERHEAD
A3320
Send
A247
Fetcham
B2039
Headley
A246
West Horsley
Walton on the Hill
Great Bookham
East Horsley
A217
West Clandon
Mickleham
B2033
Effingham
B2032
The Hermitage
A242
Burpham
East Clandon
Westhumble
Buckland
REDHILL
A25
GUILDFORD
DORKING
Brockham
Betchworth
South Nutfield
A281
REIGATE
Gomshall
A25
A248
Westcott
Shalford
Wotton
Albury
Shere

EDMONTON
CHINGFORD
CHIGWELL
Chigwell Row
Grange Hill
Hainault
Woodford Green
WOODFORD
Woodford Bridge
Havering-atte-Bower
Harold Hill
Weald
WOOD GREEN
TOTTENHAM
WALTHAMSTOW
Barkingside
Collier Row
Gidea Park
Harold Wood
Great Warley
Cranham
HORNSEY
ROMFORD
HORNCHURCH
Seven Kings
STOKE NEWINGTON
LEYTON
WANSTEAD
ILFORD
Rush Green
UPMINSTER
HACKNEY
ISLINGTON
Becontree
Elm Park
Forest Gate
BARKING
DAGENHAM
FINSBURY
BETHNAL GREEN
STRATFORD
South Hornchurch
SHOREDITCH
BOW
WEST HAM
EAST HAM
Beckton
Creekmouth
STEPNEY
CITY OF LONDON
London City Airport
RAINHAM
Aveley
Holborn
POPLAR
Blackwall Tunnel
Woolwich Ferry
Thamesmead
Wennington
BERMONDSEY
Isle of Dogs
Charlton
WOOLWICH
Belvedere
Purfleet
LAMBETH
GREENWICH
Plumstead
Abbey Wood
ERITH
West Thurrock
CAMBERWELL
DEPTFORD
Blackheath
Kidbrooke
Welling
Slade Green
Dartford Crossing
BRIXTON
LEWISHAM
Hither Green
Bexleyheath
CRAYFORD
Greenhithe
ELTHAM
BEXLEY
Stone
DARTFORD
CATFORD
New Eltham
Coldblow
STREATHAM
Dulwich
Sydenham
Mottingham
SIDCUP
North Cray
Wilmington
Bean
Bexley
West Norwood
Grove Park
Foots Cray
Hawley
Darenth
CHISLEHURST
Hextable
Sutton at Hone
South Darenth
PENGE
BROMLEY
St Paul's Cray
Swanley
Horton Kirby
BECKENHAM
Bickley
Petts Wood
Eden Park
South Norwood
St Mary Cray
Crockenhill
Hartley
Farningham
ORPINGTON
Fawkham Green
Bromley Common
Hayes
Beddington
West Wickham
CROYDON
WALLINGTON
Keston
Farnborough
Chelsfield
Eynsford
Green Street Green
West Kingsdown
Well Hill
New Addington
Pratt's Bottom
Badgers Mount
PURLEY
Selsdon
Leaves Green
Downe
Biggin Hill Airport
Halstead
Shoreham
Sanderstead
Farleigh
Kenley
COULSDON
WARLINGHAM
Biggin Hill
Cudham
Knockholt
Knockholt Pound
Otford
Kemsing
Wrotham
Heaverham
Whyteleafe
Tatsfield
Chevening
Dunton Green
Seal
Ightham
Woldingham
Chaldon
Brasted
Riverhead
CATERHAM
Westerham
Sundridge
SEVENOAKS
Ivy Hatch
Brasted Chart
Whitley Row
Merstham
Godstone
Limpsfield
Underriver
Shipbourne
Oxted
Ide Hill
Crockham Hill
Toy's Hill
Sevenoaks Weald
Hurst
Nutfield
Bletchingley
Tandridge Green
Hildenborough
Marlpit Hill
Four Elms
Chiddingstone Causeway
Leigh
Crowhurst
A10
M11
A1112
B175
A12
M25
B186
A104
A11
A107
A118
A1083
A124
B1421
A125
A1306
A13
B186
A206
A2
A205
A207
A220
A202
A3
A20
A226
A21
B258
B262
A23
A212
A223
A225
B258
A232
A20
A2022
A224
A23
B275
A21
M20
A22
A233
B269
A224
A225
M26
B2030
B269
B2024
A25
B2031
M25
A25
A227
B2026
B2042
A225
B269
B2027
A21
B245
M23
A22
Scale
0 1 2 3 4 5 6 7 8 km
0 1 2 3 4 5 miles

Key to map symbols

Roads

22a	Motorway with junction number
	Primary route – single, dual carriageway
	A road – single, dual carriageway
	B road – single, dual carriageway
	Through-route – single, dual carriageway
	Minor road – single, dual carriageway
	Road under construction
	Rural track, private road or narrow road in urban area
	Path, bridleway, byway open to all traffic, road used as public path
	Tunnel, covered road
	Gate or obstruction, car pound
P P&R	Parking, park and ride
Three Legged Cross	Junction name
	Pedestrianised or restricted access area

Public transport

	Railway with station
	London Underground station
D	Docklands Light Railway station
	Private railway station
	Tramway or miniature railway with Tramlink station
	Bus, coach station

Scale

5 inches to 1 mile   1:12672

0	220 yds	440 yds	660 yds	½ mile

0	250m	500 m	750 m	1km

Emergency services

◆ ◆ ◆	Ambulance, police, fire station
H +	Hospital, accident and emergency entrance

General features

	Market, public amenity site
i PO	Information centre, post office
VILLA House	Roman, non-Roman antiquity
100 .304	House number, spot height – metres
+	Christian place of worship
☪ ♫	Mosque, synagogue
◻	Other place of worship
	Houses, important buildings
	Woods, parkland/common
123	Adjoining page number

Leisure facilities

	Camp site, caravan site
	Golf course, picnic site, view point

Boundaries

NW6	Postcode boundaries
Westminster	County and unitary authority boundaries

Water features

Barking Creek	Water name
	Tidal water
	River or canal – major, minor
	Stream
	Water

Abbreviations

Acad	Academy	Ent	Enterprise	L Ctr	Leisure Centre	Recn Gd	Recreation Ground
Allot Gdns	Allotments	Ex H	Exhibition Hall	LC	Level Crossing	Resr	Reservoir
Bndstd	Bandstand	Fball	Football	Liby	Library	Ret Pk	Retail Park
Btcl	Botanical	Gdns	Gardens	Mkt	Market	Sch	School
Bwg Gn	Bowling	Glf C	Golf Course	Meml	Memorial	Sh Ctr	Shopping Centre
Cemy	Cemetery	Glf Crs	Golf Course	Mon	Monument	Sp	Sports
Ctr	Centre	Drv Rng	Golf Driving Range	Mus	Museum	Stad	Stadium
C Ctr	Civic Centre	Gn	Green	Nat Res	Nature Reserve	Sw Pool	Swimming Pool
CH	Club House	Gd	Ground	Obsy	Observatory	Tenn Cts	Tennis courts
Ctry Pk	Country Park	Hort	Horticultural	Pav	Pavilion	TH	Town Hall
Coll	College	Ind Est	Industrial Estate	Pk	Park	Trad Est	Trading Estate
Ct	Court	Inst	Institute	Pl Fld	Playing Field	Univ	University
Crem	Crematorium	Int	Interchange	Pal	Royal Palace	YH	Youth Hostel
Crkt	Cricket	Ct	Law Court	PH	Public House		

A1000 Potters Bar
Wrotham Park
Cockshot Hill
Ganwick Farm
Home Farm
Lower Kitt's End Farm
Kitt's End
Kitt's End Farm
Bartram's Quash
Hadley Wood
BARNET RD
Old Fold Manor
EN4
EN5
The Mount House (St Martha's Senior Sch)
Monken Hadley CE Prim Sch
Hadley Green
Convent
Bournwell Hill
Monken Hadley Common
Monken Hadley
HADLEY HIGHSTONE
ST ALBANS RD
HADLEY GN
Priddeon's Hill
London Loop
The Tudor
High Barnet
King George's Field
Tudor Sp Gd
Hadley
Cromer Road Sch
Chipping Barnet
Queen Elizabeth's Sch
High Barnet
St Catherine's Sch
BARNET HILL
HIGH ST
WOOD ST
GREAT NORTH RD
STATION RD
A411 Borehamwood, A1
A1081 Hatfield (A1(M))
Highlands Gdns
New Barnet
BARNET

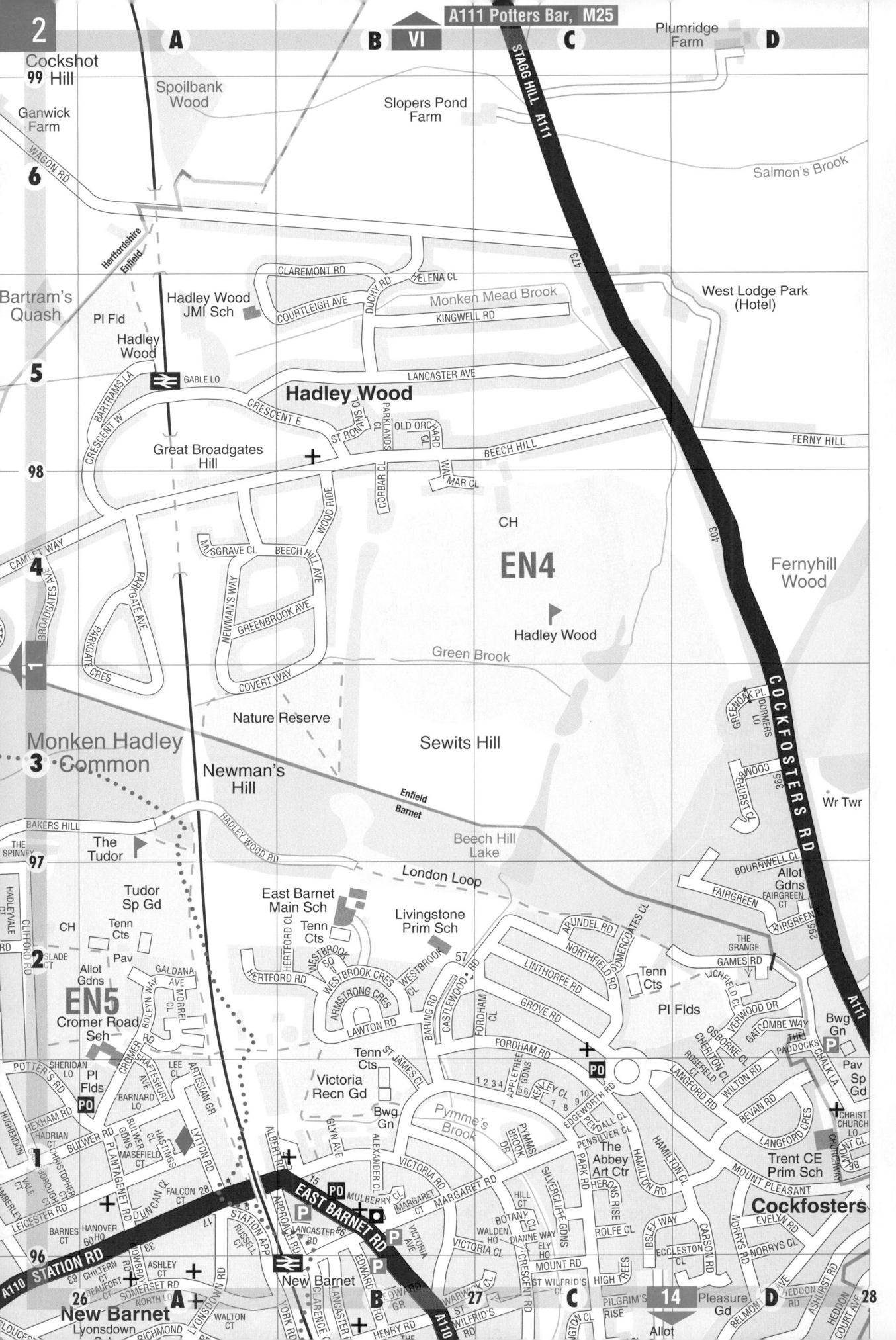
A111 Potters Bar, M25
A
B
VI
C
D
Plumridge Farm
Cockshot Hill
99
Spoilbank Wood
Slopers Pond Farm
STAGG HILL A111
Ganwick Farm
WAGON RD
6
Salmon's Brook
Hertfordshire
Enfield
A473
CLAREMONT RD
HELENA CL
DUCHY RD
West Lodge Park (Hotel)
Bartram's Quash
Hadley Wood JMI Sch
Monken Mead Brook
Pl Fld
COURTLEIGH AVE
KINGWELL RD
Hadley Wood
5
GABLE LO
LANCASTER AVE
Hadley Wood
BARTRAMS LA
CRESCENT E
CRESCENT W
ST RONANS CL
PARKLANDS CL
OLD ORCHARD CL
FERNY HILL
Great Broadgates Hill
BEECH HILL
98
WALMAR CL
CORBAR CL
WOOD RIDE
CH
CAMLET WAY
MUSGRAVE CL
BEECH HILL AVE
EN4
4
BROADGATES AVE
PARKGATE AVE
NEWMAN'S WAY
GREENBROOK AVE
403
Fernyhill Wood
Hadley Wood
PARKGATE CRES
Green Brook
1
COVERT WAY
COCKFOSTERS RD
GREENOAK PL
DORMERS LO
Nature Reserve
Monken Hadley Common
3
Sewits Hill
COOMBEHURST CL
365
Newman's Hill
Enfield
Barnet
Wr Twr
BAKERS HILL
HADLEY WOOD RD
Beech Hill Lake
THE SPINNEY
The Tudor
97
London Loop
BOURNWELL CL
Allot Gdns
FAIRGREEN
FAIRGREEN CT
Tudor Sp Gd
East Barnet Main Sch
HADLEYVALE CT
CLIFFORD RD
CH
Tenn Cts
HERTFORD CL
Tenn Cts
Livingstone Prim Sch
ARUNDEL RD
SOMERCOATES CL
295
RD
SLADE CT
2
Pav
WESTBROOK SQ
57
NORTHFIELD RD
THE GRANGE
Allot Gdns
GALDANA AVE
HERTFORD RD
WESTBROOK CRES
WESTBROOK CL
CASTLEWOOD RD
LINTHORPE RD
GAMES RD
Tenn Cts
LICHFIELD CL
A111
EN5
BOLEYN WAY
MORREL CL
ARMSTRONG CRES
BARING RD
FORDHAM CL
GROVE RD
Pl Flds
VERWOOD DR
Cromer Road Sch
LAWTON RD
GATCOMBE WAY
Bwg Gn
CROMER RD
THE PADDOCKS
P
CHALK LA
FORDHAM RD
OSBORNE CL
SHERIDAN LO
SHAFTESBURY AVE
LEE CL
ARTESIAN GR
Tenn Cts
ST JAMES CL
PO
CHERITON CL
ROSEFIELD CT
Pav
POTTER'S RD
Pl Flds
Victoria Recn Gd
1 2 3 4
APPLETREE GDNS
5 6
KENLEY CL
9 10
7 8
EDGEWORTH RD
LANGFORD RD
WILTON RD
Sp Gd
HEXHAM RD
BARNARD LO
PO
Pymme's Brook
PENDALL CL
BEVAN RD
HUGHENDON
HADRIAN CT
BULWER RD
BULWER GDNS
HASTINGS CL
LYTTON RD
Bwg Gn
PYMMS BROOK DR
PENSILVER CL
HAMILTON CL
CHRIST CHURCH LO
LANGFORD CRES
BEAUMONT CL
CHRISTOPHER CT
MASEFIELD CT
ALBERT RD
GLYN AVE
ALEXANDER CL
The Abbey Art Ctr
CHURCHWAY
1
PLANTAGENET RD
Trent CE Prim Sch
VALE CT
BOROUGH CT
FALCON CT
28
VICTORIA RD
SILVERCLIFFE GDNS
PARK RD
HAMILTON RD
MOUNT PLEASANT
LEICESTER RD
DUNCAN CL
15
PO
MULBERRY CL
MARGARET CT
MARGARET RD
HERONS RISE
HILL CT
Cockfosters
EAST BARNET RD
EVELYN RD
HANOVER HO
STATION APP
APPROACH RD
LANCASTER RD
86
P
VICTORIA AVE
BOTANY CL
IBSLEY WAY
BARNES CT
60
MOWBRAY RD
33
17
RUSSELL CT
WALDEN HO
DIANNE WAY
ROLFE CL
CARSON RD
NORRYS RD
NORRYS CL
96
VICTORIA CL
ELY HO
ECCLESTON CL
ASHLEY CT
STATION RD
A110
CHILTERN CT
63
BEAUFORT CT
SOMERSET RD
LYONSDOWN RD
New Barnet
P
EDWARD RD
MOUNT RD
CRESCENT RD
HIGH TREES
ST WILFRID'S CL
ASHURST RD
BELMONT AVE
HEDDON RD
26
NORTH LO
A
B
EDWARD GR
27
WARWICK CL
C
PILGRIM'S RISE
14
Pleasure Gd
D
28
New Barnet
WALTON CT
ST WILFRID'S RD
HEDDON COURT AVE
Lyonsdown
RICHMOND
YORK RD
CLARENCE
LANCASTER
HENRY RD
A110
Allot

A1005 Potters Bar, M25
Vault Hill Wood
Little Beechhill Wood
VI
A
B
C
D
Botany Bay Farm
Botany Bay
A1005
THE RIDGEWAY
99
Roundhedge Hill
Salmon's Brook
EN2
6
Duncan's Wood
Ash Wood
London Loop
Cuckolds Hill
Park Farm
5
FERNY HILL
Parkside Farm
Ferny Hill Farm
Obelisk
Moat Wood
P
HADLEY RD
98
Ride Wood
Camlet Hill
Leeging Beech Gutter
EN4
Rough Lot
Enfield Chase
4
4
Seedfield Spinney
Icehouse Wood
Williams Wood
Trent Country Park
Middlesex Univ Trent Park
3
Oak Wood
Shaws Wood
SHAWS WOOD COTTS
ROOKERY COTTS
97
Pav
Sp Gd
Church Wood
2
Merryhills Brook
South Lodge Farm
Triangular Wood
ENFIELD RD A110
Cemy
Trent Park Stables
EASTPOLE COTTS
P
SNAKES LA
Trent Park
Cockfosters
PO
COCKFOSTERS RD
N14
EASTPOLE COTTS
1
CH
WESTPOLE AVE
BRAMLEY RD
96
Oakwood
28
A
Southgate Sch
B
15
29
C
D
30
Pl Fld
A110
A111

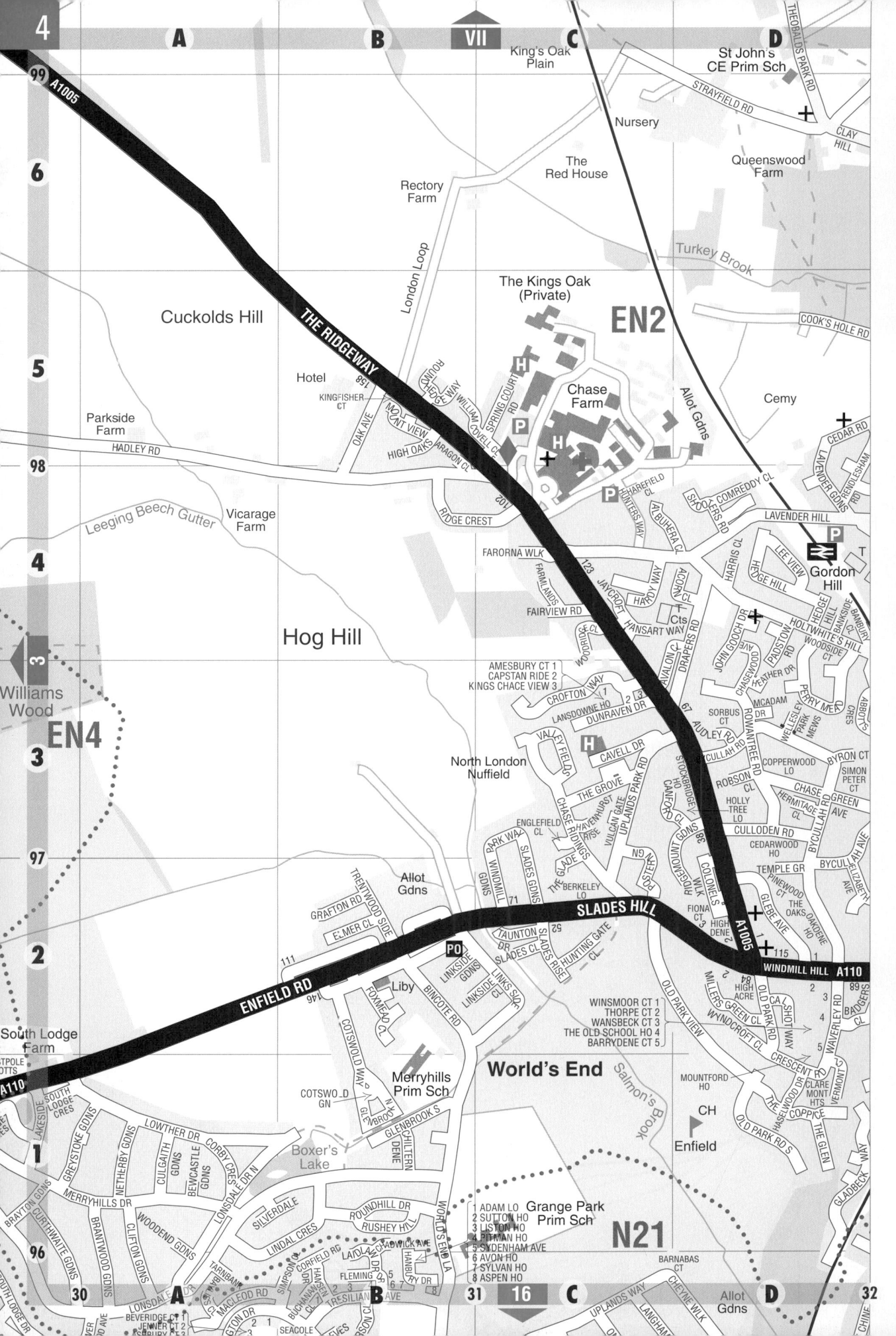
A
B
VII
C
D
99
A1005
6
5
4
3
2
1
98
97
96
30
31
32
16
King's Oak Plain
St John's CE Prim Sch
THEOBALDS PARK RD
STRAYFIELD RD
Nursery
CLAY HILL
The Red House
Queenswood Farm
Rectory Farm
London Loop
Turkey Brook
The Kings Oak (Private)
EN2
COOK'S HOLE RD
Cuckolds Hill
THE RIDGEWAY
Hotel
158
KINGFISHER CT
OAK AVE
MOUNT VIEW
ROUND HEDGE WAY
WILLIAM COVELL CL
SPRING COURT RD
HIGH OAKS
ARAGON CL
Chase Farm
Allot Gdns
Cemy
CEDAR RD
Parkside Farm
HADLEY RD
LAVENDER GDNS
RENDLESHAM RD
COMREDDY CL
HAREFIELD CL
HUNTERS WAY
ALBUHERA CL
SHOOTERS RD
LAVENDER HILL
102
RIDGE CREST
Leeging Beech Gutter
Vicarage Farm
FARORNA WLK
123
FARMLANDS
JAYCROFT
HARDY WAY
ACORN CL
HARRIS CL
LEE VIEW
HEDGE HILL
Gordon Hill
FAIRVIEW RD
Cts
HANSART WAY
DRAPERS RD
JOHN GOOCH DR
PADSTOW RD
HOLTWHITE'S HILL
BANKSIDE CL
BANBURY
WOODSIDE CT
Hog Hill
WOODRIDGE CL
AVALON CL
CHASEWOOD AVE
FEATHER DR
AMESBURY CT 1
CAPSTAN RIDE 2
KINGS CHACE VIEW 3
CROFTON WAY
LANSDOWNE HO
DUNRAVEN DR
67
SORBUS CT
AUDLEY RD
MCADAM DR
WELLESLEY PARK MEWS
PERRY MEAD
ABBOTS CRES
Williams Wood
EN4
VALLEY FIELDS
CAVELL DR
BYCULLAH RD
ROWANTREE RD
COPPERWOOD LO
BYRON CT
SIMON PETER CT
North London Nuffield
STOCKBRIDGE HO
CANFORD CL
ROBSON CL
CHASE GREEN AVE
HERMITAGE CL
THE GROVE
HAVENHURST RISE
VULCAN GATE
UPLANDS PARK RD
HOLLY TREE LO
CHASE RIDINGS
ENGLEFIELD CL
RIDGEMOUNT GDNS
CULLODEN RD
CEDARWOOD HO
BYCULLAH AVE
PARK WAY
WINDMILL GDNS
SLADES GDNS
THE GLADE
POSTERN GN
TEMPLE GR
PINEWOOD CT
THE OAKS
ELIZABETH AVE
TRENTWOOD SIDE
Allot Gdns
THE BERKELEY LO
COLONELS WLK
FIONA CT
HIGH DENE
GLEBE AVE
OAKDENE HO
GRAFTON RD
ELMER CL
71
SLADES HILL
TAUNTON DR
52
SLADES CL
SLADES RISE
HUNTING GATE CL
115
111
PO
LINKSIDE GDNS
LINKSIDE
LINKS SIDE CL
WINDMILL HILL
A110
ENFIELD RD
146
Liby
FOXMEAD CL
BINCOTE RD
OLD PARK VIEW
MILLERS GREEN CL
HIGH ACRE
OLD PARK RD
CALSHOT WAY
WAVERLEY RD
BADGERS CL
WINSMOOR CT 1
THORPE CT 2
WANSBECK CT 3
THE OLD SCHOOL HO 4
BARRYDENE CT 5
WYNDCROFT CL
CRESCENT RD
South Lodge Farm
COTSWOLD WAY
Merryhills Prim Sch
World's End
Salmon's Brook
MOUNTFORD HO
CLARE MONT HTS
VERMONT CL
COTSWOLD GN
GLENBROOK N
GLENBROOK S
CHILTERN DENE
CH
Enfield
THE HASELWOOD DR
COPPICE
THE GLEN
OLD PARK RD S
LAKESIDE
SOUTH LODGE CRES
GREYSTOKE GDNS
LOWTHER DR
CORBY CRES
NETHERBY GDNS
CULGAITH GDNS
BEWCASTLE GDNS
LONSDALE DR N
Boxer's Lake
GLADBECK WAY
MERRYHILLS DR
SILVERDALE
ROUNDHILL DR
RUSHEY HILL
WORLD'S END LA
1 ADAM LO
2 SUTTON HO
3 LISTON HO
4 PITMAN HO
5 SYDENHAM AVE
6 AVON HO
7 SYLVAN HO
8 ASPEN HO
Grange Park Prim Sch
N21
BRAYTON GDNS
CURTHWAITE GDNS
BRANTWOOD GDNS
CLIFTON GDNS
WOODEND GDNS
LINDAL CRES
CHADWICK AVE
LAIDLAW DR
HANBURY DR
FLEMING
TARNBANK
SIMPSON DR
CORFIELD RD
HANSEN DR
BUCHANAN CL
TRESILIAN AVE
LONSDALE DR
MACLEOD RD
BARNABAS CT
UPLANDS WAY
CHEYNE WLK
Allot Gdns
BEVERIDGE CT 1
JENNER CT 2
SEACOLE

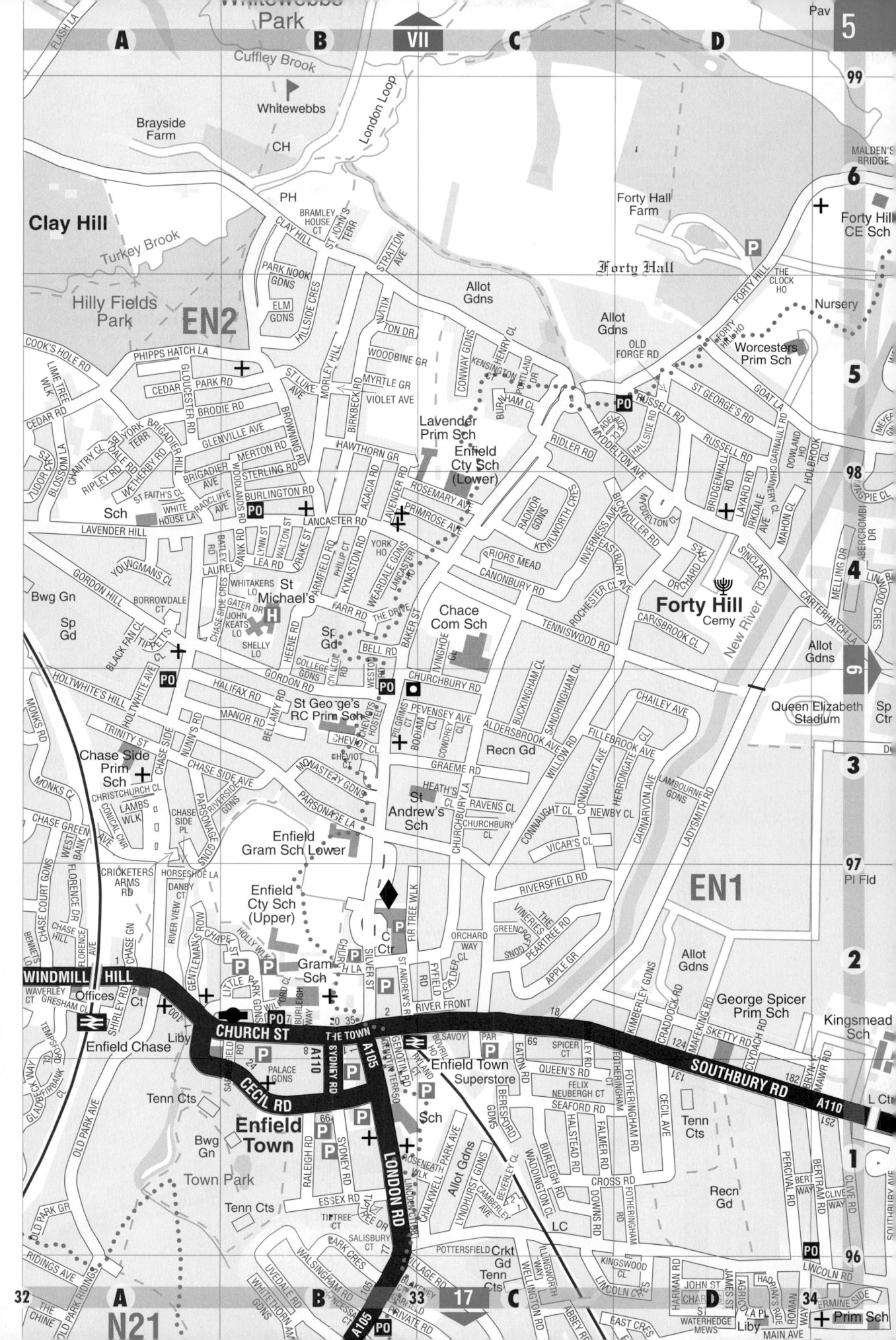
5
A
B
VII
C
D
Whitewebbs Park
Cuffley Brook
Whitewebbs
Brayside Farm
CH
London Loop
PH
Clay Hill
Turkey Brook
Hilly Fields Park
EN2
Forty Hall Farm
Forty Hall
Allot Gdns
Forty Hill CE Sch
Nursery
Worcesters Prim Sch
OLD FORGE RD
MALDEN'S BRIDGE
99
98
97
96
6
5
4
3
2
1
Lavender Prim Sch
Enfield Cty Sch (Lower)
Forty Hill
Cemy
New River
Chace Com Sch
St Michael's
St George's RC Prim Sch
St Andrew's Sch
Recn Gd
Queen Elizabeth Stadium
Sp Ctr
Bwg Gn
Sp Gd
Chase Side Prim Sch
Enfield Gram Sch Lower
Enfield Cty Sch (Upper)
C Ctr
Gram Sch
EN1
Pl Fld
Allot Gdns
George Spicer Prim Sch
Kingsmead Sch
WINDMILL HILL
CHURCH ST
THE TOWN
SOUTHBURY RD
A110
A105
LONDON RD
CECIL RD
Offices
Ct
Liby
Enfield Chase
Enfield Town
Superstore
Enfield Town
Tenn Cts
Bwg Gn
Town Park
Sch
Recn Gd
Crkt Gd
Tenn Cts
LC
Prim Sch
N21
32
33
34
17

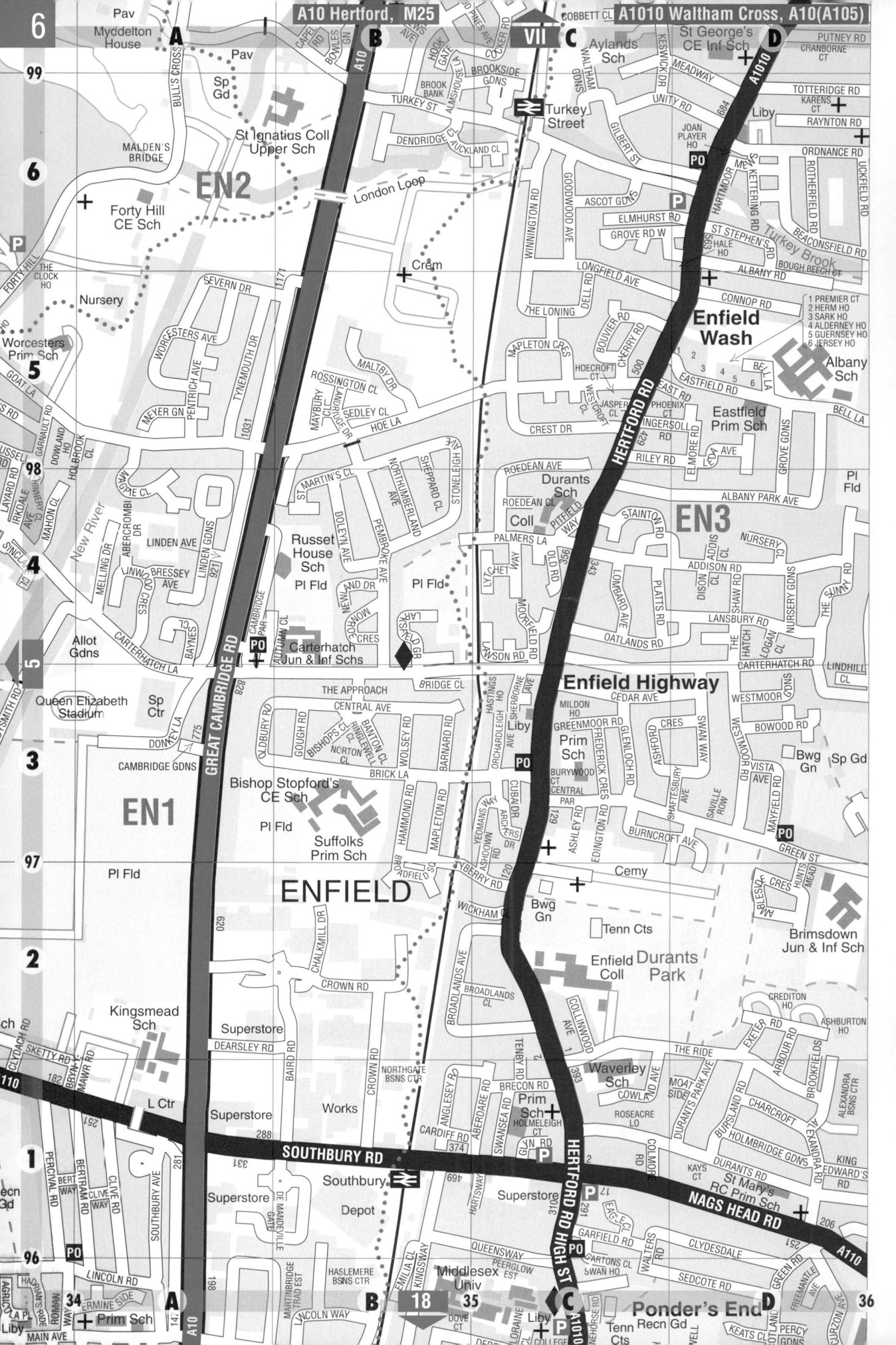
A10 Hertford, M25
VII
A1010 Waltham Cross, A10(A105)
A
B
C
D
99
6
5
98
4
5
3
97
2
1
96
Pav
Myddelton House
Bull's Cross
Sp Gd
St Ignatius Coll Upper Sch
Malden's Bridge
EN2
Forty Hill CE Sch
Forty Hill
The Clock Ho
Nursery
Worcesters Prim Sch
Goat La
London Loop
Crem
Capel Rd
Bowles Gn
Hook Gate
Almshouse La
Brook Bank
Brookside Gdns
Cocker Rd
Turkey St
Turkey Street
Dendridge Cl
Auckland Cl
Cobbett Cl
Aylands Sch
Walthan Gdns
Keswick Dr
Meadway
Unity Rd
Gilbert St
St George's CE Inf Sch
Putney Rd
Cranborne Ct
Totteridge Rd
Karens Ct
Liby
Raynton Rd
Joan Player Ho
PO
Ordnance Rd
Hartmoor Mews
Kettering Rd
Rotherfield Rd
Uckfield Rd
Winnington Rd
Goodwood Ave
Ascot Gdns
Elmhurst Rd
Grove Rd W
St Stephen's Rd
Hale Ho
Turkey Brook
Beaconsfield Rd
Albany Rd
Bough Beech Ct
Longfield Ave
Dell Rd
Connop Rd
The Loning
Enfield Wash
1 Premier Ct
2 Herm Ho
3 Sark Ho
4 Alderney Ho
5 Guernsey Ho
6 Jersey Ho
Albany Sch
Bell La
Bouvier Rd
Cherry Rd
Mapleton Cres
Hoecroft Ct
Westcroft Cl
Jasper Cl
Phoenix Ct
East Rd
Eastfield Rd
Ingersoll Rd
Eastfield Prim Sch
Crest Dr
Hertford Rd
Elmore Rd
Leda Ave
Riley Rd
Grove Gdns
Pl Fld
Severn Dr
Worcesters Ave
Tynemouth Dr
Pentrich Ave
Meyer Gn
Garnault Rd
Dowland Ho
Holbrook Cl
Hoe La
Maltby Dr
Rossington Cl
Maybury Cl
Landridge Dr
Sedley Cl
St Martin's Cl
Northumberland Ave
Sheppard Cl
Stoneleigh Ave
Roedean Ave
Durants Sch
Roedean Cl
Coll
Pitfield Way
Stainton Rd
EN3
Albany Park Ave
Nursery Cl
Addison Rd
Addis Cl
Dison Cl
Magpie Cl
Abercrombie Dr
Linden Ave
Linden Gdns
New River
Melling Dr
Linwood Cres
Bressey Ave
Layard Rd
Mahon Cl
Russet House Sch
Doleyn Ave
Pembroke Ave
Pl Fld
Palmers La
Lychet Way
Old Rd
Lombard Ave
Platts Rd
Shaw Rd
Nursery Gdns
The Sunny Rd
Newland Dr
Monroe Cres
Larksfield Gr
Moorfield Rd
Lansbury Rd
Oatlands Rd
The Hatch
Logan Cl
Allot Gdns
Carterhatch La
Baynes Cl
Cambridge Par
Autumn Cl
Carterhatch Jun & Inf Schs
Lawson Rd
Carterhatch Rd
Lindhill Cl
Great Cambridge Rd
Queen Elizabeth Stadium
Sp Ctr
The Approach
Bridge Cl
Enfield Highway
Cedar Ave
Westmoor Gdns
Donkey La
Central Ave
Oldbury Rd
Gough Rd
Bishops Cl
Ringlewell Cl
Banton Cl
Wolsey Rd
Barnard Rd
Hastings Ho
Orchardleigh Ave
Sherborne Ave
Liby
Mildon Ho
Greenmoor Rd
Frederick Cres
Glenloch Rd
Ashford Cres
Swan Way
Westmoor Rd
Bowood Rd
Cambridge Gdns
Norton Cl
Brick La
Prim Sch
Bwg Gn
Sp Gd
Vista Ave
Burywood Ct
Central Par
Shaftesbury Ave
Saville Row
Mayfield Rd
EN1
Bishop Stopford's CE Sch
Hammond Rd
Mapleton Rd
Yeomans Way
Ashdown Rd
Archers Dr
Cuba Dr
Ashley Rd
Edington Rd
Burncroft Ave
Green St
Pl Fld
Suffolks Prim Sch
Broadfield Sq
Tybery Rd
Cemy
Amblesde Cres
Hunts Mead
ENFIELD
Wickham Cl
Bwg Gn
Tenn Cts
Brimsdown Jun & Inf Sch
Chalkmill Dr
Enfield Coll
Durants Park
Broadlands Ave
Broadlands Cl
Crown Rd
Collinwood Ave
Crediton Ho
Ashburton Ho
Kingsmead Sch
Superstore
Dearsley Rd
Baird Rd
Crown Rd
Northgate Bsns Ctr
Exeter Rd
Arbour Rd
The Ride
Brookfields
Alexandra Bsns Ctr
Sch
Clydach Rd
Skerry Rd
Bryn-y-Mawr Rd
Tenby Rd
Anglesey Rd
Aberdare Rd
Brecon Rd
Waverley Sch
Cowland Ave
Moat Side
Durants Park Ave
Bursland Rd
Charcroft
A110
L Ctr
Superstore
Works
Swansea Rd
Prim Sch
Holmeleigh Ct
Roseacre Lo
Holmbridge Gdns
Alexandra Rd
Cardiff Rd
Glyn Rd
Percival Rd
Bertram Rd
Bert Way
Clive Way
Clive Rd
Southbury Ave
Southbury Rd
Hertford Rd
Colmore Rd
Kays Ct
Durants Rd
King Edward's Rd
St Mary's RC Prim Sch
Recn Gd
Superstore
De Mandeville Gate
Southbury
Depot
Hartsway
Superstore
Nags Head Rd
Eagle Cl
High St
Garfield Rd
Queensway
Peerglow Est
Walters Rd
Clydesdale
Green Rd
Lincoln Rd
Martinbridge Trad Est
Haslemere Bsns Ctr
Emilia Cl
Kingsway
Middlesex Univ
Cartons Cl
Swan Ho
Sedcote Rd
Freemantle Ave
Hadrian's Ride
Roman Way
Ermine Side
Prim Sch
Liby
Main Ave
Lincoln Way
Dove Ct
Liby
Loraine
College
Tenn Cts
Recn Gd
Ponder's End
Keats Cl
Percy Gdns
Curzon Ave
Scotland
A1010

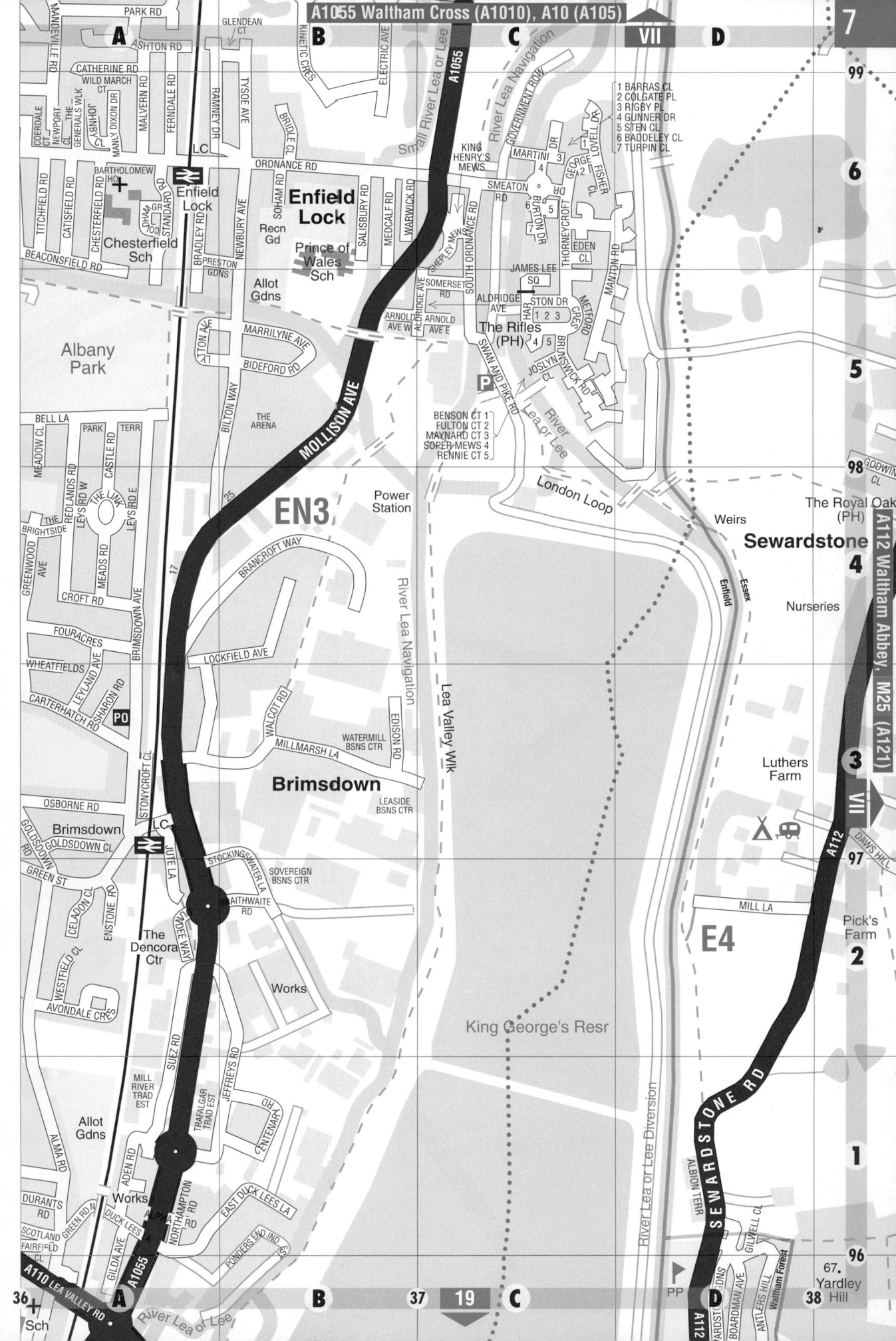

A1055 Waltham Cross (A1010), A10 (A105)
VII
A
B
C
D
PARK RD
ASHTON RD
GLENDEAN CT
MANDEVILLE RD
CATHERINE RD
WILD MARCH CT
KINETIC CRES
ELECTRIC AVE
River Lea Navigation
GOVERNMENT ROW
A1055
Small River Lea or Lee
99
1 BARRAS CL
2 COLGATE PL
3 RIGBY PL
4 GUNNER DR
5 STEN CL
6 BADDELEY CL
7 TURPIN CL
COERDALE CT
NEWPORT CL
THE GENERALS WLK
JOHNBY CL
MANLY DIXON DR
MALVERN RD
FERNDALE RD
RAMNEY DR
TYSOE AVE
BRIDLE CL
LC
ORDNANCE RD
KING HENRY'S MEWS
MARTINI DR
GEORGE LOVELL DR
FISHER CL
6
TITCHFIELD RD
CATISFIELD RD
BARTHOLOMEW HO
CHESTERFIELD RD
DHAM GR
STANDARD RD
Enfield Lock
SOHAM RD
Enfield Lock
SALISBURY RD
MEDCALF RD
WARWICK RD
SMEATON RD
BURTON DR
THORNEYCROFT DR
Recn Gd
Chesterfield Sch
Prince of Wales Sch
SHEPLEY MEWS
SOUTH ORDNANCE RD
EDEN CL
MANTON RD
BEACONSFIELD RD
BRADLEY RD
NEWBURY AVE
PRESTON GDNS
JAMES LEE SQ
Allot Gdns
SOMERSET RD
ALDRIDGE AVE
ALDRIDGE AVE
HARSTON DR
METFORD CRES
ARNOLD AVE W
ARNOLD AVE E
The Rifles (PH)
LYTTON AVE
MARRILYNE AVE
Albany Park
BIDEFORD RD
SWAN AND PIKE RD
BRUNSWICK RD
JOSLYN CL
5
P
BILTON WAY
BELL LA
PARK TERR
THE ARENA
MOLLISON AVE
BENSON CT 1
FULTON CT 2
MAYNARD CT 3
SOPER MEWS 4
RENNIE CT 5
River Lea or Lee
MEADOW CL
REDLANDS RD
LEYS RD W
CASTLE RD
THE LINK
LEYS RD E
98
GODWIN CL
London Loop
Power Station
THE BRIGHTSIDE
EN3
Weirs
The Royal Oak (PH)
Sewardstone
A112 Waltham Abbey, M25 (A121)
MEADS RD
GREENWOOD AVE
BRANCROFT WAY
River Lea Navigation
4
Enfield
Essex
CROFT RD
Nurseries
FOURACRES
BRIMSDOWN AVE
WHEATFIELDS
LOCKFIELD AVE
Lea Valley Wlk
LEYLAND AVE
SHARON RD
CARTERHATCH RD
PO
WALCOT RD
EDISON RD
WATERMILL BSNS CTR
MILLMARSH LA
STONYCROFT CL
Luthers Farm
3
Brimsdown
LEASIDE BSNS CTR
OSBORNE RD
LC
GOLDSDOWN RD
Brimsdown
GOLDSDOWN CL
JUTE LA
STOCKINGSWATER LA
SOVEREIGN BSNS CTR
GREEN ST
A112
DAWS HILL
97
CELADON CL
ENSTONE RD
BRAITHWAITE RD
MILL LA
Pick's Farm
The Dencora Ctr
RIDGE WAY
E4
WESTFIELD CL
2
Works
AVONDALE CRES
King George's Resr
SUEZ RD
JEFFREYS RD
MILL RIVER TRAD EST
TRAFALGAR TRAD EST
CENTENARY RD
SEWARDSTONE RD
Allot Gdns
River Lea or Lee Diversion
1
ALMA RD
ADEN RD
ALBION TERR
EAST DUCK LEES LA
DURANTS RD
Works
GREEN RD
DUCK LEES LA
ALPHA RD
NORTHAMPTON RD
PONDERS END IND EST
GILWELL CL
SCOTLAND GREEN RD
FAIRFIELD CL
GILDA AVE
96
Waltham Forest
67
Yardley Hill
A110 LEA VALLEY RD
36
Sch
A1055
River Lea or Lee
37
19
PP
SEWARDSTONE GDNS
BOARDMAN AVE
ANTLERS HILL
38
A112

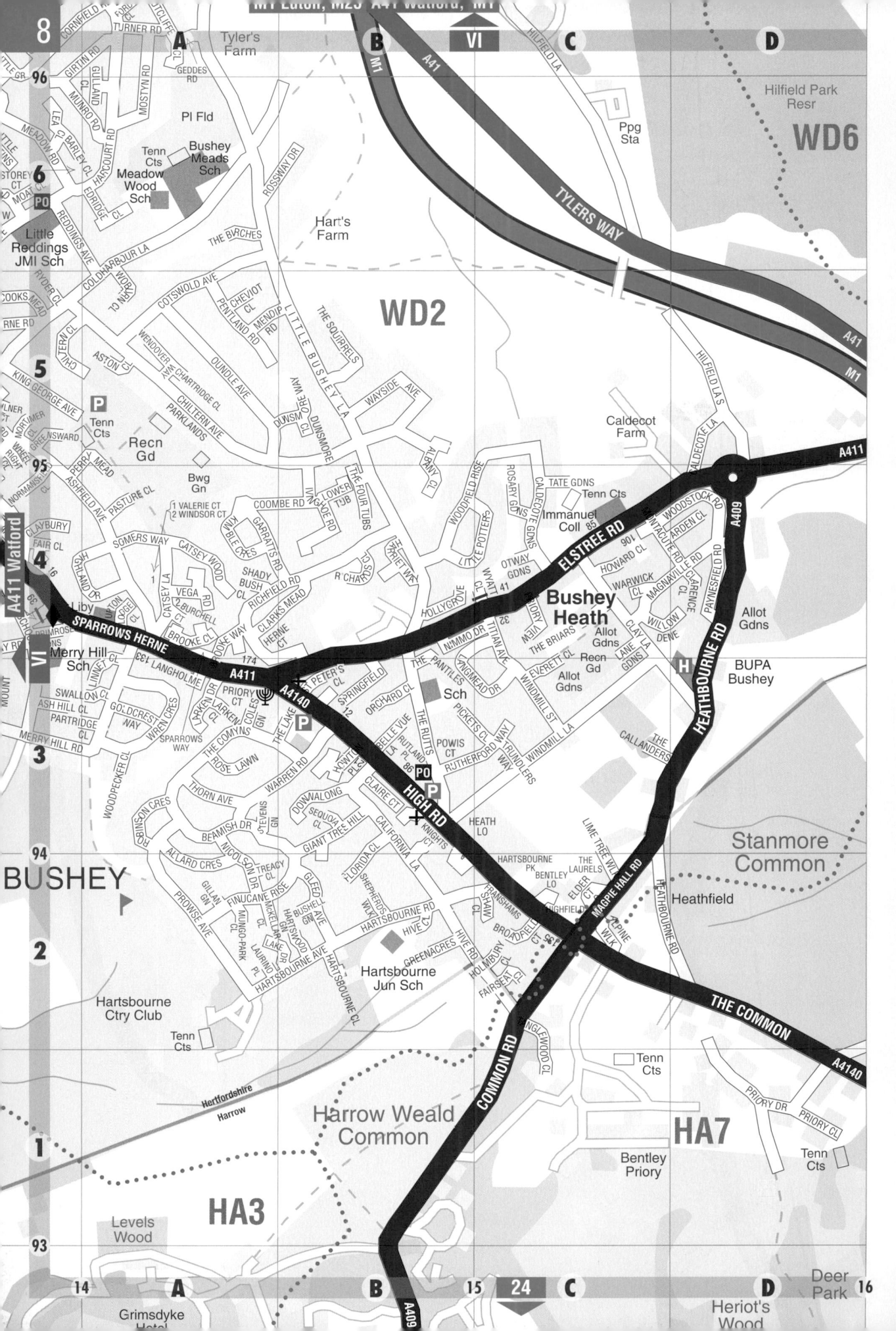
M1 Luton, M25 A41 Watford, M1
VI
A
B
C
D
Tyler's Farm
Hilfield Park Resr
WD6
Ppg Sta
Pl Fld
Bushey Meads Sch
Tenn Cts
Meadow Wood Sch
Little Reddings JMI Sch
Hart's Farm
TYLERS WAY
WD2
A41
M1
Caldecot Farm
A411
Recn Gd
Bwg Gn
Immanuel Coll
Tenn Cts
ELSTREE RD
A409
Bushey Heath
Allot Gdns
SPARROWS HERNE
A411 Watford
Liby
Merry Hill Sch
A4140
HEATHBOURNE RD
BUPA Bushey
Sch
HIGH RD
MAGPIE HALL RD
Stanmore Common
Heathfield
BUSHEY
Hartsbourne Jun Sch
Hartsbourne Ctry Club
THE COMMON
COMMON RD
Hertfordshire
Harrow
Harrow Weald Common
HA7
HA3
Bentley Priory
Levels Wood
Deer Park
Heriot's Wood
Grimsdyke Hotel
14
15
16
24
93
94
95
96
1
2
3
4
5
6

Aldenham Cntry Pk
Home Farm
Laboratory
DAGGER LA
Aldenham Resr
Sailing Club
Pav
ALDENHAM RD
Sp Gd
Tenn Cts
WD6
LANDS' END
WATFORD RD
PH
ELSTREE RD
LISMIRRANE IND PK
NORTH WESTERN AVENUE
WATFORD BY-PASS
CENTENNIAL PK
WD2
Hertfordshire
Harrow
ELSTREE HILL N
ELSTREE HILL S
HIGH ST
A5183
B5378 ALLUM LA
Cemy
THE BARTONS
ROMELAND
ST NICHOLAS CL
St Nicholas CE Sch
Elstree
NEW RD
SCHUBERT RD
FOX CL
BRITTEN CL
RODGERS CL
DELIUS CL
WEBBER CL
BEEHIVE
SULLIVAN WAY
BEETHOVEN RD
DYLAN CL
ELGAR CL
COATES RD
WEST VIEW GDNS
SUMMER GR
OAK TREE CL
GEORGES MEAD
MAY GDNS
FORTUNE LA
Tenn Cts
Edgwarebury House Farm
A411
PO
Brockleyhill Farm
Hertfordshire
Barnet
M1
A5
Sp Gd
Brockley Grange
Tenn Cts
Brockleyhill House
Royal National Orthopaedic
Works
HA7
SIR HENRY FLOYD CT
Grove Farm
Annandale
NUTT GR
BROCKLEY HILL
HA8
EDGWARE WAY (WATFORD BY-PASS)
A41
Pear Wood Cottages
Wood Farm
Pear Wood
WARREN LA
Limes House
WOOD LA
Crkt Gd
Pav
Tenn Cts
Cloisters Wood
Springbok Ho
CH
Brockley Hill
Barnet
Harrow
Tenn Cts
SPRINGFIELD CL
PARK LA
HILLTOP WAY
LITTLE COMMON
BROOMFIELD HO 1
FALLOWFIELD CT 2
HILL HO 3
WELLINGTON HO 4
FALLOWFIELD
AYLMER CL
AYLWARDS RISE
AYLMER DR
STANMORE HILL
HERIOTS CL
PINE CL
Stanmore Hall
A4140
FORGE CL
SPRING LA
DENNIS LA
GRANTHAM CL
NEWLANDS CL
HAMLYN
PIPERS GREEN LA
BROCKLEY
CHEVALIER CL
REES DR
PARTRIDGE CL
BERRY HILL
CLANLEAM RD
REENGLASS
A410
A B C D
96 6 5 95 4 3 94 2 1 93

VI
10
25

A
B
C
D
VI
96
6
5
95
4
9
3
94
2
1
93
18
19
26
20
Elstree
WOODSIDE
BLATTNER CL
B5378
ALLUM LA
NASH CL
FIR TREE CT
HILL CREST LO
DEACONS CL
CEDARS CL
OAK
ELMWOOD AVE
Allot Gdns
Sch
FURZEHILL RD
A5183
ALLUM LA
KNOWL PK
KNOWL WAY
TAUBER CL
LODGE AVE
GRANGE RD
BISHOPS AVE
CAVENDISH CRES
LAKESIDE
MELROSE AVE
TENNISON AVE
MILTON DR
B5378
Cemy
HARTFIELD AVE
DEACON'S HILL RD
London Loop
BERKELEY CL
ASCOT CL
HARTFIELD AVE
HARTFIELD CL
BYRON AVE
VALE AVE
MASEFIELD AVE
LULLINGTON GARTH
CARRINGTON AVE
THE RISE
WENTWORTH AVE
SHIREMEADE
SHERATON CL
LOWTHER CL
NICHOLAS RD
HADLEY CL
ALWYN CL
CLARE CL
BELMOR
SUMMER HILL
ELSTREE HILL N
THE BARTONS
St Nicholas CE Sch
ST NICHOLAS CL
Elstree
NEW RD
TREE CT
OAK TREE CT
GEORGES MEAD
A411
PO
DEACONS HTS
Deacons Hill
A411
Woodcock Hill
Tenn Cts
Elstree Tunnel
Abbotsbury
BARNET LA
WD6
SUMMER GR
FORTUNE LA
MAY GDNS
Tenn Cts
Edgwarebury House Farm
The Leys
Penniwells Farm
Tenn Cts
Tenn Cts
Edgwarebury Ctry Club
Hertfordshire
Barnet
NW7
M1
M1
Edgwarebury Farm
Bury Farm
Edgware Bury
EDGWAREBURY LA
Clay La
Cemy
Pav
Pl Fld
Broadfields Inf Sch
Broadfields Jun Sch
HARTLAND CL
HARTLAND DR
A41
NUTT GR
EDGWARE WAY (WATFORD BY-PASS)
HA8
WARRENS SHAWE LA
MEADFIELD
MEADFIELD GN
BUSHFIELD CL
BUSHFIELD CRES
BURRELL CL
PENTLAND AVE
HAMONDE CL
CROMARTY RD
MORAY CL
RANNOCH CL
KINGSLEY CT
TAYSIDE DR
ALDRIDGE AVE
Sch
PARSONS RD
PARSONS GR
FRANCKLYN GDNS
HARROWES MEADE
BULLESCROFT RD
GLENGALL RD
WOLMER GDNS
CROSSGATE
Edgwarebury Park
Tenn Cts
Pav
A5
Barnet
Harrow
BROCKLEY HILL
GRANTHAM CL
NEWLANDS CL
HAMLYN CL
CH
PIPERS GREEN LA
Edgwarebury
BROCKLEY AVE
HA7
BEULAH CL
CRAMMER RD
ASHFORD CT
MARLBOROUGH AVE
WYRE GR
ROSENS WLK
LYNFORD GDNS
WINDSOR AVE
BROADFIELDS AVE
PARKSIDE DR
BLACKWELL GDNS
ELMER RD
BROADHURST AVE
HURSTMEAD CT
GRENVILLE CT
A41
A410
SPUR RD
CHEVALIER CL
BROCKLEY SIDE
REES DR
PARTRIDGE CL
BERRY HILL
REENGLAS
CANONS CNR
Pl Flds
A5
SPALDING CT
GOLDSMITH CT
COLLINSON CT
POWIS
GREEN LA
GARRICK CT
MARTYN CT
STERLING AVE
HILLSI
EATON CT
RANELAGH CL
GLEN
HAZEL GDNS
THE GROVE

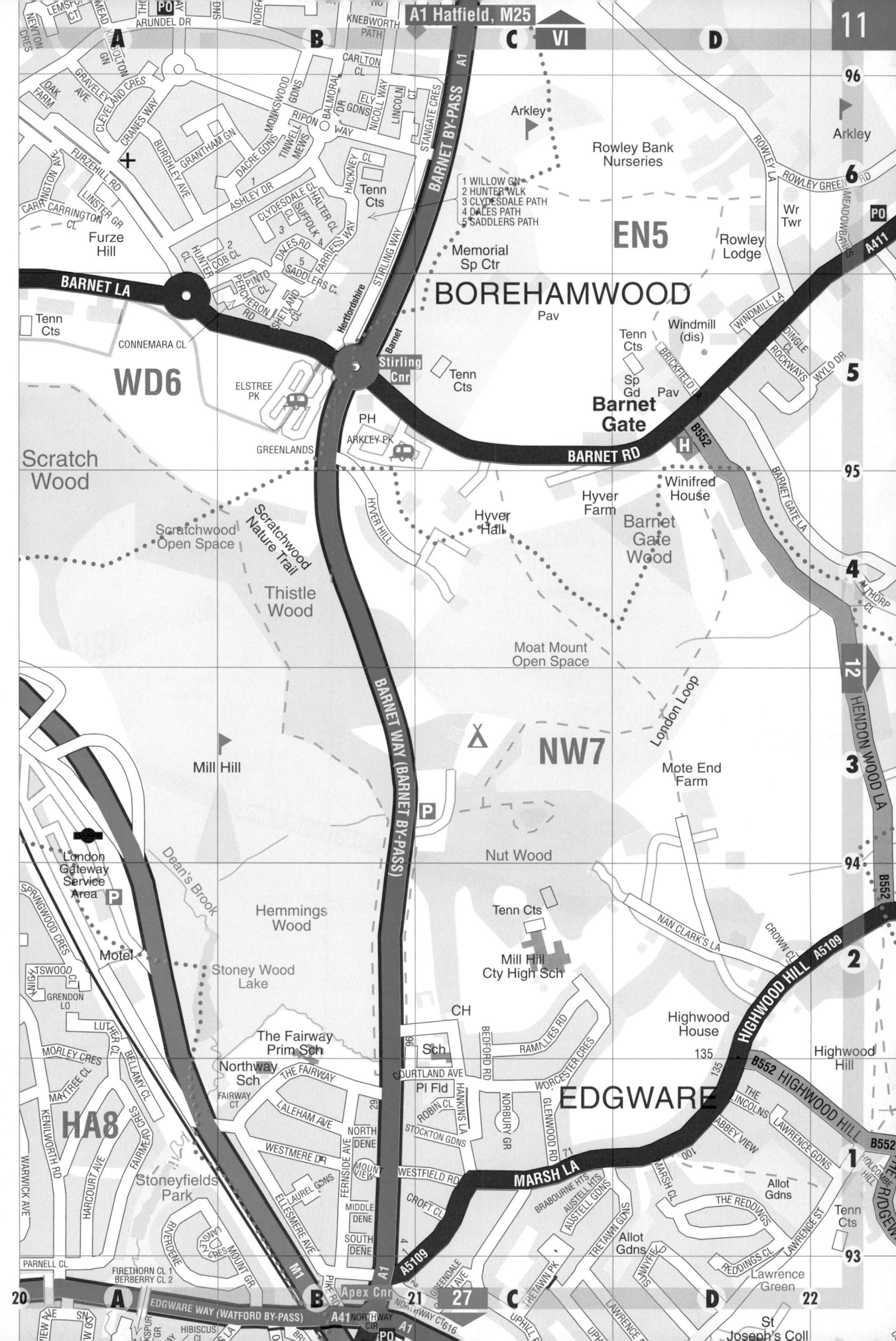
A1 Hatfield, M25
VI
A
B
C
D
96
6
5
95
4
3
94
2
1
93
20
21
22
27
12
ARUNDEL DR
KNEBWORTH PATH
CARLTON CL
NEWTON CRES
KIMBOLTON GN
GRAVELEY AVE
CLEVELAND CRES
OAK FARM
CRANES WAY
MONKSWOOD GDNS
BALMORAL DR
ELY GDNS
NICOLL WAY
LINCOLN CT
STANGATE CRES
RIPON WAY
TINWELL MEWS
GRANTHAM GN
BURGHLEY AVE
DACRE GDNS
HACKNEY CL
Tenn Cts
FURZEHILL RD
CARRINGTON AVE
CARRINGTON CL
LINSTER GR
ASHLEY DR
CLYDESDALE CL
HALTER CL
SUFFOLK CL
FARRIERS WAY
Furze Hill
HUNTER CL
COB CL
DALES RD
SADDLERS CL
PINTO CL
PERCHERON RD
SHETLAND CL
STIRLING WAY
BARNET BY-PASS
A1
1 WILLOW GN
2 HUNTER WLK
3 CLYDESDALE PATH
4 DALES PATH
5 SADDLERS PATH
Arkley
Rowley Bank Nurseries
ROWLEY LA
ROWLEY GREEN RD
MEADOWBANKS
PO
Wr Twr
Rowley Lodge
A411
EN5
Memorial Sp Ctr
BOREHAMWOOD
Pav
BARNET LA
Tenn Cts
CONNEMARA CL
Hertfordshire
Barnet
Stirling Cnr
Tenn Cts
WD6
ELSTREE PK
PH
ARKLEY PK
GREENLANDS
Windmill (dis)
WINDMILL LA
DINGLE CL
ROCKWAYS
WYLO DR
BRICKFIELD LA
Sp Gd
Barnet Gate
BARNET RD
B552
H
Scratch Wood
HYVER HILL
Hyver Hall
Hyver Farm
Winifred House
BARNET GATE LA
Barnet Gate Wood
Scratchwood Open Space
Scratchwood Nature Trail
Thistle Wood
ALTHORP CL
Moat Mount Open Space
BARNET WAY (BARNET BY-PASS)
London Loop
HENDON WOOD LA
NW7
Mill Hill
Mote End Farm
P
Nut Wood
London Gateway Service Area
Dean's Brook
Hemmings Wood
Tenn Cts
NAN CLARK'S LA
CROWN CL
SPRINGWOOD CRES
Motel
Stoney Wood Lake
Mill Hill Cty High Sch
A5109
HIGHWOOD HILL
TSWOOD CL
GRENDON LO
LUTHER CL
BELLAMY CL
CH
BEDFORD RD
RAMILLIES RD
WORCESTER CRES
Highwood House
Highwood Hill
135
The Fairway Prim Sch
Sch
MORLEY CRES
Northway Sch
THE FAIRWAY
COURTLAND AVE
Pl Fld
B552 HIGHWOOD HILL
MAYTREE CL
FAIRWAY CT
EDGWARE
THE LINCOLNS
KENILWORTH RD
HA8
LALEHAM AVE
ROBIN CL
HANKINS LA
NORBURY GR
GLENWOOD RD
ABBEY VIEW
LAWRENCE GDNS
FAIRMEAD CRES
NORTH DENE
STOCKTON GDNS
HOLCOMBE HILL
THE RIDGEWAY
WARWICK AVE
HARCOURT AVE
WESTMERE DR
MOUNT VIEW
WESTFIELD RD
MARSH LA
MARSH CL
Allot Gdns
Stoneyfields Park
LAUREL GDNS
FERNSIDE AVE
CROFT CL
BRABOURNE HTS
AUSTELL HTS
AUSTELL GDNS
THE REDDINGS
Tenn Cts
RIVERDENE
LANGLEY CRES
MOUNT GR
ELLESMERE AVE
MIDDLE DENE
SOUTH DENE
A5109
TRETAWN GDNS
Allot Gdns
LAWRENCE ST
PARNELL CL
FIRETHORN CL 1
BERBERRY CL 2
M1
PIKE RD
A1
GREENDALE
TRETAWN PK
SUNNYFIELD
REDDINGS CL
Lawrence Green
Apex Cnr
EDGWARE WAY (WATFORD BY-PASS)
A41
NORTHWAY CIR
NORTHWAY CT
PO
HIBISCUS CL
UPHILL
St Joseph's Coll

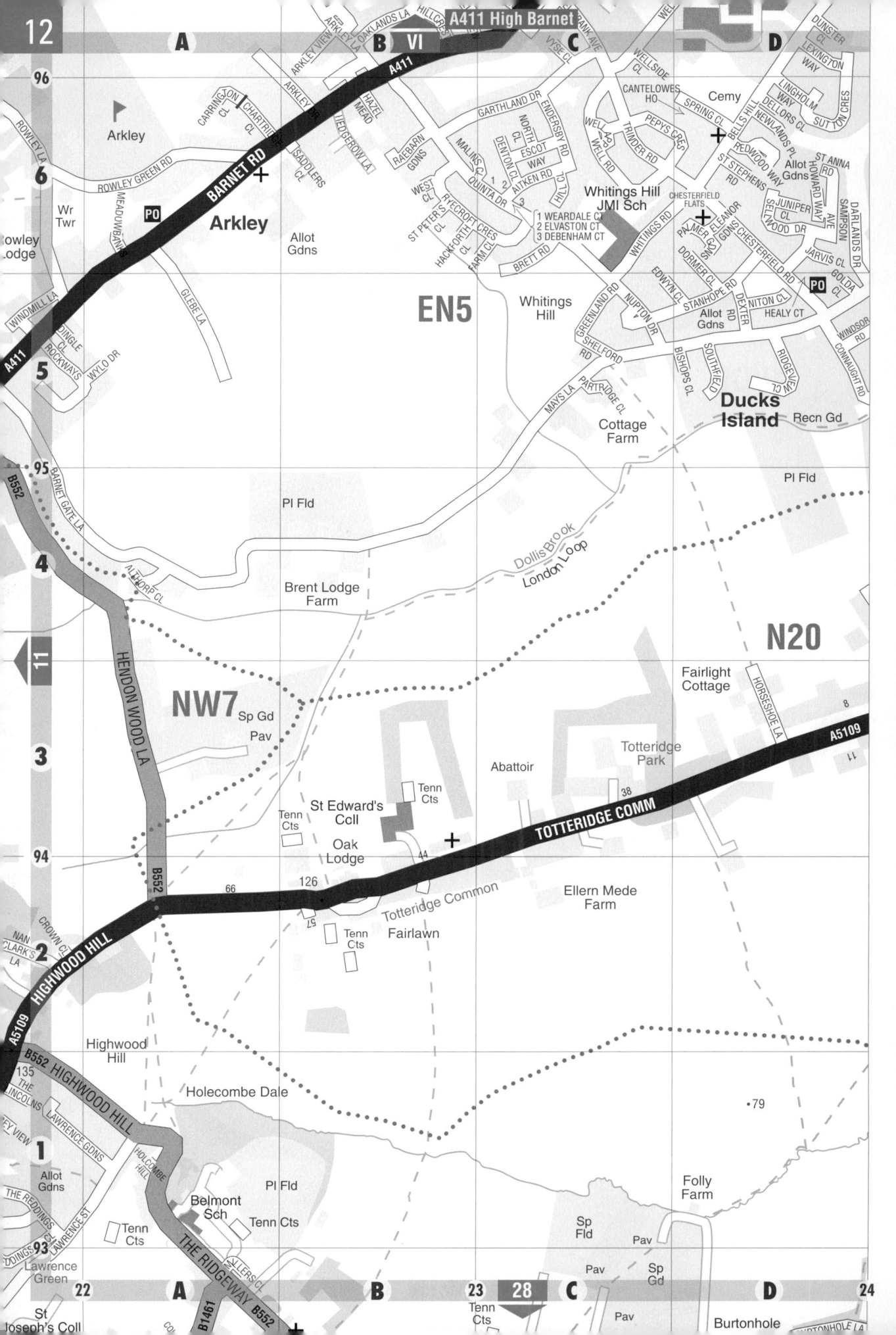

A411 High Barnet
VI
A B C D
96
6
5
95
4
11
3
94
2
1
93
22
23
28
24
Arkley
Rowley Green Rd
Barnet Rd
A411
Wr Twr
Rowley Lodge
PO
Allot Gdns
EN5
Whitings Hill
Whitings Hill JMI Sch
1 Weardale Ct
2 Elvaston Ct
3 Debenham Ct
Cantelowes Ho
Cemy
Chesterfield Flats
Allot Gdns
Ducks Island
Recn Gd
Cottage Farm
Mays La
Pl Fld
Dollis Brook
London Loop
Brent Lodge Farm
Barnet Gate La
Hendon Wood La
B552
NW7
Sp Gd
Pav
N20
Fairlight Cottage
Horseshoe La
A5109
Totteridge Park
Abattoir
Totteridge Comm
St Edward's Coll
Tenn Cts
Oak Lodge
Totteridge Common
Fairlawn
Ellern Mede Farm
Highwood Hill
Holecombe Dale
Belmont Sch
Pl Fld
Folly Farm
Sp Fld
Pav
Sp Gd
The Ridgeway
B1461
Lawrence Green
St Joseph's Coll
Burtonhole

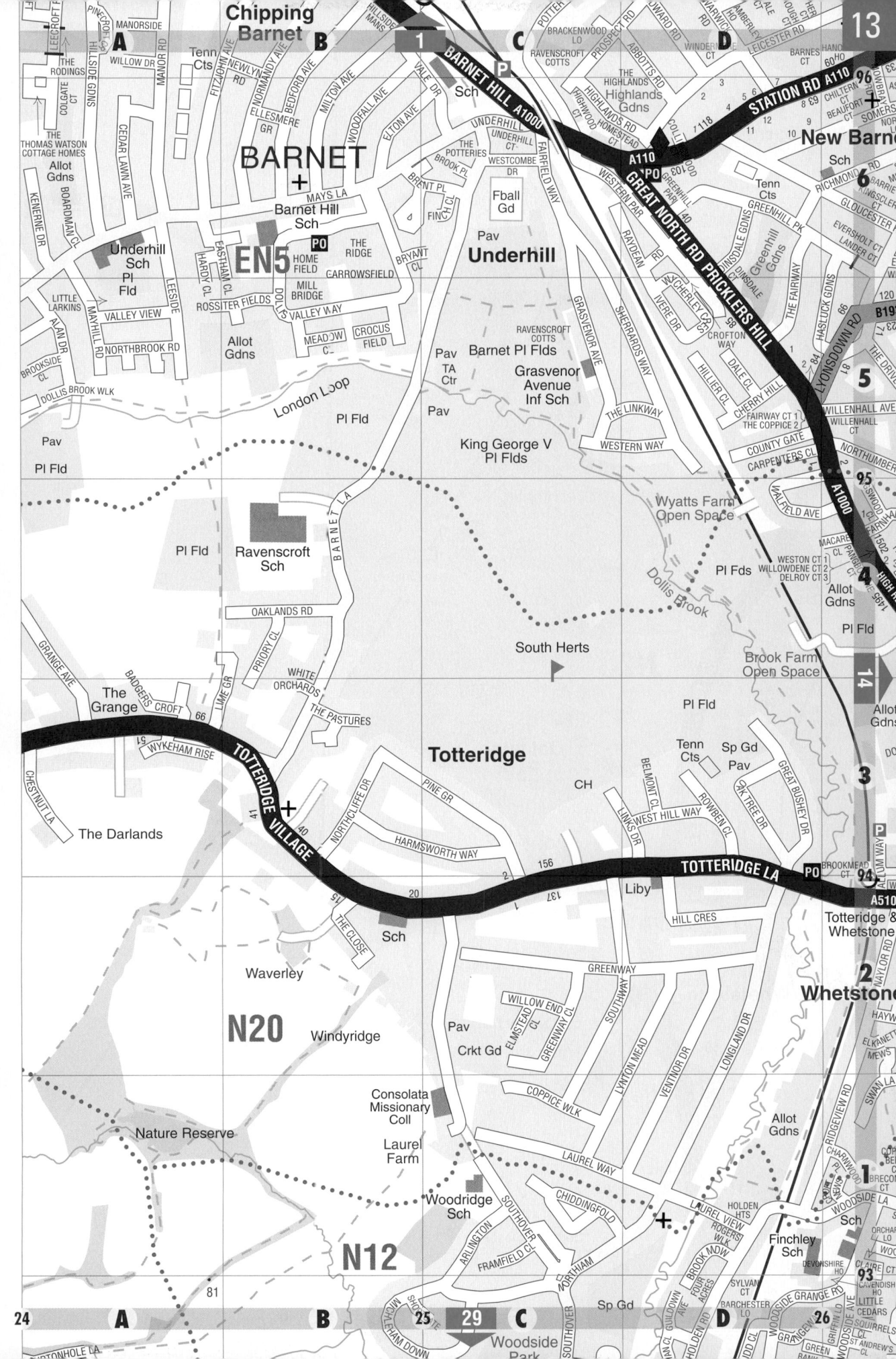
Chipping Barnet
BARNET
EN5
Underhill
New Barnet
Totteridge
Whetstone
Totteridge & Whetstone
N20
N12
BARNET HILL A1000
STATION RD A110
GREAT NORTH RD
PRICKLERS HILL
A1000
TOTTERIDGE VILLAGE
TOTTERIDGE LA
A5109
A110
B1930
MANORSIDE
WILLOW DR
THE RODINGS
COLGATE CT
HILLSIDE GDNS
MANOR RD
CEDAR LAWN AVE
THE THOMAS WATSON COTTAGE HOMES
Allot Gdns
BOARDMAN CL
KENERNE DR
Underhill Sch
Pl Fld
LEESIDE
LITTLE LARKINS
MAYHILL RD
VALLEY VIEW
NORTHBROOK RD
ALAN DR
BROOKSIDE CL
DOLLIS BROOK WLK
Tenn Cts
FITZJOHN AVE
NEWLYN RD
NORMANDY AVE
ELLESMERE GR
BEDFORD AVE
MILTON AVE
WOODFALL AVE
ELTON AVE
VALE DR
Sch
UNDERHILL
UNDERHILL CT
THE POTTERIES
WESTCOMBE DR
BROOK PL
BRENT PL
FINCH CL
MAYS LA
Barnet Hill Sch
PO
THE RIDGE
HOME FIELD
CARROWSFIELD
MILL BRIDGE
BRYANT CL
HARDY CL
EASTHAM CL
ROSSITER FIELDS
DOLLIS VALLEY WAY
MEADOW CL
CROCUS FIELD
Fball Gd
Pav
FAIRFIELD WAY
RAVENSCROFT COTTS
Barnet Pl Flds
TA Ctr
Grasvenor Avenue Inf Sch
GRASVENOR AVE
SHERRARDS WAY
THE LINKWAY
WESTERN WAY
King George V Pl Flds
London Loop
BRACKENWOOD LO
RAVENSCROFT COTTS
PROSPECT RD
ABBOTTS RD
THE HIGHLANDS
Highlands Gdns
HIGHWOOD CT
HOMESTEAD CT
WINDERMERE CT
LEICESTER RD
AMBERLEY CT
BARNES CT
CHILTERN CT
BEAUFORT CT
SOMERSET RD
WESTERN PAR
RAYDEAN RD
GREENHILL PAR
DINSDALE GDNS
Greenhill Gdns
GREENHILL PK
RICHMOND RD
GLOUCESTER RD
EVERSHOLT CT
LANDER CT
WYCHERLEY CR
IVERE DR
CROFTON WAY
HILLIER CL
DALE CL
CHERRY HILL
THE FAIRWAY
HASLUCK GDNS
LYONSDOWN RD
THE DRIVE
FAIRWAY CT
THE COPPICE
COUNTY GATE
CARPENTERS CL
WILLENHALL AVE
WILLENHALL CT
NORTHUMBERLAND RD
WALFIELD AVE
Wyatts Farm Open Space
Pl Fds
Dollis Brook
WESTON CT
WILLOWDENE CT
DELROY CT
Allot Gdns
Pl Fld
Brook Farm Open Space
Ravenscroft Sch
BARNET LA
OAKLANDS RD
PRIORY CL
WHITE ORCHARDS
THE PASTURES
GRANGE AVE
BADGERS CROFT
LIME GR
The Grange
WYKEHAM RISE
CHESTNUT LA
The Darlands
South Herts
Pl Fld
Tenn Cts
Sp Gd
Pav
CH
BELMONT CL
WEST HILL WAY
ROWBEN CL
LINKS DR
OAK TREE DR
GREAT BUSHEY DR
NORTHCLIFFE DR
PINE GR
HARMSWORTH WAY
BROOKMEAD CT
ATTLEE WAY
Liby
HILL CRES
THE CLOSE
Sch
Waverley
Windyridge
GREENWAY
WILLOW END
ELMSTEAD CL
GREENWAY CL
SOUTHWAY
LYNTON MEAD
VENTNOR DR
LONGLAND DR
Pav
Crkt Gd
COPPICE WLK
Consolata Missionary Coll
Laurel Farm
LAUREL WAY
Nature Reserve
Woodridge Sch
SOUTHOVER
CHIDDINGFOLD
LAUREL VIEW
HOLDEN HTS
ROGERS WLK
BROOK MDW
FOUR ACRES
ARLINGTON
FRAMFIELD CL
NORTHIAM
Allot Gdns
RIDGEVIEW RD
CHARNWOOD
WOODSIDE LA
Sch
Finchley Sch
DEVONSHIRE HO
NAYLOR RD
HAYWARD
ELKANETTE MEWS
SWAN LA
SYLVAN CT
BARCHESTER LO
WOODSIDE GRANGE RD
GUILDOWN AVE
HOLDEN RD
WOODSIDE AVE
GRIFFIN LO
LITTLE CEDARS
SQUIRRELS
ST ANDREWS CL
CAVENDISH HO
CLAIRE CT
MICHLEHAM DOWN
SHOOTERS
Sp Gd
Woodside Park
BURTONHOLE LA
A
B
C
D
1
2
3
4
5
6
24
25
26
93
94
95
96
14
29
81

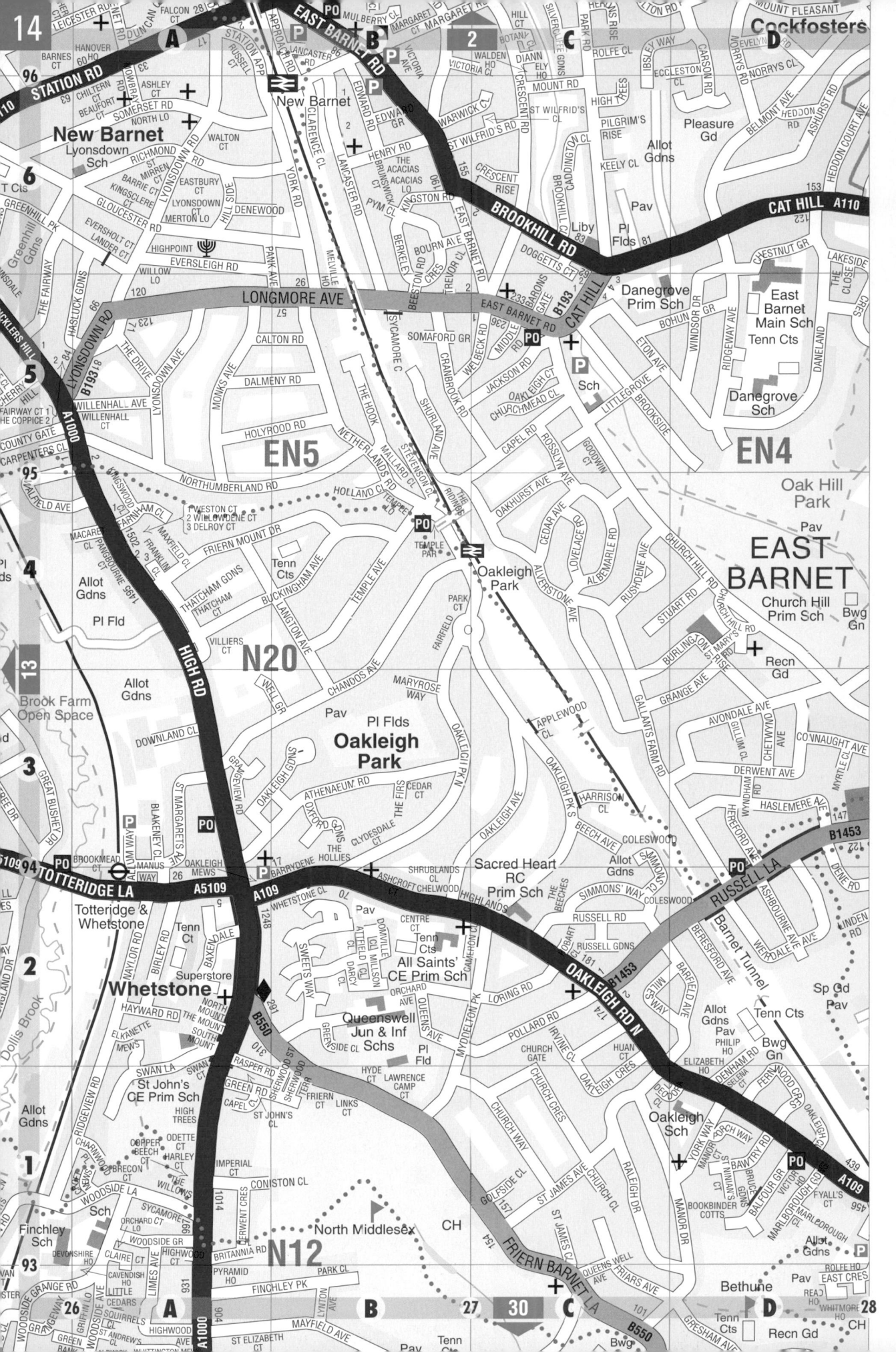
New Barnet
Cockfosters
EN5
EN4
Oak Hill Park
EAST BARNET
N20
Oakleigh Park
Whetstone
Totteridge & Whetstone
N12
North Middlesex
Bethune
Brook Farm Open Space
Danegrove Prim Sch
East Barnet Main Sch
Church Hill Prim Sch
Sacred Heart RC Prim Sch
All Saints' CE Prim Sch
Queenswell Jun & Inf Schs
St John's CE Prim Sch
Oakleigh Sch
Finchley Sch
Lyonsdown Sch
STATION RD
EAST BARNET RD
BROOKHILL RD
CAT HILL
LONGMORE AVE
HIGH RD
TOTTERIDGE LA
OAKLEIGH RD N
RUSSELL LA
FRIERN BARNET LA
FINCHLEY PK
Barnet Tunnel
A110
A1000
A5109
A109
B1453
B550
B193

13
2
30
28

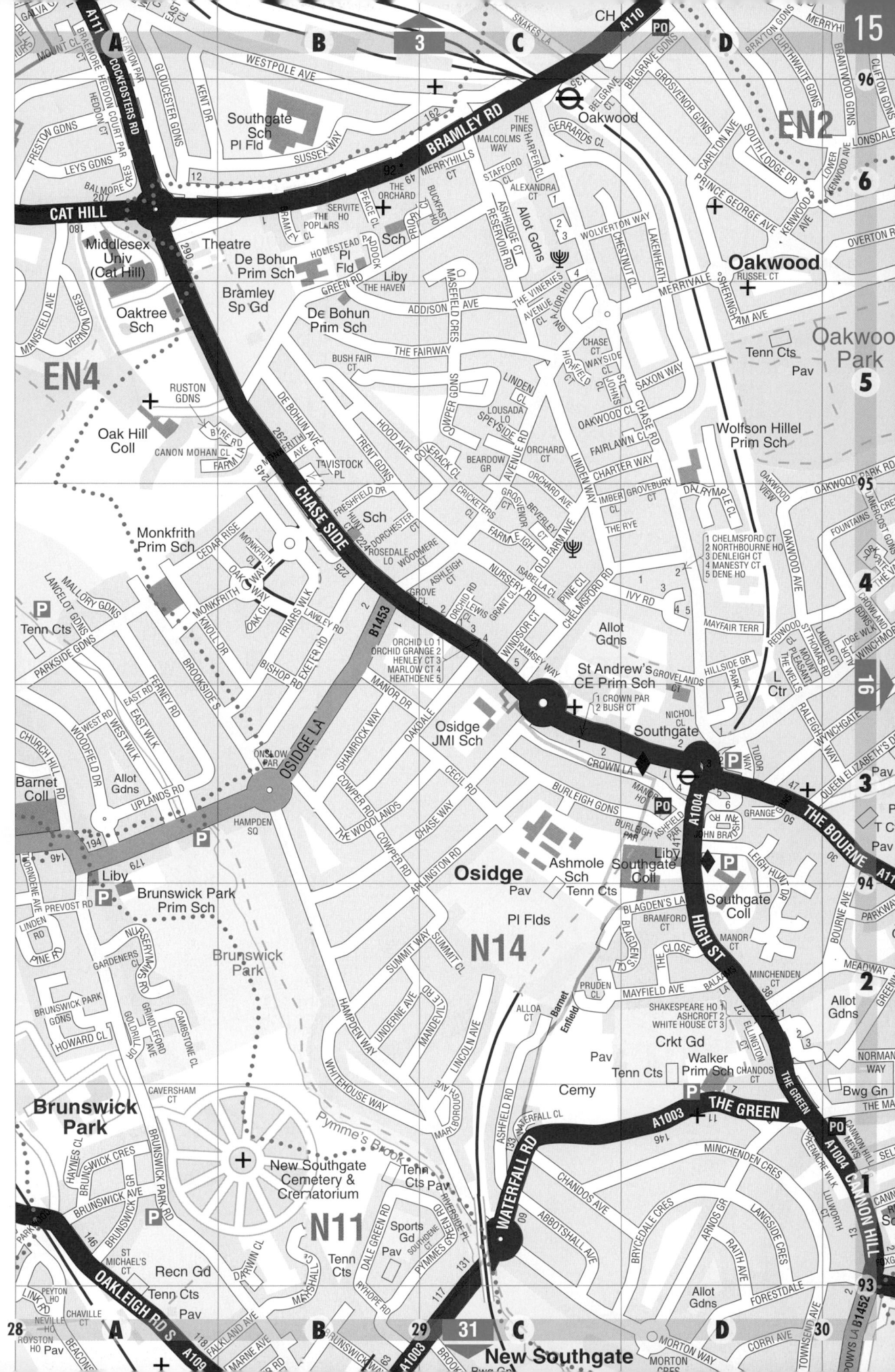
A
B
C
D
3
6
5
4
3
2
1
96
95
94
93
EN2
EN4
N14
N11
16
28
29
31
30
CAT HILL
COCKFOSTERS RD
BRAMLEY RD
CHASE SIDE
OSIDGE LA
B1453
HIGH ST
A1004
THE GREEN
A1003
WATERFALL RD
CANNON HILL
THE BOURNE
OAKLEIGH RD S
A109
A110
A111
B1452
WESTPOLE AVE
SNAKES LA
Southgate Sch
Pl Fld
SUSSEX WAY
GLOUCESTER GDNS
KENT DR
STATION PAR
HEDDON COURT PAR
FRESTON GDNS
LEYS GDNS
BALMORE CRES
MOUNT CL
Middlesex Univ (Cat Hill)
Theatre
De Bohun Prim Sch
Bramley Sp Gd
Oaktree Sch
MANSFIELD AVE
VERNON CRES
RUSTON GDNS
Oak Hill Coll
CANON MOHAN CL
FARM LA
BYRE RD
Monkfrith Prim Sch
CEDAR RISE
MONKFRITH WAY
OAK CL
FRIARS WLK
LANCELOT GDNS
MALLORY GDNS
Tenn Cts
PARKSIDE GDNS
EAST RD
FERNEY RD
WEST RD
WEST WLK
EAST WLK
WOODFIELD DR
BROOKSIDE S
CHURCH HILL RD
Barnet Coll
Allot Gdns
UPLANDS RD
ONSLOW PAR
HAMPDEN SQ
Liby
Brunswick Park Prim Sch
PREVOST RD
LINDEN RD
PINE RD
GARDENERS CL
NURSERYMANS RD
BRUNSWICK PARK GDNS
HOWARD CL
GOLDRILL DR
GRINDLEFORD AVE
CAMBSTONE CL
Brunswick Park
CAVERSHAM CT
BRUNSWICK CRES
BRUNSWICK AVE
BRUNSWICK GR
BRUNSWICK PARK RD
HAYNES CL
Recn Gd
Tenn Cts
Pav
New Southgate Cemetery & Crematorium
Pymme's Brook
Sports Gd
DALE GREEN RD
PYMMES GREEN RD
RIVERSIDE PL
RYHOPE RD
DARWIN CL
MARSHALL
FALKLAND AVE
MARNE AVE
New Southgate
MORTON WAY
CORRI AVE
TOWNSEND AVE
FORESTDALE
Allot Gdns
RAITH AVE
ARNOS GR
LANGSIDE CRES
BRYCEDALE CRES
ABBOTSHALL AVE
CHANDOS AVE
MINCHENDEN CRES
Cemy
ASHFIELD RD
WATERFALL CL
ALLOA CT
Walker Prim Sch
Crkt Gd
Tenn Cts
Pav
MAYFIELD AVE
ELLINGTON CT
BALAAMS LA
MINCHENDEN CT
Southgate Coll
Ashmole Sch
Osidge
Pl Flds
BLAGDEN'S LA
BRAMFORD CT
THE CLOSE
MANOR CT
LEIGH HUNT DR
Osidge JMI Sch
St Andrew's CE Prim Sch
Southgate
CROWN LA
BURLEIGH GDNS
Allot Gdns
IVY RD
MAYFAIR TERR
HILLSIDE GR
GROVELANDS CT
NICHOL CL
L Ctr
RALEIGH WAY
WYNCHGATE
QUEEN ELIZABETH'S DR
TUDOR WAY
GRANGE GDNS
OAKWOOD AVE
OAKWOOD PARK RD
OAKWOOD VIEW
FOUNTAINS CRES
Oakwood Park
Tenn Cts
Pav
Wolfson Hillel Prim Sch
DALRYMPLE CL
CHELMSFORD RD
OLD FARM AVE
LINDEN WAY
CHARTER WAY
FAIRLAWN CL
OAKWOOD CL
CHASE RD
SAXON WAY
Oakwood
MERRIVALE
SHERINGHAM AVE
RUSSEL CT
PRINCE GEORGE AVE
CARLTON AVE
SOUTH LODGE DR
GROSVENOR GDNS
BELGRAVE GDNS
WOLVERTON WAY
CHESTNUT CL
LAKENHEATH
Allot Gdns
ASHRIDGE CT
RESERVOIR RD
STAFFORD CL
ALEXANDRA CT
GERRARDS CL
THE PINES
MALCOLMS WAY
MERRYHILLS CT
Sch
PI Fld
Liby
THE HAVEN
ADDISON AVE
MASEFIELD CRES
THE FAIRWAY
BUSH FAIR CT
HOOD AVE
TRENT GDNS
DE BOHUN AVE
MONKFRITH AVE
TAVISTOCK PL
COWPER GDNS
LINDEN CL
LOUSADA LO
SPEYSIDE
AVENUE RD
ORCHARD CT
BEARDOW GR
CRICKETERS CL
GROSVENOR CT
BEVERLEY CT
FARM LEIGH
NURSERY RD
ISABELLA CL
PINE CL
WINDSOR CT
RAMSEY WAY
Sch
DORCHESTER CT
ROSEDALE LO
WOODMERE CT
ASHLEIGH CT
GROVE CL
ORCHID RD
LEWIS CL
GRANT CL
MANOR DR
SHAMROCK WAY
OAKDALE
CECIL RD
COWPER RD
THE WOODLANDS
CHASE WAY
ARLINGTON RD
SUMMIT WAY
SUMMIT CL
UNDERNE AVE
MANDEVILLE RD
LINCOLN AVE
HAMPDEN WAY
WHITEHOUSE WAY
MARLBOROUGH
ORCHID LO 1
ORCHID GRANGE 2
HENLEY CT 3
MARLOW CT 4
HEATHDENE 5
1 CHELMSFORD CT
2 NORTHBOURNE HO
3 DENLEIGH CT
4 MANESTY CT
5 DENE HO
1 CROWN PAR
2 BUSH CT
SHAKESPEARE HO 1
ASHCROFT 2
WHITE HOUSE CT 3
MEADWAY
NORMAN WAY
Bwg Gn
BOURNE AVE
PARKWAY
Allot Gdns
LONSDALE
OVERTON RD
CLIFTON GDNS
BRANTWOOD GDNS
CURTHWAITE GDNS
BRAYTON GDNS
MERRYHILLS
Oakwood

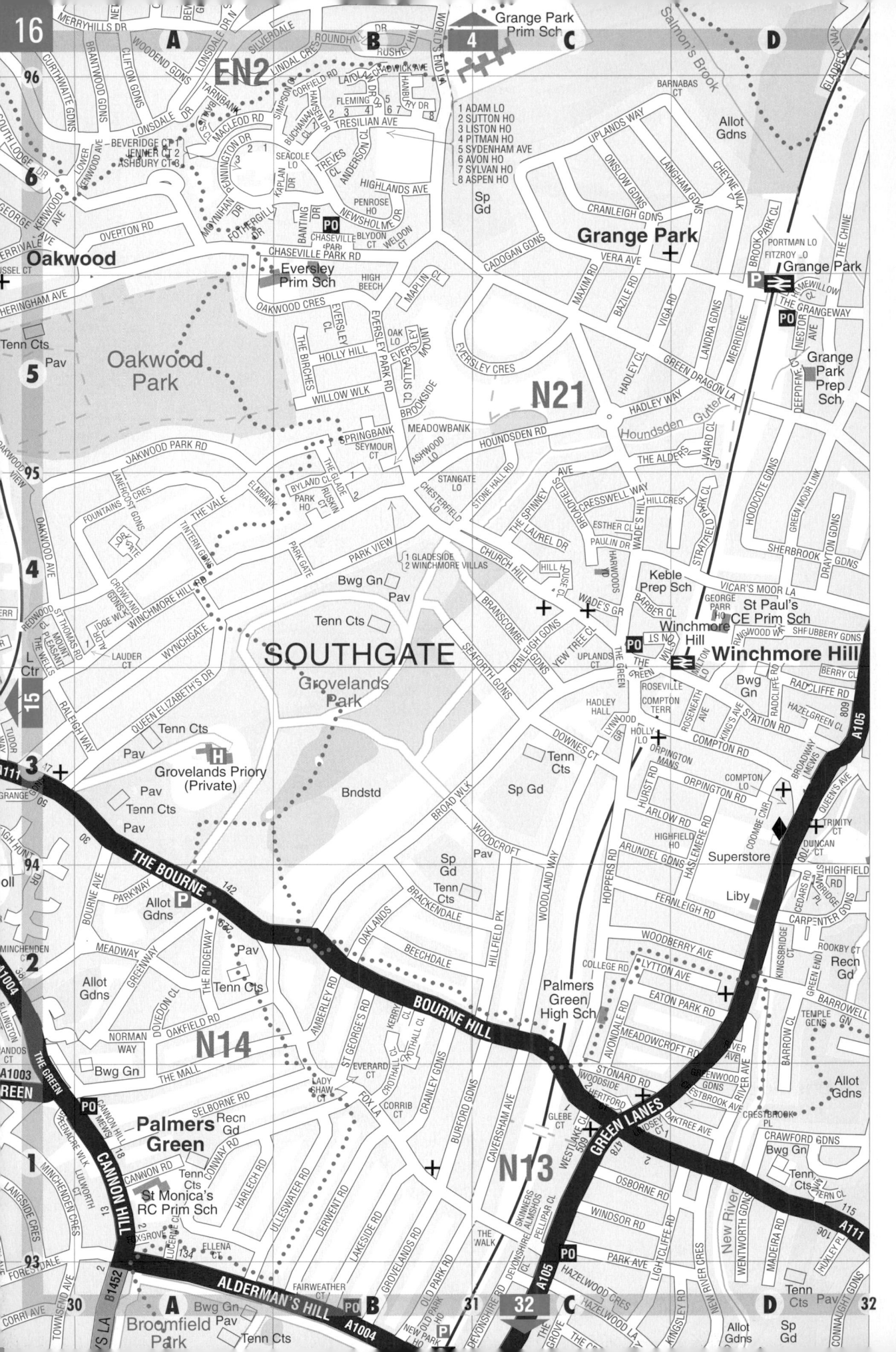
A
B
C
D
4
Grange Park Prim Sch
EN2
N21
N14
N13
Oakwood
Oakwood Park
Grange Park
Winchmore Hill
SOUTHGATE
Grovelands Park
Grovelands Priory (Private)
Palmers Green
Palmers Green High Sch
Eversley Prim Sch
Keble Prep Sch
St Paul's CE Prim Sch
Grange Park Prep Sch
St Monica's RC Prim Sch
Broomfield Park
Salmon's Brook
Houndsden Gutter
New River
THE BOURNE
BOURNE HILL
GREEN LANES
CANNON HILL
ALDERMAN'S HILL
A105
A111
A1004
A1003
B1452
CHASEVILLE PARK RD
HOUNDSDEN RD
WINCHMORE HILL RD
OAKWOOD PARK RD
GREEN DRAGON LA
1 ADAM LO
2 SUTTON HO
3 LISTON HO
4 PITMAN HO
5 SYDENHAM AVE
6 AVON HO
7 SYLVAN HO
8 ASPEN HO
1 GLADESIDE
2 WINCHMORE VILLAS
96
95
94
93
6
5
4
3
2
1
15
30
31
32

A
B
C
D
5
EN2
Bush Hill Park
CH
Town Park
Tenn Cts
ESSEX RD
TIPTREE CT
SALISBURY CT
PARK CRES
WALSINGHAM RD
UVEDALE RD
WHITETHORN GDNS
AMWELL CL
PRINCESSA CT
A105
PARK AVE
BLAKENEY CL
GARFIELD
PRIVATE RD
POTTERSFIELD
Crkt Gd
Tenn Cts
VILLAGE RD
EASTLEIGH CT
BRACKLANDS
Riverside Park
LAURA CL
FORSYTH PL
Tenn Cts
ATHOLE GDNS
WINCHESTER CL
MORTIMER DR
HAYDON CL
REGENCY CT
WALNUT GR
ADAMSRILL CL
RINGMER PL
CARRS LA
BUSH HILL
QUAKERS WLK
THE ORCHARD
ORCHARDMEDE
FAVERSHAM AVE
TEYNHAM AVE
SITTINGBOURNE AVE
MYLNE HO 1
FREAME HO 2
AISLOBIE HO 3
TRITTON HO 4
BRAIKENRIDGE HO 5
METHERELL HO 6
HALLIWICK HO 7
Bush Hill
New River
OLD PARK RIDINGS
OLD PARK GR
OLD PARK AVE
RIDINGS AVE
PARK DR
GRANGE PARK AVE
ELMSCOTT GDNS
CUNARD CRES
CLARENDON WAY
BUSH HILL
MYDDELTON GDNS
BUSH HILL RD
BERKELEY GDNS
CRANWICH AVE
BORDEN AVE
VILLAGE RD
WESTWOOD CT
COWPER GDNS
QUEEN ANNE'S GR
CONSTANCE RD
VILLAGE PARK CL
ROYAL CT
FRAMFIELD CT
QUEEN ANNE'S GDNS
LINGFIELD CL
WOODLEA LO
KENWOOD
FOXWOOD GREEN CL
WELLINGTON RD
ANSTEY LO
CANNOCK LO
DRYDEN RD
QUEEN ANNE'S PL
PARK AVE
Bush Hill Park
EDENBRIDGE RD
SUMMERHILL GR
GARDENIA RD
MANORWAY
THE BRACKENS
CROSSWAY
BRENDON WAY
BIDEFORD GDNS
ASH GR
Raglan Jun & Inf Schs
RAGLAN RD
Tenn Cts
Bwg Gn
LONGLEAT RD
SAMBROOKE CT
ABBEY RD
ILLINGWORTH WAY
DOWNS RD
FOTHERINGHAM RD
KINGSWOOD CL
LINCOLN CRES
EAST CRES
Recn Gd
LC
Bush Hill Park
INGRAM CT
WENDY CL
MELBOURNE WAY
HARMAN RD
JOHN ST
CHARLES ST
JAMES ST
AGRICOLA PL
HADRIAN'S RIDE
WATERHEDGE MEWS
Liby
MAIN AVE
SECOND AVE
FIRST AVE
THIRD AVE
TWEEDY CL
ST MARK'S RD
LADBROKE RD
MILLAIS RD
POYNTER RD
LANDSEER RD
ROMAN WAY
PERCIVAL RD
BERTRAM RD
LINCOLN RD
ERMINE SIDE
Prim Sch
96
6
LEIGHTON RD
ALBERTA RD
HAZELWOOD RD
TRINITY AVE
HAILEYBURY AVE
HARROW AVE
WOODGRANGE TERR
A10
5
LYNMOUTH AVE
BAGSHOT RD
AMBERLEY RD
COUNTISBURY AVE
DELHI RD
EN1
DIMSDALE DR
HAZEL GR
CHATSWORTH DR
95
HAMILTON AVE
Edmonton Cty Upper Sch
SENNEN RD
PORLOCK RD
LATHKILL CL
4
HAMILTON RD
HICKORY CL
EDWARD CL
LAWN CL
WARREN CRES
BURY ST
18
TRANMERE RD
DARLEY RD
HARROW DR
RUGBY AVE
FALMAN CL
BURY ST
CROYLAND RD
3
Recn Gd
Churchfield Prim Sch
LANCING GDNS
MALVERN TERR
LATYMER RD
STOWE GDNS
GLASTONBURY RD
MARLBOROUGH RD
WINCHESTER RD
CHICHESTER RD
94
BURY HALL VILLAS
LYNFORD TERR
CRAWLEY RD
LYNTON GDNS
AMBERLEY GDNS
CAMBRIDGE TERR
BURY ST W
Recn Gd
Pav
Bwg Gn
CLOVELLY GDNS
WESTVIEW CRES
RAMSCROFT CL
LITTLE BURY ST
BLAKESWARE GDNS
ALDBURY MEWS
Edmonton Cty Lower Sch
Allot Gdns
AINSLEY CL
CHURCHILL CT
GREAT CAMBRIDGE RD
Salmon's Brook
Allot Gdns
Allot Gdns
Sp Gds
Tenn Cts
Bwg Gn
Pav
RIDGE AVE
BRIDGE PAR
DEVONSHIRE GDNS
OXFORD GDNS
CAMBRIDGE GDNS
AVENUE PAR
Tenn Cts
BUSH HILL PAR
B154
Liby
Tenn Cts
RIDGE TERR
BRIDGE GATE
ELSIEDENE RD
MURLEY CT
RIVER BANK
ELM PARK RD
BEAULIEU GDNS
BLENHEIM CT
FIRS LA
PERCY RD
SOLNA RD
KENT RD
COLNE RD
YORK RD
CARLTON RD
Pav
Tenn Cts
The Paulin Gd
N21
RIDGE RD
HALSTEAD RD
ROWANTREE RD
ROWANTREE CL
HALSTEAD GDNS
FORD'S GR
FIRS PARK AVE
HYDEFIELD CL
FIRS PARK GDNS
BEVERLEY CL
FARM RD
Pl Fld
Highfield Jun & Inf Sch
BRENDON VILLAS
WELBECK VILLAS
LABURNUM GR
HYDE PARK GDNS
HYDE PARK AVE
LABURNUM GDNS
Winchmore Sch
Edmonton Cemy
Tenn Cts
CHURCH ST
HYDEFIELD CT
Recn Gd
Pav
N9
CEDARS CT
TILLOTSON RD
ARTHUR RD
STANLEY RD
STREAMSIDE CL
ST ANN'S RD
ST JOAN'S RD
CYPRUS RD
WILDFIELD GDNS
CHURCH LA
WIMBORNE RD
DURHAM RD
LICHFIELD RD
2
LAMB'S CL
MILES
RUSK WLK
COSGROVE CL
Sp Gd
Pav
FIRS LA
Firs Farm Pl Flds
KIPLING TERR
LATYMER WAY
LAMB'S TERR
WHEATLEY GDNS
The Latymer Sch
GATWARD GN
LABURNUM AVE
HAWTHORNE WAY
HYDESIDE GDNS
HYDE WAY
Latymer All Saints CE Prim Sch
ALL SAINTS CL
HYDETHORPE AVE
GRANHAM GDNS
CHAMBERLAIN RD
ROSEBERY RD
SALISBURY
B154
Sch
BARROWELL GN
Allot Gdns
FARNDALE AVE
ENSIGN DR
Allot Gdns
ASH GR
Firs Farm Prim Sch
DEANSWAY
PERRY GDNS
West Lea Sch
NORTHERN AVE
CENTRAL AVE
DUNHOLME GN
NORTHUMBERLAND GDNS
WEST CL
MALDON RD
CHAUNCEY CL
BARBOT CL
1
RAYLEIGH RD
RAYLEIGH CL
HARLOW RD
FIRSCROFT
THE LARCHES
THE FAIRWAY
Pl Fld
VICTOR VILLAS
BANSTEAD GDNS
BEXLEY GDNS
PURLEY RD
SELHURST RD
BECKENHAM GDNS
Hazelbury Jun & Inf Schs
HASELBURY RD
CHALFONT RD
CHALFONT RD
SWEET BRIAR GR
SOUTH EASTERN AVE
DUNHOLME RD
PYMMES GDNS N
PYMMES GDNS S
SUNNYSIDE RD N
LEONARD RD
SUNNYSIDE RD E
SUNNYSIDE RD S
SHRUBBERY
THE ROWANS
BIRCH AVE
N13
MYRTLE RD
CONISCLIFFE RD
BRIAR CL
HAZEL CL
RYLSTON RD
PEMBROKE RD
WESTERHAM AVE
KESTON CL
ORPINGTON GDNS
HAZELBURY LA
HAZELBURY GN
BRIARY LA
SWEET BRIAR GN
DUNHOLME LA
VICTORIA RD
PYCROFT WAY
93
HEDGE LA
NEW PARK AVE
BROMLEY RD
SHORTLANDS CL
CHEDDINGTON RD
PARK LA
PARK LA
Tatem Park
PARKSIDE TERR
N18
HUXLEY RD
TUNCOMBE RD
Pl Flds
32
A
B
33
C
D
34
A111
DORCHESTER AVE
ULSTER GDNS
Hollywood Gardens
A10
KENDAL AVE
Aylward
HENLEY RD
LOPEN WORKS
BULWER RD
SHELDON RD
WARWICK RD
SWEET BRIAR WLK
DENTON RD
Pymmes Park

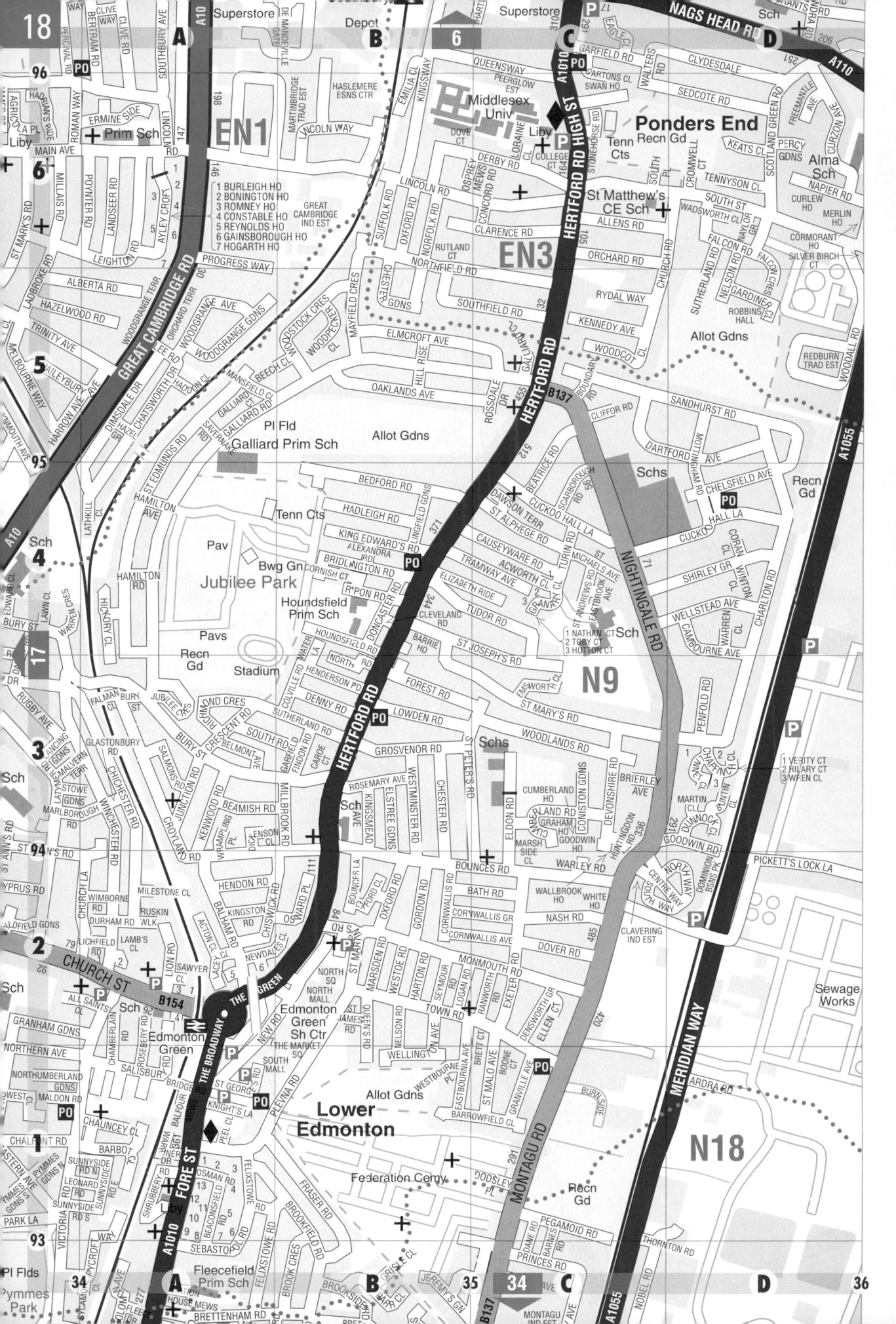

A
B
C
D
6
Superstore
Depot
Superstore
NAGS HEAD RD
A110
A10
A1010
EN1
EN3
N9
N18
Ponders End
Lower Edmonton
Middlesex Univ
Liby
Prim Sch
Recn Gd
Tenn Cts
Alma Sch
St Matthew's CE Sch
HASLEMERE ESNS CTR
GREAT CAMBRIDGE IND EST
MARTINBRIDGE TRAD EST
REDBURN TRAD EST
Allot Gdns
Pl Fld
Galliard Prim Sch
Jubilee Park
Pav
Pavs
Bwg Gn
Tenn Cts
Houndsfield Prim Sch
Stadium
Schs
Sch
Edmonton Green
Edmonton Green Sh Ctr
Fleecefield Prim Sch
Federation Cemy
Sewage Works
CLAVERING IND EST
DOMINION BSNS PK
1 BURLEIGH HO
2 BONINGTON HO
3 ROMNEY HO
4 CONSTABLE HO
5 REYNOLDS HO
6 GAINSBOROUGH HO
7 HOGARTH HO
1 NATHAN CT
2 TOBY CT
3 HUTTON CT
1 VERITY CT
2 HILARY CT
3 WREN CL
GREAT CAMBRIDGE RD
HERTFORD RD HIGH ST
HERTFORD RD
NIGHTINGALE RD
MONTAGU RD
MERIDIAN WAY
FORE ST
THE BROADWAY
THE GREEN
CHURCH ST
B154
B137
A1055
QUEENSWAY
LINCOLN WAY
LINCOLN RD
PROGRESS WAY
ALBERTA RD
HAZELWOOD RD
TRINITY AVE
MELBOURNE WAY
HARROW AVE
WOODGRANGE AVE
WOODGRANGE GDNS
WOODGRANGE TERR
ORCHARD TERR
ELMCROFT AVE
OAKLANDS AVE
HILL RISE
MAYFIELD CRES
SOUTHFIELD RD
NORTHFIELD RD
CLARENCE RD
RUTLAND CT
SUFFOLK RD
OXFORD RD
NORFOLK RD
CONCORD RD
DERBY RD
COLLEGE CT
ALLENS RD
ORCHARD RD
RYDAL WAY
KENNEDY AVE
WOODCOT CL
CHURCH RD
SOUTH ST
SUTHERLAND RD
NELSON RD
FALCON RD
GARDINER CL
SANDHURST RD
DARTFORD AVE
CHELSFIELD AVE
CUCKOO HALL LA
CORAN CL
WINTON CL
SHIRLEY GR
WELLSTEAD AVE
WARREN CL
CHARLTON RD
CAMBOURNE AVE
PENFOLD RD
BEDFORD RD
HADLEIGH RD
KING EDWARD'S RD
BRIDLINGTON RD
DONCASTER RD
CLEVELAND RD
ST JOSEPH'S RD
FOREST RD
ST MARY'S RD
WOODLANDS RD
LOWDEN RD
GROSVENOR RD
ROSEMARY AVE
WESTMINSTER RD
CHESTER RD
KINGSMEAD
ELSTREE GDNS
ELDON RD
CONISTON GDNS
DEVONSHIRE RD
BRIERLEY AVE
GOODWIN RD
BOUNCES RD
BATH RD
NASH RD
DOVER RD
CORNWALLIS AVE
MONMOUTH RD
TOWN RD
WELLINGTON AVE
BARROWFIELD CL
PICKETT'S LOCK LA
ARDRA RD
PEGAMOID RD
PRINCES RD
THORNTON RD
NOBEL RD
PLEVNA RD
FRASER RD
BROOKFIELD RD
FELIXSTOWE RD
SEBASTOPOL RD
CHAUNCEY CL
NORTHERN AVE
GRANHAM GDNS
ST ANN'S RD
MILESTONE CL
HENDON RD
BRETTENHAM RD
Pymmes Park
Pl Flds
17
34
35
36

King George's Resr
EN3
LEA VALLEY RD
Ponders End
MERIDIAN WAY
WHARF RD
VALLEYLINK EST
Works
RIVERSIDE EST
MORSON RD
River Lea or Lee
River Lea or Lea Diversion
SEWARDSTONE RD
Yardley Hill
Sch
Yardley Prim Sch
HAWKWOOD CRES
Allot Gdns
EPPING WAY
CHELWOOD CL
AMESBURY DR
REDWOOD GDNS
DELLS CL
MARKFIELD GDNS
KINGS HEAD HILL
Pole Hill
Chingford Green
LAUREL GDNS
MERRYHILL CL
MAIDA AVE
LOW HALL CL
COLLEGE GDNS
ENTERPRISE HO
A110
Lee Valley Wlk
Lee Valley L Ctr
Lee Valley Leisure
N9
River Lee Navigation
William Girling Resr
E4
Pl Fld
MANSFIELD HILL
Mansfield Park
VALLEY SIDE
WALTHAM WAY
A1037
Chingford Sch
MOUNT ECHO DR
B169 THE RIDGEWAY
Ridgeway Park
OLD CHURCH RD
Wellington Prim Sch
CHINGFORD AVE
MORELAND WAY
Cemy
PRIORY AVE
LEADALE AVE
HERIOT AVE
BRINDWOOD RD
RECTORY CL
MIDDLETON AVE
CHERRYDOWN AVE
Allot Gdns
Larkswood Sch
NEW RD
A1009
A112
Liby
PICKETT'S LOCK LA
LEE PARK WAY
MARMION AVE
36
37
38
35
7
20

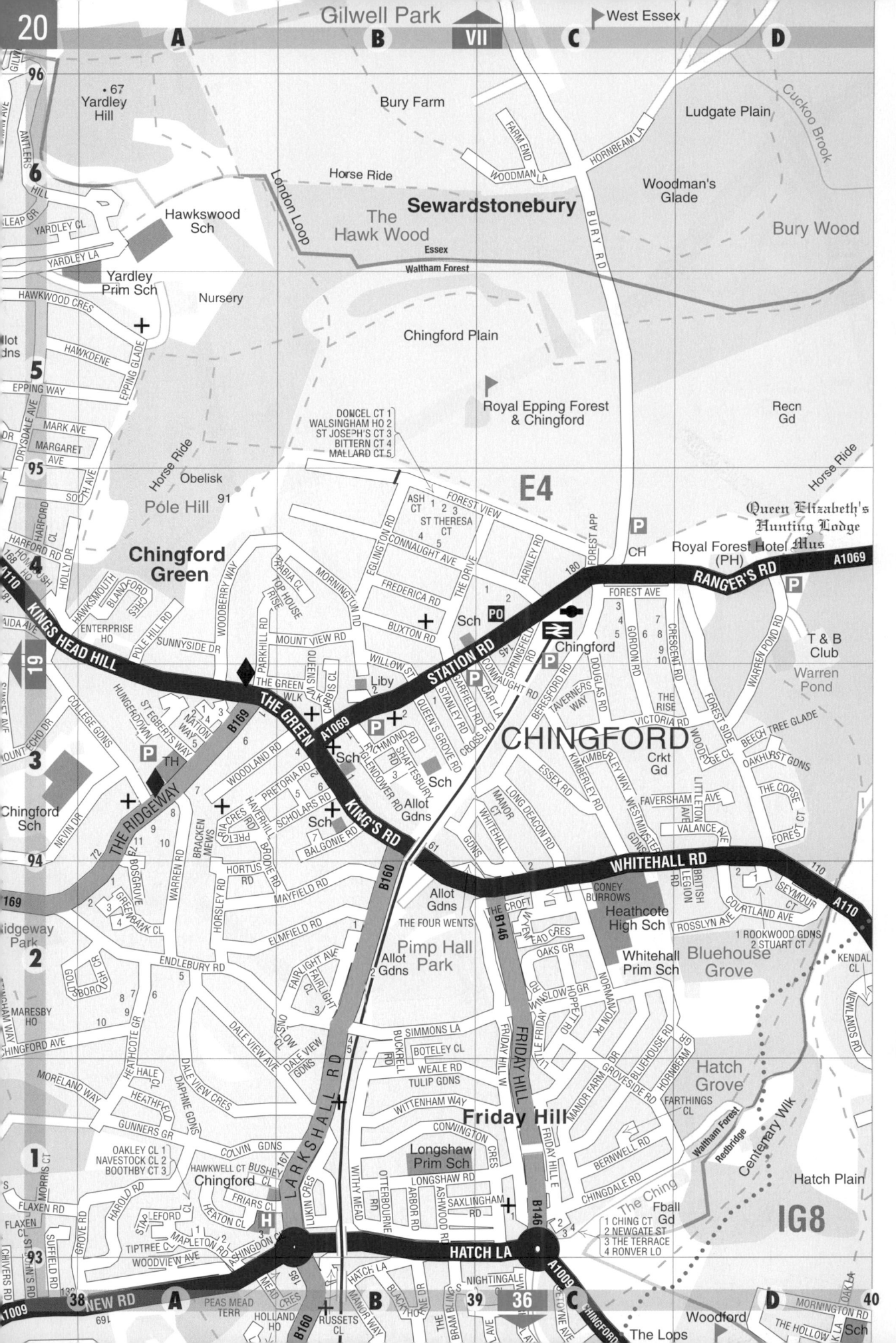
Gilwell Park
West Essex
A
B
VII
C
D
96
6
5
4
95
3
94
2
1
93
38
39
36
40
Yardley Hill
67
Bury Farm
Ludgate Plain
Cuckoo Brook
FARM END
HORNBEAM LA
WOODMAN LA
ANTLERS HILL
Horse Ride
London Loop
Woodman's Glade
Hawkswood Sch
Sewardstonebury
The Hawk Wood
Bury Wood
YARDLEY CL
YARDLEY LA
Essex
Waltham Forest
BURY RD
Yardley Prim Sch
Nursery
HAWKWOOD CRES
HAWKDENE
Chingford Plain
EPPING GLADE
EPPING WAY
Royal Epping Forest & Chingford
Recn Gd
MARK AVE
MARGARET AVE
DRYSDALE AVE
DONCEL CT 1
WALSINGHAM HO 2
ST JOSEPH'S CT 3
BITTERN CT 4
MALLARD CT 5
Horse Ride
Obelisk
SOUTH AVE
Pole Hill
91
E4
ASH CT
FOREST VIEW
ST THERESA CT
Queen Elizabeth's Hunting Lodge Mus
HARFORD CL
HARFORD RD
HOLLY DR
Chingford Green
EGLINGTON RD
CONNAUGHT AVE
FARNLEY RD
FOREST APP
CH
Royal Forest Hotel (PH)
RANGER'S RD
A1069
A110
KINGS HEAD HILL
HAWKSMOUTH
BLANDFORD CRES
WOODBERRY WAY
ARABIA CL
TOP HOUSE RISE
MORNINGTON RD
FREDERICA RD
THE DRIVE
FOREST AVE
ENTERPRISE HO
POLE HILL RD
SUNNYSIDE DR
PARKHILL RD
MOUNT VIEW RD
BUXTON RD
Sch
PO
Chingford
T & B Club
WARREN POND RD
GORDON RD
CRESCENT RD
Warren Pond
19
COLLEGE GDNS
HUNGERDOWN
ST EGBERTS WAY
NATION WAY
THE GREEN WLK
QUEENS WLK
CARBIS CL
Liby
WILLOW ST
STATION RD
GARFIELD RD
CART LA
CONNAUGHT RD
SPRINGFIELD RD
BERESFORD RD
TAVERNERS WAY
DOUGLAS RD
THE RISE
FOREST SIDE
VICTORIA RD
BEECH TREE GLADE
OAKHURST GDNS
B169
THE GREEN
MOUNT ECHO DR
TH
Sch
RICHMOND RD
SHAFTESBURY
STANLEY RD
QUEEN'S GROVE RD
CROSS RD
CHINGFORD
WOODEDGE CL
Crkt Gd
THE COPSE
KIMBERLEY WAY
KIMBERLEY RD
ESSEX RD
WOODLAND RD
PRETORIA RD
GLENDOWER RD
Allot Gdns
MANOR CT
LONG DEACON RD
FAVERSHAM AVE
LITTLETON AVE
VALANCE AVE
FOREST CT
WESTMINSTER GDNS
Chingford Sch
THE RIDGEWAY
NEVIN DR
BRACKEN MEWS
PRETORIA CRES
HAVERHILL RD
SCHOLARS RD
BALGONIE RD
KING'S RD
WHITEHALL
GDNS
WHITEHALL RD
BRITISH LEGION RD
SEYMOUR CT
HORTUS RD
BRODIE RD
B160
Allot Gdns
CONEY BURROWS
Heathcote High Sch
COURTLAND AVE
BOSGROVE
WARREN RD
HORSLEY RD
MAYFIELD RD
THE CROFT
ROSSLYN AVE
1 ROOKWOOD GDNS
2 STUART CT
Ridgeway Park
GREENBANK CL
ELMFIELD RD
THE FOUR WENTS
B146
MEAD CRES
Whitehall Prim Sch
Bluehouse Grove
KENDAL CL
ENDLEBURY RD
FAIRLIGHT AVE
FAIRLIGHT CL
Pimp Hall Park
Allot Gdns
OAKS GR
GOLDSBOROUGH CR
MARESBY HO
NORMANTON PK
HOPPETT RD
SLOWE GR
NEWLANDS RD
CHINGFORD AVE
HEATHCOTE GR
ONSLOW CL
DALE VIEW AVE
DALE VIEW GDNS
SIMMONS LA
BUCKRELL RD
BOTELEY CL
FRIDAY HILL W
FRIDAY HILL
LITTLE FRIDAY RD
BLUEHOUSE RD
GROVESIDE RD
HORNBEAM GR
MANOR FARM DR
Hatch Grove
MORELAND WAY
HALE
HEATHFIELD
DALE VIEW CRES
DAPHNE GDNS
WEALE RD
TULIP GDNS
WITTENHAM WAY
Friday Hill
FARTHINGS CL
Centenary Wlk
Waltham Forest
Redbridge
GUNNERS GR
LARKSHALL RD
CONNINGTON CRES
COLVIN GDNS
Longshaw Prim Sch
BERNWELL RD
FRIDAY HILL E
OAKLEY CL 1
NAVESTOCK CL 2
BOOTHBY CT 3
MORRIS CT
HAWKWELL CT
BUSHEY CL
Chingford
LUKIN CRES
WITHY MEAD
OTTERBOURNE RD
ARBOR RD
ASHWOOD RD
LONGSHAW RD
CHINGDALE RD
The Ching
Hatch Plain
FLAXEN RD
HAROLD RD
STAPLEFORD CL
FRIARS CL
HEATON CL
SAXLINGHAM RD
Fball Gd
1 CHING CT
2 NEWGATE ST
3 THE TERRACE
4 RONVER LO
IG8
FLAXEN CL
GROVE RD
TIPTREE C
MAPLETON RD
ASHINGDON CL
HATCH LA
SUFFIELD RD
WOODVIEW AVE
CHIVERS RD
ST JOHN'S RD
NEW RD
A1009
PEAS MEAD TERR
HOLLAND HO
RUSSETS CL
HATCH LA
MANOR WAY
BLACKTHORNE DR
NIGHTINGALE
THE BRAMBLINGS
CHINGFORD
OAK LA
MORNINGTON RD
THE HOLLOW
Woodford
The Lops
Sch

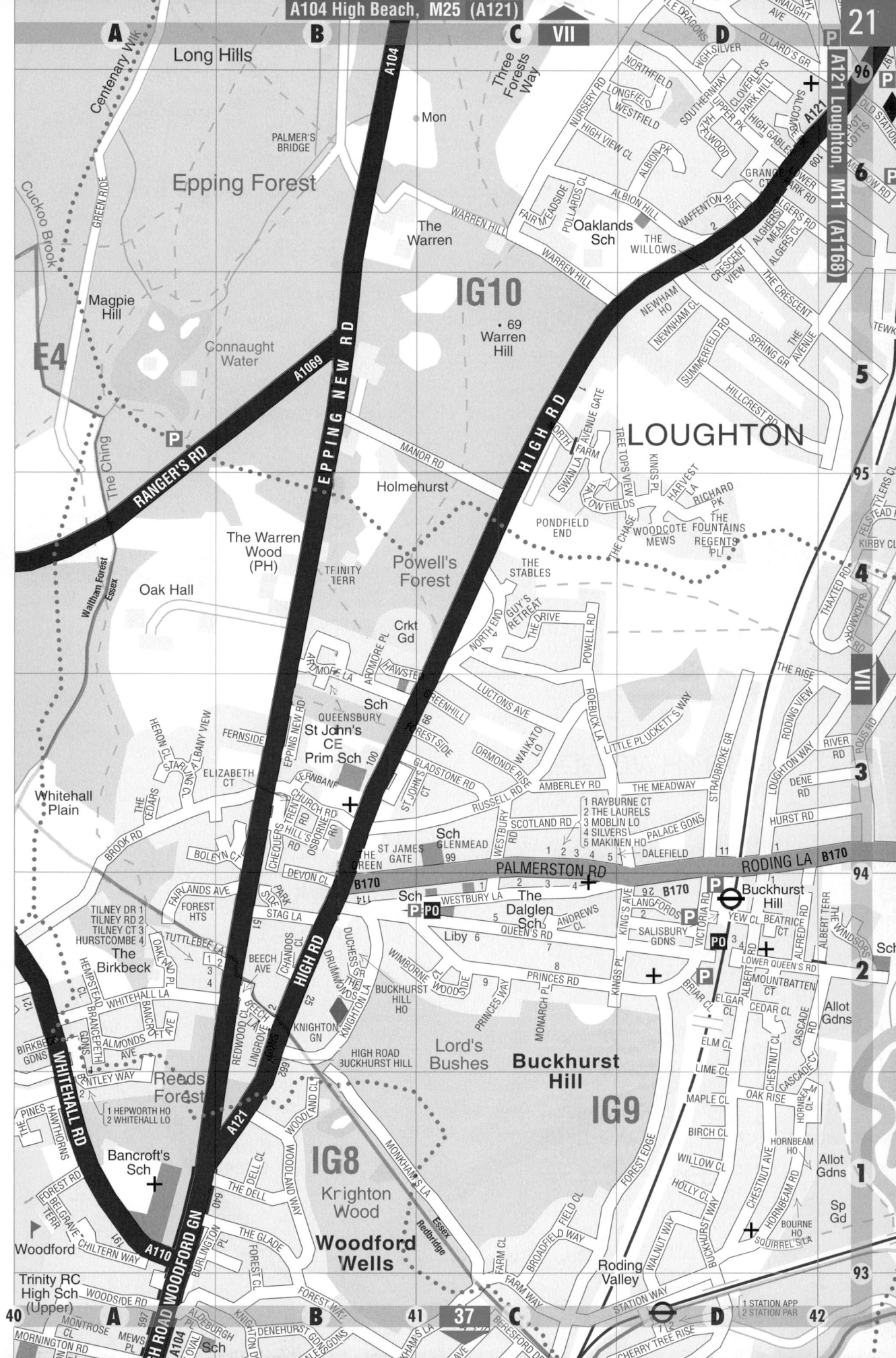
A104 High Beach, M25 (A121)
A121 Loughton, M11 (A1168)
Long Hills
Centenary Wlk
Epping Forest
Three Forests Way
Mon
Palmer's Bridge
Cuckoo Brook
Green Ride
The Warren
Magpie Hill
Connaught Water
IG10
69 Warren Hill
E4
LOUGHTON
Epping New Rd
Ranger's Rd
High Rd
Holmehurst
The Warren Wood (PH)
Powell's Forest
Oak Hall
The Ching
Waltham Forest
Essex
Crkt Gd
Oaklands Sch
The Willows
Pondfield End
The Stables
Manor Rd
Warren Hill
Sch
Queensbury
St John's CE Prim Sch
Whitehall Plain
Palmerston Rd
Roding La
B170
Buckhurst Hill
The Dalglen Sch
Liby
The Birkbeck
Reeds Forest
Lord's Bushes
Buckhurst Hill
IG9
IG8
Bancroft's Sch
Knighton Wood
Woodford Wells
Woodford
Trinity RC High Sch (Upper)
Whitehall Rd
Woodford Gn
A110
A104
Roding Valley
Station Way
Allot Gdns
Sp Gd
1 Rayburne Ct
2 The Laurels
3 Moblin Lo
4 Silvers
5 Makinen Ho
1 Hepworth Ho
2 Whitehall Lo
1 Station App
2 Station Par
Tilney Dr 1
Tilney Rd 2
Tilney Ct 3
Hurstcombe 4
Monkham's La
Redbridge
Essex
40
41
42
37
VII

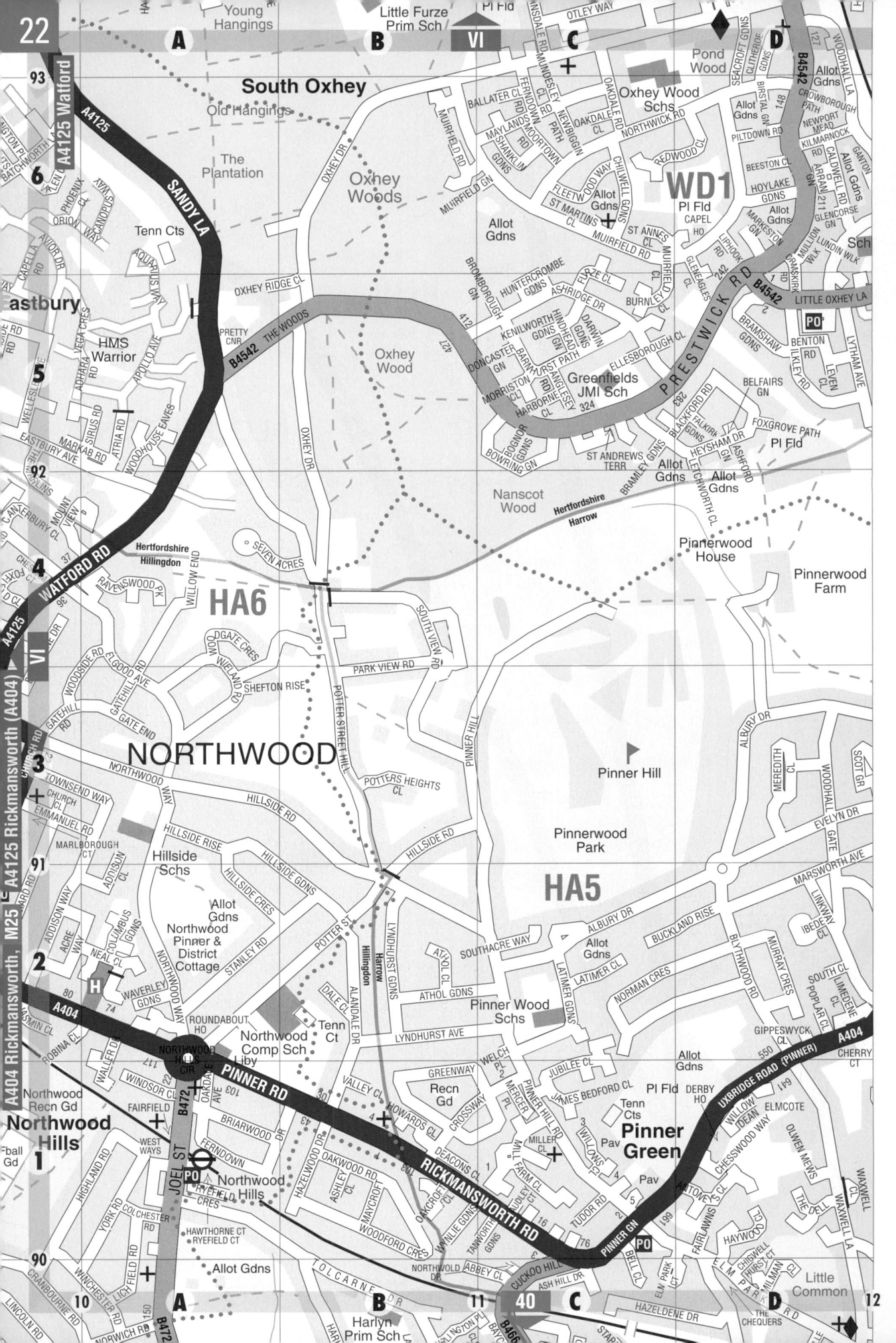
South Oxhey
Oxhey Woods
Oxhey Wood
WD1
Eastbury
HMS Warrior
HA6
NORTHWOOD
Pinner Hill
Pinnerwood Park
HA5
Pinnerwood House
Pinnerwood Farm
Nanscot Wood
Greenfields JMI Sch
Oxhey Wood Schs
Hillside Schs
Northwood Comp Sch
Pinner Wood Schs
Northwood Hills
Pinner Green
Little Common
Harlyn Prim Sch
Little Furze Prim Sch
SANDY LA
WATFORD RD
PRESTWICK RD
RICKMANSWORTH RD
PINNER RD
UXBRIDGE ROAD (PINNER)
JOEL ST
A404 Rickmansworth, M25, A4125 Rickmansworth (A404)
A4125 Watford

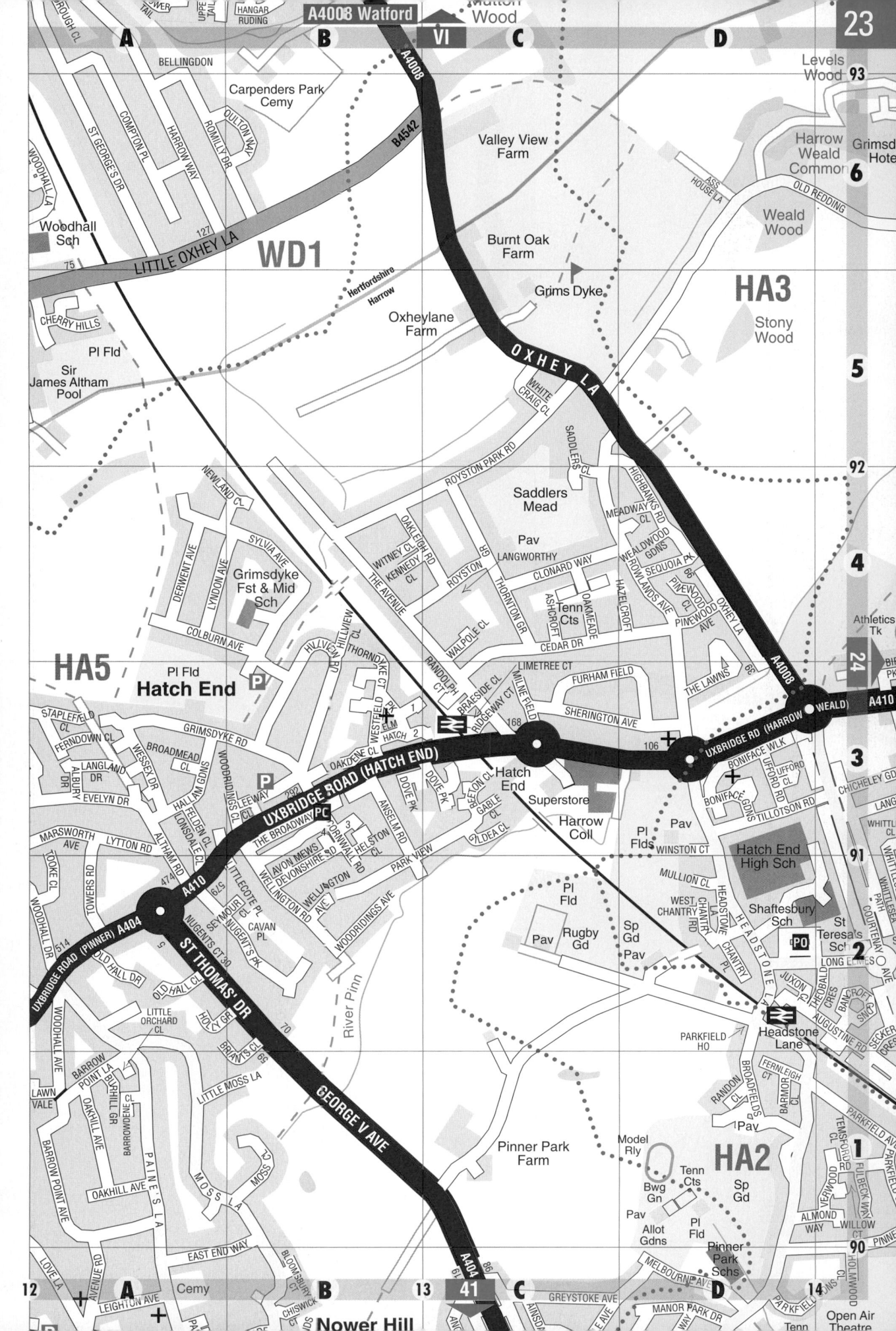
A4008 Watford
Carpenders Park Cemy
Valley View Farm
Burnt Oak Farm
Grims Dyke
Oxheylane Farm
WD1
HA3
HA5
HA2
Harrow Weald Common
Weald Wood
Stony Wood
Levels Wood
Woodhall Sch
Sir James Altham Pool
Pl Fld
Saddlers Mead
Grimsdyke Fst & Mid Sch
Hatch End
Hatch End High Sch
Harrow Coll
Superstore
Shaftesbury Sch
St Teresa's Sch
Headstone Lane
Pinner Park Farm
Pinner Park Schs
Model Rly
River Pinn
Nower Hill
Open Air Theatre
LITTLE OXHEY LA
OXHEY LA
UXBRIDGE ROAD (HATCH END)
UXBRIDGE RD (HARROW WEALD)
UXBRIDGE ROAD (PINNER)
ST THOMAS' DR
GEORGE V AVE
HEADSTONE LA
Hertfordshire
Harrow
A4008
A410
A404
B4542
12
13
14
41
24
VI
93
92
91
90
6
5
4
3
2
1
A
B
C
D

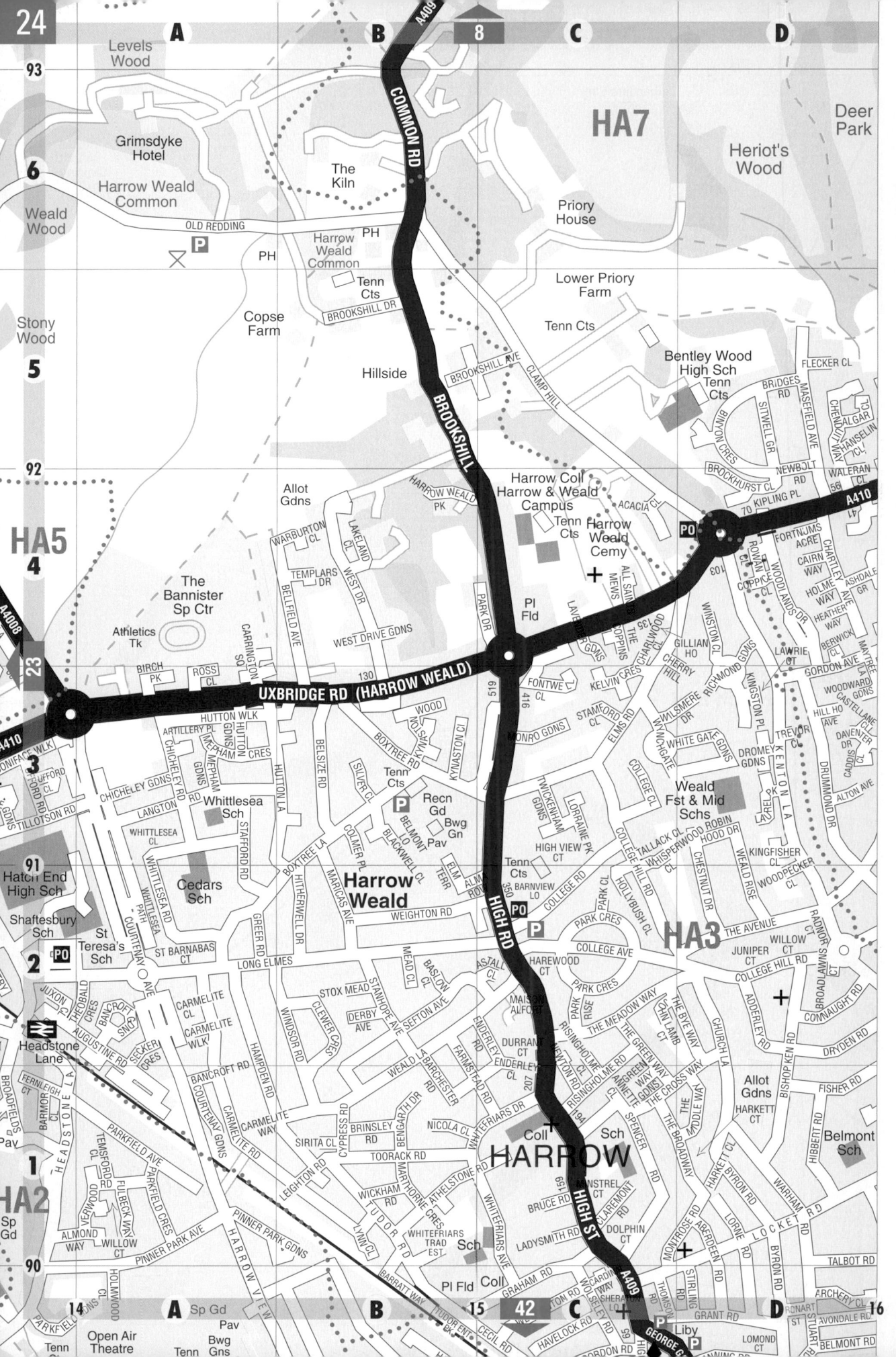

A
B
8
C
D
93
6
5
92
4
3
91
2
1
90
Levels Wood
Grimsdyke Hotel
Harrow Weald Common
Weald Wood
OLD REDDING
COMMON RD
The Kiln
HA7
Deer Park
Heriot's Wood
Priory House
Harrow Weald Common
PH
Tenn Cts
BROOKSHILL DR
Copse Farm
Stony Wood
Lower Priory Farm
Tenn Cts
Hillside
BROOKSHILL AVE
CLAMP HILL
Bentley Wood High Sch
BROOKSHILL
Harrow Coll Harrow & Weald Campus
Harrow Weald Cemy
Allot Gdns
HA5
The Bannister Sp Ctr
Athletics Tk
A4008
A410
UXBRIDGE RD (HARROW WEALD)
PARK DR
Pl Fld
A410
FLECKER CL
BRIDGES RD
MASEFIELD AVE
SITWELL GR
BINYON CRES
BROCKHURST CL
NEWBOLT RD
WALERAN CL
KIPLING PL
FORTNUMS ACRE
CAIRN WAY
HOLME WAY
HEATHER WAY
BERWICK CL
LAWRIE CT
GORDON AVE
WOODWARD GDNS
CASTELLANE CL
HILL HO AVE
DAVENTER DR
CADDIS CL
ALTON AVE
DRUMMOND DR
TREVOR CL
KENTON LA
DROMEY GDNS
Weald Fst & Mid Schs
WARBURTON CL
LAKELAND CL
TEMPLARS DR
WEST DR
BELLFIELD AVE
WEST DRIVE GDNS
CARRINGTON SQ
BIRCH PK
ROSS CL
HUTTON WLK
ARTILLERY PL
HUTTON GDNS
HUTTON CRES
MEPHAM GDNS
MEPHAM CRES
HUTTON LA
BELSIZE RD
BOXTREE RD
KYNASTON CL
SILVER CL
Tenn Cts
Recn Gd
Bwg Gn
Pav
BOXTREE LA
COLMER PL
BELMONT LO
BLACKWELL CL
MARICAS AVE
Harrow Weald
WEIGHTON RD
HIGH RD
BARNVIEW LO
HIGH VIEW CT
Whittlesea Sch
Cedars Sch
Hatch End High Sch
Shaftesbury Sch
St Teresa's Sch
CHICHELEY GDNS
CHICHELEY RD
LANGTON RD
TILLOTSON RD
WHITTLESEA CL
WHITTLESEA RD
WHITTLESEA PATH
STAFFORD RD
GREER RD
HITHERWELL DR
ST BARNABAS CT
LONG ELMES
COURTENAY AVE
CARMELITE CL
CARMELITE WLK
JUXON CL
THEOBALD CRES
BANCROFT GDNS
AUGUSTINE RD
SECKER CRES
Headstone Lane
BANCROFT RD
HAMPDEN RD
WINDSOR RD
STOX MEAD
DERBY AVE
CLEWER CRES
STANHOPE AVE
SEFTON AVE
MEAD CL
BASLOW CL
ASTALL CL
HAREWOOD CT
MAISON ALFORT
PARK CRES
COLLEGE AVE
PARK RISE
THE MEADOW WAY
HA3
THE AVENUE
JUNIPER CT
WILLOW CT
COLLEGE HILL RD
RADNOR CL
BROADLAWNS CT
CONNAUGHT RD
ADDERLEY RD
DRYDEN RD
BISHOP KEN RD
FISHER RD
Allot Gdns
HARKETT CT
HIBBERT RD
Belmont Sch
HARROW
HIGH ST
Coll
Sch
Pl Fld
Coll
BRUCE RD
LADYSMITH RD
DOLPHIN CT
MINSTREL CT
CLAREMONT RD
GRAHAM RD
A409
GEORGE GDNS
TALBOT RD
ARCHERY CL
AVONDALE RD
BELMONT RD
GRANT RD
LOMOND CT
Liby
HA2
Sp Gd
ALMOND WAY
WILLOW CT
PINNER PARK AVE
PINNER PARK GDNS
HARROW VIEW
PARKFIELD AVE
PARKFIELD CRES
TEMSFORD CL
FULBECK WAY
VERWOOD RD
HEADSTONE LA
BROADFIELDS
Pav
BARMOR CL
FERNLEIGH CT
HOLMWOOD RD
14
A
Sp Gd
B
15
42
C
D
16
Open Air Theatre
Tenn
Bwg Gns
Pav
BARRATT WAY
TUDOR ENT PK
CECIL RD
HAVELOCK RD
WOLSELEY RD
SHERATON WAY
THOMSON RD
STIRLING RD
ABERDEEN RD
MONTROSE RD
LORNE RD
LOCKET RD
BYRON RD
WARHAM RD
HARKETT CL
THE BROADWAY
THE MIDDLE WAY
SPENCER RD
WHITEFRIARS AVE
WHITEFRIARS DR
WHITEFRIARS TRAD EST
WICKHAM RD
MARTHORNE CRES
ATHELSTONE RD
TUDOR RD
LYNN CL
TOORACK RD
BRINSLEY RD
BENGARTH DR
NICOLA CL
CYPRESS RD
SIRITA CL
LEIGHTON RD
CARMELITE WAY
CARMELITE RD
COURTENAY GDNS
ENDERLEY RD
ENDERLEY CL
DURRANT CT
FARMSTEAD RD
BARCHESTER RD
WEALD LA
RISINGHOLME RD
RISINGHOLME CL
KENTON RD
THE GREEN WAY
ANNETTE CL
GREEN WAY GDNS
THE CROSS WAY
CHURCH LA
THE BYE WAY
JOHN LAMB CT
COLLEGE RD
PARK CL
HOLLYBUSH CL
COLLEGE HILL RD
TALLACK CL
WHISPERWOOD CL
ROBIN HOOD DR
CHESTNUT DR
WEALD RISE
KINGFISHER CL
WOODPECKER CL
TWICKENHAM GDNS
LORRAINE PK
MONRO GDNS
STAMFORD CL
ELMS RD
COLLEGE CL
FONTWELL CL
KELVIN CRES
CHARLWOOD CL
CHERRY HILL
WILSMERE DR
WYNCHGATE
WHITE GATE GDNS
RICHMOND GDNS
KINGSTON PL
GILLIAN HO
WINSTON CL
ROWAN CL
COPPICE CL
WOODLANDS DR
CHARTLEY AVE
ASHDALE GR
LAVENDER GDNS
ALL SAINTS MEWS
COPPINS THE
ACACIA CL
HARROW WEALD PK
ELM TERR
ALMA ROW

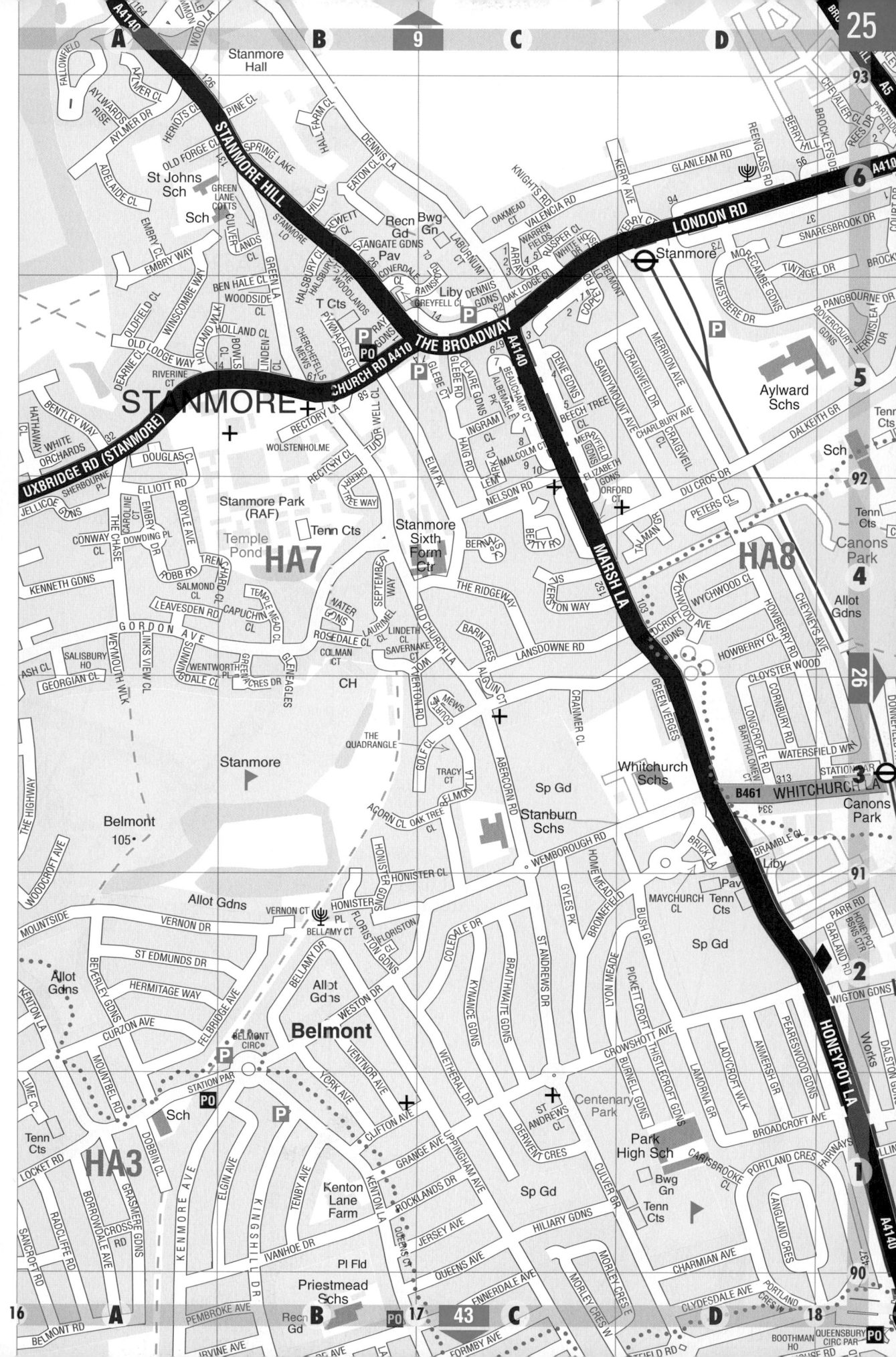
A
B
9
C
D
6
5
4
3
2
1
16
17
43
18
26
93
92
91
90
A4140
A410
A5
A5
B461
STANMORE
Stanmore Hall
FALLOWFIELD
AYLMER CL
AYLWARDS RISE
AYLMER DR
HERIOTS CL
PINE CL
STANMORE HILL
SPRING LAKE
OLD FORGE CL
ADELAIDE CL
St Johns Sch
GREEN LANE COTTS
Sch
CULVERLANDS
EMBRY CL
EMBRY WAY
WINSCOMBE WAY
BEN HALE CL
WOODSIDE CL
OLDFIELD CL
HOLLAND WLK
HOLLAND CL
OLD LODGE WAY
DEARNE CL
BOWLS
LINDEN
RIVERINE CT
GREEN LA
STANMORE LO
HALL FARM CL
DENNIS LA
EATON CL
HILL CL
HEWETT CL
STANGATE GDNS
Recn Gd
Bwg Gn
Pav
COVERDALE CL
RAINSFORD CL
LABURNUM CT
HALSBURY CL
THE WOODLANDS
T Cts
PINNACLES CL
CHERCHEFELLS MEWS
Liby
GREYFELL CL
DENNIS GDNS
THE BROADWAY
CHURCH RD A410
PO
P
GLEBE CT
GLEBE RD
CLAIRE GDNS
INGRAM CL
BEAUCHAMP CT
ALBEMARLE PK
HAIG RD
MALCOLM CT
NELSON RD
OAKMEAD CT
KNIGHTS RD
VALENCIA RD
WARREN FIELDS
RUSPER CL
ARRAN DR
WHITE HOUSE DR
OAK LODGE CL
KERRY AVE
KERRY CT
BELMONT
COPLEY RD
DENE GDNS
BEECH TREE CL
MERRYFIELD GDNS
ELIZABETH GDNS
ORFORD CT
SANDYMOUNT AVE
CRAIGWEIL DR
MERRION AVE
CHARLBURY AVE
CRAIGWEIL CL
GLANLEAM RD
REENGLASS RD
LONDON RD
Stanmore
MORECAMBE GDNS
WESTBERE DR
TINTAGEL DR
SNARESBROOK DR
COURT DR
BROCKLEY
PANGBOURNE DR
DOVERCOURT GDNS
HERONSLEA DR
CHEVALIER CL
BERRY HILL
BROCKLEYSIDE
REES DR
PARTRIDGE
Aylward Schs
DALKEITH GR
Tenn Cts
Sch
DU CROS DR
PETERS CL
TALMAN GR
Canons Park
HA8
Allot Gdns
WYCHWOOD CL
WYCHWOOD AVE
CROFT GDNS
HOWBERRY CL
HOWBERRY RD
CHEYNEYS AVE
CLOYSTER WOOD
CORNBURY RD
LONGCROFTE RD
BARTHOLOMEW CT
WATERSFIELD WAY
STATION PAR
WHITCHURCH LA
DONNEFIELD AVE
Canons Park
UXBRIDGE RD (STANMORE)
BENTLEY WAY
HATHAWAY CL
WHITE ORCHARDS
SHERBOURNE PL
JELLICOE GDNS
DOUGLAS CL
ELLIOTT RD
RECTORY LA
WOLSTENHOLME
RECTORY CL
CHERRY TREE WAY
TUDOR WELL CL
Stanmore Park (RAF)
Temple Pond
HA7
Tenn Cts
Stanmore Sixth Form Ctr
ELM PK
BERNAYS CL
BEATTY RD
CAROLINE CT
EMBRY DR
BOYLE AVE
DOWDING PL
THE CHASE
CONWAY CL
ROBB RD
TRENCHARD CL
SALMOND CL
KENNETH GDNS
LEAVESDEN RD
CAPUCHIN CL
TEMPLE MEAD CL
WATER GDNS
SEPTEMBER WAY
LAURIMEL CL
LINDETH CL
SAVERNAKE CT
ROSEDALE CL
COLMAN CT
OLD CHURCH LA
THE RIDGEWAY
VERSTON WAY
MARSH LA
BARN CRES
LANSDOWNE RD
GORDON AVE
SALISBURY HO
ASH CL
GEORGIAN CL
WEYMOUTH WLK
LINKS VIEW CL
SUNNINGDALE CL
WENTWORTH PL
GREENACRES DR
GLENEAGLES
CH
OVERTON RD
COURTMEWS
ALGUIN CT
CRANMER CL
GREEN VERGES
THE QUADRANGLE
GOLF CL
TRACY CT
BELMONT LA
ABERCORN RD
Whitchurch Schs
Sp Gd
Stanburn Schs
Stanmore
Belmont 105
THE HIGHWAY
WOODCROFT AVE
ACORN CL
OAK TREE CL
WEMBOROUGH RD
HOME MEAD
GYLES PK
BROMEFIELD
BRICK LA
MAYCHURCH CL
Pav
Tenn Cts
BRAMBLE CL
Liby
HONISTER GDNS
HONISTER CL
HONISTER PL
Allot Gdns
VERNON CT
MOUNTSIDE
VERNON DR
BELLAMY CT
FLORISTON GDNS
FLORISTON CL
COLEDALE DR
ST ANDREWS DR
BUSH GR
PARR RD
HONEYPOT BSNS CTR
GARLAND RD
Sp Gd
ST EDMUNDS DR
HERMITAGE WAY
BEVERLEY GDNS
Allot Gdns
KENTON LA
BELLAMY DR
Allot Gdns
WESTON DR
KYNANCE GDNS
BRAITHWAITE GDNS
LYON MEADE
PICKETT CROFT
WIGTON GDNS
CURZON AVE
FELBRIDGE AVE
Belmont
BELMONT CIRC
VENTNOR AVE
WETHERAL DR
CROWSHOTT AVE
THISTLECROFT GDNS
LAMORNA GR
LADYCROFT WLK
ANMERSH GR
PEAREWOOD GDNS
HONEYPOT LA
Works
DALSTON GDNS
LIME CL
MOUNTBEL RD
STATION PAR
YORK AVE
BURNELL GDNS
ST ANDREWS CL
Centenary Park
BROADCROFT AVE
Sch
Tenn Cts
HA3
DOBBIN CL
CLIFTON AVE
GRANGE AVE
UPPINGHAM AVE
DERWENT CRES
Park High Sch
CARISBROOKE CL
PORTLAND CRES
FAIRWAYS
LOCKET RD
GRASMERE GDNS
BORROWDALE AVE
CROSS RD
RADCLIFFE RD
SANCROFT RD
KENMORE AVE
ELGIN AVE
KINGSHILL DR
TENBY AVE
Kenton Lane Farm
KENTON LA
ROCKLANDS DR
Sp Gd
CULVER GR
Bwg Gn
Tenn Cts
LANGLAND CRES
JERSEY AVE
HILIARY GDNS
QUEENS CT
IVANHOE DR
Pl Fld
QUEENS AVE
MORLEY CRES
CHARMIAN AVE
Priestmead Schs
ENNERDALE AVE
MORLEY CRES W
CLYDESDALE AVE
PORTLAND CRES W
PEMBROKE AVE
Recn Gd
BELMONT RD
IRVINE AVE
FORMBY AVE
BOOTHMAN HO
QUEENSBURY CIRC PAR

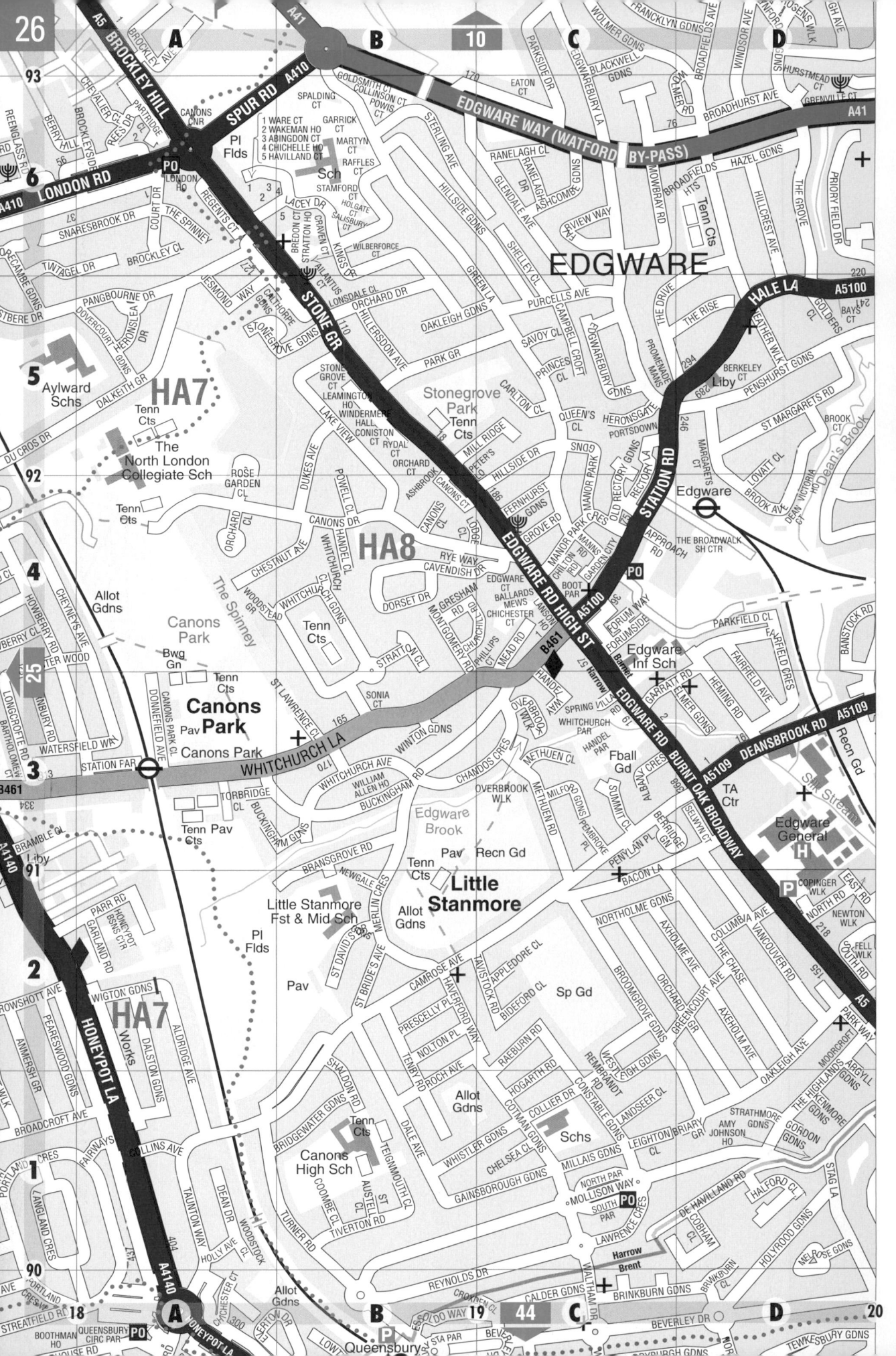
A
B
10
C
D
93
6
5
92
4
3
25
91
2
1
90
18
19
44
20
A5
A41
A410
A5100
A5109
A4140
B461
BROCKLEY HILL
SPUR RD
LONDON RD
EDGWARE WAY (WATFORD BY-PASS)
EDGWARE
STONE GR
EDGWARE RD HIGH ST
EDGWARE RD BURNT OAK BROADWAY
STATION RD
HALE LA
DEANSBROOK RD
WHITCHURCH LA
HONEYPOT LA
1 WARE CT
2 WAKEMAN HO
3 ABINGDON CT
4 CHICHELLE HO
5 HAVILLAND CT
Pl Flds
Sch
CANONS CNR
PO
LONDON HO
REGENTS CT
THE SPINNEY
SNARESBROOK DR
COURT DR
BROCKLEY CL
TINTAGEL DR
PANGBOURNE DR
JESMOND WAY
DOVERCOURT GDNS
HERONSLEA DR
DALKEITH GR
DU CROS DR
Aylward Schs
HA7
Tenn Cts
The North London Collegiate Sch
ROSE GARDEN CL
ORCHARD CL
CHESTNUT AVE
WOODSTEAD GR
The Spinney
Canons Park
Allot Gdns
Bwg Gn
Pav
STATION PAR
WATERSFIELD WAY
DONNEFIELD AVE
CANONS PARK CL
CHEYNEYS AVE
HOWBERRY RD
LONGCROFT RD
BARTHOLOMEW CL
HA8
CANONS DR
DUKES AVE
POWELL CL
HANDEL CL
WHITCHURCH GDNS
LAKE VIEW
Stonegrove Park
STONEGROVE GDNS
HILLERSDON AVE
ORCHARD DR
LONSDALE CL
KINGS DR
WILBERFORCE CT
LACEY DR
SALISBURY CT
HOLGATE CT
STAMFORD CT
RAFFLES CT
MARTYN CT
GARRICK CT
SPALDING CT
GOLDSMITH CT
COLLINSON CT
POWIS CT
STERLING AVE
HILLSIDE GDNS
GREEN LA
OAKLEIGH GDNS
PARK GR
SHELLEY CL
GLENDALE AVE
RANELAGH CL
RANELAGH DR
ASHCOMBE GDNS
FAIRVIEW WAY
PURCELLS AVE
SAVOY CL
CAMPBELL CROFT
PRINCES CL
EDGWAREBURY GDNS
CARLTON CL
QUEEN'S CL
HERONSGATE
PORTSDOWN
MILL RIDGE
HILLSIDE DR
FERNHURST GDNS
GROVE RD
MANOR PARK GDNS
MANOR PARK CRES
OLD RECTORY GDNS
RECTORY LA
CANONS CL
LODGE CL
RYE WAY
CAVENDISH DR
DORSET DR
GRESHAM RD
MONTGOMERY RD
CHURCHILL RD
PHILLIPS CT
MEAD RD
STRATTON CL
SONIA CT
ST LAWRENCE CL
WINTON GDNS
WHITCHURCH AVE
BUCKINGHAM RD
CHANDOS CRES
OVERBROOK WLK
METHUEN CL
METHUEN RD
MILFORD GDNS
PEMBROKE PL
SUMMIT CL
ALBANY CRES
BERRIDGE GN
SELWYN CT
PENYLAN PL
BACON LA
Edgware Brook
Recn Gd
Little Stanmore
Little Stanmore Fst & Mid Sch
BRANSGROVE RD
NEWGALE GDNS
MERLIN CRES
TORBRIDGE CL
BUCKINGHAM GDNS
BRAMBLE CL
Liby
PARR RD
GARLAND RD
HONEYPOT BSNS CTR
WIGTON GDNS
ROWSHOTT AVE
PEARESWOOD GDNS
AMMERSH GR
DALSTON GDNS
ALDRIDGE AVE
Works
BROADCROFT AVE
FAIRWAYS
COLLINS AVE
LANGLAND CRES
TAUNTON WAY
DEAN DR
HOLLY AVE
WOODSTOCK CL
STREATFIELD RD
QUEENSBURY CIRC PAR
BOOTHMAN HO
CHICHESTER CT
Queensbury
ST DAVID'S DR
ST BRIDE'S AVE
CAMROSE AVE
HAVERFORD WAY
TAVISTOCK RD
APPLEDORE CL
BIDEFORD CL
PRESCELLY PL
NOLTON PL
TENBY RD
ROCH AVE
RAEBURN RD
HOGARTH RD
REMBRANDT
CONSTABLE GDNS
COLLIER DR
COTMAN GDNS
Sp Gd
Schs
Allot Gdns
SHALDON RD
BRIDGEWATER GDNS
Canons High Sch
TEIGNMOUTH CL
DALE AVE
COOMBE CL
AUSTELL CL
TIVERTON RD
TURNER RD
WHISTLER GDNS
CHELSEA CL
GAINSBOROUGH GDNS
MILLAIS GDNS
NORTH PAR
MOLLISON WAY
SOUTH PAR
LAWRENCE CRES
LEIGHTON CL
LANDSEER CL
WESTLEIGH GDNS
BROOMGROVE GDNS
ORCHARD GR
GREENCOURT AVE
AXHOLME AVE
AXEHOLM AVE
THE CHASE
COLUMBIA AVE
VANCOUVER RD
NORTHOLME GDNS
OAKLEIGH AVE
BRIARY GR
AMY JOHNSON HO
STRATHMORE GDNS
GORDON GDNS
KENMORE GDNS
THE HIGHLANDS
MOORCROFT
ARGYLL GDNS
PARK WAY
STAG LA
HOLYROOD GDNS
HALFORD CL
DE HAVILLAND RD
COBHAM CL
MELROSE GDNS
REYNOLDS DR
CALDER GDNS
BRINKBURN GDNS
BRINKBURN CL
WALTHAM DR
Harrow
Brent
BEVERLEY DR
TEWKESBURY GDNS
STA PAR
Edgware Inf Sch
GARRATT RD
ELMER GDNS
HEMING RD
FAIRFIELD AVE
FAIRFIELD CRES
PARKFIELD CL
BANSTOCK RD
FORUM WAY
FORUMSIDE
SPRING VILLA RD
WHITCHURCH PAR
HANDEL PAR
Fball Gd
TA Ctr
Edgware General
COPINGER WLK
NORTH RD
NEWTON WLK
SOUTH RD
EAST RD
Edgware
THE BROADWALK SH CTR
APPROACH RD
BROOK AVE
LOVATT CL
ST MARGARETS RD
MARGARETS CT
BROOK CT
Dean's Brook
PENSHURST GDNS
BERKELEY CT
HEATHER WLK
THE RISE
THE DRIVE
PROMENADE MANS
GOLDERS CL
BAYS CT
HILLCREST AVE
THE GROVE
PRIORY FIELD DR
HAZEL GDNS
BROADFIELDS HTS
MOWBRAY RD
BROADHURST AVE
HURSTMEAD CT
GRENVILLE CT
WOLMER GDNS
FRANCKLYN GDNS
BROADFIELDS AVE
WINDSOR AVE
EDGWAREBURY LA
PARKSIDE DR
BLACKWELL GDNS
EATON CT
Silk Stream
Recn Gd

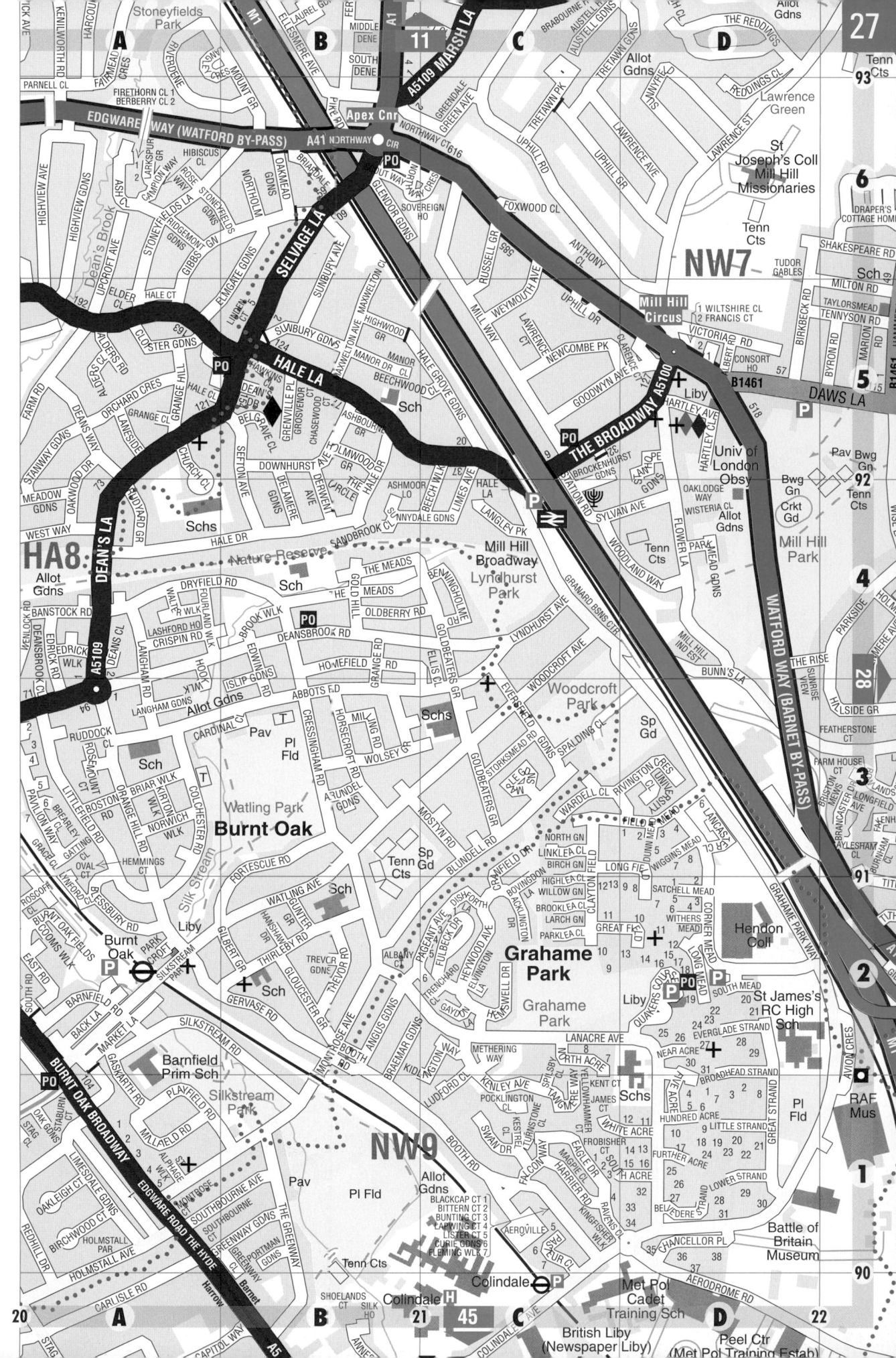

Stoneyfields Park
M1
A1
11
A5109 MARSH LA
Allot Gdns
THE REDDINGS
Tenn Cts
93
PARNELL CL
FIRETHORN CL 1
BERBERRY CL 2
EDGWARE WAY (WATFORD BY-PASS)
A41
Apex Cnr
NORTHWAY CIR
NORTHWAY CT
REDDINGS CL
Lawrence Green
St Joseph's Coll Mill Hill Missionaries
LAWRENCE ST
LAWRENCE AVE
UPHILL RD
UPHILL GR
TRETAWN PK
TRETAWN GDNS
GREEN AVE
PO
SOVEREIGN HO
GLENDOR GDNS
SELVAGE LA
FOXWOOD CL
ANTHONY CL
RUSSELL GR
DRAPER'S COTTAGE HOME
SHAKESPEARE RD
NW7
TUDOR GABLES
Sch
MILTON RD
TAYLORSMEAD
TENNYSON RD
HIGHVIEW AVE
HIGHVIEW GDNS
Dean's Brook
UPCROFT AVE
STONEYFIELDS LA
RIDGEMONT GDNS
GIBBS GN
ELMGATE GDNS
NORTHOLM
OAKMEAD GDNS
SUNBURY AVE
MAXWELTON CL
HIGHWOOD GR
WEYMOUTH AVE
UPHILL DR
Mill Hill Circus
1 WILTSHIRE CL
2 FRANCIS CT
VICTORIA RD
ALBERT RD
CONSORT HO
BIRKBECK RD
BYRON RD
MARION RD
B1461
HAMMERS LA
ELDER CL
HALE CT
CLOISTER GDNS
SUNBURY GDNS
MAXWELTON AVE
MANOR DR
MANOR CL
HALE GROVE GDNS
MILL WAY
LAWRENCE CT
NEWCOMBE PK
CLARENCE CT
GOODWYN AVE
DAWS LA
HALE LA
BEECHWOOD CL
THE BROADWAY A5100
Liby
HARTLEY AVE
HARTLEY CL
FARM RD
ALDERS CL
ALDERS RD
ORCHARD CRES
GRANGE HILL
GRANGE CL
HALE CL
DEAN'S CL
BELGRAVE CL
GRENVILLE PL
GROSVENOR CT
CHASEWOOD CT
ASHBOURNE GR
HOLMWOOD GR
THE HALE DR
DOWNHURST AVE
BROCKENHURST GDNS
STATION RD
Univ of London Obsy
Pav
Bwg Gn
Crkt Gd
92
Tenn Cts
STANWAY GDNS
DEANS WAY
LANESIDE
CHURCH CL
SEFTON AVE
DELAMERE GDNS
DERWENT AVE
THE CIRCLE
ASHMOOR LO
BEECH WLK
LIMES AVE
HALE LA
SUNNYDALE GDNS
LANGLEY PK
SYLVAN AVE
OAKLODGE WAY
WISTERIA CL
Allot Gdns
MEADOW GDNS
OAKWOOD DR
RUDYARD GR
WEST WAY
Schs
HALE DR
SANDBROOK CL
Mill Hill Broadway
WOODLAND WAY
FLOWER LA
MEAD GDNS
PARK
Mill Hill Park
HA8
Nature Reserve
DEAN'S LA
Allot Gdns
THE MEADS
Lyndhurst Park
DRYFIELD RD
Sch
GOLD HILL
BENNINGHOLME RD
GRANARD BSNS CTR
LYNDHURST AVE
4
PARKSIDE
WATFORD WAY (BARNET BY-PASS)
BANSTOCK RD
DEANSBROOK RD
EDRICK RD
EDRICK WLK
LASHFORD HO
CRISPIN RD
FOURLAND WLK
BROOK WLK
DEANSBROOK RD
OLDBERRY RD
GOLDBEATERS GR
ELLIS CL
WOODCROFT AVE
MILL HILL IND EST
BUNN'S LA
THE RISE
SUNRISE VIEW
28
A5109
DEANS CL
LANGHAM RD
HOOK WLK
EDWIN RD
ISLIP GDNS
HOMEFIELD RD
GRANGE RD
EVERSFIELD GDNS
Woodcroft Park
HILLSIDE GR
LANGHAM GDNS
Allot Gdns
ABBOTS RD
CARDINAL CL
MILLING RD
Schs
Sp Gd
FEATHERSTONE CT
RUDDOCK CL
ROSEMOUNT CT
Pav
Pl Fld
CRESSINGHAM RD
HORSECROFT RD
WOLSEY GR
STORKSMEAD RD
SPALDING CL
FARM HOUSE CT
Sch
COLCHESTER RD
BRIAR WLK
KIRTON WLK
BOSTON RD
ORANGE HILL RD
NORWICH WLK
ARUNDEL GDNS
GOLDBEATERS GR
RIVINGTON CRES
UNIVERSITY CL
WARDELL CL
FIELD MEAD
LANCASTER CL
BRISTON MEWS
BRANCASTER DR
LONGFIELD AVE
3
PAVILION WAY
LITTLEFIELD RD
BREARLEY CL
Watling Park
Burnt Oak
MOSTYN RD
BLUNDELL RD
NORTH GN
LINKLEA CL
BIRCH GN
DUNNMEAD RD
WIGGINS MEAD
AYLESHAM CL
BURNHAM CL
GRACE CL
GATTING CL
OVAL CT
HEMMINGS CT
Silk Stream
FORTESCUE RD
Tenn Cts
Sp Gd
CRANFIELD DR
LONG FIELD
HIGHLEA CL
WILLOW GN
CLAYTON FIELD
SATCHELL MEAD
91
ROSCOFF CL
LYMFORD CL
BLESSBURY RD
WATLING AVE
Sch
GUNTER GR
HANSHAW DR
DISHFORTH LA
BOVINGDON LA
ACKLINGTON DR
BROOKLEA CL
LARCH GN
PARKLEA CL
GREAT FIELD
WITHERS MEAD
CORNER MEAD
Hendon Coll
GRAHAME PARK WAY
BURNT OAK FIELDS
COOMS WLK
Liby
Burnt Oak
PARK CROFT
SILKSTREAM PARADE
GILBERT GR
THIRLEBY RD
TREVOR GDNS
TREVOR RD
ALBANY CT
PAGEANT AVE
FULBECK DR
HEYWOOD AVE
ELVINGTON LA
Grahame Park
LONG MEAD
A1
2
EAST RD
SOUTH RD
BARNFIELD RD
Sch
GERVASE RD
GLOUCESTER GR
TRENCHARD CL
GAYDON LA
HEMSWELL DR
Grahame Park
Liby
QUAKERS COURSE
SOUTH MEAD
St James's RC High Sch
BACK LA
MARKET LA
SILKSTREAM RD
MONTROSE AVE
BOOTH RD
ANGUS GDNS
BRAEMAR GDNS
KIDLINGTON WAY
METHERING WAY
LANACRE AVE
NORTH ACRE
EVERGLADE STRAND
NEAR ACRE
AVION CRES
M1
BURNT OAK BROADWAY
PO
GASKARTH RD
Barnfield Prim Sch
LUDFORD CL
KENLEY AVE
POCKLINGTON CL
SPILSBY CL
FIVE ACRE
BROADHEAD STRAND
GREAT STRAND
RAF Mus
STAG CL
OAK GDNS
STABURN
PLAYFIELD RD
Silkstream Park
MILLFIELD RD
KESTREL CL
TURNSTONE CL
THE WAY
YELLOWHAMMER CT
KENT CT
JAMES CT
Schs
WHITE ACRE
HUNDRED ACRE
LITTLE STRAND
Pl Fld
ALPHAGE WLK
NW9
SWAN DR
BOOTH RD
FROBISHER CT
SOUTH ACRE
FURTHER ACRE
LIMESDALE GDNS
OAKLEIGH CT
EDGWARE ROAD THE HYDE
MONTROSE CL
SOUTHBOURNE AVE
SOUTHBOURNE CRES
Pav
Pl Fld
Allot Gdns
FALCON WAY
EAGLE DR
MAGPIE CL
HARRIER RD
RAVENS CL
KINGFISHER WLK
LOWER STRAND
BELVEDERE STRAND
1
BIRCHWOOD CT
HOLMSTALL PAR
HOLMSTALL AVE
REDHILL DR
GREENWAY GDNS
PORTMAN GDNS
THE GREENWAY
GREENWAY CL
BLACKCAP CT 1
BITTERN CT 2
BUNTING CT 3
LAPWING CT 4
LISTER CT 5
CURIE GDNS 6
FLEMING WLK 7
AEROVILLE
PASTEUR CL
CHANCELLOR PL
Battle of Britain Museum
Tenn Cts
Colindale
Met Pol Cadet Training Sch
AERODROME RD
90
CARLISLE RD
Harrow
Barnet
SHOELANDS CT
SILK HO
Colindale
45
COLINDALE AVE
British Liby (Newspaper Liby)
Peel Ctr (Met Pol Training Estab)
CAPITOL WAY
A5
20
A
B
21
C
D
22

12

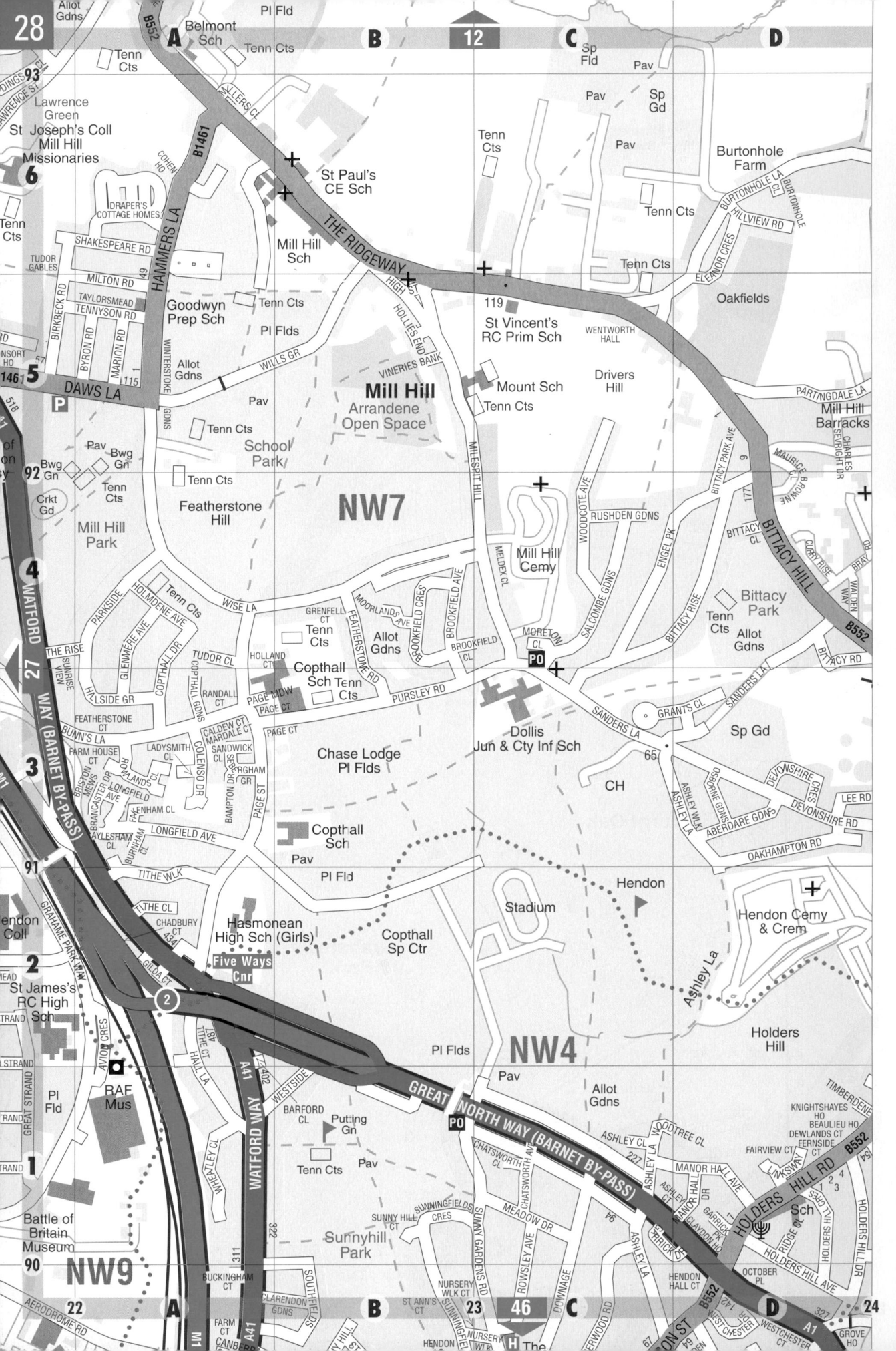
A
B
C
D
Belmont Sch
Tenn Cts
Pl Fld
Sp Fld
Pav
Sp Gd
Lawrence Green
St Joseph's Coll Mill Hill Missionaries
St Paul's CE Sch
Burtonhole Farm
THE RIDGEWAY
Mill Hill Sch
DRAPER'S COTTAGE HOMES
SHAKESPEARE RD
MILTON RD
TAYLORSMEAD
TENNYSON RD
HAMMERS LA
Goodwyn Prep Sch
St Vincent's RC Prim Sch
Oakfields
WENTWORTH HALL
Drivers Hill
DAWS LA
WILLS GR
Allot Gdns
Pl Flds
Mill Hill
Arrandene Open Space
VINERIES BANK
Mount Sch
PARTINGDALE LA
Mill Hill Barracks
School Park
Featherstone Hill
Mill Hill Park
NW7
MILESPIT HILL
RUSHDEN GDNS
BITTACY HILL
Mill Hill Cemy
Bittacy Park
WISE LA
BROOKFIELD AVE
MORETON CL
PO
SANDERS LA
GRANTS CL
Sp Gd
WATFORD WAY (BARNET BY-PASS)
PURSLEY RD
Copthall Sch
Dollis Jun & Cty Inf Sch
Chase Lodge Pl Flds
CH
DEVONSHIRE RD
LEE RD
OAKHAMPTON RD
LONGFIELD AVE
Copthall Sch
Pav
Pl Fld
Hendon
Stadium
Hendon Cemy & Crem
Hasmonean High Sch (Girls)
Five Ways Cnr
Copthall Sp Ctr
Ashley La
Holders Hill
St James's RC High Sch
NW4
Pl Flds
Pav
Allot Gdns
GREAT NORTH WAY (BARNET BY-PASS)
RAF Mus
WATFORD WAY
Putting Gn
Tenn Cts
HOLDERS HILL RD
Sch
Battle of Britain Museum
Sunnyhill Park
NW9
A1
A41
M1
B552
22
23
24
90
91
92
93
1
2
3
4
5
6
27

46

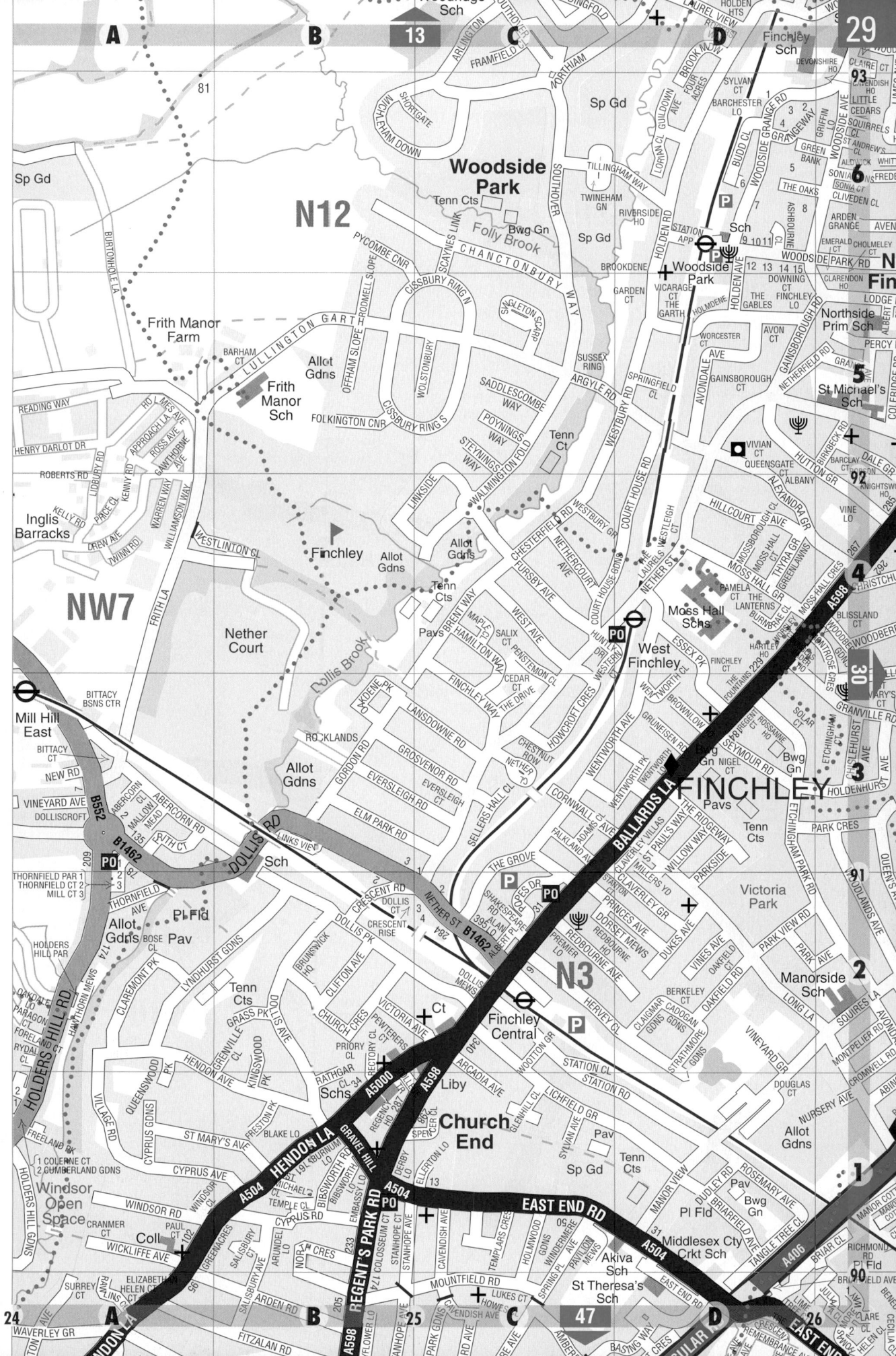

29
A
B
13
C
D
Woodside Park
N12
Frith Manor Farm
Frith Manor Sch
Allot Gdns
Sp Gd
Inglis Barracks
NW7
Nether Court
Finchley
Mill Hill East
West Finchley
Moss Hall Schs
FINCHLEY
Victoria Park
N3
Finchley Central
Church End
Manorside Sch
Windsor Open Space
Middlesex Cty Crkt Sch
Akiva Sch
St Theresa's Sch
St Michael's Sch
Northside Prim Sch
Finchley Sch
Folly Brook
Dollis Brook
BALLARDS LA
EAST END RD
HENDON LA
REGENT'S PARK RD
HOLDERS HILL RD
DOLLIS RD
NETHER ST
CHANCTONBURY WAY
LULLINGTON GARTH
HOLDEN RD
WOODSIDE PARK RD
GRAVEL HILL
A598
A504
A5000
B1462
B552
A406
30
47
24
25
26

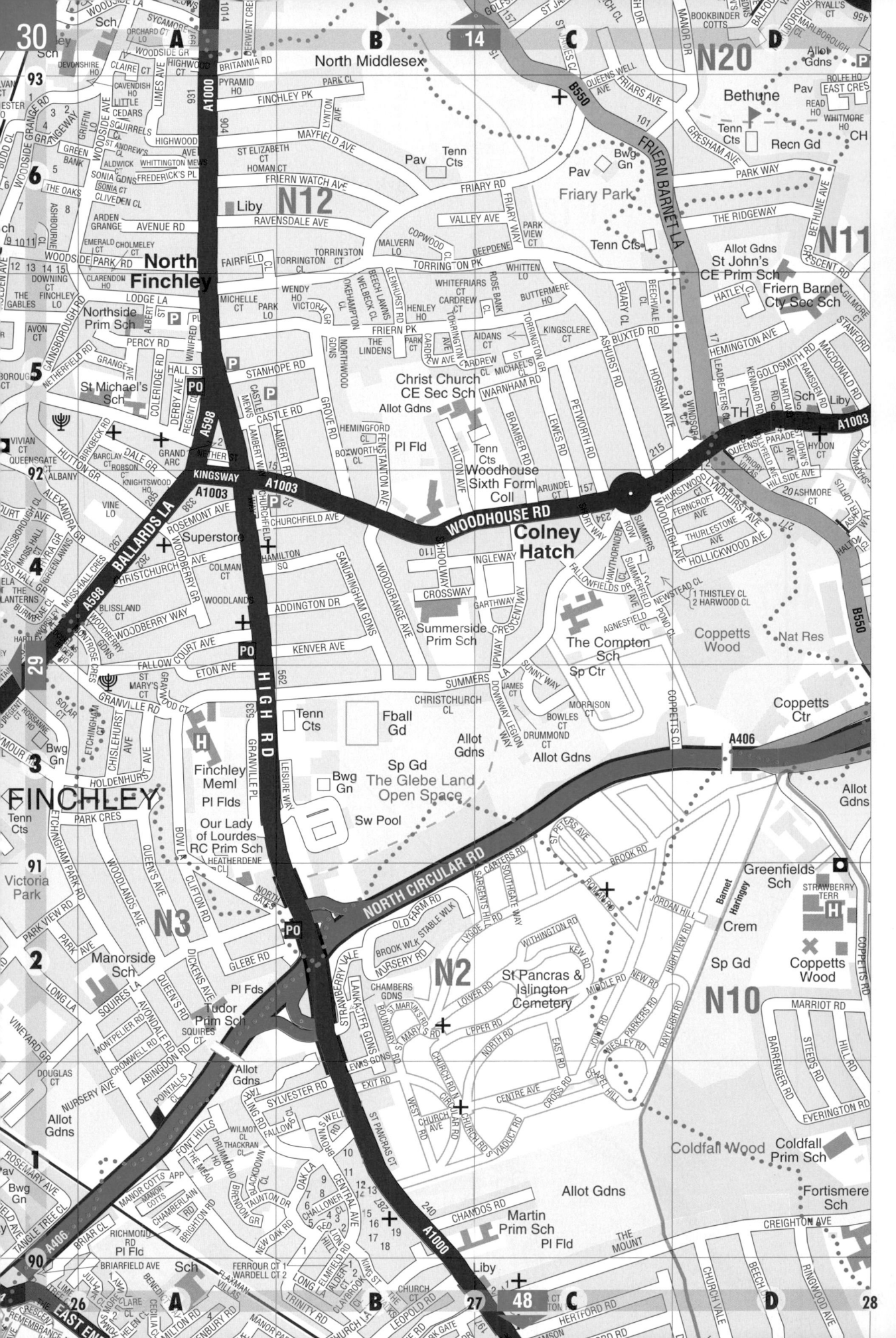

30
A
B
C
D
14
48
29
93
92
91
90
26
27
28
6
5
4
3
2
1
North Middlesex
N20
N12
N11
N10
N3
N2
North Finchley
Colney Hatch
FINCHLEY
Bethune
Friary Park
Coppetts Wood
Nat Res
Coppetts Ctr
Coldfall Wood
Victoria Park
The Glebe Land Open Space
St Pancras & Islington Cemetery
Crem
Christ Church CE Sec Sch
Woodhouse Sixth Form Coll
Summerside Prim Sch
The Compton Sch
St John's CE Prim Sch
Friern Barnet Cty Sec Sch
Northside Prim Sch
St Michael's Sch
Finchley Meml
Our Lady of Lourdes RC Prim Sch
Manorside Sch
Tudor Prim Sch
Greenfields Sch
Coldfall Prim Sch
Fortismere Sch
Martin Prim Sch
Superstore
Liby
Allot Gdns
Tenn Cts
Pl Fld
Fball Gd
Sp Gd
Sw Pool
Sp Ctr
Recn Gd
Bwg Gn
Pav
A1000
A1003
A598
A406
B550
HIGH RD
NORTH CIRCULAR RD
WOODHOUSE RD
BALLARDS LA
FRIERN BARNET LA
KINGSWAY
FRIERN PK
FRIERN WATCH AVE
RAVENSDALE AVE
TORRINGTON PK
FRIARY RD
THE RIDGEWAY
PARK WAY
SUMMERS LA
CHRISTCHURCH AVE
WOODBERRY WAY
FALLOW COURT AVE
GRANVILLE RD
HOLDENHURST AVE
ETCHINGHAM PARK RD
WOODLANDS AVE
QUEEN'S AVE
CLIFTON RD
LONG LA
CHANDOS RD
CREIGHTON AVE
THE MOUNT
COPPETTS RD
HIGH VIEW RD
BROOK RD
JORDAN HILL
EVERINGTON RD
MARRIOT RD
HILL RD
STEEDS RD
BARRENGER RD
ST PANCRAS CT
CHURCH VALE
RINGWOOD AVE
Barnet
Haringey

FRIERN BARNET
New Southgate
N11
N14
N13
N10
N22
N8
Arnos Park
Arnos Grove
Pymme's Brook
Hollickwood Park
Muswell Hill
Alexandra Palace
Alexandra Park
Bounds Green
Colney Hatch
Wood Green Tunnel
Middlesex Univ (Bounds Green)
St Martin of Porres RC Prim Sch
Hollickwood Prim Sch
Alexandra Park Sec Sch
Rhodes Avenue Prim Sch
Coppetts Wood Prim Sch
Our Lady of Muswell RC Prim Sch
Norfolk House Prep Sch
Fortismere Sch (South Wing)
Bowes Prim Sch
Broomfield Sch
The College of North East London
Superstore
Crematorium
OAKLEIGH RD S
WATERFALL RD
FRIERN BARNET RD
BOWES RD
STATION RD
TELFORD RD (NORTH CIRCULAR RD)
PINKHAM WAY NORTH CIRCULAR RD
BOUNDS GREEN RD
COLNEY HATCH LA
ALBERT RD
ALEXANDRA PARK RD
DURNSFORD RD
WILMER WAY
POWYS LA
BROWNLOW RD
MUSWELL HILL
A109
A1003
A1110
A406
B1452
B106
B550
15
32
49
28
29
30
90
91
92
93
A
B
C
D
1
2
3
4
5
6

32
A
B
16
C
D
St Monica's RC Prim Sch
HEDGE LA
A111
ALDERMAN'S HILL
A1004
B1452
POWYS LA
WILMER WAY
Broomfield Park
Bwg Gn
Pav
Tenn Cts
Bndstd
Sp Gd
Palmers Green
GREEN LANES
A105
N13
N14
Hazelwood Jun & Inf Schs
St Annes Catholic High Sch for Girls (Upper)
New River
A406
NORTH CIRCULAR RD
BOWES RD (NORTH CIRCULAR RD)
Broomfield Sch
Pl Fld
Pymme's Brook
Allot Gdns
Liby
TH
Clockhouse Junction
Tottenhall Inf Sch
St Michael-at-Bowes CE Jun Sch
Bowes Park
BROWNLOW RD
B106
N11
Enfield
Haringey
Bounds Green
A109
The College of North East London
Schs
HIGH RD
Woodside Park
St Thomas More Sch
Earlham Prim Sch
Recn Gd
N22
New River Sp & Recn Ctr
White Hart Lane Sch
BOUNDS GREEN RD
WOOD GREEN
Nightingale Gardens
Avenue Gdns
Alexandra Palace
Wood Green Common
Alexandra Prim Sch
STATION RD
B138
MAYES RD
LORDSHIP LA
Crown Ct
Noel Park Jun & Inf Schs
Noel Park
WESTBURY AVE
Crkt Gd
Alexandra Park
N8
30
31
50
HORNSEY PARK RD
Pl Fld

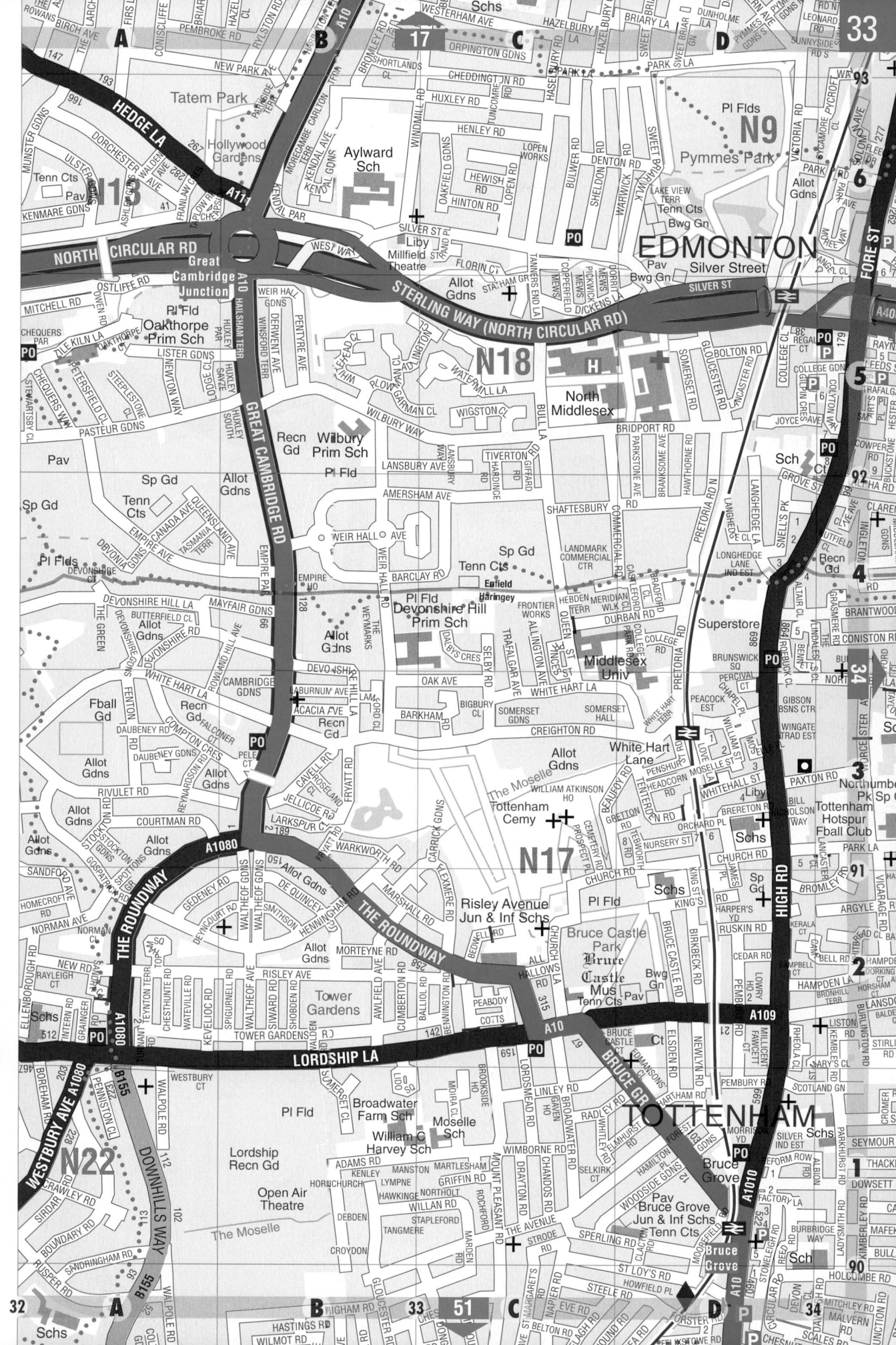

A
B
C
D
17
51
32
33
34
WESTERHAM AVE
PEMBROKE RD
BIRCH AVE
ROWANS
LARCH
FIRS LA
CONISCLIFFE
BRIAR
HAZEL CL
RYLSTON RD
ORPINGTON GDNS
HAZELBURY LA
BRIARY LA
DUNHOLME
PYMMES GDNS S
SUNNYSIDE RD S
NEW PARK AVE
SHORTLANDS CL
BROMLEY RD
CHEDDINGTON RD
PARK LA
Tatem Park
HUXLEY RD
HENLEY RD
HEDGE LA
Hollywood Gardens
Aylward Sch
WINDMILL RD
MORECAMBE TERR
CARLTON TERR
KENDAL AVE
KENDAL GDNS
KENDAL PAR
OAKFIELD GDNS
HEWISH RD
HINTON RD
LOPEN RD
LOPEN WORKS
BULWER RD
SHELDON RD
DENTON RD
WARWICK RD
SWEET BRIAR WALK
Pl Flds
N9
Pymmes Park
VICTORIA RD
SYCAMORE CL
PYCROFT WAY
93
6
Allot Gdns
LAKE VIEW TERR
Tenn Cts
Bwg Gn
PO
EDMONTON
Silver Street
Pav
Bwg Gn
SILVER ST
FORE ST
A406
N13
MUNSTER GDNS
DORCHESTER GDNS
ULSTER GDNS
Tenn Cts
Pav
KENMARE GDNS
ASHLEY GDNS
WALDEN AVE
FRANLAW CRES
A111
NORTH CIRCULAR RD
Great Cambridge Junction
A10
WEST WAY
SILVER ST
Liby
Millfield Theatre
FLORIN CT
Allot Gdns
STATHAM GR
TANNERS END LA
COPPERFIELD MEWS
PICKWICK MEWS
DORRIT MEWS
DICKENS LA
STERLING WAY (NORTH CIRCULAR RD)
OSTLIFFE RD
MITCHELL RD
OWEN RD
Pl Fld
Oakthorpe Prim Sch
CHEQUERS PAR
TILE KILN LA
OAKTHORPE
LISTER GDNS
PETERSFIELD CL
STEEPLESTONE CL
NEWTON WAY
HUXLEY PAR
HALLSHAM TERR
WEIR HALL GDNS
DERWENT AVE
WINSFORD TERR
PENTYRE AVE
WHITEHEAD CL
ADLINGTON CL
PLOWMAN CL
WATERMILL LA
N18
H
North Middlesex
SOMERSET RD
GLOUCESTER RD
BOLTON RD
LANCASTER RD
COLLEGE CL
REGAL CT
COLLEGE GDNS
GILPIN CRES
5
LEEDS ST
TRAFALGAR
JOYCE AVE
PASTEUR GDNS
HUXLEY SOUTH
GREAT CAMBRIDGE RD
Recn Gd
Wilbury Prim Sch
Pl Fld
WILBURY WAY
GARMAN CL
WIGSTON CL
BULL LA
BRIDPORT RD
LANSBURY AVE
TIVERTON RD
HARDINGE RD
GIFFARD RD
PARKSTONE AVE
BRANKSOME AVE
HAWTHORNE RD
PRETORIA RD N
LANGHEDGE LA
Sch
Ct
92
GROVE ST
COWPER RD
Pav
Sp Gd
Allot Gdns
Tenn Cts
Sp Gd
CANADA AVE
QUEENSLAND AVE
TASMANIA TERR
EMPIRE AVE
DEVONIA GDNS
AMERSHAM AVE
WEIR HALL AVE
SHAFTESBURY
COMMERCIAL RD
LANDMARK COMMERCIAL CTR
Sp Gd
Tenn Cts
LONGHEDGE LANE IND EST
SNELL'S PK
CLAREMONT
Recn Gd
4
INGLETON RD
Pl Flds
DEVONSHIRE CT
EMPIRE PAR
EMPIRE HO
BARCLAY RD
Enfield
Haringey
CASTLEFORD CL
BRADFORD CL
HEBDEN TERR
MERIDIAN WLK
DURBAN RD
FRONTIER WORKS
Superstore
BRANTWOOD
CONISTON RD
DEVONSHIRE HILL LA
MAYFAIR GDNS
BUTTERFIELD CL
DEVONSHIRE RD
THE GREEN
Allot Gdns
ROWLAND HILL AVE
Pl Fld
Devonshire Hill Prim Sch
Allot Gdns
THE WEYMARKS
WEIR HALL RD
DALBYS CRES
SELBY RD
TRAFALGAR AVE
ALLINGTON AVE
QUEEN ST
PRINCES ST
COLLEGE PARK RD
COLLEGE RD
Middlesex Univ
PRETORIA RD
BRUNSWICK SQ
PERCIVAL CT
ROEBUCK CL
BENNETTS CL
PO
34
WHITE HART LA
CAMBRIDGE GDNS
DEVONSHIRE HILL LA
LABURNUM AVE
ACACIA AVE
LAMFORD CL
OAK AVE
BARKHAM RD
BIGBURY CL
SOMERSET GDNS
SOMERSET HALL
WHITE HART LA
PEACOCK EST
CHAPEL PL
WILLIAM ST
GIBSON BSNS CTR
WINGATE TRAD EST
Fball Gd
Recn Gd
FALCONER CT
DAUBENEY RD
COMPTON CRES
Recn Gd
CREIGHTON RD
White Hart Lane
Allot Gdns
DAUBENEY GDNS
Allot Gdns
PELE CT
CAVELL RD
ROSELAND CL
FRYATT RD
The Moselle
WILLIAM ATKINSON HO
BEAUFOY RD
TENTERDEN RD
PENSHURST RD
HEADCORN RD
MOSELLE ST
WHITEHALL ST
LOVE LA
PAXTON RD
3
Northumberland Pk Sp Gd
Allot Gdns
RIVULET RD
REYNARDSON RD
JELLICOE RD
Tottenham Cemy
Liby
Tottenham Hotspur Fball Club
Allot Gdns
COURTMAN RD
LARKSPUR CL
GRETTON RD
BRERETON RD
NICHOLSON WAY
Allot Gdns
Allot Gdns
STOCKTON RD
A1080
WARKWORTH RD
CARRICK GDNS
CEMETERY RD
PROSPECT PL
TEBWORTH RD
NURSERY ST
ORCHARD PL
Schs
PARK LA
LANCASTER RD
SANDFORD AVE
GOSPATRICK RD
SPOTTONS GR
GEDENEY RD
WALTHEOF GDNS
Allot Gdns
DE QUINCEY RD
SMITHSON RD
HENNINGHAM RD
MARSHALL RD
FLEXMERE RD
N17
CHURCH RD
CHURCH RD
JAMES PL
91
BROMLEY RD
HOMECROFT RD
NORMAN AVE
THE ROUNDWAY
DEYNCOURT RD
THE ROUNDWAY
Risley Avenue Jun & Inf Schs
Pl Fld
KING'S RD
Sp Gd
HARPER'S YD
HIGH RD
ARGYLE RD
VICARAGE RD
RUSKIN RD
NORMAN CL
THOMAS SQ
Allot Gdns
MORTEYNE RD
BEDWELL RD
Bruce Castle Park
KERALA CT
ELLENBOROUGH RD
NEW RD
RAYLEIGH CT
SANDLINGS CL
RISLEY AVE
ALL HALLOWS RD
Bruce Castle Mus
BRUCE CASTLE RD
BIRKBECK RD
CEDAR RD
CAMPBELL RD
HAMPDEN RD
2
Schs
INTERN RD
GRAINGER RD
TEYNTON TERR
CHESTHUNTE RD
WATEVILLE RD
KEVELIOC RD
SPIGURNELL RD
WALTHEOF AVE
SIWARD RD
SHOBDEN RD
Tower Gardens
AWLFIELD AVE
CUMBERTON RD
BALLIOL RD
BENNINGTON RD
PEABODY COTTS
Tenn Cts
Bwg Gn
Pav
PEMBURY RD
LOWRY HO
HAMPDEN LA
BRONHILL TERR
HORSHAM CT
LANSDOWNE
TOWER GARDENS RD
A109
MILLICENT FAWCETT CT
LISTON RD
RHEOLA CL
KEMBLE RD
BURLINGTON RD
STIRLING RD
512
PO
A10
BRUCE CASTLE CT
Ct
LORDSHIP LA
PO
EDMANSONS CL
ELSDEN RD
NEWLYN RD
MARY'S CL
BOREHAM RD
WESTBURY AVE A1080
PENNISTON CL
B155
WALPOLE RD
WESTBURY CT
SOMERSET CL
LIDO SQ
MOIRA CL
BROOKSIDE HO
LORDSMEAD RD
LINLEY RD
GAVEN HO
BROADWATER RD
BRUCE GR
PEMBURY RD
HARTHAM RD
SCOTLAND GN
CROMER RD
Pl Fld
Broadwater Farm Sch
Moselle Sch
William C Harvey Sch
RADLEY RD
WHITLEY RD
ELMHURST RD
FOREST GDNS
TOTTENHAM
MORRISON YD
SILVER IND EST
Schs
PARKHURST RD
SEYMOUR
N22
Lordship Recn Gd
DOWNHILLS WAY
ADAMS RD
KENLEY
MANSTON
MARTLESHAM
GRIFFIN RD
MOUNT PLEASANT RD
WIMBORNE RD
DRAYTON RD
CHANDOS RD
SELKIRK CT
HAMILTON
Bruce Grove
A1010
REFORM ROW
ALBION RD
1
THACKERAY
CRAWLEY RD
SIRDAR RD
BOUNDARY RD
Open Air Theatre
HORNCHURCH CL
LYMPNE
HAWKINGE
NORTHOLT
WILLAN RD
ROCHFORD
WOODSIDE GDNS
Pav
Bruce Grove Jun & Inf Schs
Tenn Cts
FACTORY LA
DOWSETT RD
KIMBERLEY RD
LADYSMITH RD
MAFEKING
DEBDEN
STAPLEFORD
TANGMERE
The Moselle
THE AVENUE
STRODE RD
SPERLING RD
CLACTON RD
MOOREFIELD RD
Bruce Grove
BURBRIDGE WAY
Sch
SANDRINGHAM RD
RUSPER RD
CROYDON
MARDEN RD
ST LOY'S RD
STEELE RD
HOWFIELD PL
REED RD
DEVON RD
90
HOLCOMBE RD
MITCHLEY RD
MALVERN RD
Schs
HIGHAM RD
GLOUCESTER RD
HASTINGS RD
WILMOT RD
ST MARGARET'S RD
NAPIER RD
EVE RD
BELTON RD
FORSTER RD
STONELEIGH RD
CIRCULAR RD
SCALES RD
JUNCTION RD

A
B
C
D
18
52
33
35
36
N9
N18
N17
E17
DMONTON
Upper Edmonton
TOTTENHAM
Federation Cemy
Recn Gd
Fleecefield Prim Sch
Angel Edmonton
Angel Road
Kenninghall
Cooks Ferry
ANGEL RD (NORTH CIRCULAR RD)
MERIDIAN WAY
MONTAGU RD
FORE ST
HIGH RD
CONDUIT LA
WATERMEAD WAY
BILLET RD
BLACKHORSE LA
Raynham Prim Sch
Pl Fld
Tenn Cts
Bwg Gns
Montagu Ind Est
Lea Valley Trad Est
Superstore
Kingsway Est
Triumph Trad Est
Royal London Est
Hotspur Ind Est
Sp Gd
Northumberland Pk Sp Ctr
Tottenham Hotspur Fball Club
Northumberland Park
Coleraine Park Prim Sch
Allot Gdns
Tottenham Marshes
Lea Valley Wlk
River Lee Navigation
River Lee or Lee Diversion
Lee Flood Relief Channel
Pymme's Brook
Lockwood Resr
High Maynard Resr
Lea Valley Technopark
Down Lane Park
Millmead Ind Ctr
Chalk Bridge
Leeside Works
Leeside Trad Est
Unicorn Works
Gibson Bsns Ctr
Wingate Trad Est
Rosebery Ind Pk
Silver Ind Est
Uplands Bsns Pk
Enfield
Haringey
Waltham Forest

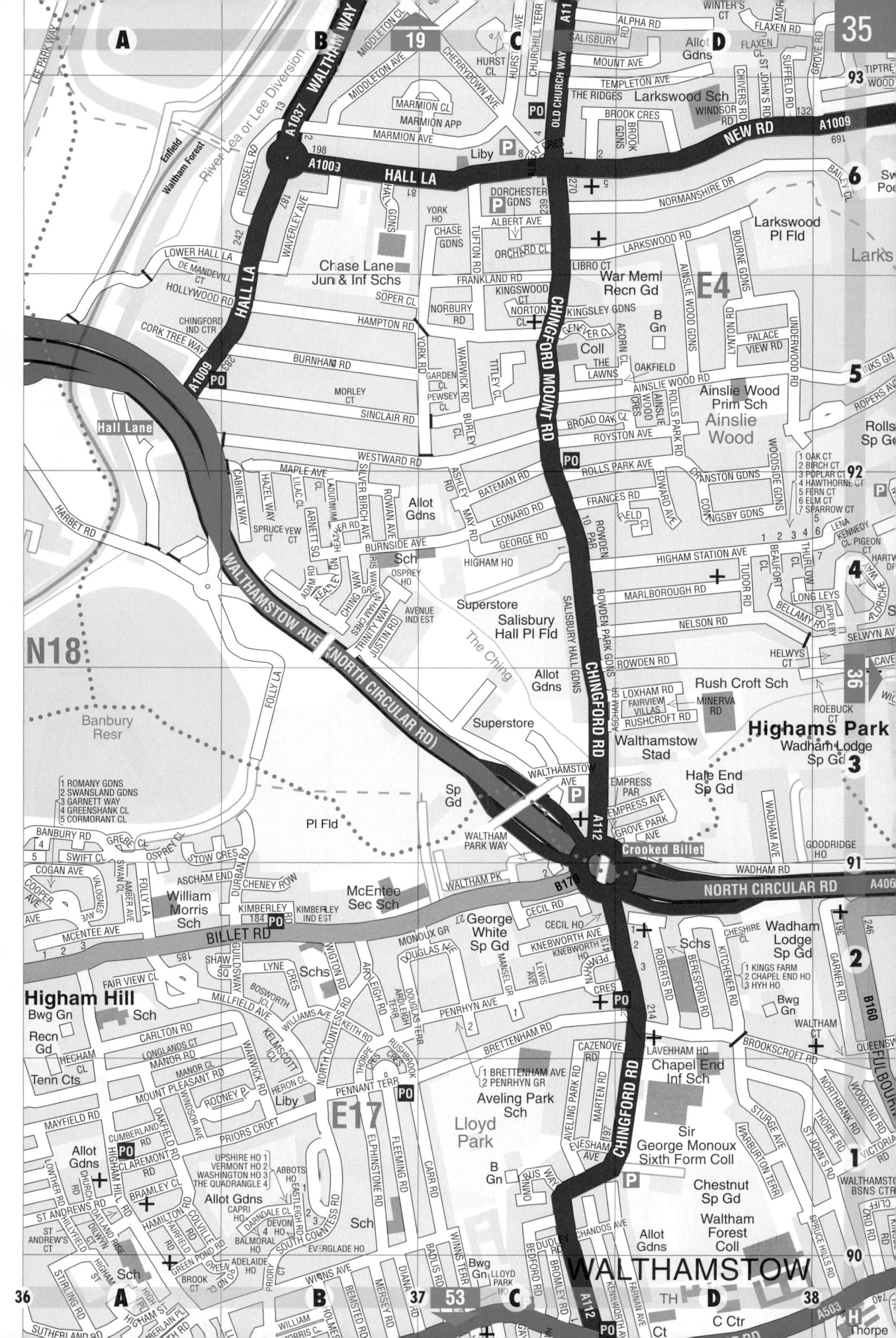
A
B
C
D
19
WALTHAM WAY
A1037
HALL LA
A1009
A1003
HALL LA
NEW RD
A1009
OLD CHURCH WAY
A11
ALPHA RD
SALISBURY
MOUNT AVE
TEMPLETON AVE
THE RIDGES
Larkswood Sch
BROOK CRES
WINDSOR RD
Allot Gdns
FLAXEN RD
FLAXEN CL
CHIVERS RD
ST JOHN'S RD
SUFFIELD RD
GROVE RD
TIPTREE
WOOD
93
6
5
4
3
2
1
92
91
90
MIDDLETON CL
MIDDLETON AVE
CHERRYDOWN AVE
HURST CL
CHURCHILL TERR
MARMION CL
MARMION APP
MARMION AVE
Liby
ALBERT CRES
DORCHESTER GDNS
ALBERT AVE
YORK HO
CHASE GDNS
TUFTON RD
ORCHARD CL
NORMANSHIRE DR
LARKSWOOD RD
Larkswood Pl Fld
LIBRO CT
War Meml Recn Gd
E4
RUSSELL RD
WAVERLEY AVE
River Lea or Lee Diversion
Enfield
Waltham Forest
LEE PARK WAY
LOWER HALL LA
DE MANDEVILLE CT
HOLLYWOOD RD
CHINGFORD IND CTR
CORK TREE WAY
Chase Lane Jun & Inf Schs
SOPER CL
HAMPTON RD
FRANKLAND RD
KINGSWOOD CT
NORBURY RD
NORTON CL
KINGSLEY GDNS
GENEVER CL
Coll
CHINGFORD MOUNT RD
THE LAWNS
OAKFIELD
ACORN CL
B Gn
AINSLIE WOOD GDNS
LYNTON RD
PALACE VIEW RD
UNDERWOOD RD
BURNHAM RD
YORK RD
WARWICK RD
GARDEN CL
PEWSEY CL
TITLEY CL
AINSLIE WOOD RD
Ainslie Wood Prim Sch
Ainslie Wood
ROLLS PARK RD
MORLEY CT
SINCLAIR RD
BURLEY CL
BROAD OAK CL
ROYSTON AVE
Hall Lane
WESTWARD RD
ROLLS PARK AVE
Rolls Sp Gd
ROPERS AVE
1 OAK CT
2 BIRCH CT
3 POPLAR CT
4 HAWTHORNE CT
5 FERN CT
6 ELM CT
7 SPARROW CT
CABINET WAY
HAZEL WAY
MAPLE AVE
LILAC CL
LABURNUM CL
SILVER BIRCH AVE
ROWAN AVE
Allot Gdns
ASHLEY RD
BATEMAN RD
CRANSTON GDNS
FRANCES RD
FIELD CL
EDWARD AVE
CONINGSBY GDNS
WOODSIDE GDNS
HARBET RD
SPRUCE CT
YEW CT
ARNETT SQ
HEATHER RD
BURNSIDE AVE
LEONARD RD
MAY RD
GEORGE RD
ROWDEN PAR
LENA KENNEDY CL
PIGEON CT
HIGHAM HO
HIGHAM STATION AVE
TUDOR RD
BEAUFORT CL
THURLOW CL
Sch
OSPREY HO
ADAM RD
KEATLEY GN
CHING WAY
IRIS WAY
GREENHAM CRES
TRINITY WAY
JUSTIN RD
AVENUE IND EST
WALTHAMSTOW AVE
Superstore
Salisbury Hall Pl Fld
MARLBOROUGH RD
NELSON RD
LONG LEYS
BELLAMY RD
APPLEBY CL
SELWYN AV
HELWYS CT
36
N18
(NORTH CIRCULAR RD)
The Ching
FOLLY LA
SALISBURY HALL GDNS
ROWDEN PARK GDNS
ROWDEN RD
Allot Gdns
CHINGFORD RD
Rush Croft Sch
LOXHAM RD
FAIRVIEW VILLAS
MINERVA RD
RUSHCROFT RD
ASCHAM DR
ROEBUCK CT
Highams Park
Banbury Resr
Superstore
Walthamstow Stad
Wadham Lodge Sp Gd
Hale End Sp Gd
WALTHAMSTOW AVE
EMPRESS PAR
EMPRESS AVE
GROVE PARK AVE
WADHAM AVE
GOODRIDGE HO
1 ROMANY GDNS
2 SWANSLAND GDNS
3 GARNETT WAY
4 GREENSHANK CL
5 CORMORANT CL
Sp Gd
Pl Fld
A112
Crooked Billet
BANBURY RD
GREBE CL
SWIFT CL
OSPREY CL
STOW CRES
DURBAN RD
WALTHAM PARK WAY
WALTHAM PK
WADHAM RD
NORTH CIRCULAR RD
A406
COGAN AVE
COOPER AVE
VALOGNES AVE
SWAN CL
AMBER AVE
FOLLY LA
ASCHAM END
CHENEY ROW
William Morris Sch
KIMBERLEY RD
KIMBERLEY IND EST
McEntee Sec Sch
B179
George White Sp Gd
CECIL RD
CECIL HO
MCENTEE AVE
BILLET RD
MONOUX GR
DOUGLAS AVE
KNEBWORTH AVE
KNEBWORTH HO
MANSEL GR
LEWIS AVE
PENRHYN CRES
ROBERTS RD
Schs
BERESFORD RD
KITCHENER RD
CHESHIRE CL
Wadham Lodge Sp Gd
GARNER RD
B160
1 KINGS FARM
2 CHAPEL END HO
3 HYH HO
Bwg Gn
WALTHAM CT
Higham Hill
Bwg Gn
Sch
Recn Gd
Tenn Cts
FAIR VIEW CL
SHAW SQ
GUILDSWAY
LYNE CRES
Schs
WIGTON RD
ARDLEIGH RD
ARDLEIGH TERR
DOUGLAS TERR
MILLFIELD AVE
BOSWORTH CL
WILLIAMS AVE
KEITH RD
PENRHYN AVE
BRETTENHAM RD
CAZENOVE RD
LAVEHHAM HO
BROOKSCROFT RD
QUEENSWAY
FULBOURNE
CARLTON RD
LONGLANDS CT
MANOR RD
HECHAM CL
MANOR CL
MOUNT PLEASANT RD
WARWICK RD
KELMSCOTT CL
NORTH COUNTESS RD
THORPE CRES
RUSHBROOK CRES
1 BRETTENHAM AVE
2 PENRHYN GR
Chapel End Inf Sch
RODNEY PL
HERON CL
Liby
PENNANT TERR
E17
Aveling Park Sch
AVELING PARK RD
MARTEN RD
NORTHBANK RD
WOODEND RD
STURGE AVE
THORPE RD
ST JOHN'S RD
VICTORIA RD
MAYFIELD RD
CUMBERLAND RD
OAKFIELD RD
WINDSOR AVE
PRIORS CROFT
Lloyd Park
EVESHAM AVE
Sir George Monoux Sixth Form Coll
WARBURTON TERR
Allot Gdns
CLAREMONT RD
HIGHAM HILL RD
UPSHIRE HO 1
VERMONT HO 2
WASHINGTON HO 3
THE QUADRANGLE 4
ABBOTS HO
ELPHINSTONE RD
FLEEMING RD
CARR RD
B Gn
OMNIBUS WAY
Chestnut Sp Gd
WALTHAMSTOW BSNS CTR
LOWTHER RD
CHURCH RD
BRAMLEY CL
Allot Gdns
EASTLEIGH RD
DARNDALE CL
CAPRI HO
ST ANDREWS RD
OATLAND RISE
HILLYFIELD
HAMILTON RD
FAIRFIELD RD
COLVILLE RD
DEVON HO
BALMORAL HO
SOUTH COUNTESS RD
Sch
CHANDOS AVE
Waltham Forest Coll
Allot Gdns
SPRUCE HILLS RD
ST ANDREW'S CT
DILWYN CT
GREEN POND RD
ADELAIDE HO
EVERGLADE HO
WINNS TERR
BADLIS RD
DUDLEY RD
BEDFORD RD
BROMLEY RD
HIGHAM ST
Sch
BROOK CT
POND CL
PRIORY CT
WINNS AVE
Bwg Gn
LLOYD PARK HO
WALTHAMSTOW
STIRLING RD
HIGH PL
BEMSTED RD
MERSEY RD
DIANA RD
KENILWORTH AVE
FARMAN AVE
TH
C Ctr
38
A503
Thorpe
HIGHAM ST
WILLIAM MORRIS CL
HOLMES
SUTHERLAND RD
37
53
36
A
B
C
D

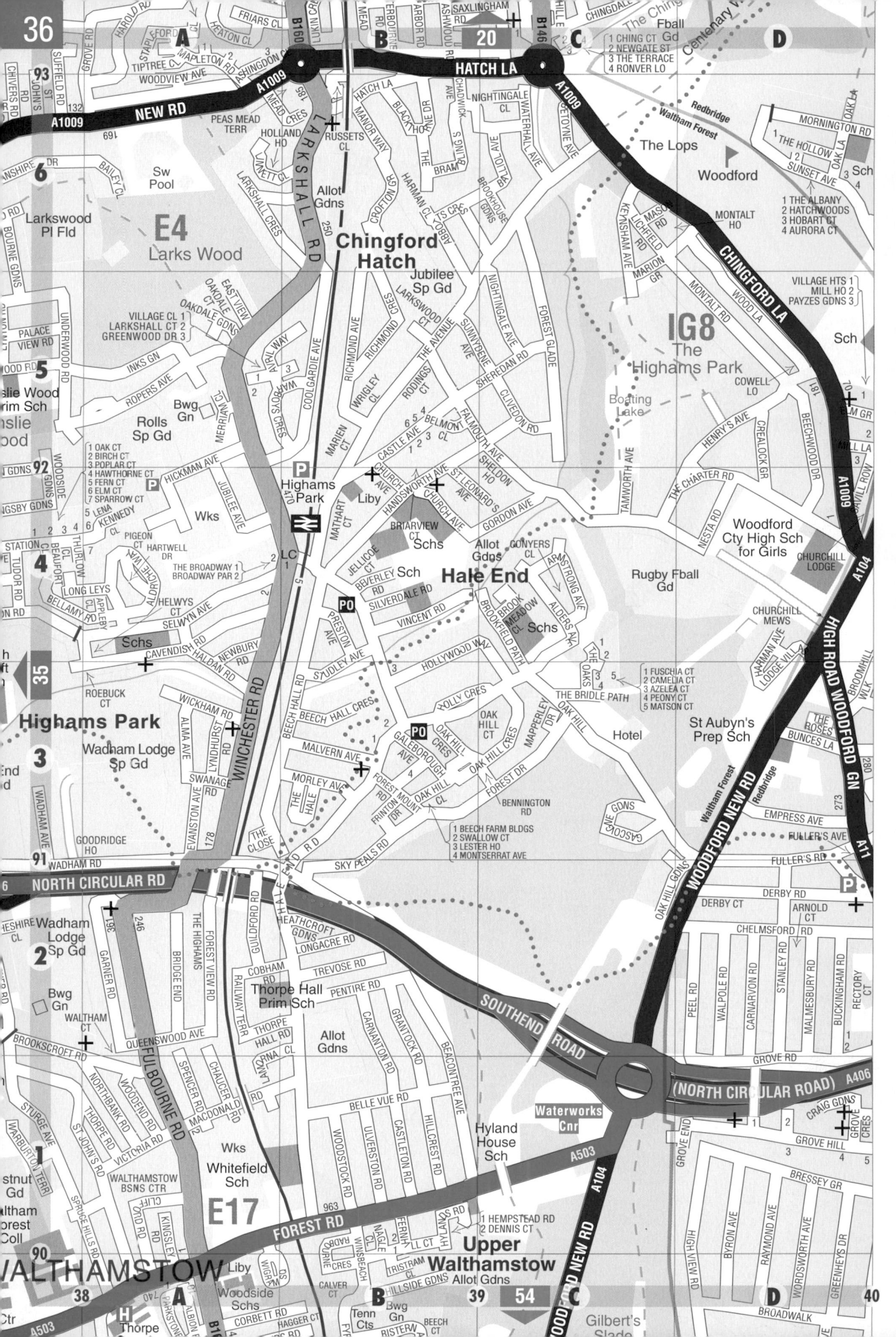
A
B
C
D
20
54
35
40
38
39
93
92
91
90
6
5
4
3
2
1
HATCH LA
NEW RD
A1009
B160
B146
Chingford Hatch
LARKSHALL RD
E4
Larks Wood
Larkswood Pl Fld
Sw Pool
Allot Gdns
Jubilee Sp Gd
Rolls Sp Gd
Bwg Gn
Wks
Highams Park
Liby
Schs
Sch
Hale End
HALE END RD
WINCHESTER RD
Highams Park
Wadham Lodge Sp Gd
NORTH CIRCULAR RD
IG8
The Highams Park
Boating Lake
The Lops
Woodford
CHINGFORD LA
Woodford Cty High Sch for Girls
CHURCHILL LODGE
Rugby Fball Gd
HIGH ROAD WOODFORD GN
A104
A11
WOODFORD NEW RD
St Aubyn's Prep Sch
Hotel
Redbridge
Waltham Forest
SOUTHEND ROAD
(NORTH CIRCULAR ROAD)
A406
Waterworks Cnr
Hyland House Sch
A503
FOREST RD
E17
Whitefield Sch
Thorpe Hall Prim Sch
FULBOURNE RD
Upper Walthamstow
Allot Gdns
WALTHAMSTOW
Woodside Schs
Wadham Lodge Sp Gd
Tenn Cts
Gilbert's Slade
Fball Gd
1 CHING CT
2 NEWGATE ST
3 THE TERRACE
4 RONVER LO
1 THE ALBANY
2 HATCHWOODS
3 HOBART CT
4 AURORA CT
VILLAGE HTS 1
MILL HO 2
PAYZES GDNS 3
VILLAGE CL 1
LARKSHALL CT 2
GREENWOOD DR 3
1 OAK CT
2 BIRCH CT
3 POPLAR CT
4 HAWTHORNE CT
5 FERN CT
6 ELM CT
7 SPARROW CT
THE BROADWAY 1
BROADWAY PAR 2
1 FUSCHIA CT
2 CAMELIA CT
3 AZELEA CT
4 PEONY CT
5 MATSON CT
1 BEECH FARM BLDGS
2 SWALLOW CT
3 LESTER HO
4 MONTSERRAT AVE
1 HEMPSTEAD RD
2 DENNIS CT

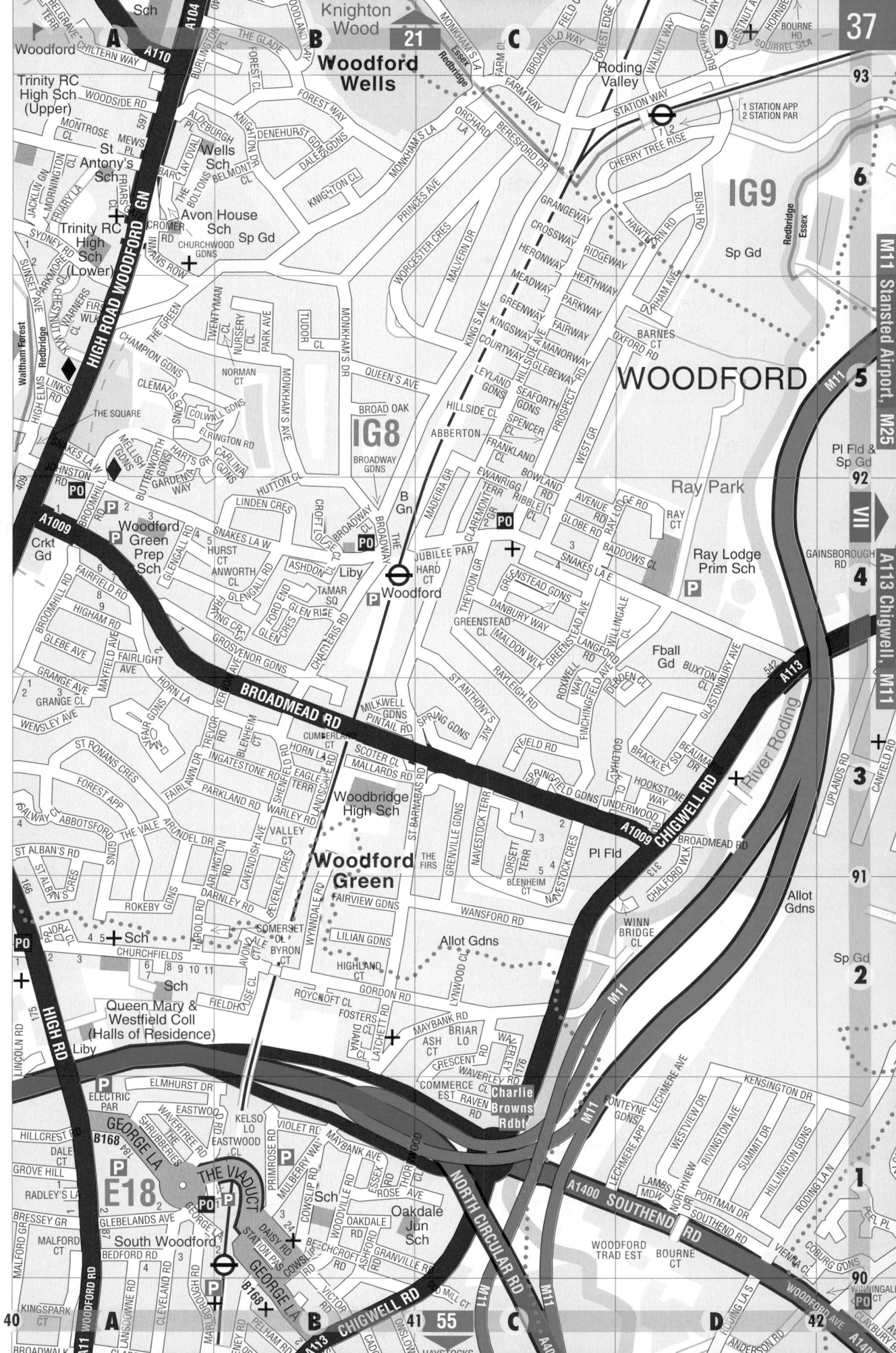
Knighton Wood
21
Woodford Wells
Woodford
Roding Valley
Trinity RC High Sch (Upper)
St Antony's Sch
Wells Sch
Avon House Sch
Trinity RC High Sch (Lower)
Sp Gd
IG9
IG8
WOODFORD
Ray Park
Ray Lodge Prim Sch
Fball Gd
Woodford Green Prep Sch
Crkt Gd
Liby
Woodbridge High Sch
Woodford Green
Allot Gdns
Pl Fld
Pl Fld & Sp Gd
Queen Mary & Westfield Coll (Halls of Residence)
Charlie Browns Rdbt
Oakdale Jun Sch
South Woodford
E18
WOODFORD TRAD EST
River Roding
HIGH ROAD WOODFORD GN
BROADMEAD RD
CHIGWELL RD
NORTH CIRCULAR RD
A1400 SOUTHEND RD
HIGH RD
GEORGE LA
THE VIADUCT
M11 Stansted Airport, M25
A113 Chigwell, M11
VII
55
HAYSTOCKS
A
B
C
D
93
6
5
92
4
3
91
2
1
90
40
41
42

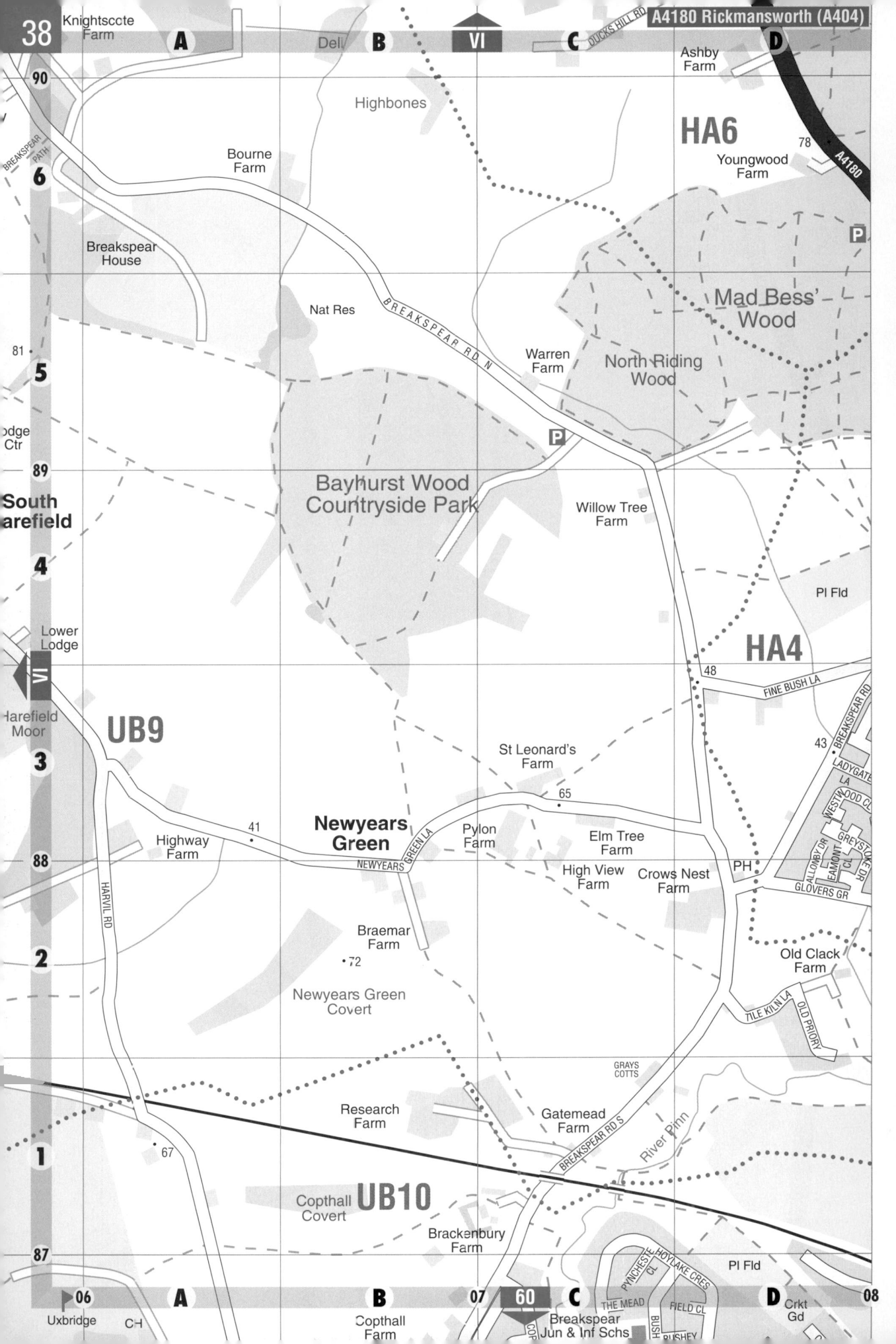
A4180 Rickmansworth (A404)
A
B
VI
C
D
Knightscote Farm
Dell
DUCKS HILL RD
Ashby Farm
90
Highbones
HA6
78
Youngwood Farm
A4180
BREAKSPEAR PATH
6
Bourne Farm
Breakspear House
P
Nat Res
BREAKSPEAR RD N
Mad Bess' Wood
81
5
Warren Farm
North Riding Wood
odge Ctr
P
89
South arefield
Bayhurst Wood Countryside Park
Willow Tree Farm
4
Pl Fld
Lower Lodge
HA4
VI
48
FINE BUSH LA
larefield Moor
UB9
BREAKSPEAR RD
43
3
St Leonard's Farm
LADYGATE LA
65
WESTWOOD CL
41
Newyears Green
GREEN LA
Pylon Farm
Elm Tree Farm
GREYSTOKE DR
Highway Farm
ALLONBY DR
EAMONT CL
88
NEWYEARS
High View Farm
Crows Nest Farm
PH
GLOVERS GR
HARVIL RD
Braemar Farm
2
72
Old Clack Farm
Newyears Green Covert
TILE KILN LA
OLD PRIORY
GRAYS COTTS
Research Farm
Gatemead Farm
1
BREAKSPEAR RD S
River Pinn
67
Copthall Covert
UB10
Brackenbury Farm
87
PYNCHESTE CL
HOYLAKE CRES
Pl Fld
06
A
B
07
60
C
D
08
Uxbridge
CH
Copthall Farm
THE MEAD
FIELD CL
BUSH
Breakspear Jun & Inf Schs
Crkt Gd

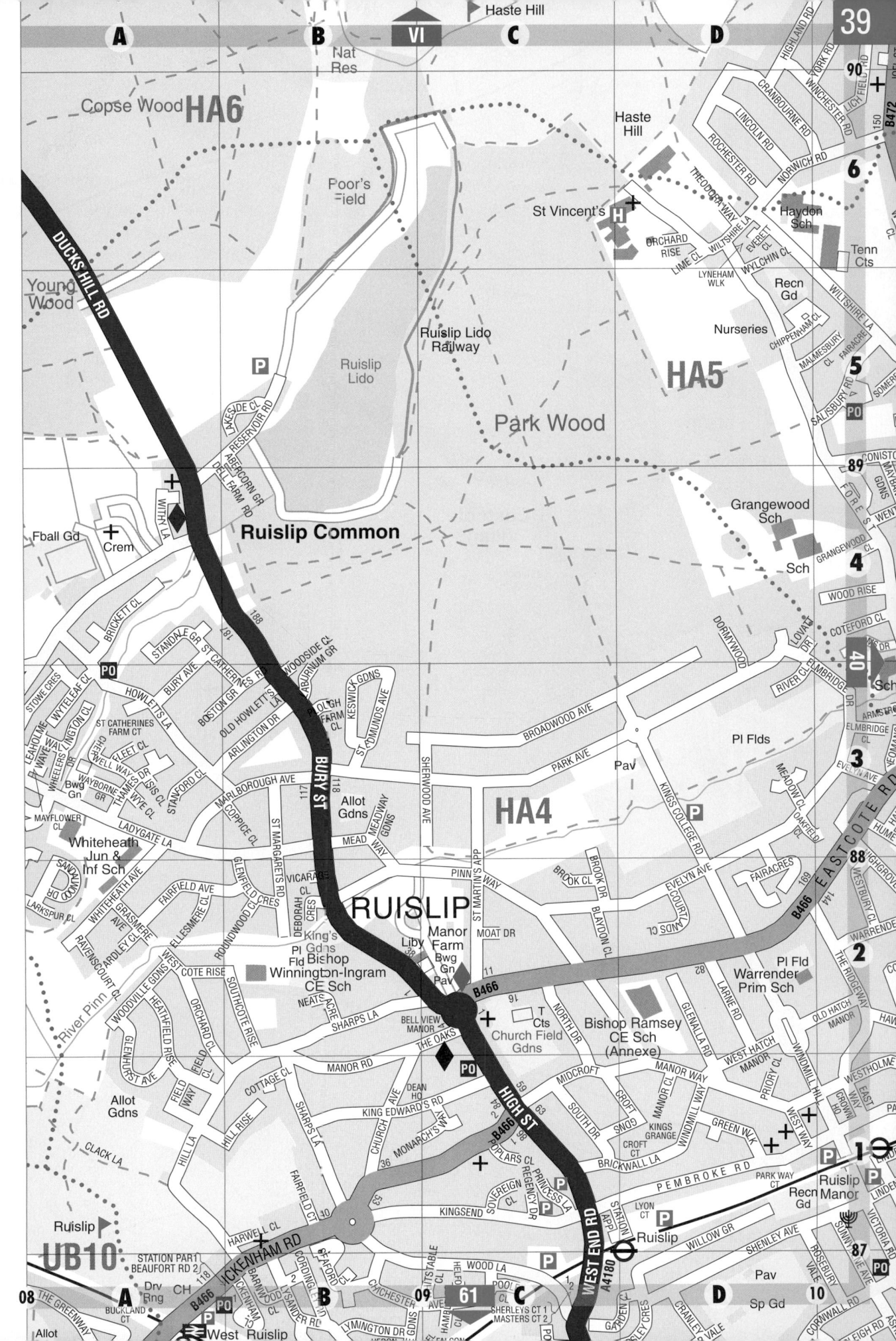
Haste Hill
VI
A
B
C
D
Nat Res
Copse Wood
HA6
Poor's Field
Haste Hill
St Vincent's
Haydon Sch
Tenn Cts
Young Wood
DUCKS HILL RD
Ruislip Lido Railway
Ruislip Lido
Recn Gd
Nurseries
HA5
Park Wood
LAKESIDE CL
RESERVOIR RD
ABERCORN GR
DELL FARM RD
WITHY LA
Ruislip Common
Fball Gd
Crem
Grangewood Sch
Sch
BRICKETT CL
STANDALE GR
ST CATHERINES RD
WOODSIDE CL
LABURNUM GR
HOWLETTS LA
BURY AVE
BOSTON GR
OLD HOWLETTS LA
ARLINGTON DR
PLOUGH FARM CL
KESWICK GDNS
ST EDMUNDS AVE
BROADWOOD AVE
DORMYWOOD
LOVAT DR
RIVER CL
ELMBRIDGE DR
ELMBRIDGE CL
Pl Flds
PARK AVE
Pav
SHERWOOD AVE
BURY ST
MARLBOROUGH AVE
STANFORD CL
COPPICE CL
ST MARGARETS RD
Allot Gdns
MEADWAY GDNS
MEAD WAY
HA4
KINGS COLLEGE RD
MEADOW CL
OAKFIELD CL
EVELYN AVE
STOWE CRES
WYTELEAF CL
ST CATHERINES FARM CT
FLEET CL
THAMES DR
ISIS CL
WYE CL
WAYBORNE GR
Bwg Gn
MAYFLOWER CL
LADYGATE LA
Whiteheath Jun & Inf Sch
SANDWOOD DR
WHITEHEATH AVE
FAIRFIELD AVE
GLENFIELD CRES
VICARAGE
DEBORAH CRES
PINN WAY
ST MARTIN'S APP
BROOK CL
BROOK DR
BLAYDON CL
COURTLANDS CL
FAIRACRES
LARKSPUR CL
GRASMERE AVE
ELLESMERE CL
ROUNDWOOD CL
RUISLIP
King's Gdns
Liby
Manor Farm
Bwg Gn
Pav
MOAT DR
B466
EASTCOTE RD
Pl Fld
Warrender Prim Sch
THE RIDGEWAY
RAVENSCOURT CL
ARDLEY CL
WEST COTE RISE
SOUTHCOTE RISE
Pl Fld
Bishop Winnington-Ingram CE Sch
NEATS ACRE
SHARPS LA
BELL VIEW MANOR
THE OAKS
Church Field Gdns
NORTH DR
Bishop Ramsey CE Sch (Annexe)
GLENALLA RD
LARNE RD
OLD HATCH MANOR
River Pinn
WOODVILLE GDNS
HEATHFIELD RISE
GLENHURST AVE
ORCHARD CL
FIELD CL
FIELD WAY
COTTAGE CL
MANOR RD
DEAN HO
KING EDWARD'S RD
MONARCH'S WAY
CHURCH AVE
HIGH ST
MIDCROFT
SOUTH DR
CROFT GDNS
MANOR CL
KINGS GRANGE
CROFT CT
WINDMILL WAY
MANOR WAY
WEST HATCH MANOR
PRIORY CL
WINDMILL HILL
GREEN WLK
WEST WAY
Allot Gdns
HILL RISE
HILL LA
SHARPS LA
CLACK LA
POPLARS CL
PRINCESS LA
BRICKWALL LA
PEMBROKE RD
PARK WAY CT
Ruislip Manor
Recn Gd
FAIRFIELD CT
SOVEREIGN CL
REGENCY DR
KINGSEND
STATION APP
LYON CT
Ruislip
WILLOW GR
SHENLEY AVE
ROSEBURY VALE
SUNNINGDALE AVE
VICTORIA RD
Ruislip
UB10
STATION PAR 1
BEAUFORT RD 2
HARWELL CL
ICKENHAM RD
CORDINGLEY RD
STAFFORD CL
WHITSTABLE CL
WOOD LA
WEST END RD
A4180
Pav
Sp Gd
08
09
10
61
Drv Rng
CH
BUCKLAND CT
THE GREENWAY
Allot
West Ruislip
CHICHESTER AVE
LYMINGTON DR
SHERLEYS CT 1
MASTERS CT 2
CRANLEY VALE
CORNWALL RD
90
89
88
87
6
5
4
3
2
1
40
Sch
ORCHARD RISE
LIME CL
WILTSHIRE LA
EVERETT CL
WYLCHIN CL
LYNEHAM WLK
THEODORA WAY
ROCHESTER RD
LINCOLN RD
CRANBOURNE RD
WINCHESTER RD
NORWICH RD
HIGHLAND RD
YORK RD
LICHFIELD RD
B472
CHIPPENHAM CL
MALMESBURY CL
FAIRACRE
SALISBURY RD
WILTSHIRE LA
FORE ST
GRANGEWOOD CL
WOOD RISE
COTEFORD CL
WESTBURY CL
B466

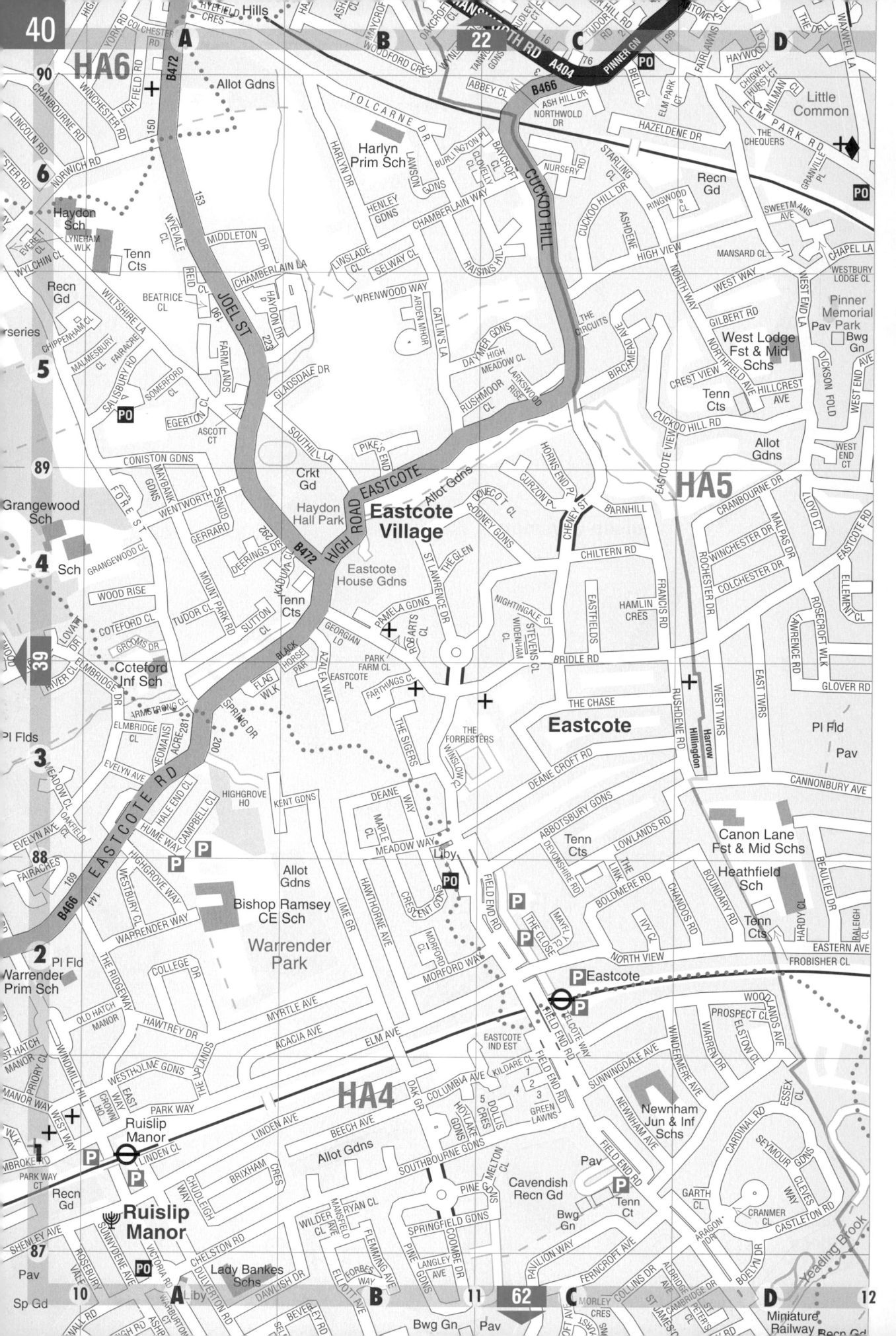
HA6
HA5
HA4
A
B
C
D
22
62
39
90
89
88
87
6
5
4
3
2
1
10
11
12
Hills
RYEFIELD CRES
YORK RD
COLCHESTER RD
LICHFIELD RD
WINCHESTER RD
CRANBOURNE RD
LINCOLN RD
NORWICH RD
Allot Gdns
B472
150
153
TOLCARNE DR
Harlyn Prim Sch
HARLYN DR
LAWSON GDNS
HENLEY GDNS
BURLINGTON PL
CLOVELLY CL
BAYCROFT CL
CHAMBERLAIN WAY
WOODFORD CRES
MAYCROFT
OAKCROFT
ABBEY CL
B466
A404
PINNER RD
PINNER GN
ASH HILL DR
NORTHWOLD DR
TUDOR RD
BELL CL
ELM PARK CT
FAIRLAWNS CL
HAYWOOD CL
CHIGWELL HURST CT
MILMAN CL
Little Common
ELM PARK RD
THE CHEQUERS
GRANVILLE PL
HAZELDENE DR
NURSERY RD
STARLING CL
CUCKOO HILL
CUCKOO HILL DR
Recn Gd
RINGWOOD CL
ASHDENE
SWEETMANS AVE
MANSARD CL
CHAPEL LA
WESTBURY LODGE CL
HIGH VIEW
NORTH WAY
WEST WAY
GILBERT RD
WEST END LA
Pinner Memorial Park
Pav
Bwg Gn
West Lodge Fst & Mid Schs
NORTHFIELD AVE
CREST VIEW
HILLCREST AVE
DICKSON FOLD
WEST END AVE
Tenn Cts
CUCKOO HILL RD
Allot Gdns
WEST END CT
Haydon Sch
LYNEHAM WLK
EVERETT CL
WYLCHIN CL
Recn Gd
WILTSHIRE LA
CHIPPENHAM CL
MALMESBURY CL
FAIRACRE
SALISBURY RD
SOMERFORD CL
PO
EGERTON CL
ASCOTT CT
BEATRICE CL
REID CL
WYEVALE CL
MIDDLETON DR
CHAMBERLAIN LA
HAYDON DR
JOEL ST
FARMLANDS
GLADSDALE DR
SOUTHILL LA
LINSLADE CL
SELWAY CL
WRENWOOD WAY
ARDEN MHOR
CATLINS LA
RAISINS HILL
THE CIRCUITS
BIRCHMEAD AVE
DAYMER GDNS
HIGH MEADOW CL
LARKSWOOD RISE
RUSHMOOR CL
PIKES END
CONISTON GDNS
MAYBANK GDNS
WENTWORTH DR
GERRARD GDNS
FORE ST
Crkt Gd
Haydon Hall Park
EASTCOTE
HIGH ROAD
Eastcote Village
Allot Gdns
DOVECOT CL
RODNEY GDNS
HORNS END PL
CURZON PL
CHENEY ST
BARNHILL
EASTCOTE VIEW
CRANBOURNE DR
WINCHESTER DR
MALPAS DR
LLOYD CT
EASTCOTE RD
Grangewood Sch
GRANGEWOOD CL
Sch
WOOD RISE
DEERINGS DR
MOUNT PARK RD
TUDOR CL
SUTTON CL
KADUNA CL
Tenn Cts
Eastcote House Gdns
ST LAWRENCE DR
THE GLEN
CHILTERN RD
EASTFIELDS
HAMLIN CRES
FRANCIS RD
ROCHESTER DR
COLCHESTER DR
ELLEMENT CL
ROSECROFT WLK
LAWRENCE RD
COTEFORD CL
LOVATT DR
GROOMS DR
Coteford Inf Sch
RIVER CL
ELMBRIDGE DR
GEORGIAN LO
BLACK HORSE PAR
AZALEA WLK
PAMELA GDNS
ROGARTS CL
PARK FARM CL
EASTCOTE PL
FARTHINGS CL
NIGHTINGALE CL
WIDENHAM CL
STEVENS CL
BRIDLE RD
FLAG WLK
ARMSTRONG CL
ELMBRIDGE CL
YEOMANS ACRE
SPRING DR
281
200
THE SIGERS
THE FORRESTERS
WINSLOW CL
THE CHASE
Eastcote
RUSHDENE RD
Hillingdon
Harrow
WEST TWRS
EAST TWRS
GLOVER RD
Pl Fld
Pav
Pl Flds
EVELYN AVE
MEADOW CL
OAKFIELD CL
EASTCOTE RD
HALE END CL
HIGHGROVE HO
KENT GDNS
DEANE WAY
MAPLE CL
MEADOW WAY
DEANE CROFT RD
ABBOTSBURY GDNS
CANNONBURY AVE
Canon Lane Fst & Mid Schs
HUME WAY
CAMPBELL CL
FAIRACRES
169
144
B466
HIGHGROVE WAY
WESTBURY CL
Allot Gdns
Liby
Tenn Cts
DEVONSHIRE RD
LOWLANDS RD
THE LINK
BOLDMERE RD
CHANDOS RD
BOUNDARY RD
Heathfield Sch
BEAULIEU DR
Bishop Ramsey CE Sch
WARRENDER WAY
HAWTHORNE AVE
CRESCENT GDNS
FIELD END RD
THE CLOSE
MAYFLY CL
IVY CL
Tenn Cts
HARDY CL
RALEIGH CL
EASTERN AVE
FROBISHER CL
Warrender Park
LIME GR
MORFORD CL
MORFORD WAY
NORTH VIEW
Eastcote
Pl Fld
Warrender Prim Sch
THE RIDGEWAY
COLLEGE DR
MYRTLE AVE
OLD HATCH MANOR
HAWTREY DR
ACACIA AVE
ELM AVE
EASTCOTE IND EST
TELCOTE WAY
WOODLANDS AVE
PROSPECT CL
ELSTON CL
WARREN DR
WINDERMERE AVE
ST HATCH MANOR
PRIORY CL
WINDMILL HILL
WESTHOLME GDNS
THE UPLANDS
KILDARE CL
COLUMBIA AVE
SUNNINGDALE AVE
MANOR WAY
WEST WAY
CROWN HO
EAST WAY
PARK WAY
OAK GR
HOYLAKE GDNS
DOLLIS CRES
GREEN LAWNS
NEWNHAM AVE
Newnham Jun & Inf Schs
ESSEX CL
CARDINAL RD
SEYMOUR GDNS
LINDEN AVE
BEECH AVE
Ruislip Manor
LINDEN CL
Allot Gdns
SOUTHBOURNE GDNS
MELTON CL
Pav
FIELD END RD
PARK WAY CT
Recn Gd
BRIXHAM CRES
CHUDLEIGH WAY
PINE GDNS
Cavendish Recn Gd
Tenn Ct
GARTH CL
CRANMER CL
CLEVES WAY
CASTLETON RD
Ruislip Manor
WILDER CL
MANSFIELD AVE
RYAN CL
SPRINGFIELD GDNS
COOMBE DR
Bwg Gn
ARAGON DR
Yeading Brook
SHENLEY AVE
SUNNYDENE AVE
ROSEBURY VALE
VICTORIA RD
CHELSTON RD
DULVERTON RD
Lady Bankes Schs
DAWLISH DR
ELLIOTT AVE
FLEMMING AVE
FORBES WAY
PINE GDNS
LANGLEY AVE
PAVILION WAY
FERNCROFT AVE
COLLINS DR
ALDRIDGE AVE
CAMBRIDGE DR
BOELYN DR
Pav
Sp Gd
Liby
BEVERLEY RD
MORLEY CRES
ST JAMES CL
ST PETERS CL
Bwg Gn
Pav
Miniature Railway
Recn Gd

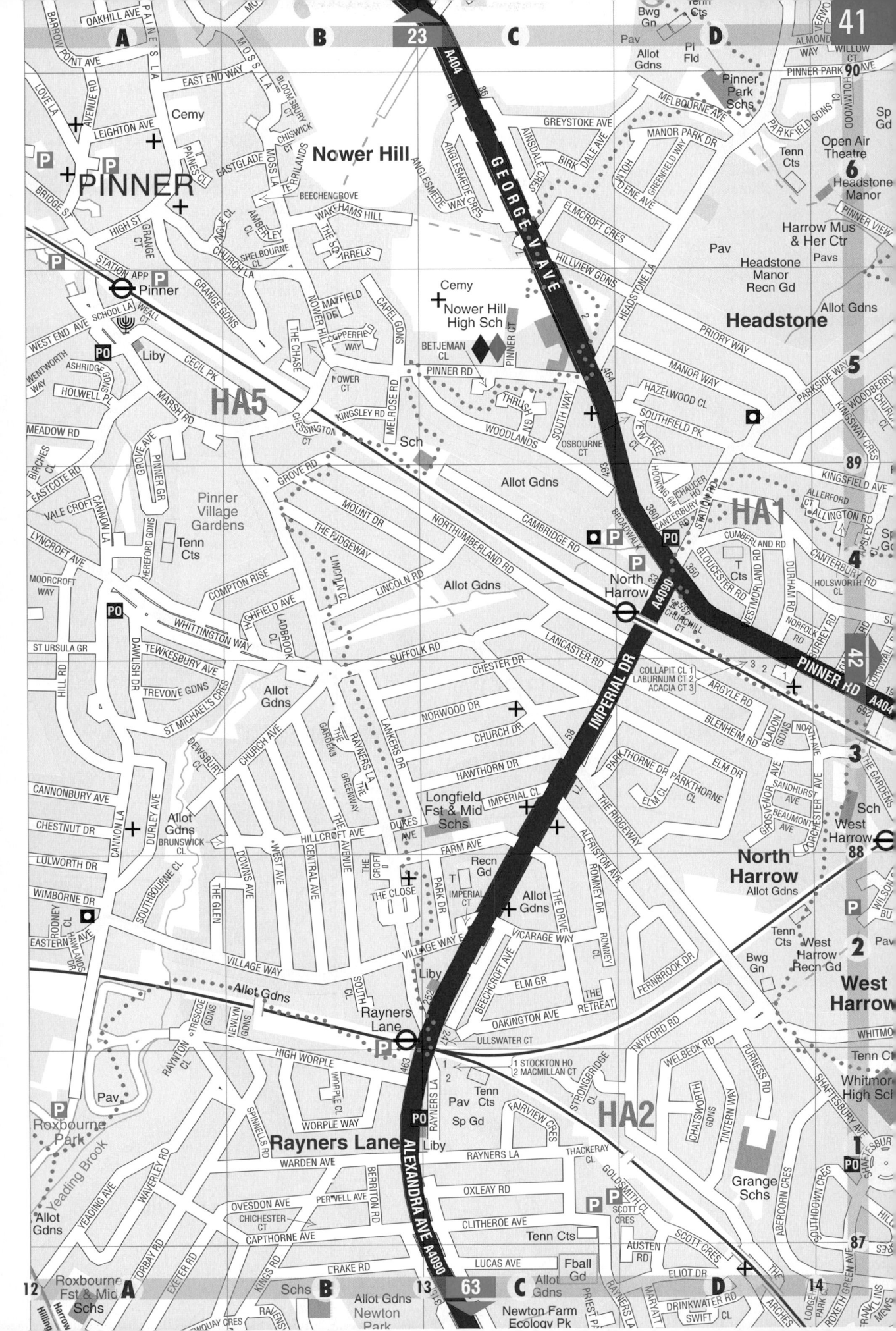

A
B
23
C
D
A404
GEORGE V AVE
PINNER
Nower Hill
HA5
HA1
HA2
Headstone
North Harrow
West Harrow
Rayners Lane
Pinner
OAKHILL AVE
BARROW POINT AVE
PAINES LA
MOSS LA
EAST END WAY
LOVE LA
AVENUE RD
LEIGHTON AVE
Cemy
BLOOMSBURY CT
CHISWICK CT
EASTGLADE
PAINES CL
TERRILANDS
BRIDGE ST
HIGH ST
GRANGE CT
ANGLE CL
AMBER CL
BEECHENGROVE
WAKEHAMS HILL
SHELBOURNE CL
THE SQUIRRELS
CHURCH LA
GRANGE GDNS
STATION APP
WEST END AVE
SCHOOL LA
WEALL CT
PO
Liby
CECIL PK
MARSH RD
WENTWORTH WAY
ASHRIDGE GDNS
HOLWELL PL
MEADOW RD
BIRCHES CL
EASTCOTE RD
VALE CROFT
CANNON LA
GROVE AVE
PINNER GR
Pinner Village Gardens
Tenn Cts
HEREFORD GDNS
LYNCROFT AVE
MOORCROFT WAY
COMPTON RISE
WHITTINGTON WAY
ST URSULA GR
HILL RD
DAWLISH DR
TEWKESBURY AVE
TREVONE GDNS
ST MICHAEL'S CRES
HIGHFIELD AVE
LADBROOK CL
Allot Gdns
DEWSBURY CL
CHURCH AVE
CANNONBURY AVE
CHESTNUT DR
DURLEY AVE
BRUNSWICK CL
LULWORTH DR
SOUTHBOURNE CL
WIMBORNE DR
RODNEY CL
HAMLANDS DR
EASTERN AVE
THE GLEN
DOWNS AVE
WEST AVE
CENTRAL AVE
THE AVENUE
HILLCROFT AVE
VILLAGE WAY
MAYFIELD DR
NOWER HILL
THE CHASE
COPPERFIELD WAY
CAPEL GDNS
NOWER CT
KINGSLEY RD
MELROSE RD
CHESSINGTON CT
GROVE RD
MOUNT DR
THE RIDGEWAY
LINCOLN CL
LINCOLN RD
NORTHUMBERLAND RD
Sch
Cemy
Nower Hill High Sch
BETJEMAN CL
PINNER CT
PINNER RD
THRUSH GN
WOODLANDS
SOUTH WAY
OSBOURNE CT
ANGLESMEDE CRES
ANGLESMEDE WAY
GREYSTOKE AVE
AINSDALE CRES
BIRKDALE AVE
ELMCROFT CRES
HILLVIEW GDNS
HEADSTONE LA
MELBOURNE AVE
MANOR PARK DR
GREENFIELD WAY
HOLMDENE AVE
Bwg Gn
Tenn Cts
Pav
Allot Gdns
Pl Fld
Pinner Park Schs
ALMOND WAY
WILLOW CT
PINNER PARK AVE
HOLLWOOD CL
PARKFIELD GDNS
Open Air Theatre
Sp Gd
Headstone Manor
PINNER VIEW
Harrow Mus & Her Ctr
Headstone Manor Recn Gd
Pavs
PRIORY WAY
MANOR WAY
HAZELWOOD CL
SOUTHFIELD PK
YEWTREE CL
PARKSIDE WAY
WOODBERRY
KINGSWAY CRES
KINGSFIELD AVE
ALLERFORD CT
ALLINGTON RD
HOOKING GN
CHAUCER HO
CANTERBURY RD
STATION RD
BROADWALK
CAMBRIDGE RD
CUMBERLAND RD
GLOUCESTER RD
WESTMORLAND RD
DURHAM RD
CANTERBURY RD
HOLSWORTH CL
NORFOLK RD
SURREY RD
CHURCHILL CT
A4090
PINNER RD
LANCASTER RD
COLLAPIT CL 1
LABURNUM CT 2
ACACIA CT 3
ARGYLE RD
BLENHEIM RD
BLADON GDNS
NORTH AVE
IMPERIAL DR
SUFFOLK RD
CHESTER DR
NORWOOD DR
CHURCH DR
HAWTHORN DR
PARKTHORNE DR
ELM DR
ELM CL
PARKTHORNE CL
THE RIDGEWAY
GROSVENOR AVE
SANDHURST AVE
BEAUMONT AVE
DORCHESTER AVE
Longfield Fst & Mid Schs
IMPERIAL CL
DUKES AVE
FARM AVE
RAYNERS LA
LANKERS DR
THE GARDENS
THE GREENWAY
THE CROFT
THE CLOSE
PARK DR
IMPERIAL CT
Recn Gd
ALFRISTON AVE
ROMNEY DR
THE DRIVE
ROMNEY CL
VICARAGE WAY
BEECHCROFT AVE
ELM GR
OAKINGTON AVE
THE RETREAT
FERNBROOK DR
ULLSWATER CT
TWYFORD RD
WELBECK RD
FURNESS RD
1 STOCKTON HO
2 MACMILLAN CT
STRONGBRIDGE CL
CHATSWORTH GDNS
TINTERN WAY
Grange Schs
ABERCORN CRES
SOUTHDOWN CRES
SHAFTESBURY AVE
Sch
Tenn Cts
West Harrow Recn Gd
Bwg Gn
WHITMORE
Whitmore High Sch
WILSON
THE GARDENS
SOUTH CL
Liby
TRESCOE GDNS
NEWLYN GDNS
RAYNTON CL
HIGH WORPLE
WORPLE CL
WORPLE WAY
SPINNELLS RD
Pav
Roxbourne Park
Yeading Brook
WAVERLEY RD
YEADING AVE
TORBAY RD
EXETER RD
KINGS RD
RAVENS
WARDEN AVE
OVESDON AVE
PERCIVALL AVE
CHICHESTER CT
CAPTHORNE AVE
BERRITON RD
DRAKE RD
ALEXANDRA AVE A4090
Pav
Sp Gd
Tenn Cts
FAIRVIEW CRES
THACKERAY CL
GOLDSMITH CL
SCOTT CRES
AUSTEN RD
SCOTT CRES
ELIOT DR
DRINKWATER RD
SWIFT CL
MARYATT
PRIEST PA
RAYNERS LA
OXLEAY RD
CLITHEROE AVE
LUCAS AVE
Fball Gd
Newton Farm Ecology Pk
Newton Park
Roxbourne Fst & Mid Schs
Schs
LODGE PARK CL
ROXETH GREEN AVE
ARCHES
12
13
14
63
42
A404
90
89
88
87
6
5
4
3
2
1

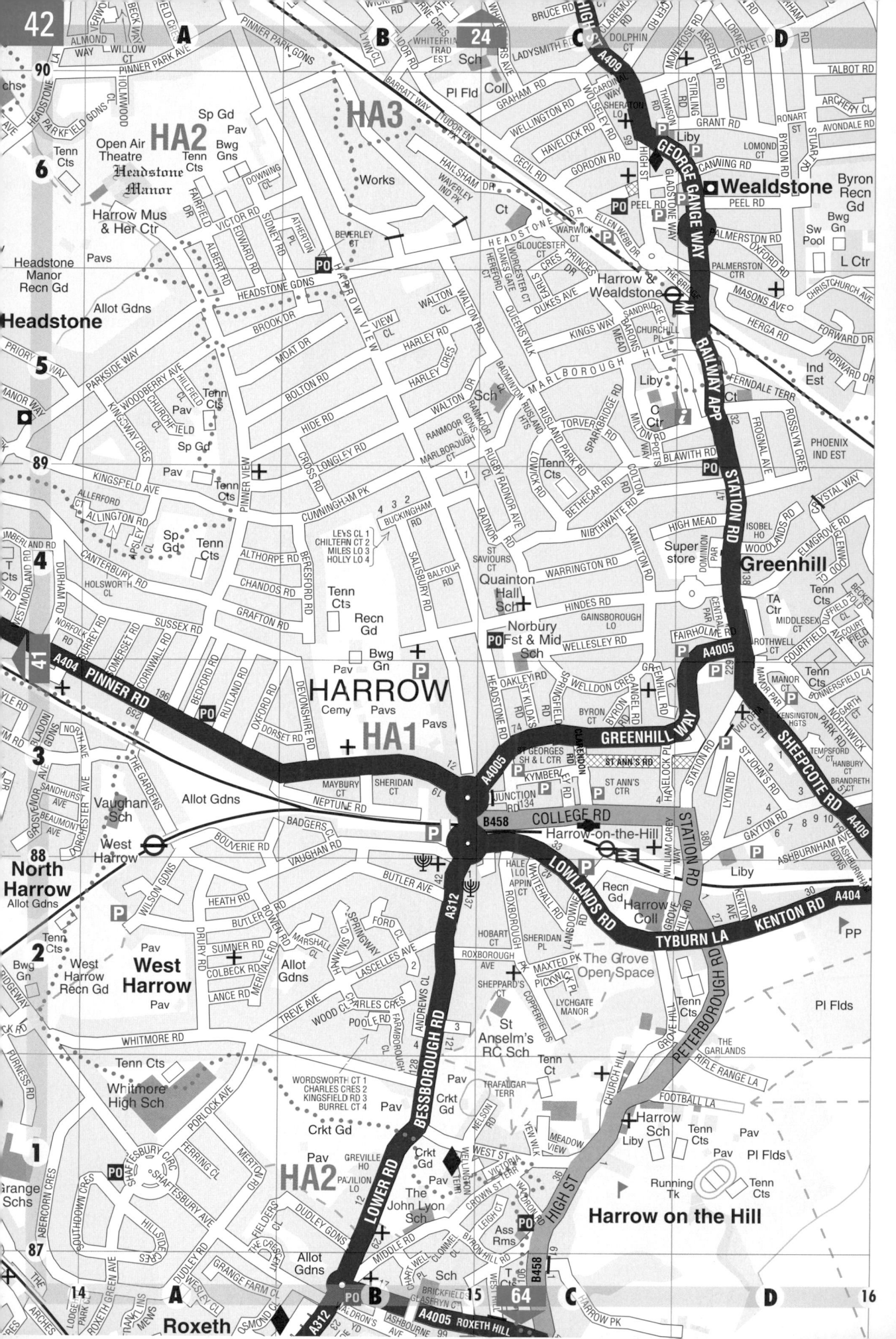

42
A
B
C
D
24
90
6
5
89
4
3
88
2
1
87
14
15
16
64
41
ALMOND WAY
WILLOW CT
VERWOOD
BECK WAY
PINNER PARK AVE
PINNER PARK GDNS
LYNN CL
TUDOR RD
WHITEFRIARS TRAD EST
Sch
BRUCE RD
LADYSMITH RD
HIGH ST
CLAREMONT RD
DOLPHIN CT
MONTROSE RD
ABERDEEN RD
LORNE RD
LOCKET RD
TALBOT RD
HEADSTONE LA
PARKFIELD GDNS
HOLMWOOD CL
BARRATT WAY
TUDOR ENT PK
Pl Fld
Coll
GRAHAM RD
WELLINGTON RD
WOLSELEY RD
CARDINAL WAY
SHERATON LO
THOMSON RD
STIRLING RD
GRANT RD
RONART ST
ARCHERY CL
AVONDALE RD
HA3
HA2
Sp Gd
Pav
Bwg Gns
Open Air Theatre
Tenn Cts
Headstone Manor
Harrow Mus & Her Ctr
DOWNING CL
FAIRFIELD DR
VICTOR RD
EDWARD RD
SIDNEY RD
ATHERTON PL
ALBERT RD
Works
HAILSHAM DR
WAVERLEY IND PK
HAVELOCK RD
CECIL RD
GORDON RD
GEORGE GANGE WAY
Liby
CANNING RD
LOMOND CT
BYRON RD
STUART RD
Wealdstone
Byron Recn Gd
PEEL RD
GLADSTONE WAY
ELLEN WEBB DR
WARWICK CT
Ct
Bwg Gn
Sw Pool
PALMERSTON RD
OXFORD RD
PALMERSTON CTR
L Ctr
BEVERLEY CT
PO
HARROW VIEW
HEADSTONE DR
GLOUCESTER CT
WORCESTER CT
DANES GATE
HEREFORD CT
EARLS CRES
PRINCES DR
Headstone Manor Recn Gd
Pavs
HEADSTONE GDNS
Allot Gdns
Harrow & Wealdstone
THE BRIDGE
MASONS AVE
CHRISTCHURCH AVE
Headstone
BROOK DR
VIEW CL
WALTON CL
WALTON RD
QUEENS WLK
DUKES AVE
KINGS WAY
SANDRIDGE CL
BARONS MEAD
CHURCHILL PL
HERGA RD
FORWARD DR
PRIORY WAY
MOAT DR
HARLEY RD
HARLEY CRES
MARLBOROUGH HILL
RAILWAY APP
Ind Est
PARKSIDE WAY
WOODBERRY AVE
HILLFIELD CL
BOLTON RD
BADMINTON CT
RUSLAND HTS
Liby
C Ctr
FERNDALE TERR
MANOR WAY
KINGSWAY CRES
CHURCHFIELD CL
Sch
RUSLAND PARK RD
SPARKBRIDGE RD
TORVER RD
MILTON RD
ROSSLYN CRES
FROGNAL AVE
HIDE RD
WALTON DR
RANMOOR GDNS
RANMOOR CL
MARLBOROUGH CT
LOWICK RD
POETS WAY
BLAWITH RD
PHOENIX IND EST
Sp Gd
KINGSFIELD AVE
PINNER VIEW
CROSS RD
LONGLEY RD
RUGBY CL
RADNOR AVE
BETHECAR RD
COLTON RD
STATION RD
CRYSTAL WAY
ALLERFORD CT
ALLINGTON RD
CUNNINGHAM PK
BUCKINGHAM RD
LEYS CL 1
CHILTERN CT 2
MILES LO 3
HOLLY LO 4
RADNOR RD
NIBTHWAITE RD
HAMILTON RD
HIGH MEAD
ISOBEL HO
WOODLANDS RD
ELMGROVE RD
GLENWOOD CL
APSLEY CL
CUMBERLAND RD
WESTMORLAND RD
DURHAM RD
CANTERBURY RD
HOLSWORTH CL
ALTHORPE RD
BERESFORD RD
SALISBURY RD
ST SAVIOURS CT
WARRINGTON RD
Super store
DOMINION PAR
Greenhill
CHANDOS RD
BALFOUR RD
Quainton Hall Sch
TA Ctr
BECKET FOLD
DUFFIELD CL
MIDDLESEX CT
GRAFTON RD
Recn Gd
HINDES RD
GAINSBOROUGH LO
CENTRAL PAR
NORFOLK RD
SURREY RD
SOMERSET RD
CORNWALL RD
SUSSEX RD
Norbury Fst & Mid Sch
WELLESLEY RD
FAIRHOLME RD
ROTHWELL CT
COURTFIELD AVE
COURTFIELD CR
A4005
A404
PINNER RD
Bwg Gn
BEDFORD RD
RUTLAND RD
OXFORD RD
DEVONSHIRE RD
HARROW
Cemy
Pavs
OAKLEY RD
ST KILDAS RD
SPRINGFIELD RD
WELLDON CRES
GRENFELL RD
MANOR PAR
Tenn Cts
BONNERSFIELD LA
KENSINGTON HGTS
NORTHWICK PARK RD
GARTH CT
BYRON CT
BYRON RD
ANGEL RD
VICTORIA TERR
HA1
HEADSTONE RD
DORSET RD
GREENHILL WAY
CLARENDON RD
SHEEPCOTE RD
TEMPSFORD CT
HANBURY CT
BRANDRETH CT
NORTH AVE
GLADSTONE GDNS
THE GARDENS
MAYBURY CT
SHERIDAN CT
ST GEORGES SH & L CTR
KYMBERLEY RD
ST ANN'S RD
HAVELOCK PL
STATION RD
LYON RD
ST JOHN'S RD
A409
SANDHURST AVE
GROSVENOR AVE
DORCHESTER AVE
BEAUMONT AVE
Vaughan Sch
Allot Gdns
NEPTUNE RD
JUNCTION RD
ST ANN'S CTR
GAYTON RD
ASHBURNHAM AVE
ASHBURNHAM GDNS
BADGERS CL
B458
COLLEGE RD
Harrow-on-the-Hill
WILLIAM CAREY WAY
West Harrow
North Harrow
Allot Gdns
BOUVERIE RD
VAUGHAN RD
BUTLER AVE
HALE LO
APPIN CT
WHITEHALL RD
LOWLANDS RD
Liby
WILSON GDNS
HEATH RD
BUTLER RD
BOWEN RD
MARSHALL CL
SPRINGWAY
FORD CL
A312
ROXBOROUGH RD
LANSDOWNE RD
Recn Gd
Harrow Coll
GROVE HILL RD
KENTON AVE
TYBURN LA
KENTON RD
PP
Tenn Cts
Bwg Gn
West Harrow Recn Gd
West Harrow
Pav
DRURY RD
SUMNER RD
COLBECK RD
MERIVALE RD
LANCE RD
HAWKINS CL
LASCELLES AVE
Allot Gdns
HOBART CT
SHERIDAN PL
ROXBOROUGH AVE
ROXBOROUGH PK
MAXTED PK
PICKWICK PL
The Grove Open Space
PETERBOROUGH RD
RIDGEWAY
TREVE AVE
WOOD CL
CHARLES CRES
POOLE RD
FARMBOROUGH CL
ANDREWS CL
BESSBOROUGH RD
SHEPPARD'S CT
COPPERFIELDS
LYCHGATE MANOR
Tenn Cts
Pl Flds
WHITMORE RD
St Anselm's RC Sch
THE GARLANDS
FURNESS RD
Whitmore High Sch
WORDSWORTH CT 1
CHARLES CRES 2
KINGSFIELD RD 3
BURREL CT 4
Pav
Crkt Gd
TRAFALGAR TERR
Tenn Ct
CHURCH HILL
RIFLE RANGE LA
FOOTBALL LA
PORLOCK AVE
NELSON RD
YEW WLK
MEADOW VIEW
Harrow Sch
Tenn Cts
Pav
Liby
Crkt Gd
Pl Flds
SHAFTESBURY CIRC
FERRING CL
MERTON RD
GREVILLE HO
Crkt Gd
WEST ST
VICTORIA TERR
WELLINGTON TERR
HIGH ST
Running Tk
Grange Schs
ABERCORN CRES
SOUTHDOWN CRES
SHAFTESBURY AVE
HILLSIDE CRES
PAVILION LO
LOWER RD
The John Lyon Sch
CROWN ST
LEIGH CT
WALDRON RD
Harrow on the Hill
DUDLEY GDNS
FIELDERS CL
THE CRESCENT
MIDDLE RD
CLONMEL CL
BYRON HILL RD
Ass Rms
DUDLEY RD
WESLEY CL
GRANGE FARM CL
Allot Gdns
CHARTWELL PL
Sch
WEST HILL
B458
THE ARCHES
LODGE PARK CL
ROXETH GREEN AVE
FRANKLINS MEWS
Roxeth
OSMOND CL
BRICKFIELDS
GLASFRYN CT
ASHBOURNE AVE
A4005
ROXETH HILL
HARROW PK

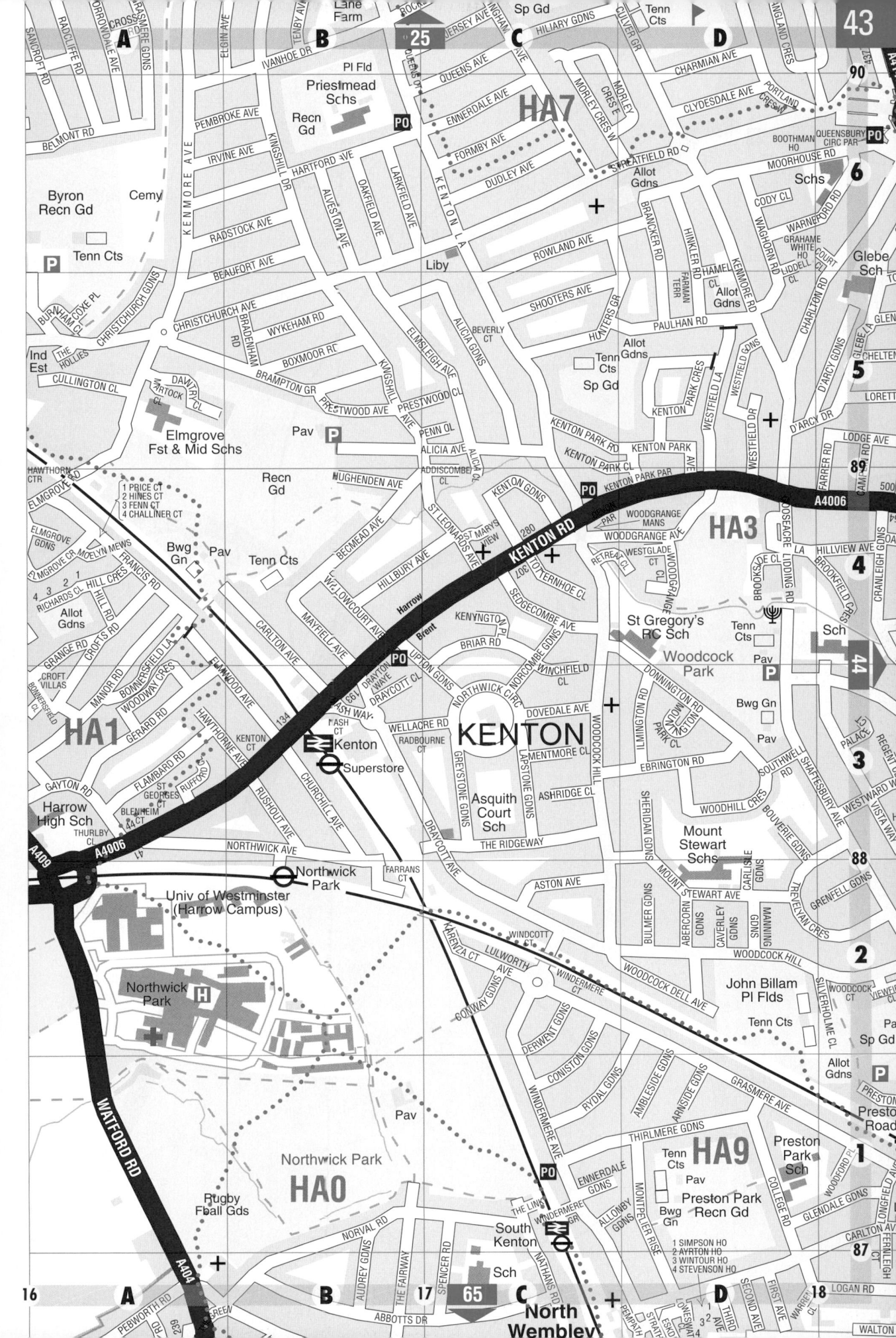
25
65
44
HA7
HA3
HA1
HA0
HA9
KENTON
A B C D
A B C D
16
17
18
90
89
88
87
6
5
4
3
2
1
Lane Farm
Sp Gd
Tenn Cts
Pl Fld
Priestmead Schs
Recn Gd
PO
Byron Recn Gd
Cemy
Tenn Cts
Liby
Allot Gdns
Schs
Glebe Sch
Ind Est
Elmgrove Fst & Mid Schs
Pav
Recn Gd
Bwg Gn
Tenn Cts
Allot Gdns
St Gregory's RC Sch
Woodcock Park
Sch
Kenton
Superstore
Asquith Court Sch
Mount Stewart Schs
Harrow High Sch
Northwick Park
Univ of Westminster (Harrow Campus)
Northwick Park
John Billam Pl Flds
Tenn Cts
Allot Gdns
Sp Gd
Preston Road
Preston Park Sch
Preston Park Recn Gd
Northwick Park
Rugby Fball Gds
South Kenton
Sch
North Wembley
A4006
A409
A404
WATFORD RD
KENTON RD
Harrow Brent
KENTON LA
KENMORE AVE
CHRISTCHURCH AVE
BRAMPTON GR
NORTHWICK AVE
NORTHWICK CIRC
WOODCOCK HILL
WOODCOCK DELL AVE
WINDERMERE AVE
GRASMERE AVE
THIRLMERE GDNS
NORVAL RD
ABBOTTS DR
1 PRICE CT
2 HINES CT
3 FENN CT
4 CHALLINER CT
1 SIMPSON HO
2 AYRTON HO
3 WINTOUR HO
4 STEVENSON HO

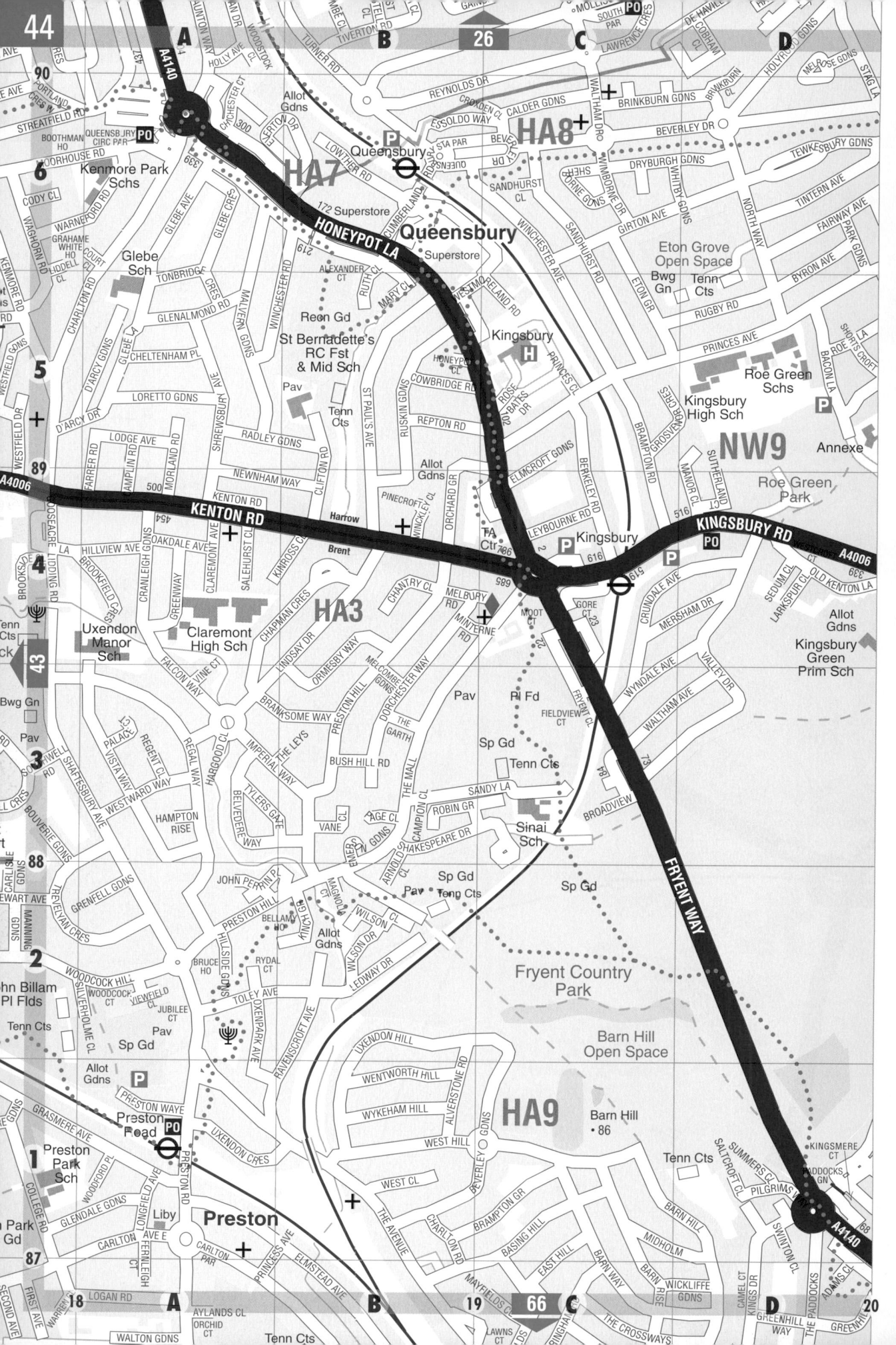
A
B
C
D
26
HA7
HA8
HA3
NW9
HA9
A4140
A4006
Queensbury
Kenmore Park Schs
Glebe Sch
HONEYPOT LA
172 Superstore
Superstore
Allot Gdns
Recn Gd
St Bernadette's RC Fst & Mid Sch
Pav
Tenn Cts
Kingsbury
Eton Grove Open Space
Bwg Gn
Roe Green Schs
Kingsbury High Sch
Annexe
Roe Green Park
KENTON RD
KINGSBURY RD
Harrow
Brent
TA Ctr
Claremont High Sch
Uxendon Manor Sch
Kingsbury Green Prim Sch
Pl Fd
Sp Gd
Sinai Sch
FRYENT WAY
Fryent Country Park
Barn Hill Open Space
Barn Hill
• 86
Preston Road
Preston Park Sch
Liby
Preston
STREATFIELD RD
MOORHOUSE RD
CODY CL
GLEBE AVE
GLEBE CRES
TONBRIDGE CRES
GLENALMOND RD
MALVERN GDNS
WINCHESTER RD
CHELTENHAM PL
LORETTO GDNS
D'ARCY DR
LODGE AVE
RADLEY GDNS
NEWNHAM WAY
OAKDALE AVE
HILLVIEW AVE
REYNOLDS DR
CALDER GDNS
BRINKBURN GDNS
BEVERLEY DR
DRYBURGH GDNS
TEWKESBURY GDNS
TINTERN AVE
FAIRWAY AVE
GIRTON AVE
RUGBY RD
PRINCES AVE
BYRON AVE
LEYBOURNE RD
ELMCROFT GDNS
REPTON RD
COWBRIDGE RD
ST PAUL'S AVE
CHANTRY CL
CHAPMAN CRES
LINDSAY DR
ORMESBY WAY
DORCHESTER WAY
BUSH HILL RD
THE MALL
SANDY LA
WYNDALE AVE
WALTHAM AVE
MERSHAM DR
CRUNDALE AVE
BROADVIEW
WESTWARD WAY
HAMPTON RISE
SHAKESPEARE DR
GRENFELL GDNS
WOODCOCK HILL
TOLEY AVE
OXENPARK AVE
RAVENSCROFT AVE
UXENDON HILL
WENTWORTH HILL
WYKEHAM HILL
WEST HILL
WEST CL
UXENDON CRES
PRESTON WAYE
GRASMERE AVE
GLENDALE GDNS
CARLTON AVE
THE AVENUE
CHARLTON RD
BRAMPTON GR
BASING HILL
EAST HILL
BARN WAY
MIDHOLM
BARN HILL
WICKLIFFE GDNS
PILGRIMS WAY
SUMMERS CL
SALTCROFT CL
THE CROSSWAYS
ELMSTEAD AVE
LOGAN RD
AYLANDS CL
WALTON GDNS
FIRST AVE
SECOND AVE
18
19
66
20
87
88
89
90
1
2
3
4
5
6
43

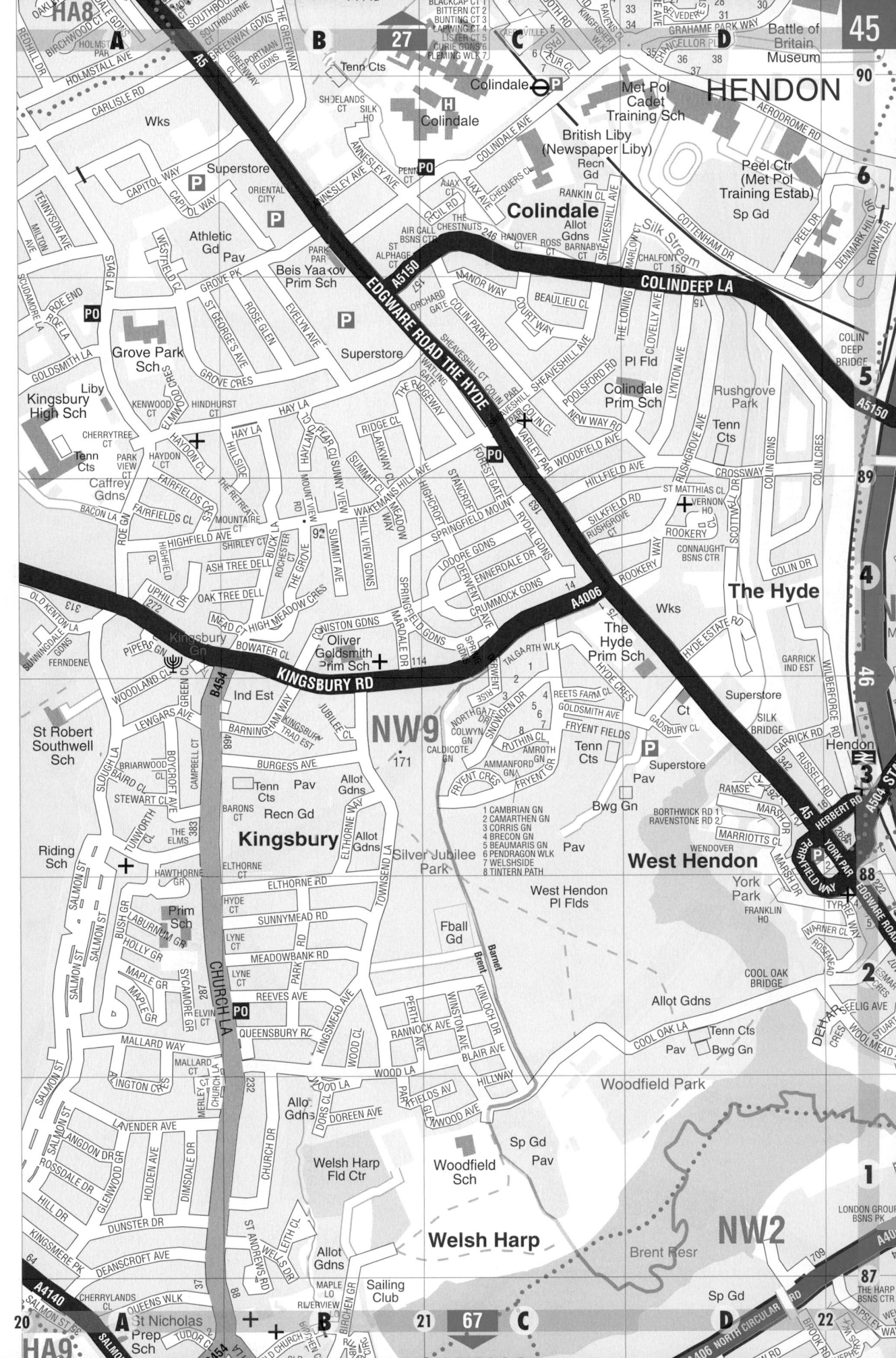
HA8
A
B
27
C
D
Battle of Britain Museum
HENDON
90
Colindale
Met Pol Cadet Training Sch
Colindale
British Liby (Newspaper Liby)
Recn Gd
Peel Ctr (Met Pol Training Estab)
Sp Gd
6
Colindale
Allot Gdns
COLINDEEP LA
EDGWARE ROAD THE HYDE
A5
A5150
A4006
CARLISLE RD
Wks
CAPITOL WAY
Superstore
ORIENTAL CITY
Athletic Gd
Pav
Beis Yaakov Prim Sch
Superstore
Grove Park Sch
Liby
Kingsbury High Sch
Tenn Cts
Caffrey Gdns
HAY LA
COLINDALE AVE
AEROFROME RD
COTTENHAM DR
Silk Stream
Pl Fld
Colindale Prim Sch
Rushgrove Park
Tenn Cts
CROSSWAY
5
COLIN DEEP BRIDGE
89
4
The Hyde
Wks
The Hyde Prim Sch
Oliver Goldsmith Prim Sch
KINGSBURY RD
Kingsbury Gn
Ind Est
NW9
B454
St Robert Southwell Sch
Superstore
SILK BRIDGE
Hendon
3
Tenn Cts
Pav
Allot Gdns
Recn Gd
Kingsbury
Allot Gdns
Silver Jubilee Park
Tenn Cts
Superstore
Pav
Bwg Gn
Pav
West Hendon
York Park
West Hendon Pl Flds
Riding Sch
Prim Sch
Fball Gd
1 CAMBRIAN GN
2 CAMARTHEN GN
3 CORRIS GN
4 BRECON GN
5 BEAUMARIS GN
6 PENDRAGON WLK
7 WELSHSIDE
8 TINTERN PATH
CHURCH LA
2
COOL OAK BRIDGE
Allot Gdns
COOL OAK LA
Tenn Cts
Pav
Bwg Gn
Woodfield Park
88
Welsh Harp Fld Ctr
Woodfield Sch
Sp Gd
Pav
1
Welsh Harp
Brent Resr
NW2
LONDON GROUP BSNS PK
87
Allot Gdns
Sailing Club
Sp Gd
A406 NORTH CIRCULAR RD
THE HARP BSNS CTR
20
A
St Nicholas Prep Sch
B
21
67
C
D
22
HA9
A4140
Barnet
Brent

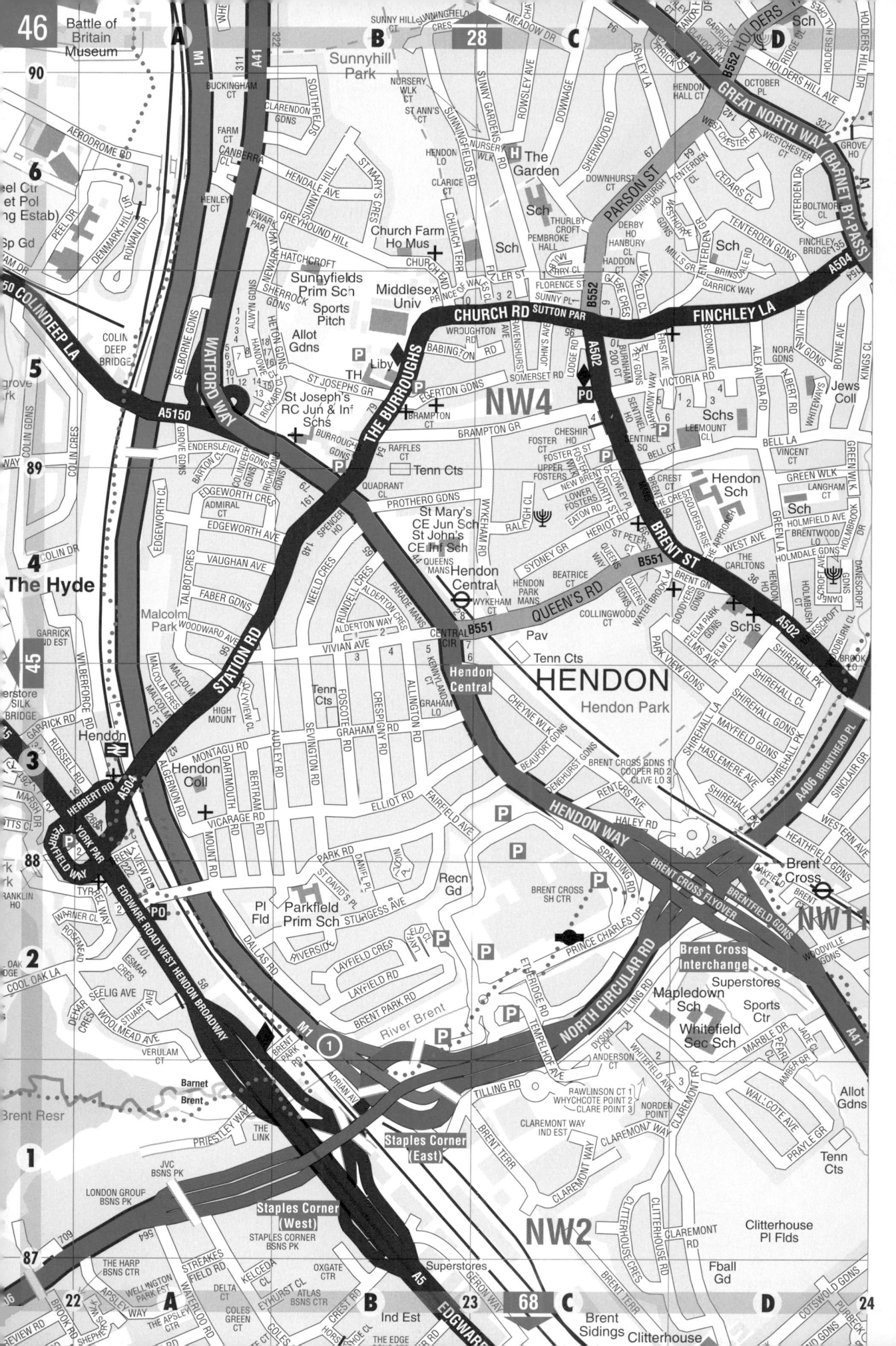
Battle of Britain Museum
A
B
28
C
D
90
Sunnyhill Park
BUCKINGHAM CT
CLARENDON GDNS
SOUTHFIELDS
FARM CT
CANBERRA CL
AERODROME RD
HENDALE AVE
SUNNY HILL
ST MARY'S CRES
NURSERY WLK CT
ST ANN'S CT
SUNNINGFIELDS RD
SUNNY GARDENS RD
ROWSLEY AVE
DOWNAGE
SHERWOOD RD
ASHLEY LA
HENDON HALL CT
OCTOBER PL
HOLDERS HILL CRES
HOLDERS HILL AVE
HOLDERS HILL DR
GREAT NORTH WAY (BARNET BY-PASS)
WESTCHESTER DR
GROVE HO
The Garden
Sch
HENDON LO
CLARICE CT
NURSERY WLK
DOWNHURST CT
PARSON ST
EDINBURGH HO
TENTERDEN CL
CEDARS CL
TENTERDEN DR
BOLTMORE CL
6
PEEL DR
DENMARK HILL DR
ROWAN DR
HENLEY CT
NEWARK PAR
GREYHOUND HILL
Church Farm Ho Mus
CHURCH TERR
THURLBY CROFT
PEMBROKE HALL
DERBY HO
HANBURY CL
HADDON CT
TENTERDEN GR
TENTERDEN GDNS
FINCHLEY BRIDGE
HATCHCROFT
Sunnyfields Prim Sch
Middlesex Univ
Sports Pitch
FULLER ST
FLORENCE ST
SUNNY PL
GLEBE CRES
LINFIELD CL
MILLS GR
BRINSDALE RD
GARRICK WAY
A504
COLINDEEP LA
COLIN DEEP BRIDGE
SELBORNE GDNS
WATFORD WAY
Allot Gdns
CHURCH RD
SUTTON PAR
FINCHLEY LA
WROUGHTON RD
BABINGTON RD
RAVENSHURST
JOHN'S AVE
LODGE RD
BURNHAM
FIRST AVE
SECOND AVE
ALEXANDRA RD
NORA GDNS
HILLVIEW GDNS
BOYNE AVE
KINGS CL
5
Liby
TH
THE BURROUGHS
ST JOSEPHS GR
EGERTON GDNS
SOMERSET RD
VICTORIA RD
ALBERT RD
WHITEWAYS
Jews Coll
A5150
St Joseph's RC Jun & Inf Schs
NW4
PO
BRAMPTON CT
BRAMPTON GR
CHESHIR HO
SENTINEL HO
SENTINEL SQ
Schs
LEEMOUNT CL
BELL LA
VINCENT CT
GROVE GDNS
ENDERSLEIGH GDNS
BARTON CL
RAFFLES CT
Tenn Cts
FOSTER CT
UPPER FOSTERS
NEW BRENT ST
BELL CT
CREST CT
Hendon Sch
GREEN WLK
LANGHAM CT
89
COLIN CRES
COLIN GDNS
EDGEWORTH CRES
ADMIRAL CT
EDGEWORTH AVE
EDGEWORTH CL
QUADRANT CL
PROTHERO GDNS
St Mary's CE Jun Sch
St John's CE Inf Sch
LOWER FOSTERS
EATON RD
HERIOT RD
ST PETER'S CT
BRENT ST
GOLDERS RISE
THE APPROACH
HOLMFIELD AVE
BRENTWOOD LO
WEST AVE
HOLMDALE GDNS
4
COLIN DR
The Hyde
VAUGHAN AVE
FABER GDNS
TALBOT CRES
SPENCER HO
NEELD CRES
QUEENS MANS
Hendon Central
WYKEHAM RD
RALEIGH CL
SYDNEY GR
QUEENS WAY
B551
BEATRICE CT
THE CARLTONS
HENDON PARK MANS
QUEEN'S RD
COLLINGWOOD CT
BRENT GN
GOODYERS GDNS
ELM PARK GDNS
Schs
A502
Malcolm Park
WOODWARD AVE
GARRICK IND EST
RUNDELL CRES
ALDERTON CRES
PARADE MANS
ALDERTON WAY
VIVIAN AVE
CENTRAL CIR
WYKEHAM CT
Pav
Tenn Cts
45
STATION RD
MALCOLM CT
MALCOLM CRES
HIGH MOUNT
Tenn Cts
FOSCOTE RD
CRESPIGNY RD
ALLINGTON RD
KENNYLAND CT
GRAHAM LO
HENDON
Hendon Park
PARK VIEW GDNS
SHIREHALL LA
SHIREHALL PK
SHIREHALL CL
SHIREHALL GDNS
MAYFIELD GDNS
HASLEMERE AVE
WILBERFORCE RD
GARRICK RD
RUSSELL RD
Hendon
AUDLEY RD
SEVINGTON RD
GRAHAM RD
CHEYNE WLK
BEAUFORT GDNS
DENEHURST GDNS
BRENT CROSS GDNS
COOPER RD
CLIVE LO
A406 BRENTHEAD PL
SINCLAIR GR
3
HERBERT RD
MONTAGU RD
DARTMOUTH RD
BERTRAM RD
Hendon Coll
ALGERNON RD
ELLIOT RD
FAIRFIELD AVE
RENTERS AVE
HENDON WAY
HALEY RD
WESTERN AVE
HEATHFIELD GDNS
YORK PAR
PERRYFIELD WAY
VICARAGE RD
MOUNT RD
PARK RD
DANIEL PL
NICOLL PL
SPALDING RD
BRENT CROSS FLYOVER
BRENTFIELD GDNS
OAKFIELD CT
Brent Cross
88
ST DAVID'S PL
Recn Gd
BRENT CROSS SH CTR
NW11
TYRREL WAY
FRANKLIN HO
WARNER CL
ROSEMEAD
PO
Pl Fld
Parkfield Prim Sch
STURGESS AVE
PRINCE CHARLES DR
Brent Cross Interchange
WOODVILLE GDNS
2
COOL OAK LA
ESMAR CRES
RIVERSIDE
LAYFIELD CRES
LAYFIELD RD
LAYFIELD CL
DALLAS RD
ETHERIDGE RD
NORTH CIRCULAR RD
TILLING RD
Superstores
Mapledown Sch
Sports Ctr
SELIG AVE
STUART AVE
WOOLMEAD AVE
DEHAR CRES
WEST HENDON BROADWAY
EDGWARE ROAD
BRENT PARK RD
BRENT PARK RD
River Brent
M1
TEMPELHOF AVE
DYSON CT
ANDERSON CT
Whitefield Sec Sch
MARBLE DR
PEARL CL
JADE CL
AMBER GR
A41
VERULAM CT
Barnet
Brent
Brent Resr
ADRIAN AV
TILLING RD
RAWLINSON CT
WHYCHCOTE POINT
CLARE POINT
WHITEFIELD AVE
NORDEN POINT
CLAREMONT RD
WALLCOTE AVE
Allot Gdns
1
PRIESTLEY WAY
THE LINK
Staples Corner (East)
BRENT TERR
CLAREMONT WAY IND EST
CLAREMONT WAY
PRAYLE GR
Tenn Cts
JVC BSNS PK
LONDON GROUP BSNS PK
Staples Corner (West)
STAPLES CORNER BSNS PK
NW2
CLITTERHOUSE CRES
CLITTERHOUSE RD
CLAREMONT RD
Clitterhouse Pl Flds
87
THE HARP BSNS CTR
STREAKES FIELD RD
KELCEDA CL
OXGATE CTR
Superstores
GERON WAY
A5
BRENT TERR
Fball Gd
WELLINGTON PARK EST
DELTA CT
EYHURST CL
ATLAS BSNS CTR
CREST RD
COTSWOLD GDNS
22
A
B
23
68
C
D
24
APSLEY WAY
THE APSLEY CTR
WATERLOO RD
COLES GREEN CT
BROOK RD
Ind Est
EDGWARE
Brent Sidings
Clitterhouse
PURBECK

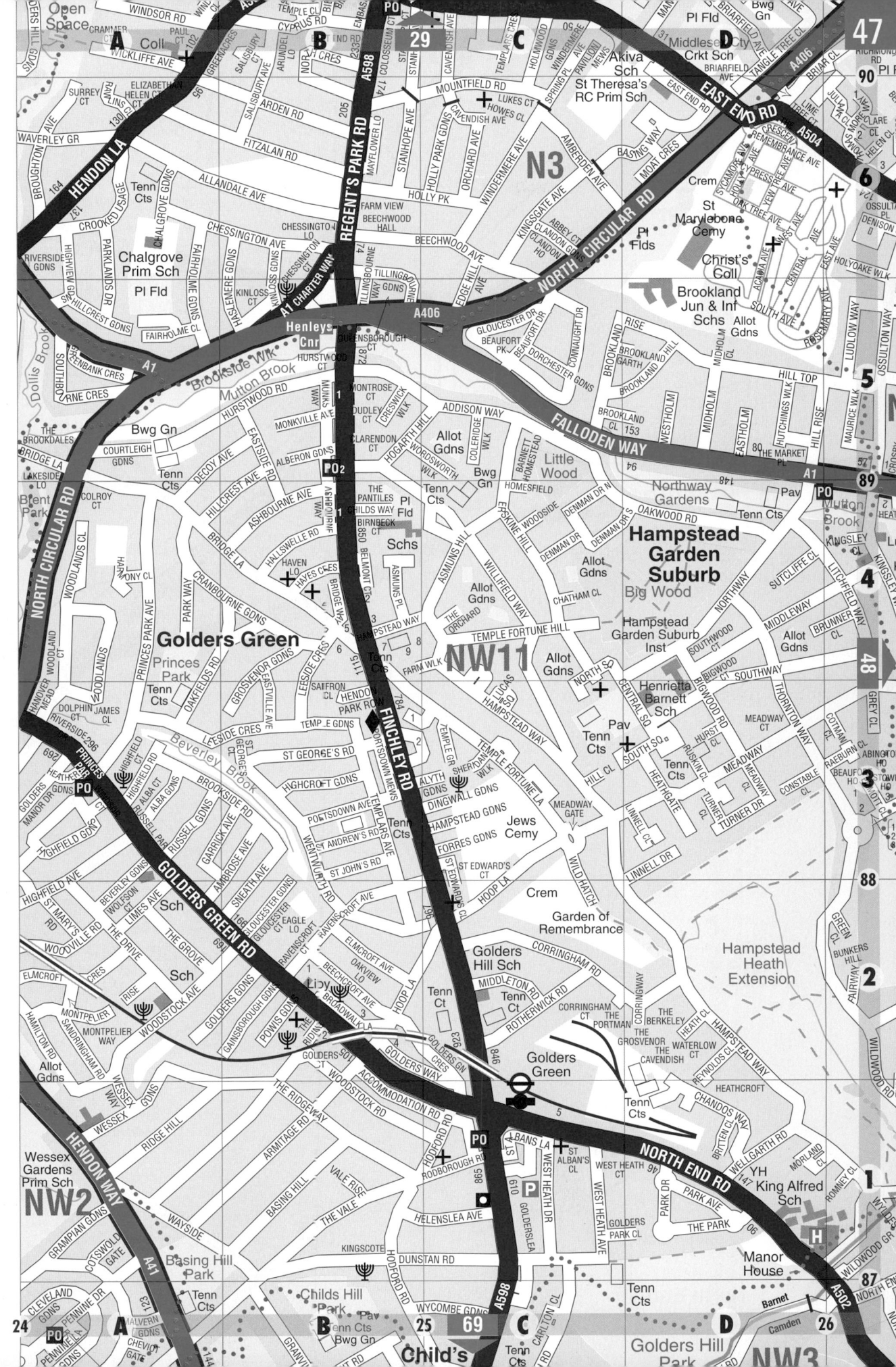

29
A
B
C
D
Open Space
Coll
WINDSOR RD
CYPRUS RD
WICKLIFFE AVE
ELIZABETH CT
HELEN CT
SURREY CT
RAWLINS CL
Middlesex Cty Crkt Sch
Pl Fld
Bwg Gn
Akiva Sch
St Theresa's RC Prim Sch
EAST END RD
A406
A504
MOUNTFIELD RD
LUKES CT
HOWES CL
CAVENDISH AVE
ARDEN RD
FITZALAN RD
WAVERLEY GR
HENDON LA
BROUGHTON AVE
REGENT'S PARK RD
A598
MAYFLOWER LO
STANHOPE AVE
HOLLY PARK GDNS
ORCHARD AVE
WINDERMERE AVE
AMBERDEN AVE
N3
BASING WAY
MOAT CRES
Crem
St Marylebone Cemy
ALLANDALE AVE
HOLLY PK
FARM VIEW
BEECHWOOD HALL
Tenn Cts
CROOKED USAGE
CHALGROVE GDNS
CHESSINGTON AVE
KINGSGATE AVE
ABBEY CT
CLANDON GDNS
NORTH CIRCULAR RD
Pl Flds
Christ's Coll
Brookland Jun & Inf Schs
Allot Gdns
Chalgrove Prim Sch
Pl Fld
RIVERSIDE GDNS
HIGHVIEW GDNS
PARKLANDS DR
FAIRHOLME GDNS
HASLEMERE GDNS
KINLOSS CT
BEECHWOOD AVE
TILLINGBOURNE GDNS
HILLCREST GDNS
FAIRHOLME CL
A1 CHARTER WAY
Henleys Cnr
QUEENSBOROUGH CT
HURSTWOOD CT
GLOUCESTER DR
BEAUFORT PK
DORCHESTER GDNS
CONNAUGHT DR
BROOKLAND RISE
BROOKLAND HILL
BROOKLAND GARTH
MIDHOLM CL
ROSEMARY AVE
LUDLOW WAY
OSSULTON WAY
HILL TOP
5
Dollis Brook
GREENBANK CRES
A1
Brookside Wlk
Mutton Brook
SOUTHBOURNE CRES
HURSTWOOD RD
MONTROSE CT
DUDLEY CT
CRESWICK WLK
MONKVILLE AVE
ADDISON WAY
FALLODEN WAY
WESTHOLM
MIDHOLM
EASTHOLM
HUTCHINGS WLK
HILL RISE
MAURICE WLK
THE MARKET PL
THE BROOKDALES
Bwg Gn
COURTLEIGH GDNS
BRIDGE LA
LAKESIDE LO
Tenn Cts
DECOY AVE
EASTSIDE RD
CLARENDON CT
ALBERON GDNS
HOGARTH HILL
WORDSWORTH WLK
Allot Gdns
COLERIDGE WLK
Bwg Gn
BARNETT HOMESTEAD
Little Wood
HOMESFIELD
Northway Gardens
Pav
Tenn Cts
89
Mutton Brook
Brent Park
COLROY CT
HILLCREST AVE
ASHBOURNE AVE
THE PANTILES
CHILDS WAY
Pl Fld
BIRNBECK CT
Schs
ASMUNS HILL
ERSKINE HILL
WOODSIDE
DENMAN DR
OAKWOOD RD
Hampstead Garden Suburb
Big Wood
KINGSLEY CL
SUTCLIFFE CL
4
NORTH CIRCULAR RD
WOODLANDS CL
HARMONY CL
BRIDGE LA
HALLSWELLE RD
HAVEN LO
HAYES CRES
BELMONT CT
ASMUNS PL
WILLIFIELD WAY
Allot Gdns
CHATHAM CL
NORTHWAY
LITCHFIELD WAY
Hampstead Garden Suburb Inst
MIDDLEWAY
Allot Gdns
BRUNNER CL
CRANBOURNE GDNS
PARK WAY
PRINCES PARK AVE
Golders Green
HAMPSTEAD WAY
THE ORCHARD
TEMPLE FORTUNE HILL
NW11
Allot Gdns
SOUTHWOOD CT
48
Princes Park
OAKFIELDS RD
GROSVENOR GDNS
LEESIDE CRES
Tenn Cts
FARM WLK
LUCAS SQ
NORTH SQ
CENTRAL SQ
Henrietta Barnett Sch
BIGWOOD RD
SOUTHWAY
THORNTON WAY
GREY CL
Tenn Cts
WOODLANDS
HANOVER MEAD
WOODLAND CT
DOLPHIN CT
JAMES CL
SAFFRON CL
HENDON PARK ROW
FINCHLEY RD
TEMPLE GDNS
EASTVILLE AVE
HAMPSTEAD WAY
Pav
Tenn Cts
MEADWAY CT
COTMAN CL
RAEBURN CL
RIVERSIDE
PRINCES PDE
LEESIDE CRES
ST GEORGES CT
ST GEORGE'S RD
TEMPLE GR
SHERIDAN WLK
TEMPLE FORTUNE LA
SOUTH SQ
HILL CL
HEATHGATE
Tenn Cts
RUSKIN CL
HURST CL
MEADWAY
TURNER CL
TURNER DR
CONSTABLE CL
ABINGTON HO
BEAUFORT HO
STOWE HO
3
Beverley Brook
HIGHFIELD CT
HIGHFIELD RD
ALBA CT
ALBA GDNS
BROOKSIDE RD
HIGHCROFT GDNS
PORTSDOWN MEWS
ALYTH GDNS
DINGWALL GDNS
MEADWAY GATE
GOLDERS MANOR DR
HEATH GDNS
RUSSELL PDE
RUSSELL GDNS
GARRICK AVE
AMBROSE AVE
PORTSDOWN AVE
Tenn Cts
HAMPSTEAD GDNS
Jews Cemy
LINNELL CL
HIGHFIELD GDNS
GOLDERS GREEN RD
SNEATH AVE
ST ANDREW'S RD
TEMPLARS AVE
FORRES GDNS
ST JOHN'S RD
ST EDWARD'S CT
WILD HATCH
LINNELL DR
88
HIGHFIELD AVE
BEVERLEY GDNS
WOLFSON CT
LIMES AVE
Sch
GLOUCESTER GDNS
WENTWORTH RD
HOOP LA
Crem
Garden of Remembrance
ST MARY'S RD
WOODVILLE RD
THE DRIVE
THE GROVE
EAGLE LO
RAVENSCROFT CT
RAVENSCROFT AVE
ELMCROFT AVE
OAKVIEW LO
Golders Hill Sch
CORRINGHAM RD
Hampstead Heath Extension
GREEN CL
BUNKERS HILL
ELMCROFT CRES
RISE
Sch
WOODSTOCK AVE
GOLDERS GDNS
BEECHCROFT AVE
Liby
BROADWALK LA
Tenn Ct
MIDDLETON RD
Tenn Ct
ROTHERWICK RD
CORRINGHAM CT
THE PORTMAN
CORRINGWAY
THE BERKELEY
HEATH CL
THE GROSVENOR
THE CAVENDISH
WATERLOW CT
HAMPSTEAD WAY
2
FAIRWAY
HAMILTON RD
MONTPELIER RISE
SANDRINGHAM RD
MONTPELIER WAY
Allot Gdns
GAINSBOROUGH GDNS
POWIS GDNS
THE RIDINGS
GOLDERS CT
GOLDERS WAY
GOLDERS GN CRES
Golders Green
REYNOLDS CL
HEATHCROFT
WILDWOOD RD
WESSEX GDNS
WESSEX WAY
RIDGE HILL
THE RIDGEWAY
WOODSTOCK RD
ACCOMMODATION RD
Tenn Cts
CHANDOS WAY
BRITTEN CL
Wessex Gardens Prim Sch
NW2
HENDON WAY
ARMITAGE RD
BASING HILL
VALE RISE
HODFORD RD
RODBOROUGH RD
ST ALBANS LA
ST ALBAN'S CL
WEST HEATH CT
WEST HEATH DR
NORTH END RD
WELLGARTH RD
YH
King Alfred Sch
MORLAND CL
ROMNEY CL
1
THE VALE
WAYSIDE
HELENSLEA AVE
GOLDERSLEA
WEST HEATH AVE
PARK DR
PARK AVE
GOLDERS PARK CL
THE PARK
H
WILDWOOD GR
GRAMPIAN GDNS
COTSWOLD GATE
Basing Hill Park
KINGSCOTE
DUNSTAN RD
Manor House
Tenn Cts
Childs Hill Park
Pav
Tenn Cts
Bwg Gn
WYCOMBE GDNS
Tenn Cts
CARLTON CL
A41
A598
A502
Barnet
Camden
NORTH END
87
CLEVELAND GDNS
PENNINE DR
MALVERN GDNS
CHEVIOT GATE
PENNINE LA
24
25
69
26
Child's
Golders Hill Park
NW3

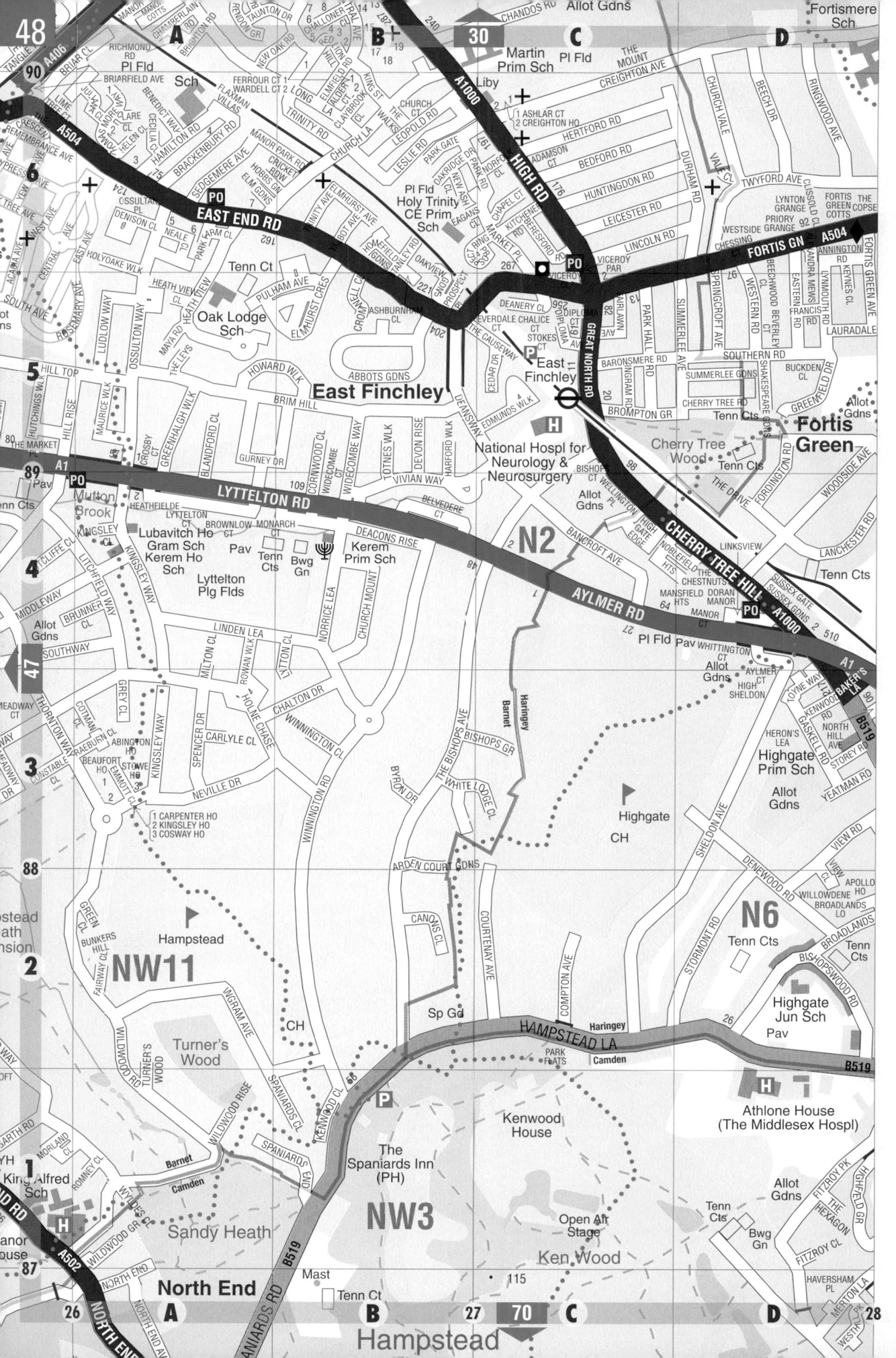
30
A
B
C
D
Fortismere Sch
Allot Gdns
Martin Prim Sch
Pl Fld
Liby
THE MOUNT
CREIGHTON AVE
1 ASHLAR CT
2 CREIGHTON HO
HERTFORD RD
BEDFORD RD
HUNTINGDON RD
LEICESTER RD
LINCOLN RD
HIGH RD
A1000
CHURCH VALE
BEECH DR
RINGWOOD AVE
DURHAM RD
TWYFORD AVE
FORTIS GN
A504
EAST END RD
A406
90
A504
RICHMOND RD
BRIAR CL
BRIARFIELD AVE
Sch
FLAXMAN VILLAS
HAMILTON RD
BRACKENBURY RD
SEDGEMERE AVE
MANOR PARK RD
CHURCH LA
TRINITY RD
LONG LA
LESLIE RD
LEOPOLD RD
PARK GATE
Pl Fld
Holy Trinity CE Prim Sch
PO
ELMHURST AVE
TRINITY AVE
TALBOT AVE
DENISON CL
HOLYOAKE WLK
CENTRAL AVE
EAST AVE
Tenn Ct
PULHAM AVE
ELMHURST CRES
Oak Lodge Sch
ROSEMARY AVE
LUDLOW WAY
OSSULTON WAY
HEATH VIEW
MAYA RD
THE LEYS
HOWARD WLK
ASHBURNHAM CL
ABBOTS GDNS
East Finchley
DEANERY CL
THE CAUSEWAY
CEDAR DR
EDMUNDS WLK
East Finchley
GREAT NORTH RD
VICEROY PAR
FAIRLAWN AVE
PARK HALL RD
SUMMERLEE AVE
SPRINGCROFT AVE
WESTERN RD
BEECHWOOD
EASTERN RD
FRANCIS RD
LAURADALE
SOUTHERN RD
BARONSMERE RD
INGRAM RD
SUMMERLEE GDNS
BUCKDEN CL
GREENFIELD DR
CHERRY TREE RD
BROMPTON GR
Tenn Cts
Fortis Green
Allot Gdns
Cherry Tree Wood
Tenn Cts
THE DRIVE
FORDINGTON RD
WOODSIDE AVE
LANCHESTER RD
5
HILL TOP
BRIM HILL
HUTCHINGS WLK
HILL RISE
MAURICE WLK
CROSBY CT
GREENHALGH WLK
BLANDFORD CL
GURNEY DR
CORNWOOD CL
WIDECOMBE WAY
TOTNES WLK
DEVON RISE
HARFORD WLK
DEANSWAY
National Hospl for Neurology & Neurosurgery
THE MARKET PL
89
A1
PO
LYTTELTON RD
VIVIAN WAY
BELVEDERE CT
Mutton Brook
Pav
Lubavitch Ho Gram Sch
Kerem Ho Sch
Pav
Tenn Cts
Bwg Gn
Kerem Prim Sch
DEACONS RISE
Lyttelton Plg Flds
KINGSLEY WAY
N2
BANCROFT AVE
Allot Gdns
CHERRY TREE HILL
LINKSVIEW
Tenn Cts
AYLMER RD
Pl Fld
Pav
PO
A1000
4
LITCHFIELD WAY
MIDDLEWAY
Allot Gdns
BRUNNER CL
SOUTHWAY
47
LINDEN LEA
NORRICE LEA
CHURCH MOUNT
MILTON CL
ROWAN WLK
LYTTON CL
HOLNE CHASE
CHALTON DR
WINNINGTON RD
WINNINGTON CL
GREY CL
THORNTON WAY
KINGSLEY WAY
SPENCER DR
CARLYLE CL
NEVILLE DR
THE BISHOPS AVE
BISHOPS GR
BYRON DR
WHITE LODGE CL
Barnet
Haringey
A1
BAKER'S LA
B519
HERON'S LEA
Highgate Prim Sch
Allot Gdns
Highgate
CH
SHELDON AVE
VIEW RD
3
1 CARPENTER HO
2 KINGSLEY HO
3 COSWAY HO
88
ARDEN COURT GDNS
CANONS CL
COURTENAY AVE
DENEWOOD RD
WILLOWDENE
BROADLANDS
N6
Tenn Cts
STORMONT RD
Tenn Cts
BISHOPSWOOD RD
Highgate Jun Sch
Pav
2
Hampstead
NW11
FAIRWAY CL
INGRAM AVE
COMPTON AVE
Sp Gd
HAMPSTEAD LA
Haringey
Camden
PARK FLATS
B519
CH
Turner's Wood
WILDWOOD RD
TURNER'S WOOD
SPANIARDS CL
WILDWOOD RISE
KENWOOD CL
Athlone House (The Middlesex Hospl)
Kenwood House
1
King Alfred Sch
MORLAND CL
ROMNEY CL
SPANIARDS END
The Spaniards Inn (PH)
Barnet
Camden
Sandy Heath
WILDWOOD GR
NW3
Allot Gdns
Tenn Cts
Bwg Gn
Open Air Stage
Ken Wood
FITZROY PK
THE HEXAGON
FITZROY CL
87
A502
NORTH END
North End
SPANIARDS RD
B519
Mast
Tenn Ct
115
HAVERSHAM PL
26
A
B
27
70
C
D
28
Hampstead

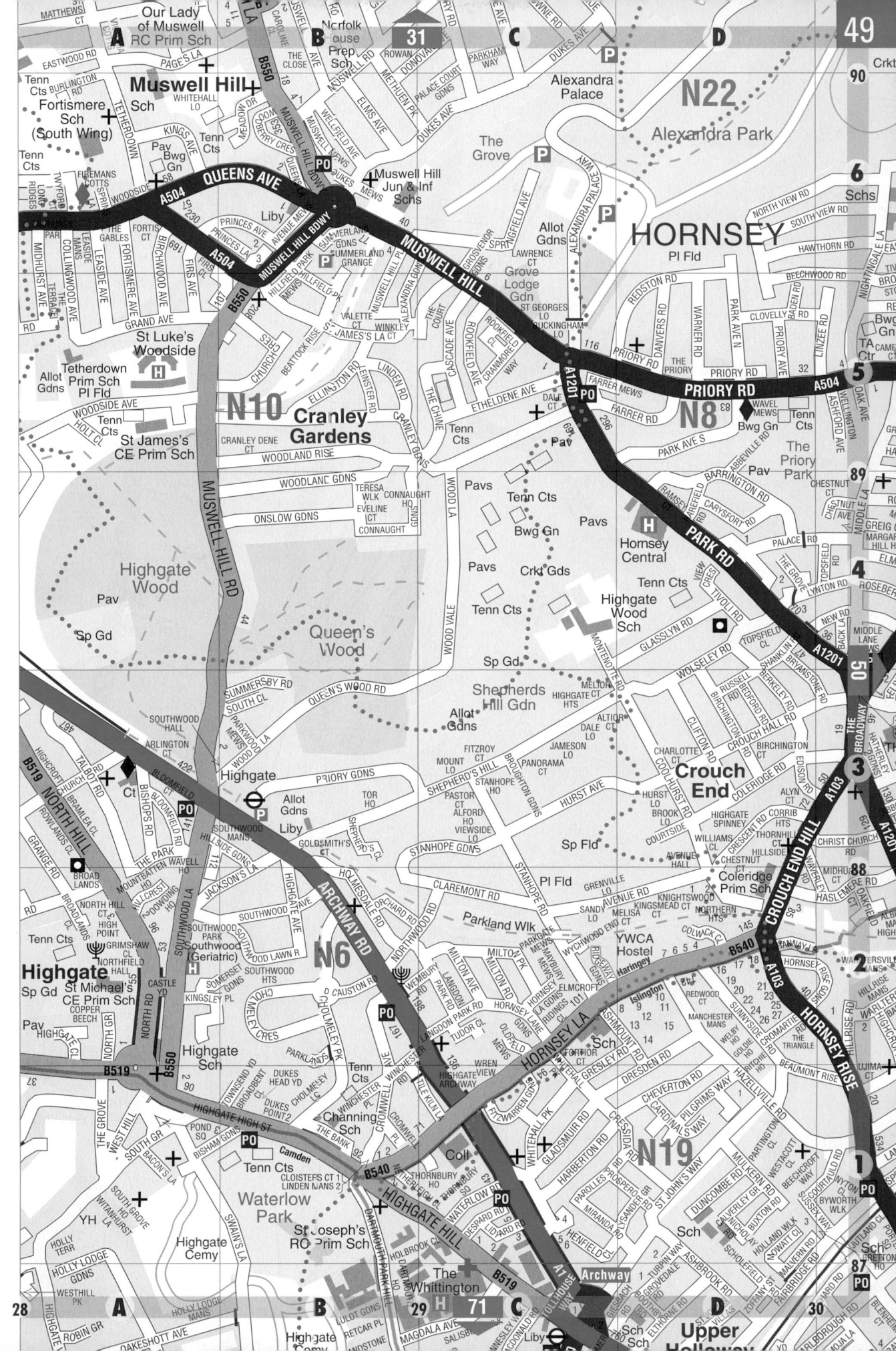
A
B
C
D
31
71
28
29
30
90
6
5
89
4
50
3
88
2
1
87
Our Lady of Muswell RC Prim Sch
Norfolk House Prep Sch
Muswell Hill
Fortismere Sch
Fortismere Sch (South Wing)
Alexandra Palace
N22
Alexandra Park
The Grove
Muswell Hill Jun & Inf Schs
HORNSEY
Pl Fld
Allot Gdns
Grove Lodge Gdn
QUEENS AVE
MUSWELL HILL
MUSWELL HILL BDWY
MUSWELL HILL RD
PRIORY RD
PARK RD
St Luke's Woodside
Tetherdown Prim Sch
N10
Cranley Gardens
N8
The Priory Park
St James's CE Prim Sch
Highgate Wood
Queen's Wood
Hornsey Central
Highgate Wood Sch
Shepherds Hill Gdn
Crouch End
Highgate
Liby
N6
ARCHWAY RD
Southwood (Geriatric)
St Michael's CE Prim Sch
Highgate Sch
Channing Sch
Waterlow Park
St Joseph's RC Prim Sch
Highgate Cemy
The Whittington
N19
YWCA Hostel
Coleridge Prim Sch
CROUCH END HILL
HORNSEY RISE
HORNSEY LA
HIGHGATE HILL
HIGHGATE HIGH ST
NORTH HILL
Parkland Wlk
Archway
Upper Holloway
A504
A1201
B550
B519
B540
A103
A1
Haringey
Islington
Camden

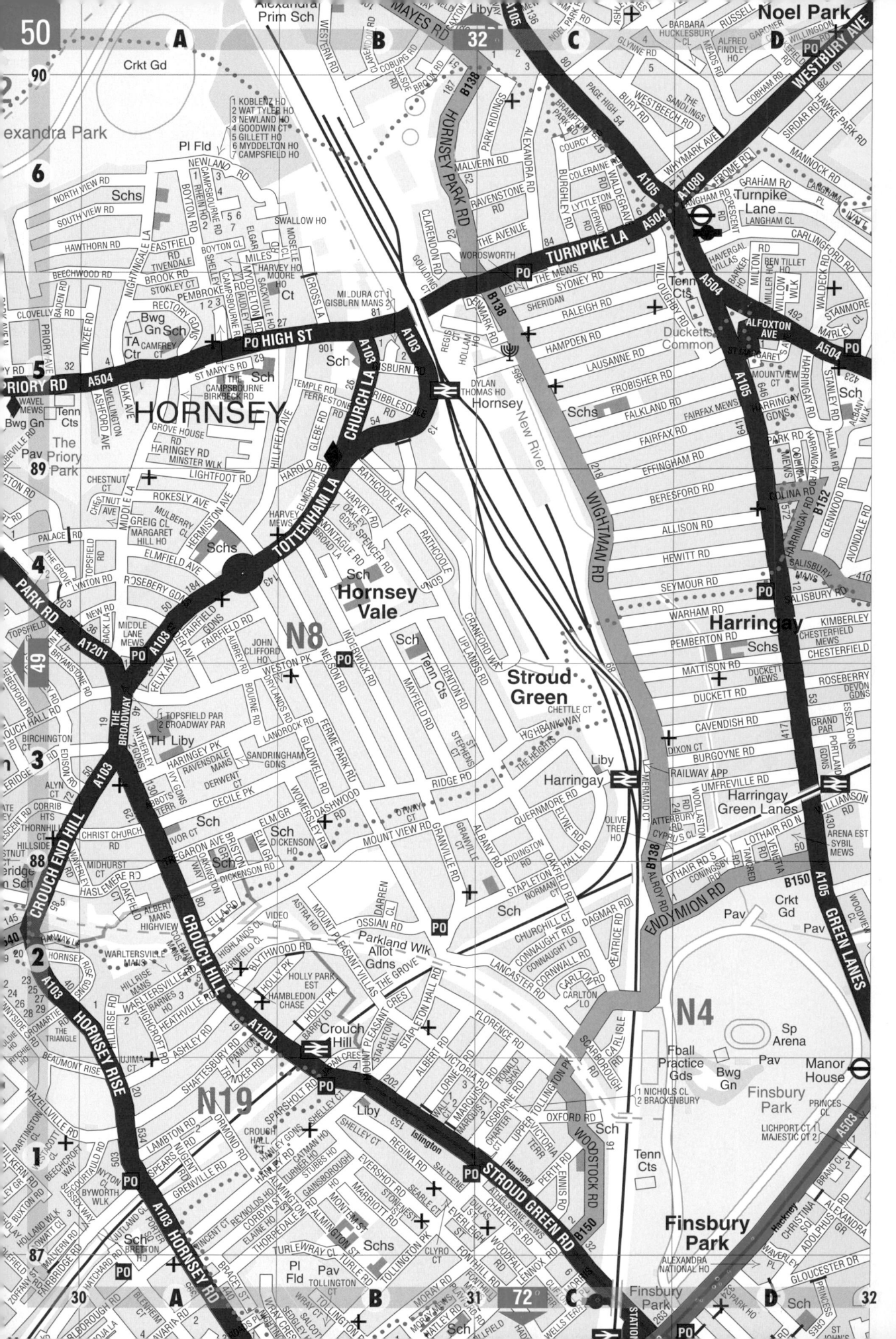
A
B
C
D
32
Noel Park
Alexandra Prim Sch
Crkt Gd
Alexandra Park
Pl Fld
1 KOBLENZ HO
2 WAT TYLER HO
3 NEWLAND HO
4 GOODWIN CT
5 GILLETT HO
6 MYDDELTON HO
7 CAMPSFIELD HO
WESTERN RD
MAYES RD
CLARENDON RD
COBURG RD
SILSOE RD
BROOK RD
HORNSEY PARK RD
B138
PARK RIDINGS
ALEXANDRA RD
BARBARA HUCKLESBURY CL
RUSSELL
ALFRED FINDLEY HO
GLYNNE RD
WESTBEECH RD
BURY RD
THE SANDLINGS
COBHAM RD
WESTBURY AVE
SIRDAR RD
HAWKE PARK RD
MANNOCK RD
WHYMARK AVE
FROME RD
GRAHAM RD
Turnpike Lane
LANGHAM CL
CARLINGFORD RD
A105
A1080
A504
TURNPIKE LA
COURCY RD
COLERAINE RD
BURGHLEY RD
LYTTLETON RD
WALDEGRAVE RD
MALVERN RD
RAVENSTONE RD
THE AVENUE
WORDSWORTH
THE MEWS
SYDNEY RD
SHERIDAN
RALEIGH RD
HAMPDEN RD
LAUSANNE RD
FROBISHER RD
FALKLAND RD
FAIRFAX MEWS
FAIRFAX RD
EFFINGHAM RD
BERESFORD RD
ALLISON RD
HEWITT RD
SEYMOUR RD
WARHAM RD
PEMBERTON RD
MATTISON RD
DUCKETT RD
CAVENDISH RD
BURGOYNE RD
RAILWAY APP
UMFREVILLE RD
WILLOUGHBY RD
Tenn Cts
Ducketts Common
ALFOXTON AVE
WALDECK RD
STANMORE
MARLEY CL
MOUNTVIEW CT
HARRINGAY GDNS
HARRINGAY RD
STANLEY RD
HALLAM RD
COLINA RD
COLINA MEWS
B152
GLENWOOD RD
AVONDALE RD
SALISBURY MANS
SALISBURY RD
Harringay
KIMBERLEY
CHESTERFIELD MEWS
CHESTERFIELD
ROSEBERRY
DEVON GDNS
GRAND PAR
PORTLAND
ESSEX GDNS
Harringay Green Lanes
WILLIAMSON RD
ARENA EST
SYBIL MEWS
LOTHAIR RD N
LOTHAIR RD S
VENETIA
TANCRED RD
CONINGSBY RD
ENDYMION RD
B150
Crkt Gd
Pav
GREEN LANES
N4
Sp Arena
Fball Practice Gds
Bwg Gn
Manor House
Finsbury Park
PRINCES CL
LICHPORT CT
MAJESTIC CT
A503
NORTH VIEW RD
SOUTH VIEW RD
HAWTHORN RD
BEECHWOOD RD
CLOVELLY RD
BADEN RD
PRIORY AVE
LINZEE RD
NEWLAND RD
BOYTON RD
CAMPSBOURNE RD
NIGHTINGALE LA
FASTFIELD RD
TIVENDALE
BROOK RD
STOKLEY CT
PEMBROKE
RECTORY GDNS
Schs
SWALLOW HO
MOSELLE CL
CROSS LA
HARVEY HO
MOORE HO
MILDURA CT
GISBURN MANS
Sch
HIGH ST
PRIORY RD
A504
Bwg Gn
TA Ctr
CAMFREY CT
ST MARY'S RD
THE CAMPSBOURNE
BIRKBECK RD
HORNSEY
WAVEL MEWS
Tenn Cts
The Priory Park
Pav
OAK AVE
WELLINGTON
ASHFORD AVE
GROVE HOUSE RD
HARINGEY RD
MINSTER WLK
LIGHTFOOT RD
CHESTNUT CT
ROKESLY AVE
MULBERRY
GREIG CL
MARGARET HILL HO
PALACE RD
ELMFIELD AVE
ROSEBERY GDNS
HERMISTON AVE
HILLFIELD AVE
GLEBE RD
HAROLD RD
TEMPLE RD
FERRESTONE RD
RIBBLESDALE RD
GISBURN RD
CHURCH LA
A103
TOTTENHAM LA
ELMCROFT
HARVEY MEWS
RATHCOOLE AVE
RATHCOOLE GDNS
OAKLEY GDNS
SPENCER RD
MONTAGUE RD
Hornsey Vale
DYLAN THOMAS HO
Hornsey
New River
WIGHTMAN RD
CRANFORD WAY
UPLANDS RD
Stroud Green
CHETTLE CT
HIGH BANK WAY
THE HEIGHTS
Liby
Harringay
MERMAID CT
ATTERBURY RD
WOOLLASTON RD
DIXON CT
CYPRUS CL
OLIVE TREE HO
PARK RD
THE GROVE
TOPSFIELD RD
LYNTON RD
NEW RD
BACK LA
MIDDLE LANE MEWS
A1207
BRYANSTONE RD
BEDFORD RD
FAIRFIELD GDNS
FAIRFIELD RD
AUBREY RD
JOHN CLIFFORD HO
N8
WESTON PK
INDERWICK RD
NELSON RD
DENTON RD
MAYFIELD RD
Sch
Tenn Cts
THE BROADWAY
HATHERLEY GDNS
1 TOPSFIELD PAR
2 BROADWAY PAR
TH Liby
HARINGEY PK
RAVENSDALE MANS
SANDRINGHAM GDNS
LANDROCK RD
GLADWELL RD
FERME PARK RD
ST STEPHENS CT
RIDGE RD
DERWENT CT
CECILE PK
IVY GDNS
ABBOTS TERR
BIRCHINGTON CT
EDISON RD
ALYN CT
CORRIB HTS
CROUCH END HILL
A103
CHRIST CHURCH RD
THORNHILL CT
HILLSIDE CT
MIDHURST CT
HASLEMERE RD
TREGARON AVE
OAKINGTON WAY
BRISTON GR
ELM GR
DICKENSON HO
DICKENSON RD
WOMERSLEY RD
DASHWOOD RD
OTWAY CT
MOUNT VIEW RD
GRANVILLE RD
GRANVILLE CT
ALBANY RD
QUERNMORE RD
ELYNE RD
ADDINGTON RD
OAKFIELD RD
STAPLETON HALL RD
NORMAN CT
Sch
ALBERT MANS
HIGHVIEW
ELLA RD
VIDEO CT
ASTRA HO
MOUNT PLEASANT VILLAS
DARREN CL
OSSIAN RD
Parkland Wlk
Allot Gdns
THE GROVE
CROUCH HILL
HORNSEY RISE GDNS
WARLTERSVILLE MANS
HILLRISE MANS
WARLTERSVILLE RD
HIGHLANDS CL
BARNFIELD CL
BLYTHWOOD RD
HOLLY PK
HOLLY PARK EST
HAMBLEDON CHASE
HOLLY LO
BARRY LO
Crouch Hill
A1201
HORNSEY RISE
A103
BARNES HO
HEATHVILLE RD
HIGHCROFT RD
ASHLEY RD
CROMARTIE RD
THE TRIANGLE
BEAUMONT RISE
HILLRISE RD
SHAFTESBURY RD
N19
PAMLION CT
DUNCAN CT
ST JOHN'S
STAPLETON HALL
ALBERT RD
VICTORIA RD
LORNE RD
MARQUIS RD
RONALD SHAW
OSBORNE RD
FLORENCE RD
CHURCHILL CT
CONNAUGHT RD
CONNAUGHT LO
CORNWALL RD
LANCASTER RD
DAGMAR RD
BEATRICE RD
CARLTON RD
CARLTON LO
CARLISLE RD
SCARBOROUGH RD
UPPER TOLLINGTON PK
1 NICHOLS CL
2 BRACKENBURY
OXFORD RD
VICTORIA TERR
WOODSTOCK RD
Sch
Tenn Cts
SPARSHOLT RD
SHELLEY CT
Liby
CROUCH HALL CT
HANLEY GDNS
CATMAN HO
TURNER HO
STUBBS HO
REGINA RD
SALTDENE
STROUD GREEN RD
Islington
Haringey
PERTH RD
ENNIS RD
B150
HAZELLVILLE RD
PARTINGTON CL
WESTCOTT CL
BEECHCROFT WAY
COURTAULD RD
NEWTON CT
BYWORTH WLK
SUSSEX WAY
LAMBTON RD
SPEARS RD
NUGENT RD
ORMOND RD
GRENVILLE RD
HORNSEY RD
A103
CORBYN ST
REYNOLDS HO
ELAINE HO
THORPEDALE RD
ALMINGTON ST
GAINSBOROUGH
EVERSHOT RD
MARRIOTT RD
STONENEST ST
SEARLE CT
EVERLEIGH ST
DULAS ST
CHARTERIS RD
ATHELSTANE MEWS
WOODFALL
LENNOX RD
Finsbury Park
ALEXANDRA NATIONAL HO
Hackney
CHRISTINA SQ
ALEXANDRA GR
ADOLPHUS RD
WAVERLEY PL
GLOUCESTER DR
PRINCESS CRES
Sch
HOLLAND WLK
ZOFFANY ST
MALVERN RD
FAIRBRIDGE RD
JUTLAND CL
PORTER
Sch
BRETTON HO
TURLEWRAY CL
TURLE RD
TOLLINGTON PK
Schs
CLYRO CT
FONTHILL RD
Pl Fld
Pav
TOLLINGTON CT
MORAY RD
BRACEY ST
PLAYFORD RD
30
31
72
32
A
B
C
D
Sch
STATION
Finsbury Park

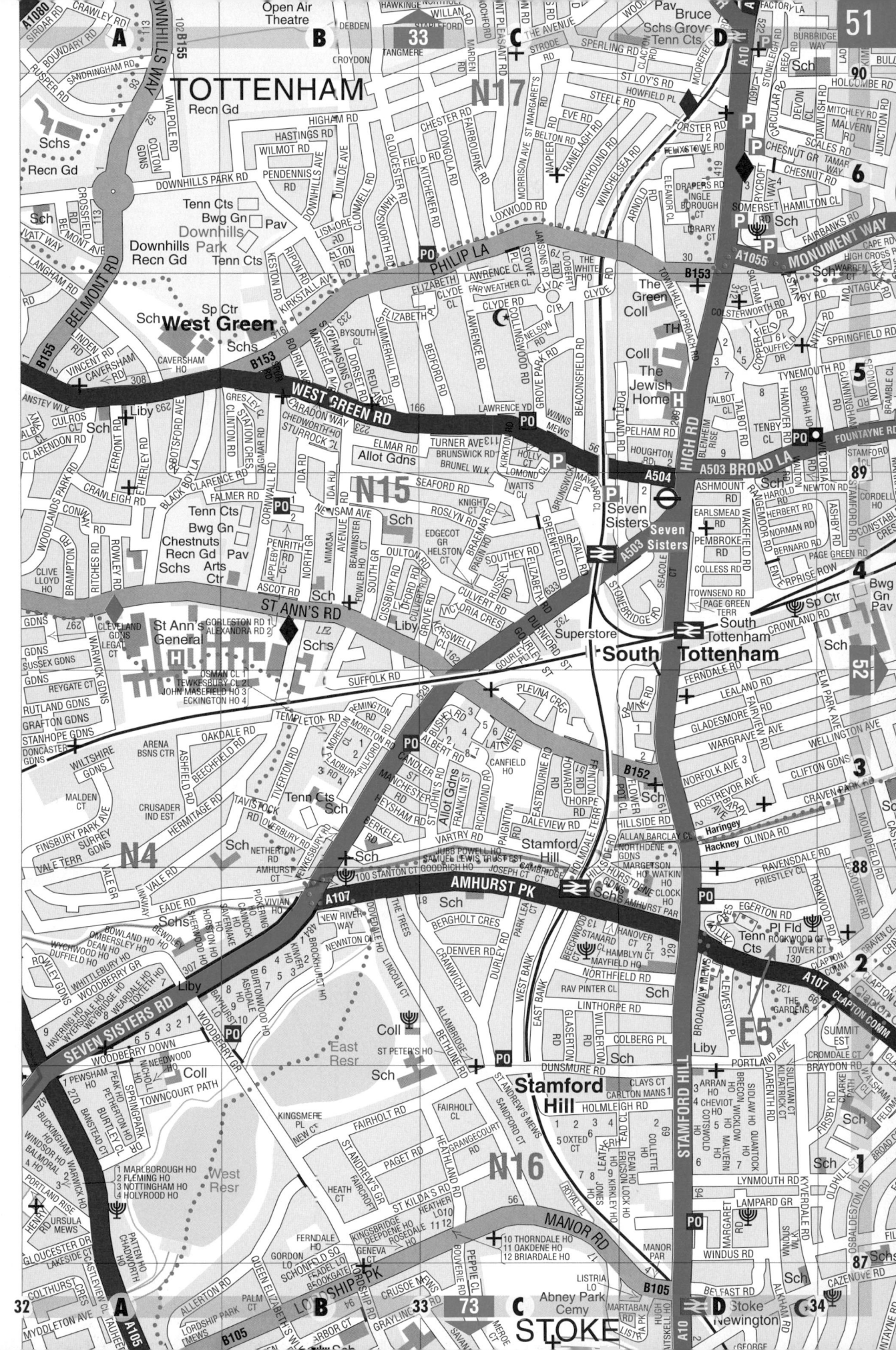
TOTTENHAM
N17
West Green
N15
Seven Sisters
South Tottenham
N4
Stamford Hill
N16
E5
STOKE
Downhills Park
Downhills Recn Gd
Chestnuts Recn Gd
St Ann's General
East Resr
West Resr
Abney Park Cemy
WEST GREEN RD
ST ANN'S RD
SEVEN SISTERS RD
AMHURST PK
HIGH RD
STAMFORD HILL
BROAD LA
MONUMENT WAY
CLAPTON COMM
MANOR RD
LORDSHIP PK
PHILIP LA
BELMONT RD
DOWNHILLS WAY
Haringey
Hackney
33
73
52
32
34

A
B
34
C
D
Lockwood Resr
Tottenham Hale
Down Lane Park
Tenn Cts
LEA VALLEY TECHNOPARK
MILLMEAD IND CTR
MILLMEAD BSNS CTR
LOCKWOOD IND PK
Allot Gdns
WATERMEAD WAY
Pymme's Brook
River Lee Navigation
River Lea or Lee Diversion
High Maynard Resr
Low Maynard Resr
Lee Flood Relief Channel
UPLANDS BSNS PK
FOREST TRAD EST
HIGHAMS LODGE BSNS CTR
Willowfield Sec Sch
Blackhorse Road
MONUMENT WAY
HALE RD
FERRY LA
N17
Sp Gd
TOTTENHAM HALE RET PK
FOUNTAYNE BSNS CTR
BROAD LA
THE HIGH CROSS CTR
ST PETERS HO
FOUNTAYNE RD
Tenn Cts
Sch
Resr No 2
Resr No 1
Resr No 4
Resr No 3
Resr No 5
Pl Flds
E17
Coppermill Prim Sch
Sp Ctr
RENSBURG VILLAS
COPPERMILL LA
Warwick Resr East
Warwick Resr West
Lee Valley Regional Park
Coppermill Stream
Water Works
Allot Gdns
Tenn Cts
Lee Flood Relief Channel
Markfield Recn Gd
Bwg Gn
Pav
N15
51
N16
River Lea or Lee
Lea Valley Walk
RAVENSDALE COM EST
WATERMINT QUAY
Pl Flds
Sp Gd
FOREST BSNS PK
LEYTON IND VILLAGE
DORMA TRAD PK
Springfield Marina
Springfield Park
Clapton Common
CLAPTON COMM
WEBB EST
FAWCETT EST
E5
Bwg Gn
1 LEA HO
2 HARRINGTON HO
3 VALLEY HO
Walthamstow Marshes
Nature Reserve
E10
Lea Valley Riding Sch
Pl Fld
Leyton Marshes
River Lea or Lee
Upper Clapton
UPPER CLAPTON RD
N16
Leeside Wharf
Lea Valley Ice Ctr
34
A
B
35
74
C
D
36

WALTHAMSTOW
E17
E10
35
75
54
36
37
38
A
B
C
D
90
89
88
87
6
5
4
3
2
1
FOREST RD
A503
A112
A104
A1006
B159
B161
HOE ST
LEA BRIDGE RD
MARKHOUSE RD
BLACKHORSE RD
CHURCH RD
A112 HIGH RD
HIGH ROAD LEYTON
LEYTON GREEN RD
ST JAMES'S ST
HIGH ST
The Bell
Walthamstow Forest Coll
Allot Gdns
Sp Gd
TH
C Ctr
Ct
Thorpe Coombe
Coll Sch
Liby
Walthamstow
Walthamstow Central
Walthamstow Queen's Road
St James Street
Queens Road Cemy
South Grove Sch
Kelmscott L Ctr
Kelmscott Sch
St Saviour's Sch
Barn Croft Sch
Sybourn Inf Sch Annexe
Church Mead Sch
St Joseph's Sch
George Mitchell Sch
The Holy Family Coll
Vestry Ho (Mus)
Tenn Cts
Fball Gd
ROXWELL TRAD PK
CROMWELL EST
FAIRWAYS BSNS PK
LEYTON BSNS CTR
ORIENT IND PK
ST ANDREWS RD
HIGHAM ST
SOUTH COUNTESS RD
WINNS AVE
BEMSTED RD
MERSEY RD
DIANA RD
BADLIS RD
WINNS TERR
BEDFORD RD
BROMLEY RD
CHANDOS AVE
FARNAN AVE
KENILWORTH AVE
SPRUCE HILLS RD
LLOYD PARK HO
SOUTH ERLAND RD
CHAMBERLAIN PL
QUEEN ELIZABETH RD
PASQUIER RD
LUTON RD
HOLMES AVE
WILLIAM MORRIS CL
BLENHEIM RD
KING EDWARD RD
TAVISTOCK AVE
CHATHAM RD
ROMA RD
BUNYAN RD
RENNESS RD
RUSSELL RD
BORWICK AVE
JEWEL RD
RUBY RD
GAYWOOD RD
PEARL RD
BROOKDALE RD
GREENLEAF RD
BYRON RD
HOWARD RD
FALMER RD
HURST RD
AUBREY RD
SEAFORD RD
THE DRIVE
PROSPECT HILL
RECTORY RD
BRANTWOOD RD
CANNING RD
MELBOURNE RD
COLERIDGE RD
COTTENHAM RD
MILTON RD
CAIRO RD
WALPOLE RD
HATHERLEY RD
WESTBURY RD
CHURCH HILL
CHURCH LA
WARNER RD
MANSFIELD RD
SOMERS RD
PALMERSTON RD
ERSKINE RD
CAMPBELL RD
GILLARDS WAY
STAINFORTH RD
EASTFIELD RD
WEST AVENUE RD
ST MARY RD
NORTHCOTE RD
PRETORIA AVE
CARISBROOKE RD
BUXTON RD
SELBORNE RD
ORFORD RD
ADDISON RD
PRIORY AVE
SECOND AVE
FIRST AVE
THIRD AVE
CEDARS AVE
MISSION GR
CRANBROOK RD
COURTENAY PL
HAZELWOOD RD
GLENTHORNE RD
COPPERMILL LA
GROSVENOR PARK RD
PEMBROKE RD
GROVE RD
COPELAND RD
FRASER RD
MERTON RD
CROMWELL RD
GRANVILLE RD
CLARENDON RD
LIVINGSTONE RD
KNOTTS GREEN RD
LYNMOUTH RD
CLACTON RD
HARTINGTON RD
MARKHOUSE AVE
ESSEX RD
FORSTER RD
SOUTH ACCESS RD
RICHMOND RD
CHELMSFORD RD
LANSDOWNE RD
SOMERSET RD
ST BARNABAS RD
WELLESLEY RD
DEVONSHIRE RD
BELGRAVE RD
VIOLET RD
IVY RD
LILY RD
BOUNDARY RD
WESTMORLAND RD
ACACIA RD
MYRTLE RD
VERULAM AVE
MARKMANOR AVE
ALEXANDRA RD
BROOMFIELD RD
FARMILO RD
ROCHDALE RD
AVONDALE RD
NORTHUMBERLAND RD
BOWDON RD
WESTERHAM RD
DUNTON RD
BICKLEY RD
SHORTLANDS RD
MELBOURNE RD
WHITNEY RD
CAPWORTH ST
QUEENS DR
WATERLOO RD
MALTA RD
BRIDGE RD
HARRIS ST
BLYTH RD
OVERTON RD
WELLINGTON RD
BURWELL RD
SANDERSTEAD RD
BELVEDERE RD
FLEMPTON RD
HEYBRIDGE WAY
MORIEUX RD
BLOXHALL RD
KETTLEBASTON RD
PERTH RD
SEYMOUR RD
CLEMENTINA RD
VIKING PL
ELM PARK RD
ARGALL WAY
RIGG APP
LAMMAS RD
TALLACK RD
ESTATE WAY
PALAMOS RD
MARCONI RD
BAIRD CL
SUNNYSIDE RD
LEASOWES RD
LEA HALL RD
RADLIX RD
MANOR RD
PARK RD
PRIMROSE RD
GOLDSMITH RD
GRANGE PARK RD
VICARAGE RD
BYRON RD
BREWSTER RD
COOPER'S LA
CRAWLEY RD
SKELTON'S LA
BEAUMONT RD
TILBURY RD
MARSH LA
CONNAUGHT CL
FRANCIS RD

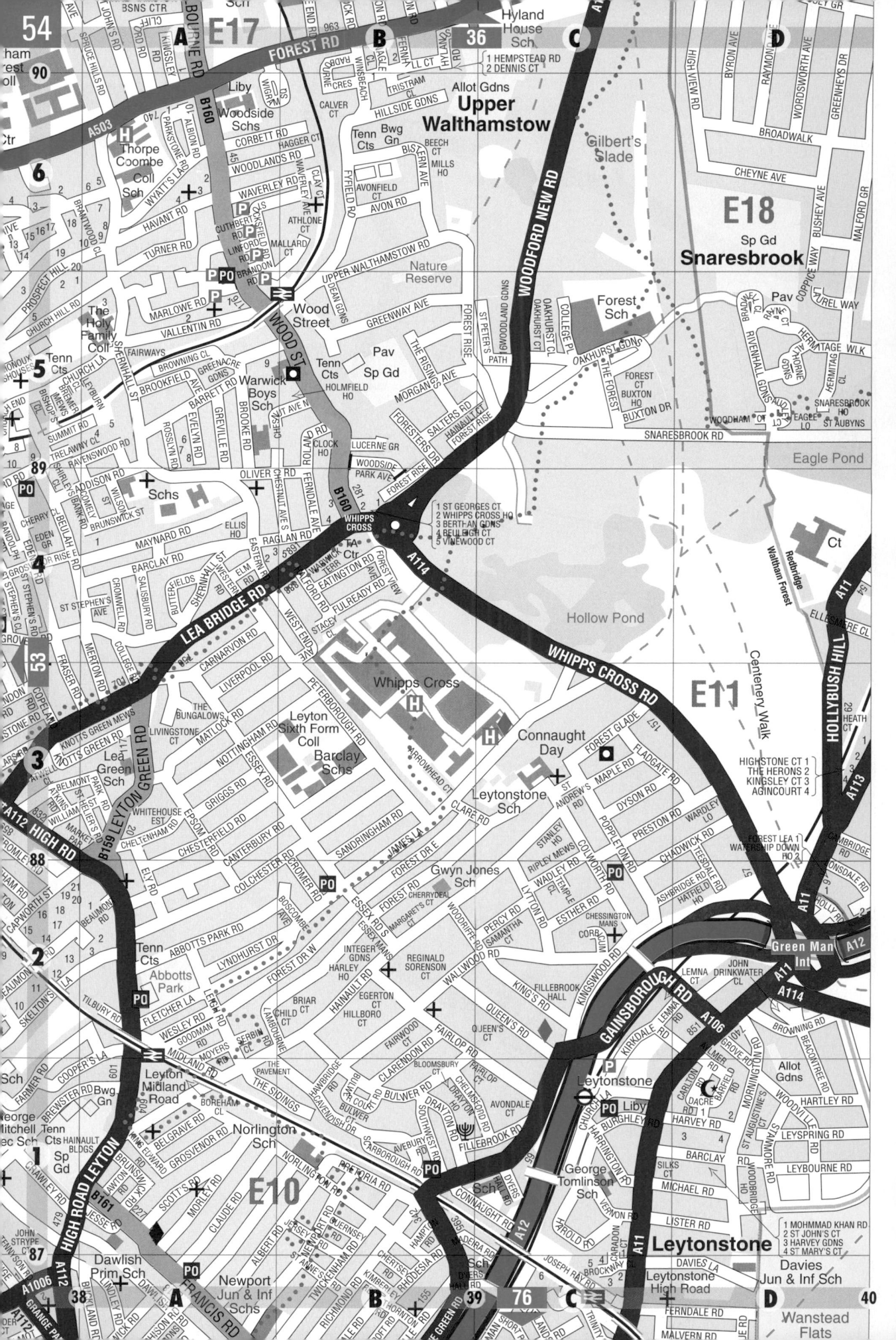
E17
FOREST RD
Hyland House Sch
36
1 HEMPSTEAD RD
2 DENNIS CT
Upper Walthamstow
Allot Gdns
Liby
Woodside Schs
Thorpe Coombe
Coll Sch
CORBETT RD
HAGGER CT
WOODLANDS RD
WAVERLEY RD
HAVANT RD
TURNER RD
BRANTWOOD RD
PROSPECT HILL
CHURCH HILL RD
A503
B160
BOURNE RD
KINGSLEY RD
SPRUCE HILLS RD
ST JOHN'S RD
BSNS CTR
WIGRAM
HILLSIDE GDNS
TRISTRAM CL
CALVER CT
WINSBEACH
Tenn Cts
Bwg Gn
BEECH CT
MILLS HO
BISTERN AVE
FYFIELD RD
AVONFIELD CT
AVON RD
ATHLONE CT
MALLARD CT
CLAY CT
WAVERLEY AVE
WYATT'S LA
CUTHBERT RD
LINFORD RD
BRANDON RD
UPPER WALTHAMSTOW RD
Nature Reserve
Wood Street
WOOD ST
GREENWAY AVE
DEAN GDNS
MARLOWE RD
VALLENTIN RD
The Holy Family Coll
FAIRWAYS
SHERNHALL ST
BROWNING CL
GREENACRE GDNS
BROOKFIELD AVE
BARRETT RD
Warwick Boys Sch
Tenn Cts
Pav
Sp Gd
HOLMFIELD HO
THE RISINGS
MORGANS AVE
FORESTERS DR
SALTERS RD
HAINAULT CT
FOREST RISE
ST PETER'S PATH
WOODLAND GDNS
WOODFORD NEW RD
Gilbert's Slade
E18
Snaresbrook
Sp Gd
BYRON AVE
RAYMOND AVE
WORDSWORTH AVE
GREENHEYS DR
HIGH VIEW RD
BROADWALK
CHEYNE AVE
BUSHEY AVE
MALFORD GR
COPPICE WAY
LAUREL WAY
Pav
HERMITAGE WLK
RIVENHALL GDNS
SNARESBROOK HO
EAGLE LO
ST AUBYNS
WOODHAM CT
SNARESBROOK RD
Eagle Pond
Forest Sch
COLLEGE PL
OAKHURST CL
OAKHURST CT
OAKHURST GDNS
THE FOREST
FOREST CT
BUXTON HO
BUXTON DR
CHURCH LA
SUMMIT RD
TRELAWNY CL
RAVENSWOOD RD
LUCERNE GR
WOODSIDE PARK AVE
CLOCK HO
ROLAND RD
ROSSLYN RD
EVELYN RD
GREVILLE RD
BROOKE RD
OLIVER RD
CHESTNUT AVE S
FERNDALE AVE
ADDISON RD
Schs
BRUNSWICK ST
BEULAH RD
MAYNARD RD
ELLIS HO
RAGLAN RD
WHIPPS CROSS
1 ST GEORGES CT
2 WHIPPS CROSS HO
3 BERTHAN GDNS
4 BEULEIGH CT
5 VINEWOOD CT
TA Ctr
A114
BARCLAY RD
EATINGTON RD
FULREADY RD
FOREST VIEW
SALISBURY RD
CROMWELL RD
ST STEPHEN'S AVE
BUTTERFIELDS
LEA BRIDGE RD
STACEY CL
WEST END AVE
Hollow Pond
Redbridge
Waltham Forest
Ct
HOLLYBUSH HILL
ELLESMERE CL
A11
53
CARNARVON RD
LIVERPOOL RD
PETERBOROUGH RD
Whipps Cross
WHIPPS CROSS RD
E11
Centenery Walk
THE BUNGALOWS
MATLOCK RD
LIVINGSTONE CT
KNOTTS GREEN MEWS
KNOTTS GREEN RD
Leyton Sixth Form Coll
Barclay Schs
NOTTINGHAM RD
ESSEX RD
Lea Green Sch
LEYTON GREEN RD
B159
Connaught Day
FOREST GLADE
FLADGATE RD
MAPLE RD
DYSON RD
PRESTON RD
ST ANDREW'S RD
Leytonstone Sch
ARROWHEAD CT
CLARE RD
HEATH CT
HIGHSTONE CT 1
THE HERONS 2
KINGSLEY CT 3
AGINCOURT 4
A113
A112 HIGH RD
WHITEHOUSE EST
CHELTENHAM RD
GRIGGS RD
EPSOM RD
CHESTERFIELD RD
CANTERBURY RD
SANDRINGHAM RD
JAMES LA
FOREST DR E
COLCHESTER RD
CROMER RD
Gwyn Jones Sch
STANLEY HO
RIPLEY MEWS
WADLEY RD
TEMPLE CL
COLWORTH RD
POPPLETON RD
CHADWICK RD
WARDLEY LO
FOREST LEA 1
WATERSHIP DOWN HO 2
CAMBRIDGE RD
LONSDALE RD
ELY RD
CAPWORTH ST
BEAUMONT RD
ABBOTTS PARK RD
LYNDHURST DR
BOSCOMBE AVE
FOREST RD
CHERRYDEAL CT
MARGARET'S CT
ESSEX RD S
ESSEX MANS
WOODRIFFE RD
PERCY RD
SAMANTHA CT
LYTTON RD
ESTHER RD
ASHBRIDGE RD
HATFIELD HO
CHESSINGTON MANS
CORBICUM
Green Man Int
A12
Tenn Cts
Abbotts Park
FOREST DR W
INTEGER GDNS
HARLEY HO
REGINALD SORENSON CT
WALLWOOD RD
KING'S RD
FILLEBROOK HALL
KINGSWOOD RD
GAINSBOROUGH RD
LEMNA CT
JOHN DRINKWATER CL
A106
BROWNING RD
TILBURY RD
FLETCHER LA
WESLEY RD
GOODMAN RD
MOYERS RD
SERBIN CL
LEIGH RD
LAMBOURNE
BRIAR CT
CHILD CT
HAINAULT RD
EGERTON CT
HILLBORO CT
QUEEN'S RD
QUEEN'S CT
FAIRLOP RD
FAIRWOOD CT
CLARENDON RD
BLOOMSBURY CT
KIRKDALE RD
ALMA RD
GROVE RD
MORNINGTON RD
BEACONTREE RD
Allot Gdns
COOPER'S LA
FARMER RD
BREWSTER RD
Bwg Gn
Leyton Midland Road
MIDLAND RD
THE PAVEMENT
THE SIDINGS
HAWBRIDGE RD
CAVENDISH DR
BULWER RD
BULWER CT
CHELMSFORD RD
DRAYTON RD
AVONDALE CT
Leytonstone
Liby
CHURCH LA
CARLTON RD
DACRE
BARFIELD RD
HARTLEY RD
WOODVILLE RD
George Mitchell Sch
Tenn Cts
HAINAULT BLDGS
Sp Gd
BOREHAM CL
BELGRAVE RD
GROSVENOR RD
Norlington Sch
SCARBOROUGH RD
AVEBURY RD
SOUTHWEST RD
FILLEBROOK RD
BURGHLEY RD
HARRINGTON RD
HARVEY RD
BARCLAY RD
ST AUGUSTINE'S CT
STANMORE RD
LEYSPRING RD
LEYBOURNE RD
CRAWLEY RD
BRUNSWICK RD
LAWTON RD
SCOTT'S RD
MORLEY RD
CLAUDE RD
E10
NORLINGTON RD
PRETORIA RD
George Tomlinson Sch
SILKS CT
MICHAEL RD
WOODBRIDGE HO
LISTER RD
VERNON RD
HAROLD RD
CONNAUGHT RD
HIGH ROAD LEYTON
B161
JESSE RD
JOHN STRYPE CT
Dawlish Prim Sch
ALBERT RD
JERSEY RD
NEWPORT RD
GUERNSEY RD
ST ANNE'S RD
TWICKENHAM RD
KIMBERLEY RD
CHERTSEY RD
RHODESIA RD
HAMPTON RD
MADEIRA RD
Sch
JOSEPH RAY RD
CARADON CL
BROCKWAY CL
Leytonstone
1 MOHMMAD KHAN RD
2 ST JOHN'S CT
3 HARVEY GDNS
4 ST MARY'S CT
DAVIES LA
Davies Jun & Inf Sch
Leytonstone High Road
Newport Jun & Inf Schs
FRANCIS RD
DAWLISH RD
LINDLEY RD
RICHMOND RD
FERNDALE RD
MALVERN RD
Wanstead Flats
A1006
A112
GRANGE PARK
87
A
38
B
39
76
C
D
40

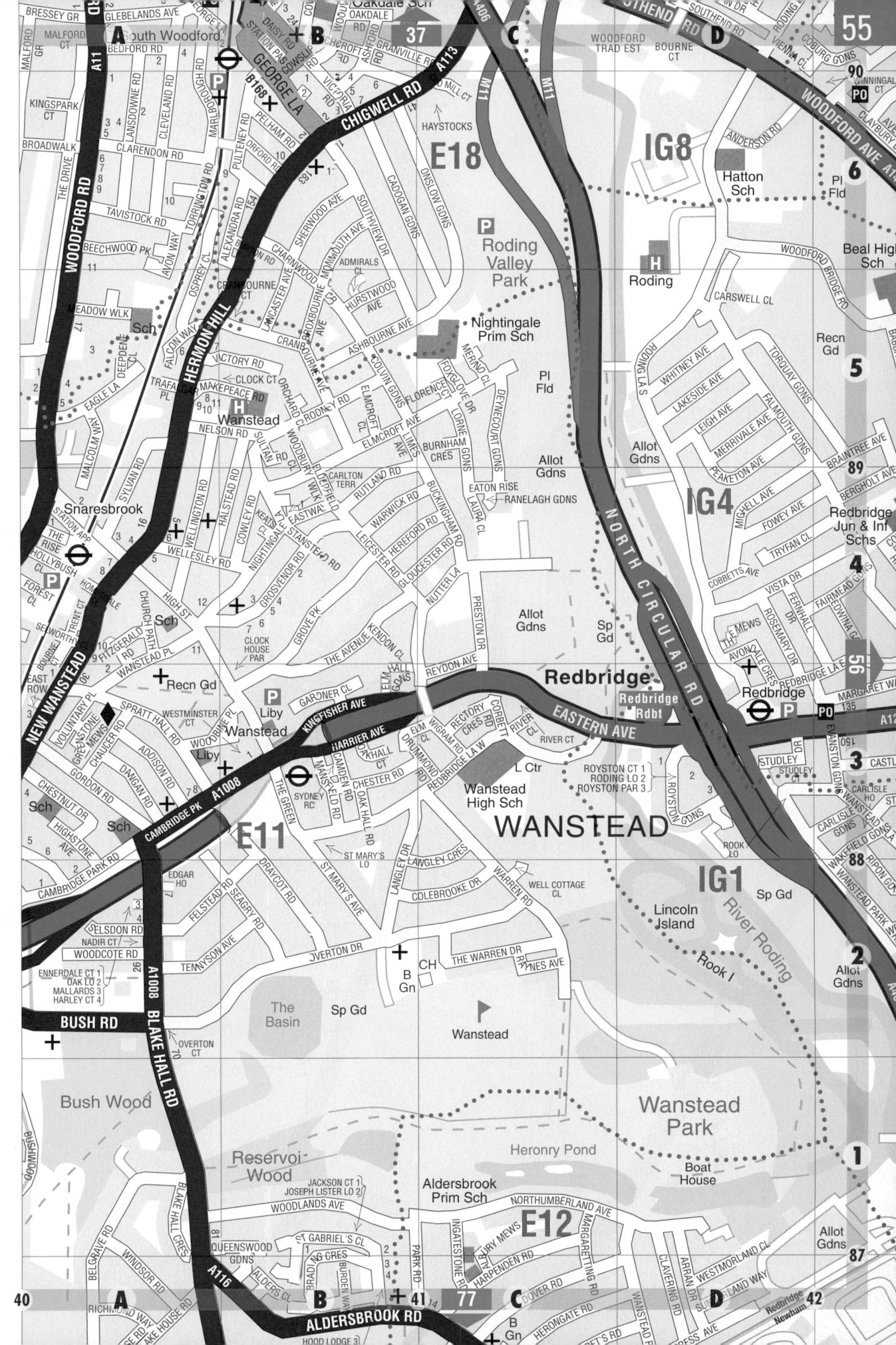
South Woodford
E18
IG8
Roding Valley Park
Nightingale Prim Sch
Hatton Sch
Roding
Beal High Sch
Wanstead
Snaresbrook
IG4
Redbridge Jun & Inf Schs
Redbridge
Redbridge Rdbt
NORTH CIRCULAR RD
EASTERN AVE
WOODFORD RD
HERMON HILL
CHIGWELL RD
GEORGE LA
WOODFORD AVE
NEW WANSTEAD
KINGFISHER AVE
HARRIER AVE
CAMBRIDGE PK
Wanstead High Sch
WANSTEAD
E11
IG1
Lincoln Island
River Roding
Rook I
The Basin
BUSH RD
BLAKE HALL RD
Bush Wood
Reservoir Wood
Heronry Pond
Wanstead Park
Boat House
Aldersbrook Prim Sch
E12
WOODLANDS AVE
NORTHUMBERLAND AVE
ALDERSBROOK RD
37
56
77
40
41
42
A
B
C
D
1
2
3
4
5
6
87
88
89
90
Redbridge
Newham

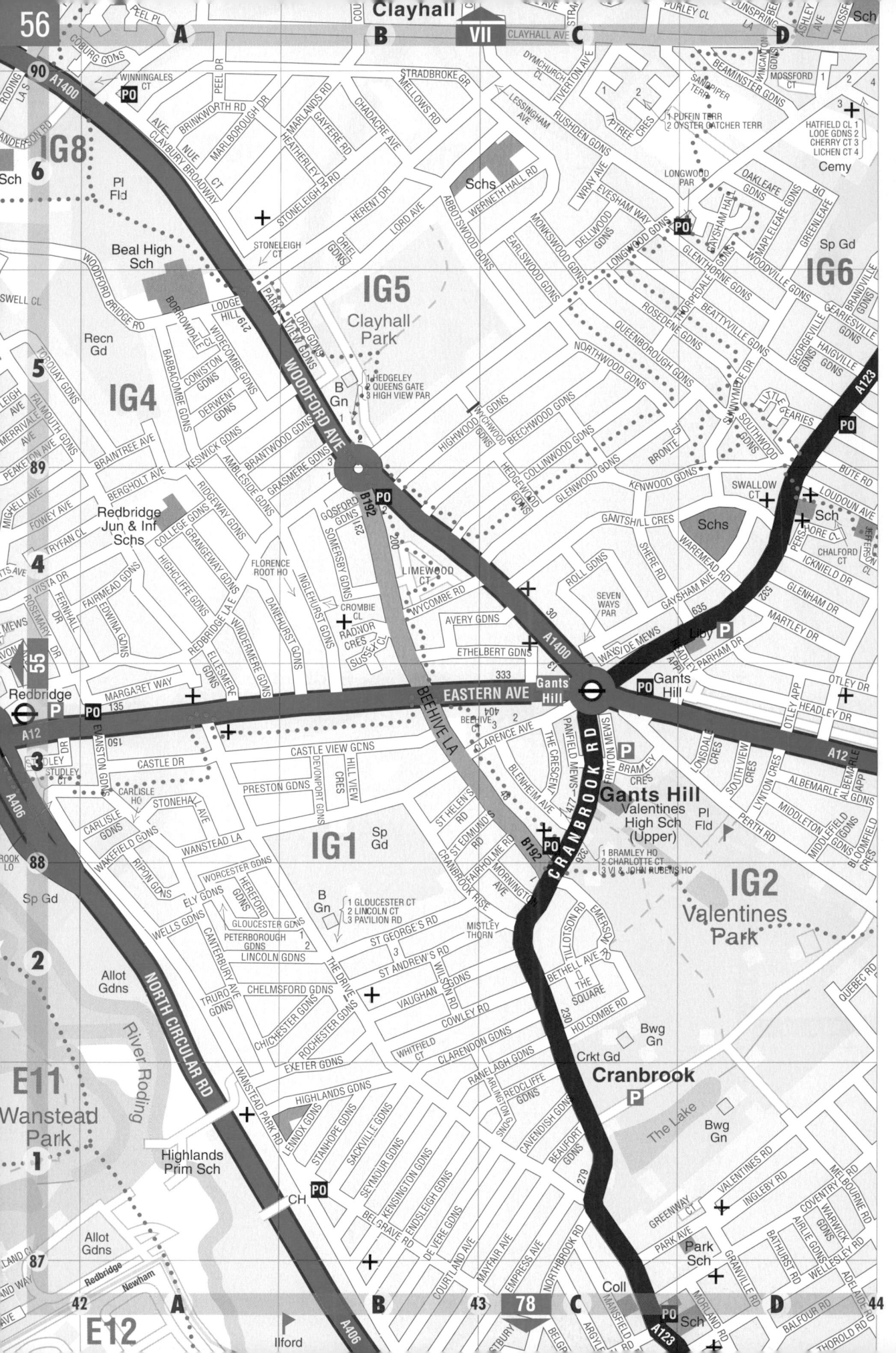

Clayhall
VII
A
B
C
D
IG8
IG5
IG4
IG6
IG1
IG2
E11
E12
Clayhall Park
Beal High Sch
Redbridge Jun & Inf Schs
Valentines Park
Gants Hill
Valentines High Sch (Upper)
Cranbrook
Wanstead Park
Highlands Prim Sch
River Roding
The Lake
WOODFORD AVE
EASTERN AVE
NORTH CIRCULAR RD
CRANBROOK RD
BEEHIVE LA
A1400
A12
A406
A123
B192
55
78
Redbridge
Newham
Ilford
42
43
44
90
89
88
87

57
A123 Chigwell, M11 (A113)
Schs
A
B
VII
C
D
Fairlop Waters
Ctry Pk
90
Fairlop Plain
Sch of Riding
PAINTERS RD
Fairlop Waters
Ilford Jewish
Prim Sch
WESTMINSTER GDNS
FREMANTLE RD
WAVERLEY GDNS
TRINITY RD
HORACE RD
MOSSFORD GN
GREEN ELMS
HIGH ST
A123
TOLLESBURY GDNS
CRAVEN GDNS
HEYBRIDGE DR
SANDRINGHAM GDNS
BARON GDNS
CRANBOURNE GDNS
TANNERS LA
SANDRINGHAM CL
Recn Gd
Ct
COURT WAY
THE VILLAGE HOME
CARLTON DR
CARLTON CT
STATION RD
Barkingside
Barkingside
IG2
Aldborough
Hall Farm
ALDBOROUGH RD
6
BARNARDO DR 1
SYCAMORE WLK 2
WALNUT CL 3
Fullwood
Prim Sch
BARTON MEADOWS
IG6
CIVIC WAY
WOODHAVEN GDNS
Fball
Gd
Aldborough Hatch
Allot
Gdns
ASTHALL GDNS
BUREFORD CL
CROWN RD
PRINCES RD
DUKE RD
MULBERRY WAY
HATLEY AVE
CORONATION CL
5
Aldborough
House Farm
ST PETERS CL
APPLEGARTH DR
SPEARPOINT GDNS
BAWDSEY AVE
NORTH CROSS RD
HASTINGS AVE
POPLAR WAY
CAMPBELL AVE
ALDWYCH AVE
WILLIAM CT
OAKS LA
CHEVIOT WAY
OAKS LA
CHILTERN RD
RAMSGILL APP
RAMSGILL DR
A12
SOUTH CROSS RD
HAMILTON AVE
SHERWOOD RD
WARREN RD
NORTHDOWN GDNS
Pl Fld
ROY GDNS
THE SHRUBBERIES
ALDBOROUGH RD N
SUNNINGHILL GDNS
89
HORNS RD
CHASE LA
1 NETLEY CT
2 SHIRLEY CT
3 KAREN TERR
4 VICTORIA COTTS
SOUTHDOWN CRES
CAMBRIAN AVE
BRENDON GDNS
LEYSWOOD DR
TORBITT WAY
SHENSTONE GDNS
VERONICA GDNS
ASHURST DR
DONINGTON AVE
EMMOTT AVE
NETLEY RD
PERKINS RD
THE WHITINGS
OAKS LA
MENDIP RD
William Torbitt
Jun & Inf
Schs
Seven Kings Water
4
Bwg
Gn
ARDWELL AVE
BIRKBECK RD
ABBEY RD
Barley
Mow
Sp Gd
HOMEFIELD AVE
STAPLEFORD AVE
GRENFELL GDNS
ALDBOROUGH CT
Sports
Gd
BROCKHAM DR
SPRINGFIELD DR
BUNTINGBRIDGE RD
PERRYMANS FARM RD
BUSH CL
CROWNFIELD AVE
AVENUE TERR
ACORN CT
SILVERDALE PAR
SILVERDALE
PARK AVE
HOLLAND RD
SELWYN AVE
58
DENHAM DR
BENTLEY DR
YOUNGS RD
ARTILLERY CL
KING GEORGE AVE
WHITES AVE
THE CLOSE
Sch
Newbury
Park
SUFFOLK CT
CANTLEY GDNS
YOXLEY DR
UPPARK DR
Newbury
Park
EASTERN AVE
HERTFORD RD
WESSEX CL
CHEPSTOW CRES
SUFFOLK RD
Seven Kings
Park
3
617
YOXLEY APP
CENTRAL PAR
NEWBURY RD
BROOK RD
NORTON CT
CHURCH RD
BUXTON RD
LYNDHURST GDNS
Bwg
Gn
MILTON CRES
EASTERNVILLE GDNS
LANCING RD
GLEBELANDS AVE
STAINFORTH RD
BRANCASTER RD
DOWNSHALL CT
DOWNSHALL AVE
EPSOM RD
Sch
CRANLEY RD
CLIFTON RD
DELL OW CL
COTSWOLD GDNS
DEVONSHIRE RD
TRILLO CT
LEICESTER GDNS
MERTON RD
BEDDINGTON RD
MORDON RD
MITCHAM RD
WALLINGTON RD
FARNHAM RD
REGENT GDNS
88
ROYAL CL
PERCY RD
QUEBEC RD
WESTERNVILLE GDNS
CRANLEY DR
LYNN RD
ST JOHNS RD
MEADS LA
NORMAN CT
AURELIA COTTS
WARDS RD
Sch
Sch
ALDBOROUGH RD S
Westwood
Rec Gd
2
MONTREAL RD
PERTH TERR
RUSSELL GDNS
RAYMOND RD
Sp Gd
Seven Kings
High Sch
MAFEKING AVE
LADYSMITH AVE
KIMBERLEY AVE
Seven Kings
ADEN RD
AUCKLAND RD
COLOMBO RD
CHARTER AVE
Allot
Gdns
GLENCOE AVE
NORFOLK RD
ELGIN RD
CAMBRIDGE RD
LANSDOWNE RD
ST ALBANS RD
PEMBROKE RD
CHESTER RD
WESTWOOD RD
BLYTHSWOOD RD
ATHOLL RD
KINGSWOOD RD
Pl Fld
COLENSO RD
SPENCER RD
BRISBANE RD
TORONTO RD
LEY ST
BENTON RD
DURBAN RD
Sch
787
A118
DUNEDIN RD
St Aidan's
Sch
MUNDON GDNS
LEEDS RD
KINGS GDNS
Allot
Gdns
BRADFORD RD
IG3
WELLESLEY RD
IG1
SIPPETTS CT
VICARAGE LA
Seven
Kings
FARLEY DR
1
Christchurch
Prim Sch
CHRISTCHURCH RD
GODDARDS WAY
Allot
Gdns
CAMERON RD
637
HIGH RD
1 BALMORAL GDNS
2 ELECTRIC PAR
ASHGROVE RD
Sch
SWINDON CL
LOMBARD AVE
BALFOUR RD
THOROLD RD
JAFFE RD
DRAYTON CL
MEISTER CL
VERNON RD
FELBRIGGE RD
1 FRANCIS ST
2 FRANCIS RD
3 ELIZABETH AVE
SALISBURY RD
SEVEN KINGS RD
87
ILFORD
CARRIAGE MEWS
MALLARD CT
HIGHBURY GDNS
HERBERT RD
LAMBOURNE RD
ELMSTEAD RD
HASLEMERE RD
MILVERTON GDNS
KENILWORTH GDNS
DARTMORE RD
475
A1083
44
A
B
45
79
C
D
46
FRANCIS AVE
REDBRIDGE ENT CTR
A118
Cemy
NORTH RD
NEW RD
CLANDON RD
EYNSFORD RD
GREEN LA
WOODSTOCK GDNS

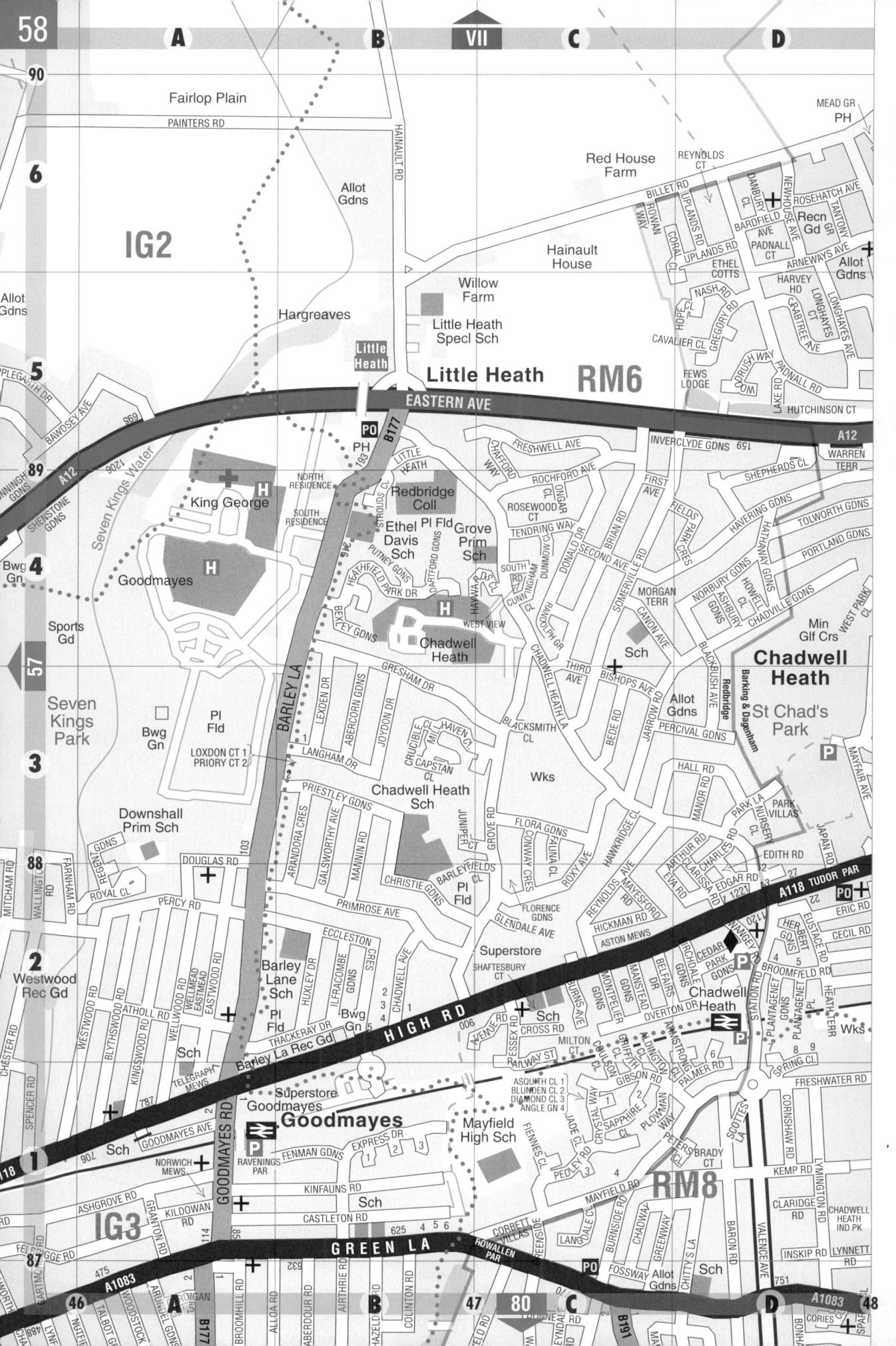
A
B
VII
C
D
90
Fairlop Plain
PAINTERS RD
HAINAULT RD
6
Allot Gdns
IG2
Red House Farm
REYNOLDS CT
MEAD GR
PH
BILLET RD
ROWAN WAY
UPLANDS RD
DANBURY CL
NEWHOUSE AVE
ROSEHATCH AVE
TANTONY GR
Recn Gd
BARDFIELD AVE
PADNALL CT
CORAL CL
UPLANDS RD
ETHEL COTTS
ARNEWAYS AVE
Allot Gdns
Hainault House
Willow Farm
HARVEY HO
NASH RD
HOPE CL
GREGORY RD
CRABTREE AVE
LONGHAYES CT
LONGHAYES AVE
CAVALIER CL
Allot Gdns
Hargreaves
Little Heath Specl Sch
Little Heath
5
PLEGARTH DR
Little Heath
RM6
FEWS LODGE
ORCHARD WAY
LAKE RD
PADNALL RD
HUTCHINSON CT
BAWDSEY AVE
EASTERN AVE
A12
PO
B177
PH
LITTLE HEATH
INVERCLYDE GDNS
WARREN TERR
89
A12
SHENSTONE GDNS
Seven Kings Water
NORTH RESIDENCE
SOUTH RESIDENCE
King George
H
Redbridge Coll
CHAFFORD WAY
FRESHWELL AVE
ROCHFORD AVE
ROSEWOOD CT
ONGAR CL
FIRST AVE
SHEPHERDS CL
FIELDS PARK CRES
HAVERING GDNS
TOLWORTH GDNS
STROUDS CL
Ethel Davis Sch
Pl Fld
Grove Prim Sch
TENDRING WAY
DUNMOW CL
DONALD DR
BRIAN RD
SECOND AVE
SOMERVILLE RD
HATHAWAY GDNS
PORTLAND GDNS
Bwg Gn
4
Goodmayes
H
PUTNEY GDNS
HEATHFIELD PARK DR
DARTFORD GDNS
SOUTH RD
CUNNINGHAM CL
HAYWARDS CL
MORGAN TERR
NORBURY GDNS
ASHBURY GDNS
HOWELL CL
CHADVILLE GDNS
WEST PARK CL
BEXLEY GDNS
H
WEST VIEW
RANDOLPH GR
CANON AVE
Min Glf Crs
Sports Gd
Chadwell Heath
Sch
57
CHADWELL HEATH LA
THIRD AVE
BISHOPS AVE
BLACKBUSH AVE
Chadwell Heath
GRESHAM DR
Seven Kings Park
Pl Fld
Bwg Gn
BARLEY LA
LEXDEN DR
ABERCORN GDNS
JOYDON DR
CRUCIBLE CL
MILL CL
HAVEN CL
BLACKSMITH CL
BEDE RD
JARROW RD
Allot Gdns
Redbridge
Barking & Dagenham
St Chad's Park
PERCIVAL GDNS
LOXDON CT 1
PRIORY CT 2
LANGHAM DR
CAPSTAN CL
Wks
HALL RD
P
MAYFAIR AVE
3
PRIESTLEY GDNS
Chadwell Heath Sch
MANOR RD
PARK LA
NURSERY CL
PARK VILLAS
Downshall Prim Sch
ARANDORA CRES
GALSWORTHY AVE
MANNIN RD
JUNIPER CT
GROVE RD
FLORA GDNS
CONWAY CRES
FAUNA CL
ROXY AVE
HAWKRIDGE CL
ARTHUR RD
CHARLES RD
JAPAN RD
REGENT GDNS
DOUGLAS RD
103
88
MITCHAM RD
WALLINGTON RD
FARNHAM RD
ROYAL CL
PERCY RD
CHRISTIE GDNS
BARLEYFIELDS CL
Pl Fld
REYNOLDS AVE
MAYESFORD RD
EVA RD
CLARISSA RD
EDGAR RD
EDITH RD
A118 TUDOR PAR
PO
ERIC RD
PRIMROSE AVE
FLORENCE GDNS
GLENDALE AVE
HICKMAN RD
ASTON MEWS
HERBERT GDNS
EUSTACE RD
CECIL RD
ECCLESTON CRES
Superstore
SHAFTESBURY CT
BURNS AVE
MONTPELIER GDNS
MANSTEAD GDNS
BELFAIRS DR
BIRCHDALE GDNS
CEDAR PARK GDNS
WANGEY RD
BROOMFIELD RD
2
Westwood Rec Gd
Barley Lane Sch
HUXLEY DR
ILFRACOMBE GDNS
CHADWELL AVE
Chadwell Heath
STATION RD
PLANTAGENET GDNS
PLANTAGENET PL
HEATH TERR
WESTWOOD RD
BLYTHSWOOD RD
ATHOLL RD
WELLWOOD RD
WELLMEAD
EASTMEAD
EASTWOOD RD
Pl Fld
Bwg Gn
HIGH RD
AVENUE RD
Sch
OVERTON DR
Wks
CHESTER RD
KINGSWOOD RD
Sch
THACKERAY DR
Barley La Rec Gd
ESSEX RD
CROSS RD
MILTON CT
RAILWAY ST
COULSON CL
GRIFFITH CL
ALDINGTON CL
ARMSTRONG CL
PALMER RD
SPRING CL
TELEGRAPH MEWS
ASQUITH CL 1
BLUNDEN CL 2
DIAMOND CL 3
ANGLE GN 4
GIBSON RD
FRESHWATER RD
SPENCER RD
Superstore
Goodmayes
Goodmayes
Mayfield High Sch
CRYSTAL WAY
SAPPHIRE CL
PLOWMAN WAY
SCOTTES LA
CORNSHAW RD
LYMINGTON RD
1
GOODMAYES AVE
Sch
GOODMAYES RD
EXPRESS DR
FENMAN GDNS
FIENNES CL
JADE CL
PETERS CL
BRADY CT
NORWICH MEWS
RAVENINGS PAR
PEDLEY RD
KEMP RD
KINFAUNS RD
Sch
MAYFIELD RD
RM8
ASHGROVE RD
KILDOWAN RD
GRANTON RD
IG3
CASTLETON RD
CORBETT VILLAS
GREENSIDE
LANGDALE CL
BURNSIDE RD
CHADWAY
GREENWAY
CHITTY'S LA
BARON RD
VALENCE AVE
CLARIDGE RD
CHADWELL HEATH IND PK
87
FELBRIGGE RD
GREEN LA
ROWALLEN PAR
PO
FOSSWAY
Allot Gdns
Sch
INSKIP RD
LYNNETT RD
A1083
46
47
80
48
A1083
CORIES CL
BROOMHILL RD
ALLOA RD
ABERDOUR RD
AIRTHRIE RD
COLINTON RD
B191
TALBOT GDNS
WOODSTOCK
ARUNDEL GDNS
B177

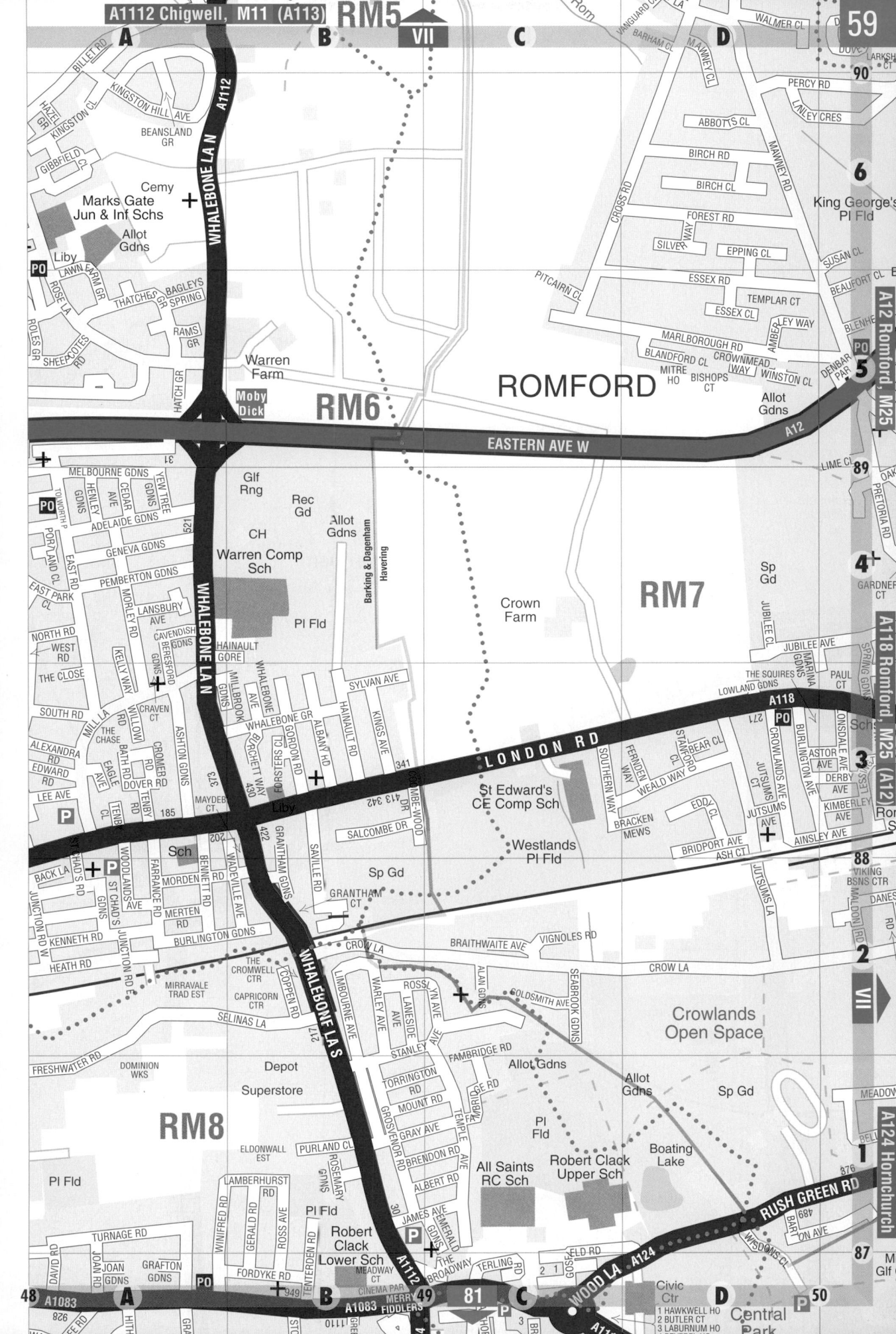
A1112 Chigwell, M11 (A113)
RM5
VII
ROMFORD
RM6
RM7
RM8
EASTERN AVE W
A12
WHALEBONE LA N
WHALEBONE LA S
LONDON RD
A118
RUSH GREEN RD
A124
WOOD LA
A1083
A1112
A12 Romford, M25
A118 Romford, M25 (A12)
A124 Hornchurch
Marks Gate Jun & Inf Schs
Cemy
Allot Gdns
Liby
Warren Farm
Moby Dick
Glf Rng
Rec Gd
CH
Warren Comp Sch
Pl Fld
Barking & Dagenham
Havering
Crown Farm
Sp Gd
St Edward's CE Comp Sch
Westlands Pl Fld
King George's Pl Fld
Crowlands Open Space
Boating Lake
Robert Clack Upper Sch
All Saints RC Sch
Robert Clack Lower Sch
Depot
Superstore
DOMINION WKS
MIRRAVALE TRAD EST
CAPRICORN CTR
THE CROMWELL CTR
ELDONWALL EST
Civic Ctr
Central Park
VIKING BSNS CTR
Mill Glf C
1 HAWKWELL HO
2 BUTLER CT
3 LABURNUM HO
48
49
50
81
87
88
89
90
1
2
3
4
5
6
A
B
C
D

A
B
38
C
D
Copthall Covert
Brackenbury Farm
Uxbridge CH
Copthall Farm
Harvil Farm
Breakspear Jun & Inf Schs
Pl Fld
Crkt Gd
Harefield Place
Ickenham
UB10
Swakeleys
Sch of the Douay Martyrs
The Douay Martyrs RC Sch (Annexe)
Swakeleys Rdbt
Vyners Sch
Park Wood
Western Ave
Swakeleys Rd
Hillingdon
Hillingdon Circus
Motel
UB8
Uxbridge Common
Ski Ctr
Uxbridge Coll
Hermitage Prim Sch
St Helens Sch
Oak Farm Jun & Inf Schs
Hillingdon Court Park (Recn Gd)
UXBRIDGE
American Com Schs
Big Clump
82
06
07
08
87
86
85
84
A40 Maidenhead (M40), M25(M40)
Long La
Freezeland Way
Park Rd

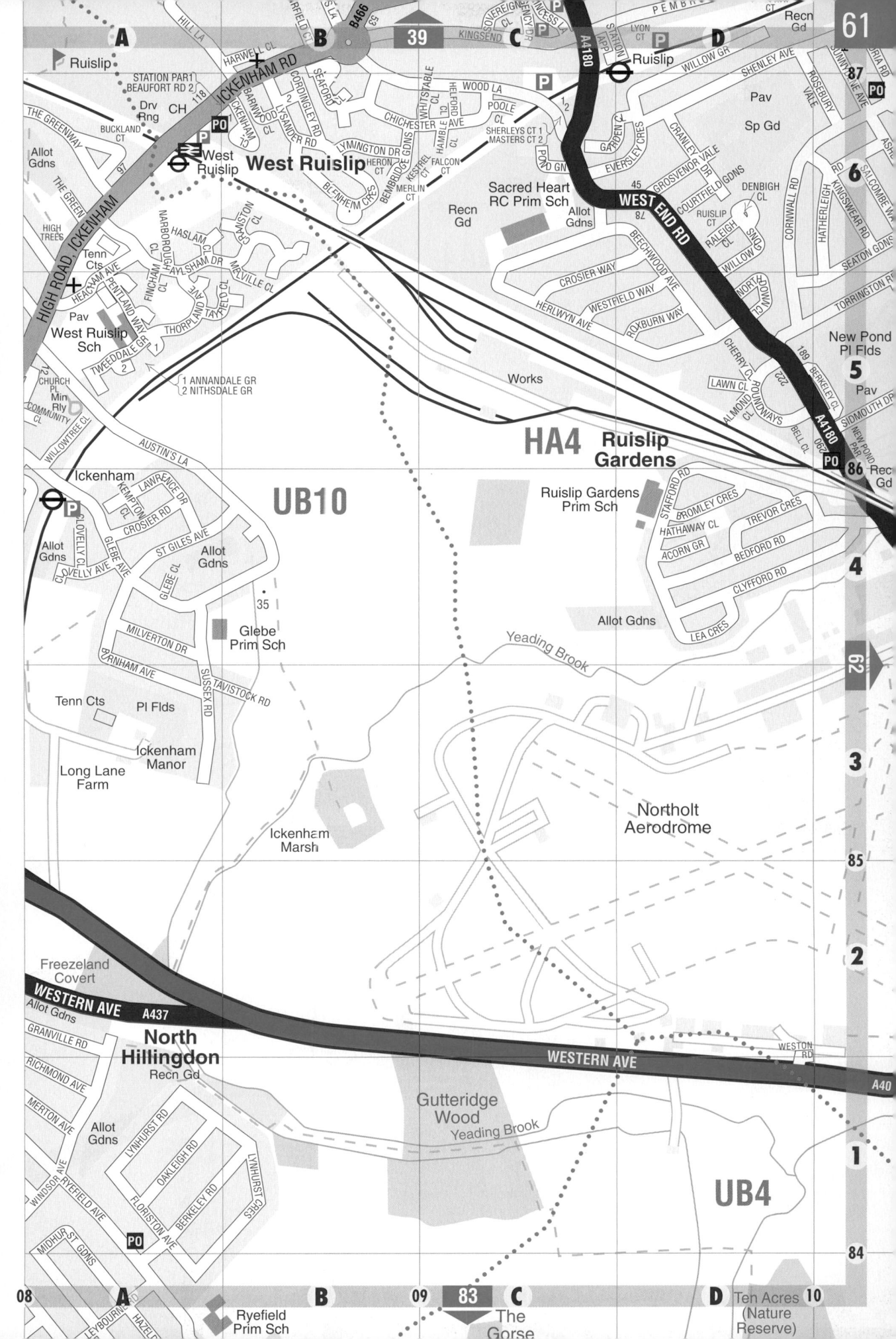
West Ruislip
Ruislip
Ruislip
Ickenham
UB10
HA4
Ruislip Gardens
Northolt Aerodrome
Ickenham Marsh
Ickenham Manor
Long Lane Farm
Freezeland Covert
North Hillingdon
Gutteridge Wood
Yeading Brook
UB4
WESTERN AVE
A437
A40
A4180
WEST END RD
ICKENHAM RD
HIGH ROAD, ICKENHAM
Sacred Heart RC Prim Sch
West Ruislip Sch
Glebe Prim Sch
Ruislip Gardens Prim Sch
Ryefield Prim Sch
Ten Acres (Nature Reserve)
The Gorse
New Pond Pl Flds

39
62
83

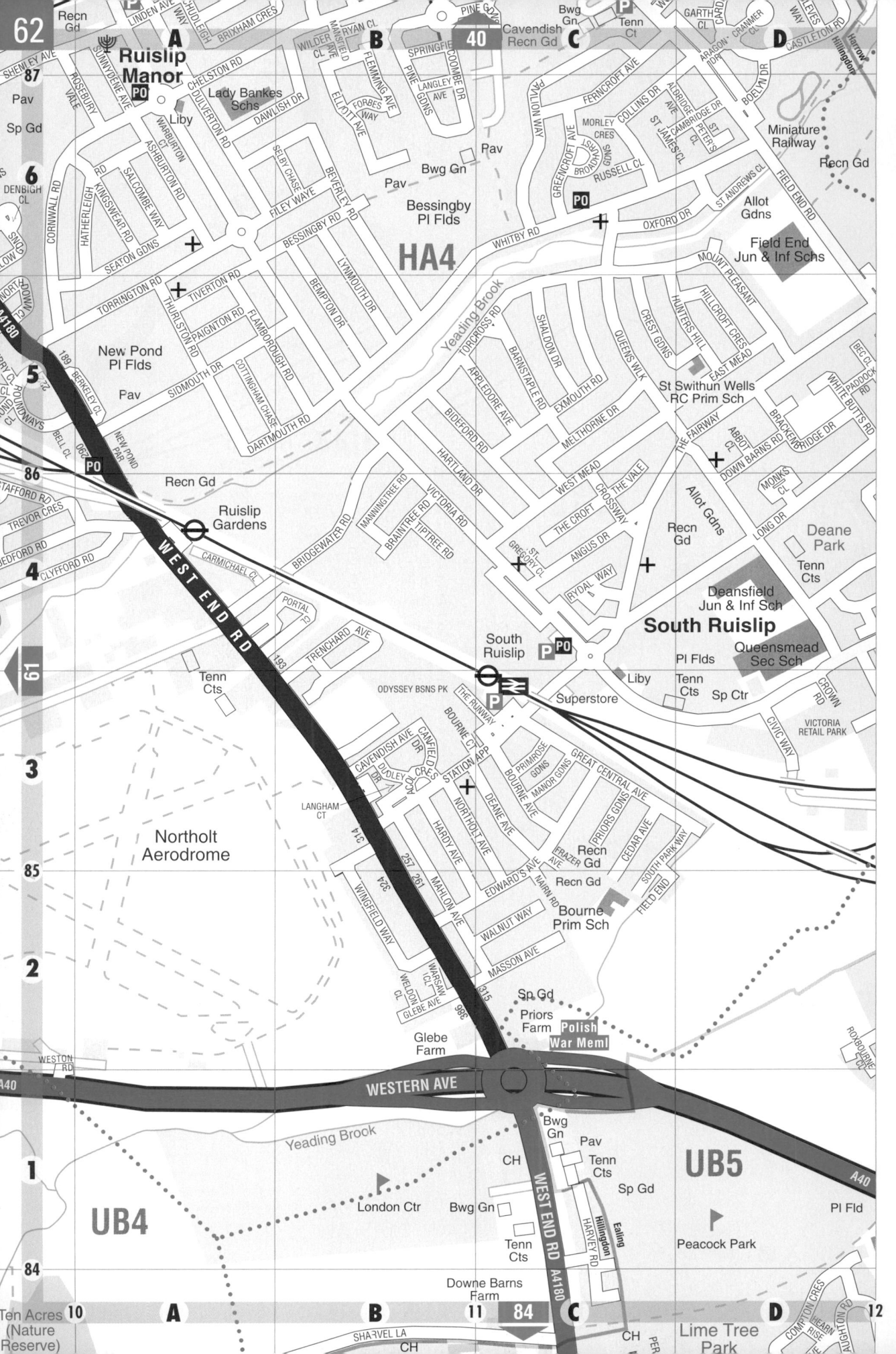

A
B
C
D
40
Recn Gd
LINDEN AVE
CHUDLEIGH
WAY
BRIXHAM CRES
WILDER CL
RYAN CL
MANSFIELD AVE
PINE GDNS
Bwg Gn
Tenn Ct
Cavendish Recn Gd
GARTH CL
CARDIGAN
ARAGON DR
CRANMER CL
LEVES WAY
CASTLETON RD
Hillingdon
Harrow
SHENLEY AVE
Ruislip Manor
87
Pav
Sp Gd
ROSEBURY VALE
SUNNYDENE AVE
PO
Liby
CHELSTON RD
DULVERTON RD
Lady Bankes Schs
DAWLISH DR
SPRINGFIELD
PINE GDNS
LANGLEY AVE
COOMBE DR
FLEMMING AVE
FORBES WAY
ELLIOTT AVE
PAVILION WAY
FERNCROFT AVE
COLLINS DR
ALDRIDGE AVE
CAMBRIDGE DR
ST PETERS CL
ST JAMES CL
BOELYN DR
Miniature Railway
Recn Gd
MORLEY CRES
GREENCROFT AVE
BROADHURST GDNS
RUSSELL CL
6
DENBIGH CL
CORNWALL RD
HATHERLEIGH RD
KINGSWEAR RD
SALCOMBE WAY
ASHBURTON RD
WARBURTON CT
SELBY CHASE
FILEY WAYE
BEVERLEY RD
Pav
Bwg Gn
Pav
Bessingby Pl Flds
PO
ST ANDREWS CL
FIELD END RD
Allot Gdns
OXFORD DR
WHITBY RD
BESSINGBY RD
SEATON GDNS
HA4
Field End Jun & Inf Schs
MOUNT PLEASANT
TORRINGTON RD
TIVERTON RD
THURLSTON RD
PAIGNTON RD
FLAMBOROUGH RD
BEMPTON DR
LYNMOUTH DR
Yeading Brook
TORCROSS RD
SHALDON DR
QUEENS WLK
CREST GDNS
HUNTERS HILL
HILLCROFT CRES
A4180
New Pond Pl Flds
189
BERKELEY CL
ROUNDWAYS
5
SIDMOUTH DR
COTTINGHAM CHASE
BARNSTAPLE RD
EXMOUTH RD
APPLEDORE AVE
EAST MEAD
St Swithun Wells RC Prim Sch
BEC CL
PADDOCK RD
WHITE BUTTS RD
Pav
DARTMOUTH RD
BIDEFORD RD
MELTHORNE DR
THE FAIRWAY
ABBOT CL
DOWN BARNS RD
BRACKENBRIDGE DR
BELL CL
NEW POND PAR
290
PO
HARTLAND DR
86
STAFFORD RD
TREVOR CRES
Recn Gd
WEST MEAD
THE VALE
CROSSWAY
MONKS CL
Allot Gdns
LONG DR
MANNINGTREE RD
VICTORIA RD
THE CROFT
Ruislip Gardens
BEDFORD RD
CLYFFORD RD
BRIDGEWATER RD
BRAINTREE RD
TIPTREE RD
ST GREGORY CL
ANGUS DR
Recn Gd
Deane Park
4
CARMICHAEL CL
WEST END RD
RYDAL WAY
Tenn Cts
Deansfield Jun & Inf Sch
PORTAL CL
TRENCHARD AVE
South Ruislip
South Ruislip
PO
Queensmead Sec Sch
Pl Flds
61
193
Tenn Cts
ODYSSEY BSNS PK
THE RUNWAY
Liby
Tenn Cts
Sp Ctr
CROWN RD
Superstore
BOURNE CT
VICTORIA RETAIL PARK
CIVIC WAY
CAVENDISH AVE
CANFIELD DR
ACOL CRES
DUDLEY DR
STATION APP
PRIMROSE GDNS
MANOR GDNS
BOURNE AVE
GREAT CENTRAL AVE
3
LANGHAM CT
NORTHOLT AVE
DEANE AVE
PRIORS GDNS
CEDAR AVE
SOUTH PARK WAY
314
HARDY AVE
Northolt Aerodrome
257
261
FRAZER AVE
Recn Gd
85
EDWARD'S AVE
NAIRN RD
Recn Gd
FIELD END
324
MAHLON AVE
WINGFIELD WAY
Bourne Prim Sch
WALNUT WAY
MASSON AVE
2
WELDON CL
WARSAW CL
GLEBE AVE
386
315
Sp Gd
Priors Farm
Polish War Meml
ROXBOURNE CL
Glebe Farm
WESTON RD
A40
WESTERN AVE
Yeading Brook
Bwg Gn
Pav
Tenn Cts
1
CH
Sp Gd
UB5
A40
London Ctr
Bwg Gn
Pl Fld
UB4
Hillingdon
Ealing
HARVEY RD
WEST END RD
Tenn Cts
Peacock Park
84
A4180
Downe Barns Farm
Ten Acres (Nature Reserve)
10
A
B
11
84
C
D
12
COMPTON CRES
HEARN RISE
SHARVEL LA
CH
CH
Lime Tree Park

63
Rayners Lane
A
B
C
D
41
Yeading Brook
Allot Gdns
YEADING AVE
WAVERLEY RD
OVESDON AVE
PERWELL AVE
CHICHESTER CT
CAPTHORNE AVE
OXLEAY RD
CLITHEROE AVE
A4090
SCOTT CRES
GOLDSMITH CL
Grange Schs
ABERCORN CRES
SOUTHDOWN CRES
87
Tenn Cts
AUSTEN RD
SCOTT CRES
WELBECK RD
Roxbourne Fst & Mid Schs
TORBAY RD
DRAKE RD
LUCAS AVE
Fball Gd
ELIOT DR
Allot Gdns
Newton Farm Schs
Allot Gdns
PRIEST PARK AVE
MARYATT AVE
DRINKWATER RD
SWIFT CL
THE ARCHES
LODGEHILL PARK CL
FRANKLINS MEWS
Newton Farm Ecology Pk
RAYNERS LA
COLES CRES
6
Roxeth
NEWQUAY CRES
WIDDICOMBE AVE
EXETER RD
LYNTON RD
LULWORTH GDNS
KINGS RD
RAVENSWOOD CRES
Newton Park
Tenn Cts
Pav
The Roxbourne
Alexandra Sch
NEWTON CL
LEAMER DR
ABBOTS DR
MONKS CL
THORNLEY DR
ROXETH GREEN AVE
EASTLEIGH AVE
EASTCOTE AVE
MAPLE AVE
STANLEY RD
Harrow
Hillingdon
Recn Gd
PARKFIELD CRES
DUNSTER WAY
LYNWOOD CL
CLOVELLY WAY
LULWORTH CL
MINEHEAD CT
JASMINE GDNS
SANDRINGHAM CRES
HA2
BARNABY CL
THE VIADUCT
ST MARGARET'S AVE
South Harrow Mkt
MALVERN AVE
MERLINS AVE
MINEHEAD RD
TITHE FARM CL
HAMILTON CRES
HODSON CL
JORDAN CL
TITHE FARM AVE
ALEXANDRA AVE
PO
CROSS RD
REVEREND CL
Cemy
BEECHWOOD AVE
BEECHWOOD GDNS
A312
5
WELL CL
RUFUS CL
LONG DR
LEAMINGTON CRES
THISTLEDENE AVE
STUART AVE
VELDENE WAY
STIVEN CRES
BODMIN CL
KINGS ROAD BGLWS
ROWE WLK
Schs
EASTCOTE LA
WINKLEY CT
1 CORNELL HO
2 MEAD FIELD
3 STRADBROOK CL
WINDSOR CRES
WINDSOR CL
ALEXANDRA CL
GROVELANDS CL
FINDON CL
CORBIN'S LA
BARNETTS CT
VALENTINE RD
Liby
WARGRAVE RD
ROYAL CRES
FIELD END RD
PRIMROSE CL
MIRREN CL
SALTER CL
ROSEBERY AVE
BROOKSIDE CL
South Harrow
PARK MEAD
PARK LA
TORRINGTON CT
TORRINGTON DR
LEATH CL
SALE RD
NORTHOLT RD
CARSDALE RD
WYVENHOE RD
86
PALACE RD
Ind Est
TREGENNA AVE
1 TREGENNA CT
2 PARK GATES
3 ARUNDEL CT
Alexandra Park
BRENDON GDNS
ROXETH GR
Schs
JUBILEE DR
PRINCES WAY
BRACKENHILL
IVY CL
LUDLOW CL
CORFE AVE
BALMORAL RD
PADDOCKS CL
WOOD END AVE
4
DIAMOND RD
THE COURT
VICTORIA RD
KENILWORTH AVE
WARWICK AVE
WALTON AVE
EARLSMEAD
CARLYON AVE
STATION PAR
WESTWOOD AVE
RAGLAN TERR
Superstores
HOLYROOD AVE
Earlsmead Fst & Mid Sch
Fball Gd
ARUNDEL DR
STROUD GATE
CADOGAN CL
Northolt Park
HA4
HOLLYDALE CL
NEW CT
DORCHESTER RD
HALSBURY RD W
Recn Gd
64
STONEFIELD CL
Ind Est
STONEFIELD WAY
BRADFIELD RD
SOMERVELL RD
1 SALISBURY CT
2 FOLKESTONE CT
3 PONTEFRACT CT
4 SEDGEFIELD CT
STATION PAR
CLAUSON AVE
T Ct
THE HEIGHTS
WINCANTON CRES
DAVENTRY GR
PETT'S HILL
ELORISTON CT
READING RD
3
MORTON CT
GREENACRE CL
DONCASTER GDNS
MARTIN DR
MALLET DR
Allot Gdns
Harrow
Ealing
DABBS HILL LA
NEWMARKET AVE
BANGOR CL
SHERIDAN TERR
WHITTON AVE W
A4090
GRAHAM CT
RABOURNMEAD DR
BAYLOR RD
SILVERDALE CL
PERCEVAL CT 1
HILL CT 2
CHURCHILL CT 3
WARWICK CT 4
LANARK CT 5
MILDRED AVE
WHEATSHEAF CL
WILSMERE DR
SANDOWN WAY
Sch
THE LINK
DONCASTER DR
EPSOM CL
HORNBEAM CL
HURST CL
KEMPTON AVE
ASCOT CL
Sch
WOOD END LA
GRAINGER CL
85
Hillingdon
Ealing
NEWBURY WAY
EASTCOTE LA
Pl Fld
PLUMPTON CL
FONTWELL CL
RIPON CL
REDCAR CL
WETHERBY CL
BAYSHILL RISE
WILSMERE DR
CARTMEL CT
NEWBURY CL
Northolt High Sch
DABBS HILL LA
HAYDOCK AVE
HAYDOCK GN
SOUTHWELL AVE
THIRSK CL
CHELTENHAM CL
HOLMWOOD CL
Masts
EGGARDON CT
LANCASTER RD
CONEYGROVE PATH 1
VINCENTS PATH 2
PRIORS FIELD 3
RIDGEWAY WLK 4
SHEPHERDS PATH 5
FARLONG PATH 6
Willow Tree Prim Sch
GOODWOOD DR
SUSSEX CRES
Allot Gdns
LEWES CL
UB5
SIVERST CL
BLENHEIM RD
2
Pl Fld
ARNOLD RD
STROUD FIELD
ATTEWOOD RD
WINNINGS WLK
BRUFFS MDW
ABBOTT CL
MILLWAY GDNS
Sch
TENBY GDNS
EASTCOTE LA N
BRIAR CRES
RIBBLESDALE AVE
GONVILLE CRES
GIRTON CL
GLAMIS WAY
NEW PARK CL
LAYMEAD CL
ACRE PATH
HOLLOWFIELD WLK
FORTUNES MEAD
COWINGS MEAD
THE FARMLANDS
WELLINGTON HO
Northolt
MANDEVILLE RD
BADMINTON CL
ORIEL WAY
CASTLE RD
FREEMAN CL
GAUNTLET CL
YEOMAN RD
ISLIP MANOR RD
EASTCOTE LA
MOAT FARM RD
Islip Manor Park
BELVUE CL
CARR RD
LORDSHIP RD
MANOR GATE
PO
PETWORTH CL
STATION PAR
SANDRINGHAM RD
BELVUE RD
BELVUE BSNS CTR
CHERRY GDNS
Allot Gdns
1
ISLIP GDNS
DUKES AVE
MANOR AVE
ALDERNEY GDNS
LYTTON CL
KINGSMEAD DR
COURT FARM RD
SUMMIT RD
Grand Union Canal Paddington Branch
Grand Union Canal Walk
FAIRWAY DR
HAREWOOD CL
HAREWOOD AVE
CHURCH LO
CHURCH RD
EALING RD
NORTHOLT
WESTERN AVE
Northolt Prim Sch
John Chilton Sch
Walford High Sch
KINGSTON CL
VICARAGE CL
CARISBROOKE CT
FORT RD
ROWDELL RD
UB6
84
TAUNTON RD
WESTWAY CT
Belvue Park
12
A
BISHOPS DR
ESKDALE AVE
B
RECTORY GDNS
13
85
C
D
14
MOORLANDS
A312
A40
SARAH CT
Golf Range
LONG DR

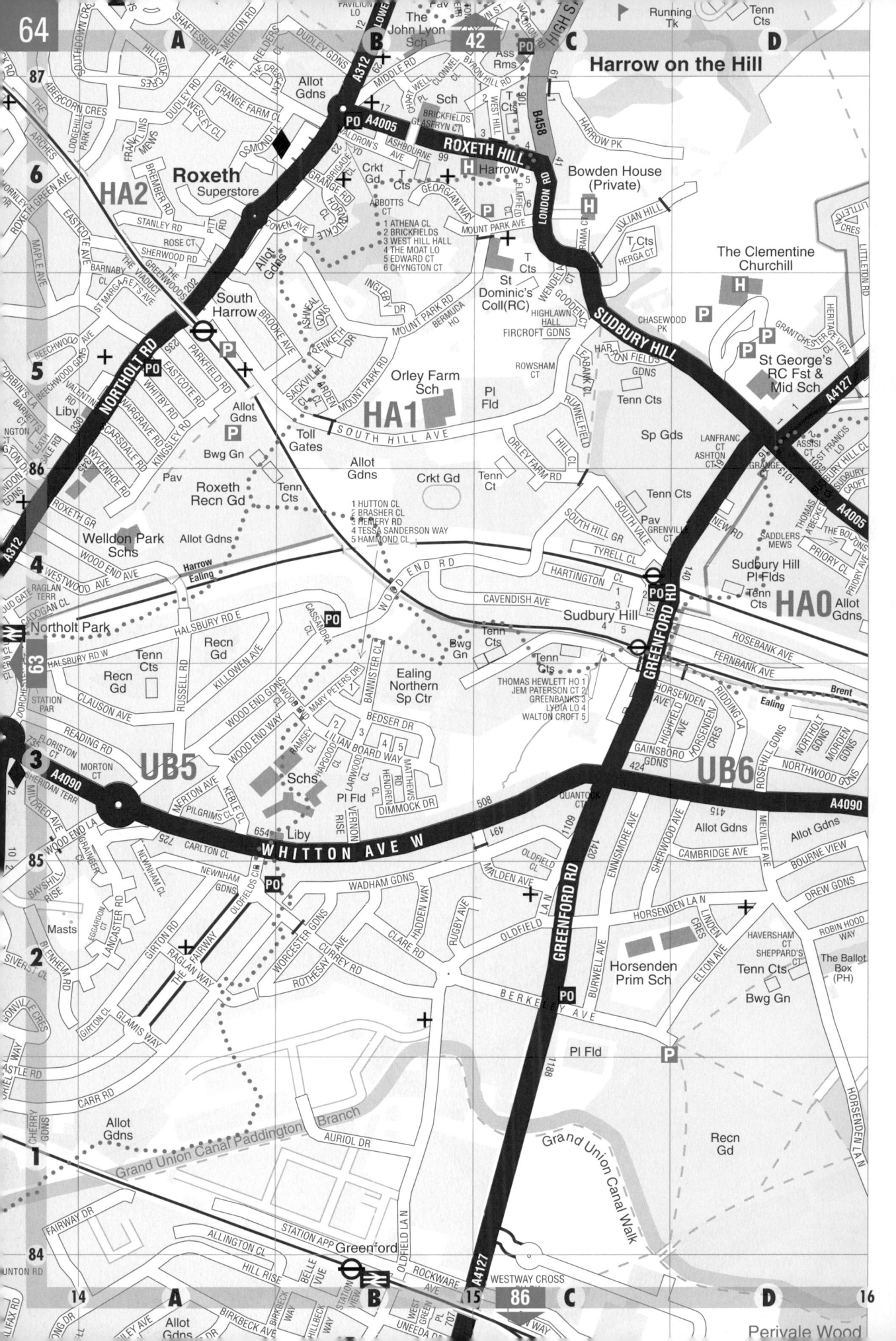
A
B
C
D
42
Harrow on the Hill
The John Lyon Sch
Running Tk
Tenn Cts
87
SHAFTESBURY AVE
MERTON RD
HILLSIDE CRES
SOUTHDOWN CRES
ABERCORN CRES
LODGEHILL PARK CL
DUDLEY RD
WESLEY CL
GRANGE FARM CL
FIELDERS CL
THE CRESCENT
DUDLEY GDNS
Allot Gdns
A312
MIDDLE RD
CHARTWELL PL
CLOMMEL CL
BYRON HILL RD
Ass Rms
Sch
WEST HILL
T Cts
HIGH ST
B458
HARROW PK
A4005
BRICKFIELDS
GLASFRYN CT
WALDRON'S YD
ASHBOURNE AVE
ROXETH HILL
Harrow
LONDON RD
Bowden House (Private)
JULIAN HILL
6
Roxeth
HA2
Superstore
BREMBER RD
FRANKLINS MEWS
OSMOND CL
ROXETH GREEN AVE
EASTCOTE AVE
STANLEY RD
ROSE CT
SHERWOOD RD
PITT RD
COWEN AVE
GRANGE RD
BRIGADE CL
HORNBUCKLE CL
Crkt Gd
T Cts
GEORGIAN WAY
ABBOTTS CT
1 ATHENA CL
2 BRICKFIELDS
3 WEST HILL HALL
4 THE MOAT LO
5 EDWARD CT
6 CHYNGTON CT
MOUNT PARK AVE
ELMFIELD CL
T Cts
St Dominic's Coll(RC)
T Cts
HERGA CT
The Clementine Churchill
LITTLETON CRES
LITTLETON RD
MAPLE AVE
BARNABY CL
THE VIADUCT
ST MARGARET'S AVE
THE GREENWOODS
Allot Gdns
South Harrow
BROOKE AVE
ASHNEAL GDNS
KENKETH DR
INGLEBY DR
MOUNT PARK RD
BERMUDA HO
WENDELA CT
GOODEN CT
HIGHLAWN HALL
FIRCROFT GDNS
SUDBURY HILL
CHASEWOOD PK
GRANTCHESTER CL
HERITAGE VIEW
St George's RC Fst & Mid Sch
A4127
5
BEECHWOOD AVE
BEECHWOOD GDNS
VALENTINE RD
NORTHOLT RD
EASTCOTE RD
WHITBY RD
PARKFIELD RD
SACKVILLE CL
ARDEN CL
MOUNT PARK RD
Orley Farm Sch
HA1
Pl Fld
ROWSHAM CT
LEABANK CL
HARROW FIELDS GDNS
Tenn Cts
RUNNELFIELD
Liby
WARGRAVE RD
CARSDALE RD
KINGSLEY RD
Allot Gdns
Toll Gates
SOUTH HILL AVE
HILL CL
ORLEY FARM RD
Sp Gds
LANFRANC CT
ASHTON CT
GRANGE CT
ASSISI CT
ST FRANCIS LO
SUDBURY HILL CL
SUDBURY CROFT
86
WYVENHOE RD
Pav
Bwg Gn
Roxeth Recn Gd
Tenn Cts
Allot Gdns
Crkt Gd
Tenn Ct
Tenn Cts
SOUTH HILL GR
SOUTH VALE
Pav
GRENVILLE CT
NEW RD
THOMAS A'BECKET CL
SADDLERS MEWS
THE BOLTONS
A4005
ROXETH GR
Welldon Park Schs
Allot Gdns
1 HUTTON CL
2 BRASHER CL
3 HEMERY RD
4 TESSA SANDERSON WAY
5 HAMMOND CL
TYRELL CL
PRIORY CL
PRIORY AVE
A312
4
WOOD END AVE
WESTWOOD AVE
Harrow
Ealing
WOOD END RD
HARTINGTON CL
Sudbury Hill Pl Flds
RAGLAN TERR
CADOGAN CL
CAVENDISH AVE
GREENFORD RD
Tenn Cts
HA0
Allot Gdns
Northolt Park
HALSBURY RD E
CASSANDRA CL
Sudbury Hill
ROSEBANK AVE
63
HALSBURY RD W
Tenn Cts
Recn Gd
KILLOWEN AVE
Tenn Cts
Bwg Gn
Tenn Cts
FERNBANK AVE
Recn Gd
RUSSELL RD
BANNISTER CL
Ealing Northern Sp Ctr
THOMAS HEWLETT HO 1
JEM PATERSON CT 2
GREENBANKS 3
LYDIA LO 4
WALTON CROFT 5
HORSENDEN AVE
RIDDING LA
Brent
Ealing
STATION PAR
CLAUSON AVE
WOOD END GDNS
MARY PETERS DR
BEDSER DR
HIGHFIELD AVE
HORSENDEN CRES
READING RD
FLORISTON CT
WOOD END WAY
RAMSEY CL
LILIAN BOARD WAY
MATTHEWS CL
GAINSBORO GDNS
ROSEHILL GDNS
NORTHOLT GDNS
MORDEN GDNS
3
MORTON CT
UB5
HAPGOOD CL
LARWOOD CL
HENDREN CL
UB6
NORTHWOOD GDNS
A4090
SHERIDAN TERR
MERTON AVE
KEBLE CL
Schs
Pl Fld
DIMMOCK DR
QUANTOCK CT
A4090
MILDRED AVE
PILGRIMS CL
VERNON RISE
Allot Gdns
Allot Gdns
WOOD END LA
GRAINGER CL
NEWNHAM CL
CARLTON CL
Liby
WHITTON AVE W
CAMBRIDGE AVE
MELVILLE AVE
BOURNE VIEW
85
BAYSHILL RISE
NEWNHAM GDNS
OLDFIELDS CIR
OLDFIELD CL
MALDEN AVE
ENNISMORE AVE
SHERWOOD AVE
WADHAM GDNS
HADDEN WAY
DREW GDNS
Masts
EGGARDON CT
LANCASTER RD
GIRTON RD
THE FAIRWAY
WORCESTER GDNS
CURREY RD
CLARE RD
RUGBY AVE
OLDFIELD LA N
GREENFORD RD
HORSENDEN LA N
LINDEN CRES
HAVERSHAM CT
ROBIN HOOD WAY
2
BLENHEIM RD
RAGLAN WAY
ROTHESAY AVE
OLDFIELD LA
BURWELL AVE
Horsenden Prim Sch
ELTON AVE
SHEPPARD'S CT
Tenn Cts
The Ballot Box (PH)
Bwg Gn
GONVILLE CRES
GIRTON CL
GLAMIS WAY
BERKELEY AVE
Pl Fld
CASTLE RD
CARR RD
HORSENDEN LA N
Recn Gd
CHERRY GDNS
Allot Gdns
Grand Union Canal Paddington Branch
AURIOL DR
Grand Union Canal Walk
1
FAIRWAY DR
STATION APP
Greenford
ALLINGTON CL
84
HILL RISE
BELLE VUE
OLDFIELD LA N
ROCKWARE AVE
A4127
WESTWAY CROSS
14
15
86
16
BIRKBECK AVE
BIRKBECK WAY
HILLBECK WAY
STATION VIEW
WEST GREEN PL
UNEEDA DR
Allot Gdns
Perivale Wood

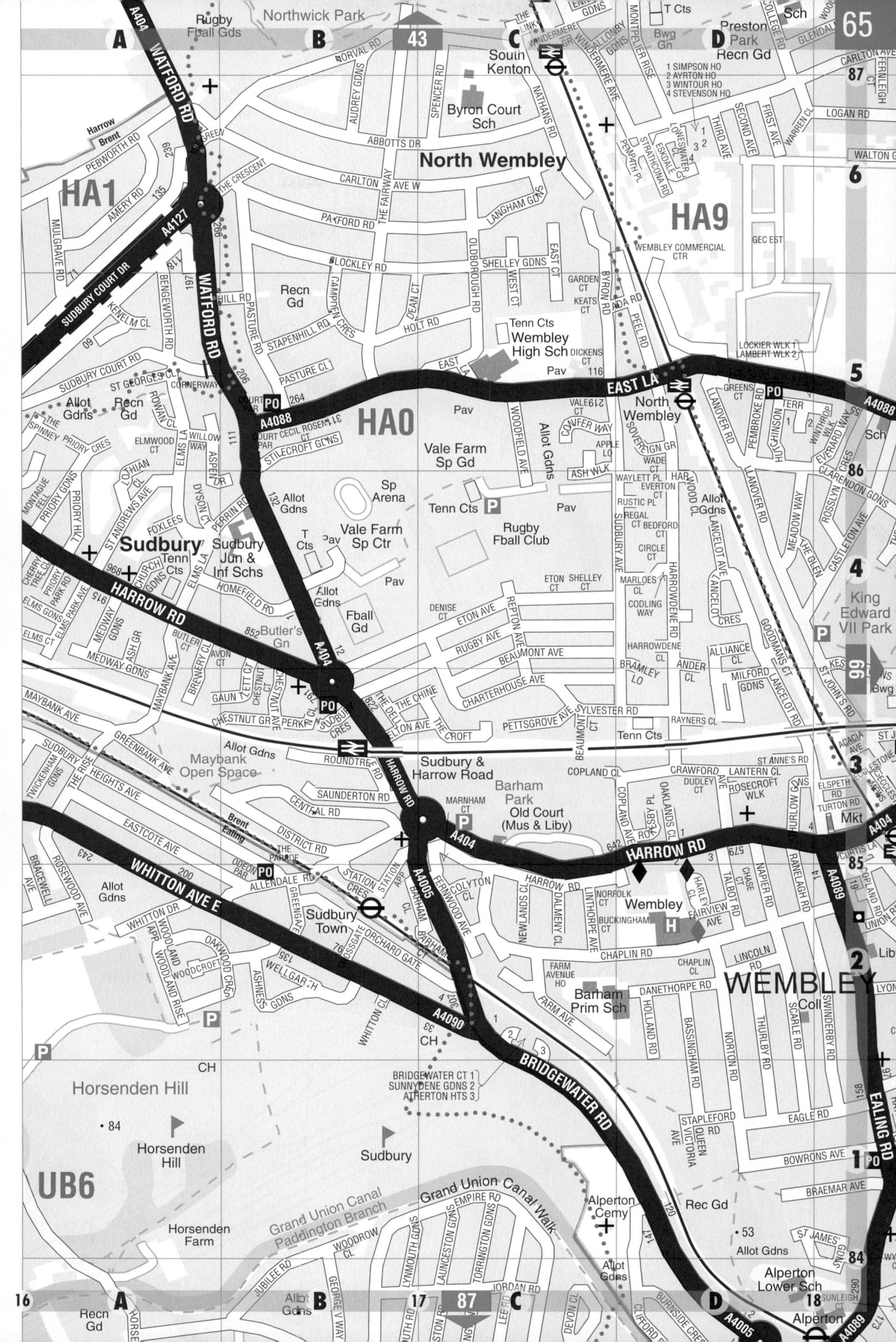

Northwick Park
43
Rugby Fball Gds
South Kenton
Preston Park Recn Gd
1 SIMPSON HO
2 AYRTON HO
3 WINTOUR HO
4 STEVENSON HO
87
CARLTON AVE
LOGAN RD
WALTON GDNS
Byron Court Sch
North Wembley
HA1
HA9
HA0
UB6
WATFORD RD
A404
A4127
SUDBURY COURT DR
NORVAL RD
AUDREY GDNS
SPENCER RD
ABBOTTS DR
CARLTON AVE W
THE CRESCENT
PEBWORTH RD
AMERY RD
MULGRAVE RD
THE FAIRWAY
PAXFORD RD
LANGHAM GDNS
BLOCKLEY RD
SHELLEY GDNS
OLDBOROUGH RD
EAST CT
WEST CT
WINDERMERE AVE
NATHANS RD
MONTPELIER RISE
STRATHCONA RD
ESKDALE CL
LOWESWATER CL
THIRD AVE
SECOND AVE
FIRST AVE
WARREN CL
WEMBLEY COMMERCIAL CTR
GEC EST
GARDEN CT
KEATS CT
BYRON RD
ADA RD
PEEL RD
Recn Gd
HILL RD
PASTURE RD
STAPENHILL RD
CAMPDEN CRES
DEAN CT
HOLT RD
Tenn Cts
Wembley High Sch
DICKENS CT
LOCKIER WLK 1
LAMBERT WLK 2
BENGEWORTH RD
KENELM CL
SUDBURY COURT RD
ST GEORGES CL
CORNERWAY
PASTURE CL
EAST LA
A4088
Pav
North Wembley
PO
Allot Gdns
Recn Gd
COURT PAR
CECIL ROSEN CT
STILECROFT GDNS
Vale Farm Sp Gd
WOODFIELD AVE
CONIFER WAY
VALE CT
APPLE LO
ASH WLK
SOVEREIGN GR
WADE CT
LLANOVER RD
GREENS CT
PEMBROKE RD
HUTCHINSON TERR
WINTHROP WLK
EVERARD WAY
Sch
THE SPINNEY
PRIORY CRES
ELMWOOD CT
ROWAN CL
WILLOW WAY
ELMS LA
ASPEN DR
LOTHIAN CL
DYSON CT
ST ANDREWS AVE
MONTAGUE FELL
PRIORY GDNS
PRIORY HILL
FOXLEES
PERRIN RD
Sp Arena
Allot Gdns
Tenn Cts
Pav
WAYLETT PL
EVERTON CT
HARWOOD CL
RUSTIC PL
REGAL CT
BEDFORD CT
CIRCLE CT
Allot Gdns
MEADOW WAY
ROSSLYN CRES
CLARENDON GDNS
86
Sudbury
Tenn Cts
Sudbury Jun & Inf Schs
T Cts
Vale Farm Sp Ctr
Rugby Fball Club
CASTLETON AVE
THE GLEN
HARROW RD
CHURCH GDNS
CHERRY TREE CL
PRIORY PARK RD
ELMS PARK AVE
ELMS GDNS
HOMEFIELD RD
Allot Gdns
Pav
Fball Gd
ETON CT
SHELLEY CT
MARLOES CL
CODLING WAY
HARROWDENE RD
LANCELOT AVE
LANCELOT CRES
King Edward VII Park
4
MEDWAY GDNS
ASH GR
Butler's Gn
BUTLER CT
AVON CT
DENISE CT
ETON AVE
RUGBY AVE
REPTON AVE
BEAUMONT AVE
HARROWDENE CL
ANDER CL
ALLIANCE CL
GOODMANS CT
MILFORD GDNS
ST JOHN'S RD
ELMS CT
MEDWAY GDNS
MAYBANK AVE
BREWERY CL
GAUNTLETT CT
CHESTNUT CT
CHARTERHOUSE AVE
BRAMLEY LO
THE CHINE
THE DELL
SYLVESTER RD
RAYNERS CL
LANCELOT RD
69
Bwg
MAYBANK AVE
CHESTNUT GR
PERKIN CL
SUDBURY CRES
FELTON AVE
THE CROFT
PETTSGROVE AVE
BEAUMONT CT
Tenn Cts
ACACIA AVE
ECCLESTONE CT
GREENBANK AVE
Allot Gdns
Maybank Open Space
ROUNDTREE RD
Sudbury & Harrow Road
COPLAND CL
CRAWFORD AVE
LANTERN CL
ST ANNE'S RD
3
SUDBURY HEIGHTS AVE
TWICKENHAM GDNS
THE RISE
SAUNDERTON RD
CENTRAL RD
Barham Park
MARNHAM CT
Old Court (Mus & Liby)
DUDLEY CT
ROSECROFT WLK
ELSPETH RD
TURTON RD
Mkt
THURLOW GDNS
DISTRICT RD
Brent
Ealing
EASTCOTE AVE
COPLAND AVE
TESBY PL
OAKLANDS CL
A4005
A4089
THE PARADE
ODEON PAR
Wembley
HARLEY CL
FAIRVIEW AVE
85
CURTIS LA
COPLAND RD
UNION RD
BRACEWELL AVE
ROSEWOOD AVE
Allot Gdns
WHITTON AVE E
ALLENDALE RD
STATION CRES
STATION APP
BARHAM CL
FERNWOOD AVE
COLYTON CL
NEWLANDS CL
DALMENY CL
LINTHORPE AVE
NORFOLK CT
BUCKINGHAM CT
TALBOT RD
CHASE CT
NAPIER RD
RANELAGH RD
WHITTON DR
WOODLAND APP
WOODLAND RISE
WOODCROFT
OAKWOOD CRES
GREENGATE
Sudbury Town
ORCHARD GATE
CHAPLIN RD
CHAPLIN CL
LINCOLN RD
Lib
2
ASHNESS GDNS
WELLGARTH
OSSGATE
A4090
WHITTON CL
FARM AVENUE HO
Barham Prim Sch
FARM AVE
DANETHORPE RD
HOLLAND RD
BASSINGHAM RD
NORTON RD
THURLBY RD
SCARLE RD
SWINDERBY RD
WEMBLEY
Coll
LYONS
CH
BRIDGEWATER RD
BRIDGEWATER CT 1
SUNNYDENE GDNS 2
ATHERTON HTS 3
CH
Horsenden Hill
84
Horsenden Hill
Sudbury
STAPLEFORD RD
QUEEN VICTORIA AVE
EAGLE RD
EALING RD
BOWRONS AVE
1
BRAEMAR AVE
Grand Union Canal Paddington Branch
Grand Union Canal
Grand Union Canal Walk
EMPIRE RD
Alperton Cemy
Rec Gd
Horsenden Farm
WOODROW CL
LYNMOUTH GDNS
LAUNCESTON GDNS
TORRINGTON GDNS
53
Allot Gdns
ST JAMES' GDNS
84
Alperton Lower Sch
Allot Gdns
JUBILEE RD
GEORGE V WAY
JORDAN RD
LEE RD
DEVON CL
CLIFFORD RD
BURNSIDE CRES
SUNLEIGH CT
16
A
Recn Gd
Allot Gdns
B
17
87
C
D
18
Alperton

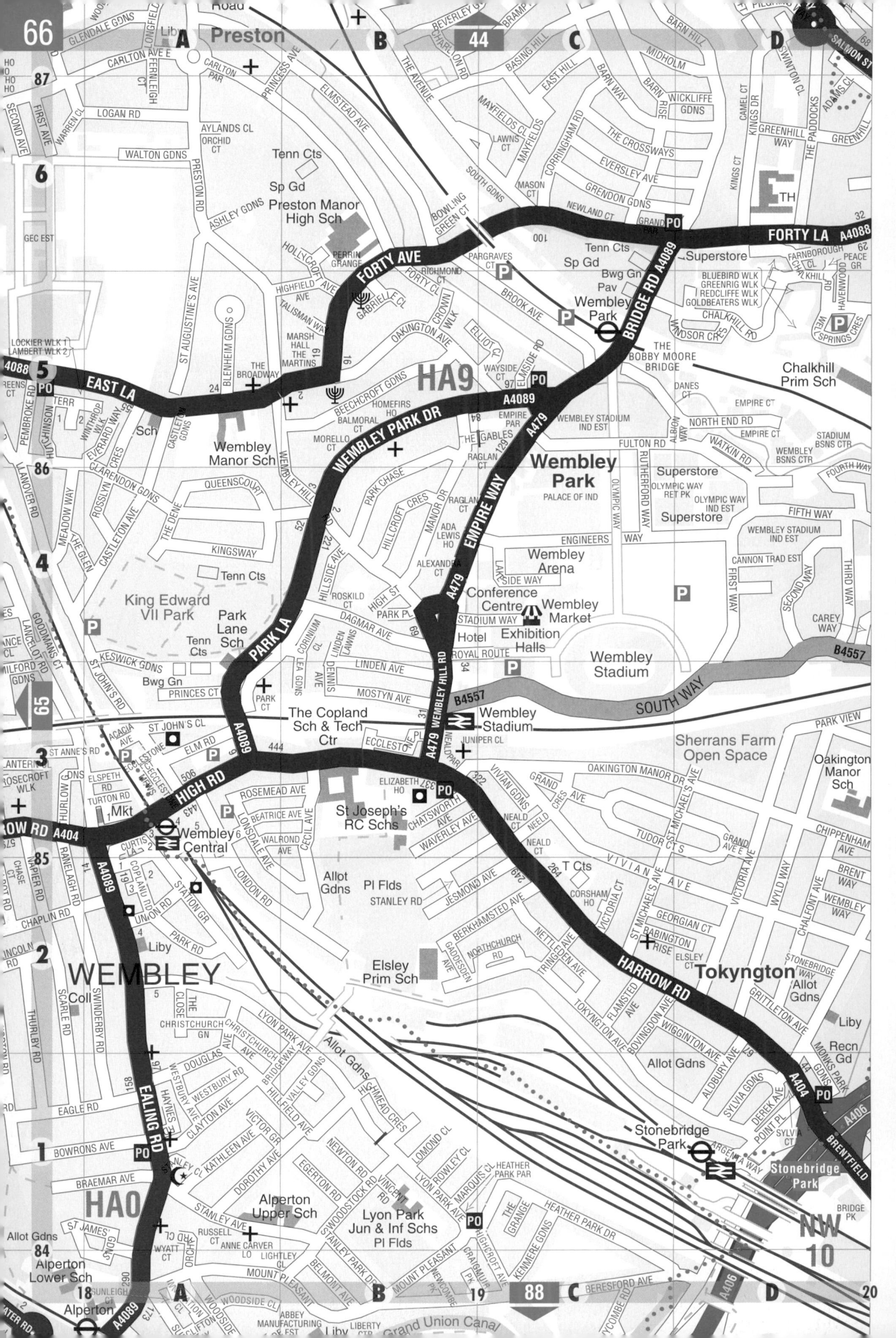
66
Preston
A
B
44
C
D
87
GLENDALE GDNS
LONGFIELD
CARLTON AVE E
FERNLEIGH CT
CARLTON PAR
PRINCESS AVE
BEVERLEY GDNS
CHARLTON RD
BRAMPTON
BARN HILL
MIDHOLM
SALMON ST
SECOND AVE
FIRST AVE
WARREN CL
LOGAN RD
AYLANDS CL
ORCHID CT
ELMSTEAD AVE
THE AVENUE
BASING HILL
EAST HILL
BARN WAY
BARN RISE
WICKLIFFE GDNS
CAMEL CT
KINGS DR
SWINTON CL
ADAMS CL
THE PADDOCKS
GREENHILL WAY
GREENHILL
WALTON GDNS
Tenn Cts
MAYFIELDS CL
LAWNS CT
MAYFIELDS
CORRINGHAM RD
THE CROSSWAYS
EVERSLEY AVE
KINGS CT
6
Sp Gd
Preston Manor High Sch
PRESTON RD
ASHLEY GDNS
SOUTH GDNS
MASON CT
GRENDON GDNS
NEWLAND CT
GRAND PAR
PO
FORTY LA
A4088
32
GEC EST
BOWLING GREEN CT
100
HOLLYCROFT AVE
PERRIN GRANGE
FORTY AVE
PARGRAVES CT
Tenn Cts
Sp Gd
Superstore
FARNBOROUGH CL
PEACE GR
RICHMOND CT
FORTY CL
Bwg Gn
Pav
BRIDGE RD A4089
BLUEBIRD WLK
GREENRIG WLK
REDCLIFFE WLK
GOLDBEATERS WLK
CHALKHILL RD
HAVENWOOD
HIGHFIELD AVE
GABRIELLE CL
BROOK AVE
Wembley Park
ST AUGUSTINE'S AVE
BLENHEIM GDNS
TALISMAN WAY
CROWN WLK
OAKINGTON AVE
ELLIOT CL
ELMSIDE RD
WINDSOR CRES
WELLSPRINGS CRES
LOCKIER WLK 1
LAMBERT WLK 2
MARSH HALL
THE MARTINS
THE BROADWAY
THE BOBBY MOORE BRIDGE
Chalkhill Prim Sch
A4088
5
PO
EAST LA
24
BEECHCROFT GDNS
HA9
WAYSIDE CT
97
PO
DANES CT
EMPIRE CT
PEMBROKE RD
HUTCHINSON TERR
WINTHROP WLK
EVERARD WAY
Sch
CASTLETON GDNS
HOMEFIRS HO
BALMORAL CT
A4089
EMPIRE PAR
WEMBLEY STADIUM IND EST
ALBION WAY
NORTH END RD
EMPIRE CT
STADIUM BSNS CTR
WEMBLEY PARK DR
MORELLO CT
THE GABLES
A479
FULTON RD
WATKIN RD
WEMBLEY BSNS CTR
Wembley Manor Sch
RAGLAN CT
Wembley Park
Superstore
FOURTH WAY
86
LLANOVER RD
CLARENDON GDNS
QUEENSCOURT
WEMBLEY HILL RD
PARK CHASE
RAGLAN CT
PALACE OF IND
OLYMPIC WAY RET PK
OLYMPIC WAY IND EST
RUTHERFORD WAY
OLYMPIC WAY
ROSSLYN CRES
MEADOW WAY
THE GLEN
CASTLETON AVE
THE DENE
HILLCROFT CRES
MANOR DR
EMPIRE WAY
FIFTH WAY
Superstore
ADA LEWIS HO
WEMBLEY STADIUM IND EST
KINGSWAY
HILLSIDE AVE
ENGINEERS WAY
Wembley Arena
CANNON TRAD EST
4
ALEXANDRA CT
LAKESIDE WAY
FIRST WAY
SECOND WAY
THIRD WAY
Tenn Cts
Conference Centre
Wembley Market
King Edward VII Park
Park Lane Sch
ROSKILD CT
HIGH ST
PARK PL
STADIUM WAY
CAREY WAY
GOODMANS CT
LANCELOT RD
Tenn Cts
PARK LA
DAGMAR AVE
Hotel
Exhibition Halls
CORINIUM CL
LINDEN LAWNS
ROYAL ROUTE
Wembley Stadium
B4557
KESWICK GDNS
LINDEN AVE
WEMBLEY HILL RD
MILFORD GDNS
ST JOHN'S RD
Bwg Gn
LEA GDNS
DENNIS AVE
MOSTYN AVE
PRINCES CT
PARK CT
B4557
SOUTH WAY
65
ST JOHN'S CL
The Copland Sch & Tech Ctr
Wembley Stadium
PARK VIEW
ACACIA AVE
ELM RD
JUNIPER CL
Sherrans Farm Open Space
ST ANNE'S RD
ECCLESTONE PL
A4089
444
ECCLESTON PL
A479
NEALDS PAR
Oakington Manor Sch
3
LANTERN CL
ROSECROFT WLK
ELSPETH RD
TURTON RD
506
HIGH RD
ROSEMEAD AVE
ELIZABETH HO
PO
322
VIVIAN GDNS
GRAND AVE
OAKINGTON MANOR DR
ST MICHAEL'S AVE
THURLOW GDNS
Mkt
443
BEATRICE AVE
St Joseph's RC Schs
CHATSWORTH AVE
NEALD CT
CHIPPENHAM AVE
ROW RD
A404
Wembley Central
LONSDALE AVE
WALROND AVE
CECIL AVE
WAVERLEY AVE
NEALD CT
TUDOR CTS
GRAND AVE E
85
RANELAGH RD
CURTIS LA
CHASE CT
NAPIER RD
COPLAND RD
A4089
LONDON RD
Allot Gdns
Pl Flds
STANLEY RD
JESMOND AVE
264
T Cts
VIVIAN AVE
BRENT WAY
STATION GR
CORSHAM HO
VICTORIA CT
VICTORIA AVE
WYLD WAY
CHALFONT AVE
WEMBLEY WAY
CHAPLIN RD
UNION RD
PARK RD
BERKHAMSTED AVE
GEORGIAN CT
Liby
NORTHCHURCH RD
NETTLEDEN AVE
BABINGTON RISE
STONEBRIDGE WAY
2
LINCOLN RD
GADDESDEN AVE
TRING AVE
ELSLEY CT
WEMBLEY
Elsley Prim Sch
HARROW RD
Tokyngton
Allot Gdns
Coll
SCARLE RD
SWINDERBY RD
THE CLOSE
GRITTLETON AVE
FLAMSTED AVE
TOKYNGTON AVE
BOVINGDON AVE
Liby
CHRISTCHURCH GN
CHRISTCHURCH AVE
LYON PARK AVE
Allot Gdns
WIGGINTON AVE
Recn Gd
THURLBY RD
DOUGLAS AVE
BRIDGEWAY
VALLEY GDNS
Allot Gdns
ALDBURY AVE
MONKS PARK
WESTBURY AVE
WESTBURY RD
HILLFIELD AVE
A404
PO
EAGLE RD
158
EALING RD
HAYNES CL
CLAYTON AVE
VICTOR GR
HIGHMEAD CRES
SYLVIA GDNS
DEREK AVE
A406
Stonebridge Park
POINT PL
SYLVIA CT
1
BOWRONS AVE
PO
KATHLEEN AVE
DOROTHY AVE
NEWTON RD
LOMOND CL
ROWLEY CL
HEATHER PARK PAR
ARGENTA WAY
BRENTFIELD
Stonebridge Park
BRAEMAR AVE
STANLEY CL
EGERTON RD
VINCENT RD
MARQUIS CL
HA0
STANLEY AVE
Alperton Upper Sch
WOODSTOCK RD
LYON PARK AVE
PO
THE GRANGE
HEATHER PARK DR
BRIDGE PK
NW 10
Allot Gdns
ST JAMES' GDNS
ORCHARD CL
RUSSELL CT
ANNE CARVER LO
Lyon Park Jun & Inf Schs
Pl Flds
KENMERE GDNS
84
WYATT CT
LIGHTLEY CL
HIGHCROFT AVE
Alperton Lower Sch
MOUNT PLEASANT
BELMONT AVE
STANLEY PARK DR
MOUNT PLEASANT
NEWCOMBE PK
CRAIGMUIR PK
18
SUNLEIGH CT
290
A
B
19
88
C
BERESFORD AVE
D
20
Alperton
A4089
WOODSIDE CL
ABBEY MANUFACTURING EST
Liby
LIBERTY CTR
Grand Union Canal
A406

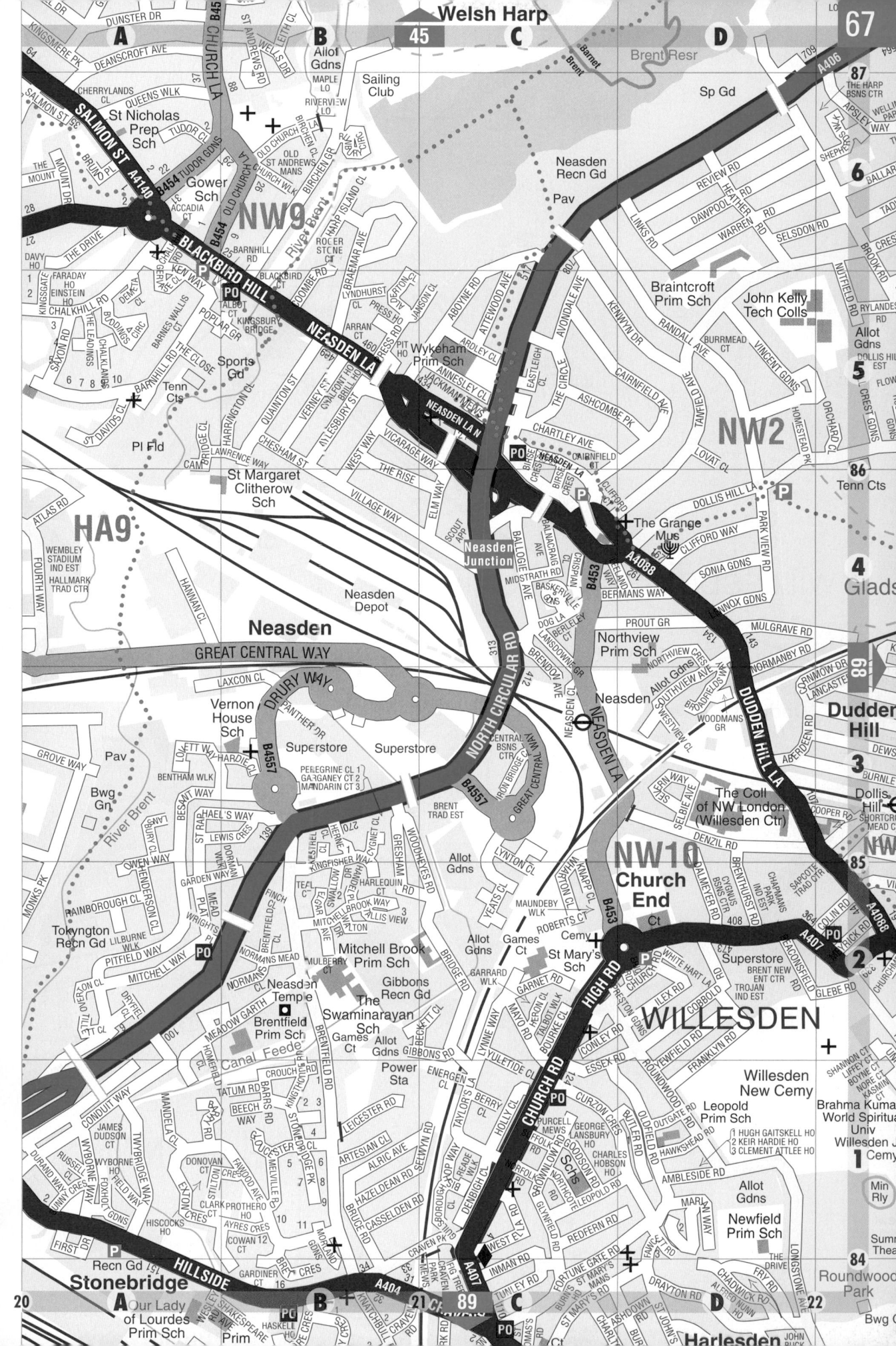
Welsh Harp
45
A
B
C
D
Brent Resr
Sailing Club
Allot Gdns
Sp Gd
St Nicholas Prep Sch
Gower Sch
NW9
SALMON ST
A4140
BLACKBIRD HILL
NEASDEN LA
CHURCH LA
B454
Neasden Recn Gd
Pav
A406
Braintcroft Prim Sch
John Kelly Tech Colls
Wykeham Prim Sch
Sports Gd
Tenn Cts
Pl Fld
St Margaret Clitherow Sch
NW2
HA9
Neasden Junction
The Grange Mus
A4088
Wembley Stadium Ind Est
Hallmark Trad Ctr
Neasden Depot
Neasden
GREAT CENTRAL WAY
NORTH CIRCULAR RD
DUDDEN HILL LA
Northview Prim Sch
Vernon House Sch
Superstore
Superstore
B4557
B453
Dudden Hill
Dollis Hill
The Coll of NW London (Willesden Ctr)
NW10
Church End
Brent Trad Est
Allot Gdns
Tokyngton Recn Gd
Mitchell Brook Prim Sch
Gibbons Recn Gd
Neasden Temple
The Swaminarayan Sch
Brentfield Prim Sch
Games Ct
Allot Gdns
Cemy
St Mary's Sch
HIGH RD
CHURCH RD
WILLESDEN
Superstore
A407
Power Sta
Canal Feeder
Willesden New Cemy
Leopold Prim Sch
Brahma Kumaris World Spiritual Univ
Allot Gdns
Newfield Prim Sch
Recn Gd
Stonebridge
HILLSIDE
A404
89
Our Lady of Lourdes Prim Sch
Harlesden
Roundwood Park
20
21
22
84
85
86
87
68
1
2
3
4
5
6

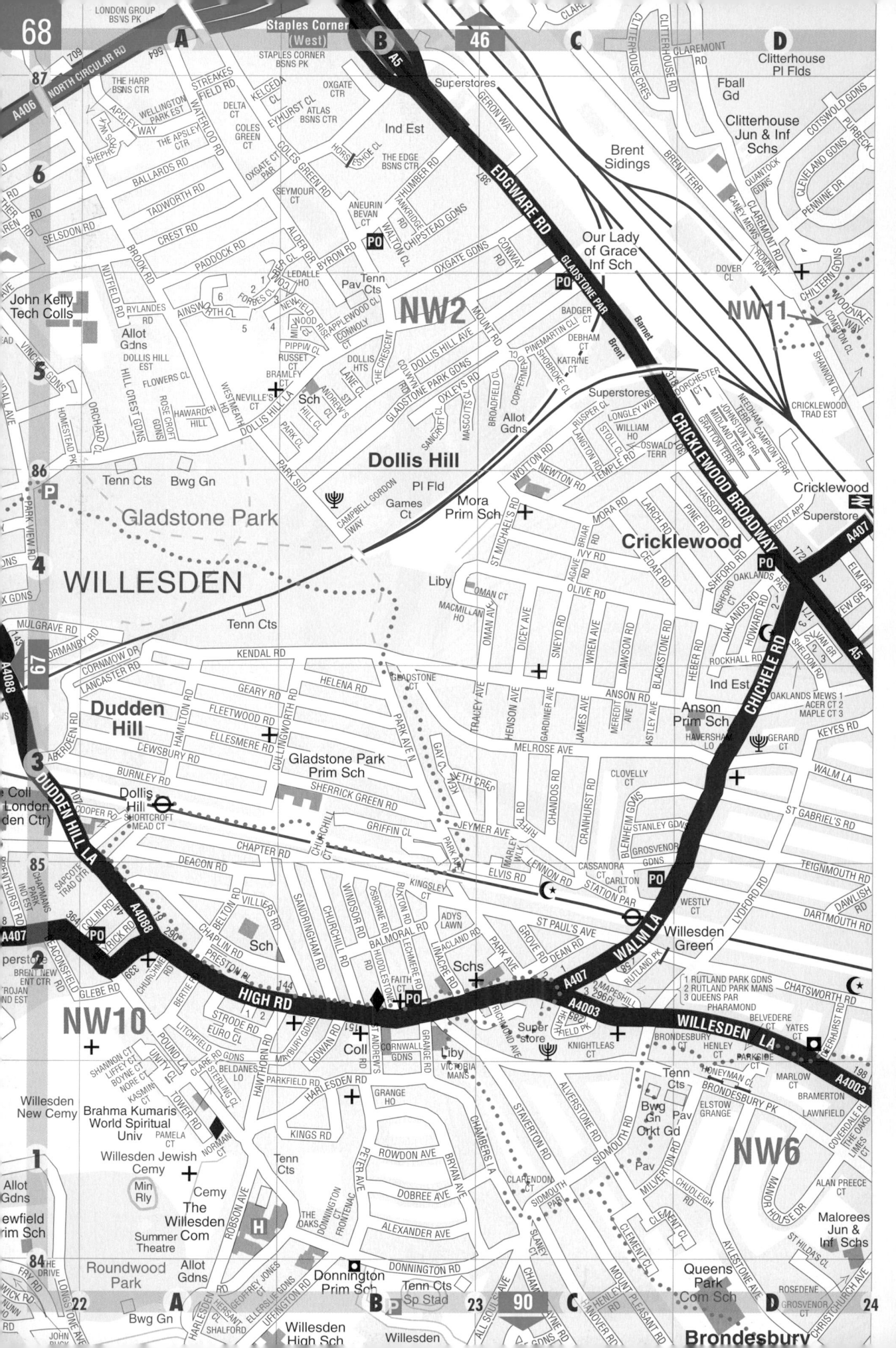
68
A
B
46
C
D
Staples Corner (West)
LONDON GROUP BSNS PK
STAPLES CORNER BSNS PK
NORTH CIRCULAR RD
A406
A5
EDGWARE RD
Superstores
GERON WAY
CLITTERHOUSE CRES
CLITTERHOUSE RD
CLAREMONT RD
Clitterhouse Pl Flds
Fball Gd
Clitterhouse Jun & Inf Schs
COTSWOLD GDNS
PURBECK DR
CLEVELAND GDNS
PENNINE DR
QUANTOCK GDNS
CANEY MEWS
CLAREMONT RD
ROMNEY ROW
DOVER CL
CHILTERN GDNS
WOODVALE WAY
COMPTON CL
SHANNON CL
NW11
CRICKLEWOOD TRAD EST
Brent Sidings
BRENT TERR
Our Lady of Grace Inf Sch
THE HARP BSNS CTR
STREAKES FIELD RD
WAUTERLOO RD
WELLINGTON PARK EST
APSLEY WAY
THE APSLEY CTR
DELTA CT
COLES GREEN CT
OXGATE CT PAR
KELCEDA CL
EYHURST CL
ATLAS BSNS CTR
OXGATE CTR
Ind Est
HORSESHOE CL
THE EDGE BSNS CTR
HUMBER RD
COLES GREEN RD
BALLARDS RD
TADWORTH RD
CREST RD
PADDOCK RD
SELSDON RD
SEYMOUR CT
ANEURIN BEVAN CT
TANKRIDGE RD
CHIPSTEAD GDNS
WALTON CL
PO
BYRON RD
ALDER GR
LEDALLE HO
OXGATE GDNS
CONWAY RD
GLADSTONE PAR
Pav
Tenn Cts
NW2
MOUNT RD
BADGER CT
DEBHAM CT
KATRINE CT
PINEMARTIN CL
SHOBROKE CL
COPPERMEAD CL
Barnet
Brent
John Kelly Tech Colls
NUTFIELD RD
BROOK RD
RYLANDES RD
AINSWORTH CL
FORBES CL
APPLEWOOD CL
CONNOLY CT
NEWFIELD RISE
MIDWOOD CL
PIPPIN CL
RUSSET CT
BRAMLFY CT
DOLLIS HTS
THE CRESCENT
COLWYN RD
DOLLIS HILL AVE
GLADSTONE PARK GDNS
OXLEYS RD
BROADFIELD CL
Allot Gdns
DOLLIS HILL EST
HILL CREST GDNS
FLOWERS CL
ROSE CROFT GDNS
HAWARDEN HILL
WESTMEATH HO
NEVILLE'S CT
DOLLIS HILL LA
Sch
ST ANDREW'S CL
SANCROFT CL
MASCOTTS CL
PARK CL
HILL CL
PARK SIDE
HOMESTEAD PK
ORCHARD CL
VINCENT GDNS
Superstores
RUSPER CL
LONGLEY WAY
WILLIAM HO
STOLL CL
LANGTON RD
OSWALD TERR
TEMPLE RD
DORCHESTER CT
JOHNSTON TERR
MIDLAND TERR
GRATTON TERR
NEEDHAM TERR
CAMPION TERR
CRICKLEWOOD BROADWAY
Dollis Hill
Pl Fld
Games Ct
CAMPBELL GORDON WAY
Tenn Cts
Bwg Gn
Gladstone Park
Mora Prim Sch
WOTTON RD
NEWTON RD
ST MICHAEL'S RD
MORA RD
LARCH RD
PINE RD
HASSOP RD
Cricklewood
Superstore
DEPOT APP
A407
WILLESDEN
Cricklewood
BRIAR RD
AGAVE RD
IVY RD
CEDAR RD
ASHFORD RD
OAKLANDS PAS
OAKLANDS RD
HOWARD RD
ELM GR
YEW GR
Liby
OMAN CT
MACMILLAN HO
OMAN AVE
DICEY AVE
SNEYD RD
OLIVE RD
WREN AVE
DAWSON RD
BLACKSTONE RD
HEBER RD
ROCKHALL RD
SHELDON RD
IVAN GR
A5
Tenn Cts
MULGRAVE RD
ORMANBY RD
CORNMOW DR
LANCASTER RD
KENDAL RD
HELENA RD
GEARY RD
GLADSTONE CT
A4088
67
Dudden Hill
HAMILTON RD
FLEETWOOD RD
ELLESMERE RD
CULLINGWORTH RD
PARK AVE N
TRACEY AVE
HENSON AVE
GARDINER AVE
JAMES AVE
MEREDITH AVE
ASTLEY AVE
ANSON RD
Ind Est
Anson Prim Sch
CHICHELE RD
OAKLANDS MEWS 1
ACER CT 2
MAPLE CT 3
KEYES RD
HAVERSHAM LO
GERARD CT
ABERDEEN RD
DEWSBURY RD
BURNLEY RD
Gladstone Park Prim Sch
GAY CL
NETH CRES
MELROSE AVE
CLOVELLY CT
WALM LA
Dollis Hill
SHERRICK GREEN RD
COOPER RD
SHORTCROFT MEAD CT
GRIFFIN CL
CHANDOS RD
CRANHURST RD
BLENHEIM GDNS
STANLEY GDNS
ST GABRIEL'S RD
DUDDEN HILL LA
CHAPTER RD
CHURCHILL CT
JEYMER AVE
PARK AVE
RIFFEL RD
MARLEY WLK
GROSVENOR GDNS
TEIGNMOUTH RD
DEACON RD
ELVIS RD
LENNON RD
CASSANORA CT
CARLTON CT
STATION PAR
PO
DAWLISH RD
SAPCOTE TRAD CTR
CHAPMANS PARK IND EST
BELTON RD
VILLIERS RD
SANDRINGHAM RD
WINDSOR RD
OSBORNE RD
BUXTON RD
KINGSLEY CT
ADYS LAWN
WESTLY CT
LYDFORD RD
DARTMOUTH RD
A407
COLIN RD
CHAPLIN RD
Sch
PRESTON PL
BALMORAL RD
ACLAND RD
ST PAUL'S AVE
GROVE RD
DEAN RD
PARK AVE
Willesden Green
RUTLAND PK
PO
BEACONSFIELD RD
CHURCHMEAD RD
BERTIE RD
HIGH RD
HUDDLESTONE RD
LEGHMERE RD
LINACRE RD
Schs
A407
A4003
MAPESHILL PL
1 RUTLAND PARK GDNS
2 RUTLAND PARK MANS
3 QUEENS PAR
PHARAMOND
CHATSWORTH RD
GLEBE RD
FAITH CT
NW10
STRODE RD
EURO CL
LITCHFIELD GDNS
POUND LA
UNITY CL
MAYBURY GDNS
GOWAN RD
Coll
ST ANDREW'S RD
CORNWALL GDNS
GRANGE RD
Liby
Super store
RICHMOND AVE
HEATHFIELD PK
KNIGHTLEAS CT
WILLESDEN LA
BRONDESBURY CT
HENLEY CT
PARKSIDE CT
BELVEDERE CT
YATES CT
DEERHURST RD
SHANNON CT
LIFFEY CT
BOYNE CT
NORE CT
KASMIN CT
CLARE RD
BELDANES LO
STERLING CL
TOWER RD
HAWTHORN RD
PARKFIELD RD
HARLESDEN RD
VICTORIA MANS
GRANGE HO
Tenn Cts
HONEYMAN CL
MARLOW CT
BRONDESBURY PK
BRAMERTON
A4003
Willesden New Cemy
Brahma Kumaris World Spiritual Univ
PAMELA CT
NORMAN CT
KINGS RD
ROWDON AVE
BRYAN AVE
CHAMBERS LA
STAVERTON RD
ALVERSTONE RD
SIDMOUTH RD
Bwg Gn
Crkt Gd
Pav
ELSTOW GRANGE
LAWNFIELD
COVERDALE PL
THE OAKS
LIMES CT
NW6
Willesden Jewish Cemy
Min Rly
Cemy
Allot Gdns
The Willesden Com
Summer Theatre
Tenn Cts
ROBSON AVE
H
PETER AVE
DOBREE AVE
CLARENDON CT
SIDMOUTH PAR
Pav
MILVERTON RD
CHUDLEIGH RD
MANOR HOUSE DR
ALAN PREECE CT
DONNINGTON CT
FRONTENAC
THE OAKS
ALEXANDER AVE
CLEMENT CL
Malorees Jun & Inf Schs
Roundwood Park
Allot Gdns
GEOFFREY JONES CT
ELLERSLIE GDNS
UFFINGTON RD
Donnington Prim Sch
DONNINGTON RD
Tenn Cts
Sp Stad
SLANEY CT
MOUNT PLEASANT RD
AYLESTONE AVE
Queens Park Com Sch
ST HILDA'S CL
ROSEDENE
GROSVENOR CT
CHRISTCHURCH AVE
22
A
B
23
90
C
D
24
Bwg Gn
HARLESDEN RD
SHALFORD
ALL SOULS AVE
HANOVER RD
Willesden High Sch
Willesden
Brondesbury

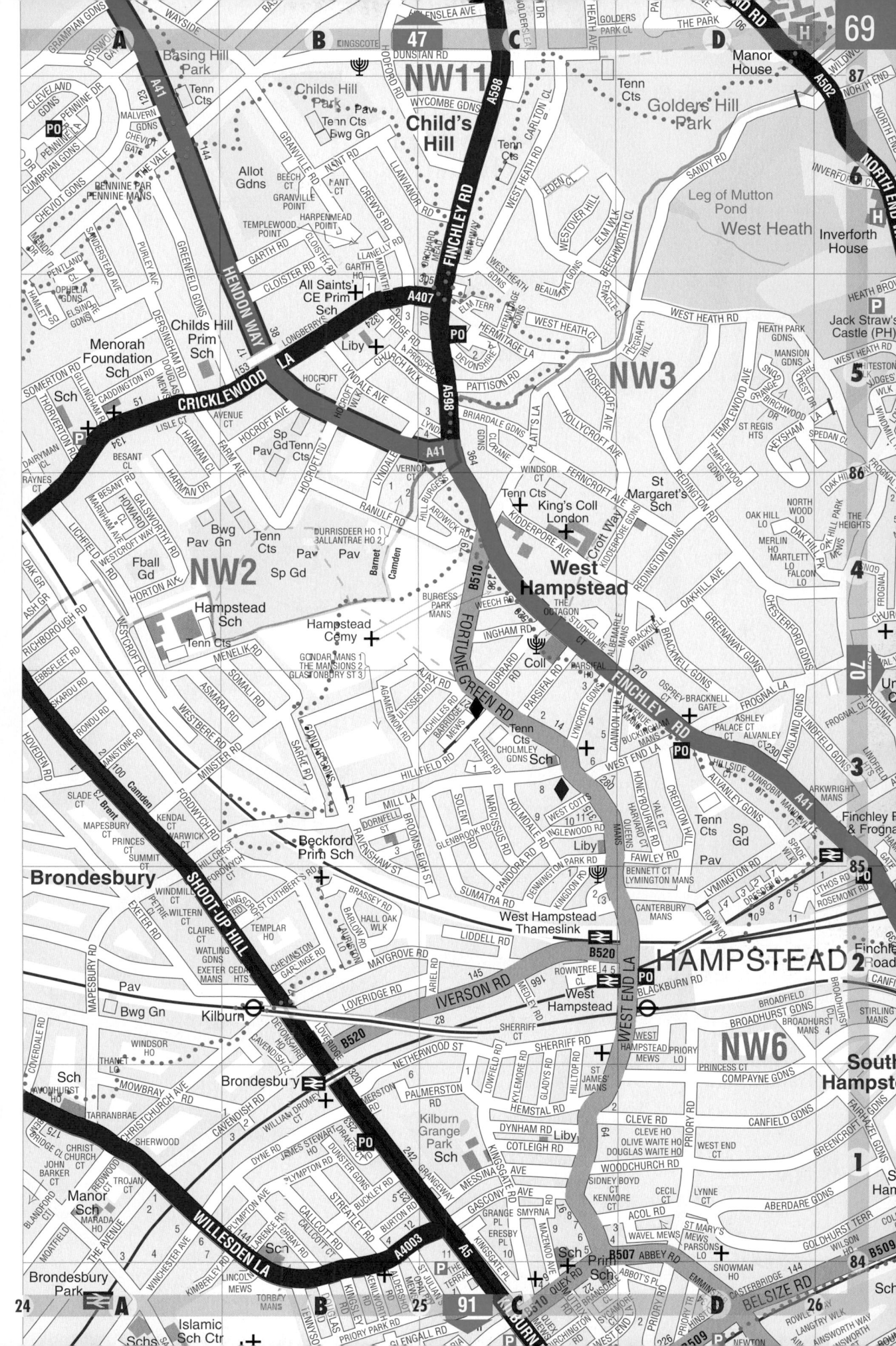
69
47
91
70
24
25
26
84
85
86
87
A
B
C
D
1
2
3
4
5
6
NW11
NW2
NW3
NW6
Child's Hill
West Hampstead
HAMPSTEAD
Brondesbury
South Hampst
Basing Hill Park
Childs Hill Park
Golders Hill Park
Manor House
Leg of Mutton Pond
West Heath
Inverforth House
Jack Straw's Castle (PH)
Allot Gdns
Tenn Cts
Pav
Bwg Gn
Sp Gd
Fball Gd
All Saints CE Prim Sch
Childs Hill Prim Sch
Menorah Foundation Sch
Hampstead Sch
Hampstead Cemy
King's Coll London
St Margaret's Sch
Beckford Prim Sch
West Hampstead Thameslink
West Hampstead
Kilburn
Brondesbury
Kilburn Grange Park
Brondesbury Park
Manor Sch
Islamic Sch Ctr
Finchley Road & Frognal
Finchley Road
Liby
Coll
Sch
Prim Sch
PO
HENDON WAY
CRICKLEWOOD LA
FINCHLEY RD
SHOOT-UP HILL
WILLESDEN LA
FORTUNE GREEN RD
WEST END LA
IVERSON RD
BELSIZE RD
KILBURN
A41
A598
A407
A5
A4003
A502
B510
B520
B507
B509
WEST HEATH RD
NORTH END RD
HEATH BROW
SANDY RD
REDINGTON RD
FROGNAL LA
FROGNAL
TEMPLEWOOD AVE
OAKHILL AVE
CHESTERFORD GDNS
GREENAWAY GDNS
ROSECROFT AVE
HOLLYCROFT AVE
FERNCROFT AVE
PLATT'S LA
KIDDERPORE AVE
KIDDERPORE GDNS
HERMITAGE LA
PATTISON RD
BRIARDALE GDNS
LLANVANOR RD
GRANVILLE RD
NANT RD
CREWYS RD
GARTH RD
CLOISTER RD
HOCROFT AVE
HOCROFT RD
LYNDALE AVE
RANULF RD
HILL BURGESS
ARDWICK RD
WESTCROFT WAY
HORTON AVE
RICHBOROUGH RD
MENELIK RD
SOMALI RD
ASMARA RD
WESTBERE RD
MINSTER RD
FORDWYCH RD
MILL LA
BURRARD RD
PARSIFAL RD
INGHAM RD
WEECH RD
HILLFIELD RD
SOLENT RD
NARCISSUS RD
HOLMDALE RD
GLENBROOK RD
PANDORA RD
SUMATRA RD
LIDDELL RD
MAYGROVE RD
LOVERIDGE RD
SHERRIFF RD
NETHERWOOD ST
PALMERSTON RD
HEMSTAL RD
DYNHAM RD
COTLEIGH RD
MESSINA AVE
GASCONY AVE
KINGSGATE RD
ABBEY RD
WOODCHURCH RD
CLEVE RD
ABERDARE GDNS
GOLDHURST TERR
BROADHURST GDNS
CANFIELD GDNS
COMPAYNE GDNS
PRIORY RD
HONEYBOURNE RD
CREDITON HILL
FAWLEY RD
LYMINGTON RD
ALVANLEY GDNS
LANGLAND GDNS
LINDFIELD GDNS
MAPESBURY RD
EXETER RD
CAVENDISH RD
MOWBRAY RD
CHRISTCHURCH AVE
WINCHESTER AVE
KIMBERLEY RD
DYNE RD
CALLCOTT RD
STREATLEY RD
BURTON RD
PRIORY PARK RD
GRANGEWAY
CRICKLEWOOD LA
BROADHURST MANS
Camden
Barnet
Brent

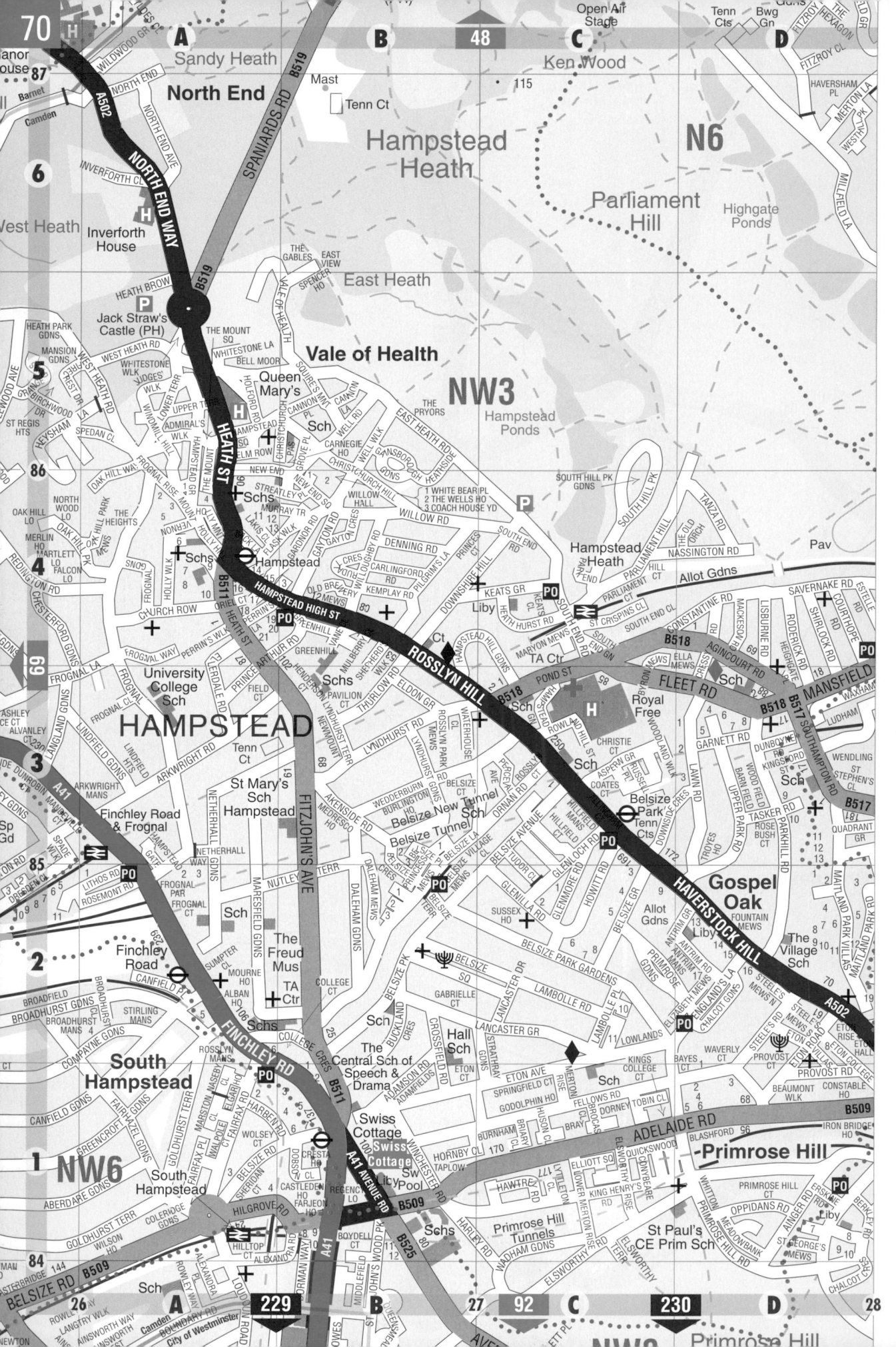
48
Open Air Stage
Tenn Cts
Bwg Gn
Sandy Heath
Ken Wood
North End
Mast
Tenn Ct
115
Hampstead Heath
N6
NORTH END WAY
SPANIARDS RD
B519
A502
Parliament Hill
Highgate Ponds
West Heath
Inverforth House
East Heath
Jack Straw's Castle (PH)
Vale of Health
NW3
Queen Mary's
Hampstead Ponds
HEATH ST
Sch
Schs
Hampstead
HAMPSTEAD HIGH ST
ROSSLYN HILL
Liby
Hampstead Heath
Allot Gdns
Pav
FLEET RD
Royal Free
MANSFIELD
HAMPSTEAD
University College Sch
Tenn Ct
St Mary's Sch Hampstead
Finchley Road & Frognal
FITZJOHN'S AVE
Belsize New Tunnel
Belsize Tunnel
Belsize Park
Tenn Cts
HAVERSTOCK HILL
Gospel Oak
Allot Gdns
The Village Sch
Finchley Road
The Freud Mus
TA Ctr
BELSIZE PARK GARDENS
Hall Sch
South Hampstead
FINCHLEY RD
The Central Sch of Speech & Drama
Swiss Cottage
ADELAIDE RD
Primrose Hill
NW6
South Hampstead
A41 AVENUE RD
Primrose Hill Tunnels
St Paul's CE Prim Sch
BELSIZE RD
229
92
230
26
27
28
A
B
C
D
1
2
3
4
5
6
84
85
86
87
69
Camden
City of Westminster

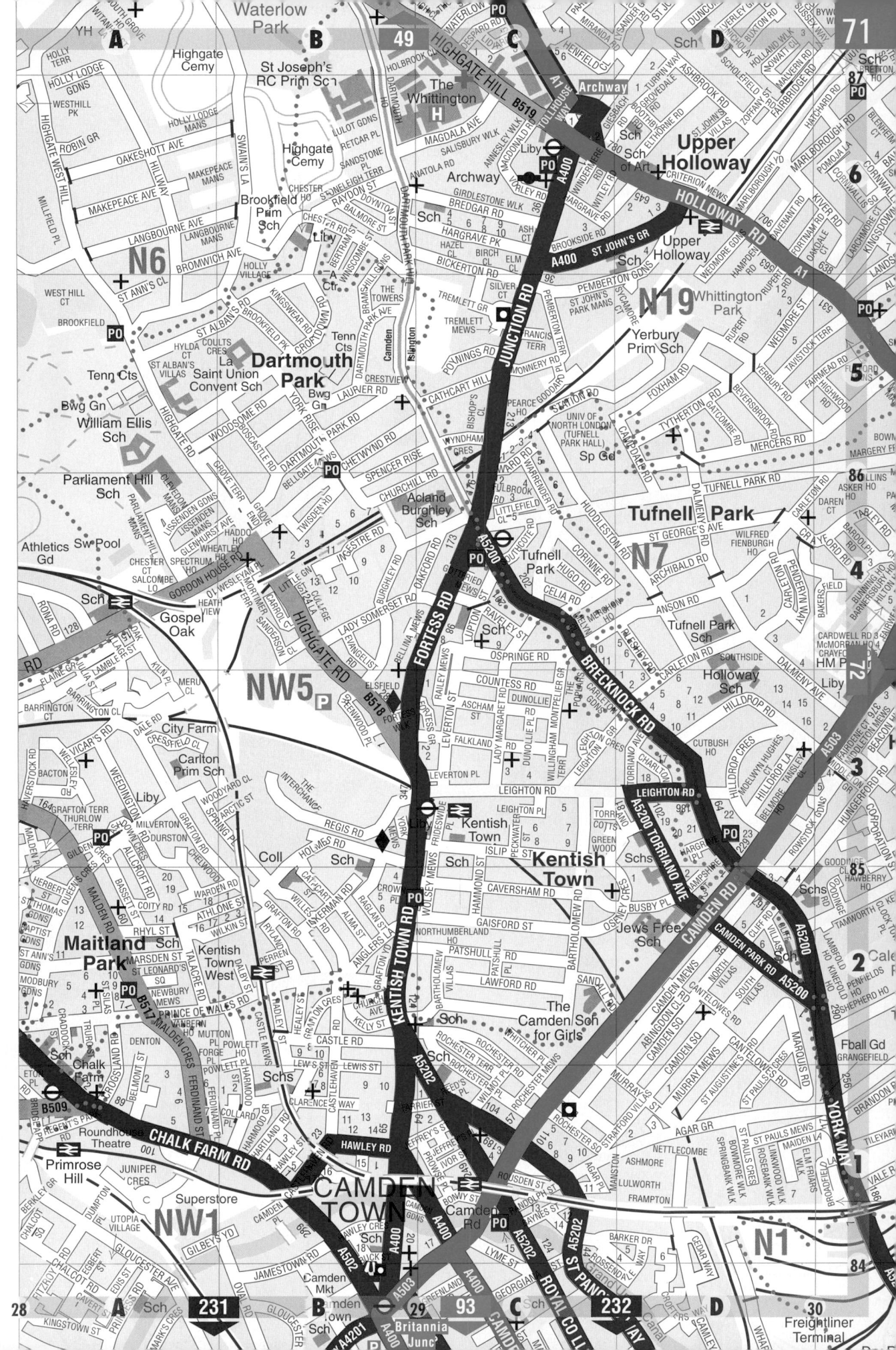

71
A
B
C
D
49
Waterlow Park
Highgate Cemy
St Joseph's RC Prim Sch
The Whittington
Highgate Hill
B519
Archway
Upper Holloway
Holloway Rd
A1
Holly Lodge Gdns
Westhill Pk
Highgate West Hill
Robin Gr
Oakeshott Ave
Makepeace Ave
Langbourne Ave
Swain's La
Hillway
Brookfield Prim Sch
Dartmouth Park Hill
Magdala Ave
Salisbury Wlk
Anatola Rd
Raydon St
Girdlestone Wlk
Bredgar Rd
Hargrave Pk
St John's Gr
A400
Holly Village
St Alban's Rd
Brookfield Pk
Kingswear Rd
Croftdown Rd
N6
N19
Whittington Park
Yerbury Prim Sch
Junction Rd
Tremlett Gr
Poynings Rd
Cathcart Hill
Monnery Rd
Pemberton Gdns
Dartmouth Park
Saint Union Convent Sch
Highgate Rd
Woodsome Rd
York Rise
Laurier Rd
Chetwynd Rd
Spencer Rise
Churchill Rd
Acland Burghley Sch
William Ellis Sch
Parliament Hill Sch
Athletics Gd
Sw Pool
Gordon House Rd
Gospel Oak
Station Rd
Univ of North London (Tufnell Park Hall)
Sp Gd
Tufnell Park Rd
Tufnell Park
St George's Ave
N7
Archibald Rd
Anson Rd
Tufnell Park Sch
Holloway Sch
Hillmarton Rd
Carleton Rd
Dalmeny Ave
Tufnell Park
Fortess Rd
A5200
Brecknock Rd
Ospringe Rd
Countess Rd
Lady Somerset Rd
Oakford Rd
NW5
B518
City Farm
Carlton Prim Sch
Leighton Rd
Kentish Town
Regis Rd
Coll
Islip St
Caversham Rd
Gaisford St
Patshull Rd
Lawford Rd
Torriano Ave
Camden Rd
Camden Park Rd
Jews Free Sch
The Camden Sch for Girls
Maitland Park
Kentish Town West
Prince of Wales Rd
Malden Rd
B517
Castle Rd
Kentish Town Rd
A5202
Hawley Rd
Chalk Farm Rd
Roundhouse Theatre
Primrose Hill
Superstore
Camden Town
Camden Rd
A400
A502
A503
NW1
Gloucester Ave
Jamestown Rd
Camden Mkt
Agar Gr
Rochester Sq
Camden Sq
St Pancras Way
Royal College St
Rousden St
Nettlecombe
Ashmore
Lulworth
Frampton
York Way
Fball Gd
Grangefield
N1
Freightliner Terminal
Britannia Junc
86
85
84
6
5
4
3
2
1
72
87
231
93
232
28
29
30

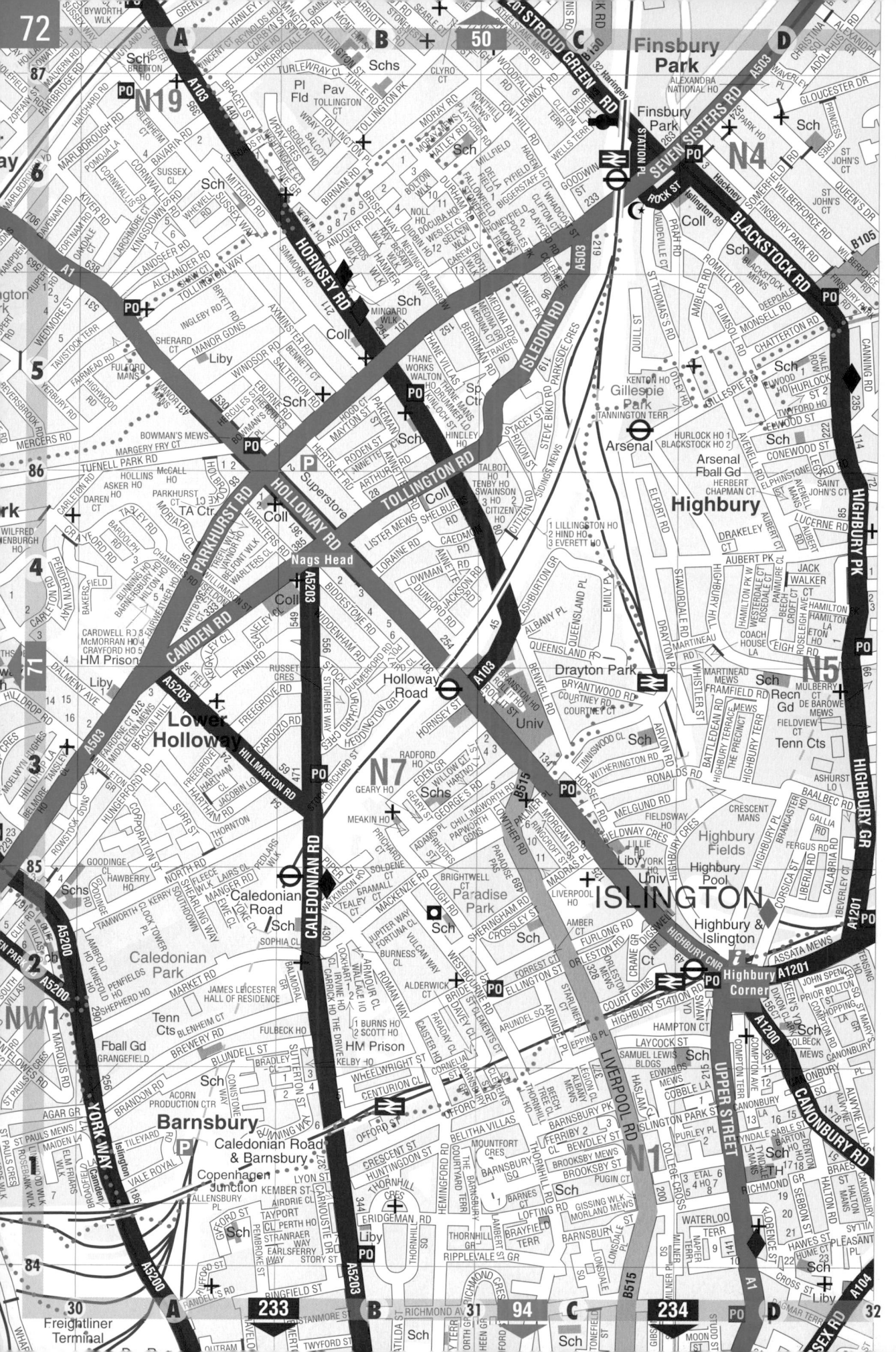
50
Finsbury Park
N19
N4
Finsbury Park
SEVEN SISTERS RD
STROUD GREEN RD
HORNSEY RD
BLACKSTOCK RD
Gillespie Park
Arsenal
Arsenal Fball Gd
Highbury
HIGHBURY PK
HIGHBURY GR
TOLLINGTON RD
HOLLOWAY RD
PARKHURST RD
CAMDEN RD
Nags Head
Holloway Road
Drayton Park
ISLEDON RD
Lower Holloway
HILLMARTON RD
N7
N5
CALEDONIAN RD
Caledonian Road
Caledonian Park
Highbury Fields
Highbury Pool
ISLINGTON
Highbury & Islington
Highbury Corner
Paradise Park
HM Prison
LIVERPOOL RD
UPPER STREET
CANONBURY RD
YORK WAY
NW1
N1
Barnsbury
Caledonian Road & Barnsbury
Copenhagen Junction
Freightliner Terminal
71
233
94
234
30
31
32
84
85
86
87

51
A
B
C
D
West Reservoir
STOKE NEWINGTON
Abney Park Cemy
Stoke Newington
N4
N16
N5
E5
E8
N1
Clissold Park
Tenn Cts
Bwg Gn
Shacklewell
Rectory Road
Recn Gd
Canonbury
Dalston Kingsland
Dalston Jct
Dalston
Kingsland
De Beauvoir Town
Essex Road
Ridley
Kingsland Basin
Tenn Cts
MANOR RD
LORDSHIP PK
LORDSHIP RD
BROWNSWOOD RD
QUEEN ELIZABETH'S WLK
STOKE NEWINGTON CHURCH ST
STOKE NEWINGTON HIGH ST
STOKE NEWINGTON RD
STAMFORD HILL
KINGSLAND HIGH ST
KINGSLAND RD
RECTORY RD
NORTHWOLD RD
STOKE NEWINGTON COMM
EVERING RD
MANSE RD
ALBION RD
CLISSOLD RD
CLISSOLD CRES
NEWINGTON GREEN RD
NEWINGTON GREEN
ST PAUL'S RD
BALLS POND RD
ESSEX RD
SOUTHGATE RD
QUEENSBRIDGE RD
DALSTON LA
NEW NORTH RD
HIGHBURY NEW PK
HIGHBURY QUADRANT
HIGHBURY GRANGE
GROSVENOR AVE
MILDMAY PK
MILDMAY GR
MILDMAY RD
AMHURST RD
SANDRINGHAM RD
MONTAGUE RD
SHACKLEWELL LA
DOWNS PARK RD
ENGLEFIELD RD
DE BEAUVOIR RD
NORTHCHURCH RD
HERTFORD RD
CULFORD RD
BALMES RD
CANAL WLK
A105
A10
A104
A1199
A1200
A1207
B104
B105
B111
B102
B108
32
33
34
235
95
74
87
86
85
84
1
2
3
4
5
6

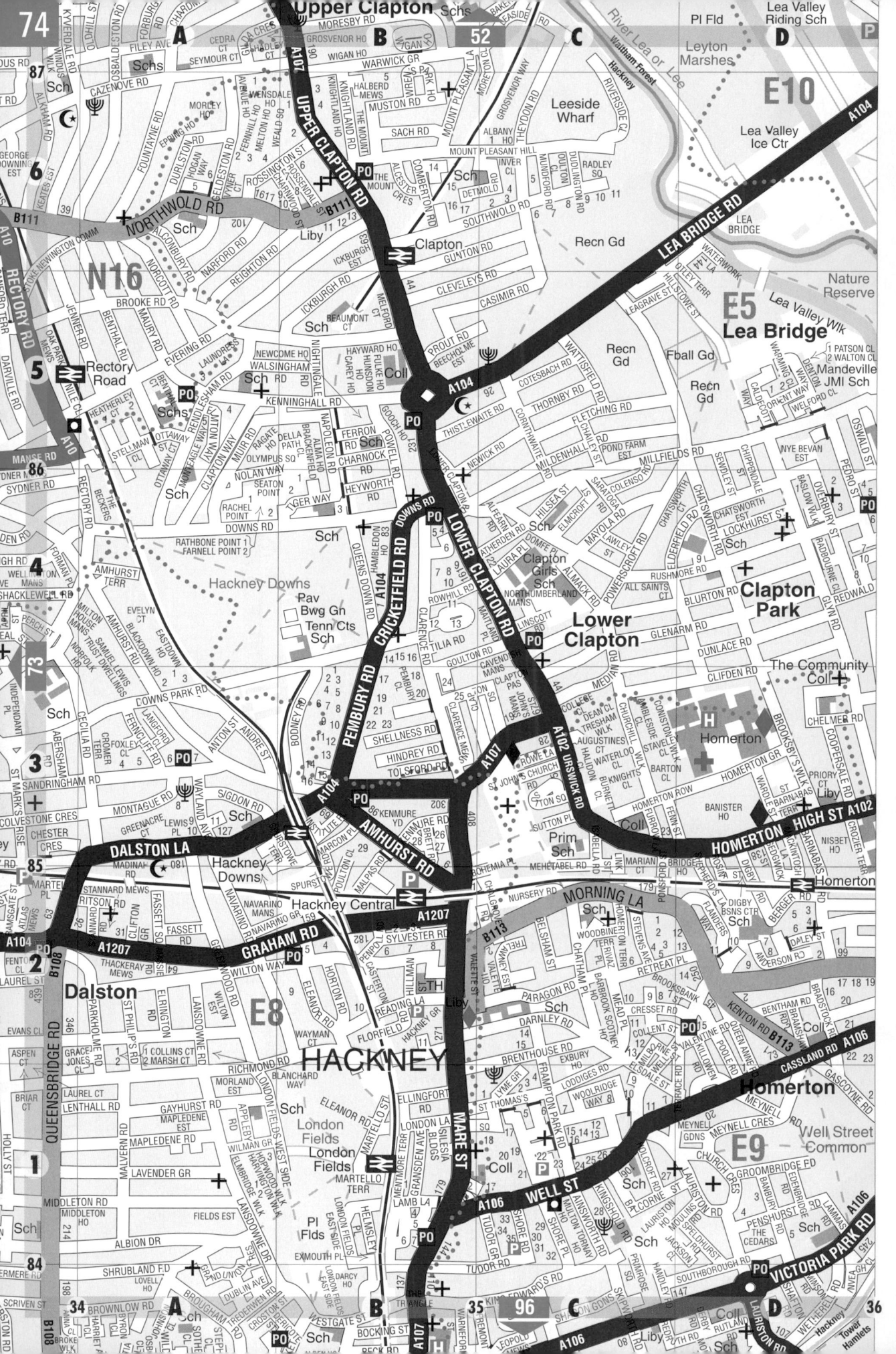
A
B
C
D
52
96
87
86
85
84
73
34
35
36
6
5
4
3
2
1
Upper Clapton
Schs
Pl Fld
Lea Valley
Riding Sch
River Lea or Lee
Waltham Forest
Hackney
Leyton
Marshes
E10
Leeside
Wharf
Lea Valley
Ice Ctr
A104
LEA BRIDGE RD
LEA
BRIDGE
Nature
Reserve
Lea Valley Wlk
E5
Lea Bridge
1 PATSON CL
2 WALTON CL
Mandeville
JMI Sch
Recn Gd
Fball Gd
N16
RECTORY RD
A10
B111
NORTHWOLD RD
STOKE NEWINGTON COMM
Sch
Schs
Rectory
Road
MANSE RD
SYDNER RD
CAZENOVE RD
ALKHAM RD
FOUNTAYNE RD
DURLSTON RD
MORESBY RD
GROSVENOR HO
WIGAN HO
WARWICK GR
A107
UPPER CLAPTON RD
KNIGHTLAND RD
HALBERD MEWS
MUSTON RD
SACH RD
MOUNT PLEASANT LA
MOUNT PLEASANT HILL
GROSVENOR WAY
THEYDON RD
RIVERSIDE CL
ALBANY HO
INVER CL
RADLEY SQ
DETMOLD RD
SOUTHWOLD RD
ROSSINGTON ST
ROSSENDALE ST
Liby
Clapton
GUNTON RD
CLEVELEYS RD
CASIMIR RD
ICKBURGH RD
ICKBURGH EST
BEAUMONT CT
PROUT RD
BEECHOLME EST
COTESBACH RD
THORNBY RD
FLETCHING RD
WATTISFIELD RD
MILDENHALL RD
POND FARM EST
MILLFIELDS RD
NEWICK RD
THISTLEWAITE RD
LOWER CLAPTON RD
Coll
PO
KENNINGHALL RD
WALSINGHAM RD
NEWCOME HO
NIGHTINGALE RD
HAYWARD HO
FERRON RD
CHARNOCK RD
HEYWORTH RD
POWELL RD
OLYMPUS SQ
NOLAN WAY
SEATON POINT
RACHEL POINT
TIGER WAY
DOWNS RD
RATHBONE POINT
FARNELL POINT
CLAPTON WAY
OTTAWAY ST
HEATHERLEY CT
STELLMAN CL
BROOKE RD
BENTHAL RD
MAURY RD
EVERING RD
REIGHTON RD
NARFORD RD
NORCOTT RD
JENNER RD
DARVILLE RD
Hackney Downs
Pav
Bwg Gn
Tenn Cts
CRICKETFIELD RD
QUEENS DOWN RD
AMHURST RD
AMHURST TERR
SHACKLEWELL RD
CECILIA RD
DOWNS PARK RD
ANDRE ST
FOXLEY CL
CROMER TERR
ABERSHAM RD
SANDRINGHAM RD
MONTAGUE RD
COLVESTONE CRES
CHESTER CRES
DALSTON LA
Hackney
Downs
STANNARD MEWS
RITSON RD
FASSETT SQ
FASSETT RD
NAVARINO RD
NAVARINO MANS
Hackney Central
PEMBURY RD
BODNEY RD
SHELLNESS RD
HINDREY RD
TOLSFORD RD
CLARENCE RD
ROWHILL RD
TILIA RD
GOULTON RD
CAVENDISH MANS
CLAPTON PAS
CLARENCE MEWS
Clapton
Girls
Sch
NORTHUMBERLAND MANS
LAURA PL
ATHERDEN RD
ALFEARN RD
HILSEA ST
ELMCROFT ST
MAYOLA RD
POWERSCROFT RD
ALL SAINTS CT
ELDERFIELD RD
RUSHMORE RD
BLURTON RD
GLENARM RD
DUNLACE RD
CLIFDEN RD
Clapton
Park
Lower
Clapton
CHATSWORTH RD
LOCKHURST ST
NYE BEVAN EST
PEDRO ST
OVERBURY ST
GLYN RD
REDWALD
The Community
Coll
CHELMER RD
Homerton
MEDIAN RD
CHURCHILL WLK
HOMERTON GR
HOMERTON ROW
BANISTER HO
A102
URSWICK RD
HOMERTON HIGH ST
A104
AMHURST RD
MEHETABEL RD
SUTTON PL
Prim
Sch
BOHEMIA PL
NURSERY RD
MORNING LA
Homerton
A1207
GRAHAM RD
SYLVESTER RD
B113
PARAGON RD
RETREAT PL
BROOKSBANK ST
KENTON RD
CASSLAND RD
A106
Homerton
MEYNELL RD
MEYNELL CRES
Well Street
Common
E9
GROOMBRIDGE RD
PENSHURST RD
VICTORIA PARK RD
SOUTHBOROUGH RD
WELL ST
Dalston
QUEENSBRIDGE RD
B108
E8
WILTON WAY
THACKERAY MEWS
ELRINGTON RD
LANSDOWNE RD
PARKHOLME RD
ST PHILIP'S RD
EVANS CL
HACKNEY
MARE ST
Liby
DARNLEY RD
BRENTHOUSE RD
LODDIGES RD
FRAMPTON PARK RD
RICHMOND RD
LAUREL CT
LENTHALL RD
GAYHURST RD
MAPLEDENE EST
MAPLEDENE RD
London
Fields
London
Fields
MARTELLO ST
MARTELLO TERR
LAVENDER GR
MIDDLETON RD
FIELDS EST
ALBION DR
SHRUBLAND RD
BROWNLOW RD
Pl
Flds
LAMB LA
EXMOUTH PL
TUDOR RD
TUDOR GR
SHORE RD
KINGSHOLD RD
KING EDWARD'S RD
WESTGATE ST
BOCKING ST
THE TRIANGLE
LAURISTON RD
HOLLY ST
SCRIVEN ST
Tower
Hamlets

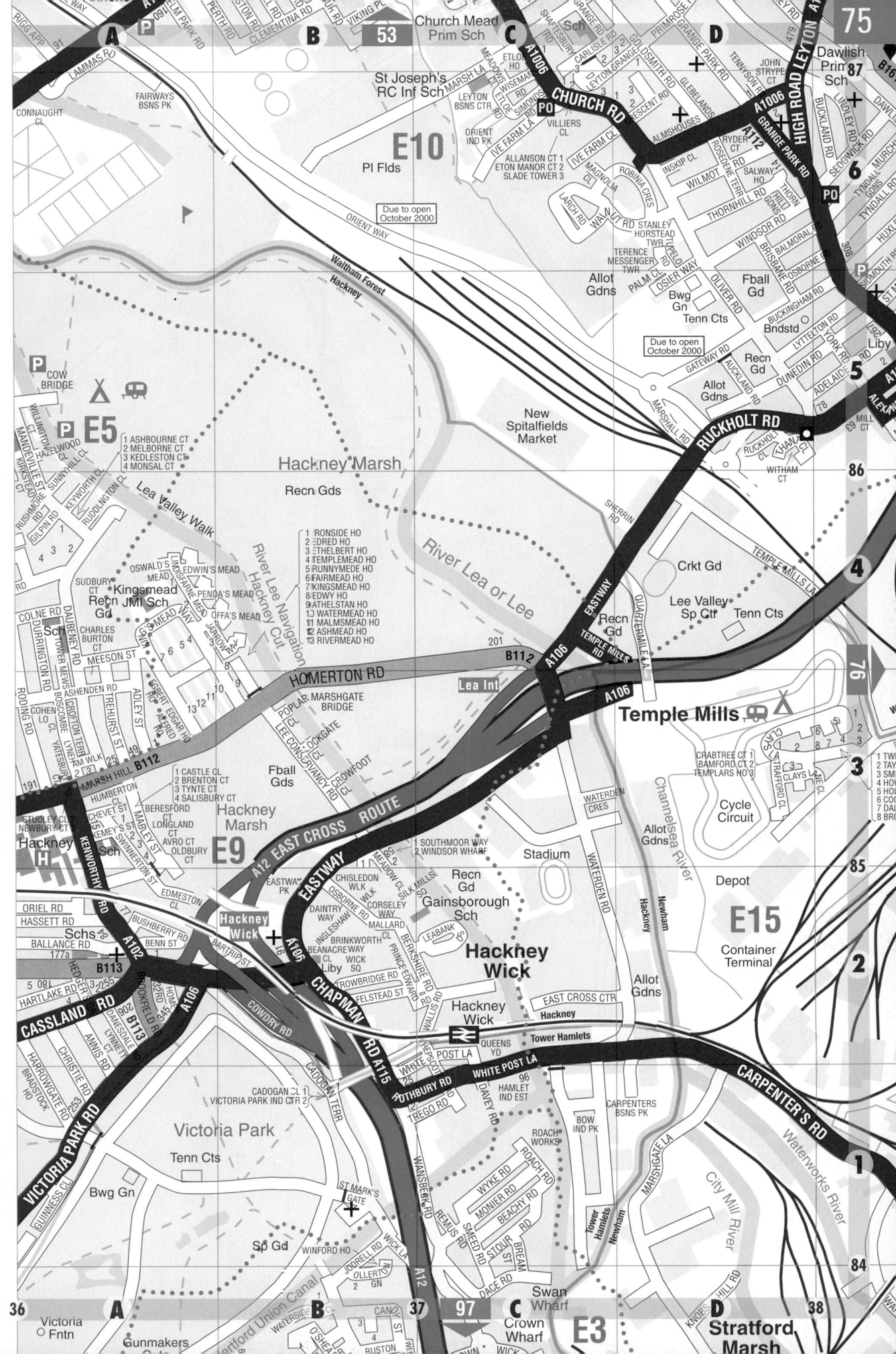
53
Church Mead Prim Sch
St Joseph's RC Inf Sch
E10
Pl Flds
CHURCH RD
A1006
HIGH ROAD LEYTON
Dawlish Prim Sch
87
GRANGE PARK RD
LEYTON BSNS CTR
ORIENT IND PK
VILLIERS CL
ALLANSON CT 1
ETON MANOR CT 2
SLADE TOWER 3
FAIRWAYS BSNS PK
CONNAUGHT CL
LAMMAS RD
Due to open October 2000
ORIENT WAY
Waltham Forest
Hackney
Allot Gdns
Bwg Gn
Tenn Cts
Fball Gd
Bndstd
Recn Gd
Liby
New Spitalfields Market
RUCKHOLT RD
WITHAM CT
86
COW BRIDGE
E5
1 ASHBOURNE CT
2 MELBORNE CT
3 KEDLESTON CT
4 MONSAL CT
Hackney Marsh
Recn Gds
Lea Valley Walk
River Lea or Lee
River Lee Navigation Hackney Cut
1 RONSIDE HO
2 EDRED HO
3 ETHELBERT HO
4 TEMPLEMEAD HO
5 RUNNYMEDE HO
6 FAIRMEAD HO
7 KINGSMEAD HO
8 EDWY HO
9 ATHELSTAN HO
10 WATERMEAD HO
11 MALMSMEAD HO
12 ASHMEAD HO
13 RIVERMEAD HO
Kingsmead JMI Sch
Recn Gd
Crkt Gd
Lee Valley Sp Ctr
Tenn Cts
TEMPLE MILLS LA
EASTWAY
A106
HOMERTON RD
B112
MARSHGATE BRIDGE
Lea Int
Temple Mills
CRABTREE CT 1
BAMFORD CT 2
TEMPLARS HO 3
Cycle Circuit
76
1 CASTLE CL
2 BRENTON CT
3 TYNTE CT
4 SALISBURY CT
Fball Gds
Hackney Marsh
E9
EAST CROSS ROUTE
A12
1 SOUTHMOOR WAY
2 WINDSOR WHARF
Stadium
Allot Gdns
Channelsea River
Depot
85
E15
Container Terminal
Hackney Wick
Recn Gd
Gainsborough Sch
Hackney Wick
CASSLAND RD
A102
B113
Schs
CHAPMAN RD A115
EAST CROSS CTR
Hackney
Tower Hamlets
WHITE POST LA
CARPENTER'S RD
CARPENTERS BSNS PK
BOW IND PK
HAMLET IND EST
CADOGAN CL 1
VICTORIA PARK IND CTR 2
Victoria Park
Tenn Cts
Bwg Gn
Sp Gd
VICTORIA PARK RD
Waterworks River
City Mill River
84
Swan Wharf
Crown Wharf
E3
Stratford Marsh
36
37
97
38
Victoria Fntn
Gunmakers
Hertford Union Canal

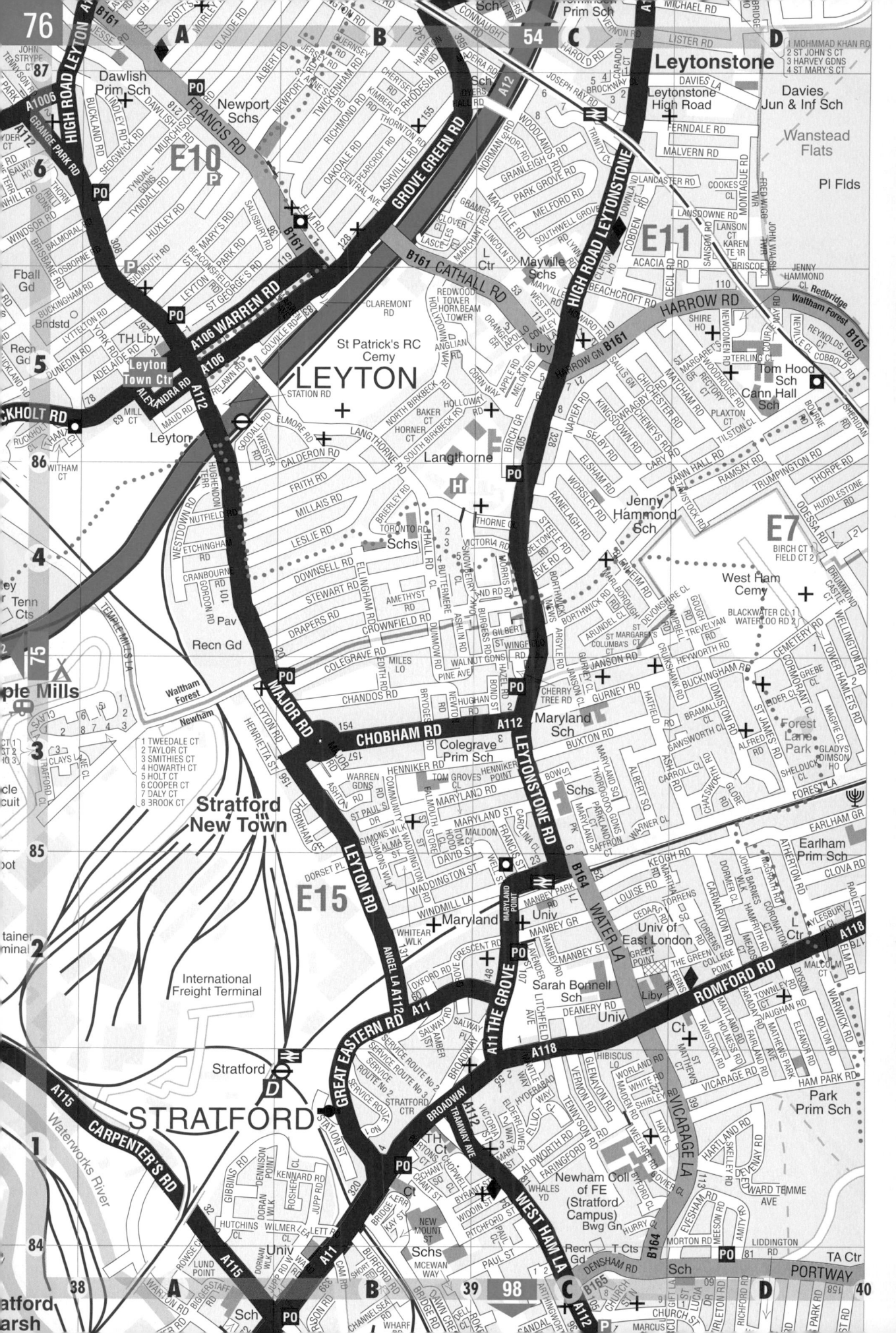
A
B
54
C
D
1 MOHMMAD KHAN RD
2 ST JOHN'S CT
3 HARVEY GDNS
4 ST MARY'S CT
Leytonstone
Davies Jun & Inf Sch
Wanstead Flats
Pl Flds
Leytonstone High Road
HIGH ROAD LEYTON
Dawlish Prim Sch
Newport Schs
E10
FRANCIS RD
GROVE GREEN RD
HIGH ROAD LEYTONSTONE
E11
HARROW RD
Redbridge
Waltham Forest
Tom Hood Sch
Cann Hall Sch
St Patrick's RC Cemy
LEYTON
A106 WARREN RD
Leyton Town Ctr
Leyton
Langthorne
Mayville Schs
CATHALL RD
Jenny Hammond Sch
E7
West Ham Cemy
Fball Gd
Bndstd
TH Liby
Recn Gd
Pav
Tenn Cts
Temple Mills
CHOBHAM RD
LEYTONSTONE RD
MAJOR RD
Maryland Sch
Colegrave Prim Sch
Forest Lane Park
1 TWEEDALE CT
2 TAYLOR CT
3 SMITHIES CT
4 HOWARTH CT
5 HOLT CT
6 COOPER CT
7 DALY CT
8 BROOK CT
Stratford New Town
E15
LEYTON RD
WATER LA
ROMFORD RD
Earlham Prim Sch
Univ of East London
Sarah Bonnell Sch
International Freight Terminal
Stratford
STRATFORD
CARPENTER'S RD
GREAT EASTERN RD
THE GROVE
BROADWAY
WEST HAM LA
VICARAGE LA
Newham Coll of FE (Stratford Campus)
Park Prim Sch
Waterworks River
PORTWAY
TA Ctr
Stratford Marsh
38
39
98
40
87
86
85
84
75
1
2
3
4
5
6

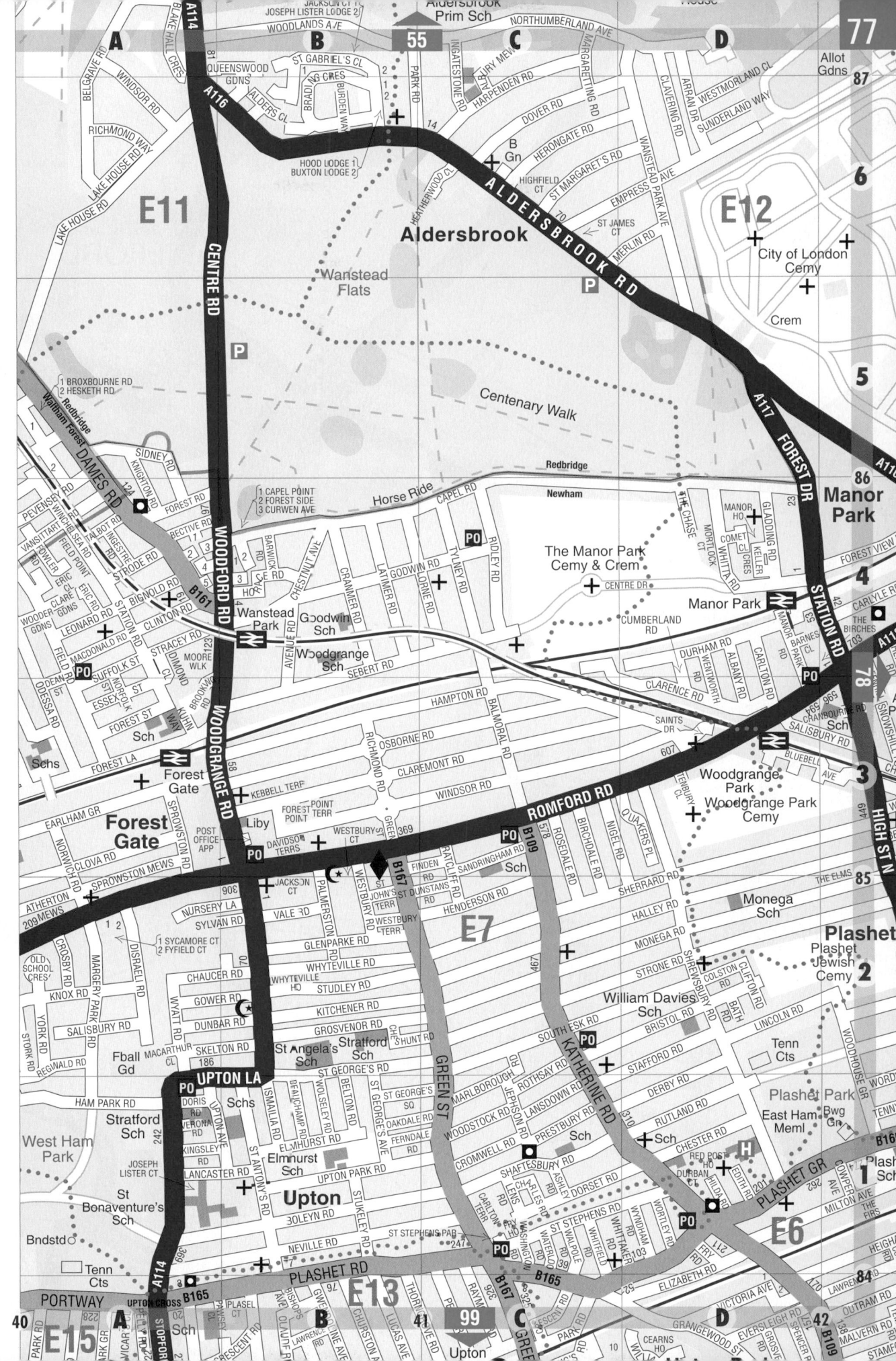
A
B
C
D
55
E11
E12
E7
E6
E13
E15
Aldersbrook
Aldersbrook Prim Sch
Wanstead Flats
Centenary Walk
Horse Ride
Redbridge
Newham
City of London Cemy
Crem
Allot Gdns
Manor Park
The Manor Park Cemy & Crem
Forest Gate
Woodgrange Park
Woodgrange Park Cemy
Wanstead Park
Goodwin Sch
Woodgrange Sch
Plashet
Plashet Jewish Cemy
Plashet Park
East Ham Meml
Monega Sch
William Davies Sch
Tenn Cts
Upton
Elmhurst Sch
St Angela's Sch
Stratford Sch
Stratford Sch
West Ham Park
St Bonaventure's Sch
Fball Gd
Bndstd
Liby
Schs
ALDERSBROOK RD
CENTRE RD
WOODFORD RD
WOODGRANGE RD
ROMFORD RD
FOREST DR
STATION RD
GREEN ST
KATHERINE RD
PLASHET RD
PLASHET GR
UPTON LA
PORTWAY
UPTON CROSS
HIGH ST N
DAMES RD
NORTHUMBERLAND AVE
WOODLANDS AVE
LAKE HOUSE RD
FOREST LA
A114
A116
A117
A118
B161
B167
B109
B165
6
5
4
3
2
1
87
86
85
84
40
41
42
78
99

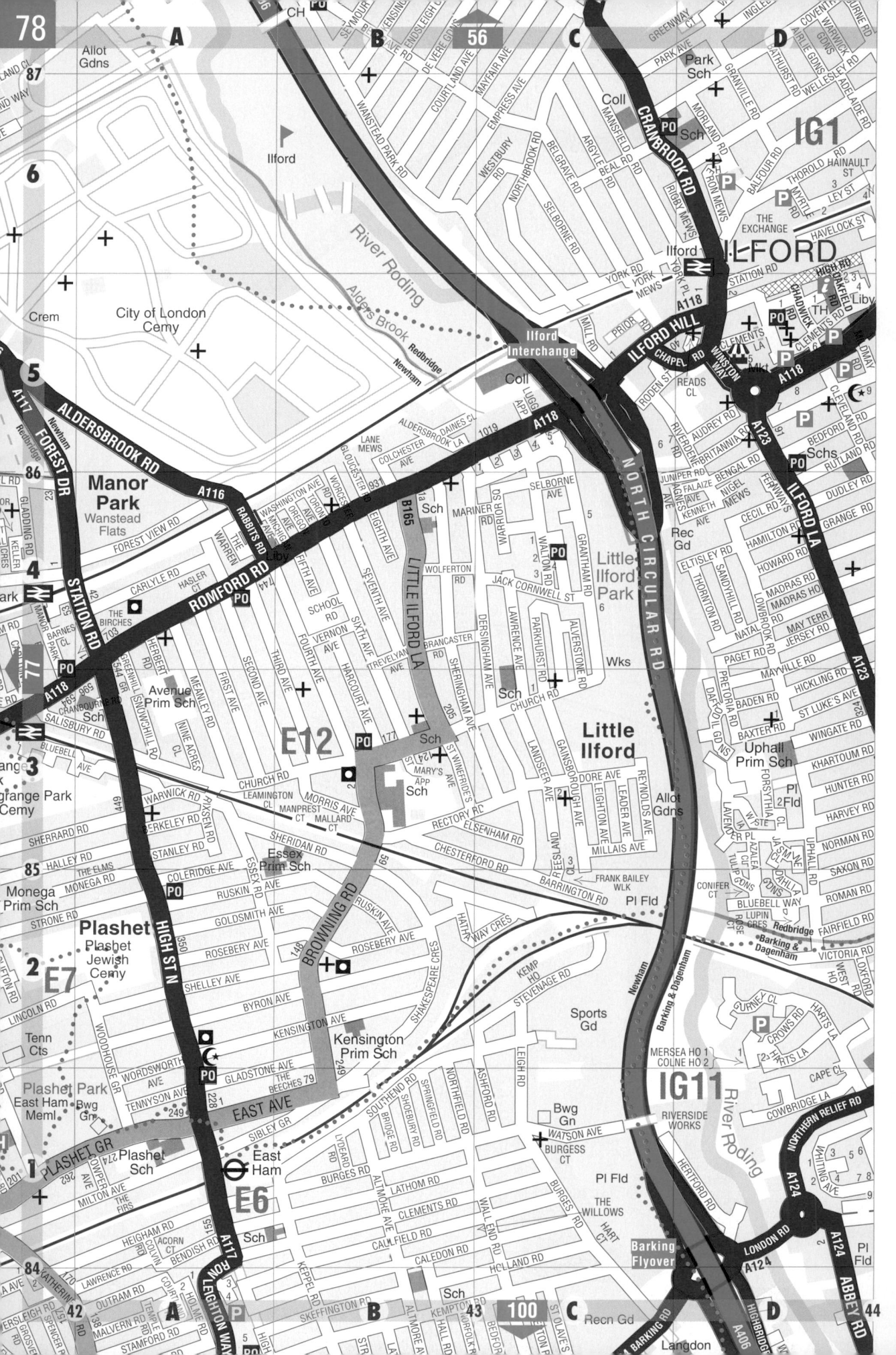
A
B
C
D
56
100
77
42
43
44
87
86
85
84
IG1
IG11
E12
E7
E6
ILFORD
Ilford
Manor Park
Wanstead Flats
Little Ilford
Little Ilford Park
Plashet
Plashet Jewish Cemy
Plashet Park
East Ham Meml
City of London Cemy
Crem
Allot Gdns
River Roding
Alders Brook
Ilford Interchange
Barking Flyover
East Ham
Redbridge
Newham
Barking & Dagenham
ROMFORD RD
ALDERSBROOK RD
NORTH CIRCULAR RD
CRANBROOK RD
ILFORD HILL
ILFORD LA
HIGH ST N
STATION RD
FOREST DR
LITTLE ILFORD LA
BROWNING RD
EAST AVE
PLASHET GR
WANSTEAD PARK RD
NORTHERN RELIEF RD
LONDON RD
ABBEY RD
RONALD LEIGHTON WAY
A118
A117
A116
A123
A124
A406
B165
Avenue Prim Sch
Essex Prim Sch
Kensington Prim Sch
Uphall Prim Sch
Monega Prim Sch
Sports Gd
Riverside Works
Rec Gd
Pl Fld
Recn Gd
Langdon
THE EXCHANGE
Tenn Cts
Coll
Sch
Wks

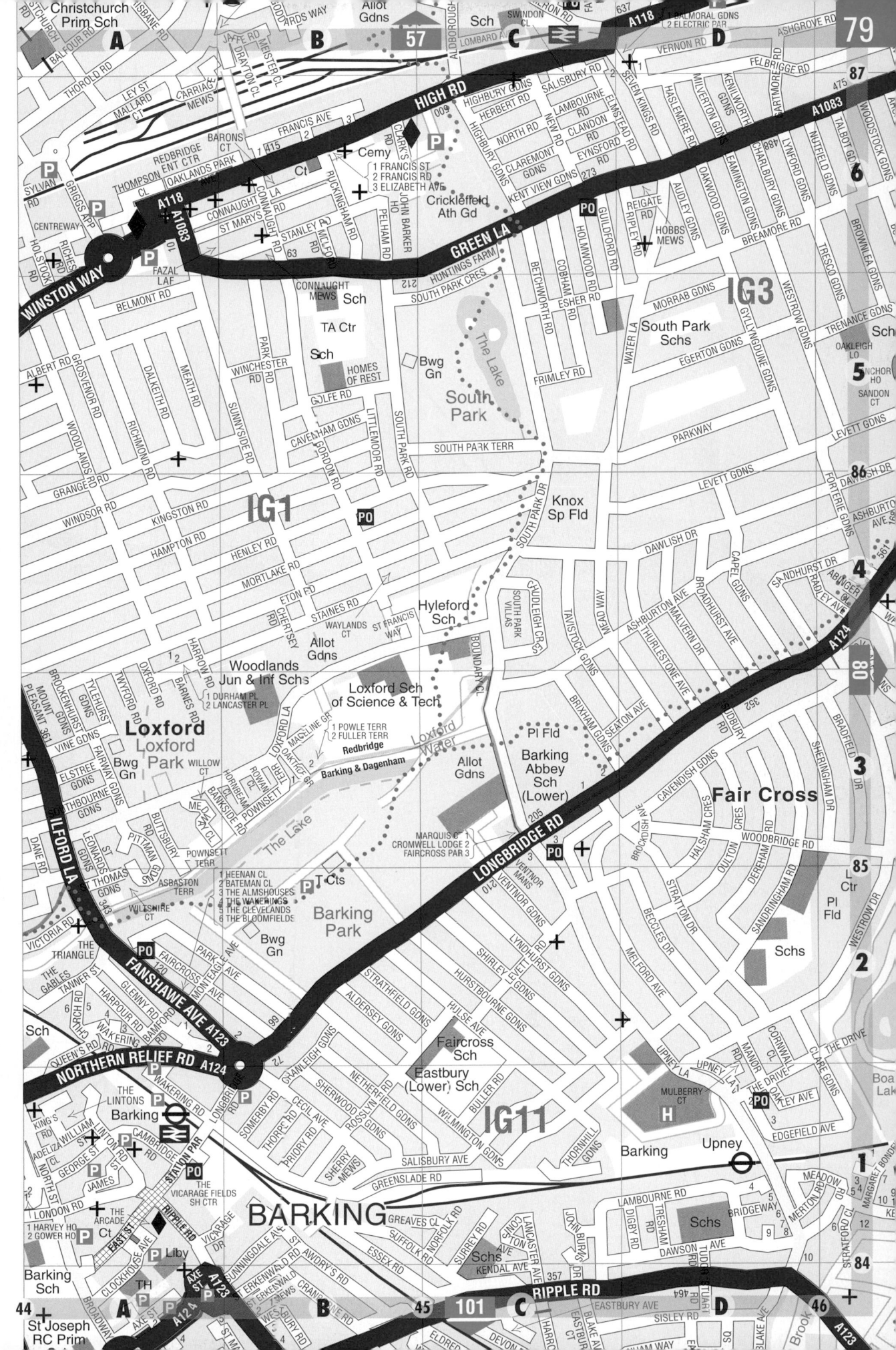
A
B
C
D
57
80
101
45
46
44
87
86
85
84
6
5
4
3
2
1
IG1
IG3
IG11
BARKING
Loxford
Fair Cross
Christchurch Prim Sch
Allot Gdns
Sch
SWINDON CL
LOMBARD AV
A118
1 BALMORAL GDNS
2 ELECTRIC PAR
ASHGROVE RD
VERNON RD
FELBRIGGE RD
SEVEN KINGS RD
HASLEMERE RD
MILVERTON GDNS
KENILWORTH GDNS
GARTMORE RD
A1083
WOODSTOCK GDNS
TALBOT GDNS
NUTFIELD GDNS
LYNFORD GDNS
CHARLBURY GDNS
LEAMINGTON GDNS
OAKWOOD GDNS
AUDLEY GDNS
HIGH RD
THOROLD RD
BALFOUR RD
LEY ST
MALLARD CT
CARRIAGE MEWS
JAFFE RD
DRAYTON CL
MEISTER CL
ALDBOROUGH RD
FRANCIS AVE
BARONS CT
REDBRIDGE ENT CTR
OAKLANDS PARK AVE
THOMPSON CL
SYLVAN RD
GRIGGS APP
CENTREWAY
CONNAUGHT RD
ST MARYS RD
STANLEY RD
MILFORD RD
BUCKINGHAM RD
PELHAM RD
JOHN BARKER HO
CLARK'S RD
Cemy
Ct
1 FRANCIS ST
2 FRANCIS RD
3 ELIZABETH AVE
Cricklefield Ath Gd
HIGHBURY GDNS
HERBERT RD
NORTH RD
CLAREMONT GDNS
KENT VIEW GDNS
SALISBURY RD
LAMBOURNE RD
CLANDON RD
EYNSFORD RD
NEW RD
ELMSTEAD RD
GREEN LA
GUILDFORD RD
HOLMWOOD RD
COBHAM RD
BETCHWORTH RD
REIGATE RD
RIPLEY RD
HOBBS MEWS
BREAMORE RD
TRESCO GDNS
BROWNLEA GDNS
WINSTON WAY
HOLSTOCK RD
RICHES RD
FAZAL LAF
HUNTINGS FARM
SOUTH PARK CRES
CONNAUGHT MEWS
Sch
TA Ctr
HOMES OF REST
BELMONT RD
ALBERT RD
GROSVENOR RD
WOODLANDS RD
RICHMOND RD
DALKEITH RD
MEATH RD
SUNNYSIDE RD
PARK RD
WINCHESTER RD
GOLFE RD
CAVENHAM GDNS
GORDON RD
LITTLEMOOR RD
SOUTH PARK RD
SOUTH PARK TERR
Bwg Gn
The Lake
South Park
ESHER RD
FRIMLEY RD
WATER LA
South Park Schs
MORRAB GDNS
GYLLYNGDUNE GDNS
WESTROW GDNS
EGERTON GDNS
TRENANCE GDNS
OAKLEIGH LO
ANCHOR HO
SANDON CT
LEVETT GDNS
PARKWAY
DAWLISH DR
FORTERIE GDNS
ASHBURTON AVE
GRANGE RD
WINDSOR RD
KINGSTON RD
HAMPTON RD
HENLEY RD
MORTLAKE RD
ETON RD
STAINES RD
CHERTSEY RD
WAYLANDS CT
ST FRANCIS WAY
Hyleford Sch
SOUTH PARK DR
Knox Sp Fld
CHUDLEIGH CRES
SOUTH PARK VILLAS
TAVISTOCK GDNS
MEAD WAY
THURLESTONE AVE
MALVERN DR
BROADHURST AVE
CAPEL GDNS
SANDHURST DR
RADLEY AVE
ABINGER CL
A124
Allot Gdns
Woodlands Jun & Inf Schs
HARROW RD
BARNES RD
1 DURHAM PL
2 LANCASTER PL
OXFORD RD
TWYFORD RD
TYLEHURST GDNS
BROCKENHURST GDNS
MOUNT PLEASANT
VINE GDNS
Loxford Park
Bwg Gn
WILLOW CT
FAIRWAY GDNS
ELSTREE GDNS
BOURNE GDNS
Loxford Sch of Science & Tech
LOXFORD LA
MACELINE GR
OAKTREE GR
1 POWLE TERR
2 FULLER TERR
Redbridge
Barking & Dagenham
Loxford Water
BOUNDARY CL
Allot Gdns
ROWAN CL
HORNBEAM CL
BANKSIDE RD
POWNSETT TERR
BRIXHAM GDNS
SEATON AVE
Pl Fld
Barking Abbey Sch (Lower)
SUDBURY RD
BRADFIELD DR
SHERINGHAM DR
CAVENDISH GDNS
ILFORD LA
DANE RD
LEONARDS GDNS
PITTMAN GDNS
BUTTSBURY RD
ASBASTON TERR
The Lake
MARQUIS CT
CROMWELL LODGE
FAIRCROSS PAR
LONGBRIDGE RD
VENTNOR MANS
VENTNOR GDNS
BROCKDISH AVE
HALSHAM CRES
OULTON CRES
WOODBRIDGE RD
DEREHAM RD
SANDRINGHAM RD
Pl Fld
Ctr
WESTROW DR
1 HEENAN CL
2 BATEMAN CL
3 THE ALMSHOUSES
4 THE WAKERINGS
5 THE CLEVELANDS
6 THE BLOOMFIELDS
T Cts
Barking Park
ST THOMAS GDNS
WILTSHIRE CT
VICTORIA RD
THE TRIANGLE
Bwg Gn
FANSHAWE AVE
A123
FAIRCROSS AVE
PARK AVE
MONTEAGLE AVE
STRATTON DR
BECCLES DR
MELFORD AVE
LYNDHURST GDNS
LEVETT GDNS
SHIRLEY GDNS
HURSTBOURNE GDNS
STRATHFIELD GDNS
ALDERSEY GDNS
Schs
THE GABLES
TANNER ST
CHURCH RD
HARPOUR RD
GLENNY RD
BAMFORD RD
WAKERING RD
QUEEN'S RD
NORTHERN RELIEF RD
HULSE AVE
Faircross Sch
Eastbury (Lower) Sch
BULLER RD
UPNEY LA
MANOR RD
CORNWALL CL
THE DRIVE
CLARE GDNS
THE OAK
LEY AVE
MULBERRY CT
H
THE LINTONS
Barking
KING'S RD
ADELIZA
WILLIAM ST
LINTON RD
CAMBRIDGE RD
LONGBRIDGE RD
SOMERBY RD
THORPE RD
CECIL AVE
PRIORY RD
ROSSLYN RD
NETHERFIELD GDNS
SHERWOOD GDNS
GRANLEIGH GDNS
WILMINGTON GDNS
THORNHILL GDNS
EDGEFIELD AVE
Barking
Upney
GEORGE ST
NORTH ST
JAMES ST
STATION PAR
THE VICARAGE FIELDS SH CTR
SHERRY MEWS
SALISBURY AVE
GREENSLADE RD
LAMBOURNE RD
DIGBY RD
TRESHAM RD
Schs
BRIDGEWAY
MEADOW RD
MERTON RD
MARGARET BONDFIELD AVE
LONDON RD
THE ARCADE
1 HARVEY HO
2 GOWER HO
Ct
RIPPLE RD
EAST ST
VICARAGE DR
GREAVES CL
NORFOLK RD
SUFFOLK RD
ESSEX RD
SURREY RD
CONSTON AVE
LANCASTER AVE
JOHN BURNS DR
DAWSON AVE
TUDOR RD
STUART RD
STRATFORD CL
Liby
CLOCKHOUSE AVE
GUNNINGDALE AVE
ST ERKENWALD RD
ST ERKENWALD MEWS
ST AWDRY'S RD
CRANLEY RD
WESTBURY RD
KENDAL AVE
Schs
RIPPLE RD
EASTBURY AVE
SISLEY RD
BLAKE AVE
Barking Sch
TH
AXE ST
A124
BROADWAY
St Joseph RC Prim
Brook
Boa Lak

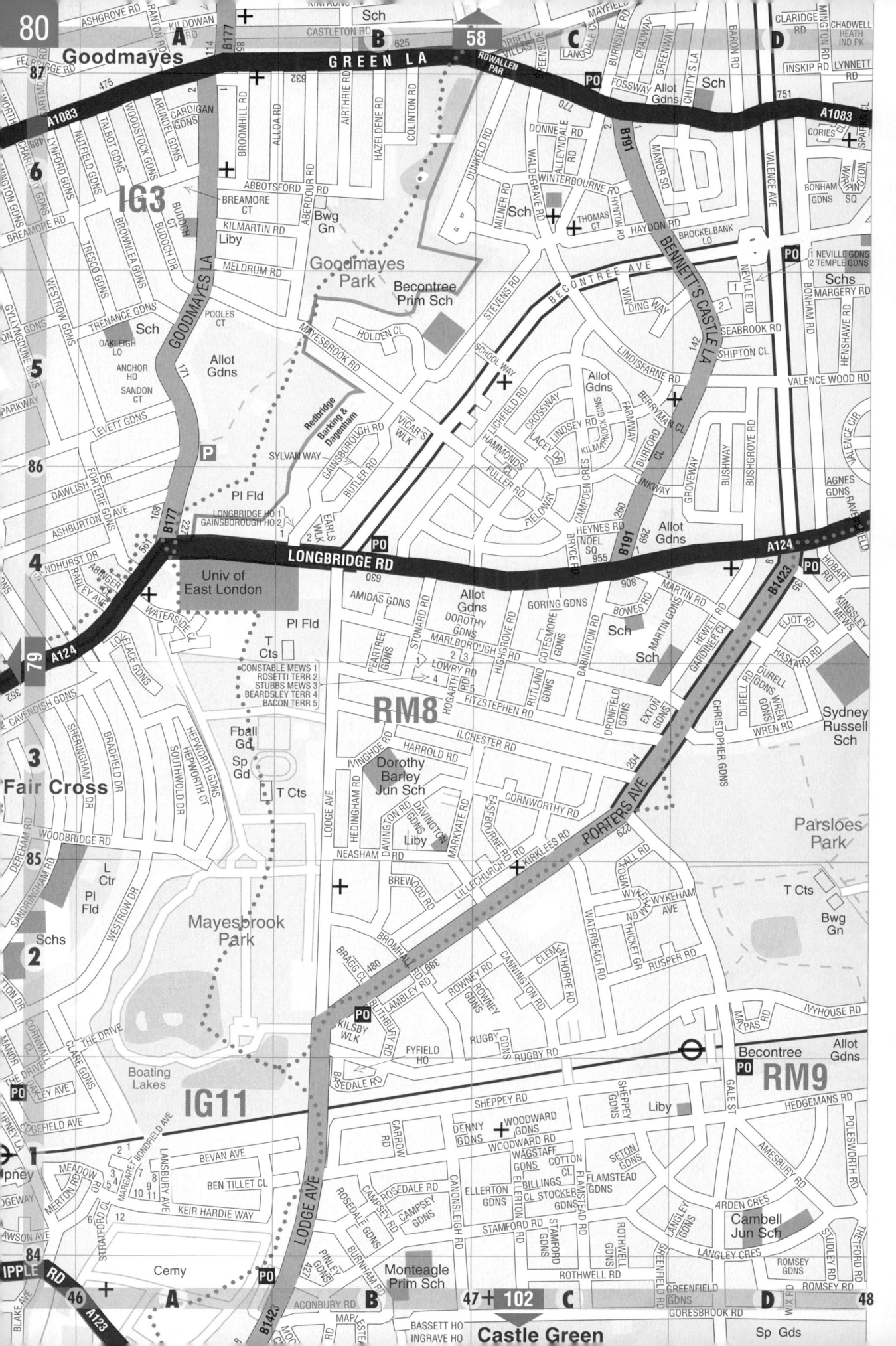
Goodmayes
GREEN LA
A1083
ASHGROVE RD
KILDOWAN RD
CASTLETON RD
Sch
58
A
B
C
D
ROWALLEN PAR
MAYFIELD
BURNSIDE RD
CHADWAY
GREENWAY
BARON RD
CLARIDGE RD
CHADWELL HEATH IND PK
LYNNETT RD
INSKIP RD
FELBRIGGE RD
CARTMORE RD
CARDIGAN GDNS
ARUNDEL GDNS
WOODSTOCK GDNS
TALBOT GDNS
NUTFIELD GDNS
LYNFORD GDNS
BROOMHILL RD
ALLOA RD
AIRTHRIE RD
HAZELDENE RD
COLINTON RD
FOSSWAY
Allot Gdns
CHITTY'S LA
DONNE RD
ALLEYNDALE RD
WALDEGRAVE RD
DUNKELD RD
MANOR SQ
VALENCE AVE
CORIES CL
SPARKS CL
WARRINGTON SQ
BONHAM GDNS
IG3
ABBOTSFORD RD
ABERDOUR RD
BREAMORE CT
BUDOCH CT
BUDOCH DR
BREAMORE RD
KILMARTIN RD
Liby
Bwg Gn
WINTERBOURNE RD
MILNER RD
THOMAS CT
HYNTON RD
HAYDON RD
BROCKELBANK LO
B191
BENNETT'S CASTLE LA
NEVILLE RD
1 NEVILLE GDNS
2 TEMPLE GDNS
Schs
MARGERY RD
BONHAM RD
HENSHAWE RD
TRESCO GDNS
BROWNLEA GDNS
WESTROW GDNS
MELDRUM RD
Goodmayes Park
Becontree Prim Sch
BECONTREE AVE
WINDING WAY
STEVENS RD
TRENANCE GDNS
POOLES CT
OAKLEIGH LO
ANCHOR HO
SANDON CT
GOODMAYES LA
Allot Gdns
MAYESBROOK RD
HOLDEN CL
SCHOOL WAY
SEABROOK RD
SHIPTON CL
LINDISFARNE RD
VALENCE WOOD RD
PARKWAY
LEVETT GDNS
Redbridge
Barking & Dagenham
VICAR'S WLK
GAINSBOROUGH RD
LICHFIELD RD
CROSSWAY
LINDSEY RD
LACEY DR
KILMARNOCK GDNS
FARMWAY
BERRYMAN CL
BURFORD CL
GROVEWAY
BUSHWAY
BUSHGROVE RD
VALENCE CIR
P
SYLVAN WAY
BUTLER RD
HAMMONDS CL
FULLER RD
CAMPDEN CRES
LINKWAY
AGNES GDNS
RAVENSFIELD
DAWLISH DR
FORTERIE GDNS
ASHBURTON AVE
Pl Fld
LONGBRIDGE HO 1
GAINSBOROUGH HO 2
EARLS WLK
FIELDWAY
HEYNES RD
NOEL SQ
BRYCE RD
Allot Gdns
B177
SANDHURST DR
ABINGER CL
RADLEY AVE
LONGBRIDGE RD
A124
PO
HOBART RD
B1423
Univ of East London
WATERSIDE CL
Pl Fld
AMIDAS GDNS
STONARD RD
Allot Gdns
DOROTHY GDNS
GORING GDNS
BOWES RD
MARTIN RD
MARTIN GDNS
HEWETT RD
KINGSLEY MEWS
ELIOT RD
HASKARD RD
79
LOVELACE GDNS
T Cts
CONSTABLE MEWS 1
ROSETTI TERR 2
STUBBS MEWS 3
BEARDSLEY TERR 4
BACON TERR 5
PEARTREE GDNS
MARLBOROUGH RD
LOWRY RD
HOGARTH RD
HIGHGROVE RD
COTESMORE GDNS
RUTLAND GDNS
BABINGTON RD
Sch
GARDINER CL
DURELL RD
DURELL GDNS
WREN GDNS
WREN RD
Sydney Russell Sch
CAVENDISH GDNS
RM8
FITZSTEPHEN RD
DRONFIELD GDNS
EXTON GDNS
CHRISTOPHER GDNS
SHERINGHAM DR
BRADFIELD DR
HEPWORTH GDNS
HEPWORTH CT
SOUTHWOLD DR
Fball Gd
Sp Gd
T Cts
IVINGHOE RD
HARROLD RD
Dorothy Barley Jun Sch
ILCHESTER RD
Fair Cross
HEDINGHAM RD
LODGE AVE
DAVINGTON RD
DAVINGTON GDNS
MARKYATE RD
EASEBOURNE RD
CORNWORTHY RD
PORTERS AVE
Parsloes Park
DEREHAM RD
WOODBRIDGE RD
NEASHAM RD
Liby
KIRKLEES RD
ROXWELL RD
SANDRINGHAM RD
L Ctr
Pl Fld
WESTROW DR
Mayesbrook Park
BREWOOD RD
LILLECHURCH RD
WYKEHAM AVE
WYKEHAM GN
T Cts
Bwg Gn
Schs
BROMHALL RD
BRAGG CL
CANNINGTON RD
CLEMENTHORPE RD
WATERBEACH RD
THICKET GR
RUSPER RD
ROWNEY RD
ROWNEY GDNS
LAMBLEY RD
BLITHBURY RD
KILSBY WLK
IVYHOUSE RD
MAYPAS RD
CORNWALL
THE DRIVE
CLARE GDNS
Boating Lakes
FYFIELD HO
RUGBY GDNS
RUGBY RD
Becontree
Allot Gdns
OAKLEY AVE
IG11
BASEDALE RD
RM9
SHEPPEY RD
SHEPPEY GDNS
Liby
HEDGEMANS RD
GALE ST
MARGARET BONDFIELD AVE
EDGEFIELD AVE
LANSBURY AVE
BEVAN AVE
DENNY GDNS
CARROW RD
WOODWARD GDNS
WOODWARD RD
WAGSTAFF GDNS
COTTON CL
SETON GDNS
POLESWORTH RD
AMESBURY RD
MEADOW RD
MERTON RD
BEN TILLET CL
ROSEDALE RD
CAMPSEY GDNS
CAMPSEY RD
CANONSLEIGH RD
ELLERTON GDNS
ELLERTON RD
BILLINGS CL
STOCKER GDNS
FLAMSTEAD RD
FLAMSTEAD GDNS
KEIR HARDIE WAY
STRATFORD CL
ROSEDALE GDNS
LODGE AVE
STAMFORD RD
STAMFORD GDNS
ROTHWELL GDNS
LANGLEY GDNS
ARDEN CRES
Cambell Jun Sch
LANGLEY CRES
THETFORD RD
STUDLEY RD
ROMSEY GDNS
ROMSEY RD
Cemy
PINLEY GDNS
BURNHAM RD
Monteagle Prim Sch
ROTHWELL RD
GREENFIELD RD
GREENFIELD GDNS
GORESBROOK RD
WIX RD
RIPPLE RD
A123
BLAKE AVE
46
ACONBURY RD
47
102
48
MAPLESTEAD
BASSETT HO
INGRAVE HO
Castle Green
Sp Gds
87
86
85
84
6
5
4
3
2
1

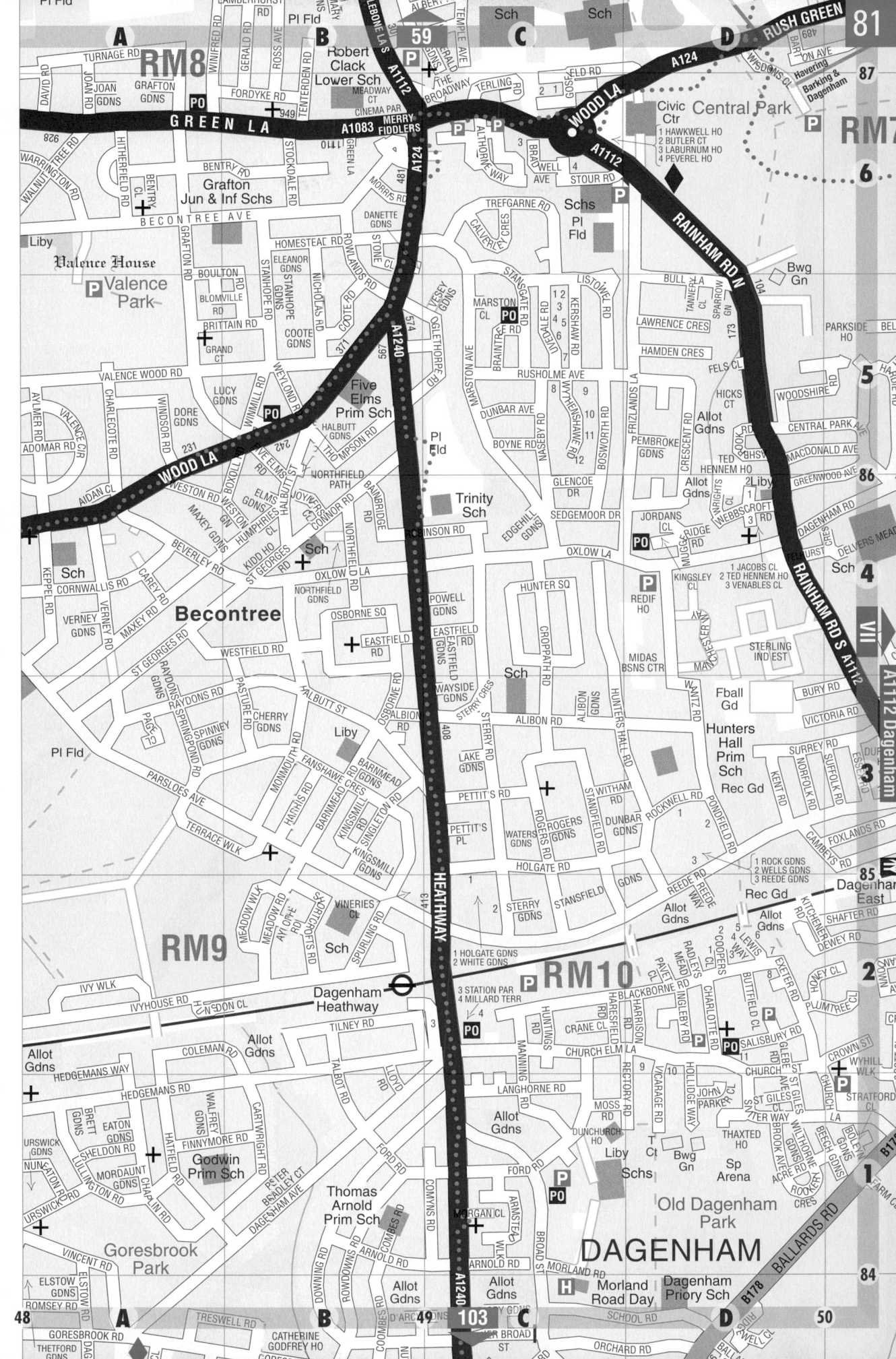
A
B
C
D
59
RUSH GREEN
RM8
TURNAGE RD
WINIFRED RD
GERALD RD
ROSS AVE
Pl Fld
Robert Clack Lower Sch
TEMPLE AVE
Sch
87
JOAN GDNS
GRAFTON GDNS
FORDYKE RD
TENTERDEN RD
MEADWAY CT
CINEMA PAR
THE BROADWAY
TERLING
WOOD LA
A124
A1112
Havering
Barking & Dagenham
Civic Ctr
Central Park
1 HAWKWELL HO
2 BUTLER CT
3 LABURNUM HO
4 PEVEREL HO
RM7
GREEN LA
A1083
MERRY FIDDLERS
949
928
WARRINGTON RD
WALNUT TREE RD
HITHERFIELD RD
BENTRY RD
BENTRY CL
STOCKDALE RD
Grafton Jun & Inf Schs
ALTHORNE WAY
BRADWELL AVE
STOUR RD
6
MORRIS RD
BECONTREE AVE
TREFGARNE RD
Schs
Pl Fld
Liby
Valence House
Valence Park
DANETTE GDNS
CALVERLEY CRES
HOMESTEAD RD
GRAFTON RD
ELEANOR GDNS
ROWLANDS RD
STONE CL
RAINHAM RD N
Bwg Gn
BOULTON RD
BLOMVILLE RD
STANHOPE RD
STANHOPE GDNS
NICHOLAS RD
VESEY GDNS
STANSGATE RD
LISTOWEL RD
BULL LA
TANNERY CL
SPARROW GN
104
BRITTAIN RD
COOTE RD
COOTE GDNS
MARSTON CL
UVEDALE RD
KERSHAW RD
LAWRENCE CRES
PARKSIDE HO
BELL
GRAND CT
A1240
OGLETHORPE RD
BRAINTREE RD
HAMDEN CRES
173
VALENCE WOOD RD
WEYLOND RD
MARSTON AVE
RUSHOLME AVE
FRIZLANDS LA
FELS CL
5
HARDIE RD
LUCY GDNS
Five Elms Prim Sch
WYTHENSHAWE RD
HICKS CT
WOODSHIRE RD
AYLMER RD
CHARLECOTE RD
WINDSOR RD
DORE GDNS
WINMILL RD
DUNBAR AVE
Allot Gdns
VALENCE CIR
HALBUTT GDNS
THOMPSON RD
Pl Fld
BOYNE RD
NASEBY RD
BOSWORTH RD
PEMBROKE GDNS
CRESCENT RD
CENTRAL PARK AVE
ADOMAR RD
231
MACDONALD AVE
FIVE ELMS RD
TED HENNEM HO
BOXOLL RD
NORTHFIELD PATH
GREENWOOD AVE
86
AIDAN CL
WESTON RD
HALBUTT ST
GLENCOE DR
Liby
WESTON GN
ELMS GDNS
JOYNERS CL
CONNOR RD
BAINBRIDGE RD
Trinity Sch
SEDGEMOOR DR
WRIGHTS CL
WEBBSCROFT RD
DAGENHAM RD
MAXEY GDNS
HUMPHRIES CL
JORDANS CL
ROBINSON RD
EDGEHILL GDNS
MUGGERIDGE RD
DELVERS MEAD
BEVERLEY RD
KIDD HO
ST GEORGES RD
Sch
NORTHFIELD RD
OXLOW LA
FELHURST CRES
4
KEPPEL RD
CAREY RD
OXLOW LA
HUNTER SQ
KINGSLEY CL
1 JACOBS CL
2 TED HENNEM HO
3 VENABLES CL
CORNWALLIS RD
NORTHFIELD GDNS
POWELL GDNS
REDIF HO
Becontree
OSBORNE SQ
VERNEY GDNS
VERNEY RD
MAXEY RD
CROPPATH RD
MANCHESTER WAY
RAINHAM RD S
VII
EASTFIELD RD
EASTFIELD GDNS
STERLING IND EST
ST GEORGES RD
WESTFIELD RD
MIDAS BSNS CTR
A1112 Dagenham
RAYDONS GDNS
RAYDONS RD
PASTURE RD
HALBUTT ST
WAYSIDE GDNS
Sch
Fball Gd
BURY RD
STERRY CRES
OSBORNE RD
ALBION RD
ALIBON GDNS
HUNTERS HALL RD
WANTZ RD
VICTORIA RD
CHERRY GDNS
Liby
ALIBON RD
408
Hunters Hall Prim Sch
SURREY RD
PAGE CL
SPINNEY GDNS
SPRINGPOND RD
Pl Fld
MONMOUTH RD
BARNMEAD GDNS
FANSHAWE CRES
LAKE GDNS
STERRY RD
Rec Gd
NORFOLK RD
SUFFOLK RD
ESSEX RD
3
KENT RD
PARSLOES AVE
HARRIS RD
BARNMEAD RD
KINGSMILL RD
SINGLETON RD
PETTIT'S RD
WITHAM RD
STANDFIELD RD
ROCKWELL RD
PONDFIELD RD
PETTIT'S PL
WATERS GDNS
ROGERS RD
ROGERS GDNS
DUNBAR GDNS
FOXLANDS RD
TERRACE WLK
KINGSMILL GDNS
CAMBEYS RD
HOLGATE RD
1 ROCK GDNS
2 WELLS GDNS
3 REEDE GDNS
85
REEDE RD
REEDE WAY
Dagenham East
STERRY GDNS
STANSFIELD RD
GDNS
Rec Gd
MEADOW WLK
MEADOW RD
AYLOFFE RD
SHORTCROFTS RD
VINERIES CL
413
Allot Gdns
KITCHENER RD
SHAFTER RD
Sch
SPURLING RD
HEATHWAY
Allot Gdns
DEWEY RD
RM9
1 HOLGATE GDNS
2 WHITE GDNS
RM10
COOPERS CL
RADLEYS MEAD
PAVET CL
LEWIS WAY
EXETER RD
2
IVY WLK
Dagenham Heathway
3 STATION PAR
4 MILLARD TERR
BLACKBORNE RD
BUTTFIELD CL
HONEY CL
IVYHOUSE RD
HUNSDON CL
HARESFIELD RD
HARRISON RD
INGLEBY RD
CHARLOTTE RD
PLUMTREE CL
TILNEY RD
HUNTINGS RD
CRANE CL
SALISBURY RD
CROWN ST
Allot Gdns
COLEMAN RD
Allot Gdns
CHURCH ELM LA
WYHILL WLK
HEDGEMANS WAY
TALBOT RD
LLOYD RD
MANNING RD
RECTORY RD
VICARAGE RD
HOLLIDGE WAY
CHURCH ST
GLEBE RD
HEDGEMANS RD
LANGHORNE RD
JOHN PARKER CL
ST GILES AVE
ST GILES CL
CHURCH LA
STRATFORD CL
BRETT GDNS
EATON GDNS
WALFREY GDNS
CARTWRIGHT RD
MOSS RD
Allot Gdns
SISLEY WAY
URSWICK GDNS
SHELDON RD
FINNYMORE RD
HATFIELD RD
Godwin Prim Sch
DUNCHURCH HO
T Ct
Bwg Gn
THAXTED HO
BROOK AVE
WILTHORNE GDNS
BEECH GDNS
BOLEYN GDNS
B178
NUNEATON RD
MORDAUNT GDNS
PETER BEADLEY CT
FORD RD
Liby
Schs
Sp Arena
1
LULLINGTON RD
CHAPLIN RD
DAGENHAM AVE
COMYNS RD
FORD RD
ACRE RD
ROOKERY CRES
FARM CL
URSWICK RD
Thomas Arnold Prim Sch
MORGAN CL
ARMSTEAD WLK
Old Dagenham Park
BALLARDS RD
Goresbrook Park
COMBES RD
DAGENHAM
VINCENT RD
DOWNING RD
ROWDOWNS RD
ARNOLD RD
ARNOLD RD
BROAD ST
MORLAND RD
ELSTOW GDNS
ELSTOW RD
Allot Gdns
Allot Gdns
Morland Road Day
Dagenham Priory Sch
84
ROMSEY RD
48
TRESWELL RD
49
103
SCHOOL RD
50
GORESBROOK RD
CATHERINE GODFREY HO
COOMBES RD
D'ARCY GDNS
BROAD ST
ORCHARD RD
THETFORD GDNS

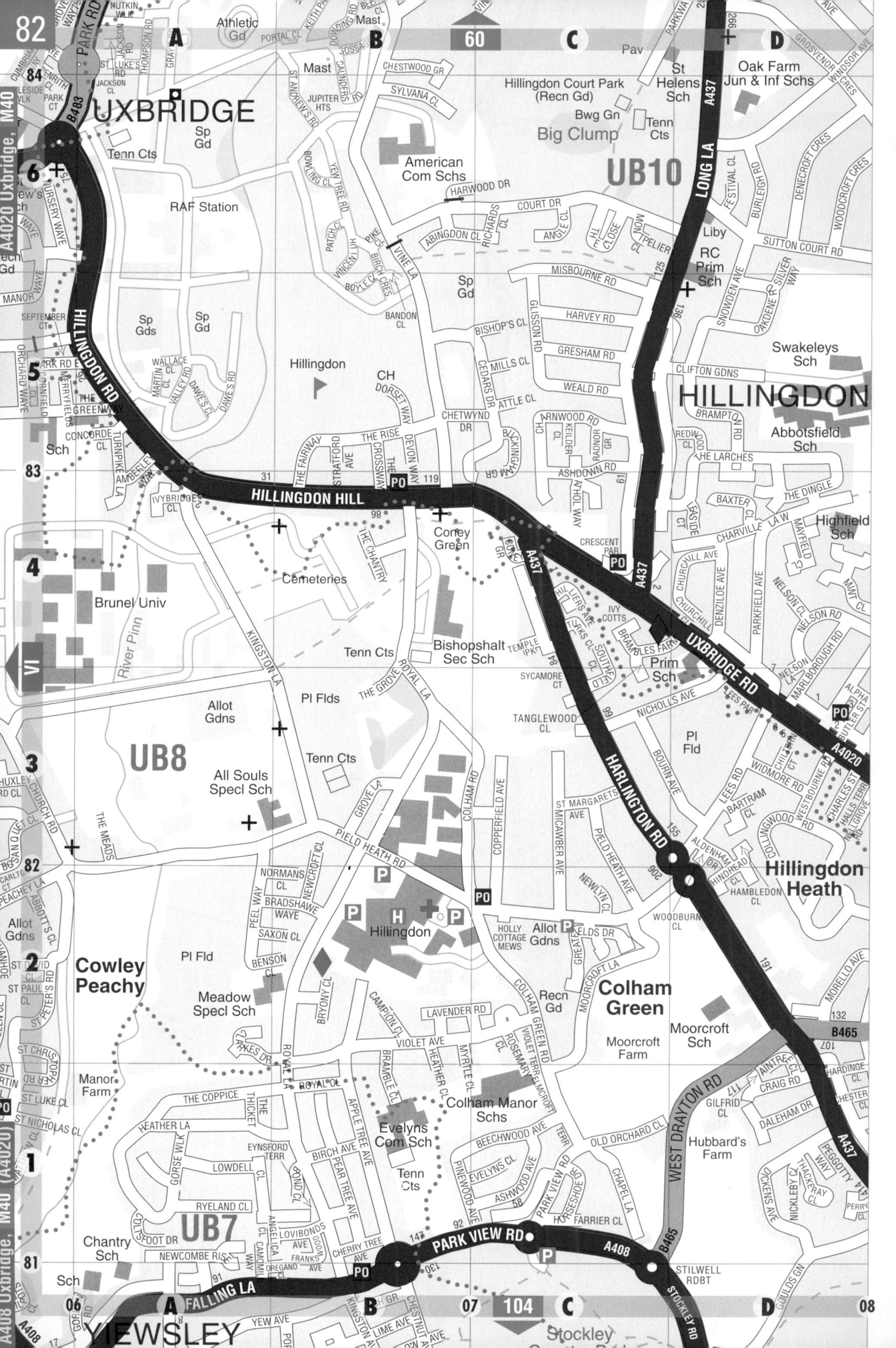
A
B
60
C
D
UXBRIDGE
HILLINGDON
Hillingdon Heath
Colham Green
Cowley Peachy
YIEWSLEY
Stockley
UB10
UB8
UB7
Hillingdon Court Park (Recn Gd)
Big Clump
RAF Station
American Com Schs
Brunel Univ
Cemeteries
Bishopshalt Sec Sch
All Souls Specl Sch
Meadow Specl Sch
Hillingdon
Colham Manor Schs
Evelyns Com Sch
Moorcroft Sch
Moorcroft Farm
Hubbard's Farm
Manor Farm
Chantry Sch
Oak Farm Jun & Inf Schs
St Helens Sch
Swakeleys Sch
Abbotsfield Sch
Highfield Sch
RC Prim Sch
Prim Sch
Coney Green
HILLINGDON HILL
HILLINGDON RD
UXBRIDGE RD
HARLINGTON RD
LONG LA
PARK VIEW RD
FALLING LA
WEST DRAYTON RD
STOCKLEY RD
PIELD HEATH RD
KINGSTON LA
ROYAL LA
COLHAM GREEN RD
A4020
A437
A408
B465
B483
STILWELL RDBT
A4020 Uxbridge, M40
A408 Uxbridge, M40 (A4020)
104
06
07
08
1
2
3
4
5
6
81
82
83
84

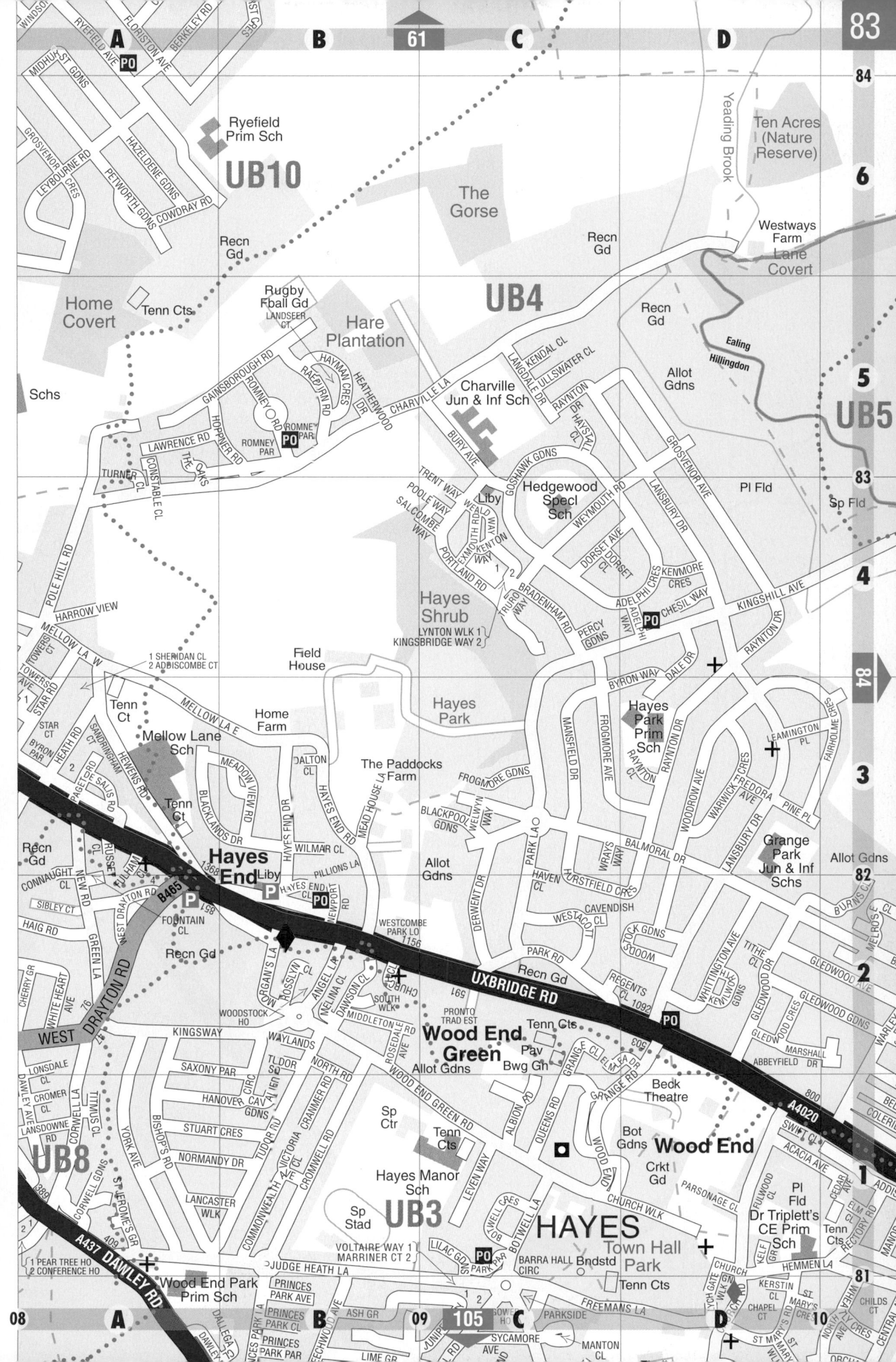
A
B
61
C
D
84
6
5
83
4
84
3
82
2
1
81
08
A
B
09
105
C
D
10
UB10
UB4
UB5
UB8
UB3
Ryefield Prim Sch
The Gorse
Ten Acres (Nature Reserve)
Yeading Brook
Westways Farm
Lane Covert
Recn Gd
Home Covert
Tenn Cts
Rugby Fball Gd
Hare Plantation
Charville Jun & Inf Sch
Ealing
Hillingdon
Allot Gdns
Schs
Hedgewood Specl Sch
Liby
Pl Fld
Sp Fld
Hayes Shrub
Field House
Hayes Park
Home Farm
Mellow Lane Sch
The Paddocks Farm
Hayes Park Prim Sch
Grange Park Jun & Inf Schs
Allot Gdns
Hayes End
UXBRIDGE RD
Wood End Green
Beck Theatre
Wood End
Bot Gdns
Crkt Gd
Sp Ctr
Hayes Manor Sch
Sp Stad
HAYES
Town Hall Park
Dr Triplett's CE Prim Sch
Wood End Park Prim Sch
WEST DRAYTON RD
A437 DAWLEY RD
A4020
B465
CHARVILLE LA
KINGSHILL AVE
MELLOW LA E
MELLOW LA W
POLE HILL RD
HARROW VIEW
KINGSWAY
JUDGE HEATH LA
CHURCH WLK
FREEMANS LA
WOOD END GREEN RD
GROSVENOR AVE
BALMORAL DR
BRADENHAM RD
RAYNTON DR
LANSBURY DR
PORTLAND RD
1 SHERIDAN CL
2 ADDISCOMBE CT
LYNTON WLK 1
KINGSBRIDGE WAY 2
VOLTAIRE WAY 1
MARRINER CT 2
1 PEAR TREE HO
2 CONFERENCE HO

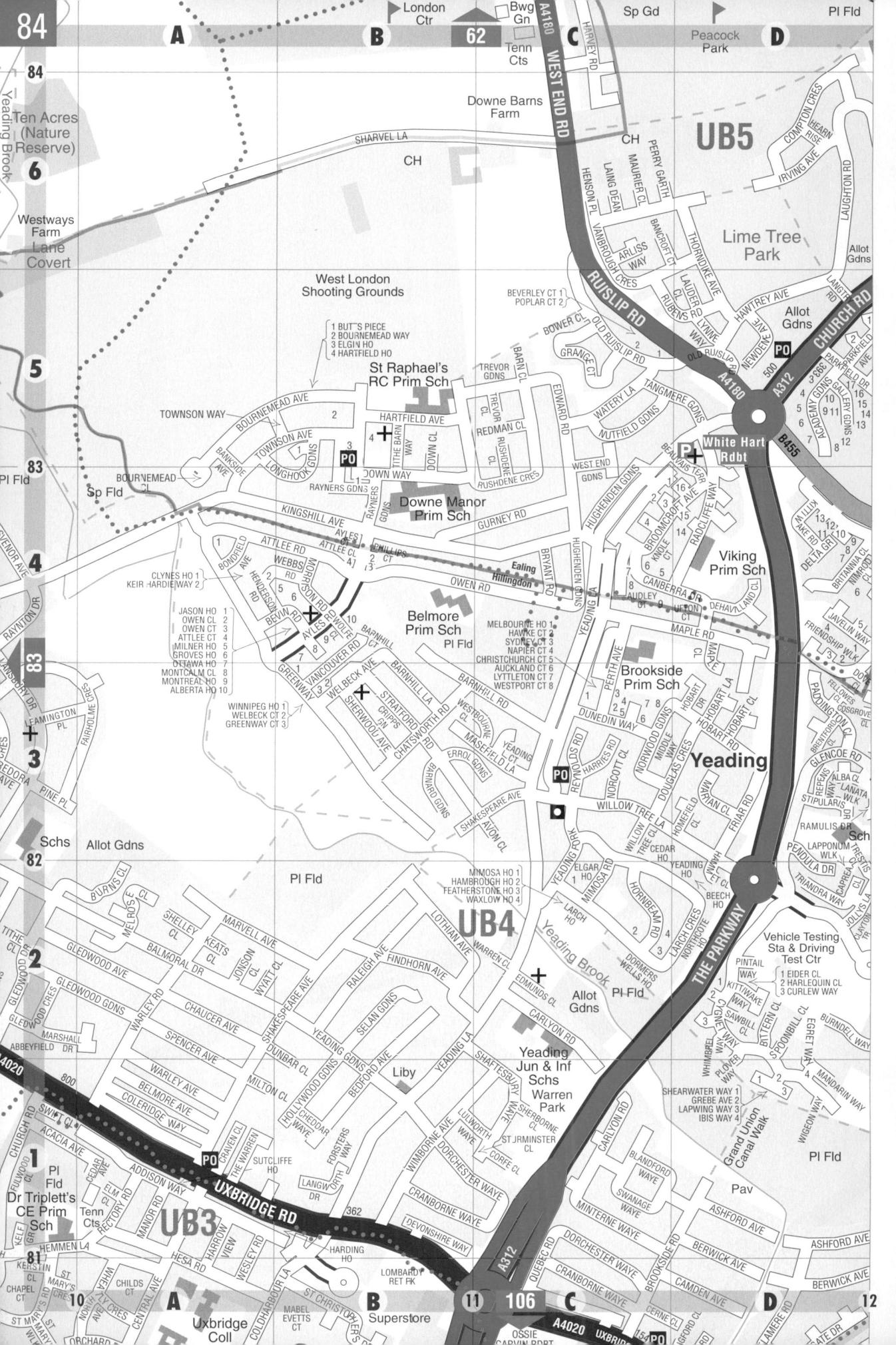
A
B
62
C
D
London Ctr
Bwg Gn
Tenn Cts
Sp Gd
Pl Fld
Peacock Park
84
Yeading Brook
Ten Acres (Nature Reserve)
6
Westways Farm
Lane Covert
WEST END RD
A4180
HARVEY RD
Downe Barns Farm
SHARVEL LA
CH
UB5
COMPTON CRES
HEARN RISE
IRVING AVE
LAUGHTON RD
PERRY GARTH
MAURIER CL
LAING DEAN
HENSON PL
VANBROUGH CRES
ARLISS WAY
BANCROFT CT
THORNDIKE AVE
LAUDER CL
RUBENS RD
LYNNE WAY
Lime Tree Park
Allot Gdns
West London Shooting Grounds
RUISLIP RD
BEVERLEY CT 1
POPLAR CT 2
HAWTREY AVE
NEWDENE AVE
CHURCH RD
A312
B455
PO
500
1 BUTTS PIECE
2 BOURNEMEAD WAY
3 ELGIN HO
4 HARTFIELD HO
5
St Raphael's RC Prim Sch
TREVOR GDNS
BARN CL
BOWER CL
GRANGE CT
OLD RUISLIP RD
WATERY LA
TANGMERE GDNS
NUTFIELD GDNS
EDWARD RD
TOWNSON WAY
BOURNEMEAD AVE
HARTFIELD AVE
TOWNSON AVE
LONGHOOK GDNS
TITHE BARN WAY
DOWN CL
REDMAN CL
RUSHDENE CL
RUSHDENE CRES
White Hart Rdbt
ACADEMY GDNS
GALLERY GDNS
PARKFIELD DR
83
Pl Fld
BOURNEMEAD CL
BANKSIDE AVE
Sp Fld
DOWN WAY
RAYNERS GDNS
RAYNERS CL
Downe Manor Prim Sch
GURNEY RD
WEST END GDNS
HUGHENDEN GDNS
BEAUVAIS TERR
BROOMCROFT AVE
RADCLIFFE WAY
KNOLE CT
Viking Prim Sch
KINGSHILL AVE
AYLES CT
ATTLEE CL
ATTLEE RD
PHILLIPS CT
BONDFIELD AVE
WEBBS RD
MORRISON RD
HENDERSON RD
BEVIN RD
AYLES RD
WOLFE CL
CLYNES HO 1
KEIR HARDIE WAY 2
4
Ealing
Hillingdon
OWEN RD
BRYANT RD
HUGHENDEN GDNS
YEADING LA
CANBERRA DR
AUDLEY CT
UFTON CT
DEHAVILLAND CL
MAPLE RD
DELTA GR
KITTIWAKE RD
BRITANNIA CL
NIMROD
JAVELIN WAY
FRIENDSHIP WLK
RAYNTON DR
JASON HO 1
OWEN CL 2
OWEN CT 3
ATTLEE CT 4
MILNER HO 5
GROVES HO 6
OTTAWA HO 7
MONTCALM CL 8
MONTREAL HO 9
ALBERTA HO 10
Belmore Prim Sch
Pl Fld
MELBOURNE HO 1
HAWKE CT 2
SYDNEY CT 3
NAPIER CT 4
CHRISTCHURCH CT 5
AUCKLAND CT 6
LYTTLETON CT 7
WESTPORT CT 8
PERTH AVE
Brookside Prim Sch
MAPLE CL
HOBART LA
HOBART CL
HOBART DR
HOBART RD
FELLOWES CL
COSGROVE CL
PADDINGTON CL
BRENTFORD CL
GLENCOE RD
83
LEAMINGTON PL
FAIRHOLME CRES
GREENWAY
VANCOUVER RD
BARNHILL CT
WELBECK AVE
BARNHILL LA
BARNHILL RD
SHERWOOD AVE
CRIPPS GN
STRATFORD RD
CHATSWORTH RD
WESTBOURNE CL
MASEFIELD LA
YEADING CT
ERROL GDNS
WINNIPEG HO 1
WELBECK CT 2
GREENWAY CT 3
DUNEDIN WAY
NORWOOD GDNS
MIDDLE WAY
DOUGLAS CRES
Yeading
REYNOLDS RD
HARRIES RD
NORCOTT CL
PO
ALBA CL
LANATA WLK
REPENS WAY
STIPULARIS DR
3
PINE PL
BARNARD GDNS
SHAKESPEARE AVE
AVON CL
WILLOW TREE LA
HOMEFIELD CL
MARIAN CL
FRIAR RD
WILLOW TREE CL
CEDAR HO
RAMULIS DR
LAPPONUM WLK
TRESTIS
Sch
PENDULA DR
CAPREA CL
TRIANDRA WAY
JOLLYS LA
Schs
Allot Gdns
82
Pl Fld
YEADING FORK
ELGAR HO
MIMOSA RD
HORNBEAM RD
LARCH CRES
NORTHCOTE HO
YEADING HO
HAMLET CL
BEECH HO
MIMOSA HO 1
HAMBROUGH HO 2
FEATHERSTONE HO 3
WAXLOW HO 4
LARCH HO
BURNS CL
MELROSE CL
SHELLEY CL
MARVELL AVE
KEATS CL
JONSON CL
WYATT CL
LOTHIAN AVE
UB4
WARREN CL
Yeading Brook
DORMERS WELLS HO
Pl Fld
THE PARKWAY
Vehicle Testing Sta & Driving Test Ctr
PINTAIL WAY
1 EIDER CL
2 HARLEQUIN CL
3 CURLEW WAY
2
TITHE CL
GLEDWOOD DR
GLEDWOOD AVE
BALMORAL DR
GLEDWOOD CRES
GLEDWOOD GDNS
WARLEY RD
CHAUCER AVE
SHAKESPEARE AVE
RALEIGH AVE
FINDHORN AVE
EDMUNDS CL
Allot Gdns
KITTIWAKE WAY
SAWBILL CL
CYGNET WAY
BITTERN CL
SPOONBILL CL
EGRET WAY
BURNDELL WAY
MARSHALL DR
ABBEYFIELD DR
SPENCER AVE
DUNBAR CL
SELAN GDNS
YEADING GDNS
CARLYON RD
Yeading Jun & Inf Schs
Warren Park
WHIMBREL WAY
PLOVER WAY
MANDARIN WAY
A4020
800
WARLEY AVE
BELMORE AVE
COLERIDGE WAY
MILTON CL
HOLLYWOOD GDNS
BEDFORD AVE
Liby
YEADING LA
SHAFTESBURY WAYE
SHERBORNE CL
SHEARWATER WAY 1
GREBE AVE 2
LAPWING WAY 3
IBIS WAY 4
Grand Union Canal Walk
WIGEON WAY
CHURCH RD
SWIFT CL
ACACIA AVE
1
Pl Fld
FULWOOD CL
CEDAR AVE
ELM CL
RECTORY RD
ADDISON WAY
PO
CRAVEN CL
THE WARREN
SUTCLIFFE HO
CHEDDAR WAYE
FORSTERS WAY
LANGWORTH DR
WIMBORNE AVE
LULWORTH WAYE
STURMINSTER CL
CORFE CL
DORCHESTER WAYE
BLANDFORD WAYE
SWANAGE WAYE
Pl Fld
Pav
Dr Triplett's CE Prim Sch
Tenn Cts
MANOR RD
UB3
UXBRIDGE RD
362
CRANBORNE WAYE
DEVONSHIRE WAY
MINTERNE WAYE
ASHFORD AVE
ASHFORD AVE
HEMMEN LA
KELF GR
81
KERSTIN CL
CHAPEL CT
ST MARY'S CRES
HESA RD
HARROW VIEW
WESLEY RD
HARDING HO
LOMBARDY RET PK
A312
QUEBEC RD
DORCHESTER WAYE
CRANBORNE WAYE
BROOKSIDE RD
BERWICK AVE
CAMDEN AVE
BERWICK AVE
10
A
WHEATLEY CRES
CHILDS CT
CENTRAL AVE
COLDHARBOUR LA
MABEL EVETTS CT
ST CHRISTOPHERS
B
Superstore
11
106
C
D
12
Uxbridge Coll
ST MARY'S RD
ORCHARD
OSSIE GARVIN RDBT
A4020
UXBRIDGE
CERNE CL
154
PO
LAMERE RD

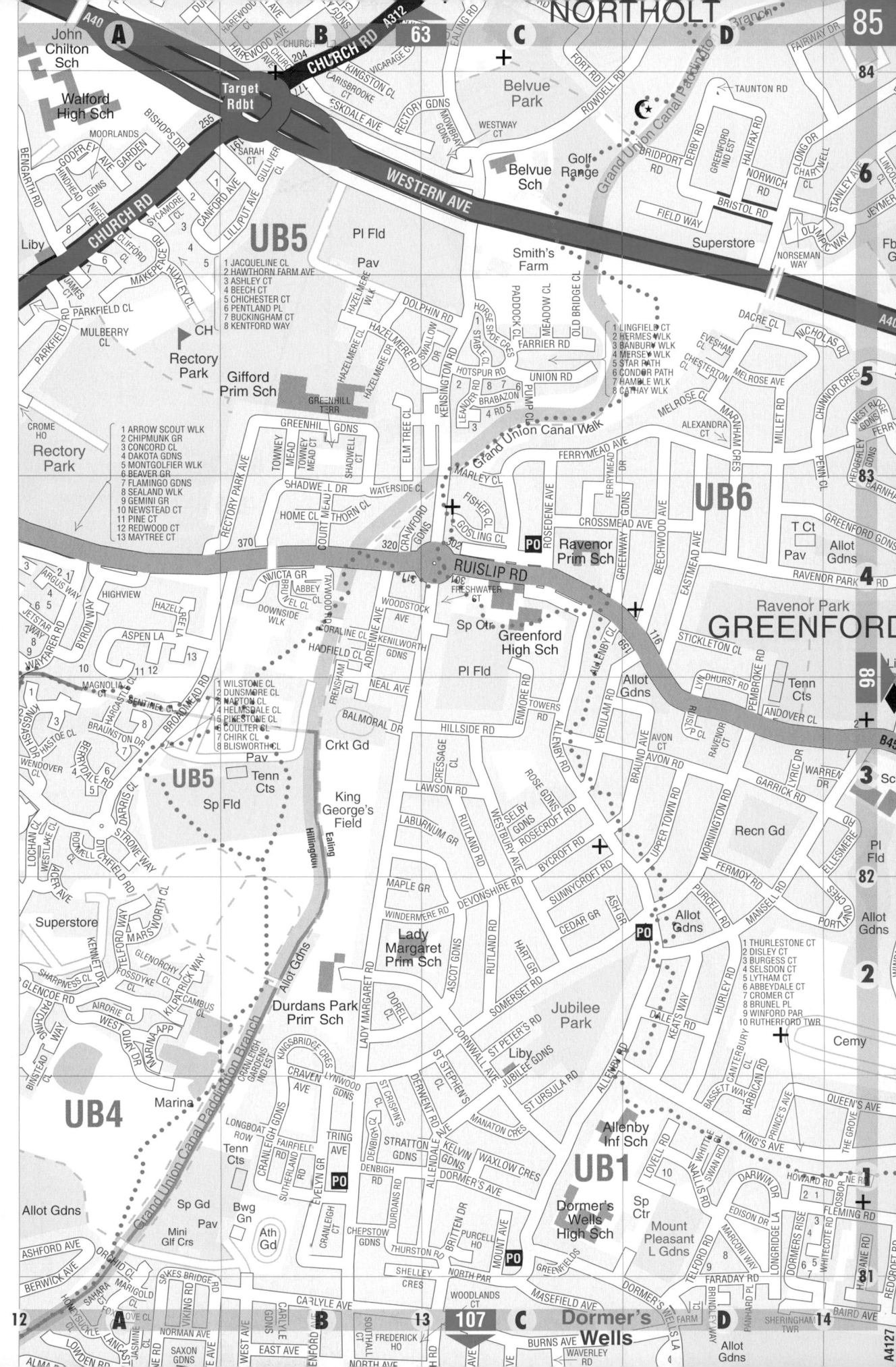
Target Rdbt
CHURCH RD
WESTERN AVE
UB5
Belvue Park
Belvue Sch
Golf Range
Grand Union Canal Paddington Branch
Walford High Sch
John Chilton Sch
Rectory Park
Gifford Prim Sch
Pl Fld
Pav
Smith's Farm
Superstore
1 JACQUELINE CL
2 HAWTHORN FARM AVE
3 ASHLEY CT
4 BEECH CT
5 CHICHESTER CT
6 PENTLAND PL
7 BUCKINGHAM CT
8 KENTFORD WAY
1 LINGFIELD CT
2 HERMES WLK
3 BANBURY WLK
4 MERSEY WLK
5 STAR PATH
6 CONDOR PATH
7 HAMBLE WLK
8 CATHAY WLK
1 ARROW SCOUT WLK
2 CHIPMUNK GR
3 CONCORD CL
4 DAKOTA GDNS
5 MONTGOLFIER WLK
6 BEAVER GR
7 FLAMINGO GDNS
8 SEALAND WLK
9 GEMINI GR
10 NEWSTEAD CT
11 PINE CT
12 REDWOOD CT
13 MAYTREE CT
Grand Union Canal Walk
RUISLIP RD
UB6
GREENFORD
Ravenor Park
Ravenor Prim Sch
Greenford High Sch
Sp Ctr
Allot Gdns
Tenn Cts
1 WILSTONE CL
2 DUNSMORE CL
3 NAPTON CL
4 HELMSDALE CL
5 PIKESTONE CL
6 COULTER CL
7 CHIRK CL
8 BLISWORTH CL
Crkt Gd
King George's Field
Sp Fld
Recn Gd
Lady Margaret Prim Sch
Jubilee Park
Durdans Park Prim Sch
1 THURLESTONE CT
2 DISLEY CT
3 BURGESS CT
4 SELSDON CT
5 LYTHAM CT
6 ABBEYDALE CT
7 CROMER CT
8 BRUNEL PL
9 WINFORD PAR
10 RUTHERFORD TWR
Cemy
UB4
Marina
UB1
Allenby Inf Sch
Dormer's Wells High Sch
Mount Pleasant L Gdns
Sp Gd
Mini Glf Crs
Dormer's Wells

A
B
C
D
64
108
85
84
83
82
81
6
5
4
3
2
1
14
15
16
Greenford
Greenford Rdbt
South Greenford
Castle Bar Park
Drayton Green
Perivale
GREENFORD
UB6
W13
W7
UB1
A40
A4127
B455
B456
WESTERN AVE
GREENFORD RD
RUISLIP RD
RUISLIP RD E
Grand Union Canal Walk
Perivale Wood
Perivale Park
Ravenor Park
Brent Valley
River Brent
Litten Nature Reserve
Oldfield Recn Gd
Oldfield Prim Sch
Selborne Prim Sch
Edward Betham Prim Sch
Coston Prim Sch
Brentside High Sch
Brentside Prim Sch
Brentside Fst Sch
Mayfield Prim Sch
Hobbayne Prim Sch
Drayton Manor High Sch
Gurnell Swimming Pool
WESTWAY CROSS SH PK
STATION APP
ALLINGTON CL
HILL RISE
ROCKWARE AVE
UNEEDA DR
BIRKBECK AVE
INGRAM WAY
DOWNING DR
COURTHOPE RD
MIDDLETON AVE
BENNETTS AVE
LYON WAY
CONWAY CRES
WOODHOUSE AVE
THAMES AVE
MEDWAY DR
HODDER DR
BARMOUTH AVE
COLWYN AVE
RHYL RD
TEES AVE
CALDER AVE
WELLAND GDNS
DARYNGTON DR
RUNNYMEDE GDNS
CAYTON RD
LEAVER GDNS
DAVID AVE
HICKS AVE
ANTHONY RD
PENIFATHER LA
WHITEOAKS LA
COSTONS LA
COSTONS AVE
WORDSWORTH AVE
SHELLEY AVE
OAKFIELD GDNS
WEDMORE RD
BETHAM RD
LOCARNO RD
CLIFTON RD
CROYDE AVE
OLDFIELD LA S
RAVENOR PARK RD
GREENFORD GDNS
BARNHAM RD
GORING WAY
FERRYMEAD GDNS
CHINNOR CRES
NICHOLAS CL
STANLEY AVE
JEYMER DR
OLYMPIC WAY
ANDOVER CL
THE BROADWAY
WARREN DR
GARRICK RD
LYRIC DR
ELLESMERE RD
OTTER RD
BINGLEY RD
STANHOPE RD
WINDMILL LA
PORTLAND CRES
QUEEN'S AVE
THE GROVE
PRINCE'S AVE
FLEMING RD
HAWTHORNE MEWS
BROOKBANK AVE
ELMBANK WAY
CUCKOO DENE
GIFFORD GDNS
BEECHMOUNT AVE
BERESFORD AVE
MAYFIELD GDNS
BRIDGE AVE
CUCKOO AVE
UPFIELD RD
GREATDOWN RD
HARP RD
COPLEY CL
BORDARS RD
WESTCOTT CRES
TEMPLEMAN RD
HIGH LA
HOBBAYNE RD
HANWAY RD
HIGHLAND AVE
STUDLAND RD
GREENFORD AVE
STEPHENSON RD
HOMEFARM RD
FRAMFIELD RD
BROWNING AVE
ELMWOOD GDNS
GROVE AVE
DRYDEN AVE
DRAYTON BRIDGE RD
COWPER RD
SHAKESPEARE RD
CUCKOO LA
CHURCH RD
PARK RD
MILL CL
STOCKDOVE WAY
WYRESDALE CRES
RIBCHESTER AVE
GURNELL GR
1 CARROWAY LA
2 DEEPWOOD LA
1 PRESTWICK CT
2 DENHAM CT
3 FULWELL CT
4 BRAMLEY CT
COLNE CT 1
DEE CT 2
HUMBER CT 3
IRWELL CT 4
TEES CT 5

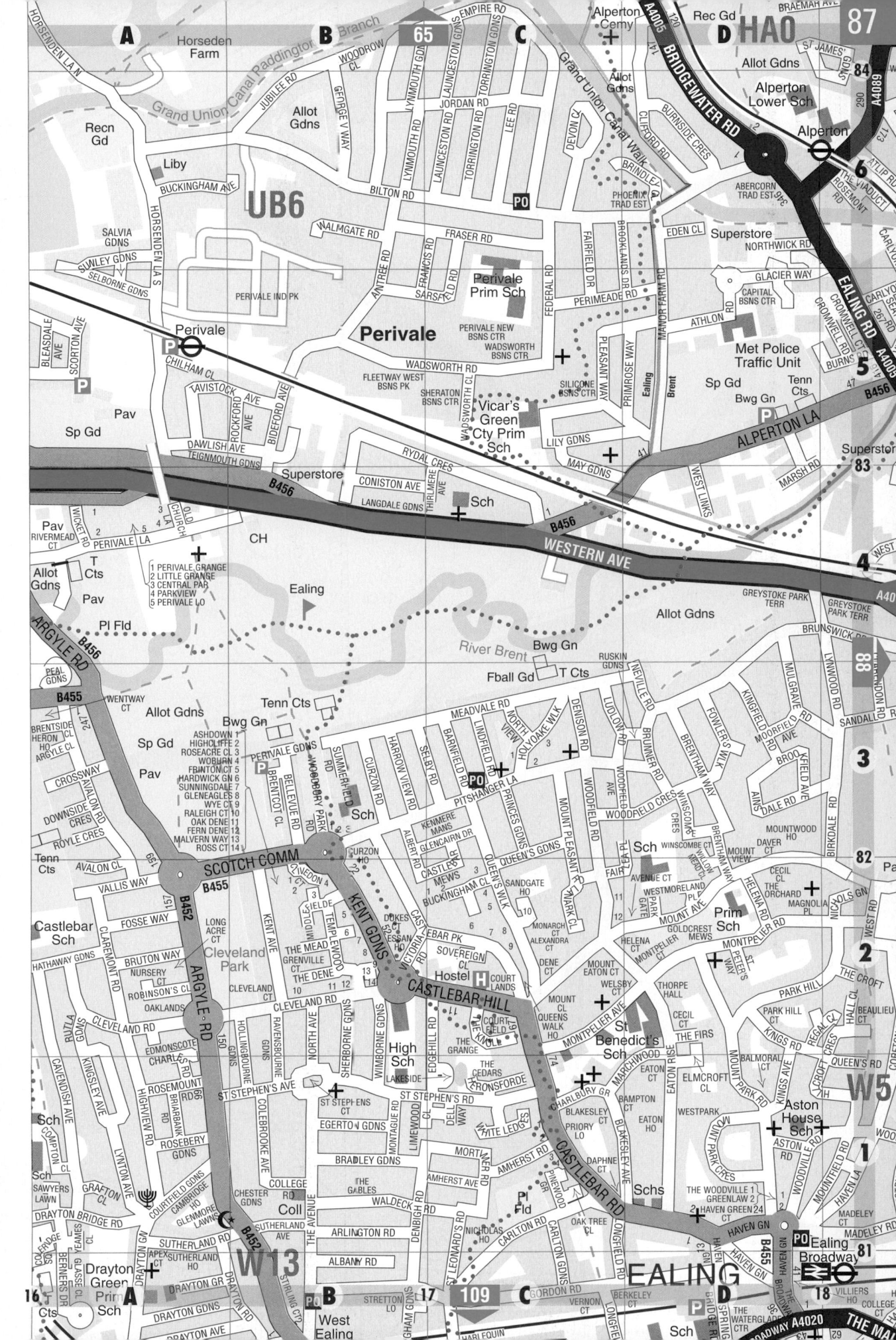

A
B
C
D
65
HA0
Horseden Farm
Grand Union Canal Paddington Branch
Recn Gd
Liby
BUCKINGHAM AVE
UB6
HORSENDEN LA N
HORSENDEN LA S
SALVIA GDNS
SUNLEY GDNS
SELBORNE GDNS
PERIVALE IND PK
JUBILEE RD
WOODROW CL
GEORGE V WAY
Allot Gdns
LYNMOUTH GDNS
LYNMOUTH RD
LAUNCESTON GDNS
LAUNCESTON RD
TORRINGTON GDNS
TORRINGTON RD
EMPIRE RD
JORDAN RD
LEE RD
BILTON RD
WALMGATE RD
FRASER RD
ANTREE RD
FRANCIS RD
SARSFELD RD
Perivale Prim Sch
Perivale
PERIVALE NEW BSNS CTR
WADSWORTH BSNS CTR
WADSWORTH RD
FLEETWAY WEST BSNS PK
SHERATON BSNS CTR
WADSWORTH CL
Vicar's Green Cty Prim Sch
FEDERAL RD
FAIRFIELD DR
PERIMEADE RD
SILICONE BSNS CTR
PLEASANT WAY
PRIMROSE WAY
LILY GDNS
MAY GDNS
Alperton Cemy
Grand Union Canal Walk
DEVON CL
Allot Gdns
CLIFFORD RD
BRINDLEY CL
PHOENIX TRAD EST
BROOKLANDS DR
MANOR FARM RD
EDEN CL
Ealing
Brent
A4005
BRIDGEWATER RD
BURNSIDE CRES
Rec Gd
BRAEMAR AVE
ST JAMES' GDNS
Allot Gdns
Alperton Lower Sch
Alperton
A4089
ABERCORN TRAD EST
ATLIP RD
THE VIADUCT
ROSEMONT RD
Superstore
NORTHWICK RD
GLACIER WAY
CAPITAL BSNS CTR
ATHLON RD
Met Police Traffic Unit
CROMWELL RD
CROMWELL CT
BURNS
EALING RD
A4005
Sp Gd
Tenn Cts
Bwg Gn
ALPERTON LA
B456
Superstore
MARSH RD
WEST LINKS
84
6
5
83
4
Perivale
BLEASDALE AVE
SCORTON AVE
CHILHAM CL
TAVISTOCK AVE
ROCKFORD AVE
BIDEFORD AVE
Pav
Sp Gd
DAWLISH AVE
TEIGNMOUTH GDNS
Superstore
RYDAL CRES
CONISTON AVE
THIRLMERE AVE
LANGDALE GDNS
Sch
B456
WESTERN AVE
A40
Pav
RIVERMEAD CT
WICKET RD
PERIVALE LA
OLD CHURCH LA
CH
T Cts
Allot Gdns
Pav
1 PERIVALE GRANGE
2 LITTLE GRANGE
3 CENTRAL PAR
4 PARKVIEW
5 PERIVALE LO
Ealing
Pl Fld
ARGYLE RD
B456
River Brent
Bwg Gn
Allot Gdns
GREYSTOKE PARK TERR
BRUNSWICK RD
RUSKIN GDNS
Fball Gd
T Cts
PEAL GDNS
B455
WENTWAY CT
Allot Gdns
Tenn Cts
Bwg Gn
Sp Gd
Pav
BRENTSIDE
HERON HO
ARGYLE CL
CROSSWAY
AVALON RD
DOWNSIDE CRES
ROYLE CRES
Tenn Cts
AVALON CL
ASHDOWN 1
HIGHCLIFFE 2
ROSEACRE CL 3
WOBURN 4
FRINTON CT 5
HARDWICK GN 6
SUNNINGDALE 7
GLENEAGLES 8
WYE CT 9
RALEIGH CT 10
OAK DENE 11
FERN DENE 12
MALVERN WAY 13
ROSS CT 14
PERIVALE GDNS
BRENTCOT CL
BELLEVUE RD
WOODBURY PARK RD
SUMMERFIELD RD
Sch
CURZON RD
HARROW VIEW RD
SELBY RD
BARNFIELD RD
LINDFIELD RD
MEADVALE RD
NORTH VIEW
HOLYOAKE WLK
DENISON RD
LUDLOW RD
NEVILLE RD
BRUNNER RD
BRENTHAM WAY
FOWLER'S WLK
KINGFIELD RD
MULGRAVE RD
LYNWOOD RD
MOORFIELD RD
AVE
BROOKFIELD AVE
AINSDALE RD
SANDALL RD
88
3
PITSHANGER LA
PRINCES GDNS
MOUNT PLEASANT RD
WOODFIELD RD
WOODFIELD AVE
WOODFIELD CRES
WINSCOMBE CRES
KENMERE MANS
GLENCAIRN DR
ALBERT RD
CASTLEBAR MEWS
QUEEN'S GDNS
QUEEN'S WLK
BUCKINGHAM CL
SANDGATE HO
Sch
FAIRLEA PL
WINSCOMBE CT
WILLOW MEAD CL
MOUNT VIEW
DAVER CT
MOUNTWOOD HO
BIRKDALE RD
82
VALLIS WAY
SCOTCH COMM
B455
CURZON HO
KENT GDNS
CLIVEDON CT
FIELDE
MIDDLEFIELDS
TEMPLEWOOD
DUKES CT
LESSAN HO
CASTLEBAR PK
AVENUE CT
WESTMORELAND PL
PARK GATE
MOUNT AVE
HELENA RD
CECIL CL
THE ORCHARD
MAGNOLIA PL
NICHOLS GN
Castlebar Sch
FOSSE WAY
LONG ACRE CT
B452
CLAREMONT RD
KENT AVE
THE MEAD
GRENVILLE CT
THE DENE
VICTORIA RD
MONARCH CT
ALEXANDRA CT
Prim Sch
GOLDCREST MEWS
MONTPELIER RD
HELENA CT
MONTPELIER CT
ST PETERS WAY
WEST RD
2
HATHAWAY GDNS
BRUTON WAY
Cleveland Park
NURSERY CT
ROBINSON'S CL
CLEVELAND CT
SOVEREIGN CL
Hostel
COURT LANDS
DENE CT
MOUNT EATON CT
WELSBY CT
THORPE HALL
THE CROFT
PARK HILL
OAKLANDS
ARGYLE RD
CLEVELAND RD
CLEVELAND RD
CASTLEBAR HILL
MOUNT CL
QUEENS WALK HO
MONTPELIER AVE
St Benedict's Sch
CECIL CT
THE FIRS
PARK HILL CT
KINGS RD
REGAL CL
HALL CL
BEAULIEU CT
RUTLAND GDNS
EDMONSCOTE
CHARLES RD
HOLLINGBOURNE GDNS
RAVENSBOURNE GDNS
NORTH AVE
SHERBORNE GDNS
WIMBORNE GDNS
High Sch
EDGEHILL RD
COURT FIELD
THE KNOLL
THE GRANGE
THE CEDARS
HERONSFORDE
MARCHWOOD
EATON CT
EATON RISE
ELMCROFT CL
BALMORAL CT
MOUNT PARK RD
QUEEN'S RD
CROFT CRES
W5
CAVENDISH AVE
KINGSLEY AVE
HIGHVIEW RD
ROSEMOUNT RD
BRIARBANK RD
ST STEPHEN'S AVE
COLEBROOKE AVE
LAKESIDE
ST STEPHENS CT
ST STEPHEN'S RD
CHARLBURY GR
BAMPTON CT
EATON HO
WESTPARK
Aston House Sch
ASTON RD
WOODVILLE RD
Sch
COMPTON CL
ROSEBERY GDNS
LYNTON AVE
EGERTON GDNS
MONTAGUE RD
LIMEWOOD CL
DELL WAY
WHITE LEDGES
BLAKESLEY CT
PRIORY LO
BLAKESLEY AVE
MOUNT PARK CRES
1
Sch
SAWYERS LAWN
GRAFTON CL
COURTFIELD GDNS
CAMBRIDGE GDNS
BRADLEY GDNS
MORTIMER RD
AMHERST RD
CASTLEBAR RD
DAPHNE CT
MOUNTFIELD RD
HAVEN LA
DRAYTON BRIDGE RD
GLENMORE LAWNS
CHESTER GDNS
COLLEGE RD
THE GABLES
AMHERST AVE
PINEWOOD GR
Pl Fld
Schs
THE WOODVILLE 1
GREENLAW 2
HAVEN GREEN CT
MADELEY CT
MADELEY RD
Coll
WALDECK RD
DENBIGH RD
THE AVENUE
NICHOLAS HO
CARLTON RD
OAK TREE CL
LONGFIELD RD
HAVEN GN
B455
COLERIDGE
YEAMES CL
BERNERS DR
GLASSE CL
DRAYTON GN
SUTHERLAND RD
SUTHERLAND AVE
APEX CT
SUTHERLAND HO
ARLINGTON RD
ALBANY RD
ST LEONARD'S RD
CARLTON GDNS
Ealing Broadway
81
Drayton Green Prim Sch
W13
B452
DRAYTON GR
DRAYTON GDNS
DRAYTON RD
STIRLING CT
West Ealing
EALING
STRETTON LO
GORDON RD
VERNON CT
BERKELEY CT
Sch
BRIDGE RD
SPRING BRIDGE RD
THE WATERGLADES
THE BROADWAY
A4020
VILLIERS HO
COLLEGE CT
THE MALL
16
17
109
18

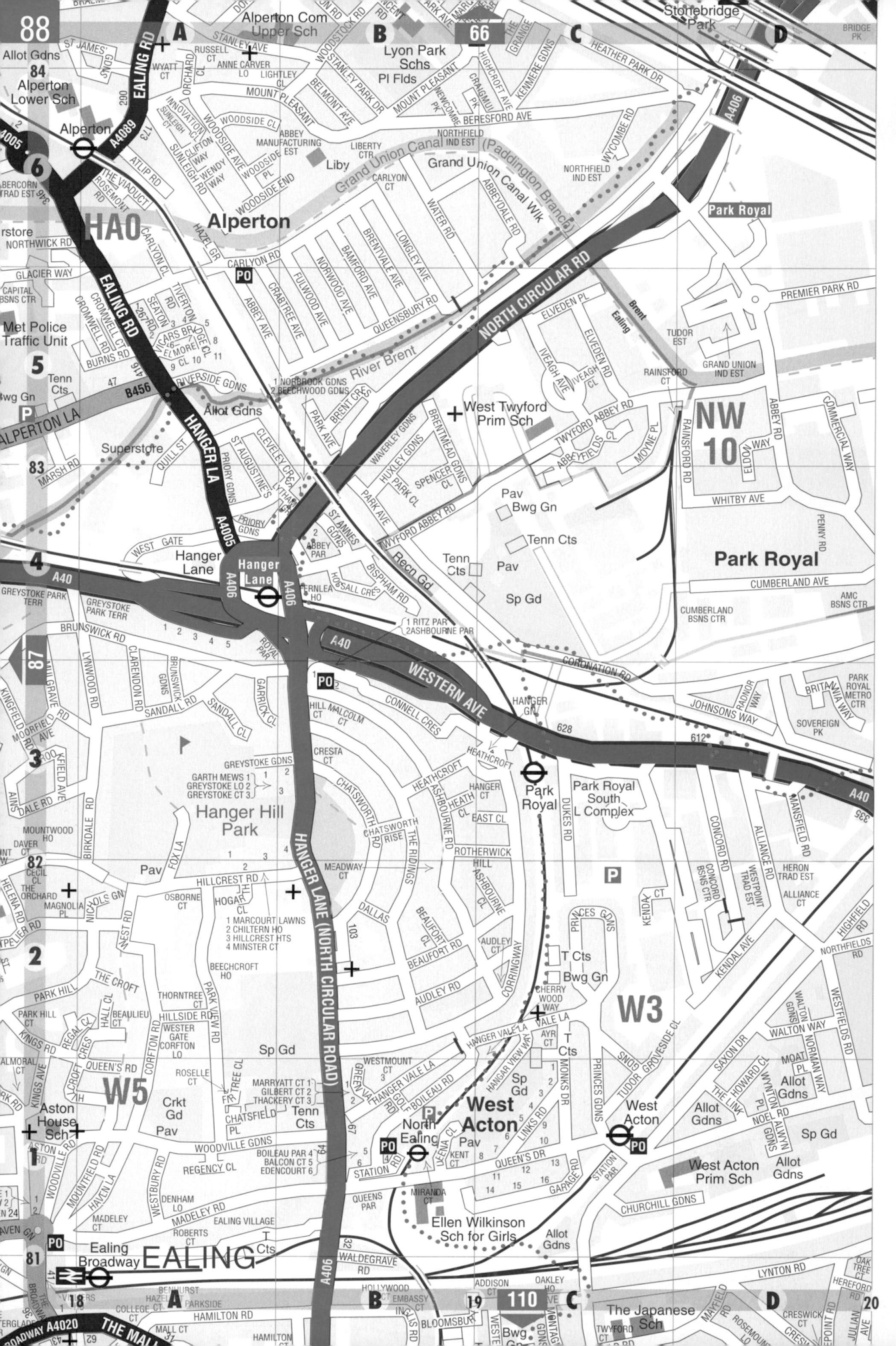

88
A
B
C
D
66
110
87
Alperton Com Upper Sch
Stonebridge Park
Lyon Park Schs Pl Flds
Allot Gdns
Alperton Lower Sch
Alperton
EALING RD
A4089
A4005
STANLEY AVE
ANNE CARVER LO
RUSSELL CT
WYATT CT
MOUNT PLEASANT
WOODSTOCK RD
HEATHER PARK DR
BERESFORD AVE
NORTHFIELD IND EST
ABBEY MANUFACTURING EST
LIBERTY CTR
Liby
Grand Union Canal (Paddington Branch)
Grand Union Canal Wlk
CARLYON CT
ALPERTON
HA0
Park Royal
WYCOMBE RD
NORTHWICK RD
GLACIER WAY
CAPITAL BSNS CTR
Met Police Traffic Unit
CARLYON RD
PO
ABBEY AVE
CRABTREE AVE
FULWOOD AVE
NORWOOD AVE
BAMFORD AVE
BRENTVALE AVE
LONGLEY AVE
WATER RD
ABBEYDALE RD
QUEENSBURY RD
NORTH CIRCULAR RD
ELVEDEN PL
ELVEDEN RD
IVEAGH AVE
IVEAGH CL
PREMIER PARK RD
TUDOR EST
GRAND UNION IND EST
RAINSFORD CT
River Brent
Tenn Cts
Bwg Gn
B456
ALPERTON LA
RIVERSIDE GDNS
Allot Gdns
West Twyford Prim Sch
TWYFORD ABBEY RD
NW 10
ABBEYFIELDS CL
MOYNE PL
RAINSFORD RD
ELDON WAY
ABBEY RD
COMMERCIAL WAY
Superstore
HANGER LA
MARSH RD
WHITBY AVE
Pav
Bwg Gn
PENNY RD
Tenn Cts
Park Royal
WEST GATE
Hanger Lane
Hanger Lane
A406
A40
Recn Gd
Sp Gd
CUMBERLAND AVE
AMC BSNS CTR
CUMBERLAND BSNS CTR
GREYSTOKE PARK TERR
BRUNSWICK RD
CORONATION RD
WESTERN AVE
HANGER GN
JOHNSONS WAY
PARK ROYAL METRO CTR
SOVEREIGN PK
CONNELL CRES
HEATHCROFT
628
612
Park Royal
Park Royal South L Complex
Hanger Hill Park
HANGER LANE (NORTH CIRCULAR ROAD)
GREYSTOKE GDNS
CHATSWORTH RD
DUKES RD
CONCORD RD
ALLIANCE RD
MANSFIELD RD
HERON TRAD EST
ALLIANCE CT
HILLCREST RD
Pav
ROTHERWICK HILL
HIGHFIELD RD
NORTHFIELDS RD
PRINCES GDNS
T Cts
Bwg Gn
W3
CORRINGWAY
AUDLEY RD
BEAUFORT RD
PARK HILL
THE CROFT
HILLSIDE RD
Sp Gd
W5
Crkt Gd
Pav
Aston House Sch
HANGER VALE LA
West Acton
North Ealing
West Acton
Sp Gd
QUEEN'S DR
Allot Gdns
West Acton Prim Sch
Sp Gd
Allot Gdns
CHURCHILL GDNS
WOODVILLE GDNS
REGENCY CL
MADELEY RD
EALING VILLAGE
Ellen Wilkinson Sch for Girls
Allot Gdns
Ealing Broadway
EALING
WALDEGRAVE RD
LYNTON RD
HAMILTON RD
The Japanese Sch
THE MALL
A4020
20

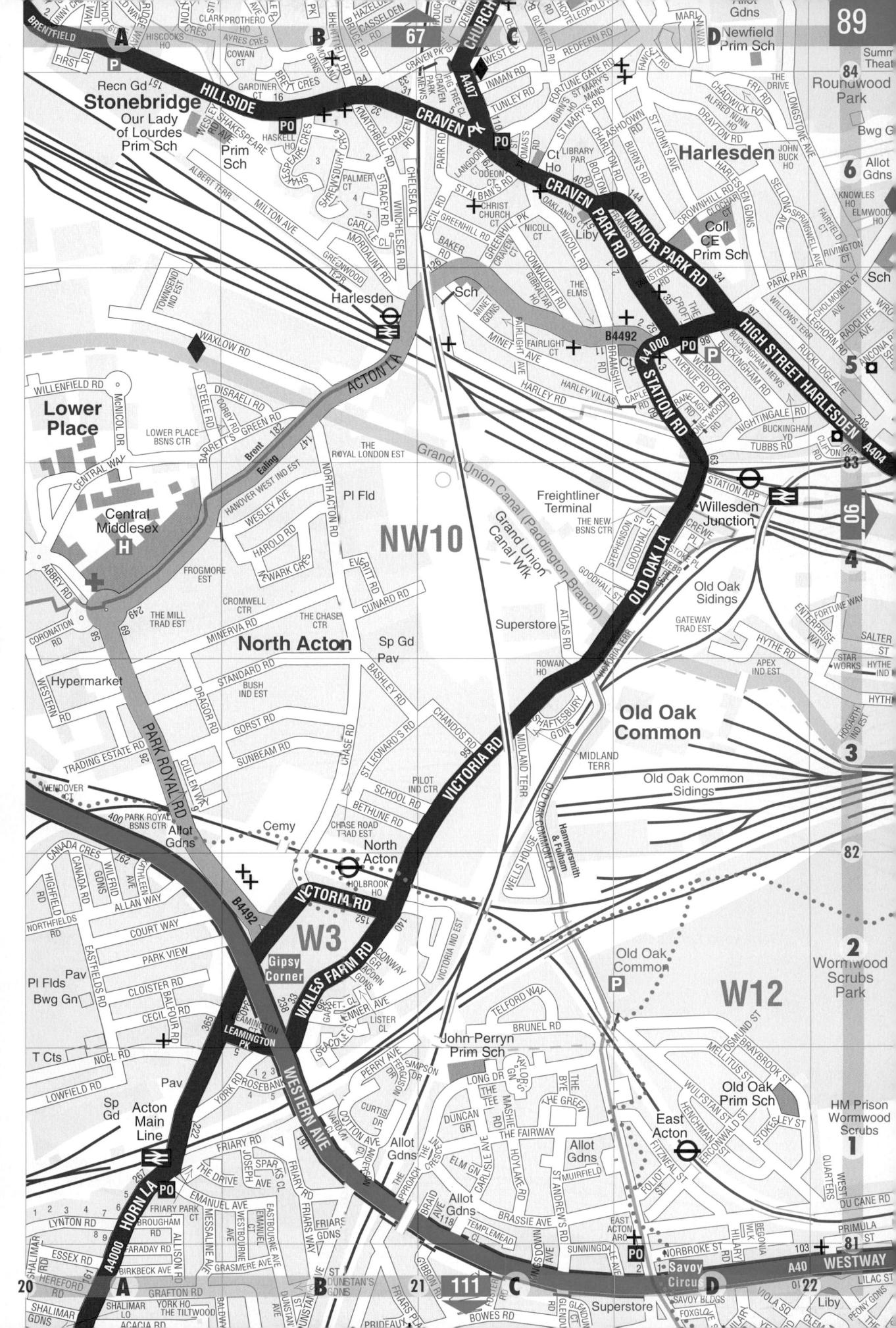

A
B
C
D
67
Stonebridge
Recn Gd
Our Lady of Lourdes Prim Sch
Shakespeare Prim Sch
HILLSIDE
CRAVEN PK
CHURCH
A407
Newfield Prim Sch
Roundwood Park
Harlesden
Bwg Gn
Allot Gdns
84
6
Coll CE Prim Sch
MANOR PARK RD
CRAVEN PARK RD
HIGH STREET HARLESDEN
A404
Harlesden
Sch
B4492
A4000
STATION RD
Liby
Ct Ho
TOWNSEND IND EST
WAXLOW RD
ACTON LA
WILLENFIELD RD
Lower Place
LOWER PLACE BSNS CTR
Brent
Ealing
THE ROYAL LONDON EST
Grand Union Canal (Paddington Branch)
Grand Union Canal Wlk
Pl Fld
NW10
Freightliner Terminal
Willesden Junction
STATION APP
83
90
5
4
Central Middlesex
H
HANOVER WEST IND EST
FROGMORE EST
CROMWELL CTR
THE MILL TRAD EST
THE CHASE CTR
North Acton
Sp Gd
Pav
Superstore
OLD OAK LA
Old Oak Sidings
GATEWAY TRAD EST
APEX IND EST
Old Oak Common
Old Oak Common Sidings
Hypermarket
BUSH IND EST
PARK ROYAL RD
PILOT IND CTR
VICTORIA RD
3
TRADING ESTATE RD
PARK ROYAL BSNS CTR
Allot Gdns
Cemy
North Acton
Hammersmith & Fulham
82
VICTORIA RD
W3
Gipsy Corner
WALES FARM RD
VICTORIA IND EST
Old Oak Common
P
W12
2
Wormwood Scrubs Park
Pl Flds
Bwg Gn
Pav
T Cts
LEAMINGTON PK
WESTERN AVE
John Perryn Prim Sch
Old Oak Prim Sch
HM Prison Wormwood Scrubs
1
Sp Gd
Acton Main Line
East Acton
Allot Gdns
PO
A4000
HORN LA
EAST ACTON ARC
Savoy Circus
A40
WESTWAY
81
Superstore
Liby
20
A
B
21
111
C
D
22

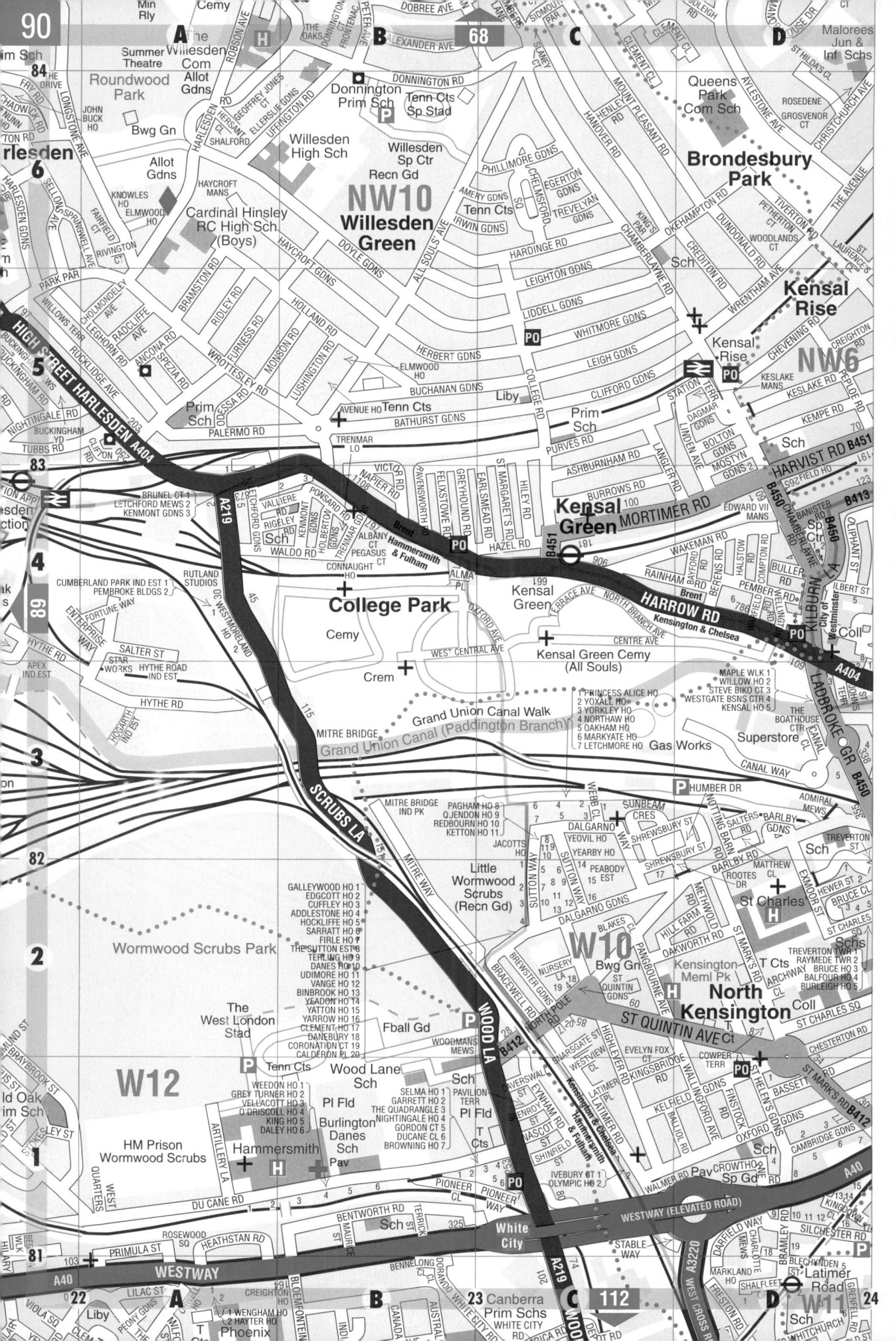

A
B
C
D
68
Min Rly
Cemy
The Willesden Com Allot Gdns
Summer Theatre
Roundwood Park
Bwg Gn
Allot Gdns
Harlesden
Donnington Prim Sch
Tenn Cts Sp Stad
Willesden High Sch
Willesden Sp Ctr Recn Gd
NW10
Willesden Green
Cardinal Hinsley RC High Sch (Boys)
Queens Park Com Sch
Brondesbury Park
Malorees Jun & Inf Schs
Kensal Rise
NW6
Tenn Cts
Sch
Prim Sch
Liby
PO
HIGH STREET HARLESDEN A404
Kensal Green
MORTIMER RD
HARROW RD
College Park
Cemy
Crem
Kensal Green
Kensal Green Cemy (All Souls)
Grand Union Canal Walk
Grand Union Canal (Paddington Branch)
MITRE BRIDGE
Gas Works
Superstore
CANAL WAY
LADBROKE GR
KILBURN LA
SCRUBS LA
A219
MITRE WAY
Little Wormwood Scrubs (Recn Gd)
Wormwood Scrubs Park
W10
North Kensington
ST QUINTIN AVE
St Charles' H
Kensington Meml Pk
The West London Stad
Fball Gd
WOOD LA
W12
HM Prison Wormwood Scrubs
Hammersmith H
Wood Lane Sch
Burlington Danes Sch
Pl Fld
DU CANE RD
WESTWAY (ELEVATED ROAD)
White City
WESTWAY
A40
A3220
Latimer Road
W11
Canberra Prim Schs
Phoenix
Liby
22
23
24
112
84
83
82
81
6
5
4
3
2
1
89

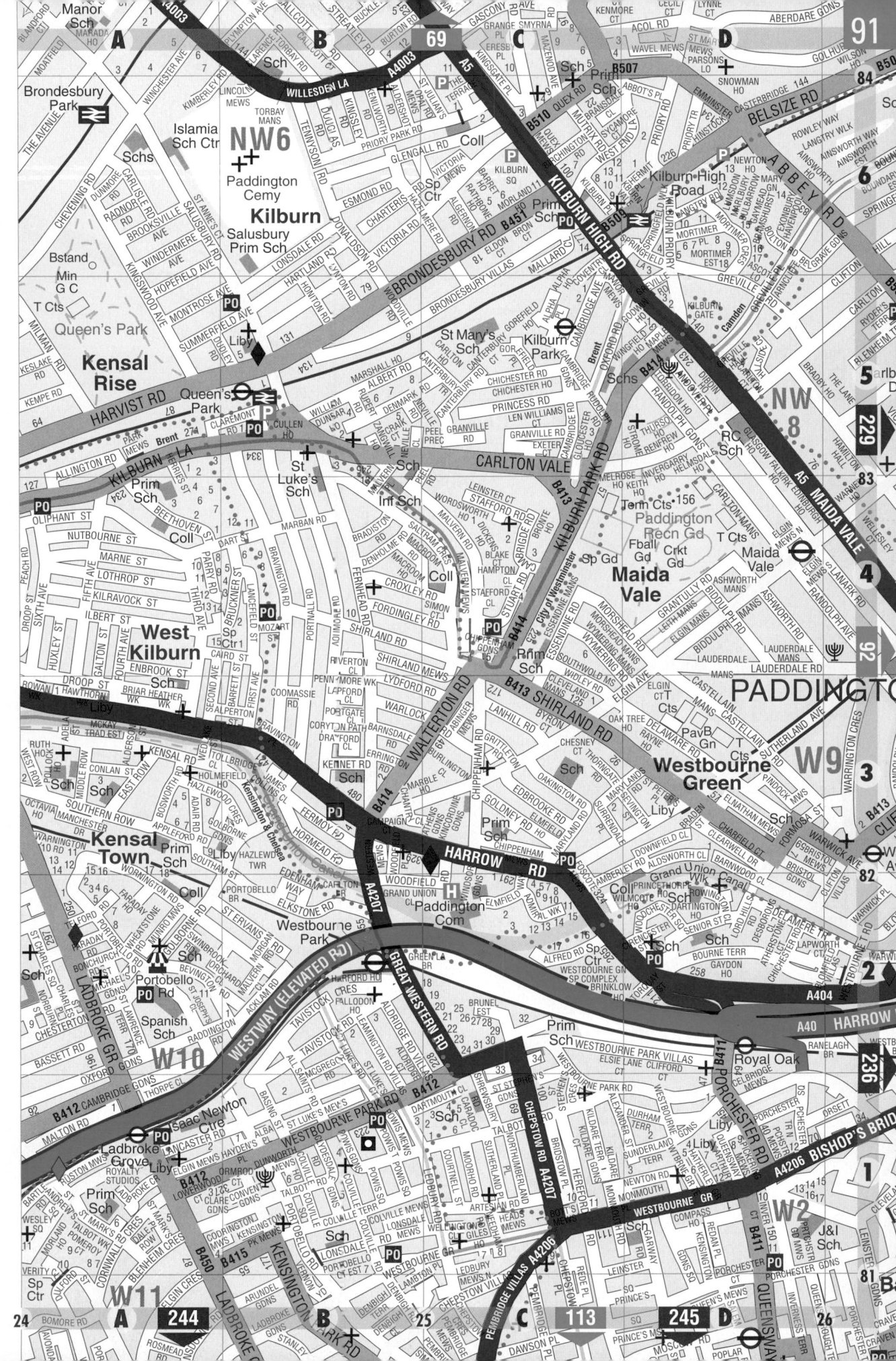

91
A
B
C
D
69
NW6
Kilburn
Brondesbury Park
Kensal Rise
Queen's Park
West Kilburn
Kensal Town
Maida Vale
Westbourne Green
PADDINGTON
NW8
W9
W10
W11
W2
KILBURN HIGH RD
MAIDA VALE
BELSIZE RD
ABBEY RD
BRONDESBURY RD
WILLESDEN LA
HARVIST RD
KILBURN LA
CARLTON VALE
KILBURN PARK RD
SHIRLAND RD
WALTERTON RD
HARROW RD
GREAT WESTERN RD
WESTWAY (ELEVATED RD)
LADBROKE GR
WESTBOURNE PARK RD
CHEPSTOW RD
PORCHESTER RD
WESTBOURNE GR
BISHOP'S BRIDGE
Grand Union Canal
Paddington Cemy
Paddington Recn Gd
Portobello Rd
Royal Oak
Ladbroke Grove
Westbourne Park
Kilburn Park
Kilburn High Road
Maida Vale
229
92
236
84
83
82
81
244
113
245
24
25
26
1
2
3
4
5
6

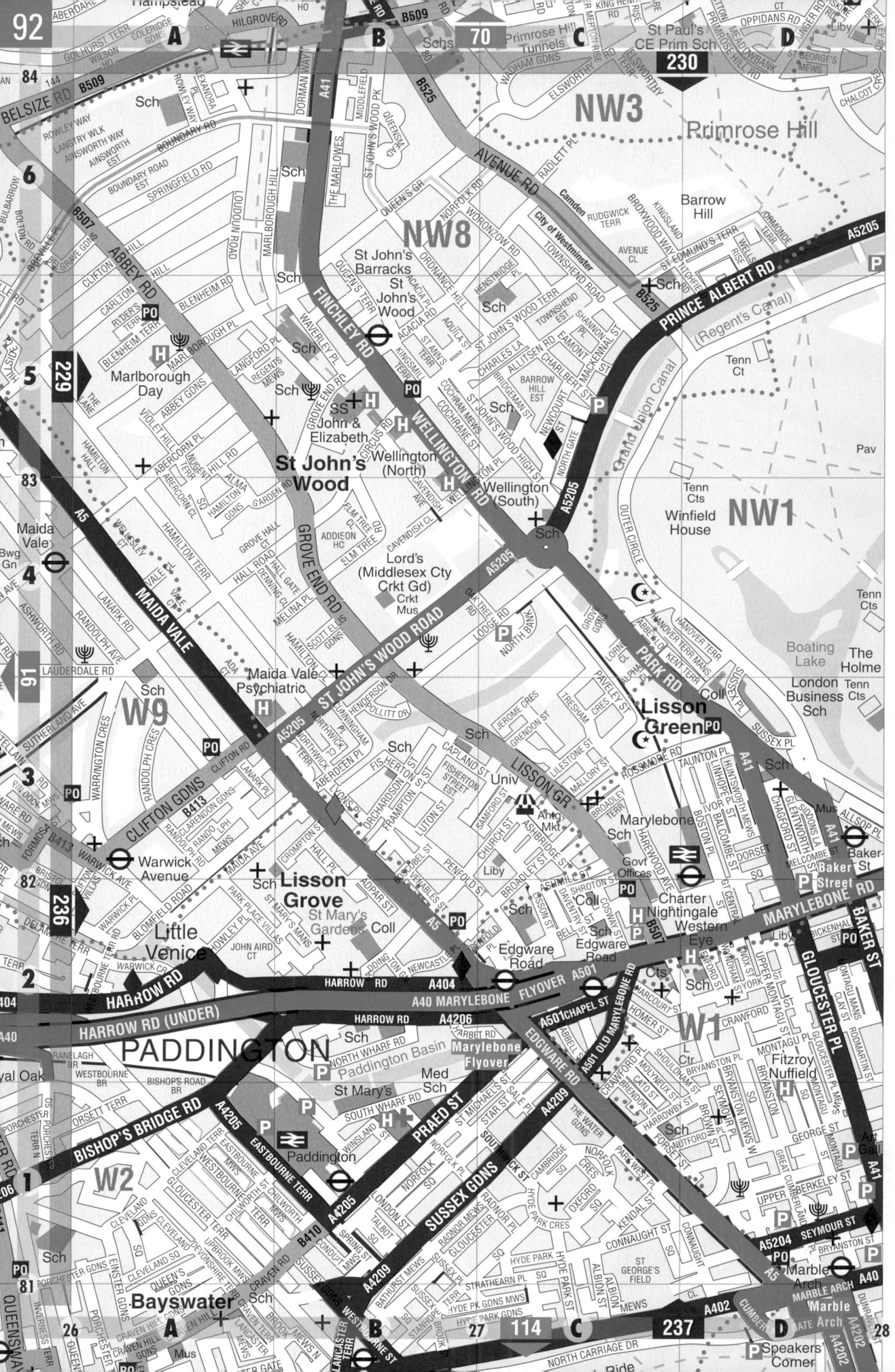

A
B
C
D
70
230
NW3
Primrose Hill
Primrose Hill Tunnels
St Paul's CE Prim Sch
BELSIZE RD
B509
HILGROVE RD
84
144
6
5
4
3
2
1
83
82
81
229
236
91
NW8
St John's Barracks
St John's Wood
FINCHLEY RD
WELLINGTON RD
AVENUE RD
PRINCE ALBERT RD
A5205
(Regent's Canal)
Grand Union Canal
Barrow Hill
Tenn Ct
Pav
NW1
Winfield House
Tenn Cts
Boating Lake
The Holme
London Business Sch
ABBEY RD
Marlborough Day
St John's Wood
SS John & Elizabeth
Wellington (North)
Wellington (South)
Lord's (Middlesex Cty Crkt Gd)
Crkt Mus
GROVE END RD
ST JOHN'S WOOD ROAD
PARK RD
Lisson Green
Maida Vale
Maida Vale Psychiatric
MAIDA VALE
W9
Warwick Avenue
CLIFTON GDNS
Lisson Grove
St Mary's Gardens
LISSON GR
Marylebone
Charter Nightingale Western Eye
MARYLEBONE RD
Baker Street
BAKER ST
Edgware Road
Little Venice
HARROW RD
A404
A40 MARYLEBONE FLYOVER
HARROW RD (UNDER)
A4206
PADDINGTON
Paddington Basin
Marylebone Flyover
St Mary's
Med Sch
W1
EDGWARE RD
GLOUCESTER PL
Fitzroy Nuffield
BISHOP'S BRIDGE RD
PRAED ST
Paddington
W2
SUSSEX GDNS
EASTBOURNE TERR
A4205
A4209
SEYMOUR ST
A5204
Marble Arch
Bayswater
26
27
28
114
237
A402
NORTH CARRIAGE DR
Speakers' Corner

93
A
B
C
D
71
231
232
Camden Town
Superstore
Camden Mkt
Britannia Junc
Prince Albert Rd
Regent's Park Rd
Gloucester Ave
Parkway
Camden High St
Camden St
Royal College St
St Pancras Way
Grand Union Canal
Regent's Canal
Freightliner Terminal
St Pancras
Pratt St
Delancey St
Albert St
Arlington Rd
Bayham St
Plender St
Crowndale Rd
Gloucester Gate Bridge
London Zoo
Mornington Crescent
Oakley Sq
Pancras Rd
Goldington St
Chalton St
St Pancras Gardens
Regents Park Barracks
NW1
Outer Circle
Broad Wlk
Albany St
Hampstead Rd
Eversholt St
Somers Town
The British Liby
Euston
Euston Road
Euston Square
Euston Underpass
Regent's Park
Refreshment Room
Cumberland Gate
Inner Circle
Open Air Theatre
Queen Mary's Gardens
New Lodge
Royal Coll of Physicians
Chester Rd
Regent's Coll
Royal Acad of Music
Pav
Tenn Cts
York Bridge
Great Portland Street
Warren Street
Park Cres
London Clinic
University Coll London
Gower St
Tottenham Court Rd
Bloomsbury
WC1
Russell Square Garden
Tavistock Sq
Gordon Sq
Woburn Pl
British Mus
Fitzrovia
BT Twr
Portland Pl
Great Portland St
Mortimer St
Goodge Street
Devonshire St
Weymouth St
New Cavendish St
Marylebone High St
Baker St
Wigmore St
Cavendish Square
Oxford St
Oxford Cir
Oxford Circus
Bond Street
MARYLEBONE
W1
Regent St
Soho
Berwick St
Charing Cross Rd
Tottenham Court Road
New Oxford St
St Giles High St
Shaftesbury Ave
Leicester Square
Carnaby St
Portman Sq
Grosvenor Sq
28
238
115
239
29
30
1
2
3
4
5
6
94

94
A
B
C
D
233
72
234
240
116
241
84
83
82
81
93
30
31
32
6
5
4
3
2
1
Freightliner Terminal
Drv Rng
Depot
MALDEN LANE BRIDGE
Grand Union Canal
(Regent's Canal)
King's Cross
NW1
King's Cross
St Pancras
Somers Town
The British Liby
YORK WAY
CALEDONIAN RD
COPENHAGEN ST
Blessed Sacrament RC Prim Sch
N1
Barnard Park
LIVERPOOL RD
Bsns Design Ctr
UPPER ST
ESSEX RD
ISLINGTON
Chapel Mkt
Angel
Pentonville
PENTONVILLE RD
King's Cross (Thameslink)
Kingsway Coll
FINSBURY
GOSWELL RD
EC1
The City Univ
ROSEBERY AVE
KING'S CROSS RD
St Pancras
EUSTON ROAD
WC1
Eastman Dental
Coram's Fields
GUILFORD ST
GRAY'S INN RD
FARRINGDON RD
CLERKENWELL RD
Clerkenwell
ST JOHN ST
Russell Square
Russell Square Garden
Bloomsbury
University Coll London
THEOBALD'S RD
Gray's Inn
Leather Lane Mkt
Farringdon
Smithfield Mkt
SOUTHAMPTON ROW
British Mus
HOLBORN
Holborn
HIGH HOLBORN
Chancery Lane
HOLBORN VIADUCT
NEW OXFORD ST
St Giles
Lincoln's Inn Fields
WC2
KINGSWAY
CHANCERY LA
Public Record Office
Royal Courts of Justice
EC4
NEWGATE
St Barts
City Thameslink
LUDGATE HILL
FLEET ST
ALDWYCH
Strand
Covent Garden
LONG ACRE
CHARING CROSS
Leicester Square
Old Covent Garden
Somerset House
Inner Temple Garden
VICTORIA EMBANKMENT

95
A
B
C
D
73
235
Essex Road
SHOREDITCH
Hoxton
Haggerston
Haggerston Park
Shoreditch Park
St Luke's
EC1
EC2
EC3
EC4
N1
E1
E2
E8
Spitalfields
Broadgate
Barbican
Barbican Arts & Con Ctr
Moorgate
Liverpool Street
Whitechapel
Aldgate
Aldgate East
Brick Lane Shoreditch
Petticoat Lane
Lloyds Bldg
Nat West Twr
Mansion House
Cannon Street
Fenchurch Street
Tower Gateway
Tower Hill
Bank
St Paul's
St Paul's Cath
Guildhall
City Road Basin
Grand Union Canal
Regent's Canal
Kingsland Basin
Old Street
NEW NORTH RD
KINGSLAND RD
HACKNEY RD
CITY RD
OLD ST
EAST RD
PITFIELD ST
SHOREDITCH HIGH ST
GREAT EASTERN ST
BISHOPSGATE
COMMERCIAL ST
LONDON WALL
ALDERSGATE ST
BUNHILL ROW
CHISWELL ST
BETHNAL GREEN RD
QUEENSBRIDGE RD
COLUMBIA RD
BRICK LA
MINORIES
GRACECHURCH ST
UPPER THAMES ST
242
117
243
96
84
83
82
81
6
5
4
3
2
1
32
33
34

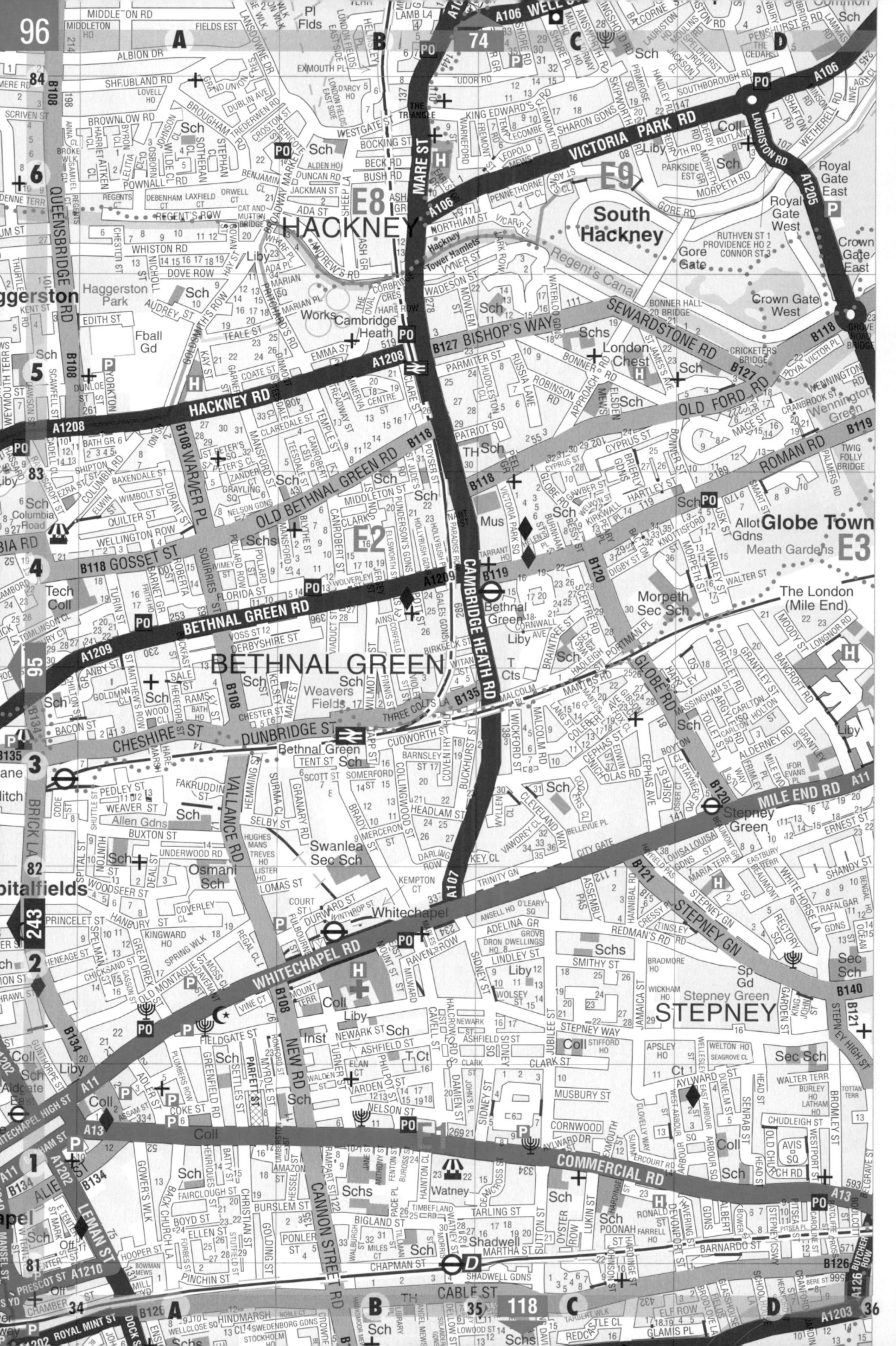

74
A
B
C
D
1
2
3
4
5
6
HACKNEY
E8
E9
South Hackney
Regent's Canal
Haggerston Park
Haggerston
Cambridge Heath
BETHNAL GREEN
E2
Bethnal Green
Weavers Fields
Globe Town
E3
Meath Gardens
The London (Mile End)
Morpeth Sec Sch
Stepney Green
STEPNEY
E1
Whitechapel
Spitalfields
Aldgate East
Shadwell
Watney
Swanlea Sec Sch
Osmani Sch
Allen Gdns
Royal Gate East
Royal Gate West
Crown Gate East
Crown Gate West
Gore Gate
London Chest
Columbia Road
Tech Coll
VICTORIA PARK RD
MARE ST
HACKNEY RD
BISHOP'S WAY
SEWARDSTONE RD
OLD FORD RD
ROMAN RD
OLD BETHNAL GREEN RD
BETHNAL GREEN RD
CAMBRIDGE HEATH RD
GOSSET ST
CHESHIRE ST
DUNBRIDGE ST
VALLANCE RD
BRICK LA
QUEENSBRIDGE RD
WARNER PL
GLOBE RD
MILE END RD
WHITECHAPEL RD
COMMERCIAL RD
NEW RD
CANNON STREET RD
CABLE ST
LEMAN ST
STEPNEY WAY
STEPNEY GN
STEPNEY HIGH ST
WHITECHAPEL HIGH ST
ROYAL MINT ST
A106
A107
A1205
A1208
A1209
A11
A13
A1202
A1210
A1203
A126
B108
B118
B119
B120
B121
B126
B127
B134
B135
B140
95
243
118
84
83
82
81
34
35
36

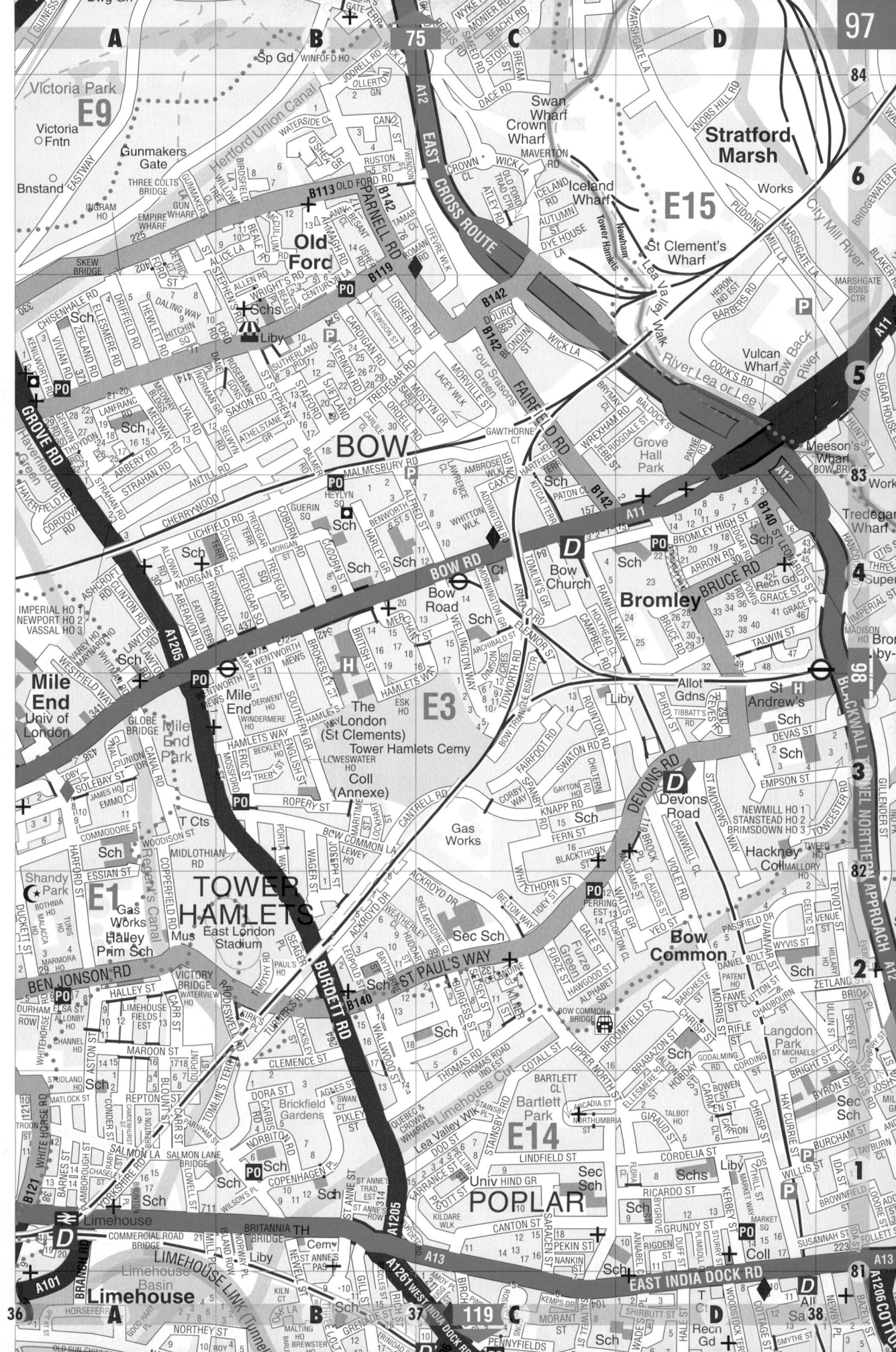
A
B
C
D
75
84
6
5
4
3
2
1
83
82
81
98
36
37
119
38
Victoria Park
E9
Victoria Fntn
Gunmakers Gate
Hertford Union Canal
Bnstand
EASTWAY
THREE COLTS BRIDGE
INGRAM HO
EMPIRE WHARF
GUN WHARF
SKEW BRIDGE
OLD FORD RD
B113
PARNELL RD
B142
Old Ford
B119
EAST CROSS ROUTE
A12
Swan Wharf
Crown Wharf
WICK LA
MAVERTON RD
Iceland Wharf
Tower Hamlets
Newham
E15
Stratford Marsh
Works
St Clement's Wharf
Lea Valley Walk
City Mill River
KNOBS HILL RD
MARSHGATE LA
MARSHGATE BSNS CTR
HERON IND EST
BARBERS RD
Vulcan Wharf
Bow Back River
River Lea or Lee
COOK'S RD
SUGAR HOUSE LA
Meeson's Wharf
BOW BRIDGE
Tredegar Wharf
A11
CHISENHALE RD
Sch
Schs
Liby
DALING WAY
ROMAN RD
GROVE RD
Haverfield Green
Four Seasons Green
FAIRFIELD RD
BOW
MALMESBURY RD
Grove Hall Park
GAWTHORNE CT
HEYLYN SQ
CHERRYWOOD
ANTILL RD
BOW RD
Bow Road
Bow Church
Bromley
BROMLEY HIGH ST
BRUCE RD
Recn Gd
ST LEONARD'S ST
A1205
Mile End
Univ of London
Mile End Park
GLOBE BRIDGE
E3
The London (St Clements)
Tower Hamlets Cemy
Coll (Annexe)
Allot Gdns
St Andrew's
BLACKWALL TUNNEL NORTHERN APPROACH
Gas Works
Devons Road
DEVONS RD
Hackney Coll
Bow Common
ST PAUL'S WAY
BURDETT RD
B140
TOWER HAMLETS
E1
Shandy Park
Gas Works
Halley Prim Sch
Mus
East London Stadium
Regent's Canal
BEN JONSON RD
VICTORY BRIDGE
Langdon Park
Sec Sch
Brickfield Gardens
Limehouse Cut
Lea Valley Wlk
Bartlett Park
E14
POPLAR
Univ
Schs
Liby
Sec Sch
Limehouse
COMMERCIAL ROAD BRIDGE
A13
EAST INDIA DOCK RD
LIMEHOUSE LINK (Tunnel)
Limehouse Basin
Cem
BRITANNIA BRIDGE
A1261 WEST INDIA DOCK RD
A101
BRANCH RD
WHITE HORSE RD
B121
Coll
All Saints
A1206
Recn Gd

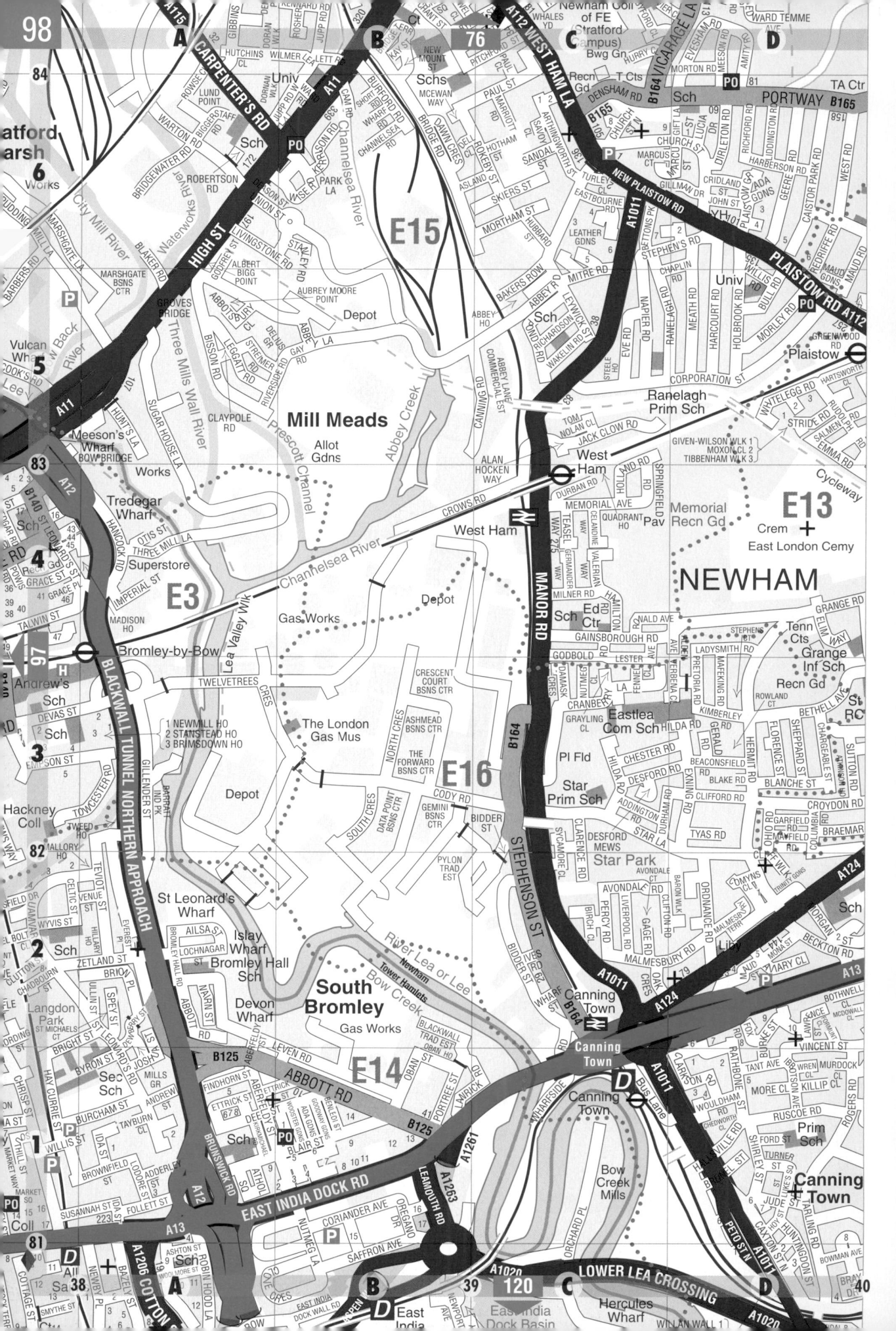

98
76
120
A
B
C
D
1
2
3
4
5
6
84
83
82
81
38
39
40
97
E15
E3
E13
E14
E16
NEWHAM
Mill Meads
Allot Gdns
South Bromley
Gas Works
Depot
Newham Coll of FE (Stratford Campus)
Bwg Gn
Univ
Schs
Sch
PO
CARPENTER'S RD
HIGH ST
A11
A12
A13
A112 WEST HAM LA
VICARAGE LA
PORTWAY
B165
NEW PLAISTOW RD
PLAISTOW RD
A1011
Plaistow
Ranelagh Prim Sch
West Ham
MANOR RD
B164
Memorial Recn Gd
Crem
East London Cemy
Cycleway
Channelsea River
Abbey Creek
Prescott Channel
Three Mills Wall River
Waterworks River
City Mill River
Bow Back River
Lea Valley Wlk
Bromley-by-Bow
BLACKWALL TUNNEL NORTHERN APPROACH
Tredegar Wharf
Meeson's Wharf
BOW BRIDGE
Superstore
The London Gas Mus
St Leonard's Wharf
Islay Wharf
Bromley Hall Sch
Devon Wharf
River Lea or Lee
Bow Creek
Newham
Tower Hamlets
ABBOTT RD
B125
EAST INDIA DOCK RD
A1261
A1263
LEAMOUTH RD
LOWER LEA CROSSING
A1020
Canning Town
Bow Creek Mills
Hercules Wharf
East India Dock Basin
STEPHENSON ST
Star Park
Star Prim Sch
Eastlea Com Sch
Grange Inf Sch
Recn Gd
Tenn Cts
Hackney Coll
Langdon Park
Sec Sch
A124
A1206
Prim Sch
Canning Town
Stratford Marsh
Vulcan Wharf
Works

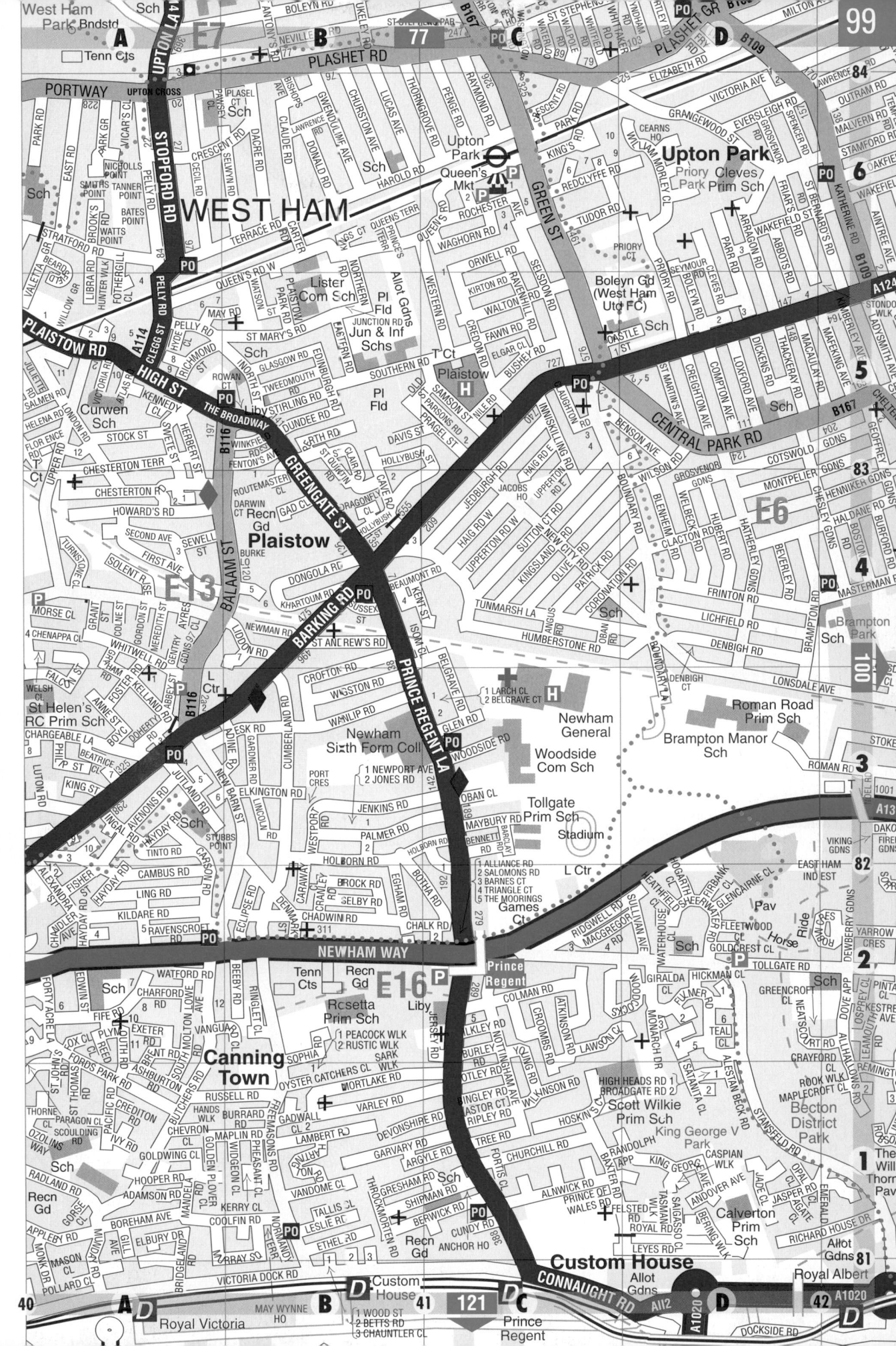
West Ham Park Bndstd
Tenn Cts
E7
77
PLASHET RD
PORTWAY
UPTON CROSS
UPTON LA
STOPFORD RD
WEST HAM
Upton Park
Queen's Mkt
GREEN ST
Upton Park
Priory Park
Cleves Prim Sch
Boleyn Gd (West Ham Utd FC)
Lister Com Sch
Allot Gdns
Jun & Inf Schs
PLAISTOW RD
HIGH ST
THE BROADWAY
Curwen Sch
Plaistow
GREENGATE ST
E13
BALAAM ST
BARKING RD
PRINCE REGENT LA
CENTRAL PARK RD
E6
Brampton Park
100
Newham General
Woodside Com Sch
Roman Road Prim Sch
Brampton Manor Sch
St Helen's RC Prim Sch
Newham Sixth Form Coll
Tollgate Prim Sch
Stadium
L Ctr
Games Ct
A13
NEWHAM WAY
Prince Regent
E16
Rosetta Prim Sch
Canning Town
Scott Wilkie Prim Sch
King George V Park
Becton District Park
The Will Thorne Pav
Calverton Prim Sch
Custom House
CONNAUGHT RD
Royal Albert
Royal Victoria
Custom House
121
Prince Regent
40
41
42
81
82
83
84
A
B
C
D
1
2
3
4
5
6

A
B
C
D
78
84
IG 11
Barking Flyover
MILTON AVE
THE FIRS
HEIGHAM RD
COLVIN RD
ACORN CT
BENDISH RD
ST N A117
CLEMENTS RD
CAULFIELD RD
CALEDON RD
HOLLAND RD
WALL END RD
BURGES RD
HART ST
THE WILLOWS
Pl Fld
LONDON RD
ABBEY RD A124
A406
HIGHBRIDGE RD
NORTH CIRCULAR RD
River Roding
WEST BANK
TOWN QUAY
TOWN QUAY WHARF
Barking Creek
FRESH WHARF RD
FRESH WHARF EST
Barking & Dagenham
Newham
HANDTROUGH WAY
LAWRENCE RD
OUTRAM RD
MALVERN RD
TEMPLE RD
STAMFORD RD
COURTLAND RD
HOLME RD
RON LEIGHTON WAY
EVERSLEIGH RD
GROSVENOR RD
SPENCER RD
B109
KEPPEL RD
ALTMORE AVE
SKEFFINGTON RD
KEMPTON RD
HALL RD
NORFOLK RD
BEDFORD RD
CALVERTON RD
ST OLAVE'S RD
Recn Gd
A124
HIGH ST N
OAKFIELD RD
WAKEFIELD ST
CAMPBELL RD
KATHERINE RD
ST BERNARD'S RD
FRIAR'S RD
STREATFEILD AVE
LATIMER AVE
THORPE RD
LLOYD RD
MYRTLE RD
CANBERRA RD
DUKES RD
DUKES CT
1 MALDON CT
2 WALL END CT
3 TRAFALGAR CT
Park
Sch
Acad
Schs
HARTLEY AVE
AINTREE AVE
WINTER AVE
ST JOHN'S RD
BARKING RD
DRAKES WALK
WELLINGTON RD
Wallend
LANGDON RD
NELSON ST
SUSSEX RD
RANELAGH RD
NAPIER RD
ARRAGON RD
WAKEFIELD ST
ABBOTS RD
TH
Liby
Coll
A117
NAVARRE RD
ST BARTHOLOMEW'S RD
NELSON ST
POULETT RD
TIPPETT CT
MARKET ST
MELBOURNE RD
TALBOT RD
PARK AVE
LANGDON CRES
Langdon Sch
Pl Fld
A124
STONDON WLK
GILLETT AVE
HOCKLEY AVE
ERNALD AVE
BARTLE AVE
HENRY RD
DORAN CT
ARTHUR RD
HOWARD RD
TILBURY RD
Flanders Pl Fld
SIDNEY ELSON WAY 1
MATHEWS AVE 2
DICKENS RD
THACKERAY RD
MACAULAY RD
MAFEKING AVE
KIMBERLEY AVE
LADYSMITH AVE
CENTRAL PARK RD
LOXFORD AVE
CHELTENHAM GDNS
Central Park
EAST HAM
Bwg Gn
Tenn Cts
SOUTHCHURCH RD
SOUTH CHURCH CT
FLANDERS RD
3 ATHELSTAN CT
4 WADHURST CT
CENTRAL PARK RD B167
COTSWOLD GDNS
GEOFFREY GDNS
RANCLIFFE RD B167
WHITE HORSE RD
GRESHAM RD
TYRONE RD
MOUNTFIELD RD
TELHAM RD
DARWELL CL
WELLSTEAD RD
EDWIN AVE
PICKERING AVE
FOLKESTONE RD
MONTPELIER GDNS
HENNIKER GDNS
CHESLEY GDNS
BASIL AVE
PULLEYNS AVE
ASCOT RD
HIGH ST S
BREDE CL
VICARAGE LA
BRIGHTON RD
PAUL ROBESON CL
HATHERLEY GDNS
HALDANE RD
BOSTON RD
BURFORD RD
BUXTON RD
EUSTACE RD
MITCHAM RD
SUNNINGDALE CL
ALEXANDRA RD
BECKET AVE
LANGTON AVE
EASTBOURNE RD
BLANEY CRES
GOOSELEY LA
Allot Gdns
BEVERLEY RD
MASTERMAN RD
MARLOW RD
MANOR FARM CT
TA Ctr
ST ALBAN'S AVE
CHARLEMONT RD
WOLSEY AVE
E6
HOLLINGTON RD
HERTFORD CT
HOLLOWAY RD
CHARLTON CT
FRINTON RD
BRAMPTON RD
Brampton Prim Sch
East Ham Jewish Cemy
SANDFORD RD
MORTIMER RD
MONMOUTH RD
JOHNSTONE RD
SKIPSEY AVE
BREAM GDNS
BURNELS AVE
Gooseley's Pl Flds
A13
A1020
LICHFIELD RD
99
Brampton Park
LONSDALE CL
SANDFORD CL 1
ST GEORGES CT 2
ST MARYS CT 3
MELFORD RD
NORMAN RD
HAMEWAY
Bwg Gn
BECKTON TRIANGLE RET PK
1 MANBROUGH AVE
2 MAGDALENE GDNS
3 MASEFIELD GDNS
4 HARTSHORN GDNS
ERIC CLARKE LA
Schs
LONSDALE AVE
BROOKS AVE
GREATFIELD AVE
Nat Res
STOKES RD
HALE RD
FABIAN ST
SAXON RD
SILVER BIRCH GDNS
CLAPS GATE LA
NOEL RD
AMY WARNE CL 1
IRIS CL 2
ROMAN RD
THE LABURNUMS
BEGONIA CL
NEWHAM WAY
Beckton Alps
Beckton Alps Ski Ctr
A13
VIKING GDNS
DAKOTA GDNS
FIREFLY GDNS
EVELYN DENNINGTON RD
Allot Gdns
EASTBURY RD
82
EAST HAM IND EST
SORREL GDNS
NIGHTINGALE WAY
Golf Range
North Beckton Prim Sch
ALPINE BSNS CTR
WHITINGS WAY
HILLCROFT RD
ROYAL DOCKS RD
CAIRNE CL
DEWBERRY GDNS
COLUMBINE AVE
REDSTART CL
EISENHOWER DR
KINGFISHER ST
BERYL AVE
PERIDOT ST
VALIANT WAY
PEMBROKE RD
HARRIER WAY
HALLYWELL CRES
BOWYER CL
ALPINE WAY
THE LONDON IND PK
HAREBELL DR
RODING RD
Pav
Horse Ride
ROBIN CRES
YARROW CRES
SWALLOW ST
BRACKEN CL
VISCOUNT DR
AMBASSADOR DR
CONCORDE DR
SOUTH ST
DERIFALL CL
PEPPER CL
COUNTY RD
TOLLGATE RD
AMBAS GDNS
ANGELICA DR
MAPLE CT
Sch
GREENCROFT CL
PINTAIL CL
OSPREY CL
KESTREL AVE
GREENWICH CRES
WAVERLEY GDNS
OLIVER GDNS
LINDEN LA
LONGAGE APP
BRADLEY STONE RD
KINGSFORD WAY
LION RD
IRELAND CL
EAST BECKTON DIST CTR
MARY ROSE MALL
MITCHELL WLK
WINSOR TERR
STONEWALL
BEAUFORT
Beckton
NEATSCOURT RD
ALLHALLOWS RD
LEAMOUTH RD
COWAN CL
LATHAM CL
CRAYFORD CL
ROOK WLK
REMINGTON RD
KIRKHAM RD
NORTHUMBERLAND RD
CHARDWELL CL
TRIUMPH RD
FROBISHER RD
SHAFTESBURY CT
NEWARK KNOK
SUDBURY
TUNNAN LEYS
WARWALL
ASHEN
DOWNINGS
COW LEAZE
HORSE LEAZE
BRADYMEAD
MAPLECROFT CL
Becton District Park
The Will Thorne Pav
BARRY RD
SALTLEY CL
DUNNOCK RD
HADLEIGH WLK
CHELMSFORD
EXETER CL
ARMSTRONG CL
Horse Ride
NEWLING CL
BRANDRETH RD
PEARL CL
SAPPHIRE CL
PEVEREL
HIDE
COVELEES WALL
TYNEMOUTH CL
OXLEAS
WHEATFIELDS
ROBSON CL
ANDREWES GDNS
CHICHESTER CL
GUILDFORD RD
SHARPER RD
BATTEN CL
PORTER RD
OAKES CL
WOOLWICH MANOR WAY
STANSFELD RD
JADE CL
OPAL CL
JASPER RD
AGATE
EMERALD
Sch
RICHARD HOUSE DR
BOULTWOOD RD
YORK CL
TRUESDALE RD
BAYNE CL
PARRY AVE
SAVAGE GDNS
New Becton Park
Tenn Cts
Bwg Gn
Winsor Prim Sch
EAST HAM MANOR WAY
BESSIE LANSBURY CL
PENNYROYAL AVE
Fball Gd
Allot Gdns
ALISON CL
TANSY CL
HEATHER CL
FERNDALE ST
TRADER RD
A117
Gallions Reach
81
E16
Allot Gdns
Pl Fld
STRAIT RD
CAMPION CL
RENFREW CL
LEAROYD GDNS
AGNES CL
BASEING CL
DEVALLS CL
FLETCHER CL
CYPRUS PL
A1020
42
ROYAL ALBERT WAY
43
122
ROYAL ALBERT RD
44
DOCKSIDE RD
Royal Albert
Beckton Park
Cyprus

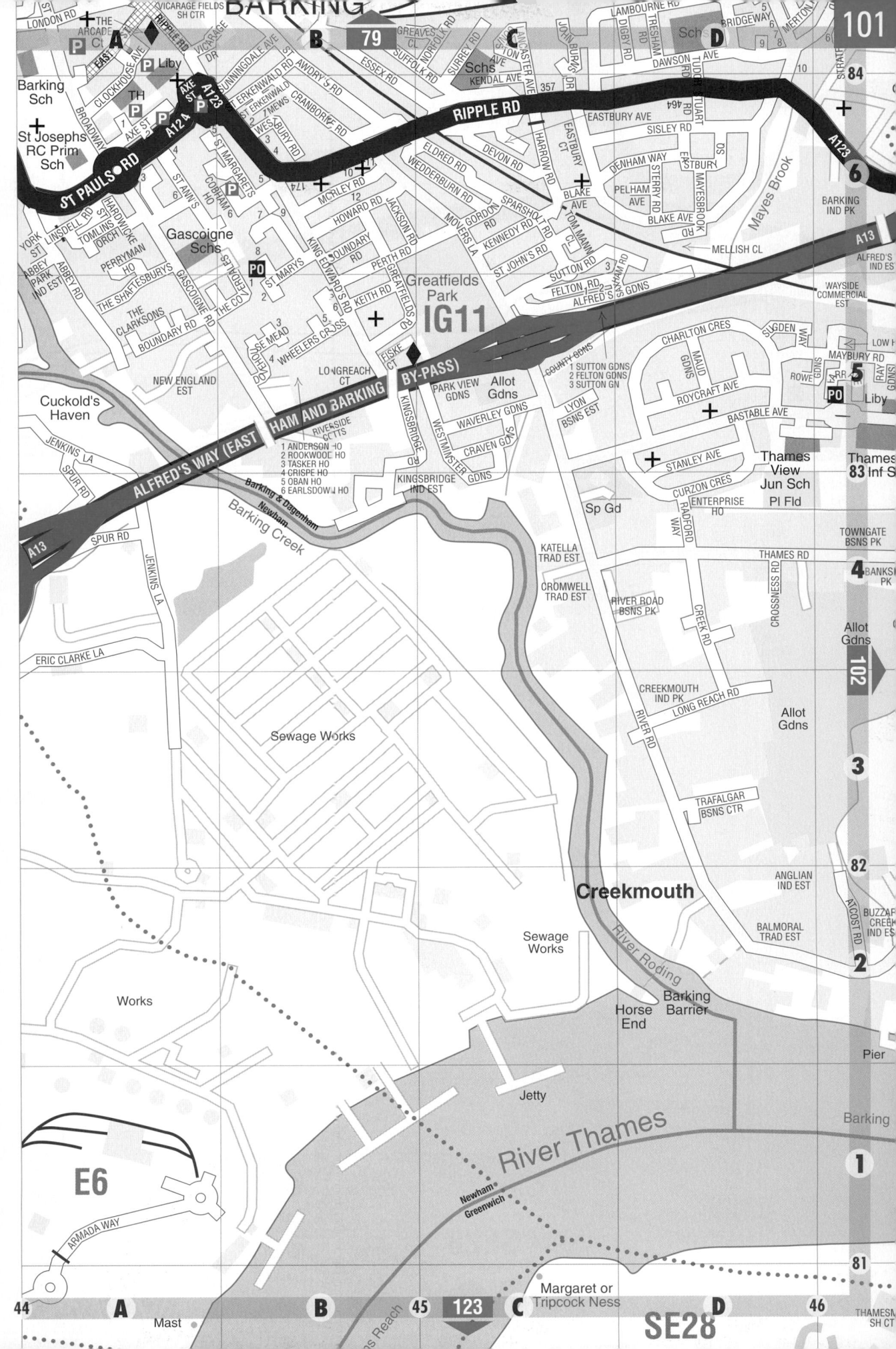
BARKING
79
IG11
RIPPLE RD
ALFRED'S WAY (EAST HAM AND BARKING BY-PASS)
A13
A123
ST PAULS RD
Barking Sch
St Josephs RC Prim Sch
Gascoigne Schs
Greatfields Park
Cuckold's Haven
Barking Creek
Sewage Works
Creekmouth
River Roding
Barking Barrier
Horse End
Jetty
River Thames
Works
E6
ARMADA WAY
Margaret or Tripcock Ness
SE28
Thames View Jun Sch
Allot Gdns
Pier
102
123
Mast

A
B
C
D
80
KEIR HARDIE WAY
LODGE AV
ROSEDALE RD
ROSEDALE GDNS
CAMPSEY RD
CAMPSEY GDNS
ELLERTON GDNS
STOCKER GDNS
STAMFORD RD
STAMFORD GDNS
ARDEN CRES
LANGLEY GDNS
LANGLEY CRES
STRATFORD CL
84
Cemy
PO
Monteagle Prim Sch
PINLEY GDNS
BURNHAM RD
ROTHWELL GDNS
ROTHWELL RD
GREENFIELD RD
GREENFIELD GDNS
ROMSEY GDNS
ROMSEY RD
STUDLEY RD
THETFORD RD
WIX RD
RIPPLE RD
ACONBURY RD
GORESBROOK RD
Ripple Road
B1423
MAPLESTEAD RD
BASSETT HO
INGRAVE HO
DUNMOW HO
Castle Green
6
Mayes Brook
CASTLE RD
MOORE CRES
A123
Rec Gd
Sp Gds
L Ctr
BARKING IND PK
A13
ALFRED'S WAY
(EAST HAM AND BARKING BY-PASS)
Works
ALFRED'S WAY IND EST
RIPPLESIDE COMMERCIAL EST
PORTLAND COMMERCIAL EST
WAYSIDE COMMERCIAL EST
MAYBELLS COMMERCIAL EST
JULIA GDNS
LEVINE GDNS
SUGDEN WAY
LOW HO
MAYBURY RD
WIVENHOE RD
BOX LA
5
ROWE GDNS
FARR AVE
RAY GDNS
ENDEAVOUR WAY
STEBBING WAY
ROXWELL RD
PO
Liby
CHELMER CRES
CROUCH AV
ABRIDGE WAY
Freightliner Terminal
BASTABLE AVE
GILSTEAD HO 1
NAVESTOCK HO 2
STANFORD HO 3
ST AIDANS CT 4
STERN CL
GREAT FLEETE WAY
KEEL CL
CALEDONIA CT
GLENMORE WAY
Thames View Jun Sch
Thames View Inf Sch
83
BLESSING WAY
SOVEREIGN RD
ALDERMAN AVE
RENWICK RD
WANDERER DR
CHOATS RD
Pl Fld
TRIUMPH HO
HAVERING WAY
STAPLEFORD WAY
TOWNGATE BSNS PK
RIVERSIDE IND EST
TWINE CL
UARY EST
GREAT GALLEY CL
5 BRECO HO
6 BELLINGHAM CT
7 ARNCROFT CT
THAMES RD
4
BANKSIDE PK
GALLIONS CL
CROSSNESS RD
City Farm & Ecological Park
IG11
CROMWELL CTR
Allot Gdns
101
Allot Gdns
3
RM9
RIVER RD
82
ANGLIAN IND EST
ATCOST RD
BUZZARD CREEK IND EST
BALMORAL TRAD EST
Pier
2
Barking & Dagenham
Greenwich
Bexley
River Thames
Gross Ness
Pier
Barking or False Point
Barking Reach
Barking & Dagenham
THAMESBANK PL
Crossway Lake Nature Reserve
1
WENTWORTH CL
WATERSMEET WAY
WOBURN CL
TURNBURY CL
MARTHAM CL
COPPERFIELD RD
DRAKE CRES
Castilion Prim Sch
Greenwich
Bexley
Green Chain Wlk
DOLPHIN CL
POINTER CL
EASTGATE CL
SUMMERTON WAY
CHERBURY CL
NICKELBY CL
GRANGE CRES
TEMPLAR DR
LONGWORTH CL
SE28
LUDHAM CL
HOVETON RD
ROLLESBY WAY
MANORDENE RD
CROSSWAY
SURLINGHAM CL
Ppg Sta
Bishop John Robinson Sch
KINGFISHER CL
WROXHAM RD
COURTLAND GR
Linton Mead Prim Sch
BERTRAND WAY
WALSHAM CL
ORMESBY CL
FLEMING WAY
HODGKINS CL
81
46
A
THAMESMEAD SH CTR
THAMESMERE DR
B
CENTRAL WAY
47
124
C
WHIMBREL CL
GARGANEY WLK
CURLEW CL
D
48
BAYLISS
CHADWICK
PO
GOLDCREST CL
HASLER CL
TAWNEY RD

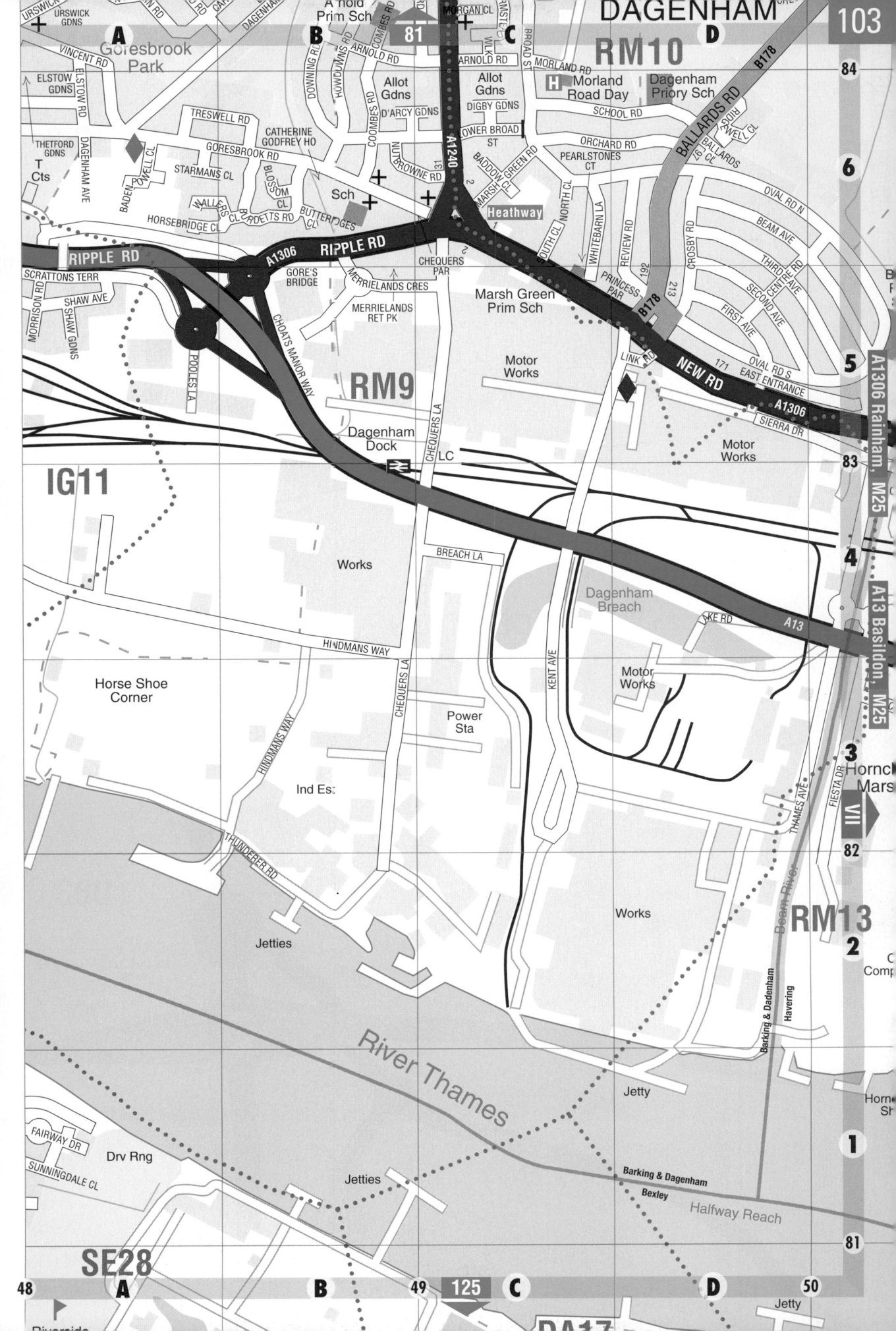
DAGENHAM
RM10
RM9
IG11
RM13
SE28
Goresbrook Park
Morland Road Day
Dagenham Priory Sch
Marsh Green Prim Sch
Dagenham Dock
Dagenham Breach
Horse Shoe Corner
Power Sta
Ind Est
Works
Motor Works
Jetties
Jetty
River Thames
Halfway Reach
Drv Rng
Heathway
RIPPLE RD
NEW RD
CHEQUERS LA
KENT AVE
HINDMANS WAY
THUNDERER RD
BREACH LA
BALLARDS RD
A13 Basildon, M25
A1306 Rainham, M25
Barking & Dagenham
Bexley
Havering
Beam River
THAMES AVE
FIESTA DR
SIERRA DR
EAST ENTRANCE
OVAL RD S
OVAL RD N
FAIRWAY DR
SUNNINGDALE CL
MERRIELANDS CRES
MERRIELANDS RET PK
CHOATS MANOR WAY
POOLES LA
SCRATTONS TERR
SHAW AVE
MORRISON RD
SHAW GDNS
GORESBROOK RD
TRESWELL RD
SCHOOL RD
ORCHARD RD
PEARLSTONES CT
WHITEBARN LA
REVIEW RD
CROSBY RD
BEAM AVE
THIRD AVE
SECOND AVE
FIRST AVE
CENTRE RD
LINK RD
PRINCESS PAR
CHEQUERS PAR
GORE'S BRIDGE
HORSEBRIDGE CL
STARMANS CL
DAGENHAM AVE
ELSTOW RD
VINCENT RD
URSWICK GDNS
THETFORD GDNS
CATHERINE GODFREY HO
NUTBROWNE RD
COOMBES RD
DOWNING RD
ARNOLD RD
D'ARCY GDNS
DIGBY GDNS
LOWER BROAD ST
MARSH GREEN RD
BADDOW CL
MORLAND RD
MORGAN CL
BROAD ST
NORTH CL
SOUTH CL
Allot Gdns
Sch
81
125
VII
84
6
5
83
4
3
82
2
1
81
48
49
50
A
B
C
D

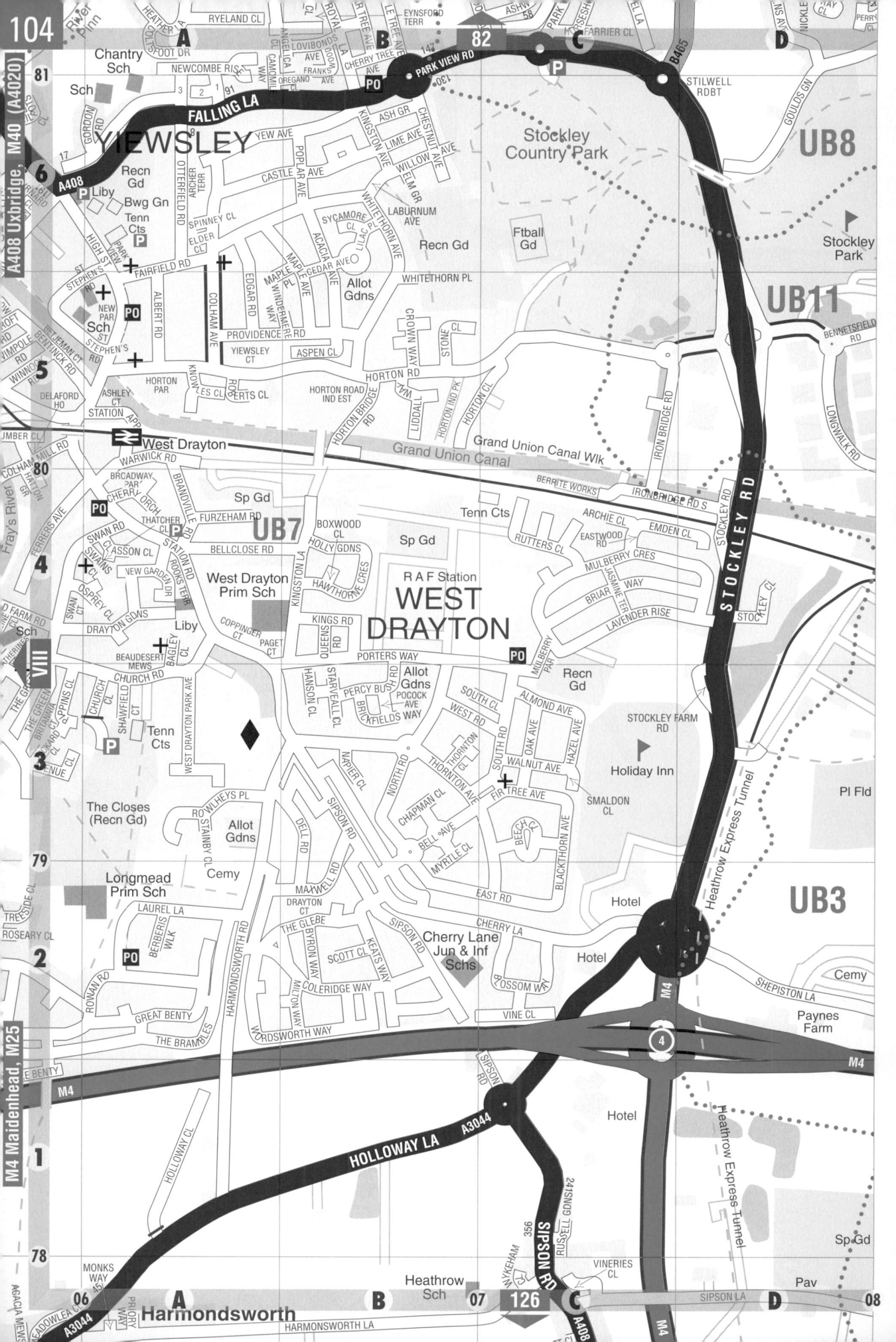
82
A
B
C
D
YIEWSLEY
WEST DRAYTON
Stockley Country Park
Stockley Park
UB8
UB11
UB7
UB3
FALLING LA
PARK VIEW RD
STILWELL RDBT
B465
A408
STOCKLEY RD
Grand Union Canal
Grand Union Canal Wlk
West Drayton
R A F Station
Chantry Sch
Recn Gd
Liby
Bwg Gn
Tenn Cts
Ftball Gd
Allot Gdns
Sp Gd
West Drayton Prim Sch
Holiday Inn
Pl Fld
The Closes (Recn Gd)
Cemy
Longmead Prim Sch
Cherry Lane Jun & Inf Schs
Hotel
Paynes Farm
Heathrow Express Tunnel
HOLLOWAY LA
A3044
SIPSON RD
M4
SHEPISTON LA
Heathrow Sch
Harmondsworth
HARMONDSWORTH LA
SIPSON LA
Pav
126
06
07
08
81
80
79
78
M4 Maidenhead, M25
A408 Uxbridge, M40 (A4020)
VIII

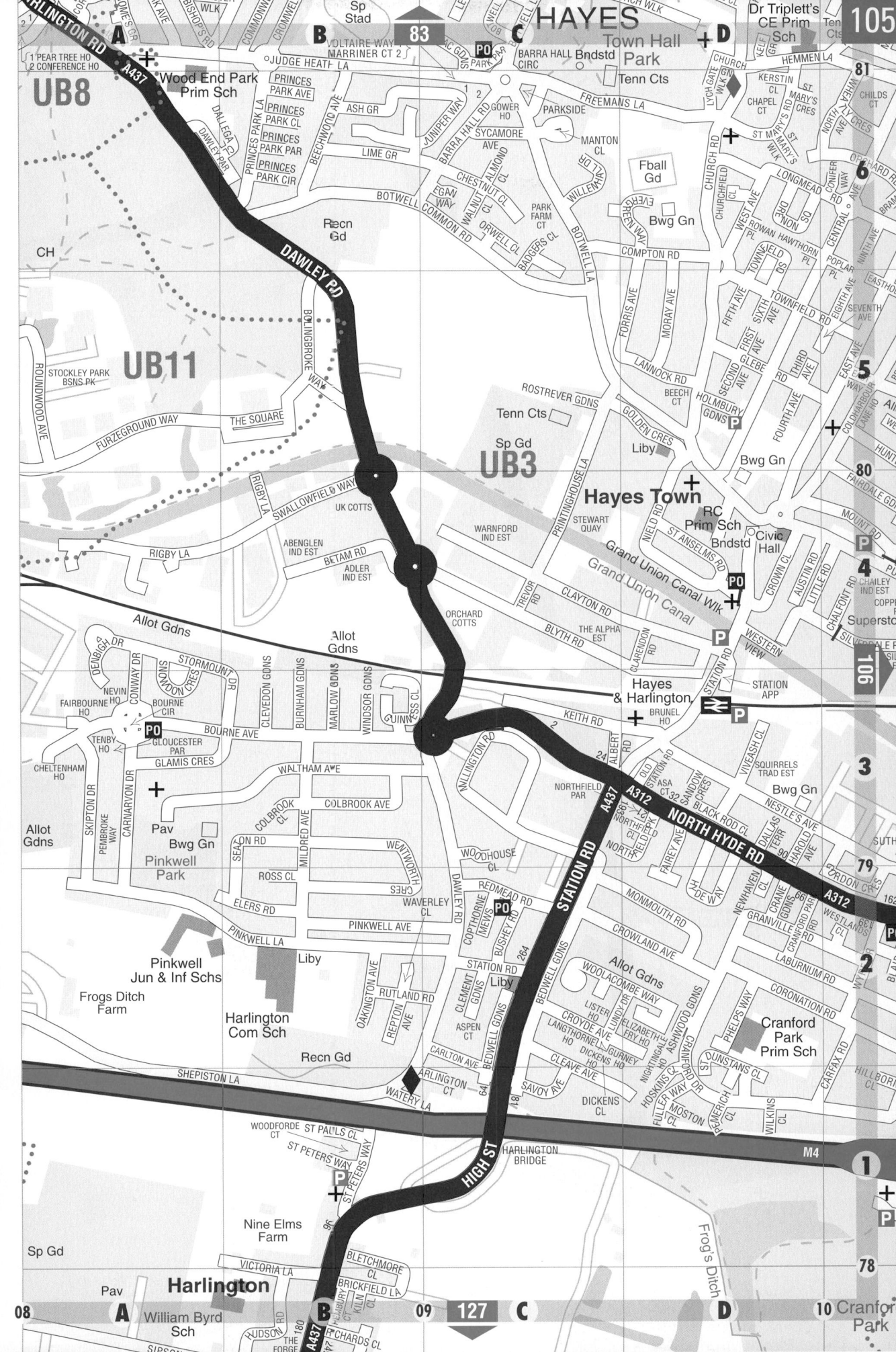
HAYES
A
B
C
D
83
Sp Stad
Dr Triplett's CE Prim Sch
Ten Cts
HARLINGTON RD
A437
BISHOP'S RD
WLK
COMMONWEALTH
CROMWELL
VOLTAIRE WAY
MARRINER CT 2
JUDGE HEATH LA
1 PEAR TREE HO
2 CONFERENCE HO
UB8
Wood End Park Prim Sch
PRINCES PARK AVE
PRINCES PARK CL
PRINCES PARK PAR
PRINCES PARK CIR
PRINCES PARK LA
DALLEGA CL
DAWLEY PAR
BEECHWOOD AVE
ASH GR
LIME GR
JUNIPER WAY
BARRA HALL RD
PO
PARK PAR
BARRA HALL CIRC
Bndstd
Town Hall Park
Tenn Cts
GOWER HO
SYCAMORE AVE
ALMOND CL
CHESTNUT CL
WALNUT CL
EGAN WAY
BOTWELL COMMON RD
ORWELL CL
BADGERS CL
PARK FARM CT
PARKSIDE
MANTON CL
WILLENHALL DR
FREEMANS LA
CHURCH RD
LYCH GATE WLK
CHURCH GN
KELF GR
HEMMEN LA
KERSTIN CL
CHAPEL CT
ST MARY'S CRES
ST MARY'S RD
ST MARY'S WLK
NORTH AVE
WHEATLEY CRES
CHILDS CT
81
Fball Gd
EVERGREEN WAY
Bwg Gn
BOTWELL LA
CHURCHFIELD CL
WEST AVE
LONGMEAD RD
DRE ON SQ
CONIFER WAY
CENTRAL AVE
ORCHARD RD
BRAMLEY
6
ROWAN PL
HAWTHORN PL
COMPTON RD
TOWNFIELD SQ
POPLAR PL
NINTH AVE
EASTHOLM
EIGHTH AVE
SEVENTH AVE
TOWNFIELD RD
FIFTH AVE
SIXTH AVE
FIRST AVE
GLEBE RD
SECOND AVE
THIRD AVE
FORRIS AVE
MORAY AVE
LANNOCK RD
BEECH CT
HOLMBURY GDNS
FOURTH AVE
EAST AVE
COLDHARBOUR LANE HO
5
Recn Gd
CH
DAWLEY RD
BOLINGBROKE WAY
UB11
STOCKLEY PARK BSNS PK
ROUNDWOOD AVE
FURZEGROUND WAY
THE SQUARE
ROSTREVER GDNS
Tenn Cts
Sp Gd
UB3
GOLDEN CRES
Liby
Bwg Gn
80
FAIRDALE GDNS
MOUNT RD
Hayes Town
PRINTINGHOUSE LA
STEWART QUAY
RC Prim Sch
NIELD RD
ST ANSELMS RD
Bndstd
Civic Hall
CROWN CL
AUSTIN RD
LITTLE RD
CHALFONT RD
CHAILEY IND EST
COPPER RD
4
Superstore
RIGBY LA
SWALLOWFIELD WAY
UK COTTS
ABENGLEN IND EST
BETAM RD
ADLER IND EST
WARNFORD IND EST
Grand Union Canal Wlk
Grand Union Canal
TREVOR RD
CLAYTON RD
ORCHARD COTTS
BLYTH RD
THE ALPHA EST
CLARENDON RD
WESTERN VIEW
SILVERDALE RD
106
Allot Gdns
Allot Gdns
DENBIGH DR
STORMOUNT DR
SNOWDON CRES
CONWAY DR
NEVIN HO
FAIRBOURNE HO
BOURNE CIR
CLEVEDON GDNS
BURNHAM GDNS
MARLOW GDNS
WINDSOR GDNS
GUINNESS CL
Hayes & Harlington
STATION RD
STATION APP
BRUNEL HO
KEITH RD
BOURNE AVE
TENBY HO
GLOUCESTER PAR
GLAMIS CRES
CHELTENHAM HO
WALTHAM AVE
WILLINGTON RD
ALBERT RD
OLD STATION RD
VIVEASH CL
SQUIRRELS TRAD EST
3
NORTHFIELD PAR
ASA CT
SANDOW CRES
A312
NORTH HYDE RD
BLACK ROD CL
Bwg Gn
NESTLE'S AVE
SKIPTON DR
CARNARVON DR
PEMBROKE WAY
COLBROOK CL
COLBROOK AVE
MILDRED AVE
NORTHFIELD PK
FAIREY AVE
DALLAS TERR
HAROLD AVE
SUTHERLAND
Allot Gdns
Pav
Bwg Gn
SEATON RD
WENTWORTH CRES
WOODHOUSE CL
HYDE WAY
NEWHAVEN CL
79
GORDON CRES
Pinkwell Park
ROSS CL
DAWLEY RD
MONMOUTH RD
CRANE GDNS
CRANFORD PARK RD
WESTLANDS CL
162
ELERS RD
WAVERLEY CL
REDMEAD RD
COPTHORNE MEWS
BUSHEY RD
PINKWELL AVE
PINKWELL LA
CROWLAND AVE
GRANVILLE RD
LABURNUM RD
Pinkwell Jun & Inf Schs
Liby
STATION RD
Liby
Allot Gdns
WOOLACOMBE WAY
2
BLAIR
Frogs Ditch Farm
OAKINGTON AVE
RUTLAND RD
CLEMENT GDNS
BEDWELL GDNS
LISTER HO
LUNDY DR
ELIZABETH FRY HO
ASHWOOD GDNS
PHELPS WAY
CORONATION RD
Harlington Com Sch
REPTON AVE
ASPEN CT
CROYDE AVE
LANGTHORNE HO
GURNEY HO
DICKENS HO
Cranford Park Prim Sch
Recn Gd
CARLTON AVE
CLEAVE AVE
NIGHTINGALE HO
CRANFORD DR
ST DUNSTANS CL
CARFAX RD
HILLBORN CL
SHEPISTON LA
HARLINGTON CT
WATERY LA
SAVOY AVE
DICKENS CL
HOSKINS CL
FULLER WAY
MOSTON CL
PEMERICH CL
WILKINS CL
WOODFORDE CT
ST PAULS CL
ST PETERS WAY
HIGH ST
HARLINGTON BRIDGE
M4
1
Nine Elms Farm
Frog's Ditch
Sp Gd
BLETCHMORE CL
VICTORIA LA
BRICKFIELD LA
KILN CL
78
Pav
Harlington
William Byrd Sch
HUDSON RD
THE FORGE
CHARDS CL
SIPSON
08
09
127
10
Cranford Park

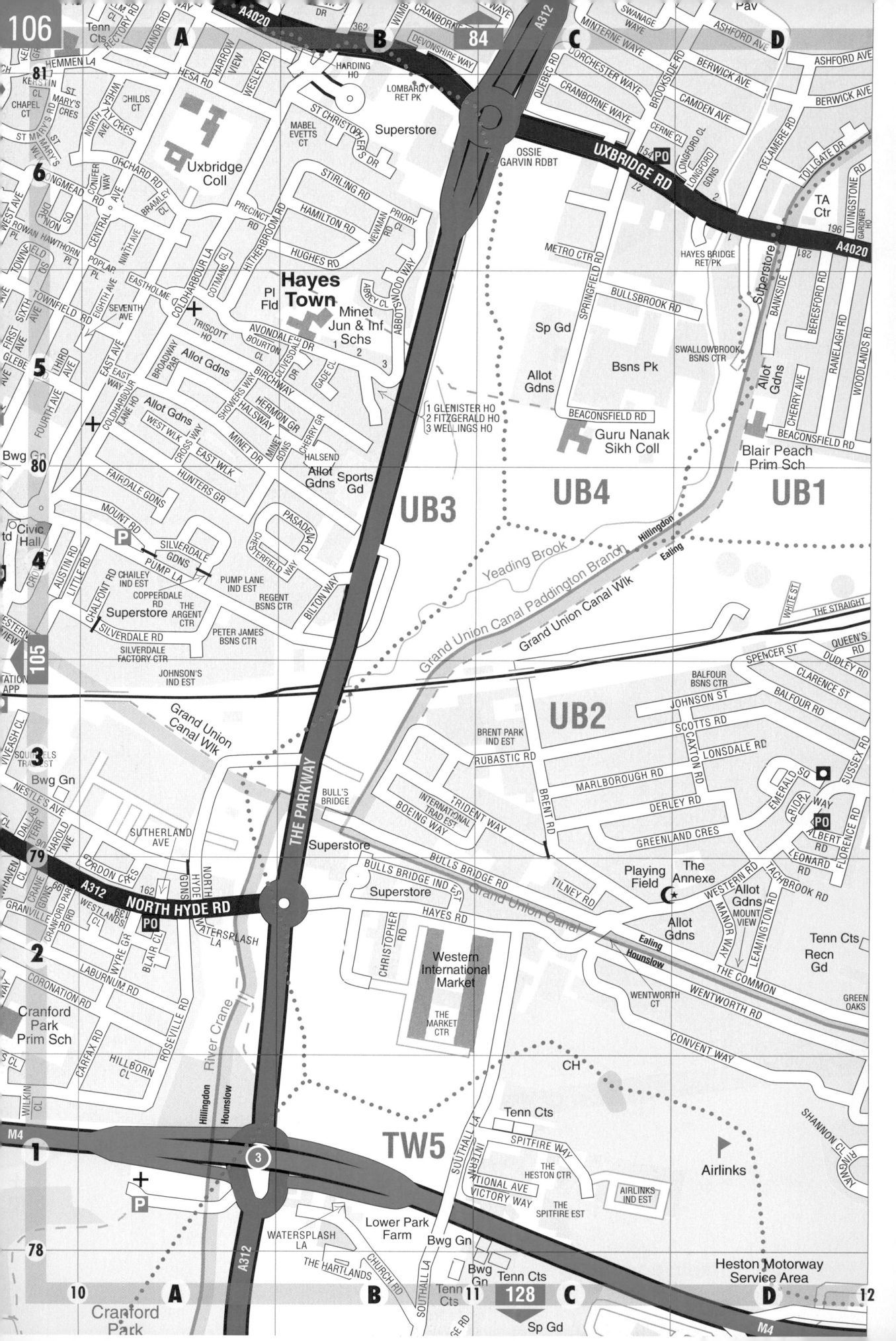
A4020
A312
84
A
B
C
D
Tenn Cts
MANOR RD
HEMMEN LA
81
KERSTIN CL
CHAPEL CT
ST MARY'S CRES
ST MARY'S RD
HESA RD
HARROW VIEW
WESLEY RD
HARDING HO
LOMBARDY RET PK
DEVONSHIRE WAY
CRANBORNE WAYE
MINTERNE WAYE
SWANAGE WAYE
ASHFORD AVE
BERWICK AVE
DORCHESTER WAYE
QUEBEC RD
BROOKSIDE RD
CAMDEN AVE
CERNE CL
LONGFORD CL
LONGFORD GDNS
DELAMERE RD
TOLLGATE DR
CHILDS CT
ORCHARD RD
ST CHRISTOPHER'S DR
MABEL EVETTS CT
Superstore
OSSIE GARVIN RDBT
UXBRIDGE RD
PO
Uxbridge Coll
6
LONGMEAD
CONIFER WAY
CENTRAL AVE
BRAMLEY CL
STIRLING RD
HAMILTON RD
PRIORY CL
NEWMAN RD
HUGHES RD
PRECINCT RD
HITHERBROOM RD
TA Ctr
LIVINGSTONE RD
GARDNER HO
A4020
HAYES BRIDGE RET PK
METRO CTR
SPRINGFIELD RD
NINTH AVE
POPLAR PL
HAWTHORN PL
ROWAN PL
EASTHOLME
COLDHARBOUR LA
COTMANS CL
Hayes Town
Pl Fld
ABBEY CL
ABBOTSWOOD WAY
BULLSBROOK RD
Superstore
BANKSIDE
BERESFORD RD
TOWNFIELD RD
EIGHTH AVE
SEVENTH AVE
SIXTH AVE
TRISCOTT HO
AVONDALE DR
BOURTON CL
Minet Jun & Inf Schs
Sp Gd
SWALLOWBROOK BSNS CTR
RANELAGH RD
WOODLANDS RD
FIRST AVE
THIRD AVE
5
EAST AVE
EAST WAY
BROADWAY PAR
Allot Gdns
BIRCHWAY
CLIVESDALE DR
GADE CL
Bsns Pk
Allot Gdns
CHERRY AVE
FOURTH AVE
COLDHARBOUR LANE HO
SHOWERS WAY
HALSWAY
HERMON GR
CHERRY GR
1 GLENISTER HO
2 FITZGERALD HO
3 WELLINGS HO
BEACONSFIELD RD
Guru Nanak Sikh Coll
BEACONSFIELD RD
Blair Peach Prim Sch
WEST WLK
CROSS WAY
EAST WLK
MINET DR
MINET GDNS
HALSEND
Bwg Gn
80
HUNTERS GR
Allot Gdns
Sports Gd
FAIRDALE GDNS
UB3
UB4
UB1
MOUNT RD
PASADENA CL
CHESTERFIELD WAY
Civic Hall
P
SILVERDALE GDNS
4
AUSTIN RD
LITTLE RD
PUMP LA
CHAILEY IND EST
PUMP LANE IND EST
BILTON WAY
REGENT BSNS CTR
Yeading Brook
Hillingdon
Ealing
Grand Union Canal Paddington Branch
Grand Union Canal Wlk
WHITE ST
THE STRAIGHT
COPPERDALE RD
CHALFONT RD
Superstore
THE ARGENT CTR
SILVERDALE RD
PETER JAMES BSNS CTR
SILVERDALE FACTORY CTR
JOHNSON'S IND EST
105
QUEEN'S RD
SPENCER ST
DUDLEY RD
CLARENCE ST
BALFOUR BSNS CTR
BALFOUR RD
JOHNSON ST
UB2
Grand Union Canal Wlk
SCOTTS RD
CAXTON RD
VIVEASH CL
3
Bwg Gn
NESTLE'S AVE
BRENT PARK IND EST
RUBASTIC RD
LONSDALE RD
SUSSEX RD
MARLBOROUGH RD
EMERALD SQ
PRIORY WAY
THE PARKWAY
BULL'S BRIDGE
INTERNATIONAL TRAD EST
TRIDENT WAY
BOEING WAY
BRENT RD
DERLEY RD
GREENLAND CRES
PO
ALBERT RD
FLORENCE RD
LEONARD RD
DALLAS TERR
HAROLD AVE
SUTHERLAND AVE
Superstore
79
GORDON CRES
A312
NORTH HYDE RD
NORTH HYDE GDNS
BULLS BRIDGE IND EST
BULLS BRIDGE RD
TILNEY RD
Playing Field
The Annexe
WESTERN RD
TACHBROOK RD
Allot Gdns
MOUNT VIEW
Superstore
HAYES RD
Grand Union Canal
Allot Gdns
WESTLANDS CL
CRANFORD PAR
GRANVILLE RD
CRANE GDNS
PO
WATERSPLASH LA
CHRISTOPHER RD
MANOR WAY
LEAMINGTON RD
Ealing
Hounslow
Tenn Cts
Recn Gd
WYRE GR
BLAIR CL
2
LABURNUM RD
CORONATION RD
Western International Market
THE COMMON
WENTWORTH CT
WENTWORTH RD
GREEN OAKS
Cranford Park Prim Sch
CARFAX RD
ROSEVILLE RD
River Crane
THE MARKET CTR
CONVENT WAY
HILLBORN CL
CH
WILKIN CL
Hillingdon
Hounslow
Tenn Cts
SHANNON CL
RINGWAY
M4
1
3
TW5
SOUTHALL LA
SPITFIRE WAY
INTERNATIONAL AVE
THE HESTON CTR
Airlinks
VICTORY WAY
AIRLINKS IND EST
THE SPITFIRE EST
P
Lower Park Farm
WATERSPLASH LA
Bwg Gn
78
A312
THE HARTLANDS
CHURCH RD
SOUTHALL LA
Bwg Gn
Tenn Cts
Heston Motorway Service Area
10
A
B
11
128
C
D
12
Cranford Park
Sp Gd
M4

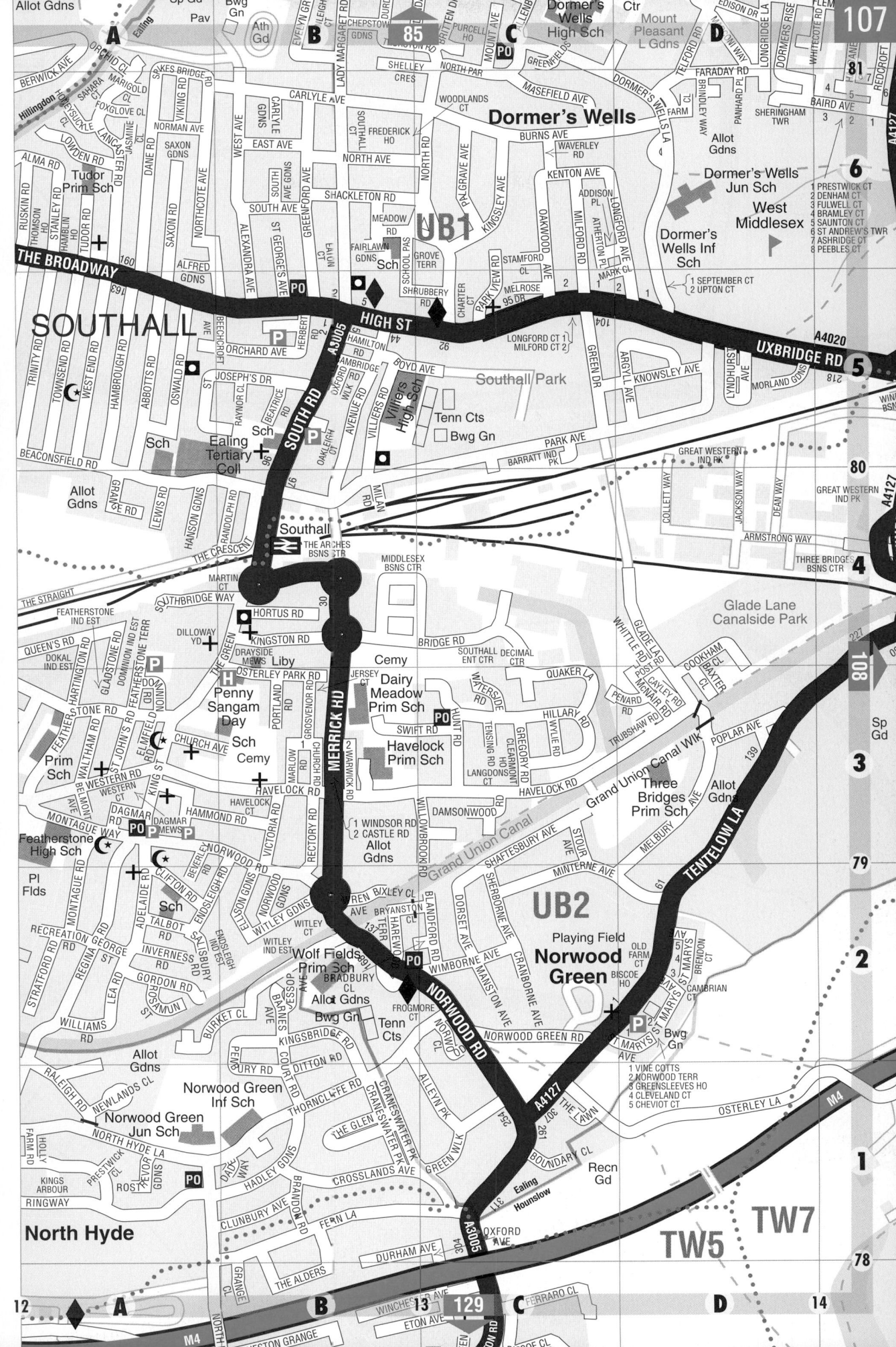
Dormer's Wells
SOUTHALL
UB1
UB2
Norwood Green
North Hyde
TW5
TW7
THE BROADWAY
HIGH ST
UXBRIDGE RD
SOUTH RD
MERRICK RD
NORWOOD RD
TENTELOW LA
Grand Union Canal
Southall Park
Glade Lane Canalside Park
1 PRESTWICK CT
2 DENHAM CT
3 FULWELL CT
4 BRAMLEY CT
5 SAUNTON CT
6 ST ANDREW'S TWR
7 ASHRIDGE CT
8 PEEBLES CT
1 SEPTEMBER CT
2 UPTON CT
1 WINDSOR RD
2 CASTLE RD
1 VINE COTTS
2 NORWOOD TERR
3 GREENSLEEVES HO
4 CLEVELAND CT
5 CHEVIOT CT
85
108
129

Brent Valley
86
Hobbayne Prim Sch
Drayton Manor High Sch
Drayton Green
Allot Gdns
West Middlesex
GREENFORD RD
Churchfields Recn Gd
Hanwell
UB1
UXBRIDGE RD
A4020
A4127
Ealing
Grand Union Canal Walk
Grand Union Canal
River Brent
City of Westminster Cemy
LOWER BOSTON RD
A4001 BOSTON RD
A3002
Glade Lane Canalside Park
107
TENTELOW LA
UB2
Sports Gd
Sp Ctr
Pl Fld
The Aviary
WINDMILL LA
W7
Elthorne Park
Elthorne Park High Sch
Osterley Lock
Trumper's Wood
M4
Osterley Park Farm
Osterley Park House
Osterley Park
TW7
Hare & Hounds (PH)
Wyke Green
SYON LA
130

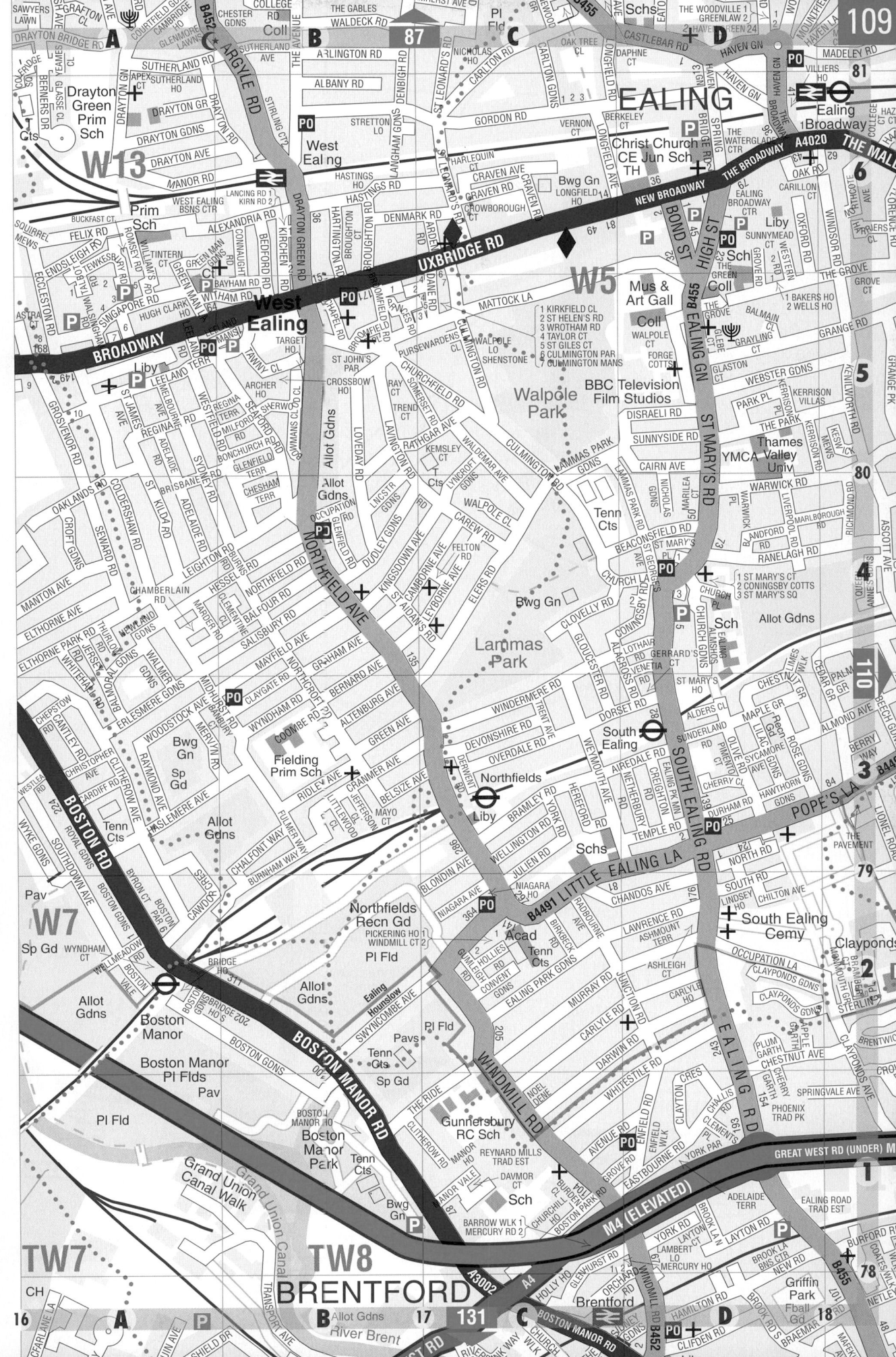
SAWYERS LAWN
GRAFTON CL
COURTFIELD GDNS
CAMBRIDGE HO
GLENMORE LAWNS
CHESTER GDNS
COLLEGE RD
Coll
THE GABLES
WALDECK RD
87
Pl Fld
B455
Schs
THE WOODVILLE 1
GREENLAW 2
DRAYTON BRIDGE RD
A
B
C
D
CASTLEBAR RD
HAVEN GREEN
HAVEN GN
MADELEY RD
VILLIERS HO
81
SUTHERLAND RD
SUTHERLAND AVE
ARLINGTON RD
NICHOLAS HO
OAK TREE CL
DAPHNE CT
APEX CT
SUTHERLAND HO
Drayton Green Prim Sch
ALBANY RD
DRAYTON GR
DRAYTON GDNS
ARGYLE RD
STIRLING CT
DENBIGH RD
CARLTON RD
CARLTON GDNS
LONGFIELD RD
EALING
Ealing Broadway
PO
STRETTON LO
GORDON RD
VERNON CT
BERKELEY CT
BRIDGE RD
SPRING
THE WATERGLADE CTR
A4020
THE MALL
West Ealing
LANGHAM GDNS
ST LEONARD'S RD
Christ Church CE Jun Sch
TH
W13
DRAYTON AVE
HARLEQUIN CT
CRAVEN AVE
CRAVEN RD
Bwg Gn
LONGFIELD HO
OAK RD
CARILLON CT
6
MANOR RD
HASTINGS HO
HASTINGS RD
NEW BROADWAY
THE BROADWAY
LANCING RD 1
KIRN RD 2
WEST EALING BSNS CTR
CROWBOROUGH CT
EALING BROADWAY CTR
Prim Sch
BUCKFAST CT
ALEXANDRIA RD
DENMARK RD
BOND ST
HIGH ST
Liby
SQUIRREL MEWS
FELIX RD
HARTINGTON RD
BROUGHTON RD
ARDEN RD
SUNNYMEAD CT
OXFORD RD
WINDSOR RD
UXBRIDGE RD
W5
Sch
ENDSLEIGH RD
TINTERN CT
GREEN MAN GDNS
KIRCHEN RD
BEDFORD RD
DRAYTON GREEN RD
GROVE RD
THE GROVE
BAYHAM RD
WITHAM RD
Mus & Art Gall
Coll
1 BAKERS HO
2 WELLS HO
SINGAPORE RD
HUGH CLARK HO
West Ealing
MATTOCK LA
GROVE CT
ASTRA CT
BROADWAY
LEELAND MANS
TARGET HO
1 KIRKFIELD CL
2 ST HELEN'S RD
3 WROTHAM RD
4 TAYLOR CT
5 ST GILES CT
6 CULMINGTON PAR
7 CULMINGTON MANS
B455
EALING GN
BALMAIN CL
GRANGE RD
GRAYLING CT
TAWNY CL
ST JOHN'S PAR
PURSEWARDENS CL
WALPOLE LO
SHENSTONE
WALPOLE CT
FORGE COTTS
GLASTON CT
WEBSTER GDNS
5
Liby
LEELAND TERR
ARCHER HO
CROSSBOW HO
CHURCHFIELD RD
CULMINGTON RD
Walpole Park
BBC Television Film Studios
KERRISON VILLAS
KENILWORTH RD
GRANGE PK
ST JAMES AVE
MELBOURNE AVE
WESTFIELD RD
REGINA TERR
MILFORD RD
SHERWOOD
BOWMANS CL
RAY CT
TREND CT
SOMERSET RD
DISRAELI RD
PARK PL
THE PARK
REGINA RD
BONCHURCH RD
GLENFIELD TERR
Allot Gdns
LOVEDAY RD
LAVINGTON RD
RATHGAR AVE
KEMSLEY CT
WALDEMAR AVE
LAMMAS PARK GDNS
SUNNYSIDE RD
ST MARY'S RD
Thames Valley Univ
YMCA
KERRISON RD
GROSVENOR RD
ADELAIDE RD
SYDNEY RD
BRISBANE RD
CHESHAM TERR
LYNGROFT GDNS
CULMINGTON RD
CAIRN AVE
80
OAKLANDS RD
COLDERSHAW RD
ST KILDA RD
Allot Gdns
LNGSTR GDNS
WALPOLE CL
LAMMAS PARK RD
NICHOLAS GDNS
MARILEA CT
WARWICK RD
WARWICK PL
LIVERPOOL RD
MARLBOROUGH RD
RICHMOND RD
CROFT GDNS
SEWARD RD
LEIGHTON RD
OCCUPATION RD
GLENFIELD RD
DUDLEY GDNS
CAREW RD
Tenn Cts
BEACONSFIELD RD
ANDFORD RD
RANELAGH RD
ASCOTT AVE
FELTON RD
KINGSDOWN AVE
CAMBORNE AVE
ELERS RD
ST MARY'S PL
ST GEORGES AVE
MANTON AVE
CHAMBERLAIN RD
BURNS AVE
HESSEL RD
NORTHFIELD RD
NORTHFIELD AVE
LEYBORNE AVE
CHURCH LA
1 ST MARY'S CT
2 CONINGSBY COTTS
3 ST MARY'S SQ
4
QUEEN ANNE'S GR
ELTHORNE AVE
BALFOUR RD
MARDER RD
CLEMENTINE CL
ST AIDAN'S RD
Bwg Gn
CLOVELLY RD
CONINGSBY RD
CHURCH PL
Sch
Allot Gdns
NEWLAND GDNS
SALISBURY RD
ELTHORNE PARK RD
THURLOW RD
JERSEY RD
MAYFIELD AVE
GRAHAM AVE
Lammas Park
GLOUCESTER RD
ALACROSS RD
LOTHAIR RD
VENETIA RD
GERRARD'S CT
CHURCH GDNS
EALING ALMSHOS
WHITEHALL RD
BALMORAL GDNS
WALMER GDNS
NORTHCROFT RD
BERNARD AVE
135
ST MARY'S HO
CHESTNUT GR
PALM GR
CEDAR GR
110
CHEPSTOW
CANTLEY RD
ERLESMERE GDNS
MIDHURST RD
CLAYGATE RD
ALTENBURG AVE
WINDERMERE RD
TRENT AVE
DORSET RD
ALDERS CL
MAPLE GR
Recn Gd
ALMOND AVE
BEECH GR
WOODSTOCK AVE
BANBURY CL
WYNDHAM RD
COOMBE RD
GREEN AVE
DEVONSHIRE RD
82
South Ealing
SUNDERLAND RD
LILAC GDNS
ROSE GDNS
BERRY WAY
CHRISTOPHER AVE
CLITHEROW AVE
RAYMOND AVE
Bwg Gn
Sp Gd
MERVYN RD
Fielding Prim Sch
CRANMER AVE
OVERDALE RD
AIREDALE RD
CREIGHTON RD
PIMENTO CT
SYCAMORE AVE
3
B4491
CARDIFF RD
HASLEMERE AVE
RIDLEY AVE
BELSIZE AVE
DERWENT RD
Northfields
WEYMOUTH AVE
NETHERBURY RD
EALING PK MN
CHERRY CL
HAWTHORN GDNS
84
POPE'S LA
LIONEL RD
WESTLEA RD
224
Tenn Cts
Allot Gdns
LITTLEWOOD CL
JEFFERSON CL
MAYO CT
Liby
BRAMLEY RD
HEREFORD RD
YORK RD
TEMPLE RD
DURHAM RD
139
THE PAVEMENT
WYKE GDNS
SOUTHDOWN AVE
ROYAL GDNS
BOSTON RD
BYRON CT
CHALFONT WAY
FULMER WAY
BURNHAM WAY
WELLINGTON RD
JULIEN RD
Schs
LITTLE EALING LA
NORTH RD
SOUTH RD
79
CAWDOR CRES
BLONDIN AVE
286
NIAGARA HO
CHANDOS AVE
LINDSEY HO
CHILTON AVE
Pav
W7
Sp Gd
WYNDHAM CT
BOSTON GDNS
BOSTON PAR
Northfields Recn Gd
PICKERING HO 1
WINDMILL CT 2
NIAGARA AVE
364
Acad
Tenn Cts
RADBOURNE AVE
BIRKBECK AVE
LAWRENCE RD
ASHMOUNT TERR
South Ealing Cemy
Claypond
WELLMEADOW RD
BOSTON VALE
BRIDGE HO
311
Pl Fld
GUMLEIGH RD
HOLLIES
CONVENT GDNS
EALING PARK GDNS
OCCUPATION LA
ASHLEIGH CT
CLAYPONDS GDNS
2
Allot Gdns
Boston Manor
202
BOSTON GDNS
Allot Gdns
Ealing
Hounslow
SWYNCOMBE AVE
Pl Fld
MURRAY RD
JUNCTION RD
CARLYLE HO
CLAYPONDS GDNS
STERLING
BRENTWICK
Boston Manor Pl Flds
Pav
BOSTON MANOR RD
Pavs
Tenn Cts
Sp Gd
205
CARLYLE RD
DARWIN RD
EALING RD
243
APPLE GARTH
PLUM GARTH
CHESTNUT AVE
CLAYPONDS AVE
WINDMILL RD
NOEL DENE
WHITESTILE RD
CLAYTON CRES
CHALLIS RD
SPRINGVALE AVE
PHOENIX TRAD PK
Pl Fld
BOSTON MANOR HO
THE RIDE
Gunnersbury RC Sch
ENFIELD RD
193
154
Boston Manor Park
Tenn Cts
CLITHEROW RD
MANOR HO
REYNARD MILLS TRAD EST
AVENUE RD
PO
ENFIELD WLK
CLEMENTS RD
YORK PAR
GREAT WEST RD (UNDER)
Grand Union Canal Walk
Grand Union Canal
MANOR VALE
DAVMOR CT
Sch
GROVE RD
EASTBOURNE RD
ADELAIDE TERR
EALING ROAD TRAD EST
1
Bwg Gn
87
BARROW WLK 1
MERCURY RD 2
CHURCHILL HO
BURDEN CL
BOSTON PARK RD
M4 (ELEVATED)
YORK RD
LAYTON CT
LAMBERT LO
MERCURY HO
BROOK LA N
LAYTON RD
BROOK LA BNS CTR
NEW RD
BURFORD RD
TW7
TW8
BRENTFORD
A3002
A4
HOLLY HO
GLENHURST RD
ORCHARD RD
WINDMILL RD
Griffin Park
Fball Gd
B455
78
CH
16
A
B
Allot Gdns
17
131
C
Brentford
D
18
River Brent
TRANSPORT AVE
BOSTON MANOR RD
B452
HAMILTON RD
CLIFDEN RD
BRAEMAR RD
SHIELD DR

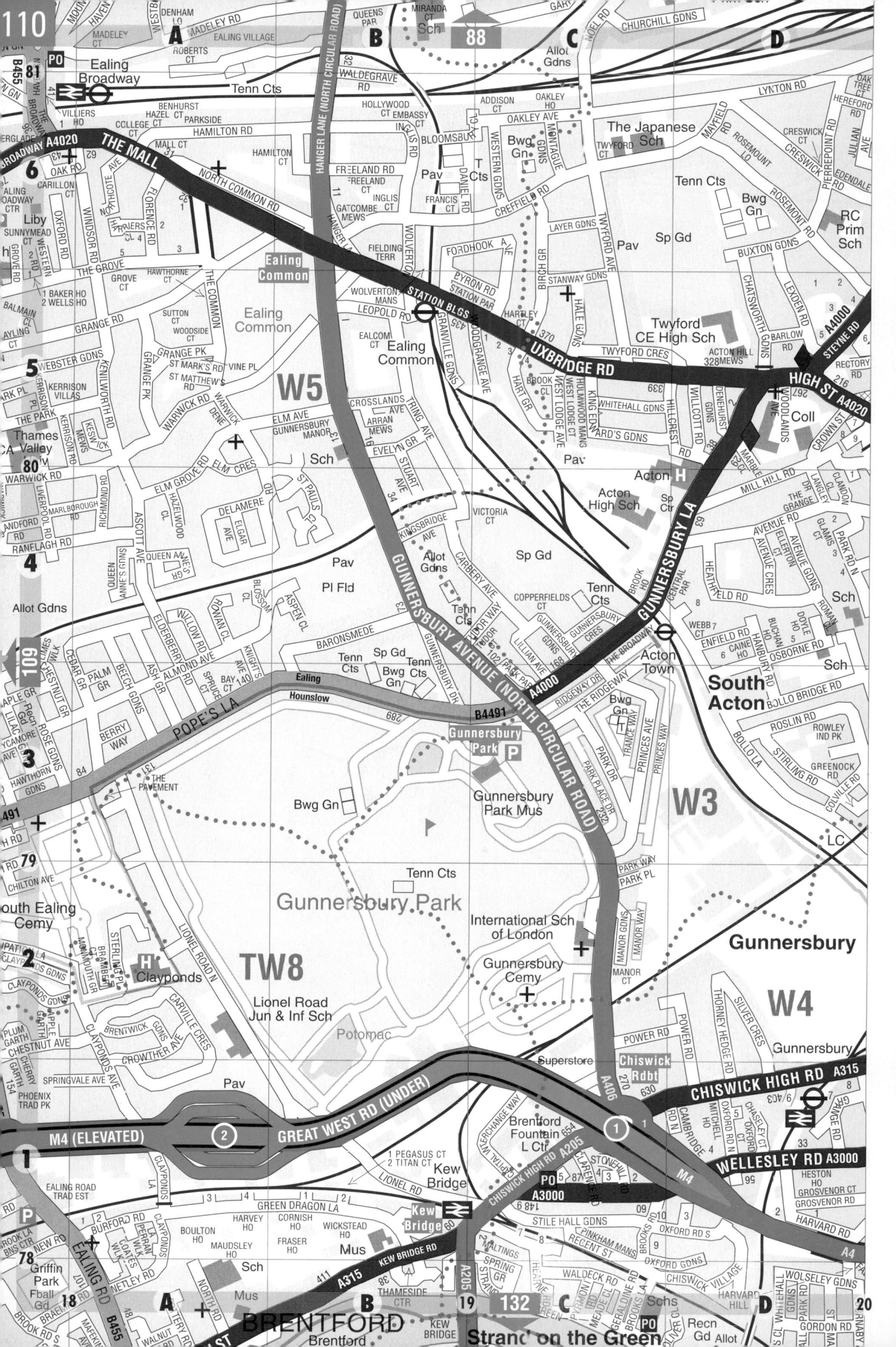
A
B
C
D
88
Ealing Broadway
Tenn Cts
Allot Gdns
MADELEY RD
EALING VILLAGE
ROBERTS CT
QUEENS PAR
MIRANDA CT
Sch
NOEL RD
CHURCHILL GDNS
WALDEGRAVE RD
HANGER LANE (NORTH CIRCULAR ROAD)
B455
VILLIERS HO
BENHURST
HAZEL CT
PARKSIDE
COLLEGE CT
HAMILTON RD
HOLLYWOOD CT
EMBASSY CT
INGLIS RD
BLOOMSBURY
ADDISON CT
OAKLEY HO
OAKLEY AVE
LYNTON RD
The Japanese Sch
TWYFORD CT
MAYFIELD RD
ROSEMOUNT LO
CRESWICK CT
CRESWICK RD
PIERREPOINT RD
HEREFORD RD
JULIAN AVE
EDENDALE RD
A4020
THE MALL
BROADWAY
MALL CT
HAMILTON CT
6
OAK RD
CARILLON CT
NORTH COMMON RD
FREELAND RD
INGLIS CT
GATCOMBE MEWS
Pav
T Cts
DANIEL RD
FRANCIS CT
Bwg Gn
WESTERN GDNS
MONTAGUE GDNS
CREFFIELD RD
Tenn Cts
Bwg Gn
ROSEMONT RD
RC Prim Sch
Liby
SUNNYMEAD CT
OXFORD RD
WINDSOR RD
FLORENCE RD
GROVE RD
WESTERN RD
THE GROVE
HAWTHORNE CT
GROVE CT
Ealing Common
FIELDING TERR
WOLVERTON
FORDHOOK AVE
LAYER GDNS
TWYFORD AVE
BIRCH GR
Pav
Sp Gd
BUXTON GDNS
CHATSWORTH GDNS
LEXDEN RD
1 BAKER HO
2 WELLS HO
BALMAIN CL
SUTTON CT
WOODSIDE CT
THE COMMON
Ealing Common
WOLVERTON MANS
STATION BLGS
LEOPOLD RD
BYRON RD
STATION PAR
STANWAY GDNS
HALE GDNS
Twyford CE High Sch
GRANGE RD
GRANGE PK
ST MARK'S RD
VINE PL
ST MATTHEW'S RD
EALCOM CT
Ealing Common
GRANVILLE GDNS
WOODGRANGE AVE
HARTLEY CT
UXBRIDGE RD
TWYFORD CRES
ACTON HILL MEWS
BARLOW RD
A4000
STEYNE RD
RECTORY RD
5
WEBSTER GDNS
KENILWORTH RD
KERRISON VILLAS
KERRISON PL
THE PARK
W5
WARWICK RD
WARWICK DENE
HART GR
BROOK CL
WEST LODGE AVE
WEST LODGE CT
HOLMWOOD MANS
KING EDW
WHITEHALL GDNS
HILLCREST RD
WILLCOTT RD
DENEHURST GDNS
WOODLANDS AVE
HIGH ST A4020
Thames Valley
KERRISON RD
KESWICK MEWS
CROSSLANDS AVE
ARRAN MEWS
ELM AVE
GUNNERSBURY MANOR
TRING AVE
Sch
Coll
CROWN ST
80
WARWICK RD
ELM GROVE RD
ELM CRES
ST PAULS CL
EVELYN GR
STUART AVE
Pav
Acton H
MARBLE CL
MILL HILL RD
LIVERPOOL RD
MARLBOROUGH RD
RICHMOND RD
HAZELWOOD CL
DELAMERE RD
ELGAR AVE
VICTORIA CT
Acton High Sch
Sp Ctr
THE GRANGE
LANGLEY DR
CLANDON CL
RANELAGH RD
ASCOTT AVE
4
QUEEN ANNE'S GR
QUEEN ANNE'S GDNS
KINGSBRIDGE AVE
Allot Gdns
CARBERY AVE
Sp Gd
GUNNERSBURY LA
AVENUE RD
AVENUE CRES
ELLERTON RD
AVENUE GDNS
GLAMIS CT
PARK RD N
Pav
Pl Fld
Allot Gdns
BLOSSOM CL
ASPEN CL
ROWAN CL
GUNNERSBURY AVENUE (NORTH CIRCULAR ROAD)
Tenn Cts
COPPERFIELDS CT
Tenn Cts
BROOK HO
CENTRAL PAR
HEATHFIELD RD
Sch
109
WILLOW RD
ELDERBERRY RD
BARONSMEDE
TUDOR WAY
GUNNERSBURY CRES
WEBB CT
BUCHAN HO
DOYLE HO
ROMAN CL
LIMES WALK
CEDAR GR
PALM GR
BEECH GDNS
ASH GR
ALMOND AVE
SPRUCE CT
BAY CT
KNIGHT'S AVE
Tenn Cts
Sp Gd
Bwg Gn
Tenn Cts
LILLIAN AVE
GUNNERSBURY GDNS
THE BROADWAY
Acton Town
ENFIELD RD
CAINE HO
HAMBURY RD
OSBORNE RD
Sch
South Acton
BOLLO BRIDGE RD
MAPLE GR
Recn Gd
LILAC
SYCAMORE AVE
ROSE GDNS
Ealing
Hounslow
POPE'S LA
B4491
A4000
RIDGEWAY DR
THE RIDGEWAY
Bwg Gn
TRANCE WAY
PRINCES AVE
PRINCES WAY
ROSLIN RD
ROWLEY IND PK
BERRY WAY
3
HAWTHORN GDNS
Gunnersbury Park
THE PAVEMENT
PARK DR
PARK PLACE DR
BOLLO LA
STIRLING RD
GREENOCK RD
COLVILLE RD
B491
Bwg Gn
Gunnersbury Park Mus
W3
79
CHILTON AVE
LC
South Ealing Cemy
Tenn Cts
PARK WAY
PARK PL
Gunnersbury Park
International Sch of London
Gunnersbury
2
STERLING PL
MONMOUTH GR
BRAMBLE
H Claypond
LIONEL ROAD N
TW8
Gunnersbury Cemy
MANOR GDNS
MANOR WAY
MANOR CT
CLAYPONDS GDNS
CLAYPONDS
CARVILLE CRES
Lionel Road Jun & Inf Sch
THORNEY HEDGE RD
SILVER CRES
W4
CHESTNUT AVE
BRENTWICK GDNS
CROWTHER AVE
CLAYPONDS AVE
Potomac
POWER RD
Gunnersbury
CHERRY GARTH
SPRINGVALE AVE
Superstore
Chiswick Rdbt
A406
CHISWICK HIGH RD
A315
PHOENIX TRAD PK
Pav
GREAT WEST RD (UNDER)
M4 (ELEVATED)
Brentford Fountain L Ctr
CAPITAL INTERCHANGE WAY
MITCHELL HO
OXFORD RD N
CHASELEY CT
OXFORD CT
GRANGE RD
1
1 PEGASUS CT
2 TITAN CT
Kew Bridge
CHISWICK HIGH RD
A205
STONEHILL RD
CLARENCE RD
M4
WELLESLEY RD A3000
EALING ROAD TRAD EST
LIONEL RD
PO
A3000
HESTON HO
GROSVENOR CT
GROSVENOR RD
HARVARD RD
P
GREEN DRAGON LA
Kew Bridge
STILE HALL GDNS
OXFORD RD S
BOULTON HO
HARVEY HO
CORNISH HO
WICKSTEAD HO
BURFORD RD
PERRAN WALK
COATES WALK
NEW RD
EALING RD
78
Griffin Park
MAUDSLEY HO
FRASER HO
Mus
KEW BRIDGE RD
MALTINGS
SPRING GR
PINKHAM MANS
RECENT ST
OXFORD GDNS
CHISWICK VILLAGE
A4
NETLEY RD
Sch
A315
Fball Gd
18
A
NORTH RD
Mus
THAMESIDE CTR
B
19
132
C
WALDECK RD
PYRMONT RD
MEADE CL
GERALDINE RD
BROOKS LA
Schs
HARVARD HILL
D
WOLSELEY GDNS
WHITEHALL GDNS
PARK RD
20
BRENTFORD
Brentford
KEW BRIDGE
Strand on the Green
PO
Recn Gd
Allot
GORDON RD
B455

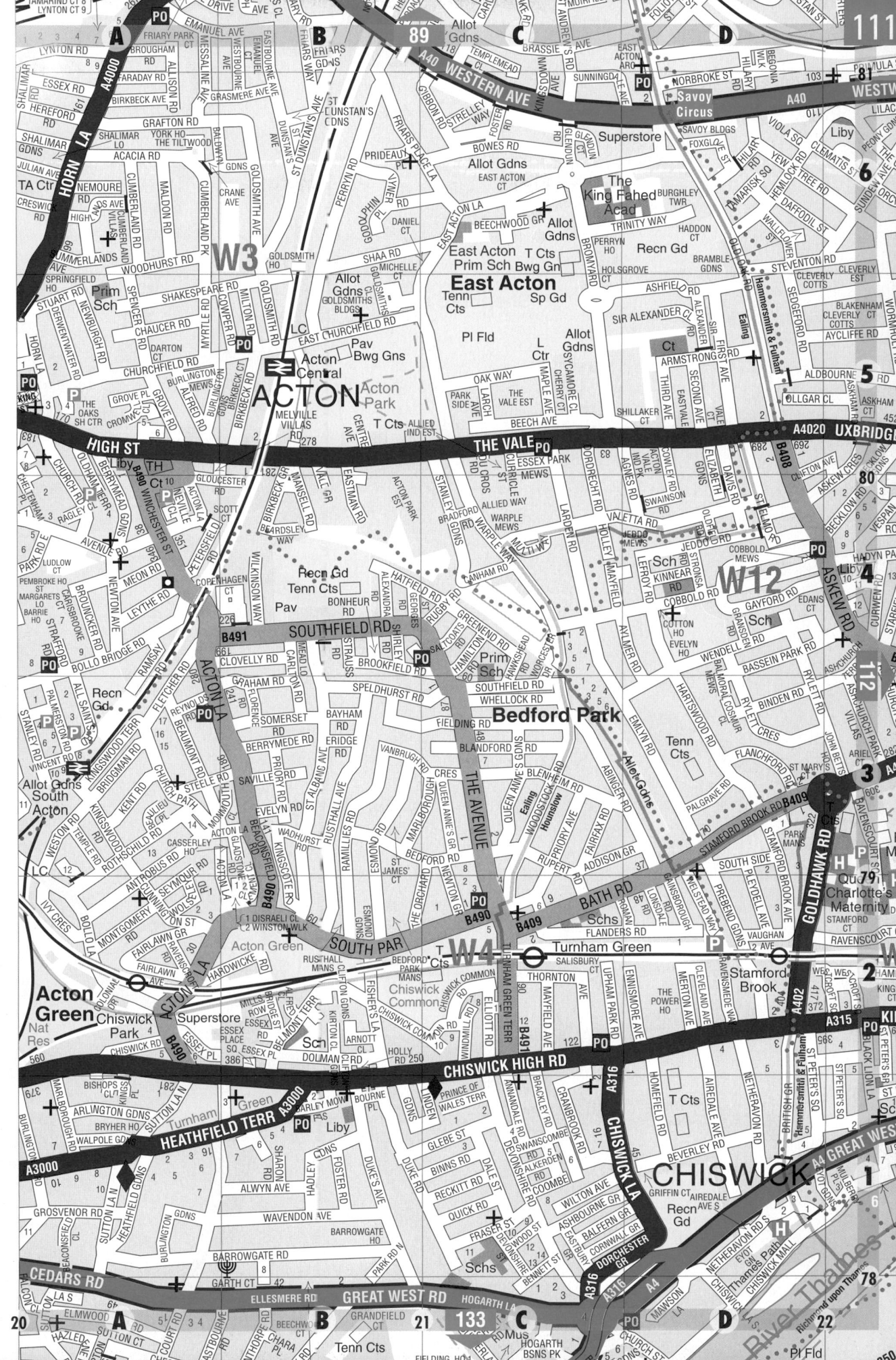
A
B
C
D
89
A40 WESTERN AVE
Savoy Circus
A40
WESTW
HORN LA
A4000
East Acton
W3
ACTON
Acton Central
Acton Park
HIGH ST
THE VALE
A4020 UXBRIDGE
B408
The King Fahed Acad
East Acton Prim Sch
Superstore
W12
B491
SOUTHFIELD RD
ACTON LA
THE AVENUE
Bedford Park
BATH RD
STAMFORD BROOK RD
B409
GOLDHAWK RD
A402
Queen Charlotte's Maternity
Turnham Green
Stamford Brook
W4
South Acton
Acton Green
Chiswick Park
SOUTH PAR
B490
CHISWICK HIGH RD
A315
HEATHFIELD TERR
A3000
CHISWICK LA
A316
CHISWICK
A4 GREAT WEST
CEDARS RD
GREAT WEST RD
River Thames
133
112
1
2
3
4
5
6
20
21
22
78
79
80
81

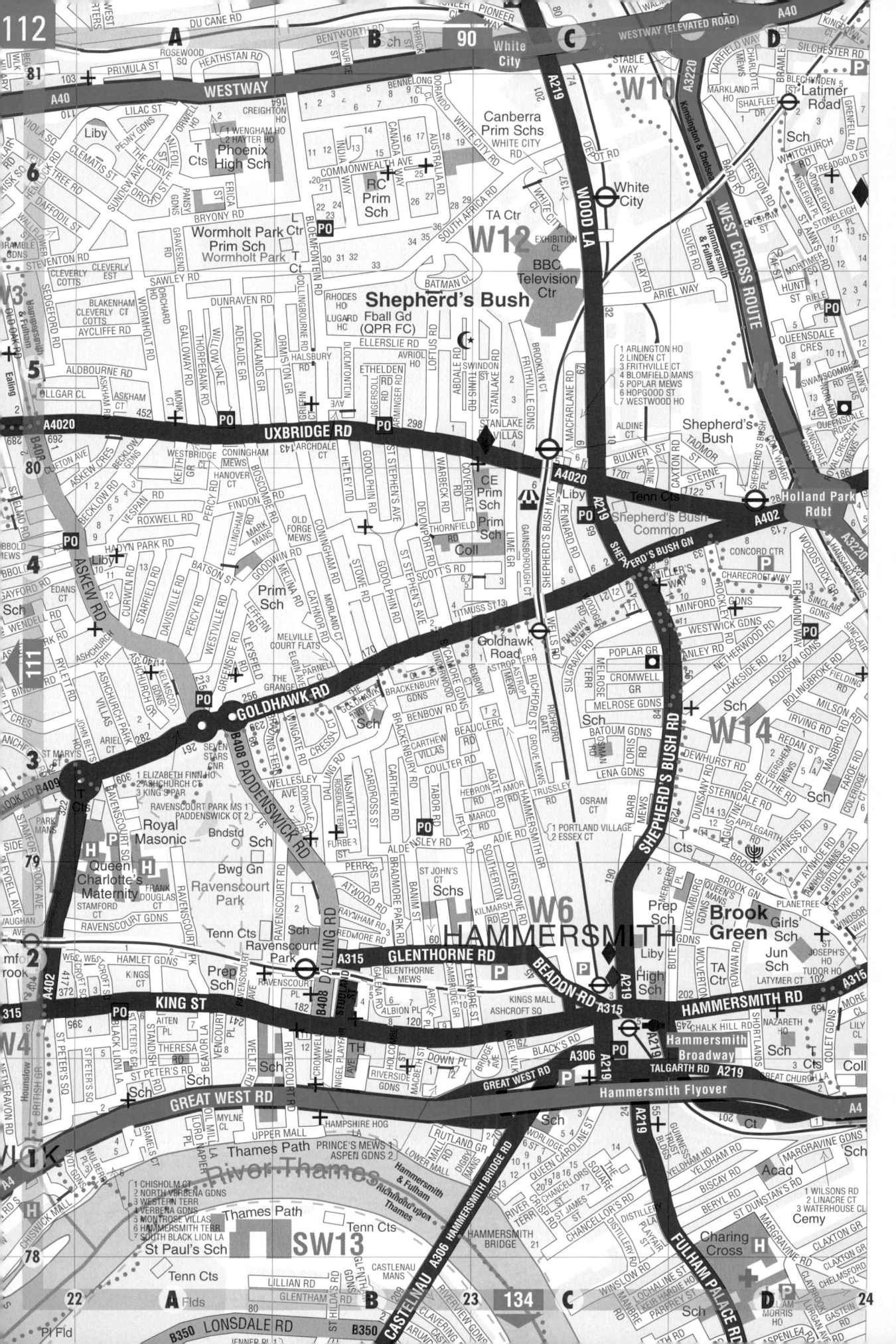

A
B
C
D
90
134
111
WESTWAY
WESTWAY (ELEVATED ROAD)
A40
White City
DU CANE RD
PRIMULA ST
HEATHSTAN RD
W10
W12
W11
W14
W6
SW13
Latimer Road
Canberra Prim Schs
WHITE CITY RD
Phoenix High Sch
Wormholt Park Prim Sch
Wormholt Park
COMMONWEALTH AVE
RC Prim Sch
BBC Television Ctr
Shepherd's Bush
Fball Gd (QPR FC)
WOOD LA
A219
WEST CROSS ROUTE
ARIEL WAY
UXBRIDGE RD
A4020
Shepherd's Bush Common
SHEPHERD'S BUSH GN
Holland Park Rdbt
A402
A3220
ASKEW RD
GOLDHAWK RD
Goldhawk Road
SHEPHERD'S BUSH RD
PADDENSWICK RD
B408
Royal Masonic
Queen Charlotte's Maternity
Ravenscourt Park
GLENTHORNE RD
A315
KING ST
HAMMERSMITH
Hammersmith Broadway
HAMMERSMITH RD
BEADON RD
TALGARTH RD
GREAT WEST RD
Hammersmith Flyover
A306
A4
Brook Green
River Thames
Thames Path
St Paul's Sch
HAMMERSMITH BRIDGE RD
HAMMERSMITH BRIDGE
CASTELNAU
FULHAM PALACE RD
Charing Cross
LONSDALE RD
B350
Cemy
1 ARLINGTON HO
2 LINDEN CT
3 FRITHVILLE CT
4 BLOMFIELD MANS
5 POPLAR MEWS
6 HOPGOOD ST
7 WESTWOOD HO
1 ELIZABETH FINN HO
2 ASHCHURCH CT
3 KING'S PAR
1 PORTLAND VILLAGE
2 ESSEX CT
1 CHISHOLM CT
2 NORTH VERBENA GDNS
3 WESTERN TERR
4 VERBENA GDNS
5 MONTROSE VILLAS
6 HAMMERSMITH TERR
7 SOUTH BLACK LION LA
1 WILSONS RD
2 LINACRE CT
3 WATERHOUSE CL
22
23
24
81
80
79
78

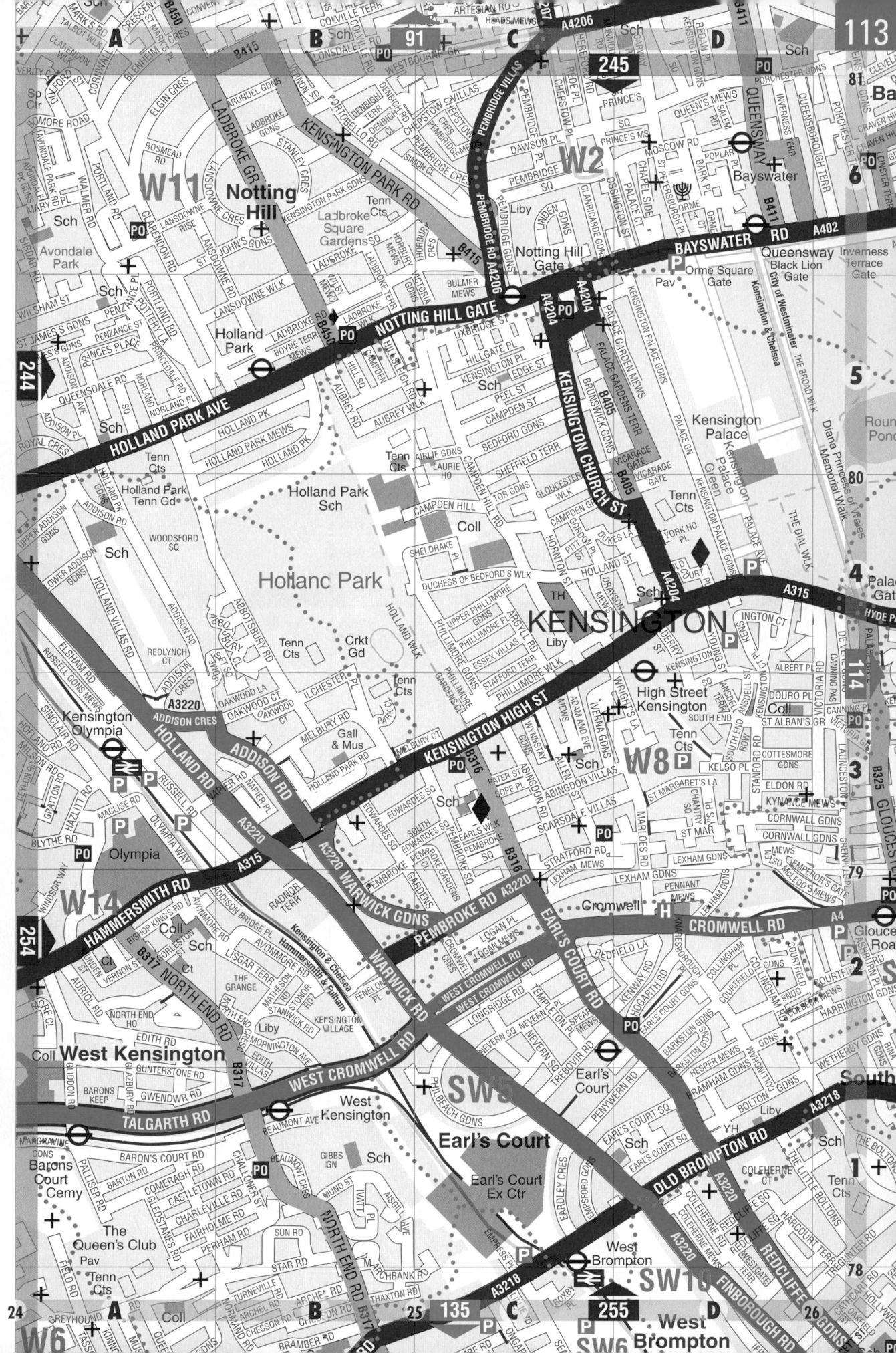
A
B
C
D
91
245
244
254
135
255
W11
W2
W8
W14
SW5
SW10
W6
SW6
Notting Hill
Holland Park
Bayswater
Notting Hill Gate
Kensington Palace
KENSINGTON
High Street Kensington
Kensington Olympia
Olympia
West Kensington
Earl's Court
Earl's Court Ex Ctr
West Brompton
Barons Court Cemy
The Queen's Club
Avondale Park
Ladbroke Square Gardens
Holland Park Sch
Holland Park Tenn Gd
Gall & Mus
Queensway
Orme Square Gate
Black Lion Gate
Inverness Terrace Gate
Diana Princess of Wales Memorial Walk
Kensington Palace Green
Cromwell
HOLLAND PARK AVE
NOTTING HILL GATE
BAYSWATER RD
KENSINGTON HIGH ST
KENSINGTON CHURCH ST
HAMMERSMITH RD
CROMWELL RD
WEST CROMWELL RD
TALGARTH RD
OLD BROMPTON RD
EARL'S COURT RD
WARWICK RD
WARWICK GDNS
PEMBROKE RD
HOLLAND RD
ADDISON RD
NORTH END RD
REDCLIFFE GDNS
FINBOROUGH RD
QUEENSWAY
LADBROKE GR
KENSINGTON PARK RD
PEMBRIDGE VILLAS
PEMBRIDGE RD
A4206
A4204
A402
A315
A3220
A4
A3218
B450
B415
B405
B411
B316
B317
B325
Kensington & Chelsea
City of Westminster
Hammersmith & Fulham
1
2
3
4
5
6
78
79
80
81
25
26
114

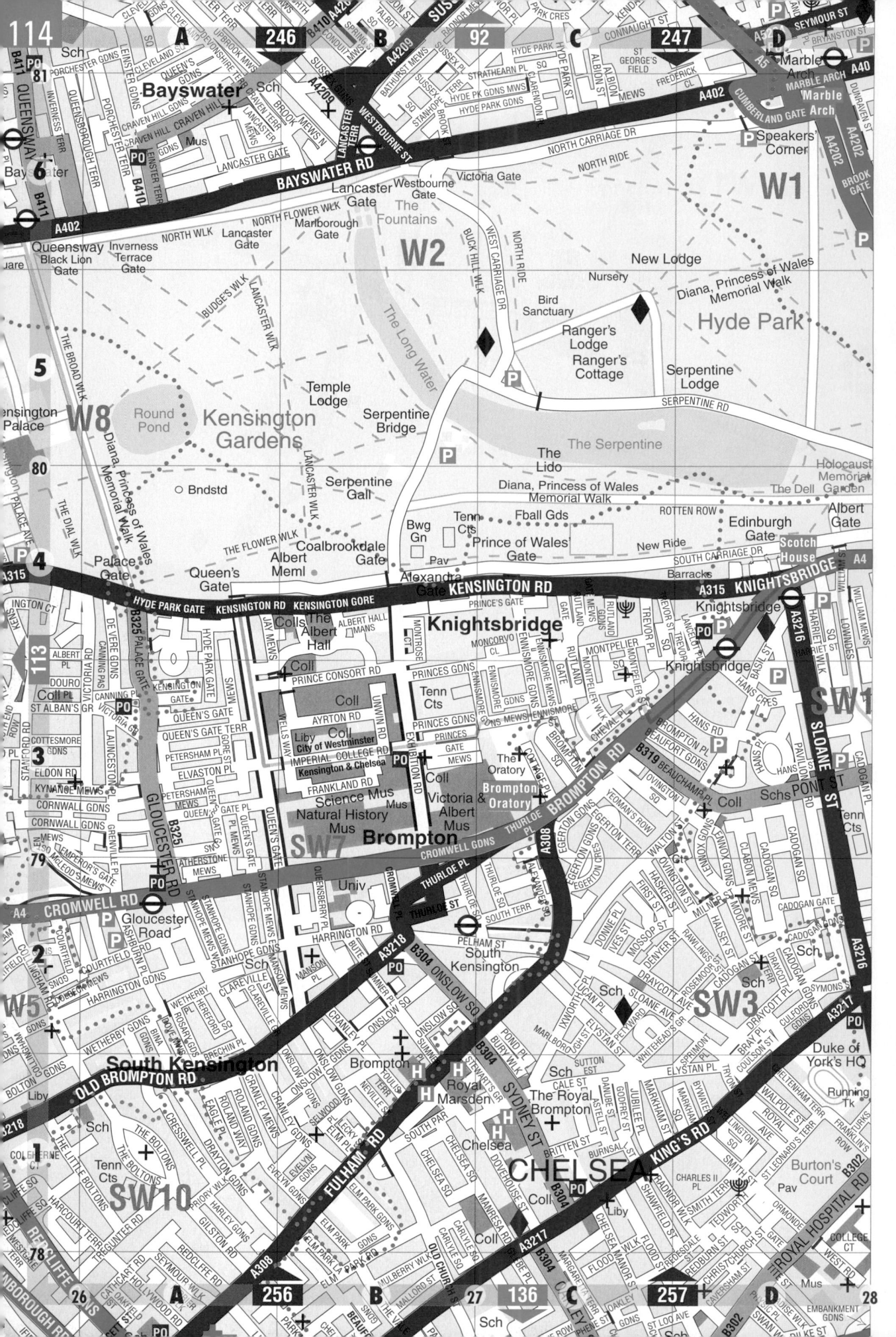

246
92
247
256
136
257
113
A
B
C
D
1
2
3
4
5
6
26
27
28
78
79
80
81
Bayswater
Queensway
Bayswater Rd
Lancaster Gate
Marble Arch
Speakers' Corner
Cumberland Gate
North Carriage Dr
North Ride
Victoria Gate
Westbourne Gate
Lancaster Gate
The Fountains
Marlborough Gate
Queensway Black Lion Gate
Inverness Terrace Gate
North Flower Wlk
North Wlk
W1
W2
W8
New Lodge
Nursery
Diana, Princess of Wales Memorial Walk
Bird Sanctuary
Ranger's Lodge
Ranger's Cottage
Hyde Park
Serpentine Lodge
Serpentine Rd
The Long Water
Buck Hill Wlk
West Carriage Dr
North Ride
Temple Lodge
Serpentine Bridge
Round Pond
Kensington Gardens
Kensington Palace
The Serpentine
The Lido
Holocaust Memorial Garden
The Dell
Serpentine Gall
Bndstd
Rotten Row
Fball Gds
Tenn Cts
Bwg Gn
Prince of Wales' Gate
Edinburgh Gate
Albert Gate
New Ride
South Carriage Dr
Coalbrookdale Gate
Albert Meml
Queen's Gate
Palace Gate
Alexandra Gate
Pav
Barracks
Scotch House
The Broad Wlk
The Dial Wlk
The Flower Wlk
Budge's Wlk
Lancaster Wlk
Kensington Rd
Knightsbridge
Hyde Park Gate
Kensington Gore
A315
A4
A402
A40
Knightsbridge
Colls
The Albert Hall
Coll
Prince Consort Rd
Princes Gdns
Imperial College Rd
City of Westminster
Kensington & Chelsea
Science Mus
Natural History Mus
Victoria & Albert Mus
Brompton Oratory
The Oratory
Brompton
Brompton Rd
SW7
SW1
SW3
SW5
SW10
Cromwell Rd
Cromwell Gdns
Thurloe Pl
Gloucester Road
Gloucester Rd
South Kensington
Old Brompton Rd
Onslow Sq
Fulham Rd
Sloane St
Pont St
Royal Marsden
The Royal Brompton
Chelsea
CHELSEA
King's Rd
Sydney St
Duke of York's HQ
Burton's Court
Royal Hospital Rd
Running Tk
The Boltons
Redcliffe Sq
Hans Cres
Cadogan Sq
Cadogan Gate
Sloane Ave
Draycott Ave
Elystan Pl
Queen's Gate
Gloucester Rd
Exhibition Rd
Harrington Rd
Pelham St
Onslow Sq
Cale St
Britten St
Chelsea Manor St
Flood St
Oakley St
Old Church St
Beaufort St
Sch
Liby
Univ
Mus

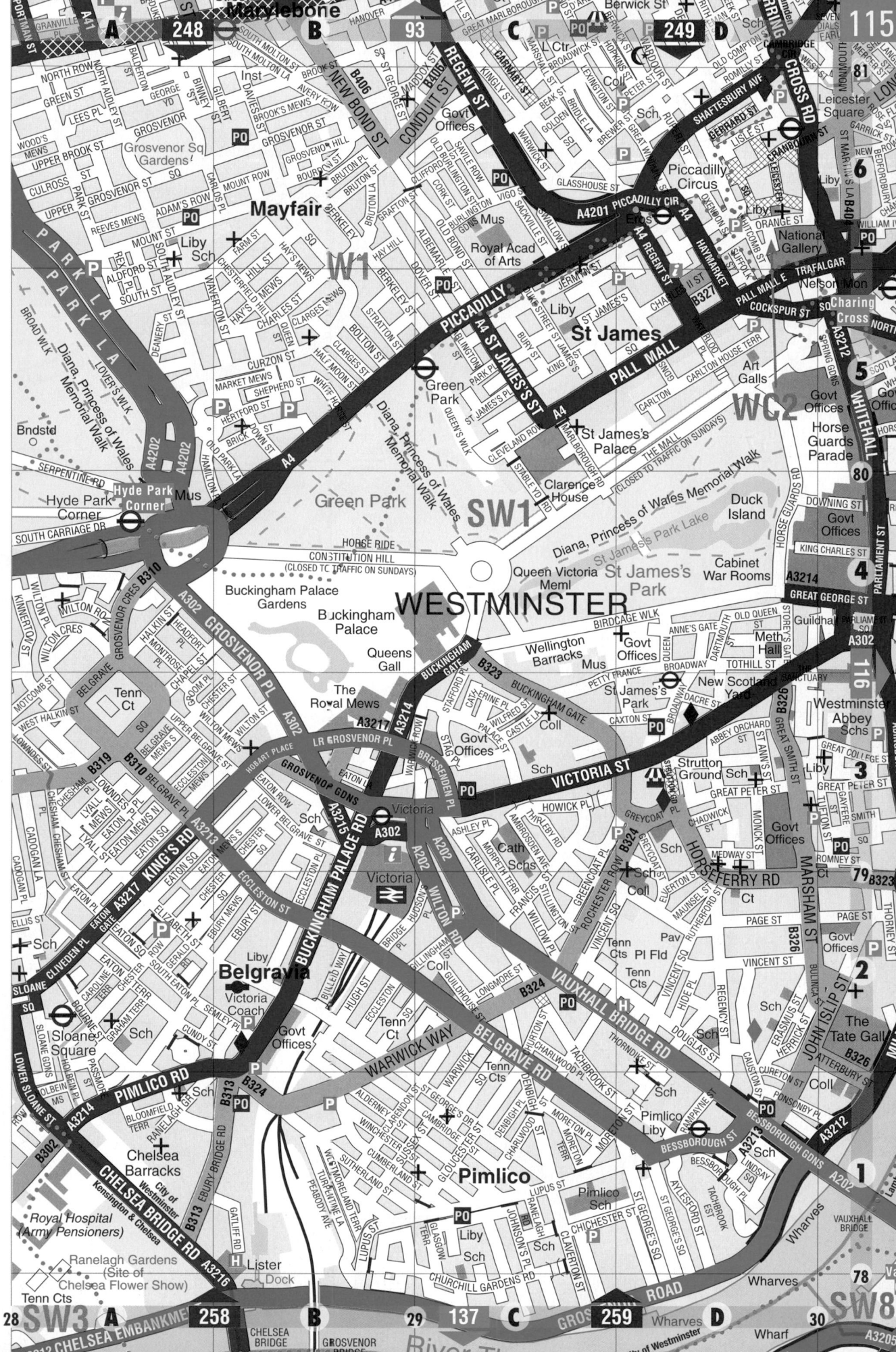
Marylebone
248
93
249
Mayfair
W1
St James
WC2
Piccadilly Circus
Leicester Square
National Gallery
Nelson Mon
Charing Cross
Green Park
St James's Palace
Clarence House
SW1
Hyde Park Corner
Buckingham Palace Gardens
Buckingham Palace
WESTMINSTER
St James's Park
Queen Victoria Meml
Cabinet War Rooms
Horse Guards Parade
Duck Island
Royal Acad of Arts
Wellington Barracks
New Scotland Yard
Westminster Abbey
The Royal Mews
Queens Gall
Victoria
Belgravia
Victoria Coach
Sloane Square
Chelsea Barracks
Royal Hospital (Army Pensioners)
Ranelagh Gardens (Site of Chelsea Flower Show)
Pimlico
The Tate Gall
PICCADILLY
PALL MALL
VICTORIA ST
REGENT ST
PARK LA
WHITEHALL
VAUXHALL BRIDGE RD
BELGRAVE RD
BUCKINGHAM PALACE RD
KING'S RD
CHELSEA BRIDGE RD
HORSEFERRY RD
MARSHAM ST
GROSVENOR PL
PIMLICO RD
WARWICK WAY
GROSVENOR RD
CHELSEA EMBANKMENT
River Thames
Lister
Dock
Wharves
City of Westminster
Kensington & Chelsea
SW3
SW8
116
258
137
259
28
29
30
A
B
C
D
1
2
3
4
5
6

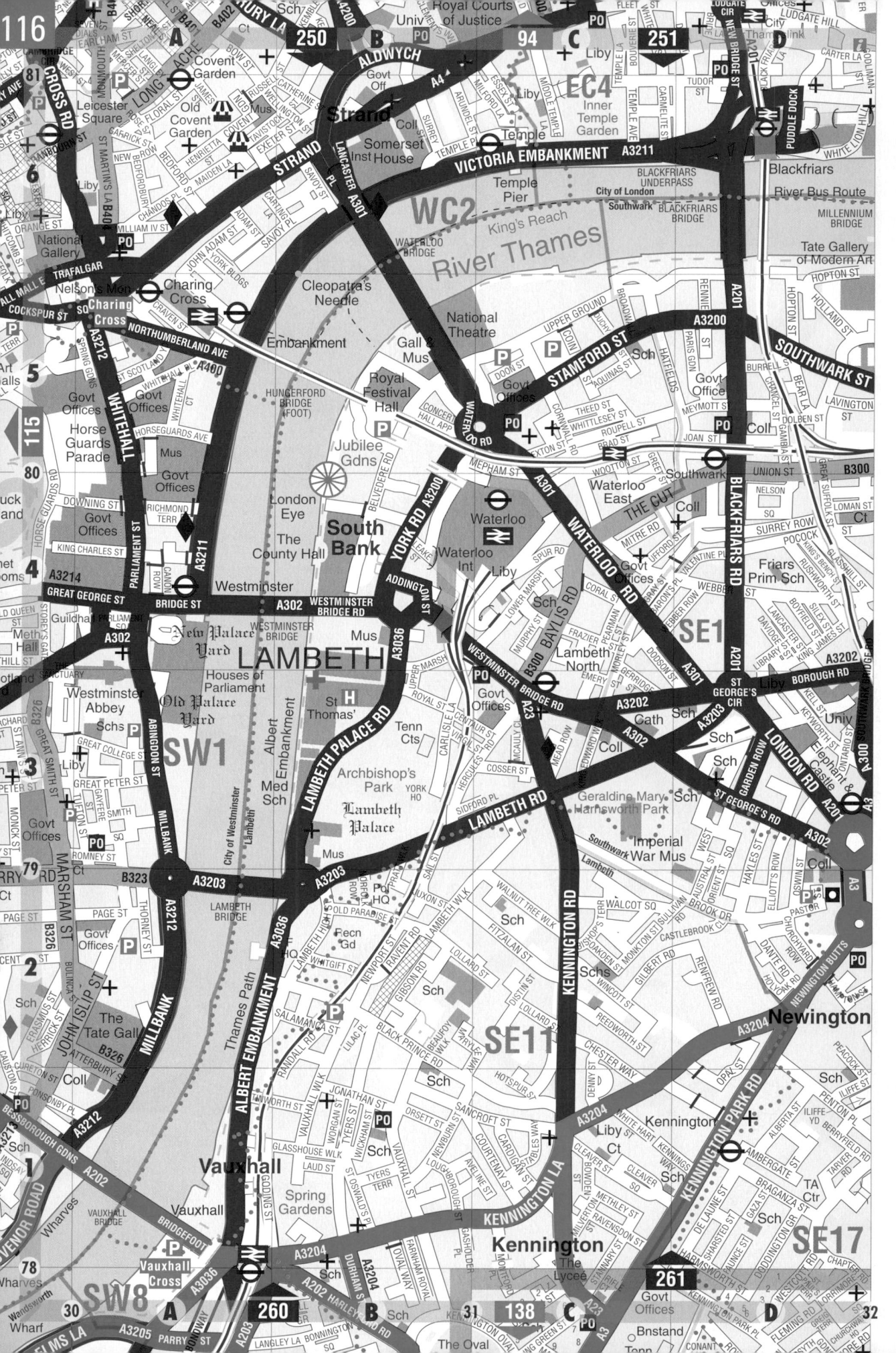
250
94
251
A
B
C
D
Royal Courts of Justice
Univ
ALDWYCH
Covent Garden
LONG ACRE
Leicester Square
Old Covent Garden
CROSS RD
Strand
STRAND
Somerset House
Govt Off
Temple
VICTORIA EMBANKMENT
A3211
EC4
Inner Temple Garden
Blackfriars
Blackfriars River Bus Route
BLACKFRIARS UNDERPASS
BLACKFRIARS BRIDGE
MILLENNIUM BRIDGE
Tate Gallery of Modern Art
Temple Pier
City of London
Southwark
WC2
King's Reach
River Thames
WATERLOO BRIDGE
National Gallery
TRAFALGAR
Nelson's Mon
Charing Cross
NORTHUMBERLAND AVE
Cleopatra's Needle
Embankment
National Theatre
Gall & Mus
Royal Festival Hall
HUNGERFORD BRIDGE (FOOT)
UPPER GROUND
STAMFORD ST
A3200
SOUTHWARK ST
BLACKFRIARS RD
A201
WHITEHALL
Govt Offices
Horse Guards Parade
HORSEGUARDS AVE
Jubilee Gdns
London Eye
The County Hall
South Bank
YORK RD
Waterloo
Waterloo Int
Waterloo East
THE CUT
WATERLOO RD
Southwark
UNION ST
B300
SE1
Friars Prim Sch
PARLIAMENT ST
Westminster
GREAT GEORGE ST
BRIDGE ST
A302
WESTMINSTER BRIDGE RD
WESTMINSTER BRIDGE
New Palace Yard
LAMBETH
Houses of Parliament
Old Palace Yard
Westminster Abbey
St Thomas'
Lambeth North
BAYLIS RD
ST GEORGE'S CIR
BOROUGH RD
LONDON RD
Elephant & Castle
SW1
Albert Embankment
LAMBETH PALACE RD
Archbishop's Park
Lambeth Palace
LAMBETH RD
Geraldine Mary Harmsworth Park
Imperial War Mus
ST GEORGE'S RD
ABINGDON ST
MILLBANK
A3203
LAMBETH BRIDGE
MARSHAM ST
KENNINGTON RD
NEWINGTON BUTTS
Newington
The Tate Gall
SE11
ALBERT EMBANKMENT
Thames Path
JOHN ISLIP ST
Vauxhall
Spring Gardens
VAUXHALL BRIDGE
KENNINGTON LA
KENNINGTON PARK RD
Kennington
SE17
BESSBOROUGH GDNS
A202
Vauxhall Cross
SW8
260
261
138
The Oval
Wharves
30
31
32
115
81
80
79
78
6
5
4
3
2
1

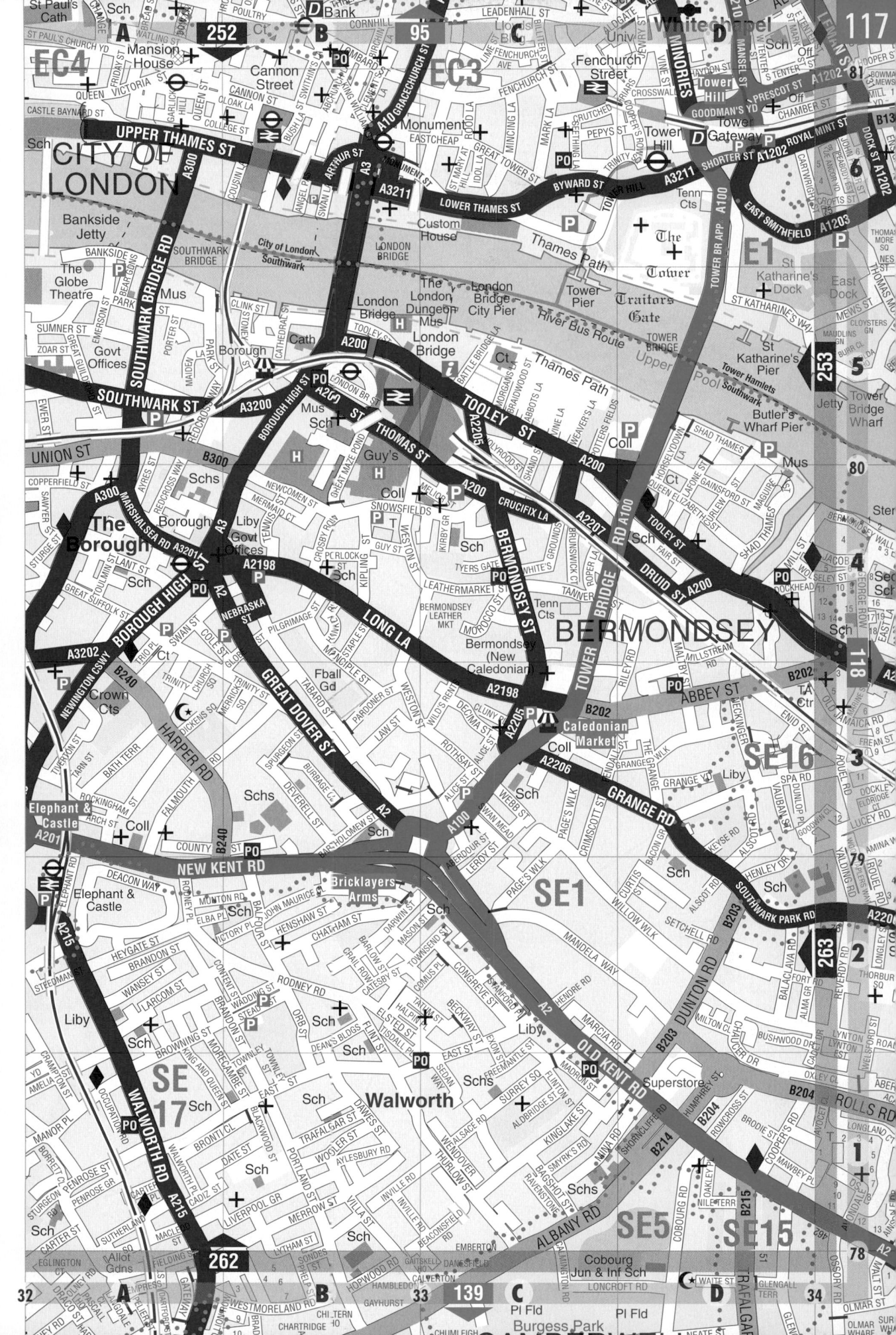
117
252
95
118
253
263
262
139
A
B
C
D
32
33
34
81
80
79
78
6
5
4
3
2
1
EC4
EC3
E1
SE1
SE16
SE17
SE5
SE15
St Paul's Cath
Mansion House
Cannon Street
Bank
Monument
Fenchurch Street
Tower Hill
Tower Gateway
Whitechapel
CITY OF LONDON
UPPER THAMES ST
LOWER THAMES ST
BYWARD ST
EAST SMITHFIELD
ROYAL MINT ST
MINORIES
GRACECHURCH ST
Custom House
LONDON BRIDGE
SOUTHWARK BRIDGE
Bankside Jetty
The Globe Theatre
Thames Path
The Tower
Traitors Gate
Tower Pier
London Bridge City Pier
River Bus Route
TOWER BRIDGE
St Katharine's Dock
East Dock
St Katharine's Pier
Butler's Wharf Pier
Tower Bridge Wharf
City of London
Southwark
Tower Hamlets
London Bridge
The London Dungeon Mus
Borough
Guy's
SOUTHWARK BRIDGE RD
SOUTHWARK ST
UNION ST
BOROUGH HIGH ST
TOOLEY ST
ST THOMAS ST
BERMONDSEY ST
LONG LA
GREAT DOVER ST
TOWER BRIDGE RD
DRUID ST
CRUCIFIX LA
The Borough
BERMONDSEY
Bermondsey Leather Mkt
Bermondsey (New Caledonian)
Caledonian Market
ABBEY ST
GRANGE RD
SOUTHWARK PARK RD
HARPER RD
NEWINGTON CSWY
Elephant & Castle
NEW KENT RD
Bricklayers Arms
OLD KENT RD
WALWORTH RD
Walworth
MANDELA WAY
DUNTON RD
ALBANY RD
Superstore
ROLLS RD
Cobourg Jun & Inf Sch
Burgess Park
Pl Fld
Allot Gdns

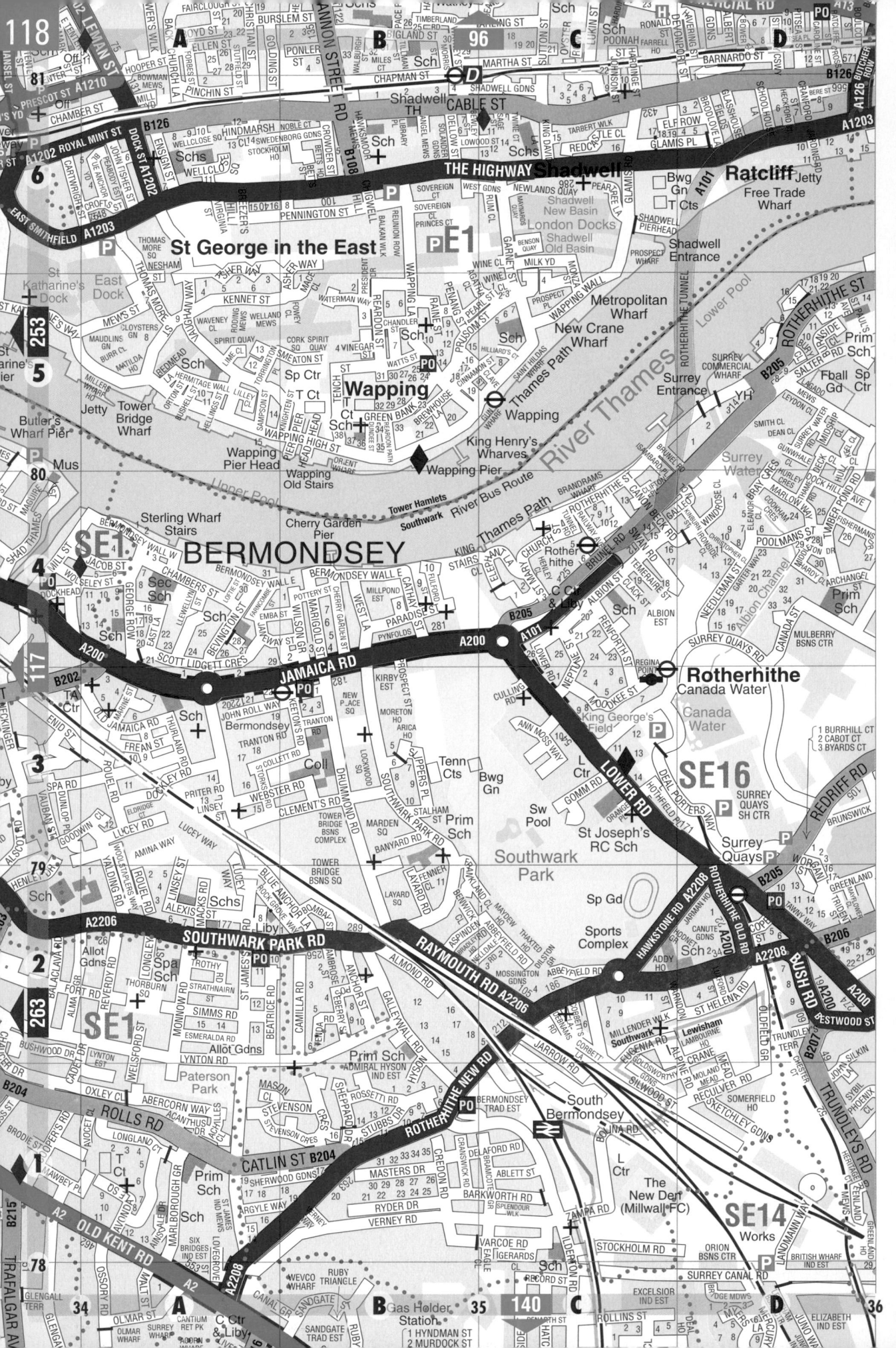
A
B
C
D
96
6
5
4
3
2
1
81
80
79
78
34
35
36
140
253
117
263
LEMAN ST
A1210
PRESCOT ST
CHAMBER ST
ROYAL MINT ST
DOCK ST A1202
B126
A1202
A1203
EAST SMITHFIELD
CANNON STREET RD
BURSLEM ST
BIGLAND ST
PONLER ST
CHAPMAN ST
MARTHA ST
SHADWELL GDNS
CABLE ST
Shadwell
HINDMARSH
WELLCLOSE SQ
SWEDENBORG GDNS
THE HIGHWAY
Shadwell
Ratcliff
Free Trade Wharf
Jetty
Shadwell New Basin
London Docks
Shadwell Old Basin
Shadwell Entrance
PENNINGTON ST
St George in the East
E1
St Katharine's Dock
East Dock
WAPPING LA
WAPPING WALL
Metropolitan Wharf
New Crane Wharf
Lower Pool
ROTHERHITHE TUNNEL
A101
Thames Path
Wapping
Wapping
WAPPING HIGH ST
Tower Bridge Wharf
Butler's Wharf Pier
Wapping Pier Head
Wapping Old Stairs
Wapping Pier
King Henry's Wharves
River Thames
Upper Pool
Tower Hamlets
Southwark
River Bus Route
Sterling Wharf Stairs
Cherry Garden Pier
SE1
BERMONDSEY
BERMONDSEY WALL W
BERMONDSEY WALL E
Surrey Entrance
SURREY COMMERCIAL WHARF
ROTHERHITHE ST
B205
Surrey Water
Rotherhithe
BRUNEL RD
SALTER RD
JAMAICA RD
A200
B202
SCOTT LIDGETT CRES
Bermondsey
Rotherhithe
Canada Water
SURREY QUAYS RD
Albion Channel
LOWER RD
SE16
REDRIFF RD
Surrey Quays
SURREY QUAYS SH CTR
Southwark Park
St Joseph's RC Sch
Sp Gd
Sports Complex
ROTHERHITHE OLD RD
HAWKSTONE RD
A2208
BUSH RD
SOUTHWARK PARK RD
A2206
RAYMOUTH RD A2206
ROTHERHITHE NEW RD
Paterson Park
ROLLS RD
B204
CATLIN ST B204
OLD KENT RD
A2
South Bermondsey
The New Den (Millwall FC)
SE14
Works
TRUNDLEYS RD
STOCKHOLM RD
SURREY CANAL RD
Gas Holder Station
1 HYNDMAN ST
2 MURDOCK ST
TRAFALGAR AV
1 BURRHILL CT
2 CABOT CT
3 BYARDS CT

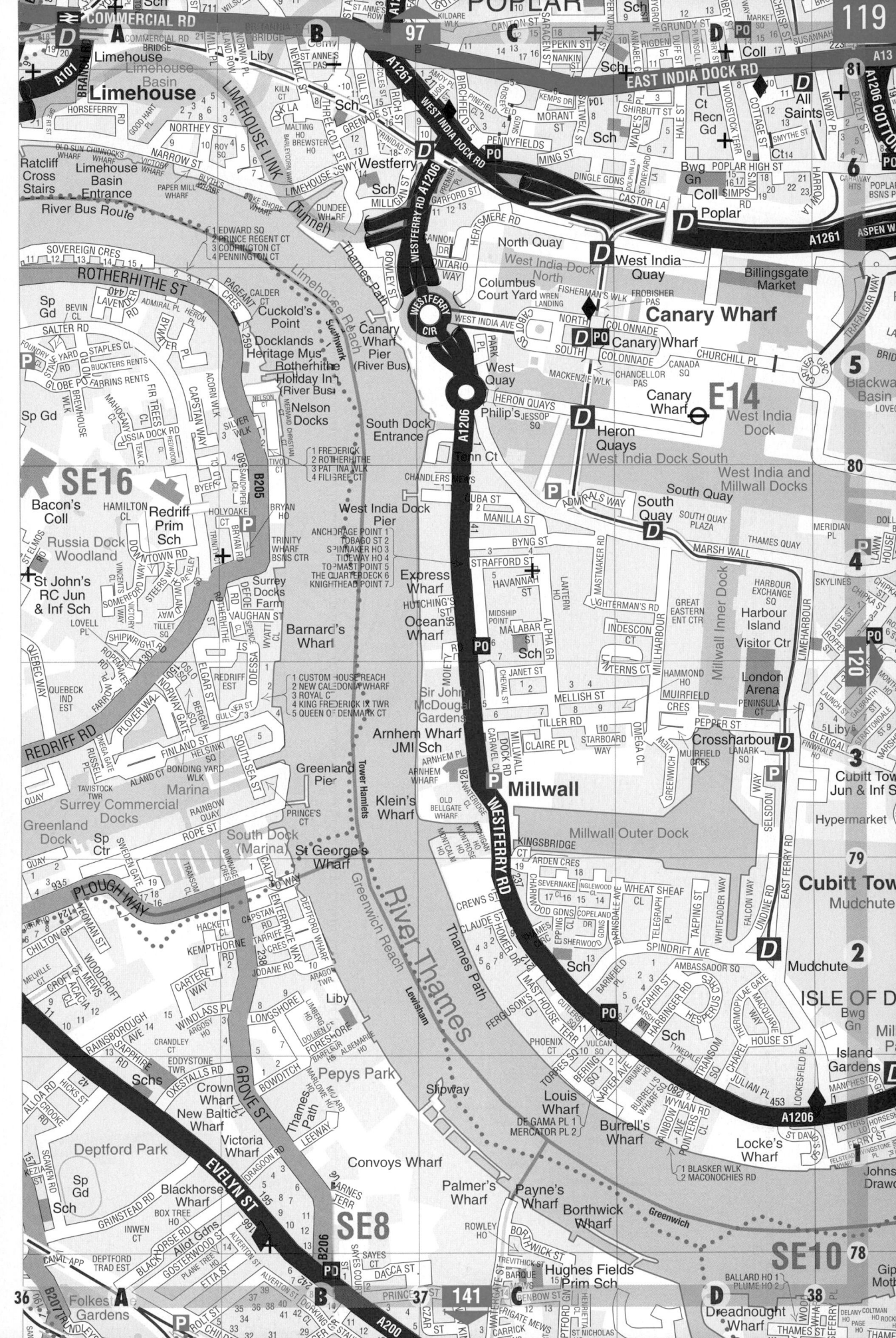
COMMERCIAL RD
POPLAR
EAST INDIA DOCK RD
Limehouse
Limehouse Basin
LIMEHOUSE LINK
Ratcliff Cross Stairs
Limehouse Basin Entrance
River Bus Route
Westferry
WESTFERRY RD
WEST INDIA DOCK RD
All Saints
POPLAR HIGH ST
Poplar
North Quay
West India Quay
West India Dock North
Billingsgate Market
Columbus Court Yard
Canary Wharf
Canary Wharf Pier (River Bus)
West Quay
Heron Quays
West India Dock
West India Dock South
E14
Blackwall Basin
ROTHERHITHE ST
Cuckold's Point
Docklands Heritage Mus
Rotherhithe Holiday Inn (River Bus)
Nelson Docks
South Dock Entrance
SE16
Bacon's Coll
Redriff Prim Sch
Russia Dock Woodland
St John's RC Jun & Inf Sch
Surrey Docks Farm
Barnard's Wharf
West India Dock Pier
Express Wharf
Ocean Wharf
Limehouse Reach
South Quay
West India and Millwall Docks
MARSH WALL
Millwall Inner Dock
Harbour Island Visitor Ctr
London Arena
Crossharbour
Sir John McDougal Gardens
Arnhem Wharf JMI Sch
Millwall
Millwall Outer Dock
Klein's Wharf
Greenland Pier
REDRIFF RD
Surrey Commercial Docks
Greenland Dock
South Dock (Marina)
St George's Wharf
PLOUGH WAY
River Thames
Greenwich Reach
Thames Path
Mudchute
Cubitt Town
ISLE OF DOGS
Island Gardens
Pepys Park
Slipway
Louis Wharf
Burrell's Wharf
Locke's Wharf
Deptford Park
EVELYN ST
GROVE ST
Convoys Wharf
Palmer's Wharf
Payne's Wharf
Borthwick Wharf
SE8
SE10
Hughes Fields Prim Sch
Dreadnought Wharf
Folkestone Gardens
A1206
A1261
A200
97
120
141
36
37
38

EAST INDIA DOCK RD
98
Creek Mills
Canning Town
A13
81
All Saints
A1206 COTTON ST
ASHTON ST
Sch
ROBIN HOOD LA
NUTMEG LA
CORIANDER AVE
OREGANO DR
SAFFRON AVE
CLOVE CRES
EAST INDIA DOCK WALL RD
East India
NAVAL ROW
QUIXLEY ST
SCOULER ST
Golf Driving Range
POPLAR BSNS PK
ASPEN WAY
A1261
A1020
LOWER LEA CROSSING
East India Dock Basin
PILGRIMS MEWS
JAMESTOWN WAY
NEWPORT AVE
Hercules Wharf
Orchard Wharf
Jetty
Blackwall Pier
Trinity Buoy Wharf
Bow Creek Wharf
Thames Wharf
WILLAN WALL
NELSON ST
FEN ST
FOSTER CT
Tower Hamlets
Newham
ORCHARD PL
PETO ST N
CAXTON ST N
A1011
HUNTINGDON ST
BOWMAN AVE
BRAY DR
DOCK RD
Brunswick Wharf
Blackwall
Blackwall Reach
BLACKWALL TUNNEL
ALBERTA HO
ST LAWRENCE ST
WARRINGTON PL
Billingsgate Mkt
Poplar Dock
TRAFALGAR WAY
A1206
PRESTON'S RD
LANDONS CL
BRIDGE HOUSE QUAY
Blackwall Basin
VANTAGE MEWS
Blackwall Stairs
Blackwall Entrance (Closed)
Blackwall Point
E16
City Airport Pier
Bugsby's Reach
Jetty
Ordnance Wharf
Millennium Dome
West India Dock
E14
LOVEGROVE WLK
LANCASTER DR
COLDHARBOUR
80
West India and Millwall Docks
MANAGERS ST
HORATIO PL
CONCORDIA WHARF
South Dock Entrance
DOLLAR BAY
GLEN TERR
MERIDIAN PL
THAMES QUAY
LAWN HOUSE CL
Jetty
River Thames
North Greenwich
TUNNEL AVE
ORDNANCE CRES
BLACKWALL TUNNEL APP
TUNNEL AVENUE TRAD EST
Delta Wharf
Victoria Deep Water Terminal
A102
Newham
Greenwich
Jetty
Jetty
RIVER WAY
RIVERSIDE IND EST
Harbour Exchange SQ
Harbour Island
Visitor Ctr
SKYLINES
CHIPKA ST
LIMEHARBOUR
119
London Arena
PENINSULA CT
PLEVNA ST
MONTFORT HO
FOLLY WALL
CAPSTAN SQ
RIVER BARGE CL
STEWART ST
NEW UNION CL
KELSON HO
DAGMAR CT
HALYARD HO
Gas Works
BLACKWALL LA
BOORD ST
Bay Wharf
GLENGALL GR
MARSHFIELD ST
Cubitt Town Jun & Inf Sch
FRANS HALS CT
VAN GOGH CT
VERMEER CT
REMBRANDT
AMSTERDAM RD
ROTTERDAM DR
LEERDAM DR
LYMINGTON LO
Pier
Primrose Wharf
Jetty
DREADNOUGHT ST
MORDEN WHARF RD
Morden Wharf
TUNNEL AVE
A2203
Hypermarket
FRIARS MEAD
JUBILEE CRES
MILLENNIUM DR
CHICHESTER WAY
MARINERS MEWS
MANCHESTER RD
Refineries
PETERBOAT CL
BUGSBYS WAY
Thames Path
79
EAST FERRY RD
SELSDON WAY
Cubitt Town
Mudchute Park
Allot Gdns
PIER ST
SEXTANT AVE
PLYMOUTH WHARF
SEYSSEL ST
KINGFIELD ST
BILLSON ST
Sch
STORERS QUAY
CALEDONIAN WHARF RD
Cubitt Town Wharf
Works
SE10
Mudchute
ISLE OF DOGS
Bwg Gn
Pl Fld
Millwall Park
STEBONDALE ST
PARSONAGE ST
EMPIRE WHARF
GROSVENOR WHARF RD
LAWRENCE TRAD EST
MAURITIUS RD
AZOF ST
Piper's Wharf
MERIDIAN HO
Island Gardens
MANCHESTER GR
SAUNDERS NESS RD
Newcastle Drawdock
CUMBERLAND MILLS SQ
Sec Sch
Badcocks Wharves
CADET PL
Lovell's Wharf
CHRISTCHURCH WAY
BELLOT ST
CE JMI Sch
BLACKWALL LA
ARMITAGE RD
HARROTT CL
MERCERS CL
TUNNEL AVE
LENTHORP RD
GLENFORTH ST
FINGAL ST
GLENISTER RD
A102
A1206
POTTERS LO
HORSESHOE CL
FERRY ST
Island Gardens
CARVEL HO
CLIPPER HO
COLLINGTON ST
BALLAST QUAY
BANNING ST
PELTON RD
Sch
A2203
A206
PO
CHEVENING RD
Johnson's Drawdock
Greenwich Footway Tunnel
Jetty
HOSKINS ST
LASSELL ST
GIBSON ST
CARADOC ST
HADRIAN ST
WHITWORTH ST
TYLER ST
COLOMB ST
Greenwich District
CALVERT RD
Prim Sch
East Greenwich Pleasaunce
78
Greenwich Pier
OLD WOOLWICH RD
TRAFALGAR RD
WOODLANDS GR
EARLSWOOD ST
WALNUT TREE RD
ANNANDALE RD
TUSKAR ST
Gipsy Moth IV
Cutty Sark
Royal Naval Coll
Sch
A206
WOODLANDS PARK RD
VANBRUGH HILL
DINSDALE RD
HUMBER RD
38
39
142
40
A
B
C
D
Cutty Sark
ROMNEY RD
THAMES ST
RESTELL CL
Maze Hill
SE3
GREENWICH
THALIA CL
1
2
3
4
5
6

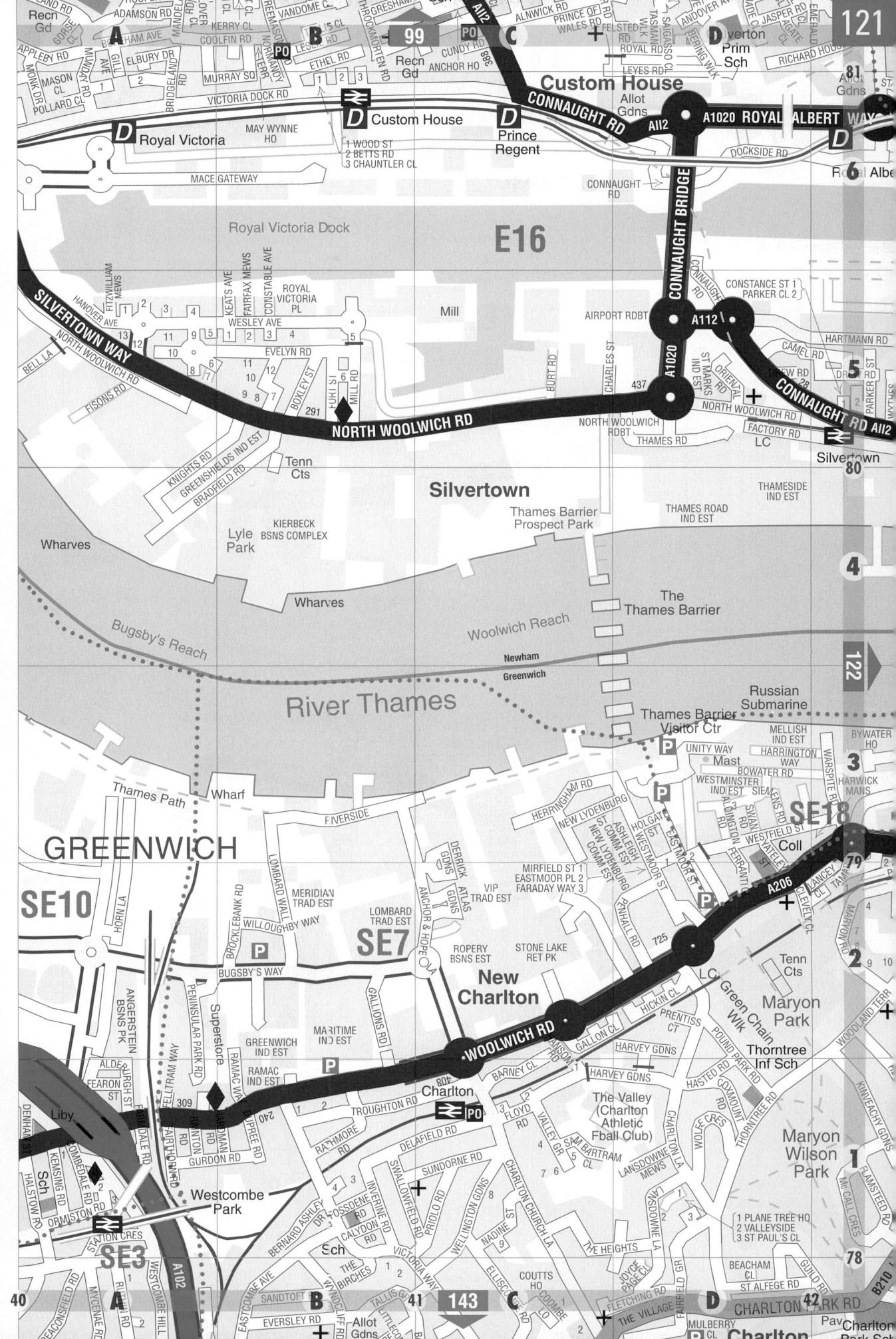
Recn Gd
ADAMSON RD
VANDOME CL
GRESHAM
ALNWICK RD
PRINCE OF WALES RD
FELSTED RD
TASMAN WLK
SAIGASSO CL
ANDOVER AVE
JASPER RD
EMERALD
Custom House
A
B
99
C
D
Keir Hardie Prim Sch
RICHARD HOUSE
81
Allot Gdns
COOLFIN RD
KERRY CL
TALLIS CL
LESLIE RD
PO
ELBURY DR
MASON CL
POLLARD CL
APPLEBY RD
MONK DR
MUNDAY RD
GILL AVE
BRIDGELAND RD
MURRAY SQ
NORMANDY TERR
ETHEL RD
THROCKMORTEN RD
Recn Gd
CUNDY RD
ANCHOR HO
ROYAL RD
LEYES RD
BERING WLK
VICTORIA DOCK RD
CONNAUGHT RD
A112
A1020 ROYAL ALBERT WAY
Royal Victoria
MAY WYNNE HO
Custom House
Prince Regent
1 WOOD ST
2 BETTS RD
3 CHAUNTLER CL
DOCKSIDE RD
6
Royal Albert
MACE GATEWAY
CONNAUGHT RD
CONNAUGHT BRIDGE
Royal Victoria Dock
E16
SILVERTOWN WAY
HANOVER AVE
FITZWILLIAM MEWS
KEATS AVE
FAIRFAX MEWS
CONSTABLE AVE
ROYAL VICTORIA PL
WESLEY AVE
EVELYN RD
Mill
AIRPORT RDBT
CONSTANCE ST 1
PARKER CL 2
A112
HARTMANN RD
CAMEL RD
BELL LA
NORTH WOOLWICH RD
FISONS RD
BOXLEY ST
PORT ST
MILL RD
BURT RD
CHARLES ST
A1020
ST MARKS IND EST
ORIENTAL RD
DREW RD
PARKER ST
5
CONNAUGHT RD A112
NORTH WOOLWICH RD
291
437
NORTH WOOLWICH RDBT
THAMES RD
FACTORY RD
LC
Silvertown
80
KNIGHTS RD
GREENSHIELDS IND EST
BRADFIELD RD
Tenn Cts
Silvertown
Thames Barrier Prospect Park
THAMESIDE IND EST
THAMES ROAD IND EST
Wharves
Lyle Park
KIERBECK BSNS COMPLEX
4
Wharves
The Thames Barrier
Bugsby's Reach
Woolwich Reach
Newham
Greenwich
122
River Thames
Russian Submarine
Thames Barrier Visitor Ctr
UNITY WAY
Mast
MELLISH IND EST
HARRINGTON WAY
BOWATER RD
WESTMINSTER IND EST
BYWATER HO
3
HARWICK MANS
WARSPITE RD
Thames Path
Wharf
RIVERSIDE
HERRINGHAM RD
NEW LYDENBURG
ST COMM EST
NEW LYDENBURG COMM EST
ASHLEIGH COMM EST
HOLGATE ST
EASTMOOR ST
WESTMOOR ST
SIEMENS RD
SWAN RD
ALDINGTON RD
FERRANTI CL
WESTFIELD ST
SE18
Coll
GREENWICH
SE10
HORN LA
LOMBARD WALL
MERIDIAN TRAD EST
DERRICK GDNS
ATLAS GDNS
VIP TRAD EST
MIRFIELD ST 1
EASTMOOR PL 2
FARADAY WAY 3
PENHALL RD
A206
YATELEY ST
LANCEY CL
CLEVELY CL
MARYON RD
79
BROCKLEBANK RD
WILLOUGHBY WAY
LOMBARD TRAD EST
SE7
ANCHOR & HOPE LA
ROPERY BSNS EST
STONE LAKE RET PK
725
Tenn Cts
2
BUGSBY'S WAY
New Charlton
LC
Green Chain Wlk
Maryon Park
WOODLAND TERR
ANGERSTEIN BSNS PK
PENINSULAR PARK RD
Superstore
GALLIONS RD
MARITIME IND EST
HICKIN CL
PRENTISS CT
WOOLWICH RD
GALLON CL
POUND PARK RD
Thorntree Inf Sch
GREENWICH IND EST
RAMAC IND EST
RAMAC WAY
HARVEY GDNS
ALDEBURGH ST
FEARON ST
FELLTRAM WAY
309
DUPREE RD
240
408
Charlton
BARNEY CL
RANSOM RD
HARVEY GDNS
HASTED RD
COXMOUNT RD
THORNTREE RD
KINVEACHY GDNS
Liby
DENHAM ST
FARMDALE RD
FAIRTHORN RD
HARDMAN RD
RATHMORE RD
TROUGHTON RD
PO
FLOYD RD
The Valley (Charlton Athletic Fball Club)
CHARLTON LA
WOLFE CRES
Maryon Wilson Park
1
KEMSING RD
COMBEDALE RD
GURDON RD
DELAFIELD RD
VALLEY GR
SAM BARTRAM CL
LANSDOWNE MEWS
Sch
Westcombe Park
SUNDORNE RD
SWALLOWFIELD RD
CHARLTON CHURCH LA
LANSDOWNE LA
FLAMSTEED RD
HALSTOW RD
ORMISTON RD
STATION CRES
SE3
A102
BERNARD ASHLEY DR
FOSSDENE RD
CALYDON RD
INVERINE RD
PRIOLO RD
WELLINGTON GDNS
NADINE ST
THE HEIGHTS
1 PLANE TREE HO
2 VALLEYSIDE
3 ST PAUL'S CL
Mc CALL CRES
78
Sch
THE BIRCHES
VICTORIA WAY
ELLISCOMBE RD
COUTTS HO
JOYCE PAGE CL
BEACHAM CL
ST ALFEGE RD
GUILD RD
B210
BEACONSFIELD RD
MYCENAE RD
RUSTON RD
WESTCOMBE HILL
EASTCOMBE AVE
SANDTOFT RD
WYNDCLIFF RD
TALLIS GR
COOMBE LA
FLETCHING RD
THE VILLAGE
FAIRFIELD GR
CHARLTON PARK RD
EVERSLEY RD
Allot Gdns
MULBERRY CL
Charlton
Charlton Park Sch

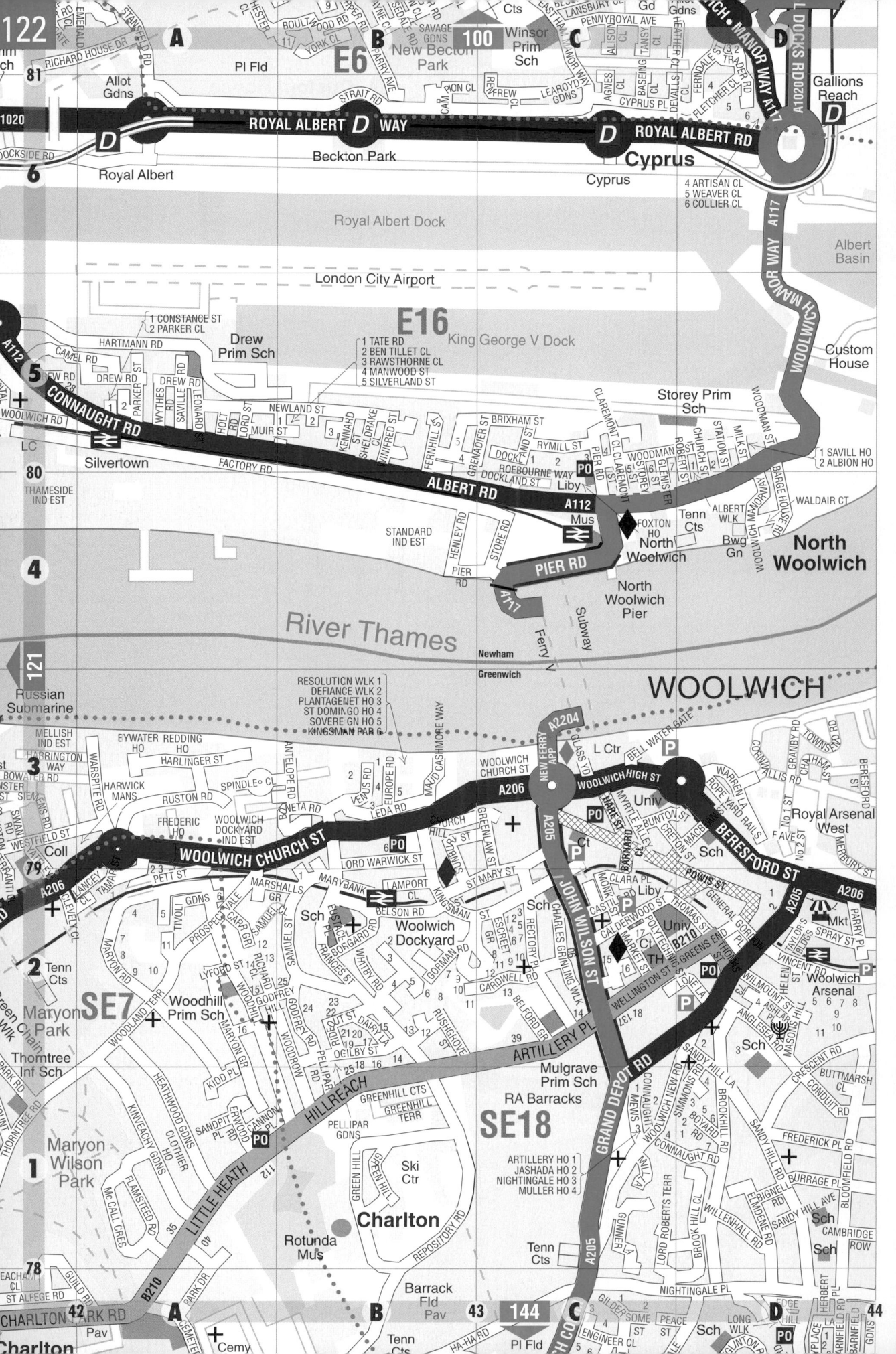
A
B
C
D
100
E6
New Beckton Park
Winsor Prim Sch
PENNYROYAL AVE
LANSBURY
RICHARD HOUSE DR
STANSFIELD RD
EMERALD
Pl Fld
BOULTWOOD RD
YORK CL
PARRY AVE
Allot Gdns
81
SAVAGE GDNS
STRAIT RD
LEAROYD GDNS
RENFREW CL
AGNES CL
BASING CL
CYPRUS PL
DEVALLS CL
FERNDALE ST
FLETCHER CL
TRADER RD
MANOR WAY A117
DOCKS RD
A1020
Gallions Reach
A1020
ROYAL ALBERT WAY
ROYAL ALBERT RD
DOCKSIDE RD
Beckton Park
Cyprus
Royal Albert
6
4 ARTISAN CL
5 WEAVER CL
6 COLLIER CL
Royal Albert Dock
Albert Basin
London City Airport
E16
King George V Dock
1 CONSTANCE ST
2 PARKER CL
HARTMANN RD
Drew Prim Sch
1 TATE RD
2 BEN TILLETT CL
3 RAWSTHORNE CL
4 MANWOOD ST
5 SILVERLAND ST
WOOLWICH MANOR WAY
Custom House
A112
CAMEL RD
DREW RD
5
CONNAUGHT RD
WOOLWICH RD
PARKER ST
WYTHES RD
SAVILLE RD
LEONARD ST
HOLT RD
LORD ST
MUIR ST
NEWLAND ST
KENNARD ST
SHELDRAKE CL
WINIFRED ST
FERNHILL ST
GRENADIER ST
BRIXHAM ST
RYMILL ST
DOCKLAND ST
ROEBOURNE WAY
CLAREMONT CL
CLAREMONT ST
PIER RD
WOODMAN ST
STOREY ST
GLENISTER ST
ROBERT ST
CHURCH ST
STATION ST
MILK ST
WOODMAN ST
Storey Prim Sch
1 SAVILL HO
2 ALBION HO
LC
Silvertown
FACTORY RD
ALBERT RD
PO
Liby
80
THAMESIDE IND EST
A112
Mus
FOXTON HO
Tenn Cts
ALBERT WLK
BARGE HOUSE RD
WALDAIR CT
Bwg Gn
STANDARD IND EST
HENLEY RD
STORE RD
PIER RD
North Woolwich
North Woolwich
4
PIER RD
A117
North Woolwich Pier
River Thames
Subway
Ferry
Newham
Greenwich
121
WOOLWICH
Russian Submarine
RESOLUTION WLK 1
DEFIANCE WLK 2
PLANTAGENET HO 3
ST DOMINGO HO 4
SOVEREIGN HO 5
KINGSMAN PAR 6
MELLISH IND EST
HARRINGTON WAY
BOWATER RD
EYWATER HO
REDDING HO
HARLINGER ST
SPINDLE CL
3
WARSPITE RD
HARWICK MANS
RUSTON RD
ANTELOPE RD
VENUS RD
EUROPE RD
CASHMORE WAY
MAUD
A2204
NEW FERRY APP
GLASS YD
L Ctr
BELL WATER GATE
WOOLWICH CHURCH ST
WOOLWICH HIGH ST
A206
LEDA RD
BONETA RD
FREDERIC HO
WOOLWICH DOCKYARD IND EST
WESTFIELD ST
Coll
79
WOOLWICH CHURCH ST
PO
CHURCH HILL
GREENLAW ST
SUNBURY ST
LORD WARWICK ST
A205
HARE ST
MYRTLE ALLEY
BUNTON ST
CRETON ST
MACBEAN ST
BARNARD CL
Univ
Ct
Sch
BERESFORD ST
WARREN LA
ROPE YARD RAILS
GRANBY RD
TOWNSEND RD
CORNWALLIS RD
CHATHAM ST
BERESFORD ST
Royal Arsenal West
No 1 ST
No 2 ST
F AVE
MERBURY ST
A206
A206
LANCEY CL
TAMAR ST
PETT ST
MARSHALLS GR
MARYBANK
LAMPORT CL
ST MARY ST
KINGSMAN ST
CLARA PL
MONK ST
CASTILE RD
Liby
POWIS ST
GENERAL GORDON PL
THOMAS ST
CALDERWOOD ST
POLYTECHNIC ST
Univ
B210
GREENS END
MARKET ST
TH
Mkt
PARRY PL
SPRAY ST
TAYLOR'S BLDGS
VINCENT RD
Woolwich Arsenal
CLEVELY CL
TIVOLI GDNS
PROSPECT VALE
CARR GR
SAMUEL CL
SAMUEL ST
Sch
EUSTACE PL
BOWGARD RD
BELSON RD
Woolwich Dockyard
ESCREET GR
RECTORY PL
CHARLES GRINLING WLK
JOHN WILSON ST
MARYON RD
2
Tenn Cts
LYFORD ST
RICHARD CL
WOODHILL
GODFREY HILL
FRANCES ST
WHITBY RD
GORMAN RD
CARDWELL RD
BELFORD GR
WELLINGTON ST
LOVE LA
WILMOUNT ST
HELEN ST
ASHLAR PL
MASONS HILL
ANGLESEA RD
SE7
Maryon Park
Green Chain Wlk
Woodhill Prim Sch
WOODLAND TERR
MARYON GR
GODFREY RD
WOODROW
RIDEOUT ST
DAIRY LA
OGILBY ST
PELLIPAR RD
RUSHGROVE ST
ARTILLERY PL
GRAND DEPOT RD
SANDY HILL LA
Sch
Thorntree Inf Sch
THORNTREE RD
PARK RD
HEATHWOOD GDNS
KIDD PL
HILLREACH
GREENHILL CTS
GREENHILL TERR
Mulgrave Prim Sch
RA Barracks
MEWS
CONNAUGHT
WOOLWICH NEW RD
SIMMONS RD
BROOKHILL RD
BOYARD RD
CRESCENT RD
BUTTMARSH CL
CONDUIT RD
KINVEACHY GDNS
CLOTHIER HO
SANDPIT PL
ERWOOD RD
CANNON
PO
PELLIPAR GDNS
SE18
CONNAUGHT RD
FREDERICK PL
Maryon Wilson Park
1
LITTLE HEATH
GREEN HILL
GREEN HILL
Ski Ctr
ARTILLERY HO 1
JASHADA HO 2
NIGHTINGALE HO 3
MULLER HO 4
GUNNER LA
LORD ROBERTS TERR
BROOK HILL CL
WILLENHALL RD
ELMDENE RD
BIGNELL RD
SANDY HILL AVE
BURRAGE PL
BLOOMFIELD RD
FLAMSTEED RD
Mc CALL CRES
35
Charlton
Rotunda Mus
REPOSITORY RD
A205
Tenn Cts
Sch
CAMBRIDGE ROW
Sch
78
BEACHAM CL
ST ALFEGE RD
GUILD RD
B210
PARK DR
Barrack Fld
NIGHTINGALE PL
HERBERT PL
42
CHARLTON PARK RD
A
B
43
144
C
GILDERSOME ST
PEACE ST
LONG WLK
D
44
Pav
Pav
Cemy
Tenn Cts
HA-HA RD
Pl Fld
ENGINEER CL
Sch
PO
Charlton

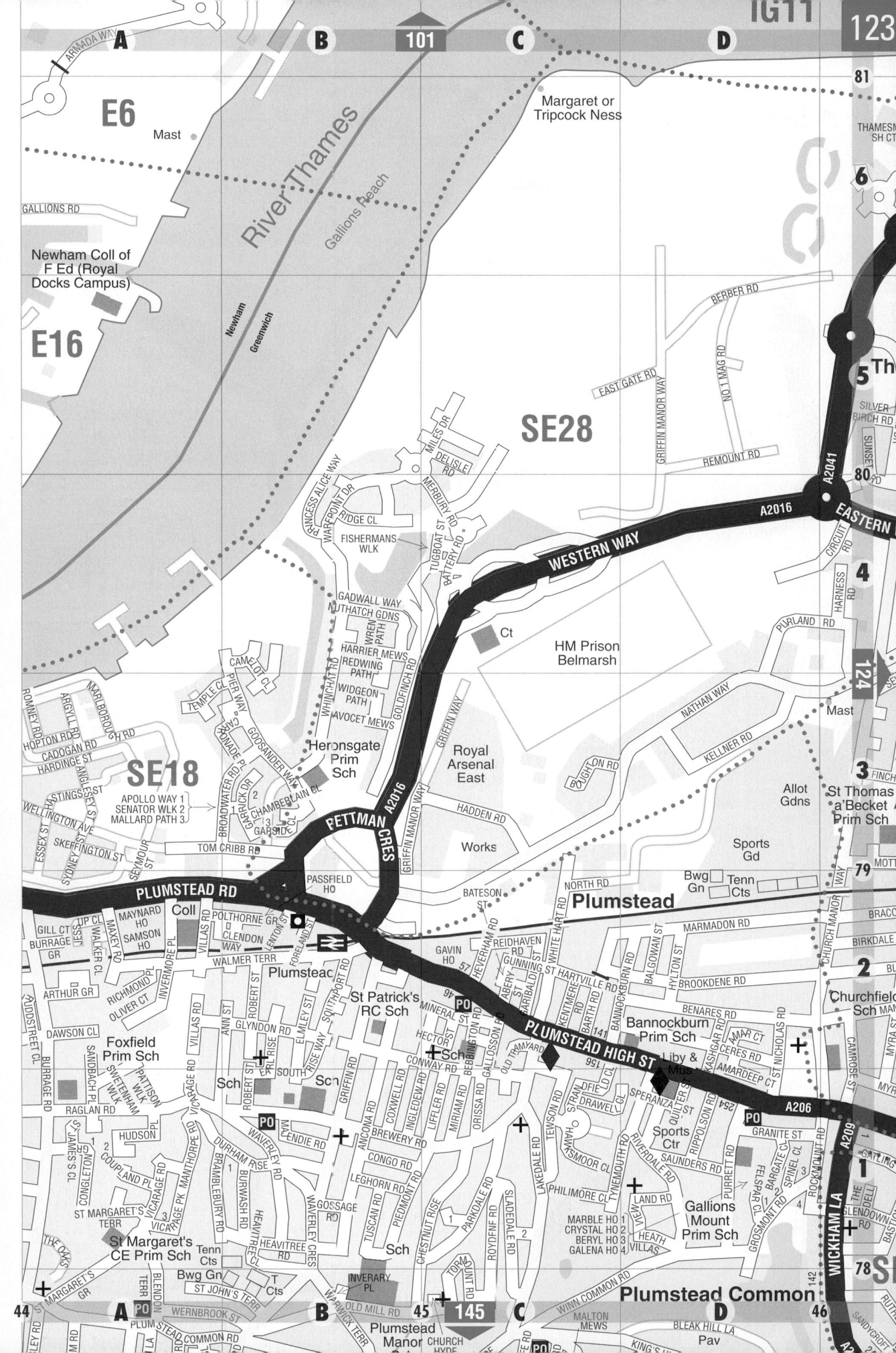

IG11
101
A
B
C
D
ARMADA WAY
E6
Mast
River Thames
Gallions Reach
Margaret or
Tripcock Ness
GALLIONS RD
Newham Coll of
F Ed (Royal
Docks Campus)
E16
Newham
Greenwich
THAMESM
SH CTR
81
6
5
80
4
3
124
79
2
1
78
BERBER RD
NO 1 MAG RD
EAST GATE RD
GRIFFIN MANOR WAY
REMOUNT RD
SE28
MILES DR
DELISLE RD
PRINCESS ALICE WAY
WARSPOINT DR
RIDGE CL
MERBURY RD
FISHERMANS WLK
TUGBOAT ST
BATTERY RD
A2016
A2041
EASTERN WAY
WESTERN WAY
CIRCUIT RD
HARNESS RD
PURLAND RD
GADWALL WAY
NUTHATCH GDNS
WREN PATH
HARRIER MEWS
REDWING PATH
WIDGEON PATH
AVOCET MEWS
WHINCHAT RD
GOLDFINCH RD
Ct
HM Prison
Belmarsh
CAMELOT CL
TEMPLE CL
PIER WAY
CARRONADE PL
GOOSANDER WAY
Heronsgate
Prim
Sch
GRIFFIN WAY
Royal
Arsenal
East
NATHAN WAY
KELLNER RD
BOUGHTON RD
Mast
Allot
Gdns
St Thomas
a'Becket
Prim Sch
ROMNEY RD
ARGYLL RD
MARLBOROUGH RD
HOPTON RD
CADOGAN RD
HARDINGE ST
SE18
ANGLESEY ST
HASTINGS ST
WELLINGTON AVE
APOLLO WAY 1
SENATOR WLK 2
MALLARD PATH 3
BROADWATER RD
GARRICK DR
CHAMBERLAIN CL
GARSIDE CL
PETTMAN CRES
GRIFFIN MANOR WAY
HADDEN RD
Works
Sports
Gd
ESSEX ST
SKEFFINGTON ST
SYDNEY ST
SEYMOUR ST
TOM CRIBB RD
PASSFIELD HO
BATESON ST
NORTH RD
Plumstead
Bwg
Gn
Tenn
Cts
PLUMSTEAD RD
MAYNARD HO
Coll
SAMSON HO
GILL CT
UP CL
BURRAGE GR
JESS ST
WALKER CL
MAXEY RD
VILLAS RD
POLTHORNE GR
CLENDON WAY
LENTON ST
FORELAND ST
INVERMORE PL
WALMER TERR
Plumstead
GAVIN HO
REIDHAVEN RD
HEVERHAM RD
GUNNING ST
ABERY ST
GARIBALDI ST
WHITE HART RD
HARTVILLE RD
MARMADON RD
BALGOWAN ST
HYLTON ST
BROOKDENE RD
CHURCH MANOR WAY
BIRKDALE
BRACON
ARTHUR GR
RICHMOND PL
OLIVER CT
ROBERT ST
ANN ST
ELMLEY ST
SOUTHPORT RD
St Patrick's
RC Sch
MINERAL ST
PO
KENTMERE RD
BARTH RD
BANNOCKBURN RD
BENARES RD
Bannockburn
Prim Sch
Churchfield
Sch
DAWSON CL
RUDDSTREET CL
Foxfield
Prim Sch
GLYNDON RD
EARL RISE
SOUTH RISE WAY
HECTOR ST
Sch
BEBBINGTON RD
GALLOSSON RD
OLD TRAMYARD
PLUMSTEAD HIGH ST
Liby &
Mus
KASHGAR RD
AMAR CT
CERES RD
AMARDEEP CT
ST NICHOLAS RD
CAMROSE ST
MYRA ST
BURRAGE RD
SANDBACH PL
SWETENHAM WLK
PATTISON WLK
VICARAGE RD
Sch
Sch
GRIFFIN RD
CONWAY RD
COXWELL RD
INGLEDEW RD
LIFFLER RD
MIRIAM RD
ORISSA RD
TEWSON RD
STRANDFIELD CL
DRAWELL CL
SPERANZA ST
QUILTER ST
RIPPOLSON RD
A206
RAGLAN RD
ST JAMES'S CL
HUDSON PL
DURHAM RISE
WAVERLEY RD
MAXENDIE RD
BREWERY RD
ANCONA RD
HAWKSMOOR CL
Sports
Ctr
GRANITE ST
A209
CONGLETON GR
COUPLAND PL
VICARAGE PK
MANTHORPE RD
BRAMBLEBURY RD
BURWASH RD
CONGO RD
LEGHORN RD
LAKEDALE RD
TYNEMOUTH RD
RIVERDALE RD
SAUNDERS RD
PURRETT RD
FELSPAR CL
BARGATE CL
SPINEL CL
ROCKMOUNT RD
WICKHAM LA
THE DELL
GLENDOWN RD
ST MARGARET'S TERR
GOSSAGE RD
HEAVITREE CL
TUSCAN RD
PIEDMONT RD
CHESTNUT RISE
PARKDALE RD
ROYDENE RD
SLADEDALE RD
PHILIMORE CL
LAND RD
MARBLE HO 1
CRYSTAL HO 2
BERYL HO 3
GALENA HO 4
HEATH VILLAS
Gallions
Mount
Prim Sch
GROSMONT RD
THE OAKS
St Margaret's
CE Prim Sch
Tenn
Cts
Bwg Gn
ST JOHN'S TERR
T
Cts
HEAVITREE RD
WAVERLEY CRES
Sch
INVERARY PL
TORMOUNT RD
WINN COMMON RD
Plumstead Common
ST MARGARET'S GR
TERR
BLENDON
WERNBROOK ST
WARWICK TERR
OLD MILL RD
145
MALTON MEWS
BLEAK HILL LA
Pav
PLUMSTEAD COMMON RD
Plumstead
Manor
CHURCH HYDE
KING'S
SANDYCROFT

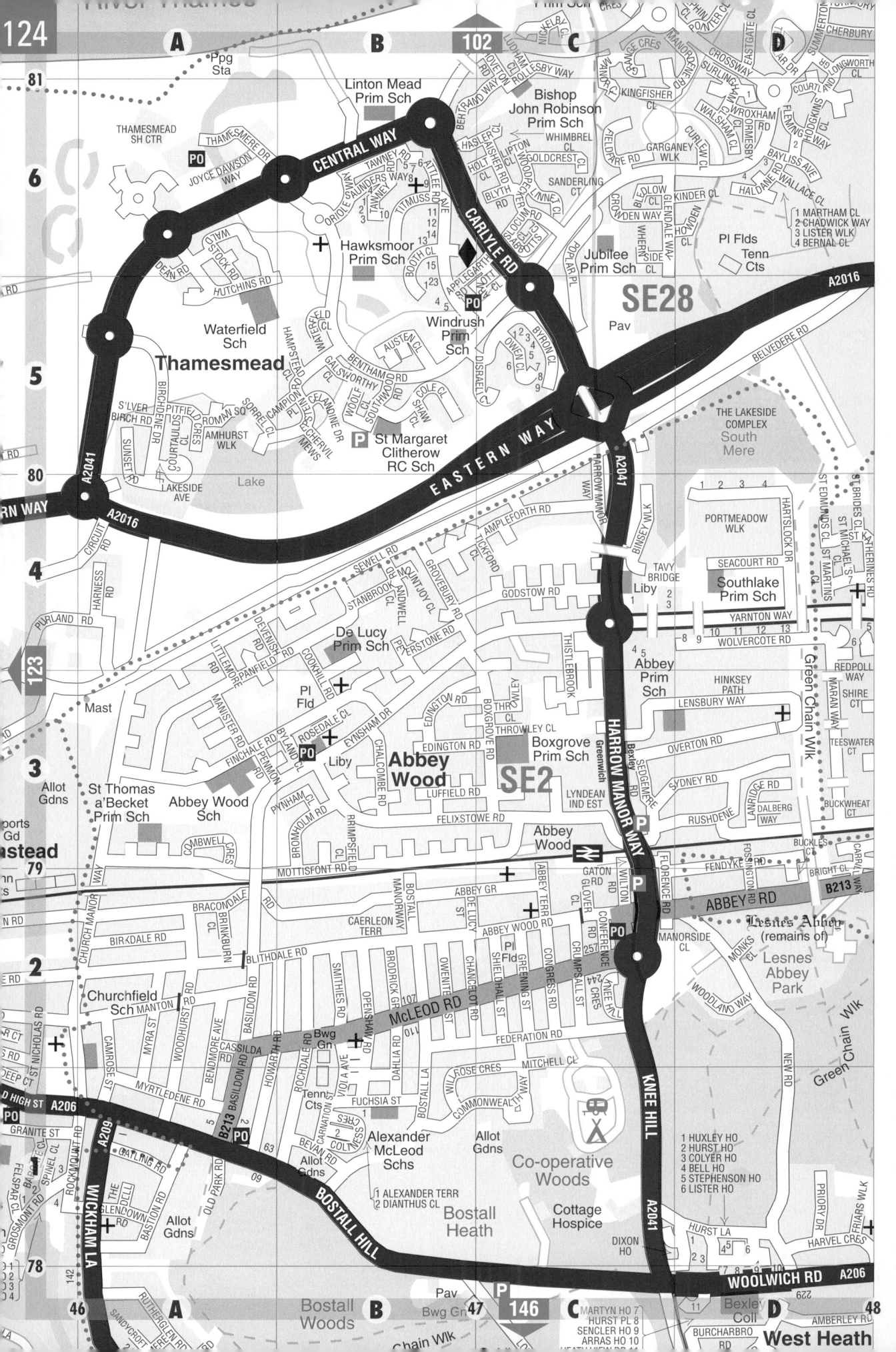

Thamesmead
Abbey Wood
SE28
SE2
CENTRAL WAY
EASTERN WAY
CARLYLE RD
HARROW MANOR WAY
KNEE HILL
BOSTALL HILL
WOOLWICH RD
WICKHAM LA
McLEOD RD
ABBEY RD
Linton Mead Prim Sch
Bishop John Robinson Prim Sch
Hawksmoor Prim Sch
Jubilee Prim Sch
Waterfield Sch
Windrush Prim Sch
St Margaret Clitherow RC Sch
THE LAKESIDE COMPLEX
South Mere
Lake
De Lucy Prim Sch
Southlake Prim Sch
Abbey Prim Sch
Boxgrove Prim Sch
St Thomas a'Becket Prim Sch
Abbey Wood Sch
Churchfield Sch
Alexander McLeod Schs
Lesnes Abbey (remains of)
Lesnes Abbey Park
Co-operative Woods
Bostall Heath
Cottage Hospice
Bostall Woods
Green Chain Wlk
West Heath
Bexley Coll
A2016
A2041
A206
A209
B213
102
123
146

A
B
103
C
D
Jetties
Barking & Dagenham
Bexley
Halfway Reach
RM13
River Thames
Jetty
81
6
Riverside
SE28
Sewage Works
BELVEDERE RD
Pl Fld
EASTERN WAY
5
80
NORMAN RD
DA18
Erith Marshes
1 CLYDESDALE HO
2 TREFOIL HO
3 TIMOTHY HO
4 MUSCOVY HO
Thamesmead Com Coll
EAST THAMESMEAD BSNS PK
KENCOT CL
WALDRIST WAY
HAILEY RD
HAILEY RD BSNS PK
PICARDY MANORWAY
ANDERSON WAY
CLAYTONVILLE TERR
ST THOMAS RD
CRABTREE MANORWAY N
BRONZE AGE WAY
B253
4
IX
A2016 Dartford(A206)
KALE RD
St John Fisher RC Prim Sch
PARKWAY
YARNTON WAY
PO
NORTHWOOD PL
LIME ROW
LEATHERBOTTLE GN
ASPEN GN
CENTURIAN WAY
WATERFIELD CL
SUTHERLAND RD
DA17
CALDY RD
ELBOURNE TRAD EST
MITCHELL CRABTREE MANORWAY S
3
KEATS RD
MAIDA RD
STATION RD N
Liby
RAILWAY PL
Belvedere
DYLAN RD
Fball Gd
GLIMPSING GN
Parkway Prim Sch
Northwood Prim Sch
DOWLING HO
Allot Gdns
ALSIKE RD
LAY MARSH CL
SHORTLANDS CL
BELVEDERE CT
GILBERT RD
PICARDY ST
NETHEWODE CT
THORNTON RD
Belvedere J & I Sch
B213
215
HALIFIELD DR
TUNSTOCK WAY
BECKETT CL
HOLCOTE CL
BLAKEMORE WAY
COPTEFIELD DR
MONARCH RD
AMBROOK RD
PAROMA RD
STATION RD
LOWER RD
79
ABBEY RD
ELSTREE GDNS
SAMPSON CL
KINGSWOOD AVE
HADLEY RD
ST AUGUSTINE'S RD
RIPLEY RD
COLEMAN RD
EDWARDS RD
SHERIDAN RD
GERTRUDE RD
LYNDON RD
B250
LOWER PARK RD
BRIGSTOCK RD
GLADESWOOD RD
Wood Side Sch
METHUEN RD
PARKSIDE RD
BELTWOOD RD
BULLBANKS RD
MAYFIELD
Tenn Cts
St Augustine's Prim Sch
Allot Gdns
UPPER ABBEY RD
STICKLAND RD
HALT ROBIN RD
HALT ROBIN LA
POPLAR MOUNT
1 BLETCHINGTON CT
2 BRUSHWOOD LODGE
2
Green Chain Wlk
UPPER SHERIDAN RD
ABBEY CRES
PICARDY RD
BUNKERS HILL
GIDEON CL
REGENT SQ
Belvedere
Frank's Park
Trinity CE Sch
A206 Dartford, M25 (A282)
MORVALE CL
HATTERSFIELD CL
DRAPER CL
CLIVE RD
RUSKIN RD
COWPER RD
KENTISH RD
VENMEAD CT
FREMANTLE RD
UPPER PARK RD
DAVID COFFER CT
HEATHDENE DR
ELMBOURNE DR
FOX HOUSE RD
HAVELOCK RD 1
NAPIER RD 2
BRAESIDE CL 3
HERON HILL
WELLINGTON RD
RAGLAN RD
MILTON RD
ORCHARD RD
PROSPECT CL
MOSSDOWN CL
CALVERT CL
Pl Fld
Lesnes Abbey Woods
LESSNESS PK
MITRE CT
EARDLEY RD
ERITH RD
A206
SMARDEN CL
BERKHAMPSTEAD RD
NELSON RD
WALDEN CL
GLOUCESTER RD
ESSENDEN RD
B250
38
UPPER HOLLY HILL RD
HOLMHURST RD
99
Bexley Coll
RUTLAND GATE
PARKSIDE LODGE
COURT AVE
EDWARD HARVEY CT
THE VIEW
TREETOPS CL
WOOLWICH RD
VANESSA WAY
HOLLY HILL RD
1
Rec Gd
Liby
Lessness Heath Prim Sch
ROBERTS RD
SALMON RD
Lessness Heath
FILSTON RD
All Gd
TYESHURST CL
CROFT CL
HAROLD AVE
FLORA ST
VICTORIA ST
ALFRED RD
ALBERT RD
BEDWELL RD
HODDESDON RD
CHESHUNT RD
STANDARD RD
WADEVILLE CL
CHAPMAN RD
LUMLEY CL
BROOK ST
RIVERDALE RD
STILES CL
HARVEL CT
Tenn Cts
Sp Gd
EVERETT WLK
FAIRMONT CL
NUXLEY RD
STAPLEY RD
LESSNESS RD
ALBANY RD
P
78
MILFORD CL
WESTERGATE RD
OSBORNE RD
BARNFIELD RD
GROSVENOR RD
WYNFORD
Allot Gdns
Cemy
SILVER SPRING CL
48
49
147
50
ORCHARD AVE
UPPER GROVE RD
WALSINGHAM WLK

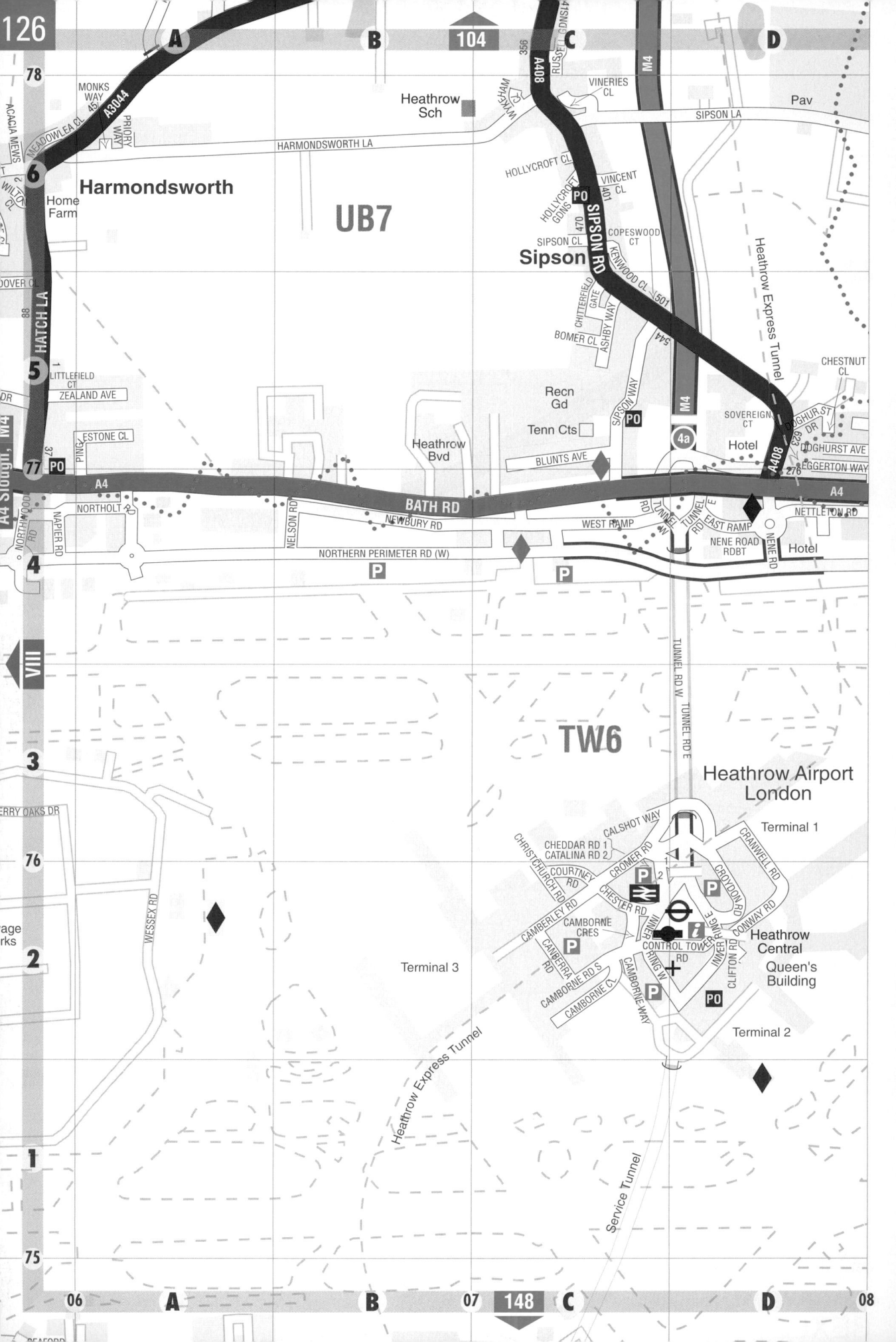

Harmondsworth

UB7

Sipson

TW6

Heathrow Airport London

Terminal 1

Terminal 3

Terminal 2

Heathrow Central
Queen's Building

Control Tower

Home Farm

Heathrow Sch

MONKS WAY

PRIORY WAY

MEADOWLEA CL

ACACIA MEWS

WILTON

A3044

HARMONDSWORTH LA

HATCH LA

A4 Slough, M4

DOVER CL

LITTLEFIELD CT

ZEALAND AVE

PINGLESTONE CL

NORTHWOOD RD

NAPIER RD

NORTHOLT

PO

A4

BATH RD

NELSON RD

NEWBURY RD

NORTHERN PERIMETER RD (W)

WEST RAMP

WESSEX RD

ERRY OAKS DR

Heathrow Express Tunnel

Service Tunnel

Heathrow Express Tunnel

Heathrow Bvd

BLUNTS AVE

Tenn Cts

Recn Gd

Sipson CL

HOLLYCROFT CL

HOLLYCROFT GDNS

PO

SIPSON RD

KENWOOD CL

SIPSON WAY

CHITTERFIELD GATE

BOMER CL

ASHBY WAY

VINCENT CL

COPESWOOD CT

VINERIES CL

SIPSON LA

RUSSELL GDNS

WYKEHAM

A408

M4

PO

4a

Hotel

SOVEREIGN CT

Heathrow Express Tunnel

CHESTNUT CL

DOGHURST DR

DOGHURST AVE

EGGERTON WAY

A408

A4

NETTLETON RD

NENE ROAD RDBT

NENE RD

Hotel

TUNNEL RD W

TUNNEL RD E

TUNNEL RD E

EAST RAMP

Pav

CALSHOT WAY

CHEDDAR RD 1

CATALINA RD 2

CROMER RD

CHRISTCHURCH RD

COURTNEY RD

CHESTER RD

CAMBERLEY RD

CAMBORNE CRES

CAMBERRA RD

CAMBORNE RD S

CAMBORNE CL

CAMBORNE WAY

INNER RING W RD

CONTROL TOWER RD

INNER RING E RD

CROYDON RD

CRANWELL RD

CONWAY RD

CLIFTON RD

PO

VIII

78

77

76

75

6

5

4

3

2

1

06   A   B   07   148   C   D   08

105
149
128
Harlington
Hatton
Hatton Cross
UB3
TW6
TW14
HIGH STREET HARLINGTON
BATH RD
A4
A437
A30
GREAT SOUTH-WEST RD
Nine Elms Farm
Sp Gd
Pav
William Byrd Sch
Harlington Lower Sch
Hotel
Hotels
Harlington Cnr
Visitor Ctr
WORLD BSNS CTR
Poultry Farm
Gravel Pits
Cranford Park
The White House
The White Hart (PH)
Frog's Ditch
River Crane
VICTORIA LA
BLETCHMORE CL
BRICKFIELD LA
PEMBURY CT
KILN CL
RICHARDS CL
HUDSON RD
THE FORGE
GOTHIC CT
FELLOWES CT
SHORTLANDS
SIPSON LA
FELBRIDGE CT
MANSE CL
MANOR LA
PONDSIDE CL
GILPIN WAY
PROVIDENCE LA
THE CRESCENT
WEST END LA
RAYWOOD CL
TASKER CL
CROFT CL
HARLINGTON CL
GRAMPIAN CL
QUANTOCK CL
WARNER CL
LITTLE ELMS
PENNINE WAY
CHEVIOT CL
HALL LA
HEATH CL
MENDIP CL
BRENDON CL
NEW RD
BROWNINGS RD
BOLTON'S LA
MONDIAL WAY
TRIUMPH CL
NORWOOD CRES
NEWALL RD
NEPTUNE RD
HATTON RD N
NORTHROP RD
NORTHERN PERIMETER RD
DAVID CL
CAROLINE PL
NOBEL DR
CRANFORD LA
WINCHESTER RD
OXFORD AVE
MALVERN RD
WINDSOR PARK RD
ETON RD
SAUNTON AVE
PENDELL AVE
ACORN GR
STRATHEARN AVE
LANGLEY CRES
CRANESWATER
PARK LA
ENFIELD ROAD RDBT
ENFIELD RD
ELGIN CRES
ELY RD
ESHER CL
EPSOM SQ
EASTERN PERIMETER RD
EASTCHURCH ROAD RDBT
EASTCHURCH RD
EXETER WAY
EXETER RD
EASTLEIGH RD
ELMDON RD
HATTON CROSS RDBT
VISCOUNT WAY
LITHGOW'S RD
SOUTHERN PERIMETER RD
HATTON RD
STEAM FARM LA
DICK TURPIN WAY
RADIUS PK
ST THERESA'S RD
ST ANTHONY'S WAY
FAGG'S RD
DOCKWELL CL
GREEN
MYRTLE AVE
WELLINGTON RD
Hillingdon
Hounslow
PO
P
180
249
324
393
499
120
104
26
78
77
76
75
6
5
4
3
2
1
08
09
10
A
B
C
D

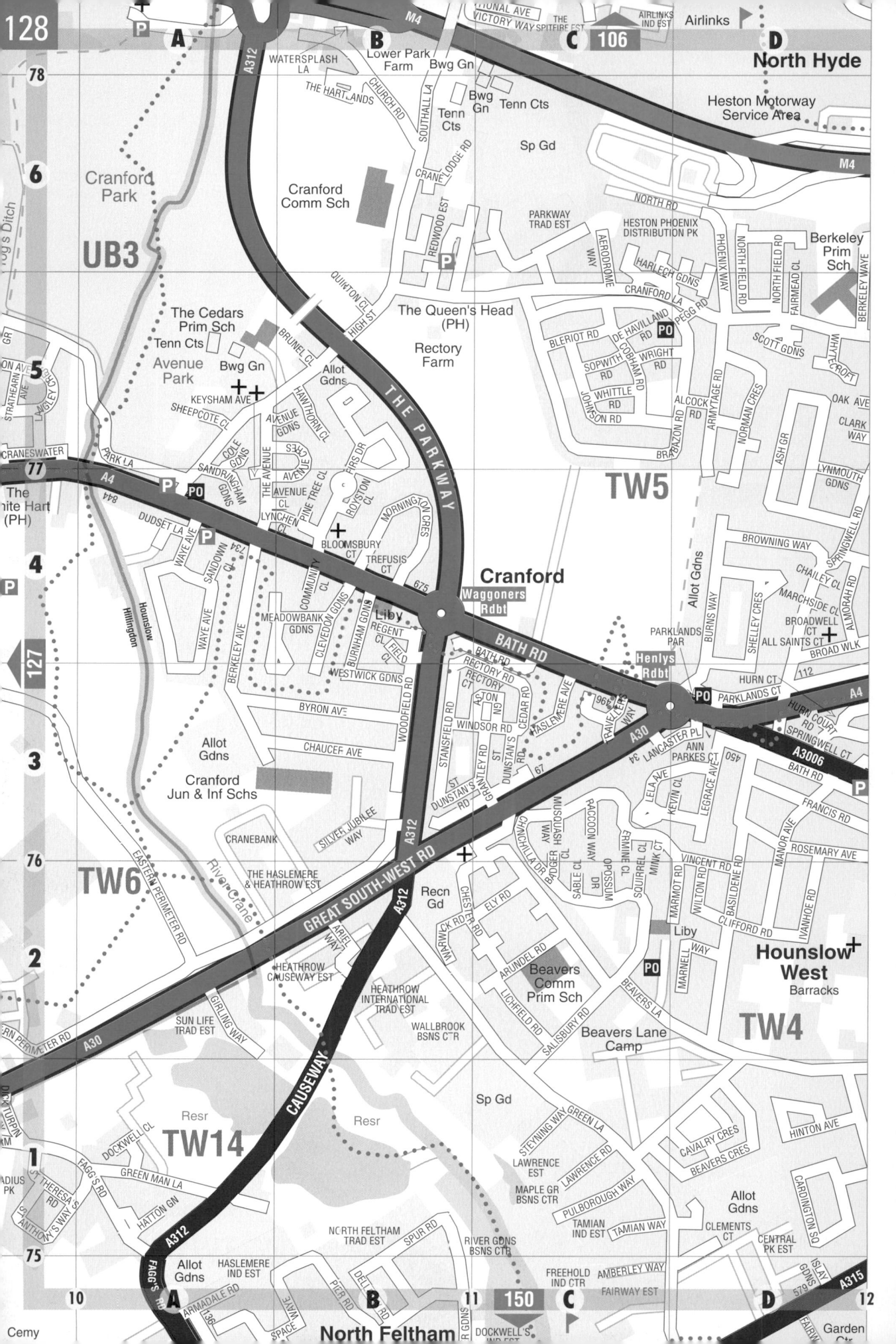
North Hyde
Heston Motorway Service Area
Cranford Park
UB3
Cranford Comm Sch
The Cedars Prim Sch
Avenue Park
The Queen's Head (PH)
Rectory Farm
TW5
Cranford
Waggoners Rdbt
Henlys Rdbt
Berkeley Prim Sch
Cranford Jun & Inf Schs
TW6
Beavers Comm Prim Sch
Beavers Lane Camp
Hounslow West
Barracks
TW4
TW14
North Feltham
THE PARKWAY
BATH RD
GREAT SOUTH-WEST RD
CAUSEWAY
106
127
150

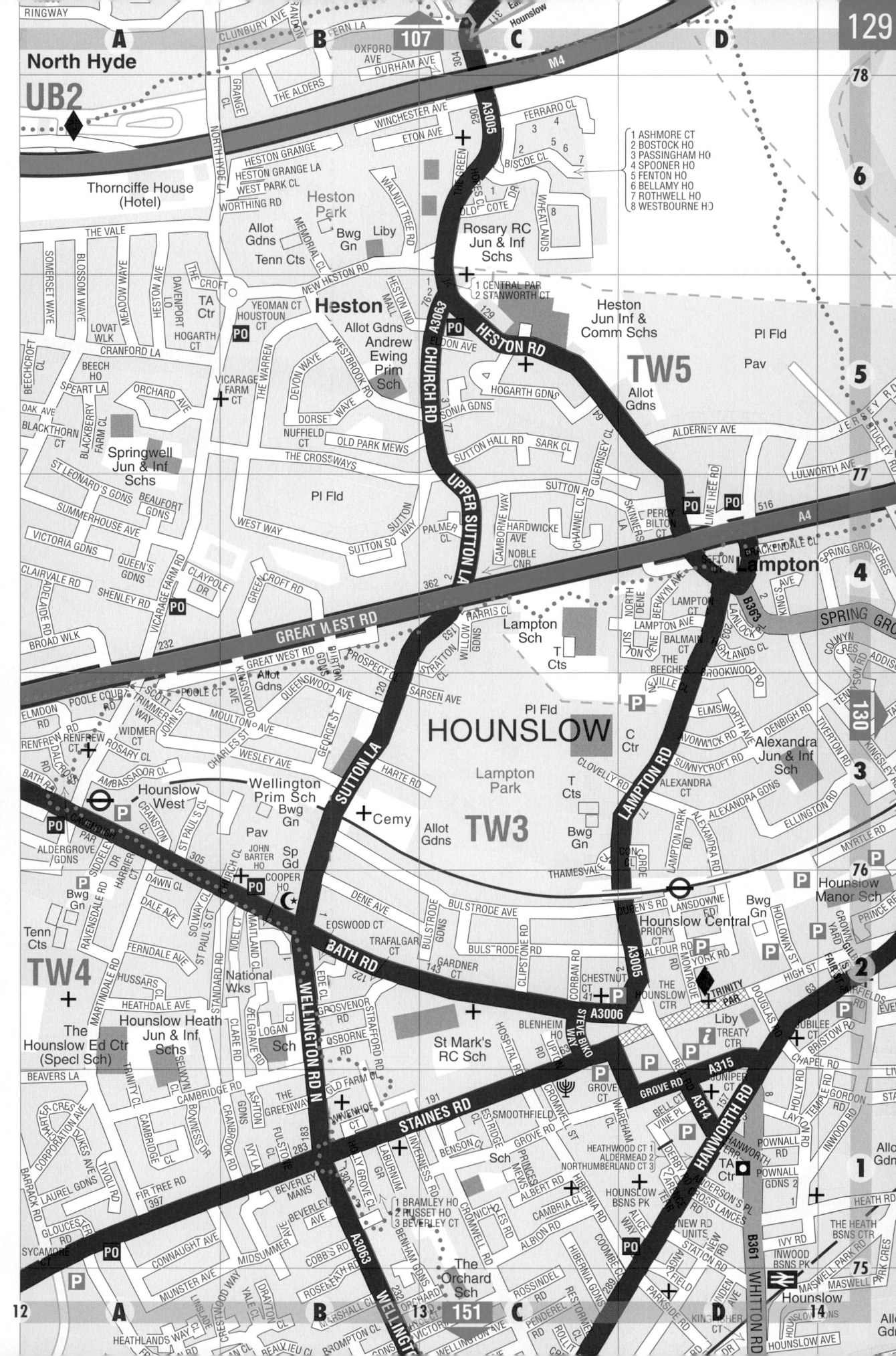
North Hyde
UB2
M4
107
A
B
C
D
78
6
5
77
4
3
76
2
1
75
130
151
12
13
14
RINGWAY
CLUNBURY AVE
FERN LA
OXFORD AVE
DURHAM AVE
THE ALDERS
GRANGE CL
WINCHESTER AVE
ETON AVE
A3005
FERRARO CL
BISCOE CL
1 ASHMORE CT
2 BOSTOCK HO
3 PASSINGHAM HO
4 SPOONER HO
5 FENTON HO
6 BELLAMY HO
7 ROTHWELL HO
8 WESTBOURNE HO
HESTON GRANGE
HESTON GRANGE LA
WEST PARK CL
WORTHING RD
Thorncliffe House (Hotel)
NORTH HYDE LA
Heston Park
WALNUT TREE RD
THE GREEN
HORSES CL
OLD COTE DR
WHEATLANDS
Rosary RC Jun & Inf Schs
THE VALE
Allot Gdns
Bwg Gn
Liby
Tenn Cts
MEMORIAL CL
NEW HESTON RD
1 CENTRAL PAR
2 STANWORTH CT
SOMERSET WAYE
BLOSSOM WAYE
MEADOW WAYE
HESTON AVE
DAVENPORT LO
THE CROFT
TA Ctr
YEOMAN CT
HOUSTOUN CT
Heston
HESTON IND MALL
A3063
Heston Jun Inf & Comm Schs
LOVAT WLK
HOGARTH CT
PO
CRANFORD LA
Allot Gdns
Andrew Ewing Prim Sch
ELDON AVE
HESTON RD
TW5
Pl Fld
Pav
BEECHCROFT CL
BEECH HO
SPEART LA
ORCHARD AVE
VICARAGE FARM CT
THE WARREN
DEVON WAYE
WESTBROOK RD
CHURCH RD
HOGARTH GDNS
Allot Gdns
JERSEY RD
STUCLEY RD
OAK AVE
BLACKTHORN CT
BLACKBERRY FARM CL
DORSET WAYE
NUFFIELD CT
SONIA GDNS
OLD PARK MEWS
SUTTON HALL RD
SARK CL
ALDERNEY AVE
GUERNSEY CL
Springwell Jun & Inf Schs
ST LEONARD'S GDNS
BEAUFORT GDNS
THE CROSSWAYS
Pl Fld
UPPER SUTTON LA
SUTTON RD
LIME TREE RD
LULWORTH AVE
SUMMERHOUSE AVE
VICTORIA GDNS
WEST WAY
SUTTON WAY
SUTTON SQ
PALMER CL
CAMBORNE WAY
HARDWICKE AVE
NOBLE CNR
CHANNEL CL
SKINNERS LA
PERCY BILTON CT
516
A4
BRACKENDALE CL
SPRING GROVE CRES
Lampton
SEFTON CT
CLAIRVALE RD
ADELAIDE RD
QUEEN'S GDNS
CLAYPOLE DR
SHENLEY RD
VICARAGE FARM RD
GREENCROFT RD
362
KING'S AVE
B363
SPRING GROVE
BROAD WLK
232
GREAT WEST RD
HARRIS CL
WILLOW GDNS
Lampton Sch
T Cts
NORTH DENE
BERWYN AVE
LAMPTON CT
LAMPTON AVE
SUTTON DENE
BALMAIN CT
HIGHLANDS CL
THE BEECHES
BROOKWOOD RD
LAWLOCK CL
COLWYN CRES
ADDISON
TENNYSON RD
PROSPECT CL
BURTON GDNS
STRATTON CL
SARSEN AVE
POOLE COURT RD
POOLE CT
SCOTT TRIMMER WAY
JOHN ST
KINGSWOOD AVE
QUEENSWOOD AVE
MOULTON AVE
NEVILLE CL
ELMSWORTH AVE
DENBIGH RD
TIVERTON RD
ELMDON RD
RENFREW RD
RENFREW CT
WIDMER CT
ROSARY CL
CHARLES ST
GEORGE ST
Pl Fld
HOUNSLOW
C Ctr
AVONWICK RD
KINGSLEY RD
Alexandra Jun & Inf Sch
DALCROSS
AMBASSADOR CL
WESLEY AVE
SUTTON LA
HARTE RD
Lampton Park
CLOVELLY RD
SUNNYCROFT RD
ALEXANDRA CT
BATH RD
Hounslow West
Wellington Prim Sch
Cemy
T Cts
LAMPTON RD
ALEXANDRA GDNS
ELLINGTON RD
CAVENDISH PAR
CRANSTON
ST PAUL'S CL
Bwg Gn
Allot Gdns
TW3
Bwg Gn
LAMPTON PARK RD
ALEXANDRA RD
ALDERGROVE GDNS
SIDDELEY DR
HARRIER CT
305
Pav
JOHN BARTER HO
Sp Gd
CONCORDE CL
MYRTLE RD
THAMESVALE CL
Hounslow Manor Sch
DAWN CL
CHURCH CL
COOPER HO
DENE AVE
QUEEN'S RD
LANSDOWNE RD
Hounslow Central
Bwg Gn
HOLLOWAY ST
CROWN YARD
PRINCE REGENT
Bwg Gn
DALE AVE
SOLWAY CL
RAVENSDALE RD
BULSTRODE AVE
EOSWOOD CT
PRIORY CT
Tenn Cts
ST PAUL'S CT
NOEL CT
MAITLAND CL
TRAFALGAR CT
BULSTRODE GDNS
BULSTRODE RD
CLIPSTONE RD
BALFOUR RD
MONTAGUE RD
YORK RD
FERNDALE AVE
A3005
TW4
National Wks
EDE CL
GARDNER CT
143
122
CORBAN RD
CHESTNUT CT
THE HOUNSLOW CTR
TRINITY PAR
HIGH ST
FAIRFIELDS
FAIR ST
HUSSARS CL
MARTINDALE RD
STANDARD RD
WELLINGTON RD N
GROSVENOR RD
STRAFFORD RD
A3006
STEVE BIKO WAY
DOUGLAS RD
63
JUBILEE CT
HEATHDALE AVE
Hounslow Heath Jun & Inf Schs
CLARE RD
BELGRAVE RD
LOGAN CL
OSBORNE RD
St Mark's RC Sch
HOSPITAL RD
BLENHEIM RD
UPTON RD
Liby
TREATY CTR
BRISTOW RD
The Hounslow Ed Ctr (Specl Sch)
Sch
A315
CHAPEL RD
BEAVERS LA
TRINITY CL
SELWYN CL
CAMBRIDGE RD
ASHTON GDNS
THE GREENWAY
OLD FARM CL
GROVE CT
WAREHAM CL
GROVE RD
JUNIPER CT
A314
HANWORTH RD
HOLLY RD
TEMPLE RD
GORDON RD
CARTER CRES
CORPORATION AVE
DUKES AVE
TIVOLI RD
CAMBRIDGE CL
BONNESS DR
CRANBROOK RD
IVANHOE CT
191
STAINES RD
SMOOTHFIELD
CROMWELL ST
BELL CT
VINE PL
LAYTON RD
INWOOD RD
BARRACK RD
LAUREL GDNS
FIR TREE RD
397
IVY LA
FULSTONE CL
283
HOLLY GROVE CL
LABURNUM GR
INVERNESS RD
BENSON CL
ESTRIDGE CL
GROVE RD
Sch
PRINCES MEWS
HEATHWOOD CT 1
ALDERMEAD 2
NORTHUMBERLAND CT 3
DERBY RD
TA Ctr
POWNALL RD
POWNALL GDNS
Allot Gdns
BEVERLEY MANS
1 BRAMLEY HO
2 RUSSET HO
3 BEVERLEY CT
CROMWELL RD
ALBERT RD
HIBERNIA RD
HOUNSLOW BSNS PK
ALICE WAY
HEATH RD
GLOUCESTER RD
SYCAMORE CT
CONNAUGHT AVE
MIDSUMMER AVE
BEVERLEY AVE
BENHAM GDNS
CAMBRIA CL
ALBION RD
HIBERNIA GDNS
COOMBE
NEW RD UNITS
ANDERSON'S PL
CROSS LANCES
STATION RD
B361
THE HEATH BSNS CTR
IVY RD
INWOOD BSNS PK
MASWELL PARK RD
MASWELL PARK CRES
MUNSTER AVE
COBB'S RD
ROSEHEATH RD
The Orchard Sch
ROSSINDEL RD
RESTORMEL
PARKSIDE RD
WHITTON RD
Hounslow
HOUNSLOW AVE
HEATHLANDS WAY
CRESTWOOD WAY
YALE CL
DRAYTON CL
MARSHALL CL
WELLINGTON RD S
PENDEREL RD
KINGFISHER CT
BROMPTON CL
Allot Gdns

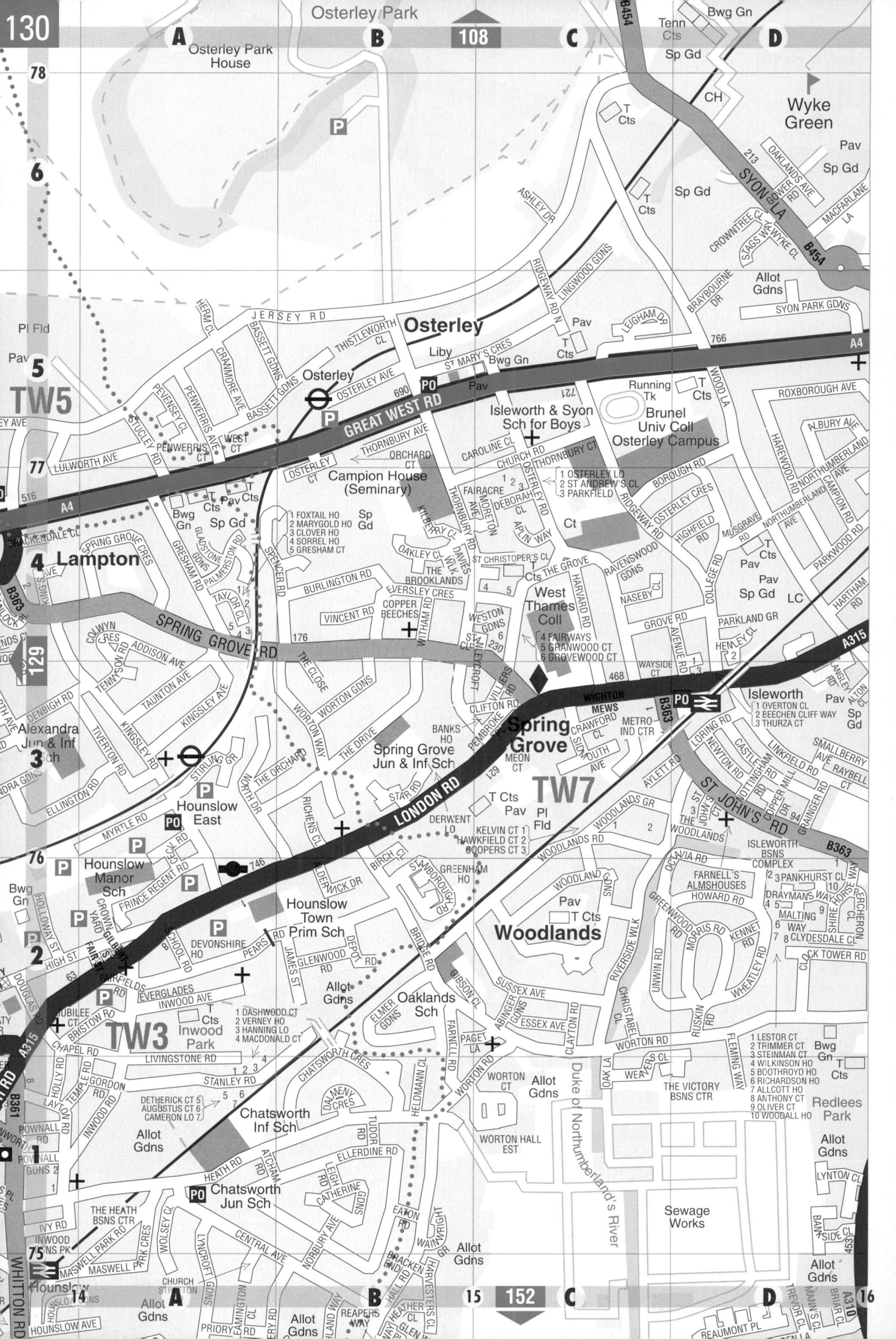

Osterley Park

Osterley Park House

Wyke Green

TW5

Osterley

Osterley Ave

GREAT WEST RD

A4

Lampton

Isleworth & Syon Sch for Boys

Brunel Univ Coll Osterley Campus

Campion House (Seminary)

1 FOXTAIL HO
2 MARYGOLD HO
3 CLOVER HO
4 SORREL HO
5 GRESHAM CT

THE BROOKLANDS

West Thames Coll

SPRING GROVE RD

COPPER BEECHES

4 FAIRWAYS
5 GRANWOOD CT
6 GROVEWOOD CT

Isleworth

1 OVERTON CL
2 BEECHEN CLIFF WAY
3 THURZA CT

Alexandra Jun & Inf Sch

Hounslow East

Spring Grove Jun & Inf Sch

LONDON RD

Spring Grove

TW7

1 KELVIN CT
2 HAWKFIELD CT
3 COOPERS CT

Woodlands

Hounslow Manor Sch

Hounslow Town Prim Sch

1 DASHWOOD CT
2 VERNEY HO
3 HANNING LO
4 MACDONALD CT

TW3

Inwood Park

Oaklands Sch

FARNELL'S ALMSHOUSES

1 LESTOR CT
2 TRIMMER CT
3 STEINMAN CT
4 WILKINSON HO
5 BOOTHROYD HO
6 RICHARDSON HO
7 ALLCOTT HO
8 ANTHONY CT
9 OLIVER CT
10 WOODALL HO

Redlees Park

Chatsworth Inf Sch

DETHERICK CT 5
AUGUSTUS CT 6
CAMERON LO 7

WORTON HALL EST

Duke of Northumberland's River

Chatsworth Jun Sch

Sewage Works

Hounslow

WHITTON RD

BRENTFORD
Brentford
Brentford End
Syon Park
Syon House
ISLEWORTH
RICHMOND
Royal Botanic Gardens
Old Deer Park
River Thames
Thames Path
Grand Union Canal
London Butterfly House
Queen Charlotte's Cottage
King's Steps Gate
Royal Mid-Surrey
Kew Obsy
Isleworth Ait
Richmond Lock
West Middlesex Univ
Brunel Univ Coll (Twickenham Campus)
Old Deer Park Recn Gd
Richmond Athletic Gd
Richmond Adult Coll
Griffin Park Fball Gd
Brentford Sch for Girls
The Green Sch for Girls
John Busch Sch
Syon Lane
TW8
TW7
TW9
TW1
GREAT WEST RD
LONDON RD
HIGH ST
BOSTON MANOR RD
SPUR RD
TWICKENHAM RD
SOUTH ST
RICHMOND RD
ST MARGARETS
SYON LA
HALF ACRE
EALING RD
TWICKENHAM RD
A4
A315
A310
A3002
A3004
A316
A307
A305
B454
B452
B363
B455
M4
Hounslow
Richmond upon Thames
1 JODRELL C
2 HOLDERNESSE RD
3 FINNEY LA
4 HANOVER TERR
5 DARCY RD
6 BLENHEIM WAY
7 MILESTONE CT
8 POYNDER LO
1 FERNEY MEADE WAY
2 TOWN FIELD WAY
3 TECK CL
4 THACKERAY CL
THE GATEWAYS 1
FITZWILLIAM HO 2
PORTLAND TERR 3
PEMBROKE VILLAS 4
109
153
132
A
B
C
D
16
17
18
78
77
76
75
6
5
4
3
2
1

A
B
C
D
110
131
154
1
2
3
4
5
6
76
77
78
75
09
148
19
20
W4
TW8
TW9
TW10
SW14
BRENTFORD
Strand on the Green
Kew
North Sheen
RICHMOND
Royal Botanic Gardens
River Thames
Brentford Ait
Lots Ait
Kew Palace
Herbarium Liby
Palm House
Temperate House
Pagoda
Arboretum
Queen Charlotte's Cottage
Kew Bridge
Kew Gardens
Kew Green
Manor Circus
Richmond Circus
Richmond
North Sheen
Chalkers Cnr
Public Record Office
Hammersmith New Cemy
North Sheen Cemy (Fulham)
Holy Trinity CE Jun Sch
Richmond Athletic Gd
The Hamlet (Day)
Griffin Park Fball Gd
Marina
Works
East Sheen Common
Pl Fld
KEW RET PK
MARLBOROUGH TRAD EST
EALING ROAD TRAD EST
THAMESIDE CTR
KEW BRIDGE RD
HIGH ST
EALING RD
KEW RD
SANDYCOMBE RD
MORTLAKE RD
LOWER RICHMOND RD
LOWER MORTLAKE RD
CLIFFORD AVE
MANOR RD
SHEEN RD
THE QUADRANT
PARADISE RD
RED LION ST
KEW GARDENS RD
NORTH RD
STATION PAR
WEST PARK RD
HIGH PARK RD
BROOMFIELD RD
LICHFIELD RD
HOLMESDALE RD
BRANSTONE RD
HATHERLEY RD
ALEXANDRA RD
WINDSOR RD
DUDLEY RD
GORDON RD
BURDETT RD
TEMPLE RD
FITZWILLIAM AVE
STANMORE RD
WINDHAM RD
RALEIGH RD
ATWOOD AVE
GARRICK RD
CHAUCER AVE
MARKSBURY AVE
HESTER TERR
DANCER RD
DARELL RD
NIMROD RD
CRANLEIGH CT
BICESTER RD
LAMBERT AVE
SOMERTON AVE
SHALSTONE RD
KINGSWAY
MANOR GR
SHEEN COURT RD
TANGIER RD
ROTHESAY AVE
WARREN AVE
BURDENSHOTT AVE
CLYDESDALE GDNS
DENEHURST GDNS
SHEEN PK
TOWNSHEND TERR
ST MARY'S GR
GRENA RD
GRENA GDNS
MANOR PK
KINGS FARM AVE
CARRINGTON RD
WORPLE WAY
ALBANY RD
HYDE RD
PRINCES RD
SHEEN COMMON DR
ORCHARD RISE
BERWYN RD
STANLEY RD
DERBY RD
COVAL LA
COVAL GDNS
WESTHAY GDNS
GRAEMESDYKE AVE
HOLMESDALE AVE
DEANHILL RD
KEW GN
BUSHWOOD RD
PRIORY RD
HAVERFIELD GDNS
MAZE RD
GLOUCESTER RD
CAMBRIDGE RD
KENT RD
KENMORE CL
CUMBERLAND RD
LEYBORNE PK
BURLINGTON AVE
BEECHWOOD AVE
RUSKIN AVE
DEFOE AVE
BESSANT DR
WEST PARK AVE
BRICK FARM CL
WEST HALL RD
MAGNOLIA CT
HAWTHORN CT
COURTLANDS AVE
TOWNMEAD RD
THAMES RD
THAMES PATH
GROVE PARK RD
GROVE PARK TERR
RIVERVIEW RD
ERNEST GDNS
HERBERT GDNS
MAGNOLIA RD
LORAINE RD
STILE HALL GDNS
OXFORD GDNS
OXFORD RD S
PINKHAM MANS
REGENT ST
CHISWICK VILLAGE
WALDECK RD
HARVARD HILL
HARVARD RD
GROSVENOR RD
WOLSELEY GDNS
BURNABY GDNS
WHITEHALL GDNS
GORDON RD
ST MARY'S GR
GREEN DRAGON LA
BURFORD RD
BRAEMAR RD
NETLEY RD
POTTERY RD
WALNUT TREE RD
ALBANY RD
FERRY LA
GOAT WHARF
TOWN MEADOW
JULIUS CT
JUSTIN CL
MARCUS CT
NUMA CT
KEW FOOT RD
SHAFTESBURY RD
EVELYN RD
JOCELYN RD
OLD DEER PARK GDNS
ROSEDALE RD
LARKFIELD RD
ST JOHN'S RD
CATHERINE DR
DUNSTABLE RD
ALTON RD
CHURCH RD
LICHFIELD GDNS
DRUMMONDS PL
PRINCE'S ST
PARKSHOT
SELWYN AVE
BEAUMONT AVE
PAGODA AVE
ST PAULS
CASTLEGATE
TRINITY RD
VICTORIA VILLAS
ST GEORGE'S RD
BARDOLPH RD
CROWN TERR
SHEFFIELD
DEE RD
WEST SHEEN VALE
CEDAR TERR
DUNCAN RD
SALISBURY RD
BLENHEIM CT 1
WOBURN CT 2
FINUCANE CT 3
TRINITY COTTS 4
1 WATCOMBE COTTS
2 CAMBRIDGE COTTS
3 WILLOW COTTS
4 THETIS TERR
1 SANDSTONE
2 BROADLANDS CT
3 FABYC HO
4 ASPEN CT
A205
A307
A315
A316
A305
A3003
A3000
A4
B353
B455
B322
Hounslow
Richmond upon Thames
Sch
Mus
PO
Recn Gd
Allot Gdns
Bwg Gn
Tenn Cts
Dv Rng
Sp Gd
Crkt Gd
Pav
LC
Liby

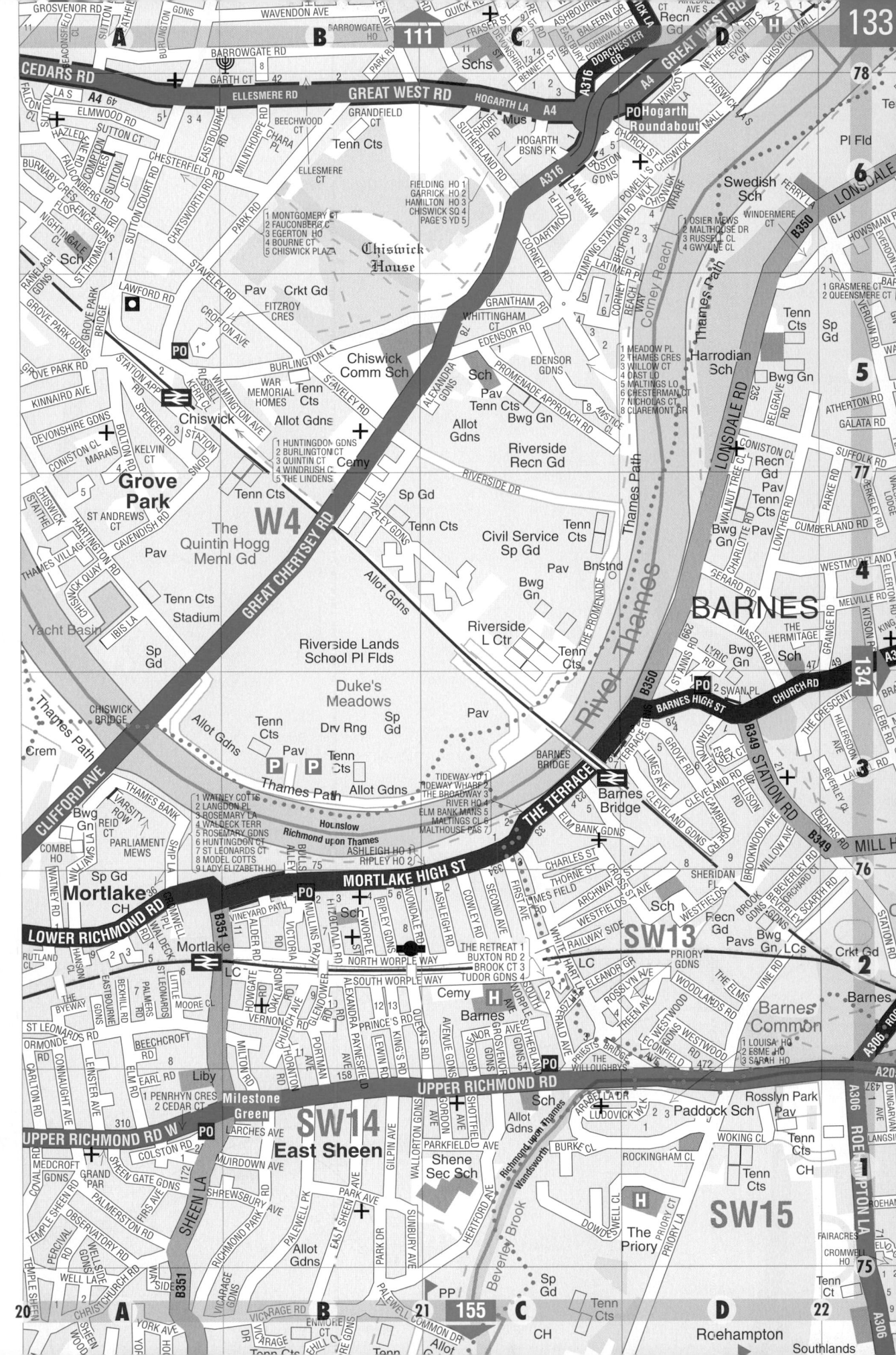
111
A
B
C
D
CEDARS RD
GREAT WEST RD
ELLESMERE RD
HOGARTH LA
A4
A316
Hogarth Roundabout
Chiswick House
Tenn Cts
Crkt Gd
Pav
Chiswick Comm Sch
Chiswick
Grove Park
W4
GREAT CHERTSEY RD
The Quintin Hogg Meml Gd
Stadium
Yacht Basin
Riverside Lands School Pl Flds
Duke's Meadows
Drv Rng
Allot Gdns
Thames Path
CHISWICK BRIDGE
Crem
CLIFFORD AVE
Riverside Recn Gd
Civil Service Sp Gd
Riverside L Ctr
River Thames
Corney Reach
BARNES BRIDGE
Barnes Bridge
THE TERRACE
BARNES
BARNES HIGH ST
CHURCH RD
LONSDALE RD
Harrodian Sch
Swedish Sch
B350
B349
STATION RD
Mortlake
MORTLAKE HIGH ST
LOWER RICHMOND RD
B351
SW13
Barnes Common
Barnes
UPPER RICHMOND RD
UPPER RICHMOND RD W
Milestone Green
SW14
East Sheen
SHEEN LA
Shene Sec Sch
Richmond upon Thames
Wandsworth
Beverley Brook
Hounslow
Paddock Sch
Rosslyn Park
The Priory
SW15
ROEHAMPTON LA
A306
A205
Roehampton
Southlands
155
134
20
21
22
78
77
76
75
6
5
4
3
2
1

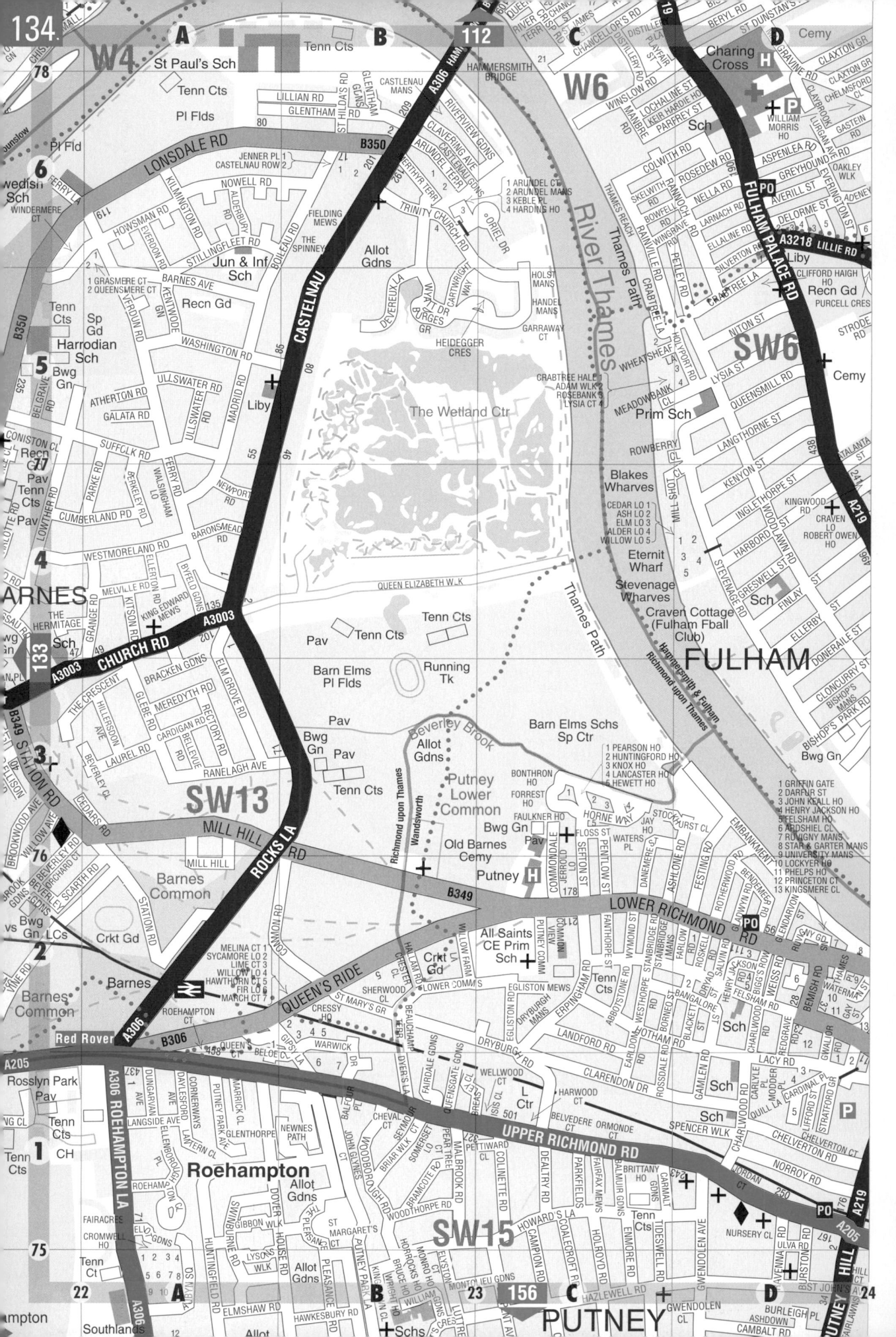
A
B
C
D
112
W4
St Paul's Sch
Tenn Cts
Pl Flds
Pl Fld
LONSDALE RD
B350
LILLIAN RD
GLENTHAM RD
CASTLENAU MANS
HAMMERSMITH BRIDGE
W6
CHANCELLOR'S RD
DISTILLERY RD
WINSLOW RD
Charing Cross
BERYL RD
ST DUNSTAN'S RD
Cemy
CLAXTON GR
GRAVINE RD
WILLIAM MORRIS HO
Sch
COLWITH RD
ROSEDEW RD
NELLA RD
FULHAM PALACE RD
ASPENLEA RD
GREYHOUND RD
OAKLEY WLK
AVERILL ST
DELORME ST
EVERINGTON ST
ADENEY
A3218 LILLIE RD
Liby
CLIFFORD HAIGH HO
Recn Gd
PURCELL CRES
STRODE RD
CRABTREE LA
River Thames
Thames Path
Thames Reach
NOWELL RD
KILMINGTON RD
ALDERBURY RD
HOWSMAN RD
EVERDON RD
STILLINGFLEET RD
Jun & Inf Sch
BOILEAU RD
FIELDING MEWS
THE SPINNEY
CASTELNAU
Allot Gdns
TRINITY CHURCH RD
1 ARUNDEL CT
2 ARUNDEL MANS
3 KEBLE PL
4 HARDINGS HO
ORIEL DR
HOLST MANS
HANDEL MANS
GARRAWAY CT
HEIDEGGER CRES
DEVEREUX LA
WYATT DR
BURGES GR
CARTWRIGHT WAY
RIVERVIEW GDNS
CLAVERING AVE
ARUNDEL TERR
MERTHYR TERR
JENNER PL 1
CASTELNAU ROW 2
Swedish Sch
WINDERMERE CT
FERRY LA
1 GRASMERE CT
2 QUEENSMERE CT
BARNES AVE
Recn Gd
VERDUN RD
KENTWODE GN
WASHINGTON RD
Tenn Cts
Sp Gd
Harrodian Sch
Bwg Gn
BELGRAVE RD
ULLSWATER RD
ATHERTON RD
GALATA RD
MADRID RD
Liby
The Wetland Ctr
CRABTREE HALL 1
ADAM WLK 2
ROSEBANK 3
LYSIA CT 4
WHEATSHEAF LA
HOLYPORT RD
MEADOWBANK CL
LYSIA ST
SW6
Cemy
QUEENSMILL RD
Prim Sch
LANGTHORNE ST
ROWBERRY CL
CONISTON CL
Recn Gd
Pav
SUFFOLK RD
PARKE RD
BERKELEY RD
WALSINGHAM LO
FERRY RD
NEWPORT RD
CUMBERLAND PD
LOWTHER RD
BARONSMEAD RD
Blakes Wharves
CEDAR LO 1
ASH LO 2
ELM LO 3
ALDER LO 4
WILLOW LO 5
MILL HOTS CL
KENYON ST
INGLETHORPE ST
KINGWOOD RD
CRAVEN LO
ROBERT OWEN HO
A219
HARBORD ST
WOODLAWN RD
Eternit Wharf
STEVENAGE RD
Stevenage Wharves
GRESWELL ST
FINLAY ST
Sch
Craven Cottage (Fulham Fball Club)
ELLERBY ST
DONERAILE ST
FULHAM
CLONCURRY ST
BISHOP'S MANS
BISHOP'S PARK RD
Bwg Gn
WESTMORELAND RD
ELLERTON RD
BYFELD GDNS
BARNES
MELVILLE RD
KITSON RD
KING EDWARD MEWS
THE HERMITAGE
GRANGE RD
Sch
133
A3003
CHURCH RD
QUEEN ELIZABETH WLK
Tenn Cts
Pav
Barn Elms Pl Flds
Running Tk
Thames Path
Hammersmith & Fulham
Richmond upon Thames
BRACKEN GDNS
THE CRESCENT
HILLERSDON AVE
GLEBE RD
MEREDYTH RD
ELM GROVE RD
CARDIGAN RD
BELLEVUE RD
RECTORY RD
LAUREL RD
RANELAGH AVE
B349
STATION RD
BEVERLEY CL
CEDARS RD
SW13
Pav
Bwg Gn
Pav
Tenn Cts
Beverley Brook
Allot Gdns
Putney Lower Common
Barn Elms Schs Sp Ctr
1 PEARSON HO
2 HUNTINGFORD HO
3 KNOX HO
4 LANCASTER HO
5 HEWETT HO
BONTHRON HO
FORREST HO
FAULKNER HO
HORNE WAY
STOCKHURST CL
EMBANKMENT
1 GRIFFIN GATE
2 DARFUR ST
3 JOHN KEALL HO
4 HENRY JACKSON HO
5 FELSHAM HO
6 ARDSHIEL CL
7 RUVIGNY MANS
8 STAR & GARTER MANS
9 UNIVERSITY MANS
10 LOCKYER HO
11 PHELPS HO
12 PRINCETON CT
13 KINGSMERE CL
MILL HILL RD
ROCKS LA
Richmond upon Thames
Wandsworth
Old Barnes Cemy
Bwg Gn
Pav
Putney
COMMONDALE
JERROLD LO
FLOSS ST
SEFTON ST
PENTLOW ST
WATERS PL
JAY HO
DANEMERE ST
ASHLONE RD
FESTING RD
ROTHERWOOD RD
BENDEMEER RD
MILL HILL
Barnes Common
Crkt Gd
STATION RD
COMMON RD
LOWER RICHMOND RD
All Saints CE Prim Sch
PUTNEY COMMON
WILLOW FARM LA
HALLAM RD
CHESTER CL
Crkt Gd
LOWER COMMON
SHERWOOD CT
QUEEN'S RIDE
ST MARY'S GR
CRESSY HO
EGLISTON MEWS
EGLISTON RD
DRYBURGH MANS
ERPINGHAM RD
Tenn Cts
ABBOTSTONE RD
WESTHORPE
STANBRIDGE RD
BORNEO ST
BLACKETT ST
BANGALORE ST
GLADWYN RD
HENRY JACKSON RD
BIGG'S ROW
WEISS RD
BEMISH RD
WATERMAN ST
GAY ST
Sch
LANDFORD RD
HOTHAM RD
MELINA CT 1
SYCAMORE LO 2
LIME CT 3
WILLOW LO 4
HAWTHORN CT 5
FIR LO 6
MARCH CT 7
Barnes
Barnes Common
Bwg Gn
LCs
ROEHAMPTON CT
Red Rover
A306
B306
QUEEN'S CT
BELOE CT
GIPSY LA
WARWICK DR
DRYBURGH RD
REDGRAVE RD
GWALIOR RD
LACY RD
A205
Rosslyn Park
Pav
Tenn Cts
Tenn Cts
CH
ROEHAMPTON LA
DUNGARVAN AVE
DAYLESFORD AVE
CORNERWAYS
PUTNEY PARK AVE
MARRICK CL
LANGSIDE AVE
ELLENBOROUGH PL
GLENTHORPE
NEWNES PATH
BALFOUR PL
JOHN GLYNES CT
CHEVAL CT
FAIRDALE GDNS
QUEENSGATE GDNS
WELLWOOD CT
L Ctr
HARWOOD CT
CLARENDON DR
ROSSDALE RD
GAMLEN RD
Sch
Sch
CARLYLE PL
MODDER PL
QUILL LA
CARDINAL PL
LIFFORD ST
STRATFORD GR
UPPER RICHMOND RD
BELVEDERE CT
ORMONDE CT
SPENCER WLK
CHELVERTON RD
NORROY RD
JORDAN CT
Roehampton
Allot Gdns
DOVER HOUSE RD
WOODBOROUGH RD
SEYMOUR
BRIAR WLK
SOMERSET
PEAR TREE
MALBROOK RD
PETTIWARD CL
COLINETTE RD
DEALTRY RD
PARKFIELDS
FAIRFAX MEWS
BALMUIR GDNS
BRITTANY HO
CARMALT GDNS
NURSERY CL
PO
SW15
WOODTHORPE RD
BRAMCOTE RD
ST MARGARET'S CT
HOWARD'S LA
CAMPION RD
COALECROFT RD
HOLROYD RD
ENMORE RD
Tenn Cts
TIDESWELL RD
GWENDOLEN AVE
RAVENNA RD
BURSTON RD
ULVA RD
PUTNEY HILL
FAIRACRES
CROMWELL HO
GIBBON WLK
SWINBURNE RD
LYSONS WLK
HUNTINGFIELD RD
Allot Gdns
PLEASANCE RD
PUTNEY PARK LA
MONTOLIEU GDNS
Tenn Ct
22
23
24
156
75
76
77
78
1
2
3
4
5
6
ELMSHAW RD
HAWKESBURY RD
HAZLEWELL RD
GWENDOLEN CL
PUTNEY
BURLEIGH PL
ASHDOWN
CAMBALT RD
ST JOHN'S AVE
Southlands
Schs
Roehampton

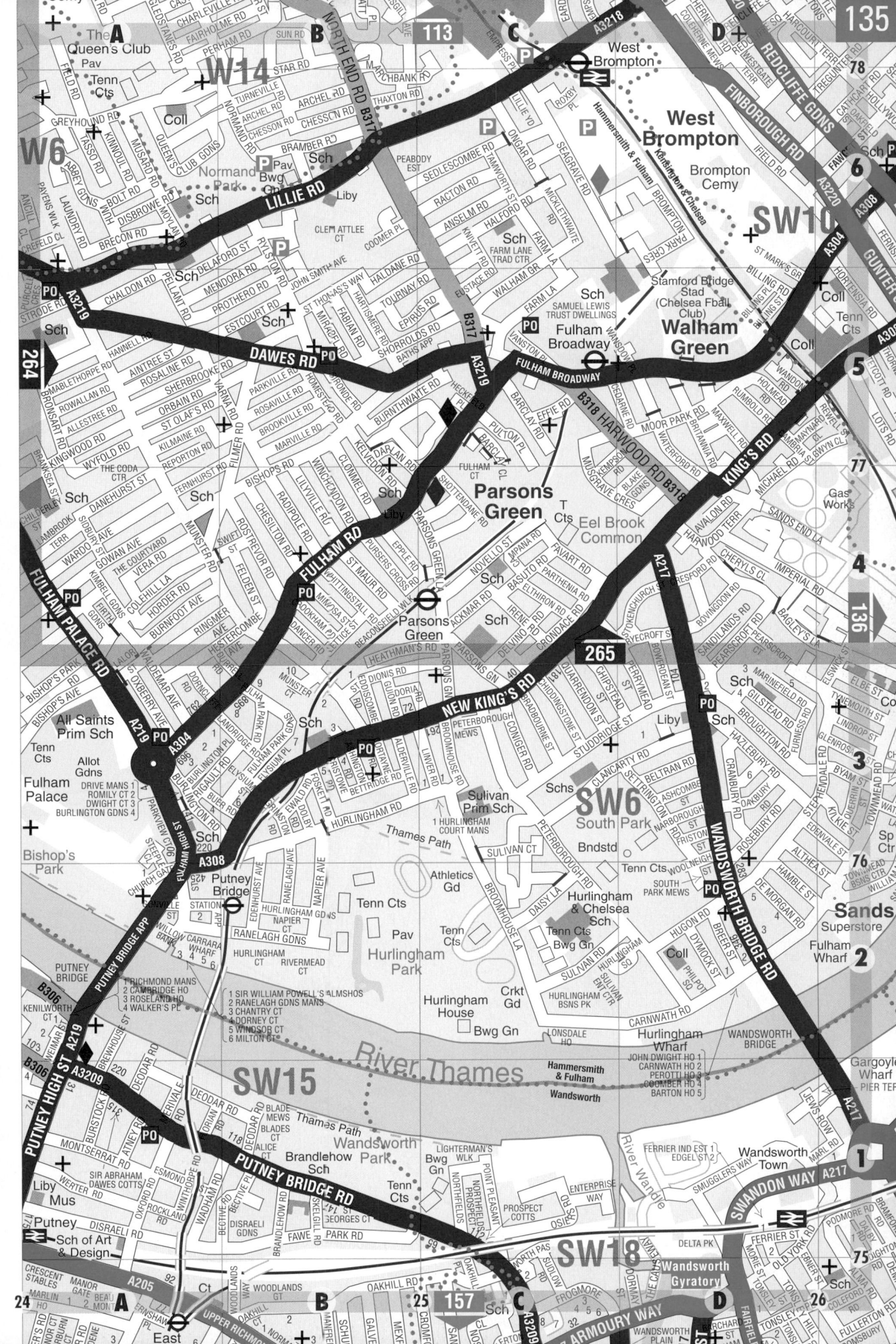
A
B
C
D
113
The Queen's Club
Pav
Tenn Cts
W14
W6
Coll
NORTH END RD
B317
LILLIE RD
Normand Park
Sch
Liby
CLEM ATTLEE CT
West Brompton
Hammersmith & Fulham
Kensington & Chelsea
Brompton Cemy
SW10
REDCLIFFE GDNS
FINBOROUGH RD
A3218
A3220
A308
A304
Stamford Bridge Stad (Chelsea Fball Club)
Walham Green
Fulham Broadway
FULHAM BROADWAY
SAMUEL LEWIS TRUST DWELLINGS
DAWES RD
A3219
264
B318 HARWOOD RD
KING'S RD
Parsons Green
Eel Brook Common
FULHAM RD
FULHAM PALACE RD
Gas Works
136
265
NEW KING'S RD
All Saints Prim Sch
Fulham Palace
Allot Gdns
Bishop's Park
Sulivan Prim Sch
SW6
South Park
Bndstd
Hurlingham & Chelsea Sch
Athletics Gd
Thames Path
Putney Bridge
Hurlingham Park
Hurlingham House
Crkt Gd
Bwg Gn
WANDSWORTH BRIDGE RD
A217
Hurlingham Wharf
WANDSWORTH BRIDGE
Sands End
Superstore
Fulham Wharf
Gargoyle Wharf
PIER TER
River Thames
SW15
Hammersmith & Fulham
Wandsworth
PUTNEY HIGH ST
A219
A3209
PUTNEY BRIDGE RD
Brandlehow Sch
Wandsworth Park
River Wandle
Wandsworth Town
SWANDON WAY
SW18
Wandsworth Gyratory
Putney Sch of Art & Design
Liby Mus
A205
UPPER RICHMOND RD
East Putney
ARMOURY WAY
157
24
25
26
75
76
77
78
1
2
3
4
5
6

A
B
114
C
D
SW10
SW3
FULHAM RD
REDCLIFFE GDNS
KING'S RD
CHELSEA EMB
Thames Path
Cadogan Pier
Chelsea Reach
ALBERT BRIDGE (SUSPENSION)
Kensington & Chelsea
Wandsworth
BATTERSEA BRIDGE
Bridge Wharf
Ransome's Dock
CHEYNE WLK
CREMORNE RD
Chelsea & Westminster
OAKLEY ST
ROYAL HOSPITAL RD
Fountain Lake
Festival Pleasure Gardens
CARRIAGE DRIVE N
CENTRAL AVE
Old Ferry Wharf
Chelsea Wharf
Cremorne Wharf
River Thames
Chelsea Creek
Gas Works
BATTERSEA BRIDGE RD
ALBERT BRIDGE RD
WESTBRIDGE RD
BATTERSEA
Hammersmith & Fulham
Wandsworth
VICARAGE CRES
SW6
135
266
267
PRINCE OF WALES DR
BATTERSEA PARK RD
Regent Wharf
LOMBARD RD
YORK RD
Heliport
Battersea Reach
Sands End
Superstore
Fulham Wharf
Sherwood Wharf
Trad Est
Gargoyle Wharf
WANDSWORTH BRIDGE
Thames Path
FALCON RD
LATCHMERE RD
SW11
Christ Church Sch
Falcon Park
Clapham Junction
ST JOHN'S HILL
BATTERSEA RISE
LAVENDER HILL
ELSPETH RD
SW18
Wandsworth Town
SWANDON WAY
EAST HILL
NORTH SIDE WANDSWORTH COMM
CLAPHAM COMMON WEST SIDE
Belleville Prim Sch
26
27
158
28
1
2
3
4
5
6
75
76
77
78

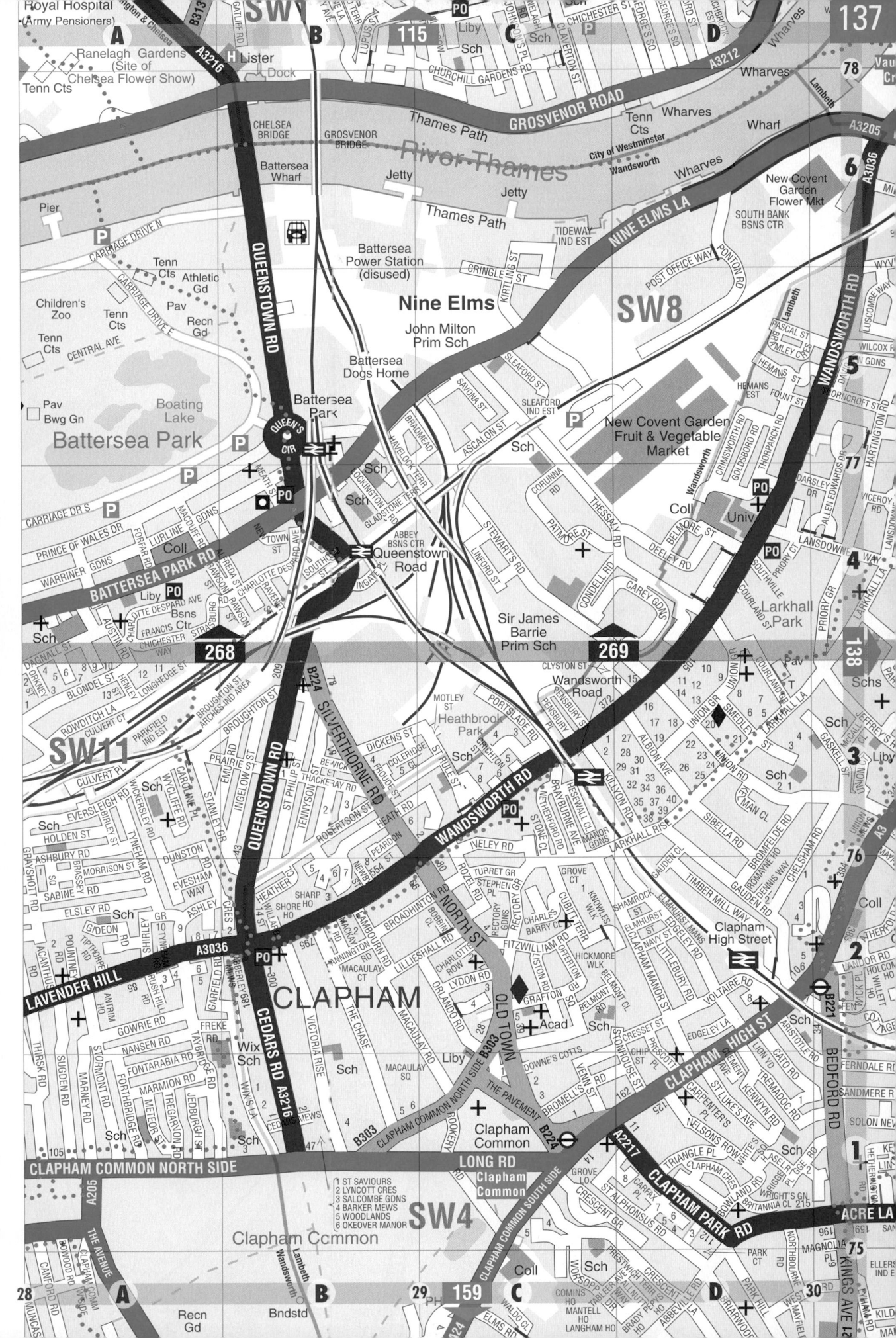
Royal Hospital (Army Pensioners)
Ranelagh Gardens (Site of Chelsea Flower Show)
Lister
Thames Path
GROSVENOR ROAD
River Thames
CHELSEA BRIDGE
GROSVENOR BRIDGE
Battersea Wharf
Jetty
City of Westminster
Wandsworth
New Covent Garden Flower Mkt
NINE ELMS LA
Battersea Power Station (disused)
Nine Elms
SW8
John Milton Prim Sch
Battersea Dogs Home
Children's Zoo
CARRIAGE DRIVE N
CENTRAL AVE
QUEENSTOWN RD
Battersea Park
Boating Lake
QUEEN'S CIR
New Covent Garden Fruit & Vegetable Market
SOUTH BANK BSNS CTR
WANDSWORTH RD
BATTERSEA PARK RD
PRINCE OF WALES DR
Queenstown Road
Sir James Barrie Prim Sch
Larkhall Park
268
269
138
SW11
SILVERTHORNE RD
Wandsworth Road
Heathbrook Park
WANDSWORTH RD
LAVENDER HILL
CEDARS RD
CLAPHAM
NORTH ST
OLD TOWN
Clapham High Street
CLAPHAM HIGH ST
BEDFORD RD
Clapham Common
CLAPHAM COMMON NORTH SIDE
LONG RD
CLAPHAM COMMON SOUTH SIDE
CLAPHAM PARK RD
ACRE LA
SW4
1 ST SAVIOURS
2 LYNCOTT CRES
3 SALCOMBE GDNS
4 BARKER MEWS
5 WOODLANDS
6 OKEOVER MANOR
Clapham Common
THE AVENUE
115
159
28
29
30
A
B
C
D
KINGS AVE

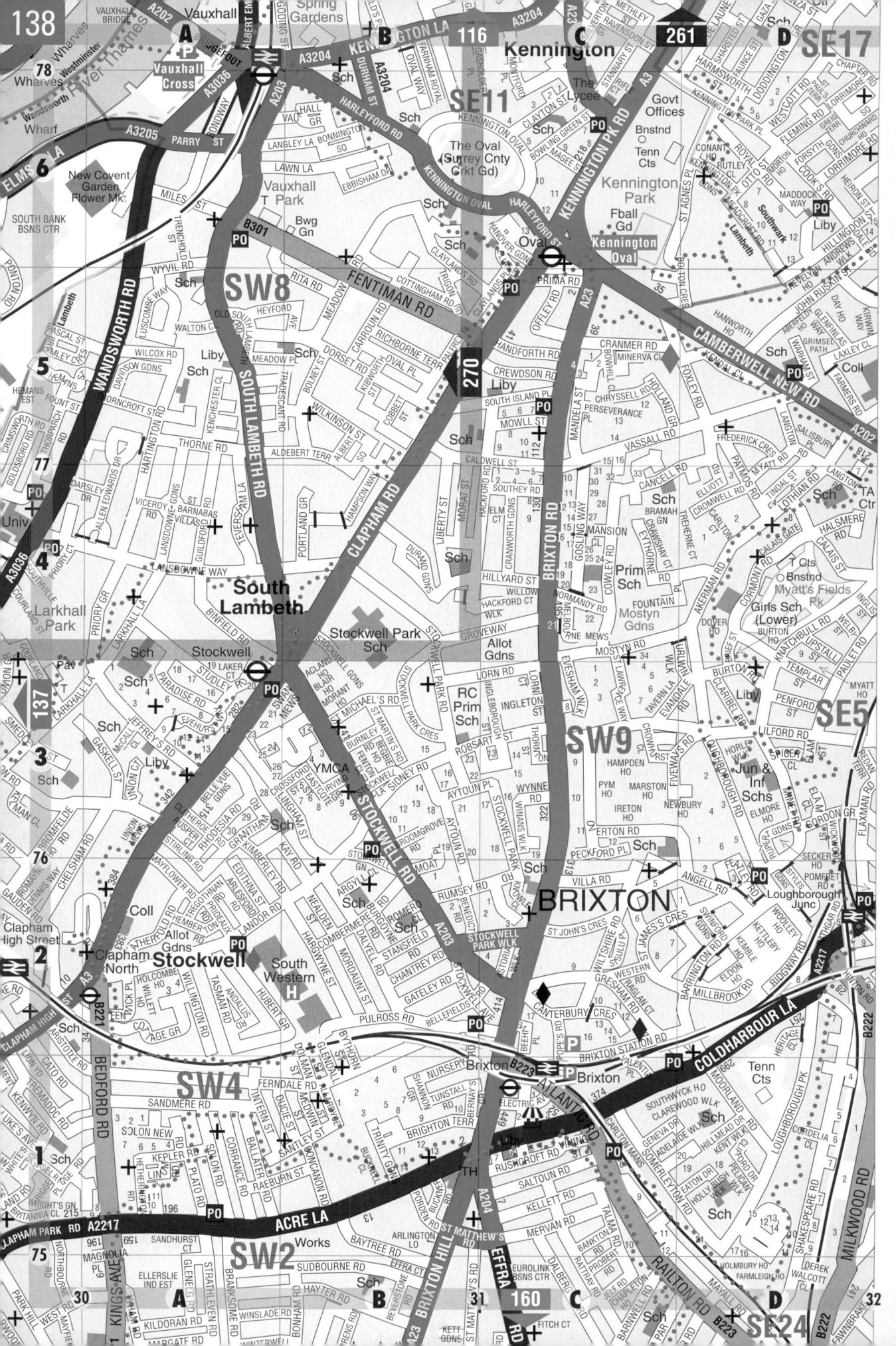
Vauxhall
Kennington
SE17
SE11
The Oval (Surrey Cnty Crkt Gd)
Vauxhall Cross
River Thames
New Covent Garden Flower Mkt
Vauxhall T Park
Kennington Park
Kennington Oval
Oval
SW8
FENTIMAN RD
WANDSWORTH RD
SOUTH LAMBETH RD
CLAPHAM RD
CAMBERWELL NEW RD
KENNINGTON PK RD
BRIXTON RD
HARLEYFORD RD
KENNINGTON OVAL
South Lambeth
Stockwell
Stockwell Park Sch
Larkhall Park
Myatt's Fields Pk
SW9
SE5
STOCKWELL RD
BRIXTON
Clapham North
Clapham High Street
Stockwell
South Western
Loughborough Junc
COLDHARBOUR LA
SW4
ACRE LA
Brixton
ATLANTIC RD
BRIXTON HILL
EFFRA RD
RAILTON RD
SW2
BEDFORD RD
MILKWOOD RD
SE24
116
261
270
137
160
30
31
32
75
76
77
78

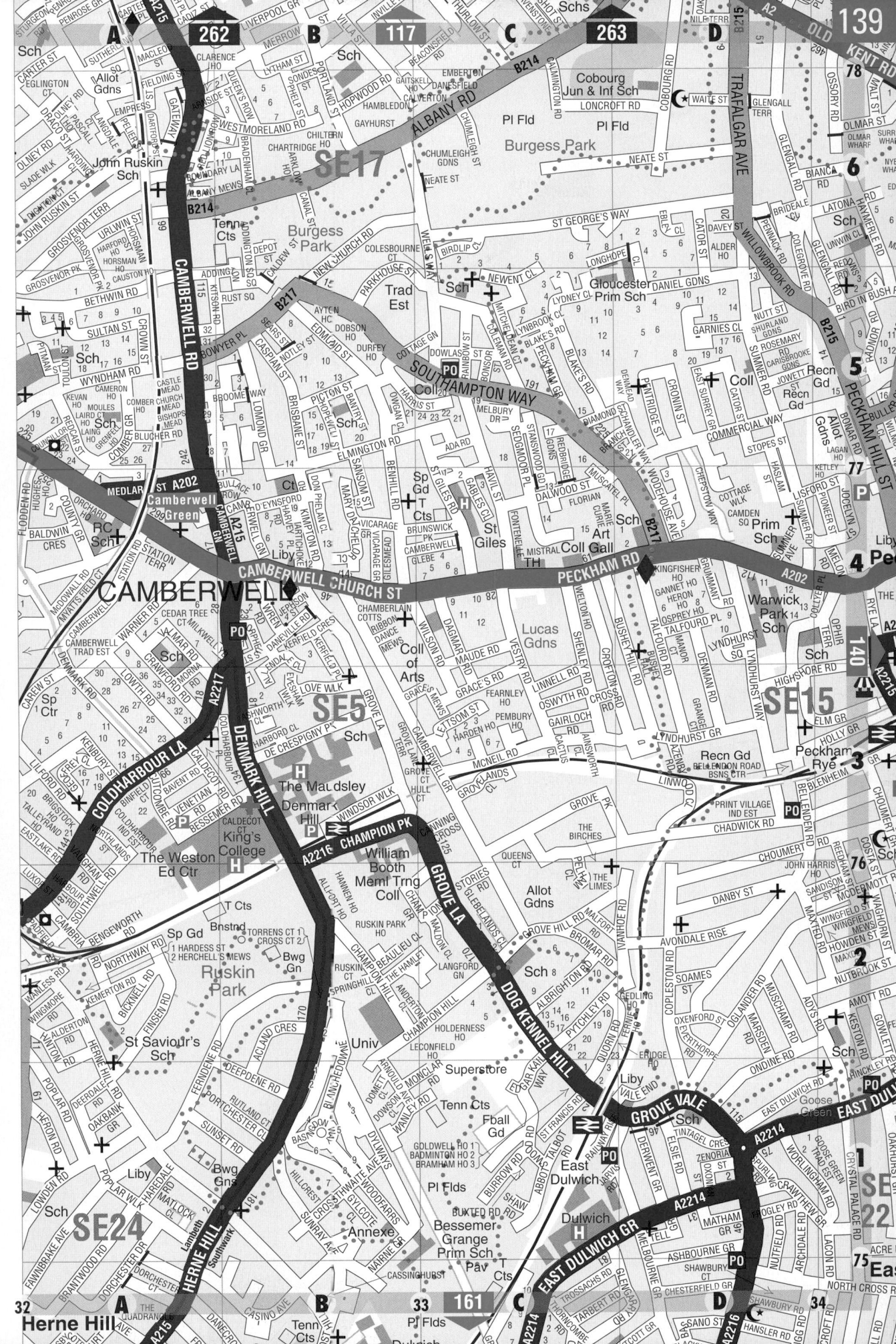
262
117
263
A
B
C
D
1
2
3
4
5
6
32
33
34
161
140
76
77
78
75
SE17
SE5
SE15
SE24
SE22
CAMBERWELL
Camberwell Green
CAMBERWELL RD
CAMBERWELL CHURCH ST
PECKHAM RD
PECKHAM HILL ST
DENMARK HILL
COLDHARBOUR LA
CHAMPION PK
GROVE LA
DOG KENNEL HILL
GROVE VALE
EAST DULWICH GR
HERNE HILL
Herne Hill
ALBANY RD
SOUTHAMPTON WAY
TRAFALGAR AVE
OLD KENT RD
ST GEORGE'S WAY
MEDLAR ST
A202
A215
A2216
A2217
A2214
A2216
B214
B215
B217
Burgess Park
Cobourg Jun & Inf Sch
Gloucester Prim Sch
John Ruskin Sch
Trad Est
Lucas Gdns
Warwick Park Sch
Peckham Rye
Recn Gd
BELLENDEN ROAD BSNS CTR
PRINT VILLAGE IND EST
The Maudsley
Denmark Hill
King's College
The Weston Ed Ctr
William Booth Meml Trng Coll
Ruskin Park
St Saviour's Sch
Coll of Arts
Art Coll Gall
St Giles
Superstore
East Dulwich
Dulwich
Bessemer Grange Prim Sch
Annexe
Univ
Goose Green
Allot Gdns
CAMBERWELL TRAD EST
Lambeth
Southwark

A
B
C
D
118
162
139
SE1
SE16
SE15
SE14
SE4
SE22
DEPTFORD
Peckham
New Cross Gate
Nunhead
East Dulwich
Peckham Rye
London Stadium (Millwall FC)
Works
ROTHERHITHE
A2208
A2
OLD KENT RD
TRAFALGAR AVE
PECKHAM PARK RD
PECKHAM HILL ST
PECKHAM HIGH ST
A202
QUEEN'S RD
B227
A2214 LAUSANNE RD
EVELINA RD
NUNHEAD LA
EAST DULWICH RD
RYE LA
A2215
B219 PECKHAM RYE
DRAKEFELL RD
B2142
KENDER ST
A202 HANOVER PK
B216
B215
Canal Bridge
Gas Holder Station
Caroline Gardens
Brimmington Park
Bridge House Meadows
Ecklington Gardens
Telegraph Hill Park
Queen's Road
New Cross
Monson Sch
Tuke Sch
Warwick Park Sch
Waverley Sch (Upper)
Friern Sch
Peckham Rye Park
Goose Green
Cemy
Allot Gdns
Bwg Gn
Ppg Sta
Water Works
ABBOTSBURY MEWS
1 HYNDMAN ST
2 MURDOCK ST
3 SKENFRITH HO
4 SARNESFIELD HO
5 PETERCHURCH HO
1 STRICKLAND CT
2 GATEFIELD CT
3 WARBURTON CT
1 MEDINA HO
2 FROME HO
3 WELLAND HO
Lewisham
Southwark
34
35
36
75
76
77
78
1
2
3
4
5
6

119
River Thames
Blackhorse Wharf
Palmer's Wharf
Payne's Wharf
Borthwick Wharf
EVELYN ST
A200
SE8
Hughes Fields Prim Sch
Dreadnought Wharf
Dowell's Wharf
Folkestone Gardens
Thames Path
CREEK RD
A200
Deptford Creek
Deptford
DEPTFORD CHURCH ST
A2209
Greenwich
GREENWICH HIGH RD
GREENWICH SOUTH ST
SE10
Fordham Park
New Cross Gate
New Cross
NEW CROSS RD
DEPTFORD BROADWAY
DEPTFORD BRIDGE
Deptford Bridge
BLACKHEATH RD
A2
NEW CROSS
SE14
LEWISHAM WAY
BROOKMILL RD
St John's
Ravensbourne River
Ravensbourne Park
Elverson Road
LOAMPIT HILL
THURSTON RD
LOAMPIT VALE
DRAKEFELL RD
B2142
Brockley
SE4
Hilly Fields Park
Prendergast Sch
BROCKLEY RD
B218
ADELAIDE AVE
Brockley
Ladywell Cemy
Brockley Cemy
LADYWELL RD
Ladywell
SE13
MOLESWORTH ST
LEWISHAM HIGH ST
LEWISHAM RD
142
163
36
37
38

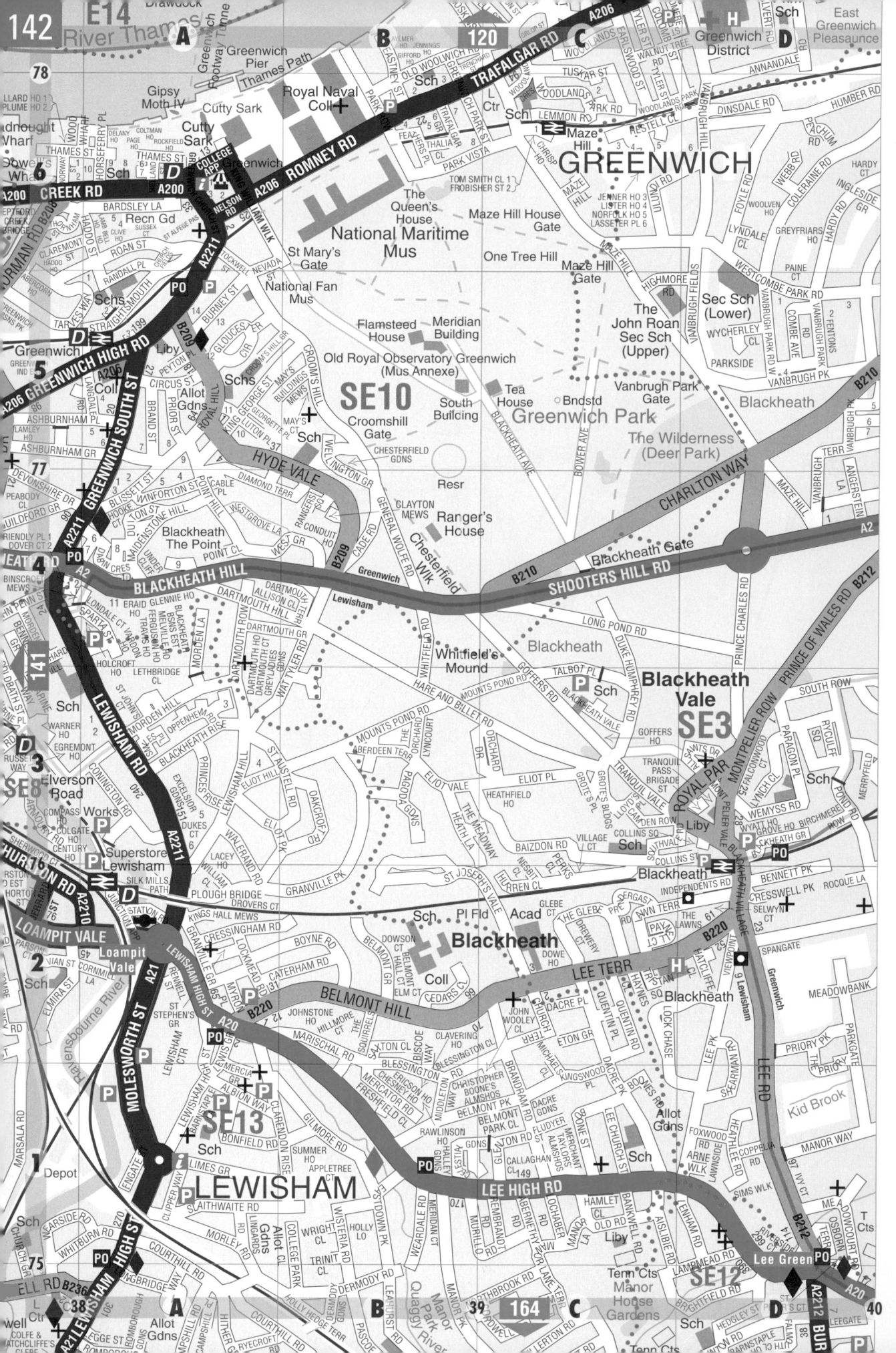
E14
River Thames
Greenwich Footway Tunnel
Greenwich Pier
Thames Path
Gipsy Moth IV
Cutty Sark
Royal Naval Coll
120
TRAFALGAR RD
ROMNEY RD
CREEK RD
GREENWICH
Maze Hill
The Queen's House
National Maritime Mus
Maze Hill House Gate
One Tree Hill
Maze Hill Gate
St Mary's Gate
National Fan Mus
Flamsteed House
Meridian Building
Old Royal Observatory Greenwich (Mus Annexe)
The John Roan Sec Sch (Upper)
Sec Sch (Lower)
Vanbrugh Park Gate
Blackheath
SE10
Croomshill Gate
South Building
Tea House
Bndstd
Greenwich Park
The Wilderness (Deer Park)
GREENWICH HIGH RD
GREENWICH SOUTH ST
HYDE VALE
CHARLTON WAY
Ranger's House
Chesterfield Wlk
Resr
Blackheath Gate
BLACKHEATH HILL
SHOOTERS HILL RD
Whitfield's Mound
Blackheath Vale
SE3
LEWISHAM RD
Elverson Road
Superstore Lewisham
Blackheath
LOAMPIT VALE
Loampit Vale
Blackheath Coll
LEE TERR
BELMONT HILL
MOLESWORTH ST
LEWISHAM HIGH ST
Ravensbourne River
SE13
LEWISHAM
LEE HIGH RD
LEE RD
Kid Brook
Tenn Cts
Manor House Gardens
SE12
Lee Green
164
A
B
C
D
1
2
3
4
5
6
38
39
40
75
76
77
78
141

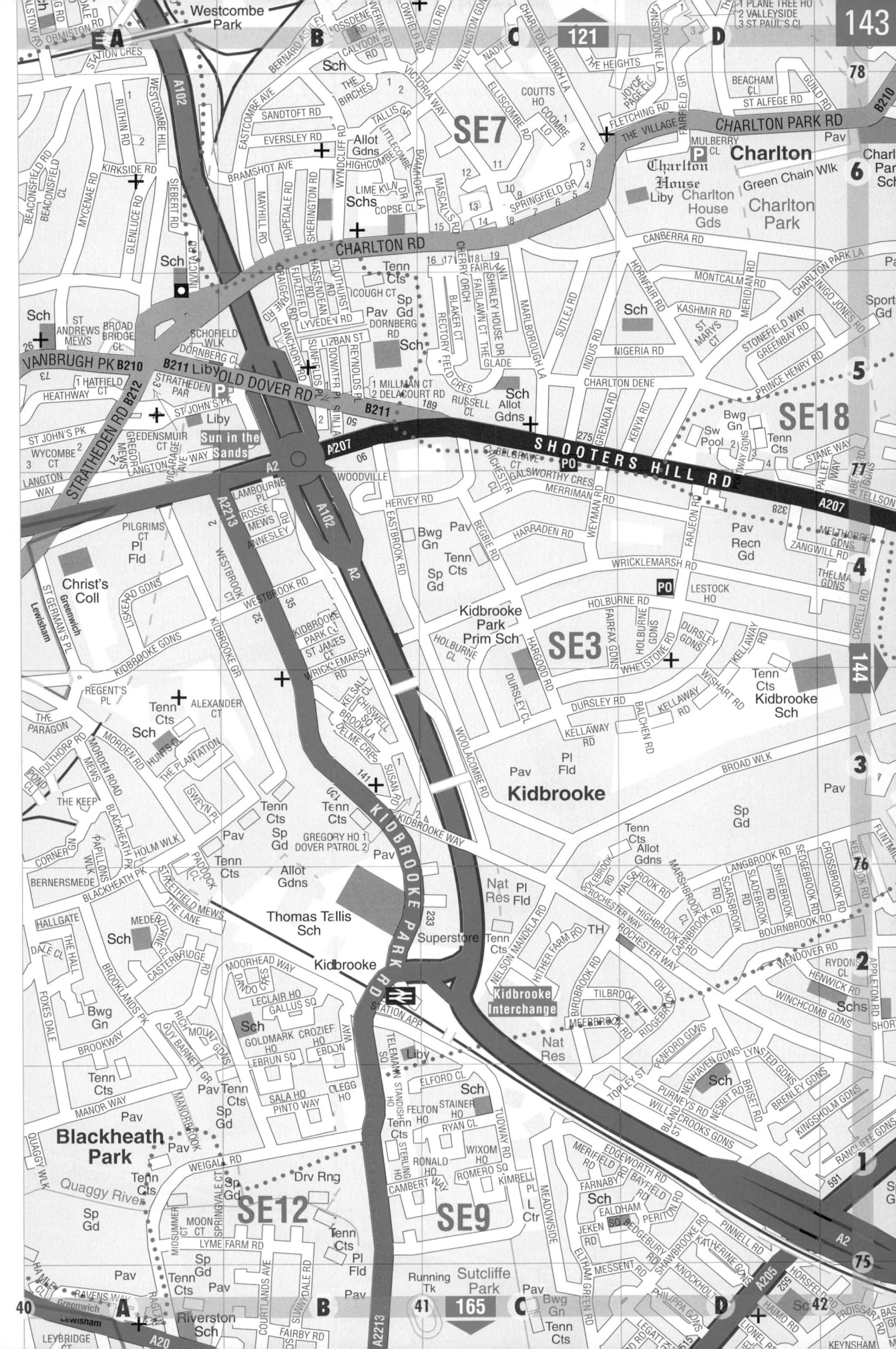

143
121
165
144
SE7
SE3
SE18
SE12
SE9
Charlton
Charlton House
Charlton House Gds
Charlton Park
Kidbrooke
Blackheath Park
Westcombe Park
Christ's Coll
Kidbrooke Park Prim Sch
Kidbrooke Sch
Thomas Tallis Sch
Kidbrooke Interchange
Sun in the Sands
Riverston Sch
Sutcliffe Park
Quaggy River
CHARLTON PARK RD
CHARLTON RD
SHOOTERS HILL RD
OLD DOVER RD
KIDBROOKE PARK RD
WESTCOMBE HILL
VANBRUGH PK
STRATHEDEN RD
WRICKLEMARSH RD
HOLBURNE RD
DURSLEY RD
BROAD WLK
ROCHESTER WAY
WENDOVER RD
WINCHCOMB GDNS
KIDBROOKE GDNS
WESTBROOK RD
KIDBROOKE GR
WOOLACOMBE RD
WEIGALL RD
MANOR WAY
BLACKHEATH PK
ELTHAM GREEN RD
EDGEWORTH RD
HORNFAIR RD
MARLBOROUGH LA
CHARLTON CHURCH LA
VICTORIA WAY

A
B
C
D
122
Rotunda Mus
Tenn Cts
Barrack Fld Pav
Charlton Park Rd
Charlton
Charlton Park Sch
Charlton Park
Green Chain Wlk
Cemy
SE7
Canberra Rd
Charlton Park La
Pav
Queen Elizabeth Sports Gd
Woolwich Stad
Woolwich Common
SE18
Stadium Rd
Shrapnel Cl
Ha-Ha Rd
Circular Way
Pl Fld
Woolwich Comm
Nightingale Pl
Nightingale Vale
Gilder
Engineer Cl
Jackson St
Kempt St
Ritter St
Schs
Sch
Long Wlk
Eglinton Rd
Westdale Rd
Ethel Brooks Ho
Cooper Ct
Barnfield
Rixon Ho
Keeble Cl
Ripon Rd
Reeves Rd
Herbert Rd
Cantwell Ho
Cantwell Rd
Dallin Rd
Highview
Eglinton Hill
Mayplace La
Brinklow Cres
Brent Rd
Santana Ho
Graham Ho
Condover Cres
Downend
Ordnance Rd
Llanover Rd
Whitworth Rd
Paget Rise
Delvan Cl
Keemor Cl
Matchless Dr
Garrison Cl
Green Chain Wlk
Academy Rd
Mansergh Cl
Baker Rd
Stane Way
Pallet Way
Aberford Gdns
Tellson Ave
Prince Imperial Rd
Red Lion La
Eaglesfield Sch
Springwater Cl
Barrington Villas
Constitution Rise
Donaldson Rd
Ankerdine Cres
Moordown
Occupation La
Riverview Hts
Bwg Gn
Eaglesfield Rd
Rayleas Cl
Shrewsbury La
Foxcroft Rd
Recn Gd
Cleanthus Rd
The Chestnuts
Cleanthus Cl
The Leas
Links View
A207
Shooters Hill Rd
Shooters Hill
Melthorpe Gdns
Zangwill Rd
Thelma Gdns
Wricklemarsh Rd
Corelli Rd
Tenn Cts
Gilbert Cl
Academy Pl
Vyvyan Ho
Hill End
Castlewood Day Sch
Campbell Cl
Craigholm
Mast
Memorial
Kenilworth Gdns
Kidbrook Sch
143
Broad Wlk
Mayday Gdns
Recn Gd
Eltham Common
Severndroog Castle
Stoney Alley
Green Chain Wlk
Jackwood
SE3
Pav
Cemy
Dunblane Rd
Allenswood Rd
Well Hall Rd
Heatherbank
Castlewood Dr
Flintmill Cres
Sedgebrook Rd
Crossbrook Rd
Kelbrook Rd
Sladebrook Rd
Birbrook Rd
Bournbrook Rd
Arbroath Rd
Ross Way
Wendover Rd
Rydons Cl
Henwick Rd
Appleton Rd
Whinyates Rd
Phineas Pett Rd
Franklin Pas
Downman Rd
Dickson Rd
Winchcomb Gdns
Schs
Shortway
Cobbett Rd
Maudslay Rd
Martin Bowes Rd
Arsenal Rd
Granby Rd
Cornwallis Wlk
Littlecroft
Crookston Rd
Grangehill Pl
Lovelace Gn
Shrapnel Rd
Brome Rd
Garnett Cl
Dairsie Rd
Deansfield Jun & Inf Schs
Rochester Way
Glenda Cl
Glenbar Cl
Glenhead Cl
Tenn Cts
Congreve Rd
Dumbreck Rd
Berryhill
Rochester Way
A208
Prince Rupert Rd
Admiral Seymour Rd
Moira Rd
Grangehill Rd
Westmount Rd
Elibank Rd
SE9
Eltham Park North
Berryhill Gdns
Brenley Gdns
Kingsholm Gdns
Rancliffe Gdns
Rickyard Path
Elmbrook Gdns
Odeon Par
Tom Coombs Cl
Tudor Par
Craigton Rd
Sch
Earlshall Rd
Well Hall Rd
Pleasaunce Ct
Kidbrooke La
Sp Gd
Pav
Tenn Cts
Well Hall Pleasaunce
Greenvale Rd
Eltham Park Gdns
Glenesk Rd
A2
Eltham
Dunvegan Rd
Well Hall Par
Bwg Gns
Eltham Park South
Horsfeld Rd
Haimo Rd
Froissart Rd
Baskerville Gdns
Tattersall Cl
Pullman Pl
Glenlea Rd
Glenlyon Rd
Glenshiel Rd
Recn Gd
Tenn Cts
Green Chain Wlk
St Mary's RC Prim
166
42
43
44

Plumstead Common
Plumstead Manor Sch
St Margaret's CE Prim Sch
SE18
Rockliffe Manor Prim Sch
Shrewsbury Park
Green Chain Wlk
Griffin Manor Spec Sch
Greenwood Sch
Shooters Hill
DA16
DOVER RD
East Wickham Prim Sch
Oxleas Wood Nature Reserve
Eastcote Prim Sch
BELLEGROVE RD
A207
Falconwood Field
SE9
Falconwood
Westwood Jun & Inf Schs
EAST ROCHESTER WAY
Eltham Warren
Crown Woods Sch
DA15
123
146
167
44
45
46
75
76
77
78

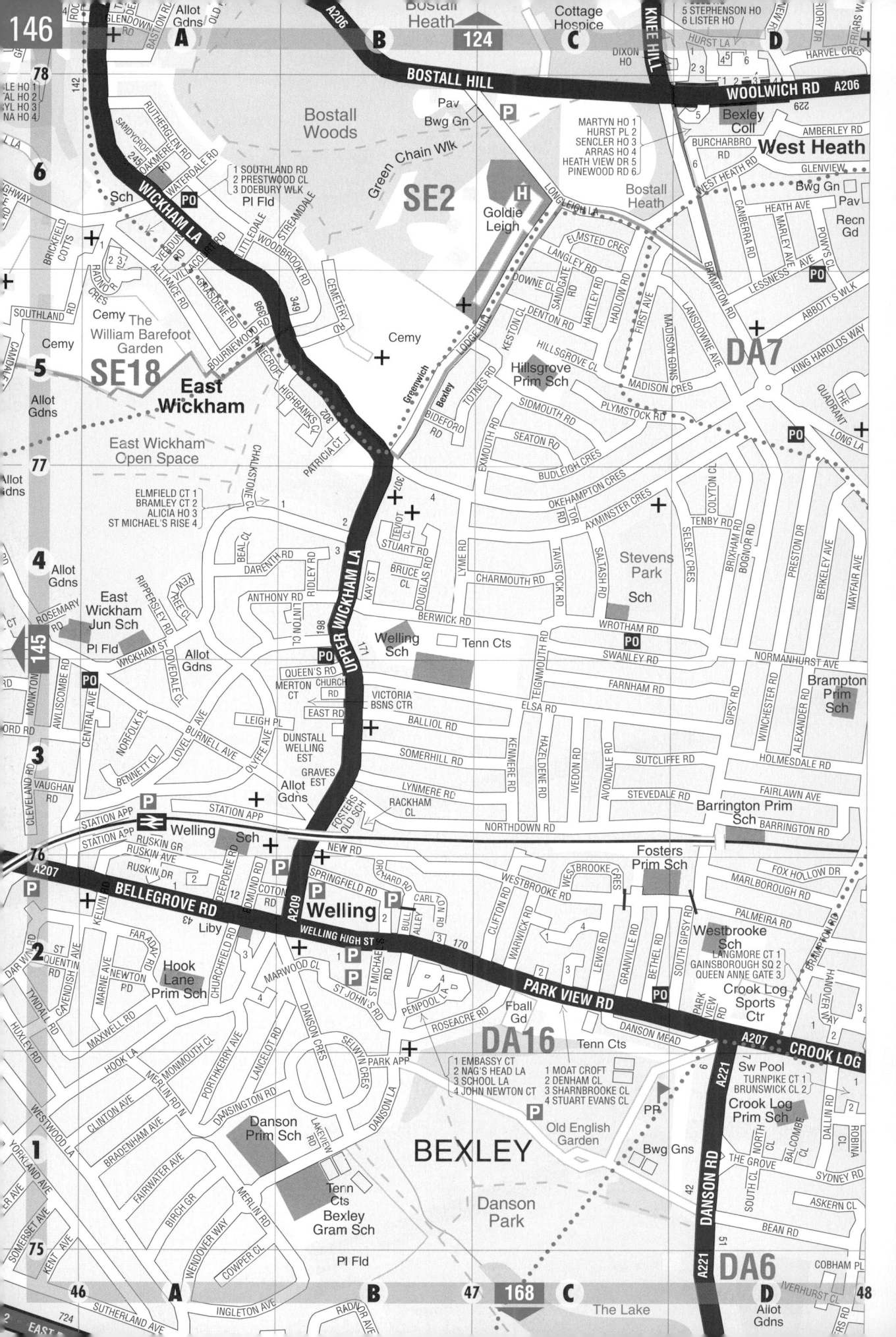
A
B
124
C
D
Bostall Heath
Cottage Hospice
KNEE HILL
5 STEPHENSON HO
6 LISTER HO
Allot Gdns
GLENDOWN RD
BASTION RD
HURST LA
DIXON HO
HARVEL CRES
78
BOSTALL HILL
WOOLWICH RD
A206
Bostall Woods
Pav
Bwg Gn
Bexley Coll
MARTYN HO 1
HURST PL 2
SENCLER HO 3
ARRAS HO 4
HEATH VIEW DR 5
PINEWOOD RD 6
AMBERLEY RD
BURCHARBRO RD
West Heath
GLENVIEW
Green Chain Wlk
RUTHERGLEN RD
SANDYCROFT
OAKMERE RD
WATERDALE RD
1 SOUTHLAND RD
2 PRESTWOOD CL
3 DOEBURY WLK
Pl Fld
6
SE2
WEST HEATH RD
Bwg Gn
Pav
Sch
PO
WICKHAM LA
Goldie Leigh
LONGLEIGH LA
Bostall Heath
HEATH AVE
Recn Gd
BRICKFIELD COTTS
VERDUN RD
VILLACOURT RD
LITTLEDALE
WOODBROOK RD
STREAMDALE
ELMSTED CRES
LANGLEY RD
CANBERRA RD
MARLEY AVE
POWYS CL
RADNOR CRES
ALLIANCE RD
GRASDENE RD
CEMETERY RD
DOWNE CL
SANDGATE RD
HARTLEY RD
HADLOW RD
FIRST AVE
LESSNESS AVE
BRAMPTON RD
ABBOTT'S WLK
SOUTHLAND RD
Cemy
The William Barefoot Garden
BOURNEWOOD RD
PINECROFT
Cemy
DENTON RD
KESTON CL
HILLSGROVE CL
MADISON GDNS
LANSDOWNE AVE
DA7
KING HAROLDS WAY
CAMDALE
5
SE18
East Wickham
LODGE HILL
Hillsgrove Prim Sch
Greenwich
Bexley
TOTNES RD
MADISON CRES
THE QUADRANT
Allot Gdns
HIGHBANKS CL
BIDEFORD RD
SIDMOUTH RD
PLYMSTOCK RD
PO
LONG LA
East Wickham Open Space
PATRICIA CT
SEATON RD
EXMOUTH RD
77
CHALKSTONE CL
BUDLEIGH CRES
Allot Gdns
ELMFIELD CT 1
BRAMLEY CT 2
ALICIA HO 3
ST MICHAEL'S RISE 4
OKEHAMPTON CRES
COLYTON CL
AXMINSTER CRES
TOR RD
TENBY RD
TEVIOT CL
STUART RD
BEAL CL
DARENTH RD
RIDLEY RD
BRUCE CL
LYME RD
TAVISTOCK RD
SALTASH RD
Stevens Park
SELSEY CRES
BRIXHAM RD
BOGNOR RD
PRESTON DR
BERKELEY AVE
MAYFAIR AVE
4
Allot Gdns
KAY ST
DOUGLAS RD
CHARMOUTH RD
East Wickham Jun Sch
RIPPERSLEY RD
NEW TREE CL
ANTHONY RD
LINTON CL
UPPER WICKHAM LA
Sch
ROSEMARY RD
BERWICK RD
TEIGNMOUTH RD
WROTHAM RD
PO
Welling Sch
Tenn Cts
145
Pl Fld
WICKHAM ST
Allot Gdns
DOVEDALE CL
QUEEN'S RD
SWANLEY RD
NORMANHURST AVE
Brampton Prim Sch
MONKTON RD
AWLISCOMBE RD
CENTRAL AVE
PO
MERTON CT
CHURCH RD
VICTORIA BSNS CTR
FARNHAM RD
EAST RD
ELSA RD
GIPSY RD
WINCHESTER RD
ALEXANDER RD
NORFOLK PL
LEIGH PL
BURNELL AVE
LOVEL AVE
OLYFFE AVE
DUNSTALL WELLING EST
BALLIOL RD
3
SOMERHILL RD
KENMERE RD
HAZELDENE RD
IVEDON RD
AVONDALE RD
SUTCLIFFE RD
HOLMESDALE RD
CLEVELAND RD
VAUGHAN RD
BENNETT CL
GRAVES EST
Allot Gdns
LYNMERE RD
STEVEDALE RD
FAIRLAWN AVE
STATION APP
P
STATION APP
RACKHAM CL
FOSTERS OLD SCH
Barrington Prim Sch
BARRINGTON RD
NORTHDOWN RD
Welling
STATION APP
RUSKIN GR
Sch
NEW RD
Fosters Prim Sch
76
A207
RUSKIN AVE
RUSKIN DR
DEEPDENE RD
EDMUND RD
ORCHARD RD
WESTBROOKE RD
WESTBROOKE CRES
FOX HOLLOW DR
MARLBOROUGH RD
BELLEGROVE RD
KELVIN RD
COTON RD
SPRINGFIELD RD
CARLTON RD
Welling
BULL ALLEY
CLIFTON RD
PALMEIRA RD
A209
Liby
WELLING HIGH ST
WARWICK RD
Westbrooke Sch
LANGMORE CT 1
GAINSBOROUGH SQ 2
QUEEN ANNE GATE 3
BRAMPTON RD
FARADAY RD
CHURCHFIELD RD
ST MICHAEL'S RD
LEWIS RD
GRANVILLE RD
BETHEL RD
SOUTH GIPSY RD
2
ST QUENTIN RD
CAVENDISH AVE
MARNE AVE
NEWTON RD
Hook Lane Prim Sch
MARWOOD CL
ST JOHN'S RD
PENPOOL LA
PARK VIEW RD
PO
PARK VIEW RD
Crook Log Sports Ctr
HANOVER WAY
TYNDALL RD
MAXWELL RD
ROSEACRE RD
Fball Gd
DA16
Tenn Cts
DANSON MEAD
A207
CROOK LOG
HUXLEY RD
HOOK LA
MONMOUTH CL
PORTHKERRY AVE
LANCELOT RD
DANSON CRES
SELWYN CRES
PARK APP
1 EMBASSY CT
2 NAG'S HEAD LA
3 SCHOOL LA
4 JOHN NEWTON CT
1 MOAT CROFT
2 DENHAM CL
3 SHARNBROOKE CL
4 STUART EVANS CL
A221
Sw Pool
TURNPIKE CT 1
BRUNSWICK CL 2
Crook Log Prim Sch
MERLIN RD N
CLINTON AVE
WESTWOOD LA
DANSINGTON RD
DANSON LA
PR
DALLIN RD
ROBINA CL
BRADENHAM AVE
Danson Prim Sch
LAKEVIEW RD
Old English Garden
NORTH CL
BALCOMBE CL
1
YORKLAND AVE
BEXLEY
Bwg Gns
THE GROVE
SYDNEY RD
FAIRWATER AVE
DANSON RD
Tenn Cts
SOUTH CL
ASKERN CL
SOMERSET AVE
BIRCH GR
WENDOVER WAY
MERLIN RD
Bexley Gram Sch
Danson Park
BEAN RD
KENT AVE
75
COWPER CL
Pl Fld
A221
DA6
COBHAM PL
46
A
B
47
168
C
D
48
IVERHURST CL
SUTHERLAND AVE
INGLETON AVE
RADNOR AVE
The Lake
Allot Gdns

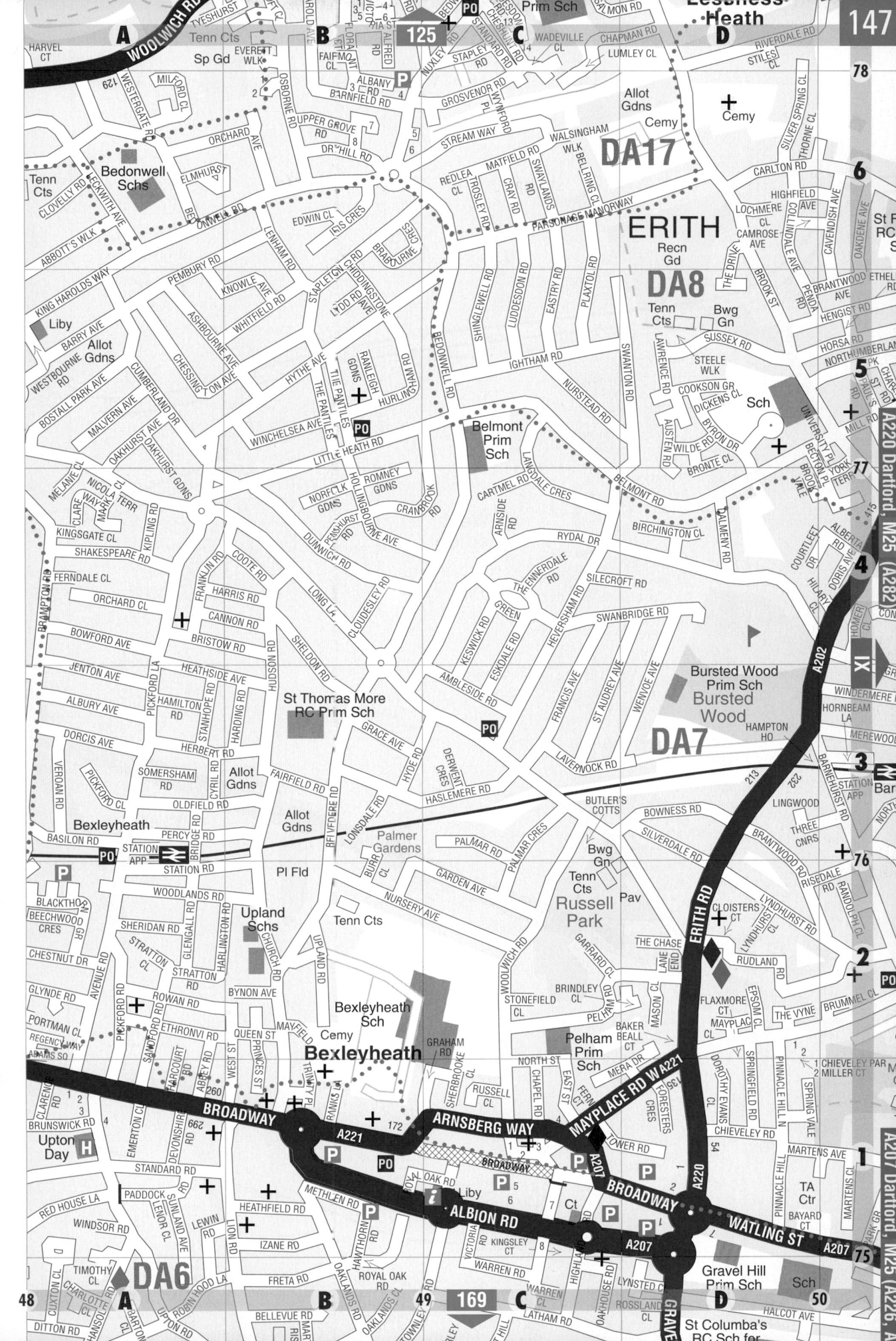

A
B
C
D
125
169
Lessness Heath
ERITH
DA17
DA8
DA7
DA6
Bexleyheath
Russell Park
Bursted Wood
Palmer Gardens
WOOLWICH RD
TYESHURST CL
Tenn Cts
Sp Gd
EVERETT WLK
HARVEL CT
WESTERGATE RD
MILFORD CL
OSBORNE RD
FAIRMONT CL
ALBANY RD
BARNFIELD RD
UPPER GROVE RD
DRY HILL RD
NUXLEY RD
STAPLEY RD
GROSVENOR RD
WYNFORD PL
STREAM WAY
Prim Sch
WADEVILLE CL
CHAPMAN RD
LUMLEY CL
RIVERDALE RD
STILES CL
Allot Gdns
Cemy
WALSINGHAM WLK
SILVER SPRING CL
THORNE CL
CARLTON RD
ORCHARD AVE
Bedonwell Schs
ELMHURST
CLOVELLY RD
BECKWITH AVE
BEDONWELL RD
ABBOTT'S WLK
EDWIN CL
IRIS CRES
BRADBOURNE CRES
REDLEA CL
MATFIELD RD
TROSLEY RD
CRAY RD
SWAYLANDS RD
BELLRING CL
PARSONAGE MANORWAY
LOCHMERE CL
HIGHFIELD AVE
COLLINDALE AVE
CAVENDISH AVE
OAKDENE AVE
CAMROSE AVE
Recn Gd
THE DRIVE
BROOK ST
KING HAROLDS WAY
PEMBURY RD
KNOWLE AVE
WHITFIELD RD
LENHAM RD
STAPLETON RD
CHIDDINGSTONE AVE
LYDD RD
SHINGLEWELL RD
LUDDESDON RD
EASTRY RD
PLAXTOL RD
Bwg Gn
SUSSEX RD
LAWRENCE RD
STEELE WLK
BRANTWOOD AVE
HENGIST RD
HORSA RD
NORTHUMBERLAND PK
Liby
BARRY AVE
WESTBOURNE RD
ASHBOURNE AVE
CHESSINGTON AVE
HYTHE AVE
RANLEIGH GDNS
HURLINGHAM RD
IGHTHAM RD
NURSTEAD RD
SWANTON RD
COOKSON GR
DICKENS CL
Sch
BOSTALL PARK AVE
CUMBERLAND DR
MALVERN AVE
THE PANTILES
TIE PANTILES
WINCHELSEA AVE
LITTLE HEATH RD
Belmont Prim Sch
AUSTEN RD
WILDE RD
BYRON DR
BRONTE CL
UNIVERSITY PL
BECTON PL
YORK TERR
BROOK VALE
MILL RD
OAKHURST AVE
OAKHURST GDNS
MELANIE CL
NICOLA TERR
MARK CL
CLARE WAY
ROMNEY GDNS
NORFOLK GDNS
HOLLINGBOURNE AVE
PENSHURST RD
CRANBROOK RD
LANGDALE CRES
CARTMEL RD
BELMONT RD
BIRCHINGTON CL
DALMENY RD
COURTLEET DR
ALBERTA RD
DORIS AVE
HILARY CL
KINGSGATE CL
KIPLING RD
SHAKESPEARE RD
FERNDALE CL
BRAMPTON RD
ORCHARD CL
FRANKLIN RD
COOTE RD
HARRIS RD
CANNON RD
BRISTOW RD
BOWFORD AVE
DUNWICH RD
LONG LA
CLOUDESLEY RD
ARNSIDE RD
RYDAL DR
THE GREEN
ENNERDALE RD
SILECROFT RD
HEVERSHAM RD
KESWICK RD
ESKDALE RD
SWANBRIDGE RD
HOMER CL
JENTON AVE
HEATHSIDE AVE
HUDSON RD
SHELDON RD
ALBURY AVE
HAMILTON RD
STANHOPE RD
HARDING RD
PICKFORD LA
St Thomas More RC Prim Sch
AMBLESIDE RD
FRANCIS AVE
ST AUDREY AVE
WENVOE AVE
Bursted Wood Prim Sch
WINDERMERE RD
HORNBEAM LA
HAMPTON HO
MEREWOOD
DORCIS AVE
HERBERT RD
GRACE AVE
HYDE RD
DERWENT CRES
LAVERNOCK RD
BARNEHURST RD
STATION APP
SOMERSHAM RD
CYRIL RD
Allot Gdns
FAIRFIELD RD
HASLEMERE RD
LONSDALE RD
BELVEDERE RD
BUTLER'S COTTS
BOWNESS RD
LINGWOOD
PICKFORD CL
OLDFIELD RD
VEROAN RD
SILVERDALE RD
BRANTWOOD RD
THREE CNRS
Bexleyheath
BASILON RD
PERCY RD
BRIDGE RD
STATION RD
PALMAR RD
PALMAR CRES
RISEDALE RD
RANDOLPH CL
Pl Fld
BURR CL
GARDEN AVE
Bwg Gn
Tenn Cts
Pav
BLACKTHORN GR
BEECHWOOD CRES
WOODLANDS RD
NURSERY AVE
SHERIDAN RD
GLENGALL RD
HARLINGTON RD
Upland Schs
CHURCH RD
UPLAND RD
Tenn Cts
CLOISTERS CT
LYNDHURST CL
LYNDHURST RD
ERITH RD
THE CHASE
LANE END
GARRARD CL
RUDLAND
CHESTNUT DR
STRATTON CL
STRATTON RD
AVENUE RD
GLYNDE RD
ROWAN RD
BYNON AVE
WOOLWICH RD
BRINDLEY CL
STONEFIELD CL
PELHAM RD
MASON CL
FLAXMORE CT
EPSOM CL
MAYPLACE CL
THE VYNE
BRUMMEL CL
PORTMAN CL
REGENCY WAY
ADAMS SQ
SANDFORD RD
ETHRONVI RD
QUEEN ST
MAYFIELD
Bexleyheath Sch
Cemy
GRAHAM RD
BAKER BEALL CT
Pelham Prim Sch
HARCOURT RD
ABBEY RD
WEST ST
PRINCES ST
TRINITY PL
SHERBROOKE CL
NORTH ST
CHAPEL RD
EAST ST
FERN CT
MERA DR
MAYPLACE RD W
FORESTERS CRES
DOROTHY EVANS CL
SPRINGFIELD RD
PINNACLE HILL N
CHIEVELEY PAR
MILLER CT
SPRING VALE
CLARENCE RD
BRUNSWICK RD
BROADWAY
DEVONSHIRE RD
RUSSELL CL
ARNSBERG WAY
TOWER RD
CHIEVELEY RD
Upton Day
EMERTON CL
STANDARD RD
RANKS LA
BROADWAY
MARTENS AVE
PINNACLE HILL
MARTENS CL
TA Ctr
BAYARD CT
RED HOUSE LA
PADDOCK CL
LENOR CL
SUNLAND AVE
HEATHFIELD RD
METHUEN RD
ROYAL OAK RD
ALBION RD
WATLING ST
WINDSOR RD
LEWIN RD
LION RD
IZANE RD
HAWTHORN RD
VICTORIA RD
KINGSLEY CT
WARREN RD
HIGHLAND RD
TIMOTHY CL
CHARLOTTE CL
FRETA RD
ROYAL OAK RD
OAKLANDS RD
WARREN CL
OAKHOUSE RD
LYNSTED CL
ROSSLAND CL
Gravel Hill Prim Sch
Sch
CUXTON CL
ROBIN HOOD LA
BELLEVUE RD
OAKLANDS CL
TOWNLEY RD
LATHAM RD
HALCOT AVE
DITTON RD
HANSOL RD
BARTON CL
UPTON RD
St Columba's RC Sch for
A220 Dartford, M25 (A282)
A207 Dartford, M25 (A226, A
A221
A207
A220
A202
78
6
5
77
4
3
76
2
1
75
48
49
50
IX

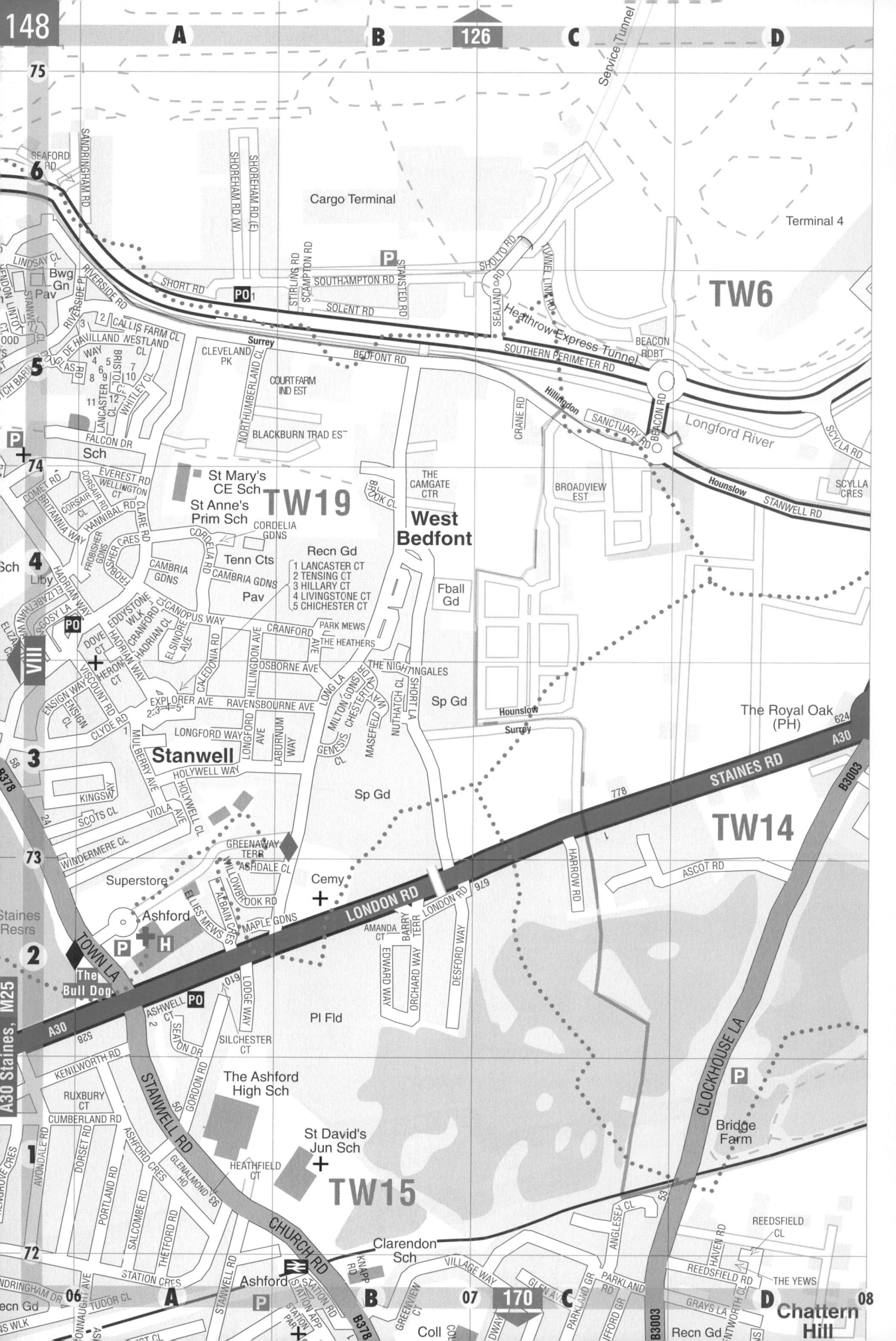

A 126 B C D

75

Service Tunnel

SEAFORD RD

6

SANDRINGHAM RD

Cargo Terminal

Terminal 4

SHOREHAM RD

SHOREHAM RD (E)

SHOREHAM RD (W)

RIVERSIDE RD

LINDSAY CL

Bwg
Gn
Pav

LONDON UNION

STANWELL BARRY

WOOD

SHORT RD

STIRLING RD

SCAMPTON RD

SOUTHAMPTON RD

SOLENT RD

STANSTED RD

P

P0 1

SHOLTO RD

SEALAND RD

TUNNEL LINK RD

Heathrow Express Tunnel

SOUTHERN PERIMETER RD

BEACON
RDBT

TW6

BEACON RD

Longford River

SCYLLA RD

5

CALLIS FARM CL

DE HAVILLAND
WESTLAND CL

WAY

2
3

AS

BRISTOL

4
6
8
9

7
10

11
12

LANCASTER RD

WHITLEY CL

CLEVELAND
PK

Surrey

NORTHUMBERLAND CL

COURT FARM
IND EST

BLACKBURN TRAD ES

BEDFONT RD

CRANE RD

Hillingdon

SANCTUARY RD

Hounslow

STANWELL RD

SCYLLA
CRES

P

74

FALCON DR

Sch

COMET RD

EVEREST RD

CORSAIR CL

WELLINGTON
CT

CLARE RD

St Mary's
CE Sch

St Anne's
Prim Sch

CORDELIA
GDNS

THE
CAMGATE
CTR

West
Bedfont

Broadview
EST

TW19

4

BRITANNIA WAY

HADRIAN WAY

FROBISHER CRES

HANNIBAL

CAMBRIA
GDNS

CORDELIA RD

CAMBRIA GDNS

Tenn Cts

Pav

Recn Gd
1 LANCASTER CT
2 TENSING CT
3 HILLARY CT
4 LIVINGSTONE CT
5 CHICHESTER CT

Fball
Gd

Sch

Liby

ELIZABETHAN WAY

ARGOSY LA

P0

DOVE
WLK

EDDYSTONE

HADRIAN WAY

CANOPUS WAY

CRANFORD CL

ELSINORE AVE

CALEDONIA RD

CRANFORD
AVE

HILLINGDON
AVE

OSBORNE AVE

PARK MEWS

THE HEATHERS

THE NIGHTINGALES

MILTON GDNS

CHESTERTON

SHORT LA

NUTHATCH CL

Sp Gd

VIII

ELIZABETH
CT

HERON CT

VISCOUNT RD

EXPLORER AVE

RAVENSBOURNE AVE

LONG LA

GENESIS

MASEFIELD

Hounslow

Surrey

The Royal Oak
(PH)

624

3

ENSIGN WAY

ENSIGN
CL

CLYDE RD

LONGFORD WAY

LONGFORD
AVE

LABURNUM
WAY

Stanwell

CL

Sp Gd

STAINES RD

A30

TW14

B3003

58

HOLYWELL WAY

B3378

73

WINDERMERE CL

KINGSW

SCOTS CL

VIOLA
AVE

HOLYWELL AVE

MULBERRY AVE

HOLYWELL CL

GREENAWAY
TERR

ASHDALE CL

WILLOWBROOK RD

Cemy

778

HARROW RD

ASCOT RD

24

Superstore

ELLIES MEWS

ALBAIN CRES

MAPLE GDNS

LONDON RD

LONDON RD

AMANDA
CT

BARRY
TERR

EDWARD WAY

ORCHARD WAY

DESFORD WAY

2

Staines
Resrs

TOWN LA

M25

P

H

Ashford

The
Bull Dog

ASHWELL
CT

LODGE WAY

P0

610

PI Fld

CLOCKHOUSE LA

P

Bridge
Farm

73

A30 Staines

A30 Staines, M25

KENILWORTH RD

RUXBURY
CT

CUMBERLAND RD

STANWELL RD

ASHFORD CRES

GORDON RD

50

SEATON DR

SILCHESTER
CT

The Ashford
High Sch

St David's
Jun Sch

1

AVONDALE RD

DORSET RD

ASHFORD RD

PORTLAND RD

SALCOMBE RD

GLENALMOND HO

HEATHFIELD
CT

TW15

72

SANDRINGHAM DR

TUDOR CL

CONNAUGHT AVE

STANWELL RD

ASHFORD CRES

CHURCH RD

Ashford

P

STATION APP

STATION RD

KNAPP RD

Clarendon
Sch

B378

GREENVIEW AVE

VILLAGE WAY

PARKLAND GR

GLEN AVE

HAVEN RD

REEDSFIELD RD

ANGLESEA CL

PARKLAND

REEDSFIELD
CL

THE YEWS

GRAYS LA

Chattern
Hill

B3003

Recn Gd

06 A B 07 170 C D 08

Coll

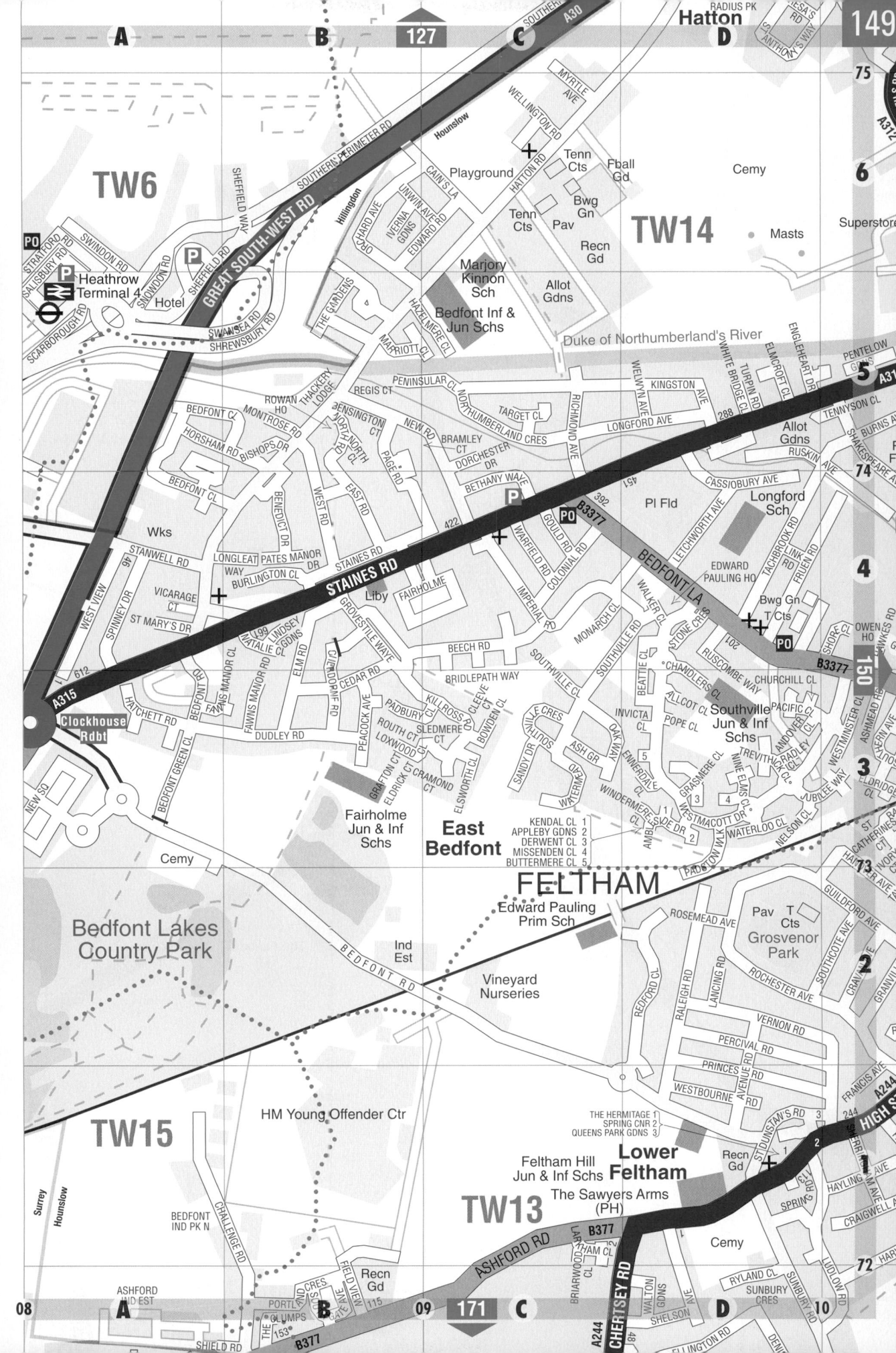
127
A
B
C
D
Hatton
RADIUS PK
75
6
5
74
4
3
73
2
72
08
09
10
171
150
TW6
TW14
TW15
TW13
A30
A312
A315
A244
B3377
B377
SOUTHERN PERIMETER RD
GREAT SOUTH-WEST RD
Hounslow
Hillingdon
SHEFFIELD WAY
SHEFFIELD RD
SWINDON RD
STRATFORD RD
SALISBURY RD
SNOWDON RD
SCARBOROUGH RD
SWANSEA RD
SHREWSBURY RD
Heathrow Terminal 4
Hotel
PO
WELLINGTON RD
MYRTLE AVE
HATTON RD
CAIN'S LA
UNWIN AVE
IVERNA GDNS
EDWARD RD
ORCHARD AVE
Playground
Tenn Cts
Fball Gd
Bwg Gn
Pav
Recn Gd
Allot Gdns
Cemy
Masts
Superstore
Marjory Kinnon Sch
Bedfont Inf & Jun Schs
THE GARDENS
HAZELMERE CL
MARRIOTT CL
Duke of Northumberland's River
ENGLEHEART DR
ELMCROFT CL
TURPIN RD
WHITE BRIDGE CL
PENTELOW GDNS
PENINSULAR CL
KINGSTON AVE
WELWYN AVE
REGIS CT
THACKERY LODGE
ROWAN HO
NORTHUMBERLAND CRES
TARGET CL
RICHMOND AVE
LONGFORD AVE
288
TENNYSON CL
BURNS AVE
Allot Gdns
RUSKIN AVE
SHAKESPEARE AVE
BEDFONT CL
MONTROSE RD
KENSINGTON CT
NORTH CT
NORTH RD
NORTH CL
NEW RD
BRAMLEY CT
DORCHESTER DR
HORSHAM RD
BISHOPS DR
PAGE RD
EAST RD
WEST RD
BENEDICT DR
BETHANY WAYE
CASSIOBURY AVE
Pl Fld
Longford Sch
451
392
422
Wks
STANWELL RD
LONGLEAT WAY
PATES MANOR DR
STAINES RD
BURLINGTON CL
STAINES RD
WARFIELD RD
GOULD RD
COLONIAL RD
BEDFONT LA
LETCHWORTH AVE
TACHBROOK RD
LINK RD
FRUEN RD
EDWARD PAULING HO
VICARAGE CT
ST MARY'S DR
SPINNEY DR
WEST VIEW
46
Liby
FAIRHOLME
IMPERIAL RD
MONARCH CL
WALKER CL
STONE CRES
Bwg Gn
T Cts
SHORE CL
OWEN HO
HAWKES RD
612
199
LINDSEY GDNS
NATALIE CL
GROVESTILE WAYE
BEECH RD
SOUTHVILLE RD
SOUTHVILLE CL
CHANDLERS CL
RUSCOMBE WAY
201
CHURCHILL CL
FAWNS MANOR CL
FAWNS MANOR RD
ELM RD
CAVENDISH RD
CEDAR RD
BRIDLEPATH WAY
BEATTIE CL
ALLCOT CL
POPE CL
Southville Jun & Inf Schs
PACIFIC CL
ANDOVER CL
WESTMINSTER CL
ASHMEAD RD
SEVERN AVE
Clockhouse Rdbt
HATCHETT RD
BEDFONT RD
DUDLEY RD
PEACOCK AVE
PADBURY CL
KILLROSS RD
CLEEVE CT
BOWDEN CL
SOUTHVILLE CRES
INVICTA CL
ROUTH CT
SLEDMERE CT
LOXWOOD CL
ASH GR
OAK WAY
ENNERDALE CL
GRASMERE CL
NINE ELMS CL
TREVITHICK CL
BRADLEY CL
JUBILEE WAY
ELDRIDGE CL
BEDFONT GREEN CL
GRAFTON CT
ELDRICK CT
CRAMOND CT
ELSWORTH CL
SANDY DR
WATERMILL WAY
WINDERMERE CL
LAKESIDE DR
AMBLESIDE DR
WESTMACOTT DR
WATERLOO CL
NELSON CL
NEW SQ
Cemy
Fairholme Jun & Inf Schs
East Bedfont
KENDAL CL 1
APPLEBY GDNS 2
DERWENT CL 3
MISSENDEN CL 4
BUTTERMERE CL 5
PADSTOW WLK
ST CATHERINES CT
HATTER AVE
IVORY CT
FELTHAM
Edward Pauling Prim Sch
ROSEMEAD AVE
Pav
T Cts
Grosvenor Park
GUILDFORD AVE
SOUTHCOTE AVE
CRAVEN AVE
GRANVILLE
Bedfont Lakes Country Park
BEDFONT RD
Ind Est
Vineyard Nurseries
REDFORD CL
RALEIGH RD
LANCING RD
ROCHESTER AVE
VERNON RD
PERCIVAL RD
PRINCES RD
AVENUE RD
WESTBOURNE RD
FRANCIS AVE
HIGH ST
HM Young Offender Ctr
THE HERMITAGE 1
SPRING CNR 2
QUEENS PARK GDNS 3
ST DUNSTAN'S RD
244
SHERRINGHAM AVE
Surrey
Hounslow
Feltham Hill Jun & Inf Schs
Lower Feltham
Recn Gd
HAYLING AVE
SPRING RD
CRAIGWELL AVE
The Sawyers Arms (PH)
BEDFONT IND PK N
CHALLENGE RD
ASHFORD RD
LARKHAM CL
BRIARWOOD CL
CHERTSEY RD
Cemy
RYLAND CL
SUNBURY CRES
SUNBURY RD
LUDLOW RD
HARVEST
ASHFORD IND EST
CRES
FIELD VIEW
GATE AVE
Recn Gd
115
PORTLAND CRES
CLUMPS
THE
153
SHIELD RD
WALTON GDNS
SHELSON AVE
ELLINGTON RD
48

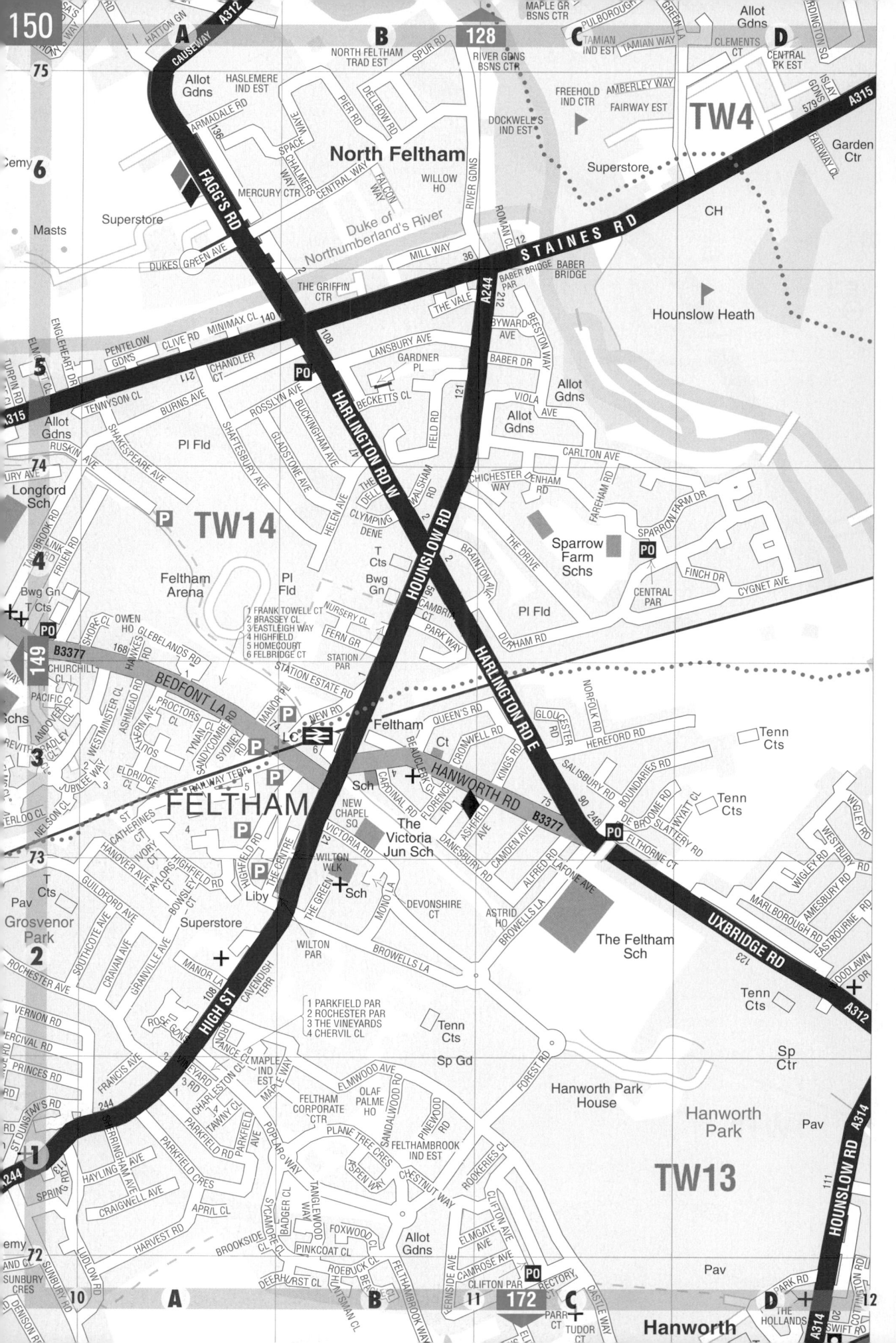

North Feltham
TW4
TW14
TW13
FELTHAM
Hanworth
Hounslow Heath
Hanworth Park
Hanworth Park House
The Feltham Sch
The Victoria Jun Sch
Sparrow Farm Schs
Feltham Arena
Feltham
STAINES RD
HARLINGTON RD W
HARLINGTON RD E
HOUNSLOW RD
HANWORTH RD
UXBRIDGE RD
HIGH ST
BEDFONT LA
FAGG'S RD
CAUSEWAY
Duke of Northumberland's River
1 FRANK TOWELL CT
2 BRASSEY CL
3 EASTLEIGH WAY
4 HIGHFIELD
5 HOMECOURT
6 FELBRIDGE CT
1 PARKFIELD PAR
2 ROCHESTER PAR
3 THE VINEYARDS
4 CHERVIL CL
128
149
172

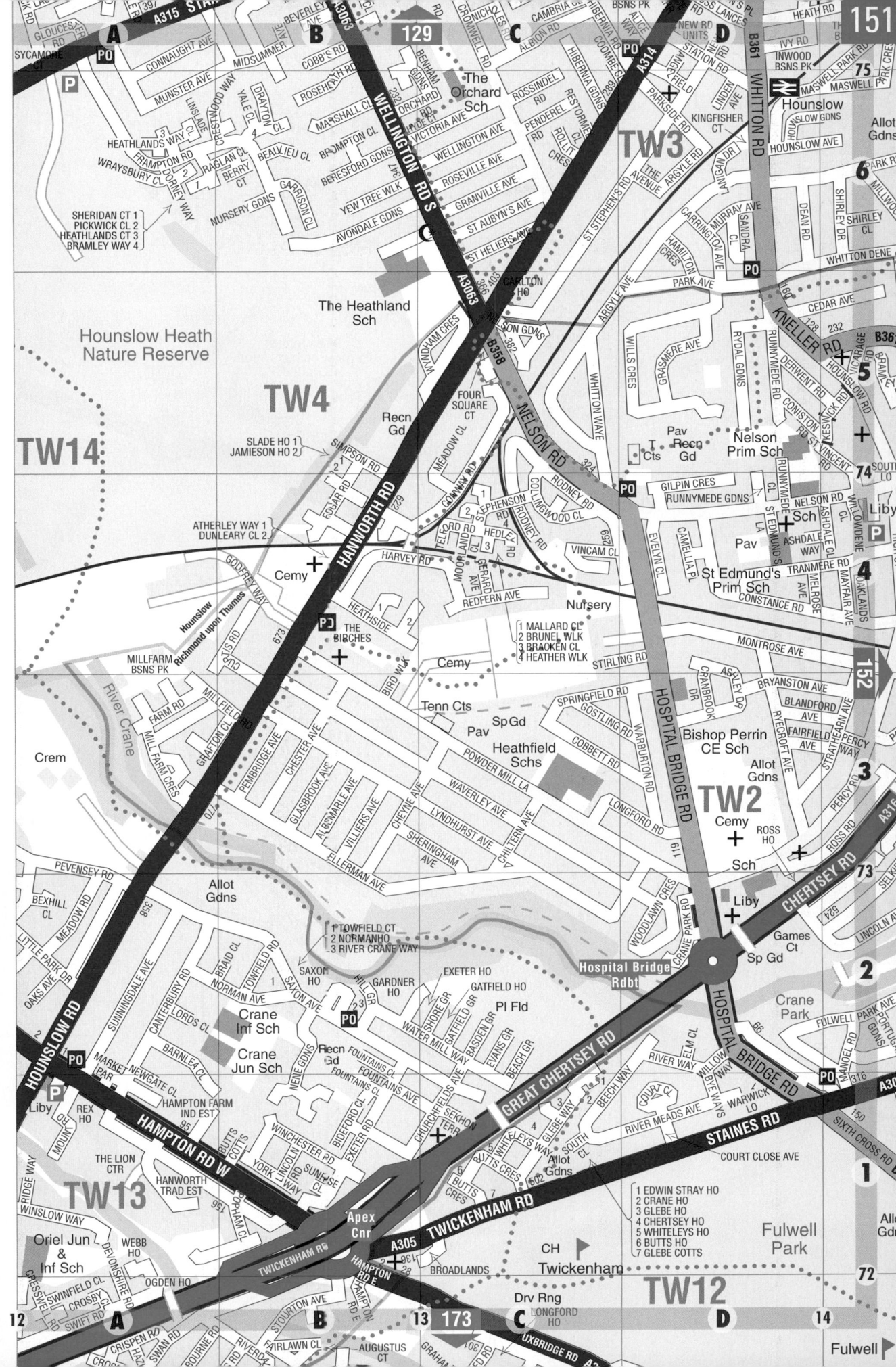
129
A
B
C
D
A315 STAINES RD
A3063
A314
B361
SYCAMORE CT
GLOUCESTER RD
CONNAUGHT AVE
MUNSTER AVE
MIDSUMMER AVE
BEVERLEY AVE
COBB'S RD
ROSEHEATH RD
MARSHALL CL
BROMPTON CL
BERESFORD GDNS
YEW TREE WLK
AVONDALE GDNS
ORCHARD RD
BENHAM GDNS
HYDE CT
VICTORIA AVE
WELLINGTON AVE
ROSEVILLE AVE
GRANVILLE AVE
ST AUBYN'S AVE
ST HELIERS AVE
WELLINGTON RD S
The Orchard Sch
CROMWELL RD
ALBION RD
CAMBRIA CL
HIBERNIA RD
HIBERNIA GDNS
COOMBE GR
ROSSINDEL RD
PENDEREL RD
RESTORMEL CL
ROLLIT CRES
TW3
ALICE WAY
NEW RD UNITS
STATION RD
AINGER FIELD
PARKSIDE RD
KINGFISHER CT
LINDEN AVE
WHITTON RD
Hounslow
INWOOD BSNS PK
IVY RD
HEATH RD
MASWELL PARK RD
MASWELL PK
HOUNSLOW AVE
SLOW GDNS
Allot Gdns
75
6
PARK RD
MILLWOOD
LINSLADE
CRESTWOOD WAY
YALE CL
DRAYTON CL
HEATHLANDS WAY
FRAMPTON RD
RAGLAN CL
BERRY CT
BEAULIEU CL
WRAYSBURY CL
DORNEY WAY
GARRISON CL
NURSERY GDNS
SHERIDAN CT 1
PICKWICK CL 2
HEATHLANDS CT 3
BRAMLEY WAY 4
ST STEPHEN'S RD
THE AVENUE
ARGYLE RD
LANIGAN DR
MURRAY AVE
SANDRA CL
CARRINGTON AVE
HAMILTON CRES
DEAN RD
SHIRLEY DR
SHIRLEY CL
WHITTON DENE
PARK AVE
CARLTON HO
The Heathland Sch
Hounslow Heath Nature Reserve
TW4
TW14
NELSON GDNS
WYNDHAM CRES
B358
FOUR SQUARE CT
Recn Gd
MEADOW CL
NELSON RD
ARGYLE AVE
WILLS CRES
GRASMERE AVE
WHITTON WAY
RYDAL GDNS
RUNNYMEDE RD
DERWENT RD
CONISTON RD
KESWICK RD
KNELLER RD
CEDAR AVE
VICARAGE
HOUNSLOW RD
BRAMLEY
5
Pav
Recn Gd
T Cts
Nelson Prim Sch
ST VINCENT RD
74
SLADE HO 1
JAMIESON HO 2
SIMPSON RD
EDGAR RD
HANWORTH RD
CONWAY RD
STEPHENSON RD
TELFORD RD
HEDLEY RD
RODNEY RD
COLLINGWOOD CL
GILPIN CRES
RUNNYMEDE GDNS
RUNNYMEDE CL
NELSON RD
ASHDALE CL
WILLOWDENE CL
Sch
Liby
ATHERLEY WAY 1
DUNLEARY CL 2
HARVEY RD
MOORLAND CL
GERARD AVE
VINCAM CL
EVELYN CL
CAMELLIA PL
ST EDMUND'S LA
Pav
ASHDALE WAY
St Edmund's Prim Sch
TRANMERE RD
HIGH ST
4
Cemy
GODFREY WAY
Hounslow
Richmond upon Thames
HEATHSIDE
THE BIRCHES
REDFERN AVE
Nursery
MELROSE AVE
MAYFAIR AVE
OAKLANDS
CONSTANCE RD
1 MALLARD CL
2 BRUNEL WLK
3 BRACKEN CL
4 HEATHER WLK
MILLFARM BSNS PK
CURTIS RD
BIRD WLK
Cemy
STIRLING RD
MONTROSE AVE
152
River Crane
FARM RD
MILLFIELD RD
MILL FARM CRES
GRAFTON CL
Tenn Cts
Sp Gd
Pav
SPRINGFIELD RD
GOSTLING RD
CRANBROOK DR
ASHLEY DR
BRYANSTON AVE
BLANDFORD AVE
FAIRFIELD AVE
PERCY WAY
Crem
PEMBRIDGE AVE
CHESTER AVE
GLASBROOK AVE
ALBEMARLE AVE
VILLIERS AVE
CHEYNE AVE
POWDER MILL LA
WAVERLEY AVE
LYNDHURST AVE
SHERINGHAM AVE
ELLERMAN AVE
CHILTERN AVE
Heathfield Schs
COBBETT RD
WARBURTON RD
LONGFORD RD
HOSPITAL BRIDGE RD
Bishop Perrin CE Sch
RYECROFT AVE
STRATHEARN AVE
Allot Gdns
TW2
Cemy
PERCY RD
3
ROSS HO
ROSS RD
A316
CHERTSEY RD
73
SELKIRK
Sch
Liby
PEVENSEY RD
BEXHILL CL
MEADOW RD
Allot Gdns
LITTLE PARK DR
OAKS AVE
WOODLAWN CRES
CRANE PARK RD
Games Ct
Sp Gd
LINCOLN AVE
1 TOWFIELD CT
2 NORMAN HO
3 RIVER CRANE WAY
SUNNINGDALE AVE
BRAID CL
TOWFIELD RD
CANTERBURY RD
NORMAN AVE
SAXON AVE
SAXON HO
HILL GR
GARDNER HO
EXETER HO
GATFIELD HO
WATER MILL WAY
GATFIELD GR
BASDEN GR
EVANS GR
BEACH GR
Pl Fld
Hospital Bridge Rdbt
Crane Park
2
FULWELL PARK AVE
PORTUGAL GDNS
HOUNSLOW RD
LORDS CL
Crane Inf Sch
Crane Jun Sch
BARNLEA CL
MARKET PAR
NEWGATE CL
HAMPTON FARM IND EST
Recn Gd
NENE GDNS
FOUNTAINS CL
FOUNTAINS AVE
GREAT CHERTSEY RD
RIVER WAY
ELM CL
WILLOW WAY
BYE WAYS
WARWICK LO
HOSPITAL BRIDGE RD
MANOEL RD
A305
Liby
REX HO
MOUNT RD
HAMPTON RD W
BUTTS COTTS
WINCHESTER RD
BIDEFORD CL
EXETER RD
CHURCHFIELDS AVE
SEKHON TERR
BEECH WAY
GLEBE WAY
WHITELEYS WAY
BUTTS CRES
SOUTH CL
Allot Gdns
COURT CL
RIVER MEADS AVE
STAINES RD
COURT CLOSE AVE
SIXTH CROSS RD
1
THE LION CTR
HANWORTH TRAD EST
TW13
RIDGE WAY
YORK
LINCOLN RD
SUNRISE CL
WAY
Apex Cnr
TWICKENHAM RD
A305
1 EDWIN STRAY HO
2 CRANE HO
3 GLEBE HO
4 CHERTSEY HO
5 WHITELEYS HO
6 BUTTS HO
7 GLEBE COTTS
Allot Gdns
Fulwell Park
WINSLOW WAY
Oriel Jun & Inf Sch
WEBB HO
DEVONSHIRE RD
CRESSWELL RD
SWINFIELD CL
CROSBY CL
SWIFT RD
OGDEN HO
TWICKENHAM RD
HAMPTON RD E
BROADLANDS
CH
Twickenham
Drv Rng
TW12
72
12
A
STOURTON AVE
B
13
173
C
LONGFORD HO
D
14
CRISPEN RD
SWAN RD
BOURNE RD
FAIRLAWN CL
AUGUSTUS CT
UXBRIDGE RD
Fulwell

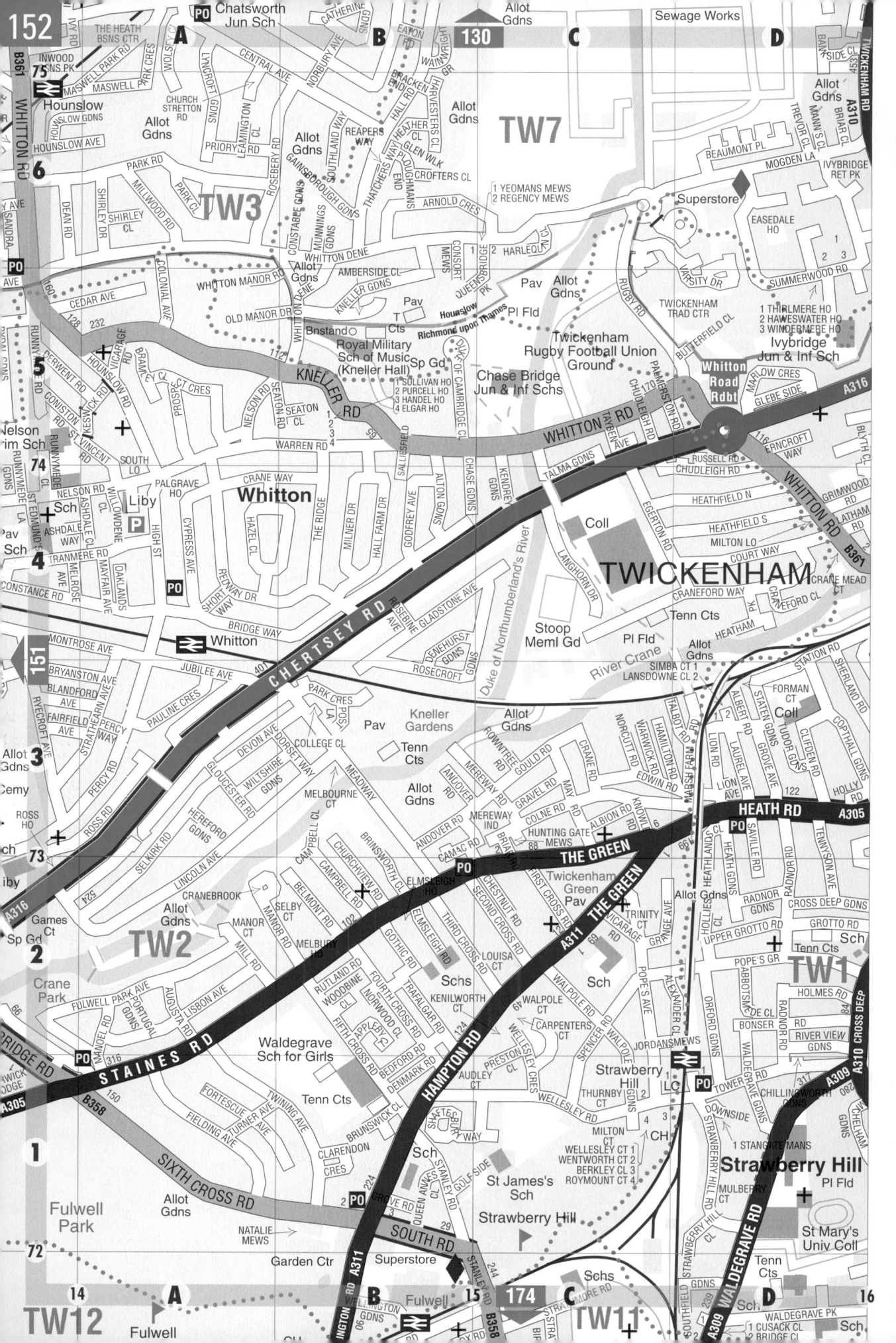

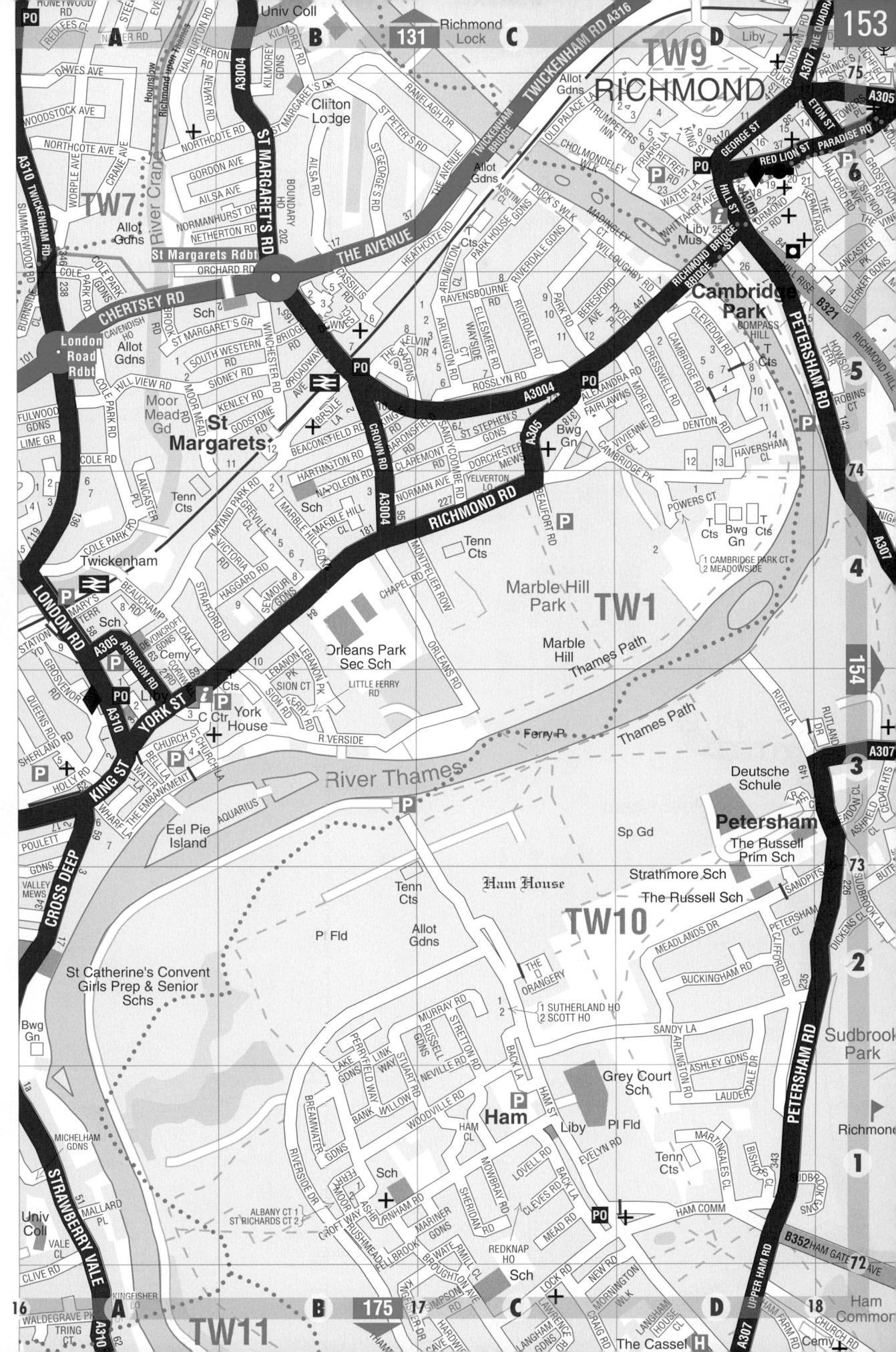

131
A
B
C
D
Univ Coll
Richmond Lock
TW9
RICHMOND
TWICKENHAM RD A316
TWICKENHAM BRIDGE
Liby
A307 THE QUADRANT
A305
GEORGE ST
RED LION ST
PARADISE RD
HILL ST
ETON ST
Allot Gdns
OLD PALACE LA
TRUMPETERS INN
CHOLMONDELEY WLK
FRIARS LA
KING ST
RETREAT RD
WATER LA
WHITTAKER AVE
Liby Mus
RICHMOND BRIDGE
BRIDGE ST
Cambridge Park
COMPASS HILL
PETERSHAM RD
B321
RICHMOND HILL
ORMOND
HERMITAGE
LANCASTER PK
ELLERKER GDNS
HALFORD RD
GROSVENOR AVE
THE VINEYARD
HILL RISE
HOWSON TERR
ROBINS CT
A3004
ST MARGARET'S RD
Clifton Lodge
RANELAGH DR
ST PETER'S RD
ST GEORGE'S RD
AILSA RD
BOUNDARY HO
THE AVENUE
HEATHCOTE RD
Allot Gdns
AUSTIN CL
DUCK'S WLK
PARK HOUSE GDNS
ARLINGTON CL
RIVERDALE GDNS
MADINGLEY CT
WILLOUGHBY RD
RAVENSBOURNE RD
ELLESMERE RD
WAYSIDE CT
RIVERDALE RD
PARK RD
BERESFORD AVE
RYDE PL
ROSSLYN RD
ALEXANDRA RD
FAIRLAWNS
CRESSWELL RD
CAMBRIDGE RD
CLEVEDON RD
DENTON RD
HAVERSHAM CL
VIVIENNE CL
CAMBRIDGE PK
Bwg Gn
TW7
DAWES AVE
WOODSTOCK AVE
NORTHCOTE AVE
NORTHCOTE RD
WORPLE AVE
CRANE AVE
HALIBURTON RD
HERON RD
NEWRY RD
GORDON AVE
AILSA AVE
NORMANHURST DR
NETHERTON RD
KILMOREY GDNS
KILMOREY RD
River Crane
A310 TWICKENHAM RD
SUMMERWOOD RD
Allot Gdns
St Margarets Rdbt
ORCHARD RD
COLE PARK GDNS
COLE PARK RD
CHERTSEY RD
London Road Rdbt
CAVENDISH HO
Sch
BROOK RD
ST MARGARET'S GR
SOUTH WESTERN RD
WINCHESTER RD
BRIDGE RD
Allot Gdns
SIDNEY RD
HILL VIEW RD
MOOR MEAD RD
KENLEY RD
GODSTONE RD
BROADWAY AVE
CASSILIS RD
THE BARONS
KELVIN DR
Moor Mead Gd
St Margarets
FULWOOD GDNS
LIME GR
COLE RD
LANCASTER PL
BRIDLE LA
BEACONSFIELD RD
CROWN RD
BARONSFIELD RD
SANDYCOMBE RD
ST STEPHEN'S GDNS
DORCHESTER MEWS
A305
HARTINGTON RD
NAPOLEON RD
CLAREMONT RD
NORMAN AVE
YELVERTON LO
Sch
MARBLE HILL CL
MARBLE HILL GDNS
AMYAND PARK RD
GREVILLE CL
RICHMOND RD
BEAUFORT RD
Tenn Cts
Tenn Cts
POWERS CT
Bwg Gn
1 CAMBRIDGE PARK CT
2 MEADOWSIDE
COLE PARK RD
Twickenham
VICTORIA RD
HAGGARD RD
SEYMOUR GDNS
STRAFFORD RD
CHAPEL RD
MONTPELIER ROW
Marble Hill Park
TW1
LONDON RD
MARY'S TERR
BEAUCHAMP RD
Sch
A305
ARRAGON RD
DEVONCROFT GDNS
OAK LA
Cemy
CORNWALL RD
STATION YD
GROSVENOR RD
Orleans Park Sec Sch
ORLEANS RD
Marble Hill
Thames Path
LEBANON PK
SION CT
LITTLE FERRY RD
Liby
YORK ST
C Ctr
York House
SION RD
FERRY RD
RIVERSIDE
Ferry P
Thames Path
RIVER LA
RUTLAND DR
A310
QUEENS RD
SHERLAND RD
HOLLY RD
KING ST
CHURCH ST
BELL LA
WATER LA
THE EMBANKMENT
CHURCH LA
River Thames
Deutsche Schule
A307
Eel Pie Island
AQUARIUS
WHARF LA
POULETT GDNS
Petersham
The Russell Prim Sch
Sp Gd
CROSS DEEP
VALLEY MEWS
Ham House
Strathmore Sch
The Russell Sch
SANDPITS RD
SUDBROOK LA
Tenn Cts
TW10
PETERSHAM CL
MEADLANDS DR
CLIFFORD RD
Pl Fld
Allot Gdns
BUCKINGHAM RD
St Catherine's Convent Girls Prep & Senior Schs
THE ORANGERY
1 SUTHERLAND HO
2 SCOTT HO
SANDY LA
PETERSHAM RD
Sudbrook Park
Bwg Gn
MURRAY RD
STRETTON RD
RUSSELL GDNS
LAKE GDNS
PERRYFIELD WAY
LINK WAY
STUART RD
NEVILLE RD
BACK LA
ARLINGTON RD
ASHLEY GDNS
DALE DR
Grey Court Sch
LAUDER CL
BANK
WILLOW
WOODVILLE RD
HAM ST
Ham
BREAMWATER GDNS
HAM CL
Liby
Pl Fld
MARTINGALES CL
Richmond
RIVERSIDE DR
Sch
MOWBRAY RD
LOVELL RD
BACK LA
EVELYN RD
Tenn Cts
BISHOPS CL
MICHELHAM GDNS
ALBANY CT 1
ST RICHARDS CT 2
CROFT WAY
ASHBURNHAM RD
SHERIDAN RD
CLEVES RD
HAM COMM
SUDBROOK GDNS
STRAWBERRY VALE
MALLARD PL
MARINER GDNS
RUSHMEAD
MEAD RD
Univ Coll
VALE CL
FELLBROOK
WATERMILL CL
REDKNAP HO
B352 HAM GATE AVE
CLIVE RD
BROUGHTON AVE
UPPER HAM RD
LOCK RD
NEW RD
Sch
MORNINGTON WLK
KINGFISHER LO
SIMPSON RD
16
175
17
18
WALDEGRAVE PK
TW11
TRING CT
A310
LAWRENCE GDNS
LANGHAM GDNS
CRAIG RD
LANGHAM HOUSE CL
The Cassel
Ham Common
Cemy
CHURCH RD
A307
154
74
73
72
75
1
2
3
4
5
6

TW9
SHEEN RD
RICHMOND
Richmond Hill
Richmond
B321
B322
B353
A305
A307
132
A
B
C
D
KINGS RD
QUEEN'S RD
FRIARS STILE RD
RICHMOND HILL
PETERSHAM RD
STAR AND GARTER HILL
SAWYER'S HILL
1 ARUNDEL HO
2 MARLBOROUGH HO
3 BUCKINGHAM HO
4 OSBOURNE HO
5 YORK HO
6 SANDRINGHAM HO
7 KENT HO
8 NORFOLK HO
9 RUNNYMEAD HO
10 CARISBROOKE HO
11 GLOUCESTER HO
Pl Fld
Allot Gdns
Christ's Sch (East Side)
Cemy
East Sheen Common
Fball Gd
Tenn Cts
Bwg Gn
SW14
The Bog
Horse Ride
Bog Lodge
Vineyard Sch
Richmond Coll
Star & Garter Home
Saw Pit Plantation
TW10
Sidmouth Wood
Petersham
Deutsche Schule
Schs
Pembroke Lodge
Petersham Park
Sudbrook Park
CH
Richmond
Pen Ponds
Pond Plantation
Pond Slade
Hamcross Plantation
KT2
Isabella Plantation
High Wood
Ham Bottom
Ham Common
HAM GATE AVE
B352
153
176
18
19
20
1
2
3
4
5
6

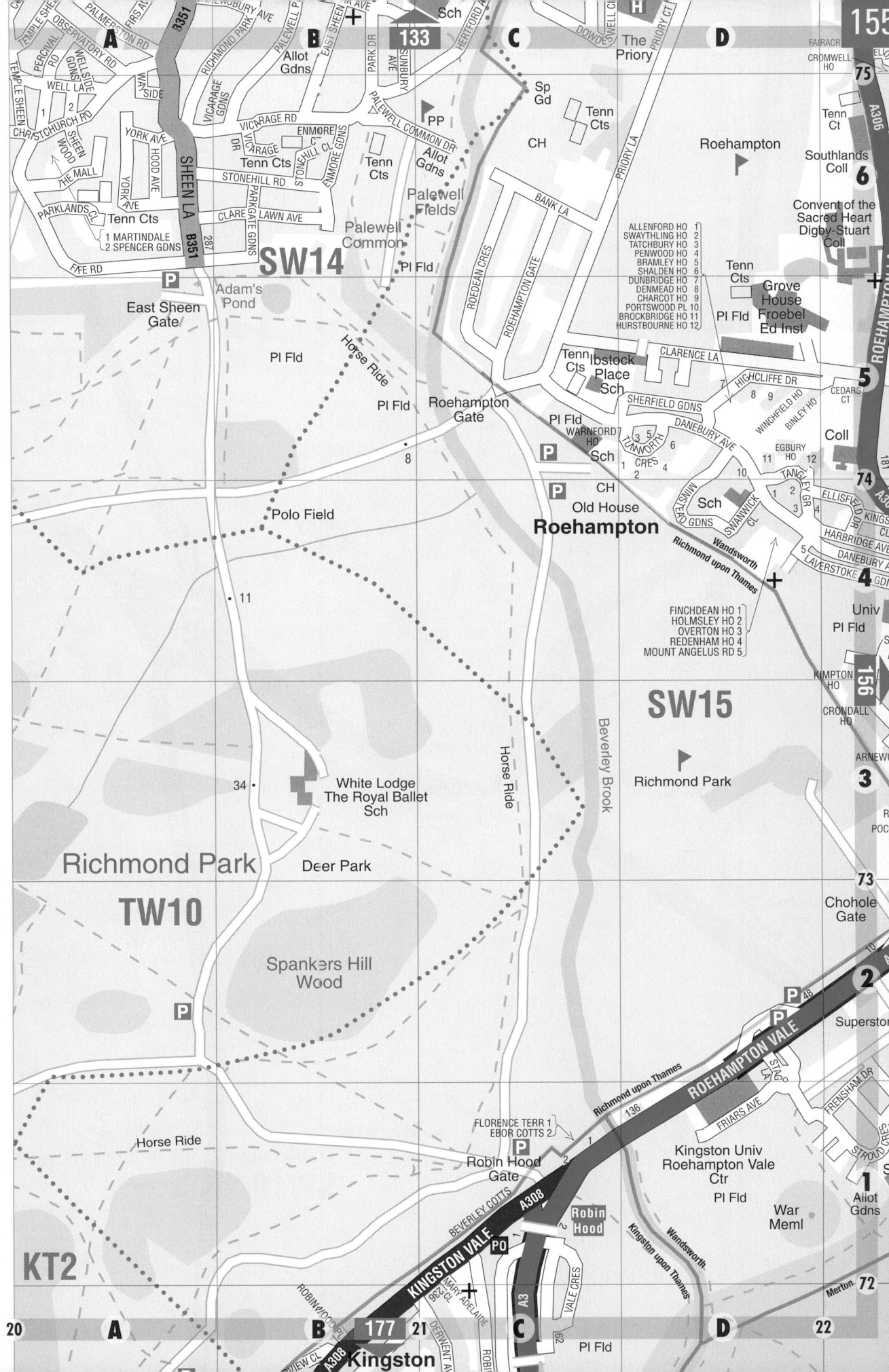
Richmond Park
Roehampton
SW14
SW15
TW10
KT2
East Sheen Gate
Adam's Pond
Palewell Common
Palewell Fields
Roehampton Gate
Polo Field
White Lodge
The Royal Ballet Sch
Deer Park
Spankers Hill Wood
Horse Ride
Beverley Brook
Robin Hood Gate
Kingston Vale
Roehampton Vale
Kingston Univ Roehampton Vale Ctr
Chohole Gate
Superstore
War Meml
The Priory
Ibstock Place Sch
Grove House Froebel Ed Inst
Convent of the Sacred Heart Digby-Stuart Coll
Southlands Coll
Old House
Kingston
ALLENFORD HO 1
SWAYTHLING HO 2
TATCHBURY HO 3
PENWOOD HO 4
BRAMLEY HO 5
SHALDEN HO 6
DUNBRIDGE HO 7
DENMEAD HO 8
CHARCOT HO 9
PORTSWOOD PL 10
BROCKBRIDGE HO 11
HURSTBOURNE HO 12
FINCHDEAN HO 1
HOLMSLEY HO 2
OVERTON HO 3
REDENHAM HO 4
MOUNT ANGELUS RD 5
FLORENCE TERR 1
EBOR COTTS 2
1 MARTINDALE
2 SPENCER GDNS
133
156
177

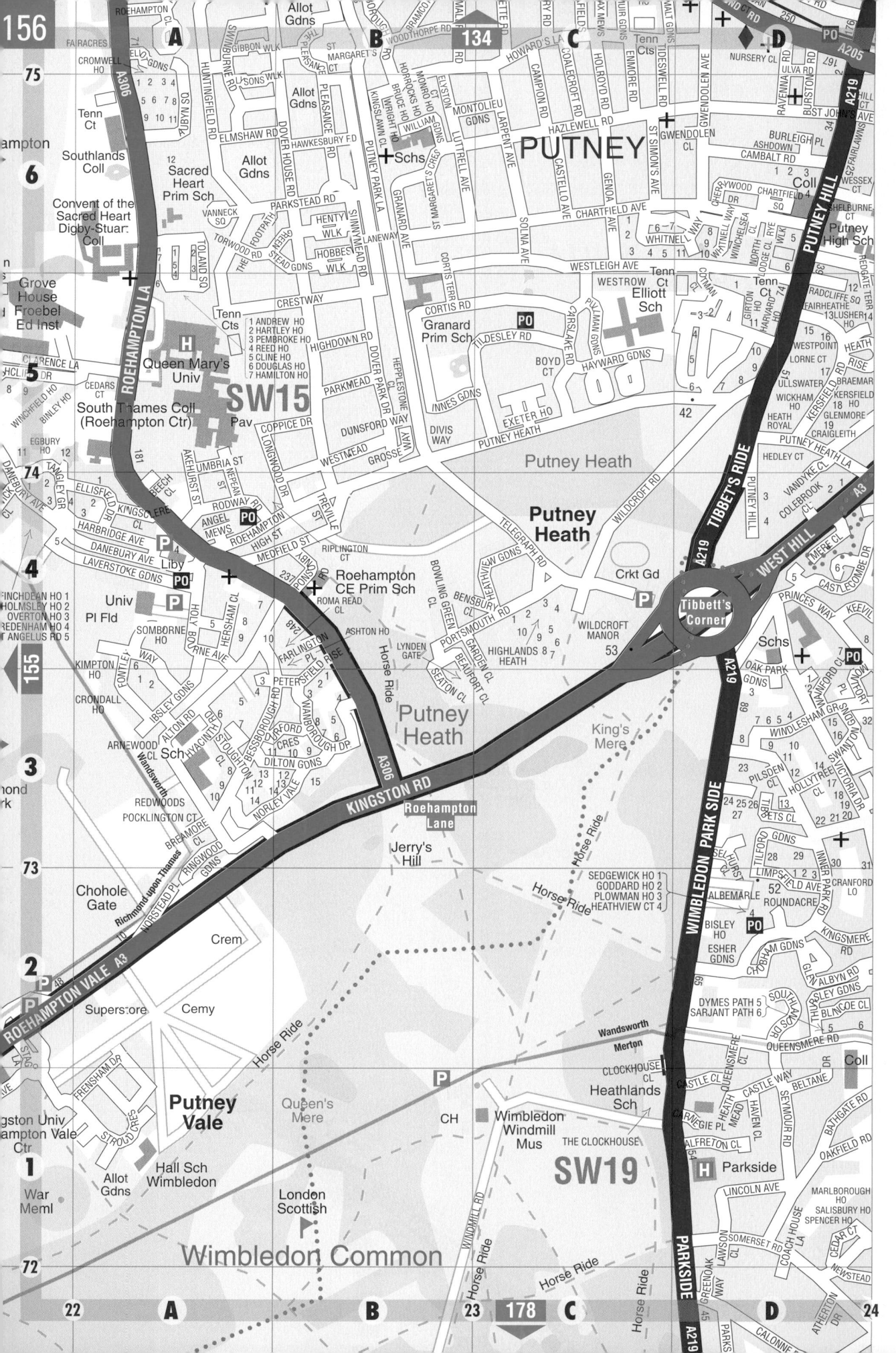

A
B
C
D
134
75
6
5
74
4
155
3
73
2
1
72
22
23
178
24
PUTNEY
SW15
SW19
Putney Heath
Putney Heath
Putney Heath
Putney Vale
Wimbledon Common
Tibbett's Corner
Roehampton Lane
Jerry's Hill
King's Mere
Queen's Mere
Chohole Gate
ROEHAMPTON LA
ROEHAMPTON VALE A3
KINGSTON RD
PUTNEY HILL
TIBBET'S RIDE
WIMBLEDON PARK SIDE
PARKSIDE
WEST HILL
PUTNEY HEATH
PUTNEY HEATH LA
WESTLEIGH AVE
CHARTFIELD AVE
HAZLEWELL RD
ST JOHN'S AVE
CAMBALT RD
BURLEIGH PL
ASHDOWN
HOWARD'S LA
WOODTHORPE RD
PUTNEY PARK LA
GRANARD AVE
DOVER HOUSE RD
DOVER PARK DR
CRESTWAY
CORTIS RD
TILDESLEY RD
HAYWARD GDNS
EXETER HO
INNES GDNS
DIVIS WAY
DUNSFORD WAY
WESTMEAD
HIGHDOWN RD
PARKMEAD
COPPICE DR
LONGWOOD DR
MEDFIELD ST
ROEHAMPTON HIGH ST
TELEGRAPH RD
WILDCROFT RD
WILDCROFT MANOR
PORTSMOUTH RD
HIGHLANDS HEATH
BOWLING GREEN CL
WINDLESHAM GR
QUEENSMERE RD
CASTLE WAY
SEYMOUR RD
BELTANE DR
LINCOLN AVE
SOMERSET RD
COACH HOUSE LA
WINDMILL RD
Queen Mary's Univ
South Thames Coll (Roehampton Ctr)
Roehampton CE Prim Sch
Granard Prim Sch
Elliott Sch
Putney High Sch
Heathlands Sch
Wimbledon Windmill Mus
THE CLOCKHOUSE
Parkside
Hall Sch Wimbledon
London Scottish
War Meml
Crem
Cemy
Superstore
Crkt Gd
Southlands Coll
Convent of the Sacred Heart Digby-Stuart Coll
Grove House Froebel Ed Inst
Sacred Heart Prim Sch
Horse Ride
Wandsworth
Merton
Richmond upon Thames

135
A
B
C
D
Putney
Sch of Art & Design
East Putney
Upper Richmond Rd
West Hill
SW15
A3
A205
A3209
A217 Armoury Way
Wandsworth Gyratory
Wandsworth High St
East Hill
Ram St
Fairfield St A217
Swandon Way
Buckhold Rd
A218
Merton Rd
Garratt La
WANDSWORTH
SW18
West Hill
Royal Hospl
Whitelands Coll, Roehampton Inst
Ronald Ross Prim Sch
Sheringdale Prim Sch
Southfields
Southfields Sch
Riversdale Prim Sch
King George's Park
River Wandle
Linden Lodge Sch
Albermarle Prim Sch
Wimbledon Park
Wimbledon Park Lake
Athletics Gd
Wimbledon Lawn Tennis Mus
The All England Lawn Tennis & Croquet Club
Wimbledon Park Prim Sch
Durnsford Rd
Garratt Park Sec Sch
Wandle Prim Sch
Earlsfield
Wimbledon Stadium Bsns Ctr
SW19
158
179
24
25
26
75
74
73
72
1
2
3
4
5
6

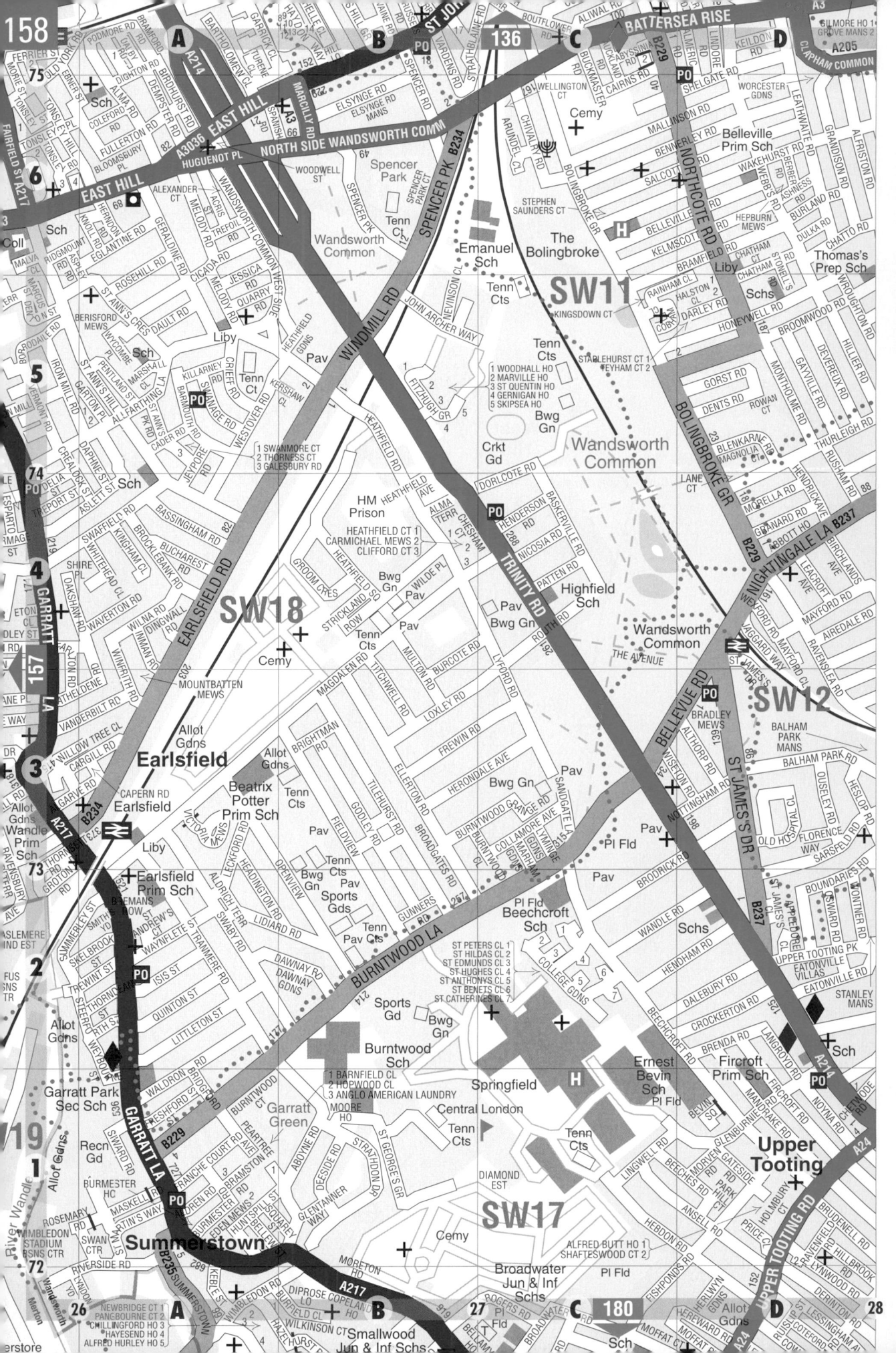

SW18
SW11
SW12
SW17
Earlsfield
Upper Tooting
Summerstown
Wandsworth Common
Spencer Park
The Bolingbroke
HM Prison
Springfield
Garratt Green
EAST HILL
TRINITY RD
WINDMILL RD
EARLSFIELD RD
BURNTWOOD LA
GARRATT LA
NIGHTINGALE LA
BOLINGBROKE GR
NORTHCOTE RD
BELLEVUE RD
UPPER TOOTING RD
BATTERSEA RISE
NORTH SIDE WANDSWORTH COMM
SPENCER PK
ST JAMES'S DR
136
157
180

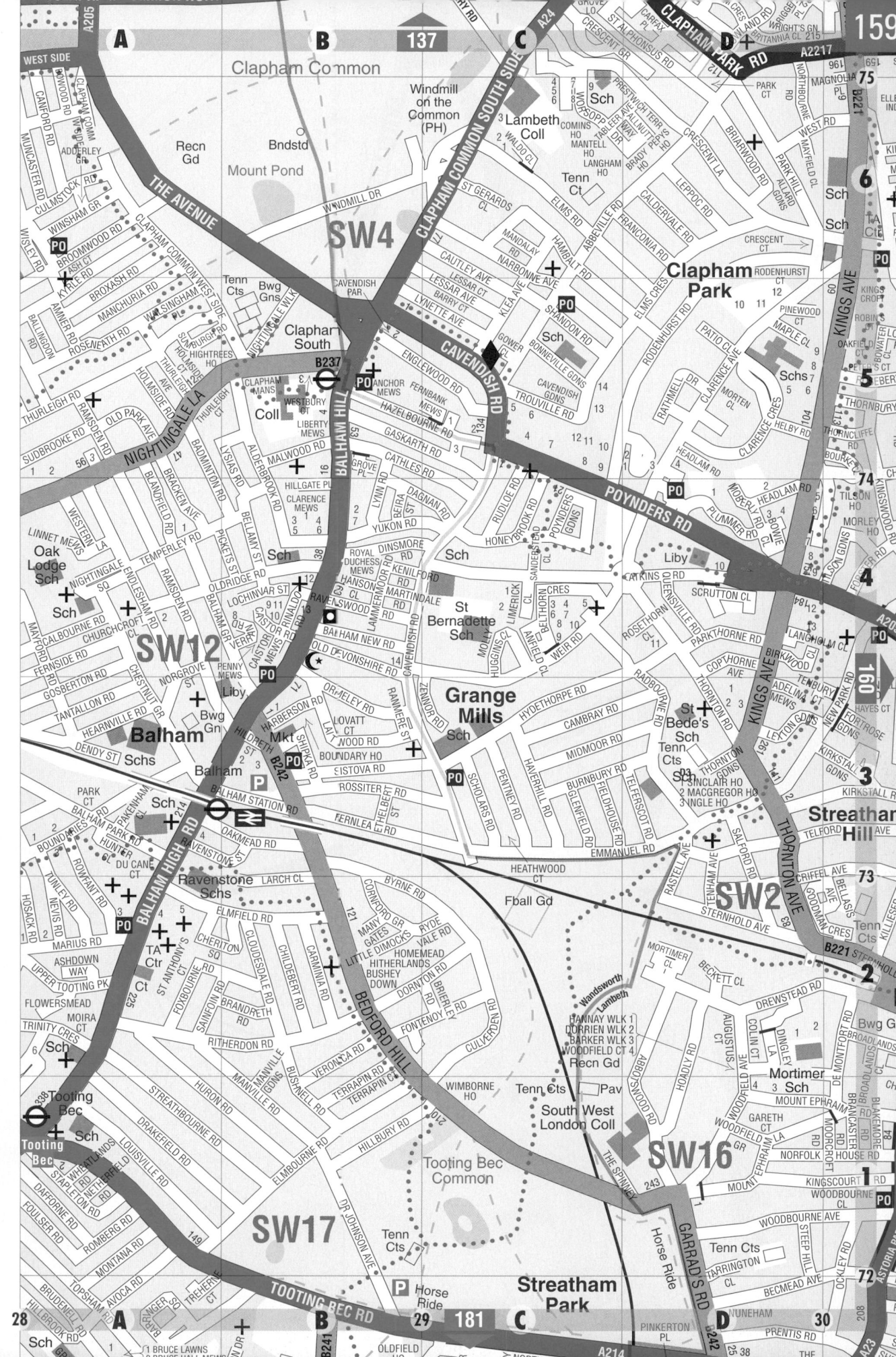

A
B
137
C
D
Clapham Common
Windmill on the Common (PH)
Bndstd
Recn Gd
Mount Pond
SW4
THE AVENUE
CLAPHAM COMMON SOUTH SIDE
CLAPHAM COMMON WEST SIDE
CLAPHAM PARK RD
A2217
A205
A24
B237
B242
B221
B241
A214
A23
WEST SIDE
WINDMILL DR
Lambeth Coll
Tenn Ct
Tenn Cts
Bwg Gns
Clapham South
CAVENDISH RD
Clapham Park
NIGHTINGALE LA
BALHAM HILL
POYNDERS RD
KINGS AVE
SW12
Oak Lodge Sch
St Bernadette Sch
Grange Mills
Balham
Schs
Liby
Mkt
BALHAM HIGH RD
BALHAM STATION RD
Ravenstone Schs
Fball Gd
SW2
Streatham Hill
THORNTON AVE
BEDFORD HILL
Wandsworth
Lambeth
Recn Gd
Mortimer Sch
South West London Coll
SW16
Tooting Bec Common
Tooting Bec
SW17
Streatham Park
Horse Ride
TOOTING BEC RD
GARRAD'S RD
160
181
28
29
30
75
74
73
72
6
5
4
3
2
1

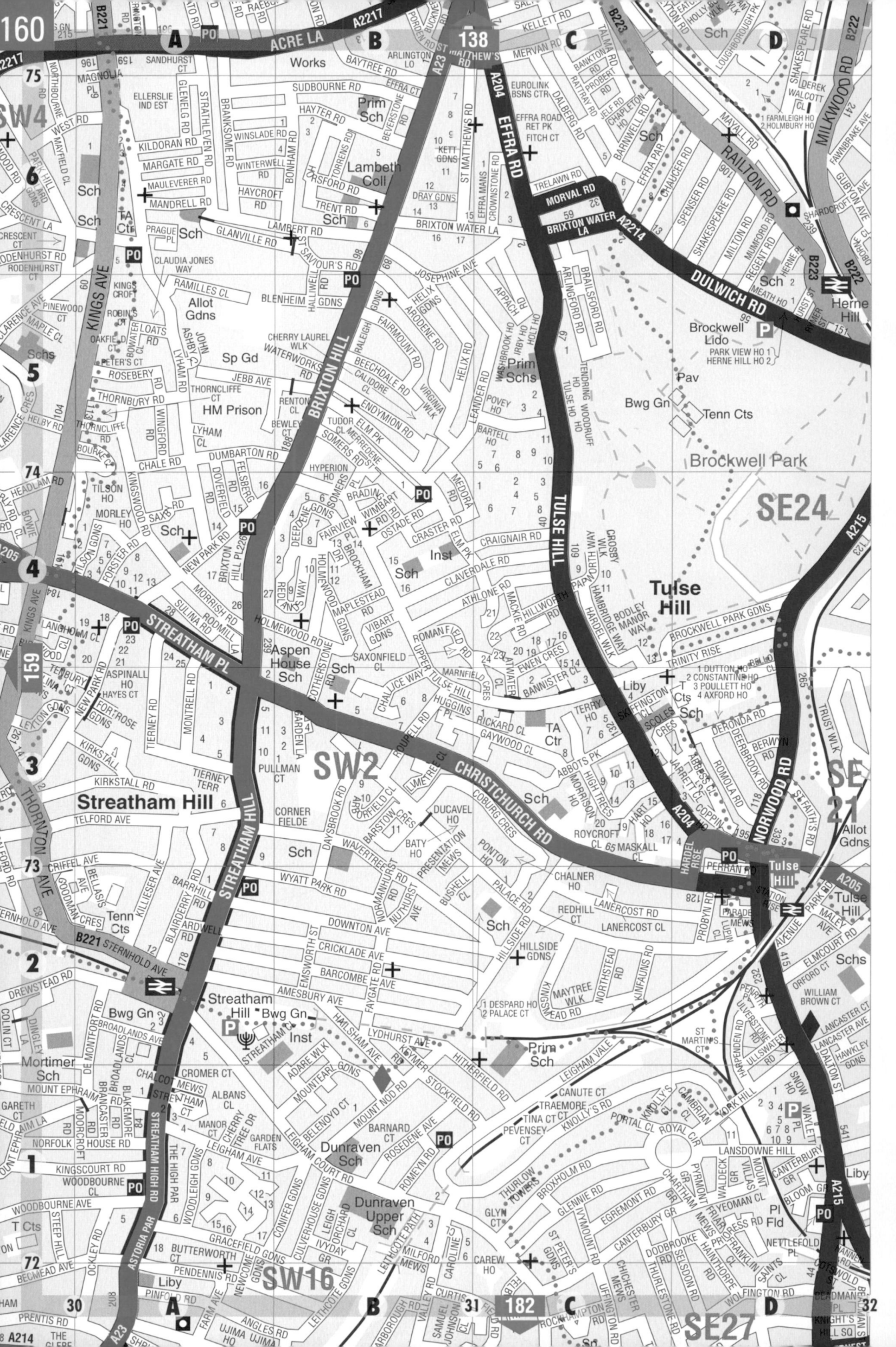
ACRE LA
BRIXTON HILL
EFFRA RD
TULSE HILL
DULWICH RD
RAILTON RD
MILKWOOD RD
STREATHAM PL
CHRISTCHURCH RD
STREATHAM HILL
STREATHAM HIGH RD
NORWOOD RD
KINGS AVE
THORNTON AVE
Streatham Hill
Brockwell Park
Tulse Hill
Brockwell Lido
HM Prison
Lambeth Coll
Aspen House Sch
Dunraven Sch
Dunraven Upper Sch
Mortimer Sch
SW2
SW4
SW16
SE24
SE27
SE 21
138
159
182

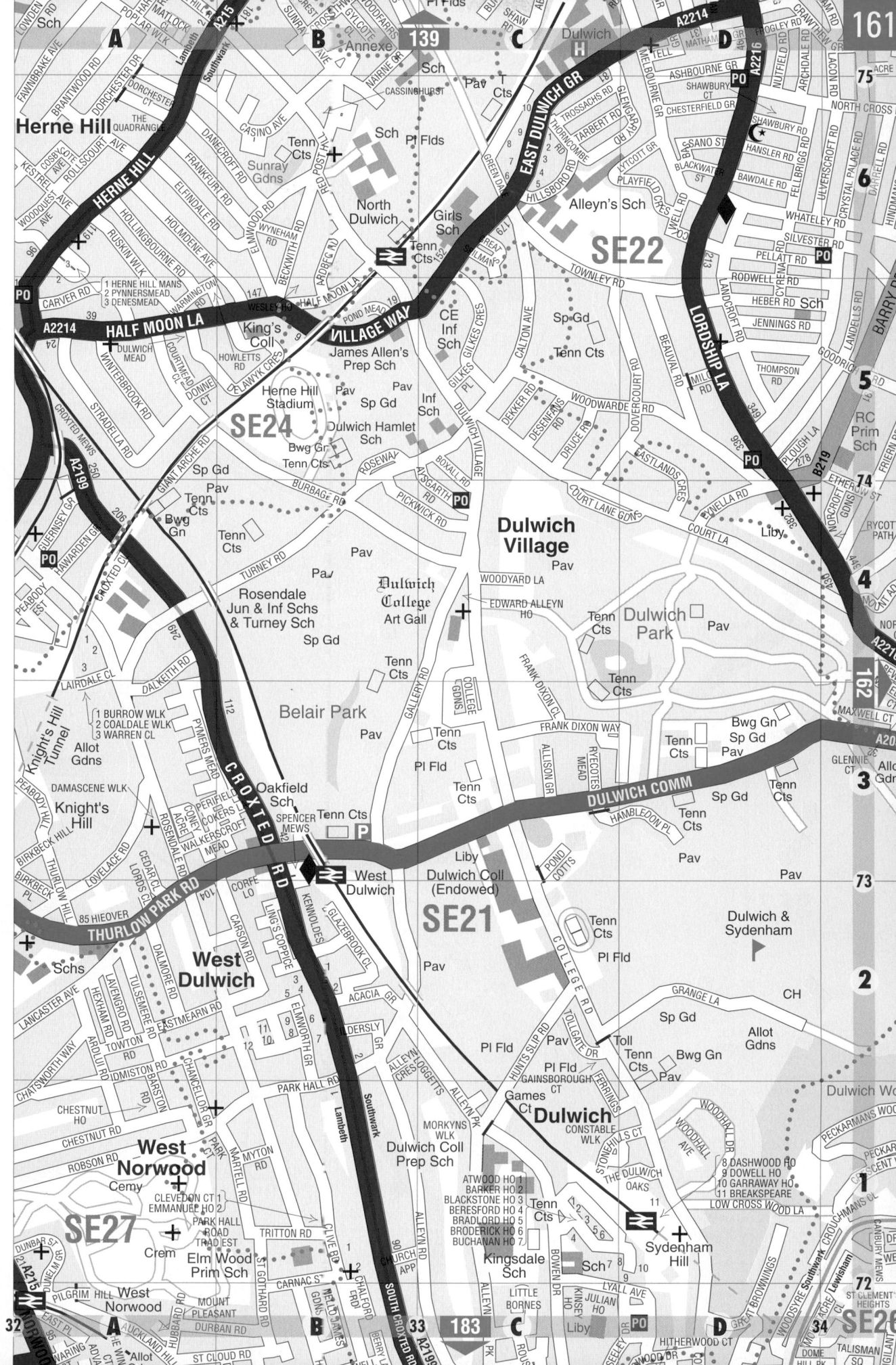
A
B
C
D
139
Herne Hill
Sunray Gdns
North Dulwich
Girls Sch
Alleyn's Sch
SE22
SE24
SE21
SE27
SE26
HERNE HILL
HALF MOON LA
VILLAGE WAY
EAST DULWICH GR
LORDSHIP LA
King's Coll
James Allen's Prep Sch
CE Inf Sch
Herne Hill Stadium
Dulwich Hamlet Sch
Dulwich Village
Dulwich College
Art Gall
Dulwich Park
Rosendale Jun & Inf Schs & Turney Sch
Belair Park
Knight's Hill Tunnel
Knight's Hill
Allot Gdns
Oakfield Sch
CROXTED RD
DULWICH COMM
THURLOW PARK RD
West Dulwich
Dulwich Coll (Endowed)
Dulwich & Sydenham
West Norwood
Cemy
Crem
Elm Wood Prim Sch
Dulwich Coll Prep Sch
Kingsdale Sch
Dulwich
Sydenham Hill
West Norwood
Dulwich Wo
RC Prim Sch
BARRY RD
A2214
A2216
A215
A2199
A205
B219
162
183
32
33
34
72
73
74
75
1
2
3
4
5
6

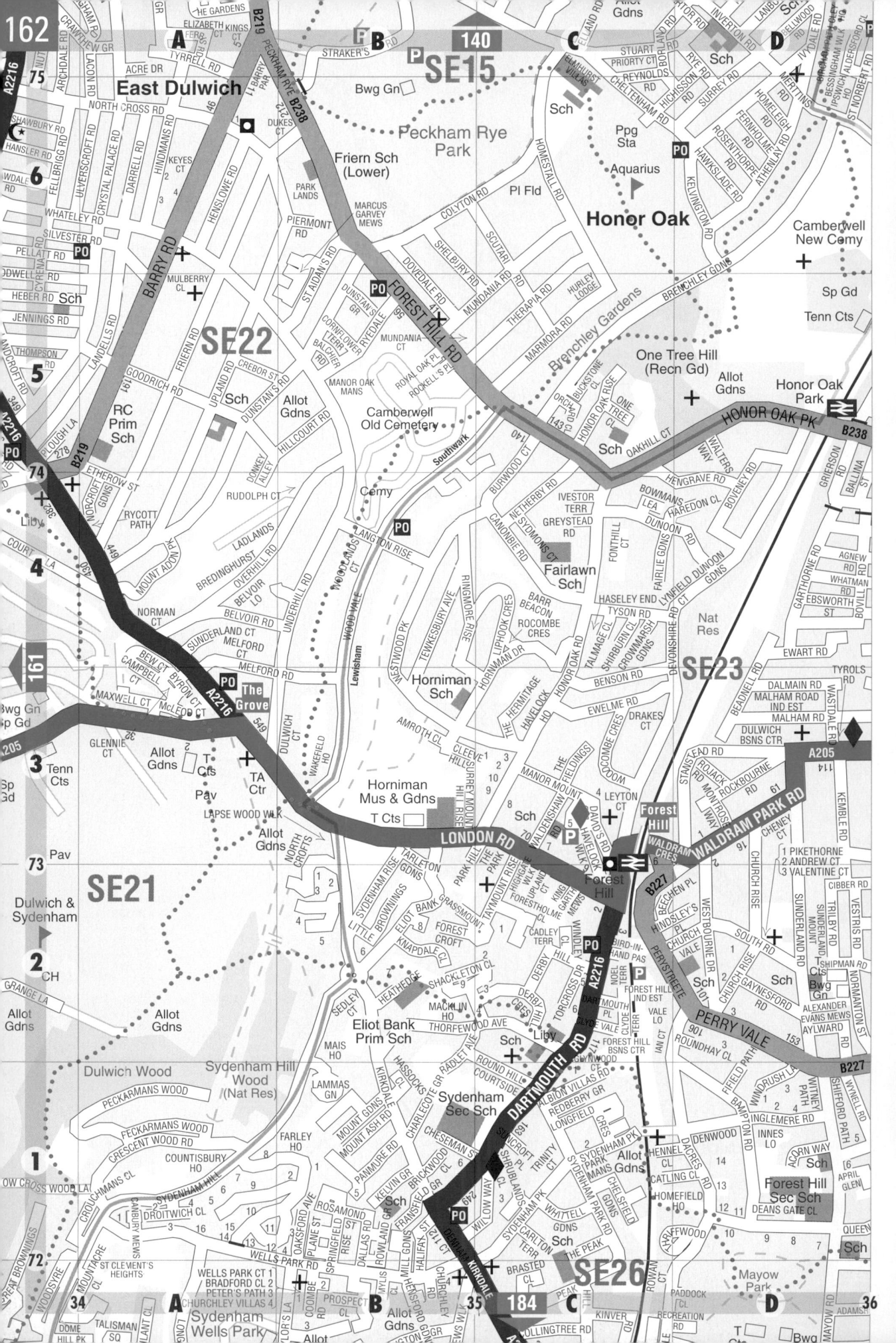
140
A
B
C
D
SE15
East Dulwich
Peckham Rye Park
Friern Sch (Lower)
Honor Oak
Camberwell New Cemy
SE22
Brenchley Gardens
One Tree Hill (Recn Gd)
Honor Oak Park
HONOR OAK PK
FOREST HILL RD
BARRY RD
Camberwell Old Cemetery
Fairlawn Sch
SE23
161
The Grove
Horniman Sch
Horniman Mus & Gdns
LONDON RD
WALDRAM PARK RD
Forest Hill
SE21
Dulwich & Sydenham
Eliot Bank Prim Sch
Dulwich Wood
Sydenham Hill Wood (Nat Res)
Sydenham Sec Sch
DARTMOUTH RD
PERRY VALE
Forest Hill Sec Sch
SE26
Sydenham Wells Park
Mayow Park
184
34
35
36
75
74
73
72
6
5
4
3
2
1

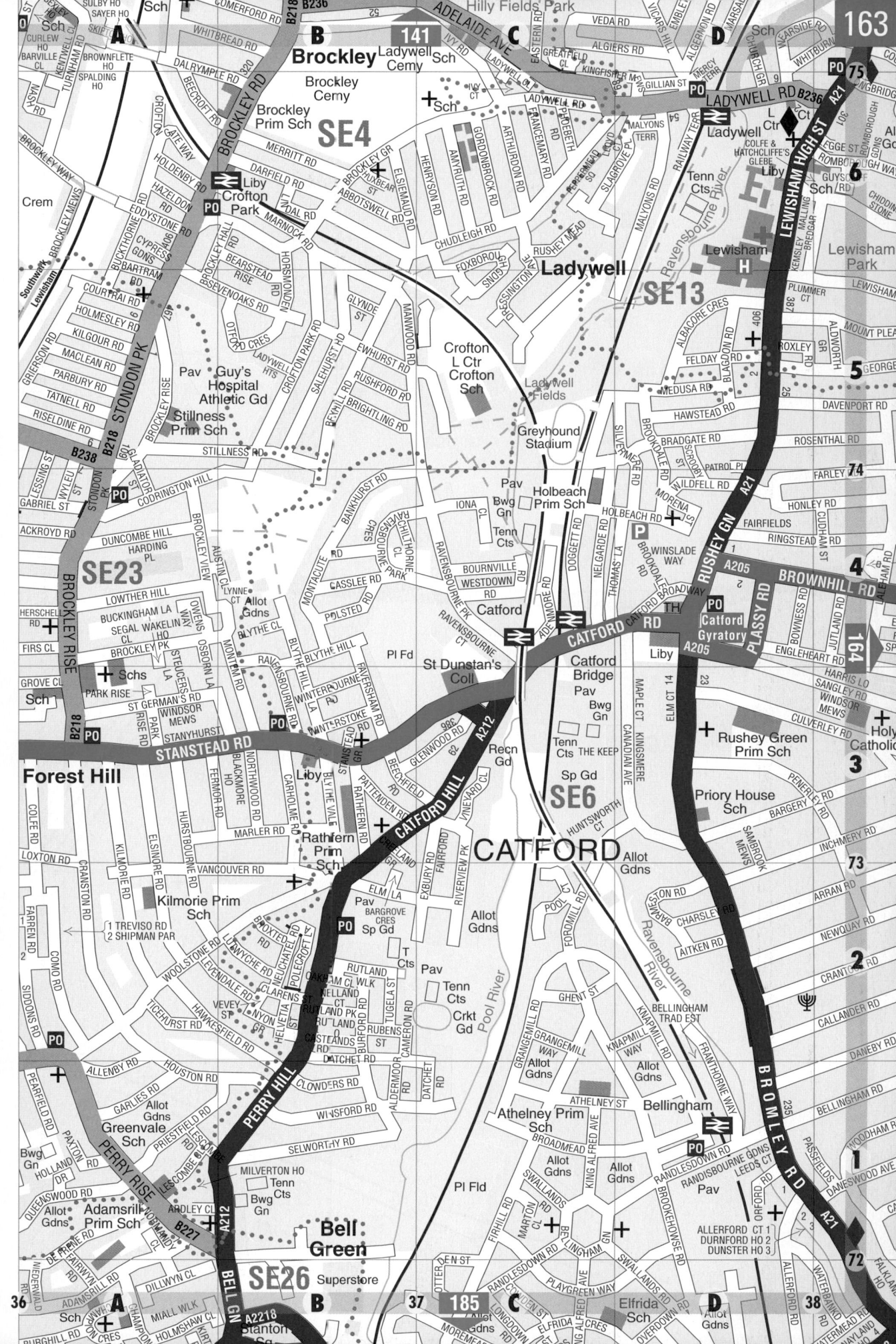
Brockley
Ladywell Cemy
Brockley Cemy
Brockley Prim Sch
SE4
Hilly Fields Park
ADELAIDE AVE
141
LADYWELL RD
Ladywell
Crofton Park
BROCKLEY RD
STONDON PK
BROCKLEY RISE
Crem
Guy's Hospital Athletic Gd
Stillness Prim Sch
STILLNESS RD
CODRINGTON HILL
Crofton L Ctr
Crofton Sch
Ladywell Fields
Greyhound Stadium
Holbeach Prim Sch
Lewisham
LEWISHAM HIGH ST
Lewisham Park
SE13
SE23
Catford
CATFORD RD
Catford Gyratory
BROWNHILL RD
RUSHEY GN
Catford Bridge
St Dunstan's Coll
STANSTEAD RD
Forest Hill
CATFORD HILL
SE6
CATFORD
Rushey Green Prim Sch
Priory House Sch
Rathfern Prim Sch
Kilmorie Prim Sch
Pool River
Ravensbourne River
Bellingham
Athelney Prim Sch
BELLINGHAM TRAD EST
BROMLEY RD
PERRY HILL
PERRY RISE
Greenvale Sch
Adamsrill Prim Sch
Bell Green
SE26
Superstore
Elfrida Sch
Stanton Sq
164
185
A
B
C
D
1
2
3
4
5
6
36
37
38
72
73
74
75

142
186
163
A
B
C
D
SE13
SE12
SE6
BR1
Hither Green
Lee
Lee Green
Southend
Lewisham Park
Mountsfield Park
Forster Park
Manor House Gardens
Manor Park
Quaggy River
LEWISHAM HIGH ST
BURNT ASH RD
BROWNHILL RD
ST MILDREDS RD
BROMLEY RD
RUSHEY GREEN
PLASSY RD
A21
A205
A2212
A20
B236
Green Chain Wlk
Brindishe Prim Sch
Sandhurst Prim Sch
Holy Cross Sch
Torridon Schs
Forster Park Sch
Catford Cty Sch
St John Baptist Sch
New Woodlands Sch
Downham Ent Ctr
Cemy
Crem
Chiltonian Ind Est
Sandhurst Mkt
Allot Gdns
Pl Fld
Pav
Bwg Gn
Tenn Cts
Sch
Liby
PO
38
39
40
72
73
74
75
1
2
3
4
5
6

143
187
166
SE3
SE9
SE12
BR1
ELTHAM RD
ELTHAM HILL
WESTHORNE AVE
SIDCUP RD
BARING RD
CHINBROOK RD
GROVE PARK RD
KIDBROOKE PARK RD
Sutcliffe Park
Horn Park
Northbrook Park
Mottingham
Mottingham Farm
Grove Park
Lee
Eltham Green
Cliftons Roundabout
Yorkshire Grey
Colfe's Sch
Riverston Sch
Eltham Green Sch
Moatbridge Sch
Eltham Hill Tech Coll for Girls
The Grange (Eltham Coll Jun Sch)
Eltham Coll Jun Sch
Malory Sec Sch
Green Chain Wlk
Quaggy River
40
41
42
75
74
73
72

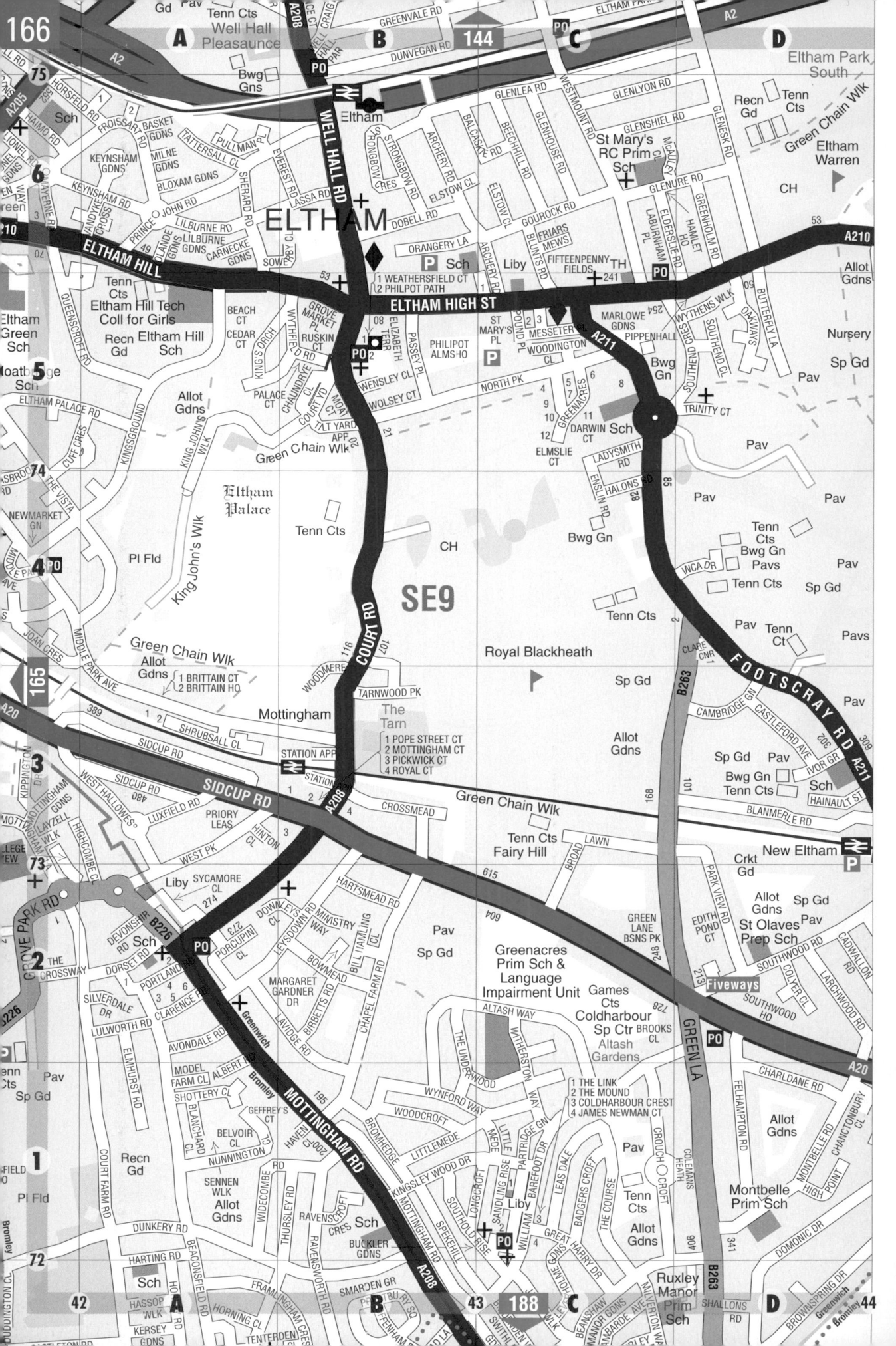
A
B
144
C
D
Well Hall Pleasaunce
Tenn Cts
A2
Greenvale Rd
Dunvegan Rd
Eltham Park South
Bwg Gns
Horsfield Rd
Froissart Rd
Basket Gdns
Tattersall Cl
Pullman Pl
Milne Gdns
Keynsham Gdns
Bloxam Gdns
Keynsham Rd
Vandyke Cross
Prince John Rd
Lilburne Rd
Lilburne Gdns
Carnecke Gdns
Sherard Rd
Everest Rd
Lassa Rd
Well Hall Rd
Eltham
ELTHAM
Strongbow Cres
Strongbow Rd
Archery Rd
Balcaskie Rd
Beechhill Rd
Glenhouse Rd
Glenlea Rd
Westmount Rd
Glenlyon Rd
Glenshiel Rd
Glenesk Rd
Glenure Rd
St Mary's RC Prim Sch
Recn Gd
Tenn Cts
Green Chain Wlk
Eltham Warren
CH
Elstow Cl
Dobell Rd
Gourock Rd
Friars Mews
Blunts Rd
Orangery La
Sch
Liby
Fifteenpenny Fields
TH
PO
Laburnham Pl
Eldersie Rd
Hamlet Ho
Greenholm Rd
A210
Allot Gdns
Eltham Hill
Eltham High St
1 Weathersfield Ct
2 Philpot Path
Tenn Cts
Eltham Hill Tech Coll for Girls
Recn Gd
Eltham Hill Sch
Eltham Green Sch
Queenscroft Rd
Beach Ct
Cedar Ct
King's Orch
Wythfield Rd
Grove Market Pl
Ruskin Ct
Elizabeth Terr
Passey Pl
Philipot Almsho
St Mary's Pl
Pound Pl
Messeter Pl
Woodington Cl
Marlowe Gdns
Pippenhall
Wythens Wlk
Southend Cres
Southend Cl
Oakways
Butterfly La
A211
Bwg Gn
Nursery
Sp Gd
Pav
North Pk
Wensley Cl
Wolsey Ct
Palace Ct
Chaundrye Cl
Court Yd
Moat Ct
Tilt Yard App
Greenacres
Darwin Ct
Sch
Trinity Ct
Eltham Palace Rd
Allot Gdns
Kingsground
Cuff Cres
King John's Wlk
Green Chain Wlk
Elmslie Ct
Ladysmith Rd
Halons Rd
Enslin Rd
The Vista
Newmarket Gn
Eltham Palace
Tenn Cts
CH
Bwg Gn
Tenn Cts
Bwg Gn
Pavs
Wica Dr
Tenn Cts
Sp Gd
Pl Fld
King John's Wlk
SE9
Court Rd
Tenn Cts
Pav
Tenn Ct
Pavs
Joan Cres
Middle Park Ave
Green Chain Wlk
Allot Gdns
1 Brittain Ct
2 Brittain Ho
Royal Blackheath
Clare Cnr
Footscray Rd
Woodmere
Tarnwood Pk
Sp Gd
B263
165
Mottingham
The Tarn
Cambridge Gn
Castleford Ave
A20
Shrubsall Cl
Sidcup Rd
1 Pope Street Ct
2 Mottingham Ct
3 Pickwick Ct
4 Royal Ct
Allot Gdns
Sp Gd
Pav
Ivor Gr
Bwg Gn
Tenn Cts
Sch
Hainault St
Kippington Dr
Mottingham Gdns
West Hallowes
Sidcup Rd
Station App
Luxfield Rd
Priory Leas
SIDCUP RD
A208
Crossmead
Green Chain Wlk
Blanmerle Rd
Layzell Wlk
Highcombe Cl
Hinton Cl
West Pk
Tenn Cts
Fairy Hill
Lawn
Broad
New Eltham
Crkt Gd
Grove Park Rd
Liby
Sycamore Cl
Hartsmead Rd
Park View Rd
Allot Gdns
Sp Gd
Devonshire Rd
B226
Sch
The Crossway
Dorset Rd
Portland Rd
Porcupine Cl
Downleys Cl
Leysdown Rd
Mimstry Way
Bill Hamling Cl
Bowmead
Margaret Gardner Dr
Chapel Farm Rd
Pav
Sp Gd
Green Lane Bsns Pk
Edith Pond Ct
St Olaves Prep Sch
Southwood Rd
Cadwallon Rd
Colyer Cl
Fiveways
Southwood Ho
Larchwood Rd
Silverdale Dr
Clarence Rd
Lulworth Rd
Greenwich
Bromley
Lavidge Rd
Birbetts Rd
Greenacres Prim Sch & Language Impairment Unit
Games Cts
Coldharbour Sp Ctr
Brooks Cl
Altash Gardens
Altash Way
Witherston Way
The Underwood
Green La
Avondale Rd
Elmhurst Rd
Model Farm Cl
Albert Rd
Shottery Cl
Blanchard Cl
Geffrey's Ct
Belvoir Cl
Nunnington Cl
Mottingham Rd
Haven
Bromhedge
Wynford Way
Woodcroft
Littlemede
Little Mede
Partridge Gn
Barefoot Dr
1 The Link
2 The Mound
3 Coldharbour Crest
4 James Newman Ct
Pav
Crouch Croft
Colemans Heath
Charldane Rd
Felhampton Rd
Allot Gdns
Montbelle Rd
Chanctonbury Cl
High Point
Montbelle Prim Sch
Recn Gd
Court Farm Rd
Sennen Wlk
Allot Gdns
Widecombe Rd
Thursley Rd
Ravenscroft Cres
Sch
Kingsley Wood Dr
Speke Hill
Southold Rise
Longcroft
Sandling Rise
William Barefoot Dr
Leas Dale
Badgers Croft
The Course
Tenn Cts
Allot Gdns
Liby
Great Harry Dr
Domonic Dr
Pl Fld
Dunkery Rd
Beaconsfield Rd
Ravensworth Rd
Buckler Gdns
Harting Rd
Sch
Hassop Wlk
Horning Cl
Framlingham Cres
Smarden Gr
Tenterden
Kersey Gdns
Ruxley Manor Prim Sch
Shallons Rd
Brownspring Dr
Beanshaw
42
43
188
44

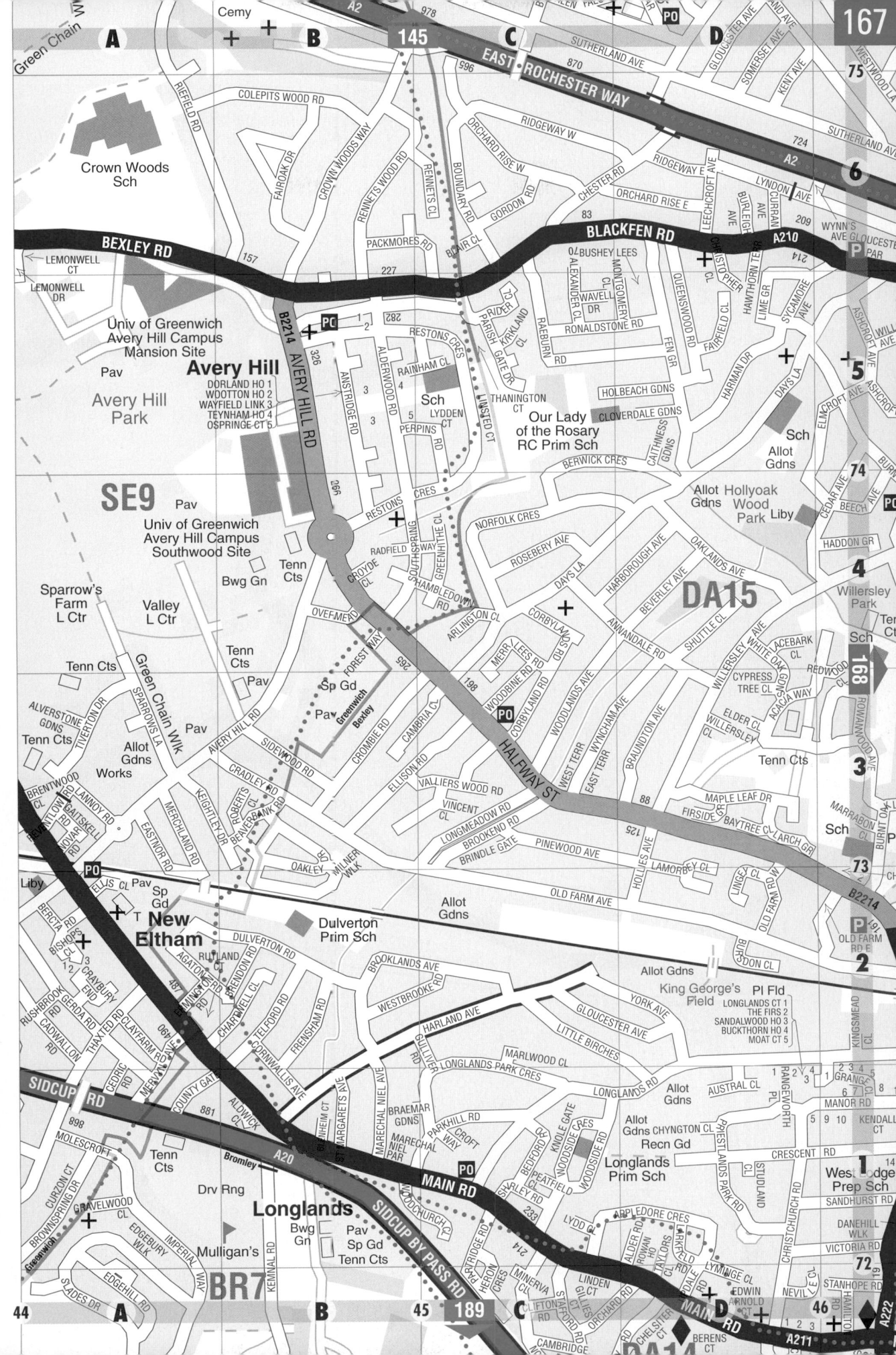
A
B
C
D
145
Cemy
Green Chain Wlk
A2
978
PO
EAST ROCHESTER WAY
SUTHERLAND AVE
870
GLOUCESTER AVE
SOMERSET AVE
KENT AVE
WESTWOOD LA
75
SUTHERLAND AVE
724
A2
6
COLEPITS WOOD RD
RIEFIELD RD
Crown Woods Sch
FAIROAK DR
CROWN WOODS WAY
RENNETS WOOD RD
RENNETS CL
BOUNDARY RD
ORCHARD RISE W
RIDGEWAY W
GORDON RD
CHESTER RD
RIDGEWAY E
ORCHARD RISE E
LEECHCROFT AVE
BURLEIGH AVE
CURRAN AVE
LYNDON AVE
209
WYNN'S AVE
GLOUCESTER PAR
BEXLEY RD
157
LEMONWELL CT
LEMONWELL DR
227
PACKMORES RD
BLAIR CL
BLACKFEN RD
83
A210
BUSHEY LEES
ALEXANDER CL
MONTGOMERY CL
WAVELL DR
CHRISTOPHER CL
HAWTHORN TERR
LIME GR
SYCAMORE AVE
QUEENSWOOD RD
FAIRFIELD CL
214
Univ of Greenwich Avery Hill Campus Mansion Site
B2214
AVERY HILL RD
326
282
RESTONS CRES
RIDER CL
PARISH GATE DR
KIRKLAND CL
RAEBURN RD
RONALDSTONE RD
FEN GR
HARMAN DR
DAYS LA
ASHCROFT AVE
WILLOW AVE
5
Pav
Avery Hill
DORLAND HO 1
WOOTTON HO 2
WAYFIELD LINK 3
TEYNHAM HO 4
OSPRINGE CT 5
Avery Hill Park
ANSTRIDGE RD
ALDERWOOD RD
RAINHAM CL
Sch
LYDDEN CT
PERPINS RD
LINSTED CT
THANINGTON CT
Our Lady of the Rosary RC Prim Sch
HOLBEACH GDNS
CLOVERDALE GDNS
CAITHNESS GDNS
BERWICK CRES
ELMCROFT AVE
Sch
Allot Gdns
74
SE9
Pav
Univ of Greenwich Avery Hill Campus Southwood Site
296
RESTONS CRES
NORFOLK CRES
Allot Gdns
Hollyoak Wood Park
Liby
CEDAR AVE
BEECH AVE
PO
HADDON GR
RADFIELD WAY
SOUTHSPRING
GREENHITHE CL
HAMBLEDOWN RD
ROSEBERY AVE
HARBOROUGH AVE
OAKLANDS AVE
4
Tenn Cts
Bwg Gn
CROYDE CL
DAYS LA
BEVERLEY AVE
DA15
Willersley Park
Sparrow's Farm L Ctr
Valley L Ctr
OVERMEAD
ARLINGTON CL
CORBYLANDS RD
ANNANDALE RD
SHUTTLE CL
Tenn Cts
Sch
Tenn Cts
Tenn Cts
FOREST WAY
265
MERRILEES RD
198
WOODBINE RD
CORBYLAND RD
WILLERSLEY AVE
LACEBARK CL
WHITE OAK GDNS
REDWOOD
168
Pav
Sp Gd
Greenwich
Bexley
CYPRESS TREE CL
ACACIA WAY
ROWANWOOD AVE
Green Chain Wlk
ALVERSTONE GDNS
TIVERTON DR
SPARROWS LA
Pav
Tenn Cts
Allot Gdns
Works
AVERY HILL RD
SIDEWOOD RD
CROMBIE RD
CAMBRIA CL
ELLISON RD
PO
HALFWAY ST
WOODLANDS AVE
WYNCHAM AVE
BRAUNDTON AVE
ELDER CL
WILLERSLEY CL
Tenn Cts
3
BRENTWOOD CL
DEVENTLOW RD
GAITSKELL RD
LANNOY RD
NOVAR RD
CRADLEY RD
KEIGHTLEY DR
ROBERTS CL
BEAVERBANK RD
MERCHLAND RD
EASTNOR RD
VALLIERS WOOD RD
VINCENT CL
LONGMEADOW RD
BROOKEND RD
BRINDLE GATE
WEST TERR
EAST TERR
88
MAPLE LEAF DR
FIRSIDE GR
BAYTREE CL
LARCH GR
MARRABON CL
Sch
BURNT OAK LA
125
HOLLIES AVE
PINEWOOD AVE
LAMORBEY CL
LINGEY CL
OLD FARM RD W
73
Liby
PO
ELLIS CL
Pav
Sp Gd
OAKLEY DR
MILNER WLK
Allot Gdns
OLD FARM AVE
B2214
BERCTA RD
BISHOPS CL
New Eltham
Dulverton Prim Sch
DULVERTON RD
P
OLD FARM RD E
BURSDON CL
2
RUTLAND CT
AGATON RD
BRENDON RD
BROOKLANDS AVE
Allot Gdns
King George's Field
Pl Fld
LONGLANDS CT 1
THE FIRS 2
SANDALWOOD HO 3
BUCKTHORN HO 4
MOAT CT 5
CRAYBURY END
RUSHBROOK RD
GERDA RD
CADWALLON RD
THAXTED RD
CLAYFARM RD
487
ELMINGTON RD
CHARTWELL CL
TELFORD RD
FRENSHAM RD
WESTBROOKE RD
HARLAND AVE
YORK AVE
GLOUCESTER AVE
LITTLE BIRCHES
KINGSMEAD CL
490
MERVYN AVE
CORNWALLIS AVE
GULLIVER RD
MARLWOOD CL
LONGLANDS PARK CRES
LONGLANDS RD
Allot Gdns
AUSTRAL CL
RANGEWORTH PL
GRANGE CL
MANOR RD
KENDALL CT
SIDCUP RD
CEDRIC RD
COUNTY GATE
881
ALDWICK CL
BLENHEIM CT
ST MARGARETS AVE
MARECHAL NIEL AVE
BRAEMAR GDNS
MARECHAL NIEL PAR
PARKHILL RD
CROFT WAY
BEDFORD RD
KNOLE GATE
WOODSIDE CRES
WOODSIDE RD
Allot Gdns
CHYNGTON CL
Recn Gd
PRIESTLANDS PARK RD
STUDLAND CL
CRESCENT RD
1
West Lodge Prep Sch
898
MOLESCROFT
Tenn Cts
Bromley
A20
PO
MAIN RD
PEATFIELD
Longlands Prim Sch
CHRISTCHURCH RD
SANDHURST RD
CURZON CT
BROWNSPRING DR
GRAVELWOOD CL
Drv Rng
Longlands
SIDCUP BY PASS RD
WOODCHURCH CL
SHIRLEY RD
233
LYDD CL
APPLEDORE CRES
DANEHILL WLK
EDGEBURY WLK
IMPERIAL WAY
Bwg Gn
Pav
Sp Gd
Tenn Cts
KEMNAL RD
214
PARTRIDGE RD
HERON CRES
MINERVA CL
ALDER RD
ROWAN CL
TAYLORS CL
LARKFIELD RD
LYMINGE CL
VICTORIA RD
72
Mulligan's
Greenwich
SLADES DR
EDGEHILL RD
BR7
LINDEN CT
GILLIES CT
EDWIN ARNOLD CT
NEVILLE CL
STANHOPE RD
HAMILTON RD
44
A
B
45
189
C
CLIFTON RD
STAFFORD RD
ORCHARD RD
CHELSITER CT
MAIN RD
D
46
BERENS CT
CAMBRIDGE
A211
A222

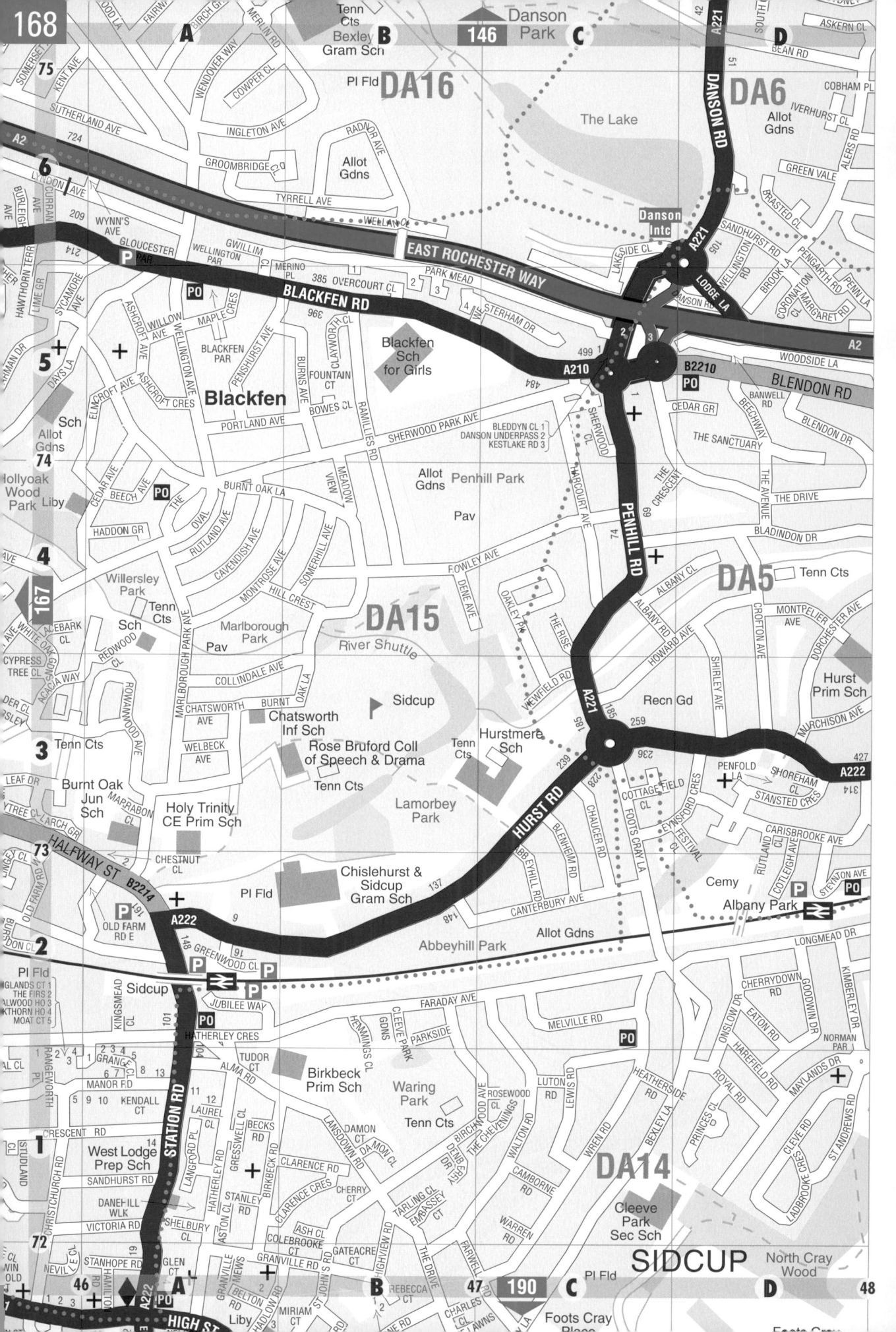

Danson Park
146
DA16
DA6
The Lake
DANSON RD
A221
EAST ROCHESTER WAY
A2
BLACKFEN RD
Blackfen
Blackfen Sch for Girls
Danson Intc
BLENDON RD
B2210
A210
Penhill Park
PENHILL RD
DA15
DA5
River Shuttle
Sidcup
Rose Bruford Coll of Speech & Drama
Chatsworth Inf Sch
Hurstmere Sch
Lamorbey Park
HURST RD
A222
Chislehurst & Sidcup Gram Sch
Holy Trinity CE Prim Sch
Burnt Oak Jun Sch
HALFWAY ST
B2214
Albany Park
Abbeyhill Park
Birkbeck Prim Sch
Waring Park
STATION RD
West Lodge Prep Sch
DA14
Cleeve Park Sec Sch
SIDCUP
North Cray Wood
Foots Cray
HIGH ST
Hurst Prim Sch
Willersley Park
Marlborough Park
Hollyoak Wood Park
167
190

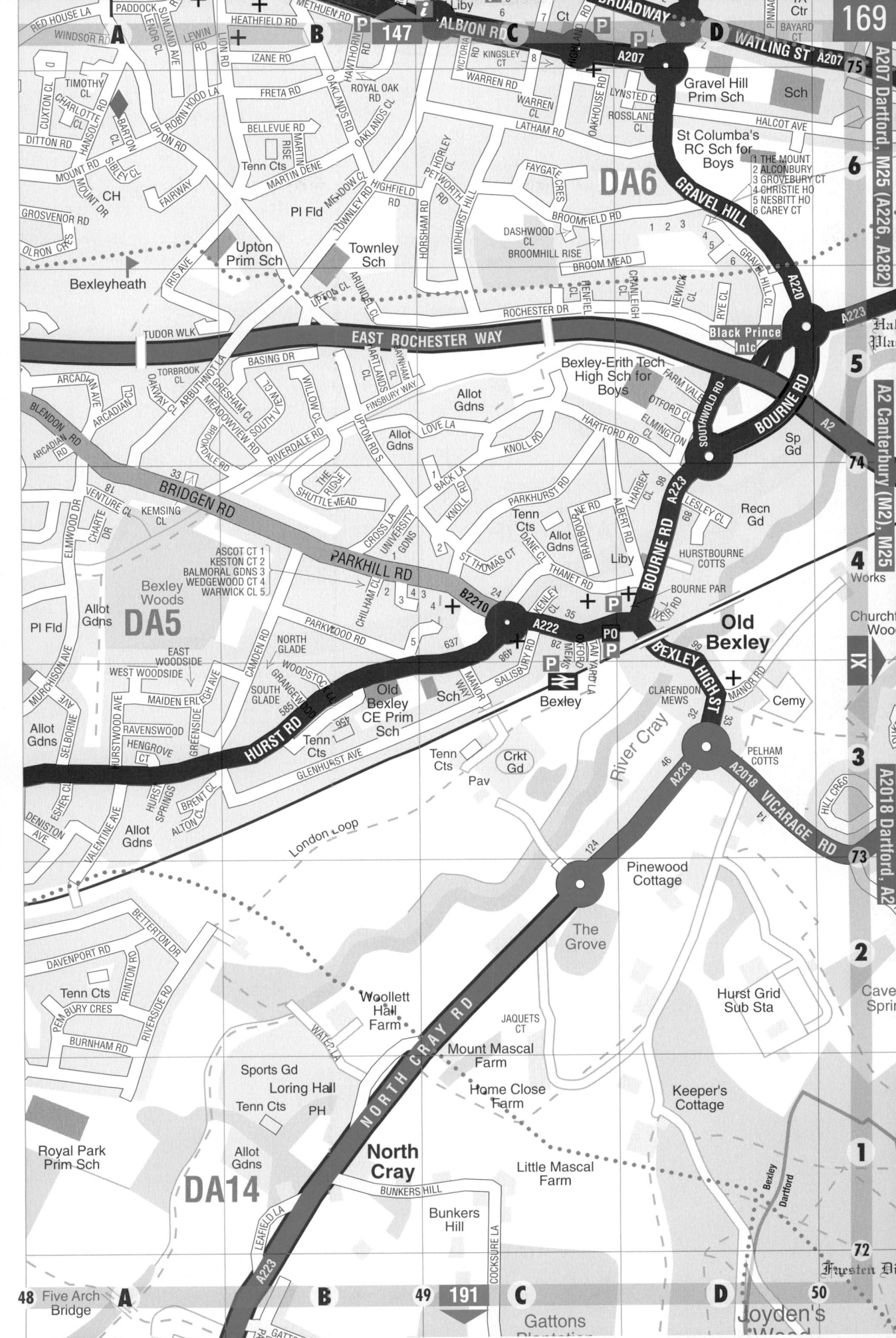
147
A
B
C
D
A207 Dartford, M25 (A226, A282)
A2 Canterbury (M2), M25
A2018 Dartford, A2
BROADWAY
WATLING ST
ALBION RD
Liby
Ct
PADDOCK
SUNLAND AVE
RED HOUSE LA
WINDSOR RD
LENOR CL
LEWIN RD
HEATHFIELD RD
METHUEN RD
IZANE RD
FRETA RD
HAWTHORN RD
ROYAL OAK RD
KINGSLEY CT
WARREN RD
WARREN CL
HIGHLAND RD
OAKHOUSE RD
LYNSTED CL
ROSSLAND CL
Gravel Hill Prim Sch
Sch
HALCOT AVE
St Columba's RC Sch for Boys
1 THE MOUNT
2 ALCONBURY
3 GROVEBURY CT
4 CHRISTIE HO
5 NESBITT HO
6 CAREY CT
GRAVEL HILL
A220
DA6
LATHAM RD
FAYGATE CRES
TIMOTHY CL
CHARLOTTE CL
CUXTON CL
BARTON CL
SIBLEY CL
HANSOL RD
DITTON RD
MOUNT RD
MOUNT DR
CH
ROBIN HOOD LA
UPTON RD
FAIRWAY
BELLEVUE RD
MARTIN RISE
MARTIN DENE
Tenn Cts
OAKLANDS RD
OAKLANDS CL
MEADOW CL
HIGHFIELD RD
HORLEY CL
PETWORTH RD
MIDHURST HILL
HORSHAM RD
TOWNLEY RD
Pl Fld
GROSVENOR RD
OLRON CRES
Bexleyheath
Upton Prim Sch
Townley Sch
IRIS AVE
UPTON CL
ARUNDEL CL
BROOMFIELD RD
DASHWOOD CL
BROOMHILL RISE
BROOM MEAD
FENFIELD CL
CRANLEIGH CL
NEWICK CL
RYE CL
GRAVEL HILL CL
ROCHESTER DR
TUDOR WLK
EAST ROCHESTER WAY
Black Prince Intc
A223
5
6
BOURNE RD
Bexley-Erith Tech High Sch for Boys
FARM VALE
OTFORD CL
ELMINGTON CL
SOUTHWOLD RD
HARTFORD RD
Sp Gd
A2
74
BASING DR
TORBROOK CL
ARCADIAN AVE
ARCADIAN CL
ARCADIAN RD
OAKWAY CL
ARBUTHNOT LA
GRESHAM CL
SOUTH VIEW CL
WILLOW CL
HARTLANDS CL
BAYNHAM CL
FINSBURY WAY
Allot Gdns
MEADOWVIEW RD
BROOKDALE RD
RIVERDALE RD
UPTON RD S
LOVE LA
KNOLL RD
BLENDON RD
BRIDGEN RD
VENTURE CL
KEMSING CL
ELMWOOD DR
CHARTE DR
THE RIDGE
SHUTTLEMEAD
BACK LA
PARKHURST RD
HARBEX CL
ALBERT RD
LESLEY CL
Recn Gd
Tenn Cts
BRADBOURNE RD
DANE CL
CROSS LA
UNIVERSITY GDNS
ST THOMAS CT
THANET RD
Liby
HURSTBOURNE COTTS
4
Works
ASCOT CT 1
KESTON CT 2
BALMORAL GDNS 3
WEDGEWOOD CT 4
WARWICK CL 5
PARKHILL RD
B2210
Bexley Woods
DA5
Allot Gdns
Pl Fld
CHILHAM CL
PARKWOOD RD
KENLEY CL
A222
BOURNE PAR
WEIR RD
Old Bexley
Church Woo
IX
PO
NORTH GLADE
EAST WOODSIDE
WEST WOODSIDE
MURCHISON AVE
SELBORNE AVE
MAIDEN ERLEGH AVE
CAMDEN RD
WOODSTOCK CT
GRANGEWOOD
SOUTH GLADE
Old Bexley CE Prim Sch
Sch
MANOR WAY
SALISBURY RD
OXFORD MEWS
TAN YARD LA
Bexley
BEXLEY HIGH ST
CLARENDON MEWS
MANOR RD
Cemy
3
HURSTWOOD AVE
RAVENSWOOD
HENGROVE CT
GREENSIDE
HURST RD
Tenn Cts
GLENHURST AVE
Tenn Cts
Crkt Gd
Pav
River Cray
PELHAM COTTS
A2018
VICARAGE RD
HILL CRES
Allot Gdns
ESHER CL
DENISTON AVE
VALENTINE AVE
HURST SPRINGS
BRENT CL
ALTON CL
Allot Gdns
London Loop
73
Pinewood Cottage
The Grove
2
BETTERTON DR
DAVENPORT RD
FRINTON RD
RIVERSIDE RD
Tenn Cts
PEMBURY CRES
BURNHAM RD
Woollett Hall Farm
WATERS LA
NORTH CRAY RD
JAQUETS CT
Mount Mascal Farm
Hurst Grid Sub Sta
Cave Sprin
Sports Gd
Loring Hall
Tenn Cts
PH
Home Close Farm
Keeper's Cottage
1
Royal Park Prim Sch
Allot Gdns
North Cray
Little Mascal Farm
DA14
BUNKERS HILL
Bunkers Hill
LEAFIELD LA
COCKSURE LA
Bexley
Dartford
72
Faesten Di
48
Five Arch Bridge
49
191
50
Gattons Plantation
Joyden's Wood

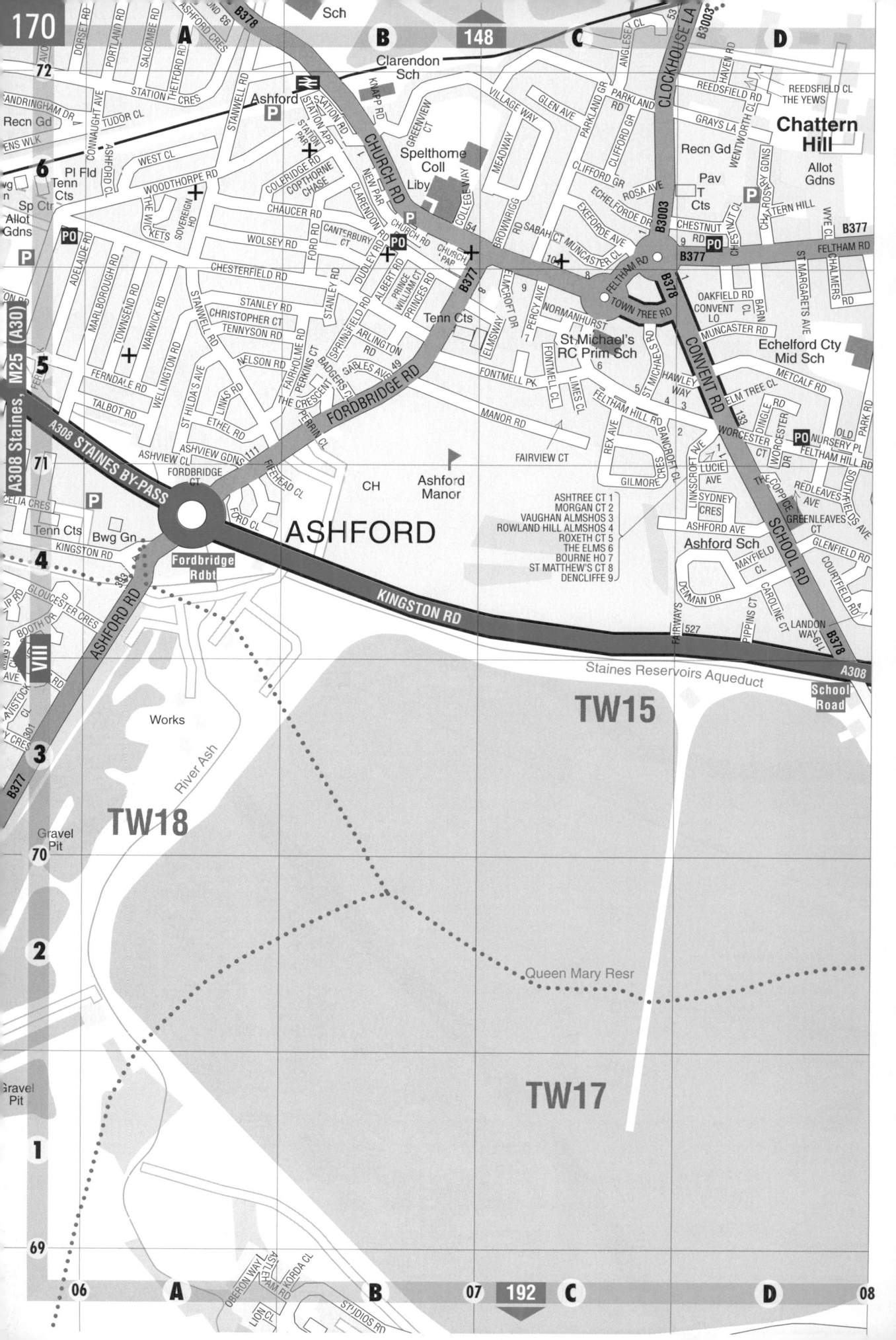
A
B
148
C
D
72
6
5
71
4
3
70
2
1
69
06
07
08
192
Sch
Clarendon
Sch
Ashford
Chattern
Hill
Recn Gd
Pl Fld
Tenn
Cts
Sp Ctr
Allot
Gdns
Spelthorne
Coll
Liby
Pav
Cts
Allot
Gdns
Tenn Cts
St Michael's
RC Prim Sch
Echelford Cty
Mid Sch
CH
Ashford
Manor
ASHFORD
Ashford Sch
Bwg Gn
Fordbridge
Rdbt
Works
River Ash
Gravel
Pit
TW18
TW15
TW17
Queen Mary Resr
Staines Reservoirs Aqueduct
School
Road
A308 Staines, M25 (A30)
A308 STAINES BY-PASS
KINGSTON RD
ASHFORD RD
FORDBRIDGE RD
CHURCH RD
CLOCKHOUSE LA
CONVENT RD
SCHOOL RD
FELTHAM RD
TOWN TREE RD
B378
B377
B3003
A308
DORSET RD
PORTLAND RD
SALCOMBE RD
THETFORD RD
ASHFORD CRES
STATION CRES
STANWELL RD
CONNAUGHT AVE
TUDOR CL
SANDRINGHAM DR
ASHFORD CL
WEST CL
WOODTHORPE RD
SOVEREIGN HO
THE WICKETS
COLERIDGE RD
COPTHORNE CHASE
CHAUCER RD
WOLSEY RD
CHESTERFIELD RD
ADELAIDE RD
MARLBOROUGH RD
TOWNSEND RD
WARWICK RD
WELLINGTON RD
STANLEY RD
CHRISTOPHER CT
TENNYSON RD
NELSON RD
FERNDALE RD
TALBOT RD
ST HILDA'S AVE
LINKS RD
ETHEL RD
ASHVIEW GDNS
ASHVIEW CL
FORDBRIDGE CT
FIFEHEAD CL
FORD CL
KINGSTON RD
GLOUCESTER CRES
BOOTH DR
CELIA CRES
STATION APP
STATION PAR
STATION RD
KNAPP RD
GREENVIEW CT
NEW PAR
CLARENDON RD
CANTERBURY CT
FORD RD
DUDLEY RD
ALBERT RD
PRINCE WILLIAM CT
PRINCES RD
CHURCH PAP
COLLEGE WAY
SPRINGFIELD RD
ARLINGTON RD
FAIRHOLME RD
PERKINS CT
BADGERS CL
GABLES AVE
THE CRESCENT
PERRIN CL
VILLAGE WAY
GLEN AVE
MEADWAY
BROWNRIGG RD
SABAH CT
ELMCROFT DR
ELMSWAY
PERCY AVE
MANOR RD
FONTMELL PK
FONTMELL CL
LIMES CL
FAIRVIEW CT
NORMANHURST
PARKLAND GR
PARKLAND RD
CLIFFORD GR
ROSA AVE
ECHELFORDE DR
EXEFORDE AVE
MUNCASTER CL
ANGLESEY CL
FELTHAM HILL RD
REX AVE
BANCROFT CL
GILMORE CRES
ST MICHAELS RD
HAWLEY WAY
LINKSCROFT AVE
LUCIE AVE
SYDNEY CRES
ASHFORD AVE
MAYFIELD CL
DENMAN DR
FAIRWAYS
PIPPINS CT
CAROLINE CT
LANDON WAY
HAVEN RD
REEDSFIELD RD
REEDSFIELD CL
THE YEWS
GRAYS LA
WENTWORTH CL
CHESTNUT RD
CHESTNUT CL
ROSARY GDNS
CHATTERN HILL
WYE CL
OAKFIELD RD
CONVENT LO
BARN CL
MUNCASTER RD
ST MARGARETS AVE
CHALMERS RD
METCALF RD
ELM TREE CL
DINGLE RD
WORCESTER DR
WORCESTER CT
NURSERY PL
OLD
PARK RD
FELTHAM HILL RD
THE COPPICE
REDLEAVES AVE
GREENLEAVES CT
SOUTHFIELDS AVE
GLENFIELD RD
COURTFIELD RD
ASHTREE CT 1
MORGAN CT 2
VAUGHAN ALMSHOS 3
ROWLAND HILL ALMSHOS 4
ROXETH CT 5
THE ELMS 6
BOURNE HO 7
ST MATTHEW'S CT 8
DENCLIFFE 9
OBERON WAY
ASTLEHAM RD
KORDA CL
LION CL
STUDIOS RD
VIII

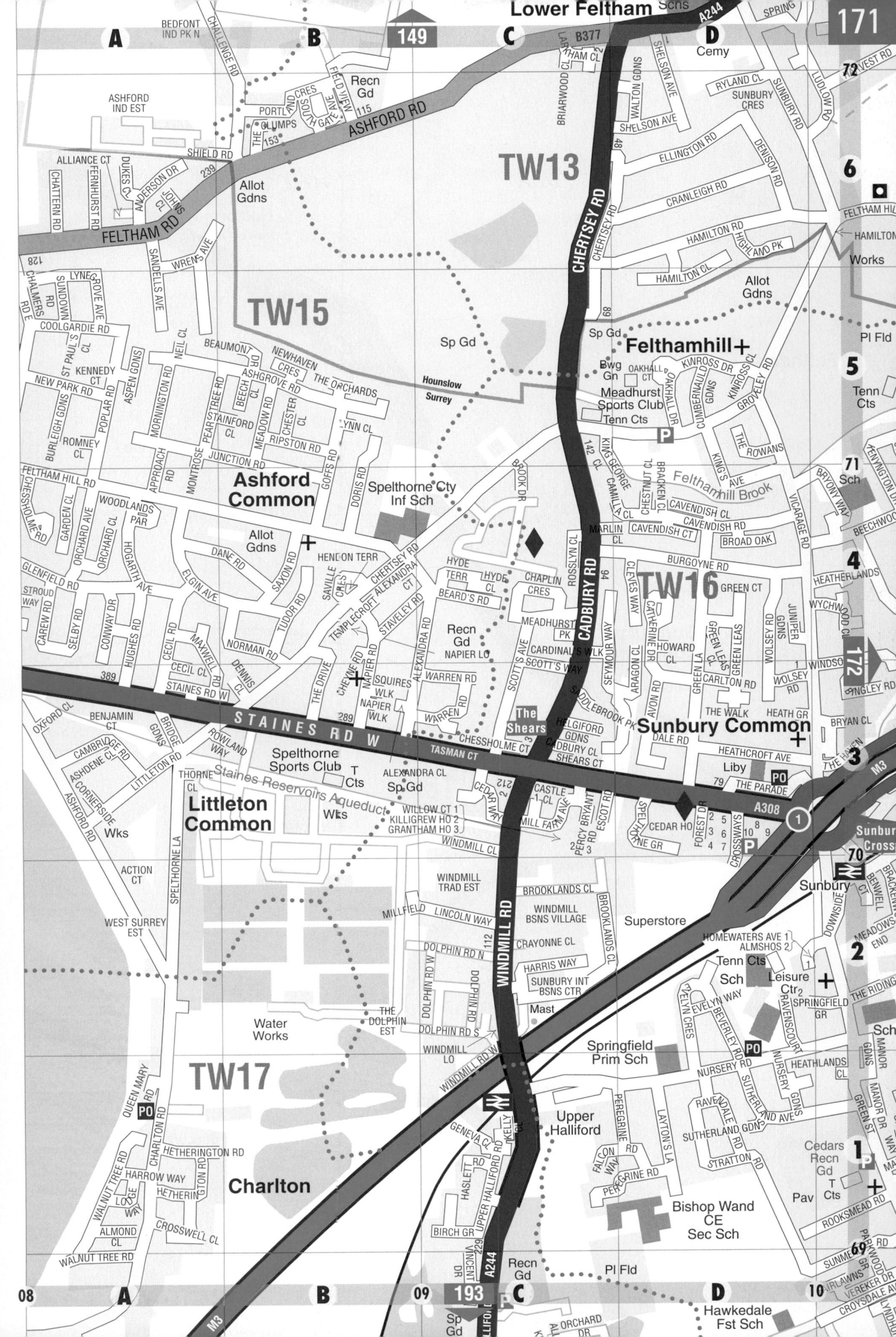
Lower Feltham
149
A
B
C
D
A244
B377
BEDFONT IND PK N
CHALLENGE RD
FIELD VIEW
Recn Gd
PORTLAND CRES
SOUTH GATE AVE
THE CLUMPS
115
153
ASHFORD RD
ASHFORD IND EST
SHIELD RD
ALLIANCE CT
DUKES CL
FERNHURST RD
CHATTERN RD
ANDERSON DR
ST JOHNS CL
239
FELTHAM RD
Allot Gdns
SANDELLS AVE
WRENS AVE
128
LYNEGROVE AVE
SUNDOWN RD
CHALMERS RD E
COOLGARDIE RD
ST PAUL'S CL
KENNEDY CT
NEW PARK RD
POPLAR RD
ASPEN GDNS
BURLEIGH GDNS
ROMNEY CL
BEAUMONT DR
NEIL CL
NEWHAVEN CRES
THE ORCHARDS
ASHGROVE RD
MORNINGTON RD
PEARTREE RD
BEECH CL
STAINFORD CL
MEADOW RD
CHESTER CL
RIPSTON RD
LYNN CL
JUNCTION RD
APPROACH RD
MONTROSE
GOFFS RD
DORIS RD
FELTHAM HILL RD
CHESSHOLME RD
GARDEN CL
ORCHARD AVE
ORCHARD CL
WOODLANDS PAR
HOGARTH AVE
Ashford Common
Spelthorne Cty Inf Sch
Allot Gdns
HENDON TERR
DANE RD
SAXON RD
GLENFIELD RD
STROUD WAY
CAREW RD
SELBY RD
CONWAY DR
HUGHES RD
ELGIN AVE
CECIL RD
MAXWELL RD
TUDOR RD
SAVILLE CRES
CHERTSEY RD
ALEXANDRA CT
TEMPLECROFT
STAVELEY RD
NORMAN RD
DENNIS CL
CECIL CL
STAINES RD W
389
THE DRIVE
CHEYNE RD
NAPIER RD
SQUIRES WLK
NAPIER WLK
289
ALEXANDRA RD
WARREN RD
Recn Gd
NAPIER LO
HYDE TERR
HYDE CL
BEARD'S RD
CHAPLIN CRES
TW13
TW15
TW16
TW17
Hounslow
Surrey
Sp Gd
CHERTSEY RD
LARKHAM CL
BRIARWOOD CL
WALTON GDNS
SHELSON AVE
Cemy
SPRING
RYLAND CL
SUNBURY CRES
SUNBURY RD
LUDLOW RD
WEST RD
72
ELLINGTON RD
DENISON RD
CRANLEIGH RD
HAMILTON RD
HIGHLAND PK
HAMILTON CL
FELTHAM HILL
HAMILTON
Works
Allot Gdns
6
Pl Fld
Sp Gd
Felthamhill
Bwg Gn
OAKHALL CT
KINROSS DR
KINROSS CL
OAKHALL DR
CUMBERNAULD GDNS
GROVELEY RD
Meadhurst Sports Club
Tenn Cts
5
Tenn Cts
THE ROWANS
KING'S AVE
KING GEORGE CL
142
CAMILLA CL
CHESTNUT CL
BRACKEN CL
Felthamhill Brook
BRYONY WAY
VICARAGE RD
71
Sch
KENNINGTON
CAVENDISH CL
CAVENDISH RD
CAVENDISH CT
MARLIN CL
BROAD OAK
BEECHWOOD
BROOK DR
ROSSLYN CL
CADBURY RD
94
CLEVES WAY
BURGOYNE RD
GREEN CT
HEATHERLANDS
4
WYCHWOOD CL
CATHERINE DR
JUNIPER GDNS
WOLSEY RD
MEADHURST PK
CARDINAL'S WLK
SCOTT'S WAY
SCOTT'S AVE
SEYMOUR WAY
ARAGON CL
HOWARD CL
GREEN LA
GREEN LEAS
GREEN LEAS CL
CARLTON RD
WOLSEY RD
WINDSOR
172
BINGLEY RD
SADDLEBROOK PK
AVON RD
THE WALK
HEATH GR
BRYAN CL
The Shears
HELGIFORD GDNS
Sunbury Common
DALE RD
CHESSHOLME CT
CADBURY CL
SHEARS CT
HEATHCROFT AVE
THE HAVEN
3
Liby
PO
79
THE PARADE
M3
A308
1
STAINES RD W
TASMAN CT
OXFORD CL
BENJAMIN CT
BRIDGE GDNS
ROWLAND WAY
CAMBRIDGE RD
ASHDENE CL
CORNERSIDE
LITTLETON RD
ASHFORD RD
Spelthorne Sports Club
T Cts
ALEXANDRA CL
Sp Gd
THORNE CL
Staines Reservoirs Aqueduct
Littleton Common
Wks
Wks
CEDAR WAY
212
CASTLE CL
MILL FARM AVE
PERCY BRYANT RD
ESCOT RD
SPELTHORNE GR
CEDAR HO
FOREST DR
CROSSWAYS
WILLOW CT 1
KILLIGREW HO 2
GRANTHAM HO 3
WINDMILL CL
Sunbury Cross
70
Sunbury
BRACKENWOOD
BENWELL CT
DOWNSIDE
ACTION CT
SPELTHORNE LA
WINDMILL TRAD EST
BROOKLANDS CL
WINDMILL BSNS VILLAGE
BROOKLANDS CL
Superstore
MILLFIELD
LINCOLN WAY
WEST SURREY EST
HOMEWATERS AVE 1
ALMSHOS 2
MEADOWS END
2
DOLPHIN RD N
112
CRAYONNE CL
HARRIS WAY
SUNBURY INT BSNS CTR
Tenn Cts
Sch
Leisure Ctr
EVELYN CRES
EVELYN WAY
SPRINGFIELD GR
THE RIDINGS
DOLPHIN RD W
DOLPHIN RD
WINDMILL RD
Mast
THE DOLPHIN EST
DOLPHIN RD S
Water Works
WINDMILL LO
Springfield Prim Sch
BEVERLEY RD
RAVENSCOURT
PO
Sch
MANOR GDNS
NURSERY RD
NURSERY GDNS
HEATHLANDS CL
QUEEN MARY RD
PO
CHARLTON RD
GENEVA CL
KELLY CL
Upper Halliford
PEREGRINE RD
LAYTON'S LA
RAVENDALE RD
SUTHERLAND AVE
SUTHERLAND GDNS
STRATTON RD
MANOR DR
GREEN ST
HETHERINGTON RD
HARROW WAY
WALNUT TREE RD
LODGE WAY
Charlton
HASLETT RD
UPPER HALLIFORD RD
FALCON WAY
PEREGRINE RD
Cedars Recn Gd
T Cts
Pav
ROOKSMEAD RD
Bishop Wand CE Sec Sch
ALMOND CL
CROSSWELL CL
BIRCH GR
229
VINCENT DR
A244
Recn Gd
Pl Fld
SUMMER
PARKWOOD GR
69
FAIRLAWNS
VEREKER DR
CROYSDALE AVE
WALNUT TREE RD
08
09
193
10
Sp Gd
ORCHARD DR
Hawkedale Fst Sch
M3

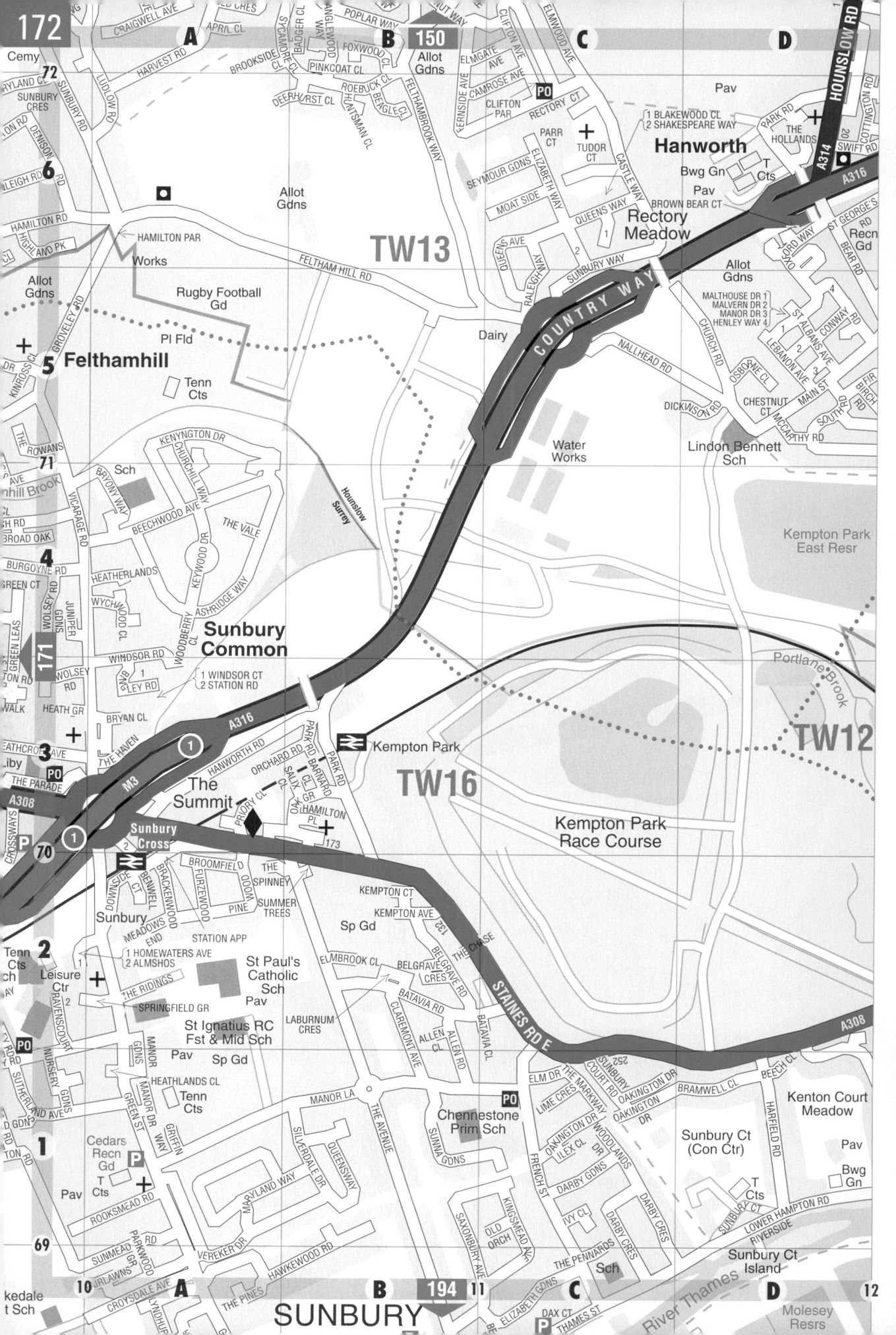

Hanworth
Felthamhill
Sunbury Common
Sunbury
TW13
TW16
TW12
Rectory Meadow
Kempton Park Race Course
Kempton Park East Resr
Kempton Park
The Summit
Sunbury Cross
Water Works
Rugby Football Gd
Lindon Bennett Sch
St Paul's Catholic Sch
St Ignatius RC Fst & Mid Sch
Chennestone Prim Sch
Sunbury Ct (Con Ctr)
Kenton Court Meadow
Sunbury Ct Island
River Thames
Molesey Resrs
Cedars Recn Gd
Leisure Ctr
COUNTRY WAY
STAINES RD E
HOUNSLOW RD
FELTHAM HILL RD
A316
A308
A314
M3
Portlane Brook
Hounslow
Surrey
150
171
173
194
SUNBURY

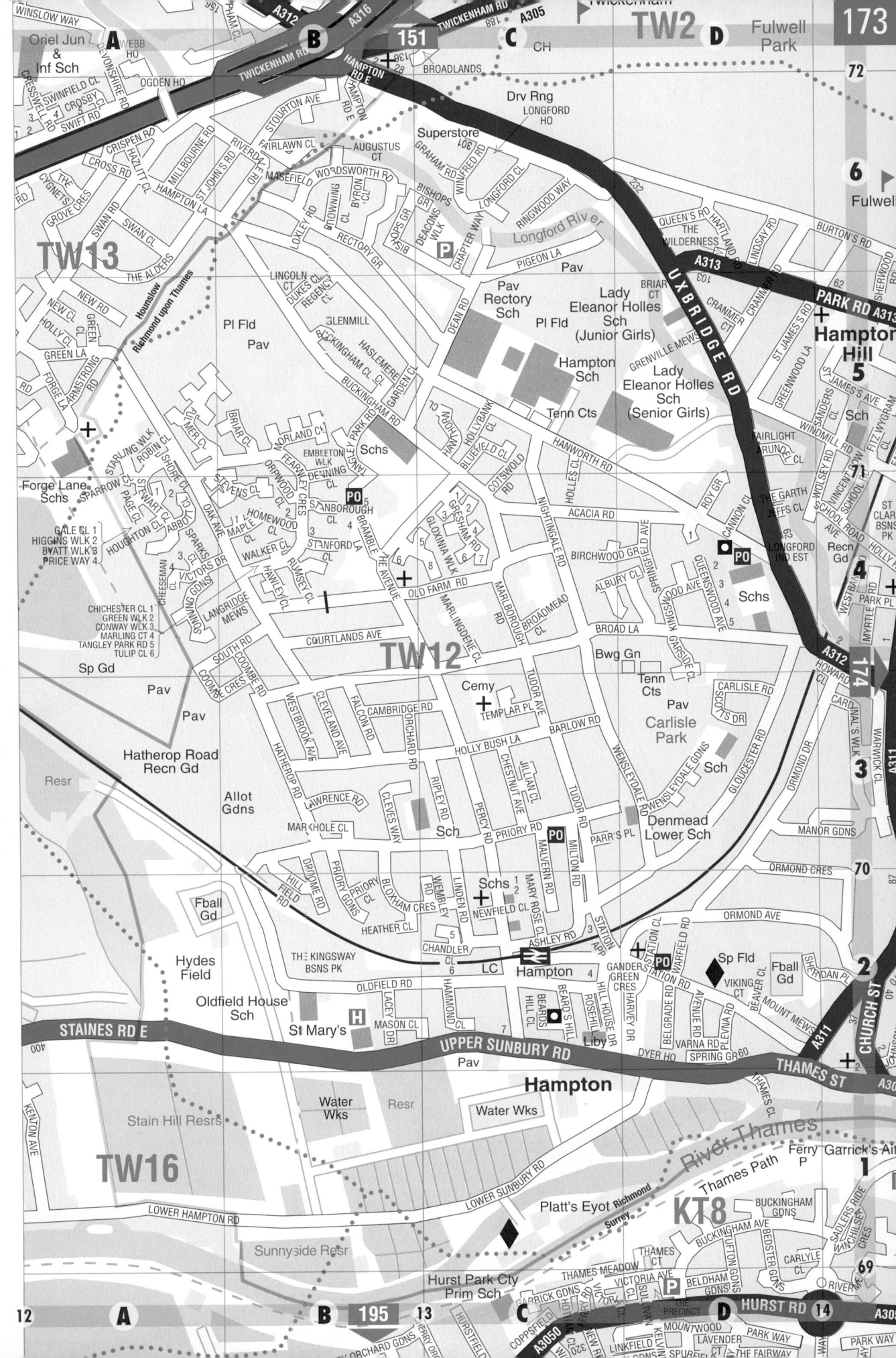
TW2
Fulwell Park
Twickenham
151
A312
A316
A305
TWICKENHAM RD
HAMPTON RD E
BROADLANDS
Oriel Jun & Inf Sch
WEBB HO
OGDEN HO
WINSLOW WAY
DEVONSHIRE RD
SWINFIELD CL
CROSBY CL
SWIFT RD
CRESSWELL RD
STOURTON AVE
Drv Rng
LONGFORD HO
Superstore
FAIRLAWN CL
AUGUSTUS CT
MASEFIELD
WORDSWORTH RD
CRISPEN RD
HAZLITT CL
CROSS RD
MILLBOURNE RD
ST JOHN'S RD
RIVERDALE RD
HAMPTON LA
THE CYGNETS
GROVE CRES
SWAN RD
SWAN CL
THE ALDERS
TW13
GRAHAM RD
WINIFRED RD
LONGFORD CL
RINGWOOD WAY
BISHOPS GR
DEACONS WLK
CHAPTER WAY
Longford River
PIGEON LA
LOXLEY RD
BROWNING CL
BYRON CL
RECTORY GR
Pav
Rectory Sch
Lady Eleanor Holles Sch (Junior Girls)
Lady Eleanor Holles Sch (Senior Girls)
Hampton Sch
Tenn Cts
Pl Fld
QUEEN'S RD
THE WILDERNESS
HARTLAND RD
LINDSAY RD
BURTON'S RD
A313
UXBRIDGE RD
CRANMER CT
CRANMER RD
BRIAR CT
GRENVILLE MEWS
PARK RD A313
Hampton Hill
Fulwell
ST JAMES'S RD
GREENWOOD LA
ST JAMES'S AVE
SANDERS CL
WINDMILL RD
FITZ WYGRAM CL
SHERWOOD RD
Sch
LINCOLN CT
DUKES CL
REGENCY CL
GLENMILL
BUCKINGHAM CL
HASLEMERE CL
GARDEN CL
BUCKINGHAM RD
DEAN RD
Hounslow
Richmond upon Thames
NEW RD
NEW CL
GREEN CL
HOLLY CL
GREEN LA
ARMSTRONG RD
FORGE LA
Forge Lane Schs
HAWTHORN CL
HOLLYBANK CL
BLUEFIELD CL
COTSWOLD RD
HANWORTH RD
HOLLES CL
ROY GR
CANNON CL
FAIRLIGHT
ARUNDEL CL
THE GARTH
JEFFS CL
WOLSEY RD
VINCENT ROW
SCHOOL RD
SCHOOL ROAD AVE
HOLLY RD
ST CLARE BSNS PK
LONGFORD IND EST
Recn Gd
WESTBANK RD
PARK PL
MYRTLE RD
STARLING WLK
ROBIN CL
SPARROW CL
STEWART CL
PAGE CL
SHORE CL
ABBOTT CL
PALMER CL
BRIAR CL
MORLAND CL
EMBLETON WLK
DENNING CL
FEARNLEY CRES
ORPWOOD CL
TANGLEY PARK RD
Schs
STEVENS CL
OAK AVE
MAPLE CL
HOMEWOOD CL
STANBOROUGH CL
BRAMBLE LA
STANFORD CL
WALKER CL
HAWLEY CL
RUMSEY CL
GALE CL 1
HIGGINS WLK 2
BYATT WLK 3
PRICE WAY 4
HOUGHTON CL
SPARKS CL
CHEESEMAN CL
VICTORS DR
SONNING GDNS
LANGRIDGE MEWS
CHICHESTER CL 1
GREEN WLK 2
CONWAY WLK 3
MARLING CT 4
TANGLEY PARK RD 5
TULIP CL 6
GRESHAM RD
GLOXINIA WLK
THE AVENUE
OLD FARM RD
ACACIA RD
NIGHTINGALE RD
BIRCHWOOD GR
SPRINGFIELD AVE
ALBURY CL
KINGSWOOD AVE
QUEENSWOOD AVE
Schs
MARLINGDENE CL
MARLBOROUGH RD
BROADMEAD CL
BROAD LA
COURTLANDS AVE
TW12
SOUTH RD
COOMBE RD
COOMBE CRES
Sp Gd
Pav
Bwg Gn
Tenn Cts
GARSIDE CL
A312
HOWARD CL
174
CARDINAL'S WLK
CARLISLE RD
SCOTT'S DR
Carlisle Park
Cemy
TEMPLAR PL
TUDOR AVE
BARLOW RD
CAMBRIDGE RD
FALCON RD
CLEVELAND AVE
WESTBROOK AVE
ORCHARD RD
HOLLY BUSH LA
Hatherop Road Recn Gd
Resr
Allot Gdns
HATHEROP RD
LAWRENCE RD
CLEVES WAY
RIPLEY RD
CHESTNUT AVE
JILLIAN CL
TUDOR RD
WENSLEYDALE RD
WENSLEYDALE GDNS
GLOUCESTER RD
ORMOND DR
WARWICK CL
A311
Sch
MARKHOLE CL
PERCY RD
PRIORY RD
MALVERN RD
MILTON RD
PARR'S PL
Denmead Lower Sch
MANOR GDNS
ORMOND CRES
HILL FIELD RD
DROMORE RD
PRIORY GDNS
PRIORY CL
BLOXHAM CRES
WEMBLEY RD
LINDEN RD
Schs
NEWFIELD CL
MARY ROSE CL
STATION APP
ASHLEY RD
ORMOND AVE
Fball Gd
HEATHER CL
CHANDLER CL
LC
Hampton
STATION CL
WARFIELD RD
GANDER GREEN CRES
STATION RD
Sp Fld
Fball Gd
SHERIDAN PL
VIKING CT
BEAVER CL
MOUNT MEWS
THE KINGSWAY BSNS PK
Hydes Field
OLDFIELD RD
LACEY DR
HAMMOND CL
BEARDS HILL CL
BEARD'S HILL
ROSEHILL
HILL HOUSE DR
HARVEY DR
BELGRADE RD
AVENUE RD
PLEVNA RD
Oldfield House Sch
St Mary's
MASON CL
Liby
VARNA RD
DYER HO
SPRING GR
STAINES RD E
UPPER SUNBURY RD
Pav
THAMES ST
THAMES CL
CHURCH ST
Hampton
Water Wks
Resr
Water Wks
Stain Hill Resrs
KENTON AVE
TW16
River Thames
Thames Path
Ferry
Garrick's Ait
LOWER SUNBURY RD
Platt's Eyot
Richmond
Surrey
KT8
BUCKINGHAM GDNS
BUCKINGHAM AVE
BEDSTER GDNS
SADLERS RIDE
WINCHILSEA CRES
LOWER HAMPTON RD
Sunnyside Resr
THAMES CT
THAMES MEADOW
VICTORIA AVE
CARLYLE CL
Hurst Park Cty Prim Sch
GARRICK GDNS
BELDHAM GDNS
THE PRECINCT
HURST RD
A3050
COPPSFIELD
MOUNTWOOD
LAVENDER CT
PARK WAY
LINKFIELD
THE FAIRWAY
ORCHARD GDNS
195
A
B
C
D
12
13
14
72
71
70
69
6
5
4
3
2
1

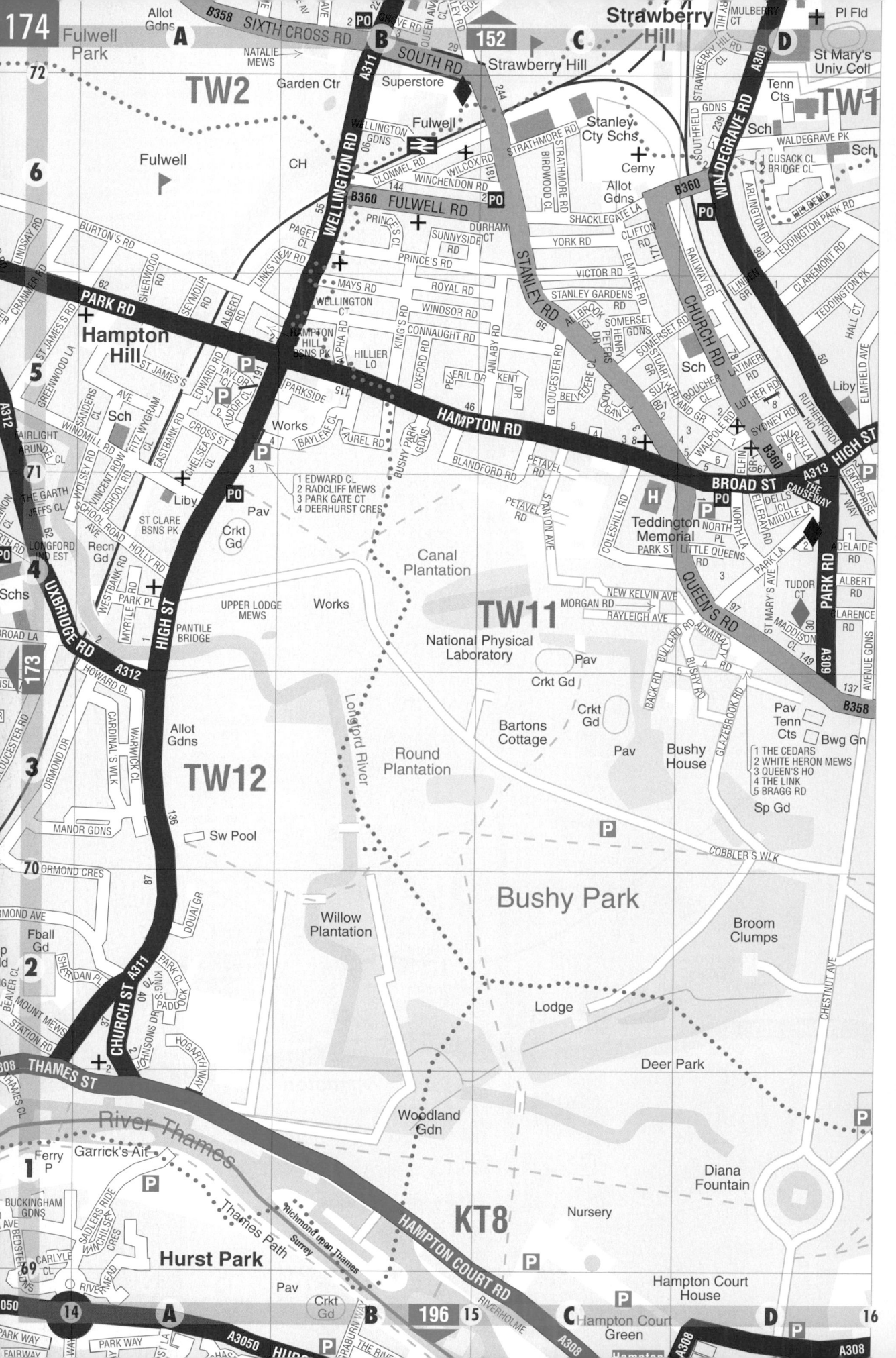
Fulwell Park
Allot Gdns
A
B358 SIXTH CROSS RD
B
152
C
Strawberry Hill
D
Pl Fld
St Mary's Univ Coll
NATALIE MEWS
TW2
Garden Ctr
SOUTH RD
Superstore
Strawberry Hill
Tenn Cts
TW1
Fulwell
WELLINGTON GDNS
WELLINGTON RD
A311
Stanley Cty Schs
STRATHMORE RD
WALDEGRAVE RD
A309
WALDEGRAVE PK
Sch
CUSACK CL
BRIDGE CL
Fulwell
CH
CLONMEL RD
WILCOX RD
Cemy
Allot Gdns
WINCHENDON RD
B360 FULWELL RD
PO
BIRDWOOD CL
STRATHMORE RD
B360
ARLINGTON RD
FIELDEND
TEDDINGTON PARK RD
BURTON'S RD
PAGET CL
PRINCE'S CL
DURHAM CT
SUNNYSIDE RD
SHACKLEGATE LA
CLIFTON RD
YORK RD
LINKS VIEW RD
PRINCE'S RD
STANLEY RD
RAILWAY RD
CLAREMONT RD
MAYS RD
ROYAL RD
VICTOR RD
TEDDINGTON PK
PARK RD
SHERWOOD RD
SEYMOUR RD
ALBERT RD
WELLINGTON CT
WINDSOR RD
STANLEY GARDENS RD
ELMTREE RD
CHURCH RD
Hampton Hill
HAMPTON HILL BSNS PK
CONNAUGHT RD
SOMERSET GDNS
SOMERSET RD
HALL CT
ST JAMES'S RD
GREENWOOD LA
ST JAMES'S
TAYLOR CL
HILLIER LO
KING'S RD
ALPHA RD
ANLABY RD
GLOUCESTER RD
BELVEDERE CL
STUART GR
Sch
LATIMER RD
ELMFIELD AVE
Liby
EDWARD RD
TUDOR CL
PARKSIDE
PEVERIL DR
KENT DR
CADOGAN CL
BOUCHER CL
LUTHER RD
SANDERS CL
AVE
Sch
FITZ WYGRAM CL
OXFORD RD
HAMPTON RD
SUTHERLAND GR
WALPOLE RD
SYDNEY RD
CHURCH LA
RUTHERFORD HO
HIGH ST
A312
FAIRLIGHT
ARUNDEL CL
WINDMILL RD
EASTBANK RD
CROSS ST
Works
BAYLEAF CL
LAUREL RD
BUSHY PARK GDNS
BLANDFORD RD
PETAVEL RD
B360
A313
BROAD ST
THE CAUSEWAY
ENTERPRISE WAY
WOLSEY RD
VINCENT ROW
SCHOOL RD
CHELSEA CL
Liby
1 EDWARD CL
2 RADCLIFF MEWS
3 PARK GATE CT
4 DEERHURST CRES
STANTON AVE
COLESHILL RD
Teddington Memorial
NORTH LA
DELLS CL
MIDDLE LA
THE GARTH
JEFFS CL
SCHOOL ROAD AVE
Pav
ST CLARE BSNS PK
Crkt Gd
NORTH PL
PARK ST
LITTLE QUEENS RD
ADELAIDE RD
LONGFORD IND EST
Recn Gd
HOLLY RD
Canal Plantation
ALBERT RD
4
Schs
UXBRIDGE RD
WESTBANK RD
MYRTLE RD
PARK PL
HIGH ST
UPPER LODGE MEWS
Works
TW11
NEW KELVIN AVE
MORGAN RD
RAYLEIGH AVE
QUEEN'S RD
ST MARY'S AVE
TUDOR CT
PARK RD
CLARENCE RD
BROAD LA
PANTILE BRIDGE
National Physical Laboratory
MADDISON CL
173
HOWARD CL
A312
BULLARD RD
ADMIRALTY RD
Pav
Crkt Gd
BUSHY RD
BACK RD
GLAZEBROOK RD
A309
AVENUE GDNS
B358
CARDINAL'S WLK
WARWICK CL
Allot Gdns
Longford River
Bartons Cottage
Crkt Gd
Pav
Bushy House
Pav
Tenn Cts
Bwg Gn
GLOUCESTER RD
ORMOND DR
TW12
Round Plantation
1 THE CEDARS
2 WHITE HERON MEWS
3 QUEEN'S HO
4 THE LINK
5 BRAGG RD
Sp Gd
MANOR GDNS
Sw Pool
COBBLER'S WLK
70
ORMOND CRES
ORMOND AVE
DOUAI GR
Bushy Park
Willow Plantation
Broom Clumps
Fball Gd
SHERIDAN PL
PARK CL
KING'S PADDOCK
CHURCH ST
A311
BEAVER CL
MOUNT MEWS
STATION RD
JOHNSONS DR
HOGARTH WAY
Lodge
CHESTNUT AVE
THAMES ST
Deer Park
THAMES CL
River Thames
Woodland Gdn
Ferry P
Garrick's Ait
Diana Fountain
BUCKINGHAM GDNS
SADLERS RIDE
WINCHILSEA CRES
Thames Path
Richmond upon Thames
Surrey
KT8
Nursery
BEDSTER GDNS
CARLYLE CL
Hurst Park
HAMPTON COURT RD
RIVERMEAD
Pav
Crkt Gd
Hampton Court House
14
A
B
196
15
RIVERHOLME
C
Hampton Court Green
D
16
PARK WAY
A3050
FAIRWAY
A308
THE RIVE
GRABURN WAY

TW1
TW10
TW11
KT1
KT2
KT8
TEDDINGTON
KINGSTON UPON THAMES
Hampton Wick
Teddington Lock
Teddington Weir
Thames Path
River Thames
Meadlands Prim Sch
Cassel
Collis Prim Sch
Sacred Heart RC Prim Sch
Teddington Sch
Normansfield
Tiffin Girls' Sch
Fern Hill Prim Sch
Kingston Coll of FEd
Warren Plantation
Oval Plantation
Heron Pond
Boating Lake
The Royal Paddocks
Bushy Lodge
Hampton Wick Pond
Old Icehouse
Athletic Gd
Marina
Recn Gd
Allot Gdns
Crkt Gd
KINGSTON RD
UPPER TEDDINGTON RD
MANOR RD
TWICKENHAM RD
STRAWBERRY VALE
HIGH ST
PARK RD
SANDY LA
HAMPTON COURT RD
UPPER HAM RD
RICHMOND RD
HORSE FAIR
WOOD ST
KINGSTON BRIDGE
OLD BRIDGE ST
CHURCH GR
LOWER HAM RD
STATION RD
CROMWELL RD
BROOM RD
KINGSTON HALL RD
SKERNE RD
153
176
197
16
17
18
A
B
C
D

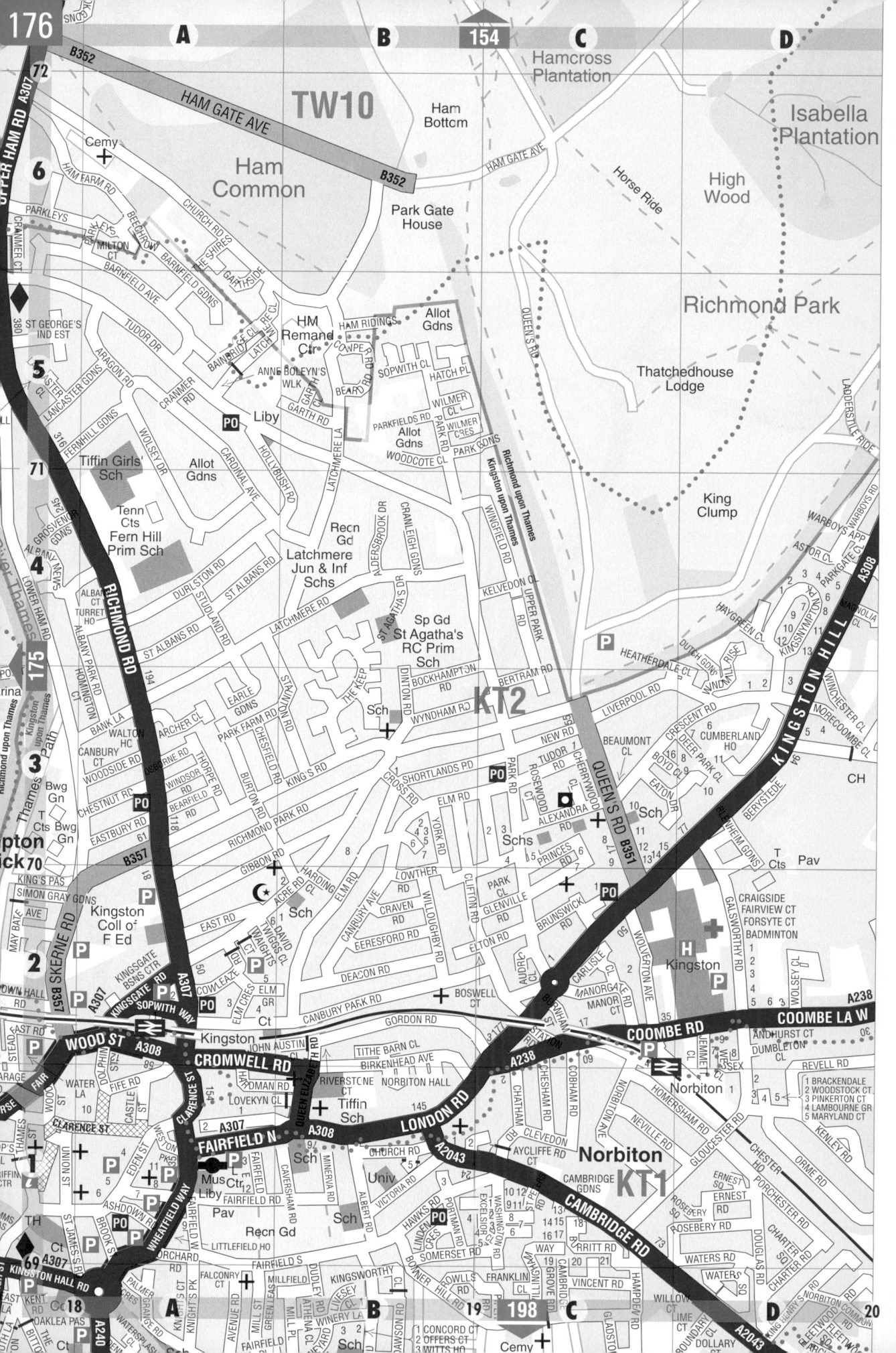

A
B
154
C
D
TW10
Ham Common
Ham Bottom
Hamcross Plantation
Isabella Plantation
High Wood
Park Gate House
Richmond Park
Thatchedhouse Lodge
King Clump
HAM GATE AVE
B352
Horse Ride
HM Remand Ctr
Allot Gdns
Liby
Tiffin Girls' Sch
Tenn Cts
Fern Hill Prim Sch
Recn Gd
Latchmere Jun & Inf Schs
Sp Gd
St Agatha's RC Prim Sch
KT2
RICHMOND RD
KINGSTON HILL
A308
QUEEN'S RD
B351
Kingston Coll of F Ed
Kingston
Norbiton
KT1
COOMBE RD
COOMBE LA W
A238
CROMWELL RD
WOOD ST
LONDON RD
CAMBRIDGE RD
A2043
FAIRFIELD N
Tiffin Sch
Mus Ctr
Liby
Recn Gd
Univ
Sch
Schs
River Thames
Thames Path
Kingston upon Thames
Richmond upon Thames
175
198

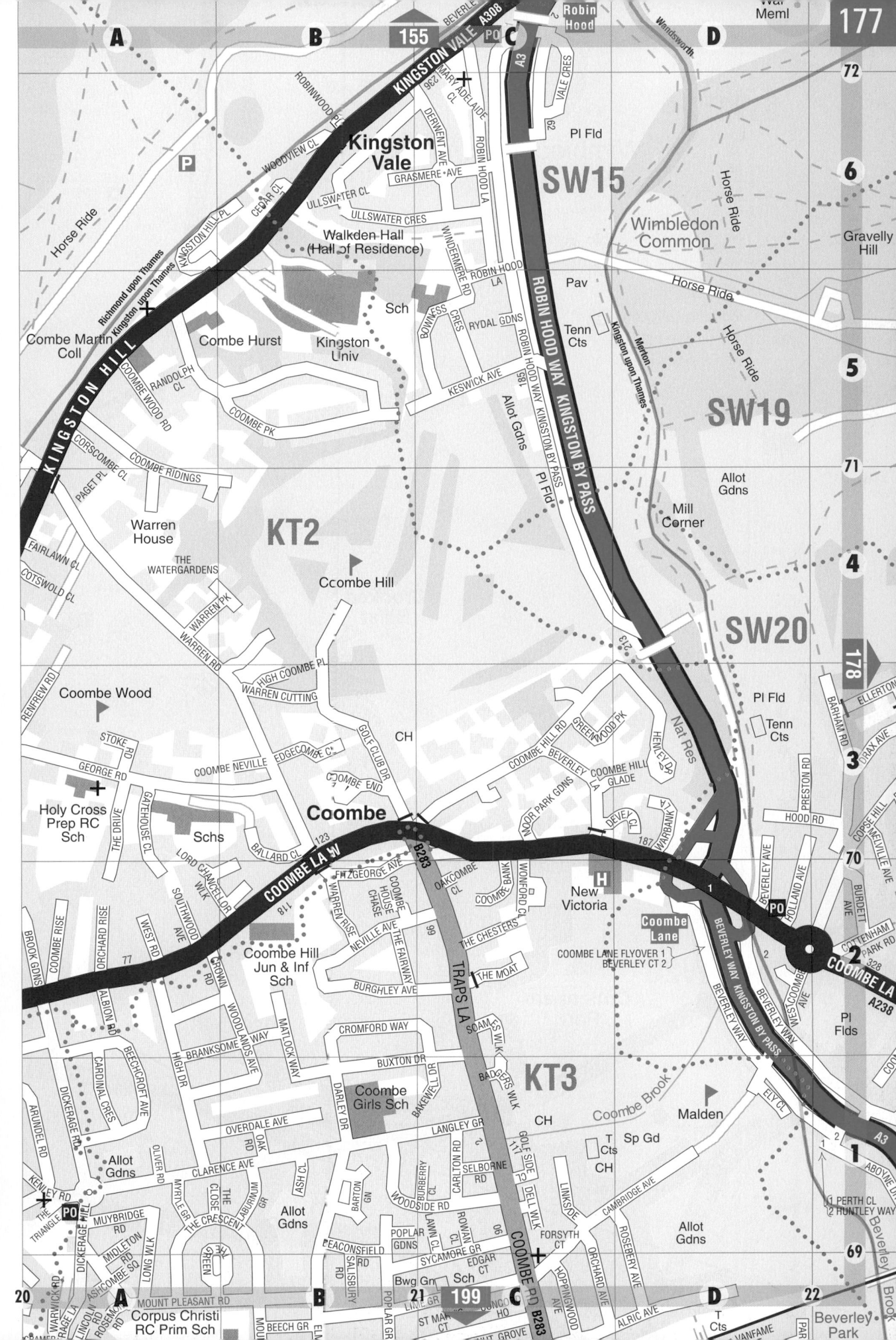
A
B
C
D
155
Robin Hood
Kingston Vale
SW15
Wimbledon Common
Horse Ride
Gravelly Hill
Walkden Hall (Hall of Residence)
Combe Martin Coll
Combe Hurst
Kingston Univ
Sch
Tenn Cts
Pav
SW19
Allot Gdns
Mill Corner
KT2
Warren House
THE WATERGARDENS
Coombe Hill
SW20
Coombe Wood
Holy Cross Prep RC Sch
Schs
Coombe
CH
New Victoria
Coombe Lane
COOMBE LANE FLYOVER 1
BEVERLEY CT 2
Coombe Hill Jun & Inf Sch
Coombe Girls Sch
KT3
Malden
Sp Gd
Allot Gdns
Pl Fld
Pl Flds
Nat Res
1 PERTH CL
2 HUNTLEY WAY
Corpus Christi RC Prim Sch
Beverley Park
KINGSTON HILL
KINGSTON VALE
ROBIN HOOD WAY KINGSTON BY PASS
COOMBE LA W
COOMBE LA
TRAPS LA
COOMBE RD
BEVERLEY WAY KINGSTON BY PASS
Wandsworth
Merton
Kingston upon Thames
Richmond upon Thames
Coombe Brook
Beverley Brook
A3
A308
A238
B283
72
6
5
71
4
3
70
2
1
69
178
20
21
22
199

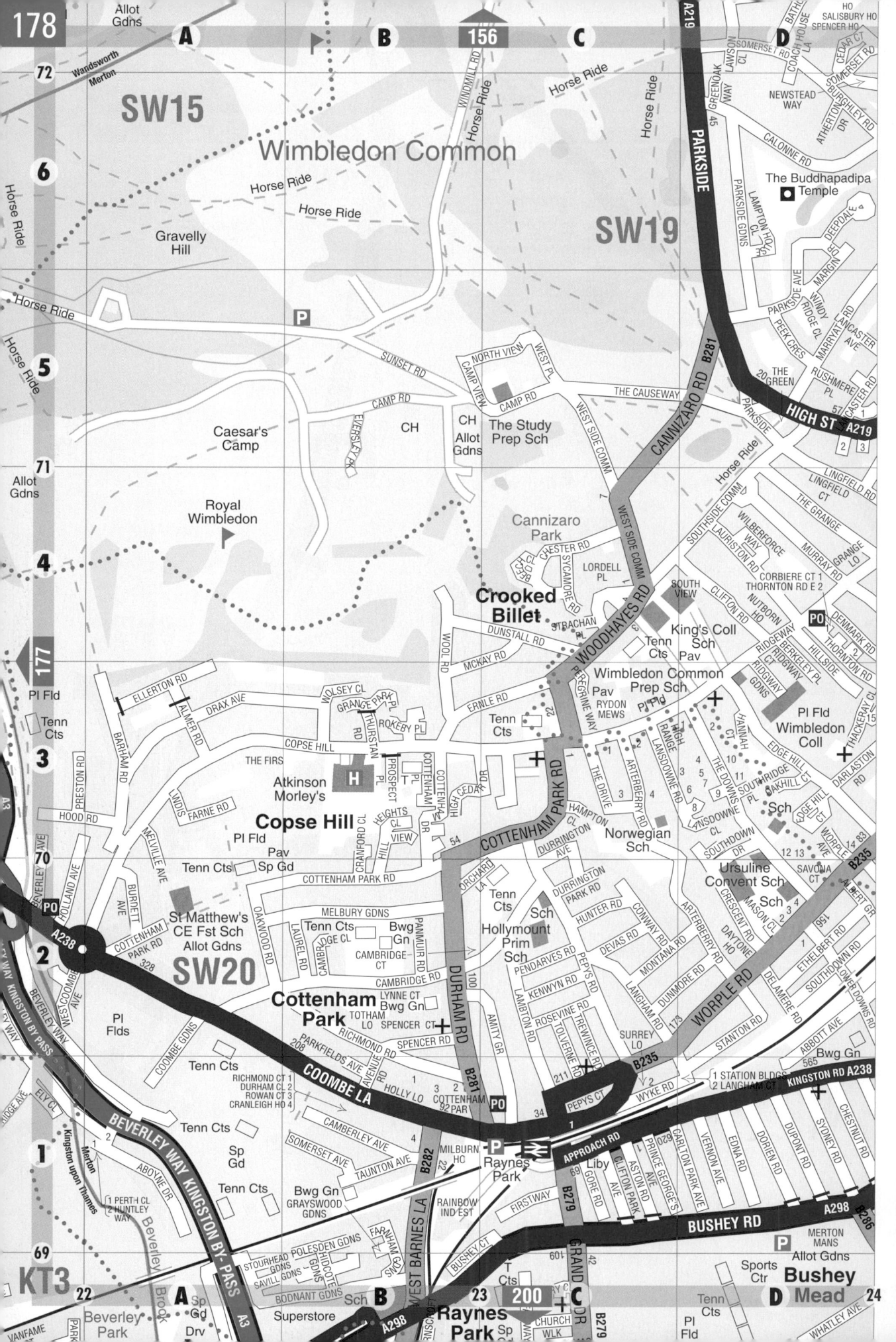
156
200
177
A
B
C
D
72
71
70
69
6
5
4
3
2
1
22
23
24
SW15
SW19
SW20
KT3
Wimbledon Common
Wandsworth
Merton
Allot Gdns
Horse Ride
Gravelly Hill
Caesar's Camp
Royal Wimbledon
WINDMILL RD
SUNSET RD
CAMP RD
EVERSLEY PK
CH
Allot Gdns
NORTH VIEW
CAMP VIEW
WEST PL
The Study Prep Sch
THE CAUSEWAY
WEST SIDE COMM
CANNIZARO RD
B281
PARKSIDE
A219
HIGH ST
SOMERSET RD
COACH HOUSE LA
LAWSON CL
GREENOAK WAY
NEWSTEAD WAY
CALONNE RD
BURGHLEY RD
ATHERTON DR
SALISBURY HO
SPENCER HO
CEDAR CT
The Buddhapadipa Temple
PARKSIDE GDNS
LAMPTON HOUSE CL
DEEPDALE
MARGIN DR
WINDY RIDGE CL
PARKSIDE AVE
PEEK CRES
MARRYAT RD
LANCASTER AVE
THE GREEN
RUSHMERE PL
LANCASTER RD
LINGFIELD RD
LINGFIELD CT
THE GRANGE
SOUTHSIDE COMM
WILBERFORCE WAY
LAURISTON RD
MURRAY RD
GRANGE LO
CORBIERE CT 1
THORNTON RD E 2
Cannizaro Park
CHESTER RD
SYCAMORE RD
LORDELL PL
Crooked Billet
STRACHAN PL
DUNSTALL RD
WOODHAYES RD
SOUTH VIEW
CLIFTON RD
NUTBORN HO
King's Coll Sch
Tenn Cts
Pav
PO
DENMARK RD
THORNTON RD
HILLSIDE
BERKELEY PL
RIDGEWAY
RIDGWAY GDNS
Wimbledon Common Prep Sch
RYDON MEWS
PI Fld
PEREGRINE WAY
Pl Fld Wimbledon Coll
THACKERAY CL
EDGE HILL
DARLASTON RD
OAKHILL CT
SOUTHRIDGE PL
EDGE HILL CT
WORPLE AVE
Sch
HANNAH CT
THE DOWNS
LANSDOWNE RD
LANSDOWNE CL
HIGH RANGE
ARTERBERRY RD
THE DRIVE
Norwegian Sch
SOUTHDOWN DR
Ursuline Convent Sch
SAVONA CT
B235
ALBERT GR
MASON CL
WOOL RD
MCKAY RD
ERNLE RD
ELLERTON RD
DRAX AVE
ALMER RD
BARHAM RD
WOLSEY CL
GRANGE PARK PL
THURSTAN RD
ROKEBY PL
COPSE HILL
THE FIRS
Atkinson Morley's
PROSPECT PL
COTTENHAM DR
HIGH CEDAR DR
COTTENHAM PARK RD
HAMPTON CL
DURRINGTON AVE
DURRINGTON PARK RD
PRESTON RD
HOOD RD
LINDIS
FARNE RD
Copse Hill
CRANFORD CL
HEIGHTS CL
HILL VIEW
Pl Fld
Pav
Tenn Cts
Sp Gd
MELVILLE AVE
BURNETT AVE
St Matthew's CE Fst Sch
Allot Gdns
COTTENHAM PARK RD
OAKWOOD RD
LAUREL RD
MELBURY GDNS
CAMBRIDGE CL
Bwg Gn
CAMBRIDGE CT
PANMUIR RD
ORCHARD LA
Hollymount Prim Sch
HUNTER RD
CONWAY RD
DEVAS RD
MONTANA RD
PENDARVES RD
PEPYS RD
KENWYN RD
ROSEVINE RD
LAMBTON RD
TOLVERNE RD
TREWINCE RD
LANGHAM RD
DUNMORE RD
SURREY LO
ARTERBERRY RD
CRESCENT RD
DAYTONE HO
WORPLE RD
DELAMERE RD
ETHELBERT RD
SOUTHDOWN RD
LOWER DOWNS RD
STANTON RD
ABBOTT AVE
Bwg Gn
HOLLAND AVE
BEVERLEY AVE
A238
COTTENHAM PARK RD
WESTCOOMBE AVE
BEVERLEY WAY
Pl Flds
CAMBRIDGE RD
Cottenham Park
LYNNE CT
TOTHAM LO
SPENCER CT
RICHMOND RD
SPENCER RD
PARKFIELDS AVE
AVENUE RD
DURHAM RD
AMITY GR
B281
COOMBE GDNS
COOMBE LA
Tenn Cts
RICHMOND CT 1
DURHAM CL 2
ROWAN CT 3
CRANLEIGH HO 4
HOLLY LO
COTTENHAM PAR
PEPYS CT
WYKE RD
1 STATION BLDGS
2 LANGHAM CT
KINGSTON RD A238
BEVERLEY WAY KINGSTON BY-PASS
ELY CL
Kingston upon Thames
Merton
ABOYNE DR
1 PERTH CL
2 HUNTLEY WAY
Beverley Brook
Sp Gd
Tenn Cts
CAMBERLEY AVE
SOMERSET AVE
TAUNTON AVE
B282
MILBURN HO
Raynes Park
APPROACH RD
Liby
GORE RD
CLIFTON PARK AVE
ASTON RD
PRINCE GEORGE'S AVE
CARLTON PARK AVE
VERNON AVE
EDNA RD
DORIEN RD
DUPONT RD
SYDNEY RD
CHESTNUT RD
Bwg Gn
GRAYSWOOD GDNS
FARNHAM GDNS
RAINBOW IND EST
FIRSTWAY
B279
BUSHEY RD
A298
B286
MERTON MANS
Allot Gdns
Sports Ctr
Bushey Mead
WEST BARNES LA
BUSHEY CT
GRAND DR
POLESDEN GDNS
STOURHEAD GDNS
SAVILL GDNS
HIDCOTE GDNS
BODNANT GDNS
Sch
Superstore
T Cts
CHURCH WLK
Raynes Park
Sp
Tenn Cts
Pl Fld
WHATLEY AVE
Beverley Park
Drv
A3

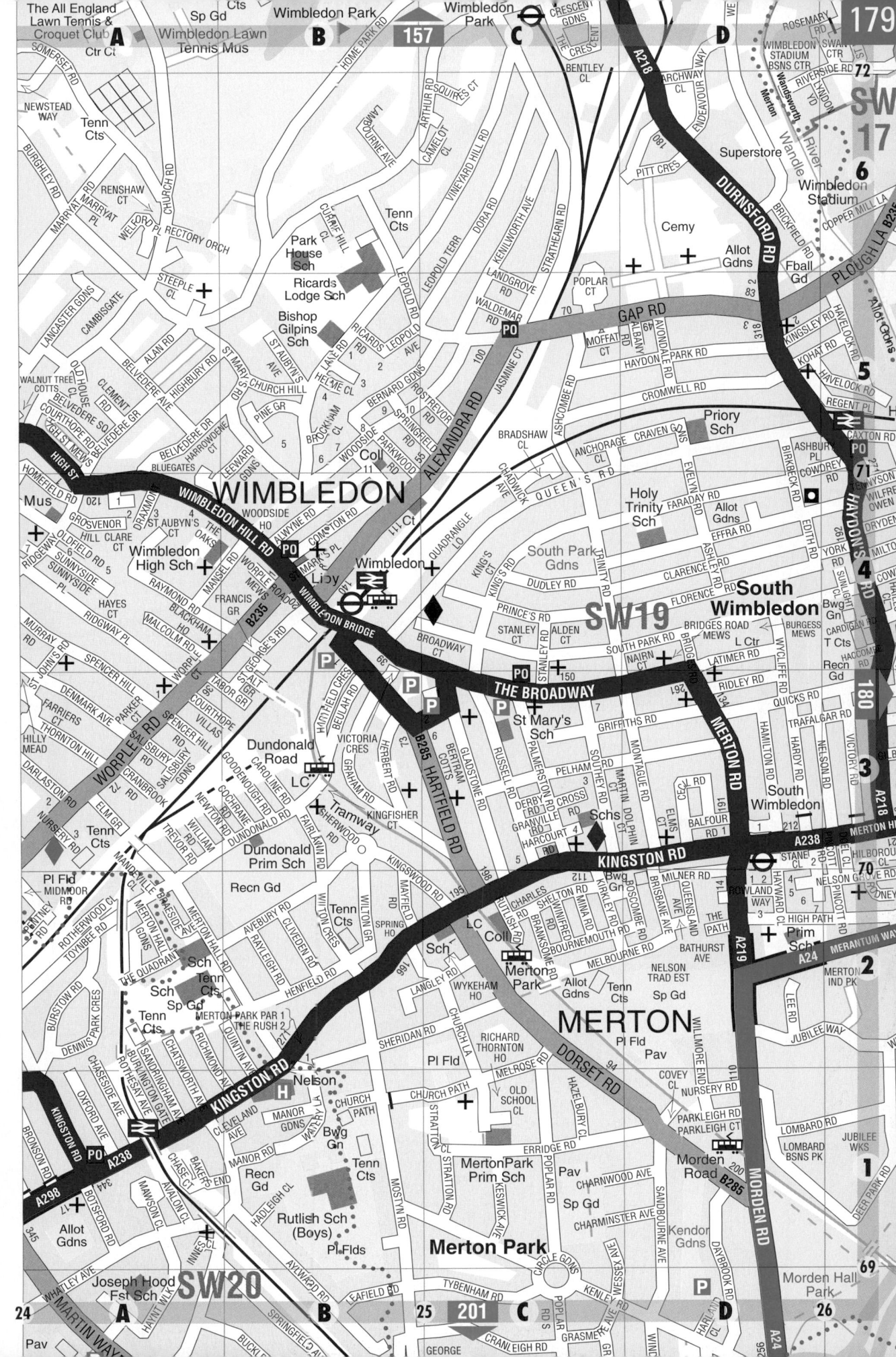
WIMBLEDON
SW19
South Wimbledon
MERTON
Merton Park
SW20
SW17
157
201
180

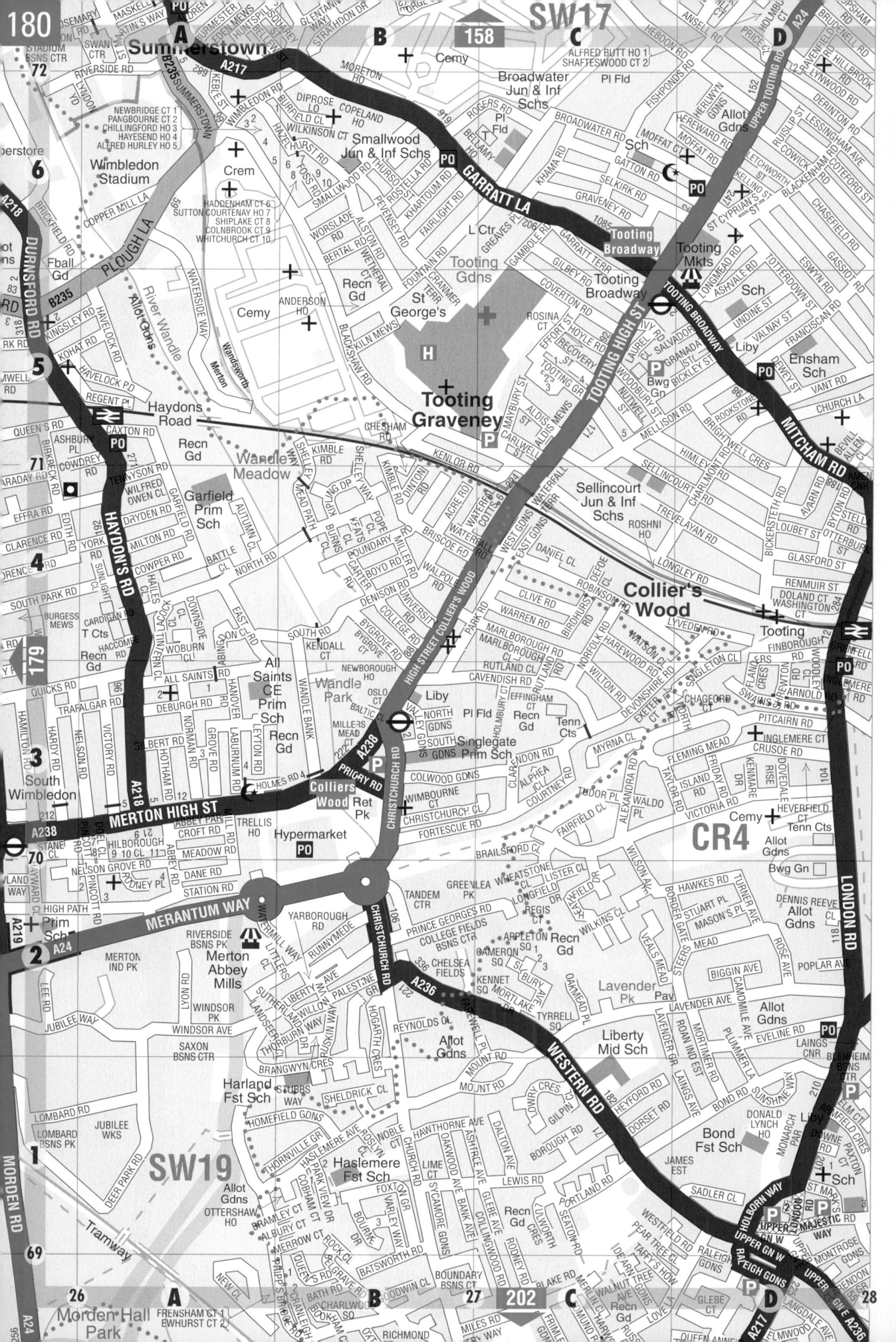
SW17
158
A
B
C
D
Summerstown
A217
Cemy
Broadwater Jun & Inf Schs
Pl Fld
Smallwood Jun & Inf Schs
GARRATT LA
Wimbledon Stadium
Crem
PLOUGH LA
DURNSFORD RD
Fball Gd
River Wandle
Cemy
Tooting Gdns
St George's
Tooting Graveney
Tooting Broadway
Tooting Mkts
TOOTING HIGH ST
UPPER TOOTING RD
TOOTING BROADWAY
Ensham Sch
MITCHAM RD
Haydons Road
Recn Gd
Wandle Meadow
Garfield Prim Sch
Sellincourt Jun & Inf Schs
HAYDON'S RD
HIGH STREET COLLIER'S WOOD
Collier's Wood
Tooting
All Saints CE Prim Sch
Wandle Park
Liby
Singlegate Prim Sch
South Wimbledon
MERTON HIGH ST
Colliers Wood
Ret Pk
Hypermarket
CHRISTCHURCH RD
CR4
LONDON RD
MERANTUM WAY
Merton Abbey Mills
WESTERN RD
Lavender Pk
Liberty Mid Sch
Harland Fst Sch
Haslemere Fst Sch
SW19
Bond Fst Sch
Tramway
MORDEN RD
Morden Hall Park
202
26
27
28
179

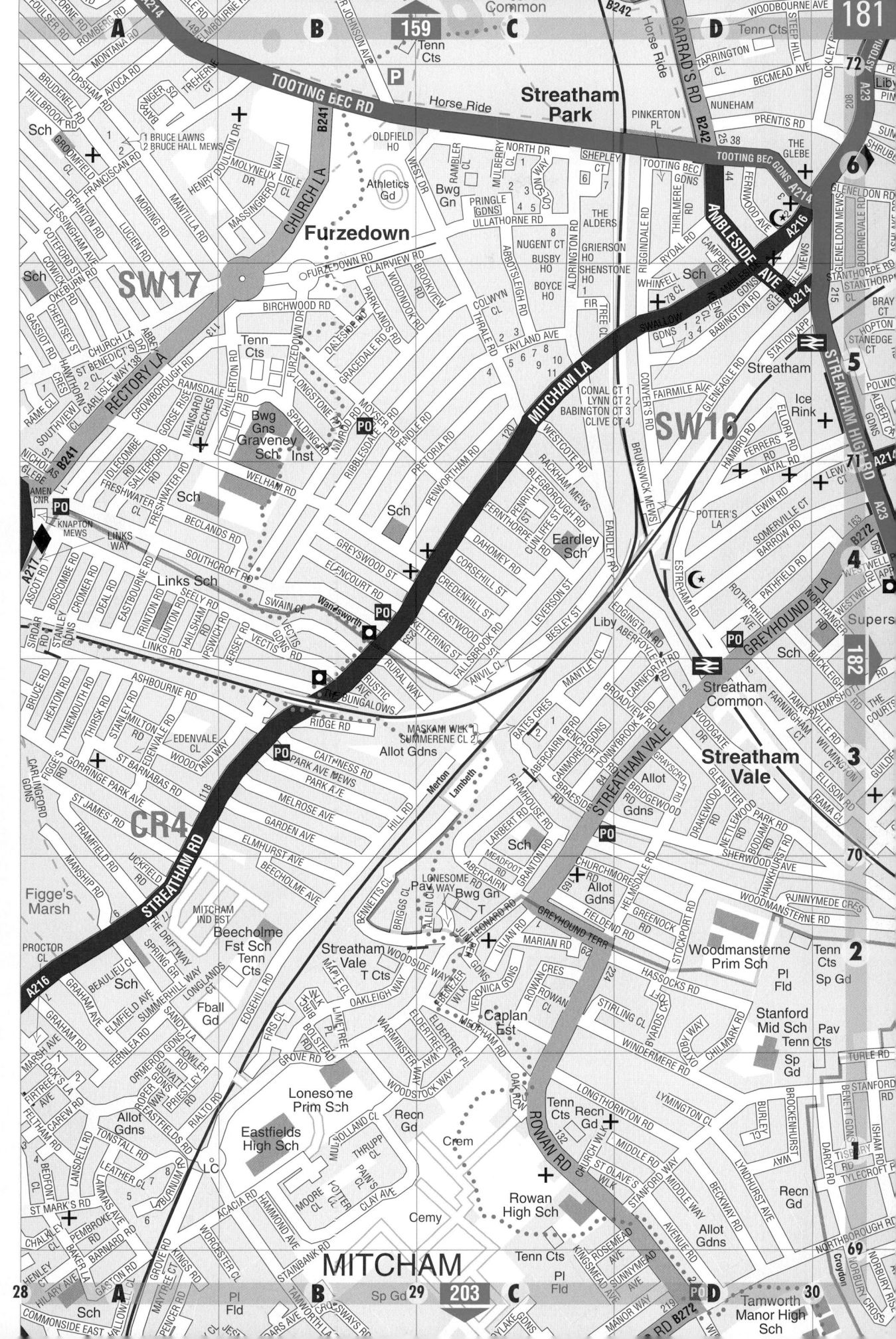
159
203
182
A
B
C
D
28
29
30
72
71
70
69
6
5
4
3
2
1
Streatham Park
Furzedown
SW17
SW16
CR4
Streatham
Streatham Common
Streatham Vale
MITCHAM
Figge's Marsh
Caplan Est
Tooting Bec Common
TOOTING BEC RD
TOOTING BEC GDNS
MITCHAM LA
STREATHAM RD
STREATHAM VALE
STREATHAM HIGH RD
GREYHOUND LA
GREYHOUND TERR
ROWAN RD
CHURCH LA
RECTORY LA
AMBLESIDE AVE
GARRAD'S RD
Horse Ride
Athletics Gd
Bwg Gn
Graveney Sch
Links Sch
Eardley Sch
Ice Rink
Woodmansterne Prim Sch
Stanford Mid Sch
Lonesome Prim Sch
Eastfields High Sch
Beecholme Fst Sch
Rowan High Sch
Tamworth Manor High Sch
Mitcham Ind Est
Crem
Cemy
Recn Gd
Allot Gdns
Tenn Cts
Sch
PO
Liby
Supers
Merton
Lambeth
Wandsworth
Croydon
FURZEDOWN RD
BIRCHWOOD RD
WELHAM RD
BECLANDS RD
SOUTHCROFT RD
LINKS RD
RIDGE RD
CAITHNESS RD
PARK AVE
MELROSE AVE
GARDEN AVE
ELMHURST AVE
BEECHOLME AVE
HILL RD
GORRINGE PARK AVE
ST JAMES' RD
FRAMFIELD RD
MANSHIP RD
GRAHAM RD
FERNLEA RD
EDGEHILL RD
GROVE RD
WOODSTOCK WAY
WINDERMERE RD
HASSOCKS RD
LONGTHORNTON RD
LYMINGTON CL
WOODMANSTERNE RD
SHERWOOD AVE
NORTHBOROUGH RD
PENWORTHAM RD
PRETORIA RD
GREYSWOOD ST
ELLENCOURT RD
KETTERING ST
RURAL WAY
FAYLAND AVE
BABINGTON RD
ESTREHAM RD
ROTHERHILL AVE
PATHFIELD RD
BARROW RD
LEWIN RD
NATAL RD
BUCKLEIGH RD
TANKERVILLE RD
ELLISON RD
DONNYBROOK RD
CANMORE GDNS
BRIDGEWOOD RD
STOCKPORT RD
CHURCHMORE RD
FIELDEND RD
ACACIA RD
HAMMOND AVE
STAINBANK RD
WORCESTER CL
TONSTALL RD
LANSDELL RD
ST MARK'S RD
COMMONSIDE EAST
ASCOT RD
BOSCOMBE RD
CROMER RD
DEAL RD
EASTBOURNE RD
ASHBOURNE RD
THIRSK RD
TYNEMOUTH RD
HEATON RD
BRUCE RD

160
204
181
A
B
C
D
1
2
3
4
5
6
69
70
71
72
30
31
32
STREATHAM
SW16
SE27
SE19
CR7
Streatham Common
Streatham
Streatham Vale
Norbury
STREATHAM HIGH RD
STREATHAM COMM N
CROWN LA
LONDON RD
GREEN LA
KNIGHT'S HILL
ASTORIA PAR
A23
A214
A215
A216
B272
B273
Dunraven Upper Sch
Sunnyhill Prim Sch
Julians Prim Sch
Bishop Thomas Grant RC Sec Sch
St Andrews RC Prim Sch
Crown Lane Prim Sch
St Joseph's RC Coll
Superstore
Immanuel Sch
South London Coll
Norbury Manor Girl's High Sch
Norbury Manor Prim Sch
Kensington Avenue Jun & Inf Schs
St James The Great RC Sch
Stanford Mid Sch
Tamworth Manor High Sch
Norwood Grove
Norbury Park
Ice Rink
Liby
Allot Gdns
Tenn Cts
Bwg Gn
Recn Gd
Pl Fld
Sp Gd
Pav
Horse Ride
NORBURY TRAD EST
THRALE ALMHOS
JAWAHAR BAGH
Lambeth
Croydon
Merton
1 ELPHINSTONE CT
2 RIDLEY CT
3 BLADON CT
4 COMMONSIDE CT
5 SANDERS HO
WOODBOURNE AVE
GRACEFIELD GDNS
BUTTERWORTH CT
PENDENNIS RD
PINFOLD RD
PRENTIS RD
BECMEAD AVE
ANGLES RD
UJIMA HO
SUNNYHILL RD
WELLFIELD RD
GLENELDON RD
STANTHORPE RD
MADEIRA RD
ST ANSELM'S CT
OAKDALE RD
BEECHCROFT CL
HOPTON RD
POLWORTH RD
NEWLANDS CT
VALLEYFIELD RD
BELLTREES GR
ETHERSTONE RD
NORMINGTON CL
ROCKHAMPTON RD
CHESTNUT CL
CHARWOOD
ST JULIAN'S FARM RD
THORNLAW RD
CASEWICK RD
TRUSLOVE RD
LAKEVIEW RD
LEAF GR
WINTON WAY
BEWLYS RD
ROXBURGH RD
DARLINGTON RD
FURNEAUX
HOLDERNESS
CANTERBURY GR
EGREMONT
WOLFINGTON RD
NETTLEFOLD PL
ERNEST
ROTHSCHILD
CHAPEL
RYECROFT RD
HOLLIES CL
GIBSON'S HILL
AVERIL GR
LEAFIELD CL
HOLLMAN GDNS
COVINGTON WAY
CRESCENT WAY
THE CHASE
HILLCOTE AVE
GROVELAND AVE
CHRISTIAN FIELDS
NORBURY HILL
BIGGINWOOD RD
CROFT RD
NORBURY CL
ST OSWALD'S RD
VIRGINIA RD
FLORIDA RD
MARYLAND RD
GEORGIA RD
KENSINGTON AVE
GOLF CL
WILLOWTREE WAY
BUCKINGHAM AVE
HAWTHORN AVE
WESTMINSTER AVE
HIGHBURY AVE
COUNTY RD
NORBURY AVE
NORBURY CRES
CRAIGNISH AVE
DALMENY AVE
DUNBAR AVE
EDERLINE AVE
MELROSE AVE
KINTYRE CL
HEATHERSET GDNS
KUALA GDNS
HEPWORTH RD
ROCHESTER CL
DANBROOK RD
COLMER RD
MARQUEEN TOWERS
HERMITAGE LA
GUILDERSFIELD RD
ARRAGON GDNS
GLENCAIRN RD
KEMPSHOTT RD
BUCKLEIGH RD
TANKERVILLE RD
WILMINGTON CT
ELLISON RD
RUNNYMEDE CRES
SOUTHBROOK RD
COLEBROOK RD
BISHOPS PARK RD
ROCHE RD
FAIRVIEW RD
ABINGDON RD
UPWOOD RD
CROINDENE RD
OAKHILL RD
SCOTT CL
THE MEWS
ST HELEN'S CRES
ST HELEN'S RD
TURLE RD
STANFORD RD
SEMLEY RD
HATCH RD
TYLECROFT RD
NEWLANDS RD
NORTON GDNS
ISHAM RD
BENETT GDNS
TISBURY RD
DARCY RD
BROCKENHURST WAY
LYNDHURST AVE
NORTHBOROUGH RD
NORBURY COURT RD
BEATRICE AVE
POLLARDS HILL N
POLLARDS WOOD RD
NORBURY CROSS
NORBURY RISE
ELGAR AVE
BEECH RD
GREYHOUND LA
WESTWELL ROAD
NORTHANGER RD
PATHFIELD RD
BARROW RD
SOMERVILLE CT
LEWIN RD
NATAL RD
FERRERS RD
ELLORA RD
STREATHAM COMM S
BALDRY GDNS
BRAXTED PK
COPLEY PK
CEDARVILLE GDNS
HEYBRIDGE AVE
COULTHURST CT
HILLDOWN RD
HEATHDENE RD
ST LEONARD'S WLK
STHRATHBROOK RD
BRIAR AVE
BEAUFORT GDNS
COURTLAND AVE
HAREFIELD RD
GRANVILLE GDNS
ACACIA RD
AOSTLE WAY
PARCHMORE WAY
WINDSOR RD
CAMDEN GDNS
THE PINES
WHITE LO
BIGGIN HILL
QUEEN MARY RD
GRECIAN CRES
PRESTON RD
ARNULL'S RD
CROWN PAR
CROWN POINT
JERVISTON GDNS
LAMBERHURST RD
GREENHURST RD
LEIGHAM COURT RD
BENHURST LA
NORMAN CT
VALLEY RD
HARBOROUGH RD
LEITHCOTE GDNS
LEITHCOTE PATH
MILFORD MEWS
CAROLINE CT
CAREW HO
ST PETER'S GDNS
CHICHESTER MEWS
THURLESTONE RD
SELSDON RD
DODBROOKE RD
HAINTHORPE RD
PRIORESS RD
YEOMAN CL
GLENNIE
IVYMOUNT RD
UFFINGTON RD
THURLBY RD
TREDWELL RD
CHEVIOT RD
CHEVIOT GDNS
ST VINCENT CL
DASSETT
CEDAR TREE GR
LINDWAY
EDGE POINT
FAIRLIGHT RD

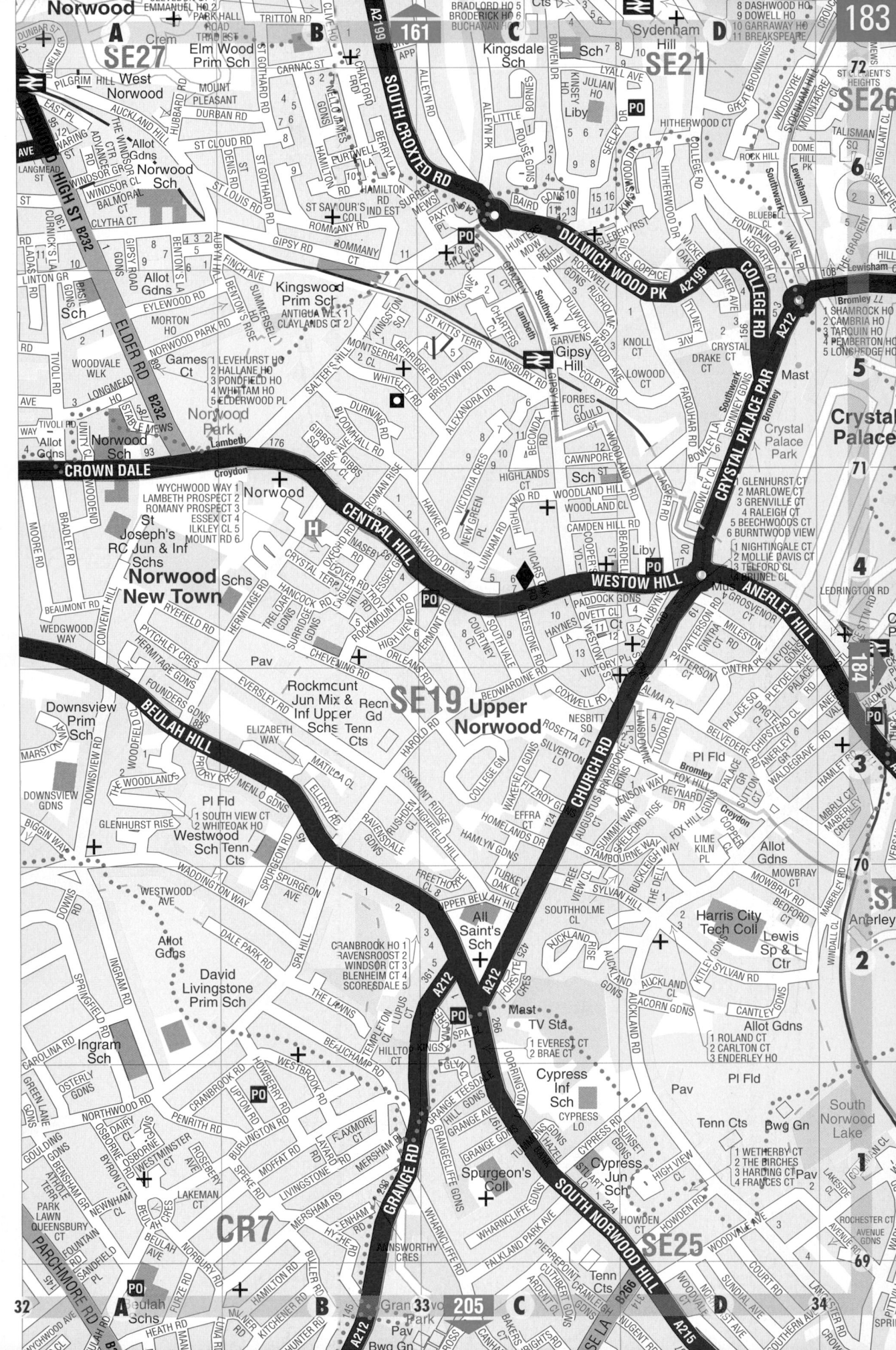
161
Norwood
A
B
C
D
SE27
West Norwood
Elm Wood Prim Sch
Kingsdale Sch
Sydenham Hill
SE21
SE26
72
8 DASHWOOD HO
9 DOWELL HO
10 GARRAWAY HO
11 BREAKSPEARE
SOUTH CROXTED RD
DULWICH WOOD PK
COLLEGE RD
CRYSTAL PALACE PAR
A2199
A212
A199
Norwood Sch
NORWOOD HIGH ST
B232
ELDER RD
Kingswood Prim Sch
Gipsy Hill
Crystal Palace
Crystal Palace Park
Mast
Norwood Park
Norwood Sch
CROWN DALE
CENTRAL HILL
WESTOW HILL
ANERLEY HILL
Norwood
St Joseph's RC Jun & Inf Schs
Norwood New Town
1 GLENHURST CT
2 MARLOWE CT
3 GRENVILLE CT
4 RALEIGH CT
5 BEECHWOODS CT
6 BURNTWOOD VIEW
1 NIGHTINGALE CT
2 MOLLIE DAVIS CT
3 TELFORD CL
4 BRUNEL CL
1 SHAMROCK HO
2 CAMBRIA HO
3 TARQUIN HO
4 PEMBERTON HO
5 LONGHEDGE HO
1 LEVEHURST HO
2 HALLANE HO
3 PONDFIELD HO
4 WHITTAM HO
5 ELDERWOOD PL
WYCHWOOD WAY 1
LAMBETH PROSPECT 2
ROMANY PROSPECT 3
ESSEX CT 4
ILKLEY CL 5
MOUNT RD 6
184
BEULAH HILL
CHURCH RD
SE19
Upper Norwood
Rockmount Jun Mix & Inf Upper Schs
Recn Gd
Tenn Cts
Downsview Prim Sch
Westwood Sch
Pl Fld
1 SOUTH VIEW CT
2 WHITEOAK HO
Allot Gdns
David Livingstone Prim Sch
Ingram Sch
All Saint's Sch
Harris City Tech Coll
Lewis Sp & L Ctr
Anerley
CRANBROOK HO 1
RAVENSROOST 2
WINDSOR CT 3
BLENHEIM CT 4
SCORESDALE 5
Mast
TV Sta
1 EVEREST CT
2 BRAE CT
1 ROLAND CT
2 CARLTON CT
3 ENDERLEY HO
Cypress Inf Sch
Cypress Jun Sch
Spurgeon's Coll
South Norwood Lake
Tenn Cts
Bwg Gn
1 WETHERBY CT
2 THE BIRCHES
3 HARDING CT
4 FRANCES CT
GRANGE RD
SOUTH NORWOOD HILL
CR7
SE25
Beulah Schs
PARCHMORE RD
1
2
3
4
5
6
70
71
69
32
33
34
205
A
B
C
D
A212
A215
B266

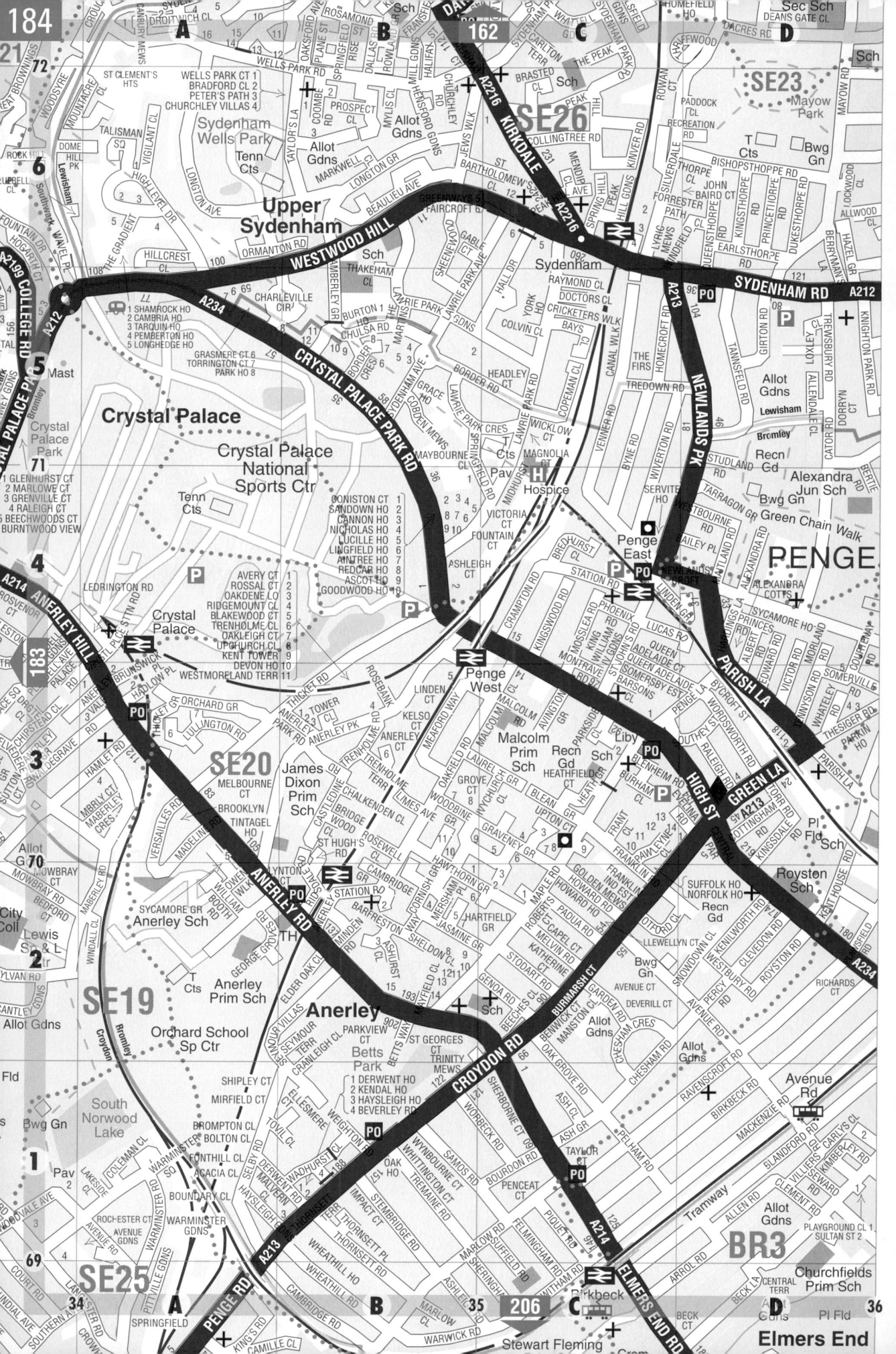
A
B
C
D
162
21
72
6
5
71
4
183
3
70
2
1
69
34
35
206
36
Upper Sydenham
Sydenham
SE26
SE23
Sydenham Wells Park
Crystal Palace
Crystal Palace Park
Crystal Palace National Sports Ctr
Crystal Palace
Penge West
Penge East
PENGE
SE20
Anerley
SE19
SE25
BR3
Birkbeck
Elmers End
Mayow Park
Alexandra Jun Sch
Green Chain Walk
James Dixon Prim Sch
Malcolm Prim Sch
Anerley Sch
Anerley Prim Sch
Orchard School Sp Ctr
South Norwood Lake
Betts Park
Royston Sch
Churchfields Prim Sch
Stewart Fleming
Avenue Rd
Hospice
WESTWOOD HILL
CRYSTAL PALACE PARK RD
KIRKDALE
SYDENHAM RD
NEWLANDS PK
ANERLEY HILL
ANERLEY RD
HIGH ST
GREEN LA
PARISH LA
CROYDON RD
ELMERS END RD
PENGE RD
COLLEGE RD
CRYSTAL PALACE PARADE
A212
A214
A234
A213
A216
A2199
WELLS PARK RD
LAWRIE PARK RD
LAWRIE PARK AVE
LAWRIE PARK GDNS
SYDENHAM AVE
BORDER RD
THICKET RD
ANERLEY PK
MELBOURNE CT
BURMARSH CT
BEECHES CL
WOODBINE GR
WINDALL CL
SELBY RD
THORNSETT RD
WHEATHILL RD
BIRKBECK RD
PELHAM RD
ALLEN RD
ARROL RD
ST JOHN'S RD
QUEEN ADELAIDE RD
VENNER RD
BYNE RD
WIVERTON RD
HOMECROFT RD
TANNSFIELD RD
GIRTON RD
KNIGHTON PARK RD
MAYOW RD
BISHOPSTHOPPE RD
EARLSTHORPE RD
DACRES RD
DEANS GATE CL
Tramway
Lewisham
Bromley
Southwark
Croydon

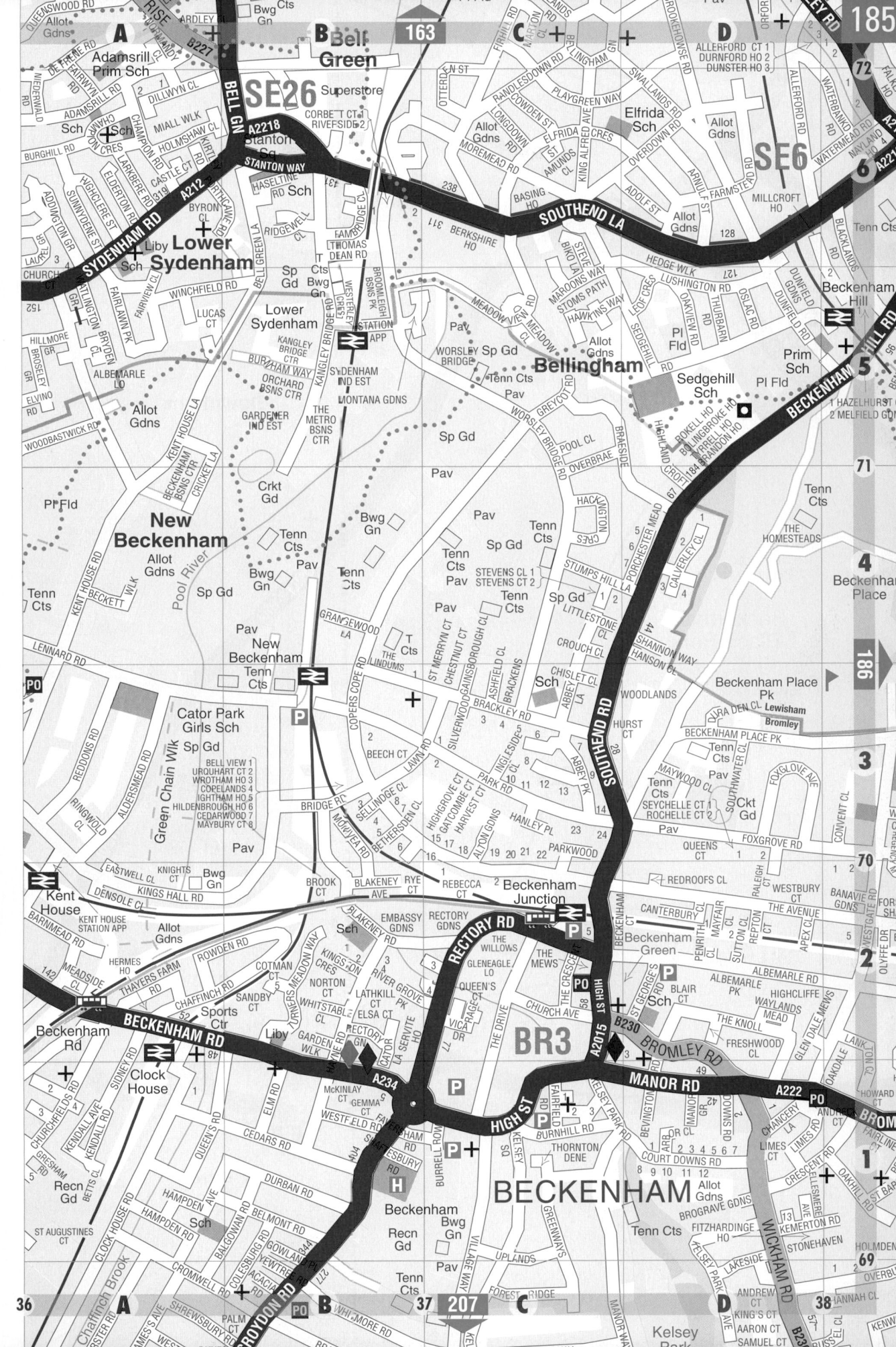
163
A
B
C
D
Bell Green
SE26
SE6
Superstore
Adamsrill Prim Sch
Lower Sydenham
New Beckenham
Bellingham
Beckenham Hill
Sedgehill Sch
Elfrida Sch
Beckenham Place
Beckenham Place Pk
Lewisham
Bromley
Cator Park Girls Sch
Green Chain Wlk
Pool River
Beckenham Junction
Kent House
Clock House
Beckenham Rd
Beckenham Green
BR3
BECKENHAM
Kelsey Park
SYDENHAM RD
SOUTHEND LA
SOUTHEND RD
BECKENHAM HILL RD
BECKENHAM RD
MANOR RD
HIGH ST
RECTORY RD
BROMLEY RD
CROYDON RD
BELL GN
STANTON WAY
WICKHAM RD
A2218
A212
A21
A2015
B230
A234
A222
B227
LENNARD RD
KENT HOUSE RD
BRACKLEY RD
PARK RD
COPERS COPE RD
WORSLEY BRIDGE RD
FOXGROVE RD
ALBEMARLE RD
KINGS HALL RD
CEDARS RD
DURBAN RD
BELMONT RD
COURT DOWNS RD
BURNHILL RD
THE AVENUE
BECKENHAM PLACE PK
186
70
71
69
72
207
36
37
38
1
2
3
4
5
6

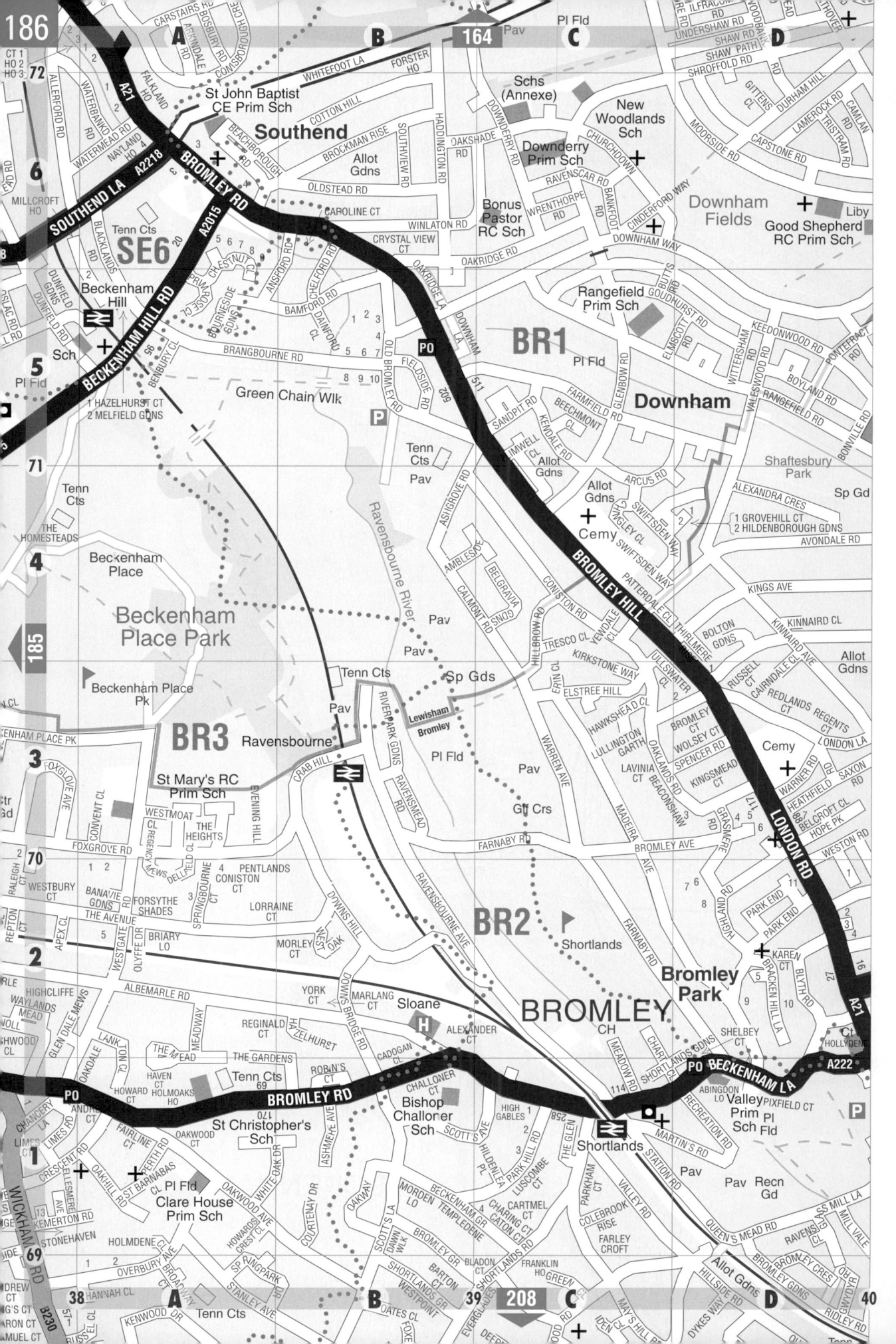
A
B
164
C
D
Pav
Pl Fld
CARSTAIRS RD
BOSBURY RD
CONISBOROUGH CRES
ARKINDALE RD
WHITEFOOT LA
FORSTER HO
ILFRACOMBE RD
UNDERSHAW RD
SHAW RD
SHAW PATH
SHROFFOLD RD
WOODBANK RD
ALLERFORD RD
WATERBANK RD
FALKLAND HO
A21
St John Baptist
CE Prim Sch
COTTON HILL
Schs
(Annexe)
New
Woodlands
Sch
GITTENS CL
DURHAM HILL
LAMEROCK RD
CAMLAN RD
TRISTRAM RD
CAPSTONE RD
MOORSIDE RD
WATERMEAD RD
NAYLAND HO
Southend
BEACHBOROUGH RD
BROCKMAN RISE
SOUTHVIEW RD
HADDINGTON RD
OAKSHADE RD
DOWNDERRY RD
Downderry
Prim Sch
CHURCHDOWN
A2218
SOUTHEND LA
BROMLEY RD
Allot
Gdns
OLDSTEAD RD
RAVENSCAR RD
WRENTHORPE RD
BANKFOOT RD
CINDERFORD WAY
Downham
Fields
Liby
Good Shepherd
RC Prim Sch
MILLCROFT HO
Tenn Cts
BLACKLANDS RD
A2015
CAROLINE CT
WINLATON RD
Bonus
Pastor
RC Sch
CRYSTAL VIEW CT
DOWNHAM WAY
SE6
CHESTNUT CL
PRIMROSE CL
ANSFORD RD
CHELFORD RD
OAKRIDGE LA
OAKRIDGE RD
BUTTS RD
Rangefield
Prim Sch
GOUDHURST RD
DUNFIELD GDNS
DUNFIELD RD
Beckenham
Hill
BECKENHAM HILL RD
BOURNESIDE GDNS
BAMFORD RD
DAINFORD CL
DOWNHAM LA
BR1
ELMSCOTT RD
WITTERSHAM RD
KEEDONWOOD RD
PONTEFRACT RD
Sch
BENBURY CL
BRANGBOURNE RD
OLD BROMLEY RD
PO
Pl Fld
GLENBOW RD
VALESWOOD RD
BOYLAND RD
RANGEFIELD RD
Pl Fld
1 HAZELHURST CT
2 MELFIELD GDNS
Green Chain Wlk
FIELDSIDE RD
209
511
SANDPIT RD
FARMFIELD RD
BEECHMONT CL
KENDALE RD
Downham
BONVILLE RD
P
Tenn
Cts
Pav
RIMWELL CL
Allot
Gdns
Shaftesbury
Park
Tenn
Cts
ASHGROVE RD
Allot
Gdns
ARCUS RD
ALEXANDRA CRES
Sp Gd
THE HOMESTEADS
Ravensbourne River
Cemy
CHINGLEY CL
SWIFTSDEN WAY
1 GROVEHILL CT
2 HILDENBOROUGH GDNS
AVONDALE RD
Beckenham
Place
AMBLESIDE
BELGRAVIA GDNS
CALMONT RD
BROMLEY HILL
PATTERDALE CL
KINGS AVE
Beckenham
Place Park
Pav
CONISTON RD
HILLBROW RD
YEWDALE CL
THIRLMERE
BOLTON GDNS
KINNAIRD CL
KINNAIRD AVE
185
Pav
TRESCO CL
KIRKSTONE WAY
ULLSWATER CL
RUSSELL CT
CAIRNDALE CL
Allot
Gdns
Beckenham Place
Pk
Tenn Cts
Sp Gds
ERIN CL
ELSTREE HILL
REDLANDS CT
REGENTS CT
Pav
RIVERPARK GDNS
Lewisham
Bromley
HAWKSHEAD CL
BROMLEY CT
WOLSEY CT
Cemy
LONDON LA
BECKENHAM PLACE PK
BR3
Ravensbourne
CRAB HILL
Pl Fld
LULLINGTON GARTH
SPENCER RD
KINGSMEAD CT
St Mary's RC
Prim Sch
RAVENSMEAD RD
Pav
WARREN AVE
LAVINIA CT
OAKLANDS RD
BEACONSHAW
WARNER RD
HEATHFIELD RD
SAXON RD
FOXGLOVE AVE
CONVENT CL
WESTMOAT CL
THE HEIGHTS
EVENING HILL
Glf Crs
MADEIRA AVE
GRASMERE RD
LONDON RD
BELCROFT CL
HOPE PK
REGENCY MEWS
DELLFIELD CL
FOXGROVE RD
FARNABY RD
BROMLEY AVE
WESTON RD
RALEIGH CT
WESTBURY CT
PENTLANDS
CONISTON CT
SPRINGBOURNE CT
DOWNS HILL
RAVENSBOURNE AVE
HIGHLAND RD
PARK END
BANAVIE GDNS
FORSYTHE SHADES
LORRAINE CT
THE AVENUE
BR2
REPTON CT
APEX CL
WESTGATE RD
OLYFFE DR
BRIARY LO
MORLEY CT
WEST OAK
Shortlands
FARNABY RD
KAREN CT
BRACKEN HILL LA
BLYTH RD
HIGHCLIFFE
ALBEMARLE RD
YORK CT
MARLANG CT
Sloane
Bromley
Park
WAYLANDS MEAD
GLEN DALE MEWS
MEADWAY
REGINALD CT
HAZELHURST
DOWNS BRIDGE RD
H
ALEXANDER CT
BROMLEY
CH
SHELBEY CT
A21
LANKTON CL
OAKDALE
THE MEAD
THE GARDENS
CADOGAN CL
CHARTWELL
SHORTLANDS GDNS
MEADOW RD
PO
BECKENHAM LA
A222
HOLLYDENE
HAVEN CT
HOLMOAKS HO
Tenn Cts
ROBIN'S CT
CHALLONER CT
ABINGDON LO
PIXFIELD CT
PO
HOWARD CT
BROMLEY RD
Bishop
Challoner
Sch
HIGH GABLES
Valley
Prim
Sch
Pl
Fld
P
CHANCERY LA
LIMES RD
OAKWOOD CT
St Christopher's
Sch
SCOTT'S AVE
HILDENLEA PL
PARK HILL RD
LUSCOMBE CT
THE GLEN
Shortlands
MARTIN'S RD
RECREATION RD
FAIRLINE CT
PERTH RD
CRESCENT RD
OAKHILL RD
ST BARNABAS CL
Pl Fld
WHITE OAK DR
ASHMERE AVE
STATION RD
Pav
Pav
Recn
Gd
ELLESMERE AVE
Clare House
Prim Sch
OAKWOOD AVE
COURTENAY DR
OAKWAY
BECKENHAM GR
MORDEN LO
TEMPLEDENE
CHARING CT
CATON CT
CARTMEL CT
PARKHAM CT
COLEBROOK RISE
FARLEY CROFT
VALLEY RD
QUEEN'S MEAD RD
MILL LA
MILL VALE
KEMERTON RD
STONEHAVEN
HOWARDS CREST CL
SCOTT'S LA
DAWN WALK
BROMLEY GR
RAVENS CL
BROMLEY CRES
WICKHAM RD
HOLMDENE CL
OVERBURY AVE
BROADWAY
SPRINGPARK DR
BARTON CT
BLADON CT
SHORTLANDS RD
FRANKLIN HO
GREEN
Allot Gdns
HILLSIDE RD
BROMLEY GDNS
GWYDYR RD
38
A
STANLEY AVE
B
39
208
C
D
40
HANNAH CL
Tenn Cts
KENWOOD DR
OATES CL
WESTPOINT
SHORTLANDS GR
EVERGLADE
FOXES
MAY'S HILL RD
DYKES WAY
RIDLEY RD
B230
72
71
70
69
6
5
4
3
2
1

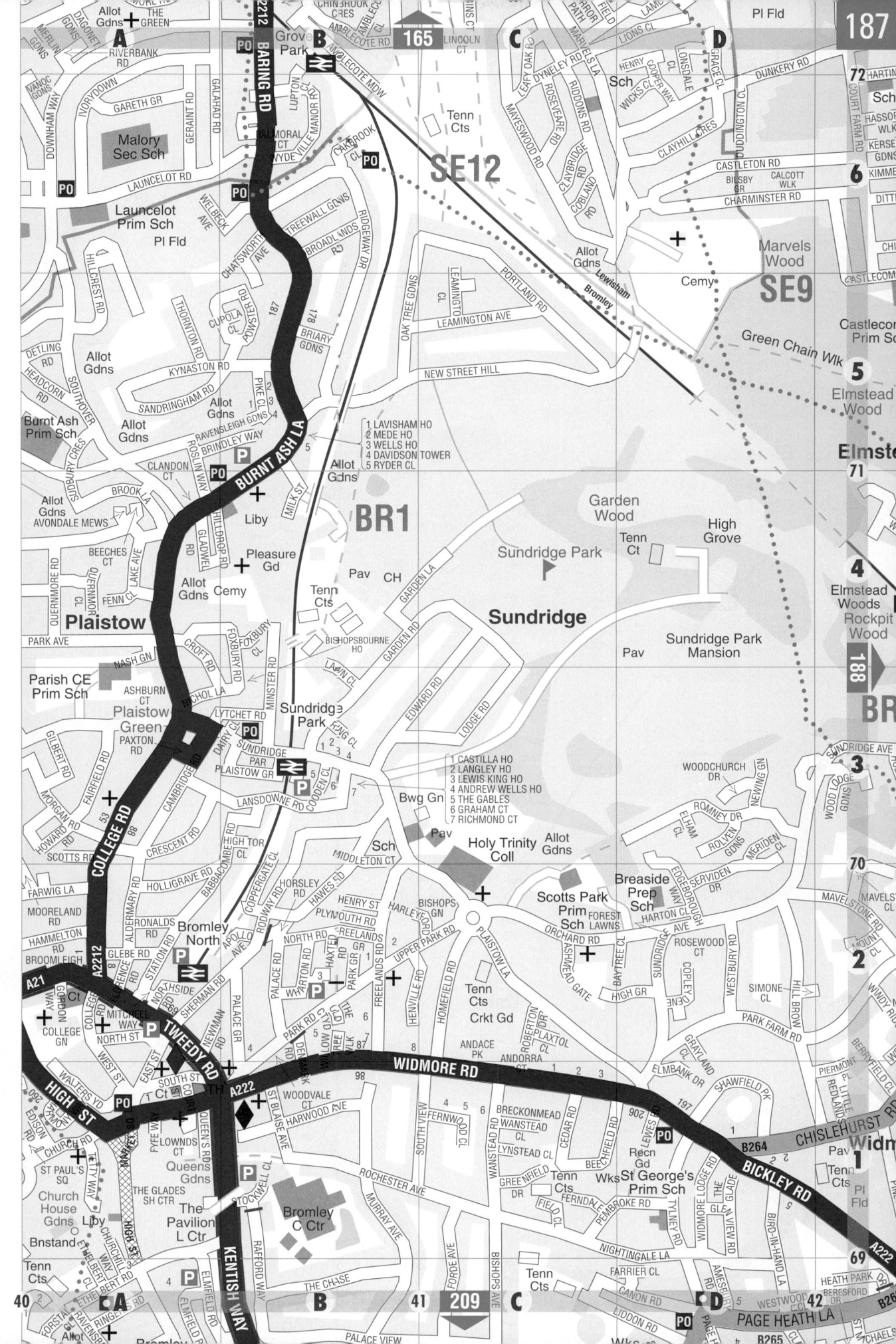
A
B
C
D
165
209
188
SE12
SE9
BR1
Grove Park
Plaistow
Sundridge
Sundridge Park
Sundridge Park Mansion
Plaistow Green
Bromley North
Malory Sec Sch
Launcelot Prim Sch
Burnt Ash Prim Sch
Parish CE Prim Sch
Holy Trinity Coll
Scotts Park Prim Sch
Breaside Prep Sch
St George's Prim Sch
Castlecombe Prim Sch
Garden Wood
High Grove
Marvels Wood
Elmstead Wood
Elmstead Woods
Rockpit Wood
Green Chain Wlk
Pleasure Gd
Bromley C Ctr
The Pavilion L Ctr
The Glades Sh Ctr
Queens Gdns
Church House Gdns
Lewisham
Bromley
BARING RD
BURNT ASH LA
COLLEGE RD
WIDMORE RD
BICKLEY RD
CHISLEHURST RD
HIGH ST
TWEEDY RD
KENTISH WAY
PAGE HEATH LA
LAUNCELOT RD
NEW STREET HILL
LEAMINGTON AVE
PORTLAND RD
OAK TREE GDNS
RIDGEWAY DR
GARDEN LA
GARDEN RD
EDWARD RD
LODGE RD
PLAISTOW LA
HOMEFIELD RD
HENVILLE RD
UPPER PARK RD
FREELANDS RD
PALACE RD
PALACE GR
ROCHESTER AVE
NIGHTINGALE LA
SUNDRIDGE AVE
ORCHARD RD
PARK FARM RD
WESTBURY RD
HILL BROW
CASTLETON RD
CHARMINSTER RD
DUNKERY RD
CLAYHILL CRES
KYNASTON RD
SANDRINGHAM RD
BRINDLEY WAY
BROOK LA
PARK AVE
NASH GN
MINSTER RD
LANSDOWNE RD
CRESCENT RD
HOLLIGRAVE RD
MOORELAND RD
HAMMELTON RD
BROOMLEIGH
GLEBE RD
STATION RD
SHERMAN RD
NEWMAN RD
MIDDLETON CT
1 LAVISHAM HO
2 MEDE HO
3 WELLS HO
4 DAVIDSON TOWER
5 RYDER CL
1 CASTILLA HO
2 LANGLEY HO
3 LEWIS KING HO
4 ANDREW WELLS HO
5 THE GABLES
6 GRAHAM CT
7 RICHMOND CT
40
41
42
69
70
71
72
1
2
3
4
5
6

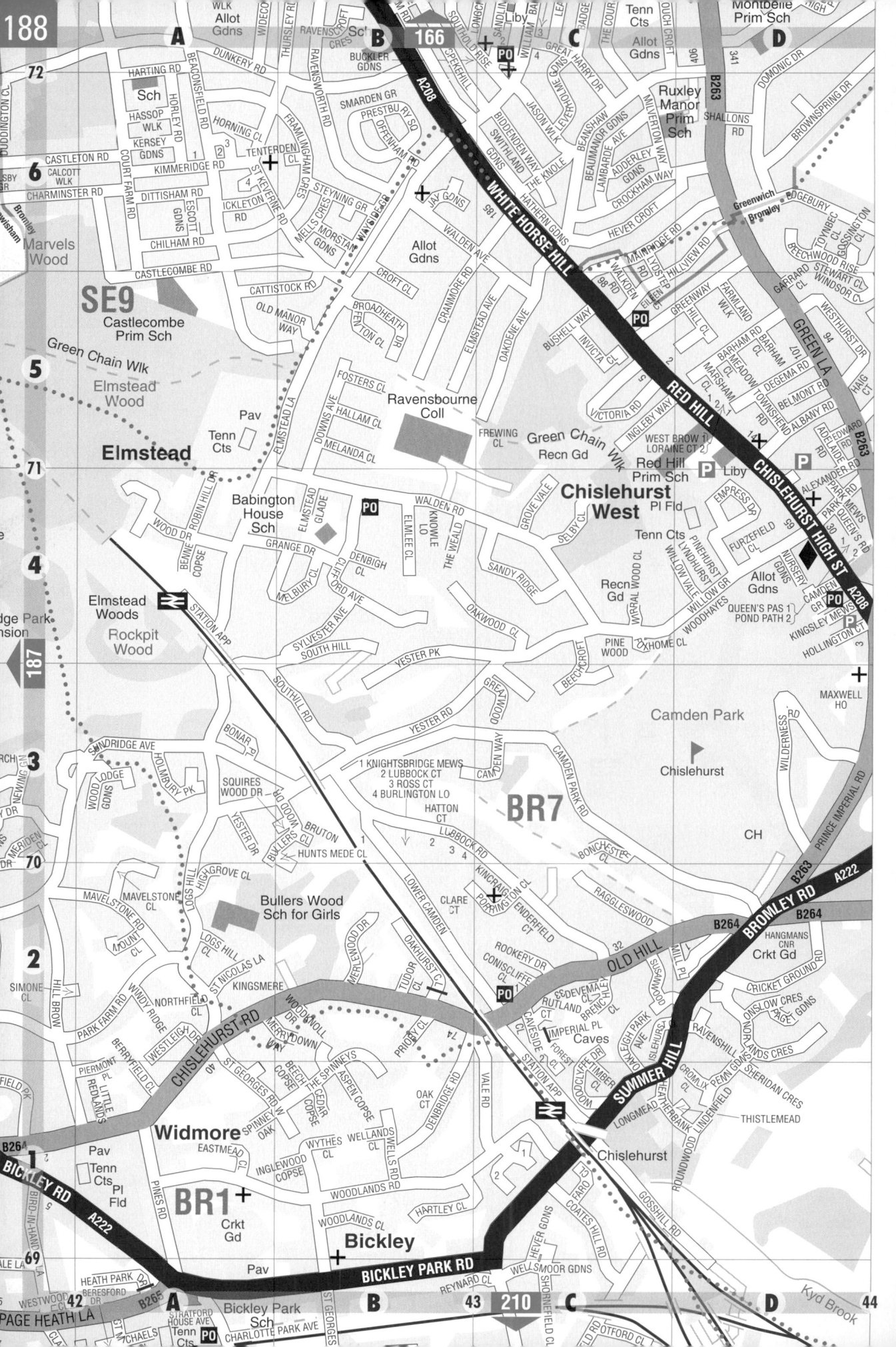
166
A
B
C
D
72
6
5
71
4
3
70
2
1
69
187
42
43
210
44
SE9
BR7
BR1
Elmstead
Chislehurst West
Widmore
Bickley
Chislehurst
Castlecombe Prim Sch
Green Chain Wlk
Elmstead Wood
Marvels Wood
Elmstead Woods
Rockpit Wood
Ravensbourne Coll
Babington House Sch
Red Hill Prim Sch
Ruxley Manor Prim Sch
Montbelle Prim Sch
Bullers Wood Sch for Girls
Camden Park
Chislehurst
Caves
Recn Gd
Allot Gdns
Tenn Cts
Pav
Crkt Gd
Pl Fld
Bickley Park Sch
WHITE HORSE HILL
RED HILL
CHISLEHURST HIGH ST
A208
B263
GREEN LA
BROMLEY RD
A222
B264
OLD HILL
SUMMER HILL
CHISLEHURST RD
BICKLEY RD
BICKLEY PARK RD
PAGE HEATH LA
B265
CASTLETON RD
KIMMERIDGE RD
CHARMINSTER RD
DITTISHAM RD
CHILHAM RD
CASTLECOMBE RD
COURT FARM RD
BEACONSFIELD RD
DUNKERY RD
HARTING RD
ELMSTEAD LA
GRANGE DR
WALDEN RD
WALDEN AVE
STATION APP
SOUTHILL RD
YESTER RD
YESTER PK
SUNDRIDGE AVE
LOWER CAMDEN
CAMDEN PARK RD
WOODLANDS RD
WILDERNESS RD
PRINCE IMPERIAL RD
GOSSHILL RD
Kyd Brook
Greenwich
Bromley
1 KNIGHTSBRIDGE MEWS
2 LUBBOCK CT
3 ROSS CT
4 BURLINGTON LO
WEST BROW 1
LORAINE CT 2
QUEEN'S PAS 1
POND PATH 2

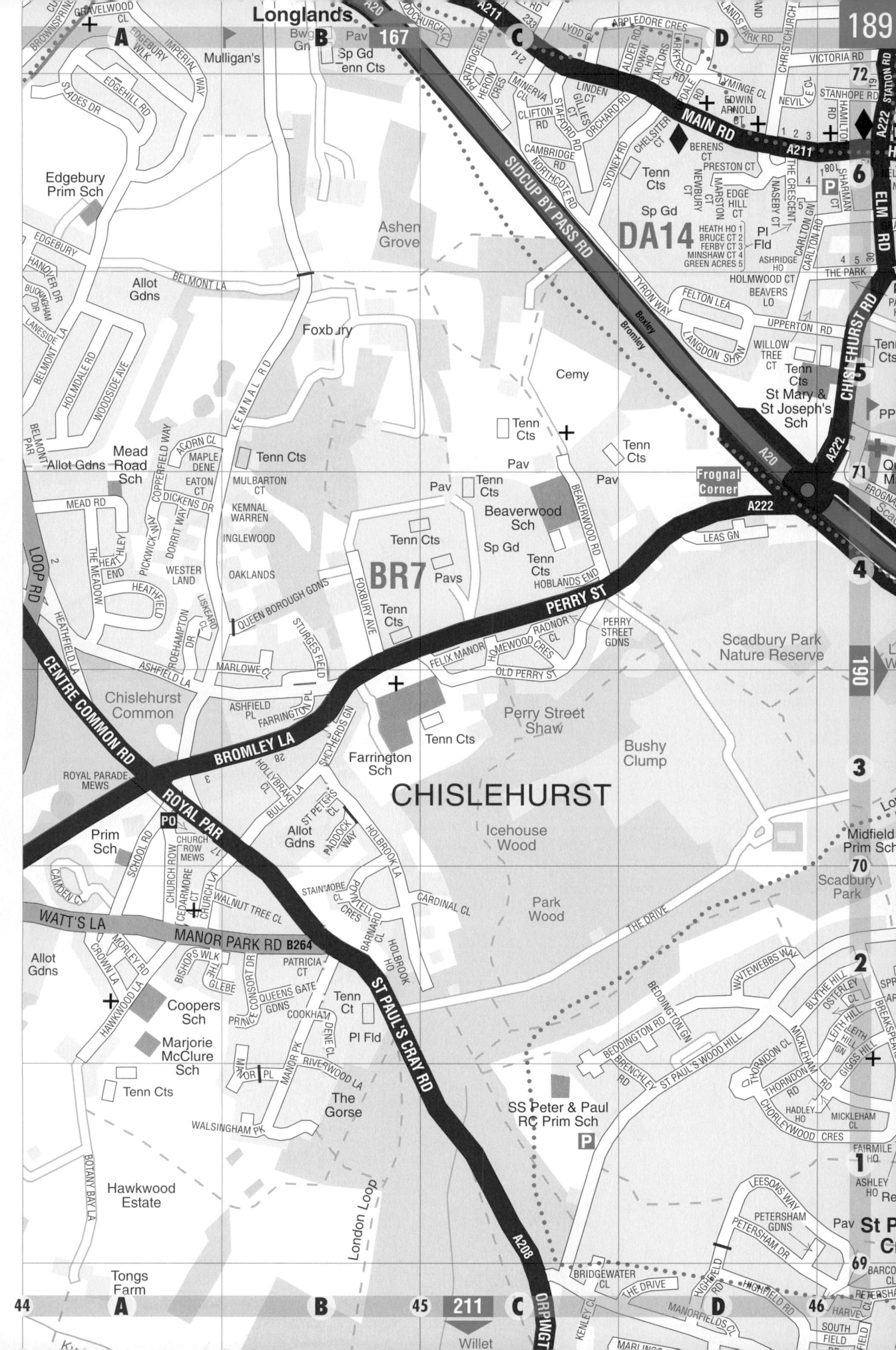
Longlands
Mulligan's
Edgebury Prim Sch
Allot Gdns
Ashen Grove
Foxbury
Cemy
Tenn Cts
Pav
Beaverwood Sch
Sp Gd
BR7
DA14
Pavs
Mead Road Sch
Allot Gdns
Chislehurst Common
Farrington Sch
CHISLEHURST
Perry Street Shaw
Bushy Clump
Scadbury Park Nature Reserve
Icehouse Wood
Park Wood
Prim Sch
Coopers Sch
Marjorie McClure Sch
The Gorse
Pl Fld
SS Peter & Paul RC Prim Sch
Hawkwood Estate
Tongs Farm
London Loop
Frognal Corner
St Mary & St Joseph's Sch
Midfield Prim Sch
Scadbury Park
SIDCUP BY PASS RD
MAIN RD
PERRY ST
BROMLEY LA
CENTRE COMMON RD
ROYAL PAR
ST PAUL'S CRAY RD
MANOR PARK RD B264
WATT'S LA
CHISLEHURST RD
ELM RD
KEMNAL RD
LOOP RD
A20
A211
A222
A208
167
190
211
44
45
46
69
70
71
72
A
B
C
D
1
2
3
4
5
6

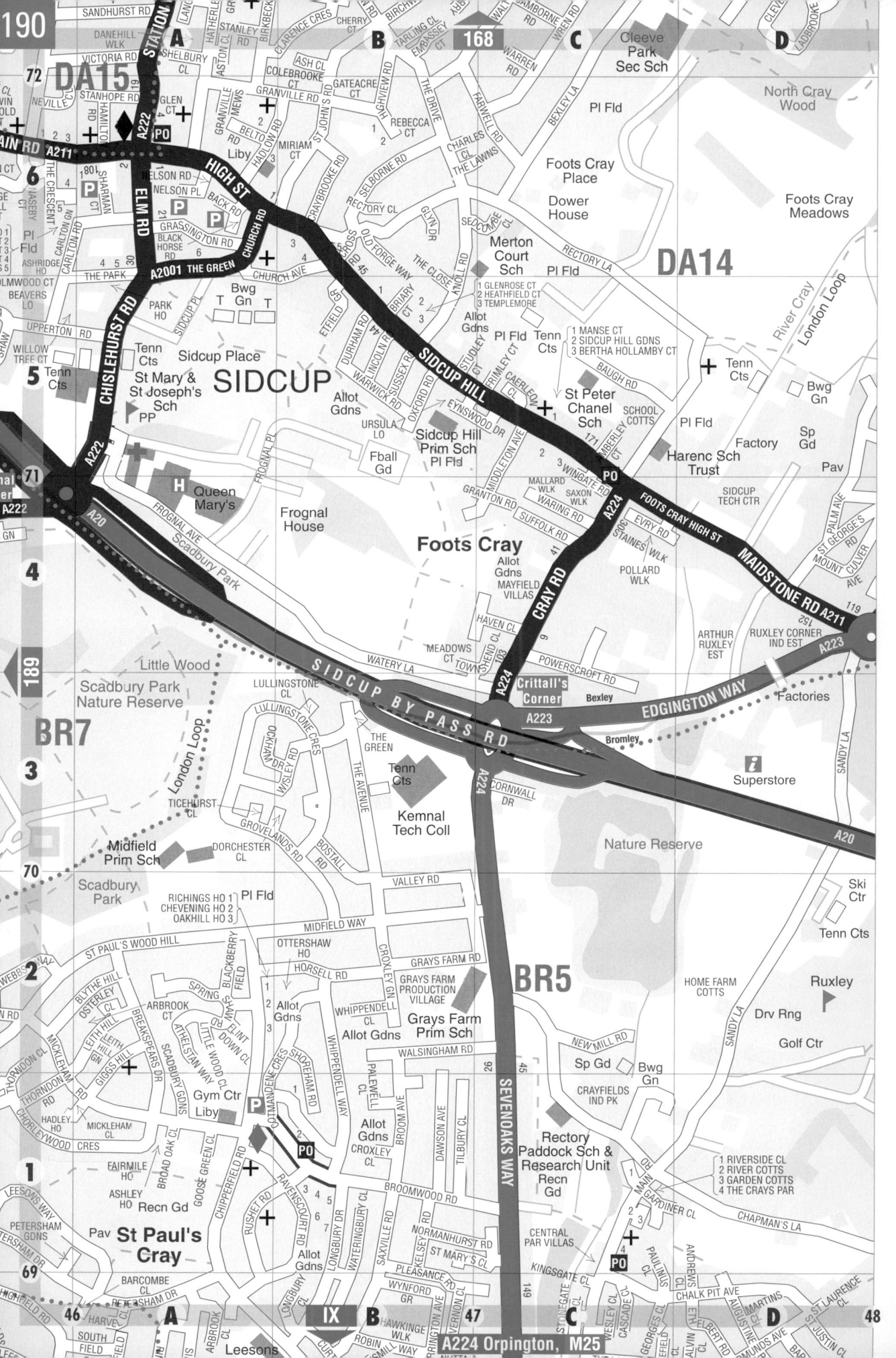

A
B
C
D
168
189
DA15
DA14
BR7
BR5
SIDCUP
Foots Cray
St Paul's Cray
Cleeve Park Sec Sch
North Cray Wood
Foots Cray Place
Dower House
Foots Cray Meadows
Merton Court Sch
Pl Fld
River Cray
London Loop
Sidcup Place
St Mary & St Joseph's Sch
Queen Mary's
Frognal House
Scadbury Park
Little Wood
Scadbury Park Nature Reserve
Sidcup Hill Prim Sch
St Peter Chanel Sch
Harenc Sch Trust
Sidcup Tech Ctr
Arthur Ruxley Est
Ruxley Corner Ind Est
Crittall's Corner
Bexley
Bromley
Factories
Superstore
Kemnal Tech Coll
Nature Reserve
Midfield Prim Sch
Grays Farm Production Village
Grays Farm Prim Sch
Home Farm Cotts
Ruxley
Drv Rng
Golf Ctr
Ski Ctr
Tenn Cts
Crayfields Ind Pk
Rectory Paddock Sch & Research Unit
Recn Gd
Central Par Villas
Gym Ctr
Liby
Allot Gdns
Bwg Gn
Sp Gd
Fball Gd
Pav
Leesons
HIGH ST
ELM RD
CHISLEHURST RD
STATION RD
SIDCUP HILL
FOOTS CRAY HIGH ST
MAIDSTONE RD A211
CRAY RD
SIDCUP BY PASS RD
EDGINGTON WAY
SEVENOAKS WAY
FROGNAL AVE
WATERY LA
RECTORY LA
BEXLEY LA
SANDY LA
MIDFIELD WAY
ST PAUL'S WOOD HILL
GRAYS FARM RD
HORSELL RD
WALSINGHAM RD
BROOMWOOD RD
CHAPMAN'S LA
A20
A222
A223
A224
A211
A2001
A224 Orpington, M25
IX
46
47
48
69
70
71
72
1
2
3
4
5
6

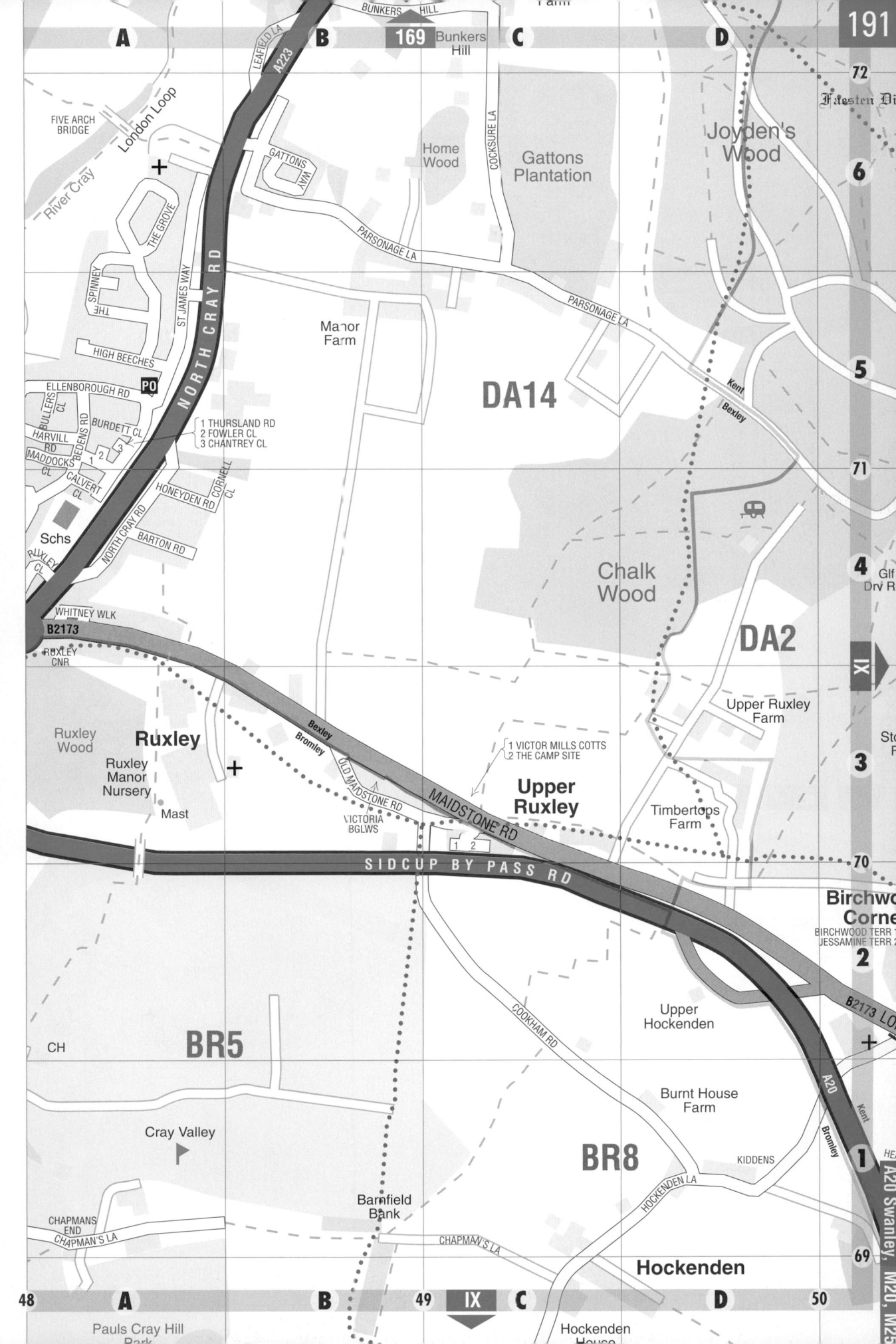
A
B
C
D
169
Bunkers Hill
BUNKERS HILL
LEAFIELD LA
A223
FIVE ARCH BRIDGE
London Loop
River Cray
GATTONS WAY
Home Wood
COCKSURE LA
Gattons Plantation
Joyden's Wood
Faesten Di
72
6
THE GROVE
PARSONAGE LA
THE SPINNEY
ST JAMES WAY
NORTH CRAY RD
Manor Farm
PARSONAGE LA
HIGH BEECHES
5
DA14
Kent
Bexley
ELLENBOROUGH RD
PO
BULLERS CL
BEDENS RD
BURDETT CL
HARVILL RD
MADDOCKS CL
CALVERT CL
1 THURSLAND RD
2 FOWLER CL
3 CHANTREY CL
HONEYDEN RD
CORNELL CL
71
Schs
NORTH CRAY RD
BARTON RD
RUXLEY CL
Chalk Wood
4
Glf Drv R
WHITNEY WLK
B2173
RUXLEY CNR
DA2
IX
Upper Ruxley Farm
Ruxley Wood
Ruxley
Ruxley Manor Nursery
Bexley
Bromley
1 VICTOR MILLS COTTS
2 THE CAMP SITE
3
OLD MAIDSTONE RD
Upper Ruxley
MAIDSTONE RD
Timbertops Farm
Mast
VICTORIA BGLWS
70
SIDCUP BY PASS RD
Birchwo Corne
BIRCHWOOD TERR
JESSAMINE TERR
2
B2173 LO
Upper Hockenden
COOKHAM RD
CH
BR5
A20
Kent
Bromley
Burnt House Farm
Cray Valley
BR8
KIDDENS
1
HOCKENDEN LA
Barnfield Bank
CHAPMANS END
CHAPMAN'S LA
CHAPMAN'S LA
Hockenden
69
A20 Swanley, M20, M25
48
49
IX
50
Pauls Cray Hill Park
Hockenden House

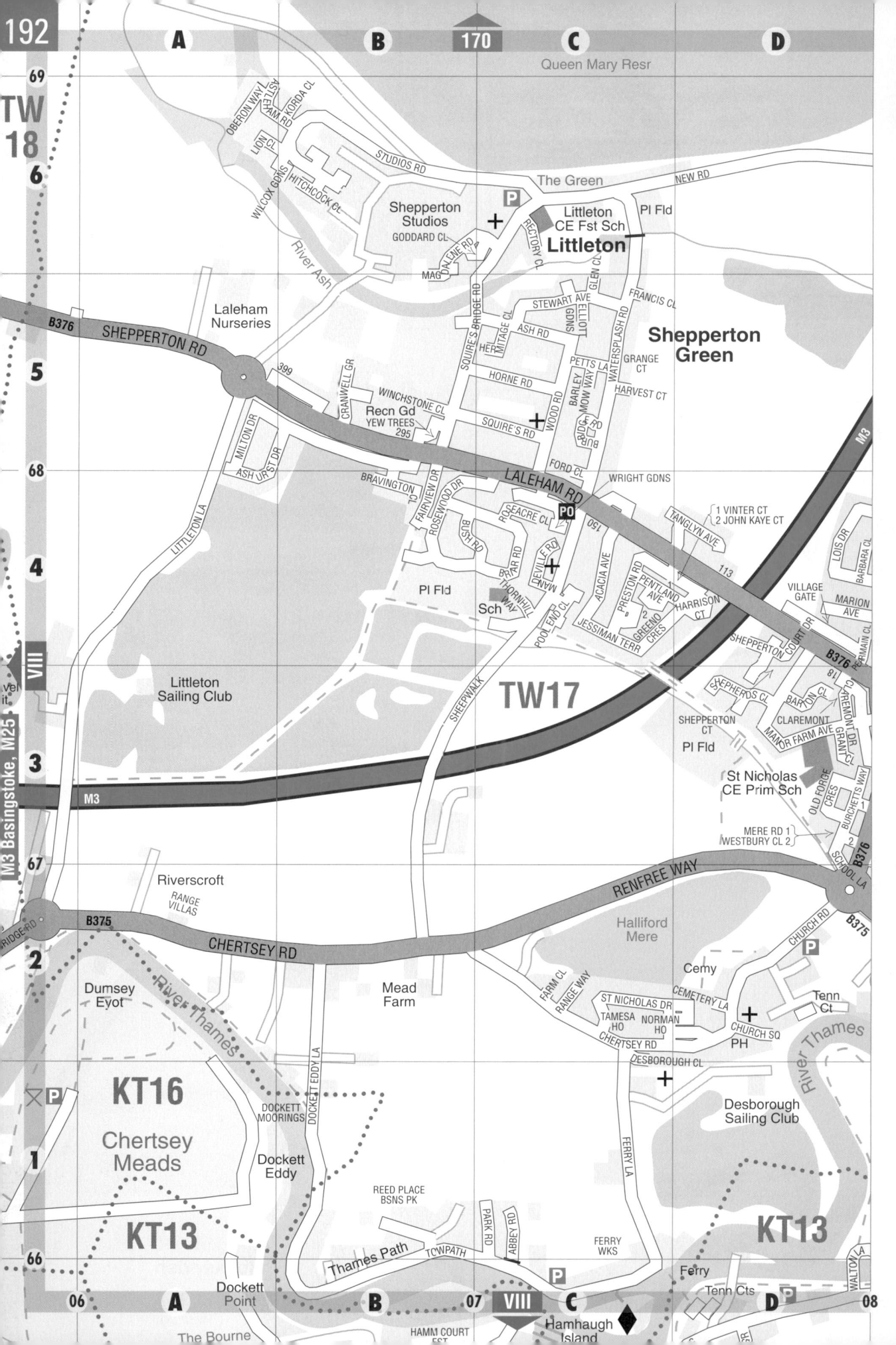
A
B
170
C
D
Queen Mary Resr
TW 18
Shepperton Studios
Littleton CE Fst Sch
Littleton
Laleham Nurseries
SHEPPERTON RD
LALEHAM RD
Shepperton Green
Recn Gd
Pl Fld
Sch
Littleton Sailing Club
TW17
M3
St Nicholas CE Prim Sch
Riverscroft
CHERTSEY RD
RENFREE WAY
Halliford Mere
Cemy
Dumsey Eyot
River Thames
Mead Farm
KT16
Chertsey Meads
Dockett Eddy
KT13
Desborough Sailing Club
Thames Path
Dockett Point
Ferry
Hamhaugh Island
The Bourne
M3 Basingstoke, M25
VIII

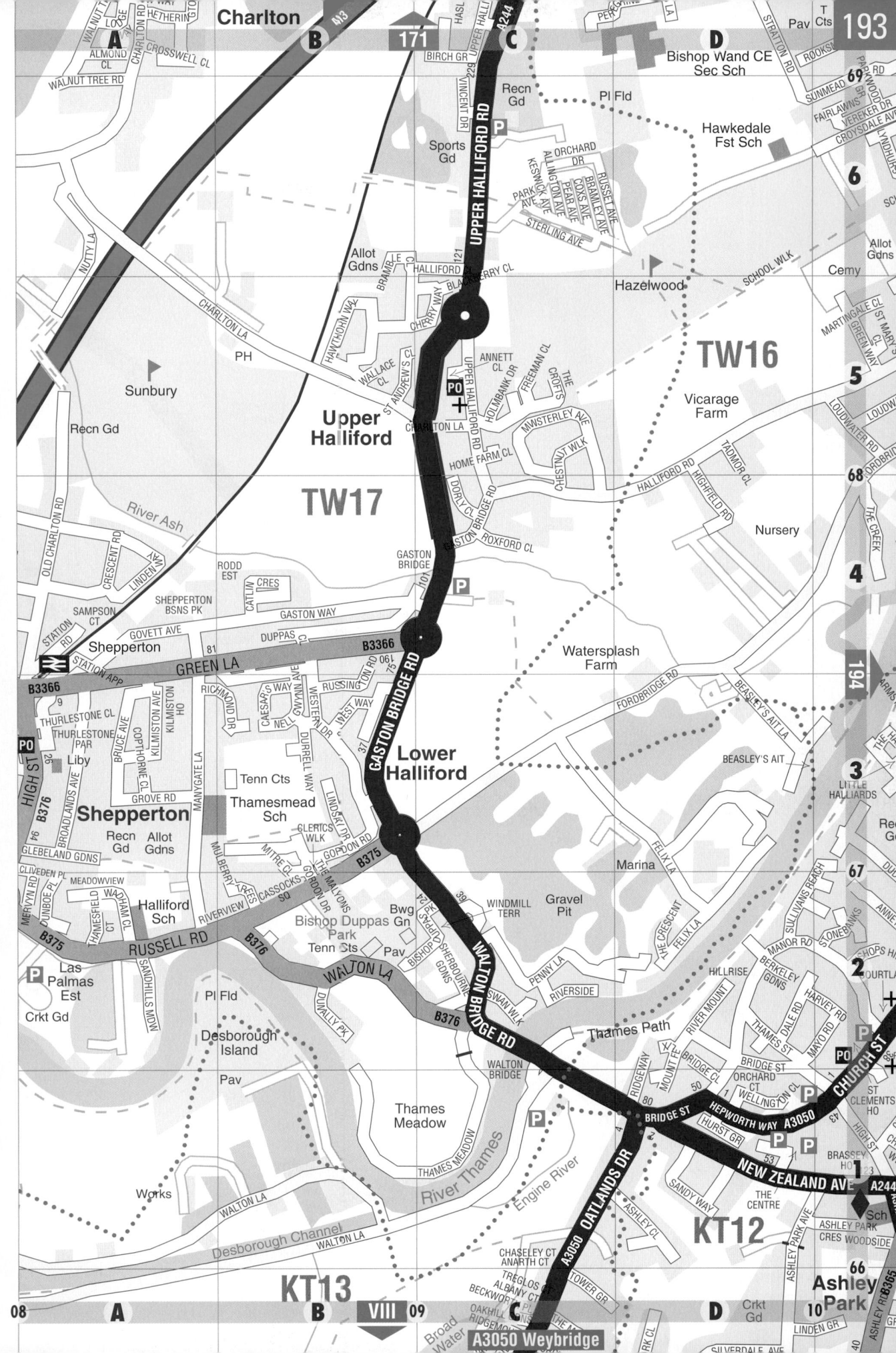
Charlton
171
A
B
C
D
A244
413
Walnut Tree Rd
Almond Cl
Crosswell Cl
Charlton Rd
Hetherington
Birch Gr
Vincent Dr
Upper Halliford Rd
Bishop Wand CE Sec Sch
Pl Fld
Recn Gd
Sports Gd
Hawkedale Fst Sch
Stratton Rd
Sunmead Rd
Fairlawns
Vereker Dr
Croysdale Ave
69
6
Orchard Dr
Allington Ave
Keswick Ave
Park Ave
Pear Ave
Coxs Ave
Bramley Ave
Russet Ave
Sterling Ave
Nutty La
Allot Gdns
Halliford Cl
Blackberry Cl
Bramble Cl
Cherry Way
Hawthorn Way
Wallace Cl
St Andrew's Cl
Charlton La
PH
Sunbury
Recn Gd
Hazelwood
School Wlk
Allot Gdns
Cemy
Martingale Cl
St Mary's Cl
Green Way
TW16
5
Annett Cl
Holmbank Dr
Freeman Cl
The Crofts
PO
Upper Halliford
Charlton La
Misterley Ave
Chestnut Wlk
Home Farm Cl
Vicarage Farm
Loudwater Rd
Halliford Rd
Tadmor Cl
Highfield Rd
68
TW17
River Ash
Old Charlton Rd
Crescent Rd
Linden Way
Dorly Cl
Gaston Bridge Rd
Roxford Cl
Gaston Bridge
Nursery
The Creek
4
Rodd Est
Catlin Cres
Shepperton Bsns Pk
Sampson Ct
Gaston Way
Station Rd
Govett Ave
Duppas Cl
B3366
Shepperton
Green La
Station App
Watersplash Farm
Fordbridge Rd
194
B3366
Thurlestone Cl
Thurlestone Par
Richmond Dr
Caesar's Way
Nell Gwynn Ave
Western Dr
Russington Rd
West Way
Kilmiston Ave
Kilmiston Ho
Bruce Ave
Copthorne Cl
Durrell Way
Gaston Bridge Rd
Beasley's Ait La
Beasley's Ait
3
Little Halliards
PO
High St
Liby
Broadlands Ave
Tenn Cts
Manygate La
Grove Rd
Lower Halliford
Shepperton
Thamesmead Sch
Lindsay Dr
B376
Recn Gd
Allot Gdns
Clerics Wlk
Gordon Rd
Glebeland Gdns
Mulberry Trees
Mitre Cl
Cassocks Sq
Gordon Dr
The Malyons
B375
Marina
Felix La
Recn Gd
67
Cliveden Pl
Meadowview
Mervyn Rd
Dunboe Pl
Thamesfield Ct
Wadham Cl
Halliford Sch
Riverview
Bishop Duppas Park
Bwg Gn
Upper Sherbourne Gdns
Windmill Terr
Gravel Pit
Sullivans Reach
Stonebanks
B375
Russell Rd
Tenn Cts
Pav
Bishop Ct
Walton Bridge Rd
The Crescent
Felix La
Manor Rd
Berkeley Gdns
Hillrise
2
Las Palmas Est
Sandhills Mdw
B376
Walton La
Dunally Pk
Penny La
Riverside
Swan Wlk
River Mount
Harvey Rd
Dale Rd
Mayo Rd
Crkt Gd
Pl Fld
B376
Thames Path
Thames St
Desborough Island
Walton Bridge
Ridgeway
Mount Pl
Bridge Cl
Bridge St
Orchard Ct
Wellington Cl
PO
Church St
St Clements Ho
Pav
Thames Meadow
Bridge St
Hepworth Way
A3050
Hurst Gr
High St
Brassey Ho
New Zealand Ave
1
A244
Thames Meadow
River Thames
Engine River
Sandy Way
The Centre
Works
Walton La
Oatlands Dr
Ashley Cl
KT12
Ashley Park Ave
Ashley Park Cres
Woodside
Desborough Channel
Walton La
A3050
Chaseley Ct
Anarth Ct
Treglos Ct
Albany Ct
Beckworth Pl
Tower Gr
66
Ashley Park
KT13
08
A
B
VIII
09
C
D
Crkt Gd
10
Linden Gr
Broad Water
A3050 Weybridge
B365

172
193
SUNBURY
TW16
TW17
KT12
KT 8
WALTON-ON-THAMES
River Thames
Thames Path
Sunbury Lock
Sunbury Ct Island
Beauclerc Cty Inf Sch
Hawkedale Fst Sch
The Walled Garden
Church Villa
Cemy
Allot Gdns
Vicarage Farm
Nursery
Wheatley's Ait
Fball Gd
Leisure Ctr
Apps Court Farm
Rivernook Farm
Bramble Hill Farm
Knight Resr
Queen Elizabeth 2 Storage Resr
Thamesfield Farm
Recn Gd
Thames View Ho
Tenn Cts
Swansmere Sch
Ashley Park
Rydens
Walton
A244 Esher
HURST RD
A3050
WALTON RD
B369
TERRACE RD
CHURCH ST
HERSHAM RD
NEW ZEALAND AVE
HIGH ST
ASHLEY RD
B365
THAMES ST
GREEN ST
SCHOOL WALK
HALLIFORD RD
FORDBRIDGE RD
WILLOW WAY
THE CREEK
WATERSIDE DR
VANBRUGH DR
COTTIMORE LA
STUART AVE
SUNBURY LA
1 RIVERMEAD HO
2 CASTLE WLK
3 ELIZABETH CT
1 LUSHINGTON HO
2 LYNDE HO
3 CROXALL HO
4 KIRBY WAY
1 RODNEY CL
2 EDGEHILL CT
3 WORCESTER CT
4 DUNBAR CT
1 RYLTON HO
2 BLATCHFORD CT
A B C D
10 11 12
1 2 3 4 5 6
66 67 68 69

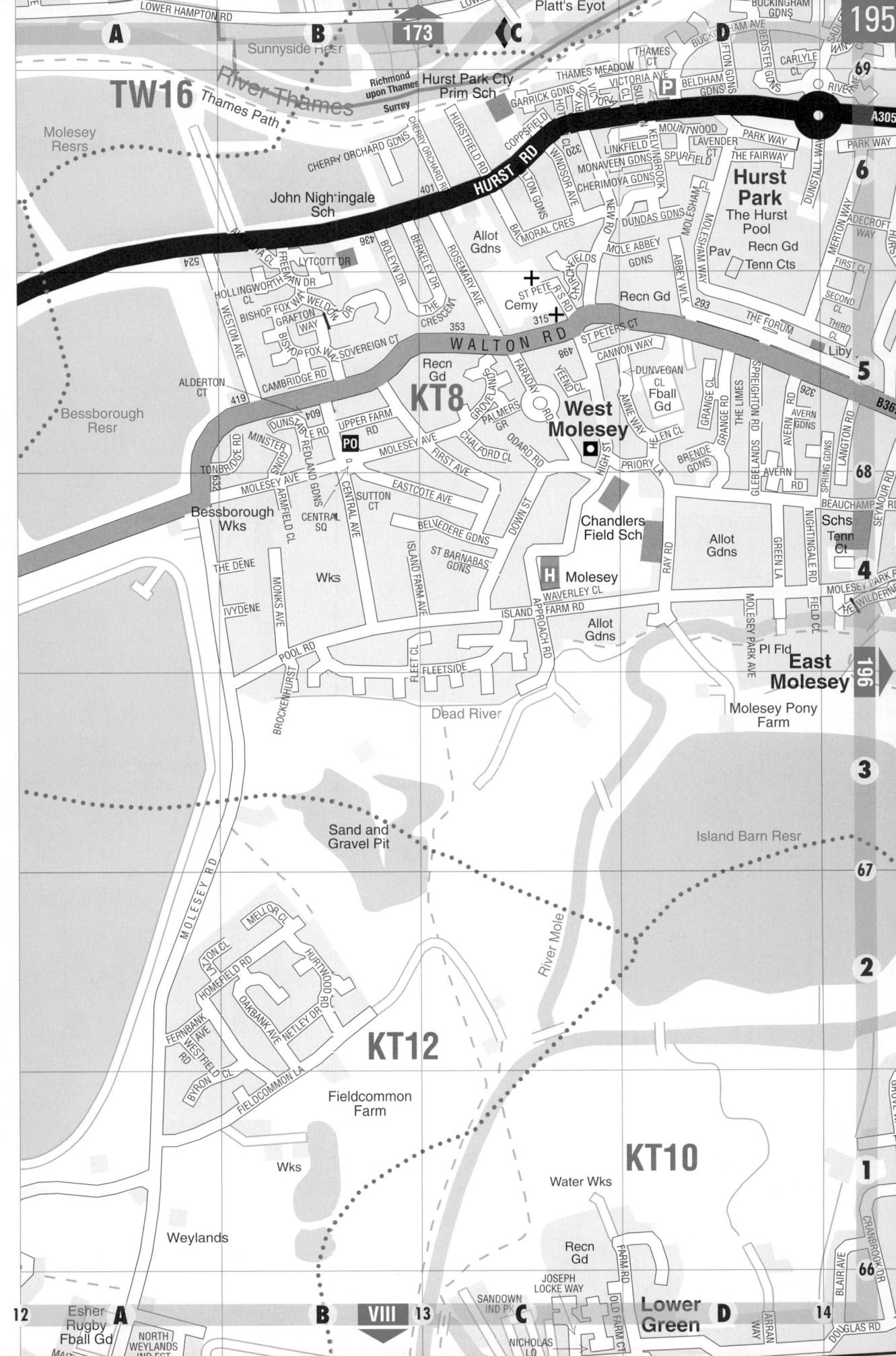

A
B
173
C
D
LOWER HAMPTON RD
Platt's Eyot
BUCKINGHAM GDNS
Sunnyside Resr
River Thames
TW16
Thames Path
Richmond upon Thames
Surrey
Hurst Park Cty Prim Sch
THAMES CT
THAMES MEADOW
VICTORIA AVE
BELDHAM GDNS
CARLYLE CL
69
A3050
Molesey Resrs
CHERRY ORCHARD GDNS
CHERRY ORCHARD RD
HURSTFIELD RD
COPPSFIELD
GARRICK GDNS
HURST RD
MOUNTWOOD
LAVENDER CT
PARK WAY
LINKFIELD
MONAVEEN GDNS
SPURFIELD
THE FAIRWAY
KELVINBROOK
CHERIMOYA GDNS
Hurst Park
The Hurst Pool
DUNSTALL WAY
6
John Nightingale Sch
BALMORAL CRES
DUNDAS GDNS
MOLESHAM CL
MOLESHAM WAY
ADECROFT WAY
MERTON WAY
Allot Gdns
MOLE ABBEY GDNS
Pav
Recn Gd
Tenn Cts
FIRST CL
LYTCOTT DR
BOLEYN DR
BERKELEY DR
ROSEMARY AVE
CHURCHFIELDS
ABBEY WLK
HOLLINGWORTH CL
FREEMAN DR
ST PETERS RD
Cemy
Recn Gd
293
SECOND CL
THE FORUM
THIRD CL
BISHOP FOX WAY
WELDON DR
GRAFTON WAY
THE CRESCENT
353
315
ST PETERS CT
Liby
WALTON RD
CANNON WAY
5
SOVEREIGN CT
DUNVEGAN CL
WESTON AVE
Recn Gd
498
YEEND CL
Fball Gd
CAMBRIDGE RD
GROVELANDS
FARADAY RD
GRANGE CL
GRANGE RD
THE LIMES
SPREIGHTON RD
AVERN RD
AVERN GDNS
B369
ALDERTON CT
KT8
PALMERS GR
West Molesey
ANNIE WAY
HELEN CL
LANGTON RD
Bessborough Resr
419
DUNSTABLE RD
UPPER FARM RD
PO
ODARD RD
MINSTER GDNS
REDLAND GDNS
MOLESEY AVE
CHALFORD CL
FIRST AVE
HIGH ST
PRIORY LA
BRENDE GDNS
GLEBELANDS
SPRING GDNS
AVERN RD
68
TONBRIDGE RD
EASTCOTE AVE
SEYMOUR RD
BEAUCHAMP RD
Bessborough Wks
ARMFIELD CL
CENTRAL SQ
CENTRAL AVE
SUTTON CT
BELVEDERE GDNS
DOWN ST
Chandlers Field Sch
Allot Gdns
GREEN LA
NIGHTINGALE RD
Schs
Tenn Ct
THE DENE
Wks
ISLAND FARM AVE
ST BARNABAS' GDNS
H
Molesey
RAY RD
4
MONKS AVE
WAVERLEY CL
MOLESEY PARK RD
THE WILDERNESS
IVYDENE
ISLAND FARM RD
APPROACH RD
Allot Gdns
FIELD CL
MOLESEY PARK AVE
Pl Fld
POOL RD
FLEET CL
FLEETSIDE
East Molesey
196
BROCKENHURST
Dead River
Molesey Pony Farm
3
Sand and Gravel Pit
Island Barn Resr
67
MOLESEY RD
MELLOR CL
LAYTON CL
HURTWOOD RD
River Mole
HOMEFIELD RD
2
OAKBANK AVE
NETLEY DR
FERNBANK AVE
WESTFIELD CL
KT12
BYRON CL
FIELDCOMMON LA
Fieldcommon Farm
GROVE WAY
KT10
Wks
1
Water Wks
CRANBROOK DR
Weylands
Recn Gd
JOSEPH LOCKE WAY
FARM RD
BLAIR AVE
66
12
Esher Rugby Fball Gd
VIII
13
SANDOWN IND PK
OLD FARM CT
Lower Green
ARRAN WAY
14
DOUGLAS RD
NORTH WEYLANDS IND EST
NICHOLAS LO

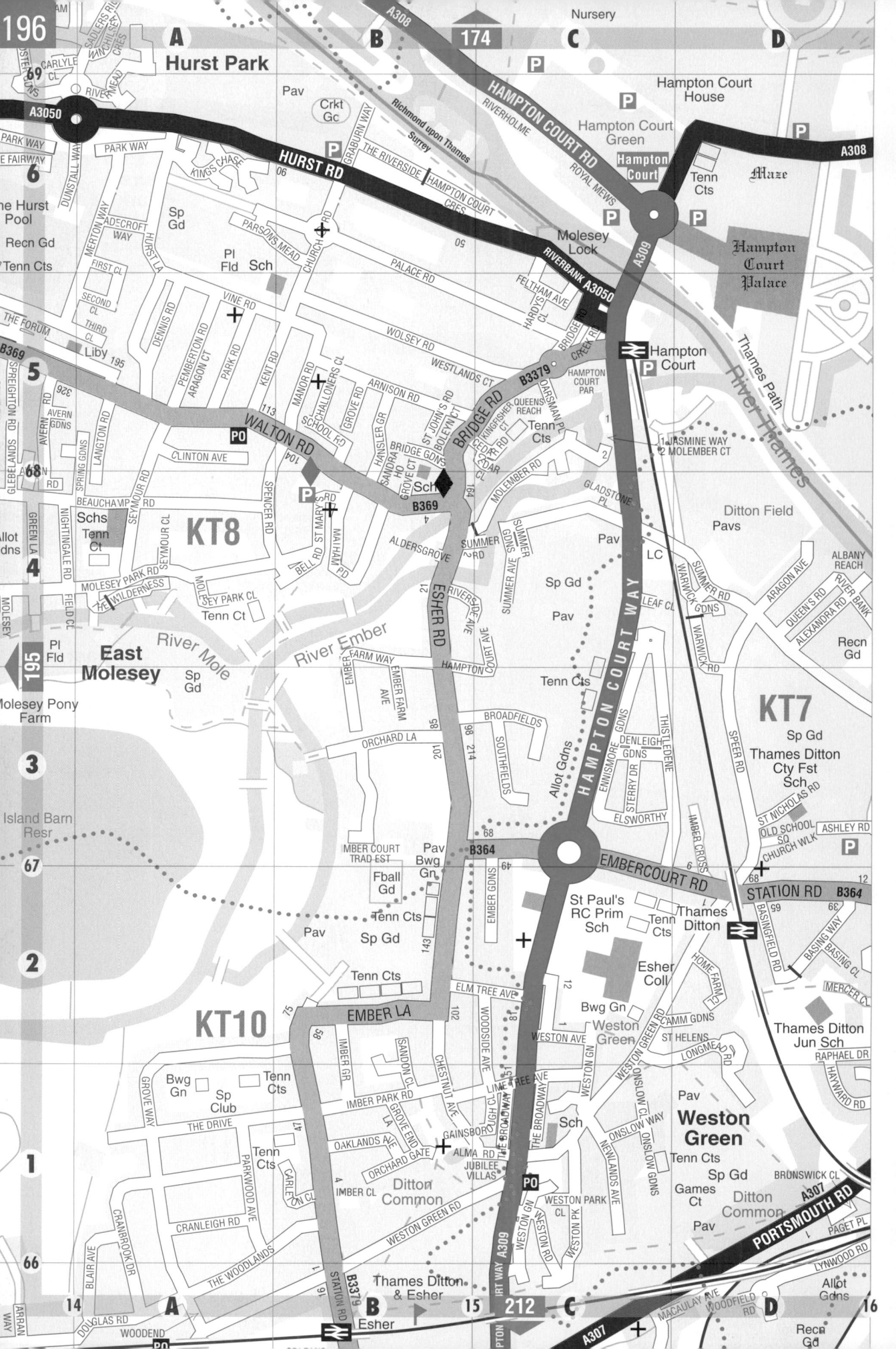

Hurst Park

174

Nursery

Hampton Court House

Hampton Court Green

Hampton Court

Maze

Tenn Cts

Hampton Court Palace

A308

A3050

Park Way

The Fairway

Park Way

The Hurst Pool

Recn Gd

Tenn Cts

Sp Gd

Liby 195

HURST RD

Sch

Pl Fld

Palace Rd

Wolsey Rd

Westlands Ct

Molesey Lock

RIVERBANK A3050

Feltham Ave

Hampton Court Par

Hampton Court

Jasmine Way
Molember Ct

Ditton Field Pavs

Albany Reach

Recn Gd

River Thames

B369

WALTON RD

PO

Sch

B369

Bridge Rd

B3379

Tenn Cts

Gladstone Pl

Pav

LC

Warwick Gdns

Summer Rd

Aragon Ave

Queen's Rd

River Bank

Alexandra Rd

KT8

East Molesey

River Mole

Tenn Ct

River Ember

Esher Rd

Summer Rd

Sp Gd

Pav

Tenn Cts

KT7

Sp Gd

Thames Ditton Cty Fst Sch

St Nicholas Rd

Old School Sq

Church Wlk

Ashley Rd

195

Molesey Pony Farm

Sp Gd

Ember Farm Way

Ember Farm Ave

Orchard La

Broadfields

Southfields

Allot Gdns

HAMPTON COURT WAY

Denleigh Gdns

Sterry Dr

Elsworthy

Speer Rd

Imber Cross

Island Barn Resr

67

Imber Court Trad Est

Fball Gd

Pav Bwg Gn

B364

EMBERCOURT RD

St Paul's RC Prim Sch

Tenn Cts

Thames Ditton

Station Rd

B364

Basingfield Rd

Basing Way

Basing Cl

Mercer Ct

2

KT10

Tenn Cts

Pav

Sp Gd

Tenn Cts

EMBER LA

Elm Tree Ave

Woodside Ave

Weston Ave

Esher Coll

Bwg Gn

Weston Green

St Helens

Home Farm

Longmead Rd

Thames Ditton Jun Sch

Raphael Dr

Hayward Rd

1

Bwg Gn

Sp Club

Tenn Cts

The Drive

Imber Gr

Imber Park Rd

Sandon Cl

Grove End La

Chestnut Ave

Lime Tree Ave

The Broadway

Weston Gn

Onslow Way

Molson Way

Sch

Pav

Games Ct

Sp Gd

Brunswick Cl

Ditton Common

Pav

A307

Tenn Cts

Grove Way

Parkwood Ave

Cranleigh Rd

Oaklands Ave

Orchard Gate

Imber Cl

Gainsborough Rd

Alma Rd

Jubilee Villas

Ditton Common

PO

Weston Gn

Weston Pk Cl

Weston Park

Newlands Ave

PORTSMOUTH RD

Paget Pl

Lynwood Rd

14

A

Woodend

Douglas Rd

B

B3379

Thames Ditton & Esher

Esher

Station Rd

15

212

A309

RT WAY

C

A307

Macaulay Ave

Woodfield Rd

16

D

Allot Gdns

Recn Gd

175
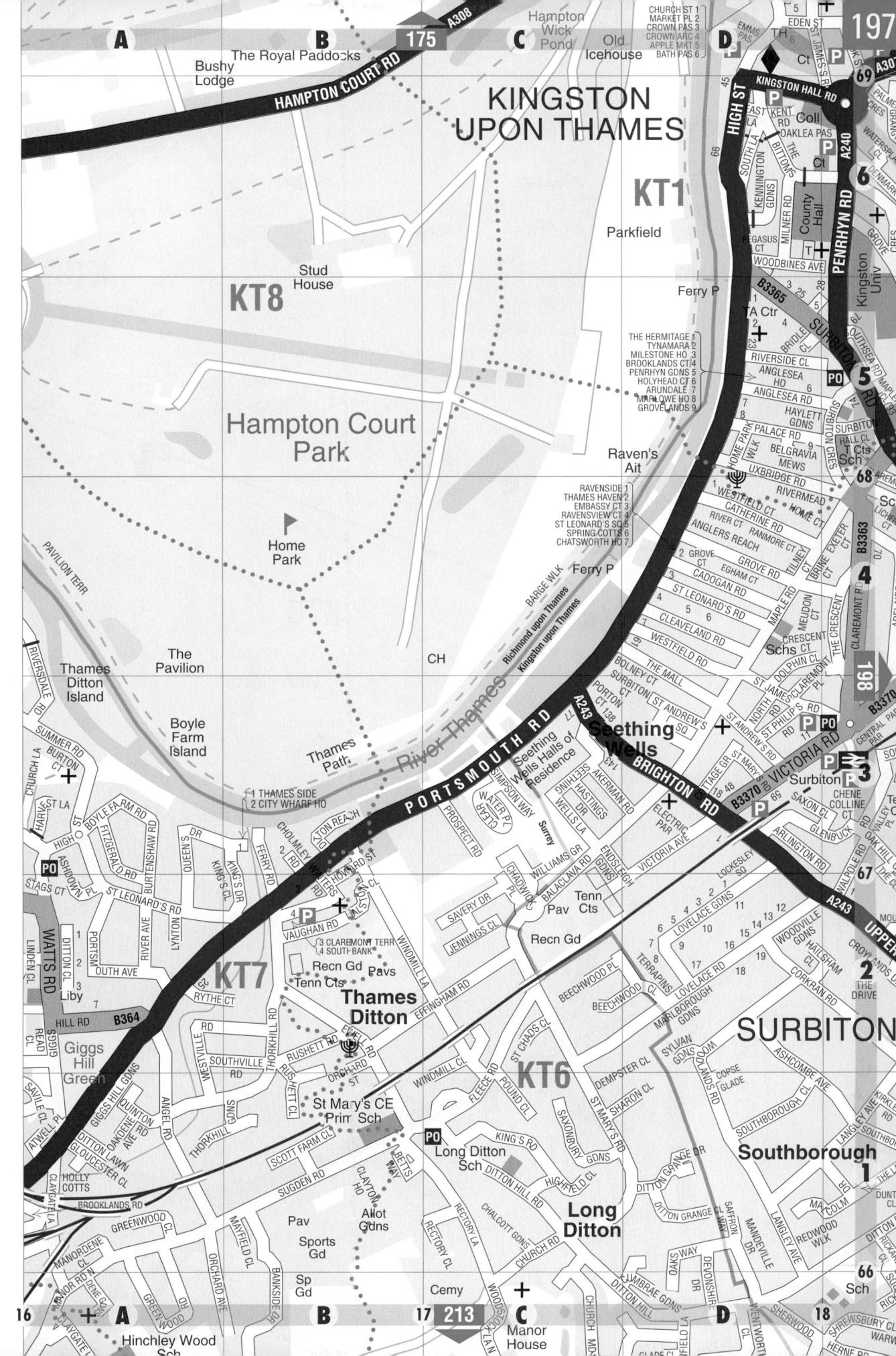

A
B
C
D
A308
HAMPTON COURT RD
Hampton Wick Pond
Old Icehouse
The Royal Paddocks
Bushy Lodge
CHURCH ST 1
MARKET PL 2
CROWN PAS 3
CROWN ARC 4
APPLE MKT 5
BATH PAS 6
EMMS PAS
TH
EDEN ST
A307
KINGSTON HALL RD
KINGSTON UPON THAMES
HIGH ST
EAST KENT RD
Coll
OAKLEA PAS
SOUTH LA
KENNINGTON GDNS
BITTOMS
THE BITTOMS
MILNER RD
County Hall
PENRHYN RD
A240
KT1
Parkfield
PEGASUS CT
WOODBINES AVE
GROVE CRES
WATERSPLASH CL
PALMER CRES
GRANGE RD
DENMARK RD
Kingston Univ
Stud House
KT8
Ferry P
B3365
TA Ctr
BRIDLE CL
SURBITON RD
SOUTHSEA RD
THE HERMITAGE 1
TYNAMARA 2
MILESTONE HO 3
BROOKLANDS CT 4
PENRHYN GDNS 5
HOLYHEAD CT 6
ARUNDALE 7
MARLOWE HO 8
GROVELANDS 9
RIVERSIDE CL
ANGLESEA HO
ANGLESEA RD
PO
MAPLE RD
HAYLETT GDNS
SURBITON CRES
PALACE RD
HOME PARK WLK
BELGRAVIA MEWS
SURBITON HALL CL
T Cts
Sch
Hampton Court Park
Raven's Ait
UXBRIDGE RD
WESTFIELD CT
RIVERMEAD
HOME CT
CATHERINE RD
RAVENSIDE 1
THAMES HAVEN 2
EMBASSY CT 3
RAVENSVIEW CT 4
ST LEONARD'S SQ 5
SPRING COTTS 6
CHATSWORTH HO 7
RIVER CT
RANMORE CT
ANGLERS REACH
GROVE CT
GROVE RD
EGHAM CT
TILNEY CT
BRINE CT
EXETER CT
B3363
CADOGAN RD
ST LEONARD'S RD
Home Park
PAVILION TERR
BARGE WLK
Ferry P
Richmond upon Thames
Kingston upon Thames
MEUDON CT
CLEAVELAND RD
WESTFIELD RD
CRESCENT CT
THE CRESCENT
CLAREMONT RD
ADELAIDE RD
Schs
DOLPHIN CL
RIVERSDALE RD
Thames Ditton Island
The Pavilion
CH
BOLNEY CT
THE MALL
SURBITON CT
ST ANDREW'S SQ
ST JAMES RD
CLAREMONT PL
NORTH RD
ST PHILIP'S RD
198
B3370
CENTRAL PAR
PORTON CT
A243
PORTSMOUTH RD
River Thames
Seething Wells
Seething Wells Halls of Residence
ST ANDREW'S RD
Boyle Farm Island
Thames Path
BRIGHTON RD
ST MARY'S RD
VICTORIA RD
SUMMER RD
BURTON CT
CHURCH LA
HARVEST LA
1 THAMES SIDE
2 CITY WHARF HO
DITTON REACH
SIMPSON WAY
CLEAR WATER PL
PROSPECT RD
SEETHING WELLS LA
HASTINGS DR
AKERMAN RD
Surrey
ELECTRIC PAR
COTTAGE GR
Surbiton
CHENE COLLINE CT
SAXON CL
GLENBUCK RD
VALLEY PL
ARLINGTON RD
OAK HILL GR
BOYLE FARM RD
HIGH ST
FITZGERALD RD
BURTENSHAW RD
QUEEN'S DR
KING'S DR
KING'S CL
FERRY RD
CHOLMLEY RD
WATERS RD
HOWARD ST
ALSTON CL
WILLIAMS GR
CHADWICK PL
BALACLAVA RD
ENDSLEIGH GDNS
VICTORIA AVE
LOCKESLEY SQ
WALPOLE RD
THE CLOSE
ASHDOWN PL
STAGS CT
ST LEONARD'S RD
RIVER AVE
LYNTON RD
VAUGHAN RD
3 CLAREMONT TERR
4 SOUTH BANK
WINDMILL LA
SAVERY DR
JENNINGS CL
Pav
Tenn Cts
Recn Gd
LOVELACE GDNS
WOODVILLE GDNS
HAILSHAM CL
CROYLANDS DR
A243
UPPER
WATTS RD
DITTON CL
LINDEN CL
PORTSMOUTH AVE
KT7
RYTHE CT
Recn Gd
Pavs
Tenn Cts
Thames Ditton
EFFINGHAM RD
TERRAPINS
BEECHWOOD PL
BEECHWOOD CL
LOVELACE RD
CORKRAN RD
THE DRIVE
Liby
HILL RD
B364
RD
READ CL
GIGGS HILL
Giggs Hill Green
WESTVILLE RD
SOUTHVILLE RD
THORKHILL RD
RUSHETT RD
RUSHETT CL
EWELL RD
ORCHARD ST
WINDMILL CL
FLEECE RD
POUND CL
ST CHADS CL
KT6
MARLBOROUGH GDNS
SURBITON
SYLVAN GDNS
WOODLANDS RD
COPSE GLADE
ASHCOMBE AVE
DEMPSTER CL
SHARON CL
ST MARY'S RD
SAXONBURY GDNS
SOUTHBOROUGH CL
KIRKLEAS RD
LANGLEY AVE
SOUTHBOROUGH
SAVILE CL
ATWELL PL
GIGGS HILL GDNS
QUINTON RD
OAKDENE AVE
THORKHILL GDNS
ANGEL RD
St Mary's CE Prim Sch
DITTON LAWN
GLOUCESTER CL
HOLLY COTTS
CLAYGATE LA
SCOTT FARM CL
PO
Long Ditton Sch
KING'S RD
DITTON HILL RD
HIGHFIELD CL
Southborough
DITTON GRANGE DR
THE LANE
DUNTON CL
BROOKLANDS RD
SUGDEN RD
BETTS WAY
CLAYTON HO
Long Ditton
DITTON GRANGE CL
SAFFRON WAY
MANDEVILLE DR
MALCOLM DR
REDWOOD WLK
DITTON RD
RICKARDS CL
GREENWOOD CL
MANORDENE CL
MANOR RD N
DENE GDNS
GREENWOOD RD
MAYFIELD CL
ORCHARD AVE
Pav
Sports Gd
Allot Gdns
RECTORY CL
RECTORY LA
CHALCOTT GDNS
CHURCH RD
OAKS WAY
DEVONSHIRE DR
BANKSIDE DR
Sp Gd
Cemy
WOODSTOCK LA N
CUMBRAE GDNS
DITTON HILL
CHURCH MDW
WENTWORTH CL
SHERWOOD
Sch
SHREWSBURY CL
WARWICK
HERNE RD
CLAYGATE
Hinchley Wood Sch
Manor House
16
17
18

213

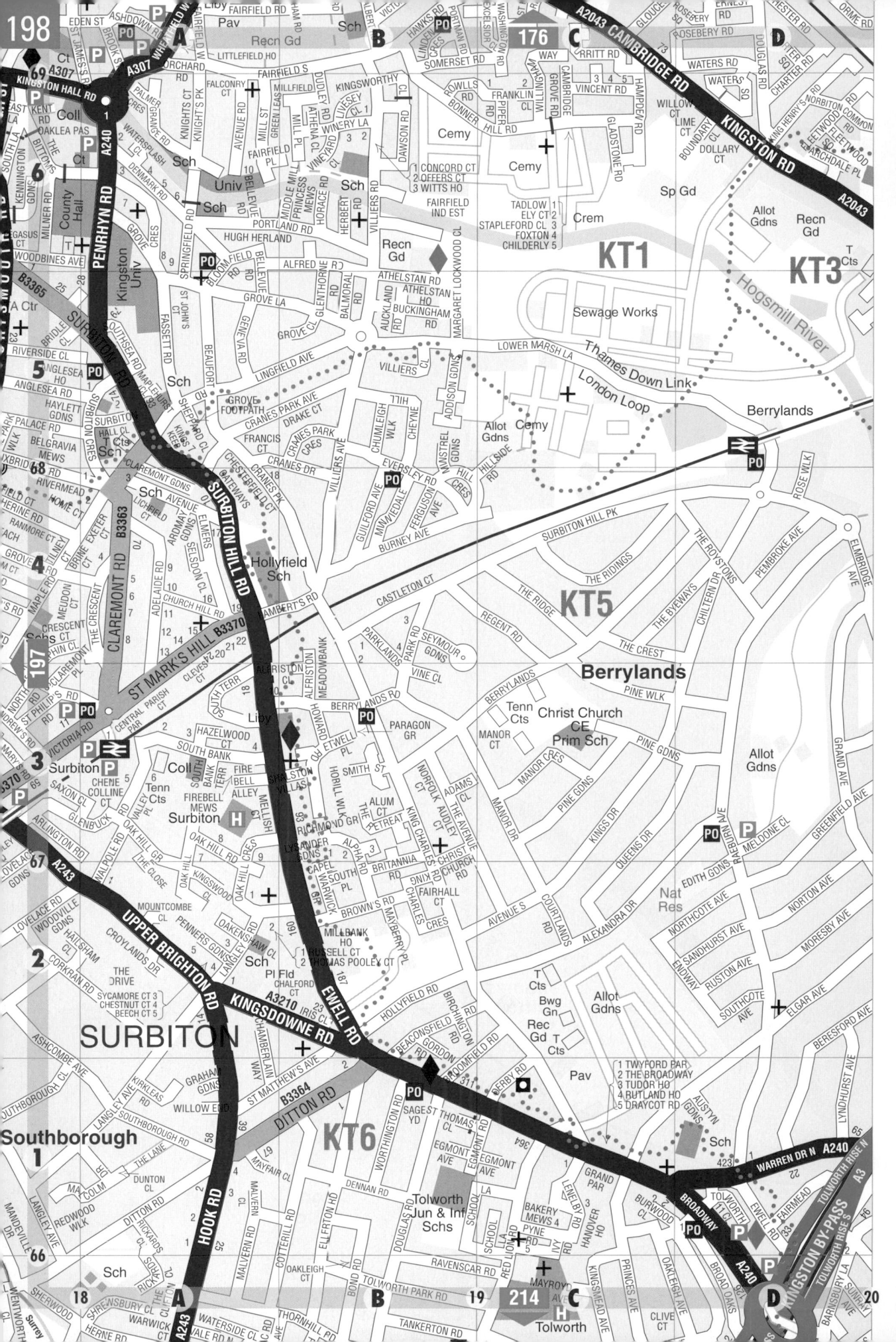
176
197
214
A
B
C
D
18
19
20
1
2
3
4
5
6
KT1
KT3
KT5
KT6
SURBITON
Southborough
Berrylands
Surbiton
Tolworth
EDEN ST
ASHDOWN RD
FAIRFIELD RD
Liby
Pav
Recn Gd
Sch
A307
WHEATFIELD WAY
A2043 CAMBRIDGE RD
KINGSTON RD
A2043
KINGSTON HALL RD
PENRHYN RD
A240
ORCHARD RD
LITTLEFIELD HO
FAIRFIELD S
KINGSWORTHY CL
SOMERSET RD
WAY
BRITT RD
VINCENT RD
ROSEBERY RD
WATERS RD
WATERS SQ
CHARTER RD
NORBITON COMMON RD
FLEETWOOD RD
FLEETWOOD SQ
BIRCHDALE PL
KING HENRY'S RD
ROWLLS RD
FRANKLIN CL
BONNER HILL RD
PIPER RD
WILLINGHAM
GROVE RD
CAMBRIDGE
GLADSTONE RD
HAMPDEN RD
WILLOW CT
LIME CT
DOLLARY CT
BOUNDARY CL
Cemy
Crem
Sp Gd
Allot Gdns
Recn Gd
1 CONCORD CT
2 OFFERS CT
3 WITTS HO
FAIRFIELD IND EST
TADLOW 1
ELY CT 2
STAPLEFORD CL 3
FOXTON 4
CHILDERLY 5
Coll
County Hall
Kingston Univ
Univ
BELLEVUE
Sch
DENMARK RD
WATERSPLASH CL
PALMER CRES
GRANGE RD
KNIGHTS CT
KNIGHT'S PK
AVENUE RD
MILL ST
GREEN LEAS
MILLFIELD
DUDLEY RD
ATHENA CL
LIVESEY CL
WINERY LA
VINEYARD CL
MILL PL
FAIRFIELD PL
MIDDLE MILL
PRINCESS MEWS
HORACE RD
HERBERT RD
VILLIERS RD
DAWSON RD
PORTLAND RD
HUGH HERLAND
SPRINGFIELD RD
BLOOMFIELD RD
ALFRED RD
Recn Gd
ATHELSTAN RD
ATHELSTAN HO
BUCKINGHAM RD
MARGARET LOCKWOOD CL
GROVE LA
GROVE CL
GLENTHORNE RD
BALMORAL RD
AUCKLAND RD
Sewage Works
Hogsmill River
LOWER MARSH LA
Thames Down Link
London Loop
Berrylands
Allot Gdns
Cemy
ST JOHN'S CT
FASSETT RD
GENEVA RD
BEAUFORT RD
LINGFIELD AVE
VILLIERS CL
ADDISON GDNS
SHEPPARD CL
GROVE FOOTPATH
CRANES PARK AVE
DRAKE CT
CRANES PARK CRES
CHUMLEIGH WLK
CHEYNE HILL
FRANCIS CT
CRANES DR
VILLIERS AVE
EVERSLEY RD
MINSTREL GDNS
HILL CRES
HILLSIDE RD
GUILFORD AVE
MINNIEDALE
FERGUSON AVE
BURNEY AVE
SURBITON HILL PK
THE RIDINGS
THE ROYSTONS
PEMBROKE AVE
ELMBRIDGE AVE
ROSE WLK
CASTLETON CT
THE RIDGE
THE BYEWAYS
CHILTERN DR
REGENT RD
THE CREST
PINE WLK
SEYMOUR GDNS
PARKLANDS
PARK RD
VINE CL
BERRYLANDS RD
BERRYLANDS
Tenn Cts
Christ Church CE Prim Sch
MANOR CT
MANOR CRES
PINE GDNS
PARAGON GR
Allot Gdns
GRAND AVE
GREENFIELD AVE
MELDONE CL
RAEBURN AVE
SURBITON RD
SOUTHSEA RD
MAPLEHURST
RIVERSIDE CL
ANGLESEA HO
ANGLESEA RD
HAYLETT GDNS
PALACE RD
BELGRAVIA MEWS
SURBITON CRES
SURBITON HALL CL
T Cts
RIVERMEAD
HOME CT
CLAREMONT GDNS
AVENUE ELMERS
LICHFIELD CT
SURBITON HILL RD
CHESTERFIELD CT
CRANES PK
GATEWAYS
ARDMAY GDNS
SELSDON CL
Hollyfield Sch
B3363
CLAREMONT RD
ADELAIDE RD
CHURCH HILL RD
LAMBERT'S RD
ST MARK'S HILL
B3370
CLEVES CT
THE CRESCENT
CRESCENT CT
MEUDON CT
MAPLE RD
TILNEY CT
EXETER CT
BRIME CT
ST PHILIP'S RD
VICTORIA RD
CENTRAL PARISH PAR
SOUTH TERR
ALFRISTON
ALFRISTON RD
MEADOWBANK
HOWARD RD
Liby
HAZELWOOD CT
SOUTH BANK
SOUTH BANK TERR
FIRE BELL ALLEY
FIREBELL MEWS
MELLISH
ETWELL PL
SMITH ST
HORILL WLK
ALUM CT
THE RETREAT
NORFOLK CT
AUDLEY CT
ADAMS CL
THE AVENUE
MANOR DR
KINGS DR
QUEENS DR
SHALSTON VILLAS
Coll
Surbiton
Tenn Cts
CHEINE COLLINE CT
SAXON CL
GLENBUCK
VALLEY PL
WALPOLE RD
OAK HILL GR
OAK HILL RD
OAK HILL CRES
OAK HILL
THE CLOSE
KINGSWOOD CL
RICHMOND GR
LYSANDER GDNS
CAPEL
SOUTH PL
ALPHA RD
BRITANNIA RD
KING CHARLES RD
CHRIST CHURCH RD
FAIRHALL CT
KING CHARLES CRES
BROWN'S RD
MAYBERRY PL
MILLBANK HO
1 RUSSELL CT
2 THOMAS POOLEY CT
AVENUE S
COURTLANDS RD
ALEXANDRA DR
EDITH GDNS
NORTHCOTE AVE
SANDHURST AVE
ENDWAY
RUSTON AVE
SOUTHCOTE AVE
ELGAR AVE
NORTON AVE
MORESBY AVE
BERESFORD AVE
LYNDHURST AVE
Nat Res
ARLINGTON RD
LOVELACE GDNS
LOVELACE RD
WOODVILLE GDNS
HAILSHAM CL
CORKRAN RD
A243
UPPER BRIGHTON RD
MOUNTCOMBE CL
PENNERS GDNS
CROYLANDS DR
OAKENSHAW CL
LANGLEY
THE DRIVE
Pl Fld
CHALFORD CT
SYCAMORE CT 3
CHESTNUT CT 4
BEECH CT 5
KINGSDOWNE RD
A3210
IRIS CL
EWELL RD
HOLLYFIELD RD
BIRCHINGTON RD
BEACONSFIELD RD
GORDON RD
BROOMFIELD RD
DERBY RD
T Cts
Bwg Gn
Rec Gd
Allot Gdns
Pav
1 TWYFORD PAR
2 THE BROADWAY
3 TUDOR HO
4 RUTLAND HO
5 DRAYCOT RD
AUSTYN GDNS
Sch
WARREN DR N
A240
TOLWORTH RISE N
A3
ASHCOMBE AVE
SOUTHBOROUGH CL
KIRKLEAS RD
GRAHAM GDNS
CHAMBERLAIN WAY
ST MATTHEW'S AVE
WILLOW END
B3364
DITTON RD
SOUTHBOROUGH RD
THE LANE
DUNTON CL
MALCOLM DR
REDWOOD WLK
LANGLEY AVE
MANDEVILLE DR
HOOK RD
MAYFAIR CL
SAGE YD
ST THOMAS CL
EGMONT AVE
EGMONT RD
DENNAN RD
WORTHINGTON RD
MALVERN RD
COTTERILL RD
ELLERTON RD
DOUGLAS RD
Tolworth Jun & Inf Schs
SCHOOL LA
BAKERY MEWS
PYNE RD
IVY RD
LENELBY RD
HANOVER HO
GRAND PAR
BURWOOD CL
BROADWAY
TOLWORTH CT
FAIRMEAD
TOLWORTH RISE S
KINGSTON BY-PASS
OAKLEIGH CT
BOND RD
RAVENSCAR RD
RED LION RD
MAYROYD AVE
KINGSMEAD AVE
PRINCES AVE
OAKLEIGH AVE
BROAD OAKS
TOLWORTH PARK RD
TANKERTON RD
CLIVE CT
BARNSBURY LA
SUNRAY AVE
RICKARDS CL
SHERWOOD
SHREWSBURY CL
THE CLIFTON
WARWICK
WATERSIDE CL
THORNHILL RD
HERNE RD
VALE RD N
WENTWORTH
Surrey
Sch

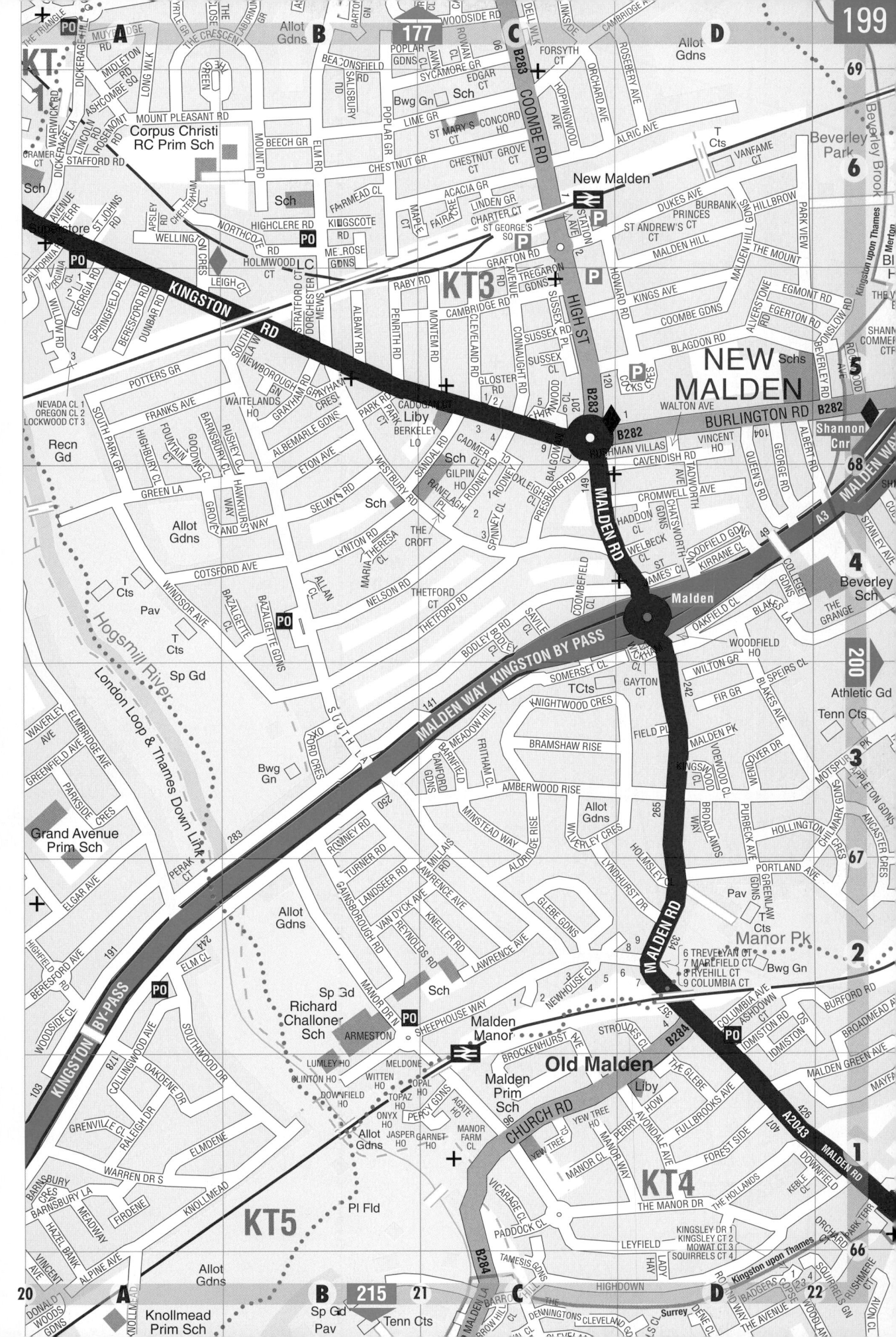

A
B
177
C
D
Allot Gdns
KT 1
MUYBRIDGE RD
DICKERAGE HILL
THE TRIANGLE
MIDLETON RD
ASHCOMBE SQ
LONG WLK
THE CRESCENT
THE GREEN
THE CLOSE
LABURNUM GR
WARWICK RD
DICKERAGE LA
LINCOLN AVE
ROSEMONT RD
MOUNT PLEASANT RD
Corpus Christi RC Prim Sch
CRAMER CT
STAFFORD RD
Sch
Superstore
CALIFORNIA RD
VIRGINIA CL
GEORGIA RD
WILLOW RD
ST JOHNS RD
AVENUE TERR
CHELTENHAM AVE
APSLEY RD
WELLINGTON CRES
NORTHCOTE RD
HIGHCLERE RD
HOLMWOOD CL
LEIGH CL
KINGSTON RD
SPRINGFIELD PL
BERESFORD RD
DUNBAR RD
NEVADA CL 1
OREGON CL 2
LOCKWOOD CT 3
BEECH GR
MOUNT RD
ELM RD
BEACONSFIELD RD
SALISBURY RD
POPLAR GDNS
POPLAR GR
SYCAMORE GR
LAWN CL
ROWAN CL
WOODSIDE RD
Bwg Gn
Sch
LIME GR
ST MARY'S CT
CONCORD HO
EDGAR CT
CHESTNUT GR
CHESTNUT CT
GROVE CT
FARMEAD CL
ACACIA GR
LINDEN GR
CHARTER CT
MAPLE CT
FAIRACRE
KINGSCOTE RD
MELROSE GDNS
ST GEORGE'S SQ
B283
COOMBE RD
DELL WLK
LINKSIDE
FORSYTH CT
HOPPINGWOOD AVE
ORCHARD AVE
ROSEBERY AVE
CAMBRIDGE AVE
ALRIC AVE
New Malden
STATION AVE
GRAFTON RD
TREGARON GDNS
RABY RD
KT3
STRATFORD CT
DORCHESTER MEWS
ALBANY RD
PENRITH RD
MONTEM RD
CAMBRIDGE RD
CLEVELAND RD
CONNAUGHT RD
SUSSEX RD
SUSSEX PL
SUSSEX CL
HIGH ST
HOWARD RD
GLOSTER RD
POTTERS GR
SOUTH LANE
NEWBOROUGH GN
GRAYHAM RD
WAITELANDS HO
GRAYHAM CRES
FRANKS AVE
PARK RD
PARK CT
CADOGAN CT
Liby
BERKELEY LO
ALBEMARLE GDNS
SOUTH PARK GR
HIGHBURY CL
FOUNTAIN CT
GOODING CL
BARNSBURY CL
RUSHEY CL
HAWKHURST WAY
Recn Gd
GREEN LA
ETON AVE
SELWYN RD
WESTBURY RD
SANDAL RD
Sch
GILPIN HO
RANELAGH PL
CADMER CL
RODNEY RD
RODNEY CL
OXLEIGH CL
PRESBURG RD
BALGOWAN CL
SHERWOOD CL
RUSHMAN VILLAS
GROVE LANE
AND WAY
Allot Gdns
THE CROFT
SPINNEY CL
LYNTON RD
MARIA THERESA CL
COTSFORD AVE
T Cts
Pav
WINDSOR AVE
BAZALGETTE CL
BAZALGETTE GDNS
ALLAN CL
NELSON RD
THETFORD CT
THETFORD RD
Hogsmill River
London Loop & Thames Down Link
Sp Gd
BODLEY RD
BODLEY CL
SAVILE CL
COOMBEFIELD CL
MALDEN WAY KINGSTON BY PASS
Malden
MALDEN RD
B282
BURLINGTON RD
WALTON AVE
CAVENDISH RD
VINCENT HO
TADWORTH AVE
CHATSWORTH GDNS
CROMWELL AVE
HADDON CL
WELBECK CL
ST JAMES' CL
WOODFIELD GDNS
KIRRANE CL
QUEEN'S RD
GEORGE RD
ALBERT RD
T Cts
VANFAME CT
DUKES AVE
BURBANK
PRINCES
ST ANDREW'S CT
MALDEN HILL
MALDEN HILL GDNS
HILLBROW
THE MOUNT
PARK VIEW
Beverley Park
Beverley Brook
KINGS AVE
COOMBE GDNS
BLAGDON RD
ALVERSTONE RD
EGMONT RD
EGERTON RD
ONSLOW RD
NEW MALDEN
Schs
BEVERLEY RD
ROCKWOOD AVE
Shannon Cnr
A3
MALDEN WAY
COLLEGE GDNS
Beverley Sch
THE GRANGE
OAKFIELD CL
BLAKES LA
WOODFIELD HO
WICKHAM CL
SOMERSET CL
GAYTON CT
TCts
WILTON GR
SPEIRS CL
FIR GR
BLAKES AVE
200
Athletic Gd
Tenn Cts
KNIGHTWOOD CRES
BRAMSHAW RISE
FIELD PL
MALDEN PK
KINGSWOOD CL
VOEWOOD CL
WOLVERTON CT
CLOVER DR
MOTSPUR PK
APPLETON GDNS
CHILMARK GDNS
ANCASTER CRES
MEADOW HILL
BARNFIELD
CANFORD GDNS
FRITHAM CL
AMBERWOOD RISE
Allot Gdns
MINSTEAD WAY
ALDRIDGE RISE
WAVERLEY CRES
BROADLANDS WAY
PURBECK AVE
HOLLINGTON CRES
HOLMSLEY CL
LYNDHURST DR
PORTLAND AVE
GREENLAW GDNS
Pav
T Cts
Manor Pk
GLEBE GDNS
6 TREVELYAN CT
7 MARLFIELD CT
8 RYEHILL CT
9 COLUMBIA CT
Bwg Gn
OXFORD CRES
Bwg Gn
WAVERLEY AVE
ELMBRIDGE AVE
GREENFIELD AVE
PARKSIDE CRES
Grand Avenue Prim Sch
ELGAR AVE
PERAK CT
ROMNEY RD
TURNER RD
LANDSEER RD
GAINSBOROUGH RD
VAN DYCK AVE
MILLAIS RD
LAWRENCE AVE
REYNOLDS RD
KNELLER RD
Allot Gdns
HIGHFIELD RD
BERESFORD AVE
ELM CL
WOODSIDE CL
KINGSTON BY-PASS
Sp Gd
Richard Challoner Sch
MANOR DR N
Sch
SHEEPHOUSE WAY
NEWHOUSE CL
ARMESTON
Malden Manor
LUMLEY HO
MELDONE
CLINTON HO
WITTEN HO
OPAL HO
DOWNFIELD HO
TOPAZ HO
ONYX HO
JASPER HO
GARNET HO
PERCY GDNS
AGATE HO
MANOR FARM CL
Allot Gdns
STROUDES CL
BROCKENHURST AVE
Old Malden
Malden Prim Sch
CHURCH RD
B284
Liby
THE GLEBE
YEW TREE HO
YEW TREE
PERRY HOW
AVONDALE AVE
MANOR WAY
MANOR CL
FULLBROOKS AVE
FOREST SIDE
COLUMBIA AVE
ASHDOWN CT
IDMISTON RD
IDMISTON SQ
BURFORD RD
BROADMEAD AVE
MALDEN GREEN AVE
MAYFAIR
A2043
MALDEN RD
DOWNFIELD CL
KEBLE CL
THE HOLLANDS
KT4
THE MANOR DR
VICARAGE CL
PADDOCK CL
TAMESIS GDNS
LEYFIELD
LADY HAY
KINGSLEY DR 1
KINGSLEY CT 2
MOWAT CT 3
SQUIRRELS CT 4
ORCHARD CT
PARK TERR
Kingston upon Thames
COLLINGWOOD AVE
OAKDENE DR
SOUTHWOOD DR
GRENVILLE CL
RALEIGH DR
ELMDENE
WARREN DR S
KNOLLMEAD
BARNSBURY CRES
BARNSBURY LA
MEADWAY
FIRDENE
HAZEL BANK
VINCENT AVE
ALPINE AVE
Pl Fld
KT5
Allot Gdns
HIGHDOWN
Kingston upon Thames
Surrey
BADGERS COPSE
THE AVENUE
WOODLANDS
SQUIRRELS GN
RUSHMERE
AVON CL
ROUND WAY
DENE CL
CLEVELAND GDNS
DENNINGTONS
BARROW HILL
MALDEN LA
20
A
B
215
21
C
D
22
Sp Gd
Pav
Tenn Cts
Knollmead Prim Sch
DONALD WOODS GDNS
KNOLLMEAD
69
6
5
68
4
3
67
2
1
66

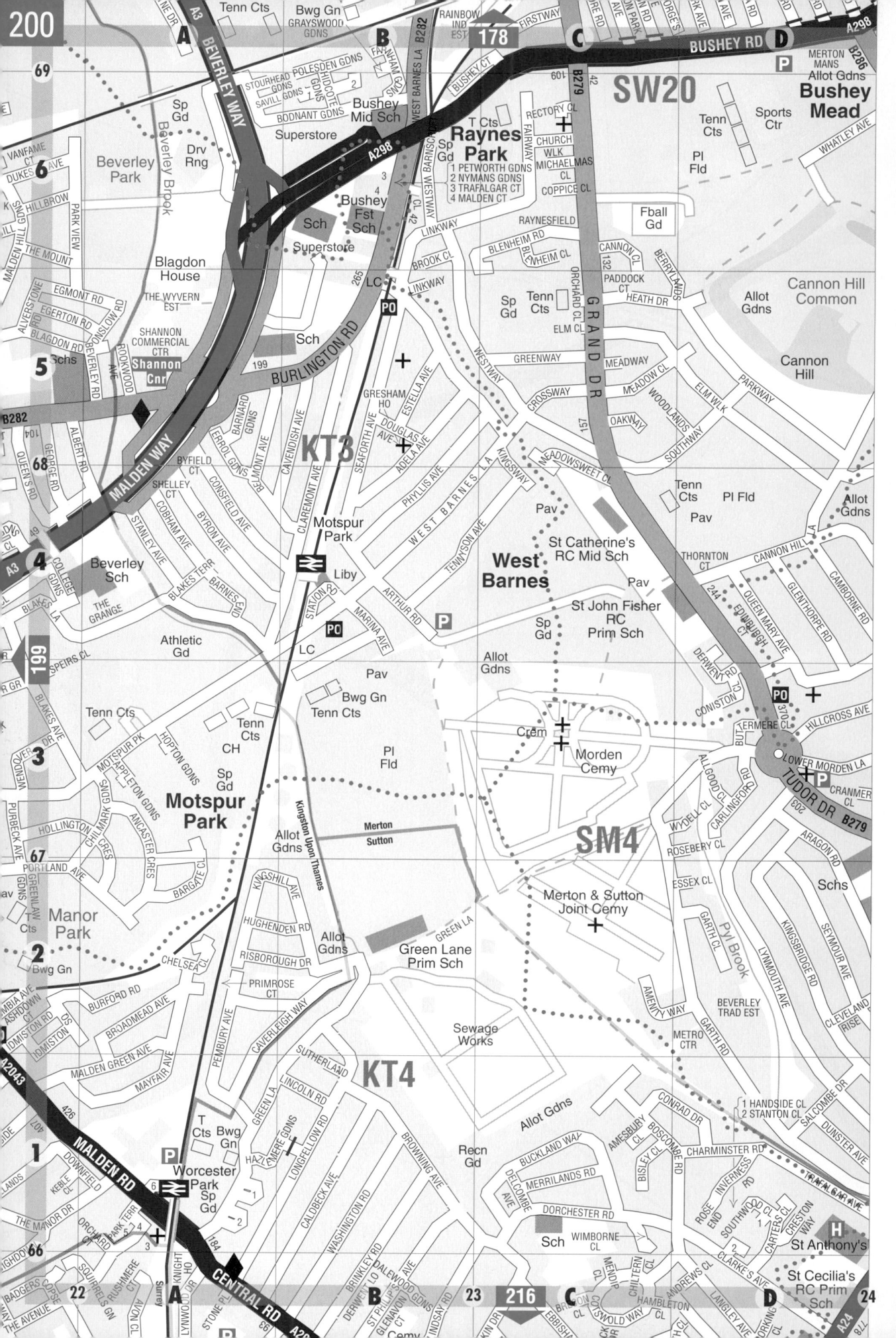

A
B
C
D
178
69
6
5
68
4
3
67
2
1
66
22
23
24
199
216
A3
BEVERLEY WAY
A298
BUSHEY RD
B282
B279
B286
SW20
KT3
SM4
KT4
Bushey Mead
Raynes Park
West Barnes
Motspur Park
Manor Park
Beverley Park
Cannon Hill Common
Cannon Hill
Blagdon House
Beverley Brook
Pyl Brook
Superstore
Bushey Mid Sch
Bushey Fst Sch
Beverley Sch
Shannon Cnr
SHANNON COMMERCIAL CTR
THE WYVERN EST
St Catherine's RC Mid Sch
St John Fisher RC Prim Sch
Morden Cemy
Merton & Sutton Joint Cemy
Green Lane Prim Sch
Sewage Works
Worcester Park
St Anthony's
St Cecilia's RC Prim Sch
Athletic Gd
Allot Gdns
Tenn Cts
Sp Gd
Pl Fld
Fball Gd
Sports Ctr
MERTON MANS Allot Gdns
BEVERLEY TRAD EST
METRO CTR
Merton
Sutton
Kingston Upon Thames
Surrey
MALDEN WAY
MALDEN RD
CENTRAL RD
BURLINGTON RD
WEST BARNES LA
GRAND DR
TUDOR DR
LOWER MORDEN LA
CANNON HILL LA
1 PETWORTH GDNS
2 NYMANS GDNS
3 TRAFALGAR CT
4 MALDEN CT
1 HANDSIDE CL
2 STANTON CL

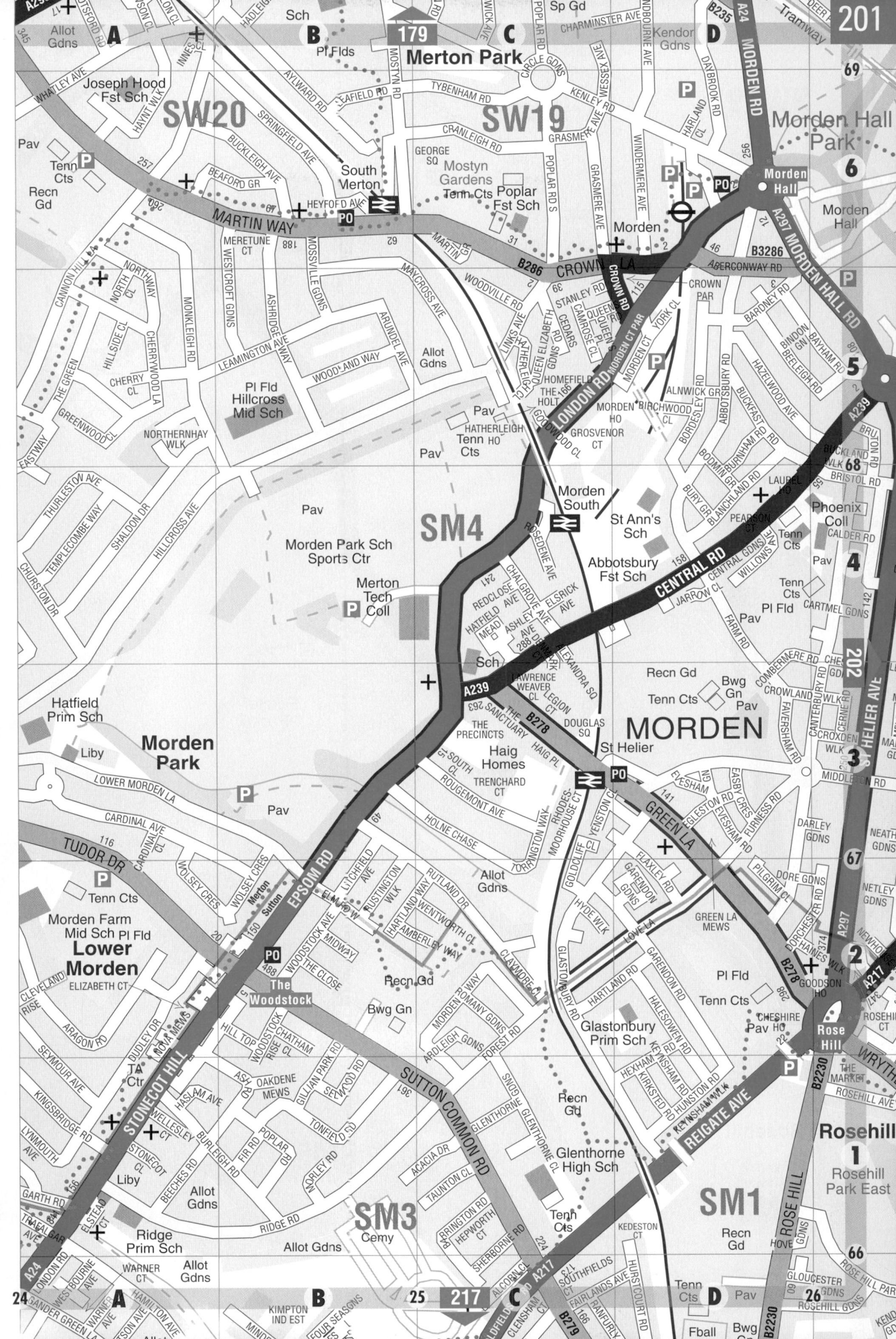
A
B
C
D
179
Merton Park
Sp Gd
Sch
Pl Flds
Allot Gdns
Kendor Gdns
Tramway
69
MORDEN RD
A24
B235
Joseph Hood Fst Sch
SW20
SW19
Morden Hall Park
Pav
Tenn Cts
Recn Gd
South Merton
GEORGE SQ
Mostyn Gardens
Tenn Cts
Poplar Fst Sch
Morden Hall
Morden Hall
6
MARTIN WAY
PO
Morden
B286
CROWN LA
B3286
ABERCONWAY RD
A297 MORDEN HALL RD
CROWN PAR
Allot Gdns
Pl Fld Hillcross Mid Sch
NORTHERNHAY WLK
LONDON RD
MORDEN CT PAR
MORDEN HO
5
A239
Pav
HATHERLEIGH HO
Tenn Cts
Pav
Morden South
St Ann's Sch
Abbotsbury Fst Sch
Pav
SM4
Morden Park Sch Sports Ctr
Merton Tech Coll
CENTRAL RD
Phoenix Coll
Tenn Cts
Pav
4
Tenn Cts
Pl Fld
Pav
68
Sch
A239
Recn Gd
Bwg Gn
Tenn Cts
Pav
202
ST HELIER AVE
Hatfield Prim Sch
Morden Park
Liby
THE PRECINCTS
Haig Homes
B278
MORDEN
St Helier
PO
3
P
Pav
LOWER MORDEN LA
CARDINAL AVE
TUDOR DR
GREEN LA
EPSOM RD
Allot Gdns
Tenn Cts
Morden Farm Mid Sch
Pl Fld
Lower Morden
67
Merton
Sutton
PO
The Woodstock
Recn Gd
Bwg Gn
GREEN LA MEWS
LOVE LA
Pl Fld
Tenn Cts
A297
2
A217
Pav
Rose Hill
STONECOT HILL
SUTTON COMMON RD
Glastonbury Prim Sch
REIGATE AVE
B2230
TA Ctr
Recn Gd
Glenthorne High Sch
Rosehill
1
Rosehill Park East
Liby
Allot Gdns
SM3
SM1
ROSE HILL
Ridge Prim Sch
Cemy
Allot Gdns
Tenn Cts
Recn Gd
66
Allot Gdns
A24
A217
24
25
217
26
KIMPTON IND EST
Tenn Cts
Pav
Fball
Bwg Gn
B279
B2230

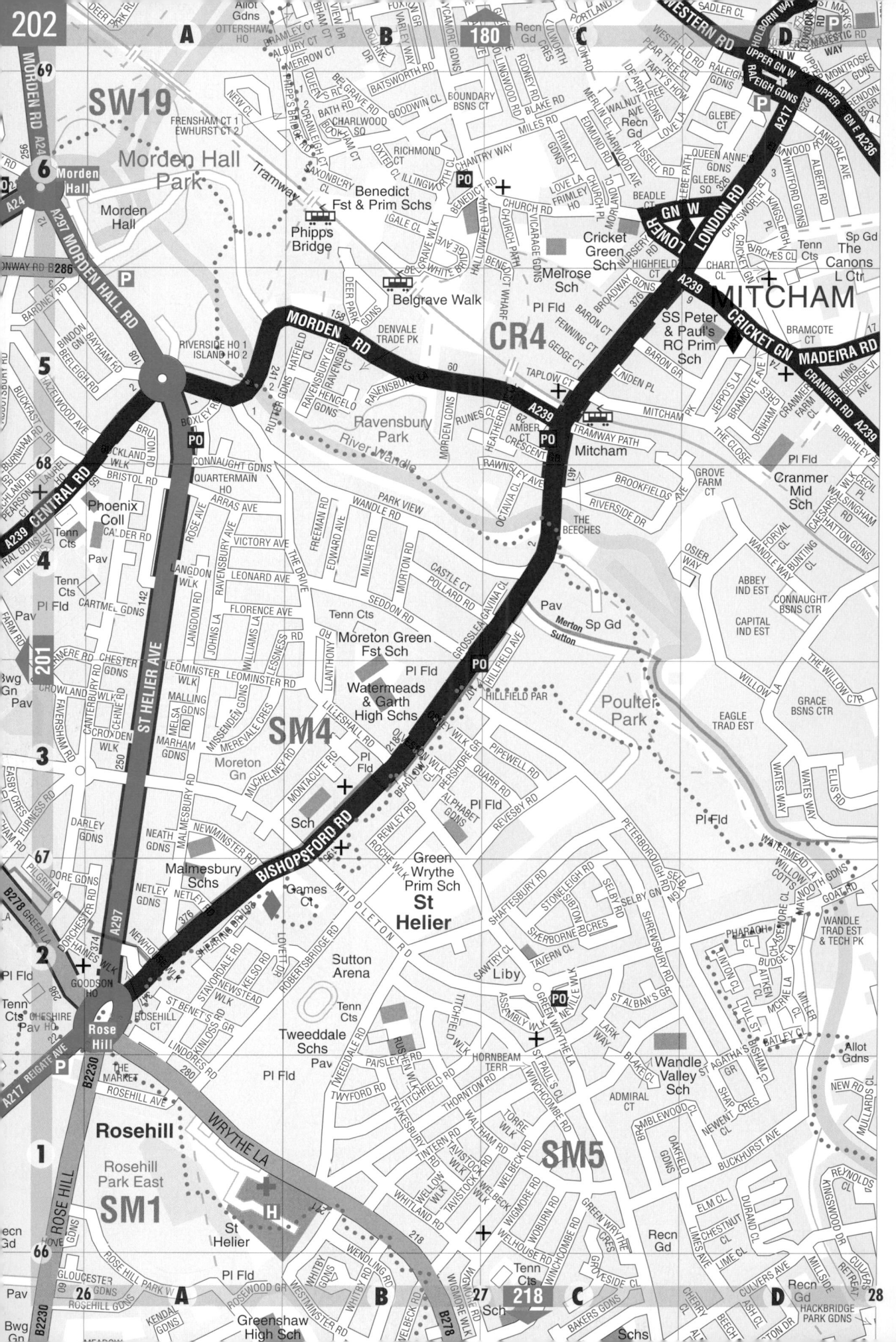
180
201
218
A
B
C
D
1
2
3
4
5
6
26
27
28
66
67
68
69
SW19
CR4
SM4
SM5
SM1
MITCHAM
Morden Hall Park
Morden Hall
Morden
Phipps Bridge
Belgrave Walk
Benedict Fst & Prim Schs
Tramway
MORDEN RD
MORDEN HALL RD
CENTRAL RD
ST HELIER AVE
BISHOPSFORD RD
LONDON RD
LOWER GN W
UPPER GN W
CRICKET GN
MADEIRA RD
CRANMER RD
WESTERN RD
Ravensbury Park
River Wandle
Mitcham
Cricket Green Sch
Melrose Sch
SS Peter & Paul's RC Prim Sch
The Canons L Ctr
Cranmer Mid Sch
Phoenix Coll
Moreton Green Fst Sch
Watermeads & Garth High Schs
Moreton Gn
Malmesbury Schs
Green Wrythe Prim Sch
St Helier
Sutton Arena
Tweeddale Schs
Poulter Park
Wandle Valley Sch
ABBEY IND EST
CAPITAL IND EST
EAGLE TRAD EST
GRACE BSNS CTR
CONNAUGHT BSNS CTR
WANDLE TRAD EST & TECH PK
DENVALE TRADE PK
Rose Hill
Rosehill
Rosehill Park East
WRYTHE LA
ROSE HILL
Greenshaw High Sch
MIDDLETON RD
Merton
Sutton

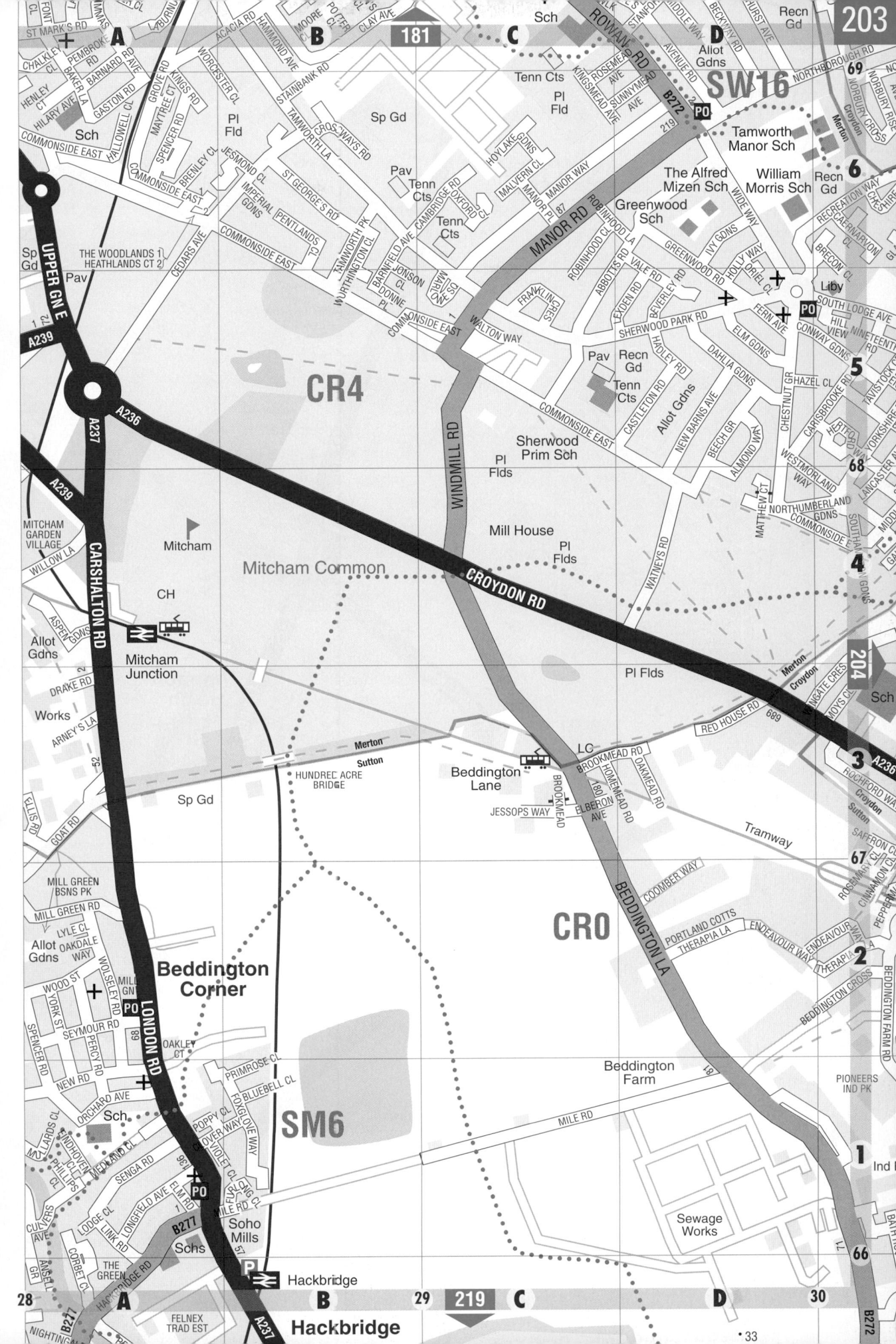

203
181
219
204
SW16
CR4
CR0
SM6
A
B
C
D
28
29
30
1
2
3
4
5
6
66
67
68
69
ST MARK'S RD
ACACIA RD
HAMMOND AVE
MOORE CL
POTTER CL
CLAY AVE
Sch
ROWAN RD
STANFORD
BECKWAY RD
AVENUE RD
Recn Gd
Allot Gdns
NORTHBOROUGH RD
NORBURY RISE
NORBURY CROSS
Tenn Cts
ROSEMEAD AVE
SUNNYMEAD AVE
KINGSMEAD AVE
Pl Fld
B272
PO
Tamworth Manor Sch
Merton
Croydon
CHALKLEY CL
PEMBROKE RD
BARNARD RD
BAKER LA
GASTON RD
HENLEY CT
HILARY AVE
HALLOWELL CL
GROVE RD
MAYTREE CT
KINGS RD
SPENCER RD
WORCESTER CL
STAINBANK RD
TAMWORTH LA
CROSSWAYS RD
Sp Gd
COMMONSIDE EAST
BRENLEY CL
JESMOND CL
IMPERIAL GDNS
ST GEORGE'S RD
PENTLANDS CL
Pav
HOYLAKE GDNS
MALVERN CL
MANOR WAY
MANOR PL
MANOR RD
ROBINHOOD LA
ROBINHOOD CL
The Alfred Mizen Sch
William Morris Sch
Greenwood Sch
WIDE WAY
RECREATION WAY
CAERNARVON CL
BRECON CL
CESHIRE
CAMBRIDGE RD
OXFORD CL
TAMWORTH PK
WORTHINGTON CL
BARNFIELD AVE
JONSON CL
DONNE PL
MARLOWE SQ
THE WOODLANDS
HEATHLANDS CT
CEDARS AVE
UPPER GN E
Sp Gd
Pav
A239
A236
A237
ABBOTTS RD
VALE RD
LEXDEN RD
BEVERLEY RD
GREENWOOD RD
IVY GDNS
HOLLY WAY
ORIEL CL
FRANKLIN CRES
WALTON WAY
SHERWOOD PARK RD
FERN AVE
ELM GDNS
DAHLIA GDNS
HADLEY RD
Liby
SOUTH LODGE AVE
HILL VIEW
NINETEENTH RD
CONWAY GDNS
HAZEL CL
CHESTNUT GR
CARISBROOKE RD
TAVISTOCK
HERTFORD WAY
YORKSHIRE
WESTMORLAND WAY
LANCASTER
NORTHUMBERLAND GDNS
COMMONSIDE E
MATTHEW CT
SOUTHAM
Recn Gd
Tenn Cts
Allot Gdns
CASTLETON RD
NEW BARNS AVE
BEECH GR
ALMOND WAY
Sherwood Prim Sch
Pl Flds
WINDMILL RD
Mill House
Mitcham
MITCHAM GARDEN VILLAGE
WILLOW LA
CARSHALTON RD
Mitcham Common
CROYDON RD
WATNEYS RD
CH
ASPEN GDNS
Allot Gdns
Mitcham Junction
DRAKE RD
Works
ARNEY'S LA
Pl Flds
RED HOUSE RD
WINGATE CRES
MOYS CL
689
Merton
Sutton
HUNDRED ACRE BRIDGE
Beddington Lane
LC
BROOKMEAD RD
HOMEMEAD RD
OAKMEAD RD
BROOKMEAD
JESSOPS WAY
ELBERON AVE
Tramway
ROCHFORD WAY
SAFFRON CL
ROSEMARY CL
CINNAMON CL
PEPPERMINT
Sp Gd
ELLIS RD
GOAT RD
MILL GREEN BSNS PK
MILL GREEN RD
LYLE CL
OAKDALE WAY
Allot Gdns
COOMBER WAY
BEDDINGTON LA
PORTLAND COTTS
THERAPIA LA
ENDEAVOUR WAY
BEDDINGTON CROSS
BEDDINGTON FARM RD
Beddington Corner
WOOD ST
YORK ST
WOLSELEY RD
MILL GN
LONDON RD
SEYMOUR RD
PERCY RD
SPENCER RD
OAKLEY CT
NEW RD
PRIMROSE CL
BLUEBELL CL
Beddington Farm
PIONEERS IND PK
ORCHARD AVE
Sch
FOXGLOVE WAY
POPPY CL
CLOVER WAY
VIOLET CL
MILE RD
MILLARDS CL
ENDHOVEN
PHILLIPS CL
MEDLAND CL
SENGA RD
FURLONG CL
LONGFIELD AVE
ELM RD
Ind Est
Sewage Works
BATH RD
CULVERS AVE
LODGE CL
LINK RD
B277
Soho Mills
Schs
ANSELL GR
CORBET CL
THE GREEN
HACKBRIDGE RD
Hackbridge
FELNEX TRAD EST
NIGHTINGALE
33

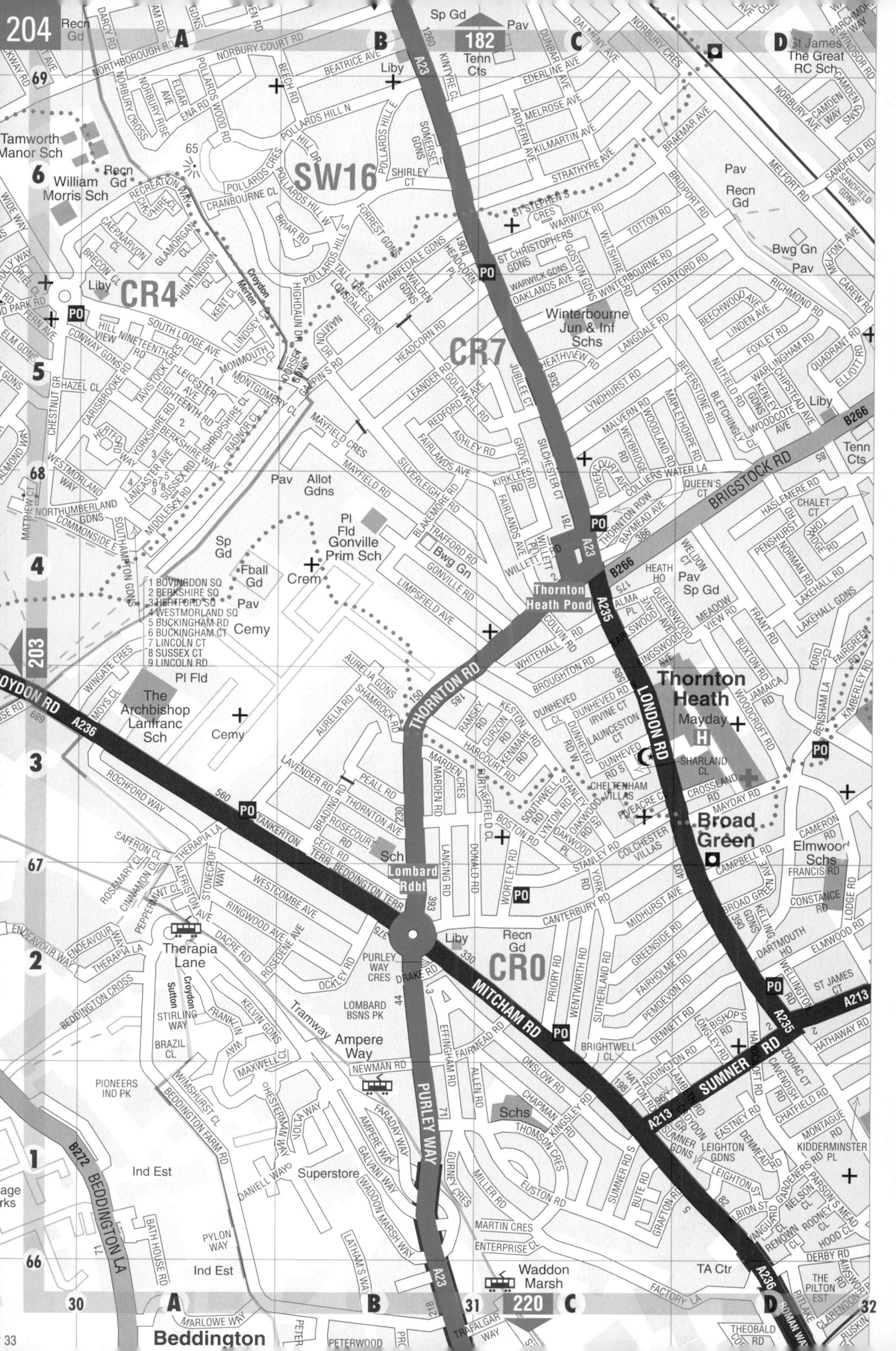
A
B
C
D
182
203
220
69
68
67
66
30
31
32
6
5
4
3
2
1
SW16
CR4
CR7
CR0
NORBURY COURT RD
NORTHBOROUGH RD
BEATRICE AVE
BEECH RD
KINTYRE CL
DUNBAR AVE
DALMENY AVE
NORBURY CRES
EDERLINE AVE
MELROSE AVE
KILMARTIN AVE
STRATHYRE AVE
BRAEMAR AVE
ARDFERN AVE
St James The Great RC Sch
NORBURY AVE
CAMDEN AVE
CAMDEN WAY
MELFORT RD
SANDFIELD RD
Sp Gd
Pav
Tenn Cts
Liby
Recn Gd
Tamworth Manor Sch
William Morris Sch
NORBURY CROSS
NORBURY RISE
ELGAR AVE
ENA RD
POLLARDS WOOD RD
POLLARDS HILL N
POLLARDS HILL E
POLLARDS HILL W
POLLARDS HILL S
POLLARDS CRES
HILL DR
SOMERSET GDNS
SHIRLEY CT
RECREATION WAY
CHESHIRE CL
CRANBOURNE CL
CAERNARVON CL
GLAMORGAN CL
BRECON CL
HUNTINGDON CL
BRIAR RD
FORREST GDNS
ST STEPHEN'S CRES
WARWICK RD
TOTTON RD
BRIDPORT RD
ST CHRISTOPHERS GDNS
WARWICK GDNS
OAKLANDS AVE
GOSTON GDNS
WILTSHIRE RD
WINTERBOURNE RD
STRATFORD RD
Bwg Gn
RICHMOND RD
CAREW RD
MELFONT AVE
Winterbourne Jun & Inf Schs
BEECHWOOD AVE
LINDEN AVE
FOXLEY RD
WARLINGHAM RD
QUADRANT RD
ELLIOTT RD
HEADCORN RD
HEADCORN PL
WALDEN GDNS
WHARFEDALE GDNS
LONSDALE GDNS
TALL TREES
HIGHDAUN DR
NIMTON DR
GALPIN'S RD
DORSET GDNS
Croydon
Merton
KENT CL
LINDSEY CT
MONMOUTH CL
MONTGOMERY CL
SOUTH LODGE AVE
HILL VIEW
NINETEENTH RD
CONWAY GDNS
CARISBROOKE RD
TAVISTOCK CRES
LEICESTER AVE
EIGHTEENTH RD
SHROPSHIRE CL
RADNOR CL
YORKSHIRE RD
BERKSHIRE WAY
HERTFORD WAY
LANCASTER AVE
SUSSEX RD
MIDDLESEX RD
WESTMORLAND WAY
NORTHUMBERLAND GDNS
COMMONSIDE E
SOUTHAMPTON GDNS
CHESTNUT GR
HAZEL CL
ELM GDNS
FERN AVE
MATTHEW CT
JUBILEE CT
HEATHVIEW RD
LANGDALE RD
LEANDER RD
GOLDWELL RD
REDFORD AVE
ASHLEY RD
FAIRLANDS AVE
SILVERLEIGH RD
MAYFIELD CRES
MAYFIELD RD
LYNDHURST RD
MALVERN RD
WEYBRIDGE RD
WOODLAND RD
MAPLETHORPE RD
BEVERSTONE RD
NUTFIELD RD
BLETCHINGLY CL
KENLEY GDNS
CHIPSTEAD AVE
WOODCOTE AVE
B266
BRIGSTOCK RD
COLLIERS WATER LA
QUEEN'S CT
DOVERCOURT AVE
THORNTON ROW
RAYMEAD AVE
HASLEMERE RD
PENSHURST RD
NORMAN RD
CHALET CT
TORRIDGE RD
LAKEHALL RD
LAKEHALL GDNS
Allot Gdns
Pl Fld
Gonville Prim Sch
BLAKEMORE RD
TRAFFORD RD
GONVILLE RD
LIMPSFIELD AVE
KIRKLEES RD
GROVE RD
FAIRLANDS AVE
SILCHESTER CT
WILLETT PL
WILLETT RD
A23
Sp Gd
Fball Gd
Crem
Cemy
1 BOVINGDON SQ
2 BERKSHIRE SQ
3 HERTFORD SQ
4 WESTMORLAND SQ
5 BUCKINGHAM RD
6 BUCKINGHAM CT
7 LINCOLN CT
8 SUSSEX CT
9 LINCOLN RD
Thornton Heath Pond
A235
HEATH HO
WELDON CT
ALMA PL
QUEENSWOOD AVE
MEADOW VIEW RD
FRANT RD
BUXTON RD
EARLSWOOD AVE
KINGSWOOD AVE
COLVIN RD
WHITEHALL RD
BROUGHTON RD
Thornton Heath
Mayday
JAMAICA RD
WOODCROFT RD
BENSHAM LA
FORD CL
FAIRGREEN RD
KIMBERLEY RD
WINGATE CRES
MOYS CL
The Archbishop Lanfranc Sch
Pl Fld
CROYDON RD
A236
AURELIA GDNS
AURELIA RD
SHAMROCK RD
THORNTON RD
RAMSEY RD
CURZON RD
KESTON RD
KENMARE RD
HARCOURT RD
DUNHEVED CL
DUNHEVED RD N
DUNHEVED RD W
DUNHEVED RD S
IRVINE CT
LAUNCESTON CT
LONDON RD
SHARLAND CL
CROSSLAND RD
MAYDAY RD
CHELTENHAM VILLAS
PURCELL CL
Broad Green
CAMERON RD
Elmwood Schs
FRANCIS RD
LODGE RD
CONSTANCE RD
ROCHFORD WAY
LAVENDER RD
PEALL RD
BRADING RD
THORNTON AVE
ROSECOURT RD
MARDEN CRES
MARDEN RD
FURTHERFIELD CL
SOUTHWELL RD
STANLEY GR
LYNTON RD
OAKWOOD RD
OAKWOOD PL
BOSTON RD
STANLEY RD
COLCHESTER VILLAS
CAMPBELL RD
BROAD GREEN AVE
KELLING GDNS
DARTMOUTH HO
ELMWOOD RD
SAFFRON CL
ROSEMARY CL
CINNAMON CL
THERAPIA LA
ALFRISTON AVE
STONECROFT WAY
TANKERTON TERR
CECIL RD
BEDDINGTON TERR
WESTCOMBE AVE
RINGWOOD AVE
Sch
Lombard Rdbt
LANCING RD
DONALD RD
WORTLEY RD
YORK RD
CANTERBURY RD
MIDHURST AVE
GREENSIDE RD
FAIRHOLME RD
PEMDEVON RD
DENNETT RD
LONGLEY RD
BISHOP'S RD
ST JAMES CT
WELLINGTON RD
A213
HATHAWAY RD
PEPPERMINT CL
ENDEAVOUR WAY
THERAPIA LA
Therapia Lane
DACRE RD
ROSEDENE AVE
OCKLEY RD
PURLEY WAY CRES
DRAKE RD
Libv
Recn Gd
MITCHAM RD
PRIORY RD
WENTWORTH RD
SUTHERLAND RD
BRIGHTWELL CL
SUMNER RD
ZODIAC CT
CAVENDISH RD
CHATFIELD RD
MONTAGUE RD
KIDDERMINSTER PL
BEDDINGTON CROSS
Sutton
Croydon
STIRLING WAY
FRANKLIN WAY
KELVIN GDNS
BRAZIL CL
MAXWELL CL
Tramway
Ampere Way
LOMBARD BSNS PK
NEWMAN RD
EFFINGHAM RD
FAIRMEAD RD
ALLEN RD
ONSLOW RD
CHAPMAN RD
KINGSLEY RD
THOMSON CRES
HATTON RD
ADDINGTON RD
LAMBETH RD
CROYDON GR
SUMNER GDNS
EASTNEY RD
LEIGHTON GDNS
DENMEAD RD
PIONEERS IND PK
WIMSHURST CL
BEDDINGTON FARM RD
CHESTERMAN WAY
VOLTA WAY
FARADAY WAY
AMPERE WAY
GALVANI WAY
PURLEY WAY
Schs
B272
BEDDINGTON LA
Ind Est
DANIELL WAY
Superstore
WADDON MARSH WAY
GURNEY CRES
MILLER RD
EUSTON RD
SUMNER RD S
BUTE RD
GRAFTON RD
LEIGHTON ST
ALBION ST
VANGUARD CL
RENOWN CL
GARDENERS RD
NELSON CL
RODNEY CL
PARSON'S MEAD
HOOD CL
BATH HOUSE RD
PYLON WAY
Ind Est
LATHAM'S WAY
MARTIN CRES
ENTERPRISE CL
Waddon Marsh
FACTORY LA
TA Ctr
DERBY RD
AINSWORTH RD
The Pilton Est
PITLAKE
CLARENDON RD
ROMAN WAY
MARLOWE WAY
Beddington
PETERWOOD
TRAFALGAR WAY
THEOBALD RD
RUSKIN

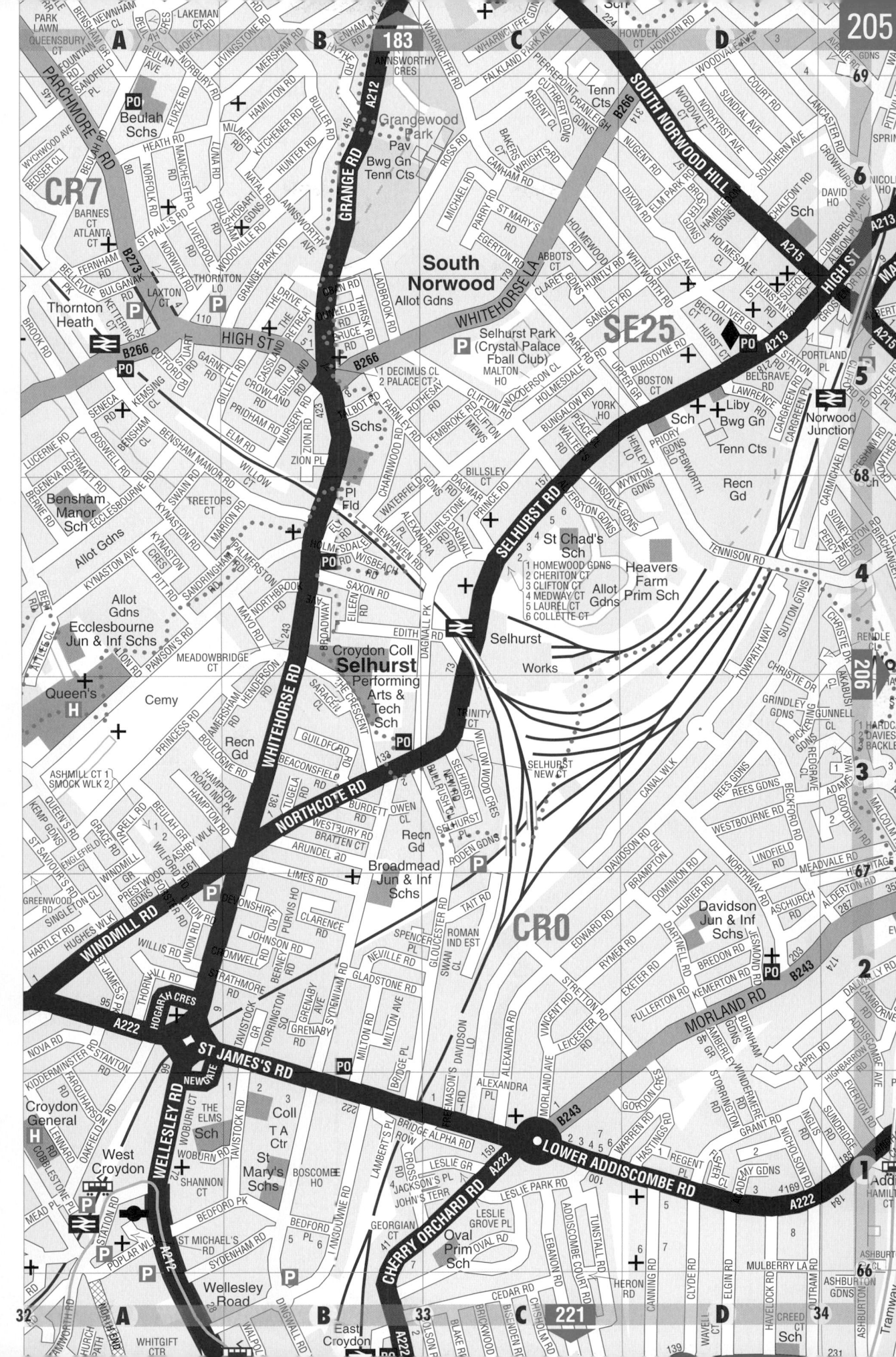
205
A
B
C
D
183
221
206
CR7
SE25
CR0
South Norwood
Selhurst
Thornton Heath
Norwood Junction
West Croydon
Wellesley Road
East Croydon
Croydon General
Beulah Schs
Grangewood Park
Bwg Gn Tenn Cts
South Norwood Allot Gdns
Selhurst Park (Crystal Palace Fball Club)
Bensham Manor Sch
Allot Gdns
Ecclesbourne Jun & Inf Schs
Queen's
Cemy
Croydon Coll
Performing Arts & Tech Sch
St Chad's Sch
Heavers Farm Prim Sch
Works
Broadmead Jun & Inf Schs
Davidson Jun & Inf Schs
Roman Ind Est
St Mary's Schs
Oval Prim Sch
Liby
Recn Gd
Tenn Cts
SOUTH NORWOOD HILL
WHITEHORSE LA
WHITEHORSE RD
GRANGE RD
HIGH ST
SELHURST RD
NORTHCOTE RD
WINDMILL RD
ST JAMES'S RD
LOWER ADDISCOMBE RD
CHERRY ORCHARD RD
MORLAND RD
WELLESLEY RD
PARCHMORE RD
BENSHAM MANOR RD
PORTLAND RD
A212
A213
A215
A222
B243
B266
B273
32
33
34
66
67
68
69
1
2
3
4
5
6
Tramway

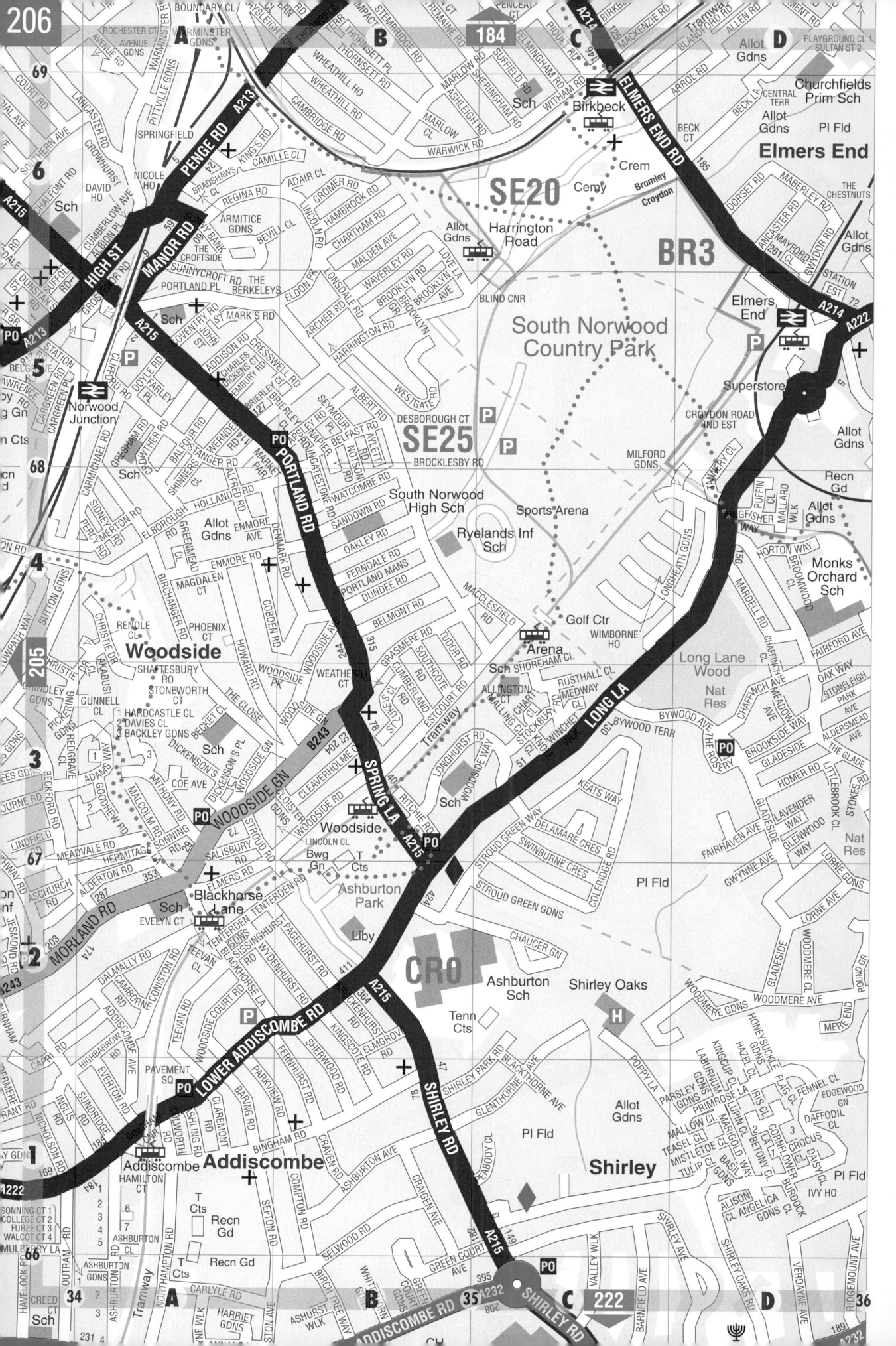
A
B
C
D
184
205
222
34
35
36
69
6
5
68
4
3
67
2
1
66
SE20
SE25
BR3
CR0
Elmers End
South Norwood Country Park
Birkbeck
Harrington Road
Norwood Junction
Woodside
Blackhorse Lane
Addiscombe
Shirley
Shirley Oaks
Elmers End
Arena
Crem
Cemy
Bromley
Croydon
Churchfields Prim Sch
Monks Orchard Sch
South Norwood High Sch
Ryelands Inf Sch
Ashburton Sch
Ashburton Park
Long Lane Wood
Sports Arena
Golf Ctr
Superstore
CROYDON ROAD IND EST
Allot Gdns
Pl Fld
Recn Gd
Nat Res
Tenn Cts
Liby
Sch
Tramway
PENGE RD
HIGH ST
MANOR RD
PORTLAND RD
SPRING LA
LONG LA
ELMERS END RD
LOWER ADDISCOMBE RD
SHIRLEY RD
WOODSIDE GN
MORLAND RD
ADDISCOMBE RD
A213
A215
A214
A222
A232
B243
WARMINSTER RD
BOUNDARY CL
THORNSETT RD
STEMBRIDGE RD
WHEATHILL RD
CAMBRIDGE RD
MARLOW RD
ASHLEIGH RD
SHERINGHAM RD
SUFFIELD RD
ELMINGHAM RD
WITHAM RD
PIQUET RD
MACKENZIE RD
BLANDFORD RD
ALLEN RD
ARROL RD
BECK LA
WARWICK RD
CAMILLE CL
KING'S RD
REGINA RD
ADAIR CL
CROMER RD
HAMBROOK RD
CHARTHAM RD
LINCOLN RD
MALDEN AVE
WAVERLEY RD
BROOKLYN RD
BROOKLYN AVE
LOVE LA
ELDON PK
LONSDALE RD
ARCHER RD
HARRINGTON RD
WESTGATE RD
ALBERT RD
BLIND CNR
DESBOROUGH CT
BROCKLESBY RD
MILFORD GDNS
TANNERY CL
PUFFIN CL
MALLARD WLK
KINGFISHER WAY
HORTON WAY
BROOMWOOD CL
MARDELL RD
CHAFFINCH RD
FAIRFORD AVE
OAK WAY
STONELEIGH PARK AVE
ALDERSMEAD AVE
BYWOOD AVE
BYWOOD TERR
THE ROSERY
BROOKSIDE WAY
GLADESIDE
HOMER RD
LITTLEBROOK CL
STOKES RD
LAVENDER WAY
GLENWOOD WAY
LORNE AVE
LORNE GDNS
FAIRHAVEN AVE
GWYNNE AVE
WOODMERE CL
WOODMERE AVE
WOODMERE GDNS
ROUND GR
MERE END
KEATS WAY
DELAMARE CRES
SWINBURNE CRES
COLERIDGE RD
STROUD GREEN WAY
STROUD GREEN GDNS
CHAUCER GN
LONGHEATH GDNS
MACCLESFIELD RD
WIMBORNE HO
SHOREHAM CL
RUSTHALL CL
MEDWAY CL
ALLINGTON CT
WINCHET WLK
LONGHURST RD
WOODSIDE WAY
ESTCOURT RD
TUDOR RD
SOUTHCOTE RD
CUMBERLAND RD
GRASMERE RD
ST LUKE'S CL
BELMONT RD
DUNDEE RD
PORTLAND MANS
FERNDALE RD
OAKLEY RD
SANDOWN RD
WATCOMBE RD
HOLLAND RD
ENMORE RD
ENMORE AVE
ELBOROUGH RD
GREENMEAD CL
MAGDALEN CT
BIRCHANGER RD
COBDEN RD
DENMARK RD
PHOENIX CT
RENDLE CL
HOWARD RD
WOODSIDE PK
WEATHERILL CT
WOODSIDE AVE
WOODSIDE GN
THE CLOSE
BECKET CL
DICKENSON'S PL
DICKENSON'S LA
SHAFTESBURY HO
STONEWORTH CT
HARDCASTLE CL
DAVIES CL
BACKLEY GDNS
ANTHONY RD
MALCOLM RD
COE AVE
GOODHEW RD
ADAMS WAY
SONNING RD
HERMITAGE LA
SALISBURY RD
STROUD RD
ELMERS RD
CLEAVERHOLME CL
CLOISTER GDNS
WOODSIDE RD
RITCHIE RD
LINCOLN CL
TENTERDEN RD
EVELYN CT
SISSINGHURST RD
WYDENHURST RD
PAGEHURST RD
BENCKENHURST RD
KINGSCOTE RD
ELMGROVE RD
SHERWOOD RD
FERNHURST RD
PARKVIEW RD
CLAREMONT RD
BARING RD
BINGHAM RD
CRAVEN RD
COMPTON RD
ASHBURTON AVE
CRAIGEN AVE
SHIRLEY PARK RD
BLACKTHORNE AVE
GLENTHORNE AVE
PEABODY CL
POPPY LA
SHIRLEY AVE
SHIRLEY OAKS RD
VERDAYNE AVE
RIDGEMOUNT AVE
BARNFIELD AVE
VALLEY WLK
GREEN COURT AVE
SELWOOD RD
SEFTON RD
IVY HO
ALISON CL
ANGELICA GDNS
BURDOCK CL
CROCUS CL
DAISY CL
DAFFODIL CL
EDGEWOOD GN
FENNEL CL
FLAG CL
HONEYSUCKLE GDNS
IRIS CL
HAZEL CL
KINGCUP CL
LABURNUM GDNS
PARSLEY GDNS
PRIMROSE LA
LUPIN CL
MARIGOLD WAY
MALLOW CL
TEASEL CL
MISTLETOE CL
TULIP CL
BASIL GDNS
BETONY CL
CORNFLOWER LA
DALMALLY RD
CAMBORNE RD
CONISTON RD
TEEVAN RD
TEEVAN CL
WOODSIDE COURT RD
BLACKHORSE LA
ADDISCOMBE AVE
HIGHBARROW RD
EVERTON RD
SUNDRIDGE RD
INGLIS RD
NICHOLSON RD
CAPRI RD
PAVEMENT SQ
HAMILTON CT
ASHBURTON CL
ASHBURTON GDNS
NORTHAMPTON RD
CARLYLE RD
HARRIET GDNS
ASHURST WLK
BIRCH TREE WAY
WHITGIFT COURT
OUTRAM RD
HAVELOCK RD
CREED CT
MULBERRY LA
SONNING CT
COLLEGE CT
FURZE CT
WALCOT CT
ALDERTON RD
ASCHURCH RD
MEADVALE RD
LINDFIELD RD
BECKFORD RD
REDGRAVE CL
PICKERING GDNS
GUNNELL CL
AKABUSI CL
CHRISTIE DR
SUTTON GDNS
CARMICHAEL RD
SIDNEY RD
PERCY RD
MERTON RD
GRESHAM RD
CROWTHER RD
BALFOUR RD
SHINNERS CL
STANGER RD
WERNDEE RD
ALFRED RD
MARKET PDE
APSLEY RD
SEYMOUR PL
BELFAST RD
AYLETT RD
NOTSON RD
ROWLANDS CL
ADDISON RD
CHARLES DICKENS CT
EMBURY RD
CRESSWELL RD
BRIERLEY CL
JOHN ST
ST MARK'S RD
COVENTRY RD
DOYLE RD
FARLEY PL
CLIFFORD RD
STATION RD
CARGREEN RD
CARGREEN PL
PORTLAND PL
THE BERKELEYS
SUNNYCROFT RD
THE CROFTSIDE
ARMITICE GDNS
BEVILL CL
BRADSHAWS CL
NICOLE HO
SPRINGFIELD
PITTVILLE GDNS
CUMBERLOW AVE
ALBION PL
CROWHURST
DAVID HO
LANCASTER RD
SOUTHERN AVE
CHALFONT RD
COURT RD
ROCHESTER CT
AVENUE GDNS
DORSET RD
MABERLEY RD
ANCASTER RD
MAYFORD CL
GWYDOR RD
STATION EST
THE CHESTNUTS
CENTRAL TERR
BECK CT
PLAYGROUND CL
SULTAN ST

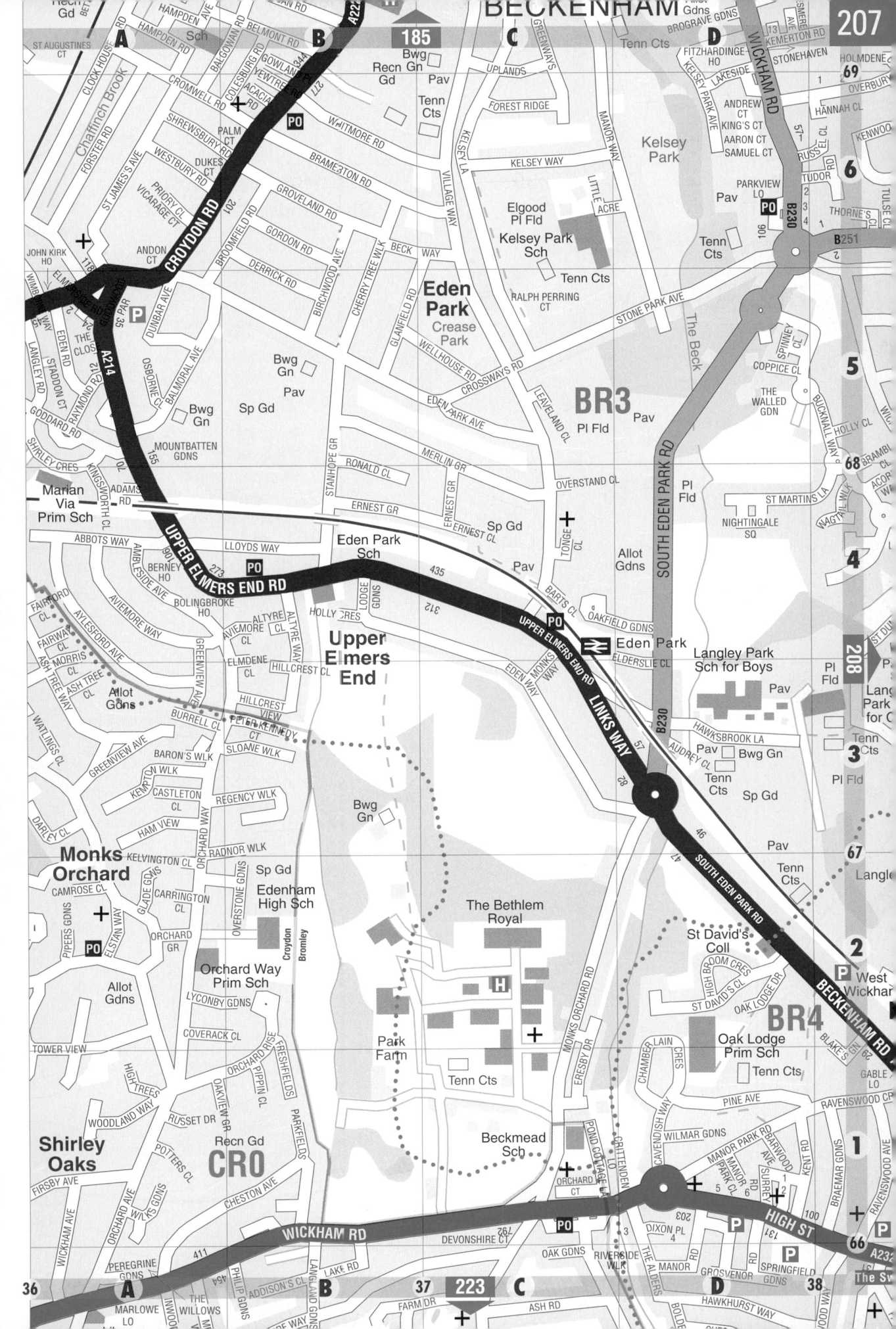
BECKENHAM
185
208
223
A
B
C
D
36
37
38
69
6
5
68
4
3
67
2
1
66
BR3
BR4
CR0
Eden Park
Upper Elmers End
Monks Orchard
Shirley Oaks
Kelsey Park
Crease Park
CROYDON RD
UPPER ELMERS END RD
LINKS WAY
SOUTH EDEN PARK RD
WICKHAM RD
BECKENHAM RD
HIGH ST
A214
A222
B230
B251
A232
Elgood Pl Fld
Kelsey Park Sch
Eden Park Sch
Edenham High Sch
Orchard Way Prim Sch
Marian Via Prim Sch
Langley Park Sch for Boys
The Bethlem Royal
St David's Coll
Oak Lodge Prim Sch
Beckmead Sch
Park Farm
West Wickham
Chaffinch Brook
The Beck
Croydon
Bromley
Allot Gdns
Recn Gd
Bwg Gn
Tenn Cts
Sp Gd
Pl Fld
Pav
PO
P
H

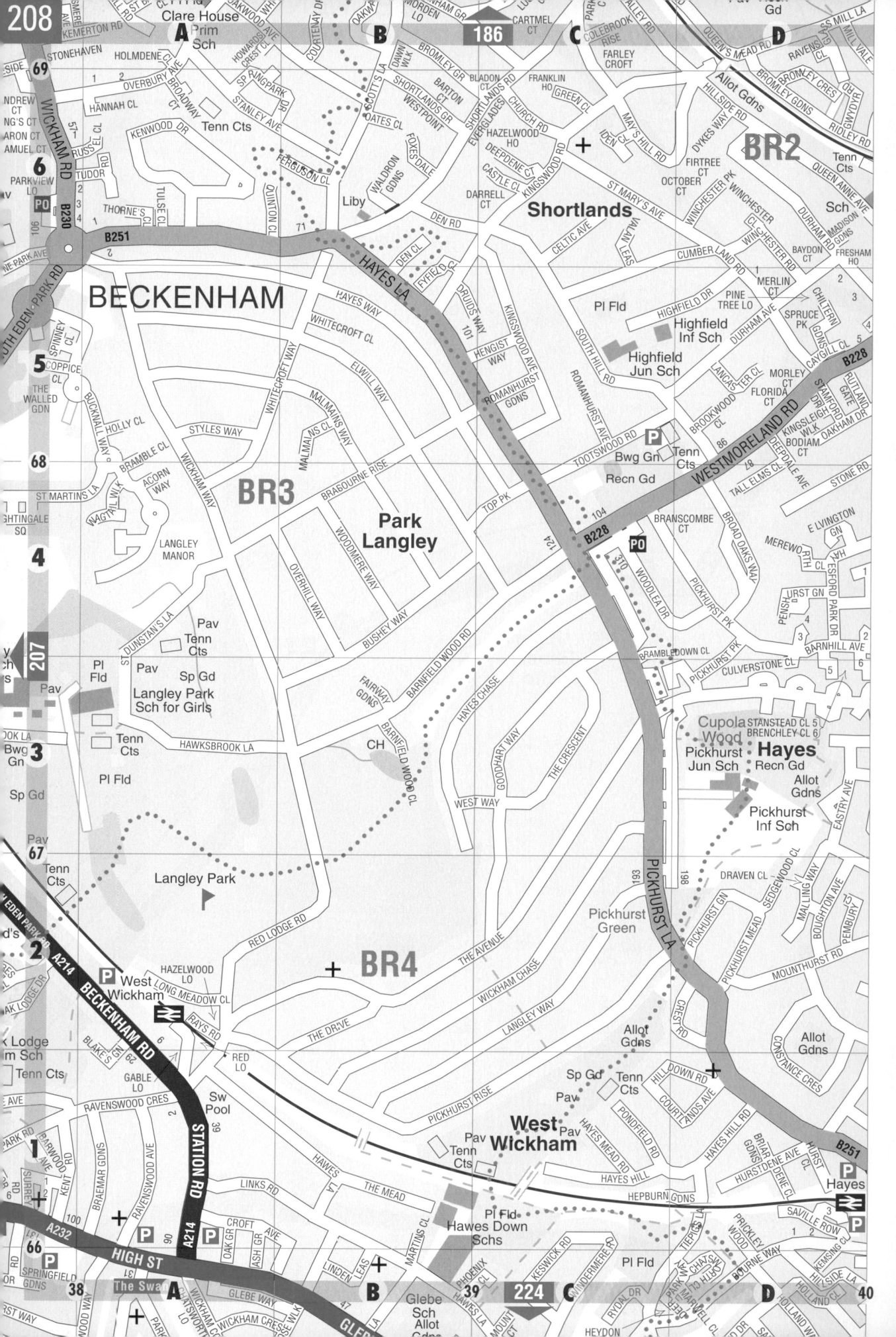

BR2

Shortlands

BECKENHAM

BR3

Park
Langley

Langley Park
Sch for Girls

Langley Park

Cupola
Wood

Pickhurst
Jun Sch

Hayes

Pickhurst
Inf Sch

Pickhurst
Green

BR4

West
Wickham

West
Wickham

Hawes Down
Schs

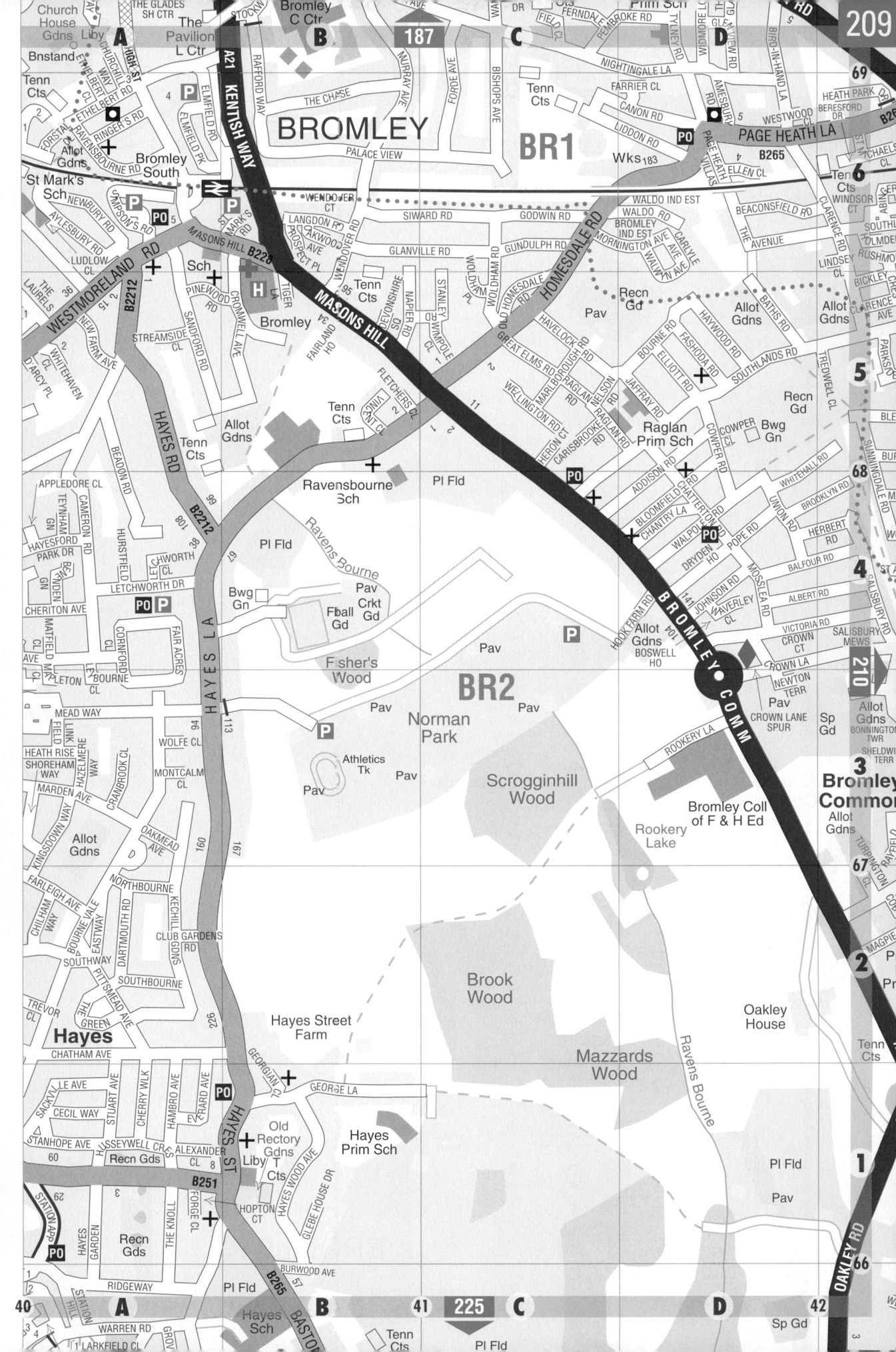
187
A
B
C
D
BROMLEY
BR1
BR2
Church House Gdns
Liby
The Glades Sh Ctr
The Pavilion L Ctr
Bromley C Ctr
Bnstand
Tenn Cts
HIGH ST
CHURCHILL WAY
ETHELBERT CL
ETHELBERT RD
RINGER'S RD
ELMFIELD RD
ELMFIELD PK
RAVENSBOURNE RD
FORSTAL CL
Allot Gdns
Bromley South
St Mark's Sch
A21
KENTISH WAY
RAFFORD WAY
THE CHASE
MURRAY AVE
FORDE AVE
BISHOPS AVE
PALACE VIEW
NIGHTINGALE LA
FARRIER CL
CANON RD
LIDDON RD
Wks
PAGE HEATH LA
PAGE HEATH VILLAS
AMESBURY RD
WESTWOOD CL
HEATH PARK DR
BERESFORD DR
B265
ELLEN CL
TYLNEY RD
WIDMORE LODGE RD
GLENVIEW RD
BIRD-IN-HAND LA
FERNDALE
PEMBROKE RD
FIELD CL
Prim Sch
NEWBURY RD
SAMPSON'S RD
AYLESBURY RD
LUDLOW CL
THE LAURELS
MASONS HILL
B228
WESTMORELAND RD
B2212
ST MARK'S RD
TIGER LA
H
Sch
Bromley
PINEWOOD RD
CROMWELL AVE
SANDFORD RD
STREAMSIDE CL
NEW FARM AVE
WHITEHAVEN CL
D'ARCY PL
WENDOVER CT
LANGDON RD
OAKWOOD AVE
PROSPECT PL
SIWARD RD
GODWIN RD
GLANVILLE RD
GUNDULPH RD
WENDOVER RD
DEVONSHIRE SQ
NAPIER RD
STANLEY RD
WIMPOLE CL
WOLDHAM PL
WOLDHAM RD
OLD HOMESDALE RD
HOMESDALE RD
WALDO IND EST
WALDO RD
BROMLEY IND EST
MORNINGTON AVE
CARLYLE AVE
WALWYN AVE
BEACONSFIELD RD
THE AVENUE
CLARENCE RD
WINDSOR CT
LINDSEY CL
Recn Gd
Pav
Allot Gdns
HAVELOCK RD
GREAT ELMS RD
MARLBOROUGH RD
RAGLAN RD
NELSON RD
WELLINGTON RD
HERON CT
CARISBROOKE RD
JAFFRAY RD
BOURNE RD
ELLIOTT RD
FASHODA RD
HAYWOOD RD
BATHS RD
SOUTHLANDS RD
TREDWELL CL
Raglan Prim Sch
COWPER CL
COWPER RD
Bwg Gn
FAIRLAND HO
FLETCHERS CL
VINCENT CL
Tenn Cts
Allot Gdns
HAYES RD
BEADON RD
Ravensbourne Sch
Pl Fld
ADDISON RD
BLOOMFIELD RD
CHATTERTON RD
CHANTRY LA
WALPOLE RD
POPE RD
DRYDEN HO
UNION RD
WHITEHALL RD
BROOKLYN RD
HERBERT RD
BALFOUR RD
ALBERT RD
VICTORIA RD
CROWN CT
CROWN LA
SALISBURY MEWS
SALISBURY RD
SUNNINGDALE RD
APPLEDORE CL
TEYNHAM GN
CAMERON RD
HAYESFORD PARK DR
BEVENDEN GN
HURSTFIELD
LETCHWORTH CL
LETCHWORTH DR
CHERITON AVE
MATFIELD CL
CORNFORD CL
FAIR ACRES
APPLETON CL
LEYBOURNE CL
HAYES LA
Ravens Bourne
Bwg Gn
Pav
Crkt Gd
Fball Gd
Fisher's Wood
Pl Fld
JOHNSON RD
WAVERLEY CL
MOSSLEA RD
HOOK FARM RD
Allot Gdns
BOSWELL HO
BROMLEY COMM
NEWTON TERR
CROWN LANE SPUR
Pav
Sp Gd
BONNINGTON TWR
SHELDWICH TERR
Bromley Common
Allot Gdns
210
MEAD WAY
LINK FIELD
HEATH RISE
SHOREHAM WAY
HAZELMERE WAY
CRANBROOK CL
WOLFE CL
MONTCALM CL
MARDEN AVE
KINGSDOWN WAY
Allot Gdns
OAKMEAD AVE
NORTHBOURNE
KECHILL GDNS
FARLEIGH AVE
CHILHAM WAY
BOURNE VALE
EASTWAY
DARTMOUTH RD
CLUB GARDENS RD
SOUTHWAY
PITTSMEAD AVE
SOUTHBOURNE
TREVOR CL
THE GREEN
Hayes
CHATHAM AVE
Norman Park
Athletics Tk
Pav
Scrogginhill Wood
ROOKERY LA
Bromley Coll of F & H Ed
Rookery Lake
TURPINGTON CL
MAGPIE
Brook Wood
Oakley House
Tenn Cts
Hayes Street Farm
Mazzards Wood
Ravens Bourne
GEORGIAN CL
GEORGE LA
SACKVILLE AVE
STUART AVE
CHERRY WLK
HAMBRO AVE
EVERARD AVE
CECIL WAY
STANHOPE AVE
HUSSEYWELL CRES
ALEXANDER CL
Recn Gds
HAYES ST
Old Rectory Gdns
Liby
T Cts
HAYES WOOD AVE
GLEBE HOUSE DR
Hayes Prim Sch
Pl Fld
Pav
B251
STATION APP
HAYES GARDEN
Recn Gds
THE KNOLL
FORGE CL
HOPTON CT
BURWOOD AVE
B265
RIDGEWAY
Pl Fld
OAKLEY RD
STATION HILL
Hayes Sch
BASTON
WARREN RD
LARKFIELD CL
Tenn Cts
Pl Fld
Sp Gd
40
41
42
225
69
6
5
68
4
3
67
2
1
66

A
B
C
D
188
BR7
Bickley
BICKLEY RD
BICKLEY PARK RD
A222
Crkt Gd
Pav
WOODLANDS CL
HARTLEY CL
COATES HILL RD
GOSSHILL RD
HEVER GDNS
WELLSMOOR GDNS
REYNARD CL
SHORNEFIELD CL
Kyd Brook
69
HEATH PARK DR
BERESFORD DR
WESTWOOD CL
B265
PAGE HEATH LA
STRATFORD HOUSE AVE
Bickley Park Sch
CHARLOTTE PARK AVE
ST GEORGES RD
ST MICHAELS CL
Tenn Cts
PO
Bickley
ST MATTHEWS DR
OTFORD CL
BARFIELD RD
GOLF RD
6
Tenn Cts
WINDSOR CT
ABINGER CL
THE PANTILES
SYLVAN WLK
NEWNHAMS CL
BEACONSFIELD RD
CLARENCE RD
SOUTHLANDS GR
HAWTHORNE RD
HAWTHORNE CL
COOMBE LEA
MEADOW CROFT
THE AVENUE
HOLMDENE CT
ARMSTRONG CL
CHADD DR
WYNCROFT CL
HURSTWOOD DR
ALBYFIELD
THORNET WOOD RD
RUSHMORE CL
LINDSEY CL
FALCON AVE
SOUTHWARK PL
ROSEMOUNT DR
Allot Gdns
BICKLEY CRES
LIME CL
AYCLIFFE CL
NORTHUMBERLAND GDNS
BLACKBROOK LA
BR1
Allot Gdns
CLARENCE AVE
OLDFIELD RD
BATHS RD
Allot Gdns
DRAPER CT
TANGLEBERRY CL
Tenn Cts
SOUTHLANDS RD
SOUTHBOROUGH RD
SPRINGFIELD RD
OLDFIELD CL
SOUTHWOOD CL
Bromley High Sch for Girls
5
TREDWELL CL
PARKSIDE AVE
PARK HILL
SPRINGFIELD GDNS
Recn Gd
P
BLENHEIM RD
CLAREMONT RD
FAIRMEAD CL
FAIRMEAD
WHITE'S MDW
Bwg Gn
SUNNINGDALE RD
BURFORD RD
HIGHFIELD RD
Thornet Wood
68
WHITEHALL RD
WALDEGRAVE RD
HOMEMEAD RD
Jubilee Country Park
BROOKLYN RD
MAYFIELD RD
WESTCOTT CL
RINGMER WAY
RIPLEY CL
UNION RD
HERBERT RD
WOODSIDE RD
THE FAIRWAY
BROOKMEAD AVE
MERTON GDNS
4
BALFOUR RD
SALISBURY RD
ST AUGUSTINE'S AVE
BIRDHAM CL
CLOISTERS AVE
MOSSLEA RD
MOORCROFT GDNS
ALBERT RD
SOUTHBOROUGH LA
FONTWELL DR
St James RC Prim Sch
MAYBURY CL
VICTORIA RD
CROWN CT
SALISBURY MEWS
DUXBERRY CL
WILLOW CL
Liby
AUSTIN AVE
HOLBROOK WAY
PARKFIELD WAY
209
CROWN LA
MAGPIE HALL LA
HOLMCROFT WAY
Southborough Prim Sch
NEWTON TERR
LAVENDER CL
STILES CL
Recn Gd
SUNRAY AVE
SOVEREIGN CT
Pav
GREEN WAY
RUSKIN WLK
BR2
CROWN LANE SPUR
Sp Gd
Allot Gdns
OXHAWTH CRES
LANGLEY GDNS
BONNINGTON TWR
Cemy
Parkfield Recn Gd
THORN CL
SHELDWICH TERR
MONS WAY
CHESHAM AVE
3
Bromley Common
TURPINGTON LA
BROOM CL
Southborough
LOVELACE AVE
NARROW WAY
MANOR WAY
SHELL CL
THE OAKS
CRESCENT DR
Coll Ed
ASH ROW
HAZEL WLK
PRESCOTT AVE
FELTON CL
Allot Gdns
MOSUL WAY
WHITEBEAM AVE
ROLLESTON AVE
RAYFIELD CL
MAGPIE HALL CL
HORNBEAM WAY
BIRCH ROW
FARINGDON AVE
A21
HOLLINGWORTH RD
67
TURPINGTON CL
LINK WAY
LABURNUM WAY
CH
Bromley
Recn Gd
COBHAM CL
LARCH WAY
ROLLESTON CL
FAIROAK CL
BROMLEY COMM
Tenn Cts
ALMOND WAY
2
Pl Fld
Recn Gd
ALMOND CL
Sparrow Wood
Prince's Plain Prim Sch
Oakley House
Allot Gdns
Pl Fld
London Loop
Tenn Cts
Prince's Plain
BR5
CHURCH LA
BARHAM CT
A233
COTTAGE AVE
PRINCE'S PLAIN
Scrubs Farm
CREDENHALL DR
BREWERY RD
Crofton Heath
Pl Fld
1
CAPEL CL
BRAMLEY CL
LENNARD RD
ARAGON CL
LOWER GRAVEL RD
BARHAM CL
LANSDOWNE AVE
SEYMOUR DR
Pav
RANDOLPH RD
BRADFORD CL
JACKSON RD
RIBSTON CL
HATHAWAY CL
DRAYTON AVE
MORLEY CL
TRINITY CL
OAKLEY RD
DAERWOOD CL
BROMLEY
66
PO
ST ANTHONY'S CT
JACKSON RD
ROSEDALE
LIME GR
CHERRY ORCHARD RD
Knowl Wood
BIRCH MEAD
COPTHORNE AVE
JASMINE CL
WISTARIA CL
42
WEALD CL
43
226
44
KNOWLE RD
POPLAR AVE
HASTINGS
FAIRBANK AVE
Sp Gd
Knowlehill

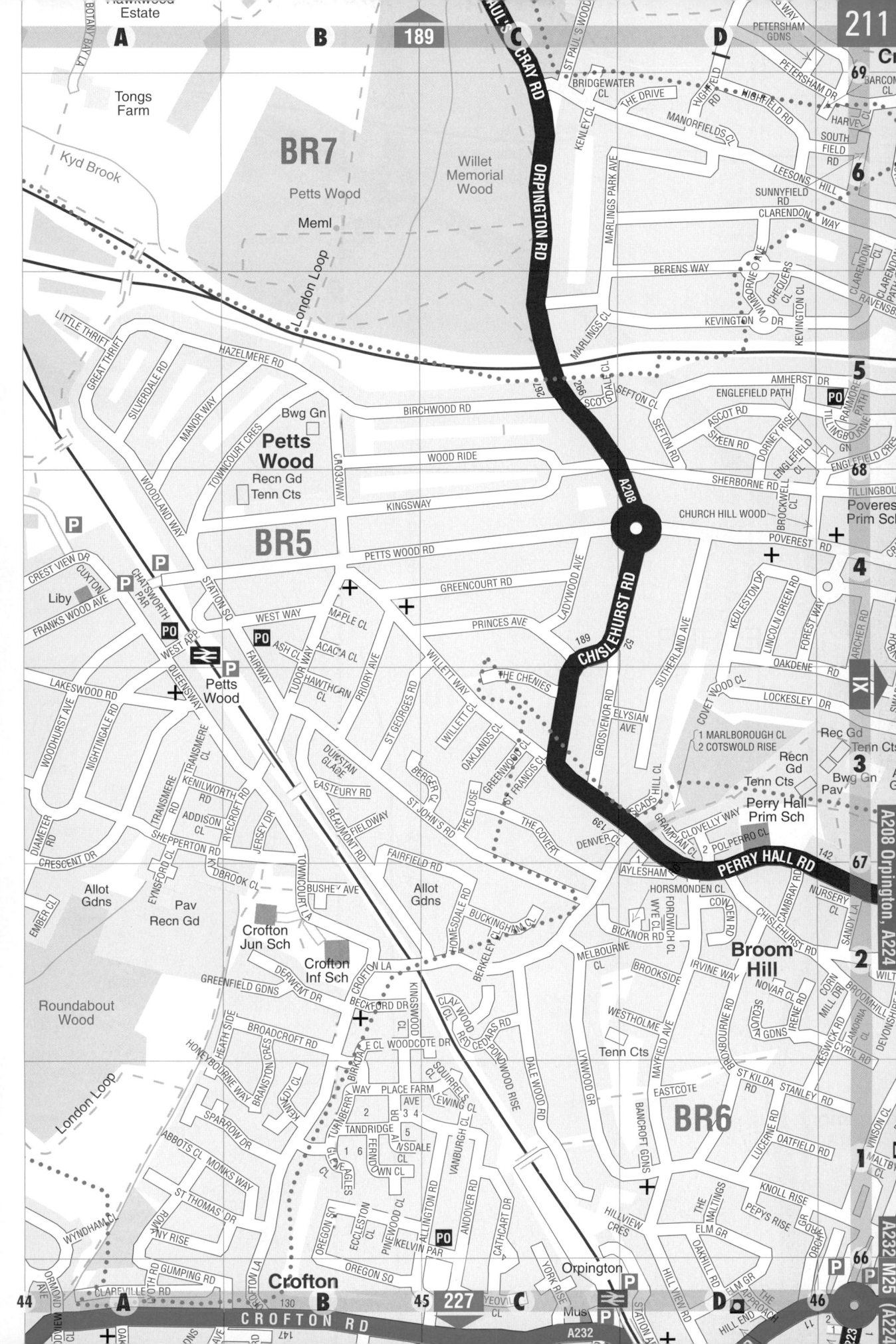

Tongs Farm
BR7
Kyd Brook
Petts Wood
Meml
Willet Memorial Wood
London Loop
ORPINGTON RD
ST PAUL'S CRAY RD
BR5
Petts Wood Recn Gd
Tenn Cts
Bwg Gn
HAZELMERE RD
BIRCHWOOD RD
WOOD RIDE
KINGSWAY
PETTS WOOD RD
GREENCOURT RD
PRINCES AVE
WEST WAY
CHISLEHURST RD
A208
SHERBORNE RD
CHURCH HILL WOOD
POVEREST RD
Poverest Prim Sch
AMHERST DR
ENGLEFIELD PATH
KEVINGTON DR
BERENS WAY
CLARENDON WAY
LEESONS HILL
MANORFIELDS CL
HIGHFIELD RD
PETERSHAM DR
BRIDGEWATER CL
THE DRIVE
MARLINGS PARK AVE
Liby
FRANKS WOOD AVE
CREST VIEW DR
Petts Wood
LAKESWOOD RD
WOODHURST AVE
NIGHTINGALE RD
Allot Gdns
Pav Recn Gd
Crofton Jun Sch
Crofton Inf Sch
Roundabout Wood
London Loop
Allot Gdns
PERRY HALL RD
Perry Hall Prim Sch
Broom Hill
BR6
Tenn Cts
MAYFIELD AVE
LYNWOOD GR
DALE WOOD RD
Orpington
Crofton
CROFTON RD
A232
A208 Orpington, A224
A232 M25 (A224)
Rec Gd
Tenn Cts
Recn Gd
Pav

189
227
IX

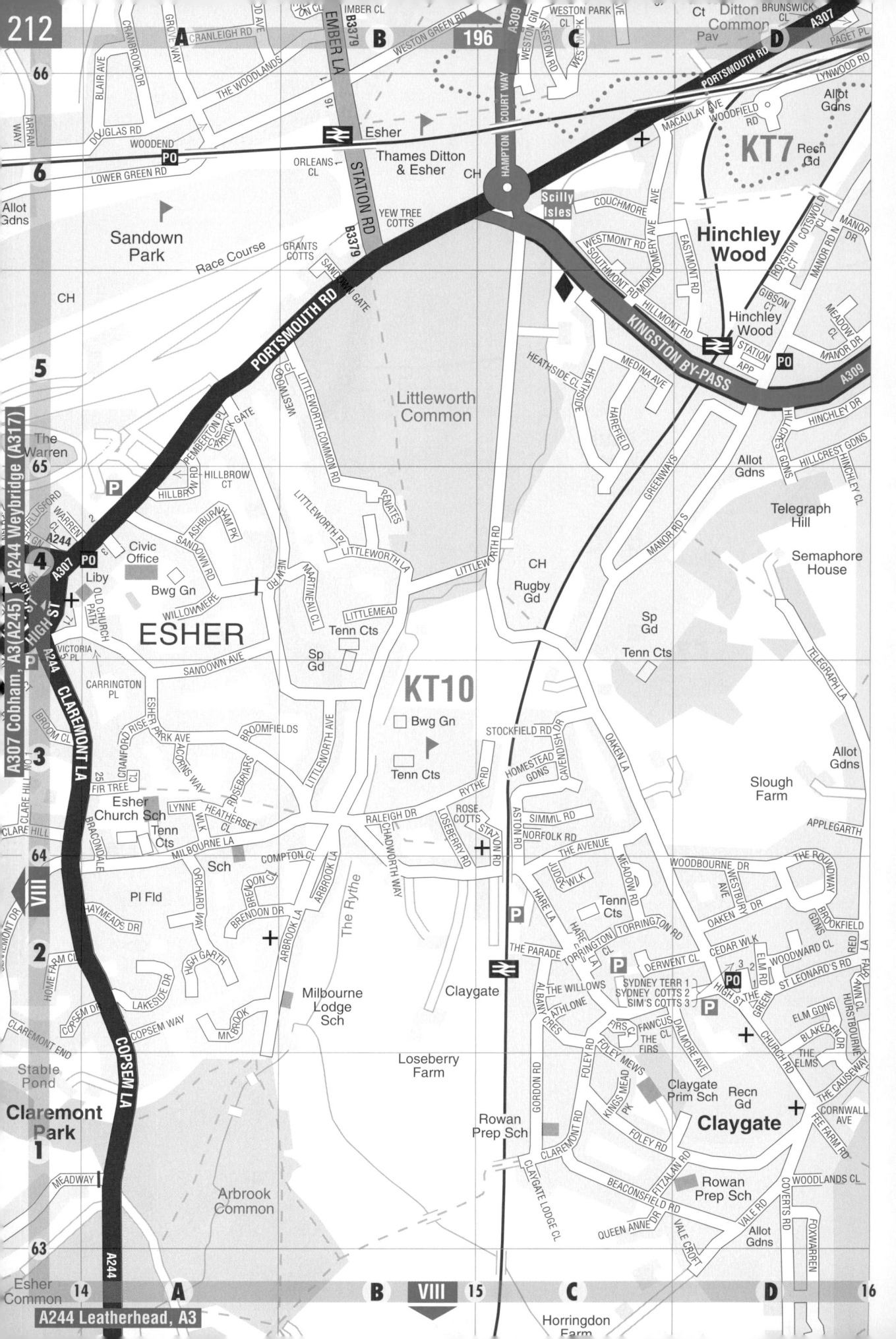
196
A
B
C
D
66
6
5
65
4
3
64
2
1
63
14
15
16
ESHER
KT10
KT7
Hinchley Wood
Claygate
Claremont Park
Sandown Park
Littleworth Common
Thames Ditton & Esher
Esher
Hinchley Wood
Claygate
Telegraph Hill
Semaphore House
Slough Farm
Loseberry Farm
Arbrook Common
Milbourne Lodge Sch
Rowan Prep Sch
Claygate Prim Sch
Esher Church Sch
Civic Office
Liby
Stable Pond
Esher Common
Horringdon Farm
Ditton Common
PORTSMOUTH RD
KINGSTON BY-PASS
CLAREMONT LA
COPSEM LA
STATION RD
EMBER LA
HAMPTON COURT WAY
LITTLEWORTH RD
A307 Cobham, A3(A245) A244 Weybridge (A317)
A244 Leatherhead, A3
VIII

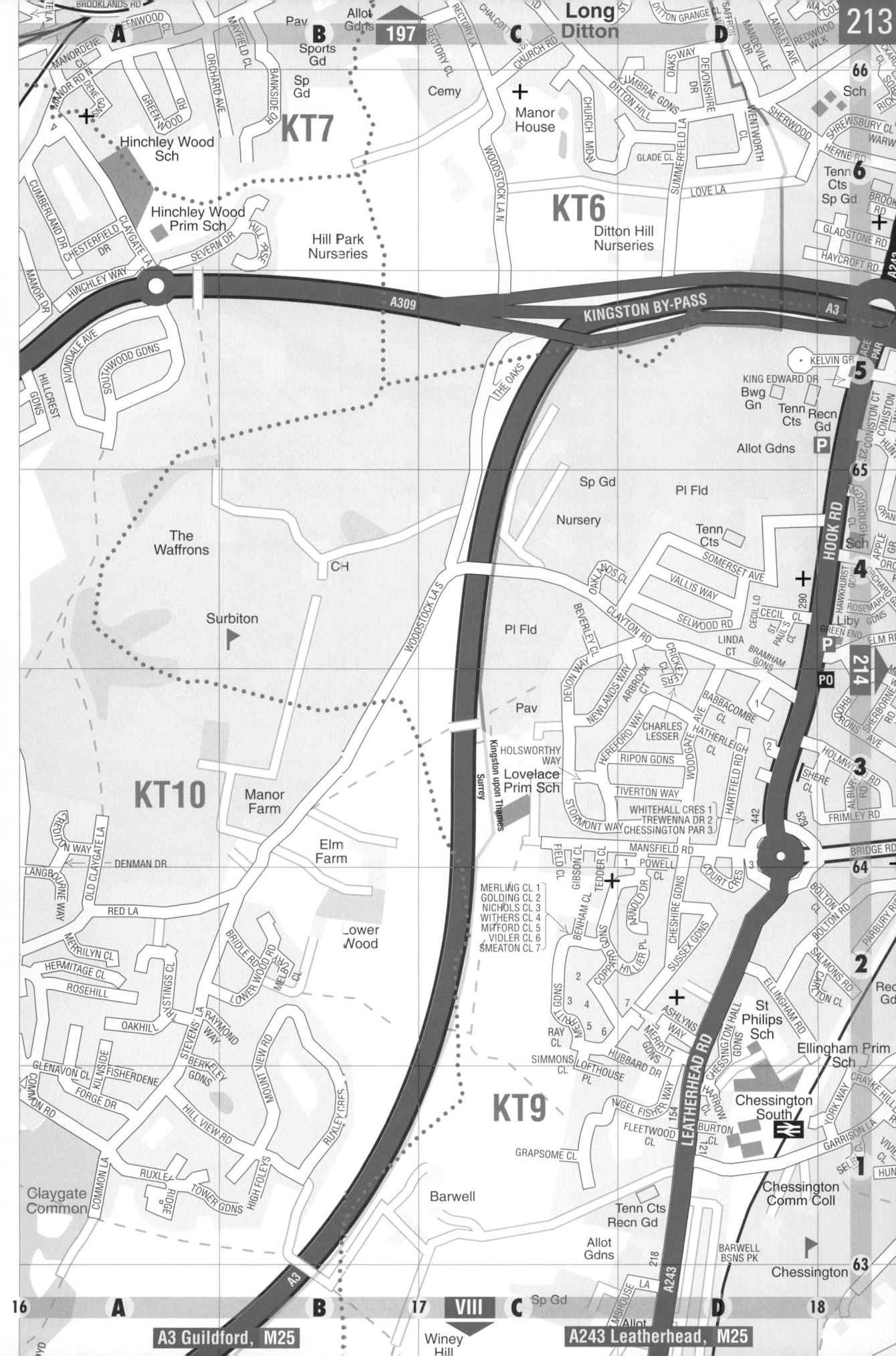
Long Ditton
KT7
KT6
KT10
KT9
Hinchley Wood Sch
Hinchley Wood Prim Sch
Hill Park Nurseries
Manor House
Ditton Hill Nurseries
KINGSTON BY-PASS
A309
A3
The Waffrons
Surbiton
Manor Farm
Elm Farm
Lower Wood
Lovelace Prim Sch
HOOK RD
LEATHERHEAD RD
St Philips Sch
Ellingham Prim Sch
Chessington South
Chessington Comm Coll
Claygate Common
Barwell
Chessington
Winey Hill
A3 Guildford, M25
A243 Leatherhead, M25
197
214
VIII

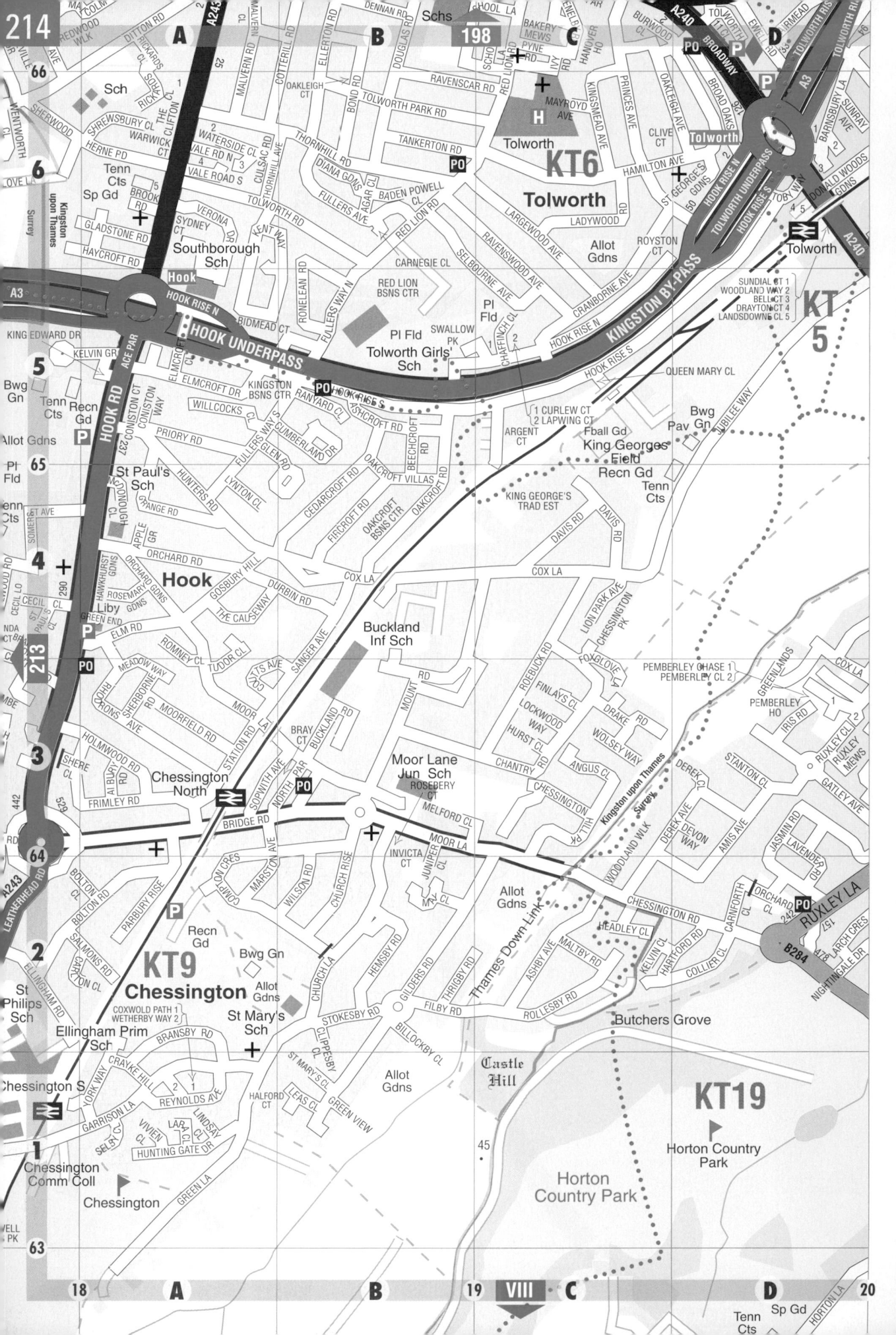
A
B
C
D
198
66
6
5
65
4
3
64
2
1
63
18
19
20
VIII
213
A243
A3
A240
Sch
Schs
DENNAN RD
SCHOOL LA
BAKERY MEWS
PYNE RD
HANOVER HO
BURWOOD CL
TOLWORTH CL
BROADWAY
EWELL RD
ORMEAD
TOLWORTH RISE
REDWOOD WLK
DITTON RD
RICKARDS CL
MALVERN RD
COTTERILL RD
ELLERTON RD
DOUGLAS RD
RED LION RD
IVY RD
KINGSMEAD AVE
PRINCES AVE
OAKLEIGH AVE
BROAD OAKS
OAKLEIGH CT
RAVENSCAR RD
TOLWORTH PARK RD
MAYROYD AVE
BOND RD
THE CLIFTON CL
SHERWOOD
WENTWORTH CL
SHREWSBURY CL
WARWICK CT
WATERSIDE CL
VALE RD N
VALE ROAD S
HERNE RD
CULSAC RD
THORNHILL AVE
THORNHILL RD
TANKERTON RD
DIANA GDNS
AGAR CL
BADEN POWELL CL
FULLERS AVE
Tolworth
KT6
CLIVE CT
HAMILTON AVE
ST GEORGE'S GDNS
HOOK RISE N
TOLWORTH UNDERPASS
HOOK RISE S
BARNSBURY LA
SUNRAY AVE
DONALD WOODS GDNS
TOBY WAY
Tenn Cts
Sp Gd
BROOK RD
LOVE LA
Kingston upon Thames
Surrey
GLADSTONE RD
VERONA DR
SYDNEY CT
TOLWORTH RD
KENT WAY
Southborough Sch
HAYCROFT RD
LARGEWOOD AVE
LADYWOOD RD
RAVENSWOOD AVE
SELBOURNE AVE
ROYSTON CT
Allot Gdns
CARNEGIE CL
RED LION BSNS CTR
RONELEAN RD
FULLERS WAY N
Hook
HOOK RISE N
HOOK UNDERPASS
BIDMEAD CT
CRANBORNE AVE
KINGSTON BY-PASS
SUNDIAL CT 1
WOODLAND WAY 2
BELL CT 3
DRAYTON CT 4
LANDSDOWNE CL 5
KT5
Pl Fld
SWALLOW PK
CHAFFINCH CL
Tolworth Girls' Sch
KING EDWARD DR
KELVIN GR
ACE PAR
ELMCROFT CL
ELMCROFT DR
KINGSTON BSNS CTR
HOOK RISE S
RANYARD CL
ASHCROFT RD
QUEEN MARY CL
JUBILEE WAY
Bwg Gn
Recn Gd
Allot Gdns
HOOK RD
CONISTON CT
CONISTON WAY
WILLCOCKS CL
FULLERS WAY S
CUMBERLAND DR
BEECHCROFT RD
1 CURLEW CT
2 LAPWING CT
ARGENT CT
Fball Gd
Pav
King Georges Field
Recn Gd
Pl Fld
PRIORY RD
GLEN RD
OAKCROFT VILLAS
OAKCROFT RD
St Paul's Sch
HUNTERS RD
LYNTON CL
CEDARCROFT RD
FIRCROFT RD
OAKCROFT BSNS CTR
KING GEORGE'S TRAD EST
DAVIS RD
GRANGE RD
APPLE GR
ORCHARD RD
GOSBURY HILL
DURBIN RD
COX LA
SOMERSET AVE
CECIL LO
CECIL CL
HAWKHURST GDNS
ORCHARD GDNS
ROSEMARY GDNS
THE CAUSEWAY
Liby
GREEN END
ELM RD
ROMNEY CL
TUDOR CL
COVERTS AVE
SANGER AVE
Buckland Inf Sch
LION PARK AVE
CHESSINGTON PK
FOXGLOVE LA
ROEBUCK RD
FINLAYS CL
LOCKWOOD WAY
HURST CL
DRAKE RD
WOLSEY WAY
PEMBERLEY CHASE 1
PEMBERLEY CL 2
GREENLANDS
PEMBERLEY HO
IRIS RD
COX LA
MEADOW WAY
SHERBORNE RD
RONS AVE
MOORFIELD RD
MOOR LA
STATION RD
BUCKLAND RD
BRAY CT
MOUNT RD
Moor Lane Jun Sch
ROSEBERY CT
CHANTRY RD
ANGUS CL
CHESSINGTON HILL PK
DEREK CL
STANTON CL
RUXLEY CL
RUXLEY MEWS
GATLEY AVE
HOLMWOOD RD
SHERE CL
ALBURY RD
FRIMLEY RD
Chessington North
SOPWITH AVE
NORTH PAR
BRIDGE RD
MELFORD CL
MOOR LA
DEREK AVE
DEVON WAY
AMIS AVE
JASMIN RD
LAVENDER RD
LEATHERHEAD RD
BOLTON CL
BOLTON RD
PARBURY RISE
COMPTON CRES
MARSTON AVE
WILSON RD
CHURCH RISE
INVICTA CT
JUNIPER CL
MAY CL
WOODLAND WLK
CHESSINGTON RD
CARNFORTH CL
ORCHARD CL
RUXLEY LA
B284
LARCH CRES
NIGHTINGALE DR
SALMONS RD
CARLTON CL
ELLINGHAM RD
KT9
Chessington
Recn Gd
Bwg Gn
Allot Gdns
CHURCH LA
HEMSBY RD
GILDERS RD
THRIGBY RD
Thames Down Link
ASHBY AVE
MALTBY RD
HEADLEY CL
KELVIN CL
HARTFORD RD
COLLIER CL
ROLLESBY RD
FILBY RD
STOKESBY RD
BILLOCKBY CL
Butchers Grove
St Philips Sch
COXWOLD PATH 1
WETHERBY WAY 2
St Mary's Sch
Ellingham Prim Sch
BRANSBY RD
CLIPPESBY CL
ST MARY'S CL
Castle Hill
Allot Gdns
KT19
Horton Country Park
YORK WAY
CRAYKE HILL
REYNOLDS AVE
LINDSAY CL
HALFORD CT
LEAS CL
GREEN VIEW
Chessington S
GARRISON LA
VIVIEN CL
LARA CL
SELBY CL
HUNTING GATE DR
Chessington Comm Coll
Chessington
GREEN LA
Horton Country Park
Sp Gd
Tenn Cts
HORTON LA

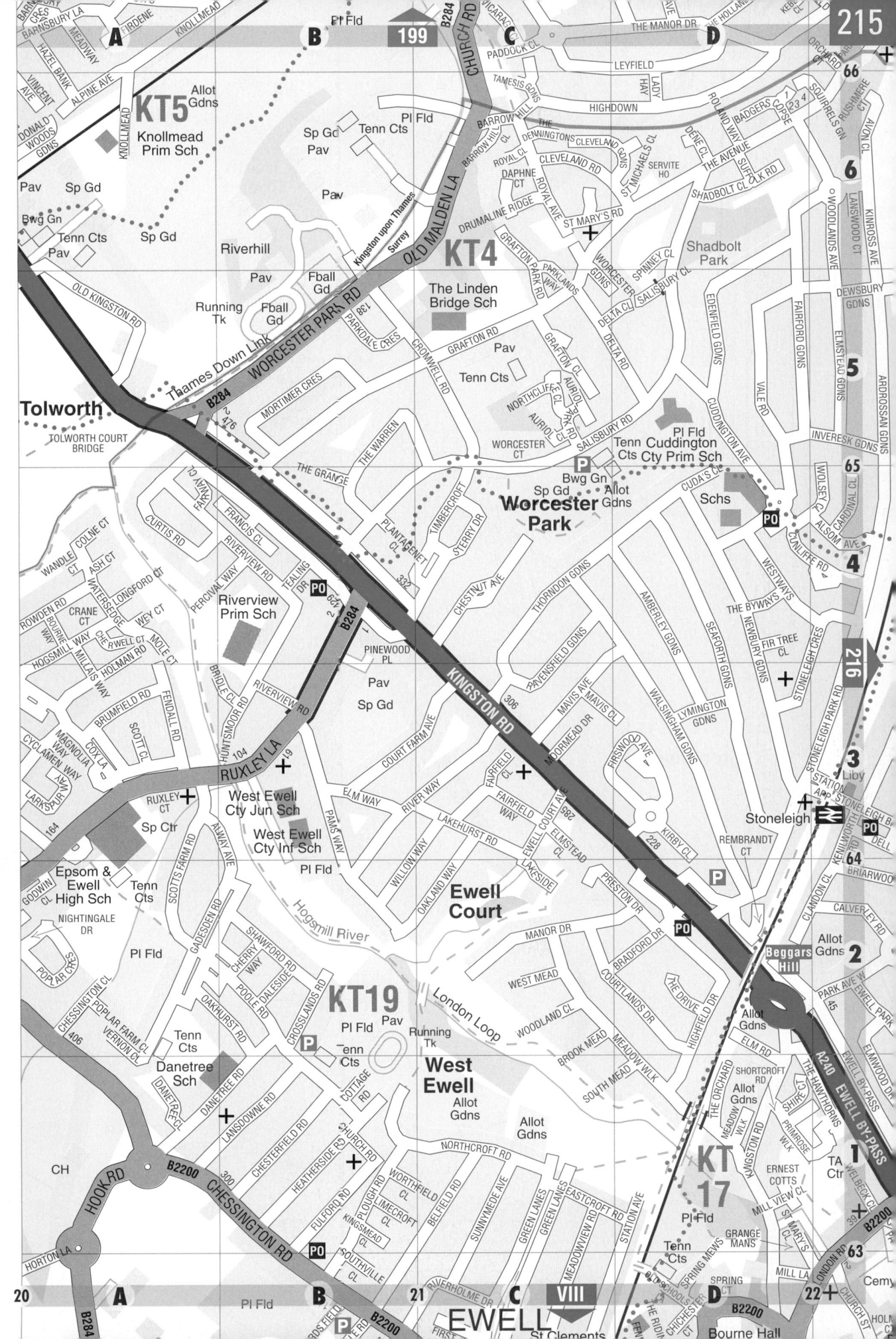
A
B
C
D
199
VIII
216
20
21
22
66
6
5
65
4
3
64
2
1
63
KT5
KT4
KT19
KT 17
Tolworth
Worcester Park
Ewell Court
West Ewell
Stoneleigh
Beggars Hill
EWELL
Knollmead Prim Sch
Riverhill
The Linden Bridge Sch
Shadbolt Park
Cuddington Cty Prim Sch
Riverview Prim Sch
West Ewell Cty Jun Sch
West Ewell Cty Inf Sch
Epsom & Ewell High Sch
Danetree Sch
Servite Ho
Bourne Hall
St Clements
Kingston upon Thames
Surrey
Thames Down Link
London Loop
Hogsmill River
TOLWORTH COURT BRIDGE
KINGSTON RD
OLD MALDEN LA
WORCESTER PARK RD
CHURCH RD
RUXLEY LA
CHESSINGTON RD
HOOK RD
EWELL BY-PASS
A240
B284
B2200
OLD KINGSTON RD
MORTIMER CRES
PARKDALE CRES
CROMWELL RD
GRAFTON RD
THE WARREN
THE GRANGE
SALISBURY RD
DELTA RD
CUDDINGTON AVE
EDENFIELD GDNS
FAIRFORD GDNS
ELMSTEAD GDNS
VALE RD
INVERESK GDNS
ARDROSSAN GDNS
KINROSS AVE
WOODLANDS AVE
LANSWOOD CT
DEWSBURY GDNS
THE AVENUE
SHADBOLT CL
HIGHDOWN
LEYFIELD
THE MANOR DR
PADDOCK CL
TAMESIS GDNS
BARROW HILL
DRUMALINE RIDGE
ROYAL AVE
ST MARY'S RD
CLEVELAND RD
CHESTNUT AVE
THORNDON GDNS
AMBERLEY GDNS
SEAFORTH GDNS
NEWBURY GDNS
WESTWAYS
THE BYWAYS
STONELEIGH CRES
STONELEIGH PARK RD
RAVENSFIELD GDNS
MAVIS AVE
MOORMEAD DR
WALSINGHAM GDNS
LYMINGTON GDNS
FIRSWOOD AVE
KIRBY CL
REMBRANDT CT
COURT FARM AVE
ELM WAY
RIVER WAY
LAKEHURST RD
FAIRFIELD WAY
EWELL COURT AVE
ELMSTEAD CL
PRESTON DR
MANOR DR
WEST MEAD
BRADFORD DR
COURTLANDS DR
THE DRIVE
HIGHFIELD DR
WOODLAND CL
BROOK MEAD
MEADOW WLK
SOUTH MEAD
RIVERVIEW RD
FRANCIS CL
CURTIS RD
PERCIVAL WAY
HUNTSMOOR RD
BRIDLE CL
PINEWOOD PL
HOGSMILL WAY
HOLMAN RD
BRUMFIELD RD
FENDALL RD
SCOTT CL
MAGNOLIA WAY
CYCLAMEN WAY
LARKSPUR WAY
SCOTTS FARM RD
GADESDEN RD
SHAWFORD RD
CHERRY WAY
DALESIDE
POOLE RD
OAKHURST RD
CROSSLANDS RD
CHESSINGTON CL
POPLAR FARM CL
VERNON CL
POPLAR CRES
NIGHTINGALE DR
DANETREE RD
LANSDOWNE RD
CHESTERFIELD RD
HEATHERSIDE RD
CHURCH RD
FULFORD RD
PLOUGH RD
WORTHFIELD CL
BELFIELD RD
NORTHCROFT RD
SUNNYMEDE AVE
GREEN LANES
EASTCROFT RD
MEADOWVIEW RD
STATION AVE
SOUTHVILLE CL
KINGSMEAD CL
LIMECROFT CL
RIVERHOLME DR
THE ORCHARD
SHORTCROFT RD
MEADOW WLK
KINGSTON RD
ELM RD
THE HAWTHORNS
PRIMROSE WLK
ERNEST COTTS
MILL VIEW CL
GRANGE MANS
SPRING MEWS
MILL LA
LONDON RD
HORTON LA
CH
Pl Fld
Sp Gd
Pav
Tenn Cts
Bwg Gn
Fball Gd
Running Tk
Allot Gdns
Sp Ctr
Schs
Liby
TA Ctr
Cemy
PO
P

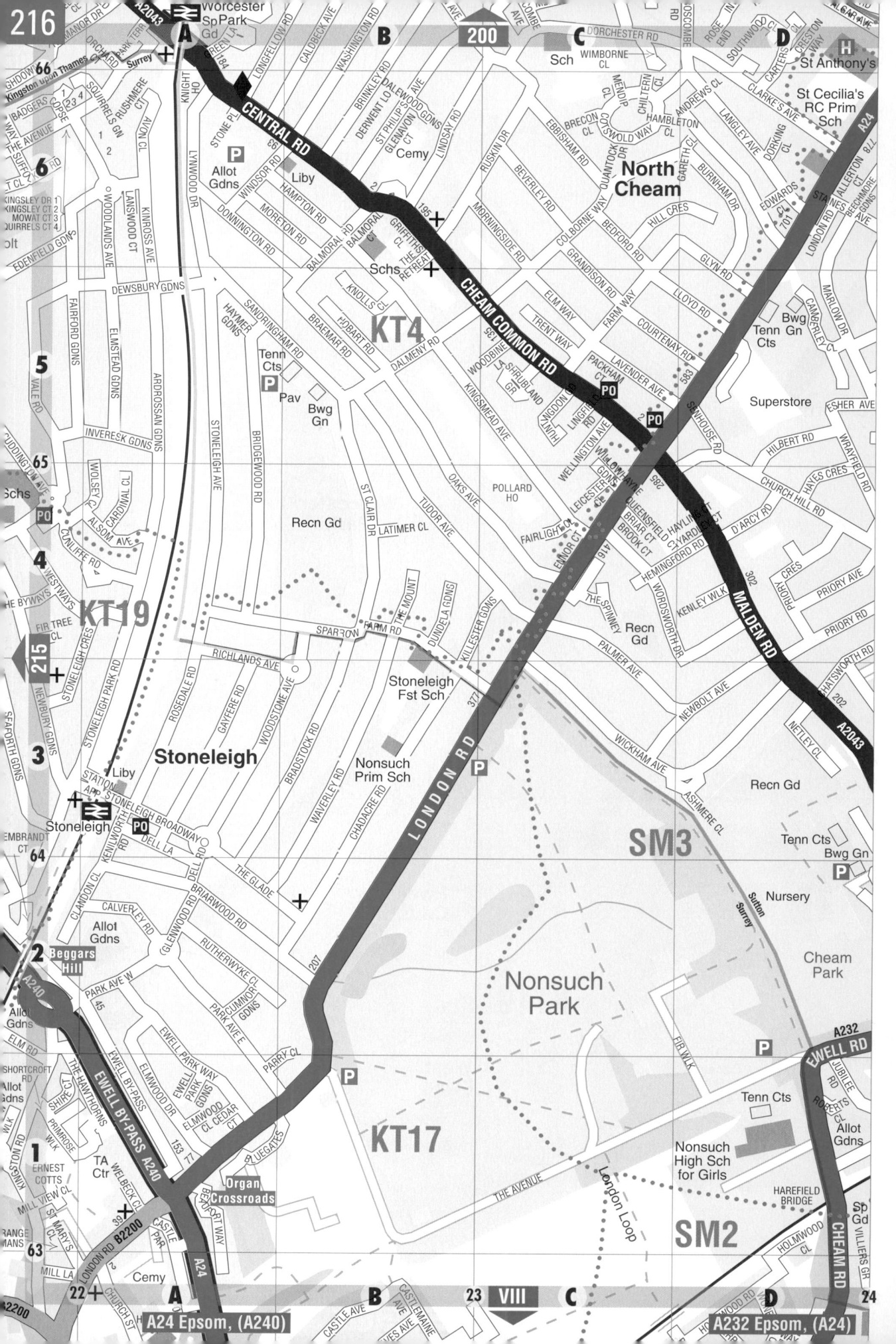

A
B
200
C
D
Worcester Park
Sp Gd
Sch
St Anthony's
St Cecilia's RC Prim Sch
Kingston upon Thames
Surrey
CENTRAL RD
CHEAM COMMON RD
MALDEN RD
LONDON RD
North Cheam
KT4
KT19
SM3
SM2
KT17
Allot Gdns
Liby
Cemy
Schs
Tenn Cts
Pav
Bwg Gn
Recn Gd
POLLARD HO
Superstore
Stoneleigh
Stoneleigh Fst Sch
Nonsuch Prim Sch
Nonsuch Park
Cheam Park
Nursery
Nonsuch High Sch for Girls
London Loop
HAREFIELD BRIDGE
Beggars Hill
Organ Crossroads
TA Ctr
EWELL BY-PASS A240
EWELL RD
CHEAM RD
DORCHESTER RD
RUSKIN DR
BEVERLEY RD
MORNINGSIDE RD
COLBORNE WAY
BEDFORD RD
GRANDISON RD
FARM WAY
LLOYD RD
COURTENAY RD
LAVENDER AVE
SENHOUSE RD
HILBERT RD
CHURCH HILL RD
D'ARCY RD
PRIORY CRES
PRIORY AVE
PRIORY RD
CHATSWORTH RD
NETLEY CL
KINGSMEAD AVE
OAKS AVE
TUDOR AVE
ST CLAIR DR
LATIMER CL
SPARROW FARM RD
THE MOUNT
DUNDELA GDNS
KILLESTER GDNS
PALMER AVE
NEWBOLT AVE
WICKHAM AVE
ASHMERE CL
RICHLANDS AVE
ROSEDALE RD
GAYFERE RD
WOODSTONE AVE
BRADSTOCK RD
WAVERLEY RD
CHADACRE RD
STONELEIGH AVE
BRIDGEWOOD RD
SANDRINGHAM RD
BRAEMAR RD
HOBART RD
DALMENY RD
DEWSBURY GDNS
FAIRFORD GDNS
ELMSTEAD GDNS
ARDROSSAN GDNS
INVERESK GDNS
VALE RD
STONELEIGH PARK RD
STONELEIGH BROADWAY
KENILWORTH RD
DELL LA
DELL RD
THE GLADE
BRIARWOOD RD
CALVERLEY RD
GLENWOOD RD
RUTHERWYKE CL
PARK AVE W
PARK AVE E
CUMNOR GDNS
EWELL PARK WAY
ELMWOOD DR
PARRY CL
BLUEGATES
BEAUFORT WAY
CASTLE PAR
THE AVENUE
FIR WLK
HOLMWOOD CL
A24 Epsom, (A240)
A232 Epsom, (A24)
23
VIII
24
22
215
66
65
64
63

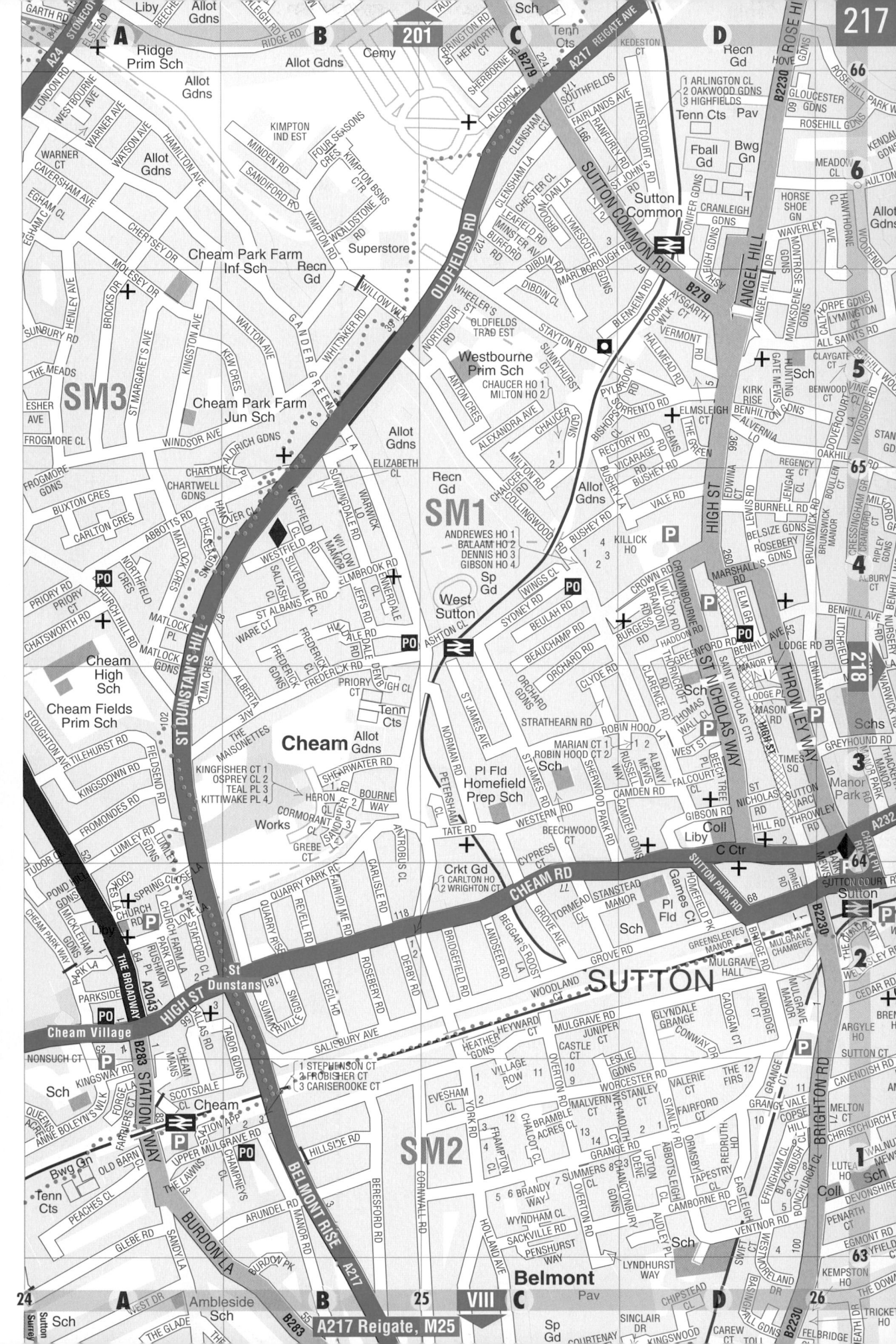
A
B
C
D
201
GARTH RD
STONECOT
ELSTEAD CT
Liby
BEECHES
Allot Gdns
Ridge Prim Sch
RIDGE RD
Allot Gdns
Cemy
BARRINGTON RD
HEPWORTH CT
SHERBORNE RD
B279
A217 REIGATE AVE
Sch
Tenn Cts
224
KEDESTON CT
Recn Gd
ROSE HILL
HOVE GDNS
66
ROSE HILL PARK W
A24
LONDON RD
WESTBOURNE AVE
WARNER AVE
WATSON AVE
HAMILTON AVE
Allot Gdns
WARNER CT
CAVERSHAM AVE
EGHAM CL
KIMPTON IND EST
FOUR SEASONS CRES
KIMPTON BSNS CTR
MINDEN RD
SANDIFORD RD
KIMPTON RD
WALDSTONE RD
Superstore
ALCORN CL
CLENSHAM CT
SOUTHFIELDS CT
FAIRLANDS AVE
RANFURLY RD
HURSTCOURT RD
ST JOHN'S RD
1 ARLINGTON CL
2 OAKWOOD GDNS
3 HIGHFIELDS
Tenn Cts
Pav
Fball Gd
Bwg Gn
B2230
GLOUCESTER GDNS
ROSEHILL GDNS
KENDAL GDNS
MEADOW CL
6
AULTON
HORSE SHOE GN
Allot Gdns
HAWTHORNE
WOODEND
CLENSHAM LA
CHESTER CL
LOAN LA
BROOM
LYMESCOTE
LEAFIELD RD
MINSTER AV
BURFORD RD
SUTTON COMMON RD
Sutton Common
CONIFER GDNS
CRANLEIGH GDNS
ANGEL HILL
WAVERLEY AVE
MONTROSE GDNS
MONKSDENE GDNS
Cheam Park Farm Inf Sch
Recn Gd
MOLESEY DR
CHERTSEY DR
HENLEY AVE
BROCKS DR
SUNBURY RD
WALTON AVE
GANDER GREEN LA
WHITTAKER RD
WILLOW WLK
OLDFIELDS RD
WHEELER'S LA
DIBDIN RD
DIBDIN CL
MARLBOROUGH RD
BLENHEIM RD
COOMBE WLK
AYSGARTH CT
VERMONT RD
HALLMEAD RD
B279
ANGEL HILL DR
CALTHORPE GDNS
LYMINGTON CT
ALL SAINTS RD
THE MEADS
SM3
ST MARGARET'S AVE
KINGSTON AVE
KEW CRES
ESHER AVE
Cheam Park Farm Jun Sch
NORTHSPUR RD
OLDFIELDS TRAD EST
Westbourne Prim Sch
ANTON CRES
SUNNYHURST CL
STAYTON RD
CHAUCER HO 1
MILTON HO 2
PYLBROOK RD
SORRENTO RD
BISHOPSFORD
ELMSLEIGH CT
GATE MEWS
HUNTING
KIRK RISE
CLAYGATE CT
5
Sch
BENWOOD CT
BENHILTON GDNS
VINE CL
WOODSIDE RD
DOVERCOURT LA
ALVERNIA LO
FROGMORE CL
WINDSOR AVE
ALDRICH GDNS
ALEXANDRA AVE
CHAUCER GDNS
MILTON RD
Allot Gdns
ELIZABETH CL
RECTORY RD
VICARAGE RD
BUSHEY RD
DEANS
THE GREEN
OAKHILL
REGENCY CT
JENGAR CL
65
STAN GDNS
FROGMORE GDNS
CHARTWELL PL
CHARTWELL GDNS
SUNNINGDALE RD
WARWICK
Recn Gd
SM1
CHAUCER RD
COLLINGWOOD RD
Allot Gdns
VALE RD
HIGH ST
EDWINA CT
LEWIS RD
BURNELL RD
BOULLEN CT
CRESSINGHAM GR
MILFORD GDNS
BUXTON CRES
CARLTON CRES
ABBOTTS RD
MATLOCK CRES
HANOVER CL
CHELSEA GDNS
WESTFIELD CL
WESTFIELD RD
WILLOW MANOR
SILVERDALE RD
ELMBROOK RD
JEFFS RD
FINDERDALE CL
ANDREWES HO 1
BALAAM HO 2
DENNIS HO 3
GIBSON HO 4
BUSHEY LA
KILLICK HO
BELSIZE GDNS
ROSEBERY GDNS
BRUNSWICK MANOR
CRANFORD CL
RIPLEY GDNS
4
ALBURY CT
NORTHFIELD CRES
PRIORY RD
PRIORY CT
CHURCH HILL RD
CHATSWORTH RD
MATLOCK PL
SALTASH CL
ST ALBANS RD
WARE CT
Sp Gd
West Sutton
WINGS CL
SYDNEY RD
BEULAH RD
CROWN RD
CROWNBOURNE CT
WILCOX RD
BRANDON
MARSHALL'S RD
ELM GR
BENHILL AVE
LITCHFIELD
NURSERY
Cheam High Sch
MATLOCK GDNS
ALMA CRES
ALBERTA AVE
FREDERICK GDNS
FREDERICK CL
FREDERICK RD
ASHTON CL
BEAUCHAMP RD
ORCHARD RD
BURGESS RD
HADDON RD
GREENFORD RD
MANOR PL
LODGE RD
LODGE PL
THORNCROFT RD
CLARENCE RD
ST NICHOLAS WAY
SAINT NICHOLAS CTR
THROWLEY WAY
LENHAM RD
218
WARWICK
Cheam Fields Prim Sch
STOUGHTON AVE
TILEHURST RD
THE MAISONETTES
PRIORY CT
DENBIGH CL
Tenn Cts
ST JAMES AVE
NORMAN RD
ORCHARD GDNS
CLYDE RD
STRATHEARN RD
ROBIN HOOD LA
THOMAS WALL CL
MASON RD
Schs
GREYHOUND RD
THACKERAY
3
MANOR PARK
Manor Park
KINGSDOWN RD
FIELDSEND RD
ST DUNSTAN'S HILL
Cheam
Allot Gdns
KINGFISHER CT 1
OSPREY CL 2
TEAL PL 3
KITTIWAKE PL 4
SHEARWATER RD
BOURNE WAY
HERON CL
Pl Fld
Homefield Prep Sch
PETERSHAM CL
MARIAN CT 1
ROBIN HOOD CT 2
Sch
RUSSELL WAY
ALBANY MEWS
WEST ST
FALCOURT CL
BEECH TREE PL
ST NICHOLAS RD
TIMES SQ
SUTTON ARC
FROMONDES RD
CORMORANT CL
SANDPIPER RD
Works
GREBE CT
ANTROBUS CL
TATE RD
WESTERN RD
ST JAMES RD
SHERWOOD PARK RD
CAMDEN RD
CAMDEN GDNS
BEECHWOOD CT
GIBSON RD
Coll
Liby
HILL RD
THROWLEY RD
C Ctr
A232
CHALK PIT RD
64
LUMLEY RD
LUMLEY GDNS
TUDOR CL
POND HILL GDNS
MICKLEHAM GDNS
CHEAM PARK WAY
SPRING CLOSE LA
CHURCH RD
CHURCH FARM LA
STAFFORD CL
QUARRY PARK RD
FAIRLIE RD
CARLISLE RD
Crkt Gd
1 CARLTON HO
2 WRIGHTON CT
CHEAM RD
CYPRESS CT
STANSTEAD MANOR
TORMEAD CL
GROVE AVE
Games Ct
Pl Fld
HOMEFIELD PK
SUTTON PARK RD
SUTTON COURT RD
Sutton
Liby
THE BROADWAY
QUARRY RISE
REVELL RD
FAIRHOLME RD
DERBY RD
BRIDGEFIELD RD
LANDSEER RD
BEGGAR'S ROOST LA
Sch
GROVE RD
GREENSLEEVES MANOR
BRIDGE RD
MULGRAVE CHAMBERS
THE QUADRANT
2
WESTLEY RD
PARK LA
RUSHMON PL
A2043
HIGH ST
St Dunstans
SUMMERVILLE GDNS
CECIL RD
ROSEBERY RD
WOODLAND CT
SUTTON
MULGRAVE HALL
CEDAR RD
PARKSIDE
DALLAS RD
TABOR GDNS
SALISBURY AVE
HEYWARD CT
HEATHER GDNS
MULGRAVE RD
JUNIPER CT
GLYNDALE GRANGE
CADOGAN CT
TANDRIDGE CT
MULGRAVE MANOR
ARGYLE HO
Cheam Village
NONSUCH CT
B283
STATION WAY
CHEAM MANS
CASTLE CT
LESLIE GDNS
CONWAY DR
SUTTON CT
KINGSWAY RD
SCOTSDALE
Cheam
1 STEPHENSON CT
2 FROBISHER CT
3 CARISBROOKE CT
VILLAGE ROW
WORCESTER RD
VALERIE CT
THE FIRS
GRANGE CT
CAVENDISH RD
Sch
FORGE LA
QUEENS ACRE
ANNE BOLEYN'S WLK
FARRIERS CT
STATION APP
UPPER MULGRAVE RD
EVESHAM CL
YORK RD
CHALCOT CL
BRAMBLE ACRES CL
MALVERN CT
WEYMOUTH CT
STANLEY CT
STANLEY RD
FAIRFORD CT
GRANGE VALE
COPSE HILL
MELTON CT
CHRISTCHURCH PK
Bwg Gn
OLD BARN
THE LAWNS
CHAMPNEYS CL
HILLSIDE RD
SM2
FRAMPTON CL
GRANGE RD
UPTON DENE
ABBOTSLEIGH RD
ORMSBY
REDRUTH HO
TAPESTRY CL
EFFINGHAM CL
BLACKBUSH CL
BRIGHTON RD
WALNUT MEWS
LUTEA HO
Sch
Coll
Tenn Cts
PEACHES CL
SUMMERS CL
CHANCTONBURY GDNS
CAMBORNE RD
EASTLEIGH CL
BONCHURCH CL
DEVONSHIRE
PENARTH CT
BURDON LA
ARUNDEL RD
MANOR RD
BELMONT RISE
BERESFORD RD
CORNWALL RD
HOLLAND AVE
BRANDY WAY
WYNDHAM CL
SACKVILLE RD
PENSHURST WAY
OVERTON RD
AUDLEY PL
VENTNOR RD
WESTMORELAND
EGMONT RD
GLEBE RD
SANDY LA
BURDON PK
LYNDHURST WAY
Sch
SWIFT CT
BASINGHALL GDNS
63
KEMPSTON HO
THE DOWNS
Belmont
24
25
26
VIII
A
B
C
D
WEST DR
Ambleside Sch
Sch
B283
A217 Reigate, M25
Pav
CHIPSTEAD CL
Sp Gd
SINCLAIR DR
KINGSWOOD
COURTENAY
CAREW CT
FELBRIDGE
TRICKETT HO
Sutton Surrey

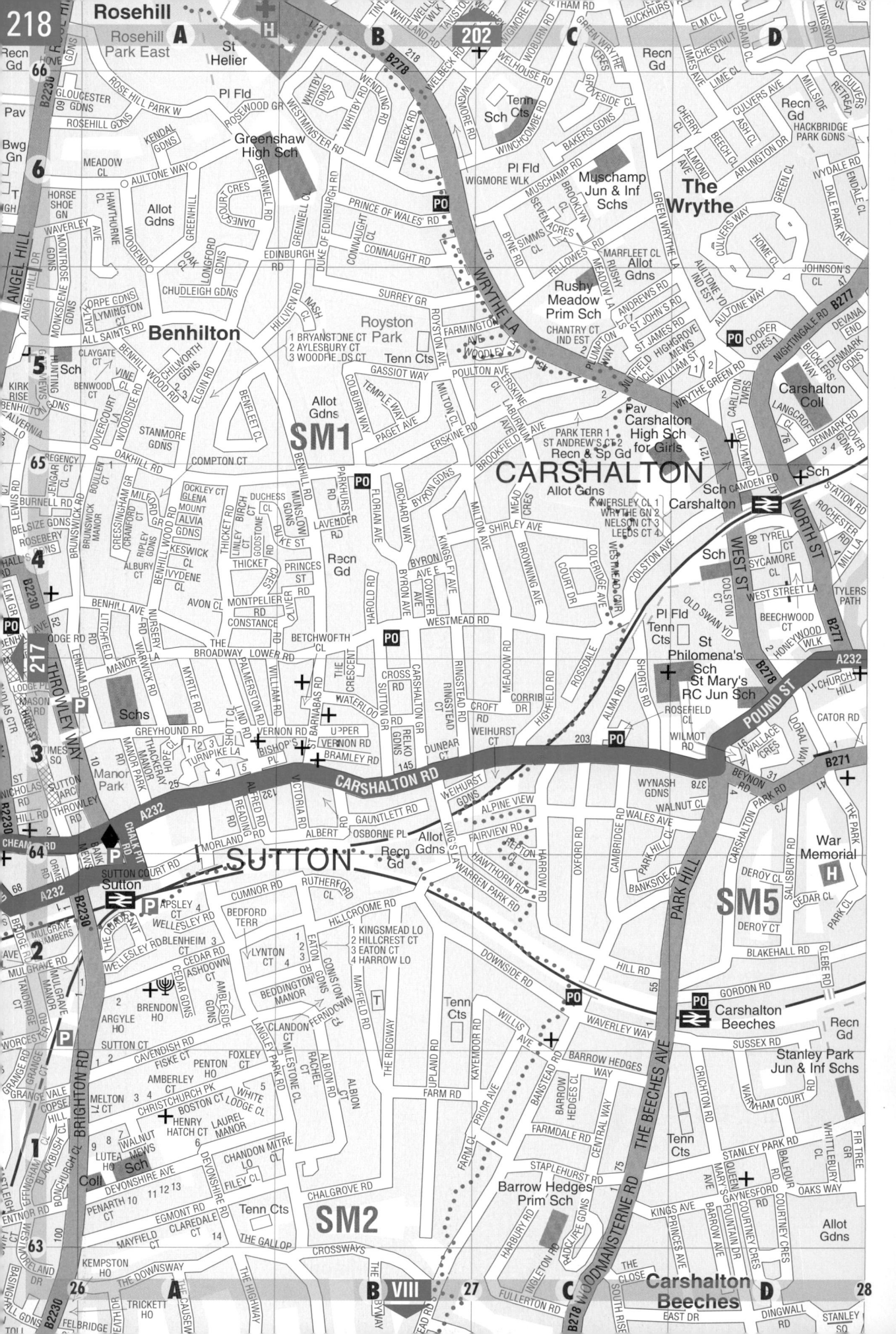
Rosehill
Rosehill Park East
St Helier
202
The Wrythe
Muschamp Jun & Inf Schs
Greenshaw High Sch
Benhilton
Royston Park
SM1
CARSHALTON
Carshalton High Sch for Girls
Rushy Meadow Prim Sch
Carshalton Coll
St Philomena's Sch
St Mary's RC Jun Sch
Carshalton
SUTTON
Sutton
Manor Park
SM5
War Memorial
Carshalton Beeches
Stanley Park Jun & Inf Schs
Barrow Hedges Prim Sch
SM2
Carshalton Beeches
217
VIII
26
27
28
A
B
C
D
1
2
3
4
5
6
63
64
65
66
ANGEL HILL
THROWLEY WAY
BRIGHTON RD
CARSHALTON RD
WRYTHE LA
PARK HILL
THE BEECHES AVE
WOODMANSTERNE RD
POUND ST
NORTH ST
WEST ST
CHEAM RD
A232
B278
B277
B2230
B271
1 BRYANSTONE CT
2 AYLESBURY CT
3 WOODFIELDS CT
1 KINGSMEAD LO
2 HILLCREST CT
3 EATON CT
4 HARROW LO

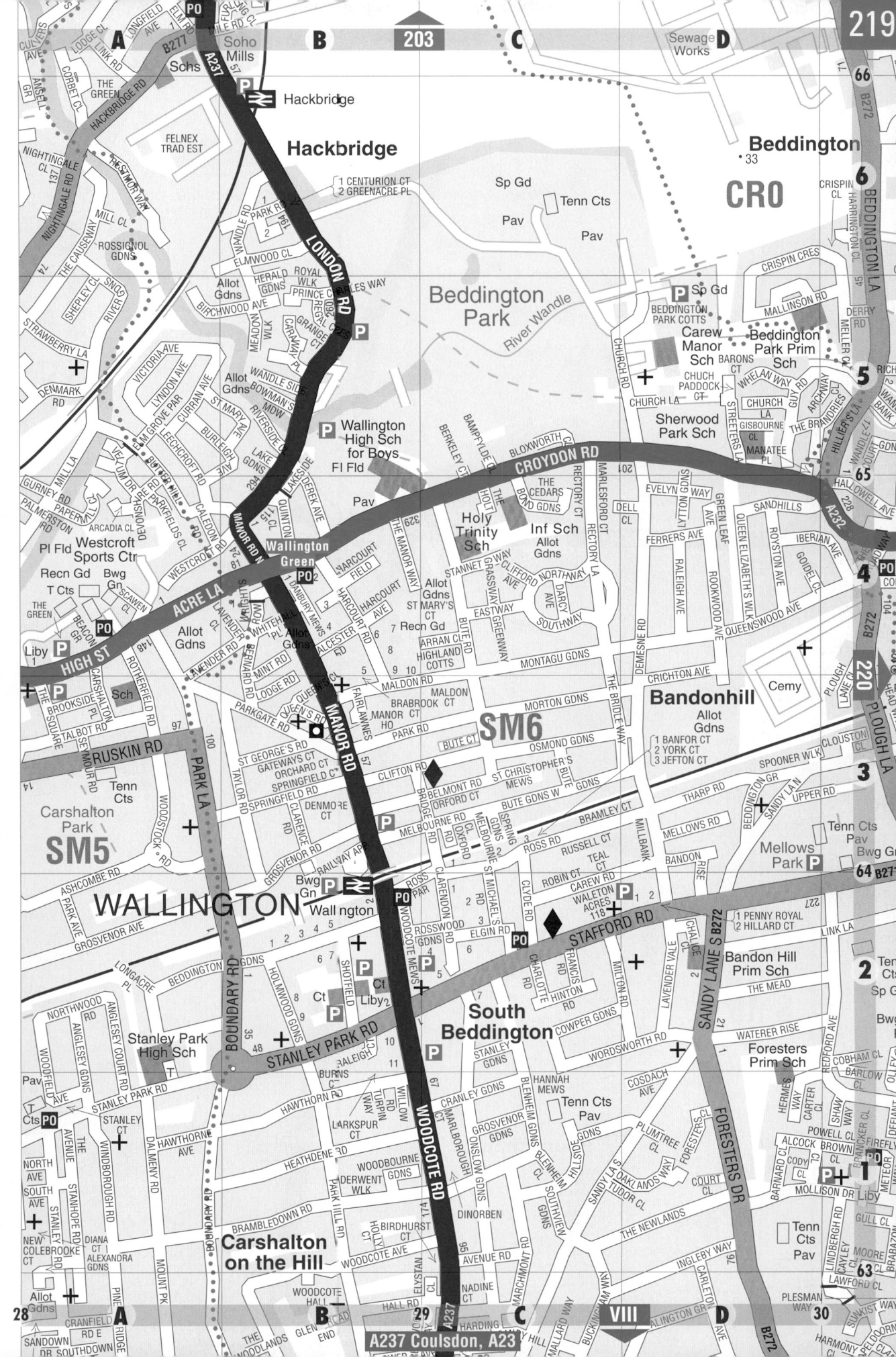
203
A
B
C
D
Sewage Works
Soho Mills
Schs
B277
A237
Hackbridge
FELNEX TRAD EST
Hackbridge
Beddington
33
CR0
Sp Gd
Tenn Cts
Pav
Pav
1 CENTURION CT
2 GREENACRE PL
LONDON RD
HACKBRIDGE RD
NIGHTINGALE CL
NIGHTINGALE RD
RESTMOR WAY
MILL CL
ROSSIGNOL GDNS
THE CAUSEWAY
SHEPLEY CL
STRAWBERRY LA
DENMARK RD
ELMWOOD CL
HERALD GDNS
ROYAL WLK
PRINCE CHARLES WAY
Allot Gdns
BIRCHWOOD AVE
MEADOW WLK
CARAWAY PL
GRANGE CT
REGAL CRES
Beddington Park
River Wandle
VICTORIA AVE
LYNDON AVE
CURRAN AVE
ST MARY AVE
BURLEIGH AVE
ELM GROVE PAR
LEECHCROFT RD
WANDLE SIDE
BOWMAN'S MDW
RIVERSIDE CL
LAKE GDNS
Wallington High Sch for Boys
Fl Fld
Pav
LAKESIDE
DEREK AVE
QUINTON CL
MANOR RD N
Wallington Green
CROYDON RD
BLOXWORTH CL
BERKELEY CT
BAMPFYLDE CL
HOLT THE
BOND GDNS
THE CEDARS
RECTORY CT
MARLESFORD CT
CHURCH RD
CHURCH LA
Carew Manor Sch
Beddington Park Prim Sch
BEDDINGTON PARK COTTS
CHUCH PADDOCK CT
BARONS CT
WHELAN WAY
CHURCH LA
GISBOURNE CL
MANATEE PL
Sherwood Park Sch
THE BRANDRIES
HILLIER'S LA
CRISPIN CL
CRISPIN CRES
HARRINGTON CL
BEDDINGTON LA
MALLINSON RD
DERRY RD
MELLER CL
B272
66
6
5
65
4
3
2
1
64
63
A232
HALLOWELL AVE
SANDHILLS
IBERIAN AVE
GOIDEL CL
ROYSTON AVE
QUEEN ELIZABETH'S WLK
GREEN LEAF AVE
EVELYN WAY
LYTTON GDNS
DELL CL
FERRERS AVE
RALEIGH AVE
ROOKWOOD AVE
QUEENSWOOD AVE
Holy Trinity Sch
Inf Sch
Allot Gdns
GURNEY RD
PAPERMILL CL
PALMERSTON RD
ARCADIA CL
DEVONSHIRE RD
PARKFIELDS CL
CALEDON RD
WESTCROFT RD
Pl Fld
Westcroft Sports Ctr
Recn Gd
Bwg Gn
T Cts
THE GREEN
BEACON GR
Liby
HIGH ST
ACRE LA
SCAWEN CL
Allot Gdns
LAVENDER CL
LAVENDER RD
BERNARD RD
WRIGHTS ROW
WHITEHALL PL
DANBURY MEWS
HARCOURT FIELD
HARCOURT AVE
HARCOURT RD
ALCESTER RD
THE MANOR WAY
Allot Gdns
ST MARY'S CT
Recn Gd
STANNET WAY
GRASSWAY
CLIFFORD AVE
NORTHWAY
DARCY AVE
SOUTHWAY
EASTWAY
GREENWAY
ARRAN CL
HIGHLAND COTTS
BUTE RD
MONTAGU GDNS
DEMESNE RD
CRICHTON AVE
Cemy
PLOUGH LANE CL
PLOUGH LA
220
MINT RD
LODGE RD
MALDON RD
MALDON CT
BRABROOK CT
MANOR HO
FAIRLAWNES
QUEEN'S CL
QUEEN'S RD
PARKGATE RD
PARK RD
MANOR RD
ROTHERFIELD RD
CARSHALTON PL
BROOKSIDE
THE SQUARE
Sch
TALBOT RD
SEYMOUR RD
MORTON GDNS
THE BRIDLE WAY
Bandonhill
Allot Gdns
SM6
BUTE CT
OSMOND GDNS
1 BANFOR CT
2 YORK CT
3 JEFTON CT
CLOUSTON CL
SPOONER WLK
RUSKIN RD
PARK LA
Tenn Cts
Carshalton Park
SM5
WOODSTOCK RD
ST GEORGE'S RD
GATEWAYS CT
ORCHARD CT
SPRINGFIELD CT
SPRINGFIELD RD
TAYLOR RD
CLARENCE RD
DENMORE CT
CLIFTON RD
BELMONT RD
ORFORD CT
ST CHRISTOPHER'S MEWS
BUTE GDNS
BUTE GDNS W
BRAMLEY CT
MILLBANK
THARP RD
BEDDINGTON GR
SANDY LA N
UPPER RD
MELLOWS RD
Tenn Cts
Pav
Bwg Gn
Mellows Park
B271
GROSVENOR RD
RAILWAY APP
MELBOURNE RD
BRIDGE RD
OXFORD CL
SPRING GDNS
ROSS RD
RUSSELL CT
TEAL CT
BANDON RISE
ASHCOMBE RD
PARK AVE
WALLINGTON
Bwg Gn
Wallington
ROSS PAR
CLARENDON RD
ST MICHAEL'S RD
CLYDE RD
ROBIN CT
CAREW RD
WALETON ACRES
PENNY ROYAL
HILLARD CT
LINK LA
GROSVENOR AVE
ROSSWOOD GDNS
WOODCOTE MEWS
ELGIN RD
STAFFORD RD
CHALICE CL
SANDY LANE S
LONGACRE PL
BEDDINGTON GDNS
HOLMWOOD GDNS
SHOTFIELD
Ct
Liby
CHARLOTTE RD
FRANCIS RD
HINTON RD
MILTON RD
LAVENDER VALE
Bandon Hill Prim Sch
THE MEAD
NORTHWOOD RD
ANGLESEY GDNS
ANGLESEY COURT RD
WOODFIELD AVE
Stanley Park High Sch
BOUNDARY RD
STANLEY PARK RD
RALEIGH
South Beddington
COWPER GDNS
WORDSWORTH RD
WATERER RISE
Foresters Prim Sch
REDFORD AVE
COBHAM CL
BARLOW CL
Pav
BURNS CL
HAWTHORN RD
TURPIN WAY
WILLOW RD
STANLEY GDNS
HANNAH MEWS
COSDACH AVE
HERMES WAY
CARTER CL
SHAW WAY
STANLEY CT
HAWTHORNE AVE
LARKSPUR CT
CRANLEY GDNS
MARLBOROUGH CT
GROSVENOR GDNS
BLENHEIM GDNS
Tenn Cts Pav
HILLSIDE GDNS
PLUMTREE CL
FORESTERS CL
FORESTERS DR
POWELL CL
ALCOCK CL
BROWN CL
FIREFLY
NORTH AVE
SOUTH AVE
STANHOPE RD
WINDBOROUGH RD
DALMENY RD
HEATHDENE RD
WOODBOURNE GDNS
DERWENT WLK
WOODCOTE RD
ONSLOW GDNS
BLENHEIM CL
SANDY LA S
OAKLANDS WAY
TUDOR CL
COURT CL
BARNARD CL
CODY CL
MOLLISON DR
Liby
METEOR WAY
GULL CL
NEW COLEBROOKE CT
DIANA CT
ALEXANDRA GDNS
STANLEY RD
BRAMBLEDOWN RD
PARK HILL RD
HOLLY CT
BIRDHURST CT
DINORBEN
SOUTHVIEW GDNS
THE NEWLANDS
Tenn Cts Pav
LINDBERGH RD
CAYLEY CL
MOORE CL
BRABAZON
Carshalton on the Hill
WOODCOTE AVE
AVENUE RD
MARCHMONT RD
INGLEBY WAY
CARLETON AVE
LAWFORD CL
MOUNT PK
PINE RIDGE
Allot Gdns
WOODCOTE HALL
ELYSTAN CL
NADINE CT
HALL RD
MALLARD WAY
BUCKINGHAM WAY
PLESMAN WAY
SUNKIST WAY
HARMONY CL
SELDORN
CRANFIELD RD E
SANDOWN DR
SOUTHDOWN RD
THE WOODLANDS
GLEN RD END
HARDING
A237 Coulsdon, A23
VIII
28
29
30

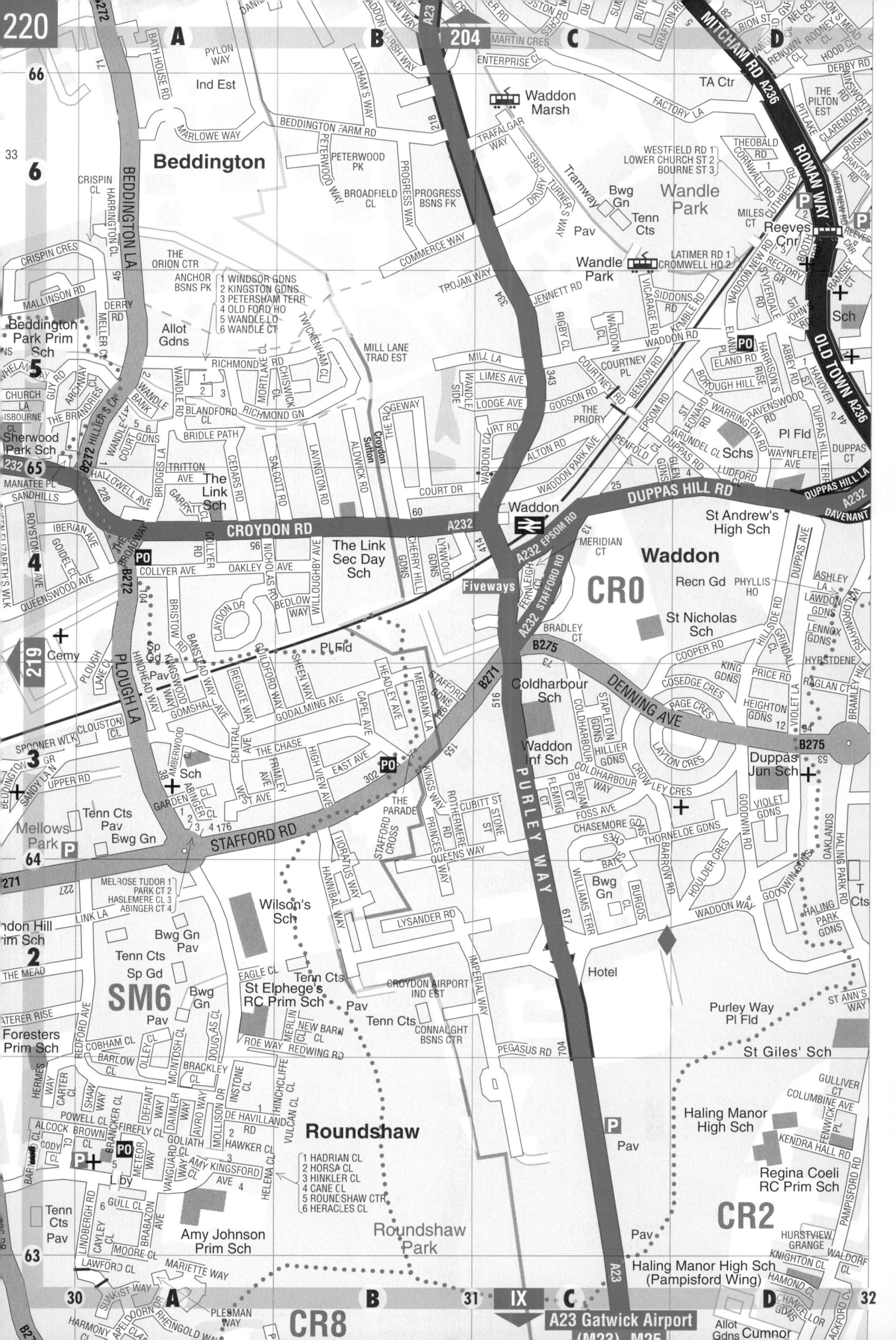

204
Beddington
Wandle Park
Waddon
CR0
SM6
Roundshaw
CR2
CR8
BEDDINGTON LA
PLOUGH LA
CROYDON RD
PURLEY WAY
STAFFORD RD
DUPPAS HILL RD
DENNING AVE
MITCHAM RD A236
ROMAN WAY
OLD TOWN A236
Waddon Marsh
Wandle Park
Reeves Cnr
Waddon
Fiveways
219
IX
A23 Gatwick Airport

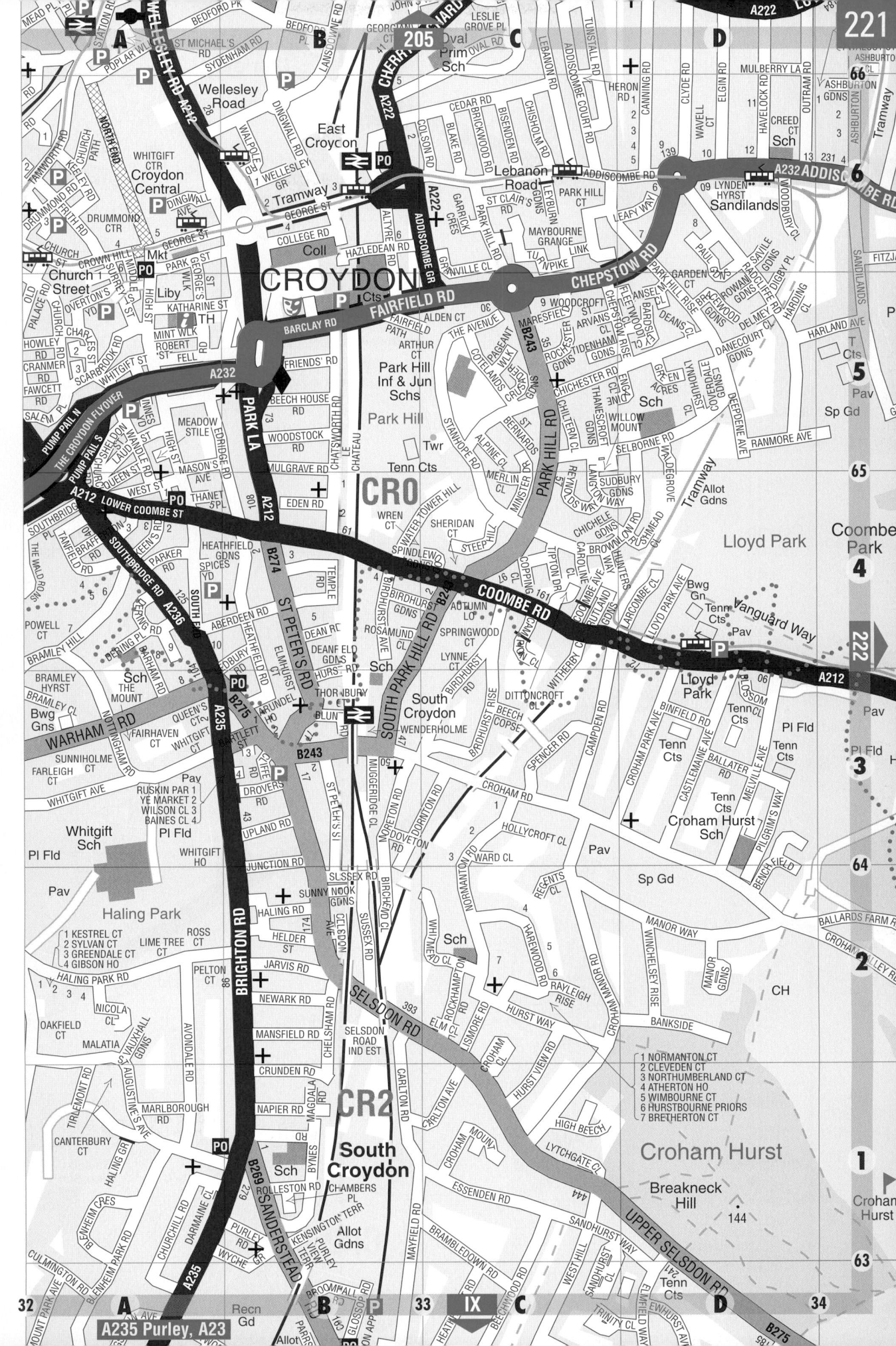
A
B
C
D
205
A222
6
5
65
4
222
3
64
2
1
63
32
33
IX
34
A235 Purley, A23
Wellesley Road
East Croydon
Croydon Central
WHITGIFT CTR
Tramway
Lebanon Road
Sandilands
CROYDON
Church Street
Coll
Mkt
Liby
TH
Park Hill Inf & Jun Schs
Park Hill
Twr
Tenn Cts
CR0
Lloyd Park
Coombe Park
Vanguard Way
Allot Gdns
South Croydon
Whitgift Sch
Haling Park
Pl Fld
Pav
Sp Gd
Croham Hurst Sch
Croham Hurst
Breakneck Hill
144
CR2
Sch
WELLESLEY RD
A212
CHERRY ORCHARD RD
ADDISCOMBE RD
A232
FAIRFIELD RD
CHEPSTOW RD
BARCLAY RD
PARK LA
THE CROYDON FLYOVER
LOWER COOMBE ST
COOMBE RD
PARK HILL RD
B243
SOUTH PARK HILL RD
ST PETER'S RD
B274
SOUTH END
A236
SOUTHBRIDGE RD
WARHAM RD
A235
BRIGHTON RD
SELSDON RD
UPPER SELSDON RD
B275
SANDERSTEAD RD
B269
CROHAM RD
MANOR WAY
ADDISCOMBE GR
GEORGE ST
1 KESTREL CT
2 SYLVAN CT
3 GREENDALE CT
4 GIBSON HO
RUSKIN PAR 1
YE MARKET 2
WILSON CL 3
BAINES CL 4
1 NORMANTON CT
2 CLEVEDEN CT
3 NORTHUMBERLAND CT
4 ATHERTON HO
5 WIMBOURNE CT
6 HURSTBOURNE PRIORS
7 BRETHERTON CT

Addiscombe

206

Shirley

A B C D

6 A232

A232 WEST WAY

Trinity Sch

Pl Fld

Pav

Tenn Cts

1 SONNING CT
2 COLLEGE CT
3 FURZE CT
4 WALCOT CT

Pl Fld

Bwg Gn

Shirley Park

Oaks Farm

CR0

Windmill (dis)

Coloma Convent Girls Sch

Shirley High Sch

London Loop

Upper Shirley

5

65

Lloyd Park

Coombe Park

Coombe Farm

Pl Fld

Addington Hills

132

4

221 A212

COOMBE RD

P Tramway

P

P

Pav

Hotel

Pl Fld

Pl Fld

Vanguard Way

COOMBE LA

Combe Lane

3

Tenn Cts

Tenn Cts

Royal Russell Sch (Ballards)

Sp Gd

Pav

Heathfield Tramway

A212

64

2

CH

Ballards Farm Rd

Ballards Rise

Hollingsworth Rd

Ballards Way

Ballards Way

Riesco Dr

Bramley Bank

Nat Res

London Loop

Pl Fld

Croham Hurst

1

Croham Hurst

Ruffetts Cl

Crest Rd

The Ruffetts

Croham Valley Rd

The Gallop

Chapel View

Chestnut Gr

Farley Rd

Littleheath Rd

Vanguard Way

Warren Ave

Shepherds Way

Tedder Rd

Broadcoombe

Edgecoombe

Selsdon High Sch

Sp Ctr

Moss Gdns

Freelands Ave

Heather Way

CR2

63

B275

34 A 35 IX C 36

A B D

Littleheath Woods

Ingham Rd

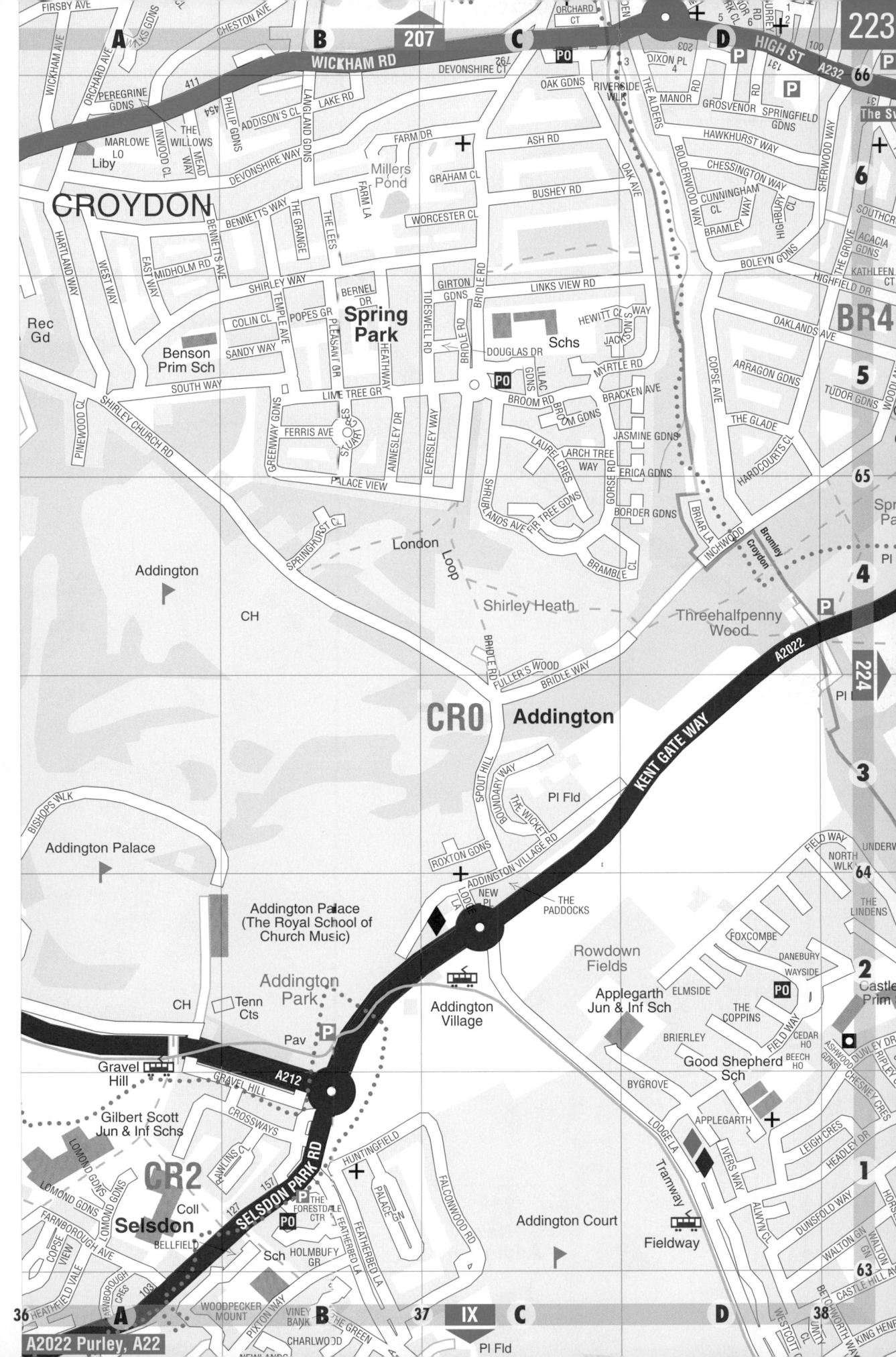

207
A
B
C
D
WICKHAM RD
HIGH ST
A232
CROYDON
Spring Park
Schs
Benson Prim Sch
Rec Gd
Millers Pond
BR4
London Loop
Shirley Heath
Threehalfpenny Wood
Addington
CH
CR0
Addington
KENT GATE WAY
A2022
Pl Fld
224
Addington Palace
Addington Palace (The Royal School of Church Music)
Addington Park
Tenn Cts
Pav
Gravel Hill
A212
Addington Village
Rowdown Fields
Applegarth Jun & Inf Sch
Good Shepherd Sch
Gilbert Scott Jun & Inf Schs
CR2
Selsdon
Coll
SELSDON PARK RD
Addington Court
Fieldway
Tramway
6
5
4
3
2
1
66
65
64
63
36
37
38
IX
A2022 Purley, A22

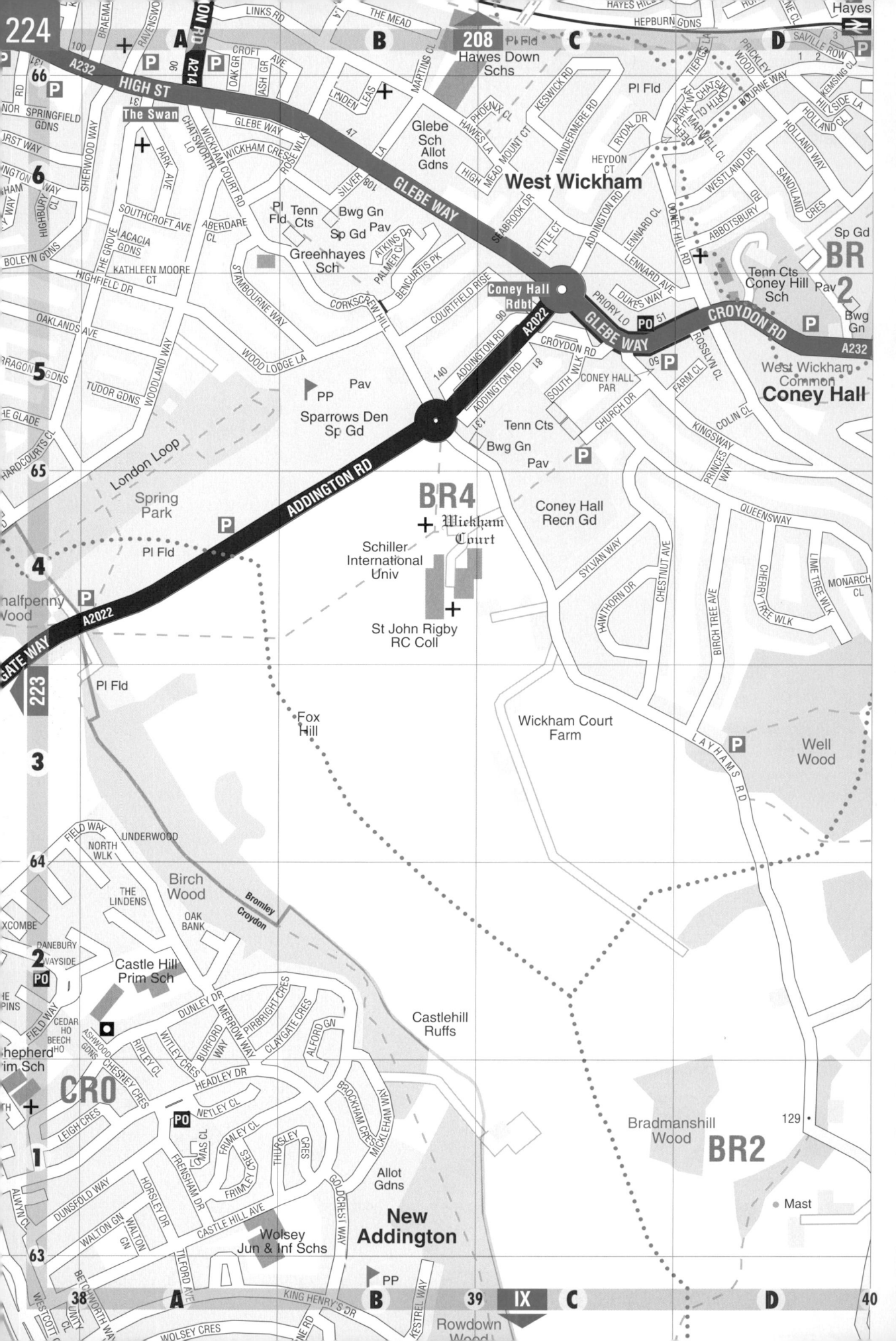

West Wickham
Coney Hall
New Addington
HIGH ST
GLEBE WAY
CROYDON RD
ADDINGTON RD
A232
A2022
A214
Coney Hall Rdbt
BR4
BR2
CR0
Wickham Court
Schiller International Univ
St John Rigby RC Coll
Spring Park
London Loop
Sparrows Den Sp Gd
Greenhayes Sch
Glebe Sch Allot Gdns
Hawes Down Schs
Coney Hill Sch
West Wickham Common
Coney Hall Recn Gd
Wickham Court Farm
Well Wood
Fox Hill
Birch Wood
Castle Hill Prim Sch
Castlehill Ruffs
Bradmanshill Wood
Wolsey Jun & Inf Schs
Rowdown Wood
The Swan
Hayes
LAYHAMS RD
Bromley
Croydon
208
223
IX

209
A
B
C
D
Recn Gds
RIDGEWAY
WARREN RD
1 LARKFIELD CL
2 WENTWORTH CL
3 HAWTHORNDENE CL
4 HAWTHORNDENE RD
5 WARREN WOOD CL
HAYES CL
PRESTONS RD
Pl Fld
Hayes Sch
BURWOOD AVE
B265
Tenn Cts
Bwg Gn
Pav Baston Sch
Pav
Sp Gd
Tenn Cts
REDGATE DR
Pl Fld
Pav
Tenn Cts
Barnet Wood
BARNET WOOD RD
Keston Mark
Pav
Pl Fld
Ravens Wood Boys Sch
Sp Gd
OAKLEY RD
A233
Ravens Bourne
BASTON RD
FIVE ELMS RD
SIMPSON'S COTTS
Colyers Wood
Hayes Court
WEST COMMON RD
Hayes Common
THE DRIFT
Allot Gdns
CROYDON RD
A232
HARVEST BANK RD
ROBINS GR
HARTFIELD CRES
BASTON MANOR RD
London Loop
QUIET NOOK
PHOENIX DR
THE AVENUE
THANET DR
THE DALE
RUSHLEY CL
MARK CL
HARVEST BANK RD
HARTFIELD RD
RODNEY GDNS
LAWRENCE RD
GATES GREEN RD
Hast Hill
Wickham Common Prim Sch
Pl Fld
BR4
Baston Manor
COMMONSIDE
OAKFIELD LA
BEECHWOOD DR
BROCK DENE DR
HASSOCK WOOD
LONGDON WOOD
STOUR CL
WINDMILL DR
KESTON GDNS
LAKES RD
Keston
SWIRES SHAW
COLLIERS WOOD
POULTERS WOOD
ROLVENDEN WAY
PH
PO
KESTON AVE
Keston CE Prim Sch
226
Rouse Farm
FOX LA
HERITAGE HILL
HEATHFIELD CL
LEAFY GR
GREYS PARK CL
REGENTS DR
HEATHFIELD RD
FISHPONDS RD
London Loop
BR2
Windmill
Keston Common
WESTERHAM RD
Nash
NORTH POLE LA
NASH LA
Fuller's Wood
James's Wood
JACKASS LA
ROMAN MAUSOLEUM
Keston Court
RECTORY RD
CHURCH RD
Milchden
LAYHAMS RD
BLACKNESS LA
DOWNE RD
40
41
IX
42
A233 Biggin Hill

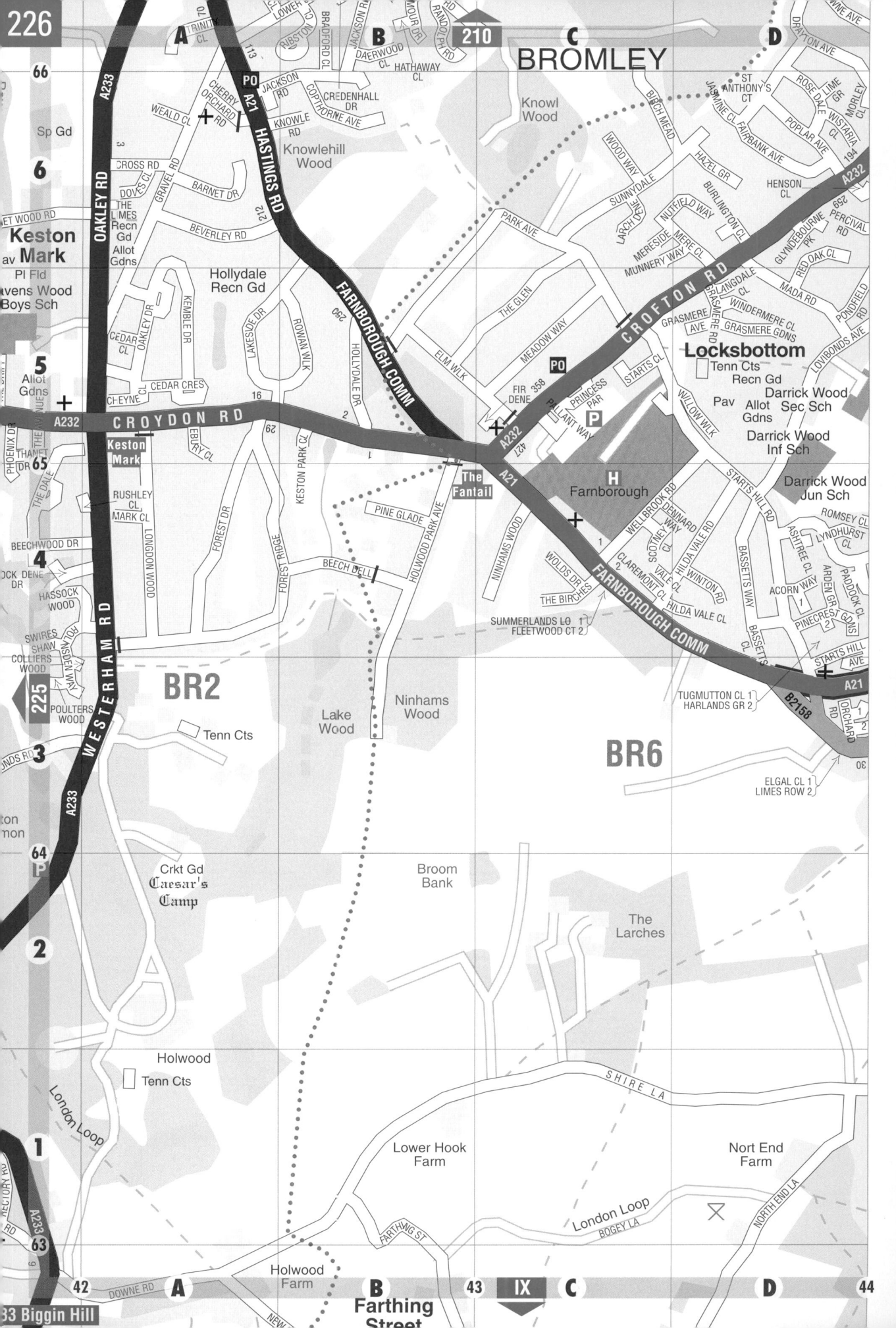
BROMLEY
Keston Mark
Locksbottom
BR2
BR6
OAKLEY RD
WESTERHAM RD
HASTINGS RD
FARNBOROUGH COMM
CROYDON RD
CROFTON RD
Knowl Wood
Knowlehill Wood
Hollydale Recn Gd
Lake Wood
Ninhams Wood
Farnborough
Darrick Wood Sec Sch
Darrick Wood Inf Sch
Darrick Wood Jun Sch
Tenn Cts
Recn Gd
Allot Gdns
Crkt Gd
Caesar's Camp
Broom Bank
The Larches
Holwood
Lower Hook Farm
Nort End Farm
Holwood Farm
London Loop
SHIRE LA
BOGEY LA
FARTHING ST
NORTH END LA
DOWNE RD
Farthing Street
The Fantail
SUMMERLANDS LO 1
FLEETWOOD CT 2
TUGMUTTON CL 1
HARLANDS GR 2
ELGAL CL 1
LIMES ROW 2
A233
A21
A232
B2158
210
225
IX
A B C D
66 65 64 63
42 43 44

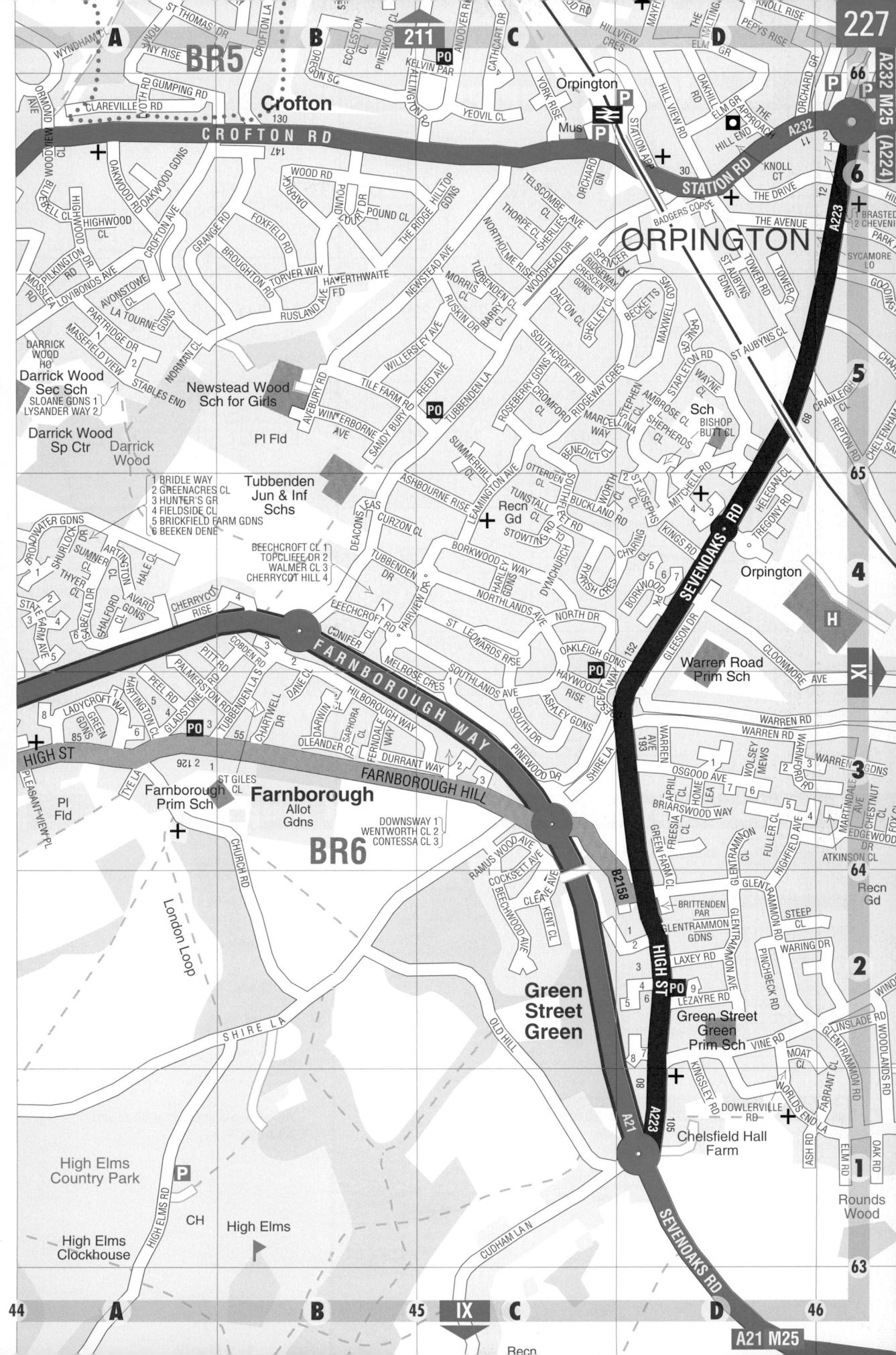
A
B
C
D
211
BR5
Crofton
CROFTON RD
Orpington
Mus
STATION RD
ORPINGTON
A232
A223
A232 M25 (A224)
66
6
5
65
4
3
64
2
1
63
Darrick Wood Sec Sch
Darrick Wood Sp Ctr
Darrick Wood
Newstead Wood Sch for Girls
Pl Fld
Tubbenden Jun & Inf Schs
Recn Gd
Sch
Orpington
Warren Road Prim Sch
IX
FARNBOROUGH WAY
HIGH ST
FARNBOROUGH HILL
Farnborough Prim Sch
Farnborough
Allot Gdns
BR6
B2158
London Loop
Green Street Green
Green Street Green Prim Sch
Chelsfield Hall Farm
SEVENOAKS RD
A21
High Elms Country Park
CH
High Elms
High Elms Clockhouse
Rounds Wood
SHIRE LA
OLD HILL
CUDHAM LA N
CHURCH RD
HIGH ELMS RD
1 BRIDLE WAY
2 GREENACRES CL
3 HUNTER'S GR
4 FIELDSIDE CL
5 BRICKFIELD FARM GDNS
6 BEEKEN DENE
BEECHCROFT CL 1
TOPCLIFFE DR 2
WALMER CL 3
CHERRYCOT HILL 4
DOWNSWAY 1
WENTWORTH CL 2
CONTESSA CL 3
SLOANE GDNS 1
LYSANDER WAY 2
44
45
46
A21 M25
Recn

Key to enlarged map pages

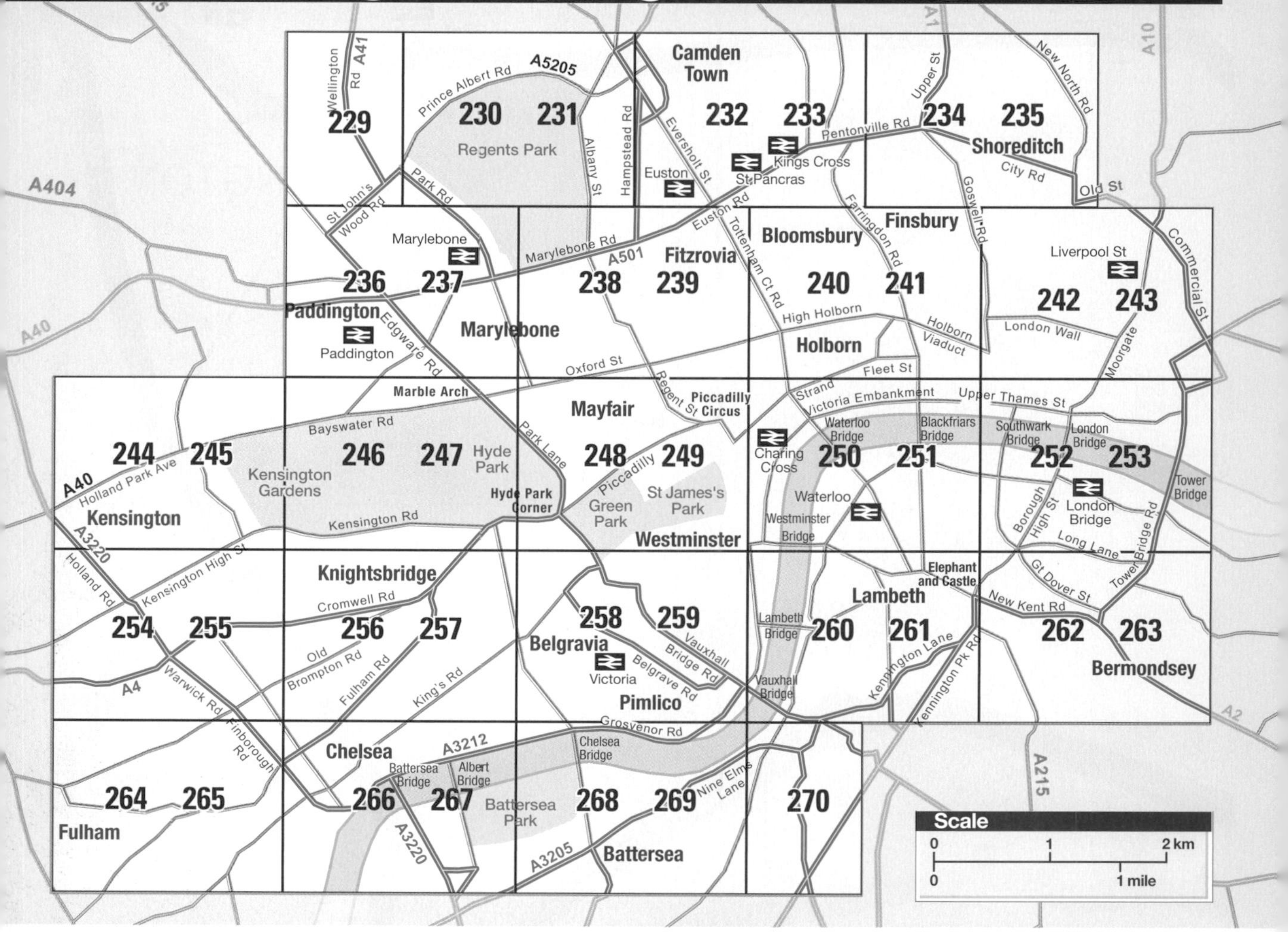

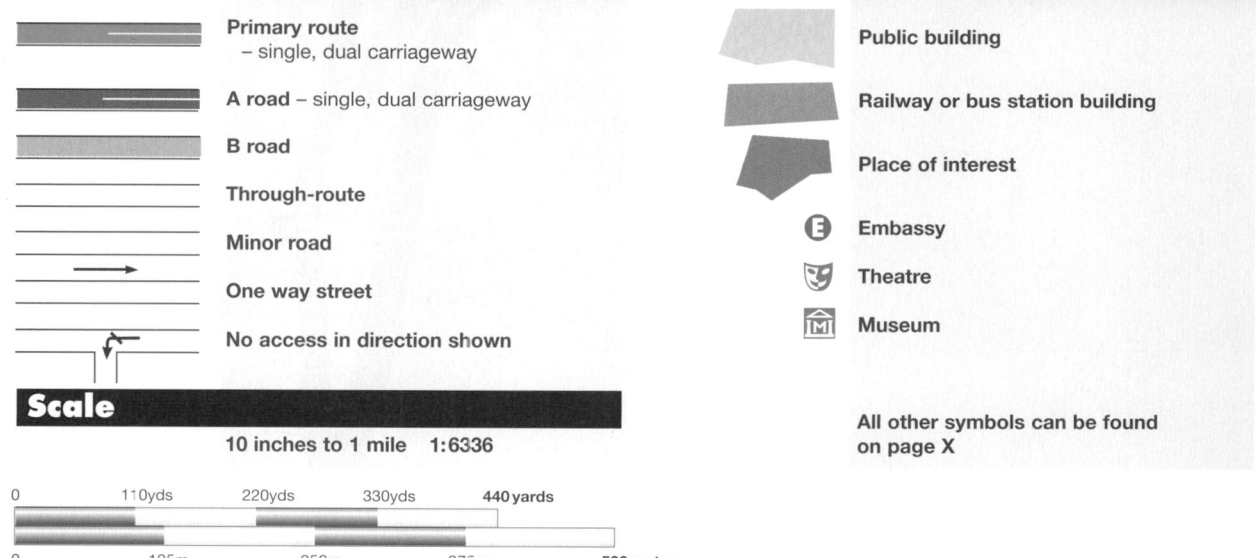

| 229 | 230 | 231 | 232 | 233 | 234 | 235 Shoreditch |

Wellington Rd A41 · Prince Albert Rd · A5205 · Regents Park · Hampstead Rd · Albany St · Eversholt St · Euston · St Pancras · Kings Cross · Pentonville Rd · Upper St · New North Rd · A1 · A10 · Goswell Rd · City Rd · Old St · Commercial St

Camden Town

A404 · A40

| 236 | 237 | 238 | 239 | 240 | 241 | 242 | 243 |

Marylebone · Marylebone Rd · A501 · Fitzrovia · Bloomsbury · Finsbury · Liverpool St · Paddington · Edgware Rd · Marylebone · Oxford St · High Holborn · Holborn · Holborn Viaduct · London Wall · Moorgate · Fleet St · Tottenham Ct Rd · Euston Rd · Regent St · Gower St · Farringdon Rd · St John's Wood Rd · Park Rd

Marble Arch · Bayswater Rd · Park Lane · Mayfair · Piccadilly Circus · Strand · Victoria Embankment · Upper Thames St

| 244 | 245 | 246 | 247 | 248 | 249 | 250 | 251 | 252 | 253 |

Kensington · Kensington Gardens · Hyde Park · Hyde Park Corner · Green Park · St James's Park · Charing Cross · Waterloo Bridge · Blackfriars Bridge · Southwark Bridge · London Bridge · Tower Bridge · Holland Park Ave · A40 · Kensington Rd · Piccadilly · Westminster · Waterloo · Westminster Bridge · Lambeth Bridge · Borough High St · Long Lane · A3220

| 254 | 255 | 256 | 257 | 258 | 259 | 260 | 261 | 262 | 263 |

Knightsbridge · Cromwell Rd · Old Brompton Rd · Fulham Rd · King's Rd · Belgravia · Victoria · Belgrave Rd · Vauxhall Bridge Rd · Pimlico · Vauxhall Bridge · Lambeth · Elephant and Castle · New Kent Rd · Gt Dover St · Bermondsey · Kennington Lane · Kennington Pk Rd · Tower Bridge Rd · Holland Rd · Kensington High St · A4 · Warwick Rd · Finborough Rd · A3220 · A2

| 264 | 265 | 266 | 267 | 268 | 269 | 270 |

Fulham · Chelsea · A3212 · Battersea Bridge · Albert Bridge · Battersea Park · Chelsea Bridge · Grosvenor Rd · Nine Elms Lane · A3220 · A3205 · Battersea · A215

Scale

| 0 | 1 | 2 km |
| 0 | | 1 mile |

Additional symbols on enlarged maps

Primary route
– single, dual carriageway

A road – single, dual carriageway

B road

Through-route

Minor road

One way street

No access in direction shown

Public building

Railway or bus station building

Place of interest

E **Embassy**

Theatre

M **Museum**

All other symbols can be found on page X

Scale

10 inches to 1 mile   1:6336

| 0 | 110yds | 220yds | 330yds | 440 yards |

| 0 | 125m | 250m | 375m | 500 metres |

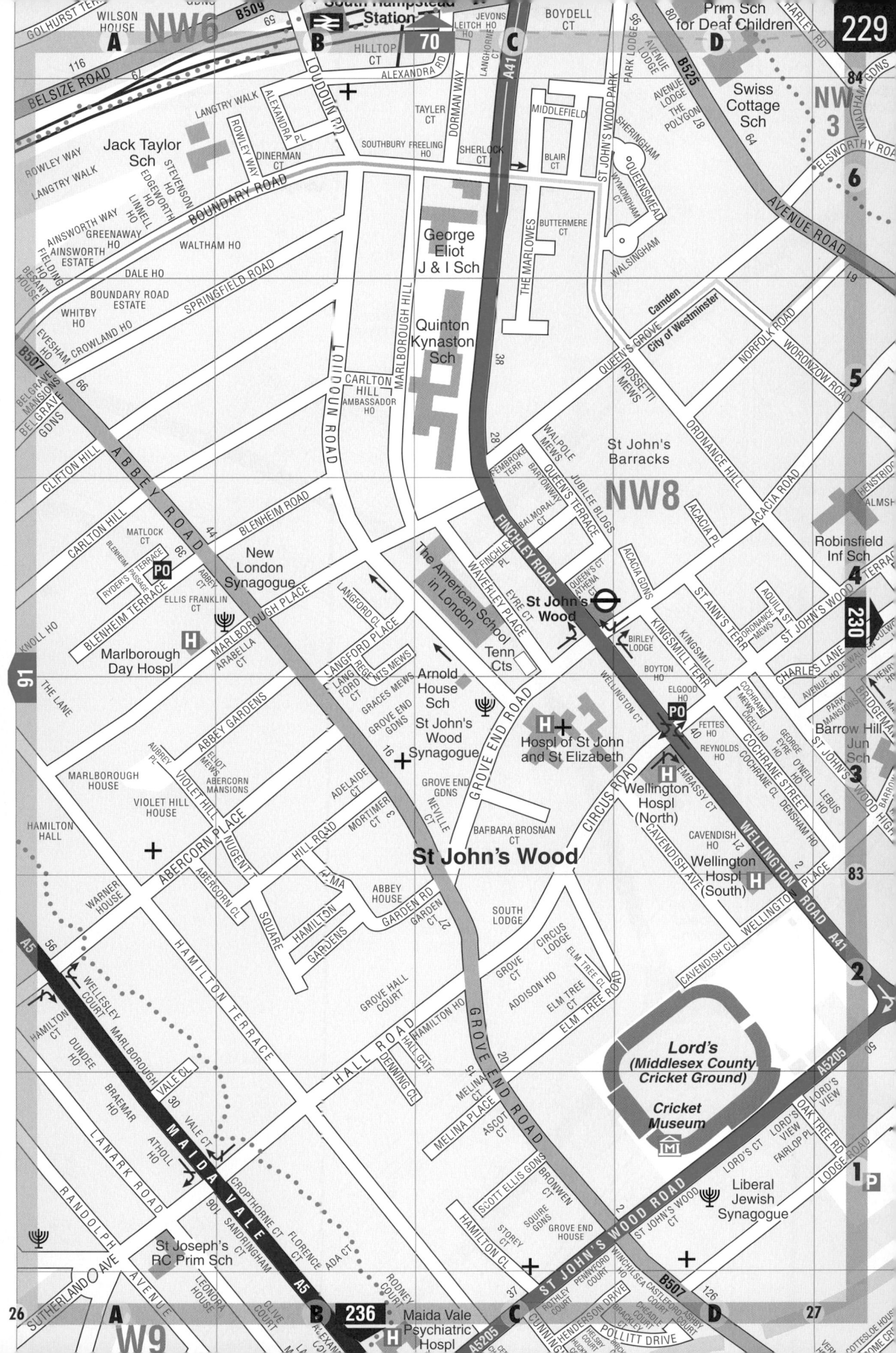
NW6
NW8
NW3
W9
St John's Wood
South Hampstead Station
St John's Wood
Lord's (Middlesex County Cricket Ground)
Cricket Museum
Jack Taylor Sch
George Eliot J & I Sch
Quinton Kynaston Sch
Swiss Cottage Sch
Prim Sch for Deaf Children
St John's Barracks
Robinsfield Inf Sch
New London Synagogue
Marlborough Day Hospl
The American School in London
Arnold House Sch
St John's Wood Synagogue
Hospl of St John and St Elizabeth
Wellington Hospl (North)
Wellington Hospl (South)
Barrow Hill Jun Sch
Liberal Jewish Synagogue
St Joseph's RC Prim Sch
Maida Vale Psychiatric Hospl
Tenn Cts
ABBEY ROAD
FINCHLEY ROAD
WELLINGTON ROAD
GROVE END ROAD
ST JOHN'S WOOD ROAD
MAIDA VALE
BOUNDARY ROAD
BELSIZE ROAD
LOUDOUN ROAD
AVENUE ROAD
ACACIA ROAD
HAMILTON TERRACE
SPRINGFIELD ROAD
MARLBOROUGH PLACE
ABERCORN PLACE
HALL ROAD
CIRCUS ROAD
ELM TREE ROAD
QUEEN'S GROVE
Camden
City of Westminster
70
230
236
91
26
27
83
84
A B C D
1 2 3 4 5 6

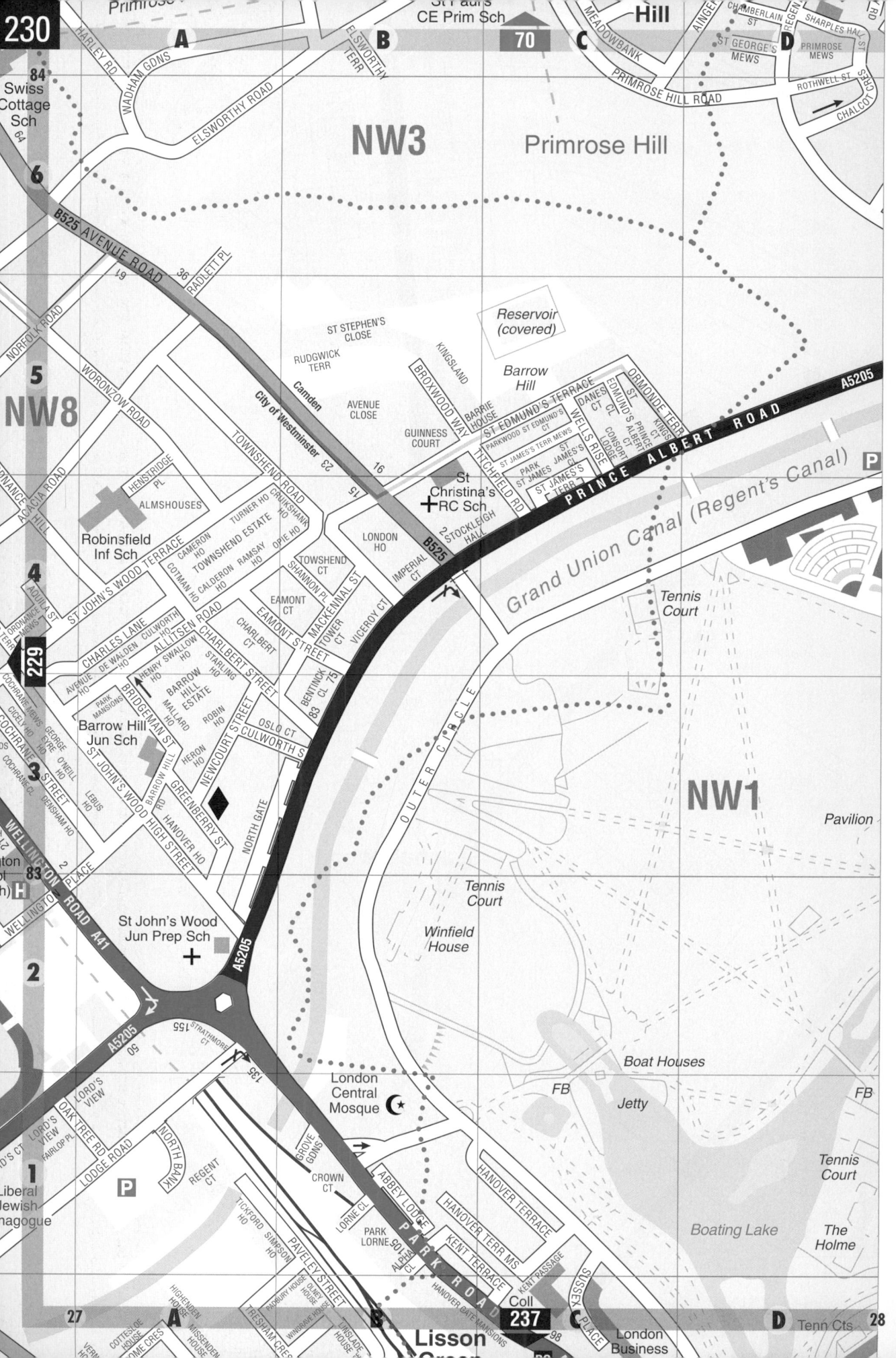

St Paul's
CE Prim Sch

Hill

CHAMBERLAIN ST
REGEN

SHARPLES HALL ST

St GEORGE'S
MEWS

PRIMROSE
MEWS

ROTHWELL ST

CHALCOT CRES

NW3

Primrose Hill

PRIMROSE HILL ROAD

A

B

70

C

D

MEADOWBANK

AINGE

84
Swiss
Cottage
Sch

64

6

B525 AVENUE ROAD

RADLETT PL

36

61

HARLEY RD

WADHAM GDNS

ELSWORTHY ROAD

ELSWORTHY TERR

Reservoir
(covered)

Barrow
Hill

NORFOLK ROAD

5

NW8

WORONZOW ROAD

ACACIA ROAD

City of Westminster

Camden

ST STEPHEN'S
CLOSE

RUDGWICK
TERR

AVENUE
CLOSE

KINGSLAND

BROXWOOD WAY

BARRIE
HOUSE

GUINNESS
COURT

ST EDMUND'S TERRACE

TITCHFIELD RD

ORMONDE TERR

A5205

PRINCE ALBERT ROAD

St
Christina's
RC Sch

WELLS RISE

DANES
CT

KINGS

EDMUND'S ALBERT
CT

CONSORT
LODGE

St
PRINCE
ALBERT
CT

PARKWOOD ST EDMUND'S
CT

PARK
ST JAMES'S
TERR

ST JAMES'S
TERR MEWS

ST JAMES'S
TERR

DS

HENSTRIDGE
PL

ALMSHOUSES

Robinsfield
Inf Sch

TOWNSHEND ROAD

CAMERON
HO

TURNER HO

CRUIKSHANK
HO

OPIE HO

RAMSAY
HO

TOWNSHEND ESTATE

COTMAN HO

CALDERON
HO

LONDON
HO

TOWNSHEND
CT

SHANNON PL

MACKENNAL ST

IMPERIAL
CT

B525

2

STOCKLEIGH
HALL

4

AQUILA ST

ORDNANCE
HILL

ST JOHN'S WOOD TERRACE

CHARLES LANE

AVENUE

DE WALDEN
HO

CULWORTH

ALLITSEN ROAD

CHARLBERT STREET

EAMONT
CT

CHARLBERT
CT

EAMONT STREET

TOWER
CT

VICEROY CT

Tennis
Court

Grand Union Canal (Regent's Canal)

P

229

COCHRANE MEWS

GEORGE
EYRE

O'NEILL

HENRY SWALLOW
HO

MALLARD

STARLING
HO

BENTINCK
CL

75

OUTER CIRCLE

3

COCHRANE
STREET

CGELY HO

JENSHAM HO

PARK
MANSIONS

BRIDGEMAN ST

BARROW
HILL ESTATE

ROBIN
HO

OSLO CT

83

NW1

Barrow Hill
Jun Sch

ST JOHN'S WOOD HIGH STREET

LEBUS
HO

HERON
HO

HANOVER HO

BARROW HILL

GREENBERRY ST

NEWCOURT STREET

CULWORTH S

NORTH GATE

CULWORTH ST

Pavilion

WELLINGTON ROAD

WELLINGTON
PLACE

2

83

H

A41

St John's Wood
Jun Prep Sch

A5205

Tennis
Court

Winfield
House

27

A5205

50

STRATHMORE
CT

155

135

London
Central
Mosque

Boat Houses

FB

Jetty

FB

Tennis
Court

1

Liberal
Jewish
nagogue

LORD'S VIEW

OAK TREE RD

FAIRLOP PL

LODGE ROAD

P

NORTH BANK

REGENT
CT

GROVE
GDNS

CROWN
CT

ABBEY LODGE

TICKFORD

SIMPSON

LORNE CL

PARK
LORNE

ALPHA
CL

Boating Lake

The
Holme

HIGHEND

PAVELEY STREET

HANOVER TERR MS

HANOVER TERRACE

KENT TERRACE

KENT PASSAGE

HANOVER GATE MANSIONS

HANOVER GATE

SUSSEX
PLACE

Tennis
Court

27

A

B

237

C

D

Tenn Cts

28

Lisson

Coll

London
Business

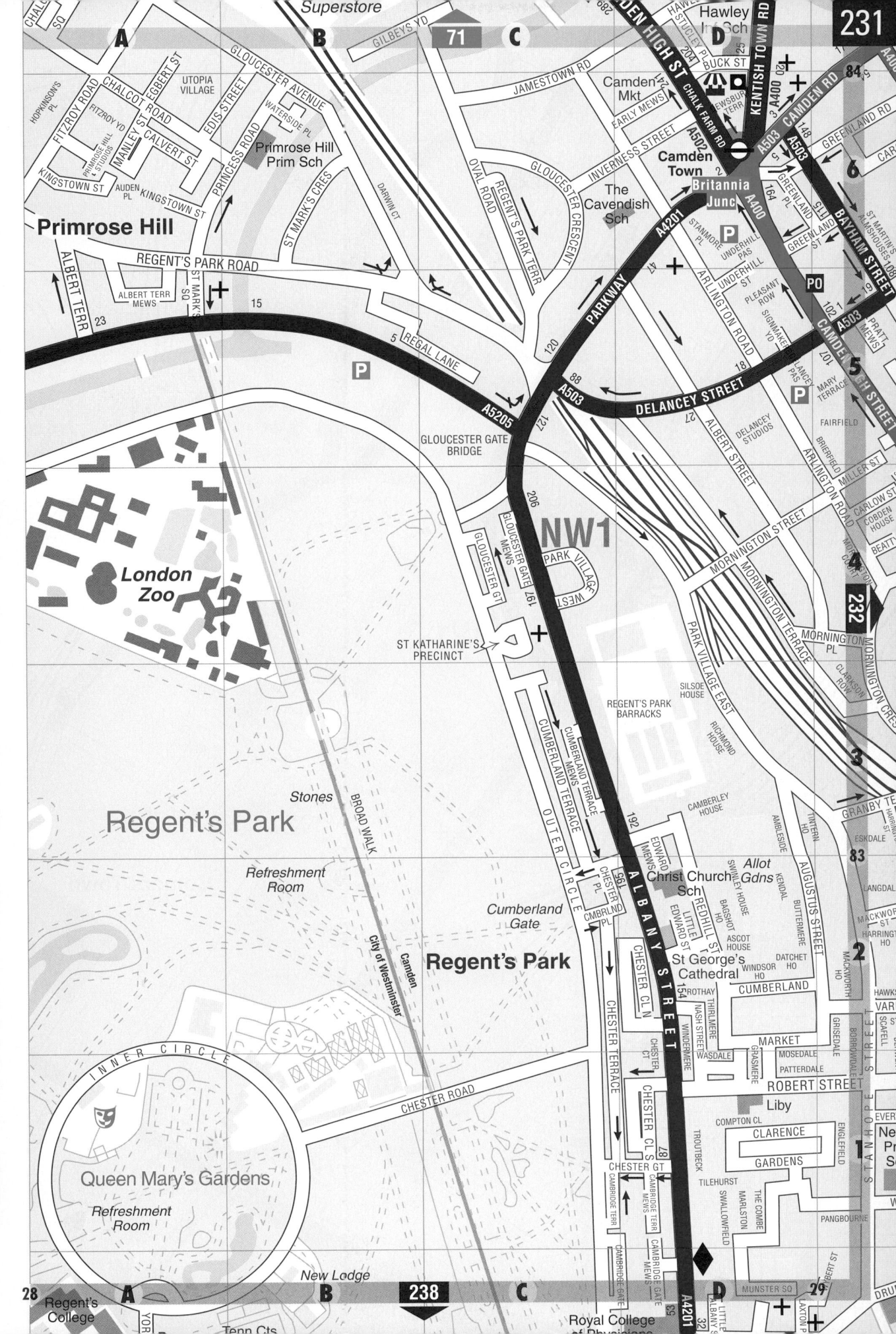

Superstore
A
B
C
D
71
GILBEYS YD
GLOUCESTER AVENUE
UTOPIA VILLAGE
EGBERT ST
EDIS STREET
CHALCOT ROAD
FITZROY ROAD
FITZROY YD
HOPKINSON'S PL
MANLEY ST
CALVERT ST
PRINCESS ROAD
WATERSIDE PL
Primrose Hill Prim Sch
KINGSTOWN ST
AUDEN PL
Primrose Hill
REGENT'S PARK ROAD
ALBERT TERR
ALBERT TERR MEWS
ST MARK'S SQ
ST MARK'S CRES
DARWIN CT
JAMESTOWN RD
OVAL ROAD
REGENT'S PARK TERR
GLOUCESTER CRESCENT
INVERNESS STREET
EARLY MEWS
Camden Mkt
Hawley Inf Sch
BUCK ST
CAMDEN HIGH ST
CHALK FARM RD
KENTISH TOWN RD
CAMDEN RD
A400
A502
A503
Camden Town
Britannia Junc
The Cavendish Sch
GREENLAND RD
GREENLAND PL
GREENLAND ST
BAYHAM STREET
ST MARTIN'S ALMSHOUSES
PO
STANMORE PL
UNDERHILL PAS
UNDERHILL ST
PLEASANT ROW
SIGNMAKERS YD
DELANCEY PAS
PRATT MEWS
PARKWAY
A4201
ARLINGTON ROAD
REGAL LANE
A5205
DELANCEY STREET
ALBERT STREET
DELANCEY STUDIOS
MARY TERRACE
FAIRFIELD
BRIERFIELD
MILLER ST
CARLOW ST
COBDEN HOUSE
GLOUCESTER GATE BRIDGE
NW1
London Zoo
GLOUCESTER GT
GLOUCESTER GATE MEWS
PARK VILLAGE WEST
MORNINGTON STREET
MORNINGTON TERRACE
MORNINGTON PL
MORNINGTON CRES
CLARKSON ROW
232
ST KATHARINE'S PRECINCT
PARK VILLAGE EAST
SILSOE HOUSE
REGENT'S PARK BARRACKS
RICHMOND HOUSE
CUMBERLAND TERRACE MEWS
CUMBERLAND TERRACE
OUTER CIRCLE
BROAD WALK
Stones
Regent's Park
CAMBERLEY HOUSE
GRANBY TER
ESKDALE
AMBLESIDE
TINTERN HO
EDWARD MEWS
Christ Church Sch
Allot Gdns
SWINLEY HOUSE
KENDAL
AUGUSTUS STREET
BUTTERMERE
LANGDALE
Refreshment Room
Cumberland Gate
CHESTER PL
CMBRLND PL
ALBANY STREET
LITTLE EDWARD ST
REDHILL ST
BAGSHOT HO
ASCOT HOUSE
MACKWORTH ST
MACKWORTH HO
City of Westminster
Camden
Regent's Park
CHESTER CL N
St George's Cathedral
WINDSOR HO
DATCHET HO
ROTHAY
CUMBERLAND
CHESTER TERRACE
NASH STREET
THIRLMERE
WINDERMERE
MARKET
GRISEDALE
BORROWDALE
STANHOPE STREET
SCAFELL
CHESTER CT
WASDALE
GRASMERE
MOSEDALE
PATTERDALE
INNER CIRCLE
CHESTER ROAD
ROBERT STREET
Liby
COMPTON CL
CHESTER CL S
CLARENCE GARDENS
ENGLEFIELD
TROUTBECK
Queen Mary's Gardens
CHESTER GT
TILEHURST
SWALLOWFIELD
MARLSTON
THE COMBE
PANGBOURNE
Refreshment Room
CAMBRIDGE TERR
CAMBRIDGE TERR MEWS
CAMBRIDGE GATE
CAMBRIDGE GATE MEWS
New Lodge
238
28
Regent's College
MUNSTER SQ
ALBANY ST
LITTLE ALBANY ST
29
Royal College of Physicians

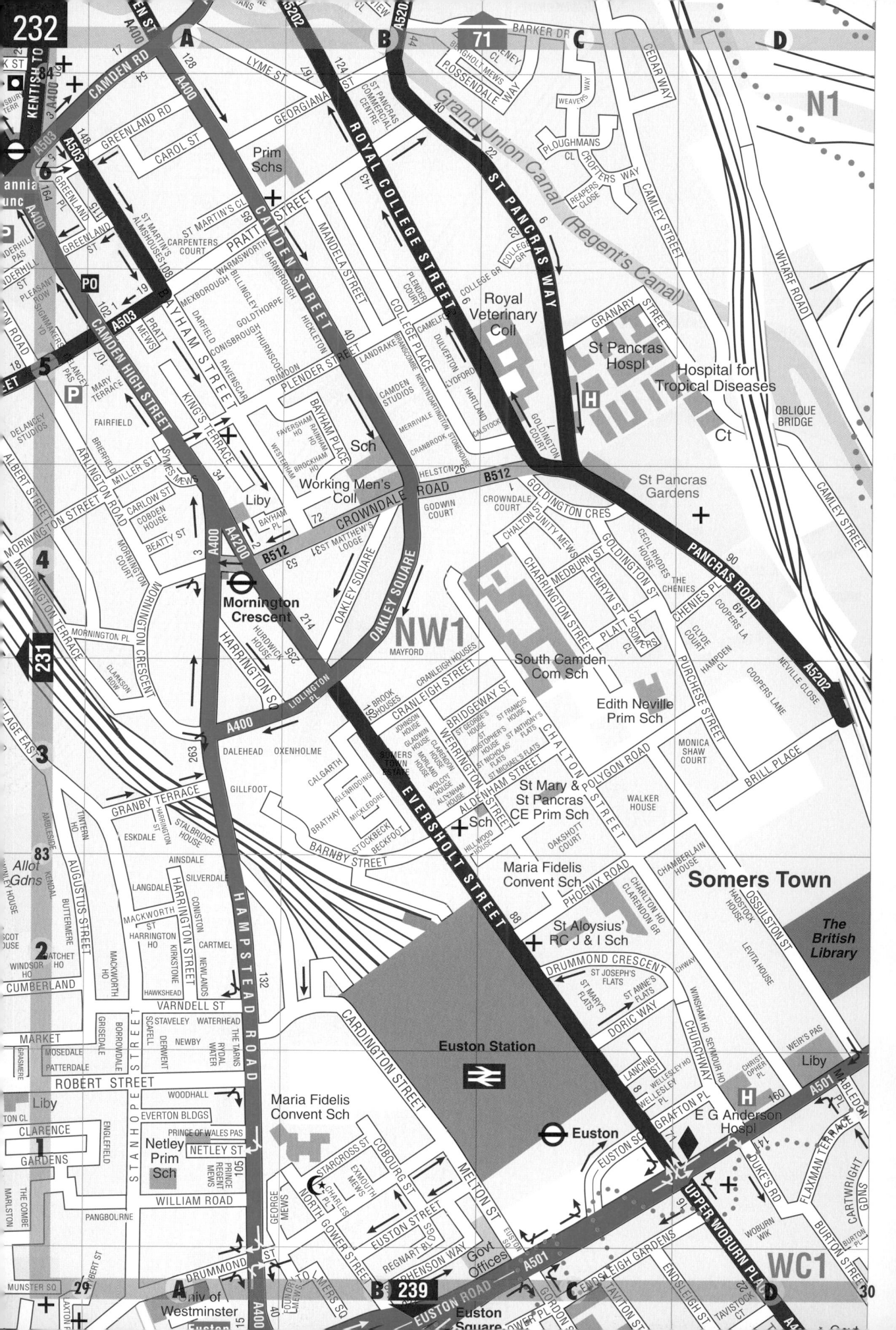
A
B
C
D
71
N1
NW1
WC1
231
239
30
CAMDEN RD
KENTISH TOWN
LYME ST
GEORGIANA ST
GREENLAND RD
CAROL ST
Prim Schs
ST PANCRAS COMMERCIAL CENTRE
ROYAL COLLEGE STREET
ST PANCRAS WAY
Grand Union Canal (Regent's Canal)
BARKER DR
ROSSENDALE WAY
CEDAR WAY
WEAVERS WAY
PLOUGHMANS CL
CROFTERS WAY
REAPERS CLOSE
CAMLEY STREET
WHARF ROAD
GREENLAND PL
GREENLAND ST
ST MARTIN'S CL
ST MARTIN'S ALMSHOUSES
CARPENTERS COURT
PRATT STREET
CAMDEN STREET
MANDELA STREET
PLENDER COURT
COLLEGE PLACE
COLLEGE GR
Royal Veterinary Coll
GRANARY STREET
St Pancras Hospl
Hospital for Tropical Diseases
OBLIQUE BRIDGE
Ct
PLEASANT ROW
PO
A503
CAMDEN HIGH STREET
PRATT MEWS
BAYHAM STREET
MEXBOROUGH
WARMSWORTH
BILLINGLEY
BARNBROUGH
DARFIELD
CONISBROUGH
GOLDTHORPE
THURNSCOE
RAVENSCAR
TRIMDON
HICKLETON
PLENDER STREET
LANDRAKE
CAMELFORD
DULVERTON
LYDFORD
HARTLAND
CALSTOCK
GOLDINGTON COURT
CAMDEN STUDIOS
MERRIVALE
CRANBROOK
STONEHOUSE
DELANCEY PAS
MARY TERRACE
DELANCEY STUDIOS
FAIRFIELD
ALBERT STREET
ARLINGTON ROAD
BRIERFIELD
MILLER ST
KING'S TERRACE
SYMES MEWS
FAVERSHAM HO
RAINHAM HO
WESTERHAM
BROCKHAM HO
BAYHAM PLACE
Sch
Working Men's Coll
Liby
HELSTON
B512
CROWNDALE ROAD
CROWNDALE COURT
GODWIN COURT
GOLDINGTON CRES
St Pancras Gardens
PANCRAS ROAD
CAMLEY STREET
MORNINGTON STREET
CARLOW ST
COBDEN HOUSE
BEATTY ST
BAYHAM PL
ST MATTHEW'S LODGE
A4200
A400
MORNINGTON COURT
MORNINGTON CRESCENT
Mornington Crescent
OAKLEY SQUARE
CHALTON ST
UNITY MEWS
CHARRINGTON STREET
MEDBURN ST
PENRYN ST
GOLDINGTON ST
CECIL RHODES HOUSE
THE CHENIES
CHENIES PL
COOPERS LA
PLATT ST
SOMERS CL
MORNINGTON TERRACE
MORNINGTON PL
CLARKSON ROW
HURDWICK HOUSE
HARRINGTON SQ
MAYFORD
CRANLEIGH HOUSES
CRANLEIGH STREET
South Camden Com Sch
CLYDE COURT
HAMPDEN CL
COOPERS LANE
NEVILLE CLOSE
A5202
LIDLINGTON PL
BROOK HOUSES
JOHNSON HOUSE
GLADWIN HOUSE
CLARENDON HOUSE
BRIDGEWAY ST
WERRINGTON STREET
Edith Neville Prim Sch
PURCHESE STREET
MONICA SHAW COURT
BRILL PLACE
DALEHEAD
OXENHOLME
SOMERS TOWN ESTATE
CALGARTH
GLENRIDDING
MICKLEDORE
ALDENHAM STREET
CHALTON STREET
POLYGON ROAD
St Mary & St Pancras CE Prim Sch
WALKER HOUSE
GILLFOOT
GRANBY TERRACE
TINTERN HO
ESKDALE
HARRINGTON ST
STALBRIDGE HOUSE
BRATHAY
STOCKBECK
BECKFOOT
EVERSHOLT STREET
OAKSHOTT COURT
BARNBY STREET
HILLWOOD HOUSE
AINSDALE
SILVERDALE
Allot Gdns
AUGUSTUS STREET
LANGDALE
HARRINGTON STREET
Maria Fidelis Convent Sch
PHOENIX ROAD
CHARLTON HO
CLARENDON GR
CHAMBERLAIN HOUSE
Somers Town
HADSTOCK HOUSE
OSSULSTON ST
The British Library
MACKWORTH
ST HARRINGTON HO
CONISTON
CARTMEL
BUTTERMERE
HATCHET HO
WINDSOR HO
MACKWORTH HO
KIRKSTONE
NEWLANDS
HAMPSTEAD ROAD
St Aloysius' RC J & I Sch
DRUMMOND CRESCENT
ST JOSEPH'S FLATS
ST MARY'S FLATS
ST ANNE'S FLATS
DORIC WAY
LEVITA HOUSE
CUMBERLAND
HAWKSHEAD
VARNDELL ST
MARKET
GRISEDALE
BORROWDALE
STAVELEY
WATERHEAD
SCAFELL
NEWBY
RYDAL WATER
THE TARNS
DERWENT
MOSEDALE
PATTERDALE
GRASMERE
STANHOPE STREET
CARDINGTON STREET
Euston Station
CHURCHWAY
WINSHAM HO
SEYMOUR HO
CHRISTOPHER PL
WEIR'S PAS
LANCING ST
WELLESLEY PL
ROBERT STREET
WOODHALL
EVERTON BLDGS
PRINCE OF WALES PAS
NETLEY ST
Netley Prim Sch
PRINCE REGENT MEWS
WILLIAM ROAD
PANGBOURNE
CLARENCE GARDENS
ENGLEFIELD
Liby
MARLSTON
THE COMBE
GRAFTON PL
E G Anderson Hospl
Euston
EUSTON SQ
MABLEDON PL
A501
DUKE'S RD
FLAXMAN TERRACE
CARTWRIGHT GDNS
COBOURG ST
STARCROSS ST
EXMOUTH MEWS
CHARLES PL
NORTH GOWER STREET
GEORGE MEWS
EUSTON STREET
MELTON ST
REGNART BLDGS
STEPHENSON WAY
Govt Offices
UPPER WOBURN PLACE
WOBURN WLK
BURTON STREET
BURTON PL
ENDSLEIGH GARDENS
ENDSLEIGH ST
TAVITON ST
TAVISTOCK CT
DRUMMOND ST
MUNSTER SQ
Univ of Westminster
FOUNDRY MEWS
EVERSHOLT SQ
EUSTON ROAD
Euston Square
GORDON ST

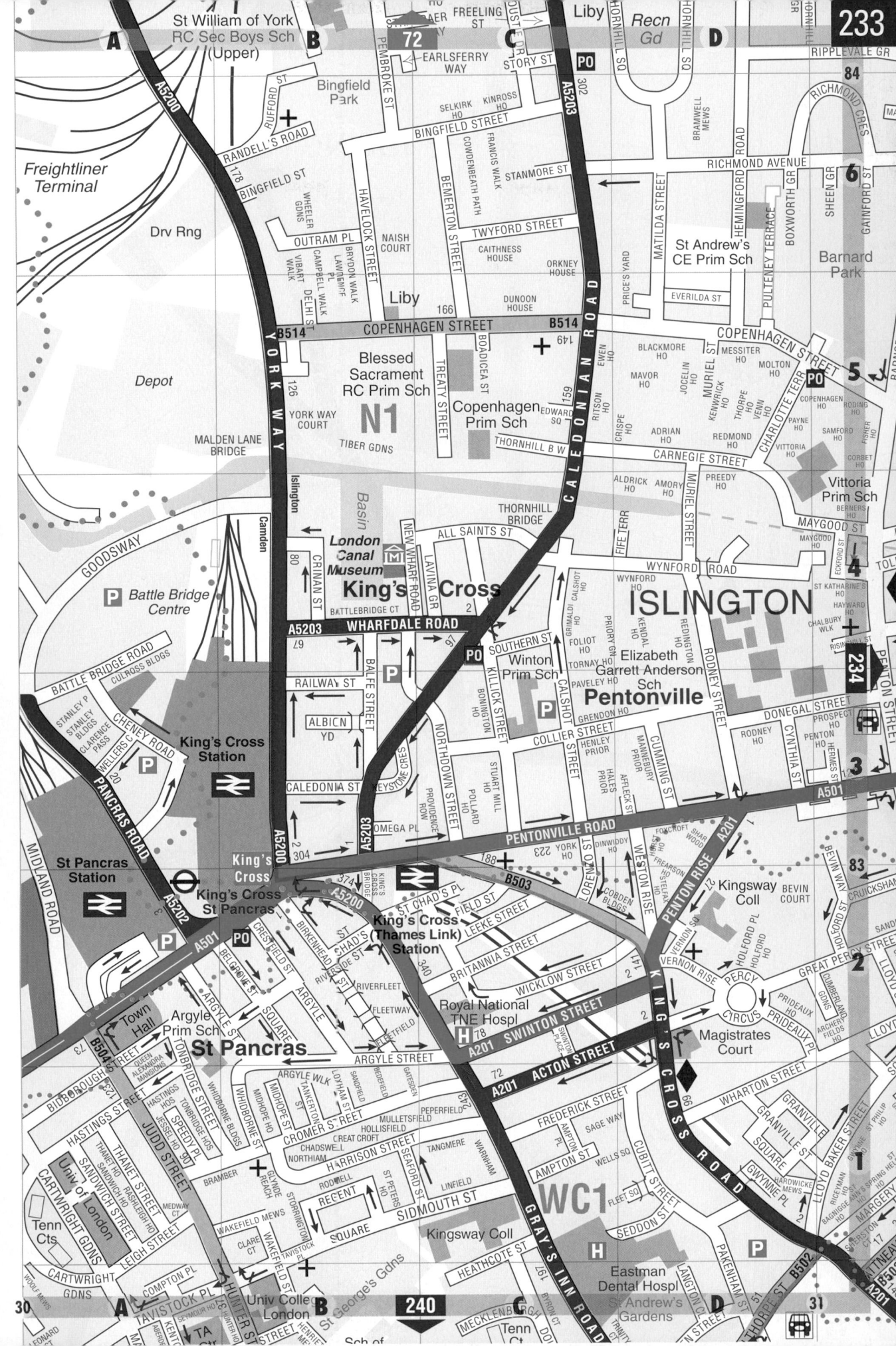
72
240
234
A
B
C
D
6
5
4
3
2
1
84
83
30
31
St William of York RC Sec Boys Sch (Upper)
Freightliner Terminal
Drv Rng
Depot
Bingfield Park
Liby
Recn Gd
FREELING ST
EARLSFERRY WAY
STORY ST
PEMBROKE ST
RUFFORD ST
RANDELL'S ROAD
BINGFIELD ST
BINGFIELD STREET
SELKIRK HO
KINROSS HO
COWDENBEATH PATH
FRANCIS WALK
STANMORE ST
BEMERTON STREET
TWYFORD STREET
HAVELOCK STREET
NAISH COURT
CAITHNESS HOUSE
ORKNEY HOUSE
DUNOON HOUSE
OUTRAM PL
WHEELER GDNS
VIBART WALK
CAMPBELL WALK
BRYDON WALK
DELHI ST
HORNHILL SQ
BRAMWELL MEWS
RICHMOND AVENUE
RICHMOND CRES
RIPPLEVALE GR
HEMINGFORD ROAD
MATILDA STREET
BOXWORTH GR
SHEEN GR
GAINFORD ST
PULTENEY TERRACE
PRICE'S YARD
EVERILDA ST
St Andrew's CE Prim Sch
Barnard Park
A5200
A5203
A5202
A201
A501
B514
B503
B504
B502
COPENHAGEN STREET
YORK WAY
CALEDONIAN ROAD
Blessed Sacrament RC Prim Sch
N1
TREATY STREET
BOADICEA ST
Copenhagen Prim Sch
YORK WAY COURT
TIBER GDNS
MALDEN LANE BRIDGE
EDWARD SQ
THORNHILL B W
EWEN HO
RITSON HO
CRISPE HO
BLACKMORE HO
MAVOR HO
ADRIAN HO
JOCELIN HO
MURIEL ST
KENWRICK HO
THORPE HO
VENN HO
MESSITER HO
MOLTON HO
REDMOND HO
CHARLOTTE TERR
COPENHAGEN HO
RODING HO
PAYNE HO
SAMFORD HO
FISHER HO
VITTORIA HO
CORBET HO
Vittoria Prim Sch
CARNEGIE STREET
ALDRICK HO
AMORY HO
PREEDY HO
MURIEL STREET
MAYGOOD ST
Islington
Camden
Basin
London Canal Museum
King's Cross
THORNHILL BRIDGE
ALL SAINTS ST
NEW WHARF ROAD
LAVINA GR
CRINAN ST
BATTLEBRIDGE CT
FIFE TERR
WYNFORD ROAD
WYNFORD HO
ISLINGTON
GOODSWAY
Battle Bridge Centre
WHARFDALE ROAD
CALSHOT HO
GRIMALDI HO
FOLIOT HO
PRIORY GN
KENDAL HO
REDINGTON HO
RODNEY STREET
Elizabeth Garrett Anderson Sch
Pentonville
TORNAY HO
PAVELEY HO
GRENDON HO
SOUTHERN ST
Winton Prim Sch
KILLICK STREET
BONINGTON HO
BALFE STREET
RAILWAY ST
ALBION YD
CALSHOT STREET
BATTLE BRIDGE ROAD
CULROSS BLDGS
STANLEY P
STANLEY BLDGS
CLARENCE PASS
CHENEY ROAD
WELLERS C
King's Cross Station
PANCRAS ROAD
CALEDONIA ST
KEYSTONE CRES
PROVIDENCE ROW
NORTHDOWN STREET
POLLARD HO
STUART MILL HO
COLLIER STREET
HENLEY PRIOR
MANNEBURY PRIOR
HALES PRIOR
AFFLECK ST
CUMMING ST
DONEGAL STREET
RODNEY HO
CYNTHIA ST
PROSPECT HO
PENTON HO
HERMES ST
PENTON STREET
ST KATHARINE'S HO
HAYWARD HO
CHALBURY WLK
RISINGHILL ST
ECKFORD ST
MAYGOOD HO
OMEGA PL
PENTONVILLE ROAD
MIDLAND ROAD
St Pancras Station
King's Cross
King's Cross St Pancras
YORK HO
DINWIDDY HO
LORENZO ST
WESTON RISE
FOXCROFT
SHARWOOD
HAMBLIN HO
FREARSON HO
STELFAX HO
COBDEN BLDGS
PENTON RISE
Kingsway Coll
BEVIN COURT
BEVIN WAY
HOLFORD ST
HOLFORD PL
HOLFORD HO
CRUICKSHANK
GREAT PERCY STREET
CUMBERLAND GDNS
LLOYD
VERNON SQ
VERNON RISE
PERCY CIRCUS
PRIDEAUX HO
PRIDEAUX PL
ARCHERY FIELDS HO
Magistrates Court
KING'S CROSS BRIDGE
ST CHAD'S PL
FIELD ST
LEEKE STREET
King's Cross (Thames Link) Station
BRITANNIA STREET
WICKLOW STREET
CRESTFIELD ST
BIRKENHEAD ST
ST CHAD'S ST
BELGROVE ST
RIVERSIDE ST
RIVERFLEET
FLEETWAY
FLEETFIELD
Royal National TNE Hospl
SWINTON STREET
SWINTON PLACE
ACTON STREET
ARGYLE SQUARE
ARGYLE ST
Town Hall
Argyle Prim Sch
St Pancras
ARGYLE STREET
ARGYLE WLK
QUEEN ALEXANDRA MANSIONS
BIDBOROUGH STREET
TONBRIDGE STREET
WHIDBORNE BLDGS
WHIDBORNE ST
MIDHOPE HO
MIDHOPE ST
TANKERTON ST
LOXHAM ST
SANDFIELD
BEDEFIELD
GATESDEN
HASTINGS HOS
HASTINGS STREET
TONBRIDGE HOS
SPEEDY PL
JESSEL HO
JUDD STREET
CROMER STREET
PEPERFIELD
MULLETSFIELD
HOLLISFIELD
GREAT CROFT
CHADSWELL
NORTHIAM
HARRISON STREET
TANGMERE
WARNHAM
FREDERICK STREET
SAGE WAY
AMPTON PL
AMPTON ST
WELLS SQ
CUBITT STREET
KING'S CROSS ROAD
WHARTON STREET
GRANVILLE SQUARE
GRANVILLE ST
GWYNNE PL
HARDWICKE MEWS
LLOYD BAKER STREET
RICEYMAN HO
BAGNIGGE HO
ANN'S SPRING HO
ST PHILIP HO
MARGERY
SHERSTON CT
THANET STREET
THANET HO
SANDWICH HO
SANDWICH STREET
RASHLEIGH HO
Univ of London
CARTWRIGHT GDNS
Tenn Cts
MEDWAY CT
LEIGH STREET
BRAMBER
GLYNDE REACH
RODMELL
REGENT SQUARE
ST PETERS HO
SEAFORD ST
LINFIELD
SIDMOUTH ST
WC1
FLEET SQ
SEDDON ST
WAKEFIELD MEWS
STORRINGTON
WAKEFIELD ST
CLARE CT
TAVISTOCK PL
Kingsway Coll
HEATHCOTE ST
GRAY'S INN ROAD
Eastman Dental Hospl
St Andrew's Gardens
LANGTON CL
PAKENHAM ST
THORPE ST
CARTWRIGHT GDNS
COMPTON PL
TAVISTOCK PL
HUNTER ST
SEYMOUR HO
Univ Coll London
St George's Gdns
MECKLENBURGH
BYRON CT
Tenn
WOOLF MEWS
LEONARD CT
TA Ctr

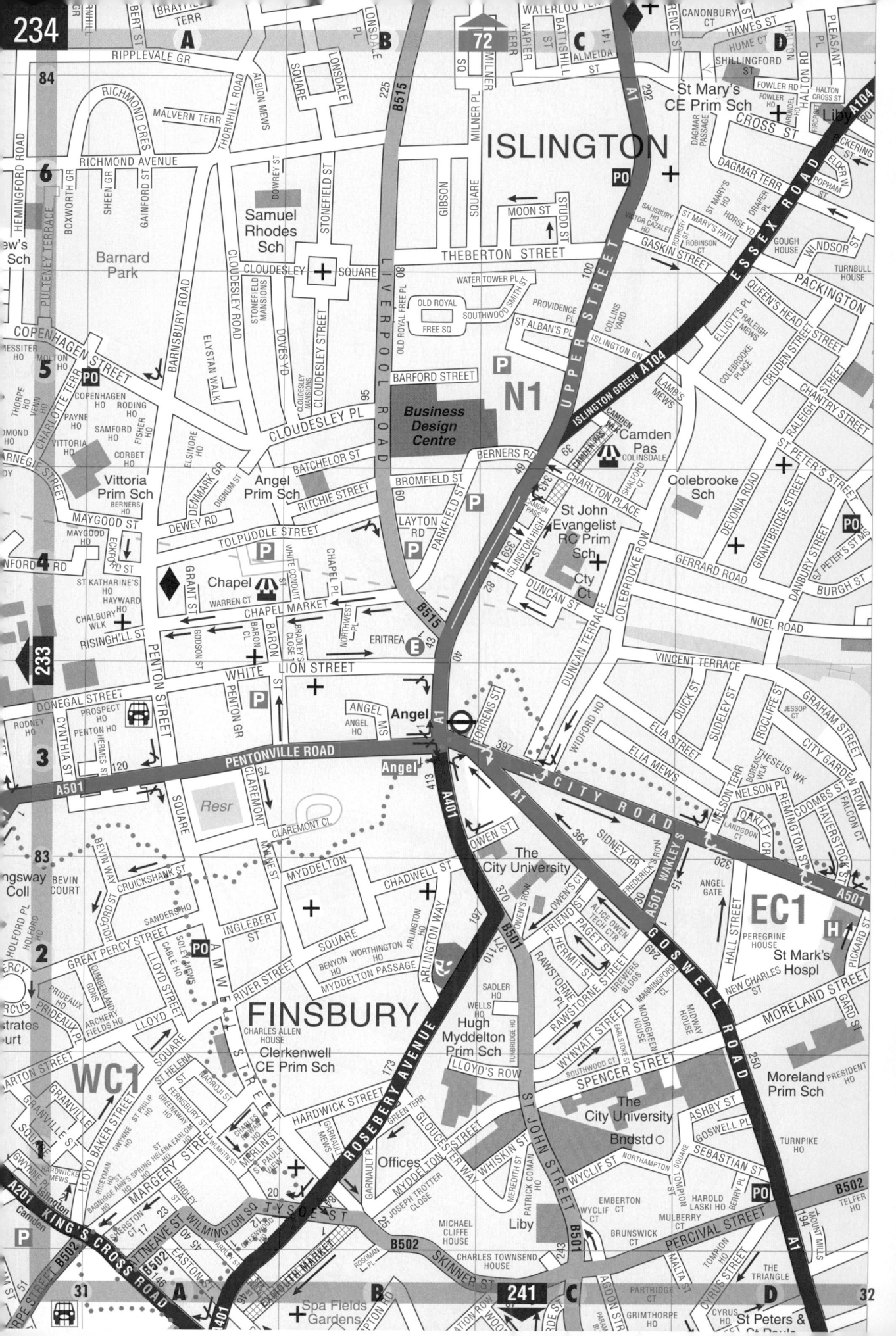
ISLINGTON
FINSBURY
N1
EC1
WC1
Samuel Rhodes Sch
Barnard Park
Vittoria Prim Sch
Angel Prim Sch
Business Design Centre
Camden Pas
Colebrooke Sch
St John Evangelist RC Prim Sch
Cty Ct
Chapel
Angel
The City University
St Mary's CE Prim Sch
St Mark's Hospl
Hugh Myddelton Prim Sch
Clerkenwell CE Prim Sch
Moreland Prim Sch
Offices
Bndstd
Liby
Spa Fields Gardens
PENTONVILLE ROAD
CITY ROAD
GOSWELL ROAD
ROSEBERY AVENUE
UPPER STREET
LIVERPOOL ROAD
ESSEX ROAD
ISLINGTON GREEN A104
ST JOHN STREET
KING'S CROSS ROAD
AMWELL STREET
WHITE LION STREET
CHAPEL MARKET
COPENHAGEN STREET
CLOUDESLEY SQUARE
BARNSBURY ROAD
RICHMOND AVENUE
THEBERTON STREET
SPENCER STREET
MYDDELTON SQUARE
PERCIVAL STREET
SKINNER ST
72
233
241

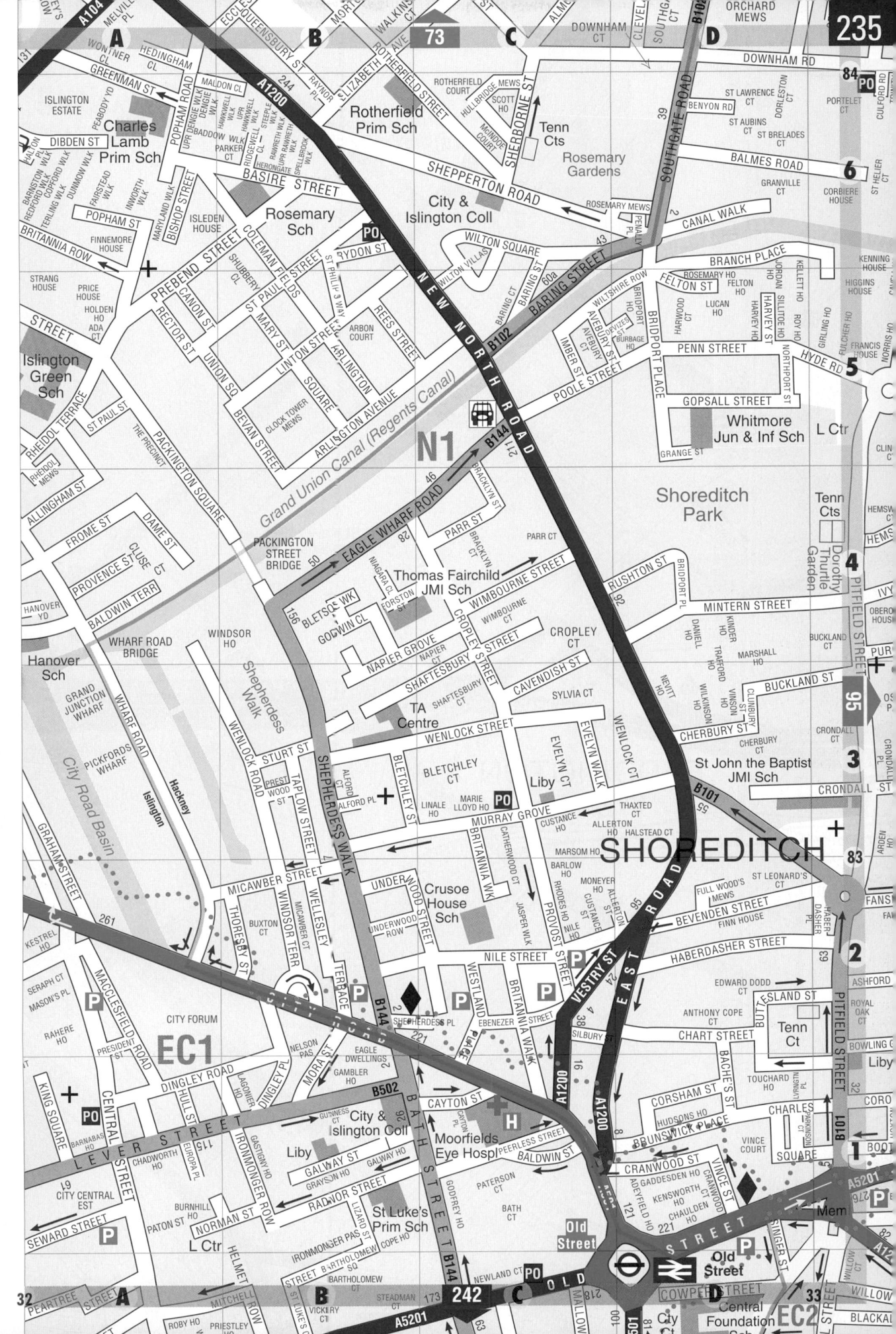
73
95
242
A
B
C
D
1
2
3
4
5
6
N1
EC1
EC2
SHOREDITCH
Grand Union Canal (Regents Canal)
City Road Basin
NEW NORTH ROAD
EAST ROAD
CITY ROAD
OLD STREET
SOUTHGATE ROAD
PITFIELD STREET
SHEPHERDESS WALK
BATH STREET
EAGLE WHARF ROAD
BARING STREET
SHEPPERTON ROAD
DOWNHAM RD
BALMES ROAD
CANAL WALK
BRANCH PLACE
PENN STREET
HYDE RD
POOLE STREET
GOPSALL STREET
MINTERN STREET
RUSHTON ST
WIMBOURNE STREET
SHAFTESBURY STREET
CAVENDISH ST
WENLOCK STREET
WENLOCK ROAD
MURRAY GROVE
CHERBURY ST
BUCKLAND ST
CRONDALL ST
BEVENDEN STREET
HABERDASHER STREET
NILE STREET
VESTRY ST
CHART STREET
CORSHAM ST
BRUNSWICK PLACE
CRANWOOD ST
CHARLES SQUARE
MICAWBER STREET
PACKINGTON SQUARE
WHARF ROAD
BASIRE STREET
PREBEND STREET
COLEMAN FIELDS
LINTON STREET
ARLINGTON AVENUE
BRITANNIA ROW
POPHAM ST
GREENMAN ST
ROTHERFIELD STREET
SHERBORNE ST
DINGLEY ROAD
LEVER STREET
CENTRAL STREET
GOSWELL ROAD
SEWARD STREET
RADNOR STREET
IRONMONGER ROW
MACCLESFIELD ROAD
GRAHAM STREET
Rotherfield Prim Sch
Charles Lamb Prim Sch
Rosemary Sch
City & Islington Coll
Islington Green Sch
Rosemary Gardens
Whitmore Jun & Inf Sch
Shoreditch Park
Thomas Fairchild JMI Sch
St John the Baptist JMI Sch
Hanover Sch
Crusoe House Sch
Moorfields Eye Hospl
St Luke's Prim Sch
Central Foundation Sch
TA Centre
Shepherdess Walk
Dorothy Thurtle Garden
Tenn Cts
Liby
L Ctr
PO
Old Street
CITY FORUM
PACKINGTON STREET BRIDGE
WHARF ROAD BRIDGE
Islington
Hackney
A1200
A5201
B144
B101
B102
B502

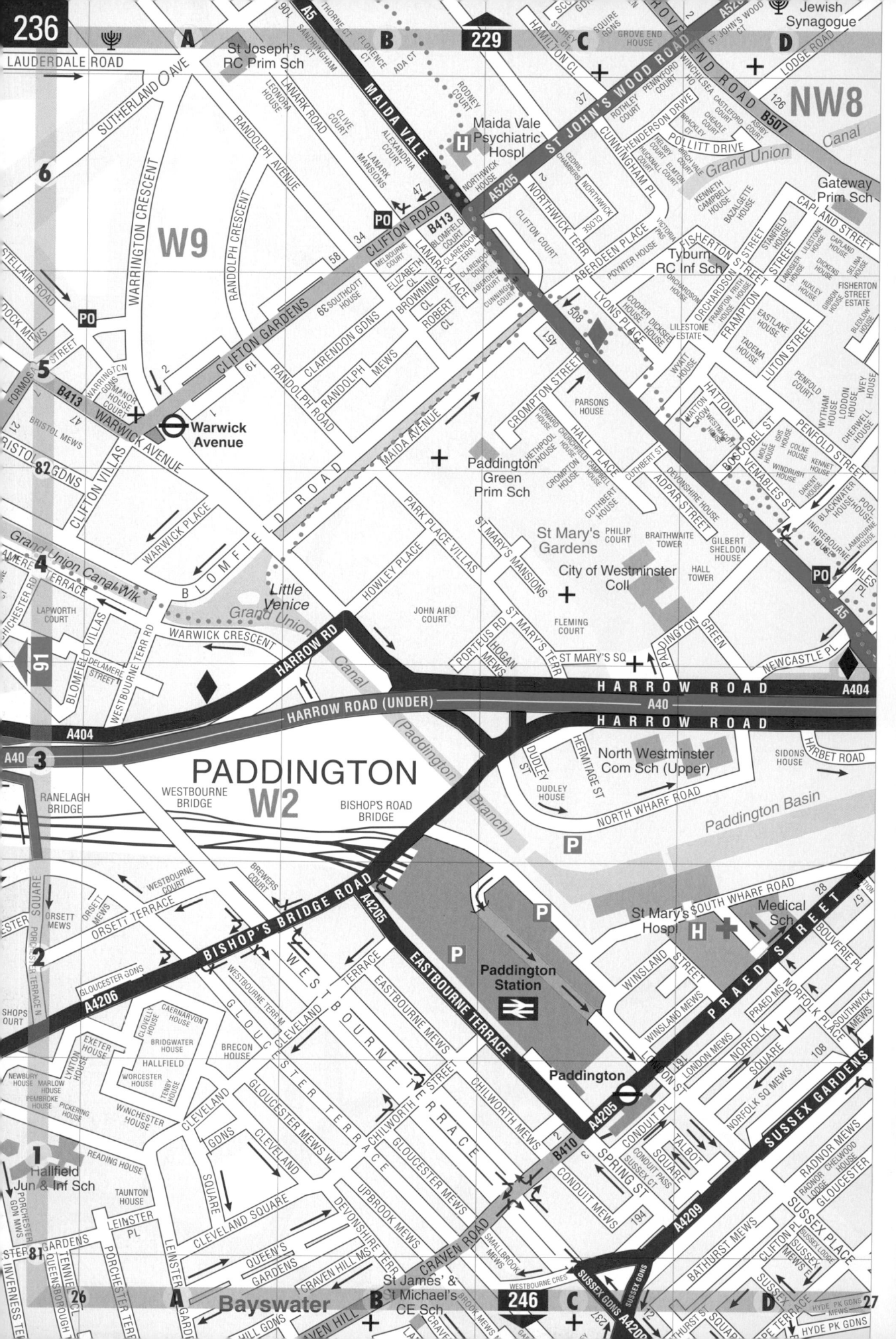
A
B
229
C
D
1
2
3
4
5
6
LAUDERDALE ROAD
St Joseph's RC Prim Sch
Jewish Synagogue
NW8
W9
W2
PADDINGTON
MAIDA VALE
A5
Maida Vale Psychiatric Hospl
ST JOHN'S WOOD ROAD
A5205
GROVE END ROAD
B507
Grand Union Canal
Gateway Prim Sch
SUTHERLAND AVE
WARRINGTON CRESCENT
RANDOLPH CRESCENT
RANDOLPH AVENUE
LANARK ROAD
CLIFTON ROAD
B413
CLIFTON GARDENS
CLARENDON GDNS
RANDOLPH MEWS
RANDOLPH ROAD
Warwick Avenue
WARWICK AVENUE
CLIFTON VILLAS
WARWICK PLACE
BLOMFIELD ROAD
MAIDA AVENUE
Little Venice
Grand Union Canal Wlk
WARWICK CRESCENT
HARROW RD
HARROW ROAD
HARROW ROAD (UNDER)
A404
A40
Paddington Green Prim Sch
St Mary's Gardens
City of Westminster Coll
Tyburn RC Inf Sch
ABERDEEN PLACE
CROMPTON STREET
HALL PLACE
LYONS PLACE
FISHERTON STREET
ORCHARDSON STREET
FRAMPTON STREET
LUTON STREET
CAPLAND STREET
PENFOLD STREET
VENABLES ST
BOSCOBEL ST
HATTON ST
NEWCASTLE PL
PADDINGTON GREEN
ST MARY'S SQ
ST MARY'S TERR
PORTEUS RD
HOWLEY PLACE
PARK PLACE VILLAS
North Westminster Com Sch (Upper)
NORTH WHARF ROAD
HARBET ROAD
Paddington Basin
RANELAGH BRIDGE
WESTBOURNE BRIDGE
BISHOP'S ROAD BRIDGE
BISHOP'S BRIDGE ROAD
A4206
A4205
EASTBOURNE TERRACE
Paddington Station
Paddington
St Mary's Hospl
Medical Sch
SOUTH WHARF ROAD
PRAED STREET
WINSLAND STREET
NORFOLK PLACE
NORFOLK SQUARE
SUSSEX GARDENS
A4209
WESTBOURNE TERRACE
GLOUCESTER TERRACE
CHILWORTH STREET
CLEVELAND SQUARE
ORSETT TERRACE
PORCHESTER SQUARE
Hallfield Jun & Inf Sch
CRAVEN ROAD
B410
SPRING ST
CONDUIT MEWS
SUSSEX PLACE
Bayswater
St James' & St Michael's CE Sch
246
26
27
81
82
91

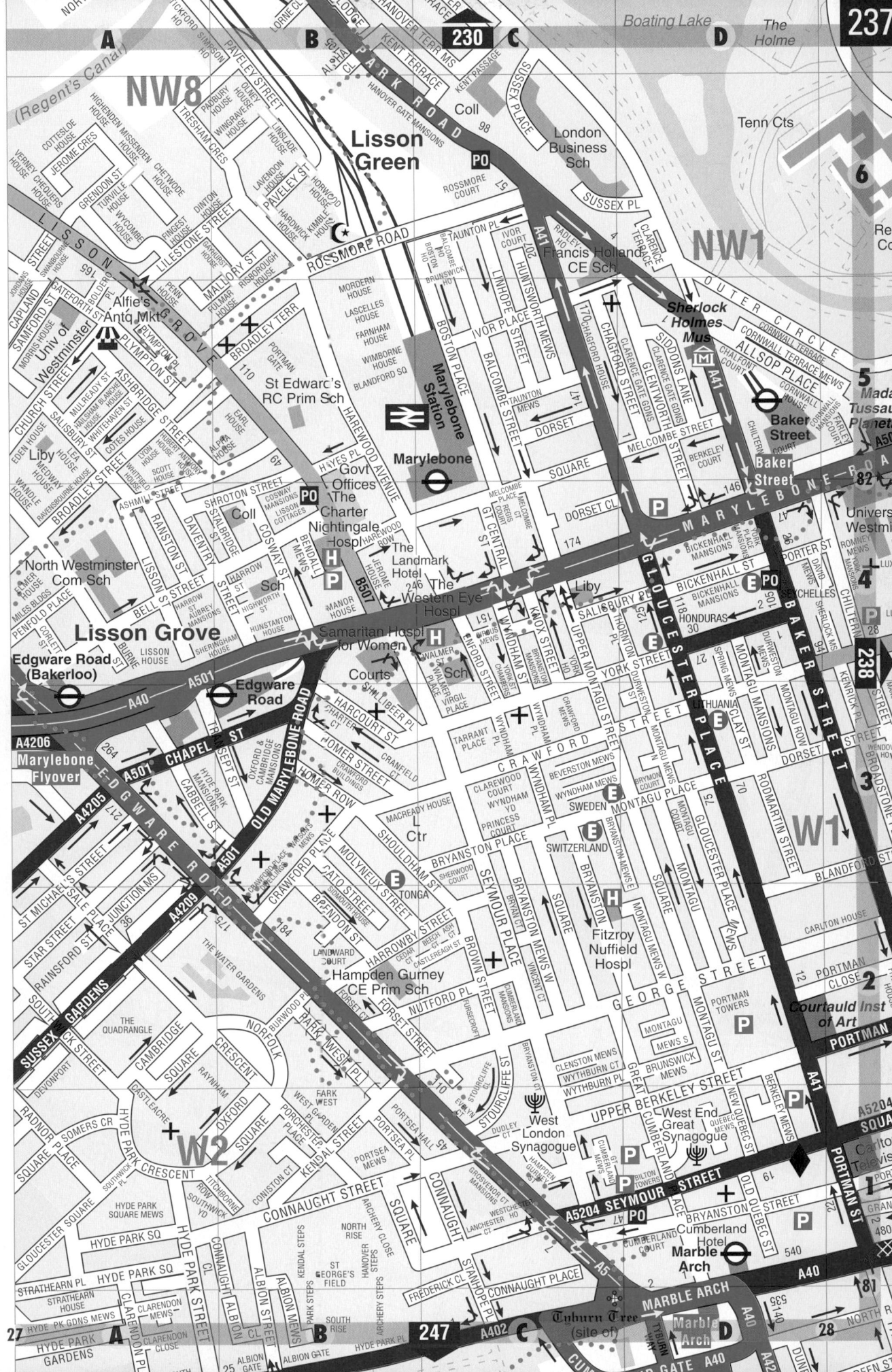
A
B
C
D
230
Boating Lake
The Holme
NW8
(Regent's Canal)
Lisson Green
PARK ROAD
KENT TERRACE
HANOVER TERR MS
HANOVER GATE MANSIONS
KENT PASSAGE
SUSSEX PLACE
Coll
London Business Sch
Tenn Cts
6
Reg Coll
SUSSEX PL
ROSSMORE COURT
ROSSMORE ROAD
TAUNTON PL
IVOR COURT
RADLEY MS
CLARENCE TERRACE
NW1
Francis Holland CE Sch
OUTER CIRCLE
CORNWALL TERRACE
CORNWALL TERRACE MEWS
ALLSOP PLACE
Sherlock Holmes Mus
5
Madame Tussauds Planetarium
Baker Street
CHILTERN COURT
A501
MARYLEBONE ROAD
University of Westminster
PAVELEY STREET
PAVELEY ST
TRESHAM CRES
LILESTONE STREET
MALLORY ST
LISSON GROVE
Alfie's Antq Mkt
Univ of Westminster
BROADLEY TERR
PORTMAN GATE
MORDERN HOUSE
LASCELLES HOUSE
FARNHAM HOUSE
WIMBORNE HOUSE
BLANDFORD SQ
Marylebone Station
Marylebone
St Edward's RC Prim Sch
HAREWOOD AVENUE
BOSTON PLACE
BALCOMBE STREET
LINHOPE STREET
IVOR PLACE
HUNTSWORTH MEWS
DORSET SQUARE
CHAGFORD STREET
CLARENCE GATE GDNS
GLENTWORTH STREET
SIDDONS LANE
MELCOMBE STREET
BERKELEY COURT
DORSET CL
A41
CHURCH STREET
SALISBURY ST
ASHBRIDGE STREET
Liby
HAYES PL
Govt Offices
The Charter Nightingale Hospl
The Landmark Hotel
The Western Eye Hospl
SHROTON STREET
COSWAY MANSIONS
LISSON COTTAGES
Coll
BROADLEY STREET
RANSTON ST
DAVENTRY
STALBRIDGE
COSWAY ST
BENDALL MEWS
North Westminster Com Sch
BELL STREET
Sch
PENFOLD PLACE
Lisson Grove
Edgware Road (Bakerloo)
Edgware Road
A40
Samaritan Hospl for Women
Courts
Sch
GLOUCESTER PLACE
BICKENHALL MANSIONS
BICKENHALL ST
PORTER ST
SEYCHELLES
HONDURAS
SALISBURY PL
YORK STREET
UPPER MONTAGU STREET
CHILTERN ST
4
238
LITHUANIA
CLAY ST
MONTAGU MANSIONS
DORSET ST
A4206
Marylebone Flyover
CHAPEL ST
TRANSEPT ST
OLD MARYLEBONE ROAD
HARCOURT ST
HOMER STREET
CRAWFORD STREET
WYNDHAM PL
TARRANT PLACE
BEVERSTON MEWS
WYNDHAM MEWS
SWEDEN
MONTAGU PLACE
3
A4205
EDGWARE ROAD
CABBELL ST
HOMER ROW
MACREADY HOUSE
L Ctr
SHOULDHAM ST
MOLYNEUX STREET
BRYANSTON PLACE
SWITZERLAND
BRYANSTON SQUARE
RODMARTIN STREET
W1
BLANDFORD STR
ST MICHAEL'S STREET
A4209
CRAWFORD PLACE
CATO STREET
TONGA
SEYMOUR PLACE
MONTAGU SQUARE
Fitzroy Nuffield Hospl
CARLTON HOUSE
STAR STREET
RAINSFORD ST
THE WATER GARDENS
HARROWBY STREET
Hampden Gurney CE Prim Sch
BROWN STREET
GEORGE STREET
PORTMAN TOWERS
PORTMAN CLOSE
2
Courtauld Inst of Art
SUSSEX GARDENS
THE QUADRANGLE
CAMBRIDGE SQUARE
NORFOLK CRESCENT
NUTFORD PL
FORSET STREET
PARK WEST PL
MONTAGU MEWS S
MONTAGU ST
PORTMAN
SOUTHWICK STREET
DEVONPORT
RAYNHAM
STOURCLIFFE ST
CLENSTON MEWS
WYTHBURN PL
BRUNSWICK MEWS
UPPER BERKELEY STREET
BERKELEY MEWS
A5204
RADNOR PLACE
SOMERS CR
HYDE PARK CRESCENT
OXFORD SQUARE
W2
PORCHESTER PLACE
KENDAL STREET
PORTSEA MEWS
PORTSEA PL
West London Synagogue
West End Great Synagogue
GREAT CUMBERLAND PLACE
NEW QUEBEC ST
PORTMAN ST
SEYMOUR STREET
HYDE PARK SQUARE MEWS
GLOUCESTER SQUARE
CONNAUGHT STREET
CONNAUGHT SQUARE
BRYANSTON STREET
OLD QUEBEC ST
1
HYDE PARK SQ
NORTH RISE
ST GEORGE'S FIELD
Cumberland Hotel
Marble Arch
HYDE PARK PL
STRATHEARN PL
HYDE PARK STREET
CONNAUGHT PLACE
A5
MARBLE ARCH
HYDE PARK GARDENS
ALBION STREET
SOUTH RISE
247
A402
Tyburn Tree (site of)
NORTH ROW
27
28

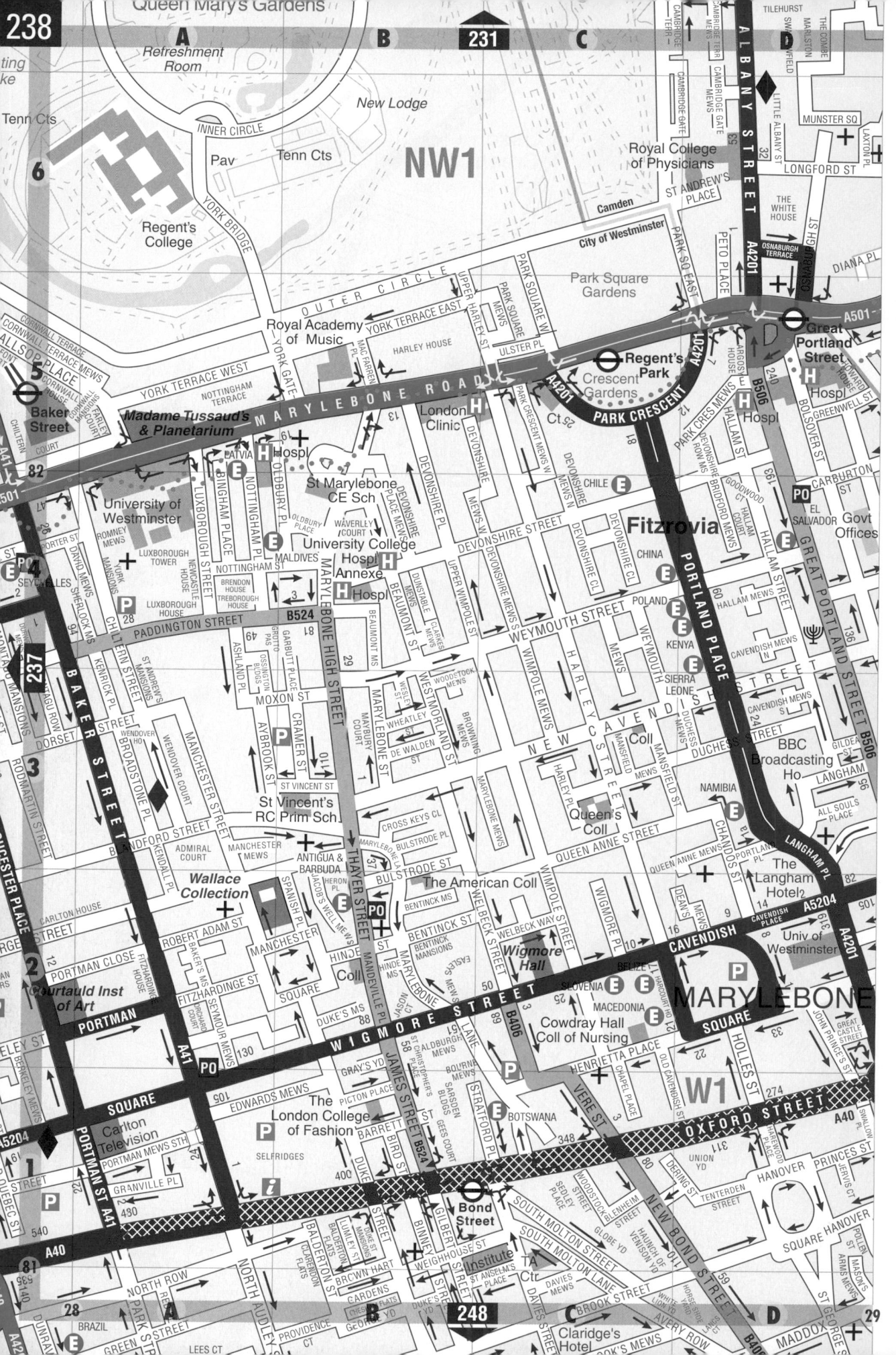
231
A
B
C
D
Queen Mary's Gardens
Refreshment Room
New Lodge
Inner Circle
Tenn Cts
Pav
NW1
Regent's College
York Bridge
Royal College of Physicians
Albany Street
A4201
Little Albany St
Munster Sq
Longford St
Laxton Pl
St Andrew's Place
Camden
City of Westminster
The White House
Osnaburgh St
Osnaburgh Terrace
Diana Pl
Peto Place
Park Sq East
Park Square Gardens
Outer Circle
York Terrace East
Upper Harley St
Park Square Mews
Park Square W
Ulster Pl
Royal Academy of Music
Harley House
York Terrace West
Nottingham Terrace
York Gate
Marylebone Road
Regent's Park
Crescent Gardens
Park Crescent
Great Portland Street
A501
Hospl
Cornwall Terrace
Cornwall Terrace Mews
Allsop Place
Baker Street
Madame Tussaud's & Planetarium
London Clinic
Devonshire Pl
Devonshire Mews W
Park Crescent Mews W
Park Crescent Mews E
Bolsover St
Greenwell St
Carburton St
El Salvador
Govt Offices
University of Westminster
Latvia
St Marylebone CE Sch
Chile
Fitzrovia
Portland Place
Great Portland Street
B506
Hallam St
Hallam Mews
Bridford Mews
Devonshire Street
Devonshire Cl
China
Poland
Kenya
Sierra Leone
Weymouth Street
Weymouth Mews
University College Hospl Annexe
Maldives
Nottingham St
Luxborough Tower
Luxborough House
Luxborough St
Bingham Place
Nottingham Pl
Oldbury Pl
Waverley Court
Porter St
David Mews
Sherlock Mews
Seychelles
Paddington Street
B524
Marylebone High Street
Beaumont St
Upper Wimpole St
Wimpole Mews
Harley Street
Cavendish Mews N
Cavendish Mews S
New Cavendish Street
Duchess Street
BBC Broadcasting Ho
Langham
All Souls Place
Gildea St
Chiltern Street
Kenrick Pl
Dorset Street
Baker Street
Manchester Street
Broadstone Pl
Wendover Court
Moxon St
Aybrook St
Cramer St
St Vincent St
St Vincent's RC Prim Sch
Westmorland St
Marylebone St
De Walden St
Wheatley St
Browning Mews
Mansfield St
Mansfield Mews
Coll
Queen's Coll
Harley Pl
Namibia
Chandos St
Queen Anne Street
Queen Anne Mews
Portland Pl
Langham Pl
The Langham Hotel
Rodmartin Street
Gloucester Place
Blandford Street
Admiral Court
Manchester Mews
Antigua & Barbuda
Cross Keys Cl
Bulstrode Pl
Bulstrode St
Marylebone La
Thayer Street
Heron Pl
The American Coll
Marylebone Mews
Wigmore Pl
Dean's Mews
Cavendish Place
A5204
Univ of Westminster
Wallace Collection
Carlton House
Robert Adam St
Manchester Square
Spanish Pl
Jacob's Well Mews
Bentinck Ms
Bentinck St
Bentinck Mansions
Welbeck Street
Welbeck Way
Wimpole Street
Wigmore Hall
Cavendish
Belize
Slovenia
Macedonia
Marylebone
Portman Close
Fitzhardinge St
Fitzhardinge House
Baker's Ms
Seymour Mews
Orchard Court
Hinde St
Hinde Ms
Duke's Ms
Mandeville Pl
Jason Ct
Easley's Mews
Courtauld Inst of Art
Portman
Wigmore Street
B406
Cowdray Hall Coll of Nursing
Square
Holles St
John Prince's St
Great Castle Street
Henrietta Place
Chapel Place
Old Cavendish St
W1
Berkeley Mews
Square
Carlton Television
Portman Mews Sth
Portman St
A41
Edwards Mews
Gray's Yd
James Street
Aldburgh Mews
St Christopher's Place
Bourne Mews
Sarsden Bldgs
Stratford Pl
Botswana
Vere St
Oxford Street
A40
Swallow Pl
Harewood Place
Union Yd
The London College of Fashion
Picton Place
Barrett St
Bird St
Gees Court
Selfridges
Granville Pl
Quebec St
Duke Street
Bond Street
South Molton Street
South Molton Lane
Woodstock Street
Sedley Place
Blenheim Street
Globe Yd
Haunch of Venison Yd
New Bond Street
Dering St
Tenterden Street
Hanover Square
Princes St
Jervis Ct
Pollen St
Mason's Arms Mews
North Audley Street
Balderton St
Balderton Flats
Clarendon Flats
Lumley St
Duke St Mansions
Brown Hart Gardens
Binney St
Gilbert Street
Weighhouse St
Institute
TA Ctr
St Anselm's Place
Davies Mews
Davies Street
Brook Street
Avery Row
North Row
Park St
Brazil
Green Street
Lees Ct
Providence Ct
George Yd
Chesterfield Flats
Duke's Yd
Claridge's Hotel
Maddox St
St George St
248
237
1
2
3
4
5
6
28
29
A42

NW1
232
WC1
W1
WC2
240
249
A
B
C
D
1
2
3
4
5
6
29
30
WILLIAM ROAD
PANGBOURNE
STANHOPE
WYBERT ST
DRUMMOND ST
NORTH GOWER STREET
EUSTON STREET
REGNART BLDGS
STEPHENSON WAY
Govt Offices
TOLMERS SQ
FOUNDRY MEWS
EUSTON ROAD
Euston Square
Univ of Westminster
Euston Underpass
Euston Twr
TRITON SQ
GOWER PLACE
GOWER CT
GORDON STREET
ENDSLEIGH GARDENS
ENDSLEIGH ST
ENDSLEIGH PLACE
TAVISTOCK CT
UPPER WOBURN PL
WOBURN WLK
BURTON STREET
CARTWRIGHT GDNS
FLAXMAN
TAVISTOCK SQUARE
Tavistock Square Gdn
Govt Offices
TAVITON STREET
GORDON SQUARE
Gordon Square Gdn
Warren Street
BEAUMONT PLACE
University College London
H
WARREN STREET
FITZROY STREET
GRAFTON MS
GRAFTON WAY
WHITFIELD PLACE
FITZROY CT
CONWAY ST
RICHARDSON'S MEWS
FITZROY SQ
St Luke's Hospl
WARREN MS
CROATIA
MOZAMBIQUE
London Foot Hospl
CLEVELAND STREET
PARAMOUNT CT
UNIVERSITY STREET
University College Hospl
MIDFORD PL
IRVINE CT
MORTIMER MARKET
CAPPER ST
SHROPSHIRE PL
HUNTLEY STREET
CHENIES MEWS
Royal Ear Hospl
MALET PL
BYNG PL
WOBURN SQUARE
TORRINGTON SQUARE
BEDFORD WAY
University College London
THORNHAUGH ST
RUSSELL SQUARE
Bloom
Russell Gar
A4200
WOBURN PL
CORAM HO
THACKERAY HO
DICKENS HO
Govt Offices
GOWER STREET
TOTTENHAM COURT ROAD
TORRINGTON PLACE
MULLARD HO
BROCK HO
RIDGMOUNT GDNS
MALET STREET
CYPRESS PL
HOWLAND MEWS E
MAPLE PL
MAPLE ST
CONWAY MEWS
BROMLEY PL
GRAFTON WAY
HOLCROFT COURT
CLIPSTONE MEWS
BT Tower
CLEVELAND MEWS
HOWLAND ST
NORTHCOURT
WHITFIELD ST
CHITTY ST
CHARLOTTE MEWS
WHITFIELD GDNS
ALFRED MS
NORTH CRES
CHENIES STREET
RIDGMOUNT ST
KEPPEL ST
MONTAGUE PLACE
B506
CLIPSTONE ST
Univ of Westminster
University College London
Middlesex Hospl Annexe
Goodge Street
ALFRED PLACE
RIDGMOUNT PL
HANSON STREET
OGLE STREET
Sch of Nursing
All Souls Sch
CHARLOTTE STREET
TOTTENHAM MS
TOTTENHAM ST
SCALA ST
STORE STREET
GOWER MEWS
PO
British Museum
GOSFIELD ST
GREAT TITCHFIELD ST
FOLEY STREET
CANDOVER ST
RIDING HOUSE STREET
Camden
City of Westminster
Middlesex Hospital
GOODGE ST A5204
GOODGE PL
COLVILLE PL
KIRKMAN PL
WHITFIELD ST
WINDMILL ST
SOUTH CR
BAYLEY ST
BEDFORD SQUARE
BLOOMSBURY STREET
MIDDLETON BLDGS
BOURLET CL
NASSAU ST
Univ of Westminster
BYWELL PL
CHARLOTTE PLACE
RATHBONE ST
PERCY PAS
PERCY STREET
MORWELL STREET
ADELINE PL
BEDFORD AVENUE
BEDFORD COURT MANSIONS
GREAT RUSSELL
B506
LITTLE TITCHFIELD ST
NEWMAN PAS
PERCY MEWS
STEPHEN MS
STEPHEN ST
Time Out Magazine
DYOTT ST
COPTIC
Liby
Law Ct
BTH'S PL
WELLS STREET
Univ of Westminster
WELLS MEWS
BERNERS MEWS
BERNERS ST
NEWMAN STREET
GRESSE ST
Birkbeck Coll
RATHBONE PL
EVELYN YD
HANWAY PL
HANWAY STREET
BARBADOS
E
BAINBRIDGE ST
LITTLE PORTLAND ST
MARYLEBONE PASSAGE
EASTCASTLE STREET
BERNERS PL
Talk Radio Ltd
PERRY'S PL
Tottenham Court Road
ST GILES' CIRCUS
A40
NEW OX
A400
MARGARET STREET
MARGARET COURT
MARKET PLACE
ADAM AND EVE CT
WINSLEY ST
SOHO ST
FALCON CT
BERWICK MEWS
FALCON BERG
Centre Point
ANDREW BORDE ST
EARNSHAW ST
BUCKNALL
ST GILES CT
ST GILES HIGH ST
GT CASTLE ST
PO
MKT CT
OXFORD STREET
GT CHAPEL ST
FAREHAM ST
HOLLEN ST
DIADEM CT
SOHO SQUARE
SUTTON ROW
GOSLETT YARD
ORANGE YD
DENMARK PL
DENMARK ST
FLITCROFT ST
ST GILES PAS
PENDRELL HO
NEW COMPTON ST
A401
B404
OXFORD CIRCUS
Oxford Circus
HILLS PL
OXFORD CIRCUS AVE
RAMILLIES PLACE
RAMILLIES ST
NOEL ST
SHERATON ST
CARLISLE ST
Soho
GREEK ST
BATEMAN'S BLDGS
MANETTE ST
WEDGEWOOD MEWS
PHOENIX ST
STACEY ST
LITTLE ARGYLL STREET
ARGYLL ST
Law Ct
GREAT MARLBOROUGH STREET
POLAND STREET
P
D'ARBLAY ST
PORTLAND MEWS
WARDOUR MEWS
BERWICK STREET
ST ANNE'S CT
CHAPONE PL
DEAN STREET
ROYALTY MEWS
Sch of Art and Design
CHARING CROSS ROAD
GREEK CT
CAMBRIDGE CIRCUS
MONMOUTH STREET
SEVEN DIALS
TOWER ST
ST
LITTLE MARLBOROUGH ST
FOUBERT'S PLACE
NEWBURGH STREET
MARSHALL STREET
L Ctr
SANDRINGHAM CT
DUFOUR'S PL
PO
LIVONIA ST
Berwick Street
WARDOUR STREET
DUCK LA
FLAXMAN CT
RICHMOND BLDGS
RICHMOND MEWS
BATEMAN ST
FRITH ST
MOOR ST
WEST ST
LITCHFIELD STREET
SANDRINGHAM FLATS
81
Carnaby Street
GANTON ST
KINGLY STREET
BROADWICK ST
INGESTRE PLACE
HOPKINS ST
KEMP'S CT
BLORE CT
MEARD ST
BOURCHIER ST
OLD COMPTON STREET
ROMILLY STREET
SHAFTESBURY AVENUE A401
REGENT STREET
A4201
B406
CONDUIT ST
MILL ST
NEW BRLGTN PL
KINGLY CT
BEAK STREET
UPPER JAMES ST
LEXINGTON STREET
SILVER PL
Westminster
GT PULTENEY
BRIDLE
CHANCEL CT
TISBURY CT
WINNETT ST
HORSE AND DOLPHIN YD
GERRARD PL
NEWPORT
UPPER ST MARTIN'S LANE
WELLINGTON CT

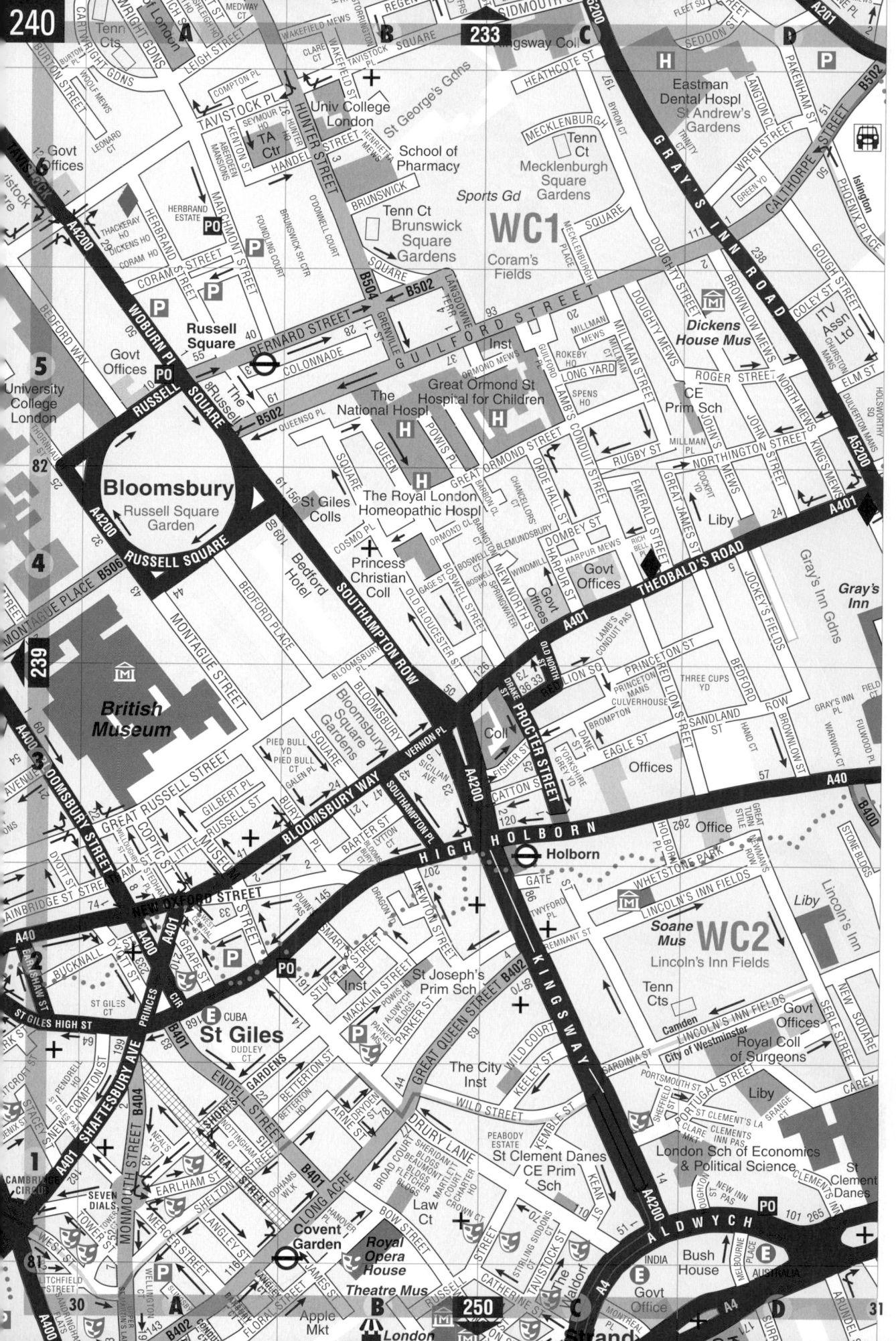
233
250
239
A
B
C
D
1
2
3
4
5
6
Tavistock Sq
Tenn Cts
Univ College London
St George's Gdns
School of Pharmacy
Kingsway Coll
Eastman Dental Hospl
St Andrew's Gardens
Mecklenburgh Square Gardens
Sports Gd
Tenn Ct
Brunswick Square Gardens
WC1
Coram's Fields
Govt Offices
University College London
Russell Square
Bloomsbury
Russell Square Garden
The National Hospl
Great Ormond St Hospital for Children
The Royal London Homeopathic Hospl
St Giles Colls
Princess Christian Coll
Bedford Hotel
Dickens House Mus
ITV Assn Ltd
CE Prim Sch
Liby
Gray's Inn
Gray's Inn Gdns
British Museum
Bloomsbury Square Gardens
Coll
Offices
Office
Holborn
Soane Mus
WC2
Lincoln's Inn Fields
Lincoln's Inn
Tenn Cts
Govt Offices
Royal Coll of Surgeons
Camden
City of Westminster
St Giles
St Joseph's Prim Sch
Inst
The City Inst
Peabody Estate
St Clement Danes CE Prim Sch
London Sch of Economics & Political Science
St Clement Danes
Law Ct
Covent Garden
Royal Opera House
Theatre Mus
Apple Mkt
London
Strand
Bush House
India
Australia
Govt Office
Islington
TAVISTOCK PL
HUNTER STREET
HANDEL ST
BRUNSWICK SQUARE
GUILFORD STREET
BERNARD STREET
WOBURN PL
SOUTHAMPTON ROW
RUSSELL SQUARE
MONTAGUE PLACE
MONTAGUE STREET
BEDFORD PLACE
BEDFORD WAY
GRAY'S INN ROAD
THEOBALD'S ROAD
LAMB'S CONDUIT STREET
GREAT ORMOND STREET
DOUGHTY STREET
MECKLENBURGH SQUARE
CALTHORPE STREET
ROGER STREET
NORTHINGTON STREET
JOHN STREET
RED LION SQ
RED LION STREET
PROCTER STREET
EAGLE ST
HIGH HOLBORN
NEW OXFORD STREET
BLOOMSBURY WAY
BLOOMSBURY STREET
GREAT RUSSELL STREET
BLOOMSBURY SQUARE
KINGSWAY
GREAT QUEEN STREET
LINCOLN'S INN FIELDS
PORTUGAL STREET
ALDWYCH
DRURY LANE
LONG ACRE
BOW STREET
ENDELL STREET
SHAFTESBURY AVE
MONMOUTH STREET
NEAL STREET
EARLHAM ST
ST GILES HIGH ST
WILD STREET
SEVEN DIALS
A4200
A401
A40
A400
A5200
A4
B502
B504
B506
B401
B402
B404

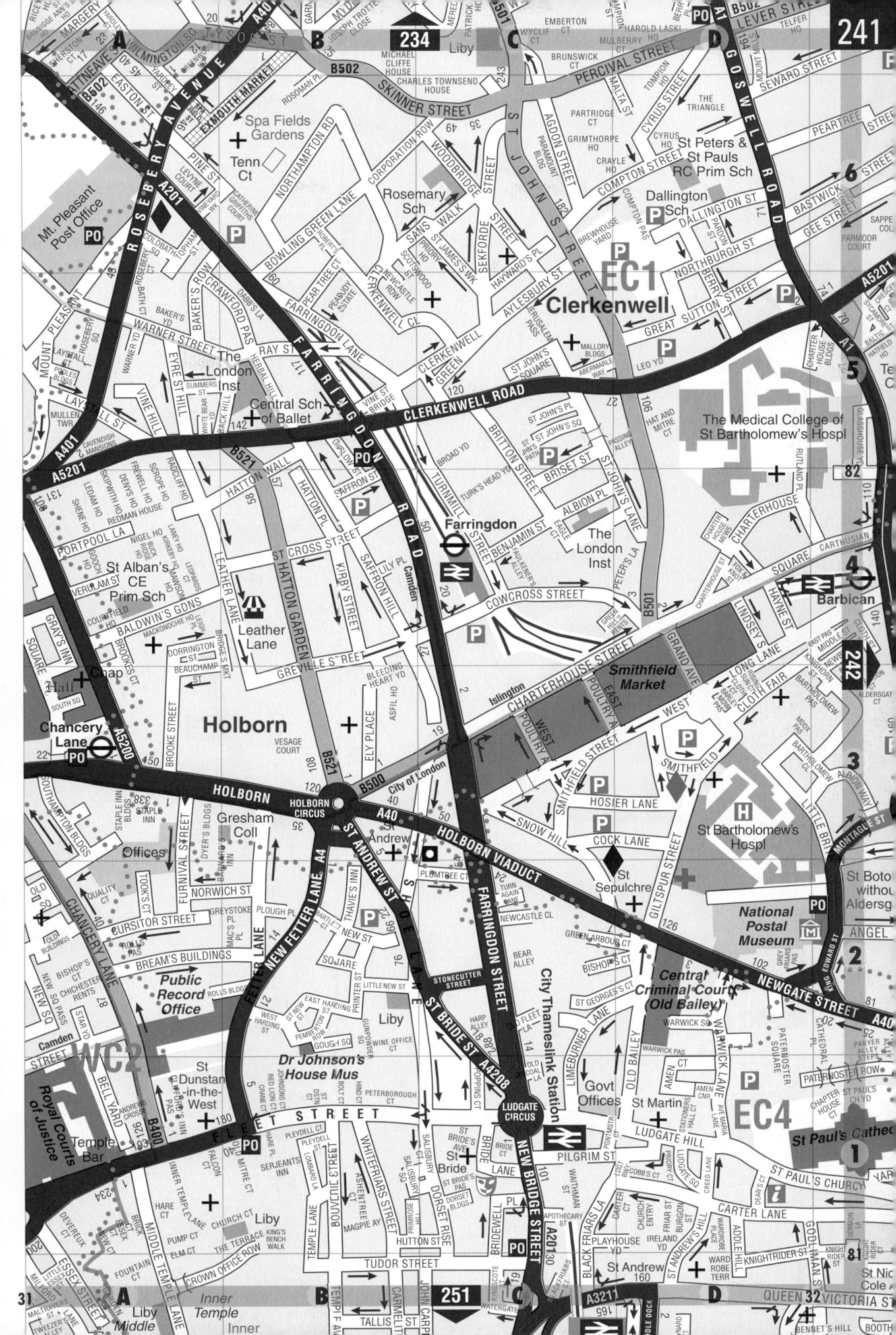

241
234
242
251
31
32
A
B
C
D
1
2
3
4
5
6
Clerkenwell
EC1
Holborn
EC4
WC2
Spa Fields Gardens
Mt. Pleasant Post Office
Rosemary Sch
Dallington Sch
St Peters & St Pauls RC Prim Sch
The Medical College of St Bartholomew's Hospl
The London Inst
Central Sch of Ballet
Farringdon
Barbican
Smithfield Market
St Alban's CE Prim Sch
Leather Lane
Chancery Lane
Gresham Coll
Holborn Circus
St Andrew
St Bartholomew's Hospl
St Sepulchre
National Postal Museum
Central Criminal Court (Old Bailey)
City Thameslink Station
Public Record Office
Dr Johnson's House Mus
Royal Courts of Justice
Temple Bar
St Dunstan-in-the-West
St Bride
Ludgate Circus
St Martin
Govt Offices
St Paul's Cathedral
Inner Temple
Middle Temple
Clerkenwell Road
Farringdon Road
Rosebery Avenue
Goswell Road
St John Street
Holborn Viaduct
Farringdon Street
Fleet Street
New Bridge Street
Newgate Street
Ludgate Hill
Charterhouse Street
Cowcross Street
Percival Street
Skinner Street
Compton Street
Chancery Lane
Fetter Lane
New Fetter Lane
Shoe Lane
St Bride St
Hatton Garden
Greville Street
Queen Victoria St

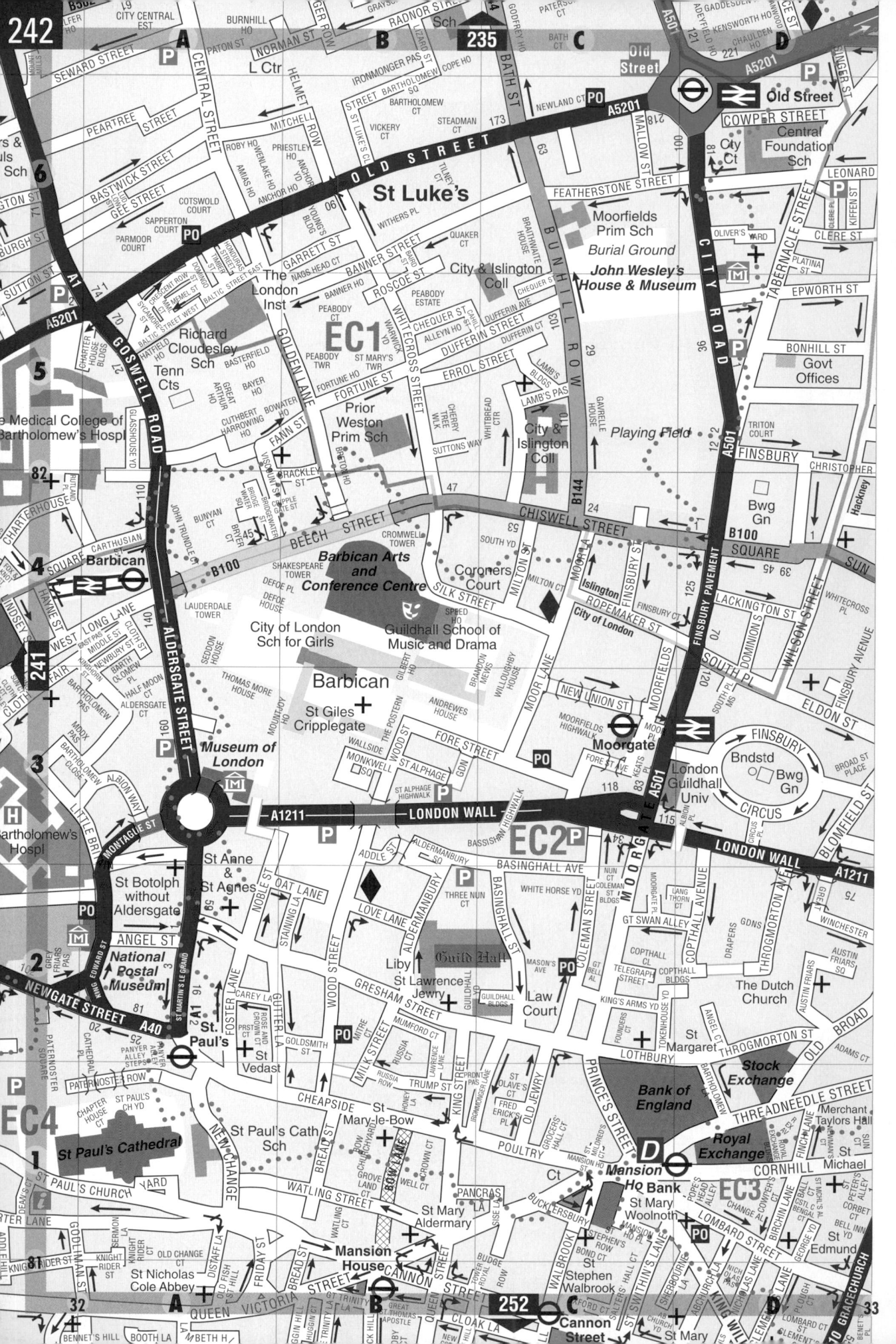

St Luke's
OLD STREET
EC1
EC2
EC3
EC4
GOSWELL ROAD
ALDERSGATE STREET
CITY ROAD
BUNHILL ROW
CHISWELL STREET
BEECH STREET
LONDON WALL
Barbican Arts and Conference Centre
Guildhall School of Music and Drama
City of London Sch for Girls
Barbican
St Giles Cripplegate
Museum of London
National Postal Museum
St Paul's Cathedral
Bank of England
Royal Exchange
Stock Exchange
Guild Hall
Moorgate
Old Street
Mansion House
Cannon Street
St Paul's
Bank
John Wesley's House & Museum
Moorfields Prim Sch
Burial Ground
City & Islington Coll
Prior Weston Prim Sch
Richard Cloudesley Sch
The London Inst
Coroners Court
London Guildhall Univ
Finsbury Circus
The Dutch Church
St Botolph without Aldersgate
St Anne & St Agnes
St Lawrence Jewry
St Mary-le-Bow
St Mary Aldermary
St Mary Woolnoth
St Stephen Walbrook
St Nicholas Cole Abbey
St Vedast
St Margaret
St Michael
St Edmund
Merchant Taylors Hall
Law Court
Govt Offices
Central Foundation Sch
Playing Field
CHEAPSIDE
QUEEN VICTORIA STREET
CANNON STREET
NEWGATE STREET
MOORGATE
FINSBURY PAVEMENT
THREADNEEDLE STREET
LOMBARD STREET
CORNHILL
POULTRY
WOOD STREET
ALDERMANBURY
COLEMAN STREET
BASINGHALL ST
GRESHAM STREET
WATLING STREET
ST PAUL'S CHURCH YARD

235
241
252

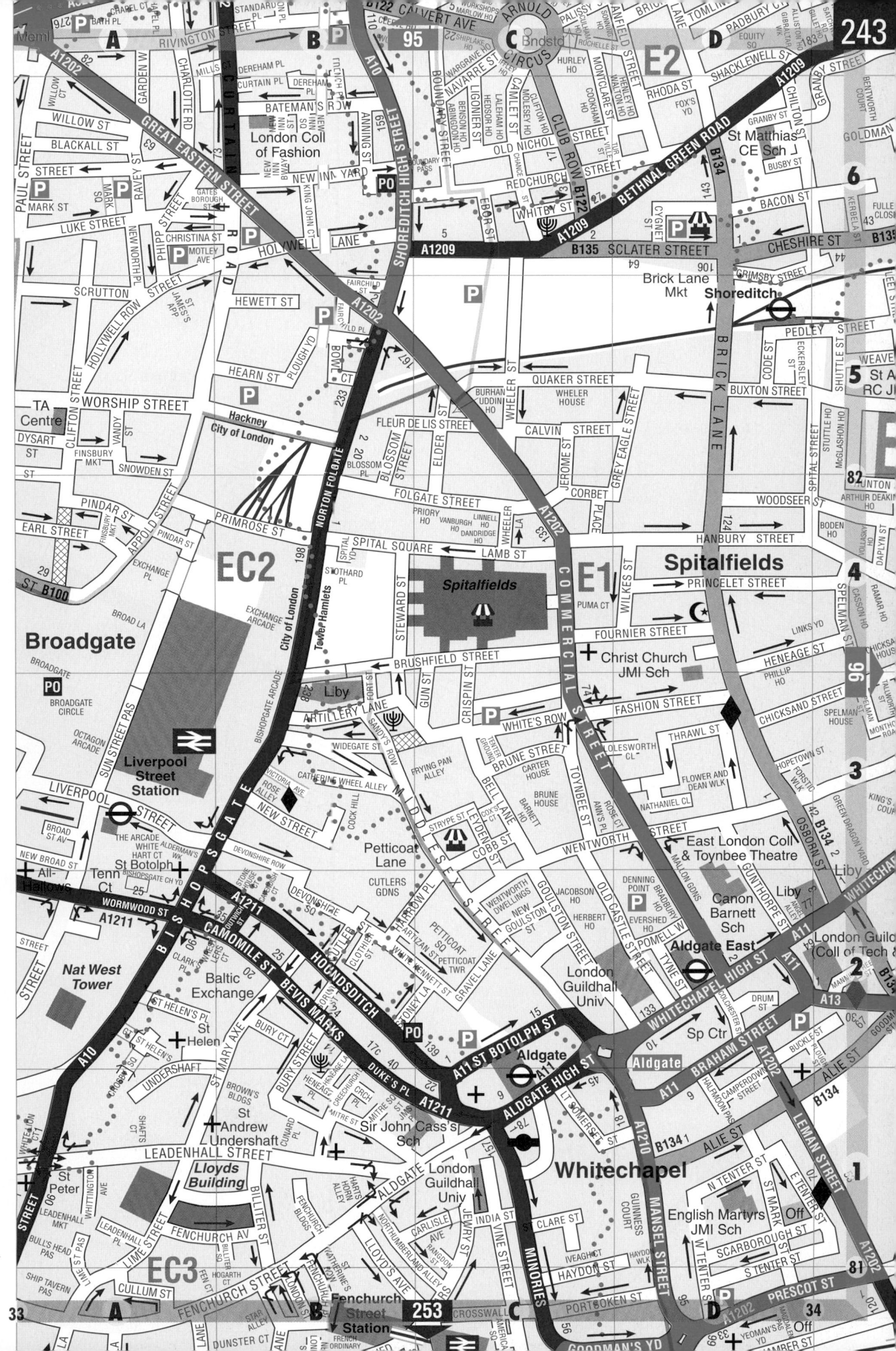
95
E2
ARNOLD CIRCUS
CALVERT AVE
RIVINGTON STREET
GREAT EASTERN STREET
CURTAIN ROAD
SHOREDITCH HIGH STREET
BOUNDARY STREET
BETHNAL GREEN ROAD
CLUB ROW
REDCHURCH STREET
OLD NICHOL STREET
London Coll of Fashion
St Matthias CE Sch
SCLATER STREET
CHESHIRE ST
HOLYWELL LANE
Brick Lane Mkt
Shoreditch
BRICK LANE
QUAKER STREET
BUXTON STREET
WORSHIP STREET
TA Centre
Hackney
City of London
NORTON FOLGATE
FOLGATE STREET
CALVIN STREET
WOODSEER ST
HANBURY STREET
PRIMROSE ST
SPITAL SQUARE
LAMB ST
EC2
E1
Spitalfields
PRINCELET STREET
FOURNIER STREET
COMMERCIAL STREET
Broadgate
BRUSHFIELD STREET
Christ Church JMI Sch
HENEAGE ST
FASHION STREET
Liverpool Street Station
LIVERPOOL STREET
BISHOPSGATE
MIDDLESEX STREET
Petticoat Lane
WENTWORTH STREET
East London Coll & Toynbee Theatre
Canon Barnett Sch
Aldgate East
WHITECHAPEL HIGH STREET
London Guildhall Univ
WORMWOOD ST
CAMOMILE ST
HOUNDSDITCH
BEVIS MARKS
Nat West Tower
Baltic Exchange
ST BOTOLPH ST
Aldgate
ALDGATE HIGH ST
St Helen
St Andrew Undershaft
LEADENHALL STREET
Lloyds Building
Sir John Cass's Sch
Whitechapel
MINORIES
MANSEL STREET
LEMAN STREET
ALIE ST
English Martyrs JMI Sch
FENCHURCH AV
FENCHURCH STREET
EC3
Fenchurch Street Station
PRESCOT ST
253
96
A
B
C
D
1
2
3
4
5
6

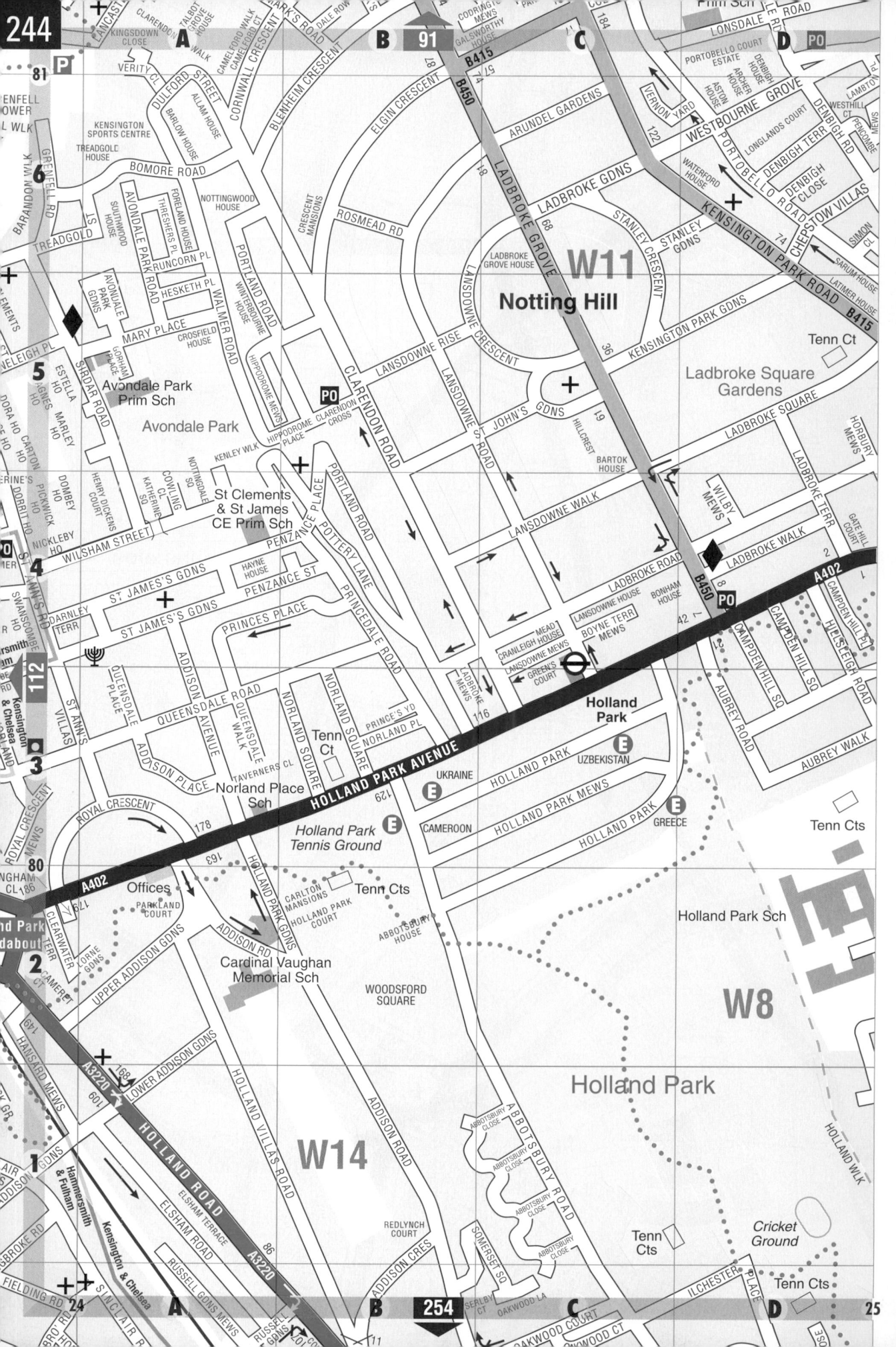
Notting Hill
W11
W14
W8
Holland Park
Ladbroke Square Gardens
Avondale Park
Avondale Park Prim Sch
St Clements & St James CE Prim Sch
Norland Place Sch
Cardinal Vaughan Memorial Sch
Holland Park Sch
Holland Park Tennis Ground
Holland Park
HOLLAND PARK AVENUE
HOLLAND ROAD
LADBROKE GROVE
KENSINGTON PARK ROAD
WESTBOURNE GROVE
PORTOBELLO ROAD
CLARENDON ROAD
PORTLAND ROAD
WALMER ROAD
ADDISON AVENUE
QUEENSDALE ROAD
ST JAMES'S GDNS
LANSDOWNE CRESCENT
LANSDOWNE RISE
LANSDOWNE WALK
LADBROKE ROAD
LADBROKE SQUARE
LADBROKE GDNS
STANLEY CRESCENT
ELGIN CRESCENT
BLENHEIM CRESCENT
ROSMEAD RD
ARUNDEL GARDENS
BOMORE ROAD
MARY PLACE
WILSHAM STREET
PENZANCE PLACE
POTTERY LANE
PRINCEDALE ROAD
NORLAND SQUARE
ROYAL CRESCENT
ADDISON PLACE
HOLLAND VILLAS ROAD
ADDISON ROAD
ABBOTSBURY ROAD
UPPER ADDISON GDNS
LOWER ADDISON GDNS
ELSHAM ROAD
AUBREY ROAD
AUBREY WALK
CAMPDEN HILL SQ
HILLSLEIGH ROAD
HOLLAND WLK
ILCHESTER PLACE
OAKWOOD COURT
Tenn Cts
Cricket Ground
UKRAINE
UZBEKISTAN
CAMEROON
GREECE
A402
A3220
B450
B415
91
112
254
A B C D
1 2 3 4 5 6
Kensington & Chelsea
Hammersmith & Fulham

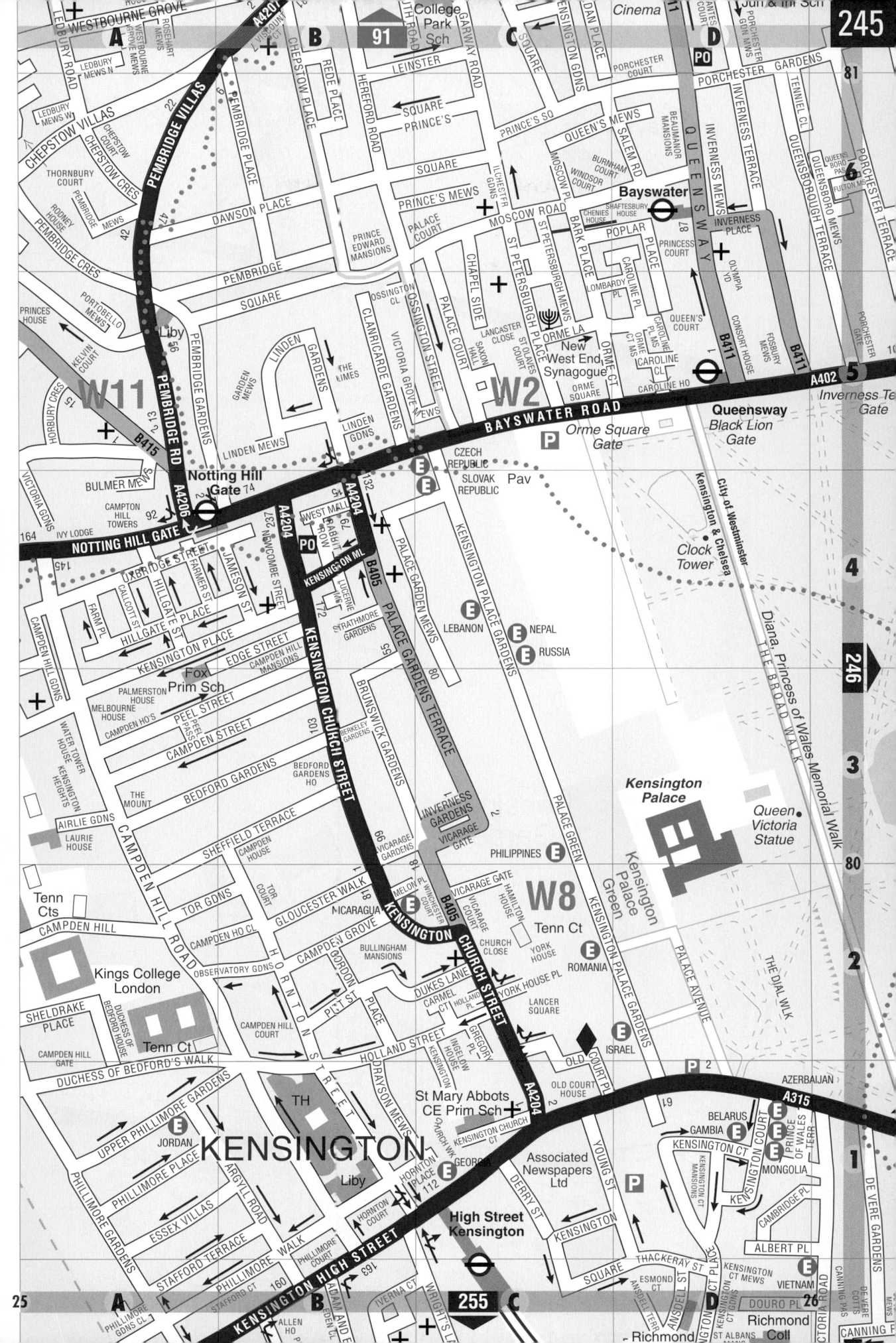

A
B
C
D
91
College Park Sch
Cinema
WESTBOURNE GROVE
LEDBURY ROAD
LEDBURY MEWS N
LEDBURY MEWS W
WESTBOURNE GROVE MEWS
ROSEHART MEWS
CHEPSTOW VILLAS
CHEPSTOW COURT
CHEPSTOW CRES
THORNBURY COURT
RODNEY HOUSE
PEMBRIDGE MEWS
PEMBRIDGE CRES
PEMBRIDGE VILLAS
PEMBRIDGE PLACE
REDE PLACE
CHEPSTOW PLACE
HEREFORD ROAD
GARWAY ROAD
LEINSTER SQUARE
PRINCE'S SQUARE
PRINCE'S MEWS
DAWSON PLACE
PEMBRIDGE SQUARE
PRINCE EDWARD MANSIONS
PALACE COURT
KENSINGTON GDNS SQUARE
PORCHESTER COURT
PORCHESTER GARDENS
PRINCE'S SQ
QUEEN'S MEWS
SALEM RD
BEAUMANOR MANSIONS
QUEENSWAY
INVERNESS MEWS
INVERNESS TERRACE
TENNIEL CL
QUEENSBOROUGH TERRACE
QUEENSBOROUGH MEWS
PORCHESTER TERRACE
BURNHAM COURT
WINDSOR COURT
MOSCOW PL
MOSCOW ROAD
ILCHESTER GDNS
Bayswater
CHENIES HOUSE
SHAFTESBURY HOUSE
POPLAR PLACE
BARK PLACE
INVERNESS PLACE
PRINCESS COURT
OLYMPIA YD
LOMBARDY PL
CAROLINE PL
CAROLINE PL MS
ST PETERSBURGH PLACE
ST PETERSBURGH MEWS
CHAPEL SIDE
OSSINGTON CL
OSSINGTON STREET
CLANRICARDE GARDENS
VICTORIA GROVE MEWS
LANCASTER CLOSE
SAXON HALL
ST OLAVES COURT
ORME LA
New West End Synagogue
ORME CT
ORME CT MS
CAROLINE CL
CAROLINE HO
QUEEN'S COURT
CONSORT HOUSE
FOSBURY MEWS
PORCHESTER GATE
B411
A402
ORME SQUARE
W2
W11
PORTOBELLO MEWS
PRINCES HOUSE
KELVIN COURT
HORBURY CRES
PEMBRIDGE GARDENS
PEMBRIDGE RD
GARDEN MEWS
LINDEN GARDENS
LINDEN MEWS
LINDEN GDNS
THE LIMES
Liby
B415
BAYSWATER ROAD
Orme Square Gate
Queensway
Black Lion Gate
Inverness Terrace Gate
CZECH REPUBLIC
SLOVAK REPUBLIC
Pav
Notting Hill Gate
BULMER MEWS
VICTORIA GDNS
CAMPTON HILL TOWERS
IVY LODGE
NOTTING HILL GATE
A4206
A4204
WEST MALL
RABBIT ROW
PO
KENSINGTON ML
B405
UXBRIDGE STREET
HILLGATE STREET
FARMER ST
JAMESON ST
NEWCOMBE STREET
CALLCOTT ST
FARM PL
HILLGATE PLACE
KENSINGTON PLACE
EDGE STREET
CAMPDEN HILL MANSIONS
LUCERNE MS
STRATHMORE GARDENS
PALACE GARDEN MEWS
PALACE GARDENS TERRACE
KENSINGTON PALACE GARDENS
Kensington & Chelsea
City of Westminster
Clock Tower
Diana, Princess of Wales Memorial Walk
THE BROAD WALK
LEBANON
NEPAL
RUSSIA
CAMPDEN HILL GDNS
Fox Prim Sch
PALMERSTON HOUSE
MELBOURNE HOUSE
CAMPDEN HO'S
PEEL STREET
PEEL PASS
CAMPDEN STREET
KENSINGTON CHURCH STREET
BRUNSWICK GARDENS
BERKELEY GARDENS
BEDFORD GARDENS HO
BEDFORD GARDENS
WATER TOWER HOUSE
KENSINGTON HEIGHTS
THE MOUNT
AIRLIE GDNS
LAURIE HOUSE
SHEFFIELD TERRACE
CAMPDEN HOUSE
INVERNESS GARDENS
VICARAGE GATE
VICARAGE GARDENS
PALACE GREEN
Kensington Palace
Queen Victoria Statue
Kensington Palace Green
PHILIPPINES
Tenn Cts
CAMPDEN HILL
TOR GDNS
TOR COURT
GLOUCESTER WALK
MELON PL
WINCHESTER COURT
NICARAGUA
HAMILTON HOUSE
W8
Tenn Ct
CAMPDEN HO CL
CAMPDEN HILL ROAD
CAMPDEN GROVE
BULLINGHAM MANSIONS
CHURCH CLOSE
YORK HOUSE
ROMANIA
Kings College London
OBSERVATORY GDNS
HORNTON STREET
GORDON PLACE
PITT ST
DUKES LANE
CARMEL CT
HOLLAND PL
YORK HOUSE PL
LANCER SQUARE
PALACE AVENUE
THE DIAL WALK
SHELDRAKE PLACE
DUCHESS OF BEDFORD HOUSE
CAMPDEN HILL COURT
CAMPDEN HILL GATE
HOLLAND STREET
INGELOW HOUSE
GREGORY PL
ISRAEL
OLD COURT PL
OLD COURT HOUSE
DUCHESS OF BEDFORD'S WALK
UPPER PHILLIMORE GARDENS
DRAYSON MEWS
St Mary Abbots CE Prim Sch
KENSINGTON CHURCH CT
CHURCH WK
AZERBAIJAN
A315
BELARUS
GAMBIA
KENSINGTON COURT
PRINCE OF WALES TERR
KENSINGTON CT MANSIONS
MONGOLIA
JORDAN
KENSINGTON
TH
Liby
GEORGIA
HORNTON PLACE
Associated Newspapers Ltd
YOUNG ST
DERRY ST
CAMBRIDGE PL
DE VERE GARDENS
PHILLIMORE PLACE
ARGYLL ROAD
HORNTON COURT
High Street Kensington
KENSINGTON SQUARE
ALBERT PL
PHILLIMORE GARDENS
ESSEX VILLAS
STAFFORD TERRACE
PHILLIMORE WALK
PHILLIMORE COURT
THACKERAY ST
ESMOND CT
ANSDELL ST
KENSINGTON CT MEWS
VIETNAM
KENSINGTON HIGH STREET
STAFFORD CT
PHILLIMORE GDNS CL
ALLEN HO
ADAM AND EVE
IVERNA CT
WRIGHT'S LA
255
ANSDELL TERR
KENSINGTON CT GDNS
ST ALBANS
DOURO PL
VICTORIA ROAD
CANNING PAS
DE VERE COTTS
CANNING PL
Richmond
Richmond Coll
246
1
2
3
4
5
6
80
81
25
26

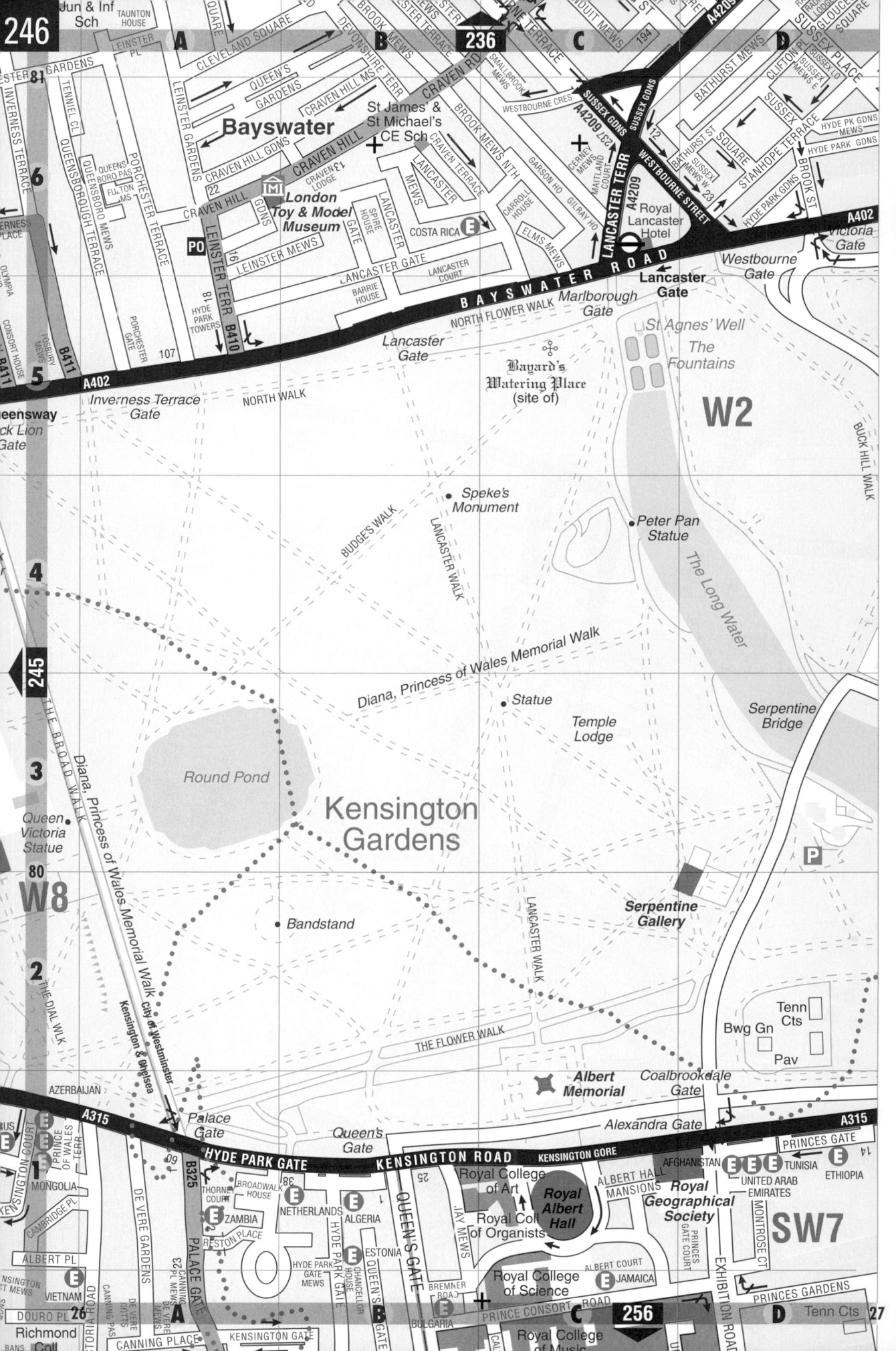
Bayswater
London Toy & Model Museum
Kensington Gardens
Round Pond
The Long Water
Serpentine Gallery
Albert Memorial
Royal Albert Hall
Royal Geographical Society
W2
W8
SW7
BAYSWATER ROAD
KENSINGTON ROAD
HYDE PARK GATE
KENSINGTON GORE
Lancaster Gate
Marlborough Gate
Speke's Monument
Peter Pan Statue
Diana, Princess of Wales Memorial Walk
Serpentine Bridge
Bandstand
THE FLOWER WALK
Palace Gate
Queen's Gate
Alexandra Gate
Coalbrookdale Gate
Royal College of Art
Royal College of Organists
Royal College of Science
236
245
256

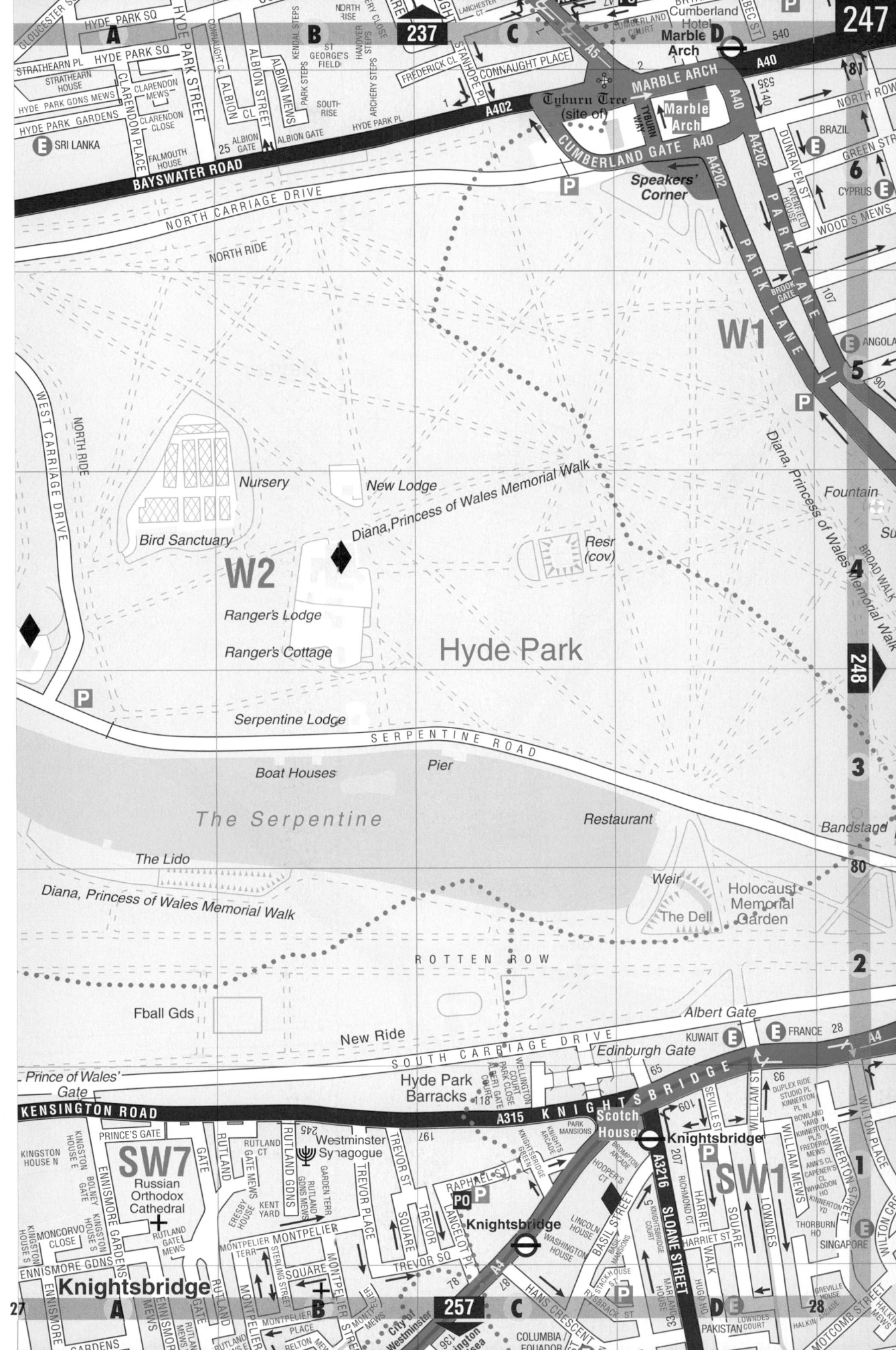

A **B** 237 **C** **D**

STRATHEARN PL
HYDE PARK SQ
STRATHEARN
HOUSE
HYDE PARK GDNS MEWS
HYDE PARK GARDENS
CLARENDON PLACE
CLARENDON
MEWS
CLARENDON
CLOSE
FALMOUTH
HOUSE
ALBION
STREET
ALBION
CL
ALBION MEWS
PARK STEPS
ST GEORGE'S
FIELD
HANOVER
TERR
NORTH
RISE
KENDAL STEPS
ARCHERY STEPS
SOUTH-
RISE
FREDERICK CL
STANHOPE PL
CONNAUGHT PLACE
Lanchester CT
Cumberland
Hotel
BRITA
Marble
Arch
CUMBERLAND
COURT
DEC ST
540
E SRI LANKA
25 ALBION
GATE
ALBION GATE
25
HYDE PARK PL
Tyburn Tree
(site of)
MARBLE ARCH
TYBURN WAY
Marble
Arch
CUMBERLAND GATE A40
A40
A4202
A40
DUNRAVEN ST
ALFRED
PLACE
NORTH ROW
BRAZIL
E
GREEN STREET
E
6
CYPRUS

BAYSWATER ROAD

NORTH CARRIAGE DRIVE

Speakers'
Corner
A4202
WOOD'S MEWS

NORTH RIDE

WEST CARRIAGE DRIVE

NORTH RIDE

W1

BROOK
GATE
107

PARK LANE

E ANGOLA
5
90

Diana, Princess of Wales Memorial Walk

P

Nursery
New Lodge
Diana, Princess of Wales Memorial Walk
Fountain
Su

Bird Sanctuary
W2
◆
Resr
(cov)
4

BROAD WALK

Ranger's Lodge
Ranger's Cottage
Hyde Park
248 ►

◆

Serpentine Lodge
P

SERPENTINE ROAD

Boat Houses
Pier
3

The Serpentine
Restaurant
Bandstand

The Lido
Weir
The Dell
Holocaust
Memorial
Garden
80

Diana, Princess of Wales Memorial Walk

ROTTEN ROW
2

Fball Gds

New Ride
Albert Gate
KUWAIT **E** **E** FRANCE 28
A4

SOUTH CARRIAGE DRIVE
Edinburgh Gate

Prince of Wales'
Gate
Hyde Park
Barracks
118
WELLINGTON
W COURT
PARK CLOSE
ALBERT GATE CT
65
Scotch
House
KNIGHTSBRIDGE
P
Knightsbridge
DUPLEX RIDE
STUDIO PL
KINNERTON
PL N
BOWLAND
YARD
KINNERTON
PL S
FREDERIC
MEWS
ANN'S CL
WILLIAM MEWS
WHADDON
HO
KINNERTON
YD
1

KENSINGTON ROAD
A315 KNIGHTSBRIDGE
A3216
SEVILLE ST
WILLIAM ST
KINNERTON STREET
WILTON PLACE

PRINCE'S GATE
KINGSTON
HOUSE N
SW7
Russian
Orthodox
Cathedral
KINGSTON
HOUSE E
ENNISMORE GARDENS
BOLNEY GATE
RUTLAND GATE
RUTLAND GATE
RUTLAND
GDNS
245
Westminster
Synagogue
TREVOR ST
TREVOR PLACE
LANCELOT PL
RAPHAEL ST
197
Knightsbridge
BROMPTON
ARCADE
KNIGHTSBRIDGE GREEN
PARK
MANSIONS
LINCOLN
HOUSE
£6
RICHMOND
MEWS
207
SW1
SLOANE STREET
HARRIET WALK
LOWNDES
SQUARE
HUGO'S
THORBURN
HOUSE
SINGAPORE
E

KINGSTON
HOUSE S
MONCORVO
CLOSE
ENNISMORE GDNS
Knightsbridge
RUTLAND
GATE MEWS
KENT
YARD
ERESBY
HOUSE
MONTPELIER
SQUARE
MONTPELIER
TERR
MONTPELIER
MEWS
TREVOR
SQUARE
78
Knightsbridge
WASHINGTON
HOUSE
BASIL STREET
LINCOLN
HOUSE
RYSBRACK
ST
STACK
HOUSE
MARLBROOK
HO
PAKISTAN

Knightsbridge
RUTLAND ST
MONTPELIER WALK
MONTPELIER
STREET
TREVOR SQ
HANS CRESCENT
COLUMBIA
EQUADOR
City of
Westminster
Kensington
Chelsea
LOWNDES
COURT
MOTCOMBE STREET
HALKIN ARCADE

SW7
A
27
B
257
C
D
E
28

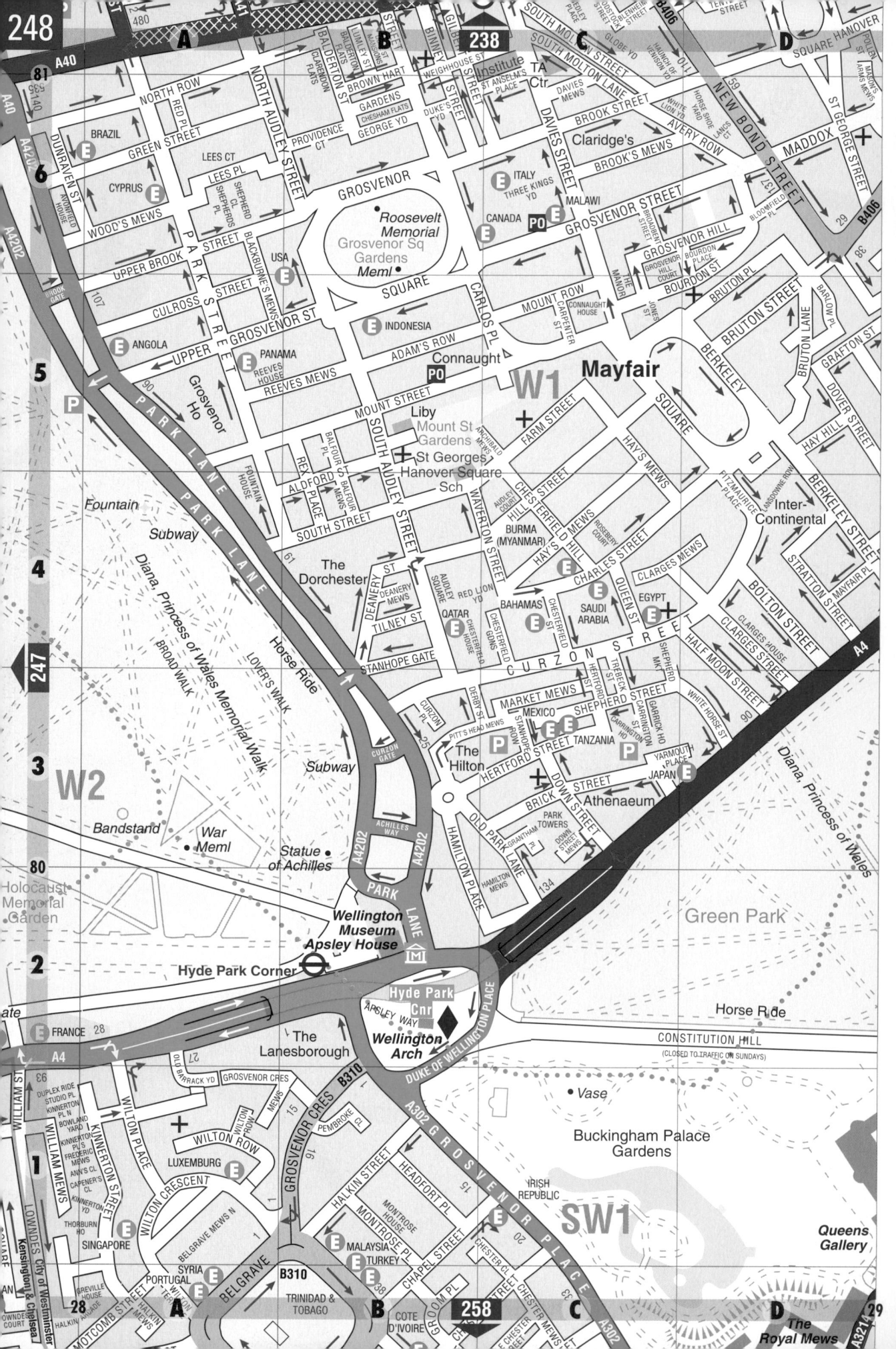

Mayfair
W1
W2
SW1
Grosvenor Sq Gardens
Roosevelt Memorial
Hyde Park Corner
Wellington Museum
Apsley House
Wellington Arch
Green Park
Buckingham Palace Gardens
Queens Gallery
The Royal Mews
The Dorchester
The Hilton
The Lanesborough
Claridge's
Connaught
Inter-Continental
Athenaeum
PARK LANE
GROSVENOR SQUARE
SOUTH AUDLEY STREET
NORTH AUDLEY STREET
CURZON STREET
PICCADILLY
CONSTITUTION HILL
(CLOSED TO TRAFFIC ON SUNDAYS)
GROSVENOR PLACE
BERKELEY SQUARE
NEW BOND STREET
Diana, Princess of Wales Memorial Walk
Horse Ride
Statue of Achilles
Holocaust Memorial Garden
Bandstand
War Meml
Fountain
Subway
238
247
258

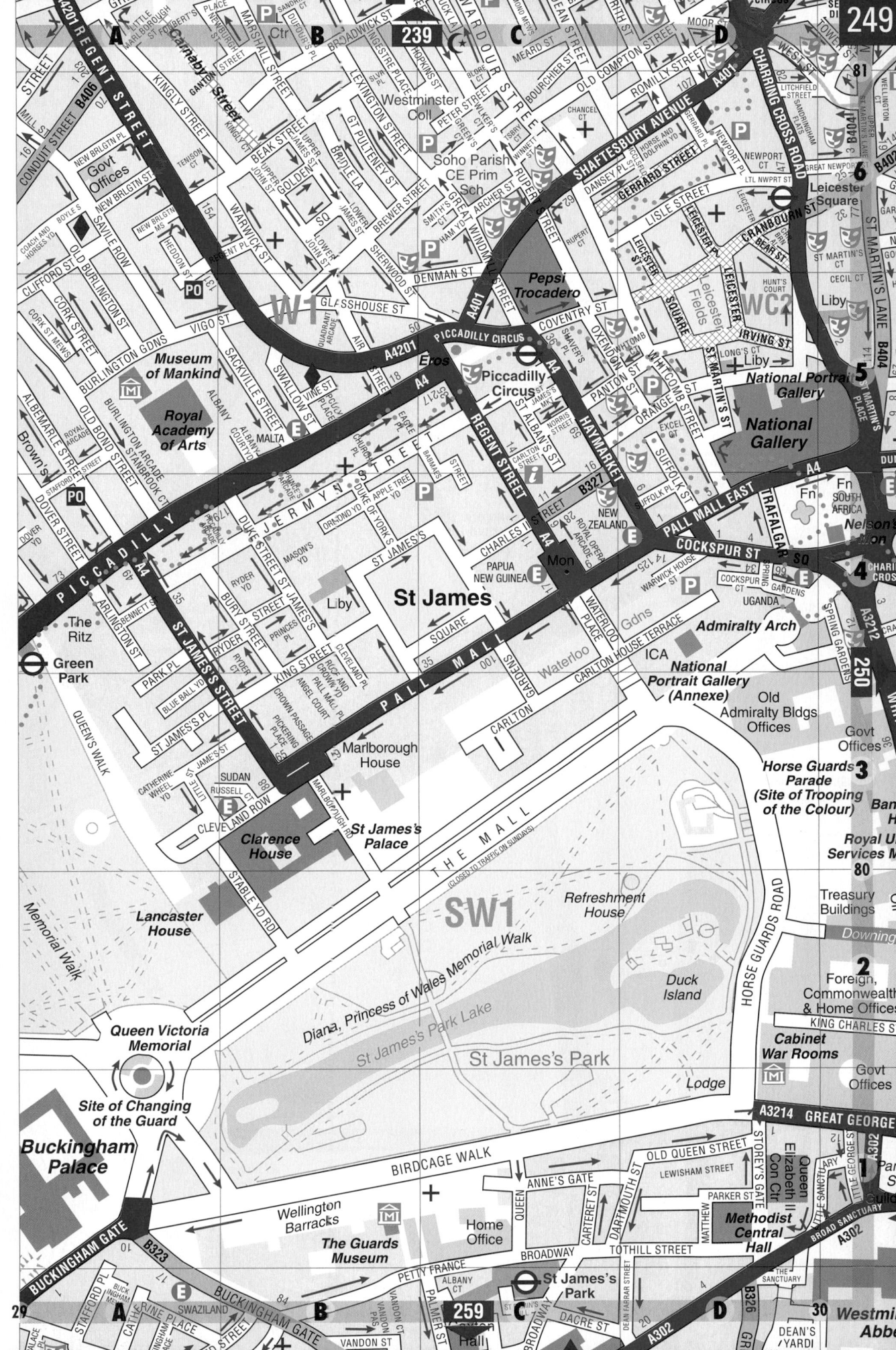
239
REGENT STREET
Carnaby Street
SHAFTESBURY AVENUE
CHARRING CROSS ROAD
Westminster Coll
Soho Parish CE Prim Sch
Govt Offices
W1
WC2
PICCADILLY CIRCUS
Pepsi Trocadero
Eros
Piccadilly Circus
Museum of Mankind
Royal Academy of Arts
Leicester Square
Leicester Fields
National Portrait Gallery
National Gallery
HAYMARKET
PALL MALL EAST
TRAFALGAR SQ
COCKSPUR ST
PICCADILLY
JERMYN STREET
St James
The Ritz
Green Park
PALL MALL
Admiralty Arch
ICA
National Portrait Gallery (Annexe)
Old Admiralty Bldgs Offices
Horse Guards Parade (Site of Trooping of the Colour)
Marlborough House
St James's Palace
Clarence House
Lancaster House
THE MALL
SW1
Refreshment House
Duck Island
Diana, Princess of Wales Memorial Walk
St James's Park Lake
St James's Park
Queen Victoria Memorial
Site of Changing of the Guard
Buckingham Palace
BIRDCAGE WALK
Wellington Barracks
The Guards Museum
Home Office
Methodist Central Hall
Cabinet War Rooms
Treasury Buildings
Foreign, Commonwealth & Home Offices
HORSE GUARDS ROAD
GREAT GEORGE
St James's Park
259
250

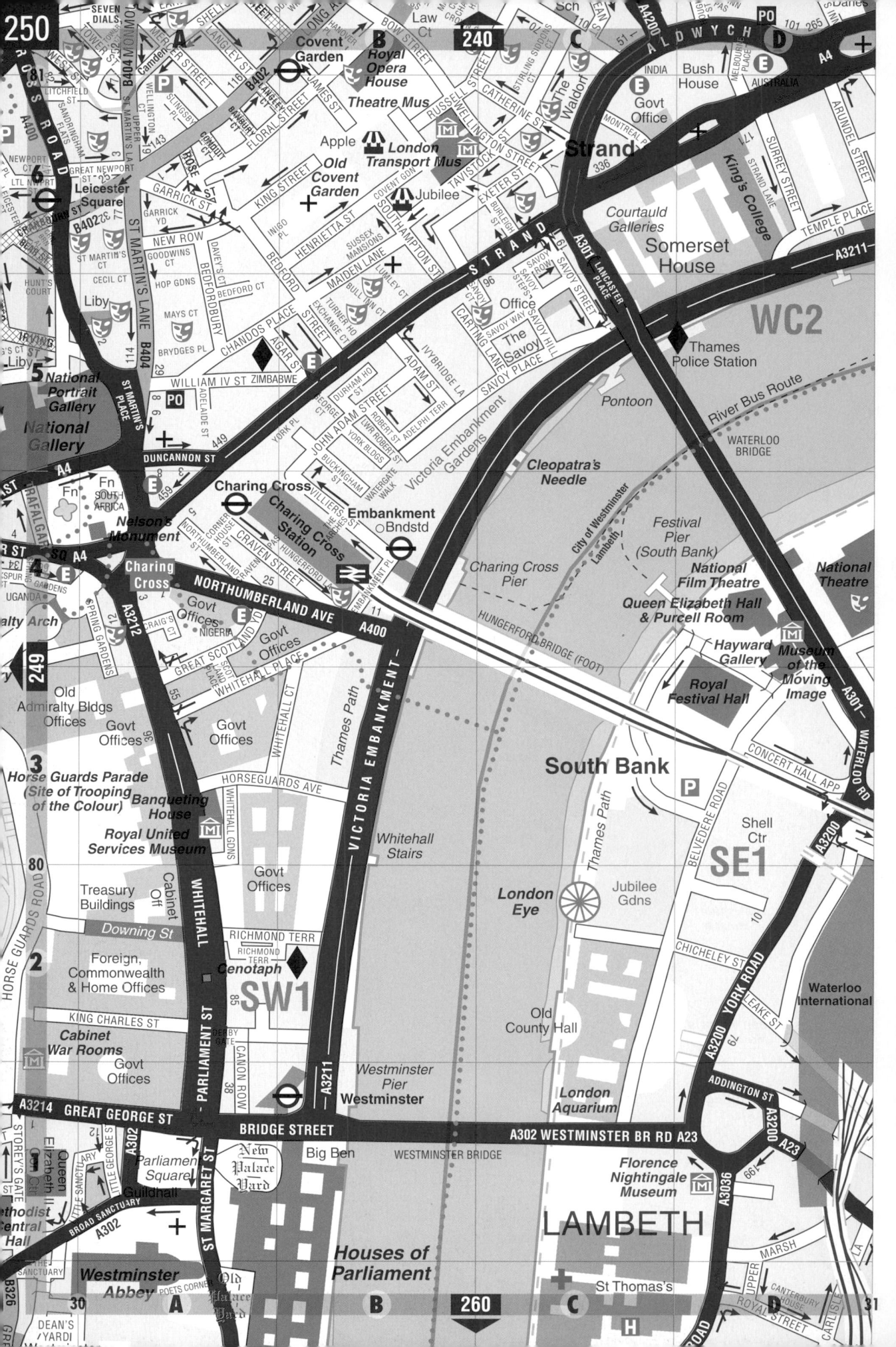

SEVEN DIALS

Covent Garden

Royal Opera House

Theatre Mus

240

Strand

Apple

London Transport Mus

Old Covent Garden

Jubilee

Leicester Square

Courtauld Galleries

Somerset House

WC2

Thames Police Station

National Portrait Gallery

National Gallery

PO

Zimbabwe

River Bus Route

WATERLOO BRIDGE

Cleopatra's Needle

Pontoon

Charing Cross

Charing Cross Station

Embankment Bndstd

Nelson's Monument

Charing Cross

NORTHUMBERLAND AVE

Festival Pier (South Bank)

Charing Cross Pier

National Film Theatre

Queen Elizabeth Hall & Purcell Room

National Theatre

249

Govt Offices NIGERIA

Govt Offices

Hungerford Bridge (Foot)

Hayward Gallery

Museum of the Moving Image

Royal Festival Hall

Old Admiralty Bldgs Offices

Govt Offices

South Bank

SE1

Horse Guards Parade (Site of Trooping of the Colour)

Banqueting House

Royal United Services Museum

Govt Offices

Shell Ctr

Thames Path

Whitehall Stairs

London Eye

Jubilee Gdns

Treasury Buildings

Downing St

CHICHELEY ST

Waterloo International

Foreign, Commonwealth & Home Offices

Cenotaph

SW1

Govt Offices

Old County Hall

YORK ROAD

King Charles St

Cabinet War Rooms

Govt Offices

Westminster Pier Westminster

London Aquarium

GREAT GEORGE ST

BRIDGE STREET

A302 WESTMINSTER BR RD A23

Parliament Square

New Palace Yard

Big Ben

WESTMINSTER BRIDGE

Florence Nightingale Museum

Guildhall

LAMBETH

Methodist Central Hall

Westminster Abbey

Houses of Parliament

St Thomas's

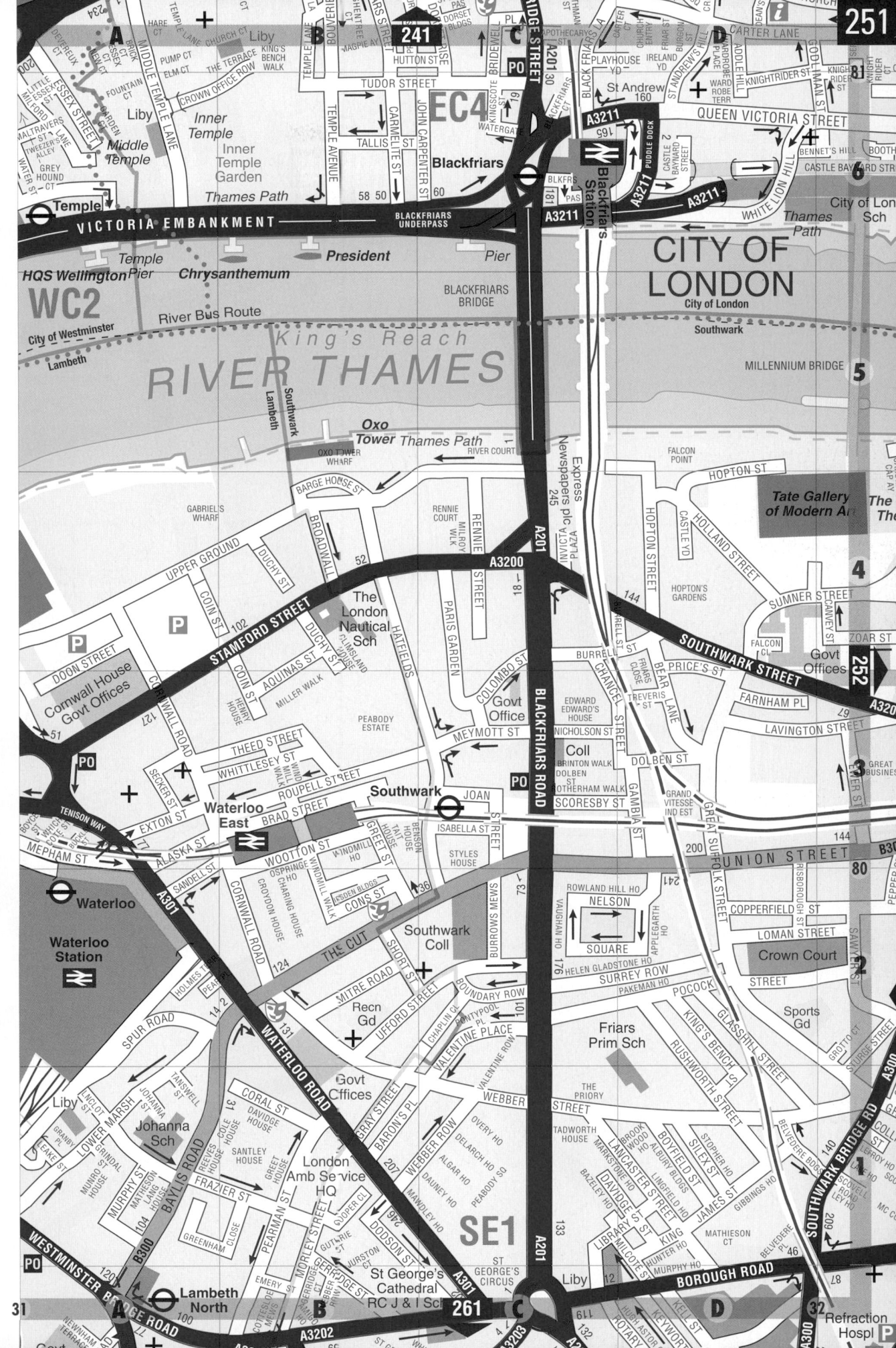
241
EC4
Inner Temple
Inner Temple Garden
Middle Temple
Temple
Thames Path
VICTORIA EMBANKMENT
BLACKFRIARS UNDERPASS
Blackfriars
Blackfriars Station
QUEEN VICTORIA STREET
CARTER LANE
St Andrew
Temple Pier
HQS Wellington
Chrysanthemum
President
Pier
WC2
BLACKFRIARS BRIDGE
CITY OF LONDON
City of London
River Bus Route
City of Westminster
Lambeth
Southwark
King's Reach
RIVER THAMES
MILLENNIUM BRIDGE
Oxo Tower
OXO TOWER WHARF
Thames Path
Tate Gallery of Modern Art
UPPER GROUND
STAMFORD STREET
The London Nautical Sch
Cornwall House Govt Offices
SOUTHWARK STREET
BLACKFRIARS ROAD
Govt Office
Govt Offices
252
Southwark
Waterloo East
Waterloo
Waterloo Station
UNION STREET
NELSON SQUARE
Southwark Coll
THE CUT
Crown Court
Sports Gd
Friars Prim Sch
WATERLOO ROAD
Recn Gd
Govt Offices
Johanna Sch
London Amb Service HQ
St George's Cathedral RC J & I Sch
SE1
ST GEORGE'S CIRCUS
BOROUGH ROAD
SOUTHWARK BRIDGE RD
WESTMINSTER BRIDGE ROAD
Lambeth North
261
Refraction Hospl
31

242
251
262
A
B
C
D
81
6
5
4
3
80
2
1
32
33
EC4
EC3
SE1
CITY OF
LONDON
Watling Street
St Mary Aldermary
Mansion House
Pancras La
Bucklersbury
St Mary Woolnoth
Lombard Street
St Edmund
Godliman St
Knightrider St
Knight Rider St
Old Change Ct
Distaff La
Friday St
Bread St
Old Fish St Hill
St Nicholas Cole Abbey
Queen Victoria Street
Cannon Street
Queen Street
Budge Row
Walbrook
St Stephen Walbrook
Bond Ct
Oxford Ct
St Swithin's Lane
Salters' Hall Ct
Sherbourne La
Abchurch La
Nicholas Lane
Clement's Lane
Plough Ct
Gracechurch
King William Street
Cannon Street
St Mary
St Clement
Lombard Ct
Talbot Ct
Monument
The Monument
Pudding La
Fish St H
A10
Bennet's Hill
Booth La
Lambeth H
Castle Baynard Street
White Lion Hill
Huggin Hill
Little Trinity La
Gt Trinity La
Great St Thomas Apostle
Garlick Hill
Doby Ct
Skinners La
St James
College Street
Cloak Lane
New Cstl Ct
College Hill
St Michael
Dowgate Hill
Cannon Street Station
Bush Lane
Suffolk La
Laurence Pountney Hill
Laurence Pountney La
Martin Lane
Arthur St
A3211
Upper Thames Street
High Timber St
Broken Wf
Gardners La
Stew Lane
Queen's Quay
Queenhithe
Kennett Wf La
Vintners Ct
Queen St Pl
A300
Bell Wharf La
Cousin Lane
Allhallows La
Angel Pass
Swan Lane
A3
City of London Sch
Norfolk Ho
Queenhithe Stairs
Thames Path
Southwark Bridge Stairs
City of London
Southwark
Millennium Bridge
Southwark Bridge
Bankside Jetty
Princess Elizabeth
Swan Lane Pier
River Bus Route
St Magnus London Bridge
London Bridge
Bankside
Cardinal Cap Ay
The Globe Theatre
New Globe Wlk
Bear Gdns
Rose Alley
Tate Gallery of Modern Art
The Financial Times Ltd
Shakespeare's Globe Theatre (site of)
Old London Bridge (site of)
Park Street
Bank End
Clink St
Winchester Sq
Montague Cl
Southwark Cathedral
Emerson St
Bear Gardens Mus
Sumner Street
Canvey St
Falcon Cl
Zoar St
Gov Offices
Sumner Bldgs
Great Guildford Street
Anchor Terrace
Old Theatre Ct
Porter St
Perkins Square
Gatehouse Sq
Riverside Workshops
Stoney St
Winchester Walk
Cathedral St
Borough
Rochester Wk
Borough Market
Green Dragon Ct
Bedale St
Tooley St
Bridge Yd
The London Dungeon
A200
Duke St Hill
Railway Approach
London Br St
London Bridge
Joiner St
Peabody Estate
Southwark Bridge Office Village
Maiden Lane
Lucy Brown Ho
A3200
Southwark Street
Farnham Pl
Lavington Street
Thrale St
Redcross Way
Bridge Road
Great Guilford Business Square
Ewer St
Keppel Row
Wardens Gr
America St
Omeara St
King's Head Yd
White Hart Yd
George Inn Yd
Talbot Yd
Calvert's Buildings
Margaret's Court
Maidstone Bldgs
Queen's Head Yd
Kentish Bldgs
Guy's Evelina Hospl Sch
Guy's
St Thomas Street
London Bridge Station
Stainer St
Union Street
B300
Risborough St
Pepper St
Thorold Ho
Trelawney Ho
Farnham Ho
Tomline Ho
Doyce St
Southwark
Ayres Street
Pattison House
Redcross Way
Cathedral Sch of St Saviour & St Mary Overie Prim Sch
St Joseph's RC J & I Sch
Great Maze Pond
Copperfield St
Loman Street
Sawyer St
Crown Court
Pocock Street
The Borough
Quilp St
Clennam St
Dorrit St
Babington House
Little Dorrit Ct
Disney St
Disney Pl
Little Dorrit Park
A3201 Marshalsea Road
Borough High Street
Newcomen Street
Betsham Ho
Mermaid Ct
Chapel Ct
Tennis Street
Northfleet Ho
Bowling Green Pl
Chaloner Ct
Kellow Ho
Liby
Boughton Ho
Crosby Ct
Baden Pl
Crosby Row
City Banking Coll
Snowsfields
Hamilton Sq
Weston Street
Tenn Cts
Sarah Swift Ho
Guy Street
Sports Gd
Grotto Ct
Sturge Street
Mint St
Caleb St
Weller St
Douglas Buildings
Trundle St
Angel Pl
Govt Offices
Brenley Ho
Balin Ho
Plantain Pl
Eynsford Ho
Porlock St
Kipling Street
Hamlet Way
Mulvaney Way
Burwash Ho
Sudrey St
Bittern St
Lant House
Toulmin St
Lant Street
Sanctuary St
Vine Yd
Wall's Alley
Borough
A3201
A2198
A2
Pickwick Street
Bittern Ho
Charles Dickens Prim Sch
Redman House
Silvester St
Nebraska Street
Beormund Sch
Long Lane
Lockyer St
Lockyer Estate
Simla Ho
Webber Street
Great Suffolk Street
Collinson St
Collinson Ct
Collinson Walk
Lefroy Ho
Lake Ho
Scovell Road
Scovell Cres
Mc Coid Way
Borough Square
Stones End St
Belvedere Bdgs
Sterry St
Pilgrimage
Harbledown Ho
Halling Ho
Hankey Place
Munro Ho
Aylesford Ho
Medway Ho
Strood Ho
Staple Street
Crayford Ho
Rudyard Ct
Dunsterville Way
Heldar Ct
Lenham Ho
Kemsing Ho
Hulme Place
Avon Place
Swan Street
Cole Street
Great Dover Street
Abinger Ho
Tabard Gardens
Rochester Ho
Manciple Street
Otford Ho
Becket Ho
Selborne Ho
Tabard Street
Globe St
Shere Ho
Borough Road
A3202
King's Pl
Trio Place
Cty Ct
Trinity Street
Church Sq
Gloucester Ct
Harper Road
B240
Eastwell Ho
Elim St
Fball Gd
Becket St
Inner London & Southwark
Causeway

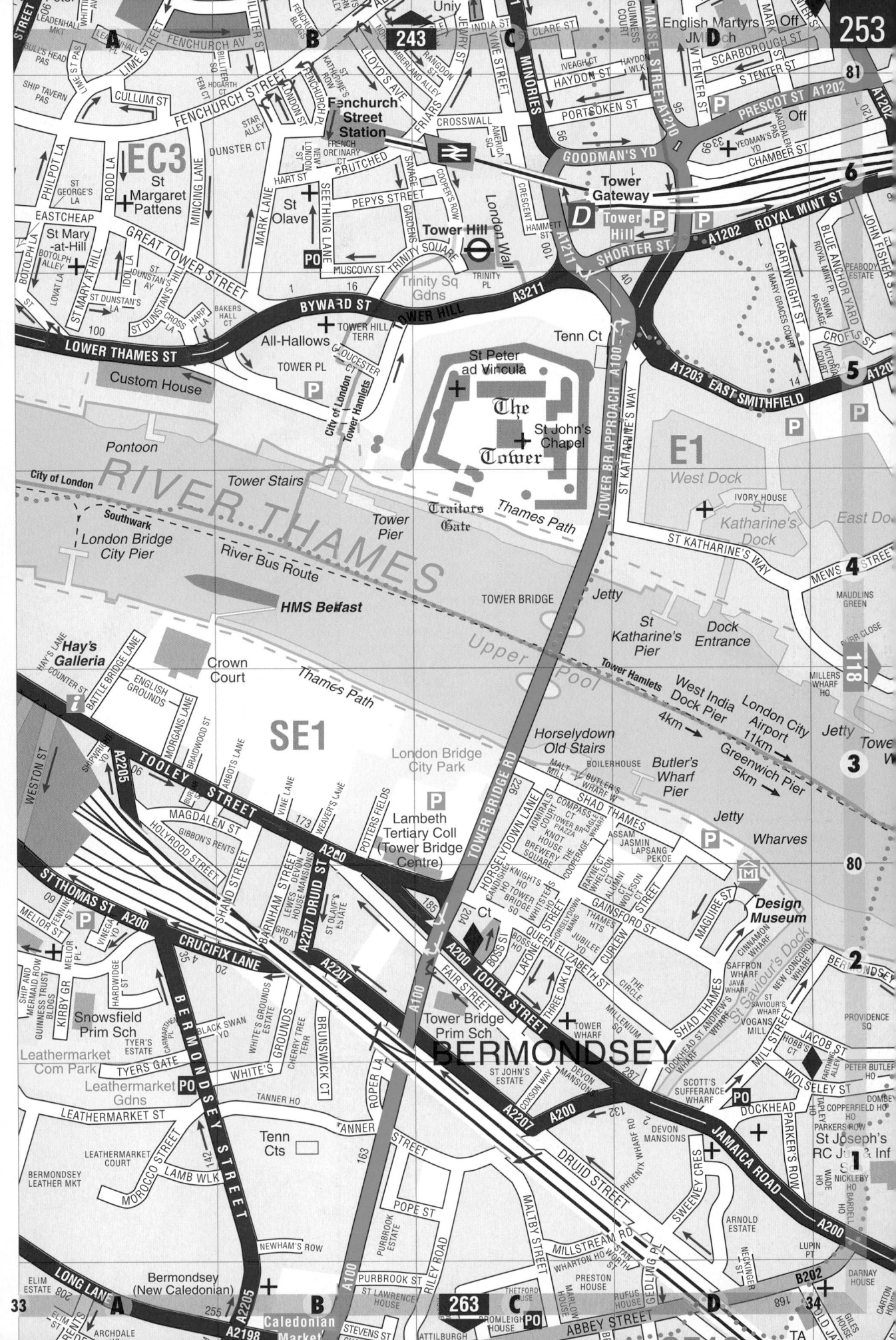

EC3

St Margaret Pattens

St Mary-at-Hill

St Olave

Tower Hill

Fenchurch Street Station

FENCHURCH STREET

Tower Gateway

Tower Hill

SHORTER ST

A1211

GOODMAN'S YD

PRESCOT ST A1202

ROYAL MINT ST

A1202

A1203 EAST SMITHFIELD

E1

West Dock

St Katharine's Dock

Ivory House

BYWARD ST

LOWER THAMES ST

Custom House

City of London
Tower Hamlets

All-Hallows

TOWER PL

City of London
Tower Hamlets

The Tower

St Peter ad Vincula

St John's Chapel

Thames Path

ST KATHARINE'S WAY

ST KATHARINE'S WAY

MAUDLINS GREEN

RIVER THAMES

Pontoon

Tower Stairs

Tower Pier

Traitors Gate

Southwark

London Bridge City Pier

River Bus Route

HMS Belfast

TOWER BRIDGE

Jetty

St Katharine's Pier

Dock Entrance

West India Dock Pier

London City Airport 11km

Greenwich Pier 5km

Jetty

Upper Pool

Tower Hamlets

4km

Hay's Galleria

Crown Court

Thames Path

London Bridge City Park

Horselydown Old Stairs

Boilerhouse

Butler's Wharf Pier

Jetty

Wharves

SE1

Lambeth Tertiary Coll (Tower Bridge Centre)

SHAD THAMES

Design Museum

St Saviour's Dock

TOOLEY STREET

ST THOMAS ST A200

CRUCIFIX LANE

DRUID ST A250

A2207

TOWER BRIDGE RD

A200 TOOLEY STREET

Queen Elizabeth St

THE CIRCLE

Saffron Wharf
Java Wharf
New Concordia Wharf
Vogans Mill

BERMONDSEY

Snowsfield Prim Sch

Leathermarket Com Park

Leathermarket Gdns

BERMONDSEY STREET

Tower Bridge Prim Sch

Tower Wharf

St John's Estate

Devon Mansions

Millenium Sq

Shad Thames Wharf
Dockhead Wharf
St Andrews Wharf

Scott's Sufferance Wharf

JAMAICA ROAD A200

St Joseph's RC Jun & Inf Sch

Leathermarket Leather Mkt

LEATHERMARKET ST

Tenn Cts

Tanner Ho

DRUID STREET

Coxson Way

A2207

MILL STREET

WOLSELEY ST

DOCKHEAD

PARKERS ROW

LONG LANE

Bermondsey (New Caledonian)

A2205

A100

PURBROOK ST

A2198

Caledonian Market

263

ABBEY STREET

B202

34

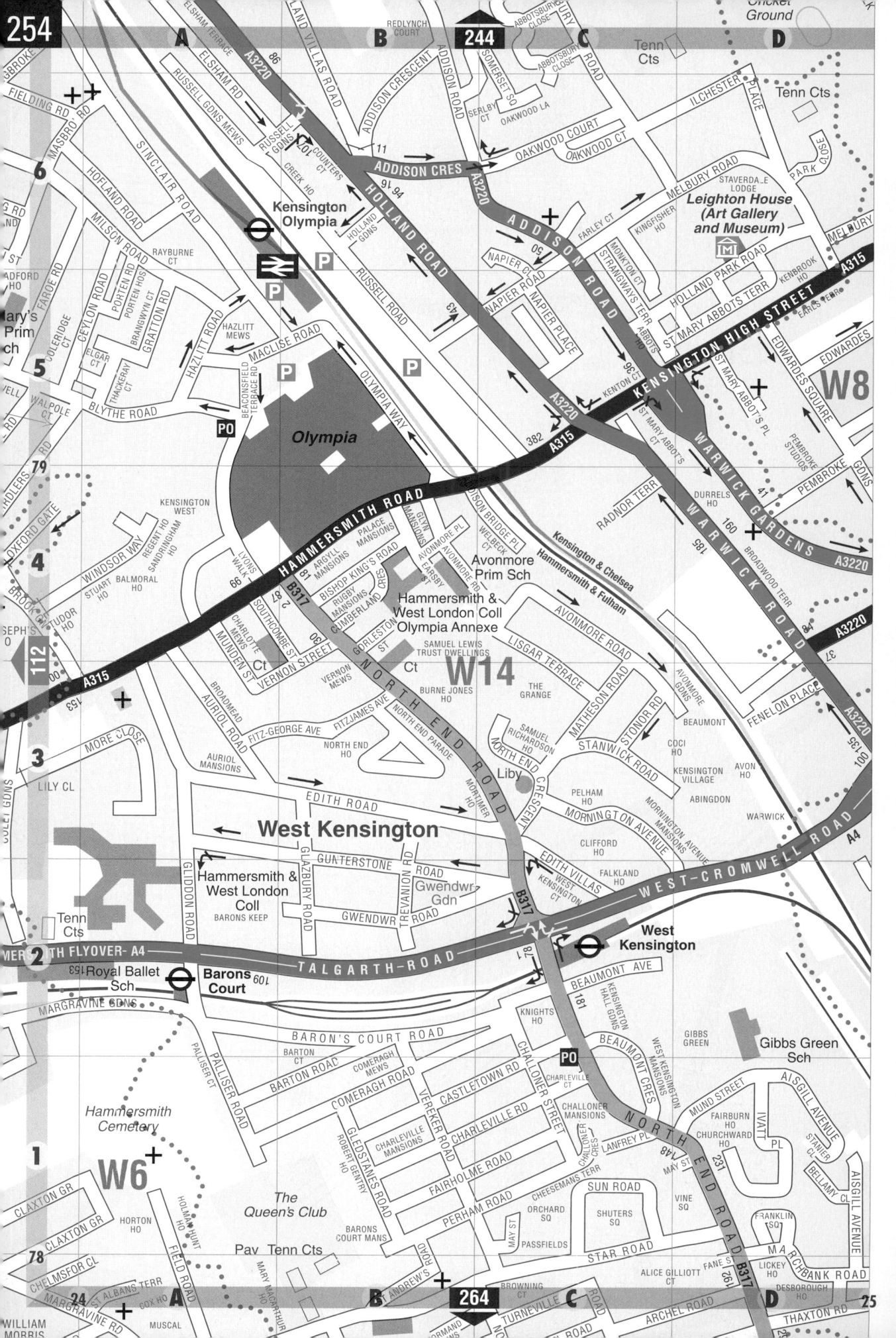
A
B
C
D
244
264
112
Kensington Olympia
Olympia
Leighton House (Art Gallery and Museum)
KENSINGTON HIGH STREET
HOLLAND ROAD
ADDISON ROAD
ADDISON CRES
HAMMERSMITH ROAD
NORTH END ROAD
WARWICK ROAD
WARWICK GARDENS
WEST CROMWELL ROAD
TALGARTH ROAD
HAMMERSMITH FLYOVER A4
W14
W8
W6
West Kensington
Avonmore Prim Sch
Hammersmith & West London Coll Olympia Annexe
Hammersmith & West London Coll
Kensington & Chelsea
Hammersmith & Fulham
Royal Ballet Sch
Barons Court
Gibbs Green Sch
Hammersmith Cemetery
The Queen's Club
Pav Tenn Cts
Tenn Cts
EDITH ROAD
GUNTERSTONE ROAD
GWENDWR ROAD
BARON'S COURT ROAD
COMERAGH ROAD
CHALLONER STREET
SUN ROAD
STAR ROAD
MARCHBANK ROAD
AISGILL AVENUE
BLYTHE ROAD
SINCLAIR ROAD
MORNINGTON AVENUE
AVONMORE ROAD
LISGAR TERRACE
MATHESON ROAD
STANWICK ROAD
BEAUMONT CRES
PALLISER ROAD
GLIDDON ROAD
GLAZBURY ROAD
ARCHEL ROAD
THAXTON RD
1
2
3
4
5
6
A3220
A315
A4
B317

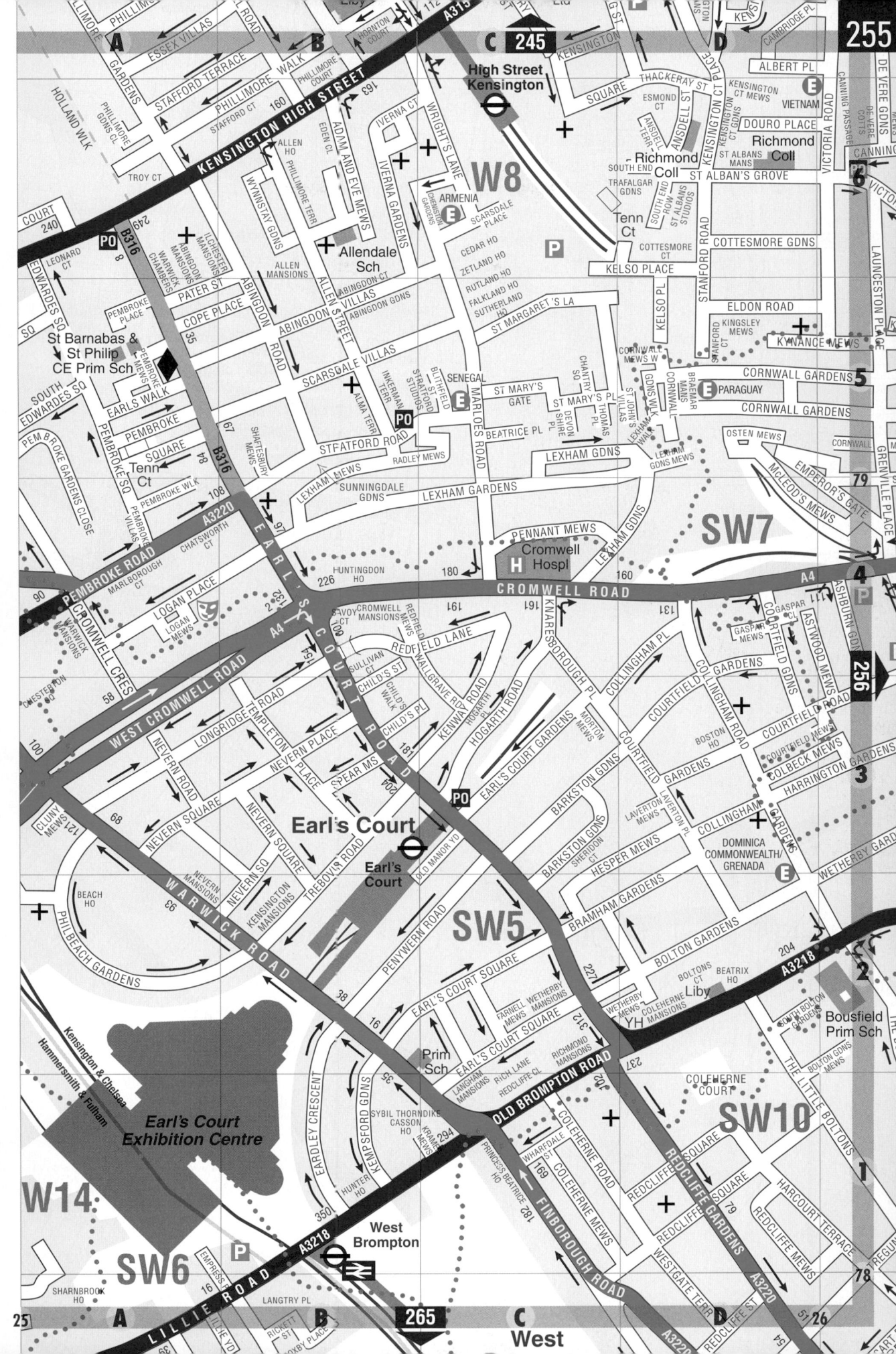
A
B
C
D
245
High Street Kensington
W8
Richmond Coll
Allendale Sch
Tenn Ct
St Barnabas & St Philip CE Prim Sch
SW7
Cromwell Hospl
Earl's Court
SW5
SW10
Earl's Court Exhibition Centre
W14
SW6
West Brompton
Prim Sch
Bousfield Prim Sch
Liby
YH
Kensington & Chelsea
Hammersmith & Fulham
KENSINGTON HIGH STREET
PHILLIMORE WALK
PHILLIMORE GARDENS
STAFFORD TERRACE
ESSEX VILLAS
HOLLAND WLK
ABINGDON ROAD
ABINGDON VILLAS
ALLEN STREET
SCARSDALE VILLAS
WRIGHT'S LANE
IVERNA GARDENS
ADAM AND EVE MEWS
KENSINGTON SQUARE
THACKERAY ST
ALBERT PL
DOURO PLACE
VICTORIA ROAD
ST ALBAN'S GROVE
COTTESMORE GDNS
KELSO PLACE
ELDON ROAD
KYNANCE MEWS
CORNWALL GARDENS
STANFORD ROAD
LAUNCESTON PLACE
MARLOES ROAD
ST MARY'S GATE
LEXHAM GDNS
LEXHAM GARDENS
PENNANT MEWS
STRATFORD ROAD
PEMBROKE SQUARE
PEMBROKE ROAD
EARLS WALK
LOGAN PLACE
CROMWELL ROAD
CROMWELL CRES
WEST CROMWELL ROAD
EARL'S COURT ROAD
REDFIELD LANE
CHILD'S PL
NEVERN PLACE
NEVERN SQUARE
NEVERN ROAD
TREBOVIR ROAD
WARWICK ROAD
PHILBEACH GARDENS
PENYWERN ROAD
EARL'S COURT SQUARE
EARL'S COURT GARDENS
BARKSTON GDNS
HOGARTH ROAD
KNARESBOROUGH PL
COLLINGHAM PL
COURTFIELD GARDENS
COURTFIELD ROAD
COLLINGHAM ROAD
COLLINGHAM GARDENS
HARRINGTON GARDENS
WETHERBY GARDENS
ASHBURN GDNS
GRENVILLE PLACE
EMPEROR'S GATE
McLEOD'S MEWS
BRAMHAM GARDENS
BOLTON GARDENS
HESPER MEWS
OLD BROMPTON ROAD
REDCLIFFE GARDENS
REDCLIFFE SQUARE
FINBOROUGH ROAD
COLEHERNE ROAD
COLEHERNE MEWS
THE LITTLE BOLTONS
HARCOURT TERRACE
REDCLIFFE MEWS
WESTGATE TERR
EARDLEY CRESCENT
KEMPSFORD GDNS
LILLIE ROAD
A3218
A3220
A4
B316
265
West

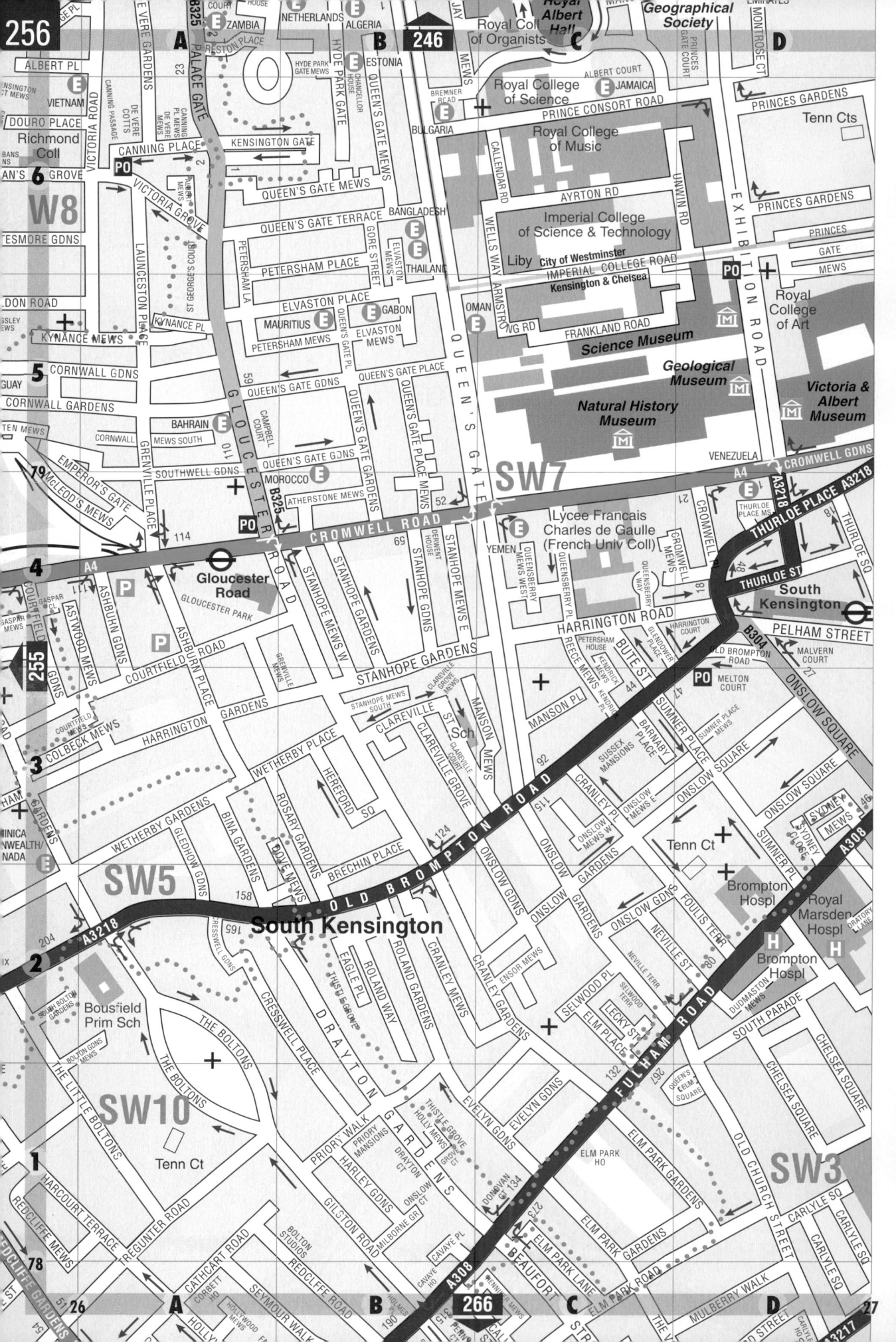
246
255
266
A
B
C
D
6
5
4
3
2
1
W8
SW7
SW5
SW10
SW3
Royal Albert Hall
Royal Coll of Organists
Geographical Society
Royal College of Science
Royal College of Music
Imperial College of Science & Technology
Liby
City of Westminster
Kensington & Chelsea
Royal College of Art
Science Museum
Geological Museum
Natural History Museum
Victoria & Albert Museum
Lycee Francais Charles de Gaulle (French Univ Coll)
Richmond Coll
Gloucester Road
South Kensington
Brompton Hospl
Royal Marsden Hospl
Bousfield Prim Sch
Tenn Cts
Tenn Ct
Sch
ZAMBIA
NETHERLANDS
ALGERIA
ESTONIA
VIETNAM
JAMAICA
BULGARIA
BANGLADESH
THAILAND
MAURITIUS
GABON
OMAN
BAHRAIN
MOROCCO
YEMEN
VENEZUELA
PALACE GATE
KENSINGTON GATE
CANNING PLACE
VICTORIA GROVE
VICTORIA ROAD
QUEEN'S GATE MEWS
QUEEN'S GATE TERRACE
PETERSHAM PLACE
ELVASTON PLACE
QUEEN'S GATE GDNS
QUEEN'S GATE PLACE
QUEEN'S GATE GARDENS
QUEEN'S GATE
GLOUCESTER ROAD
CROMWELL ROAD
PRINCE CONSORT ROAD
PRINCES GARDENS
EXHIBITION ROAD
IMPERIAL COLLEGE ROAD
FRANKLAND ROAD
AYRTON RD
CROMWELL GDNS
THURLOE PLACE
THURLOE ST
PELHAM STREET
HARRINGTON ROAD
STANHOPE GARDENS
ONSLOW SQUARE
OLD BROMPTON ROAD
FULHAM ROAD
DRAYTON GARDENS
CRESSWELL PLACE
THE BOLTONS
THE LITTLE BOLTONS
REDCLIFFE GARDENS
TREGUNTER ROAD
EVELYN GDNS
ELM PARK GARDENS
OLD CHURCH STREET
CHELSEA SQUARE
SOUTH PARADE
CARLYLE SQ
MULBERRY WALK
BEAUFORT ST
KYNANCE MEWS
CORNWALL GARDENS
COURTFIELD ROAD
HARRINGTON GARDENS
WETHERBY GARDENS
COLBECK MEWS
LAUNCESTON PLACE
GRENVILLE PLACE
A4
A3218
A308
B325
B304
PO

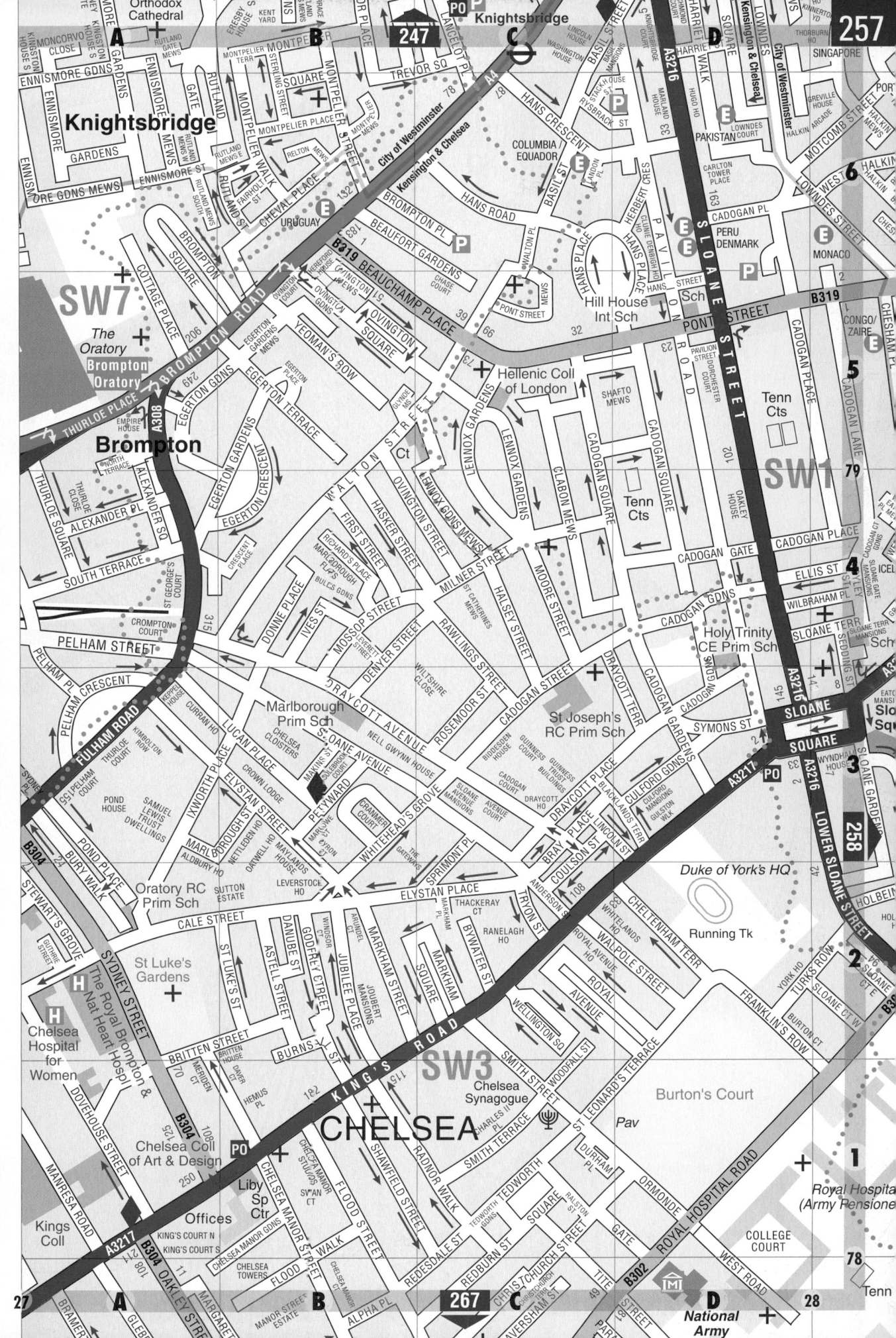
Orthodox Cathedral
Knightsbridge
247
Knightsbridge
Kensington & Chelsea
City of Westminster
SINGAPORE
MONCORVO CLOSE
ENNISMORE GDNS
ENNISMORE GARDENS
ENNISMORE MEWS
ENNISMORE ST
ENNISMORE GDNS MEWS
RUTLAND GATE
RUTLAND GATE MEWS
MONTPELIER TERR
MONTPELIER SQUARE
MONTPELIER STREET
MONTPELIER PLACE
MONTPELIER WALK
MONTPELIER MEWS
STERLING STREET
TREVOR SQ
RUTLAND MEWS E
RUTLAND MEWS W
RUTLAND MEWS SOUTH
RUTLAND ST
FAIRHOLT ST
CHEVAL PLACE
RELTON MEWS
URUGUAY
HANS CRESCENT
HANS ROAD
HANS PLACE
HANS ST
BASIL ST
STACKHOUSE ST
RYSBRACK ST
COLUMBIA / EQUADOR
LANDON PL
HERBERT CRES
CLUNIE DENBIGH HO
PAVILION ROAD
HARRIET WALK
HUGO HO
MARLAND HOUSE
LOWNDES COURT
PAKISTAN
CARLTON TOWER PLACE
CADOGAN PL
PERU
DENMARK
MONACO
HALKIN ARCADE
MOTCOMB STREET
LOWNDES STREET
WEST HALKIN ST
GREVILLE HOUSE
BROMPTON SQUARE
BROMPTON PL
BEAUFORT GARDENS
CHASE COURT
BEAUCHAMP PLACE
B319
WALTON PL
WALTON STREET
PONT STREET
Hill House Int Sch
CONGO / ZAIRE
CHESHAM PL
SW7
The Oratory
Brompton Oratory
COTTAGE PLACE
OVINGTON MEWS
OVINGTON GDNS
OVINGTON COURT
OVINGTON SQUARE
OVINGTON STREET
HEREFORD HOUSE
EGERTON GARDENS MEWS
EGERTON GDNS
EGERTON GARDENS
EGERTON TERRACE
EGERTON PLACE
EGERTON CRESCENT
YEOMAN'S ROW
BROMPTON ROAD
THURLOE PLACE
EMPIRE HOUSE
Brompton
A308
NORTH TERRACE
THURLOE SQUARE
THURLOE CLOSE
ALEXANDER PL
ALEXANDER SQ
SOUTH TERRACE
CRESCENT PLACE
ST GEORGE'S COURT
GLYNDE MS
Hellenic Coll of London
LENNOX GARDENS
LENNOX GDNS MEWS
SHAFTO MEWS
CLABON MEWS
CADOGAN SQUARE
Tenn Cts
PAVILION STREET
DORCHESTER COURT
OAKLEY HOUSE
Tenn Cts
SW1
CADOGAN PLACE
CADOGAN LANE
CADOGAN GATE
ELLIS ST
WILBRAHAM PL
SLOANE TERR
SLOANE TERR MANSIONS
SEDDING ST
Sch
Holy Trinity CE Prim Sch
CADOGAN GDNS
Ct
FIRST STREET
HASKER STREET
RICHARD'S PLACE
MARLBOROUGH FLATS
BULLS GDNS
MILNER STREET
ST CATHERINES MEWS
HALSEY STREET
MOORE STREET
DONNE PLACE
IVES ST
MOSSOP STREET
LEVERETT STREET
DENYER STREET
RAWLINGS STREET
WILTSHIRE CLOSE
CROMPTON COURT
PELHAM STREET
PELHAM PL
PELHAM CRESCENT
FULHAM ROAD
KEPPEL HOUSE
CURRAN HO
KIMBOLTON ROW
THURLOE COURT
DRAYCOTT AVENUE
Marlborough Prim Sch
CHELSEA CLOISTERS
ROSEMOOR ST
CADOGAN STREET
DRAYCOTT TERR
St Joseph's RC Prim Sch
SYMONS ST
SLOANE SQUARE
WYNDHAM HOUSE
SLOANE GARDENS
LUCAN PLACE
CROWN LODGE
SLOANE AVENUE
NELL GWYNN HOUSE
MAKINS ST
COLEBROOK COURT
BIDDESDEN HOUSE
GUINNESS COURT
GUINNESS TRUST BUILDINGS
CADOGAN COURT
DRAYCOTT HO
DRAYCOTT PLACE
BLACKLANDS TERR
CULFORD GDNS
CULFORD MANSIONS
GULSTON WLK
A3217
PO
A3216
LOWER SLOANE STREET
258
SYDNEY PL
PELHAM COURT
POND HOUSE
SAMUEL LEWIS TRUST DWELLINGS
IXWORTH PLACE
ELYSTAN STREET
PETYWARD
CRANMER COURT
MARLOWE CT
BYRON CT
WHITEHEAD'S GROVE
SLOANE AVENUE MANSIONS
AVENUE COURT
BRAY PLACE
LINCOLN ST
COULSON ST
ANDERSON ST
Duke of York's HQ
B304
POND PLACE
BURY WALK
MARLBOROUGH ST
ALDBURY HO
NETTLEDEN HO
OATWELL HO
MAYLANDS HOUSE
LEVERSTOCK HO
THE GATEWAYS
SPRIMONT PL
Oratory RC Prim Sch
SUTTON ESTATE
ELYSTAN PLACE
THACKERAY CT
MARKHAM PL
RANELAGH HO
TRYON ST
WHITELANDS HO
CHELTENHAM TERR
Running Tk
HOLBEIN
STEWART'S GROVE
GUTHRIE STREET
CALE STREET
DANUBE ST
WINDSOR CT
ARUNDEL CT
BYWATER ST
ROYAL AVENUE HO
WALPOLE STREET
ROYAL AVENUE
YORK HO
TURKS ROW
SLOANE CT E
SLOANE CT W
BURTON CT
FRANKLIN'S ROW
SYDNEY STREET
St Luke's Gardens
ST LUKE'S ST
ASTELL STREET
GODFREY ST
JUBILEE PLACE
JOUBERT MANSIONS
MARKHAM STREET
MARKHAM SQUARE
MARKHAM
The Royal Brompton & Nat Heart Hospl
H
Chelsea Hospital for Women
WELLINGTON SQ
BRITTEN STREET
BRITTEN HOUSE
MERIDEN CT
DAVER CT
BURNSALL ST
KING'S ROAD
SW3
SMITH STREET
WOODFALL ST
ST LEONARD'S TERRACE
Burton's Court
DOVEHOUSE STREET
HEMUS PL
Chelsea Synagogue
CHARLES II PL
SMITH TERRACE
Pav
CHELSEA
Chelsea Coll of Art & Design
PO
Liby Sp Ctr
CHELSEA MANOR STUDIOS
SWAN CT
SHAWFIELD STREET
RADNOR WALK
TEDWORTH SQUARE
RALSTON ST
DURHAM PL
ORMONDE GATE
ROYAL HOSPITAL ROAD
Royal Hospital (Army Pensioners)
MANRESA ROAD
Offices
KING'S COURT N
KING'S COURT S
CHELSEA MANOR GDNS
CHELSEA MANOR STREET
FLOOD STREET
FLOOD WALK
TEDWORTH GDNS
CHRISTCHURCH STREET
COLLEGE COURT
Kings Coll
A3217
B304
OAKLEY STREET
CHELSEA TOWERS
CHELSEA MANOR CT
REDESDALE ST
REDBURN ST
TITE STREET
B302
WEST ROAD
Tenn
BRAMERTON
GLEBE
MARGARETTA
MANOR STREET ESTATE
ALPHA PL
267
CHRISTCHURCH TERR
FLAXMAN
PARADISE
National Army
A B C D
1 2 3 4 5 6
27 28 78 79

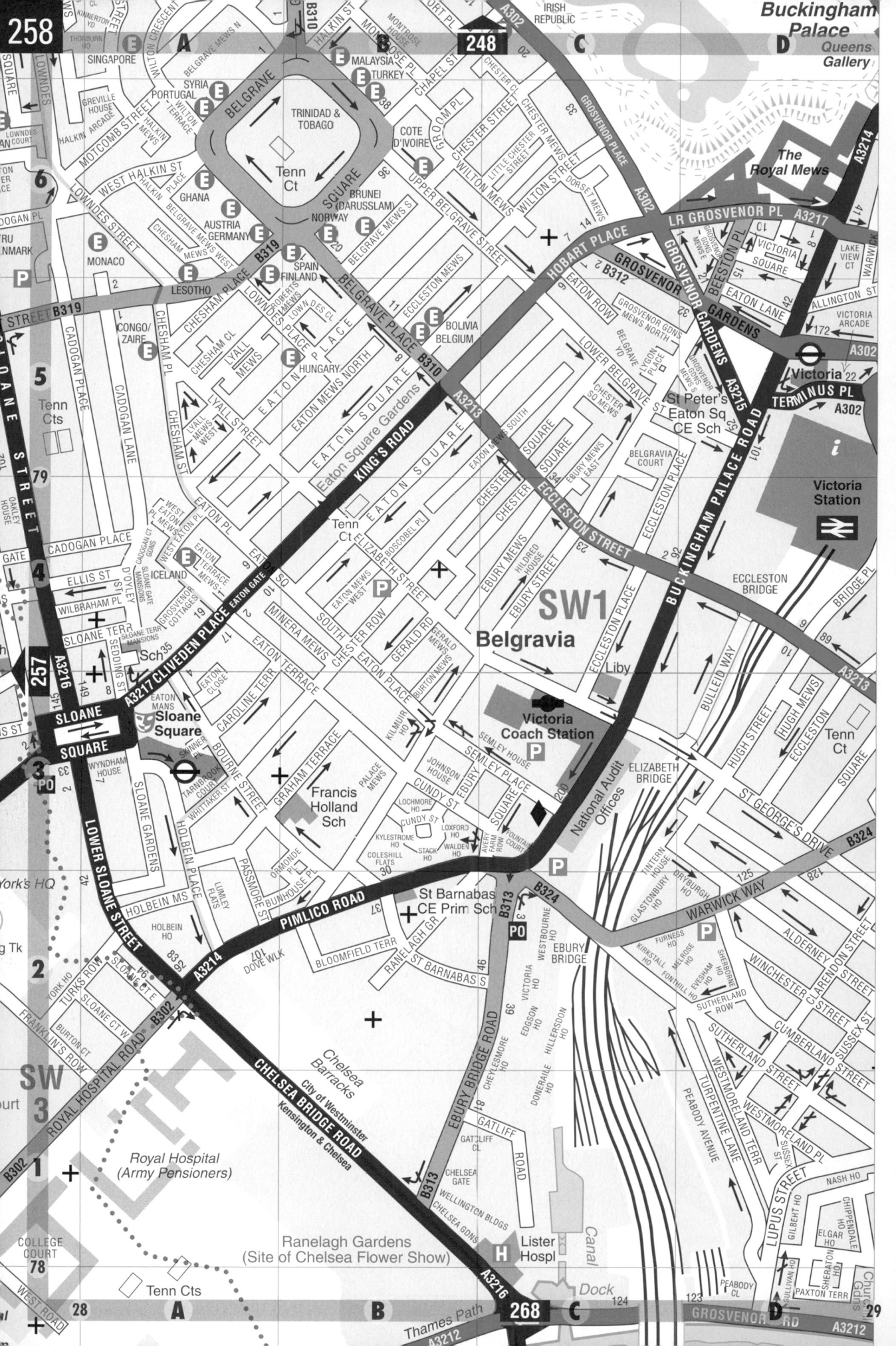
Buckingham Palace
Queens Gallery
The Royal Mews
Victoria Station
Victoria Coach Station
Belgravia
SW1
SW3
Sloane Square
Eaton Square Gardens
Chelsea Barracks
Royal Hospital (Army Pensioners)
Ranelagh Gardens (Site of Chelsea Flower Show)
Lister Hospl
Francis Holland Sch
St Barnabas CE Prim Sch
St Peter's Eaton Sq CE Sch
National Audit Offices
BELGRAVE SQUARE
EATON SQUARE
CHESTER SQUARE
KING'S ROAD
BUCKINGHAM PALACE ROAD
GROSVENOR PLACE
GROSVENOR GARDENS
ECCLESTON STREET
PIMLICO ROAD
LOWER SLOANE STREET
CHELSEA BRIDGE ROAD
EBURY BRIDGE ROAD
ROYAL HOSPITAL ROAD
WARWICK WAY
ST GEORGE'S DRIVE
LOWNDES STREET
SLOANE STREET
CLIVEDEN PLACE
HOBART PLACE
LR GROSVENOR PL
TERMINUS PL
ELIZABETH STREET
BELGRAVE PLACE
UPPER BELGRAVE STREET
LOWER BELGRAVE STREET
ECCLESTON PLACE
EBURY STREET
GROSVENOR RD
Thames Path
248
257
268

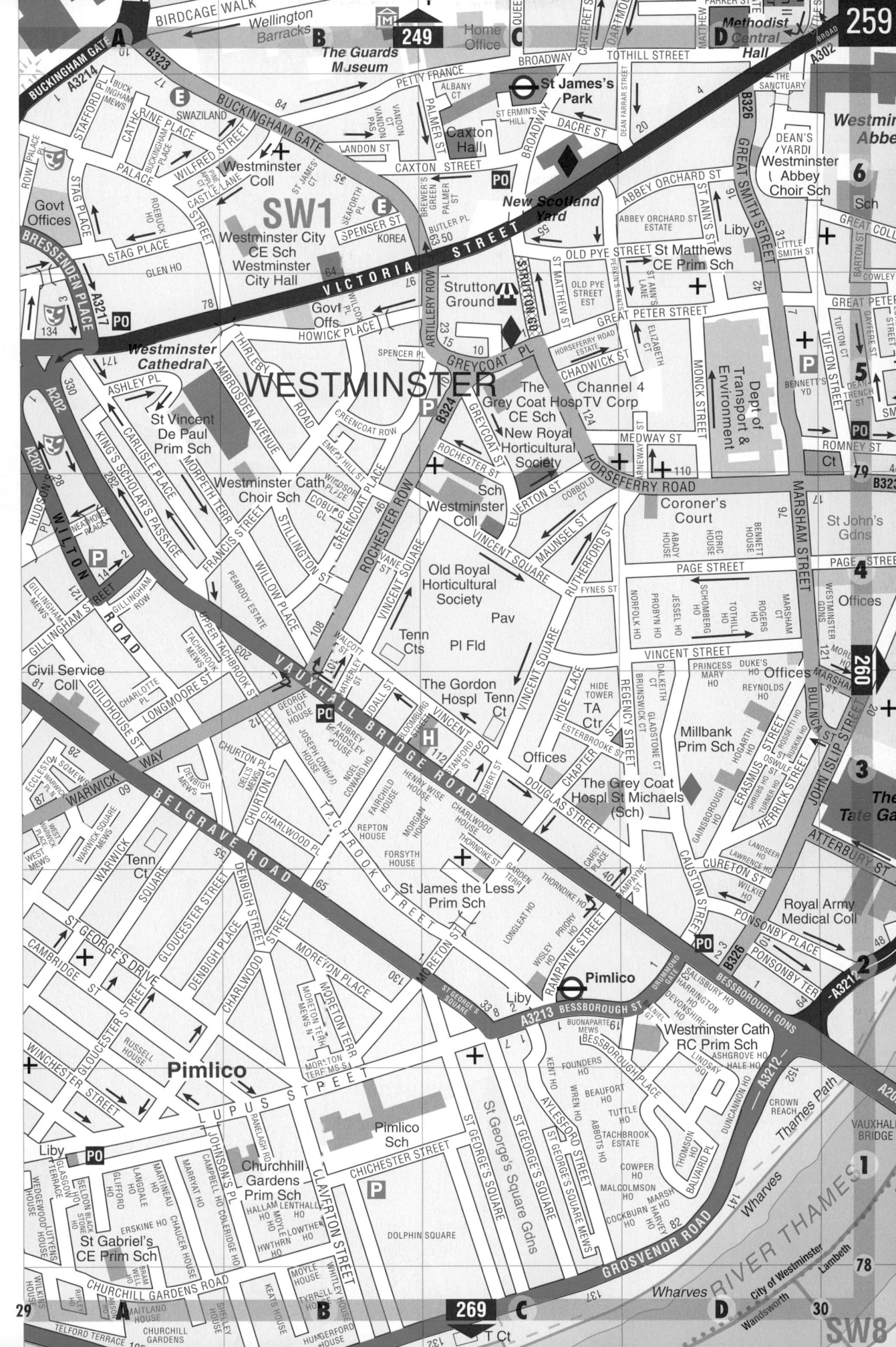
BIRDCAGE WALK
Wellington Barracks
249
Home Office
The Guards Museum
Methodist Central Hall
BUCKINGHAM GATE
PETTY FRANCE
BROADWAY
TOTHILL STREET
St James's Park
Caxton Hall
CAXTON STREET
Westminster Coll
DACRE ST
New Scotland Yard
ABBEY ORCHARD ST
GREAT SMITH STREET
Dean's Yard
Westminster Abbey Choir Sch
SW1
Westminster City CE Sch
Westminster City Hall
Govt Offices
STAG PLACE
BRESSENDEN PLACE
VICTORIA STREET
Strutton Ground
OLD PYE STREET
St Matthews CE Prim Sch
Liby
GREAT PETER STREET
Govt Offs
HOWICK PLACE
Westminster Cathedral
GREYCOAT PL
WESTMINSTER
The Grey Coat Hosp CE Sch
Channel 4 TV Corp
Dept of Transport & Environment
MONCK STREET
New Royal Horticultural Society
St Vincent De Paul Prim Sch
ASHLEY PL
AMBROSDEN AVENUE
ROCHESTER ROW
HORSEFERRY ROAD
MARSHAM STREET
Westminster Cath Choir Sch
Westminster Coll
Coroner's Court
St John's Gdns
VINCENT SQUARE
Old Royal Horticultural Society
Pav
Pl Fld
Tenn Cts
WILTON ROAD
FRANCIS STREET
PAGE STREET
VINCENT STREET
Offices
260
Civil Service Coll
VAUXHALL BRIDGE ROAD
The Gordon Hospl
Tenn Ct
TA Ctr
Millbank Prim Sch
JOHN ISLIP STREET
The Tate Ga
WARWICK WAY
BELGRAVE ROAD
The Grey Coat Hospl St Michaels (Sch)
DOUGLAS STREET
ATTERBURY ST
Tenn Ct
St James the Less Prim Sch
Royal Army Medical Coll
ST GEORGE'S DRIVE
PONSONBY PLACE
Pimlico
BESSBOROUGH ST
BESSBOROUGH GDNS
Westminster Cath RC Prim Sch
Pimlico
LUPUS STREET
Pimlico Sch
CHICHESTER STREET
St George's Square Gdns
Churchhill Gardens Prim Sch
St Gabriel's CE Prim Sch
CLAVERTON STREET
DOLPHIN SQUARE
GROSVENOR ROAD
RIVER THAMES
Thames Path
Wharves
VAUXHALL BRIDGE
CHURCHILL GARDENS ROAD
269
City of Westminster
Lambeth
Wandsworth
SW8

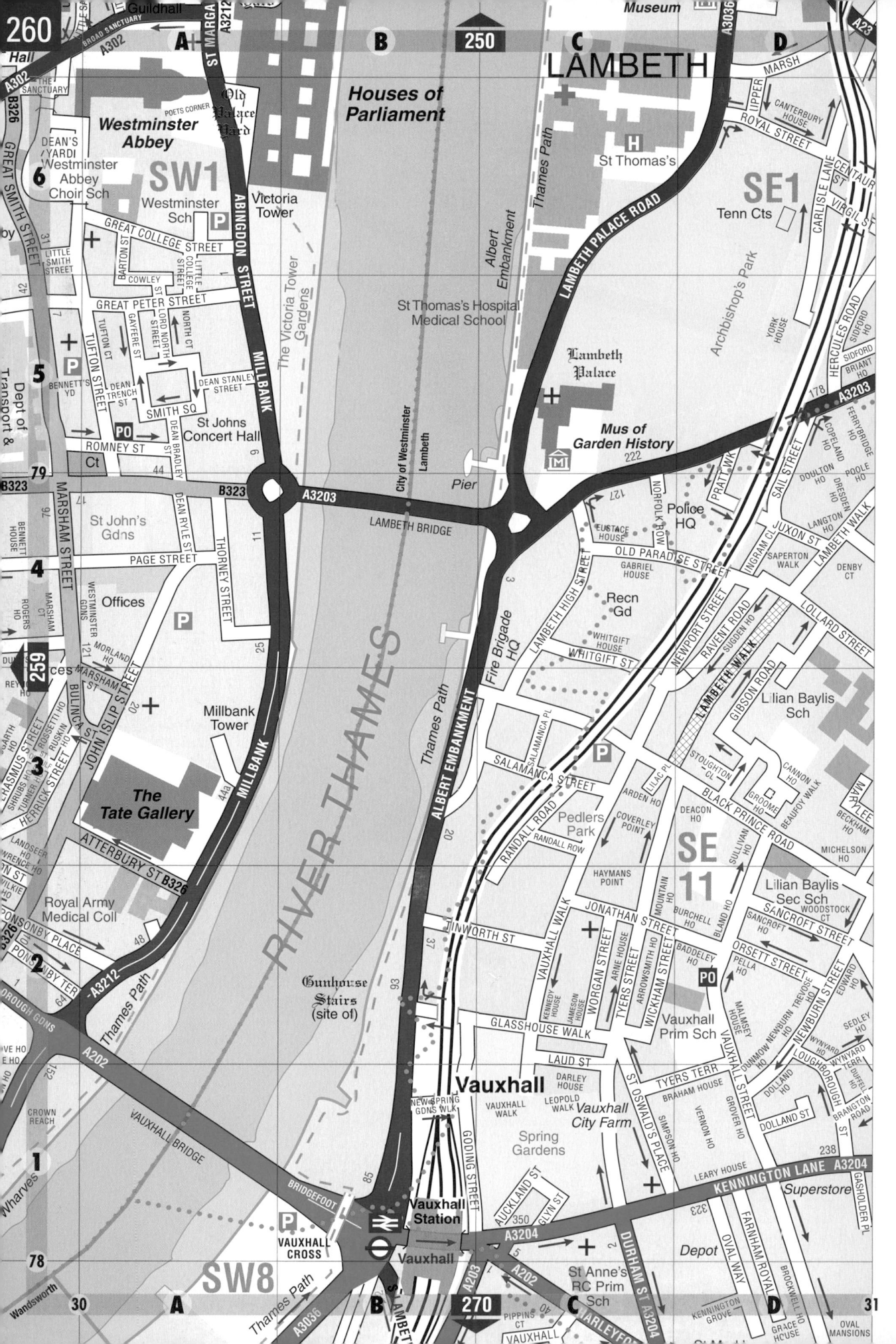
LAMBETH
Houses of Parliament
Westminster Abbey
SW1
Westminster Abbey Choir Sch
Westminster Sch
Victoria Tower
St Thomas's
SE1
Tenn Cts
Archbishop's Park
Lambeth Palace
Mus of Garden History
St Thomas's Hospital Medical School
The Victoria Tower Gardens
Albert Embankment
Thames Path
LAMBETH PALACE ROAD
ABINGDON STREET
MILLBANK
GREAT COLLEGE STREET
GREAT PETER STREET
St Johns Concert Hall
St John's Gdns
PAGE STREET
THORNEY STREET
MARSHAM STREET
Offices
Millbank Tower
The Tate Gallery
ATTERBURY ST
Royal Army Medical Coll
PONSONBY PLACE
RIVER THAMES
LAMBETH BRIDGE
Pier
Police HQ
OLD PARADISE STREET
Recn Gd
Fire Brigade HQ
LAMBETH HIGH STREET
Lilian Baylis Sch
SALAMANCA STREET
BLACK PRINCE ROAD
Pedlers Park
SE 11
Lilian Baylis Sec Sch
SANCROFT STREET
JONATHAN STREET
TINWORTH ST
GLASSHOUSE WALK
Vauxhall Prim Sch
Vauxhall
Vauxhall City Farm
Spring Gardens
Gunhorse Stairs (site of)
VAUXHALL BRIDGE
Vauxhall Station
VAUXHALL CROSS
SW8
KENNINGTON LANE
Superstore
Depot
St Anne's RC Prim Sch
DURHAM ST
A3203
A3204
A202
A3212
A3036
B323
B326
A302
A23

250
259
270

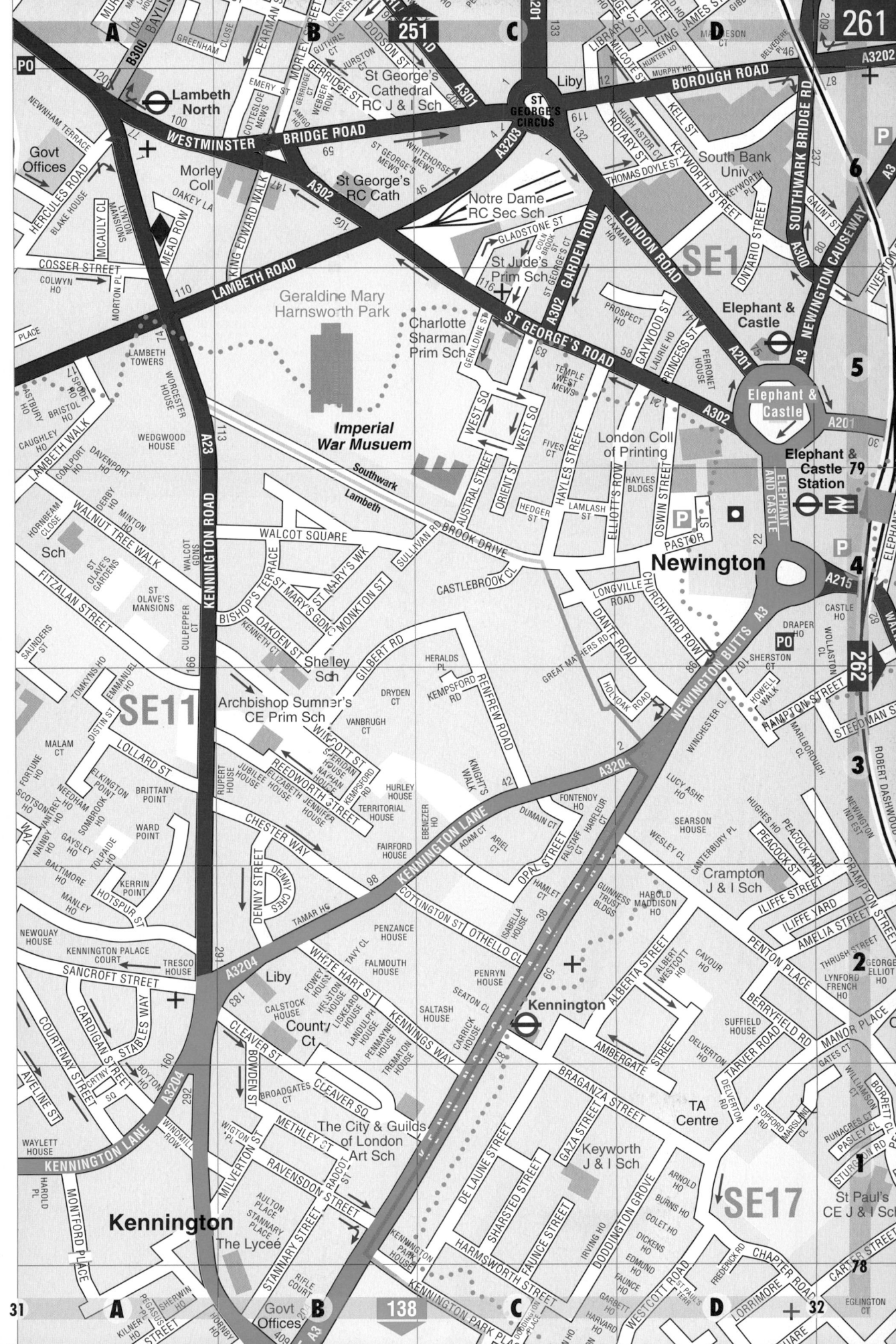
251
Lambeth North
Westminster Bridge Road
St George's Circus
Borough Road
St George's Cathedral RC J & I Sch
St George's RC Cath
Notre Dame RC Sec Sch
Lambeth Road
Geraldine Mary Harmsworth Park
Imperial War Museum
St George's Road
Elephant & Castle
Elephant & Castle Station
London Road
South Bank Univ
SE1
London Coll of Printing
Newington
Kennington Road
SE11
Archbishop Sumner's CE Prim Sch
Shelley Sch
Charlotte Sharman Prim Sch
St Jude's Prim Sch
Newington Butts
Kennington Lane
Kennington Park Road
Kennington
Crampton J & I Sch
The City & Guilds of London Art Sch
Keyworth J & I Sch
TA Centre
SE17
St Paul's CE J & I Sch
The Lyceé
Govt Offices
262
138
31
32

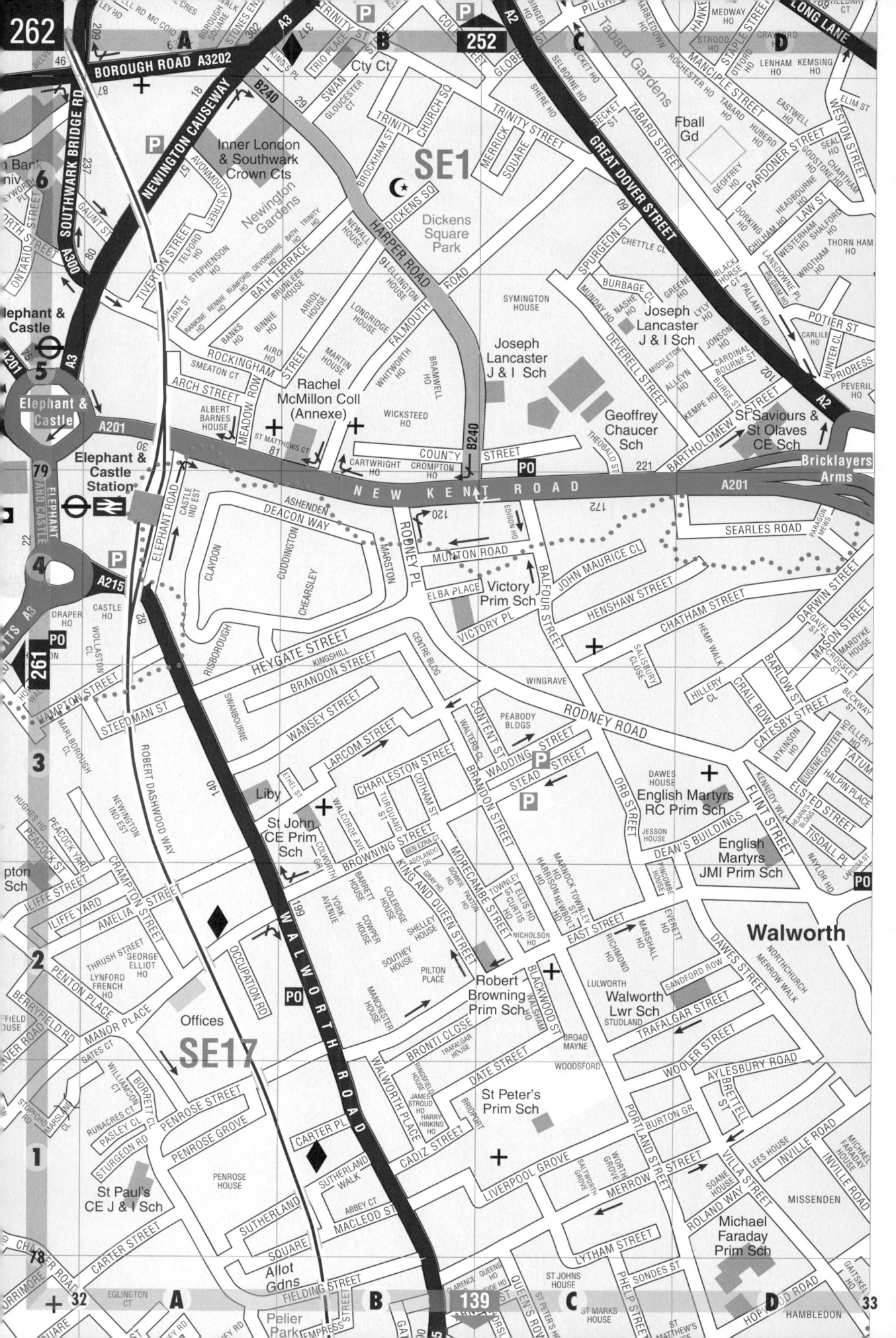
A
B
C
D
252
139
261
BOROUGH ROAD A3202
NEWINGTON CAUSEWAY
SOUTHWARK BRIDGE RD
A300
GREAT DOVER STREET
A2
LONG LANE
Tabard Gardens
Fball Gd
SE1
Inner London & Southwark Crown Cts
Newington Gardens
Dickens Square Park
HARPER ROAD
B240
TRINITY STREET
TRINITY CHURCH SQ
MERRICK SQUARE
DICKENS SQ
TABARD STREET
Elephant & Castle
Elephant & Castle Station
A201
NEW KENT ROAD
Bricklayers Arms
Rachel McMillon Coll (Annexe)
Joseph Lancaster J & I Sch
Geoffrey Chaucer Sch
St Saviours & St Olaves CE Sch
Victory Prim Sch
HEYGATE STREET
RODNEY ROAD
A215
WALWORTH ROAD
English Martyrs RC Prim Sch
English Martyrs JMI Prim Sch
Walworth
St John CE Prim Sch
Liby
Robert Browning Prim Sch
Walworth Lwr Sch
Offices
SE17
St Peter's Prim Sch
St Paul's CE J & I Sch
Michael Faraday Prim Sch
Allot Gdns
Pelier Park
PO
P
32
33

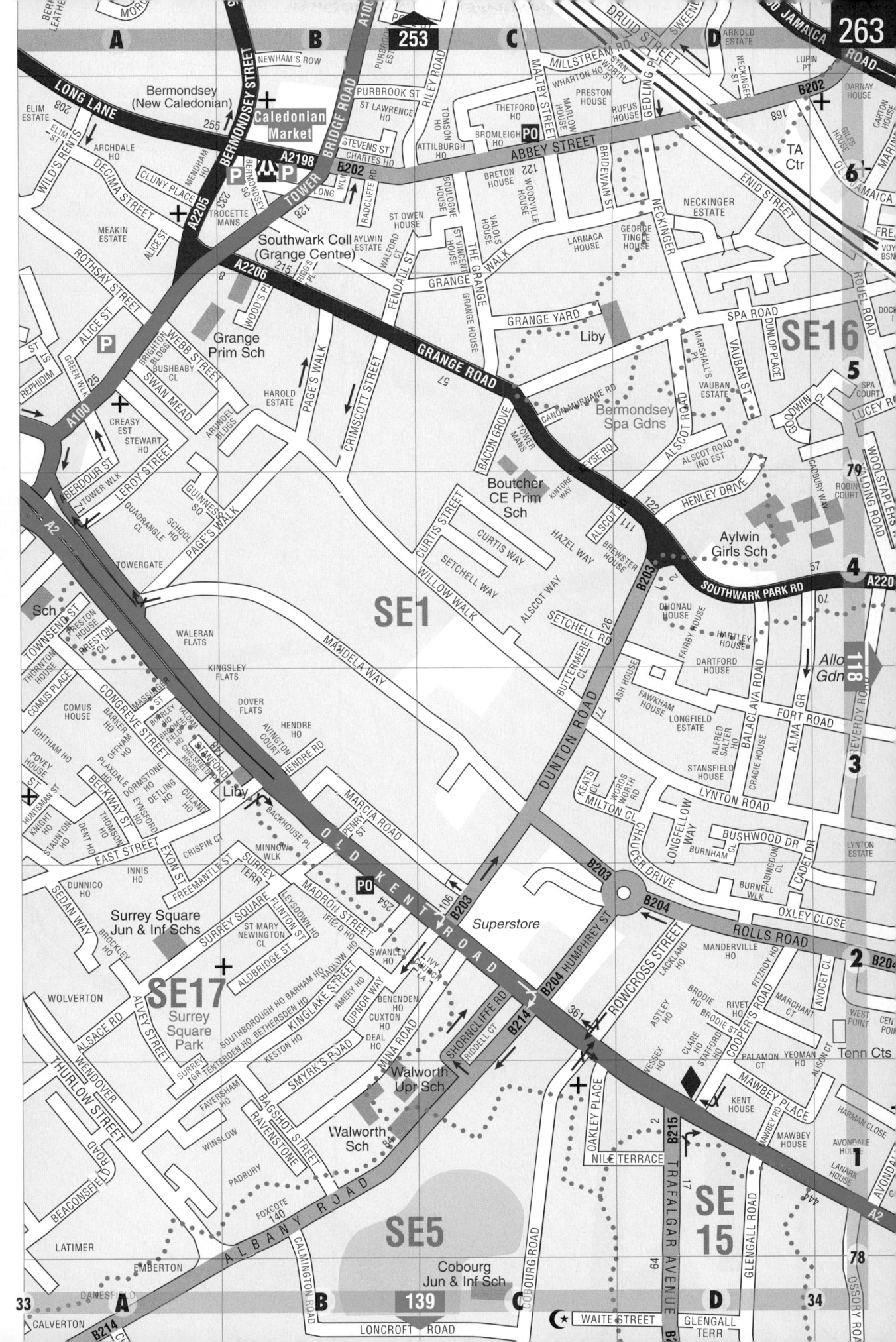
A
B
C
D
253
139
33
34
118
78
79
SE1
SE16
SE17
SE5
SE 15
LONG LANE
BERMONDSEY STREET
TOWER BRIDGE ROAD
Bermondsey (New Caledonian)
Caledonian Market
ABBEY STREET
GRANGE ROAD
DRUID STREET
JAMAICA ROAD
SOUTHWARK PARK RD
OLD KENT ROAD
ALBANY ROAD
DUNTON ROAD
ROLLS ROAD
TRAFALGAR AVENUE
COBOURG ROAD
Southwark Coll (Grange Centre)
Grange Prim Sch
Boutcher CE Prim Sch
Aylwin Girls Sch
Bermondsey Spa Gdns
Surrey Square Jun & Inf Schs
Surrey Square Park
Walworth Upr Sch
Walworth Sch
Cobourg Jun & Inf Sch
Superstore
Tenn Cts
TA Ctr
Liby
MANDELA WAY
WILLOW WALK
SPA ROAD
LYNTON ROAD
FORT ROAD
OXLEY CLOSE
ROWCROSS STREET
HUMPHREY ST
MARCIA ROAD
EAST STREET
SURREY SQUARE
THURLOW STREET
GLENGALL ROAD
WAITE STREET
LONCROFT ROAD
CALMINGTON ROAD
NILE TERRACE
OAKLEY PLACE
MAWBEY PLACE
COOPER'S ROAD
CHAUCER DRIVE
NECKINGER ESTATE
ENID STREET
PAGE'S WALK
CRIMSCOTT STREET
ROTHSAY STREET
DECIMA STREET
ALSCOT ROAD
HENLEY DRIVE
BALACLAVA ROAD
CONGREVE STREET
KINGLAKE STREET
SMYRK'S ROAD
MINA ROAD
BAGSHOT STREET
ALSACE RD
ALVEY STREET
BEACONSFIELD ROAD
WENDOVER
LATIMER
EMBERTON
CALVERTON
PADBURY
WINSLOW
FOXCOTE
WOLVERTON

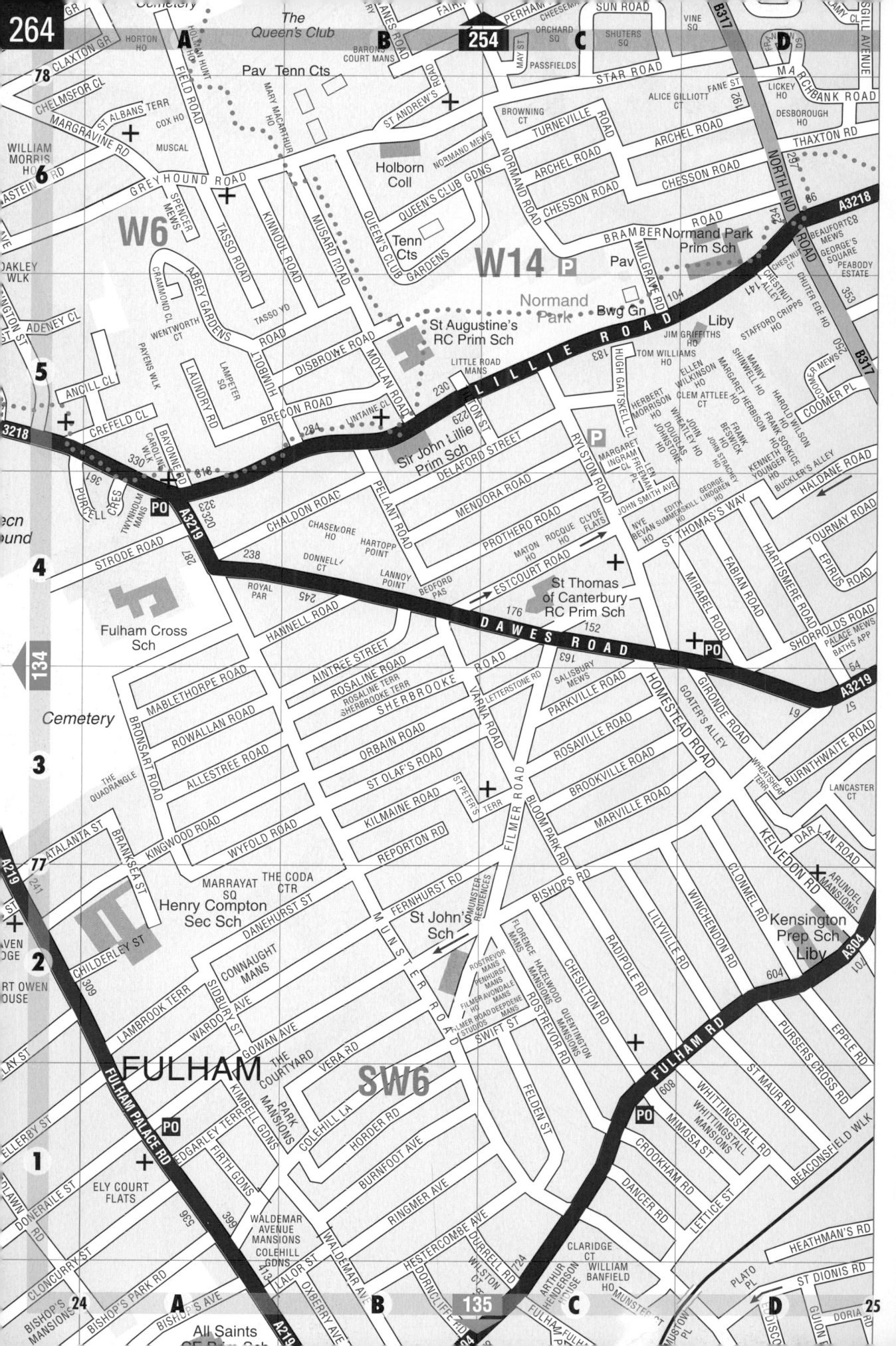
The Queen's Club
254
A
B
C
D
HORTON HO
BARONS COURT MANS
CLAXTON GR
CHELMSFORD CL
ST ALBANS TERR
MARGRAVINE RD
COX HO
MUSCAL
WILLIAM MORRIS HO
FIELD ROAD
HOLMAN HUNT HO
MARY MACARTHUR HO
Pav Tenn Cts
ST ANDREW'S ROAD
PERHAM
CHEESEMAN
ORCHARD SQ
MAY ST
PASSFIELDS
SUN ROAD
SHUTERS SQ
VINE SQ
STAR ROAD
B317
FANE ST
ALICE GILLIOTT CT
LICKEY HO
MARCHBANK ROAD
DESBOROUGH HO
GILL AVENUE
THAXTON RD
BROWNING CT
TURNEVILLE ROAD
ARCHEL ROAD
NORTH END ROAD
NORMAND MEWS
Holborn Coll
QUEEN'S CLUB GDNS
NORMAND ROAD
CHESSON ROAD
GREYHOUND ROAD
SPENCER MEWS
TASSO ROAD
KINNOUL ROAD
MUSARD ROAD
QUEEN'S CLUB GARDENS
Tenn Cts
W6
W14
P
BRAMBER ROAD
Normand Park Prim Sch
A3218
BEAUFORT MEWS
GEORGE'S SQUARE
PEABODY ESTATE
CHESTNUT CT
CHESTNUT ALLEY
CHUTER EDE HO
OAKLEY WLK
ABBEY GARDENS
CRAMMOND CL
WENTWORTH CT
TASSO YD
HUMBOLDT ROAD
Pav
Normand Park
Bwg Gn
MULGRAVE RD
Liby
ADENEY CL
ANCILL CL
PAYENS WLK
LAUNDRY RD
LAMPETER SQ
DISBROWE ROAD
St Augustine's RC Prim Sch
LILLIE ROAD
JIM GRIFFITHS HO
STAFFORD CRIPPS HO
TOM WILLIAMS HO
LITTLE ROAD MANS
HUGH GAITSKELL CL
ELLEN WILKINSON HO
MARGARET HERBISON HO
MANNY SHINWELL HO
HAROLD WILSON HO
COOMER MEWS
COOMER PL
CREFELD CL
BRECON ROAD
LINTAINE CL
MOYLAN ROAD
HERBERT MORRISON HO
CLEM ATTLEE CT
DOUGLAS JOHNSTONE HO
JOHN WHEATLEY HO
FRANK BESWICK HO
FRANK SOSKICE HO
KENNETH YOUNGER HO
BUCKLER'S ALLEY
HALDANE ROAD
CAROLINE WLK
BAYONNE RD
Sir John Lillie Prim Sch
DELAFORD STREET
RYLSTON ROAD
MARGARET INGRAM CL
LEN FREEMAN PL
JOHN STRACHEY HO
GEORGE LINDGREN HO
JOHN SMITH AVE
PURCELL CRES
TWYNHOLM MANS
PO
A3219
CHALDON ROAD
PELLANT ROAD
MENDORA ROAD
PROTHERO ROAD
CLYDE FLATS
NYE BEVAN HO
EDITH SUMMERSKILL HO
ST THOMAS'S WAY
TOURNAY ROAD
CHASEMORE HO
HARTOPP POINT
MATON HO
ROCQUE HO
ESTCOURT ROAD
STRODE ROAD
DONNELL CT
LANNOY POINT
BEDFORD PAS
ROYAL PAR
St Thomas of Canterbury RC Prim Sch
FABIAN ROAD
MIRABEL ROAD
HARTISMERE ROAD
EPIRUS ROAD
Fulham Cross Sch
HANNELL ROAD
DAWES ROAD
SHORROLDS ROAD
PALACE MEWS
BATHS APP
134
AINTREE STREET
ROSALINE ROAD
ROSALINE TERR
SHERBROOKE TERR
SHERBROOKE ROAD
LETTERSTONE RD
SALISBURY MEWS
PARKVILLE ROAD
HOMESTEAD ROAD
GOATER'S ALLEY
GIRONDE ROAD
MABLETHORPE ROAD
ROWALLAN ROAD
VARNA ROAD
ORBAIN ROAD
ROSAVILLE ROAD
WHEATSHEAF TERR
BURNTHWAITE ROAD
Cemetery
BRONSART ROAD
ALLESTREE ROAD
ST OLAF'S ROAD
BROOKVILLE ROAD
THE QUADRANGLE
KILMAINE ROAD
ST PETER'S TERR
FILMER ROAD
BLOOM PARK RD
MARVILLE ROAD
LANCASTER CT
ATALANTA ST
BRANKSEA ST
KINGWOOD ROAD
WYFOLD ROAD
REPORTON RD
KELVEDON RD
DARLAN ROAD
CLONMEL RD
WINCHENDON RD
LILYVILLE RD
ARUNDEL MANSIONS
MARRAYAT SQ
THE CODA CTR
FERNHURST RD
MUNSTER RESIDENCES
BISHOPS RD
Henry Compton Sec Sch
DANEHURST ST
St John's Sch
FLORENCE MANS
RADIPOLE RD
Kensington Prep Sch
Liby
A304
CHILDERLEY ST
CONNAUGHT MANS
MUNSTER ROAD
ROSTREVOR MANS
PENHURST MANS
AVONDALE MANS
HAZELWOOD MANSIONS
CHESILTON RD
FILMER HO
DEEPDENE MANS
FILMER ROAD STUDIOS
QUENTINGTON MANSIONS
LAMBROOK TERR
SIDBURY ST
WARDO AVE
GOWAN AVE
SWIFT ST
ROSTREVOR RD
FULHAM RD
PURSERS CROSS RD
EPPLE RD
FULHAM
THE COURTYARD
VERA RD
SW6
FELDEN ST
ST MAUR RD
WHITTINGSTALL RD
WHITTINGSTALL MANSIONS
KIMBELL GDNS
PARK MANSIONS
COLEHILL LA
HORDER RD
MIMOSA ST
CROOKHAM RD
BEACONSFIELD WLK
FULHAM PALACE RD
EDGARLEY TERR
FIRTH GDNS
BURNFOOT AVE
DANCER RD
LETTICE ST
ELLERBY ST
DONERAILE ST
ELY COURT FLATS
RINGMER AVE
WALDEMAR AVENUE MANSIONS
COLEHILL GDNS
HESTERCOMBE AVE
DURRELL RD
CLARIDGE CT
WILLIAM BANFIELD HO
HEATHMAN'S RD
ARTHUR HENDERSON HOUSE
PLATO PL
ST DIONIS RD
CLONCURRY ST
BISHOP'S PARK RD
LALOR ST
WALDEMAR AVE
OXBERRY AVE
DORNCLIFFE RD
WILSTON CT
MUNSTER CT
BISHOP'S MANSIONS
BISHOP'S AVE
135
All Saints
MUSTOW PL
DORIA RD
GUION RD
24
25
1
2
3
4
5
6

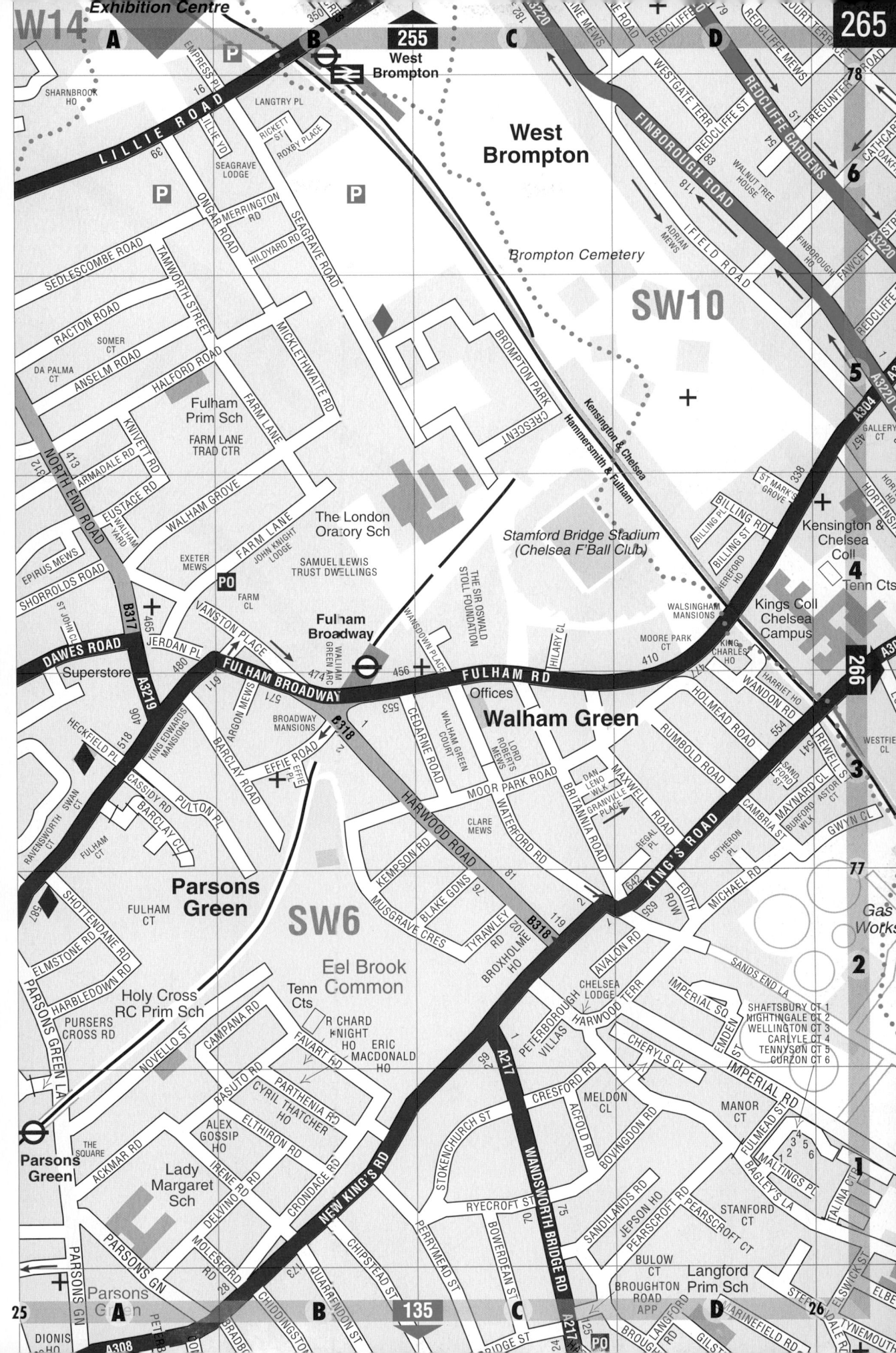
W14
Exhibition Centre
255
West Brompton
West Brompton
Brompton Cemetery
SW10
LILLIE ROAD
NORTH END ROAD
FINBOROUGH ROAD
REDCLIFFE GARDENS
Fulham Prim Sch
The London Oratory Sch
Stamford Bridge Stadium (Chelsea F'Ball Club)
Kensington & Chelsea
Hammersmith & Fulham
Fulham Broadway
FULHAM BROADWAY
FULHAM RD
Walham Green
Kensington & Chelsea Coll
Kings Coll Chelsea Campus
266
Parsons Green
SW6
Eel Brook Common
KING'S ROAD
NEW KING'S RD
WANDSWORTH BRIDGE RD
Holy Cross RC Prim Sch
Lady Margaret Sch
Langford Prim Sch
Gas Works
Parsons Green
135

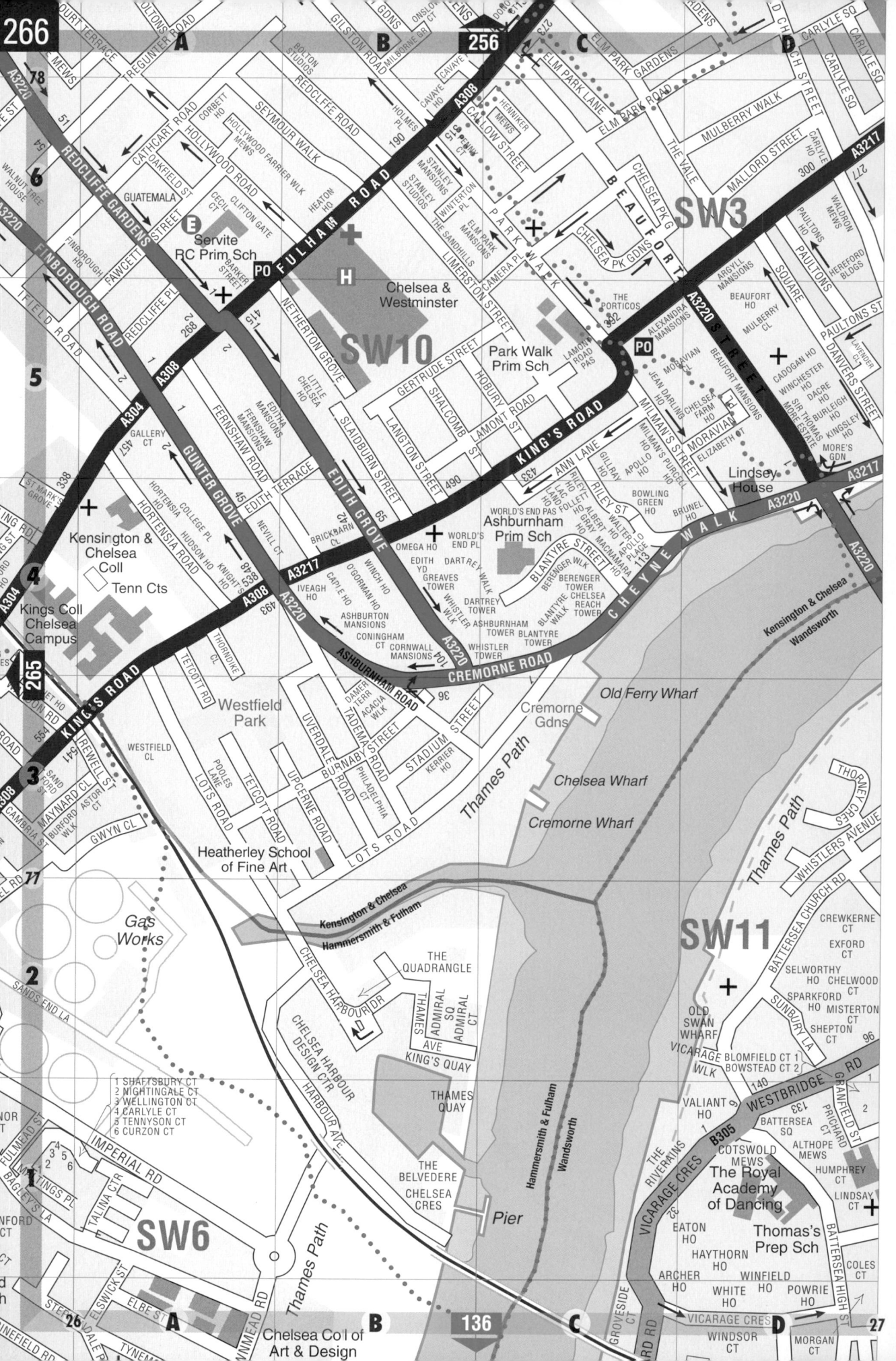

A   B   256   C   D

78

54

6

Servite
RC Prim Sch

SW3

SW10

Chelsea &
Westminster

H

Park Walk
Prim Sch

5

SW10

Ashburnham
Prim Sch

Lindsey
House

4

Kensington &
Chelsea
Coll

Tenn Cts

World's End
Est

Kings Coll
Chelsea
Campus

265

Westfield
Park

Kensington & Chelsea
Wandsworth

3

Old Ferry Wharf

Cremorne
Gdns

Thames Path

Chelsea Wharf

Cremorne Wharf

77

Heatherley School
of Fine Art

Kensington & Chelsea
Hammersmith & Fulham

SW11

Gas
Works

2

1 SHAFTSBURY CT
2 NIGHTINGALE CT
3 WELLINGTON CT
4 CARLYLE CT
5 TENNYSON CT
6 CURZON CT

THE
QUADRANGLE

Old
Swan
Wharf

The Royal
Academy
of Dancing

1

Chelsea Harbour
Design Ctr

King's Quay

THE
BELVEDERE
CHELSEA
CRES

Thames
Quay

Hammersmith & Fulham
Wandsworth

Thomas's
Prep Sch

SW6

Pier

Thames Path

26   A   B   136   C   Vicarage Cres   D   27

Chelsea Coll of
Art & Design

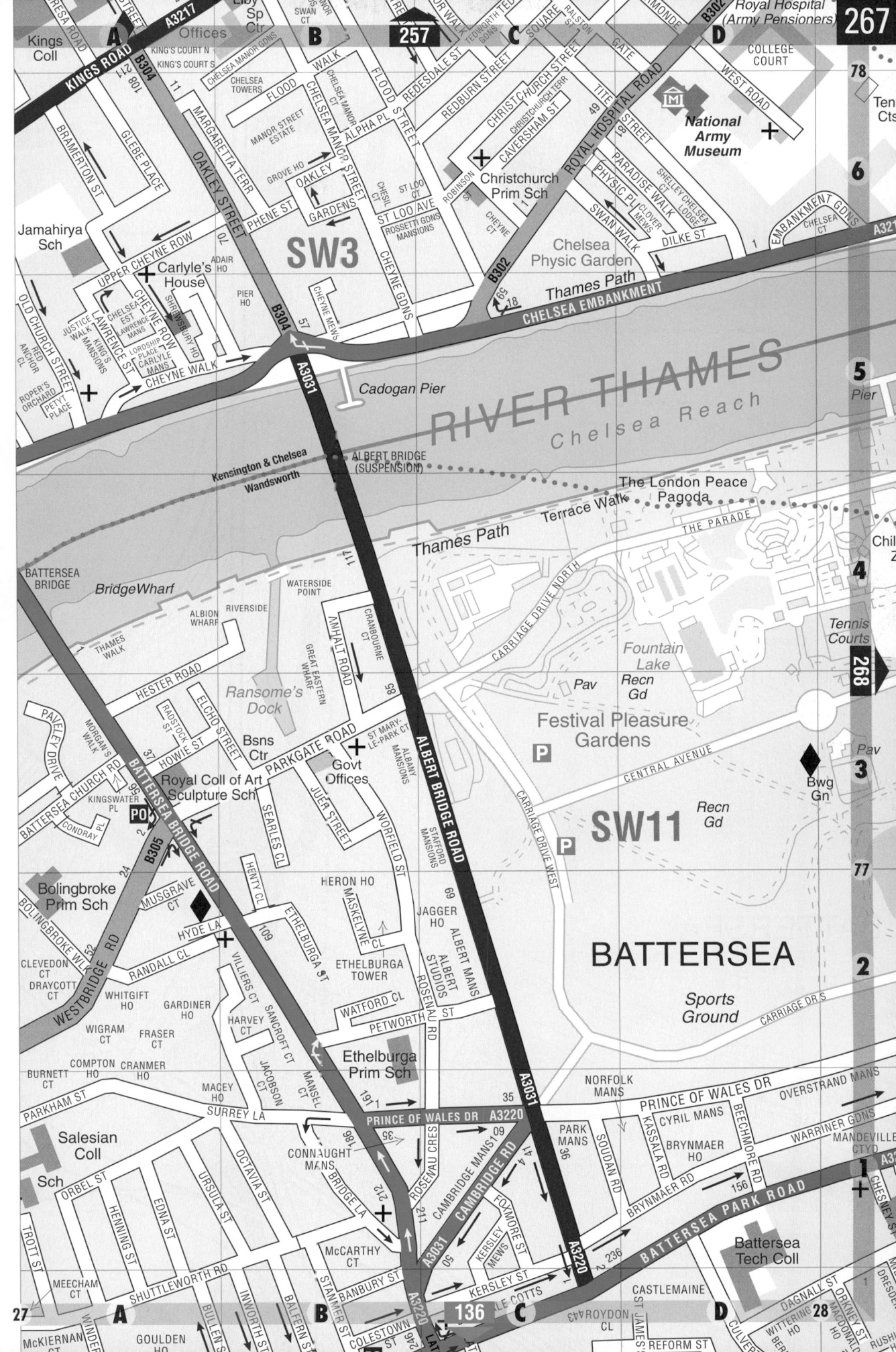
257
136
268
Kings Coll
KINGS ROAD
A3217
Offices
KING'S COURT N
KING'S COURT S
CHELSEA MANOR GDNS
CHELSEA TOWERS
FLOOD WALK
FLOOD ST
MANOR STREET ESTATE
CHELSEA MANOR ST
ALPHA PL
REDESDALE ST
REDBURN STREET
CHRISTCHURCH STREET
CHRISTCHURCH TERR
CAVERSHAM ST
TITE STREET
ROYAL HOSPITAL ROAD
Royal Hospital (Army Pensioners)
COLLEGE COURT
WEST ROAD
National Army Museum
Tenn Cts
B302
B304
BRAMERTON ST
GLEBE PLACE
MARGARETTA TERR
OAKLEY STREET
GROVE HO
OAKLEY GARDENS
CHESIL CT
ST LOO CT
ST LOO AVE
ROSSETTI GDNS MANSIONS
ROBINSON ST
Christchurch Prim Sch
CHEYNE CT
PHYSIC PL
PARADISE WALK
SHELLEY CT
CHELSEA LODGE
CLOVER MEWS
SWAN WALK
DILKE ST
EMBANKMENT GDNS
CHELSEA CT
Jamahirya Sch
UPPER CHEYNE ROW
Carlyle's House
ADAIR HO
PHENE ST
SW3
Chelsea Physic Garden
Thames Path
CHELSEA EMBANKMENT
PIER HO
CHEYNE MEWS
CHEYNE GDNS
OLD CHURCH STREET
JUSTICE WALK
LAWRENCE ST
CHELSEA EST
LAWRENCE MANS
CHEYNE ROW
SHREWSBURY HO
LORDSHIP PLACE
CARLYLE MANS
KING'S MANSIONS
RED ANCHOR CL
ROPER'S ORCHARD
PETYT PLACE
CHEYNE WALK
A3031
Cadogan Pier
RIVER THAMES
Chelsea Reach
Pier
Kensington & Chelsea
Wandsworth
ALBERT BRIDGE (SUSPENSION)
The London Peace Pagoda
Terrace Walk
THE PARADE
Thames Path
BATTERSEA BRIDGE
BridgeWharf
WATERSIDE POINT
ALBION WHARF
RIVERSIDE
THAMES WALK
HESTER ROAD
Ransome's Dock
GREAT EASTERN WHARF
ANHALT ROAD
CRANBOURNE CT
CARRIAGE DRIVE NORTH
Fountain Lake
Tennis Courts
Pav
Recn Gd
Festival Pleasure Gardens
PAVELEY DRIVE
MORGAN'S WALK
RADSTOCK ST
ELCHO STREET
HOWIE ST
Bsns Ctr
PARKGATE ROAD
ST MARY-LE-PARK CT
Govt Offices
ALBANY MANSIONS
ALBERT BRIDGE ROAD
CENTRAL AVENUE
Bwg Gn
BATTERSEA CHURCH RD
KINGSWATER PL
Royal Coll of Art Sculpture Sch
BATTERSEA BRIDGE ROAD
CONDRAY PL
PO
SEARLES CL
JUER STREET
WORFIELD ST
STAFFORD MANSIONS
CARRIAGE DRIVE WEST
SW11
B305
Bolingbroke Prim Sch
BOLINGBROKE WLK
MUSGRAVE CT
HYDE LA
HENTY CL
HERON HO
MASKELYNE CL
JAGGER HO
ETHELBURGA ST
VILLIERS CT
ETHELBURGA TOWER
ALBERT STUDIOS
ALBERT MANS
BATTERSEA
CLEVEDON CT
DRAYCOTT CT
RANDALL CL
WESTBRIDGE RD
WHITGIFT HO
GARDINER HO
HARVEY CT
SANCROFT CT
WATFORD CL
ROSENAU RD
PETWORTH ST
Sports Ground
CARRIAGE DR S
WIGRAM CT
FRASER CT
COMPTON HO
CRANMER HO
BURNETT CT
JACOBSON CT
Ethelburga Prim Sch
MANSEL CT
NORFOLK MANS
PARKHAM ST
MACEY HO
SURREY LA
PRINCE OF WALES DR
A3220
OVERSTRAND MANS
PARK MANS
SOUDAN RD
KASSALA RD
CYRIL MANS
BEECHMORE RD
WARRINER GDNS
MANDEVILLE CTYD
Salesian Coll
Sch
CONNAUGHT MANS
BRIDGE LA
ROSENAU CRES
CAMBRIDGE MANS
CAMBRIDGE RD
BRYNMAER HO
BRYNMAER RD
ORBEL ST
HENNING ST
EDNA ST
URSULA ST
OCTAVIA ST
FOXMORE ST
KERSLEY MEWS
BATTERSEA PARK ROAD
CHESNEY ST
Battersea Tech Coll
TROTT ST
MEECHAM CT
SHUTTLEWORTH RD
McCARTHY CT
BANBURY ST
KERSLEY ST
LE COTTS
CASTLEMAINE
DAGNALL ST
ORKNEY ST
MACDONALD HO
WITTERING HO
DRESDEN
McKIERNAN CT
WINDER
GOULDEN HO
BULLEN ST
INWORTH ST
BALFERN ST
STANMER ST
COLESTOWN ST
ROYDON CL
ST JAMES'S
REFORM ST
CULVERT
RUSHL
A B C D
1 2 3 4 5 6
27 28 77 78

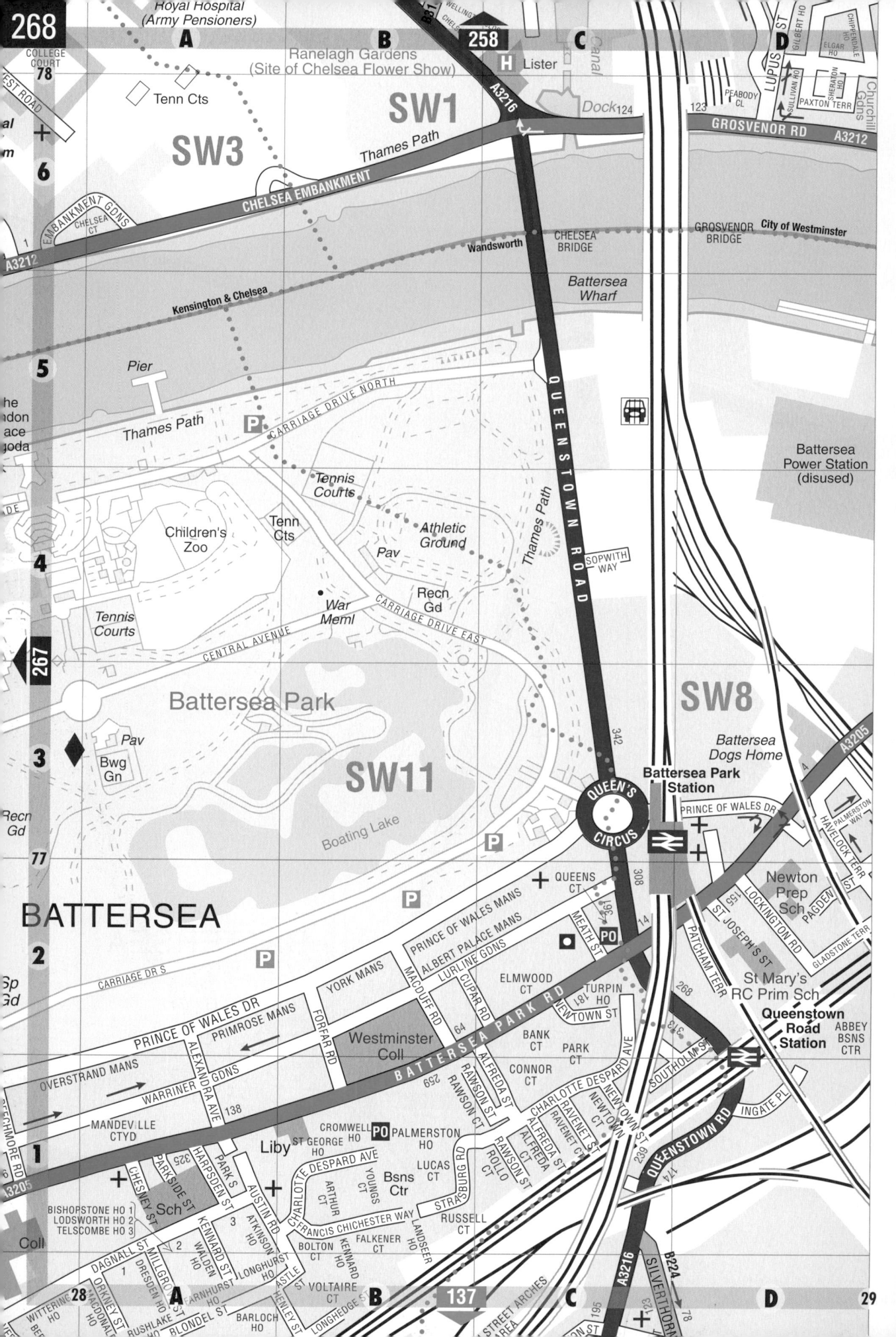
Royal Hospital
(Army Pensioners)
Ranelagh Gardens
(Site of Chelsea Flower Show)
Lister
Tenn Cts
SW1
SW3
Dock
GROSVENOR RD
A3212
Thames Path
CHELSEA EMBANKMENT
EMBANKMENT GDNS
CHELSEA CT
CHELSEA BRIDGE
GROSVENOR BRIDGE
City of Westminster
Wandsworth
Kensington & Chelsea
Battersea Wharf
Pier
Thames Path
CARRIAGE DRIVE NORTH
QUEENSTOWN ROAD
Battersea Power Station (disused)
Tennis Courts
Tenn Cts
Children's Zoo
Athletic Ground
Pav
Thames Path
SOPWITH WAY
Recn Gd
War Meml
CARRIAGE DRIVE EAST
Tennis Courts
CENTRAL AVENUE
Battersea Park
SW8
Battersea Dogs Home
A3205
Pav
Bwg Gn
SW11
Battersea Park Station
QUEEN'S CIRCUS
PRINCE OF WALES DR
Boating Lake
QUEENS CT
Newton Prep Sch
LOCKINGTON RD
HAVELOCK TERR
PALMERSTON WAY
PAGDEN ST
GLADSTONE TERR
BATTERSEA
PRINCE OF WALES MANS
ALBERT PALACE MANS
MEATH ST
LURLINE GDNS
ST JOSEPH'S ST
PATCHAM TERR
St Mary's RC Prim Sch
Queenstown Road Station
ABBEY BSNS CTR
CARRIAGE DR S
YORK MANS
MACDUFF RD
CUPAR RD
ELMWOOD CT
TURPIN HO
NEWTOWN ST
PRINCE OF WALES DR
PRIMROSE MANS
FORFAR RD
BATTERSEA PARK RD
BANK CT
PARK CT
Westminster Coll
SOUTHOLM ST
OVERSTRAND MANS
ALEXANDRA AVE
GDNS
WARRINER
RAWSON CT
RAWSON ST
ALFREDA ST
CONNOR CT
CHARLOTTE DESPARD AVE
RAVENET ST
RAVENET CT
NEWTOWN CT
NEWTOWN ST
QUEENSTOWN RD
INGATE PL
MANDEVILLE CTYD
CROMWELL HO
PALMERSTON HO
ST GEORGE HO
Liby
ROLLO CT
RAWSON ST
ALFREDA CT
ALFREDA ST
HARPSDEN ST
PARKSIDE ST
PARK S
CHESNEY ST
Sch
CHARLOTTE DESPARD AVE
ARTHUR CT
YOUNGS CT
Bsns Ctr
LUCAS CT
STRASBURG RD
AUSTIN RD
BISHOPSTONE HO
LODSWORTH HO
TELSCOMBE HO
KENNARD ST
WALDEN HO
ATKINSON HO
FRANCIS CHICHESTER WAY
LANDSEER HO
RUSSELL CT
Coll
DAGNALL ST
MILLGROVE ST
DRESDEN HO
LONGHURST HO
BOLTON CT
KENNARD HO
FALKENER CT
ASTLE ST
VOLTAIRE CT
A3216
B224
SILVERTHORNE
STREET ARCHES AREA
WITTERING HO
ORKNEY ST
FARNHURST HO
RUSHLAKE HO
BLONDEL ST
BARLOCH HO
HENLEY ST
LONGHEDGE ST
COLLEGE COURT
Recn Gd
Sp Gd
LUPUS ST
GILBERT HO
CHIPPENDALE HO
ELGAR HO
SULLIVAN HO
SHERATON HO
PAXTON TERR
PEABODY CL
Churchill Gdns
A B C D
1 2 3 4 5 6
77 78 28 29
258 267 137

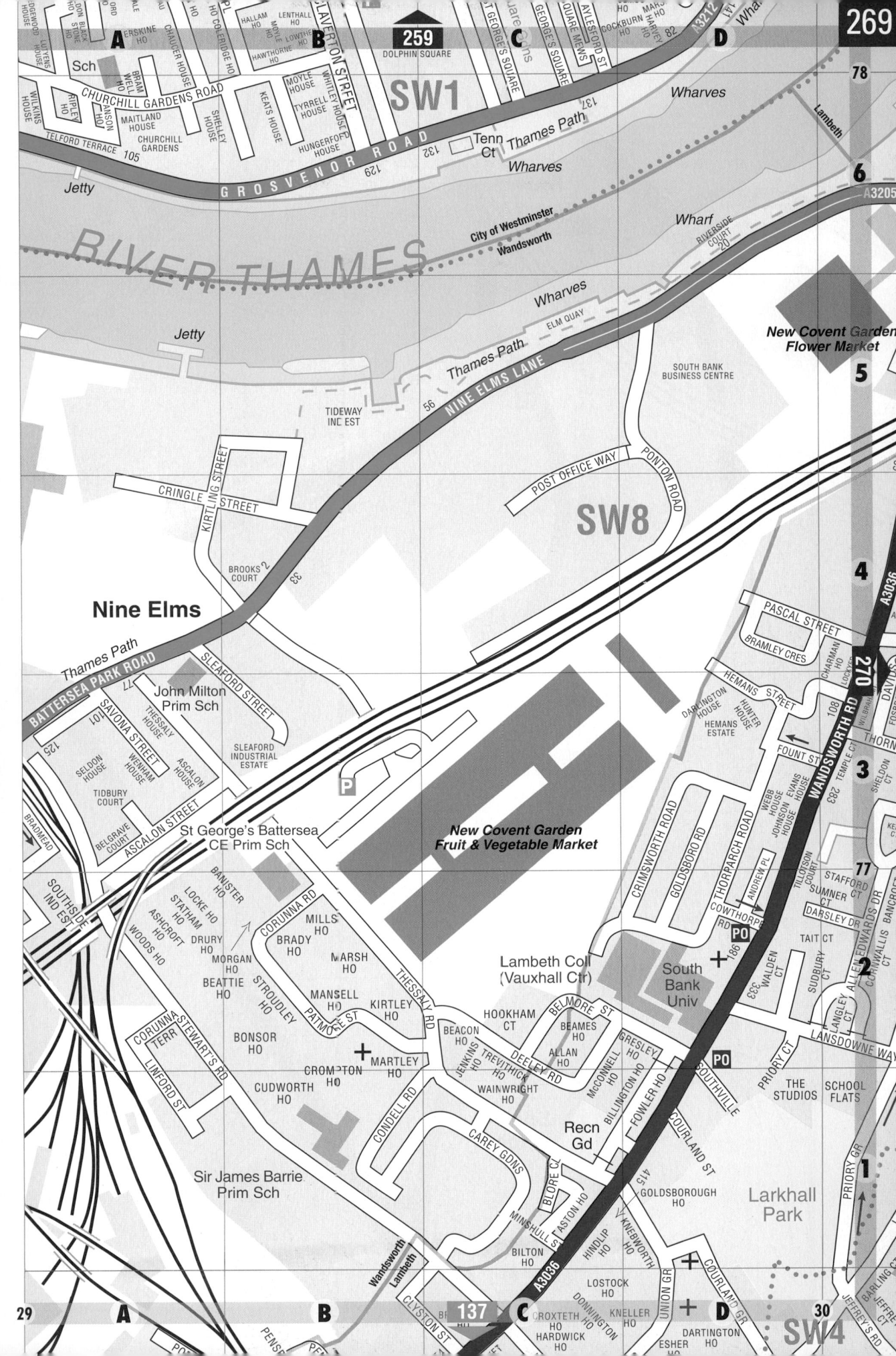
259
DOLPHIN SQUARE
A
B
C
D
SW1
CHURCHILL GARDENS ROAD
TELFORD TERRACE
CHURCHILL GARDENS
GROSVENOR ROAD
CLAVERTON STREET
ST GEORGE'S SQUARE
AYLESFORD ST
Thames Path
Wharves
Tenn Ct
Jetty
RIVER THAMES
City of Westminster
Wandsworth
Wharf
RIVERSIDE COURT
Lambeth
A3212
A3205
ELM QUAY
NINE ELMS LANE
TIDEWAY IND EST
SOUTH BANK BUSINESS CENTRE
New Covent Garden Flower Market
POST OFFICE WAY
PONTON ROAD
SW8
CRINGLE STREET
KIRTLING STREET
BROOKS COURT
Nine Elms
BATTERSEA PARK ROAD
SLEAFORD STREET
John Milton Prim Sch
SAVONA STREET
SLEAFORD INDUSTRIAL ESTATE
ASCALON STREET
TIDBURY COURT
BELGRAVE COURT
St George's Battersea CE Prim Sch
New Covent Garden Fruit & Vegetable Market
PASCAL STREET
BRAMLEY CRES
HEMANS STREET
HEMANS ESTATE
FOUNT ST
CRIMSWORTH ROAD
GOLDSBORO RD
THORPARCH ROAD
ANDREW PL
COWTHORPE RD
WANDSWORTH RD
A3036
270
SOUTHSIDE IND EST
BRADMEAD
CORUNNA RD
THESSALY RD
PATMORE ST
STEWART'S RD
CORUNNA TERR
LINFORD ST
Lambeth Coll (Vauxhall Ctr)
South Bank Univ
BELMORE ST
DEELEY RD
HOOKHAM CT
CONDELL RD
CAREY GDNS
Recn Gd
BLORE CL
COURLAND ST
SOUTHVILLE
LANSDOWNE WAY
PRIORY CT
THE STUDIOS
SCHOOL FLATS
Sir James Barrie Prim Sch
Larkhall Park
PRIORY GR
GOLDSBOROUGH HO
UNION GR
COURLAND GR
CLYSTON ST
Wandsworth
Lambeth
137
29
30
SW4
1
2
3
4
5
6

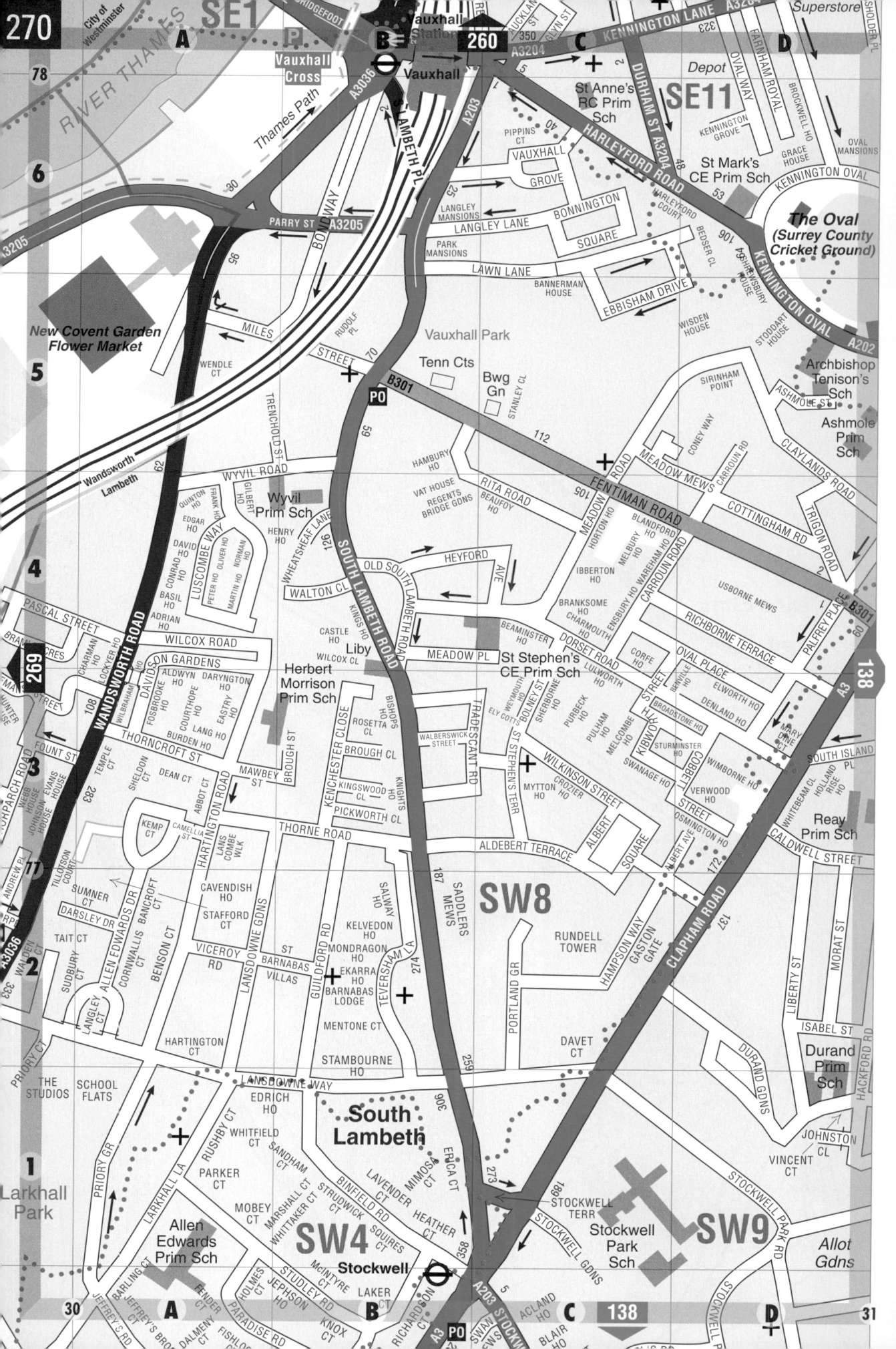
SE1
SE11
SW8
SW4
SW9
Vauxhall Station
Vauxhall Cross
Vauxhall
RIVER THAMES
Thames Path
New Covent Garden Flower Market
Vauxhall Park
Tenn Cts
Bwg Gn
St Anne's RC Prim Sch
St Mark's CE Prim Sch
The Oval (Surrey County Cricket Ground)
Archbishop Tenison's Sch
Ashmole Prim Sch
Wyvil Prim Sch
Herbert Morrison Prim Sch
St Stephen's CE Prim Sch
Reay Prim Sch
Durand Prim Sch
Allen Edwards Prim Sch
Stockwell Park Sch
South Lambeth
Stockwell
Larkhall Park
Allot Gdns
Depot
Superstore
Liby
KENNINGTON LANE
HARLEYFORD ROAD
KENNINGTON OVAL
DURHAM ST
SOUTH LAMBETH ROAD
WANDSWORTH ROAD
FENTIMAN ROAD
CLAPHAM ROAD
LANSDOWNE WAY
STOCKWELL PARK RD
WILKINSON STREET
ALDEBERT TERRACE
THORNE ROAD
PARRY ST
BOND WAY
LAMBETH PL
LAWN LANE
LANGLEY LANE
VAUXHALL GROVE
BONNINGTON SQUARE
EBBISHAM DRIVE
MILES STREET
WYVIL ROAD
PASCAL STREET
WILCOX ROAD
DAVIDSON GARDENS
THORNCROFT ST
HARTINGTON ROAD
LANSDOWNE GDNS
GUILDFORD RD
VICEROY RD
ST BARNABAS VILLAS
TEVERSHAM LA
OLD SOUTH LAMBETH ROAD
HEYFORD AVE
MEADOW PL
MEADOW ROAD
RITA ROAD
CARROUN ROAD
DORSET ROAD
RICHBORNE TERRACE
OVAL PLACE
CLAYLANDS ROAD
TRIGON ROAD
COTTINGHAM RD
USBORNE MEWS
PALFREY PLACE
CALDWELL STREET
SOUTH ISLAND PL
LIBERTY ST
MORAT ST
DURAND GDNS
RUNDELL TOWER
PORTLAND GR
HAMPSON WAY
GASTON GATE
ALBERT SQUARE
COBBETT STREET
TRADESCANT RD
STOCKWELL TERR
STOCKWELL GDNS
LARKHALL LA
PRIORY GR
BINFIELD RD
STUDLEY RD
PARADISE RD
A3036
A203
A3204
A3205
A202
A3
B301
260
269
138
30
31

Index

Church Rd **6** Beckenham BR2.........**53** C6 **228** C6

Place name
May be abbreviated on the map

Location number
Present when a number indicates the place's position in a crowded area of mapping

Locality, town or village
Shown when more than one place (outside London postal districts) has the same name

Postcode district
District for the indexed place

Standard scale reference
Page number and grid reference for the standard mapping

Enlarged scale reference
Page number and grid reference for the central London enlarged mapping, underlined in red

Public and commercial buildings are highlighted in **magenta**

Places of interest are highlighted in **blue** with a star★

Index of Localities, towns and villages

A

Abbey Wood 124 B3
Acton 111 B5
Acton Green 111 A2
Addington 223 C3
Addiscombe 206 A1
Aldborough Hatch 57 C5
Aldersbrook 77 C6
Alperton 88 A6
Anerley 184 B2
Arkley 12 A6
Ashford 170 B4
Ashford Common 171 B4
Avery Hill 167 B5

B

Balham 159 A3
Bandonhill 219 D3
Barbican 95 A2
Barking 79 B1
Barkingside 57 A6
Barnes 133 D4
Barnet 13 B6
Barnet Gate 11 D5
Barnsbury 72 A1
Battersea 136 D4
Bayswater 114 A6
Beckenham 185 C1
Beckton 100 D2
Becontree 81 A4
Beddington 220 A6
Beddington Corner 203 A2
Bedford Park 111 C3
Belgravia 115 B2
Bell Green 163 B1
Bellingham 185 C5
Belmont 25 B2
Belsize Park 70 C3
Belvedere 125 D2
Benhilton 218 A5
Bermondsey 118 A4
Berrylands 198 C3
Bethnal Green 96 B4
Bexley 146 B1
Bexleyheath 147 B2
Bickley 188 B1
Blackfen 168 A5
Blackheath 142 C2
Blackheath Park 143 A1
Blackheath Vale 142 D3
Blackwall 120 B6
Bloomsbury 93 D2
Borehamwood 11 C5
Borough The 117 A4
Bow 97 B5
Bow Common 97 D2
Bowes Park 32 A4
Brent Cross 46 D2
Brentford 131 B6
Brentford End 131 C4
Brimsdown 7 B3
Brixton 138 C2
Broad Green 204 D3
Broadgate 95 C2
Brockley 141 B1
Bromley 186 C2
Bromley (Tower Hamlets) 97 D4
Bromley Common 210 A3
Bromley Park 186 D2
Brompton 114 B3
Brondesbury 69 A2
Brondesbury Park 90 D6
Brook Green 112 D2
Broom Hill 211 D2
Brunswick Park 15 A1
Buckhurst Hill 21 C2
Burnt Oak 27 B3
Bush Hill Park 17 C5
Bushey 8 A2
Bushey Heath 8 C4
Bushey Mead 200 D6

C

Camberwell 139 A4
Camden Town 71 B1
Canary Wharf 119 D5
Canning Town 99 B1
Canonbury 73 A2
Canons Park 26 A3
Carshalton 218 C4
Carshalton Beeches 218 D1
Carshalton on the Hill 219 B1
Castle Green 102 C6
Catford 163 C3
Chadwell Heath 58 D4
Charlton (Greenwich) 143 D6
Charlton (Surrey) 171 B1
Chattern Hill 170 D6
Cheam 217 B3
Chelsea 114 C1
Chertsey Meads 192 A1
Chessington 214 A2
Child's Hill 69 C6
Chingford 20 C3
Chingford Green 20 A4
Chingford Hatch 36 B6
Chipping Barnet 1 B1
Chislehurst 189 C3
Chislehurst West 188 C4
Chiswick 111 D1
Church End (Barnet) 29 C1
Church End (Brent) 67 D2
City of London 117 A6
Clapham 137 B2
Clapham Common 137 B1
Clapham Junction 136 C1
Clapham Park 159 D6
Clapton Park 74 D4
Clay Hill 5 A6
Claygate 212 D1
Clayhall 56 B6
Clerkenwell 94 D3
Cockfosters 2 D1
Colham Green 82 C2
Colindale 45 C6
College Park 90 B4
Collier's Wood 180 C4
Colney Hatch 30 C4
Coney Hall 224 D5
Coombe 177 B3
Copse Hill 178 B3
Cottenham Park 178 B2
Covent Garden 116 A6
Cowley Peachy 82 A2
Cranbrook 56 C1
Cranford 128 C4
Cranley Gardens 49 B5
Creekmouth 101 D2
Cricklewood 68 D4
Crofton 227 B6
Crooked Billet 178 C4
Crouch End 49 D3
Croydon 221 B5
Crystal Palace 184 A5
Cubitt Town 120 A2
Custom House 121 C6
Cyprus 122 C6

D

Dagenham 81 D1
Dalston 74 A2
Dartmouth Park 71 B5
De Beauvoir Town 73 C1
Deacons Hill 10 C5
Deptford 140 D6
Dollis Hill 68 B5
Dormer's Wells 107 C6
Downham 186 C5
Ducks Island 12 D5
Dudden Hill 68 A3
Dulwich 161 C1
Dulwich Village 161 C4

E

Ealing 109 D6
Earl's Court 113 C1
Earlsfield 158 A3
East Acton 111 C5
East Barnet 14 D4
East Bedfont 149 C3
East Dulwich 162 A6
East Finchley 48 B5
East Ham 100 A5
East Molesey 196 A4
East Sheen 133 B1
East Wickham 146 A5
Eastbury 22 A5
Eastcote 40 C3
Eastcote Village 40 B4
Eden Park 207 C5
Edgware 26 C6
Edgware Bury 10 B3
Edmonton 33 D6
Elmers End 206 D6
Elmstead 188 A5
Elstree 10 A5
Eltham 166 B6
Enfield 6 B2
Enfield Highway 6 C3
Enfield Lock 7 B6
Enfield Town 5 B1
Enfield Wash 6 D5
Erith 147 D6
Esher 212 A4
Euston 93 C4
Ewell 215 C1

F

Fair Cross 79 D3
Falconwood 145 C1
Farnborough 227 B3
Farthing Street 226 B1
Feltham 150 A3
Felthamhill 171 D5
Finchley 29 D3
Finsbury 94 C4
Finsbury Park 50 D1
Fitzrovia 93 C1
Foots Cray 190 B4
Forest Gate 77 A3
Forest Hill 163 A3
Fortis Green 48 D5
Forty Hill 5 D4
Friday Hill 20 C1
Friern Barnet 31 A6
Fulham 134 D4
Furzedown 181 B6

G

Gants Hill 56 C3
Globe Town 96 D4
Golders Green 47 B4
Goodmayes 58 B1
Gospel Oak 70 D2
Grahame Park 27 C2
Grange Park 16 C6
Green Street Green 227 C2
Greenford 86 A4
Greenhill 42 D4
Greenwich 142 C6
Grove Park (Hounslow) 133 A4
Grove Park (Lewisham) 165 B1
Gunnersbury 110 D2

H

Hackbridge 219 B6
Hackney 74 B2
Hackney Wick 75 C2
Hadley 1 B2
Hadley Wood 2 B5
Haggerston 95 D5
Hale End 36 C4
Ham 153 C1
Hammersmith 112 C2
Hampstead 70 A3
Hampstead Garden Suburb 47 D4
Hampton 173 C1
Hampton Court 196 C5
Hampton Hill 174 A5
Hampton Wick 175 D3
Hanwell 108 D5
Hanworth 172 D6
Harlesden 89 D6
Harlington 127 A6
Harmondsworth 126 A6
Harringay 50 D4
Harrow 42 B3
Harrow on the Hill 42 C1
Harrow Weald 24 B2
Hatch End 23 A3
Hatton 127 D1
Hayes (Bromley) 209 A2
Hayes (Hillingdon) 83 C1
Hayes End 83 B3
Hayes Town 106 B5
Headstone 41 D5
Hendon 46 C3
Herne Hill 161 A6
Heston 129 B5
High Barnet 1 A2
Higham Hill 35 A2
Highams Park 36 A3
Highbury 72 D4
Highgate 49 A2
Hillingdon 82 D5
Hillingdon Heath 82 D2
Hinchley Wood 212 D6
Hither Green 164 C5
Holborn 94 C2
Homerton 74 D1
Honor Oak 162 C6
Hook 214 A4
Hornsey 50 A5
Hornsey Vale 50 B4
Hounslow 129 C3
Hounslow West 128 D2
Hoxton 95 C5
Hurst Park 174 A1
Hyde Park 114 D5
Hyde The 45 D4

I

Ickenham 60 C4
Ilford 78 D6
Isle of Dogs 120 A2
Isleworth 131 B2
Islington 72 D2

K

Kennington 116 C1
Kensal Green 90 C4
Kensal Rise 91 A5
Kensal Town 91 A3
Kensington 113 C4
Kentish Town 71 C3
Kenton 43 C3
Keston 225 D4
Keston Mark 225 D6
Kew 132 C6
Kidbrooke 143 C3
Kilburn 91 B6
King's Cross 94 A5
Kingsbury 45 B3
Kingsland 73 C2
Kingston Upon Thames 197 C6
Kingston Vale 177 B6
Kitts End 1 A5
Knightsbridge 114 C4

L

Ladywell 163 C6
Lambeth 116 B4
Lampton 129 D4
Lea Bridge 74 D5
Lee 74 D5
Lessness Heath 125 D1
Lewisham 142 A1
Leyton 76 B5
Leytonstone 54 D1
Limehouse 119 A6
Lisson Green 92 C3
Lisson Grove 92 B2
Little Heath 58 B5
Little Ilford 78 C3
Little Stanmore 26 B2
Littleton 192 C6
Littleton Common 171 B3
Locksbottom 226 D5
London City Airport 122 B5
Long Ditton 197 C1
Longlands 167 B1
Loughton 21 D5
Lower Clapton 74 C4
Lower Edmonton 18 B1
Lower Feltham 149 D1
Lower Green 195 D1
Lower Halliford 193 C3
Lower Holloway 72 A3
Lower Morden 201 A2
Lower Place 89 A5
Lower Sydenham 185 A6
Loxford 79 A3

M

Maida Vale 91 D4
Maitland Park 71 A2
Manor Park 78 A4
Marylebone 93 B1
Mayfair 115 B6
Merton 179 C2
Merton Park 179 C1
Mile End 97 A3
Mill Hill 28 B5
Mill Meads 98 B5
Millwall 119 C3
Mitcham 202 D5
Monken Hadley 1 A3
Monks Orchard 207 A3
Morden 201 D3
Morden Park 201 A3
Mortlake 133 A2
Motspur Park 200 A3
Mottingham 165 D2
Muswell Hill 49 A6

N

Nash 225 A2
Neasden 67 B4
New Addington 224 B1
New Barnet 14 A6
New Beckenham 185 A4
New Charlton 121 C2

New Cross ... 141 B4
New Cross Gate ... 140 D4
New Eltham ... 167 A2
New Malden ... 199 D5
New Southgate ... 31 C6
Newbury Park ... 57 B3
Newham ... 98 D4
Newington ... 116 D2
Newyears Green ... 38 B3
Nine Elms ... 137 C5
Noel Park ... 32 D1
Norbiton ... 176 C1
Norbury ... 182 C2
North Acton ... 89 B4
North Cheam ... 216 C6
North Cray ... 169 B1
North End ... 70 A6
North Feltham ... 150 B6
North Finchley ... 30 A6
North Harrow ... 41 D2
North Hillingdon ... 61 A2
North Hyde ... 107 A1
North Kensington ... 90 D2
North Sheen ... 132 C3
North Wembley ... 65 C6
North Woolwich ... 122 D4
Northolt ... 63 C1
Northwood ... 22 A3
Northwood Hills ... 22 A1
Norwood Green ... 107 C2
Norwood New Town 183 A4
Notting Hill ... 113 B6
Nower Hill ... 41 B6
Nunhead ... 140 C1

O

Oakleigh Park ... 14 B3
Oakwood ... 15 D6
Old Bexley ... 169 D4
Old Ford ... 97 B6
Old Malden ... 199 C1
Old Oak Common ... 89 D3
Orpington ... 227 D6
Osidge ... 15 C3
Osterley ... 130 B5

P

Paddington ... 92 A2
Palmers Green ... 16 A1
Park Langley ... 208 B4
Park Royal ... 88 D4
Parsons Green ... 135 C4
Peckham ... 140 A4
Penge ... 184 D4
Pentonville ... 94 B5
Perivale ... 87 B5
Petersham ... 153 D3
Petts Wood ... 211 B5
Pimlico ... 115 C1
Pinner ... 41 A6
Pinner Green ... 22 C1
Pinnerwood Park ... 22 C3
Plaistow (Bromley) ... 187 A4
Plaistow (Newham) ... 99 B4
Plashet ... 78 A2
Plumstead ... 123 C2
Plumstead Common 145 D6
Ponders End ... 18 D6
Poplar ... 97 C1
Preston ... 44 A1
Primrose Hill ... 70 D1
Putney ... 156 C6
Putney Heath ... 156 C6
Putney Vale ... 156 A1

Q

Queensbury ... 44 B6

R

Ratcliff ... 118 D6
Rayners Lane ... 41 B1
Raynes Park ... 200 C6
Redbridge ... 55 D3
Regent's Park ... 93 B4
Richmond ... 154 A6
Richmond Hill ... 154 A5
Richmond Park ... 155 A3
Roehampton ... 155 C4
Romford ... 59 C5
Rosehill ... 202 A1
Rotherhithe ... 118 D3
Roundshaw ... 220 B1
Roxeth ... 64 A6
Ruislip ... 39 B2
Ruislip Common ... 39 B4
Ruislip Gardens ... 61 D5
Ruislip Manor ... 40 A1
Ruxley ... 191 A3

S

Sands End ... 136 A2
Seething Wells ... 197 D3
Selhurst ... 205 B4
Selsdon ... 223 A1
Seven Kings ... 57 D2
Sewardstonebury ... 20 C6
Shacklewell ... 73 D4
Shadwell ... 118 C6
Shepherd's Bush ... 112 B5
Shepperton ... 193 A3
Shepperton Green ... 192 D5
Shirley ... 206 C1
Shooters Hill ... 145 A4
Shoreditch ... 95 B5
Shortlands ... 208 C6
Sidcup ... 190 A5
Silvertown ... 121 C4
Sipson ... 126 C6
Snaresbrook ... 54 D6
Soho ... 93 D1
Somers Town ... 93 D4
South Acton ... 110 D3
South Bank ... 116 B4
South Beddington ... 219 C2
South Bromley ... 98 B2
South Croydon ... 221 B1
South Hackney ... 96 C6
South Hampstead ... 70 A1
South Harrow ... 63 D5
South Kensington ... 114 A1
South Lambeth ... 138 A4
South Norwood ... 205 C6
South Oxhey ... 22 B6
South Ruislip ... 62 D4
South Tottenham ... 51 D4
South Wimbledon ... 179 D4
Southall ... 107 A5
Southborough (Bromley) ... 210 B3
Southborough (Kingston Upon Thames) ... 197 D1
Southend ... 186 B6
Southfields ... 157 C3
Southgate ... 16 B4
Southwark ... 117 B5
Spitalfields ... 95 D2
Spring Grove ... 130 C3
Spring Park ... 223 B5
St George in the East 118 A6
St Giles ... 94 A1
St Helier ... 202 B2
St James ... 115 C5
St John's ... 141 C3
St John's Wood ... 92 B5
St Luke's ... 95 A3
St Margarets ... 153 A5
St Pancras ... 94 A4
St Paul's Cray ... 190 A1
Stamford Hill ... 51 C1
Stanmore ... 25 B2
Stanwell ... 148 A3
Stepney ... 96 D2
Stockwell ... 138 A2
Stoke Newington ... 73 C6
Stonebridge ... 89 A6
Stoneleigh ... 216 A3
Strand ... 116 B6
Strand on the Green 132 C6
Stratford ... 76 A1
Stratford Marsh ... 97 D6
Stratford New Town ... 76 A3
Strawberry Hill ... 152 D1
Streatham ... 182 A4
Streatham Hill ... 160 A3
Streatham Park ... 181 C6
Streatham Vale ... 181 D3
Stroud Green ... 50 C3
Sudbury ... 65 A4
Summerstown ... 158 A1
Sunbury ... 194 B6
Sunbury Common ... 171 D3
Sundridge ... 187 C4
Surbiton ... 198 A2
Sutton ... 218 A1
Syon Park ... 131 B4

T

Teddington ... 175 C5
Temple Mills ... 75 D3
Thames Ditton ... 197 B2
Thamesmead ... 124 A5
Thornton Heath ... 204 D3
Tokyngton ... 66 D2
Tolworth ... 214 C6
Tooting ... 180 D4
Tooting Graveney ... 180 B5
Tottenham ... 33 D1
Tottenham Hale ... 52 A6
Totteridge ... 13 C3
Tower Hamlets ... 97 B2
Tufnell Park ... 71 D4
Tulse Hill ... 160 D4
Twickenham ... 152 D4

U

Underhill ... 13 C6
Upper Clapton ... 52 B1
Upper Edmonton ... 34 B5
Upper Elmers End ... 207 B4
Upper Halliford ... 193 B5
Upper Holloway ... 71 D6
Upper Norwood ... 183 C3
Upper Ruxley ... 191 C3
Upper Shirley ... 222 D4
Upper Sydenham ... 184 A6
Upper Tooting ... 158 D1
Upper Walthamstow ... 54 C6
Upton ... 77 B1
Upton Park ... 99 D6
Uxbridge ... 82 A6

V

Vale of Health ... 70 B5
Vauxhall ... 116 A1

W

Waddon ... 220 D4
Walham Green ... 135 D5
Wallend ... 100 C6
Wallington ... 219 A2
Walthamstow ... 53 D6
Walton-on-Thames ... 194 C2
Walworth ... 117 B1
Wandsworth ... 157 C5
Wanstead ... 55 C3
Wapping ... 118 B5
Waterloo ... 116 C4
Wealdstone ... 42 D6
Welling ... 146 B2
Welsh Harp ... 45 C1
Wembley ... 66 A2
Wembley Park ... 66 C5
West Acton ... 88 C1
West Barnes ... 200 C4
West Bedfont ... 148 C4
West Brompton ... 135 D6
West Drayton ... 104 B4
West Dulwich ... 161 A2
West Ealing ... 109 B5
West Ewell ... 215 C1
West Green ... 51 A5
West Ham ... 99 B6
West Hampstead ... 69 C4
West Harrow ... 42 A2
West Heath ... 146 D6
West Hendon ... 45 D3
West Hill ... 157 B5
West Kensington ... 113 A2
West Kilburn ... 91 A4
West Molesey ... 195 C5
West Norwood ... 161 A1
West Ruislip ... 61 B6
West Wickham ... 224 C6
Westbourne Green ... 91 D3
Westminster ... 115 C4
Weston Green ... 196 D1
Whetstone ... 14 A2
Whitechapel ... 95 D1
Whitton ... 152 A4
Widmore ... 188 A1
Willesden ... 68 A4
Willesden Green ... 90 B6
Wimbledon ... 179 B4
Wimbledon Park ... 157 B2
Winchmore Hill ... 16 D4
Wood End ... 83 D1
Wood End Green ... 83 C2
Wood Green ... 32 B2
Woodford ... 37 D5
Woodford Green ... 37 B3
Woodford Wells ... 21 B1
Woodlands ... 130 C2
Woodside ... 206 A4
Woodside Park ... 29 C6
Woolwich ... 122 D3
Worcester Park ... 215 C4
World's End ... 4 C1
Wrythe The ... 218 D6

Y

Yeading ... 84 D3
Yiewsley ... 104 A6

Abbreviations used in the index

Abbreviation	Meaning
Acad	Academy
App	Approach
Arc	Arcade
Art Gall	Art Gallery
Ave	Avenue
Bglws	Bungalows
Bldgs	Buildings
Bsns Ctr	Business Centre
Bsns Pk	Business Park
Bvd	Boulevard
Cath	Cathedral, Catholic
CE	Church of England
Cemy	Cemetery
Cir	Circus
Circ	Circle
Cl	Close
Cnr	Corner
Coll	College
Com	Community
Comm	Common
Comp	Comprehensive
Con Ctr	Conference Centre
Cotts	Cottages
Cres	Crescent
Cswy	Causeway
Ct	Court
Ctr	Centre
Crkt	Cricket
Ctry Pk	Country Park
Cty	County
Ctyd	Courtyard
Dr	Drive
Ent Ctr	Enterprise Centre
Ent Pk	Enterprise Park
Est	Estate
Ex Ctr	Exhibition Centre
Ex Hall	Exhibition Hall
Fst	First
Gdn	Garden
Gdns	Gardens
Gn	Green
Gr	Grove
Gram	Grammar
Her Ctr	Heritage Centre
Ho	House
Hospl	Hospital
Hts	Heights
Ind Est	Industrial Estate
Inf	Infant
Inst	Institute
Int	International
Intc	Interchange
Jun	Junior
Junc	Junction
La	Lane
L Ctr	Leisure Centre
Liby	Library
Mans	Mansions
Mdw/s	Meadow/s
Meml	Memorial
Mid	Middle
Mix	Mixed
Mkt	Market
Mon	Monument
Mus	Museum
Obsy	Observatory
Orch	Orchard
Par	Parade
Pas	Passage
Pav	Pavilion
Pk	Park
Pl	Place
Prec	Precinct
Prep	Preparatory
Prim	Primary
Prom	Promenade
RC	Roman Catholic
Rd	Road
Rdbt	Roundabout
Ret Pk	Retail Park
Sch	School
Sec	Secondary
Sh Ctr	Shopping Centre
Sp	Sports
Specl	Special
Sports Ctr	Sports Centre
Sq	Square
St	Street, Saint
Sta	Station
Stad	Stadium
Tech	Technical/Technology
Terr	Terrace
Trad Est	Trading Estate
Twr/s	Tower/s
Univ	University
Wlk	Walk
Yd	Yard

A

Aaron Ct BR3 207 D6
Abady Ho SW1 259 D4
Abberton IG8 37 C5
Abbess Cl 11 E6 100 A2
SW2 160 D3
Abbeville Mews 3
SW4 137 D1
Abbeville Rd N8 49 D5
SW4 159 C6
Abbey Ave HA0 88 A5
Abbey Bsns Ctr
SW8 137 B4 268 D2
Abbey Cl Hayes UB3 106 B5
Northolt UB5 85 B4
Pinner HA5 40 C6
Abbey Cres DA17 125 C2
Abbey Ct N3 47 C6
NW8 229 A4
SE17 262 B1
6 W12 111 C3
Abbey Dr SW17 181 A5
Abbey Gdns NW8 92 A5 229 B3
9 SE16 118 A2
W6 135 A6 264 A5
Abbey Gr SE2 124 B2
Abbey Ho E15 98 C5
NW8 229 B2
Abbey Ind Est CR4 202 D4
Abbey La E15 98 B5
Beckenham BR3 185 C3
Abbey Lane Commercial Est
E15 98 C5
Abbey Lo NW8 230 B1
1 W5 109 C6
Abbey Manufacturing Est
HA0 88 B6
Abbey Orchard St
SW1 115 D3 259 D6
Abbey Orchard Street Est
SW1 259 D6
Abbey Par NW10 88 B4
SW19 180 A3
Abbey Park Ind Est
IG11 101 A6
Abbey Pk BR3 185 C3
Abbey Prim Sch SE2 124 C3
Abbey Rd E15 98 C5
NW6 69 D1
NW8 92 A5 229 A4
NW10 88 D5
SW19 180 A2
Barking IG11 100 D6
Bexleyheath DA6,DA7 147 A1
Croydon CR0 220 D5
Enfield EN1 17 C6
Erith DA17 125 A3
Ilford IG2 57 B4
Lower Halliford TW17 192 C1
Abbey St E13 99 A3
SE1 117 D3 263 C6
Abbey Terr SE2 124 C2
Abbey View NW7 11 D1
Abbey Wlk KT8 195 D5
Abbey Wood Rd SE2 124 C2
Abbey Wood Sch SE2 124 A3
Abbey Wood Sta SE2 124 C3
Abbeydale Ct 6 UB1 85 D1
Abbeydale Rd HA0 88 C6
Abbeyfield UB4 83 D2
Abbeyfield Rd SE16 118 C2
Abbeyfields Cl NW10 88 C5
Abbeyhill Rd DA15 168 C2
Abbot Cl HA4 62 D5
Abbot Ct SW8 270 A3
Abbot Ho 13 E14 119 D6
Abbot St E8 73 D2
Abbots Cl BR5 211 A1
Abbots Ct SE25 205 C6
Abbots Dr HA2 63 C6
Abbots Gdns N2 48 B5
Abbots Gn CR0,CR2 222 D2
Abbots Ho E17 35 B1
SW1 259 C1
W14 254 C5
Abbots La SE1 117 C5 253 B3
Abbots Pk SW2 160 C3
Abbot's Pl NW6 91 D6
Abbots Rd E6 99 D6
Burnt Oak HA8 27 B3
Abbots Terr N8 50 A3
Abbots Way BR3 207 A4
Abbotsbury Cl E15 98 A5
W14 113 B4 244 C1
Abbotsbury Fst Sch
SM4 201 D4
Abbotsbury Gdns HA5 40 C3
Abbotsbury Ho W14 244 B2
Abbotsbury Mews SE15 140 C2
Abbotsbury Rd
W14 113 B4 244 C1
Coney Hall BR2,BR4 224 D6
Morden SM4 201 D5
Abbotsfield Sch UB10 82 D5
Abbotsford Ave N15 51 A5
Abbotsford Gdns IG8 37 A3
Abbotsford Rd IG3 80 B6
Abbotshade Rd 15
SE16 118 D5
Abbotshall Ave N14 15 C1
Abbotshall Rd SE6 164 B2
Abbotsleigh Cl SM2 217 D1
Abbotsleigh Rd SW16 181 C5
Abbotsmede Cl TW1 152 D2
Abbotstone Ho 4 E5 74 A6
Abbotstone Rd SW15 134 C2
Abbotswell Rd SE4 163 B6
Abbotswood Cl 7
DA17 125 A3
Abbotswood Gdns IG5 56 B6
Abbotswood Rd SE22 139 C1
SW16 159 D1
Abbotswood Way UB3 106 B5
Abbott Ave SW20 178 D2
Abbott Cl
Hampton TW12 173 A4
Northolt UB5 63 B2
Abbott Ho SW12 158 D4
Abbott Rd E14 98 B1
Abbotts Cl N1 73 A2
SE28 124 C6
Romford RM7 59 D6
Abbotts Cres E4 36 B6
Enfield EN2 4 D3
Abbotts Ct HA2 64 B6
Abbotts Dr HA0 65 B6
Abbotts Park Rd E10 54 A2
Abbotts Rd Barnet EN5 1 D1
Cheam SM1,SM2 217 A4
Mitcham CR4 203 C5
Southall UB1 107 A5
Abbott's Wlk DA7 146 D5
Abchurch La
EC2,EC4 117 B6 252 D6
Abchurch Yd EC4 252 C6
Abdale Rd W12 112 B5
Abel Ho 7 SE11 138 C6
Abenglen Ind Est UB3 105 B4
Aberavon Rd E3 97 A4
Abercairn Rd SW16 181 C3
Aberconway Rd SM4 201 D5
Abercorn Cl NW7 29 A3
NW8 92 A4 229 A2
Abercorn Cres HA2 41 D1
Abercorn Gdns
Harrow HA3 43 D2
Ilford RM6 58 B3
Abercorn Gr HA4 39 B5
Abercorn Ho SE10 141 D5
Abercorn Mans NW8 229 B3
Abercorn Pl
NW8 92 A5 229 A3
Abercorn Rd NW7 29 A3
Stanmore HA7 25 C3
Abercorn Trad Est HA0 87 D6
Abercorn Way SE1 118 A1
Abercrombie Dr EN1 6 A4
Abercrombie Ho 1
W12 112 B6
Abercrombie St SW11 136 C3
Aberdale Ct 22 SE16 118 D4
Aberdare Cl BR4 224 A6
Aberdare Gdns NW6 69 D1
NW7 28 D3
Aberdare Rd EN3 6 C1
Aberdeen Ct N5 73 A3
W2 236 C5
Aberdeen La N5 73 A3
Aberdeen Mans WC1 240 A6
Aberdeen Par N18 34 B5
Aberdeen Pk N5 73 A3
Aberdeen Pl
NW8 92 B3 236 C6
Aberdeen Rd N5 73 A4
N18 34 B5
NW10 67 D3
Croydon CR0 221 B4
Harrow HA3 24 D1
Aberdeen Terr SE3 142 B3
Aberdour Rd IG3 80 B6
Aberdour St
SE1 117 C3 263 A4
Aberfeldy Ho SE5 138 D5
Aberfeldy St E14 98 A1
Aberford Gdns SE18 144 A4
Aberfoyle Rd SW16 181 D4
Abergeldie Rd SE12 165 B5
Abernethy Rd SE13 142 C1
Abersham Rd E8 73 D3
Abery St SE18 123 C2
Abingdon W14 254 D3
Abingdon Cl NW1 71 D2
SE1 263 D2
SW19 180 A4
Hillingdon UB10 82 B6
Abingdon Ct W8 255 B5
Edgware HA8 26 A6
Abingdon Gdns W8 255 B5
Abingdon Ho E2 243 C6
Abingdon Lo BR2 186 D1
Abingdon Mans W8 255 A6
Abingdon Rd N3 30 A1
SW16 182 A2
W8 113 C3 255 B5
Abingdon St
SW1 116 A3 260 A6
Abingdon Villas
W8 113 C3 255 B5
Abinger Cl Barking IG11 80 A4
Bromley BR1 210 A6
Wallington SM6 220 A3
Abinger Ct 3 W5 109 C6
Wallington SM6 220 A3
Abinger Gdns TW7 130 C2
Abinger Gr SE8 141 B6
Abinger Ho SE1 252 C1
2 Kingston u T KT2 176 D3
Abinger Mews W9 91 C3
Abinger Rd W4 111 C3
Abington Ho NW11 48 A3
Ablett St SE16 118 C1
Abney Park Cemetery*
N16 73 C6
Abney Park Ct N16 73 D6
Aborfield 6 NW5 71 C3
Aboyne Dr SW20 178 A1
Aboyne Rd NW10 67 C5
SW17 158 B1
Abridge Way IG11 102 B5
Abyssinia Cl SW11 136 C1
Abyssinia Rd SW11 136 C1
Acacia Ave N2 47 D6
N17 33 B3
Brentford TW8 131 B5
Hayes UB3 83 D1
Littleton TW17 192 C4
Ruislip HA4 40 B2
Wembley HA9 66 A3
Yiewsley UB7 104 B6
Acacia Bsns Ctr 1 E11 76 C5
Acacia Cl SE8 119 A2
SE20 184 A1
Harrow Weald HA7 24 C4
Petts Wood BR5 211 B4
Acacia Ct 5 SW16 182 C5
Harrow HA1 41 D3
Acacia Dr SM3 201 C1
Acacia Gdns NW8 229 D4
West Wickham BR4 224 A6
Acacia Gr SE21 161 B2
Kingston u T KT3 199 C6
Acacia Ho N16 73 B6
N22 32 C2
1 New Malden KT3 199 C5
Acacia Pl NW8 92 B5 229 D4
Acacia Rd E11 76 C6
E17 53 A3
N22 32 C2
NW8 92 B5 229 D4
SW16 182 A2
W3 111 A6
Beckenham BR3 207 B6
Enfield EN2 5 B4
Hampton TW12 173 C4
Mitcham CR4 181 B1
Acacia Way DA15 167 D3
Acacia Wlk SW10 266 B3
Acacias Lo EN4 14 B6
Acacias The EN4 14 B6
Academy Ct 13 E2 96 C4
Academy Gdns
Croydon CR0 205 D1
Northolt UB5 84 D5
Academy Pl SE18 144 C4
Academy Rd SE18 144 B5
Academy The 2 N19 49 C1
Acanthus Dr SE1 118 A1
Acanthus Rd SW11 137 A2
Accadia Ct NW9 67 A6
Accommodation Rd
NW11 47 B1
Ace Par KT9 214 A5
Acer Ave UB4 85 A2
Acer Ct NW2 68 D4
Acfold Rd SW6 265 C1
Achilles Cl SE1 118 A1
Achilles Ho 16 E2 96 B5
Achilles Rd NW6 69 C3
Achilles St SE14 141 A5
Achilles Way W1 248 B3
Acklam Rd W10 91 B2
Acklington Dr NW9 27 C2
Ackmar Rd
SW6 135 C4 265 A1
Ackroyd Dr E3 97 C2
Ackroyd Rd SE23 163 A4
Acland Burghley Sch
NW5 71 B4
Acland Cl SE18 145 B5
Acland Cres SE5 139 B2
Acland Ho SW9 138 B3
Acland Rd NW2 68 B2
Acol Cres HA4 62 B3
Acol Ct 3 NW6 69 C1
Acol Rd NW6 69 D1
Aconbury Rd RM9 102 B6
Acorn Cl E4 35 D5
Chislehurst West BR7 189 A5
Enfield EN2 4 D4
1 Hampton TW12 173 D4
Stanmore HA7 25 B3
Acorn Ct E6 78 A1
Ilford IG2 57 C4
Acorn Gdns SE19 183 D2
W3 89 B2
Acorn Gr Harlington UB3 127 D5
Ruislip HA4 61 D4
Acorn Par 7 SE15 140 B5
Acorn Production Ctr
N7 72 A1
Acorn Way SE23 162 D1
Orpington BR6 226 D4
Acorn Wharf SE1 140 A6
Acorn Wlk SE16 119 A5
Acorns The 21 SW19 156 D3
Acorns Way KT10 212 A3
Acre Dr SE22 140 A1
Acre La SW2 138 B1
Carshalton SM5 219 A4
Acre Path UB5 63 A2
Acre Rd SW19 180 B4
Dagenham RM10 81 D1
Kingston u T KT2 176 B2
Acre Way HA6 22 A2
Acrefield Ho 4 NW4 46 D5
Acris St SW18 158 A6
Action Ct TW15 171 A2
Acton Central Ind Est 4
W3 110 D5
Acton Central Sta W3 111 B5
Acton Cl N9 18 A2
Acton High Sch W3 110 C4
Acton Hill Mews W3 110 D5
Acton Ho 16 E8 95 D6
5 W3 89 A1
Acton Hospl W3 110 C4
Acton La NW10 89 B5
W3 111 A4
W4 111 A2
Acton Main Line Sta W3 89 A1
Acton Mews E8 95 D6
Acton Park Est W3 111 B4
Acton St WC1 94 B4 233 C1
Acton Town Sta W3 110 C4
Acton Vale Ind Pk W3 111 D5
Acuba Ho SW18 157 D3
Acuba Rd SW18 157 D2
Acworth Cl N9 18 C4
Acworth Ho 1 SE18 144 D6
Ada Ct N1 235 A5
W9 92 A4 229 B1
Ada Gdns E14 98 B1
E15 98 D6
Ada Ho 23 E2 96 A6
Ada Kennedy Ct 6
SE10 142 A5
Ada Lewis Ho HA9 66 B4
Ada Pl E2 96 A6
Ada Rd SE5 139 C5
Wembley HA0,HA9 65 D5
Ada St E8 96 B6
Adair Cl SE25 206 B6
Adair Ho SW3 267 B6
Adair Rd W10 91 A3
Adair Twr 7 W10 91 A3
Adam & Eve Ct W1 239 B2
Adam & Eve Mews
W8 113 C3 255 B6
Adam Ct SE11 261 C3
Adam Lo N21 16 B6
Adam Rd E4 35 B4
Adam St WC2 116 A6 250 B5
Adam Wlk SW6 134 C5
Adamfields NW3 70 B1
Adams Cl N3 29 C3
NW9 66 D6
Surbiton KT5 198 B3
Adams Ct E17 53 A3
EC2 242 D2
Adams Gardens Est 5
SE16 118 C4
Adams Ho 3 E14 98 B1
3 SW16 181 C5
Adams Mews N22 32 B3
Adams Pl N7 72 B3
Adams Rd N17 33 B1
Beckenham BR3 207 A4
Adam's Row
W1 115 A6 248 B5
Adams Sq DA6 147 A2
Adams Way CR0 206 A3
Adams Wlk 11 KT1 176 A1
Adamson Ct N2 48 C6
Adamson Rd E16 99 A1
NW3 70 B1
Adamsrill Cl EN1 17 B5
Adamsrill Prim Sch
SE26 163 A1
Adamsrill Rd SE26 185 A6
Adare Wlk SW16,SW2 160 B2
Adcot Wlk 6 BR6 227 D4
Adderley Gdns SE9 188 C6
Adderley Gr SW11 159 A6
Adderley Rd HA3 24 D2
Adderley St E14 98 A1
Addey & Stanhope Sch
SE14 141 C4
Addey Ho SE8 141 B5
Addington Ct 7 SW14 133 B2
Addington Dr N12 30 B4
Addington Gr SE26 185 A6
Addington Ho 13 SW9 138 B3
Addington Palace (The Royal
Sch of Church Music)
CR9 223 B2
Addington Rd E3 97 C4
E16 98 C3
N4 50 C3
Thornton Heath CR0 204 C1
West Wickham BR4 224 C6
West Wickham BR4,CR0 224 B4
Addington Sq SE5 139 B5
Addington St
SE1 116 B4 250 D1
Addington Village Rd
CR0 223 C3
Addington Village Sta
CR0 223 C2
Addis Cl EN3 6 D4
Addiscombe Ave CR0 206 A2
Addiscombe Cl HA3 43 C4
Addiscombe Court Rd
CR0 221 C6
Addiscombe Ct UB10 83 A3
Addiscombe Rd CR0 222 B6
Addiscombe Sta CR0 206 A1
Addison Ave N14 15 C5
W11 113 A5 244 A3
Hounslow TW3 130 A4
Addison Bridge Pl
W14 113 B2 254 C4
Addison Cl
Northwood HA6 22 A2
Petts Wood BR5 211 A3
Addison Cres
W14 113 A3 254 B6
Addison Ct W5 110 C6
Addison Dr SE12 165 B6
Addison Gdns W14 112 D3
Kingston u T KT5 198 B5
Addison Gr W4 111 C3
Addison Ho NW8 92 B4 229 C2
Addison Park Mans 12
W14 112 D4
Addison Pl W11 113 A5 244 A3
Southall UB1 107 C6
Addison Prim Sch W14 112 D3
Addison Rd E11 55 A3
E17 54 A4
SE25 206 A5
W14 113 B3 254 C6
Bromley BR2 209 D4
Enfield EN3 6 D4
Teddington TW11 175 B4
Addison Way NW11 47 C5
Hayes UB3 84 A1
HA6 22 A2
Addison's Cl CR0 223 B6
Addle Hill EC4 241 D1
Addle St EC2 242 B3
Addlestone Ho W10 90 C2
Addy Ho SE16 118 C2
Adecroft Way KT8 196 A6
Adela Ave KT3 200 B5
Adela Ho 9 W6 112 C1
Adela St W10 91 A3
Adelaide Ave SE4 141 C1
Adelaide Cl Enfield EN1 5 C5
Stanmore HA7 25 A6
Adelaide Ct NW8 229 B3
W7 108 D4
15 Beckenham BR3 185 C3
Adelaide Gdns RM6 59 A4
Adelaide Gr W12 112 A5
Adelaide Ho E17 53 B6
Adelaide Rd E10 76 A5
NW3 70 C1
2 SW18 157 C6
W13 109 A4
Ashford TW15 170 A6
Chislehurst West BR7 188 D5
Heston TW5 129 A4
Ilford IG1 78 D6
Kingston u T KT6 198 A4
Richmond TW9 132 B1
Southall UB2 107 A2
Teddington TW11 174 D4
Adelaide St WC2 250 A5
Adelaide Terr TW8 109 D1
Adelaide Wlk SW9 138 C1
Adelina Gr E1 96 C2
Adelina Mews SW12 159 D3
Adeline Pl WC1 93 D2 239 D3
Adeliza Cl IG11 79 A1
Adelphi Cres UB4 83 D4
Adelphi Ct 20 SE16 118 D4
Adelphi Terr WC2 250 B5
Adelphi Way UB4 83 D4
Aden Gr N16 73 B4
Aden Ho 12 E1 96 D2
Aden Lo N16 73 B4
Aden Rd Enfield EN3 7 A1
Ilford IG1 57 A2
Adeney Cl W6 134 D6
Adenmore Rd SE6 163 C4
Adeyfield Ho EC1 235 D1
Adhara Rd HA6 22 A5
Adie Rd W6 112 C3
Adine Rd E13 99 B3
Adisham Ho 4 E5 74 B3
7 SE20 184 C3
Adler Ind Est UB3 105 B4
Adler St E1 96 A1
Adley St E5 75 A3
Adlington Cl N18 33 C5
Admaston Rd SE18 145 A6
Admiral Ct NW4 46 A4
SW10 136 A4 266 B2
W1 238 A3
Carshalton SM5 202 C1
Admiral Ho TW11 175 A6
Admiral Hyson Ind Est
SE16 118 B1
Admiral Mews W10 90 D3
Admiral Pl SE16 119 A5
Admiral Seymour Rd
SE9 144 B1
Admiral Sq
SW10 136 A4 266 B2
Admiral St SE8 141 C4
Admiral Wlk W9 91 C2
Admirals Cl E18 55 B5
Admirals Ct 3 E6 100 D1
SE1 253 C3
32 SW19 156 D3
Admirals Way E14 119 C4
Admiral's Wlk NW3 70 A5
Admiralty Arch* SW1 249 D4
Admiralty Cl 1 SE8 141 C4
Admiralty Rd TW11 174 D4
Adolf St SE6 185 D6
Adolphus Rd N4 50 D1
Adolphus St SE8 141 B5
Adomar Rd RM8 81 A5
Adpar St W2 92 B2 236 C4
Adrian Ave NW2 46 B1
Adrian Bolt Ho 2 E2 96 B4
Adrian Ho N1 233 D5
SW8 270 A4
Adrian Mews SW10 265 D6
Adriatic Ho 18 E1 96 D3
Adrienne Ave UB1 85 B4
Adron Ho 9 SE16 118 C2
Adstock Ho 5 N1 72 D1
ADT Coll SW15 157 B6
Advance Rd SE27 183 A6
Advent Way N18 34 D5
Adys Lawn NW2 68 B2
Adys Rd SE15 139 D2
Aerodrome Rd NW4,NW9 45 D6
Aerodrome Way TW5 128 C6
Aeroville NW9 27 C1
Affleck St N1 233 D3
Afghan Rd SW11 136 C3
Agamemnon Rd NW6 69 B3
Agar Cl KT6 214 B6
Agar Gr NW1 71 D1
Agar Ho 6 KT1 198 A6
Agar Pl NW1 71 C1
Agar St WC2 250 B5
Agate Cl E16 99 D1
Agate Ho 12 SE26 184 B5
New Malden KT4 199 C1
Agate Rd W6 112 C3
Agatha Cl E1 118 C5
Agaton Rd BR7,SE9 167 A2
Agave Rd NW2 68 C4
Agdon St EC1 94 D3 241 C6
Agincourt E11 54 D3
Agincourt Rd NW3 70 D4
Agnes Ave IG1 78 D4
Agnes Cl E6 122 C6
Agnes Ct 11 SW18 136 B1
Agnes Gdns RM8 80 D4
Agnes Ho 13 W11 112 D6
Agnes Rd W3 111 D4
Agnes St E14 97 B1
Agnesfield Cl N12 30 C4
Agnew Rd SE23 162 D4
Agricola Pl EN1 17 D6
Aidan Cl RM8 81 A4
Aidans Ct N12 30 C5
Aigburth Mans 5 SW9 138 C5
Ailantus Ct HA8 26 B5
Ailsa Ave TW1 153 B6
Ailsa Rd TW1 153 B6
Ailsa St E14 98 A2
Ainger Rd NW3 70 D1
Ainsdale NW1 232 A2
Ainsdale Cl BR6 211 B1
Ainsdale Cres HA5 41 C6
Ainsdale Dr SE1 118 A1
Ainsdale Rd W5 87 D3
Ainsley Ave RM7 59 D3
Ainsley Cl N9 17 C3
Ainsley St E2 96 B4
Ainsley Wood Prim Sch
E4 35 D5
Ainslie Ct 2 HA0 88 A5
Ainslie Wood Cres E4 35 D5
Ainslie Wood Gdns E4 35 D5
Ainslie Wood Rd E4 35 B5
Ainsty St 14 SE16 118 C4
Ainsworth Cl NW2 68 A5
SE5 139 C3
Ainsworth Est
NW8 92 A6 229 A6
Ainsworth Ho NW8 91 D6
Ainsworth Rd E9 74 C1
Croydon CR0 220 D6
Ainsworth Way
NW8 92 A6 229 A6
Aintree Ave E6 100 A6
Aintree Cl UB8 82 D2
Aintree Ho SE26 184 B4
Aintree Rd UB6 87 B5
Aintree St SW6 135 A5 264 B4
Air Call Bsns Ctr NW9 45 C6
Air St W1 249 B5
Airborne Ho 10 SM6 219 B4
Aird Ho SE1 262 A5
Airdrie Cl N1 72 B1
Hayes UB4 85 A2
Airedale Ave W4 111 D1
Airedale Ave S W4 111 D1
Airedale Rd SW12 158 D4
W5 109 D3
Airlie Gdns W8 113 C5 245 A3
Ilford IG1 56 D1
Airlinks Ind Est TW5 106 C1
Airport Rdbt E16 121 D5
Airthrie Rd IG3 80 B6
Aisgill Ave SW5 113 B1 254 D1
Aisher Rd SE28 124 C6
Aislibie Rd SE12 142 C1
Aislobie Ho N21 17 B5
Aiten Pl W6 112 A2
Aithan Ho 9 E14 97 B1
Aitken Cl E8 96 A6
Carshalton CR4 202 D2
Aitken Rd SE6 163 D2
Ducks Island EN5 12 C6
Ajax Ave NW9 45 C6
Ajax Ho 15 E2 96 B5
Ajax Rd NW6 69 C3
Akabusi Cl SE25 206 A3
Akbar Ho 7 E14 119 D2
Akehurst St SW15 156 A4
Akenside Ct 3 NW3 70 B3
Akenside Rd NW3 70 B3
Akerman Rd SW9 138 D4
Kingston u T KT6 197 C3
Akintaro Ho 7 SE8 141 B6
Akiva Sch N3 29 D1
Al Sadiq & Al Zahra Schs
NW6 91 A6
Alabama St SE18 145 C5
Alacross Rd W5 109 D4
Alan Dr EN5 13 A5
Alan Gdns RM7 59 C2
Alan Hocken Way E15 98 C5
Alan Lo N3 29 C2
Alan Preece Ct NW6 68 D1

Alan Rd SW19 179 A5
Alanbrooke Ho 2 SE18 144 A5
Aland Ct SE16 119 A3
Alandale Dr HA5 22 B2
Alanthus Cl SE12 165 A5
Alaska St SE1 251 A3
Alba Cl UB4 84 D3
Alba Gdns NW11 47 A3
Alba Pl W11 91 B1
Albacore Cres SE13 163 D5
Albain Cres TW15 148 A2
Alban Ho NW3 70 A2
Albans Cl SW16 160 A1
Albany N12 29 D4
W1 249 A5
Albany Cl N15 50 D5
SW14 132 D1
Bexley DA5 168 D4
Bushey WD2 8 B5
Ickenham UB10 60 C3
Albany Cres
Claygate KT10 212 C2
Edgware HA8 26 C3
Albany Ct E10 53 C2
NW10 90 B4
SW1 259 C6
Burnt Oak HA8 27 B2
Kingston u T KT2 176 A4
Richmond TW10 153 B1
E4 19 D5
Albany Ctyd W1 249 B5
Albany Ho E5 74 C6
6 Brentford TW8 132 A6
Albany Mans SW11 267 B3
Albany Mews N1 72 C1
SE5 139 A6
Kingston u T KT2 175 D4
Sutton SM1 217 D3
Albany Par 4 TW8 132 A6
Albany Park Ave EN3 6 D4
Albany Park Rd KT2 176 A4
Albany Park Sta DA14 168 D2
Albany Pl N7 72 C4
Brentford TW8 131 D6
Albany Rd E10 53 C2
E12 77 D4
E17 53 A3
N4 50 C3
N18 34 C5
SE5 139 C6
SW19 179 D5
W13 109 B6
Brentford TW8 131 D6
Chislehurst West BR7 188 D5
Dagenham RM6 59 B3
Enfield EN3 6 D5
Erith DA17 147 B6
New Malden KT3 199 B5
Richmond TW10 154 A6
Sidcup DA5 168 C4
Albany Reach KT7 196 D4
Albany Sch EN3 6 D5
Albany St NW1 93 B4 231 D2
Albany Terr 6 TW10 154 B6
Albany The IG8 36 D6
Albany View IG9 21 A3
Albany Wlk N15 50 D5
Albatross 31 NW9 27 D1
Albatross St SE18 145 C5
Albemarle SW19 156 D2
Albemarle App IG2 56 D3
Albemarle Ave TW2 151 B3
Albemarle Gdns
Ilford IG2 56 D3
New Malden KT3 199 B5
Albemarle Ho SE8 119 B2
Albemarle Lo SE26 185 A5
Albemarle Mans NW3 69 D4
Albemarle Pk
Beckenham BR3 185 D2
Stanmore HA7 25 C5
Albemarle Rd
Beckenham BR2,BR3 186 A2
East Barnet EN4 14 C4
Albemarle St
W1 115 C6 249 A5
Albemarle Way EC1 241 C5
Albermarle Ho 3 SW9 138 C2
Albermarle Prim Sch
SW19 157 A2
Albermarle Prim Sch
(Annexe) SW19 157 A3
Alberon Gdns NW11 47 B5
Albert Ave E4 35 C6
SW8 270 C3
Albert Barnes Ho SE1 262 A5
Albert Bigg Point E15 98 A6
Albert Bridge Rd
SW11 136 D5 267 C3
Albert Carr Gdns SW16 182 A5
Albert Cl 11 E9 96 B6
N22 31 D2
Albert Cotts 2 E1 96 A2
Albert Cres E4 35 C6
Albert Ct SW7 246 C1
9 SW19 157 A3
Albert Dr SW19 157 A3
Albert Emb SE1 116 A2 260 B3
Albert Gate Ct SW1 247 C1
Albert Gdns E1 96 D1
Albert Gr SW20 178 D2
Albert Gray Ho SW10 266 C4
Albert Hall Mans
SW7 114 B4 246 C1
Albert Ho 5 E18 55 B6
Albert Mans N8 50 A2
SW11 267 C2
Albert Memorial*
SW7 114 B4 246 C1
Albert Mews W8 256 A6
Albert Palace Mans
SW11 268 B2
Albert Pl N3 29 C2
W8 113 D4 245 D1
Albert Rd E10 54 A1
E16 122 B4
E17 53 C4
4 E18 55 B6
N4 50 B2
N15 51 C3
N22 31 C2
NW4 46 D5
NW6 91 B5
NW7 27 D5
SE9 166 A1
SE20 184 D4
SE25 206 B5
W5 87 B3
Ashford TW15 170 B5
Bromley BR2 209 D4
Buckhurst Hill IG9 21 D2
Dagenham RM8 59 C1
East Barnet EN4 2 A1
Erith DA17 125 B1
Hampton TW12 174 A5
Harrow HA2 42 A6
Hayes UB3 105 C3
Hounslow TW3 129 C1
Ilford IG1 79 A5
Kingston u T KT1 176 B1
Mitcham CR4 202 D6
New Malden KT3 199 D5
Old Bexley DA5 169 D4
Richmond TW10 154 B6
Southall UB2 106 D3
Sutton SM1 218 B3
Teddington TW11 174 D4
Twickenham TW1 152 D3
Yiewsley UB7 104 A5
Albert Sq E15 76 C3
SW8 138 B5 270 C3
Albert St N12 30 A5
NW1 93 B6 231 D5
Albert Starr Ho 7 SE8 118 D2
Albert Studios SW11 267 C2
Albert Terr NW1 93 A6 231 A5
NW10 89 A6
Buckhurst Hill IG9 21 D2
Albert Terr Mews NW1 231 A5
Albert Victoria Ho N22 32 C2
Albert Westcott Ho
SE17 261 D2
Albert Whicher Ho 8
E17 54 A5
Albert Wlk E16 122 D4
Alberta Ave SM1 217 B3
Alberta Ct 1 TW10 154 B6
Alberta Ho E14 120 A5
Hayes UB4 84 B4
Alberta Rd Enfield EN1 18 A5
Erith DA7 147 D4
Alberta St SE17 116 D1 261 D2
Albion Ave N10 31 A2
SW8 137 D3
Albion Cl W2 247 B6
Albion Ct 2 SE7 122 A2
7 W6 112 B2
Sutton SM2 218 B1
Albion Dr E8 74 A1
Albion Est SE16 118 C4
Albion Gate W2 247 B6
Albion Gdns 1 W6 112 B2
Albion Gr N16 73 C4
Albion Hill IG10 21 D6
Albion Ho E16 122 D5
Albion Jun & Inf Sch
SE16 118 C4
Albion Mews N1 234 A6
W2 114 C6 247 B6
6 W6 112 B2
Albion Pk IG10 21 D6
Albion Pl EC1 241 C4
EC2 242 D3
SE25 206 A6
W6 112 B2
Albion Rd E17 54 A6
N16 73 B4
N17 34 A1
Bexleyheath DA6 147 C1
Hayes UB3 83 C1
Hounslow TW3 129 C1
Kingston u T KT2 177 A2
Sutton SM2 218 B1
Twickenham TW2 152 C3
Albion Sq E8 73 D1
Albion St SE16 118 C4
W2 114 C6 247 B6
Thornton Heath CR0 204 D1
Albion Terr E4 7 D1
E8 73 D1
Albion Villas Rd SE23,
SE26 162 C1
Albion Way EC1 242 A3
SE13 142 A1
Wembley HA9 66 C5
Albion Wharf SW11 267 A4
Albion Yd N1 233 B3
Albon Ho SE14 141 B4
SW18 157 D5
Albrighton Rd SE5,SE22 139 C2
Albuhera Cl EN2 4 C4
Albury Ave
Bexleyheath DA7 147 A3
Albury Ave *continued*
Hounslow TW7 130 D5
Albury Bldgs SE1 251 D1
Albury Cl TW12 173 D4
Albury Ct
4 Croydon CR0 221 A4
Mitcham CR4 180 B1
6 Northolt UB5 84 C4
Sutton SM1 218 A4
Albury Dr HA5 22 D3
Albury Lo 7 SW2 160 B4
Albury Mews E12 77 C6
Albury Rd KT9 214 A3
Albury St SE8 141 C6
Albyfield BR1 210 B6
Albyn Rd SE8 141 C4
Alcester Cres E5 74 B6
Alcester Ct 4 SM6 219 B4
Alcester Rd SM6 219 B4
Alcock Cl SM6 219 D1
Alcock Rd TW5 128 D5
Alconbury DA6 169 D6
Alconbury Rd E5 74 A6
Alcorn Cl SM3 217 C6
Alcott Cl W7 86 D2
Aldborough Ct E4 19 D1
Ilford IG2 57 D4
Aldborough Rd IG2 57 D6
Aldborough Rd N IG2 57 D4
Aldborough Rd S IG3 57 C2
Aldbourne Rd W12 112 A5
Aldbridge St
SE17 117 C1 263 B2
Aldburgh Mews W1 238 B2
Aldbury Ave HA9 66 D1
Aldbury Ho SW3 257 A3
Aldbury Mews N9 17 B4
Aldebert Terr
SW8 138 B5 270 C3
Aldeburgh Cl 16 E5 74 B6
Aldeburgh Pl IG8 37 A6
Aldeburgh St SE18 121 A1
Alden Ave E15 98 D4
Alden Ct SW19 179 C4
South Croydon CR0 221 C5
Alden Ho E8 96 B6
Aldenham Ctry Pk WD6 9 B6
Aldenham Dr UB8 82 D3
Aldenham Ho NW1 232 B3
Aldenham Rd WD6 9 C6
Aldenham St
NW1 93 D5 232 C3
Aldensley Rd W6 112 B3
Alder Ct N2 48 B6
3 SW16 182 C5
Alder Gr NW2 68 B6
Alder Ho 1 NW3 70 D2
SE4 141 C2
SE15 139 D6
Alder Lo SW6 134 D4
Alder Mews 9 N19 71 C6
Alder Rd SW14 133 B2
Sidcup DA14 167 D1
Alderbrook Prim Sch
SW12 159 B4
Alderbrook Rd SW12 159 B5
Alderbury Rd SW13 134 A6
Aldergrove Gdns TW4 129 A3
Aldergrove Ho 3 E5 74 A6
Alderholt Way 9 SE15 139 C5
Alderley Ho 36 SW8 137 D3
Alderman Ave IG11 102 A4
Alderman Judge Mall 6
KT1 176 A1
Aldermanbury
EC2 95 A1 242 B2
Aldermanbury Sq EC2 242 B3
Alderman's Hill N13 32 B6
Alderman's Wlk EC2 243 A3
Aldermary Rd BR1 187 A2
Aldermead 2 TW3 129 D1
Aldermoor Rd SE6 163 B1
Alderney Ave TW5 129 D5
Alderney Gdns UB5 63 B1
Alderney Ho 16 N1 73 A2
Enfield EN3 6 D5
Alderney Rd E1 96 D3
Alderney St
SW1 115 B1 258 D2
Alders Ave IG8 36 C4
Alders Cl E11 77 B6
W5 109 D3
Edgware HA8 27 A5
Alders Ct N17 52 B5
Alders Rd HA8 27 A5
Alders The N21 16 C5
SW16 181 C6
Feltham TW13 173 A6
Heston TW5 129 B6
West Wickham BR4 223 D6
Aldersbrook Ave EN1 5 C3
Aldersbrook Dr KT2 176 B4
Aldersbrook House Coll of
Railway Tech E12 78 C5
Aldersbrook La E12 78 B5
Aldersbrook Prim Sch
E12 77 C6
Aldersbrook Rd E12,E11 77 C6
Aldersey Gdns IG11 79 B2
Aldersford Cl SE4 140 D1
Aldersgate Ct EC1 242 A3
Aldersgate St
EC1 95 A2 242 A3
Aldersgrove KT8 196 B4
Aldersgrove Ave SE9,
SE12 165 D1
Aldershot Rd NW6 91 B6
Aldersmead Ave CR0 206 D3
Aldersmead Rd BR3 185 A3
Alderson Pl UB2 108 A5
Alderson St W10 91 A3
Alderton 9 KT2 176 D2
Alderton Cl NW10 67 B5
Alderton Cres NW4 46 B4
Alderton Ct KT8 195 B5
Alderton Rd SE24 139 A2
Croydon CR0 206 A2
Alderton Way NW4 46 B4
Alderville Rd SW6 135 B3
Alderwick Ct N7 72 B2
Alderwick Dr TW3 130 B2
Alderwood Prim Sch
SE9 167 C5
Alderwood Rd SE9 167 B5
Aldford St W1 115 A5 248 B4
Aldgate EC3 95 C1 243 B1
Aldgate East Sta
E1 95 D1 243 D2
Aldgate High St
EC3 95 D1 243 C1
Aldgate Sta EC3 95 D1 243 C1
Aldham Hall 1 E11 55 A3
Aldham Ho SE4 141 B4
Aldine Ct W12 112 C5
Aldine St W12 112 C4
Aldington Cl RM8 58 C1
Aldington Ct 1 E8 74 A1
Aldington Rd SE18 121 D3
Aldis Mews SW17 180 C5
Aldis St SW17 180 C5
Aldred Rd NW6 69 C3
Aldren Rd SW17 158 A1
Aldrich Gdns SM3 217 B5
Aldrich Terr SW18 158 A2
Aldriche Way E4 36 A4
Aldrick Ho N1 233 D4
Aldridge Ave
Edgware HA8 10 D1
Enfield EN3 7 C5
Ruislip HA4 62 D6
Stanmore HA7 26 A2
Aldridge Ct W11 91 B2
Aldridge Rd Villas W11 91 B2
Aldridge Rise KT3 199 C3
Aldridge Wlk N14 16 A4
Aldrington Rd SW16 181 C6
Aldsworth Cl W9 91 D3
Aldwick Cl BR7 167 B1
Aldwick Ct N12 30 A6
Aldwick Rd CR0 220 B4
Aldworth Gr SE13 164 A5
Aldworth Rd E15 76 C1
Aldwych WC2 94 B1 240 D1
Aldwych Ave IG6 57 A5
Aldwych Bldgs WC2 240 B2
Aldwyn Ho SW8 270 A3
Alers Rd DA6 168 D6
Alesia Cl N22 32 A3
Alestan Beck Rd E16 99 D1
Alex Gossip Ho SW6 265 A1
Alexander Ave NW10 68 B1
Alexander Cl Barnet EN4 2 B1
Hayes BR2 209 A1
Sidcup DA15 167 C5
Southall UB2 108 A5
Twickenham TW2 152 D2
Alexander Ct SE3 143 B3
SW18 158 A6
Beckenham BR3 186 B2
Stanmore HA7 44 B6
14 Surbiton KT6 197 D2
Alexander Evans Mews
SE23 162 D2
Alexander Ho 9 E14 119 C3
Alexander McLeod Jun Sch
SE2 124 B1
Alexander McLeod Prim Sch
SE2 124 B1
Alexander Mews 2 W2 91 D1
Alexander Pl SW7 257 A4
Alexander Rd N19 72 A6
Bexley DA16 146 D3
Chislehurst West BR7 188 D5
Alexander Sq
SW3 114 C2 257 A4
Alexander St W2 91 C1
Alexander Terr SE2 124 B1
Alexandra Ave N22 31 D2
SW11 268 A1
Harrow HA2 63 C5
Southall UB1 107 B6
Sutton SM1 217 C5
Alexandra Bsns Ctr EN3 6 D1
Alexandra Cl
Ashford TW15 171 B3
Harrow HA2 63 D5
Alexandra Cotts SE14 141 B4
SE20 184 D4
Alexandra Cres BR1 186 D4
Alexandra Ct N14 15 C6
4 N16 73 D4
W5 87 C2
W9 236 B6
5 W12 112 A4
Ashford TW15 171 B4
Greenford UB6 85 D5
Hounslow TW3 129 D3
Wembley HA9 66 B4
Alexandra Dr SE19 183 C5
Surbiton KT5 198 C2
Alexandra Gdns N10 49 B5
W4 133 C5
Hounslow TW3 129 D3
Wallington SM5 219 A1
Alexandra Gr N4 50 D1
N12 29 D4
Alexandra Ho 18 W6 112 C1
Alexandra Inf Sch
Kingston u T KT2 176 C3
Penge BR3 184 D3
Alexandra Jun & Inf Sch
TW3 129 D3
Alexandra Jun Sch
SE26 184 D4
Alexandra Mans 6 NW6 69 C3
SW3 266 C5
Alexandra Mews N2 48 D6
Alexandra National Ho
N4 72 D6
Alexandra Palace* N22 31 D1
Alexandra Palace Sta
N22 32 A1
Alexandra Palace Way
N10 49 C6
Alexandra Park Rd N10,
N22 31 D2
Alexandra Park Sec Sch
N22 31 C2
Alexandra Pl
NW8 92 A6 229 B6
SE25 205 B4
Croydon CR0 205 C1
Alexandra Prim Sch N22 32 B1
Alexandra Rd E6 100 C4
E10 76 A5
E17 53 B2
E18 55 B6
N8,N22 50 C6
N9 18 B4
N10 31 B3
N15 51 B4
NW4 46 D5
NW8 70 B1
SE26 184 D4
SW14 133 B2
SW19 180 C3
SW19 179 C5
W4 111 B4
Ashford TW15 171 C4
10 Brentford TW8 131 D6
Croydon CR0 205 C2
Dagenham RM6 59 A3
Enfield EN3 6 D1
Hounslow TW3 129 D3
Kingston u T KT2 176 C3
Richmond TW9 132 B3
Thames Ditton KT7 196 D4
Twickenham TW1 153 C5
Alexandra Sch HA2 63 C6
Alexandra Sq SM4 201 C4
Alexandra St E16 99 A2
5 SE14 141 A5
Alexandra Wlk 8 SE19 183 C5
Alexandria Rd W13 109 B6
Alexis St SE16 118 A2
Alfearn Rd E5 74 C4
Alford Ct N1 235 B3
5 Sutton SM2 217 D1
Alford Gn CR0 224 B2
Alford Ho N6 49 C3
6 SE18 144 D6
Alford Pl N1 235 B3
Alfoxton Ave N8,N15 50 D5
Alfred Butt Ho SW17 158 D1
Alfred Cl W4 111 B2
Alfred Findley Ho N22 32 D1
Alfred Gdns UB1 107 A6
Alfred Ho E9 75 A3
Alfred Hurley Ho SW17 180 A6
Alfred Mews W1,WC1 239 C4
Alfred Mizen Prim Sch The
CR4 203 D6
Alfred Nunn Ho NW10 89 D6
Alfred Pl WC1 93 D2 239 C4
Alfred Prior Ho 6 E12 78 C4
Alfred Rd E15 76 D3
SE25 206 A4
W2 91 C2
W3 111 A5
Buckhurst Hill IG9 21 D2
Erith DA17 125 B1
Feltham TW13 150 C2
Kingston u T KT1 198 B6
Sutton SM1 218 A3
Alfred Salter Ho SE1 263 D3
Alfred Salter Prim Sch
SE16 118 D4
Alfred St E3 97 B4
Alfred Villas 9 E17 54 A5
Alfreda Ct SW11 268 C1
Alfreda St SW11 137 B4 268 C1
Alfred's Gdns IG11 101 C5
Alfred's Way (East Ham &
Barking By-Pass)
IG11 101 B5
Alfred's Way Ind Est
IG11 102 A6
Alfreton Cl SW19 156 D1
Alfriston KT5 198 B3
Alfriston Ave Harrow HA2 41 C2
Thornton Heath CR0 204 A2
Alfriston Cl KT5 198 B3
Alfriston Rd SW11 158 D6
Algar Cl Harrow HA7 24 D5
Isleworth TW7 131 A2
Algar Ho SE1 251 C1
Algar Rd TW7 131 A2
Algarve Rd SW18 157 D3
Algernon Rd NW4 46 A3
NW6 91 C6
SE13 141 D1
Algers Cl IG10 21 D6
Algers Rd IG10 21 D6
Alghers Mead IG10 21 D6
Algiers Rd SE13 141 C1
Alguin Ct HA7 25 C3
Alibon Gdns RM10 81 C3
Alibon Rd RM10 81 C3
Alice Ct SW15 135 B1
Alice Gilliott Ct W14 264 D6
Alice La E3 97 B6
Alice Mews 8 TW11 174 D5
Alice Owen Tech Ctr
EC1 234 C2
Alice Shepherd Ho 7
E14 120 A4
Alice St SE1 117 C3 263 A5
Alice Thompson Cl
SE12 165 C2
Alice Walker Cl 8
SE24 138 D1
Alice Way TW3 129 D1
Alicia Ave HA3 43 C5
Alicia Cl HA3 43 C5
Alicia Gdns HA3 43 C5
Alicia Ho DA16 146 B4
Alie St E1 95 D1 243 D1
Alington Cres NW9 45 A1
Alison Cl E6 100 C1
Croydon CR0 206 D1
Alison Ct 1 SE1 118 A1
Aliwal Rd SW11 136 C1
Alkerden Rd W4 111 C1
Alkham Rd N16 73 D6
All England Lawn Tennis &
Croquet Club The
SW19 157 A1
All Hallows Rd N17 33 C2
All Saints' Benhilton CE Prim
Sch SM1 217 D5
All Saints Carshalton CE Sch
SM5 219 A3
All Saints CE Prim Sch
SW6 135 A3
SW15 134 C2
SW19 180 A3
All Saints' CE Prim Sch
N20 14 B2
NW2 69 B5
SE3 142 C3
All Saints' Cl N9 18 A2
All Saints Ct 9 E1 118 C6
E5 74 C4
Heston TW5 128 D4
All Saints Dr SE3 142 D3
All Saints Mews HA3 24 C4
All Saints Pas SW18 157 C6
All Saint's Prim Sch
SE19 183 C2
All Saints RC Sch RM8 59 C1
All Saints Rd SW19 180 A3
W11 91 B1
Sutton SM1 218 A5
All Saints' Rd W3 111 A3
All Saints St N1 94 B5 233 C4
All Saints Sta E14 119 D6
All Saints Twr 18 E10 53 D2
All Souls' Ave NW10 90 B6
All Souls CE Prim Sch
W1 93 C2 239 A4
All Souls Pl W1 238 D3
All Souls Specl Sch UB8 82 A4
Allam Ho W11 244 A6
Allan Barclay Cl N15 51 D3
Allan Cl KT3 199 B4
Allan Ho SW8 269 C2
Allan Way W3 89 A2
Allanbridge N16 51 C2
Allandale Ave N3 47 B6
Allanson Ct E10 75 C6
Allard Cres WD2 8 A2
Allard Gdns SW4 159 D6
Allardyce St SW4,SW9 138 B1
Allbrook Cl TW11 174 C5
Allbrook Ho 4 SW15 156 A4
Allcot Cl TW14 149 D3
Allcott Ho TW7 130 D2
Allcroft Rd NW5 71 A2
Allen Cl Streatham CR4 181 C2
Sunbury TW16 172 B2
Allen Ct E17 53 C3
Allen Edwards Dr
SW8 138 A4 270 A2
Allen Edwards Prim Sch
SW4 138 A4 270 A1
Allen Ho W8 255 B6
Allen Mans W8 255 B6
Allen Rd E3 97 B5
N16 73 C4
Penge BR3 184 D1
Sunbury TW16 172 B1
Thornton Heath CR0 204 C1
Allen St W8 113 C3 255 B5
Allenby Cl UB6 85 C4
Allenby Inf Sch UB1 85 D1
Allenby Rd SE23 163 A1
Southall UB1 85 C3
Allendale Ave UB1 85 C1
Allendale Cl SE5 139 B4
SE26 184 D5
Allendale Rd UB6 65 B2
Allendale Sch
W8 113 C3 255 B6
Allenford Ho 1 SW15 155 D5
Allens Rd EN3 18 C6
Allensbury Pl NW1 72 A1
7 NW1 71 D1
Allenswood 12 SW19 157 A3
Allenswood Rd SE9 144 B3
Allerdale Ho 7 N4 51 B2
Allerford Ct SE6 163 D1
Harrow HA2 42 A4

Allerford Rd SE6 185 D6
Allerton Ct SM3 216 D6
Allerton Ho N1 235 D3
4 SW19 180 A3
Allerton Rd N16 73 A6
Allerton St N1 235 D2
Allerton Wlk 11 N7 72 B6
Allestree Rd
SW6 135 A5 264 A3
Alleyn Cres SE21 161 B2
Alleyn Ho EC1 242 B5
SE1 262 C5
Alleyn Pk SE21 161 C1
Southall UB2 107 C1
Alleyn Rd SE21 161 C1
Alleyndale Rd RM8 80 C6
Alleyn's Sch SE22 161 C6
Allfarthing La SW18 158 A5
Allfarthing Prim Sch
SW18 158 A5
Allgood Cl SM4 200 D3
Allgood St 10 E2 95 D5
Allhallows La EC4 252 C5
Allhallows Rd E6 100 A1
Alliance Cl HA0 65 D4
Alliance Ct W3 88 D2
Ashford TW15 171 A6
Alliance Rd E16 99 C2
SE18 146 A5
W3 88 D3
Allied Ind Est W3 111 C5
Allied Way W3 111 C4
Allingham Cl W7 108 D6
Allingham Ct NW3 70 C3
Allingham St N1 95 A5 235 A4
Allington Ave N17 33 C4
Sunbury TW17 193 C6
Allington Cl 3 SW19 178 D5
Northolt UB6 64 A1
Allington Ct 6 SW8 137 C3
Croydon CR0 206 C3
Allington Rd NW4 46 B3
W10 91 A5
Harrow HA2 42 A4
Orpington BR6 211 C1
Allington St SW1 258 D5
Allison Cl SE10 142 A4
Allison Gr SE21 161 C3
Allison Rd N8 50 D4
W3 111 A6
Alliston Ho 27 E2 95 D4
Allitsen Rd NW8 92 C5 230 A4
Allnutt Way SW4 159 D6
Alloa Ct N14 15 C2
Alloa Rd SE8 119 A1
Ilford IG3 80 A6
Allom Ct 11 SW4 138 A3
Allonby Dr HA4 38 D2
Allonby Gdns HA9 43 C1
Allonby Ho E14 97 A2
Alloway Rd E3 97 A4
Allport Ho SE5 139 B2
Allsop Pl NW1 92 D3 237 D5
Allum La Elstree WD6 10 A6
WD6 10 A6
Allum Way N20 14 A3
Allwood Cl SE26 184 D6
Alma Ave E4 36 A3
Alma Birk Ho 1 NW6 69 B1
Alma Cl N10 31 B2
Alma Cres SM1 217 A3
Alma Gr SE1 117 D2 263 D3
Alma Ho E5 74 B5
2 N9 34 A6
7 Brentford TW8 132 A6
Alma Pl NW10 90 B4
SE19 183 D3
Thornton Heath CR7 204 C4
Alma Prim Sch SE16 118 A2
Enfield EN3 18 D6
Alma Rd N10 31 B3
SW18 158 A6
Carshalton SM5 218 C3
Enfield EN3 7 A1
Sidcup DA14 168 A1
Southall UB1 107 A6
Thames Ditton KT10,KT7 196 C1
Alma Row HA3 24 B2
Alma Sq NW8 92 A4 229 B2
Alma St E15 76 B2
NW5 71 B2
Alma Terr SW18 158 B4
W8 255 B5
Almack Rd E5 74 C4
Almeida St 10 N1 72 D1
Almer Rd SW20 178 A3
Almeric Rd SW11 136 D1
Almington St N4 50 B1
Almond Ave W5 110 A3
Carshalton SM5 218 D6
Uxbridge UB10 60 D5
West Drayton UB7 104 C3
Almond Cl SE15 140 A3
Bromley BR2 210 C2
Charlton TW17 171 A1
Hayes UB3 105 C6
Ruislip HA4 61 D5
Almond Gr TW8 131 B5
Almond Ho SE4 141 B3
Almond Rd N17 34 A3
SE16 118 B2
Almond Way
Bromley BR2 210 C2
Harrow HA2 24 A1
Mitcham CR4 203 D5
Almonds Ave IG9 21 A2
Almondsbury Ct 7
SE15 139 C5
Almorah Rd N1 73 B1
Heston TW5 128 D4
Almshouse La EN1 6 B6
Almshouses E10 75 D6
Sunbury TW16 171 D2
Almshouses The IG11 79 A2
Alnmouth Ct 10 UB1 86 A1
Alnwick 8 N17 34 B3
Alnwick Gr SM4 201 D5
Alnwick Rd E16 99 C1
SE12 165 B4
Alonso Ct 4 DA17 125 C1
Alperton Com Lower Sch
HA0 87 D6
Alperton Com Upper Sch
HA0 66 B1
Alperton La UB6 87 D5
Alperton St W10 91 B3
Alperton Sta HA0 88 A6
Alpha Bsns Ctr E17 53 B4
Alpha Cl NW8 92 C4 230 B1
Alpha Ct 6 NW5 71 B2
Alpha Est The UB3 105 C4
Alpha Gr E14 119 C4
Alpha Ho NW6 91 C5
NW8 237 B5
Alpha Pl NW6 91 C5
SW3 136 C6 267 B6
Alpha Rd E4 19 D1
N18 34 A4
SE14 141 B4
Croydon CR0 205 C1
Enfield EN3 7 A1
Hillingdon UB10 82 D3
Surbiton KT5 198 B3
Teddington TW12 174 B5
Alpha St SE15 140 A3
Alphabet Gdns SM5 202 B3
Alphabet Sq E3 97 C2
Alphea Cl SW19 180 C3
Alpine Ave KT5 215 A6
Alpine Bsns Ctr E6 100 C2
Alpine Cl CR0 221 C5
Alpine Copse 2 BR1 188 C1
Alpine Rd SE16 118 D1
Walton-on-T KT12 194 A2
Alpine View SM1 218 C3
Alpine Way E6 100 C2
Alpine Wlk HA7 8 C2
Alric Ave NW10 67 B1
New Malden KT3 199 D6
Alroy Rd N4 50 C2
Alsace Rd SE17 117 C1 263 A2
Alscot Rd SE1 117 D3 263 D5
Alscot Road Ind Est
SE1 263 D5
Alscot Way SE1 263 C4
Alsike Rd DA18 125 A3
Alsom Ave KT19,KT4 216 A4
Alston Cl KT7 197 B2
Alston Ct EN5 1 A2
Alston Rd N18 34 B5
SW17 180 B6
High Barnet EN5 1 A2
Alt Gr SW19 179 A3
Altair Cl N17 33 D4
Altash Way SE9 166 C2
Altenburg Ave W13 109 B3
Altenburg Gdns SW11 136 D1
Altham Rd HA5 23 A3
Althea St SW6 135 D2
Althorpe Mews SW11 266 D1
Althorne Gdns E18 54 D5
Althorne Way RM10 81 C6
Althorp Cl EN5 12 A4
Althorp Rd SW17 158 D3
Althorpe Rd HA1 42 A4
Altior Ct N6 49 C3
Altmore Ave E6 100 B6
Altmore Inf Sch E6 100 B6
Alton Ave HA7 24 D3
Alton Cl Isleworth TW7 130 D3
Sidcup DA5 169 A3
Alton Ct 18 BR3 185 C3
Alton Gdns
Beckenham BR3 185 C3
Twickenham TW2 152 B4
Alton Ho 3 E3 97 D4
Alton Rd N17 51 B6
SW15 156 A3
Croydon CR0 220 C5
Richmond TW10,TW9 132 A1
Alton St E14 97 D2
Altyre Cl BR3 207 B4
Altyre Rd CR0 221 B6
Altyre Way BR3 207 B4
Alum Ct KT5 198 B3
Alumni Ct SE1 253 D2
Alvanley Ct NW3 69 D3
Alvanley Gdns NW6 69 D3
Alvanley Ho 14 SW9 138 C4
Alverston Gdns SE25 205 C4
Alverstone Ave
SW18,SW19 157 C2
East Barnet EN4 14 C4
Alverstone Gdns SE9 167 A3
Alverstone Ho 11 SE11 138 C6
Alverstone Rd E12 78 C4
NW2 68 C1
New Malden KT3 199 D5
Wembley HA9 44 B1
Alverton St SE8 141 B6
Alveston Ave HA3 43 B6
Alvey St SE17 263 A2
Alvia Gdns SM1 218 A4
Alvington Cres E8 73 D3
Alway Ave KT19 215 B3
Alwold Cres SE12 165 C5
Alwyn Ave W4 111 B1
Alwyn Cl Deacons Hill WD6 10 B5
New Addington CR0 223 D1
Alwyn Gdns NW9 46 A5
W3 88 C1
Alwyne La N1 72 D1
Alwyne Pl N1 73 A1
Alwyne Rd N1 73 A1
SW19 179 B4
W7 108 C6
Alwyne Sq N1 73 A2
Alwyne Villas N1 72 D1
Alyn Ct N8 49 D3
Alyth Gdns NW11 47 C3
Alzette Ho 11 E2 96 D5
Amalgamated Dr TW8 131 B6
Amanda Ct TW15 148 B2
Amar Ct SE18 123 D2
Amardeep Ct SE18 123 D1
Amazon St E1 96 B1
Ambassador Cl TW3 129 A3
Ambassador Ct 9 NW6 69 C3
Ambassador Gdns E6 100 B2
Ambassador Ho NW8 229 B5
Ambassador Sq E14 119 D2
Amber Ave E17 35 A2
Amber Ct N7 72 C2
NW9 45 C6
Mitcham CR4 202 C5
Amber Gr NW2 46 D1
Amber St E15 76 B2
Amberden Ave N3 47 C6
Ambergate St
SE17 116 D1 261 D2
Amberley Cl
2 Orpington BR6 227 D3
Pinner HA5 41 B6
Amberley Ct 2 SW9 138 D2
Foots Cray DA14 190 C5
Sutton SM2 218 A1
Amberley Gdns
Enfield EN1 17 C4
Worcester Pk KT19 215 D4
Amberley Gr SE26 184 B5
Croydon CR0 205 D2
Amberley Ho EN5 1 D1
Amberley Rd E10 53 D2
N13 16 B2
SE2 146 D6
W9 91 C2
Buckhurst Hill IG9 21 C3
Enfield EN1 17 D5
Amberley Way
Heston TW4 150 C6
Morden SM4 201 B2
Romford RM7 59 D5
Uxbridge UB10 82 A5
Amberside Cl TW2 152 B5
Amberwood Cl SM6 220 A3
Amberwood Rise KT3 199 C3
Amblecote Cl SE12 165 B1
Amblecote Mdw SE12 165 B1
Amblecote Rd SE12 165 B1
Ambler JMI Sch N4 72 D6
Ambler Rd N4 72 D5
Ambleside NW1 231 D3
13 SW19 157 A3
Catford BR1 186 B4
Ambleside Ave SW16 181 D6
Beckenham BR3 207 A4
Walton-on-T KT12 194 C1
Ambleside Cl E9 74 C3
E10 53 D2
Ambleside Cres EN3 6 D2
Ambleside Cty Jun Sch
KT12 194 C1
Ambleside Dr TW14 149 D3
Ambleside Gdns SW16 181 D5
Redbridge IG4 56 A4
Sutton SM2 218 A2
Wembley HA9 43 D1
Ambleside Point 1
SE15 140 C5
Ambleside Rd NW10 67 D1
Bexleyheath DA7 147 C3
Ambrook Rd DA17 125 C3
Ambrosden Ave
SW1 115 C3 259 B5
Ambrose Ave NW11 47 B3
Ambrose Cl 6 E6 100 B2
Orpington BR6 227 D5
Ambrose Ho 9 E14 97 C2
Ambrose Mews 2
SW11 136 D3
Ambrose St SE16 118 B2
Ambrose Wlk E3 97 C5
AMC Bsns Ctr NW10 88 D4
Amelia Ho 5 W6 112 C1
Amelia St SE17 117 A1 262 A2
Amen Cnr EC4 241 D1
SW17 181 A4
Amen Ct EC4 94 D1 241 D1
Amenity Way SM4 200 C2
America Sq EC3 253 C6
America St SE1 252 A3
American Coll The
W1 93 A1 238 B2
American Com Schs
UB10 82 B6
American Sch in London The
NW8 92 B5 229 C4
Amerland Rd SW18 157 B5
Amersham Ave N18 33 B4
Amersham Gr SE14 141 B5
Amersham Rd SE14 141 B4
Thornton Heath CR0 205 B3
Amersham Vale SE14,
SE8 141 B5
Amery Gdns NW10 90 B6
Amery Ho SE17 263 B2
Amery Rd HA1 65 A6
Ames Cotts 14 E3 97 A2
Ames Ho 10 E2 96 D5
Amesbury Ave SW2 160 B2
Amesbury Cl KT4 200 C1
Amesbury Ct EN2 4 C3
Amesbury Dr E4 19 D5
Amesbury Rd
Bromley BR1 209 D6
Dagenham RM9 80 D1
Feltham TW13 150 D2
Amesbury Twr 4 SW8 137 C3
Amethyst Rd E15 76 B4
Amherst Ave W13 87 C1
Amherst Dr BR5 211 D5
Amherst Gdns 2 W13 87 C1
Amherst JMI Sch E8 74 A3
Amherst Rd W13 87 C1
Amhurst Ct N4 51 B2
Amhurst Gdns TW7 131 A3
Amhurst Par N16 51 D2
Amhurst Pk N4,N16 51 C2
Amhurst Rd E8,N16 74 A4
Amhurst Terr E8 74 A4
Amhurst Wlk SE28 124 A5
Amias Ho EC1 242 A6
Amidas Gdns RM8 80 B4
Amiel St 17 E1 96 C3
Amies St SW11 136 D2
Amigo Ho SE1 261 B6
Amina Way SE16 118 A3
Amis Ave KT19 214 D3
Amity Gr SW20 178 C2
Amity Rd E15 76 D1
Ammanford Gn NW9 45 C3
Amner Rd SW11 159 A5
Amor Rd W6 112 C3
Amory Ho N1 233 D4
Amott Rd SE15 140 A2
Amoy Pl E14 119 C6
Ampere Way
Croydon CR0 204 B1
Croydon CR0 204 B1
Ampleforth Rd SE2 124 C4
Ampton Pl WC1 233 C1
Ampton St WC1 94 B4 233 C1
Amroth Cl SE23 162 B3
Amroth Gn NW9 45 C3
Amstel Ct 11 SE15 139 D5
Amsterdam Rd E14 120 A3
Amundsen Ho 5 NW10 67 B1
Amwell Cl EN2 17 B6
Amwell St EC1 94 C4 234 A2
Amy Cl SM6 220 A1
Amy Johnson Ho HA8 26 D1
Amy Johnson Prim Sch
SM6 220 A1
Amy Warne Cl E6 100 A3
Amyand Cotts 12 TW1 153 B5
Amyand Park Gdns 2
TW1 153 B4
Amyand Park Rd TW1 153 B4
Amyruth Rd SE4 163 C6
Anarth Ct KT13 193 C1
Anatola Rd N19 71 C6
Ancaster Cres KT3 200 A3
Ancaster Rd BR3 206 D6
Ancaster St SE18 145 C5
Anchor & Hope La SE7 121 C2
Anchor Bsns Pk CR0,
SM6 220 A5
Anchor Ct 5 EN1 17 C6
Anchor Ho E16 99 C1
EC1 242 A6
Ilford IG3 80 A5
Anchor Mews SW12 159 B5
Anchor St SE16 118 B2
Anchor Terr SE1 252 B4
Anchor Yd EC1 242 B6
Anchorage Cl SW19 179 C5
Anchorage Point E14 119 C4
Ancill Cl W6 135 A6 264 A5
Ancona Rd NW10 90 A5
SE18 123 B1
Andace Pk BR1 187 C2
Andalus Rd SW9 138 A2
Andaman Ho 3 E1 97 A2
Ander Cl HA0 65 D4
Anderson Cl N21 16 B6
W3 89 B1
Anderson Ct NW2 46 C2
Anderson Dr TW15 171 A6
Anderson Ho 10 E14 120 A6
SW17 180 B5
Barking IG11 101 B5
Anderson Rd E9 74 D2
Woodford IG8 55 D6
Anderson St SW3 257 C2
Anderson Way DA17 125 D4
Anderson's Pl TW3 129 D1
Anderton Cl SE5 139 B2
Anderton Ct N22 31 D1
Andhurst Ct KT2 176 D2
Andon Ct BR3 207 A6
Andorra Ct BR1 187 C2
Andover Ave E16 99 D1
Andover Cl
East Bedfont TW14 149 D3
Greenford UB6 85 D3
Andover Ho 5 N7 72 B6
Andover Pl NW6 91 D5
Andover Rd N7 72 B6
Orpington BR6 211 C1
Twickenham TW2 152 B3
Andoversford Ct 7
SE15 139 C6
Andre St E8 74 A3
Andreck Ct BR3 186 A1
Andrew Borde St WC2 239 D2
Andrew Ct SE23 162 D2
Beckenham BR3 207 D6
Andrew Ewing Prim Sch
TW5 129 B5
Andrew Ho SE4 141 B3
SW15 156 A6
Andrew Marvell Ho 12
N16 73 C4
Andrew Pl SW8 269 D2
Andrew Reed Ho SW18 157 A4
Andrew St E14 98 A1
Andrew Wells Ho BR1 187 B3
Andrewes Gdns E6 100 A1
Andrewes Ho EC2 242 B3
Sutton SM1 217 C4
Andrews Cl
Buckhurst Hill IG9 21 C2
Harrow HA1 42 B2
North Cheam KT4 216 D6
St Paul's Cray BR5 190 D1
Andrews Crosse WC2 241 A1
Andrews Ct 2 W7 108 C5
Andrew's Rd E8 96 B6
Andrews Wlk SE17 138 D6
Andringham Lo 4 BR1 187 B2
Andrula Ct N22 32 D2
Andwell Cl SE2 124 B4
Anerley Ct SE20 184 B3
Anerley Gr SE19 183 D3
Anerley Hill SE19 183 D4
Anerley Park Rd SE20 184 B3
Anerley Pk SE20 184 B3
Anerley Prim Sch SE20 184 A2
Anerley Rd SE20 184 B2
Anerley Sch SE20 184 A2
Anerley Sta SE20 184 B2
Anerley Station Rd
SE20 184 B2
Anerley Vale SE19 184 A3
Aneurin Bevan Ct NW2 68 B6
Aneurin Bevan Ho N11 31 D3
Anfield Cl SW12 159 C4
Angel Alley E1 243 D2
Angel Cl N18 34 A6
Angel Corner Par 6
N18 34 A6
Angel Ct EC2 242 D2
SW1 249 B3
Angel Edmonton N18 34 A5
Angel Gate EC1 234 D2
Angel Hill SM1 217 D5
Angel Hill Dr SM1 217 D5
Angel Ho N1 234 B3
Angel La E15 76 B2
Hayes UB3 83 B2
Angel Mews E1 118 B6
N1 234 B3
SW15 156 A4
Angel Pas EC4 117 B6 252 C5
Angel Pl 1 N18 34 A5
SE1 252 C2
Angel Prim Sch
N1 94 C5 234 B4
Angel Rd Harrow HA1 42 C3
Thames Ditton KT7 197 A1
Angel Rd (North Circular Rd)
N18 34 B5
Angel Rd Works N18 34 C5
Angel Road Sta N18 34 C5
Angel St EC1 95 A1 242 A2
Angel Sta EC1 94 C5 234 B3
Angel Wlk W6 112 C2
Angela Ct 2 SE23 162 C3
Angela Davis Ind Est 21
SW9 138 D1
Angelfield TW3 151 D6
Angelica Cl UB7 82 B1
Angelica Dr E6 100 C2
Angelica Gdns CR0 206 D1
Angelina Ho 2 SE15 140 A4
Angell Park Gdns 5
SW9 138 C2
Angell Rd SW9 138 D2
Angerstein Bsns Pk
SE10 121 A2
Angerstein La SE3 142 D4
Angle Cl UB10 82 C6
Angle Gn RM8 58 C1
Anglebury 5 W2 91 C1
Anglers La NW5 71 B2
Anglers Reach KT6 197 D4
Angles Rd SW16 182 A6
Anglesea Ave 4 SE18 122 D2
Anglesea Ho KT1 197 D5
Anglesea Rd SE18 122 D2
Kingston u T KT1 197 D5
Anglesey Cl TW15 148 C1
Anglesey Court Rd
SM5 219 A2
Anglesey Ct W7 86 D3
Anglesey Gdns SM5 219 A2
Anglesey Ho 9 E14 97 C1
Anglesey Rd Enfield EN3 6 B1
South Oxhey WD1 22 C5
Anglesey St SE18 123 A3
Anglesmede Cres HA5 41 C6
Anglesmede Way HA5 41 C6
Anglia Cl N17 34 B3
Anglia Ho 15 E14 97 A1
Anglian Ind Est IG11 101 D2
Anglian Rd E11 76 B5
Anglo American Laundry
SW17 158 A1
Anglo Rd 24 E3 97 B5
Angrave Ct 4 E8 95 D6
Angrave Pas 5 E8 95 D6
Angus Cl KT9 214 C3
Angus Dr HA4 62 C4
Angus Gdns NW9 27 B2
Angus Ho 12 SW12 159 D4
Angus Rd E13 99 C4
Angus St SE14 141 A5
Anhalt Rd SW11 136 C5 267 B4
Ankerdine Cres SE18 144 D4
Anlaby Rd TW11 174 C5
Anley Rd W14 112 D4
Anmersh Gr HA7 25 D2
Ann La SW10 136 B6 266 C5
Ann Moss Way SE16 118 C3
Ann Parkes Ct TW5 128 D3
Ann St SE18 123 B2
Ann Stroud Ct SE12 165 A6
Anna Cl E8 95 D6
Anna Neagle Cl 2 E7 77 A4
Annabel Cl E14 97 D1
Annandale Gr UB10 61 A5
Annandale Prim Sch
SE10 120 D1
Annandale Rd SE10 120 D1
W4 111 C1
Croydon CR0 222 A6
Sidcup DA15 167 D4
Anne Boleyn's Wlk
Cheam SM3 217 A1
Kingston u T KT2 176 A5
Anne Carver Lo HA0 66 A1
Anne Goodman Ho 3
E1 96 C1
Anne Kerr Ct 18 SW15 156 D5
Anne St E13 99 A3
Anne Way KT8 195 D5
Annesley Ave NW9 45 B6
Annesley Cl NW10 67 C5
Annesley Dr CR0 223 B5
Annesley Ho 15 SW9 138 C5
31 SW9 138 C4
Annesley Rd SE3 143 B4
Annesley Wlk N19 71 C6
Annett Cl TW17 193 C5
Annett Rd KT12 194 A2
Annette Cl HA3 24 C1
Annette Cres 5 N1 73 A1
Annette Ct N7 72 B5
Annette Rd N7 72 B4
Annie Besant Cl E3 97 B6
Annie Taylor Ho 1 E12 78 C4
Anning St E2 243 B6
Annington Rd N2 48 D6
Annis Rd E9 75 A2
Ann's Cl SW1 248 A1
Ann's Pl E1 243 C3
Annsworthy Ave CR7 205 B6
Annsworthy Cres CR7 183 B1
Annunciation RC Inf Sch The
HA8 27 B2
Annunciation RC Jun Sch
The HA8 27 B4
Ansar Gdns E17 53 B4
Ansdell Rd SE15 140 C3
Ansdell St W8 113 D3 255 D6
Ansdell Terr
W8 113 D3 255 D6
Ansell Gr SM5 203 A1
Ansell Ho E1 96 C2
Ansell Rd SW17 158 D1
Anselm Cl CR0 221 D5
Anselm Rd SW6 135 C6 265 A5
Hatch End HA5 23 B3
Ansford Rd BR1,SE6 186 B6
Ansleigh Pl W11 112 D6
Anslie Wlk 8 SW12 159 B4
Anson 30 NW9 27 D1
Anson Ho 6 E1 97 A3
SW1 269 A6
Anson Prim Sch NW2 68 D3
Anson Rd N7 71 D4
NW2 68 C3
Anstey Ct 6 W3 110 D4
Anstey Ho 8 E9 96 C6
Anstey Lo EN1 17 C5
Anstey Rd SE15 140 A2
Anstey Wlk N15 51 A5
Anstice Cl W4 133 C5
Anstridge Rd SE9 167 B5
Antelope Rd SE18 122 B3
Antenor Ho 11 E2 96 B5
Anthony Cl NW7 27 C6
Anthony Cope Ct N1 235 D2
Anthony Ct TW7 130 D2
Anthony Ho NW8 237 A5
Anthony Rd SE25 206 A3
Bexley DA16 146 A4
Greenford UB6 86 C4
Anthony St E1 96 B1
Antigua Wlk SE19 183 B5
Antill Rd E3 97 A4
N15 52 A5
Antill Terr 5 E1 96 D1
Antlers Hill E4 19 D6
Anton Cres SM1 217 C5
Anton St E8 74 A3
Antoneys Cl HA5 22 D1
Antony Ho 4 SE14 140 D5
2 SE16 118 C2
Antrim Gr NW3 70 D2
Antrim Ho 8 E3 97 B6
SW11 137 A2
Antrim Mans NW3 70 D2
Antrim Rd NW3 70 D2
Antrobus Cl SM1 217 B3

Antrobus Rd W4 111 A3
Anvil Cl SW16 181 C3
Anvil Ho 10 N9 18 A1
Anvil Rd TW16 194 A6
Anworth Cl IG8 37 B4
Apex Cl BR3 185 D2
Apex Cnr NW7 27 B6
Feltham TW13 151 B1
Apex Ct W13 87 A1
Apex Ind Est NW10 89 D3
Aphrodite Ct 2 E14 119 C2
Aplin Way TW7 130 C4
Apollo Ave Bromley BR1 187 B2
Eastbury HA6 22 A5
Apollo Ho 31 E2 96 B5
N6 48 D2
SW10 266 C5
Apollo Ind Bsns Ctr 23
SE8 140 D6
Apollo Pl E11 76 C5
SW10 266 C4
Apollo Studios 18 NW5 71 D3
Apollo Way SE18 123 B3
Apostle Way CR7 182 D1
Apothecary St EC4 241 C1
Appach Rd SW2 160 C5
Appin Ct HA1 42 C2
Apple Garth TW8 109 D2
Apple Gr
Chessington KT9 214 A4
Enfield EN1 5 C2
Apple Lo HA0 65 C5
Apple Mkt WC2 250 B6
Kingston u T KT1 175 D1
Apple Rd E11 76 C5
Apple Tree Ave UB7 82 B1
Apple Tree Yd SW1 249 B4
Appleby Cl E4 36 A4
N15 51 B4
Twickenham TW2 152 B2
Appleby Gdns TW14 149 D3
Appleby Rd E8 74 A1
E16 99 A1
Appleby St E2 95 D5
Appledore Ave HA4 62 C5
Appledore Cl
SW12,SW17 158 D2
Edgware HA8 26 C2
Hayes BR2 209 A4
Appledore Cres DA14,
DA15 167 D1
Appleford 8 NW5 71 C3
Appleford Ho 6 W10 91 A3
Appleford Rd W10 91 A3
Applegarth
Claygate KT10 212 D3
New Addington CR0 223 D1
Applegarth Dr IG2 57 D5
Applegarth Ho SE1 251 D2
8 SE15 140 A5
Applegarth Jun & Inf Sch
CR0 223 D2
Applegarth Rd SE28 124 C6
W14 112 D3
Appleshaw Ho 4 SE5 139 C2
Appleton Gdns KT3 200 A3
Appleton Rd SE9 144 A2
Appleton Sq CR4 180 C2
Appletree Cl 5 SE20 184 B2
Appletree Ct SE13 142 B1
Appletree Gdns EN4 2 C1
Applewood Cl N20 14 C3
NW2 68 B5
Appold St EC2 95 C2 243 A4
Appollo Ct 7 SW9 138 C4
Apprentice Way 6 E5 74 B4
Approach Cl N16 73 C4
Approach La NW7 29 A5
Approach Rd E2 96 C5
SW20 178 C1
Ashford TW15 171 A4
East Molesey KT8 195 C4
Edgware HA8 26 C4
New Barnet EN4,EN5 2 B1
Approach The NW4 46 D4
W3 89 B1
Enfield EN1 6 B3
Orpington BR6 227 D6
Aprey Gdns NW4 46 C5
April Cl W7 108 C6
Feltham TW13 150 A1
Orpington BR6 227 D3
April Ct 20 E2 96 A5
April Glen SE23 162 D1
April St E8 73 D4
Apsley Cl HA2 42 A4
Apsley Ct SM2 218 A2
Apsley Ctr The NW2 68 A6
Apsley Ho E1 96 C2
Apsley Rd SE25 206 B5
Kingston u T KT3 199 A6
Apsley Way NW2 68 A6
W1 248 B2
Aquarius TW1 153 B3
Aquarius Way HA6 22 A6
Aquila St NW8 92 B5 229 D4
Aquinas St SE1 116 C5 251 B3
Arabella Ct NW8 229 B4
Arabella Dr SW15 133 C1
Arabia Cl E4 20 B4
Arabian Ho 8 E1 97 A3
Arabin Rd SE4 141 B1
Aragon Ave KT7 196 D4
Aragon Cl Ashford TW16 171 D3
Enfield EN2 4 B5
Aragon Cl *continued*
Keston Mark BR2 210 B1
Aragon Ct KT8 196 A5
Aragon Dr HA4 40 D1
Aragon Rd
Kingston u T KT2 176 A5
West Barnes SM4 201 A2
Aragon Twr SE8 119 B2
Arakan Ho 4 N16 73 B4
Aral Ho 14 E1 96 D3
Arandora Cres RM6 58 B2
Arapiles Ho 6 E14 98 B1
Arbery Rd E3 97 A5
Arbon Ct N1 235 B5
Arbor Cl BR3 185 D1
Arbor Ct N16 73 B6
Arbor Rd E4 20 B1
Arborfield Ho 6 E14 119 C6
Arbour Ho 8 E1 96 D1
Arbour Rd EN3 6 D2
Arbour Sq E1 96 D1
Arbourfield Cl SW2 160 B3
Arbroath Rd SE9 144 A2
Arbrook Ct
Chessington KT9 213 D3
St Paul's Cray BR5 190 A2
Arbrook La KT10 212 B2
Arbury Terr 3 SE26 162 B1
Arbuthnot La DA5 169 A5
Arbuthnot Rd SE14 140 D3
Arbutus St E8 95 D6
Arcade Ho 7 NW11 47 B4
Arcade The E17 53 C5
EC2 243 A3
1 N7 72 A4
2 SE9 166 C5
Barking IG11 79 A1
Arcadia Ave N3 29 C2
Arcadia Cl SM5 219 A4
Arcadia St E14 97 C1
Arcadian Ave DA5 169 A5
Arcadian Cl DA5 169 A5
Arcadian Gdns N22 32 C3
Arcadian Rd DA5 169 A5
Arch St SE1 117 A3 262 A5
Archangel St SE16 118 D4
Archbishop Lanfranc Sch
The CR0 204 A3
Archbishop Michael Ramsey
Tech Coll SE5 138 D5
Archbishop Sumner's CE
Prim Sch SE11 116 C2 261 B3
Archbishop Tenison's Sch
SE11 138 B6 270 D5
South Croydon CR0 221 D5
Archbishop's Pl 1 SW2 160 B4
Archdale Ct W12 112 B5
Archdale Ho SE1 263 A6
Archdale Pl KT3 198 D6
Archdale Rd SE22 139 D1
Archdeacon Cambridge's CE
Prim Sch TW2 152 C2
Archel Rd W14 135 B6 264 C6
Archer Cl KT2 176 A3
Archer Ho 25 N1 95 C6
1 SW11 136 B3
W11 244 D6
W13 109 B5
Archer Rd SE25 206 B5
Archer Sq SE14 141 A6
Archer St W1 249 C6
Archer Terr UB7 104 A6
Archers Dr EN3 6 C3
Archers Lo 14 SE16 118 A1
Archery Cl W2 237 B1
Harrow HA3 42 D6
Archery Fields Ho WC1 234 A2
Archery Rd SE9 166 B6
Archery Steps W2 247 B6
Arches Bsns Ctr The
UB2 107 B4
Arches The WC2 250 B4
Harrow HA2 63 C6
Archibald Mews W1 248 C5
Archibald Rd N7 71 D4
Archibald St E3 97 C4
Archie Cl UB7 104 C4
Archway N19 71 C6
Archway Bsns Ctr 5
N19 71 D5
Archway Cl SW19 179 D6
W10 90 D2
Wallington SM6 220 A5
Archway Hts 5 N19 49 C1
Archway Rd N6 49 B2
Archway St SW13,SW14 133 C2
Archway Sta N19 71 C6
Arcola St E8 73 D3
Arctic St NW5 71 B3
Arcus Rd BR1 186 C4
Ardbeg Rd SE24 161 B6
Arden 17 SW19 156 D3
Arden Cl Bushey WD2 8 D4
Harrow HA1 64 B5
Arden Court Gdns N2 48 B3
Arden Cres E14 119 C2
Dagenham RM9 80 D1
Arden Gr BR6 226 D4
Arden Grange N12 30 A6
Arden Ho 21 N1 95 C5
SE11 260 C3
29 SW9 138 A3
Arden Mhor HA5 40 B5
Arden Rd N3 47 B6
W13 109 C6
Ardent Cl SE25 205 C6
Ardent Ho 28 E3 97 A5
Ardfern Ave SW16 204 C6
Ardfillan Rd SE6 164 B2
Ardgowan Rd SE6 164 C3
Ardilaun Rd N5 73 A4
Ardingly Cl CR0 222 D5
Ardleigh Gdns SM3 201 C2
Ardleigh Ho 4 IG11 101 A6
Ardleigh Rd E17 35 B2
N1 73 C2
Ardleigh Terr E17 35 B2
Ardley Cl NW10 67 C5
SE6 163 A1
Ruislip HA4 39 A2
Ardlui Rd SE27 161 A2
Ardmay Gdns KT6 198 A4
Ardmere Rd SE13 164 B5
Ardmore La IG9 21 B4
Ardmore Pl IG9 21 B4
Ardoch Rd SE6 164 B2
Ardra Rd N9 18 D1
Ardrossan Gdns KT4 216 A5
Ardshiel Cl SW15 134 D2
Ardwell Ave IG6 57 A4
Ardwell Rd SW2 160 A2
Ardwick Rd NW2 69 C4
Arena Bsns Ctr N4 51 A3
Arena Est N4 50 D3
Arena Sta SE25 206 C4
Arena The EN3 7 B5
Ares Ct 8 E14 119 C2
Arethusa Ho 8 E14 119 D2
Argall Ave E10 52 D1
Argall Ho 3 DA18 125 A3
Argall Way E10 53 A1
Argent Ct KT6 214 C5
Argent Ctr The UB3 106 A4
Argenta Way NW10 66 D1
Argon Mews SW6 265 B3
Argon Rd N18 34 D5
Argos Ct 5 SW9 138 C4
Argos Ho 8 E2 96 B5
Argosy Ho SE8 119 A2
W1 238 D5
Argus Way UB5 85 A4
Argyle Ave
Isleworth TW2,TW3 151 C5
Twickenham TW3 151 C5
Argyle Cl W13 87 A3
Argyle Ho E14 120 A3
Sutton SM2 218 A2
Argyle Pl W6 112 B2
Argyle Prim Sch WC1 233 A2
Argyle Rd E1 96 D3
E15 76 C4
E16 99 B1
N12 29 C5
N17 34 A2
N18 34 A6
W13 87 A2
Harrow HA2 41 D3
Hounslow TW3 151 D6
Ilford IG1 78 C6
Argyle Sq WC1 94 A4 233 B2
Argyle St WC1 94 A4 233 B2
Argyle Way SE16 118 A1
Argyle Wlk WC1 233 B1
Argyll Ave UB1 107 D5
Argyll Cl SW9 138 B2
Argyll Ct 15 SW2 160 A4
Argyll Gdns HA8 26 D2
Argyll Mans SW3 266 D6
W14 254 B4
Argyll Rd SE18 123 A3
W8 113 C4 245 B1
Argyll St W1 93 C1 239 A1
Arica Ho SE16 118 B3
Arica Rd SE4 141 A2
Ariel Ct SE11 261 C3
W12 112 A3
5 Belvedere DA17 125 C1
Ariel Rd NW6 69 C2
Ariel Way W12 112 C5
Hounslow TW4 128 B2
Aristotle Rd SW4 137 D2
Arkansas Ho 21 N19 49 D2
Arkell Gr SW16 182 D3
Arkindale Rd SE6 164 A1
Arkley Cres E17 53 B4
Arkley Dr EN5 12 B6
Arkley Pk EN5 11 B5
Arkley Rd E17 53 B4
Arklow Ho SE17 139 B6
Arklow Mews 4 KT6 214 A6
Arklow Rd SE14 141 B6
Arklow Road Trad Est
SE14 141 B6
Arkwright Ho 23 SW2 160 A4
Arkwright Mans NW3 70 A3
Arkwright Rd NW3 70 A3
Arlesey Cl SW15 157 A6
Arlesford Rd SW9 138 A2
Arlingford Rd SW2 160 C5
Arlington N12 13 C1
Arlington Ave N1 95 A6 235 B5
Arlington Cl
Sidcup DA15 167 C4
Sutton SM1 217 C6
Twickenham TW1 153 C5
Arlington Ct N6 49 A3
Hayes UB3 105 B1
4 Twickenham TW1 153 C5
Arlington Dr
Carshalton SM5 218 D6
Ruislip HA4 39 B3
Arlington Gdns W4 111 A1
Ilford IG1 56 C1
Arlington Ho EC1 234 B2
3 SE8 141 B6
W12 112 B5
Arlington Lo SW2 138 B1
Arlington Park Mans 1
W4 111 A1
Arlington Pl 7 SE10 142 A5
Arlington Rd N14 15 C3
NW1 93 B6 231 D5
W13 87 B1
Ashford TW15 170 B5
Richmond TW10 153 D2
Surbiton KT6 197 D3
Teddington TW11 174 D6
Twickenham TW1 153 C5
Woodford IG8 37 B3
Arlington Sq N1 95 A6 235 B5
Arlington St
SW1 115 C5 249 A4
Arlington Way
EC1 94 C4 234 B2
Arliss Way UB5 84 C6
Arlow Rd N21 16 C3
Armada Ct 11 SE8 141 C6
Armada St 10 SE8 141 C6
Armada Way E6 101 A1
Armadale Cl N17 52 B5
Armadale Rd SW6 265 A5
Feltham TW14 150 A6
Armagh Rd E3 97 B6
Armeston KT3 199 B2
Armfield Cl KT8 195 B4
Armfield Cotts 3
SW19 180 D1
Armfield Cres CR4 180 D1
Armfield Rd EN2 5 B4
Arminger Rd W12 112 B5
Armitage Rd NW11 47 B1
SE10 120 D1
Armitice Gdns SE25 206 A6
Armour Cl N7 72 B2
Armoury Rd SE8 141 D3
Armoury Way SW18 157 C6
Armsby Ho 15 E1 96 C2
Armstead Wlk RM10 81 C1
Armstrong Ave IG8 36 C4
Armstrong Cl E6 100 B1
Bromley BR1 210 A6
Dagenham RM8 58 D2
Pinner HA5 40 A3
Walton-on-T KT12 194 A3
Armstrong Cres EN4 2 B2
Armstrong Ct W13 86 D2
Armstrong Ho 8 SW15 156 D5
Armstrong Rd SW7 256 C5
W3 111 D5
Feltham TW13 173 A5
Armstrong Way UB2 107 D4
Armytage Rd TW5 128 D5
Arnal Cres SW18 157 A4
Arncliffe NW6 91 D6
Arncroft Ct IG11 102 B4
Arne Gr BR6 227 D5
Arne Ho SE11 260 C2
Arne St WC2 94 A1 240 B1
Arne Wlk SE3 142 D1
Arnett Sq E4 35 B4
Arneway St SW1 259 D5
Arneways Ave RM6 58 D6
Arnewood Cl SW15 156 A3
Arney's La CR4 203 A3
Arngask Rd SE6 164 B4
Arnhem Pl E14 119 C3
Arnhem Way 3 SE22 161 C6
Arnhem Wharf E14 119 C3
Arnhem Wharf JMI Sch
E14 119 C3
Arnison Rd KT8 196 B5
Arnold Ave E EN3 7 C5
Arnold Ave W EN3 7 B5
Arnold Cir E2 95 D4
Arnold Cl HA3 44 B2
Arnold Cres TW7 152 B6
Arnold Ct E18 36 D2
Arnold Dr KT9 213 D2
Arnold Est SE1 253 D1
Arnold Gdns N13 32 D5
Arnold Ho 9 N16 73 C5
SE17 261 D1
Arnold House Sch
NW8 92 B5 229 C3
Arnold Rd E3 97 C4
N15 51 D6
SW17 180 D3
Dagenham RM10 81 C1
Northolt UB5 63 A2
Arnos Gr N14 15 D1
Arnos Grove Ct 4 N11 31 C5
Arnos Grove Sta N11 31 C6
Arnos Rd N11 31 C6
Arnot Ho 27 SE5 139 A5
Arnott Cl SE28 124 C5
W4 111 B2
Arnould Ave SE5 139 B1
Arnsberg Way DA7 147 C1
Arnside Gdns HA9 43 D1
Arnside Ho 2 SE17 139 B6
Arnside Rd DA7 147 C4
Arnside St SE17 139 A6
Arnulf St SE6 185 D6
Arnull's Rd SW16 182 D4
Arodene Rd SW2 160 B5
Arosa Rd 4 TW1 153 D5
Arragon Gdns SW16 182 A3
West Wickham BR4 223 D5
Arragon Rd E6 99 D6
SW18 157 C3
Twickenham TW1 153 A4
3 Twickenham TW1 153 A3
Arran Cl SM6 219 C4
Arran Ct 32 NW9 27 D1
Arran Ct *continued*
NW10 67 B5
Arran Dr E12 77 D6
Stanmore HA7 25 C6
Arran Ho N16 51 D1
Arran Mews W5 110 B5
Arran Rd SE6 164 A2
Arran Wlk N1 73 A1
Arrandene Ho 3 BR5 190 B1
Arras Ave SM4 202 A4
Arras Ho SE2 146 D6
Arrol Ho SE1 262 B5
Arrol Rd BR3 206 D6
Arrow Ho 24 N1 95 C6
Arrow Rd E3 97 D4
Arrow Scout Wlk UB5 85 A6
Arrowe Ct 7 E5 74 B4
Arrowhead Ct E11 54 B3
Arrowsmith Ho SE11 260 C2
Arsenal Rd SE9 144 B2
Arsenal Sta N5 72 C5
Artemis Ct 6 E14 119 C2
Arterberry Rd SW20,
SW19 178 D2
Artesian Cl NW10 67 B1
Artesian Gr EN5 2 A1
Artesian Rd W2 91 C1
Arthingworth St E15 98 C6
Arthur Ct SW11 268 B1
W2 91 D1
10 W10 90 D1
Croydon CR0 221 B5
Arthur Deakin Ho 1 E1 96 A2
Arthur Gr SE18 123 A2
Arthur Henderson Ho
9 N19 49 D2
6 SW6 135 B3
Arthur Newton Ho 20
SW11 136 B2
Arthur Rd E6 100 B5
N7 72 B4
N9 17 D2
SW19 179 C6
Dagenham RM6 58 D3
6 Kingston u T KT2 176 C3
West Barnes KT3 200 B4
Arthur Ruxley Est DA14 190 D4
Arthur St EC4 117 B6 252 D6
Arthur Wade Ho 7 E2 95 D4
Arthur Walls Ho 3 E12 78 C5
Arthurdon Rd SE4 163 C6
Artichoke Hill 8 E1 118 B6
Artichoke Mews 5 SE5 139 B4
Artichoke Pl SE5 139 B4
Artillery Cl IG2 57 A3
Artillery Ho SE18 122 C1
Artillery La E1 95 C2 243 B3
W12 90 A1
Artillery Pl SE18 122 C2
Harrow HA3 24 A3
Artillery Row SW1 259 C5
Artington Cl BR6 227 A4
Artisan Cl E16 122 D6
Artizan St E1 243 B2
Arton Wilson Ho 12
SW15 156 A6
Arts Educational Schs The
W4 111 C2
Arun Ho 5 KT2 175 D2
Arundale KT1 197 D5
Arundel Ave SM4 201 B5
Arundel Bldgs SE1 263 B5
Arundel Cl E15 76 C4
SW11 158 C6
Bexley DA5 169 B5
Croydon CR0 220 D5
Hampton TW12 173 D5
Arundel Ct N12 30 C4
N17 34 A2
SW3 257 B2
SW13 134 B6
SW15 156 D6
4 Beckenham BR2 186 C1
2 Bexleyheath DA6 147 A1
Harrow HA2 63 C4
Arundel Dr Harrow HA2 63 C4
Woodford IG8 37 A3
Arundel Gdns N21 16 C3
W11 113 B6 244 C6
Burnt Oak HA8 27 B3
Ilford IG3 80 A6
Arundel Gr N16 73 C3
Arundel Ho N1 94 D6 234 D6
3 W3 110 D4
Croydon CR0 221 B3
Arundel Lo N3 29 B1
Arundel Mans SW6 264 D2
SW13 134 B6
Arundel Pl N1,N7 72 C2
Arundel Rd Belmont SM2 217 B1
Cockfosters EN4 2 C2
Hounslow TW4 128 C2
Kingston u T KT1 177 A1
Thornton Heath CR0 205 B3
Arundel Sq N7 72 C2
Arundel St WC2 116 B6 250 D6
Arundel Terr SW13 134 B6
Arvon Rd N5 72 C3
Asa Ct UB3 105 D3
Asaph Ho SE14 141 B4
Asbaston Terr IG11 79 A2
Ascalon Ct 16 SW2 160 B4
Ascalon Ho SW8 269 A3
Ascalon St SW8 137 C5 269 A3
Ascham Dr E4 35 C3
Ascham End E17 35 A2
Ascham St NW5 71 C3
Aschurch Rd CR0 205 D2
Ascot Cl Deacons Hill WD6 10 C6
Northolt UB5 63 C3
Ascot Ct NW8 229 C1
8 SW4 138 A1
Sidcup DA5 169 B4
Ascot Gdns Enfield EN3 6 C6
Southall UB1 85 C2
Ascot Ho NW1 231 D2
SE26 184 B4
6 W4 111 A1
1 W9 91 C2
Ascot Lo NW6 91 D5
Ascot Par 9 SW4 138 A1
Ascot Rd E6 100 B4
N15 51 B4
N18 34 A6
SW17 181 A4
East Bedfont TW14 148 D2
St Paul's Cray BR5 211 D5
Ascott Ave W5 110 A4
Ascott Ct HA5 40 A5
Asfil Ho EC1 241 B3
Ash Cl SE20 184 C1
Carshalton SM5 218 D6
Edgware HA8 27 A6
Kingston u T KT3 177 B1
Petts Wood BR5 211 B4
Sidcup DA14 168 B1
Stanmore HA7 25 A4
Ash Ct E4 20 B4
E18 37 C2
N19 71 C6
SE12 165 A4
SW11 159 A6
2 SW16 182 C5
W1 237 C2
Romford RM7 59 D3
West Ewell KT19 215 A4
Ash Gr E8 96 B6
N13 17 A1
NW2 69 A4
SE12 165 A3
SE20 184 C1
W5 110 A3
East Bedfont TW14 149 C3
Enfield EN1 17 C4
Hayes UB3 105 B6
Heston TW5 128 D5
Southall UB1 85 C2
Wembley HA0 65 A4
West Wickham BR4 208 A1
Yiewsley UB7 104 B6
Ash Hill Dr HA5 40 C6
Ash Ho 8 E14 120 A4
SE1 263 D3
Ash Lo SW6 134 D4
2 Ashford TW16 171 D3
Ash Rd E15 76 D3
Cheam SM3 201 B1
Croydon CR0 223 C6
Littleton TW17 192 C5
Orpington BR6 227 D1
Ash Row BR2 210 C3
Ash Tree Cl Croydon CR0 207 A3
1 Surbiton KT6 198 A1
Ash Tree Dell NW9 45 B4
Ash Tree Way CR0 207 A3
Ash Wlk HA0 65 C4
Ashbourne Ave E18 55 B5
N20 14 D2
NW11 47 B4
Bexley DA7 147 A5
Harrow HA2 64 B6
Ashbourne Cl N12 29 D6
W5 88 C2
Ashbourne Ct E5 75 A4
11 N12 29 D6
Ashbourne Gr NW7 27 B5
SE22 139 D1
W4 111 C1
Ashbourne Par 2 NW11 47 B5
W5 88 B3
Ashbourne Rd W5 88 B3
Mitcham CR4 181 A3
Ashbourne Rise BR6 227 C4
Ashbourne Terr 1
SW19 179 C3
Ashbourne Way NW11 47 B4
Ashbridge Rd E11 54 D2
Ashbridge St
NW8 92 C3 237 A5
Ashbrook HA8 26 B4
Ashbrook Rd N19 71 D6
Dagenham RM10 81 D5
Ashburn Ct BR1 187 A3
Ashburn Gdns SW7 256 A4
Ashburn Pl
SW7 114 A2 256 A3
Ashburnham Ave HA1 42 D3
Ashburnham Cl N2 48 B5
Ashburnham Gdns HA1 42 D3
Ashburnham Gr SE10 141 D5
Ashburnham Pk KT10 212 A4
Ashburnham Pl SE10 141 D5
Ashburnham Prim Sch
SW10 136 B5 266 C4
Ashburnham Rd NW10 90 C5
SW10 136 A5 266 B3
Richmond TW10 153 B1
Ashburnham Retreat 6
SE10 141 D5
Ashburnham Twr SW10 266 C4
Ashburton Ave
Croydon CR0 206 B1
Ilford IG3 79 D4
Ashburton Cl CR0 206 A1
Ashburton Gdns CR0 222 A6
Ashburton Gr N7 72 C4

Ashburton Ho EN3 ....6 D2
Ashburton Jun & Inf Sch
CR0 ....206 B3
Ashburton Mans SW10 .266 B4
Ashburton Rd E16 .....99 A1
Croydon CR0 .....222 A6
Ruislip HA4 .....62 A6
Ashburton Sch CR0 ....206 B2
Ashburton Terr 2 E13 ..99 A5
Ashbury Ct N21 .....16 A6
Ashbury Dr UB10 .....60 D5
Ashbury Gdns RM6 .....58 D4
Ashbury Pl SW19 .....179 D5
Ashby Ave KT19,KT9 ....214 C2
Ashby Ct NW8 .....236 D6
Ashby Gr N1 .....73 A1
Ashby Grange 7 SM6 .219 C2
Ashby Ho 8 N1 .....73 A1
6 SW9 .....138 D3
Ashby Mews SE4 .....141 B3
Ashby Rd N15 .....52 A4
SE4 .....141 B3
Ashby St EC1 ...94 D4 234 D1
Ashby Way UB7 .....126 C5
Ashby Wlk CR0 .....205 A3
Ashchurch Ct W12 ....112 A3
Ashchurch Gr W12 ....112 A3
Ashchurch Park Villas
W12 .....112 A3
Ashchurch Terr W12 ...112 A3
Ashcombe Ave KT6 ....197 D2
Ashcombe Ct 4 SW15 .157 A6
Ashcombe Gdns HA8 ...26 C6
Ashcombe Ho 39 E3 ...97 D4
Ashcombe Pk NW2 .....67 C5
Ashcombe Rd SW19 ...179 C5
Wallington SM5 .....219 A2
Ashcombe Sq KT3 .....199 A6
Ashcombe St SW6 .....135 D3
Ashcroft N14 .....15 D2
Hatch End HA5 .....23 C4
Ashcroft Ave DA15 .....168 A5
Ashcroft Cres DA15 ....168 A5
Ashcroft Ct N20 .....14 B2
5 SE9 .....166 C5
Ashcroft Ho SW8 .....269 A2
Ashcroft Rd E3 .....97 A4
Chessington KT9 .....214 B5
Ashcroft Sq W6 .....112 C2
Ashdale Cl
Stanwell TW19 .....148 A2
Twickenham TW2 .....152 A4
Ashdale Gr HA7 .....24 D4
Ashdale Ho N4 .....51 B2
Ashdale Rd SE12 .....165 B3
Ashdale Way TW2 .....151 D4
Ashdene 6 SE15 .....140 B5
Pinner HA5 .....40 C6
Ashdene Cl TW15 .....171 A3
Ashdon Cl IG8 .....37 B4
Ashdown SW15 .....156 D6
W13 .....87 B2
Ashdown Cl 13 BR3 ....185 D1
Ashdown Cres NW5 .....71 A3
Ashdown Ct
New Malden KT4 .....199 D2
Sutton SM2 .....218 A2
Ashdown Ho 7 E5 .....74 A6
Ashdown Pl KT7 .....197 A2
Ashdown Rd NW10 .....89 D6
Enfield EN3 .....6 C3
Hillingdon UB10 .....82 C5
Kingston u T KT1 .....176 A1
Ashdown Way SW17 ...159 A2
Ashdown Wlk 15 E14 ..119 C2
Ashdowne Ct N17 .....34 A2
Ashe Ho 8 TW1 .....153 D5
Ashen E6 .....100 C1
Ashen Gr SW19 .....157 C2
Ashenden SE17 .....262 B4
Ashenden Rd E5 .....75 A3
Ashentree Ct EC4 .....241 B1
Asher Loftus Way N11 ..30 D4
Asher Way E1 .....118 A6
Ashfield Ave Bushey WD2 .8 A4
Feltham TW13 .....150 B3
Ashfield Cl
Beckenham BR3 .....185 C3
Richmond TW10 .....154 A3
Ashfield Ho 5 N5 .....73 A3
Ashfield La BR7 .....189 A3
Ashfield Par N14 .....15 D3
Ashfield Pl BR7 .....189 B3
Ashfield Rd N4 .....51 A3
N14 .....15 C1
W3 .....111 D5
Ashfield St E1 .....96 B2
Ashford Ave N8 .....50 A5
Ashford TW15 .....170 D4
Hayes UB4 .....84 D1
Ashford CE Fst & Mid Sch
TW15 .....170 D4
Ashford Cl E17 .....53 B3
Ashford TW15 .....170 A6
Ashford Cres
Ashford TW15 .....148 A1
Enfield EN3 .....6 C3
Ashford Ct NW2 .....68 D4
Edgware HA8 .....26 C5
Ashford Gn WD1 .....22 D5
Ashford High Sch The
TW15 .....148 A1
Ashford Ho 11 SE8 ....141 B6
14 SW9 .....138 D1
Ashford Hospl TW15 ...148 A2
Ashford Ind Est TW15 ..171 A6
Ashford Rd E6 .....78 C1
E18 .....37 B1
Ashford Rd *continued*
NW2 .....68 D4
Feltham TW13,TW15 ....171 B6
Littleton TW15,TW17 ....171 A3
Staines TW18 .....170 A4
Ashford St N1 .....95 C4
Ashgrove Ct 2 W9 .....91 C2
Ashgrove Ho SW1 .....259 D2
Ashgrove Rd
Ashford TW15 .....171 B5
Catford BR1 .....186 B4
Ilford IG3 .....58 A1
Ashingdon Cl E4 .....20 A1
Ashington 1 NW5 .....71 B2
Ashington Ho 16 E1 ....96 B3
Ashington Rd SW6 .....135 B3
Ashlake Rd SW16 .....182 A6
Ashland Pl W1 .....238 A4
Ashlar Ct N2 .....48 C6
Ashlar Pl SE18 .....122 D2
Ashleigh Commercial Est
SE7 .....121 D3
Ashleigh Ct N14 .....15 C4
SE26 .....184 B4
W5 .....109 D2
Ashleigh Gdns SM1 ....217 D6
Ashleigh Ho SW14 .....133 C2
Ashleigh Point 8 SE26 162 D1
Ashleigh Rd SE20 .....206 B6
SW14 .....133 B2
Ashley Ave SM4 .....201 C4
Ashley Cl NW4 .....28 C1
Oatlands Pk KT12,KT13 ..193 D1
Pinner Green HA5 .....22 B1
Ashley Cres N22 .....32 C1
SW11 .....137 A2
Ashley Ct 19 N16 .....73 C3
NW3 .....69 D3
NW4 .....28 C1
New Barnet EN5 .....14 A6
Northolt UB5 .....85 A6
Yiewsley UB7 .....104 A5
Ashley Dr
Borehamwood WD6 .....11 B6
Hounslow TW7 .....130 C6
Twickenham TW2 .....151 D3
Ashley Gdns N13 .....33 A6
Orpington BR6 .....227 C3
Richmond TW10 .....153 D2
Wembley HA9 .....66 A6
Ashley Ho BR5 .....190 A1
Ashley Inf Sch KT12 ....194 A1
Ashley La NW4 .....28 C1
NW7 .....28 D3
Croydon CR0 .....220 D4
Ashley Park Ave KT12 .193 D1
Ashley Park Cres KT12 .194 A1
Ashley Pl SW1 .115 C3 259 A5
Ashley Rd E4 .....35 C4
E7 .....77 C1
N17 .....52 A6
N19 .....50 A2
SW19 .....179 D4
Enfield EN3 .....6 C3
Hampton TW12 .....173 C2
Richmond TW9 .....132 A2
Thames Ditton KT7 .....196 D3
Thornton Heath CR7 .....204 B5
Walton-on-T KT12 .....194 A1
Ashley Wlk NW7 .....28 D3
Ashlin Rd E15 .....76 B4
Ashling Rd CR0 .....206 A1
Ashlone Rd SW15 .....134 D2
Ashlyns Way KT9 .....213 D2
Ashmead 4 N14 .....15 C6
Ashmead Bsns Ctr E16 ..98 B3
Ashmead Gate BR1 .....187 C2
Ashmead Ho E9 .....75 A3
Ashmead Prim Sch SE8 141 C3
Ashmead Rd SE8 .....141 C3
East Bedfont TW14 .....150 A3
Ashmere Ave BR3 .....186 B1
Ashmere Cl SM3 .....216 D3
Ashmere Gr 11 SW2,
SW4 .....138 A1
Ashmere Ho 10 SW2 ...138 A1
Ashmill Ct CR0 .....205 A3
Ashmill St NW8 .92 C2 237 A4
Ashmole Prim Sch
SW8 .....138 B6 270 D5
Ashmole Sch N14 .....15 C3
Ashmole St SW8 .....270 D5
Ashmoor Lo NW7 .....27 B4
Ashmore NW1 .....71 D1
Ashmore Ct N11 .....30 D4
Heston TW5 .....129 C6
Ashmore Gr DA16 .....145 C2
Ashmore Rd W9 .....91 B4
Ashmount Prim Sch N6 .49 C2
Ashmount Rd N15 .....51 D4
N19 .....49 D2
Ashmount Terr W5 ....109 D2
Ashneal Gdns HA1 .....64 B5
Ashness Gdns UB6 .....65 B2
Ashness Rd SW11 .....158 D6
Ashpark Ho 4 E14 .....97 B1
Ashridge Cl HA3 .....43 C3
Ashridge Cres SE18 ....145 A5
Ashridge Ct N14 .....15 C6
Southall UB1 .....108 A6
Ashridge Dr WD1 .....22 C5
Ashridge Gdns N13 .....32 A5
Pinner HA5 .....41 A5
Ashridge Ho DA14 .....189 D6
Ashridge Way
Ashford TW16 .....172 A4
Merton SM4 .....201 B5
Ashtead Ct 15 SW19 ...156 D3
Ashtead Rd E5 .....52 A2
Ashton Cl SM1 .....217 C4
Ashton Ct
1 Beckenham BR3 .....185 B2
Harrow HA1 .....64 D5
Ashton Gdns
Dagenham RM6 .....59 A3
Hounslow TW4 .....129 B1
Ashton Ho 13 SW9 .....138 C5
SW15 .....156 B4
Ashton Rd E15 .....76 B3
Ashton St E14 .....120 A6
Ashtree Ave CR4 .....180 B1
Ashtree Cl BR6 .....226 D4
Ashtree Ct TW15 .....170 D5
Ashurst Cl SE20 .....184 B2
Ashurst Dr Ilford IG2,IG6 .57 A4
Littleton TW17 .....192 A4
Ashurst Lo N5 .....72 D3
Ashurst Rd N12 .....30 C5
East Barnet EN4 .....14 D6
Ashurst Wlk CR0 .....222 B6
Ashvale Rd SW17 .....180 D5
Ashview Cl TW15 .....170 A5
Ashview Gdns TW15 ....170 A5
Ashville Rd E11 .....76 B6
Ashwater Rd SE12 .....165 A3
Ashway Ctr 5 KT2 .....176 A2
Ashwell Cl 8 E6 .....100 A1
Ashwell Ct TW15 .....148 A2
Ashwin St E8 .....73 D2
Ashwood Ave UB8 .....82 C1
Ashwood Gdns
Hayes UB3 .....105 D2
New Addington CR0 ....224 A2
Ashwood Ho 5 NW4 .....46 C5
Ashwood Lo N21 .....16 B5
Ashwood Pk 6 SM2 ....217 C1
Ashwood Rd E4 .....20 B1
Ashworth Cl SE5 .....139 B3
Ashworth Mans W9 .....91 D4
Ashworth Rd W9 .....91 D4
Aske Ho 2 N1 .....95 C4
Aske St N1 .....95 C4
Asker Ho N7 .....72 A4
Askern Cl DA6 .....146 D1
Askew Cres W12 .....112 A4
Askew Mans 14 W12 ...112 A4
Askew Rd W12 .....112 A4
Askham Ct W12 .....112 A5
Askham Lo 5 SE12 .....165 A4
Askham Rd W12 .....112 A5
Askill Dr SW15 .....157 A6
Asland Rd E15 .....98 B6
Aslett St SW18 .....158 A4
Asmara Rd NW2 .....69 A3
Asmuns Hill NW11 .....47 C4
Asmuns Pl NW11 .....47 B4
Asolando Dr SE17 .....262 B3
Aspen Cl 10 N19 .....71 C6
W5 .....110 B4
Yiewsley UB7 .....104 B5
Aspen Copse BR1 .....188 B1
Aspen Ct E8 .....73 D2
Hayes UB3 .....105 C2
Richmond TW9 .....132 C5
Aspen Dr HA0 .....65 A5
Aspen Gdns W6 .....112 B1
Ashford TW15 .....171 A5
Mitcham CR4 .....203 A4
Aspen Gn DA18 .....125 B3
Aspen Ho N21 .....16 B6
4 NW3 .....70 D2
8 SE15 .....140 C6
2 Sidcup DA15 .....168 A1
Aspen House Sch SW2 .160 B4
Aspen La UB5 .....85 A4
Aspen Way E14 .....120 A6
Feltham TW13 .....150 B1
Aspenlea Rd W6 .....134 D6
Aspern Gr NW3 .....70 C3
Aspinall Ho SW12 .....160 A3
Aspinall Rd SE4 .....140 D2
Aspinden Rd SE16 .....118 B2
Aspley Rd SW18 .....157 D6
Asplins Rd N17 .....34 B2
Asquith Cl RM8 .....58 C1
Asquith Court Sch HA3 .43 C3
Ass House La HA3 .....23 D6
Assam SE1 .....253 D3
Assam St E1 .....96 A1
Assata Mews N1 .....72 D2
Assembly Pas E1 .....96 C2
Assembly Wlk SM5 ....202 C2
Assheton-Bennett Ho 15
KT6 .....198 A4
Assisi Ct HA0 .....64 D5
Astall Cl HA3 .....24 C2
Astbury Ho SE11 .....261 A5
Astbury Rd SE15 .....140 C4
Aste St E14 .....120 A4
Astell St SW3 ..114 C1 257 B2
Asteys Row 3 N1 .....73 A1
Asthall Gdns IG6 .....57 A5
Astins Ho 4 E17 .....53 D5
Astle St SW11 .....137 A3
Astleham Rd TW17 .....192 A6
Astley Ave NW2 .....68 C3
Astley Ho SE1 .....263 D2
8 SE27 .....183 A6
Aston Ave HA3 .....43 C2
Aston Cl Bushey WD2 .....8 A5
Sidcup DA14 .....168 A1
Aston Gn TW5 .....128 C3
Aston Ho SW8 .....269 C1
W11 .....244 D6
Aston House Sch W5 ...87 D1
Aston Mews RM6 .....58 C2
Aston Rd SW20 .....178 C1
W5 .....87 D1
Claygate KT10 .....212 C3
Aston St E14 .....97 A2
Astonville St SW18 ....157 C3
Astor Ave RM7 .....59 D3
Astor Cl KT2 .....176 D4
Astor Ct E16 .....99 C1
SW6 .....266 A3
Astoria Mans 13 SW16 .160 A1
Astoria Par SW16 .....160 A1
Astoria Wlk SW9 .....138 C2
Astra Ct W13 .....109 A5
Astra Ho 4 E3 .....97 B4
N4 .....50 B2
Astrid Ho TW13 .....150 C2
Astrop Mews W6 .....112 C3
Astrop Terr W6 .....112 C4
Astwood Mews SW7 ...256 A4
Asylum Rd SE15 .....140 B5
Atalanta St
SW6 .....134 D5 264 A3
Atbara Ct TW11 .....175 B4
Atbara Rd TW11 .....175 B4
Atcham Rd TW3 .....130 A1
Atcost Rd IG11 .....102 A2
Atheldene Rd SW18 ...158 A3
Athelney Prim Sch SE6 163 C1
Athelney St SE6 .....163 C1
Athelstan Ct E6 .....100 C5
Athelstan Gdns 6 NW6 .69 A1
Athelstan Ho E9 .....75 B3
N16 .....73 C4
Kingston u T KT1 .....198 B5
Athelstan House Sch
TW12 .....173 C2
Athelstan Rd KT1 .....198 B5
Athelstan Way BR5 ....190 A2
Athelstane Gr E3 .....97 B5
Athelstane Mews N4 ...50 C1
Athelstone Rd HA3 .....24 B1
Athena Cl Harrow HA2 ..64 C6
Kingston u T KT1 .....198 B6
Athena Ct NW8 .....229 C4
Athenaeum Pl 3 N10 ...49 B6
Athenaeum Rd N20 .....14 B3
Athenia Ho 7 E14 .....98 B1
Athenlay Rd SE15 .....162 D6
Athenoeum Ct N5 .....73 A4
Athens Gdns W9 .....91 C3
Atherden Rd E5 .....74 C4
Atherfield Ct SW18 ....157 D5
Atherfold Rd SW9 .....138 A2
Atherley Way TW4 .....151 B4
Atherstone Ct W2 .....91 D2
Atherstone Mews
SW7 .....114 A2 256 B4
Atherton Dr SW19 .....178 D6
Atherton Ho CR2 .....221 C2
Atherton Hts HA0 .....65 C2
Atherton Mews E7 .....77 A2
Atherton Pl Harrow HA2 .42 B6
Southall UB1 .....107 C6
Atherton Rd E7 .....76 D2
SW13 .....134 A5
Atherton St SW11 .....136 C3
Athlon Rd HA0 .....87 D5
Athlone KT10 .....212 C2
Athlone Cl 24 E5 .....74 B3
Athlone Ct E17 .....54 B6
Athlone Ho 9 E1 .....96 C1
16 NW5 .....71 A2
Athlone House (The
Middlesex Hospl) N6 ..48 D1
Athlone Rd SW2 .....160 C4
Athlone St NW5 .....71 A2
Athol Cl HA5 .....22 B2
Athol Gdns HA5 .....22 B2
Athol Sq E14 .....98 A1
Athol Way UB10 .....82 C4
Athole Gdns EN1 .....17 C6
Athole Terr CR7 .....183 A1
Atholl Ho W9 .....229 A1
Atholl Rd IG3 .....58 A2
Atkins Dr BR4 .....224 B6
Atkins Rd E10 .....53 D3
SW4,SW12 .....159 D4
Atkinson Ct 3 E10 .....53 D2
Atkinson Ho 13 E2 .....96 A5
E13 .....98 D3
SE17 .....262 D3
SW11 .....268 A1
Atkinson Morley's Hospl
SW20 .....178 B3
Atkinson Rd E16 .....99 C2
Atlanta Ct CR7 .....205 A6
Atlantic Ho 4 E1 .....97 A2
4 SW15 .....157 B6
Atlantic Rd SW2,SW9,
SE24 .....138 C1
Atlas Bsns Ctr NW2 ....68 B6
Atlas Gdns SE7 .....121 C2
Atlas Mews E8 .....73 D2
Atlas Rd E13 .....99 A5
N11 .....31 A4
NW10 .....89 C4
Wembley HA9 .....67 A4
Atley Rd E3 .....97 C6
Atlip Rd HA0 .....88 A6
Atney Rd SW15 .....135 A1
Atria Rd HA6 .....22 A5
Atterbury Rd N4 .....50 D3
Atterbury St
SW1 .....116 A2 260 A3
Attewood Ave NW10 ....67 C5
Attewood Rd UB5 .....63 A2
Attfield Cl N20 .....14 B2
Attilburgh Ho SE1 .....263 C6
Attle Cl UB10 .....82 C5
Attleborough Ct 4
SE21 .....162 B2
Attlee Cl Hayes UB4 ....84 B4
Thornton Heath CR7 ....205 A4
Attlee Ct UB4 .....84 B4
Attlee Rd SE28 .....124 B6
Hayes UB4 .....84 B4
Attlee Terr 3 E17 .....53 D5
Attneave St WC1 .....234 A1
Atwater Cl SW2 .....160 C3
Atwell Cl E10 .....53 D3
Atwell Pl KT7 .....197 A1
Atwell Rd 4 SE15 .....140 A3
Atwood Ave TW9 .....132 C3
Atwood Ho SE21 .....161 C1
Atwood Rd W6 .....112 B2
Aubert Ct N5 .....72 D4
Aubert Pk N5 .....72 D4
Aubert Rd N5 .....72 D4
Aubrey Beardsley Ho
SW1 .....259 B3
Aubrey Mans NW1 .....237 A4
Aubrey Moore Point E15 98 A5
Aubrey Pl NW8 .....229 A3
Aubrey Rd E17 .....53 D6
N8 .....50 A4
W14 .....113 B5 244 D3
Aubrey Wlk
W14 .....113 B5 244 D3
Auburn Cl SE14 .....141 A5
Aubyn Hill SE27 .....183 B6
Aubyn Sq SW15 .....156 A6
Auckland Cl SE19 .....183 D2
Enfield EN1 .....6 B6
Auckland Ct UB4 .....84 C3
Auckland Gdns SE19 ..183 D2
Auckland Hill SE27 ....183 A6
Auckland Ho 11 W12 ..112 B6
Auckland Rd E10 .....75 D5
SE19 .....183 D2
SW11 .....136 C1
Ilford IG1 .....57 A2
Kingston u T KT1 .....198 B5
Auckland Rise SE19 ...183 C2
Auckland St SE11 .....260 C1
Audax 29 NW9 .....27 D1
Auden Pl NW1 .....231 A6
Audley Cl N10 .....31 B3
Audley Ct E11,E18 .....54 D5
W1 .....248 C4
W5 .....88 C2
Northolt UB5 .....84 C4
Pinner Green HA5 .....22 C1
Surbiton KT5 .....198 B3
Twickenham TW2 .....152 B1
Audley Dr 3 E16 .....121 B5
Audley Gdns IG3 .....79 D6
Audley Ho 11 E5 .....74 C6
N8 .....50 A5
Audley Pl SM2 .....217 D1
Audley Rd NW4 .....46 B3
W5 .....88 B2
Enfield EN2 .....4 D3
Richmond TW10 .....154 B6
Audley Sq W1 .....248 B4
Audrey Cl BR3 .....207 D3
Audrey Gdns HA0 .....65 B6
Audrey Rd IG1 .....78 D5
Audrey St E2 .....96 A5
Audric Cl KT2 .....176 C2
Augurs La 3 E13 .....99 B4
Augusta Cl KT8 .....195 B6
Augusta Rd TW2 .....152 A2
Augustas Cl W12 .....112 B3
Augustine Rd W14 ....112 D3
Harrow HA3 .....24 A2
Augustines Ct E9 .....74 C3
Augustus Cl TW8 .....131 D5
Augustus Ct SE19 .....183 C3
SW16 .....159 D2
8 SW19 .....157 A3
Feltham TW12 .....173 B6
Hounslow TW3 .....130 A1
Augustus Rd SW19 ....157 A3
Augustus St NW1 93 B4 231 D2
Aulton Pl SE11 .....261 B1
Aultone Way
Carshalton SM5 .....218 D5
Sutton SM1 .....218 A6
Aultone Yd Ind Est
SM5 .....218 D5
Aurelia Cotts IG2 .....57 A2
Aurelia Gdns CR0 .....204 B3
Aurelia Rd CR0 .....204 B3
Auriga Mews N1 .....73 B3
Auriol Cl KT4 .....215 C5
Auriol Cty Jun Sch
KT19 .....215 D4
Auriol Dr Greenford UB6 ..64 B1
Hillingdon UB10 .....60 D2
Auriol Mans W14 .....254 A3
Auriol Park Rd KT4 ....215 C5
Auriol Rd W14 .113 A2 254 A3
Aurora Ct IG8 .....36 D6
Austell Gdns NW7 .....11 C1
Austell Hts NW7 .....11 C1
Austen Cl SE28 .....124 B5
Austen Ho 2 NW6 .....91 C4
Austen Rd Erith DA8 ....147 D5
Harrow HA2 .....63 D6
Austin Ave BR1,BR2 ....210 A4
Austin Cl SE23 .....163 B4
Isleworth TW1 .....153 C6
Austin Ct 10 E6 .....99 C6
9 Enfield EN1 .....17 C6
Austin Friars EC2 .....242 D2
Austin Friars Sq EC2 ..242 D2
Austin Ho 1 SE14 .....141 B5
6 SW2 .....160 B6
19 Kingston u T KT6 ....198 A4
Austin Rd SW11 137 A4 268 A1
Hayes UB3 .....105 D4
Austin St E2 .....95 D4
Austins Ct SE15 .....140 A2
Austin's La UB10 .....61 A5
Austral Cl DA15 .....167 D1
Austral St SE11 116 D2 261 C4
Australia Rd W12 .....112 B6
Austyn Gdns KT5 .....198 D1
Autumn Cl SW19 .....180 A4
Enfield EN1 .....6 A4
Autumn Lo CR2 .....221 C4
Autumn St E3 .....97 C6
Avalon Cl SW20 .....179 A1
W13 .....87 A2
Enfield EN2 .....4 C3
Avalon Rd SW6 135 D4 265 C2
W13 .....87 A3
Avard Gdns BR6 .....227 A4
Avarn Rd SW17 .....180 D4
Ave Maria La EC4 .....241 D1
Avebury Ct N1 .....235 C5
Avebury Rd E11 .....54 B1
SW19 .....179 B2
Orpington BR6 .....227 B5
Avebury St N1 .....235 C5
Aveley Ct 15 E5 .....74 B6
Aveley Mans 1 IG11 ...78 D1
Aveline St SE11 116 C1 261 A1
Aveling Park Rd E17 ...35 C1
Aveling Park Sch E17 ..35 C1
Avenell Mans N5 .....72 D4
Avenell Rd N5 .....72 D5
Avenfield Ho W1 .....247 D6
Avening Rd SW18 .....157 C4
Avening Terr SW18 ....157 C4
Avenons Rd E13 .....99 A3
Avenue Cl N14 .....15 C5
NW8 .....92 C6 230 B5
Cranford TW5 .....128 B4
Avenue Cres W3 .....110 D4
Cranford TW5 .....128 B5
Avenue Ct NW2 .....69 A5
SE20 .....184 C2
SW3 .....257 C3
W5 .....87 D2
Redbridge IG5 .....56 A6
Avenue Elmers KT6 ....198 A4
Avenue Gate IG10 .....21 C5
Avenue Gdns SE25 .....184 A1
SW14 .....133 C2
W3 .....110 D4
Cranford TW5 .....128 B5
Teddington TW11 .....174 D4
Avenue Hall N6 .....49 D3
Avenue Ho N16 .....74 A6
NW8 .....230 A3
NW10 .....90 B5
Avenue Ind Est E4 .....35 B4
Avenue Lo 12 NW8 .....70 B1
Avenue Mans N10 .....31 C1
NW3 .....69 D3
Avenue Mews N10 .....49 B6
Avenue Par N21 .....17 B4
Sunbury TW16 .....194 B6
Avenue Park Rd SE21,
SE27 .....160 D2
Avenue Prim Sch E12 ...78 A3
Avenue Rd E7 .....77 B4
N6 .....49 D2
N12 .....30 A6
N14 .....15 C5
N15 .....51 B4
NW8 .....92 C6 230 A6
NW10 .....89 D5
SE25 .....184 A1
SW16 .....181 D1
SW20 .....178 B1
W3 .....110 D4
Bexleyheath DA6,DA7 ...147 A2
Brentford TW8 .....109 C1
Feltham TW13 .....149 D1
Hampton TW12 .....173 D2
Hounslow TW7 .....130 D4
Ilford RM6 .....58 C2
Kingston u T KT1 .....198 A6
New Malden KT3 .....199 C5
Pinner HA5 .....41 A6
South Norwood BR3,SE20 184 D2
Southall UB1 .....107 B5
Teddington TW11 .....175 A4
Wallington SM6 .....219 C1
Woodford IG8 .....37 C4
Avenue Rd Sta BR3 ....184 D1
Avenue S KT5 .....198 C2
Avenue Terr Ilford IG2 ...57 C3
Kingston u T KT3 .....199 A6
Avenue The E4 .....36 B5
E11 .....55 B4
N8 .....50 C6
N10 .....31 C1
N11 .....31 B5
N17 .....33 C1
NW6 .....91 A6
SW4 .....159 A6
SW18,SW12 .....158 C4
W4 .....111 C3
W13 .....87 B1
Beckenham BR3 .....186 A2
Bexley DA5 .....168 D4
Bromley BR1 .....209 D6
8 Buckhurst Hill IG9 ....21 C2

Avenue The *continued*
Claygate KT10 212 C3
Cranford TW5 128 A4
Hampton TW12 173 B4
High Barnet EN5 1 A2
Hounslow TW3 151 D6
Keston Mark BR2 225 D5
Loughton IG10 21 D5
Old Malden KT4 215 D6
Orpington BR6 227 D6
Pinner HA5 41 B3
Pinner HA5 23 B4
Richmond TW9 132 B3
South Croydon CR0 221 C5
St Paul's Cray BR5 190 B3
Stoneleigh KT17,SM3 216 C1
Sunbury TW16 172 B1
Surbiton KT5 198 B3
Twickenham TW1 153 B6
Uxbridge UB10 60 D5
Wallington SM5 219 A1
Wembley HA9 44 B1
West Wickham BR4 208 C2
4 Worcester Pk KT4 200 A1
Averil Gr SW16 182 D4
Averill St W6 134 D6
Avern Gdns KT8 195 D5
Avern Rd KT8 195 D5
Avery Ct SE20 184 B3
Avery Farm Row SW1 258 C3
Avery Gdns IG2 56 B4
Avery Hill Coll (Mile End Annexe) E3 97 B3
Avery Hill Rd SE9 167 B3
Avery Row W1 115 B6 248 D6
Aviary Cl E16 98 D2
Aviemore Cl BR3 207 B4
Aviemore Way BR3 207 A4
Avigdor (Jewish) JMI Sch N16 73 B6
Avignon Rd SE4 140 D2
Avington Ct SE1 263 B3
Avington Gr SE20 184 C3
Avion Cres NW7,NW9 28 A2
Avis Sq E1 96 D1
Avoca Rd SW17 181 A6
Avocet Cl SE1 118 A1
Avocet Mews SE28 123 B3
Avon Cl Hayes UB4 84 C3
Sutton SM1 218 A4
Worcester Pk KT4 216 A6
Avon Ct N12 29 D5
11 SW15 157 A6
1 W3 89 A1
Southall UB6 85 D3
Wembley HA0 65 A4
Avon Ho 14 N16 73 B4
N21 16 B6
W14 254 D3
7 Kingston u T KT2 175 D2
Avon House Sch IG8 37 A6
Avon Mews HA5 23 B2
Avon Pl SE1 252 B1
Avon Rd E17 54 B6
SE4 141 C2
Ashford TW16 171 D3
Southall UB6 85 D3
Avon Way E18 55 A6
Avondale Ave N12 29 D5
NW2 67 C5
Barnet EN4 14 D3
Hinchley Wood KT10 213 A5
New Malden KT4 199 D1
Avondale Cres Enfield EN3 7 A2
Redbridge IG4 55 D4
Avondale Ct E11 54 C1
E16 98 C2
E18 37 B2
9 Sutton SM2 218 A1
Avondale Dr UB3 106 B5
Avondale Gdns TW4 151 B6
Avondale Ho 10 SE1 118 A1
6 SW14 133 B2
Avondale Mans SW6 264 C2
Avondale Mews BR1 187 A4
Avondale Park Gdns W11 113 A6 244 A5
Avondale Park Prim Sch W11 113 A6 244 A5
Avondale Park Rd W11 113 A6 244 A6
Avondale Rd E16 98 C2
E17 53 C2
N3 30 A2
N13 16 C2
N15 50 D4
SE9 166 A2
SW14 133 B2
SW19 179 D5
Bexley DA16 146 C3
Bromley BR1 186 D4
Harrow HA3 42 D6
South Croydon CR2 221 A2
Avondale Rise SE15 139 D2
Avondale Sq SE1 118 A1
Avonfield Ct E17 54 B6
Avonhurst Ho NW6 69 A1
Avonley Rd SE14 140 C5
Avonmore Gdns W14 254 D3
Avonmore Pl W14 254 B4
Avonmore Prim Sch W14 113 A2 254 B4
Avonmore Rd W14 113 B2 254 C4
Avonmouth St SE1 262 A6
Avonstowe Cl BR6 227 A5
Avonwick Rd TW3 129 D3
Avril Way E4 36 A5
Avriol Ho W12 112 B5
Avro Ct E9 75 A3
Avro Way SM6 220 A1
Awlfield Ave N17 33 B2
Awliscombe Rd DA16 145 D3
Axe St IG11 101 A6
Axeholm Ave HA8 26 D2
Axford Ho SW2 160 D3
Axminster Cres DA16 146 C4
Axminster Rd N7 72 B5
Aybrook St W1 93 A2 238 A3
Aycliffe Cl BR1 210 B5
Aycliffe Ct KT1 176 C1
Aycliffe Rd W12 112 A5
Ayerst Ct 1 E10 54 A2
Aylands Cl HA9 66 A6
Ayles Ct UB4 84 B4
Ayles Rd UB4 84 B4
Aylesbury Cl E7 76 D2
Aylesbury Ct SM1 218 A5
Aylesbury Ho 13 SE15 140 A6
Aylesbury Rd SE17 117 B1 262 D1
Bromley BR2 209 A6
Aylesbury St EC1 94 D3 241 C5
NW10 67 B5
Aylesford Ave BR3 207 A4
Aylesford Ho SE1 252 D1
Aylesford St SW1 115 D1 259 C1
Aylesham Centre The SE15 140 A4
Aylesham Cl NW7 28 A3
Aylesham Rd BR6 211 D2
Aylestone Ave NW6 90 D6
Aylett Rd SE25 206 B5
Hounslow TW7 130 C3
Ayley Croft EN1 18 A6
Aylmer Cl HA7 25 A6
Aylmer Ct N2 48 D4
Aylmer Dr HA7 25 A6
Aylmer Ho SE10 120 B1
Aylmer Rd E11 54 D1
N2 48 C4
W12 111 D4
Dagenham RM8 81 A5
Aylofte Rd RM9 81 B2
Aylsham Dr UB10 61 A6
Aylton Est 22 SE16 118 C4
Aylward Fst & Mid Sch HA7 25 D5
Aylward Ho 18 E14 97 A2
Aylward Rd SE23 162 D2
SW20 201 B6
Aylward Sch N18 33 B6
Aylward St E1 96 D1
Aylwards Rise HA7 25 A6
Aylwin Est SE1 263 B6
Aylwin Girls Sch SE1 117 D2 263 D4
Aynhoe Mans W14 112 D2
Aynhoe Rd W14 112 D3
Ayr Ct W3 88 C2
Ayres Cl E13 99 A4
Ayres Cres NW10 67 B1
Ayres St SE1 117 A4 252 B2
Aysome Rd N16 73 C5
Ayrton Gould Ho 9 E2 96 D4
Ayrton Ho HA9 65 D6
Ayrton Rd SW7 114 B3 256 C6
Aysgarth Ct SM1 217 D5
Aysgarth Rd SE21 161 C4
Ayston Ho 15 SE8 118 D2
Ayton Ho SE5 139 B5
Aytoun Ct 17 SW9 138 B3
Aytoun Pl SW9 138 B3
Aytoun Rd SW9 138 B3
Azalea Cl W7 108 D5
Ilford IG1 78 D3
Azalea Ct W7 108 D5
Azalea Ho SE14 141 B5
Azalea Wlk HA5 40 B3
Azelea Ct IG8 36 C3
Azenby Rd SE15 139 D3
Azof St SE10 120 C2
Azov Ho 9 E1 97 A3

B

B Sky B Hq TW7 131 A6
Baalbec Rd N5 72 D3
Babbacombe Cl KT9 213 D3
Babbacombe Gdns IG4 56 A5
Babbacombe Rd BR1 187 A2
Baber Bridge Par TW14 150 C5
Baber Dr TW14 150 C5
Babington Ct SW16 181 D5
WC1 240 B4
Babington Ho SE1 252 B2
Babington House Sch BR7 188 B4
Babington Rd NW4 46 B5
SW16 181 D5
Dagenham RM8 80 C4
Babington Rise HA9 66 C2
Babmaes St SW1 249 C5
Bacchus Wlk 12 N1 95 C5
Bache's St N1 95 B4 235 D1
Back Church La E1 96 A1
Back Hill EC1 241 B5
Back La N8 50 A4
NW3 70 A4
Brentford TW8 131 D6
Burnt Oak HA8 27 A2
Back La *continued*
Dagenham RM6 59 A2
Old Bexley DA5 169 C4
Richmond TW10 153 C2
Back Rd Sidcup DA14 190 A6
Teddington TW11 174 C3
Backhouse Pl SE1 263 B3
Backley Gdns SE25 206 A3
Bacon Gr SE1 117 D3 263 C5
Bacon La NW9 44 D5
Edgware HA8 26 C2
Bacon St E2 95 D3 243 D6
Bacon Terr RM8 80 B3
Bacon's Coll SE16 119 A4
Bacon's La N6 49 A1
Bacton NW5 71 A3
Bacton St E2 96 C4
Baddeley Cl EN3 7 C6
Baddeley Ho SE11 260 D2
Baddow Cl RM10 103 C6
Baddow Wlk N1 235 A6
Baddows Cl IG8 37 D4
Baden Ct N11 31 D3
Baden Pl SE1 252 C2
Baden Powell Cl Dagenham RM9 103 A6
Surbiton KT6 214 B6
Baden Powell Ho 11 DA17 125 C3
Baden Powell JMI Sch E5 74 B5
Baden Rd N8 49 D5
Ilford IG1 78 D3
Badger Cl Feltham TW13 150 B1
Hounslow TW4 128 C2
Badger Ct NW2 68 C5
Badgers Cl Ashford TW15 170 B5
Enfield EN2 4 D2
Harrow HA1 42 B3
Hayes UB3 105 C6
Badgers Copse Orpington BR6 227 D6
Worcester Pk KT4 215 D6
Badgers Croft N20 13 A3
SE9 166 C1
Badgers Wlk KT3 177 C1
Badlis Rd E17 53 C6
Badminton KT2 176 D2
Badminton Cl Harrow HA1 42 C5
Northolt UB5 63 C2
Badminton Ct 9 N4 51 A2
Badminton Ho SE22 139 C1
Badminton Mews 10 E16 121 A5
Badminton Rd SW12 159 A5
Badric Ct SW11 136 B3
Badsworth Rd 3 SE5 139 A4
Bagley Cl UB7 104 A4
Bagley's La SW6 135 D4 265 D1
Bagleys Spring RM6 59 A5
Bagnigge Ho WC1 234 A1
Bagshot Ho NW1 231 D2
Bagshot Rd EN1 17 D5
Bagshot St SE17 117 C1 263 B1
Baildon 28 E2 96 C5
Baildon St SE8 141 B5
Bailey Cl E4 36 A6
N11 31 D3
Bailey Ct 4 E4 36 B5
9 W12 112 A4
Bailey Ho 11 SE26 184 B5
Bailey Mews W4 132 D6
Bailey Pl SE26 184 D4
Bain Ho 23 SW9 138 A3
Bainbridge cl KT2 176 A5
Bainbridge Rd RM9 81 B4
Bainbridge St WC1 239 D2
Baines Cl CR2 221 B3
Baird Ave UB1 108 A6
Baird Cl E10 53 C1
NW9 45 A3
Baird Gdns SE19 183 C6
Baird Ho 29 W12 112 B6
12 Belvedere DA17 125 C3
Baird Rd EN1 6 B1
Baird St EC1 242 B6
Baizdon Rd SE3 142 C3
Baker Beall Ct DA7 147 D2
Baker Ct E11 76 B5
Baker Ho 12 E3 97 D4
W7 108 D5
Baker La CR4 203 A6
Baker Rd NW10 89 C6
SE18 144 A4
Baker St W1 92 D2 237 D4
Enfield EN1 5 B4
Baker Street W1 92 D2 237 D4
Baker Street Sta NW1 92 D3 237 D5
Bakers' Almshouses E10 53 D3
Bakers Ave E17 53 D3
Bakers Ct SE25 205 C6
Bakers End SW20 179 A1
Bakers Field N7 72 A4
Bakers Gdns SM5 218 C6
Bakers Hall Ct EC3 253 B5
Bakers Hill E5 52 C1
Barnet EN5 1 D3
Bakers Ho W5 109 D5
Baker's La N6 48 D3
Bakers Mews 9 BR6 227 D2
Baker's Mews W1 238 A2
Bakers Rents 13 E2 95 D4
Bakers Row E15 98 C5
Baker's Row EC1 94 C3 241 A5
Baker's Yd EC1 241 A5
Bakery Mews KT6 198 C1
Bakewell Dr KT3 177 C1
Balaam Ho SM1 217 C4
Balaam St E13 99 B4
Balaams La N14 15 D2
Balaclava Rd SE1 117 D2 263 D3
Long Ditton KT6 197 C2
Balcaskie Rd SE9 166 B6
Balchen Rd SE3 143 D3
Balchier Rd SE22 162 B5
Balcombe Cl DA6 146 D1
Balcombe Ho NW1 237 C6
3 SW2 160 B3
Balcombe St NW1 92 D3 237 C5
Balcon Ct W5 88 B1
Balcorne St E9 74 C1
Balder Rise SE12 165 B2
Balderton Flats W1 238 B1
Balderton St W1 93 A1 238 B1
Baldewyne Ct N17 34 A2
Baldock Ho 32 SE5 139 A3
Baldock St E3 97 D5
Baldrey Ho 1 SE10 120 D1
Baldry Gdns SW16 182 B4
Baldwin Cres SE5 139 A4
Baldwin Ho 15 SW2 160 C3
Baldwin St EC1 235 C1
Baldwin Terr N1 95 A5 235 A4
Baldwin's Gdns EC1 94 C2 241 A4
Baldwyn Gdns W3 111 B6
Bales Coll W10 90 D4
Balfe St N1 94 A5 233 B3
Balfern Gr W4 111 C1
Balfern St SW11 136 C3
Balfour Ave W7 108 D5
Balfour Bsns Ctr UB2 106 D3
Balfour Gr N20 14 D1
Balfour Ho W10 90 D2
Balfour Mews N9 18 A1
W1 248 B4
Balfour Pl SW15 134 B1
W1 248 B5
Balfour Rd N5 73 A4
SE25 206 A5
SW19 179 D3
W3 89 A2
W13 109 B4
Bromley BR2 209 D4
Harrow HA1 42 B4
Hounslow TW3 129 D2
Ilford IG1 57 A1
Southall UB2 106 D3
Wallington SM5 218 D1
Balfour St SE17 117 B2 262 C4
Balfron Twr 2 E14 98 A1
Balgonie Rd E4 20 B3
Balgowan Cl KT3 199 C5
Balgowan Prim Sch BR3 185 A1
Balgowan Rd BR3 185 B1
Balgowan St SE18 123 D2
Balham Gr SW12 159 A4
Balham High Rd SW12, SW17 159 A3
Balham Hill SW12 159 B5
Balham New Rd SW12 159 B4
Balham Park Mans SW12 158 D3
Balham Park Rd SW12, SW17 159 A3
Balham Rd N9 18 A2
Balham Sta SW12 159 B3
Balham Station Rd SW12 159 B3
Balin Ho SE1 252 C2
Balkan Wlk E1 118 B6
Ball Ct EC3 242 D1
Ballamore Rd BR1 165 A1
Ballance Rd E9 75 A2
Ballantine St SW18 136 A1
Ballantrae Ho NW2 69 B4
Ballard Cl KT2 177 B3
Ballard Ho SE10 141 D6
Ballards Cl RM10 103 D6
Ballards Farm Rd CR0, CR2 222 A2
Ballards La N3 29 D3
Ballards Mews HA8 26 C4
Ballards Rd NW2 68 A6
Dagenham RM10 103 D6
Ballards Rise CR2 222 A2
Ballards Way CR0,CR2 222 B2
Ballast Quay SE10 120 B1
Ballater Cl WD1 22 C6
Ballater Rd SW2,SW4 138 A1
South Croydon CR2 221 D3
Ballin Ct 9 E14 120 A4
Ballina St SE23 162 D4
Ballingdon Rd SW11 159 A5
Ballinger Point 18 E3 97 D4
Balliol Ave E4 36 C6
Balliol Ho 11 SW15 156 D5
Balliol Rd N17 33 C2
W10 90 D1
Bexley DA16 146 B3
Balloch Rd SE6 164 B2
Ballogie Ave NW10 67 C4
Ballow Cl 23 SE5 139 C5
Ball's Pond Pl 8 N1 73 B2
Ball's Pond Rd N1 73 C2
Balmain Cl W5 109 D5
Balmain Ct TW3 129 D4
Balman Ho 3 SE16 118 D2
Balmer Rd E3 97 B5
Balmes Rd N1 95 B6 235 D6
Balmoral Ave N11 31 B5
Beckenham BR3 207 A5
Balmoral Cl 1 SW15 156 D5
Balmoral Cres KT8 195 C6
Balmoral Ct NW8 229 C4
SE12 187 B6
21 SE16 118 D5
SE27 183 A6
W5 87 D1
11 Belmont SM2 217 C1
North Cheam KT4 216 B6
Wembley HA9 66 B5
Balmoral Dr Borehamwood WD6 11 B6
Hayes UB4 83 D3
Southall UB1 85 B3
Balmoral Gdns W13 109 A3
Ilford IG3 57 D1
Sidcup DA5 169 B4
Balmoral Gr N7 72 B2
Balmoral Ho E17 35 B1
N4 51 A1
W14 254 A4
Balmoral Mews W12 111 D3
Balmoral Rd E7 77 C3
E10 75 D6
NW2 68 B2
Harrow HA2 63 C4
Kingston u T KT1 198 B5
North Cheam KT4 216 B6
Balmoral Trad Est IG11 101 D2
Balmore Cres EN4 15 A6
Balmore St N19 71 B6
Balmuir Gdns SW15 134 C1
Balnacraig Ave NW10 67 C4
Balniel Gate SW1 259 D2
Balsam Ho 8 E14 119 D6
Baltic Cl SW19 180 B3
Baltic Ho 7 SE5 139 A3
Baltic St E EC1 95 A3 242 A5
Baltic St W EC1 95 A3 242 A5
Baltimore Ho SE11 261 A2
Baltimore Pl DA16 145 D3
Balvaird Pl SW1 259 D1
Balvernie Gr SW18 157 C4
Bamber Ho 5 IG11 101 A6
Bamborough Gdns 12 W12 112 C4
Bamburgh 9 N17 34 B3
Bamford Ave HA0 88 B5
Bamford Ct E15 75 D3
Bamford Rd Barking IG11 79 A2
Catford BR1 186 B5
Bampfylde Cl SM6 219 C5
Bampton Ct W5 87 D1
Bampton Dr NW7 28 A3
Bampton Rd SE23 162 D1
Banavie Gdns BR3 186 A2
Banbury Cl EN2 4 D4
Banbury Ct W13 109 A3
WC2 250 A6
8 Belmont SM2 217 C1
Banbury Ho 5 E9 74 D1
Banbury Rd E9 74 D1
E17 35 A3
Banbury St 3 SW11 136 C3
Banbury Wlk UB5 85 C5
Banchory Rd SE3 143 B5
Bancroft Ave N2 48 C4
Woodford IG9 21 A2
Bancroft Cl TW15 170 C5
Bancroft Ct SW8 270 A2
Northolt UB5 84 C6
Bancroft Gdns Harrow HA3 24 A2
Orpington BR6 211 D1
Bancroft Ho 10 E1 96 C3
Bancroft Rd E1 96 D3
Harrow HA3 24 A1
Bancroft's Sch IG8 21 A1
Bandon Cl UB10 82 B5
Bandon Hill Prim Sch SM6 219 D2
Bandon Rise SM6 219 D3
Banff Ho 1 NW3 70 C2
Banfor Ct SM6 219 C3
Bangabandhu JMI Sch E2 96 C4
Bangalore St SW15 134 D2
Bangor Cl UB5 63 D3
Banim St W6 112 B2
Banister Ho E9 74 D3
SW8 269 B2
15 W10 91 A4
Banister Rd W10 90 D4
Bank Ave CR4 180 B1
Bank Ct SW11 268 C2
Bank End SE1 252 B4
Bank La SW15 155 C6
Kingston u T KT2 176 A3
Bank Mews SM1 218 A2
Bank of England★ EC2 242 C1
Bank Par N11 31 B5
Bank Sta EC3 95 B1 242 D1
Bank The N6 49 B1
Bank Willow TW10 153 B1
Bankfoot Rd BR1 186 C6
Bankhurst Rd SE6 163 B4
Banks Ho SE1 262 A5
Hounslow TW7 130 C3
Banks La DA6 147 B1
Banksia Rd N18 34 D5
Bankside SE1 252 B4
SE1 117 A6 252 A5
Enfield EN2 4 D4
South Croydon CR2 221 D2
Bankside *continued*
Southall UB1 106 D5
Bankside Ave UB5 84 A5
Bankside Cl Carshalton SM5 218 C2
Isleworth TW7 130 D1
Bankside Dr KT7 213 B6
Bankside Pk IG11 102 A4
Bankside Rd IG1 79 B3
Bankside Way 6 SE19 183 C4
Bankton Rd SW2 138 C1
Bankwell Rd SE13 142 C1
Banner Ho EC1 242 B5
Banner St EC1 95 A3 242 B6
Bannerman Ho SW8 270 C5
Banning Ho 4 SW19 156 D3
Banning St SE10 120 C1
Bannister Cl SW2 160 C3
Greenford UB6 64 B3
Bannister Ho 28 SE14 140 D6
Bannister Sports Ctr The HA3 24 A4
Bannockburn Prim Sch SE18 123 D2
Bannockburn Rd SE18 123 D2
Banqueting House★ SW1 250 A3
Banstead Ct N4 51 A1
Banstead Gdns N9 17 C1
Banstead Rd SM2,SM5 218 C1
Banstead St SE15 140 C2
Banstead Way SM6 220 A3
Banstock Rd HA8 26 D4
Banting Dr N21 16 B6
Banting Ho 6 NW2 68 A5
Bantock Ho 14 W10 91 A4
Banton Cl EN1 6 B3
Bantry Ho 13 E1 96 D3
Bantry St SE5 139 B5
Banwell Rd DA5 168 D5
Banyan Ho 8 NW3 69 D2
Banyard Rd SE16 118 B3
Baptist Gdns NW5 71 A2
Barandon Wlk 6 W11 112 D6
Barb Mews W6 112 C3
Barbanel Ho 19 E1 96 C3
Barbara Brosnan Ct NW8 229 C3
Barbara Cl TW17 192 D4
Barbara Hucklesbury Cl N22 32 D1
Barbara Martin Ho 1 N11 31 C5
Barbara Ward Ct 3 E11 76 C6
Barbauld Rd N16 73 C5
Barber Beaumont Ho 21 E1 96 D4
Barber Cl N21 16 C4
Barbers Alley 1 E13 99 B4
Barbers Rd E15 97 D5
Barbican★ EC2 95 A2 242 B3
Barbican Arts & Con Ctr EC2 95 A2 242 B4
Barbican Rd UB1 85 D1
Barbican Sta EC1 95 A2 242 A4
Barbon Cl WC1 240 C4
Barbot Cl N9 18 A1
Barbrook Ho E9 74 C2
Barchard St SW18 157 D6
Barchester Cl W7 108 D5
Barchester Lo N12 29 D6
Barchester Rd HA3 24 B1
Barchester St E14 97 D2
Barclay Cl SW6 135 C5 265 A3
Barclay Ct N12 30 A5
Barclay Ho 21 E9 74 C1
Barclay Jun & Inf Schs E10 54 B3
Barclay Oval IG8 37 A6
Barclay Rd E11 54 D1
E13 99 C3
E17 54 A4
N18 33 B4
SW6 135 C5 265 B3
Croydon CR0 221 B5
Barcombe Ave SW2 160 B2
Bard Rd W10 112 D6
Bardell Ho 14 SE1 118 A4
Barden St SE18 145 C5
Bardfield Ave RM6 58 D6
Bardney Rd SM4 201 D5
Bardolph Rd N7 72 A4
Richmond TW9 132 B2
Bardsey Pl 35 E1 96 C3
Bardsey Wlk 2 N1 73 A2
Bardsley Cl CR0 221 D5
Bardsley Ho 5 SE10 142 A6
Bardsley La SE10 142 A6
Barents Ho 10 E1 96 D3
Barfett St W10 91 B3
Barfield Ave N20 14 D2
Barfield Rd E11 54 D1
Bromley BR1,BR7 210 C6
Barfleur Ho SE8 119 B2
Barford Cl NW4 28 A2
Barford Ho 19 E3 97 B5
Barford St N1 94 C6 234 B5
Barforth Rd SE15 140 B2
Barfreston Way SE20 184 B2
Bargate Cl SE18 123 D1
New Malden KT3 200 A2
Barge House Rd E16 122 D4
Barge House St SE1 251 B4
Barge Wlk KT1,KT6,KT7 197 B3
Bargery Rd SE6 163 D3
Bargrove Cl 8 SE20 184 A3
Bargrove Cres SE6 163 B2

Barham Cl
Chislehurst West BR7 ... 188 D5
Keston Mark BR2 ... 210 A1
Wembley HA0 ... 65 C2
Barham Ct N12 ... 29 B5
8 Croydon CR2 ... 221 A4
Keston Mark BR2 ... 210 A1
Wembley HA0 ... 65 C2
Barham Ho SE17 ... 263 B2
Barham Prim Sch HA0 ... 65 C2
Barham Rd SW20 ... 178 A3
Chislehurst West BR7 ... 188 D5
Croydon CR2 ... 221 A3
Baring Cl SE12 ... 165 A2
Baring Ct N1 ... 235 C5
Baring Ho 11 E14 ... 97 C1
Baring Prim Sch SE12 ... 165 A4
Baring Rd SE12 ... 165 A2
Cockfosters EN4 ... 2 B2
Croydon CR0 ... 206 A1
Baring St N1 ... 95 B6 235 C5
Bark Pl W2 ... 113 D6 245 C6
Barker Dr NW1 ... 71 D1
Barker Ho N15 ... 50 D5
SE17 ... 263 A3
SE21 ... 161 C1
Barker Mews SW4 ... 137 B1
Barker St SW10 ... 266 A6
Barker Wlk SW16 ... 159 D1
Barkham Rd N17 ... 33 C3
Barking Abbey Comp Sch
IG11 ... 79 D2
Barking Abbey Comp Sch
(Lower Sch) IG11 ... 79 C3
Barking CE Prim Sch
IG11 ... 79 A1
Barking Flyover IG11 ... 78 D1
Barking Hospl IG11 ... 79 D1
Barking Ind Pk IG11 ... 102 A6
Barking Rd E6 ... 100 B6
E13 ... 99 B4
Barking Sta IG11 ... 79 A1
Barkingside Sta IG6 ... 57 B6
Barkston Gdns
SW5 ... 113 D2 255 C3
Barkway Ct N4 ... 73 A6
Barkwith Ho 27 SE14 ... 140 D6
Barkworth Rd SE16 ... 118 C1
Barlborough St SE14 ... 140 D5
Barlby Gdns W10 ... 90 D3
Barlby Prim Sch W10 ... 90 D3
Barlby Rd W10 ... 90 D2
Barley Cl WD2 ... 8 A6
Barley La IG3 ... 58 B3
Barley Lane Prim Sch
RM6 ... 58 B2
Barley Mow Pas EC1 ... 241 D3
W4 ... 111 B1
Barley Mow Way TW17 192 C5
Barleycorn Way E14 ... 119 B6
Barleyfields Cl RM6 ... 58 C2
Barling 6 NW1 ... 71 B1
Barling Ct 1 SW4 ... 138 A3
Barlings Ho 2 SE4 ... 140 D1
Barloch Ho 13 SW11 ... 137 A3
Barlow Cl SM6 ... 220 A1
Barlow Ho N1 ... 235 C2
14 SE16 ... 118 B2
W11 ... 244 A6
Barlow Pl W1 ... 248 D5
Barlow Rd NW6 ... 69 B2
W3 ... 110 D5
Hampton TW12 ... 173 C3
Barlow St SE17 117 B2 262 D3
Barmeston Rd SE6 ... 163 D2
Barmor Cl HA2 ... 23 D1
Barmouth Ave UB6 ... 86 D5
Barmouth Ho 6 N7 ... 72 B6
Barmouth Rd SW18 ... 158 A5
Croydon CR0 ... 222 D6
Barn Cl 19 NW5 ... 71 D3
Ashford TW15 ... 170 D5
Northolt UB5 ... 84 C5
Barn Cres HA7 ... 25 C4
Barn Croft Prim Sch E17 53 A3
Barn Field NW3 ... 70 D3
Barn Hill HA9 ... 44 D1
Barn Rise HA9 ... 66 C6
Barn St N16 ... 73 C6
Barn Way HA9 ... 66 C6
Barnabas Ct N21 ... 16 D6
Barnabas Ho EC1 ... 235 A1
Barnabas Lo SW8 ... 270 B2
Barnabas Rd E9 ... 74 D3
Barnaby Cl HA2 ... 64 A6
Barnaby Ct NW9 ... 45 C6
Barnaby Pl SW7 ... 256 C3
Barnard Cl SE18 ... 122 C3
Chislehurst BR7 ... 189 B2
Sunbury TW16 ... 172 B3
Wallington SM6 ... 219 D1
Barnard Ct SW16 ... 160 B1
Barnard Gdns Hayes UB4 84 B3
West Barnes KT3 ... 200 A5
Barnard Hill N10 ... 31 B2
Barnard Ho 17 E2 ... 96 B4
Barnard Lo 10 W9 ... 91 C2
New Barnet EN5 ... 2 A1
Barnard Mews SW11 ... 136 C1
Barnard Rd SW11 ... 136 C1
Enfield EN1 ... 6 B3
Mitcham CR4 ... 181 A1
Barnardo Dr IG6 ... 57 A5
Barnardo Gdns 1 E1 ... 118 D6
Barnardo St E1 ... 96 D1
Barnard's Inn EC4 ... 241 B2
Barnbrough NW1 ... 232 A5
Barnby Sq 1 E15 ... 98 C6
Barnby St 2 E15 ... 98 C6
NW1 ... 93 C4 232 B2
Barnehurst Rd DA7 ... 147 D3
Barnersbury Ho N7 ... 72 A4
Barnes Ave SW13 ... 134 A5
Southall UB2 ... 107 B2
Barnes Bridge Sta
SW13 ... 133 C3
Barnes Cl E12 ... 77 D4
Barnes Common SW13 134 A2
Barnes Ct E16 ... 99 C2
N1 ... 72 C1
N22 ... 32 A3
New Barnet EN5 ... 1 D1
South Norwood CR7 ... 205 A6
Woodford IG8 ... 37 D5
Barnes End KT3 ... 200 A4
Barnes High St SW13 ... 133 D3
Barnes Ho 14 E2 ... 96 C5
N19 ... 50 A2
26 SE14 ... 140 D6
8 Barking IG11 ... 101 B6
Barnes Hospl SW14 ... 133 C2
Barnes Rd N18 ... 34 C6
Barking IG1 ... 79 A3
Barnes St E14 ... 97 A1
Barnes Sta SW13 ... 134 A2
Barnes Terr SE8 ... 119 B1
Barnes Wallis Ct HA9 ... 67 A5
Barnet Coll EN4 ... 15 A3
Barnet Coll of F Ed EN5 ... 1 B1
Barnet Dr BR2 ... 226 A6
Barnet Gate La
Borehamwood EN5 ... 11 D4
EN5 ... 11 D4
Barnet Gr E2 ... 96 A4
Barnet Hill EN5 ... 1 C1
Barnet Hill JMI Prim Sch
EN5 ... 13 B6
Barnet Ho 38 SE5 ... 139 A3
Barnet La Barnet EN5,N20 13 B4
Deacons Hill WD6 ... 10 B5
Barnet Mus EN5 ... 1 A1
Barnet Rd Barnet EN5 ... 1 B5
Borehamwood EN5 ... 11 C5
Barnet Trad Est EN5 ... 1 B2
Barnet Way (Barnet By-Pass)
EN5,NW7,WD6 ... 11 B3
Barnet Wood Rd BR2 ... 225 C6
Barnett Ho E1 ... 243 C3
Barnett Homestead
NW11 ... 47 C5
Barnett St 8 E1 ... 96 B1
Barnetts Ct HA2 ... 63 D5
Barney Cl SE7 ... 121 C1
Barnfield KT3 ... 199 C3
Barnfield Ave
Croydon CR0 ... 222 C6
Kingston u T KT2 ... 176 A5
Mitcham CR4 ... 203 B6
Barnfield Cl N4 ... 50 A2
SW17 ... 158 A1
Barnfield Gdns SE18 ... 144 D6
Kingston u T KT2 ... 176 A5
Barnfield Pl E14 ... 119 C2
Barnfield Prim Sch HA8 ... 27 A2
Barnfield Rd SE18 ... 144 D6
W5 ... 87 C3
Burnt Oak HA8 ... 27 A2
Erith DA17 ... 147 B6
Barnfield Wood Cl BR3 208 B3
Barnfield Wood Rd
BR3 ... 208 B3
Barnham Rd UB6 ... 86 A4
Barnham St SE1 ... 253 B2
Barnhill HA5 ... 40 C4
Barnhill Ave BR2 ... 208 D4
Barnhill Ct UB4 ... 84 B4
Barnhill La UB4 ... 84 B4
Barnhill Rd Hayes UB4 ... 84 C3
Wembley HA9 ... 67 A5
Barnhurst Path WD1 ... 22 C5
Barningham Way NW9 ... 45 B3
Barnlea Cl TW13 ... 151 A2
Barnmead Gdns RM9 ... 81 B3
Barnmead Rd
Dagenham RM9 ... 81 B3
Penge BR3 ... 185 A2
Barnsbury Cl KT3 ... 199 A5
Barnsbury Cres KT5 ... 199 A1
Barnsbury Gr N7 ... 72 B1
Barnsbury Ho 12 SW4 ... 159 D5
Barnsbury La KT5 ... 199 A1
Barnsbury Pk N1 ... 72 C1
Barnsbury Rd N1 94 C6 234 A5
Barnsbury Sq N1 ... 72 C1
Barnsbury St N1 ... 72 C1
Barnsbury Terr N1 ... 72 B1
Barnscroft SW20 ... 200 B6
Barnsdale Ave E14 ... 119 C2
Barnsdale Rd W9 ... 91 B3
Barnsley St E1 ... 96 B3
Barnstaple Ho SE12 ... 164 D6
Barnstaple La SE13 ... 142 A1
Barnstaple Rd HA4 ... 62 C5
Barnston Wlk N1 ... 235 A6
Barnview Lo HA3 ... 24 C2
Barnwell Ho 1 SE5 ... 139 C4
Barnwell Rd SW2 ... 160 C6
Barnwood Cl W9 ... 91 D3
Ruislip HA4 ... 61 B6
Baron Cl N1 ... 234 A4
N11 ... 31 B5
Baron Ct CR4 ... 202 C5
Baron Gdns IG6 ... 57 A6
Baron Gr CR4 ... 202 C5
Baron Rd RM8 ... 58 D1
Baron St N1 ... 94 C5 234 A4
Baron Wlk E16 ... 98 D2
Baroness Rd 5 E2 ... 95 D4
Baronet Gr N17 ... 34 A2
Baronet Rd N17 ... 34 A2
Barons Court Mans
W14 ... 254 B1
Baron's Court Rd
W14 ... 113 A1 254 B2
Barons Court Sta
W14 ... 113 A1 254 A2
Barons Ct NW9 ... 45 B3
Ilford IG1 ... 79 B6
Wallington SM6 ... 219 D5
Barons Gate 13 W4 ... 111 A3
East Barnet EN4 ... 14 C5
Barons Keep
W14 ... 113 A1 254 A2
Barons Lo 8 E14 ... 120 A2
Barons Mead HA1 ... 42 C5
Baron's Pl SE1 ... 116 C4 251 B1
Barons The TW1 ... 153 B5
Baron's Wlk CR0 ... 207 A3
Baronsfield Rd TW1 ... 153 B5
Baronsmead Rd SW13 ... 134 A4
Baronsmede W5 ... 110 B4
Baronsmere Ct 7 EN5 ... 1 A1
Baronsmere Rd N2 ... 48 C5
Barque Mews SE8 ... 141 C6
Barr Beacon SE23 ... 162 C4
Barra Hall Cir UB3 ... 83 C1
Barra Hall Rd UB3 ... 105 C6
Barrack Rd TW4 ... 129 A1
Barras Cl EN3 ... 7 C6
Barratt Ave N22 ... 32 B1
Barratt Ho 15 N1 ... 72 D1
Barratt Ind Pk E3 ... 98 A3
Southall UB1 ... 107 C5
Barratt Way HA3 ... 42 B6
Barrenger Rd N10 ... 30 D1
Barret Ho NW6 ... 91 C6
2 SW9 ... 138 C2
Barrett Ho SE17 ... 262 B2
Barrett Rd E17 ... 54 A5
Barrett St W1 ... 93 A1 238 B1
Barrett's Gr N16 ... 73 C3
Barrett's Green Rd NW10 89 B5
Barrhill Rd SW2 ... 160 A2
Barridge Mews NW6 ... 69 C3
Barrie Ct EN5 ... 14 A6
Barrie Ho N9 ... 18 B4
8 N16 ... 73 C5
NW8 ... 230 B5
W2 ... 246 B5
W3 ... 111 A4
Barriedale SE14 ... 141 A3
Barringer Sq SW17 ... 181 A6
Barrington Cl NW5 ... 71 A3
Barrington Ct 4 N10 ... 31 B1
NW5 ... 71 A3
Barrington Prim Sch
DA16 ... 146 D3
Barrington Rd E12 ... 78 C2
N8 ... 49 D4
SW9 ... 138 D2
Bexley DA16 ... 146 D3
Cheam SM3 ... 201 C1
Barrington Villas SE18 ... 144 C4
Barrington Wlk 9
SE19 ... 183 C4
Barrow Ave SM5 ... 218 D1
Barrow Cl N21 ... 16 D2
Barrow Ct 6 SE6 ... 164 D3
Barrow Hedges Cl SM5 218 C1
Barrow Hedges Prim Sch
SM5 ... 218 C1
Barrow Hedges Way
SM5 ... 218 C1
Barrow Hill KT4 ... 215 C6
Barrow Hill Cl KT4 ... 215 C6
Barrow Hill Est
NW8 ... 92 C5 230 A3
Barrow Hill Jun Sch
NW8 ... 92 C5 230 A3
Barrow Hill Rd NW8 ... 230 A3
Barrow Point Ave HA5 ... 23 A1
Barrow Point La HA5 ... 23 A1
Barrow Rd SW16 ... 181 D4
Croydon CR0 ... 220 C3
Barrow Wlk TW8 ... 109 C1
Barrowdene Cl HA5 ... 23 A1
Barrowell Gn N21 ... 17 A2
Barrowfield Cl N9 ... 18 C1
Barrowgate Ho W4 ... 111 B1
Barrowgate Rd W4 ... 111 B1
Barrs Rd NW10 ... 67 B1
Barry Ave N15 ... 51 D3
Bexley DA7 ... 147 A5
Barry Cl BR6 ... 227 C5
Barry Ct SW4 ... 159 C5
Barry Ho 4 SE16 ... 118 B1
Barry Lo N4 ... 50 B2
Barry Par SE22 ... 140 A1
Barry Rd E6 ... 100 A1
NW10 ... 67 A1
SE22 ... 162 A6
Barry Terr TW15 ... 148 B2
Barrydene N20 ... 14 B2
Barrydene Ct EN2 ... 4 D2
Barset Rd SE15 ... 140 C2
Barsons Cl SE20 ... 184 C3
Barston Rd SE27 ... 161 A1
Barstow Cres SW2 ... 160 B3
Bartell Ho SW2 ... 160 C5
Barter St WC1 ... 94 A2 240 B3
Barth Rd SE18 ... 123 C2
Bartholomew Cl EC1 ... 242 A3
SW18 ... 136 A1
Bartholomew Ct EC1 ... 242 B6
Bartholomew Ct *continued*
Edgware HA8 ... 25 D3
Bartholomew Ho
23 SE5 ... 139 A3
Enfield EN3 ... 7 A6
Bartholomew La EC2 ... 242 D1
Bartholomew Pas EC1 ... 241 D3
Bartholomew Pl EC1 ... 242 A3
Bartholomew Rd NW5 ... 71 C2
Bartholomew Sq 18 E1 ... 96 B3
Bartholomew St
SE1 ... 117 B3 262 D5
Bartholomew Villas
NW5 ... 71 C2
Bartle Ave E6 ... 100 A5
Bartle Rd W11 ... 91 A1
Bartlett Cl E14 ... 97 C1
Bartlett Ct EC4 ... 241 B2
Bartlett St CR2 ... 221 B3
Bartletts Ho 10 RM10 ... 81 D2
Bartok Ho W11 ... 244 C5
Bartolomew Sq EC1 ... 242 B6
Barton Ave RM7 ... 59 D1
Barton Cl 2 E6 ... 100 B1
E9 ... 74 C3
NW4 ... 46 A5
SE15 ... 140 B2
Bexley DA6 ... 169 A6
Shepperton TW17 ... 192 D3
Barton Ct 10 SW4 ... 138 A3
W14 ... 254 B2
Beckenham BR2 ... 208 B6
Barton Gn KT3 ... 177 B1
Barton Ho 8 E3 ... 97 D4
N1 ... 72 D1
SW6 ... 135 D2
Barton Mdws IG6 ... 57 A5
Barton Rd W14 ... 113 A1 254 B1
Ruxley DA14 ... 191 A4
Barton St SW1 ... 260 A6
Bartons The WD6 ... 9 D5
Bartonway NW8 ... 229 C4
Bartram Cl UB8 ... 82 D3
Bartram Rd SE4 ... 163 A5
Bartrams La EN4 ... 2 A5
Bartrip St E9 ... 75 B2
Barts Cl BR3 ... 207 C4
Barville Cl SE4 ... 141 A1
Barwell Ho 6 E2 ... 96 A3
Barwick Ho 7 W3 ... 111 A4
Barwick Rd E7 ... 77 B4
Barwood Ave BR4 ... 207 D1
Basden Gr TW13 ... 151 C2
Basedale Rd RM9 ... 80 B1
Baseing Cl E6 ... 122 C6
Bashley Rd NW10 ... 89 B3
Basil Ave E6 ... 100 A4
Basil Gdns SE27 ... 183 A5
Croydon CR0 ... 206 D1
Basil Ho 14 E1 ... 96 A1
SW8 ... 270 A4
Basil Mans SW1 ... 247 C1
Basil Spence Ho N22 ... 32 B2
Basil St SW1 ... 114 D3 247 C1
SW1,SW3 ... 114 D3 257 C6
Basildene Rd TW4,TW5 128 D2
Basildon Rd SE2 ... 124 A1
Basilon Rd DA7 ... 147 A3
Basing Cl KT7 ... 196 D2
Basing Ct 12 SE15 ... 139 D4
Basing Dr DA5 ... 169 B5
Basing Hill NW11 ... 47 B1
Wembley HA9 ... 44 C1
Basing Ho SE6 ... 185 C6
7 Barking IG11 ... 101 B6
Basing House Yd 23 E2 ... 95 C4
Basing Pl E2 ... 95 C4
Basing St W11 ... 91 B1
Basing Way N3 ... 47 D6
Thames Ditton KT7 ... 196 D2
Basingdon Way SE5 ... 139 B1
Basingfield Rd KT7 ... 196 D2
Basinghall Ave
EC2 ... 95 B1 242 C2
Basinghall St
EC2 ... 95 B1 242 C2
Basire St N1 ... 95 A6 235 B6
Baskerville Gdns NW10 ... 67 C4
Baskerville Rd SW18 ... 158 C4
Basket Gdns SE9 ... 166 A6
Baslow Cl HA3 ... 24 B2
Baslow Wlk E5 ... 74 D4
Basnett Rd 8 SW11 ... 137 A2
Basque Ct 21 SE16 ... 118 D4
Bassano St SE22 ... 161 D6
Bassant Rd SE18 ... 145 D6
Bassein Park Rd W12 ... 111 D4
Bassett Gdns TW7 ... 130 A5
Bassett Ho RM9 ... 102 B6
Bassett Rd W10 ... 90 D1
Bassett St NW5 ... 71 A2
Bassett Way UB1 ... 85 D1
Bassetts Cl BR6 ... 226 D4
Bassetts Way BR6 ... 226 D4
Bassingbourn Ho 3 N1 ... 72 D1
Bassingham Rd SW18 ... 158 A4
Wembley HA0 ... 65 D2
Bassishaw Highwalk
EC2 ... 242 C3
Basswood Cl SE15 ... 140 B2
Bastable Ave IG11 ... 102 A5
Basterfield Ho EC1 ... 242 A5
Bastion Rd SE18,SE2 ... 124 A1
Baston Manor Rd BR2,
BR4 ... 225 B4
Baston Rd BR2 ... 225 B5
Baston Sch BR2 ... 225 B6
Bastwick St EC1 ... 95 A3 242 A6
Basuto Rd SW6 135 C4 265 B1
Batavia Cl TW16 ... 172 C2
Batavia Ho 1 SE14 ... 141 A5
Batavia Mews 3 SE14 ... 141 A5
Batavia Rd SE14 ... 141 A5
Sunbury TW16 ... 172 B2
Batchelor St N1 ... 94 C6 234 B5
Bate St 10 E14 ... 119 B6
Bateman Cl IG11 ... 79 A2
Bateman Ho 8 SE17 ... 138 D6
Bateman Rd E4 ... 35 C4
Bateman St W1 ... 93 D1 239 C1
Bateman's Bldgs W1 ... 239 C1
Bateman's Row
EC2 ... 95 C3 243 B6
Bates Cres SW16 ... 181 C3
Croydon CR0 ... 220 C3
Bates Point E13 ... 99 A6
Bateson St SE18 ... 123 C2
Bath Cl SE15 ... 140 B5
Bath Ct EC1 ... 241 A5
EC1 ... 235 C1
3 SE26 ... 162 A1
Bath Gr E2 ... 96 A5
Bath Ho E2 ... 96 A3
SE1 ... 262 B6
Bath House Rd CR0 ... 204 A1
Bath Pas KT1 ... 175 D1
Bath Pl 11 EC2 ... 95 C4
14 W6 ... 112 C1
Hadley EN5 ... 1 B2
Bath Rd E7 ... 77 D2
N9 ... 18 C2
W4 ... 111 C2
Dagenham RM6 ... 59 A3
Harlington TW6,UB7,TW5 127 B4
Harmondsworth TW6,UB7 126 B4
Hounslow TW3,TW4,TW5 128 C4
Bath St EC1 ... 95 B4 235 C1
Bath Terr SE1 ... 117 A3 262 A6
Bathgate Ho 8 SW9 ... 138 D4
Bathgate Rd SW19 ... 156 D1
Baths App SW6 135 B5 264 D4
Baths Rd BR1,BR2 ... 209 D5
Bathurst Ave SW19 ... 179 D2
Bathurst Gdns NW10 ... 90 B5
Bathurst Ho 2 W12 ... 112 B6
Bathurst Mews
W2 ... 114 B6 246 D6
Bathurst Rd IG1 ... 56 D1
Bathurst St W2 ... 246 D6
Bathway 17 SE18 ... 122 C2
Batley Cl CR4 ... 202 D2
Batley Pl 3 N16 ... 73 D5
Batley Rd N16 ... 73 D5
Enfield EN2 ... 5 B4
Batman Cl W12 ... 112 B5
Batoum Gdns W6 ... 112 C3
Batson Ho 21 E1 ... 96 A1
Batson St W12 ... 112 A4
Batsworth Rd CR4 ... 202 B6
Batten Cl E6 ... 100 B1
Batten Ho 8 E17 ... 53 D6
7 SW4 ... 159 C6
13 W10 ... 91 A4
Batten St SW11 ... 136 C2
Battenberg Wlk 10
SE19 ... 183 C5
Battersby Rd SE6 ... 164 B1
Battersea Bridge Rd
SW11 ... 136 C5 267 A3
Battersea Church Rd
SW11 ... 136 B4 266 D2
Battersea Dogs Home
SW8 ... 137 B5 268 D3
Battersea High St
SW11 ... 136 B3 266 D1
6 SW11 ... 136 B3
Battersea Park*
SW11 ... 137 A5 268 A3
Battersea Park Rd
SW11,SW8 ... 267 D1
Battersea Park Sta
SW8 ... 137 B5 268 C3
Battersea Power Station(dis)
SW8 ... 137 B6 268 D6
Battersea Rise SW11 ... 136 C1
Battersea Sq SW11 ... 266 D1
Battersea Tech Coll
SW11 ... 136 D4 267 D1
Battery Rd SE28 ... 123 C4
Battishill St 9 N1 ... 72 D1
Battle Bridge Ctr NW1 ... 233 A4
Battle Bridge La
SE1 ... 117 C5 253 A3
Battle Bridge Rd
NW1 ... 94 A5 233 A4
Battle Cl SW19 ... 180 A4
Battle Ho 8 SE15 ... 140 A6
Battle of Britain Mus*
NW9 ... 27 D1
Battlebridge Ct NW1 ... 233 B4
Battledean Rd N5 ... 72 D3
Batty St E1 ... 96 A1
Baty Ho SW2 ... 160 B3
Baudwin Rd SE6 ... 164 C2
Baugh Rd DA14 ... 190 C5
Baulk The SW18 ... 157 C4
Bavant Rd SW16 ... 182 B1
Bavaria Rd N19 ... 72 A6
Bavent Rd SE5 ... 139 A3
Bawdale Rd SE22 ... 161 D6
Bawdsey Ave IG2 ... 57 D5
Bawtree Rd SE14 ... 141 A5
Bawtry Rd N20 ... 14 D1
Baxendale N20 ... 14 A2
Baxendale St E2 ... 96 A4
Baxter Cl Hillingdon UB10 ... 82 D4
Baxter Cl *continued*
Southall UB2 ... 107 D3
Baxter Ho 11 E3 ... 97 D4
Baxter Rd E16 ... 99 C1
N1 ... 73 B2
N18 ... 34 B6
Ilford IG1 ... 78 D3
Bay Ct 7 E1 ... 96 D3
W5 ... 110 A3
Bayard Ct DA7 ... 147 D1
Baycliffe Ho 8 E9 ... 74 D2
Baycroft Cl HA5 ... 40 C6
Baydon Ct BR2 ... 208 D6
Bayer Ho EC1 ... 242 A5
Bayes Ct NW3 ... 70 D1
Bayeux Ho 10 SE7 ... 143 C6
Bayfield Ho 3 SE4 ... 140 D1
Bayfield Rd SE9 ... 143 D1
Bayford Rd NW10 ... 90 D4
Bayford St 5 E8 ... 74 B1
Bayford St Ind Ctr 4 E8 74 B1
Bayham Pl NW1 ... 93 C6 232 B5
Bayham Rd W4 ... 111 B3
W13 ... 109 B5
Morden SM4 ... 202 A5
Bayham St NW1 ... 93 C6 232 A5
Bayhurst Lo N4 ... 51 A2
Bayhurst Wood Countryside
Park UB9 ... 38 B4
Bayleaf Cl TW12 ... 174 B5
Bayley St WC1 ... 239 C3
Baylis Rd SE1 ... 116 C4 251 A1
Bayliss Ave SE28 ... 124 D6
Bayliss Cl N21 ... 16 A6
Bayne Cl E6 ... 100 B1
Baynes Cl EN1 ... 6 A4
Baynes Mews 2 NW3 ... 70 B2
Baynes St NW1 ... 71 C1
Baynham Cl DA5 ... 169 B5
Bayon Ho 27 N19 ... 49 D2
Bayonne Rd W6 ... 264 A5
Bays Cl SE26 ... 184 C5
Bays Ct HA8 ... 26 D5
Bayshill Rise UB5 ... 63 D2
Bayston Rd N16 ... 73 D5
Bayswater Rd
W2 ... 114 B6 246 C5
Bayswater Sta
W2 ... 113 D6 245 D6
Baythorne St 5 E3 ... 97 B2
Bayton Ct 2 E8 ... 74 A1
Baytree Cl Bromley BR1 ... 187 D2
Sidcup DA15 ... 167 D3
Baytree Ho E4 ... 19 D4
Baytree Rd SW2 ... 138 B1
Bazalgette Cl KT3 ... 199 B4
Bazalgette Gdns KT3 ... 199 B4
Bazalgette Ho NW8 ... 236 D6
Bazeley Ho SE1 ... 251 C1
Bazely St E14 ... 120 A6
Bazile Rd N21 ... 16 C5
BBC Television Ctr
W12 ... 112 C5
Beach Ct SE9 ... 166 A5
Beach Gr TW13 ... 151 C2
Beach Ho SW5 ... 255 A2
Beacham Cl SE7 ... 143 D6
Beachborough Rd BR1 186 A6
Beachcroft Rd E11 ... 76 C5
Beachy Rd E3 ... 75 C1
Beacon Gate SE14 ... 140 D2
Beacon Gr SM5 ... 219 A4
Beacon Hill N7 ... 72 A3
Beacon Ho 19 SE5 ... 139 C5
10 SE26 ... 184 B5
SW8 ... 269 C2
Beacon House Sch W5 110 B5
Beacon Rd SE13 ... 164 B5
Stanwell TW19,TW6 ... 148 C5
Beacon Rdbt TW6 ... 148 C5
Beaconfield Terrace Rd
W14 ... 254 A5
Beacons Wlk 10 E6 ... 100 A2
Beaconsfield Cl N11 ... 31 A5
SE3 ... 143 A6
W4 ... 111 A1
Beaconsfield Ct N11 ... 31 A5
Beaconsfield Par 1
SE9 ... 188 A6
Beaconsfield Prim Sch
UB2 ... 107 A5
Beaconsfield Rd E10 ... 76 A5
E16 ... 98 D3
E17 ... 53 B3
N9 ... 18 A1
N11 ... 31 A6
N15 ... 51 C5
NW10 ... 67 D2
SE3 ... 143 A5
SE9 ... 188 A6
SE17 ... 117 C1 263 A1
W4 ... 111 B3
W5 ... 109 D4
Bromley BR1 ... 209 D6
Claygate KT10 ... 212 C1
Enfield EN3 ... 6 D6
Hayes UB4 ... 106 C5
Kingston u T KT3 ... 177 B1
Southall UB1 ... 107 A5
Surbiton KT5 ... 198 B2
Thornton Heath CR0 ... 205 B3
Twickenham TW1 ... 153 B5
Beaconsfield Wlk
SW6 ... 135 B4 264 D1
Beaconshaw BR1 ... 186 C3

Beacontree Ave E17 36 B1
Beacontree Rd E11 54 D2
Beadle Ct CR4 202 C6
Beadlow Cl SM4 202 B3
Beadman Pl SE27 182 D6
Beadman St SE27 182 D6
Beadnell Rd SE23 162 D3
Beadon Rd W6 112 C2
Hayes BR2 209 A4
Beaford Gr SW20 201 B6
Beagle Cl TW13 172 B6
Beak St W1 115 C6 249 B6
Beal Cl DA16 146 A4
Beal High Sch IG5 56 A5
Beal Rd IG1 78 C6
Beale Cl N13 32 D5
Beale Ho 7 SW9 138 B3
Beale Pl E3 97 B5
Beale Rd E3 97 B6
Beam Ave RM10 103 D6
Beames Ho SW8 269 C2
Beaminster Ct N15 51 B4
Beaminster Gdns IG6 56 D6
Beaminster Ho SW8 270 C4
Beamish Dr WD2 8 A3
Beamish Ho 5 SE16 118 C2
Beamish Rd N9 18 A3
Bean Rd DA6 146 D1
Beanacre Cl E9 75 B2
Beanshaw SE9 188 C6
Beansland Gr RM6 59 A6
Bear Alley EC4 241 C2
Bear Cl RM7 59 D3
Bear Croft Ho 6 SW6 135 B3
Bear Gardens Mus
SE1 117 A5 252 A4
Bear Gdns SE1 117 A5 252 A4
Bear La SE1 116 D5 251 D3
Bear Rd TW13 172 D6
Bear St WC2 249 D6
Beard Rd TW10 176 B5
Beardell St SE19 183 D4
Beardow Gr N14 15 C5
Beard's Hill TW12 173 C2
Beards Hill Cl TW12 173 C2
Beard's Rd TW15,TW16 171 C4
Beardsfield E13 99 A5
Beardsley Terr RM8 80 B3
Beardsley Way W3 111 B4
Bearfield Rd KT2 176 A3
Bearstead Rise SE4 163 B6
Bearsted Terr 2 BR3 185 C2
Beasley's Ait La TW15,
TW17 193 D3
Beatrice Ave SW16 182 B1
Wembley HA9 66 A3
Beatrice Cl E13 99 A3
Pinner HA5 40 A5
Beatrice Ct NW4 46 C4
Buckhurst Hill IG9 21 D2
Beatrice Ho 1 SW2 160 B6
4 W6 112 C1
Beatrice Pl W8 255 C5
Beatrice Rd E17 53 C4
N4 50 C2
N9 18 C4
SE1 118 A2
2 Richmond TW10 154 B6
Southall UB1 107 B5
Beatrice Tate Sch E2 96 B4
Beatrice Webb Ho 3 E3 97 A5
Beatrix Ho SW5 255 D2
Beatrix Potter Prim Sch
SW18 158 A3
Beattie Cl TW14 149 D3
Beattie Ho SW8 269 B2
Beattock Rise N10 49 B5
Beatty Rd N16 73 C4
Stanmore HA7 25 C4
Beatty St NW1 232 A4
Beattyville Gdns IG6 56 D5
Beauchamp Cl 16 W4 111 A3
Beauchamp Ct HA7 25 C5
Beauchamp Pl
SW3 114 C3 257 B5
Beauchamp Rd E7 77 B1
SE19 183 B2
SW11 136 D1
East Molesey KT8 196 A4
Sutton SM1 217 C4
Twickenham TW1 153 A4
Beauchamp St EC1 241 A3
Beauchamp Terr SW15 134 B2
Beauclerc Cty Inf Sch
TW16 194 C6
Beauclerc Rd W6 112 B3
Beauclere Ho 1 SM2 218 A1
Beauclerk Cl TW13 150 B3
Beauclerk Ho 10 SW16 160 A1
Beaudesert Mews UB7 104 A4
Beaufort E6 100 C2
Beaufort Ave HA3 43 B6
Beaufort Cl E4 35 D4
SW19 156 B4
W5 88 B2
Beaufort Ct N11 31 B5
New Barnet EN5 14 A6
Richmond TW10 175 C6
Beaufort Dr NW11 47 C5
Beaufort Gdns NW4 46 C3
SW3 114 C3 257 B6
SW16 182 B3
Heston TW5 129 A4
Ilford IG1 56 C1
Beaufort Ho 7 N15 51 D5
Beaufort Ho *continued*
NW11 48 A3
SW1 259 C1
SW3 266 D5
SW11 136 C3
1 SW20 178 D2
Beaufort Mans SW3 266 D5
Beaufort Mews SW6 264 D6
Beaufort Pk NW11 47 C5
Beaufort Rd W5 88 B2
Kingston u T KT1,KT5,KT6 198 A5
Richmond TW10 175 C6
Ruislip HA4 61 B6
Twickenham TW1 153 C4
Beaufort St
SW3 136 B6 266 C6
Beaufort Way KT17 216 A1
Beaufoy Ho 3 SE27 160 D1
SW8 270 C4
Beaufoy Rd N17 33 C3
Beaufoy Wlk
SE11 116 B2 260 D3
Beaulieu Ave 1 E16 121 B5
SE26 184 B6
Beaulieu Cl NW9 45 C5
SE5 139 B2
Hounslow TW4 151 B6
Mitcham CR4 181 A2
13 Twickenham TW1 153 D5
Beaulieu Ct W5 88 A2
Beaulieu Dr HA5 40 D2
Beaulieu Gdns N21 17 A4
Beaulieu Ho NW4 28 D1
Beaulieu Pl W4 111 A3
Beaumanor Gdns SE9 188 C6
Beaumanor Mans W2 245 D6
Beaumaris 4 N11 32 A4
Beaumaris Dr IG8 37 D3
Beaumaris Gn NW9 45 C3
Beaumaris Twr 2 W3 110 D4
Beaumont SW15 157 A6
W14 254 D3
Beaumont Ave
W14 113 B1 254 C2
Harrow HA2 41 D2
Richmond TW9 132 B2
Wembley HA0 65 C4
Beaumont Bldgs WC2 240 B1
Beaumont Cl KT2 176 C3
Beaumont Cres
W14 113 B1 254 C1
Beaumont Ct E5 74 B5
10 NW9 27 D1
10 W4 111 A1
6 Mitcham CR4 181 A1
Wembley HA0 65 C3
Beaumont Dr TW15 171 B5
Beaumont Gdns NW3 69 C5
Beaumont Gr E1 96 D3
Beaumont Ho 11 E10 53 D2
1 SW2 160 A3
SW19 157 C1
Beaumont Mews W1 238 B4
Beaumont Pl
NW1,WC1,W1 93 C3 239 B6
Hadley EN5 1 B4
Isleworth TW7 152 D6
Beaumont Prim Sch E10 53 D1
Beaumont Rd E10 53 D2
E13 99 B4
SE19 183 A4
SW15,SW19 157 A4
W4 111 A3
Orpington BR5,BR6 211 B3
Beaumont Rise N19 49 D1
Beaumont Sq E1 96 D2
Beaumont St W1 238 B4
Beaumont Terr 1 SE13 164 C4
Beaumont Wlk NW3 70 D1
Beauvais Terr UB5 84 D4
Beauval Rd SE22 161 D5
Beauvale 6 NW1 71 A1
Beaver Cl 9 SE20 184 A3
Hampton TW12 173 D2
Beaver Gr UB5 85 A4
Beaverbank Rd DA15,
SE9 167 B3
Beavers Comm Prim Sch
TW4 128 C2
Beavers Cres TW4 128 D1
Beavers La TW4 128 C2
Beavers Lo DA14 189 D5
Beaverwood Rd BR7 189 C4
Beaverwood Sch for Girls
BR7 189 C4
Beavis Ho N16 73 C5
Beavor La W6 112 A1
Bebbington Rd SE18 123 C2
Beblets Cl 4 BR6 227 D3
Bec Cl HA4 62 D5
Beccles Dr IG11 79 D2
Beccles St E14 119 B6
Bechervaise Ct 2 E10 53 D1
Beck Cl SE13 141 D4
Beck Ct BR3 206 D6
Beck Ho N16 73 C5
4 N18 34 A5
Beck La BR3 206 D6
Beck Rd E8 96 B6
Beck River Pk 3 BR3 185 C2
Beck Way BR3 207 B6
Beckenham Bsns Ctr
BR3 185 A4
Beckenham Ct BR3 185 C2
Beckenham Gdns N9 17 C1
Beckenham Gr BR2 186 B1
Beckenham Hill Rd
BR3,SE6 186 A5
Beckenham Hill Sta
SE6 186 A5
Beckenham Hospl BR3 185 B1
Beckenham Junction Sta
BR3 185 C2
Beckenham La BR1,BR2 186 D1
Beckenham Place Pk
BR3 185 D3
Beckenham Rd
Beckenham BR3 185 A2
West Wickham BR3,BR4 208 A2
Beckenham Rd Sta
BR3 185 A2
Beckers The N16 74 A4
Becket Ave E6 100 C4
Becket Cl SE25 206 A3
2 SW19 179 D2
Becket Fold HA1 42 D4
Becket Ho SE1 252 C1
Becket Rd N18 34 C6
Becket St SE1 262 C6
Beckett Cl NW10 67 C2
SW16 159 D2
Erith DA17 125 B3
Beckett Ho 12 E1 96 C2
28 SW9 138 A3
Beckett Wlk BR3 185 A4
Becketts Cl
Feltham TW14 150 B5
Orpington BR6 227 D5
Becketts Pl KT1 175 D2
Beckfoot NW1 232 B3
Beckford Dr BR5,BR6 211 B2
Beckford Ho 18 N16 73 C3
Beckford Prim Sch NW6 69 B3
Beckford Rd CR0 205 D3
Beckham Ho SE11 260 D3
Beckington 18 NW5 71 A2
Beckley Ho E3 97 B3
Becklow Gdns W12 112 A5
1 W12 112 A4
Becklow Mews 7 W12 112 A4
Becklow Rd W12 112 A4
Beckmead Sch BR3 207 C1
Becks Rd DA14 168 A1
Beckton Alps E6 100 C3
Beckton Alps Ski Ctr
E6 100 C3
Beckton Park Sta E16 122 B6
Beckton Rd E16 98 D2
Beckton Spec Sch E16 99 D2
Beckton Sta E6 100 C2
Beckton Triangle Ret Pk
E6 100 D3
Beckway Rd SW16 181 D1
Beckway St
SE17 117 C2 263 A3
Beckwith Ho 22 E2 96 B5
Beckwith Rd SE24 161 B6
Beclands Rd SW17 181 A4
Becmead Ave SW16 181 D6
Harrow HA3 43 B4
Becondale Rd SE19 183 C5
Becontree Ave RM8 80 C5
Becontree Prim Sch
RM8 80 B5
Becontree Sta RM9 80 D2
Bective Pl SW15 135 B1
Bective Rd E7 77 A4
SW15 135 B1
Becton Pl DA7,DA8 147 D5
Bedale Rd EN2 5 A5
Bedale St SE1 252 C3
Beddington Cross CR0 204 A2
Beddington Farm Rd
CR0 204 A1
Beddington Gdns SM5,
SM6 219 A2
Beddington Gn BR5 189 D2
Beddington Gr SM6 219 D3
Beddington Inf Sch
SM6 219 C4
Beddington La
Wallington CR0 220 A6
CR0 203 D2
Beddington Lane Sta
CR0 203 C2
Beddington Manor
SM2 218 B2
Beddington Park Cotts
SM6 219 D5
Beddington Park Prim Sch
CR0 219 D5
Beddington Rd Ilford IG3 57 D2
St Paul's Cray BR5 189 D2
Beddington Terr CR0 204 B2
Bede Cl HA5 22 D2
Bede Ho SE14 141 B4
5 SW15 156 D5
Bede Rd RM6 58 C3
Bedefield WC1 233 B1
Bedelsford Sch KT1 198 A6
Bedens Rd DA14 191 A5
Bedfont Cl
East Bedfont TW14 149 A5
Mitcham CR4 181 A1
Bedfont Green Cl TW14 149 A3
Bedfont Ind Pk N TW15 149 A1
Bedfont Inf Sch TW14 149 C5
Bedfont Jun Sch TW14 149 C5
Bedfont La TW14,TW13 149 D4
Bedfont Lakes Ctry Pk
TW14 149 A2
Bedfont Rd
Feltham TW13,TW14 149 B2
Stanwell TW19 148 B5
Bedford Ave
WC1 93 D2 239 D3
Bedford Ave *continued*
Barnet EN5 13 B6
Hayes UB4 84 B1
Bedford Cl N10 31 A3
W4 133 D6
Bedford Cnr 3 W4 111 C2
Bedford Court Mans
WC1 239 D3
Bedford Ct SE19 183 D2
WC2 250 A5
6 Richmond TW9 132 B1
Wembley HA0 65 D4
Bedford Gardens Ho
W8 245 B3
Bedford Gdns
W8 113 C5 245 B3
Bedford Hill SW12 159 B2
Bedford Ho 7 SW4 138 A1
2 W4 111 C2
Bedford Park Cnr 5
W4 111 C2
Bedford Park Mans W4 111 B2
Bedford Pas SW6 264 B4
Bedford Pk CR0 205 A1
Bedford Pl WC1 94 A2 240 A4
Croydon CR0 205 B1
Bedford Rd E6 100 C6
E17 53 C6
E18 37 A1
N2 48 C6
N8 49 D3
N9 18 B4
N15 51 C5
N22 32 A1
NW7 11 C1
SW2,SW4 138 A1
W4 111 C3
W13 109 B6
Harrow HA1 42 A3
Ilford IG1 78 D5
North Cheam KT4 216 C6
Ruislip HA4 61 D4
Sidcup DA15 167 C1
Twickenham TW2 152 B1
Bedford Row
WC1 94 B2 240 D3
Bedford Sq WC1 93 D2 239 D3
Bedford St WC2 116 A6 250 B5
Bedford Terr SM2 218 A2
Bedford Way
WC1 93 D3 239 D5
Bedfordbury
WC2 116 A6 250 A5
Bedgebury Gdns SW19 157 A2
Bedgebury Rd SE9 143 D1
Bedivere Rd BR1 165 A1
Bedlow Way CR0 220 B4
Bedonwell Inf Sch SE2 147 A6
Bedonwell Jun Sch
DA17 147 A6
Bedonwell Rd
Bexley DA7,DA17 147 A6
Erith DA7 147 C5
Bedser Cl SE11 270 D6
South Norwood CR7 205 A6
Bedser Ct 7 SW4 138 A3
Bedser Dr UB6 64 B3
Bedster Gdns KT8 195 D6
Bedwardine Rd SE19 183 C3
Bedwell Ct 4 RM6 58 D2
Bedwell Gdns UB3 105 C2
Bedwell Ho 19 SW9 138 C3
Bedwell Rd N17 33 C2
Belvedere DA17 125 C1
Beeby Rd E16 99 B2
Beech Ave N20 14 C3
W3 111 C5
Brentford TW8 131 B5
Chigwell IG9 21 B2
Ruislip HA4 40 B1
Sidcup DA15 168 A4
Beech Cl N9 18 B5
SE8 141 B6
SW15 156 A4
SW19 178 C4
Ashford TW15 171 B5
Carshalton SM5 218 D6
Sunbury TW16 172 D1
West Drayton UB7 104 C3
Beech Copse
Bromley BR1 188 B1
South Croydon CR2 221 C3
Beech Croft Ct N5 72 D4
Beech Ct 6 E12 78 C5
E17 54 B6
NW2 69 B6
4 SW16 182 C5
W1 237 C2
Beckenham BR3 185 B3
3 Buckhurst Hill IG9 21 D2
Hayes UB3 105 D5
Northolt UB5 85 A6
Surbiton KT6 198 A2
Teddington TW11 175 C4
Beech Dell BR2,BR6 226 B4
Beech Dr N2 48 D6
Beech Farm Bldgs IG8 36 B3
Beech Gdns W5 110 A3
Dagenham RM10 81 D1
Beech Gr
Kingston u T KT3 199 B6
Mitcham CR4 203 D5
Beech Hall Cres E4 36 B3
Beech Hall Rd E4 36 B3
Beech Hill EN4 2 C5
Beech Hill Ave EN4 2 B4
Beech Ho 5 N16 73 B6
6 NW3 70 D2
Beech Ho *continued*
16 SE16 118 C4
Hayes UB4 84 D2
Heston TW5 129 A5
New Addington CR0 223 D2
7 Sidcup DA15 168 A1
Beech House Rd CR0 221 B5
Beech La IG9 21 B2
Beech Lawns N12 30 B5
Beech Rd N11 32 A4
SW16 204 B6
East Bedfont TW14 149 C4
Beech St EC2 95 A2 242 B4
Beech Tree Cl N1 72 C1
Stanmore HA7 25 C5
Beech Tree Glade E4 20 D3
Beech Tree Pl SM1 217 D3
Beech Way NW10 67 B1
Twickenham TW2 151 C1
Beech Wlk NW7 27 C4
Beechcroft
Chislehurst West BR7 188 C3
3 Kingston u T KT2 176 D2
Beechcroft Ave NW11 47 B2
Harrow HA2 41 C2
Kingston u T KT1,KT3 177 A1
Southall UB1 107 B5
Beechcroft Cl SW16 182 B5
Heston TW5 129 A5
Orpington BR6 227 B4
Beechcroft Ct 6 N12 29 D6
3 NW11 47 B2
Beechcroft Gdns HA9 66 B5
Beechcroft Ho W5 88 A2
Beechcroft Lo 6 SM2 218 A1
Beechcroft Mans SW16 182 B5
Beechcroft Rd E18 37 B1
SW14 133 A2
SW17 158 C2
Chessington KT9 214 B5
Orpington BR6 227 B4
Beechcroft Sch SW17 158 C2
Beechcroft Way N19 49 D1
Beechdale N21 16 B2
Beechdale Rd SW2 160 B5
Beechdene 4 SE15 140 B4
Beechen Cliff Way
TW7 130 D3
Beechen Pl SE23 162 C2
Beechengrove HA5 41 B6
Beeches Ave The SM5 218 C1
Beeches Cl SE20 184 C2
Beeches Ct BR1 187 A4
Beeches Rd SW17 158 D1
Cheam SM3 201 A1
Beeches The E12 78 B1
1 N19 50 A1
N20 14 C2
Hounslow TW3 129 D4
Mitcham CR4 202 C4
Beechey Ho 30 E1 118 B5
Beechfield Cotts 3
BR1 187 C1
Beechfield Ct 7 CR2 221 A4
Beechfield Rd N4 51 A3
SE6 163 B3
Bromley BR1 187 C1
Beechhill Rd SE9 166 C6
Beechmont Cl BR1 186 C5
Beechmore Gdns SM3 216 D6
Beechmore Rd
SW11 136 D4 267 D1
Beechmount Ave W7 86 C2
Beecholme 19 N12 29 D6
Beecholme Ave CR4 181 B2
Beecholme Est E5 74 B5
Beecholme Fst Sch
CR4 181 B2
Beechrow KT2 176 A6
Beechvale Cl N12 30 C5
Beechway DA5 168 D5
Beechwood Ave N3 47 C6
Ashford TW16 172 A4
Greenford UB6 85 D4
Harrow HA2 63 D5
Hayes UB3 105 B6
Hillingdon UB8 82 C1
Orpington BR6 227 C2
Richmond TW9 132 C4
Ruislip HA4 61 D6
Thornton Heath CR7 204 D5
Beechwood Cl N2 48 D5
NW7 27 C5
Surbiton KT6 197 D2
Beechwood Cres DA7 147 A2
Beechwood Ct N16 51 C2
W4 133 B6
Carshalton SM5 218 D4
Sutton SM1 217 C3
Beechwood Dr
Keston BR2 225 D4
Woodford IG8 36 D5
Beechwood Gdns NW10 88 B4
Harrow HA2 63 D5
Ilford IG5 56 C5
Beechwood Gr W3 111 C6
Beechwood Hall N3 47 B6
Beechwood Ho 22 E2 96 A5
Beechwood Mews 2 N9 18 A2
Beechwood Pk E18 55 A6
Beechwood Pl KT6 197 C2
Beechwood Rd E8 73 D2
N8 50 A5
South Croydon CR2 221 C1
Beechwood Rise BR7 188 D6
Beechwoods Ct SE19 183 D5
Beechworth Cl NW3 69 C6
Beecroft Rd SE4 163 A6
Beehive Cl E8 73 D1
Elstree WD6 9 D5
Hillingdon UB10 60 B1
Beehive Ct IG1,IG2 56 B3
Beehive La IG1 56 B3
Beehive Pl SW9 138 C2
Beeken Dene BR6 227 A4
Beeleigh Rd SM4 201 D5
Beeston Cl 5 E8 74 A3
South Oxhey WD1 22 D6
Beeston Pl SW1 258 D6
Beeston Rd EN4 14 B5
Beeston Way TW14 150 C5
Beeston's Ho SE15 140 B2
Beethoven Rd WD6 9 D5
Beethoven St W10 91 A4
Beeton Cl HA5 23 C3
Begbie Ho SW9 138 B3
Begbie Rd SE3 143 C4
Beggars Hill KT17 215 D2
Beggar's Roost La SM1,
SM2 217 C2
Begonia Cl E6 100 B3
Begonia Pl 1 TW12 173 C4
Begonia Wlk W12 89 D1
Beira St SW12 159 B4
Beis Rachel D'Satmar Girls
Sch N16 51 C2
Beis Yaakov Prim Sch
NW9 45 B6
Bekesbourne St 19 E14 97 A1
Belcroft Cl BR1 186 D3
Beldanes Lo NW10 68 A1
Beldham Gdns KT8 195 D6
Belenoyd Ct SW16 160 B1
Belfairs Dr RM6 58 C2
Belfairs Gn WD1 22 D5
Belfast Rd N16 73 D6
SE25 206 B5
Belfield Rd KT19 215 C1
Belfont Wlk N7 72 A4
Belford Gr SE18 122 C2
Belford Ho 7 E8 95 D6
Belfort Rd SE15 140 C3
Belfry Cl 33 SE16 118 B1
Belgrade Ho N16 73 C4
Belgrade Rd N16 73 C4
Hampton TW12 173 D2
Belgrave Cl N14 15 C6
NW7 27 B5
1 W3 111 A4
Belgrave Cres TW16 172 B2
Belgrave Ct E13 99 C3
SE3 143 C5
SW8 269 A3
8 W4 111 A1
Belgrave Gdns N14 3 D1
NW8 91 D6
1 Stanmore HA7 25 C5
Belgrave Mans NW8 229 A5
Belgrave Mews N SW1 248 A1
Belgrave Mews S
SW1 115 A3 258 B6
Belgrave Mews W SW1 258 A6
Belgrave Pl
SW1 115 A3 258 B5
Belgrave Rd E10 54 A1
E11 55 A1
E13 99 C3
E17 53 C3
SE25 205 D5
SW1 115 C2 259 A3
SW13 133 D5
Hounslow TW4 129 B2
Ilford IG1 56 B1
Mitcham CR4 202 B6
Sunbury TW16 172 B2
Belgrave Sq
SW1 115 A3 258 A6
Belgrave St E1 96 D1
Belgrave Terr IG8 21 A1
Belgrave Wlk CR4 202 B6
Belgrave Wlk Sta CR4 202 B5
Belgrave Yd SW1 258 C5
Belgravia Cl EN5 1 B2
Belgravia Ct SW1 258 C5
Belgravia Gdns BR1 186 C4
Belgravia Ho 11 SW4 159 D5
Teddington TW11 175 C3
Belgravia Mews KT1 197 D5
Belgrove St WC1 233 B2
Belham Wlk 13 SE5 139 B4
Belinda Rd 8 SW9 138 D2
Belitha Villas N1 72 C1
Bell Ave UB7 104 B3
Bell Cl Pinner HA5 40 C6
Ruislip HA4 61 D5
Bell Ct NW4 46 C5
Hounslow TW3 129 D1
Tolworth KT5 214 D6
Bell Dr SW18 157 A4
Bell Gn SE26 185 B6
Bell Green La SE26 185 B6
Bell Ho SE2 124 D1
SE10 142 A6
15 SW2 160 C4
6 Dagenham RM10 81 D2
Bell Ind Est 2 W4 111 A2
Bell Inn Yd EC3 242 D1
Bell La E1 95 D2 243 C3
E16 121 A5
NW4 46 D5
Enfield EN3 6 D5
Twickenham TW1 153 A3
Bell Lane Prim Sch NW4 46 D5
Bell Meadow SE19 183 C6
Bell Moor NW3 70 A5
Bell Rd East Molesey KT8 196 B4

Bell Rd *continued*
Enfield EN1 5 B4
Hounslow TW3 129 D1
Bell St NW1 92 C2 237 A4
Bell The E17 53 C6
Bell View BR3 185 B3
Bell View Manor HA4 39 C2
Bell Water Gate SE18 122 C3
Bell Wharf La EC4 252 B6
Bell Yd WC2 94 C1 241 A1
Bellamy Cl SW5 254 D1
Edgware HA8 11 A1
Uxbridge UB10 60 C5
Bellamy Ct HA7 25 B2
Bellamy Dr HA7 25 B2
Bellamy Ho SW17 180 B6
Harrow HA3 44 A2
Heston TW5 129 C6
Bellamy Rd E4 35 D4
Enfield EN2 5 B3
Bellamy St SW12 159 B4
Bellamy's Ct 16 SE16 118 D5
Bellasis Ave SW2 160 A2
Bellclose Rd UB7 104 A4
Belle Staines Pleasaunce E4 19 C2
Belle Vue UB6 86 B6
Belle Vue Gdns SW9 138 A3
Belle Vue La WD2 8 B3
Belle Vue Rd E17 36 B1
Bellefields Rd SW9 138 B2
Bellegrove Cl DA16 145 D3
Bellegrove Par DA16 145 D2
Bellegrove Rd DA16 145 D3
Bellenden Prim Sch SE15 140 A3
Bellenden Rd SE15 139 D3
Bellendon Road Bsns Ctr SE15 139 D3
Belleville Prim Sch SW11 158 D6
Belleville Rd SW11 158 D6
Bellevue Pk CR7 205 A5
Bellevue Pl E1 96 C3
Bellevue Rd N11 31 A5
SW13 134 A3
SW17 158 D3
W13 87 B3
Bexley DA6 169 B6
Kingston u T KT1 198 A6
Bellew St SW17 158 A1
Bellfield CR0 223 B1
Bellfield Ave HA3 24 B4
Bellflower Cl 2 E6 100 A2
Bellgate Mews NW5 71 B5
Bellhill 6 CR0 221 A6
Bellina Mews NW5 71 C4
Bellingham 10 N17 34 B3
Bellingham Ct IG11 102 B4
Bellingham Gn SE6 163 C1
Bellingham Rd SE6 164 A1
Bellingham Sta SE6 163 D1
Bellingham Trad Est SE6 163 D2
Bellmore Ct 5 CR0 205 D1
Bello Cl SE24,SW2 160 D3
Bellot Gdns 1 SE10 120 C1
Bellot St SE10 120 C1
Bellring Cl DA17 147 C6
Bells Hill EN5 12 D6
Belltrees Gr 1 SW16 182 C5
Bellview Mews N11 31 A5
Bellwood Rd SE15 140 D1
Belmont Ave N9 18 A3
N13 32 B5
N17 51 A6
Bexley DA16 145 C2
East Barnet EN4 14 D6
Southall UB2 107 A3
Wembley HA0 88 B6
West Barnes KT3 200 A5
Belmont Circ HA3 25 B2
Belmont Cl E4 36 B5
N20 13 D3
SW4 137 C2
Cockfosters EN4 2 D1
Uxbridge UB8 60 A2
Woodford IG8 37 B6
Belmont Ct N5 73 A4
6 N16 51 C1
NW11 47 B4
Belmont Fst & Mid Sch HA3 24 D1
Belmont Gr SE13 142 B2
Belmont Hall Ct SE13 142 B2
Belmont Hill SE13 142 B2
Belmont Jun & Inf Sch W4 111 B2
Belmont Jun & Inf Schs N22 51 A6
Belmont La
Chislehurst West BR7 189 A5
Stanmore HA7 25 C3
Belmont Lo Harrow HA3 24 B3
Stanmore HA7 25 C6
Belmont Par 2 NW11 47 B4
Chislehurst West BR7 189 A5
Belmont Park Cl SE13 142 C1
Belmont Park Rd E10 53 D3
Belmont Pk SE13 142 C1
Belmont Prim Sch DA7 147 C5
Belmont Rd N15,N17 51 A5
SE25 206 B4
SW4 137 C2
Beckenham BR3 185 B1
Chislehurst West BR7 188 D5
Erith DA8 147 D4
Harrow HA3 43 A6

Belmont Rd *continued*
Ilford IG1 79 A5
Twickenham TW2 152 B2
Uxbridge UB8 60 A2
Wallington SM6 219 C3
Belmont Rise SM1,SM2 217 B1
Belmont Sch NW7 12 A1
Belmont St NW1 71 A1
Belmont Terr W4 111 B2
Belmor WD6 10 C5
Belmore Ave UB4 84 A1
Belmore Ho N7 71 D3
Belmore Prim Sch UB4 84 B4
Belmore St SW8 137 D4 269 C2
Beloe Cl SW15 134 A1
Belsham St E9 74 C2
Belsize Ave N13 32 B4
NW3 70 C3
W13 109 B3
Belsize Court Garages 1 NW3 70 B3
Belsize Cres NW3 70 B2
Belsize Ct NW3 70 B3
Belsize Gdns SM1 217 D4
Belsize Gr NW3 70 C2
Belsize La NW3 70 B3
Belsize Mews NW3 70 B2
Belsize Park Gdns NW3 70 C2
Belsize Park Mews 1 NW3 70 B2
Belsize Park Sta NW3 70 C3
Belsize Pk NW3 70 B2
Belsize Pl NW3 70 B3
Belsize Rd NW6 91 D6
NW8 229 A6
Harrow HA3 24 B3
Belsize Sq NW3 70 B2
Belsize Terr NW3 70 B2
Belson Rd SE18 122 B2
Beltane Dr SW19 156 D1
Belthorn Cres SW12 159 C4
Belton Rd E7 77 B1
E11 76 C4
N17 51 C6
NW2 68 A2
Sidcup DA14 190 A6
Belton Way E3 97 C2
Beltran Rd SW6 135 D3
Belvedere Ave SW19 179 A5
Belvedere Bldgs SE1 251 D1
Belvedere Cl TW11 174 C5
Belvedere Ct N2 48 B4
NW2 68 D2
7 SW4 159 D5
SW15 134 C1
Erith DA17 125 B3
8 Kingston u T KT2 176 C3
Belvedere Dr SW19 179 A5
Belvedere Gdns KT8 195 C4
Belvedere Gr SW19 179 A5
Belvedere Jun & Inf Sch DA17 125 D3
Belvedere Mews SE15 140 C2
Belvedere Pl SE1 251 D1
Belvedere Rd E10 53 A1
SE1 116 B4 250 D3
SE19 183 D3
SE28 124 D5
W7 108 D3
Bexley DA7 147 B3
Belvedere Sq SW19 179 A5
Belvedere Sta DA17 125 D3
Belvedere Strand NW9 27 D1
Belvedere The SW10 266 B1
Belvedere Way HA3 44 A3
Belvoir Cl SE9 166 A1
Belvoir Lo SE22 162 A4
Belvoir Rd SE22 162 A4
Belvue Bsns Ctr UB5 63 D1
Belvue Cl UB5 63 C1
Belvue Rd UB5 63 C1
Belvue Sch UB5 85 C6
Bembridge Cl NW6 69 A1
Bembridge Gdns HA4 61 B6
Bembridge Ho 8 SE8 119 B2
SW18 157 D5
Bemersyde Point 6 E13 99 B4
Bemerton St N1 94 B6 233 C6
Bemish Rd SW15 134 D2
Bempton Dr HA4 62 B5
Bemsted Rd E17 53 B6
Ben Ezra Ct SE17 262 B3
Ben Hale Cl HA7 25 B5
Ben Jonson Ct 30 N1 95 C5
Ben Jonson JMI Sch E1 97 A3
Ben Jonson Rd E1 97 A2
Ben Smith Way 21 SE16 118 A3
Ben Tillet Cl E16 122 B5
Barking IG11 80 A1
Ben Tillet Ho N15 50 D6
Benabo Ct 6 E8 74 A3
Benares Rd SE18,SE2 123 D2
Benbow Ct W6 112 B3
Benbow Ho 12 SE8 141 C6
Benbow Rd W6 112 B3
Benbow St SE8 141 C6
Benbury Cl BR1 186 A5
Bence Ho 13 SE8 119 A2
Bench Field CR2 221 D3
Bencroft Rd SW16 181 C3
Bencurtis Pk BR4 224 B6
Bendall Mews NW1 237 B4
Bendemeer Rd SW15 134 D2
Benden Ho SE13 164 A6
Bendish Rd E6 78 A1
Bendmore Ave SE2 124 A2

Bendon Valley SW18 157 D4
Benedict Cl
9 Erith DA17 125 A3
Orpington BR6 227 C5
Benedict Dr TW14 149 B4
Benedict Fst Sch CR4 202 B6
Benedict Prim Sch CR4 202 B6
Benedict Rd SW9 138 B2
Mitcham CR4 202 B6
Benedict Way N2 48 A6
Benedict Wharf CR4 202 C6
Benenden Gn BR2 209 A4
Benenden Ho SE17 263 B2
Benett Gdns SW16 182 A1
Benfleet Cl SM1 218 A5
Benfleet Ct 6 E8 95 D6
Bengal Ct EC3 242 D1
Bengal Ho E1 96 D2
Bengal Rd IG1 78 D5
Bengarth Dr HA3 24 B1
Bengarth Rd UB5 85 A6
Bengeworth Rd SE5 139 A2
Harrow HA1 65 A5
Benham Cl 1 SW11 136 B2
Chessington KT9 213 C2
Benham Gdns TW3,TW4 151 B6
Benham Rd W7 86 C2
Benham's Pl 8 NW3 70 A4
Benhill Ave SM1 218 A4
Benhill Rd SE5 139 B4
Carshalton SM1 218 B4
Benhill Wood Rd SM1 218 A4
Benhilton Gdns SM1 217 D5
Benhurst Ct 12 SE20 184 B2
SW16 182 C5
W5 110 A6
Benhurst La SW16 182 C5
Benin St SE13 164 B4
Benjafield Cl N18 34 B6
Benjamin Cl E8 96 A6
Benjamin Ct 4 W7 108 C5
4 Erith DA17 147 B6
Littleton TW15 171 A3
Benjamin St EC1 241 C4
Benledi St E14 98 B1
Benn Ho 7 SE7 121 C1
Benn St E9 75 A2
Bennelong Cl W12 90 B1
Bennerley Rd SW11 158 D6
Bennet Cl KT1 175 C2
Bennet's Hill EC4 251 D6
Bennets Lo EN2 5 A2
Bennetsfield Rd UB11 104 D5
Bennett Cl DA16 146 A3
Bennett Ct N7 72 B5
NW6 69 D2
7 W3 110 D4
Bennett Gr SE13 141 D4
Bennett Ho SW1 259 D4
2 SW4 159 D4
Bennett Pk SE3 142 D2
Bennett Rd E13 99 C3
Dagenham RM6 59 A2
Bennett St SW1 249 A4
W4 111 C1
Bennetts Ave
Croydon CR0 223 A6
Greenford UB6 86 C6
Bennett's Castle La RM8 80 D5
Bennetts Cl N17 33 D4
Mitcham CR4,SW16 181 B2
Bennetts Copse BR7 188 A4
Bennetts Way CR0 223 B6
Bennett's Yd SW1 259 D5
Benningholme Rd HA8 27 C4
Bennington Rd N17 33 C2
Chingford IG8 36 C3
Bensbury Cl SW15 156 C4
Bensham Cl CR7 205 A5
Bensham Gr CR7 183 A1
Bensham La CR0,CR7 204 D3
Bensham Manor Rd CR7 205 A5
Bensham Manor Sch CR7 205 A4
Bensington Ct TW14 149 B5
Bensley Cl 7 N11 30 D5
Benson Ave E13,E6 99 D5
Benson Cl Hillingdon UB8 82 A2
Hounslow TW3 129 C1
Benson Ct 1 N19 71 C4
SW8 270 A2
Enfield EN3 7 C5
Benson Ho E2 243 C6
SE1 251 B3
Benson Prim sch CR0 223 A5
Benson Quay E1 118 C6
Benson Rd SE23 162 C3
Croydon CR0 220 C5
Bentall Sh Ctr The 10 KT2 176 A1
Bentfield Gdns SE9 165 D1
Benthal Ct N16 74 A5
Benthal JMI Schs N16 74 A5
Benthal Rd N16 74 A5
Bentham Ct 10 N1 73 A1
Bentham Rd E9 74 D2
SE28 124 B5
Bentham Wlk NW10 67 A3
Bentinck Cl NW8 230 B3
Bentinck Ho 4 W12 112 B6
Bentinck Mans W1 238 B2
Bentinck Mews W1 238 B2
Bentinck Rd UB7 104 A5
Bentinck St W1 93 A1 238 B2
Bentley Cl SW19 157 C1
Bentley Dr IG2 57 A3
Bentley Ho 6 E3 97 C3

Bentley Ho *continued*
4 SE5 139 C4
Bentley Lo WD2 8 C2
Bentley Mews EN1 17 B5
Bentley Rd N1 73 C2
Bentley Way
Stanmore HA7 25 A5
Woodford IG8 21 A1
Bentley Wood High Sch HA7 24 D5
Benton Rd Ilford IG1,IG2 57 B1
South Oxhey WD1 22 D5
Benton's La SE27 183 A6
Benton's Rise SE27 183 B5
Bentry Cl RM8 81 A6
Bentry Rd RM8 81 B6
Bentworth Ct 1 E2 96 A3
Bentworth Prim Sch W12 90 B1
Bentworth Rd W12 90 B1
Benville Ho SW8 270 D3
Benwell Ct TW16 172 A2
Benwell Rd N7 72 C3
Benwick Cl SE16 118 B2
Benwick Ct SE20 184 C2
Benwood Ct SM1 218 A5
Benworth St E3 97 B4
Benyon Ho EC1 234 B2
Benyon Rd N1 95 B6 235 D6
Beormund Sch SE1 117 B4 252 D1
Berber Rd SE28 123 D5
SW11 158 D6
Berberis Ho 15 E3 97 C2
Berberis Wlk UB7 104 A2
Berberry Cl HA8 27 A6
Bercta Rd SE9 167 A2
Bere St E1 118 D6
Berebinder Ho 17 E3 97 B5
Berenger Twr SW10 266 C4
Berenger Wlk SW10 266 C4
Berens Ct DA14 189 D6
Berens Rd NW10 90 D4
Berens Way BR5,BR7 211 D6
Beresford Ave N20 14 D2
W7 86 C2
Tolworth KT5 199 A2
Twickenham TW1 153 C5
Wembley HA0 88 C6
Beresford Ct E9 75 A3
11 Twickenham TW1 153 C5
Beresford Dr
Bromley BR1 210 A6
Woodford IG8 37 C6
Beresford Gdns
Dagenham RM6 59 A4
Enfield EN1 5 C1
Hounslow TW4 151 B6
Beresford Ho SE21 161 C1
Beresford Lo N4 73 B3
Beresford Rd E4 20 C3
E17 35 D2
N2 48 C6
N5 73 B3
N8 50 D4
Belmont SM2 217 B1
Harrow HA1 42 B4
Kingston u T KT2 176 B2
Kingston u T KT3 199 A5
Southall UB1 106 D5
Beresford Square Market Pl
1 SE18 122 D2
Beresford St SE18 122 D3
Beresford Terr 3 N5 73 A3
Berestede Rd 4 W6 111 D1
Bergen Ho 1 SE5 139 A3
Bergen Sq SE16 119 A3
Berger Cl BR5 211 C3
Berger JMI Sch E9 74 D2
Berger Rd E9 74 D2
Berghem Mews W14 112 D3
Bergholt Ave IG4 56 A4
Bergholt Cres N16 51 C2
Bergholt Mews 4 NW1 71 D1
Bering Sq E14 119 C1
Bering Wlk E16 99 D1
Berisford Mews SW18 158 A5
Berkeley Ave
Bexley DA16 146 D4
Cranford TW4 128 A3
Northolt UB6 64 C2
Berkeley Cl
Broom Hill BR5,BR6 211 C2
Deacons Hill WD6 10 C6
Ruislip HA4 62 A5
Berkeley Cres EN4 14 B6
Berkeley Ct N3 29 D2
NW1 237 D5
1 NW11 47 B2
10 SW2 160 C3
W5 109 C6
Edgware HA8 26 D5
Wallington SM6 219 C4
Berkeley Dr KT8 195 C6
Berkeley Gdns N21 17 B4
W8 245 B3
Claygate KT10 213 A2
Walton-on-T KT12 193 D2
Berkeley Ho 17 E3 97 C4
8 SE8 119 B1
11 Brentford TW8 131 D6
Berkeley Lo Enfield EN2 4 C2
KT3 199 C5
Berkeley Mews W1 237 D1
Berkeley Pl SW19 178 D4
Berkeley Prim Sch TW5 128 D5
Berkeley Rd E12 78 A3

Berkeley Rd *continued*
N8 49 D3
N15 51 B3
NW9 44 C4
SW13 134 A4
Hillingdon UB10 61 A1
Berkeley Sq W1 115 B6 248 D5
Berkeley St W1 115 B5 248 D4
Berkeley The NW11 47 D2
Berkeley Waye TW5 128 D5
Berkeley Wlk 1 N7 72 B6
Berkeleys The SE25 206 A5
Berkerley Ct SW15 156 D6
Berkhampstead Rd DA17 125 C1
Berkhamsted Ave HA9 66 C2
Berkley Cl TW2 152 C1
Berkley Ct 6 TW1 153 A4
Berkley Gr NW1 71 A1
Berkley Mews TW16 194 C6
Berkley Rd NW1 70 D1
Berkshire Ct 1 W7 86 D3
Berkshire Gdns N13 32 C4
N18 34 B5
Berkshire Ho SE6 185 C6
Berkshire Rd E9 75 B2
Berkshire Sq CR4 204 A5
Berkshire Way CR4 204 A5
Berleley Ct NW10 67 C4
Bermans Way NW10 67 D4
Bermondsey Leather Mkt SE1 253 A1
Bermondsey Mkt* SE1 117 C3 263 B8
Bermondsey Sq SE1 263 B6
Bermondsey St SE1 117 C4 253 A1
Bermondsey Sta SE16 118 A3
Bermondsey Trad Est SE16 118 C1
Bermondsey Wall E SE16 118 B4
Bermondsey Wall W SE1,SE16 118 A4
Bermuda Ho HA1 64 B5
Bernal Cl SE28 124 D6
Bernard Angell Ho 4 SE10 142 B6
Bernard Ashley Dr SE7 121 B1
Bernard Ave W13 109 B3
Bernard Cassidy St 4 E16 98 D2
Bernard Gdns SW19 179 B5
Bernard Rd N15 51 D4
Wallington SM5,SM6 219 B4
Bernard Shaw Ct 3 NW1 71 C1
Bernard Shaw Ho 2 NW10 89 B6
Bernard St WC1 94 A3 240 B5
Bernays Cl HA7 25 C4
Bernay's Gr SW9 138 B1
Berne Rd CR7 205 A4
Bernel Dr CR0 223 B5
Berners Dr W13 109 A6
Berners Ho N1 234 A4
Berners Mews W1 93 C2 239 B3
Berners Pl W1 239 B2
Berners Rd N1 234 C5
N22 32 C1
Berners St W1 93 C1 239 B2
Bernersmede SE3 143 A2
Berney Ho BR3 207 A4
Berney Rd CR0 205 B2
Bernwell Rd E4 20 C1
Bernwood Ho 6 N4 51 B2
Berridge Gn HA8 26 C3
Berridge Rd SE19 183 C5
Berriman Rd N7 72 B5
Berrite Works UB7 104 C4
Berriton Rd HA2 41 B1
Berry Cl N21 16 D3
NW10 67 C1
Berry Ct TW4 151 B6
Berry Field Cl 8 E17 53 D5
Berry Hill HA7 25 D6
Berry Ho 25 E1 96 B3
10 SW11 136 D3
Berry La SE21 183 B6
Berry Pl EC1 234 D1
Berry St EC1 241 D5
Berry Way W5 110 A3
Berrybank Cl 4 E4 20 A2
Berrydale Rd UB4 85 A3
Berryfield Cl BR1 188 A1
Berryfield Rd SE17 116 D1 261 D2
Berryhill SE9 144 D1
Berryhill Gdns SE9 144 D1
Berrylands SW20 200 C5
Tolworth KT5 198 C3
Berrylands Ct 7 SM2 217 D1
Berrylands Rd KT5 198 B3
Berrylands Sta KT5 198 D5
Berryman Cl RM8 80 C5
Berryman's La SE26 184 D6
Berrymead Gdns W3 111 A4
Berrymede Inf Sch W3 110 D4
Berrymede Jun Sch W3 110 D4
Berrymede Rd W4 111 B3
Bert Rd CR7 205 A4
Bert Reilly Ho 1 SE18 123 B1
Bert Way EN1 5 D1
Bertal Rd SW17 180 B6
Bertha Hollamby Ct DA14 190 C5

Bertha Neubergh Ho 1 SE5 139 A4
Berthan Gdns E17 54 B4
Berthon St SE8 141 C6
Bertie Rd NW10 68 A2
SE26 184 D4
Bertram Cotts SW19 179 C3
Bertram House Sch SW17 159 A2
Bertram Rd NW4 46 A3
Enfield EN1 6 A1
Kingston u T KT2 176 C3
Bertram St N19 71 B6
Bertrand Ho 11 SW16 160 A1
Bertrand St SE13 141 D2
Bertrand Way SE28 124 C6
Berwick Ave UB4 106 D6
Berwick Cl HA7 24 D4
Berwick Cres DA15 167 C5
Berwick Ho 10 N2 30 B1
Berwick Rd E16 99 C1
N22 32 D2
Bexley DA16 146 B4
Berwick St W1 93 C1 239 B1
Berwyn Ave TW3 129 D4
Berwyn Ho 3 N16 51 D1
Berwyn Rd SE24 160 D3
SW14,TW10 132 D1
Beryl Ave E6 100 A2
Beryl Harding Ho 3 SW19 178 D3
Beryl Ho SE18 123 D1
Beryl Rd W6 112 D1
Berystede KT2 176 D3
Besant Cl NW2 69 A5
Besant Ct N1 73 B3
15 SE28 124 B6
Besant Ho NW8 229 A5
Besant Rd NW2 69 A4
Besant Way NW10 67 A3
Besant Wlk N7 72 B6
Besford Ho 25 E2 96 A5
Besley St SW16 181 C4
Bessant Dr TW9 132 D4
Bessborough Gdns SW1 115 D1 259 D2
Bessborough Pl SW1 115 D1 259 D2
Bessborough Rd SW15 156 A3
Harrow HA1 42 B1
Bessborough St SW1 115 D1 259 C2
Bessborough Wks KT8 195 B4
Bessemer Ct 5 NW1 71 C1
Bessemer Grange Prim Sch SE5 139 C1
Bessemer Park Ind Est 3 SE24 138 D1
Bessemer Rd SE5 139 A3
Bessie Lansbury Cl E6 100 C1
Bessingby Rd HA4 62 B6
Bessingham Wlk SE4 162 D6
Besson St SE14 140 D4
Bessy St E2 96 C4
Bestwood St SE8 118 D2
Beswick Mews 1 NW6 69 D2
Betam Rd UB3 105 B4
Betchworth Cl SM1 218 B3
Betchworth Ho 8 N7 71 D3
Betchworth Rd IG3 79 C5
Beth Jacob Gram Sch NW4 46 D5
Betham Rd UB6 86 B4
Bethany Waye TW14 149 C4
Bethecar Rd HA1 42 C4
Bethel Rd DA16 146 C2
Bethell Ave E13,E16 98 D3
Ilford IG1 56 C2
Bethersden Cl BR3 185 B3
Bethersden Ho SE17 263 B2
Bethesda Ct 8 SE20 184 C3
Bethlehem Ho 13 E14 119 B6
Bethlem Royal Hospl The BR3 207 C2
Bethnal Green Museum of Childhood* E2 96 C4
Bethnal Green Rd E1,E2 243 D6
E2 96 A4
Bethnal Green Sta E1 96 B3
E2 96 C4
Bethnal Green Tech Coll E2 95 D4
Bethune Ave N11 30 D6
Bethune Rd N16 51 C2
NW10 89 B3
Bethwin Rd SE5 139 A5
Betjeman Cl HA5 41 C5
Betony Cl CR0 206 D1
Betoyne Ave E4 36 C6
Betsham Ho SE1 252 C2
Betspath Ho 6 N11 31 C5
Betstyle Ho 2 N10 31 A3
Betstyle Rd N11 31 B6
Betterton Dr DA14 169 A2
Betterton Ho WC2 240 B1
Betterton St WC2 94 A1 240 B1
Bettons Pk E15 98 C6
Bettridge Rd SW6 135 B3
Betts Cl BR3 185 A1
Betts Ho E1 118 B6
Betts Mews E17 53 B3
Betts Rd E16 121 B6
Betts St E1 118 B6
Betts Way SE20 184 B2

Betts Way *continued*
Long Ditton KT6 197 B1
Bettswood Ct 15 SE20 184 B2
Betty May Gray Ho 1
E14 120 A2
Beulah Ave CR7 183 A1
Beulah Cl HA8 10 D1
Beulah Cres CR7 183 A1
Beulah Gr CR0 205 A3
Beulah Hill SE19 183 A3
Beulah Inf Sch CR7 205 A6
Beulah Jun Sch CR7 205 A6
Beulah Rd E17 53 D4
SW19 179 B3
South Norwood CR7 205 A6
Sutton SM1 217 C4
Beuleigh Ct E17 54 B4
Bev Callender Cl 4
SW8 137 B2
Bevan Ave IG11 80 A1
Bevan Ct Croydon CR0 220 C3
9 Twickenham TW1 153 D5
Bevan Rd SE2 124 B1
Cockfosters EN4 2 D1
Bevan St N1 95 A6 235 B5
Bevenden St N1 95 B4 235 D2
Bevercote Wlk 1 DA17 147 B6
Beveridge Ct N21 16 A6
1 SE28 124 B6
Beverley Ave SW20 177 D2
Hounslow TW4 129 B1
Sidcup DA15 167 D4
Beverley Cl N21 17 A3
6 SW11 136 B1
SW13 134 A3
Chessington KT9 213 C4
Enfield EN1 5 C1
Beverley Cotts SW15 155 C1
Beverley Cres IG8 37 B2
Beverley Ct N2 48 D5
N5 72 D2
N14 15 C4
SE4 141 B2
SW20 177 D2
9 W4 111 A1
5 W12 111 C4
Harrow HA2 42 B6
Hounslow TW4 129 B1
Northolt UB5 84 C5
Beverley Dr HA8 44 C6
Beverley Gdns NW11 47 A2
SW13 133 D2
2 North Cheam KT4 200 A1
Stanmore HA7 25 A2
Wembley HA9 44 C1
Beverley Ho 5 BR1 186 B5
Beverley Hyrst 10 CR0 221 D6
Beverley La KT2 177 C3
Beverley Lo 6 TW10 154 A6
Beverley Mans TW4 129 B1
Beverley Path 9 SW13 133 D3
Beverley Prim Sch
SE10 142 A5
Beverley Rd E4 36 B4
E6 99 D4
SE20 184 B1
SW13 133 D2
W4 111 D1
Dagenham RM9 81 A4
Keston Mark BR2 226 A6
Mitcham CR4 203 D5
New Malden KT3 200 A5
North Cheam KT4 216 C6
Ruislip HA4 62 B6
Southall UB2 107 A3
Sunbury TW16 171 D2
Teddington KT1 175 C2
Beverley Sch KT3 200 A4
Beverley Trad Est SM4 200 D2
Beverley Way KT3,SW20,
KT2 177 D2
Beverley Way (Kingston By
Pass) KT3,SW20 200 A6
Beverly Ct HA3 43 C5
Beversbrook Rd N19 71 D5
Beverston Mews NW1 237 C3
Beverstone Rd SW2 160 B6
Thornton Heath CR7 204 D5
Bevill Allen Cl SW17 180 D5
Bevill Cl SE25 206 A6
Bevin Cl SE16 119 A5
Bevin Ct WC1 233 D2
Bevin Ho 35 E2 96 C4
7 E3 97 C4
Bevin Rd UB4 84 B4
Bevin Sq SW17 158 D1
Bevin Way WC1 234 A2
Bevington Prim Sch
W10 91 A2
Bevington Rd W10 91 A2
Beckenham BR3 185 D1
Bevington St SE16 118 A4
Bevis Marks EC3 95 C1 243 B2
Bew Ct SE21 162 A4
Bewcastle Gdns EN2 4 A1
Bewdley Ho N4 51 A2
Bewdley St N1 72 C1
Bewick St SW8 137 B3
Bewley Ct SW2 160 B5
Bewley Ho 7 E1 118 B6
Bewley St E1 118 B6
Bewlys Rd SE27 182 D5
Bexhill Cl TW13 151 A2
Bexhill Rd N11 31 D5
SE4 163 B5
Bexhill Rd *continued*
SW14 133 A2
Bexhill Wlk 6 E15 98 C6
Bexley Coll SE2 146 D6
Bexley Coll Erith Rd Campus
DA17 125 D1
Bexley Gdns N9 17 B1
Ilford RM6 58 B4
Bexley Gram Mix Sch
DA16 146 B1
Bexley High St DA5 169 D3
Bexley Ho SE4 141 A1
Bexley La DA14 168 C1
Bexley Rd SE9 167 A6
Bexley Sta DA5 169 C3
Bexley-Erith Tech High Sch
for Boys DA5 169 D5
Bexleyheath Sch DA7 147 B2
Bexleyheath Sta DA7 147 A3
Beynon Rd SM5 218 D3
Bianca Rd SE1,SE15 140 A6
Bibsworth Lo N3 29 B1
Bibsworth Rd N3 29 B1
Bicester Rd TW9 132 D2
Bickenhall Mans W1 237 D4
Bickenhall St
W1 92 D2 237 D4
Bickersteth Rd SW17 180 D4
Bickerton Rd N19 71 C6
Bickley Cres BR1 210 A5
Bickley Ct 1 HA7 25 C6
Bickley Park Rd BR1,
BR7 210 B6
Bickley Park Sch BR1 210 A6
Bickley Rd E10 53 D2
Bromley BR1 187 D1
Bickley St SW17 180 D5
Bickley Sta BR1 210 A6
Bicknell Ho 23 E1 96 A1
Bicknell Rd SE5 139 A2
Bicknoller Rd EN1 5 D4
Bicknor Ho 2 E5 74 B3
Bicknor Rd BR6 211 D2
Bidborough Cl 3 BR2 208 D4
Bidborough St
N1,WC1 94 A4 233 A1
Biddenden Way SE9 188 C6
Biddenham Ho 18 SE16 118 D2
Bidder St E16 98 C2
Biddesden Ho SW3 257 C3
Biddestone Rd N7 72 B4
Biddulph Ho 23 SE18 122 B2
Biddulph Mans W9 91 D4
Biddulph Rd W9 91 D4
Bideford Ave UB6 87 B5
Bideford Cl Edgware HA8 26 C2
Feltham TW13 151 B1
Bideford Gdns EN1 17 C4
Bideford Rd
Bexley DA16 146 B5
Catford BR1 164 D1
Enfield EN3 7 B5
Ruislip HA4 62 B5
Bidmead Ct KT6 214 A5
Bidwell Gdns N11 31 C3
Bidwell St SE15 140 B4
Big Ben* SW1 250 B1
Big Hill E5 52 B1
Bigbury Cl N17 33 C3
Biggerstaff Rd E15 98 A6
Biggerstaff St N4 72 C6
Biggin Ave CR4 180 D2
Biggin Hill SE19 182 D3
Biggin Hill Cl KT2 175 C5
Biggin Way SE19 183 A3
Bigginwood Rd SW16 182 D2
Bigg's Row SW15 134 D2
Bigland Green JMI Sch
E1 96 B1
Bigland St E1 96 B1
Bignell Rd SE18 122 D1
Bignold Rd E7 77 A4
Bigwood Ct NW11 47 D4
Bigwood Rd NW11 47 D3
Bilberry Ho 13 E3 97 C2
Bill Hamling Cl SE9 166 B2
Bill Nicholson Way N17 33 D3
Billet Rd E17 35 B2
Ilford RM6 58 C6
Billetts Hart Cl W7 108 C4
Billing Ho 6 E1 96 D1
Billing Pl SW10 135 D5 265 D4
Billing Rd
SW10 135 D5 265 D4
Billing St SW10 135 D5 265 D4
Billingford Cl SE4 140 D1
Billingley NW1 232 A5
Billings Cl RM9 80 C1
Billingsgate Mkt E14 119 D5
Billington Ho SW8 269 D1
Billington Rd SE14 140 D5
Billiter Sq EC3 243 B1
Billiter St EC3 95 C1 243 B1
Billockby Cl KT9 214 B2
Billsley Ct SE25 205 C5
Billson St E14 120 A2
Bilsby Gr SE9 187 D6
Bilton Ho SW8 269 C1
Bilton Rd UB6 87 B6
Bilton Twrs W1 237 D1
Bilton Way Enfield EN3 7 B5
Hayes UB3 106 B4
Bina Gdns SW5 114 A2 256 A3
Binbrook Ho W10 90 C2
Bincote Rd EN2 4 B2
Binden Rd W12 111 D3
Bindon Gn SM4 201 D5
Binfield Ct SE5 139 A3
Binfield Rd
SW4 138 A4 270 B1
South Croydon CR2 221 D3
Bingfield St N1 94 B6 233 C6
Bingham Cnr CR0 206 A1
Bingham Pl W1 93 A2 238 A4
Bingham Point 11 SE18 122 D2
Bingham Rd CR0 206 B1
Bingham St N1 73 B2
Bingley Rd E16 99 C1
Ashford TW16 172 A3
Southall UB6 86 A2
Binley Ho SW15 155 D5
Binney St W1 93 A1 238 B1
Binnie Ho SE1 262 A5
Binns Rd W4 111 C1
Binns Terr 3 W4 111 C1
Binsey Wlk 1 SE2 124 C4
Binstead Cl UB4 85 A2
Binstead Ho SW18 157 D5
Binyon Cres HA7 24 D5
Binyon Ho 8 N16 73 C4
Birbetts Rd SE9 166 B2
Birch Ave N13 17 A1
Hillingdon UB7 82 B1
Birch Cl E16 98 C2
N19 71 C6
SE15 140 A3
Brentford TW8 131 B5
Buckhurst Hill IG9 21 D1
Hounslow TW3 130 B3
Romford RM7 59 D6
Teddington TW11 175 A5
Birch Cres UB10 82 B6
Birch Ct E4 35 D4
E7 76 D4
Sutton SM1 218 A4
9 Wallington SM6 219 B4
Birch Gn NW9 27 C3
Birch Gr E11 76 C5
SE12 164 D4
W3 110 C6
Bexley DA16 146 A1
Upper Halliford TW17 171 C1
Birch Hill CR0 222 D3
Birch Ho SE14 141 B4
8 SW2 160 C5
Birch Mead BR2,BR6 226 C6
Birch Pk HA3 24 A3
Birch Rd Feltham TW13 172 D5
Romford RM7 59 D6
Birch Row BR2 210 C3
Birch Tree Ave BR4 224 D4
Birch Tree Ho 16 SE7 143 C6
Birch Tree Way CR0 222 B6
Birch Vale Ct NW8 236 D6
Birch Wlk CR4 181 B2
Bircham Path SE4 140 D1
Birchanger Rd SE25 206 A4
Birchdale Gdns RM6 58 D2
Birchdale Rd E7 77 C3
Birchdene Dr SE28 124 A5
Birchdown Ho 32 E3 97 D4
Birchen Cl NW9 67 B6
Birchen Gr NW9 67 B6
Birchend Cl CR2 221 B2
Birches Cl Mitcham CR4 202 D6
Pinner HA5 41 A4
Birches The E12 78 A4
N21 16 B5
SE5 139 C3
SE7 143 B6
SE25 183 D1
2 Beckenham BR2 208 D5
Bushey WD2 8 A6
Locksbottom BR6 226 C4
Twickenham TW4 151 B4
Birchfield Ho 2 E14 119 C6
Birchfield St E14 119 C6
Birchin La EC3 242 D1
Birchington Cl DA7 147 D4
Birchington Ct N8 49 D3
2 NW6 91 D6
Birchington Ho 1 E5 74 B3
Birchington Rd N8 49 D3
NW6 91 C6
Surbiton KT5 198 B2
Birchlands Ave SW12 158 D4
Birchmead Ave HA5 40 C5
Birchmere Lo 18 SE16 118 B1
Birchmere Row SE3 142 D3
Birchmore Wlk N5 73 A5
Birchway UB3 106 A5
Birchwood Ave N10 49 A6
Beckenham BR3 207 B5
Hackbridge SM5,SM6 219 B5
Sidcup DA14 168 C1
Birchwood Cl SM4 201 D5
Birchwood Ct N13 32 D5
Burnt Oak HA8 27 A1
Birchwood Dr NW3 69 D5
Birchwood Gr TW12 173 C4
Birchwood Rd SW17 181 B5
St Paul's Cray BR5 211 C5
Bird In Bush Rd SE15 140 A5
Bird In Hand Yd 14 NW3 70 A4
Bird St W1 238 B1
Bird Wlk TW2 151 B3
Birdbrook Rd SE3,SE9 143 C2
Birdcage Wlk
SW1 115 D4 249 C1
Birdham Cl BR1 210 A4
Birdhurst Ave CR2 221 B4
Birdhurst Ct SM6 219 C1
Birdhurst Gdns CR2 221 B4
Birdhurst Rd SW18 158 A6
SW19 180 C4
South Croydon CR2 221 C3
Birdhurst Rise CR2 221 C3
Bird-in-Hand La BR1 187 D1
Bird-In-Hand Pas SE23 162 C2
Birdlip Cl SE15 139 C6
Birdsall Ho 5 SE5 139 C2
Birdsfield La E3 97 B6
Birdwood Cl TW11 174 C6
Birkbeck Ave W3 111 A6
Greenford UB6 86 A6
Birkbeck Coll
W1 93 D1 239 C2
Birkbeck Ct W3 111 B5
Birkbeck Gdns IG8 21 A2
Birkbeck Gr W3 111 B4
Birkbeck Hill SE21 160 D3
Birkbeck Mews 5 E8 73 D3
Birkbeck Pl SE21 161 A2
Birkbeck Prim Sch
DA14 168 B1
Birkbeck Rd E8 73 D3
N8 50 A5
N12 30 A5
N17 33 D2
NW7 27 D5
SW19 179 D4
W3 111 B5
W5 109 C2
Enfield EN2 5 B5
Ilford IG2 57 B4
Penge BR3 184 D1
Sidcup DA14 168 A1
Birkbeck St E2 96 B4
Birkbeck Sta SE20 206 C6
Birkbeck Way UB6 86 B6
Birkdale Ave HA5 41 C6
Birkdale Cl 30 SE16 118 B1
Orpington BR6 211 B2
Birkdale Ct 3 UB1 86 A1
Birkdale Gdns CR0 222 D4
Birkdale Rd SE2 124 A2
W5 88 A3
Birkenhead Ave KT2 176 B2
Birkenhead Ho 11 N7 72 C3
Birkenhead St
WC1 94 A4 233 B2
Birkhall Rd SE6 164 B2
Birkwood Cl SW12 159 D4
Birley Lo NW8 229 D4
Birley Rd N20 14 A2
Birley St SW11 137 A3
Birling Ho 4 SE20 184 C3
Birnam Rd N4 72 B6
Birnbeck Ct NW11 47 B4
Birrell Ho 9 SW9 138 B3
Birse Cres NW10 67 C4
Birstal Gn WD1 22 D6
Birstall Rd N15 51 C4
Birtwhistle Ho 5 E3 97 B6
Biscay Ho 11 E1 96 D3
Biscay Rd W6 112 D1
Biscoe Cl TW5 129 C6
Biscoe Ho UB2 107 D2
Biscoe Way SE13 142 B2
Biscott Ho 3 E3 97 D3
Bisenden Rd CR0 221 C6
Bisham Cl CR4 202 D1
Bisham Gdns N6 49 A1
Bishop Butt Cl BR6 227 D5
Bishop Challoner Sch
BR2 186 B1
Bishop Challoner Sec Sch
E1 96 C1
Bishop Douglass RC High
Sch N2 48 A6
Bishop Duppa's Almshouses
7 TW10 154 A6
Bishop Duppas Pk
TW17 193 C2
Bishop Fox Way KT8 195 B5
Bishop Gilpins Prim Sch
SW19 179 B5
Bishop John Robinson Prim
Sch SE28 124 C6
Bishop Ken Rd HA3 24 D2
Bishop King's Rd
W14 113 A2 254 B4
Bishop Perrin CE Sch
TW2 151 D3
Bishop Ramsey CE Sch
HA4 40 A2
Bishop Ramsey CE Sch
(Annexe) HA4 39 D2
Bishop Rd N14 15 B4
Bishop St N1 95 A6 235 A6
Bishop Stopford's CE Sch
EN1 6 B3
Bishop Thomas Grant RC Sec
Sch SW16 182 B5
Bishop Wand CE Sec Sch
TW16 171 D1
Bishop Way NW10 67 C1
Bishop Wilfred Wood Cl
SE15 140 A3
Bishop Wilfred Wood Ct 2
E13 99 C5
Bishop Winnington-Ingram
CE Sch HA4 39 B2
Bishopgate 32 N1 95 C6
Bishops Ave E13 99 B6
Bromley BR1 209 C6
Dagenham RM6 58 C3
Deacons Hill WD6 10 B6
Bishop's Ave SW6 135 A3
Bishops Ave The N2 48 B3
Bishop's Bridge Rd
W2 92 A1 236 A2
Bishops Cl SE9 167 A2
W4 111 A1
Bishops Cl *continued*
Ducks Island EN5 12 D5
Enfield EN1 6 B3
Richmond TW10 153 D1
Sutton SM1 217 C5
Bishop's Cl E17 53 D5
N19 71 C5
Hillingdon UB10 82 C5
Bishops Ct N2 48 C5
12 W2 91 D1
1 Ashford TW16 171 D3
Romford RM7 59 D5
Bishop's Ct EC4 241 C2
WC2 241 A2
Bishops Dr
East Bedfont TW14 149 B5
Northolt UB5 85 A6
Bishops Gn BR1 187 C2
Bishops Gr N2 48 C3
Hampton TW12 173 B6
Bishop's Hall KT1 175 D1
Bishops Hill KT12 194 A2
Bishops Ho SW8 270 B3
Bishop's Mans SW6 134 D3
Bishops Mead SE5 139 A5
Bishops Park Rd SW16 182 A2
Bishop's Park Rd SW6 134 D3
Bishop's Pl SM1 218 A3
Bishops Rd N6 49 A3
SW6 135 B4 264 C2
Bishop's Rd W7 108 C4
Hayes UB3 83 A1
Thornton Heath CR0 204 D2
Bishop's Terr
SE11 116 C2 261 B4
Bishop's Way E2 96 C5
Bishops Wlk
Chislehurst BR7 189 A2
South Croydon CR0,CR9 223 A3
Bishopsbourne Ho BR1 187 B3
Bishopscourt 8 CR0 221 D6
Bishopsdale Ho 8 NW6 91 C6
Bishopsford Rd SM4 202 B3
Bishopsgate EC2 95 C1 243 A2
Bishopsgate Arcade E1 243 B3
Bishopsgate Church Yd
EC2 243 A2
Bishopshalt Sec Sch
UB8 82 B4
Bishopsthorpe Rd SE26 184 D6
Bishopstone Ho 4
SW11 137 A3
Bishopswood Rd N6 48 D2
Bisley Cl KT4 200 C1
Bisley Ho SW19 156 D2
Bispham Rd NW10 88 B4
Bissextile Ho SE13 141 D3
Bisson Rd E15 98 A5
Bistern Ave E17 54 B6
Bittacy Bsns Ctr NW7 29 A3
Bittacy Cl NW7 28 D4
Bittacy Ct NW7 29 A3
Bittacy Hill NW7 28 D4
Bittacy Park Ave NW7 28 D5
Bittacy Rd NW7 28 D4
Bittacy Rise NW7 28 D4
Bittern Cl UB4 84 D2
Bittern Ct E4 20 B4
NW9 27 C1
8 SE8 141 C6
Bittern Ho SE1 252 A1
Bittern St SE1 252 A1
Bittoms The KT1 197 D6
Bixley Cl UB2 107 B2
Black Boy La N15 51 A4
Black Fan Cl EN2 5 A4
Black Friars La
EC4 94 D1 241 C1
Black Horse Ct SE1 262 D6
Black Horse Par HA5 40 B4
Black Horse Rd DA14 190 A6
Black Lion La W6 112 A2
Black Lion Mews 4
W6 112 A2
Black Prince Intc DA5 169 D5
Black Prince Rd
SE1,SE11 116 B2 260 D3
Black Rod Cl UB3 105 D3
Black Roof Ho 9 SE5 138 D4
Black Swan Yd SE1 253 A2
Blackall St EC2 243 A6
Blackberry Cl TW17 193 C5
Blackberry Farm Cl
TW5 129 A5
Blackberry Field BR5 190 A2
Blackbird Ct NW9 67 B5
Blackbird Hill NW9 67 B5
Blackborne Rd RM10 81 D2
Blackbrook La BR1,BR2 210 C5
Blackburn 28 NW9 27 D1
Blackburn Rd NW6 69 D2
Blackburn Trad Est
TW19 148 B5
Blackburne's Mews W1 248 A5
Blackbush Ave RM6 58 D4
Blackbush Cl SM2 217 D1
Blackcap Ct NW9 27 C1
Blackdown Cl N2 30 A1
Blackdown Ho E8 74 A4
Blackenham Rd SW17 180 D6
Blackett St SW15 134 D2
Blackfen Par DA15 168 A5
Blackfen Rd DA15 168 B5
Blackfen Sch for Girls
DA15 168 B5
Blackford Rd WD1 22 D5
Blackfriars Bridge EC4 251 C5
Blackfriars Ct EC4 251 C6
Blackfriars Pas EC4 251 C6
Blackfriars Rd
SE1 116 D4 251 C3
Blackfriars Sta
EC4 116 D6 251 C6
Blackfriars Underpass
EC4 116 C6 251 B6
Blackham Ho SW19 179 A4
Blackheath SE3 142 C4
Blackheath Ave SE3 142 C5
Blackheath Bluecoat CE Sch
SE3 143 B5
Blackheath Bsns Est
SE10 142 A4
Blackheath Gr SE3 142 D3
Blackheath High Sch
SE3 143 A5
Blackheath High Sch (Girls)
SE3 142 D3
Blackheath High Sch GPDST
(Jun Dept) SE3 143 A3
Blackheath Hill SE10 142 A4
Blackheath Hospl SE3 142 C2
Blackheath Pk SE3 143 A2
Blackheath Rd SE10 141 D4
Blackheath Rise SE13 142 A3
Blackheath Sta SE3 142 D2
Blackheath Vale SE3 142 C3
Blackheath Village SE3 142 D3
Blackhorse La E17 34 D1
Croydon CR0 206 A2
Blackhorse La Sta CR0 206 A2
Blackhorse Mews E17 52 D6
Blackhorse Rd E17 53 A5
SE8 141 A6
Blackhorse Road E17 52 D5
Blackhorse Road Sta
E17 52 D5
Blacklands Dr UB4 83 A3
Blacklands Rd SE6 186 A6
Blacklands Terr SW3 257 D3
Blackmore Ave UB1 108 B5
Blackmore Ho N1 233 D5
SE23 163 B3
2 SW18 157 D6
Blackmore Twr 1 W3 111 A3
Blackmore's Gr TW11 175 A4
Blackness La BR2 225 D1
Blackpool Gdns UB4 83 C3
Blackpool Rd SE15 140 B3
Black's Rd W6 112 C2
Blackshaw Rd SW17 180 B5
Blacksmith Cl RM6 58 C3
Blacksmiths Ho 7 E17 53 C5
Blackstock Ho N5 72 D5
Blackstock Mews N4 72 D5
Blackstock Rd N4,N5 72 D6
Blackstone Ho SE21 161 C1
SW1 259 A1
Blackstone Rd NW2 68 C4
Blackthorn Ave UB7 104 C3
Blackthorn Ct 4 E15 76 B4
19 SE15 139 D5
6 SW16 182 C5
Heston TW5 129 A5
Blackthorn Gr DA7 147 A2
Blackthorn St E3 97 C3
Blackthorne Ave CR0 206 C1
Blackthorne Dr E4 36 B6
Blacktree Mews 12
SW9 138 C2
Blackwall La SE10 120 D2
Blackwall Sta E14 120 A6
Blackwall Trad Est E14 98 B2
Blackwall Tunnel E14,
SE10 120 B5
Blackwall Tunnel App
SE10 120 C4
Blackwall Tunnel Northern
Approach E14,E3 98 A3
Blackwall Way E14 120 A6
Blackwater Cl E7 76 D4
Blackwater Ho NW8 236 D4
Blackwater St SE22 161 D6
Blackwell Cl 10 E5 74 D4
Harrow HA3 24 B3
Blackwell Gdns HA8 10 C1
Blackwell Ho 3 SW4 159 D5
Blackwood Ho 11 E1 96 B3
Blackwood St
SE17 117 B1 262 C2
Blade Mews SW15 135 B1
Bladen Ho 4 E1 96 D1
Blades Ct SW15 135 B1
Blades Ho 12 SE11 138 C6
Bladindon Dr DA5 168 D4
Bladon Ct SW16 182 A4
Beckenham BR2 208 C6
Bladon Gdns HA2 41 D3
Blagden's Cl N14 15 D2
Blagden's La N14 15 D2
Blagdon Ct W7 108 C6
Blagdon Rd SE13 163 D5
New Malden KT3 199 D5
Blagdon Wlk TW11 175 C4
Blagrove Rd 1 W10 91 B2
Blair Ave NW9 45 C2
Thames Ditton KT10 212 A6
Blair Cl N1 73 A2
Hayes UB3 106 A2
Sidcup DA15 167 C6
Blair Ct NW8 229 C6
7 SE6 164 D3
Beckenham BR3 185 D2
Blair Ho SW9 138 B3
Blair Peach Prim Sch
UB1 106 D5
Blair St E14 98 B1

Blairderry Rd SW2 160 A2
Blake Ave IG11 101 D6
Blake Cl Bexley DA16 145 C4
Carshalton SM5 202 C1
Blake Ct NW6 91 C4
8 SE16 118 B1
Blake Gdns
SW6 135 D4 265 C2
Blake Hall Cres E11 55 A1
Blake Hall Rd E11 55 A2
Blake Ho 14 N16 73 C4
1 N19 71 D3
SE1 261 A6
2 SE8 141 C6
6 Beckenham BR3 185 D4
Blake Lo N3 29 B1
Blake Rd E16 98 D3
N11 31 C3
Croydon CR0 221 C6
Mitcham CR4 202 C6
Blakeden Dr KT10 212 D2
Blakehall Rd SM5 218 D2
Blakemore Rd SW16 160 A1
Thornton Heath CR7 204 B4
Blakemore Way DA17 125 A3
Blakeney Ave BR3 185 B2
Blakeney Cl 4 E8 74 A3
N20 14 A3
5 NW1 71 D1
Blakeney Ct EN2 17 B6
Blakeney Rd BR3 185 B2
Blakenham Ct W12 112 A5
Blaker Ct SE7 143 C5
Blaker Rd E15 98 A6
Blakes Ave KT3 199 D3
Blakes Cl W10 90 C2
Blake's Gn BR4 208 A1
Blakes La KT3 199 D4
Blake's Rd SE15 139 C5
Blakes Terr KT3 200 A4
Blakesley Ave W5 87 C1
Blakesley Ct W5 87 C1
Blakesley Ho 4 E12 78 C5
Blakesware Gdns N9 17 B4
Blakewood Cl TW13 172 C6
Blakewood Ct SE20 184 B3
Blanca Ho 16 N1 95 C5
Blanch Cl SE15 140 C5
Blanchard Cl SE9 166 A1
Blanchard Ho 7 TW1 153 D5
Blanchard Way E8 74 A2
Blanche Ho NW8 237 A5
Blanche Nevile Sch The
N15 51 D6
Blanche St E16 98 D3
Blanchedowne SE5 139 B1
Blanchland Rd SM4 201 D4
Bland Ho SE11 260 D2
Bland St SE9 143 D1
Blandfield Rd SW12 159 A4
Blandford Ave
2 Penge BR3 185 A1
Twickenham TW2 151 D3
Blandford Cl N2 48 A5
Romford RM7 59 D5
Wallington CR0 220 A5
Blandford Cres E4 20 A4
Blandford Ct 6 N1 73 C1
NW6 69 A1
Blandford Ho SW8 270 C4
Blandford Rd W4 111 C3
W5 109 D4
Penge BR3 184 D1
Southall UB2 107 C2
Teddington TW11 174 C5
Blandford Sq NW1 237 B5
Blandford St W1 93 A2 238 A3
Blandford Waye UB4 84 C1
Blaney Cres E6 100 D4
Blaney Pl 1 N7 72 C3
Blanmerle Rd SE9 166 D3
Blann Cl SE9 165 D5
Blantyre St
SW10 136 B5 266 C4
Blantyre Twr SW10 266 C4
Blantyre Wlk
SW10 136 B5 266 C4
Blashford NW3 70 D1
Blashford St SE13 164 B4
Blasker Wlk E14 119 D1
Blatchford Ct KT12 194 A1
Blatchford Ho 8 RM10 81 C5
Blawith Rd HA1 42 D5
Blaxland Ho 12 W12 112 B6
Blaydon Cl HA4 39 C2
Blaydon Ct 4 UB5 63 C2
Blaydon Wlk N17 34 B3
Bleak Hill La SE18 145 D6
Blean Gr SE20 184 C3
Bleasdale Ave UB6 87 A5
Blechynden Ho 17 W10 90 D1
Blechynden St W10 112 D6
Bleddyn Cl DA15 168 C5
Bledlow Cl SE28 124 C6
Bledlow Ho NW8 236 D5
Bledlow Rise UB6 86 A5
Bleeding Heart Yd EC1 241 B3
Blegborough Rd SW16 181 C4
Blemundsbury WC1 240 C4
Blendon Dr DA5 168 D5
Blendon Path 7 BR1 186 D3
Blendon Rd DA5 168 D5
Blendon Terr SE18 145 A6
Blendworth Point 4
SW15 156 B3
Blendworth Way 11
SE15 139 C5
Blenheim 26 SW19 156 D3
Blenheim Ave IG2 56 C3
Blenheim Bsns Ctr CR4 180 D1
Blenheim Cl N21 17 A3
SW20 200 C6
Greenford UB6 86 B5
Wallington SM6 219 C1
Blenheim Cr
W11 113 A6 244 B6
Blenheim Cres W11 91 A1
Ruislip HA4 61 B6
South Croydon CR2 221 A1
Blenheim Ct N7 72 A2
N19 72 A6
17 SE16 118 D5
SE19 183 C2
Harrow HA3 43 A3
Longlands DA15 167 B1
Richmond TW9 132 B2
Sutton SM2 218 A2
Woodford IG8 37 B3
Woodford IG8 37 C2
Blenheim Dr DA16 145 D4
Blenheim Gdns NW2 68 C3
SW2 160 B5
Kingston u T KT2 176 D3
Wallington SM6 219 C1
Wembley HA9 66 A5
Blenheim Gr SE15 140 A3
Blenheim Ho 6 N9 18 A1
Hounslow TW3 129 C2
Blenheim Par 2 UB10 82 D3
Blenheim Park Rd CR2 221 A1
Blenheim Pas NW8 229 A4
Blenheim Rd E6 99 D4
E15 76 C4
E17 53 A6
NW8 92 A5 229 B4
SE20 184 C3
SW20 200 C6
W4 111 C3
Bromley BR1,BR2 210 A5
Harrow HA2 41 D3
Northolt UB5 63 D2
Sidcup DA15 168 C3
Sutton SM1 217 D5
Blenheim Rise N15 51 D5
Blenheim St W1 238 C1
Blenheim Terr
NW8 92 A5 229 A4
Blenheim Way TW7 131 A4
Blenkarne Rd SW11 158 D5
Bleriot 27 NW9 27 D1
Bleriot Rd TW5 128 C5
Blessbury Rd HA8 27 A2
Blessed Dominic RC Prim
Sch NW9 27 D1
Blessed John Roche RC Sec
Sch E14 97 C1
Blessed Sacrament RC Prim
Sch N1 94 B6 233 C5
Blessing Way IG11 102 C5
Blessington Cl SE13 142 B2
Blessington Rd SE13 142 B1
Bletchingly Cl CR7 204 D5
Bletchington Ct DA17 125 C2
Bletchley Ct N1 235 C3
Bletchley St N1 95 A5 235 B3
Bletchmore Cl UB3 105 B1
Bletsoe Wlk N1 235 B4
Blewbury Ho 3 SE2 124 C4
Blick Ho 1 SE16 118 C3
Bligh Ho 4 SE27 183 A6
Blincoe Cl SW19 156 D2
Blind Cnr SE25 206 C5
Blissett St SE10 142 A4
Blissland Ct N12 30 A4
Bliss Ct W4 85 A3
Blisworth Cl UB4 85 A3
Blisworth Ho 12 E2 96 A6
Blithbury Rd RM9 80 B2
Blithdale Rd SE2 124 A2
Blithfield St W8 255 C5
Blockley Rd HA0 65 B6
Bloemfontein Ave W12 112 B5
Bloemfontein Rd W12 112 B6
Blomfield Ct SW11 266 D2
W9 236 B6
Blomfield Mans W12 112 C5
Blomfield Rd W9 92 A2 236 A4
Blomfield St EC2 95 B2 242 D3
Blomfield Villas W2 91 D2
W9 236 A4
Blomville Rd RM8 81 A5
Blondel St SW11 137 A3
Blondin Ave W5 109 C3
Blondin St E3 97 C5
Bloom Gr SE27 160 D1
Bloom Park Rd SW6 264 C3
Bloomburg St SW1 259 B3
Bloomfield Cres IG2 56 D3
Bloomfield Ct N6 49 A3
Bloomfield Ho 17 E1 96 A2
Bloomfield Pl W1 248 D6
Bloomfield Rd N6 49 A3
SE18 122 D1
Bromley BR2 209 D4
Kingston u T KT1 198 A6
Bloomfield Terr
SW1 115 A1 258 B2
Bloomfields The IG11 79 A2
Bloomhall Rd SE19 183 B5
Bloomsbury Cl W5 110 B6
Bloomsbury Ct E11 54 B1
WC1 240 B3
Cranford TW5 128 B4
Pinner HA5 41 B6
Bloomsbury Ho 10
SW4 159 D5
Bloomsbury Pl SW18 158 A6
Bloomsbury Pl *continued*
WC1 240 B3
Bloomsbury Sq
WC1 94 A2 240 B3
Bloomsbury St
WC1 93 D2 239 D3
Bloomsbury Way
WC1 94 A2 240 B3
Blore Cl SW8 269 C1
Blore Ct W1 249 C6
Blossom Cl W5 110 A4
Dagenham RM9 103 B6
South Croydon CR2 221 D3
Blossom La EN2 5 A4
Blossom Pl E1 243 B5
Blossom St E1 95 C3 243 B5
Blossom Way
Hillingdon UB10 60 B1
West Drayton UB7 104 C2
Blossom Waye TW5 129 A5
Blount Ho 16 E14 97 A2
Blount St E14 97 A1
Bloxam Gdns SE9 166 A6
Bloxhall Rd E10 53 B1
Bloxham Cres TW12 173 B2
Bloxworth Cl SM6 219 C5
Blucher Rd SE5 139 A5
Blue Anchor Alley 4
TW9 132 A1
Blue Anchor La SE16 118 B2
Blue Anchor Yd E1 118 A6
Blue Ball Yd SW1 249 A3
Blue Gate Field JMI Schs
E1 118 C6
Blue Sch The TW7 131 A2
Bluebell Ave E12 78 A3
Bluebell Cl SE26 183 D6
Orpington BR6 227 A6
Wallington SM6 203 B1
Bluebell Way IG1 78 D2
Bluebird Wlk HA9 66 D5
Bluefield Cl TW12 173 C5
Bluegates SW19 179 A5
Stoneleigh KT17 216 A1
Bluehouse Rd E4 20 C1
Blundell Rd HA8 27 C3
Blundell St N7 72 A2
Blunden Cl RM8 58 C1
Blunt Rd CR0 221 B3
Blunts Ave UB7 126 C5
Blunts Rd SE9 166 C6
Blurton Rd E5 74 D4
Blydon Ct N21 16 B6
Blyth Cl 4 E14 120 B2
Twickenham TW1 152 D5
Blyth Rd E17 53 B2
SE23 124 C6
Bromley BR1 186 D2
Hayes UB3 105 C4
Blythe Cl SE23 163 B4
Blythe Hill SE6 163 B4
St Paul's Cray BR5 190 A2
Blythe Hill La SE6 163 B3
Blythe Ho 8 SE11 138 C6
Blythe Mews 2 W14 112 D3
Blythe Rd W14 112 D3 254 A5
Blythe St E2 96 B4
Blythe Vale SE6 163 B3
Blythendale Ho 11 E2 96 A5
Blyth's Wharf E14 119 A6
Blythswood Rd IG3 58 A2
Blythwood Pk 10 BR1 186 D2
Blythwood Rd N4 50 A2
Pinner Green HA5 22 D2
Boadicea St N1 233 C5
Boardoak Ho 18 NW6 91 D6
Boardman Ave E4 19 D6
Boardman Cl EN5 13 A6
Boarhound 25 NW9 27 D1
Boarley Ho SE17 263 A3
Boat Lifter Way 19
SE16 119 A2
Boathouse Ctr The W10 90 D3
Bob Anker Cl 1 E13 99 A4
Bob Marley Way 11
SE24 138 C1
Bobbin Cl SW4 137 C2
Bobby Moore Bridge The
HA9 66 C5
Babington Ct
WC1 94 A2 240 B4
Bockhampton Rd KT2 176 B3
Bocking St E8 96 B6
Boddicott Cl SW19 157 A2
Boddington Ho SE14 140 C4
Boden Ho 4 E1 96 A2
Bodeney Ho 10 SE5 139 C4
Bodiam Cl EN1 5 C3
Bodiam Ct BR2 208 D5
Bodiam Rd SW16 181 D3
Bodington Ct 2 W12 112 D4
Bodley Cl KT3 199 C4
Bodley Manor Way
SE24 160 C4
Bodley Rd KT3 199 C4
Bodmin 26 NW9 27 D1
Bodmin Cl HA2 63 B5
Bodmin Gr SM4 201 D4
Bodmin St SW18 157 C3
Bodnant Gdns SW20 200 B6
Bodney Mans 14 E8 74 B3
Bodney Rd E5,E8 74 B3
Boeing Way UB2 106 B3
Boelyn Dr HA4 62 D6
Boevey Path 2 DA17 147 B6
Bognor Gdns WD1 22 C5
Bognor Rd DA16 146 D4
Bohemia Pl 1 E8 74 B2
Bohun Gr EN4 14 D5
Boileau Par W5 88 B1
Boileau Rd SW13 134 B6
W5 88 B1
Boilerhouse SE1 253 C3
Boisseau Ho 27 E1 96 C2
Bolden St SE8 141 D3
Boldero Pl NW8 237 A5
Bolderwood Way BR4 223 D6
Boldmere Rd HA5 40 C2
Boleyn Ave EN1 6 B4
Boleyn Ct E17 53 C5
Buckhurst Hill IG9 21 B3
East Molesey KT8 196 B5
Boleyn Dr KT8 195 B6
Boleyn Gdns BR4 223 D6
Boleyn Ground(Upton Park)
(West Ham United FC)
E13,E6 99 D5
Boleyn Rd E6 99 D5
E7 77 B1
N16 73 C3
Boleyn Way EN5 2 A2
Bolina Rd SE16 118 C1
Bolingbroke Gr SW11 158 D5
Bolingbroke Ho
Beckenham BR3 207 A4
Catford BR3 185 D5
Bolingbroke Hospl The
SW11 158 C6
Bolingbroke Prim Sch
SW11 136 C4 267 A2
Bolingbroke Rd W14 112 D3
Bolingbroke Way UB11,
UB3 105 B5
Bolingbroke Wlk
SW11 136 C4 267 A2
Bollo Bridge Rd W3 111 A4
Bollo Ct 2 W3 111 A3
Bollo La W3 110 D3
Bolney Ct KT6 197 D4
Bolney Gate SW7 247 A1
Bolney St SW8 138 B5 270 C3
Bolsover St W1 93 B3 238 D5
Bolstead Rd CR4 181 B2
Bolster Gr N22 31 D2
Bolt Ct EC4 241 B1
Boltmore Cl NW4 46 D6
Bolton Cl SE20 184 A1
Chessington KT9 214 A2
Bolton Cres SE5 138 D5
Bolton Ct SW11 268 B1
Bolton Gdns NW10 90 D5
SW5 113 D1 255 D2
Bromley BR1 186 D4
Teddington TW11 175 A4
Bolton Gdns Mews
SW10 256 A2
Bolton Ho 4 SE10 120 C1
Bolton Rd E15 76 D2
N18 33 D5
NW8 91 D6
NW10 89 C6
W4 133 A5
Chessington KT9 214 A2
Harrow HA1 42 B5
Bolton St W1 115 B5 248 D4
Bolton Studios SW10 256 B1
Bolton Wlk N7 72 B6
Boltons Ct SW5 255 D2
Bolton's La TW6,UB7 127 A5
Boltons The
SW10 114 A1 256 A2
Wembley HA0 64 D4
Woodford IG8 37 A6
Bombay St SE16 118 B2
Bomer Cl UB7 126 C5
Bomore Rd
W11 113 A6 244 A6
Bonar Pl BR7 188 A3
Bonar Rd SE15 140 A5
Bonchester Cl BR7 188 C3
Bonchurch Cl SM2 217 D1
Bonchurch Rd W10 91 A2
W13 109 B5
Bond Cl UB7 82 B1
Bond Ct EC4 242 C1
Bond Fst Sch CR4 180 D1
Bond Gdns SM6 219 C4
Bond Ho 4 NW6 91 B5
Bond Rd Mitcham CR4 180 D1
Surbiton KT6 214 B6
Bond St E15 76 C3
W5 109 D6
Bond Street Sta
W1 93 B1 238 B1
Bondfield Ave UB4 84 A4
Bondfield Rd 4 E6 100 B2
Bonding Yard Wlk
SE16 119 A3
Bondway SW8 138 A6 270 B6
Boneta Rd SE18 122 B3
Bonfield Rd SE13 142 A1
Bonham Gdns RM8 80 D6
Bonham Ho W11 244 C4
Bonham Rd SW2 160 B6
Dagenham RM8 80 D5
Bonheur Rd W4 111 B4
Bonhill St EC2 95 B3 242 D5
Boniface Gdns HA3 23 D3
Boniface Rd UB10 60 D5
Boniface Wlk HA3 23 D3
Bonington Ho N1 233 C3
Enfield EN1 18 A6
Bonne Marche Terr Mews 18
SE27 183 C6
Bonner Hill Rd KT1 198 C6
Bonner Ho 3 SW15 156 A6
Bonner JMI Sch E2 96 C4
Bonner Rd E2 96 C5
Bonner St E2 96 C5
Bonnersfield Cl HA1 43 A3
Bonnersfield La
Harrow HA1 42 D3
Harrow HA1,HA3 43 A3
Bonneville Gdns SW4 159 C5
Bonneville Prim Sch
SW4 159 C5
Bonnington Ct 15 UB5 84 D5
Bonnington Sq
SW8 138 B6 270 C6
Bonnington Twr BR2 210 A3
Bonny St NW1 71 C1
Bonser Rd TW1 152 D2
Bonsor Ho SW8 269 B2
Bonsor St SE5 139 C5
Bonthron Ho SW15 134 C3
Bonus Pastor RC Sch
BR1 186 C6
Bonville Gdns 17 NW4 46 A5
Bonville Rd BR1 186 D5
Bookbinder Cotts N20 14 D1
Booker Cl 15 E3 97 B2
Booker Rd 5 N18 34 A5
Bookham Ct CR4 202 B6
Boone Ct N9 18 C1
Boone St SE13 142 C1
Boones Rd SE13 142 C1
Boord St SE10 120 C3
Boot Par HA8 26 C4
Boot St N1 95 C4
Booth Cl 10 E9 96 B6
SE28 124 B6
Booth Ho 2 SW2 160 C4
Booth La EC4 252 A6
Booth Rd NW9 27 C1
Croydon CR0 220 D6
Boothby Ct E4 20 A1
Boothby Ho 2 SW16 181 C5
Boothby Rd N19 71 D6
Boothman Ho HA3 43 D6
Boothroyd Ho TW7 130 D2
Booth's Pl W1 239 B3
Bordars Rd W7 86 D2
Bordars Wlk W7 86 C2
Borden Ave EN1 17 B5
Border Cres SE26 184 B5
Border Gate CR4 180 D2
Border Gdns CR0 223 D4
Border Rd SE26 184 B5
Bordesley Rd SM4 201 D5
Bordon Wlk 5 SW15 156 A4
Boreas Wlk N1 234 D3
Boreham Ave E16 99 A1
Boreham Cl E11 54 A1
Boreham Rd N22 33 A1
Boreman Ho 10 SE10 142 A6
Borgard Ho 3 SE18 144 A4
Borgard Rd SE18 122 B2
Borkwood Pk BR6 227 D4
Borkwood Way BR6 227 C4
Borland Rd SE15 140 C1
Teddington TW11 175 B3
Borneo St SW15 134 C2
Borough High St
SE1 117 B5 252 C2
Borough Hill CR0 220 D5
Borough Mkt* SE1 252 C3
Borough Rd
SE1 116 D3 261 D6
Hounslow TW7 130 D4
7 Kingston u T KT2 176 C3
Mitcham CR4 180 C1
Borough Sq SE1 252 A1
Borough Sta The
SE1 117 A4 252 B1
Borrett Cl SE17 117 A1 262 A1
Borrodaile Rd SW18 157 D5
Borrowdale NW1 232 A1
Borrowdale Ave HA3 25 A1
Borrowdale Cl IG4 56 A5
Borrowdale Ct EN2 5 A4
Borthwick Mews E15 76 C4
Borthwick Rd E15 76 C4
NW9 45 D3
Borthwick St SE8 119 C1
Borwick Ave E17 53 B6
Bosbury Rd SE6 164 A1
Boscastle Rd NW5 71 B5
Boscobel Ho 4 E8 74 B2
Boscobel Pl SW1 258 B4
Boscobel St NW8 92 B3 236 D5
Boscombe Ave E10 54 B2
Boscombe Cl E5 75 A3
Boscombe Gdns SW16 182 A4
Boscombe Ho CR0 205 B1
Boscombe Rd SW17 181 A4
SW19 179 D2
W12 112 A4
North Cheam KT4 200 D1
Bose Cl N3 29 A2
Bosgrove E4 20 A2
Boss Ho SE1 253 C2
Boss St SE1 253 C2
Bostall Hill SE2 124 B1
Bostall La SE2 124 B1
Bostall Manorway SE2 124 B2
Bostall Park Ave DA7 147 A5
Bostall Rd BR5 190 B3
Bostock Ho TW5 129 C6
Boston Bsns Pk W7 108 C3
Boston Ct SE25 205 D5
Sutton SM2 218 A1
Boston Gdns W4 133 C6
W7 109 A2
Brentford TW8 109 B2
Boston Gr HA4 39 A3
Boston Ho NW1 237 C6
25 SE5 139 A3
SW5 255 D3
Boston Manor Ho TW8 109 B1
Boston Manor Rd TW8 109 B1
Boston Manor Sta TW8 109 B2
Boston Par W7 109 A2
Boston Park Rd TW8 109 C1
Boston Pl NW1 92 D3 237 C5
Boston Rd E6 100 A4
W7 109 A3
Burnt Oak HA8 27 A3
Thornton Heath CR0 204 C3
Boston Vale W7 109 A2
Bostonthorpe Rd W7 108 C4
Boswell Ct 9 W14 112 D3
WC1 240 B4
Kingston u T KT2 176 C2
Boswell Ho 5 SW16 181 C5
WC1 240 B4
Bromley BR2 209 D4
Boswell Rd CR7 205 A5
Boswell St WC1 94 A2 240 B4
Boswood Ct TW4 129 B2
Bosworth Cl E17 35 B2
Bosworth Ho 4 W10 91 A3
Bosworth Rd N11 31 D4
W10 91 A3
Barnet EN5 1 C2
Dagenham RM10 81 C5
Botany Bay La BR7 189 A1
Botany Cl EN4 2 C1
Boteley Cl E4 20 B2
Botha Rd E13 99 C2
Botham Cl 6 HA8 27 A3
Bothnia Ho E1 97 A2
Bothwell Cl E16 98 D2
Bothwell St 4 W6 134 D6
Botolph Alley EC3 253 A6
Botolph La EC3 253 A6
Botsford Rd SW20 179 A1
Bott's Mews W2 91 C1
Botwell Common Rd
UB3 105 C6
Botwell Cres UB3 83 C1
Botwell House RC Prim Sch
UB3 105 D4
Botwell La UB3 105 C6
Boucher Cl TW11 174 D5
Bouchier Ho 6 N2 30 B1
Bough Beech Ct EN3 6 D6
Boughton Ave BR2 208 D2
Boughton Ho SE1 252 C2
Boughton Rd SE28 123 C3
Boulcott St E1 96 D1
Boulevard The 4
SW17 159 A2
Boullen Ct SM1 218 A4
Boulogne Ho SE1 263 C6
Boulogne Rd CR0 205 A3
Boulter Ho SE14 140 C4
Boulton Ho TW8 110 A1
Boulton Rd RM8 81 B6
Boultwood Rd E6 100 B1
Bounces La N9 18 B2
Bounces Rd N9 18 C2
Boundaries Mans 3
SW12 159 A3
Boundaries Rd SW12 159 A3
Feltham TW13 150 C3
Boundary Ave E17 53 B2
Boundary Bsns Ct CR4 202 B6
Boundary Cl SE20 184 A1
Hadley EN5 1 B4
Ilford IG3 79 C4
Kingston u T KT1 198 D6
Southall UB2 107 C1
Boundary Ct 3 N18 33 D4
Boundary Ho 1 SE5 139 A5
SW12 159 B3
Isleworth TW1 153 B6
Boundary La E13,E6 99 D3
SE17 139 A6
Boundary Pas E2 243 C6
Boundary Rd E13 99 D4
E17 53 C3
N2 30 B3
N9 18 C5
N22 33 A1
NW8 92 A6 229 B6
SW19 180 B4
Barking IG11 101 A5
Barking IG11 101 B6
Pinner HA5 40 D2
Sidcup DA15 167 C6
Wallington SM5,SM6,SM5,
SM6 219 A1
Boundary Road Est
NW8 92 A6 229 A5
Boundary Row SE1 251 C2
Boundary St E2 95 D3 243 C6
Boundary Way CR0 223 C3
Boundfield Rd SE6 164 C2
Bounds Green Ct N11 31 D4
Bounds Green Ind Est
N11 31 C4
Bounds Green Jun & Inf Schs
N11 32 A3
Bounds Green Rd N11 31 D4
N22 32 A2
Bounds Green Sta N11 31 D3
Bourbon Ho 9 SE6 186 A6
Bourchier St W1 249 C6
Bourdillon Ct 2 SE9 166 A2

Bourdon Pl W1 248 D6
Bourdon Rd SE20 184 C1
Bourdon St W1 115 B6 248 D5
Bourke Cl NW10 67 C2
SW4 160 A5
Bourlet Cl W1 239 A3
Bourn Ave N15 51 B5
Hillingdon UB8 82 C3
New Barnet EN4 14 B6
Bournbrook Rd SE3,SE9 143 D2
Bourne Ave N14 16 A2
Hayes UB3 105 B3
Ruislip HA4 62 C3
Bourne Cir UB3 105 A3
Bourne Ct E11 55 A4
W4 133 A6
Ruislip HA4 62 B3
Woodford IG8 37 D1
Bourne Dr CR4 180 B1
Bourne Gdns E4 35 D6
Bourne Hill N13 16 B2
Bourne Ho 1 NW2 68 A5
5 SW4 137 C1
Ashford TW15 170 C5
Buckhurst Hill IG9 21 D1
Bourne Mews W1 238 B1
Bourne Par DA5 169 D4
Bourne Pl W4 111 B1
Bourne Prim Sch HA4 62 C2
Bourne Rd E7,E11 76 D5
N8 50 A3
Bromley BR2 209 D5
Old Bexley DA5 169 D5
Bourne St SW1 115 A2 258 A3
Croydon CR0 220 D6
Bourne Terr W2 91 D2
Bourne The N14 16 A2
Bourne Vale BR2 208 D1
Bourne View UB6 64 D3
Bourne Way Cheam SM1 217 B3
Coney Hall BR2,BR4 224 D6
West Ewell KT19 215 A4
Bournemead Ave UB5 84 A5
Bournemead Cl UB5 84 A4
Bournemead Way UB5 84 B5
Bournemouth Cl SE15 140 A3
Bournemouth Rd SE15 140 A3
SW19 179 C2
Bournes Ho 4 N15 51 C3
Bourneside 5 N14 15 D3
Bourneside Cres 6 N14 15 D3
Bourneside Gdns SE6 186 A5
Bournevale Rd SW16 182 A6
Bournewood Rd SE18, SE2 146 A5
Bournville Rd SE6 163 C4
Bournwell Cl EN4 2 D3
Bourton Cl UB3 106 A5
Bousfield Prim Sch SW10 114 A1 256 A2
Bousfield Rd SE14 140 D3
Boutcher CE Prim Sch SE1 117 D2 263 C4
Boutflower Rd SW11 136 C1
Bouverie Gdns HA3 43 D3
Bouverie Mews N16 73 C6
Bouverie Pl W2 236 D2
Bouverie Rd N16 73 C6
Harrow HA1 42 A3
Bouverie St EC4 94 C1 241 B1
Bouvier Rd EN3 6 C5
Boveney Rd SE23 162 D4
Bovill Rd SE23 162 D4
Bovingdon Ave HA9 66 C2
Bovingdon Cl 3 N19 71 C6
Bovingdon La NW9 27 C2
Bovingdon Rd SW6 135 D4 265 D1
Bovingdon Sq CR4 204 A5
Bovril Ho EN1 5 C2
Bow Boys Sec Sch E3 97 C4
Bow Brook The 20 E2 96 D5
Bow Church Sta E3 97 C4
Bow Churchyard EC2, EC4 242 B1
Bow Common La E3 97 B3
Bow Ind Pk E15 75 C1
Bow La EC2,EC4 95 A1 242 B1
N12 30 A3
Bow Rd E3 97 C4
Bow Road Sta E3 97 C4
Bow St E15 76 C3
WC2 94 A1 240 B1
Bow Triangle Bsns Ctr E3 97 C3
Bowater Cl NW9 45 B4
SW2 160 A5
Bowater Ho EC1 242 B5
Bowater Pl SE3 143 B5
Bowater Rd SE18 121 D3
Bowden Cl TW14 149 C3
Bowden Ho 29 E3 97 D4
Bowden House Hospl (Private) HA1 64 C6
Bowden St SE11 116 C1 261 B1
Bowditch SE8 119 B1
Bowdon Rd E17 53 C2
Bowen Ct 2 N5 72 D4
Bowen Dr SE21 161 C1
Bowen Rd HA1 42 A2
Bowen St E14 97 D1
Bower Ave SE3 142 C5
Bower Cl UB5 84 C5
Bower Ho SE14 140 D4
Bower St E1 96 D1
Bowerdean St SW6 135 D3
Bowerman Ave SE14 141 A6
Bowerman Ct 1 N19 71 D6
Bowers Ho 5 IG11 78 D1
Bowers Wlk 1 E6 100 B1
Bowes Cl DA15 168 B5
Bowes Park Sta N22 32 A3
Bowes Prim Sch N11 31 D5
Bowes Rd N11 31 C5
W3 111 C6
Dagenham RM8 80 C4
Walton-on-T KT12 194 B1
Bowes Rd (North Circular Rd) N13 32 A5
Bowfell Rd W6 134 C6
Bowford Ave DA7 147 A4
Bowhill Cl SW9 138 C5
Bowie Cl SW4 159 D4
Bowl Ct EC2 243 B5
Bowland Ho N4 51 A2
Bowland Rd SW4 137 D1
Woodford IG8 37 C4
Bowland Yd SW1 247 D1
Bowles Ct N12 30 C3
Bowles Rd 1 SE1 140 A6
Bowley Cl SE19 183 D4
Bowley Ho 6 SE16 118 A3
Bowley La SE19 183 D5
Bowley St E14 119 B6
Bowling Cl UB10 82 B6
Bowling Green Cl SW19 156 B4
Bowling Green Ct HA9 66 B6
Bowling Green Ho SW10 266 C4
Bowling Green La EC1 94 C3 241 B6
Bowling Green Pl SE1 252 C2
Bowling Green Row 1 SE18 122 B2
Bowling Green St SE11 138 C6
Bowling Green Wlk N1 95 C4
Bowls Cl HA7 25 B5
Bowman Ave E16 120 D6
Bowman Mews E1 118 A6
SW18 157 B3
Bowmans Cl W13 109 B5
Bowmans Lea SE23 162 C4
Bowman's Meadow SM6 219 B5
Bowman's Mews N7 72 A5
Bowman's Pl N7 72 A5
Bowmead SE9 166 B2
Bowmore Wlk NW1 71 D1
Bowness Cl 5 E8 73 D2
Bowness Cres KT2, SW15 177 C5
Bowness Dr TW4 129 A1
Bowness Ho SE15 140 C5
Bowness Rd SE6 163 D4
Bexleyheath DA7 147 D3
Bowood Rd SW11 159 A6
Enfield EN3 6 D3
Bowring Gn WD1 22 C5
Bowrons Ave HA0 65 D1
Bowry Ho 14 E14 97 B2
Bowsley Ct TW13 150 A2
Bowsprit Point 5 E14 119 C3
Bowstead Ct SW11 266 D1
Bowyer Cl E6 100 B2
Bowyer Ct 4 E4 20 A3
Bowyer Ho 28 N1 95 C6
SW18 157 D5
Bowyer Pl SE5 139 A5
Bowyer St 15 SE5 139 A5
Box La IG11 102 C5
Box Tree Ho SE8 119 A1
Boxall Rd SE21 161 C5
Boxgrove Prim Sch SE2 124 C3
Boxgrove Rd SE2 124 C3
Boxley Ho 3 E5 74 B3
Boxley Rd SM4 202 A5
Boxley St E16 121 B5
Boxmoor Ho 16 E2 96 A6
9 W11 112 D5
Boxmoor Rd HA3 43 B5
Boxoll Rd RM9 81 B5
Boxshall Ho 7 SE18 144 D6
Boxtree La HA3 24 B3
Boxtree Rd HA3 24 B3
Boxwood Cl UB7 104 B4
Boxworth Cl N12 30 B5
Boxworth Gr N1 94 B6 233 D6
Boyard Rd SE18 122 D1
Boyce Ho SW16 181 C5
1 W10 91 B4
Boyce St SE1 251 A3
Boyce Way E13 99 A3
Boycroft Ave NW9 45 A3
Boyd Ave UB1 107 B5
Boyd Cl KT2 176 C3
Boyd Ct SW15 156 C5
Boyd Rd SW19 180 B4
Boyd St E1 96 A1
Boydell Ct NW8 70 B1
Boyden Ho 8 E17 54 A6
Boyfield St SE1 116 D4 251 D1
Boyland Rd BR1 186 D5
Boyle Ave HA7 25 A4
Boyle Cl UB10 82 B5
Boyle Farm Rd KT7 197 A3
Boyle Ho 13 DA17 125 C3
Boyle St W1 249 A6
Boyne Ave NW4 46 D5
Boyne Ct NW10 68 A1
Boyne Ho 10 E5 74 B6
Boyne Rd SE13 142 B2
Boyne Rd *continued*
Dagenham RM10 81 C5
Boyne Terr Mews W11 113 B5 244 C4
Boyson Rd 10 SE17 139 B6
Boyton Cl E1 96 D3
N8 50 A6
Boyton Ho NW8 229 D4
SE11 261 A1
Boyton Rd N8 50 A6
Brabant Rd N22 32 B1
Brabazon Ave SM6 220 A1
Brabazon Rd
Heston TW5 128 D5
Northolt UB5 85 C5
Brabazon St E14 97 D2
Brabner Ho 2 E2 96 A4
Brabourn Gr SE15 140 C3
Brabourne Cl 7 SE19 183 C5
Brabourne Cres DA7 147 B6
Brabourne Hts NW7 11 C1
Brabourne Rise BR3 208 B4
Brabrook Ct SM6 219 B3
Brabstone Ho 2 UB6 86 D5
Bracer Ho 1 N1 95 C5
Bracewell Ave UB6 65 A2
Bracewell Rd W10 90 C2
Bracewood Gdns CR0 221 D5
Bracey St N4 72 A6
Bracken Ave SW12 159 A4
Croydon CR0 223 C5
Bracken Cl E6 100 B2
Ashford TW16 171 D4
Twickenham TW4 151 C4
Bracken End TW7 152 B6
Bracken Gdns SW13 134 A3
Bracken Hill Cl 5 BR1 186 D2
Bracken Hill La BR1 186 D2
Bracken Ho 14 E3 97 C2
Bracken Mews E4 20 A3
Romford RM7 59 D3
Bracken The E4 20 A2
Brackenbridge Dr HA4 62 D5
Brackenbury N4 50 B1
Brackenbury Gdns W6 112 B3
Brackenbury Prim Sch W6 112 B3
Brackenbury Rd N2 48 A6
W6 112 B3
Brackendale N21 16 B2
Kingston u T KT1 176 D1
Brackendale Cl TW5 129 D4
Brackendale Ct 2 BR3 185 C3
Brackenfield Cl E5 74 B5
Brackenhill HA4 63 A4
Brackens BR3 185 C3
Brackens The EN1 17 C4
Brackenwood TW16 172 A2
Brackenwood Lo EN5 1 C1
Brackley Cl SM6 220 A1
Brackley Ct NW8 236 D6
Brackley Rd W4 111 C1
Beckenham BR3 185 C3
Brackley Sq IG8 37 D3
Brackley St EC1 242 B4
Brackley Terr 6 W4 111 C1
Bracklyn Ct N1 235 C4
Bracklyn St N1 235 C4
Bracknell Cl N22 32 C2
Bracknell Gate NW3 69 D3
Bracknell Gdns NW3 69 D4
Bracknell Way NW3 69 D4
Bracondale KT10 212 A3
Bracondale Rd SE2 124 A2
Brad St SE1 116 C5 251 B3
Bradbeer Ho 24 E2 96 C4
Bradbourne Rd DA5 169 C4
Bradbourne St SW6 135 C3
Bradbury Cl UB2 107 B2
Bradbury Ct 2 SE3 143 A5
Bradbury Ho E1 243 D2
Bradbury St 28 N16 73 C3
Bradby Ho NW8 91 D5
Braddock Ho 9 NW6 91 D6
Braddon Rd TW9 132 B2
Braddyll St SE10 120 C1
Braden St W9 91 D3
Bradenham 11 SE17 139 B6
Bradenham Ave DA16 146 A1
Bradenham Cl SE17 139 B6
Bradenham Rd
Harrow HA3 43 B5
Hayes UB4 83 C4
Bradfield Ct 14 NW1 71 B1
Bradfield Dr IG11 80 A3
Bradfield Ho 15 SW8 137 D3
Bradfield Rd E16 121 B4
Ruislip HA4 63 A3
Bradford Cl N17 33 D4
SE26 184 B6
Keston Mark BR2 210 B1
Bradford Dr KT19 215 D2
Bradford Ho 4 W14 112 D3
Bradford Rd W3 111 C4
Ilford IG1 57 C1
Bradgate Rd SE6 163 D5
Brading Cres E11 77 B6
Brading Rd SW2 160 B4
Thornton Heath CR0 204 B3
Brading Terr W12 112 A3
Bradiston Rd W9 91 B4
Bradley Cl N7 72 B2
Bradley Ct CR0 220 C4
Bradley Gdns W13 87 B1
Bradley Ho 4 E2 96 B5
1 E3 97 D4
SE16 118 B2
Bradley Mews SW12 158 D3
Bradley Rd N22 32 B1
SE19 183 A4
Enfield EN3 7 A6
Bradley Stone Rd E6 100 B2
Bradley's Cl N1 234 B4
Bradlord Ho SE21 161 C1
Bradman Row 7 HA8 27 A3
Bradmead SW8 137 C5 269 A3
Bradmore Ho E1 96 C2
Bradmore Park Rd W6 112 B2
Bradon 24 NW9 27 D1
Bradshaw Cl SW19 179 C4
Bradshaw Waye UB8 82 B2
Bradshaws Cl SE25 206 A6
Bradsole Ho 13 BR3 185 C3
Bradstock Ho E9 75 A1
Bradstock Rd E9 74 D2
Ewell KT17 216 B3
Bradwell Ave RM10 81 C6
Bradwell Cl E18 54 D5
Bradwell Ho 9 E17 53 D6
6 NW6 91 D6
Bradwell Mews 5 N18 34 A6
Brady Ct RM8 58 D1
Brady Ho SW4 159 D6
SW8 269 B2
Brady St E1 96 B3
Bradymead E6 100 D1
Brae Ct SE25 183 C2
2 Kingston u T KT2 176 C2
Braeburn Ct 1 EN4 2 C1
Braefoot Ct SW15 156 D6
Braemar SW15 156 D5
Braemar Ave N22 32 A2
NW10 67 B6
SW18,SW19 157 C2
Thornton Heath CR7 204 D6
Wembley HA0 66 A1
Braemar Ct 5 SE6 164 D3
4 Brentford TW8 131 D6
Braemar Gdns NW9 27 B2
Longlands DA15 167 B1
West Wickham BR4 208 A1
Braemar Ho W9 229 A1
Teddington TW11 175 B5
Braemar Mans W8 255 D5
Braemar Rd E13 98 D3
N15 51 C4
Brentford TW8 131 D6
North Cheam KT4 216 B5
Braemore Ct EN4 3 A1
Braemore Ho 21 SE15 140 A5
Braes St N1 72 D1
Braeside BR3 185 D5
Braeside Ave SW19 179 A2
Braeside Cl HA5 23 C3
Braeside Rd SW16 181 C3
Braeside Sch
Buckhurst Hill IG9 21 B3
Buckhurst Hill IG9 21 C2
Braesyde Cl DA17 125 B2
Brafferton Rd CR0 221 A4
Braganza St SE17 116 D1 261 C1
Bragg Cl RM8 80 B2
Bragg Rd TW11 174 D4
Braham Ho SE11 260 D1
Braham St E1 243 D2
Brahma Kumaris World Spiritual Univ NW10 68 A1
Braid Ave W3 89 C1
Braid Cl TW13 151 B2
Braid Ho SE10 142 A4
Braidwood Rd SE6 164 B3
Braidwood St SE1 117 C5 253 A3
Braikenridge Ho N21 17 B5
Brailsford Cl SW19 180 C3
Brailsford Rd SW2 160 C5
Braintcroft Prim Sch NW2 67 D5
Brainton Ave TW14 150 C4
Braintree Ave IG4 56 A5
Braintree Ho 5 E1 96 C3
Braintree Rd
Dagenham RM10 81 C5
Ruislip HA4 62 B4
Braintree St E2 96 C4
Braithwaite Ave RM7 59 C2
Braithwaite Gdns HA7 25 C2
Braithwaite Ho 14 E14 98 B1
EC1 242 C6
Braithwaite Rd EN3 7 B2
Braithwaite Twr W2 236 C4
Bramah Gn SW9 138 C4
Bramall Cl E15 76 D3
Bramall Ct N7 72 B2
Bramber WC1 233 A1
Bramber Ct TW8 110 A2
Bramber Rd N12 30 C5
W14 135 B6 264 C6
Bramble Acres Cl SM2 217 C1
Bramble Cl N15 52 A5
Croydon CR0 223 D4
Hillingdon UB8 82 B1
Stanmore HA7 25 D3
Upper Halliford TW17 193 B6
Bramble Gdns W12 111 D6
Bramble Ho 12 E3 97 C2
Bramble La TW12 173 B4
Bramblebury Rd SE18 123 A1
Brambledown 4 N4 50 A2
Brambledown Cl BR2, BR4 208 C4
Brambledown Rd
South Croydon CR2 221 C1
Wallington SM5,SM6 219 B1
Brambles Cl TW7,TW8 131 B5
Brambles Farm Dr UB10 82 C4
Brambles The 8 SW19 179 B5
West Drayton UB7 104 A2
Bramblewood Cl SM5 202 C1
Brambling Ct 25 SE8 141 B6
Bramblings The E4 36 B6
Bramcote Ave CR4 202 D5
Bramcote Ct CR4 202 D5
Bramcote Gr SE16 118 C1
Bramcote Rd SW15 134 B1
Bramdean Cres SE12 165 A3
Bramdean Gdns SE12 165 A3
Bramerton NW6 68 D1
Bramerton Rd BR3 207 B6
Bramerton St SW3 136 C6 267 A6
Bramfield Ct N4 73 A6
Bramfield Rd SW11 158 D6
Bramford Ct N14 15 D2
Bramford Rd SW18 136 A1
Bramham Gdns SW5 113 D1 255 D2
Chessington KT9 213 D4
Bramham Ho SE22 139 C1
Bramhope La SE7 143 B6
Bramlands Cl SW11 136 C2
Bramlea Cl N6 49 A3
Bramley Ave TW17 193 C6
Bramley Cl E17 35 A1
N14 15 B6
Bromley BR6 210 D1
Croydon CR2 221 A3
Hayes UB3 106 A6
Twickenham TW2 152 A5
Bramley Cres SW8 137 D5 269 D4
Ilford IG2 56 C3
Bramley Ct 9 E4 20 A3
NW2 68 B5
Bexley DA16 146 B4
2 Cockfosters EN4 2 C1
East Bedfont TW14 149 C5
Mitcham CR4 180 B1
Southall UB1 108 A6
Wallington SM6 219 C3
Bramley Gdns WD1 22 C5
Bramley Hill CR2 221 A4
Bramley Ho 5 SW15 155 D5
10 W10 90 D1
Hounslow TW3 129 B1
Ilford IG2 56 C3
1 Kingston u T KT2 176 D3
Bramley House Ct EN2 5 B6
Bramley Lo HA0 65 D4
Bramley Rd N14 15 C6
W5 109 C3
W10 90 D1
Carshalton SM1 218 B3
Bramley Way
Hounslow TW4 151 B6
West Wickham BR4 223 D6
Bramleyhyrst CR2 221 A3
Brampton Cl 14 E5 74 B6
Brampton Ct NW4 46 B5
Brampton Gr NW4 46 C5
Harrow HA3 43 B5
Wembley HA9 44 C1
Brampton La 4 NW4 46 C5
Brampton Manor Sch E6 99 D3
Brampton Park Rd N22 50 D6
Brampton Prim Sch E6 100 A4
Bexley DA16 146 D3
Brampton Rd E6 99 D4
N15 51 A4
NW9 44 C5
Bexley DA7 147 A4
Croydon CR0 205 D3
Hillingdon UB10 82 D5
Bramshaw Gdns WD1 22 D5
Bramshaw Rd E9 74 D2
Bramshaw Rise KT3 199 C3
Bramshill Gdns NW5 71 B5
Bramshill Rd NW10 89 D5
Bramshot Ave SE7 143 B6
Bramshott Ct 3 KT6 198 A3
Bramshurst NW8 91 D6
Bramston Rd NW10 90 A5
SW17 158 A1
Bramwell Cl TW16 172 D1
Bramwell Ho SE1 262 B5
SW1 269 A6
Bramwell Mews N1 233 D6
Brancaster Dr NW7 28 A3
Brancaster Ho 22 E1 96 D4
N5 72 D3
Brancaster Rd E12 78 B4
SW16 160 A1
Ilford IG2 57 C3
Brancepeth Gdns IG9 21 A2
Branch Pl N1 95 B6 235 D6
Branch Rd E14 119 A6
Branch St SE15 139 C5
Brancker Cl SM6 220 A1
Brancker Rd HA3 43 D6
Brancroft Way EN3 7 B4
Brand Cl N4 50 D1
Brand St SE10 142 A5
Brandlehow Prim Sch SW15 135 B1
Brandlehow Rd SW15 135 B1
Brandon Ho BR3 185 D5
Brandon Mews EC2 242 C4
Brandon Rd E17 54 A6
N7 72 A1
Southall UB2 107 B1
Sutton SM1 217 D4
Brandon St SE17 117 A2 262 B3
Brandram Rd SE13 142 C1
Brandrams Wharf SE16 118 C4
Brandreth Ct HA1 42 D3
Brandreth Rd E6 100 B1
SW17 159 B2
Brandries The SM6 219 D5
Brandville Gdns IG6 56 D5
Brandville Rd UB7 104 A4
Brandy Way SM2 217 C1
Brangbourne Rd BR1 186 A5
Brangton Rd SE11 260 D1
Brangwyn Cres SW19 180 B1
Brangwyn Ct W14 254 A5
Branham Ho 1 SE18 122 D1
Branksea St SW6 135 A3 264 A3
Branksome Ave N18 33 D5
Branksome Cl KT12 194 D1
Branksome Ct 6 N2 48 A6
Branksome Ho SW8 270 C4
Branksome Rd SW2 160 A6
SW19 179 C2
Branksome Way
Harrow HA3 44 B3
Kingston u T KT3 177 B2
Bransby Ct 4 N16 73 C4
Bransby Rd KT9 214 A2
Branscombe NW1 232 B5
Branscombe Ct BR2 208 C4
Branscombe Gdns N21 16 C4
Branscombe St SE13 141 D2
Bransdale Cl NW6 91 C6
Bransgrove Rd HA8 26 B3
Branston Cres BR5 211 B1
Branston Ho N7 72 C3
Branstone Ct 9 TW9 132 B4
Branstone Rd TW9 132 B4
Brants Wlk W7 86 C3
Brantwood Ave
Erith DA8 147 D5
Isleworth TW7 131 A1
Brantwood Cl E17 53 D6
Brantwood Gdns
Enfield EN2 16 A6
Redbridge IG4 56 A5
Brantwood Ho 9 SE5 139 A5
Brantwood Rd N17 34 A4
SE24 161 A6
Bexleyheath DA7 147 D2
Brasher Cl UB6 64 B3
Brass Talley Alley 31 SE16 118 D4
Brassett Point 3 E15 98 C6
Brassey Cl TW14 150 A3
Brassey Ho 1 E14 119 D2
Walton-on-T KT12 194 A1
Brassey Rd NW6 69 B2
Brassey Sq SW11 137 A2
Brassie Ave W3 89 C1
Brasted Cl SE26 184 C6
Bexleyheath DA6 168 D6
Brasted Lo 11 BR3 185 C3
Brathay NW1 232 B3
Brathway Rd SW18 157 C4
Bratley St 12 E1 96 A3
Bratten Ct CR0 205 B3
Braund Ave UB6 85 D3
Braundton Ave DA15 167 D3
Braunston Dr UB4 85 A3
Bravington Cl TW17 192 B4
Bravington Pl W9 91 B3
Bravington Rd W9 91 B4
Brawne Ho 12 SE17 138 D6
Braxfield Rd SE4 141 B1
Braxted Pk SW16 182 B4
Bray NW3 70 C1
Bray Cres SE16 118 D4
Bray Ct SW16 182 A5
Chessington KT9 214 B3
Bray Dr E16 120 D6
Bray Pl SW3 114 D2 257 C3
Bray Rd NW7 28 D4
Brayard's Rd SE15 140 B3
Braybourne Dr TW7 130 D5
Braybrook St W12 89 D1
Braybrooke Gdns SE19 183 C3
Brayburne Ave SW4 137 C3
Braycourt Ave KT12 194 C2
Braydon Rd N16 52 A1
Brayfield Terr N1 72 C1
Brayford Sq 12 E1 96 C1
Brayton Gdns EN2 3 D1
Braywick Ct 9 KT2 176 C3
Braywood Rd SE9 145 B1
Brazil Cl CR0 204 A2
Breach La RM9 103 C4
Bread St EC2,EC4 242 B1
Breakspear Jun & Inf Schs UB10 60 C6
Breakspear Rd HA4,UB9 38 D3
Breakspear Rd N UB9 38 B5
Breakspear Rd S UB9, UB10 38 C1
Breakspeare SE21 161 D1
Breakspears Dr BR5 190 A2
Breakspears Mews SE4 141 C3
Breakspears Rd SE4 141 C2
Breakwell Ct 16 W10 91 A3
Bream Cl N17 52 B5
Bream Gdns E6 100 C4
Bream St E3 75 C1
Breamore Cl SW15 156 A3
Breamore Ct IG3 80 A6
Breamore Rd IG3 79 D6
Bream's Bldgs EC4 94 C1 241 A2

Breamwater Gdns
TW10 .... 153 B1
Brearley Cl Burnt Oak HA8 27 A3
Uxbridge UB8 .... 60 A2
Breaside Prep Sch BR1 187 D2
Breasley Cl SW15 .... 134 B1
Brechin Pl SW7 114 A2 256 B3
Brecknock Prim Sch
NW1 .... 71 D2
Brecknock Rd N19 .... 71 D3
Breckonmead BR1 .... 187 C1
Breco Ho IG11 .... 102 B4
Brecon Cl Mitcham CR4 .204 A6
North Cheam KT4 .... 216 C6
Brecon Ct N12 .... 14 A1
7 SE9 .... 166 C5
Brecon Gn NW9 .... 45 C3
Brecon Ho N16 .... 51 D1
SW18 .... 157 C4
W2 .... 236 A2
Brecon Rd W6 .135 A6 264 B5
Enfield EN3 .... 6 C1
Brede Cl E6 .... 100 C4
Bredel Ho 1 E14 .... 97 C2
Bredgar SE13 .... 163 D6
Bredgar Rd N19 .... 71 C6
Bredhurst Cl SE20 .... 184 C4
Bredinghurst SE22 .... 162 A4
Bredinghurst Sch SE15 140 D1
Bredon Ct HA8 .... 26 B6
Bredon Rd CR0 .... 205 D2
Breer St SW6 .... 135 D2
Breezer's Ct 15 E1 .... 118 A6
Breezer's Hill E1 .... 118 A6
Bremans Row SW18 .... 158 A2
Brember Rd HA2 .... 64 A6
Bremer Mews E17 .... 53 D5
Bremner Rd SW7 .... 256 B6
Brenchley Cl
Chislehurst West BR7 .. 188 C2
Hayes BR2 .... 208 D3
Brenchley Gdns SE15,
SE22,SE23 .... 162 D5
Brenchley Rd BR5 .... 189 D1
Brenda Rd SW17 .... 158 D2
Brende Gdns KT8 .... 195 D5
Brendon Ave NW10 .... 67 C4
Brendon Cl Esher KT10 .212 A2
Harlington UB7 .... 127 A5
Brendon Ct UB2 .... 107 D2
Brendon Dr KT10 .... 212 A2
Brendon Gdns
Harrow HA2 .... 63 D4
Ilford IG2 .... 57 C4
Brendon Gr N2 .... 30 A1
Brendon Ho SM2 .... 218 A2
Brendon Ho W1 .... 238 A4
Brendon Rd
Dagenham RM8 .... 59 C1
New Eltham BR7 .... 167 B2
Brendon St W1 ..92 C1 237 B2
Brendon Villas N21 .... 17 A3
Brendon Way EN1 .... 17 C4
Brenley Cl CR4 .... 203 A6
Brenley Gdns SE9 .... 143 D1
Brenley Ho SE1 .... 252 C2
Brent Cl DA5 .... 169 A3
Brent Cres NW10 .... 88 B5
Brent Cross Flyover
NW2,NW4 .... 46 D2
Brent Cross Gdns NW4 .46 D3
Brent Cross Interchange
NW2,NW4 .... 46 D2
Brent Cross Sh Ctr NW4 46 C2
Brent Cross Sta NW11 ..46 D2
Brent Ct NW11 .... 46 D2
W7 .... 108 B6
5 W12 .... 111 C3
Brent Gn NW4 .... 46 D4
Brent Ho 15 E9 .... 74 C2
3 Catford BR1 .... 186 B5
Brent Knoll Spec Sch
SE26 .... 162 D1
Brent Lea TW8 .... 131 C5
Brent Mans NW4 .... 46 C4
Brent New Ent Ctr NW10 67 D2
Brent Park Ind Est UB2 106 C3
Brent Park Rd NW4 .... 46 B2
Brent Pl EN5 .... 13 B6
Brent Rd E16 .... 99 A2
SE18 .... 144 D5
Brentford TW8 .... 131 C6
Southall UB2 .... 106 C3
Brent St NW4 .... 46 C4
Brent Terr NW2 .... 46 C1
NW2 .... 68 D6
Brent Trad Est NW10 .... 67 C3
Brent View Rd NW9 .... 46 A2
Brent Way N3 .... 29 C4
Brentford TW8 .... 131 D5
Wembley HA9 .... 66 D2
Brentcot Cl W13 .... 87 B3
Brentfield NW10 .... 66 D1
Brentfield Cl NW10 .... 67 B2
Brentfield Gdns NW2 ...46 D2
Brentfield Ho 6 NW10 ..67 B1
Brentfield Prim Sch
NW10 .... 67 B2
Brentfield Rd NW10 .... 67 B2
Brentford Bsns Ctr
TW8 .... 131 C5
Brentford Cl UB4 .... 84 D3
Brentford Fountain Leisure
Centre W4 .... 110 C1
Brentford Sch for Girls
TW8 .... 131 D6
Brentford Sta TW8 .... 131 C6
Brentford v 6 TW1 .... 153 B4
Brentham Way W5 .... 87 D3
Brenthouse Rd E9 .... 74 C2
Brenthurst Rd NW10 .... 67 D2
Brentmead Cl W7 .... 108 C6
Brentmead Gdns NW10 .88 B5
Brenton Ct E9 .... 75 A3
Brenton St E14 .... 97 A1
Brentside TW8 .... 131 C6
Brentside Cl W13 .... 87 A3
Brentside Executive Ctr
TW8 .... 131 B6
Brentside Fst Sch W7 ...86 C2
Brentside High Sch W7 .86 C3
Brentside Prim Sch W7 .86 C3
Brentvale Ave
Southall UB1 .... 108 B5
Wembley HA0 .... 88 B6
Brentwaters Bsns Pk
TW8 .... 131 C5
Brentwick Gdns TW8 ..110 A2
Brentwood Cl SE9 .... 167 A3
Brentwood Ho 2 SE18 143 D5
Brentwood Lo NW4 .... 46 D4
Brereton Ho 4 SW2 ...160 C4
Brereton Rd N17 .... 33 D3
Bressenden Pl
SW1 .... 115 C3 259 A6
Bressey Ave EN1 .... 6 A4
Bressey Gr E18 .... 36 D1
Bretherton Ct CR2 .... 221 C2
Breton Ho EC2 .... 242 B5
SE1 .... 263 C6
Brett Cl N16 .... 73 C6
15 Northolt UB5 .... 84 D4
Brett Cres NW10 .... 89 B6
Brett Ct N9 .... 18 C2
Brett Gdns RM9 .... 81 A1
Brett Ho 1 SW15 .... 156 D4
Brett House Cl 2
SW15 .... 156 D4
Brett Manor E8 .... 74 B3
Brett Pas 28 E8 .... 74 B3
Brett Rd E8 .... 74 B3
Ducks Island EN5 .... 12 C6
Brettell St SE17 .... 262 D1
Brettenham Ave E17 .... 35 C2
Brettenham Prim Sch
N18 .... 34 A6
Brettenham Rd E17 .... 35 C2
N18 .... 34 A6
Brettinghurst 7 SE1 ..118 A1
Bretton Ho N19 .... 50 A1
Brewer St W1 ..115 C6 249 B6
Brewers Bldgs EC1 .... 234 C2
Brewers Ct W2 .... 236 A2
Brewer's Gn SW1 .... 259 C6
Brewers La 11 TW9 ...153 D6
Brewery Cl HA0 .... 65 A4
Brewery Mews Bsns Ctr 1
TW7 .... 131 A2
Brewery Rd N7 .... 72 A2
SE18 .... 123 B1
Keston Mark BR2 .... 210 A1
Brewery Sq SE1 .... 253 C3
Brewhouse La E1 .... 118 B5
Brewhouse Rd 3 SE18 122 B2
Brewhouse St SW15 ...135 A2
Brewhouse Wlk SE16 ..119 A5
Brewhouse Yd EC1 .... 241 C6
Brewood Rd RM8 .... 80 B2
Brewster Gdns W10 .... 90 C2
Brewster Ho E14 .... 119 B6
SE1 .... 263 D4
Brewster Rd E10 .... 53 D1
Brian Ct N10 .... 31 B2
Brian Rd RM6 .... 58 C4
Briant Ho SE1 .... 260 D5
Briant St SE14 .... 140 D5
Briants Cl HA5 .... 23 B1
Briar Ave SW16 .... 182 B3
Briar Cl N2 .... 30 A1
N13 .... 17 A1
Buckhurst Hill IG9 .... 21 D2
Hampton TW12 .... 173 B5
Isleworth TW7 .... 152 D6
Briar Cres UB5 .... 63 D2
Briar Ct E8 .... 73 D1
E11 .... 54 B2
Cheam SM3 .... 216 C4
Hampton TW12 .... 173 D5
Briar Gdns BR2 .... 208 D1
Briar La CR0 .... 223 D4
Briar Lo E18 .... 37 C2
Briar Rd NW2 .... 68 C4
SW16 .... 204 B6
Harrow HA3 .... 43 C4
Littleton TW17 .... 192 C4
Twickenham TW2 .... 152 C3
Briar Way UB7 .... 104 C4
Briar Wlk SW15 .... 134 B1
W10 .... 91 A3
Burnt Oak HA8 .... 27 A3
Briarbank Rd W13 .... 87 A1
Briardale SW19 .... 157 B3
Edgware HA8 .... 27 B6
Briardale Gdns NW3 .... 69 C5
Briardale Ho N16 .... 51 C1
Briarfield Ave N2 .... 47 D6
N3 .... 29 D1
Briars Cl 11 N17 .... 34 B3
Briars The WD2 .... 8 C4
Briarswood Way BR6 ..227 D3
Briarview Ct E4 .... 36 B4
Briarwood Cl NW9 .... 45 A3
Feltham TW13 .... 149 C1
Briarwood Ct 5 KT4 ..200 A1
Briarwood Dr HA6 .... 22 A1
Briarwood Rd SW4 ....159 D6
Briarwood Rd *continued*
Stoneleigh KT17 .... 216 A2
Briary Cl NW3 .... 70 C1
Briary Ct DA14 .... 190 B5
Briary Gdns BR1 .... 187 B5
Briary Gr HA8 .... 26 D1
Briary La N9 .... 17 D1
Briary Lo BR3 .... 186 A2
Brick Ct EC4 .... 241 A1
Brick Farm Cl TW9 .... 132 D4
Brick La E1 .... 95 D3 243 D5
E2 .... 95 D4
Enfield EN1 .... 6 B3
Stanmore HA7 .... 25 D3
Brick St W1 ....115 B5 248 C3
Brickbarn Cl SW10 .... 266 B4
Brickett Cl HA4 .... 39 A4
Brickfield Cl TW8 .... 131 C5
Brickfield Cotts SE18 ..145 D6
Brickfield Farm Gdns
BR6 .... 227 A4
Brickfield La
Borehamwood EN5 .... 11 D5
Harlington UB3 .... 127 B6
Brickfield Rd SW19 ...179 D6
South Norwood CR7,
SW16 .... 182 D2
Brickfields HA2 .... 64 B6
Brickfields Way UB7 ...104 B3
Bricklayers Arms SE1 .262 D5
Brickwall La HA4 .... 39 D1
Brickwood Cl SE26 .... 162 B1
Brickwood Rd CR0 .... 221 C6
Brickworth Ho 26 SW9 138 C4
Bride Ct EC4 .... 241 C1
Bride La EC4 ....94 D1 241 C1
Bride St N7 .... 72 B2
Brideale Cl SE15 .... 139 D6
Bridewain St SE1 .... 263 C6
Bridewell Pl 20 E1 .... 118 B5
EC4 .... 241 C1
Bridford Mews W1 .... 238 D4
Bridge App NW3 .... 71 A1
Bridge Ave W6 .... 112 C1
W7 .... 86 B2
Bridge Avenue Mans 1
W6 .... 112 C1
Bridge Cl 13 W10 .... 90 D1
Enfield EN1 .... 6 B3
Lower Halliford KT12 ...193 D1
Teddington TW11 .... 174 D6
Bridge Ct E10 .... 53 B2
Bridge Dr N13 .... 32 B6
Bridge End E17 .... 36 A2
Bridge Field Ho 7 W2 .91 D1
Bridge Gate N21 .... 17 A4
Bridge Gdns
East Molesey KT8 .... 196 B5
Littleton TW15 .... 171 A3
Bridge Ho E9 .... 74 D3
1 NW1 .... 71 A1
SE4 .... 141 B1
Brentford TW8 .... 109 A2
Bridge Ho S TW8 .... 109 A2
Bridge House Quay
E14 .... 120 A5
Bridge La NW11 .... 47 B4
SW11 ....136 C4 267 B1
Bridge Meadows SE14 .140 D6
Bridge Par N21 .... 17 A4
Bridge Pk NW10 .... 66 D1
7 SW18 .... 157 C6
Bridge Pl SW1 .115 B2 258 D4
Croydon CR0 .... 205 B1
Bridge Rd E6 .... 78 B1
E15 .... 98 B6
E17 .... 53 B2
N9 .... 18 A1
N22 .... 32 A2
NW10 .... 67 C2
Beckenham BR3 .... 185 B3
Bexleyheath DA7 .... 147 A3
Chessington KT9 .... 214 A3
East Molesey KT8 .... 196 C5
Hounslow TW3 .... 130 B2
Isleworth TW3,TW7 .... 130 B2
Southall UB2 .... 107 C4
Sutton SM2 .... 217 D2
Twickenham TW1 .... 153 B5
Wallington SM6 .... 219 C3
Wembley HA9 .... 66 C5
Bridge Row CR0 .... 205 B1
Bridge St SW1 .116 A4 250 B1
W4 .... 111 B2
Pinner HA5 .... 41 A6
Richmond TW10 .... 153 D6
Walton-on-T KT12 .... 193 D2
Bridge Terr E15 .... 76 B1
Bridge The HA3 .... 42 D5
Bridge Way NW11 .... 47 B4
Twickenham TW2 .... 152 A4
Uxbridge UB10 .... 60 D3
Bridge Wharf 18 E2 .... 96 D5
Bridge Yd SE1 .... 252 D4
Bridgefield Rd SM1,
SM2 .... 217 C2
Bridgefoot SE1 .116 A1 260 B1
Bridgeland Rd E16 .... 121 A6
Bridgeman Ho 19 E9 .... 74 C1
Bridgeman Rd N1 .... 72 B1
Teddington TW11 .... 175 A4
Bridgeman St
NW8 .... 92 C5 230 A3
Bridgen Ho 15 E1 .... 96 B1
Bridgen Rd DA5 .... 169 A4
Bridgend Rd SW18 .... 136 A1
Bridgenhall Rd EN1 .... 5 D4
Bridgeport Pl 4 E1 ...118 A5
Bridges Ct SW11 .... 136 B3
Bridges Ho 15 SE5 .... 139 B5
Bridges La CR0 .... 220 A4
Bridges Rd SW19 .... 179 D4
Harrow HA7 .... 24 D5
Bridges Road Mews
SW19 .... 179 D4
Bridgetown Cl 5 SE19 183 C5
Bridgeview 2 W6 .... 112 C1
Bridgewater Cl BR5,BR7 211 C6
Bridgewater Ct HA0 .... 65 C2
Bridgewater Gdns HA8 ..26 B1
Bridgewater Rd E15 .... 98 A6
Ruislip HA4 .... 62 B4
Wembley HA0 .... 65 C1
Bridgewater Sq EC2 ...242 A4
Bridgewater St EC2 .... 242 A4
Bridgeway Barking IG11 .79 D1
Wembley HA0 .... 66 B1
Bridgeway St
NW1 .... 93 C5 232 B3
Bridgewood Cl SE20 ...184 B3
Bridgewood Rd SW16 .181 D3
Stoneleigh KT17,KT4 ...216 A4
Bridgford St SW17,
SW18 .... 158 A1
Bridgman Rd W4 .... 111 A3
Bridgnorth Ho 10 SE15 140 A6
Bridgwater Ho W2 .... 236 A2
Bridle Cl Enfield EN3 .... 7 B6
Kingston u T KT1 .... 197 D5
Sunbury TW16 .... 194 A6
West Ewell KT19 .... 215 B3
Bridle La W1 ..115 C6 249 B6
Twickenham TW1 .... 153 B5
Bridle Path CR0 .... 220 A5
Bridle Path The IG8 .... 36 C3
Bridle Rd Addington CR0 223 C4
Claygate KT10 .... 213 B2
Croydon CR0 .... 223 C5
Pinner HA5 .... 40 C4
Bridle Way Croydon CR0 223 C3
Orpington BR6 .... 227 A4
Bridle Way The SM6 ...219 C3
Bridlepath Way TW14 ..149 C3
Bridlington Ho SW18 ..136 A1
Bridlington Rd N9 .... 18 B4
Bridport SE17 .... 262 B1
Bridport Ave RM7 .... 59 D3
Bridport Ho N1 .... 235 D5
6 N18 .... 34 A5
Bridport Pl N1 ..95 B6 235 D5
Bridport Rd N18 .... 33 D5
Greenford UB6 .... 85 D6
Thornton Heath CR7 .... 204 D6
Bridstow Pl W2 .... 91 C1
Brief St SE5 .... 138 D4
Brierfield NW1 .... 232 A5
Brierley CR0 .... 223 D2
Brierley Ave N9 .... 18 C3
Brierley Cl SE25 .... 206 A5
Brierley Ct W7 .... 108 C6
Brierley Rd E11 .... 76 B4
SW12 .... 159 C2
Brierly Gdns E2 .... 96 C5
Brig Mews SE8 .... 141 C6
Brigade Cl HA2 .... 64 B6
Brigade St SE3 .... 142 D3
Brigadier Ave EN2 .... 5 A4
Brigadier Hill EN2 .... 5 A5
Briggeford Cl 5 E5 .... 74 A6
Briggs Cl CR4 .... 181 B2
Briggs Ho 20 E2 .... 95 D4
Bright Cl DA17 .... 124 D2
Bright Ct 8 SE28 .... 124 C5
Bright St E14 .... 97 D2
Brightfield Rd SE12 ...164 D6
Brightling Rd SE4 .... 163 B5
Brightlingsea Pl 5 E14 119 B6
Brightman Rd SW18 ....158 B3
Brighton Ave E17 .... 53 B4
Brighton Bldgs SE1 ....263 A5
Brighton Cl UB10 .... 60 D1
Brighton Ct SW15 .... 157 B5
Brighton Dr 3 UB5 .... 63 C2
Brighton Gr SE14 .... 141 A4
Brighton Ho 7 SE5 .... 139 B4
Brighton Rd E6 .... 100 C4
N2 .... 30 A1
N16 .... 73 C4
Kingston u T KT6 .... 197 D3
South Croydon CR2 .... 221 B2
Sutton SM1,SM2 .... 217 D1
Sutton SM2 .... 218 A1
Brighton Terr SW9 .... 138 B1
Brightside Rd SE13 .... 164 B5
Brightside The EN3 .... 7 A4
Brightwell Cl CR0 .... 204 C1
Brightwell Cres SW17 .180 D5
Brightwell Ct N7 .... 72 B3
Brightwells 1 SW6 ....135 D3
Brigstock Ho SE5 .... 139 A3
Brigstock Rd
Belvedere DA17 .... 125 D2
Thornton Heath CR7 ....204 D4
Brill Ho NW10 .... 67 B5
Brill Pl NW1 ....93 D5 232 D3
Brim Hill N2 .... 48 B5
Brimpsfield Cl SE2 .... 124 B3
Brimsdown Ave EN3 .... 7 A4
Brimsdown Ho E3 .... 98 A3
Brimsdown Jun & Inf Sch
EN3 .... 6 D2
Brimsdown Sta EN3 .... 7 A3
Brimstone Ho 3 E15 ....76 C1
Brindishe Prim Sch
SE12 .... 164 D6
Brindle Gate DA15 .... 167 C3
Brindley Cl
Bexleyheath DA7 .... 147 C2
Wembley HA0 .... 87 D6
Brindley Ho 22 SW12 ..160 A4
Brindley St SE14 .... 141 B4
Brindley Way
Plaistow BR1 .... 187 B5
Southall UB1 .... 107 D6
Brindwood Rd E4 .... 19 C1
Brine Ct KT6 .... 197 D4
Brine Ho 10 E3 .... 97 A5
Brinkburn Cl SE2 .... 124 A2
Edgware HA8 .... 44 D6
Brinkburn Gdns HA8 ....44 C6
Brinkley 18 KT1 .... 176 C1
Brinkley Rd KT4 .... 216 B6
Brinklow Cres SE18 ....144 D5
Brinklow Ho W2 .... 91 D2
Brinkworth Rd IG5 .... 56 A6
Brinkworth Way E9 .... 75 B2
Brinsdale Rd NW4 .... 46 D6
Brinsley Ho 17 E1 .... 96 C1
Brinsley Rd HA3 .... 24 B1
Brinsley St 29 E1 .... 96 B1
Brinsworth Cl TW2 .... 152 B2
Brinton Wlk SE1 .... 251 C3
Brion Pl E14 .... 98 A2
Brisbane Ave SW19 ....179 D2
Brisbane Ct N10 .... 31 B3
Brisbane Ho 3 W12 ...112 B6
Brisbane Rd E10 .... 75 D6
W13 .... 109 A4
Ilford IG1 .... 57 A1
Brisbane St SE5 .... 139 B5
Briscoe Cl E11 .... 76 D6
Briscoe Rd SW19 .... 180 B4
Briset Prim Sch SE9 ..143 D1
Briset Rd SE9 .... 143 D1
Briset St EC1 ....94 D3 241 C5
Briset Way N7 .... 72 B6
Bristol Cl TW19 .... 148 A5
Bristol Ct 11 TW19 .... 148 A5
Bristol Gdns W9 .... 91 D3
Bristol Ho 1 IG11 .... 80 A1
SE11 .... 261 A5
Bristol Mews W9 .... 91 D3
Bristol Park Rd 1 E17 ..53 A5
Bristol Rd E7 .... 77 D2
Greenford UB6 .... 85 D6
Morden SM4 .... 202 A4
Briston Gr N8 .... 50 A3
Briston Mews NW7 .... 28 A3
Bristow Rd SE19 .... 183 C5
Bexley DA7 .... 147 A4
Hounslow TW3 .... 130 A2
Wallington CR0 .... 220 A4
Britannia Cl SW4 .... 137 D1
Northolt UB5 .... 84 D4
Britannia Gate 12 E16 .121 A5
Britannia Junc NW1 ...231 D6
Britannia Rd 11 E14 ...119 C2
N12 .... 14 A1
SW6 ....135 D5 265 C3
Ilford IG1 .... 78 D5
Surbiton KT5 .... 198 B2
Britannia Row
N1 .... 95 A6 235 A6
Britannia St WC1 94 B4 233 C2
Britannia Way NW10 ....88 D3
TW19 .... 148 A4
Britannia Wlk N1 .... 235 C2
British Gr W4 .... 111 D1
British Grove Pas 2
W4 .... 111 D1
British Grove S 3 W4 .111 D1
British Home & Hospl for
Incurables SE27 .... 182 D5
British Legion Rd E4 .... 20 D2
British Library (Newspaper
Library) NW9 .... 45 C6
British Library The★
WC1 .... 93 D4 232 D2
British Mus★
WC1 .... 94 A2 240 A3
British St E3 .... 97 B4
British Wharf Ind Est
SE14 .... 140 D6
Britley Ho 10 E14 .... 97 B1
Brittain Ct SE9 .... 166 A3
Brittain Ho SE9 .... 166 A3
Brittain Rd RM8 .... 81 B5
Brittany Ho SW15 .... 134 C1
Brittany Point SE11 ....261 A3
Britten Cl NW11 .... 47 D1
Elstree WD6 .... 9 D5
Britten Dr UB1 .... 85 C1
Britten Ho SW3 .... 257 B2
Britten St SW3 .114 C1 257 A2
Brittenden Cl 1 BR6 ..227 D2
Brittenden Par BR6 ....227 D2
Britton Cl SE6 .... 164 B4
Britton St EC1 ...94 D2 241 C5
Brixham Cres HA4 .... 40 A1
Brixham Gdns IG3 .... 79 C3
Brixham Rd DA16 .... 146 D4
Brixham St E16 .... 122 C5
Brixton Day Coll SW9 ..138 A2
Brixton Hill SW2 .... 160 B5
Brixton Hill Ct 5 SW2 .160 B6
Brixton Hill Pl SW2 ....160 A4
Brixton Mkt SW9 .... 138 C1
Brixton Oval 7 SW2 ...138 C1
Brixton Rd SW9 .... 138 C4
Brixton Sta SW9 .... 138 C1
Brixton Station Rd
SW9 .... 138 C2
Brixton Water La SW2 .160 B6
Broad Berry Ct N18 .... 34 B5
Broad Bridge Cl SE3 ...143 A5
Broad Common Est N16 52 A1
Broad Ct WC2 .... 240 B1
Broad Green Ave CR0 .204 D2
Broad La EC2 .... 243 A4
N8 .... 50 B4
N15 .... 51 D5
N15 .... 52 A5
Hampton TW12 .... 173 C4
Broad Lawn SE9 .... 166 C3
Broad Oak
Ashford TW16 .... 171 D4
Woodford IG8 .... 37 B5
Broad Oak Cl E4 .... 35 C5
St Paul's Cray BR5 .... 190 A1
Broad Oaks KT6 .... 214 D6
Broad Oaks Way BR2 ..208 D4
Broad Sanctuary SW1 .250 A1
Broad St Dagenham RM10 81 C1
Teddington TW11 .... 174 D4
Broad St Ave EC2 .... 243 A3
Broad St Pl EC2 .... 242 D3
Broad Wlk N21 .... 16 B3
NW1 ....93 A5 231 B3
SE3,SE18 .... 144 A3
W1 ....115 A5 248 A4
Heston TW5 .... 129 A4
Richmond TW9 .... 132 B5
Broad Wlk The
W8 ....113 D5 245 D3
Broad Yd EC1 .... 241 C5
Broadacre Cl UB10 .... 60 D5
Broadbent Cl N6 .... 49 B1
Broadbent St W1 .... 248 C6
Broadcoombe CR2 .... 222 D1
Broadcroft Ave HA7 .... 25 D1
Broadcroft Rd BR5 .... 211 B2
Broadfield NW6 .... 69 D2
Broadfield Cl NW2 .... 68 C5
Croydon CR0 .... 220 B6
Broadfield Ct WD2 .... 8 C2
Broadfield La NW1 .... 72 A1
Broadfield Rd SE6 .... 164 C3
Broadfield Sq EN1 .... 6 B3
Broadfield Way IG9 .... 21 C1
Broadfields Harrow HA2 23 D1
Thames Ditton KT8 .... 196 C3
Broadfields Ave N21 .... 16 C4
Edgware HA8 .... 10 D1
Broadfields Hts HA8 ....26 D6
Broadfields Inf Sch HA8 10 C2
Broadfields Jun Sch
HA8 .... 10 D2
Broadfields Way NW10 ..67 B3
Broadford Ho 11 E1 .... 97 A3
Broadgate EC2 ..95 C2 243 A4
Broadgate Circ
EC2 .... 95 C2 243 A3
Broadgate Rd E16 .... 99 D1
Broadgates Ave EN4 .... 1 D4
Broadgates Ct SE11 ....261 B1
Broadgates Rd SW18 ..158 B3
Broadhead Strand NW9 .27 D2
Broadheath Dr BR7 ....188 B5
Broadhinton Rd SW4 ..137 C2
Broadhurst Ave
Edgware HA8 .... 26 D6
Ilford IG3 .... 79 D4
Broadhurst Cl NW6 .... 70 A2
9 Richmond TW10 .... 154 B6
Broadhurst Gdns NW6 ..69 D2
Ruislip HA4 .... 62 C6
Broadhurst Mans NW6 ..69 D2
Broadlands N6 .... 49 A2
Feltham TW13 .... 151 C1
Broadlands Ave SW16 .160 A2
Enfield EN3 .... 6 B2
Shepperton TW17 .... 193 A3
Broadlands Cl N6 .... 49 A2
SW16 .... 160 A2
Enfield EN3 .... 6 C2
Broadlands Ct TW9 ....132 C5
Broadlands Lo N6 .... 48 D2
Broadlands Mans 2
SW16 .... 160 A2
Broadlands Rd N6 .... 48 D2
Plaistow BR1 .... 187 B6
Broadlands Way KT3 .199 D3
Broadlawns Ct HA3 .... 24 D2
Broadley St NW8 92 C2 237 A4
Broadley Terr
NW1 .... 92 C3 237 B5
Broadmayne SE17 .... 262 C2
Broadmead SE6 .... 163 C1
W14 .... 254 A3
Broadmead Ave KT4 ...200 A2
Broadmead Cl
Hampton TW12 .... 173 C4
Hatch End HA5 .... 23 A3
Broadmead Ct 6 IG8 ...37 A4
Broadmead Inf Sch
CR0 .... 205 B2
Broadmead Jun Sch
CR0 .... 205 B3
Broadmead Rd
Northolt UB5 .... 85 A3
Woodford IG8 .... 37 B3
Broadoak Ct 9 SW9 ...138 C2
Broadoak Ho 18 NW6 ...91 D6
Broadstone Ho SW8 ...270 C3
Broadstone Pl W1 .... 238 A3
Broadview NW9 .... 44 C3
Broadview Est TW19 ...148 C4
Broadview Rd SW16 ...181 D3
Broadwalk E18 .... 54 D6

Broadwalk *continued*
Harrow HA2 41 D4
Broadwalk Ho SW7 246 A1
Broadwalk La NW11 47 B2
Broadwalk Sh Ctr The HA8 26 D4
Broadwall SE1 116 C5 251 B4
Broadwater Farm Prim Sch N17 33 B1
Broadwater Gdns BR6 227 A4
Broadwater Inf Sch SW17 180 C6
Broadwater Jun Sch SW17 180 C6
Broadwater Rd N17 33 C1
SE18 123 B3
SW17 180 C6
Broadway E15 76 B1
SW1 115 D3 259 C6
W7 108 C5
W13 109 A5
Barking IG11 101 A6
Bexley DA6 147 B1
Bexleyheath DA6,DA7 147 C1
Tolworth KT6 198 D1
Broadway Arc 3 W6 112 C2
Broadway Ave
Thornton Heath CR0 205 B4
Twickenham TW1 153 B5
Broadway Bldgs 5 W7 108 C5
Broadway Cl IG8 37 B4
Broadway Ct SW19 179 C4
Beckenham BR3 208 A6
Broadway Gdns
Mitcham CR4 202 C5
Woodford IG8 37 B4
Broadway Ho 2 E8 96 B6
Broadway Mans SW6 265 B3
Broadway Market E8 96 B6
Broadway Market Mews 21 E8 96 A6
Broadway Mews E5 51 D2
N21 16 D3
Broadway Par E4 36 A4
N8 50 A3
Hayes UB3 106 A5
West Drayton UB7 104 A4
Broadway Sh Ctr 5 DA6 147 C1
Broadway The E4 36 B4
E13 99 B5
N8 50 A3
N9 18 A1
N11 31 A5
2 N14 15 D3
N22 32 C1
NW7 27 D5
SW13 133 C3
SW19 179 C3
W3 110 C4
W5 109 D6
Cheam SM3 217 A2
Dagenham RM8 81 C6
Greenford UB6 86 A3
Harrow HA3 24 D1
Hatch End HA5 23 B3
Southall UB1 107 A6
Stanmore HA7 25 C5
Sutton SM1 218 A4
Thames Ditton KT10 196 C1
Tolworth KT6 198 C1
Wallington SM6 220 A4
Wembley HA9 66 A5
Woodford IG8 37 B4
Broadwell Ct TW5 128 D4
Broadwick St W1 93 C1 239 B1
Broadwood Ave HA4 39 C3
Broadwood Terr W14 254 D4
Brocas Cl NW3 70 C1
Brock Ho WC1 239 C4
Brock Pl E3 97 D3
Brock Rd E13 99 B2
Brock St SE15 140 C2
Brockbridge Ho 11 SW15 155 D5
Brockdene Dr BR2 225 D4
Brockdish Ave IG11 79 D3
Brockelbank Lo RM8 80 D6
Brockenhurst KT8 195 B3
Brockenhurst Ave KT4 199 C1
Brockenhurst Gdns NW7 27 C5
Barking IG1 79 A3
Brockenhurst Rd CR0 206 B2
Brockenhurst Way SW16 181 D1
Brocket Ho 15 SW8 137 D3
Brockham Cl SW19 179 B5
Brockham Cres CR0 224 B1
Brockham Ct 6 SM2 217 D1
Brockham Dr SW2 160 B4
Ilford IG2 57 A4
Brockham Ho NW1 232 B5
11 SW2 160 B4
Brockham St SE1 262 B6
Brockhurst Cl HA7 24 D4
Brockhurst Ho N4 51 B2
Brockill Cres SE4 141 A1
Brocklebank Ho 7 E16 122 C5
Brocklebank Rd SE7 121 B2
SW18 158 A4
Brocklehurst St SE14 140 D5
Brocklesby Rd SE25 206 B5
Brockley Ave HA7 10 A1
Brockley Cl HA7 26 A6
Brockley Cross SE4 141 B2
Brockley Cross Bsns Ctr SE4 141 A2
Brockley Gdns SE4 141 B3
Brockley Gr SE4 163 B6
Brockley Hall Rd SE4 163 A6
Brockley Hill HA7,HA8 9 D2
Brockley Ho SE17 263 A2
Brockley Mews SE4 163 A6
Brockley Pk SE23 163 A4
Brockley Prim Sch SE4 163 B6
Brockley Rd SE4 163 B6
Brockley Rise SE23 163 A4
Brockley Sta SE4 141 A2
Brockley View SE23 163 A4
Brockley Way SE4 163 A6
Brockleyside HA7 26 A6
Brockman Rise BR1 186 B6
Brockmer Ho 5 E1 118 B6
Brocks Dr SM3 217 A5
Brockshot Cl 11 TW8 131 D6
Brockway Cl E11 76 C6
Brockweir 29 E2 96 C5
Brockwell Cl BR5 211 D4
Brockwell Ct 2 SW2 160 C6
Brockwell Ho SE11 270 D6
Brockwell Park SE24 160 D5
Brockwell Park Gdns SE24 160 D4
Brockwell Prim Schs SW2 160 C5
Brockworth 8 KT2 176 D2
Broderick Ho SE21 161 C1
Brodia Rd N16 73 C5
Brodick Ho 11 E3 97 B5
Brodie Ho SE1 263 D2
7 Wallington SM6 219 B4
Brodie Rd E4 20 A2
Enfield EN2 5 A5
Brodie St SE1 117 D1 263 D2
Brodlove La E1 118 D6
Brodrick Gr SE2 124 B2
Brodrick Rd SW17 158 C2
Brograve Gdns BR3 185 D1
Broke Wlk E8 95 D6
11 E8 96 A6
Broken Wharf EC4 252 A6
Brokesley St E3 97 B4
Bromar Rd SE5 139 C2
Bromborough Gn WD1 22 C5
Brome Ho 5 SE18 144 A4
Brome Rd SE9 144 B2
Bromefield HA7 25 C2
Bromehead St 8 E1 96 C1
Bromell's Rd SW4 137 C1
Bromfelde Rd SW4 137 D3
Bromfield Ct 20 SE16 118 A3
Bromfield St N1 234 B4
Bromhall Rd RM8 80 B2
Bromhedge SE9 166 B1
Bromholm Rd SE2 124 B3
Bromleigh Ct 1 SE21, SE22 162 B2
Bromleigh Ho SE1 263 C6
Bromley Ave BR1 186 C3
Bromley Coll of F & H Ed BR2 209 D3
Bromley Comm BR2 209 D4
Bromley Cres
Bromley BR2 208 D6
Ruislip HA4 61 D4
Bromley Ct SE13 164 B6
Bromley BR1 186 D3
Bromley Gdns BR2 208 D6
Bromley Gr BR2 186 B1
Bromley Hall Rd E14 98 A2
Bromley Hall Sch E14 98 A2
Bromley High Sch for Girls BR1 210 C5
Bromley High St E3 97 D4
Bromley Hill BR1 186 C4
Bromley Hospl BR1 209 B5
Bromley Ind Est BR1 209 D6
Bromley La BR7 189 B3
Bromley Lo 2 W3 89 A1
Bromley Manor Mans 3 BR1 209 A6
Bromley North Sta BR1 187 A2
Bromley Pk 11 BR1 186 D2
Bromley Pl W1 239 A4
Bromley Rd E10 53 D3
E17 53 C6
N17 34 A2
N18 17 B1
SE6 163 D1
Beckenham BR2,BR3 186 B1
Beckenham BR3 185 D2
Chislehurst BR7 188 D2
Bromley Road Infs Sch BR3 185 D2
Bromley South Sta BR2 209 A6
Bromley St E1 96 D1
Bromley-by-Bow Sta E3 97 D4
Brompton WC1 240 C3
Brompton Arc SW1 247 D1
Brompton Cl SE20 184 A1
Hounslow TW4 151 B6
Brompton Ct 4 HA7 25 C6
Brompton Gr N2 48 C5
Brompton Ho 3 N9 34 A6
Brompton Hospl SW3 114 B1 256 D2
Brompton Oratory SW3 114 C3 257 A5
Brompton Park Cres SW6 135 D6 265 C5
Brompton Pl SW3 114 C3 257 B6
Brompton Rd SW3 114 C3 257 A5
Brompton Sq SW3 114 C3 257 A6
Bromstone Ho 10 SW9 138 C4
Bromwich Ave N6 71 A6
Bromwich Ho 3 TW10 154 A5
Bromyard Ave W3 111 C6
Bromyard Ho 3 SE15 140 B5
Bron Ct NW6 91 C6
Brondesbury Ct NW2 68 D2
Brondesbury Mews 11 NW6 69 C1
Brondesbury Park Sta NW6 91 A6
Brondesbury Pk NW2 68 D1
Brondesbury Rd NW6 91 C5
Brondesbury Sta NW6 69 B1
Brondesbury Villas NW6 91 C5
Bronhill Terr N17 34 A2
Bronsart Rd SW6 135 A5 264 A3
Bronson Rd SW20 179 A1
Bronte Cl 1 E7 77 A4
Erith DA8 147 D5
Ilford IG2 56 C5
Bronte Ct 8 W14 112 D3
Bronte Ho 6 N16 73 C3
NW6 91 C4
Bronti Cl SE17 117 A1 262 B2
Bronwen Ct NW8 229 C1
Bronze Age Way DA17 125 D4
Bronze St SE8 141 C5
Brook Ave
Dagenham RM10 81 D1
Edgware HA8 26 D4
Wembley HA9 66 C5
Brook Bank EN1 6 B6
Brook Cl SW20 200 B6
W3 110 C5
Ruislip HA4 39 C2
Stanwell TW19 148 B4
Brook Cres E4 35 D6
N9 34 B6
Brook Ct 2 E11 76 C5
E15 76 A3
E17 53 A6
SW14 133 C2
Beckenham BR3 185 B2
5 Brentford TW8 131 D6
Cheam SM3 216 C4
Edgware HA8 26 D5
Brook Dr SE11 116 D2 261 C4
Ashford TW16 171 C4
Harrow HA1 42 A5
Ruislip HA4 39 C2
Brook Gate W1 114 D6 247 D5
Brook Gdns E4 35 D6
SW13 133 D2
Kingston u T KT2 177 A2
Brook Gn W6 112 D2
Brook Green Flats 11 W14 112 D3
Brook Hill Cl SE18 122 D1
Brook Ho 3 N9 18 A1
3 SW4 159 C6
W3 110 C4
4 W6 112 C2
3 Twickenham TW1 153 A4
Brook Hos NW1 232 B3
Brook La SE3 143 B3
Bexley DA5 168 D5
Plaistow BR1 187 A4
Brook La Bns Ctr TW8 109 D1
Brook La N
Brentford TW8 109 D1
3 Brentford TW8 131 D6
Brook Lo N8 49 D3
NW4 46 D4
Brook Mdw N12 13 D1
Brook Mead KT19 215 C2
Brook Meadow Cl IG8 36 C4
Brook Mews N W2 114 B6 246 B6
Brook Park Cl N21 16 D6
Brook Pl EN5 13 C6
Brook Rd N8 50 A5
N12 30 C3
N22 50 B6
NW2 68 A6
Buckhurst Hill IG9 21 A3
Ilford IG2 57 C3
Surbiton KT6 214 A6
Thornton Heath CR7 205 A5
Twickenham TW1 153 A5
Brook Rd S TW8 131 D6
Brook St 8 N17 33 D1
W1 115 B6 248 C6
W2 114 B6 246 D6
Erith DA8 147 D5
Kingston u T KT1 176 A1
Brook Vale DA7,DA8 147 D4
Brook Wlk N2 30 B2
Burnt Oak HA8 27 B4
Brookbank Ave W7 86 B2
Brookbank Rd SE13 141 D2
Brookdale N11 31 C6
Brookdale Rd E17 53 C6
SE6 163 D4
SE6 163 D5
Sidcup DA5 169 A5
Brookdales The NW4 47 A5
Brookdene N12 29 D6
Brookdene Rd SE18,SE2 123 D2
Brooke Ave HA2 64 A5
Brooke Cl WD2 8 A4
Brooke Ct 7 KT2 175 D6
Brooke Rd E5,N16 74 A5
Brooke Rd *continued*
E17 54 A5
Brooke St EC1 94 C2 241 A3
Brooke Way WD2 8 A4
Brookehowse Rd SE6 163 D1
Brookes Ct EC1 241 A4
Brooke's Mkt EC1 241 B4
Brookfield 1 N4 72 C6
N6 71 A5
Brookfield Ave E17 54 A5
NW7 28 B4
W5 87 D3
Carshalton SM1,SM5 218 C5
Brookfield Cl NW7 28 B4
Brookfield Cres NW7 28 B4
Harrow HA3 44 A4
Brookfield Ct UB6 86 A4
1 N12 29 D6
Brookfield Gdns KT10 212 D2
Brookfield House Sch IG8 36 C4
Brookfield Path IG8 36 C4
Brookfield Pk NW5 71 B5
Brookfield Prim Sch N19 71 B6
Brookfield Rd E9 75 A2
N9 18 B1
W4 111 B4
Brookfields EN3 6 D1
Brookfields Ave CR4 202 C4
Brookgate N16 73 B6
Brookhill Cl EN4 14 C6
Brookhill Ct 2 EN4 14 C5
Brookhill Rd SE18 122 D1
Barnet EN4 14 C6
Brookhouse Gdns E4 36 C6
Brooking Rd E7 77 A3
Brookland Cl NW11 47 C5
Brookland Garth NW11 47 D5
Brookland Hill NW11 47 D5
Brookland Jun & Inf Schs NW11 47 D5
Brookland Rise NW11 47 C5
Brooklands Ave SW18 157 D2
New Eltham DA15 167 B2
Brooklands Cl TW16 171 C2
Brooklands Court Apartments 3 NW6 69 B1
Brooklands Ct N21 17 B6
Kingston u T KT1 197 D5
2 Mitcham CR4 180 B1
2 NW6 69 B1
Brooklands Dr UB6 87 D6
Brooklands Pk SE3 143 A2
Brooklands Prim Sch SE3 143 A2
Brooklands Rd KT7 197 A1
Brooklands The TW7 130 B4
Brooklea Cl NW9 27 C2
Brooklyn SE20 184 A3
Brooklyn Ave SE25 206 B5
Brooklyn Cl SM5 218 C6
Brooklyn Ct W12 112 C5
Brooklyn Gr SE25 206 B5
Brooklyn Rd SE25 206 B5
Bromley BR2 210 A4
Brookmarsh Ind Est SE10 141 D5
Brookmead CR0 203 C3
Brookmead Ave BR1, BR2 210 B4
Brookmead Ct N20 14 A2
Brookmead Rd CR0 203 C3
Brookmill Rd SE8 141 C4
Brooks Ave E6 100 B3
Brooks Cl SE9 166 C2
Brooks Ct 3 SW4 138 A3
SW8 269 B4
Brooks Ho 6 SW2 160 C3
Brooks La W4 132 C6
Brook's Mans 5 IG3 58 B1
Brook's Mews W1 115 B6 248 C6
Brook's Par 6 IG3 58 B1
Brooks Rd W4 110 C1
Brook's Rd E13 99 A6
Brooksbank Ho 7 E9 74 C2
Brooksbank St 9 E9 74 C2
Brooksby Mews N1 72 C1
Brooksby St N1 72 C1
Brooksby's Wlk E9 74 D3
Brookscroft Rd E17 35 D2
Brookshill HA3 24 B5
Brookshill Ave HA3 24 C5
Brookshill Dr HA3 24 B5
Brookside N21 16 B5
Broom Hill BR6 211 D2
East Barnet EN4 14 C5
Wallington SM5 219 A3
Brookside Cl Barnet EN5 13 A5
Feltham TW13 150 A1
Harrow HA3 43 D4
South Harrow HA2,HA4 63 A4
Brookside Cres 1 KT4 200 A1
Brookside Gdns EN1 6 C6
Brookside Ho N17 33 C1
Brookside Prim Sch UB4 84 C4
Brookside Rd N9 34 B6
N19 71 C6
NW11 47 B3
Hayes UB4 106 C6
Brookside S EN4 15 A4
Brookside Way
Croydon CR0 206 D3
Uxbridge UB10 60 B1
Brookstone Ct SE15 140 B1
Brooksville Ave NW6 91 A6
Brookview Ct 11 EN1 17 C6
Brookview Rd SW16 181 C5
Brookville Rd SW6 135 B5 264 C3
Brookway SE3 143 A2
Brookwood Ave SW13 133 D3
Brookwood Cl BR2 208 D5
Brookwood Ho SE1 251 D1
Brookwood Rd SW18 157 C3
Hounslow TW3 129 D4
Broom Ave BR5 190 B1
Broom Cl Bromley BR2 210 A3
Teddington KT1,TW11 175 D3
Broom Gdns CR0 223 C5
Broom Lock TW11 175 C4
Broom Mead DA6 169 C6
Broom Pk KT1 175 D3
Broom Rd Croydon CR0 223 C5
Richmond TW11 175 C5
Teddington KT1,TW11 175 C4
Broom Water TW11 175 C5
Broom Water W TW11 175 C5
Broomcroft Ave UB5 84 C4
Broome Ct 3 TW9 132 C4
Broome Ho 7 E5 74 B3
Broome Rd TW12 173 B2
Broome Way SE5 139 B5
Broomfield E17 53 B2
7 NW1 71 A1
Sunbury TW16 172 A2
Broomfield Ave N13 32 B5
Broomfield Cotts N13 32 A5
Broomfield Ct N13 32 A5
Broomfield Ho SE17 263 A3
4 St Paul's Cray BR5 190 B1
Stanmore HA7 9 A1
Broomfield House Sch TW9 132 B4
Broomfield La N13 32 B6
Broomfield Pl W13 109 B5
Broomfield Rd N13 32 A5
W13 109 B5
Beckenham BR3 207 B6
Bexleyheath DA6 169 C6
Dagenham RM6 58 D2
Richmond TW9 132 B4
Surbiton KT5 198 B1
Teddington TW11 175 C4
Broomfield Sch N14 31 D5
Broomfield St E14 97 D2
Broomfields KT10 212 A3
Broomgrove Gdns HA8 26 C2
Broomgrove Rd SW9 138 B3
Broomhill Ct 2 IG8 37 A4
Broomhill Rd SW18 157 C6
Broom Hill BR6 211 D2
Ilford IG3 80 A6
Woodford IG8 37 A4
Broomhill Rise DA6 169 C6
Broomhill Wlk IG8 36 D3
Broomhouse La SW6 135 C2
Broomhouse Rd SW6 135 C3
Broomleigh BR1 187 A2
Broomleigh Bsns Pk SE26 185 B5
Broomloan La SM1 217 C6
Broomsleigh St NW6 69 B3
Broomwood Cl CR0 206 D4
Broomwood Rd SW11 159 A6
St Paul's Cray BR5 190 B1
Broseley Gr SE26 185 A5
Broster Gdns SE25 205 D6
Brough Cl SW8 270 B3
Kingston u T KT2 175 D5
Brough St SW8 270 B3
Brougham Rd E8 96 A6
W3 89 A1
Brougham St SW11 136 D3
Broughton Ave N3 47 A6
Richmond TW10 175 C6
Broughton Ct W13 109 B6
Broughton Dr 20 SW9 138 D1
Broughton Gdns N6 49 C3
Broughton Rd SW6 135 D3
W13 109 B6
Orpington BR6 227 B6
Thornton Heath CR7 204 C3
Broughton Road App 2 SW6 135 D3
Broughton St SW8 137 B3
Broughton Street Arches Ind Area SW11 137 A3
Brouncker Rd W3 111 A4
Browells La TW13 150 B2
Brown Bear Ct TW13 172 D6
Brown Cl SM6 220 A1
Brown Hart Gdns W1 248 B6
Brown St W1 92 D1 237 C2
Browne Ho 13 SE8 141 C5
9 SE26 184 B5
Brownfield St E14 98 A1
Brownflete Ho SE4 141 A1
Browngraves Rd UB7 127 A5
Brownhill Rd SE6 164 A4
Browning Ave W7 86 D1
Carshalton SM1 218 C4
North Cheam KT4 200 B1
Browning Cl E17 54 A5
W9 236 B5
Bexley DA16 145 C4
Hampton TW12 173 B6
Browning Ct W14 264 C6
Browning Ho 10 N16 73 C4
W12 90 C1
Browning Mews W1 238 B3
Browning Rd E11 54 D2
E12 78 B2
Enfield EN2 5 B5
Browning St SE17 117 A2 262 B3
Browning Way TW5 128 D4
Brownlea Gdns IG3 80 A6
Brownlow Ct N2 48 A4
1 N11 32 A4
Brownlow Ho 7 SE16 118 A4
Brownlow Mews WC1 94 B3 240 D5
Brownlow Rd 3 E7 77 A4
E8 96 A6
N3 29 D3
N11 32 A4
NW10 67 C1
6 W13 109 A5
South Croydon CR0 221 D4
Brownlow St WC1 94 B2 240 D3
Brownrigg Rd TW15 170 C6
Brown's Bldgs EC3 243 B1
Brown's Rd E17 53 C6
Surbiton KT5,KT6 198 B2
Brownspring Dr SE9 166 D1
Brownswell Rd N2 30 B1
Brownswood Rd N4 73 A6
Broxash Rd SW11 159 A5
Broxbourne Ave E18 55 B5
Broxbourne Ho 1 E3 97 D3
Broxbourne Rd E7 77 A5
Broom Hill BR6 211 D2
Broxholm Rd SE27, SW16 160 C1
Broxholme Ho SW6 265 C2
Broxted Rd SE6 163 B2
Broxwood Way NW8 92 C6 230 B5
Bruce Ave TW17 193 A3
Bruce Castle Ct N17 33 C2
Bruce Castle Mus N17 33 C2
Bruce Castle Rd N17 33 D2
Bruce Cl W10 90 D2
Bexley DA16 146 B4
Bruce Ct DA15 189 D6
Bruce Gdns N20 14 D1
Bruce Glasier Ho 13 N19 49 D2
Bruce Gr N17 33 D1
Bruce Grove N17 33 D1
Bruce Grove Jun & Inf Schs N17 33 D1
Bruce Grove Sta N17 33 D1
Bruce Hall Mews SW17 181 A6
Bruce Ho 4 SW4 159 D5
SW15 156 B6
W10 90 D2
Harrow HA3 44 A2
Bruce Lawns SW17 181 A6
Bruce Rd E3 97 D4
NW10 67 B1
SE25 205 B5
Harrow HA3 24 C1
High Barnet EN5 1 A2
Mitcham CR4 181 A3
Bruckner St W10 91 B4
Brudenell Rd SW17 181 A6
Bruffs Meadow UB5 63 A2
Bruges Pl 15 NW1 71 C1
Brumfield Rd KT19 215 A3
Brune Ho E1 243 C3
Brune St E1 95 D2 243 C3
Brunel Cl SE19 183 D4
Cranford TW5 128 B5
Northolt UB5 85 B4
Brunel Ct NW10 90 A4
8 SW13 133 D3
Brunel Est W2 91 C2
Brunel Ho E14 119 D1
4 NW5 71 B4
25 SW2 160 A4
SW10 266 D4
Hayes UB3 105 D3
Brunel Pl 8 UB1 85 D1
Brunel Rd SE16 118 C5
W3 89 C2
Brunel St E16 98 D1
Brunel Univ UB8 82 A4
Brunel Univ Coll (Twickenham Campus) TW1 131 B1
Brunel Univ Coll Osterley Campus TW7 130 D5
Brunel Wlk N15 51 C5
Twickenham TW4 151 C4
Brunlees Ho SE1 262 B5
Brunner Cl NW11 48 A4
Brunner Ho 6 SE6 186 A6
Brunner Rd E17 53 B4
W5 87 D3
Bruno Pl NW9 67 A6
Brunswick Ave N11 15 A1
Brunswick Cl
Bexley DA6 146 D1
Pinner HA5 41 A3
Thames Ditton KT7 196 D1
Twickenham TW2 152 B1
Brunswick Cres N11 15 A1
Brunswick Ct EC1 234 C1
SE1 117 C4 253 B2
2 SE19 184 A3
SW1 259 D3
2 SW19 179 A3
Kingston u T KT2 175 D4
New Barnet EN4 14 B6
Brunswick Gdns W5 88 A3
W8 113 C5 245 B3
Brunswick Gr N11 15 A1
Brunswick Ho 4 E2 95 D5
N3 29 B2
NW1 237 C6

Brunswick Lo 6 E4 20 A2
Brunswick Manor SM1 218 A4
Brunswick Mews SW16 181 D4
W1 237 D2
Brunswick Park Gdns
N11 15 A2
Brunswick Park Prim Sch
N14 15 A2
SE5 139 B5
Brunswick Park Rd N11 15 A1
Brunswick Pk SE5 139 C4
Brunswick Pl N1 95 B4 235 D1
SE19 184 A3
Brunswick Quay SE16 118 D3
Brunswick Rd E10 54 A1
E14 98 A1
N15 51 C5
W5 88 A4
Bexleyheath DA6 147 A1
Enfield EN3 7 C5
Kingston u T KT2 176 C2
Sutton SM1 217 D4
Brunswick Sh Ctr
WC1 94 A3 240 B6
Brunswick Sq N17 33 D4
WC1 94 A3 240 B6
Brunswick St E17 54 A4
Brunswick Villas 2
SE5 139 C4
Brunswick Way N11 31 B6
Brunton Pl E14 97 A1
Brushfield St E1 95 D2 243 C4
Brushwood Ho 4 E14 97 D2
Brushwood Lo DA17 125 C2
Brussels Rd SW11 136 B1
Bruton Cl BR7 188 B3
Bruton La W1 115 B6 248 D5
Bruton Pl W1 115 B6 248 D5
Bruton Rd SM4 202 A5
Bruton St W1 115 B6 248 D5
Bruton Way W13 87 A2
Bryan Ave NW10 68 B1
Bryan Cl TW16 172 A3
Bryan Ct W1 237 C2
Bryan Ho SE16 119 B4
Bryan Rd SE16 119 B4
Bryanston Ave TW2 151 D3
Bryanston Cl UB2 107 B2
Bryanston Ct W1 237 C2
Bryanston Ho 11 SE15 139 D4
Bryanston Mans W1 237 C4
Bryanston Mews E W1 237 C3
Bryanston Mews W
W1 92 D1 237 C2
Bryanston Pl W1 92 D2 237 C3
Bryanston Sq
W1 92 D1 237 C2
Bryanston St W1 92 D1 237 D1
Bryanstone Ct SM1 218 A5
Bryanstone Rd N8 49 D4
Bryant Cl EN5 13 B6
Bryant Ct E2 95 D5
Bryant Rd UB5 84 C4
Bryant St E15 76 C1
Bryantwood Rd N5,N7 72 C3
Bryce Ho 25 SE14 140 D6
Bryce Rd RM8 80 C4
Brycedale Cres N14 15 D1
Brydale Ho 2 SE16 118 D2
Bryden Cl SE26 185 A5
Brydges Pl WC2 250 A5
Brydges Rd E15 76 B3
Brydon Wlk N1 233 B6
Bryer Ct EC2 242 A4
Bryett Rd N7 72 A5
Bryher Ho W4 111 A1
Brymay Cl E3 97 C5
Brymon Ct W1 237 D3
Brynmaer Ho SW11 267 D1
Brynmaer Rd
SW11 136 D4 267 D1
Bryn-y-Mawr Rd EN1 5 D1
Bryony Cl UB8 82 B2
Bryony Rd W12 112 A6
Bryony Way TW16 172 A4
BT Telecom Twr*
W1 93 C2 239 A4
Buccleuch Ho E5 52 A2
Buchan Ho W3 110 D4
Buchan Rd SE15 140 C2
Buchanan Cl N21 16 B6
Buchanan Ct 16 SE16 118 D2
Buchanan Gdns NW10 90 B5
Buchanan Ho SE21 161 C1
SW18 157 C4
Bucharest Rd SW18 158 A4
Buck Hill Wlk
W2 114 B6 246 D5
Buck La NW9 45 B4
Buck St NW1 71 B1
Buckden Cl N2 48 D5
SE12 165 A5
Buckfast Ct W13 109 A6
Buckfast Ho N14 15 C6
Buckfast Rd SM4 201 D5
Buckfast St E2 96 A4
Buckhold Rd SW18 157 C5
Buckhurst Ave CR4,SM5 202 D1
Buckhurst Hill Ho IG9 21 B2
Buckhurst Hill Sta IG9 21 D2
Buckhurst Ho 15 N7 71 D3
Buckhurst St E1 96 B3
Buckhurst Way IG9 21 D1
Buckingham Ave N20 14 B4
Bexley DA16 145 C1
East Molesey KT8 173 D1
Feltham TW14 150 B5
South Norwood CR7 182 C2
Buckingham Ave *continued*
Wembley UB6 87 A6
Buckingham Cl W5 87 C2
Broom Hill BR5 211 C2
Enfield EN1 5 C3
Hampton TW12 173 B5
Buckingham Ct NW4 46 A6
2 W7 86 D3
Mitcham CR4 204 A4
Northolt UB5 85 A6
Wembley HA0 65 C2
Buckingham Dr BR7 189 A5
Buckingham Gate
SW1 115 C3 259 B6
Buckingham Gdns
Edgware HA8 26 B3
Hampton KT8 173 D1
South Norwood CR7 182 C1
Buckingham Gr UB10 82 C5
Buckingham Ho N4 51 A1
1 W3 88 C1
Richmond TW10 154 C6
Buckingham La SE23 163 A4
Buckingham Lo N10 49 C5
Buckingham Mans NW6 69 D3
Buckingham Mews
NW10 89 D5
SW1 259 A6
Buckingham Palace*
SW1 115 C4 249 A1
Buckingham Palace Rd
SW1 115 B2 258 D4
Buckingham Pl SW1 259 A6
Buckingham Prim Sch
TW12 173 B5
Buckingham Rd E10 75 D5
E11 55 C4
E15 76 D3
E18 36 D2
N1 73 C2
N22 32 A2
NW10 89 D5
Edgware HA8 26 B3
Hampton TW12,TW13 173 B5
Harrow HA1 42 B4
Ilford IG1 79 B6
Kingston u T KT1 198 B5
Mitcham CR4 204 A4
Richmond TW10 153 D2
Buckingham St WC2 250 B5
Buckingham Way SM6 219 C1
Buckingham Yd NW10 89 D5
Buckland Cres NW3 70 B2
Buckland Ct 6 N1 95 C5
Uxbridge UB10 61 A6
Buckland Inf Sch KT9 214 B4
Buckland Rd E10 76 A6
Chessington KT9 214 B3
Orpington BR6 227 C4
Buckland Rise HA5 22 D2
Buckland St N1 95 B5 235 D3
Buckland Way KT4 200 C1
Buckland Wlk 2 W3 111 A4
Morden SM4 202 A5
Bucklands Rd TW11 175 C4
Buckle St E1 243 D2
9 E1 96 A1
Buckleigh Ave SW20 201 B6
Buckleigh Rd SW16 182 A3
Buckleigh Way SE19 183 D3
Buckler Gdns SE9 166 B1
Buckler's Alley SW6 264 D4
Bucklers' Way SM5 218 D5
Bucklersbury EC2,EC4 242 C1
Buckles Ct DA17 124 D2
Buckley Ct 5 NW6 69 B1
Buckley Rd NW6 69 B1
Buckley St SE1 251 A3
Buckmaster Ho 1 N7 72 B4
1 SW9 138 C2
Buckmaster Rd SW11 136 C1
Bucknall St WC1 240 A2
Bucknell Cl SW2 138 B1
Buckner Rd SW2 138 B1
Buckrell Rd E4 20 B2
Buckridge Ho EC1 241 A4
Buckshead Ho 19 W2 91 C2
Buckstone Cl SE23 162 C5
Buckstone Rd N18 34 A5
Buckters Rents SE16 119 A5
Buckthorn Ho DA15 167 D1
Buckthorne Rd SE4 163 A6
Buckwheat Ct DA18 124 D3
Budd Cl N12 29 D6
Buddings Circ HA9 67 A5
Budge La CR4 202 D2
Budge Row EC4 242 C1
Budge's Wlk
W2 114 A5 246 B4
Budleigh Cres DA16 146 C4
Budleigh Ho 19 SE15 140 A5
Budoch Ct IG3 80 A6
Budoch Dr IG3 80 A6
Buer Rd SW6 135 A3
Bugsbys Way SE10 120 D2
Bugsby's Way SE7,SE10 121 B2
Buick Ho 4 E3 97 C3
Bulbarrow NW8 91 D6
Bulganak Rd CR7 205 A5
Bulinca St SW1 115 D2 259 D3
Bull Alley DA16 146 B2
Bull Dog The (Juct)
TW15 148 A2
Bull Inn Ct WC2 250 B5
Bull La N18 33 C5
Chislehurst BR7 189 B3
Dagenham RM10 81 D5
Bull Rd E15 98 D5
Bull Yd SE15 140 A4
Bullace Row SE5 139 B4
Bullard Rd TW11 174 D4
Bullards Pl 13 E2 96 D4
Bulleid Way
SW1 115 B2 258 D3
Bullen Ho 13 E1 96 B3
Bullen St SW11 136 C3
Buller Cl SE15 140 A5
Buller Rd N17 34 A1
N22 32 C1
NW10 90 D4
Barking IG11 79 C1
South Norwood CR7 205 B6
Bullers Cl DA14 191 A5
Bullers Wood Dr BR7 188 B3
Bullers Wood Sch for Girls
BR7 188 B2
Bullescroft Rd HA8 10 D1
Bullfinch Ct 3 SE21 161 B2
Bullingham Mans W8 245 B2
Bullivant St 9 E14 120 A6
Bullrush Cl CR0 205 C3
Bulls Alley SW14 133 B3
Bulls Bridge Ind Est
UB2 106 B2
Bulls Bridge Rd UB2 106 B2
Bull's Cross EN1,EN2 6 A6
Bull's Gdns SW3 257 B4
Bulls Head Pas EC3 243 A1
Bullsbrook Rd UB4 106 C5
Bulmer Gdns HA3 43 D2
Bulmer Mews
W11 113 C5 245 A4
Bulow Ct 3 SW6 135 D3
Bulstrode Ave TW3 129 C2
Bulstrode Gdns TW3 129 C2
Bulstrode Pl W1 238 B3
Bulstrode Rd TW3 129 C2
Bulstrode St W1 93 A1 238 B2
Bulwer Court Rd E11 54 B1
Bulwer Ct E11 54 B1
Bulwer Gdns EN5 2 A1
Bulwer Rd E11 54 B1
N18 33 C6
New Barnet EN5 2 A1
Bulwer St W12 112 C5
Bunbury Ho SE15 140 A5
Bunces La IG8 36 D3
Bungalow Rd SE25 205 C5
Bungalows The E10 54 A3
SW16 181 B3
Bunhill Row EC1 95 B3 242 C5
Bunhouse Pl SW1 258 B2
Bunkers Hill NW11 48 A2
Sidcup DA14 169 B1
Bunker's Hill DA17 125 C2
Bunning Ho N7 72 A4
Bunning Way N7 72 B1
Bunn's La NW7 27 D4
Bunsen Ho 1 E3 97 A5
Bunsen St 2 E3 97 A5
Bunting Cl N9 18 D3
Mitcham CR4 202 D4
Bunting Ct NW9 27 C1
Buntingbridge Rd IG2 57 B4
Bunton St SE18 122 C3
Bunyan Ct EC2 242 A4
Bunyan Rd E17 53 A6
Buonaparte Mews SW1 259 C2
BUPA Bushey Hospl WD2 8 D3
Burbage Cl SE1 117 B3 262 C5
Burbage Ho N1 235 D5
16 SE14 140 D6
Burbage Jun & Inf Sch
N1 95 C5
Burbage Rd SE21,SE24 161 B4
Burbank KT3 199 D6
Burberry Cl KT3 177 C1
Burbidge Rd TW17 192 C5
Burbridge Way N17 34 A1
Burcham St E14 98 A1
Burcharbro Rd SE2 146 D6
Burchell Ct WD2 8 A4
Burchell Ho SE11 260 D2
Burchell Rd E10 53 D1
SE15 140 B4
Burchett Way RM6 59 B3
Burchetts Way TW17 192 D3
Burcote Rd SW18 158 B4
Burden Cl TW8 109 C1
Burden Ho SW8 270 A3
Burden Way E11 77 B6
Burdenshott Ave TW10 132 D1
Burder Cl N1 73 C2
Burder Rd N1 73 C2
Burdett Ave SW20 178 A2
Burdett Cl 2 W7 108 D5
Ruxley DA14 191 A5
Burdett Coutts CE Prim Sch
SW1 115 D2 259 C4
Burdett Mews 4 W2 91 D1
Burdett Rd E3 97 B2
Richmond TW9 132 B2
Thornton Heath CR0 205 B3
Burdetts Rd RM9 103 B6
Burdock Cl CR0 206 D1
Burdock Rd N17 52 A6
Burdon La SM2 217 A1
Burdon Pk SM2 217 B1
Bure Ct 10 EN5 13 D6
Burfield Cl SW17 180 B6
Burford Cl
Dagenham RM8 80 C5
Ickenham UB10 60 A4
Ilford IG6 57 A5
Burford Gdns N13 16 B1
Burford Ho 11 SW9 138 B3
Burford Ho *continued*
1 Brentford TW8 110 A1
Burford Rd E6 100 A4
E15 98 B6
SE6 163 B2
Brentford TW8 110 A1
Bromley BR1 210 A5
New Malden KT4 200 A2
Sutton SM1 217 C6
Burford Way CR0 224 A2
Burford Wlk SW6 265 D3
Burgate Ct 10 SW9 138 C2
Burge St SE1 262 D5
Burges Gr SW13 134 B5
Burges Rd E6 78 B1
Burgess Ave NW9 45 B3
Burgess Cl 4 TW13 173 A6
Burgess Ct E12 78 C1
3 Southall UB1 85 D1
Burgess Ho 3 SE5 139 A5
Burgess Mews SW19 179 D4
Burgess Park Mans NW6 69 C4
Burgess Rd E15 76 C4
Sutton SM1 217 D4
Burgess St E14 97 C2
Burgh St N1 94 D5 234 D4
Burghill Rd SE26 185 A6
Burghley Ave
Borehamwood WD6 11 A6
Kingston u T KT3 177 B2
Burghley Ho SW19 157 A1
Burghley Pl CR4 202 D5
Burghley Rd E11 54 C1
N8 50 C6
NW5 71 B4
SW19 179 A6
Burghley Twr W3 111 D6
Burgon St EC4 241 D1
Burgos Cl CR0 220 C2
Burgos Gr SE10 141 D4
Burgoyne Rd N4 50 D3
SE25 205 D5
SW9 138 B2
Ashford TW16 171 D4
Burham Cl SE20 184 C3
Burhan Uddin Ho E1 243 C5
Burhill Gr HA5 23 A1
Buriton Ho 9 SW15 156 B3
Burke Cl SW15 133 C1
Burke Ho 1 SW11 136 B1
Burke Lo E13 99 B4
Burke St E16 98 D2
Burket Cl UB2 107 B2
Burland Rd SW11 158 D6
Burleigh Ave
Bexley DA15 167 D6
Hackbridge SM6 219 B5
Burleigh Ct N17 34 A4
Burleigh Gdns N14 15 C3
Ashford TW15 171 A5
Burleigh Ho SW3 266 D5
W10 90 D2
Enfield EN1 18 A6
Burleigh Par N14 15 D3
Burleigh Pl SW15 156 D6
Burleigh Rd Cheam SM3 201 A1
Enfield EN1 5 C1
Hillingdon UB10 82 D6
Burleigh St WC2 250 C6
Burleigh Way EN2 5 B2
Burleigh Wlk SE6 164 A3
Burley Cl E4 35 C5
SW16 181 D1
Burley Ho E1 96 D1
Burley Rd E16 99 C2
Burlington Arc W1 249 A5
Burlington Ave
Richmond TW9 132 C4
Romford RM7 59 D3
Burlington Cl 5 E6 100 A1
W9 91 C3
East Bedfont TW14 149 B4
Orpington BR6 226 D6
Burlington Ct W4 133 A5
Burlington Danes Sch
W12 90 B1
Burlington Gate SW20 179 A1
Burlington Gdns SW6 135 A3
W1 115 C6 249 A5
W3 111 A5
W4 111 A1
Dagenham RM6 59 A2
Burlington Ho NW3 70 B3
Burlington Jun Sch
KT3 199 D5
Burlington La W4 133 B5
Burlington Lo BR7 188 B3
Burlington Mews
1 SW15 157 B6
W3 111 A5
Burlington Pl SW6 135 A3
Pinner HA5 40 B6
Woodford IG8 21 A1
Burlington Rd N10 49 A6
N17 34 A2
SW6 135 A3
W4 111 A1
Enfield EN2 5 B4
Hounslow TW7 130 B4
New Malden KT3 199 D5
South Norwood CR7 183 B1
Burlington Rise EN4 14 D4
Burma Rd N16 73 B4
Burma Terr 11 SE19 183 C5
Burmarsh 6 NW5 71 A2
Burmarsh Ct SE20 184 C2
Burmester Ho SW17 158 A1
Burmester Rd SW17 158 A1
Burn Side N9 18 C1
Burnaby Cres W4 133 A6
Burnaby Ct 27 SE16 118 A4
Burnaby Gdns W4 132 D6
Burnaby St
SW10 136 A5 266 B3
Burnand Ho 3 W14 112 D3
Burnaston Ho 5 E5 74 A5
Burnbrae Cl N12 29 D4
Burnbury Rd SW12 159 C3
Burncroft Ave EN3 6 C3
Burndell Way UB4 84 D2
Burne Jones Ho W14 254 B3
Burne St NW1 237 A4
Burnell Ave Bexley DA16 146 A3
Richmond TW10 175 C5
Burnell Gdns HA7 25 D1
Burnell Ho 19 SW2 160 C3
Burnell Rd SM1 217 D4
Burnell Wlk SE1 263 D2
Burnels Ave E6 100 C4
Burness Cl N7 72 B2
Burnett Cl E9 74 C3
Burnett Ct SW11 267 A1
Burnett Ho 5 SE13 142 A3
Burney Ave KT5 198 B4
Burney Ho 4 SW16 181 C5
Burney St SE10 142 A5
Burnfoot Ave
SW6 135 A4 264 B1
Burnham NW3 70 C1
Burnham Ave UB10 61 A4
Burnham Cl NW7 28 A3
SE1 263 D3
Enfield EN1 5 C5
Harrow HA3 43 A5
Burnham Cres E11 55 C5
Burnham Ct NW4 46 C5
W2 245 D6
Burnham Dr KT4 216 D6
Burnham Est 8 E2 96 C4
Burnham Gdns
Cranford TW4 128 B4
Croydon CR0 205 D2
Hayes UB3 105 B3
Burnham Rd E4 35 B5
Dagenham RM9 102 B6
Morden SM4 201 D5
Sidcup DA14 169 A2
Burnham St E2 96 C4
Kingston u T KT2 176 C2
Burnham Way SE26 185 B5
W13 109 B3
Burnhill Ho EC1 235 A1
Burnhill Rd BR3 185 C1
Burnley Cl WD1 22 C5
Burnley Rd NW10 68 A3
SW9 138 B3
Burns Ave Bexley DA15 168 B5
Dagenham RM6 58 C2
Feltham TW14 150 A5
Southall UB1 107 C6
Burns Cl SW17 180 B4
Bexley DA16 145 D4
Hayes UB4 84 A2
Burns Ct SM6 219 B1
Burns Ho 18 E2 96 C4
N7 72 B2
11 N16 73 C4
SE17 261 D1
Burn's Ho NW10 89 C6
Burns Rd SW11 136 D3
W13 109 B4
Wembley HA0 88 A5
Burn's Rd NW10 89 D6
Burns Way TW5 128 D4
Burnsall St SW3 114 C1 257 B2
Burnside Ave E4 35 B4
Burnside Cl SE16 118 D5
Barnet EN5 1 C2
Twickenham TW1 153 A5
Burnside Cres HA0 87 D6
Burnside Rd RM8 58 C1
Burnt Ash Hill SE12 165 A3
Burnt Ash La BR1,SE12 187 B5
Burnt Ash Prim Sch
BR1 187 A5
Burnt Ash Rd SE12 164 D6
Burnt Oak Broadway
HA8 26 D2
Burnt Oak Fields HA8 27 A2
Burnt Oak Jun Sch
DA15 168 A3
Burnt Oak La DA15 168 B3
Burnt Oak Sta HA8 27 A2
Burnthwaite Rd
SW6 135 B5 264 D3
Burntwood Cl SW18 158 C3
Burntwood Ct SW17 158 A1
Burntwood Grange Rd
SW18 158 C3
Burntwood La SW17 158 B2
Burntwood Sch SW17 158 B2
Burntwood View SE19 183 D5
Buross St E1 96 B1
Burr Cl E1 118 A5
Bexley DA7 147 B2
Burr Rd SW18 157 C4
Burrage Ct 17 SE16 118 D2
Burrage Gr SE18 123 A2
Burrage Pl SE18 122 D1
Burrage Rd SE18 123 A1
Burrard Ho 11 E2 96 C5
Burrard Rd E16 99 B1
NW6 69 C4
Burrel Ct HA1 42 B2
Burrell Cl Croydon CR0 207 A3
Edgware HA8 10 D2
Burrell Ho 4 TW1 153 B4
Burrell Row BR3 185 C1
Burrell St SE1 116 D5 251 C4
Burrell Twrs E10 53 C2
Burrells 9 BR3 185 D1
Burrell's Wharf Sq E14 119 D1
Burrhill Ct SE16 118 D3
Burritt Rd KT1 176 C1
Burrmead Ct NW2 67 D5
Burroughs Gdns NW4 46 B5
Burroughs The NW4 46 B5
Burrow Ho 19 SW9 138 B3
Burrow Rd SE22 139 C1
Burrow Wlk SE21 161 A4
Burrows Mews SE1 251 C2
Burrows Rd NW10 90 C4
Bursar St SE1 253 A3
Bursdon Cl DA15 167 D2
Bursland Rd EN3 6 D1
Burslem St E1 96 A1
Bursted Wood Prim Sch
DA7 147 D3
Burstock Rd SW15 135 A1
Burston Rd SW15 156 D6
Burstow Rd SW20 179 A2
Burt Rd E16 121 C5
Burtenshaw Rd KT7 197 A3
Burtley Cl N4 51 A1
Burton Bank N1 73 B1
Burton Cl KT9 213 D1
Burton Ct SW3 257 D2
Thames Ditton KT7 197 A3
Burton Dr EN3 7 C6
Burton Gdns TW5 129 B4
Burton Gr SE17 262 C1
Burton Ho SE5 138 D4
6 SE16 118 B4
SE26 184 B5
Burton La 3 SW9 138 C3
6 SW9 138 C3
Burton Lo 5 SW15 157 B6
Burton Mews SW1 258 B3
Burton Pl WC1 232 D1
Burton Rd E18 55 B6
NW6 69 B1
SW9 138 D3
8 SW9 138 C3
Kingston u T KT2 176 A3
Burton St WC1 93 D3 239 D6
Burtonhole Cl NW7 28 D6
Burtonhole La NW7 28 D6
Burtons Ct E15 76 B1
Burton's Rd TW12 174 A6
Burtonwood Ho N4 51 B2
Burtt Ho 6 N1 95 C4
Burtwell La SE21,SE27 183 B6
Burwash Ho SE1 252 D1
Burwash Rd SE18 123 B1
Burwell 2 KT1 176 C1
Burwell Ave UB6 64 C2
Burwell Cl 25 E1 96 B1
Burwell Rd E10 53 A1
Burwell Wlk 14 E3 97 C3
Burwood Ave BR2 225 B6
Burwood Cl KT6 198 C1
Burwood Ct SE23 162 C4
Burwood Ho 11 SW9 138 D1
Burwood Pl W2 237 B2
Bury Ave Hayes UB4 83 C5
Ruislip HA4 39 A3
Bury Cl SE16 118 D5
Bury Ct EC3 243 B2
Bury Gr SM4 201 D4
Bury Hall Villas N9 17 D4
Bury Pl WC1 94 A2 240 B3
Bury Rd E4 20 C6
N22 50 C6
Dagenham RM10 81 D3
Bury St EC3 95 C1 243 B2
N9 18 A3
SW1 115 C5 249 B4
Ruislip HA4 39 B3
Bury St W N9 17 C4
Bury Wlk SW3 114 C1 257 A2
Burywood Ct EN3 6 C3
Busbridge Ho 16 E14 97 C2
Busby Ho SW16 181 C6
Busby Pl NW5 71 D2
Busby St E2 243 D6
Busch Cl TW7 131 B4
Busch Cnr TW7 131 B4
Bush Cl IG2 57 B4
Bush Cotts 12 SW18 157 C6
Bush Ct N14 15 C3
7 W12 112 D4
Bush Fair Ct N14 15 B5
Bush Gr NW9 45 A2
Stanmore HA7 25 D2
Bush Hill N21 17 A5
Bush Hill Par EN1 17 B4
Bush Hill Park Sta EN1 17 D5
Bush Hill Prim & Inf Sch
EN1 18 A6
Bush Hill Rd N21 17 B5
Harrow HA3 44 B3
Bush La EC4 117 B6 252 C6
Bush Rd E8 96 B6
E11 55 A2
SE8 118 D2
Littleton TW17 192 B4
Richmond TW9 132 B6
Woodford IG9 37 D6
Bushbaby Cl SE1 263 A5
Bushberry Rd E9 75 A2
Bushell Cl SW2 160 B2

Bushell Gn WD2 . . . . .8 B2
Bushell Ho 3 SE27 . . . .183 A6
Bushell St E1 . . . . .118 A5
Bushey Ave E18 . . . . .54 D6
  Orpington BR5 . . . . .211 B2
Bushey CI E4 . . . . .20 A1
  Ickenham UB10 . . . . .60 C6
Bushey Ct SW20 . . . . .178 B1
Bushey Down SW12 . . . .159 B2
Bushey Fst Sch KT3 . . . .200 B6
Bushey Hall SE5 . . . . .139 D4
Bushey Heath JMI Prim Sch
  WD2 . . . . .8 B3
Bushey Hill Rd SE5 . . . . .139 D4
Bushey Ho SE12 . . . . .165 C1
Bushey La SM1 . . . . .217 C4
Bushey Lees DA15 . . . . . .167 D5
Bushey Mead Sch SW20 .200 B6
Bushey Mid Sch SW20 . .200 B6
Bushey Rd E13 . . . . .99 C5
  N15 . . . . .51 C3
  SW20 . . . . .178 D1
  Croydon CR0 . . . . .223 C6
  Hayes UB3 . . . . .105 C2
  Ickenham UB10 . . . . .60 C6
  Sutton SM1 . . . . .217 C4
Bushey Way BR3 . . . . .208 B4
Bushfield CI HA8 . . . . .10 D1
Bushfield Cres HA8 . . . . . .10 D2
Bushfield Ho N5 . . . . .73 A3
Bushgrove Rd RM8 . . . . . .80 D5
Bushmead CI 6 N15 . . . . .51 D5
Bushmoor Cres SE18 . . . .144 D5
Bushnell Rd SW17 . . . . . .159 B1
Bushway RM8 . . . . .80 D5
Bushwood E11 . . . . .55 A1
Bushwood Dr
  SE1 . . . . .117 D2 263 D3
Bushwood Rd TW9 . . . . . .132 C6
Bushy Ct KT1 . . . . .175 C2
Bushy Park Gdns TW12 .174 B5
Bushy Park Rd TW11 . . . .175 B3
Bushy Rd TW11 . . . . .174 D3
Business Design Ctr*
  N1 . . . . .94 C6 234 B5
Buspace Studios 3 W10 91 A3
Butcher Row E1 . . . . .96 D1
Butchers Rd E16 . . . . .99 A1
Bute Ave TW10 . . . . .154 A2
Bute Ct SM6 . . . . .219 C3
Bute Gdns W6 . . . . .112 D2
  Wallington SM6 . . . . . . .219 C3
Bute Gdns W SM6 . . . . . .219 C3
Bute House Prep Sch
  W6 . . . . .112 D2
Bute Rd Ilford IG6 . . . . . . .56 D4
  Thornton Heath CR0 . . . .204 C1
  Wallington SM6 . . . . . . .219 C4
Bute St SW7 . . . .114 32 256 C4
Butfield Ho 6 E9 . . . . . . .74 C2
Butler Ave HA1 . . . . .42 B2
Butler Ct Dagenham RM8 .81 C6
  Wembley HA0 . . . . .65 A4
Butler Ho 32 E2 . . . . .96 C4
  13 E14 . . . . .97 B1
  5 SW9 . . . . .138 D4
Butler PI SW1 . . . . . . .259 C6
Butler Rd NW10 . . . . .67 D1
  Dagenham RM8 . . . . .80 B4
  Harrow HA1 . . . . .42 A2
Butler St 33 E2 . . . . .96 C4
  Hillingdon UB10 . . . . .82 D3
Butler's Cotts DA7 . . . . . .147 C3
Butler's Wharf W SE1 . .253 C2
Butley Ct 7 E3 . . . . .97 A5
Butter Hill SM5,SM6 . . . .219 A4
Butterfield CI N17 . . . . . . .33 A4
  1 SE16 . . . . .118 B4
  Twickenham TW1 . . . . . .152 B5
Butterfield Sq 10 E6 . . . .100 B1
Butterfields E17 . . . . .54 A4
Butterfly La SE9 . . . . .166 D5
Butterfly Wlk 2 SE5 . . . .139 B4
Butteridges Ct RM9 . . . . .103 B6
Buttermere NW1 . . . . .231 D2
Buttermere CI E11 . . . . . . .76 B4
  SE1 . . . . .263 C3
  East Bedfont TW14 . . . . .149 D3
  West Barnes SM4 . . . . . .200 D3
Buttermere Ct NW8 . . . . .229 C3
Buttermere Dr SW15 . . . .157 A6
Buttermere Ho 11 E3 . . . .97 B4
  N12 . . . . .30 C5
Buttermere Wlk 9 E8 . . . .73 D2
Butterwick W6 . . . . .112 C2
Butterworth Gdns IG8 . . .37 A5
Buttesland St N1 95 B4 235 D2
Buttfield CI RM10 . . . . .81 D2
Buttmarsh CI SE18 . . . . . .122 C1
Buttsbury Rd IG1 . . . . .79 A3
Buttermere Wlk 9 E8 . . . .73 D2
Butts Cotts TW13 . . . . . . .151 B1
Butts Cres TW13 . . . . . . .151 C1
Butts Ho TW13 . . . . .151 C1
Butts Piece UB5 . . . . .84 B5
Butts Rd BR1 . . . . .186 C5
Butts The TW8 . . . . .131 D6
Buttsbury Rd IG1 . . . . .79 A3
Buxlow Prep Sch HA9 . . . .66 A5
Buxted Rd E8 . . . . .73 D1
  N12 . . . . .30 C5
  SE22 . . . . .139 C1
Buxton CI IG8 . . . . .37 D4
Buxton Cres SM3 . . . .217 A4
Buxton Ct N1 . . . . . . .235 B2

Buxton Dr E11 . . . . .54 C5
  Kingston u T KT3 . . . . . .177 B1
Buxton Gdns W3 . . . . . . .110 C6
Buxton Ho E11 . . . . .54 C5
  3 SW11 . . . . .136 B1
Buxton Lo E11 . . . . .77 B6
Buxton Rd E4 . . . . .20 A4
  E6 . . . . .100 A4
  E15 . . . . .76 C3
  E17 . . . . .53 A5
  N19 . . . . .49 D1
  NW2 . . . . .68 B2
  SW14 . . . . .133 C2
  Ilford IG2 . . . . .57 C3
  Thornton Heath CR7 . . . .204 D4
Buxton St E1 . . . .96 A3 243 D5
Buzzard Creek Ind Est
  IG11 . . . . .102 A2
Byam Shaw Sch of Art
  N19 . . . . .71 C6
Byam St SW6 . . . . .136 A3
Byards Croft SW16 . . . . .181 D2
Byards Ct SE16 . . . . .118 C3
Byas Ho 3 E3 . . . . .97 B4
Byatt Wlk TW12 . . . . .173 A6
Bychurch End 9 TW11 174 D5
Bycroft Rd UB1 . . . . .85 C3
Bycroft St SE20 . . . . .184 D3
Bycullah Ave EN2 . . . . .4 D3
Bycullah Rd EN2 . . . . .4 D3
Bye The W3 . . . . .89 C1
Bye Way The HA3 . . . . . . .24 D2
Bye Ways TW2 . . . . .151 D1
Byefield CI SE16 . . . . .119 A4
Byelands CI 12 SE16 . . . .118 D5
Byeway The SW14 . . . . . .133 A2
Byeways The KT5 . . . . . . .198 D4
Byfeld Gdns SW13 . . . . . .134 A4
Byfield Ct KT3 . . . . .200 B5
Byfield Rd TW7 . . . . .131 A2
Byford CI E15 . . . . .76 C1
Bygrove CR0 . . . . .223 D1
Bygrove Ct SW19 . . . . . . .180 B4
Bygrove Prim Sch E14 . . .97 C1
Bygrove Rd SW19 . . . . . .180 B4
Bygrove St E14 . . . . .97 C1
Byland CI N21 . . . . .16 B4
  SE2 . . . . .124 B3
Byne Rd SE26 . . . . .184 C5
  Carshalton SM5 . . . . . . .218 C6
Bynes Rd CR2 . . . . .221 B1
Byng PI WC1 . . . .93 D3 239 C5
Byng St E14 . . . . .119 C4
Bynon Ave DA7 . . . . .147 B2
Byre Rd N14 . . . . .15 B5
Byrne Ho 11 SW2 . . . . . . .160 B6
Byrne Rd SW12 . . . . .159 B2
Byron Ave E12 . . . . .78 A2
  E18 . . . . .36 D1
  NW9 . . . . .44 D6
  Carshalton SM1 . . . . . . .218 B4
  Cranford TW4 . . . . .128 B3
  West Barnes KT3 . . . . . .200 A4
Byron Ave E SM1 . . . . . . .218 B4
Byron CI E8 . . . . .96 A6
  SE26 . . . . .185 A6
  SE28 . . . . .124 C5
  Hampton TW12 . . . . . . .173 B6
  Walton-on-T KT12 . . . . .195 A1
Byron Court Prim Sch
  HA0 . . . . .65 C4
Byron Ct 11 E11 . . . . .55 A5
  E18 . . . . .37 B2
  3 NW6 . . . . .70 A1
  SE21 . . . . .162 A3
  SW3 . . . . .257 B3
  W7 . . . . .109 A2
  W9 . . . . .91 C3
  WC1 . . . . .240 C6
  Enfield EN2 . . . . .4 D3
  Harrow HA1 . . . . .42 C3
  1 Richmond TW10 . . . . .175 D6
  South Norwood CR7 . . . .183 A1
Byron Dr N2 . . . . .48 B3
  Erith DA8 . . . . .147 D5
Byron Gdns SM1 . . . . .218 B4
Byron Hill Rd HA1,HA2 . . .64 C6
Byron Ho 5 BR3 . . . . .185 D4
Byron Mews NW3 . . . . . . .70 C4
Byron Par UB10 . . . . .83 A3
Byron Rd E10 . . . . .53 D1
  E17 . . . . .53 C6
  NW2 . . . . .68 B6
  NW7 . . . . .28 A5
  W5 . . . . .110 B5
  Harrow HA1 . . . . .42 C4
  Harrow HA3 . . . . .24 D1
  Wembley HA0 . . . . .65 C5
Byron St E14 . . . . .98 A1
Byron Way Hayes UB4 . . .83 D3
  Northolt UB5 . . . . .85 A4
  West Drayton UB7 . . . . .104 B2
Bysouth CI N15 . . . . .51 B5
Bythorn St SW9 . . . . .138 B1
Byton Rd SW17 . . . . .180 D4
Byward Ave TW14 . . . . . .150 C5
Byward St EC3 . .117 C6 253 B5
Bywater Ho SE18 . . . . . . .122 A3
Bywater PI SE16 . . . . .119 A5
Bywater St
  SW3 . . . . .114 D1 257 C2
Byways The KT19 . . . . . . .215 D4
Bywell PI W1 . . . . .239 A3
Bywood Ave CR0 . . . . . . .206 D3
Bywood Terr CR0 . . . . . . .206 D3
Byworth Wlk N19 . . . . . . .50 A1

C

Cabbell St NW1 .92 C2 237 A3
Cabinet Off SW1 . . . . .250 A2
Cabinet War Rooms*
  SW1 . . . . .115 D4 249 D2
Cable Ho WC1 . . . . . . .234 A2
Cable PI SE10 . . . . .142 A4
Cable St E1 . . . . .118 B6
Cabot Ct SE16 . . . . .118 D3
Cabot Sq E14 . . . . .119 C5
Cabot Way 3 E6 . . . . .99 D2
Cabul Rd SW11 . . . . .136 C3
Cactus CI SE5 . . . . .139 C3
Cadbury CI
  Ashford TW16 . . . . .171 C3
  Isleworth TW7 . . . . .131 A4
Cadbury Rd TW16 . . . . . .171 C4
Cadbury Way 1 SE16 . . .118 A2
Caddington CI EN4 . . . . . .14 C6
Caddington Rd NW2 . . . . .69 A5
Caddis CI HA7 . . . . .24 D3
Cade Rd SE10 . . . . .142 B4
Cade Tyler Ho 10 SE10 . .142 A4
Cadell CI E2 . . . . .95 D5
Cadell Ho 12 E2 . . . . .95 D5
Cader Rd SW18 . . . . .158 A5
Cadet Dr SE1 . . . .117 D1 263 D2
Cadet PI SE10 . . . . .120 C1
Cadiz St SE17 . . . .117 A1 262 B1
Cadley Terr SE23 . . . . . . .162 C2
Cadmer CI KT3 . . . . .199 C5
Cadmore Ho 4 N1 . . . . . . .72 C1
Cadmus CI 5 SW4 . . . . . .138 C4
Cadnam Point 15 SW15 156 B3
Cadogan CI E9 . . . . .75 B1
  Beckenham BR3 . . . . . . .186 B1
  Harrow HA2 . . . . .63 D4
  Teddington TW11 . . . . . .174 C5
Cadogan Ct SW3 . . . . .257 C3
  Sutton SM2 . . . . .217 D2
  KT3 . . . . .199 C5
Cadogan Ct Gdns SW1 .258 A4
Cadogan Gate
  SW1 . . . . .114 D2 257 D4
Cadogan Gdns E18 . . . . . .55 B6
  N3 . . . . .29 C2
  N21 . . . . .16 C6
  SW3 . . . . .114 D2 257 D3
Cadogan Ho SW3 . . . .266 D5
Cadogan La
  SW1 . . . . .115 A3 258 A5
Cadogan PI
  SW1 . . . . .114 D3 257 D5
Cadogan Rd SE18 . . . . . . .123 A3
  Kingston u T KT6 . . . . . .197 D4
Cadogan Sq
  SW1 . . . . .114 D3 257 D5
Cadogan St
  SW3 . . . . .114 D2 257 C3
Cadogan Terr E9 . . . . .75 B1
Cadoxton Ave 3 N15 . . . .51 D3
Cadwallon Rd SE9 . . . . . .167 A2
Caedmon Rd N7 . . . . .72 B4
Caerleon CI DA14 . . . . . . .190 C5
Caerleon Terr SE2 . . . . . .124 B2
Caernarvon CI CR4 . . . . . .204 A6
Caernarvon Ct 3 KT5 . . . .198 B4
Caernarvon Ho
  SW1 . . . . .256 A2
Caesar's Way TW17 . . . . .193 B3
Caesars Wlk CR4 . . . . . . .202 D4
Cahill St EC1 . . . . .242 B5
Cahir St E14 . . . . .119 D2
Cain Ct 2 W5 . . . . .87 C2
Caine Ho W3 . . . . .110 D4
Cain's La TW14 . . . . .149 C6
Caird St W10 . . . . .91 B4
Cairn Ave W5 . . . . .109 D5
Cairn Way HA7 . . . . .24 D4
Cairndale CI BR1 . . . . . . .186 D3
Cairnfield Ave NW2 . . . . . .67 D5
Cairnfield Ct NW2 . . . . . . .67 C5
Cairns Ho 3 N7 . . . . .72 B4
Cairns Rd SW11 . . . . .158 C6
Cairo New Rd CR0 . . . . . .220 D6
Cairo Rd E17 . . . . .53 C5
Caister Ho N7 . . . . .72 B2
  10 SW2 . . . . .159 B4
Caister Ho 5 E15 . . . . .98 D6
Caistor Mews SW12 . . . . .159 B4
Caistor Park Rd E15 . . . . . .98 D6
Caistor Rd SW12 . . . . . . .159 B4
Caithness Ho N1 . . . . .233 C6
Caithness Gdns DA15 . . .167 D5
Caithness Rd W14 . . . . . .112 D3
  Mitcham CR4 . . . . .181 B3
Calabria Rd N5 . . . . .72 D2
Calais Gate SE5 . . . . .138 D4
Calais St SE5 . . . . .138 D4
Calbourne Rd SW12 . . . . .159 A4
Calcott Wlk SE9 . . . . .187 D6
Calcraft Ho 10 E2 . . . . . . .96 C5
Caldbeck Ave KT4 . . . . . .200 B1
Caldecot Ct SE5 . . . . .139 A3
Caldecot Rd SE5 . . . . .139 A3
Caldecote 11 KT1 . . . . . .176 C1
Caldecote Gdns WD2 . . . . .8 C4
Caldecott Way E5 . . . . . . .74 D6
Calder Ave UB6 . . . . .86 D5
Calder CI EN1 . . . . .5 C5
Calder Ct SE16 . . . . .119 B5
Calder Gdns HA8 . . . . .44 C6
Calder Rd SM4 . . . . .202 A4
Calderon Ho NW8 . . . .230 A4
Calderon PI W10 . . . . .90 C2

Calderon Rd E11 . . . . .76 B5
Caldervale Rd SW4 . . . . . .159 D6
Calderwood St SE18 . . . .122 C2
Caldew Ct NW7 . . . . .28 A3
Caldew St SE5 . . . . .139 B5
Caldicote Gn NW9 . . . . . . .45 C3
Caldwell Rd WD1 . . . . .22 C2
Caldwell St
  SW9 . . . . .138 B5 270 D3
Caldy Rd DA17 . . . . .125 D3
Caldy Wlk 15 N1 . . . . .73 A2
Cale St SW3 . . . .114 C1 257 A2
Caleb St SE1 . . . . .252 B2
Caledon Rd E6 . . . . .78 B1
  Carshalton SM5,SM6 . . .219 A4
Caledonia Ct IG11 . . . . . .102 C5
Caledonia Ho 17 E14 . . . .97 A1
Caledonia Rd TW19 . . . . .148 A3
Caledonia St N1 . . . . .233 B3
Caledonian CI 3 IG3 . . . . .58 B1
Caledonian Market
  SE1 . . . . .117 C3 263 B6
Caledonian Rd
  N1 . . . . .94 B6 233 C5
  N7 . . . . .72 B2
Caledonian Road &
  Barnsbury Sta N7 . . . . . . .72 B1
Caledonian Road Sta N7 72 B2
Caledonian Wharf Rd
  E14 . . . . .120 B2
Caletock Way SE10 . . . . .120 D1
Calgarth NW1 . . . . . . .232 B3
Calgary Ct 24 SE16 . . . . .118 C4
Caliban Twr 3 N1 . . . . . . .95 C5
Calico Ho 4 SW11 . . . . . .136 A2
Calico Row 5 SW11 . . . . .136 A2
Calidore CI SW2 . . . . .160 B5
California La WD2 . . . . .8 B3
California Rd KT3 . . . . . . .199 A6
Callaby Terr 11 N1 . . . . . .73 B2
Callaghan Ct SW3 . . . . . .142 C1
Callahan Cotts 8 E1 . . . . .96 C2
Callander Rd SE6 . . . . . . .164 A2
Callanders The WD2 . . . . . .8 C3
Callard Ave N13 . . . . .32 D6
Callcott Ct NW6 . . . . .69 B1
Callcott Rd NW6 . . . . .69 B1
Callcott St W8 . . . . . . .245 A4
Callendar Rd SW7 . . . .256 C6
Callingham CI 7 E14 . . . . .97 B2
Callingham Ho 1 SW4 138 C4
Callis Farm CI TW19 . . . . .148 A5
Callis Rd E17 . . . . .53 B3
Callonfield 3 E17 . . . . .53 A5
Callow St SW3 . .136 B6 266 C6
Calmington Rd SE5 . . . . . .139 C6
Calmont Rd BR1 . . . . .186 C4
Calmore Mews SE15 . . . .140 B4
Calonne Rd SW19 . . . . . .178 D6
Calshot Ho N1 . . . . . . .233 A2
Calshot Rd TW6 . . . . .126 C3
Calshot St N1 . . .94 B5 233 C3
Calshot Way Enfield EN2 . .4 D2
  Harlington TW6 . . . . .126 C3
Calstock NW1 . . . . . . .232 C5
Calstock Ho SE11 . . . .261 B2
Calthorpe Gdns
  Edgware HA8 . . . . .26 B5
  Sutton SM1 . . . . .218 A5
Calthorpe St
  WC1 . . . . .94 B3 240 D6
Calton Ave SE21 . . . . .161 C5
Calton Rd EN5 . . . . .14 B5
Calver 13 NW5 . . . . .71 B4
Calver Ct E17 . . . . .54 B6
Calverley CI BR3 . . . . .185 D4
Calverley Cres RM10 . . . . .81 C6
Calverley Gr N19 . . . . .49 D1
Calverley Rd KT17 . . . . . .216 A2
Calvert Ave E2 . . . . .95 C4
Calvert CI
  Belvedere DA17 . . . . . . .125 D2
  Ruxley DA14 . . . . .191 A4
Calvert Ct 11 N19 . . . . . . .49 C1
  5 Richmond TW9 . . . . .132 B1
Calvert Ho 9 W12 . . . . . .112 B6
Calvert Rd SE10 . . . . .120 D1
Calvert St NW1 . .93 A6 231 A6
Calverton SE5 . . . . .139 C6
Calverton Prim Sch E16 . .99 D1
Calverton Rd E6 . . . . .100 C4
Calvert's Bldgs SE1 . . .252 C3
Calvin St E1 . . . . .95 D3 243 C5
Calydon Rd SE7 . . . . .121 B1
Calypso Way SE8,SE16 . .119 B2
Cam Ct 2 SE15 . . . . .139 D6
Cam Rd E15 . . . . .98 B6
Camac Rd TW2 . . . . .152 B3
Camarthen Gn NW9 . . . . . .45 C3
Cambalt Ho 3 SW15 . . . .156 D6
Cambalt Rd SW15 . . . . . .156 D6
Cambell Jun Sch RM9 . . . .80 D1
Cambell Wlk N1 . . . . . .233 B6
Camber Ho 4 SE15 . . . . .140 C6
Camberley Ave SW20 . . . .178 B1
  Enfield EN1 . . . . .5 C1
Camberley CI SM3 . . . . . .216 D5
Camberley Ct 3 SM2 . . . .217 D1
Camberley Ho NW1 . . .231 D3
Camberley Rd TW6 . . . . . .126 C3
Cambert Way SE9 . . . . . . .143 B1
Camberwell Church St
  SE5 . . . . .139 B4
Camberwell Coll of Arts
  SE5 . . . . .139 C4
  SE15 . . . . .139 D5
Camberwell Glebe SE5 . .139 C4
Camberwell Gn SE5 . . . . .139 B4

Camberwell Gr SE5 . . . .139 C3
Camberwell Green SE5 139 A4
Camberwell New Rd
  SW9 . . . . .138 D5
Camberwell Rd SE5 . . . . .139 A5
Camberwell Station Rd
  SE5 . . . . .139 A4
Camberwell Trad Est
  SE5 . . . . .139 A4
Cambeys Rd RM10 . . . . . . .81 D3
Cambisgate SW19 . . . . . .179 A5
Camborne Ave W13 . . . . .109 C4
Camborne Ct TW6 . . . . . .126 C2
Camborne Cres TW6 . . . .126 C2
Camborne Rd SW18 . . . . .157 C4
  Belmont SM2 . . . . .217 D1
  Bexley DA16 . . . . .145 D3
  Croydon CR0 . . . . .206 A2
  Sidcup DA14 . . . . .168 C1
  West Barnes SM4 . . . . . .200 D4
Camborne Rd S TW6 . . . .126 C2
Camborne Way
  Harmondsworth TW6 . . .126 C2
  Heston TW5 . . . . .129 C4
Cambourne Ave N9 . . . . . .18 D4
Cambourne Mews 6
  W11 . . . . .91 A1
Cambray Rd SW12 . . . . . .159 C3
  Broom Hill BR3 . . . . .211 D2
Cambria 6 BR3 . . . . .185 D1
Cambria CI
  Hounslow TW3 . . . . .129 C1
  Sidcup DA15 . . . . .167 C3
Cambria Ct TW14 . . . . . . .150 B4
Cambria Gdns TW19 . . . .148 A4
Cambria Ho 16 E14 . . . . . .97 A1
Cambria Rd SE5 . . . . .139 A2
  SE26 . . . . .184 A6
Cambria St
  SW6 . . . . .135 D5 265 D3
Cambrian Ave IG2 . . . . . . .57 C4
Cambrian Cl SE27 . . . . . .160 D1
Cambrian Ct UB2 . . . . . . .107 D2
Cambrian Gn NW9 . . . . . . .45 C4
Cambrian Rd E10 . . . . .53 C1
  Richmond TW10 . . . . . . .154 B5
Cambridge Ave NW6 . . . . .91 C5
  Greenford UB6 . . . . .64 D3
  Kingston u T KT3,KT2 . . .177 D1
  New Malden KT3 . . . . . .199 C5
  Richmond TW9 . . . . .132 C5
  Sidcup DA14 . . . . .189 C6
  Southall UB1 . . . . .107 A5
  Teddington TW11 . . . . . .175 A5
  Twickenham TW1 . . . . . .153 D5
  Walton-on-T KT12 . . . . .195 A1
Cambridge Rd N W4 . . . . .110 D1
Cambridge Rd S 3 W4 110 D1
Cambridge Row SE18 . . . .122 D1
Cambridge Sch W6 . . . . .112 B2
Cambridge Sq
  W2 . . . . .92 C1 237 A2
Cambridge St
  SW1 . . . . .115 C1 259 A2
Cambridge Terr N9 . . . . . .17 D4
  NW1 . . . . .231 C1
Cambridge Terr Mews
  NW1 . . . . .231 D1
Cambstone CI N11 . . . . . .15 A2
Cambus CI UB4 . . . . .85 A2
Cambus Rd E16 . . . . .99 A2
Camdale Rd SE18 . . . . .145 D5
Camden Ave
  Feltham TW13 . . . . .150 C3
  Hayes UB4 . . . . .106 D6
Camden CI BR7 . . . . .189 A2
Camden Ct 5 DA17 . . . . .125 C1
Camden Gdns NW1 . . . . . .71 B1
  South Norwood CR7 . . . .204 D6
  Sutton SM1 . . . . .217 D3
Camden Gr BR7 . . . . .188 D4
Camden High St
  NW1 . . . . .93 C6 232 A5
Camden Hill Rd SE19 . . . .183 C4
Camden Ho 6 SE8 . . . . . .119 B6
Camden Jun Sch SM5 . . .218 D4
Camden Lock PI NW1 . . . .71 B1
Camden Mews 71 D2
Camden Mkt*
  NW1 . . . . .93 B6 231 D6
Camden Park Rd NW1 . . . .71 D2
  Chislehurst West BR7 . . .188 C3
Camden Pas N1 .94 D6 234 C5
Camden Rd E11 . . . . .55 B3
  E17 . . . . .53 B6
  NW1 . . . . .71 D2 231 D6
  Carshalton SM5 . . . . . . .218 D4
  Sidcup DA5 . . . . .169 B4
  Sutton SM1 . . . . .217 D3
Camden Road Sta NW1 . .71 C1
Camden Row SE3 . . . . . .142 C3
Camden Sch for Girls The
  NW5 . . . . .71 C2
Camden Sq NW1 . . . . .71 D2
  SE15 . . . . .140 C4
Camden St NW1 . .93 C6 232 B5
Camden Studios NW1 . .232 B5
Camden Town Sta
  NW1 . . . . .93 B6 231 D6
Camden Way
  Chislehurst West BR7 . . .188 C3
  South Norwood CR7 . . . .204 D6
Camden Wlk N1 . . . . . .234 C5
Camdenhurst St E14 . . . . .97 A1
Cameford Ct 20 SW12 . . .160 A4
Camel CI KT2 . . . . .175 D5
Camel Ct HA9 . . . . .66 C6
Camel Rd E16 . . . . .121 D5
Camelford NW1 . . . . . .232 B3
Camelford Ct 7 W11 . . . . .91 A1
Camelford Wlk 8 W11 . . . .91 A1
Camelia Ct IG8 . . . . .36 C4
Camelia Ct 20 BR3 . . . . . .185 D1
Camellia Ho SE8 . . . . .141 B5
Camellia PI TW2 . . . . .151 D4
Camellia St SW8 . . . . .270 A3
Camelot CI SE18 . . . . .123 B4
  SW19 . . . . .179 C6
Camelot Ho N1 . . . . .71 D2
Camelot Prim Sch SE15 140 B6
Camera PI SW10 . . . . . .266 C6
Cameret Ct 6 W11 . . . . . .112 C4
Cameron CI N18 . . . . .34 B5
  N20 . . . . .14 C2
Cameron Ct 3 SW19 . . . .157 A3
Cameron Ho NW8 . . . .230 A4
  SE5 . . . . .139 A4
  8 Bromley BR1 . . . . . . .186 D2
Cameron Lo TW3 . . . . . . .130 A1
Cameron Rd SE6 . . . . .163 B2
  Hayes BR2 . . . . .209 A4
  Ilford IG3 . . . . .57 C1
  Thornton Heath CR0 . . . .204 D3
Cameron Sq CR4 . . . . . . .180 C2
Camerton CI 8 E8 . . . . . . .73 D2
Camfrey Ct N8 . . . . .50 A5
Camgate Ctr The TW19 148 B4
Camilla CI TW16 . . . . .171 D4
Camilla Ct 14 SM2 . . . . . .217 C1
Camilla Rd SE16 . . . . .118 B2
Camille CI SE25 . . . . .206 A6
Camlan Rd BR1 . . . . .186 D6
Camlet St E2 . . . . .243 C6
Camlet Way TW4 . . . . . . .128 D4
Camley St NW1 . .93 D5 232 D4
Camm Gdns
  5 Kingston u T KT1 . . . .176 C1
  Thames Ditton KT7 . . . . .196 C2
Camomile Ave CR4 . . . . . .180 C2
Camomile St EC3 95 C1 243 B2
Camomile Way UB7 . . . . . .82 A1
Camp Rd SW19 . . . . .178 C6
Camp Site The BR8 . . . . .191 C3

Camp View SW19 178 B5
Campaign Ct W9 91 B3
Campana Rd
SW6 135 C4 265 B2
Campbell Ave IG6 57 A5
Campbell Cl SE18 144 C4
SW16 181 D6
Ruislip HA4 40 A3
Twickenham TW2 152 B3
Campbell Croft HA8 26 C5
Campbell Ct N17 33 D2
NW9 45 A3
SE21 162 A3
SW7 256 A5
W7 108 C6
Campbell Gordon Way
NW2 68 B4
Campbell Ho SW1 259 A1
W2 236 C5
30 W12 112 B6
6 Wallington SM6 219 B4
Campbell Rd E3 97 C4
E6 100 A6
E15 76 D4
E17 53 B5
N17 34 A2
W7 108 C6
Thornton Heath CR0 204 D3
Twickenham TW2 152 B2
Campdale Rd N7 71 D5
Campden Cres
Dagenham RM8 80 C4
Wembley HA0 65 B5
Campden Gr
W8 113 C4 245 B2
Campden Hill
W8 113 C4 245 A2
Campden Hill Ct W8 245 B2
Campden Hill Gate W8 245 A2
Campden Hill Gdns W8 245 A4
Campden Hill Mans
W8 245 B4
Campden Hill Pl W14 244 D4
Campden Hill Rd
W8 113 C4 245 A2
Campden Hill Sq
W14 113 B5 244 D4
Campden Ho 4 NW6 70 B1
W8 245 B3
Campden Hos W8 245 A3
Campden House Cl W8 245 B2
Campden Rd
Ickenham UB10 60 B4
South Croydon CR2 221 C3
Campden St
W8 113 C5 245 A3
Campe Ho 1 N10 31 A3
Campen Cl SW19 157 A2
Camperdown St E1 243 D1
Campfield Rd SE9 165 D4
Campion Cl E6 122 B6
Harrow HA3 44 B3
Hillingdon UB8 82 B2
South Croydon CR2 221 C4
Campion Ct 10 HA0 88 A5
Campion Ho 15 N16 73 C3
Campion House (Seminary)
TW7 130 B4
Campion Pl SE28 124 B5
Campion Rd SW15 156 C6
Hounslow TW7 130 D4
Campion Terr NW2 68 D5
Campion Way HA8 27 A6
Camplin Rd HA3 44 A4
Camplin St SE14 140 D5
Campsbourne Ho 3 N8 50 A5
Campsbourne Jun & Inf Schs
N8 50 A5
Campsbourne Rd N8 50 A5
N8 50 A6
Campsbourne The N8 50 A5
Campsey Gdns RM9 80 B1
Campsey Rd RM9 80 B1
Campsfield Ho N8 50 A6
Campsfield Rd N8 50 A6
Campshill Pl SE13 164 A6
Campshill Rd SE13 164 A6
Campton Hill Twrs W8 245 A4
Campus Rd E17 53 B3
Camrose Ave
Edgware HA8 26 B2
Erith DA8 147 D6
Feltham TW13 172 C6
Camrose Cl Croydon CR0 207 A2
Morden SM4 201 C5
Camrose St SE2 124 A2
Camsey Ho 8 SW2 160 B6
Canada Ave N18 33 A4
Canada Cres W3 89 A3
Canada Gdns SE13 164 A6
Canada Rd W3 89 A2
Canada Sq E14 119 D5
Canada St SE16 118 D4
Canada Way W12 112 B6
Canadian Ave SE6 163 D3
Canal App SE8 141 A6
Canal Bridge SE15 140 A6
Canal Cl E1 97 A3
W10 90 D3
Canal Gr SE15 140 B6
Canal Path 22 E2 95 D6
Canal Rd E1 97 A3
Canal St SE5 139 B6
Canal Way W10 90 D3
Canal Wlk N1 95 B6 235 D6
SE26 184 C5
Croydon CR0 205 D3
Canalside Studios 31 N1 95 C6
Canary Wharf★ E14 119 D5
Canary Wharf Pier (River
Bus) E14 119 B5
Canary Wharf Sta E14 119 C5
Canberra Cl NW4 46 A6
Canberra Dr UB4 84 C4
Canberra Prim Schs
W12 112 B6
Canberra Rd E6 100 B6
SE7 143 D6
Bexley DA7 146 D6
Harlington TW6 126 C2
Canbury Ave KT2 176 B2
Canbury Bsns Pk 3
KT2 176 A2
Canbury Ct KT2 176 A3
Canbury Mews SE26 162 A1
Canbury Park Rd KT2 176 B2
Cancell Rd SW9 138 C4
Candahar Rd SW11 136 C3
Candida Ct 9 NW1 71 B1
Candishe Ho SE1 253 C2
Candler St N15 51 B3
Candover St W1 239 A3
Candy St E3 97 B6
Cane Cl SM6 220 A1
Caney Mews NW2 68 D6
Canfield Dr HA4 62 B3
Canfield Gdns NW6 69 D1
Canfield Ho N15 51 C3
Canfield Pl NW6 70 A2
Canford Ave UB5 85 A6
Canford Cl EN2 4 C3
Canford Gdns KT3 199 C3
Canford Pl TW11 175 C4
Canford Rd SW11 159 A6
Canham Rd SE25 205 C6
W3 111 C4
Canmore Gdns SW16 181 C3
Cann Hall Prim Sch E11 76 D5
Cann Hall Rd E11 76 D4
Canning Cres N22 32 B2
Canning Cross SE5 139 C3
Canning Ct N22 32 B2
Canning Ho 23 W12 112 B6
Canning Pas
W8 114 A3 256 A6
Canning Pl W8 114 A3 256 A6
Canning Pl Mews W8 256 A6
Canning Rd E15 98 C5
E17 53 A6
N5 72 D5
Croydon CR0 221 D6
Harrow HA3 42 D6
Canning Town E16 98 C2
Canning Town Sta E16 98 C2
Cannington 14 NW5 71 A2
Cannington Rd RM9 80 C2
Cannizaro Rd SW19 178 D5
Cannock Ho N4 51 B2
Cannock Lo EN1 17 C5
Cannon Cl SW20 200 C6
Hampton TW12 173 D4
Cannon Dr E14 119 C6
Cannon Hill N14 16 A1
NW6 69 C3
Cannon Hill La SM4,
SW20 201 A5
Cannon Hill Mews N14 16 A1
Cannon Ho SE11 260 D3
SE26 184 B4
Cannon La NW3 70 B5
Pinner HA5 41 A3
Cannon Pl NW3 70 B5
SE7 122 A1
Cannon Rd N14 16 A1
Erith DA7 147 B4
Cannon St EC4 117 B6 252 B6
Cannon Street Rd E1 96 B1
Cannon Street Sta
EC4 117 B6 252 C6
Cannon Trad Est HA9 66 D4
Cannon Way KT8 195 D5
Cannon Wharf Bsns Ctr 12
SE8 119 A2
Cannonbury Ave HA5 40 D3
Canon Ave RM6 58 C4
Canon Barnett CE Prim Sch
E1 95 D1 243 D2
Canon Beck Rd SE16 118 C4
Canon Lane Fst & Mid Schs
HA5 40 D3
Canon Mohan Cl N14 15 B5
Canon Murnane Rd
SE1 263 C5
Canon Palmer RC High Sch
IG3 57 C1
Canon Rd BR1 209 D6
Canon Row
SW1 116 A4 250 A1
Canon St N1 95 A6 235 A5
Canonbie Rd SE23 162 C4
Canonbury Cres N1 73 A1
Canonbury Ct 21 N1 72 D1
Canonbury Gr N1 73 A1
Canonbury La N1 72 D1
Canonbury Pk N N1 73 A2
Canonbury Pk S N1 73 A2
Canonbury Pl N1 72 D2
Canonbury Prim Sch N1 72 D2
Canonbury Rd N1 72 D1
Enfield EN1 5 C4
Canonbury Sq N1 72 D1
Canonbury St N1 73 A1
Canonbury Sta N1,N5 73 A3
Canonbury Villas N1 72 D1
Canons Cl N2 48 B2
Edgware HA8 26 B4
Canons Cnr HA8 26 A6
Canons Ct HA8 26 B4
Canons Dr HA8 26 B4
Canons High Sch HA8 26 B1
Canons L Ctr The CR4 202 D5
Canons Park Cl HA8 26 A3
Canons Park Sta HA8 26 A3
Canon's Wlk CR0 222 D5
Canonsleigh Rd RM9 80 B1
Canopus Way
Eastbury HA6 22 A6
Stanwell TW19 148 A4
Canrobert St E2 96 B4
Cantelowes Ho EN5 12 D6
Cantelowes Rd NW1 71 D2
Canterbury SE13 164 A6
Canterbury Ave
Redbridge IG1 56 A2
Sidcup DA14,DA15 168 C2
Canterbury Cl 7 E6 100 B1
18 SE5 139 A3
Beckenham BR3 185 D2
Southall UB6 85 D2
Canterbury Cres SW9 138 C2
Canterbury Ct NW6 91 C5
15 NW9 27 D1
NW11 47 A3
Ashford TW15 170 B6
South Croydon CR2 221 A1
Canterbury Gr SE27,
SW16 160 C1
Canterbury Ho 6 E3 97 D4
SE1 260 D6
2 Barking IG11 80 A1
Canterbury Ind Pk 15
SE15 140 C6
Canterbury Mans NW6 69 D2
Canterbury Pl SE17 261 D3
Canterbury Rd E10 54 A3
NW6 91 C5
Feltham TW13 151 A2
Harrow HA1,HA2 42 A4
Morden SM4 202 A3
Thornton Heath CR0 204 C2
Canterbury Terr NW6 91 C5
Cantium Ret Pk SE1 140 A6
Cantley Gdns SE19 183 D2
Ilford IG2 57 A3
Cantley Rd W7 109 A3
Canton St E14 97 C1
Cantrell Rd E3 97 C3
Cantwell Ho SE18 144 D5
Cantwell Rd SE18 144 D5
Canute Ct SW16 160 C1
Canute Gdns SE16 118 D2
Canvey St SE1 252 A4
Cape Cl IG11 78 D1
Cape Rd N17 52 A6
Capel KT5 198 B2
Capel Ave SM6 220 B3
Capel Cl N20 14 A1
Keston Mark BR2 210 A1
Capel Ct SE20 184 C2
Capel Gdns Ilford IG3 79 D4
Pinner HA5 41 B5
Capel Ho 17 E9 74 C1
South Oxhey WD1 22 D6
Capel Lo 12 SW2 160 B4
5 Richmond TW9 132 B4
Capel Point E7 77 B4
Capel Rd E7,E12 77 C4
East Barnet EN4 14 C5
Capella Ho SE7 143 B6
Capener's Cl SW1 248 A1
Capern Rd SW18 158 A3
Capital Bsns Ctr HA0 87 D5
Capital Ind Est CR4 202 D4
Capital Interchange Way
TW8 110 C1
Capital Wharf 15 E1 118 A5
Capitol Way NW9 45 A6
Caplan Est CR4 181 C2
Capland Ho NW8 236 D6
Capland St NW8 92 B3 236 D6
Caple Ho SW10 266 B4
Caple Rd NW10 89 D5
Capper St WC1 93 C3 239 B5
Caprea Cl UB4 84 D2
Capri Ho E17 35 B1
Capri Rd CR0 205 D2
Capricorn Ctr RM8 59 B2
Capstan Cl RM6 58 B3
Capstan Ho 5 E14 120 A2
Capstan Rd SE8 119 B2
Capstan Ride EN2 4 C3
Capstan Sq E14 120 A4
Capstan Way SE16 119 A5
Capstone Rd BR1 186 D6
Capthorne Ave HA2 41 B1
Capuchin Cl HA7 25 B4
Capulet Mews 1 E16 121 A5
Capworth St E10 53 D2
Caradoc Cl W2 91 C1
Caradoc Evans Cl 1 N11 31 B5
Caradoc St SE10 120 C1
Caradon Ct E11 54 C1
7 Twickenham TW1 153 C5
Caradon Way N15 51 B5
Caravel Cl E14 119 C3
Caravel Mews 14 SE8 141 C6
Caravelle Gdns 1 UB5 84 D4
Caraway Cl E13 99 B2
Caraway Hts E14 120 A6
Caraway Pl SM6 219 B5
Carberry Rd 12 SE19 183 C4
Carbery Ave W3 110 B4
Carbis Cl E4 20 B3
Carbis Rd E14 97 B1
Carbroke Ho 10 E9 96 C6
Carburton St W1 93 B3 238 D5
Cardale St 1 E14 120 A3
Carden Rd SE15 140 B2
Cardiff Ho 9 SE15 140 A6
Cardiff Rd W7 109 A3
Enfield EN3 6 B1
Cardiff St SE18 145 C5
Cardigan Ct 8 W7 86 D3
Cardigan Gdns IG3 80 A6
Cardigan Rd E3 97 B5
SW13 134 A3
SW19 180 A4
Richmond TW10 154 A5
Cardigan St
SE11 116 C1 261 A2
Cardigan Wlk 12 N1 73 A1
Cardinal Ave
Kingston u T KT2 176 A4
West Barnes SM4 201 A3
Cardinal Bourne St
SE1 262 D5
Cardinal Cap Alley SE1 252 A4
Cardinal Cl Burnt Oak HA8 27 B3
Chislehurst BR7 189 B2
West Barnes SM4 201 A3
Worcester Pk KT19,KT4 216 A4
Cardinal Cres KT3 177 A1
Cardinal Dr KT12 194 D1
Cardinal Hinsley RC High Sch
(Boys) NW10 90 A6
Cardinal Pl SW15 134 D1
Cardinal Pole Sch (Lower)
E9 74 D1
Cardinal Pole Sch (Upper)
E9 75 A3
Cardinal Rd
Feltham TW13 150 B3
Ruislip HA4 40 D1
Cardinal Road Inf Sch
TW13 150 B3
Cardinal Vaughan Memorial
Sch W14 244 A2
Cardinal Way HA3 42 C6
Cardinal Wiseman RC High
Sch
Greenford UB6 86 A2
Greenford UB6 86 A3
Cardinals Way N19 49 D1
Cardinal's Wlk
Ashford TW16 171 C4
Hampton TW12 174 A3
Cardine Mews SE15 140 B5
Cardington Sq TW4 128 D1
Cardington St
NW1 93 C4 232 B1
Cardozo Rd N7 72 A3
Cardrew Ave N12 30 B5
Cardrew Cl N12 30 B5
Cardrew Ct N12 30 B5
Cardross St W6 112 B3
Cardwell Prim Sch
SE18 122 B2
Cardwell Rd N7 72 A4
SE18 122 C2
Career Ct 11 SE16 118 D4
Carew Cl N7 72 B6
Carew Ct 15 SE14 140 D6
Carew Ho 24 SE18 122 B2
SW16 160 C1
Carew Manor Sch SM6 219 D5
Carew Rd N17 34 A1
W13 109 C4
Ashford TW15 171 A4
Mitcham CR4 181 A1
Thornton Heath CR7 204 D5
Wallington SM6 219 C2
Carew St SE5 139 A3
Carey Ct 20 SE5 139 A5
Bexleyheath DA6 169 D6
Carey Gdns
SW8 137 D4 269 C1
Carey Ho E5 74 B5
Carey La EC2 242 A2
Carey Pl SW1 259 C3
Carey Rd RM9 81 A4
Carey St WC2 94 B1 240 D1
Carey Way HA9 66 D4
Carfax Pl SW4 137 D1
Carfax Rd UB3 106 A2
Carfree Cl 3 N1 72 C1
Cargill Rd SW18 158 A3
Cargreen Pl SE25 205 D5
Cargreen Rd SE25 205 D5
Cargrey Ho 9 HA7 25 C5
Carholme Rd SE23 163 B3
Carillon Ct W5 109 D6
Carisbrook 2 N10 31 B1
Carisbrook Cl EN1 5 D4
Carisbrook Ct 1 SW16 160 B1
Carisbrooke Ave DA5 168 D3
Carisbrooke Cl HA7 25 D1
Carisbrooke Ct W3 111 A4
Belmont SM2 217 B1
Northolt UB5 85 B6
Carisbrooke Gdns SE15 139 D5
Carisbrooke Ho TW10 154 C6
Carisbrooke Rd E17 53 A4
Bromley BR2 209 C5
Mitcham CR4 204 A5
Carleton Ave SM6 219 D1
Carleton Cl KT10 196 B1
Carleton Gdns N19 71 C3
Carleton Rd N7 71 D4
Carlile Cl E3 97 B5
Carlile Ho SE1 262 D5
Carlina Gdns IG8 37 B5
Carlingford Gdns CR4 181 A3
Carlingford Rd N15 50 D6
NW3 70 B4
West Barnes SM4 200 D3
Carlisle Ave EC3 243 C1
W3 89 C1
Carlisle Cl KT2 176 C2
Carlisle Gdns
Harrow HA3 43 D2
Redbridge IG1 56 A3
Carlisle Ho IG1 56 A3
Carlisle Inf Sch TW12 173 D4
Carlisle La SE1 116 B3 260 D6
Carlisle Pl N11 31 B6
SW1 115 C3 259 A5
Carlisle Rd E10 53 C1
N4 50 C2
NW6 91 A6
NW9 45 A6
Cheam SM1 217 B2
Hampton TW12 173 D3
Carlisle St W1 93 D1 239 C1
Carlisle Way SW17 181 A5
Carlisle Wlk 6 E8 73 D2
Carlos Pl W1 115 B6 248 C5
Carlow St NW1 232 A4
Carlton Ave N14 15 D6
Feltham TW14 150 C5
Harrow HA3 43 B4
Hayes UB3 105 C2
South Croydon CR2 221 C1
Carlton Ave E HA9 44 A1
Carlton Ave W HA0 65 B6
Carlton Cl NW3 69 C6
Chessington KT9 213 D2
Edgware HA8 26 C5
Northolt UB5 64 A3
Carlton Cres SM3 217 A4
Carlton Ct NW2 68 C2
NW6 91 D5
SE19 183 D2
11 SE20 184 B2
SW9 138 D4
Ilford IG6 57 B6
Carlton Dr SW15 157 A6
Ilford IG6 57 B6
Carlton Gdns
SW1 115 D5 249 C3
W5 109 C6
Carlton Gn DA14 189 D6
Carlton Gr SE15 140 B4
8 SE15 140 B5
Carlton Hill NW8 92 A5 229 A4
Carlton Ho N21 17 A3
NW6 91 C5
8 NW6 91 B5
W1 237 D2
Cheam SM1 217 B2
Hounslow TW4 151 C5
Carlton House Terr
SW1 115 D5 249 D4
Carlton Lo N4 50 C2
Carlton Mans N16 51 D1
7 NW6 69 C1
SW9 138 C1
W9 91 D4
W14 244 B2
Carlton Par HA9 44 A1
Carlton Park Ave SW20 178 D1
Carlton Prim Sch NW5 71 A3
Carlton Rd E11 54 D1
E12 77 D4
E17 35 A2
N4 50 C2
N11 31 A5
SW14 133 A1
W4 111 B4
W5 87 C1
Ashford TW16 171 D3
Bexley DA16 146 B2
Erith DA8 147 D6
Kingston u T KT3 177 C1
Sidcup DA14 189 D6
South Croydon CR2 221 B1
Walton-on-T KT12 194 B2
Carlton Sq E1 96 D3
Carlton St SW1 249 C5
Carlton Terr E7 77 C1
E11 55 B4
N18 33 B6
SE26 162 C1
Carlton Tower Pl SW1 257 D6
Carlton Twrs SM5 218 D5
Carlton Vale NW6 91 C5
Carlton Vale Inf Sch
NW6 91 B4
Carltons The NW4 46 D4
5 SW15 157 A6
Carlwell St SW17 180 C5
Carlyle Ave Bromley BR1 209 D6
Southall UB1 107 B6
Carlyle Cl N2 48 A3
NW10 89 B6
Hampton KT8 173 D1
Carlyle Ct SW6 265 D1
Carlyle Gdns UB1 107 B6
Carlyle Ho 12 N16 73 C5
4 SE5 139 A5
SW3 266 D6
W5 109 D2
Carlyle Mans SW3 267 A5
Carlyle Pl SW15 134 D1
Carlyle Rd E12 78 A4
SE28 124 C6
W5 109 C2
Croydon CR0 222 A6
Carlyle Sq SW3 114 B1 256 D1
Carlyle's Ho SW3 267 A5
Carlyon Ave HA2 63 C4
Carlyon Cl HA0 88 A6
Carlyon Ct HA0 88 B6
Carlyon Mans 1 HA0 88 A5
Carlyon Rd Hayes UB4 84 C1
Hayes UB4 84 C2
Wembley HA0 88 A6
Carlys Cl BR3 184 D1
Carmalt Gdns SW15 134 C1
Carmarthen Ct 4 W7 86 D3
Carmarthen Ho 8
SW15 156 C4
Carmarthen Pl SE1 253 A2
Carmel Ct W8 245 C2
Carmelite Cl HA3 24 A2
Carmelite Rd HA3 24 A1
Carmelite St
EC4 116 C6 251 B6
Carmelite Way HA3 24 A1
Carmelite Wlk HA3 24 A2
Carmen St E14 97 D1
Carmichael Cl 9 SW11 136 B2
Ruislip HA4 62 A4
Carmichael Ct 5 SW13 133 D3
Carmichael Ho 6 E14 120 A6
17 SE21 183 C6
Carmichael Mews
SW18 158 B4
Carmichael Rd SE25 206 A5
Carminia Rd SW17 159 B2
Carnaby St★ W1 93 C1 239 A1
Carnac St SE21,SE27 161 B1
Carnanton Rd E17 36 B2
Carnarvon Ave EN1 5 D3
Carnarvon Dr UB3 105 A3
Carnarvon Rd E10 54 A4
E15 76 D2
E18 36 D2
High Barnet EN5 1 A2
Carnation St SE2 124 B1
Carnbrook Rd SE3 143 D2
Carnecke Gdns SE9 166 A6
Carnegie Cl KT6 214 B6
Carnegie Ho NW3 70 B5
Carnegie Pl SW19 156 D1
Carnegie St N1 94 B6 233 D5
Carnforth Cl KT19 214 D2
Carnforth Rd SW16 181 D3
Carnicot Ho 9 SE15 140 B4
Carnoustie Dr N1 72 B1
Carnwath Ho SW6 135 D2
Carnwath Rd SW6 135 D2
Caroe Ct N9 18 B3
Carol St NW1 93 C6 232 A6
Carole Ho 18 SE20 184 B2
Carolina Cl E15 76 C3
Carolina Rd CR7 183 A2
Caroline Cl N10 31 B1
SW16 160 B1
W2 245 D5
Hounslow TW7 130 C5
South Croydon CR0 221 C4
Caroline Ct NW11 47 A3
SE6 186 B6
Ashford TW15 170 D4
Stanmore HA7 25 A4
17 Surbiton KT6 197 D2
Caroline Gdns E2 95 C4
Caroline Ho W2 245 D5
20 W6 112 C1
Caroline Martyn Ho 8
N19 49 D2
Caroline Pl SW11 137 A3
W2 245 D5
Harlington UB3 127 C5
Caroline Pl Mews W2 245 D5
Caroline Rd SW19 179 B3
Caroline St E1 96 D1
Caroline Terr
SW1 115 A2 258 A3
Caroline Wlk W6 264 A5
Caronia Ct 4 SE16 119 A2
Carpenter Gdns N21 16 D2
Carpenter Ho 10 E14 97 C2
6 N19 71 D4
NW11 48 A3
Carpenter St W1 248 C5
Carpenters Bsns Pk E15 75 D1
Carpenters Cl EN5 13 D5
Carpenters Ct NW1 232 A6
5 Dagenham RM10 81 D2
Twickenham TW2 152 C2
Carpenter's Pl SW4 137 D1
Carpenters Prim Sch
E15 98 A6
Carpenter's Rd E15 75 D1
Carr Gr SE18 122 A2
Carr Rd E17 35 C1
Northolt UB5 64 A1
Carr St E14 97 A2
Carrara Wharf SW6 135 A2
Carrara Wlk 19 SW9 138 D1
Carriage Dr E
SW11 137 A5 268 B4
Carriage Dr N
SW8 137 A6 268 B5
SW11 136 D5 267 C4
Carriage Dr S
SW11 137 A4 268 A2
Carriage Dr W
SW11 136 D5 267 C3
Carriage Mews IG1 79 A6
Carrick Cl TW7 131 A2
Carrick Gate KT10 212 A5
Carrick Gdns N17 33 C3
Carrick Ho N7 72 B2

Carrick Ho *continued*
SE11 261 C2
Carrick Mews SE8 141 C6
Carrill Way DA17 124 D3
Carrington Ave
Borehamwood WD6 10 D6
Isleworth TW3 151 D6
Carrington Cl Arkley EN5 12 A6
Borehamwood WD6 11 A6
Croydon CR0 207 A2
Carrington Gdns 4 E7 77 A4
Carrington Ho W1 248 C3
Carrington Lo 3 TW10 154 A6
Carrington Pl KT10 212 A4
Carrington Rd TW10 132 C1
Carrington Sq HA3 24 A3
Carrington St W1 248 C3
Carrol Cl NW5 71 B4
Carroll Cl E15 76 D3
Carroll Ho W2 246 C6
Carron Cl E14 97 D1
Carronade Pl SE18 123 B3
Carroun Rd
SW8 138 B5 270 C4
Carrow Rd RM9 80 B1
Carroway La UB6 86 B4
Carrs La N21 17 B6
Carshalton Beeches Sta
SM5 218 D2
Carshalton Coll SM5 218 D5
Carshalton Gr SM1 218 B3
Carshalton High Sch for Boys
SM5 218 C6
Carshalton High Sch for Girls
SM5 218 C5
Carshalton Park Rd
SM5 218 D3
Carshalton Pl SM5 219 A3
Carshalton Rd
Mitcham CR4 203 A4
Sutton SM1,SM5 218 B3
Carshalton Sta SM5 218 D4
Carshalton, Beddington & Wallington War Memorial Hospl SM5 218 D2
Carslake Rd SW15 156 C5
Carson Rd E16 99 A2
SE21 161 B2
Cockfosters EN4 2 D1
Carstairs Rd SE6 164 A1
Carston Cl SE12 164 D6
Carswell Cl IG1 55 D5
Carswell Rd SE6 164 A4
Cart La E4 20 C3
Carter Cl SM6 219 D1
Carter Ct EC4 241 D1
Carter Ho E1 243 C3
Carter La EC4 94 D1 241 D1
Carter Pl SE17 117 A1 262 B1
Carter Rd E13 99 B6
SW19 180 B4
Carter St SE17 117 A1 262 A1
Carteret Ho 8 W12 112 B6
Carteret St SW1 249 C1
Carteret Way SE8 119 A2
Carterhatch Jun & Inf Schs
EN1 6 B4
Carterhatch La EN1 6 A4
Carterhatch Rd EN3 6 D4
Carters Cl 2 NW5 71 D2
North Cheam KT4 200 D1
Carters Hill Cl SE9 165 C3
Carters Rd N2 30 C3
Carter's Yd SW18 157 C6
Carthew Rd W6 112 B3
Carthew Villas W6 112 B3
Carthusian St EC1 242 A4
Cartier Circ E14 120 A5
Carting La WC2 116 A6 250 B5
Cartmel NW1 232 A2
Cartmel Cl N17 34 B3
Cartmel Ct
Beckenham BR2 186 C1
Northolt UB5 63 A2
Cartmel Gdns SM4 202 A4
Cartmel Rd DA7 147 C4
Carton Ho 2 NW2 68 A5
4 SE16 118 A3
12 W11 112 D6
Cartwright Gdns
WC1 94 A4 233 A1
Cartwright Ho SE1 262 B5
Cartwright Rd RM9 81 B1
Cartwright St
E1 117 D5 253 D5
Cartwright Way SW13 134 B5
Carvel Ho E14 120 A1
Carver Rd SE24 161 A5
Carville Cres TW8 110 A2
Cary Rd E11 76 C5
Caryl Ho 6 SW19 156 D3
Carysfort Rd N8 49 D4
N16 73 B4
Casby Ho 7 SE16 118 A3
Cascade Ave N10 49 C5
Cascade Cl IG9 21 D2
Cascade Rd IG9 21 D2
Casella Rd SE14 140 D5
Casewick Rd SE27 182 D6
Casimir Rd E5 74 C5
Casino Ave SE24 161 B6
Caspian Ho 7 E1 96 D2
Caspian St SE5 139 B5
Caspian Wlk E16 99 D1
Cass Ho 23 E9 74 D2
Cassandra Cl UB5 64 B4
Cassanora Ct NW2 68 C2
Cassel Hospl TW10 175 D6
Casselden Rd NW10 67 B1
Cassell Ho 21 SW9 138 A3
Casserley Ho W4 111 B3
Cassidy Rd SW6 265 A3
Cassilda Rd SE2 124 A2
Cassilis Rd TW1 153 B5
Cassinghurst SE24 161 B6
Cassiobury Ave TW14 149 D4
Cassiobury Rd E17 53 A4
Cassland Rd E9 74 D2
South Norwood CR7 205 B5
Casslee Rd SE6 163 B4
Cassocks Sq TW17 193 B2
Casson Ho 10 E1 96 A2
Casson St E1 96 A2
Castalia Sq 6 E14 120 A4
Castell Ho 11 SE8 141 C5
Castellain Mans W9 91 D3
Castellain Rd W9 91 D3
Castellane Cl HA7 24 D3
Castello Ave SW15 156 C6
Castelnau SW13 134 B5
Casterbridge NW6 91 D6
3 W11 91 C1
Casterbridge Rd SE3 143 A2
Casterton St E8 74 B2
Castile Rd SE18 122 C2
Castilion Prim Sch
SE28 102 C1
Castilla Ho BR1 187 B3
Castillon Rd SE6 164 C2
Castlands Rd SE6 163 B2
Castle Ave E4 36 B5
Yiewsley UB7 104 B6
Castle Bar Park Sta W7 86 D2
Castle Baynard St
EC4 117 A6 252 A6
Castle Cl E9 75 A3
SW19 156 D1
Beckenham BR2 208 C6
Charlton TW16 171 C3
Castle Ct EC3 242 D1
SE26 185 A6
Belmont SM2 217 C2
Morden SM4 202 B4
Castle Dr IG4 56 A3
Castle Hill Ave CR0 224 A1
Castle Hill Prim Sch
CR0 224 A2
Castle Ho 3 E4 36 B5
SE1 262 A4
SW8 270 B4
10 Belmont SM2 217 C1
Castle Ind Est SE17 262 A4
Castle La SW1 115 C3 259 A6
Castle Mead SE5 139 A5
Castle Mews N12 30 A5
NW1 71 B2
Castle Par KT17 216 A1
Castle Pl 8 W4 111 C2
Castle Point 3 E13 99 C5
Castle Rd N12 30 B5
NW1 71 B2
Dagenham RM9 102 B6
Enfield EN3 7 A5
Isleworth TW7 130 D3
Northolt UB5 63 D1
Southall UB2 107 B3
Castle St E6 99 C5
Kingston u T KT2 176 A1
Castle View Gdns IG1 56 B3
Castle Way SW19 156 D1
Feltham TW13 172 C6
Castle Wlk TW16 194 C6
Castle Yd N6 49 A2
SE1 251 D4
17 Richmond TW10 153 D6
Castleacre W2 237 A1
Castlebar Ct 5 W5 87 C2
Castlebar Hill W5 87 C2
Castlebar Mews W5 87 C2
Castlebar Pk W5 87 B2
Castlebar Rd W5 87 C1
Castlebar Sch W13 87 A2
Castlebrook Cl
SE11 116 D2 261 C4
Castlecombe Dr SW19 156 D4
Castlecombe Prim Sch
SE9 188 A5
Castlecombe Rd SE9 188 A6
Castleden Ho NW6 70 B1
Castledine Rd SE20 184 B3
Castleford Ave SE9 166 D3
Castleford Cl N17 33 D4
Castleford Ct NW8 236 D6
Castlefrank Ho 21 N1 95 C4
Castlegate TW9 132 B2
Castlehaven Rd NW1 71 B1
Castleigh Ct EN2 17 B6
Castlemaine 8 SW11 136 D3
Castlemaine Ave CR2 221 D3
Castlenau Gdns SW13 134 B6
Castlenau Mans SW13 134 B6
Castlenau Row SW13 134 B6
Castlereagh St W1 237 C2
Castleton Ave HA9 66 A4
Castleton Cl CR0 207 A3
Castleton Ct KT5 198 B4
Castleton Gdns HA9 66 A5
Castleton Ho 2 E14 120 A2
Castleton Rd E17 36 B1
SE12,SE9 187 D6
Ilford IG3 58 B1
Mitcham CR4 203 D5
Ruislip HA4 40 D1
Castletown Rd
W14 113 A1 254 B1
Castleview Cl N4 73 A6
Castlewood Day Hospl
SE18 144 C4
Castlewood Dr SE9 144 B3
Castlewood Rd N16 52 A3
New Barnet EN4 2 B2
Castor La E14 119 D6
Cat Hill EN4 14 D6
Catalina Rd TW6 126 C2
Caterham Rd SE13 142 B2
Catesby Ho 25 E9 74 C1
Catesby St SE17 117 B2 262 D3
Catford Bridge Sta SE6 163 C4
Catford Broadway SE6 163 D4
Catford Cty Sch SE6 164 A1
Catford Cty Sch (Annexe)
BR1 186 C6
Catford Gyratory SE6 163 D4
Catford Hill SE6 163 C3
Catford Rd SE6 163 C4
Catford Sta SE6 163 C4
Cathall Rd E11 76 B5
Cathay Ho SE16 118 B4
Cathay St 9 SE16 118 B4
Cathay Wlk UB5 85 C5
Cathcart Dr BR6 211 C1
Cathcart Hill N19 71 C5
Cathcart Rd
SW10 136 A6 266 A6
Cathcart St NW5 71 B2
Cathedral Pl EC4 242 A2
Cathedral Sch of St Saviour & St Mary Overie Prim Sch
SE1 117 A4 252 B2
Cathedral St
SE1 117 B5 252 C4
Catherall Rd N5,N16 73 A5
Catherine Baird Ct 12
SW12 159 B4
Catherine Ct 2 N14 15 C6
3 SW19 179 B5
1 Ilford IG2 57 A3
Catherine Dr
Ashford TW16 171 D4
Richmond TW9 132 A1
Catherine Gdns TW3 130 B1
Catherine Godfrey Ho
RM9 103 B6
Catherine Gr SE10 141 D4
Catherine Griffiths Ct
EC1 241 B6
Catherine Ho 16 N1 95 C6
Brentford TW7 131 B4
Catherine Pl
SW1 115 C3 259 A6
Catherine Rd Enfield EN3 7 A6
Kingston u T KT6 197 D4
Catherine St
WC2 116 B6 250 C6
Catherine Wheel Alley
E1 243 B3
Catherine Wheel Rd
TW8 131 D5
Catherine Wheel Yd
SW1 249 A3
Catherwood Ct N1 235 C3
Cathles Rd SW12 159 B5
Cathnor Rd W12 112 B4
Catinthia Ct 5 SE8 119 A2
Catisfield Rd EN3 7 A6
Catlin Cres TW17 193 B4
Catlin St SE16 118 B1
Catling Cl SE23 162 D1
Catlin's La HA5 40 B5
Catman Ho N4 50 B1
Cato Rd SW4 137 D1
Cato St W1 92 C1 237 B2
Caton Ct BR2 186 C1
Cator La BR3 185 B2
Cator Park Girls Sch
BR3 185 A3
Cator Rd SE20,SE26 184 D5
Carshalton SM5 218 D3
Cator St SE15 139 D6
SE15 139 D6
Catsey La WD2 8 A4
Catsey Wood WD2 8 A4
Catterick Cl N11 31 A4
Cattistock Rd SE9 188 B5
Cattley Cl EN5 1 A1
Catton St WC1 240 C3
Caughley Ho SE11 261 A5
Caulfield Ct 12 NW1 71 C1
Caulfield Rd E6 78 B1
SE15 140 B3
Causeway TW14,TW4 128 B1
Causeway The N2 48 C5
SW18 157 D6
SW19 178 C5
Carshalton SM5 219 A6
Chessington KT9 214 A4
Claygate KT10 212 D1
Teddington TW11 174 D4
Causeyware Rd N9 18 C4
Causton Cotts 3 E14 97 A1
Causton Ho SE5 139 A5
Causton Rd N6 49 B2
Causton St
SW1 115 D1 259 D2
Cautley Ave SW4 159 C6
Cavalier Cl RM6 58 D5
Cavalier Gdns UB3 83 B1
Cavalry Cres TW4 128 D1
Cavalry Gdns SW15 157 B6
Cavan Ho 7 E3 97 B6
Cavan Pl HA5 23 B2
Cavaye Ho SW10 266 B6
Cavaye Pl SW10 256 B1
Cave Rd E13 99 B4
Richmond TW10 175 C6
Cavell Dr EN2 4 C3
Cavell Ho 8 N1 95 C6
Cavell Rd N17 33 B3
Cavell St E1 96 B2
Cavendish Ave N3 29 C1
NW8 92 B5 229 D3
W13 87 A1
Bexley DA16 145 D2
Harrow HA1 64 C4
Ruislip HA4 62 B3
Sidcup DA15 168 A4
West Barnes KT3 200 B5
Woodford IG8 37 B3
Cavendish Cl N18 34 B5
NW6 69 B2
NW8 92 B4 229 D2
3 SW15 157 A6
Ashford TW16 171 D4
Hayes UB4 83 C2
Cavendish Cres
Deacons Hill WD6 10 C6
WD6 10 C6
Cavendish Ct 5 E4 20 C4
EC2 243 B2
Ashford TW16 171 D4
Cavendish Dr E11 54 B1
Claygate KT10 212 C3
Edgware HA8 26 B4
Cavendish Gdns SW4 159 C5
Barking IG11 79 D3
Dagenham RM6 59 A4
Ilford IG1 56 C1
Cavendish Ho N12 30 A6
NW8 229 D3
SW8 270 A2
Twickenham TW1 153 A5
Cavendish Jun & Inf Sch
W4 133 C5
Cavendish Mans E5 74 C4
EC1 241 A5
8 NW6 69 C3
2 SW12 159 C5
Cavendish Mews N W1 238 D4
Cavendish Mews S W1 238 D3
Cavendish Par SW12 159 B5
Hounslow TW4 129 A3
Cavendish Pl W1 238 D2
Cavendish Rd E4 36 A4
N4 50 D3
N18 34 B5
NW6 69 B1
SW12 159 C5
SW19 180 C3
W4 133 A4
Ashford TW16 171 D4
New Malden KT3 199 D5
Sutton SM2 218 A1
Thornton Heath CR0 204 D1
Cavendish Sch W13 87 A1
Cavendish Sch The
NW1 93 B6 231 D6
Cavendish Sq
W1 93 B1 238 D2
Cavendish St N1 95 B5 235 C3
Cavendish Terr 10 E3 97 B4
Feltham TW13 150 A2
Cavendish The NW11 47 D2
Cavendish Way BR4 207 D1
Cavenham Gdns IG1 79 B5
Caverleigh Way KT4 200 B2
Caverley Gdns HA3 43 D2
Caversham Ave N13 16 C1
Cheam SM3 217 A6
Caversham Ct N11 15 A1
Caversham Ho N15 51 A5
7 SE15 140 A6
8 Kingston u T KT1 176 A1
Caversham Rd N15 51 A5
NW5 71 C2
Kingston u T KT1 176 B1
Caversham St
SW3 136 D6 267 C6
Caverswall St W12 90 C1
Caveside Cl BR7 188 C2
Cavour Ho SE17 261 D2
Cawdor Cres W7 109 A2
Cawnpore St SE19 183 C5
Cawston Ct 6 BR1 186 D3
Caxton Gr E3 97 C4
Caxton Hall SW1 259 C6
Caxton Rd N22 32 B1
SW19 180 A5
W12 112 D4
Southall UB2 106 D3
Caxton St SW1 115 D3 259 C6
Caxton St N E16 98 D1
Cayford Ho 1 NW3 70 D3
Caygill Cl BR2 208 D5
Cayley Cl SM6 220 A1
Cayley Rd UB2 107 D3
Cayley Sch E14 97 A1
Cayton Pl EC1 235 C1
Cayton Rd UB6 86 C5
Cayton St EC1 235 C1
Cazenove Mans 1 N16 74 A6
Cazenove Rd E17 35 C2
N16 74 A6
Cearns Ho E6 99 D6
Cecil Ave Barking IG11 79 B1
Enfield EN1 5 D1
Wembley HA9 66 B3
Cecil Cl W5 87 D2
Ashford TW15 171 A3
Chessington KT9 213 D4
Cecil Ct NW6 69 D1
SW10 266 A6
W5 87 D2
WC2 250 A5
12 Croydon CR0 221 D6
Cecil Ho 6 E5 74 C6
E17 35 C2
Cecil Lo KT9 213 D4
Cecil Mans 2 SW17 159 A2
Cecil Pk HA5 41 A5
Cecil Pl CR4 202 D4
Cecil Rd E11 76 C5
E13 99 A6
E17 35 C2
N10 31 B1
N14 15 C3
NW9 45 C6
NW10 89 C6
SW19 179 D3
W3 89 A2
Ashford TW15 171 A4
Cheam SM1,SM2 217 B2
Dagenham RM6 58 D2
Enfield EN2 5 B1
Harrow HA3 42 C6
Hounslow TW3 130 A3
Ilford IG1 78 D4
Thornton Heath CR0 204 B3
Cecil Rhodes Ho NW1 232 C4
Cecil Rosen Ct HA0 65 B5
Cecil Way BR2 209 A1
Cecile Pk N8 50 A3
Cecilia Cl N2 48 A6
Cecilia Rd E8 74 A3
Cedar Ave Barnet EN4 14 C4
Dagenham RM6 59 A4
Enfield EN3 6 C3
Hayes UB3 84 A1
Ruislip HA4 62 C3
Sidcup DA15 168 A4
Twickenham TW2 152 A5
Yiewsley UB7 104 B6
Cedar Cl SE21 161 A2
Buckhurst Hill IG9 21 D2
East Molesey KT8 196 C5
Keston Mark BR2 226 A5
Kingston u T KT2 177 B6
Wallington SM5 218 D2
Cedar Copse BR1 188 B1
Cedar Cres BR2 226 A5
Cedar Ct 6 E11 55 B4
5 E18 37 A2
N1 73 A1
N3 29 C3
1 N10 31 B1
5 N11 31 C5
N20 14 B3
19 SE7 143 C6
SE9 166 A5
SW14 133 A1
SW19 156 D1
W1 237 B2
7 Brentford TW8 131 D6
Stoneleigh KT17 216 A1
3 Sutton SM2 218 A2
Cedar Dr N2 48 C5
Hatch End HA5 23 C4
Cedar Gdns SM2 218 A2
Cedar Gr W5 110 A3
Bexley DA5 168 D5
Southall UB1 85 C2
Cedar Grange 10 EN1 17 C6
Cedar Ho 6 E14 120 A4
N22 32 C2
SE14 140 D4
16 SE16 118 D4
W8 255 C6
Charlton TW16 171 D3
Hayes UB4 84 C3
New Addington CR0 223 D2
Cedar Hts NW2 69 B2
Richmond TW10 154 A3
Cedar Lawn Ave EN5 13 A6
Cedar Lo SW6 134 D4
Cedar Mount SE9 165 D3
Cedar Park Gdns RM6 58 D2
Cedar Park Rd EN2 5 A5
Cedar Pl 3 SE7 121 C1
Cedar Rd N17 33 D2
NW2 68 C4
Bromley BR1 187 C1
Cranford TW5 128 C3
Croydon CR0 221 C6
East Bedfont TW14 149 B3
East Molesey KT8 196 C5
Enfield EN2 5 A5
Sutton SM2 218 A2
Cedar Rise N14 15 A4
Cedar Terr
9 Dagenham RM8 58 D2
Richmond TW9 132 A1
Cedar Tree Ct SE5 139 A4
Cedar Tree Gr SE27 182 D5
Cedar Way NW1 71 D1 232 C6
Ashford TW16 171 C3
Cedar Wlk KT10 212 D2
Cedarcroft Rd KT9 214 B4
Cedarhurst Dr SE9 165 C6
Cedarmore Ct BR7 189 A2
Cedarne Rd
SW6 135 D5 265 C3
Cedars Ave E17 53 C4
Mitcham CR4 203 A6
Cedars Cl NW4 46 D6
SE13 142 B2
Cedars Ct N9 17 D2
SW15 156 A5
Cedars Dr UB10 82 C5
Cedars Fst & Mid Sch
HA3 24 A2
Cedars Ho 15 E17 53 D6
5 SW27 182 D5
Cedars Mews SW4 137 B1
Cedars Prim Sch The
TW5 128 A5
Cedars Rd E15 76 C2
4 N9 18 A2
N21 16 D2
SW4 137 B1
SW13 134 A3
W4 111 C1
Beckenham BR3 185 B1
Morden SM4 201 C5
Teddington KT8 175 C2
Wallington CR0 220 A4
Cedars The E9 74 D1
W13 87 C1
Buckhurst Hill IG9 21 A3
4 Kingston u T KT2 176 D2
Teddington TW11 174 D4
Wallington SM6 219 C4
Cedarville Gdns SW16 182 B4
Cedarwood BR3 185 B3
Cedarwood Ho EN2 4 D3
Cedra Ct N16 52 A1
Cedric Chambers NW8 236 C6
Cedric Rd SE9 167 A1
Celadon Cl EN3 7 A2
Celandine Cl E3,E14 97 C2
Celandine Dr E8 73 D1
SE28 124 B5
Celandine Way E15 98 C4
Celbridge Mews W2 91 D1
Celendine Ct E4 19 D1
Celestial Gdns SE13 142 B1
Celia Ct 7 TW9 132 B4
Celia Ho 10 N1 95 C5
Celia Rd N19 71 C4
Celtic Ave BR2 208 C6
Celtic St E14 97 D2
Cemetery La SE7 144 A6
Lower Halliford TW17 192 D2
Cemetery Rd E7 76 D4
N17 33 C3
SE2 146 B5
Cenacle Cl NW3 69 C5
Cenotaph* SW1 250 A2
Centaur Ct 3 TW8 110 A1
Centaur St SE1 116 B3 260 D6
Centaurs Bsns Pk TW7 131 A6
Centenary Rd EN3 7 B1
Centennial Pk HA7,WD6 9 C4
Central Ave E11 76 B6
N2 30 B1
N2 47 D6
N9 17 D1
SW11 136 D5 267 D3
Bexley DA16 146 A3
East Molesey KT8 195 B4
Enfield EN1 6 B3
Hayes UB3 106 A6
Isleworth TW3,TW7 130 A1
Pinner HA5 41 B2
Wallington SM6 220 A3
Central Bsns Ctr NW10 67 C3
Central Cir NW4 46 B4
Central Criminal Court (Old Bailey)* EC4 94 D1 241 D2
Central Ct 2 SE18 122 D2
Central Foundation Lower Sch E3 97 A4
Central Foundation Sch
EC2 95 B3 242 D6
Central Foundation Upper Sch E3 97 B4
Central Gdns SM4 201 D4
Central Hill SE19 183 B4
Central Mans 8 NW4 46 B4
Central Middlesex Hospl
NW10 89 A4
Central Par 8 E17 53 C5
SE20 184 D3
W3 110 D4
Ealing UB6 87 A4
Enfield EN3 6 C3
Feltham TW14 150 C4
Harrow HA1 42 D4
Heston TW5 129 C5
Ilford IG2 57 B3
Kingston u T KT6 198 A3
Central Par Villas BR5 190 C1
Central Park Ave RM10 81 D5
Central Park Prim Sch
E6 99 D5
Central Park Rd E6 99 D5
Central Pk Est TW4 128 D1
Central Public Health Laboratories NW9 45 C6
Central Rd Morden SM4 201 D4
North Cheam KT4 216 A6
Wembley HA0 65 B3
Central Sch of Speech & Drama The NW3 70 B1
Central School of Ballet
EC1 94 C3 241 B5
Central Sq NW11 47 D3
East Molesey KT8 195 B5
4 Wembley HA9 66 A3
Central St EC1 95 A4 235 A1
Central St Martins Coll of Art & Design (The London Inst)
WC1 94 B2 240 C3
Central St Martin's Sch of Art & Design W1 93 D1 239 D1
Central Terr BR3 206 D6
Central Way NW10 89 A4

Central Way *continued*
SE28 124 B6
Feltham TW14 150 B6
Sutton SM5 218 C1
Centre Ave N2 30 C1
NW10 90 C4
W3 111 B5
Centre Bldg SE17 262 B4
Centre Common Rd
BR7 189 A3
Centre Ct N20 14 B2
Centre Dr E7 77 C4
Centre Hts 5 NW3 70 B1
Centre Point 3 SE1 118 A1
Centre Rd E11,E7 77 A6
Dagenham RM10 103 D5
Centre St E2 96 B5
Centre The
Feltham TW13 150 B2
Walton-on-T KT12 193 D1
Centre Way N9 18 D2
Centreway IG1 79 A6
Centurian Way DA18 125 C3
Centurion Cl N7 72 B1
Centurion Ct SM6 219 B6
Centurion Ho 2 RM10 81 D2
Centurion La E3 97 B5
Century Ho SE13 141 D3
Century Rd E17 53 A6
Cephas Ave E1 96 C3
Cephas Ho 8 E1 96 C3
Cephas St E1 96 C3
Ceres Rd SE18 123 D2
Cerise Rd SE15 140 A4
Cerne Cl UB4 106 C6
Cerne Rd SM4 202 A3
Cerney Mews W2 246 C6
Cervantes Ct 11 W2 91 D1
Ceylon Rd W14 254 A5
6 W14 112 D3
Chace Com Sch EN1 5 C4
Chadacre Ave IG5 56 B6
Chadacre Rd KT17 216 B3
Chadbourn St E14 97 D2
Chadbury Ct NW7 28 A2
Chadd Dr BR1 210 A6
Chaddacre Ho 10 SW9 138 D1
Chadston Ho 17 N1 72 D1
Chadswell WC1 233 B1
Chadview Ct 2 RM6 58 D2
Chadville Gdns RM6 58 D4
Chadway RM8 58 C1
Chadwell Ave RM6 58 B2
Chadwell Heath Hospl
RM6 58 B4
Chadwell Heath Ind Pk
RM8 58 D1
Chadwell Heath La RM6 58 C3
Chadwell Heath Sch
RM6 58 B3
Chadwell Heath Sta
RM6 58 D2
Chadwell Prim Sch RM6 58 C2
Chadwell St EC1 94 C4 234 B2
Chadwick Ave E4 36 B6
SW19 179 C4
Chadwick Cl 12 W7 86 D2
Teddington TW11 175 A4
Chadwick Ct 4 SE28 124 B5
Chadwick Pl KT6 197 C2
Chadwick Rd E11 54 D3
NW10 89 D6
SE15 139 D3
Ilford IG1 78 D5
Chadwick St
SW1 115 D3 259 C5
Chadwick Way SE28 124 D6
Chadwin Rd E13 99 B2
Chadworth Ho EC1 235 A1
N4 51 A1
Chadworth Way KT10 212 B3
Chaffey Ho 6 SE7 121 C1
Chaffinch Ave CR0 206 D3
Chaffinch Cl N9 18 D3
Croydon CR0 206 D3
Tolworth KT6 214 C5
Chaffinch Rd BR3 185 A2
Chafford Way RM6 58 C5
Chagford Ct SW19 180 C3
Chagford Ho 33 E3 97 D4
NW1 237 C5
Chagford St
NW1 92 D3 237 D5
Chailey Ave EN1 5 D3
Chailey Cl TW5 128 D4
Chailey Ind Est UB3 106 A4
Chailey St E5 74 C5
Chalbury Ho 8 SW9 138 B1
Chalbury Wlk N1 234 A4
Chalcombe Rd SE2 124 B3
Chalcot Cl SM2 217 C1
Chalcot Cres
NW1 92 D6 230 D6
Chalcot Gdns NW3 70 D2
Chalcot Mews SW16 160 A1
Chalcot Rd NW1 93 A6 231 A6
Chalcot Sch NW1 71 B1
Chalcot Sq NW1 71 A1
Chalcott Gdns KT6 197 C1
Chalcroft Rd SE13 164 C6
Chaldon Rd
SW6 135 A5 264 B4
Chale Rd SW2 160 A5
Chalet Ct CR7 204 D4
Chalfont Ave HA9 66 D2
Chalfont Ct NW1 237 D5
NW9 45 D6
3 Belvedere DA17 125 C1
Chalfont Gn N9 17 C1
Chalfont Ho NW10 67 B5
2 SE16 118 B3
Chalfont Rd N9 17 D1
SE25 205 D6
Hayes UB3 106 A4
Chalfont Way W13 109 B3
Chalfont Wlk 3 HA5 22 C1
Chalford Cl KT8 195 C5
Chalford Ct 15 SW15 156 D5
Ilford IG2 56 D4
Surbiton KT6 198 B2
Chalford Rd SE21 183 B6
Chalford Wlk IG8 37 D3
Chalgrove Ave SM4 201 C4
Chalgrove Gdns N3 47 A6
Chalgrove Prim Sch N3 47 A6
Chalgrove Rd E8,E9 74 C2
N17 34 B2
Sutton SM2 218 B1
Chalice Cl SM6 219 D2
Chalice Ct N2 48 C5
Chalk Farm Rd
NW1 71 A1 231 D6
Chalk Farm Sta NW3 71 A1
Chalk Hill Rd W6 112 D2
Chalk La EN4 2 D1
Chalk Pit Ave BR5 190 C1
Chalk Pit Rd SM1 218 A3
Chalk Rd E13 99 C2
Chalkenden Cl SE20 184 B3
Chalkers Cnr TW9 132 D2
Chalkhill Prim Sch HA9 66 D5
Chalkhill Rd HA9 67 A5
Chalklands HA9 67 A5
Chalkley Cl CR4 181 A1
Chalkmill Dr EN1 6 B2
Chalkstone Cl DA16 146 A4
Chalkwell Ho 9 E1 96 D1
Chalkwell Park Ave EN1 5 C1
Challenge Rd TW15 149 B1
Challenger Ho 7 E14 119 A6
Challice Way SW2 160 B3
Challin St 1 SE20 184 C2
Challiner Ct HA1 43 A4
Challis Rd TW8 109 D1
Challoner Cl N2 30 B1
Challoner Cres W14 254 C1
Challoner Ct BR2 186 B1
Challoner Mans W14 254 C1
Challoner St
W14 113 B1 254 C1
Challoners Cl KT8 196 B5
Chalmers Ho E17 53 D4
13 SW11 136 A2
Chalmers Rd TW15 170 D5
Chalmers Rd E TW15 171 A5
Chalmers Way TW14 150 B6
Chalmer's Wlk 14 SE17 138 D6
Chalner Ho SW2 160 C3
Chaloner Ct SE1 252 C2
Chalsey Rd SE4 141 B1
Chalton Dr N2 48 B3
Chalton St NW1 93 D5 232 C3
Chamber St E1 117 D6 253 D6
Chamberlain Cl SE18 123 B3
Chamberlain Cotts SE5 139 B4
Chamberlain Cres BR4 207 D2
Chamberlain Ho 5 E1 118 C6
NW1 232 D2
Chamberlain La HA5 40 A5
Chamberlain Pl E17 53 A6
Chamberlain Rd N2 30 A1
N9 18 A2
W13 109 A4
Chamberlain St 7 NW1 70 D1
Chamberlain Way
Pinner HA5 40 B6
Surbiton KT6 198 A2
Chamberlain Wlk 5
TW13 173 A6
Chamberlayne Mans 3
NW10 90 D4
Chamberlayne Rd NW10 90 C6
Chambers Gdns N2 30 B2
Chambers Ho 2 SW16 181 C6
Chambers La NW10 68 C1
Chambers Pl CR2 221 B1
Chambers Rd N7 72 A4
Chambers St SE16 118 A4
Chambon Pl 7 W6 112 A2
Chambord Ho 24 E2 95 D4
Chambord St E2 95 D4
Chamomile Ct E17 53 C3
Champion Cres SE26 185 A6
Champion Gdns IG8 37 A5
Champion Gr SE5 139 B2
Champion Hill SE5 139 B2
Champion Pk SE5 139 B3
Champion Rd SE26 185 A6
Champlain Ho 26 W12 112 B6
Champness Cl 9 SE27 183 B6
Champneys Cl SM2 217 B1
Chance St E2 243 C6
Chancel Ct W1 249 C6
Chancel St SE1 116 D5 251 C3
Chancellor Gr SE21 161 A1
Chancellor Ho 29 E1 118 B5
SW7 256 B6
Chancellor Pas E14 119 C5
Chancellor Pl NW9 27 D1
Chancellors' Ct WC1 240 C4
Chancellor's Rd W6 112 C1
Chancellors St W6 112 C1
Chancellors Wharf 21
W6 112 C1
Chancelot Rd SE2 124 B2
Chancery Bldgs 13 E1 118 C6
Chancery La EC4 94 C1 241 A2
Beckenham BR3 185 D1
Chancery Lane Sta
WC1 94 C2 241 A3
Chanctonbury Cl SE9 166 D1
Chanctonbury Gdns
SM2 217 D1
Chanctonbury Way N12 29 C6
Chandler Ave E16 99 A2
Chandler Cl TW12 173 C2
Chandler Ct
Feltham TW14 150 A5
2 Tolworth KT5 198 D1
8 Wallington SM6 219 B2
Chandler St E1 118 B5
Chandler Way SE15 139 D5
Chandlers Cl TW14 149 D4
Chandlers Field Sch
KT8 195 C4
Chandlers Mews E14 119 C4
Chandlers Way 11 SE24 160 C4
Chandon Lo SM2 218 A1
Chandos Ave E17 35 C1
N14 15 C1
N20 14 B3
W5 109 D2
Chandos Cl IG9 21 B2
Chandos Cres HA8 26 C3
Chandos Ct N14 15 D2
Chandos Pl
WC2 116 A6 250 A5
Chandos Rd E15 76 B3
N2 30 C1
N17 33 C1
NW2 68 C3
NW10 89 C3
Harrow HA1 42 A4
Pinner HA5 40 D2
Chandos St W1 93 B2 238 D3
Chandos Way NW11 47 D1
Change Alley EC3 242 D1
Channel Cl TW5 129 C4
Channel Ho E14 97 A2
Channelsea Rd E15 98 B6
Channing Sch N6 49 B1
Channon Ct 3 KT6 198 A4
Chant Sq E15 76 B1
Chant St E15 76 B1
Chantrey Cl DA14 191 A5
Chantrey Rd SW9 138 B2
Chantry Cl W9 91 B3
Enfield EN2 5 A5
Harrow HA3 44 B4
Chantry Ct SW6 135 A2
Chantry Ct Ind Est SM5 218 C5
Chantry La BR2 209 D4
Chantry Pl HA3 23 D2
Chantry Rd
Chessington KT9 214 C3
Harrow HA3 23 D2
Chantry Sch UB7 104 A6
Chantry Sq W8 113 D3 255 C5
Chantry St N1 94 D6 234 D5
Chantry The 3 E4 20 A3
Hillingdon UB8 82 B4
Chantry Way CR4 202 B6
Chapel Ct 12 EC2 95 C4
N2 48 C6
SE1 252 C2
Hayes UB3 105 D6
Chapel End Ho E17 35 D2
Chapel End Inf Sch E17 35 D2
Chapel End Jun Sch E17 35 D2
Chapel Farm Rd SE9 166 B2
Chapel Hill N2 30 C1
Chapel House St E14 119 D2
Chapel La
5 Dagenham RM6 58 D2
Hillingdon UB8 82 C1
Pinner HA5 40 D6
Chapel Market
N1 94 C5 234 A4
Chapel Pl 13 EC2 95 C4
N1 234 B4
N17 33 D3
W1 238 C1
Chapel Rd SE27 182 D6
W13 109 B5
Bexleyheath DA7 147 C1
Hounslow TW3 129 D2
Ilford IG1 78 D5
Twickenham TW1 153 B4
Chapel Side
W2 113 D6 245 C5
Chapel St NW1 92 C2 237 A3
SW1 115 A4 248 B1
Enfield EN2 5 B2
Chapel View CR2 222 C1
Chapleton Ho SW2 160 C6
Chaplin Cl SE1 251 C2
Wembley HA0 65 D2
Chaplin Cres TW16 171 C4
Chaplin Ho 6 SW9 138 C1
Chaplin Rd E15 98 D6
2 N17 51 D6
NW2 68 A2
Dagenham RM9 81 A1
Wembley HA0 65 D2
Chapman Cl UB7 104 B3
Chapman Cres HA3 44 B4
Chapman Gn N22 32 C2
Chapman Ho 26 E1 96 B1
2 SE27 160 D1
Chapman Rd E9 75 B2
Belvedere DA17 125 D1
Thornton Heath CR0 204 C1
Chapman St E1 118 B6
Chapmans End BR5 191 A1
Chapman's La BR5 190 D1
Chapmans Park Ind Est
NW10 67 D2
Chapone Pl W1 239 C1
Chapter Cl 15 W4 111 A3
Hillingdon UB10 60 B1
Chapter House Ct EC4 242 A1
Chapter Rd NW2 68 A3
SE17 116 D1 261 D1
Chapter St SW1 259 C3
Chapter Way TW12 173 C6
Chara Pl W4 133 B6
Charcot Ho 9 SW15 155 D5
Charcroft Ct 11 W14 112 D4
Charcroft Gdns EN3 6 D1
Chard Ho 7 N7 72 B6
Chardin Ho 30 SW9 138 C4
Chardin Rd 11 W4 111 C2
Chardmore Rd N16 52 A1
Chardwell Cl E6 100 B1
Charecroft Way W12 112 D4
Charfield Ct W9 91 D3
Charford Rd E16 99 A2
Chargeable La E13 99 A3
Chargeable St E16 98 D3
Chargrove Cl 24 SE16 118 D4
Charing Cl BR6 227 D4
Charing Cross
SW1 116 A5 250 A4
Charing Cross Hospl
W6 112 D1
Charing Cross Pier
WC2 250 B4
Charing Cross Rd
WC2 93 D1 239 D1
Charing Cross Sta
WC2 116 A5 250 B4
Charing Ct BR2 186 C1
Charing Ho SE1 251 B2
Charity Sch Hall The N9 18 A2
Charlbert Ct NW8 230 A4
Charlbert St
NW8 92 C5 230 A4
Charlbury Ave HA7 25 D5
Charlbury Gdns IG3 79 D6
Charlbury Gr W5 87 C1
Charlbury Ho 1 E12 78 C5
Charlbury Rd UB10 60 B5
Charldane Rd SE9 166 D1
Charlecote Gr SE26 162 B1
Charlecote Rd RM8 81 A5
Charlemont Rd E6 100 C4
Charles Allen Ho EC1 234 A2
Charles Auffray Ho 26
E1 96 C2
Charles Barry Cl SW4 137 C2
Charles Bradlaugh Ho 2
N17 34 B3
Charles Burton Ct E5 75 A4
Charles Cl DA14 190 B6
Charles Coveney Way 4
SE15 139 D4
Charles Cres HA1 42 B2
Charles Ct 5 TW11 174 C5
Charles Darwin Ho 8
E2 96 B4
Charles Dickens Ct
SE25 206 A5
Charles Dickens Ho 1
E2 96 B4
Charles Dickens Prim Sch
SE1 117 A4 252 A1
Charles Edward Brooke Girls
Sch (Lower) SE5 138 D4
Charles Edward Brooke Girls
Sch (Upper) SW9 138 D4
Charles Flemmell Mews 8
E16 121 A5
Charles Grinling Wlk
SE18 122 C2
Charles Ho 1 N17 33 D3
Charles Hobson Ho
NW10 67 C1
Charles Hocking Ho 8
W3 111 A4
Charles II Pl
SW3 114 D1 257 C1
Charles II St
SW1 115 D5 249 C4
Charles La NW8 92 C5 230 A4
Charles Lamb Prim Sch
N1 95 A6 235 A6
Charles Lesser KT9 213 D3
Charles Mackenzie Ho 7
SE16 118 A2
Charles Mills Ct SW16 182 A4
Charles Pl NW1 232 B1
Charles Rd E7 77 C1
SW19 179 C2
W13 87 A1
Dagenham RM6 58 D3
Charles Rowan Ho
WC1 234 A1
Charles Sevright Dr
NW7 28 D5
Charles Sq N1 95 B4 235 D1
Charles St E16 121 C5
SW13 133 C3
W1 115 B5 248 C4
Croydon CR0 221 A5
Enfield EN1 17 D6
Hillingdon UB10 82 D3
Hounslow TW3 129 B3
Charles Staunton Ho 3
SE27 183 B6
Charles Townsend Ho
EC1 241 C6
Charles Winchup Rd 2
E16 121 B5
Charlesfield SE12 165 C1
Charleston Cl TW13 150 A1
Charleston St SE17 262 B3
Charlesworth Ho 2 E14 97 C1
Charleville Cir SE26 184 A5
Charleville Ct SW5 254 C1
Charleville Mans W14 254 B1
Charleville Rd
W14 113 A1 254 C1
Charlie Browns Rdbt
E18 37 C1
Charlmont Rd SW17 180 D4
Charlotte Cl DA6 169 A6
Charlotte Ct N8 49 D3
Ilford IG2 56 C3
5 Wembley HA0 66 A2
Charlotte Despard Ave
SW11 137 A4 268 B1
SW11 137 B4 268 C1
Charlotte Ho 12 W6 112 C1
Charlotte Mews W1 239 B4
W10 90 D1
W14 254 A4
Charlotte Park Ave
BR1 210 A6
Charlotte Pl SW1 259 A3
W1 239 B3
Charlotte Rd EC2 95 C3 243 A6
SW13 133 D4
Dagenham RM10 81 D2
Wallington SM6 219 C2
Charlotte Row SW4 137 C2
Charlotte Sharman Prim Sch
SE11 116 D3 261 C5
Charlotte Sq 5 TW10 154 B5
Charlotte St W1 93 C2 239 B4
Charlotte Terr
N1 94 B6 233 D5
Charlow Cl SW6 136 A3
Charlton Church La
SE7 121 C1
Charlton Cl UB10 60 D6
Charlton Cres IG11 101 D5
Charlton Ct 25 E2 95 D6
E6 100 B4
17 N7 71 D3
Charlton Dene SE7 143 D5
Charlton Ho NW1 232 C2
5 Brentford TW8 132 A6
Charlton King's Rd NW5 71 D3
Charlton La SE7 121 D1
Upper Halliford TW17 193 B5
TW17 193 C5
Charlton Lo 1 NW11 47 B3
Charlton Manor Prim Sch
SE7 143 D5
Charlton Park La SE7 144 A6
Charlton Park Rd SE7 143 D6
Charlton Park Sch SE7 144 A6
Charlton Pl N1 94 D5 234 C4
Charlton Rd N9 18 D4
NW10 89 C6
SE3,SE7 143 B6
Charlton TW17 171 A1
Harrow HA3 43 D5
Wembley HA9 44 B1
Charlton Way SE10,SE3 142 C4
Charlwood Cl HA3 24 C4
Charlwood Ho SW1 259 C3
1 SW2 160 B3
Charlwood Pl
SW1 115 C2 259 B3
Charlwood Rd SW15 134 D1
Charlwood Sq CR4 202 B6
Charlwood St
SW1 115 C1 259 B2
Charlwood Terr 5
SW15 134 D1
Charman Ho SW8 270 A4
Charmian Ave HA7 25 D1
Charmian Ho 19 N1 95 C5
Charminster Ave SW19 179 D1
Charminster Ct 3 KT6 197 D2
Charminster Rd
SE12,SE9 187 D6
North Cheam KT4 200 D1
Charmouth Ct TW10 154 B6
Charmouth Ho SW8 270 C4
Charmouth Rd DA16 146 C4
Charnock Ho 22 W12 112 B6
Charnock Rd E5 74 B5
Charnwood Ave SW19 179 D1
Charnwood Cl KT3 199 C5
Charnwood Dr E18 55 B5
Charnwood Gdns E14 119 C2
Charnwood Ho 9 E5 74 B6
Charnwood Pl N20 14 A1
Charnwood Rd SE25 205 B5
Hillingdon UB10 82 C5
Charnwood St E5 74 B6
Charrington Rd 2 CR0 221 A6
Charrington St
NW1 93 D5 232 C4
Charsley Rd SE6 163 D2
Chart Cl Bromley BR2 186 C2
Croydon CR0 206 C3
Mitcham CR4 202 D6
Chart St N1 95 B4 235 D2
Charter Ave IG2 57 B2
Charter Cres TW4 129 A1
Charter Ct N4 50 C1
W1 237 B3
Kingston u T KT3 199 C6
Southall UB1 107 C5
Charter Dr DA5 169 A4
Charter Ho WC2 240 B1
Charter Nightingale Hospl
The NW1 92 C2 237 B4
Charter Rd KT1 198 D6
Charter Rd The IG8 36 D4
Charter Sq KT1 176 D1
Charter Way N14 15 D5
NW3 47 B5
Charterhouse Ave HA0 65 C3
Charterhouse Bldgs
EC1 242 A5
Charterhouse Mews
EC1 241 D4
Charterhouse Sq
EC1 94 D2 241 D4
Charterhouse St EC1 241 C3
Charteris Rd N4 50 C1
NW6 91 B6
Woodford IG8 37 B4
Charters Cl SE19 183 C5
Chartes Ho SE1 263 B6
Chartfield Ave SW15 156 C6
Chartfield Sch SW15 156 B6
Chartfield Sq SW15 156 D6
Chartham Ct 13 SW9 138 C2
Chartham Gr SE27 160 D1
Chartham Ho SE1 262 D6
Chartham Rd SE25 206 B6
Chartley Ave NW2 67 C5
Harrow HA7 24 D4
Charton Cl 5 DA17 147 B6
Chartres Ct UB6 86 B5
Chartridge SE17 139 B6
Chartridge Cl Arkley EN5 12 A6
Bushey WD2 8 A5
Chartridge Ct 6 HA7 25 C5
Chartwell 25 SW19 156 D3
Chartwell Cl
2 Croydon CR0 205 B1
Greenford UB6 85 D6
New Eltham BR7,DA15 167 B2
Chartwell Ct
8 Chipping Barnet EN5 1 A1
2 Woodford IG8 37 A3
Chartwell Dr BR6 227 B3
Chartwell Gdns SM3 217 A4
Chartwell Lo 5 BR3 185 C3
Chartwell Pl Cheam SM3 217 B4
Harrow HA2 64 B6
Chartwell Way 3 SE20 184 B2
Charville Ct 8 HA1 42 D3
Charville Jun & Inf Sch
UB4 83 C5
Charville La UB4 83 C5
Charville La W UB10 82 D4
Charwood SW16 182 C6
Chase Bridge Inf Sch
TW2 152 C5
Chase Bridge Jun Sch
TW2 152 C5
Chase Court Gdns EN2 5 A2
Chase Ct N14 15 C5
SW3 257 C5
SW20 179 A1
Isleworth TW7 131 A3
Wembley HA0 65 D2
Chase Ctr The NW10 89 B4
Chase Farm Hospl EN2 4 C5
Chase Gdns E4 35 C6
Twickenham TW2 152 B4
Chase Gn EN2 5 A2
Chase Green Ave EN2 5 A3
Chase Hill EN2 5 A2
Chase La IG6 57 B4
Chase Lane Inf Sch E4 35 B6
Chase Lane Jun Sch E4 35 B6
Chase Rd N14 15 D5
NW10 89 B3
Chase Ridings EN2 4 C3
Chase Road Trad Est
NW10 89 B3
Chase Side N14 15 B4
Enfield EN2 5 A3
Chase Side Ave EN2 5 A3
Chase Side Cres EN2 5 A4
Chase Side Pl EN2 5 A3
Chase Side Prim Sch EN2 5 A3
Chase The E12 77 D4
SW4 137 B2
SW16 182 C3
Bexleyheath DA7 147 D2
Bromley BR1 209 B6
Edgware HA8 26 D2
Ickenham UB10 60 C3
Loughton IG10 21 D4
Pinner HA5 40 C3
Pinner HA5 41 B5
Stanmore HA7 25 A4
Sunbury TW16 172 B2
Wallington CR0,SM6 220 B3
RM6 59 A3
Chase Way N14 15 C3
Chasefield Rd SW17 180 D6
Chaseley Ct W4 110 D1
Oatlands Pk KT13 193 C1
Chaseley St E14 97 A1
Chasemore Cl CR4 202 D2
Chasemore Gdns CR0 220 C3
Chasemore Ho SW6 264 B4
Chaseside Ave SW20 179 A1
Chaseville Par N21 16 B6
Chaseville Park Rd N21 16 B6
Chasewood Ave EN2 4 D3
Chasewood Ct NW7 27 B5
Chasewood Pk HA1 64 C5
Chater Ho 6 E2 96 D4

Chatfield Rd SW11 136 A2
Thornton Heath CR0 204 D1
Chatham Ave BR2 209 A2
Chatham Cl NW11 47 C4
Cheam SM3 201 B2
Chatham Ct SW11 158 D6
Chatham Ho 7 SE5 139 C3
22 SE18 122 B2
Chatham Pl E9 74 C2
Chatham Rd E17 53 A6
1 E18 36 D1
SW11 158 D6
Kingston u T KT1,KT2 176 C1
Chatham St
SE17 117 B2 262 D4
SE18 122 D3
Chatsfield Pl W5 88 A1
Chatsworth Ave NW4 28 C1
SW20 179 A1
Plaistow BR1 187 B6
Sidcup DA15 168 A3
Wembley HA9 66 B3
Chatsworth Cl NW4 28 C1
Coney Hall BR2,BR4 224 D6
Chatsworth Cres TW3,
TW7 130 B2
Chatsworth Ct E5 74 D4
W8 255 A4
5 Stanmore HA7 25 C5
Chatsworth Dr EN1 18 A5
Chatsworth Est E5 74 D4
Chatsworth Gdns W3 110 D5
Harrow HA2 41 D1
New Malden KT3 199 D4
Chatsworth Ho
2 Bromley BR2 209 A5
Kingston u T KT6 197 D4
Chatsworth Inf Sch
Isleworth TW3 130 A1
Sidcup DA15 168 A3
Chatsworth Jun Sch
TW3 130 A1
Chatsworth Lo 1 W4 111 B1
West Wickham BR4 224 A6
Chatsworth Par BR5 211 A4
Chatsworth Pl
Mitcham CR4 202 D6
Teddington TW11 175 A6
Chatsworth Rd E5 74 D4
E15 76 D3
NW2 68 D2
W4 133 A6
W5 88 B3
Cheam SM3 217 A4
Croydon CR0 221 B5
Hayes UB4 84 B3
Chatsworth Rise W5 88 B3
Chatsworth Way SE27 161 A1
Chattenden Ho 8 N4 51 B2
Chattern Hill TW15 170 D6
Chattern Rd TW15 171 A6
Chatterton Ct TW9 132 B3
Chatterton Rd N4 72 D5
Bromley BR2 209 D4
Chatto Rd SW11 158 D6
Chatton Ct 5 NW9 46 A5
Chaucer Ave
Cranford TW4 128 B3
Hayes UB4 84 A2
Richmond TW9 132 C3
Chaucer Cl N11 31 D5
Chaucer Ct 17 N16 73 C4
12 New Barnet EN5 13 D6
Chaucer Dr SE1 117 D2 263 D3
Chaucer Gdns SM1 217 C5
Chaucer Gn CR0 206 C2
Chaucer H SM1 217 C5
Chaucer Ho 2 SE27 183 A6
SW1 259 A1
Harrow HA2 41 D4
Chaucer Rd E7 77 A2
E11 55 A3
E17 36 A1
SE24 160 D6
W3 111 A5
Ashford TW15 170 B6
Bexley DA16 145 D4
Sidcup DA15 168 C3
Sutton SM1 217 C4
Chaulden Ho EC1 235 D1
Chauncey Cl N9 18 A1
Chaundrye Cl SE9 166 B5
Chauntler Cl E16 121 B6
Chaville Ct N11 31 A6
Cheadle Ct NW8 236 D6
Cheadle Ho 11 E14 97 B1
Cheam Common Inf Sch
KT4 216 B6
Cheam Common Jun Sch
KT4 216 B6
Cheam Common Rd
KT4 216 C5
Cheam Court Flats 1
SM3 217 A2
Cheam Fields Prim Sch
SM3 217 A3
Cheam High Sch SM3 217 A4
Cheam Mans SM3 217 A1
Cheam Park Farm Inf Sch
SM3 217 A5
Cheam Park Farm Jun Sch
SM3 217 A5
Cheam Park Way SM3 217 A2
Cheam Rd Cheam SM1 217 C2
East Ewell SM2,SM3 216 D1
Cheam St 4 SE15 140 B2
Cheam Sta SM2 217 A1
Cheam Village SM3 217 A2
Cheapside EC2 95 A1 242 B1
N13 32 C6
Chearsley SE17 262 B4
Cheddar Cl N11 31 A4
Cheddar Rd TW6 126 C3
Cheddar Waye UB4 84 B1
Cheddington Ho 9 E2 96 A6
Cheddington Rd N18 33 C6
Chedworth Cl E16 98 D1
Chedworth Ho 2 E5 74 A6
N15 51 B5
Cheeseman Cl TW12 173 A4
Cheesemans Terr W14 254 C1
Chelford Rd BR1 186 B5
Chelmer Cres IG11 102 B5
Chelmer Rd E9 74 D3
Chelmsford Cl E6 100 B1
W6 134 D6
Chelmsford Ct N14 15 D4
Chelmsford Gdns IG1 56 B2
Chelmsford Ho 5 N7 72 B4
Chelmsford Rd E11 54 B1
E17 53 C3
E18 36 D2
N14 15 C4
Chelmsford Sq NW10 90 C6
Chelsea & Westminster
Hospl SW10 136 A6 266 B5
Chelsea Barracks
SW1 115 A1 258 B1
Chelsea Bridge
SW1 137 B6 268 C6
Chelsea Bridge Rd
SW1 115 A1 258 B1
Chelsea Cl NW10 89 B6
Edgware HA8 26 C1
Hampton TW12 174 A5
New Malden KT4 200 A2
Chelsea Cloisters SW3 257 B3
Chelsea Coll of Art & Design
SW3 114 C1 257 A1
SW6 135 D2
SW6 136 A3
Chelsea Cres SW10 266 B1
Chelsea Ct 8 E4 20 A3
SW3 268 A6
Chelsea Emb
SW3 136 D6 267 C5
Chelsea Est SW3 267 A5
Chelsea Farm Ho SW10 266 D5
Chelsea Fields SW19 180 B2
Chelsea Gate SW1 258 B1
Chelsea Gdns SW1 258 B1
Cheam SM3 217 A4
Chelsea Harbour Design Ctr
SW10 266 B2
Chelsea Harbour Dr
SW10 136 A4 266 B2
Chelsea Hospl for Women
SW3 114 C1 257 A2
Chelsea Lo SW3 267 D6
SW6 265 C2
Chelsea Manor Ct SW3 267 B6
Chelsea Manor Gdns
SW3 257 B1
Chelsea Manor St
SW3 114 C1 257 B1
Chelsea Manor Studios
SW3 257 B1
Chelsea Park Gdns
SW3 136 B6 266 C6
Chelsea Physic Gdn*
SW1 115 A1 267 C6
Chelsea Reach Twr
SW10 266 C4
Chelsea Sq
SW3 114 B1 256 D1
Chelsea Twrs SW3 267 B6
Chelsfield Ave N9 18 D4
Chelsfield Gdns SE26 162 C1
Chelsfield Ho SE17 263 A3
Chelsfield Point 3 E9 74 D1
Chelsham Ho 1 SW4 137 D2
Chelsham Rd SW4 137 D2
South Croydon CR2 221 B2
Chelsiter Ct DA14 189 D6
Chelston Ct 2 E11 55 B4
Chelston Rd HA4 40 A1
Chelsworth Dr SE18 145 B6
Cheltenham Ave 8
TW1 153 A4
Cheltenham Cl
Kingston u T KT3 199 A6
Northolt UB5 63 D2
Cheltenham Ct 8 HA7 25 C5
Cheltenham Gdns E6 100 A5
Cheltenham Ho UB3 105 A3
Cheltenham Pl 1 W3 110 D4
Harrow HA3 44 A5
Cheltenham Rd E10 54 A3
SE15 162 C6
Cheltenham Terr
SW3 114 D1 257 D2
Cheltenham Villas CR7 204 C3
Chelverton Ct SW15 134 D1
Chelverton Rd SW15 134 D1
Chelwood N20 14 B2
NW5 71 A3
Chelwood Cl E4 19 D5
Chelwood Ct SW11 266 D2
Chelwood Gdns TW9 132 C3
Chelwood Ho W2 236 D1
Chenappa Cl E13 99 A4
Chenduit Way HA7 24 D5
Chene Colline Ct KT6 198 A3
Cheney Ct SE23 162 D3
Cheney Rd NW1 94 A5 233 A3
Cheney Row E17 35 B2
Cheney St HA5 40 C4
Cheneys Rd E11 76 C5
Chenies Ho W2 245 C6
Chenies Mews WC1 239 C5
Chenies Pl NW1 232 D4
Chenies St WC1 93 D2 239 C4
Chenies The NW1 232 D4
Orpington BR5,BR6 211 C3
Cheniston Gdns W8 255 C6
Chennestone Cty Prim Sch
TW16 172 B1
Chepstow Cl SW15 157 A6
Chepstow Cres
W11 113 C6 245 A6
Ilford IG3 57 C3
Chepstow Ct W11 245 A6
Chepstow Gdns UB1 85 B1
Chepstow Pl
W2 113 C6 245 B6
Chepstow Rd W2 91 C1
W7 109 A3
Croydon CR0 221 D6
Chepstow Rise CR0 221 C5
Chepstow Villas
W11 113 C6 245 A6
Chepstow Way SE15 139 D4
Chequer St EC1 95 A3 242 B5
Chequers IG9 21 B3
Chequers Cl NW9 45 C6
St Paul's Cray BR5 211 D5
Chequers Ct 7 CR0 205 D1
Chequers Ho NW8 237 A6
Chequers La RM9 103 C5
Chequers Par N13 33 A5
Dagenham RM9 103 C6
Chequers The HA5 40 D6
Chequers Way N13 32 D5
Cherbury Cl SE28 102 D1
Cherbury Ct N1 235 D3
Cherbury St N1 95 B5 235 D3
Cherchefells Mews HA7 25 B5
Cherimoya Gdns KT8 195 D6
Cherington Rd W7 108 D5
Cheriton Ave BR2 209 A4
Cheriton Cl 10 W5 87 C2
Cockfosters EN4 2 D1
Cheriton Ct 4 SE12 165 A4
SE25 205 C4
Walton-on-T KT12 194 C1
Cheriton Dr SE18 145 B6
Cheriton Ho 9 E5 74 B3
Cheriton Sq SW17 159 A2
Cherry Ave UB1 106 D5
Cherry Blossom Cl N13 32 D5
Cherry Cl E17 53 D4
7 SW2 160 C4
W5 109 D3
Carshalton SM5 218 D6
Merton SM4 201 A5
Ruislip HA4 61 D5
Cherry Cres TW8 131 B5
Cherry Croft Gdns 2
HA5 23 B3
Cherry Ct W3 111 C5
Ilford IG6 56 D6
Pinner Green HA5 22 D2
Sidcup DA14 168 B1
Cherry Garden Ho 5
SE16 118 B4
Cherry Garden Specl Sch
SE16 118 A2
Cherry Garden St SE16 118 B4
Cherry Garth TW8 109 D1
Cherry Gdns
Dagenham RM9 81 B3
Northolt UB5 63 D1
Cherry Gr Hayes UB3 106 B5
Hillingdon UB8 83 A2
Cherry Hill
Harrow Weald HA3 24 C4
New Barnet EN5 13 D5
Cherry Hill Gdns CR0 220 B4
Cherry Hills WD1 23 A5
Cherry La UB7 104 C2
Cherry Lane Jun & Inf Schs
UB7 104 B2
Cherry Laurel Wlk SW2 160 B5
Cherry Orch SE7 143 C6
West Drayton UB7 104 A4
Cherry Orchard Gdns
5 Croydon CR0 221 B6
7 Croydon CR0 205 B1
East Molesey KT8 195 B6
Cherry Orchard Prim Sch
SE7 143 C5
Cherry Orchard Rd
Croydon CR0 205 C1
East Molesey KT8 195 C6
Keston Mark BR2 226 A6
Cherry Rd EN3 6 C5
Cherry Tree Ave UB7 82 B1
Cherry Tree Cl HA0 65 A4
Cherry Tree Ct 3 E18 36 D1
17 SE7 143 C6
Cherry Tree Dr SW16 160 A1
Cherry Tree Hill N6 48 D4
Cherry Tree Ho SE14 141 B3
Cherry Tree Rd E15 76 C3
N2 48 D5
Cherry Tree Rise IG9 37 D6
Cherry Tree Terr SE1 253 B2
Cherry Tree Way HA7 25 B4
Cherry Tree Wlk EC1 242 B5
Beckenham BR3 207 B5
Coney Hall BR4 224 D4
Cherry Way
Upper Halliford TW17 193 C5
West Ewell KT19 215 B2
Cherry Wlk BR2 209 A1
Cherry Wood Way W5 88 C2
Cherrycot Hill BR6 227 B4
Cherrycot Rise BR6 227 A4
Cherrydeal Ct E11 54 B2
Cherrydown Ave E4 19 C1
Cherrydown Cl E4 19 C1
Cherrydown Rd DA14 168 D2
Cherrylands Cl NW9 67 A6
Cherrytree Ct NW9 45 A5
Cherrytree Ho 8 W10 90 D4
Cherrywood Cl E3 97 A4
Kingston u T KT2 176 C3
Cherrywood Ct 1
TW11 175 A5
Cherrywood Dr SW15 156 D6
Cherrywood La SM4,
SW20 201 A5
Chertsey Ct SW14 132 D2
Chertsey Dr SM3 217 A6
Chertsey Ho 37 E2 95 D4
Feltham TW13 151 C1
Chertsey Rd E11 76 B6
Ashford TW15,TW16 171 B4
Feltham TW13,TW16 171 B4
Feltham TW13,TW16 171 C6
Ilford IG1 79 B4
Shepperton TW17 192 A2
Shepperton TW17 192 C2
Twickenham TW2 152 B4
Chertsey St SW17 181 A5
Chervil Cl TW13 150 A1
Chervil Mews SE28 124 B5
Cherwell Ct
Teddington KT1 175 D3
West Ewell KT19 215 A4
Cherwell Ho NW8 236 D5
Cherwell Way HA4 39 A3
Cheryls Cl SW6 135 D4 265 D2
Cheseman St SE26 162 B1
Chesfield Rd KT2 176 A3
Chesham Ave BR2,BR5 210 D3
Chesham Cl SW1 258 A5
Chesham Cres SE20 184 C2
Chesham Ct SW18 158 B4
Chesham Flats W1 248 B6
Chesham Mews SW1 258 A6
Chesham Pl
SW1 115 A3 258 A5
Chesham Rd SE20 184 C2
Kingston u T KT1,KT2 176 C1
Chesham St NW10 67 B5
SW1 115 A3 258 A5
Chesham Terr W13 109 B4
Cheshir Ho NW4 46 C5
Cheshire Cl E17 35 D2
Mitcham CR4,SW16 204 A6
Cheshire Gdns KT9 213 D2
Cheshire Ho SM4 201 D2
Cheshire Rd N22 32 B4
Cheshire St E2 95 D3 243 D6
Chesholm Rd N16 73 C5
Cheshunt Ho 7 NW6 91 D6
Cheshunt Rd E7 77 B2
Belvedere DA17 125 C1
Chesil Ct 18 E2 96 C5
SW3 267 B6
Chesil Way UB4 83 D4
Chesilton Rd
SW6 135 B4 264 C2
Chesley Gdns E6 100 A4
Chesney Cres CR0 224 A1
Chesney Ct W9 91 C3
Chesney Ho SE13 142 B1
Chesney St SW11 268 A1
Chesnut Ave N E17 54 B5
Chesnut Gr N17 51 D6
Chesnut Rd N17 51 D6
Chessholme Ct TW16 171 C3
Chessholme Rd TW15 171 A4
Chessing Ct N2 48 D6
Chessington Ave N3 47 B6
Bexley DA7 147 A5
Chessington Cl KT19 215 A2
Chessington Comm Coll
KT9 213 D1
Chessington Ct N3 47 B6
Pinner HA5 41 B5
Chessington Hall Gdns
KT9 213 D1
Chessington Hill Pk
KT9 214 C3
Chessington Ho 19
SW8 137 D3
Chessington Lo N3 47 B6
Chessington Mans E10 53 C2
E11 54 C2
Chessington North Sta
KT9 214 A3
Chessington Par KT9 213 D3
Chessington Park KT9 214 C4
Chessington Pk KT9 214 C4
Chessington Rd KT19 215 B1
Chessington South Sta
KT9 213 D1
Chessington Way BR4 223 D6
Chesson Rd
W14 135 B6 264 D6
Chesswood Way HA5 22 D1
Chestbrook Ct 12 EN1 17 C6
Chester Ave
Richmond TW10 154 B5
Twickenham TW2 151 B3
Chester Cl SW1 248 C1
SW13 134 B2
Chester Cl *continued*
Ashford TW15 171 B5
Hayes UB8 82 D1
1 Richmond TW10 154 B5
Sutton SM1 217 C6
Chester Close N NW1 231 D2
Chester Close S NW1 231 D1
Chester Cres E8 73 D3
Chester Ct NW1 231 D1
NW5 71 A4
4 SE5 139 B5
SE8 118 D1
2 W3 88 C1
Chester Dr HA2 41 C3
Chester Gate NW1 231 D1
Chester Gdns W13 87 B1
Enfield EN3 18 B5
Morden SM4 202 A3
Chester Ho N19 71 B6
1 SE8 141 B6
Kingston u T KT1 176 D1
Chester Mews SW1 258 C6
Chester Pl NW1 231 C2
Chester Rd E7 77 D1
E11 55 B3
E16 98 C3
E17 52 D4
N9 18 B3
N17 51 C6
N19 71 B6
NW1 93 B4 231 C2
SW19,SW20 178 C4
Harlington TW6 126 C2
Hounslow TW4 128 B2
Ilford IG3 57 D2
Sidcup DA15 167 C6
Chester Row
SW1 115 A2 258 B4
Chester Sq SW1 115 B2 258 C4
Chester Sq Mews SW1 258 C5
Chester St E2 96 A3
E2 96 A6
SW1 115 A3 258 B6
Chester Terr
NW1 93 B4 231 C2
Chester Way
SE11 116 C2 261 B3
Chesterfield Ct KT6 198 A4
Chesterfield Dr KT10 213 A6
Chesterfield Flats EN5 12 D6
Chesterfield Gdns N4 50 D4
SE10 142 B5
W1 248 C4
Chesterfield Gr SE22 161 D6
Chesterfield Hill
W1 115 B5 248 C4
Chesterfield Ho
6 SW16 181 C5
W1 248 B4
Chesterfield Lo N21 16 B4
Chesterfield Mews N4 50 D4
Chesterfield Rd E10 54 A3
N3 29 C4
W4 133 A6
Ashford TW15 170 A5
Ducks Island EN5 12 D6
Enfield EN3 7 A6
West Ewell KT19 215 B1
Chesterfield Sch EN3 7 A6
Chesterfield St W1 248 C4
Chesterfield Way SE15 140 C5
Hayes UB3 106 A4
Chesterford Gdns NW3 69 D4
Chesterford Ho 4
SE18 143 D5
Chesterford Rd E12 78 B3
Chesterman Ct W4 133 C5
Chesters The KT3 177 C2
Chesterton Cl SW18 157 C6
Greenford UB6 85 D5
Chesterton Dr TW19 148 B3
Chesterton Ho 21 SW11 136 B2
3 W10 91 A2
Chesterton Prim Sch
SW11 137 A4 268 A1
Chesterton Rd E13 99 A4
W10 91 A2
Chesterton Sq W8 255 A3
Chesterton Terr E13 99 A4
6 Kingston u T KT1 176 C1
Chesthunte Rd N17 33 A2
Chestnut Alley SW6 264 D5
Chestnut Ave E7 77 B4
N8 50 A4
11 SW14 133 B2
Brentford TW8 109 D2
Buckhurst Hill IG9 21 D1
Coney Hall BR4 224 C4
Edgware HA8 26 B4
Hampton KT8,KT11 174 D2
Hampton TW12 173 C3
Thames Ditton KT10 196 B1
Wembley HA0 65 B3
Worcester Pk KT19 215 C4
Yiewsley UB7 104 B6
Chestnut Ave S E17 54 B4
Chestnut Cl N14 15 D6
1 N16 73 B6
SE6 186 A6
SE14 141 B4
SW16 182 C6
Ashford TW15 170 D6
Ashford TW16 171 D4
Buckhurst Hill IG9 21 D2
Carshalton SM5 202 D1
Harlington UB7 126 D5
Hayes UB3 105 C6
Sidcup DA15 168 A2
Chestnut Ct N8 49 D3
N8 50 A4
SW6 264 D6
Beckenham BR3 185 C3
5 Croydon CR0 221 A4
Feltham TW13 172 D5
Hounslow TW3 129 C2
Kingston u T KT3 199 C6
Surbiton KT6 198 A2
Wembley HA0 65 B3
Chestnut Dr E11 55 A3
Bexleyheath DA7 147 A2
Harrow HA3 24 D2
Pinner HA5 41 A3
Chestnut Gr SW12 159 A3
W5 109 D3
East Barnet EN4 14 D6
Isleworth TW7 131 A1
Kingston u T KT3 199 B6
Mitcham CR4 203 D5
South Croydon CR2 222 B1
Wembley HA0 65 B3
Chestnut Grove Sch
SW12 159 A3
Chestnut Ho 7 NW3 70 D2
SE4 141 B2
SE27 161 A1
1 W4 111 C2
Chestnut La N20 13 A3
Chestnut Rd SE21,SE27 161 A1
SW20 178 D1
Ashford TW15 170 D6
Kingston u T KT2 176 A3
Twickenham TW2 152 C2
Chestnut Rise SE18 123 C1
Chestnut Row N3 29 C3
Chestnut Way TW13 150 B1
Chestnut Wlk
Upper Halliford TW17 193 C5
Woodford IG8 37 A5
Chestnuts Ct 3 E17 54 A6
Chestnuts The N2 48 D4
1 N5 72 D4
NW9 45 C6
SE18 144 D4
3 Erith DA17 125 B1
Penge BR3 206 D6
Uxbridge UB10 60 A1
Walton-on-T KT12 194 B1
Cheston Ave CR0 207 B1
Chestwood Gr UB10 60 B1
Chettle Cl SE1 262 C6
Chettle Ct N8 50 C3
Chetwode Ho NW8 237 A6
Chetwode Rd SW17 158 D1
Chetwood Wlk 13 E6 100 A2
Chetwynd Ave EN4 14 D3
Chetwynd Dr UB10 82 B5
Chetwynd Rd NW5 71 B5
Cheval Ct SW15 134 B1
Cheval Pl SW7 114 C3 257 B6
Cheval St E14 119 C3
Chevalier Cl HA7 26 A6
Cheveney Wlk 2 BR2 209 A6
Chevening Ho BR5 190 A2
Chevening Rd NW6 91 A6
SE10 120 D1
SE19 183 B4
Chevenings The DA14 168 C1
Cheverell Ho 24 E2 96 A5
Cheverton Rd N19 49 D1
Chevet St E9 75 A3
Chevington NW2 69 B2
Cheviot 4 N17 34 B3
Cheviot Cl Bushey WD2 8 A5
Enfield EN1 5 B3
Harlington UB3 127 B5
Cheviot Ct 16 SE14 140 C5
Enfield EN2 5 B3
Southall UB2 107 D2
Cheviot Gate NW2 69 A6
Cheviot Gdns NW2 69 A6
SE27 182 D6
Cheviot Ho N16 51 D1
Cheviot Rd SE27 182 D5
Cheviot Way IG2 57 C5
Cheviots Hostel EN1 5 B3
Chevron Cl E16 99 A1
Chevy Rd UB2 108 A4
Chewton Rd E17 53 A5
Cheylesmore Ho SW1 258 C2
Cheyne Ave E18 54 D6
Twickenham TW2 151 B3
Cheyne Cl 6 NW4 46 B4
Keston Mark BR2 226 A5
Cheyne Ct SW3 267 C6
1 Croydon CR0 221 D6
4 Wallington SM6 219 B2
Cheyne Gdns
SW3 136 C6 267 B5
Cheyne Hill KT5 198 B5
Cheyne Mews
SW3 136 C6 267 B5
Cheyne Path W7 86 D1
Cheyne Rd TW15 171 B4
Cheyne Row
SW3 136 C6 267 A5
Cheyne Wlk N21 16 D6
NW4 46 C3
SW10 136 B5 266 C4
Croydon CR0 222 A6
Cheyney Ho 2 E9 74 D2
Cheyneys Ave HA8 25 D4
Chichele Gdns CR0 221 C4
Chichele Rd NW2 68 D3
Chicheley Gdns HA3 24 A3
Chicheley Rd HA3 24 A3
Chicheley St SE1 250 D2

Chichelle Ho HA8 26 B6
Chichester Ave HA4 61 B6
Chichester Cl E6 100 A1
SE3 143 C4
Hampton TW12 173 B4
Chichester Ct
Edgware HA8 26 C4
Harrow HA2 41 B1
Northolt UB5 85 A6
3 Old Bexley DA5 169 C4
Stanmore HA7 44 A6
Stanwell TW19 148 A3
Chichester Gdns IG1 56 B2
Chichester Ho NW6 91 C5
2 Kingston u T KT2 176 D2
Chichester Mews SE27 182 C6
Chichester Rd E11 76 C5
N9 18 A3
NW6 91 C5
W2 91 D2
South Croydon CR0 221 C5
Chichester Rents WC2 241 A2
Chichester St
SW1 115 C1 259 B1
Chichester Way E14 120 B2
Feltham TW14 150 C4
Chicksand Ho 13 E1 96 A2
Chicksand St E1 95 D2 243 D3
Chiddingfold N12 13 C1
Chiddingstone SE13 164 A6
Chiddingstone Ave DA7 147 B5
Chiddingstone St SW6 135 C3
Chieveley Par DA7 147 D2
Chieveley Rd DA7 147 D1
Chignell Pl 7 W13 109 A5
Chigwell Hill E1 118 B6
Chigwell Hurst Ct HA5 40 D6
Chigwell Rd E18 55 B6
Woodford IG8 37 D3
Chilam Ho 5 SE15 140 C6
Chilchester Ct 3 BR3 207 D6
Chilcombe Ho 6 SW15 156 A4
Chilcot Cl 13 E14 97 D1
Child Ct E11 54 B2
Childebert Rd SW17 159 B2
Childeric Prim Sch
SE14 141 A5
Childeric Rd SE14 141 A5
Childerley St
SW6 135 A4 264 A2
Childerly KT1 198 C6
Childers St SE8 141 B6
Childs Ct UB3 106 A6
Childs Hill Prim Sch
NW2 69 A5
Childs La 11 SE19 183 C4
Child's Pl SW5 255 B3
Child's St SW5 255 B3
Childs Way NW11 47 B4
Child's Wlk SW5 255 B3
Chilham Cl Sidcup DA5 169 B4
Wembley UB6 87 A5
Chilham Ct 14 SW9 138 C2
Chilham Ho SE1 262 D6
Chilham Rd SE9 188 A6
Chilham Way BR2 209 A2
Chillerton Rd SW17 181 B5
Chillingford Ho SW17 180 A6
Chillingworth Gdns
TW1 152 D1
Chillingworth Rd N7 72 C3
Chilmark Gdns KT3 200 A3
Chilmark Rd SW16 181 D2
Chiltern Ave Bushey WD2 8 A5
Twickenham TW2 151 C3
Chiltern Cl
Ickenham UB10 60 C6
North Cheam KT4 216 C6
South Croydon CR0 221 C5
WD2 8 A5
Chiltern Ct N10 31 A1
NW1 237 D5
11 SE9 166 C5
15 SE14 140 C5
Harrow HA1 42 B4
Hillingdon UB8 82 D3
New Barnet EN5 14 A6
Chiltern Dene EN2 4 B1
Chiltern Dr KT5 198 D4
Chiltern Gdns NW2 68 D5
Beckenham BR2 208 D5
Chiltern Ho 5 N9 18 A1
5 N16 51 D1
SE17 139 B6
W5 88 A2
4 W10 91 A2
Chiltern Rd E3 97 C3
Ilford IG2 57 C4
Pinner HA5 40 C4
Chiltern St W1 93 A2 238 A4
Chiltern Way IG8 21 A1
Chilthorne Cl SE6 163 B4
Chilton Ave W5 109 D2
Chilton Gr SE8 119 A2
Chilton Rd Edgware HA8 26 C4
Richmond TW9 132 C2
Chilton St E2 95 D3 243 D6
Chiltonian Ind Est SE12 164 D5
Chiltons The 1 E18 37 A1
Chilver St SE10 120 D1
Chilwell Gdns WD1 22 C6
Chilworth Ct 8 SW19 156 D3
Chilworth Gdns SM1 218 A5
Chilworth Mews
W2 92 B1 236 C1
Chilworth St W2 92 A1 236 B1
Chimes Ave N13 32 D6
Chimney Ct 23 E1 118 B5
Chimneys Ct 2 SW19 178 C3
China Ct 1 E1 118 B5
Chinbrook Cres SE12 165 B1
Chinbrook Rd SE12 165 B1
Chinchilla Dr TW4 128 C3
Chindit Ho 11 N16 73 B4
Chine The N10 49 C5
N21 16 D6
Wembley HA0 65 B3
Ching Ct E4 20 C1
Ching Way E4 35 B4
Chingdale Rd E4 20 C1
Chingford Ave E4 19 D2
Chingford CE Inf Sch E4 20 B3
Chingford CE Jun Sch
E4 20 B3
Chingford Hall Prim Sch
E4 35 B4
Chingford Hospl E4 20 A1
Chingford Ind Ctr E4 35 A5
Chingford La IG8 36 D5
Chingford Mount Rd E4 35 C5
Chingford Rd E4 35 C3
E17 35 D1
Chingford Sch E4 19 D3
Chingford Sta E4 20 C4
Chingley Cl BR1 186 C4
Chinnery Cl EN1 5 D4
Chinnocks Wharf E14 119 A6
Chinnor Cres UB6 86 A5
Chip St SW4 137 D1
Chipka St E14 120 A4
Chipley St SE14 141 A6
Chipmunk Gr UB5 85 A4
Chippendale Ho SW1 258 D1
Chippendale St E5 74 D5
Chippenham 4 KT1 176 B1
Chippenham Ave HA9 66 D3
Chippenham Cl HA5 39 D5
Chippenham Gdns NW6 91 C4
Chippenham Mews W9 91 C3
Chippenham Rd W9 91 C3
Chipperfield Rd BR5 190 A1
Chipping Cl EN5 1 A2
Chipstead Ave CR7 204 D5
Chipstead Cl SE19 183 D3
Chipstead Gdns NW2 68 B6
Chipstead Ho 4 SW2 160 A3
Chipstead St SW6 135 C3
Chirk Cl UB4 85 A3
Chisenhale JMI Sch E3 97 A5
Chisenhale Rd E3 97 A5
Chisholm Ct W6 112 A1
Chisholm Rd
Croydon CR0 221 C6
13 Richmond TW10 154 B5
Chisledon Wlk E9 75 B2
Chislehurst & Sidcup Gram
Sch DA15 168 B2
Chislehurst Ave N12 30 A3
Chislehurst CE Prim Sch
BR7 189 A3
Chislehurst High St
BR7 188 D4
Chislehurst Rd
Bromley BR1,BR7 188 A2
Broom Hill BR6 211 D2
Petts Wood BR5,BR6,BR7 211 C4
Richmond TW10 154 A6
Sidcup DA14 190 A5
Chislehurst Sta BR7 188 C1
Chislet 5 NW5 71 A2
Chislet Cl BR3 185 C3
Chisley Rd 5 N15 51 C3
Chiswell Sq SE3 143 B3
Chiswell St EC1 95 B2 242 C4
Chiswick Cl CR0 220 B5
Chiswick Comm Sch
W4 133 B5
Chiswick Common Rd
W4 111 B2
Chiswick Ct HA5 41 B6
Chiswick High Rd W4 111 C2
Chiswick High Road (North
Circular Rd) W4 110 C1
Chiswick House* W4 133 B6
Chiswick La W4 111 C1
Chiswick La S W4 133 D6
Chiswick Mall W4 111 D1
Chiswick Maternity Hospl
W4 111 D1
Chiswick Park Sta W4 111 A2
Chiswick Plaza W4 133 A6
Chiswick Quay W4 133 A4
Chiswick Rd N9 18 A2
W4 111 A2
Chiswick Rdbt W4 110 C1
Chiswick Sq W4 133 C6
Chiswick Sta W4 133 A5
Chiswick Staithe W4 133 A4
Chiswick Terr 6 W4 111 A2
Chiswick Village W4 132 D6
Chiswick Wharf W4 133 D6
Chitterfield Gate UB7 126 C5
Chitty St W1 93 C2 239 B4
Chitty's La RM8 80 D6
Chivalry Rd SW11 158 C6
Chivelston 27 SW19 156 D3
Chivenor Gr KT2 175 D5
Chivers Rd E4 35 D6
Choats Manor Way
RM9 103 B5
Choats Rd IG11 102 D4
Chobham Gdns SW19 156 D2
Chobham Rd E15 76 B3
Cholmeley Cres N6 49 B2
Cholmeley Ct N12 30 A6
Cholmeley Lo N6 49 B1
Cholmeley Pk N6 49 B2
Cholmley Gdns NW6 69 C3
Cholmley Rd KT7 197 B3
Cholmondeley Ave
NW10 90 A5
Cholmondeley Wlk
TW9 153 C6
Chopin's Ct 13 E1 118 B5
Chopwell Cl E15 76 B1
Chorleywood Cres BR5 190 A1
Choumert Gr SE15 140 A3
Choumert Rd SE15 139 D3
Choumert Sq 2 SE15 140 A3
Chow Sq 2 E8 73 D3
Chrisp Ho SE10 142 C6
Chrisp St E14 97 D1
Christ Church Bentinck CE
Prim Sch NW1 92 C2 237 B4
Christ Church CE Inf Sch
KT3 199 C6
Christ Church CE JMI Sch
SE10 120 C1
SE18 144 C4
Christ Church CE Jun Sch
W5 109 D6
Kingston u T KT3 199 B6
Christ Church CE Prim Sch
NW1 93 B4 231 D2
NW3 70 B5
SW2 160 B3
SW9 138 C4
Tolworth KT5 198 C3
Christ Church CE Sec Sch
N12 30 B5
Christ Church Ct NW6 69 A1
NW10 89 C6
Christ Church JMI Sch
E1 95 D2 243 D3
Christ Church La EN5 1 A3
Christ Church Prim Sch
SE23 162 D2
SW11 136 C2
Christ Church Rd N8 50 A3
1 Beckenham BR3 185 C1
Surbiton KT5 198 B3
Christ Church Sq 4 E9 96 C6
Christ the King Coll
SE13 142 B2
Christ the King RC Fst Sch
TW19 148 A5
Christ the King RC Prim Sch
N4 72 B6
Christabel Cl TW7 130 C2
Christchurch Ave N12 30 A4
NW6 69 A1
Harrow HA3 42 D5
4 Teddington TW11 175 A5
Wembley HA0 66 A2
Christchurch Cl N12 30 B3
SW19 180 B3
Enfield EN2 5 A3
Christchurch Ct UB4 84 C3
Christchurch Gdns HA3 43 A5
Christchurch Gn HA0 66 A2
Christchurch Hill NW3 70 B4
Christchurch Ho 2
SW2 160 A3
Christchurch Lo EN4 2 D1
Christchurch Pas NW3 70 A5
Christchurch Pk SM2 218 A1
Christchurch Prim Sch
NW6 69 B1
SW3 136 D6 267 C6
Ilford IG1 57 A1
Christchurch Rd SW14 155 A6
SW19 180 B3
Harlington TW6 126 C2
Ilford IG1 57 A1
Sidcup DA15 167 D1
Christchurch St
SW3 136 D6 267 C6
Christchurch Terr SW3 267 C6
Christchurch Way SE10 120 C1
Christian Ct SE16 119 B5
Christian Fields SW16 182 C3
Christian St E1 96 A1
Christie Ct 1 N19 72 A6
NW3 70 C3
Christie Dr SE25 206 A4
Christie Gdns RM6 58 B2
Christie Ho 2 SE10 120 D1
Bexleyheath DA6 169 D6
4 West Wickham BR4 207 D1
Christie Rd E9 75 A2
Christina Sq N4 50 D1
Christina St EC2 243 A6
Christopher Ave W7 109 A3
Christopher Boone's
Almshouses SE13 142 B1
Christopher Cl SE16 118 D4
Bexley DA15 167 D6
Christopher Ct
Ashford TW15 170 A5
Barnet EN5 1 D1
6 Croydon CR0 206 A1
Christopher Gdns RM9 80 D3
Christopher Ho 2 N6 49 D2
Christopher Pl NW1 232 D1
Christopher Rd UB2 106 B2
Christopher St
EC2 95 B3 242 D5
Christ's Coll NW11 47 D6
SE3 143 A4
Christ's Coll Upper Sch
N3 29 B1
Christ's Sch (East Side)
SW14 133 B2
Christ's Sch (West Side)
TW10 154 B6
Chryssell Rd SW9 138 C5
Chubworthy St SE14 141 A6
Chuch Paddock Ct
SM6 219 D5
Chudleigh 1 DA14 190 B6
Chudleigh Cres IG3 79 C4
Chudleigh Gdns SM1 218 A5
Chudleigh Rd NW6 68 D1
SE4 163 C6
Twickenham TW1,TW2 152 D4
Chudleigh St E1 96 D1
Chudleigh Way HA4 40 A1
Chulsa Rd SE26 184 B5
Chumleigh Gdns SE5 139 C6
Chumleigh St SE5 139 C6
Chumleigh Wlk KT5 198 B5
Church Almshouses 8
TW9 132 B1
Church App SE21 161 B1
Church Ave E4 36 B4
N2 30 B2
NW1 71 B2
SW14 133 B2
Beckenham BR3 185 C2
Northolt UB5 63 B1
Pinner HA5 41 B3
Ruislip HA4 39 B1
Sidcup DA14 190 B5
Southall UB2 107 A3
Church Cl N20 14 C1
W8 245 C2
Edgware HA8 27 A5
Hayes UB4 83 B2
Hounslow TW4 129 B3
West Drayton UB7 104 A3
Church Cres E9 74 D1
N3 29 B2
N10 49 B5
N20 14 C1
Church Ct EC4 241 B1
N2 48 B6
SE26 185 A5
Church Dr NW9 45 B1
Coney Hall BR4 224 C5
Harrow HA2 41 C3
Church Elm La RM10 81 C2
Church End E17 53 D5
NW4 46 B6
Church Entry EC4 241 D1
Church Farm House Mus
NW4 46 B6
Church Farm La SM3 217 A2
Church Garth 3 N19 71 D6
Church Gate N20 14 C2
SW6 135 A2
Church Gdns W5 109 D4
Wembley HA0 65 A4
Church Gn 4 SW9 138 C3
Hayes UB3 83 D1
Church Gr SE13 163 D6
Teddington KT1 175 C1
Church Green Ho 1
W4 111 A2
Church Hill E17 53 D5
N21 16 C4
SE18 122 B3
SW19 179 B5
Harrow HA1 42 C1
Wallington SM5 218 D3
Church Hill Prim Sch
EN4 14 D4
Church Hill Rd E17 53 D5
Cheam SM1,SM3 217 A4
East Barnet EN4 14 D4
Kingston u T KT6 198 A4
Church Hill Wood BR5 211 D4
Church Hyde SE18 145 C6
Church La E11 54 C1
E17 53 D5
N2 48 B6
N8 50 B5
N9 18 A2
N17 33 C2
NW9 45 B2
SW17 181 A5
W5 109 D4
Chessington KT9 214 B2
Chislehurst BR7 189 A2
Dagenham RM10 81 D1
Enfield EN1 5 B2
Harrow HA3 24 D2
Keston Mark BR2 210 A1
Pinner HA5 41 B6
Teddington TW11 174 D5
Thames Ditton KT7 197 A3
Twickenham TW1 153 A3
Wallington SM6 219 D5
SW19 179 C2
Church Lo UB5 63 B1
Church Manor Way
SE18,SE2 124 A2
Church Mdw KT6 213 C6
Church Mead SE5 139 A5
Church Mead Inf Sch
E10 53 C1
Church Mead Jun Sch
E10 53 C1
Church Mount N2 48 B4
Church Par TW15 170 B6
Church Path E11 55 A4
E17 53 D5
SW19 179 C1
W4 111 A3
Croydon CR0 221 A6
Mitcham CR4 202 C6
Church Pl SW1 249 B5
Church Pl *continued*
W5 109 D4
Mitcham CR4 202 C6
Uxbridge UB10 61 A5
Church Rd E10 75 C6
E12 78 A3
E17 35 A1
N6 49 A3
N17 33 D3
NW4 46 C5
NW10 67 C1
SE19 183 C3
SW13 134 A4
SW19 179 A6
W3 111 A4
W7 108 C6
Ashford TW15 170 B6
Barking IG11 79 A2
Beckenham BR2 208 C6
Bexley DA6,DA7 147 B2
Bexley DA16 146 B3
Bromley BR1,BR2 187 A1
Buckhurst Hill IG9 21 B3
Cheam SM3 217 A2
Claygate KT10 212 D1
Cranford TW5 128 B6
Croydon CR0 221 A5
East Molesey KT8 196 B6
Enfield EN3 18 C6
Feltham TW13 172 D5
Hayes UB3 105 D6
Heston TW5 129 C5
Hounslow TW7 130 C5
Ilford IG2 57 C3
Keston BR2 225 D1
Kingston u T KT1 176 B1
Long Ditton KT6 197 C1
Lower Halliford TW17 192 D2
Mitcham CR4,SW19 180 B1
New Malden KT4 199 C1
Northolt UB5 85 A6
Orpington BR6 227 B3
Richmond TW10 176 A6
Richmond TW10,TW9 154 A6
Sidcup DA14 190 A6
Southall UB2 107 B3
Stanmore HA7 25 B5
Teddington TW11 174 D5
Uxbridge UB8 82 A3
Wallington SM6 219 D5
West Drayton UB7 104 A3
West Ewell KT19 215 B1
CR4 202 C6
Church Rd N N2 30 B2
Church Rd S N2 30 B2
Church Rise SE23 162 D2
Chessington KT9 214 B2
Church Row NW3 70 A4
Chislehurst BR7 189 A2
Church Row Mews BR7 189 A3
Church Sq TW17 192 D2
Church St E15 98 D6
E16 122 D5
N9 17 C2
NW8 92 C3 237 A5
W4 133 D6
Croydon CR0 221 A6
Dagenham RM10 81 D2
Enfield EN2 5 B2
Hampton TW12 174 A2
Isleworth TW7 131 B3
Kingston u T KT1 175 D1
Sunbury TW16 194 B6
Twickenham TW1 153 A3
Walton-on-T KT12 194 A2
Church St N E15 98 C6
Church St Sta CR0 221 A6
Church Stretton Rd
TW3 152 A6
Church Terr NW4 46 B6
SE13 142 C2
20 Richmond TW10 153 D6
Church Vale N2 48 D6
SE23 162 D2
Church Villa TW16 194 B6
Church Way N20 14 C1
Church Wlk N16 73 B4
NW2 69 B5
NW9 67 B6
SW16 181 C1
SW20 200 C6
Brentford TW8 131 C6
Hayes UB3 83 D1
15 Richmond TW10 153 D6
Thames Ditton KT7 196 D3
Walton-on-T KT12 194 A1
Churchbank E17 53 C5
Churchbury Cl EN1 5 C3
Churchbury La EN1 5 C3
Churchbury Rd SE9 165 D4
Enfield EN1 5 C3
Churchcroft Cl SW12 159 A4
Churchdale Ct 1 W4 110 D1
Churchdown BR1 186 C6
Churchfield Ave N12 30 B4
Churchfield Cl
Harrow HA2 42 A5
Hayes UB3 105 D6
Churchfield Ho W2 236 C5
Churchfield Mans 5
SW6 135 B3
Churchfield Prim Sch
N9 17 D3
Churchfield Rd W3 111 A5
W7 108 C4
W13 109 C5
Bexley DA16 146 A2
Walton-on-T KT12 194 A1
Churchfield Sch SE2 124 A2
Churchfield Way N12 30 A4
Churchfields E18 37 A2
SE10 142 A6
East Molesey KT8 195 C6
Churchfields Ave TW13 151 C1
Churchfields Inf Sch
E18 37 A2
Churchfields Jun Sch
E18 37 A2
Churchfields Prim Sch
BR3 206 D6
Churchfields Rd BR3 185 A1
Churchill Ave
Harrow HA3 43 B3
Hillingdon UB10 82 D4
Churchill Cl
East Bedfont TW14 149 D3
Hillingdon UB10 82 D4
Churchill Ct N4 50 C2
N9 17 B3
NW2 68 B3
4 Farnborough BR6 227 A3
Harrow HA2 41 D4
7 Ilford IG1 78 D5
Northolt UB5 63 C3
Churchill Gardens Prim Sch
SW1 115 C1 259 B1
Churchill Gdns
SW1 137 C6 269 A6
W3 88 C1
Churchill Gdns Rd
SW1 137 C6 269 A6
Churchill Ho TW8 109 C1
Churchill Lo IG8 36 D4
Churchill Mews IG8 36 D4
Churchill Pl E14 119 D5
Harrow HA1 42 C5
Churchill Rd E16 99 C1
NW2 68 B2
NW5 71 B4
Edgware HA8 26 C4
South Croydon CR2 221 A1
Churchill Terr E4 19 C1
Churchill Way
Ashford TW16 172 A4
Bromley BR1 187 A1
Churchill Wlk E9 74 C3
Churchley Rd SE26 184 B6
Churchley Villas SE26 184 B6
Churchmead Cl EN4 14 C5
Churchmead Rd NW10 68 A2
Churchmore Rd SW16 181 D2
Churchview Rd TW2 152 B2
Churchward Ho SE17 138 D6
SW5 254 D1
Churchway NW1 232 D2
Cockfosters EN4 2 D1
Churchwood Gdns IG8 37 A6
Churchyard Row
SE11 116 D2 261 D4
Churnfield 2 N4 72 C6
Churston Ave E13 99 B6
Churston Cl 17 SW2 160 C3
Churston Dr SM4 201 A4
Churston Gdns N11 31 C4
Churston Mans WC1 240 D5
Churton Pl SW1 259 B3
Churton St SW1 115 C2 259 B3
Chute Ho 18 SW9 138 C3
Chuter Ede Ho SW6 264 D5
Chyngton Cl DA15 167 D1
Chyngton Ct HA1 64 C6
Cibber Rd SE23 162 D2
Cicada Rd SW18 158 A6
Cicely Ho NW8 229 D3
Cicely Rd SE15 140 A4
Cinderford Way BR1 186 C6
Cinema Par RM8 81 B6
Cinnamon Cl CR0 204 A2
Cinnamon Row 3
SW11 136 A2
Cinnamon St E1 118 B5
Cinnamon Wharf SE1 253 D2
Cintra Ct SE19 183 D4
Cintra Pk SE19 183 D3
Circle Ct HA0 65 D4
Circle Gdns SW19 179 C1
Circle Ho 12 E14 98 B1
Circle The NW2 67 C5
NW7 27 B4
SE1 253 D2
Circuit Rd SE28 124 A4
Circuits The HA5 40 C5
Circular Rd N2 30 B2
N17 51 D6
Circular Way SE18 144 C6
Circus Lo NW8 229 C2
Circus Mews W1 237 C4
Circus Pl EC2 242 D3
Circus Rd NW8 92 B5 229 C3
Circus St SE10 142 A5
Cirencester St W2 91 D2
Cirrus 17 NW9 27 D1
Cissbury Ho 6 SE26 162 A1
Cissbury Rd N15 51 B4
Cissbury Ring N N12 29 C5
Cissbury Ring S N12 29 B5
Citizen Ho N7 72 C4
Citizen Rd N7 72 C4
Citron Terr 3 SE15 140 B2
Citrus Ho 14 SE8 119 B1
City & Guilds of London Art
Sch The SE11 116 C1 261 B1

City & Islington Coll
EC1 95 A4 235 B1
EC1 95 B3 242 C5
N1 95 B6 235 C6
N4 72 D6
N7 72 B4
N7 72 B5
City Airport Pier E16 120 D5
City Banking Coll
SE1 117 B4 252 D2
City Bsns Ctr 28 SE16 118 C4
City Central Est EC1 235 A1
City Forum EC1 95 A4 235 A2
City Garden Row
N1 94 D5 234 D3
City Gate E1 96 C3
City Institute The
WC2 94 B1 240 C1
City Literature Inst The
WC2 94 A1 240 B2
City of London Sch
EC4 117 A6 252 A6
City of London Sch for Girls
EC2 95 A2 242 B4
City of Westminster Coll
W10 91 A4
City of Westminster Coll
NW1 92 C2 237 B4
W2 92 B2 236 C4
W9 91 C4
City Prospect 5 SE19 183 C4
City Rd EC1 95 A4 235 B2
City Thameslink Sta
EC4 94 D1 241 C1
City Univ The
EC1 94 D4 234 C1
EC1 94 D4 234 C2
City Wharf Ho KT7 197 B3
Civic Way Ilford IG6 57 A5
Ruislip HA4 62 D3
Civil Service Coll
SW1 115 C2 259 A3
Clabon Mews
SW1 114 D2 257 C4
Clack St SE16 118 C4
Clacton Rd E6 99 D4
E17 53 A3
N17 33 D1
Claigmar Gdns N3 29 D2
Claire Ct N12 14 A1
NW2 69 A2
Bushey WD2 8 B3
Claire Gdns HA7 25 C5
Claire Pl E14 119 C3
Clairvale Rd TW5 129 A4
Clairview Rd SW16 181 B5
Clairville Gdns W7 108 C5
Clairville Point 12 SE23 162 D1
Clamp Hill HA7 24 C5
Clancarty Rd SW6 135 C3
Clandon Cl W3 110 D4
Stoneleigh KT17 216 A2
Clandon Ct Plaistow BR1 187 A4
Sutton SM2 218 B2
Clandon Gdns N3 47 C6
Clandon Ho N3 47 C6
12 Kingston u T KT2 176 D4
Clandon Rd IG3 79 C6
Clandon St SE8 141 C3
Clanfield Ho 12 SW15 156 A3
Clanfield Way 12 SE15 139 C5
Clanricarde Gdns
W2 113 C6 245 B5
Clapham Common★
SW4 137 C1
Clapham Common North Side SW4 137 A1
Clapham Common South Side SW4 159 C6
Clapham Common Sta
SW4 137 C1
Clapham Common West Side
SW4,SW11 136 D1
SW11 159 A6
Clapham Court Terr 2
SW4 160 A6
Clapham Cres SW4 137 D1
Clapham Ct 3 SW4 160 A6
Clapham High St SW4 137 D1
Clapham High Street Sta
SW4 137 D2
Clapham Junction Est
SW11 136 C1
Clapham Junction Sta
SW11 136 C1
Clapham Manor Ct 1
SW4 137 C2
Clapham Manor Prim Sch
SW4 137 C2
Clapham Manor St
SW4 137 D2
Clapham Mans SW4 159 B5
Clapham North Sta
SW4 138 A2
Clapham Park Rd SW4 137 D1
Clapham Park Sch
SW4 160 A6
Clapham Park Terr 4
SW2 160 A6
Clapham Rd
SW9 138 B4 270 D2
Clapham South Sta
SW4 159 B5
Claps Gate La E6 100 D3
Clapton Comm E5 52 A2
Clapton Girls Sch E5 74 C4
Clapton Ho 7 E5 74 C6
Clapton Pas E5 74 C3
Clapton Sq E5 74 C3
Clapton Sta E5 74 B6
Clapton Terr E5 52 A1
Clapton Way E5 74 A5
Clara Grant JMI Sch E3 97 C3
Clara Pl SE18 122 C2
Clare Cl N2 48 A6
Deacons Hill WD6 10 B5
Clare Cnr SE9 166 D4
Clare Ct SW19 179 A4
WC1 233 B1
Bromley BR7 188 B2
Clare Gdns E7 77 A4
W11 91 A1
Barking IG11 80 A1
Clare Grant Ho 3 E14 119 C3
Clare Ho 6 E3 97 B6
SE1 263 D2
4 Burnt Oak HA8 27 A1
Clare House Prim Sch
BR3 186 A1
Clare La N1 73 A1
Clare Lawn Ave SW14 155 B6
Clare Mews SW6 265 C3
Clare Mkt WC2 240 D1
Clare Point NW2 46 D1
Clare Rd E11 54 B3
NW10 90 A6
SE14 141 B4
Hounslow TW4 129 B2
Northolt UB6 64 B2
Stanwell TW19 148 A4
Clare St E2 96 B5
Clare Way DA7 147 A4
Claredale Ct SM2 218 A1
Claredale Ho 3 E2 96 B5
Claredale St E2 96 A5
Claremont 1 SW15 157 A6
Shepperton TW17 192 D3
Claremont Ave
Harrow HA3 44 A4
Sunbury TW16 172 B2
West Barnes KT3 200 B4
Claremont Cl E16 122 C5
N1 94 C5 234 B3
4 SW2 160 B3
Locksbottom BR6 226 C4
Claremont Ct 1 W9 91 B5
Claremont Dr TW17 192 D3
Claremont Gdns
Ilford IG3 79 C6
Kingston u T KT6 198 A4
Claremont Gr W4 133 C5
Woodford IG8 37 C4
Claremont High Sch
HA3 44 A4
Claremont Hts EN2 4 D1
Claremont La KT10 212 A3
Claremont Pk N3 29 A2
Claremont Pl KT6 197 D3
Claremont Rd E7 77 C3
E7 76 B5
E17 35 A1
N6 49 C2
NW2 68 D6
W9 91 B5
W13 87 A2
Barnet EN4 2 B6
Bromley BR1 210 B5
Claygate KT10 212 C1
Croydon CR0 206 A1
Harrow HA3 24 C1
Kingston u T KT6 198 A4
Teddington TW11 174 D6
Twickenham TW1 153 C5
Claremont Sq N1 94 C5 234 A3
Claremont St E16 122 C4
N18 34 A4
SE10 141 D6
Claremont Terr KT7 197 B2
Claremont Way NW2 46 C1
Claremont Way Ind Est
NW2 46 C1
Clarence Ave SW4 159 D5
Bromley BR1,BR2 210 A5
Ilford IG2 56 C3
Kingston u T KT3 177 B1
Clarence Cl Bushey WD2 8 D4
New Barnet EN4 14 B6
Clarence Cres DA14 168 B1
Clarence Ct NW7 27 D5
10 W6 112 B2
Clarence Gate Gdns
NW1 237 D5
Clarence Gdns
NW1 93 B4 231 D1
Clarence Ho SE17 139 A6
Clarence House★
SW1 115 C5 249 B3
Clarence La SW15 155 D5
Clarence Mews E5 74 B3
1 SE16 118 D5
SW12 159 B4
Clarence Pas NW1 233 A3
Clarence Pl 25 E5 74 B3
Clarence Rd E5 74 B3
E12 77 D3
E16 98 C3
E17 34 D1
N15 51 A4
N22 32 A3
NW6 69 B1
SE9 166 A2
SW19 179 D4
W4 110 C1
Clarence Rd *continued*
Bexleyheath DA6 147 A1
Bromley BR1,BR2 210 A6
Enfield EN3 18 C6
Richmond TW9 132 C4
Sidcup DA14 168 B1
Sutton SM1 217 D3
Teddington TW11 175 A4
Thornton Heath CR0 205 B2
Wallington SM6 219 B3
Clarence St
Kingston u T KT1,KT2 176 A1
5 Richmond TW9 132 A1
Southall UB2 106 D3
Clarence Terr NW1 237 D6
Hounslow TW3 129 D1
Clarence Way NW1 71 B1
Clarence Wlk 9 SW4 138 A3
Clarendon Cl W2 247 A6
Clarendon Cres TW2 152 B1
Clarendon Cross W11 244 B5
Clarendon Ct NW2 68 C1
NW11 47 B5
W9 236 B6
1 Richmond TW9 132 C4
Clarendon Cty Prim Sch
TW15 170 B6
Clarendon Dr SW15 134 C1
Clarendon Flats W1 238 B1
Clarendon Gdns NW4 46 B6
W9 92 A3 236 B5
Redbridge IG1 56 B2
Wembley HA9 66 A4
Clarendon Gr NW1 232 C2
Mitcham CR4 202 D6
Clarendon Ho N12 30 A5
NW1 232 B3
Clarendon Mews W2 247 A6
Old Bexley DA5 169 D3
Clarendon Pl
W2 114 C6 247 A6
Clarendon Rd E11 54 B1
E17 53 D3
E18 55 A6
N8 50 B6
N15 51 A5
N18 34 A5
N22 32 B1
SW19 180 C3
W5 88 A3
W11 113 A6 244 B5
Ashford TW15 170 B6
Croydon CR0 220 D6
Harrow HA1 42 C3
Hayes UB3 105 D4
Wallington SM6 219 C2
Clarendon Rise SE13 142 A1
Clarendon Sch TW12 173 D4
Clarendon St
SW1 115 B1 258 D2
Clarendon Terr W9 236 B6
Clarendon Way N21 17 A5
St Paul's Cray BR5,BR7 211 D6
Clarendon Wlk 10 W11 91 A1
Clarens St SE6 163 B2
Claret Gdns SE25 205 C5
Clareville Ct SW7 256 B3
Clareville Gr
SW7 114 A2 256 B3
Clareville Grove Mews
SW7 256 B3
Clareville Rd BR5,BR6 227 A6
Clareville St
SW7 114 A2 256 B3
Clarewood Ct W1 237 C3
Clarewood Wlk SW9 138 C1
Clarges Ho W1 248 D4
Clarges Mews
W1 115 B5 248 C4
Clarges St W1 115 B5 248 D4
Claribel Rd SW9 138 D3
Clarice Ct NW4 46 B6
Claridge Ct SW6 264 C1
Claridge Rd RM8 58 D1
Clarissa Ho 7 E14 97 D1
Clarissa Rd RM6 58 D2
Clarissa St E8 95 D6
Clark Ct NW10 67 A1
Clark Lawrence Ct 11
SW11 136 B2
Clark St E1 96 C2
Clark Way TW5 128 D5
Clarke Ho 2 SW4 137 C2
Clarke Mans 8 IG11 79 D1
Clarke Path N16 52 A1
Clarke's Ave KT4,SM3 216 D6
Clarkes Dr UB8 82 A2
Clarkes Mews W1 238 B4
Clarks Mead WD2 8 B4
Clark's Pl EC2 243 A2
Clark's Rd IG1 79 B6
Clarkson Ho SW11 136 B1
Clarkson Rd E16 98 D1
Clarkson Row NW1 232 A3
Clarkson St E2 96 B4
Clarksons The IG11 101 A5
Classic Mans 33 E9 74 C1
Classinghall Ho 14
SW15 156 D5
Classon Cl UB7 104 A4
Claude Rd E10 54 A1
E13 99 B6
SE15 140 B3
Claude St E14 119 C2
Claudia Jones Way
SW2 160 A5
Claudia Pl SW19 157 A3
Claughton Rd E13 99 C5
Clauson Ave UB5 64 A3
Clave St E1 118 C5
Clavell St 7 SE10 142 A6
Claverdale Rd SW2 160 C4
Clavering Ave SW13 134 B6
Clavering Cl TW1 175 A6
Clavering Ho SE13 142 B1
Clavering Ind Est N9 18 C2
Clavering Rd E12 77 D6
Claverley Gr N3 29 D2
Claverley Villas N3 29 D3
Claverton St
SW1 115 C1 259 B1
Claxton Gr W6 112 D1 254 A1
Clay Ave CR4 181 B1
Clay Ct E17 54 B6
Clay Hill EN2 5 B6
Clay La WD2 8 C4
Clay St W1 92 D2 237 D3
Clay Wood Cl BR6 211 C2
Claybank Gr SE13 141 D2
Clayborne Mews 2
SE19 183 D3
Claybridge Rd SE12 187 C6
Claybrook Cl N2 48 B6
Claybrook Rd W6 134 D6
Claybury Broadway IG5 56 A6
Claydon SE17 262 A4
Claydon Dr CR0 220 A4
Claydon Ho NW4 28 D1
Clayfarm Rd SE9 167 A2
Claygate Cres CR0 224 B2
Claygate La
Hinchley Wood KT10 213 A6
Thames Ditton KT7 197 A1
Claygate Lodge Cl
KT10 212 C1
Claygate Prim Sch
KT10 212 C1
Claygate Rd W13 109 B3
Claygate Sta KT10 212 C2
Clayhall Ct 16 E3 97 B5
Clayhill Cres SE12,SE9 187 D6
Claylands Ct SE19 183 B5
Claylands Pl SW8 138 C5
Claylands Rd
SW8 138 B6 270 D5
Claymill Ho 2 SE18 123 A1
Claymore Cl SM3,SM4 201 C2
Claypole Ct E17 53 C4
Claypole Dr TW5 129 A4
Claypole Rd E15 98 A5
Clayponds Ave TW8 110 A2
Clayponds Gdns W5 109 D2
Clayponds Hospl & Day Treatment Ctr TW8 110 A2
Clayponds La TW8 110 A1
Clays Ct N16 51 D1
Clays La E15 75 D3
Clays Lane Cl E15 75 D3
Clayton 22 NW9 27 D1
Clayton Ave HA0 66 A1
Clayton Cl 3 E6 100 B1
Clayton Cres TW8 109 D1
Clayton Ct N16 52 A2
Clayton Field NW9 27 C2
Clayton Ho 22 E9 74 C1
Hinchley Wood KT7 197 B1
Clayton Mews SE10 142 B4
Clayton Rd SE15 140 A4
Chessington KT10,KT9 213 D4
Hayes UB3 105 C4
Isleworth TW7 130 C2
Clayton St SE11 138 C6
Clayton Terr UB4 84 D2
Claytonville Terr DA17 125 D4
Clayworth Cl DA15 168 B5
Cleanthus Cl SE18 144 D4
Cleanthus Rd SE18 144 D4
Clear Water Pl KT6 197 C3
Clearbrook Way 13 E1 96 C1
Clearmont Ho UB2 107 C3
Clearwater Ho 9 TW10 154 A6
Clearwater Terr 4
W11 112 D4
Clearwell Dr W9 91 D3
Cleave Ave Hayes UB3 105 C2
Orpington BR6 227 C2
Cleaveland Rd KT6 197 D4
Cleaver Ho 6 NW3 70 D1
Cleaver Sq SE11 116 C1 261 B1
Cleaver St SE11 116 C1 261 B2
Cleaverholme Cl SE25 206 B3
Cleave's Almshos 1
KT2 176 A1
Cleeve Ct N10 31 B3
East Bedfont TW14 149 C3
Cleeve Hill SE23 162 B3
Cleeve Ho 16 E2 95 C4
Cleeve Park Gdns DA14 168 B2
Cleeve Park Sec Sch
DA14 168 C1
Cleeve Workshops 15 E2 95 C4
Clegg Ho SE3 143 B1
Clegg St 16 E1 118 B5
E13 99 A5
Cleland Ho 20 E2 96 C5
Clem Attlee Ct
SW6 135 B6 264 D5
Clematis Gdns IG8 37 A5
Clematis St W12 112 A6
Clemence St E14 97 B2
Clement Attlee Ho
NW10 67 D1
Clement Ave SW4 137 D1
Clement Cl NW6 68 C1
W4 111 B2
Clement Gdns UB3 105 C2
Clement Ho 14 SE8 119 A2
W10 90 C2
Clement Rd SW19 179 A5
Penge BR3 184 D1
Clementhorpe Rd RM9 80 C2
Clementina Rd E10 53 B1
Clementine Churchill Hospl The HA1 64 D5
Clementine Cl W13 109 B4
Clements Ave 1 E16 121 A6
Clements Ct
Hounslow TW4 128 D1
5 Ilford IG1 78 D5
Clements Inn
WC2 94 B1 240 D1
Clements Inn Pas WC2 240 D1
Clements La IG1 78 D5
Clement's La
EC2,EC4 117 B6 252 D6
Clements Pl TW8 109 D1
Clements Rd E6 78 B1
Ilford IG1 78 D5
Clement's Rd SE16 118 B3
Clemson Ho 9 E8 95 D6
Clendon Way SE18 123 B2
Clenham St SE1 252 B2
Clensham Ct SM3 217 C6
Clensham La SM1 217 C6
Clenston Mews W1 237 C2
Clent Ho 4 N16 51 D1
Cleopatra's Needle★
WC2 116 B5 250 C5
Clephane Rd 6 N1 73 A2
Clephane Rd N N1 73 A2
Clephane Rd S N1 73 B2
Clere Pl EC2 242 D6
Clere St EC2 95 B3 242 D6
Clerics Wlk TW17 193 B3
Clerkenwell Cl
EC1 94 C3 241 B5
Clerkenwell Gn
EC1 94 D3 241 C5
Clerkenwell Parochial CE Prim Sch EC1 94 C4 234 A2
Clerkenwell Rd
EC1 94 D3 241 C5
Clermont Rd E9 96 C6
Cleve Ho NW6 69 D1
Cleve Rd NW6 69 D1
Sidcup DA14 168 D1
Cleveden Ct CR2 221 C3
Clevedon Ct SE21 161 B1
SW11 267 A2
Clevedon Gdns
Cranford TW5 128 B4
Hayes UB3 105 B3
Clevedon Mans NW5 71 A4
Clevedon Rd SE20 184 D2
Kingston u T KT1 176 C1
Twickenham TW1 153 D5
Cleveland Ave SW20 179 B1
W4 111 D2
Hampton TW12 173 B3
Cleveland Cres WD6 11 A6
Cleveland Ct W13 87 B2
Southall UB2 107 D2
Cleveland Gdns N4,N15 51 A4
NW2 68 D6
SW13 133 D3
W2 92 A1 236 A1
Worcester Pk KT4 215 D6
Cleveland Gr 33 E1 96 C3
Cleveland Ho 7 N2 30 B1
Cleveland Inf Sch IG1 78 D5
Cleveland Jun Schs IG1 78 D5
Cleveland Mans 4 NW6 69 B1
8 SW9 138 C5
W9 91 C3
Cleveland Mews W1 239 A4
Cleveland Park Ave E17 53 C5
Cleveland Park Cres E17 53 C5
Cleveland Pk TW19 148 A5
Cleveland Pl SW1 249 B4
Cleveland Rd E18 55 A6
N1 73 B1
N9 18 B4
SW13 133 D3
14 W4 111 A3
W13 87 B2
Bexley DA16 145 D3
Ilford IG1 78 D5
Isleworth TW7 131 A1
New Malden KT3 199 C5
Worcester Pk KT4 215 C6
Cleveland Rise SM4 200 D2
Cleveland Row
SW1 115 C5 249 B3
Cleveland Sq W2 92 A1 236 A1
Cleveland St W1 93 C3 239 A5
Cleveland Terr
W2 92 A1 236 B2
Cleveland Way E1 96 C3
Clevelands The IG11 79 A2
Cleveley Cres W5 88 B5
Cleveleys Rd E5 74 B5
Clevely Cl SE7 121 D2
Clevendon Cl N16 73 D5
Cleverly Cotts W12 111 D5
Cleverly Est W12 112 A6
Cleves Ct KT6 198 A3
Cleves Prim Sch E6 99 D6
Cleves Rd E6 99 D5
Richmond TW10 153 C1
Cleves Way
Ashford TW16 171 D4
Hampton TW12 173 B3
Ruislip HA4 40 D1
Clewer Cres HA3 24 B2
Clewer Ct 2 E10 53 C1
Clewer Ho 8 SE2 124 D4
Cley Ho SE4 140 D1
Clichy Ho 22 E1 96 C2
Clifden Centre (Richmond Adult & Community Coll)
TW1 152 D3
Clifden Ho 6 TW8 131 D6
Clifden Rd E5 74 D3
Brentford TW8 131 D6
Twickenham TW1 152 D3
Cliff Ct 5 NW1 71 D2
Cliff Rd NW1 71 D2
Cliff Terr SE8 141 C3
Cliff Villas NW1 71 D2
Cliff Wlk E16 98 D2
Cliffe Ho 4 SE10 120 D1
Cliffe Rd CR2 221 B3
Cliffe Wlk 2 SM1 218 A3
Clifford Ave
Chislehurst West BR7 188 B4
Wallington SM6 219 C4
SW14,TW10,TW9 133 A3
Clifford Cl UB5 85 A6
Clifford Ct NW10 67 C4
SW18 158 B4
W2 91 D2
Clifford Dr SW9 138 D1
Clifford Gdns NW10 90 C5
Clifford Gr TW15 170 C6
Clifford Haigh Ho SW6 134 D5
Clifford Ho W14 254 C3
2 Beckenham BR3 185 D4
Clifford Rd E16 98 D3
E17 36 A1
N9 18 C5
SE25 206 A5
Barnet EN5 1 D2
Hounslow TW4 128 D2
Richmond TW10 153 D2
Wembley HA0 87 D6
Clifford St W1 115 C6 249 A5
Clifford Way NW10 67 D4
Clifford's Inn Pas EC4 241 A1
Cliffsend Ho 23 SW9 138 C4
Cliffview Rd SE13 141 C2
Clifton Ave E17 52 D6
N3 29 B2
W12 111 D5
Feltham TW13 150 C1
Stanmore HA7 25 B1
Wembley HA9 66 B2
Clifton Cl 8 BR6 227 A3
Clifton Cres SE15 140 B5
Clifton Ct N4 72 C6
NW8 236 C6
SE15 140 B5
SE25 205 C4
SW15 156 D6
2 Beckenham BR3 185 D2
9 Stanwell TW19 148 A5
3 Woodford IG8 37 A4
Clifton Gate SW10 266 A6
Clifton Gdns N15 51 D3
2 NW11 47 B3
W4 111 B2
W9 92 A3 236 A5
Enfield EN2 16 A6
Hillingdon UB10 82 D5
Clifton Gr E8 74 A2
Clifton Hill NW8 92 A6 229 A5
Clifton Ho E2 243 C6
E11 76 C6
Clifton Lodge (Brunel Univ Coll Twickenham Campus)
TW1 153 B6
Clifton Mans 4 SW9 138 C1
Clifton Mews SE25 205 C5
Clifton Par TW13 172 C6
Clifton Park Ave SW20 178 C1
Clifton Pl SE16 118 C4
W2 236 D1
Clifton Prim Sch UB2 107 A2
Clifton Rd E7 77 D2
E16 98 C2
N3 30 A2
N8 49 D3
N22 31 C2
NW10 90 A5
SE25 205 C5
SW19 178 D4
W9 92 A3 236 B6
Bexley DA16 146 C2
Greenford UB6 86 B3
Harlington TW6 126 D2
Harrow HA3 44 B4
Hounslow TW7 130 C3
Ilford IG2 57 B3
Kingston u T KT2 176 B2
Sidcup DA14 189 C6
Southall UB2 107 A2
Teddington TW11 174 C6
Wallington SM6 219 B3
Clifton Rise SE14 141 A5
Clifton St EC2 95 C3 243 A5
Clifton Terr N4 72 C6
Clifton The KT6 214 A6
Clifton Villas W9 92 A2 236 A4
Clifton Way SE15 140 C5
Wembley HA0 88 A6
Cliftons Roundabout
SE9,SE12 165 C5
Cliftonville Ct SE12 165 A3
Climsland Ho SE1 251 B4
Clinch Ct 11 E16 99 A2
Cline Ho SW15 156 A4
Cline Rd N11 31 C4
Clinger Ct N1 95 C6

Clink St SE1 117 B5 252 C4
Clinton Ave Bexley DA16 146 A1
East Molesey KT8 196 A5
Clinton Ho
New Malden KT3 199 B1
6 Surbiton KT6 197 D2
Clinton Rd E3 97 A4
E7 77 A4
N15 51 B5
Clipper Cl 3 SE16 118 D4
Clipper Ho E14 120 A1
Clipper Way SE13 142 A1
Clippesby Cl KT9 214 B2
Clipstone Ho 10 SW15 156 A6
Clipstone Mews W1 239 A4
Clipstone Rd TW3 129 C2
Clipstone St W1 93 C2 239 A4
Clissold Cl N2 48 D6
Clissold Cres N16 73 B4
Clissold Ct N4 73 A6
Clissold Ho 4 N16 73 B6
Clissold Rd N16 73 B5
Clitheroe Ave HA2 41 C1
Clitheroe Gdns WD1 22 D6
Clitheroe Rd SW9 138 A3
Clitherow Ave W7 109 A3
Clitherow Rd TW8 109 C1
Clitterhouse Cres NW2 46 C1
Clitterhouse Jun & Inf Schs
NW2 68 D6
Clitterhouse Rd NW2 46 C1
Clive Ave N18 34 A4
Clive Ct SW16 181 D5
W9 236 B6
Tolworth KT6 214 C6
Clive Ho SE10 142 A6
18 SW8 137 D3
3 Croydon CR0 205 D1
Clive Lloyd Ho N15 51 A4
Clive Lo NW4 46 D3
Clive Rd SE21,SE27 161 B1
SW19 180 C4
Belvedere DA17 125 C2
Enfield EN1 6 A1
Feltham TW14 150 A5
Teddington TW1 175 A6
Clive Way EN1 6 A1
Cliveden Cl N12 30 A6
Cliveden Pl
SW1 115 A2 258 A4
Shepperton TW17 193 A3
Cliveden Rd SW19 179 B2
Clivedon Ct W13 87 B2
Clivedon Rd E4 36 C5
Clivesdale Dr UB3 106 B5
Cloak La EC4 117 B6 252 C6
Clochar Ct NW10 89 D6
Clock Ct E11 55 B5
Clock Ho E17 54 B5
N16 51 D2
Clock Ho The EN2 5 D6
Clock House Ct 1 BR3 185 A1
Clock House Par E11 55 B3
Clock House Rd BR3 185 A1
Clock House Sta BR3 185 A2
Clock Tower Mews N1 235 B5
Clock Tower Pl N7 72 A2
Clock Tower Rd TW7 130 D2
Clockhouse Ave IG11 101 A6
Clockhouse Cl SW19 156 C2
Clockhouse Junc N13 32 C5
Clockhouse La TW14,
TW15 148 D2
Clockhouse Par N13 32 C5
Clockhouse Pl SW15 157 A5
Clockhouse Rdbt TW14 149 A3
Clockhouse The SW19 156 C1
Cloister Cl TW11 175 B5
Cloister Gdns SE25 206 B3
Edgware HA8 27 A5
Cloister Rd NW2 69 B6
W3 89 A2
Cloisters Ave BR1,BR2 210 B4
Cloisters Ct N6 49 B1
Bexleyheath DA7 147 D2
Cloisters The 22 SW9 138 C4
Clonard Way HA5 23 C4
Clonbrock Rd N16 73 C4
Cloncurry St SW6 134 D3
Clone Ct 4 W12 111 C3
Clone The 5 KT2 176 D3
Clonmel Cl HA2 42 B1
Clonmel Rd
SW6 135 B4 264 D2
Teddington TW11,TW12 174 B6
Clonmell Rd N17 51 B6
Clonmore St SW18 157 B3
Cloonmore Ave BR6 227 D4
Clorane Gdns NW3 69 C5
Close The E4 36 A3
N10 31 B1
N14 15 D2
N20 13 B2
SE25 206 A3
Beckenham BR3 207 A5
Cheam SM3 201 B2
Dagenham RM6 59 A3
East Barnet EN4 14 D6
Hillingdon UB10 82 C6
Hounslow TW7 130 B3
Ilford IG2 57 C3
Kingston u T KT3 177 A1
Mitcham CR4 202 D5
Mortlake TW9 132 D2
1 Old Bexley DA5 169 C4
Orpington BR5 211 C3
Pinner HA5 40 C2
Pinner HA5 41 B2
Close The *continued*
Sidcup DA14 190 B5
Surbiton KT6 198 A3
Wembley HA0 66 A2
Wembley HA9 67 A5
Cloth Ct EC1 241 D3
Cloth Fair EC1 94 D2 241 D3
Cloth St EC1 95 A2 242 A4
Clothier Ho SE7 122 A1
Clothier St EC3 243 B2
Clothworkers Rd SE18 145 B5
Cloudesdale Rd SW17 159 B2
Cloudesley Mans N1 234 B5
Cloudesley Pl N1 94 C6 234 B5
Cloudesley Rd
N1 94 C6 234 A5
Erith DA7 147 B4
Cloudesley Sq
N1 94 C6 234 B6
Cloudesley St N1 94 C6 234 B5
Clouston Cl SM6 220 A3
Clova Rd E7 77 A3
Clove Cres E14 120 B6
Clove St 9 E13 99 A3
Clovelly Ave NW9 45 D5
Uxbridge UB10 61 A4
Clovelly Cl Pinner HA5 40 C6
Uxbridge UB10 61 A4
Clovelly Ct NW2 68 C3
Clovelly Gdns EN1 17 C4
Clovelly Ho W2 236 A2
Clovelly Rd N8 49 D5
W4 111 B4
W5 109 C4
Bexley DA7 147 A6
Hounslow TW3 129 C3
Clovelly Way E1 96 C1
Broom Hill BR6 211 D3
Harrow HA2 63 B6
Clover Cl E11 76 B6
Clover Ho TW3 130 A4
Clover Mews SW3 267 D6
Clover Way SM6 203 A1
Cloverdale Gdns DA15 167 D5
Cloverleys IG10 21 D6
Clowders Rd SE6 163 B1
Clowes Ho 3 SW4 138 A1
Clowser Cl 4 SM1 218 A3
Cloyster Wood HA8 25 D4
Cloysters Gn E1 118 A5
Club Gardens Rd BR2 209 A2
Club Row E2 95 D3 243 C6
Clumps The TW15 171 B6
Clunbury Ave UB2 107 B1
Clunbury St N1 235 D3
Clunie Ho SW1 257 D6
Cluny Mews SW5 255 A3
Cluny Pl SE1 117 C3 263 A6
Cluse Ct N1 235 A4
Clutton St E14 97 D2
Clydach Rd EN1 5 D1
Clyde Cir N15 51 C5
Clyde Ct NW1 232 D4
Clyde Flats SW6 264 C4
Clyde Ho 9 KT2 175 D2
Clyde Pl E10 53 D2
Clyde Rd N15 51 C5
N22 31 D2
Croydon CR0 221 D6
Stanwell TW19 148 A3
Sutton SM1 217 C3
Wallington SM6 219 C2
Clyde St SE8 141 B6
Clyde Terr SE23 162 C2
Clyde Vale SE23 162 C2
Clydesdale EN3 6 D1
Clydesdale Ave HA7 43 D6
Clydesdale Cl
Borehamwood WD6 11 B6
Isleworth TW7 130 D2
Clydesdale Ct N20 14 B3
Clydesdale Gdns TW10 132 D1
Clydesdale Ho 4 W11 91 B1
Erith DA18 125 A4
Clydesdale Path WD6 11 B6
Clydesdale Rd W11 91 B1
Clyfford Rd HA4 61 D4
Clymping Dene TW14 150 B4
Clynes Ho 3 E2 96 D4
6 Dagenham RM10 81 C5
Hayes UB4 84 A4
Clyro Ct N4 50 B1
Clyston St SW8 137 C3
Clytha Ct SE27 183 A6
Coach & Horses Yd W1 249 A6
Coach House La N5 72 D4
SW19 156 D1
Coach House Yd NW3 70 B4
Coal Wharf Rd W12 112 D5
Coalbrook Mans 3
SW12 159 B3
Coaldale Wlk SE21 161 A4
Coalecroft Rd SW15 156 C6
Coalport Ho SE11 261 A4
Coate St E2 96 A5
Coates Ct NW3 70 C3
Coates Hill Rd BR1 188 C1
Coates Rd WD6 9 D4
Coates Wlk TW8 110 A1
Cob Cl WD6 11 A6
Cobb St E1 243 C3
Cobbett Rd SE9 144 A2
Twickenham TW2 151 C3
Cobbett St SW8 138 B5 270 D3
Cobbetts Ave IG4 55 D4
Cobble La N1 72 D1
Cobble Mews N4,N5 73 A5
Cobbler's Wlk
Teddington KT1,TW11 175 A2
Teddington TW11 174 D3
Cobblestone Pl CR0 205 A1
Cobbold Ct SW1 259 C4
Cobbold Mews W12 111 D4
Cobbold Rd E11 76 D5
NW10 67 D2
W12 111 D4
Cobb's Ct EC4 241 D1
Cobb's Hall 1 SW6 134 D6
Cobb's Rd TW4 129 B1
Cobden Bldgs WC1 233 C2
Cobden Ct 9 SE28 124 C5
Cobden Ho 7 E2 96 A4
NW1 232 A4
Cobden Mews SE26 184 B5
Cobden Rd E11 76 C6
SE25 206 A4
Orpington BR6 227 B4
Cobham 21 NW9 27 D1
Cobham Ave KT3 200 A4
Cobham Cl SW11 158 C5
2 Bexley DA15 168 B5
Bromley BR2 210 A2
Edgware HA8 26 D1
Wallington SM6 220 A2
Cobham Ct CR4 180 B1
Cobham Ho IG11 101 A6
Cobham Mews 3 NW1 71 D1
Cobham Pl DA6 168 D6
Cobham Rd E17 36 A2
N22 50 D6
Heston TW5 128 C5
Ilford IG3 79 C5
Kingston u T KT1,KT2 176 C1
Cobland Rd SE12 187 C6
Coborn Rd E3 97 B4
Coborn St E3 97 B4
Cobourg Jun & Inf Sch
SE5 139 D6
Cobourg Rd SE5 139 D6
Cobourg St NW1 93 C4 232 B1
Coburg Cl SW1 259 B4
Coburg Cres SW2 160 C3
Coburg Dwellings 10
E1 118 C6
Coburg Gdns IG5 37 D1
Coburg Rd N22 32 B1
Coburn Mews 9 E3 97 B4
Cochrane Cl NW8 229 D3
Cochrane Ct 3 E10 53 C1
Cochrane Mews
NW8 92 B5 229 D3
Cochrane Rd SW19 179 B3
Cochrane St
NW8 92 B5 229 D3
Coci Ho W14 254 D3
Cock Hill E1 243 B3
Cock La EC1 94 D2 241 D3
Cockburn Ho SW1 259 D1
Cockerell Rd E17 53 A3
Cockfosters Par EN4 3 A1
Cockfosters Rd EN4 2 D3
Cockfosters Sta EN4 3 A1
Cockpit Yd WC1 240 D4
Cocks Cres KT3 199 D5
Cocksett Ave BR6 227 C2
Cockspur Ct SW1 249 D4
Cockspur St
SW1 115 D5 249 D4
Cocksure La DA14 191 C6
Coda Ctr The
SW6 135 A4 264 B2
Code St E1 95 D3 243 D5
Codicote Ho 22 SE8 118 D2
Codicote Terr N4 73 A6
Codling Cl 13 E1 118 A5
Codling Way HA0 65 D4
Codrington Ct SE16 119 A5
Codrington Hill SE23 163 A4
Codrington Ho 7 E1 96 B3
Codrington Mews W11 91 A1
Cody Cl Harrow HA3 43 D6
Wallington SM6 219 D1
Cody Rd E16 98 B3
Coe Ave SE25 206 A3
Coerdale Ct EN3 7 A6
Coe's Alley EN5 1 A1
Cogan Ave E17 35 A2
Cohen Ho NW7 28 A6
Cohen Lo E5 75 A3
Coin St SE1 116 C5 251 A4
Coity Rd NW5 71 A2
Coke St E1 96 A1
Cokers La SE21 161 B3
Colab Ct N22 32 C2
Colas Mews 7 NW6 91 C6
Colbeck Mews N1 72 D2
SW5 113 D2 255 D3
Colbeck Rd HA1 42 A2
Colberg Pl N16 51 D2
Colbert 1 SE5 139 D4
Colborne Ho 7 E14 119 C6
Colborne Way KT4 216 C6
Colbrook Ave UB3 105 B3
Colbrook Cl UB3 105 B3
Colburn Ave HA5 23 A4
Colburn Way SM1 218 B5
Colby Rd SE19 183 C5
Walton-on-T KT12 194 A1
Colchester Ave E12 78 B5
Colchester Dr HA5 40 D4
Colchester Ho 17 SW8 137 D3
Colchester Rd E10 54 A2
E17 53 C3
Burnt Oak HA8 27 A3
Northwood Hills HA6 22 A1
Colchester St E1 243 D2
Colchester Villas CR7 204 C3
Coldbath Sq EC1 241 A6
Coldbath St SE13 141 D3
Coldblow La SE14 140 D6
Coldershaw Rd W13 109 A4
Coldfall Ave N10 31 A1
Coldfall Prim Sch N10 30 D1
Coldham Ct N22 32 D2
Coldham Gr EN3 7 A6
Coldharbour E14 120 A5
Coldharbour Crest SE9 166 C1
Coldharbour Ind Est
SE5 139 A3
Coldharbour La SW9 138 D2
Bushey WD2 8 A6
Hayes UB3 106 A5
Coldharbour Lane Ho
UB3 106 A5
Coldharbour Pl SE5 139 B3
Coldharbour Rd CR0 220 C3
Coldharbour Sch CR9 220 C3
Coldharbour Sports Ctr
SE9 166 C2
Coldharbour Way CR0 220 C3
Coldstream Gdns SW18 157 B5
Cole Cl SE28 124 B5
Cole Court Lo 7 TW1 153 A4
Cole Gdns TW5 128 A5
Cole Ho SE1 251 B1
Cole Park Gdns TW1 153 A5
Cole Park Rd TW1 153 A5
Cole Park View 2 TW1 153 A5
Cole Rd TW1 153 A5
Cole St SE1 117 A4 252 B1
Colebert Ave E1 96 C3
Colebert Ho 20 E1 96 C3
Colebrook Cl SW19 156 D4
Colebrook Ct SW3 257 B3
Colebrook Ho 1 E14 97 D1
Colebrook Rd SW16 182 A2
Colebrook Rise BR2 186 C1
Colebrook Way N11 31 B5
Colebrooke Ave W13 87 B1
Colebrooke Ct DA14 190 B6
Colebrooke Dr E11 55 C2
Colebrooke Pl N1 234 D5
Colebrooke Row
N1 94 D5 234 C4
Colebrooke Sch
N1 94 D5 234 D4
Coleby Path 21 SE5 139 B5
Colechurch Ho 8 SE1 118 A1
Coledale Dr HA7 25 C2
Coleford Rd SW18 158 A6
Colegrave Prim Sch E15 76 B3
Colegrave Rd E15 76 B3
Colegrove Rd SE15 139 D6
Coleherne Ct
SW10 113 D1 255 D1
Coleherne Mans SW5 255 D2
Coleherne Mews
SW10 113 D1 255 C1
Coleherne Rd
SW10 113 D1 255 C1
Colehill Gdns SW6 264 A1
Colehill La SW6 135 A4 264 B1
Coleman Cl SE25 184 A1
Coleman Ct SW18 157 C4
Coleman Fields
N1 95 A6 235 B6
Coleman Mans N19 50 A2
Coleman Rd SE5 139 C5
Belvedere DA17 125 C2
Dagenham RM9 81 A2
Coleman St EC2 95 B1 242 C2
Coleman St Bldgs EC2 242 C2
Colemans Heath SE9 166 D1
Colenso Dr NW7 28 A3
Colenso Rd E5 74 C4
Ilford IG2 57 C2
Colepits Wood Rd SE9 167 B6
Coleraine Park Prim Sch
N17 34 B2
Coleraine Rd N8,N22 50 C6
SE3 142 D6
Coleridge Ave E12 78 A2
Carshalton SM1 218 C4
Coleridge Cl SW8 137 B3
Coleridge Ct W14 112 D3
11 New Barnet EN5 13 D6
2 Richmond TW10 175 D6
Coleridge Gdns NW6 70 A1
Coleridge Ho SE17 262 B2
SW1 259 B1
Coleridge Prim Sch N8 49 D2
Coleridge Rd E17 53 B5
N4,N7 72 C6
N8 49 D3
N12 30 A5
Ashford TW15 170 B6
Croydon CR0 206 C2
Coleridge Sq W13 87 A1
Coleridge Way
Hayes UB4 84 A1
West Drayton UB7 104 B2
Coleridge Wlk NW11 47 C5
Colerne Ct NW4 29 A1
Coles Cres HA2 63 D6
Coles Ct SW11 266 D1
Coles Gn WD2 8 A3
Coles Green Ct NW2 68 A6
Coles Green Rd NW2 68 B6
Colesbourne Ct SE5 139 C5
Colesburg Rd BR3 185 B1
Coleshill Flats SW1 258 B3
Coleshill Rd TW11 174 C4
Colestown St 4 SW11 136 C3
Coleswood N20 14 C3
Colesworth Ho 1 HA8 27 A1
Colet Cl N13 32 D4
Colet Gdns W14 112 D2
Colet Ho SE17 261 D1
Colette Ct 5 SE16 118 D4
Coley St WC1 94 B3 240 D5
Colfe & Hatchcliffe's Glebe
SE13 163 D6
Colfe Rd SE23 163 A3
Colfe's Sch SE12 165 B5
Colgate Ct EN5 13 A6
Colgate Ho SE13 141 D3
Colgate Pl EN3 7 C6
Colham Ave UB7 104 A5
Colham Green Rd UB8 82 C2
Colham Manor Jun & Inf
Schs UB8 82 C1
Colham Rd UB8 82 B3
Colin Blanchard Ho
SE4 141 C3
Colin Cl NW9 45 C5
Coney Hall BR4 224 D5
Croydon CR0 223 B5
Colin Cres NW9 45 D5
Colin Ct SW16 159 D2
Colin Dr NW9 45 D4
Colin Gdns NW9 45 D5
Colin Par NW9 45 C5
Colin Park Rd NW9 45 C5
Colin Rd NW10 68 A2
Colin Winter Ho 37 E1 96 C3
Colina Mews N8,N15 50 D5
Colina Rd N8,N15 50 D4
Colindale Ave NW9 45 C6
Colindale Hospl NW9 45 C6
Colindale Prim Sch
NW9 45 D5
Colindale Sta NW9 45 C6
Colindeep Gdns NW4 46 A5
Colindeep La NW9,NW4 45 D5
Colinette Rd SW15 134 C1
Colinsdale N1 234 C5
Colinton Rd IG3 80 B6
Coliston Pass SW18 157 C4
Coliston Rd SW18 157 C4
Coll of Liberal Arts
SM1 217 D3
Coll of North East London
The N15 51 D5
Coll of NW London
(Willesden Centre) The
NW10 67 D3
Coll Sharp Ct 42 E2 95 D4
Collamore Ave SW18 158 C3
Collapit Cl HA1 41 D3
Collard Pl NW1 71 B1
College App SE10 142 A6
College Ave HA3 24 C2
College Cl E5 74 C3
N18 33 D5
Harrow Weald HA3 24 C3
Twickenham TW2 152 B3
College Cres NW3 70 B2
College Cross N1 72 C1
College Ct NW3 70 B2
SW3 114 D1 257 D1
W5 110 A6
3 W6 112 C1
Croydon CR0 222 A6
Enfield EN3 18 C6
College Dr HA4 40 A2
College Fields Bsns Ctr
SW19 180 C2
College Gdns E4 20 A3
N18 34 A5
SE21 161 C3
SW17 158 C2
Enfield EN2 5 B4
New Malden KT3 199 D4
Redbridge IG4 56 A4
College Gn SE19 183 C3
Plaistow BR1 187 A2
College Gr NW1 232 C6
College Hill EC4 252 B6
College Hill Rd HA3 24 C3
College La NW5 71 B4
College of North East
London The N11 31 D3
College Park Cl SE13 142 B1
College Park Rd N17 33 D4
College Park Sch W2 91 D1
College Pl E17 54 C5
NW1 93 C6 232 B5
SW10 266 A4
College Point E15 76 D2
College Rd E17 54 A4
N17 33 D4
N21 16 C2
NW10 90 C5
SE19,SE21 161 C2
SW19 180 B4
W13 87 B1
Croydon CR0 221 B6
Enfield EN2 5 B3
Harrow HA1 42 C3
Harrow HA3 24 C2
Hounslow TW7 130 D4
Plaistow BR1 187 A3
Wembley HA9 43 D1
College Rdbt 1 KT1 198 A6
College St EC4 117 A6 252 B6
College Terr E3 97 B4
N3 29 B1
College View SE9 165 D3
College Way TW15 170 B6
College Wlk 10 KT1 198 A6
Collent Ho 12 E9 74 C2
Collent St E9 74 C2
Collerston Ho SE10 120 D1
Colless Rd N15 51 D4
Collett Rd SE16 118 A3
Collett Way UB2 107 D4
Collette Ct SE25 205 C4
Collette Ho N16 51 D1
Colley Ho 12 N7 71 D3
Collier Cl E16 122 D6
West Ewell KT19 214 D2
Collier Dr HA8 26 C1
Collier St N1 94 B5 233 C3
Colliers Water La CR7 204 C4
Colliers Wood SW19 180 B3
Keston BR2 225 D3
Collier's Wood Sta
SW19 180 B3
Collindale Ave
Erith DA8 147 D6
Sidcup DA15 168 A3
Collingbourne Rd W12 112 B5
Collingham Gdns
SW5 113 D2 255 D3
Collingham Pl
SW5 113 D2 255 D4
Collingham Rd
SW5 113 D2 255 D3
Collings Cl N22 32 B4
Collington Ho SE7 143 B6
Collington St SE10 120 B1
Collingtree Rd SE26 184 C6
Collingwood Ave N10 49 A5
Tolworth KT5 199 A1
Collingwood Cl 2 SE20 184 B2
Twickenham TW2,TW4 151 C4
Collingwood Ct NW4 46 C4
New Barnet EN5 13 D6
Collingwood Ho 27 E1 96 B3
Collingwood Rd N15 51 C5
Hillingdon UB8 82 D3
Mitcham CR4 202 C6
Sutton SM1 217 C4
Collingwood St E1 96 B3
Collins Ave HA7 26 A1
Collins Ct E8 74 A2
Collins Dr HA4 62 C6
Collins Ho 4 E14 120 A6
6 SE10 120 D1
8 Barking IG11 78 D1
Collins Rd N5,N16 73 A4
Collins Sq SE3 142 D3
Collins St SE3 142 C3
Collins Yd N1 234 C5
Collinson Ct SE1 252 A1
Edgware HA8 26 B6
Collinson Ho 13 SE15 140 A5
Collinson St SE1 252 A1
Collinson Wlk SE1 252 A1
Collinwood Ave EN3 6 C2
Collinwood Gdns IG5 56 C5
Collis Prim Sch TW11 175 B4
Coll's Rd SE15 140 C4
Collyer Ave CR0 220 A4
Collyer Pl SE15 140 A4
Collyer Rd CR0 220 A4
Colman Ct N12 30 A4
Stanmore HA7 25 B4
Colman Rd E16 99 C2
Colmans Wharf 6 E14 97 D2
Colmar Cl 3 E1 96 D3
Colmer Pl HA3 24 B3
Colmer Rd SW16 182 A3
Colmore Rd EN3 6 C1
Colnbrook Ct SW17 180 B6
Colnbrook St SE1 261 C6
Colne Ct W7 86 B1
West Ewell KT19 215 A4
Colne Ho NW8 236 D5
Barking IG11 78 D2
Colne Rd E5 75 A4
N21 17 B4
Twickenham TW1,TW2 152 C3
Colne St E13 99 A4
Colney Hatch N10 31 A3
Colney Hatch La N10 31 A3
Cologne Rd SW11 136 B1
Coloma Convent Girls Sch
CR0 222 D5
Colomb St SE10 120 C1
Colombo Rd IG1 57 A2
Colombo St SE1 251 C3
Colonades The 4 SE5 139 B4
Colonels Wlk EN2 4 D2
Colonial Ave TW2 152 A5
Colonial Dr W4 111 A2
Colonial Rd TW14 149 C4
Colonnade WC1 240 B5
Colonnades The 6 E8 74 B2
Colosseum Ct N3 29 B1
Colroy Ct NW4 47 A4
Colson Rd CR0 221 C6
Colson Way SW16 181 C6
Colstead Ho 28 E1 96 B1
Colsterworth Rd N15 51 D5
Colston Ave SM1,SM5 218 C4
Colston Ct SM5 218 D4
Colston Rd E7 77 D2
SW14 133 A1
Colthurst Cres N4 73 A6
Coltman Ho 1 E14 97 A1
SE10 142 A6
Coltness Cres SE2 124 B1
Colton Gdns N17 51 A6
Colton Rd HA1 42 C4
Coltsfoot Dr UB7 82 A1

Columba Ho SE14 .....141 B4
Columbia Ave
Edgware HA8 ....26 D2
New Malden KT4 ....199 D2
Ruislip HA4 ....40 B1
Columbia Ct KT3 ......199 D2
Columbia Ho 16 E3 .....97 C4
Columbia JMI Sch E2 ...95 D4
Columbia Point 7
SE16 ....118 C3
Columbia Rd E2 ....95 D4
E13 ....98 D3
Columbine Ave E6 ......100 A2
Croydon CR2 ....220 D1
Columbus Gdns HA6 ....22 A2
Colveiw Ct SE9 ....165 D3
Colverson Ho 11 E1 .....96 C2
Colvestone Cres E8 .....73 D3
Colvestone JMI Sch E8 .73 D3
Colville Gdns W11 ......91 B1
Colville Ho 2 E2 ....96 C6
W11 ....91 B1
Colville Mews W11 .....91 B1
Colville Pl W1 ....239 B3
Colville Prim Sch W11 ..91 B1
Colville Rd E11 ....76 A5
E17 ....35 A1
N9 ....18 B3
W3 ....110 D3
W11 ....91 B1
Colville Sq W11 ....91 B1
Colville Sq Mews 6
W11 ....91 B1
Colville Terr W11 ....91 B1
Colvin Cl SE26 ....184 C5
Colvin Gdns E4 ....20 A1
E11 ....55 B5
Colvin Rd E6 ....78 A1
Thornton Heath CR7 ....204 C4
Colwall Gdns IG8 ....37 A5
Colwall Ho 18 SW9 .....138 B3
Colwell Rd SE22 ....161 D6
Colwick Cl N6 ....49 D2
Colwith Rd W6 ....134 C6
Colwood Gdns SW19 ...180 B3
Colworth Gr SE17 ......262 B3
Colworth Rd E11 ....54 C2
Croydon CR0 ....206 A1
Colwyn Ave UB6 ....86 D5
Colwyn Cl SW16 ....181 C5
Colwyn Cres TW3 ......130 A4
Colwyn Gn NW9 ....45 C3
Colwyn Ho SE1 ....261 A5
Colwyn Rd NW2 ....68 B5
Colyer Cl SE9 ....166 D2
Colyer Ho SE2 ....124 D1
Colyton Cl Bexley DA16 .146 D4
Wembley HA0 ....65 C2
Colyton Rd SE22 ....162 B6
Colyton Way N18 ....34 A5
Com Coll Sixth Form Ctr The
E9 ....74 D2
Com Coll The E5 ....74 B5
Combe Ave SE3 ....142 D5
Combe Ho SW14 ....133 A3
20 W2 ....91 C2
Combe Hurst KT2 .....177 A5
Combe Lane Sta CR0 ..222 C3
Combe Martin Coll KT2 177 A5
Combe Mews 4 SE3 ...142 D5
Combe The NW1 ....231 D1
Combedale Rd SE10 ...121 A1
Combemartin Rd SW18 157 A3
Comber Cl NW2 ....68 B6
Comber Gr SE5 ....139 A5
Comber Grove Jun & Inf Sch
SE5 ....139 A5
Comber Ho SE5 ....139 A5
Combermere Rd SW9 ..138 B2
Morden SM4 ....201 D4
Comberton 10 KT1 .....176 C1
Comberton Rd E5 ....74 B6
Combes Rd RM9 ....81 B1
Combeside SE18 ....145 D5
Combwell Cres SE2 ....124 A3
Comely Bank Rd E17 ...54 A4
Comer Cres UB2 ....108 A4
Comeragh Mews W14 .254 B1
Comeragh Rd
W14 ....113 A1 254 B1
Comerford Rd SE4 .....141 B1
Comet Cl E12 ....77 D4
Comet Pl SE8 ....141 C5
Comet St SE8 ....141 C5
Comins Ho SW4 ....159 C6
Commerce Est E18 ......37 C1
Commerce Rd N22 ......32 B2
Brentford TW8 ....131 C5
Commerce Way CR0 ...220 B6
Commercial Rd E1 ....96 C1
N18 ....33 C4
Commercial St
E1 ....95 C2 243 C4
Commercial Way NW10 .88 D5
SE15 ....140 A5
Commerell Pl SE10 ....120 D1
Commerell St SE10 ....120 C1
Commodore Ct SE8 ....270 A1
Commodore Ho 7 E14 120 A6
Commodore St E1 ......97 A3
Common La KT10 ......213 A1
Common Rd SW13 .....134 A2
Bushey HA7 ....8 C1
Claygate KT10 ....213 A1
Common The W5 ......110 A5
Common The continued
Bushey HA7 ....8 D2
Southall UB2 ....106 D2
Common View SW15 ...134 C2
Commondale SW15 ....134 C2
Commonside BR2 .....225 C4
Commonside Ct SW16 .182 A4
Commonside E CR4 ...203 B6
Commonwealth Ave
21 W12 ....112 B6
Hayes UB3 ....83 B1
Commonwealth Rd N17 .34 A3
Commonwealth Way
SE2 ....124 C1
Community Cl
Cranford TW5 ....128 B4
Uxbridge UB10 ....61 A5
Community Coll The E9 .74 D3
E9 ....96 D6
Community Rd E15 .....76 B3
Greenford UB6 ....86 A6
Como Rd SE23 ....163 A2
Compania Bldg 12 E1 .118 D6
Compass Ct SE1 ......253 C3
Compass Hill TW10 ...153 D5
Compass Ho SE8 ......141 D3
W2 ....91 D1
Compass Point 9 E14 .119 C6
Compayne Gdns NW6 ..69 D1
Compton Ave E6 ....99 D5
N1 ....72 D2
N6 ....48 C2
Compton Cl NW1 ......231 D1
NW11 ....68 D5
W13 ....87 A1
5 Burnt Oak HA8 ....27 A3
Esher KT10 ....212 B3
Compton Cres N17 .....33 A3
W4 ....133 A6
Chessington KT9 ......214 A2
Northolt UB5 ....84 D6
Compton Ct 9 SE19 ...183 C5
Sutton SM1 ....218 A4
Compton Ho SW11 ....267 A2
Compton Lo N21 ....16 D3
Compton Pas EC1 .....241 D6
Compton Pl WC1 ......240 A6
South Oxhey WD1 ......23 A6
Compton Rd N1 ....72 D2
N21 ....16 D3
NW10 ....90 D4
SW19 ....179 B4
Croydon CR0 ....206 B1
Hayes UB3 ....105 D6
Compton Rise HA5 .....41 B4
Compton Sch The N12 ..30 C4
Compton St EC1 94 D3 241 D6
Compton Terr N1 ....72 D2
N21 ....16 C3
Comreddy Cl EN2 ....4 D4
Comus Ho SE17 ....263 A3
Comus Pl SE17 .117 C2 263 A3
Comyn Rd SW11 ....136 C1
Comyns Cl E16 ....98 D2
Comyns Rd RM9 ....81 C1
Comyns The WD2 ....8 A3
Conal Ct SW16 ....181 D5
Conant Ho SE11 ....138 D6
Conant Mews 1 E1 ....118 A6
Concanon Rd SW2,SW4 138 B1
Concert Hall App
SE1 ....116 B5 250 D3
Concord Bsns Ctr W3 ...88 D2
Concord Cl UB5 ....85 A4
Concord Ct KT1 ....198 B6
Concord Ctr W12 .....112 D4
Concord Ho 5 N17 ......33 D3
Kingston u T KT3 ......199 C6
Concord Rd W3 ....88 D3
Enfield EN3 ....18 C6
Concorde Cl
Hounslow TW3 ....129 D3
Uxbridge UB10 ....82 A5
Concorde Dr E6 ....100 B2
Concordia Wharf E14 ..120 A5
Concourse The 7 N9 ...18 A2
Condell Rd SW8 137 C4 269 B1
Conder St E14 ....97 A1
Condor Path UB5 ....85 C5
Condover Cres SE18 ..144 D5
Condray Pl SW11 ......267 A3
Conduit Ct WC2 ....250 A6
Conduit Ho SE10 ......142 B4
Conduit La N18 ....34 C5
South Croydon CR0 ....222 A3
Conduit Mews
W2 ....92 B1 236 C1
Conduit Pas W2 ....236 C1
Conduit Pl W2 ....236 C1
Conduit Rd SE18 ......122 D1
Conduit St W1 .115 C6 249 A6
Conduit Way NW10 .....67 A1
Conewood St N5 ....72 D5
Coney Acre SE21 .....161 A3
Coney Burrows E4 ......20 C2
Coney Gr UB8 ....82 C4
Coney Hall Par BR4 ...224 C5
Coney Hall Rdbt BR4 .224 C5
Coney Hill Rd BR4 ....224 D6
Coney Hill Sch BR2 ...224 D5
Coney Way SW8 ......270 D5
Coneygrove Path UB5 ..63 A2
Conference Cl 3 E4 ....20 A2
Conference Ho UB8 .....83 A1
Conference Rd SE2 ...124 C2
Congers Ho SE8 ......141 C5
Congleton Gr SE18 ....123 A1
Congo Rd SE18 ....123 B1
Congress Rd SE2 ......124 C2
Congreve Ho 10 N16 ....73 C3
Congreve Rd SE9 ......144 B2
Congreve St
SE17 ....117 C2 263 A3
Congreve Wlk 6 E16 ...99 D2
Conical Cnr EN2 ....5 A3
Conifer Cl BR6 ....227 B4
Conifer Ct 23 SW19 ....156 D3
Ilford IG1 ....78 D2
Conifer Gdns SW16 ...160 B1
Enfield EN1 ....17 C5
Sutton SM1 ....217 D6
Conifer Ho SE4 ....141 B1
Conifer Way Hayes UB3 .106 A6
Wembley HA0 ....65 C5
Conifers Cl TW11 ......175 C3
Coniger Rd SW6 ....135 C3
Coningham Ct SW10 ..266 B4
Coningham Mews W12 112 A5
Coningham Rd W12 ...112 B4
Coningsby Cotts W5 ..109 D4
Coningsby Ct 4 CR4 ..181 A1
Coningsby Gdns E4 ....35 D4
Coningsby Rd N4 ....50 D2
W5 ....109 D4
Conington Rd SE13 ....142 A3
Conisbee Ct 3 N14 .....15 C6
Conisborough Cres
SE6 ....164 A1
Conisbrough NW1 .....232 A5
Coniscliffe Cl BR7 .....188 C2
Coniscliffe Rd N13 .....17 A1
Coniston NW1 ....232 A2
Coniston Ave
Barking IG11 ....79 C1
Bexley DA16 ....145 C2
Ealing UB6 ....87 B4
Coniston Cl N20 ....14 A1
SW13 ....133 D5
W4 ....133 A5
West Barnes SM4 .....200 D3
Coniston Ct 6 SE16 ...118 D4
SE26 ....184 B4
W2 ....237 B1
Beckenham BR3 ......186 A2
Chessington KT9 ......214 A5
Edgware HA8 ....26 B5
3 Wallington SM6 .....219 B4
Coniston Gdns N9 .....18 C3
NW9 ....45 B4
Pinner HA5 ....40 A5
Redbridge IG4 ....56 A5
Sutton SM2 ....218 B2
Wembley HA9 ....43 C1
Coniston Ho 13 E3 .....97 B4
18 SE5 ....139 A5
Coniston Rd N10 ....31 B1
N17 ....34 A4
Catford BR1 ....186 C4
Croydon CR0 ....206 A2
Twickenham TW2 ......151 D5
Coniston Way KT9 ....214 A5
Coniston Wlk E9 ....74 C3
Conistone Way N7 .....72 A1
Conlan St W10 ....91 A3
Conley Rd NW10 ....67 C2
Conley St SE10 ....120 C1
Connaught Ave E4 .....20 B4
SW14 ....133 A1
Ashford TW15 ....170 A6
East Barnet EN4 ....14 D3
Enfield EN1 ....5 C3
Hounslow TW4 ....129 A1
Connaught Br E16 .....121 D6
Connaught Bsns Ctr
NW9 ....45 D4
Mitcham CR4 ....202 D4
Wallington CR0 ....220 B2
Connaught Cl E10 ......75 A6
W2 ....237 B1
Carshalton SM1 ......218 B6
Enfield EN1 ....5 C3
Hillingdon UB8 ....83 A3
Connaught Ct 1 E4 ....20 C4
10 E17 ....53 D5
Connaught Day Hospl
E11 ....54 C3
Connaught Dr NW11 ...47 C5
Connaught Gdns N10 ..49 B4
N13 ....32 D6
Morden SM4 ....202 A5
Connaught Girls Sch
E11 ....54 C1
Connaught Girls Sch
(Annexe) E11 ....76 C6
Connaught Grange N13 .32 D6
Connaught Ho N10 ......49 B4
NW10 ....90 B4
W1 ....248 C5
Connaught La IG1 ......79 B6
Connaught Lo N4 ....50 C2
Connaught Mans 15 N16 73 B4
SW6 ....264 A2
3 SW9 ....138 C1
SW11 ....267 B1
Connaught Mews SE18 122 C1
Ilford IG1 ....79 B6
Connaught Pl W2 .....237 C1
Connaught Rd E4 ......20 C3
E11 ....54 B1
E16 ....121 C6
E16 ....121 D5
E17 ....53 C4
N4 ....50 C2
NW10 ....89 C5
SE18 ....122 D1
W13 ....109 B6
Connaught Rd continued
Carshalton SM1 ......218 B6
Ducks Island EN5 ......12 D5
Harrow HA3 ....24 D2
Ilford IG1 ....79 B6
New Malden KT3 ......199 C5
5 Richmond TW10 .....154 B6
Teddington TW11,TW12 .174 B5
Connaught Sq
W2 ....92 D1 237 C1
Connaught St
W2 ....92 C1 237 B1
Connaught Way N13 ....32 D6
Connell Cres W5 ....88 B3
Connell Ct 6 SE14 .....140 D6
Connell Ho 6 SM6 .....219 C2
Connemara Cl WD6 .....11 B5
Connett Ho 5 E2 ....96 B5
Connington 5 KT1 ....176 C1
Connington Cres E4 ....20 B1
Connoly Ct NW2 ....68 B5
Connop Rd EN3 ....6 D5
Connor Ct SW11 ....268 C1
Connor Rd RM9 ....81 B4
Connor St E9 ....96 D6
Conolly Rd W7 ....108 C5
Conrad Dr KT4 ....200 D1
Conrad Ho 12 N16 ......73 C3
8 SE16 ....119 A6
SW8 ....270 A4
Cons St SE1 ....251 B2
Consfield Ave KT3 ....200 A4
Consolata Missionary Coll
N20 ....13 C1
Consort Ho NW7 ....27 D5
W2 ....245 D5
Consort Lo NW8 ....230 C5
Consort Mews TW7 ....152 B6
Consort Rd SE15 ......140 B3
Constable Ave E16 ....121 B5
Constable Cl NW11 .....47 D3
Hayes UB4 ....83 A5
Constable Cres N15 ....52 A4
Constable Ct 11 SE16 ..118 B1
Constable Gdns
Edgware HA8 ....26 C1
Isleworth TW7 ....152 B6
Constable Ho NW3 ......70 D1
Enfield EN1 ....18 A6
14 Northolt UB5 ....84 D5
Constable Mews RM8 ...80 B4
Constable Wlk SE21 ...161 C1
Constance Cres BR2 ...208 D1
Constance Rd Enfield EN1 17 C5
Sutton SM1 ....218 A4
Thornton Heath CR0 ...204 D2
Twickenham TW2 ......151 D4
Constance St E16 .....122 A5
Constant Ho 23 E14 ...119 D6
Constantine Ho SW2 ..160 D3
Constantine Rd NW3 ....70 C4
Constitution Hill
SW1,W1 ....115 B4 248 D2
Constitution Rise SE18 144 C4
Consul Ho 5 E3 ....97 C3
Content St SE17 117 B2 262 C3
Contessa Cl BR6 ......227 C3
Control Tower Rd TW6 .126 D2
Convair Wlk 11 UB5 ....84 D4
Convent Cl BR3 ....186 A3
Convent Gdns W5 .....109 C2
W11 ....91 B1
Convent Hill SE19 .....183 A4
Convent Lo TW15 .....170 D5
Convent of Jesus & Mary CE
Inf Sch NW2 ....68 C2
Convent of Jesus & Mary
Language Coll for Girls The
NW10 ....89 D6
Convent of the Sacred Heart
Digby-Stuart Coll
SW15 ....155 D6
Convent Rd TW15 .....170 D5
Convent Way UB2 .....106 D2
Conway Cl HA7 ....25 A4
Conway Cres Ilford RM6 .58 C3
Wembley UB6 ....86 C5
Conway Dr
Ashford TW15 ....171 A4
Hayes UB3 ....105 A3
Sutton SM2 ....217 D2
Conway Gdns Enfield EN2 .5 C5
Mitcham CR4 ....204 A5
Wembley HA9 ....43 C2
Conway Gr W3 ....89 B2
Conway Ho 5 E14 .....119 D2
6 SW2 ....160 A3
Conway Jun & Inf Sch
SE18 ....123 C2
Conway Mews W1 .....239 A5
Conway Rd N14 ....16 A1
N15 ....51 A4
NW2 ....68 C6
SE18 ....123 C2
SW20 ....178 C2
Feltham TW13 ....172 D5
Harlington TW6 ....126 D2
Twickenham TW4 .....151 C4
Conway St W1 ..93 C3 239 A5
Conway Wlk TW12 ....173 B4
Conybeare NW3 ....70 C1
Conyer St 19 E3 ....97 A5
Conyers Cl IG8 ....36 C4
Conyer's Rd SW16 ....181 D5
Cooden Cl BR1 ....187 B3
Cookes Cl E11 ....76 D6
Cookes La SM3 ....217 A2
Cookham Cl UB2 ......107 D4
Cookham Cres SE16 ...118 D4
Cookham Dene Cl BR7 .189 B2
Cookham Ho E2 ....243 C6
Cookham Rd BR8 .....191 C2
Cookhill Rd SE2 ......124 B3
Cooks Ferry N18 ....34 D5
Cook's Hole Rd EN2 ......5 A5
Cook's Rd E15 ....97 D5
SE17 ....138 D6
Cookson Gr DA8 ......147 D5
Cool Oak La NW9 ....45 D2
Coolfin Rd E16 ....99 B1
Coolgardie Ave E4 ......36 B5
Coolgardie Rd TW15 ..171 A5
Coolhurst Rd N8 ....49 D3
Coomassie Rd W9 ....91 B3
Coombe Ave CR0 ......221 C4
Coombe Bank KT2,KT3 .177 C2
Coombe Cl Edgware HA8 .26 B1
Hounslow TW3 ....129 C1
Coombe Cnr N21 ....16 D3
Coombe Cres TW12 ...173 A3
Coombe Ct
2 Beckenham BR3 .....185 B2
3 Croydon CR0 ....221 B4
Coombe Dr HA4 ....40 B1
Coombe End KT2 ......177 B3
Coombe Gdns SW20 ...178 A2
New Malden KT3 ......199 D5
Coombe Girls Sch KT3 .177 B1
Coombe Hill Glade KT2 177 C3
Coombe Hill Inf Sch
KT3 ....177 B2
Coombe Hill Jun Sch
KT3 ....177 B2
Coombe Hill Rd KT2 ...177 C3
Coombe Ho 13 N7 ....71 D3
Coombe House Chase
KT3 ....177 B2
Coombe La SW20 .....178 B1
South Croydon CR0 ....222 B3
Coombe La W KT2 .....177 B2
Coombe Lane SW20 ...177 D2
Coombe Lane Flyover
SW20 ....177 D2
Coombe Lea BR1 ......210 A6
Coombe Lo SE7 ....143 C6
Coombe Neville KT2 ...177 B3
Coombe Pk KT2 ....177 B5
Coombe Rd N22 ....32 C2
NW10 ....67 B5
SE26 ....184 B6
W13 ....109 B3
Bushey WD2 ....8 B4
Croydon CR0,CR2 .....221 C4
Hampton TW12 ....173 B4
Kingston u T KT2 .....176 C2
Kingston u T KT3 .....199 C6
Coombe Ridings KT2 ..177 A5
Coombe Rise KT2 .....177 A2
Coombe Wlk SM1 .....217 D5
Coombe Wood Rd KT2 .177 A5
Coombefield Cl KT3 ...199 C4
Coombehurst Cl EN4 .....2 D3
Coomber Ho SW6 .....135 D2
Coomber Way CR0 ....203 D2
Coombes Rd RM9 .....103 B6
Coombe-Wood Dr RM6 .59 B3
Coombs St N1 ....234 D3
Coomer Mews SW6 ...264 D5
Coomer Pl SW6 135 B6 264 D5
Cooms Wlk HA8 ....27 A2
Cooper Ave E17 ....35 A2
Cooper Cl SE1 ....251 B1
Cooper Cres SM5 .....218 D5
Cooper Ct E15 ....76 A3
SE18 ....144 D6
Cooper Ho NW8 ....236 C5
7 SW27 ....182 D5
Hounslow TW4 ....129 B2
Cooper Rd NW4 ....46 D3
NW10 ....68 A3
Croydon CR0,CR9 .....220 D4
Cooper St 10 E16 ....98 D2
Cooperage Cl 5 N17 ....33 D4
Cooperage The SE1 ...253 C3
Coopers Cl E1 ....96 C3
Dagenham RM10 ....81 D2
Coopers Ct TW7 ......130 D3
Coopers La NW1 ......232 D3
SE12 ....165 B2
Cooper's La E10 ....54 A1
Coopers' Lane Prim Sch
SE12 ....165 B2
Cooper's Rd
SE1 ....117 D1 263 D2
Cooper's Row
EC3 ....117 D6 253 C6
Coopers Sch BR7 ......189 A2
Cooper's Yd SE19 .....183 C4
Coopersale Rd E9 ......74 D3
Coopersole Cl 3 IG8 ...37 C3
Coote Gdns RM8 ....81 B5
Coote Rd Dagenham RM8 .81 B5
Erith DA7 ....147 B4
Cope Ho EC1 ....235 B1
Cope Pl W8 ....113 C3 255 A5
Cope St SE16 ....118 D2
Cope Yd 6 E1 ....118 A5
Copeland Dr E14 ......119 C2
Copeland Ho SE11 .....260 D5
SW17 ....180 B6
Copeland Rd E17 ....53 D3
SE15 ....140 B3
Copelands BR3 ....185 B3
Copeman Cl SE26 .....184 C5
Copenhagen Ct W4 ....111 B4
Copenhagen Ho N1 ...234 A5
Copenhagen Pl E14 .....97 B1
Copenhagen Prim Sch
N1 ....94 B6 233 C5
Copenhagen St
N1 ....94 B6 233 C5
Copers Cope Rd BR3 ..185 B3
Copeswood Ct UB7 ....126 C5
Copford Wlk N1 ....235 A6
Copinger Wlk HA8 ......26 D2
Copland Ave HA0 ....65 D3
Copland Cl HA0 ....65 C3
Copland Com Sch & Tech Ctr
The HA9 ....66 B3
Copland Mews 3 HA0 ..66 A2
Copland Rd HA0 ....66 A2
Copleston Rd SE15 ....139 D2
Copley Cl 18 SE17 .....138 D6
W7 ....86 D2
Copley Dene BR1 ......187 D2
Copley Pk SW16 ......182 B4
Copley Rd HA7 ....25 C5
Copnor Way 14 SE15 ..139 C5
Coppard Gdns KT9 ....213 C2
Coppedhall 1 SE21 ...161 B2
Coppelia Rd SE3 ......142 D1
Coppen Rd RM8 ....59 B2
Copper Beech N6 ....49 A2
Copper Beech Ct N20 ..14 A1
Copper Beeches TW7 ..130 B4
Copper Cl SE19 ....183 D3
Copper Mill Dr TW7 ...130 D3
Copper Mill La SW17 ..180 A6
Copperas St SE8 ......141 D6
Copperdale Rd UB3 ...106 A4
Copperfield Ave UB8 ....82 C3
Copperfield Dr N15 .....51 D5
Copperfield Ho 10 SE1 .118 A4
Copperfield Mews N18 .33 C5
Copperfield Rd E3 ......97 A2
SE28 ....102 C1
Copperfield St
SE1 ....117 A4 252 A2
Copperfield Way
Chislehurst West BR7 ..189 A4
Pinner HA5 ....41 B5
Copperfields
5 Beckenham BR3 .....186 A2
Harrow HA1 ....42 C2
Copperfields Ct W3 ...110 C4
Coppergate Cl BR1 ....187 B2
Coppermead Cl NW2 ...68 C5
Coppermill La E17 ......52 D4
Coppermill Prim Sch
E17 ....52 D4
Copperwood Lo EN2 .....4 D3
Coppetts Cl N12 ....30 D3
Coppetts Ctr N12 ....30 D3
Coppetts Rd N10 ....30 D2
Coppetts Wood Hospl
N10 ....30 D2
Coppetts Wood Prim Sch
N10 ....31 A2
Coppice Cl SW20 .....200 C6
Harrow HA7 ....24 D4
Ruislip HA4 ....39 B3
Coppice Dr SW15 .....156 B5
Coppice The
Ashford TW15 ....170 D4
Enfield EN2 ....4 D1
Hillingdon UB7 ....82 A1
New Barnet EN5 ....13 D5
Coppice Way E18 ....54 D6
Coppice Wlk N20 ....13 C1
Coppies Gr N11 ....31 B6
Coppin Ho SW2 ....160 D3
Copping Cl CR0 ....221 C4
Coppinger Ct UB7 ....104 A4
Coppins The
Harrow Weald HA3 .....24 C4
New Addington CR0 ...223 D2
2 RM6 ....58 B2
Coppock Cl SW11 .....136 C3
Coppsfield KT8 ....195 C6
Copse Ave BR4 ....223 D5
Copse Cl SE7 ....143 B6
Copse Ct SW15 ....157 A6
Copse Glade KT6 ......197 D1
Copse Hill SW20 ......178 B3
Sutton SM2 ....217 D1
Copse The E4 ....20 D3
N2 ....48 D6
Copse View CR2 ......223 A1
Copsem Dr KT10 ......212 A2
Copsem La KT10 ......212 A1
Copsem Way KT10 .....212 A2
Coptefield Dr DA17 ....125 A3
Copthall Ave EC2 95 B1 242 D2
Copthall Bldgs EC2 ...242 D2
Copthall Cl EC2 ....242 C2
Copthall Dr NW7 ....28 A4
Copthall Gdns NW7 ....28 A3
Twickenham TW1 ......152 D3
Copthall Rd E UB10 ....60 C5
Copthall Rd W UB10 ...60 C6
Copthall Sch NW7 ......28 B3
Copthall Sports Ctr NW4 28 B2
Copthorne Ave SW12 ..159 D4
Keston Mark BR2 .....226 B6
Copthorne Chase TW15 170 B6
Copthorne Cl TW17 ...193 A3
Copthorne Mews UB3 .105 C2
Coptic St WC1 ..94 A2 240 A3
Copton Cl E3 ....97 C2
Copwood Cl N12 ....30 B6
Coral Cl RM6 ....58 C6
Coral Ho 5 E1 ....97 A3
Coral St SE1 ...116 C4 251 B1
Coraline Cl UB1 ....85 B4

Coralline Wlk 4 SE2 ..124 C4
Coram Ho 9 W4 ..111 C1
WC1 ..240 A6
Coram St WC1 ..94 A3 240 A5
Coran Cl N9 ..18 D4
Corban Rd TW3 ..129 C2
Corbar Cl EN4 ..2 B4
Corbet Cl CR4,SM6 ..219 A6
Corbet Ct EC3 ..242 D1
Corbet Ho N1 ..234 A5
Corbet Pl E1 ..95 D2 243 C4
Corbett Ct SE26 ..185 B6
Corbett Gr N22 ..32 A3
Corbett Ho SW10 ..266 A6
Corbett Rd E11 ..55 C3
E17 ..54 A6
Corbett Villas RM8 ..58 C1
Corbett's La SE16 ..118 C2
Corbicum E11 ..54 C2
Corbiere Ct SW19 ..178 D4
Corbiere Ho 5 N1 ..95 C6
Corbin Ho 7 E3 ..97 D4
Corbin's La HA2 ..63 D5
Corbridge 5 N17 ..34 B3
Corbridge Cres E2 ..96 B5
Corby Cres EN2 ..4 A1
Corby Rd NW10 ..89 B5
Corby Way E3 ..97 C3
Corbyland Rd DA15 ..167 C3
Corbylands Rd DA15 ..167 C4
Corbyn St N4,N19 ..50 A1
Cord Way 7 E14 ..119 C3
Cordelia Cl SE24 ..138 D1
Cordelia Gdns TW19 ..148 A4
Cordelia Ho 26 N1 ..95 C5
Cordelia Rd TW19 ..148 A4
Cordelia St E14 ..97 D1
Cordell Ho N15 ..51 D4
Cording St E14 ..97 D2
Cordingley Rd HA4 ..61 B6
Cordova Rd E3 ..97 A4
Cordwain Ho 7 N18 ..34 A5
Cordwainers Coll E8 ..74 B1
Cordwainers Ct 18 E9 ..74 C1
Cordwainers Wlk 9 E13 99 A5
Cordwell Rd SE13 ..164 C6
Corelli Rd SE3 ..144 A4
Corfe Ave HA2 ..63 C4
Corfe Cl UB4 ..84 C1
Corfe Ho SW8 ..270 C4
Corfe Lo SE21 ..161 B2
Corfe Twr 6 W3 ..111 A4
Corfield Rd N21 ..16 B6
Corfield St E2 ..96 B4
Corfton Lo W5 ..88 A2
Corfton Rd W5 ..88 A2
Coriander Ave E14 ..98 B1
Cories Cl RM8 ..80 D6
Corigan Ct 5 E11 ..76 C6
Corinium Cl HA9 ..66 B4
Corinne Rd N19 ..71 C4
Cork Sq E1 ..118 B5
Cork St W1 ..115 C6 249 A5
Cork St Mews W1 ..249 A5
Cork Tree Ho 3 SW27 ..182 D5
Cork Tree Way E4 ..35 A5
Corkran Rd KT6 ..198 A2
Corkscrew Hill BR4 ..224 B5
Corlett St NW1 ..237 A4
Cormont Rd SE5 ..138 D4
Cormorant Cl E7 ..76 D3
E17 ..35 A3
Cheam SM1 ..217 B3
Cormorant Ct 34 SE8 ..141 B6
12 SE21 ..161 B2
Cormorant Ho EN3 ..18 D6
Corn Way E11 ..76 C5
Cornbury Ho 5 SE8 ..141 B6
Cornbury Rd HA8 ..25 D3
Cornel Ho 4 DA15 ..168 A1
Cornelia St N7 ..72 B2
Cornell Cl DA14 ..191 A4
Cornell Ho HA2 ..63 B5
Corner Fielde SW2 ..160 B3
Corner Gn SE3 ..143 A3
Corner House St WC2 ..250 A4
Corner Mead NW9 ..27 D2
Cornerside TW15 ..171 A3
Cornerways SW15 ..134 A1
Harrow HA1 ..65 A5
Corney Rd W4 ..133 C6
Corney Reach Way W4 133 C5
Cornflower La CR0 ..206 D1
Cornflower Terr SE22 ..162 B5
Cornford Cl BR2 ..209 A4
Cornford Gr SW12 ..159 B2
Cornhill EC3 ..95 B1 242 D1
Cornick Ho 7 SE16 ..118 B3
Cornish Ct N9 ..18 B4
Cornish Gr SE20 ..184 B2
Cornish Ho 7 SE17 ..138 D6
Brentford TW8 ..110 B1
Cornmill La SE13 ..142 A2
Cornmow Dr NW10 ..68 A3
Cornshaw Rd RM8 ..58 D1
Cornthwaite Rd E5 ..74 C5
Cornwall Ave E2 ..96 C4
N3 ..29 C3
N22 ..32 A2
Bexley DA16 ..145 D2
Claygate KT10 ..212 D1
Southall UB1 ..85 C2
Cornwall Cl Barking IG11 79 D2
3 Hatch End HA5 ..23 B3
Cornwall Cres W11 ..91 A1
Cornwall Ct 5 W7 ..86 D3
Cornwall Dr BR5 ..190 C3
Cornwall Gdns NW10 ..68 B2
Cornwall Gdns *continued*
SW7 ..113 D3 255 D5
Cornwall Gdns Wlk
SW7 ..255 D5
Cornwall Gr W4 ..111 C1
Cornwall Ho NW1 ..237 D5
3 SW15 ..156 C4
Cornwall Mans NW1 ..237 D5
SW10 ..266 B4
Cornwall Mews S SW7 256 A5
Cornwall Mews W SW7 255 D5
Cornwall Rd N4 ..50 C2
N15 ..51 B4
N18 ..34 A5
SE1 ..116 C5 251 B2
Belmont SM2 ..217 B1
Harrow HA1 ..42 A3
Hatch End HA5 ..23 B3
Ruislip HA4 ..61 D6
Thornton Heath CR0 ..220 D6
Twickenham TW1 ..153 A3
Cornwall St 4 E1 ..118 B6
Cornwall Terr NW1 ..237 D5
Cornwall Terr Mews
NW1 ..237 D5
Cornwallis Ave N9 ..18 C2
New Eltham DA15 ..167 B2
Cornwallis Ct SW8 ..270 A2
Cornwallis Gr N9 ..18 C2
Cornwallis Ho 24 W12 ..112 B6
Cornwallis Rd E17 ..52 D5
N9 ..18 B2
N19 ..72 A6
SE18 ..122 D3
Dagenham RM9 ..81 A4
Cornwallis Sq N19 ..72 A6
Cornwallis Wlk SE9 ..144 B2
Cornwell Ct 21 E10 ..53 D2
Cornwood Cl N2 ..48 B5
Cornwood Dr E1 ..96 C1
Cornworthy Rd RM8 ..80 C3
Corona Rd SE12 ..165 A4
Coronation Ave 1 N16 ..73 D4
Coronation Cl
Bexley DA5 ..168 D5
Ilford IG6 ..57 A5
Coronation Ct E15 ..76 D2
W10 ..90 C2
Coronation Rd E13 ..99 C4
NW10 ..88 C3
Hayes UB3 ..105 D2
Coronet Par 4 HA0 ..66 A2
Coronet St N1 ..95 C4
Corporation Ave TW4 ..129 A1
Corporation Row EC1 ..241 B6
Corporation St E15 ..98 D5
N7 ..72 A3
Corpus Christi RC Prim Sch
SW2 ..160 B6
Kingston u T KT3 ..199 A6
Corrance Rd SW2,SW4 ..138 A1
Corri Ave N14 ..31 D6
Corrib Ct N13 ..16 B1
Corrib Dr SM1 ..218 C3
Corrib Hts N8 ..49 D3
Corringham Ct NW11 ..47 C2
Corringham Ho 10 E1 ..96 D1
Corringham Rd NW11 ..47 C2
Wembley HA9 ..66 C6
Corringway NW11 ..47 D2
W5 ..88 C2
Corris Gn NW9 ..45 C3
Corry Ho 2 E14 ..119 D6
Corsair Cl TW19 ..148 A4
Corsair Rd TW19 ..148 A4
Corscombe Cl KT2 ..177 A5
Corsehill St SW16 ..181 C4
Corseley Way E9 ..75 B2
Corsham Ho HA9 ..66 C2
Corsham St N1 ..95 B4 235 D1
Corsica St N5 ..72 D2
Cortayne Rd SW6 ..135 B3
Cortis Rd SW15 ..156 B5
Cortis Terr SW15 ..156 B5
Corunna Rd
SW8 ..137 C4 269 B2
Corunna Terr SW8 ..269 A2
Corvette Sq 5 SE10 ..142 B6
Corwell Gdns UB8 ..83 A1
Corwell La UB8 ..83 A1
Coryton Path W9 ..91 B3
Cosbycote Ave SE24 ..161 A6
Cosdach Ave SM6 ..219 D1
Cosedge Cres CR0,CR9 ..220 D3
Cosgrove Cl N21 ..17 A2
Hayes UB4 ..84 D3
Cosgrove Ho 11 E2 ..96 A6
Cosmo Pl WC1 ..240 B4
Cosmur Cl W12 ..111 D3
Cossall Wlk SE15 ..140 B4
Cosser St SE1 ..116 C3 261 A6
Costa St SE15 ..140 A3
Coston Prim Sch UB6 ..86 A4
Coston Wlk 4 SE4 ..140 D1
Costons Ave UB6 ..86 B4
Costons La UB6 ..86 B4
Cosway Ho NW11 ..48 A3
Cosway Mans NW1 ..237 B4
Cosway St NW1 ..92 C2 237 B4
Cotall St E14 ..97 C2
Coteford Cl HA5 ..40 A4
Coteford Inf Sch HA5 ..40 A3
Coteford Jun Sch HA5 ..39 D4
Coteford St SW17 ..181 A6
Cotelands CR0 ..221 C5
Cotes Ho NW8 ..237 A5
Cotesbach Rd E5 ..74 C5
Cotesmore Gdns RM8 ..80 C4
Cotford Rd CR7 ..205 A5
Cotham St SE17 ..262 B3
Cotherstone Rd SW2 ..160 B3
Cotleigh Ave DA5 ..168 D2
Cotleigh Rd NW6 ..69 C1
Cotman Cl NW11 ..48 A3
SW15 ..156 D6
Cotman Ct BR3 ..185 B2
Cotman Gdns HA8 ..26 C1
Cotman Ho NW8 ..230 A4
6 Northolt UB5 ..84 D5
Cotmandene Cres BR5 ..190 A1
Cotmans Cl UB3 ..106 A5
Coton Rd DA16 ..146 A2
Cotsford Ave KT3 ..199 B4
Cotswold Ave WD2 ..8 A5
Cotswold Cl N11 ..31 A6
Hinchley Wood KT10 ..212 D6
Kingston u T KT2 ..177 A4
Cotswold Ct EC1 ..242 A6
3 Wembley UB6 ..86 D5
Cotswold Gate NW2 ..47 A1
Cotswold Gdns E6 ..99 D5
NW2 ..68 D6
Ilford IG2 ..57 B2
Cotswold Gn EN2 ..4 B1
Cotswold Ho N16 ..51 D1
Cotswold Mews SW11 ..266 D1
Cotswold Rd TW12 ..173 C4
Cotswold Rise BR6 ..211 D3
Cotswold St SE27 ..182 D6
Cotswold Way Enfield EN2 ..4 B2
North Cheam KT4 ..216 C6
Cottage Ave BR2 ..210 A1
Cottage Cl HA4 ..39 B1
Cottage Field Cl DA14,
DA15 ..168 C3
Cottage Gn SE5 ..139 B5
Cottage Gr SW9 ..138 A2
Kingston u T KT6 ..197 D3
Cottage Pl SW3 114 C3 257 A5
Cottage Rd KT19 ..215 B1
Cottage St E14 ..119 D6
Cottage Wlk 2 N16 ..73 D5
SE15 ..139 D4
Cottages The UB10 ..60 D5
Cottenham Dr NW9 ..45 D6
SW20 ..178 B3
Cottenham Ho 4 N19 ..72 A6
Cottenham Par SW20 ..178 B1
Cottenham Park Rd
SW20 ..178 C3
Cottenham Pl SW20 ..178 B3
Cottenham Rd E17 ..53 B5
Cotterill Rd KT6 ..198 B1
Cottesbrook St 9 SE14 141 A5
Cottesloe Ho NW8 ..237 A6
Cottesloe Mews SE1 ..261 B6
Cottesmore Ct W8 ..255 D6
Cottesmore Gdns
W8 ..113 D3 255 D6
Cottimore Ave KT12 ..194 B1
Cottimore Cres KT12 ..194 B2
Cottimore La
Walton-on-T KT12 ..194 B2
Walton-on-T KT12 ..194 D1
Cottimore Terr KT12 ..194 B2
Cottingham Chase HA4 ..62 A5
Cottingham Rd SE20 ..184 D3
SW8 ..138 B5 270 D4
Cottington Rd TW13 ..172 D6
Cottington St SE11 ..261 C2
Cotton Ave W3 ..89 B1
Cotton Cl RM9 ..80 C1
Cotton Hill BR1 ..186 B6
Cotton Ho 18 SW12 ..160 A4
W12 ..111 D4
Cotton Row SW11 ..136 B2
Cotton St E14 ..120 A6
Cottongrass Cl 1 CR0 ..206 D1
Cotton's Gdns E2 ..95 C4
Cottons La SE1 ..252 D4
Cotts Cl 18 W7 ..86 D2
Couchman Ho 8 SW4 ..159 C5
Couchmore Ave KT10 ..212 C6
Coulgate St SE4 ..141 A2
Coulsdon Ct 3 N8 ..49 D4
Coulsdon Ho 5 SW2 ..160 A3
Coulsdon Rd RM8 ..58 C1
Coulson St
SW3 ..114 D1 257 C2
Coulter Cl UB4 ..85 A3
Coulter Rd W6 ..112 B3
Coulthurst Ct SW16 ..182 A3
Coults Cres NW5 ..71 A5
Councillor St SE5 ..139 A5
Counter St SE1 ..253 A3
Counters Ct W14 ..254 B6
Countess Rd NW5 ..71 C3
Countisbury Ave EN1 ..17 D4
Countisbury Ho SE26 ..162 A1
Country Way TW13,
TW16 ..172 C5
County Gate
New Barnet EN5 ..13 D5
New Eltham BR7 ..167 A1
County Gdns IG11 ..101 C5
County Gr SE5 ..139 A4
County Ho 9 SW9 ..138 C4
County Par TW8 ..131 D5
County Rd E6 ..100 D2
South Norwood CR7 ..182 D1
County St SE1 ..117 A3 262 B5
Coupland Pl SE18 ..123 A1
Courcy Rd N8,N22 ..50 C6
Courier Ho 17 SW2 ..160 C4
Courland Gr SW8 ..137 D3
Courland St
SW8 ..137 D4 269 D1
Course The SE9 ..166 C1
Court Ave DA17 ..125 B1
Court Cl Harrow HA3 ..44 A6
Twickenham TW13,TW2 ..151 D1
Wallington SM6 ..219 D1
Court Close Ave TW13,
TW2 ..151 D1
Court Cres KT9 ..213 D2
Court Downs Rd BR3 ..185 D1
Court Dr Carshalton SM1 218 C4
Croydon CR0 ..220 B4
Hillingdon UB10 ..82 C6
Stanmore HA7 ..26 A6
Court Farm Ave KT19 ..215 B3
Court Farm Ind Est
TW19 ..148 B5
Court Farm Rd SE9 ..166 A1
Northolt UB5 ..63 C1
Court Gdns N7 ..72 C2
Court House Gdns N3 ..29 C4
Court House Rd N12 ..29 D4
Court La SE21 ..161 D4
Court Lands W5 ..87 C2
Court Lane Gdns SE21 ..161 C4
Court Lo 11 DA17 ..125 C1
Court Mans 8 W6 ..112 A2
Court Mead UB5 ..85 B4
Court Par HA0 ..65 B5
Court Rd SE9 ..166 B4
SE25 ..205 D6
Southall UB2 ..107 B1
Uxbridge UB10 ..60 D4
Court Royal SW15 ..157 A6
Court St E1 ..96 B2
Bromley BR1 ..187 A1
Court The N10 ..49 C5
Ruislip HA4 ..63 A4
Court Way NW9 ..45 C5
W3 ..89 A2
Ilford IG6 ..57 A6
Twickenham TW1,TW2 ..152 D4
Court Yd SE9 ..166 B5
Courtauld Galleries★
WC2 ..250 C6
Courtauld Ho 11 E2 ..96 A5
Courtauld Inst of Art
W1 ..237 D2
Courtauld Rd N19 ..50 A1
Courtaulds Cl SE28 ..124 A5
Courten Mews HA7 ..25 C3
Courtenay Ave N6 ..48 C2
Harrow HA3 ..24 A2
Courtenay Dr BR3 ..186 B1
Courtenay Gdns HA3 ..24 A1
Courtenay Mews E17 ..53 A4
Courtenay Pl E17 ..53 A4
Courtenay Rd E11 ..76 D5
E17 ..52 D5
North Cheam KT4,SM3 ..216 C5
Penge BR3,SE20 ..184 D4
Courtenay Sq SE11 ..261 A1
Courtenay St
SE11 ..116 C1 261 A2
Courtfield W13 ..87 C2
Courtfield Ave HA1 ..42 D4
Courtfield Cres HA1 ..42 D4
Courtfield Gdns
SW5 ..113 D2 255 D3
W13 ..87 A1
Ruislip HA4 ..61 D6
Courtfield Ho EC1 ..241 A4
Courtfield Mews SW7 ..255 D3
Courtfield Rd
SW7 ..114 A2 256 A3
Ashford TW15 ..170 D4
Courtfield Rise BR4 ..224 B5
Courthill Rd SE13 ..142 A1
Courthope Ho 14 SE16 ..118 C3
SW8 ..270 A3
Courthope Rd NW3 ..70 D4
SW19 ..179 A5
Greenford UB6 ..86 B5
Courthope Villas SW19 179 A3
Courtland Ave E4 ..20 D2
NW7 ..11 C1
SW16 ..182 B3
Ilford IG1 ..78 B6
Courtland Gr SE28 ..124 D6
Courtland Prim Sch
NW7 ..11 C2
Courtland Rd E6 ..100 A6
Courtlands 5 E5 ..52 B1
11 Beckenham BR3 ..185 D1
Richmond TW10 ..154 C6
10 Sutton SM2 ..217 D1
Walton-on-T KT12 ..194 A2
Courtlands Ave SE12 ..165 B6
Hampton TW12 ..173 B4
Richmond TW9 ..132 D3
West Wickham BR2 ..208 D1
Courtlands Cl HA4 ..39 D2
Courtlands Dr KT19 ..215 D2
Courtlands Rd KT5 ..198 C2
Courtleet Dr DA7 ..147 D4
Courtleigh 6 NW11 ..47 B4
Courtleigh Ave EN4 ..2 B5
Courtleigh Gdns NW11 ..47 A5
Courtman Rd N17 ..33 A3
Courtmead Cl SE24 ..161 A5
Courtnell St W2 ..91 C1
Courtney Cl SE19 ..183 C4
Courtney Cres SM5 ..218 D1
Courtney Ct N7 ..72 C3
Courtney Ho 1 NW4 ..46 C5
Courtney Pl CR0 ..220 C5
Courtney Rd N7 ..72 C3
Courtney Rd *continued*
SW19 ..180 C3
Croydon CR0 ..220 C5
Harlington TW6 ..126 C2
Courtrai Rd SE23 ..163 A5
Courts The SW16 ..182 A3
Courtside N8 ..49 D3
SE23 ..162 C1
Courtville Ho 11 W10 ..91 A4
Courtway IG8 ..37 C5
Courtyard The N1 ..72 B1
SW6 ..135 A4 264 A1
13 SW18 ..136 B1
Cousin La EC4 ..117 B6 252 C5
Cousins Cl 2 UB7 ..104 A6
Cousins Ct 2 NW9 ..46 A5
Couthurst Rd SE3 ..143 B5
Coutts Ave KT9 ..214 A3
Coutts Ho SE7 ..143 C6
Couzens Ho 9 E3 ..97 B2
Coval Gdns SW14 ..132 D1
Coval La SW14 ..132 D1
Coval Rd SW14 ..133 A1
Covelees Wall E6 ..100 C1
Covent Garden Sta
WC2 ..94 A1 240 B1
Covent Gdn★
WC2 ..116 A6 250 B6
Coventry Cl 9 E6 ..100 B1
NW6 ..91 C6
Coventry Rd E1 ..96 B3
SE25 ..206 A5
Ilford IG1 ..56 D1
Coventry St W1 ..249 C5
Coverack Cl N14 ..15 C5
Croydon CR0 ..207 A2
Coverdale Cl HA7 ..25 B5
Coverdale Gdns CR0 ..221 D5
Coverdale Pl NW6 ..68 D1
Coverdale Rd N11 ..31 A4
NW2 ..69 A2
W12 ..112 B4
Coverdales The IG11 ..101 B5
Coverham Ho 5 SE4 ..140 D1
Coverley Cl E1 ..96 A2
Coverley Point SE11 ..260 C3
Covert The BR5,BR6 ..211 C3
Covert Way EN4 ..2 A3
Coverton Rd SW17 ..180 C5
Coverts Rd KT10 ..212 D1
Covet Wood Cl BR5 ..211 D3
Covey Cl SW19 ..179 D1
Covington Gdns SW16 ..182 D3
Covington Way SW16 ..182 C3
SW16 ..182 D3
Cow Leaze E6 ..100 C1
Cowan Cl E6 ..100 A2
Cowan Ct NW10 ..67 B1
Cowbridge La IG11 ..78 D1
Cowbridge Rd HA3 ..44 B5
Cowcross St EC1 94 D2 241 C4
Cowden Rd BR6 ..211 D2
Cowden St SE6 ..185 C6
Cowdenbeath Path N1 233 C6
Cowdray Hall Coll of Nursing
W1 ..93 B1 238 C2
Cowdray Ho 23 SE22 ..139 C2
Cowdray Rd UB10 ..83 A6
Cowdrey Cl EN1 ..5 C3
Cowdrey Rd SW19 ..180 A5
Cowdry Rd E9 ..75 B2
Cowell Lo E4 ..36 D5
Cowen Ave HA2 ..64 B6
Cowen Ho 4 SE18 ..144 D6
Cowgate Rd UB6 ..86 B4
Cowick Rd SW17 ..180 D6
Cowings Mead UB5 ..63 A2
Cowland Ave EN3 ..6 C1
Cowleaze Rd KT2 ..176 A2
Cowley La E11 ..76 C5
Cowley Pl NW4 ..46 C4
Cowley Rd E11 ..55 B4
SW9 ..138 C4
16 SW9 ..138 C5
SW14 ..133 C2
W3 ..111 D5
Redbridge IG1 ..56 B2
Cowley St SW1 ..260 A5
Cowling Cl W11 ..244 A4
Cowper Ave E6 ..78 A1
Carshalton SM1 ..218 B4
Cowper Cl Bexley DA16 ..168 A6
Bromley BR2 ..209 D5
Cowper Gdns N14 ..15 C5
Wallington SM6 ..219 C2
Cowper Ho SE17 ..262 B2
SW1 ..259 D1
Cowper Rd N14 ..15 B3
N16 ..73 C4
N18 ..34 A5
SW19 ..180 A4
W3 ..111 B5
W7 ..108 D6
Belvedere DA17 ..125 C2
Bromley BR2 ..209 D5
Richmond TW10 ..176 B5
Cowper St EC1,
EC2 ..95 B3 242 D6
Cowper Terr W10 ..90 D2
Cowper's Ct EC3 ..242 D1
Cowslip Cl UB10 ..60 A1
Cowslip Rd E18 ..37 B1
Cowthorpe Rd SW8 ..269 D2
Cox Ct 3 EN4 ..2 C1
Cox Ho W6 ..264 A6
Cox La Chessington KT9 ..214 B4
West Ewell KT19 ..215 A3
Coxe Pl HA3 ..43 A5
Coxmount Rd SE7 ..121 D1
Coxs Ave TW17 ..193 C6
Cox's Ct E1 ..243 C3
Coxson Way SE1 ..253 C1
Coxwell Rd SE18 ..123 B1
SE19 ..183 C3
Coxwold Path KT9 ..214 A1
Coysh Ct 8 SW15 ..157 A6
Crab Hill BR3 ..186 B3
Crabbs Croft Cl 7 BR6 227 A3
Crabtree Ave Ilford RM6 ..58 D5
Wembley HA0 ..88 B5
Crabtree Cl E2 ..95 D5
Crabtree Ct E15 ..75 D3
Crabtree Hall SW6 ..134 C5
Crabtree La SW6 ..134 D5
Craddock Rd EN1 ..5 D2
Craddock St NW5 ..71 A2
Cradley Rd DA15,SE9 ..167 B3
Craig Gdns E18 ..36 D1
Craig Park Rd N18 ..34 B6
Craig Rd Hayes UB8 ..82 D1
Richmond TW10 ..175 C6
Craigen Ave CR0 ..206 B1
Craigerne Rd SE3 ..143 B5
Craigholm SE18 ..144 C4
Craigie Ho SE1 ..263 D3
Craigleith SW15 ..156 D5
Craigmuir Pk HA0 ..88 B6
Craignair Rd SW2 ..160 C4
Craignish Ave SW16 ..182 B1
Craig's Ct SW1 ..250 A4
Craigside KT2 ..176 D2
Craigton Rd SE9 ..144 B1
Craigweil Cl HA7 ..25 D5
Craigweil Dr HA7 ..25 D5
Craigwell Ave TW13 ..150 A1
Craik Ct NW6 ..91 B5
Crail Row SE17 117 B2 262 D3
Cramer Ct KT3 ..199 A6
Cramer St W1 ..93 A2 238 B3
Crammond Cl W6 ..264 A5
Cramond Ct TW14 ..149 C3
Crampton Jun & Inf Sch
SE17 ..116 D1 261 D2
Crampton Rd SE20 ..184 C4
Crampton St
SE17 ..117 A1 262 A2
Cranberry Cl 2 UB5 ..84 D5
Cranberry La E16 ..98 C3
Cranborne Ave
Southall UB2 ..107 C2
Tolworth KT6,KT9 ..214 C5
Cranborne Rd IG11 ..101 B6
Cranborne Waye
Hayes UB4 ..84 B1
Hayes UB4 ..106 C6
Cranbourn Alley WC2 ..249 D6
Cranbourn Ho 4 SE16 ..118 B4
Cranbourn St
WC2 ..115 D6 249 D6
Cranbourne Ave E11 ..55 B5
E11,E18 ..55 B5
Cranbourne Cl SW16 ..204 A6
Cranbourne Ct E18 ..55 B5
SW11 ..267 B4
Cranbourne Dr HA5 ..40 D4
Cranbourne Gdns NW11 47 B4
Ilford IG6 ..57 A6
Cranbourne Rd E12 ..78 A3
E15 ..76 A4
N10 ..31 B1
Northwood HA6 ..39 D6
Cranbrook NW1 ..232 B5
Cranbrook Cl BR2 ..209 A3
Cranbrook Coll (Boys)
IG1 ..78 C6
Cranbrook Ct 8 TW8 ..131 D6
Cranbrook Dr
Thames Ditton KT10 ..196 A1
Twickenham TW2 ..151 D3
Cranbrook Ho 5 E5 ..74 B3
SE19 ..183 B2
Cranbrook Mews E17 ..53 B4
Cranbrook Pk N22 ..32 C2
Cranbrook Point 11
E16 ..121 B5
Cranbrook Rd SE8 ..141 C4
SW19 ..179 A3
W4 ..111 C1
Erith DA7 ..147 B4
Hounslow TW4 ..129 B1
Ilford IG1,IG2 ..56 C3
New Barnet EN4 ..14 B5
South Norwood CR7 ..183 A1
Cranbrook Rise IG1 ..56 B2
Cranbrook St E2 ..96 D5
Cranbury Rd SW6 ..135 D3
Crandale Ho 8 E5 ..74 B3
Crandley Ct SE8 ..119 A2
Crane Ave W3 ..111 A6
Isleworth TW7 ..153 A6
Crane Cl RM10 ..81 C2
Crane Ct EC4 ..241 B1
7 W12 ..111 C4
West Ewell KT19 ..215 A4
Crane Gdns UB3 ..105 D2
Crane Gr N7 ..72 C2
Crane Ho 22 E3 ..97 A5
9 SE15 ..139 D4
9 Catford BR1 ..186 B5
Feltham TW13 ..151 C1
Crane Inf Sch TW13 ..151 B2
Crane Jun Sch TW13 ..151 B2
Crane Lodge Rd TW5 ..128 B6

Crane Mead SE16 118 D2
Crane Mead Ct TW1 152 D4
Crane Park Rd TW2 151 D2
Crane Rd Stanwell TW19 148 C5
Twickenham TW2 152 C3
Crane St 5 SE15 139 D4
Crane Way TW2 152 D4
Cranebrook TW2 152 A2
Craneford Cl TW2 152 D4
Craneford Way TW2 152 D4
Cranes Dr KT5 198 B5
Cranes Park Ave KT5, KT6 198 B5
Cranes Park Cres KT5 198 B5
Cranes Pk KT5,KT6 198 A4
Cranes Way WD6 11 A6
Craneswater TW6 127 D5
Craneswater Pk UB2 107 B1
Cranfield Ct NW1 237 B3
2 Woodford IG8 37 A6
Cranfield Dr NW9 27 C3
Cranfield Rd SE4 141 B2
Cranford Ave N13 32 A5
Stanwell TW19 148 B4
Cranford Cl SW20 178 B3
Stanwell TW19 148 A4
Cranford Comm Sch TW5 128 B6
Cranford Cotts 8 E1 118 D6
Cranford Ct SM1 218 A4
Cranford Dr UB3 105 D2
Cranford Jun & Inf Schs TW4 128 B3
Cranford La
Harlington UB3 127 C5
Hatton TW6 127 D2
Hatton TW6 127 D4
Heston TW5 128 C5
Cranford Lo SW19 156 D2
Cranford Park Prim Sch UB3 105 D2
Cranford Park Rd UB3 105 D2
Cranford Rise KT10 212 A3
Cranford St E1 118 D6
Cranford Way N8 50 C4
Cranhurst Rd NW2 68 C3
Cranleigh W11 244 C4
Cranleigh Cl SE20 184 B1
Old Bexley DA5 169 D5
Cranleigh Ct 4 N16 51 C1
Mitcham CR4 202 B6
Richmond TW9 132 C2
Southall UB1 85 B1
Cranleigh Gardens Ind Est UB1 85 B2
Cranleigh Gdns N21 16 C6
SE25 205 C6
Barking IG11 79 B2
Harrow HA3 44 A4
Kingston u T KT2 176 B4
Southall UB1 85 B1
Sutton SM1 217 D6
Cranleigh Ho SW20 178 B1
Cranleigh Hos NW1 232 B3
Cranleigh Mews SW11 136 D3
Cranleigh Rd N15 51 A4
SW19 201 C6
Feltham TW13 171 D6
Thames Ditton KT10 196 A1
Cranleigh St NW1 93 C5 232 B3
Cranley Dene Ct N10 49 B5
Cranley Dr Ilford IG2 57 A2
Ruislip HA4 61 D6
Cranley Gdns N10 49 B5
N13 16 B1
SW7 114 B1 256 C2
Wallington SM6 219 C1
Cranley Mews SW7 114 A1 256 B2
Cranley Par 2 SE9 188 A6
Cranley Pl SW7 114 B2 256 C3
Cranley Rd E13 99 B2
Ilford IG2 57 A2
Cranmer Ave W13 109 B3
Cranmer Cl Ruislip HA4 40 D1
Stanmore HA7 25 C3
West Barnes SM4 200 D3
Cranmer Ct N3 29 A1
SW3 257 B3
Hampton TW12 173 D5
Kingston u T KT2 175 D6
Cranmer Farm Cl CR4 202 D5
Cranmer Ho SW11 267 A2
Cranmer Mid Sch CR4 202 D5
Cranmer Rd E7 77 B4
SW9 138 C5
Croydon CR0 221 A5
Edgware HA8 10 D1
Hampton TW12 173 D5
Hayes UB3 83 B1
Kingston u T KT2 176 A5
Mitcham CR4 202 D5
Cranmer Terr SW17 180 B5
Cranmore Ave TW7 130 A5
Cranmore Rd
Catford BR1 164 D1
Chislehurst West BR7 188 B5
Cranmore Way N10 49 C5
Cranston Cl
Hounslow TW3,TW4 129 A3
Uxbridge UB10 61 B6
Cranston Gdns E4 35 D4
Cranston Rd SE23 163 A2
Cranswick Rd SE16 118 B1
Crantock Rd SE6 164 A2
Cranwell Cl E3 97 D3
Cranwell Ct 6 NW9 27 D3
Croydon CR0 222 D6
Cranwell Gr TW17 192 B5
Cranwell Rd TW6 126 D3
Cranwich Ave N21 17 B4
Cranwich Rd N16 51 C2
Cranwood Ct EC1 235 D1
Cranwood St EC1 95 B4 235 D1
Cranworth Cres 7 E4 20 B3
Cranworth Gdns SW9 138 C4
Cranworth Ho 6 N7 72 B4
Craster Rd SW2 160 B4
Craston Ho 2 SE5 139 C3
Crathie Rd SE12 165 B5
Crathorne Ho N2 30 B1
Cravan Ave TW13 150 A2
Craven Ave W5 109 C6
Southall UB1 85 B2
Craven Cl N16 52 A2
Hayes UB4 84 A1
Craven Cottage (Fulham FC) SW6 134 D4
Craven Ct NW10 89 C6
Dagenham RM6 59 A3
Edgware HA8 26 B6
Craven Gdns SW19 179 D5
Barking IG11 101 C5
Ilford IG6 57 B6
Craven Hill W2 114 A6 246 B6
Craven Hill Gdns W2 114 A6 246 A6
Craven Hill Mews W2 246 B6
Craven Ho 13 N2 30 B1
2 SW14 133 B2
Craven Lo SW6 134 D4
W2 246 B6
Craven Mews 6 SW11 137 A2
Craven Park JMI Sch N16 52 A3
Craven Park Mews NW10 89 C6
Craven Park Rd N15 52 A3
NW10 89 C6
Craven Pas WC2 250 A4
Craven Pk NW10 89 C6
Craven Rd NW10 89 B6
W2 92 A1 236 B1
W5 109 C6
Croydon CR0 206 B1
Kingston u T KT2 176 B2
Craven St WC2 116 A5 250 A4
Craven Terr W2 114 A6 246 B6
Craven Wlk E5,N16 52 A2
Crawford Ave HA0 65 D3
Crawford Bldgs NW1 237 B3
Crawford Cl TW7 130 C3
Crawford Gdns N13 16 D1
Northolt UB5 85 B4
Crawford Jun & Inf Sch SE5 139 A4
Crawford Mews W1 237 C3
Crawford Pas EC1 241 B5
Crawford Pl W1 92 C2 237 B3
Crawford Place Dwellings NW1 237 B3
Crawford Point 4 E16 98 D1
Crawford Rd SE5 139 A3
Crawford St W1 92 D2 237 C3
Crawley Rd E10 53 D1
N22 33 A1
Enfield EN1 17 D4
Crawshay Ct SW9 138 C4
Crawshay Cy SW9 138 C4
Crawshay Ho 13 N16 73 B4
Crawthew Gr SE22 139 D1
Cray Rd Erith DA17 147 C6
Foots Cray DA14 190 C4
Craybrooke Rd DA14 190 B6
Craybury End SE9 167 A2
Crayfields Ind Pk BR5 190 C1
Crayford Cl E6 100 A1
Crayford Ho N7 72 A4
SE1 252 D1
Crayford Rd N7 72 A4
Crayke Hill KT9 214 A1
Crayle Ho EC1 241 D6
Crayonne Cl TW16 171 C2
Crays Par The BR5 190 C1
Crealock Gr IG8 36 D5
Crealock St SW18 157 D5
Creasy Est SE1 263 A5
Crebor St SE22 162 A5
Credenhall Dr BR2 210 B1
Credenhill Ho 2 SE15 140 B5
Credenhill St SW16 181 C4
Crediton Hill NW6 69 D3
Crediton Ho EN3 6 D2
Crediton Rd E16 99 A1
NW10 90 D6
Crediton Way KT10 213 A3
Credon Rd E13 99 C5
SE16 118 B1
Creechurch La EC3 243 B1
Creechurch Pl EC3 243 B1
Creed Ho SE15 140 B2
Creed La EC4 241 D1
Creek Ho W14 254 B6
Creek Rd SE10,SE8 141 D6
Barking IG11 101 D4
East Molesey KT8 196 C5
Creek The TW16 194 A4
Creekmouth Ind Pk IG11 101 D3
Creekside SE8 141 D5
Creeland Gr SE6 163 B3
Crefeld Cl W6 135 A6 264 A5
Creffield Rd W3,W5 110 C6
Creighton Ave E6 99 D5
N2,N10 30 D1
Creighton Ho N2 48 C6
W12 112 A6
Creighton Rd N17 33 C3
NW6 90 D5
W5 109 D3
Cremer Bsns Ctr 8 E2 95 D5
Cremer Ho 9 SE8 141 C5
Cremer St E2 95 D5
Cremorne Rd SW10 136 B5 266 C4
Creon Ct 3 SW9 138 C4
Crescent EC3 253 C6
Crescent Court Bsns Ctr E16 98 B3
Crescent Ct SW4 159 D6
Kingston u T KT6 197 D4
14 Sidcup DA15 168 A1
Crescent Dr BR5 211 A3
Crescent E EN4 2 A5
Crescent Gdns SW19 157 C1
Ruislip HA4 40 B2
Crescent Gr SW4 137 C1
Mitcham CR4 202 C5
Crescent Ho SE13 141 D3
Crescent La SW4 159 D6
Crescent Mans N5 72 D3
W11 244 B6
Crescent Par UB10 82 C4
Crescent Pl SW3 257 B4
Crescent Rd E4 20 C4
E6 99 C6
E10 75 D6
E13 99 A6
E18 37 C2
N3 29 B2
N8 49 D3
N9 18 A3
N11 30 D6
N15 50 D6
N22 31 D2
SE18 122 D2
SW20 178 D2
Barnet EN4 14 C6
Beckenham BR3 185 D1
Dagenham RM10 81 D5
Enfield EN2 4 D1
Kingston u T KT2 176 D3
Plaistow BR1 187 A3
Shepperton TW17 193 A4
Sidcup DA15 167 D1
Crescent Rise N3 29 B2
3 N3 29 C2
N22 31 D2
Barnet EN4 14 C6
Crescent Row EC1 242 A5
Crescent St N1 72 B1
Crescent Stables SW15 157 A6
Crescent The E17 53 A4
N2 47 D6
N11 31 A6
NW2 68 B5
SW13 134 A3
SW19 157 C1
W3 89 C1
Ashford TW15 170 B5
Barnet EN5 1 D3
Beckenham BR3 185 C2
Bexley DA5 168 C4
Carshalton SM1 218 B3
East Molesey KT8 195 C5
Harlington UB7 127 B5
Harrow HA2 42 A1
Ilford IG2 56 C3
Kingston u T KT3 177 A1
Kingston u T KT6 198 A4
Loughton IG10 21 D5
Lower Halliford TW17 193 D2
Sidcup DA14 189 D6
Southall UB1 107 A4
Thornton Heath CR0 205 B3
Wembley HA0 65 B6
West Wickham BR4 208 C3
Crescent View IG10 21 D6
Crescent W EN4 2 A5
Crescent Way SE4 141 C2
SW16 182 C3
Orpington BR6 227 C3
Crescent Wood Rd SE21,SE26 162 A1
Crescentway N12 30 C4
Cresford Rd SW6 135 D4 265 C1
Crespigny Rd NW4 46 B3
Cressage Cl UB1 85 C3
Cressage Ho 9 TW8 132 A6
Cressall Ho 8 E14 119 C3
Cresset Ho 8 E9 74 C2
Cresset Rd E9 74 C2
Cresset St SW4 137 D2
Cressfield Cl NW5 71 A3
Cressida Rd N19 49 D1
Cressingham Ct 1 DA17 125 C3
Cressingham Gr SM1 218 A4
Cressingham Rd SE13 142 A2
Burnt Oak HA8 27 B3
Cressington Cl 4 N16 73 C3
Cresswell Gdns SW5 256 A2
Cresswell Pk SE3 142 D2
Cresswell Pl SW10 114 A1 256 B2
Cresswell Rd SE25 206 A5
Feltham TW13 173 A6
Twickenham TW1 153 D5
Cresswell Way N21 16 C4
Cressy Ct 6 E1 96 C2
W6 112 B3
Cressy Ho SW13 134 B2
Cressy Hos 7 E1 96 C2
Cressy Pl E1 96 C2
Cressy Rd NW3 70 D4
Crest Ct NW4 46 C4
Crest Dr EN3 6 C5
Crest Gdns HA4 62 C5
Crest Rd NW2 68 A6
South Croydon CR2 222 B1
West Wickham BR2 208 D2
Crest The N13 32 C6
NW4 46 C4
10 SW27 182 D5
Kingston u T KT5 198 C4
Crest View HA5 40 D5
Crest View Dr BR5 211 A4
Cresta Ct W5 88 B3
Cresta Ho 7 E3 97 C3
NW6 70 B1
Crestbrook Ave N13 16 D1
Crestbrook Pl N13 16 D1
Crestfield St N1,WC1 233 B2
Creston Way KT4 200 D1
Crestview NW5 71 B5
Crestway SW15 156 B5
Crestwood Way TW4 151 A6
Creswick Ct W3 110 D6
Creswick Rd W3 110 D6
Creswick Wlk 6 E3 97 C4
NW11 47 B5
Creton St SE18 122 C3
Crewdson Rd SW9 138 C5
Crewe Pl NW10 89 D4
Crewkerne Ct SW11 266 D2
Crews St E14 119 C2
Crewys Rd NW2 69 B6
SE15 140 B3
Crichton Ave SM6 219 D4
Crichton Rd SM5 218 D1
Crichton St SW8 137 C3
Cricket Gn CR4 202 D5
Cricket Green Sch CR4 202 C6
Cricket Ground Rd BR7 188 D2
Cricket La BR3 185 A4
Cricket Row N2 48 B6
Cricketers Arms Rd EN2 5 A3
Cricketers Cl N14 15 C4
Chessington KT9 213 D4
Cricketers Mews 4 SW18 157 D6
Cricketers Wlk SE26 184 C5
Cricketfield Rd E5 74 B4
Cricklade Ave SW2 160 B2
Cricklewood Broadway NW2 68 D4
Cricklewood La NW2 69 B5
Cricklewood Sta NW2 68 D4
Cricklewood Trad Est NW2 68 D5
Cridland St E15 98 D6
Crieff Ct TW11,KT8 175 C3
Crieff Rd SW18 158 A5
Criffel Ave SW2 159 D3
Crimscott St SE1 117 C3 263 B5
Crimsworth Rd SW8 137 D5 269 D3
Crinan St N1 94 A5 233 B4
Cringle St SW8 137 C5 269 A4
Cripplegate St EC1 242 B4
Cripps Gn UB4 84 B3
Crisp Rd W6 112 C1
Crispe Ho N1 233 D5
Barking IG11 101 B5
Crispen Rd TW13 173 A6
Crispian Cl NW10 67 C4
Crispin Cl SM6 220 A6
Crispin Cres SM6 219 D6
Crispin Ct SE17 263 A3
Crispin Rd HA8 27 A4
Crispin St E1 95 D2 243 C3
Cristowe Rd SW6 135 B3
Criterion Mews N19 71 D6
Crittall's Corner DA14 190 C3
Crittenden Lo BR4 207 C1
Crockerton Rd SW17 158 D2
Crockham Way SE9 188 C6
Crocus Cl CR0 206 D1
Crocus Field EN5 13 B5
Croft Ave BR4 208 A1
Croft Cl NW7 11 C1
Chislehurst West BR7 188 B5
Erith DA17 125 B1
Harlington UB7 127 A5
Hillingdon UB10 60 C1
Croft Ct HA4 39 D1
Croft Gdns W7 109 A4
Ruislip HA4 39 D1
Croft Ho SW15 157 A5
12 W10 91 A4
Croft Lodge Cl IG8 37 B4
Croft Mews N12 14 A1
Croft Rd SW16 182 C3
SW19 180 A3
Carshalton SM1 218 C3
Enfield EN3 7 A4
Plaistow BR1 187 A4
Croft St SE8 119 A2
Croft The E4 20 C2
NW10 89 D5
W5 88 A2
Chipping Barnet EN5 1 A1
Heston TW5 129 A5
New Malden KT3 199 C4
Pinner HA5 41 B2
Croft The *continued*
Ruislip HA4 62 C4
Wembley HA0 65 C3
Croft Villas HA1 43 A3
Croft Way
Richmond TW10 153 B1
Sidcup DA15 167 C1
Croftdown Rd NW5 71 B5
Crofters Cl TW7 152 B6
Crofters Ct 9 SE8 119 A2
Crofters Way NW1 93 D6 232 C6
Crofton Ave W4 133 B5
Bexley DA5 168 D4
Orpington BR6 227 A6
Crofton Gate Way SE4 163 A6
Crofton Gr E4 36 B6
Crofton Inf Sch BR5 211 B2
Crofton Jun Sch BR5 211 B2
Crofton L Ctr SE4 163 C5
Crofton La BR5,BR6 211 B2
Crofton Park Rd SE4 163 B5
Crofton Park Sta SE4 163 B6
Crofton Rd E13 99 B3
SE5 139 C3
Locksbottom BR6 226 C5
Crofton Sch SE4 163 C5
Crofton Terr E5 75 A3
Richmond TW9 132 B1
Crofton Way Enfield EN2 4 C3
New Barnet EN5 13 D5
Crofts Ho 19 E2 96 A5
Crofts Rd HA1 43 A4
Crofts St E1 118 A6
Crofts The TW17 193 C5
Croftside The SE25 206 A6
Crogsland Rd NW1 71 A1
Croham Cl CR2 221 C1
Croham Hurst Sch CR2 221 D3
Croham Manor Rd CR2 221 C2
Croham Mount CR2 221 C1
Croham Park Ave CR2 221 D3
Croham Rd CR2 221 C3
Croham Valley Rd CR2 222 B1
Croindene Rd SW16 182 A2
Crokesley Ho 2 HA8 27 A1
Cromartie Rd N19 49 D2
Cromarty Ct 8 BR1 187 C1
Cromarty Ho 8 E1 97 A2
Cromarty Rd HA8 10 D2
Cromberdale Ct N17 34 A2
Crombie Cl IG4 56 B4
Crombie Mews 5 SW11 136 C3
Crombie Rd DA15 167 B3
Cromdale Ct N16 51 D2
Crome Ho UB5 85 A5
Cromer Cl UB8 83 A1
Cromer Ct SW16 160 A1
SW18 157 B5
7 Southall UB1 85 D1
Cromer Pl 5 BR6 211 B1
Cromer Rd E10 54 B2
N17 34 A1
SE25 206 B6
SW17 181 A4
Dagenham RM6 59 A3
Harlington TW6 126 C3
New Barnet EN5 2 A2
Woodford IG8 37 A6
Cromer Road Prim Sch EN5 2 A2
Cromer St WC1 94 A4 233 B1
Cromer Terr E8 74 A3
Cromer Villas Rd SW18 157 B5
Cromford Cl BR6 227 C5
Cromford Path 1 E5 74 D4
Cromford Rd SW18 157 C6
Cromford Way KT3 177 B2
Cromlix Cl BR7 188 D1
Crompton Ct SW3 257 A4
Crompton Ho SE1 262 B5
SW8 269 B1
W2 236 C5
Crompton St W2 92 B3 236 C5
Cromwell Ave N6 49 B1
W6 112 B2
Bromley BR2 209 B5
New Malden KT3 199 D4
Cromwell Cl N2 48 B5
W3 111 A5
2 W4 110 D1
Walton-on-T KT12 194 B1
Cromwell Cres SW5 113 C2 255 A4
Cromwell Ct Enfield EN3 18 D6
15 Kingston u T KT2 176 C3
Wembley HA0 88 A5
Cromwell Ctr NW10 89 B4
Barking IG11 102 A4
Cromwell Ctr The RM8 59 B2
Cromwell Est E10 53 A1
Cromwell Gdns SW7 114 B3 256 D5
Cromwell Gr W6 112 C3
Cromwell Ho SW11 268 B1
SW15 134 A1
Croydon CR0 220 D5
Cromwell Hospl SW5 113 D2 255 C4
Cromwell Lo 36 E1 96 C3
Barking IG11 79 C3
Cromwell Mans SW5 255 B4
Cromwell Mews SW7 256 D4
Cromwell Pl N6 49 B1
SW7 114 B2 256 D4
SW14 133 A2
5 W3 111 A5
Cromwell Rd E7 77 C1
E17 54 A4
N3 30 A2
N10 31 A3
SW7 256 B4
SW9 138 D4
SW19 179 D5
Beckenham BR3 207 A6
Feltham TW13 150 B3
Hayes UB3 83 B1
Hounslow TW3 129 C1
Kingston u T KT2 176 A2
Teddington TW11 175 A4
Thornton Heath CR0 205 B2
Wembley HA0 88 A5
Worcester Pk KT4 215 C5
Cromwell St TW3 129 C1
Cromwell Trad Est IG11 101 C4
Cromwell Twr EC2 242 B4
Crondace Rd SW6 135 C4 265 B1
Crondall Ct 7 N1 95 C5
Crondall Ho SW15 156 A3
Crondall Pl 15 N1 95 C5
Crondall St N1 95 C5
Crone Ct 5 NW6 91 B5
Cronin St SE15 139 D5
Crook Log DA6 146 D1
Crook Log Prim Sch DA6 146 D1
Crook Log Sports Ctr DA16 146 D2
Crooke Rd SE8 119 A1
Crooked Billet E4 35 C3
Crooked Billet Yd 19 E2 95 C4
Crooked Usage N3 47 A6
Crookham Rd SW6 135 B4 264 C1
Crookston Rd SE9 144 C2
Croombs Rd E16 99 C2
Croom's Hill SE10 142 B5
Croom's Hill Gr SE10 142 A5
Cropley Ct N1 235 C4
Cropley St N1 95 B5 235 C4
Croppath Rd RM10 81 C4
Cropthorne Ct W9 229 B1
Crosbie 10 NW9 27 D1
Crosbie Ho 20 E17 53 D6
Crosby Cl TW13 173 A6
Crosby Ct N2 48 A5
SE1 252 C2
Crosby Rd E7 77 A2
Dagenham RM10 103 D6
Crosby Row SE1 117 B4 252 C2
Crosby Sq EC3 243 A2
Crosby Wlk 3 E8 73 D2
SE24 160 C4
Crosfield Ct 3 W10 90 D1
Crosfield Ho W11 244 A5
Crosier Rd UB10 61 A4
Crosier Way HA4 61 C5
Crosland Pl 5 SW11 137 A2
Cross Cl SE15 140 B3
Cross Ct SE5 139 B2
11 SE28 124 B6
Cross Deep TW1 153 A2
Cross Deep Gdns TW1 152 D2
Cross Keys Cl 5 N9 18 A2
W1 238 B3
Cross La EC3 253 A5
N8 50 B5
Sidcup DA5 169 B4
Cross Lances Rd TW3 129 D1
Cross Rd E4 20 C3
N2 30 C1
N11 31 B5
N22 32 C3
SE5 139 C3
SW19 179 C3
Carshalton SM1 218 B3
Croydon CR0 205 B1
Dagenham RM6 58 C2
Enfield EN1 5 C1
Feltham TW13 173 A6
Harrow HA1 42 B4
Harrow HA2 63 D5
Harrow HA3 25 A1
Keston Mark BR2 226 A6
Kingston u T KT2 176 B3
Romford RM7 59 C6
Sidcup DA14 190 B6
Cross St N1 94 D6 234 D6
2 N18 34 A5
SW13 133 C2
Hampton TW12 174 A5
Cross Way UB3 106 A5
Cross Way The HA3 24 C1
Crossbow Ho 15 N1 95 C6
W13 109 B5
Crossbrook Rd SE3 144 A2
Crossfield Rd N17 51 A6
NW3 70 B2
Crossfield St SE8 141 C5
Crossford St SW9 138 B3
Crossgate
Deacons Hill HA8 10 C1
Wembley UB6 65 B2
Crossharbour & London Arena Sta E14 119 D3
Crossland Rd CR7 204 D3
Crosslands Ave W5 110 B5
Southall UB2 107 B1
Crosslands Rd KT19 215 B2
Crossleigh Ct 3 SE14 141 B5
Crosslet St SE17 262 D4
Crosslet Vale SE10 141 D4

Crossley St N7 72 C2
Crossman Hos 19 SW12 160 A4
Crossmead SE9 166 B3
Crossmead Ave UB6 85 C4
Crossmount Ho 13 SE5 139 A5
Crossness Rd IG11 101 D4
Crossthwaite Ave SE5, SE24 139 B1
Crosswall EC3 117 D6 253 C6
Crossway E8,N16 73 C3
N12 30 B4
NW9 45 D5
SE28 102 D1
W13 87 A3
Dagenham RM8 80 C5
Enfield EN1 17 C4
Petts Wood BR5 211 B4
Pinner Green HA5 22 B1
Ruislip HA4 62 C4
West Barnes KT3,SW20 200 C5
Woodford IG8 37 C6
Crossway Ct SE4 141 A3
Crossway Par N22 32 D3
Crossway The N22 32 D3
SE9 165 D2
Hillingdon UB10 82 B5
Crossways
Charlton TW16 171 D3
South Croydon CR2 223 B1
Sutton SM2 218 B1
Crossways Rd
Beckenham BR3 207 C5
Mitcham CR4 203 B6
Crossways The
Heston TW5 129 B5
Wembley HA9 66 C6
Crosswell Cl TW17 171 A1
Croston St E8 96 A6
Crosts La N22 32 C3
Crothall Cl N13 16 B1
Crouch Ave IG11 102 B5
Crouch Cl BR3 185 C4
Crouch Croft SE9 166 C1
Crouch End Hill N8 49 D2
Crouch Hall Ct N19 50 A1
Crouch Hall Rd N8 49 D3
Crouch Hill N4,N8,N19 50 A2
Crouch Rd NW10 67 B1
Crouchmans Cl SE21, SE26 162 A1
Crow La RM7,RM8 59 D2
Crowborough Ct W13 109 C6
Crowborough Path WD1 22 D6
Crowborough Rd SW17 181 A5
Crowden Way SE28 124 C6
Crowder St E1 118 B6
Crowfield Ho N5 73 A4
Crowfoot Cl E9 75 B3
Crowhurst SE25 206 A6
Crowhurst Cl SW9 138 C3
Crowhurst Ct N17 34 B2
Crowhurst Ho 21 SW9 138 B3
Crowland Ave UB3 105 D2
Crowland Gdns N14 16 A4
Crowland Ho NW8 229 A5
Crowland Prim Sch N15 52 A4
Crowland Rd N15 51 D4
South Norwood CR7 205 B5
Crowland Terr N1 73 B1
Crowland Wlk SM4 202 A3
Crowlands Ave RM7 59 D3
Crowley Cres CR0 220 C3
Crowline Wlk 1 N1 73 A2
Crowmarsh Gdns SE23 162 C4
Crown Arc KT1 175 D1
Crown Bldgs 4 E4 20 B3
Crown Cl E3 97 C6
NW6 69 D2
NW7 11 D2
Hayes UB3 105 D4
Walton-on-T KT12 194 C2
Crown Ct EC4 242 B1
6 N10 31 A3
NW8 230 B1
SE12 165 B5
4 SW15 134 D1
WC2 240 B1
Bromley BR1 209 D4
3 Twickenham TW1 153 B4
Crown Dale SE19 183 A5
Crown Hill CR0 221 A5
Crown Ho HA4 40 A1
Crown La N14 15 C3
SE19,SW16 182 C5
Bromley BR2 209 D4
Chislehurst BR7 189 A2
Merton SM4 201 C6
Crown Lane Gdns SE27 182 C5
Crown Lane Prim Sch SE27 182 D5
Crown Lane Spur BR2 209 D3
Crown Lo SW3 257 B3
Crown Mews 3 E13 99 C6
Crown Office Row EC4 251 A6
Crown Par N14 15 C3
SE19 182 D4
Morden SM4 201 D5
Crown Pas SW1 249 B3
Kingston u T KT1 175 D1
Crown Pl NW5 71 B2
Crown Point SE19 182 D4
Crown Rd N10 31 A3
Enfield EN1 6 B2
Ilford IG6 57 B5
Kingston u T KT3 177 A2
Morden SM4 201 D5
Ruislip HA4 62 D3
Sutton SM1 217 D4
Crown Rd *continued*
Twickenham TW1 153 B5
Crown Reach SW1 259 D1
Crown St SE5 139 A5
W3 110 D5
Dagenham RM10 81 D2
Harrow HA2 42 C1
Crown Terr TW9 132 B1
Crown Way UB7 104 B5
Crown Wlk HA9 66 B5
Crown Woods Sch SE9 167 A6
Crown Woods Way SE9 167 B6
Crown Yard TW3 130 A2
Crownbourne Ct SM1 217 D4
Crowndale Ct NW1 232 C4
Crowndale Rd NW1 93 C5 232 B4
Crownfield Ave IG2 57 C4
Crownfield Rd E15 76 B4
Crownhill Rd NW10 89 D6
Crownleigh Ct SW2 160 C6
Crownmead Way RM7 59 D5
Crownstone Ct 1 SW2 160 C6
Crownstone Rd SW2 160 C6
Crowntree Cl TW7 130 D6
Crows Rd E15 98 B4
Barking IG11 78 D2
Crowshott Ave HA7 25 D2
Crowther Ave TW8 110 A2
Crowther Rd SE25 206 A5
Crowthorne Cl SW18 157 B3
Crowthorne Rd W10 90 D1
Croxall Ho KT12 194 C3
Croxden Cl HA8 44 C6
Croxden Wlk SM4 202 A3
Croxford Gdns N22 32 D3
Croxley Cl BR5 190 B1
Croxley Gn BR5 190 B2
Croxley Rd W9 91 B4
Croxted Cl SE21 161 A4
Croxted Mews SE24 161 A5
Croxted Rd SE21,SE24 161 B3
Croxteth Ho 11 SW8 137 D3
Croxton 17 KT1 176 C1
Croyde Ave
Greenford UB6 86 A4
Hayes UB3 105 C2
Croyde Cl SE9 167 B4
Croydon N17 33 B1
Croydon Airport Ind Est CR0 220 B2
Croydon Central Sta CR0 221 A6
Croydon Coll CR0 221 B6
Croydon Coll (Selhurst Tertiary Ctr) SE25 205 B4
Croydon Coll Annexe CR0 205 B1
Croydon Flyover The CR0 221 A5
Croydon General Hospl CR0 205 A1
Croydon Gr CR0 204 D1
Croydon Ho SE1 251 B2
Croydon Rd E13 98 D3
SE20 184 C2
Beckenham BR3 207 A6
Coney Hall BR2,BR4 224 D5
Croydon CR0 220 B4
Harlington TW6 126 D2
Keston Mark BR2,BR4, BR6 225 C5
Mitcham CR0,CR4 203 C4
Wallington CR0,SM5,SM6 219 C5
Croydon Rd Ind Est BR3 206 D5
Croyland Rd N9 18 A3
Croylands Dr KT6 198 A2
Croysdale Ave TW16 194 A6
Crozier Ho SE3 143 B2
SW8 270 C3
Crozier Terr E9 74 D3
Crucible Cl RM6 58 B3
Crucifix La SE1 117 C4 253 A2
Cruden Ho 23 E3 97 B5
11 SE17 138 D6
Cruden St N1 94 D6 234 D5
Cruickshank St WC1 234 A2
Cruikshank Ho NW8 230 B4
Cruikshank Rd E15 76 C3
Crummock Gdns NW9 45 C4
Crumpsall St SE2 124 C2
Crundale Ave NW9 44 C4
Crunden Rd CR2 221 B1
Crusader Gdns CR0 221 C5
Crusader Ind Est N4 51 A3
Crusoe House Sch N1 95 B4 235 C2
Crusoe Mews N16 73 B6
Crusoe Rd CR4 180 D3
Crutched Friars EC3 117 C6 253 B6
Crutchfield La KT12 194 B1
Crutchley Rd SE6 164 C2
Crystal Ct SE19 183 D5
Crystal Ho SE18 123 D1
Crystal Palace National Sports Ctr SE20 184 A4
Crystal Palace Par SE19 183 D5
Crystal Palace Park Rd SE26 184 B5
Crystal Palace Rd SE22 162 A6
Crystal Palace Sta SE19 184 A4
Crystal Palace Station Rd SE19 184 A4
Crystal Terr SE19 183 B4
Crystal View Ct BR1 186 B6
Crystal Way
Dagenham RM8 58 C1
Harrow HA1 42 D4
Cuba Dr EN3 6 C3
Cuba St E14 119 C4
Cubitt Ho 4 SW4 159 C5
Cubitt Sq UB2 108 A5
Cubitt St WC1 94 B4 233 D1
Croydon CR0 220 B3
Cubitt Terr SW4 137 C2
Cubitt Town Jun & Inf Sch E14 120 A3
Cuckoo Ave W7 86 C3
Cuckoo Dene W7 86 B2
Cuckoo Hall La N9 18 D4
Cuckoo Hill HA5 40 C6
Cuckoo Hill Dr HA5 40 C6
Cuckoo Hill Rd HA5 40 D5
Cuckoo La W7 108 C6
Cuckoo Prim Sch N9 18 D4
Cuda's Cl KT19 215 D4
Cuddington SE17 262 B4
Cuddington Ave KT19, KT4 215 D5
Cuddington Cty Prim Sch KT4 215 D5
Cudham La N BR6 227 C1
Cudham St SE6 164 A4
Cudworth Ho SW8 269 B1
Cudworth St E1 96 B3
Cuff Cres SE9 165 D5
Cuff Point 12 E2 95 D4
Cuffley Ho W10 90 C2
Culand Ho SE17 263 A3
Culford Gdns SW3 114 D2 257 D3
Culford Gr N1 73 C2
Culford Mans SW3 257 D3
Culford Mews N1 73 C2
Culford Rd N1 95 C6
N1 73 C2
Culgaith Gdns EN2 4 A1
Culham Ho 33 E2 95 D4
21 W2 91 C2
Cullen Ho W9 91 B5
Cullen Way NW10 89 A3
Culling Rd SE16 118 C3
Cullington Cl HA3 43 A5
Cullingworth Rd NW10 68 B3
Culloden Cl 15 SE16 118 A1
Culloden JMI Sch E14 98 A1
Culloden Rd EN2 4 D3
Cullum St EC3 253 A6
Culmington Mans W13 109 C6
Culmington Par W13 109 C6
Culmington Rd W13,W5 109 C5
South Croydon CR2 221 A1
Culmore Rd SE15 140 C5
Culmstock Rd SW11 159 A6
Culpepper Ct SE11 261 A4
Culpepper Ho 5 E14 97 A1
Culross Bldgs NW1 233 A4
Culross Cl N15 51 A5
Culross St W1 115 A6 248 A5
Culsac Rd KT6 214 A6
Culver Ct SW18 157 D5
Culver Gr HA7 25 C1
Culverden Rd SW12 159 C2
Culverhouse WC1 240 C3
Culverhouse Gdns SW16 160 B1
Culverlands Cl HA7 25 B6
Culverley Rd SE6 164 A3
Culvers Ave SM5,CR4 218 D6
Culvers House Prim Sch CR4 203 A1
Culvers Retreat SM5 218 D6
Culvers Way SM5 218 D6
Culverstone Cl BR2 208 D4
Culvert Ct SW11 137 A3
Culvert Pl SW11 137 A3
Culvert Rd N15 51 C4
SW11 136 D3
Culverton Ct 5 DA14 190 A6
Culworth Ho NW8 230 A4
Culworth St NW8 230 A3
Cumber Ho SW18 157 C3
Cumberland Ave NW10 88 D4
Bexley DA16 145 D1
Cumberland Bsns Ctr NW10 88 D4
Cumberland Cl E8 73 D2
8 SW20 178 D3
2 Twickenham TW1 153 B5
Cumberland Comp Sch E16 99 A2
Cumberland Cres W14 254 B4
Cumberland Ct W1 237 D1
4 Croydon CR0 205 B1
Woodford IG8 37 B3
Cumberland Dr
Bexley DA7 147 A5
Chessington KT9 214 B5
Hinchley Wood KT10 213 A6
Cumberland Gate W1 114 D6 247 D6
Cumberland Gdns NW4 29 A1
WC1 234 A2
Cumberland Ho N9 18 C3
1 SW15 156 C4
Kingston u T KT2 176 D3
Cumberland Mans
7 NW6 69 C3
W1 237 C2
Cumberland Market NW1 93 B4 231 D2
Cumberland Mills Sq E14 120 B1
Cumberland Park Ind Est NW10 90 A4
Cumberland Pk W3 111 A6
Cumberland Pl NW1 231 C2
SE6 164 D3
Sunbury TW16 194 A5
Cumberland Rd E12 77 D4
E13 99 B3
E17 35 A1
N9 18 C3
N22 32 B1
SE25 206 B3
SW13 134 A4
W3 111 A6
W7 108 D4
Ashford TW15 148 A1
Beckenham BR2 208 D6
Harrow HA1 41 D4
Richmond TW9 132 C5
Stanmore HA7,HA8 44 B6
Cumberland Sch E16 98 D2
Cumberland St SW1 115 B1 258 D2
Cumberland Terr NW1 231 C3
Cumberland Terrace Mews NW1 231 C3
Cumberland Villas W3 111 A6
Cumberlow Ave SE25 206 A6
Cumbernauld Gdns TW16 171 D5
Cumberton Rd N17 33 B2
Cumbrae Gdns KT6 213 D6
Cumbria Ho 2 SW15 157 B6
Cumbrian Gdns NW2 69 A6
Cumming St N1 233 D3
Cumnor Cl 23 SW9 138 B3
Cumnor Gdns KT17 216 A2
Cumnor Rd SM2 218 A2
Cunard Cres N21 17 B5
Cunard Pl EC3 243 B1
Cunard Rd NW10 89 B4
Cunard Wlk 3 SE16 119 A2
Cundy Rd E16 99 C1
Cundy St SW1 115 A2 258 B3
Cunliffe Rd KT19 215 D4
Cunliffe St SW16 181 C4
Cunningham Cl
Ilford RM6 58 C4
West Wickham BR4 223 D6
Cunningham Ct W2 236 C5
Cunningham Ho 16 SE5 139 B5
Cunningham Pk HA1 42 B4
Cunningham Pl NW8 92 B3 236 C6
Cunningham Rd N15 52 A5
Cunnington St W4 111 A2
Cupar Rd SW11 268 B2
Cupola Cl BR1 187 B5
Cureton St SW1 115 D2 259 D3
Curfew Ho 3 IG11 101 A6
Curie Gdns NW9 27 C1
Curie Ho 1 HA9 67 A5
Curlew Cl SE28 124 D6
Curlew Ct KT6 214 C5
Curlew Ho SE4 141 A1
6 SE15 139 D4
Enfield EN3 18 D6
Curlew St SE1 117 D4 253 D2
Curlew Way UB4 84 D2
Curnick's La SE27 183 A6
Curran Ave Bexley DA15 167 D6
Hackbridge SM6 219 A5
Curran Ho SW3 257 A3
Currey Rd UB6 64 B2
Curricle St W3 111 C5
Currie Hill Cl SW19 179 B6
Curry Rise NW7 28 D4
Cursitor St EC4 94 C1 241 A2
Curtain Pl EC2 243 B6
Curtain Rd EC2 95 C3 243 B6
Curthwaite Gdns EN2 15 D6
Curtis Dr W3 89 B1
Curtis Field Rd SW16 182 C6
Curtis Ho 7 N11 31 C5
SE17 262 C2
Curtis La HA0 66 A3
Curtis Rd
Twickenham TW4 151 B4
West Ewell KT19 215 A4
Curtis St SE1 117 D2 263 C4
Curtis Way SE1 263 C4
7 SE28 124 B6
Curtlington Ho 3 HA8 27 A1
Curve The W12 112 A6
Curwen Ave E7 77 B4
Curwen Rd W12 112 A4
Curwen Sch E13 99 A5
Curzon Ave Enfield EN3 18 D6
Stanmore HA7 25 A2
Curzon Cl BR6 227 B4
Curzon Cres NW10 67 C1
Barking IG11 101 D4
Curzon Ct SE9 167 A1
SW6 265 D1
Curzon Gate W1 248 B3
Curzon Ho W5 87 B3
Curzon Pl W1 248 B3
Pinner HA5 40 C4
Curzon Rd N10 31 B1
W5 87 B3
Thornton Heath CR7 204 C3
Curzon St W1 115 B5 248 C4
Cusack Cl TW1 174 D6
Custance Ho N1 235 C3
Custance St N1 235 C2
Custom House EC3 117 C6 253 A5
Custom House Reach SE16 119 B3
Custom House Sta E16 121 B6
Cut The SE1 116 C4 251 B2
Cutbush Ho N7 71 D3
Cutcombe Mans 22 SE5 139 A3
Cutcombe Rd SE5 139 A3
Cuthbert Gdns SE25 205 C6
Cuthbert Harrowing Ho EC1 242 A5
Cuthbert Ho W2 236 C4
Cuthbert Rd E17 54 A6
8 N18 34 A6
Croydon CR0 220 D6
Cuthbert St W2 236 C5
Cuthill Wlk 3 SE5 139 B4
Cutler St EC2 243 B2
Cutlers Gdns EC2 243 B2
Cutlers Sq E14 119 C2
Cutty Sark★ SE10 142 A6
Cutty Sark Sta SE10 142 A6
Cuxton BR5 211 A4
Cuxton Cl DA6 169 A6
Cuxton Ho SE17 263 B2
Cyclamen Cl 4 TW12 173 C4
Cyclamen Way KT19 215 A3
Cyclops Mews 9 E14 119 C2
Cygnet Ave TW14 150 D4
Cygnet Cl NW10 67 B3
Cygnet St E1 243 D6
Cygnet Way UB4 84 D2
Cygnets The TW13 173 A6
Cygnus Bsns Ctr NW10 67 D2
Cymbeline Ct 6 HA1 42 D3
Cyns Ct 5 E11 55 A3
Cynthia St N1 233 D3
Cypress Ave N2 47 D6
Twickenham TW2 152 A4
Cypress Ct 5 E11 76 B4
7 SW16 182 C5
Cheam SM1 217 C2
Cypress Gdns SE4 163 A6
Cypress Ho SE14 140 D4
Cypress Inf Sch SE25 183 C1
Cypress Jun Sch SE25 183 C1
Cypress Lo SE25 183 C1
Cypress Pl W1 239 B5
Cypress Rd SE25 183 C1
Harrow HA3 24 B1
Cypress Tree Cl DA15 167 D3
Cyprus Ave N3 29 A1
Cyprus Cl N4 50 C3
Cyprus Gdns N3 29 A1
Cyprus Pl 24 E2 96 C5
E6 122 C6
Cyprus Rd N3 29 B1
N9 17 D2
Cyprus St E2 96 C5
Cyprus Sta E6 122 C6
Cyrena Rd SE22 161 D6
Cyril Jackson JMI Sch E14 119 B6
Cyril Jackson Sch E14 119 B6
Cyril Lo 2 DA14 190 A6
Cyril Mans SW11 267 D1
Cyril Rd DA7 147 A3
Cyril Smith Ho N13 32 B5
Cyril Thatcher Ho SW6 265 B1
Cyrus Ho EC1 241 D6
Cyrus St EC1 94 D3 241 D6
Czar St SE8 141 C6

D

Da Palma Ct SW6 265 A5
Da Vinci Ct 12 SE16 118 B1
Dabbs Hill La UB5 63 C3
Dabb's La EC1 241 B5
Dabin Cres SE10 142 A4
Dacca St SE8 141 B6
Dace Rd E3 97 C6
Dacre Cl UB6 85 D5
Dacre Gdns SE13 142 C1
Borehamwood WD6 11 B6
Dacre Ho SW3 266 D5
Dacre Pk SE13 142 C1
Dacre Pl SE13 142 C2
Dacre Rd E11 54 D1
E13 99 B6
Croydon CR0 204 A2
Dacre St SW1 115 D3 259 C6
Dacres Rd SE23 162 D1
Dade Way UB2 107 B1
Daerwood Cl BR2 210 B1
Daffodil Cl Croydon CR0 206 D1
7 Hampton TW12 173 C4
Daffodil Gdns IG1 78 D3
Daffodil St W12 111 D6
Dafforne Rd SW17 159 A1
Dagenham Ave RM9 103 A6
Dagenham Dock Sta RM9 103 B5
Dagenham East Sta RM10 81 D3
Dagenham Heathway Sta RM9 81 B2
Dagenham Priory Comp Sch RM10 103 D6
Dagenham Rd E10 53 B1
RM10 81 D4
Dagger La WD2,WD6 9 A6
Dagmar Ave HA9 66 B4
Dagmar Ct E14 120 A3
Dagmar Gdns NW10 90 D5
Dagmar Mews UB2 107 A3
Dagmar Pas N1 234 D6
Dagmar Rd N4 50 C2
N15 51 B5
N22 31 D2
SE5 139 C4
SE25 205 C4
4 Kingston u T KT2 176 C3
Southall UB2 107 A3
Dagmar Terr N1 94 D6 234 D6
Dagnall Pk SE25 205 C4
Dagnall Rd SE25 205 C4
Dagnall St SW11 137 A4 268 A1
Dagnan Rd SW12 159 C4
Dagobert Ho 25 E1 96 C2
Dagonet Gdns BR1 165 A1
Dagonet Rd BR1 165 A1
Dahlia Gdns Ilford IG1 78 D2
Mitcham CR4 203 D5
Dahlia Rd SE2 124 B2
Dahomey Rd SW16 181 C4
Daimler Ho 8 E3 97 C3
Daimler Way SM6 220 A1
Daines Cl E12 78 B5
Dainford Cl BR1 186 B5
Dainton Cl 2 BR1 187 B2
Dainton Ho 22 W2 91 C2
Daintry Cl HA3 43 A5
Daintry Way E9 75 B2
Dairsie Ct 2 BR1 187 C1
Dairsie Rd SE9 144 C2
Dairy Cl Bromley BR1 187 B3
South Norwood CR7 183 A1
Dairy La SE18 122 B2
Dairy Meadow Prim Sch UB2 107 B3
Dairyman Cl NW2 69 A5
Daisy Cl CR0 206 D1
Daisy Dormer Ct 11 SW9 138 B1
Daisy La SW6 135 C2
Daisy Rd E18 37 B1
Dakota Gdns E6 100 A3
Northolt UB5 85 A4
Dalberg Rd SW2 160 C6
Dalberg Way SE2 124 D3
Dalbury Ho 6 SW9 138 B1
Dalby Rd SW18 136 A1
Dalby St NW5 71 B2
Dalbys Cres N17 33 C4
Dalcross Rd TW4,TW5 129 A3
Dale Ave Edgware HA8 26 B1
Hounslow TW4 129 A2
Dale Cl SE3 143 A2
New Barnet EN5 13 D5
Northwood HA5 22 B2
Dale Croft N4 73 A5
Dale Ct E18 37 A1
N8 49 C5
3 Kingston u T KT2 176 B3
Dale Dr UB4 83 D4
Dale Gdns IG8 37 B6
Dale Gr N12 30 A5
Dale Green Rd N11 15 B1
Dale Ho NW8 229 A6
SE4 141 A1
Dale Lo N6 49 C3
Dale Park Ave SM5 218 D6
Dale Park Rd SE19 183 B2
Dale Rd NW5 71 A3
SE17 138 D6
Ashford TW16 171 D3
Cheam SM1 217 B4
Southall UB6 85 D2
Walton-on-T KT12 193 D2
Dale Row W11 91 A1
Dale St W4 111 C1
Dale The BR2 225 D4
Dale View Ave E4 20 A2
Dale View Cres E4 20 A1
Dale View Gdns E4 20 B1
Dale Wood Rd BR6 211 C1
Dalebury Rd SW17 158 D2
Dalefield IG9 21 D3
Dalehead NW1 232 A3
Daleham Dr UB8 82 D1
Daleham Gdns NW3 70 B2
Daleham Mews NW3 70 B2
Dalemain Ho 5 SW8 137 D3
Dalemain Mews 13 E16 121 A5
Dales Path WD6 11 B6
Dales Rd WD6 11 B6
Daleside Rd SW17 181 B5
West Ewell KT19 215 B2
Daleview Rd N15 51 C3
Dalewood Gdns KT4 216 B6
Daley Ho W12 90 B1
Daley St E9 74 D2
Daley Thompson Way 7 SW8 137 B2
Dalgarno Gdns W10 90 C2
Dalgarno Way W10 90 C3
Dalglen Sch The IG9 21 C2
Daling Way E3 97 A5
Dalkeith Ct SW1 259 D3
Dalkeith Gr HA7 26 A5
Dalkeith Ho 6 SW9 138 D4
Dalkeith Rd SE21 161 A4
Ilford IG1 79 A5
Dallas Rd NW4 46 A2
SE26 162 B1
W5 88 B2
Cheam SM3 217 A2
Dallas Terr UB3 105 D3

Dallega Cl UB3 . . . . .105 B6
Dallin Rd SE18 . . . . .144 D5
 Bexley DA6 . . . . .146 D1
Dalling Rd W6 . . . . .112 B2
Dallinger Rd SE12 . . . .164 D5
Dallington Sch
 EC1 . . . . .94 D3 241 D6
Dallington St
 EC1 . . . . .94 D3 241 D6
Dalmain Prim Sch
 SE23 . . . . .163 A3
Dalmain Rd SE23 . . . . .162 D3
Dalmally Rd CR0 . . . . .206 A2
Dalmeny Ave N7 . . . . . .71 D4
 SW16 . . . . .182 C1
Dalmeny Cl HA0 . . . . . . .65 C2
Dalmeny Cres TW3 . . .130 B1
Dalmeny Ct 4 SW4 . . . .138 A3
Dalmeny Rd N7 . . . . . . .71 D4
 Erith DA7,DA8 . . . . . . .147 D4
 New Barnet EN5 . . . . . . .14 A5
 North Cheam KT4 . . . . .216 B5
 Wallington SM5 . . . . . . .219 A1
Dalmeyer Rd NW10 . . . .67 D2
Dalmore Ave KT10 . . . .212 D2
Dalmore Rd SE21 . . . . .161 A2
Dalrymple Cl N14 . . . . . .15 D4
Dalrymple Rd SE4 . . . .141 A1
Dalston Gdns HA7 . . . . .26 A1
Dalston Jct E8 . . . . .73 C2
Dalston Kingsland Sta
 E8 . . . . .73 D3
Dalston La E8 . . . . .74 A3
Dalton Ave CR4 . . . . . . .180 C1
Dalton Cl Hayes UB4 . . . .83 B3
 Orpington BR6 . . . . .227 C5
Dalton Ho 9 E3 . . . . .97 A5
 19 SE14 . . . . .140 D6
 7 SW1 . . . . .159 B4
Dalton St SE27 . . . . . . .160 D1
Dalwood St SE5 . . . . . .139 C4
Daly Ct E15 . . . . .76 A3
Dalyell Rd SW9 . . . . . . .138 A2
Damascene Wlk SE21 . .161 A3
Damask Cres E16 . . . . . .98 C3
Dame St N1 . . .95 A5 235 A4
Damer Ho 9 TW10 . . . .154 B6
Damer Terr SW10 . . . . .266 B3
Dames Rd E7 . . . . .77 A5
Damien Ct 20 E1 . . . . . . .96 B1
Damien St E1 . . . . .96 B1
Damon Cl DA14 . . . . . . .168 A1
Damon Ct DA14 . . . . . . .168 B1
Damory Ho 1 SE16 . . . .118 C2
Damsonwood Rd UB2 . .107 C3
Dan Bryant Ho 5
 SW12 . . . . .159 C4
Dan Leno Wlk SW6 . . . .265 C3
Danbrook Rd SW16 . . . .182 A3
Danbury Cl RM6 . . . . . . .58 D6
Danbury Mans 3 IG11 . .78 C1
Danbury Mews SM5,
 SM6 . . . . .219 B4
Danbury St N1 . .94 D5 234 D4
Danbury Way IG8 . . . . . .37 C4
Danby Cl EN2 . . . . .5 A2
Danby Ho 22 E9 . . . . . . .74 C1
 3 W10 . . . . .91 B4
Danby St SE15 . . . . . . .139 D2
Dancer Rd SW6 135 B4 264 C1
 Mortlake TW9 . . . . .132 C2
Dando Cres SE3 . . . . . .143 B2
Dandridge Cl SE10 . . . .120 D1
Dandridge Ho E1 . . . . . .243 C4
Dane Cl Old Bexley DA5 .169 C4
 Orpington BR6 . . . . .227 B3
Dane Ho 15 SE5 . . . . . .139 A3
Dane Pl E3 . . . . .97 B5
Dane Rd N18 . . . . .18 C1
 SW19 . . . . .180 A4
 W13 . . . . .109 C5
 Ashford TW15 . . . . .171 B4
 Ilford IG1 . . . . .79 A3
 Southall UB1 . . . . .107 A6
Dane St WC1 . . . . .240 C3
Danebury W10 . . . . .90 C2
 New Addington CR0 . . . .223 D2
Danebury Ave SW15 . . .155 D5
Danebury Prim Sch
 SW15 . . . . .155 D4
Daneby Rd SE6 . . . . . . .164 A2
Danecourt Gdns CR0 . . .221 D5
Danecroft Rd SE24 . . . .161 B6
Danegrove Prim Sch
 EN4 . . . . .14 C5
Danehill Wlk DA14 . . . .168 A1
Danehurst TW8 . . . . . . .131 C5
Danehurst Gdns IG4 . . . .56 B4
Danehurst St
 SW6 . . . . . . .135 A4 264 A2
Daneland EN4 . . . . .14 D5
Danemead Gr UB5 . . . . .63 D3
Danemere St SW15 . . . .134 C2
Danes Ct 3 HA9 . . . . . .230 C5
 Wembley HA9 . . . . .66 D5
Danes Gate HA1 . . . . . . .42 C6
Danes Ho W10 . . . . .90 C2
Danesbury Rd TW13 . . .150 B3
Danescombe SE12 . . . . .165 A3
Danescourt Cres SM1 . .218 A6
Danescroft NW4 . . . . . . .46 D4
Danescroft Ave NW4 . . .46 D4
Danescroft Gdns NW4 . .46 D4
Danesdale Rd E9 . . . . . .75 A2

Danesfield SE5 . . . . . . .139 C6
Daneswood Ave SE6 . . .164 A1
Danethorpe Rd HA0 . . . . .65 D2
Danetree Cl KT19 . . . . .215 A1
Danetree Rd KT19 . . . . .215 A1
Danetree Sch KT19 . . . .215 A1
Danette Gdns RM8 . . . . .81 B6
Daneville Rd SE5 . . . . .139 B4
Danford Ho 9 N11 . . . . . .31 C5
Dangan Rd E11 . . . . .55 A3
Daniel Bolt Cl E14 . . . . .97 D2
Daniel Cl N18 . . . . .34 C6
 SW17 . . . . .180 C4
Daniel Ct 8 NW9 . . . . . .27 C2
 W3 . . . . .111 C2
 3 Beckenham BR3 . . . .185 C3
Daniel Gdns SE15 . . . . .139 D5
Daniel Pl NW4 . . . . .46 B2
Daniel Way CR0 . . . . . . .204 B1
Daniell Ho N1 . . . . .235 C4
Daniell Way CR0 . . . . . .204 B1
Daniel's Rd SE15 . . . . . .140 C2
Dansey Pl W1 . . . . .249 C6
Dansington Rd DA16 . . .146 A1
Danson Cres DA16 . . . . .146 B2
Danson Intc DA5,DA6 . .168 C5
Danson La DA16 . . . . . .146 B1
Danson Mead DA16 . . . .146 C2
Danson Prim Sch DA16 146 A1
Danson Rd DA5,DA6,
 DA15 . . . . .168 D6
Danson Underpass
 DA15 . . . . .168 D6
Dante Rd SE11 .116 D2 261 C4
Danube Ct 12 SE15 . . . .139 D5
Danube St SW3 114 C1 257 B2
Danvers Ho 22 E1 . . . . . .96 A1
Danvers Rd N8 . . . . .49 D5
Danvers St SW3 136 B6 266 D5
Daphne Ct W5 . . . . .87 C1
 Worcester Pk KT4 . . . . .215 C6
Daphne Gdns E4 . . . . . . .20 A1
Daphne Ho N22 . . . . . . .32 C2
Daphne St SW18 . . . . . .158 A5
Daplyn St 6 E1 . . . . .96 A2
Darby Cres SW19 . . . . .172 C1
Darby Gdns TW16 . . . . .172 C1
Darcy Ave SM6 . . . . . . .219 C4
Darcy Ct N20 . . . . .14 B2
D'arcy Dr HA3 . . . . .43 D5
D'arcy Gdns
 Dagenham RM9 . . . . . . .103 B6
 Harrow HA3 . . . . .44 A5
D'arcy Ho E8 . . . . .96 B6
D'arcy Pl BR2 . . . . .209 A5
Darcy Rd SW16 . . . . . . .182 A1
 Isleworth TW7 . . . . .131 A4
D'arcy Rd SM3 . . . . . . .216 D4
Dare Ct 2 E10 . . . . .54 A2
Darell Prim Sch TW9 . .132 C2
Darell Rd TW9 . . . . .132 C2
Daren Ct N7 . . . . .72 A4
Darent Ho NW8 . . . . . . .236 D4
 3 Catford BR1 . . . . . . .186 B5
Darenth Rd N16 . . . . . . .51 D1
 Bexley DA16 . . . . .146 A4
Darfield NW1 . . . . .232 A5
Darfield Rd SE4 . . . . . . .163 B6
Darfield Way W10 . . . . . .90 D1
Darfur St SW15 . . . . . . .134 D2
Dargate Cl SE19 . . . . . .183 D3
Darien Ho 8 E1 . . . . .96 D2
 17 SW11 . . . . .136 B2
Darien Rd SW11 . . . . . .136 B2
Daring Ho 21 E3 . . . . . . .97 A5
Darlan Rd SW6 135 B5 264 D3
Darland Ct SW15 . . . . . .157 B5
Darlands Dr EN5 . . . . . . .12 D6
Darlaston Rd SW19 . . . .179 A3
Darley Cl CR0 . . . . .207 A3
Darley Dr KT3 . . . . .177 B1
Darley Gdns SM4 . . . . .201 B3
Darley Ho SE11 . . . . . . .260 C1
Darley Rd N9 . . . . .17 C3
 SW11 . . . . .158 D5
Darling Ho 5 TW1 . . . . .153 D5
Darling Rd SE4 . . . . .141 C2
Darling Row E1 . . . . .96 B3
Darlington Ct 8 SE6 . . .164 D3
Darlington Ho SW8 . . . . .269 D3
 2 Surbiton KT6 . . . . . . .197 D2
Darlington Rd SE27 . . . .182 D5
Darmaine Cl CR2 . . . . . .221 A1
Darnay Ho 3 SE16 . . . . .118 A3
Darndale Cl E17 . . . . . . .35 B1
Darnell Ho 4 SE10 . . . .142 A4
 9 SE10 . . . . .142 A5
Darnley Ho 9 E14 . . . . . .97 A1
Darnley Rd E9 . . . . .74 C2
 Woodford IG8 . . . . .37 B2
Darnley Terr 12 W11 . . .112 C5
Darrell Ct BR2 . . . . .208 C6
Darrell Rd SE22 . . . . . . .162 A6
Darren Cl N4 . . . . .50 B2
Darrick Wood Ho BR6 .227 A5
Darrick Wood Inf Sch
 BR6 . . . . .226 D4
Darrick Wood Jun Sch
 BR6 . . . . .226 D4
Darrick Wood Rd BR6 .227 B6
Darrick Wood Sec Sch
 BR6 . . . . .226 D4
Darrick Wood Sports Ctr
 BR6 . . . . .227 C6
Darris Cl UB4 . . . . .85 A3
Darsingham Inf Sch E12 78 C3
Darsley Dr SW8 138 A4 270 A2

Dart St W10 . . . . .91 B4
Dartford Ave N9 . . . . . . .18 D5
Dartford Gdns RM6 . . . . .58 A4
Dartford Ho SE1 . . . . . . .263 D4
Dartford St SE17 . . . . . .139 A6
Dartington NW1 . . . . . . .232 B5
Dartington Ho 7 SW8 . .137 D3
 W2 . . . . .91 D2
Dartle Ct 26 SE16 . . . . .118 A4
Dartmoor Wlk 17 E14 . .119 C2
Dartmouth Cl W11 . . . . .91 C1
Dartmouth Gr SE10 . . . .142 A4
Dartmouth Hill SE10 . . .142 A4
Dartmouth Ho N19 . . . . .71 B6
 SE10 . . . . .142 A3
 Thornton Heath CR0 . . . .204 D2
Dartmouth Park Ave
 NW5 . . . . .71 B6
Dartmouth Park Hill N19 71 B6
Dartmouth Park Rd NW5 71 B5
Dartmouth Pl SE23 . . . .162 C2
 W4 . . . . .133 C4
Dartmouth Rd NW2 . . . . .68 D2
 N4 . . . . .46 A3
 SE23,SE26 . . . . .162 C1
 Hayes BR2 . . . . .209 A4
 Ruislip HA4 . . . . .62 A5
Dartmouth Row SE10 . .142 A4
Dartmouth St
 SW1 . . . . . . .115 D4 249 D1
Dartmouth Terr SE10 . .142 B4
Dartnell Rd CR0 . . . . . . .205 D2
Darton Ct W3 . . . . .111 A5
Dartrey Twr SW10 . . . . .266 C4
Dartrey Wlk
 SW10 . . . . . . .136 A5 266 B4
Darul Ammah Private Sch
 E1 . . . . .96 B1
Darville Ho N16 . . . . .73 D5
Darwell Cl E6 . . . . .100 C5
Darwin Cl N11 . . . . .15 B1
 Orpington BR6 . . . . .227 B3
Darwin Ct E13 . . . . .99 B4
 NW1 . . . . .231 B6
 SE5 . . . . .166 C5
Darwin Dr UB1 . . . . .85 D1
Darwin Gdns WD1 . . . . . .22 C5
Darwin Ho 2 HA9 . . . . . .67 A5
Darwin Rd N22 . . . . .32 C1
 W5 . . . . .109 C2
 Bexy DA16 . . . . .145 D2
Darwin St SE17 117 B2 262 D4
Daryngton Dr UB6 . . . . . .86 C5
Daryngton Ho SW8 . . . . .270 A3
Dashwood Cl DA6 . . . . .169 C6
Dashwood Ct TW3 . . . . .130 A1
Dashwood Ho SE21 . . . .161 D1
Dashwood Rd N8 . . . . . . .50 B3
Dassett Rd SE27 . . . . . .182 D5
Data Point Bsns Ctr E16 98 B3
Datchelor Pl 14 SE5 . . .139 B4
Datchet Ho NW1 . . . . . .231 D2
Datchet Rd SE6 . . . . . . .163 B2
Datchett Ho 40 E2 . . . . .95 D4
Datchwood Ct N4 . . . . . .73 A5
Datchworth Ct 7 EN1 . .17 C6
Datchworth Ho 8 N1 . . .72 D1
Date St SE17 . . .117 B1 262 C1
Daubeney Gdns N17 . . . .33 A3
Daubeney JMI Sch E5 . .75 A4
Daubeney Rd E5 . . . . . . .75 A4
 N17 . . . . .33 A3
Daubeney Twr 2 SE8 . .119 B1
Dault Rd SW18 . . . . . . .158 A5
Dauney Ho SE1 . . . . . . .251 C1
Dave Adams Ho 7 E3 . .97 B5
Dave Porter Hts SW19 .157 A4
Davenant Ho 18 E1 . . . . .96 A1
Davenant Rd N19 . . . . . .71 D6
 Croydon CR0,CR9 . . . . .220 D4
Davenant St E1 . . . . .96 A2
Davenport Cl TW11 . . . .175 A4
Davenport Ho SE11 . . . .261 A5
Davenport Lo TW5 . . . . .129 A5
Davenport Rd SE6 . . . . .164 A5
 Sidcup DA14 . . . . .169 A2
Daventer Dr HA7 . . . . . .24 D3
Daventry Ave E17 . . . . . .53 C3
Daventry St NW1 92 C4 237 A4
Daver Ct SW3 . . . . .257 B1
 W5 . . . . .87 D3
Davern Cl SE10 . . . . . . .120 C2
Davet Ct SW8 . . . . .270 C2
Davey Cl N7 . . . . .72 B2
Davey Lo 2 N1 . . . . .72 C1
Davey Rd E9 . . . . .75 C1
Davey St SE15 . . . . .139 D6
Davey's Ct WC2 . . . . . . .250 A6
David Ave UB6 . . . . .86 C5
David Cl UB3 . . . . .127 C5
David Coffer Ct DA17 . .125 D2
David Devine Ho 7 E8 . .74 A3
David Ho 3 E14 . . . . .97 D2
 SE25 . . . . .206 A6
 8 SW15 . . . . .156 A6
David Lee Point 4 E15 . .98 C6
David Livingstone Prim Sch
 CR7 . . . . .183 A2
David Mews W1 . . . . . . .237 D4
David Rd RM8 . . . . .81 A6
David St E15 . . . . .76 B3
David Twiggs Cl KT2 . . .176 A2
Davidge Ho SE1 . . . . . . .251 B1
David's Rd SE23 . . . . . . .162 C3

Davidson Gdns
 SW8 . . . . . . .138 A5 270 A4
Davidson Ho 7 N19 . . . . .71 C4
Davidson Inf Sch CR0 . .205 D2
Davidson Jun Sch CR0 .205 D2
Davidson Lo CR0 . . . . . .205 D2
Davidson Rd CR0 . . . . . .206 A3
Davidson Terrs E7 . . . . . .77 B3
Davidson Twr BR1 . . . . .187 B5
Davies Cl CR0 . . . . .206 A2
Davies Jun & Inf Sch
 E11 . . . . .76 B6
Davies La E11 . . . . .76 B6
Davies Mews W1 . . . . . .248 C6
Davies St W1 . . .115 B6 248 C6
Davies Walk TW7 . . . . . .130 B4
Davington Gdns RM8 . . . .80 B3
Davington Rd RM8 . . . . . .80 B3
Davis Ho W12 . . . . .112 B6
Davis Rd W3 . . . . .111 D4
 Chessington KT9 . . . . . .214 C4
Davis St E13 . . . . .99 B5
Davisville Rd W12 . . . . .112 A4
Davmor Ct TW8 . . . . . . .109 C1
Davy Ho HA7 . . . . .67 A6
Dawes Ave TW7 . . . . . . .131 A1
Dawes Cl UB10 . . . . .82 A5
Dawes Ho SE17 . . . . . . .262 C3
Dawes Rd SW6 .135 B5 264 C4
Dawes St SE17 .117 B1 262 D2
Dawley Ave UB8 . . . . . . .83 A1
Dawley Par UB3 . . . . . . .105 A6
Dawley Rd Hayes UB3 . .105 B6
 Hayes Town UB3 . . . . . .105 C2
Dawlish Ave N13 . . . . . . .32 A5
 SW18 . . . . .157 D2
Dawlish Dr Ilford IG3 . . . .79 C4
 Pinner HA5 . . . . .41 A3
 Ruislip HA4 . . . . .62 B6
Dawlish Prim Sch E10 . .54 A1
Dawlish Rd E10 . . . . .54 A1
 Hampton TW12 . . . . . . .173 C5
 Isleworth TW3 . . . . .151 B4
 N17 . . . . .52 A6
 NW2 . . . . .68 D2
Dawn Cl TW4 . . . . .129 A2
Dawn Cres E15 . . . . .98 B6
Dawn Wlk BR2 . . . . .186 B1
Dawnay Gdns SW18 . . . .158 B2
Dawnay Rd SW18 . . . . . .158 B2
 SW17,SW18 . . . . .158 B2
Dawpool Rd NW2 . . . . . .67 D6
Daws Ho 35 W12 . . . . . .112 B6
Daws La NW7 . . . . .27 A6
Dawson Ave Barking IG11 79 D1
 St Paul's Cray BR5 . . . . .190 B1
Dawson Cl SE18 . . . . . . .123 A2
 Hayes UB3 . . . . .83 B2
Dawson Gdns 9 IG11 . .79 D1
Dawson Ho 2 E2 . . . . . . .96 C4
 5 SE5 . . . . .139 A5
Dawson Pl W2 . .113 C6 245 B6
Dawson Rd NW2 . . . . . . .68 C4
 Kingston u T KT1 . . . . . .198 B6
Dawson St E2 . . . . .95 D5
Dawson Terr N9 . . . . .18 C4
 South Croydon CR0 . . . .221 D5
Dax Ct TW16 . . . . .194 C6
Day Ho SE5 . . . . .138 D5
 2 SE5 . . . . .139 A5
Daybrook Rd SW19 . . . .201 D6
Daylesford Ave SW15 . .134 A1
Daymer Gdns HA5 . . . . . .40 C5
Daynor Ho 4 NW6 . . . . . .91 C2
Days La DA15 . . . . .167 C4
Days Lane Prim Sch
 DA15 . . . . .167 D5
Daysbrook Rd SW2 . . . .160 B3
Dayton Gr SE15 . . . . . . .140 C4
Daytone Rd SW20 . . . . .178 D2
De Barowe Mews N5 . . . .72 D3
De Beauvoir Cres 1 . . . .95 C6
De Beauvoir Ct N1 . . . . .73 B3
De Beauvoir JMI Sch N1 73 C2
De Beauvoir Pl 5 N1 . . .73 C2
De Beauvoir Rd N1 . . . . .73 C1
De Beauvoir Sq N1 . . . . .73 C1
De Bohun Ave N14 . . . . .15 B5
De Bohun Prim Sch N14 15 B6
De Broome Rd TW13 . . .150 C3
De Burgh Ho 10 SW19 .180 A3
De Crespigny Pk SE5 . .139 B4
De Frene Rd SE26 . . . . .163 A1
De Gama Pl E14 . . . . . . .119 C1
De Havilland Rd
 Edgware HA8 . . . . .26 D1
 Heston TW5 . . . . .128 C5
 Wallington SM6 . . . . . . .220 A1
De Havilland Way
 TW19 . . . . .148 A5
De Laune St
 SE17 . . . . . . .116 D1 261 C1
De Lucy Prim Sch SE2 .124 B4
De Lucy St SE2 . . . . .124 B2
De Mandeville Ct E4 . . . .35 A6
De Mandeville Gate EN1 . .6 B1
De Montfort Par 1
 SW16 . . . . .160 A1
De Montfort Rd SW16 . .160 A2
De Morgan Rd SW6 . . . .135 D2
De Quincey Mews 3
 E16 . . . . .121 A5
De Quincey Rd N17 . . . . .33 B2
De Salis Rd UB10 . . . . . .83 A3
De Vere Cotts W8 . . . . . .256 A6
De Vere Gdns
 W8 . . . . .114 A4 246 A1
 Redbridge IG1 . . . . .56 B1
De Vere Mews W8 . . . . .256 A6

De Walden Ho NW8 . . . .230 A4
De Walden St W1 . . . . . .238 B3
Deacon Ho 7 SE11 . . . . .260 D3
Deacon Mews N1 . . . . . . .73 B1
Deacon Rd NW2 . . . . . . .68 A2
 Kingston u T KT2 . . . . . .176 B2
Deacon Way
 SE17 . . . . . . .117 A2 262 B4
Deaconess Ct 4 N15 . . .51 D5
Deacons Cl HA5 . . . . . . .40 C2
Deacon's Hill Rd WD6 . .10 C6
Deacons Hts WD6 . . . . . .10 C5
Deacons Leas BR6 . . . . .227 B4
Deacons Rise N2 . . . . . . .48 B4
Deacons Wlk TW12 . . . .173 C6
Deal Ct 13 NW9 . . . . .27 D1
 7 Southall UB1 . . . . . . .86 A1
Deal Ho SE15 . . . . .140 D6
 SE17 . . . . .263 B2
Deal Porters Way SE16 118 C3
Deal Rd SW17 . . . . .181 A4
Deal St E1 . . . . .96 A2
Deal Wlk 3 SW9 . . . . . .138 C5
Dealtry Rd SW15 . . . . . .134 C1
Dean Bradley St 1 SW1 .260 A5
Dean Cl E9 . . . . .74 C3
 SE16 . . . . .118 D5
 Hillingdon UB10 . . . . . . .60 B1
Dean Ct SW8 . . . . .270 A3
 Edgware HA8 . . . . .26 A4
 10 Kingston u T KT2 . . .176 C3
 Wembley HA0 . . . . .65 B5
Dean Dr HA7 . . . . .26 A1
Dean Farrar St SW1 . . . .259 D6
Dean Gdns E17 . . . . .54 B5
Dean Ho 18 E1 . . . . .96 C1
 N4 . . . . .51 A2
 N16 . . . . .51 D1
 Ruislip HA4 . . . . .39 B1
Dean Rd NW2 . . . . .68 C2
 SE28 . . . . .124 A6
 Croydon CR0 . . . . .221 B6
 Hampton TW12 . . . . . . .173 C5
 Isleworth TW3 . . . . .151 D6
Dean Ryle St SW1 . . . . .260 A4
Dean St E7 . . . . .77 A3
 W1 . . . . .93 D1 239 C1
Dean Stanley St 1 SW1 .260 A5
Dean Trench St SW1 . . . .260 A5
Dean Way UB2 . . . . .107 D4
Deancross St E1 . . . . . . .96 C1
Deane Ave HA4 . . . . .62 C3
Deane Croft Rd HA5 . . . .40 C3
Deane Way HA4 . . . . .40 B3
Deanery Cl N2 . . . . .48 C5
Deanery Mews W1 . . . . .248 B4
Deanery Rd E15 . . . . .76 C2
Deanery St W1 . .115 A5 248 B4
Deanfield Gdns CR0 . . . .221 B4
Deanhill Ct 2 SW14 . . . .132 C1
Deanhill Rd SW14 . . . . .132 C1
Dean's Bldgs
 SE17 . . . . . . .117 B2 262 D3
Deans Cl W4 . . . . .132 D6
 Burnt Oak HA8 . . . . .27 A4
 South Croydon CR0 . . . .221 D5
Dean's Ct EC4 . . . . .241 D1
Deans Dr N13 . . . . .32 D4
Dean's Dr HA8 . . . . .27 B5
Dean's Gate Cl SE23 . . .162 D1
Dean's La HA8 . . . . .27 A4
Dean's Mews W1 . . . . . .238 C2
Deans Rd SM1 . . . . .217 D5
Dean's Rd W7 . . . . .108 C4
Deans Way HA8 . . . . .27 A5
Dean's Yd SW1 . . . . .259 D6
Deansbrook Cl HA8 . . . . .27 A3
Deansbrook Jun & Inf Schs
 HA8,NW7 . . . . .27 A4
Deansbrook Rd
 Burnt Oak HA8 . . . . .27 B4
 Stanmore HA8 . . . . .26 D3
Deanscroft Ave NW9 . . . .45 A1
Deansfield Inf Sch SE9 144 C2
Deansfield Jun & Inf Sch
 HA4 . . . . .62 D4
Deansfield Jun Sch
 SE9 . . . . .144 C2
Deanshanger Ho 21
 SE8 . . . . .118 D2
Deansway N2 . . . . .48 B5
 N9 . . . . .17 C1
Deanswood N11 . . . . .31 D4
Dearmer Ho 6 SW2 . . . .160 C4
De'arn Gdns CR4 . . . . . .202 C6
Dearne Cl HA7 . . . . .25 A5
Dearsley Rd EN1 . . . . .6 A2
Deason St E15 . . . . .98 A6
Deauville Ct 4 SE16 . . . .118 D4
 14 SW4 . . . . .159 C5
Deauville Mans 13 SW4 159 C5
Debdale Ho 20 E2 . . . . . .96 A6
Debden N17 . . . . .33 B1
Debden Cl
 Kingston u T KT2 . . . . . .175 D5
 Woodford IG8 . . . . .37 D3
Debenham Ct E8 . . . . . . .96 A6
 Ducks Island EN5 . . . . . .12 C6
Debham Ct NW2 . . . . . . .68 C5
Debnams Rd SE16 . . . . .118 C2
Deborah Cl TW7 . . . . . . .130 C4
Deborah Cres HA4 . . . . . .39 B2
Deborah Ct 7 E18 . . . . . .55 B6
Deburgh Rd SW19 . . . . .180 A3
Decima St SE1 . .117 C3 263 A6
Decimal Ctr UB2 . . . . . . .107 C4
Decimus Cl CR7 . . . . . . .205 B5

Deck Cl SE16 . . . . .118 D5
Decoy Ave NW11 . . . . . . .47 A5
Dedham Ho 1 SE6 . . . . .186 A6
Dee Ct W7 . . . . .86 B1
Dee Rd TW9 . . . . .132 B1
Dee St E14 . . . . .98 A1
Deeley Rd SW8 137 D4 269 C2
Deena Cl W3 . . . . .88 B1
Deepdale N4 . . . . .72 A6
 SW19 . . . . .178 D6
Deepdale Ave BR2 . . . . .208 D5
Deepdale Cl N11 . . . . . . .31 A4
Deepdale Ct 4 CR0 . . . .221 D4
Deepdene N12 . . . . .30 C6
Deepdene Ave CR0 . . . . .221 D5
Deepdene Cl E11 . . . . . . .55 A5
Deepdene Ct N21 . . . . . .16 C5
 Beckenham BR2 . . . . . . .208 C6
Deepdene Gdns SW2 . . .160 B4
Deepdene Ho N3 . . . . . . .51 B1
Deepdene Lo 5 SW2 . . .160 B4
Deepdene Mans SW6 . . .264 C2
Deepdene Point 9
 SE26 . . . . .162 B1
Deepdene Rd SE5,SE24 .139 B1
 Bexley DA16 . . . . .146 A2
Deepwell Ct 7 TW7 . . . .131 A4
Deepwood La UB6 . . . . . .86 B4
Deer Lo SW6 . . . . .135 A2
Deer Park Cl KT2 . . . . . .176 D3
Deer Park Gdns CR4 . . .202 B5
Deer Park Rd SW19 . . . .180 A1
Deer Park Way BR4 . . . .224 D2
Deerbrook Rd SE24,
 SW2 . . . . .160 D3
Deerdale Rd SE24 . . . . .139 A1
Deerhurst 7 KT2 . . . . . .176 D2
Deerhurst Cl TW13 . . . . .172 B6
Deerhurst Cres TW12 . .174 A5
Deerhurst Ho 6 SE15 . .140 A6
Deerhurst Rd NW2 . . . . . .68 D2
 SW16 . . . . .182 B5
Deerings Dr HA5 . . . . . . .40 A4
Deerleap Gr E4 . . . . .19 D6
Deeside Rd SW17 . . . . .158 B1
Defiance Wlk SE18 . . . . .122 B3
Defiant 18 NW9 . . . . .27 D1
Defiant Way SM6 . . . . . .220 A1
Defoe Cl SW17 . . . . .180 C4
Defoe Ho EC2 . . . . .242 A4
 5 N16 . . . . .73 C5
Defoe Pl EC2 . . . . .242 A4
Defoe Rd N16 . . . . .73 C5
 SE16 . . . . .119 B4
Degema Rd BR7 . . . . . . .188 D5
Dehar Cres NW9 . . . . . . .46 A2
Dehavilland Cl UB5 . . . . .84 D4
Dekker Ho 19 SE5 . . . . .139 B5
Dekker Rd SE21 . . . . . . .161 C5
Delacourt Rd SE3 . . . . . .143 B5
Delafield Ho 18 E1 . . . . .96 A1
Delafield Rd SE7 . . . . . .121 C1
 SE16 . . . . .118 A4
Delaford St
 SW6 . . . . .135 B6 264 B5
Delamare Cres CR0 . . . .206 C3
Delamere Gdns NW7 . . . .27 A4
Delamere Ho 4 N4 . . . . .51 B2
Delamere Rd SW20 . . . .178 D2
 W5 . . . . .110 A4
 Hayes UB4 . . . . .106 D6
Delamere St W2 . . . . . . .236 A3
Delamere Terr W2 . . . . . .91 D2
Delancey Pas NW1 . . . . .231 D5
Delancey St NW1 93 B6 231 D5
Delancey Studios NW1 .231 D5
Delany Ho SE10 . . . . . . .142 A6
Delarch Ho SE1 . . . . . . .251 C1
Delaware Rd W9 . . . . . . .91 D3
Delcombe Ave KT4 . . . . .200 C1
Delft Ho 8 KT2 . . . . .176 B3
Delft Way 2 SE22 . . . . .161 C6
Delhi Rd EN1 . . . . .17 D4
Delhi St N1 . . . . .94 A5 233 B5
Delia St SW18 . . . . .157 D4
Delisle Rd SE28 . . . . . . .123 C5
Delius Cl WD6 . . . . .9 C5
Delius Gr E15 . . . . .98 A5
Dell Cl E15 . . . . .98 B6
 Wallington SM6 . . . . . . .219 D4
 Woodford IG8 . . . . .21 B1
Dell La KT17 . . . . .216 A3
Dell Rd Enfield EN3 . . . . . .6 C5
 Stoneleigh KT17 . . . . . .216 A2
 West Drayton UB7 . . . . .104 B3
Dell The SE2 . . . . .124 A1
 SE19 . . . . .183 D2
 Brentford TW8 . . . . .131 C6
 Feltham TW14 . . . . .150 B4
 Pinner Green HA5 . . . . . .22 D1
 Wembley HA0 . . . . .65 B3
 Woodford IG8 . . . . .21 B1
Dell Way W13 . . . . .87 C1
Dell Wlk KT3 . . . . .177 C1
Della Path E5 . . . . .74 B5
Dellafield N4 . . . . .72 C6
Dellbow Rd TW14 . . . . . .150 B6
Dellfield Cl BR3 . . . . . . .186 A2
Dellors Cl EN5 . . . . .12 D6
Dellow Cl IG2 . . . . .57 B2
Dellow Ho 6 E1 . . . . . . .118 B6
Dellow St E1 . . . . .118 B6
Dells Cl E4 . . . . .19 D4
 Teddington TW11 . . . . . .174 D4
Dell's Mews SW1 . . . . . .259 B3
Dellwood Gdns IG5 . . . . .56 C6

Delmane Ho 4 E14 97 A1
Delme Cres SE3 143 B3
Delmey Cl CR0 221 D5
Deloraine Ho SE8 141 C4
Deloraine St SE8 141 C4
Delorme St W6 134 D6
Delphian Ct 5 SW16 182 C6
Delroy Ct N20 14 A4
Delta Bldg 4 E14 98 A1
Delta Cl KT4 215 D5
Delta Ct NW2 68 A6
Delta Gr UB5 84 D4
Delta Pk SW18 135 D1
Delta Rd KT4 215 C5
Delta St 3 E2 96 A4
Delvan Cl SE18 144 C5
Delverton Ho SE17 261 D2
Delverton Rd SE17 261 D1
Delvino Rd SW6 135 C4 265 B1
Demesne Rd SM6 219 D4
Demeta Cl HA9 67 A5
Dempster Cl KT6 197 C1
Dempster Rd SW18 158 A6
Den Cl BR2,BR3 208 B6
Den Rd BR2 208 B6
Denberry Dr DA14 168 B1
Denbigh Cl NW10 67 C1
W11 113 B6 244 D6
Cheam SM1 217 B3
Chislehurst West BR7 188 B4
Ruislip HA4 61 D6
Southall UB1 85 B1
Denbigh Ct E6 99 D4
1 W7 86 D2
Denbigh Dr UB3 105 A4
Denbigh Gdns TW10 154 B6
Denbigh Ho SW1 257 D6
W11 244 D6
7 W11 91 B1
Denbigh Mews SW1 259 A3
Denbigh Pl
SW1 115 C1 259 A2
Denbigh Rd E6 99 D4
W11 113 B6 244 D6
W13 87 B1
Hounslow TW3 129 D3
Southall UB1 85 B1
Denbigh St
SW1 115 C1 259 B2
Denbigh Terr
W11 113 B6 244 D6
Denbridge Rd BR1,BR7 188 B1
Denbury Ho 48 E3 97 D4
Denby Ct SE11 260 D4
Dence Ho 20 E2 96 A4
Denchworth Ho 15
SW9 138 C3
Dencliffe TW15 170 C5
Dendridge Cl EN1 6 B6
Dendy St SW12 159 A3
Dene Ave Hounslow TW3 129 B2
Sidcup DA15 168 B4
Dene Cl SE4 141 A1
Hayes BR2 208 D1
Worcester Pk KT4 215 D6
Dene Ct W5 87 C2
W7 108 D4
Dene Gdns
Hinchley Wood KT7 213 A6
Stanmore HA7 25 C5
Dene Ho N14 15 D4
Dene Mans 1 NW6 69 C2
Dene Rd N11 14 D2
Buckhurst Hill IG9 21 D3
Dene The W13 87 B2
East Molesey KT12,KT8 195 B4
South Croydon CR0 222 D4
Wembley HA9 66 A4
Denecroft Cres UB10 82 D6
Denehurst Gdns NW4 46 C3
W3 110 D5
Mortlake TW10 132 C1
Twickenham TW2 152 B4
Woodford IG8 37 B6
Denesmead SE24 161 A6
Denewood EN5 14 A6
Denewood Rd N6 48 D2
Dengie Wlk N1 235 A6
Denham Cl DA16 146 C2
Denham Cres CR4 202 D5
Denham Ct SE26 162 B1
Southall UB1 108 A6
Denham Dr IG2 57 A3
Denham Ho 32 W12 112 B6
Denham Lo W5 88 A1
Denham Rd N20 14 D1
Feltham TW14 150 C4
Denham St SE10 121 A1
Denham Way IG11 101 D6
Denholme Rd W9 91 B4
Denise Ct HA0 65 C4
Denison Cl N2 48 A6
Denison Rd SW19 180 B4
W5 87 C3
Feltham TW13 171 D6
Deniston Ave DA5 169 A3
Denland Ho SW8 270 D3
Denleigh Ct N14 15 D4
Denleigh Gdns N21 16 C4
Thames Ditton KT7 196 C3
Denman Dr NW11 47 C4
Ashford TW15 170 D4
Claygate KT10 213 A3
Denman Dr N NW11 47 C4
Denman Dr S NW11 47 C4
Denman Ho N16 73 C6
Denman Rd SE15 139 D3
Denman St W1 249 C5
Denmark Ave SW19 179 A3
Denmark Ct SM4 201 C4
Denmark Gdns SM5 218 D5
Denmark Gr N1 234 A4
Denmark Hill SE5 139 B3
Denmark Hill Dr NW9 46 A6
Denmark Hill Sta SE5 139 B3
Denmark Ho 9 SE7 122 A2
Denmark Mans 14 SE5 139 A3
Denmark Pl WC2 239 D2
Denmark Rd N8 50 C5
NW6 91 B5
SE5 139 A3
SE25 206 B4
SW19 178 D4
W13 109 B6
Bromley BR1 187 B2
Carshalton SM5 218 D5
Kingston u T KT1 198 A6
Twickenham TW2 152 B1
Denmark St 6 E11 76 C5
E13 99 B2
N17 34 B3
WC2 239 D2
Denmead Ho 8 SW15 155 D5
Denmead Lower Sch
TW12 173 D3
Denmead Rd CR0 204 D1
Denmead Upper Sch
TW12 173 D3
Denmead Way SE15 139 D5
Denmore Ct SM6 219 B3
Dennan Rd KT6 198 B1
Dennard Way BR6 226 C4
Denne Terr E8 95 D6
Denner Rd E4 19 C2
Dennett Rd CR0 204 C2
Dennett's Gr SE14 140 D3
Dennett's Rd SE14 140 C4
Denning Ave CR0 220 C3
Denning Cl NW8 92 A4 229 B1
Hampton TW12 173 B5
Denning Point E1 243 D2
Denning Rd NW3 70 B4
Dennington Cl 17 E5 74 B6
Dennington Park Rd
NW6 69 C2
Denningtons The KT4 215 C6
Dennis Ave HA9 66 B3
Dennis Cl TW15 171 B3
Dennis Ct E17 36 B1
Dennis Gdns HA7 25 C5
Dennis Ho 4 E3 97 B5
Sutton SM1 217 C4
Dennis La HA7 25 B6
Dennis Par 1 N14 15 D3
Dennis Park Cres
SW20 179 A2
Dennis Rd KT8 196 A5
Dennis Reeve Cl CR4 180 D2
Dennis Way SW4 137 D2
Dennison Ho 8 E14 97 C1
Dennison Point E15 76 A1
Denny Cl 15 E6 100 A2
Denny Cres SE11 261 B2
Denny Gdns RM9 80 B1
Denny Rd N9 18 B3
Denny St SE11 116 C1 261 B2
Densham Ho NW8 229 D3
Densham Rd E15 98 C6
Densole Cl BR3 185 A2
Denstone Ho 5 SE15 140 A6
Densworth Gr N9 18 C2
Dent Ho SE17 263 A3
Denton NW1 71 A2
Denton Cl EN5 12 C6
Denton Ho N1 72 D1
Denton Rd N8 50 B3
N18 33 C6
Bexley DA16 146 C5
Twickenham TW1 153 D5
Denton St SW18 157 D5
Denton Way E5 74 D5
Dents Rd SW11 158 D5
Denvale Trade Pk CR4 202 B5
Denver Cl BR6 211 C3
Denver Rd N16 51 C2
Denwood SE23 162 D1
Denyer Ho 1 NW5 71 B4
Denyer St SW3 114 C2 257 B4
Denys Ho EC1 241 A4
Denzil Rd NW10 67 D3
Denziloe Ave UB10 82 D4
Deodar Rd SW15 135 A1
Deodora Cl N20 14 D1
Depot App NW2 68 D4
Depot Rd W12 112 C6
Hounslow TW3,TW7 130 B2
Depot St SE5 139 B6
Dept of Transport &
Environment SW1 259 D5
Deptford Bridge SE8 141 C4
Deptford Bridge Sta
SE8 141 C4
Deptford Broadway
SE8,SE14 141 C4
Deptford Church St
SE8 141 C5
Deptford Ferry Rd 12
E14 119 C2
Deptford Gn SE8 141 C6
Deptford Green Sch
SE14 141 B5
Deptford Green Sch
(Annexe) SE14 141 A5
Deptford High St SE8 141 C5
Deptford Park Prim Schs
SE8 119 A1
Deptford Sta SE8 141 C5
Deptford Trad Est SE8 141 A6
Deptford Wharf SE8 119 B2
Derby Ave N12 30 A5
Harrow HA3 24 B2
Romford RM7 59 D3
Derby Ct 8 E5 74 D4
E18 36 D2
Derby Gate SW1 250 A2
Derby Hill SE23 162 C2
Derby Hill Cres SE23 162 C2
Derby Ho NW4 46 C6
SE11 261 A4
Pinner Green HA5 22 D1
Derby Lo N3 29 B1
Derby Rd E7 77 D1
E9 96 D6
E18 36 D2
N18 34 C5
SW14 132 D1
SW19 179 C3
Cheam SM1,SM2 217 B2
Enfield EN3 18 C6
Greenford UB6 85 D6
Hounslow TW3 129 D1
Surbiton KT5,KT6 198 C1
Thornton Heath CR0 204 D1
Derby St W1 248 B3
Derbyshire St E2 96 A4
Dereham Ho 7 SE4 140 D1
Dereham Pl EC2 243 B6
Dereham Rd IG11 79 D3
Derek Ave
Hackbridge SM6 219 B4
Wembley HA9 66 D1
West Ewell KT19 214 D3
Derek Cl KT19 214 D3
Derek Walcott Cl SE24 160 D6
Deri Dene Cl 2 TW19 148 A5
Dericote St E8 96 B6
Derifall Cl E6 100 B2
Dering Pl CR0 221 A4
Dering Rd CR0 221 A4
Dering St W1 238 D1
Derinton Rd SW17 181 A6
Derley Rd UB2 106 D3
Dermody Gdns SE13 164 B6
Dermody Rd SE13 164 B6
Deronda Rd SE24,SW2 160 D3
Deroy Cl SM5 218 D2
Deroy Ct SM5 218 D2
Derrick Gdns SE7 121 C2
Derrick Ho 13 SW2 160 C3
Derrick Rd BR3 207 B5
Derry Rd CR0,SM6 220 A5
Derry St W8 113 D4 245 C1
Derrycombe Ho 18 W2 91 C2
W11 91 B2
Dersingham Ave E12 78 C4
Dersingham Rd NW2 69 A5
Derwent NW1 232 A1
Derwent Ave N18 33 B5
NW7 27 B4
NW9 45 C4
SW15 177 C6
Barnet EN4 14 D3
Hatch End HA5 23 A4
Uxbridge UB10 60 C5
Derwent Cl
Claygate KT10 212 D2
East Bedfont TW14 149 D3
Derwent Cres N20 14 A1
Bexleyheath DA7 147 C3
Stanmore HA7 25 C1
Derwent Ct N8 50 A3
8 SE16 118 D4
2 W6 112 A2
Derwent Dr Hayes UB4 83 C2
Orpington BR5 211 B2
Derwent Gdns
Redbridge IG4 56 A5
Wembley HA9 43 C2
Derwent Gr SE22 139 D1
Derwent Ho E3 97 B3
SE20 184 B1
SW7 256 B4
Derwent Lo
Hounslow TW7 130 B3
North Cheam KT4 216 B6
Derwent Rd N13 16 B1
SE20 184 B1
W5 109 C3
Southall UB1 85 B1
Twickenham TW2 151 D5
West Barnes SM4 200 D3
Derwent Rise NW9 45 C3
Derwent St SE10 120 C1
Derwent Wlk SM6 219 B1
Derwentwater Mans 2
W3 111 A5
Derwentwater Prim Sch
W3 111 A5
Derwentwater Rd W3 111 A5
Desborough Cl W2 91 D2
Lower Halliford TW17 192 C2
Desborough Ct SE25 206 B5
Desborough Ho W14 264 D6
Desenfans Rd SE21 161 C5
Desford Mews E16 98 C3
Desford Rd E16 98 C3
Desford Way TW15 148 B2
Design Mus*
SE1 117 D4 253 D2
Desmond Ho 4 EN4 14 C5
Desmond St SE14 141 A6
Despard Ho SW2 160 C2
Despard Rd N19 49 C1
Dessouter 19 NW9 27 D1
Detherick Ct TW3 130 A1
Dethick Ct E3 97 A6
Detling Ho SE17 263 A3
Detling Rd BR1 187 A5
Detmold Rd E5 74 C6
Deutsche Schule TW10 153 D3
Devalls Cl E6 122 C6
Devana End SM5 218 D5
Devas Rd SW20 178 C2
Devas St E3 97 D3
Devema Cl BR7 188 C2
Devenay Rd E15 76 D1
Devenish Rd SE2 124 A4
Deventer Cres 8 SE22 161 C6
Deverell St SE1 117 B3 262 C5
Devereux Ct WC2 241 A1
Devereux Ho 7 SW15 156 A6
Devereux La SW13 134 B5
Devereux Rd SW11 158 D5
Deverill Ct SE20 184 C2
Devey Cl KT2 177 B5
Devitt Ho 4 E14 119 D6
Devizes St N1 235 D5
Devon Ave TW2 152 A3
Devon Cl N17 51 D6
Buckhurst Hill IG9 21 B2
Wembley UB6 87 C6
Devon Ct 3 W3 88 C1
2 W7 86 D2
Devon Gdns N4 50 D3
Devon Ho 5 E11 55 A5
E17 35 B1
SE20 184 B3
Devon Mans SE1 253 B2
SE1 253 C1
SE1 253 D1
Devon Par HA3 43 C4
Devon Rd IG11 101 C6
Devon Rise N2 48 B5
Devon St SE15 140 B6
Devon Way
Chessington KT9 213 C3
Hillingdon UB10 82 B5
West Ewell KT19 214 D3
Devon Waye TW5 129 B5
Devoncroft Gdns TW1 153 A4
Devonhurst Pl 4 W4 111 B1
Devonia Gdns N18 33 A4
Devonia Rd N1 94 D5 234 D4
Devonport W2 237 A2
Devonport Gdns IG1 56 B3
Devonport Ho 23 W2 91 C2
Devonport Rd W12 112 B4
Devonport St E1 96 D1
Devons Rd E3 97 D3
Devons Road Sta E3 97 D3
Devonshire Ave SM2 218 A1
Devonshire Cl E15 76 C4
N13 32 C6
W1 238 C4
Devonshire Cres NW7 28 D3
Devonshire Ct N17 33 A4
Croydon CR0 207 C1
Feltham TW13 150 B2
6 Richmond TW9 132 B4
Devonshire Dr SE10 141 D4
Long Ditton KT6 213 D6
Devonshire Gdns N17 33 A4
N21 17 A4
W4 133 A5
Devonshire Gr SE15 140 B6
Devonshire Hall 14 E9 74 C2
Devonshire Hill La N17 33 A4
Devonshire Hill Prim Sch
N17 33 B4
Devonshire Ho N12 14 A1
NW6 69 B2
SE1 262 A6
SW1 259 D2
14 SW12 159 B4
2 SW15 156 C4
W2 236 D4
Hounslow TW3 130 A2
10 Sutton SM2 218 A1
Devonshire Hospl
W1 93 A2 238 B4
Devonshire Mews 2
W4 111 C1
Devonshire Mews N
W1 238 C4
Devonshire Mews S
W1 238 C4
Devonshire Mews W
W1 238 B4
Devonshire Pl NW2 69 C5
W1 93 A2 238 B4
W8 255 C5
Devonshire Place Mews
W1 238 B4
Devonshire Prim Sch
SM2 218 A1
Devonshire Rd E16 99 B1
E17 53 C3
N9 18 C3
N13 32 C6
N17 33 A4
NW7 28 D3
SE9 166 A2
SE23 162 C4
SW17,SW19 180 C3
W4 111 C1
W5 109 C3
Bexleyheath DA6 147 A1
Feltham TW13 173 A6
Hackbridge SM5,SM6 219 A4
Harrow HA1 42 B3
Ilford IG2 57 C2
Pinner HA5 23 B2
Devonshire Rd *continued*
Pinner HA5 40 C2
Southall UB1 85 C2
Sutton SM2 218 A1
Thornton Heath CR0 205 B2
Devonshire Row EC2 243 B3
Devonshire Row Mews
W1 238 D5
Devonshire Sq
EC2 95 C1 243 B2
Bromley BR2 209 B5
Devonshire St
W1 93 B2 238 C4
W4 111 C1
Devonshire Terr
W2 92 A1 236 B1
Devonshire Way
Croydon CR0,CR9 223 B6
Hayes UB4 84 B1
Dewar Ho 2 SW17 180 C5
Dewar St SE15 140 A2
Dewberry Gdns E6 100 A2
Dewberry St E14 98 A2
Dewey Rd N1 94 C5 234 A4
Dagenham RM10 81 D2
Dewey St SW17 180 D5
Dewhurst Rd W14 112 D3
Dewlands Ct NW4 28 D1
Dewsbury Cl HA5 41 A3
Dewsbury Ct 5 W4 111 A2
Dewsbury Gdns KT4 216 A5
Dewsbury Rd NW10 68 A3
Dewsbury Terr NW1 231 D6
Dexter Ho 2 DA18 125 A3
Dexter Rd EN5 12 D5
Deyncourt Rd N17 33 A2
Deynecourt Gdns E11 55 C5
D'eynsford Rd SE5 139 B4
Dhonau Ho SE16 263 D4
Diadem Ct W1 239 C2
Dial Wlk The
W8 113 D4 245 D2
Diameter Rd BR5 211 A3
Diamond Cl RM8 58 C1
Diamond Est SW17 158 C1
Diamond Ho 20 E3 97 A5
Diamond Rd HA4 63 A4
Diamond St SE15 139 C5
Diamond Terr SE10 142 A4
Diana Cl E18 37 B2
Diana Ct SM5 219 A1
Diana Gdns KT6 214 B6
Diana Ho 4 SW2 160 B6
Diana Pl NW1 238 D6
Diana Rd E17 53 B6
Diana, Princess of Wales
Mml Wlk W2 114 A5 246 A3
Dianne Ct SE12 165 A3
Dianne Way EN4 2 C1
Dianthus Cl SE2 124 B1
Dibden Ho 16 SE5 139 C5
Dibden St N1 95 A6 235 A6
Dibdin Cl SM1 217 C5
Dibdin Ho W9 91 D5
Dibdin Rd SM1 217 C6
Dicey Ave NW2 68 C4
Dick Sheppard Sch
SE24 160 C4
Dick Turpin Way TW14 127 D1
Dickens Ave N3 30 A2
Hayes UB8 82 D1
Dickens Cl Erith DA8 147 D5
Hayes UB3 105 C2
Richmond TW10 154 A2
Dickens Ct 10 E11 55 A5
Wembley HA0 65 C5
Dickens Dr BR7 189 A4
Dickens Ho NW6 91 C4
NW8 236 D6
SE17 261 D1
WC1 240 A6
3 Erith DA17 125 B1
Hayes UB3 105 C2
Dickens House Mus
WC1 94 B3 240 D5
Dickens La N18 33 C5
Dickens Rd E6 99 D5
Dickens Sq SE1 117 A3 262 B6
Dickens St SW8 137 B3
Dickenson Cl N9 18 A3
Dickenson Ho N8 50 B3
Dickenson Rd N8 50 A2
Dickenson's La SE25 206 A3
Dickenson's Pl SE25 206 A3
Dickerage Hill
Kingston u T KT3 199 A6
KT3 177 A1
Dickerage La KT3 199 A6
Dickerage Rd KT1,KT2,
KT3 177 A1
Dickinson Ho 21 E2 96 A4
Dickinson Rd TW13 172 D5
Dicksee Ho NW8 236 C5
Dickson Fold HA5 40 D5
Dickson Ho 13 E1 96 B1
9 SE18 144 A4
Dickson Rd SE9 144 A2
Didbin Ho N7 72 B6
Didsbury Cl E6 100 B6
Digby Bsns Ctr E9 74 D2
Digby Cres N4 73 A6
Digby Gdns RM10 103 C6
Digby Mans W6 112 C1
Digby Pl CR0 221 D5
Digby Rd E9 74 D2
Barking IG11 79 D1
Digby St E2 96 C4
Diggon St 16 E1 96 D2
Dighton Ct SE17 139 A6
Dighton Rd SW18 136 A1
Dignum St N1 234 A4
Digswell St N7 72 C2
Dilhorne Cl SE12 165 B1
Dilke St SW3 136 D6 267 D6
Dilloway Yd UB2 107 A4
Dillwyn Cl SE26 185 A6
Dilston Cl 1 UB5 84 C4
Dilston Gr SE16 118 C2
Dilton Gdns SW15 156 B3
Dilwyn Ct E17 35 A1
Dimes Pl 9 W6 112 B2
Dimmock Dr UB6 64 B3
Dimond Cl E7 77 A4
Dimsdale Dr NW9 45 A1
Enfield EN1 18 A5
Dimsdale Wlk 4 E13 99 A5
Dimson Cres E3 97 C4
Dinerman Ct NW8 229 B6
Dingle Ct EN5 11 D5
Dingle Gdns E14 119 C6
Dingle Rd TW15 170 D5
Dingle The UB10 82 D4
Dingley La SW16 159 D2
Dingley Pl EC1 95 A4 235 B1
Dingley Rd EC1 95 A4 235 A1
Dingwall Ave CR0 221 A6
Dingwall Gdns NW11 47 C3
Dingwall Rd SW18 158 A4
Croydon CR0 221 B6
Dinmont Ho 28 E2 96 A5
Dinmont St 1 E2 96 B5
Dinmore Ho 7 E9 96 C6
Dinnington Ho 17 E1 96 B3
Dinorben SM6 219 C1
Dinsdale Ct EN5 13 D6
Dinsdale Gdns SE25 205 C4
New Barnet EN5 13 D6
Dinsdale Rd SE3 142 D6
Dinsmore Rd SW12 159 B4
Dinton Ho NW8 237 A6
Dinton Rd SW19 180 B4
Kingston u T KT2 176 B3
Dinwiddy Ho N1 233 C3
Diploma Ave N2 48 C5
Diploma Ct N2 48 C5
Dirleton Rd E15 98 D6
Disbrowe Rd
W6 135 A6 264 B5
Discovery Bsns Pk 13
SE16 118 A3
Discovery Ho 1 E14 120 A6
Dishforth La NW9 27 C2
Disley Ct 2 UB1 85 D1
Disney Pl SE1 252 B2
Disney St SE1 252 B2
Dison Cl EN3 6 D4
Disraeli Cl SE28 124 C5
W4 111 B2
Disraeli Gdns SW15 135 B1
Disraeli Rd E7 77 A2
NW10 89 B5
SW15 135 A1
W5 109 D5
Diss St E2 95 D4
Distaff La EC4 252 A6
Distillery La W6 112 C1
Distillery Rd W6 112 C1
Distillery Wlk 14 TW8 132 A6
Distin St SE11 116 C2 261 A3
District Rd HA0 65 B3
Ditchburn St E14 120 A6
Ditchfield Rd UB4 85 A3
Dittisham Rd SE9 188 A6
Ditton Cl KT7 197 A2
Ditton Grange Cl KT6 197 D1
Ditton Grange Dr KT6 197 D1
Ditton Hill KT6 213 D6
Ditton Hill Rd KT6 197 C1
Ditton Ho 10 E5 74 B3
Ditton Lawn KT7 197 A1
Ditton Pl 6 SE20 184 B2
Ditton Rd Bexley DA6 169 A6
Southall UB2 107 B1
Surbiton KT6 198 B1
Ditton Reach KT7 197 B3
Dittoncroft Cl CR0 221 C4
Divis Way SW15 156 B5
Dixon Cl 4 E6 100 B1
Dixon Clark Ct N1 72 D2
Dixon Ct N4 50 C3
Dixon Ho SE2 124 C1
Dixon Pl BR4 207 D1
Dixon Rd SE14 141 A4
SE25 205 D6
Dobbin Cl HA3 25 A1
Dobell Rd SE9 166 B6
Dobree Ave NW10 68 B1
Dobson Cl NW6 70 B1
Dobson Ho SE5 139 B5
18 SE14 140 D6
Doby Ct EC4 252 B6
Dock Hill Ave SE16 118 D4
Dock Offices 12 SE16 118 C3
Dock Rd E16 120 D6
Brentford TW8 131 D5
Dock St E1 118 A6
Dockers Tanner Rd 19
E14 119 C2
Dockett Eddy La KT16,
TW17 192 B1
Dockett Moorings KT16 192 B1
Dockhead SE1 117 D4 253 D1
Dockhead Wharf SE1 253 D2

Dockland St E16 122 C5
Docklands Heritage Mus SE16 119 B5
Dockley Rd SE16 118 A3
Dockley Road Ind Est 11 SE16 118 A3
Dockside Rd E16 121 D6
Dockwell Cl TW14 128 A1
Dockwell's Ind Est TW14 150 C6
Doctor Spurstowe Almshos 9 E8 74 B2
Doctors Cl SE26 184 C5
Docura Ho N7 72 B6
Docwra's Bldgs N1 73 C2
Dod St E14 97 C1
Dodbrooke Rd SE27 160 D1
Dodd Ho 18 SE16 118 B2
Doddington Gr SE17 116 D1 261 D1
Doddington Pl 4 SE17 138 D6
Dodsley Pl N9 18 C1
Dodson St SE1 116 C4 251 B1
Doebury Wlk SE18 146 A6
Doel Cl SW19 180 A3
Dog Kennel Hill SE22 139 C2
Dog Kennel Hill Jun & Inf Sch SE22 139 C2
Dog La NW10 67 C4
Doggett Rd SE6 163 C4
Doggetts Ct EN4 14 C6
Doghurst Ave UB3 126 D5
Doghurst Dr UB7 126 D5
Dogrose Ct 14 NW9 46 A5
Doherty Rd E13 99 A3
Dokal Ind Est UB2 107 A4
Doland Ct SW17 180 D4
Dolben Ct SE8 119 B2
Dolben St SE1 116 D5 251 D3
Dolby Rd SW6 135 B3
Dolland Ho SE11 260 D1
Dolland St SE11 260 D1
Dollar Bay E14 120 A4
Dollary Ct KT3 198 D6
Dollis Ave N3 29 B2
Dollis Brook Wlk EN5 13 A5
Dollis Cres HA4 40 C1
Dollis Ct N3 29 B2
Dollis Hill Ave NW2 68 B5
Dollis Hill Est NW2 68 A5
Dollis Hill La NW2 68 A5
Dollis Hill Sta NW2 68 A3
Dollis Hts NW2 68 B5
Dollis Jun & Cty Inf Sch NW7 28 C3
Dollis Mews N3 29 C2
Dollis Pk N3 29 B2
Dollis Rd N3,NW7 29 B3
Dollis Valley Way EN5 13 B5
Dolliscroft NW7 29 A3
Dolman Rd W4 111 B2
Dolman St SW4 138 B1
Dolphin Cl 2 SE16 118 D4
SE28 102 D1
Kingston u T KT6 197 D4
Dolphin Ct N7 71 D4
NW11 47 A3
SW19 179 C3
Harrow HA3 24 C1
2 Wallington SM6 219 B2
Dolphin Est The TW16 171 B2
Dolphin La E14 119 D6
Dolphin Rd
Charlton TW16 171 C2
Northolt UB5 85 B5
Dolphin Rd N TW16 171 C2
Dolphin Rd S TW16 171 C2
Dolphin Rd W TW16 171 C2
Dolphin Sq SW1 259 B1
Dolphin St KT2 176 A2
Dolphin Twr 21 SE8 141 B6
Dombey Ho 9 SE1 118 A4
4 W11 112 D5
Dombey St WC1 240 C4
Dome Hill Pk SE26 183 D6
Domelton Ho SW18 157 D5
Domett Cl SE5 139 B1
Domfe Pl E5 74 C4
Domingo St EC1 242 A5
Dominica Cl 6 E6 99 D5
Dominion Bsns Pk N9 18 D2
Dominion Ind Est UB2 107 A4
Dominion Par HA1 42 D4
Dominion Rd
Croydon CR0 205 D2
Southall UB2 107 A3
Dominion St EC2 95 B2 242 D4
Dominion Wks RM8 59 A1
Domonic Dr SE9 166 D1
Domville Cl N20 14 B2
Don Phelan Cl SE5 139 B4
Donaghue Cotts 13 E14 97 A2
Donald Dr RM6 58 C4
Donald Lynch Ho CR4 180 D1
Donald Rd E13 99 B6
Thornton Heath CR0 204 B2
Donald Woods Gdns KT5 215 A6
Donaldson Rd NW6 91 B6
SE18 144 C4
Doncaster Dr UB5 63 B3
Doncaster Gdns N4 51 A3
Northolt UB5 63 B3
Doncaster Gn WD1 22 C5
Doncaster Rd N9 18 B4
Doncel Ct E4 20 B4
Donegal Ho 2 E1 96 C3
Donegal St N1 94 B5 233 D3
Doneraile Ho SW1 258 C1
Doneraile St SW6 134 D4
Dongola Rd E13 99 B4
N17 51 C6
Dongola Rd W 5 E13 99 B4
Donington Ave IG6 57 A4
Donkey Alley SE22 162 A5
Donkey La EN1 6 A3
Donkin Ho 15 SE16 118 B2
Donne Ct SE24 161 A5
Donne Ho 7 E14 97 C1
18 N16 73 B4
14 SE14 140 D6
Donne Pl SW3 114 C2 257 B4
Mitcham CR4 203 B5
Donne Rd RM8 80 C6
Donnefield Ave HA8 26 A3
Donnelly Ct SW6 264 B4
Donnington Ct 11 NW1 71 B1
NW10 68 B1
Donnington Ho 12 SW8 137 D3
Donnington Prim Sch NW10 90 B6
Donnington Rd NW10 90 B6
Harrow HA3 43 D3
North Cheam KT4 216 A6
Donnybrook Rd SW16 181 D3
Donovan Ave N10 31 C1
Donovan Ct NW10 67 A1
SW7 256 C1
Donovan Ho 3 E1 118 C6
Doon St SE1 116 C5 251 A4
Doone Cl TW11 175 A4
Dora Ho 1 E14 97 B1
11 W11 112 D6
Dora Rd SW19 179 C6
Dora St E14 97 B1
Doradus Ct 20 SW19 156 D3
Doral Way SM5 218 D3
Doran Ct E6 100 B5
Doran Gr SE18 145 C5
Doran Manor N2 48 D4
Doran Wlk E15 76 A1
Dorando Cl W12 112 B6
Dorcas Ct 9 SW18 136 B1
Dorchester Ave N13 33 A6
Bexley DA5 168 D4
Harrow HA2 42 A3
Dorchester Cl
Northolt UB5 63 D3
St Paul's Cray BR5 190 B3
Dorchester Ct 2 E18 36 D2
1 N1 73 C1
1 N10 49 B6
N14 15 B4
NW2 68 D5
SE24 161 A6
SW1 257 D5
5 SW16 160 A2
Dorchester Dr SE24 161 A6
Feltham TW14 149 C5
Dorchester Gdns E4 35 C6
NW11 47 C5
Dorchester Gr W4 111 D1
Dorchester Mews
New Malden KT3 199 B5
Twickenham TW1 153 C5
Dorchester Prim Sch KT4 200 C1
Dorchester Rd
Cheam SM4 202 A2
North Cheam KT4 200 C1
Northolt UB5 63 D3
Dorchester Way HA3 44 B3
Dorchester Waye
Hayes UB4 84 B1
Hayes UB4 84 C1
Dorcis Ave DA7 147 A3
Dordrecht Rd W3 111 C5
Dore Ave E12 78 C3
Dore Gdns
Dagenham RM8 81 A5
Morden SM4 201 D2
Doreen Ave NW9 45 B1
Doreen Capstan Ho 3 E11 76 C5
Dorell Cl UB1 85 B2
Doria Rd SW6 135 B3
Doric Ho 7 E2 96 D5
Doric Way NW1 93 D4 232 C2
Dorien Rd SW20 178 D1
Doris Emmerton Ct SW18 136 A1
Doris Rd E7 77 A1
Ashford TW15 171 B4
Dorking Cl SE8 141 B6
North Cheam KT4 216 D6
Dorking Ct N17 34 A2
Dorking Ho SE1 262 D6
Dorland Ho SE9 167 B5
Dorlcote Rd SW18 158 C4
Dorleston Ct N1 235 D6
Dorly Cl TW17 193 C4
Dorma Trad Pk E10 52 D1
Dorman Pl 6 N9 18 A2
Dorman Way NW8 92 B6 229 C6
Dorman Wlk NW10 67 B2
Dormay St SW18 157 D6
Dormer Cl E15 76 D2
Ducks Island EN5 12 D6
Dormer's Ave UB1 85 C1
Dormers Lo EN4 2 D3
Dormers Rise UB1 85 D1
Dormer's Wells High Sch UB1 85 C1
Dormers Wells Ho UB4 84 C2
Dormer's Wells Inf Sch UB1 107 D6
Dormer's Wells Jun Sch UB1 107 D5
Dormer's Wells La UB1 107 C5
Dormstone Ho SE17 263 A3
Dormywood HA4 39 D4
Dornan Wlk E15 98 A6
Dornberg Cl SE3 143 A5
Dornberg Rd SE3 143 B5
Dorncliffe Rd SW6 135 A3
Dorney NW3 70 C1
Dorney Ct SW6 135 A2
Dorney Rise BR5 211 D5
Dorney Way TW4 151 A6
Dornfell St NW6 69 B3
Dornoch Ho 25 E3 97 B5
Dornton Rd SW12,SW17 159 C2
South Croydon CR2 221 C3
Dorothy Ave HA0 66 A1
Dorothy Barley Jun Sch RM8 80 B3
Dorothy Charrington Ho 1 SE22 162 A6
Dorothy Evans Cl DA7 147 D1
Dorothy Gdns RM8 80 B4
Dorothy Rd SW11 136 D2
Dorrien Wlk SW16 159 D2
Dorrington Ct SE25 183 C1
Dorrington Point 20 E3 97 D4
Dorrington St EC1 241 A4
Dorrit Ho 2 W11 112 D5
Dorrit Mews N18 33 C5
Dorrit St SE1 252 B2
Dorrit Way BR7 189 A4
Dorryn Ct SE26 184 D5
Dors Cl NW9 45 B1
Dorset Ave Bexley DA16 145 D1
Hayes UB4 83 C4
Southall UB2 107 C2
Dorset Bldgs EC4 241 C1
Dorset Cl NW1 237 C4
Hayes UB4 83 C4
Dorset Ct 3 W7 86 D2
3 N1 73 C1
Dorset Dr HA8 26 B4
Dorset Gdns SW16 204 B5
Dorset Ho 1 SE20 184 B2
Dorset Mans 2 W6 134 D6
Dorset Mews N3 29 C2
SW1 258 C6
Dorset Pl E15 76 B2
Dorset Rd E7 77 C1
N15 51 B5
N22 32 A2
SE9 166 A2
SW8 138 B5 270 C4
SW19 179 C1
W5 109 D3
Ashford TW15 148 A1
Harrow HA1 42 A3
Mitcham CR4 180 C1
Penge BR3 206 D6
Dorset Rise EC4 94 D1 241 C1
Dorset Road Inf Sch SE9 166 A2
Dorset Sq NW1 92 D3 237 C5
Dorset St W1 92 D2 237 D3
Dorset Way
Hillingdon UB10 82 B5
Twickenham TW2 152 B3
Dorset Waye TW5 129 B5
Dorville Cres W6 112 B3
Dorville Rd SE12 165 A6
Dothill Rd SE18 145 A5
Douai Gr TW12 174 A2
Douay Martyrs RC Sch (Annexe) The UB10 60 D3
Doughty Ct 11 E1 118 B5
Doughty Mews WC1 94 B3 240 C5
Doughty St WC1 94 B3 240 C5
Douglas 20 NW9 27 D1
Douglas Ave E17 35 C2
Wembley HA0 66 A1
West Barnes KT3 200 B5
Douglas Bader Ho N3 29 D4
Douglas Bldgs SE1 252 B2
Douglas Cl Stanmore HA7 25 A5
Wallington SM6 220 A2
Douglas Cres UB4 84 D3
Douglas Ct N3 29 D1
5 NW6 69 C1
Douglas Dr CR0 223 C5
Douglas Gracey Ho SW18 157 A4
Douglas Ho SW15 156 A5
Isleworth TW1 153 B6
Douglas Johnstone Ho SW6 264 C5
Douglas Mews NW2 69 A5
Douglas Rd E4 20 C3
5 E16 99 A2
N1 73 A1
N22 32 C2
NW6 91 B6
Bexley DA16 146 B4
Hounslow TW3 129 D2
Ilford IG3 58 A3
Kingston u T KT1 176 D1
Stanwell TW19 148 A5
Surbiton KT6 198 B1
Thames Ditton KT10 212 A6
Douglas Rd N N1 73 A2
Douglas Rd S N1 73 A2
Douglas Robinson Ct SW16 182 A3
Douglas Sq SM4 201 C3
Douglas St SW1 115 D2 259 C3
Douglas Terr E17 35 B2
Douglas Waite Ho NW6 69 D1
Douglas Way SE8 141 B5
Doulton Ho SE11 260 D4
Doulton Mews 4 NW6 69 D2
Dounesforth Gdns SW18 157 D3
Douro Pl W8 113 D3 255 D6
Douro St E3 97 C5
Douthwaite Sq 12 E1 118 A5
Dove App E6 100 A2
Dove Cl UB5 84 D3
Dove Ct Enfield EN3 18 B6
Stanwell TW19 148 A4
Dove House Gdns E4 19 C2
Dove Mews SW7 114 A2 256 B2
Dove Pk HA5 23 C3
Dove Rd N1 73 B2
Dove Row E2 96 A6
Dove Wlk SW1 258 A2
Dovecot Cl HA5 40 C4
Dovecote Gdns 8 SW14 133 B2
Dovedale Ave HA3 43 C3
Dovedale Cl DA16 146 A3
Dovedale Cotts 6 SW11 136 D3
Dovedale Ho N16 51 B2
Dovedale Rd SE22 162 B5
Dovedale Rise CR4 180 D3
Dovedon Cl N14 16 A2
Dovehouse Mead IG11 101 B5
Dovehouse St SW3 114 C1 257 A1
Dover Cl NW2 68 D6
Dover Ct SE10 141 D4
Dover Flats SE1 263 B3
Dover Gdns SM5 218 D5
Dover Ho SE5 138 D4
11 SE15 140 C6
14 SE20 184 B2
7 Beckenham BR3 185 C3
Dover House Rd SW15 156 B6
Dover Mans 17 SW9 138 C2
Dover Park Dr SW15 156 B5
Dover Patrol SE3 143 C3
Dover Rd E12 77 C6
N9 18 C2
SE18 145 A3
SE19 183 B4
Dagenham RM6 59 A3
Dover St W1 115 C5 249 A4
Dover Terr TW9 132 C3
Dover Yd W1 249 A4
Dovercourt Ave CR7 204 C5
Dovercourt Gdns HA7 26 A5
Dovercourt La SM1 218 A5
Dovercourt Rd SE22 161 D5
Doverfield Rd SW2 160 A4
Doveridge Gdns N13 32 D6
Doves Cl BR2 226 A6
Doves Yd N1 94 C6 234 A5
Doveton Ho 6 E1 96 C3
Doveton Rd CR2 221 B3
Doveton St 7 E1 96 C3
Dowanhill Rd SE6 164 B3
Dowdeswell Cl SW15 133 C1
Dowding Ho N6 49 A2
Dowding Pl HA7 25 A4
Dowding Rd UB10 60 B1
Dowe Ho SE3 142 C2
Dowell Ho SE21 161 D1
Dowes Ho 13 SW16 160 A1
Dowgate Hill EC4 252 C6
Dowland Ho EN1 5 D5
Dowlas St SE5 139 C5
Dowler Ct 8 KT2 176 B2
Dowlerville Rd BR6 227 D2
Dowling Ho DA17 125 B3
Dowman Cl 2 SW19 179 D3
Down Barns Rd HA4 62 D5
Down Cl UB5 84 B5
Down Hall Rd KT2 175 D2
Down Lane Jun Sch N17 34 A1
Down Pl W6 112 B1
Down Rd TW11 175 B4
Down St W1 115 B5 248 C3
East Molesey KT8 195 C4
Down St Mews W1 248 C3
Down Way UB5 84 B4
Downage NW4 46 C6
Downalong WD2 8 B3
Downbarton Ho 11 SW9 138 C4
Downbury Mews 13 SW18 157 C6
Downderry Prim Sch BR1 186 C6
Downderry Rd BR1 186 C6
Downe Cl DA16 146 C5
Downe Ho 9 SE7 143 C6
Downe Manor Prim Sch UB5 84 B4
Downe Rd CR4 180 D1
Downend SE18 144 D5
Downend Ct 8 SE15 139 C6
Downer's Cotts SW4 137 C1
Downes Cl TW1 153 B5
Downes Ct N21 16 C3
Downey Ho 6 E1 96 D3
Downfield KT4 200 A1
Downfield Cl W9 91 D3
Downfield Ho KT3 199 B1
Downham Ct N1 73 B1
Downham Ent Ctr SE6 164 D2
Downham La BR1 186 B5
Downham Rd N1 73 B1
Downham Way BR1 186 C6
Downhills Ave N17 51 B6
Downhills Jun & Inf Schs N15 51 B5
Downhills Park Rd N17 51 A6
Downhills Way N17 33 A1
Downhurst Ave NW7 27 B5
Downhurst Ct NW4 46 C6
Downing Cl HA2 42 A6
Downing Ct N12 29 D5
Downing Dr UB6 86 C6
Downing Ho 4 SW15 156 A6
3 SW19 179 C3
2 W10 90 D1
Downing Rd RM9 81 B1
Downing St* SW1 116 A4 250 A2
Downings E6 100 C1
Downland Cl N20 14 A3
Downland Ct E11 76 C6
Downleys Cl SE9 166 B2
Downman Rd SE9 144 A2
Downs Ave
Chislehurst West BR7 188 B5
Pinner HA5 41 B2
Downs Bridge Rd BR3 186 B2
Downs Ct 16 E8 74 B3
12 SW19 178 D3
Downs Hill BR2,BR3 186 B2
Downs La 3 E5 74 B4
Downs Park Rd E5,E8 74 A3
Downs Rd E5,N16 74 A4
Beckenham BR3 185 D1
Enfield EN1 5 C1
South Norwood CR7 183 A2
Downs Side JMI Sch E5 74 A4
Downs The SW19,SW20 178 D3
Downs View TW7 131 A4
Downs View Lo 9 KT6 198 A3
Downsell Jun & Inf Schs E15 76 B4
Downsell Rd E15 76 B4
Downsfield Rd E17 53 A3
Downshall Ave IG3 57 C3
Downshall Ct IG3 57 C3
Downshall Jun Sch IG1 57 C2
Downshall Prim Sch
Ilford IG3 57 C2
Ilford IG3 58 A3
Downshire Hill NW3 70 B4
Downside 2 SW15 157 A6
Twickenham TW1 152 D1
Downside Cl SW19 180 A4
Downside Cres NW3 70 C3
W13 87 A3
Downside Rd SM2 218 C2
Downside Wlk UB5 85 B4
Downsview Gdns SE19 183 A3
Downsview Prim Sch SE19 183 A3
Downsview Rd SE19 183 A3
Downsview Sch E5 74 B4
Downsway BR6 227 C3
Downsway The SM2 218 A1
Downton Ave SW2 160 B2
Downtown Rd SE16 119 A4
Downway N12 30 C3
Dowrey St N1 234 A6
Dowsett Rd N17 34 A1
Dowson Cl SE5 139 B1
Dowson Ct SE13 142 B2
Dowson Ho 7 E1 96 D1
Doyce St SE1 252 A2
Doyle Gdns NW10 90 B6
Doyle Ho W3 110 D4
Doyle Rd SE25 206 A5
D'Oyley St SW1 258 A4
Doynton St N19 71 B6
Dr Johnson Ave SW17 159 B1
Dr Johnson's House EC4 241 B1
Dr Triplett's CE Prim Sch UB3 83 D1
Draco St SE17 139 A6
Dragon Yd WC1 240 B2
Dragonfly Cl E13 99 B4
Dragoon Rd SE8 119 B1
Dragor Rd NW10 89 A3
Drake Cl 30 SE16 118 D4
Drake Cres SE28 102 C1
Drake Croft N16 73 B6
Drake Ct SE19 183 D5
5 W12 112 B4
Kingston u T KT5 198 B5
Drake Ho 17 E1 96 C2
2 E14 119 A6
Drake Rd SE4 141 C2
Chessington KT9 214 C3
Harrow HA2 63 B6
Mitcham CR4 203 A3
Thornton Heath CR0 204 B2
Drake St WC1 240 C3
Enfield EN2 5 B4
Drakefell Rd SE4,SE14 140 D2
Drakefield Rd SW17 159 A1
Drakeley Ct N5 72 D4
Drakes Ct SE23 162 C3
Drakes Ctyd NW6 69 B1
Drakes Wlk E6 100 B6
Drakewood Rd SW16 181 D3
Draldo Ho 6 SW15 157 A6
Draper Cl DA17 125 B2
Draper Ct BR1 210 A5
Draper Ho SE1 261 D4
Draper Pl N1 234 D6
Drapers Almshouses 4 E3 97 C4
Draper's Cottage Homes NW7 28 A6
Drapers Gdns EC2 242 D2
Drapers Rd E15 76 B4
N17 51 D6
Enfield EN2 4 D4
Drappers Way 8 SE16 118 A2
Drawell Cl SE18 123 C1
Drax Ave SW20 178 A3
Draxmont SW19 179 A4
Dray Gdns SW2 160 B6
Draycot Rd E11 55 B2
Tolworth KT6 198 C1
Draycott Ave SW3 114 C2 257 B3
Kenton HA3 43 C3
Draycott Cl HA3 43 B3
Draycott Ct SW11 267 A2
Draycott Ho SW3 257 C3
Draycott Pl SW3 114 D2 257 C3
Draycott Terr SW3 114 D2 257 D3
Draymans Way TW7 130 D2
Drayside Mews UB2 107 B4
Drayson Mews W8 113 C4 245 B1
Drayton Ave W13 109 A6
Bromley BR6 210 D1
Drayton Bridge Rd W7,W13 108 D6
W13 87 A1
Drayton Cl
Hounslow TW4 151 B6
Ilford IG1 57 B1
Drayton Ct SW10 256 B1
Tolworth KT5 214 D6
West Drayton UB7 104 B2
Drayton Gdns N21 16 D4
SW10 114 A1 256 B1
W13 109 A6
West Drayton UB7 104 A4
Drayton Gn W13 109 A6
Drayton Gr W13 109 A6
Drayton Green Prim Sch W13 109 A6
Drayton Green Rd W13 109 B6
Drayton Green Sta W7 86 D1
Drayton Ho E11 54 B1
14 SE5 139 B5
Drayton Manor High Sch W7 86 D1
Drayton Park Prim Sch N5 72 C3
Drayton Park Sta N5 72 C3
Drayton Pk N5,N7 72 C4
Drayton Rd E11 54 B1
N17 33 C1
NW10 89 D6
W13 109 B6
Croydon CR0 220 D6
Drayton Sch The N15 52 A3
Drayton Waye HA3 43 B3
Dreadnought St SE10 120 C3
Drenon Sq UB3 105 D6
Dresden Cl NW6 69 D2
Dresden Ho SE11 260 D4
5 SW11 137 A3
Dresden Rd N19 49 D1
Dressington Ave SE4 163 C5
Drew Ave NW7 29 A4
Drew Gdns UB6 64 D2
Drew Ho 12 SW16 160 A1
Drew Prim Sch E16 122 A5
Drew Rd E16 121 D5
E16 122 A5
Drewery Ct SE3 142 C2
Drewett Ho 19 E1 96 A1
Drewstead Rd SW16 159 D2
Driffield Ct 4 NW9 27 C2
Driffield Rd E3 97 A5
Drift The BR2 225 D5
Driftway Ho 15 E3 97 B5
Driftway The CR4 181 A2
Drinkwater Ho 11 SE5 139 B5
Drinkwater Rd HA2 63 D6
Drive Mans SW6 135 A3
Drive The E4 20 B4
E17 53 D6
E18 55 A6
N3 29 C3
N6 48 D4
N7 72 B2
N11 31 D4
NW10 89 D6
NW11 47 A2
SW19,SW20 178 C3
W3 89 A1
Ashford TW15 171 B3
Barking IG11 79 D1
Beckenham BR3 185 C2
Bexley DA5 168 D4
Buckhurst Hill IG9 21 C4
Chislehurst BR7 189 D2
Edgware HA8 26 C5
Enfield EN2 5 B4
Erith DA8 147 D6
Feltham TW14 150 C4
Harrow HA2 41 C2
High Barnet EN5 1 A2
Hounslow TW3,TW7 130 B3
Ickenham UB10 60 A5
Kingston u T KT2 177 A3
Morden SM4 202 B4

Drive The *continued*
New Barnet EN5 14 A5
Orpington BR6 227 D6
Redbridge IG1 56 B2
Sidcup DA14 190 B6
South Norwood CR7 205 B5
St Paul's Cray BR7 211 D6
Surbiton KT6 198 A2
Thames Ditton KT10 196 A1
Wembley HA9 67 A6
West Ewell KT19 215 D2
West Wickham BR4 208 B2
IG11 80 A2
Droitwich Cl SE26 162 A1
Dromey Gdns HA3 24 D3
Dromore Rd SW15 157 A5
Dron Ho E1 96 C2
Dronfield Gdns RM8 80 C3
Droop St W10 91 A3
Drovers Ct SE13 142 A2
3 Kingston u T KT1 176 A1
Drovers Pl SE15 140 B5
Drovers Rd CR2 221 B3
Druce Rd SE21 161 C5
Druid St SE1 117 D4 253 C1
Druids Way BR2 208 B5
Drum St E1 243 D2
Drumaline Ridge KT4 215 C6
Drummer Lo N7 72 B5
Drummond Castle Ct E7 76 D4
Drummond Cres
NW1 93 D4 232 C2
Drummond Ct N12 30 C3
Drummond Ctr CR0 221 A6
Drummond Dr HA7 24 D3
Drummond Gate SW1 259 D2
Drummond Ho 12 E2 96 A5
N2 30 A1
11 SE18 122 C2
Drummond Rd E11 55 C3
SE16 118 B3
Croydon CR0 221 A6
Drummond St
NW1 93 C3 239 A6
Drummonds Pl TW9 132 A1
Drummonds The IG9 21 B2
Drury Cres CR0 220 C6
Drury Ho SW8 269 A2
Drury Lane WC2 94 A1 240 B1
Drury Rd HA1 42 A2
Drury Way NW10 67 B3
Dryad St SW15 134 D2
Dryburgh Gdns NW9 44 C6
Dryburgh Ho SW1 258 D2
Dryburgh Mans SW15 134 C2
Dryburgh Rd SW15 134 C2
Dryden Ave W7 86 D1
Dryden Ct SE11 261 B3
11 Richmond TW10 175 D6
Dryden Ho 16 N16 73 C5
6 SE5 139 C4
Bromley BR2 209 D4
Dryden Rd SW19 180 A4
Bexley DA16,SE18 145 D4
Enfield EN1 17 D5
Harrow HA3 24 D2
Dryden St WC2 240 B1
Dryer's Bldgs EC1 241 A3
Dryfield Cl NW10 67 A2
Dryfield Rd HA8 27 A4
Dryfield Wlk 1 SE8 141 C6
Dryhill Rd DA17 147 B6
Dryland Ave 5 BR6 227 D4
Drylands Rd N8 50 A3
Drysdale Ave E4 19 D5
Drysdale Flats 3 E8 73 D3
Drysdale Ho 20 E2 95 C4
Drysdale Pl N1 95 C4
Drysdale St N1 95 C4
Du Burstow Terr W7 108 C4
Du Cane Ct SW12 159 A3
Du Cane Rd W12 90 A1
Du Cros Dr HA7 25 D4
Du Cros Rd W3 111 C5
Du Maurier Ho 2 NW3 70 D3
Dublin Ave E8 96 A6
Ducal St 25 E2 95 D4
Ducane Cl W12 90 C1
Ducavel Ho SW2 160 B3
Duchess Cl N11 31 B5
Sutton SM1 218 A4
Duchess Gr IG9 21 B2
Duchess Mews W1 238 D3
Duchess of Bedford Ho
W8 245 A2
Duchess of Bedford's Wlk
W8 113 C4 245 A1
Duchess St W1 93 B2 238 D3
Duchy Rd EN4 2 B5
Duchy St SE1 116 C5 251 B4
Ducie Ho 8 SE7 143 C6
2 SW15 156 C6
Ducie St SW4 138 B1
Duck La W1 239 C1
Duck Lees La EN3 7 A1
Duckett Mews N4 50 D3
Duckett Rd N4 50 D3
Duckett St E1 97 A2
Ducks Hill Rd HA4,HA6 39 A5
Duck's Wlk TW1 153 C6
Dudden Hill La NW10 67 D3
Duddington Cl SE9 187 D6
Dudley Ave HA3,HA7 43 C6
Dudley Ct 9 E11 55 A4
NW11 47 B5
W1 237 C1
WC2 240 A2
Wembley HA0 65 D3
Dudley Dr Ruislip HA4 62 B3
West Barnes SM4 201 A2
Dudley Gdns W13 109 B4
Harrow HA2 42 B1
Dudley Ho 14 SW9 138 C3
W2 236 C3
Dudley Rd E17 35 C1
N3 29 D1
NW6 91 B5
SW19 179 C4
Ashford TW15 170 B6
East Bedfont TW14 149 B3
Harrow HA2 64 A6
Ilford IG1 78 D4
Kingston u T KT1 198 B6
Richmond TW9 132 B3
Southall UB2 106 D3
Walton-on-T KT12 194 A2
Dudley St W2 236 C3
Dudlington Rd E5 74 C6
Dudmaston Mews SW3 256 D2
Dudset La TW5 128 A4
Duff St E14 97 D1
Duffell Ho SE11 260 D1
Dufferin Ave EC1 242 C5
Dufferin Ct EC1 242 C5
Dufferin St EC1 95 A3 242 B5
Duffield Cl HA1 42 D4
Duffield Dr N15 51 D5
Duffield Ho N4 51 A2
Dufour's Pl W1 239 B1
Dugdale Ho 10 N7 71 D3
Duke Humphrey Rd
SE3 142 C3
Duke Of Cambridge Cl
TW2 152 B5
Duke Of Edinburgh Rd
SM1 218 B6
Duke of Wellington Pl
SW1,W1 248 B2
Duke of York St SW1 249 B4
Duke Rd W4 111 B1
Ilford IG6 57 B5
Duke Shore Wharf E14 119 B6
Duke St W1 93 A1 238 B1
Richmond TW10,TW9 153 D6
Sutton SM1 218 B4
Duke St Hill SE1 252 D4
Duke St Mans W1 238 B1
Duke St St James's
SW1 115 C5 249 B4
Dukes Ave N3 29 D2
N10 49 C6
Edgware HA8 26 B5
Harrow HA1 42 C5
Harrow HA2,HA5 41 B3
Hounslow TW4 129 A1
New Malden KT3 199 D6
Northolt UB5 63 A1
Richmond KT2,TW10 175 D6
Duke's Ave W4 111 B1
Dukes Cl Ashford TW15 171 A6
Hampton TW12 173 B5
Dukes Ct E6 100 C6
SE13 142 A3
SE22 162 B6
W13 87 B2
Beckenham BR3 207 A6
Dukes Gate 4 W4 111 A2
Dukes Green Ave TW14 150 A6
Dukes Head Yd N6 49 B1
Duke's Ho SW1 259 D4
Dukes La W8 113 D4 245 C2
Dukes Mews N10 49 B6
Duke's Mews W1 238 B2
Duke's Pl EC3 95 C1 243 B1
Dukes Point N6 49 B1
Dukes Rd E6 100 C6
W3 88 C3
Duke's Rd WC1 93 D4 232 D1
Dukes Ride UB10 60 A4
Dukes Way BR4 224 C5
Duke's Yd W1 248 B6
Dukesthorpe Rd SE26 184 D6
Dulas St N4 50 B1
Dulford St W11 113 A6 244 A6
Dulka Rd SW11 158 D6
Dulverton NW1 232 B5
Dulverton Ct 12 KT6 198 A4
Dulverton Mans WC1 240 D5
Dulverton Prim Sch
DA15 167 B2
Dulverton Rd
New Eltham DA15,DA15 167 B2
Ruislip HA4 62 A6
Dulwich Bsns Ctr SE23 162 D3
Dulwich Coll (Endowed)
SE21 161 C2
Dulwich Coll Picture Gall
SE21 161 C4
Dulwich Coll Prep Sch
SE21 161 C1
Dulwich Comm SE21 161 C3
Dulwich Ct SE22 162 B3
Dulwich Hamlet Jun & Inf
Sch SE21 161 B5
Dulwich High Sch for Boys
SE24 161 B6
Dulwich Hospl SE22 139 C1
Dulwich Mead SE24 161 A5
Dulwich Mews 1 SE22 139 D1
Dulwich Oaks The
SE21 161 D1
Dulwich Rd SE24 160 D5
Dulwich Village SE21 161 C5
Dulwich Village CE Inf Sch
SE21 161 C5
Dulwich Wood Ave
SE19 183 C5
Dulwich Wood Pk SE19 183 C6
Dumain Ct SE11 261 C3
Dumbarton Ct 16 SW2 160 A4
Dumbarton Rd SW2 160 A5
Dumbleton Cl KT2 176 D2
Dumbreck Rd SE9 144 C2
Dumont Rd N16 73 C5
Dumphreys Ho 5 SW4 159 D4
Dumpton Pl NW1 71 A1
Dunally Pk TW17 193 B2
Dunbar Ave SW16 182 C1
Beckenham BR3 207 A5
Dagenham RM10 81 C5
Dunbar Cl UB4 84 A2
Dunbar Ct 3 N12 29 D6
Carshalton SM1 218 B3
Walton-on-T KT12 194 C1
Dunbar Gdns RM10 81 D3
Dunbar Rd E7 77 A2
N22 32 D2
Kingston u T KT3 199 A5
Dunbar St SE27 161 A1
Dunblane Rd SE9 144 A3
Dunboe Pl TW17 193 A2
Dunboyne Rd NW3 70 D3
Dunbridge Ho 7 SW15 155 D5
Dunbridge St E2 96 B3
Duncan Cl EN5 2 A1
Duncan Ct N21 16 D3
Duncan Gr W3 89 C1
Duncan Ho 3 NW3 70 D1
Duncan Rd E8 96 B6
Richmond TW9 132 A1
Duncan St N1 94 D5 234 C4
Duncan Terr N1 94 D5 234 C4
Duncannon Ho SW1 259 D1
Duncannon St WC2 250 A5
Dunch St 30 E1 96 B1
Dunchurch Ho RM10 81 C1
Duncombe Hill SE23 163 A4
Duncombe Ho 7 SW19 156 D3
Duncombe Prim Sch
N19 50 A1
Duncombe Rd N19 49 D1
Duncrievie Rd SE13 164 B5
Duncroft SE18 145 C5
Dundalk Ho 2 E1 96 C1
Dundalk Rd SE4 141 A2
Dundas Gdns KT8 195 D6
Dundas Ho 12 E2 96 C5
Dundas Rd SE15 140 C3
Dundee Ct 36 E1 118 B5
Dundee Ho W9 229 A2
Dundee Rd E13 99 B5
SE25 206 B4
Dundee St E1 118 B5
Dundee Way EN3 7 A2
Dundee Wharf E14 119 B6
Dundela Gdns KT17,KT4 216 B4
Dundonald Cl 6 E6 100 A1
Dundonald Prim Sch
SW19 179 B3
Dundonald Rd NW10 90 D6
SW19 179 B3
Dundonald Road Sta
SW19 179 B3
Dundry Ho 8 SE26 162 A1
Duneaves HA1 64 C5
Dunedin Rd E10 75 D5
Ilford IG1 57 A1
Dunedin Way UB4 84 C3
Dunelm Gr SE27 161 A1
Dunelm St E1 96 D1
Dunfield Gdns SE6 185 D5
Dunfield Rd SE6 185 D5
Dunford Rd N7 72 B4
Dungarvan Ave SW15 134 A1
Dungeness Ho SW18 136 A1
Dunheved Cl CR7 204 C3
Dunheved Rd N CR7 204 C3
Dunheved Rd S CR7 204 C3
Dunheved Rd W CR7 204 C3
Dunhill Point 12 SW15 156 B3
Dunholme Gn N9 17 D1
Dunholme La N9 17 D1
Dunholme Rd N9 17 D1
Dunkeld Ho 13 E14 98 B1
Dunkeld Rd SE25 205 B5
Dagenham RM8 80 C6
Dunkery Rd SE9 166 A1
Dunkirk St 12 SE27 183 A6
Dunlace Rd E5 74 D4
Dunleary Cl TW4 151 B4
Dunley Dr CR0 224 A2
Dunlin Ct 11 SE21 161 B2
Dunlin Ho 13 SE16 118 D2
Dunloe Ave N17 51 B6
Dunloe Ct 7 E2 95 D5
Dunloe St E2 95 D5
Dunlop Pl SE16 117 D3 263 D5
Dunlop Point 10 E16 121 B5
Dunmore Point 15 E2 95 D4
Dunmore Rd NW6 91 A6
SW20 178 D2
Dunmow Cl
3 Feltham TW13 173 A6
Ilford RM6 58 C4
Dunmow Ho SE11 260 D2
Dagenham RM9 102 B6
Dunmow Rd E15 76 B4
Dunmow Wlk N1 235 A6
Dunn Mead NW9 27 D3
Dunn St E8 73 D3
Dunnage Cres SE16 119 A2
Dunnet Ho 26 E3 97 B5
Dunnico Ho SE17 263 A2
Dunnock Cl N9 18 D3
Dunnock Ct 10 SE21 161 B2
Dunnock Rd E6 100 A1
Dunn's Pas WC1 240 B2
Dunollie Pl NW5 71 C3
Dunollie Rd NW5 71 C3
Dunoon Gdns SE23 162 D4
Dunoon Ho N1 233 C5
Dunoon Rd SE23 162 C4
Dunraven Dr EN2 4 C3
Dunraven Ho 12 TW9 132 B4
Dunraven Lower Sch
SW16 160 B1
Dunraven Rd W12 112 A5
Dunraven St
W1 114 D6 247 D6
Dunraven Upper Sch
SW16 160 B1
Dunrobin Ct NW3 69 D3
Dunsany Rd W14 112 D3
Dunsfold Ct 9 SM2 217 D1
Dunsfold Ho 4 SW2 160 B4
10 Kingston u T KT2 176 D4
Dunsfold Way CR0 223 D1
Dunsford Ct 4 HA5 23 B3
Dunsford Way SW15 156 B5
Dunsmore Cl Bushey WD2 8 B5
Hayes UB4 85 A3
Dunsmore Rd KT12 194 B3
Dunsmore Way WD2 8 B5
Dunsmure Rd N16 51 C1
Dunstable Ct 3 SE3 143 A5
Dunstable Mews W1 238 B4
Dunstable Rd
East Molesey KT8 195 B5
Richmond TW10,TW9 132 A1
Dunstall Ho 9 SE15 140 A4
Dunstall Rd SW19,SW20 178 C4
Dunstall Way KT8 195 D6
Dunstall Welling Est
DA16 146 B3
Dunstan Cl 2 N2 48 A6
Dunstan Glade BR5 211 B3
Dunstan Ho SE4 141 B3
Dunstan Hos 5 E1 96 C2
Dunstan Rd NW11 47 C1
Dunstan's Gr SE22 162 B5
Dunstan's Rd SE22 162 A5
Dunster Ave SM4 200 D1
Dunster Ct EC3 253 B6
Dunster Dr NW9 45 A1
Dunster Gdns NW6 69 B1
Dunster Ho SE6 163 D1
Dunster Way HA2 63 A5
Dunsterville Way SE1 252 D1
Dunston Rd E8 95 D6
SW11 137 A3
Dunston St E8 95 D6
Dunton Cl KT6 198 A1
Dunton Ct 5 SE26 162 B2
Dunton Ho 14 SW16 160 A1
Dunton Rd E10 53 D2
SE1 117 D2 263 C3
Duntshill Rd SW18 157 D3
Dunvegan Cl KT8 195 D5
Dunvegan Rd SE9 144 B1
Dunwich Rd DA7 147 B4
Dunworth Mews W11 91 B1
Duplex Ride SW1 247 D1
Dupont Rd SW20 178 D1
Dupont St E14 97 A2
Duppas Ave CR0 220 D4
Duppas Cl TW17 193 B4
Duppas Ct CR0 220 D5
Duppas Hill La CR0 220 D4
Duppas Hill Rd CR0 220 D4
Duppas Hill Terr CR0 220 D5
Duppas Jun Sch CR0 220 D3
Duppas Rd CR0 220 D5
Dupree Rd SE7 121 B1
Dura Den Cl BR3 185 D3
Durand Cl SM5 202 D1
Durand Gdns
SW9 138 B4 270 D1
Durand Prim Sch
SW9 138 B4 270 D1
Durand Way NW10 67 A1
Durant St E2 96 A4
Durants Park Ave EN3 6 D1
Durants Rd EN3 6 D1
Durants Sch EN3 6 C4
Durban Ct E7 77 D1
Durban Ho 28 W12 112 B6
Durban Rd E15 98 C4
E17 35 B2
N17 33 D4
SE27 183 B6
Beckenham BR3 185 B1
Ilford IG2 57 C1
Durbin Ho 18 N9 18 A1
Durbin Rd KT9 214 B4
Durdans Ho 1 NW1 71 C1
Durdans Park Prim Sch
UB1 85 B2
Durdans Rd UB1 85 B1
Durell Gdns RM9 80 D3
Durell Rd RM9 80 D3
Durfey Ho SE5 139 B5
Durford Cres SW15 156 B3
Durham Ave
Beckenham BR2 208 D5
Hounslow TW5 107 B1
Woodford IG8 37 D5
Durham Cl SW20 178 B1
Durham Ct 3 NW6 91 C5
Teddington TW11 174 C6
Durham Hill BR1 186 D6
Durham Ho 3 IG11 80 A1
Durham House St WC2 250 B5
Durham Pl SW3 257 C1
Ilford IG1 79 A4
Durham Rd E12 77 D4
E16 98 C3
N2 48 D6
N4,N7 72 B6
N9 18 A2
SW20 178 B2
W5 109 D3
Beckenham BR2 208 D6
Feltham TW14 150 C4
Harrow HA1 41 D4
Sidcup DA14 190 B5
Durham Rise SE18 123 B1
Durham Row E1 97 A2
Durham St SE11 138 B6 270 C6
Durham Terr W2 91 D1
Durley Ave HA5 41 A3
Durley Rd N16 51 C2
Durlock Ho 16 SW9 138 C4
Durlston Rd E5 74 A6
Kingston u T KT2 176 A4
Durnford Ho SE6 163 D1
Durnford St N15 51 C4
3 SE10 142 A6
Durning Rd SE19 183 B5
Durnsford Ave SW18,
SW19 157 C2
Durnsford Rd N11 31 D3
SW18,SW19 157 C1
Durrant Ct HA3 24 C2
Durrant Way BR6 227 B3
Durrell Rd SW6 264 C1
Durrell Way TW17 193 B3
Durrels Ho W14 254 D4
Durrington Ave SW20 178 C3
Durrington Park Rd
SW20 178 C2
Durrington Rd E5 75 A4
Durrington Twr 3
SW8 137 C3
Durrisdeer Ho NW2 69 B4
Dursley Cl SE3 143 C3
Dursley Ct 2 SE15 139 C5
Dursley Gdns SE3 143 D4
Dursley Rd SE3 143 C3
Durston NW5 71 A3
Durston House Middleton's
Sch W5 87 D1
Durston House Prep Sch
W5 87 D1
Durward St E1 96 B2
Durweston Mews W1 237 D4
Durweston St W1 237 D3
Dury Rd EN5 1 B3
Dutch Gdns KT2 176 D4
Dutch Yd SW18 157 C6
Dutton Ho SW2 160 D3
Dutton St SE10 142 A4
Duxberry Cl BR2 210 A4
Duxford 21 KT1 176 C1
Duxford Ho 12 SE2 124 D4
Dwight Ct SW6 135 A3
Dycer Ho 19 E9 74 D2
Dye House La E3 97 C6
Dyer Ho TW12 173 D2
Dyers Hall Rd E11 54 C1
E11 76 B6
Dyer's La SW15 134 B1
Dyke Ct E17 53 B4
Dykes Ct 11 SW2 160 B3
Dykes Way BR2 208 D6
Dylan Cl WD6 9 D4
Dylan Rd 2 SE24 138 D1
Belvedere DA17 125 C3
Dylan Thomas Ho N8 50 B5
Dylways SE5 139 B1
Dymchurch Cl
Orpington BR6 227 C4
Redbridge IG5 56 C6
Dymchurch Ho 12 E5 74 B3
Dymes Path SW19 156 D2
Dymock Ct 3 SE15 139 C5
Dymock St SW6 135 D2
Dyne Rd NW6 69 B1
Dyneley Rd SE12 165 C1
Dynevor Rd N16 73 D5
Richmond TW10 154 A6
Dynham Rd NW6 69 C1
Dyott St WC1 239 D2
WC1,WC2 94 A1 240 A2
Dysart Ave KT2,TW10 175 C6
Dysart Sch KT2 175 D6
Dysart St EC2 95 C3 243 A5
Dyson Ct NW2 46 C2
Wembley HA0 65 A4
Dyson Ho 3 SE10 120 D1
Dyson Rd E11 54 C3
E15 76 D2
Dyson's Rd N18 34 B4

E

Eade Rd N4 51 A2
Eagans Cl N2 48 B6
Eagle Ave RM6 59 A3
Eagle Cl SE16 118 C1
Enfield EN3 6 C1
Wallington SM6 220 A2
Eagle Ct 6 E11 55 A5
EC1 241 C4
9 SE21 161 B2
Eagle Dr NW9 27 C1
Eagle Dwellings EC1 235 B2
Eagle Hill SE19 183 B4
Eagle Ho 22 E1 96 B3
Eagle Hts 10 SW11 136 C2
Eagle La E11 55 A5
Eagle Lo E11 54 D5
NW11 47 B2
Eagle Mans N16 73 D3
Eagle Mews N1 73 C2
Eagle Pl SW1 249 B5
SW7 114 A1 256 B2
Eagle Rd HA0 65 D1
Eagle St WC1 94 B2 240 C3
Eagle Terr IG8 37 B3
Eagle Trad Est CR4 202 D3
Eagle Wharf SE1 253 C3
Eagle Wharf Rd
N1 95 A5 235 B4
Eaglesfield Rd SE18 144 D4
Eaglesfield Sch SE18 144 C4
Ealcom Ct W5 110 B5
Ealdham Prim Sch SE9 143 C1
Ealdham Sq SE9 143 C1
Ealing Almshouses W5 109 D4
Ealing Broadway Ctr
W5 109 D6
Ealing Broadway Sta
W5 109 D6
Ealing Coll W13 87 B1
Ealing Common W5 110 B6
Ealing Common Sta
W5 110 B5
Ealing Gn W5 109 D5
Ealing Hospl UB1,UB2 108 B4
Ealing Park Gdns W5 109 C2
Ealing Park Mans W5 109 D3
Ealing Rd Brentford TW8 109 D2
Northolt UB5 63 C1
Wembley HA0 66 A1
Ealing Road Trad Est
TW8 109 D1
Ealing Tertiary Coll
W3 110 D5
W5 109 D5
Southall UB1 107 A5
Ealing Village W5 88 A1
Eamann Casey Ho 34
SW9 138 C4
Eamont Cl HA4 38 D2
Eamont Ct NW8 230 B4
Eamont St NW8 92 C5 230 B4
Eardley Cres
SW5 113 C1 255 B1
Eardley Point 9 SE18 122 D2
Eardley Prim Sch SW16 181 C4
Eardley Rd SW16 181 C4
Belvedere DA17 125 C1
Earl Cl N11 31 B5
Earl Ho NW1 237 B5
Earl Rd SW14 133 A1
Earl Rise SE18 123 B2
Earl St EC2 95 C2 243 A4
Earldom Rd SW15 134 C1
Earle Gdns KT2 176 A3
Earlham Gr E7 77 A3
N22 32 B3
Earlham Prim Sch E7 76 D3
Earlham Prim Schs N22 32 C3
Earlham St WC2 94 A1 240 A1
Earlom Ho WC1 234 A1
Earl's Court Ex Ctr SW5 255 A1
Earl's Court Gdns
SW5 113 D2 255 C3
Earl's Court Rd
SW5,W8 113 C2 255 B4
Earl's Court Sq
SW5 113 D1 255 C2
Earl's Court Sta
SW5 113 C2 255 B3
Earls Cres HA1 42 C5
Earls Terr W8 254 D5
Earls Wlk W8 113 C3 255 A5
Barking RM8 80 B4
Earlsdown Ho IG11 101 B5
Earlsferry Way N1 72 A1
Earlsfield Prim Sch
SW18 158 A2
Earlsfield Rd SW18 158 A4
Earlsfield Sta SW18 158 A3
Earlshall Rd SE9 144 C1
Earlsmead HA2 63 B4
Earlsmead Fst & Mid Sch
HA2 63 B4
Earlsmead Prim Sch
N15 51 D5
Earlsmead Rd N15 51 D4
NW10 90 C4
Earlsthorpe Mews 3
SW12 159 A5
Earlsthorpe Rd SE26 184 D6
Earlstoke St EC1 234 C2
Earlston Gr E9 96 B6
Earlswood Ave CR7 204 C4
Earlswood Cl 10 SE10 120 C1
Earlswood Gdns IG5 56 C6
Earlswood Ho 2 SW2 160 B3
Earlswood St SE10 120 C1
Early Mews NW1 231 D6
Earnshaw St WC1,WC2 239 D2
Earsby St W14 254 B4
Easby Cres SM4 201 D3
Easebourne Rd RM8 80 C3
Easedale Ho TW7 152 D6
Eashing Point 5 SW15 156 B3
Easleys Mews W1 238 B2
East Acton Arc W3 89 D1
East Acton Ct W3 111 C6
East Acton La W3 111 C6

East Acton Prim Sch
W3 ... 111 C6
East Acton Sta W12 ... 89 D1
East Arbour St E1 ... 96 D1
East Ave E12 ... 78 A1
E17 ... 53 D5
NW2 ... 48 A6
Hayes UB3 ... 106 A5
Southall UB1 ... 107 B6
Wallington CR0 ... 220 B3
East Bank N16 ... 51 C2
East Barnet Main Sch
East Barnet EN4 ... 14 D5
New Barnet EN4 ... 2 B2
East Barnet Rd EN4 ... 2 B1
East Beckton District Ctr
E6 ... 100 B2
East Block 5 E1 ... 118 D6
East Churchfield Rd
W3 ... 111 B5
East Cl W5 ... 88 C3
Cockfosters EN4 ... 3 A1
Greenford UB6 ... 86 A5
East Cres N11 ... 30 D6
Enfield EN1 ... 17 D6
East Cross Ctr E15 ... 75 C2
East Cross Route E3 ... 97 C6
E9 ... 75 B3
East Croydon Sta CR0 . 221 B6
East Ct HA0 ... 65 C6
East Dr BR3 ... 208 A4
East Duck Lees La EN3 ... 7 B1
East Dulwich Gr SE22 .. 161 C6
East Dulwich Rd SE15,
SE22 ... 140 A1
East Dulwich Sta SE22 . 139 C1
East End Rd N2 ... 48 A6
N3 ... 29 C1
N3 ... 47 D6
East End Way HA5 ... 41 A6
East Entrance RM10 ... 103 D5
East Ferry Rd E14 ... 119 D2
East Finchley Sta N2 ... 48 C5
East Gate Rd SE28 ... 123 D5
East Gdns SW17 ... 180 C4
East Ham Ind Est E6 ... 100 A2
East Ham Manor Way
E6 ... 100 C1
East Ham Meml Hospl
E7 ... 77 D1
East Ham Sta E6 ... 78 A1
East Harding St EC4 ... 241 B2
East Heath Rd NW3 ... 70 B5
East Hill SW18 ... 158 A6
Wembley HA9 ... 44 C1
East India Bldgs 8 E14 119 C6
East India Dock Basin
E14 ... 120 C6
East India Dock Rd E14 119 D6
East India Dock Road Tunnel
17 E14 ... 98 B1
East India Dock Wall Rd
E14 ... 120 B6
East India Sta E14 ... 120 B6
East La SE16 ... 118 A4
Kingston u T KT1 ... 197 D6
Wembley HA0,HA9 ... 65 D5
East London Coll & Toynbee
Theatre E1 ... 95 D2 243 D3
East London Stadium E3 97 B2
East Mascalls 15 SE7 . 143 C6
East Mead HA4 ... 62 D5
East Mount St E1 ... 96 B2
East Park Cl RM6 ... 59 A4
East Pas EC1 ... 242 A4
East Pl SE27 ... 183 A6
East Point 4 SE1 ... 118 A1
East Poultry Ave EC1 .. 241 C3
East Putney Sta SW15 . 157 A6
East Ramp TW6 ... 126 D4
East Rd E15 ... 99 A6
N1 ... 95 B4 235 D2
N2 ... 30 C2
SW19 ... 180 A4
Bexley DA16 ... 146 B3
Burnt Oak HA8 ... 27 A2
Dagenham RM6 ... 59 A4
East Barnet EN4 ... 15 A3
East Bedfont TW14 ... 149 B4
Enfield EN3 ... 6 C5
Kingston u T KT2 ... 176 A2
West Drayton UB7 ... 104 C2
East Rochester Way
DA5,DA15,DA16,SE9 ... 168 B6
East Row E11 ... 55 A3
W10 ... 91 A3
East Sheen Ave SW14 .. 133 B1
East Sheen Prim Sch
SW14 ... 133 C1
East Smithfield
E1 ... 117 D6 253 D5
East St SE17 ... 117 B1 262 C2
Barking IG11 ... 79 A1
Bexleyheath DA7 ... 147 C1
Brentford TW8 ... 131 C5
Bromley BR1 ... 187 A1
East Surrey Gr SE15 ... 139 D5
East Tenter St
E1 ... 95 D1 243 D1
East Terr DA15 ... 167 C3
East Thamesmead Bsns Pk
DA18 ... 125 B4
East Towers HA5 ... 40 D3
East View E4 ... 36 A5
NW3 ... 70 B6
East View *continued*
Hadley EN5 ... 1 B2
East Way Croydon CR0 .. 223 A5
Hayes UB3 ... 106 A5
Ruislip HA4 ... 40 A1
East Wickham Jun Sch
DA16 ... 146 A4
East Wickham Prim Sch
DA16 ... 145 D4
East Wlk East Barnet EN4 . 15 A3
Hayes UB3 ... 106 A5
East Woodside DA5 ... 169 A3
Eastbank Rd TW12 ... 174 A5
Eastbourne Ave W3 ... 89 B1
Eastbourne Gdns SW14 133 A2
Eastbourne Mews
W2 ... 92 A1 236 B2
Eastbourne Rd E6 ... 100 C4
E15 ... 98 C6
N15 ... 51 C3
SW17 ... 181 A4
W4 ... 133 A6
Brentford TW8 ... 109 D1
Feltham TW13 ... 150 D2
Eastbourne Terr
W2 ... 92 A1 236 B2
Eastbournia Ave N9 ... 18 B1
Eastbrook Ave N9 ... 18 C4
Eastbrook Rd SE3 ... 143 B4
Eastbury Ave
Barking IG11 ... 101 C6
Enfield EN1 ... 5 D4
HA6 ... 22 A5
Eastbury Comp (Lower) Sch
IG11 ... 79 B1
Eastbury Comp Sch
IG11 ... 79 D1
Eastbury Ct
Barking IG11 ... 101 C6
New Barnet EN5 ... 14 A6
Eastbury Gr W4 ... 111 C1
Eastbury Inf Sch IG11 .. 79 D1
Eastbury Rd E6 ... 100 C3
Kingston u T KT2 ... 176 A3
Eastbury Sq IG11 ... 101 D6
Eastbury Terr E1 ... 96 D3
Eastcastle St W1 93 C1 239 B2
Eastcheap EC3 . 117 C6 253 A6
Eastchurch Rd TW6 ... 127 C2
Eastchurch Road Rdbt
TW6 ... 127 C3
Eastcombe Ave SE7 ... 143 B6
Eastcote BR6 ... 211 D1
Eastcote Ave
East Molesey KT8 ... 195 C4
Greenford UB6 ... 65 A3
Harrow HA2 ... 64 A6
Eastcote Ind Est HA4 ... 40 C2
Eastcote La Harrow HA2 . 63 C5
Northolt UB5 ... 63 B2
Eastcote La N UB5 ... 63 C2
Eastcote Pl HA5 ... 40 B3
Eastcote Prim Sch
DA16 ... 145 B2
Eastcote Rd Bexley DA16 145 B3
Harrow HA2 ... 64 A5
Pinner HA5 ... 40 D4
Ruislip HA4 ... 40 A3
Eastcote St SW9 ... 138 B3
Eastcote Sta HA5 ... 40 C2
Eastcote View HA5 ... 40 C3
Eastcourt Ind Sch IG3 .. 58 A1
Eastcroft Rd KT19 ... 215 C1
Eastdown Ho E8 ... 74 A4
Eastdown Pk SE13 ... 142 B1
Eastern Ave E11 ... 55 C3
Ilford IG2 ... 57 B3
Pinner HA5 ... 40 D2
Redbridge IG1,IG2,IG4, ... 56 B3
Eastern Ave W RM7 ... 59 C5
Eastern Perimeter Rd
TW14 ... 127 D3
Eastern Rd E13 ... 99 B5
E17 ... 54 A4
N2 ... 48 D5
N22 ... 32 A2
SE4 ... 141 C1
Eastern Way SE28 ... 124 B4
Easternville Gdns IG2 .. 57 A3
Eastfield Gdns RM10 ... 81 C4
Eastfield Prim Sch EN3 . 6 D5
Eastfield Rd E17 ... 53 C5
N8 ... 50 A6
Dagenham RM9 ... 81 B4
Dagenham RM10 ... 81 C4
Enfield EN3 ... 6 D5
Eastfields HA5 ... 40 C4
Eastfields High Sch
CR4 ... 181 B1
Eastfields Rd W3 ... 89 A2
Mitcham CR4 ... 181 A1
Eastgate Cl SE28 ... 102 D1
Eastglade HA5 ... 41 B6
Eastham Cl EN5 ... 13 B6
Eastholm NW11 ... 47 D5
Eastholme UB3 ... 106 A5
Eastlake Ho NW8 ... 236 D5
Eastlake Rd SE5 ... 139 A3
Eastlands Cres SE21 ... 161 D5
Eastlea Com Sch E16 ... 98 C3
Eastleigh Ave HA2 ... 63 D6
Eastleigh Cl NW2 ... 67 C5
Sutton SM2 ... 217 D1
Eastleigh Rd E17 ... 35 B1
Hatton TW6 ... 127 D2
Eastleigh Way TW14 ... 150 A3
Eastleigh Wlk 9 SW15 156 A4
Eastman Dental Hospl
WC1 ... 94 B4 240 C6
Eastman Ho 7 SW4 ... 159 C5
Eastman Rd W3 ... 111 B4
Eastmead IG3 ... 58 A2
Eastmead Ave UB6 ... 85 D4
Eastmead Cl BR1 ... 188 A1
Eastmearn Rd SE21,
SE27 ... 161 A2
Eastmont Rd KT10 ... 212 D6
Eastmoor Pl SE7 ... 121 D3
Eastmoor St SE7 ... 121 D3
Eastney Rd CR0 ... 204 D1
Eastney St SE10 ... 120 B1
Eastnor Rd SE9 ... 167 A3
Easton Ho 4 SE27 ... 160 D1
Easton St WC1 ... 241 A6
Eastpole Cotts N14 ... 3 D1
Eastry Ave BR2 ... 208 D3
Eastry Ho SW8 ... 270 A3
Eastry Rd DA8 ... 147 C5
Eastside Rd NW11 ... 47 B5
Eastvale W3 ... 111 D5
Eastview Ave SE18 ... 145 C5
Eastville Ave NW11 ... 47 A3
Eastway E3,E9 ... 97 A6
E9,E10 ... 75 C4
E11 ... 55 B4
Hayes BR2 ... 209 A2
Merton SM4,SW20 ... 201 A5
Wallington SM6 ... 219 C4
Eastway Pk E9 ... 75 B2
Eastwell Cl BR3 ... 185 A2
Eastwell Ho SE1 ... 262 D6
Eastwick Ct 2 SW19 ... 156 D3
Eastwood Cl E18 ... 37 A1
7 N17 ... 34 B3
Eastwood Rd E18 ... 37 A1
N10 ... 31 A1
Ilford IG3 ... 58 A2
West Drayton UB7 ... 104 C4
Eastwood St SW16 ... 181 C4
Eatington Rd E10 ... 54 B4
Eaton Cl SW1 ... 258 A3
Stanmore HA7 ... 25 B6
Eaton Ct W5 ... 87 D1
Chislehurst West BR7 ... 189 A4
Edgware HA8 ... 26 C6
Southall UB1 ... 107 B6
Sutton SM2 ... 218 B2
Eaton Dr SW9 ... 138 D1
Kingston u T KT2 ... 176 C3
Eaton Gate
SW1 ... 115 A2 258 A4
Eaton Gdns RM9 ... 81 A1
Eaton Ho SW11 ... 266 D1
W5 ... 87 D1
Eaton House The Manor Sch
SW4 ... 137 B1
Eaton La SW1 .. 115 B3 258 D5
Eaton Mans SW1 ... 258 A3
Eaton Mews N
SW1 ... 115 A3 258 B5
Eaton Mews S
SW1 ... 115 B3 258 C5
Eaton Mews W SW1 ... 258 B4
Eaton Park Rd N13 ... 16 D2
Eaton Pl SW1 . 115 A3 258 B5
Eaton Rd NW4 ... 46 C4
Enfield EN1 ... 5 C1
Isleworth TW3,TW7 ... 130 B1
Sidcup DA14 ... 168 D2
Sutton SM2 ... 218 B2
Eaton Rise E11 ... 55 C4
W5 ... 87 D1
Eaton Row SW1 115 B3 258 C5
Eaton Sq SW1 .. 115 A3 258 B5
Eaton Terr E3 ... 97 A4
SW1 ... 115 A2 258 B4
Eaton Terr Mews SW1 . 258 A4
Eatons Mead E4 ... 19 C2
Eatonville Rd SW17 ... 158 D2
Eatonville Villas SW17 . 158 D2
Ebbisham Dr
SW8 ... 138 B6 270 C5
Ebbisham Rd KT4 ... 216 C6
Ebbsfleet Rd NW2 ... 69 A4
Ebdon Way SE3 ... 143 B2
Ebenezer Ho SE11 ... 261 C3
Ebenezer Mussel Ho 5
E2 ... 96 C5
Ebenezer St N1 ... 235 C2
Ebenezer Wlk CR4 ... 181 C2
Ebley Cl SE15 ... 139 D6
Ebner St SW18 ... 157 D6
Ebony Ho 10 NW3 ... 69 D2
Ebor Cotts SW15 ... 155 C1
Ebor St E1,E2 ... 243 C6
Ebrington Rd HA3 ... 43 D3
Ebsworth St SE23 ... 162 D4
Eburne Rd N7 ... 72 A5
Ebury Bridge Rd
SW1 ... 115 A1 258 B1
Ebury Cl BR2 ... 226 A5
Ebury Mews
SW1 ... 115 B2 258 C4
Ebury Mews E SW1 ... 258 C5
Ebury Sq SW1 ... 258 B3
Ebury St SW1 . 115 B2 258 C4
Eccles Rd SW11 ... 136 D1
Ecclesbourne Cl N13 ... 32 C5
Ecclesbourne Gdns N13 32 C5
Ecclesbourne Inf Sch
CR7 ... 205 A4
Ecclesbourne Jun Sch
CR7 ... 205 A4
Ecclesbourne Prim Sch
N1 ... 73 B1
Ecclesbourne Rd N1 ... 73 A1
Thornton Heath CR7 ... 205 A4
Eccleshill 3 BR2 ... 208 D5
Eccleston Cl
Cockfosters EN4 ... 2 D1
Orpington BR6 ... 211 B1
Eccleston Cres RM6 ... 58 B2
Eccleston Ho 1 SW2 .. 160 C5
Eccleston Mews
SW1 ... 115 A3 258 B5
Eccleston Pl
SW1 ... 115 B2 258 C4
Eccleston Rd W13 ... 109 A5
Eccleston Sq
SW1 ... 115 B2 258 D3
Eccleston Sq Mews
SW1 ... 259 A3
Eccleston St
SW1 ... 115 B2 258 C4
Ecclestone Ct HA9 ... 66 A3
Ecclestone Mews HA9 .. 66 A3
Ecclestone Pl HA9 ... 66 B3
Echelford Cty Mid Sch
TW15 ... 170 D5
Echelforde Dr TW15 ... 170 C6
Echo Hts E4 ... 19 D3
Eckersley St E1 ... 243 D5
8 E2 ... 96 A3
Eckford St N1 ... 234 A4
Eckington Ho N15 ... 51 B3
Eckstein Rd SW11 ... 136 C1
Eclipse Rd E13 ... 99 B2
Ector Rd SE6 ... 164 C2
Edam Ct 11 DA14 ... 168 A1
Edans Ct W12 ... 111 D4
Edbrooke Rd W9 ... 91 C3
Eddisbury Ho 7 SE26 . 162 A1
Eddiscombe Rd SW6 ... 135 B3
Eddy Cl RM7 ... 59 D3
Eddystone Rd SE4 ... 163 A6
Eddystone Twr SE8 ... 119 A1
Eddystone Wlk TW19 ... 148 A4
Ede Cl TW4 ... 129 B2
Eden Cl NW3 ... 69 C6
W8 ... 255 B6
Holdbrook EN3 ... 7 C6
Wembley HA0 ... 87 D6
Eden Gr E17 ... 53 D4
N7 ... 72 B3
Eden Ho NW8 ... 237 A5
15 SW11 ... 136 C2
Eden Mews SW17 ... 158 A1
Eden Park Ave BR3 ... 207 C4
Eden Park Sch BR3 ... 207 B4
Eden Park Sta BR3 ... 207 C4
Eden Rd E17 ... 53 D4
SE27 ... 182 D5
Croydon CR0 ... 221 B4
Penge BR3 ... 185 A2
Eden St KT1,KT2 ... 176 A1
Eden Way BR3 ... 207 C3
Eden Wlk 5 KT1 ... 176 A1
Edenbridge Cl 29 SE16 . 118 B1
Edenbridge Rd E9 ... 74 D1
Enfield EN1 ... 17 C5
Edencourt W5 ... 88 B1
Edencourt Rd SW16 ... 181 B4
Edendale W3 ... 110 D6
Edenfield Gdns KT4 ... 215 D5
Edenham High Sch
CR0 ... 207 B2
Edenham Way W10 ... 91 B2
Edenhurst Ave SW6 ... 135 B2
Edensmuir Ct SE3 ... 143 A5
Edensor Gdns W4 ... 133 C5
Edensor Rd W4 ... 133 C5
Edenvale Cl CR4 ... 181 A3
Edenvale Rd CR4 ... 181 A3
Edenvale St SW6 ... 136 A3
Ederline Ave SW16 ... 182 C1
Edgar Ct KT3 ... 199 C6
Edgar Ho E9 ... 75 A3
E11 ... 55 A2
SW8 ... 270 A4
Edgar Kail Way SE22 .. 139 C1
Edgar Rd E3 ... 97 D4
Dagenham RM6 ... 58 D2
Twickenham TW4 ... 151 B4
Yiewsley UB7 ... 104 A5
Edgarley Terr SW6 ... 264 A1
Edgcott Ho W10 ... 90 C2
Edge Bsns Ctr The NW2 . 68 B6
Edge Hill SE18 ... 144 D6
SW19 ... 178 D3
Edge Hill Ave N3 ... 47 C5
Edge Hill Ct SW19 ... 178 D3
Sidcup DA14 ... 189 D6
Edge Point Cl SE27 ... 182 D5
Edge St W8 ... 113 C5 245 B4
Edgeborough Way BR1 187 D2
Edgebury BR7,SE9 ... 188 D6
Edgebury Prim Sch
BR7 ... 189 A6
Edgebury Wlk BR7 ... 167 A1
Edgecombe Ho 4 SE5 . 139 C3
SW19 ... 157 A4
Edgecoombe CR2 ... 222 C1
Edgecot Gr N15 ... 51 C4
Edgecote Cl 7 W3 ... 111 A5
Edgecumbe Ct 2 CR0 . 206 A1
Edgefield Ave IG11 ... 79 D1
Edgefield Ct 2 IG11 ... 79 D1
Edgehill Ct KT12 ... 194 C1
Edgehill Gdns RM10 ... 81 C4
Edgehill Ho 4 SW9 ... 138 D3
Edgehill Rd W13 ... 87 C2
Chislehurst West BR7 ... 189 A6
Edgehill Rd *continued*
Mitcham CR4 ... 181 B2
Edgel St SW18 ... 135 D1
Edgeley La SW4 ... 137 D2
Edgeley Rd SW4 ... 137 D2
Edgewood Dr BR6 ... 227 D3
Edgewood Gn CR0 ... 206 D1
Edgeworth Ave NW4 ... 46 A4
Edgeworth Cl NW4 ... 46 A4
Edgeworth Cres NW4 ... 46 A4
Edgeworth Ct 10 EN4 ... 2 C1
Edgeworth Ho NW8 ... 229 A6
Edgeworth Rd SE9 ... 143 D1
Barnet EN4 ... 2 C1
Edgington Rd SW16 ... 181 D4
Edgington Way DA14 ... 190 D3
Edgson Ho SW1 ... 258 C2
Edgware Ct HA8 ... 26 C4
Edgware General Hospl
HA8 ... 26 D3
Edgware Inf Sch HA8 ... 26 C4
Edgware Rd NW2 ... 68 C6
W1,W2,NW1,NW8 92 C2 237 A3
Edgware Rd Burnt Oak
Broadway HA8 ... 26 D3
Edgware Rd High St
HA8 ... 26 C4
Edgware Road Sta
(Bakerloo)
NW1 ... 92 C2 237 A3
Edgware Road Sta
(Met,Distr,Circle)
NW1 ... 237 B3
Edgware Road The Hyde
NW9 ... 45 C5
Edgware Road West Hendon
Broadway NW9 ... 46 A2
Edgware Sch The HA8 .. 26 B6
Edgware Sta HA8 ... 26 D4
Edgware Way (Watford
By-Pass) HA8 ... 26 C6
Edgwarebury Ct HA8 ... 26 C5
Edgwarebury Gdns HA8 . 26 C5
Edgwarebury La HA8 ... 10 C2
Edinburgh Cl 7 E2 ... 96 C5
Uxbridge UB10 ... 60 D4
Edinburgh Ct 1 SE6 ... 164 D3
10 SE16 ... 118 D5
2 Kingston u T KT1 ... 198 A6
West Barnes SM4 ... 200 D4
Edinburgh Dr UB10 ... 60 D4
Edinburgh Ho NW4 ... 46 C6
3 W3 ... 89 B1
W9 ... 91 D4
Edinburgh Prim Sch E17 53 B4
Edinburgh Rd E13 ... 99 B5
E17 ... 53 C4
N18 ... 34 A5
W7 ... 108 D4
Carshalton SM1 ... 218 B6
Edington 20 NW5 ... 71 A2
Edington Rd SE2 ... 124 B3
Enfield EN3 ... 6 C3
Edis St NW1 ... 93 A6 231 B6
Edison Cl E17 ... 53 C4
Edison Dr UB1 ... 85 D1
Edison Gr SE18 ... 145 D5
Edison Ho SE1 ... 262 C4
10 Wembley HA9 ... 67 A5
Edison Rd N8 ... 49 D3
Bexley DA16 ... 145 D4
Brimsdown EN3 ... 7 B3
Bromley BR2 ... 187 A1
Edith Gdns KT5 ... 198 D2
Edith Gr SW10 . 136 A5 266 B4
Edith Ho 6 W6 ... 112 C1
Edith Neville Prim Sch
NW1 ... 93 D5 232 C3
Edith Pond Ct SE9 ... 166 D2
Edith Ramsay Ho 2 E1 . 97 A2
Edith Rd E6 ... 77 D1
E15 ... 76 B3
N11 ... 31 D3
SE25 ... 205 B4
SW19 ... 179 D4
W14 ... 113 A2 254 B3
Romford RM6 ... 58 D2
Edith Row SW6 ... 265 D2
Edith St E2 ... 96 A5
Edith Summerskill Ho
SW6 ... 264 C4
Edith Terr
SW10 ... 136 A5 266 A4
Edith Villas
W14 ... 113 B2 254 C2
Edith Yd SW10 ... 266 B4
Editha Mans SW10 ... 266 A5
Edithna St SW9 ... 138 A2
Edmansons' Cl N17 ... 33 D2
Edmeston Cl E9 ... 75 A2
Edmond Ct SE14 ... 140 C4
Edmonscote W13 ... 87 A2
Edmonton Coll of F Ed
EN3 ... 6 C4
Edmonton Ct 5 SE16 ... 118 C3
Edmonton Cty Lower Sch
N9 ... 17 C3
Edmonton Cty Upper Sch
EN1 ... 17 D4
Edmonton Green Sh Ctr
N9 ... 18 B2
Edmonton Green Sta N9 18 A2
Edmund Ho SE14 ... 141 B4
SE17 ... 261 D1
Edmund Rd Bexley DA16 146 A2
Mitcham CR4 ... 202 C6
Edmund St SE5 ... 139 B5
Edmund Waller Jun & Inf
Schs SE14 ... 140 D3
Edmunds Cl UB4 ... 84 C2
Edmunds Wlk N2 ... 48 C5
Edmundson Ho 10
SE18 ... 122 C2
Edna Rd SW20 ... 178 D1
Edna St SW11 .. 136 C4 267 A1
Ednam Ho SE15 ... 140 A6
Edred Ho E9 ... 75 A4
Edric Ho SW1 ... 259 D4
Edric Rd SE14 ... 140 D5
Edrich Ho SW4 ... 270 A1
Edrick Rd HA8 ... 27 A4
Edrick Wlk HA8 ... 27 A4
Edridge Cl WD2 ... 8 A6
Edridge Ho 9 SE27 ... 160 D1
Edridge Rd CR0 ... 221 B5
Edward Alleyn Ho SE21 161 C4
Edward Ave E4 ... 35 D4
Morden SM4 ... 202 B4
Edward Betham CE Prim Sch
UB6 ... 86 A5
Edward Cl N9 ... 17 D4
Hampton TW12 ... 174 A5
Edward Ct 2 E16 ... 99 A2
2 W5 ... 87 B3
Harrow HA1 ... 64 C6
Edward Dodd Ct N1 ... 235 D2
Edward Edward's Ho
SE1 ... 251 C3
Edward Friend Ho 6
N16 ... 73 C5
Edward Gr EN4 ... 14 B6
Edward Harvey Ct DA17 125 B1
Edward Ho SE11 ... 260 D2
W2 ... 236 C5
Edward Kennedy Ho 18
W10 ... 91 A3
Edward Mann Cl 12 E1 .. 96 D1
Edward Mans 7 IG11 .. 79 D1
Edward Mews NW1 ... 231 D3
Edward Pauling Ho
TW14 ... 149 D4
Edward Pauling Prim Sch
TW13 ... 149 C2
Edward Pinner Ct 5
KT6 ... 214 A6
Edward Pl SE8 ... 141 B6
Edward Rd E17 ... 52 D4
SE20 ... 184 D4
Bromley BR1 ... 187 C3
Chislehurst West BR7 ... 188 D5
Croydon CR0 ... 205 C2
Dagenham RM6 ... 59 A3
Hampton TW12 ... 174 A5
Harrow HA2 ... 42 A6
Hatton TW14 ... 149 C6
New Barnet EN4 ... 14 B6
Northolt UB5 ... 84 C5
Edward Redhead Jun & Inf
Sch E17 ... 53 A6
Edward Robinson Ho 3
SE14 ... 140 D5
Edward Sq N1 ... 233 C5
SE16 ... 119 A5
Edward St 10 E16 ... 99 A3
SE14 ... 141 B5
Edward Temme Ave E15 76 D1
Edward Tyler Rd SE12 .. 165 C2
Edward VII Mans NW10 . 90 D4
Edward Way TW15 ... 148 B2
Edward Wilson Prim Sch
W2 ... 91 D2
Edwardes Sq
W8 ... 113 B3 254 D5
Edward's Ave HA4 ... 62 C2
Edwards Cl KT4 ... 216 D6
Edward's Cotts 11 N1 .. 72 D1
Edwards Dr N11 ... 31 D3
Edward's La N16 ... 73 C6
Edwards Mews N1 ... 72 C1
W1 ... 93 A1 238 A1
Edwards Rd DA17 ... 125 C2
Edwin Arnold Ct DA15 . 189 D6
Edwin Ave E6 ... 100 C5
Edwin Cl DA7 ... 147 B6
Edwin Ho SE15 ... 140 A5
Edwin Rd Burnt Oak HA8 27 B4
Twickenham TW1,TW2 ... 152 C3
Edwin St E1 ... 96 C3
E16 ... 99 A2
Edwin Stray Ho TW13 . 151 C1
Edwin Ware Ct 2 HA5 .. 22 C1
Edwina Ct SM1 ... 217 D4
Edwina Gdns IG4 ... 56 A4
Edwin's Mead E9 ... 75 A4
Edwy Ho E9 ... 75 B4
Edwyn Cl EN5 ... 12 D5
Edwyn Ho SW18 ... 157 D5
Eel Pie Island* TW1 .. 153 A3
Effie Pl SW6 ... 265 B3
Effie Rd SW6 .. 135 C5 265 B3
Effingham Cl SM2 ... 217 D1
Effingham Ct SW19 ... 180 C3
Effingham Ho 37 SW8 . 137 D3
9 Kingston u T KT2 ... 176 D4
Effingham Lo 1 KT6 .. 198 A4
Effingham Rd N8 ... 50 C5
SE12 ... 164 D6
Thames Ditton KT6,KT7 .. 197 C2
Thornton Heath CR0 ... 204 B2
Effort St SW17 ... 180 C5
Effra Ct SE19 ... 183 C3
SW2 ... 160 B6
Effra Mans SW2 ... 160 C6
Effra Par SW2 ... 160 C6
Effra Rd SW2 ... 160 C6

Effra Rd *continued*
SW19 179 D4
Effra Road Ret Pk SW2 160 C6
Egan Way UB3 105 C6
Egbert Ho E9 75 A3
Egbert St NW1 93 A6 231 A6
Egbury Ho SW15 155 D5
Egerton Cl HA5 40 A5
Egerton Cres
SW3 114 C2 257 B4
Egerton Ct E11 54 B2
5 Richmond TW10 154 A6
Egerton Dr SE10 141 D4
Egerton Gdns NW4 46 B5
NW10 90 C6
SW3 114 C3 257 A5
W13 87 B1
Ilford IG3 79 D5
Egerton Gdns Mews
SW3 257 B5
Egerton Ho W4 133 A6
Egerton Pl SW3 257 B5
Egerton Rd N16 51 D2
SE25 205 C6
New Malden KT3 199 D5
Twickenham TW2 152 C4
Wembley HA0 66 B1
Egerton Terr
SW3 114 C3 257 B5
Eggardon Ct UB5 64 A2
Eggerton Way UB3 126 D5
Egham Cl SW19 157 A2
Cheam SM3 217 A6
Egham Cres SM3 217 A6
Egham Ct KT6 197 D4
Egham Rd E13 99 B2
Eglantine Rd SW18 158 A6
Egleston Rd SM4 201 D3
Eglington Ct SE17 139 A6
Eglington Rd E4 20 B4
Eglinton Hill SE18 144 D5
Eglinton Inf Sch SE18 144 C6
Eglinton Jun Sch SE18 144 C6
Eglinton Rd SE18 144 D6
Egliston Mews SW15 134 C2
Egliston Rd SW15 134 C2
Egmont Ave KT6 198 B1
Egmont Rd
New Malden KT3 199 D5
Surbiton KT6 198 C1
Sutton SM2 218 A1
Walton-on-T KT12 194 B2
Egmont St SE14 140 D5
Egremont Ho SE13 141 D3
Egremont Rd SE27 160 C1
Egret Ho 11 SE16 118 D2
Egret Way UB4 84 D2
Eider Cl E7 76 D3
Hayes UB4 84 D2
Eighteenth Rd CR4 204 A5
Eighth Ave E12 78 B4
Hayes UB3 106 A5
Eileen Ct BR7 188 C5
Eileen Rd SE25 205 B4
Eindhoven Cl SM5 203 A1
Einstein Ho HA9 67 A5
Eisenhower Dr E6 100 A2
Eisenhower Ho KT8 175 C2
Ekarra Ho SW8 270 B2
Elaine Ct 13 NW3 70 D2
Elaine Gr NW5 71 A3
Elaine Ho N4 50 A1
Elam Cl SE5 138 D3
Elam St SE5 138 D3
Elan Ct E1 96 B2
Eland Pl CR0 220 D5
Eland Rd SW11 136 D2
Croydon CR0 220 D5
Elba Pl SE17 117 A2 262 B4
Elbe St SW6 136 A3
Elberon Ave CR0 203 C3
Elborough Rd SE25 206 A4
Elborough St SW18 157 C3
Elbourne Trad Est
DA17 125 D3
Elbury Dr E16 99 A1
Elcho St SW11 136 C5 267 B3
Elcot Ave SE15 140 B5
Elder Ave N8 50 A4
Elder Cl Edgware HA8 27 A5
Sidcup DA15 167 D3
Yiewsley UB7 104 A6
Elder Ct 39 SE8 141 B6
Bushey WD2 8 C2
Elder Gdns 9 SE27 183 A6
Elder Oak Cl SE20 184 B2
Elder Rd SE27 183 A5
Elder St E1 95 D3 243 C5
Elder Wlk N1 234 D6
Elderberry Gr 10 SE27 183 A6
Elderberry Rd W5 110 A4
Elderfield Ho 3 E14 119 C6
Elderfield Rd E5 74 C4
Elderfield Wlk E11 55 B4
Elderflower Way E15 76 C1
Elderslie Cl BR3 207 D3
Elderslie Rd SE9 166 C6
Elderton Rd SE26 185 A6
Eldertree Pl CR4 181 C2
Eldertree Way CR4 181 C2
Elderwood Pl SE27 183 A5
Eldon Ave Croydon CR0 222 C6
Heston TW5 129 C5
Eldon Ct NW6 91 C6
Eldon Gr NW3 70 B3
Eldon Ho SW9 138 D2
Eldon Jun & Inf Schs N9 18 C3
Eldon Pk SE25 206 B5
Eldon Rd E17 53 B5
N9 18 C3
N22 32 D2
W8 113 D3 255 D5
Eldon St EC2 95 B2 242 D3
Eldon Way NW10 88 D5
Eldonwall Est RM8 59 B1
Eldred Rd IG11 101 C6
Eldrick Ct TW14 149 B3
Eldridge Cl TW14 150 A3
Eldridge Ct SE16 118 A3
Eleanor Cl N15 51 D6
SE16 118 D4
Eleanor Cres NW7 28 D6
Eleanor Ct 13 E2 96 A6
Eleanor Gdns
Dagenham RM8 81 B6
Ducks Island EN5 12 D6
Eleanor Gr SW13 133 C2
Uxbridge UB10 60 D5
Eleanor Ho 1 NW5 71 C3
6 SW19 179 D2
18 W6 112 C1
Eleanor Palmer Prim Sch
NW5 71 C4
Eleanor Rathbone Ho 1
N6 49 D2
Eleanor Rd E8 74 B1
E8 74 B2
E15 76 D2
N11 32 A4
Eleanor Smith Sch E13 99 B5
Eleanor St E3 97 C4
Eleanor Wlk 25 SE18 122 B2
Electric Ave SW9 138 C1
Enfield EN3 7 B6
Electric Ho 12 E3 97 C4
Electric La 2 SW9 138 C1
Electric Mans 1 SW9 138 C1
Electric Par E18 37 A1
Ilford IG3 57 D1
Kingston u T KT6 197 D3
Elephant & Castle SE1 261 D4
SE1 117 A3 261 D5
Elephant & Castle Sta
SE1 116 D3 261 D5
SE17 117 A2 262 A4
Elephant La SE16 118 C4
Elephant Rd
SE17 117 A2 262 A4
Elers Rd W13 109 C4
Hayes UB3 105 B2
Eley Rd N18 34 D5
Eley's Est N18 34 D6
Elf Row E1 118 C6
Elfin Gr TW11 174 D5
Elfindale Rd SE24 161 A6
Elford Cl SE9 143 C1
Elfort Rd N5 72 C4
Elfrida Cres SE6 185 C6
Elfrida Inf & Jun Sch
SE6 185 C6
Elfwine Rd W7 86 C2
Elgal Cl BR6 226 D3
Elgar N8 50 A6
Elgar Ave NW10 67 B2
SW16 204 A6
W5 110 A4
Tolworth KT5,KT6 198 D2
Elgar Cl E13 99 C5
SE8 141 C5
Buckhurst Hill IG9 21 D2
Elstree WD6 9 D4
Ickenham UB10 60 C6
Elgar Ct W14 254 A5
Elgar Ho NW6 70 A1
SW1 258 D1
Hayes UB4 84 C2
Twickenham TW2 152 B5
Elgar St SE16 119 A3
Elgin Ave W9 91 D3
W12 112 B3
Ashford TW15 171 A4
Harrow HA3 25 B1
Elgin Cres W11 113 A6 244 B6
Harlington TW6 127 C3
Elgin Ct W9 91 D3
6 Croydon CR0 221 A4
Elgin Ho 8 E14 97 D1
Northolt UB5 84 B5
Elgin Mans W9 91 D4
Elgin Mews W11 91 A1
Elgin Mews N W9 91 D4
Elgin Mews S W9 91 D4
Elgin Rd N22 31 C1
Croydon CR0 221 D6
Ilford IG3 57 C2
Sutton SM1 218 A5
Wallington SM6 219 C2
Elgood Ave HA6 22 A3
Elgood Ho NW8 229 D3
Elham Cl BR1 187 D3
Elham Ho 18 E5 74 B3
Elia Mews N1 94 D5 234 C3
Elia St N1 94 D5 234 C3
Elias Pl SW8 138 C6
Elibank Rd SE9 144 C1
Elim Est SE1 263 A6
Elim St SE1 263 A6
Elim Way E13 98 D4
Eliot Bank SE23,SE26 162 B2
Eliot Bank Prim Sch
SE23 162 B2
Eliot Ct SW18 157 D5
Eliot Dr HA2 63 D6
Eliot Gdns SW15 134 A1
Eliot Hill SE13 142 A3
Eliot Ho 10 TW10 154 B5
Eliot Mews NW8 229 A3
Eliot Pk SE13 142 A3
Eliot Pl SE3 142 C3
Eliot Rd RM9 80 D4
Eliot Vale SE3 142 B3
Elizabeth Ave N1 73 B1 235 B6
Enfield EN2 4 D2
Ilford IG1 79 B6
Elizabeth Barnes Ct 5
SW6 135 D3
Elizabeth Blackwell Ho
N22 32 C2
Elizabeth Cl 12 E14 97 D1
W9 236 B5
Sutton SM1 217 B6
Elizabeth Clyde Cl N15 51 C5
Elizabeth Cotts 5 TW9 132 C4
Elizabeth Ct 6 E18 37 A2
SE22 140 A1
SW1 259 D5
SW10 266 D5
Buckhurst Hill IG9 21 B3
Sunbury TW16 194 C6
3 Teddington TW11 174 C5
West Barnes SM4 201 A2
2 Woodford IG8 37 C3
Elizabeth Finn Ho W12 112 A3
Elizabeth Fry Ho UB3 105 D2
Elizabeth Garrett Anderson
Ho 9 DA17 125 C3
Elizabeth Garrett Anderson
Hospl NW1 93 D4 232 D1
Elizabeth Garrett Anderson
Sch N1 94 B5 233 D4
Elizabeth Gdns W3 111 D5
Stanmore HA7 25 C5
Sunbury TW16 194 C6
Elizabeth Ho 46 E3 97 D4
N20 14 D1
SE11 261 B3
15 W6 112 C1
Wembley HA9 66 B3
Elizabeth Ind Est SE14 140 D6
Elizabeth Kenny Ho N1 73 A2
Elizabeth Mews NW3 70 D2
Elizabeth Pl N15 51 B5
Elizabeth Rd E6 99 D6
N15 51 C4
Elizabeth Ride N9 18 B4
Elizabeth Selby Inf Sch
E2 96 A4
Elizabeth Sq 18 SE16 119 A6
Elizabeth St
SW1 115 A2 258 B4
Elizabeth Terr SE9 166 B5
Elizabeth Way SE19 183 B3
Feltham TW13 172 C6
Elizabethan Ct N3 47 A6
Elkanette Mews N20 14 A2
Elkington Point SE11 261 A3
Elkington Rd E13 99 B3
Elkstone Ct 1 SE15 139 C6
Elkstone Rd W10 91 B2
Ella Mews NW3 70 D4
Ella Rd N4,N8 50 A2
Ellacombe Ho 1 SW2 160 C4
Ellaline Rd W6 134 D6
Ellanby Cres N18 34 B5
Elland Ho 12 E14 97 B1
Elland Rd SE15 140 C1
Ellement Cl HA5 40 D4
Ellen Cl BR1 209 D6
Ellen Ct 6 E4 20 A3
N9 18 C2
Ellen Miller Ho 2 E17 54 A4
Ellen St E1 96 A1
Ellen Webb Dr HA3 42 C6
Ellen Wilkinson Ho
7 E2 96 D4
SW6 264 D5
12 Dagenham RM10 81 C5
Ellen Wilkinson Prim Sch
E6 100 A2
Ellen Wilkinson Sch for Girls
W3 88 B1
Ellena Ct N14 16 A1
Ellenborough Ct N22 32 D2
Ellenborough Ho 5
W12 112 B6
Ellenborough Pl SW15 134 A1
Ellenborough Rd N22 33 A2
Ruxley DA14 191 A5
Elleray Rd TW11 174 D4
Ellerby St SW6 134 D4
Ellerdale Rd NW3 70 A3
Ellerdale St SE13 141 D2
Ellerdine Rd TW3 130 B1
Ellerker Gdns TW10 154 A5
Ellerman Ave TW2,TW4 151 B3
Ellerslie Ct 6 SM6 219 B2
Ellerslie Gdns NW10 90 A6
Ellerslie Ind Est SW2 160 A6
Ellerslie Rd W12 112 B5
Ellerton Ct W3 110 D4
Ellerton Gdns RM9 80 C1
Ellerton Lo N3 29 C1
Ellerton Rd SW13 134 A4
SW17,SW18 158 B3
SW20 178 A3
Dagenham RM9 80 C1
Surbiton KT6 198 B1
Ellery Ho SE17 262 D3
Ellery Rd SE19 183 B3
Ellery St SE15 140 B3
Ellesborough Cl WD1 22 C5
Ellesmere Ave NW7 11 B1
Beckenham BR3 185 D1
Ellesmere Cl E11 54 D4
Ellesmere Cl *continued*
Ruislip HA4 39 A2
Ellesmere Ct SE12 165 A3
SE20 184 B1
W4 133 B6
Ellesmere Gdns IG4 56 A3
Ellesmere Gr EN5 13 B6
Ellesmere Rd E3 97 A5
NW10 68 A3
Southall UB6 86 A3
Twickenham TW1 153 C5
Ellesmere Rd (Great West
Rd) W4 133 B6
Ellesmere St E14 97 D1
Ellies Mews TW15 148 A2
Ellingfort Rd E8 74 B1
Ellingham Prim Sch
KT9 213 D1
Ellingham Rd E15 76 B4
W12 112 A4
Chessington KT9 213 D2
Ellington Ct N14 15 D2
Ellington Ho SE1 262 B5
Ellington Rd N10 49 B5
Feltham TW13 171 D6
Hounslow TW3 129 D3
Ellington St N7 72 C2
Elliot Cl E15 76 C1
Wembley HA9 66 C5
Elliot Ct 5 N15 51 D5
Elliot Rd NW4 46 B3
SW9 138 D5
Elliott Ave HA4 62 B6
Elliott Gdns TW17 192 C5
Elliott Rd SW9 138 D4
W4 111 C2
Bromley BR2 209 D5
Stanmore HA7 25 A4
Thornton Heath CR7 204 D5
Elliott Sch SW15 156 C5
Elliott Sq NW3 70 C1
Elliott's Pl N1 234 D5
Elliott's Row
SE11 116 D2 261 D4
Ellis Cl SE9 167 A2
Burnt Oak HA8 27 C4
Ellis Ct W7 86 D2
Ellis Franklin Ct NW8 229 A4
Ellis Ho E17 54 A4
SE17 262 C2
Ellis Rd Mitcham CR4 202 D3
Southall UB2 108 A5
Ellis St SW1 115 A2 258 A4
Elliscombe Mount 11
SE7 143 C6
Elliscombe Rd SE7 143 C6
Ellisfield Dr SW15 156 A4
Ellison Gdns UB2 107 B2
Ellison Ho 1 SE13 142 A3
Ellison Rd SW13 133 D3
SW16 182 A3
New Eltham DA15 167 B3
Elliston Ho 14 SE18 122 C2
Ellora Rd SW16 181 D5
Ellswood Ct 18 KT6 197 D2
Ellsworth St E2 96 B4
Ellwood Ct 1 W9 91 D3
Elm Ave W5 110 B5
Ruislip HA4 40 B2
Elm Bank Gdns SW13 133 C3
Elm Bank Mans SW13 133 C3
Elm Cl E11 55 B3
N19 71 C6
NW4 46 D4
SW20 200 C5
Buckhurst Hill IG9 21 D2
Carshalton SM5 202 D1
Harrow HA2 41 D3
Hayes UB3 84 A1
South Croydon CR2 221 C2
Tolworth KT5 199 A2
Twickenham TW13,TW2 151 D2
Elm Court Sch SE27 161 A2
Elm Cres W5 110 A4
Kingston u T KT2 176 A2
Elm Ct E4 36 A4
EC4 251 A6
4 N3 29 C2
SE6 163 D3
SE13 142 B2
SW9 138 C4
5 Charlton TW16 171 D3
Mitcham CR4 180 D1
Elm Dr Harrow HA2 41 D3
Sunbury TW16 172 C1
Elm Friars Wlk NW1 71 D1
Elm Gdns N2 48 A6
Claygate KT10 212 D2
Enfield EN2 5 B5
Mitcham CR4 203 D5
Elm Gn W3 89 C1
Elm Gr N8 50 A3
NW2 68 D4
SE15 140 A3
SW19 179 A3
Harrow HA2 41 C2
Kingston u T KT2 176 A2
Orpington BR6 211 D1
Sutton SM1 217 D4
Woodford IG8 36 D5
Yiewsley UB7 104 B6
Elm Grove Par SM6 219 A5
Elm Grove Rd SW13 134 A3
W5 110 A4
Elm Hall Gdns E11 55 B3
Elm Hatch HA5 23 B3
Elm Ho 4 E14 120 A4
2 Kingston u T KT2 176 B3
Elm La SE6 163 B2
Elm Lawn Cl UB8 60 A1
Elm Lo SW6 134 D4
Elm Park Ave N15 52 A3
Elm Park Ct HA5 40 C6
Elm Park Gdns NW4 46 D4
SW10 114 B1 256 C1
Elm Park Ho SW10 256 C1
Elm Park La
SW3 114 B1 256 C1
Elm Park Mans SW10 266 B6
Elm Park Rd E10 53 A1
N3 29 B3
N21 17 A4
SE25 205 D6
SW3 136 B6 266 C6
Pinner HA5 40 D6
Elm Pk SW2 160 B4
Stanmore HA7 25 C5
Elm Pl SW7 114 B1 256 C2
Elm Quay SW8 269 C5
Elm Rd E7 76 D2
E11 76 B6
E17 54 A4
N22 32 D2
SW14 133 A1
Beckenham BR3 185 B1
Carshalton SM6 203 A1
Chessington KT9 214 A4
Chipping Barnet EN5 1 B1
Claygate KT10 212 D2
East Bedfont TW14 149 B4
Kingston u T KT2 176 B2
Kingston u T KT3 199 B6
Sidcup DA14 190 A6
South Norwood CR7 205 B5
Stoneleigh KT17 215 D2
Wembley HA9 66 A3
Elm Rd W SM4 201 B2
Elm Row NW3 70 A5
Elm St WC1 94 B3 240 D5
Elm Terr NW2 69 C5
3 SE9 166 C5
Harrow HA3 24 B2
Elm Tree Ave KT10 196 C2
Elm Tree Cl NW8 92 B4 229 C2
Ashford TW15 170 D5
Northolt UB5 85 B5
Elm Tree Ct NW8 229 C2
5 SE5 139 A4
18 SE7 143 C6
Elm Tree Rd
NW8 92 B4 229 C2
Elm Way N11 31 A4
NW10 67 C4
North Cheam KT4 216 C5
West Ewell KT19 215 B3
Elm Wlk NW3 69 C6
SW20 200 D5
Locksbottom BR6 226 B5
Elm Wood Prim Sch
SE27 161 B1
Elmar Rd N15 51 B5
Elmbank N14 16 A4
Elmbank Dr BR1 187 D1
Elmbank Way W7 86 B2
Elmbourne Dr DA17 125 D2
Elmbourne Rd SW17 159 B1
Elmbridge Ave KT5 199 A3
Elmbridge Cl HA4 40 A3
Elmbridge Dr HA4 40 A3
Elmbridge Wlk E8 74 A1
Elmbrook 2 E18 55 A6
Elmbrook Cl TW16 172 B2
Elmbrook Gdns SE9 144 A1
Elmbrook Rd SM1 217 B4
Elmcote HA5 22 D1
Elmcourt Rd SE21,SE27 160 D2
Elmcroft N6 49 C2
N8 50 B4
Elmcroft Ave E11 55 B5
N9 18 B5
NW11 47 B2
Sidcup DA15 168 A5
Elmcroft Cl E11 55 B5
W5 87 D1
Chessington KT9 214 A5
Feltham TW14 149 D5
Elmcroft Cres NW11 47 A2
Harrow HA2 41 C6
Elmcroft Dr
Ashford TW15 170 C5
Chessington KT9 214 A5
Elmcroft Gdns NW9 44 C4
Elmcroft St E5 74 C4
Elmcroft Terr UB8 82 C1
Elmdale Rd N13 32 B5
Elmdene KT5 199 A1
Elmdene Cl BR3 207 B4
Elmdene Rd SE18 122 D1
Elmdon Rd Hatton TW6 127 D2
Hounslow TW5 129 A3
Elmer Cl EN2 4 B2
Elmer Ct SW6 135 A3
Elmer Gdns Edgware HA8 26 D3
Isleworth TW7 130 B2
Elmer Ho NW1 237 A4
Elmer Rd SE6 164 A4
Elmer's Dr TW11 175 B4
Elmers End Rd BR3,
SE20 206 C6
Elmers End Sta BR3 206 D5
Elmers Rd SE25 206 A2
Elmerside Rd BR3 207 A5
Elmfield Ave N8 50 A4
Mitcham CR4 181 A2
Teddington TW11 174 D5
Elmfield Cl HA1 64 C6
Elmfield Ct DA16 146 B4
Elmfield Ho 17 N2 30 B1
6 N5 73 A3
W9 91 C3
Elmfield Mans 5 SW17 159 A2
Elmfield Pk BR1 209 A6
Elmfield Rd E4 20 B2
E17 52 D3
N2 48 B6
SW17 159 B2
Bromley BR1 209 A6
Southall UB2 107 A3
Elmfield Way W9 91 C2
South Croydon CR2 221 D1
Elmgate Ave TW13 150 C1
Elmgate Gdns HA8 27 B6
Elmgreen Cl 8 E15 98 C6
Elmgrove Cres HA1 43 A4
Elmgrove Fst & Mid Schs
HA3 43 A5
Elmgrove Gdns HA1 43 A4
Elmgrove Rd
Croydon CR0 206 B2
Harrow HA1 42 D4
Elmhurst DA17 147 A6
Elmhurst Ave N2 48 B6
Mitcham CR4 181 B3
Elmhurst Cres N2 48 B5
Elmhurst Ct CR0 221 B3
Elmhurst Dr E18 37 A1
Elmhurst Lo 3 SM2 218 A1
Elmhurst Mans SW4 137 D2
Elmhurst Prim Sch E7 77 B1
Elmhurst Rd E7 77 B1
N17 33 D1
SE9 166 A1
Enfield EN3 6 C6
Elmhurst Sch for Boys
CR2 221 B3
Elmhurst St SW4 137 D2
Elmhurst Villas SE15 140 C1
Elmington Cl DA5 169 D5
Elmington Rd SE5 139 B5
Elmira St SE13 141 D2
Elmlea Dr UB3 83 D2
Elmlee Cl BR7 188 B4
Elmley Cl 12 E6 100 A2
Elmley St SE18 123 B2
Elmore Cl HA0 88 A5
Elmore Ho SW9 138 D3
Elmore Rd E11 76 B5
Enfield EN3 6 D5
Elmore St N1 73 B1
Elms Ave N10 49 B6
NW4 46 D4
Elms Cotts 1 CR4 180 D1
Elms Cres SW4 159 D5
Elms Ct SW19 179 D3
Wembley HA0 65 A4
Elms Gdns
Dagenham RM9 81 B4
Wembley HA0 65 A4
Elms La HA0 65 A5
Elms Mews W2 246 C6
Elms Park Ave HA0 65 A4
Elms Rd SW4 159 C6
Harrow Weald HA3 24 C3
Elms The E12 78 A2
NW9 45 A3
NW10 89 C5
SW13 133 D2
Ashford TW15 170 C5
Claygate KT10 212 D1
Croydon CR0 205 A1
Elmscott Gdns N21 17 A5
Elmscott Rd BR1 186 D5
Elmsdale Rd E17 53 B5
Elmshaw Rd SW15 156 A6
Elmside CR0 223 D2
Elmside Rd HA9 66 C5
Elmsleigh Ave HA3 43 C5
Elmsleigh Ct SM1 217 D5
Elmsleigh Ho TW2 152 B2
Elmsleigh Rd TW2 152 B2
Elmslie Ct SE9 166 C5
Elmslie Point 2 E3 97 B2
Elmstead Ave
Chislehurst West BR7 188 B5
Wembley HA9 66 B6
Elmstead Cl N20 13 C2
West Ewell KT19 215 C3
Elmstead Gdns KT4 216 A5
Elmstead Glade BR7 188 B4
Elmstead La BR7 188 B5
Elmstead Rd IG3 79 D6
Elmstead Woods Sta
BR7 188 A4
Elmsted Cres DA16 146 C6
Elmstone Rd SW6 265 A2
Elmsway TW15 170 C5
Elmsworth Ave TW3 129 D3
Elmton Ct NW8 236 C6
Elmton Way E5 74 A5
Elmtree Rd TW11 174 C5
Elmwood Ave N13 32 A5
Feltham TW13 150 B1
Harrow HA3 43 B3
Elmwood Cl
Hackbridge SM6 219 B6
Stoneleigh KT17 216 A1
Elmwood Cres NW9 45 A5
Elmwood Ct SW11 268 C2
HA0 65 A5
Elmwood Dr Sidcup DA5 169 A4
Stoneleigh KT17 216 A1

Elmwood Gdns W7 . . . . .86 C1
Elmwood Ho NW10 . . . . . .90 A6
NW10 . . . . .90 B5
Elmwood Inf Sch CR0 .204 D3
Elmwood Jun Sch CR0 .204 D2
Elmwood Rd SE24 . . . .161 B6
W4 . . . . .133 A4
Mitcham CR4 . . . . .202 D6
Thornton Heath CR7 . . . . .204 D2
Elmworth Gr SE21 . . . .161 B2
Elnathan Mews W9 . . . . .91 B3
Elphinstone Ct SW16 . .182 A4
Elphinstone Rd E7 . . . . .35 B1
Elphinstone St N5 . . . . .72 D4
Elrington Rd E8 . . . . .74 A2
Woodford IG8 . . . . .37 A5
Elsa Ct BR3 . . . . .185 B2
Elsa Rd DA16 . . . . .146 C3
Elsa St E1 . . . . .97 A2
Elsdale St E9 . . . . .74 C2
Elsden Mews E2 . . . . . . .96 C5
Elsden Rd N17 . . . . .33 D2
Elsenham Rd E12 . . . . . .78 C3
Elsenham St SW18
SW19 . . . . .157 B2
Elsfield NW5 . . . . .71 B3
Elsham Rd E11 . . . . .76 C4
W14 . . . . .113 A4 244 A1
Elsham Terr W14 . . . . .244 A1
Elsie La Ct W2 . . . . .91 D2
Elsie Rd SE22 . . . . .139 D1
Elsiedene Rd N21 . . . . . .17 A4
Elsinore Ave TW19 . . . .148 A4
Elsinore Gdns NW2 . . . .69 A5
Elsley Ct HA9 . . . . .66 D2
Elsinore Ho N1 . . . . . . .234 A5
E5 . . . . .139 A3
SE7 . . . . .122 A1
Elsinore Rd SE23 . . . . .163 A3
Elsinore Way TW9 . . . .132 D2
Elsley Ct HA9 . . . . .66 D2
Elsley Prim Sch HA9 . . .66 B3
Elsley Rd SW11 . . . . . .137 A2
Elsley Rd SW11 . . . . . .137 A2
Elspeth Rd SW11 . . . . .136 D1
Wembley HA0 . . . . .66 A3
Elsrick Ave SM4 . . . . . .201 C4
Elstan Way CR0 . . . . . .207 A2
Elstead Ho 9 SW2 . . . .160 B4
Elsted St SE17 . . .117 B2 262 D3
Elstow Cl SE9 . . . . .166 B6
Ruislip HA4 . . . . .40 D2
Elstow Gdns RM9 . . . . .103 A4
Elstow Grange NW6 . . . .68 D1
Elstow Rd RM9 . . . . . . .103 A6
Elstree Gdns N9 . . . . . . .18 B3
Erith DA18 . . . . .125 A2
Ilford IG1 . . . . .79 A3
Elstree Hill BR1 . . . . . .186 C3
Elstree Hill N WD6 . . . . . .9 A4
Elstree Hill S WD6 . . . . . .9 D4
Elstree Ho 3 HA7 . . . . . .25 C6
Elstree Pk WD6 . . . . . . .11 B5
Elstree Rd Bushey WD2 . .8 C4
Elstree WD6 . . . . .9 A5
Elswick Rd SE13 . . . . . .141 D3
Elswick St SW6 . . . . . . .136 A3
Elsworth Cl TW14 . . . . .149 C3
Elsworthy KT7 . . . . .196 C3
Elsworthy Rd
NW3 . . . . .92 C6 230 A6
Elsworthy Rise NW3 . . . .70 C1
Elsworthy Terr NW3 . . . .70 C1
Elsynge Rd SW18 . . . . .158 B6
Elsynge Road Mans
SW18 . . . . .158 B6
Eltham CE JMI Sch SE9 166 B6
Eltham Coll Jun Sch
SE9 . . . . .165 D2
Eltham Green Rd SE9 .165 C6
Eltham Green Sch SE9 165 D5
Eltham High St SE9 . . .166 B5
Eltham Hill SE9 . . . . . .166 A6
Eltham Hill Sch SE9 . . .166 A5
Eltham Hill Tech Coll for
Girls SE9 . . . . .166 A5
Eltham Palace ★ SE9 . .166 A4
Eltham Palace Rd SE9 .165 D5
Eltham Park Gdns SE9 .144 C1
Eltham Rd SE9,SE12 . . .165 B6
Eltham Sta SE9 . . . . . .166 B6
Elthiron Rd
SW6 . . . . .135 C4 265 B1
Elthorne Ave W7 . . . . .109 A4
Elthorne Ct NW9 . . . . . .45 B3
Feltham TW13 . . . . .150 C3
Elthorne Park High Sch
W7 . . . . .108 D3
Elthorne Park Rd W7 . .109 A4
Elthorne Rd N19 . . . . . . .71 D6
NW9 . . . . .45 B2
Elthorne Way NW9 . . . . .45 B3
Elthruda Rd SE13 . . . . .164 B5
Eltisley Rd IG1 . . . . .78 D4
Elton Ave Barnet EN5 . . .13 B6
Wembley HA0 . . . . .65 B3
Wembley UB6 . . . . .64 D2
Elton Cl KT1 . . . . .175 C3
Elton Ho 3 E3 . . . . .97 B6
Elton Lo 4 W5 . . . . . . .110 A6
Elton Pl N16 . . . . .73 C3
Elton Rd KT2 . . . . .176 C2
Elton St 11 N16 . . . . . . .73 C3
Eltringham St SW18 . . .136 A1

Elvaston Ct EN5 . . . . . . .12 C6
Elvaston Mews SW7 . . .256 B6
Elvaston Pl
SW7 . . . . .114 A3 256 B5
Elveden Ho 17 SW9 . . .138 D1
Elveden Pl NW10 . . . . . .88 C5
Elveden Rd NW10 . . . . . .88 C5
Elvendon Rd N13 . . . . . .32 A4
Elver Gdns 6 E2 . . . . . . .96 A4
Elverson Rd SE8 . . . . . .141 D3
Elverson Rd Sta SE8 . .141 D3
Elverton St
SW1 . . . . .115 D2 259 C4
Elvin Cl N9 . . . . .45 A2
Elvin Ho 2 E9 . . . . .74 C2
Elvington Gn BR2 . . . . .208 D4
Elvington La SW9 . . . . . .27 C2
Elvino Rd SE26 . . . . . . .185 A5
Elvis Rd NW2 . . . . .68 C2
Elwill Way BR3 . . . . . . .208 B5
Elwin St E2 . . . . .96 A4
Elwood Ho N5 . . . . .72 D5
Elwood St N4,N5 . . . . . .72 D5
Elworth Ho SW8 . . . . . .270 D3
Elwyn Gdns SE12 . . . . .165 A4
Ely Cl SW20 . . . . .177 D1
Ely Cottages SW8 . . . . .270 D1
Ely Court Flats SW6 . . .264 A1
Ely Ct KT1 . . . . .198 C6
Ely Gdns
Borehamwood WD6 . . . . .11 B6
Redbridge IG1 . . . . .56 A2
Ely Ho 22 SE15 . . . . . . .140 A5
Barnet EN4 . . . . .2 C1
Ely Pl EC1 . . . . .94 C2 241 B3
Ely Rd E10 . . . . .54 A2
Hatton TW6 . . . . .127 D3
Hounslow TW4 . . . . .128 C2
Thornton Heath CR0 . . . .205 B4
Elyne Rd N4 . . . . .50 C3
Elysian Ave BR5 . . . . . .211 D3
Elysium Gate 7 SW6 . .135 B3
Elysium Pl SW6 . . . . . .135 B3
Elysium St SW6 . . . . . . .72 D5
Elystan Pl SW3 114 D1 257 C2
Elystan St SW3 .114 C2 257 B3
Elystan Wlk N1 . . . . . . .234 A5
Elyston Ct SW15 . . . . . .156 B6
Emanuel Ave W3 . . . . . .89 A1
Emanuel Ct W3 . . . . . . .89 B1
Emanuel Sch SW11 . . .158 C6
Emba St SE16 . . . . .118 A4
Embankment SW15 . . .134 D3
Embankment Gdns
SW3 . . . . .136 D6 267 D6
Embankment Pl WC2 . .250 B4
Embankment Sta
WC2 . . . . .116 A5 250 B4
Embankment The TW1 .153 A3
Embassey Ct DA14 . . . .168 B1
Embassy Ct 7 E18 . . . . .55 A6
N11 . . . . .31 D4
NW8 . . . . .229 D3
Bexley DA16 . . . . .146 B2
Kingston u T KT6 . . . . . .197 D4
7 Wallington SM6 . . . . .219 B2
W5 . . . . .110 B6
Embassy Gdns BR3 . . . .185 B2
Embassy Ho 2 NW6 . . . .69 C1
Embassy Lo N3 . . . . .29 B1
Ember Cl BR5 . . . . .211 A2
Ember Ct 14 NW9 . . . . . .27 D1
2 W12 . . . . .111 C3
Ember Farm Ave KT8 . .196 B3
Ember Farm Way KT8 . .196 B4
Ember Gdns KT10,KT8 . .196 C2
Ember Ho 8 BR1 . . . . . .186 B5
Ember La KT10,KT8 . . . .196 B2
Embercourt Rd KT10,
KT7,KT8 . . . . .196 C3
Emberson Ho 7 E17 . . . .54 A1
Emberton SE5 . . . . .139 C6
Emberton Ct EC1 . . . . .234 C1
Embleton Rd SE13 . . . .141 D1
Embleton Wlk TW12 . . .173 B5
Embley Point 2 E5 . . . . .74 B4
Embry Cl HA7 . . . . .25 A6
Embry Dr HA7 . . . . .25 A4
Embry Way HA7 . . . . . . .25 A6
Emden Cl UB7 . . . . .104 C4
Emden St SW6 . . . . . . .265 D2
Emerald Cl E16 . . . . . . .100 A1
Emerald Ct N1 . . . . .30 A6
Emerald Gdns RM8 . . . .59 C1
Emerald Sq UB2 . . . . . .106 D3
Emerald St WC1 .94 B2 240 C4
Emerson Gdns HA3 . . . .44 B3
Emerson Ho N16 . . . . . . .73 C3
Emerson Rd IG1 . . . . . . .56 C2
Emerson St SE1 117 A5 252 A4
Emerton Cl DA6 . . . . . . .147 A1
Emery Hill St SW1 . . . .259 B5
Emery St SE1 . . .116 C3 261 B6
Emilia Ct EN3 . . . . .18 B6
Emily Pl N7 . . . . .72 C4
Emily St 7 E16 . . . . .98 D1
Emlyn Gdns 3 W12 . . .111 C3
Emlyn Rd W12 . . . . .111 D3
Emma Rd E13 . . . . .98 D5
Emma St E2 . . . . .96 B5
Emmanuel CE Prim Sch
NW6 . . . . .69 C2
Emmanuel Ct 9 E10 . . . .53 D2
Emmanuel Ho SE11 . . .261 A3
SE21 . . . . .161 B1
Emmanuel Rd SW12 . . .159 D3
HA6 . . . . .22 A3
Emmeline Ct KT12 . . . .194 C2

Emminster NW6 . . . . . . .91 D6
Emmott Ave IG6 . . . . . . .57 A4
Emmott Cl E1 . . . . .97 A3
NW11 . . . . .48 A3
Emms Pas KT1 . . . . . . .175 D1
Emperor's Gate
SW7 . . . . .114 A2 256 A4
Empingham Ho 20 SE8 118 D2
Empire Ave N18 . . . . . . .33 A4
Empire Ct HA9 . . . . .66 D5
Empire Ho N18 . . . . .33 B4
W8 . . . . .257 A5
Empire Par N18 . . . . . . .33 B4
Wembley HA9 . . . . .66 C5
Empire Rd UB6 . . . . .65 C1
Empire Way HA9 . . . . . . .66 C4
Empire Wharf E3 . . . . . .97 A6
Empire Wharf Rd E14 . .120 B2
Empress Ave E4 . . . . . . .35 D3
E12 . . . . .77 D6
Ilford IG1 . . . . .78 C4
Woodford IG8 . . . . .36 D3
Empress Dr BR7 . . . . . .188 D4
Empress Par E4 . . . . . . .35 C3
Empress Pl
SW5 . . . . .113 C1 255 A1
Empress St SE17 . . . . . .139 A6
Empson St E3 . . . . .97 D3
Emsworth Cl N9 . . . . . . .18 C3
Emsworth Ho SW2 . . . .160 B2
Emu Rd SW8 . . . . .137 B3
Ena Rd SW16 . . . . .204 A6
Enard Ho 27 E3 . . . . . . .97 B5
Enbrook St W10 . . . . . . .91 A4
Endale Cl SM5 . . . . .218 D6
Endeavour Way SW19 .179 D6
Barking IG11 . . . . .102 A5
Wallington CR0 . . . . .204 A2
Endell St WC2 . . .94 A1 240 A1
Enderby St SE10 . . . . . .120 C1
Enderfield Ct BR7 . . . . .188 C2
Enderley Cl HA3 . . . . . . .24 C2
Enderley Ho SE19 . . . . .183 D1
Enderley Rd HA3 . . . . . .24 C2
Endersby Rd EN5 . . . . . .12 C5
Endersleigh Gdns NW4 . .46 A5
Endlebury Ct 3 E4 . . . . .20 B2
Endlebury Rd E4 . . . . . . .20 B2
Endlesham Ct 2 SW12 159 A4
Endlesham Rd SW12 . . .159 A4
Endsleigh Gdns
WC1 . . . . .93 D3 239 C6
Kingston u T KT6 . . . . . .197 C3
Redbridge IG1 . . . . .56 D1
Endsleigh Ind Est UB2 .107 B2
Endsleigh Mans 4
SW16 . . . . .160 A1
Endsleigh Pl WC1 . . . . .239 D6
Endsleigh Rd W13 . . . .109 A3
Southall UB2 . . . . .107 A2
Endsleigh St
WC1 . . . . .93 D3 239 D6
Endway KT5 . . . . .198 D2
Endwell Rd SE4 . . . . . . .141 A3
Endymion Rd N4 . . . . . . .50 D2
SW2 . . . . .160 B5
Energen Cl NW10 . . . . . .67 C1
Enfield Chase Sta EN2 . . .5 A2
Enfield Cloisters 7 N1 . .95 C4
Enfield Coll EN3 . . . . .6 C2
Enfield Cty Sch (Lower)
EN2 . . . . .5 C4
Enfield Cty Sch (Upper)
EN2 . . . . .5 B2
Enfield Gram Sch Lower
EN1 . . . . .5 B3
Enfield Ho 24 SW9 . . . .138 A3
Enfield Lock Sta EN3 . . . .7 A6
Enfield Rd E8,N1 . . . . . .73 C1
W3 . . . . .110 D4
Brentford TW8 . . . . .109 D1
Enfield EN2 . . . . .4 A2
Harlington TW6 . . . . .127 C3
Enfield Town Sta EN1 . . . .5 B2
Enfield Upper Gram Sch
EN2 . . . . .5 B2
Enfield Wlk TW8 . . . . . .109 D1
Enford St W1 . . .92 D2 237 C4
Engadine Cl CR0 . . . . . .221 D5
Engadine St SW18 . . . .157 C3
Engate St SE13 . . . . . . .142 A1
Engel Pk NW7 . . . . .28 C4
Engineer Cl SE18 . . . . .144 C6
Engineers Way HA9 . . . .66 C4
England's La NW3 . . . . . .70 D2
Englefield NW1 . . . . . . .232 A1
Englefie d Cl Enfield EN2 . .4 C3
St Paul's Cray BR5 . . . . . .211 D5
Thornton Heath CR0 . . . .205 A3
Englefield Path BR5 . . .211 D5
Englefield Rd N1 . . . . . . .73 C1
Englefield Rd N1 . . . . . . .73 C1
Engleheart Dr TW14 . . .149 D5
Engleheart Rd SE6 . . . .164 A4
Englewood Rd SW12 . . .159 C5
English Grounds SE1 . .253 A2
English Martyrs JMI Prim
Sch SE1 . . . . . . .117 B2 262 D3
English Martyrs JMI Sch
E1 . . . . .95 D1 243 D1
English Martyrs RC Sec Sch
SE17 . . . . .117 B2 262 D3
Enid St SE16 . . .117 B3 263 D6
Enid Stacy Ho 11 N19 . . .49 D2
Enmore Ave SE25 . . . . .206 A4
Enmore Ct SW14 . . . . . .155 B6
Enmore Gdns SW14 . . .155 B6

Enmore Rd SE25 . . . . . .206 A4
SW15 . . . . .156 C6
Southall UB1 . . . . .85 C3
Ennerdale Ave HA3,HA7 .43 C6
Ennerdale Cl
Cheam SM1 . . . . .217 B4
East Bedfont TW14 . . . . .149 D3
Ennerdale Ct E11 . . . . . .55 A2
Ennerdale Dr NW9 . . . . .45 C4
Ennerdale Gdns HA9 . . .43 C5
Ennerdale Ho 3 N4 . . . . .51 B2
Ennerdale Rd DA7 . . . . .147 C4
Richmond TW9 . . . . .132 B2
Ennerdale Prim Sch
SE13 . . . . .164 B6
Ennersdale Rd SE13 . . .164 B6
Ennis Ho 16 E14 . . . . . . .97 D1
Ennis Rd N4 . . . . .50 C1
SE18 . . . . .145 A1
Ennismore Ave W4 . . . .111 D2
Greenford UB6 . . . . .64 C3
Ennismore Gdns
SW7 . . . . .114 C3 257 A6
Thames Ditton KT7 . . . . .196 C3
Ennismore Gdns Mews
SW7 . . . . .114 C3 257 A6
Ennismore Mews
SW7 . . . . .114 C3 257 A6
Ennismore St
SW7 . . . . .114 C3 257 A6
Ennor Ct KT4 . . . . .216 C4
Ensbury Ho SW8 . . . . . .270 C4
Ensham Sch SW17 . . . .180 C5
Ensham Sec Sch (Annexe)
SW17 . . . . .180 C6
Ensign Cl TW19 . . . . . .148 A3
Ensign Dr N13 . . . . .17 A1
Ensign Ind Ctr 7 E1 . . .118 A6
Ensign St E1 . . . . .118 A6
Ensign Way TW19 . . . . .148 A3
Enslin Rd SE9 . . . . .166 C4
Ensor Mews SW7 . . . . .256 C2
Enstone Rd Enfield EN3 . . .7 A2
Ickenham UB10 . . . . .60 A5
Enterprise Ct CR0 . . . . .204 C1
Enterprise Ho E4 . . . . . .20 A4
Barking IG11 . . . . .101 D4
Walton-on-T KT12 . . . . . .194 D4
Enterprise Row N15 . . . .51 D4
Enterprise Way NW10 . . .90 A4
SW18 . . . . .135 C1
Teddington TW11 . . . . . .174 D4
Enterprize Way SE8 . . .119 B2
Epirus Mews SW6 . . . . .265 A4
Epirus Rd SW6 .135 B5 264 D4
Epping Cl E14 . . . . .119 C2
Romford RM7 . . . . .59 D6
Epping Forest IG10 . . . . .21 B6
Epping Glade E4 . . . . . . .20 A5
Epping Ho E5 . . . . .74 A6
Epping New Rd IG9 . . . . .21 B5
Epping Pl N1 . . . . .72 C2
Epping Way E4 . . . . .19 D6
Epple Rd SW6 .135 B4 264 D2
Epsom & Ewell High Sch
KT19 . . . . .215 A3
Epsom Cl
Bexleyheath DA7 . . . . . .147 D2
Northolt UB5 . . . . .63 B3
Epsom Rd E10 . . . . .54 A3
Croydon CR0 . . . . .220 C4
Ilford IG3 . . . . .57 D3
Morden SM4 . . . . .201 B2
Epsom Sq TW6 . . . . . . .127 D3
Epstein Rd SE28 . . . . . .124 B5
Epworth Rd TW7,TW8 . .131 B5
Epworth St EC2 .95 B3 242 D5
Equity Sq 24 E2 . . . . . . .95 D4
Erasmus St
SW1 . . . . .115 D2 259 D3
Erconwald St W12 . . . . . .89 D1
Eresby Dr BR3 . . . . .207 C1
Eresby Ho SW7 . . . . . . .247 B1
Eresby Pl NW6 . . . . .69 C1
Eric Cl E7 . . . . .77 A4
Eric Clarke La IG11 . . . .101 A4
Eric Fletcher Ct 7 N1 . . .73 A1
Eric Macdonald Ho
SE9 . . . . .265 B1
Eric Rd E7 . . . . .77 A4
NW10 . . . . .67 D2
Romford RM6 . . . . .58 D2
Eric Shipman Terr 2
E13 . . . . .99 A3
Eric St E3 . . . . .97 B3
Eric Wilkins Ho 19 SE1 118 A1
Erica Ct SW4 . . . . .270 D1
Erica Gdns CR0 . . . . . . .223 D5
Erica Ho N22 . . . . .32 C2
Erica St W12 . . . . .112 A6
Ericcson Cl SW18 . . . . .157 C6
Ericson Ho N16 . . . . .51 D1
SE13 . . . . .142 B1
Eridge Ho SE22 . . . . . . .139 D2
Eridge Rd W4 . . . . .111 B3
Erin Cl BR1 . . . . .186 C3
Erindale SE18 . . . . .145 B6
Erindale Ct 11 BR3 . . . .185 C2
Erindale Terr SE18 . . . .145 B6
Erith Rd Belvedere DA17 125 D1
Bexleyheath DA7 . . . . . .147 D2
Erlanger Rd SE14 . . . . .140 D3
Erlesmere Gdns W13 . .109 A3
Ermine Cl TW4 . . . . .128 C3
Ermine Ho 3 N17 . . . . . .33 D3
Ermine Rd N15 . . . . .51 D3
SE13 . . . . .141 D1

Ermine Side EN1 . . . . . .18 A6
Ermington Rd BR7,SE9 .167 A2
Ernald Ave E6 . . . . .100 A5
Erncroft Way TW1 . . . . .152 D5
Ernest Ave SE27 . . . . . .182 D6
Ernest Bevin Sch SW17 158 C1
Ernest Cl BR3 . . . . .207 C4
Ernest Cotts KT17 . . . . .215 D5
Ernest Gdns W4 . . . . . .132 D6
Ernest Gr BR3 . . . . .207 B4
Ernest Rd KT1 . . . . .176 D1
Ernest Richards Twr E17 53 B3
Ernest Simmonds Ho
SE14 . . . . .140 C3
Ernest Sq KT1 . . . . .176 D1
Ernest St E1 . . . . .96 D3
Ernle Rd SW20 . . . . . . .178 C3
Ernshaw Pl SW15 . . . . .157 A6
Eros (Shaftesbury Meml)
W1 . . . . .115 D6 249 C5
Erpingham Rd SW15 . . .134 C2
Erridge Rd SW19 . . . . . .179 C1
Errington Rd W9 . . . . . . .91 B3
Errol Gdns Hayes UB4 . .84 B3
West Barnes KT3 . . . . . . .200 A5
Errol St EC1 . . . .95 A3 242 B5
Erroll Rd RM6 . . . . .58 B4
Erskine Cl SM1 . . . . . . .218 C5
Erskine Cres N17 . . . . . .52 B5
Erskine Hill NW11 . . . . . .47 C4
Erskine Ho 7 SE7 . . . . .143 C6
SW1 . . . . .259 A1
Erskine Rd E17 . . . . .53 B5
NW3 . . . . .70 D1
Carshalton SM1,SM5 . . . .218 B5
Erwood Rd SE7 . . . . . . .122 A1
Esam Way SW16 . . . . . .182 C5
Escot Rd TW16 . . . . . . .171 C3
Escot Way EN5 . . . . .12 C6
Escreet Gr SE18 . . . . . .122 C2
Escuan Lo N5 . . . . .73 A1
Esher Ave Cheam SM3 .216 D5
Walton-on-T KT12 . . . . . .194 A1
Esher Church Sch KT10 212 A3
Esher Cl DA5 . . . . .169 A3
Esher Coll KT7 . . . . . . .196 C2
Esher Cres TW6 . . . . . .127 D3
Esher Gdns SW19 . . . . .156 C2
Esher Ho 8 SW8 . . . . . .137 D3
Esher Mews 4 CR4 . . . .202 C6
Esher Park Ave KT10 . .212 A3
Esher Rd
East Molesey KT8 . . . . . .196 B4
Ilford IG3 . . . . .79 C5
Esher Sta KT10 . . . . . . .212 B6
Esk Ho E3 . . . . .97 B3
Esk Rd E13 . . . . .99 B3
Eskdale NW1 . . . . .232 A3
Eskdale Ave UB5 . . . . . . .85 B6
Eskdale Cl HA9 . . . . .65 D6
Eskdale Rd DA7 . . . . . . .147 C4
Esk Ho N5 . . . . .73 A1
Esmar Cres NW9 . . . . . . .46 A2
Esme Ho SW15 . . . . . . .133 D1
Esmeralda Rd SE1 . . . . .118 A2
Esmond Ct W8 . . . . .255 D6
Esmond Gdns W4 . . . . .111 B2
Esmond Rd NW6 . . . . . . .91 B6
W4 . . . . .111 B3
Esmond St SW15 . . . . . .135 A1
Esparto St SW18 . . . . . .157 C4
Espedair St SW8 . . . . . .269 D4
Essan Ho W13 . . . . .87 B2
Essenden Rd
Belvedere DA17 . . . . . . .125 C1
South Croydon CR2 . . . . .221 C1
Essendine Mans W9 . . . .91 C4
Essendine Prim Sch W9 91 C4
Essendine Rd W9 . . . . . .91 C4
Essex Ave TW7 . . . . . . .130 C2
Essex Cl E17 . . . . .53 A5
Romford RM7 . . . . .59 D5
Ruislip HA4 . . . . .40 D1
West Barnes SM4 . . . . . .200 D2
Essex Ct EC4 . . . . .241 A1
SE19 . . . . .183 B4
SW13 . . . . .133 D3
W6 . . . . .112 C3
Essex Gdns N4 . . . . .50 D3
Essex Gr SE19 . . . . .183 B4
Essex Ho 2 E14 . . . . . . .97 D1
4 W3 . . . . .88 C1
Essex Lo 5 N10 . . . . . . .31 B4
Essex Mans E11 . . . . . . .54 B4
Essex Park Mews W3 . .111 C5
Essex Pk N3 . . . . .29 C4
Essex Pl W4 . . . . .111 A2
Essex Place Sq W4 . . . .111 B2
Essex Prim Sch E12 . . . .78 A3
Essex Rd E4 . . . . .20 C3
E10 . . . . .54 A3
E12 . . . . .78 A2
E17 . . . . .53 A3
E18 . . . . .37 B1
N1 . . . . .73 A1 234 D6
NW10 . . . . .67 C1
W3 . . . . .111 A6
W4 . . . . .111 B1
Barking IG11 . . . . .79 B1
Dagenham RM6 . . . . .58 C2
Enfield EN2 . . . . .5 B1
Romford RM7 . . . . .59 D5
Essex Rd S E11 . . . . .54 B2
Essex Road Sta N1 . . . . .73 A1
Essex St E7 . . . . .77 A3
WC2 . . . . .116 A5 251 A6
Essex Twr 4 SE20 . . . . .184 B2
Essex Villas W8 113 C4 245 A1

Essian St E1 . . . . .97 A2
Essington St SW15 . . . .157 A5
Essoldo Way HA8 . . . . . .44 B6
Estate Way E10 . . . . .53 B1
Este Rd SW11 . . . . .136 C2
Estcourt Rd SE25 . . . . .206 B3
SW6 . . . . .135 B5 264 C4
Estella Ave KT3 . . . . . . .200 B5
Estella Ho W11 . . . . . . .112 C6
Estelle Rd NW3 . . . . .70 D4
Esterbrooke St SW1 . . .259 C3
Esther Cl N21 . . . . .16 C4
Esther Rd E11 . . . . .54 C2
Estoria Cl 22 SW2 . . . . .160 C4
Estreham Rd SW16 . . . .181 D5
Estridge Cl TW3 . . . . . .129 C1
Estuary Cl IG11 . . . . . . .102 B4
Eswyn Rd SW17 . . . . . .180 D5
Etal Ho N1 . . . . .72 D1
Etchingham Ct N12 . . . . .30 A3
Etchingham Park Rd N3 .29 D3
Etchingham Rd E15 . . . . .76 A4
Etfield Gr DA14 . . . . . . .190 B5
Ethel Brooks Ho SE18 .144 D6
Ethel Cotts RM6 . . . . . . .58 B4
Ethel Davis Sch RM6 . . .58 B4
Ethel Rankin Ct 8 SW6 135 B3
Ethel Rd E16 . . . . .99 B1
Ashford TW15 . . . . .170 A5
Ethel St SE17 . . . . .262 B3
Ethelbert Ct BR1 . . . . . .209 A6
Ethelbert Gdns IG2 . . . .56 C4
Ethelbert Ho E9 . . . . . . .75 A4
Ethelbert Rd SW20 . . . .178 C2
Bromley BR1,BR2 . . . . . .209 A6
Ethelbert St SW12 . . . .159 B3
Ethelburga Prim Sch
SW11 . . . . . . .136 C4 267 B2
Ethelburga St
SW11 . . . . . . .136 C4 267 B2
Ethelburga Twr SW11 . .267 B2
Ethelden Rd W12 . . . . .112 B5
Etheldene Ave N10 . . . . .49 C5
Ethelworth Ct 4 SW2 . .160 C3
Etheridge Rd NW2 . . . . . .46 C2
Etherley Rd N15 . . . . . . .51 A4
Etherow St SE22 . . . . . .162 A4
Etherstone Grn SW16 . .182 C6
Etherstone Rd SW16 . . .182 C6
Ethnard Rd SE15 . . . . . .140 B6
Ethronvi Rd DA7 . . . . . .147 A2
Etloe Ho E10 . . . . .53 C1
Etloe Rd E10 . . . . .75 C6
Eton Ave N12 . . . . .30 A3
NW3 . . . . .70 C1
East Barnet EN4 . . . . .14 C5
Heston TW5 . . . . .129 C6
New Malden KT3 . . . . . . .199 B5
Wembley HA0 . . . . .65 C4
Eton Cl SW18 . . . . .157 D4
Eton College Rd NW3 . . .70 D2
Eton Ct NW3 . . . . .70 B1
Eton Garages 11 NW3 . .70 C2
Eton Gr NW9 . . . . .44 C5
SE13 . . . . .142 C2
Eton Hall NW3 . . . . .70 D2
Eton Ho N5 . . . . .72 D4
Eton Manor Ct E10 . . . . .75 C6
Eton Pl NW1 . . . . .71 A1
Eton Rd NW3 . . . . .70 D2
Harlington UB3 . . . . .127 D5
Ilford IG1 . . . . .79 B4
Eton Rise NW3 . . . . .70 D2
Eton St TW10 . . . . .154 A6
Eton Villas NW3 . . . . . . .70 D2
Etta St SE8 . . . . .141 A6
Ettrick Ho 8 E5 . . . . .74 B6
Ettrick St E14 . . . . .98 A1
Etwell Pl KT5 . . . . .198 B3
Eugene Cotter Ho SE17 262 D3
Eugenia Rd SE16 . . . . . .118 C2
Eureka Rd 8 KT1 . . . . . .176 C1
Euro Bsns Ctr 3 E15 . . .98 B6
Euro Cl NW10 . . . . .68 A2
Eurolink Bsns Ctr SW2 160 C6
Europa Pl EC1 . . . . .235 A1
Europe Rd SE18 . . . . . .122 B3
Eustace Ho SE11 . . . . . .260 C4
Eustace Pl SE18 . . . . . .122 B2
Eustace Rd E6 . . . . .100 A4
SW6 . . . . .135 C5 265 A4
Romford RM6 . . . . .58 D2
Euston Rd NW1 . . .93 D3 239 B6
Thornton Heath CR0 . . . .204 C1
Euston Sq NW1 . . . . . . .232 C1
Euston Square Sta
WC1 . . . . .93 D3 239 B6
Euston St NW1 . . .93 C4 232 B1
Euston Sta NW1 .93 C4 232 C1
Euston Underpass NW1 239 A6
Eva Rd RM6 . . . . .58 D2
Evandale Rd SW9 . . . . .138 C3
Evangelist Rd NW5 . . . . .71 B4
Evans Cl E8 . . . . .73 D2
E15 . . . . .98 C5
NW10 . . . . .67 C6
W4 . . . . .111 A6
Evans Gr TW13 . . . . . . .151 C2
Evans Ho SW8 . . . . .269 D3
34 W12 . . . . .112 B6
Evans Rd SE6 . . . . .164 C2
Evanston Ave E4 . . . . . . .36 A3
Evanston Gdns IG4 . . . . .56 A3
Eve Rd E11 . . . . .76 C4
E15 . . . . .98 C5
N17 . . . . .51 C6
Isleworth TW7 . . . . .131 A1
Evelina Mans 8 SE5 . . .139 B5
Evelina Rd SE15 . . . . . .140 C3
SE20 . . . . .184 D3

Eveline Ct N10 49 B4
Eveline Lowe Prim Sch SE1 118 A1
Eveline Rd CR4 180 D2
Evelyn Ave NW9 45 B5
Ruislip HA4 39 D2
Evelyn Cl TW2 151 D4
Evelyn Cres TW16 171 D2
Evelyn Ct E8 74 A4
N1 235 C3
W1 237 C1
Croydon CR0 206 A2
Evelyn Denington Ct 2 N1 72 D1
Evelyn Denington Rd E6 100 A3
Evelyn Dr HA5 22 D3
Evelyn Fox Ct W10 90 C2
Evelyn Gdns SW7 114 B1 256 C1
Richmond TW9 132 A1
Evelyn Gr W5 110 B5
Southall UB1 85 B1
Evelyn Ho 3 SW2 160 B6
W12 111 D4
Evelyn Rd E16 121 B5
E17 54 A5
SW19 179 D4
W4 111 B3
Cockfosters EN4 2 D1
Richmond TW9 132 A2
Richmond TW10 153 C1
Evelyn St SE8 119 A1
Evelyn Terr TW9 132 A2
Evelyn Way
Sunbury TW16 171 D2
Wallington SM6 219 D4
Evelyn Wlk N1 95 B5 235 C3
Evelyn Yd W1 239 C2
Evelyns Cl UB8 82 C1
Evelyns Com Sch UB7 82 B1
Evening Hill BR3 186 A3
Evenlode Ho 5 SE2 124 C4
Evenwood Cl SW15 157 A6
Everard Ave BR2 209 A1
Everard Ct N13 16 B1
Everard Ho 24 E1 96 A1
Everard Way HA9 66 A5
Everatt Cl SW18 157 B6
Everdale Ct N2 48 C5
Everdon Rd SW13 134 A6
Everest Ct 6 SE9 166 A2
SE19 183 C2
Everest Pl E14 98 A2
Everest Rd SE9 166 B6
Stanwell TW19 148 A4
Everett Cl Bushey WD2 8 C3
Pinner HA5 39 D6
Everett Ho N7 72 C4
SE17 262 C2
Everett Wlk DA17 125 B1
Everglade Ho E17 35 B1
Everglade Strand NW9 27 D2
Everglades
Beckenham BR2 208 C6
Hounslow TW3 130 A2
Evergreen Way UB3 105 D6
Everilda St N1 233 D5
Evering Rd E5,N16 74 A5
Everington Rd N10 30 D1
Everington St W6 134 D6
Everitt Rd NW10 89 B4
Everleigh St N4 50 B1
Eversfield Ct SE12 165 B2
Eversfield Gdns HA8, NW7 27 C3
Eversfield Rd TW9 132 B3
Evershed Ho E1 243 D2
Eversholt Ct EN5 14 A6
Eversholt St NW1 93 C4 232 B3
Evershot Rd N4 50 B1
Eversleigh Ct N3 29 C3
Eversleigh Rd E6 99 D6
N3 29 B3
SW11 137 A3
New Barnet EN5 14 A6
Eversley Ave HA9 66 C6
Eversley Cl N21 16 B5
Eversley Cres N21 16 C5
Hounslow TW7 130 B4
Ruislip HA4 61 D6
Eversley Ho 18 E2 96 A4
Eversley Mount N21 16 B5
Eversley Park Rd N21 16 B5
Eversley Pk SW19 178 B5
Eversley Prim Sch N21 16 B5
Eversley Rd SE7 143 B6
SE19 183 B3
Kingston u T KT5 198 B4
Eversley Way CR0 223 C5
Everthorpe Rd SE15 139 D2
Everton Bldgs NW1 232 A1
Everton Ct HA0 65 D4
Everton Dr HA7 44 A6
Everton Rd CR0 206 A1
Evesham Ave E17 35 C1
Evesham Cl
Belmont SM2 217 C1
Greenford UB6 85 D5
Evesham Ct 2 W13 109 A5
Evesham Gn SM4 201 D3
Evesham Ho 1 E2 96 C5
NW8 229 A5
SW1 258 D2
Evesham Rd E15 76 D1
N11 31 D5
Morden SM4 201 D3
Evesham St W11 112 D6
Evesham Way SW11 137 A2
Ilford IG5 56 C6
Evesham Wlk SE5 139 B3
SW9 138 C3
Evry Rd DA14 190 C4
Ewald Rd SW6 135 B3
Ewanrigg Terr IG8 37 C5
Ewart Gr N22 32 C2
Ewart Pl 10 E3 97 B5
Ewart Rd SE23 162 D4
Ewe Cl N7 72 A2
Ewell By-Pass KT17 216 A1
Ewell Court Ave KT19 215 C3
Ewell Park Gdns KT17 216 A1
Ewell Park Way KT17 216 A1
Ewell Rd
Cheam SM2,SM3 216 D2
Surbiton KT5,KT6 198 B2
Thames Ditton KT6,KT7 197 B2
Tolworth KT6 198 D1
Ewelme Rd SE23 162 C3
Ewen Cres SW2 160 C4
Ewen Ho N1 233 C5
Ewer St SE1 117 A5 252 A3
Ewhurst 19 SW15 156 D5
Ewhurst Ct CR4 202 B6
Ewhurst Ho 29 E1 96 C2
Ewhurst Rd SE4 163 B5
Exbury Ho E9 74 C2
4 SW9 138 B1
Exbury Rd SE6 163 C2
Excel Ct WC2 249 D5
Excelsior Cl KT1 176 C1
Excelsior Gdns SE13 142 A3
Excelsior Ind Est SE16 140 C6
Exchange Arc EC2 243 B4
Exchange Ct WC2 250 B5
Exchange Mans 2 NW11 47 B2
Exchange Pl EC2 243 A4
Exchange The IG1 78 D6
Exeforde Ave TW15 170 C6
Exeter Cl E6 100 B1
Exeter Ct NW6 91 C5
SW19 180 C3
Kingston u T KT6 198 A4
Exeter Gdns IG1 56 B1
Exeter Ho 11 SE15 140 A6
SW15 156 C5
W2 236 A2
7 Barking IG11 80 A1
Feltham TW13 151 C2
Exeter Mans NW2 69 A2
Exeter Mews SW6 265 A4
Exeter Rd E16 99 A2
E17 53 C4
N9 18 C2
N14 15 B4
NW2 69 A2
Bexley DA16 145 D3
Croydon CR0 205 D2
Dagenham RM10 81 D2
Enfield EN3 6 D2
Feltham TW13 151 B1
Harlington TW6 127 C2
Harrow HA2 63 A6
Exeter St WC2 116 B6 250 C6
Exeter Way 2 SE14 141 B5
Harlington TW6 127 C3
Exford Ct SW11 266 D2
Exford Gdns SE12 165 B3
Exford Rd SE12 165 B3
Exhibition Cl W12 112 C6
Exhibition Rd
SW7 114 B3 256 D6
Exmoor Ho 23 E3 97 A5
Exmoor St W10 90 D2
Exmouth Ho 6 E14 119 D2
Exmouth Market
EC1 94 C3 241 B6
Exmouth Mews NW1 232 B1
Exmouth Pl E8 74 B1
Exmouth Rd E17 53 B4
Bexley DA16 146 C5
Hayes UB4 83 C4
Ruislip HA4 62 C5
Exmouth St E1 96 C1
Exning Rd E16 98 D3
Exon St SE17 117 C2 263 A3
Exonbury NW8 91 D6
Explorer Ave TW19 148 A3
Express Dr IG3 58 B1
Exton Cres NW10 67 A1
Exton Gdns RM8 80 C3
Exton St SE1 116 C5 251 A3
Eyebright Cl 3 CR0 206 D1
Eyhurst Cl NW2 68 A6
Eylewood Rd SE27 183 A5
Eynella Rd SE21 161 D4
Eynham Rd W12 90 C1
Eynsford Cl BR5 211 A3
Eynsford Cres DA5, DA14 168 D3
Eynsford Ho SE1 252 C2
12 SE15 140 C6
SE17 263 A3
Eynsford Rd IG3 79 C6
Eynsford Terr UB7 82 B1
Eynsham Dr SE2 124 B3
Eynswood Dr DA14 190 C5
Eyot Gdns W6 111 D1
Eyot Gn W4 111 D1
Eyre Ct NW8 229 C4
Eyre St Hill EC1 94 C3 241 A5
Eysham Ct 8 EN5 13 D6
Eythorne Rd SW9 138 C4
Ezra St E2 95 D4

F

F Ave SE18 122 D3
Faber Gdns NW4 46 A4
Fabian Rd SW6 135 B5 264 D4
Fabian St E6 100 B3
Fabyc Ho TW9 132 C5
Factory La N17 33 D1
Croydon CR0 220 D6
Factory Rd E16 122 A5
Factory Yd W7 108 C5
Fagg's Rd TW14 150 A6
Fair Acres BR2 209 A4
Fair Green Ct 1 CR4 202 D6
Fair Lea Pl W5 87 C2
Fair St SE1 117 D4 253 C2
Hounslow TW3 130 A2
Fair View Cl E17 35 A2
Fairacre Hounslow TW7 130 B4
Kingston u T KT3 199 C6
Pinner HA5 40 A5
Fairacres SW15 134 A1
Ruislip HA4 39 D2
Fairbairn Gn 1 SW9 138 D4
Fairbank Ave BR6 226 D6
Fairbanks Rd N17 52 A6
Fairbourne Ho UB3 105 A3
Fairbourne Rd N17 51 C6
Fairbridge Rd N19 71 D6
Fairbrook Cl N13 32 C5
Fairbrook Rd N13 32 C4
Fairburn Ct SW15 157 A6
Fairburn Ho 9 N16 51 C1
SW5 254 D1
Fairby Ho SE1 263 D4
Fairby Rd SE12 165 B6
Faircharm Trad Est SE8 141 D5
Fairchild Cl 6 SW11 136 B3
Fairchild Ho 13 E9 74 C1
5 N1 95 C4
SW1 259 B3
Fairchild Pl EC2 243 B5
Fairchild St EC2 243 B5
Fairclough St E1 96 A1
Faircourt 14 NW3 70 D2
Faircroft N16 51 B1
SE26 184 C6
Faircross Ave IG11 79 A2
Faircross Par IG11 79 C3
Faircross Sch IG11 79 C2
Fairdale Gdns SW15 134 B1
Hayes UB3 106 A4
Fairdene Ct N7 72 A3
Fairey Ave UB3 105 D3
Fairfax Cl KT12 194 B1
Fairfax Gdns SE3 143 C4
Fairfax Ho 12 SW9 138 C3
6 SW15 156 A6
5 W5 88 A4
Fairfax Mews E16 121 B5
N8 50 D5
SW15 134 C1
Fairfax Pl NW6 70 A1
Fairfax Rd N8 50 C5
NW6 70 A1
W4 111 C3
Teddington TW11 175 B3
Fairfax Way N10 31 A3
Fairfield 4 E1 96 C2
N20 14 B4
NW1 232 A5
Northwood Hills HA6 22 A1
Fairfield Ave NW4 46 B3
Edgware HA8 26 D3
Ruislip HA4 39 A2
Twickenham TW2 151 D3
Fairfield Cl N12 30 A6
SW19 180 C3
Enfield EN3 7 A1
Sidcup DA15 167 D5
West Ewell KT19 215 C3
Fairfield Cres HA8 26 D4
Fairfield Ct NW10 90 A6
1 SW18 157 D6
Ruislip HA4 39 B1
8 Woodford IG8 37 A4
Fairfield Dr SW18 157 D6
Harrow HA2 42 A6
Wembley UB6 87 C6
Fairfield E KT1 176 A1
Fairfield Gdns N8 50 A4
Fairfield Gr SE7 143 D6
Fairfield Ind Est KT1 198 B6
Fairfield N KT1,KT2 176 A1
Fairfield Path CR0 221 B5
Fairfield Pl KT1 198 A6
Fairfield Rd E3 97 C5
E17 35 A1
N8 50 A4
N18 34 A6
Beckenham BR3 185 C1
Bexley DA7 147 B3
Ilford IG1 78 D2
Kingston u T KT1 176 A1
Orpington BR5 211 B3
Plaistow BR1 187 A3
South Croydon CR0 221 C5
Southall UB1 85 B1
Woodford IG8 37 A4
Yiewsley UB7 104 A6
Fairfield S KT1 176 B1
Fairfield St SW18 157 D6
Fairfield W KT1 176 A1
Fairfield Way Barnet EN5 13 C6
West Ewell KT19 215 C3
Fairfields SE6 163 D4
Fairfields Cl NW9 45 A4
Fairfields Cres NW9 45 A4
Fairfields Rd TW3 130 A2
Fairfoot Rd E3 97 C3
Fairford SE6 163 C3
Fairford Ave CR0 206 D4
Fairford Cl CR0 207 A4
Fairford Ct SM2 217 D1
Fairford Gdns KT4 215 D5
Fairford Ho SE11 261 B3
Fairgreen EN4 2 D2
Fairgreen Ct EN4 2 D2
Fairgreen E EN4 2 D2
Fairgreen Rd CR7 204 D4
Fairhall Ct KT6 198 B2
Fairhaven Ave CR0 206 D3
Fairhaven Ct CR2 221 A3
Fairhazel Gdns NW6 70 A1
Fairheathe SW15 156 D5
Fairholme TW14 149 C4
Fairholme Cl N3 47 A5
Fairholme Cres UB4 84 A3
Fairholme Gdns N3 47 A5
Fairholme Ho 3 KT3 199 C5
Fairholme Jun & Inf Schs TW14 149 B3
Fairholme Rd
W14 113 A1 254 B1
Ashford TW15 170 B5
Cheam SM1 217 B2
Harrow HA1 42 D4
Ilford IG1 56 C2
Thornton Heath CR0 204 C2
Fairholt Cl N16 51 C1
Fairholt Rd N16 51 B1
Fairholt St SW7 257 B6
Fairhurst 4 NW6 70 A2
Fairland Ho BR2 209 B5
Fairland Rd E15 76 D1
Fairlands Ave
Buckhurst Hill IG9 21 A2
Sutton SM1 217 C6
Thornton Heath CR7 204 C4
Fairlands Ct 6 SE9 166 C5
Fairlawn SE7 143 C6
Fairlawn Ave N2 48 C5
W4 111 A2
Bexley DA16 146 D3
Fairlawn Cl N14 15 D5
Claygate KT10 212 D2
Feltham TW13 173 B6
Kingston u T KT2 177 A4
Fairlawn Ct SE7 143 C5
3 W4 111 A2
Fairlawn Dr IG8 37 A3
Fairlawn Gdns UB1 107 B6
Fairlawn Gr W4 111 A2
Fairlawn Mans SE14 140 D4
Fairlawn Pk SE26 185 A5
Fairlawn Prim Sch SE23 162 C4
Fairlawn Prim Sch Annexe SE23 162 C3
Fairlawn Rd SW19 179 B3
Fairlawnes SM6 219 B3
Fairlawns 10 E4 20 A2
3 N11 32 A4
SW15 156 D6
Pinner Green WD1 22 D1
Sunbury TW16 194 A6
Twickenham TW1 153 C5
Fairlea Pl W5 87 D3
Fairleas 12 BR3 185 D1
Fairlie Ct 22 E3 97 D4
1 N7 71 D4
Fairlie Gdns SE23 162 C4
Fairlight TW12 173 D5
Fairlight Ave E4 20 B2
NW10 89 C5
Woodford IG8 37 A4
Fairlight Cl E4 20 B2
North Cheam KT4 216 C4
Fairlight Ct NW10 89 C5
Greenford UB6 86 B5
Fairlight Rd SW17 180 B6
Fairline Ct BR3 186 A1
Fairlop Ct E11 54 C1
Fairlop Pl NW8 229 D1
Fairlop Rd E11 54 B2
Fairmark Dr UB10 60 C2
Fairmead Bromley BR1 210 B5
Tolworth KT5,KT6 198 D1
Fairmead Cl
Bromley BR1 210 B5
Heston TW5 128 D5
Kingston u T KT3 199 B6
Fairmead Cres HA8 11 A1
Fairmead Ct 3 E4 20 C4
Fairmead Gdns IG4 56 A4
Fairmead Ho E9 75 A4
Fairmead Rd N7,N19 72 A5
Thornton Heath CR0 204 C2
Fairmeadside IG10 21 C6
Fairmile Ave SW16 181 D5
Fairmile Ho
St Paul's Cray BR5 190 A1
Teddington TW11 175 A6
Fairmont Cl DA17 125 B1
Fairmont Ho 1 E3 97 C3
Fairmount Rd SW2 160 B5
Fairoak Cl BR5 210 D2
Fairoak Dr SE9 167 B6
Fairseat Cl WD2 8 C2
Fairstead Lo 4 IG8 37 A4
Fairstead Wlk N1 235 A6
Fairthorn Rd SE7,SE10 121 A1
Fairview Ave HA0 65 D2
Fairview Cl SE26 185 A5
Fairview Cres HA2 41 C1
Fairview Ct NW4 28 D1
Ashford TW15 170 C5
Kingston u T KT2 176 D2
Fairview Dr
Littleton TW17 192 B4
Orpington BR6 227 B4
Fairview Gdns IG8 37 B2
Fairview Ho 14 SW2 160 B4
Fairview Pl SW2 160 B4
Fairview Rd N15 51 D3
SW16 182 B2
Carshalton SM1,SM5 218 C3
Enfield EN2 4 C4
Fairview Villas E4 35 D3
Fairview Way HA8 26 C6
Fairwall Ho 9 SE5 139 C4
Fairwater Ave DA16 146 A1
Fairwater Ho TW11 175 A6
Fairway SW20 200 C6
Bexley DA6 169 A6
Petts Wood BR5 211 B4
Woodford IG8 37 C5
Fairway Ave NW9 44 D6
Fairway Cl NW11 48 A2
Croydon CR0 207 A4
Hounslow TW4 150 D6
West Ewell KT19 215 A4
Fairway Ct NW7 11 B1
12 SE9 166 C5
13 SE16 118 D4
New Barnet EN5 13 D5
Fairway Dr SE28 103 A1
Greenford UB6 63 D1
Fairway Est TW4 150 C6
Fairway Gdns
Beckenham BR3 208 B3
Ilford IG1 79 A3
Fairway Prim Sch The NW7 11 B2
Fairway The N13 17 B1
N14 15 C5
NW7 11 B1
W3 89 C1
Bromley BR1,BR2 210 B4
East Molesey KT8 195 D6
Hillingdon UB10 82 B5
Kingston u T KT3 177 B2
New Barnet EN5 13 D5
Northolt UB5 64 A2
Ruislip HA4 62 D5
Wembley HA0 65 B6
Fairways E17 54 A5
Ashford TW15 170 D4
4 Hounslow TW7 130 C4
Stanmore HA7 26 A1
Teddington TW11 175 D3
Fairways Bsns Pk E10 75 A6
Fairweather Cl N15 51 C5
Fairweather Ct N13 32 B6
Fairweather Ho N7 72 A4
Fairweather Rd N16 52 A3
Fairwood Ct E11 54 B2
Fairwyn Rd SE26 185 A6
Faith Ct NW2 68 B2
Faithfull Ho N5 73 A3
Fakenham Cl NW7 28 A3
5 Northolt UB5 63 C2
Fakruddin St E1 96 A3
Falaize Ave IG1 78 D4
Falcon Ave BR1 210 A5
Falcon Cl SE1 251 D4
W4 133 A6
Falcon Cres EN3 18 D6
Falcon Ct 6 E18 55 B6
EC4 241 A1
N1 234 D3
8 SE21 161 B2
New Barnet EN5 2 A1
Ruislip HA4 61 C6
Falcon Dr TW19 148 A5
Falcon Gr SW11 136 C2
Falcon Ho 10 SE15 139 D4
Falcon La SW11 136 C2
Falcon Lo NW3 69 D4
11 W9 91 C2
Falcon Point SE1 251 D5
Falcon Rd SW11 136 C2
Enfield EN3 18 D6
Hampton TW12 173 B3
Falcon St E13 99 A3
Falcon Terr SW11 136 C2
Falcon Way E11 55 A5
E14 119 D2
NW9 27 C1
Feltham TW14 150 B6
Harrow HA3 44 A3
Sunbury TW16 171 C1
Falconberg Ct W1 239 D2
Falconberg Mews W1 239 D2
Falconbrook Prim Sch SW11 136 B2
Falconer Ct N17 33 A3
Falconer Wlk 12 N7 72 B6
Falconhurst 4 KT6 198 A4
Falconry Ct KT1 198 A6
Falconwood Ave DA16 145 C3
Falconwood Ct SE3 142 D3
Falconwood Par DA16 145 D1
Falconwood Rd CR0 223 C1
Falconwood Sta SE9 145 B1
Falcourt Cl SM1 217 D3
Falkener Ct SW11 268 B1
Falkirk Ct 11 SE16 118 D5
Falkirk Gdns WD1 22 D5
Falkirk Ho W9 91 D4
Falkirk St N1 95 C5
Falkland Ave N3 29 C3
Falkland Ave *continued*
N11 31 B6
Falkland Ho SE6 186 A6
W8 255 C5
W14 254 C2
Falkland Park Ave SE25 183 C1
Falkland Pl 2 NW5 71 C3
Falkland Rd N8 50 C5
NW5 71 C3
Monken Hadley EN5 1 A3
Falladon Ho W11 91 B2
Falling La UB7 104 A6
Falloden Way NW11 47 C5
Fallodon Ho 6 SW8 137 D3
Fallow Court Ave N12 30 A4
Fallow Ct 16 SE16 118 A1
Fallow Fields IG10 21 C4
Fallowfield N4 72 B6
Stanmore HA7 9 A1
Fallowfield Ct HA7 9 A1
Fallowfields Dr N12 30 C4
Fallows Cl N2 30 B1
Fallsbrook Rd SW16 181 C4
Falman Cl N9 18 A3
Falmer Rd E17 53 D6
N15 51 B4
Enfield EN1 5 C1
Falmouth Ave E4 36 C5
Falmouth Cl N22 32 B3
SE12 164 D6
Falmouth Gdns IG4 55 D5
Falmouth Ho SE11 261 B2
W2 247 A6
Falmouth Rd
SE1 117 A3 262 B5
Falmouth St E15 76 B3
Falstaff Ct SE11 261 C3
Falstaff Ho 18 N1 95 C5
Fambridge Cl SE26 185 B6
Fambridge Rd RM8 59 C1
Fane Ho 3 E2 96 C6
Fane St W14 264 D6
Fann St EC1 95 A3 242 B5
Fanshaw Ho 6 E17 53 D6
Fanshaw St N1 95 C4
Fanshawe Ave IG11 79 A2
Fanshawe Cres RM9 81 B3
Fanshawe Rd TW10 175 C6
Fantail The BR6 226 B5
Fanthorpe St SW15 134 C2
Faraday Ave DA14 168 B2
Faraday Cl N7 72 B2
Faraday Ho 6 E14 119 B6
6 NW5 71 B4
2 SW12 159 B4
W10 91 A2
4 Belvedere DA17 125 C3
5 Hampton TW12 173 D4
Wembley HA9 67 A5
Faraday Rd E15 76 D2
SW19 179 D4
W3 111 A6
W10 91 A2
Bexley DA16 146 A2
East Molesey KT8 195 C5
Southall UB1 107 D6
Faraday Way SE18 121 D3
Croydon CR0 204 B1
Fareham Ho 15 SW15 156 A3
Fareham Rd TW14 150 C4
Fareham St W1 239 C2
Farewell Pl CR4 180 C2
Faringdon Ave BR2 210 C3
Faringford Rd E15 76 C1
Farjeon Ho NW6 70 B1
Farjeon Rd SE3 143 D4
Farleigh Ave BR2 209 A2
Farleigh Ct CR2 221 A3
Farleigh Ho 7 KT2 176 D4
Farleigh Pl N16 73 D4
Farleigh Rd N16 73 D4
Farley Croft BR2 186 C1
Farley Ct NW1 238 A5
W14 254 C6
Farley Dr IG3 57 C1
Farley Ho SE26 162 B1
Farley Pl SE25 206 A5
Farley Rd SE6 164 A4
South Croydon CR2 222 B1
Farleycroft 1 CR0 206 A1
Farlington Pl SW15 156 B4
Farlong Path UB5 63 A2
Farlow Rd SW15 134 D2
Farlton Rd SW18 157 D4
Farm Ave NW2 69 B5
SW16 182 A6
Harrow HA2,HA5 41 C3
Wembley HA0 65 C2
Farm Avenue Ho HA0 65 C2
Farm Cl SW6 265 B4
Buckhurst Hill IG9 21 C1
Coney Hall BR4 224 D5
Ducks Island EN5 12 C6
Lower Halliford TW17 192 C2
Southall UB1 107 D6
Sutton SM2 218 B1
Uxbridge UB10 60 D6
Farm Cotts E17 53 A3
Farm Ct NW4 46 A6
Farm Dr CR0 223 B6
Farm End E4 20 C6
Farm House Ct NW7 28 A3
Farm La N14 15 B5
SW6 135 C5 265 B4

Farm La *continued*
Croydon CR0 223 B6
Farm Lane Trad Ctr
SW6 135 C6 265 B5
Farm Pl W8 245 A4
Farm Rd N21 17 A3
Morden SM4 201 D4
Sutton SM2 218 B1
Twickenham TW4 151 A3
KT10 195 C1
Farm St W1 115 B6 248 C5
Farm Vale DA5 169 D5
Farm View N3 47 B6
Farm Way
Buckhurst Hill IG9 37 C6
North Cheam KT4 216 C5
Farm Wlk NW11 47 C4
Farman Terr HA3 43 D5
Farmborough Cl HA1 42 B2
Farmcote Rd SE12 165 A3
Farmdale Rd SE10 121 A1
Sutton SM5 218 C1
Farmer Ho 4 SE15 118 B3
Farmer Rd E10 53 D1
Farmer St W8 245 A4
Farmers Rd SE5 138 D5
Farmfield Rd BR1 186 C5
Farmhouse Rd SW16 181 C3
Farmilo Rd E17 53 C2
Farmington Ave SM1 218 B5
Farmland Wlk BR7 188 D5
Farmlands Enfield EN2 4 C4
Pinner HA5 40 A5
Farmlands The UB5 63 C2
Farmleigh N14 15 C4
Farmleigh Ho SW9 160 D6
Farmstead Rd SE6 185 D6
Harrow HA3 24 B1
Farmway RM8 80 C5
Farnaby Ho 2 W10 91 B4
Farnaby Rd SE9 143 C1
Bromley BR1 186 C2
Farnan Ave E17 53 D6
Farnan Rd SW16 182 A5
Farnborough Ave E17 53 A6
Selsdon CR2 223 A1
Farnborough Cl HA9 66 D6
Farnborough Comm
Keston Mark BR2,BR6 226 B5
Locksbottom BR6 226 C4
Farnborough Cres
3 Coney Hall BR2 208 D1
Selsdon CR2 223 A1
Farnborough Ct 2 BR6 227 A3
Farnborough Hill BR6 227 C3
Farnborough Ho 1
SW15 156 A3
Farnborough Hospl
BR6 226 C4
Farnborough Prim Sch
BR6 227 A3
Farnborough Way
10 SE15 139 C5
Orpington BR6 227 B3
Farncombe St SE16 118 A4
Farndale Ave N13 17 A1
Farndale Cres UB6 86 A4
Farndale Ho 1 NW6 91 D6
Farnell Mews SW5 255 C2
Farnell Point E5 74 A4
Farnell Rd TW7 130 B2
Farnell's Almshouses
TW7 130 D3
Farnfield Ho 12 SW2 160 B6
Farnham Cl N20 14 A4
Farnham Ct 2 N16 51 C1
2 Cheam SM3 217 A2
1 Southall UB1 86 A1
Farnham Gdns SW20 178 B1
Farnham Ho NW1 237 B5
SE1 252 A3
Farnham Pl SE1 251 D3
Farnham Rd
Bexley DA16 146 C3
Ilford IG3 57 D2
Farnham Royal
SE11 116 B1 260 D1
Farnhurst Ho 7 SW11 137 A3
Farningham Ct SW16 181 D3
Farningham Ho 9 N4 51 B2
Farningham Rd N17 34 A3
Farnley Ho 13 SW8 137 D3
Farnley Rd E4 20 C4
SE25 205 B5
Farnsworth Ho 8
SW27 182 D5
Farnworth Ho 5 E14 120 B2
Faro Cl BR1 188 C1
Faroe Rd W14 112 D3
Farorna Wlk EN2 4 C4
Farquhar Rd SE19 183 D5
SW19 157 C1
Farquharson Rd CR0 205 A1
Farr Ave IG11 102 A5
Farr Rd EN2 5 B4
Farrance Rd RM6 59 A2
Farrance St E14 97 C1
Farrans Ct HA3 43 B2
Farrant Ave N22 32 D1
Farrant Cl BR6 227 D1
Farrant Ho 15 SW11 136 B2
Farrell Ho E1 96 C1
Farren Rd SE23 163 A2
Farrer Ho SE8 141 C5
Farrer Mews N8 49 C5
Farrer Rd N8 49 D5
Harrow HA3 44 A5
Farrer's Pl CR0 222 D4
Farrier Cl Bromley BR1 209 D6
Hillingdon UB8 82 C1
Farrier Rd UB5 85 C5
Farrier St NW1 71 C1
Farrier Wlk
SW10 136 A6 266 A6
Farriers Ct SW19 179 A3
Belmont SM2 217 A1
Farriers Way WD6 11 B6
Farringdon La
EC1 94 C3 241 B5
Farringdon Rd
EC1 94 C3 241 B5
Farringdon St
EC4 94 D1 241 C2
Farringdon Sta
EC1 94 D2 241 C4
Farrington Girls' Sch
BR7 189 B3
Farrington Ho 12 SE18 122 C2
Farrington Pl BR7 189 B3
Farrins Rents SE16 119 A5
Farrow La SE14 140 C5
Farrow Pl SE16 119 A3
Farthing Alley 5 SE1 118 A4
Farthing Fields 8 E1 118 B5
Farthing St BR6 226 B1
Farthings Cl E4 20 C1
Pinner HA5 40 B3
Farthings The 1 KT2 176 C2
Farwell Rd DA14 190 C6
Farwig La BR1 187 A2
Fashion St E1 95 D2 243 D3
Fashoda Rd BR2 209 D5
Fassett Rd E8 74 A2
Kingston u T KT1 198 A5
Fassett Sq E8 74 A2
Fauconberg Ct W4 133 A6
Fauconberg Rd W4 133 A6
Faulkner Cl 6 RM8 58 D2
Faulkner Ho SW15 134 C3
Faulkner St SE14 140 C4
Faulkner's Alley EC1 241 C4
Fauna Cl RM6 58 C3
Faunce Ho 1 SE17 138 D6
Faunce St SE17 116 D1 261 C1
Favart Rd SW6 135 C4 265 B2
Faversham Ave E4 20 D3
Enfield EN1 17 B5
Faversham Ho NW1 232 B5
SE17 263 A1
Faversham Rd SE6 163 B3
Beckenham BR3 185 B1
Morden SM4 201 D3
Fawcett Cl SW11 136 B3
SW16 182 C6
Fawcett Est E5 52 A1
Fawcett Ho 23 SW9 138 A3
Fawcett Rd NW10 67 D1
Croydon CR0 221 A5
Fawcett St
SW10 136 A6 266 A6
Fawcus Cl KT10 212 C2
Fawe Park Rd SW15 135 B1
Fawe St E14 97 D2
Fawkham Ho SE1 263 D3
Fawley Lo 2 E14 120 B2
Fawley Rd NW6 69 D3
Fawn Rd E13 99 C5
Fawnbrake Ave SE24 161 A6
Fawns Manor Cl TW14 149 A3
Fawns Manor Rd TW14 149 B3
Fawood Ave NW10 67 B1
Fayetville Ho 20 N19 49 D2
Faygate Cres DA6 169 C6
Faygate Rd SW2 160 B2
Fayland Ave SW16 181 C5
Fazal Laf IG1 79 A6
Fearnley Cres TW12 173 B4
Fearnley Ho SE5 139 C3
Fearon St SE10 121 A1
Featherbed La CR0 223 B1
Feathers Pl SE10 142 B6
Featherstone Ave 4
SE23 162 C2
Featherstone Ct NW7 28 A3
Featherstone High Sch
UB2 107 A2
Featherstone Ho UB4 84 C2
Featherstone Ind Est
UB2 107 A3
Featherstone Prim Sch
UB2 107 A3
Featherstone Rd NW7 28 B4
Southall UB2 107 A3
Featherstone St
EC1 95 B3 242 C6
Featherstone Terr UB2 107 A3
Featley Rd SW9 138 D2
Federal Rd UB6 87 C5
Federation Rd SE2 124 C2
Fee Farm Rd KT10 212 D1
Felbridge Ave HA7 25 B2
Felbridge Cl SW16 182 C6
Felbridge Ct
East Bedfont TW14 150 B3
Harlington UB3 127 B6
Felbridge Ho 22 SE22 139 C2
Felbrigge Rd IG3 57 D1
Felday Rd SE13 163 D5
Felden Cl HA5 23 A3
Felden St SW6 135 B4 264 C1
Feldman Cl N16 52 A1
Felgate Mews 4 W6 112 B2
Felhampton Rd SE9 166 D1
Felhurst Cres RM10 81 D4
Feline Ct 1 EN4 14 C5
Felix Ave N8 50 A3
Felix Ct E17 53 D4
Felix La TW17 193 D3
Felix Manor BR7 189 C4
Felix Neubergh Ct EN1 5 C1
Felix Rd W13 109 A6
Walton-on-T KT12 194 A3
Felix St 19 E2 96 B5
Felixstowe Rd N9 34 A6
N17 51 D6
NW10 90 B4
SE2 124 B3
Fell Rd CR0 221 A5
Fell Wlk HA8 26 D2
Fellbrigg Rd SE22 161 D6
Fellbrigg St 21 E1 96 B3
Fellbrook TW10 153 B1
Fellmongers Yd 3 CR0 221 A5
Fellowes Cl UB4 84 D3
Fellowes Ct UB3 127 B6
Fellowes Rd SM1,SM5 218 C6
Fellows Ct E2 95 D5
Fellows Rd NW3 70 C1
Fells Haugh 6 W3 89 A1
Felltram Way SE7 121 A1
Felmersham Cl 2 SW4 137 D1
Felmingham Rd SE20 184 C1
Felnex Trad Est SM6 219 A6
Fels Cl RM10 81 D5
Felsberg Rd SW2 160 A4
Felsham Ho SW15 134 D2
Felsham Rd SW15 134 D2
Felspar Cl SE18 123 D1
Felstead Rd E11 55 A2
Felstead St E9 75 B2
Felstead Wharf E14 120 A1
Felsted Rd E16 99 D1
Feltham Ave KT8 196 C5
Feltham Corporate Ctr
TW13 150 B1
Feltham Hill Jun & Inf Schs
TW13 149 D1
Feltham Hill Rd
Ashford TW15 171 A4
Feltham TW13 172 B6
Feltham Rd
Ashford TW15 171 A6
Mitcham CR4 181 A1
Feltham Sch The TW13 150 C2
Feltham Sta TW13 150 B3
Felthambrook Ind Est
TW13 150 B1
Felthambrook Way
TW13 172 B5
Felton Cl BR5 210 D3
Felton Gdns IG11 101 C5
Felton Ho N1 235 D5
SE9 143 C1
Felton Lea DA14 189 D5
Felton Rd W13 109 C4
Barking IG11 101 C5
Felton St N1 95 B6 235 D5
Fen Ct EC3 253 A6
Fen Gr DA15 167 D5
Fen St E16 120 D6
Fenchurch 34 N1 95 C6
Fenchurch Ave
EC3 95 C1 243 A1
Fenchurch Bldgs EC3 243 B1
Fenchurch Pl EC3 253 B6
Fenchurch St
EC3 117 C6 253 B6
Fenchurch Street Sta
EC3 117 C6 253 B6
Fendall Rd KT19 215 A3
Fendall St SE1 117 C3 263 B5
Fender Ct 5 SW4 138 A3
Fendt Cl 8 E16 120 D6
Fendyke Rd SE2,DA17 124 D3
Fenelon Pl W14 113 B2 254 D3
Fenham Rd SE15 140 B5
Fenman Ct N17 34 B2
Fenman Gdns IG3 58 B1
Fenn Cl BR1 187 A4
Fenn Ct HA1 43 A4
Fenn St E9 74 C3
Fennel Cl E16 98 C3
Croydon CR0 206 D1
Fennell St SE18 144 C6
Fenner Cl SE16 118 B2
Fenner Ho 23 E1 118 B5
Fenner Sq 10 SW11 136 B2
Fenning Ct CR4 202 C5
Fenning St SE1 253 A2
Fenstanton Ave N12 30 B5
Fenstanton Prim Sch
SW2 160 C3
Fentiman Rd
SW8 138 B5 270 C4
Fenton Cl E8 73 D2
SW9 138 B3
Chislehurst West BR7 188 B5
Fenton Ho SE14 141 A5
Heston TW5 129 C6
Fenton Rd N17 33 A3
Fenton St E1 96 B1
Fentons SE3 142 D5
Fenton's Ave E13 99 B5
Fenwick Cl 16 SE18 144 C6
Fenwick Gr SE15 140 A2
Fenwick Pl SW9 138 A2
Croydon CR2 220 D1
Fenwick Rd SE15 140 A2
Ferby Ct DA15 189 D6
Ferdinand Ho 1 NW1 71 B1
Ferdinand Pl NW1 71 A1
Ferdinand St NW1 71 A1
Fergus Rd N5 72 D3
Ferguson Ave KT5 198 B4
Ferguson Cl BR2,BR3 208 B6
Ferguson Dr W3 89 B1
Ferguson Ho SE10 142 A4
Ferguson's Cl E14 119 C2
Fermain Ct E N1 95 C6
Fermain Ct N N1 95 C6
Fermain Ct W N1 95 C6
Ferme Park Rd N4,N8 50 B3
Fermor Rd SE23 163 A3
Fermoy Rd W9 91 B3
Southall UB6 85 D3
Fern Ave CR4 203 D5
Fern Cl 8 N1 95 C5
Fern Ct E4 36 A4
SE14 140 D3
Bexleyheath DA7 147 C1
Fern Dene W13 87 B2
Fern Gr TW14 150 B4
Fern Hill Pl 8 BR6 227 A3
Fern La TW5 107 B1
Fern Lo 13 SW16 182 C5
Fern St E3 97 C3
Fern Wlk 17 SE16 118 A1
Fernbank IG9 21 B3
Fernbank Ave
Walton-on-T KT12 195 A2
Wembley HA0 64 D3
Fernbank Mews SW12 159 C5
Fernbrook Dr HA2 41 D2
Fernbrook Rd SE13 164 C5
Ferncliff Rd E8 74 A3
Ferncroft Ave N12 30 D4
NW3 69 C4
Ruislip HA4 62 C6
Ferndale BR1 187 C1
Ferndale Ave E17 54 B4
Hounslow TW4 129 A2
Ferndale Cl DA7 147 A4
Ferndale Ct 3 SE3 142 D5
Ferndale Ho N16 51 B1
Ferndale Rd E7 77 B1
E11 76 D6
N15 51 D4
SE25 206 B4
SW4,SW9 138 B1
Ashford TW15 170 A5
Enfield EN3 7 A6
Ferndale St E6 100 D1
Ferndale Terr HA1 42 D5
Ferndale Way BR6 227 B3
Fernden Way RM7 59 D3
Ferndene NW9 45 A4
Ferndene Rd SE24 139 A1
Ferndown 6 E18 55 A6
5 Kingston u T KT6 198 A4
Northwood Hills HA6 22 A1
Ferndown Cl
Hatch End HA5 23 A3
Orpington BR6 211 B1
Sutton SM2 218 B2
Ferndown Ct 6 UB1 86 A1
Ferndown Rd SE9 165 D4
South Oxhey WD1 22 C6
Ferney Meade Way
TW7 131 A3
Ferney Rd EN4 15 A3
Fernhall Dr IG1 55 D4
Fernham Rd CR7 205 A6
Fernhead Rd W9 91 B4
Fernhill Ct E17 36 B1
Kingston u T KT2 175 D5
Fernhill Gdns KT2 176 A5
Fernhill Ho E5 74 A6
Fernhill St E16 122 B5
Fernholme Rd SE15 162 D6
Fernhurst Gdns HA8 26 C4
Fernhurst Rd
SW6 135 A4 264 B2
Ashford TW15 171 A6
Croydon CR0 206 B1
Fernie Ho SE22 139 D2
Fernlea Ho NW10 88 B4
Fernlea Rd SW12 159 B3
Mitcham CR4 181 A2
Fernleigh Cl CR0 220 C4
Fernleigh Ct Harrow HA2 23 D1
Wembley HA9 44 A1
Fernleigh Rd N21 16 D2
Ferns Rd E15 76 D2
Fernsbury St WC1 234 A1
Fernshaw Mans SW10 266 A5
Fernshaw Rd
SW10 136 A6 266 A5
Fernside IG9 21 B3
Fernside Ave NW7 11 B1
Feltham TW13 172 B6
Fernside Ct NW4 28 D1
Fernside Rd SW12 159 A4
Fernthorpe Rd SW16 181 C4
Ferntower Rd N5 73 B3
Fernways IG1 78 D4
Fernwood N22 32 A3
SW19 157 B3
Fernwood Ave SW16 181 D6
Wembley HA0 65 C2
Fernwood Cl BR1 187 C1
Fernwood Cres N20 14 D1
Ferny Hill EN4 3 A5
Ferranti Cl SE18 121 D3
Ferraro Cl TW5 129 C6
Ferrers Ave
Wallington SM6 219 D4
West Drayton UB7 104 A4
Ferrers Rd SW16 181 D5
Ferrestone Rd N8 50 B5
Ferriby Cl N1 72 C1
Ferrier Ind Est SW18 135 D1
Ferrier Point 6 E16 99 A2
Ferrier St SW18 135 D1
Ferring Cl HA2 42 A1
Ferrings SE21 161 C1
Ferris Ave CR0 223 B5
Ferris Rd SE22 140 A1
Ferron Rd E5 74 B5
Ferrour Ct N2 48 B6
Ferry Ho E5 52 B1
Ferry La N17 52 B5
SW13 133 D6
Brentford TW8 132 A6
Lower Halliford TW17 192 C1
Richmond TW9 132 B6
Ferry Lane Prim Sch
N17 52 B5
Ferry Rd SW13 134 A4
East Molesey KT8 195 C6
Richmond TW11 175 B5
Thames Ditton KT7 197 B3
Twickenham TW1 153 B3
Ferry Sq 1 TW8 132 A6
Ferry St E14 120 A1
Ferry Wks TW17 192 C1
Ferrybridge Ho SE11 260 D5
Ferrymead Ave UB6 85 C5
Ferrymead Dr UB6 85 C5
Ferrymead Gdns UB6 86 A5
Ferrymoor TW10 153 B1
Festing Rd SW15 134 D2
Festival Cl
Hillingdon UB10 82 D6
Sidcup DA5 168 D3
Festival Pier SE1 250 C4
Festival Pleasure Gdns
SW11 136 D5 267 C3
Fetter La EC4 94 C1 241 B2
Fettes Ho NW8 229 D3
Fews Lodge RM6 58 D5
Ffinch St SE8 141 C5
Field Cl E4 35 D4
Bromley BR1 187 C1
Buckhurst Hill IG9 21 C1
Chessington KT9 213 C3
Cranford TW4 128 B4
East Molesey KT8 195 D4
Harlington UB7 127 A5
Ruislip HA4 39 A1
Uxbridge UB10 60 D6
Field Ct N7 72 A3
NW3 70 A3
SW19 157 C1
WC1 240 D3
Field End HA4 62 C2
Field End Jun & Inf Schs
HA4 62 D6
Field End Rd HA5,HA4 40 C1
Field Ho 4 N9 34 A6
Field La Brentford TW8 131 C5
Teddington TW11 175 A5
Field Mead NW9,NW7 27 D3
Field Pl KT3 199 D3
Field Point E7 77 A4
Field Rd E7 77 A4
N17 51 C6
W6 135 A6 264 A6
Feltham TW14 150 B5
Field St WC1 233 C2
Field View TW13 171 B6
Field Way NW10 67 A1
Greenford UB6 85 D6
New Addington CR0 223 D2
Ruislip HA4 39 A1
Fieldcommon La KT12 195 B1
Fieldend TW11 174 D6
Fieldend Rd SW16 181 C2
Fielders Cl 2 Enfield EN1 5 C1
Harrow HA2 42 A1
Fieldfare Rd SE28 124 C6
Fieldgate Mans 23 E1 96 A2
Fieldgate St E1 96 A2
Fieldhouse Cl E18 37 B2
Fieldhouse Rd SW12 159 C3
Fielding Ave TW2 152 A1
Fielding Ho 3 NW6 91 C4
NW8 229 A6
W4 133 C6
Fielding Mews SW13 134 B6
Fielding Prim Sch W13 109 B3
Fielding Rd W4 111 C3
W14 112 D3
Fielding St SE17 139 A6
Fielding Terr W5 110 B6
Fieldings The SE23 162 C3
Fields Est E8 74 A1
Fields Park Cres RM6 58 D4
Fieldsend Rd SM3 217 A3
Fieldside Cl BR6 227 A4
Fieldside Rd BR1 186 B5
Fieldsway Ho N5 72 C3
Fieldview SW17,SW18 158 B3
Fieldview Ct N5 72 D3
NW9 44 C3
Fieldway Dagenham RM8 80 C4
Orpington BR5 211 B3
Fieldway Cres N5,N7 72 C3
Fieldway Sta CR0 223 D1
Fieldwick Ho 14 E9 74 D2
Fiennes Cl RM8 58 C1
Fife Ct 5 W3 88 C1
Fife Rd E16 99 A2
N22 32 D3
SW14 155 A6
Kingston u T KT2 176 A1
Fife Terr N1 233 D4
Fifehead Cl TW15 170 A4
Fifield Path SE23 162 D1
Fifteenpenny Fields
SE9 166 C6
Fifth Ave E12 78 B4
W10 91 A4
Hayes UB3 105 D5
Fifth Cross Rd TW2 152 B2
Fifth Way HA9 66 D4
Fig Tree Cl NW10 89 C6
Figge's Rd CR4 181 A3
Filanco Ct W7 108 D5
Filby Rd KT9 214 B2
Filey Ave N16 52 A1
Filey Cl SM2 218 A1
Filey Ho SW18 136 A1
Filey Waye HA4 62 B6
Filigree Ct SE16 119 B5
Fillebrook Ave EN1 5 D3
Fillebrook Hall E11 54 C2
Fillebrook Rd E11 54 C1
Filmer Ho SW6 264 B2
Filmer Rd SW6 135 B5 264 C3
Filmer Road Studios
SW6 264 B2
Filston Rd DA8 125 D1
Filton Ct 10 SE14 140 C5
Finborough Ho SW10 266 A6
Finborough Rd
SW10 135 D6 265 D6
SW17 180 D4
Finch Ave SE27 183 B6
Finch Cl NW10 67 B2
Barnet EN5 13 C6
Finch Dr TW14 150 D4
Finch Ho 1 SE8 141 D5
Finch La EC2,EC3 242 D1
Finch Lo 15 W9 91 C2
Finch Mews 3 SE15 139 D4
Finchale Rd SE2 124 A3
Fincham Cl UB10 61 A5
Finchdean Ho SW15 155 D4
Finchingfield Ave IG8 37 C3
Finchley Cath High Sch
N12 13 D1
Finchley Central Sta N3 29 C2
Finchley Ct N3 29 D4
Finchley La NW4 46 D5
Finchley Lo N12 29 D5
Finchley Memorial Hospl
N12 30 A3
Finchley Pk N12 30 B6
Finchley Pl NW8 229 C4
Finchley Rd NW3 70 A2
NW8 229 C4
NW11 47 B3
Finchley Road & Frognal Sta
NW3 70 A3
Finchley Road Sta NW3 70 A2
Finchley Way N3 29 C3
Finch's Ct 9 E14 119 D6
Finden Rd E7 77 C3
Findhorn Ave UB4 84 B2
Findhorn St E14 98 A1
Findon Cl SW18 157 C5
Harrow HA2 63 D5
Findon Rd N9 18 B3
W12 112 A4
Fine Bush La HA4 38 D3
Fineran Ct 16 SW11 136 B1
Fingal St SE10 120 D1
Fingest Ho NW8 237 A6
Finians Cl UB10 60 B1
Finland Rd SE4 141 A2
Finland St SE16 119 A3
Finlay St SW6 134 D4
Finlays Cl KT9 214 C3
Finley Ct 21 SE5 139 A5
Finmere Ho 1 N4 51 A2
Finn Ho N1 235 D2
Finnemore Ho N1 235 A6
Finney La TW7 131 A4
Finnis St E2 96 B3
Finnymore Rd RM9 81 A1
Finsbury Ave EC2 242 D3
Finsbury Cir EC2 95 B2 242 D3
Finsbury Cotts N22 32 A3
Finsbury Ct EC2 242 C4
Finsbury Ho N22 32 A2
Finsbury Market EC2 243 A4
Finsbury Mkt EC2 243 A5
Finsbury Park Ave N4 51 A3
Finsbury Park Rd N4,N5 72 D6
Finsbury Park Sta N4 72 C6
Finsbury Pavement
EC2 95 B2 242 D4
Finsbury Rd N22 32 B2
Finsbury Sq EC2 95 B2 242 D4
Finsbury St EC2 242 C4
Finsbury Way DA5 169 B5
Finsen Rd SE5 139 A2
Finstock Rd W10 90 D1
Finton House Sch
SW17 158 D2
Finucane Ct TW9 132 B2
Finucane Rise WD2 8 A2
Finwhale Ho E14 119 D3
Fiona Ct 9 NW6 91 B5
Enfield EN2 4 D2
Fir Cl KT12 194 A2
Fir Dene BR6 226 C5
Fir Gr KT3 199 D3
Fir Lo SW15 134 B1
Fir Rd Cheam SM3 201 B1
Feltham TW13 172 D5
Fir Tree Ave UB7 104 C3
Fir Tree Cl SW16 181 C5
W5 88 A1
Esher KT10 212 A3

Fir Tree Cl *continued*
5 Orpington BR6 ... 227 D3
Worcester Pk KT19 ... 215 D4
Fir Tree Gdns CR0 ... 223 C4
Fir Tree Gr SM5 ... 218 D1
Fir Tree Ho 11 SE14 ... 140 C5
Fir Tree Rd TW4 ... 129 A1
Fir Tree Wlk EN1 ... 5 B2
Fir Trees Cl SE16 ... 119 A5
Fir Wlk KT17,SM3 ... 216 D2
Firbank Cl E16 ... 99 D2
Enfield EN2 ... 5 A1
Firbank Rd SE15 ... 140 B3
Fircroft N1 ... 94 D6 234 D6
Fircroft Gdns HA1 ... 64 C5
Fircroft Prim Sch
SW17 ... 158 D1
Fircroft Rd SW17 ... 158 D1
Chessington KT9 ... 214 B4
Firdene KT5 ... 199 A1
Fire Bell Alley KT6 ... 198 A3
Fire Station Alley EN5 ... 1 A3
Fire Station Mews 3
BR3 ... 185 D2
Firebell Mews KT6 ... 198 A3
Firecrest Dr NW3 ... 69 D5
Firefly 7 NW9 ... 27 D1
Firefly Cl SM6 ... 220 A1
Firefly Gdns E6 ... 100 A3
Firemans Cotts N10 ... 49 A6
Fireman's Flats N22 ... 32 A2
Firethorn Cl HA8 ... 27 A6
Firhill Rd SE6 ... 163 C1
Firle Ho W10 ... 90 C2
Firmston Ho 9 SW14 ... 133 B2
Firs Ave N10 ... 49 A5
N11 ... 31 A4
SW14 ... 133 A1
Firs Cl N10 ... 49 A6
SE23 ... 163 A4
Claygate KT10 ... 212 C2
Mitcham CR4 ... 181 B2
Firs Dr TW5 ... 128 B5
Firs Farm Prim Sch N13 17 B1
Firs Ho N22 ... 32 C3
Firs La N13,N21 ... 17 A2
Firs Park Ave N21 ... 17 B3
Firs Park Gdns N21 ... 17 B3
Firs The E6 ... 78 A1
N20 ... 14 B3
SE26 ... 184 C5
2 SE26 ... 184 B5
SW20 ... 178 A3
W5 ... 87 D2
Claygate KT10 ... 212 C2
Sidcup DA15 ... 167 D1
Sutton SM2 ... 217 D1
IG8 ... 37 C3
Firs Wlk IG8 ... 37 A5
Firsby Ave CR0 ... 207 A1
Firsby Rd N16 ... 52 A1
Firscroft N13 ... 17 A1
Firside Gr DA15 ... 167 D3
First Ave E12 ... 78 A3
E13 ... 99 A4
E17 ... 53 D4
N18 ... 34 C6
NW4 ... 46 C5
SW14 ... 133 C2
W3 ... 111 D5
W10 ... 91 B3
Bexley DA7 ... 146 C5
Dagenham RM10 ... 103 D5
East Molesey KT8 ... 195 C5
Enfield EN1 ... 17 D6
Hayes UB3 ... 105 D5
Ilford RM6 ... 58 C4
Walton-on-T KT12 ... 194 B3
Wembley HA9 ... 65 D6
First Cl KT8 ... 196 A6
First Cross Rd TW2 ... 152 C2
First Dr NW10 ... 67 A1
First St SW3 ... 114 C2 257 B4
First Way HA9 ... 66 D4
Firstway SW20 ... 178 C1
Firswood Ave KT19 ... 215 D3
Firth Gdns SW6 135 A4 264 A1
Firtree Ave CR4 ... 181 A1
Firtree Ct BR2 ... 208 D6
Fish St Hill EC3 ... 252 D5
Fisher Cl Croydon CR0 ... 205 D1
Greenford UB6 ... 85 C4
EN3 ... 7 C6
Fisher Ho 8 E1 ... 118 C6
N1 ... 234 A5
2 N19 ... 71 C5
13 SE18 ... 122 C2
Fisher Rd HA3 ... 24 D1
Fisher St E16 ... 99 A2
WC1 ... 240 C3
Fisherdene KT10 ... 213 A1
Fisherman Cl TW10 ... 175 C6
Fishermans Dr SE16 ... 118 D4
Fishermans Wlk SE28 ... 123 C4
Fisherman's Wlk E14 ... 119 C5
Fishers Ct SE14 ... 140 D4
4 Teddington TW11 ... 174 D5
Fisher's La W4 ... 111 B2
Fisherton St
NW8 ... 92 B3 236 D6
Fisherton Street Est
NW8 ... 92 B3 236 D5
Fishlock Ct 6 SW4 ... 138 A3
Fishponds Rd SW17 ... 180 C6
Keston BR2 ... 225 D3
Fiske Ct N17 ... 34 A2
1 SW19 ... 180 A3
Barking IG11 ... 101 B5

Fiske Ct *continued*
Sutton SM2 ... 218 A1
Fisons Rd E16 ... 121 A5
Fitch Ct SW2 ... 160 C6
8 Mitcham CR4 ... 181 A1
Fitz Wygram Cl TW12 ... 174 A5
Fitzalan Rd N3 ... 47 B6
Claygate KT10 ... 212 C1
Fitzalan St SE11 116 C2 261 A4
Fitzgeorge Ave KT2,KT3 177 B2
Fitz-George Ave W14 ... 254 A3
Fitzgerald Ave SW14 ... 133 C2
Fitzgerald Ct 1 E10 ... 53 D1
Fitzgerald Ho 14 E14 ... 97 D1
16 SW9 ... 138 C3
Hayes UB3 ... 106 B5
Fitzgerald Rd E11 ... 55 A4
SW14 ... 133 B2
Thames Ditton KT7 ... 197 A3
Fitzhardinge Ho W1 ... 238 A2
Beckenham BR3 ... 185 D1
Fitzhardinge St W1 ... 238 A2
Fitzherbert Ho 11 TW10 154 B5
Fitzhugh Gr SW18 ... 158 B5
Fitzjames Ave W14 ... 254 B3
Croydon CR0 ... 222 A6
Fitzjohn Ave EN5 ... 1 B1
Fitzjohn's Ave NW3 ... 70 B3
Fitzjohns Prim Sch NW3 70 B3
Fitzmaurice Ho 17 SE16 118 B2
Fitzmaurice Pl W1 ... 248 D4
Fitzneal St W12 ... 89 D1
Fitzroy Cl N6 ... 48 D1
Fitzroy Cres W4 ... 133 B5
Fitzroy Ct N6 ... 49 C3
W1 ... 239 B5
Fitzroy Gdns SE19 ... 183 C3
Fitzroy Ho 14 E14 ... 97 B1
SE1 ... 263 D2
Fitzroy Lo N21 ... 16 D6
Fitzroy Mews W1 ... 239 A5
Fitzroy Nuffield Hospl
W1 ... 92 D1 237 C2
Fitzroy Pk N6 ... 48 D1
Fitzroy Rd NW1 ... 93 A6 231 A6
Fitzroy Sq W1 ... 239 A5
Fitzroy St W1 ... 93 C3 239 A5
Fitzroy Yd NW1 ... 231 A6
Fitzsimmons Ct 1 NW10 89 B6
Fitzstephen Rd RM8 ... 80 C3
Fitzwarren Gdns N19 ... 49 C1
Fitzwilliam Ave TW9 ... 132 B3
Fitzwilliam Ho TW9 ... 131 D1
Fitzwilliam Hts 1 SE23 162 C2
Fitzwilliam Mews E16 ... 121 A5
Fitzwilliam Rd SW4 ... 137 C2
Five Acre NW9 ... 27 D2
Five Elms Prim Sch RM8 81 B5
Five Elms Rd
Dagenham RM9 ... 81 B5
Keston BR2 ... 225 C5
Five Ways Cnr NW4 ... 28 A2
Fiveacre Cl CR7 ... 204 C3
Fives Ct SE11 ... 261 C5
Fiveways SE9 ... 166 D2
Croydon CR0 ... 220 C4
Fiveways Rd SW9 ... 138 C3
Flack Ct 14 E10 ... 53 D2
Fladbury Rd N15 ... 51 B3
Fladgate Rd E11 ... 54 C3
Flag Cl CR0 ... 206 D1
Flag Wlk HA5 ... 40 A3
Flambard Rd HA1,HA3 ... 43 A3
Flamborough Ho 11
SE15 ... 140 A4
Flamborough Rd HA4 ... 62 A5
Flamborough St E14 ... 97 A1
Flamingo Ct 2 SE8 ... 141 C5
Flamingo Gdns UB5 ... 85 A4
Flamstead Gdns RM9 ... 80 C1
Flamstead Rd RM9 ... 80 C1
Flamsted Ave HA9 ... 66 C2
Flamsteed House SE10 142 B5
Flamsteed Rd SE7 ... 122 A1
Flanchford Rd W12 ... 111 D3
Flanders Cres SW17 ... 180 D4
Flanders Ct E17 ... 53 A3
Flanders Mans 1 W4 ... 111 D2
Flanders Rd E6 ... 100 C5
W4 ... 111 C2
Flanders Way E9 ... 74 D2
Flank St 6 E1 ... 118 A6
Flansham Ho 2 E14 ... 97 B1
Flash La EN2 ... 5 A6
Flask Wlk NW3 ... 70 B4
Flatford Ho 2 SE6 ... 186 A6
Flavell Mews SE10 ... 120 C1
Flaxen Cl E4 ... 19 D1
Flaxen Rd E4 ... 19 D1
Flaxley Rd SM4 ... 201 D2
Flaxman Ct W1 ... 239 C1
12 Belvedere DA17 ... 125 C1
Flaxman Ho SE1 ... 261 D6
10 W4 ... 111 C1
Flaxman Rd SE5 ... 138 D3
Flaxman Terr
WC1 ... 93 D4 232 D1
Flaxman Villas N2 ... 48 A6
Flaxmore Ct
Bexleyheath DA7 ... 147 D2
South Norwood CR7 ... 183 B1
Flaxton Rd SE18 ... 145 C5
Flecker Cl HA7 ... 24 D5
Flecker Ho 6 SE5 ... 139 B5
Fleece Dr N9 ... 34 A6
Fleece Rd KT6 ... 197 C1
Fleece Wlk N7 ... 72 A2

Fleecefield Prim Sch
N18 ... 34 A6
Fleeming Cl E17 ... 35 B1
Fleeming Rd E17 ... 35 B1
Fleet Cl
East Molesey KT8 ... 195 B4
Ruislip HA4 ... 39 A3
Fleet Ct 1 W12 ... 111 C3
Fleet Ho 4 E14 ... 119 A6
6 SW2 ... 160 C6
Fleet Prim Sch NW3 ... 70 D3
Fleet Rd NW3 ... 70 D3
Fleet Sq WC1 ... 233 D1
Fleet St EC4 ... 94 C1 241 B1
Fleet Street Hill 11 E1 ... 96 A3
Fleet Terr SE6 ... 164 A4
Fleetfield WC1 ... 233 B2
Fleetside KT8 ... 195 C4
Fleetway WC1 ... 233 B2
Fleetway West Bsns Pk
UB6 ... 87 B5
Fleetwood Cl E16 ... 99 D2
Chessington KT9 ... 213 D1
South Croydon CR0 ... 221 D5
Fleetwood Ct 1 E6 ... 100 B2
Locksbottom BR6 ... 226 C4
8 Stanwell TW19 ... 148 A5
Fleetwood Rd NW10 ... 68 A3
Kingston u T KT3 ... 198 D6
Fleetwood Sq KT3 ... 198 D6
Fleetwood St N16 ... 73 C6
Fleetwood Way WD1 ... 22 C6
Fleming Ct W2 ... 236 C4
Croydon CR0 ... 220 C3
Fleming Dr N21 ... 16 B6
Fleming Ho N4 ... 51 A1
8 SE16 ... 118 A4
8 Wembley HA9 ... 67 A5
Fleming Mead CR4 ... 180 D3
Fleming Rd SE17 ... 138 D6
Southall UB1 ... 86 A1
Fleming Way SE28 ... 124 D6
Isleworth TW7 ... 130 D1
Fleming Wlk NW9 ... 27 C1
Flemming Ave HA4 ... 62 B6
Flempton Rd E10 ... 53 A1
Fletcher Bldgs WC2 ... 240 B1
Fletcher Ct 9 NW5 ... 71 B4
Fletcher Ho 22 N1 ... 95 C6
16 N16 ... 73 C4
Fletcher La E10 ... 54 A2
Fletcher Path 7 SE8 ... 141 C5
Fletcher Rd W4 ... 111 A3
Fletcher St 10 E1 ... 118 A6
Fletchers Cl BR2 ... 209 B5
Fletching Rd E5 ... 74 C5
SE7 ... 143 D6
Fletton Rd N11 ... 32 A3
Fleur Gates 7 SW19 ... 156 D4
Flexmere Rd N17 ... 33 C2
Flimwell Cl BR1 ... 186 C5
Flinders Ho 23 E1 ... 118 B5
Flint Cl 8 BR6 ... 227 D2
Flint Down Cl BR5 ... 190 A2
Flint St SE17 ... 117 B2 262 D3
Flintmill Cres SE3,SE9 ... 144 A3
Flinton St SE17 ... 117 C1 263 B2
Flitcroft St WC2 ... 239 D1
Flitton Ho 7 N1 ... 72 D1
Flock Mill Pl SW18 ... 157 D3
Flockton St 17 SE16 ... 118 A4
3 SE16 ... 118 A4
Flodden Rd SE5 ... 139 A4
Flood La 4 TW1 ... 153 A3
Flood St SW3 ... 136 C6 267 B6
Flood Wlk SW3 136 C6 267 B6
Flora Cl E14 ... 97 D1
Flora Gardens Prim Sch
W6 ... 112 B2
Flora Gdns 2 W6 ... 112 B2
Ilford RM6 ... 58 C3
Flora St DA17 ... 125 B1
Floral St WC2 ... 116 A6 250 A6
Florence Ave Enfield EN2 ... 5 A2
Morden SM4 ... 202 A4
Florence Cl KT12 ... 194 B2
Florence Ct 4 E5 ... 74 A5
E11 ... 55 C5
5 SW19 ... 179 A4
W9 ... 229 B1
Florence Dr EN2 ... 5 A2
Florence Gdns W4 ... 133 A6
Dagenham RM6 ... 58 C2
Florence Ho 20 SE16 ... 118 B1
2 SE18 ... 144 B4
2 SW2 ... 160 B6
7 SW18 ... 136 B1
10 W11 ... 112 D6
5 Kingston u T KT2 ... 176 B3
Florence Mans 4 NW4 ... 46 B4
SW6 ... 264 C2
Florence Nightingale Ho 11
N1 ... 73 A2
Florence Nightingale Mus
SE1 ... 250 D1
Florence Rd 8 E6 ... 99 C6
E13 ... 99 A5
N4 ... 50 C2
SE2 ... 124 C2
SE14 ... 141 B4
SW19 ... 179 D4
W4 ... 111 B3
W5 ... 110 A6
Feltham TW13 ... 150 B3
6 Kingston u T KT2 ... 176 B3
5 Penge BR3 ... 185 A1
Plaistow BR1 ... 187 A2
Southall UB2 ... 106 D3

Florence Rd *continued*
Walton-on-T KT12 ... 194 B2
Florence Root Ho IG4 ... 56 B4
Florence St E16 ... 98 D3
N1 ... 72 D1
NW4 ... 46 C5
Florence Terr SE14 ... 141 B4
SW15 ... 155 C1
Florence Way SW12 ... 158 D3
Florentine Ho 3 IG1 ... 78 D6
Flores Ho 10 E1 ... 96 D2
Florfield Rd E8 ... 74 B2
Florian SE5 ... 139 C4
Florian Ave SM1 ... 218 B4
Florian Rd SW15 ... 135 A1
Florida Cl WD2 ... 8 B2
Florida Ct BR2 ... 208 D5
Florida Rd CR7 ... 182 D2
Florida St E2 ... 96 A4
Florin Ct N18 ... 33 C6
Floriston Ave UB10 ... 61 A1
Floriston Cl HA7 ... 25 B2
Floriston Ct UB5 ... 63 D3
Floriston Gdns HA7 ... 25 B2
Florys Ct 7 SW19 ... 157 A3
Floss St SW15 ... 134 C3
Flower & Dean Wlk E1 243 D3
Flower La NW7 ... 27 D4
Flower Pot Cl N15 ... 51 D3
Flower Wlk The
SW7 ... 114 A4 246 B2
Flowers Cl NW2 ... 68 A5
Flowers Mews 1 N19 ... 71 C6
Flowersmead SW17 ... 159 A2
Floyd Rd SE7 ... 121 C1
Fludyer St SE13 ... 142 C1
Fluer De Lis St E1 ... 243 C5
Flynn Ct 12 E14 ... 119 C6
Foley Ho 19 E1 ... 96 C1
Foley Mews KT10 ... 212 C2
Foley Rd KT10 ... 212 C1
Foley St W1 ... 93 C2 239 A3
Folgate St E1 ... 95 D2 243 C4
Foliot Ho N1 ... 233 C4
Foliot St W12 ... 89 D1
Folkestone Ct UB5 ... 63 D3
Folkestone Rd E6 ... 100 C4
E17 ... 53 D5
N18 ... 34 A6
Folkingham La 6 NW9 ... 27 C2
Folkington Cnr N12 ... 29 B5
Folland 6 NW9 ... 27 D1
Follett Ho SW10 ... 266 C4
Follett St E14 ... 98 A1
Folly La E4 ... 35 B3
E17 ... 35 A2
Folly Wall E14 ... 120 A4
Font Hills N2 ... 30 A1
Fontaine Ct 3 BR3 ... 185 B2
Fontaine Rd SW16 ... 182 B3
Fontarabia Rd SW11 ... 137 A1
Fontenelle SE5 ... 139 C4
Fontenoy Ho SE11 ... 261 C3
Fontenoy Rd SW12,
SW17 ... 159 C2
Fonteyne Gdns IG8 ... 37 D1
Fonthill Cl SE20 ... 184 A1
Fonthill Ct SE23 ... 162 C4
Fonthill Ho SW1 ... 258 D2
Fonthill Mews N4 ... 72 B6
Fonthill Rd N4 ... 72 C6
Fontley Way SW15 ... 156 A4
Fontmell Cl TW15 ... 170 C5
Fontmell Pk TW15 ... 170 C5
Fontwell Cl
Harrow Weald HA3 ... 24 C3
Northolt UB5 ... 63 C2
Fontwell Dr BR2 ... 210 C4
Football La HA1 ... 42 C1
Footpath The SW15 ... 156 A6
Foots Cray High St
DA14 ... 190 D4
Foots Cray La DA14,
DA15 ... 168 C3
Footscray Rd SE9 ... 166 D3
Forber Ho 25 E2 ... 96 C4
Forbes Cl NW2 ... 68 A5
Forbes Ct SE19 ... 183 C5
Forbes Ho 2 W4 ... 110 C1
Forbes St E1 ... 96 A1
Forbes Way HA4 ... 62 B6
Forburg Rd N16 ... 52 A1
Ford Cl 11 E3 ... 97 A5
Ashford TW15 ... 170 A4
Harrow HA1 ... 42 B2
Littleton TW17 ... 192 C4
Thornton Heath CR7 ... 204 D4
Ford End IG8 ... 37 B4
Ford Ho 2 SE18 ... 122 D1
2 New Barnet EN5 ... 13 D6
Ford Rd E3 ... 97 B5
Ashford TW15 ... 170 B6
Dagenham RM10 ... 81 C1
Ford Sq E1 ... 96 B2
Ford St E3 ... 97 A5
E16 ... 98 D1
Fordbridge Ct TW15 ... 170 A4
Fordbridge Rd
Ashford TW15 ... 170 B5
Upper Halliford TW16,
TW17 ... 193 D3
TW16 ... 194 A5
Fordbridge Rdbt TW15 170 A4
Fordcombe 13 NW5 ... 71 A2
Forde Ave BR1 ... 209 C6
Fordel Rd SE6 ... 164 B3
Fordham 4 KT1 ... 176 C1
Fordham Cl EN4 ... 2 C2

Fordham Rd EN4 ... 2 C2
Fordham St 7 E1 ... 96 A1
Fordhook Ave W5 ... 110 C6
Fordingley Rd W9 ... 91 B4
Fordington Ho 2 SE26 162 B1
Fordington Rd N6 ... 48 D5
Fordmill Rd SE6 ... 163 C2
Ford's Gr N21 ... 17 A3
Fords Park Rd E16 ... 99 A1
Fordwich Cl BR6 ... 211 D2
Fordwych Ct NW2 ... 69 A2
Fordwych Rd NW2 ... 69 A3
Fordyce Ho 3 SW16 ... 181 C6
Fordyce Rd SE13 ... 164 A6
Fordyke Rd RM8 ... 81 B6
Fore St EC2 ... 95 A2 242 B3
N18 ... 34 A6
Pinner HA5 ... 40 A4
Fore St Ave EC2 ... 242 C3
Foreign, Commonwealth &
Home Offices SW1 ... 250 A2
Foreland Ct NW4 ... 29 A2
Foreland Ho W11 ... 244 A6
Foreland St SE18 ... 123 B2
Foreshore SE8 ... 119 B2
Forest App E4 ... 20 C4
Woodford IG8 ... 37 A3
Forest Ave E4 ... 20 C4
Forest Bsns Pk E17 ... 52 D2
Forest Cl E11 ... 55 A4
Chislehurst West BR7 ... 188 C2
Woodford IG8 ... 37 B6
Forest Croft SE23 ... 162 B2
Forest Ct E4 ... 20 D3
E11 ... 54 C5
12 N12 ... 29 D6
Forest Dene Ct 2 SM2 218 A2
Forest Dr E12 ... 77 D5
Charlton TW16 ... 171 D3
Chingford IG8 ... 36 C3
Keston Mark BR2 ... 226 A4
Forest Dr E E11 ... 54 B3
Forest Dr W E11 ... 54 B2
Forest Edge IG9 ... 21 D1
Forest Gate NW9 ... 45 C4
Forest Gate Com Sch E7 77 A3
Forest Gate Sta E7 ... 77 A3
Forest Gdns N17 ... 33 D1
Forest Glade E4 ... 36 C5
E11 ... 54 C3
Forest Gr E8 ... 73 D2
Forest Hill SE23 ... 162 C3
Forest Hill Bsns Ctr
SE23 ... 162 C2
Forest Hill Ct 6 SE26 ... 162 B1
Forest Hill Ind Est SE23 162 C2
Forest Hill Rd SE22 ... 162 B5
Forest Hill Sec Sch
SE23 ... 162 D1
Forest Hill Sta SE23 ... 162 C2
Forest Ho 9 E4 ... 20 C4
Forest Hts IG9 ... 21 A2
Forest La E7,E15 ... 76 D3
Forest Lawns BR1 ... 187 C2
Forest Lea E11 ... 54 D2
Forest Lo 1 SE23 ... 162 C1
Forest Mount Rd IG8 ... 36 B3
Forest Point E7 ... 77 B3
Forest Rd E7 ... 77 A4
E8 ... 73 D2
E11 ... 54 B2
E17 ... 53 C6
N9 ... 18 B3
Cheam SM3,SM4 ... 201 C2
Feltham TW13 ... 150 C2
Richmond TW9 ... 132 C5
Romford RM7 ... 59 D6
Woodford IG8 ... 21 A1
Forest Ridge
Beckenham BR3 ... 207 C6
Keston Mark BR2 ... 226 B4
Forest Rise E17 ... 54 B5
Forest Sch E17 ... 54 C5
Forest Side E4 ... 20 D3
E7 ... 77 B4
Buckhurst Hill IG9 ... 21 C3
New Malden KT4 ... 199 D1
Forest St E7 ... 77 A3
Forest The E11 ... 54 C5
Forest Trad Est E17 ... 52 D6
Forest View E4 ... 20 B4
Forest View Ave E10 ... 54 B4
Forest View Rd E12 ... 78 A4
E17 ... 36 A2
Forest Way 6 N19 ... 71 C6
Avery Hill DA15 ... 167 B4
Broom Hill BR5 ... 211 D4
Woodford IG8 ... 37 B6
Forestdale N14 ... 31 D6
Forestdale Ctr The CR0 223 B1
Forester Rd SE15 ... 140 B2
Foresters Cl SM6 ... 219 D1
Foresters Cres DA7 ... 147 D1
Foresters Dr E17 ... 54 B5
Wallington SM6 ... 219 D1
Foresters Prim Sch
SM6 ... 219 D2
Forestholme Cl SE23 ... 162 C2
Forfar Rd N22 ... 32 D2
SW11 ... 137 A4 268 B2
Forge Cl BR2 ... 209 A1
Forge Cotts W5 ... 109 D5
Forge Dr KT10 ... 213 A1
Forge La Cheam SM3 ... 217 A1
Feltham TW13 ... 173 A5
Sunbury TW16 ... 194 A6
Forge Lane Inf Sch
TW13 ... 173 A5

Forge Lane Jun Sch
TW13 ... 173 A5
Forge Pl NW1 ... 71 A2
Forge The UB3 ... 127 B6
Forman Ct TW1 ... 152 D3
Forman Gr 2 UB5 ... 84 D4
Forman Ho SE4 ... 140 D1
Forman Pl N16 ... 73 D4
Formby Ave HA3,HA7 ... 43 C6
Formby Ct 9 N7 ... 72 C3
Formosa Ho 1 E1 ... 97 A3
Formosa St W9 ... 91 D3
Formunt Cl E16 ... 98 D2
Forres Gdns NW11 ... 47 C3
Forrest Ct N7 ... 72 C2
Forrest Gdns SW16 ... 204 B6
Forrest Ho SW15 ... 134 C3
Forrester Path SE26 ... 184 C6
Forresters The HA5 ... 40 B3
Forris Ave UB3 ... 105 D5
Forset Ct W1 ... 237 B2
Forset St W1 ... 92 C1 237 B2
Forstal Cl BR2 ... 209 A6
Forster Ho SE6 ... 164 B1
Forster Park Sch SE6 ... 164 C1
Forster Rd E17 ... 53 A3
N17 ... 51 D6
SW2 ... 160 A4
Beckenham BR3 ... 207 A6
Thornton Heath CR0 ... 205 A2
Forsters Cl RM6 ... 59 B3
Forsters Way UB4 ... 84 B1
Forstic Wlk E1 ... 243 D3
Forston St N1 ... 95 A5 235 B4
Forsyte Cres SE19 ... 183 C2
Forsyte Ct KT2 ... 176 D2
Forsyth Ct KT3 ... 177 C1
Forsyth Gdns SE17 ... 138 D6
Forsyth Ho 14 E9 ... 74 C1
SW1 ... 259 B3
Forsyth Pl EN1 ... 17 C6
Forsythe Shades BR3 ... 186 A2
Forsythia Cl IG1 ... 78 D3
Forsythia Ho SE4 ... 141 A2
Fort Rd SE1 ... 117 D2 263 D3
Northolt UB5 ... 63 C1
Fort St E1 ... 243 B3
E16 ... 121 B5
Forterie Gdns IG3 ... 80 A4
Fortescue Ave 1 E8 ... 74 B1
Twickenham TW2 ... 152 A1
Fortescue Rd SW19 ... 180 B3
Burnt Oak HA8 ... 27 B3
Fortess Gr NW5 ... 71 C3
Fortess Rd NW5 ... 71 C4
Fortess Wlk NW5 ... 71 B3
Forth Ho 29 E3 ... 97 B5
Forthbridge Rd SW11 ... 137 A1
Forties The 9 NW5 ... 71 C3
Fortior Ct N6 ... 49 C2
Fortis Cl E16 ... 99 C1
Fortis Ct N10 ... 49 A6
Fortis Gn N2,N10 ... 48 D6
Fortis Green Ave N2 ... 48 D5
Fortis Green Cotts N2 ... 48 D6
Fortismere Ave N10 ... 49 A6
Fortismere Sch N10 ... 30 D1
Fortismere Sch (South Wing)
N10 ... 49 A6
Fortnam Rd N19 ... 71 D6
Fortnums Acre HA7 ... 24 D4
Fortrose Gdns SW12,
SW2 ... 160 A3
Fortuna Cl N7 ... 72 B2
Fortune Gate Rd NW10 ... 89 C6
Fortune Green Rd NW6 ... 69 C4
Fortune Ho EC1 ... 242 B5
SE11 ... 261 A3
Fortune La WD6 ... 9 D5
Fortune St EC1 ... 95 A3 242 B5
Fortune Way NW10 ... 90 A4
Fortunes Mead UB5 ... 63 A2
Forty Acre La E16 ... 99 A2
Forty Ave HA9 ... 66 B6
Forty Cl HA9 ... 66 B5
Forty Hall EN2 ... 5 D6
Forty Hill EN2 ... 5 D5
Forty Hill CE Sch EN2 ... 6 A6
Forty Hill Ho EN1 ... 5 D5
Forty La HA9 ... 66 D6
Forum The KT8 ... 195 D5
Forum Way HA8 ... 26 C4
Forumside HA8 ... 26 C4
Forval Cl CR4 ... 202 D4
Forward Bsns Ctr The
E16 ... 98 B3
Forward Dr HA3 ... 42 D5
Fosbroke Ho SW8 ... 270 A3
Fosbury Ho 7 SW9 ... 138 B1
Fosbury Mews W2 ... 245 D5
Foscote Mews W9 ... 91 C2
Foscote Rd NW4 ... 46 B3
Foskett Ho 16 N2 ... 30 B1
Foskett Rd SW6 ... 135 B3
Foss Ave CR0,CR9 ... 220 C3
Foss Rd SW17 ... 180 B6
Fossdene Prim Sch
SE7 ... 121 B1
Fossdene Rd SE7 ... 121 B1
Fossdyke Cl UB4 ... 85 A2
Fosse Way W13 ... 87 A2
Fossil Rd SE13 ... 141 C2
Fossington Rd DA17 ... 124 D2
Fossway RM8 ... 80 C6
Foster Ct E16 ... 120 D6

Foster Ct *continued*
4 NW1 .....71 C1
NW4 .....46 C5
Foster Ho SE14 .....141 B4
Foster La EC2 ...95 A1 242 A2
Foster Rd E13 .....99 A3
W3 .....111 C6
W4 .....111 B1
Foster St NW4 .....46 C5
Foster Wlk NW4 .....46 C5
Fosters Cl E18 .....37 B2
Chislehurst West BR7 ...188 B5
Fosters Old Sch DA16 ..146 B3
Fosters Prim Sch DA16 146 C2
Fothergill Cl E13 .....99 A5
Fothergill Dr N21 .....16 A6
Fotheringham Ct EN1 ....5 D1
Fotheringham Rd EN1 ....5 D1
Foubert's Pl W1 .....239 A1
Foulden Rd N16 .....73 D4
Foulden Terr N16 .....73 D4
Foulis Terr
SW7 .....114 B1 256 D2
Foulser Rd SW17 .....159 A1
Foulsham Rd CR7 .....205 B6
Foundary Ho 7 E14 ....97 D2
Founder Cl 2 E6 .....100 D1
Founders Ct EC2 .....242 C2
Founders Gdns SE19 ..183 A3
Founders Ho SW1 .....259 C2
Foundling Ct WC1 .....240 A6
Foundry Cl SE16 .....119 A5
Foundry Mews NW1 ...239 B6
Fount St SW8 ..137 D5 269 D3
Fountain Cl UB8 .....83 A2
Fountain Ct EC4 .....251 A6
SE26 .....184 C4
SW1 .....258 C3
Bexley DA15 .....168 B5
New Malden KT3 .....199 A5
Fountain Dr SE19 .....183 D6
Wallington SM5 .....218 D1
Fountain Green Sq 31
SE16 .....118 A4
Fountain Ho 1 NW6 ....69 A1
30 SE16 .....118 A4
W1 .....248 A4
Fountain Mews 1 N5 ..73 A4
NW3 .....70 D2
Fountain Pl SW9 .....138 C4
Fountain Rd SW17 .....180 B6
South Norwood CR7 ....183 A1
Fountains Ave TW13 ...151 B1
Fountains Cl TW13 .....151 B1
Fountains Cres N14 .....16 A4
Fountains The N3 .....29 D3
Loughton IG10 .....21 D4
Fountayne Bsns Ctr N15 52 A5
Fountayne Rd N15 .....52 A5
N16 .....74 A6
Four Acres N12 .....29 D6
Four Seasons Cres
SM3 .....217 B6
Four Square Ct TW4 ...151 C5
Four Tubs The WD2 .....8 B4
Four Wents The E4 .....20 B2
Fouracres EN3 .....7 A4
Fourland Wlk HA8 .....27 A4
Fournier St E1 ..95 D2 243 D4
Fourth Ave E12 .....78 B4
W10 .....91 A4
Hayes UB3 .....105 D5
Fourth Cross Rd TW2 ..152 B2
Fourth Way Wembley HA9 66 D4
Wembley HA9 .....67 A4
Fourways 2 CR0 .....221 D6
Fovant Ct 5 SW8 .....137 C3
Fowey Ave IG4 .....55 D4
Fowey Cl E1 .....118 B5
Fowey Ho SE11 .....261 B2
Fowler Cl SW11 .....136 B2
Ruxley DA14 .....191 A5
Fowler Ho N1 ..94 D6 234 D6
N15 .....51 B4
5 SE5 .....139 C3
SW8 .....269 D1
Fowler Rd E7 .....77 A4
N1 .....94 D6 234 D6
Mitcham CR4 .....181 A1
Fowler's Wlk W5 .....87 D3
Fownes St SW11 .....136 C2
Fox & Knot St EC1 .....241 D4
Fox Cl E1 .....96 C3
E16 .....99 A2
Elstree WD6 .....9 D5
Fox Gr KT12 .....194 B2
Fox Hill SE19 .....183 D3
Fox Hill Gdns SE19 ....183 D3
Fox Ho 2 SW11 .....136 B1
Fox Hollow Cl 1 SE18 .123 C1
Fox Hollow Dr DA16 ...146 D2
Fox House Rd DA17 ...125 D1
Fox La N13 .....16 B1
W5 .....88 A3
Keston BR2 .....225 C3
Fox Prim Sch
W8 .....113 C5 245 A3
Fox Rd E16 .....98 D2
Foxberry Ct SE4 .....141 B1
Foxberry Rd SE4 .....141 A2
Foxborough Gdns SE4 .163 C6
Foxbourne Rd SW17 ...159 A2
Foxbury Ave BR7 .....189 B4
Foxbury Cl BR1 .....187 B4
Foxbury Rd BR1 .....187 B4
Foxcombe CR0 .....223 D2
Foxcombe Cl 1 E6 .....99 D5
Foxcombe Rd 6 SW15 156 A3
Foxcote SE5 .....263 B1
Foxcroft N1 .....233 D3
Foxcroft Rd SE18 .....144 D4
Foxes Dale SE3 .....143 A2
Beckenham BR2 .....208 B6
Foxfield Prim Sch SE18 123 A2
Foxfield Rd BR6 .....227 B6
Foxglove Ave BR3 .....185 D3
Foxglove Cl UB1 .....107 A6
Foxglove Ct 11 HA0 ....88 A5
Foxglove Dr E11 .....55 C5
Foxglove La KT9 .....214 C4
Foxglove St W12 .....111 D6
Foxglove Way SM6 .....203 B1
Foxgrove N14 .....16 A1
Foxgrove Path WD1 ....22 D5
Foxgrove Rd BR3 .....186 A3
Foxham Rd N19 .....71 D5
Foxhole Rd 2 SE9 .....166 A6
Foxholt Gdns NW10 ....67 A1
Foxhome Cl BR7 .....188 C4
Foxlands Rd RM10 .....81 D3
Foxlees HA0 .....65 A4
Foxley Cl E8 .....74 A3
Foxley Ct SM2 .....218 A1
Foxley Ho 4 E3 .....97 D4
Foxley Rd SW9 .....138 D5
Thornton Heath CR7 .....204 D5
Foxley Sq 3 SW9 .....138 D4
Foxmead Cl EN2 .....4 B2
Foxmore St SW11 .....267 C1
Fox's Yd E2 .....243 D6
Foxtail Ho TW3 .....130 A4
Foxton KT1 .....198 C6
Foxton Gr CR4 .....180 B1
Foxton Ho E16 .....122 C4
Foxwarren KT10 .....212 D1
Foxwell Mews SE4 .....141 A2
Foxwell St SE4 .....141 A2
Foxwood Cl NW7 .....27 C6
Feltham TW13 .....150 B1
Foxwood Green Cl EN1 .17 C5
Foxwood Rd SE3 .....142 D1
Foyle Rd N17 .....34 A2
SE3 .....142 D6
Fradel Lo N16 .....51 B1
Framfield Cl N12 .....13 C1
Framfield Ct EN1 .....17 C5
Framfield Rd N5 .....72 D3
W7 .....86 D1
Mitcham CR4 .....181 A3
Framlingham Cl 2 E5 ..74 C6
Framlingham Cres SE9 188 B6
Frampton NW1 .....71 D1
Frampton Cl SM2 .....217 C1
Frampton Ct 3 W3 .....111 A4
Frampton Ho NW8 ....236 D5
Frampton Park Rd E9 ..74 C1
Frampton Rd TW4 .....151 A6
Frampton St
NW8 .....92 B3 236 D5
Francemary Rd SE4 ...163 C6
Frances Ct E17 .....53 C3
SE25 .....183 D1
Frances Grey Ho 15 E1 .96 D2
Frances Rd E4 .....35 C4
Frances St SE18 .....122 B2
Franche Court Rd
SW17 .....158 A1
Francis Ave
Bexleyheath DA7 .....147 C3
Feltham TW13 .....150 A1
Ilford IG1 .....79 B6
Francis Barber Cl
SW16 .....182 B6
Francis Chichester Way
SW11 .....137 A4 268 B1
Francis Cl 6 E14 .....120 B2
Littleton TW17 .....192 C5
West Ewell KT19 .....215 B4
Francis Ct NW7 .....27 D5
12 SE14 .....140 D6
W5 .....110 B6
Kingston u T KT5 .....198 A5
Francis Gr SW19 .....179 B4
Francis Ho 11 N1 .....95 C6
NW10 .....89 D6
Francis Holland CE School
For Girls NW1 .92 D3 237 C6
Francis Holland Sch
SW1 .....115 A2 258 B3
Francis Rd E10 .....76 A6
N2 .....48 D5
Harrow HA1 .....43 A4
Hounslow TW4 .....128 D3
Ilford IG1 .....79 B6
Pinner HA5 .....40 C4
Thornton Heath CR0 ....204 D2
Wallington SM6 .....219 C2
Wembley UB6 .....87 C6
Francis Snary Lo 11
SW18 .....157 C6
Francis St E15 .....76 C3
SW1 .....115 C2 259 B4
Ilford IG1 .....79 B6
Francis Terr N19 .....71 C5
Francis Wlk N1 .....233 C6
Franciscan Prim Sch
SW17 .....181 A5
Franciscan Rd SW17 ...181 A6
Francklyn Gdns HA8 ....10 C1
Franconia Rd SW4 .....159 D6
Frank Bailey Wlk E12 ...78 C2
Frank Barnes Prim Sch for
Deaf Children NW3 ....70 B1
Frank Beswick Ho SW6 264 D5
Frank Burton Cl 4 SE7 121 B1
Frank Dixon Cl SE21 ...161 C3
Frank Dixon Way SE21 .161 C3
Frank Douglas Ct W6 ..112 A2
Frank Ho SW8 .....270 A4
Frank Slater Ho 4 IG3 .58 B1
Frank Soskice Ho SW6 264 D5
Frank St 5 E13 .....99 A3
Frank Towell Ct TW14 .150 A3
Frank Whymark Ho 4
SE16 .....118 C4
Frankfurt Rd SE24 .....161 A6
Frankham Ho 8 SE8 ..141 C5
Frankham St SE8 .....141 C5
Frankland Cl SE16 .....118 B2
Woodford IG8 .....37 C5
Frankland Ho 4 SW12 .159 B4
Frankland Rd E4 .....35 C5
SW7 .....114 B3 256 C5
Franklin Cl N20 .....14 A4
SE13 .....141 D4
SE27 .....160 D1
Kingston u T KT1 .....198 C6
Franklin Cres CR4 .....203 C5
Franklin Ho 26 E1 .....118 B5
NW9 .....45 D2
Beckenham BR2 .....208 C6
Franklin Ind Est SE20 ..184 C2
Franklin Pas SE9 .....144 A2
Franklin Rd SE20 .....184 C3
Bexley DA7 .....147 A4
Walton-on-T KT12 .....194 A3
Franklin Sq SW5 .....254 D1
Franklin St 43 E3 .....97 D4
N15 .....51 C3
Franklin Way CR0 .....204 A2
Franklins Mews HA2 ....64 A6
Franklin's Row
SW3 .....114 D1 257 D2
Franklyn Rd NW10 .....67 D2
Walton-on-T KT12 .....194 B3
Franks Ave KT3 .....199 A5
Franks Ho TW7 .....131 B1
Franks Wood Ave BR2,
BR5 .....211 A4
Frankswood Ave UB7 ...82 B1
Franlaw Cres N13 .....33 A6
Frans Hals Ct E14 .....120 B3
Fransfield Gr SE26 ....162 B1
Franshams WD2 .....8 C2
Frant Cl SE20 .....184 C3
Frant Rd CR7 .....204 D4
Franthorne Way SE6 ..163 D1
Fraser Cl 3 E6 .....100 A1
Fraser Ct SW11 .....267 A2
Fraser Ho 3 SE18 .....122 C2
40 SW8 .....137 D3
Brentford TW8 .....110 B1
Fraser Rd E17 .....53 D3
N9 .....18 B1
Wembley UB6 .....87 C6
Fraser Regnart Ct 12
NW5 .....70 D3
Fraser St W4 .....111 C1
Fraserburgh Ho 28 E3 ..97 B5
Frating Cres IG8 .....37 B4
Frazer Ave HA4 .....62 C3
Frazier St SE1 .116 C4 251 A1
Freame Ho N21 .....17 B5
Frean St SE16 .....118 A3
Frearson Ho WC1 .....233 D2
Fred Wigg Twr E11 .....76 D6
Freda Corbett Cl 9
SE15 .....140 A5
Frederic Ho SE7 .....122 A3
Frederic Mews SW1 ...248 A1
Frederic St E17 .....53 A4
Frederica Rd E4 .....20 B4
Frederica St 4 N7 .....72 B1
Frederick SE16 .....119 B5
Frederick Charrington Ho 3
E1 .....96 C3
Frederick Cl
W2 .....114 D6 247 C6
Cheam SM1 .....217 B3
Frederick Cres SW9 ...138 D5
Enfield EN3 .....6 C3
Frederick Gdns SM1 ...217 B3
Frederick Ho UB1 .....107 B6
Frederick Pl SE18 .....122 D1
Frederick Rd SM1 .....217 B3
Frederick Sq 11 SE16 ..119 A6
Frederick St
WC1 .....94 B4 233 C1
Frederick Terr E8 .....73 D1
Frederick's Pl EC2 .....242 C1
N12 .....30 A6
Frederick's Row EC1 ...234 C2
Fredora Ave UB4 .....83 D3
Freedom Cl E17 .....53 A5
Freedom St SW11 .....136 D3
Freegrove Rd N7 .....72 A3
Freehold Ind Ctr TW4 .150 C6
Freeland Ct W5 .....110 B6
Freeland Pk N3 .....29 A1
Freeland Rd W5 .....110 B6
Freelands Ave CR2 ....222 D1
Freelands Gr BR1 .....187 B2
Freelands Rd BR1 .....187 B2
Freeling Ho NW8 .....229 C6
Freeling St 7 N1 .....72 B1
Freeman Cl Northolt UB5 .63 A1
Upper Halliford TW17 ...193 C5
Freeman Dr KT8 .....195 B5
Freeman Ho 13 SW2 ...160 A4
Freeman Rd SM4 .....202 B4
Freemans La UB3 .....105 C6
Freemantle Ave EN3 ....18 D6
Freemantle St
SE17 .....117 C1 263 A2
Freemasons Rd E16 .....99 B1
Freemason's Rd CR0 ...205 C1
Freemens Hos 1 SW9 .138 B1
Freesia Cl BR6 .....227 D3
Freethorpe Cl SE19 ....183 C2
Freezeland Way UB10 ...60 D2
Freke Rd SW11 .....137 A2
Fremantle Ho 14 E1 ....96 B3
Fremantle Rd
Belvedere DA17 .....125 C2
Ilford IG6 .....57 A6
Fremont St E9 .....96 C6
French Ordinary Ct EC3 253 B6
French Pl E1 .....243 B6
French St TW16 .....172 C1
Frendsbury Rd SE4 ....141 A1
Frensham Cl UB1 .....85 B4
Frensham Ct N5 .....73 A3
4 NW9 .....46 A5
Mitcham CR4 .....202 B6
Frensham Dr SW15 .....156 A2
New Addington CR0 .....224 A1
Frensham Ho 7 KT6 ...198 A4
Frensham Rd DA15 .....167 B2
Frensham St SE15 .....140 A6
Frere St 6 SW11 .....136 C3
Fresh Wharf Est IG11 ..100 D6
Fresh Wharf Rd IG11 ..100 D5
Fresham Ho BR2 .....208 D6
Freshfield Ave E8 .....73 D1
Freshfield Cl SE13 .....142 B1
Freshfield Dr N14 .....15 B4
Freshfields CR0 .....207 B1
Freshford St SW17,
SW18 .....158 A1
Freshwater Cl SW17 ...181 A4
Freshwater Ct UB1 .....85 C4
Freshwater Rd SW17 ..181 A4
Dagenham RM8 .....59 A1
Freshwell Ave RM6 .....58 C5
Freshwood Cl BR3 .....185 D2
Freston Gdns EN4 .....15 A6
Freston Pk N3 .....29 B1
Freston Rd W10,W11 ...112 D6
Freswick Ho 6 SE8 ...119 A2
Freta Rd DA6 .....169 B6
Freud Mus The NW3 ....70 A2
Frewell Ho EC1 .....241 A4
Frewin Rd SW18 .....158 B3
Frewing Cl BR7 .....188 C5
Friar Mews SE27 .....160 D1
Friar Rd UB4 .....84 D3
Friar St EC4 .....241 D1
Friars Ave N20 .....30 C6
SW15 .....155 D1
Friars Cl E4 .....20 A1
SE1 .....251 D3
16 Northolt UB5 .....84 D4
Friars Ct 5 SM6 .....219 B4
Friars Gate Cl IG8 .....37 A6
Friars Gdns W3 .....89 B1
Friars La TW9 .....153 D6
Friars Mead E14 .....120 A3
Friars Mews SE9 .....166 C6
Friars Place La W3 ....111 B6
Friars Prim Sch
SE1 .....116 D4 251 D1
Friar's Rd E6 .....99 D6
Friars Stile Pl 9 TW10 154 A5
Friars Stile Rd TW10 ..154 A5
Friars Way W3 .....89 B1
Friars Wlk N14 .....15 B4
SE2 .....124 D1
Friary Cl N12 .....30 C5
Friary La IG8 .....37 A6
Friary Park Ct W3 .....89 A1
Friary Rd N12 .....30 C6
SE15 .....140 A5
W3 .....89 B1
Friary Way N12 .....30 C6
Friday Hill E4 .....20 C1
Friday Hill E E4 .....20 C1
Friday Hill W E4 .....20 C2
Friday Rd CR4 .....180 D3
Friday St EC4 ...117 A6 252 A6
Frideswide Pl NW5 .....71 C3
Friend St EC1 ...94 D4 234 C2
Friendly Pl SE13 .....141 D4
Friendly St SE8 .....141 C4
Friendly Street Mews
SE8 .....141 C3
Friends' Rd CR0 .....221 B5
Friendship Wlk UB5 ....84 D4
Friern Barnet Cty Sec Sch
N11 .....30 D5
Friern Barnet La N20 ...30 C6
Friern Barnet Rd N11 ...31 A5
Friern Ct N20 .....14 B1
Friern Mount Dr N20 ...14 A4
Friern Pk N12 .....30 B5
Friern Rd SE22 .....162 A5
Friern Sch (Lower)
SE22 .....162 B6
Friern Watch Ave N12 ..30 B6
Frigate Ho 6 E14 .....120 A2
Frigate Mews SE8 .....141 C6
Frimley Ave SM6 .....220 B3
Frimley Cl SW19 .....157 A2
New Addington CR0 .....224 A1
Frimley Cres CR0 .....224 A1
Frimley Ct DA14 .....190 C5
Frimley Gdns CR4 .....202 C6
Frimley Ho CR4 .....202 C6
Frimley Rd
Chessington KT9 .....214 A3
Frimley Rd *continued*
Ilford IG3 .....79 C5
Frimley Way E1 .....96 D3
Frinstead Ho 1 W10 ..112 D6
Frinton Ct W13 .....87 B2
Frinton Dr IG8 .....36 B3
Frinton Mews IG2 .....56 C3
Frinton Rd E6 .....99 D4
N15 .....51 C3
SW17 .....181 A4
Sidcup DA14 .....169 A2
Friston St SW6 .....135 D3
Friswell Pl 1 DA7 .....147 C1
Frith Ct NW7 .....29 A3
Frith Ho E2 .....96 A4
NW8 .....236 D5
Frith La NW7 .....29 A4
Frith Manor Sch N12 ...29 B5
Frith Rd E11 .....76 B4
Croydon CR0 .....221 A6
Frith St W1 ....93 D1 239 C1
Fritham Cl KT3 .....199 C3
Frithville Ct W12 .....112 C5
Frithville Gdns W12 ...112 C5
Frizlands La RM10 .....81 D5
Frobisher Cl HA5 .....40 D2
Frobisher Cres TW19 ..148 A4
Frobisher Ct NW9 .....27 C1
6 SE23 .....162 B2
3 W12 .....112 C4
Belmont SM2 .....217 B1
Frobisher Gdns TW19 ..148 A4
Frobisher Ho 27 E1 ....118 B5
3 W5 .....88 A4
Frobisher Pas E14 .....119 C5
Frobisher Rd N8 .....50 C5
Frobisher Sq 1 SE10 ..142 B6
Frobisher St SE10 .....142 C6
Frogley Rd SE22 .....139 D1
Frogmore SW18 .....157 C6
Frogmore Ave UB4 .....83 C3
Frogmore Cl SM3 .....217 A5
Frogmore Ct UB2 .....107 B2
Frogmore Est NW10 ....89 A4
Frogmore Gdns
Cheam SM3 .....217 A4
Hayes UB4 .....83 C3
Frogmore Ind Est N5 ...73 A4
Frognal NW3 .....70 A3
Frognal Ave Harrow HA1 .42 D5
Sidcup DA14 .....190 A4
Frognal Cl NW3 .....70 A3
Frognal Corner BR7 ...189 D4
Frognal Ct NW3 .....70 A2
Frognal Gdns NW3 .....70 A4
Frognal La NW3 .....69 D3
Frognal Par NW3 .....70 A2
Frognal Pl DA14 .....190 A5
Frognal Rise NW3 .....70 A4
Frognal Way NW3 .....70 A4
Froissart Rd SE9 .....166 A6
Frome Ho SE15 .....140 C1
Frome Rd N22 .....50 D6
Frome St N1 ....95 A5 235 A4
Fromondes Rd SM3 ...217 A3
Frontenac NW10 .....68 B1
Frontier Works N17 .....33 C4
Froude St SW8 .....137 B3
Fruen Rd TW14 .....149 D4
Fry Ho E6 .....77 C1
Fry Rd E6 .....77 D1
NW10 .....89 D6
Fryatt Rd N17 .....33 B3
Frye Ct E3 .....97 B4
Fryent Cl NW9 .....44 C3
Fryent Cres NW9 .....45 C3
Fryent Ctry Park HA3,
HA9 .....44 C2
Fryent Fields NW9 .....45 C3
Fryent Gr NW9 .....45 C3
Fryent Prim Sch NW9 ...45 A2
Fryent Way HA9,NW9 ....44 D2
Frying Pan Alley E1 ...243 C3
Fryston Ave CR0 .....222 A6
Fuchsia St SE2 .....124 B1
Fulbeck Dr NW9 .....27 C2
Fulbeck Ho N7 .....72 B2
Fulbeck Way HA2 .....24 A1
Fulbourn 9 KT1 .....176 C1
Fulbourne Rd E17 .....36 A1
Fulbourne St E1 .....96 B2
Fulbrook Rd N19 .....71 C4
Fulcher Ho 10 N1 .....95 C6
13 SE8 .....119 B1
Fulford Mans N19 .....72 A5
Fulford Rd KT19 .....215 B1
Fulford St SE16 .....118 B4
Fulham Broadway
SW6 .....135 C5 265 B3
Fulham Broadway Sta
SW6 .....135 C5 265 B4
Fulham Cl UB10 .....83 A3
Fulham Cross Sch
SW6 .....135 A5 264 A4
Fulham Ct SW6 135 C4 265 A2
Fulham High St SW6 ..135 A3
Fulham Palace* SW6 .135 A3
Fulham Palace Rd
SW6 .....135 A4 264 A1
W6 .....134 D6
Fulham Park Gdns SW6 135 B3
Fulham Park Rd SW6 ..135 B3
Fulham Prep Sch The
SW6 .....135 A3
Fulham Prim Sch
SW6 .....135 C6 265 A5
Fulham Rd SW6 135 B4 264 D2
SW10 .....136 A6 266 B6
Fulke Ho E5 .....74 B5
Fullbrooks Ave KT4 ....199 D1
Fuller Cl 3 E2 .....96 A3
Orpington BR6 .....227 D3
Fuller Rd RM8 .....80 C4
Fuller St NW4 .....46 C5
Fuller Terr IG1 .....79 B3
Fuller Way UB3 .....105 D1
Fullers Ave KT6 .....214 B6
Fuller's Ave IG8 .....36 D3
Fullers Cotts N22 .....32 B3
Fullers Ho 6 SW18 ....157 C6
Fuller's Rd E18 .....36 D3
Fullers Way N KT6 .....214 B5
Fullers Way S KT9 .....214 A5
Fuller's Wood CR0 .....223 C3
Fullerton Ct TW11 .....175 A4
Fullerton Rd SW18 .....158 A6
Croydon CR0 .....205 D2
Fullwood Prim Sch IG6 .57 A5
Fullwood's Mews N1 ...235 D2
Fulmar Ct 5 SE21 .....161 B2
Fulmar Ho NW8 .....237 B5
12 SE16 .....118 D2
Fulmead St SW6 .....265 D1
Fulmer Cl TW12 .....173 A5
Fulmer Rd E16 .....99 D2
Fulmer Way W13 .....109 B3
Fulneck 1 E1 .....96 C2
Fulready Rd E10 .....54 B4
Fulstone Cl TW4 .....129 B1
Fulthorp Rd SE3 .....143 A3
Fulton Ct EN3 .....7 C5
Fulton Mews W2 .....246 A6
Fulton Rd HA9 .....66 C5
Fulwell Ct UB1 .....108 A6
Fulwell Park Ave TW2 .152 A2
Fulwell Rd TW11,TW12 .174 B6
Fulwell Sta TW11 .....174 B6
Fulwood Ave HA0 .....88 B5
Fulwood Cl UB3 .....83 D1
Fulwood Gdns TW1 ....153 A5
Fulwood Pl WC1 .....240 D3
Fulwood Wlk SW19 ....157 A3
Furber St W6 .....112 B3
Furham Field HA5 .....23 C3
Furley Ho 7 SE15 .....140 A5
Furley Rd SE15 .....140 A5
Furlong Cl SM6 .....203 B1
Furlong Rd N7 .....72 C2
Furmage St SW18 .....157 D4
Furneaux Ave SE27 ....182 D5
Furness Ho SW1 .....258 C2
Furness Lo 4 SW14 ...132 D1
Furness Rd NW10 .....90 A5
SW6 .....135 D3
Harrow HA2 .....41 D1
Morden SM4 .....201 D3
Furnival St EC4 ..94 C1 241 A2
Furrow La E9 .....74 C3
Furrows The KT12 .....194 C1
Fursby Ave N3 .....29 C4
Fursecroft W1 .....237 C2
Further Acre NW9 .....27 D1
Further Green Rd SE6 .164 C3
Furtherfield Cl CR0 ....204 C3
Furze Cl WD1 .....22 C5
Furze Ct CR0 .....222 A6
Furze Inf Sch RM6 .....59 A3
Furze Rd CR7 .....205 A6
Furze St E3 .....97 C2
Furzedown Dr SW17 ...181 B5
Furzedown Prim Sch
SW17 .....181 A4
Furzedown Rd SW17 ...181 B5
Furzefield Cl BR7 .....188 D4
Furzefield Rd SE3 .....143 B5
Furzeground Way UB11 105 A5
Furzeham Rd UB7 .....104 A4
Furzehill Rd
Borehamwood WD6 .....11 A6
WD6 .....11 A6
Furzeland Ho 2 KT3 ..199 C2
Furzewood TW16 .....172 A2
Fuschia Ct IG8 .....36 C4
Fyfe Way BR1 .....187 A1
Fyfield N4 .....72 C6
Fyfield Cl BR2,BR3 .....208 B5
Fyfield Ct E7 .....77 A2
Fyfield Ho RM9 .....80 B1
Fyfield Rd E17 .....54 B6
6 SW9 .....138 C2
Enfield EN1 .....5 C2
Woodford IG8 .....37 C3
Fynes St SW1 .....259 C4

G

Gable Cl HA5 .....23 C3
Gable Ct SE26 .....184 B6
Gable Ho 12 W4 .....111 C2
Gable Lo Barnet EN4 .....2 A5
West Wickham BR4 .....208 A1
Gables Ave TW15 .....170 B5
Gables Cl SE5 .....139 C4
SE12 .....165 A3
Gables The N10 .....49 A6
N12 .....29 D5
NW3 .....70 B6
3 SW4 .....137 C2
W13 .....87 B1
Barking IG11 .....79 A2
Bromley BR1 .....187 B3
Wembley HA9 .....66 B5
Gabriel Cl 1 TW13 ....173 A6
Gabriel Ho SE11 .....260 C4
Gabriel St SE23 .....163 A4

Gabrielle Cl HA9 66 B5
Gabrielle Ct NW3 70 B2
Gabriel's Wharf SE1 251 A4
Gad Cl E13 99 B4
Gaddesden Ave HA9 66 B2
Gaddesden Ho EC1 235 D1
Gade Cl UB3 106 B5
Gadesden Rd KT19 215 A2
Gadsbury Cl NW9 45 D3
Gadsden Ho 6 E9 74 D2
8 W10 91 A3
Gadwall Cl E16 99 B1
Gadwall Way SE28 123 B4
Gagarin Ho SW11 136 B2
Gage Rd E16 98 C2
Gage St WC1 240 B4
Gainford Ho 18 E2 96 B4
Gainford St N1 94 C6 234 A6
Gainsboro Gdns UB6 64 C3
Gainsborough Ave E12 78 C3
Gainsborough Cl
Beckenham BR3 185 C3
Thames Ditton KT10 196 C1
Gainsborough Ct N12 29 D5
6 SE16 118 B1
SE21 161 C2
W12 112 C4
Barnet EN5 1 D1
Gainsborough Gdns
NW3 70 B5
NW11 47 B2
Edgware HA8 26 C1
Isleworth TW7 152 B6
Gainsborough Ho
5 E14 119 A6
N4 50 B1
3 NW3 70 A4
SW1 259 D3
Barking RM8 80 B4
Enfield EN1 18 A6
Gainsborough Lo HA1 42 C4
Gainsborough Mews 5
SE26 162 B1
Gainsborough Prim Sch
E9 75 C2
E15 98 C4
Gainsborough Rd E11 54 C2
E15 98 C4
N12 29 D5
W4 111 D2
Dagenham RM8 80 B5
Hayes UB4 83 B5
New Malden KT3 199 B2
Richmond TW9 132 B2
Gainsborough Sq DA7 146 D2
Gainsborough Twr 8
UB5 84 D5
Gainsford Rd E17 53 B5
Gainsford St
SE1 117 D4 253 D2
Gairloch Ho 2 NW1 71 D1
Gairloch Rd SE5 139 C3
Gaisford St NW5 71 C2
Gaitskell Ct SW11 136 C3
Gaitskell Ho 2 E6 99 D6
3 E17 53 D6
SE17 139 B6
Gaitskell Rd SE9 167 A3
Galahad Rd BR1 187 A6
Galata Rd SW13 134 A5
Galatea Sq SE15 140 B2
Galba Ct 1 TW8 131 D5
Galbraith St E14 120 A3
Galdana Ave EN5 2 A2
Gale Cl Hampton TW12 173 A4
Mitcham CR4 202 B6
Gale Ho 10 SW2 160 B6
Gale St E3 97 C2
Dagenham RM9 80 D1
Galeborough Ave IG8 36 B3
Galen Pl WC1 240 B3
Galena Ho SE18 123 D1
5 W6 112 B2
Galena Rd W6 112 B2
Gales Gdns E2 96 B4
Galesbury Rd SW18 158 A5
Galgate Cl 4 SW19 157 A3
Gallants Farm Rd EN4 14 C3
Galleon Cl SE16 118 D4
Galleon Ho 7 E14 120 A2
Gallery Ct SW10 266 A5
Gallery Gdns UB5 84 D5
Gallery Rd SE21 161 B3
Galleywall Prim Sch
SE16 118 B2
Galleywall Rd SE16 118 B2
Galleywall Road Trad Est 12
SE16 118 B2
Galleywood Ho W10 90 C2
Gallia Rd N5 72 D3
Galliard Cl N9 18 C5
Galliard Ct N9 18 A5
Galliard Prim Sch N9 18 A5
Galliard Rd N9 18 A5
Gallions Cl IG11 102 A4
Gallions Mount Prim Sch
SE18 123 D1
Gallions Rd E16 123 A6
SE7 121 A2
Gallions Reach Sta E16 122 D6
Gallon Cl SE7 121 C2
Gallop The
South Croydon CR2 222 B1
Sutton SM2 218 A1
Gallosson Rd SE18 123 C2
Galloway Path 5 CR0 221 B4
Galloway Rd W12 112 A5
Gallus Cl N21 16 B5
Gallus Sq SE3 143 B2
Galpin's Rd CR4,CR7 204 B5
Galsworthy Ave RM6 58 B2
Galsworthy Cl SE28 124 B5
Galsworthy Cres SE3 143 C4
Galsworthy Ho 4 W11 91 A1
Galsworthy Rd NW2 69 A4
Kingston u T KT2 176 D2
Galton Ho 1 SE18 144 B4
Galton St W10 91 A4
Galva Cl EN4 3 A1
Galvani Way CR0 204 B1
Galveston Ho 2 E1 97 A3
Galveston Rd SW15 157 B6
Galway Cl 28 SE16 118 B1
Galway Ho 6 E1 96 D2
EC1 235 B1
Galway St EC1 95 A4 235 B1
Galy 5 NW9 27 D1
Gambetta St 3 SW8 137 B3
Gambia St SE1 116 D5 251 D3
Gambler Ho EC1 235 B1
Gambole Rd SW17 180 C6
Games Ho 6 SE7 143 C6
Games Rd EN4 2 D2
Gamlen Rd SW15 134 D1
Gander Green Cres
TW12 173 C2
Gander Green La KT4,
SM1,SM3 217 B5
Gandhi Cl E17 53 C3
Ganley Ct 19 SW11 136 B2
Gannet Ct 4 SE21 161 B2
Gannet Ho SE15 139 D4
Ganton St W1 239 B1
Ganton Wlk WD1 22 D6
Gants Hill IG2 56 C3
Gants Hill Sta IG2 56 C3
Gantshill Cres IG2 56 C4
Gap Rd SW19 179 D5
Garage Rd W3 88 C1
Garbett Ho 2 SE17 138 D6
Garbutt Pl W1 238 B3
Gard St EC1 234 D2
Garden Ave
Bexleyheath DA7 147 C2
Mitcham CR4 181 B3
Garden City HA8 26 C4
Garden Cl E4 35 C5
SE12 165 B1
SW15 156 B4
Ashford TW15 171 A4
Hampton TW12 173 B5
Northolt UB5 85 A6
Ruislip HA4 61 D6
Wallington SM6 220 A3
Garden Cotts BR5 190 C1
Garden Ct EC4 251 A6
N12 29 D5
NW8 229 C2
10 SE9 166 C5
12 W4 111 A3
5 Belmont SM2 217 C1
4 Richmond TW9 132 B4
South Croydon CR0 221 D5
4 Stanmore HA7 25 C5
Wembley HA0 65 C5
Garden Flats SW16 160 A1
Garden Ho 2 N2 30 B1
12 SW9 138 A3
Garden Hospl The NW4 46 C6
Garden La SW2 160 B3
Plaistow BR1 187 B4
Garden Lodge Ct N2 48 B6
Garden Mews W2 245 B5
Garden Rd NW8 92 A4 229 B2
SE20 184 C2
Mortlake TW9 132 C2
Plaistow BR1 187 B4
Walton-on-T KT12 194 B2
Garden Row
SE1 116 D3 261 C6
Garden Royal 16 SW15 156 D5
Garden St E1 96 D2
Garden Suburb Jun & Inf
Schs NW11 47 B4
Garden Terr SW1 259 C2
SW7 247 B1
Garden Way NW10 67 A2
Garden Wlk EC2 95 C3 243 A6
Beckenham BR3 185 B2
Gardeners Cl N11 15 A2
Gardeners Rd CR0 204 D1
Gardenia Ct 1 BR3 185 C3
Gardenia Rd EN1 17 C5
Gardenia Way IG8 37 A5
Gardens The N16 51 D2
SE22 140 A1
Beckenham BR3 186 A2
Harrow HA1,HA2 42 A3
Hatton TW14 149 B5
Pinner HA5 41 B3
Gardiner Ave NW2 68 C3
Gardiner Cl
Dagenham RM8 80 D4
Enfield EN3 18 D5
St Paul's Cray BR5 190 C1
Gardiner Ct NW10 89 B6
Gardiner Ho 3 SE18 144 A5
SW11 267 A2
Gardner Cl E11 55 B3
Gardner Ct N5 73 A4
N22 32 D1
Hounslow TW3 129 C2
Gardner Ho
Feltham TW13 151 B2
Southall UB1 106 D6
Gardner Ind Est SE26 185 B5
Gardner Pl TW14 150 B5
Gardner Rd E13 99 B3
Gardners La EC4 252 A6
Gardnor Mans 10 NW3 70 A4
Gardnor Rd NW3 70 B4
Garendon Gdns SM4 201 D2
Garendon Rd SM4 201 D2
Garenne Ct 10 E4 20 A3
Gareth Cl KT4 216 D6
Gareth Ct SW16 159 D1
Gareth Gr BR1 187 A6
Garfield N9 18 B3
Enfield EN2 17 B6
Garfield Prim Sch N11 31 C5
SW19 180 A4
Garfield Rd E4 20 B3
E13 98 D3
SW11 137 A2
SW19 180 A4
Enfield EN3 6 C1
2 Twickenham TW1 153 A3
Garford St E14 119 C6
Garganey Ct NW10 67 B2
Garganey Wlk SE28 124 C6
Garibaldi St SE18 123 C2
Garland Ho N16 73 B5
Garland Rd SE18 145 B5
Stanmore HA7 26 A2
Garlands Ct 2 CR0 221 B4
Garlands The HA1 42 D2
Garlick Hill EC4 117 A6 252 B6
Garlies Rd SE23 163 A1
Garlinge Ho 12 SW9 138 C4
Garlinge Rd NW2 69 B2
Garman Cl N18 33 B5
Garman Rd N17 34 C3
Garnault Mews EC1 234 B1
Garnault Pl EC1 234 B1
Garnault Rd EN1 5 D5
Garner Rd E17 36 A2
Garner St E2 96 A5
Garnet Ho KT4 199 B1
Garnet Rd NW10 67 C2
South Norwood CR7 205 B5
Garnet St E1 118 C6
Garnet Wlk 8 E6 100 A2
Garnett Cl SE9 144 B2
Garnett Ho 5 NW3 70 D3
Garnett Rd NW3 70 D3
Garnett Way E17 35 A2
Garnham Cl 2 N16 73 D6
Garnham St 1 N16 73 D6
Garnies Cl SE15 139 D5
Garrads Rd SW16 159 D1
Garrard Cl
Bexleyheath DA7 147 C2
Chislehurst West BR7 188 D5
Garrard Wlk NW10 67 C2
Garratt Cl CR0 220 A4
Garratt Ho 8 N16 51 C1
Garratt La SW17,SW18 180 C6
SW18 157 D3
Garratt Park Sec Sch
SW18 158 A1
Garratt Rd HA8 26 C3
Garratt Terr SW17 180 C6
Garratts Rd WD2 8 A4
Garraway Ct SW13 134 C5
Garraway Ho SE21 161 D1
Garrett Cl W3 89 B2
Garrett Ho W12 90 B1
Teddington TW11 175 B4
Garrett St EC1 95 A3 242 B6
Garrick Ave NW11 47 A3
Garrick Cl SW18 136 A1
W5 88 A3
1 Richmond TW9 153 D6
Garrick Cres CR0 221 C6
Garrick Ct HA8 26 B6
Garrick Dr NW4 28 C1
SE18 123 B3
Garrick Gdns KT8 195 C6
Garrick Ho 7 SW16 181 C5
W1 248 C3
W4 133 C6
2 Kingston u T KT1 198 A5
Garrick Ind Est NW9 45 D4
Garrick Pk NW4 28 D1
Garrick Rd NW9 45 D3
Richmond TW9 132 C3
Southall UB6 85 D3
Garrick St WC2 116 A6 250 A6
Garrick Way NW4 46 D5
Garrick Yd WC2 250 A6
Garrick's Ait KT8 174 A1
Garrison Cl SE18 144 C5
Hounslow TW4 151 B6
Garrison La KT9 214 A1
Garrowsfield EN5 13 B6
Garsdale Cl N11 31 A4
Garside Cl SE28 123 B3
Hampton TW12 173 D4
Garsington Mews SE4 141 B2
Garson Ho W2 246 C6
Garston Ho 6 N1 72 D1
Garter Way SE16 118 D4
Garth Cl Kingston u T KT2 176 B5
Ruislip HA4 40 D1
West Barnes SM4 200 D2
Garth Ct W4 133 B6
Harrow HA1 42 D3
Garth High Sch SM4 202 B3
Garth Ho NW2 69 B6
Garth Mews W5 88 A3
Garth Rd NW2 69 B6
8 W4 111 B1
Kingston u T KT2 176 B5
West Barnes SM4 200 D2
Garth The N12 29 D5
Hampton TW12 173 D4
Harrow HA3 44 B3
Garthland Dr EN5 12 C6
Garthorne Rd SE23 162 D4
Garthside TW10 176 A5
Garthway N12 30 C4
Gartmoor Gdns SW19 157 B3
Gartmore Rd IG3 79 D6
Garton Ho 6 N6 49 D2
Garton Pl SW18 158 A5
Gartons Cl EN3 6 C1
Gartons Way SW11 136 A2
Garvary Rd E16 99 B1
Garvens SE19 183 C5
Garway Rd W2 91 D1
Gascoigne Gdns IG8 36 C3
Gascoigne Jun & Inf Schs
IG11 101 A6
Gascoigne Pl 17 E2 95 D4
Gascoigne Rd IG11 101 A5
Gascony Ave NW6 69 C1
Gascoyne Ho 2 E9 74 D1
Gascoyne Rd E9 74 D1
Gaselee St E14 120 A6
Gasholder Pl
SE11 116 B1 260 D1
Gaskarth Rd SW12 159 B5
Burnt Oak HA8 27 A1
Gaskell Rd N6 48 D3
Gaskell St SW4 138 A3
Gaskin Ho N16 73 B5
Gaskin St N1 94 D6 234 C6
Gaspar Cl SW7 255 D4
Gaspar Mews SW5 255 D4
Gassiot Rd SW17 180 D6
Gassiot Way SM1 218 B5
Gasson Ho 24 SE14 140 D6
Gastein Rd W6 134 D6
Gastigny Ho EC1 235 B1
Gaston Bell Cl TW9 132 B2
Gaston Bridge Rd
TW17 193 B3
Gaston Gate SW8 270 C2
Gaston Rd CR4 203 A6
Gaston Way TW17 193 B4
Gataker Ho 5 SE16 118 B3
Gataker St 6 SE16 118 B3
Gatcliff Cl SW1 258 B1
Gatcombe Ct BR3 185 C3
Gatcombe Ho 20 SE22 139 C2
Gatcombe Mews W5 110 B6
Gatcombe Rd 9 E16 121 A5
N19 71 D5
Gatcombe Way EN4 2 D2
Gate End HA6 22 A3
Gate Hill Ct W11 244 D4
Gate Ho 4 KT6 198 A1
Gate Mews
SW7 114 C4 247 B1
Gate St WC2 94 B1 240 C2
Gateacre Ct DA14 190 B6
Gatebeck Ho 21 SE22 139 C2
Gatefield Ct SE15 140 A2
Gateforth St NW8 237 A5
Gatehill Rd HA6 22 A3
Gatehouse Cl KT2 177 A3
Gatehouse Sch E2 96 D5
Gatehouse Sq SE1 252 B4
Gateley Ho 6 SE4 140 D1
Gateley Rd SW9 138 B2
Gater Dr EN2 5 B4
Gates 4 NW9 27 D1
Gates Ct SE17 262 A2
Gates Green Rd
Coney Hall BR4 224 D5
Hayes BR2,BR4 225 A4
Gatesborough St EC2 243 A6
Gatesden WC1 233 B1
Gateside Rd SW17 158 D1
Gatestone Ct 10 SE19 183 C4
Gatestone Rd SE19 183 C4
Gateway SE17 139 A6
Gateway Ho 6 IG11 101 A6
Gateway Mews 4 E8 73 D3
Gateway Prim Sch
NW8 92 B3 236 D6
Gateway Rd E10 75 D5
Gateway Trad Est NW10 89 D4
Gateways KT6 198 A4
Gateways Ct SM6 219 B3
Gateways The SW3 257 B3
Richmond TW9 131 D1
Gatfield Gr TW13 151 C2
Gatfield Ho TW13 151 C2
Gathorne Rd N22 32 C2
Gathorne St 19 E2 96 D5
Gatley Ave KT19 214 D3
Gatliff Rd SW1 115 B1 258 C1
Gatling Rd SE18,SE2 124 A1
Gaton Rd SE2 124 C3
Gatting Cl HA8 27 A3
Gatting Way UB8 60 A2
Gatton Rd SW17 180 C6
Gattons Way DA14 191 B6
Gatward Cl N21 16 D5
Gatward Gn N9 17 D2
Gatwick Ho 3 E14 97 B1
Gatwick Rd SW18 157 B4
Gauden Cl SW4 137 D2
Gauden Rd SW4 137 D2
Gaugin Ct 13 SE16 118 B1
Gaunt St SE1 262 A6
Gauntlet 1 NW9 27 D1
Gauntlet Cl UB5 63 A1
Gauntlett Ct HA0 65 B3
Gauntlett Rd SM1 218 B3
Gautrey Rd SE15 140 C3
Gautrey Sq 5 E6 100 B1
Gavel St SE17 262 D4
Gaven Ho N17 33 C1
Gavestone Cres SE12 165 B4
Gavestone Rd SE12 165 B4
Gaviller Pl 4 E5 74 B4
Gavin Ho SE18 123 C2
Gavina Cl SM4 202 C4
Gavrelle Ho EC1 242 C5
Gawber St E2 96 C4
Gawsworth Cl E15 76 D3
Gawthorne Ave NW7 29 A5
Gawthorne Ct E3 97 C5
Gay Cl NW2 68 B3
Gay Ho N16 73 C3
Gay Rd E15 98 B5
Gay St SW15 134 D2
Gaydon Ho W2 91 D2
Gaydon La NW9 27 C2
Gayfere Rd Redbridge IG5 56 B6
Stoneleigh KT17 216 A3
Gayfere St SW1 116 A3 260 A5
Gayford Rd W12 111 D4
Gayhurst SE17 139 B6
Gayhurst Ct 9 UB5 84 C4
Gayhurst Ho NW8 237 B6
Gayhurst JMI Sch E8 74 A1
Gayhurst Rd E8 74 A1
Gaylor Rd UB5 63 B3
Gaymead NW8 91 D6
Gaynesford Rd SE23 162 D2
Wallington SM5 218 D1
Gaysham Ave IG2 56 D4
Gaysham Hall IG5 56 D6
Gaysley Ho SE11 261 A3
Gayton Cres NW3 70 B4
Gayton Ct 3 Harrow HA1 42 D3
New Malden KT3 199 D4
Gayton Ho E3 97 C3
Gayton Rd NW3 70 B4
Harrow HA1 43 A3
Gayville Rd SW11 158 D5
Gaywood Cl SW2 160 C3
Gaywood Rd E17 53 C6
Gaywood St SE1 261 D5
Gaza St SE17 116 D1 261 C1
Gaze Ho 10 E14 98 B1
Gean Ct 3 E11 76 B4
Gearies Inf Sch IG2 56 D4
Gearies Jun Sch IG2 56 D4
Geariesville Gdns IG6 56 D5
Geary Ho N7 72 B3
Geary Rd NW10 68 A3
Geary St N7 72 B3
GEC Est HA9 65 D6
Geddes Pl 3 DA7 147 C1
Gedeney Rd N17 33 A2
Gedge Ct CR4 202 C5
Gedling Ho SE22 139 D2
Gedling Pl SE1 263 D6
Gee St EC1 95 A3 242 A6
Geere Rd E15 98 D6
Gees Ct W1 238 B1
Geffrey's Ct SE9 166 A1
Geffrye Ct N1 95 C5
Geffrye Mus* E2 95 D5
Geffrye St E2 95 D5
Geldart Rd SE15 140 B5
Geldeston Rd E5 74 A6
Gell Cl UB10 60 B5
Gellatly Rd SE14 140 D3
Gemini Bsns Ctr E16 98 B3
Gemini Gr UB5 85 A4
Gemini Ho SW15 134 D1
Gemma Ct BR3 185 B1
General Gordon Pl
SE18 122 D2
General Wolfe Rd SE10 142 B4
Generals Wlk The EN3 7 A6
Genesis Cl TW19 148 B3
Genesta Rd SE18 145 A6
Geneva Cl TW17 171 C1
Geneva Ct N16 51 B1
1 SW15 156 D6
Geneva Dr SW9 138 C1
Geneva Gdns RM6 59 A4
Geneva Rd
Kingston u T KT1 198 A5
Thornton Heath CR7 205 A4
Genever Cl E4 35 C5
Genista Rd N18 34 B5
Genoa Ave SW15 156 C6
Genoa Ho 19 E1 96 D3
Genoa Rd SE20 184 C2
Genotin Rd EN1 5 B2
Genotin Terr EN1 5 B2
Gentleman's Row EN2 5 A2
Gentry Gdns E13 99 A4
Geoffrey Chaucer Sch
SE1 117 B3 262 C5
Geoffrey Cl SE5 139 A3
Geoffrey Ct SE4 141 B2
Geoffrey Gdns E6 100 A5
Geoffrey Ho SE1 262 D6
Geoffrey Jones Ct NW10 90 A6
Geoffrey Rd SE4 141 B2
Geological Mus
SW7 114 B3 256 D5
George Akass Ho 3
SE18 123 A1
George Beard Rd 10
SE8 119 B2
George Beare Lo 9
SW4 159 C6
George Belt Ho 8 E2 96 D4
George Comberton Wlk 3
E12 78 C3
George Cres N10 31 A3
George Ct WC2 250 B5
George Downing Est
N16 73 D6
George Eliot Ho SW1 259 B3
George Eliot Jun & Inf Sch
NW8 92 B6 229 C6
George Elliot Ho SE17 262 A2
George Elliston Ho 12
SE1 118 A1
George Eyre Ho NW8 229 D3
George Gange Way HA3 42 D6
George Green's Sec Sch
E14 120 A1
George Groves Rd
SE20 184 A2
George Ho 8 SE26 184 B5
George Inn Yd SE1 252 C3
George La E18 37 A1
E18 55 B6
SE13 164 A5
Hayes BR2 209 B1
George Lansbury Ho
7 E3 97 B4
N22 32 C2
NW10 67 C1
George Lashwood Ct 12
SW9 138 B1
George Leybourne Ho 9
E1 118 A6
George Lindgren Ho
SW6 264 D4
George Loveless Ho 4
E2 95 D4
George Lovell Dr EN3 7 C6
George Mews NW1 232 A1
George Mitchell Sec Sch
E10 53 D1
George Orwell Sch N4 50 B1
George Parr Ho N21 16 D4
George Rd E4 35 C4
Kingston u T KT2 177 A3
New Malden KT3 199 D4
George Row SE16 118 A4
George Spicer Prim Sch
EN1 5 D2
George Sq SW19 201 C6
George St 6 E16 98 D1
W1 92 D1 237 D2
W7 108 C5
Barking IG11 79 A1
Croydon CR0 221 B6
Hounslow TW3,TW5 129 B3
Richmond TW10 153 D6
Southall UB2 107 A2
George Tingle Ho SE1 263 D6
George Tomlinson Prim Sch
E11 54 C1
George V Ave HA2,HA5 41 C6
George V Way UB6 87 B6
George Vale Ho 32 E2 96 A5
George Walter Ho 7
SE16 118 C2
George Wyver Cl SW18 157 A4
George Yd EC3 242 D1
W1 115 A6 248 B6
Georges Mead WD6 10 A5
George's Rd N7 72 B3
George's Sq SW6 264 D6
Georgetown Cl 4 SE19 183 C5
Georgette Pl SE10 142 A5
Georgeville Gdns IG6 56 D5
Georgia Rd
Kingston u T KT3 199 A5
South Norwood CR7 182 D2
Georgian Cl Hayes BR2 209 B1
Ickenham UB10 60 A4
Stanmore HA7 25 A3
Georgian Ct 19 E9 96 C6
3 NW4 46 B4
Croydon CR0 205 B1
Wembley HA9 66 D2
Georgian Lo HA5 40 B4
Georgian Way HA1 64 B6
Georgiana St
NW1 93 C6 232 B6
Georgina Ct 5 TW1 153 C5
Georgina Gdns 10 E2 95 D4
Geraint Rd BR1 187 A6
Gerald Mews SW1 258 B4
Gerald Rd E16 98 D3
SW1 115 A2 258 B4
Dagenham RM8 59 B1
Geraldine Ct 6 NW9 46 A5
Geraldine Rd SW18 158 A6
W4 132 C6
Geraldine St SE11 261 C5
Gerard Ave TW4 151 C4
Gerard Ct NW2 68 D3
Gerard Rd SW13 133 D4
Harrow HA1 43 A3
Gerards Cl SE16 118 C1
Gerboa Ct 6 E4 36 B5
Gerda Rd SE9 167 A2
Germander Way E15 98 C4
Gernigan Ho SW18 158 B5
Gernon Rd E3 97 A5
Geron Way NW2 68 C6
Gerrard Gdns HA5 40 A4
Gerrard Ho 5 SE14 140 D5
Gerrard Pl W1 249 D6
Gerrard Rd N1 94 D5 234 D4
Gerrard St W1 115 D6 249 D6
Gerrards Cl N14 15 C6
Gerrard's Ct W5 109 D3
Gerridge Ct SE1 261 B6

Gerridge St SE1 116 C3 261 B6
Gertrude Rd DA17 125 C2
Gertrude St
SW10 136 A6 266 B5
Gervase Cl HA9 67 A5
Gervase Rd HA8 27 B2
Gervase St SE15 140 B5
Ghent St SE6 163 C2
Ghent Way E8 73 D2
Giant Arches Rd SE24 161 A5
Giant Tree Hill WD2 8 B3
Gibbards Cott 1 IG11 79 D1
Gibbfield Cl RM6 59 A6
Gibbings Ho SE1 251 D1
Gibbins Rd E15 76 A1
Gibbon Ho NW8 236 D5
Gibbon Rd SE15 140 C3
W3 111 C6
Kingston u T KT2 176 A3
Gibbon Wlk SW15 134 A1
Gibbons Rd NW10 67 C2
Gibbon's Rents SE1 253 A3
Gibbs Ave SE19 183 B5
Gibbs Cl SE19 183 B5
Gibbs Gn W14 113 B1 254 D2
Edgware HA8 27 A6
Gibbs Green Sch
W14 113 B1 254 D2
Gibbs Ho 6 SW12 159 B4
2 Bromley BR1 186 D2
Gibbs Rd N18 34 C6
Gibbs Sq SE19 183 B5
Gibraltar Ho NW10 89 C5
Gibraltar Wlk 28 E2 95 D4
Gibson Bsns Ctr N17 33 D3
Gibson Cl E1 96 C3
Chessington KT9 213 C3
Isleworth TW7 130 B2
Gibson Ct KT10 212 D5
Gibson Gdns N16 73 D6
Gibson Ho Croydon CR2 221 A2
Sutton SM1 217 C4
Gibson Rd SE11 260 D3
Dagenham RM8 58 C1
Ickenham UB10 60 B4
Sutton SM1 217 D3
Gibson Sq N1 94 C6 234 B6
Gibson St SE10 120 C1
Gibson's Hill SW16 182 C3
SW16 182 C4
Gideon Cl DA17 125 D2
Gideon Rd SW11 137 A2
Giesbach Rd N19 71 D6
Giffard Rd N18 33 C4
Giffen Square Mkt SE8 141 C5
Giffin St SE8 141 C5
Gifford Gdns W7 86 C2
Gifford Ho SE10 120 B1
5 SW4 137 D1
Gifford Prim Sch UB5 85 B5
Gifford St N1 72 A1
Gift La E15 98 D6
Giggs Hill BR5 190 A2
Giggs Hill Gdns KT7 197 A1
Giggs Hill Rd KT7 197 A2
Gilbert Cl SE18 144 B4
1 SW19 179 D2
Gilbert Ct W5 88 B1
Gilbert Gr HA8 27 B2
Gilbert Ho 5 E2 96 D4
5 E17 54 A6
EC2 242 B3
SE8 141 C6
SW1 258 D1
SW8 270 A4
Gilbert Pl WC1 94 A2 240 A3
Gilbert Rd SE11 116 C2 261 B4
SW19 180 A3
Belvedere DA17 125 C3
Pinner HA5 40 D5
Plaistow BR1 187 A3
Gilbert Scott Jun & Inf Sch
CR2 223 A1
Gilbert Sheldon Ho W2 236 D4
Gilbert St E15 76 C4
W1 93 A1 238 B1
Enfield EN3 6 C6
Hounslow TW3 130 A2
Gilbertson Ho 4 E14 119 C3
Gilbey Cl UB10 60 D4
Gilbey Rd SW17 180 C5
Gilbeys Yd NW1 71 A1
Gilbourne Rd SE18 145 D6
Gilby Ho 5 E9 74 D2
Gilda Ave EN3 19 A6
Gilda Cres N16 52 A1
Gilda Ct NW7 28 A2
Gildea Cl HA5 23 C3
Gildea St W1 238 D3
Gilden Cres NW5 71 A3
Gilders Rd KT9 214 B2
Gildersome St SE18 144 C6
Giles Coppice SE19 183 D6
Giles Ho 5 SE16 118 A3
W11 91 C1
Gilesmead SE5 139 B4
Gilfrid Cl UB8 82 D1
Gilkes Cres SE21 161 C5
Gilkes Pl SE21 161 C5
Gill Ave E16 99 A1
Gill Ct SE18 123 A2
Gill St E14 119 B6
Gillam Ho 6 SE16 118 C2
Gillan Ct SE12 165 B1
Gillan Gn WD2 8 A2
Gillards Mews 6 E17 53 C5
Gillards Way E17 53 C5
Gillender St E3 98 A3
Gillespie Prim Sch N5 72 D5
Gillespie Rd N4,N5 72 D5
Gillett Ave E6 100 A5
Gillett Ho N8 50 A6
Gillett Pl 27 E8 73 C3
Gillett Rd CR7 205 B5
Gillett St E8,N16 73 C3
Gillette Cnr TW7 131 A5
Gillfoot NW1 232 A3
Gillham Terr N17 34 A3
Gillian Ho HA3 24 C4
Gillian Park Rd SM3 201 B1
Gillian St SE13 163 D6
Gillies Ct DA14 189 C6
Gillies Ho NW6 70 B1
Gilling Ct 5 NW3 70 C2
Gillingham Mews SW1 259 A4
Gillingham Rd NW2 69 A5
Gillingham Row SW1 259 A4
Gillingham St
SW1 115 C2 259 A4
Gillings Ct EN5 1 A1
Gillison Wlk 19 SE16 118 A3
Gillman Dr E15 98 D6
Gillman Ho 23 E2 96 A5
Gillray Ho SW10 266 C5
Gillum Cl EN4 14 D3
Gilmore Cl UB10 60 C5
Gilmore Cres TW15 170 C4
Gilmore Ct N11 30 D5
Gilmore Ho SW4 136 D1
Gilmore Rd SE13 142 B1
Gilpin Ave SW14 133 B1
Gilpin Cl CR4 180 C1
Gilpin Cres N18 33 D5
Twickenham TW2 151 D4
Gilpin Ho 9 N9 18 A1
KT3 199 C4
Gilpin Rd E5 75 A4
Gilpin Way UB3 127 B5
Gilray Ho W2 246 C6
Gilsland Rd CR7 205 B5
Gilstead Ho IG11 102 B5
Gilstead Rd SW6 135 D3
Gilston Rd
SW10 114 A1 256 B1
Gilton Rd SE6 164 C1
Giltspur St EC1 94 D1 241 D2
Gilwell Cl E4 7 D1
Gilwell Ct 8 E5 74 B4
Gippeswyck Cl HA5 22 D2
Gipsy Corner W3 89 B2
Gipsy Hill SE19 183 C5
Gipsy Hill Sta SE19 183 C5
Gipsy La SW15 134 B2
Gipsy Moth IV SE10 142 A6
Gipsy Rd SE27 183 B6
Bexley DA16 146 D3
Gipsy Road Gdns SE27 183 A6
Giralda Cl E16 99 D2
Giraud St E14 97 D1
Girdlers Rd W14 112 D2
Girdlestone Wlk N19 71 C6
Girdwood Rd SW18,
SW19 157 A4
Girling Ho 9 N1 95 C6
Girling Way TW14 128 A2
Gironde Rd
SW6 135 B5 264 D3
Girtin Ho 5 UB5 84 D5
Girton Ave NW9 44 C6
Girton Cl UB5 64 A2
Girton Gdns CR0 223 C5
Girton Ho SW15 156 D5
Girton Rd SE26 184 D5
Northolt UB5 64 A2
Girton Villas 6 W10 90 D1
Gisbourne Cl SM6 219 D5
Gisburn Mans N8 50 B5
Gisburn Rd N8 50 B5
Gissing Wlk N1 72 C1
Gittens Cl BR1 186 D6
Given-Wilson Wlk E13 98 D5
Glacier Way HA0 87 D5
Gladbeck Way EN2 4 D1
Gladding Rd E12 77 D4
Glade Cl KT6 213 D6
Glade Gdns CR0 207 A2
Glade La UB2 107 D4
Glade The N21 16 B4
SE7 143 C5
Bromley BR1 187 D1
Croydon CR0 206 D3
Enfield EN2 4 C3
Stoneleigh KT17 216 A2
West Wickham BR4 223 D5
Woodford IG8 21 B1
Glades Sh Ctr The BR1 187 A1
Gladeside N21 16 B4
Croydon CR0 206 D3
Gladesmore Com Sch
N15 52 A4
Gladesmore Rd N15 51 D3
Gladeswood Rd DA17 125 D2
Gladiator St SE23 163 A4
Glading Terr N16 73 D5
Gladioli Cl 6 TW12 173 C4
Gladsdale Dr HA5 40 B5
Gladsmuir Rd N19 49 C1
Monken Hadley EN5 1 A3
Gladstone Ave E12 78 A1
N22 32 D1
Feltham TW14 150 B5
Twickenham TW2 152 B4
Gladstone Ct NW2 68 B3
Gladstone Ct *continued*
SW1 259 D3
5 SW19 179 C3
Gladstone Gdns TW3 130 A4
Gladstone Ho 14 E14 97 C1
Gladstone Mews N22 32 C2
3 SE20 184 C3
Gladstone Par NW2 68 C5
Gladstone Park Gdns
NW2 68 B5
Gladstone Park Prim Sch
NW10 68 B3
Gladstone Pl KT8 196 C4
Gladstone Rd SW19 179 C3
W4 111 B3
Buckhurst Hill IG9 21 C3
Croydon CR0 205 B2
Farnborough BR6 227 A3
Kingston u T KT1 198 C6
Southall UB2 107 A4
Surbiton KT6 214 A6
Gladstone St SE1 261 C6
Gladstone Terr
SW8 137 B4 268 D2
Gladstone Way HA3 42 C6
Gladwell Rd N8 50 B3
Plaistow BR1 187 A4
Gladwin Ho NW1 232 B3
Gladwyn Rd SW15 134 D2
Gladys Dimson Ho E7 76 D3
Gladys Rd NW6 69 C1
Glaisher St 2 SE10 142 A5
Glamis Cres UB3 105 A3
Glamis Ct W3 110 D4
Glamis Est 3 E1 118 D6
Glamis Pl E1 118 C6
Glamis Rd E1 118 C6
Glamis Way UB5 64 A2
Glamorgan Cl CR4,
SW16 204 A6
Glamorgan Ct 4 W7 86 D2
Glamorgan Rd KT1 175 C3
Glanfield Rd BR3 207 B5
Glanleam Rd HA7 25 D6
Glanville Ho 4 SW12 159 C4
Glanville Rd SW2 160 A6
Bromley BR2 209 B6
Glasbrook Ave TW2 151 B3
Glasbrook Rd SE9 165 D4
Glasbury Ho 5 SW9 138 B1
Glaserton Rd N16 51 C2
Glasford St SW17 180 D4
Glasfryn Ct HA2 64 B6
Glasgow Ho W9 91 D5
Glasgow Rd E13 99 B5
N18 34 B5
Glasgow Terr
SW1 115 C1 259 A1
Glass St 4 E2 96 B3
Glass Yd SE18 122 C3
Glasse Cl W13 109 A6
Glasshill St SE1 116 D4 251 D2
Glasshouse Fields E1 118 D6
Glasshouse St
W1 115 C6 249 B5
Glasshouse Wlk
SE11 116 B1 260 C2
Glasshouse Yd EC1 242 A5
Glasslyn Rd N8 49 D4
Glassmill La BR2 186 D1
Glaston Ct W5 109 D5
Glastonbury Ave IG8 37 D4
Glastonbury Ct 12 SE14 140 C5
1 W13 109 A5
Glastonbury Ho SW1 258 C2
Glastonbury Prim Sch
SM4 201 D2
Glastonbury Rd N9 18 A3
Morden SM4 201 C2
Glastonbury St NW6 69 B3
Glaucus St E3 97 D2
Glazbury Rd
W14 113 A1 254 B2
Glazebrook Cl SE21 161 B2
Glazebrook Rd TW11 174 D3
Glebe Ave Enfield EN2 4 D2
Harrow HA3 44 A6
Mitcham CR4 180 C1
Ruislip HA4 62 B2
Uxbridge UB10 61 A4
Woodford IG8 37 A4
Glebe Cl 1 W4 111 C1
Uxbridge UB10 61 A4
Glebe Cotts TW13 151 C1
Glebe Cres NW4 46 C5
Harrow HA3 44 A6
Glebe Ct N13 16 C1
SE3 142 C2
W5 109 D5
W7 108 B6
Mitcham CR4 202 D6
Stanmore HA7 25 C5
Glebe Fst & Mid Sch
HA3 44 A5
Glebe Gdns KT3 199 C2
Glebe Ho 8 SE16 118 B3
7 SE18 122 C2
Feltham TW13 151 C1
Glebe House Dr BR2 209 B1
Glebe La Arkley EN5 12 A5
Harrow HA3 44 A5
Glebe Path CR4 202 D6
Glebe Pl SW3 136 C6 267 A6
Glebe Prim Sch UB10 61 B4
Glebe Rd E8 73 D1
N3 30 A2
N8 50 B5
NW10 68 A2
Glebe Rd *continued*
SW13 134 A3
Belmont SM2 217 A1
Dagenham RM10 81 D2
Hayes UB3 105 D5
Plaistow BR1 187 A2
Stanmore HA7 25 C5
Wallington SM5 218 D2
Glebe Sch BR4 224 B6
Glebe Side TW1 152 D5
Glebe Sq CR4 202 D6
Glebe St W4 111 C1
Glebe Terr 15 E3 97 D4
Glebe The SE3 142 C2
SW16 181 D6
Chislehurst BR7 189 A2
New Malden KT4 199 D1
West Drayton UB7 104 B2
Glebe Way
Feltham TW13 151 C1
West Wickham BR4 224 B6
Glebehyrst SE19 183 C6
Glebeland Gdns TW17 193 A3
Glebelands E10 75 D6
East Molesey KT8 195 D5
Glebelands Ave E18 37 A1
Ilford IG2 57 B2
Glebelands Cl SE5 139 C2
Glebelands Rd TW14 150 A4
Glebeway IG8 37 C5
Gledhow Gdns SW5 256 A3
Gledstanes Rd
W14 113 A1 254 B1
Gledwood Ave UB4 84 A2
Gledwood Cres UB4 83 D2
Gledwood Dr UB4 83 D2
Gledwood Gdns UB4 84 A2
Gleed Ave WD2 8 B2
Gleeson Dr BR6 227 D4
Glegg Pl 3 SW15 134 D1
Glen Albyn Rd SW19 156 D2
Glen Ave TW15 170 C6
Glen Cl TW17 192 C5
Glen Cres IG8 37 B4
Glen Ct 9 SE20 184 B2
5 Bromley BR1 186 D3
Sidcup DA14 190 A6
Glen Dale Mews BR3 185 D2
Glen Gdns CR0 220 C4
Glen Ho 6 E16 122 C5
SW1 259 A6
Glen Rd E13 99 C3
E17 53 B4
Chessington KT9 214 A5
Glen Rise IG8 37 B4
Glen Terr E14 120 A4
Glen The
Beckenham BR2 186 C1
Croydon CR0 222 D5
Enfield EN2 4 D1
Locksbottom BR6 226 C5
Pinner HA5 40 B4
Pinner HA5 41 A2
Southall UB2 107 B1
Wembley HA9 65 D4
Glen View Rd BR1 187 D1
Glen Wlk TW7 152 B6
Glena Mount SM1 218 A4
Glenaffric Ave E14 120 B2
Glenalla Rd HA4 39 D2
Glenalmond Ho
2 SW15 156 D5
Ashford TW15 148 A1
Glenalmond Rd HA3 44 A5
Glenalvon Way 5 SE7 122 A2
Glenarm Rd E5 74 D4
Glenavon Cl KT10 213 A1
Glenavon Ct KT4 216 B6
Glenavon Lo 4 E18 55 A6
Glenavon Rd E15 76 C1
Glenbarr Cl SE9 144 D2
Glenbow Rd BR1 186 C5
Glenbrook N EN2 4 B1
Glenbrook Rd NW6 69 C3
Glenbrook S EN2 4 B1
Glenbuck Ct 6 KT6 198 A3
Glenbuck Rd KT6 198 A3
Glenburnie Rd SW17 158 D1
Glencairn Dr W5 87 C3
Glencairn Rd SW16 182 A3
Glencairne Cl E16 99 D2
Glencoe Ave IG2 57 C2
Glencoe Dr RM10 81 C4
Glencoe Mans 6 SW9 138 C5
Glencoe Rd UB4 84 D3
Glencorse Gn WD1 22 D6
Glendale Ave N22 32 C3
Dagenham RM6 58 C2
Edgware HA8 26 C6
Glendale Cl SE9 144 C2
Glendale Gdns HA9 44 A1
Glendale Way SE28 124 C6
Glendall St SW9 138 B1
Glendarvon St SW15 134 D2
Glendish Rd N17 34 B2
Glendor Gdns NW7 27 B6
Glendower Gdns 10
SW14 133 B2
Glendower Pl SW7 256 C4
Glendower Rd E4 20 B3
SW14 133 B2
Glendown Ho 2 E8 74 A3
Glendown Rd SE2 124 A1
Glendun Ct W3 111 C6
Glendun Rd W3 111 C6
Gleneagle Lo BR3 185 C2
Gleneagle Mews SW16 181 D5
Gleneagle Rd SW16 181 D5
Gleneagles W13 87 B2
Stanmore HA7 25 B4
Gleneagles Cl 21 SE16 118 B1
Orpington BR6 211 B1
South Oxhey WD1 22 D6
Gleneagles Ct 3 TW11 175 A5
Gleneagles Gn 1 BR6 211 B1
Gleneagles Twr 2 UB1 86 A1
Gleneldon Mews SW16 182 A6
Gleneldon Rd SW16 182 A6
Glenelg Rd SW2 160 A6
Glenesk Rd SE9 144 D1
Glenfarg Rd SE6 164 B3
Glenfield Cres HA4 39 B2
Glenfield Rd SW12 159 C3
W13 109 B4
Ashford TW15 171 A4
Glenfield Terr W13 109 B4
Glenfinlas Way SE5 138 D5
Glenforth St SE10 120 D1
Glengall Gr E14 120 A3
Glengall Pass 2 NW6 91 C6
Glengall Rd NW6 91 B6
SE15 139 D6
Bexleyheath DA7 147 A2
Edgware HA8 10 D1
Woodford IG8 37 B4
Glengall Terr SE15 139 D6
Glengarnock Ave E14 120 A2
Glengarry Rd SE22 161 D6
Glenham Dr IG2 56 D4
Glenhead Cl SE9 144 D2
Glenhill Cl N3 29 C1
Glenhouse Rd SE9 166 C6
Glenhurst 4 BR3 186 A2
Glenhurst Ave NW5 71 A4
Ruislip HA4 39 A1
Sidcup DA5 169 B3
Glenhurst Ct SE19 183 D5
Glenhurst Rd N12 30 B5
Brentford TW8 109 C1
Glenhurst Rise SE19 183 A3
Glenilla Rd NW3 70 C2
Glenister Ho UB3 106 B5
Glenister Park Rd
SW16 181 D3
Glenister Rd SE10 120 D1
Glenister St E16 122 C5
Glenlea Rd SE9 166 C6
Glenloch Ct 2 NW3 70 C2
Glenloch Rd NW3 70 C3
Enfield EN3 6 C3
Glenluce Rd SE3 143 A6
Glenlyon Rd SE9 166 C6
Glenmead IG9 21 C3
Glenmere Ave NW7 28 A4
Glenmill TW12 173 B5
Glenmore SW15 156 D5
Glenmore Ho 6 TW10 154 A5
Glenmore Lawns W13 87 A1
Glenmore Rd NW3 70 C2
Bexley DA16 145 D4
Glenmore Way IG11 102 A5
Glenmount Path 1
SE18 123 A1
Glennie Ct SE21 162 A3
Glennie Ho SE10 142 A4
Glennie Rd SE27,SW16 160 C1
Glenny Rd IG11 79 A2
Glenorchy Cl UB4 85 A2
Glenparke Rd E7 77 B2
Glenridding NW1 232 B3
Glenrosa St SW6 136 A3
Glenrose Ct DA14 190 B5
Glenroy St W12 90 C1
Glensdale Rd SE4 141 B2
Glenshaw Mans 7
SW9 138 C5
Glenshiel Rd SE9 166 C6
Glentanner Way SW17 158 B1
Glentham Gdns SW13 134 B6
Glentham Rd SW13 134 B6
Glenthorne Ave CR0 206 C1
Glenthorne Cl SM3 201 C1
Glenthorne Gdns
Cheam SM3 201 C1
Ilford IG6 56 D5
Glenthorne High Sch
SM3 201 C1
Glenthorne Mews W6 112 B2
Glenthorne Rd E17 53 A4
N11 31 A5
W6 112 B2
Kingston u T KT1 198 B5
Glenthorpe SW15 134 A1
Glenthorpe Rd SM4 200 D4
Glenton Rd SE13 142 C1
Glentrammon Ave BR6 227 D2
Glentrammon Cl BR6 227 D3
Glentrammon Gdns
BR6 227 D2
Glentrammon Rd BR6 227 D2
Glentworth St
NW1 92 D3 237 D5
Glenure Rd SE9 166 C6
Glenview SE2 146 D6
Glenville Ave EN2 5 A5
Glenville Gr SE8 141 B5
Glenville Mews SW18 157 C4
Glenville Rd KT2 176 C2
Glenwood Ave NW9 45 C1
Glenwood Cl HA1 42 D4
Glenwood Ct 5 E18 55 A6
4 Sidcup DA14 190 A6
Glenwood Gdns IG2 56 C4
Glenwood Gr NW9 45 A1
Glenwood Ho 3 EN5 13 D6
Glenwood Rd N15 50 D4
Glenwood Rd *continued*
NW7 11 C1
SE5 163 C3
Hounslow TW3 130 B2
Stoneleigh KT17 216 A2
Glenwood Way CR0 206 D3
Glenworth Ave E14 120 B2
Gliddon Rd
W14 113 A1 254 A2
Glifford Ho SW1 259 A1
Glimpsing Gn DA18 125 A3
Glisson Rd UB10 82 C5
Globe JMI Sch E2 96 C4
Globe Pond Rd SE16 119 A5
Globe Rd E1,E2 96 C3
E15 76 D3
Woodford IG8 37 C4
Globe St SE1 117 B4 252 C1
Globe Terr 9 E2 96 C4
Globe Theatre The★
SE1 252 A5
Globe Yd W1 238 C1
Gloster Rd KT3 199 C5
Gloucester Ave
NW1 71 A1 231 B6
Bexley DA16 145 D1
Sidcup DA15 167 C2
Gloucester Cir SE10 142 A5
Gloucester Cl NW10 67 B1
Thames Ditton KT7 197 A1
Gloucester Cres
NW1 93 B6 231 C6
Staines TW18 170 A4
Gloucester Ct EC3 253 B5
NW11 47 B2
SE1 262 B6
6 W3 88 C1
5 W7 86 D2
Harrow HA1 42 C6
Redbridge IG1 56 B2
Richmond TW9 132 C5
8 Surbiton KT6 197 D2
Gloucester Dr N4 72 D6
NW11 47 C5
Gloucester Gate NW1 231 C4
Gloucester Gate Mews
NW1 231 C4
Gloucester Gdns NW11 47 B2
W2 236 A2
Cockfosters EN4 15 A6
Redbridge IG1 56 A2
Sutton SM1 217 D6
Gloucester Gr HA8 27 B2
Gloucester Ho NW6 91 C5
Richmond TW10 154 C6
Gloucester Lo 5 CR0 221 D6
Gloucester Mews W2 236 B1
Gloucester Mews W
W2 236 B1
Gloucester Par
Bexley DA15 168 A6
Hayes UB3 105 A3
Gloucester Pk SW7 256 A4
Gloucester Pl
W1 92 D2 237 D4
Gloucester Pl Mews
W1 92 D2 237 D3
Gloucester Prim Sch
SE15 139 C5
Gloucester Rd E10 53 C2
E11 55 C4
E12 78 B4
E17 34 D1
N17 51 B6
N18 33 D5
SW7 114 A3 256 A4
W3 111 A4
W5 109 C4
Croydon CR0 205 C2
Enfield EN2 5 A5
Erith DA17 125 B1
Feltham TW13 150 C3
Hampton TW12 173 D3
Harrow HA1 41 D4
Hounslow TW4 129 A1
Kingston u T KT1,KT2 176 D1
New Barnet EN5 14 A6
Richmond TW9 132 C5
Teddington TW11 174 C5
Twickenham TW2 152 A3
Gloucester Road Sta
SW7 114 A2 256 A4
Gloucester Sq 6 E2 96 A6
W2 92 C1 237 A1
Gloucester St
SW1 115 C1 259 A2
Gloucester Terr
W2 92 A1 236 B1
Gloucester Way EC1 234 B1
Gloucester Wlk
W8 113 C4 245 B2
Glover Cl SE2 124 C2
Glover Dr N18 34 C4
Glover Ho 2 NW6 70 A1
SE15 140 B1
Glover Rd HA5 40 D3
Glovers Gr HA4 38 D2
Gloxinia Wlk TW12 173 C4
Glycena Rd SW11 136 D2
Glyn Ave EN4 2 B1
Glyn Cl SE25 183 C2
Glyn Ct SE27 160 C1
Glyn Dr DA14 190 B6
Glyn Mans W14 254 B4
Glyn Rd E5 74 D4
Enfield EN3 6 C1
North Cheam KT4,SM3 216 D6
Glyn St SE11 260 C1

Glyndale Grange SM2 217 D2
Glynde Mews SW3 257 B5
Glynde Rd DA7 147 A2
Glynde Reach WC1 233 B1
Glynde St SE4 163 B5
Glyndebourne Ct 5 UB5 84 C4
Glyndebourne Pk BR6 226 D6
Glyndon Rd SE18 123 B2
Glynfield Rd NW10 67 C1
Glynne Rd N22 32 C1
Glynwood Ct SE23 162 C2
Goat La EN1 5 D5
Goat Rd CR4 202 D2
Goat Wharf TW8 132 A6
Goater's Alley SW6 264 D3
Godalming Ave SM6 220 B3
Godalming Rd E14 97 D2
Godbold Rd E15 98 C4
Goddard Cl TW17 192 B6
Goddard Ho SW19 156 D2
Goddard Pl N19 71 C5
Goddard Rd BR3 207 A5
Goddards Way IG1 57 B1
Goddarts Ho E17 53 C6
Godfrey Ave Northolt UB5 85 A6
Twickenham TW2 152 B4
Godfrey Hill SE18 122 A2
Godfrey Ho EC1 235 C1
Godfrey Rd SE18 122 B2
Godfrey St E15 98 A5
SW3 114 C1 257 B2
Godfrey Way TW4 151 B4
Goding St SE11 116 A1 260 B1
Godley Rd SW18 158 B3
Godliman St EC4 252 A6
Godman Rd SE15 140 B3
Godolphin & Latymer Sch
W6 112 B2
Godolphin Cl N13 32 D4
Godolphin Ho NW3 70 C1
7 SW2 160 C3
Godolphin Pl W3 111 B6
Godolphin Rd W12 112 B4
Godson Rd CR0 220 C5
Godson St N1 234 A4
Godstone Ct 1 N16 51 C1
Godstone Ho SE1 262 D6
1 Kingston u T KT2 176 D4
Godstone Rd
Sutton SM1 218 A4
Twickenham TW1 153 B5
Godstow Rd SE2 124 C4
Godwin Cl N1 235 B4
West Ewell KT19 215 A2
Godwin Ct NW1 232 B4
Godwin Ho 2 E2 95 D5
NW6 91 D5
6 SE18 144 B4
Godwin Prim Sch RM9 81 A1
Godwin Rd E7 77 B4
Bromley BR1,BR2 209 C6
Goffers Ho SE3 142 C3
Goffers Rd SE3,SE13 142 C3
Goffs Rd TW15 171 B4
Goffton Ho 14 SW9 138 B3
Goidel Cl SM6 219 D4
Golborne Gdns W10 91 B3
5 W10 91 A3
Golborne Mews 9 W10 91 A2
Golborne Rd W10 91 A2
Gold Hill HA8 27 B4
Golda Cl EN5 12 D5
Goldbeaters Gr HA8 27 C3
Goldbeaters Prim Sch
HA8 27 B2
Goldbeaters Wlk
Wembley HA9 66 D5
3 Wembley HA9 67 A5
Goldcliff Cl SM4 201 C2
Goldcrest Cl E16 99 D2
SE28 124 C6
Goldcrest Mews W5 87 D2
Goldcrest Way
Bushey WD2 8 A3
New Addington CR0 224 B1
Golden Cres UB3 105 D5
Golden Ct W7 108 C6
4 Cockfosters EN4 2 C1
10 Richmond TW9 153 D6
Golden Hind Pl 4 SE8 119 B2
Golden La EC1 95 A3 242 B5
Golden Manor W7 108 C6
Golden Mews SE20 184 C2
Golden Par 2 E17 54 A6
Golden Plover Cl E16 99 A1
Golden Sq W1 115 C6 249 B6
Golders Cl HA8 26 D5
Golders Ct NW11 47 B2
Golders Gdns NW11 47 B2
Golders Green Cres
NW11 47 C2
Golders Green Rd NW11 47 A2
Golders Green Sta NW11 47 C1
Golders Hill Sch NW11 47 C2
Golders Manor Dr NW11 47 A3
Golders Park Cl NW11 47 C1
Golders Rise NW4 46 D4
Golders Way NW11 47 B2
Golderslea NW11 47 C1
Golderton 2 NW4 46 C5
Goldfinch Rd SE28 123 B3
Goldhawk Ind Est The
W6 112 B3
Goldhawk Mews 2
W12 112 B4
Goldhawk Rd W12 112 A3
Goldhawk Road Sta
W12 112 C4
Goldhaze Cl IG8 37 D3
Goldhurst Terr NW6 70 A1
Goldie Ho N19 49 D2
Goldie Leigh Hospl SE2 146 C6
Golding Cl KT9 213 C2
Golding Ct 7 IG1 78 C5
Golding St E1 96 A1
Golding Terr 17 E1 96 A1
Goldington Cres NW1 232 C4
Goldington Ct NW1 232 C5
Goldington St
NW1 93 D5 232 C4
Goldman Cl E2 96 A3
Goldmark Ho SE3 143 B2
Goldney Rd W9 91 C3
Goldrill Dr N11 15 A2
Goldsboro Rd
SW8 137 D5 269 D3
Goldsborough Cres E4 20 A2
Goldsborough Ho SW8 269 D1
Goldsdown Cl EN3 7 A3
Goldsdown Rd EN3 7 A3
Goldsmid St 2 SE18 123 C1
Goldsmith Ave E12 78 A2
NW9 45 C3
W3 111 B6
Romford RM7 59 C2
Goldsmith Cl HA2 41 D1
Goldsmith Ct HA8 26 B6
Goldsmith Ho W3 111 B6
Goldsmith La NW9 45 A5
Goldsmith Rd E10 53 D1
E17 34 D1
N11 30 D5
SE15 140 A4
Goldsmith St EC2 242 B2
Goldsmiths Bldgs W3 111 B5
Goldsmiths Cl W3 111 B5
Goldsmith's Ct N6 49 B3
Goldsmith's Pl 4 NW6 91 D6
Goldsmith's Row E2 96 A5
Goldsmith's Sq 16 E2 96 A5
Goldsworthy Gdns
SE16 118 C1
Goldthorpe NW1 232 A5
Goldwell Ho SE22 139 C1
Goldwell Rd CR7 204 B5
Goldwin Cl SE14 140 C4
Goldwing Cl E16 99 A1
Golf Cl SW16 182 C2
Stanmore HA7 25 C3
Golf Club Dr KT2 177 B3
Golf Rd W5 88 B1
Bromley BR1 210 C6
Golf Side TW2 152 B1
Golf Side Cl KT3 177 C1
Golfe Rd IG1 79 B5
Golfside Cl N20 14 C1
Goliath Cl SM6 220 A1
Gollogly Terr 9 SE7 121 C1
Gomer Gdns TW11 175 A4
Gomer Pl TW11 175 A4
Gomm Rd SE16 118 C3
Gomshall Ave SM6 220 A3
Gondar Gdns NW6 69 B3
Gondar Mans NW6 69 B3
Gonson St SE8 141 D6
Gonston Cl SW19 157 A2
Gonville Cres UB5 63 D2
Gonville Ho 6 SW15 156 D5
Gonville Prim Sch CR7 204 B4
Gonville Rd CR7 204 B4
Gonville St SW6 135 A2
Gooch Ho E5 74 B5
EC1 241 A4
Good Hart Pl E14 119 A6
Good Shepherd RC Prim Sch
New Addington CR0 223 D1
Plaistow BR1 186 D6
Goodall Ho 10 SE4 140 D1
Goodall Rd E11 76 A5
Goodbehere Ho 7
SE27 183 A6
Gooden Ct HA1 64 C5
Goodenough Rd SW19 179 B3
Goodfaith Ho 16 E14 119 D6
Goodge Pl W1 239 B3
Goodge St W1 93 C2 239 B3
Goodge Street Sta
W1 93 D2 239 C4
Goodhall St NW10 89 D4
Goodhart Way BR4 208 C3
Goodhew Rd CR0 206 A3
Goodhope Ho 15 E14 119 D6
Gooding Cl KT3 199 A4
Gooding Ho 4 SE7 121 C1
Goodinge Cl N7 72 A2
Goodinge Rd N7 72 A2
Goodland Ho 1 KT3 199 C2
Goodman Cres SW2 159 D2
Goodman Rd E10 54 A2
Goodmans Ct HA0 65 D4
Goodman's Stile 12 E1 96 A1
Goodman's Yd
E1,EC3 117 D6 253 C6
Goodmayes Ave IG3 58 A2
Goodmayes Hospl IG3 58 A4
Goodmayes La IG3 80 A5
Goodmayes Prim Sch
IG3 58 B1
Goodmayes Rd IG3 58 A1
Goodmayes Sta IG3 58 A1
Goodrich Ct 9 W10 90 D1
Goodrich Ho 21 E2 96 C5
N16 51 C2
Goodrich Prim Sch
SE22 162 A5
Goodrich Rd SE22 162 A5
Goodridge Ho E17 36 A3
Goodson Ho SM4 202 A2
Goodson Rd NW10 67 C1
Goodsway NW1 94 A5 233 A4
Goodway Gdns E14 98 B1
Goodwill Ho 19 E14 119 D6
Goodwin Cl
SE16 117 D3 263 D5
Mitcham CR4 202 B6
Goodwin Ct N8 50 A6
East Barnet EN4 14 C5
Goodwin Dr DA14 168 D2
Goodwin Gdns CR0,CR2 220 D2
Goodwin Ho N9 18 C3
2 SE15 140 B2
Goodwin Jun Sch E7 77 B4
Goodwin Rd N9 18 D3
W12 112 A4
Croydon CR0 220 D3
Goodwin St N4 72 C6
Goodwins Ct WC2 250 A6
Goodwood Ave EN3 6 C6
Goodwood Cl SM4 201 C5
Goodwood Ct W1 238 D4
Goodwood Dr UB5 63 C2
Goodwood Ho SE26 184 B4
3 W4 111 A1
Goodwood Mans 4
SW9 138 C2
Goodwood Par BR3 207 A5
Goodwood Rd SE14 141 A5
Goodwyn Ave NW7 27 C5
Goodwyn Prep Sch NW7 28 A5
Goodwyn's Vale N10 31 B2
Goodyear Ho 8 N2 30 B1
Goodyers Gdns NW4 46 D4
Goosander Ct 34 NW9 27 D1
33 SE8 141 B6
Goosander Way SE18,
SE28 123 B3
Goose Green Cl BR5 190 A1
Goose Green Trad Est
SE22 140 A1
Goose Sq 8 E6 100 B1
Gooseacre La HA3 43 D4
Gooseley La E6 100 C4
Goossens Cl 1 SM1 218 A3
Gophir La EC4 252 C6
Gopsall St N1 95 B6 235 D5
Gordon Ave E4 36 C4
SW14 133 C1
Isleworth TW1 153 B6
Stanmore HA7 25 A4
Gordon Cl E17 53 C3
Gordon Cres
Croydon CR0 205 D1
Hayes UB3 106 A2
Gordon Ct W12 90 C1
Gordon Dr TW17 193 B2
Gordon Gdns HA8 26 D1
Gordon Gr SE5 138 D3
Gordon Hill EN2 5 A4
Gordon Hill Sta EN2 4 D4
Gordon Ho 16 E1 118 C6
3 SE10 141 D5
SE12 165 A4
2 W5 88 A4
Gordon Hospl The
SW1 115 D2 259 C3
Gordon House Rd NW5 71 A4
Gordon Inf Sch IG1 79 B5
Gordon Lo N16 51 B1
Gordon Pl W8 113 C4 245 B2
Gordon Prim Sch SE9 144 B1
Gordon Rd E4 20 C4
E11 55 A3
E15 76 A4
E18 37 B2
N3 29 B3
N9 18 B2
N11 31 D3
SE15 140 B3
W4 132 D6
W13 109 C6
Ashford TW15 148 A1
Barking IG11 101 C6
Beckenham BR3 207 B6
Claygate KT10 212 C1
Dagenham RM6 59 B3
Enfield EN2 5 B3
Harrow HA3 42 C6
Hillingdon UB7 104 A6
Hounslow TW3 130 A1
Ilford IG1 79 B5
Kingston u T KT2 176 B2
Richmond TW9 132 B3
Shepperton TW17 193 B3
Sidcup DA15 167 C6
Southall UB2 107 A2
Surbiton KT5 198 B2
Wallington SM5 218 D2
Gordon Sq WC1 93 D3 239 D6
Gordon St E13 99 A4
WC1 93 D3 239 C6
Gordon Way
Chipping Barnet EN5 1 B1
Plaistow BR1 187 A2
Gordonbrock Jun & Inf Sch
SE4 163 C6
Gordonbrock Rd SE4 163 C6
Gordondale Rd SW18,
SW19 157 C2
Gore Ct NW9 44 C4
Gore Rd E9 96 C6
SW20 178 C1
Gore St SW7 114 A3 256 B6
Gorefield Ho NW6 91 C5
Gorefield Pl NW6 91 C5
Goresbrook Rd RM9 102 D6
Gorham Ho 12 SW4 159 C5
Gorham Pl W11 244 A5
Goring Gdns RM8 80 C4
Goring Rd N11 32 A4
Goring St EC3 243 B2
Goring Way UB6 86 A5
Gorleston Rd N15 51 B4
Gorleston St
W14 113 A2 254 B4
Gorman Rd SE18 122 B2
Gorringe Park Ave CR4 181 A3
Gorringe Park Mid Sch
CR4 181 A2
Gorse Cl E16 99 A1
Gorse Rd CR0 223 C5
Gorse Rise SW17 181 A5
Gorse Wlk UB7 82 A1
Gorsefield Ho 5 E14 119 C6
Gorst Rd NW10 89 B3
SW11 158 D5
Gorsuch Pl 1 E2 95 D4
Gorsuch St E2 95 D4
Gosberton Rd SW12 159 A3
Gosbury Hill KT9 214 A4
Gosfield Rd RM8 59 C1
Gosfield St W1 93 C2 239 A3
Gosford Gdns IG4 56 B4
Gosford Ho 21 E3 97 B5
Goshawk Gdns UB4 83 C5
Goslett Yd WC2 239 D2
Gosling Cl UB6 85 C4
Gosling Ho 1 E1 118 C6
Gosling Way SW9 138 C4
Gospatrick Rd N17 33 A2
Gospel Oak Prim Sch
NW5 71 A4
Gospel Oak Sta NW5 71 A4
Gosport Ho 9 SW15 156 A3
Gosport Rd E17 53 B4
Gosport Way 5 SE15 139 D5
Gosport Wlk N17 52 B5
Gossage Rd SE18 123 B1
Hillingdon UB10 60 B1
Gosset St E2 96 A4
Gosshill Rd BR7 188 C1
Gossington Cl BR7 188 D6
Gosterwood St SE8 141 A6
Gostling Rd TW2 151 C3
Goston Gdns CR7 204 C6
Goswell Pl EC1 234 D1
Goswell Rd EC1 94 D4 234 D2
Gothic Ct 16 SE5 139 A5
Harlington UB3 127 B6
Gothic Rd TW2 152 B2
Gottfried Mews NW5 71 C4
Goudhurst Ho 10 SE20 184 C3
Goudhurst Rd BR1 186 D5
Gough Ho N1 234 D6
4 Kingston u T KT1 176 A1
Gough Rd E15 76 D4
Enfield EN1 6 B4
Gough Sq EC4 94 C1 241 B2
Gough St WC1 94 B3 240 D5
Gough Wlk 10 E14 97 C1
Gould Ct SE19 183 C5
Gould Rd
East Bedfont TW14 149 C4
Twickenham TW2 152 C3
Gould Terr 26 E8 74 B3
Goulden Ho SW11 136 C3
Goulding Ct N8 50 B5
Goulding Gdns CR7 183 A1
Gouldman Ho 30 E1 96 C3
Gould's Gn UB8 104 D6
Goulston St E1 95 D1 243 C2
Goulton Rd E5 74 B4
Gourley Pl N15 51 C4
Gourley St N15 51 C4
Gourock Rd SE9 166 C6
Govan St E2 96 A6
Gover Ct 8 SW4 138 A3
Government Row EN3 7 C6
Govett Ave TW17 193 A4
Govier Cl E15 76 C1
Gowan Ave
SW6 135 A4 264 A2
Gowan Ho 22 E2 95 D4
Gowan Lea 4 E18 55 A5
Gowan Rd NW10 68 B2
Gower Cl SW4 159 C5
Gower Ct WC1 239 C6
Gower Ho 12 E17 53 D6
SE17 262 B2
Barking IG11 79 A1
Hayes UB3 105 C6
Gower Mews WC1 239 D4
Gower Pl NW1,
WC1 93 D3 239 C6
Gower Rd E7 77 A2
Hounslow TW7 130 D6
Gower Sch NW9 67 A6
Gower St WC1 93 D3 239 C5
Gower's Wlk E1 96 A1
Gowland Pl BR3 185 B1
Gowlett Rd SE15 140 A2
Gowrie Rd SW11 137 A2
Graburn Way KT8 196 B6
Grace Ave DA7 147 B3
Grace Bsns Ctr CR4 202 D3
Grace Cl SE9 165 D1
Burnt Oak HA8 27 A3
Grace Ho SE11 270 D6
SE26 184 B5
Grace Jones Cl E8 74 A2
Grace Path SE26 184 C6
Grace Pl E3 97 D4
Grace Rd CR0 205 A3
Grace St E3 97 D4
Gracechurch St EC2,
EC4 252 D6
Gracedale Rd SW16 181 B5
Gracefield Gdns SW16 160 A1
Gracehill 2 E1 96 C2
Graces Mews NW8 229 B3
Grace's Mews SE5 139 C3
Grace's Rd SE5 139 C3
Gradient The SE26 184 A6
Graeme Rd EN1 5 C3
Graemesdyke Ave
SW14 132 D1
Grafton Cl W13 87 A1
Twickenham TW4 151 B3
Worcester Pk KT4 215 C5
Grafton Cres NW1 71 B2
Grafton Ct 10 E8 74 A3
East Bedfont TW14 149 B3
Grafton Gdns N4 51 A3
Dagenham RM8 81 A6
Grafton Ho 15 E3 97 C4
12 SE8 119 B1
Grafton Jun & Inf Schs
RM8 81 B6
Grafton Mews W1 239 A5
Grafton Park Rd KT4 215 C6
Grafton Pl NW1 93 D4 232 D1
Grafton Prim Sch N7 72 A5
Grafton Rd NW5 71 A3
W3 111 A6
Dagenham RM8 81 A6
Enfield EN2 4 B2
Harrow HA1 42 A4
Kingston u T KT3 199 C6
Thornton Heath CR0 204 C1
Worcester Pk KT4 215 C5
Grafton Sq SW4 137 C2
Grafton St W1 115 B6 248 D5
Grafton Terr NW5 71 A3
Grafton Way W1 239 B5
East Molesey KT8 195 B5
Grafton Yd NW5 71 B2
Graham Ave W13 109 B4
Mitcham CR4 181 A2
Graham Cl CR0 223 C6
Graham Ct 5 SE14 140 D6
Bromley BR1 187 B3
Northolt UB5 63 B3
Graham Gdns KT6 198 A1
Graham Ho N9 18 C3
7 N19 71 D4
SE18 144 D5
5 SW12 159 B4
Graham Lo NW4 46 B3
Graham Mans 2 E8 74 B2
11 Barking IG11 80 A1
Graham Rd E8 74 A2
E13 99 A3
N15 50 D6
NW4 46 B3
SW19 179 B3
W4 111 B3
Bexleyheath DA7 147 C1
Hampton TW12 173 C6
Harrow HA3 42 C6
Mitcham CR4 181 A2
Graham St N1 94 D5 234 D3
Graham Terr
SW1 115 A2 258 B3
Grahame Park Jun & Inf
Schs NW9 27 D2
Grahame Park Way NW7,
NW9 27 D2
Grahame White Ho HA3 43 D6
Grainger Cl UB5 64 A3
Grainger Ct 22 SE5 139 A5
Grainger Rd N22 33 A2
Isleworth TW7 130 D3
Gramer Cl E11 76 B6
Grampian Cl
Broom Hill BR6 211 D3
Harlington UB3 127 B5
Grampian Gdns NW2 47 A1
Grampians The 10 W14 112 D4
Granada St SW17 180 D5
Granard Ave SW15 156 B6
Granard Bsns Ctr NW7 27 C4
Granard Ho 20 E9 74 D2
Granard Prim Sch
SW15 156 B5
Granard Rd SW11,SW12 158 D4
Granary Cl N9 18 C4
Granary Ct 3 RM6 58 D2
Granary Rd E1 96 B3
Granary St NW1 93 D6 232 C5
Granby Ho 14 SE18 122 B2
Granby Pl SE1 251 A1
Granby Rd SE9 144 B2
SE18 122 D3
Granby St E2 96 A3 243 D6
Granby Terr
NW1 93 C5 232 A3
Grand Arc N12 30 A5
Grand Ave EC1 241 D4
N10 49 A5
Tolworth KT5 198 D3
Wembley HA9 66 C3
Grand Ave E HA9 66 D3
Grand Avenue Prim Sch
KT5 199 A3
Grand Avenue Prim Sch
(Upper Sch) KT5 199 A3
Grand Ct RM8 81 A5
Grand Depot Rd SE18 122 C1
Grand Dr Southall UB2 108 A4
West Barnes SM4,SW20 200 C5
Grand Junction Wharf
N1 235 A3
Grand Par SW14 133 A1
Tolworth KT6 198 C1
Wembley HA9 66 C6
N4 50 D3
Grand Union Cl W9 91 B2
Grand Union Cres E8 96 A6
Grand Union Ind Est
NW10 88 D5
Grand Vitesse Ind Est
SE1 251 D3
Granden Rd SW16 182 A1
Grandfield Ct W4 133 B6
Grandison Rd SW11 158 D6
North Cheam KT4 216 C5
Granfield St SW11 266 D1
Grange Ave N12 30 A5
N20 13 A4
SE25 183 C1
East Barnet EN4 14 D3
Stanmore HA7 25 C1
Twickenham TW2 152 C2
Woodford IG8 37 A3
Grange Cl
East Molesey KT8 195 D5
Edgware HA8 27 A5
Hayes UB3 83 C2
Heston TW5 129 B6
Sidcup DA15 168 A1
Woodford IG8 37 A3
Grange Cres SE28 102 C1
Grange Ct SE15 139 D3
WC2 240 D1
Hackbridge SM6 219 B5
Littleton TW17 192 C5
Loughton IG10 21 D6
Northolt UB5 84 C5
Pinner HA5 41 A6
Sutton SM2 217 D1
HA1 64 D5
Grange Dr BR7 188 B4
Grange Farm Cl HA2 64 A6
Grange Fst & Mid Schs
HA2 41 D1
Grange Gdns N14 15 D3
NW3 69 D5
SE25 183 C1
Pinner HA5 41 A5
Grange Gr N1 73 A2
Grange Hill SE25 183 C1
Edgware HA8 27 A5
Grange Ho NW10 68 B1
SE1 263 C5
6 Barking IG11 101 B6
Grange Inf Sch E13 98 D4
Grange La SE21 161 D2
Grange Lo SW19 178 D4
Grange Mans KT17 215 D1
Grange Mills SW12 159 C3
Grange Mus of Community
History The NW10 67 C4
Grange Park Ave N21 17 A5
Grange Park Jun & Inf Schs
UB4 83 D3
Grange Park Pl SW20 178 B3
Grange Park Prep Sch
N21 16 D5
Grange Park Rd E10 53 D1
South Norwood CR7 205 B6
Grange Park Sta N21 16 D5
Grange Pk W5 110 A5
Grange Pl NW6 69 C1
Grange Prim Sch
SE1 117 C3 263 A5
W5 109 D4
Grange Rd E10 53 C1
E13 98 D4
E17 53 A4
N6 49 A3
N17 34 A4
NW10 68 B2
SE1 117 D3 263 C5
SE19,SE25 183 B1
SW13 134 A4
W4 110 D1
W5 110 A5
Belmont SM2 217 C1
Burnt Oak HA8 27 B4
Chessington KT9 214 A4
Deacons Hill WD6 10 B6
East Molesey KT8 195 D5
Harrow HA1 43 A4
Harrow HA2 64 B6
Hayes UB3 83 C1
Ilford IG1 79 A4
Kingston u T KT1 198 A6
Orpington BR6 227 A6
Southall UB1 107 A4
Grange St N1 235 D5
Grange The 3 E17 53 A4
3 E18 55 A6
19 NW3 70 D2
SE1 117 D3 263 C5
SW19 178 D4
W3 110 D4
7 W4 110 D1
W12 112 B3
W13 87 C2
W14 113 B2 254 C3
Cockfosters EN4 2 D2
Croydon CR0 223 B6
New Malden KT3 200 A4
Wembley HA0 66 C1
Worcester Pk KT19 215 B4

Grange The(Eltham Coll Jun Sch) SE9 ... 165 D3
Grange Vale SM2 ... 217 D1
Grange Wlk
SE1 ... 117 D3 263 C5
Grange Yd SE1 . 117 D3 263 C5
Grangecliffe Gdns
SE25 ... 183 C1
Grangecourt Rd N16 ... 51 C1
Grangefield NW1 ... 72 A1
Grangehill Pl SE9 ... 144 B2
Grangehill Rd SE9 ... 144 B1
Grangemill 11 NW5 ... 71 B4
Grangemill Rd SE6 ... 163 C2
Grangemill Way SE6 ... 163 C2
Grangeview Rd N20 ... 14 A3
Grangeway N12 ... 29 D6
NW6 ... 69 C1
Woodford IG8 ... 37 C6
Grangeway Gdns IG4 ... 56 A4
Grangeway The N21 ... 16 D5
Grangewood DA5 ... 169 B3
Grangewood Cl HA5 ... 40 A4
Grangewood Ind Sch E7 77 D1
Grangewood La BR3 ... 185 B4
Grangewood Sch HA5 ... 39 D4
Grangewood St E6 ... 99 D6
Granham Gdns N9 ... 17 D2
Granite St SE18 ... 123 D1
Granleigh Rd E11 ... 76 C6
Gransden Ave E8 ... 74 B1
Gransden Ho 1 SE8 ... 119 B1
Gransden Rd W12 ... 111 D4
Grant Cl N14 ... 15 C4
Shepperton TW17 ... 192 D3
Grant Ct 2 E4 ... 20 A3
11 NW9 ... 27 D1
Grant Ho 38 SW8 ... 137 D3
Grant Pl 2 CR0 ... 205 D1
Grant Rd SW11 ... 136 C2
Croydon CR0 ... 205 D1
Harrow HA3 ... 42 D6
Grant St E13 ... 99 A4
N1 ... 234 A4
Grant Way TW7,TW3 ... 131 A6
Grantbridge St
N1 ... 94 D5 234 D4
Grantchester 12 KT1 ... 176 C1
Grantchester Cl HA1 ... 64 D5
Grantham Cl HA8 ... 10 A1
Grantham Ct 9 SE16 ... 118 D4
Dagenham RM6 ... 59 B2
Grantham Gdns RM6 ... 59 B2
Grantham Gn WD6 ... 11 A6
Grantham Ho 12 SE15 ... 140 A6
Ashford TW16 ... 171 C3
Grantham Pl W1 ... 248 C3
Grantham Rd E12 ... 78 C4
SW9 ... 138 A3
W4 ... 133 C5
Grantley Ho 2 SE14 ... 140 D6
5 SW19 ... 156 D3
Grantley Rd TW4,TW5 ... 128 C3
Grantley St E1 ... 96 D3
Grantock Rd E17 ... 36 B2
Granton Rd SW16 ... 181 C2
Foots Cray DA14 ... 190 C4
Ilford IG3 ... 58 A1
Grants Cl NW7 ... 28 D3
Grants Cotts KT10 ... 212 B6
Grantully Rd W9 ... 91 D4
Granville Ave N9 ... 18 C1
Feltham TW13 ... 150 A2
Hounslow TW3,TW4 ... 151 C6
Granville Cl CR0 ... 221 C6
Granville Ct N1 ... 235 D6
N4 ... 50 B3
8 SE14 ... 141 A5
Granville Gdns SW16 ... 182 B3
W5 ... 110 B5
Granville Gr SE13 ... 142 A2
Granville Ho 13 E14 ... 97 C1
Granville Mans 8 W12 112 C4
Granville Mews DA14 .. 190 A6
Granville Pk SE13 ... 142 B2
Granville Pl N12 ... 30 A3
SW6 ... 265 C3
W1 ... 93 A1 238 A1
Pinner HA5 ... 40 D6
Granville Point NW2 ... 69 B6
Granville Rd E17 ... 53 D3
E18 ... 37 B1
N4,N8 ... 50 B3
N12 ... 30 A3
N13 ... 32 B4
N22 ... 32 D2
NW2 ... 69 B6
NW6 ... 91 C5
SW18 ... 157 B4
SW19 ... 179 C3
Bexley DA16 ... 146 C2
Hayes UB3 ... 105 D2
Hillingdon UB10 ... 60 D2
Ilford IG1 ... 78 D6
Sidcup DA14 ... 190 B6
Granville Sq 8 SE15 ... 139 C5
WC1 ... 94 B4 233 D1
Granville St WC1 ... 233 D1
Granwood Ct 5 TW7 ... 130 C4
Grape St WC2 ... 240 A2
Grapsome Cl KT9 ... 213 C1
Grasdene Rd SE18,SE2 ... 146 A5
Grasmere NW1 ... 231 D1
Grasmere Ave SW15 ... 177 C6
SW19 ... 201 C6
Grasmere Ave *continued*
W3 ... 111 B6
Orpington BR6 ... 226 D5
Ruislip HA4 ... 39 A2
Twickenham TW3 ... 151 D5
Wembley HA9 ... 43 D1
Grasmere Cl TW14 ... 149 D3
Grasmere Ct N22 ... 32 B4
SE26 ... 184 A5
SW13 ... 134 A6
Grasmere Gdns
Harrow HA3 ... 25 A1
Orpington BR6 ... 226 D5
Redbridge IG4 ... 56 B4
Grasmere Ho 19 N16 ... 73 B4
Grasmere JMI Sch N16 .73 B4
Grasmere Point 2
SE15 ... 140 C5
Grasmere Rd 3 E13 ... 99 A5
N10 ... 31 B2
N17 ... 34 A4
SE25 ... 206 B4
SW16 ... 182 B5
Bromley BR1 ... 186 D3
Orpington BR6 ... 226 D5
Grass Pk N3 ... 29 B2
Grassington Cl N11 ... 31 A4
Grassington Rd DA14 .. 190 A6
Grassmere Ct 6 EN1 ... 17 C6
Grassmount SE23 ... 162 B2
Grassway SM6 ... 219 C4
Grasvenor Ave EN5 ... 13 C5
Grasvenor Avenue Inf Sch
EN5 ... 13 C5
Grately Ho 10 SW15 ... 156 B3
Gratton Rd W14 113 A3 254 A5
Gratton Terr NW2 ... 68 D5
Gravel Hill N3 ... 29 B1
Bexleyheath DA6 ... 169 D6
South Croydon CR0,CR2 ... 223 B1
Gravel Hill Cl DA5,DA6 .169 D5
Gravel Hill Prim Sch
DA6 ... 169 D6
Gravel Hill Sta CR0 ... 223 A2
Gravel La E1 ... 95 D1 243 C2
Gravel Rd
Keston Mark BR2 ... 226 A6
Twickenham TW2 ... 152 C3
Graveley 18 KT1 ... 176 C1
Graveley Ave WD6 ... 11 A6
Graveley Ho 7 SE8 ... 119 A2
Gravelwood Cl BR7 ... 167 A1
Gravenel Gdns 5
SW17 ... 180 C5
Graveney Gr SE20 ... 184 C3
Graveney Rd SW17 ... 180 C6
Graveney Sch SW17 ... 181 B5
Graves Est DA16 ... 146 B3
Gravesend Rd W12 ... 112 A6
Gray Ave RM8 ... 59 B1
Gray Ct 8 KT2 ... 175 D6
Gray Ho SE17 ... 262 B2
Gray St SE1 ... 116 C4 251 B1
Grayfriars Pas EC1 ... 241 D2
Grayham Cres KT3 ... 199 B5
Grayham Rd KT3 ... 199 B5
Grayland Cl BR1 ... 187 D2
Grayling Cl E16 ... 98 C3
Grayling Ct N17 ... 52 B5
W5 ... 109 D5
Grayling Rd N16 ... 73 B6
Grayling Sq E2 ... 96 A4
Grays Cotts UB9 ... 38 C1
Grays Farm Prim Sch
BR5 ... 190 B2
Grays Farm Production Village BR5 ... 190 B2
Grays Farm Rd BR5 ... 190 B2
Gray's Inn* WC1 94 B2 240 D4
Gray's Inn Pl WC1 ... 240 D3
Gray's Inn Rd
WC1 ... 94 B3 240 D6
Gray's Inn Sq
WC1 ... 94 C2 241 A4
Grays La TW15 ... 170 D6
Gray's Rd UB10 ... 60 A1
Gray's Yd W1 ... 238 B2
Grayscroft Rd SW16 ... 181 D3
Grayshott Rd SW11 ... 137 A2
Grayson Ho EC1 ... 235 B1
Grayswood Gdns SW20 178 B1
Grayswood Point 14
SW15 ... 156 A3
Graywood Ct N12 ... 30 A3
Grazebrook JMI Sch
N16 ... 73 C6
Grazebrook Rd N16 ... 73 B6
Grazely Ct SE19 ... 183 C5
Great Arthur Ho EC1 ... 242 A5
Great Bell Alley EC2 ... 242 C2
Great Benty UB7 ... 104 A2
Great Brownings SE21 .183 D6
Great Bushey Dr N20 ... 13 D3
Great Cambridge Ind Est
EN1 ... 18 B6
Great Cambridge Junction
N13,N18 ... 33 B6
Great Cambridge Rd
N9,N18 ... 17 B1
Enfield EN1 ... 6 A3
Great Castle St W1 ... 239 A2
Great Central Ave HA4 ... 62 C3
Great Central St
NW1 ... 92 D2 237 C4
Great Central Way NW10 67 B4
Great Chapel St
W1 ... 93 D1 239 C2
Great Chertsey Rd
SW14,W4 ... 133 B4
Feltham TW13,TW2 ... 151 C1
Great Church La W6 ... 112 D1
Great College St
SW1 ... 116 A3 260 A6
Great Croft WC1 ... 233 B1
Great Cumberland Mews
W1 ... 237 C1
Great Cumberland Pl
W1 ... 92 D1 237 D1
Great Dover St
SE1 ... 117 B3 262 C6
Great Eastern Bldgs 10
E8 ... 74 B2
Great Eastern Ent Ctr
E14 ... 119 D4
Great Eastern Rd E15 ... 76 B2
Great Eastern St
EC2 ... 95 C3 243 A6
Great Eastern Wharf
SW11 ... 267 B3
Great Elms Rd BR2 ... 209 C5
Great Field 7 NW5 ... 71 C3
NW9 ... 27 D2
Great Fleete Way IG11 102 C5
Great Galley Cl IG11 ... 102 C4
Great George St
SW1 ... 116 A4 250 A1
Great Guildford St
SE1 ... 117 A5 252 A3
Great Guilford Bsns Sq
SE1 ... 252 A3
Great Harry Dr SE9 ... 166 C1
Great James St WC1 ... 240 C4
Great Marlborough St
W1 ... 93 C1 239 A1
Great Mathers Rd SE11 261 C4
Great Maze Pond
SE1 ... 117 B4 252 D2
Great New St
EC4 ... 94 C1 241 B2
Great Newport St WC2 250 A6
Great North Rd N2 ... 48 C5
High Barnet EN5 ... 13 D6
New Barnet EN5 ... 1 A2
Great North Way (Barnet By-Pass) NW4 ... 46 D6
Great Ormond St
WC1 ... 94 B3 240 C5
Great Ormond St Hospl for Children WC1 .. 94 B3 240 C5
Great Percy St
WC1 ... 94 C4 234 A2
Great Peter St
SW1 ... 115 D3 259 D5
Great Portland St
W1 ... 93 B2 238 D4
Great Portland Street Sta
W1 ... 93 B3 238 D5
Great Pulteney St W1 ... 249 B6
Great Queen St
WC2 ... 94 A1 240 B2
Great Russell St
WC1 ... 94 A2 240 A3
Great Scotland Yd
SW1,WC2 ... 116 A5 250 A4
Great Smith St
SW1 ... 115 D3 259 D6
Great South-West Rd
East Bedfont TW14,TW6,
TW4,TW5 ... 149 B6
Feltham TW6,TW14,TW4 .127 B6
Hounslow TW5 ... 128 B2
Great Spilmans SE22 ... 161 C6
Great St Helen's EC3 ... 243 A2
Great St Thomas Apostle
EC4 ... 252 B6
Great Strand NW9 ... 27 D1
Great Suffolk St
SE1 ... 116 D4 251 D3
Great Sutton St
EC1 ... 94 D3 241 D5
Great Swan Alley EC2 ... 242 C2
Great Thrift BR5 ... 211 A5
Great Titchfield St
W1 ... 93 C2 239 A3
Great Tower St
EC3 ... 117 C6 253 A6
Great Trinity La EC4 ... 252 B6
Great Turnstile WC2 ... 240 D3
Great West Rd W4,W6 ... 133 B6
Brentford TW7,TW8 ... 131 B6
Hounslow TW5 ... 129 B4
Hounslow TW5,TW7 ... 130 B5
Hounslow TW7,TW8 ... 129 B4
Great West Road Cedars Rd
W4 ... 133 A6
Great West Road Hogarth La
W4 ... 133 C6
Great West Trad Est
TW8 ... 131 B6
Great Western Ind Pk
Southall UB1 ... 107 D5
Southall UB2 ... 108 A4
Great Western Rd W2,
W9 ... 91 B2
Great Winchester St
EC2 ... 95 B1 242 D2
Great Windmill St
W1 ... 115 D6 249 C6
Great Yd SE1 ... 253 B2
Greatdown Rd W7 ... 86 D2
Greatfield Ave E6 ... 100 B3
Greatfield Cl 4 N19 ... 71 C4
SE4 ... 141 C1
Greatfields Dr UB8 ... 82 C2
Greatfields Rd IG11 ... 101 B5
Greatham Wlk 8 SW15 156 A3
Greatorex Ho 12 E1 ... 96 A2
Greatorex St E1 ... 96 A2
Greatstone Ho 13 SE20 184 C3
Greatwood BR7 ... 188 C3
Greaves Cl IG11 ... 79 C1
Greaves Cotts 12 E14 ... 97 A2
Greaves Pl SW17 ... 180 C6
Greaves Twr SW10 ... 266 B4
Grebe 3 NW9 ... 27 D1
Grebe Ave UB4 ... 84 D1
Grebe Cl E7 ... 76 D3
E17 ... 35 A3
Grebe Ct 11 E14 ... 120 A4
33 SE8 ... 141 B6
Cheam SM1 ... 217 B3
Grebe Terr 4 KT1 ... 198 A6
Grecian Cres SE19 ... 182 D4
Greek Ct W1 ... 239 D1
Greek St W1 ... 93 D1 239 D1
Green Acres
Sidcup DA14 ... 189 D6
South Croydon CR0 ... 221 D5
Green Arbour Ct EC1 ... 241 C2
Green Ave NW7 ... 27 C6
W13 ... 109 B3
Green Bank E1 ... 118 B5
N12 ... 29 D6
Green CE Prim Sch The
N17 ... 51 D6
Green CE Sch Holy Trinity (Infants' Annexe) The
N15 ... 51 D5
Green Cl NW9 ... 45 A3
NW11 ... 48 A2
Beckenham BR2 ... 208 C6
Carshalton SM5 ... 218 D6
Feltham TW13 ... 173 A5
Green Court Ave CR0 ... 222 B6
Green Court Gdns CR0 ... 222 B6
Green Ct TW16 ... 171 D4
Green Dale SE22 ... 161 C6
Green Dr UB1 ... 107 C5
Green Dragon Ct SE1 ... 252 C3
Green Dragon Jun & Inf Sch
TW8 ... 132 A6
Green Dragon La N21 ... 16 D5
Brentford TW8 ... 110 B1
Green Dragon Yd 21 E1 .96 A2
Green Elms IG6 ... 57 A6
Green End N21 ... 16 D2
Chessington KT9 ... 214 A4
Green Farm Cl BR6 ... 227 D3
Green Gdns BR6 ... 227 A3
Green Hedges 8 TW1 .153 C5
Green Hill SE18 ... 122 B1
Green Ho The 5 SW19 157 A3
Green Hundred Rd
SE15 ... 140 A6
Green La NW4 ... 46 D4
SE9 ... 166 D1
SE20 ... 184 D3
W7 ... 108 C4
Ashford TW16 ... 171 D4
Chessington KT9 ... 214 A1
Dagenham RM8 ... 81 B6
East Molesey KT8 ... 195 D4
Feltham TW13 ... 173 A5
Hillingdon UB8 ... 83 A2
Hounslow TW4 ... 128 C1
Ilford IG1 ... 79 C6
Ilford IG1,IG3,RM8, ... 58 B1
Ilford IG3 ... 79 C6
Morden SM4 ... 201 D3
New Malden KT3 ... 199 A4
North Cheam KT4 ... 200 A1
Shepperton TW17 ... 193 A4
South Norwood CR7,
SW16 ... 182 C2
Stanmore HA7 ... 25 B5
Stanmore HA8 ... 26 C5
Green Lane Bsns Pk
SE9 ... 166 C2
Green Lane Cotts HA7 ... 25 B6
Green Lane Gdns CR7 .183 A1
Green Lane Mews SM4 201 D3
Green Lane Prim Sch
KT4 ... 200 B2
Green Lanes N4,N8,N15 ... 50 D2
N13 ... 16 C1
West Ewell KT19 ... 215 C1
Green Lawns 8 SE18 ... 122 D2
Ruislip HA4 ... 40 C1
Green Leaf Ave SM6 ... 219 D4
Green Leas
Ashford TW16 ... 171 D4
Kingston u T KT1 ... 198 A6
Green Leas Cl TW16 ... 171 D4
Green Man Gdns W13 .109 A6
Green Man Intc E11 ... 54 D2
Green Man La W13 ... 109 A5
Feltham TW14 ... 128 A1
Green Moor Link N21 ... 16 D4
Green Oaks UB2 ... 106 D2
Green Park
SW1,W1 ... 115 B4 248 D2
Green Park Sta
W1 ... 115 C5 249 A4
Green Point E15 ... 76 C2
Green Pond Cl E17 ... 53 B6
Green Pond Rd E17 ... 53 A6
Green Rd N14 ... 15 B5
N20 ... 14 A1
Green Ride IG10,E4 ... 21 A6
Green Sch for Girls The
TW7 ... 131 A4
Green St E7 ... 77 C1
E13 ... 99 C6
Green St *continued*
W1 ... 115 A6 248 A6
Enfield EN3 ... 6 D3
Sunbury TW16 ... 172 A1
Green Street Green Prim Sch
BR6 ... 227 D2
Green Terr EC1 ... 234 B1
Green The E4 ... 20 B3
E11 ... 55 B3
E15 ... 76 D2
N9 ... 18 A2
N14 ... 15 D1
N17 ... 33 A4
N21 ... 16 C4
SW19 ... 178 D5
W3 ... 89 C1
W5 ... 109 D6
Bexley DA16 ... 145 C1
Carshalton SM5 ... 219 A4
Carshalton SM6 ... 219 A6
Catford BR1 ... 165 A1
Claygate KT10 ... 212 D2
Erith DA7 ... 147 C4
Feltham TW13 ... 150 B2
Hayes BR2 ... 209 A2
Heston TW5 ... 129 C6
Kingston u T KT3 ... 177 A1
Merton SM4 ... 201 A5
7 Richmond TW9 ... 153 D6
Sidcup DA14 ... 190 A6
Southall UB2 ... 107 B4
St Paul's Cray BR5 ... 190 B3
Sutton SM1 ... 217 D5
Twickenham TW2 ... 152 C2
Uxbridge UB10 ... 61 A6
Wembley HA0 ... 65 A6
Woodford IG8 ... 37 A5
IG9 ... 21 B3
Green Vale W5 ... 88 B1
Bexleyheath DA6 ... 168 D6
Green Verges HA7 ... 25 D3
Green View KT9 ... 214 B1
Green Way SE9 ... 165 D6
Bromley BR2 ... 210 A3
Sunbury TW16 ... 194 A5
Green Way Gdns HA3 ... 24 C1
Green Way The HA3 ... 24 C2
Green Wlk NW4 ... 46 D4
SE1 ... 263 A5
Hampton TW12 ... 173 B4
Ruislip HA4 ... 39 D1
Southall UB2 ... 107 C1
Green Wlk The E4 ... 20 B3
Green Wood NW5 ... 71 C3
Green Wrythe Cres
SM5 ... 202 C1
Green Wrythe La SM5 .202 C2
Green Wrythe Prim Sch
SM5 ... 202 B3
Green Yd WC1 ... 240 D6
Greenacre Cl Barnet EN5 .. 1 B5
Northolt UB5 ... 63 B3
Greenacre Ct E8 ... 74 A3
Greenacre Gdns E17 ... 54 A5
Greenacre Pl SM6 ... 219 B6
Greenacre Sq 26 SE16 .118 D4
Greenacre Wlk N14 ... 15 D1
Greenacres N3 ... 29 A1
SE9 ... 166 C5
Bushey WD2 ... 8 B2
Greenacres Ave UB10 ... 60 C5
Greenacres Cl BR6 ... 227 A4
Greenacres Dr HA7 ... 25 B3
Greenacres Prim Sch
SE9 ... 166 C2
Greenaway Gdns NW3 .. 69 D4
Greenaway Ho NW8 ... 229 A6
WC1 ... 234 A1
Greenaway Terr TW19 .148 A3
Greenbank Ave HA0 ... 65 A3
Greenbank Cl E4 ... 20 A2
Greenbank Cres NW4 ... 47 A5
Greenbank Lo 2 BR7 .. 188 C2
Greenbanks HA1 ... 64 C4
Greenbay Rd SE7 ... 143 D5
Greenberry St NW8 ... 230 A3
Greenbrook Ave EN4 ... 2 A4
Greencoat Pl
SW1 ... 115 C2 259 B4
Greencoat Row SW1 ... 259 B5
Greencourt Ave HA8 ... 26 D2
Greencourt Rd BR5 ... 211 C4
Greencroft Ave HA4 ... 62 C6
Greencroft Cl E16 ... 99 D2
Greencroft Gdns NW6 ... 70 A1
Enfield EN1 ... 5 C2
Greencroft Rd TW5 ... 129 B4
Greendale NW7 ... 27 C6
Greendale Ct CR2 ... 221 A2
Greene Ct 20 SE14 ... 140 D6
Greene Ho SE1 ... 262 C5
Greenend Rd W4 ... 111 C4
Greener Ho 3 SW4 ... 137 D2
Greenfield Ave KT5 ... 198 D3
Greenfield Dr N2 ... 48 D5
Bromley BR1 ... 187 C1
Greenfield Gdns NW2 ... 69 A5
Dagenham RM9 ... 102 D6
Orpington BR5 ... 211 B2
Greenfield Ho 28 SW19 156 D3
Greenfield Rd E1 ... 96 A1
N15 ... 51 C4
Dagenham RM9 ... 102 C6
Greenfield Way HA2 ... 41 D6
Greenfields UB1 ... 85 C1
Greenfields JMI Sch
WD1 ... 22 C5
Greenfields Sch N10 ... 30 D2
Greenford Ave W7 ... 86 C1
Southall UB1 ... 107 B6
Greenford Gdns UB6 ... 86 A4
Greenford High Sch UB6 85 C4
Greenford Ind Est UB6 .. 85 D6
Greenford Rd
Greenford UB6,UB1 ... 64 C2
Sutton SM1 ... 217 D4
Greenford Rdbt UB6 ... 86 B5
Greenford Sta UB6 ... 86 B6
Greengate UB6 ... 65 B2
Greengate St E13 ... 99 B4
Greenhalgh Wlk N2 ... 48 A5
Greenham Cl SE1 ... 251 A1
Greenham Cres E4 ... 35 B4
Greenham Ho 6 E9 ... 96 C6
Isleworth TW7 ... 130 B2
Greenham Rd N10 ... 31 A1
Greenhayes Sch BR4 .. 224 A6
Greenheath Bsns Ctr 3
E2 ... 96 B3
Greenheys Dr E18 ... 54 D6
Greenhill NW3 ... 70 B4
Buckhurst Hill IG9 ... 21 C3
Sutton SM1 ... 218 A6
Wembley HA9 ... 66 D6
Greenhill Cts SE7 ... 122 B1
Greenhill Gdns UB5 ... 85 B5
Greenhill Gr E12 ... 78 A4
Greenhill Par EN5 ... 13 D6
Greenhill Pk NW10 ... 89 C6
New Barnet EN5 ... 13 D6
Greenhill Rd NW10 ... 89 C6
Harrow HA1 ... 42 C3
Greenhill Terr SE18 ... 122 B1
Northolt UB5 ... 85 B5
Greenhill Way
Harrow HA1 ... 42 C3
Wembley HA9 ... 66 D6
Greenhill's Rents EC1 .. 241 C4
Greenhills Terr 16 N1 ... 73 B2
Greenhithe Cl SE9 ... 167 C4
Greenholm Rd SE9 ... 166 D6
Greenhurst Rd SE27 ... 182 C5
Greening St SE2 ... 124 C2
Greenland Cres UB2 ... 106 D3
Greenland Ho 4 E1 ... 97 A3
SE8 ... 118 D1
Greenland Mews SE8 .. 118 D1
Greenland Pl NW1 ... 231 D6
Greenland Quay SE16 .118 D2
Greenland Rd
NW1 ... 93 C6 232 A6
Ducks Island EN5 ... 12 C5
Greenland St NW1 ... 231 D6
Greenlands
Borehamwood WD6 ... 11 B5
West Ewell KT19 ... 214 D3
Greenlaw Ct W5 ... 87 D1
Greenlaw Gdns KT3 ... 199 D2
Greenlaw St SE18 ... 122 C3
Greenlawns N12 ... 29 D4
Greenlea Pk SW19 ... 180 C2
Greenleaf Cl 8 SW2 ... 160 C4
Greenleaf Prim Sch E17 53 B6
Greenleaf Rd 6 E6 ... 99 C6
E17 ... 53 B6
Greenleafe Dr IG6 ... 56 D6
Greenleaves Ct TW15 .. 170 D4
Greenman St N1 95 A6 235 A6
Greenmead Cl SE25 ... 206 A4
Greenmead Sch SW15 .156 B6
Greenmoor Rd EN3 ... 6 C3
Greeno Cres TW17 ... 192 C4
Greenoak Pl EN4 ... 2 D3
Greenoak Way SW19 .. 178 D6
Greenock Rd SW16 ... 181 D2
11 W3 ... 111 A3
Greenrig Wlk
Wembley HA9 ... 66 D5
4 Wembley HA9 ... 67 A5
Greens Ct W1 ... 249 C6
Wembley HA9 ... 65 D5
Green's Ct W11 ... 244 C3
Greens End SE18 ... 122 D2
Greenshank Cl E17 ... 35 A3
Greenshields Ind Est
E16 ... 121 B5
Greenside Dagenham RM8 58 C1
Sidcup DA5 ... 169 A3
Greenside Cl N20 ... 14 B2
SE6 ... 164 B2
Greenside Prim Sch
W12 ... 112 A4
Greenside Rd W12 ... 112 A4
Thornton Heath CR0 ... 204 C2
Greenslade Prim Sch
SE18 ... 145 B6
Greenslade Rd IG11 ... 79 B1
Greensleeves Ho UB2 .107 D2
Greensleeves Manor
SM2 ... 217 D2
Greenstead Ave IG8 ... 37 C4
Greenstead Cl IG8 ... 37 C4
Greenstead Gdns SW15 156 B6
Woodford IG8 ... 37 C4
Greenstone Mews E11 .. 55 A3
Greenstreet Hill SE4 ... 140 D2
Greenvale Rd SE9 ... 144 C1
Greenvale Specl Sch
SE23 ... 163 A1
Greenview Ave CR0 ... 207 A3
Greenview Ct TW15 ... 170 B6
Greenway N14 ... 16 A2
N20 ... 13 C2
SW20 ... 200 C5
Chislehurst West BR7 .. 188 D5
Dagenham RM8 ... 58 C1

Greenway *continued*
Hayes UB4 ... 84 B3
Kenton HA3 ... 44 A4
Pinner Green HA5 ... 22 B1
Wallington SM6 ... 219 C4
Woodford IG8 ... 37 C5
Greenway Ave E17 ... 54 B5
Greenway Cl N4 ... 73 A6
N11 ... 31 A4
1 N15 ... 51 D5
N20 ... 13 C2
NW9 ... 27 B1
Greenway Ct Hayes UB4 ... 84 B3
Ilford IG1 ... 56 D1
Greenway Gdns NW9 ... 27 B1
Croydon CR0 ... 223 B5
Greenford UB6 ... 85 D4
Greenway The NW9 ... 27 B1
Hounslow TW4 ... 129 B1
Pinner HA5 ... 41 B3
Uxbridge UB8 ... 82 A5
Uxbridge UB10 ... 61 A6
Greenways SE26 ... 184 C6
Beckenham BR3 ... 185 C1
Hinchley Wood KT10 ... 212 C4
Greenways The 1 TW1 153 A5
Greenwell St W1 ... 238 D5
Greenwich Bsns Ctr
SE10 ... 141 D5
Greenwich Bsns Pk
SE10 ... 141 D5
Greenwich Church St
SE10 ... 142 A6
Greenwich Cres E6 ... 100 A2
Greenwich Ct 18 E1 ... 96 B1
Greenwich District Hospl
SE10 ... 120 D1
Greenwich High Rd
SE10 ... 141 D5
Greenwich Ind Est SE7 121 B2
SE10 ... 141 D5
Greenwich Mkt 1
SE10 ... 142 A6
Greenwich Park SE10 ... 142 C5
Greenwich Park Sch
SE10 ... 142 A5
Greenwich Park St
SE10 ... 142 B6
Greenwich South St
SE10 ... 142 A4
Greenwich Sta SE10 ... 141 D5
Greenwich View E14 ... 119 D3
Greenwood 8 SW19 ... 156 D4
3 Woodford IG8 ... 37 A3
Greenwood Ave
Dagenham RM10 ... 81 D4
Enfield EN3 ... 7 A4
Greenwood Cl
Hinchley Wood KT7 ... 197 A1
Merton SM4 ... 201 A5
Orpington BR5,BR6 ... 211 C3
Sidcup DA15 ... 168 A2
Greenwood Dr E4 ... 36 B5
Greenwood Gdns N13 ... 16 D1
Greenwood Ho N22 ... 32 C2
8 SE4 ... 140 D1
WC1 ... 234 A1
Greenwood La TW12 ... 173 D5
Greenwood Mans 9
IG11 ... 80 A1
Greenwood Pk KT2 ... 177 C3
Greenwood Pl NW5 ... 71 B3
Greenwood Prim Sch
Greenford UB6 ... 64 B3
Mitcham CR4 ... 203 D6
Northolt UB5 ... 64 A3
Greenwood Rd E8 ... 74 A2
E13 ... 98 D5
Hinchley Wood KT7 ... 213 A6
Isleworth TW7 ... 130 D2
Mitcham CR4 ... 203 D6
Thornton Heath CR0 ... 205 A2
Greenwood Sch SE18 ... 145 C4
Greenwood Terr NW10 ... 89 B5
Greenwoods The HA2 ... 64 A5
Greer Rd HA3 ... 24 A2
Greet Ho SE1 ... 251 B1
Greet St SE1 ... 116 C5 251 B3
Gregor Mews SE3 ... 143 A5
Gregory Cres SE9 ... 165 D4
Gregory Ho SE3 ... 143 B3
Gregory Pl W8 ... 245 C2
Gregory Rd Ilford RM6 ... 58 D5
Southall UB2 ... 107 C3
Greig Cl N8 ... 50 A4
Greig Terr SE17 ... 138 D6
Grena Gdns TW9 ... 132 B1
Grena Rd TW10,TW9 ... 132 B1
Grenaby Ave CR0 ... 205 B2
Grenaby Rd CR0 ... 205 B2
Grenada Ho 18 E14 ... 119 B6
Grenada Rd SE7 ... 143 C5
Grenade St E14 ... 119 B6
Grenadier St E16 ... 122 C5
Grendon Gdns HA9 ... 66 C6
Grendon Ho 29 E9 ... 74 C1
N1 ... 233 C3
Grendon Lo HA8 ... 11 A2
Grendon St NW8 92 C3 237 A6
Grenfell Ct NW7 ... 28 B4
Grenfell Gdns
Harrow HA3 ... 44 A2
Ilford IG2 ... 57 D4
Grenfell Ho SE5 ... 139 A5
Grenfell Rd W11 ... 112 D6
Mitcham CR4,SW17 ... 180 D4
Grenfell Sch E1 ... 96 B1
Grenfell Twr 5 W11 ... 112 D6
Grenfell Wlk 4 W11 ... 112 D6
Grengate Lo 2 E13 ... 99 B4
Grennell Cl SM1 ... 218 B6
Grennell Rd SM1 ... 218 A6
Grenoble Gdns N13 ... 32 C4
Grenville Cl N3 ... 29 B2
Tolworth KT5 ... 199 A1
Grenville Ct SE19 ... 183 D5
W13 ... 87 B2
Edgware HA8 ... 26 D6
Harrow HA1 ... 64 C4
Grenville Gdns IG8 ... 37 C3
Grenville Ho 24 E3 ... 97 A5
4 SE8 ... 141 C6
Grenville Lo N6 ... 49 C2
Grenville Mews SW7 ... 256 A3
Hampton TW12 ... 173 D5
Grenville Pl NW7 ... 27 B5
SW7 ... 114 A2 256 A4
Grenville Rd N19 ... 50 A1
Grenville St WC1 ... 240 B5
Gresham Almshouses 3
SW9 ... 138 B1
Gresham Ave N20 ... 30 D6
Gresham Cl Bexley DA5 ... 169 B5
Enfield EN2 ... 5 A2
Gresham Coll
EC1 ... 94 C2 241 B3
Gresham Ct TW3 ... 130 A4
Gresham Dr RM6 ... 58 B3
Gresham Ho
2 Teddington TW11 ... 174 D5
3 Thames Ditton KT7 ... 197 A2
West Barnes KT3 ... 200 B5
Gresham Rd E6 ... 100 B5
E16 ... 99 B1
NW10 ... 67 B3
SE25 ... 206 A5
SW9 ... 138 C2
Edgware HA8 ... 26 B4
Hampton TW12 ... 173 C4
Hillingdon UB10 ... 82 C5
Hounslow TW3,TW5 ... 130 A4
Penge BR3 ... 185 A1
Gresham St EC2 . 95 A1 242 B2
Gresham Way SW19 ... 157 C1
Gresham Way Est
SW19 ... 157 D1
Gresley Cl E17 ... 53 A3
N15 ... 51 B5
Gresley Ho SW8 ... 269 D2
Gresley Rd N19 ... 49 C2
Gresse St W1 ... 93 D1 239 C2
Gressenhall Rd SW18 ... 157 B4
Gresswell Cl DA14 ... 168 A1
Greswell St SW6 ... 134 D4
Gretton Ho 2 E2 ... 96 C4
Gretton Rd N17 ... 33 D3
Greville Cl TW1 ... 153 B4
Greville Hall NW6 ... 91 D5
Greville Ho SW1 ... 258 A6
SW15 ... 134 D2
HA2 ... 42 B1
Greville Lo 14 N12 ... 29 D6
5 W2 ... 91 D1
Greville Mews 3 NW6 ... 91 D6
Greville Pl W9 ... 91 D5
Greville Rd E17 ... 54 A5
NW6 ... 91 D5
Richmond TW10 ... 154 B5
Greville St EC1 ... 94 C2 241 B4
Grey Cl NW11 ... 48 A3
Grey Coat Hospital CE Sch
The SW1 ... 115 D3 259 C5
Grey Coat Hospital St
Michaels The
SW1 ... 115 D2 259 C3
Grey Court Sch TW10 ... 153 C1
Grey Eagle St E1 95 D3 243 D5
Grey Ho 27 W12 ... 112 B6
Grey Turner Ho W12 ... 90 A1
Greycoat Pl
SW1 ... 115 D3 259 C5
Greycoat St
SW1 ... 115 D3 259 C5
Greycot Rd BR3 ... 185 C5
Greyfell Cl HA7 ... 25 B5
Greyfriars 16 SE26 ... 162 A1
Greyfriars Ho SE3 ... 142 D6
Greyhound Ct WC2 ... 251 A6
Greyhound Hill NW4 ... 46 B6
Greyhound La SW16 ... 181 D4
Greyhound Rd N17 ... 51 C6
NW10 ... 90 B4
W6 ... 135 A6 264 A6
Sutton SM1 ... 218 A3
Greyhound Terr SW16 ... 181 C2
Greyladies Gdns SE10 ... 142 A3
Greys Park Cl BR2 ... 225 D3
Greystead Rd SE23 ... 162 C4
Greystoke Ave HA5 ... 41 C6
Greystoke Ct W5 ... 88 B3
Greystoke Dr HA4 ... 38 D3
Greystoke Gdns W5 ... 88 B3
Enfield EN2 ... 3 D1
Greystoke Ho SE15 ... 140 A6
Greystoke Lo W5 ... 88 B3
Greystoke Park Terr W5 . 88 A4
Greystoke Pl EC4 ... 241 B2
Greystone Gdns HA3 ... 43 C3
Greyswood St SW16 ... 181 B4
Grice Ct N1 ... 73 A2
Grierson Ho SW16 ... 181 C6
Grierson Rd SE23 ... 162 D4
Griffin Cl NW10 ... 68 B3
Griffin Ct W4 ... 111 D1
W12 ... 112 B5
8 Brentford TW8 ... 132 A6
Griffin Ctr KT1 ... 175 D1
Griffin Ctr The TW14 ... 150 B5
Griffin Gate SW15 ... 134 D2
Griffin Lo N12 ... 30 A6
Griffin Manor Spec Sch
SE18 ... 145 C4
Griffin Manor Way
Plumstead SE28 ... 123 B3
Thamesmead SE28 ... 123 D5
Griffin Rd N17 ... 33 C1
SE18 ... 123 B1
Griffin Way SE28 ... 123 C3
Sunbury TW16 ... 172 A1
Griffith Cl RM8 ... 58 C1
Griffiths Cl KT4 ... 216 B6
Griffiths Ho 2 SE18 ... 144 D6
Griffiths Rd SW19 ... 179 D3
Grifton Ho 3 SW11 ... 136 C2
Griggs App IG1 ... 79 A6
Grigg's Pl SE1 ... 263 B5
Griggs Rd E10 ... 54 A3
Grimaldi Ho N1 ... 233 C4
Grimsby St E2 ... 243 D6
7 E2 ... 96 A3
Grimsdyke Fst & Mid Sch
HA5 ... 23 B4
Grimsdyke Rd HA5 ... 23 A3
Grimsel Path SE5 ... 138 D5
Grimshaw Cl N6 ... 49 A2
Grimston Rd SW6 ... 135 B3
Grimthorpe Ho EC1 ... 241 C6
Grimwade Ave CR0 ... 222 A5
Grimwade Cl SE15 ... 140 C2
Grimwood Rd TW1 ... 152 D4
Grindal St SE1 ... 251 A1
Grindall Cl CR0 ... 220 D4
Grindall Ho 25 E1 ... 96 B3
Grindleford Ave N11 ... 15 A2
Grindley Gdns CR0 ... 205 D3
Grindley Ho 3 E3 ... 97 B2
Grinling Gibbons Prim Sch
SE8 ... 141 B6
Grinling Ho 6 SE18 ... 122 C2
Grinling Pl SE8 ... 141 C6
Grinstead Rd SE8 ... 119 A1
Grisedale NW1 ... 232 A2
Grisle Cl N9 ... 34 B6
Grittleton Ave HA9 ... 66 D2
Grittleton Rd W9 ... 91 C3
Grizedale Terr 8 SE23 ... 162 B2
Grocers' Hall Ct EC2 ... 242 C1
Groom Cres SW18 ... 158 B4
Groom Pl SW1 . 115 A3 258 B6
Groombridge Cl DA16 ... 168 A6
Groombridge Ho 1
SE20 ... 184 D3
Groombridge Rd E9 ... 74 D1
Groome Ho SE11 ... 260 D3
Groomfield Cl SW17 ... 181 A6
Grooms Dr HA5 ... 40 A4
Grosmont Rd SE18 ... 123 D1
Grosse Way SW15 ... 156 B5
Grosslea SM4 ... 202 B4
Grosvenor Ave N5 ... 73 A3
SW14 ... 133 C2
Harrow HA2 ... 41 D3
Hayes UB4 ... 83 D5
Richmond TW10 ... 154 A6
Wallington SM5,SM6 ... 219 A2
Grosvenor Bridge
SW1 ... 137 B6 268 D6
Grosvenor Cotts SW1 ... 258 A4
Grosvenor Cres NW9 ... 44 C5
SW1 ... 115 A4 248 B1
Hillingdon UB10 ... 82 D6
Grosvenor Cres Mews
SW1 ... 248 A1
Grosvenor Ct E10 ... 53 D1
3 E11 ... 55 B4
N14 ... 15 C4
NW6 ... 90 D6
NW7 ... 27 B5
SE19 ... 183 D4
SW15 ... 157 A6
2 SW19 ... 179 A4
4 W3 ... 110 C5
W4 ... 110 D1
3 W5 ... 110 A6
Morden SM4 ... 201 C5
2 Richmond TW10 ... 154 B5
1 Sutton SM2 ... 218 A2
Teddington TW11 ... 175 A4
Grosvenor Ct Mans W2 237 C1
Grosvenor Gdns E6 ... 99 D4
N10 ... 49 C6
N14 ... 15 D6
NW2 ... 68 C3
NW11 ... 47 B4
SW1 ... 115 B3 258 D5
SW14 ... 133 C2
Kingston u T KT2 ... 175 D4
Wallington SM6 ... 219 C1
Woodford IG8 ... 37 B4
Grosvenor Gdns Mews E
SW1 ... 258 D6
Grosvenor Gdns Mews N
SW1 ... 258 C5
Grosvenor Gdns Mews S
SW1 ... 258 D5
Grosvenor Hill SW19 ... 179 A4
W1 ... 115 B6 248 C6
Grosvenor Hill Ct W1 ... 248 C6
Grosvenor Ho E5 ... 52 A1
Grosvenor Lo 4 E18 ... 36 D1
Grosvenor Par 1 W5 ... 110 C5
Grosvenor Park SE5 ... 139 A5
Grosvenor Park Rd E17 . 53 D4
Grosvenor Pk SE5 ... 139 A6
Grosvenor Pl
SW1 ... 115 B4 248 C1
Grosvenor Rd E6 ... 99 D6
E7 ... 77 B2
E10 ... 54 A1
E11 ... 55 B4
N3 ... 29 C3
N9 ... 18 B3
N10 ... 31 B2
SE25 ... 206 A5
SW1 ... 137 C6 269 B6
W4 ... 111 A1
W7 ... 109 A5
Bexley DA6 ... 169 A6
Brentford TW8 ... 131 D6
Dagenham RM8 ... 59 B1
Erith DA17 ... 147 C6
Hounslow TW3,TW4 ... 129 B2
Ilford IG1 ... 79 A5
Orpington BR5,BR6 ... 211 C3
Richmond TW10 ... 154 A6
Southall UB2 ... 107 B3
Twickenham TW1 ... 153 A3
Wallington SM6 ... 219 B3
West Wickham BR4 ... 223 D6
Grosvenor Residences 1
W14 ... 112 D3
Grosvenor Rise E E17 ... 53 D4
Grosvenor Sq
W1 ... 115 A6 248 B6
Grosvenor St
W1 ... 115 B6 248 C6
Grosvenor Terr SE5 ... 139 A6
Grosvenor The NW11 ... 47 D2
Grosvenor Vale HA4 ... 61 D6
Grosvenor Way E5 ... 74 C6
Grosvernor Wharf Rd
E14 ... 120 B2
Grote's Bldgs SE3 ... 142 C3
Grote's Pl SE3 ... 142 C3
Groton Rd SW18 ... 157 D2
Grotto Ct SE1 ... 252 A2
Grotto Pas W1 ... 238 A4
Grotto Rd TW1 ... 152 D2
Grove Ave N10 ... 31 C1
W7 ... 86 C1
Pinner HA5 ... 41 A5
Sutton SM1,SM2 ... 217 C2
Twickenham TW1 ... 152 D3
Grove Cl N14 ... 15 B4
SE23 ... 163 A3
Hayes BR2 ... 225 A6
Ickenham UB10 ... 60 C3
Kingston u T KT1 ... 198 B5
Grove Cres E18 ... 36 D1
NW9 ... 45 B5
Feltham TW13 ... 173 A6
Kingston u T KT1 ... 198 A6
Walton-on-T KT12 ... 194 B2
Grove Crescent Rd E15 . 76 B2
Grove Ct NW8 ... 229 C2
SE5 ... 139 C3
SE20 ... 184 B3
3 SE26 ... 185 A6
SW4 ... 137 C2
SW10 ... 256 B1
W5 ... 110 A5
East Molesey KT8 ... 196 B4
Hadley EN5 ... 1 B2
Hounslow TW3 ... 129 C1
8 Kingston u T KT1 ... 198 A6
Kingston u T KT3 ... 199 C6
Kingston u T KT6 ... 197 D4
Grove Dwellings E1 ... 96 C2
Grove End E18 ... 36 D1
NW5 ... 71 B4
Grove End Gdns NW8 ... 229 B3
Grove End Ho NW8 ... 229 C1
Grove End La KT10 ... 196 B1
Grove End Rd
NW8 ... 92 B4 229 C1
Grove Farm Ct CR4 ... 202 D4
Grove Footpath KT5 ... 198 A5
Grove Gdns NW4 ... 46 A5
NW8 ... 92 C4 230 B1
Enfield EN3 ... 6 D5
Teddington TW11 ... 175 A6
Grove Green Rd E11 ... 76 B6
Grove Hall Ct
NW8 ... 92 A4 229 B2
Grove Hill E18 ... 36 D1
Harrow HA1 ... 42 C2
Grove Hill Rd SE5 ... 139 C2
Harrow HA1 ... 42 D2
Grove Ho N3 ... 46 D6
SE3 ... 142 D3
SW3 ... 267 B6
Walton-on-T KT12 ... 194 B2
Grove House Froebel Ed Inst
SW15 ... 155 D5
Grove House Prim Sch
SE27 ... 160 D2
Grove House Rd N8 ... 50 A5
Grove Jun & Inf Sch
W4 ... 133 A6
Grove La SE5 ... 139 C2
Hillingdon UB8 ... 82 B3
Kingston u T KT1 ... 198 A5
Grove Lane Terr SE5 ... 139 B3
Grove Lo SW4 ... 137 C1
Grove Mans 3 N16 ... 52 A1
SW4 ... 136 D1
2 W6 ... 112 C4
Grove Market Pl SE9 ... 166 B5
Grove Mews W6 ... 112 C3
Grove Park Ave E4 ... 35 D3
Grove Park Bridge W4 133 A5
Grove Park Gdns W4 ... 133 A5
Grove Park Rd N15 ... 51 C5
SE9,SE12 ... 165 D2
W4 ... 132 D5
Grove Park Sch NW9 ... 45 A5
Grove Park Sta SE12 ... 165 B1
Grove Park Terr W4 ... 132 D6
Grove Pk E11 ... 55 B4
NW9 ... 45 B5
SE5 ... 139 C3
Grove Pl NW3 ... 70 B5
SW12 ... 159 B5
W3 ... 111 A5
Grove Prim Sch RM6 ... 58 C4
Grove Rd E3 ... 97 A5
E4 ... 20 A1
E11 ... 54 D2
E17 ... 53 D4
E18 ... 36 D1
N11 ... 31 B5
N12 ... 30 B5
N15 ... 51 C4
NW2 ... 68 C2
SW13 ... 133 D3
SW19 ... 180 A3
W3 ... 111 A5
W5 ... 109 D6
Brentford TW8 ... 109 C1
Cockfosters EN4 ... 2 C2
East Molesey KT8 ... 196 B5
Edgware HA8 ... 26 C4
8 Erith DA17 ... 147 B6
Hounslow TW3 ... 129 C1
Hounslow TW7 ... 130 C4
Ilford RM6 ... 58 C3
Kingston u T KT6 ... 197 D4
Mitcham CR4 ... 181 B1
Pinner HA5 ... 41 B4
Richmond TW10 ... 154 B5
Shepperton TW17 ... 193 A3
Sutton SM2 ... 217 C2
Thornton Heath CR7 ... 204 C5
Twickenham TW2 ... 152 B1
Uxbridge UB8 ... 60 A1
Grove Rd Prim Sch
TW3 ... 129 C1
Grove Rd W EN3 ... 6 C6
Grove St N18 ... 33 D4
SE8 ... 119 B1
Grove Terr NW5 ... 71 B4
Southall UB1 ... 107 C6
Teddington TW11 ... 175 A6
Grove The E15 ... 76 C2
N3 ... 29 C3
N4 ... 50 B2
N6 ... 49 A1
N8 ... 49 D4
N13 ... 32 C6
NW9 ... 45 B4
NW11 ... 47 A2
SE21 ... 162 A3
W5 ... 110 A5
Bexley DA6 ... 146 D1
Edgware HA8 ... 26 D6
Enfield EN2 ... 4 C3
Hillingdon UB8 ... 82 B3
Hounslow TW7 ... 130 C4
Ickenham UB10 ... 60 C3
Sidcup DA14 ... 191 A6
Southall UB6 ... 86 A1
Teddington TW11 ... 175 A6
1 Twickenham TW1 ... 153 B5
Walton-on-T KT12 ... 194 B2
West Wickham BR4 ... 224 A6
Grove Vale SE22 ... 139 D1
Chislehurst West BR7 ... 188 C4
Grove Vale Prim Sch
SE22 ... 139 D1
Grove Way
Thames Ditton KT10 ... 196 A1
Wembley HA9 ... 67 A3
Grovebury Ct N14 ... 15 D4
Bexleyheath DA6 ... 169 D6
Grovebury Rd SE2 ... 124 B4
Grovedale Rd N19 ... 71 D6
Grovefield 1 N11 ... 31 B6
Grovehill Ct BR1 ... 186 D4
Groveland Ave SW16 ... 182 B3
Groveland Ct EC4 ... 242 B1
Groveland Rd BR3 ... 207 B6
Groveland Way KT3 ... 199 B4
Grovelands
East Molesey KT8 ... 195 C5
Kingston u T KT1 ... 197 D5
Grovelands Cl SE5 ... 139 C3
Harrow HA2 ... 63 D5
Grovelands Ct N14 ... 15 D4
Grovelands Priory (Private
Hospl) N14 ... 16 A3
Grovelands Rd N13 ... 16 B1
N15 ... 52 A3
St Paul's Cray BR5 ... 190 A3
Grovelands Sch KT12 ... 194 B3
Groveley Ho 7 N4 ... 51 A2
Groveley Rd TW13,
TW16 ... 171 D5
Grover Ct SE13 ... 141 D3
Grover Ho SE11 ... 260 D1
4 SW4 ... 159 C6
Groves Ho UB4 ... 84 B4
Groveside Cl W3 ... 88 C1
Carshalton SM5 ... 218 C6
Groveside Ct SW11 ... 136 B3
Groveside Rd E4 ... 20 C1
Grovestile Waye TW14 ... 149 B4
Groveway SW9 . 138 B4 270 D1
Dagenham RM8 ... 80 D4
Grovewood 9 TW9 ... 132 C4
Grovewood Ct 6 TW7 ... 130 C4
Grummant Rd SE15 ... 139 D4
Grundy St E14 ... 97 D1
Gruneisen Rd N3 ... 29 D3
Guardian Angels RC JMI Sch
E3 ... 97 A4
Guardian Ct SE12 ... 164 C6
Guards Mus The
SW1 ... 115 C4 249 B1
Gubyon Ave SE24 ... 160 D6
Guerin Sq E3 ... 97 B4
Guernsey Cl TW5 ... 129 C5
Guernsey Gr SE24 ... 161 A4
Guernsey Ho 9 N1 ... 73 A2
Enfield EN3 ... 6 D5
Guernsey Rd E11 ... 54 B1
8 N1 ... 73 A2
Guibal Rd SE12 ... 165 B3
Guild Hall★ EC2 . 95 A1 242 B2
Guild Rd SE7 ... 143 D6
Guildersfield Rd SW16 ... 182 A3
Guildford Ave TW13 ... 150 A2
Guildford Gr SE10 ... 141 D4
Guildford Ho 24 SE5 ... 139 A3
Guildford Rd E6 ... 100 B1
E17 ... 36 A2
SW8 ... 138 A4 270 B2
Ilford IG3 ... 79 C6
Thornton Heath CR0 ... 205 B3
Guildford Way SM6 ... 220 A3
Guildhall Bldgs EC2 ... 242 C2
Guildhall Sch Music & Drama
EC2 ... 95 A2 242 B4
Guildhall Yd EC2 ... 242 B2
Guildhouse St
SW1 ... 115 C2 259 A3
Guildown Ave N12 ... 29 D6
Guildsway E17 ... 35 B2
Guilford Ave KT5 ... 198 B4
Guilford Pl WC1 ... 240 C5
Guilford St WC1 . 94 A3 240 B5
Guilfoyle 2 NW9 ... 27 D1
Guillemot Ct 28 SE8 ... 141 B6
Guilsborough Cl NW10 ... 67 C1
Guinness Cl E9 ... 75 A1
Hayes UB3 ... 105 B3
Guinness Ct E1 ... 243 D1
EC1 ... 235 B1
NW8 ... 230 B5
SW3 ... 257 C3
6 Croydon CR0 ... 221 D6
Guinness Sq SE1 ... 263 A4
Guinness Trust Bldgs
7 E2 ... 96 A5
SE1 ... 253 A2
SE11 ... 261 C2
SW3 ... 257 C3
W6 ... 112 C1
Guion Rd SW6 ... 135 B3
Gujarat Ho 1 N16 ... 73 C5
Gull Cl SM6 ... 220 A1
Gulland Cl WD2 ... 8 A6
Gulland Wlk 20 N1 ... 73 A2
Gullane Ho 22 E3 ... 97 B5
Gulliver Cl UB5 ... 85 B6
Gulliver Ct CR2 ... 220 D1
Gulliver Rd DA15 ... 167 C2
Gulliver St SE16 ... 119 B3
Gulston Wlk SW3 ... 257 D3
Gumleigh Rd W5 ... 109 C2
Gumley Gdns TW7 ... 131 A2
Gumley House Convent Sch
for Girls TW7 ... 131 A2
Gumping Rd BR5 ... 227 A6
Gun St E1 ... 243 C3
Gun Wharf E1 ... 118 C5
E3 ... 97 A6
Gundulph Rd BR2 ... 209 C6
Gunmakers La E3 ... 97 A6
Gunnell Cl SE25 ... 206 A3
Gunnell Ct 3 CR4 ... 180 C2
Gunnels Ct & Hastingwood
Ct 6 IG9 ... 21 C2
Gunner Dr EN3 ... 7 C6
Gunner La SE18 ... 122 C1
Gunners Gr E4 ... 20 A1
Gunners Rd SW18 ... 158 B2
Gunnersbury Avenue (North
Circular Rd) W3 ... 110 C3
Gunnersbury Cl 8 W4 110 D1
Gunnersbury Cres W3 ... 110 C4
Gunnersbury Ct 8 W3 110 D4
Gunnersbury Dr W5 ... 110 B4
Gunnersbury Gdns W3 110 C4
Gunnersbury La W3 ... 110 C4
Gunnersbury Manor
W5 ... 110 B5
Gunnersbury Mews 6
W4 ... 110 D1
Gunnersbury Park W3 ... 110 C3
Gunnersbury Park Mus
W3 ... 110 C3
Gunnersbury RC Sch
TW8 ... 109 C1
Gunnersbury Sta W4 ... 110 D1
Gunning St SE18 ... 123 C2
Gunpowder Sq EC4 ... 241 B2
Gunstor Rd N16 ... 73 C4
Gunter Gr SW6 . 136 A5 266 A4
Burnt Oak HA8 ... 27 B2
Gunterstone Rd
W14 ... 113 A1 254 B2
Gunthorpe St E1 95 D1 243 D2
Gunton Rd E5 ... 74 B6
SW17 ... 181 A4
Gunwhale Cl SE16 ... 118 D5

Gurdon Ho 3 E14 ... 97 C1
Gurdon Rd SE7 ... 121 A1
Gurnell Gr W13 ... 86 D3
Gurney Cl E15 ... 76 C3
E17 ... 34 D2
Barking IG11 ... 78 D2
Gurney Cres CR0 ... 204 B1
Gurney Dr N2 ... 48 A5
Gurney Ho 14 E2 ... 96 A5
3 W2 ... 91 D1
Hayes UB3 ... 105 C2
Gurney Rd E15 ... 76 C3
Carshalton SM5 ... 219 A4
Northolt UB5 ... 84 C4
Guru Nanak Sikh Coll
UB4 ... 106 C5
Guthrie Ct SE1 ... 251 B1
Guthrie St SW3 ... 257 A2
Gutter La EC2 ... 95 A1 242 A2
Guy Barnett Gr SE3 ... 143 A2
Guy Rd CR0,SM6 ... 219 D5
Guy St SE1 ... 117 B4 252 D2
Guyatt Gdns CR4 ... 181 A1
Guy's Evelina Hospl Sch
SE1 ... 117 B5 252 D3
Guy's Hospl SE1 117 B5 252 D2
Guy's Retreat IG9 ... 21 C4
Guyscliff Rd SE13 ... 164 A6
Gwalior Ho N14 ... 15 C5
Gwalior Rd SW15 ... 134 D2
Gwendolen Ave SW15 . 156 D6
Gwendolen Cl SW15 ... 156 D6
Gwendoline Ave E13 ... 99 B6
Gwendwr Rd
W14 ... 113 A1 254 B2
Gwent Ct 13 SE16 ... 118 D5
Gwillim Cl DA15 ... 168 A6
Gwilym Maries Ho 11 E2 96 B4
Gwydor Rd BR3 ... 206 D6
Gwydyr Rd BR2 ... 208 D6
Gwyn Cl SW6 .. 136 A5 266 A3
Gwyn Jones Prim Sch
E11 ... 54 B2
Gwynne Ave CR0 ... 206 D2
Gwynne Cl W4 ... 133 D6
Gwynne Ho 3 E11 ... 55 A4
6 SW2 ... 160 B3
WC1 ... 234 A1
Gwynne Pl WC1 ... 233 D1
Gwynne Rd SW11 ... 136 B3
Gye Ho 2 SW4 ... 138 A1
Gylcote Cl SE5 ... 139 B1
Gyles Pk HA7 ... 25 C2
Gyllyngdune Gdns IG3 .. 79 D5

H

Haarlem Rd 12 W14 ... 112 D3
Haberdasher Pl 4 N1 .. 95 C4
Haberdasher St
N1 ... 95 B4 235 D2
Haberdashers' Aske's
Hatcham Coll SE14 ... 141 A4
Haberdashers' Aske's
Hatcham Coll (Boys)
SE4 ... 141 A3
Habington Ho 9 SE5 .. 139 B5
Haccombe Rd SW19 ... 180 A4
Hackbridge Inf Sch
SM6 ... 203 A1
Hackbridge Jun Sch
SM6 ... 203 A1
Hackbridge Park Gdns
SM5 ... 218 D6
Hackbridge Rd SM5,
SM6 ... 219 A6
Hackbridge Sta SM6 ... 219 B6
Hackett Cl SE8 ... 119 B2
Hackford Rd
SW9 ... 138 C4 270 D2
Hackford Wlk SW9 ... 138 C4
Hackforth Cl EN5 ... 12 B6
Hackington Cres BR3 .. 185 C4
Hackney Central Sta E8 . 74 B2
Hackney Cl WD6 ... 11 B6
Hackney Coll (Poplar Centre)
E3 ... 97 D3
Hackney Com Coll N1 .. 95 C4
N4 ... 51 A2
Hackney Downs Sch E5,
E8 ... 74 A3
Hackney Downs Sta E8 . 74 B3
Hackney Free & Parochial CE
Sch (Secondary) E9 ... 74 C2
Hackney Gr E8 ... 74 B2
Hackney Hospl E9 ... 75 A3
Hackney Rd E2 ... 96 A5
Hackney Wick E9 ... 75 B2
Hackney Wick Sta E9 .. 75 C2
Hackworth Point 24 E3 . 97 D4
Hadden Rd SE28 ... 123 C3
Hadden Way UB6 ... 64 B2
Haddenham Ct SW17 .. 180 B6
Haddington Ct 4 SE10 141 D5
Haddington Rd BR1 ... 186 B6
Haddo Ho NW5 ... 71 B4
SE10 ... 141 D6
Haddo St SE10 ... 142 A6
Haddon Cl Enfield EN1 ... 18 A5
New Malden KT3 ... 199 D4
Haddon Ct NW4 ... 46 C6
W3 ... 111 D6
Haddon Gr DA15 ... 168 A4
Haddon Rd SM1 ... 217 D4
Haden Ct N4 ... 72 C6
Hadfield Cl UB1 ... 85 B4
Hadfield Ho 26 E1 ... 96 A1
Hadleigh Cl 16 E1 ... 96 C3
SW20 ... 179 B1
Hadleigh Ct 8 E4 ... 20 C4
Hadleigh Ho 15 E1 ... 96 C3
Hadleigh Lo 5 IG8 ... 37 A4
Hadleigh Rd N9 ... 18 B4
Hadleigh St E2 ... 96 C4
Hadleigh Wlk 1 E6 ... 100 A1
Hadley Cl N21 ... 16 C5
Deacons Hill WD6 ... 10 B5
Hadley Ct N16 ... 52 A1
Hadley Gdns W4 ... 111 B1
Southall UB2 ... 107 B1
Hadley Gn EN5 ... 1 B3
Hadley Gn W EN5 ... 1 B3
Hadley Gr EN5 ... 1 A3
Hadley Green Rd EN5 ... 1 B3
Hadley Hall N21 ... 16 C3
Hadley Highstone EN5 ... 1 B4
Hadley Ho BR5 ... 189 D1
Hadley Rd Barnet EN5 ... 1 D2
Enfield EN2 ... 4 A5
Erith DA17 ... 125 B2
Mitcham CR4 ... 203 D5
Hadley Ridge EN5 ... 1 B2
Hadley St NW1 ... 71 B2
Hadley Way N21 ... 16 C5
Hadley Wood JMI Sch
EN4 ... 2 A5
Hadley Wood Rd
Barnet EN4 ... 2 A3
Barnet EN5 ... 1 C3
Hadley Wood Sta EN4 ... 2 A5
Hadleyvale Ct EN5 ... 1 D2
Hadlow Ho SE17 ... 263 B2
Hadlow Pl SE19 ... 184 A3
Hadlow Rd Bexley DA16 . 146 C5
Sidcup DA14 ... 190 A6
Hadrian Cl
Stanwell TW19 ... 148 A4
Wallington SM6 ... 220 A1
Hadrian Ct SE4 ... 141 C2
Barnet EN5 ... 1 D1
1 Belmont SM2 ... 217 D1
Hadrian Est 30 E2 ... 96 A5
Hadrian St SE10 ... 120 C1
Hadrian Way TW19 ... 148 A4
Hadrian's Ride EN1 ... 17 D6
Hadstock Ho NW1 ... 232 D2
Hadyn Park Ct 13 W12 . 112 A4
Hadyn Park Rd W12 ... 112 A4
Hafer Rd SW11 ... 136 D1
Hafton Rd SE6 ... 164 C2
Haggard Rd TW1 ... 153 B4
Hagger Ct E17 ... 54 B6
Haggerston Rd E8 ... 95 D6
Haggerston Sch E2 ... 95 D5
Hague JMI Sch E2 ... 96 B3
Hague St 12 E2 ... 96 A4
Ha-Ha Rd SE7,SE18 ... 144 B6
Haig Ct BR7 ... 188 D5
Haig Ho 4 E2 ... 96 A5
Haig Pl SM4 ... 201 C3
Haig Rd Hillingdon UB8 ... 83 A2
Stanmore HA7 ... 25 C5
Haig Rd E E13 ... 99 C5
Haig Rd W E13 ... 99 C4
Haigville Gdns IG6 ... 56 D5
Hailes Cl SW19 ... 180 A4
Hailey Rd DA18 ... 125 C4
Hailey Rd Bsns Pk
DA18 ... 125 C4
Haileybury Ave EN1 ... 17 D5
Hailsham Ave SW2 ... 160 B2
Hailsham Cl KT6 ... 197 D2
Hailsham Dr HA1 ... 42 B6
Hailsham Ho NW8 ... 237 A5
Hailsham Rd SW17 ... 181 A4
Hailsham Terr N18 ... 33 B5
Haimo Prim Sch SE9 .. 165 D6
Haimo Rd SE9 ... 165 D6
Hainault Bldgs E10 ... 54 A1
Hainault Bridge Par 4
IG1 ... 78 D6
Hainault Ct E17 ... 54 B5
Hainault Gore RM6 ... 59 A4
Hainault Rd E11 ... 54 B2
Dagenham RM6 ... 59 A3
Ilford RM6 ... 58 B6
Hainault St SE9 ... 166 D3
Ilford IG1 ... 78 D6
Haines Wlk SM4 ... 201 D2
Hainford Cl SE4 ... 140 D1
Haining Cl 3 W4 ... 110 C1
Hainthorpe Rd SE27 .. 182 D6
Hainton Cl E1 ... 96 B1
Halberd Mews E5 ... 74 B6
Halbutt Gdns RM9 ... 81 B5
Halbutt St Dagenham RM9 81 B3
Dagenham RM9 ... 81 B5
Halcomb St N1 ... 95 C6
Halcot Ave DA6 ... 169 D6
Halcrow St E1 ... 96 B2
Halcyon 3 EN1 ... 17 C6
Haldan Rd E4 ... 36 A4
Haldane Cl N10 ... 31 B3
Haldane Pl SW18 ... 157 D3
Haldane Rd E6 ... 100 A4
SE28 ... 124 D6
SW6 ... 135 B6 264 D5
Southall UB1 ... 86 A1
Haldon Rd SW18 ... 157 B5
Hale Cl E4 ... 20 A1
Edgware HA8 ... 27 A5
Orpington BR6 ... 227 A4
Hale Ct HA8 ... 27 A5
Hale Dr NW7 ... 27 B4
Hale End Cl HA4 ... 40 A3
Hale End Rd E17 ... 36 B2
Hale Gdns N17 ... 52 A6
W3 ... 110 C5
Hale Grove Gdns NW7 .. 27 C5
Hale Ho SW1 ... 259 D2
Enfield EN3 ... 6 D6
Hale La NW7,HA8 ... 27 B5
Hale Lo HA1 ... 42 C2
Hale Rd E6 ... 100 A3
N17 ... 52 A6
Hale St E14 ... 119 D6
Hale The E4 ... 36 B3
N17 ... 52 A6
Hale Wlk W7 ... 86 C2
Halefield Rd N17 ... 34 B2
Hales Ct 5 TW11 ... 175 A5
Hales Ho 3 SW12 ... 159 B4
Hales Prior N1 ... 233 C3
Hales St SE8 ... 141 C5
Halesowen Rd SM4 ... 201 D2
Halesworth Cl 3 E5 ... 74 C6
Halesworth Rd SE13 ... 141 D2
Haley Rd NW4 ... 46 C3
Half Acre TW8 ... 131 D6
Half Acre Mews TW8 .. 131 D6
Half Acre Rd W7 ... 108 C5
Half Moon Ct EC1 ... 242 A3
Half Moon La SE24 ... 161 A5
Half Moon St
W1 ... 115 B5 248 D3
Halfmoon Pas E1 ... 243 D1
Halford Cl HA8 ... 26 D1
Halford Ct KT9 ... 214 A1
Halford Ho 9 SW15 .. 156 D6
Halford Rd E10 ... 54 B4
SW6 ... 135 C6 265 A5
Ickenham UB10 ... 60 C3
Richmond TW10 ... 154 A6
Halfway St DA15 ... 167 C3
Haliburton Rd TW1,TW7 131 A1
Haliday Ho N1 ... 73 B2
Haliday Wlk 4 N1 ... 73 B2
Halidon Cl E9 ... 74 C3
Halifax 8 NW9 ... 27 D1
Halifax Rd Enfield EN2 ... 5 B3
Greenford UB6 ... 85 D6
Halifax St SE26 ... 162 B1
Halifield Dr DA17 ... 125 A3
Haling Gr CR2 ... 221 A1
Haling Manor High Sch
CR2 ... 220 D1
Haling Park Gdns CR2 . 220 D2
Haling Park Rd CR2 ... 221 A2
Haling Rd CR2 ... 221 B2
Haliwell Ho 8 NW6 ... 91 D6
Halkett Ho 1 E2 ... 96 C6
Halkin Arc SW1 114 D3 257 D6
Halkin Mews SW1 ... 258 A6
Halkin Pl SW1 ... 258 A6
Halkin St SW1 .. 115 A4 248 B1
Hall Cl W5 ... 88 A2
Hall Ct TW11 ... 174 D5
Hall Dr SE26 ... 184 C5
W7 ... 86 C1
Hall Farm Cl HA7 ... 25 B6
Hall Farm Dr TW2 ... 152 B4
Hall Gate NW8 .. 92 A4 229 B2
Hall Gdns E4 ... 35 B6
Hall Jun Sch The NW3 .. 70 B2
Hall La E4 ... 35 B5
NW4 ... 28 A1
Harlington UB3 ... 127 B5
Hall Lane E4 ... 35 A5
Hall Oak Wlk NW6 ... 69 B2
Hall Pl W2 ... 92 B3 236 C5
Hall Rd E6 ... 100 B6
E15 ... 76 B4
NW8 ... 92 A4 229 B2
Ilford RM6 ... 58 D3
Isleworth TW7 ... 152 B6
Hall Sch NW3 ... 70 B2
Hall Sch Wimbledon
SW15 ... 156 A1
Hall St EC1 ... 94 D4 234 D2
N12 ... 30 A5
Hall The SE3 ... 143 A2
Hall Twr W2 ... 236 D4
Hall View SE9 ... 165 D2
Hallam Cl BR7 ... 188 B5
Hallam Ct W1 ... 238 D4
Hallam Gdns HA5 ... 23 A3
Hallam Ho SW1 ... 259 B1
17 SW9 ... 138 C4
Hallam Mews W1 ... 238 D4
Hallam Rd N15 ... 50 D5
SW13 ... 134 B2
Hallam St W1 .. 93 B2 238 D4
Hallane Ho SE27 ... 183 A5
Halley Gdns SE13 ... 142 B1
Halley Ho 15 E2 ... 96 A5
8 SE10 ... 120 D1
Halley Prim Sch E14 ... 97 A2
Halley Rd E7,E12 ... 77 D2
Halley St E14 ... 97 A2
Hallfield W2 ... 236 A1
Hallfield Jun & Inf Sch
W2 ... 91 D1
Hallgate SE3 ... 143 A2
Halliards The KT12 ... 194 A3
Halliday Ho 29 E1 ... 96 A1
Halliday Sq UB2 ... 108 B5
Halliford Cl TW17 ... 193 C6
Halliford Rd
Sunbury TW16 ... 194 A5
Upper Halliford TW16,
TW17 ... 193 D5
Halliford Sch TW17 ... 193 A2
Halliford St N1 ... 73 B1
Halling Ho SE1 ... 252 D1
Halliwell Ct 4 SE22 ... 162 A6
Halliwell Rd SW2 ... 160 B5
Halliwick Court Par 2
N12 ... 30 D5
Halliwick Ct 1 N12 ... 30 D5
Halliwick Ho N21 ... 17 B5
Halliwick Rd N10 ... 31 A2
Hallmark Trad Ctr HA9 .. 67 A4
Hallmead Rd SM1 ... 217 D5
Hallowell Ave CR0 ... 220 A4
Hallowell Cl CR4 ... 203 A6
Hallowfield Way CR4 .. 202 C6
Halls Terr UB10 ... 82 D3
Hallside Rd EN1 ... 5 D5
Hallsville Prim Sch E16 . 99 A1
Hallsville Rd E16 ... 98 D1
Hallswelle Par 1 NW11 . 47 B4
Hallswelle Rd NW11 ... 47 B4
Hallywell Cres E6 ... 100 B2
Halons Rd SE9 ... 166 C4
Halpin Pl SE17 . 117 B2 262 D3
Halsbrook Rd SE3 ... 143 D2
Halsbury Cl HA7 ... 25 B6
Halsbury Ct HA7 ... 25 B6
Halsbury Ho 4 N7 ... 72 B4
Halsbury Rd W12 ... 112 B5
Halsbury Rd E UB5 ... 64 A4
Halsbury Rd W UB5 ... 63 D3
Halsend UB3 ... 106 B5
Halsey St SW3 . 114 D2 257 C4
Halsham Cres IG11 ... 79 D3
Halsmere Rd SE5 ... 138 D4
Halstead Cl 2 CR0 ... 221 A5
Halstead Ct N1 ... 235 D3
Halstead Gdns N21 ... 17 B3
Halstead Rd E11 ... 55 B4
N21 ... 17 B3
Enfield EN1 ... 5 C1
Halston Cl SW11 ... 158 D5
Halstow 12 NW5 ... 71 A2
Halstow Prim Sch SE10 121 A1
Halstow Rd NW10 ... 90 D4
SE3,SE10 ... 121 A1
Halsway UB3 ... 106 A5
Halt Robin La DA17 ... 125 D2
Halt Robin Rd DA17 ... 125 D2
Halter Cl WD6 ... 11 B6
Halton Cl N11 ... 30 D4
Halton Cross St
N1 ... 94 D6 234 D6
Halton Ho 23 N1 ... 72 D1
Halton Mans N1 ... 72 D1
Halton Pl N1 ... 235 A6
Halton Rd N1 .. 72 D1 234 D6
Haltone Ho 1 SW4 ... 137 D3
Halyard Ho E14 ... 120 A3
Ham Cl TW10 ... 153 C1
Ham Comm TW10 ... 153 D1
Ham Ct 12 NW9 ... 27 D1
Ham Farm Rd KT2,
TW10 ... 176 A6
Ham Gate Ave TW10 ... 176 A6
Ham House TW10 ... 153 C2
Ham Park Rd E15 ... 76 D1
Ham Ridings TW10 ... 176 B5
Ham Shades Cl 1
DA15 ... 168 A1
Ham St TW10 ... 153 C1
Ham The TW8 ... 131 C5
Ham View CR0 ... 207 A3
Ham Yd W1 ... 249 C6
Hamara Ghar 5 E13 ... 99 C6
Hambalt Rd SW4 ... 159 C6
Hamble Cl HA4 ... 61 C6
Hamble Ct KT1 ... 175 D3
Hamble St SW6 ... 135 D2
Hamble Wlk UB5 ... 85 C5
Hambledon SE17 ... 139 B6
Hambledon Chase N4 .. 50 A2
Hambledon Cl UB8 ... 82 D3
Hambledon Ct 5 W5 .. 110 A6
9 Wallington SM6 ... 219 B2
Hambledon Gdns SE25 205 D6
Hambledon Ho E5 ... 74 B4
2 Kingston u T KT2 ... 176 D4
Hambledon Pl SE21 ... 161 D3
Hambledon Rd SW18 .. 157 B4
Hambledown Rd SE9 .. 167 C4
Hambleton Cl KT4 ... 216 C6
Hambley Ho 5 SE16 ... 118 B2
Hamblin Ho UB1 ... 107 A6
Hamblyn Ct N16 ... 51 D2
Hambridge Way SW2 .. 160 C4
Hambro Ave BR2 ... 209 A1
Hambro Rd SW16 ... 181 D5
Hambrook Ct 12 NW5 ... 71 B4
Hambrook Rd SE25 ... 206 B6
Hambrough Ho UB4 ... 84 C2
Hambrough Prim Sch
UB1 ... 107 B5
Hambrough Rd UB1 .. 107 A5
Hambury Ho SW8 ... 270 B5
Hamden Cres RM10 ... 81 D5
Hamel Cl HA3 ... 43 D5
Hamers Ho 19 SW2 ... 160 C4
Hameway E6 ... 100 C3
Hamfrith Rd E15 ... 76 D2
Hamilton Ave N9 ... 18 A4
Cheam SM3 ... 217 A6
Ilford IG6 ... 57 A4
Tolworth KT6,SM3 ... 214 C6
Hamilton Cl N17 ... 51 D6
NW8 ... 92 B4 229 C1
Hamilton Cl *continued*
SE16 ... 119 A4
Ashford TW13 ... 171 D5
Cockfosters EN4 ... 2 D1
Hamilton Cres N13 ... 32 C6
Harrow HA2 ... 63 B5
Hounslow TW3 ... 151 D6
Hamilton Ct 9 SE6 ... 164 D3
W5 ... 110 B6
W9 ... 229 A2
Croydon CR0 ... 206 A1
Hamilton Gdns
NW8 ... 92 A4 229 B2
Hamilton Hall
NW8 ... 92 A5 229 A3
Hamilton Ho 18 E3 ... 97 B4
1 E14 ... 119 B6
NW8 ... 229 C2
SW15 ... 156 A6
W4 ... 133 C6
W8 ... 245 C2
10 Richmond TW9 ... 132 C4
Hamilton La N5 ... 72 D4
Hamilton Lo 32 E1 ... 96 C3
Hamilton Mews W1 ... 248 C2
Hamilton Par TW13 ... 172 A6
Hamilton Pk N5 ... 72 D4
Hamilton Pk W N5 ... 72 D4
Hamilton Pl N17 ... 33 D1
W1 ... 115 A5 248 B3
Sunbury TW16 ... 172 B3
Hamilton Rd E15 ... 98 C4
E17 ... 35 A1
N2 ... 48 A6
N9 ... 18 A4
NW10 ... 68 A3
NW11 ... 47 A2
SE27 ... 183 B6
SW19 ... 179 D3
W4 ... 111 C4
W5 ... 110 A6
Bexleyheath DA7 ... 147 A3
Brentford TW8 ... 131 D6
Cockfosters EN4 ... 2 C1
Feltham TW13 ... 171 D6
Harrow HA1 ... 42 C4
Hayes UB3 ... 106 B6
Ilford IG1 ... 78 D4
Sidcup DA15 ... 190 A6
South Norwood CR7 ... 205 B6
Southall UB1 ... 107 B5
Twickenham TW2 ... 152 C3
Hamilton Road Ctr E15 . 98 C4
Hamilton Road Ind Est
SE27 ... 183 B6
Hamilton Road Mews 1
SW19 ... 179 D3
Hamilton Sq N12 ... 30 A4
SE1 ... 252 D2
Hamilton St SE8 ... 141 C6
Hamilton Terr
NW8 ... 92 A4 229 B2
Hamilton Way N3 ... 29 C4
N13 ... 32 D6
Hamlea Cl SE12 ... 165 A6
Hamlet (Day) Hospl The
TW9 ... 132 A2
Hamlet Cl SE13 ... 142 C1
Hamlet Ct SE11 ... 261 C2
1 W6 ... 112 A2
14 Enfield EN1 ... 17 C6
Hamlet Gdns W6 ... 112 A2
Hamlet Ho SE9 ... 166 C6
Hamlet Ind Est E9 ... 75 C1
Hamlet Rd SE19 ... 184 A3
Hamlet Sq NW2 ... 69 A5
Hamlet The SE5 ... 139 B2
Hamlet Way SE1 ... 252 D2
Hamlets Way E3 ... 97 B3
Hamlin Cres HA5 ... 40 C4
Hamlyn Cl HA8 ... 10 A1
Hamlyn Gdns SE19 ... 183 C3
Hammelton Ct 4 BR1 . 186 D2
Hammelton Gn 2 SW9 138 D4
Hammelton Rd BR1 ... 187 A2
Hammers La NW7 ... 28 A6
Hammersley Ho 8
SE14 ... 140 C5
Hammersmith & West
London Coll
W12 ... 112 B4
W14 ... 113 A1 254 A2
Hammersmith & West
London Coll Olympia
Annexe W14 .. 113 A2 254 B4
Hammersmith Bridge Rd
W6,SW13 ... 112 C1
Hammersmith Broadway 5
W6 ... 112 C2
Hammersmith Flyover
W6 ... 112 C1
Hammersmith Gr W6 .. 112 C3
Hammersmith Hospl
W12 ... 90 B1
Hammersmith Rd W6 . 112 D2
W14 ... 254 B4
Hammersmith Sta W6 . 112 C2
Hammersmith Terr W6 112 A1
Hammet Cl UB4 ... 84 D2
Hammett St EC3 ... 253 C6
Hammond Ave CR4 ... 181 B1
Hammond Cl
Greenford UB6 ... 64 B3
Hampton TW12 ... 173 C2
Hammond Ct 1 E10 ... 75 D6
1 E17 ... 53 A4
Hammond Ho E14 ... 119 D3
10 SE14 ... 140 C5
Hammond Lo 6 W9 ... 91 C2
Hammond Rd Enfield EN1 . 6 B3
Southall UB2 ... 107 A3
Hammond St NW5 ... 71 C2
Hammond Way 2 SE28 124 B6
Hammonds Cl RM8 ... 80 C5
Hamond Sq N1 ... 95 C5
Hamonde Cl HA8 ... 10 D2
Hampden Ave BR3 ... 185 A1
Hampden Cl NW1 ... 232 D4
Hampden Ct 5 N10 ... 31 A3
Hampden Gurney CE Prim
Sch W1 ... 92 C1 237 B2
Hampden Gurney St
W1 ... 237 C1
Hampden Ho SW9 ... 138 C3
Hampden La N17 ... 34 A2
Hampden Rd N8 ... 50 C5
N10 ... 31 A3
N17 ... 34 A2
N19 ... 71 D6
Beckenham BR3 ... 185 A1
Harrow HA3 ... 24 A1
Kingston u T KT1 ... 198 C6
Hampden Sq N14 ... 15 B3
Hampden Way N14 ... 15 B2
Hampshire Cl N18 ... 34 B5
Hampshire Ct 6 SW13 133 D3
Hampshire Hog La 11
W6 ... 112 B2
Hampshire Rd N22 ... 32 B3
Hampshire St NW5 ... 71 D2
Hampson Way
SW8 ... 138 B4 270 C2
Hampstead Cl SE28 ... 124 B5
Hampstead Garden Suburb
Inst NW11 ... 47 D4
Hampstead Gate NW3 .. 70 A3
Hampstead Gdns NW11 . 47 C3
Hampstead Gn NW3 ... 70 C3
Hampstead Gr NW3 ... 70 A5
Hampstead Heath*
NW3 ... 70 B6
Hampstead Heath Sta
NW3 ... 70 C4
Hampstead High St NW3 70 B4
Hampstead Hill Gdns
NW3 ... 70 C4
Hampstead Hill Sch
NW3 ... 70 C3
Hampstead La N6 ... 48 C2
Hampstead Parochial CE Sch
NW3 ... 70 A4
Hampstead Rd
NW1 ... 93 C4 232 A2
Hampstead Sch NW2 ... 69 A4
Hampstead Sq NW3 ... 70 A5
Hampstead Sta NW3 ... 70 A4
Hampstead Way NW11 .. 47 C3
Hampstead West 4
NW6 ... 69 C2
Hampstead Wlk 1 E3 .. 97 B6
Hampton Cl N11 ... 31 B5
NW6 ... 91 C4
SW20 ... 178 C3
Hampton Court KT8 ... 196 C6
Hampton Court Ave
KT8 ... 196 C3
Hampton Court Cres
KT8 ... 196 B6
Hampton Court Palace*
KT8 ... 196 D6
Hampton Court Par
KT8 ... 196 C5
Hampton Court Rd KT1,
KT8 ... 197 B6
Hampton Court Sta
KT8 ... 196 C5
Hampton Court Way
KT10,KT7,KT8 ... 196 C3
Hampton Ct N1 ... 72 D2
N22 ... 31 C2
19 SE16 ... 118 D5
Hampton Farm Ind Est
TW13 ... 151 A1
Hampton Hill Bsns Pk
TW12 ... 174 A5
Hampton Hill Jun Mix Sch
TW12 ... 174 A5
Hampton Ho DA7 ... 147 D3
Hampton Inf Sch TW12 173 C3
Hampton Jun Sch
TW12 ... 173 C2
Hampton La TW13 ... 173 A6
Hampton Rd E4 ... 35 B5
E7 ... 77 C3
E11 ... 54 B1
Ilford IG1 ... 79 A4
North Cheam KT4 ... 216 B6
Teddington TW11,TW12 . 174 C5
Thornton Heath CR0 ... 205 A3
Twickenham TW2 ... 152 B1
Hampton Rd E TW13 .. 151 B1
Hampton Rd W TW13 .. 151 A1
Hampton Rise HA3 ... 44 A3
Hampton Road Ind Pk
CR0 ... 205 A3
Hampton Sch TW12 ... 173 C5
Hampton St
SE1 ... 116 D2 261 D3
Hampton Sta TW12 ... 173 C2
Hampton Wick Inf Sch
KT1 ... 175 D3
Hampton Wick Sta KT1 175 C2
Hanameel St 6 E16 ... 121 A5
7 E16 ... 121 B5
Hanbury Cl NW4 ... 46 C6
Hanbury Ct HA1 ... 42 D3

Hanbury Dr N21 ... 16 B6
Hanbury Ho 8 E1 ... 96 A2
Hanbury Rd N17 ... 34 B1
W3 ... 110 D4
Hanbury St E1 .. 96 A2 243 D4
Hancock Nunn Ho 1 NW3 ... 70 D1
Hancock Rd E3 ... 98 A4
SE19 ... 183 B4
Hancocke Ho 4 E17 ... 53 D6
Hand Ct WC1 ... 240 D3
Handa Wlk 3 N1 ... 73 A2
Handcroft Rd CR0 ... 204 D1
Handel Cl HA8 ... 26 B4
Handel Ho TW2 ... 152 B5
Handel Mans SW13 ... 134 C5
Handel Par HA8 ... 26 C3
Handel Pl NW10 ... 67 B2
Handel St WC1 .. 94 A3 240 B6
Handel Way HA8 ... 26 C3
Handen Rd SE12 ... 164 D6
Handforth Rd SW9 ... 138 C5
6 Ilford IG1 ... 78 D5
Handley Rd E9 ... 96 C6
Handowe Cl NW4 ... 46 A5
Hands Wlk E16 ... 99 A1
Handside Cl KT4 ... 200 D1
Handsworth Ave E4 ... 36 B4
Handsworth Prim Sch E4 ... 36 B4
Handsworth Rd N17 ... 51 B6
Handtrough Way IG11 . 100 D5
Hanford Cl SW18 ... 157 C3
Hangar View Way W3 ... 88 C2
Hanger Ct W5 ... 88 C3
Hanger Gn W5 ... 88 C3
Hanger La W5 ... 88 A5
Hanger La (North Circular Rd) W5 ... 88 A5
Hanger Lane W5 ... 88 A4
Hanger Lane (North Circular Rd) W5 ... 88 B2
Hanger Lane Sta W5 ... 88 A4
Hanger Vale La W5 ... 88 B1
Hangmans Cnr BR7 ... 188 D2
Hankey Pl SE1 . 117 B4 252 D1
Hankins La NW7 ... 11 C1
Hanley Gdns N4 ... 50 B1
Hanley Pl BR3 ... 185 C3
Hanley Rd N4,N19 ... 50 A1
Hanmer Wlk N7 ... 72 B6
Hannah Cl BR3 ... 208 A6
Hannah Ct SW19 ... 178 D3
Hannah Mary Way 15 SE1 ... 118 A2
Hannah Mews SM6 ... 219 C1
Hannan Cl NW10 ... 67 A4
Hannay La N8 ... 49 D2
Hannay Wlk SW16 ... 159 D2
Hannell Rd SW6 135 A5 264 B4
Hannen Ho SE5 ... 139 B2
Hannen Rd SE27 ... 160 D1
Hannibal Rd E1 ... 96 C2
Stanwell TW19 ... 148 A4
Hannibal Way CR0 ... 220 B2
Hanning Lo TW3 ... 130 A1
Hannington Rd SW4 ... 137 B2
Hanover Ave E16 ... 121 A5
Feltham TW13 ... 150 A2
Hanover Circ UB3 ... 83 B1
Hanover Cl Cheam SM3 . 217 B4
Richmond TW9 ... 132 C5
Hanover Ct N16 ... 51 D2
NW9 ... 45 C6
1 SE19 ... 184 A3
W12 ... 112 A5
Hanover Dr BR7 ... 189 A6
Hanover Gate Mans NW1 ... 237 B6
Hanover Gdns SE11 ... 138 C6
Hanover Ho NW8 ... 230 A3
New Barnet EN5 ... 2 A1
Tolworth KT6 ... 198 C1
Hanover Mans 5 SW2 . 160 C6
Hanover Mead NW11 ... 47 A4
Hanover Pk SE15 ... 140 A4
Hanover Pl WC2 ... 240 B1
Hanover Rd N15 ... 51 D5
NW10 ... 90 C6
SW19 ... 180 A3
Hanover Sch N1 . 95 A5 235 A4
Hanover Sq W1 . 93 B1 238 D1
Hanover St W1 .. 93 B1 238 D1
Croydon CR0 ... 220 D5
Hanover Steps W2 ... 237 B1
Hanover Terr NW1 ... 92 D4 230 C1
Isleworth TW7 ... 131 A4
Hanover Terr Mews NW1 ... 92 C4 230 B1
Hanover Way DA7 ... 146 D2
Hanover West Ind Est NW10 ... 89 B4
Hanover Yd N1 ... 235 A4
Hans Cres SW1 114 D3 257 C6
Hans Pl SW1 .. 114 D3 257 C6
Hans Rd SW3 .. 114 D3 257 C6
Hans St SW1 .. 114 D3 257 D5
Hansard Mews W14 ... 112 D4
Hansart Way EN2 ... 4 C4
Hanselin Cl HA7 ... 24 D5
Hansen Dr N21 ... 16 B6
Hanshaw Dr HA8 ... 27 B2
Hansler Gr KT8 ... 196 B5
Hansler Rd SE22 ... 161 D6
Hansol Rd DA6 ... 169 A6
Hansom Terr 1 BR1 ... 187 B2
Hanson Cl SW12 ... 159 B4
Hanson Cl *continued*
SW14 ... 133 A2
Beckenham BR3 ... 185 D4
West Drayton UB7 ... 104 B3
Hanson Ct E17 ... 53 D3
Hanson Gdns UB1 ... 107 A4
Hanson Ho 2 E1 ... 118 A6
Hanson St W1 .. 93 C2 239 A4
Hanway Ho 25 SW9 ... 138 C4
Hanway Pl W1 ... 239 C2
Hanway Rd W7 ... 86 C1
Hanway St W1 ... 239 C2
Hanwell Ho 24 W2 ... 91 C2
Hanwell Sta W7 ... 108 C6
Hanworth Ho SE5 ... 138 D5
Hanworth Rd
Feltham TW13 ... 150 B3
Hampton TW12 ... 173 C5
Hounslow TW3,TW4 ... 129 D1
Sunbury TW16 ... 172 A3
Twickenham TW4 ... 151 B4
Hanworth Terr TW3 ... 129 D1
Hanworth Trad Est TW13 ... 151 A1
Hapgood Cl UB6 ... 64 B3
Harben Rd NW6 ... 70 A1
Harberson Rd E15 ... 98 D6
SW12 ... 159 B3
Harberton Rd N19 ... 49 C1
Harbet Rd N18 ... 35 A4
W2 ... 92 B2 236 D3
Harbex Cl DA5 ... 169 D4
Harbin Ho 5 SW2 ... 160 C3
Harbinger JMI Sch E14 119 D2
Harbinger Rd E14 ... 119 D2
Harbledown Ho SE1 ... 252 C1
Harbledown Rd SW6 .. 265 A2
Harbord Cl SE5 ... 139 B3
Harbord Ho 5 SE16 ... 118 D2
Harbord St SW6 ... 134 D4
Harborne Cl WD1 ... 22 C5
Harborough Ave DA15 . 167 D4
Harborough Rd SW16 .. 182 B6
Harborough Sch N19 .. 71 D6
Harbour Ave SW10 ... 136 A4 266 B1
Harbour Exchange Sq E14 ... 119 D4
Harbour Rd SE5 ... 139 A2
Harbridge Ave SW15 .. 156 A4
Harbury Rd SM5 ... 218 C1
Harbut Rd SW11 ... 136 B1
Harcastle Cl UB4 ... 85 A3
Harcombe Rd N16 ... 73 C5
Harcourt Ave E12 ... 78 B3
Edgware HA8 ... 11 A1
Sidcup DA14,DA15 ... 168 C4
Wallington SM6 ... 219 B4
Harcourt Cl TW7 ... 131 A2
Harcourt Field SM6 ... 219 B4
Harcourt Ho 5 E4 ... 36 B5
27 SW8 ... 137 D3
W1 ... 238 C2
Harcourt Lo 2 SM6 ... 219 B4
Harcourt Rd E15 ... 98 D5
N22 ... 31 D2
SE4 ... 141 B2
SW19 ... 179 C3
Bexleyheath DA6,DA7 ... 147 A1
Bushey WD2 ... 8 A6
Thornton Heath CR7 ... 204 C3
Wallington SM6 ... 219 B4
Harcourt St W1 . 92 C2 237 B3
Harcourt Terr SW10 ... 113 D1 255 D1
Hard Ct IG8 ... 37 C4
Hardcastle Cl SE25 ... 206 A3
Hardcastle Ho 8 SE15 . 140 A4
Hardcourts Cl BR4 ... 223 D5
Hardel Rise SW2 ... 160 D3
Hardel Wlk SE24,SW2 .. 160 C4
Harden Ct 1 SE7 ... 122 A2
Harden Ho SE5 ... 139 C3
Harders Rd SE15 ... 140 B3
Hardess St SE24 ... 139 A2
Hardham Ho 5 SW2 ... 160 C5
Hardie Cl NW10 ... 67 B3
Harding Cl SE17 ... 139 A6
Kingston u T KT2 ... 176 B2
South Croydon CR0 ... 221 D5
Harding Ct SE25 ... 183 D1
Harding Ho 16 SE18 ... 122 B2
SW13 ... 134 B6
Hayes UB3 ... 84 B1
Harding Pl SE23 ... 163 A4
Harding Rd DA7 ... 147 B3
Hardinge Cl UB8 ... 82 D1
Hardinge Rd N18 ... 33 C4
NW10 ... 90 C6
Hardinge St E1 ... 96 C1
SE18 ... 123 A3
Hardings La SE20 ... 184 D4
Hardington 2 NW1 ... 71 A1
Hardman Rd SE7 ... 121 B1
Kingston u T KT2 ... 176 A1
Hardwick Cl 7 HA7 ... 25 C5
Hardwick Ct 8 E11 ... 55 A3
Hardwick Gn W13 ... 87 B2
Hardwick Ho NW8 ... 237 B6
14 SW8 ... 137 D3
Hardwick St EC1 94 C4 234 B1
Hardwicke Ave TW5 ... 129 C4
Hardwicke Ho 14 E3 ... 97 D4
Hardwicke Mews WC1 . 233 D1
Hardwicke Rd N13 ... 32 A4
W4 ... 111 B2
Richmond TW10 ... 175 C6
Hardwicke St IG11 ... 101 A6
Hardwick's Way SW18 . 157 C6
Hardwidge St SE1 ... 253 A2
Hardy Ave 4 E16 ... 121 A5
Ruislip HA4 ... 62 B3
Hardy Cl SE16 ... 118 D4
Barnet EN5 ... 13 A6
Pinner HA5 ... 40 D2
Hardy Cotts 2 SE10 ... 142 B6
Hardy Ct 9 E11 ... 55 A5
SE3 ... 142 D6
Hardy Pas N22 ... 32 C1
Hardy Rd SE3 ... 142 D6
SW19 ... 179 D3
Hardy Way EN2 ... 4 C4
Hardyng Ho 4 E17 ... 53 A5
Hardys Cl KT8 ... 196 C5
Hare & Billet Rd SE3 ... 142 B3
Hare Ct EC4 ... 241 A1
Hare La KT10 ... 212 C2
Hare Marsh E2 ... 96 A3
Hare Pl EC4 ... 241 B1
Hare Row E2 ... 96 B5
Hare St SE18 ... 122 C3
Hare Wlk N1 ... 95 C5
Harebell Dr E6 ... 100 C2
Harecourt Rd N1 ... 73 A2
Haredale Ho 22 SE16 ... 118 A4
Haredale Rd SE24 ... 139 A1
Haredon Cl SE23 ... 162 D4
Harefield KT10 ... 212 C5
Harefield Cl EN2 ... 4 C4
Harefield Ct 6 SW19 ... 179 C3
Harefield Mews SE4 ... 141 B2
Harefield Rd N8 ... 49 D4
SE4 ... 141 B2
SW16 ... 182 B3
Sidcup DA14 ... 168 D1
Uxbridge UB8 ... 60 A3
Harenc Sch Trust DA14 190 C5
Haresfield Rd RM10 ... 81 C2
Harewood Ave NW1 ... 92 C3 237 B5
Northolt UB5 ... 63 B1
Harewood Cl UB5 ... 63 B1
Harewood Ct HA3 ... 24 C2
Harewood Pl W1 ... 238 D1
Harewood Rd SW19 ... 180 C4
Hounslow TW7 ... 130 D4
South Croydon CR2 ... 221 C2
Harewood Row NW1 ... 237 B4
Harewood Terr UB2 ... 107 B2
Harfield Gdns 1 SE5 ... 139 C2
Harfield Rd TW16 ... 172 D1
Harfleur Ct SE11 ... 261 C3
Harford Cl E4 ... 19 D4
Harford Ho SE5 ... 139 A6
W11 ... 91 B2
Harford Rd E4 ... 19 D4
Harford St E1 ... 97 A3
Harford Wlk N2 ... 48 B5
Hargood Cl HA3 ... 44 A3
Hargood Rd SE3 ... 143 C4
Hargrave Mans 2 N19 .. 71 D6
Hargrave Park Prim Sch N19 ... 71 C6
Hargrave Pk N19 ... 71 C6
Hargrave Pl N7 ... 71 D3
Hargrave Rd N19 ... 71 C6
Hargraves Ho 14 W12 .. 112 B6
Hargwyne St SW9 ... 138 B2
Haringey Pk N8 ... 50 A3
Haringey Rd N8 ... 50 A5
Harington Terr N18 ... 17 B1
Harket Cl HA3 ... 24 D1
Harkness Ho 20 E1 ... 96 A1
Harland Ave
Sidcup DA15 ... 167 C2
South Croydon CR0 ... 222 A5
Harland Cl SW19 ... 201 D6
Harland Fst Sch CR4 ... 180 B1
Harland Rd SE12 ... 165 A3
Harlands Gr BR6 ... 226 D4
Harlech Ct 1 SE23 ... 162 C3
Harlech Gdns TW5 ... 128 C5
Harlech Rd N14 ... 16 A1
Harlech Twr 5 W3 ... 111 A4
Harlequin Ave TW8 ... 131 A6
Harlequin Cl Hayes UB4 . 84 D2
Isleworth TW7 ... 152 C6
Harlequin Ct NW10 ... 67 B2
W5 ... 109 C6
Harlequin Ho 1 DA18 ... 125 A3
Harlequin Rd TW11 ... 175 B3
Harlescott Rd SE15 ... 140 D1
Harlesden Gdns NW10 .. 89 D6
Harlesden Prim Sch NW10 ... 89 C5
Harlesden Rd NW10 ... 90 A6
Harlesden Sta NW10 ... 89 B5
Harleston Cl 4 E5 ... 74 C6
Harley Cl HA0 ... 65 D2
Harley Cres HA1 ... 42 B5
Harley Ct E11 ... 55 A2
N20 ... 14 A1
Harley Gdns SW10 ... 114 A1 256 B1
Orpington BR6 ... 227 C4
Harley Gr E3 ... 97 B4
Harley Ho E11 ... 54 B2
NW1 ... 238 B5
Harley Pl W1 ... 93 B2 238 C3
Harley Rd NW3 ... 70 B1
NW10 ... 89 C5
Harrow HA1 ... 42 B5
Harley St W1 ... 93 B2 238 C3
Harley Villas NW10 ... 89 C5
Harleyford BR1 ... 187 C2
Harleyford Ct SW8 ... 270 C6
Harleyford Manor 8 W3 ... 111 A5
Harleyford Rd SE11 ... 138 B6 270 C6
Harleyford St SE11 ... 138 C6
Harling Ct 3 SW11 ... 136 D3
Harlinger St SE18 ... 122 A3
Harlington Bridge UB3 105 C1
Harlington Cl UB7 ... 127 A5
Harlington Cnr UB3 ... 127 B4
Harlington Com Sch UB3 ... 105 B2
Harlington Lower Sch UB7 ... 127 A5
Harlington Rd
Bexleyheath DA7 ... 147 A2
Hillingdon UB8 ... 82 C3
Harlington Rd E TW13, TW14 ... 150 C3
Harlington Rd W TW14 150 B5
Harlow Mans 2 IG11 ... 78 D1
Harlow Rd N13 ... 17 B1
Harlowe Ho 13 E8 ... 95 D6
Harlyn Dr HA5 ... 40 B6
Harlyn Prim Sch HA5 ... 40 B6
Harlynwood 19 SE5 ... 139 A5
Harman Ave IG8 ... 36 D4
Harman Cl E4 ... 36 B6
NW2 ... 69 A5
9 SE1 ... 118 A1
Harman Dr NW2 ... 69 A4
Sidcup DA15 ... 167 D5
Harman Rd EN1 ... 17 D6
Harmon Ho 6 SE8 ... 119 B2
Harmondsworth La UB7 ... 126 B6
Harmondsworth Rd UB7 ... 104 A2
Harmony Cl NW11 ... 47 A4
Harmony Way NW4 ... 46 C5
Bromley BR1 ... 187 A1
Harmood Gr NW1 ... 71 B1
Harmood Ho 2 NW1 ... 71 B1
Harmood St NW1 ... 71 B1
Harmsworth St SE17 ... 116 D1 261 C1
Harmsworth Way N20 .. 13 C3
Harness Rd SE28 ... 124 A4
Harold Ave Erith DA17 .. 125 B1
Hayes UB3 ... 105 D3
Harold Ct 14 SE16 ... 118 D4
Harold Est SE1 ... 263 B5
Harold Gibbons Ct 12 SE7 ... 143 C6
Harold Ho 16 E2 ... 96 D5
Harold Laski Ho EC1 .. 234 D1
Harold Maddison Ho SE17 ... 261 D2
Harold Pl SE11 ... 261 A1
Harold Rd E4 ... 20 A1
E11 ... 54 C1
E13 ... 99 B6
N8 ... 50 B5
N15 ... 51 D4
NW10 ... 89 B4
SE19 ... 183 B3
Carshalton SM1 ... 218 B4
Woodford IG8 ... 37 A2
Harold Wilson Ho SW6 264 D5
Haroldstone Rd E17 ... 53 A4
Harp Alley EC4 ... 241 C2
Harp Bsns Ctr The NW2 . 68 A6
Harp Island Cl NW10 ... 67 B6
Harp La EC3 ... 253 A5
Harp Rd W7 ... 86 D2
Harpenden Rd E12 ... 77 C6
SE27,SW16 ... 160 D2
Harpenmead Point NW2 69 B6
Harper Cl N14 ... 15 C6
Harper Ho 3 SW9 ... 138 D2
Harper Rd E6 ... 100 B1
SE1 ... 117 A3 262 B6
Harper's Yd N17 ... 33 D2
Harpley Sch E1 ... 96 D3
Harpley Sq E1 ... 96 D3
Harpour Rd IG11 ... 79 A2
Harpsden St SW11 ... 268 A1
Harpur Mews WC1 ... 240 C4
Harpur St WC1 .. 94 B2 240 C4
Harraden Rd SE3 ... 143 C4
Harrier Ave E11 ... 55 B3
Harrier Ct TW4 ... 129 A3
Harrier Ho 9 SW11 ... 136 C2
Harrier Mews SE28 ... 123 B4
Harrier Rd NW9 ... 27 C1
Harrier Way E6 ... 100 B2
Harriers Cl W5 ... 110 A6
Harries Rd UB4 ... 84 C3
Harriet Cl E8 ... 96 A6
Harriet Gdns CR0 ... 222 A6
Harriet Ho SW6 ... 265 D3
Harriet St SW1 114 D4 247 D1
Harriet Tubman Cl 21 SW2 ... 160 C4
Harriet Way WD2 ... 8 B4
Harriet Wlk SW1 ... 114 D4 247 D1
Harringay Gdns N8 ... 50 D5
Harringay Green Lanes Sta N4 ... 50 D3
Harringay Rd N15 ... 50 D5
Harringay Sta N4 ... 50 C3
Harrington Cl NW10 ... 67 B5
Wallington CR0 ... 220 A6
Harrington Ct SW7 ... 256 D4
9 W9 ... 91 B4
6 Croydon CR0 ... 221 B6
Harrington Gdns SW7 ... 114 A2 256 A3
Harrington Hill E5 ... 52 B1
Harrington Hill Prim Sch E5 ... 52 B1
Harrington Ho E5 ... 52 C1
NW1 ... 232 A2
SW1 ... 259 D2
Harrington Rd E11 ... 54 C1
SE25 ... 206 B5
SW7 ... 114 B2 256 C4
Harrington Rd Sta SE25 ... 206 C6
Harrington Sq NW1 ... 93 C5 232 A3
Harrington St NW1 ... 93 C4 232 A2
Harrington Way SE18 .. 121 D3
Harriott Cl SE10 ... 120 D2
Harriott Ho 11 E1 ... 96 C1
Harris City Tech Coll SE19 ... 183 D2
Harris Cl Enfield EN2 ... 4 D4
Hounslow TW5 ... 129 C4
Harris Cotts 1 E15 ... 98 D6
Harris Ho 10 E3 ... 97 C4
8 SW9 ... 138 C2
Harris Lo SE6 ... 164 A3
Harris Rd Dagenham RM9 . 81 B3
Erith DA7 ... 147 B4
Harris St E17 ... 53 B2
SE5 ... 139 B5
Harris Way TW16 ... 171 C2
Harrison Cl N20 ... 14 C3
Harrison Ct TW17 ... 192 D4
Harrison Ho SE17 ... 262 C2
Harrison Rd RM10 ... 81 D2
Harrison St WC1 94 A4 233 B1
Harrisons Ct 1 SE14 ... 140 D6
Harrison's Rise CR0 ... 220 D5
Harrodian Sch SW13 .. 133 D5
Harrogate Ct 2 SE26 ... 162 A1
Harrold Ho 1 NW3 ... 70 A1
Harrold Rd RM8 ... 80 B3
Harrow & Wealdstone Sta HA1 ... 42 C5
Harrow Ave EN1 ... 17 D5
Harrow Cl KT9 ... 213 D1
Harrow Coll Harrow HA1 . 42 C2
Hatch End HA5 ... 23 C3
Harrow Coll Harrow & Weald Campus HA3 ... 24 C4
Harrow Dr N9 ... 17 D3
Harrow Fields Gdns HA1 64 C5
Harrow Gn E11 ... 76 C5
Harrow High Sch HA1 ... 43 A3
Harrow Hospl HA2 ... 64 C6
Harrow La E14 ... 120 A6
Harrow Lo SM2 ... 218 B2
Harrow Manor Way SE2 ... 124 C3
Harrow Mus & Her Ctr HA2 ... 42 A6
Harrow Pk HA1 ... 64 C6
Harrow Pl E1 ... 95 C1 243 B2
Harrow Rd 2 E6 ... 100 A6
E11 ... 76 D5
W2 ... 92 A2 236 B3
W2,W9 ... 91 C3
Ashford TW15 ... 148 C2
Barking IG11 ... 101 C6
Carshalton SM1,SM2,SM5 218 C2
Ilford IG1 ... 79 A4
Sudbury HA0 ... 65 A4
Wembley HA0 ... 65 D3
Wembley HA9 ... 66 C2
Harrow Sch HA1 ... 42 C1
Harrow St NW1 ... 237 A4
Harrow View
Harrow HA1,HA2 ... 42 B5
Hayes UB3 ... 84 A1
Hillingdon UB10 ... 83 A4
Harrow View Rd W5 ... 87 B3
Harrow Way
Charlton TW17 ... 171 A1
South Oxhey WD1 ... 23 A6
Harrow Weald Pk HA3 .. 24 B4
Harroway Rd SW11 ... 136 B3
Harrowby St W1 92 C1 237 B2
Harrowdene Cl HA0 ... 65 D4
Harrowdene Ct SW19 .. 179 A5
Harrowdene Gdns TW11 ... 175 A3
Harrowdene Rd HA0 ... 65 D4
Harrowes Meade HA8 ... 10 C1
Harrowgate Ho 22 E9 ... 74 D2
Harrowgate Rd E9 ... 75 A1
Harrow-on-the-Hill Sta HA1 ... 42 C3
Harry & Abe Sherman Rosh Pinar Prim Sch HA8 ... 10 D1
Harry Ct 15 NW9 ... 46 A5
Harry Gosling JMI Sch E1 ... 96 A1
Harry Hinkins Ho SE17 . 262 B1
Harry Lambourn Ho 10 SE15 ... 140 B5
Harston 15 KT1 ... 176 C1
Harston Dr EN3 ... 7 C5
Hart Ct E12 ... 78 C1
Hart Gr W5 ... 110 C5
Southall UB1 ... 85 C2
Hart Grove Ct 3 W5 .. 110 C5
Hart Ho SW2 ... 160 C3
Hart Lo EN5 ... 1 A2
Hart St EC3 ... 253 B6
Harte Rd TW3 ... 129 B3
Hartfield Ave
Deacons Hill WD6 ... 10 C6
Northolt UB5 ... 84 B5
Hartfield Cl WD6 ... 10 C6
Hartfield Cres SW19 ... 179 B3
Coney Hall BR4 ... 225 A5
Hartfield Gr SE20 ... 184 C2
Hartfield Ho UB5 ... 84 B5
Hartfield Rd SW19 ... 179 C3
Chessington KT9 ... 213 D3
Hayes BR4 ... 225 A4
Hartfield Terr E3 ... 97 C5
Hartford Ave HA3 ... 43 B6
Hartford Rd
Bexleyheath DA5 ... 169 C5
West Ewell KT19 ... 214 D2
Hartham Cl N7 ... 72 A3
Isleworth TW7 ... 131 A4
Hartham Rd N7 ... 72 A3
N17 ... 33 D1
Isleworth TW7 ... 131 A4
Harting Rd SE9 ... 166 A1
Hartington Cl
Farnborough BR6 ... 227 A3
Harrow HA1 ... 64 C4
Hartington Ct SW8 ... 270 A2
W4 ... 132 D5
Hartington Rd E16 ... 99 B1
E17 ... 53 A3
SW8 ... 138 A5 270 A3
W4 ... 133 A4
W13 ... 109 B6
Southall UB2 ... 107 A3
Twickenham TW1 ... 153 B5
Hartismere Rd SW6 ... 135 B5 264 D4
Hartlake Rd E9 ... 75 A2
Hartland NW1 ... 232 B5
Hartland Cl N21 ... 17 A5
Deacons Hill HA8 ... 10 C2
Hartland Ct 5 N11 ... 30 D5
Hartland Dr
Deacons Hill HA8 ... 10 C2
Ruislip HA4 ... 62 B4
Hartland Rd E15 ... 76 D1
N11 ... 30 D5
NW1 ... 71 B1
NW6 ... 91 B6
Cheam SM4 ... 201 D2
Hampton TW12 ... 173 D6
Isleworth TW7 ... 131 A2
Hartland Way
Croydon CR0 ... 223 A6
Morden SM4 ... 201 B2
Hartlands Cl DA5 ... 169 B5
Hartlands The TW5 ... 128 B6
Hartley Ave E6 ... 100 A6
NW7 ... 27 D5
Hartley Cl NW7 ... 27 D5
Bromley BR1 ... 188 B1
Hartley Ct W5 ... 110 C5
Hartley Ho N3 ... 29 D4
SE1 ... 263 D4
SW15 ... 156 A6
Hartley Prim Schs E6 .. 100 A6
Hartley Rd E11 ... 54 D1
Bexley DA16 ... 146 C5
Thornton Heath CR0 ... 205 A2
Hartley St E2 ... 96 C4
Hartmann Rd E16 ... 122 A5
Hartmoor Mews EN3 ... 6 D6
Hartnoll Ho 4 N7 ... 72 C3
Hartnoll St N7 ... 72 B3
Harton Cl BR1 ... 187 D2
Harton Lo 2 SE8 ... 141 C4
Harton Rd N9 ... 18 B2
Harton St SE8 ... 141 C4
Hartopp Ct N16 ... 73 C5
Hartopp Point SW6 ... 264 B4
Harts Gr IG8 ... 37 A5
Harts La IG11 ... 78 D2
Hart's La SE14 ... 141 A4
Hartsbourne Ave WD2 ... 8 B2
Hartsbourne Cl WD2 ... 8 B2
Hartsbourne Ct 5 UB1 . 86 A1
Hartsbourne Jun Sch WD2 ... 8 B2
Hartsbourne Pk WD2 ... 8 C2
Hartsbourne Rd WD2 ... 8 B2
Hartshill Cl UB10 ... 60 D2
Hartshorn Alley EC3 ... 243 B1
Hartshorn Gdns E6 ... 100 C3
Hartslock Dr SE2 ... 124 D4
Hartsmead Rd SE9 ... 166 B2
Hartsway EN3 ... 6 C1
Hartswood Gn WD2 ... 8 B2
Hartswood Ho 10 SW2 . 160 A3
Hartswood Rd W12 ... 111 D3
Hartsworth Cl E13 ... 98 D5
Hartville Rd SE18 ... 123 C2
Hartwell Dr E4 ... 36 A4
Hartwell Ho 2 SE7 ... 121 B1
Hartwell St E8 ... 73 D2
Harvard Ct NW6 ... 69 D3
9 SE9 ... 166 C5
Harvard Hill W4 ... 132 D6
Harvard Ho 3 SE17 ... 138 D6
SW15 ... 156 D5
Harvard Mans 18 SW11 136 B1
Harvard Rd SE13 ... 164 A6
W4 ... 110 D1
11 W4 ... 111 A1
Hounslow TW7 ... 130 C4
Harvel Cres SE2 ... 124 D1
Harvest Bank Rd BR4 .. 225 A5

Harvest Ct
Beckenham BR3 .185 C3
Littleton TW17 .192 C5
Harvest La Loughton IG10 21 D4
Thames Ditton KT7 .197 A3
Harvest Rd TW13 .150 A1
Harvesters Cl TW7 .152 B6
Harvey Ct E17 .53 C4
SW11 .267 B2
Harvey Dr TW12 .173 C2
Harvey Gdns E11 .54 D1
SE7 .121 C1
Harvey Ho 10 E1 .96 B3
N1 .235 D5
N8 .50 A6
SW1 .259 D1
Barking IG11 .79 A1
Brentford TW8 .110 A1
Ilford RM6 .58 D5
Harvey Lo 8 W9 .91 C2
Harvey Mews N8 .50 B4
Harvey Point 7 E16 .99 A2
Harvey Rd E11 .54 D1
N8 .50 B4
15 SE5 .139 B4
Hillingdon UB10 .82 C5
Ilford IG1 .78 D3
Ruislip UB5 .62 C1
Twickenham TW4 .151 B4
Walton-on-T KT12 .194 A2
Harvey St N1 .235 D5
Harvil Rd UB9,UB10 .38 A2
Harvill Rd DA14 .191 A5
Harvington Sch W5 .87 D1
Harvington Wlk E8 .74 A1
Harvist Rd NW6 .91 A5
Harwell Cl HA4 .39 B1
Harwick Mans SE13 .122 A3
Harwood Ave
Bromley BR1 .187 B1
Mitcham CR4 .202 C6
Harwood Cl N12 .30 C4
Wembley HA0 .65 D4
Harwood Ct N1 .235 D5
SW15 .134 C1
Harwood Dr UB10 .82 B6
Harwood Rd
SW6 .135 D5 265 C3
Harwood Terr
SW6 .135 D4 265 C2
Harwoods Yd N21 .16 C4
Hascombe Ho 11 SW15 156 B3
Hascombe Terr 2 SE5 .139 B3
Haselbury Rd N9 .17 C1
Haseley End SE23 .162 C4
Haselrigge Prim Sch
SW4 .137 D1
Haselrigge Rd SW4 .137 D1
Haseltine Prim Sch
SE26 .185 B6
Haseltine Rd SE26 .185 B6
Haselwood Dr EN2 .4 D1
Haskard Rd RM9 .80 D4
Haskell Ho NW10 .89 B6
Hasker St SW3 .114 C2 257 B4
Haslam Ave SM3 .201 A1
Haslam Cl N1 .72 C1
Uxbridge UB10 .61 A6
Haslam Ct N11 .31 B6
Haslam Ho 1 N1 .73 A1
Haslam St SE15 .139 D4
Haslemere & Heathrow Est
The TW4 .128 B2
Haslemere Ave NW4 .46 D3
SW18 .157 D2
W13 .109 A3
Cranford TW5 .128 C3
East Barnet EN4 .14 D3
Mitcham CR4,SW19 .180 B1
Haslemere Bsns Ctr EN1 18 B6
Haslemere Cl
Hampton TW12 .173 B5
Wallington SM6 .220 A3
Haslemere Ct 5 N16 .51 C1
Haslemere Fst Sch CR4 180 B1
Haslemere Gdns N3 .47 B5
Haslemere Ind Est
SW18 .157 D2
Feltham TW14 .150 A6
Haslemere Rd N8 .50 A2
N21 .16 D3
Bexleyheath DA7 .147 C3
Ilford IG3 .79 D6
Thornton Heath CR7 .204 D4
Hasler Cl SE28 .124 C6
Hasler Ct E12 .78 A4
Haslett Rd TW17 .171 C1
Hasluck Gdns EN5 .14 A5
Hasmonean High Sch (Boys)
NW4 .28 D1
Hasmonean High Sch (Girls)
NW7 .28 A2
Hasmonean Prim Sch
NW4 .46 D4
Hassard St E2 .95 D5
Hassendean Rd SE3 .143 B5
Hassett Rd E9 .75 A2
Hassock Wood BR2 .225 D4
Hassocks Cl SE23,SE26 .162 B1
Hassocks Rd SW16 .181 D2
Hassop Rd NW2 .68 D4
Hassop Wlk SE9 .188 A6
Hasted Rd SE7 .121 D1
Hastings Ave IG6 .57 A5
Hastings Cl 16 SE15 .140 A5
Hastings Cl *continued*
New Barnet EN5 .2 A1
Hastings Dr KT6 .197 C3
Hastings Ho N17 .34 A2
11 SE18 .122 B2
18 W12 .112 B6
W13 .109 B6
Enfield EN3 .6 C3
Hastings Hos WC1 .233 A1
Hastings Pl 1 CR0 .205 D1
Hastings Rd N11 .31 D5
N17 .51 B6
W13 .109 B6
Croydon CR0 .205 D1
Keston Mark BR2 .226 A6
Hastings St SE18 .123 A3
WC1 .94 A4 233 A1
Hastingwood Ct E17 .53 D4
Hastingwood Trad Est
N18 .34 D4
Hastoe Cl UB4 .85 A3
Hat & Mitre Ct EC1 .241 D5
Hatch End High Sch
HA3 .23 D2
Hatch End Sta HA5 .23 C3
Hatch Gr RM6 .59 A5
Hatch La E4 .20 C1
Hatch Pl TW10 .176 B5
Hatch Rd SW16 .182 A1
Hatch The EN3 .6 D4
Hatcham Mews Bsns Ctr
SE14 .140 D4
Hatcham Park Mews
SE14 .140 D4
Hatcham Park Rd SE14 140 D4
Hatcham Rd SE15 .140 C6
Hatcham Wood Sch
SE4 .141 A3
Hatchard Rd N19 .72 A6
Hatchcroft NW4 .46 B6
Hatchett Rd TW14 .149 A3
Hatchfield Ho 8 N15 .51 C3
Hatchwoods IG8 .36 D6
Hatcliffe Almshouses 8
SE10 .120 C1
Hatcliffe Cl SE3 .142 D2
Hatcliffe St SE10 .120 D1
Hatfield Cl SE14 .140 D5
Ilford IG6 .56 D6
Mitcham CR4 .202 B5
Hatfield Ct SE3 .143 A5
8 Northolt UB5 .84 C4
Hatfield Ho E11 .54 D2
EC1 .242 A5
16 Kingston u T KT6 .198 A4
Hatfield Mead SM4 .201 C4
Hatfield Prim Sch SM4 201 A3
Hatfield Rd E15 .76 C3
W4 .111 B4
10 W13,W7 .109 A5
Dagenham RM9 .81 A1
Hatfields SE1 .116 C5 251 B4
Hathaway Cl
Keston Mark BR2 .210 B1
Ruislip HA4 .61 D4
Stanmore HA7 .25 A5
Hathaway Cres E12 .78 C2
Hathaway Gdns W13 .87 A2
Dagenham RM6 .58 D4
Hathaway Ho 3 N1 .95 C4
Hathaway Prim Sch
W13 .86 D2
Hathaway Rd CR0 .204 D2
Hatherleigh Cl
Chessington KT9 .213 D3
Morden SM4 .201 C5
Hatherleigh Ho SM4 .201 C5
Hatherleigh Rd HA4 .62 A6
Hatherley Cres DA14 .168 A2
Hatherley Ct 6 W2 .91 D1
Hatherley Gdns E6 .99 D4
N8 .50 A3
Hatherley Gr W2 .91 D1
Hatherley Ho 2 E17 .53 C5
Hatherley Mews E17 .53 C5
Hatherley Rd E17 .53 C5
Richmond TW9 .132 B4
Sidcup DA14 .168 A1
Hatherley St SW1 .259 B3
Hathern Gdns SE9 .188 C6
Hatherop Rd TW12 .173 B3
Hathersage Ct N1 .73 B3
Hathersley Ho 3 SW2 .160 C4
Hathorne Cl 3 SE15 .140 B3
Hathway Ho 3 SE15 .140 C3
Hathway St 4 SE15 .140 C3
Hatley Ave IG6 .57 A5
Hatley Cl N11 .30 D5
Hatley Rd N4,N7 .72 B6
Hatteraick St 6 SE16 .118 C4
Hattersfield Cl DA17 .125 B2
Hatton Cl SE18 .145 B5
Hatton Cross Rdbt
TW6 .127 D2
Hatton Cross Sta TW6 .127 D1
Hatton Ct BR7 .188 B3
Hatton Gdn EC1 .94 C2 241 B4
Hatton Gdns CR4 .202 D4
Hatton Gn TW14 .128 A1
Hatton Ho 13 E1 .118 A6
Hatton Pl EC1 .241 B4
Hatton Rd
Hatton TW14,TW6 .149 C6
Thornton Heath CR0 .204 C1
Hatton Rd N TW6 .127 B4
Hatton Row NW8 .236 D5
Hatton Sch IG8 .55 D6
Hatton St NW8 .236 D5
Hatton Wall EC1 .94 C2 241 B4
Haughmond 4 N12 .29 D6
Haunch of Venison Yd
W1 .238 C1
Hauteville Court Gdns 2
W6 .111 D3
Havana Rd SW18,SW19 .157 C2
Havannah St E14 .119 C4
Havant Rd E17 .54 A6
Havant Way 8 SE15 .139 D5
Havelock Cl 13 W12 .112 B6
Havelock Ct UB2 .107 B3
Havelock Hall 8 CR0 .205 D1
Havelock Ho SE23 .162 C3
4 Croydon CR0 .205 D1
Havelock Pl HA1 .42 C3
Havelock Prim Sch
UB2 .107 B3
Havelock Rd N17 .34 A1
SW19 .180 A5
Bromley BR2 .209 C5
Croydon CR0 .221 D6
Erith DA17 .125 B2
Harrow HA3 .42 C6
Southall UB2 .107 C3
Havelock St N1 .94 A6 233 B6
Ilford IG1 .78 D6
Havelock Terr
SW8 .137 B5 268 D3
Havelock Wlk SE23 .162 C2
Haven Cl SE9 .166 B1
SW19 .156 D1
Foots Cray DA14 .190 C4
Hayes UB4 .83 C3
Haven Ct BR3 .186 A1
Haven Gn W5 .87 D1
Haven Green Ct W5 .87 D1
Haven La W5 .88 A1
Haven Lo NW11 .47 B4
7 SE18 .122 D2
15 Enfield EN1 .17 C6
Haven Rd TW15 .148 D1
Haven St 17 NW1 .71 B1
Haven The N14 .15 B5
Ashford TW16 .172 A3
Richmond TW9 .132 C2
Havenhurst Rise EN2 .4 C3
Havenpool NW8 .91 D6
Havenwood HA9 .66 D5
Havercourt 3 NW3 .70 C2
Haverfield Gdns TW9 .132 C5
Haverfield Rd E3 .97 A4
Haverford Way HA8 .26 B2
Havergal Villas N15 .50 D6
Haverhill Rd E4 .20 A3
SW12 .159 C3
Havering 8 NW1 .71 B1
Havering Gdns RM6 .58 D4
Havering Ho N4 .51 A2
Havering St E1 .96 D1
Havering Way IG11 .102 B4
Haverley 14 SW20 .178 D3
Haversham Cl TW1 .153 D5
Haversham Ct UB6 .64 D2
Haversham Lo NW2 .68 D3
Haversham Pl N6 .70 D6
Haverstock Ct 2 BR5 .190 B1
Haverstock Hill NW3 .70 D2
Haverstock Rd NW5 .71 A3
Haverstock Sch NW1 .71 A2
Haverstock St
N1 .94 D5 234 D3
Haverthwaite Rd BR6 .227 B5
Havil St SE5 .139 C4
Havilland Ct HA8 .26 B6
Havisham Ho 23 SE16 .118 A4
Havisham Pl SW16 .182 D3
Hawarden Gr SE24 .161 A4
Hawarden Hill NW2 .68 A5
Hawarden Rd E17 .52 D5
Hawberry Ho N7 .72 A2
Hawbridge Rd E11 .54 B1
Hawes Down Schs BR4 208 B1
Hawes La BR4 .224 C6
Hawes Rd N18 .34 B4
Bromley BR1 .187 B2
Hawes St N1 .72 D1
Haweswater Ho TW1 .152 D6
Hawfinch 29 NW9 .27 D2
Hawgood St E3 .97 C2
Hawk Ho 7 SW11 .136 C2
Hawkdene E4 .20 A5
Hawke Ct UB4 .84 C3
Hawke Ho 20 E1 .96 D3
Hawke Park Rd N22 .50 D6
Hawke Pl 29 SE16 .118 D4
Hawke Rd SE19 .183 C4
Hawke Twr 4 SE14 .141 A6
Hawkedale Fst Sch
TW16 .193 D6
Hawker 28 NW9 .27 D2
Hawker Cl SM6 .220 A1
Hawker Ct 14 KT2 .176 C3
Hawkes Rd
East Bedfont TW14 .150 A4
Mitcham CR4 .180 D2
Hawkesbury Rd SW15 .156 B6
Hawkesfield Rd SE23 .163 B2
Hawkesley Cl TW1 .175 A6
Hawkesworth Ho 5
SW4 .159 C5
Hawkewood Rd TW16 .194 A6
Hawkfield Ct TW7 .130 C3
Hawkhurst Gdns KT9 .214 A4
Hawkhurst Rd SW16 .181 D2
Hawkhurst Way
New Malden KT3 .199 B4
West Wickham BR4 .223 D6
Hawkinge N17 .33 B1
Hawkins Cl NW7 .27 B5
Harrow HA1 .42 B2
Hawkins Ho 3 SE8 .141 C6
Hawkins Rd TW11 .175 B4
Hawkins Way SE6 .185 C5
Hawkley Gdns SE27 .160 D2
Hawkridge 16 NW5 .71 A2
Hawkridge Cl RM6 .58 C3
Hawks Mews 10 SE10 .142 A5
Hawks Rd KT1 .176 B1
Hawksbrook La BR3 .208 A3
Hawkshead NW1 .232 A2
Hawkshead Cl BR1 .186 C3
Hawkshead Rd NW10 .67 D1
W4 .111 C4
Hawkslade Rd SE15 .162 D6
Hawksley Rd N16 .73 C5
Hawksmoor Cl 2 E6 .100 A1
SE18 .123 C1
Hawksmoor Ho 10 E14 .97 A2
Hawksmoor Mews E1 .118 B6
Hawksmoor Prim Sch
SE28 .124 B6
Hawksmoor St 5 W6 .134 D6
Hawksmouth E4 .20 A4
Hawkstone Rd SE16 .118 C2
Hawkswood Sch E4 .20 A6
Hawkwell Ct E4 .20 A1
Hawkwell Ho RM8 .81 C6
Hawkwell Wlk N1 .235 B6
Hawkwood Cres E4 .19 D5
Hawkwood La BR7 .189 A2
Hawkwood Mount 1 E5 52 B1
Hawlands Dr HA5 .41 A2
Hawley Cl TW12 .173 B4
Hawley Cres NW1 .71 B1
Hawley Inf Sch NW1 .71 B1
Hawley Mews 4 NW1 .71 B1
Hawley Rd N18 .34 D5
3 NW1 .71 B1
Hawley St NW1 .71 B1
Hawley Way TW15 .170 D5
Haworth Ct E15 .76 A3
Haworth Ho 7 SW2 .160 C5
Hawstead Rd SE6 .163 D5
Hawsted IG9 .21 B4
Hawthorn Ave N13 .32 A5
South Norwood CR7 .182 D2
Hawthorn Cl
Cranford TW5 .128 B5
Hampton TW12 .173 C5
Orpington BR5 .211 B3
Hawthorn Cres SW17 .181 A5
Hawthorn Ct SW15 .134 B2
8 SW16 .182 C5
Richmond TW9 .132 D4
Hawthorn Ctr HA1 .43 A4
Hawthorn Dr
Coney Hall BR4 .224 C4
Harrow HA2 .41 C3
Hawthorn Farm Ave UB5 85 A6
Hawthorn Gdns W5 .109 D3
Hawthorn Gr SE20 .184 B2
Enfield EN2 .5 B5
Hawthorn Hatch TW8 .131 B5
Hawthorn Mews NW7 .29 A2
Hawthorn Pl UB3 .105 D6
Hawthorn Rd N8 .50 A6
NW10 .68 A1
Bexley DA6 .147 B1
Brentford TW8 .131 B5
Carshalton SM1,SM2,SM5 218 C2
Wallington SM5,SM6 .219 B1
Woodford IG9 .37 D6
Hawthorn Terr DA15 .167 D6
Hawthorn Way TW17 .193 B5
Hawthorn Wlk W10 .91 A3
Hawthornden Cl N12 .30 C4
Hawthorndene Cl BR2 .225 A6
Hawthorndene Rd BR2 .225 A6
Hawthorne Ave
Harrow HA3 .43 A3
Mitcham CR4 .180 B1
Ruislip HA4 .40 B2
Wallington SM5 .219 A1
Hawthorne Cl N1 .73 C2
Bromley BR1 .210 B6
Sutton SM1 .218 A6
Hawthorne Cres UB7 .104 B4
Hawthorne Ct E4 .35 D4
W5 .110 A5
Northwood Hills HA6 .22 A1
Hawthorne Gr NW9 .45 A2
Hawthorne Ho SW1 .259 B1
Hawthorne Mews UB6 .86 A1
Hawthorne Rd E17 .53 C6
N18 .33 D5
Bromley BR1 .210 B6
Hawthorne Way N9 .17 D2
Hawthorns IG8 .21 A1
Hawthorns The KT17 .216 A1
Hawtrey Ave UB5 .84 D5
Hawtrey Dr HA4 .40 B2
Hawtrey Rd NW3 .70 C1
Haxted Rd BR1 .187 B2
Hay Cl E15 .76 D1
Hay Currie St E14 .97 D1
Hay Hill W1 .115 B6 248 D5
Hay La NW9 .45 B5
Hay St E2 .96 A6
Haybridge Ho 1 E5 .74 C6
Haycroft Gdns NW10 .90 B6
Haycroft Mans NW10 .90 A6
Haycroft Rd SW2 .160 A6
Surbiton KT6 .214 A6
Hayday Rd E16 .99 A2
Hayden's Pl W11 .91 B1
Haydock Ave UB5 .63 C2
Haydock Gn UB5 .63 C2
Haydock Green Flats 2
UB5 .63 C2
Haydon Cl NW9 .45 A5
Enfield EN1 .17 C6
Haydon Ct NW9 .45 A5
Haydon Dr HA5 .40 A5
Haydon Ho W7 .108 D5
Teddington TW11 .175 C3
Haydon Park Rd SW19 .179 D5
Haydon Rd RM8 .80 C6
Haydon Sch HA5 .39 D6
Haydon St E1,
EC3 .117 D6 253 C6
Haydon Way SW11 .136 B1
Haydon Wlk E1 .243 D1
Haydon's Rd SW19 .180 A4
Haydons Road Sta
SW19 .180 A5
Hayes & Harlington Sta
UB3 .105 D3
Hayes Bridge Ret Pk
UB4 .106 D6
Hayes Chase BR4 .208 C3
Hayes Cl BR2 .225 A6
Hayes Cres NW11 .47 B4
Cheam SM3 .216 D4
Hayes Ct 28 SE5 .139 A5
SW12 .160 A3
SW19 .179 A4
Hayes End Cl UB4 .83 B2
Hayes End Dr UB4 .83 B3
Hayes End Rd UB4 .83 B3
Hayes Garden BR2 .209 A1
Hayes Hill BR2 .208 C1
Hayes Hill Rd BR2 .208 D1
Hayes La
Beckenham BR2,BR3 .208 B5
Hayes BR2 .209 A4
Hayes Manor Sch UB3 .83 C1
Hayes Mead Rd BR2 .208 C1
Hayes Park Prim Sch
UB4 .83 D3
Hayes Pl NW1 .237 B5
Hayes Prim Sch BR2 .209 B1
Hayes Rd Bromley BR2 .209 A5
Southall UB2 .106 B2
Hayes Sch BR2 .225 B6
Hayes St BR2 .209 B1
Hayes Sta BR2 .208 D1
Hayes Way BR3 .208 B5
Hayes Wood Ave BR2 .209 B1
Hayesend Ho SW17 .180 A6
Hayesford Park Dr BR2 208 D4
Hayfield Ho 38 E1 .96 C3
Hayfield Pas E1 .96 C3
Haygarth Pl 2 SW19 .178 D5
Haygreen Cl KT2 .176 D4
Hayland Cl NW9 .45 B5
Hayles Bldgs SE11 .261 D4
Hayles St SE11 .116 D3 261 C4
Haylett Gdns KT1 .197 D5
Hayling Ave TW13 .150 A1
Hayling Cl 20 N16 .73 C3
Hayling Ct SM3 .216 C4
Haymaker Cl UB10 .60 B1
Hayman Cres UB4 .83 B5
Haymans Point SE11 .260 C2
Haymarket
SW1 .115 D6 249 C5
Haymeads Dr KT10 .212 A2
Haymer Gdns KT4 .216 A5
Haymerle Ho 6 SE15 .140 A6
Haymerle Rd SE15 .140 A6
Haymerle Sch SE15 .140 A6
Haymill Cl UB6 .86 D4
Hayne Ho W11 .244 A4
Hayne Rd BR3 .185 B2
Hayne St EC1 .94 D2 241 D4
Haynes Cl N11 .15 A1
N17 .34 B3
SE3 .142 C2
Haynes Ho 3 E9 .74 D2
Haynes La SE19 .183 C4
Haynes Rd HA0 .66 A1
Haynt Wlk SW20 .201 A6
Hay's Galleria SE1 .253 A4
Hay's La SE1 .253 A4
Hay's Mews W1 115 B6 248 C4
Haysleigh Gdns SE20 .184 A1
Haysleigh Ho SE20 .184 B1
Haystall Cl UB4 .83 C5
Haystocks E18 .55 C6
Hayter Ho W12 .112 A6
Hayter Rd SW2 .160 B6
Haythorn Ho
SW11 .136 B4 266 D1
Hayward Cl SW19 .179 D2
Hayward Ct 18 SW4 .138 A3
Hayward Gallery★
SE1 .116 B5 250 D4
Hayward Gdns SW15 .156 C5
Hayward Ho E5 .74 B5
N1 .234 A4
Hayward Rd N20 .14 A2
Thames Ditton KT7 .196 D1
Haywards Cl RM6 .58 C4
Hayward's Pl EC1 .241 C6
Haywood Cl HA5 .22 D1
Haywood Lo 23 N7 .71 D3
N11 .31 D4
Haywood Rd BR2 .209 D5
Haywood Rise BR6 .227 C3
Hazel Ave UB7 .104 C3
Hazel Bank SE25 .183 C1
Tolworth KT5 .199 A1
Hazel Cl N13 .17 B1
Hazel Cl *continued*
N19 .71 C6
SE15 .140 A3
Brentford TW8 .131 B5
Croydon CR0 .206 D1
Mitcham CR4 .203 D5
Twickenham TW2 .152 A4
Hazel Ct 9 SW16 .182 C5
W5 .110 A6
Hazel Gdns HA8 .26 D6
Hazel Gr SE26 .184 D6
Dagenham RM6 .59 A6
Enfield EN1 .18 A5
Orpington BR6 .226 D6
Wembley HA0 .88 A6
Hazel Ho 12 NW3 .70 D2
SE4 .141 B2
Hazel Mead EN5 .12 B6
Hazel Rd E15 .76 C3
NW10 .90 C4
Hazel Way E4 .35 B4
SE1 .263 C4
Hazel Wlk BR2 .210 C3
Hazelbank Rd SE6 .164 C2
Hazelbourne Rd SW12 .159 B5
Hazelbury Cl SW19 .179 C1
Hazelbury Gn N9 .17 C1
Hazelbury Inf Sch N9 .17 C1
Hazelbury Jun Sch N9 .17 C1
Hazelbury La N9 .17 C1
Hazelcroft HA5 .23 D4
Hazelcroft Cl UB10 .60 B1
Hazeldean Rd NW10 .67 B1
Hazeldene Dr HA5 .40 C6
Hazeldene Gdns UB10 .83 A6
Hazeldene Rd
Bexley DA16 .146 C3
Ilford IG3 .80 B6
Hazeldon Rd SE4 .163 A6
Hazelgreen Cl N21 .16 D3
Hazelhurst BR3 .186 B2
Hazelhurst Ct SE6 .186 A5
Hazelhurst Rd SW17 .180 B6
Hazelhurst Sch SW20 .178 D2
Hazellville Rd N19 .49 D1
Hazelmere Cl
Hatton TW14 .149 C5
Northolt UB5 .85 B5
Hazelmere Ct 10 SW2 .160 B3
Hazelmere Dr UB5 .85 B5
Hazelmere Rd NW6 .91 B6
Northolt UB5 .85 B5
Petts Wood BR5 .211 B5
Hazelmere Way BR2 .209 A3
Hazelmere Wlk UB5 .85 B5
Hazeltree La UB5 .85 A4
Hazelwood IG10 .21 D6
Hazelwood Ave SM4 .201 D5
Hazelwood Cl E5 .75 A5
W5 .110 A4
Harrow HA2 .41 D5
Hazelwood Cres N13 .32 C6
Hazelwood Ct 1 NW10 .67 C5
Surbiton KT6 .198 A3
Hazelwood Dr HA5 .22 B1
Hazelwood Ho N13 .32 D6
11 SE8 .119 A2
Beckenham BR2 .208 C6
Hazelwood Jun & Inf Schs
N13 .32 C6
Hazelwood La N13 .32 C6
Hazelwood Lo BR4 .208 A2
Hazelwood Mans SW6 .264 C2
Hazelwood Rd E17 .53 A4
Enfield EN1 .17 D5
Hazlebury Rd SW6 .135 D3
Hazledean Rd CR0 .221 B6
Hazledene Rd W4 .133 A6
Hazlemere Gdns KT4 .200 A1
Hazlewell Rd SW15 .156 C6
Hazlewood Cres W10 .91 A3
Hazlewood Twr W10 .91 B3
Hazlitt Cl TW13 .173 A6
Hazlitt Ct 4 SE28 .124 C5
Hazlitt Mews W14 .254 A5
Hazlitt Rd W14 .113 A3 254 A5
Heacham Ave UB10 .61 A5
Head St E1 .96 D1
Headbourne Ho SE1 .262 D6
Headcorn 10 NW5 .71 A2
Headcorn Pl CR7 .204 B5
Headcorn Rd N17 .33 D3
Plaistow BR1 .187 A5
Thornton Heath CR7 .204 B5
Headfort Pl
SW1 .115 A4 248 B1
Headington Rd SW18 .158 A2
Headlam Rd SW4 .159 D4
Headlam St E1 .96 B3
Headley App IG2 .56 D4
Headley Ave CR0,SM6 .220 B3
Headley Cl KT19 .214 C2
Headley Ct SE26 .184 C5
Headley Dr Ilford IG2 .56 D3
New Addington CR0 .224 A1
Headley Ho 5 BR5 .190 B1
Heads Mews W11 .91 C1
Headstone Dr HA1,HA3 .42 C6
Headstone Gdns HA2 .42 A5
Headstone La
Harrow HA2 .41 D5
Harrow HA2,HA3 .23 D2
Headstone Lane Sta
HA3 .23 D2
Headstone Rd HA1 .42 C3
Headway Cl TW10 .175 C6
Heald St SE8,SE14 .141 C4
Healey Ho 2 E3 .97 C3

Healey St NW1 ...71 B2
Healy Ct EN5 ...12 D5
Healy Dr 1 BR6 ...227 D4
Healy Ho 12 SW9 ...138 C5
Heanor Ct 4 E5 ...74 D4
Hearn Rise UB5 ...84 D6
Hearn St EC2 ...95 C3 243 B5
Hearne Rd W4 ...132 C6
Hearn's Bldgs SE17 ...262 D3
Hearnshaw Ho 9 E14 ...97 A2
Hearnville Prim Sch
SW12 ...159 A3
Hearnville Rd SW12 ...159 A3
Heath Ave DA7 ...147 A6
Heath Brow NW3 ...70 A5
Heath Bsns Ctr The
TW3 ...130 A1
Heath Cl NW11 ...47 D2
W5 ...88 B3
Harlington UB3 ...127 B5
Heath Ct E11 ...54 D3
N16 ...51 B1
2 NW3 ...70 A2
Uxbridge UB8 ...60 A1
Heath Dr SW20 ...200 C5
Heath Gdns TW1 ...152 D2
Heath Gr SE20 ...184 C3
Ashford TW16 ...171 D3
Heath Ho Sidcup DA15 ...189 D6
Thornton Heath CR7 ...204 C4
Uxbridge UB10 ...60 D4
Heath Hurst Rd NW3 ...70 C4
Heath La SE3 ...142 B3
Heath Lo WD2 ...8 B3
Heath Mans 4 NW3 ...70 A4
SW15 ...156 D5
Heath Mead SW19 ...156 D1
Heath Park Dr BR1 ...210 A6
Heath Park Gdns NW3 ...69 D5
Heath Rd SW8 ...137 B3
Dagenham RM6 ...59 A2
Harrow HA1 ...42 A2
Hillingdon UB10 ...83 A3
Isleworth TW3,TW7 ...130 A1
South Norwood CR7 ...205 A6
Twickenham TW1 ...152 D3
Heath Rise SW15 ...156 D5
Hayes BR2 ...208 D3
Heath Royal SW15 ...156 D5
Heath Side BR5 ...211 A2
Heath St NW3 ...70 A5
Heath Terr RM6 ...58 D2
Heath The W7 ...108 C5
Heath View N2 ...48 A5
NW5 ...71 A4
Heath View Cl N2 ...48 A5
Heath View Dr SE2 ...146 D6
Heath Villas SE18 ...123 D1
Heatham Pk TW2 ...152 D4
Heathbourne Rd WD2,HA7 8 D3
Heathbrook Prim Sch
SW4 ...137 C3
Heathcote Gr E4 ...20 A2
Heathcote High Sch E4 .20 C2
Heathcote Rd TW1 ...153 B6
Heathcote St
WC1 ...94 B4 233 C1
Heathcroft NW11 ...47 D1
W5 ...88 B3
Heathcroft Ave TW16 ...171 D3
Heathcroft Gdns E4 ...36 B2
Heathdale Ave TW4 ...129 A2
Heathdene N14 ...15 C4
Heathdene Dr DA17 ...125 D2
Heathdene Rd SW16 ...182 B3
Wallington SM5,SM6 ...219 B1
Heathedge SE23,SE26 ...162 B2
Heather Cl E6 ...100 C1
SE13 ...164 B3
SW8 ...137 B2
Hampton TW12 ...173 B2
Hillingdon UB8 ...82 B2
Isleworth TW7 ...152 B6
Heather Ct SW4 ...270 B1
Heather Dr EN2 ...4 D3
Heather Gdns NW11 ...47 A3
Sutton SM2 ...217 C2
Heather Ho 7 E14 ...98 A1
Heather La UB7 ...82 A1
Heather Lo N16 ...51 C1
Heather Park Dr HA0 ...66 C1
Heather Park Par HA0 ...66 B1
Heather Rd E4 ...35 B4
NW2 ...67 D6
SE12 ...165 A3
Heather Way HA7 ...24 D4
Heather Wlk W10 ...91 A3
Edgware HA8 ...26 D5
Twickenham TW4 ...151 C4
Heatherbank SE9 ...144 B3
Bickley BR7 ...188 C1
Heatherdale Cl KT2 ...176 D3
Heatherdene Cl N12 ...30 A2
Mitcham CR4 ...202 C5
Heatherdene Mans 2
TW1 ...153 D5
Heatherlands TW16 ...172 A4
Heatherley Ct N16 ...74 A5
Heatherley Dr IG5 ...56 B6
Heatherley Sch of Fine Art
SW10 ...266 B3
Heathers The TW19 ...148 B4
Heatherset Cl KT10 ...212 A3
Heatherset Gdns SW16 182 B3
Heatherside Rd
Sidcup DA14 ...168 C1
West Ewell KT19 ...215 B1
Heatherwood Cl E12 ...77 C6
Heatherwood Dr UB4 ...83 B5
Heathfield E4 ...20 A1
Chislehurst West BR7 ...189 A4
Heathfield Ave SW18 ...158 B4
Heathfield Cl E16 ...99 D2
Keston BR2 ...225 C3
Heathfield Ct SE20 ...184 C3
SW18 ...158 B4
5 W4 ...111 B1
Ashford TW15 ...148 A1
Sidcup DA14 ...190 B5
Heathfield Dr CR4 ...180 C2
Heathfield Gdns NW11 ...46 D3
SW18 ...158 B5
W4 ...111 A1
Croydon CR0 ...221 B4
Heathfield Ho SE3 ...142 C3
Heathfield Inf Sch TW2 151 C3
Heathfield Jun Sch
TW2 ...151 C3
Heathfield La BR7 ...189 A4
Heathfield N TW1,TW2 ...152 D4
Heathfield Park Dr RM6 .58 B4
Heathfield Pk NW2 ...68 C2
Heathfield Rd SW18 ...158 B5
W3 ...110 D4
Bexley DA6 ...147 B1
Bromley BR1 ...186 D3
Croydon CR0 ...221 B4
Keston BR2 ...225 D3
Heathfield Rise HA4 ...39 A2
Heathfield S TW1,TW2 ...152 D4
Heathfield Sch HA5 ...40 D2
Heathfield Sq SW18 ...158 B4
Heathfield Terr SE18 ...145 D6
W4 ...111 B1
Heathfield Vale CR2 ...223 A1
Heathfielde N2 ...48 A4
Heathgate NW11 ...47 D3
Heathland Rd N16 ...51 C1
Heathland Sch The
TW4 ...151 B5
Heathlands Cl
Sunbury TW16 ...172 A1
Twickenham TW1 ...152 D3
Heathlands Ct
Hounslow TW4 ...151 A6
Mitcham CR4 ...203 A6
Heathlands Sch SW19 ...156 C1
Heathlands Way TW4 ...151 A6
Heathlee Rd SE3 ...142 D1
Heathley End BR7 ...189 A4
Heathman's Rd
SW6 ...135 B4 264 D1
Heathmere Prim Sch
SW15 ...156 A3
Heathpool Ct 8 E1 ...96 B3
Heathrow Airport London
TW6 ...126 D3
Heathrow Bvd UB7 ...126 B5
Heathrow Causeway Est
TW4 ...128 B2
Heathrow Central Sta
TW6 ...126 D2
Heathrow International Trad
Est TW4 ...128 B2
Heathrow Sch UB7 ...126 B6
Heathrow Terminal 4 Sta
TW6 ...149 A5
Heath's Cl EN1 ...5 C3
Heathshot 8 TW10 ...154 A5
Heathside NW3 ...70 B4
Hinchley Wood KT10 ...212 C5
Twickenham TW4 ...151 B4
Heathside Ave DA7 ...147 A3
Heathside Cl KT10 ...212 C5
Heathside Prep Sch
NW3 ...70 A4
Heathstan Rd W12 ...90 A1
Heathview Ct SW19 ...156 D2
Heathview Gdns SW15 ...156 C4
Heathview Rd CR7 ...204 C5
Heathville Rd N4,N19 ...50 A2
Heathwall St SW11 ...136 D2
Heathway SE3 ...143 A5
6 SE3 ...142 D5
Croydon CR0 ...223 B5
Dagenham RM10 ...81 C2
Dagenham RM10 ...103 C6
Woodford IG8 ...37 C5
Heathway Ct NW3 ...69 C6
Heathwood Ct SW12 ...159 C3
1 Hounslow TW3 ...129 D1
Heathwood Gdns SE7 ...122 A1
Heathwood Point 7
SE26 ...162 D1
Heaton Cl E4 ...20 A1
Heaton Ho 6 SE15 ...140 B3
SW10 ...266 B6
Heaton Rd SE15 ...140 B3
Mitcham CR4 ...181 A3
Heaver Rd 24 SW11 ...136 B2
Heavers Farm Prim Sch
SE25 ...205 D4
Heavitree Cl SE18 ...123 B1
Heavitree Rd SE18 ...123 B1
Hebden Ct 22 E2 ...95 D6
Hebden Terr N17 ...33 C4
Hebdon Rd SW17 ...158 C1
Heber Prim Sch SE22 ...161 D5
Heber Rd NW2 ...68 D4
SE22 ...161 D5
Hebron Rd W6 ...112 B3
Hecham Cl E17 ...35 A2
Heckfield Pl
SW6 ...135 C5 265 A3
Heckford St E1 ...118 D6
Hector 31 NW9 ...27 D2
Hector Ct 1 SW9 ...138 C4
SW15 ...156 D6
Hector Ho 14 E2 ...96 B5
Hector St SE18 ...123 C2
Heddington Gr N7 ...72 B3
Heddon Cl TW7 ...131 A1
Heddon Court Ave EN4 .14 D6
Heddon Court Par EN4 ...15 A6
Heddon Ct EN4 ...15 A6
Heddon Rd EN4 ...14 D6
Heddon St W1 ...249 A6
Hedge Hill EN2 ...4 D4
Hedge La N13 ...17 A1
Hedge Wlk SE6 ...185 D6
Hedgeley IG4 ...56 B5
Hedgemans Rd RM9 ...81 A1
Hedgemans Way RM9 ...81 A2
Hedgemoor Ct 1 E4 ...36 B5
Hedger St SE11 ...261 C4
Hedgerley Gdns UB6 ...86 A5
Hedgerow La EN5 ...12 B6
Hedger's Gr E9 ...75 A2
Hedgewood Gdns IG5 ...56 C4
Hedgewood Specl Sch
UB4 ...83 C4
Hedgley St SE12 ...164 D6
Hedingham Cl 6 N1 ...73 A1
Hedingham Rd RM8 ...80 B3
Hedley Ct SW15 ...156 D5
Hedley Ho E14 ...120 A3
Hedley Rd TW4 ...151 C4
Hedley Row N5,N16 ...73 B3
Hedsor Ho E2 ...243 C6
Heenan Cl IG11 ...79 A2
Heene Rd EN2 ...5 B4
Heidegger Cres SW13 ...134 B5
Heigham Rd E6 ...78 A1
Heighgate Pl NW3 ...70 D4
Heighton Gdns CR0 ...220 D3
Heights Cl SW20 ...178 B3
Heights The N4 ...50 C3
NW3 ...70 A4
SE7 ...121 C1
Beckenham BR3 ...186 A3
Northolt UB5 ...63 C3
Heiron St SE17 ...138 D6
Helby Rd SW4 ...159 D5
Heldar Ct SE1 ...252 D1
Helder Gr SE12 ...164 D4
Helder St CR2 ...221 B2
Heldmann Cl TW7 ...130 B1
Helegan Cl BR6 ...227 D4
Helen Ave TW14 ...150 B4
Helen Cl N2 ...48 A6
East Molesey KT8 ...195 D5
Helen Ct N3 ...47 A6
Helen Gladstone Ho
SE1 ...251 C2
Helen Ho 9 E2 ...96 B5
Helen Mackay Ho 9 E14 98 B1
Helen Peele Cotts 10
SE16 ...118 C3
Helen St SE18 ...122 D2
Helen Taylor Ho 5
SE16 ...118 A2
Helena Cl Barnet EN4 ...2 B5
Wallington SM6 ...220 A1
Helena Ct W5 ...87 D2
Helena Rd E13 ...99 A5
E17 ...53 C4
NW10 ...68 B3
W5 ...87 D2
Helena Sq 12 SE16 ...119 A6
Helen's Pl E2 ...96 C4
Helenslea Ave NW11 ...47 C1
Helford Cl HA4 ...61 C6
Helgiford Gdns TW16 ...171 C3
Heliport Est The SW11 ...136 B3
Helix Gdns SW2 ...160 B5
Helix Ho TW7 ...131 B3
Helix Rd SW2 ...160 B5
Hellenic Coll of London
SW1 ...114 D3 257 C5
Hellings St E1 ...118 A5
Helme Cl SW19 ...179 B5
Helmet Row EC1 ...242 B6
Helmsdale Cl UB4 ...85 A3
Helmsdale Ho NW6 ...91 D5
Helmsdale Rd SW16 ...181 D2
Helmsley 10 E18 ...55 A6
Helmsley Pl E8 ...74 B1
Helmsley St 7 E8 ...74 B1
Helsby Ct NW8 ...236 C6
Helsinki Sq SE16 ...119 A3
Helston NW1 ...232 B4
Helston Cl HA5 ...23 B3
Helston Ct N15 ...51 C4
Helston Ho SE11 ...261 B2
Helvetia St SE6 ...163 B2
Helwys Ct E4 ...36 A4
Hemans Est
SW8 ...137 D5 269 D3
Hemans St
SW8 ...137 D5 269 D3
Hemberton Rd SW9 ...138 A2
Hemery Rd UB6 ...64 B3
Heming Rd HA8 ...26 D3
Hemingford Cl N12 ...30 B5
Hemingford Rd
N1 ...72 B1 233 D6
Cheam SM3 ...216 C4
Hemington Ave N11 ...30 D5
Hemlington Ho 11 E14 ...97 A2
Hemlock Rd W12 ...111 D6
Hemmen La UB3 ...83 D1
Hemming Cl 5 TW12 ...173 C2
Hemming St E1 ...96 A3
Hemmings Cl DA14 ...168 B2
Hemmings Ct HA8 ...27 A3
Hemp Wlk SE17 ...262 D4
Hempstead Cl IG9 ...21 A2
Hempstead Rd E17 ...36 B1
Hemstal Rd NW6 ...69 C1
Hemswell Dr NW9 ...27 C2
Hemsworth Ct N1 ...95 C5
Hemsworth St N1 ...95 C5
Hemus Pl SW3 ...257 B1
Henchman St W12 ...89 D1
Hendale Ave NW4 ...46 B6
Hendale Ho 13 E5 ...74 B6
Henderson Cl NW10 ...67 A2
Henderson Ct NW3 ...70 B3
8 SE14 ...140 D6
Henderson Dr
NW8 ...92 B3 236 C6
Henderson Ho 7 RM10 ...81 C5
Henderson Rd E7 ...77 C2
N9 ...18 B3
SW18 ...158 C4
Hayes UB4 ...84 A4
Thornton Heath CR0 ...205 B3
Hendfield Ct 5 SM6 ...219 B2
Hendham Rd SW17 ...158 D2
Hendon Ave N3 ...29 A2
Hendon Central NW4 ...46 B4
Hendon Central Sta
NW4 ...46 B4
Hendon Coll NW9 ...27 D2
Hendon Coll (School of
English) NW4 ...46 A3
Hendon Hall Ct NW4 ...46 D6
Hendon Ho NW4 ...46 D4
Hendon La N3 ...29 B1
Hendon Lo NW4 ...46 B6
Hendon Park Mans NW4 46 C4
Hendon Park Row NW11 47 B3
Hendon Prep Sch NW4 ...46 D6
Hendon Rd N9 ...18 A2
Hendon Sch NW4 ...46 D4
Hendon Sta NW4 ...46 A3
Hendon Terr TW15 ...171 B4
Hendon Way NW2 ...46 C3
Hendon Wood La NW7 ...12 A3
Hendre Ho SE1 ...263 B3
Hendre Rd SE1 .117 C2 263 B3
Hendren Cl UB6 ...64 B3
Hendrick Ave SW12 ...158 D4
Heneage La EC3 ...243 B1
Heneage Pl EC3 ...243 B1
Heneage St E1 ...95 D2 243 D4
Henfield Cl N19 ...49 C1
Bexleyheath DA5 ...169 C5
Henfield Rd SW19,SW20 179 B2
Hengelo Gdns CR4 ...202 B5
Hengist Rd SE12 ...165 B4
Erith DA8 ...147 D5
Hengist Way BR2,BR3 ...208 C5
Hengrave Rd SE23 ...162 D4
Hengrove Ct DA5 ...169 A3
Henley Ave SM3 ...217 A5
Henley Cl SE16 ...118 C4
Greenford UB6 ...86 A5
Hounslow TW7 ...130 D4
Henley Ct N14 ...15 C4
NW2 ...68 D2
NW4 ...46 A6
SE15 ...140 A2
Mitcham CR4 ...203 A6
Henley Dr SE1 .117 D2 263 D4
Kingston u T KT2 ...177 D3
Henley Gdns
Dagenham RM6 ...59 A4
Pinner HA5 ...40 B6
Henley Ho E2 ...243 D6
N12 ...30 B5
Henley Lo E17 ...53 B4
SE25 ...205 D5
Henley Prior N1 ...233 C3
Henley Rd E16 ...122 B4
N18 ...33 C6
NW10 ...90 C6
Ilford IG1 ...79 B4
Henley St SW11 ...137 A3
Henley Way TW13 ...172 D5
Henleys Cnr NW11 ...47 B5
Henlys Rdbt TW5 ...128 C3
Hennel Cl SE23 ...162 C1
Henniker Gdns E6 ...100 A4
Henniker Mews SW3 ...266 C6
Henniker Point E15 ...76 C3
Henniker Rd E15 ...76 B3
Henning St
SW11 ...136 C4 267 A1
Henningham Rd N17 ...33 B2
Henrietta Barnett Sch
NW11 ...47 D3
Henrietta Cl SE8 ...141 C6
Henrietta Ho 3 N15 ...51 C3
11 W6 ...112 C1
Henrietta Mews WC1 ...240 B6
Henrietta Pl W1 .93 B1 238 C2
Henrietta St E15 ...76 A3
WC2 ...116 A6 250 B6
Henriques St E1 ...96 A1
Henry Cavendish Prim Sch
SW12 ...159 C3
Henry Cl EN2 ...5 C5
Henry Compton Sec Sch
SW6 ...135 A4 264 A2
Henry Cooper Way
SE12 ...187 D6
Henry Darlot Dr NW7 ...29 A5
Henry Dickens Ct W11 ...244 A4
Henry Doulton Dr
SW17 ...181 B6
Henry Fawcett Prim Sch
SE11 ...138 C6
Henry Green Prim Sch
RM8 ...80 D6
Henry Hatch Ct SM2 ...218 A1
Henry Ho NW8 ...230 A4
SE1 ...251 B3
SW8 ...270 A4
Henry Jackson Ho
SW15 ...134 D2
Henry Jackson Rd
SW15 ...134 D2
Henry Maynard Inf Sch
E17 ...54 A4
Henry Maynard Jun Sch
E17 ...54 A4
Henry Peters Dr TW11 .174 C5
Henry Rd E6 ...100 A5
N4 ...51 A1
New Barnet EN4 ...14 B6
Henry St BR1 ...187 B2
Henry Wise Ho SW1 ...259 B3
Henry's Ave IG8 ...36 D5
Henryson Rd SE4 ...163 C6
Hensford Gdns SE26 ...184 B6
Henshall Point 19 E3 ...97 D4
Henshall St N1 ...73 B2
Henshaw St
SE17 ...117 B2 262 C4
Henshawe Rd RM8 ...80 D5
Henslow Ho 11 SE15 ...140 A5
Henslowe Rd SE22 ...162 A6
Henson Ave NW2 ...68 C3
Henson Cl BR6 ...226 D6
Henson Ct 3 N5 ...73 A4
Henson Pl UB5 ...84 C6
Henstridge Pl
NW8 ...92 C5 230 A4
Henty Cl SW11 .136 C4 267 B2
Henty Wlk SW15 ...156 B6
Henville Rd BR1 ...187 B2
Henwick Prim Sch SE9 144 A2
Henwick Rd SE9 ...144 A2
Hepburn Gdns BR2 ...208 D1
Hepburn Mews SW11 ...158 D6
Hepple Cl TW7 ...131 B3
Hepplestone Cl SW15 ...156 B5
Hepscott Rd E9 ...75 C1
Hepworth Ct
Barking IG11 ...80 A3
Cheam SM3 ...201 C1
Hepworth Gdns IG11 ...80 A3
Hepworth Ho IG8 ...21 A1
Hepworth Rd SW16 ...182 A3
Hepworth Way KT12 ...193 D1
Hera Ct 7 E14 ...119 C2
Heracles 30 NW9 ...27 D2
Heracles Cl SM6 ...220 A1
Herald Gdns SM6 ...219 B5
Herald St 5 E2 ...96 B3
Heralds Pl SE11 ...261 C4
Herbal Hill EC1 ...241 B5
Herbert Chapman Ct N5 72 D4
Herbert Cres SW1 ...257 D6
Herbert Gdns NW10 ...90 B5
W4 ...132 D6
Romford RM6 ...58 D2
Herbert Ho E1 ...243 C2
Herbert Morrison Ho
SW6 ...264 C5
Herbert Morrison Prim Sch
SW8 ...138 A5 270 B3
Herbert Pl SE18 ...144 D6
Herbert Rd E12 ...78 A4
E17 ...53 B2
N11 ...32 A3
N15 ...51 D4
NW9 ...46 A3
SE18 ...144 D6
SW19 ...179 B3
Bexleyheath DA7 ...147 A3
Bromley BR2 ...210 A4
Ilford IG3 ...79 C6
Kingston u T KT1 ...198 B6
Southall UB1 ...107 B5
Herbert St E13 ...99 A5
NW5 ...71 A2
Herbrand Est
WC1 ...94 A3 240 A6
Herbrand St
WC1 ...94 A3 240 A6
Hercies Rd UB10 ...60 C2
Hercules Pl N7 ...72 A5
Hercules Rd
SE1 ...116 B3 260 D5
Hercules St N7 ...72 A5
Hercules Twr SE14 ...141 A6
Hereford Ave EN4 ...14 D3
Hereford Bldgs SW3 ...266 D6
Hereford Ct 6 W7 ...86 D2
12 Belmont SM2 ...217 C1
6 Croydon CR0 ...205 D1
Harrow HA1 ...42 C6
Hereford Gdns SE13 ...164 C6
Pinner HA5 ...41 A4
Redbridge IG1 ...56 A2
Twickenham TW2 ...152 A3
Hereford Ho 26 SE5 ...139 A3
7 SE18 ...122 B2
5 SW2 ...138 C1
SW3 ...257 B6
SW10 ...265 D4
7 W3 ...88 C1
Hereford Mans 10 W2 ...91 C1
Hereford Mews 11 W2 ...91 C1
Hereford Pl SE14 ...141 B5
Hereford Rd E11 ...55 B4
W2 ...91 C1 245 B6
Hereford Rd *continued*
W3 ...111 A6
W5 ...109 C3
Feltham TW13 ...150 C3
Hereford Retreat 5
SE15 ...140 A5
Hereford Sq
SW7 ...114 A2 256 B3
Hereford St E2 ...96 A3
Hereford Way KT9 ...213 D3
Herent Dr IG5 ...56 B6
Hereward Gdns N13 ...32 C5
Hereward Rd SW17 ...180 D6
Herga Ct HA1 ...64 C6
Herga Rd HA3 ...42 D5
Heriot Ave E4 ...19 C2
Heriot Rd NW4 ...46 C4
Heriots Cl HA7 ...25 A6
Heritage Cl SW9 ...138 D2
Heritage Ct SE8 ...118 D1
Heritage Hill BR2 ...225 C3
Heritage Ho 22 SW19 ...156 D3
Heritage View HA1 ...64 D5
Herlwyn Ave HA4 ...61 C5
Herlwyn Gdns SW17 ...180 D6
Herm Cl TW7 ...130 A5
Herm Ho 10 N1 ...73 A2
Enfield EN3 ...6 D5
Hermes Ct 4 SW9 ...138 C4
Hermes Ho BR3 ...185 A2
Hermes St N1 ...234 A3
Hermes Way SM6 ...219 D1
Hermes Wlk UB5 ...85 C5
Hermiston Ave N8 ...50 A4
Hermit Pl NW6 ...91 D6
Hermit Rd E16 ...98 D3
Hermit St EC1 ...234 C2
Hermitage Cl E18 ...54 D5
Claygate KT10 ...213 A2
Enfield EN2 ...4 D3
Littleton TW17 ...192 C5
Hermitage Ct 14 E1 ...118 A5
3 E18 ...55 A5
2 NW2 ...69 C5
Hermitage Gdns NW2 ...69 C5
SE19 ...183 A3
Hermitage JMI Sch E1 118 A5
Hermitage La NW2 ...69 C5
SW16 ...182 B3
Croydon CR0 ...206 A3
Hermitage Rd N4,N15 ...51 A3
SE19 ...183 B4
Hermitage Row 9 E8 ...74 A3
Hermitage St W2 ...236 C3
Hermitage The SE23 ...162 C3
SW13 ...133 D4
Feltham TW13 ...149 D1
Kingston u T KT1 ...197 D5
Richmond TW10 ...154 A6
Uxbridge UB8 ...60 A2
Hermitage Wall E1 ...118 A5
Hermitage Way HA7 ...25 A2
Hermitage Wlk E18 ...54 D5
Hermon Gr UB3 ...106 A5
Hermon Hill E11 ...55 A5
Herndon Rd SW18 ...158 A6
Herne Cl NW10 ...67 B3
Herne Ct WD2 ...8 A4
Herne Hill SE24 ...161 A6
Herne Hill Ho SE24 ...160 D5
Herne Hill Mans SE24 ...161 A5
Herne Hill Rd SE24 ...139 A1
Herne Hill Sta SE24 ...160 D5
Herne Hill Stadium
SE24 ...161 B5
Herne Mews N18 ...34 A6
Herne Pl SE24 ...160 D6
Herne Rd KT6 ...214 A6
Heron Cl E17 ...35 B1
NW10 ...67 C2
Buckhurst Hill IG9 ...21 A3
Cheam SM1 ...217 B3
Heron Cres DA14 ...189 C6
Heron Ct 14 E14 ...120 A3
6 SE21 ...161 B2
9 SE23 ...162 C3
Bromley BR2 ...209 C5
5 Kingston u T KT1 ...198 A6
Ruislip HA4 ...61 B6
Stanwell TW19 ...148 A3
Heron Dr N4 ...73 A6
Heron Hill DA17 ...125 B2
Heron Ho NW8 ...230 A3
SE15 ...139 D4
SW11 ...267 B2
W13 ...87 A3
Teddington KT1 ...175 C2
Heron Ind Est E15 ...97 D5
Heron Mews IG1 ...78 D6
Heron Pl SE16 ...119 A5
W1 ...238 B2
Heron Quays E14 ...119 C5
Heron Quays Sta E14 ...119 C5
Heron Rd SE24 ...139 A1
Croydon CR0 ...221 C6
Isleworth TW1 ...131 B1
Heron Sq 25 TW10 ...153 D6
Heron Trad Est W3 ...88 D2
Herondale Ave SW18 ...158 C3
Herongate N1 ...235 B6
Herongate Rd E12 ...77 C6
Heron's Lea N6 ...48 D3
Herons Pl TW7 ...131 B2
Herons Rise EN4 ...2 C1
Herons The E11 ...54 D3

Heronsforde W13 . . . . .87 C1
Heronsgate HA8 . . . . .26 C5
Heronsgate Prim Sch
  SE28 . . . . .123 B3
Heronslea Dr HA7 . . . . .26 A1
Heronway IG8 . . . . .37 C6
Herrick Ct **4** TW10 . . .175 D6
Herrick Ho **17** N16 . . . .73 B4
  18 SE5 . . . . .139 B5
Herrick Rd N5 . . . . .73 A5
Herrick St SW1 115 D2 **259 D3**
Herries St W10 . . . . .91 A5
Herringham Rd SE7 . . . . . .121 C3
Herrongate Cl EN1 . . . . .5 D3
Hersant Cl NW10 . . . . .90 A6
Herschell Rd SE23 . . . . . . .163 A4
Herschell's Mews SE5 . . . .139 A2
Hersham Cl SW15 . . . . . . .156 A4
Hersham Rd KT12 . . . . . . .194 A1
Hershell Ct **1** SW14 . . .132 D1
Hertford Ave SW14 . . . . . .133 C1
Hertford Cl EN4 . . . . .2 B2
Hertford Ct E6 . . . . .100 B4
  N13 . . . . .16 C1
  16 SW11 . . . . .136 C2
Hertford Lo **10** SW19 . . .157 A3
Hertford Pl W1 . . . .**239 B5**
Hertford Rd N1 . . . . .95 C6
  N2 . . . . .48 C6
  N9 . . . . .18 B3
  Barking IG11 . . . . .78 C1
  Barnet EN4 . . . . .2 A2
  Enfield EN3 . . . . .6 C5
  Ilford IG2 . . . . .57 C3
Hertford Rd High S: EN3 18 B3
Hertford Sq CR4 . . . . .204 A5
Hertford St W1 115 B5 **248 C3**
Hertford Way CR4 . . . . . . .204 A5
Hertford Wlk **13** DA17 . .125 C1
Hertmitage The **4**
  SE13 . . . . .142 A3
Hertslet Rd N7 . . . . .72 B5
Hertsmere Rd E14 . . . . . . .119 C6
Hertswood Ct **1** EN5 . . . . .1 A1
Hervey Cl N3 . . . . .29 C2
Hervey Park Rd E17 . . . . . . .53 A5
Hervey Rd SE3 . . . . .143 B4
Hesa Rd UB3 . . . . .106 A6
Hesewall Ct SW14 . . . . . . .137 C3
Hesketh Pl W11 . . . .**244 A5**
Hesketh Rd E7 . . . . .77 A5
Heslop Ct **1** SW12 . . . . .159 A3
Heslop Rd SW12 . . . . .158 D3
Hesper Mews
  SW5 . . . . .113 D2 **255 C3**
Hesperus Cres E14 . . . . . .119 D2
Hessel Rd W13 . . . . .109 B4
Hessel St E1 . . . . .96 B1
Hester Rd N18 . . . . .34 A5
  SW11 . . . . . . .136 C5 **267 A3**
Hester Terr TW9 . . . . .132 C2
Hestercombe Ave
  SW6 . . . . .135 34 **264 B3**
Hesterman Way CR0 . . . . .204 B1
Heston Ave TW5 . . . . .129 A5
Heston Comm Sch
  TW5 . . . . .129 C5
Heston Ctr The TW5 . . . . .106 C1
Heston Grange TW5 . . . . . .129 B6
Heston Grange La TW5 129 B6
Heston Ho **5** SE8 . . . . . .141 C4
  W4 . . . . .110 A5
Heston Ind Mall TW5 . . . . .129 B5
Heston Inf Sch TW5 . . . . . .129 C5
Heston Jun Sch TW5 . . . . .129 C5
Heston Phoenix Distribution
  Pk TW5 . . . . .128 C6
Heston Rd TW5 . . . . .129 C5
Heston St SE14 . . . . .141 C4
Hetherington Rd
  SW2,SW4 . . . . .138 A1
  Charlton TW17 . . . . . . .171 A1
Hetherington Way UB10 60 A4
Hethpool Ho W2 . . . .**236 C5**
Hetley Gdns **1** SE19 . . .183 D3
Hetley Rd W12 . . . . .112 B4
Heton Gdns NW4 . . . . .46 A5
Hevelius Cl SE10 . . . . .120 D1
Hever Croft SE9 . . . . .188 C6
Hever Gdns BR1 . . . . .188 C1
Hever Ho SE15 . . . . .140 D6
Heverfield Ct CR4 . . . . . . .180 D3
Heverham Rd SE18 . . . . . .123 E1
Heversham Ho SE15 . . . . .140 C6
Heversham Rd DA7 . . . . . .147 C4
Hewens Rd UB4 . . . . .83 A3
Hewer Ho **6** SW4 . . . . . .159 C6
Hewer St W10 . . . . .90 D2
Hewes Ho E17 . . . . .52 D5
Hewett Cl HA7 . . . . .25 B6
Hewett Ho **7** SE18 . . . .122 D1
Hewett Rd RM8 . . . . .80 D4
Hewett St EC2 . . .95 C3 **243 B5**
Hewish Rd N18 . . . . .33 C6
Hewison St E3 . . . . .97 B5
Hewitt Ave N22 . . . . .32 D1
Hewitt Cl CR0 . . . . .223 C6
Hewitt Ho **2** E4 . . . . . . .36 B5
Hewitt Rd N8 . . . . .50 D4
Hewlett Rd E3 . . . . .97 A5
Hewling Ho **1** N16 . . . .73 C3
Hewtt Ho SE15 . . . . .140 C6
Hexagon The N6 . . . . .48 D1
Hexal Rd SE6 . . . . .164 C1
Hexham Gdns TW7 . . . . . .131 A5

Hexham Rd SE27 . . . . . . .161 A2
  Barnet EN5 . . . . .1 D1
  Cheam SM4 . . . . .201 D1
Hey Bridge **9** NW1 . . . . .71 B2
Heybourne Rd N17 . . . . .34 B3
Heybridge Ave SW16 . . . . .182 A3
Heybridge Dr IG6 . . . . .57 B6
Heybridge Way E10 . . . . . . .53 B1
Heydon Ct BR4 . . . . .224 C6
Heydon Ho SE14 . . . . .140 C4
Heyford Ave
  SW8 . . . . .138 A5 **270 B4**
  SW20 . . . . .201 B4
Heyford Rd CR4 . . . . .180 C1
Heygate St
  SE17 . . . . . . .117 A2 **262 B4**
Heylyn Sq E3 . . . . .97 B4
Heynes Rd RM8 . . . . .80 C4
Heysham Dr WD1 . . . . .22 D5
Heysham La NW3 . . . . .69 D5
Heysham Rd N15 . . . . .51 B3
Heythorp St SW18 . . . . . . .157 B2
Heythrop Dr UB10 . . . . .60 B4
Heyward Ct SW2 . . . . .217 C2
Heywood Ave NW9 . . . . . . .27 C2
Heywood Ct **2** HA7 . . . .25 C5
Heywood Ho **11** SE14 . .140 D6
  6 SW2 . . . . .160 C5
Heyworth Rd E5 . . . . .74 B4
  E15 . . . . .76 D4
Hibbert Rd E17 . . . . .53 B2
  Harrow HA3 . . . . .24 D1
Hibbert St SW11 . . . . .136 B2
Hibernia Gdns TW3 . . . . . .151 C3
Hibernia Point **11** SE2 . .124 C4
Hibernia Rd TW3 . . . . .129 C1
Hibiscus Cl HA8 . . . . .27 A6
Hibiscus Lo E15 . . . . .76 C1
Hichisson Rd SE15 . . . . . . .162 C6
Hickes Ho **6** NW6 . . . . .70 B1
Hickey's Almshouses **7**
  TW9 . . . . .132 B1
Hickin Cl SE7 . . . . .121 D2
Hickin St **2** E14 . . . . . . .120 A3
Hickleton Ho **1** W10 . .**232 B5**
Hickling Ho **10** SE16 . . .118 B3
Hickling Rd IG1 . . . . .78 D3
Hickman Ave E4 . . . . .36 A4
Hickman Cl E16 . . . . .99 D2
Hickman Rd RM6 . . . . .58 C2
Hickmore Wlk SW4 . . . . . .137 C2
Hickory Cl N9 . . . . .18 A4
Hicks Ave UB6 . . . . .86 C4
Hicks Cl SW11 . . . . .136 C2
Hicks Ct RM10 . . . . .81 D5
Hicks St SE8 . . . . .119 A1
Hidaburn Ct **8** SW16 . . .181 C6
Hidcote Gdns SW20 . . . . . .200 B6
Hidcote Ho **11** SM2 . . . .218 A1
Hide E6 . . . . .100 C1
Hide Pl SW1 . . . .115 D2 **259 C3**
Hide Rd HA1 . . . . .42 B5
Hide Twr SW1 . . . .**259 C3**
Hieover SE21 . . . . .161 A2
Higgins Ho **7** N1 . . . . . .95 C6
Higgins Wlk TW12 . . . . . . .173 A4
Higginson Ho **2** NW3 . . .70 D1
Higgs Ind Est **9** SE24 . .138 D2
High Acre EN2 . . . . .4 D2
High Ashton **11** KT2 . . . .176 D3
High Barnet Sta EN5 . . . . . . .1 C1
  South Croydon CR2 . . . .221 C1
High Beech N21 . . . . .16 B5
High Beeches DA14 . . . . . .191 A5
High Birch Ct **7** EN4 . . . . .2 C1
High Broom Cres BR4 . . . .207 D2
High Cedar Dr SW20 . . . . .178 B3
High Coombe Pl KT2 . . . . .177 B3
High Cross Ctr The N15 . . . .52 A5
High Cross Rd N17 . . . . .52 A6
High Dene EN2 . . . . .4 D2
High Dr KT2,KT3 . . . . .177 A1
High Elms IG8 . . . . .37 A5
High Elms Rd BR6 . . . . . . .227 A4
High Foleys KT10 . . . . .213 B1
High Gables
  Beckenham BR2 . . . . . . .186 C1
  Loughton IG10 . . . . .21 D6
High Garth KT10 . . . . .212 A2
High Gate Edge N2 . . . . . . .48 C3
High Gr SE18 . . . . .145 B4
  Bromley BR1 . . . . .187 D2
High Hill Ferry **3** E5 . . . .52 B1
High Holborn
  WC1 . . . . .94 B2 **240 C3**
High La W7 . . . . .86 B1
High Level Dr SE26 . . . . . .184 A6
High Limes **2** SE19 . . . .183 C4
High London S N6 . . . . .49 D2
High Mead Harrow HA1 . . . .42 D4
  West Wickham BR4 . . . .224 C6
High Meadow Cl HA5 . . . . . .40 C5
High Meadow Cres NW9 45 B4
High Meads Rd E16 . . . . . . .99 D1
High Mount NW4 . . . . .46 A3
High Oaks EN2 . . . . .4 B5
High Par The SW16 . . . . . .160 A1
High Park Ave TW9 . . . . . .132 C4
High Park Rd TW9 . . . . . . .132 C4
High Path SW19 . . . . .180 A2
High Point N6 . . . . .49 A2
  SE9 . . . . .166 D1
High Range SW20 . . . . . . .178 C3
High Rd E10 . . . . .53 D3
  E18 . . . . .37 A2
  N2 . . . . .48 C6
  N2,N12 . . . . .30 A3
  N11 . . . . .31 B5

High Rd continued
  N15,N17 . . . . .51 D5
  N17 . . . . .33 D2
  N20 . . . . .14 A4
  N22 . . . . .32 B3
  NW10 . . . . .68 A2
  Buckhurst Hill IG9,IG10 . .21 C5
  Bushey WD2 . . . . .8 B3
  Dagenham RM6 . . . . .58 B2
  Harrow Weald HA3 . . . . . .24 C3
  Ilford IG1 . . . . .78 D6
  Ilford IG1,IG3 . . . . .79 C6
  Ilford IG3 . . . . .57 D1
  Loughton IG8,IG9 . . . . . . .21 B2
  Wembley HA0,HA9 . . . . .66 A3
High Ridge N10 . . . . .31 B2
High Road Eastcote HA5 40 B4
High Road Leyton E10 . . . . .75 D6
High Road Leytonstone
  E11 . . . . .76 D3
High Road Woodford Gn
  IG8 . . . . .37 A6
High Road, Ickenham
  UB10 . . . . .61 A6
High Sheldon N6 . . . . .48 D3
High Silver IG10 . . . . .21 D6
High St E11 . . . . .55 A4
  E13 . . . . .99 A5
  E15 . . . . .98 A6
  E17 . . . . .53 B5
  N8 . . . . .50 B5
  N14 . . . . .15 D2
  NW7 . . . . .28 B5
  SE20 . . . . .184 D3
  SE25 . . . . .206 A5
  SW19 . . . . .178 D5
  W3 . . . . .110 D5
  W5 . . . . .109 D6
  Beckenham BR3 . . . . . . .185 C1
  Brentford TW8 . . . . .132 A6
  Bromley BR1 . . . . .187 A1
  Carshalton SM5 . . . . . . .219 A4
  Cheam SM1,KT17 . . . . . .217 A2
  Chipping Barnet EN5 . . . . .1 B1
  Claygate KT10 . . . . .212 D2
  Cranford TW5 . . . . .128 B5
  Croydon CR0 . . . . .221 A5
  East Molesey KT8 . . . . . .195 C5
  Elstree WD6 . . . . .9 D5
  Farnborough BR6 . . . . . .227 A3
  Feltham TW13 . . . . .150 A2
  Green St Grn BR6 . . . . . .227 D2
  Harlington UB3 . . . . .127 B6
  Harrow HA1 . . . . .42 C1
  Hounslow TW3 . . . . .129 D2
  Ilford IG6 . . . . .57 A6
  Kingston u T KT1 . . . . . .197 D6
  New Malden KT3 . . . . . . .199 C5
  Pinner HA5 . . . . .39 C1
  Ruislip HA4 . . . . .39 C1
  Shepperton TW17 . . . . . .193 A3
  Sidcup DA14 . . . . .190 A6
  South Norwood CR7 . . . .205 B5
  Southall UB1 . . . . .107 B5
  Sutton SM1 . . . . .217 D4
  Sutton SM1,SM5 . . . . . .217 D3
  Teddington KT1 . . . . . . .175 D2
  Teddington TW11 . . . . . .175 A4
  Teddington TW12 . . . . . .174 A4
  Thames Ditton KT7 . . . . .197 A3
  Twickenham TW2 . . . . . .152 A4
  Walton-on-T KT12 . . . . . .194 A1
  Wealdstone HA3 . . . . . . .42 C6
  Wemb ey HA9 . . . . .66 B4
  West Wickham BR4 . . . .207 D1
  Yiewsley UB7 . . . . .104 B5
High St Mews SW19 . . . . .179 A5
High St N E6 . . . . .100 A6
  E12 . . . . .78 A2
High St S E6 . . . . .100 A5
High St Collier's Wood
  SW17,SW19 . . . . .180 B4
High Street Harlesden
  NW10 . . . . .89 D5
High Street Harlington
  TW6 . . . . .127 B5
High Street Kensington Sta
  W8 . . . . .113 D2 **245 C5**
High The SW16 . . . . .181 D5
High Timber St EC4 . . . . .**252 A6**
High Tor Cl BR1 . . . . .187 B3
High Trees N20 . . . . .14 A1
  SW2 . . . . .160 C3
  Barnet EN4 . . . . .14 C6
  Croydon CR0 . . . . .207 A1
  Uxbridge UB10 . . . . .61 A6
High View Ave CR0,SM6 220 B3
High View **1** SE19 . . . . .183 D1
  Loughton IG10 . . . . .21 C4
High View HA3 . . . . .24 A3
High View Par **1** IG4 . . .56 B4
High View Prim Sch
  SW11 . . . . .136 B1
  Wallington SM6 . . . . . . .220 A3
High View Rd E18 . . . . .54 D6
  N10 . . . . .30 D2
  SE19 . . . . .183 B4
High Wigsell TW11 . . . . . . .175 A5
High Worple HA2 . . . . .41 B5
Higham St **7** IG8 . . . . . .37 A4
Higham Hill Ho E17 . . . . . . .34 D2
Higham Hill Rd E17 . . . . . . .35 A1
Higham Ho **6** E4 . . . . . .35 C4
Higham Pl E17 . . . . .53 A6
Higham Rd N17 . . . . .51 B6
  Woodford IG8 . . . . .37 A4

Higham St E17 . . . . .53 A6
Higham Station Ave E4 . .35 D4
Highams Lodge Bsns Ctr
  E17 . . . . .52 D6
Highams Park Sch E4 . . . . .36 B4
Highams Park Sta E4 . . . . .36 B4
Highams The E17 . . . . .36 A2
Highbank Way N8 . . . . .50 C3
Highbanks Cl DA16 . . . . . .146 B5
Highbanks Rd HA5 . . . . .24 D1
Highbarrow Rd CR0 . . . . . .206 A1
Highbridge Ct **13** SE14 .140 C5
Highbridge Rd IG11 . . . . . .100 D6
Highbrook Rd SE3 . . . . . . .143 D2
Highbury & Islington Sta
  N1 . . . . .72 D2
Highbury (Arsenal FC)
  N5 . . . . .72 D5
Highbury Ave CR7 . . . . . . .182 D1
Highbury Cl
  New Malden KT3 . . . . . . .199 A4
  West Wickham BR4 . . . .223 D6
Highbury Cnr N5 . . . . .72 C2
Highbury Corner N5 . . . . . .72 C2
Highbury Cres N5 . . . . .72 C2
Highbury Fields Sch N5 72 D3
Highbury Gdns IG3 . . . . . . .79 C6
Highbury Gr N5 . . . . .72 D2
Highbury Grange N5 . . . . . .72 D3
Highbury Grove Ct N5 . . . . .72 C2
Highbury Grove Sch N5 73 A3
Highbury Hill N5 . . . . .72 C4
Highbury New Pk N5 . . . . . .73 A4
Highbury Pk N5 . . . . .72 D4
Highbury Pl N5 . . . . .72 C2
Highbury Quadrant N5 73 A5
Highbury Quadrant Prim Sch
  N5 . . . . .73 A4
Highbury Rd SW19 . . . . . .179 A5
Highbury Station Rd N1 72 C2
Highbury Terr N5 . . . . .72 C2
Highbury Terrace Mews
  N5 . . . . .72 D3
Highclere Rd KT3 . . . . .199 B6
Highclere St SE26 . . . . . . .185 A6
Highcliffe W13 . . . . .87 B2
Highcliffe Dr SW15 . . . . . .155 D5
Highcliffe Gdns IG4 . . . . . . .56 A4
Highcombe SE7 . . . . .143 B6
Highcombe Cl SE9 . . . . . . .166 A3
Highcroft N6 . . . . .49 A3
  NW9 . . . . .45 C4
  2 Kingston u T KT5 . . .198 A4
Highcroft Ave HA0 . . . . .88 C6
Highcroft Gdns NW11 . . . . .47 B3
Highcroft Rd N19 . . . . .50 A2
Highcross Way **4**
  SW15 . . . . .156 A3
Highdaun Dr SW16 . . . . . .204 B5
Highdown KT4 . . . . .215 D6
Highdown Rd SW15 . . . . . .156 B5
Highenden Ho NW8 . . . .**237 A6**
Highfield Bushey WD2 . . . . . .8 A3
  Feltham TW14 . . . . .150 A3
Highfield Ave NW9 . . . . .45 A4
  NW11 . . . . .47 A2
  Erith DA8 . . . . .147 D6
  Greenford UB6 . . . . .64 D3
  Orpington BR6 . . . . .227 D3
  Pinner HA5 . . . . .41 B4
  Wembley HA9 . . . . .66 B5
Highfield Cl N22 . . . . .32 C2
  NW9 . . . . .45 A4
  SE13 . . . . .164 C5
  Long Ditton KT6 . . . . . . .197 C1
Highfield Ct E12 . . . . .77 C6
  N14 . . . . .15 C5
  NW11 . . . . .47 A3
  Mitcham CR4 . . . . .202 C5
Highfield Dr
  Beckenham BR2 . . . . . . .208 D5
  Ickenham UB10 . . . . .60 A5
  West Ewell KT19 . . . . . .215 D2
  West Wickham BR4 . . . .224 A5
Highfield Gdns NW11 . . . . .47 A3
Highfield Gr **1** SE20 . . . .48 D1
Highfield Hill SE19 . . . . . . .183 C3
Highfield Ho **1** N21 . . . .16 D3
Highfield Inf Sch BR2 . . . .208 C5
Highfield Jun & Inf Sch
  N21 . . . . .16 D3
Highfield Jun Sch BR2 . . .208 C5
Highfield Prim Sch
  UB10 . . . . .82 D4
Highfield Rd N21 . . . . .16 D2
  NW11 . . . . .47 A3
  W3 . . . . .89 A2
  Bexley DA6 . . . . .169 B6
  Bromley BR1 . . . . .210 B5
  Carshalton SM1 . . . . . . .218 C3
  Feltham TW13 . . . . .150 A2
  Hounslow TW7 . . . . .130 D4
  St Paul's Cray BR5,BR7 .211 D6
  Tolworth KT5 . . . . .199 A2
  Upper Halliford TW19 . . .193 D4
  Walton-on-T KT12 . . . . . .194 A1
Highfield Sch SW18 . . . . . .158 C4
Highfields SM1 . . . . .217 C6
Highgate Archway N6 . . . . .49 C1
Highgate Ave N6 . . . . .49 B2
Highgate Cemetery*
  N19 . . . . .71 B6
Highgate Cl N6 . . . . .49 A2
Highgate High St N6 . . . . . .49 B1
Highgate Hill N19 . . . . .49 C1
Highgate Ho **11** SE26 . .162 A1
Highgate Hts N6 . . . . .49 C3

Higham St E17 . . . . .53 A6
Highgate Jun Sch N6 . . . .48 D2
Highgate Prim Sch N6 . . .48 D3
Highgate Rd NW5 . . . . .71 B4
Highgate Sch N6 . . . . .49 A3
Highgate Spinney N8 . . . . . .49 D3
Highgate Sta N6 . . . . .49 B3
Highgate West Hill N6 . . . . .71 A6
Highgate Wlk SE23 . . . . . .162 C2
Highgate Wood Sch N8 . .49 C4
Highgrove Cl N11 . . . . .31 A5
  Bromley BR7 . . . . .188 A2
Highgrove Ct BR3 . . . . . . .185 C3
Highgrove Ho HA4 . . . . .40 A3
Highgrove Mews SM5 . . . .218 D5
Highgrove Point **2** NW3 70 A4
Highgrove Rd RM8 . . . . .80 C4
Highgrove Way HA4 . . . . . . .40 A2
Highland Ave W7 . . . . .86 C1
Highland Cotts SM6 . . . . . .219 C4
Highland Croft BR3 . . . . . .185 D4
Highland Ct E18 . . . . .37 B2
Highland Dr WD2 . . . . .8 A4
Highland Lo **3** SE19 . . . .183 D3
Highland Pk TW13 . . . . . . .171 D6
Highland Rd SE19 . . . . . . .183 C4
  Bexleyheath DA6 . . . . . .147 C1
  Bromley BR1 . . . . .186 D2
  Northwood Hills HA6 . . . . .22 A1
Highlands N20 . . . . .14 B2
Highlands Ave N21 . . . . .16 B6
  W3 . . . . .111 A6
Highlands Cl N4 . . . . .50 A2
  Hounslow TW3 . . . . .129 D4
Highlands Ct SE19 . . . . . . .183 C4
Highlands Gdns IG1 . . . . . . .56 B1
Highlands Heath SW15 156 C4
Highlands Prim Sch IG1 56 B1
Highlands Rd N5 . . . . .73 A4
  Barnet EN5 . . . . .13 C1
  Edgware HA8 . . . . .26 D1
Highlands The Barnet EN5 . .1 D1
Highlawn Hall HA1 . . . . .64 C5
Highlea Cl NW9 . . . . .27 C2
Highlever Rd W10 . . . . .90 C2
Highmead **9** N18 . . . . . .34 A5
Highmead Cres HA0 . . . . . .66 B1
Highmore Rd SE3 . . . . .142 C5
Highpoint EN5 . . . . .14 A6
Highshore Rd SE15 . . . . . .139 D3
Highshore Sch SE15 . . . . .139 D4
Highstone Ave E11 . . . . . . .55 A3
Highstone Ct E11 . . . . .55 A4
Highstone Mans **15** NW1 71 C1
Hightrees Ct W7 . . . . .108 C6
Hightrees Ho SW12 . . . . . .159 A5
Highview N8 . . . . .50 A2
  SE18 . . . . .144 D5
  Northolt UB5 . . . . .85 A4
Highview Ave HA8 . . . . .27 A6
Highview Ct **2** SW19 . . .157 A3
Highview Gdns N3 . . . . .47 A6
  N11 . . . . .31 C5
  Edgware HA8 . . . . .27 A6
Highview Rd W13 . . . . .87 A1
  Sidcup DA14 . . . . .190 B6
Highway Bsns Pk The **7**
  E1 . . . . .118 D6
Highway The E1 . . . . .118 C6
  Stanmore HA7 . . . . .25 A3
Highway Trad Ctr The **6**
  E1 . . . . .118 D6
Highwood Ave N12 . . . . . . .30 A6
Highwood Cl BR6 . . . . .227 A6
Highwood Ct N12 . . . . .14 A1
  Barnet EN5 . . . . .13 C6
Highwood Dr BR6 . . . . . . .227 A6
Highwood Gr NW7 . . . . .27 B5
Highwood Hill NW7 . . . . . . .11 D2
Highwood Rd N19 . . . . .72 A5
Highworth Rd N11 . . . . .31 D5
Highworth St NW1 . . . . . .**237 B4**
Hilary Ave CR4 . . . . .203 A6
Hilary Cl SW6 . . . .**265 C4**
  Erith DA7 . . . . .147 D4
Hilary Ct N9 . . . . .18 D3
Hilary Rd W12 . . . . .111 D6
Hilbert Rd SM3 . . . . .216 D5
Hilborough Cl SW19 . . . . . .180 A3
Hilborough Ct **1** E8 . . . . .95 D6
Hilborough Rd **1** E8 . . . . .73 D1
Hilborough Way BR6 . . . . .227 B3
Hilda Rd E6 . . . . .77 D1
  E16 . . . . .98 D3
Hilda Terr **2** SW9 . . . . .138 C3
Hilda Vale Cl BR6 . . . . .226 D4
Hilda Vale Rd BR6 . . . . . . .226 D4
Hildenborough Gdns
  BR1 . . . . .186 D4
Hildenbrough Ho BR3 . . . .185 B3
Hildenlea Pl BR2 . . . . .186 C1
Hilditch Ho **7** TW10 . . . .154 B5
Hildred Ho SW1 . . . .**258 C4**
Hildreth Street Mews **2**
  SW12 . . . . .159 B3
Hildyard Rd SW6 . . . .**265 B6**
Hiley Rd NW10 . . . . .90 C4
Hilfield La WD2 . . . . .8 C6
Hilfield La S WD2 . . . . .8 D5
Hilgrove Rd NW6 . . . . .70 A1
Hiliary Gdns HA7 . . . . .25 C1
Hillary Ct **3** SE9 . . . . . . .166 A2
  Stanwell TW19 . . . . .148 A3
Hillary Ho E14 . . . . .98 A2
Hillary Rd UB2 . . . . .107 C3
Hillary Rise EN5 . . . . .1 C1
Hillbeck Cl SE15 . . . . .140 C5
  SE15 . . . . .140 C6
Hillbeck Way UB6 . . . . .86 B6
Hillbrook Prim Sch &
  Hillcroft Sch Annexe
  SW17 . . . . .181 A6
Hillbrook Rd SW17 . . . . . .181 A6
Hillbrow
  New Malden KT3 . . . . . . .199 D6
  7 Richmond TW10 . . . .154 A5
Hillbrow Ct KT10 . . . . .212 A4
Hillbrow Rd Catford BR1 186 C4
  Esher KT10 . . . . .212 A4
Hillbury Ave HA3 . . . . .43 B4
Hillbury Rd SW17 . . . . .159 B1
Hillcote Ave SW16 . . . . . . .182 C5
Hillcourt Ave N12 . . . . .29 D4
Hillcourt Rd SE22 . . . . . . .162 B5
Hillcrest N6 . . . . .49 A2
  N21 . . . . .16 C4
  SE24 . . . . .139 B1
  W11 . . . .**244 C5**
Hillcrest Ave NW11 . . . . . . .47 A4
  Edgware HA8 . . . . .26 C6
  Pinner HA5 . . . . .40 D5
Hillcrest Cl SE26 . . . . .184 A6
  Beckenham BR3 . . . . . . .207 B3
Hillcrest Ct NW2 . . . . .69 A3
  Sutton SM2 . . . . .218 B2
Hillcrest Gdns N3 . . . . .47 A5
  Hinchley Wood KT10 . . . .212 D5
Hillcrest Hts W5 . . . . .88 A3
Hillcrest Rd E17 . . . . .36 B1
  E18 . . . . .37 A1
  W3 . . . . .110 D5
  W5 . . . . .88 A2
  Loughton IG10 . . . . .21 D5
Hillcrest View BR3 . . . . . . .207 B3
Hillcroft Ave HA5 . . . . .41 B3
  Wembley HA9 . . . . .66 B4
Hillcroft Rd E6 . . . . .100 D2

Hill Cl continued
  Ducks Island EN5 . . . . . .12 C6
  Harrow HA1 . . . . .64 C5
  Stanmore HA7 . . . . .25 B6
Hill Cres N20 . . . . .13 D2
  Harrow HA1 . . . . .43 A4
  Kingston u T KT5 . . . . . .198 B4
  North Cheam KT4 . . . . . .216 C6
Hill Crest DA15 . . . . .168 B4
Hill Crest Gdns NW2 . . . . . .68 C4
Hill Ct NW3 . . . . .70 C4
  SW15 . . . . .156 D6
  W5 . . . . .88 B3
  Barnet EN4 . . . . .2 C1
  8 Kingston u T KT2 . . .176 D3
  12 Kingston u T KT6 . .198 A4
  Northolt UB5 . . . . .63 C3
Hill Dr NW9 . . . . .45 A1
  SW16 . . . . .204 B6
Hill End BR6 . . . . .227 D6
Hill Farm Rd W10 . . . . .90 D2
Hill Field Rd TW12 . . . . . . .173 B2
Hill Gr W13 . . . . .151 B2
Hill Ho E5 . . . . .52 B1
  Stanmore HA7 . . . . .9 A1
Hill House Ave HA7 . . . . . . .24 D3
Hill House Cl N21 . . . . .16 C4
Hill House Dr TW12 . . . . . .173 C2
Hill House Int Jun Sch
  SW1 . . . . .114 D3 **257 D5**
Hill House Rd SW16 . . . . .182 B5
Hill La HA4 . . . . .39 A1
Hill Lo SW11 . . . . .136 B1
Hill Rd N10 . . . . .30 D2
  NW8 . . . . .92 A5 **229 B3**
  Carshalton SM5 . . . . . . .218 C2
  Harrow HA1 . . . . .43 A4
  Mitcham CR4 . . . . .181 B3
  Pinner HA5 . . . . .41 A3
  Sutton SM1 . . . . .217 D3
  Wembley HA0 . . . . .65 B5
Hill Rise N9 . . . . .18 B5
  NW11 . . . . .47 D5
  SE23 . . . . .162 B3
  Greenford UB6 . . . . .86 A6
  Hinchley Wood KT10 . . . .213 B6
  Richmond TW10 . . . . . . .153 D6
  Ruislip HA4 . . . . .39 B1
Hill Side EN5 . . . . .1 A4
Hill St W1 . . . . . . .115 B6 **248 C4**
  Richmond TW10 . . . . . . .153 D6
Hill Top NW11 . . . . .47 D5
  Cheam SM3 . . . . .201 B2
Hill View CR4 . . . . .204 A5
Hill View Cres IG1 . . . . .56 B3
Hill View Dr DA16 . . . . .145 C3
Hill View Gdns NW9 . . . . . .45 B4
Hill View Rd
  Claygate KT10 . . . . .213 A1
  Orpington BR6 . . . . .227 D6
  Twickenham TW1 . . . . . .153 A5
Hill Wood Ho NW1 . . . . .**232 C3**
Hillard Ct SM6 . . . . .219 D2
Hillary Cres KT12 . . . . .194 C1
Hillary Ct **3** SE9 . . . . . . .166 A2
  Stanwell TW19 . . . . .148 A3
Hillary Ho E14 . . . . .98 A2
Hillary Rd UB2 . . . . .107 C3
Hillary Rise EN5 . . . . .1 C1
Hillbeck Cl SE15 . . . . .140 C5
  SE15 . . . . .140 C6
Hillbeck Way UB6 . . . . .86 B6
Hillborne Cl UB3 . . . . .106 A1
Hillboro Ct E11 . . . . .54 B2
  1 E18 . . . . .36 D2
Hillbrook Prim Sch &
  Hillcroft Sch Annexe
  SW17 . . . . .181 A6
Hillbrook Rd SW17 . . . . . .181 A6
Hillbrow
  New Malden KT3 . . . . . . .199 D6
  7 Richmond TW10 . . . .154 A5
Hillbrow Ct KT10 . . . . .212 A4
Hillbrow Rd Catford BR1 186 C4
  Esher KT10 . . . . .212 A4
Hillbury Ave HA3 . . . . .43 B4
Hillbury Rd SW17 . . . . .159 B1
Hillcote Ave SW16 . . . . . . .182 C5
Hillcourt Ave N12 . . . . .29 D4
Hillcourt Rd SE22 . . . . . . .162 B5
Hillcrest N6 . . . . .49 A2
  N21 . . . . .16 C4
  SE24 . . . . .139 B1
  W11 . . . .**244 C5**
Hillcrest Ave NW11 . . . . . . .47 A4
  Edgware HA8 . . . . .26 C6
  Pinner HA5 . . . . .40 D5
Hillcrest Cl SE26 . . . . .184 A6
  Beckenham BR3 . . . . . . .207 B3
Hillcrest Ct NW2 . . . . .69 A3
  Sutton SM2 . . . . .218 B2
Hillcrest Gdns N3 . . . . .47 A5
  Hinchley Wood KT10 . . . .212 D5
Hillcrest Hts W5 . . . . .88 A3
Hillcrest Rd E17 . . . . .36 B1
  E18 . . . . .37 A1
  W3 . . . . .110 D5
  W5 . . . . .88 A2
  Loughton IG10 . . . . .21 D5
Hillcrest View BR3 . . . . . . .207 B3
Hillcroft Ave HA5 . . . . .41 B3
  Wembley HA9 . . . . .66 B4
Hillcroft Rd E6 . . . . .100 D2

Hillcroome Rd SM2 ....218 B2
Hillcross Ave SM4 .....201 A4
Hillcross Mid Sch SM4 .201 B5
Hilldale Rd SM1 ....217 B4
Hilldown Ct SW16 ......182 A3
Hilldown Rd SW16 ......182 B3
Coney Hall BR2 ....208 D1
Hilldrop Cres N7 ....71 D3
Hilldrop Est 4 N7 ......71 D4
Hilldrop La N7 ....71 D3
Hilldrop Rd N7 ....71 D3
Plaistow BR1 ....187 B4
Hillersdon Ave SW13 ...134 A3
Edgware HA8 ....26 B5
Hillersdon Ho SW1 ....258 C2
Hillery Cl SE17 ....262 D3
Hillfield Ave N8 ....50 A5
NW9 ....45 C5
Carshalton SM4 ....202 C4
Wembley HA0 ....66 B1
Hillfield Cl HA2 ....42 A5
Hillfield Ct NW3 ....70 C3
Hillfield Ho N5 ....73 A3
Hillfield Mans NW3 .....70 C3
Hillfield Par SM4 ......202 B3
Hillfield Park Mews N10 49 B5
Hillfield Pk N10 ....49 B5
N21 ....16 C2
Hillfield Rd NW6 ....69 C3
Hillgate Pl SW12 ......159 B4
W8 ....113 C5 245 A4
Hillgate St W8 ....245 A4
Hilliard Ho 15 E1 ......118 B5
Hilliard's Ct E1 ....118 C5
Hillier Cl EN5 ....13 D5
Hillier Gdns CR0 ......220 C3
Hillier Ho 1 NW1 ....71 D1
Hillier Lo TW12 ....174 B5
Hillier Pl KT9 ....213 D2
Hillier Rd SW11 ....158 D5
Hilliers Ave UB8 ....82 C4
Hillier's La CR0,SM6 ....220 A5
Hillingdon Ave TW19 ...148 A3
Hillingdon Circus UB10 .60 D2
Hillingdon Hill UB10 ....82 B4
Hillingdon Hospl UB8 ..82 B2
Hillingdon Par 6 UB10 .82 D3
Hillingdon Prim Sch
UB10 ....82 D4
Hillingdon Rd UB10 .....82 A5
Hillingdon St SE17 ....138 D6
Hillingdon Sta UB10 ....60 D3
Hillington Gdns IG8 ....37 D1
Hillman Cl UB8 ....60 A3
Hillman St E8 ....74 B2
Hillmarton Rd N7 ....72 A3
Hillmead Dr SW9 ......138 D1
Hillmead Prim Sch
SW9 ....138 D1
Hillmont Rd KT10 ......212 C5
Hillmore Ct SE13 ......142 B2
Hillmore Gr SE26 ......185 A5
Hillreach SE7,SE18 ....122 B1
Hillrise KT12 ....193 D2
Hillrise Mans N19 ......50 A2
Hillrise Rd N19 ....50 A2
Hills Mews 2 W5 ....110 A6
Hills Pl W1 ....239 A1
Hill's Rd IG9 ....21 B3
Hillsboro Rd SE22 .....161 C6
Hillsborough Ct 11 NW6 91 D6
Hillsgrove Cl DA16 ....146 C5
Hillsgrove Prim Sch
DA16 ....146 C5
Hillside N8 ....49 D3
NW9 ....45 B5
NW10 ....89 B6
SW19 ....178 D4
Hillside Ave N11 ....30 D4
Wembley HA9 ....66 B4
Woodford IG8 ....37 C5
Hillside Cl NW8 ....91 D5
Merton SM4 ....201 A5
Woodford IG8 ....37 C5
Hillside Cres Enfield EN2 ..5 B5
Harrow HA2 ....42 A1
Northwood HA6 ....22 A2
Hillside Ct NW3 ....69 D3
7 Kingston u T KT2 ....176 D3
Hillside Dr HA8 ....26 C5
Hillside Gdns E17 ....54 B6
N6 ....49 B3
SW2 ....160 C2
Chipping Barnet EN5 ......1 A1
Edgware HA8 ....26 B6
Harrow HA3 ....44 A2
Northwood HA6 ....22 B2
Wallington SM6 ....219 C1
Hillside Gr N14 ....15 D4
NW7 ....28 A3
Hillside Jun Inf Schs
HA6 ....22 A3
Hillside La BR2 ....224 D6
Hillside Mans EN5 ....1 B1
Hillside Rd N15 ....51 C3
SW2 ....160 C2
W5 ....88 A2
Beckenham BR2 ....208 D6
Belmont SM2 ....217 B1
Croydon CR0 ....220 D4
Kingston u T KT5 .....198 C4
Northwood HA6,HA5 .....22 B3
Southall UB1 ....85 C3
Hillside Rise HA6 ....22 A3
Hillsleigh Rd
W14 ....113 B5 244 D4
Hillstone Ct 5 E3 ....97 D3
Hillstowe St E5 ....74 C5
Hilltop 7 E17 ....53 D6
Hilltop Ct NW8 ....70 A1
SE19 ....183 B2
12 SW18 ....136 B1
Hilltop Gdns BR6 ......227 C6
Hilltop Ho 7 N6 ....49 D2
Hilltop Rd NW6 ....69 C1
Hilltop Way HA7 ....9 A1
Hillview SW20 ....178 B3
Hillview Ave HA3 ....44 A4
Hillview Cl HA5 ....23 B4
Hillview Cres BR6 .....211 D1
Hillview Ct SE19 ......183 C6
Hillview Gdns NW4 .....46 D5
Harrow HA2 ....41 C5
Hillview Rd NW7 ....28 D6
Chislehurst West BR7 ...188 D6
Hatch End HA5 ....23 B4
Sutton SM1 ....218 B5
Hillway N6 ....71 A6
NW9 ....45 C1
Hillworth 7 BR3 ....185 D1
Hillworth Rd SW2 ......160 C4
Hilly Fields Cres SE4 ..141 C2
Hilly Mead SW19 ......179 A3
Hillyard Rd W7 ....86 C2
Hillyard St SW9 ....138 C4
Hillyfield E17 ....35 A1
Hilsea Point 7 SW15 ..156 B3
Hilsea St E5 ....74 C4
Hilton Ave N12 ....30 B5
Hilton Ho N7 ....72 A4
9 SE4 ....140 D1
4 W13 ....87 C1
Hilversum Cres 10
SE22 ....161 C6
Himley Rd SW17 ......180 D4
Hinchcliffe Cl SM6 .....220 B1
Hinchley Cl KT10 ......212 D5
Hinchley Dr KT10 ......212 D5
Hinchley Way KT10 ....213 A5
Hinchley Wood Prim Sch
KT10 ....213 A6
Hinchley Wood Sch
KT10 ....213 A6
Hinchley Wood Sta
KT10 ....212 D5
Hinckley Rd SE15 .....140 A1
Hind Ct EC4 ....241 B1
Hind Gr E14 ....97 C1
Hind Ho N7 ....72 C4
13 SE14 ....140 D6
Hinde Mews W1 ....238 B2
Hinde St W1 ....93 A1 238 B2
Hindes Rd HA1 ....42 C4
Hindhead Cl UB8 ....82 D2
Hindhead Gdns UB5 ....85 A6
Hindhead Gn WD1 ......22 C5
Hindhead Point 6
SW15 ....156 B3
Hindhead Way SM6 ....220 A3
Hindhurst Ct NW9 ......45 A5
Hindle Ho E8 ....73 D3
Hindley Ho N7 ....72 B5
Hindlip Ho SW8 ....269 C1
Hindmans Rd SE22 ....162 A6
Hindmans Way RM9 ...103 B3
Hindmarsh Cl E1 ......118 A6
Hindrey Rd E5 ....74 B3
Hindsley's Pl SE23 ....162 C2
Hines Ct HA1 ....43 A4
Hinkler Cl SM6 ....220 A1
Hinkler Rd HA3 ....43 D6
Hinksey Path SE2 ......124 D3
Hinstock NW6 ....91 D6
Hinstock Rd SE18 .....145 A5
Hinton Ave TW4 ....128 D1
Hinton Cl SE9 ....166 A3
Hinton Ct 3 E10 ....75 D6
Hinton Rd N18 ....33 C6
SE24 ....138 D2
Wallington SM6 ....219 C2
Hippodrome Mews
W11 ....244 A5
Hippodrome Pl W11 ...244 B5
Hiscocks Ho NW10 .....67 A1
Hitcham Rd E17 ....53 B2
Hitchcock Cl TW17 ....192 B6
Hitchin Sq E3 ....97 A5
Hither Farm Rd SE3 ...143 C2
Hither Green Hospl
SE13 ....164 B5
Hither Green La SE13 .164 B5
Hither Green Prim Sch
SE13 ....164 B5
Hither Green Sta SE13 .164 C5
Hitherbroom Rd UB3 ..106 A6
Hitherfield Prim Sch
SW2 ....160 C2
Hitherfield Rd
SW16,SW27 ....160 C1
Dagenham RM8 ....81 A6
Hitherlands SW12 .....159 B2
Hitherwell Dr HA3 ......24 B2
Hitherwood Ct SE21 ...183 D6
Hitherwood Dr SE19 ...183 D6
Hive Cl WD2 ....8 B2
Hive Rd WD2 ....8 C2
HM Prison Wormwood
Scrubs W12 ....90 A1
HMS Belfast* SE1 .....253 B4
Hoadly Rd SW16 ......159 D2
Hobart Cl N20 ....14 C2
Hayes UB4 ....84 D3
Hobart Ct Harrow HA1 ...42 C2
Woodford IG8 ....36 D6
Hobart Dr UB4 ....84 D3
Hobart Gdns CR7 ......205 B6
Hobart La UB4 ....84 D3
Hobart Pl SW1 .115 B3 258 C6
Richmond TW10 ....154 B4
Hobart Rd Dagenham RM9 80 D4
Hayes UB4 ....84 D3
North Cheam KT4 ......216 B5
Hobbayne Prim Sch W7 86 D1
Hobbayne Rd W7 ....86 B1
Hobbes Wlk SW15 .....156 B6
Hobb's Ct SE1 ....253 D2
Hobbs Gn N2 ....48 A6
Hobbs Mews IG3 ....79 D6
Hobbs' Pl N1 ....95 C6
Hobbs Rd 5 SE27 ......183 A6
Hobday St E14 ....97 D1
Hobill Wlk KT5 ....198 B3
Hoblands End BR7 ....189 C4
Hobsons Pl 7 E1 ....96 A2
Hobury St SW10 136 B6 266 C5
Hockenden La BR5,BR8 191 D1
Hocker St 21 E2 ....95 D4
Hockington Ct 7 EN5 ...13 D6
Hockley Ave E6 ....100 A5
Hockley Ct 2 E18 ....37 A2
Hockley Ho 4 E9 ....74 C2
Hockliffe Ho W10 ....90 C2
Hockney Ct 1 SE16 ...118 B1
Hockworth Ho 7 N16 ...51 C1
Hocroft Ave NW2 ....69 B5
Hocroft Ct NW2 ....69 B5
Hocroft Rd NW2 ....69 B5
Hocroft Wlk NW2 ....69 B5
Hodder Dr UB6 ....86 D5
Hoddesdon Rd DA17 ...125 C1
Hodford Rd NW11 ....47 B1
Hodgkins Cl SE28 .....124 D6
Hodister Cl 28 SE5 .....139 A5
Hodnet Grove SE16 ...118 D2
Hodson Cl HA2 ....63 B5
Hoe La EN1 ....6 B5
Hoe St E17 ....53 C4
Hoecroft Ct EN3 ....6 C5
Hofland Rd
W14 ....113 A3 254 A6
Hogan Mews W2 ......236 C4
Hogan Way E5 ....74 A6
Hogarth Ave TW15 ....171 A4
Hogarth Bsns Pk W4 ..133 C6
Hogarth Cl E16 ....99 D2
W5 ....88 A2
Hogarth Cres SW19 ...180 B2
Thornton Heath CR0 ...205 A2
Hogarth Ct 15 E1 ....96 A1
EC3 ....253 B6
6 NW1 ....71 C1
SE19 ....183 D6
Heston TW5 ....129 A5
Hogarth Gdns TW5 ....129 C5
Hogarth Hill NW11 .....47 B5
Hogarth Ho 6 SE27 ...183 A6
SW1 ....259 D3
Enfield EN1 ....18 A6
13 Northolt UB5 ....84 D5
Hogarth Ind Est NW10 ..90 A3
Hogarth La W4 ....133 C6
Hogarth Pl SW5 ....255 C3
Hogarth Prim Sch W4 .111 C1
Hogarth Rd
SW5 ....113 D2 255 C3
Dagenham RM8 ....80 B3
Edgware HA8 ....26 C1
Hogarth Roundabout
W4 ....133 C6
Hogarth Way TW12 ...174 A2
Hogsmill Way KT19 ...215 A4
Holbeach Gdns DA15 ..167 D5
Holbeach Mews 1
SW12 ....159 B3
Holbeach Prim Sch
SE6 ....163 C4
Holbeach Rd SE6 .....163 D4
Holbeck Row SE15 ....140 A5
Holbein Ho SW1 ......258 A2
10 Stanmore HA7 ....25 C5
Holbein Mews
SW1 ....115 A1 258 A2
Holbein Pl SW1 115 A2 258 A3
Holberry Ho 5 SE21 ...183 C6
Holberton Gdns NW10 ..90 B4
Holborn EC1 ....94 C2 241 B3
Holborn Cir EC1 .94 C2 241 B3
Holborn Coll
W14 ....135 A6 264 B6
Holborn Pl WC1 ....240 C3
Holborn Rd E13 ....99 B3
Holborn Sta WC1 94 B2 240 C3
Holborn Way CR4 .....180 D1
Holbrook Cl N19 ....49 B1
Enfield EN1 ....6 A5
Holbrook Ho 5 SW2 ...160 B3
W3 ....89 B2
Chislehurst BR7 ....189 B2
Holbrook La BR7 ......189 B3
Holbrook Rd E15 ....98 D5
Holbrook Way BR2 ....210 B4
Holbrooke Ct N7 ....72 A4
Holburn 33 N1 ....95 C6
Holburn Viaduct
EC1 ....94 D2 241 C3
Holburne Cl SE3 ......143 C4
Holburne Gdns SE3 ...143 D4
Holburne Rd SE3 ......143 D4
Holcombe Hill NW7 .....12 A1
Holcombe Ho SW9 ....138 A2
Holcombe Rd N17 ....52 A6
1 N17 ....51 D6
Ilford IG1 ....56 C2
Holcombe St W6 ....112 B2
Holcote Cl DA17 ....125 A3
Holcroft Ct W1 ....239 A4
Holcroft Ho SE10 .....142 A4
SW11 ....136 B2
Holcroft Rd E9 ....74 C1
Holden Ave N12 ....29 D5
NW9 ....45 A1
Holden Cl RM8 ....80 B5
Holden Ho N1 ....235 A5
12 SE8 ....141 C5
Holden Hts N12 ....13 D1
Holden Lo N11 ....31 C5
Holden Rd N12 ....29 D6
Holden St SW11 ......137 A3
Holdenby Rd SE4 .....163 A6
Holdenhurst Ave N12 ...30 A3
Holderness Ho SE5 ...139 C2
Holderness Way SE27 .182 D5
Holdernesse Rd
6 SW17 ....159 A2
Isleworth TW7 ....131 A4
Holders Hill Ave NW4 ..46 D6
Holders Hill Cres NW4 ..28 D1
Holders Hill Dr NW4 ....28 D1
Holders Hill Gdns NW4 .29 A2
Holders Hill Par NW7 ...29 A2
Holders Hill Rd NW4 ....28 D1
NW4,NW7 ....29 A2
Holdsworth Ho 5 SW2 160 C4
Holford Ho 6 SE16 ....118 B2
WC1 ....233 D2
Holford Pl WC1 ....233 D2
Holford Rd NW3 ....70 A5
Holford St WC1 ....234 A2
Holgate Ave SW11 ....136 B2
Holgate Ct HA8 ....26 B6
Holgate Gdns RM10 ....81 C2
Holgate Rd RM10 ....81 C3
Holgate St SE7 ....121 D3
Hollam Ho N8 ....50 B5
Holland Ave SW20 ....177 D2
Belmont SM2 ....217 C1
Holland Cl
Coney Hall BR2 ....224 D6
New Barnet EN5 ....14 B4
Stanmore HA7 ....25 B5
Holland Ct 6 E17 ....54 A5
NW7 ....28 A4
Holland Dr SE23 ......163 A1
Holland Gdns W14 ....254 B6
Holland Gr SW9 ......138 C5
Holland Ho E4 ....36 A6
Holland Park
W11 ....113 B5 244 C3
Holland Park Ave
W11 ....113 A5 244 B3
Ilford IG3 ....57 D4
Holland Park Ct W14 ..244 B2
Holland Park Gdns
W14 ....113 A4 244 A2
Holland Park Mews
W11 ....113 B5 244 C3
Holland Park Rd
W14 ....113 B3 254 D5
Holland Park Rdbt
W12 ....112 D4
Holland Park Sch
W8 ....113 B4 244 D2
Holland Park Sta
W11 ....113 B5 244 C3
Holland Pl W8 ....245 C2
Holland Rd E6 ....78 C1
E15 ....98 C4
NW10 ....90 B5
SE25 ....206 A4
W14 ....113 A3 254 B6
Wembley HA0 ....65 D2
Holland Rise Ho SW9 ..270 D3
Holland St SE1 .116 D5 251 D4
W8 ....113 C4 245 B2
Holland Villas Rd
W14 ....113 A4 244 A1
Holland Way BR2 .....224 D6
Holland Wlk N19 ....49 D1
W14 ....113 B4 244 D1
Stanmore HA7 ....25 A5
Hollands The
Feltham TW13 ....172 D6
New Malden KT4 ......199 D1
Hollar Rd N16 ....73 D5
Hollen St W1 ....239 C2
Holles Cl TW12 ....173 C5
Holles Ho 9 SW9 .....138 C3
Holles St W1 ....93 B1 238 D2
Holley Rd W3 ....111 C4
Hollickwood Ave N12 ...30 D4
Hollickwood Prim Sch
N10 ....31 B3
Holliday Sq 7 SW11 ...136 B2
Hollidge Way RM10 ....81 D1
Hollies Ave DA15 .....167 D3
Hollies Cl SW16 ......182 C4
Twickenham TW1 .....152 D2
Hollies End NW7 ....28 B5
Hollies Rd W5 ....109 C2
Hollies The 7 E11 ......55 A4
N20 ....14 B3
Harrow HA3 ....43 A5
Hollies Way 1 SW12 ..159 A4
Holligrave Rd BR1 ....187 A2
Hollingbourne Ave DA7 147 B4
Hollingbourne Gdns
W13 ....87 B2
Hollingbourne Rd SE24 161 A6
Hollingbury Ct 1 E17 ...53 D6
Hollingsworth Rd CR0 .222 B2
Hollington Cres KT3 ...199 D3
Hollington Ct BR7 .....188 D4
Hollington Rd E6 ......100 B4
N17 ....34 A1
Hollingworth Cl KT8 ...195 B5
Hollingworth Ct 7 KT6 197 D2
Hollingworth Rd BR2,
BR5 ....210 D2
Hollins Ho N7 ....72 A4
Hollisfield WC1 ....233 B1
Hollman Gdns SW16 ...182 D4
Hollow The IG8 ....36 D6
Holloway Cl UB7 ......104 A1
Holloway La UB7 ......104 B1
Holloway Rd E6 ....100 B4
E11 ....76 B5
N7 ....72 B4
N19 ....71 D6
Holloway Road Sta N7 ..72 B3
Holloway Sch N7 ....71 D3
Holloway St TW3 .....129 D2
Hollowfield Wlk UB5 ...63 A2
Holly Ave N2 ....47 D6
Stanmore HA7 ....26 A1
Walton-on-T KT12 .....194 D1
Holly Berry La 6 NW3 ..70 A4
Holly Bush La TW12 ...173 C3
Holly Bush Vale 9 NW3 .70 A4
Holly Bush Wlk SW9 ...138 D1
Holly Cl NW10 ....67 C1
Buckhurst Hill IG9 .....21 D1
Feltham TW13 ....173 A5
Holly Cott KT7 ....197 A1
Holly Cottage Mews UB8 82 C2
Holly Cres
Beckenham BR3 ....207 B4
Chingford IG8 ....36 B3
Holly Ct N15 ....51 C5
9 Belmont SM2 ....217 C1
4 Sidcup DA14 ....190 B6
Wallington SM6 ....219 B1
Holly Dale Prim Sch
SE15 ....140 C3
Holly Dr E4 ....19 D4
Holly Farm Rd UB2 ....107 A1
Holly Gdns UB7 ....104 B4
Holly Gr NW9 ....45 A2
SE15 ....140 A3
Hatch End HA5 ....23 A2
Holly Grove Cl TW3 ...129 B1
Holly Hedge Terr SE13 .164 B6
Holly Hill N21 ....16 B5
NW3 ....70 A4
Holly Hill Rd DA8,DA17 .125 D1
Holly Ho TW8 ....131 C6
Holly Lo N21 ....16 C3
SE13 ....142 B1
4 SW19 ....179 A4
SW20 ....178 B1
Harrow HA1 ....42 B4
Holly Lodge Gdns N6 ...49 A1
Holly Lodge Mans N6 ...71 A6
Holly Mews SW10 .....256 B1
Holly Mount NW3 ......70 A4
Holly Park Est N4 ....50 B2
Holly Park Gdns N3 ....47 C6
Holly Park Prim Sch
N11 ....31 A5
Holly Park Rd N11 ......31 A5
W7 ....108 D5
Holly Pk N3 ....47 C6
N4 ....50 B2
Holly Rd E11 ....54 D2
W4 ....111 B2
Hampton TW12 ....174 A4
Hounslow TW3 ....129 D1
Twickenham TW1 .....153 A3
Holly St E8 ....73 D1
Holly Terr N6 ....49 A1
Holly Tree Ho SE4 ....141 B2
Holly Tree Lo EN2 ....4 D3
Holly Village N6 ....71 B6
Holly Way CR4 ....203 D6
Holly Wlk NW3 ....70 A4
Enfield EN2 ....5 B2
Hollybank Cl TW12 ....173 C5
Hollybrake Cl BR7 ....189 B3
Hollybush Cl E11 ....55 A4
Harrow HA3 ....24 C2
Hollybush Gdns E2 .....96 B4
Hollybush Hill E11 ......54 D3
Hollybush Ho 23 E2 ....96 B4
Hollybush Pl E2 ....96 B4
Hollybush Rd KT2 .....176 A4
Hollybush St E13 ....99 B4
Hollycroft Ave NW3 ....69 C5
Wembley HA9 ....66 B5
Hollycroft Cl
Harmondsworth UB7 ...126 C6
South Croydon CR2 ....221 C3
Hollycroft Gdns UB7 ...126 C6
Hollydale Cl UB5 ....63 D4
Hollydale Dr BR2 ......226 B5
Hollydale Rd SE15 ....140 C3
Hollydene SE13 ....164 B5
5 SE15 ....140 B4
Bromley BR1 ....186 D2
Hollydown Way E11 ....76 B5
Hollyfield Ave N11 .....30 D5
Hollyfield Rd KT5 .....198 B2
Hollyfield Sch KT6 ....198 A4
Hollygrove WD2 ....8 B4
Hollymead SM5 ....218 D5
Hollymount Cl 9 SE10 142 A4
Hollymount Prim Sch
SW20 ....178 C2
Hollytree Cl SW19 ....156 D3
Hollyview Cl NW4 ......46 A3
Hollywell Row
EC2 ....95 C3 243 A5
Hollywood Ct W5 ......110 B6
Hollywood Gdns UB4 ....84 B1
Hollywood Mews SW10 266 A6
Hollywood Rd E4 ....35 A5
SW10 ....136 A6 266 A6
Hollywood Way IG8 .....36 B4
Holm Ct SE12 ....165 B1
Holm Gr UB10 ....60 C1
Holm Oak Cl SW15 ....157 B5
Holm Wlk SE3 ....143 A3
Holman Ho 2 E2 ....96 D4
Holman Hunt Ho W14 ..254 A1
Holman Rd SW11 ......136 B3
West Ewell KT19 ....215 A3
Holmbank Dr TW17 ....193 C5
Holmbridge Gdns EN3 ...6 D1
Holmbrook Dr NW4 ....46 D4
Holmbury Cl WD2 ....8 C2
Holmbury Ct SW17 ....158 D1
SW19 ....180 C3
Holmbury Gdns UB3 ...105 D5
Holmbury Gr CR0 ......223 B1
Holmbury Ho SW9 ....160 D6
Holmbury Manor 6
DA14 ....190 A6
Holmbury Pk BR7 .....188 A3
Holmbury View 2 E5 ....52 B1
Holmbush Ct NW4 ......46 D4
Holmbush Rd SW15 ...157 A5
Holmcote Gdns N5 .....73 A3
Holmcroft Ho 9 E17 ....53 D5
Holmcroft Way BR2 ...210 B4
Holmdale Gdns NW4 ...46 D4
Holmdale Rd NW6 ......69 C3
Chislehurst West BR7 ..189 A5
Holmdale Terr N15 .....51 C3
Holmdene N12 ....29 D5
Holmdene Ave NW7 ....28 A4
SE24 ....161 A6
Harrow HA2 ....41 D6
Holmdene Cl BR3 .....186 A1
Holmdene Ct BR1 .....210 A6
Holme Lacey Rd SE12 .164 D5
Holme Rd E6 ....100 A6
Holme Way HA7 ....24 D4
Holmead Rd
SW6 ....135 D5 265 D3
Holmefield Ho W10 .....91 A3
Holmeleigh Ct EN3 ......6 C1
Holmes Ave E17 ....53 B6
NW7 ....29 A5
Holmes Ct 5 E4 ....20 B2
18 SW4 ....138 A3
17 W4 ....111 A3
Holmes Pl SW10 ......266 B6
Holmes Rd NW5 ....71 B3
SW19 ....180 A3
Twickenham TW1 .....152 D2
Holmes Terr SE1 ......251 A2
Holmesdale Ave SW14 .132 D1
Holmesdale Cl SE25 ...205 D6
Holmesdale Ho 12 NW6 .91 C6
Holmesdale Rd N6 ......49 B2
SE25 ....205 C5
Bexley DA16 ....146 D3
Richmond TW9 ....132 B4
Teddington TW11 .....175 C4
Thornton Heath CR0 ...205 B4
Holmesley Rd SE23 ...163 A5
Holmeswood Ct 3 N22 .32 C1
Holmewood Gdns SW2 160 B4
Holmewood Rd SE25 ..205 C6
SW2 ....160 B4
Holmfield Ave NW4 ....46 D4
Holmfield Ct 4 NW3 ....70 C2
Holmfield Ho E17 ....54 B5
Holmhurst SE13 ....164 B5
Holmhurst Rd DA17 ...125 D1
Holmlea Ct 1 CR0 ....221 B4
Holmleigh JMI Sch N16 .51 C1
Holmleigh Rd N16 ......51 C1
Holmoaks Ho BR3 .....186 A1
Holmsbury Ho 6 N7 ....71 D3
Holmsdale Ho 21 E14 ..119 D6
6 N11 ....31 B6
Holmshaw Cl SE26 ....185 A6
Holmside Ct SW12 ....159 A5
Holmside Rd SW12 ....159 A5
Holmsley Cl KT3 ......199 D2
Holmsley Ho SW15 ....155 D4
Holmstall Ave HA8 ......27 A1
Holmstall Par HA8 ......27 A1
Holmwood 2 KT5 .....198 B3
Holmwood Cl
Cheam SM2 ....216 D1
Harrow HA2 ....42 A6
Northolt UB5 ....63 D2
Holmwood Ct 3 N16 ....51 D2
Sidcup DA14 ....189 D5
KT3 ....199 B6
Holmwood Gdns N3 ....29 C1
Wallington SM6 ....219 B2
Holmwood Gr NW7 .....27 B5
Holmwood Mans W3 ..110 C5
Holmwood Rd
Chessington KT9 ......214 A3
Ilford IG3 ....79 C6
Holne Chase N2 ....48 A3
Morden SM4 ....201 C3
Holness Rd E15 ....76 D2
Holocaust Meml Gdn
W2 ....114 D4 247 D2
Holroyd Rd SW15 .....156 C6
Holsgrove Ct W3 ......111 C5
Holst Mans SW13 .....134 C5

Holstein Way 6 DA18 125 A3
Holstock Rd IG1 79 A6
Holsworth Cl HA2 42 A4
Holsworthy Ho 49 E3 97 D4
Holsworthy Way KT9 213 C3
Holt Cl N10 49 A5
SE28 124 C6
Holt Ct E15 76 A3
Holt Ho SW2 160 C5
Holt Rd E16 122 A5
Wembley HA0 65 C5
Holt The Morden SM4 201 C5
Wallington SM6 219 C4
Holtoake Ct 1 W5 87 C3
Holtoake Ho 3 W5 87 C3
Holton St E1 96 D3
Holtwhite Ave EN2 5 A3
Holtwhite's Hill EN2 4 D4
Holwell Pl HA5 41 A5
Holwood Park Ave BR2, BR6 226 B4
Holwood Pl 7 SW4 137 D1
Holy Cross RC Convent Sch KT3 199 C4
Holy Cross RC Prep Sch KT2 177 A3
Holy Cross RC Prim Sch SE6 164 A3
SW6 135 C4 265 A2
Holy Family Coll The E17 54 A5
E17 54 A6
Holy Family RC JMI Sch E14 119 C6
Holy Family RC Prim Sch SE9 143 C1
Holy Ghost & St Stephen RC Prim Sch The W12 111 D4
Holy Ghost RC Prim Sch SW12 159 A4
Holy Innocents RC Prim Sch BR6 227 D5
Holy Trinity CE Inf Sch SW17 158 D2
Holy Trinity CE Jun Sch Mortlake TW10 132 C1
Wallington SM6 219 C4
Holy Trinity CE Prim Sch N2 48 B6
NW1 71 B1
NW3 70 A2
SE23 162 C2
SW1 114 D2 257 D4
SW1 115 A2 258 A4
SW2 160 B4
SW19 179 D4
Sidcup DA15 168 A3
Holy Trinity Coll BR1 187 C2
Holy Trinity Dalston CE JMI Sch E8 73 D2
Holybourne Ave SW15 156 A4
Holyhead Cl E3 97 C4
3 E6 100 B2
Holyhead Ct KT1 197 D5
Holyoak Rd SE11 116 D2 261 D3
Holyoake Ct SE16 119 B4
Holyoake Wlk N2 48 A6
W5 87 C3
Holyport Rd SW6 134 D5
Holyrood Ave HA2 63 B4
Holyrood Gdns HA8 26 D1
Holyrood Ho N4 50 D1
Holyrood Mews 11 E16 121 A5
Holyrood Rd EN5 14 B5
Holyrood St SE1 117 C5 253 A3
Holywell Cl 2 SE3 143 A6
35 SE16 118 B1
Stanwell TW19 148 A3
Holywell La EC2 243 B6
Holywell Way TW19 148 A3
Homan Ct N12 30 A6
Homan Ho 6 SW4 159 D4
Home Cl Carshalton SM5 218 D6
Northolt UB5 85 B4
Home Ct KT6 197 D4
Home Farm Cl Thames Ditton KT7 196 D2
Upper Halliford TW17 193 C5
Home Farm Cotts BR5 190 D2
Home Field EN5 13 B6
Home Lea BR6 227 D3
Home Mead HA7 25 C2
Home Office SW1 249 C1
Home Park Rd SW19 157 B1
Home Park Wlk KT1 197 D5
Home Rd SW11 136 C3
Homebush Ho E4 19 D4
Homecoppice Ho 1 BR1 186 D3
Homecourt TW14 150 A3
Homecroft Rd N22 33 A2
SE26 184 C5
Homefarm Rd W7 86 D1
Homefield SM4 201 C5
Homefield Ave IG2 57 C4
Homefield Cl NW10 67 A2
Hayes UB4 84 D3
Homefield Ct NW4 46 C5
Homefield Gdns N2 48 B6
Mitcham CR4,SW19 180 B1
Homefield Ho SE23 162 D1
Homefield Pk SM1,SM2 217 D2
Homefield Prep Sch SM1 217 C3
Homefield Rd SW19 179 A4
W4 111 D1
Bromley BR1 187 C2
Burnt Oak HA8 27 B4
Walton-on-T KT12 195 A2
Wembley HA0 65 B4
Homefield St 14 N1 95 C5
Homefirs Ho HA9 66 B5
Homelands Dr SE19 183 C3
Homeleigh Ct 8 SW16 160 A1
Homeleigh Rd SE15 162 D6
Homemead SW12 159 B2
Homemead Rd Bromley BR2 210 B4
Wallington CR0 203 C3
Homer Dr E14 119 C2
Homer Rd E9 75 A2
Croydon CR0 206 D3
Homer Row W1 237 B3
Homer St W1 92 C2 237 B3
Homersham Rd KT1 176 D1
Homerton Coll of Technology E9 74 C3
Homerton Gr E9 74 D3
Homerton High St E9 74 D3
Homerton Hospl E9 74 D3
Homerton Rd E9 75 B3
Homerton Row E9 74 C3
Homerton Sta E9 74 D2
Homerton Terr E9 74 C2
Homes Of Rest (CE Temperance Society) IG1 79 B5
Homesdale Cl E11 55 A4
Homesdale Rd Bromley BR1,BR2 209 C6
Broom Hill BR5,BR6 211 C2
Homesfield NW11 47 C4
Homestall Rd SE22 162 C6
Homestead Ct EN5 13 C6
Homestead Gdns KT10 212 C3
Homestead Paddock N14 15 B6
Homestead Pk NW2 67 D5
Homestead Rd SW6 135 B5 264 D3
Dagenham RM8 81 B6
Homestead The N11 31 B6
Homesteads The BR3 185 D4
Homewalk Ho SE26 184 C6
Homewaters Ave TW16 171 D2
Homewillow Cl N21 16 D5
Homewood Cl TW12 173 B4
Homewood Cres BR7 189 C4
Homewood Gdns SE25 205 C4
Homewoods 2 SW12 159 C4
Homildon Ho 10 SE26 162 A1
Homington Ct KT2 176 A3
Honduras St EC1 242 A6
Honey Cl RM10 81 D2
Honey Hill UB10 60 B1
Honey La EC2 242 B1
Honeybourne Rd NW6 69 D3
Honeybourne Way BR5 211 B1
Honeybrook Rd SW12, SW4 159 C4
Honeycroft Hill UB10 60 A1
Honeyden Rd DA14 191 A4
Honeyfield N4 72 C6
Honeyman Cl NW6 68 D1
Honeypot Bsns Ctr HA7 26 A2
Honeypot Cl NW9 44 B5
Honeypot La HA3,HA7, NW9 44 B6
Honeysett Rd 1 N17 33 D1
Honeysuckle Cl UB1 107 A6
Honeysuckle Ct 2 SE12 165 A4
Honeysuckle Gdns CR0 206 D1
Honeywell Jun & Inf Schs SW11 158 D5
Honeywell Rd SW11 158 D5
Honeywood Ho 5 SE15 140 A4
Honeywood Rd NW10 89 D5
Isleworth TW7 131 A1
Honeywood Wlk SM5 218 D4
Honister Cl HA7 25 B2
Honister Gdns HA7 25 B2
Honister Pl HA7 25 B2
Honiton Gdns 1 SE15 140 C3
Honiton Ho 30 SE5 139 A3
Honiton Rd NW6 91 B5
Bexley DA16 145 D3
Honley Rd SE6 163 D4
Honor Oak Park Sta SE23 162 D5
Honor Oak Pk SE23 162 D5
Honor Oak Rd SE23 162 C4
Honor Oak Rise SE23 162 C5
Honwell Ho 2 W2 91 C2
Hood Ave N14 15 B5
SW14 155 A6
Hood Cl CR0 204 D1
Hood Ct N7 72 B5
Hood Ho 17 SE5 139 B5
Hood Lo E11 77 B6
Hood Rd SW20 177 D3
Hoodcote Gdns N21 16 D4
Hook KT6 214 A5
Hook Farm Rd BR2 209 D4
Hook Ho 9 SW27 182 D5
Hook La DA16 146 A1
Hook Lane Prim Sch DA16 146 A2
Hook Rd Chessington KT6 214 A5
Epsom KT19,KT17 215 A1
Surbiton KT6,KT9 214 A5
Hook Rise N Surbiton KT6 214 A5
Tolworth KT6,KT9 214 D6
Hook Rise S KT6,KT9 214 D6
Hook Rise South KT6 214 A5
Hook The EN5 14 B5
Hook Underpass KT6 214 A5
Hook Wlk HA8 27 A4
Hooke Ct SE10 142 A4
Hooke Ho 30 E3 97 A5
Hooker's Rd E17 52 D6
Hookham Ct SW8 269 C2
Hooking Gn HA2 41 D4
Hooks Cl SE15 140 B4
Hookstone Way IG8 37 D3
Hoop La NW11 47 C2
Hooper Ho 8 SW18 157 B6
Hooper Rd E16 99 A1
Hooper St E1 96 A1
Hooper's Ct SW1 247 C1
Hooper's Mews 4 W3 111 A5
Hoover Ho 5 SE6 186 A6
Hop Gdns WC2 250 A5
Hope Cl N1 73 A2
SE12 165 B1
2 Brentford TW8 110 A1
Ilford RM6 58 D5
Sutton SM1 218 A3
1 Woodford IG8 37 C4
Hope Pk BR1 186 D3
Hope St SW11 136 B2
Hopedale Rd SE7 143 B6
Hopefield 3 W7 108 D5
Hopefield Ave NW6 91 A5
Hopes Cl TW5 129 C6
Hopetown St E1 243 D3
Hopewell St SE5 139 B5
Hopgood St W12 112 C5
Hopkins Cl N10 31 A3
Hopkins Ho 12 E14 97 C1
Hopkins St W1 93 D1 239 C1
Hopkinson Ho 1 SW11 137 A3
Hopkinson's Pl NW1 231 A6
Hoppers Rd N21 16 C2
Hoppett Rd E4 20 C2
Hopping La N1 72 D2
Hoppingwood Ave KT3 199 C6
Hoppner Rd UB4 83 B5
Hopton Ct BR2 209 A1
Hopton Gdns KT3 200 A3
Hopton Ho 5 SW9 138 D3
Hopton Rd SE18 123 A3
SW16 182 A5
Hopton St SE1 116 D5 251 D4
Hopton's Gdns SE1 251 D4
Hopwood Cl SW17 158 A1
Hopwood Rd SE17 139 B6
Hopwood Wlk E8 74 A1
Horace Rd E7 77 B4
Ilford IG6 57 A6
Kingston u T KT1 198 B6
Horatio Ho 18 E2 95 D5
Horatio Pl E14 120 A5
Horatio St 11 E2 95 D5
Horatius Way CR0 220 B2
Horbury Cres W11 113 C6 245 A5
Horbury Mews W11 113 B6 244 D5
Horder Rd SW6 135 A4 264 B1
Hordle Promenade E 14 SE15 139 D5
Hordle Promenade N 3 SE15 139 D5
Hordle Promenade S 7 SE15 139 D5
Hordle Promenade W 13 SE15 139 C5
Horizon Sch N16 73 C4
Horle Wlk SE5 138 D3
Horley Cl DA6 169 C6
Horley Rd SE9 188 A6
Hormead Rd W9 91 B3
Horn La SE10 121 A2
W3 89 A1
Woodford IG8 37 A3
Horn Park Cl SE12 165 B6
Horn Park La SE12 165 B5
Horn Park Prim Sch SE12 165 B4
Hornbeam Cl SE11 261 A4
Buckhurst Hill IG9 21 D1
Northolt UB5 63 B3
Hornbeam Cres TW8 131 B5
Hornbeam Gr E4 20 D1
Hornbeam Ho 2 NW3 70 D2
Buckhurst Hill IG9 21 D1
6 Sidcup DA15 168 A1
Hornbeam La E4 20 C6
Hornbeam Rd Buckhurst Hill IG9 21 D1
Hayes UB4 84 C2
Hornbeam Terr SM5 202 C1
Hornbeam Twr E11 76 B5
Hornbeam Way BR2 210 C3
Hornbeams Rise N11 31 A4
Hornblower Cl 2 SE16 119 A2
Hornbuckle Cl HA2 64 B6
Hornby Cl NW3 70 B1
Hornby Ho 6 SE11 138 C6
Horncastle Cl SE12 165 A4
Horncastle Rd SE12 165 A4
Hornchurch N17 33 B1
Hornchurch Cl KT2 175 D6
Horndean Cl 3 SW15 156 A3
Horne Ho 7 SE18 144 A4
Horne Rd TW17 192 C5
Horne Way SW15 134 C3
Horner Ct E11 76 B5
Horner Hos 18 N1 95 C6
Horner La 3 CR4 180 B1
Hornfair Rd SE7 143 D5
Horniman Dr SE23 162 C4
Horniman Grange 7 SE23 162 C3
Horniman Mus & Gdns SE23 162 B3
Horniman Prim Sch SE23 162 B3
Horning Cl SE9 188 A6
Horns End Pl HA5 40 C4
Horns Rd IG2,IG6 57 A4
Hornsey Central Hospl N8 49 D4
Hornsey La N6 49 C2
Hornsey Lane Gdns N6 49 C2
Hornsey Park Rd N8 50 B6
Hornsey Rd N7,N19 72 B6
Hornsey Rise Gdns N19 50 A2
Hornsey Sch for Girls N8 50 B4
Hornsey St N7 72 B3
Hornsey Sta N8 50 B5
Hornshay St SE15 140 C6
Hornton Ct W8 245 B1
Hornton Pl W8 245 B1
Hornton St W8 113 C4 245 B2
Horrocks Ho SW15 156 B6
Horsa Cl SM6 220 A1
Horsa Rd SE12 165 C4
Erith DA8 147 D5
Horse & Dolphin Yd W1 249 D6
Horse Fair KT1 175 D1
Horse Guards Par* SW1 115 D5 249 D3
Horse Guards Rd SW1 115 D4 249 D2
Horse Leaze E6 100 C1
Horse Shoe Cres UB5 85 C5
Horse Shoe Gn SM1 217 D6
Horse Shoe Yd W1 248 D6
Horse Yd N1 234 D6
Horsebridge Cl RM9 103 A6
Horsecroft Rd HA8 27 B3
Horseferry Pl SE10 142 A6
Horseferry Rd E14 119 A6
SW1 115 D2 259 D4
Horseferry Rd Est SW1 259 C5
Horseguards Ave SW1 116 A5 250 A3
Horsell Rd N5 72 C3
St Paul's Cray BR5 190 B2
Horselydown La SE1 117 D5 253 C3
Horselydown Mans SE1 253 C2
Horsenden Ave UB6 64 D3
Horsenden Cres UB6 64 D3
Horsenden La N Wembley UB6 64 C2
Wembley UB6 64 D1
Horsenden La S UB6 87 A6
Horsenden Prim Sch UB6 64 C2
Horsendon Ho 11 N7 71 D3
Horseshoe Cl E14 120 A1
NW2 68 B6
Horseshoe Dr UB8 82 C1
Horseshoe La N20 12 D3
Enfield EN2 5 A2
Horsfeld Gdns 1 SE9 166 A6
Horsfeld Rd SE9 165 D6
Horsfield Ho 2 N1 73 A1
Horsford Rd SW2 160 B6
Horsham Ave N12 30 C5
Horsham Ct N17 34 A2
Horsham Rd Bexleyheath DA6 169 C6
East Bedfont TW14 149 A5
Horsley Dr Kingston u T KT2 175 D5
New Addington CR0 224 A1
Horsley Ho 11 SE4 140 D1
Horsley Rd E4 20 A2
Bromley BR1 187 B2
Horsley St 3 SE17 139 B6
Horsman Ho SE5 139 A6
Horsman St SE5 139 A6
Horsmonden Cl BR6 211 D2
Horsmonden Rd SE4 163 B5
Horston Ho N4 51 A2
Hortensia Ho SW10 266 A4
Hortensia Rd SW10 136 A5 266 A4
Horticultural Pl 6 W4 111 B1
Horton Ave NW2 69 A4
Horton Bridge Rd UB7 104 B5
Horton Cl UB7 104 B5
Horton Ctry Park KT19 214 C1
Horton Ho 18 SE15 140 C6
SW8 270 C4
W14 254 A1
Horton Ind Pk UB7 104 B5
Horton La KT19 215 A1
Horton Par UB7 104 A5
Horton Rd E8 74 B2
Yiewsley UB7 104 B5
Horton Road Ind Est UB7 104 B5
Horton St SE13 141 D2
Horton Way CR0 206 D4
Hortus Rd E4 20 A2
Hortus Rd *continued* Southall UB2 107 B4
Horwood Ho 24 E2 96 B4
NW8 237 B6
Hosack Rd SW12,SW17 159 A2
Hoser Ave SE12 165 A2
Hosier La EC1 94 D2 241 D3
Hoskins Cl UB3 105 D1
Hoskin's Cl E16 99 C1
Hoskins St SE10 120 B1
Hospital Bridge Rd TW2 151 D3
Hospital Bridge Rdbt TW2 151 D2
Hospital of the Holy Trinity (Almshouses) 5 CR0 221 A6
Hospital Rd TW3 129 C2
Hospital Way SE13 164 B3
Hospl for Tropical Diseases NW1 232 C5
Hospl of St John & St Elizabeth NW8 92 B5 229 C3
Hotham Cl KT8 195 C6
Hotham Prim Sch SW15 134 D1
Hotham Rd SW15 134 C2
SW19 180 A3
Hotham Road Mews 12 SW19 180 A3
Hotham St E15 98 C6
Hothfield Pl SE16 118 C3
Hotspur Ind Est N17 34 B4
Hotspur Rd UB5 85 C5
Hotspur St SE11 116 C1 261 A2
Houblon Rd TW10 154 A6
Houghton Cl 10 E8 73 D2
Hampton TW12 173 A4
Houghton Rd N15 51 D5
Houghton St WC2 240 D1
Houlder Cres CR0 220 D2
Houndsden Rd N21 16 C5
Houndsditch EC3 95 C1 243 B2
Houndsfield Prim Sch N9 18 B4
Houndsfield Rd N9 18 B4
Hounslow Ave TW3 151 D6
Hounslow Bsns Pk TW3 129 D1
Hounslow Central Sta TW3 129 D2
Hounslow Ctr The TW3 129 D2
Hounslow East Sta TW3 130 A3
Hounslow Ed Ctr (Specl Sch) The TW4 129 A2
Hounslow Gdns TW3 151 D6
Hounslow Heath Jun & Inf Schs TW4 129 A2
Hounslow Heath Nature Reserve TW4 151 A5
Hounslow Manor Sch TW3 130 A2
Hounslow Rd Feltham TW13 151 A2
Twickenham TW2,TW3 152 A5
TW14 150 B4
Hounslow Sta TW3 151 D6
Hounslow Town Prim Sch TW3 130 B2
Hounslow West Sta TW3 129 A3
Houses of Parliament* SW1 116 A3 260 B6
Housman Way 20 SE5 139 B5
Houston Ct 3 CR0 205 C1
Houston Rd SE23 163 A1
Houstoun Ct TW5 129 B5
Hove Ave E17 53 B4
Hove Gdns SM1 201 D1
Hoveden Rd NW2 69 A3
Hovenden Ho 6 SE21 183 C6
Hoveton Rd SE28 102 C1
Howard Ave DA5 168 C4
Howard Cl N11 15 A2
NW2 69 A4
W3 88 D1
Ashford TW16 171 D4
Bushey WD2 8 C4
Hampton TW12 174 A4
Howard Ct SE15 140 A2
12 Barking IG11 101 B6
Beckenham BR3 186 A1
Howard Ho 8 E5 74 C6
14 SE8 141 B6
SE20 184 C2
7 SW9 138 C2
W1 238 D5
Howard Mans E17 53 D6
Howard Prim Sch CR0 221 A4
Howard Rd E6 100 B5
E11 76 C5
E17 53 D6
N15 51 C3
N16 73 B4
NW2 68 D4
SE20 184 C2
SE25 206 A3
Barking IG11 101 B6
Ilford IG1 78 D4
Isleworth TW7 130 D2
New Malden KT3 199 D5
Plaistow BR1 187 A3
Southall UB1 85 D1
Surbiton KT5 198 B3
Howard St KT7 197 B3
Howard Way EN5 12 D6
Howard Wlk N2 48 B5
Howards Cl HA5 22 B1
Howards Crest Cl BR3 186 A1
Howard's La SW15 134 C1
Howard's Rd E13 99 A4
Howarth Rd SE2 124 A2
Howberry Cl HA8 25 D4
Howberry Rd South Norwood CR7 183 B1
Stanmore HA7,H8 25 D4
Howbury Rd SE15 140 C2
Howcroft Cres N3 29 C3
Howcroft Ho 3 E3 97 B4
Howcroft La UB6 86 B4
Howden Cl SE28 124 D6
Howden Ct SE25 183 D1
Howden Rd SE25 183 D1
Howden St SE15 140 A2
Howell Cl RM6 58 D4
Howell Ct 2 E10 53 D2
Howell Ho 5 N7 71 D3
Howell Wlk SE1 261 D3
Howes Cl N3 47 C6
Howfield Pl N17 51 D6
Howgate Rd SW14 133 B2
Howick Pl SW1 115 C3 259 B5
Howie St SW11 136 C5 267 A3
Howitt Cl 6 NW3 70 C2
Howitt Rd NW3 70 C2
Howland Ho 9 SW16 160 A1
Howland Mews E W1 239 B4
Howland St W1 93 C2 239 B4
Howland Way SE16 119 A4
Howletts La HA4 39 A3
Howletts Rd SE24 161 A5
Howley Pl W2 92 A2 236 B4
Howley Rd CR0 221 A5
Howmic Ct 1 TW1 153 C5
How's St E2 95 D5
Howsman Rd SW13 134 A6
Howson Rd SE4 141 A1
Howson Terr TW10 154 A5
Howton Pl WD2 8 A3
Hoxton Mkt 10 N1 95 C4
Hoxton Sq N1 95 C4
Hoxton St N1 95 C5
Hoy St E16 98 D1
Hoylake Cres UB10 60 D6
Hoylake Gdns Mitcham CR4 203 C6
Ruislip HA4 40 B1
South Oxhey WD1 22 D6
Hoylake Rd W3 89 C1
Hoyland Cl 4 SE15 140 B5
Hoyle Rd SW17 180 C5
Huan Ct N20 14 C2
Hubbard Dr KT9 213 D2
Hubbard Rd SE27 183 A6
Hubbard St E15 98 C6
Huberd Ho SE1 262 D6
Hubert Gr SW9 138 A2
Hubert Ho NW8 237 A5
Hubert Rd E6 99 D4
Hucknall Ct NW8 236 C6
Huddart St E3 97 B2
Huddleston Cl E2 96 C5
Huddleston Rd N7 71 C4
Huddlestone Rd E7 76 D4
NW2 68 B2
Hudson 27 NW9 27 D2
Hudson Cl 15 W12 112 B6
Hudson Ct 4 SW19 179 D2
Hudson Ho SW10 266 A4
5 W11 91 A1
Hudson Pl SE18 123 A1
Hudson Rd Erith DA7 147 B4
Harlington UB7 127 B6
Hudsons Ho N1 235 D1
Hudson's Pl SW1 115 C2 259 A4
Huggin Ct EC4 252 B6
Huggin Hill EC4 252 B6
Huggins Ho 8 E3 97 C4
Huggins Pl SW2 160 B3
Hugh Astor Ct SE1 261 D6
Hugh Clark Ho W13 109 A5
Hugh Gaitskell Cl SW6 264 C5
Hugh Gaitskell Ho N16 73 D6
NW10 67 D1
Hugh Herland KT1 198 A6
Hugh Mews SW1 258 D3
Hugh Morgan Ho 5 SW4 137 D2
Hugh Myddelton Prim Sch EC1 94 C4 234 B1
Hugh Platt Ho 29 E2 96 B5
Hugh St SW1 115 B2 258 D3
Hughan Rd E15 76 B3
Hughenden Ave HA3 43 B4
Hughenden Gdns UB5 84 C4
Hughenden Rd KT4 200 A2
Hughendon EN5 1 D1
Hughendon Terr E15 76 A4
Hughes Fields Prim Sch SE8 141 C6
Hughes Ho 28 E2 96 C4
SE5 139 A4
15 SE8 141 C6
SE17 261 D3
Hughes Mans E1 96 A3
Hughes Rd Ashford TW15 171 A4
Hayes UB3 106 B6
Hughes Terr 6 E16 98 D2
Hughes Wlk CR0 205 A2
Hugo Ho SW1 257 D6
Hugo Rd N19 71 C4
Hugon Rd SW6 135 D2
Huguenot Pl SW18 158 A6

Huguenot Sq SE15 ... 140 B2
Hull Cl SE16 ... 118 D5
Hull Ct SE5 ... 139 B3
Hull St EC1 ... 235 A1
Hullbridge Mews N1 ... 235 C6
Hulme Pl SE1 ... 252 B1
Hulse Ave IG11 ... 79 C2
Humber Ct W7 ... 86 B1
Humber Dr W10 ... 90 D3
Humber Rd NW2 ... 68 B6
SE3 ... 142 D6
Humberstone Rd E13 ... 99 C4
Humberton Cl E9 ... 75 A3
Humbolt Rd W6 135 A6 264 A5
Hume Ct N1 ... 72 D1
Hume Ho 14 W11 ... 112 D5
Hume Way HA4 ... 40 A3
Humes Ave W7 ... 108 D4
Humphrey Ct SW11 ... 266 D1
Humphrey St
SE1 ... 117 D1 263 C2
Humphries Cl RM9 ... 81 B4
Humphry Ho 10 SW15 ... 156 D6
Hundred Acre NW9 ... 27 D1
Hungerdown E4 ... 20 A3
Hungerford Bridge
WC2 ... 250 C4
Hungerford Ho SW1 ... 269 B6
Hungerford Inf Sch N7 ... 72 A2
Hungerford Jun & Inf Schs
N7 ... 71 D2
Hungerford La WC2 ... 250 B4
Hungerford Prim Sch
N7 ... 72 A2
Hungerford Rd N7 ... 72 A3
4 N7 ... 71 D2
Hungerford St 24 E1 ... 96 B1
Hunsdon Cl RM9 ... 81 A2
Hunsdon Ho E5 ... 74 B5
Hunsdon Rd SE14 ... 140 D5
Hunslett St 27 E2 ... 96 C5
Hunstanton Ho NW1 ... 237 B4
Hunston Rd SM4 ... 201 D1
Hunt Ct N14 ... 15 B4
11 Northolt UB5 ... 84 D5
Hunt Rd UB2 ... 107 C3
Hunt St W11 ... 112 D5
Hunter Cl SE1 ... 262 D5
SW12 ... 159 A3
Borehamwood WD6 ... 11 A6
Hunter Ct 8 SE5 ... 139 B1
Hunter Ho 1 N19 ... 71 C5
SE1 ... 251 D1
SW5 ... 255 B1
SW8 ... 269 D3
WC1 ... 240 B6
Hunter Lo 9 W9 ... 91 C2
Hunter Rd SW20 ... 178 C2
Ilford IG1 ... 78 D3
South Norwood CR7 ... 205 B6
Hunter Sq RM10 ... 81 C4
Hunter St WC1 ... 94 A3 240 B6
Hunter Wlk E13 ... 99 A5
Borehamwood WD6 ... 11 B6
Huntercrombe Gdns
WD1 ... 22 C5
Hunters Ct 5 TW9 ... 153 D6
Hunters Gr Harrow HA3 ... 43 C5
Hayes UB3 ... 106 A4
Hunter's Gr BR6 ... 227 A4
Hunters Hall Prim Sch
RM10 ... 81 D3
Hunters Hall Rd RM10 ... 81 C3
Hunters Hill HA4 ... 62 D5
Hunters Lo 10 DA15 ... 168 A1
Hunters Mdw SE19 ... 183 C6
Hunters Rd KT9 ... 214 A4
Hunters The 2 BR3 ... 186 A2
Hunters Way Enfield EN2 ... 4 C4
South Croydon CR0 ... 221 C4
Hunting Gate Cl EN2 ... 4 C2
Hunting Gate Dr KT9 ... 214 A1
Hunting Gate Mews
Sutton SM1 ... 217 D5
Twickenham TW2 ... 152 C3
Huntingdon Cl CR4,
SW16 ... 204 A5
Huntingdon Ct SW14 ... 133 A2
Huntingdon Gdns W4 ... 133 A5
North Cheam KT4 ... 216 C5
Huntingdon Ho SW5 ... 255 B4
Huntingdon Rd N2 ... 48 C6
N9 ... 18 C3
Huntingdon St E16 ... 98 D1
N1 ... 72 B1
Huntingfield CR0 ... 223 B1
Huntingfield Rd SW15 ... 156 A6
Huntingford Ho SW15 ... 134 C3
Huntings Farm IG1 ... 79 C6
Huntings Rd RM10 ... 81 C2
Huntley Ho 7 SE21 ... 183 C6
Huntley St WC1 ... 93 D3 239 C5
Huntley Way SW20 ... 178 A1
Huntly Dr N3 ... 29 C4
Huntly Rd SE25 ... 205 C5
Hunton St E1 ... 96 A2
Hunts Cl SE3 ... 143 A3
Hunt's Ct WC2 ... 249 D5
Hunt's La E15 ... 98 A5
Hunts Mead EN3 ... 6 D2
Hunts Mede Cl BR7 ... 188 B3
Hunts Slip Rd SE21 ... 161 C2
Huntshaw Ho 37 E3 ... 97 D4
Huntsman Cl TW13 ... 172 B6
Huntsman St SE17 ... 263 A3
Huntsmoor Rd KT19 ... 215 B3
Huntspill St SW17 ... 158 A1
Huntsworth Ct SE6 ... 163 C3
Huntsworth Mews
NW1 ... 92 D3 237 C5
Hurdwick Ho NW1 ... 232 A4
Hurleston Ho 11 SE8 ... 119 B1
Hurley Cres SE16 ... 118 D4
Hurley Ct 1 W5 ... 87 C1
Hurley Ho 34 E2 ... 95 D4
SE11 ... 261 B3
Hurley Lo SE22 ... 162 C5
Hurley Rd UB6 ... 85 D2
Hurlingham & Chelsea Sch
SW6 ... 135 C2
Hurlingham Bsns Pk
SW6 ... 135 C2
Hurlingham Court Mans
SW6 ... 135 C3
Hurlingham Ct SW6 ... 135 B2
Hurlingham Gdns SW6 135 B2
Hurlingham Rd SW6 ... 135 B3
Erith DA7 ... 147 B5
Hurlingham Sq SW6 ... 135 D2
Hurlock Ho N5 ... 72 D5
Hurlock St N5 ... 72 D5
Hurlstone Rd SE25 ... 205 C4
Hurn Court Rd TW5 ... 128 D3
Hurn Ct TW5 ... 128 D3
Huron Cl 5 BR6 ... 227 D2
Huron Rd SW17 ... 159 A1
Hurren Cl SE3 ... 142 C2
Hurry Cl E15 ... 76 C1
Hursley Ct 11 KT6 ... 197 D2
Hurst Ave E4 ... 19 C1
N6 ... 49 C3
Hurst Cl E4 ... 19 C1
NW11 ... 47 D3
Chessington KT9 ... 214 C3
Hayes BR2 ... 208 D1
Northolt UB5 ... 63 B3
Hurst Ct SE25 ... 205 D5
Beckenham BR3 ... 185 C3
Woodford IG8 ... 37 B4
Hurst Gr KT12 ... 193 D1
Hurst Ho N1 ... 233 D3
SE2 ... 124 D1
7 SE26 ... 184 B5
Hurst La SE2 ... 124 D1
East Molesey KT8 ... 196 A6
Hurst Lo N8 ... 49 D3
Hurst Park Cty Prim Sch
KT8 ... 195 C6
Hurst Pl SE2 ... 146 D6
Hurst Prim Sch DA5 ... 168 D3
Hurst Rd E17 ... 53 D6
N21 ... 16 C3
Buckhurst Hill IG9 ... 21 D3
Croydon CR0 ... 221 B3
East Molesey KT8,KT12 ... 195 C6
Sidcup DA5,DA15 ... 168 C3
Walton-on-T KT8&KT12 ... 194 D5
Hurst Rise EN5 ... 1 C2
Hurst Springs DA5 ... 169 A3
Hurst St SE24 ... 160 D5
Hurst View Rd CR2 ... 221 C1
Hurst Way CR2 ... 221 C2
Hurstbourne KT10 ... 212 D2
Hurstbourne Cotts DA5 169 D4
Hurstbourne Gdns IG11 ... 79 C2
Hurstbourne Ho 12
SW15 ... 155 D5
Hurstbourne Priors
CR2 ... 221 C2
Hurstbourne Rd SE23 ... 163 A3
Hurstcombe IG9 ... 21 A2
Hurstcourt Rd SM1 ... 217 D6
Hurstdene Ave BR2 ... 208 D1
Hurstdene Gdns N15 ... 51 C2
Hurstfield BR2 ... 209 A4
Hurstfield Cres UB4 ... 83 C2
Hurstfield Rd KT8 ... 195 C6
Hurstmead Ct HA8 ... 26 D6
Hurstmere Sch DA15 ... 168 C3
Hurstview Grange CR2 220 D1
Hurstway Wlk 2 W11 ... 112 D6
Hurstwood Ave E18 ... 55 B5
Sidcup DA5 ... 169 A3
Hurstwood Ct N12 ... 30 C4
NW11 ... 47 B5
Hurstwood Dr BR1 ... 210 B6
Hurstwood Rd NW11 ... 47 B5
Hurtwood Rd KT12 ... 195 B2
Husbourne Ho 8 SE8 ... 119 A2
Huson Cl NW3 ... 70 C1
Hussars Cl TW4 ... 129 A2
Husseywell Cres BR2 ... 209 A1
Hutching's St E14 ... 119 C4
Hutchings Wlk NW11 ... 47 D5
Hutchins Cl E15 ... 76 A1
Hutchins Ho 8 SW4 ... 159 D4
Hutchins Rd SE28 ... 124 A5
Hutchinson Ct RM6 ... 58 D5
Hutchinson Ho 9 SE14 140 C5
Hutchinson Terr HA9 ... 65 D5
Hutton Cl Greenford UB6 ... 64 B3
Woodford IG8 ... 37 B4
Hutton Ct 3 N4 ... 50 B1
N9 ... 18 C4
1 W5 ... 87 C2
Hutton Gdns HA3 ... 24 A3
Hutton Gr N12 ... 29 D5
Hutton Ho 22 E2 ... 96 A4
Hutton La HA3 ... 24 A3
Hutton Row 4 HA8 ... 27 A3
Hutton St EC4 ... 241 B1
Hutton Wlk HA3 ... 24 A3
Huxbear St SE4 ... 163 B6
Huxley Cl UB5 ... 85 A6
Huxley Dr RM6 ... 58 B2
Huxley Gdns NW10 ... 88 B5
Huxley Ho NW8 ... 236 D5
SE2 ... 124 D1
4 SW9 ... 138 B3
Huxley Par N18 ... 33 B5
Huxley Pl N13 ... 16 D1
Huxley Rd E10 ... 76 A6
N18 ... 33 C6
Bexley DA16 ... 145 D2
Huxley Sayze N18 ... 33 B5
Huxley South N18 ... 33 B5
Huxley St W10 ... 91 A4
Hyacinth Cl 3 TW12 ... 173 C4
Hyacinth Dr UB10 ... 60 A1
Hyacinth Rd SW15 ... 156 A3
Hyde Cl E13 ... 99 A5
Ashford TW16 ... 171 C4
Hadley EN5 ... 1 B2
Hyde Cres NW9 ... 45 C4
Hyde Ct N20 ... 14 B1
NW9 ... 45 B2
Hounslow TW4 ... 151 B6
Hyde Estate Rd NW9 ... 45 D4
Hyde Farm Sch SW12 ... 159 D3
Hyde La SW11 ... 136 C4 267 A2
Hyde Park*
W2 ... 114 D5 247 C3
Hyde Park Ave N21 ... 17 B3
Hyde Park Cnr SW1 ... 248 B2
Hyde Park Corner Sta
SW1 ... 115 A4 248 B2
Hyde Park Cres
W2 ... 92 C1 237 A1
Hyde Park Gate
SW7 ... 114 A4 246 A1
SW7 ... 114 A4 246 B1
Hyde Park Gate Mews
SW7 ... 246 B1
Hyde Park Gdns N21 ... 17 A3
W2 ... 114 C6 246 D6
Hyde Park Gdns Mews
W2 ... 114 C6 247 A6
Hyde Park Mans NW1 ... 237 A3
Hyde Park Pl W2 ... 247 B6
Hyde Park Sq
W2 ... 92 C1 237 A1
Hyde Park Square Mews
W2 ... 237 A1
Hyde Park St W2 92 C1 237 A1
Hyde Park Twrs W2 ... 246 A5
Hyde Prim Sch The NW9 45 D3
Hyde Rd N1 ... 95 C6
Bexley DA7 ... 147 B3
Richmond TW10 ... 154 B6
Hyde St SE8 ... 141 C6
Hyde Terr TW15,TW16 ... 171 C4
Hyde Vale SE10 ... 142 A5
Hyde Way N9 ... 17 D2
Hayes UB3 ... 105 D2
Hyde Wlk SM4 ... 201 C2
Hydefield Cl N21 ... 17 B3
Hydefield Ct N9 ... 17 C2
Hyderabad Way E15 ... 76 C1
Hydes Pl 12 N1 ... 72 D1
Hydeside Gdns N9 ... 17 D2
Hydethorpe Ave N9 ... 17 D2
Hydethorpe Rd SW12 ... 159 C3
Hydon Ct N11 ... 30 D5
Hyh Ho E17 ... 35 D2
Hyland House Sch E17 ... 36 B1
Hylands Rd E17 ... 36 B1
Hylda Ct NW5 ... 71 A5
Hyleford Sch IG3 ... 79 C4
Hylton St SE18 ... 123 D2
Hyndewood 14 SE23 ... 162 D1
Hyndman Ho 5 N19 ... 71 D4
5 Dagenham RM10 ... 81 C5
Hyndman St SE15 ... 140 B6
Hynton Rd RM8 ... 80 C6
Hyperion Ho 23 E3 ... 97 A5
SW2 ... 160 B4
Hyrstdene CR0 ... 220 D4
Hyson Rd SE16 ... 118 B1
Hythe Ave DA7 ... 147 B5
Hythe Cl N18 ... 34 A6
Hythe Ho 7 SE16 ... 118 C4
Hythe Rd NW10 ... 90 A3
South Norwood CR7 ... 183 B1
Hythe Road Ind Est
NW10 ... 90 A3
Hyver Hill NW7 ... 11 B4

I

Ian Ct SE23 ... 162 C2
Ibberton Ho SW8 ... 270 C4
Ibbotson Ave E16 ... 98 D1
Ibbott St 22 E1 ... 96 C3
Iberia Ho 17 N19 ... 49 D2
Iberian Ave CR0,SM6 ... 220 A4
Ibis Ct 16 SE8 ... 141 B6
Ibis La W4 ... 133 A4
Ibis Way UB4 ... 84 D1
Ibrox Ct 3 IG9 ... 21 C2
Ibsley Gdns SW15 ... 156 A3
Ibsley Way EN4 ... 2 C1
Ibstock Place Sch
SW15 ... 155 C5
Icarus Ho 16 E3 ... 97 B4
Iceland Rd E3 ... 97 C6
Ickburgh Est E5 ... 74 B6
Ickburgh Rd E5 ... 74 B5
Ickburgh Sch E5 ... 74 B5
Ickenham Cl HA4 ... 61 B6
Ickenham Rd HA4 ... 39 B1
Ickenham Sta UB10 ... 61 A4
Ickleton Rd SE9 ... 188 A6
Icknield Dr IG2 ... 56 D4
Ickworth Park Rd E17 ... 53 A5
Icough Ct SE3 ... 143 B5
Ida Rd N15 ... 51 B5
Ida St E14 ... 98 A1
Iden Cl BR2 ... 208 C6
Idlecombe Rd SW17 ... 181 A4
Idmiston Rd E15 ... 76 D3
SE21,SE27 ... 161 A2
New Malden KT4 ... 199 D2
Idmiston Sq KT4 ... 199 D2
Idol La EC3 ... 117 C6 253 A5
Idonia St SE8 ... 141 C5
Iffley Ho 47 E2 ... 95 D4
Iffley Rd W6 ... 112 B3
Ifield Ho SE17 ... 263 B2
Ifield Rd SW10 ... 135 D6 265 D6
Ifor Evans Pl E1 ... 96 D3
Ightham Ho SE17 ... 263 A3
Beckenham BR3 ... 185 B3
Ightham Rd DA8 ... 147 C5
Ilbert St W10 ... 91 A4
Ilchester Gdns W2 ... 245 C6
Ilchester Mans W8 ... 255 A6
Ilchester Pl
W14 ... 113 B3 254 D6
Ilchester Rd RM8 ... 80 C3
Ildersly Gr SE21 ... 161 B2
Ilderton Jun & Inf Sch
SE16 ... 118 C1
Ilderton Rd SE15,SE16 ... 140 C6
Ilex Cl TW16 ... 172 C1
Ilex Rd NW10 ... 67 D2
Ilex Way SW16 ... 182 C5
Ilford Hill IG1 ... 78 C5
Ilford Ho 14 N1 ... 73 B2
Ilford Interchange IG1 ... 78 C5
Ilford Jewish Prim Sch
IG6 ... 57 B6
Ilford La IG1 ... 78 D4
Ilford Prep Sch IG3 ... 58 A1
Ilford Sta IG1 ... 78 D6
Ilford Ursuline High Sch
IG1 ... 78 D6
Ilfracombe Gdns RM6 ... 58 B2
Ilfracombe Rd BR1 ... 164 D1
Iliffe St SE17 ... 116 D1 261 D2
Iliffe Yd SE17 ... 116 D1 261 D2
Ilkeston Ct 7 E5 ... 74 D4
Ilkley Cl SE19 ... 183 B4
Ilkley Rd E16 ... 99 C2
South Oxhey WD1 ... 22 D5
Illingworth Cl CR4 ... 202 B6
Illingworth Way EN1 ... 17 C6
Ilmington Rd HA3 ... 43 D3
Ilminster Gdns SW11 ... 136 C1
Ilsley Ct 8 SW8 ... 137 C3
Imber Cl N14 ... 15 C4
Thames Ditton KT7 ... 196 B1
Imber Court Trad Est
KT8 ... 196 B3
Imber Cross KT7 ... 196 D3
Imber Ct 4 SE9 ... 166 C5
Imber Gr KT10 ... 196 B2
Imber Park Rd KT10 ... 196 B1
Imber St N1 ... 235 C5
Immanuel & St Andrew CE
Prim Sch SW16 ... 182 A4
Immanuel Coll WD2 ... 8 C4
Impact Ct SE20 ... 184 B1
Imperial Ave 5 N16 ... 73 C4
Imperial Cl HA2 ... 41 C3
Imperial Coll of Science &
Technology
SW7 ... 114 B3 256 C6
Imperial College Rd
SW7 ... 114 B3 256 C6
Imperial Ct N20 ... 14 A1
NW8 ... 230 B4
HA2 ... 41 C2
Imperial Dr HA2 ... 41 C3
Imperial Gdns CR4 ... 203 B6
Imperial Ho E3 ... 97 A4
2 E14 ... 119 B6
Imperial Mews 5 E6 ... 99 D5
Imperial Pl BR7 ... 188 C2
Imperial Rd N22 ... 32 A2
SW6 ... 265 D1
East Bedfont TW14 ... 149 C4
Imperial Sq SW6 ... 265 D2
Imperial St E3 ... 98 A4
Imperial Twrs 3 NW3 ... 70 A2
Imperial War Mus*
SE1,SE11 ... 116 C3 261 B5
Imperial Way
Croydon CR0,CR9 ... 220 C2
Harrow HA3 ... 44 A3
New Eltham BR7,SE9 ... 167 A1
Impington 19 KT1 ... 176 C1
Inca Dr SE9 ... 166 D4
Inchmery Rd SE6 ... 164 A3
Inchwood BR4,CR0 ... 223 D4
Independant Jewish Day Sch
NW4 ... 46 D4
Independant Pl E8 ... 73 D3
Independents Rd SE3 ... 142 D2
Inderwick Rd N8 ... 50 B4
Indescon Ct E14 ... 119 D4
India St EC3 ... 243 C1
India Way W12 ... 112 B6
Indigo Mews N16 ... 73 B5
Indus Ct 15 SE15 ... 139 D5
Indus Rd SE7 ... 143 C5
Ingal Rd E13 ... 99 A3
Ingate Pl SW8 ... 137 B4 268 D1
Ingatestone Rd E12 ... 55 C1
SE25 ... 206 B5
Woodford IG8 ... 37 B3
Ingelow Ho W8 ... 245 C2
Ingelow St SW8 ... 137 B3
Ingersoll Rd W12 ... 112 B5
Enfield EN3 ... 6 C5
Ingestre Pl W1 ... 239 B1
Ingestre Rd E7 ... 77 A4
NW5 ... 71 B4
Ingham Rd NW6 ... 69 C4
Ingle Cl HA5 ... 41 B6
Ingle Ho 3 SW12 ... 159 D3
Inglebert St EC1 ... 94 C4 234 A2
Ingleborough Ct N17 ... 51 D6
Ingleborough St SW9 ... 138 C3
Ingleby Dr HA1 ... 64 B5
Ingleby Rd N7 ... 72 A5
Dagenham RM10 ... 81 D2
Ilford IG1 ... 56 D1
Ingleby Way
Chislehurst West BR7 ... 188 C5
Wallington SM6 ... 219 D1
Ingledew Rd SE18 ... 123 B1
Inglefield Sq 12 E1 ... 118 B5
Inglehurst Gdns IG4 ... 56 B4
Inglemere Ct CR4,SW17 180 D3
Inglemere Rd SE23 ... 162 D1
Mitcham CR4,SW17 ... 180 D3
Ingleshaw Wlk E9 ... 75 B2
Ingleside Cl BR3 ... 185 C3
Ingleside Gr SE3 ... 142 D6
Inglethorpe Ho 6 E5 ... 74 A6
Inglethorpe St SW6 ... 134 D4
Ingleton Ave DA16 ... 168 A6
Ingleton Rd N18 ... 34 A4
Ingleton St SW9 ... 138 C3
Ingleway N12 ... 30 C4
Inglewood BR7 ... 189 B4
Inglewood Cl E14 ... 119 C2
Inglewood Copse BR1 ... 188 B1
Inglewood Ct 3 BR1 ... 186 D3
Inglewood Mans 11 NW6 69 C3
Inglewood Rd NW6 ... 69 C3
Inglis Ct W5 ... 110 B6
Inglis Ho 1 SW15 ... 156 C6
Inglis Rd W5 ... 110 B6
Croydon CR0 ... 205 D1
Inglis St SE5 ... 138 D4
Ingram Ave NW11 ... 48 A2
Ingram Cl SE11 ... 260 D4
Stanmore HA7 ... 25 C5
Ingram Ct EN1 ... 17 D5
Ingram High Sch for Boys
CR7 ... 183 A2
Ingram Ho E3 ... 97 A6
Teddington KT8 ... 175 C2
Ingram Lo 8 SW4 ... 159 D5
Ingram Rd N2 ... 48 C5
South Norwood CR7 ... 183 A2
Ingram Way UB6 ... 86 B6
Ingrave Ho RM9 ... 102 B6
Ingrave St SW11 ... 136 C2
Ingrebourne Ct E4 ... 19 D2
Ingrebourne Ho NW8 ... 236 D4
2 Catford BR1 ... 186 B5
Ingress St 4 W4 ... 111 C1
Inigo Jones Rd SE7 ... 144 A5
Inigo Pl WC2 ... 250 A6
Inkerman Rd NW5 ... 71 B2
Inkerman Terr W8 ... 255 B5
Inks Gn E4 ... 36 A5
Inkster Ho 8 SW11 ... 136 C2
Inman Rd NW10 ... 89 C6
SW18 ... 158 A4
Inmans Row IG8 ... 37 A6
Inner Circ NW1 ... 93 A4 231 A2
Inner Park Rd SW19 ... 156 D2
Inner Ring E TW6 ... 126 D2
Inner Ring W TW6 ... 126 C2
Inner Temple EC4 ... 251 A6
Inner Temple La EC4 ... 241 A1
Innes Cl SW20 ... 179 A1
Innes Gdns SW15 ... 156 B5
Innes Lo SE23 ... 162 D1
Innes Yd CR0 ... 221 A5
Innis Ho SE17 ... 263 A2
Inniskilling Rd E13 ... 99 C5
Innovation Cl HA0 ... 88 A6
Inskip Cl E10 ... 75 D6
Inskip Rd RM8 ... 58 D1
Insley Ho 13 E3 ... 97 D4
Inst for Child Health
WC1 ... 94 B3 240 C5
Institute Pl E8 ... 74 B3
Instone Cl SM6 ... 220 A1
Integer Gdns E11 ... 54 B2
Interchange The NW5 ... 71 B3
International Ave TW5 ... 106 C1
International Sch of London
W3 ... 110 C2
International Trad Est
UB2 ... 106 B3
Inveagh Cl E9 ... 96 D6
Inver Cl E5 ... 74 C6
Inver Ct W2 ... 91 D1
Inverary Pl SE18 ... 145 B6
Inverclyde Gdns RM6 ... 58 D5
Inveresk Gdns KT4 ... 216 A5
Inverforth Cl NW3 ... 70 A6
Inverforth House Hospl
NW3 ... 70 A6
Inverforth Rd N11 ... 31 B5
Invergarry Ho NW6 ... 91 D5
Inverine Rd SE7 ... 121 B1
Invermore Pl SE18 ... 123 A2
Inverness Ave EN1 ... 5 C4
Inverness Ct 10 SE6 ... 164 D3
8 W3 ... 88 C1
Inverness Gdns W8 ... 245 C3
Inverness Mews W2 ... 245 D6
Inverness Pl W2 ... 245 D6
Inverness Rd N18 ... 34 B5
Hounslow TW3 ... 129 C1
North Cheam KT4 ... 200 D1
Southall UB2 ... 107 A2
Inverness St NW1 ... 231 D6
Inverness Terr
W2 ... 113 D6 245 D6
Inverton Rd SE15 ... 140 D1
Invicta Cl
Chislehurst West BR7 ... 188 C5
East Bedfont TW14 ... 149 D3
Invicta Ct KT9 ... 214 B3
Invicta Gr UB5 ... 85 B4
Invicta Plaza SE1 ... 251 C4
Invicta Prim Sch SE3 ... 143 A5
Invicta Rd SE3,SE7 ... 143 A6
Inville Rd SE17 ... 117 B1 262 D1
Inwen Ct SE8 ... 119 A1
Inwood Ave TW3 ... 130 A2
Inwood Bsns Pk TW3 ... 129 D1
Inwood Cl CR0 ... 223 A6
Inwood Ct 10 NW1 ... 71 C1
Inwood Ho 19 SE22 ... 139 C2
Inwood Rd TW3 ... 130 A1
Inworth St SW11 ... 136 C3
Inworth Wlk N1 ... 235 A6
Ion Sq 8 E2 ... 96 A5
Iona Cl SE6 ... 163 C4
Ionian Ho 22 E1 ... 96 D3
Ipsden Bldgs SE1 ... 251 B2
Ipswich Ho SE4 ... 162 D6
Ipswich Rd SW17 ... 181 A4
Irby Ho SW2 ... 160 C5
Ireland Cl E6 ... 100 B2
Ireland Pl N22 ... 32 A3
Ireland Yd EC4 ... 241 D1
Irene Rd SW6 ... 135 C4 265 B1
Broom Hill BR6 ... 211 D2
Ireton Cl N10 ... 31 A3
Ireton Ho SW9 ... 138 C3
Ireton St 12 E3 ... 97 C3
Iris Ave DA5 ... 169 A5
Iris Cl E6 ... 100 A3
Croydon CR0 ... 206 D1
Surbiton KT6 ... 198 B2
Iris Cres DA7 ... 147 B6
Iris Rd KT19 ... 214 D3
Iris Way E4 ... 35 B4
Irkdale Ave EN1 ... 5 D4
Iroko Ho 7 NW3 ... 69 D2
Iron Bridge Cl NW10 ... 67 C3
Southall UB2 ... 108 A5
Iron Bridge Ho NW3 ... 70 D1
Iron Bridge Rd UB11 ... 104 C5
Iron Mill Pl SW18 ... 157 D5
Iron Mill Rd SW18 ... 157 D5
Ironbridge Rd S UB7 ... 104 C4
Ironmonger La
EC2 ... 95 B1 242 C1
Ironmonger Pas EC1 ... 235 B1
Ironmonger Row
EC1 ... 95 A4 235 B1
Ironmonger's Pl 13 E14 119 C2
Ironside Cl SE16 ... 118 D4
Ironside Ho E9 ... 75 A4
Irvine Ave HA3 ... 43 B6
Irvine Cl N20 ... 14 C2
Irvine Ct W1 ... 239 B5
Thornton Heath CR7 ... 204 C3
Irvine Ho 2 E14 ... 97 D2
N7 ... 72 B2
Irvine Way BR6 ... 211 D2
Irving Ave UB5 ... 84 D6
Irving Ct N22 ... 32 D2
Irving Gr SW9 ... 138 B3
Irving Ho SE17 ... 261 C1
Irving Mews N1 ... 73 A2
Irving Rd W14 ... 112 D3
Irving St WC2 ... 249 D5
Irwell Ct W7 ... 86 B1
Irwell Est 25 SE16 ... 118 C4
Irwin Ave SE18 ... 145 C5
Irwin Cl UB10 ... 60 C5
Irwin Gdns NW10 ... 90 B6
Isaac Newton Ctr W11 ... 91 A1
Isabel St SW9 ... 270 D2
Isabella Cl N14 ... 15 C4
Isabella Ct 8 TW10 ... 154 B5
Isabella Dr BR6 ... 227 A4
Isabella Ho SE11 ... 261 C2
19 W6 ... 112 C1
Isabella Rd E9 ... 74 C3
Isabella St SE1 ... 251 C3
Isambard Mews E14 ... 120 A3
Isambard Pl SE16 ... 118 C5
Isel Way 4 SE22 ... 161 C6
Iseldon Ct N7 ... 72 A4
Isham Rd SW16 ... 182 A1
Isis Cl SW15 ... 134 C1
Ruislip HA4 ... 39 A3
Isis Ct W4 ... 132 D5
Isis Ho 2 N18 ... 33 D4
NW8 ... 236 D5
Isis St SW18 ... 158 A2
Isla Rd SE18 ... 145 A6
Islamia Sch Ctr NW6 ... 91 A6
Islamic Coll for Advanced
Studies NW10 ... 68 B2
Island Farm Ave KT8 ... 195 B4
Island Farm Rd KT8 ... 195 C4
Island Gardens Sta E14 120 A1
Island Ho SW19 ... 202 A5
Island Rd CR4 ... 180 D3
Island Row E14 ... 97 B1
Islay Gdns TW4 ... 150 D6

Isleden Ho N1 235 A6
Isledon Rd N4,N7 72 C5
Islehurst Cl BR7 188 C2
Isleworth & Syon Sch for Boys TW7 130 C5
Isleworth Bsns Complex TW7 130 D3
Isleworth Sta TW7 130 D3
Isleworth Town Sch TW7 131 A3
Islington Est N1 95 A6 235 A6
Islington Gn N1 94 D6 234 C5
Islington Green Sch N1 95 A6 235 A5
Islington High St N1 94 D5 234 C4
Islington Park Mews 1 N1 72 D1
Islington Park St N1 72 D1
Islington Sixth Form Ctr N7 72 C4
Islip Gdns Burnt Oak HA8 27 B3
Northolt UB5 63 A1
Islip Manor Rd UB5 63 A1
Islip St NW5 71 C3
Ismailia Rd E7 77 B1
Isobel Ho
10 Charlton TW16 171 D3
Harrow HA1 42 D4
Isokon Flats 3 NW3 70 D3
Isom Cl E13 99 B4
Ivanhoe Dr HA3 25 B1
Ivanhoe Ho 32 E3 97 A5
11 SW12 159 B4
Ivanhoe Rd SE5 139 D2
Hounslow TW4 128 D2
Ivatt Pl W14 113 B1 254 D1
Ivatt Way N17 50 D6
Ive Farm Cl E10 75 C6
Ive Farm La E10 75 C6
Iveagh Ave NW10 88 C5
Iveagh Cl NW10 88 C5
Iveagh Ct EC3 243 C1
4 Beckenham BR3 207 D6
Iveagh Ho 2 SW9 138 D3
SW10 266 B4
Ivebury Ct W10 90 C1
Ivedon Rd DA16 146 C3
Iveley Rd SW4 137 C3
Iver Ct N1 73 A2
Ivere Dr EN5 13 D5
Iverhurst Cl DA6 168 D6
Iverna Ct W8 255 B6
Iverna Gdns W8 113 C3 255 B6
Hatton TW14 149 B6
Ivers Way CR0 223 D1
Iverson Rd NW6 69 C2
Ives Rd E16 98 C2
Ives St SW3 114 C2 257 B4
Ivestor Terr SE23 162 C4
Ivimey St E2 96 A4
Ivinghoe Cl EN1 5 C4
Ivinghoe Ho 14 N7 71 D3
Ivinghoe Rd Bushey WD23 8 B4
Dagenham RM8 80 B3
Ivor Ct N8 50 A3
NW1 237 C6
Ivor Gr SE9 166 D3
Ivor Pl NW1 92 D3 237 C5
Ivor St NW1 71 C1
Ivories The N1 73 A1
Ivory Ct TW13 150 A3
Ivory Ho E1 253 D4
9 SW11 136 A2
Ivorydown BR1 187 A6
Ivy Church La SE1,SE17 263 C2
Ivy Cl Harrow HA2 63 B4
Pinner HA5 40 C2
Sunbury TW16 172 C1
Ivy Cotts UB10 82 C4
Ivy Cres W4 111 A2
Ivy Ct SE3 142 D1
SE13 163 C6
18 SE16 118 A1
Ivy Gdns N8 50 A3
Mitcham CR4 203 D6
Ivy Ho 6 E5 52 B1
Croydon CR0 206 D1
Ivy La TW4 129 B1
Ivy Lo W8 245 A4
Ivy Rd E16 99 A1
E17 53 C3
N14 15 D4
NW2 68 C4
SE4 141 C1
SW17 180 C5
Hounslow TW3 129 D1
Tolworth KT6 198 C1
Ivy St N1 95 C5
Ivy Terr 3 IG2 57 A3
Ivy Wlk RM9 81 A2
Ivybridge Cl
Hillingdon UB8 82 A4
2 Twickenham TW1 153 A4
Ivybridge Ct 1 BR7 188 C2
Ivybridge Ho 18 SE22 139 C2
Ivybridge Jun & Inf Sch TW1 152 D5
Ivybridge La WC2 250 B5
Ivybridge Ret Pk TW7 152 D6
Ivychurch Cl SE20 184 C3
Ivydale Jun & Inf Sch SE15 140 D1
Ivydale Rd SE15 140 D1
Carshalton SM5 218 D6
Ivyday Gr SW16 160 B1
Ivydene KT12,KT8 195 B4
Ivydene Cl SM1 218 A4
Ivyhouse Rd
Dagenham RM9 81 A2
Uxbridge UB10 60 D5
Ivymount Rd SE27 160 C1
Ixworth Pl SW3 114 C2 257 A3
Izane Rd DA6 147 B1

J

Jack Ashley Ct 5 NW9 27 C2
Jack Barnett Way N22 32 B1
Jack Clow Rd E15 98 C5
Jack Cook Ho 9 IG11 78 D1
Jack Cornwell St E12 78 C4
Jack Taylor Sch NW8 92 A6 229 A6
Jack Tizard Sch SW6 134 D4
Jack Walker Ct N5 72 D4
Jackass La BR2 225 C2
Jacklin Gn IG8 37 A6
Jackman Ho 24 E1 118 B5
Jackman Mews NW2 67 C5
Jackman St E8 96 B6
Jackson Cl E9 74 D1
Uxbridge UB10 60 A1
Jackson Ct E7 77 B2
E11 55 B1
Jackson Ho 16 SW11 136 B2
Jackson Rd N7 72 B4
Barking IG11 101 B6
East Barnet EN4 14 C5
Keston Mark BR2 226 B6
Uxbridge UB10 60 A1
Jackson St SE18 144 C6
Jackson Way UB2 107 D4
Jackson's La N6 49 B2
Jackson's Pl CR0 205 C1
Jackson's Way CR0 223 C5
Jacob Ho 5 DA18 124 D4
Jacob Mans 1 E1 96 B1
Jacob St SE1 118 A4
Jacobin Lo N7 72 A3
Jacobs Cl RM10 81 D4
Jacobs Ho E13 99 C4
Jacob's Well Mews W1 238 B2
Jacobson Ct SW11 267 B1
Jacobson Ho E1 243 C2
Jacotts Ho W10 90 C3
Jacqueline Cl UB5 85 A6
Jade Cl E16 99 D1
NW2 46 D2
Dagenham RM8 58 C1
Jaffe Rd IG1 57 B1
Jaffray Rd BR2 209 D5
Jaggard Way SW12 158 D4
Jagger Ho SW11 267 C2
Jago Cl SE18 145 A6
Jamahirya Sch SW3 136 C6 267 A6
Jamaica Rd SE1 253 D1
SE16 118 B3
Thornton Heath CR7 204 D3
Jamaica St E1 96 C2
James Allen's Girls' Sch SE22 161 C6
James Allen's Prep Sch SE21 161 B5
James Anderson Ct 29 E2 95 C5
James Ave NW2 68 C3
Dagenham RM8 59 B1
James Bedford Cl HA5 22 C1
James Boswell Cl 1 SW16 182 C6
James Brine Ho 6 E2 95 D4
James Campbell Ho 2 E2 96 C5
James Cl 8 E13 99 A5
NW11 47 A3
James Collins Cl W9 91 B3
James Ct 4 E4 20 B2
3 E18 37 B1
N12 30 C3
NW9 27 C1
Northolt UB5 85 A5
James Dixon Prim Sch SE20 184 B3
James Docherty Ho 4 E2 96 C5
James Dudson Ct NW10 67 A1
James Est CR4 180 D1
James Gdns N22 32 D3
James Hammett Ho 9 E2 95 D5
James Ho E1 97 A3
33 SE16 118 D4
James Joyes Wlk 7 SE24 138 D1
James La E10,E11 54 B3
James Lee Sq EN3 7 C5
James Leicester Hall of Residence N7 72 A2
James Lind Ho 5 SE8 119 B2
James Middleton Ho 20 E2 96 B4
James Newman Ct SE9 166 C1
James Pl N17 33 D2
James St W1 93 A1 238 B1
WC2 116 A6 250 B6
Barking IG11 79 A1
Enfield EN1 17 D6
Hounslow TW3 130 B2
James Stewart Ho NW6 69 B1
James Stroud Ho SE17 262 B1
James Wolfe Jun & Inf Sch SE10 142 A5
Jameson Ct 6 E2 96 C5
Jameson Ho SE11 260 C2
Jameson Lo N6 49 C3
Jameson St W8 245 B4
Jamestown Rd NW1 93 B6 231 C6
Jamestown Way E14 120 B6
Jamieson Ho TW4 151 B5
Jane Sabina Colard's Almshouses 1 E17 54 A4
Jane St E1 96 B1
Janet Ct 4 DA7 147 C1
Janet St E14 119 C3
Janeway Pl 2 SE16 118 B4
Janeway St SE16 118 A4
Janice Mews 3 IG1 78 D5
Jansen Wlk SW11 136 B1
Janson Cl E15 76 C3
NW10 67 C5
Janson Rd E15 76 C3
Jansons Rd N15 51 C6
Japan Cres N4 50 B1
Japan Rd RM6 58 D3
Japanese Sch The W3 110 C6
Jaquets Ct DA5 169 C2
Jardine Rd E1 118 D6
Jarman Ho 13 E1 96 C2
SE16 118 D2
Jarret Ho 1 E3 97 C4
Jarrett Cl SW2 160 D3
Jarrow Cl SM4 201 D4
Jarrow Rd N17 52 B5
SE16 118 C1
Ilford RM6 58 C3
Jarrow Way E9 75 A4
Jarvis Cl
1 Barking IG11 101 B6
Ducks Island EN5 12 D6
Jarvis Ct 2 SE10 142 A4
Jarvis Ho 3 SE15 140 A4
Jarvis Rd SE22 139 C1
South Croydon CR2 221 B2
Jashada Ho SE18 122 C1
Jasmin SE1 253 D3
Jasmin Ho SE4 141 B2
Jasmin Lo 17 SE16 118 B1
Jasmin Rd KT19 214 D3
Jasmine Cl Ilford IG1 78 D3
Orpington BR6 226 D6
Southall UB1 107 A6
Jasmine Ct SE12 165 A5
11 Wallington SM6 219 B2
Jasmine Gdns
Harrow HA2 63 C6
West Wickham CR0 223 D5
Jasmine Gr SE20 184 B2
Jasmine Terr UB7 104 C4
Jasmine Way KT7 196 C5
Jason Ct 2 SW9 138 C4
W1 238 B2
Jason Ho UB5 84 B4
Jason Wlk SE9 188 C6
Jasper Cl EN3 6 C5
Jasper Ho KT4 199 B1
Jasper Rd E16 99 D1
SE19 183 D4
Jasper Wlk N1 235 C2
Java Wharf SE1 253 D2
Javelin Way UB5 84 D4
Jawahar Bagh SW16 182 D4
Jay Gdns BR7 188 B6
Jay Ho SW15 134 C3
Jay Mews SW7 114 A4 246 B1
Jaycroft EN2 4 C4
Jayson Ct 7 CR0 206 A1
Jean Darling Ho SW10 266 C5
Jean Ho 3 SW17 180 C5
Jean Humbert Ho 2 SE27 183 B6
Jean Pardies Ho 21 E1 96 C2
Jebb Ave SW2 160 A5
Jebb St E3 97 C5
Jedburgh Rd E13 99 C4
Jedburgh St SW11 137 A1
Jeddo Mews W12 111 D4
Jeddo Rd W12 111 D4
Jefferies Ho 12 NW10 67 B1
Jefferson Cl W13 109 B3
Ilford IG2 56 D4
Jefferson Wlk 13 SE18 144 C6
Jeffrey Row SE12 165 B6
Jeffrey's Ct 2 SW4 138 A3
Jeffrey's Pl NW1 71 C1
Jeffreys Rd EN3 7 B1
Jeffrey's Rd SW4 138 A3
Jeffrey's St NW1 71 C1
Jeffs Cl TW12 173 D4
Jeffs Rd SM1 217 B4
Jefton Ct SM6 219 C3
Jeger Ave E2 95 D6
Jeken Rd SE9 143 C1
Jelf Rd SW2 160 C6
Jellicoe Ct E4 36 B4
Jellicoe Gdns HA7 25 A4
Jellicoe Ho 5 E2 96 A5
11 SW15 156 D6
Jellicoe Rd 4 E13 99 A3
N17 33 B3
Jem Paterson Ct HA1 64 C4
Jemmett Cl KT2 176 D2
Jemotts Ct 9 SE14 140 D6
Jengar Cl SM1 217 D4
Jenkins Ho SW8 269 C2
Jenkins La IG11 101 A4
Jenkins Rd E13 99 B3
Jenkinson Ho 12 E2 96 D4
Jenner Ave W3 89 B2
Jenner Ct N21 16 A6
Jenner Ho SE3 142 C6
5 Belvedere DA17 125 C3
Jenner Pl SW13 134 B6
Jenner Rd N16 73 D5
Jennett Rd CR0 220 C5
Jennifer Ho SE11 261 B3
Jennifer Rd BR1 164 D1
Jennings Cl KT6 197 C2
Jennings Ho SE10 120 B1
Jennings Rd SE22 161 D5
Jenny Hammond Cl E11 76 D5
Jenny Hammond Prim Sch E11 76 C4
Jensen Ho 10 E3 97 C3
Jenson Way SE19 183 D3
Jenton Ave DA7 147 A3
Jephson Ho 6 SE17 138 D6
17 SW4 138 A3
Jephson Rd E7 77 C1
Jephson St SE5 139 B4
Jephtha Rd SW18 157 C5
Jeppo's La CR4 202 D5
Jerdan Pl SW6 265 A4
Jeremiah St 11 E14 97 D1
Jeremy Bentham Ho 9 E2 96 A4
Jeremy's Gn N18 34 C6
Jermyn St SW1 115 C5 249 B4
Jerningham Ct SE14 141 A4
Jerningham Rd SE14 141 A4
Jerome Cres NW8 92 C3 237 A6
Jerome Ct 2 N11 31 C5
Jerome Ho 8 E14 97 A1
NW1 237 B4
Kingston u T KT1 175 D1
Jerome St E1 95 D3 243 C5
Jerome Twr 5 W3 110 D4
Jerrard St SE13 141 D2
Jerrold Lo SW15 134 C2
Jerrold St 24 N1 95 C5
Jersey Ave HA7 25 C1
Jersey Ct UB2 107 B3
Jersey Dr BR5 211 B3
Jersey Ho 12 N1 73 A2
Enfield EN3 6 D5
Jersey Rd E11 54 B1
E16 99 C1
N1 73 A2
SW17 181 B4
W7 109 A4
Hounslow TW5,TW7 130 B5
Ilford IG1 78 D4
Jersey St E2 96 B4
Jerusalem Pas EC1 241 C5
Jervis Bay Ho 8 E14 98 B1
Jervis Ct W1 238 D1
9 Dagenham RM10 81 D2
Jerviston Gdns SW16 182 C4
Jesmond Ave HA9 66 B2
Jesmond Cl CR4 203 B6
Jesmond Rd CR0 205 D2
Jesmond Way HA7 26 A5
Jessam Ave E5 52 B1
Jessamine Rd W7 108 D5
Jesse Rd E10 54 A1
Jessel Ho SW1 259 D4
WC1 233 A1
Jessica Rd SW18 158 A6
Jessie Blythe La 2 N19 50 A2
Jessie's Cotts E17 53 A3
Jessiman Terr TW17 192 C4
Jesson Ho SE17 262 C3
Jessop Ave UB2 107 B2
Jessop Ct N1 234 D3
Jessop Prim Sch SE24 139 A1
Jessop Sq E14 119 C5
Jessops Way CR0 203 C3
Jessup Cl SE18 123 A2
Jeston Ho 10 SE27 160 D1
Jethou Ho 13 N1 73 A2
Jetstar Way UB5 85 A4
Jevington Way SE12 165 B3
Jevons Ho 9 NW8 70 B1
Jewel Rd E17 53 C6
Jewell Ho 3 SW12 159 C4
Jewish Home & Hospl at Tottenham The N15 51 D5
Jewry St EC3 95 D1 243 C1
Jews Coll NW4 46 D5
Jews Free Sch NW1 71 D2
Jews Row SW18 136 A1
Jews Wlk SE26 184 B6
Jeymer Ave NW2 68 C3
Jeymer Dr UB6 86 A6
Jeypore Rd SW18 158 A5
Jillian Cl TW12 173 C3
Jim Bradley Cl 16 SE18 122 C2
Jim Griffiths Ho SW6 264 D5
Joan Cres SE9 165 D4
Joan Gdns RM8 81 A6
Joan Player Ho EN3 6 D6
Joan Rd RM8 81 A6
Joan St SE1 116 D5 251 C3
Joanna Ho 7 W6 112 C1
Jocelin Ho N1 233 D5
Jocelyn Rd TW9 132 A2
Jocelyn St SE15 140 A4
Jockey's Fields WC1 94 B2 240 D4
Jodane Rd SE8 119 B2
Jodrell Cl TW7 131 A4
Jodrell Rd E3 75 B1
Joe Hunte Ct 2 SW27 182 D5
Joel St HA5,HA6 40 A5
Johanna Prim Sch SE1 116 C4 251 A1
Johanna St SE1 251 A1
John Adam St WC2 116 A6 250 B5
John Aird Ct W2 92 A2 236 B4
John Archer Way SW18 158 B5
John Ashby Cl SW2 160 A5
John Austin Cl KT2 176 B2
John Baird Ct SE26 184 D6
John Baird Ho 14 SE20 184 C3
John Ball Prim Sch SE3 142 C3
John Barker Ct NW6 69 A1
John Barker Ho IG1 79 B6
John Barnes Wlk E15 76 D2
John Barter Ho TW3 129 B3
John Betts' Ho W12 112 A3
John Bond Ho 2 E3 97 B5
John Bradshaw Rd N14 15 D3
John Brent Ho 8 SE8 118 D2
John Buck Ho NW10 89 D6
John Burns Dr IG11 79 C1
John Burns Prim Sch SW11 137 A3
John Busch Sch TW7 131 B4
John Campbell Rd 26 N16 73 C3
John Carpenter St EC4 251 C6
John Cartwright Ho 7 E2 96 B4
John Chilton Sch UB5 63 A1
John Clifford Ho N8 50 A3
John Cornwell VC Ho 5 E12 78 C4
John Dee Ho 3 SW14 133 B2
John Donne Jun & Inf Sch SE15 140 B4
John Drinkwater Cl E11 54 D2
John Dwight Ho SW6 135 D2
John F. Kennedy Sch E15 98 B6
John Felton Rd 16 SE16 118 A4
John Fielden Ho 10 E2 96 B4
John Fisher St E1 118 A6
John Glynes Ct SW15 134 B1
John Gooch Dr EN2 4 D4
John Harris Ho SE15 140 A2
John Hunt Ct 5 SE9 166 A2
John Islip St SW1 116 A2 260 A3
John Kaye Ct TW17 192 C4
John Keall Ho SW15 134 D2
John Keats Lo EN2 5 B4
John Keats Sec & Prim Sch NW8 70 B1
John Keble CE Prim Sch NW10 89 D6
John Kelly Tech Colls NW2 67 D5
John Kennedy Ct 1 N1 73 B2
John Kennedy Ho 1 SE16 118 D2
John Kennedy Lo 2 N1 73 B2
John King Ct 4 N19 71 D6
John Kirk Ho 22 SW11 136 B2
5 SW16 160 A1
Beckenham BR3 207 A5
John Knight Lo SW6 265 B4
John Lamb Ct HA3 24 C2
John Loughborough Sch The N17 33 D1
John Lyon Sch The HA2 42 B1
John Masefield Ho N15 51 B3
John Maurice Cl SE17 117 B2 262 C4
John McDonald Ho 3 E14 120 A3
John McKenna Wlk 17 SE16 118 A3
John Milton Prim Sch SW8 137 C5 269 A3
John Nettleford Ho 14 E2 96 B4
John Newton Ct DA16 146 B2
John Nightingale Sch KT8 195 B6
John Orwell Sports Ctr E1 118 B5
John Parker Cl RM10 81 D1
John Parker Sq 8 SW11 136 B2
John Parry Ct 28 N1 95 C5
John Paul II RC Sec Sch SW19 156 D4
John Penn St SE13 141 D4
John Perrin Pl HA3 44 A2
John Perryn Prim Sch W3 89 C1
John Prince's St W1 238 D2
John Pritchard Ho 14 E1 96 A3
John Ratcliffe Ho 5 NW6 91 C4
John Rennie Wlk 1 E1 118 C5
John Roan Sec Sch (Lower) The SE3 142 D5
John Roan Sec Sch (Upper) The SE3 142 C5
John Roll Way SE16 118 A3
John Ruskin Jun & Inf Sch SE5 139 A6
John Ruskin Sixth Form Coll CR2 223 A1
John Ruskin St SE5 139 A6
John Scurr Ho 20 E14 97 A1
John Scurr JMI Sch E1 96 C3
John Silkin La SE8 118 D1
John Smith Ave SW6 135 B5 264 C4
John Spencer Sq N1 72 D2
John St E15 98 D6
SE25 206 A5
WC1 94 B3 240 D5
Enfield EN1 17 D6
Hounslow TW3,TW5 129 A3
John Steiner Jun Sch SE4 141 A2
John Strachey Ho SW6 264 D5
John Strype Ct E10 53 D1
John Trundle Ct EC2 242 A4
John Tucker Ho 2 E14 119 C3
John Walsh Twr E11 76 D6
John Wesley Ct 5 TW1 153 A3
John Wesley's House & Mus EC1 242 D6
John Wheatley Ho
14 N19 49 D2
SW6 264 D5
John William Cl 12 KT2 175 D2
John Williams Cl SE14 140 D6
John Wilson St SE18 122 C2
John Wooley Cl SE13 142 C1
Johnby Cl EN3 7 A6
John's Ave NW4 46 C5
Johns Cl TW15 171 A6
Johns La SM4 202 A4
John's Mews WC1 94 B3 240 D5
John's Pl E1 96 B1
Johns Terr CR0 205 C1
Johnson Cl E8 96 A6
Johnson Ct 10 SW18 136 B1
Johnson Ho 14 E2 96 A4
NW1 232 B3
SW1 258 B3
SW8 269 D3
Johnson Lo 12 W9 91 C2
Johnson Rd
Bromley BR2 209 D4
Heston TW5 128 C5
Thornton Heath CR0 205 B2
Johnson St E1 96 C1
Southall UB2 106 D3
Johnson's Cl SM5 218 D5
Johnsons Ct EC4 241 B1
Johnsons Dr TW12 174 A2
Johnson's Ind Est UB3 106 A3
Johnson's Pl SW1 115 C1 259 A1
Johnsons Way NW10 88 D3
Johnston Cl SW9 270 D1
Johnston Rd IG8 37 A5
Johnston Terr NW2 68 D5
Johnstone Ho SE13 142 B2
Johnstone Rd E6 100 B4
Johson Ho 5 SW15 156 A6
Joiner St SE1 252 D3
Joiners Arms Yd 1 SE5 139 B4
Joint Rd N10 30 C2
Jolles Ho 9 E3 97 D4
Jollys La UB4 84 D2
Jonathan Ct 9 W4 111 C2
Jonathan St SE11 116 B1 260 C2
Jones Ho 4 E14 98 B1
N16 51 C1
Jones Rd E13 99 B3
Jones St W1 248 C5
Jones Wlk 6 TW10 154 B5
Jonquil Gdns 5 TW12 173 C4
Jonson Cl Hayes UB4 84 A2
Mitcham CR4 203 B6
Jonson Ho 16 N16 73 B4
SE1 262 D5
Jordan Cl HA2 63 B5
Jordan Ct SW15 134 D1
Jordan Hill N10 30 C2
Jordan Ho N1 235 D5
12 SE4 140 D1
Jordan Rd UB6 87 C6
Jordans Cl RM10 81 D4
Jordans Ho NW8 237 A5
Jordans Mews TW11 152 C2
Joscoyne Ho 6 E1 96 B1
Josef Perrin Ho 1 SE27 183 B6
Joseph Ave W3 89 B1
Joseph Clarke Sch E4 36 B4
Joseph Conrad Ho SW1 259 B3
Joseph Ct N16 51 C2
Joseph Hood Fst Sch SW20 201 A6
Joseph Irwin Ho 11 E14 119 B6
Joseph Lancaster Jun & Inf Sch SE1 117 B3 262 C5
Joseph Lister Ct E7 77 A1
Joseph Lister Lo E11 55 B1
Joseph Powell Cl 1 SW12 159 C5
Joseph Priestley Ho 12 E2 96 B4
Joseph Ray Rd E11 76 C6
Joseph St E3 97 B3
Joseph Tritton Prim Sch SW18 136 A1
Joseph Trotter Cl EC1 234 B1
Josephine Ave SW2 160 B6
Joshua St E14 98 A1
Joslyn Cl EN3 7 C5
Josseline Ct 8 E3 97 A5
Joubert Mans SW3 257 B2
Joubert St SW11 136 D3

Jowett Ho 27 SW9 ....138 A3
Jowett St SE15 ....139 D5
Joyce Ave N18 ....33 D5
Joyce Butler Ho N22 ....32 B2
Joyce Dawson Way
SE28 ....124 A6
Joyce Page Cl SE7 ....143 D6
Joydon Dr RM6 ....58 B3
Joyners Cl RM9 ....81 B4
Joystone Ct 8 EN4 ....2 C1
Jubb Powell Ho N15 ....51 C3
Jubet Ho 9 N16 ....73 B4
Jubilee Ave E4 ....36 A4
Romford RM7 ....59 D4
Twickenham TW2 ....152 A3
Jubilee Bldgs NW8 ....229 C4
Jubilee Cl NW9 ....45 B3
Pinner Green HA5 ....22 C1
Romford RM7 ....59 D4
Teddington KT1 ....175 C2
Jubilee Cres E14 ....120 A3
N9 ....18 A3
Jubilee Ct Harrow HA3 ....44 A2
Hounslow TW3 ....129 D2
Thornton Heath CR7 ....204 C5
Jubilee Ctry Pk BR2 ....210 D4
Jubilee Dr HA4 ....63 A4
Jubilee Gdns UB1 ....85 C1
Jubilee Ho SE11 ....261 B3
3 Hampton TW12 ....173 C2
Jubilee JMI Sch N16 ....52 A1
Jubilee Mans 10 E1 ....96 C1
Jubilee Mkt WC2 ....250 B6
Jubilee Par IG8 ....37 C4
Jubilee Pl SW3 114 C1 257 B2
Jubilee Prim Sch SE28 124 C6
Jubilee Rd Cheam SM3 .216 D1
Wembley UB6 ....87 B6
Jubilee St E1 ....96 C2
Jubilee The 2 SE10 ....141 D5
Jubilee Villas KT10 ....196 C1
Jubilee Way SW19 ....179 D2
East Bedfont TW14 ....150 A3
Sidcup DA14 ....168 A2
Tolworth KT4,KT9 ....214 D5
Jubilee Wks SW19 ....180 A1
Jubilee Yd SE1 ....253 C2
Judd St WC1 ....94 A4 233 A1
Jude St E16 ....98 D1
Judge Heath La UB3 ....83 B1
Judge Wlk KT10 ....212 C2
Judges' Wlk NW3 ....70 A5
Juer St SW11 ..136 C5 267 B3
Julia Ct E17 ....53 D4
Julia Gdns IG11 ....102 D5
Julia St NW5 ....71 A3
Julian Ave W3 ....110 D6
Julian Cl EN5 ....1 D2
Julian Hill HA1 ....64 C6
Julian Ho SE21 ....183 C6
Julian Pl E14 ....119 D1
Julian Taylor Path 7
SE23 ....162 B2
Juliana Cl N2 ....48 A6
Julians Prim Sch SW16 182 C6
Julie Garfield Mews 4
E16 ....121 B5
Julien Rd W5 ....109 C3
Juliet Ho 11 N1 ....95 C5
Juliette Rd E13 ....99 A5
Julius Ct TW8 ....132 A5
Junction App SE13 ....142 A2
SW11 ....136 C2
Junction Mews W2 ....237 A2
Junction Pl W2 ....236 D2
Junction Rd E13 ....99 B5
N9 ....18 A3
N17 ....52 A6
N19 ....71 C5
Ashford TW15 ....171 B5
Brentford TW8 ....109 D2
Croydon CR2 ....221 B3
Harrow HA1 ....42 C3
Junction Rd E RM6 ....59 A2
Junction Rd W RM6 ....59 A2
Juniper Cl
Chessington KT9 ....214 B3
Ducks Island EN5 ....12 D6
Wembley HA9 ....66 C3
Juniper Cres NW1 ....71 A1
Juniper Ct N16 ....73 B6
12 W5 ....87 C2
Belmont SM2 ....217 C2
Harrow HA3 ....24 D2
Hounslow TW3 ....129 D1
Ilford RM6 ....58 C3
Juniper Gdns
Ashford TW16 ....171 D4
Mitcham CR4 ....181 C2
Juniper La E6 ....100 A2
Juniper Rd IG1 ....78 D4
Juniper St 15 E1 ....118 C6
Juniper Way UB3 ....105 C6
Juno Ct 11 SW9 ....138 C5
Juno Way SE14 ....140 D6
Juno Way Ind Est SE14 140 D6
Jupiter Ct 10 SW9 ....138 C5
8 Northolt UB5 ....84 D4
Jupiter Hts UB10 ....82 B6
Jupiter Way N7 ....72 B2
Jupp Rd E15 ....76 B1
Jupp Rd W E15 ....98 B6
Jura Ho SE16 ....119 A2
Jurston Ct SE1 ....251 B1
Justice Wlk SW3 ....267 A5
Justin Cl TW8 ....131 D5
Justin Rd E4 ....35 B4
Jute La EN3 ....7 A2
Jutland Cl N19 ....50 A1
Jutland Ho 4 SE5 ....139 A3
10 SE7 ....122 A2
Jutland Rd E13 ....99 A3
SE6 ....164 A4
Jutsums Ave RM7 ....59 D3
Jutsums Ct RM7 ....59 D3
Jutsums La RM7 ....59 D2
Juxon Cl HA3 ....23 D2
Juxon St SE11 .116 B2 260 D4
JVC Bsns Pk NW2 ....46 A1

K

Kaduna Cl HA5 ....40 B4
Kale Rd DA18 ....125 A4
Kambala Rd SW11 ....136 B2
Kangley Bridge Ctr
SE26 ....185 B5
Kangley Bridge Rd
SE26 ....185 B5
Kaplan Dr N21 ....16 B6
Karen Ct 2 SE5 ....139 C2
Bromley BR1 ....186 D2
Karen Ho 7 N16 ....73 B4
Karen Terr E11 ....76 D6
Ilford IG2 ....57 B4
Karens Ct EN3 ....6 D6
Karenza Ct HA9 ....43 C2
Karoline Gdns UB6 ....86 B5
Kashgar Rd SE18 ....123 D2
Kashmir Rd SE7 ....143 D5
Kasmin Ct NW10 ....68 A1
Kassala Rd
SW11 ....136 D4 267 D1
Katella Trad Est IG11 ..101 C4
Katharine Rd 1 TW1 ..153 A3
Katharine St CR0 ....221 A5
Katherine Cl 3 SE16 ..118 D5
Katherine Ct SE20 ....184 C2
10 SE23 ....162 C3
Katherine Gdns SE9 ..143 D1
Katherine Ho 15 W10 ....91 A3
Katherine Rd E6,E7 ....77 C1
Katherine Sq W11 ....244 A4
Katherine's Wlk 1
W11 ....112 D5
Kathleen Ave W3 ....89 A2
Wembley HA0 ....66 A1
Kathleen Ferrier Ct 4
N17 ....33 D3
Kathleen Moore Ct
BR4 ....224 A6
Kathleen Rd SW11 ....136 D2
Katie Rance Ct 8 SE18 122 B2
Katrine Ct NW2 ....68 C5
Kay Rd SW9 ....138 B3
Kay St E2 ....96 A5
E15 ....76 B1
Bexley DA16 ....146 B4
Kayemoor Rd SM2 ....218 C2
Kays Ct EN3 ....6 D1
Kean Ho 5 SE17 ....138 D6
Kean St WC2 ....94 B1 240 C1
Keates Est N16 ....73 D6
Keatley Gn E4 ....35 B4
Keats Ave E16 ....121 B5
Keats Cl E11 ....55 B4
NW3 ....70 C4
SE1 ....263 C3
SW19 ....180 B4
Enfield EN3 ....18 D6
Hayes UB4 ....84 A2
Keats Ct HA0 ....65 C5
Keats Gr NW3 ....70 C4
Keats Ho 22 E2 ....96 C4
30 SE5 ....139 A5
SW1 ....269 B6
7 Beckenham BR3 ....185 D4
Keats Par 3 N9 ....18 A2
Keats Pl EC2 ....242 C3
Keats Rd DA16 ....145 D4
Keats Way Croydon CR0 .206 C3
Southall UB6 ....85 D2
West Drayton UB7 ....104 B2
Kebbell Terr E7 ....77 B3
Keble Cl
New Malden KT4 ....199 D1
Northolt UB5 ....64 A3
Keble Ho 4 SW15 ....156 D5
Keble Pl SW13 ....134 B6
Keble Prep Sch N21 ....16 C4
Keble St SW17 ....180 A6
Kechill Gdns BR2 ....209 A2
Kedeston Ct SM3 ....201 D1
Kedge Ho 10 E14 ....119 C3
Kedleston Ct E5 ....75 A4
Kedleston Dr BR5 ....211 D4
Kedleston Wlk 21 E2 ....96 B4
Kedyngton Ho 5 HA8 ....27 A1
Keeble Cl SE18 ....144 D6
Keedonwood Rd BR1 ..186 D5
Keel Cl SE16 ....118 D5
Barking IG11 ....102 C5
Keeley Rd CR0 ....221 A6
Keeley St WC2 ..94 B1 240 C1
Keeling Ho 2 TW11 ..174 C5
Keeling Rd SE9 ....165 D6
Keely Cl EN4 ....14 C6
Keemor Cl SE18 ....144 C5
Keens Cl SW16 ....181 D5
Keen's Rd CR0 ....221 A4
Keen's Yd N1 ....72 D2
Keep The SE3 ....143 A3
SE6 ....163 C3
Kingston u T KT2 ....176 B3
Keeper Wharf E1 ....118 D6
Keepers Mews TW11 ..175 C4
Keeton's Rd SE16 ....118 B3
Keevil Dr SW19 ....157 A4
Keighley Cl N7 ....72 A4
Keightley Dr SE9 ....167 A3
Keilder Cl UB10 ....82 C5
Keildon Rd SW11 ....136 D1
Keir Hardie Est E5 ....52 B1
Keir Hardie Ho 15 N19 ..49 D2
NW10 ....67 D1
W6 ....134 D6
Keir Hardie Way
Barking IG11 ....80 A1
Hayes UB4 ....84 A4
Keir Hardy Ho 6 DA17 125 C3
Keith Connor Cl 5
SW8 ....137 B2
Keith Gr W12 ....112 A5
Keith Ho NW6 ....91 D5
Keith Park Rd UB10 ....60 B1
Keith Rd E17 ....35 B2
Barking IG11 ....101 B5
Hayes UB3 ....105 C3
Keith Sutton Ho 3 SE9 167 A2
Kelbrook Rd SE3 ....144 A2
Kelby Ho N7 ....72 B2
Kelceda Cl NW2 ....68 A6
Kelf Gr UB3 ....83 D1
Kelfield Ct 1 W10 ....90 D1
Kelfield Gdns W10 ....90 D1
Kelham Ho 10 SE18 ....144 D6
Kell St SE1 ....116 D3 261 D6
Kelland Cl 1 N8 ....49 D4
Kelland Rd E13 ....99 A3
Kellaway Rd SE3 ....143 D3
Keller Cres E12 ....77 D4
Kellerton Rd SE13 ....164 C6
Kellett Ho N1 ....235 D5
Kellett Rd SW2 ....138 C1
Kelling Gdns CR0 ....204 D2
Kellino St SW17 ....180 D6
Kellner Rd SE28 ....123 D3
Kellow Ho SE1 ....252 C2
Kelly Cl TW17 ....171 C1
Kelly Ct 11 E14 ....119 C6
Kelly Rd NW7 ....29 A4
Kelly St NW1 ....71 B2
Kelly Way RM6 ....59 A3
Kelman Cl SW4 ....137 D3
Kelmore Gr SE22 ....140 A1
Kelmscott 5 SE23 ....162 D1
Kelmscott Cl E17 ....35 B2
Kelmscott Ct 2 HA7 ....25 C6
Kelmscott Gdns W12 ..112 A3
Kelmscott L Ctr E17 ....53 B3
Kelmscott Rd SW11 ....158 D6
Kelmscott Sec Sch E17 .53 B3
Kelross Rd N5 ....73 A4
Kelsall Cl SE3 ....143 B3
Kelsey Gate 8 BR3 ....185 D1
Kelsey La BR3 ....207 C6
Kelsey Park Ave BR3 ..185 D1
Kelsey Park Rd BR3 ..185 C1
Kelsey Park Sch BR3 ..207 C6
Kelsey Rd BR5 ....190 B1
Kelsey Sq BR3 ....185 C1
Kelsey St E2 ....96 A3
Kelsey Way BR3 ....207 C6
Kelshall Ct N4 ....73 A6
Kelso Ct SE20 ....184 B3
Kelso Lo E18 ....37 B1
Kelso Pl W8 ..113 D3 255 D6
Kelso Rd SM5 ....202 A2
Kelson Ho E14 ....120 A3
Kelvedon Cl KT2 ....176 C4
Kelvedon Ho SW8 ....270 B2
Kelvedon Rd
SW6 ....135 B5 264 D3
Kelvin Ave N13 ....32 B4
Kelvin Cl KT19 ....214 C2
Kelvin Cres HA3 ....24 C3
Kelvin Ct 7 SE20 ....184 B2
W4 ....133 A5
W11 ....245 A5
Isleworth TW7 ....130 C3
8 Twickenham TW1 ....153 B5
Kelvin Dr TW1 ....153 B5
Kelvin Gdns
Croydon CR0 ....204 A2
Southall UB1 ....85 C1
Kelvin Gr SE26 ....162 B1
Chessington KT6 ....214 A5
Kelvin Grove Prim Sch
SE23 ....163 A3
SE26 ....162 B1
Kelvin Ho 3 DA17 ....125 C3
Kelvin Par BR6 ....211 C1
Kelvin Rd N5 ....73 A4
Bexley DA16 ....146 A2
Kelvinbrook KT8 ....195 D6
Kelvington Cl CR0 ....207 A2
Kelvington Rd SE15 ..162 D6
Kelyway Ho 20 SW2 ..160 C4
Kember St N1 ....72 B1
Kemble Ct 1 SE15 ....139 C5
Kemble Dr BR2 ....226 A5
Kemble Ho SW9 ....138 D2
Kemble Rd N17 ....34 A2
SE23 ....162 D3
Croydon CR0 ....220 D5
Kemble St WC2 .94 B1 240 C1
Kemerton Rd SE5 ....139 A2
Beckenham BR3 ....185 D1
Croydon CR0 ....205 D2
Kemey's St E9 ....75 A3
Kemnal Rd BR7 ....189 B5
Kemnal Tech Coll BR5 .190 B3
Kemnal Warren BR7 ..189 B4
Kemp 24 NW9 ....27 D2
Kemp Ct SW8 ....270 A3
Kemp Gdns CR0 ....205 A3
Kemp Ho 1 E2 ....96 D5
E6 ....78 C2
Kemp Rd RM8 ....58 D1
Kempe Ho SE1 ....262 D5
Kempe Rd NW6 ....90 D5
Kempis Way 5 SE22 ..161 C6
Kemplay Rd NW3 ....70 B4
Kemps Ct NW2 ....68 D5
Kemp's Ct W1 ....239 C1
Kemps Dr E14 ....119 C6
Kempsford Gdns
SW5 ....113 C1 255 B1
Kempsford Rd SE11 ....261 B3
Kempshott Rd SW16 ..182 A3
Kempson Rd
SW6 ....135 C5 265 B3
Kempt St SE18 ....144 C6
Kempthorne Rd SE8 ..119 B2
Kempton Ave
Northolt UB5 ....63 C3
Sunbury TW16 ....172 B2
Kempton Cl UB10 ....61 A4
Kempton Ct E1 ....96 B2
Sunbury TW16 ....172 B2
Kempton Ho 13 N1 ....95 C6
Kempton Park Race Course
TW16 ....172 C3
Kempton Park Sta
TW16 ....172 B3
Kempton Rd E6 ....100 B6
Kempton Wlk CR0 ....207 A3
Kemsford Rd SE11 ....261 C3
Kemsing Cl
Coney Hall BR2 ....224 D6
Sidcup DA5 ....169 A4
Thornton Heath CR7 ....205 A5
Kemsing Ho SE1 ....252 D1
Kemsing Rd SE10 ....121 A1
Kemsley SE13 ....163 D6
Kemsley Ct W13 ....109 C5
Ken Way HA9 ....67 A5
Ken Wilson Ho 17 E2 ....96 A5
Kenbrook Ho 5 NW5 ....71 C3
W14 ....254 D5
Kenbury Cl UB10 ....60 C5
Kenbury Gdns 10 SE5 ..139 A3
Kenbury Mans 18 SE5 ..139 A3
Kenbury St SE5 ....139 A3
Kenchester Cl
SW8 ....138 A5 270 B3
Kencot Cl DA18 ....125 B4
Kendal NW1 ....231 D2
Kendal Ave N18 ....33 B6
W3 ....88 D2
Barking IG11 ....101 C6
Kendal Cl SE5 ....138 D5
East Bedfont TW14 ....149 D3
Hayes UB4 ....83 C5
Woodford IG8 ....20 D2
Kendal Ct 11 E4 ....20 A3
NW2 ....69 A3
W3 ....88 C2
7 Croydon CR0 ....205 C1
Kendal Gdns N18 ....33 B6
Sutton SM1 ....218 A6
Kendal Ho 32 E9 ....74 C1
N1 ....233 D4
SE20 ....184 B1
5 Croydon CR0 ....205 C1
Kendal Par N18 ....33 B6
Kendal Pl SW15 ....157 B6
Kendal Rd NW10 ....68 A4
Kendal St W2 ....92 C1 237 B1
Kendal Steps W2 ....237 B1
Kendale Rd BR1 ....186 C5
Kendall Ave BR3 ....185 A1
Kendall Ct 5 SE19 ....183 D3
3 SE22 ....162 A6
SW19 ....180 B4
Sidcup DA15 ....168 A1
Kendall Ho SE12 ....164 D4
Kendall Lo 5 BR1 ....187 B2
Kendall Pl W1 ....238 A3
Kendall Rd
Isleworth TW7 ....131 A3
Penge BR3 ....185 A1
Kendalmere Cl N10 ....31 B2
Kender Prim Sch SE14 .140 C4
Kender St SE14 ....140 C4
Kendoa Rd 1 SW4 ....137 D1
Kendon Cl E11 ....55 B4
Kendra Hall Rd CR2 ..220 D1
Kendrey Gdns TW2 ....152 C4
Kendrick Mews SW7 ..256 C3
Kendrick Pl SW7 ....256 C3
Kenelm Cl HA1 ....65 A5
Kenerne Dr EN5 ....13 A6
Kenilford Rd SW12 ....159 B4
Kenilworth Ave E17 ....53 C6
SW19 ....179 C6
Harrow HA2 ....63 B4
Kenilworth Cres EN1 ....5 C4
Kenilworth Ct 7 E4 ....20 A2
SW6 ....135 A2
Twickenham TW2 ....152 C2
Kenilworth Gdns SE18 .144 D3
Hayes UB4 ....83 D2
Ilford IG3 ....79 D6
South Oxhey WD1 ....22 C5
Southall UB1 ....85 B4
Kenilworth Rd E3 ....97 A5
NW6 ....91 B6
SE20 ....184 D2
W5 ....110 A5
Ashford TW15,TW19 ....148 A1
Kenilworth Rd *continued*
Edgware HA8 ....11 A1
Petts Wood BR5 ....211 A3
Stoneleigh KT17 ....216 A3
Kenilworth Terr 3
SM2 ....217 C1
Kenley N17 ....33 B1
Kenley Ave NW9 ....27 C1
Kenley Cl Barnet EN4 ....2 C1
Old Bexley DA5 ....169 C4
St Paul's Cray BR7 ....211 C6
Kenley Gdns CR7 ....204 D5
Kenley Ho
5 Croydon CR0 ....206 A1
6 St Paul's Cray BR5 ..190 B1
Kenley Rd SW19 ....201 C6
Kingston u T KT1,KT3 ..176 D1
Twickenham TW1 ....153 B5
Kenley Wlk W11 ....244 A5
Cheam SM3 ....216 D4
Kenlor Rd SW17 ....180 B5
Kenmare Ct 5 HA7 ....25 C6
Kenmare Dr CR4 ....180 D3
Kenmare Gdns N13 ....33 A6
Kenmare Mans NW6 ....69 B3
Kenmare Rd CR7 ....204 C3
Kenmere Gdns HA0 ....88 C6
Kenmere Mans W5 ....87 C3
Kenmere Rd DA16 ....146 C3
Kenmont Gdns NW10 ....90 B4
Kenmont Prim Sch
NW10 ....90 B4
Kenmore Ave HA3 ....43 A6
Kenmore Cl TW9 ....132 C5
Kenmore Cres UB4 ....83 D4
Kenmore Ct NW6 ....69 C1
Kenmore Gdns HA8 ....26 D1
Kenmore Park Fst & Mid
Schs HA3 ....44 A6
Kenmore Rd HA3 ....43 D5
Kenmure Rd E8 ....74 B3
Kenmure Yd E8 ....74 B3
Kennacraig Cl 7 E16 ..121 A5
Kennard Ho 11 SW11 ..137 A3
Kennard Mans 6 N11 ....30 D5
Kennard Rd E15 ....76 B1
N11 ....30 D5
Kennard St E16 ....122 B5
9 SW11 ....137 A3
Kennedy Ave EN3 ....18 C5
Kennedy Cl E13 ....99 A5
Hatch End HA5 ....23 B4
1 Mitcham CR4 ....181 A1
Orpington BR5 ....211 B1
Kennedy Cox Ho 9 E16 .98 D2
Kennedy Ct TW15 ....171 A5
Kennedy Ho SE11 ....260 C2
Kennedy Rd W7 ....86 C2
Barking IG11 ....101 C6
Kennedy Wlk SE17 ....262 D3
Kennet Cl SW11 ....136 B1
Kennet Dr UB4 ....85 A2
Kennet Ho NW8 ....236 D5
Kennet Rd W9 ....91 B3
Isleworth TW7 ....130 D2
Kennet Sq CR4 ....180 C2
Kennet St E1 ....118 A5
Kennet Wharf La EC4 .252 B6
Kenneth Ave IG1 ....78 D4
Kenneth Campbell Ho
NW8 ....236 D6
Kenneth Cres NW2 ....68 B3
Kenneth Ct SE11 ....261 B4
Kenneth Gdns HA7 ....25 A4
Kenneth Moor Rd 4
IG1 ....78 D5
Kenneth Rd RM6 ....59 A2
Kenneth Robbins Ho 1
N17 ....34 B3
Kenneth Younger Ho
SW6 ....264 D5
Kenning Ho 6 N1 ....95 C6
Kenning St 12 SE16 ....118 C4
Kenninghall N18 ....34 C5
Kenninghall Rd E5 ....74 B5
N18 ....34 C5
Kennings Way
SE11 ....116 C1 261 B2
Kennington Gdns KT1 .197 D6
Kennington Gr SE11 ..270 D6
Kennington La
SE11 ....116 C1 260 D1
Kennington Oval
SE11 ....138 C6 270 D5
Kennington Palace Ct
SE11 ....261 A2
Kennington Park Gdns
SE17 ....138 D6
Kennington Park Ho
SE11 ....261 B1
Kennington Park Pl
SE11 ....138 D6
Kennington Park Rd
SE11 ....116 D1 261 C2
Kennington Rd
SE11 ....116 C2 261 A3
Kennington Sta
SE17 ....116 D1 261 C2
Kennoldes SE21 ....161 B2
Kenny Rd NW7 ....29 A5
Kennyland Lo NW4 ....46 B3
Kenrick Pl W1 ....238 A3
Kensal Green Cemetery (All
Souls)* NW10 ....90 C4
Kensal Green Sta NW10 .90 C4
Kensal Ho W10 ....90 D3
Kensal Rd W10 ....91 A3
Kensal Rise Prim Sch
NW6 ....90 D5
Kensal Rise Sta NW10 ..90 D5
Kensington & Chelsea Coll
SW10 ....136 A5 266 A4
W10 ....91 A2
Kensington Ave E12 ....78 B2
South Norwood CR7 ....182 C2
Kensington Avenue Inf Sch
CR7 ....182 C2
Kensington Avenue Jun Sch
CR7 ....182 C2
Kensington Church Ct
W8 ....245 C1
Kensington Church St
W8 ....113 C5 245 B3
Kensington Church Wlk
W8 ....245 C1
Kensington Cl N11 ....31 A4
Kensington Court Mans
W8 ....245 D1
Kensington Court Mews
W8 ....255 D6
Kensington Court Pl
W8 ....113 D3 255 D6
Kensington Ct
W8 ....113 D4 245 D1
Enfield EN2 ....5 C5
Kensington Ct Gdns
W8 ....255 D6
Kensington Dr IG8 ....37 D1
Kensington Gardens
W2 ....114 A5 246 B3
Kensington Gate
W8 ....114 A3 256 A6
Kensington Gdns IG1 ....56 B1
Kensington Gdns Sq W2 91 D1
Kensington Gore
SW7 ....114 B4 246 C1
Kensington Hall Gdns
W14 ....254 C2
Kensington Hgts HA1 ....42 D3
Kensington High St
W8 ....113 C3 255 B6
Kensington Ho 8 NW5 .71 C3
Kensington Hts W8 ....245 A3
Kensington Mall W8 ..245 B4
Kensington Mans SW5 255 B2
Kensington Olympia Sta
W14 ....113 A3 254 A6
Kensington Palace*
W8 ....113 D5 245 D3
Kensington Palace Gdns
W8 ....113 D5 245 C4
Kensington Park Gdns
W11 ....113 B6 244 D5
Kensington Park Mews
W11 ....91 B1
Kensington Park Rd
W11 ....113 B6 244 D6
Kensington Pl
W8 ....113 C5 245 A4
Kensington Prep Sch
SW6 ....135 B4 264 D2
Kensington Prim Sch
E12 ....78 B2
Kensington Rd
SW7 ....114 C4 246 B1
Northolt UB5 ....85 C5
Kensington Sports Ctr
W11 ....244 A6
Kensington Sq
W8 ....113 D4 245 C1
Kensington Terr CR2 ..221 B1
Kensington Village
W14 ....113 B2 254 D3
Kensington W W14 ....254 A4
Kensworth Ho EC1 ....235 D1
Kent Ave W13 ....87 B2
Bexley DA16 ....167 D6
Dagenham RM9 ....103 C3
Kent Cl
Mitcham CR4,SW16 ....204 A5
Orpington BR6 ....227 C2
Kent Ct 3 E2 ....95 D5
NW9 ....27 C1
W3 ....88 B1
Kent Dr Cockfosters EN4 .15 A6
Teddington TW11 ....174 C5
Kent Gate Way CR0 ....223 D3
Kent Gdns W13 ....87 B2
Ruislip HA4 ....40 B3
Kent Ho SE1 ....263 D1
SW1 ....259 C1
13 W4 ....111 C1
Richmond TW10 ....154 C6
Kent House La BR3 ....185 A5
Kent House Rd BR3 ....185 A4
Kent House Sta BR3 ....185 A2
Kent House Station App
BR3 ....184 D2
Kent Lo 9 SW19 ....156 D3
Kent Pas NW1 ....237 C6
Kent Rd N21 ....17 B4
W4 ....111 A3
Dagenham RM10 ....81 D3
East Molesey KT8 ....196 A5
Kingston u T KT1 ....197 D6
Richmond TW9 ....132 C5
West Wickham BR4 ....207 D1
Kent St E2 ....95 D5
E13 ....99 B4
Kent Terr NW1 ...92 C4 230 B1
Kent Twr SE20 ....184 B3
Kent View Gdns IG3 ....79 C6

Kent Way KT6 214 B6
Kent Wlk SW9 138 D1
Kent Yard SW7 247 B1
Kentford Way UB5 85 A6
Kentish Bldgs SE1 252 C3
Kentish Rd DA17 125 C2
Kentish Town CE Prim Sch
NW5 71 C3
Kentish Town Rd NW1 71 B2
Kentish Town Sta NW5 71 C3
Kentish Town West Sta
NW5 71 B2
Kentish Way BR1,BR2 209 B6
Kentmere Ho SE15 140 C6
Kentmere Rd SE18 123 C2
Kenton Ave Harrow HA1 42 D2
Southall UB1 107 C6
Sunbury TW16 173 A1
Kenton Ct 2 SE26 185 A6
W14 254 C5
Harrow HA3 43 B3
3 Richmond TW10 153 D5
Kenton Gdns HA3 43 C4
Kenton Ho 21 E1 96 C3
N5 72 C5
Kenton La Harrow HA3 24 D3
Kenton HA3 43 C6
Kenton Park Ave HA3 43 D5
Kenton Park Cl HA3 43 C4
Kenton Park Cres HA3 43 D5
Kenton Park Par HA3 43 D4
Kenton Park Rd HA3 43 C5
Kenton Rd E9 74 D2
Harrow HA3 43 C4
Kenton St WC1 240 A6
Kenton Sta HA3 43 B3
Kenton Way UB4 83 C4
Kentwell Cl SE4 141 A1
Kentwode Gn SW13 134 A5
Kenver Ave N12 30 B4
Kenward Rd SE9 165 D6
Kenway Rd
SW5 113 D2 255 C3
Kenwood EN1 17 C5
Kenwood Ave N14 15 D6
Kenwood Cl NW3 48 B1
Harmondsworth UB7 126 C6
Kenwood Ct NW9 45 A5
Kenwood Dr BR3 208 A6
Kenwood Gdns 2 E18 55 B6
Ilford IG2 56 C4
Kenwood Ho* NW3 48 C1
15 SW9 138 D1
Kenwood Rd N6 48 D3
N9 18 A3
Kenworthy Rd E9 75 A2
Kenwrick Ho N1 233 D5
Kenwyn Dr NW2 67 D5
Kenwyn Rd SW4 137 D1
SW20 178 C2
Kenya Rd SE7 143 D5
Kenyngton Dr TW16 172 A5
Kenyngton Manor Prim Sch
TW16 172 A4
Kenyngton Pl HA3 43 C4
Kenyon Ho 31 SE5 139 A5
Kenyon St SW6 134 D4
Keogh Rd E15 76 D2
Kepler Ho 9 SE10 120 D1
Kepler Rd SW2,SW4 138 A1
Keppel Ho 5 SE8 119 B1
SW3 257 A3
Keppel Rd E6 100 B6
Dagenham RM9 81 A4
Keppel Row SE1 252 A3
Keppel St WC1 239 D4
Kerala Ct N17 33 D2
Kerbela St 2 E2 96 A3
Kerbey St E14 97 D1
Kerem House Sch N2 48 A4
Kerem Prim Sch N2 48 B4
Kerfield Cres SE5 139 B4
Kerfield Pl SE5 139 B4
Kerridge Ct N1 73 C2
Kerrier Ho SW10 266 B3
Kerrin Point SE11 261 A2
Kerrington Ct 7 W12 112 C4
Kerrison Pl W5 109 D5
Kerrison Rd E15 98 B6
SW11 136 C2
W5 109 D5
Kerrison Villas W5 109 D5
Kerry N7 72 A2
Kerry Ave HA7 25 D6
Kerry Cl E16 99 B1
N13 16 B2
Kerry Ct HA7 25 D6
Kerry Ho 5 E1 96 C1
Kerry Path SE8 141 B6
Kerry Rd SE8 141 B6
Kerscott Ho 30 E3 97 D4
Kersey Gdns SE9 188 A6
Kersfield Ho SW15 156 D5
Kersfield Rd SW15 156 D5
Kershaw Cl SW18 158 B5
Kershaw Ho 7 SE27 160 D1
Kershaw Rd RM10 81 C5
Kersley Mews SW11 267 C1
Kersley Rd N16 73 C5
Kersley St SW11 136 D3
Kerstin Cl UB3 105 D6
Kerswell Cl N15 51 C4
Kerwick Cl 1 N7 72 B1
Keslake Mans NW10 90 D5
Keslake Rd NW6 90 D5
Kessock Cl N17 52 B4
Kestlake Rd DA5 168 C5
Keston Ave BR2 225 C3
Keston CE Prim Sch
BR2 225 D3
Keston Cl N18 17 B1
Bexley DA16 146 C5
Keston Ct DA5 169 B4
Keston Gdns BR2 225 C4
Keston Ho SE17 263 B2
Keston Mark BR2 226 A5
Keston Park Cl BR2 226 B5
Keston Rd N17 51 B5
SE15 140 A2
Thornton Heath CR7 204 C3
Kestral Ho EC1 235 A2
Kestrel Ave E6 100 A2
SE24 161 A6
Kestrel Cl NW9 27 C1
NW10 67 B3
Kingston u T KT2 175 D6
Kestrel Ct E17 34 D1
27 SE8 141 B6
Croydon CR2 221 A2
Ruislip HA4 61 B6
Kestrel Ho 4 SW11 136 C2
Enfield EN3 19 A6
Kestrel Pl SE14 141 A6
Keswick Ave SW19 179 C1
Kingston u T KT2,SW15 177 C5
Upper Halliford TW17 193 C6
Keswick Cl SM1 218 A4
Keswick Ct 18 SE6 164 D3
2 SE22 162 A6
Keswick Dr EN3 6 C6
Keswick Gdns
Redbridge IG4 56 A5
Ruislip HA4 39 B3
Wembley HA9 66 A4
Keswick Ho 8 SE5 139 A4
Keswick Hts 9 SW15 157 A6
Keswick Lo E8 73 D2
Keswick Mews W5 110 A5
Keswick Rd SW15 157 A6
Erith DA7 147 C4
Orpington BR6 211 D1
Twickenham TW2 152 A5
West Wickham BR4 224 C6
Ketley Ho SE15 140 A4
Kett Gdns SW2 160 B6
Kettering Ct CR7 205 A5
Kettering Rd EN3 6 D6
Kettering St SW16 181 C4
Kettlebaston Rd E10 53 B1
Kettleby Ho SW9 138 D2
Kettlewell Cl N11 31 A4
Ketton Ho W10 90 C3
Kevan Ct 6 E17 53 D5
Kevan Ho SE5 139 A5
Kevelioc Rd N17 33 A2
Kevin Cl TW4 128 D3
Kevington Cl BR5 211 D5
Kevington Dr BR5,BR7 211 D5
Kew Bridge TW8 110 B1
Kew Bridge Ct 8 W4 110 C1
Kew Bridge Rd TW8 110 B1
Kew Bridge Sta TW8 110 B1
Kew Bridge Steam Mus
TW8 110 B1
Kew Cres SM3 217 B5
Kew Foot Rd TW9 132 A2
Kew Gardens Rd TW9 132 C4
Kew Gardens Sta TW9 132 C4
Kew Gardens(Royal
Botanic)* TW9 132 A4
Kew Gn TW9 132 B6
Kew Green TW9 132 C5
Kew Lo 11 TW9 132 B4
Kew Obsy TW9 131 C2
Kew Palace TW9 132 A5
Kew Rd N2 30 C2
Richmond TW9,W4 132 B4
Kew Ret Pk TW9 132 D4
Key Cl E1 96 B3
Key Ho 9 SE11 138 C6
Keyes Ct SE22 162 A6
Keyes Rd NW2 68 D3
Keyham Ho 31 W2 91 C2
Keymer Rd SW2 160 B2
Keynes Cl N2 48 D6
Keynes Ct 9 SE28 124 B6
Keynsham Ave IG8 36 C6
Keynsham Gdns SE9 166 A6
Keynsham Ho 2 N4 51 A2
Keynsham Rd SE9 166 A6
Cheam SM4 201 D1
Keynsham Wlk SM4 201 D1
Keyse Rd SE1 117 D3 263 C5
Keysham Ave TW5 128 A4
Keystone Cres N1 233 B3
Keywood Dr TW16 172 A4
Keyworth Cl E5 75 A4
Keyworth Jun & Inf Sch
SE17 116 D1 261 C1
Keyworth Pl SE1 261 D6
Keyworth St
SE1 116 D3 261 D6
Kezia St SE8 119 A1
Khama Rd SW17 180 C6
Khartoum Rd E13 99 B4
SW17 180 B6
Ilford IG1 78 D3
Khyber Rd SW11 136 C3
Kibworth St
SW8 138 B5 270 C3
Kidbrooke Gdns SE3 143 A4
Kidbrooke Gr SE3 143 B4
Kidbrooke Interchange
SE3 143 C2
Kidbrooke La SE9 144 A1
Kidbrooke Park Cl SE3 143 B4
Kidbrooke Park Prim Sch
SE3 143 C4
Kidbrooke Park Rd
SE12,SE3 143 B2
Kidbrooke Sch SE3 143 D3
Kidbrooke Sta SE3 143 B2
Kidbrooke Way SE3 143 B3
Kidd Ho RM9 81 B4
Kidd Pl SE7 122 A1
Kiddens BR8 191 D1
Kidderminster Pl CR0 204 D1
Kidderminster Rd CR0 205 A2
Kidderpore Ave NW3 69 C4
Kidderpore Gdns NW3 69 C4
Kidlington Way NW9 27 C2
Kidron Way 18 E9 96 C6
Kierbeck Bsns Complex
E16 121 B4
Kiffen St EC2 242 D6
Kilberry Cl TW7 130 B4
Kilbrennan Ho 5 E14 98 A1
Kilburn Bridge 14 NW6 91 C6
Kilburn Gate NW6 91 D5
Kilburn High Rd NW6 91 C6
Kilburn High Road Sta
NW6 91 D6
Kilburn Ho 13 W9 91 B4
Kilburn La W10 91 A5
Kilburn Park Jun Sch
NW6 91 B5
Kilburn Park Rd NW6 91 C4
Kilburn Park Sta NW6 91 C5
Kilburn Pl NW6 91 C6
Kilburn Priory NW6 91 D6
Kilburn Sq NW6 91 C6
Kilburn Sta NW2 69 B2
Kilburn Vale NW6 91 D6
Kilburn Vale Est 13 NW6 91 C6
Kildare Cl HA4 40 C1
Kildare Ct W2 91 C1
Kildare Gdns W2 91 C1
Kildare Rd E16 99 A2
Kildare Terr W2 91 C1
Kildare Wlk E14 97 C1
Kildoran Rd SW2 160 A6
Kildowan Rd IG3 58 A1
Kilgour Rd SE23 163 A5
Kilkie St SW6 136 A3
Killarney Rd SW18 158 A5
Killearn Rd SE6 164 B3
Killester Gdns KT17,KT4 216 B4
Killick Ho SM1 217 D4
Killick St N1 94 B5 233 C3
Killieser Ave SW2 160 A2
Killigrew Ho TW16 171 C3
Killip Cl E16 98 D1
Killowen Ave UB5 64 A3
Killowen Rd E9 74 D2
Killross Rd TW14 149 B3
Killyon Rd SW8 137 C3
Kilmaine Rd
SW6 135 A5 264 B3
Kilmarnock Gdns RM8 80 C5
Kilmarnock Rd WD1 22 D6
Kilmarsh Rd W6 112 C2
Kilmartin Ave SW16 204 C6
Kilmartin Rd IG3 80 A6
Kilmington Rd SW13 134 A6
Kilmiston Ave TW17 193 A3
Kilmiston Ho TW17 193 A3
Kilmore Ho 17 E14 97 D1
Kilmorey Gdns TW1 131 B1
Kilmorey Rd TW1 131 B1
Kilmorie Prim Sch
SE23 163 A2
Kilmorie Rd SE23 163 A2
Kilmuir Ho SW1 258 B3
Kiln Cl UB3 127 B6
Kiln Ct E14 119 B6
Kiln Mews SW17 180 B5
Kiln Pl NW5 71 A3
Kilner Ho 3 SE11 138 C6
Kilner St E14 97 C2
Kilnside KT10 213 A1
Kiloh Ct 1 SW11 136 C2
Kilpatrick Ct N16 51 D1
Kilpatrick Way UB4 85 A2
Kilpeck Ho 3 N4 51 A2
Kilravock St W10 91 A4
Kilronan 5 W3 89 B1
Kilross Rd TW14 149 C3
Kilsby Wlk RM9 80 B2
Kilsha Rd KT12 194 C3
Kilvinton Dr EN2 5 B5
Kimbell Gdns
SW6 135 A4 264 A1
Kimbell Pl SE9 143 C1
Kimber Ctr The SW18 157 C4
Kimber Ho 11 SE18 144 D6
Kimber Rd SW18 157 D4
Kimberley Ave E6 100 A5
SE15 140 C2
Ilford IG2 57 C2
Kimberley Dr DA14 168 D2
Kimberley Gate 2 BR1 186 D3
Kimberley Gdns N4 50 D4
Enfield EN1 5 D2
Kimberley Ho 7 E14 120 A3
Kimberley Ind Est E17 35 B2
Kimberley Rd E4 20 C3
E11 76 B6
E16 98 D3
E17 35 B2
N17 34 A1
Kimberley Rd *continued*
N18 34 B4
NW6 91 A6
SW9 138 A2
Penge BR3 184 D1
Thornton Heath CR0 204 D3
Kimberley Way E4 20 C3
Kimberley Wlk KT12 194 B2
Kimble Cres WD2 8 A4
Kimble Ho 1 N7 72 A3
NW8 237 B6
Kimble Rd SW17 180 B4
SW17 180 B5
Kimbolton Cl SE12 164 D5
Kimbolton Row SW3 257 A3
Kimm Ho 16 E17 53 D6
Kimmeridge Gdns 3
SE9 188 A6
Kimmeridge Rd SE9 188 A6
Kimpton Bsns Ctr SM3 217 B6
Kimpton Ct 12 SE5 139 B4
Kimpton Ho SW15 156 A4
Kimpton Ind Est SM3 217 B6
Kimpton Rd SE5 139 B4
Cheam SM3 217 B6
Kinburn St SE16 118 D4
Kincaid Rd SE15 140 B5
Kincardine Gdns W9 91 C3
Kinch Gr HA3,HA9 44 B2
Kincraig BR7 188 C2
Kindell Ho 4 SW14 133 B2
Kinder Cl SE28 124 D6
Kinder Ho N1 235 D4
Kinder St 9 E1 96 B1
Kindersley Ho 27 E1 96 A1
Kinefold Ho N7 72 A2
Kinetic Cres EN3 7 B6
Kinfauns Rd SW2 160 C2
Ilford IG3 58 B1
King & Queen Cl 4
SE9 188 A6
King & Queen St
SE17 117 A1 262 B2
King Alfred Ave SE6 185 C6
King Alfred Sch NW11 47 D1
King Arthur Cl SE15 140 C5
King Athelstan Prim Sch
KT1 198 B6
King Charles Cres KT5 198 B2
King Charles Ho SW6 265 D4
King Charles' Rd KT5,
KT6 198 B3
King Charles St
SW1 116 A4 250 A2
King Charles Wlk 6
SW19 157 A3
King Ct 15 E10 53 D2
King David La E1 118 C6
King Edward Dr KT6 214 A5
King Edward Mans 12
E8 96 B6
King Edward Mews
SW13 134 A4
King Edward Rd E10 54 A1
E17 53 A6
Barnet EN5 1 D1
King Edward St EC1 242 A2
King Edward The Third
Mews 8 SE16 118 B4
King Edward Wlk
SE1 116 C3 261 B6
King Edward's Gdns
W3 110 C5
King Edward's Gr TW11 175 C4
King Edwards Mans
SW6 265 A3
King Edward's Rd E9 96 C6
N9 18 B4
Barking IG11 101 B5
Enfield EN3 6 D1
Ruislip HA4 39 B1
King Fahad Acad The
W5 109 C2
King Fahed Acad The
W3 111 D6
King Frederick IX Ct
SE16 119 B3
King Garth Mews SE23 162 C2
King Gdns CR0 220 D3
King George Ave E16 99 D1
Ilford IG2 57 B3
Walton-on-T KT12 194 D1
King George Cl TW16 171 C5
King George Hospl IG3 58 A4
King George Sq TW10 154 B5
King George St SE10 142 A5
King George VI Ave
CR4 202 D5
King George's Trad Est
KT9 214 C4
King Harolds Way DA7 147 A5
King Henry Mews 7
BR6 227 D3
King Henry St N16 73 C3
King Henry's Mews EN3 7 C6
King Henry's Rd NW3 70 C1
Kingston u T KT1,KT3 198 D6
King Henry's Wlk N1 73 C2
King Henry's Yd 5 N16 73 C3
King Ho W12 90 B1
King James St
SE1 116 D4 251 D1
King John Ct EC2 243 B6
King John St E1 96 D2
King John's Wlk SE9 166 A5
King Sq EC1 95 A4 235 A1
King St E13 99 A3
EC2 95 A1 242 B1
King St *continued*
N2 48 B6
N17 33 D2
SW1 115 C5 249 B4
W3 111 A5
W6 112 A2
WC2 250 A6
Richmond TW9 153 D6
Southall UB2 107 A3
Twickenham TW1 153 A3
King Stairs Cl SE16 118 B4
King Street Cloisters 8
W6 112 B2
King Street Par 6 TW1 153 A3
King William IV Gdns
SE20 184 C4
King William La 3
SE10 120 C1
King William St
EC4 117 B6 252 D6
King William Wlk SE10 142 A6
Kingcup Cl CR0 206 D1
Kingdon Ho 8 E14 120 A3
Kingdon Rd NW6 69 C2
Kingfield Rd W5 87 D3
Kingfield St E14 120 A2
Kingfisher Ave E11 55 B3
Kingfisher Cl SE28 124 C6
Harrow HA3 24 D3
Kingfisher Ct 12 E14 120 A4
11 SW11 136 C2
SW19 179 B3
SW19 157 A2
Cheam SM1 217 B3
East Molesey KT8 196 C5
Enfield EN2 4 B5
Isleworth TW3 151 D6
Kingfisher Dr TW10 175 B6
Kingfisher Ho SE15 139 D4
W14 254 C6
Kingfisher Lo TW11 175 A6
Kingfisher Mews SE13 163 D6
Kingfisher Sports Ctr The 12
KT1 176 A1
Kingfisher Sq 10 SE8 141 B6
Kingfisher St E6 100 A2
Kingfisher Way NW10 67 B3
Croydon CR0 206 D4
Kingfisher Wlk NW9 27 C1
Kingham Cl SW18 158 A4
3 W11 112 D4
Kinghorn St EC1 242 A3
Kinglake St
SE17 117 C1 263 B2
Kingly Ct W1 249 B6
Kingly St W1 115 C6 249 A6
Kings Acre Prim Sch
SW4 160 A6
Kings Arbour UB2 107 A1
King's Arms Ct 22 E1 96 A2
King's Arms Yd EC2 242 C2
Kings Ave N10 49 A6
SW4 160 A5
W5 87 D1
Bromley BR1 186 D4
Dagenham RM6 59 B3
New Malden KT3 199 D5
Wallington SM5 218 D1
King's Ave N21 16 D3
Ashford TW16 171 D4
Buckhurst Hill IG9 21 D2
Hounslow TW3,TW5 129 D4
Southall UB1 85 D1
Woodford IG8 37 C5
King's Bench St
SE1 116 D4 251 D2
Kings Bench Wlk EC4 241 B1
Kings Chace View EN2 4 C3
Kings Chase KT8 196 A6
Kings Cl NW4 46 D5
Walton-on-T KT12 194 B1
King's Cl E10 53 D2
Thames Ditton KT7 197 A2
King's Coll SE24 161 B5
WC2 116 B6 250 D6
Kings Coll Chelsea Campus
(Univ of London)
SW10 135 D5 265 D4
Kings Coll London W8 245 A2
Kings Coll London (Chelsea
Campus) SW3 114 C1 257 A1
King's Coll Sch SW19 178 D4
Kings College Ct NW3 70 C1
King's College Hospl
SE5 139 B3
King's College London
NW3 69 C4
Kings College Rd HA4 39 D3
King's Court N SW3 257 A1
King's Court S SW3 257 A1
King's Cres N4,N5 73 A5
King's Cross WC1 94 A4 233 B2
King's Cross (Thames Link)
Sta WC1 233 B2
King's Cross Bridge
WC1 233 B2
King's Cross Rd
WC1 94 B4 233 D1
King's Cross Sta
N1 94 A5 233 B3
King's Cross, St Pancras
N1 233 A2
Kings Ct E13 99 B6
6 N7 72 B1
NW8 230 C5
SE22 140 A1
10 SW15 156 A4
W6 112 A2
Kings Ct *continued*
2 Buckhurst Hill IG9 21 D2
16 Kingston u T KT2 176 C3
3 Wallington SM6 219 B2
Wembley HA9 66 D6
King's Ct SW19 179 C4
9 W5 87 C2
Beckenham BR3 207 D6
Kings Dr Edgware HA8 26 B6
Surbiton KT5 198 C3
Wembley HA9 66 D6
King's Dr KT7 197 B2
Kings Farm E17 35 D2
Kings Farm Ave TW10 132 C1
Kings Gdns IG1 57 B1
King's Gdns 6 NW6 69 C1
King's Gr SE15 140 B4
SE15 140 B5
Kings Grange HA4 39 D1
Kings Hall Mews SE13 142 A2
Kings Hall Rd BR3 185 A2
Kings Head Hill E4 19 D4
King's Head Yd SE1 252 C3
King's Highway SE18,
SE2 145 D6
Kings Ho SW8 270 B4
King's House Jun Sch
TW10 154 B6
King's House Sch TW10 154 B6
Kings Keep KT6 198 A5
King's Keep 6 SW15 156 D6
King's La SM1,SM2 218 B3
Kings Mall W6 112 C2
King's Mans SW3 267 A5
Kings Mead Pk KT10 212 C1
King's Mead Way E5,E9 75 A4
King's Mews 1 SW4 160 A6
WC1 94 B3 240 D5
Kings Oak Hospl (Private)
The EN2 4 C5
King's Orch SE9 166 A5
King's Paddock TW12 174 A2
King's Par NW10 90 C6
W12 112 A3
King's Pas KT2 175 D2
Kings Pl W4 111 A2
Buckhurst Hill IG9 21 D2
Loughton IG10 21 D4
King's Pl SE1 252 A1
King's Quay SW10 266 B2
Kings Rd N22 32 B2
NW10 68 B1
W5 87 D2
Feltham TW13 150 C3
Harrow HA2 63 B6
Mitcham CR4 203 A6
Orpington BR6 227 D4
Richmond TW10,TW9 154 B6
Walton-on-T KT12 194 B1
West Drayton UB7 104 B4
King's Rd E4 20 B3
E6 99 C6
E11 54 C2
N17 33 D2
N18 34 A6
SE25 206 A6
SW3 257 B1
SW10 136 B6 266 C5
SW14 133 B2
SW19 179 C4
Barking IG11 79 A1
Kingston u T KT2 176 B3
Long Ditton KT6 197 C1
Teddington TW11,TW12 174 B5
Twickenham TW1 153 B5
Kings Ride Gate TW10 132 C1
Kings Road Bglws HA2 63 B5
King's Scholars' Pas
SW1 259 A4
King's Terr NW1 93 C6 232 A5
8 Isleworth TW7 131 A2
Kings Way Croydon CR0 220 B3
Harrow HA1 42 C5
Kings Wood Ct 4 NW6 69 C1
Kingsand Rd SE12 165 A2
Kingsash Dr UB4 85 A3
Kingsbridge N16 51 B1
Kingsbridge Ave W3 110 B4
Kingsbridge Cres UB1 85 B2
Kingsbridge Ct E14 119 C2
N21 16 D2
Kingsbridge Ho 10
SE20 184 B2
Kingsbridge Ind Est
IG11 101 C4
Kingsbridge Rd W10 90 C1
Barking IG11 101 B5
Southall UB2 107 B2
Walton-on-T KT12 194 B2
West Barnes SM4 200 D2
Kingsbridge Way UB4 83 C4
Kingsbury Green Prim Sch
NW9 44 D4
Kingsbury High Sch
NW9 44 D5
NW9 45 A5
Kingsbury High Sch Annexe
NW9 44 D5
Kingsbury Hospl NW9 44 C5
Kingsbury Rd N1 73 C2
NW9 44 D4
Kingsbury Sta NW9 44 C4
Kingsbury Terr N1 73 C2
Kingsbury Trad Est NW9 45 B3
Kingsclere Cl SW15 156 A4
Kingsclere Ct N12 30 C5
New Barnet EN5 14 A6
Kingscliffe Gdns SW19 157 B3

Kingscote NW11 47 B1
Kingscote Rd W4 111 B3
Croydon CR0 206 B2
Kingston u T KT3 199 B6
Kingscote St EC4 251 C6
Kingscourt Rd SW16 160 A1
Kingscroft SW4 160 A5
Kingscroft Rd NW2 69 B2
Kingsdale Gdns W11 112 D5
Kingsdale Rd SE18 145 D6
SE20 184 D3
Kingsdale Sch SE21 161 C1
Kingsdown 1 SW19 178 D3
Kingsdown Ave W3 111 C6
W13 109 B4
Kingsdown Cl 28 SE16 118 B1
W10 90 D1
11 W11 91 A1
Kingsdown Ct SW11 158 C5
Kingsdown Ho 1 E8 74 A3
Kingsdown Rd E11 76 C5
3 N19 72 A6
Cheam SM3 217 A3
Kingsdown Way BR2 209 A3
Kingsdowne Rd KT6 198 B2
Kingsend HA4 39 C1
Kingsfield Ave HA1,HA2 42 A4
Kingsfield Ho 18 N16 73 C5
SE9 165 D1
Kingsfield Rd HA1 42 B2
Kingsford Ave SM6 220 A1
Kingsford St NW5 70 D3
Kingsford Way E6 100 B2
Kingsgate HA9 67 A5
Kingsgate Ave N3 47 C6
Kingsgate Bsns Ctr KT2 176 A2
Kingsgate Cl Bexley DA7 147 A4
St Paul's Cray BR5 190 C1
Kingsgate Est N1 73 C2
Kingsgate Ho 29 SW9 138 C4
Kingsgate Jun & Inf Sch
NW6 69 C1
Kingsgate Pl NW6 69 C1
Kingsgate Rd NW6 69 C1
Kingston u T KT2 176 A2
Kingsground SE9 166 A5
Kingshill SE17 262 B4
Kingshill Ave Harrow HA3 43 B5
Hayes UB4 83 D4
New Malden KT4 200 B2
Northolt UB5 84 B4
Kingshill Ct 6 EN5 1 A1
Kingshill Dr HA3 43 B6
Kingshold Rd E9 74 C1
Kingsholm Gdns SE9 144 A1
Kingshurst Rd SE12 165 A4
Kingsland NW8 92 C6 230 B5
Kingsland Gn 1 E8,N1 73 C2
Kingsland High St E8 73 D3
Kingsland Pas 2 E8 73 C2
Kingsland Rd E2 95 C5
E13 99 C4
Kingsland Sch E8 73 D3
Kingsland Sh Ctr E8 73 D2
Kingslawn Cl SW15 156 B6
Kingslee Ct 12 SM2 217 D1
Kingsleigh Pl CR4 202 D6
Kingsleigh Wlk BR2 208 D5
Kingsley Ave W13 87 A1
Carshalton SM1 218 B4
Hounslow TW3 130 A3
Southall UB1 107 C6
Kingsley Cl N2 48 A4
Dagenham RM10 81 D4
Kingsley Ct E11 54 D3
N22 32 B3
NW2 68 B2
1 SE28 124 C5
Bexleyheath DA6 147 C1
Edgware HA8 10 D2
2 Worcester Pk KT4 215 D6
Kingsley Dr 1 KT4 215 D6
Kingsley Flats SE1 263 B3
Kingsley Gdns E4 35 C5
Kingsley Grange 1 E11 55 A4
Kingsley Ho NW11 47 D3
SW3 266 D5
3 SW4 137 D3
8 Kingston u T KT6 198 A4
Kingsley Inf Sch CR9 204 C1
Kingsley Jun Sch CR9 204 C1
Kingsley Mews W8 255 D5
Chislehurst West BR7 188 D4
Dagenham RM9 80 D4
Kingsley Pl N6 49 A2
Kingsley Rd E7 77 A1
E17 36 A1
N13 32 D6
NW6 91 B6
SW19 179 D5
Harrow HA2 64 A5
Hounslow TW3 130 A3
Orpington BR6 227 D1
Pinner HA5 41 B5
Thornton Heath CR0 204 C1
Kingsley St SW11 136 D2
Kingsley Way N2 48 A4
Kingsley Wood Dr SE9 166 B1
Kingslyn Cres SE19 183 C2
Kingsman Par SE18 122 B3
Kingsman St SE18 122 B2
Kingsmead Barnet EN5 1 C1
Richmond TW10 154 B5
Kingsmead Ave N9 18 B3
NW9 45 B2
Mitcham CR4 203 C6
North Cheam KT4 216 B5
Sunbury TW16 172 C1
Kingsmead Ave *continued*
Tolworth KT6 214 C6
Kingsmead Cl
Sidcup DA15 168 A2
Teddington TW11 175 B4
West Ewell KT19 215 B1
Kingsmead Ct N6 49 D2
Bromley BR1 186 D3
Kingsmead Dr UB5 63 B1
Kingsmead Ho E9 75 A4
Kingsmead JMI Sch E9 75 A4
Kingsmead Lo 9 E4 20 A2
Sutton SM2 218 B2
Kingsmead Rd SW2 160 C2
Kingsmead Sch EN1 6 A2
Kingsmere SE6 163 D3
Bromley BR7 188 A2
Kingsmere Cl SW15 134 D2
Kingsmere Ct NW9 44 D1
Kingsmere Pk NW9 45 A1
Kingsmere Pl N16 51 B1
Kingsmere Rd SW19 156 D2
Kingsmill NW8 92 B5 229 D4
Kingsmill Gdns RM9 81 B3
Kingsmill Rd RM9 81 B3
Kingsmill Terr
NW8 92 B5 229 D4
Kingsnorth Ho 18 W10 90 D1
Kingsnympton Pk KT2 176 D4
Kingspark Ct E18 55 A6
Kingsridge SW19 157 A2
Kingsthorpe Rd SE26 184 D6
Kingston Ave
Cheam SM3 217 A5
Feltham TW14 149 D5
Yiewsley UB7 104 B6
Kingston Bsns Ctr KT9 214 B5
Kingston By - Pass KT6 214 C5
Kingston By-Pass KT6,
KT7,KT9 213 C5
Kingston Cl
Dagenham RM6 59 A6
Northolt UB5 85 B6
Teddington TW11 175 B4
Kingston Coll of F Ed
KT1 197 D6
Kingston Coll of F Ed (M V
Annex) KT2 176 A2
Kingston Cres BR3 185 B2
Kingston Gdns CR0 220 A5
Kingston Gram Sch
KT2 176 B1
Kingston Hall Rd KT1 197 D6
Kingston Hill KT2 177 A5
Kingston Hill Ave RM6 59 A6
Kingston Hill Pl KT2,
TW10 177 A6
Kingston Ho 2 NW6 69 A1
Kingston Ho E SW7 247 A1
Kingston Ho N SW7 247 A1
Kingston Ho S SW7 247 A1
Kingston Hospl KT2 176 D2
Kingston La
Hillingdon UB8 82 A4
Teddington TW11 175 B4
West Drayton UB7 104 B4
Kingston Lo 2 KT3 199 C5
Kingston Mus KT1 176 A1
Kingston Pl HA3 24 D3
Kingston Poly (Gipsy Hill Ctr)
KT2 177 B5
Kingston Rd N9 18 A2
SW15,SW19 156 B3
SW19,SW20 179 B1
Ashford TW15 170 A4
Ashford TW15,TW17 170 B4
Ewell KT17,KT19,KT4,KT5,
KT6 215 C3
Ilford IG1 79 A4
Kingston u T KT1,KT3 199 A5
New Barnet EN4 14 B6
New Malden KT3 199 A5
Southall UB2 107 B4
Teddington TW11 175 B4
KT17 215 D1
Kingston Sq SE19 183 B5
Kingston Sta KT2 176 A2
Kingston Univ
Kingston u T KT1 198 A6
Kingston u T KT2 177 B5
Kingston Univ Annex
KT1 176 B1
Kingston Univ Roehampton
Vale Ctr SW15 155 D1
Kingston Vale SW15 155 C1
Kingstown St
NW1 93 A6 231 A6
Kingswater Pl SW11 267 A3
Kingsway N12 30 A4
SW14,TW9 132 D2
WC2 94 B1 240 C2
Coney Hall BR4 224 D5
Enfield EN3 18 B6
Hayes UB3 83 A2
Petts Wood BR5 211 B4
Stanwell TW19 148 A3
Wembley HA9 66 A4
West Barnes KT3 200 C4
Woodford IG8 37 C5
Kingsway Bsns Pk The
TW12 173 B2
Kingsway Coll NW5 71 B2
WC1 94 B4 233 D2
WC1 94 B4 233 C1
Kingsway Cres HA2 42 A5
Kingsway Est N18 34 D4
Kingsway Rd SM3 217 A1
Kingswear Ho 5 SE23 162 C2
Kingswear Rd NW5 71 B5
Ruislip HA4 62 A6
Kingswood 32 E2 96 C5
Kingswood Ave NW6 91 A5
Beckenham BR2,BR3 208 C5
Erith DA17 125 B2
Hampton TW12 173 D4
Hounslow TW3,TW5 129 B3
Thornton Heath CR7 204 C4
Kingswood Cl N20 14 A4
SW8 270 B3
Enfield EN1 17 D6
New Malden KT3 199 D3
Orpington BR6 211 B2
Surbiton KT6 198 A2
Kingswood Ct E4 35 C5
7 Richmond TW10 154 B6
Kingswood Dr
SE19,SE21 183 D6
Carshalton SM5 202 D1
Kingswood Ho 3 KT2 176 D4
Kingswood Pk N3 29 B1
Kingswood Pl SE13 142 C1
Kingswood Prim Sch
SE27 183 B5
Kingswood Rd E11 54 C2
SE20 184 C4
SW2 160 A5
SW19 179 B2
W4 111 A3
Beckenham BR2 208 C6
Ilford IG3 58 A2
Kingswood Terr W4 111 A3
Kingswood Way SM6 220 A3
Kingsworth Cl BR3 207 A4
Kingsworthy Cl KT1 198 B6
Kingthorpe Rd NW10 67 B1
Kingthorpe Terr 1
NW10 67 B1
Kington Ho 16 NW6 91 D6
Kingward Ho E1 96 A2
Kingwell Rd EN4 2 B5
Kingwood Rd
SW6 135 A5 264 A3
Kinlet Rd SE18 145 A4
Kinloch Dr NW9 45 C2
Kinloch St N7 72 B5
Kinloss Ct NW3 47 B5
Kinloss Gdns NW3 47 B5
Kinloss Rd SM5 202 A2
Kinnaird Ave W4 133 A5
Bromley BR1 186 D4
Kinnaird Cl BR1 186 D4
Kinnear Ct 2 SW20 178 D2
Kinnear Rd W12 111 D4
Kinnerton Pl N SW1 247 D1
Kinnerton Pl S SW1 247 D1
Kinnerton St
SW1 115 A4 248 A1
Kinnerton Yd SW1 248 A1
Kinnoul Rd W6 135 A6 264 A6
Kinnoull Mans 10 E5 74 B4
Kinross Ave KT4 216 A6
Kinross Cl Ashford TW16 171 D5
Harrow HA3 44 B4
Kinross Ct 1 SE6 164 D2
Kinross Dr TW16 171 D5
Kinross Ho N1 233 C6
Kinsale Rd SE15 140 A2
Kinsey Ho SE21 183 C6
Kinsham Ho 4 E2 96 A3
Kintore Way SE1 263 C4
Kintyre Cl SW16 204 B6
Kintyre Ct 17 SW2 160 A4
Kinveachy Gdns SE7 122 A1
Kinver Ho N4 51 B2
Kinver Rd SE26 184 C6
Kipling Ct W7 108 D6
Kipling Dr SW17 180 B4
Kipling Ho 29 SE5 139 A5
Kipling Pl HA7 24 D4
Kipling Rd DA7 147 A4
Kipling St SE1 117 B4 252 D2
Kipling Terr N9 17 B2
Kipling Twr 3 W3 111 A3
Kippington Dr SE9 165 D3
Kirby Cl KT19 215 D3
Kirby Est SE16 118 B3
Kirby Gr SE1 117 C4 253 A2
Kirby St EC1 94 C2 241 B4
Kirby Way KT12 194 C3
Kirchen Rd W13 109 B6
Kirk La SE18 145 A6
Kirk Rd E17 53 B3
Kirk Rise SM1 217 D5
Kirkby Cl N11 31 A4
Kirkdale SE26 162 B1
Kirkdale Rd E11 54 C2
Kirkeby Ho EC1 241 A4
Kirkfield Cl W13 109 B5
Kirkham Rd E6 100 A1
Kirkham St SE18 145 C6
Kirkland Cl DA15 167 C5
Kirkland Wlk 4 E8 73 D2
Kirkleas Rd KT6 198 A1
Kirklees Rd
Dagenham RM8 80 C3
Thornton Heath CR7 204 C4
Kirkley Ho N16 51 C1
Kirkley Rd SW19 179 C2
Kirkman Pl W1 239 C3
Kirkmichael Rd E14 98 A1
Kirk's Pl E3 97 B2
Kirkside Rd SE3 143 A6
Kirkstall Ave N17 51 B5
Kirkstall Gdns SW2 160 A3
Kirkstall Ho SW1 258 C2
Kirkstall Rd SW2 160 A3
Kirkstead Ct E5 75 A4
Kirksted Rd SM4 201 D1
Kirkstone NW1 232 A2
Kirkstone Way BR1 186 C3
Kirkton Lo SW18 157 D5
Kirkton Rd N15 51 C5
Kirkwall Pl E2 96 C4
Kirkwood Rd SE15 140 B3
Kirn Rd W13 109 B6
Kirrane Cl KT3 199 D4
Kirtley Ho SW8 269 B2
Kirtley Rd SE26 185 A6
Kirtling St SW8 137 C5 269 A4
Kirton Cl W4 111 B2
Kirton Gdns 23 E2 95 D4
Kirton Rd E13 99 C5
Kirton Wlk HA8 27 A3
Kirwin Way SE5 138 D5
Kitcat Terr E3 97 C4
Kitchener Rd E7 77 B2
E17 35 D2
N2 48 C6
N17 51 C6
Dagenham RM10 81 D2
South Norwood CR7 205 B6
Kite Ho 5 SW11 136 C2
Kitley Gdns SE19 183 D2
Kitson Rd SE5 139 A5
SW13 134 A4
Kittiwake Ct 26 SE8 141 B6
Kittiwake Pl SM1 217 B3
Kittiwake Rd UB5 84 D4
Kittiwake Way UB4 84 D2
Kitto Rd SE14 140 D3
Kitt's End Rd EN5 1 A6
Kiver Rd N19 72 A6
Klea Ave SW4 159 C5
Kleffens Ct 2 SE3 142 D5
Knaggs Ho 1 TW11 174 C5
Knapdale Cl SE23 162 B2
Knapmill Rd SE6 163 D2
Knapmill Way SE6 163 D2
Knapp Cl NW10 67 C2
Knapp Rd E3 97 C3
Ashford TW15 170 B6
Knapton Mews SW17 181 A4
Knaresborough Dr
SW18 157 D3
Knaresborough Ho 4
N4 51 A2
Knaresborough Pl
SW5 113 D2 255 C4
Knatchbull Rd NW10 89 B6
SE5 138 D4
Knebworth Ave E17 35 C2
Knebworth Ho E17 35 C2
2 N16 73 C4
SW8 269 D1
Knebworth Rd 3 N16 73 C4
Knee Hill SE2 124 C1
Knee Hill Cres SE2 124 C2
Kneller Gdns TW7 152 B5
Kneller Ho 9 SW8 137 D3
4 Northolt UB5 84 D5
Kneller Rd SE4 141 A1
New Malden KT3 199 C2
Twickenham TW2 152 B5
Knight Ct 1 E4 20 A3
N15 51 C4
Knight Ho SE17 263 A3
Knighten St E1 118 B5
Knighthead Point E14 119 C4
Knightland Ho E5 74 B6
Knightland Rd E5 74 B6
Knightleas Ct NW2 68 C2
Knighton Cl
Croydon CR2 220 D1
Woodford IG8 37 B6
Knighton Dr IG8 37 B6
Knighton Gn IG9 21 B2
Knighton La IG9 21 B2
Knighton Park Rd SE26 184 D5
Knighton Rd E7 77 A4
Knightrider Ct EC4 252 A6
Knightrider St EC4 251 D6
Knights Arc SW1 247 C1
Knight's Ave W5 110 A4
Knights Cl E9 74 C3
Knights Ct Bushey WD2 8 B3
Kingston u T KT1 198 A6
Penge BR3 185 A2
Knight's Hill SE19,SE27 182 D6
Knight's Hill Sq SE27 182 D6
Knights Ho SE1 253 C2
SW5 254 C2
SW8 270 B3
Knight's Ho SW10 266 A4
Knight's La N9 18 A1
Knight's Pk KT1 198 A6
Knights Rd E16 121 A4
Stanmore HA7 25 C6
Knight's Wlk SE11 261 C3
Knightsbridge
SW1,SW7 114 D4 247 C1
Knightsbridge Ct SW1 247 D1
Knightsbridge Gn SW1 247 C1
Knightsbridge Mews
BR7 188 B3
Knightsbridge Sta
SW1 114 D4 247 C1
SW1 114 D4 247 D1
Knightshayes Ho NW4 28 D1
Knightswood Cl HA8 11 A2
Knightswood Ct N6 49 D2
Knightswood Ho N12 30 A4
Knightwood Cres KT3 199 C3
Knivett Rd SW6 135 C6 265 A5
Knobs Hill Rd E15 97 D6
Knockholt Rd SE9 165 D6
Knole Cl CR0 206 C3
Knole Ct UB5 84 C4
Knole Gate DA15 167 C1
Knole The SE9 188 C6
Knoll Ct SE19 183 D5
Orpington BR6 227 D6
Knoll Dr N14 15 A4
Knoll Ho NW8 229 A4
Knoll Rd SW18 158 A6
Bexleyheath DA5 169 C5
Sidcup DA14 190 B6
Knoll Rise BR6 211 D1
Knoll The W13 87 C2
Beckenham BR3 185 D2
Hayes BR2 209 A1
Knollmead KT4,KT5 199 A1
Knollmead Prim Sch
KT5 215 A6
Knolls Cl KT4 216 B5
Knolly's Cl SE27,SW16 160 C1
Knolly's Rd SE27,SW16 160 C1
Knot Ho SE1 253 C3
Knottisford St E2 96 C4
Knotts Green Mews E10 54 A3
Knotts Green Rd E10 54 A3
Knowl Pk WD6 10 A6
Knowl Way WD6 10 B6
Knowlden Ho 4 E1 118 C6
Knowle Ave DA7 147 B5
Knowle Cl SW9 138 C2
Knowle Lo BR7 188 B4
Knowle Rd
Keston Mark BR2 226 A6
Twickenham TW2 152 C3
Knowles Cl UB7 104 A5
Knowles Ct 7 HA1 42 D3
Knowles Hill Cres SE13 164 B6
Knowles Ho NW10 90 A6
SW18 157 D5
Knowles Wlk SW4 137 C2
Knowlton Gn 1 BR2 208 D4
Knowlton Ho 32 SW9 138 C4
Knowsley Ave UB1 107 D5
Knowsley Rd SW11 136 D3
Knox Ct 16 SW4 138 A3
Knox Ho SW15 134 C3
Knox Rd E7 77 A2
Knox St W1 92 D2 237 C4
Knoyle St SE14 141 A6
Kobi Nazrul Prim Sch
E1 96 A1
Koblenz Ho N8 50 A6
Kohat Rd SW19 179 D5
Korda Cl TW17 192 B6
Kossuth St SE10 120 C1
Kramer Mews SW5 255 C1
Kreedman Wlk 8 E8 74 A3
Kreisel Wlk TW9 132 B6
Kuala Gdns SW16 182 B2
Kuhn Way E7 77 A3
Kwesi Johnson Ct 4
N22 32 C1
Kydbrook Cl BR5 211 A2
Kylemore Cl 3 E6 99 D5
Kylemore Ct 4 W12 112 A4
Kylemore Rd NW6 69 C1
Kylestrome Ho SW1 258 B3
Kymberley Rd HA1 42 C3
Kynance Gdns HA7 25 C2
Kynance Mews
SW7 113 D3 255 D5
Kynance Pl SW7 256 A5
Kynaston Ave CR7 205 A4
Kynaston Cl HA3 24 B3
Kynaston Cres CR7 205 A4
Kynaston Ho 7 SW2 160 B3
Kynaston Rd N16 73 C5
Enfield EN2 5 B4
Plaistow BR1 187 A5
Thornton Heath CR7 205 A4
Kynaston Wood HA3 24 B3
Kynersley Cl SM5 218 D5
Kynoch Rd N18 34 D6
Kyrle Rd SW11 159 A5
Kyverdale Rd N16 51 D1

L

La Retraite RC Girls Sch
SW12 159 C4
La Saint Union Convent Sch
NW5 71 A5
La Tourne Gdns BR6 227 A5
Laburnam Ct 12 SW16 182 C5
Laburnham Cl 5 SE15 140 C5
Laburnham Ho SE4 141 B3
Laburnham Pl SE9 166 C6
Laburnum Ave N9 17 D2
N17 33 B3
Carshalton SM1 218 C5
Yiewsley UB7 104 B6
Laburnum Cl E4 35 B4
N11 31 A4
Laburnum Cres TW16 172 B2
Laburnum Ct 26 E2 95 D6
Harrow HA1 41 D3
5 Mitcham CR4 181 A1
Stanmore HA7 25 C6
Laburnum Gdns N21 17 A2
Croydon CR0 206 D1
Laburnum Gr N21 17 A2
NW9 45 A2
Hounslow TW3 129 B1
Kingston u T KT3 177 B1
Ruislip HA4 39 B3
Southall UB1 85 B3
Laburnum Ho 6 N16 73 B6
Dagenham RM10 81 C6
Laburnum JMI Sch E2 95 D6
Laburnum Lo N3 29 B1
Laburnum Rd SW19 180 A3
Hayes UB3 105 D2
Mitcham CR4 181 A1
Laburnum St E2 95 D6
Laburnum Way
Bromley BR2 210 D2
Stanwell TW19 148 B3
Laburnums The E6 100 A3
Lacebark Cl DA15 167 D4
Lacey Cl N9 18 A2
Lacey Dr Dagenham RM8 80 C5
Edgware HA8 26 B6
Hampton TW12 173 B2
Lacey Ho 6 SE13 142 A3
Lacey Wlk E3 97 C5
Lacine Ct 12 SE16 118 D4
Lackington St EC2 242 D4
Lackland Ho SE1 263 D2
Lacland Ho SW10 266 C4
Lacock Cl SW19 180 A4
Lacock Ct 3 W13 109 A5
Lacon Rd SE22 140 A1
Lacy Rd SW15 134 D1
Ladas Rd SE27 183 A5
Ladbroke Cres W11 91 A1
Ladbroke Gdns
W11 113 B6 244 C6
Ladbroke Gr W10 91 A2
W11 113 B6 244 C6
Ladbroke Grove Ho
W11 244 C6
Ladbroke Grove Sta
W10 91 A1
Ladbroke Mews W11 244 B3
Ladbroke Rd
W11 113 B5 244 C4
Enfield EN1 17 D5
Ladbroke Sq
W11 113 B6 244 D5
Ladbroke Terr
W11 113 B5 244 D4
Ladbroke Wlk
W11 113 B5 244 D4
Ladbrook Cl HA5 41 B4
Ladbrook Rd SE25 205 B5
Ladbrooke Cres DA14 168 D1
Ladderstile Ride KT2,
TW10 176 D5
Ladderswood Way N11 31 C5
Ladlands SE22 162 A4
Lady Bankes Jun & Inf Schs
HA4 62 A6
Lady Booth Rd 7 KT1 176 A1
Lady Eleanor Holles Sch The
(Jun Girls) TW12 173 D5
Lady Eleanor Holles Sch The
(Senior Girls) TW12 173 D5
Lady Elizabeth Ho
SW14 133 A2
Lady Hay KT4 215 D6
Lady Margaret Prim Sch
UB1 85 B2
Lady Margaret Rd NW5 71 C3
Southall UB1 85 B2
Lady Margaret Sch
SW6 135 C4 265 A1
Lady Shaw Ct N13 16 B1
Lady Somerset Rd NW5 71 B4
Ladybower Ct 6 E5 74 D4
Ladycroft Gdns 6 BR6 227 A3
Ladycroft Rd SE13 141 D2
Ladycroft Way BR6 227 A3
Ladycroft Wlk HA7 25 D1
Ladygate La HA4 39 A3
Ladysmith Ave E6 100 A5
Ilford IG2 57 C2
Ladysmith Cl NW7 28 A3
Ladysmith Rd E16 98 D4
N17 34 A1
N18 34 B5
SE9 166 C5
Enfield EN1 5 D3
Harrow HA3 24 C1
Ladywell Cl SE4 141 C1
Ladywell Ho 7 BR5 190 B1
Ladywell Hts SE4 163 B5
Ladywell Rd SE13 163 D6
Ladywell St 4 E15 98 D6
Ladywell Sta SE13 163 D6
Ladywood Ave BR5 211 C4
Ladywood Rd KT6 214 C6
Lafitte Ho 22 N19 49 D2
Lafone Ave TW13 150 C2
Lafone Ho 11 SW2 160 A4
Lafone St SE1 117 D4 253 C2
Lagado Mews SE16 118 D5
Lagan Ho SE15 140 A5
1 SE15 140 A4
Lagonda Ho 11 E3 97 C3
Lagonier Ho EC1 235 B1
Laidlaw Dr N21 16 B6
Laindon Ho 6 N16 51 D1
Laing Dean UB5 84 C6
Laing Ho SE5 139 A5
Laings Ave CR4 180 D1
Laings Cnr CR4 180 D2
Lainlock Pl TW3 129 D4
Lainson St SW18 157 C4
Laird Ho SE5 139 A5
Lairdale Cl SE21 161 A4
Lairs Cl N7 72 A2

Laitwood Rd SW12 159 B3
Lakanal 14 SE5 139 C4
Lake Ave BR1 187 A4
Lake Bsns Ctr N17 34 A3
Lake Cl 6 SW19 179 B5
Lake Dr WD2 8 B2
Lake Gdns
Dagenham RM10 81 C3
Hackbridge SM6 219 B5
Richmond TW10 153 B2
Lake Ho SE1 252 A1
4 SW27 182 D5
Lake House Rd E11 77 A6
Lake Rd SW19 179 B5
Croydon CR0 223 B6
Dagenham RM9 103 D4
Ilford RM6 58 D5
Lake The WD2 8 B3
Lake View HA8 26 B5
Lake View Ct SW1 258 D6
Lake View Terr N18 33 D6
Lakedale Rd SE18 123 C1
Lakefield Rd N22 32 D1
Lakehall Gdns CR7 204 D4
Lakehall Rd CR7 204 D4
Lakehurst Rd KT19 215 C3
Lakeland Cl HA3 24 B4
Lakeman Ct CR7 183 A1
Lakenheath N14 15 D6
Laker Ct SW4 138 A3
Laker Pl SW15 157 A5
Lakes Rd BR2 225 C3
Lakeside W13 87 C1
Beckenham BR3 207 D6
Deacons Hill WD6 10 C6
Enfield EN2 3 D1
Hackbridge SM6 219 B4
10 Kingston u T KT2 176 D3
West Ewell KT19 215 C2
Lakeside Ave SE28 124 A5
Redbridge IG4 55 D5
Lakeside Cl SE25 184 A1
Ruislip HA4 39 B5
Sidcup DA15 168 C6
Lakeside Complex The
SE2 124 D5
Lakeside Cres EN4 14 D6
Lakeside Ct N4 51 A1
Lakeside Dr Esher KT10 212 A2
Keston Mark BR2 226 A5
Lakeside Lo NW4 47 A5
Lakeside Rd N13 16 B1
W14 112 D3
Lakeside Way HA9 66 C4
Lakeswood Rd BR5 211 A3
Lakeview 23 E3 96 D5
Lakeview Rd SE27 182 D5
Bexley DA16 146 B1
Lakis Cl NW3 70 A4
Laleham Ave NW7 11 B1
Laleham Ho E2 243 C6
Laleham Rd SE6 164 A4
Littleton TW17 192 C4
Lamb Ho 11 SE5 139 B4
28 SE5 139 A5
SE10 142 A6
Lamb La E8 74 B1
Lamb St E1 95 D2 243 C4
Lamb Wlk SE1 253 A1
Lambarde Ave SE9 188 C6
Lamberhurst Ho 14
SE15 140 C6
Lamberhurst Rd SE27 182 C5
Dagenham RM8 59 B1
Lambert Ave TW9 132 D2
Lambert Ho 19 N19 49 D2
17 SW9 138 C3
Lambert Lo TW8 109 D1
Lambert Rd E16 99 B1
N12 30 B5
SW2 160 B6
Lambert St N1 72 C1
Lambert Way N12 30 A5
Lambert Wlk HA9 65 D5
Lambert's Pl CR0 205 B1
Lambert's Rd KT6 198 B4
Lambeth Coll SW2 160 B6
Lambeth Coll (Clapham Ctr)
SW4 159 C6
Lambeth Coll (Tower Bridge
Ctr) SE1 117 C5 253 B3
Lambeth Coll (Vauxhall Ctr)
SW8 137 D4 269 C2
Lambeth Ct 8 SW18 157 C6
Lambeth High St
SE1 116 B2 260 C4
Lambeth Hill EC4 252 A6
Lambeth Inst Strand Ctr
SW2 160 B4
Lambeth North Sta
SE1 116 C3 261 A6
Lambeth Palace*
SE1 116 B3 260 C5
Lambeth Palace Rd
SE1 116 B3 260 C6
Lambeth Prospect
SE19 183 B4
Lambeth Rd
SE1 116 C3 261 B5
Thornton Heath CR0 204 D1
Lambeth Twrs SE11 261 A5
Lambeth Wlk
SE11 116 B2 260 D4
Lambfold Ho N7 72 A2
Lamble St NW5 71 A4
Lambley Rd RM9 80 B2
Lambolle Pl NW3 70 C2
Lambolle Rd NW3 70 C2
Lambourn Cl 9 NW5 71 C4
W7 108 D4
Lambourn Rd SW4 137 B2
Lambourne Ave SW19 179 B6
Lambourne Ct 5 IG8 37 C3
Lambourne Gdns E4 19 C2
4 Barking IG11 79 D1
Enfield EN1 5 D3
Lambourne Gr KT1 176 D1
Lambourne Ho NW8 236 D4
SE16 118 D2
Lambourne Pl SE3 143 B4
Lambourne Rd E11 54 A2
Barking IG11 79 D1
Ilford IG3 79 C6
Lambrook Ho 12 SE15 140 A4
Lambrook Terr
SW6 135 A4 264 A2
Lamb's Bldgs EC1 242 C5
Lamb's Cl N9 18 A2
Lamb's Conduit Pas
WC1 240 C4
Lamb's Conduit St
WC1 94 B3 240 C5
Lambs Mdw IG8 37 D1
Lamb's Mews N1 234 C5
Lamb's Pas EC1 95 B3 242 C5
Lamb's Terr N9 17 B2
Lambs Wlk EN2 5 A3
Lambscroft Ave SE9,
SE12 165 D1
Lambton Ct 2 N19 50 A1
Lambton Pl W11 244 D6
Lambton Rd N19 50 A1
SW20 178 C2
Lamerock Rd BR1 186 D6
Lamerton Lo 10 TW9 132 B4
Lamerton St 9 SE8 141 C6
Lamford Cl N17 33 B3
Lamington St 3 W6 112 B2
Lamlash St SE11 261 C4
Lamley Ho SE10 141 D5
Lammas Ave CR4 181 A1
Lammas Gn SE26 162 B1
Lammas Park Gdns W5 109 C5
Lammas Park Rd W5 109 D4
Lammas Rd E9 74 D1
E10 53 A1
Richmond TW10 175 C6
Lammermoor Rd SW12 159 B4
Lamont Rd
SW10 136 B6 266 C5
Lamont Rd Pas SW10 266 C5
Lamorbey Cl DA15 167 D2
Lamorna Cl E17 36 A2
Lamorna Gr HA7 25 D1
Lampard Gr N16 51 D1
Lampern Sq 8 E2 96 A4
Lampeter Sq W6 264 A5
Lamplighter Cl 31 E1 96 C3
Lampmead Rd SE12 142 D1
Lamport Cl SE18 122 B2
Lamps Ct 10 SE5 139 A5
Lampson Ho 6 N19 71 C4
Lampton Ave TW5 129 D4
Lampton Ct TW5 129 D4
Lampton House Cl
SW19 178 D6
Lampton Park Rd TW3 129 D3
Lampton Rd TW3,TW5 129 D3
Lampton Sch TW5 129 C4
Lanacre Ave NW9 27 C2
Lanain Ct SE12 164 D4
Lanark Cl W5 87 C2
Lanark Ct UB5 63 C3
Lanark Ho 11 SE1 118 A1
Lanark Mans W9 236 B6
6 W12 112 C4
Lanark Pl W9 92 A3 236 B6
Lanark Rd W9 92 A4 229 A1
Lanark Sq E14 119 D3
Lanata Wlk UB4 84 D3
Lanbury Rd SE15 140 D1
Lancashire Ct W1 248 D6
Lancaster Ave E18 55 B5
SE21,SE27 161 A2
SW19 178 D5
Barking IG11 101 C6
Barnet EN4 2 B5
Mitcham CR4 204 A4
Lancaster Cl 9 N1 73 C1
N17 34 A3
NW9 27 D3
W2 245 C5
Beckenham BR2 208 D5
Kingston u T KT2 175 D5
Stanwell TW19 148 A5
Lancaster Cotts 1
TW10 154 A5
Lancaster Ct SE27 160 D2
SW6 264 D3
W2 246 B6
1 Belmont SM2 217 C1
Stanwell TW19 148 A3
Walton-on-T KT12 194 B2
Lancaster Dr E14 120 A5
NW3 70 C2
Lancaster Gate
W2 114 A6 246 B6
Lancaster Gate Sta
W2 114 B6 246 C6
Lancaster Gdns SW19 179 A5
W13 109 B4
Kingston u T KT2 175 D5
Lancaster Gr NW3 70 C2
Lancaster Ho SW15 134 C3
SW18 157 D4
Enfield EN2 5 B4
Lancaster House SW1 249 A2
Lancaster Lo 2 W11 91 A1
Lancaster Mews
3 SW18 157 D5
W2 114 A6 246 B6
2 Richmond TW10 154 A5
Lancaster Pk TW10 154 A6
Lancaster Pl 1 SW19 178 D5
WC2 116 B6 250 C5
Hounslow TW5 128 D3
Ilford IG1 79 A4
Twickenham TW1 153 A4
Lancaster Rd E7 77 A1
E11 76 C6
E17 34 D1
N4 50 C2
N11 31 D4
N18 33 D5
NW10 68 A3
SE25 206 A6
W11 91 A1
Enfield EN2 5 B4
Harrow HA2 41 C4
New Barnet EN4 14 B6
Northolt UB5 64 A2
Southall UB1 107 A6
SW19 178 D5
Lancaster Road Ind Est 2
EN4 14 B6
Lancaster St
SE1 116 D4 251 D1
Lancaster Stables 10
NW3 70 C2
Lancaster Terr
W2 114 B6 246 C6
Lancaster Wlk
W2 114 A5 246 B4
Hayes UB3 83 A1
Lancasterian Jun & Inf Schs
N17 33 D2
Lance Rd HA1 42 A2
Lancefield Ct 1 NW6 91 A5
Lancefield Ho SE15 140 B2
Lancefield St W10 91 B4
Lancell St N16 73 C6
Lancelot Ave HA0 65 D4
Lancelot Cres HA0 65 D4
Lancelot Gdns EN4 15 A4
Lancelot Par 4 HA0 65 D3
Lancelot Pl
SW7 114 D4 247 C1
Lancelot Rd
Bexley DA16 146 A2
Wembley HA0 65 D3
Lancer Sq W8 245 C2
Lancey Cl SE7 122 A2
Lanchester Ct W2 237 C1
Lanchester Rd N6 48 D4
Lancing Gdns N9 17 D3
Lancing Rd W13 109 B6
Feltham TW13 149 D2
Ilford IG2 57 B2
Thornton Heath CR0 204 B2
Lancing St NW1 232 C1
Lancresse Ct N1 95 C6
Landale Ho 13 SE16 118 C3
Landcroft Rd SE22 161 D5
Landells Rd SE22 162 A5
Lander Ct EN5 14 A6
Landford Rd SW15 134 C2
Landgrove Rd SW19 179 C5
Landin Ho 1 E14 97 C1
Landleys Field 21 N7 71 D3
Landmann Ho 16 SE16 118 C2
Landmann Way SE14 118 D1
Landmark Commercial Ctr
N18 33 C4
Landon Pl SW1 257 C6
Landon Way TW15 170 D4
Landon Wlk 14 E14 119 D6
Landons Cl E14 120 A5
Landor Ct N16 73 C3
Landor Ho 7 SE5 139 B5
Landor Rd SW9 138 A2
Landor Wlk 11 W12 112 A4
Landra Gdns N21 16 D5
Landrake NW1 232 B5
Landridge Dr EN1 6 B5
Landridge Rd SW6 135 B3
Landrock Rd N8 50 B3
Lands' End WD6 9 D5
Landscape Rd IG8 37 B3
Landsdowne Cl KT5 214 D6
Landseer Ave E12 78 C3
Landseer Cl SW19 180 B2
Edgware HA8 26 C1
Landseer Ct UB4 83 B5
Landseer Ho NW8 236 D6
SW1 259 D3
SW11 268 B1
17 Northolt UB5 84 D5
Landseer Rd N19 72 A6
Cheam SM1,SM2 217 C2
Enfield EN1 18 A6
New Malden KT3 199 B2
Landstead Rd SE18 145 B5
Landulph Ho SE11 261 B2
Landward Ct W1 237 B2
Lane Cl NW2 68 B5
Lane Ct SW11 158 D4
Lane End DA7 147 D2
Lane Gdns WD2 8 C4
Lane Mews E12 78 B5
Lane The NW8 92 A5 229 A3
SE3 143 A2
Lanercost Cl SW2 160 C2
Lanercost Gdns N14 16 A4
Lanercost Rd SW2 160 C2
Laneside HA8 27 A5
Laneside Ave RM8 59 B2
Laneway SW15 156 B6
Laney Ho EC1 241 A4
Lanfranc Ct HA1 64 D5
Lanfranc Rd E3 97 A5
Lanfrey Pl W14 254 C1
Lang Ho 3 N19 71 C5
SW8 270 A3
Lang St E1 96 C3
Langbourne Ave N6 71 A6
Langbourne Ct E17 53 A3
Langbourne Ho 7 SW2 160 C6
Langbourne Mans N6 71 A6
Langbourne Prim Sch
SE21 161 C1
Langbourne Way KT10 213 A2
Langbrook Rd SE3 143 D3
Langcroft Cl SM5 218 D5
Langdale NW1 232 A2
Langdale Ave CR4 202 D6
Langdale Cl SE17 139 A6
SW14 132 D1
Dagenham RM8 58 C1
Orpington BR6 226 D5
Langdale Cres DA7 147 C4
Langdale Ct 3 W5 87 C2
9 Ilford IG1 78 D5
Langdale Dr UB4 83 C5
Langdale Gdns UB6 87 B4
Langdale Ho SW1 259 A1
Langdale Rd SE10 142 A5
Thornton Heath CR7 204 C5
Langdale St 3 E1 96 B1
Langdon Cres E6 100 C5
Langdon Ct EC1 234 D3
NW10 89 C6
Langdon Dr NW9 45 A1
Langdon Ho 1 E14 98 A1
Langdon Park Rd N6 49 C2
Langdon Park Sec Sch
E14 98 A1
Langdon Pl SW14 133 A2
Langdon Rd E6 100 C6
Bromley BR2 209 B6
Morden SM4 202 A4
Langdon Sch E6 100 D6
Langdon Shaw DA14 189 D5
Langdon Way 14 SE1 118 A2
Langdon Wlk SM4 202 A4
Langdons Ct UB2 107 C3
Langford Cl E8 74 A3
7 N15 51 C3
NW8 229 B4
Langford Cres EN4 2 D1
Langford Ct NW8 229 B3
Langford Gn SE5 139 C2
Langford Ho 5 SE8 141 C6
Langford Pl NW8 92 A5 229 B4
Sidcup DA14 168 A1
Langford Prim Sch
SW6 135 D3
Langford Rd 4 SW6 135 D3
Cockfosters EN4 2 D1
Woodford IG8 37 C4
Langfords IG9 21 D2
Langham Cl N15 50 D6
Langham Ct NW4 46 D4
4 SW15 156 D6
SW20 178 C1
Ruislip HA4 62 B3
12 Twickenham TW1 153 C5
Langham Dr RM6 58 B3
Langham Gdns N21 16 D6
W13 109 B6
Burnt Oak HA8 27 A3
Richmond TW10 175 C6
Wembley HA0 65 C6
Langham Ho SW4 159 C6
Langham House Cl
TW10 175 D6
Langham Mans SW5 255 C1
Langham Pl N15 50 D6
W1 93 B2 238 D3
W4 133 C6
Langham Rd N15 51 A6
SW20 178 C2
Burnt Oak HA8 27 A4
Teddington TW11 175 B4
Langham Sch The N15 51 A5
Langham St W1 93 B2 238 D3
Langhedge Cl N18 33 D4
Langhedge La N18 33 D4
Langholm Cl SW12 159 D4
Langholme WD2 8 A3
Langhorn Dr TW2 152 C4
Langhorne Ct 10 NW8 70 B1
Langhorne Ho 5 SE7 143 C6
Langhorne Rd RM10 81 C1
Langhurst Ho 10 SW11 137 A3
Langland Cres HA7 25 D1
Langland Dr HA5 23 A3
Langland Gdns NW3 69 D3
Croydon CR0 223 B6
Langland Ho 10 SE5 139 B5
Langler Rd NW10 90 C5
Langley Ave
North Cheam KT4,SM3 216 D6
Ruislip HA4 62 B6
Surbiton KT6 198 A1
Langley Cres E11 55 C2
Dagenham RM9 80 D1
Edgware HA8 11 A1
Harlington UB3 127 D5
Langley Ct SW8 270 A2
Langley Ct *continued*
WC2 250 A6
Langley Dr E11 55 B2
W3 110 D4
Langley Gdns
Dagenham RM9 80 D1
Petts Wood BR5 210 D3
Langley Gr KT3 177 C1
Langley Ho 11 E5 74 B3
Bromley BR1 187 B3
Langley La SW8 138 A6 270 B6
Langley Mans SW8 270 B6
Langley Park Rd SM1,
SM2 218 A1
Langley Park Sch for Boys
BR3 207 D3
Langley Park Sch for Girls
BR3 208 A3
Langley Pk NW7 27 C4
Langley Rd SW19 179 C2
Beckenham BR3 207 A5
Bexley DA16 146 C6
Isleworth TW7 130 D3
Surbiton KT6 198 A2
Langley Row EN5 1 B4
Langley St WC2 94 A1 240 A1
Langley Way BR4 208 C2
Langmead Dr WD2 8 B3
Langmead Ho 34 E3 97 D4
Langmead St SE27 183 A6
Langmore Ct DA7 146 D2
Langmore Ho 28 E1 96 A1
Langport Ct KT12 194 C1
Langport Ho 1 SW9 138 D3
Langridge 15 NW5 71 A2
Langridge Mews TW12 173 B4
Langroyd Rd SW17 158 D2
Langside Ave SW15 134 A1
Langside Cres N14 15 D1
Langston Hughes Cl 5
SE24 138 D1
Langthorn Ct EC2 242 D2
Langthorne Ct 4 SE6 186 A6
Langthorne Ho UB3 105 C2
Langthorne Hospl E11 76 B5
Langthorne Rd E11 76 B5
Langthorne St SW6 134 D5
Langton Ave E6 100 C4
N20 14 B4
Langton Cl WC1 94 B3 240 D6
Langton Ct SW15 157 B5
Langton Ho SE11 260 D4
5 SW16 181 C6
Langton Pl SW18 157 C3
Langton Rd NW2 68 C5
SW9 138 D5
East Molesey KT8 196 A5
Harrow HA3 24 A3
Langton Rise SE22,SE23 162 B4
Langton St
SW10 136 A6 266 B5
Langton Way SE3 143 A5
South Croydon CR0 221 C4
Langtry Pl SW6 265 B6
Langtry Rd NW8 91 D6
Northolt UB5 84 D5
Langtry Wlk NW8 91 D6
NW8 92 A6 229 A6
Langwood Chase TW11 175 C4
Langworth Dr UB4 84 B1
Langworthy HA5 23 C4
Lanherne Ho 7 SW19 178 D3
Lanhill Rd W9 91 C3
Lanier Rd SE13 164 B5
Lanigan Dr TW3 151 D6
Lankaster Gdns N2 30 B2
Lankers Dr HA2 41 B3
Lankton Cl BR3 186 A2
Lanner Ho 2 SW11 136 C2
Lannock Rd UB3 105 D5
Lannoy Point SW6 264 B4
Lannoy Rd SE9 167 A3
Lanrick Rd E14 98 C1
Lanridge Rd SE2 124 D3
Lansbury Ave N18 33 C5
Barking IG11 80 A1
Dagenham RM6 59 A4
Feltham TW14 150 B5
Lansbury Cl NW10 67 A3
Lansbury Ct 4 SE28 124 B6
Lansbury Dr UB4 83 D3
Lansbury Gdns 1 E14 98 B1
Lansbury Ho 5 DA17 125 B1
Lansbury Rd EN3 6 D4
Lansbury Way N18 33 C5
Lanscombe Wlk SW8 270 A3
Lansdell Rd CR4 181 A1
Lansdown Cl KT12 194 C1
Lansdown Ho 29 SE5 139 A3
Lansdown Rd E7 77 C1
Sidcup DA14 168 B1
Lansdowne SW15 157 A6
Lansdowne Ave
Bexley DA7 146 D5
Bromley BR6 210 D1
Lansdowne Cl SW20 178 D3
Twickenham TW1 152 D3
Lansdowne Copse 1
KT4 216 A6
Lansdowne Cres
W11 113 A6 244 B5
Lansdowne Ct 2 KT4 216 A6
Lansdowne Dr E8 74 A1
Lansdowne Gdns
SW8 138 A4 270 A2
Lansdowne Gr NW10 67 C4
Lansdowne Hill SE27 160 D1
Lansdowne Ho W11 244 C4
Lansdowne Ho *continued*
Enfield EN2 4 C3
Lansdowne La SE7 121 D1
Lansdowne Mews SE7 121 D1
W11 244 C4
Lansdowne Pl SE1 262 D6
SE19 183 D3
Lansdowne Rd E4 19 C2
E8 74 A2
E11 76 D6
E17 53 C3
E18 55 A6
N3 29 C3
N10 31 C1
N17 34 A2
SW19,SW20 178 C3
W11 113 A6 244 B5
Bromley BR1 187 B3
Croydon CR0 205 B1
Harrow HA1 42 C2
Hayes UB8 83 A1
Hounslow TW3 129 D2
Ilford IG3 57 D2
Stanmore HA7 25 C4
West Ewell KT19 215 B1
Lansdowne Rise
W11 113 A6 244 B5
Lansdowne Row W1 248 D4
Lansdowne Sch SW9 138 B2
Lansdowne Terr WC1 240 B5
Lansdowne Way
SW4,SW8 138 A4 270 B1
Lansdowne Wlk
W11 113 B5 244 C4
Lansdowne Wood Cl 11
SE27 160 D1
Lansfield Ave N18 34 A6
Lanson Ct E11 76 D6
Lanson Ho HA8 26 C4
Lanswood Ct KT4 216 A6
Lant Ho SE1 252 A1
Lant St SE1 117 A4 252 B1
Lantern Cl SW15 134 A1
Wembley HA0 65 D3
Lantern Ct 4 SW20 178 D2
Lantern Ho E14 119 C4
Lanterns Ct E14 119 C3
Lanterns The N12 29 D4
Lantry Ct 1 W3 110 D5
Lanvanor Rd SE15 140 C3
Lanyard Ho 3 SE8 119 B2
Lapford Cl W9 91 B3
Lapponum Wlk UB4 84 D2
Lapsang SE1 253 D3
Lapse Wood Wlk SE22 162 B3
Lapstone Gdns HA3 43 C3
Lapwing Ct NW9 27 C1
Tolworth KT6 214 C5
Lapwing Twr 31 SE8 141 B6
Lapwing Way UB4 84 D1
Lapworth 2 N11 31 B6
Lapworth Ct W2 91 D2
Lara Cl SE13 164 A5
Chessington KT9 214 A1
Larbert Rd SW16 181 C3
Larch Ave W3 111 C5
Larch Cl E13 99 C3
N11 31 A3
7 N19 71 C6
15 SE8 141 B6
SW12 159 B2
Larch Cres Hayes UB4 84 D2
West Ewell KT19 214 D2
Larch Dene BR6 226 C6
Larch Gn NW9 27 C2
Larch Gr DA15 167 D3
Larch Ho 17 SE16 118 C4
Hayes UB4 84 C2
Larch Rd E10 75 C6
NW2 68 C4
Larch Tree Way CR0 223 C5
Larch Way BR2 210 C2
Larches Ave SW14 133 B1
Larches The N13 17 A1
Hillingdon UB10 82 D5
Larchfield Ho 2 N5 73 A3
Larchmore Ct N19 72 A6
Larchvale Ct 4 SM2 217 D1
Larchwood Rd SE9 166 D2
Larcom St SE17 117 A2 262 B3
Larcombe Cl CR0 221 D4
Larden Rd W3 111 C4
Largewood Ave KT6 214 C6
Larissa St SE17 262 D3
Lark Hall Inf Sch SW4 137 D3
Lark Hall Jun & Inf Sch
SW4 138 A3
Lark Row E2 96 C6
Lark Way SM5 202 C2
Larkbere Rd SE26 185 A6
Larken Cl WD2 8 A3
Larken Dr WD2 8 A3
Larkfield Ave HA3 43 B6
Larkfield Cl BR2 225 A6
Larkfield Rd
Richmond TW9 132 A1
Sidcup DA14 167 D1
Larkhall La
SW4 138 A4 270 A1
Larkhall Rise SW4 137 D3
Larkham Cl TW13 149 C1
Larksfield Gr EN1 6 B4
Larkshall Bsns Ctr 2 E4 20 B2
Larkshall Cres E4 36 A6
Larkshall Ct E4 36 A5
Larkshall Rd E4 36 B6
Larkspur Cl 4 E6 100 A2
N17 33 B3

Lar – Len 329

Larkspur Cl *continued*
NW9 44 D4
Ruislip HA4 39 A2
Larkspur Ct SM6 219 B1
Larkspur Gr HA8 27 A6
Larkspur Way KT19 215 A3
Larkswood Ct E4 36 B5
Larkswood Jun & Inf Sch
E4 35 D6
Larkswood Rd E4 35 D6
Larkswood Rise HA5 40 C5
Larkway Cl NW9 45 B5
Larmenier RC Inf Sch
W6 112 D2
Larnaca Ho SE1 263 C6
Larnach Rd W6 134 D6
Larne Rd HA4 39 D2
Larpent Ave SW15 156 C6
Larwood Cl UB6 64 B3
Lasborough Ct 6 SE15 139 C5
Lascelles Ave HA1 42 B2
Lascelles Cl E11 76 B6
Lascelles Ho NW1 237 B5
Lascott's Rd N22 32 B4
Lashford Ho HA8 27 A4
Lassa Rd SE9 166 B6
Lassell St SE10 120 B1
Lasseter Pl SE3 142 D6
Latchett Rd E18 37 B2
Latchingdon Ct E17 52 D5
Latchmere Cl KT2,TW10 176 A5
Latchmere Jun & Inf Schs
KT2 176 B4
Latchmere La KT2,TW10 176 B5
Latchmere Rd KT2 176 B4
Latchmere St 5 SW11 136 D3
Lateward Rd TW8 131 D6
Latham Cl E6 100 A1
4 Twickenham TW1 153 A4
Latham Ct 2 N11 32 A4
7 Northolt UB5 84 D4
Latham Ho E1 96 D1
18 E17 53 D6
Latham Rd
Bexleyheath DA6 169 C6
Twickenham TW1 152 D4
Latham's Way CR0 220 B6
Lathkill Cl EN1 18 A4
Lathkill Ct BR3 185 B2
Lathom Jun Sch E6 78 A1
Lathom Rd E6 78 B1
Lathwood Ho 6 SE26 184 B5
Latimer SE17 263 A1
Latimer Ave E6 100 B6
Latimer Cl
North Cheam KT4 216 B4
Northwood HA5 22 C2
Latimer Gdns HA5 22 C2
Latimer Ho 11 E9 74 D2
W11 244 D5
Latimer Pl W4 133 C6
W10 90 C1
Latimer Rd E7 77 B4
N15 51 C3
SW19 179 D4
W10 90 C1
Barnet EN5 1 D2
Croydon CR0 220 D5
Teddington TW11 174 D5
Latimer Road Sta W10 112 D6
Latona Rd SE15 140 A6
Latton Cl KT12 195 A2
Latymer All Saints CE Prim
Sch N9 17 D2
Latymer Ct W6 112 D2
Latymer Rd N9 17 D3
Latymer Sch The N9 17 C2
Latymer Upper Sch W6 112 A1
Latymer Way N9 17 C2
Laud St SE11 116 B1 260 C2
Croydon CR0 221 A5
Lauder Cl UB5 84 D5
Lauder Ct N14 16 A4
Lauderdale Dr TW10 153 D1
Lauderdale Mans W9 91 D4
Lauderdale Rd W9 91 D4
Lauderdale Twr EC2 242 A4
Laughton Ho 11 SW2 160 C5
Laughton Rd UB5 84 D6
Launcelot Prim Sch
BR1 187 A6
Launcelot Rd BR1,SE12 187 A6
Launcelot St SE1 251 A1
Launceston Ct CR7 204 C3
Launceston Gdns UB6 65 C1
Launceston Pl
W8 114 A3 256 A5
Launceston Rd UB6 87 C6
Launch St E14 120 A3
Laundress La N16 74 A5
Laundry Rd W6 135 A6 264 A5
Laura Cl E11 55 C4
Enfield EN1 17 C6
Laura Pl E5 74 C4
Lauradale Rd N2 48 D5
Laurel Ave TW1 152 D3
Laurel Bank Gdns 3
SW6 135 B3
Laurel Bank Rd EN2 5 B4
Laurel Cl 5 N19 71 C6
SW17 180 C5
Sidcup DA14 168 A1
Laurel Cres CR0 223 C5
Laurel Ct E8 73 D2
SE25 205 C4
2 SW15 156 D6
8 Wembley HA0 88 A5
Laurel Dr N21 16 C4
Laurel Gdns E4 19 D4
NW7 11 B1
W7 108 C5
Hounslow TW4 129 A1
Laurel Gr SE20 184 C3
SE26 185 A6
Laurel Ho 5 NW3 69 D2
9 SE8 141 B6
Morden SM4 201 D4
Laurel La UB7 104 A2
Laurel Manor SM2 218 A1
Laurel Mead Ct 8 E18 37 A2
Laurel Pk HA3 24 D3
Laurel Rd SW13 134 A3
SW20 178 B2
Teddington TW12 174 B5
Laurel St E8 73 D2
Laurel View N12 13 D1
Laurel Way E18 54 D5
N20 13 C1
Laurels The N3 29 D4
8 Bromley BR1 187 B2
Bromley BR2 209 A5
Bushey WD2 8 C2
8 DA17 125 C1
IG9 21 C3
Laurence Ct E10 53 D2
Laurence Mews 12
W12 112 A4
Laurence Pountney Hill
EC4 252 C6
Laurence Pountney La
EC4 252 D6
Laurie Gr SE14 141 A4
Laurie Ho SE1 261 D5
W8 113 C5 245 A3
Laurie Rd W7 86 C2
Laurier Rd NW5 71 B5
Croydon CR0 205 D2
Laurimel Cl HA7 25 B4
Laurino Pl WD2 8 A2
Lauriston Ho E9 74 D1
Lauriston JMI Sch E9 96 D6
Lauriston Lo NW6 69 B2
Lauriston Rd E9 74 D1
SW19 178 D4
Lausanne Rd N8 50 C5
SE15 140 C4
Lavehham Ho E17 35 D2
Lavell St N16 73 B4
Lavender Ave NW9 45 A1
Mitcham CR4 180 D2
North Cheam KT4,SM3 216 C5
Lavender Cl SW3 266 D5
Bromley BR2 210 A3
Wallington SM5 219 B4
Lavender Ct SW4 270 B1
East Molesey KT8 195 D6
Lavender Gdns SW11 136 D1
Enfield EN2 4 D4
Harrow Weald HA3 24 C4
Lavender Gr E8 74 A1
Mitcham CR4 180 C2
Lavender Hill SW11 137 A2
Enfield EN2 4 D4
Lavender Ho 14 SE16 118 D5
Lavender Pl IG1 78 D3
Lavender Prim Sch EN2 5 C5
Lavender Rd SE16 119 A5
SW11 136 B2
Carshalton SM1 218 B4
Enfield EN2 5 B4
Hillingdon UB8 82 B2
Thornton Heath CR0 204 B3
Wallington SM5 219 A4
West Ewell KT19 214 D2
Lavender Rise UB7 104 C4
Lavender St E15 76 C2
Lavender Sweep SW11 136 D1
Lavender Terr 12 SW11 136 C2
Lavender Vale SM6 219 D2
Lavender Way CR0 206 D3
Lavender Wlk SW11 136 D1
Lavendon Ho NW8 237 B6
Lavengro Rd SE27 161 A2
Lavenham Ho E17 35 C2
Lavenham Rd SW18 157 C3
Lavernock Rd DA7 147 C3
Lavers Rd N16 73 C5
Laverstoke Gdns SW15 156 A4
Laverton Mews SW5 255 D3
Laverton Pl SW5 255 D3
Lavidge Rd SE9 166 B2
Lavina Gr N1 233 C4
Lavington Rd W13 109 B5
Croydon CR0 220 B4
Lavington St
SE1 116 D5 251 D3
Lavinia Ct BR1 186 C3
Lavisham Ho BR1 187 B5
Law St SE1 117 B3 262 D6
Lawdale Jun Sch E2 96 A4
Lawdon Gdns CR0 220 D4
Lawford Cl SM6 220 A1
Lawford Rd N1 73 C1
NW5 71 C2
W4 133 A5
Lawless Ho 5 E14 120 A6
Lawless St 11 E14 119 D6
Lawley Ho 10 TW1 153 D5
Lawley Rd N14 15 B4
Lawley St E5 74 C4
Lawman Ct 2 TW9 132 B4
Lawn Cl N9 17 D4
Bromley BR1 187 B3
Kingston u T KT3 177 C1
Ruislip HA4 61 D5
Lawn Cres TW9 132 C3
Lawn Farm Gr RM6 59 A5
Lawn Gdns W7 108 C5
Lawn House Cl E14 120 A4
Lawn La SW8 138 B6 270 C6
Lawn Rd NW3 70 D3
Beckenham BR3 185 B3
Lawn Terr SE3 142 C2
Lawn The UB2 107 C1
Lawn Vale HA5 23 A1
Lawnfield NW6 68 D1
Lawns Ct HA9 66 C6
Lawns The E4 35 C5
N16 73 C3
SE3 142 D2
SE19 183 B2
1 SW19 179 B5
Belmont SM2 217 A1
Harrow HA5 23 D3
Sidcup DA14 190 B6
Lawnside SE3 142 D1
Lawrence Ave E12 78 C4
N13 32 D6
NW7 27 D6
New Malden KT3 199 C2
Lawrence Camp Ct N20 14 B1
Lawrence Cl E3 97 C5
N15 51 C5
6 W12 112 B6
Lawrence Cres
Dagenham RM10 81 D5
Edgware HA8 26 C1
Lawrence Ct N10 49 C6
N16 73 D5
NW7 27 C5
4 W3 111 A3
Lawrence Dr UB10 61 A4
Lawrence Est TW4 128 C1
Lawrence Gdns NW7 11 D1
Lawrence Hill E4 19 C2
Lawrence Ho N22 32 B4
SW1 259 D3
Lawrence La EC2 242 B2
Lawrence Mans SW3 267 A5
Lawrence Pl N1 233 B6
Lawrence Rd E6 100 A6
E13 99 B6
N15 51 C5
N18 34 B6
SE25 205 D5
W5 109 D2
Erith DA8 147 D5
Hampton TW12 173 B3
Hayes BR4 225 A4
Hayes UB4 83 A5
Hounslow TW4 128 C1
Pinner HA5 40 D4
Richmond TW10 175 C6
Lawrence St E16 98 D2
NW7 27 D6
SW3 136 C6 267 A5
Lawrence Trad Est
SE10 120 C2
Lawrence Way NW10 67 B5
Lawrence Weaver Cl
SM4 201 C3
Lawrence Yd N15 51 C5
Lawrence's Bldgs 1
N16 73 D5
Lawrie Ct HA3 24 D3
Lawrie Park Ave SE26 184 B5
Lawrie Park Cres SE26 184 B5
Lawrie Park Gdns SE26 184 B5
Lawrie Park Rd SE26 184 C5
Lawson Cl E16 99 C2
SW19 156 D1
Lawson Ct 1 N4 50 B1
13 Surbiton KT6 197 D2
Lawson Gdns HA5 40 B6
Lawson Ho 1 SE18 144 C6
17 W12 112 B6
Lawson Rd Enfield EN3 6 C4
Southall UB1 85 C3
Lawton Rd E3 97 A4
E10 54 A1
New Barnet EN4 2 B2
Laxcon Cl NW10 67 B3
Laxey Rd BR6 227 D2
Laxfield Ct E8 96 A6
Laxley Cl SE5 138 D5
Laxton Ct CR7 205 A5
Laxton Path 1 SE4 140 D1
Laxton Pl NW1 238 D6
Layard Rd SE16 118 B2
Enfield EN1 5 D4
South Norwood CR7 183 B1
Layard Sq SE16 118 B2
Laycock Prim Sch N1 72 D2
Laycock St N1 72 C2
Layer Gdns W3 110 C6
Layfield Cl NW4 46 B2
Layfield Cres NW4 46 B2
Layfield Ho 1 SE10 121 A1
Layfield Rd NW4 46 B2
Layhams Rd BR2,BR4,
CR6 224 D3
Laymarsh Cl DA17 125 B3
Laymead Cl UB5 63 A2
Laystall Ct EC1 241 A5
Laystall St EC1 241 A5
Layton Cres CR0 220 D3
Layton Ct TW8 109 D1
Layton Ho 11 E9 96 C6
Layton Pl TW9 132 C4
Layton Rd N1 234 B4
Brentford TW8 109 D1
Hounslow TW3 129 D1
Layton's La TW16 171 D1
Layzell Wlk SE9 165 D3
Lazar Wlk 2 N7 72 B6
Le Chateau CR0 221 B5
Le May Ave SE12 165 B1
Le Moal Ho 23 E1 96 C2
Lea Bridge Rd E10 53 C2
Lea Cres HA4 61 D4
Lea Ct 1 E4 20 A2
2 E13 99 A4
3 W12 111 C4
3 Hillingdon UB10 82 D3
Lea Gdns HA9 66 B4
Lea Green Sch E10 54 A3
Lea Hall Gdns E10 53 C1
Lea Hall Rd E10 53 C1
Lea Ho E5 52 C1
2 N9 18 A1
NW8 237 A5
Lea Int E9 75 C3
Lea Rd
2 Beckenham BR3 185 C1
Enfield EN2 5 B4
Southall UB2 107 A2
Lea Valley Prim Sch N17 34 A3
Lea Valley Rd EN3 19 B5
Lea Valley Riding Sch
E10 52 D1
Lea Valley Technopark
N17 52 A6
Lea Valley Trad Est N18 34 D5
Lea View Ho E5 52 B1
Leabank Cl HA1 64 C5
Leabank Sq E9 75 C2
Leabank View N15 52 A3
Leabourne Rd N16 52 A2
Leacroft Ave SW12 158 D4
Leacroft Cl 3 UB7 104 A6
Leadale Ave E4 19 C2
Leadale Rd N16 52 A3
Leadbeaters Cl N11 30 D5
Leadbetter Ct 10 NW10 67 B1
Leadenhall Mkt EC3 243 A1
Leadenhall Pl EC3 243 A1
Leadenhall St
EC3 95 C1 243 A1
Leadenham Ct 15 E3 97 C3
Leader Ave E12 78 C3
Leadings The HA9 67 A5
Leaf Cl KT7,KT8 196 C4
Leaf Gr SE27 182 C5
Leafield Cl SW16 182 D4
Leafield La DA14 169 B1
Leafield Rd SW19,SW20 201 B6
Sutton SM1 217 C6
Leafy Gr BR2 225 C3
Leafy Oak Rd SE12 165 C1
Leafy Way CR0 221 D6
Leagrave St E5 74 C5
Leaholme Waye HA4 39 A3
Leahurst Rd SE13 164 C6
Leake St SE1 116 B4 250 D2
SE1 251 A1
Lealand Rd N15 51 D3
Leamington Ave E17 53 C4
Bromley BR1 187 C5
Merton SM4 201 B5
Orpington BR6 227 C4
Leamington Cl E12 78 A3
Bromley BR1 187 C5
Isleworth TW3 152 A6
Leamington Cres HA2 63 B5
Leamington Ct 4 SE26 162 A1
W3 89 B2
Leamington Gdns IG3 79 D6
Leamington Ho 3 W11 91 B2
Edgware HA8 26 B5
Leamington Pk W3 89 B2
Leamington Pl UB4 83 D3
Leamington Rd UB2 106 D2
Leamington Rd Villas
W11 91 B2
Leamington Villas SE13 164 C6
Leamore St W6 112 C2
Leamouth Rd E6 100 A2
E14 98 B1
Leander Ct 27 E9 74 C1
7 NW9 27 C2
SE8 141 C4
5 Surbiton KT6 197 D2
Leander Rd SW2 160 C5
Northolt UB5 85 C5
Thornton Heath CR7 204 B5
Learner Dr HA2 63 C6
Learoyd Gdns E6 122 C6
Leary Ho SE11 260 D1
Leas Cl KT9 214 B1
Leas Dale SE9 166 C1
Leas Gn BR7 189 D4
Leas The SE18 144 D4
Leaside Ave N10 49 A5
Leaside Bsns Ctr EN3 7 B3
Leaside Ct UB10 82 D4
Leaside Ho 4 E5 52 B1
Leaside Mans N10 49 A6
Leaside Rd E5 52 C1
Leasowes Rd E10 53 C1
Leather Cl CR4 181 A1
Leather Gdns E15 98 C6
Leather La EC1 94 C2 241 B4
Leatherbottle Gn DA18 125 B3
Leatherdale St 29 E1 96 C3
Leatherhead Cl N16 51 D1
Leatherhead Rd KT9 213 D1
Leathermarket Ct SE1 253 A1
Leathermarket St
SE1 117 C4 253 A1
Leathersellers Cl EN5 1 A2
Leathsale Rd HA2 63 D5
Leathwaite Rd SW11 158 D6
Leathwell Rd SE8 141 D3
Leaveland Cl BR3 207 C5
Leaver Gdns UB6 86 C5
Leavesden Rd HA7 25 A4
Leaview Ct 7 E4 20 A3
Lebanon Ave TW13 172 D5
Lebanon Ct 10 TW1 153 B4
Lebanon Gdns SW18 157 C5
Lebanon Pk TW1 153 B4
Lebanon Rd SW18 157 C6
Croydon CR0 205 C1
Lebanon Road Sta CR0 221 C6
Lebrun Sq SE3 143 B2
Lebus Ho NW8 230 A3
Lechmere App IG8 37 D1
Lechmere Ave IG8 37 D1
Lechmere Rd NW2 68 B2
Leckford Rd SW18 158 A3
Leckhampton Pl 23
SW2 160 C4
Leckwith Ave DA17 147 A6
Lecky St SW7 114 B1 256 C2
Leclair Ho SE3 143 B2
L'Ecole des Petits SW6 135 D3
Leconfield Ave SW13,
SW15 133 D2
Leconfield Ho SE5 139 C2
Leconfield Rd N5 73 B4
Leda Ave EN3 6 D5
Leda Ct 9 SW9 138 C5
Leda Rd SE18 122 B3
Ledalle Ho NW2 68 B5
Ledam Ho EC1 241 A4
Ledbury Ho 12 SE22 139 C2
Ledbury Mews N W11 91 C1
Ledbury Mews W W11 245 A6
Ledbury Pl 10 CR0 221 A4
Ledbury Rd W11 91 C1
Croydon CR0 221 B4
Ledbury St SE15 140 A5
Ledo Ho 1 N16 73 B4
Ledrington Rd SE19 184 A4
Ledway Dr HA9 44 B2
Lee Ave RM6 59 A3
Lee CE Prim Sch SE13 142 C1
Lee Church St SE13 142 C1
Lee Cl E17 34 D2
New Barnet EN5 2 A1
Lee Conservancy Rd E9 75 B3
Lee Green SE12 142 D1
Lee High Rd SE12,SE13 142 C1
Lee Ho 3 N19 71 D3
Lee Manor Prim Sch
SE13 164 C5
Lee Park Way N9,N18 19 A1
Lee Pk SE3 142 D2
Lee Rd NW7 28 D3
SE3 142 D1
SW19 179 D2
Enfield EN1 18 A5
Wembley UB6 87 C6
Lee St E8 95 D6
Lee Sta SE12 165 A5
Lee Terr SE3 142 C2
Lee Valley L Ctr N9 19 A3
Lee Valley Sp Ctr E15 75 D4
Lee View EN2 4 D4
Leechcroft Ave DA15 167 D6
Leechcroft Rd SM6 219 A5
Leecroft Rd EN5 1 A1
Leeds Ct SE6 163 D1
Carshalton SM5 218 D5
Leeds Rd IG1 57 B1
Leeds St N18 34 A5
Leegate SE12 164 D6
Leeke St WC1 94 B4 233 C2
Leeland Mans W13 109 A5
Leeland Rd W13 109 A5
Leeland Terr W13 109 A5
Leeland Way NW10 67 D4
Leemount Cl NW4 46 D5
Leerdam Dr E14 120 A3
Lees Ct W1 248 A6
Lees Ho SE17 262 D1
Lees Par UB10 82 D3
Lees Pl W1 115 A6 248 A6
Lees Rd UB8 82 D3
Lees The CR0 223 B6
Leeside EN5 13 A5
Leeside Cres NW11 47 B4
Leeside Ind Est N17 34 B3
Leeside Rd N17 34 B4
Leeside Trad Est N17 34 C3
Leeside Works N17 34 C3
Leeson Ho 7 TW1 153 B4
Leeson Rd 12 SE24 138 C1
Leesons Hill BR5,BR7 211 D6
Leesons Way BR5 189 D1
Leet Ct N16 73 B4
Leeve Ho 7 W9 91 B4
Leeward Ct 3 E1 118 A5
Leeward Gdns SW19 179 B5
Leeway SE8 119 B1
Leeway Cl HA5 23 B3
Leewood Cl SE12 165 A5
Lefevre Wlk E3 97 C6
Leff Ho 7 NW6 69 A1
Leffern Rd W12 112 A4
Lefroy Ho SE1 252 A1
Lefroy Rd W12 111 D4
Legard Rd N5 72 D5
Legat Ct N4 51 A4
Legatt Rd SE9 165 D6
Leggatt Rd E15 98 A5
Legge St SE13 164 A6
Leghorn Rd NW10 90 A5
SE18 123 B1
Legion Cl N1 72 C1
Legion Ct SM4 201 C3
Legion Rd UB6 86 A5
Legion Way N12 30 C3
Legrace Ave TW4,TW5 128 D3
Leicester Ave CR4 204 A5
Leicester Cl KT4 216 C4
Leicester Ct WC2 249 D6
11 Twickenham TW1 153 D5
Leicester Gdns IG3 57 C2
Leicester Ho 4 SW9 138 D2
5 SW15 156 C4
2 Thames Ditton KT7 197 A2
Leicester Pl WC2 249 D6
Leicester Rd E11 55 B4
N2 48 C6
NW10 67 B1
Croydon CR0 205 C2
New Barnet EN5 1 D1
Leicester Sq*
WC2 115 D6 249 D5
Leicester Square Sta
WC2 115 D6 249 D6
Leicester St WC2 249 D6
Leigh Ave IG4 55 D5
Leigh Cl KT3 199 B5
Leigh Cres CR0 223 D1
Leigh Ct 3 E18 37 A1
Harrow HA2 42 C1
Leigh Gdns NW10 90 C5
Leigh Ho 9 SW15 156 A6
4 Kingston u T KT2 176 D4
Leigh Hunt Dr N14 15 D3
Leigh Orchard Cl SW16 160 B1
Leigh Pl EC1 241 A4
Bexley DA16 146 A3
Leigh Rd E6 78 C2
E10 54 A2
N5 72 D4
Isleworth TW3 130 B1
Leigh St WC1 94 A4 233 A1
Leigham Ave SW16 160 A1
Leigham Court Rd
SW16,SW21 182 C6
Leigham Dr TW7 130 C5
Leigham Hall 3 SW16 160 A1
Leigham Hall Par 2
SW16 160 A1
Leigham Vale SE27,
SW16,SW2 160 C2
Leighfield Ho 5 N4 51 A2
Leighton Ave E12 78 C3
Pinner HA5 41 A6
Leighton Cl HA8 26 C1
Leighton Cres NW5 71 C3
Leighton Gdns NW10 90 C5
Thornton Heath CR0 204 D1
Leighton Gr NW5 71 C3
Leighton Ho 7 KT6 198 A3
Leighton House (Art Gall &
Mus) W14 254 D6
Leighton Pl NW5 71 C3
Leighton Rd NW5 71 C3
W13 109 A4
Enfield EN1 18 A6
Harrow HA3 24 B1
Leighton St CR0 204 D1
Leila Parnell Pl 14 SE7 143 C6
Leinster Ave SW14 133 A1
Leinster Ct NW6 91 C4
Leinster Gdns
W2 114 A6 246 A6
Leinster Mews W2 246 A6
Leinster Pl W2 236 A1
Leinster Rd N10 49 B5
Leinster Sq W2 91 D1
Leinster Terr W2 246 A6
Leisure Way N12 30 B3
Leitch Ho 8 NW8 70 B1
Leith Cl NW9 45 B1
Leith Hill BR5 190 A2
Leith Hill Gn BR5 190 A2
Leith Ho 7 N7 71 D3
13 SW2 160 B4
Leith Mans W9 91 D4
Leith Rd N22 32 D2
Leith Towers 11 SM2 217 D1
Leith Yd 3 NW6 91 C6
Leithcote Gdns SW16 182 B6
Leithcote Path SW16 160 B1
Lela Ave TW4,TW5 128 C3
Lelitia Cl E8 96 A6
Lelland Ho 8 SE7 122 A2
Lely Ho 3 UB5 84 D5
Leman St E1 96 A1
Lemark Cl HA7 25 C4
Lemmon Rd SE10 142 C6
Lemna Ct E11 54 C2
Lemna Rd E11 54 C2
Lemonwell Ct SE9 167 A6
Lemonwell Dr SE9 167 A6
Lemsford Cl N15 52 A4
Lemsford Ct N4 73 A6
Len Clifton Ho 18 SE18 122 B2
Len Freeman Pl SW6 264 C5
Len Williams Ct NW6 91 C5
Lena Gardens Prim Sch
W6 112 C3
Lena Gdns W6 112 C3
Lena Kennedy Cl E4 36 A4
Lendal Terr 7 SW4 137 D2
Lenelby Rd KT6 198 C1
Lenham 11 NW5 71 A2
Lenham Ho SE1 252 D1
Lenham Rd SE12 142 D1
Erith DA7 147 B6

Lenham Rd *continued*
South Norwood CR7 ... 183 B1
Sutton SM1 ... 218 A3
Lennard Ave BR4 ... 224 C6
Lennard Cl BR4 ... 224 C6
Lennard Rd
Keston Mark BR2 ... 210 B1
Penge BR3 ... 185 A4
Thornton Heath CR0 ... 205 A1
Lennon Rd NW2 ... 68 C2
Lennox Gdns NW10 ... 67 D4
SW1 ... 114 D3 257 C5
Croydon CR0 ... 220 D4
Redbridge IG1 ... 56 B1
Lennox Gdns Mews
SW1 ... 257 C4
Lennox Ho 10 E9 ... 74 C2
7 Belvedere DA17 ... 125 C3
Lennox Rd E17 ... 53 C3
N4,N7 ... 72 C6
Lenor Cl DA6 ... 147 A1
Lens Rd E7 ... 77 C1
Lensbury Way SE2 ... 124 D3
Lenthall Ho SW1 ... 259 B1
Lenthall Rd E8 ... 74 A1
Lenthorp Rd SE10 ... 120 D2
Lentmead Rd BR1 ... 164 D1
Lenton Rise TW9 ... 132 A2
Lenton St SE18 ... 123 B2
Leo Ct 4 TW8 ... 131 D5
Leo St SE15 ... 140 B5
Leo Yd EC1 ... 241 D5
Leof Cres SE6 ... 185 D5
Leominster Rd SM4 ... 202 A3
Leominster Wlk SM4 ... 202 A3
Leonard Ave SM4 ... 202 A4
Leonard Ct W8 ... 255 A6
WC1 ... 240 A6
Leonard Day Ho 3 NW5 71 B2
Leonard Pl 6 N16 ... 73 C4
Leonard Rd E4 ... 35 C4
E7 ... 77 A4
N9 ... 18 A1
Mitcham CR4,SW16 ... 181 C2
Southall UB2 ... 106 D2
Leonard Robbins Path 3
SE28 ... 124 B6
Leonard St E16 ... 122 A5
EC2 ... 95 B3 242 D6
Leonora Ho W9 ... 236 A6
Leontine Cl SE15 ... 140 A5
Leopards Ct EC1 ... 241 A4
Leopold Ave SW19 ... 179 B5
Leopold Bldgs 14 E2 ... 95 D4
Leopold Mews E9 ... 96 C6
Leopold Prim Sch NW10 67 D1
Leopold Rd E17 ... 53 C4
N2 ... 48 B6
N18 ... 34 B5
NW10 ... 67 C1
SW19 ... 179 B5
W5 ... 110 B5
Leopold St E3 ... 97 B2
Leopold Terr SW19 ... 179 C5
Leopold Wlk SE11 ... 260 C1
Leppoc Rd SW4 ... 159 D6
Leroy St SE1 ... 117 C2 263 A4
Lerwick Ct 4 EN1 ... 17 C6
Lerwick Ho SW18 ... 136 A1
Lescombe Cl SE23 ... 163 A1
Lescombe Rd SE23,SE6 163 A1
Lesley Cl DA5 ... 169 D4
Lesley Ct 8 SM6 ... 219 B4
Leslie Gdns SM2 ... 217 C1
Leslie Gr CR0 ... 205 C1
Leslie Grove Pl CR0 ... 205 C1
Leslie Park Rd CR0 ... 205 C1
Leslie Rd E11 ... 76 B4
E16 ... 99 B1
N2 ... 48 B6
Leslie Smith Sq 7
SE18 ... 144 C6
Lessar Ave SW4 ... 159 C5
Lessar Ct SW4 ... 159 C5
Lessing St SE23 ... 163 A4
Lessingham Ave SW17 . 181 A6
Ilford IG5 ... 56 C6
Lessness Ave DA7 ... 146 D5
Lessness Heath Prim Sch
DA17 ... 125 C1
Lessness Pk DA17 ... 125 C1
Lessness Rd
Belvedere DA17 ... 125 C1
Morden SM4 ... 202 A4
Lester Ave E16 ... 98 C3
Lester Ct 12 E3 ... 97 D4
Lester Ho IG8 ... 36 B3
Lestock Ho SE3 ... 143 D4
Lestor Ct TW7 ... 130 D2
Leswin Pl N16 ... 73 D5
Leswin Rd N16 ... 73 D5
Letchford Gdns NW10 ... 90 A4
Letchford Mews NW10 ... 90 A4
Letchmore Ho W10 ... 90 C3
Letchworth Ave TW14 . 149 D4
Letchworth Cl
Hayes BR2 ... 209 A4
South Oxhey WD1 ... 22 D5
Letchworth Dr BR2 ... 209 A4
Letchworth St SW17 ... 180 D6
Lethbridge Cl SE13 ... 142 A3
Lett Rd E15 ... 76 B1
Letterstone Rd SW6 ... 264 C3
Lettice St SW6 . 135 B4 264 D1
Lettsom St SE5 ... 139 C3
Lettsom Wlk 1 E13 ... 99 A5
Leucha Rd E17 ... 53 A4
Levana Cl SW19 ... 157 A3
Levant Ho 17 E1 ... 96 D3
Levehurst Ho SE27 ... 183 A5
Levehurst Way SW4,
SW9 ... 138 A3
Leven Cl WD1 ... 22 D5
Leven Rd E14 ... 98 B1
Leven Way UB3 ... 83 C1
Levendale Rd SE23 ... 163 B2
Lever Ct 15 E9 ... 74 D2
Lever St EC1 ... 95 A4 235 A1
Leverett St SW3 ... 257 B4
Leverholme Gdns SE9 . 188 C6
Leverington Pl N1 ... 235 D1
Leverson St SW16 ... 181 C4
Leverstock Ho SW3 ... 257 B2
Leverton Pl NW5 ... 71 C3
Leverton St NW5 ... 71 C3
Levett Gdns IG3 ... 80 A5
Levett Ho 8 SW16 ... 181 C5
Levett Rd IG11 ... 79 C2
Levine Gdns IG11 ... 102 D5
Levison Way 2 N19 ... 49 D1
Levita Ho NW1 ... 232 D2
Levyne Ct EC1 ... 241 A6
Lewes Cl UB5 ... 63 C2
Lewes Ct 3 CR4 ... 202 D6
Lewes Ho SE1 ... 253 B2
SE15 ... 140 A6
Lewes Rd N12 ... 30 C5
Bromley BR1 ... 187 D1
Lewesdon Cl 13 SW19 . 156 D3
Leweston Pl N16 ... 51 D2
Lewey Ho E3 ... 97 B3
Lewgars Ave NW9 ... 45 A3
Lewin Ct SW16 ... 182 A4
Lewin Rd SW14 ... 133 B2
SW16 ... 181 D4
Bexleyheath DA6 ... 147 A1
Lewing Cl BR6 ... 211 C1
Lewis Ave E17 ... 35 C2
Lewis Cl N14 ... 15 C4
Lewis Cres NW10 ... 67 B3
Lewis Ct 5 SE16 ... 118 B1
Lewis Gdns N2 ... 30 B1
Lewis Gr SE13 ... 142 A2
Lewis King Ho BR1 ... 187 B3
Lewis Pl E8 ... 74 A3
Lewis Rd Bexley DA16 .. 146 C2
Mitcham CR4 ... 180 C1
18 Richmond TW10 ... 153 D6
Sidcup DA14 ... 168 C1
Southall UB1 ... 107 A4
Sutton SM1 ... 217 D4
Lewis Silkin Ho 9
SE15 ... 140 C6
Lewis Sports & L Ctr
SE19 ... 183 D2
Lewis St NW1 ... 71 B2
Lewis Way RM10 ... 81 D2
Lewisham Bridge Prim Sch
SE13 ... 141 D2
Lewisham Bsns Ctr
SE14 ... 140 D6
Lewisham Coll SE4 ... 141 C3
Lewisham Ctr SE13 ... 142 A2
Lewisham High St
SE13 ... 163 D6
Lewisham Hill SE13 ... 142 A3
Lewisham Hospl SE13 . 163 D6
Lewisham Pk SE13 ... 164 A5
Lewisham Rd SE13 ... 142 A3
Lewisham St SW1 ... 249 D1
Lewisham Sta SE13 ... 142 A2
Lewisham Way SE4,
SE14 ... 141 B4
Lexden Dr RM6 ... 58 B3
Lexden Rd W3 ... 110 D5
Mitcham CR4 ... 203 D5
Lexfield Ho N5 ... 73 A4
Lexham Gardens Mews
W8 ... 255 D5
Lexham Gdns
W8 ... 113 D2 255 C4
Lexham Ho 9 IG11 ... 101 B6
Lexham Mews
W8 ... 113 C2 255 B4
Lexham Wlk W8 ... 255 D5
Lexington St
W1 ... 115 C6 249 B6
Lexton Gdns SW12 ... 159 D3
Ley Ho SE1 ... 252 A1
Ley St Ilford IG1 ... 78 D6
Ilford IG1,IG2 ... 57 B1
Leyborne Ave W13 ... 109 C4
Leyborne Pk TW9 ... 132 C4
Leybourne Cl BR2 ... 209 A3
Leybourne Ho 15 E14 ... 97 B1
19 SE15 ... 140 C6
Leybourne Rd E11 ... 54 D1
16 NW1 ... 71 B1
NW9 ... 44 C4
Hillingdon UB10 ... 83 A6
Leybourne St 5 NW1 ... 71 B1
Leybridge Ct SE12 ... 165 A6
Leyburn Cl E17 ... 53 D5
Leyburn Gdns CR0 ... 221 C6
Leyburn Gr N18 ... 34 A4
Leyburn Ho 1 SE18 ... 144 A5
Leyburn Rd N18 ... 34 B4
Leyden Mans 3 N19 ... 50 A2
Leyden St E1 ... 95 D2 243 C3
Leydon Cl SE16 ... 118 D5
Leyes Rd E16 ... 99 D1
Leyfield KT4 ... 199 D1
Leyland Ave EN3 ... 7 A3
Leyland Gdns IG8 ... 37 C5
Leyland Ho 5 E14 ... 119 D6
Leyland Rd SE12 ... 165 A6
Leylands SW18 ... 157 B5
Leylang Rd SE14 ... 140 D5
Leys Cl HA1 ... 42 B4
Leys Ct 10 SW9 ... 138 C3
Leys Gdns EN4 ... 15 A6
Leys Rd E EN3 ... 7 A4
Leys Rd W EN3 ... 7 A4
Leys The N2 ... 48 A5
Harrow HA3 ... 44 B3
Leysdown 9 NW5 ... 71 A2
Leysdown Ho SE17 ... 263 B2
Leysdown Rd SE9 ... 166 B2
Leysfield Rd W12 ... 112 A4
Leyspring Rd E11 ... 54 D1
Leyswood Dr IG2 ... 57 C4
Leythe Rd W3 ... 111 A4
Leyton Bsns Ctr E10 ... 75 C6
Leyton Ct SE23 ... 162 C3
Leyton Grange E10 ... 53 C1
Leyton Green Rd E10 ... 54 A3
Leyton Ind Village E10 .. 52 D2
Leyton Midland Road Sta
E10 ... 54 A2
Leyton Park Rd E10 ... 76 A5
Leyton Rd E15 ... 76 B2
SW19 ... 180 A3
Leyton Sixth Form Coll
E10 ... 54 B3
Leyton Sta E11 ... 76 A5
Leyton Stadium (Leyton
Orient FC) E10 ... 75 D5
Leyton Town Ctr E10 ... 76 A5
Leytonstone High Road Sta
E11 ... 76 C6
Leytonstone Rd E15 ... 76 C3
Leytonstone Sec Sch
E11 ... 54 C3
Leytonstone Sta E11 ... 54 C1
Leywick St E15 ... 98 C5
Lezayre Rd BR6 ... 227 D2
Liardet St SE14 ... 141 A6
Liberia Rd N5 ... 72 D2
Liberty Ave SW19 ... 180 B2
Liberty Ctr HA0 ... 88 B6
Liberty Mews SW12 ... 159 B5
Liberty Mid Sch CR4 ... 180 C1
Liberty St SW9 . 138 B4 270 D2
Libra Ct E4 ... 35 C6
Libra Rd 6 E3 ... 97 B5
E13 ... 99 A5
Library Ct N17 ... 51 D6
Library Mans 4 W12 .. 112 C4
Library Par NW10 ... 89 C6
Library Pl E1 ... 118 B6
Library St SE1 . 116 D4 251 D1
Lichdale Cl 7 BR6 ... 227 D4
Lichen Ct IG6 ... 56 D6
Lichfield Cl EN4 ... 2 D2
Lichfield Ct
Kingston u T KT6 ... 198 A4
Richmond TW9 ... 132 A1
Lichfield Gdns TW10,
TW9 ... 154 A6
Lichfield Gr N3 ... 29 C1
Lichfield Ho 28 SE5 ... 139 A3
Lichfield Rd E3 ... 97 A4
E6 ... 99 D4
N9 ... 18 A2
NW2 ... 69 A4
Dagenham RM8 ... 80 C5
Hounslow TW4 ... 128 C2
Northwood HA6 ... 40 A6
Richmond TW9 ... 132 B4
Woodford IG8 ... 36 C6
Lichfield Terr 1 TW9 ... 154 A6
Lichport Ct N4 ... 50 D1
Lickey Ho W14 ... 264 D6
Lidbury Rd NW7 ... 29 A4
Lidcote Gdns 22 SW9 ... 138 B3
Liddall Way UB7 ... 104 B5
Liddell Cl HA3 ... 43 D6
Liddell Gdns NW10 ... 90 C5
Liddell Rd NW6 ... 69 C2
Lidding Rd HA3 ... 43 D4
Liddington Rd E15 ... 98 D6
Liddlesdale Ho E 6
KT2 ... 176 D2
Liddlesdale Ho W 5
KT2 ... 176 D2
Liddon Rd E13 ... 99 B4
Bromley BR1 ... 209 D6
Liden Cl E10,E17 ... 53 B1
Lidfield Rd N16 ... 73 B4
Lidgate Rd 21 SE15 ... 139 D5
Lidiard Rd SW18 ... 158 A2
Lidlington Pl NW1 ... 232 B3
Lido Sq N17 ... 33 B1
Lidyard Rd N19 ... 49 C1
Liffey Ct NW10 ... 68 A1
Liffler Rd SE18 ... 123 C1
Lifford St SW15 ... 134 D1
Lightcliffe Rd N13 ... 16 C1
Lighter Cl 16 SE16 ... 119 A2
Lighterman Mews 13 E1 96 D1
Lighterman's Rd E14 .. 119 D4
Lighterman's Wlk
SW18 ... 135 C1
Lightfoot Rd N8 ... 50 A4
Lightley Cl HA0 ... 88 B6
Ligonier St E2 ... 243 C6
Lilac Cl E4 ... 35 B4
Lilac Ct 4 E13 ... 99 C6
Lilac Gdns W5 ... 109 D3
Croydon CR0 ... 223 C5
Hayes UB3 ... 83 C1
Lilac Ho SE4 ... 141 B2
Lilac Pl SE11 ... 116 B2 260 C3
Yiewsley UB7 ... 104 B6
Lilac St W12 ... 112 A6
Lilburn Ct SW15 ... 134 D2
Lilburne Gdns SE9 ... 166 A6
Lilburne Rd SE9 ... 166 A6
Lilburne Wlk NW10 ... 67 A2
Lile Cres W7 ... 86 C2
Lilestone Est NW8 ... 236 D5
Lilestone Ho NW8 ... 236 D6
Lilestone St NW8 92 C3 237 A6
Lilford Ho 21 SE5 ... 139 A3
Lilford Rd SE5 ... 138 D3
Lilian Barker Cl SE12 .. 165 A6
Lilian Baylis Ho N1 ... 73 A2
Lilian Baylis Sch
SE11 ... 116 B2 260 D3
Lilian Baylis Sec Sch
SE11 ... 116 B1 260 D2
Lilian Board Way UB6 ... 64 B3
Lilian Gdns IG8 ... 37 B2
Lilian Rd SW16 ... 181 C2
Lilian Rolfe Ho 5 SE27 183 B6
Lillechurch Rd RM8 ... 80 C2
Lilleshall Rd SM4 ... 202 B3
Lilley Cl E1 ... 118 A5
Lillian Ave W3 ... 110 C4
Lillian Cl 14 N16 ... 73 C5
Lillian Rd SW13 ... 134 B6
Lillie Ho N5 ... 72 C3
Lillie Rd SW6 .. 135 B6 264 C5
Lillie Yd SW6 .. 135 C6 265 A6
Lillieshall Rd SW4 ... 137 C2
Lillington Ho N7 ... 72 C4
Lilliput Ave UB5 ... 85 B6
Lillywhite 21 NW9 ... 27 D2
Lily Cl W14 ... 112 D2
Lily Gdns HA0 ... 87 C5
Lily Pl EC1 ... 241 B4
Lily Rd E17 ... 53 C3
Lilyville Rd SW6 135 B4 264 C2
Limavady Ho 18 SE18 .. 122 C2
Limberg Ho SE8 ... 119 B2
Limborough Ho 5 E14 ... 97 C2
Limbourne Ave RM8 ... 59 B2
Limburg Rd SW11 ... 136 C1
Lime Ave UB7 ... 104 B6
Lime Cl E1 ... 118 A5
Bromley BR1 ... 210 A5
Buckhurst Hill IG9 ... 21 D2
Carshalton SM5 ... 218 D6
Harrow HA3 ... 25 A1
Pinner HA5 ... 39 D6
Lime Cres TW16 ... 172 C1
Lime Ct 8 E11 ... 76 C6
SW15 ... 134 B2
9 Harrow HA1 ... 42 D3
Kingston u T KT3 ... 198 D6
Mitcham CR4 ... 180 B1
Lime Gr N20 ... 13 B3
W12 ... 112 C4
Hayes UB3 ... 105 B6
Kingston u T KT3 ... 199 C6
Orpington BR6 ... 226 D6
Ruislip HA4 ... 40 B2
Sidcup DA15 ... 167 D5
Twickenham TW1 ... 153 A5
Lime Kiln Dr SE7 ... 143 B6
Lime Lo 3 TW16 ... 171 D3
Lime Row DA18 ... 125 B3
Lime St E17 ... 53 A5
EC3 ... 95 C1 243 A1
Lime St Pas EC3 ... 253 A6
Lime Terr W7 ... 108 C6
Lime Tree Ave KT10,
KT7 ... 196 C1
Lime Tree Ct N2 ... 47 D6
Croydon CR2 ... 221 A2
Lime Tree Gr CR0 ... 223 B5
Lime Tree Rd TW5 ... 129 D4
Lime Tree Wlk
Bushey WD2 ... 8 C2
Coney Hall BR4 ... 224 D4
Enfield EN2 ... 5 A5
Limeburner La
EC4 ... 94 D1 241 C2
Limecroft Cl KT19 ... 215 B1
Limedene Cl HA5 ... 22 D2
Limeharbour E14 ... 119 D4
Limehouse Cswy E14 .. 119 B6
Limehouse Cut 5 E14 .. 97 D2
Limehouse Fields Est
E14 ... 97 A2
Limehouse Link (Tunnel)
E14 ... 119 B6
Limehouse Sta E14 ... 97 A1
Limekiln Pl SE19 ... 183 D3
Limerick Cl SW12 ... 159 C4
Limerick Ct 1 SW12 ... 159 C4
Limerston St
SW10 ... 136 A6 266 B5
Limes Ave E11 ... 55 B5
N12 ... 30 A6
NW7 ... 27 C4
NW11 ... 47 A2
SE20 ... 184 B3
SW13 ... 133 D3
Carshalton SM5 ... 202 D1
Croydon CR0 ... 220 C5
Limes Ave The N11 ... 31 C5
Limes Cl 3 N11 ... 31 C5
Ashford TW15 ... 170 C5
Limes Ct NW6 ... 68 D1
Beckenham BR3 ... 185 D1
Limes Field Rd SW14 .. 133 C2
Limes Gdns SW18 ... 157 C5
Limes Gr SE13 ... 142 A1
Limes Rd
Beckenham BR3 ... 185 D1
Thornton Heath CR0 ... 205 B2
Limes Row BR6 ... 226 D3
Limes The SE5 ... 139 C2
W2 ... 245 B5
East Molesey KT8 ... 195 D5
Keston Mark BR2 ... 226 A6
Limes Wlk SE15 ... 140 C1
W5 ... 109 D4
Limesdale Gdns HA8 ... 27 A1
Limesford Rd SE15 ... 140 D1
Limetree Cl SW2 ... 160 B3
Limetree Ct HA5 ... 23 C3
Limetree Pl CR4 ... 181 B2
Limetree Wlk 2 SW17 . 181 A5
Limewood Cl E17 ... 53 B5
W13 ... 87 B1
Limewood Ct IG2,IG4 ... 56 B4
Limpsfield Ave SW19 .. 156 D2
Thornton Heath CR7 ... 204 B4
Limscott Ho 35 E3 ... 97 D4
Linacre Ct W6 ... 112 D1
Linacre Rd NW2 ... 68 B2
Linale Ho N1 ... 235 C3
Linberry Wlk 2 SE8 ... 119 B2
Linchmere Rd SE12 ... 164 D4
Lincoln Ave N14 ... 15 C2
SW19 ... 156 D1
Twickenham TW2 ... 152 A2
Lincoln Cl SE25 ... 206 B3
Greenford UB6 ... 86 A6
Harrow HA2 ... 41 B4
Lincoln Cres EN1 ... 17 D6
Lincoln Ct N16 ... 51 B2
SE12 ... 165 C1
Borehamwood WD6 ... 11 B6
Enfield EN2 ... 5 B1
Hampton TW12 ... 173 B5
2 Ilford IG2 ... 57 A3
Mitcham CR4 ... 204 A4
Redbridge IG1 ... 56 B2
Lincoln Gdns IG1 ... 56 A2
Lincoln Green Rd BR5 . 211 D4
Lincoln Ho SW1 ... 247 C1
10 SW15 ... 157 A6
Lincoln Lo 10 BR3 ... 185 D1
Lincoln Mews NW6 ... 91 B6
Lincoln Rd E7 ... 77 D2
E13 ... 99 B3
E18 ... 37 A2
N2 ... 48 C6
SE25 ... 206 B6
Enfield EN1,EN3 ... 18 B6
Feltham TW13 ... 151 B1
Harrow HA2,HA5 ... 41 B4
Kingston u T KT3 ... 199 A6
Mitcham CR4 ... 204 A4
North Cheam KT4 ... 200 B1
Northwood HA6 ... 39 D6
Sidcup DA14 ... 190 B5
Wembley HA0 ... 65 D2
Lincoln St E11 ... 76 C6
SW3 ... 257 C3
Lincoln Terr 4 SM2 ... 217 C1
Lincoln Way
Charlton TW16 ... 171 C2
Enfield EN1 ... 18 B6
Lincoln's Inn*
WC2 ... 94 B1 240 D2
Lincoln's Inn Fields
WC2 ... 94 B1 240 D2
Lincolns The NW7 ... 11 D1
Lincombe Rd BR1 ... 164 D1
Lind Rd SM1 ... 218 A3
Lind St SE8 ... 141 D3
Linda Ct KT9 ... 213 D4
Lindal Cres EN2 ... 4 B1
Lindal Ct 1 E18 ... 37 A2
Lindal Rd SE4 ... 163 B6
Lindale SW19 ... 157 A2
Lindales The N17 ... 33 D4
Lindbergh Rd SM6 ... 220 A1
Linden Ave NW10 ... 90 D5
Enfield EN1 ... 6 A4
Hounslow TW3 ... 151 D6
Ruislip HA4 ... 40 A1
Thornton Heath CR7 ... 204 D5
Wembley HA9 ... 66 B3
Linden Bridge Sch KT4 215 C5
Linden Cl N14 ... 15 C5
Ruislip HA4 ... 40 A1
Stanmore HA7 ... 25 B5
Thames Ditton KT7 ... 197 A2
Linden Cotts 6 SW19 .. 179 A4
Linden Cres
Kingston u T KT1 ... 176 B1
Wembley UB6 ... 64 D2
Woodford IG8 ... 37 B4
Linden Ct NW7 ... 27 B5
SE20 ... 184 B3
8 SW18 ... 136 B1
W12 ... 112 C5
1 Beckenham BR3 ... 207 D6
Sidcup DA14 ... 189 C6
Linden Gdns
W2 ... 113 C6 245 B5
W4 ... 111 B1
Enfield EN1 ... 6 A4
Linden Gr SE15 ... 140 C2
SE20 ... 184 C4
Kingston u T KT3 ... 199 C6
Teddington TW11 ... 174 D5
Linden Ho 10 SE8 ... 141 B6
5 SE15 ... 140 B2
Linden Lawns HA9 ... 66 B4
Linden Lea N2 ... 48 A4
Linden Leas BR4 ... 224 B6
Linden Lodge Sch
SW19 ... 157 A3
Linden Mans N6 ... 49 B1
Linden Mews N1 ... 73 B3
W2 ... 245 B5
Linden Pl CR4 ... 202 C5
Linden Rd N10 ... 49 B5
N11 ... 15 A2
N15 ... 51 A5
Hampton TW12 ... 173 C2
Linden Way N14 ... 15 C5
Shepperton TW17 ... 193 A4
Lindenfield BR7 ... 188 D1
Lindenlea Ct E17 ... 53 B5
Lindens The 5 E17 ... 53 D5
N12 ... 30 B5
W4 ... 133 A4
New Addington CR0 ... 224 A2
Lindeth Cl HA7 ... 25 B4
Lindfield Gdns NW3 ... 70 A3
Lindfield Hts NW3 ... 70 A3
Lindfield Rd W5 ... 87 C3
Croydon CR0 ... 205 D3
Lindfield St E14 ... 97 C1
Lindhill Cl EN3 ... 6 D3
Lindholme Ct 3 NW9 ... 27 C2
Lindisfarne Mead E9 ... 75 A4
Lindisfarne Rd SW20 .. 178 A3
Dagenham RM8 ... 80 C5
Lindley Ct KT1 ... 175 C2
Lindley Ho 12 SE15 ... 140 A5
Lindley Pl TW9 ... 132 C4
Lindley Rd E10 ... 76 A6
Lindley St E1 ... 96 C2
Lindo St SE15 ... 140 C3
Lindon Bennett Sch
TW13 ... 172 D5
Lindop Ho 7 E3 ... 97 A3
Lindore Rd SW11 ... 136 D1
Lindores Rd SM5 ... 202 A1
Lindrop St SW6 ... 136 A3
Lindsay Cl KT9 ... 214 A1
Lindsay Ct SW11 ... 266 D1
Lindsay Dr Harrow HA3 .. 44 B4
Shepperton TW17 ... 193 B3
Lindsay Ho 2 SE18 ... 122 C2
Lindsay Rd
Hampton TW12 ... 173 D6
North Cheam KT4 ... 216 B6
Lindsay Sq
SW1 ... 115 D1 259 D2
Lindsell St 6 SE10 ... 142 A4
Lindsey Cl Bromley BR1 . 210 A6
Mitcham CR4,SW16 ... 204 A5
Lindsey Ct N13 ... 16 C1
Lindsey Gdns TW14 ... 149 B4
Lindsey Ho SW10 ... 266 D4
W5 ... 109 D2
Lindsey Mews 18 N1 ... 73 A1
Lindsey Rd RM8 ... 80 C5
Lindsey St EC1 .. 94 D2 241 D4
Lindum Rd TW11 ... 175 C3
Lindums The BR3 ... 185 B4
Lindway SE27 ... 182 D5
Lindwood Cl 8 E6 ... 100 B2
Linfield WC1 ... 233 C1
Linfield Cl NW4 ... 46 C5
Linford Ct 1 CR4 ... 180 C2
Linford Ho 17 E2 ... 96 A6
Linford Rd E17 ... 54 A6
Linford St SW8 . 137 C4 269 A1
Ling Rd E16 ... 99 A2
Lingard Ho 9 E14 ... 120 A3
Lingards Rd SE13 ... 142 A1
Lingey Cl DA15 ... 167 D2
Lingfield Ave KT1,KT5 .. 198 B5
Lingfield Cl EN1 ... 17 C5
Lingfield Cres SE9,DA16 145 B1
Lingfield Ct SW19 ... 178 D4
Northolt UB5 ... 85 C5
Lingfield Gdns N9 ... 18 B4
Lingfield Ho SE1 ... 251 D1
SE26 ... 184 B4
5 W4 ... 111 A1
Lingfield Rd SW19 ... 178 D4
North Cheam KT4 ... 216 C5
Lingham St SW9 ... 138 B3
Lingholm Way EN5 ... 12 D6
Lingrove Gdns IG9 ... 21 B2
Ling's Coppice SE21 .. 161 B2
Lingwell Rd SW17 ... 158 C1
Lingwood DA7 ... 147 D3
Lingwood Gdns TW7 .. 130 C5
Lingwood Rd E5 ... 52 A2
Linhope St NW1 . 92 D3 237 C5
Link Field BR2 ... 209 A3
Link La SM6 ... 220 A2
Link Prim Day Sch The
CR0 ... 220 A4
Link Rd N11 ... 31 A6
Carshalton SM6 ... 203 A1
Dagenham RM9 ... 103 D5
East Bedfont TW14 ... 149 D4
Link Sec Day Sch The
CR0 ... 220 B4
Link St E9 ... 74 C2
Link The NW2 ... 46 A1
SE9 ... 166 C1
W3 ... 88 D1
Enfield EN3 ... 7 A4
Northolt UB5 ... 63 B3
Pinner HA5 ... 40 C2
Teddington TW11 ... 174 D4
Wembley HA0 ... 43 C1
Link Way Bromley BR2 .. 210 A2
Richmond TW10 ... 153 B2
Linkenholt Mans 3
W6 ... 111 D2

Linkfield KT8 .... 195 D6
Linkfield Rd TW7 ...... 130 D3
Linklea Cl NW9 .... 27 C3
Links Ave SM4 .... 201 C5
Links Ct N20 .... 14 B1
Links Dr N20 .... 13 D3
Links Gdns SW16 ...... 182 C3
Links Prim Sch SW17 .. 181 A4
Links Rd NW2 .... 67 D6
SW16 .... 181 A4
W3 .... 88 C1
Ashford TW15 .... 170 A5
West Wickham BR4 ..... 208 A1
Woodford IG8 .... 37 A5
Links Side EN2 .... 4 C2
Links The E17 .... 53 A5
Links View N3 .... 29 B3
SE18 .... 144 D4
Links View Cl HA7 ...... 25 A4
Links View Rd
Croydon CR0 .... 223 C5
Hampton TW12 .... 174 A6
Links Way SW17 .... 181 A4
Beckenham BR3 .... 207 C3
Links Yd E1 .... 243 D4
9 E1 .... 96 A2
Linkscroft Ave TW15 ... 170 D4
Linkside N12 .... 29 C4
Kingston u T KT3 ..... 177 C1
Linkside Cl EN2 .... 4 C2
Linkside Gdns EN2 ...... 4 B2
Linksview N2 .... 48 D4
Linksway NW4 .... 28 D1
Linkway N4 .... 51 A2
SW20 .... 200 B6
Dagenham RM8 .... 80 C4
Pinner Green HA5 ...... 22 D2
Linkway The EN5 .... 13 D5
Linkwood Wlk NW1 ..... 71 D1
Linley Cres RM7 .... 59 D6
Linley Ct 1 SE21 ...... 183 C6
Sutton SM1 .... 218 A4
Linley Rd N17 .... 33 C1
Linnell Cl NW11 .... 47 D3
Linnell Dr NW11 .... 47 D3
Linnell Ho E1 .... 243 C4
NW8 .... 229 A6
Linnell Rd N18 .... 34 A5
SE5 .... 139 C3
Linnet Cl N9 .... 18 D3
SE28 .... 124 C6
Bushey WD2 .... 8 A3
Linnet Mews SW12 .... 159 A4
Linnett Cl E4 .... 36 A6
Linom Rd SW4 .... 138 A1
Linscott Rd E5 .... 74 C4
Linsdell Rd IG11 ...... 101 A6
Linsey St SE16 .... 118 A2
SE16 .... 118 A3
Linslade Cl
Hounslow TW4 .... 151 A6
Pinner HA5 .... 40 B6
Linslade Ho 10 E2 ...... 96 A6
NW8 .... 237 B6
Linstead St 1 NW6 ..... 69 C1
Linstead Way SW18,
SW19 .... 157 A4
Linsted Ct SE9,DA15 .... 167 C5
Linster Gr WD6 .... 11 A6
Lintaine Cl W6 .... 264 B5
Linthorpe Ave HA0 ...... 65 C2
Linthorpe Rd N16 ...... 51 C2
Cockfosters EN4 .... 2 C2
Linton Cl 2 SE7 .... 121 C1
Bexley DA16 .... 146 B4
Carshalton CR4 .... 202 D2
Linton Gdns E6 .... 100 A1
Linton Gr SE27 .... 183 A5
Linton Ho 2 E3 .... 97 C2
Linton Mead Prim Sch
SE28 .... 124 B6
Linton Rd IG11 .... 79 A1
Linton St N1 .... 95 A6 235 B5
Lintons The IG11 .... 79 A1
Linver Rd SW6 .... 135 C3
Linwood Cl SE5 .... 139 D3
Linwood Cres EN1 .... 6 A4
Linzee Rd N8 .... 50 A5
Lion Ave TW1 .... 152 D3
Lion Cl TW17 .... 192 A6
Lion Ct 12 NW9 .... 46 A5
Lion Ctr The TW13 .... 151 A1
Lion Gate Gdns TW9 ... 132 B2
Lion Mills 33 E2 .... 96 A5
Lion Park Ave KT9 ..... 214 C4
Lion Rd E6 .... 100 B2
N9 .... 18 A2
Bexley DA6 .... 147 B1
Thornton Heath CR0 .... 205 A4
Twickenham TW1,TW2 .. 152 D3
Lion Way TW8 .... 131 D5
Lion Wharf Rd TW7 .... 131 B2
Lion Yd SW4 .... 137 D1
Lionel Gdns SE9 ...... 165 D6
Lionel Ho N22 .... 32 B4
5 W10 .... 91 A2
Lionel Mans 14 W14 ... 112 D3
Lionel Rd SE9 .... 165 D6
Brentford TW8 .... 110 B1
Lionel Road Jun & Inf Sch
TW8 .... 110 A2
Lionel Road N TW8 .... 110 A2
Lions Cl SE12 .... 165 D1
Liphook Cres SE23 .... 162 C4
Liphook Rd WD1 .... 22 D6
Lipton Cl SE28 .... 124 C6
Lipton Rd 8 E1 .... 96 D1
Lisa Lo 5 EN5 .... 13 D6
Lisbon Ave TW2 .... 152 A2
Lisburne Rd NW3 .... 70 D4
Lisford St SE15 .... 139 D4
Lisgar Terr W14 113 B2 254 C4
Liskeard Cl BR7 .... 189 A4
Liskeard Gdns SE3 .... 143 A4
Liskeard Ho SE11 ..... 261 B2
Lisle Cl SW17 .... 181 B6
Lisle Ct NW2 .... 69 A5
Lisle St WC2 ... 115 D6 249 D6
Lismirrane Ind Pk WD6 ... 9 B5
Lismore 9 SW19 ...... 179 B5
Lismore Cl TW7 .... 131 A3
Lismore Rd N17 .... 51 B6
South Croydon CR2 .... 221 C2
Lismore Wlk 4 N1 ...... 73 A2
Lisselton Ho 3 NW4 .... 46 D5
Lissenden Gdns NW5 ... 71 A4
Lissenden Mans NW5 ... 71 A4
Lisson Cotts NW1 ..... 237 B4
Lisson Gr NW1,
NW8 .... 92 C3 237 A6
Lisson Ho NW1 .... 237 A4
Lisson St NW1 .. 92 C2 237 A4
Lister Cl SW19 .... 180 C2
W3 .... 89 B2
Lister Com Sch E13 ..... 99 B5
Lister Ct N16 .... 73 C6
NW9 .... 27 C1
Lister Gdns N18 .... 33 A5
Lister Ho E1 .... 96 A2
SE2 .... 124 D1
SE3 .... 142 C6
Hayes UB3 .... 105 C2
9 Wembley HA9 .... 67 A5
Lister Hospl
SW1 .... 115 B1 258 C1
Lister Mews N7 .... 72 B4
Lister Rd E11 .... 54 D1
Lister Wlk SE28 .... 124 D6
Liston Ho N21 .... 16 B6
Liston Rd N17 .... 34 A2
SW4 .... 137 C2
Liston Way 1 IG8 ...... 37 C3
Listowel Cl 2 SW9 .... 138 C5
Listowel Rd RM10 ...... 81 C5
Listria Lo N16 .... 73 D6
Listria Pk N16 .... 73 D6
Litcham Ho 23 E1 .... 96 D4
Litchfield Ave E15 ...... 76 C2
Morden SM4 .... 201 B2
Litchfield Ct E17 .... 53 C3
Litchfield Gdns NW10 ... 68 A2
Litchfield Rd SM1 ..... 218 A4
Litchfield St WC2 ..... 249 D6
Litchfield Way NW11 .... 48 A4
Lithgow's Rd TW14,TW6 127 D1
Lithos Rd NW3 .... 70 A2
Little Acre BR3 .... 207 C6
Little Albany St NW1 .. 238 D6
Little Argyll St W1 .... 239 A1
Little Birches DA15 .... 167 C2
Little Boltons The
SW10 .... 255 D1
Little Bornes SE21 ..... 183 C6
Little Britain EC1 ...... 242 A3
Little Brownings SE23 . 162 B2
Little Bury St N9 .... 17 C4
Little Bushey La WD2 ... 8 B5
Little Cedars N12 .... 30 A6
Little Chelsea Ho SW10 266 B5
Little Chester St SW1 . 258 C6
Little College St SW1 . 260 A6
Little Combe Cl 13
SW15 .... 156 D5
Little Common HA7 ...... 9 A1
Little Ct BR4 .... 224 C6
Little Dimocks SW12 ... 159 B2
Little Dorrit Ct SE1 .... 252 B2
Little Ealing La W5 .... 109 C2
Little Ealing Prim Sch
W5 .... 109 C3
Little Edward St NW1 .. 231 D2
Little Elms UB3 .... 127 B5
Little Essex St WC2 ... 251 A6
Little Ferry Rd TW1 ... 153 B3
Little Friday Rd E4 ..... 20 C2
Little Gearies IG6 ...... 56 D5
Little George St SW1 .. 250 A1
Little Grange UB6 ...... 87 A4
Little Green St NW5 .... 71 B4
Little Halliards KT12 ... 194 A3
Little Heath SE7 .... 122 A1
Ilford RM6 .... 58 B5
Little Heath Rd DA7 ... 147 B5
Little Heath Specl Sch
RM6 .... 58 B5
Little Holt 8 E11 .... 55 A4
Little Ilford La E12 ..... 78 B4
Little Ilford Sec Sch E12 78 B3
Little Larkins EN5 ...... 13 A5
Little Marlborough St
W1 .... 239 A1
Little Moss La HA5 ..... 23 A1
Little New St EC4 ..... 241 B2
Little Newport St WC2 . 249 D6
Little Orchard Cl HA5 ... 23 A1
Little Oxhey La WD1 ... 23 A6
Little Park Dr TW13 ... 151 A2
Little Park Gdns EN2 .... 5 B2
Little Pluckett's Way
IG9 .... 21 D3
Little Portland St W1 .. 239 A2
Little Potters WD2 .... 8 C4
Little Queens Rd TW11 174 D4
Little Rd UB3 .... 105 D4
Little Redlands BR1 ... 188 A1
Little Road Mans SW6 . 264 B5
Little Russell St WC1 .. 240 A3
Little Sanctuary SW1 .. 250 A1
Little Smith St SW1 ... 259 D6
Little Somerset St E1 .. 243 C1
Little St James's St
SW1 .... 249 A3
Little St Leonards
SW14 .... 133 A2
Little Stanmore Fst & Mid
Sch HA8 .... 26 B2
Little Strand NW9 ...... 27 D1
Little Thrift BR5 ...... 211 A5
Little Titchfield St W1 . 239 A3
Little Trinity La EC4 ... 252 B6
Little Venice★
W9 .... 92 A2 236 A4
Little Wood Cl BR5 .... 190 A2
Littlebourne 2 SE13 ... 164 C4
Littlebrook Cl CR0 .... 206 D3
Littlebury Rd SW4 .... 137 D2
Littlecombe SE7 .... 143 B6
Littlecote Cl SW19 .... 157 A4
Littlecote Pl HA5 .... 23 B2
Littlecroft SE9 .... 144 C2
Littledale SE2 .... 146 A6
Littlefield Cl N19 .... 71 C4
9 Kingston u T KT1 .... 176 A1
Littlefield Ct UB7 ..... 126 A5
Littlefield Ho KT1 ..... 176 A1
Littlefield Rd HA8 ...... 27 A3
Littlegrove EN4 .... 14 C5
Littlegrove Ct 3 EN4 .. 14 C5
Littleheath Rd CR2 .... 222 B1
Littlejohn Rd W7 .... 86 D1
Littlemead KT10 ...... 212 B4
Littlemede SE9 .... 166 B1
Littlemoor Rd IG1 ...... 79 B5
Littlemore Rd SE2 .... 124 A4
Littlers Cl SW19 ...... 180 B2
Littlestone Cl BR3 .... 185 C4
Littleton Ave E4 .... 20 D3
Littleton CE Fst Sch
TW17 .... 192 C6
Littleton Cres HA1 ..... 64 D6
Littleton La TW17,TW18 192 A4
Littleton Rd Harrow HA1 64 D6
Littleton TW15,TW17 .... 171 A3
Littleton St SW18 ..... 158 A2
Littlewood SE13 ...... 164 A5
Littlewood Cl W13 .... 109 B3
Littleworth Ave KT10 .. 212 B3
Littleworth Common Rd
KT10 .... 212 B5
Littleworth La KT10 ... 212 B4
Littleworth Pl KT10 ... 212 B4
Littleworth Rd KT10 ... 212 C4
Livermere Ct 3 E8 ...... 95 D6
Livermere Rd E8 .... 95 D6
Liverpool Gr
SE17 .... 117 B1 262 C1
Liverpool Ho N7 .... 72 C2
Liverpool Rd E10 ...... 54 A3
E16 .... 98 C2
N1 .... 234 B5
N1,N7 .... 72 C1
W5 .... 109 D4
Kingston u T KT2 ...... 176 C3
South Norwood CR7 .... 205 A6
Liverpool St EC2 95 C2 243 A3
Liverpool Street Sta
EC2 .... 95 C2 243 A3
Livesey Cl KT1 .... 198 B6
Livesey Mus SE15 ..... 140 B6
Livesey Pl SE15 .... 140 A6
Livingstone Ct E10 ..... 54 A3
Monken Hadley EN5 ...... 1 A3
Stanwell TW19 .... 148 A3
Livingstone Ho 16 SE5 . 139 A5
Livingstone Lo 18 W9 .. 91 C2
Livingstone Pl E14 .... 120 A1
Livingstone Prim Sch EN4 2 B2
Livingstone Rd E15 .... 98 A6
E17 .... 53 D3
N13 .... 32 A5
14 SW11 .... 136 B2
Hounslow TW3 .... 130 A1
South Norwood CR7 .... 183 B1
Southall UB1 .... 106 D6
Livonia St W1 .... 239 B1
Lizard St EC1 .... 95 A4 235 B1
Lizban St SE3 .... 143 B5
Llandovery Ho 1 E14 .. 120 A4
Llanelly Rd NW2 .... 69 B6
Llanover Ct HA9 .... 65 D4
Llanover Rd SE18 ..... 144 C5
Llanthony Rd SM4 .... 202 B4
Llanvanor Rd NW2 ..... 69 B6
Llewellyn Ct SE20 .... 184 C2
Llewellyn St SE16 .... 118 A4
Lloyd Ave SW16 .... 182 A2
Lloyd Baker St
WC1 .... 94 C4 234 A1
Lloyd Ct SE13 .... 163 D6
5 SE27 .... 160 D1
Pinner HA5 .... 40 D4
Lloyd Ho N16 .... 73 B5
10 SE18 .... 122 B2
3 Beckenham BR3 ..... 185 D4
Lloyd Park Ave CR0 .... 221 D4
Lloyd Park Ho E17 ...... 53 C6
Lloyd Park Sta CR0 ... 221 D4
Lloyd Rd E6 .... 100 B6
E17 .... 52 D5
Dagenham RM9 .... 81 B1
North Cheam KT4,SM3 . 216 D5
Lloyd Sq WC1 .... 94 C4 234 A2
Lloyd St WC1 .... 94 C4 234 A2
Lloyd Villas SE4 .... 141 C3
Lloyd's Ave EC3 .... 243 B1
Lloyd's Bldg★
EC3 .... 95 C1 243 A1
Lloyd's Pl SE3 .... 142 C3
Lloyd's Row EC1 .94 D4 234 C1
Lloyds Way BR3 .... 207 B4
Loampit Hill SE13 ..... 141 D3
Loampit Vale SE13 .... 142 A2
Loanda Cl 17 E8 .... 95 D6
Loanda Ho SE15 .... 140 C2
Loats Rd SW2 .... 160 A5
Lobelia Cl 5 E6 .... 100 A2
Locarno Rd 6 W3 ..... 111 A5
Greenford UB6 .... 86 B3
Lochaber Rd SE13 .... 142 C1
Lochaline St W6 ...... 134 C6
Lochan Cl UB4 .... 85 A3
Lochbie 5 N4 .... 50 A2
Lochinvar St SW12 .... 159 B4
Lochleven Ho 9 N2 ..... 30 B1
Lochmere Cl DA8 ..... 147 D6
Lochmore Ho SW1 .... 258 B3
Lochnagar St E14 ...... 98 A2
Lock Chase SE3 .... 142 C2
Lock Cl UB2 .... 108 A4
Lock Ho N16 .... 51 D1
Lock Rd TW10 .... 175 C6
Lock View Ct 9 E14 ... 119 A6
Lockbridge Ct 3 W9 ... 91 C2
Locke Ho SW8 .... 269 A2
Lockesfield Pl E14 .... 119 D1
Lockesley Dr BR5 ..... 211 D3
Lockesley Sq KT6 ..... 197 D3
Locket Rd HA3 .... 24 D1
Lockfield Ave EN3 .... 7 B4
Lockgate Cl E9 .... 75 B3
Lockhart Cl N7 .... 72 B2
Lockhart Lo 4 E4 ...... 20 C4
Lockhart St E3 .... 97 B3
Lockhurst St E5 .... 74 D4
Lockier Wlk HA9 .... 65 D5
Lockington Rd
SW8 .... 137 B4 268 D2
Lockmead Rd N15 ...... 52 A3
SE13 .... 142 A2
Lock's La CR4 .... 181 A1
Locksley St E14 .... 97 B2
Locksmeade Rd TW10 . 175 C6
Lockwood Cl SE26 .... 184 D6
Lockwood Ct KT3 ..... 199 A5
Lockwood Ho 10 SE11 . 138 C6
Lockwood Ind Pk N17 ... 52 B6
Lockwood Sq SE16 .... 118 B3
Lockwood Way E17 ..... 34 D1
Chessington KT9 ...... 214 C3
Lockyer Est SE1 ...... 252 D1
Lockyer Ho 7 SE10 .... 120 D1
SW8 .... 270 A4
SW15 .... 134 D2
Lockyer St SE1 .... 252 D1
Locton Gn 4 E3 .... 97 B6
Lodden Lo 13 SM2 .... 218 A1
Loddiges Ho 5 E9 ...... 74 C1
Loddiges Rd E9 .... 74 C1
Loddon Ho NW8 .... 236 D5
Loder St SE15 .... 140 C5
Lodge Ave Croydon CR0 220 C5
Dagenham RM8,RM9,IG11 . 80 B3
Deacons Hill WD6 .... 10 B6
Harrow HA3 .... 44 A5
Lodge Cl N18 .... 33 A5
Brentford TW7 .... 131 B4
Carshalton SM6 .... 203 A1
Edgware HA8 .... 26 C4
Lodge Ct 3 HA0 .... 66 A3
Lodge Dr N13 .... 32 C6
Lodge Gdns BR3 ...... 207 B4
Lodge Hill Bexley DA16 . 146 B5
Redbridge IG4 .... 56 A5
Lodge La N12 .... 30 A5
Beckenham BR3 .... 207 D5
Bexley DA5 .... 168 D5
New Addington CR0 .... 223 D1
Lodge Pl SM1 .... 217 D3
Lodge Rd NW4 .... 46 C5
NW8 .... 92 C4 230 A1
Bromley BR1 .... 187 C3
Sutton SM1 .... 217 D3
Thornton Heath CR0 .... 204 D2
Wallington SM6 .... 219 B3
Lodge Villas IG8 .... 36 D4
Lodge Way
Ashford TW15 .... 148 A2
Charlton TW17 .... 171 A1
Lodgehill Park Cl HA2 .. 63 D6
Lodore Gdns NW9 ...... 45 C4
Lodore Gn UB10 .... 60 A5
Lodore St E14 .... 98 A1
Lodsworth Ho SW11 ... 268 A1
Lofthouse Pl KT9 ..... 213 C2
Loftie St SE16 .... 118 A4
Lofting Rd N1 .... 72 C1
Loftus Rd W12 .... 112 B5
Loftus Rd (Queens Park
Rangers FC) W12 .... 112 B5
Logan Cl Enfield EN3 ..... 6 D4
Hounslow TW4 .... 129 B2
Logan Mews W8 .... 255 A4
Logan Pl W8 ... 113 C2 255 A4
Logan Rd N9 .... 18 B2
Wembley HA9 .... 66 A6
Loggetts SE21 .... 161 C2
Logs Hill BR1,BR7 ..... 188 A2
Logs Hill Cl BR7 ...... 188 A2
Lohmann Ho 5 SE11 ... 138 C6
Lois Dr TW17 .... 192 D4
Lolesworth Cl E1 ..... 243 D3
Lollard St SE11 116 C2 261 A3
Loman St SE1 .. 116 D4 251 D2
Lomas Cl CR0 .... 224 A1
Lomas St E1 .... 96 A2
Lombard Ave Enfield EN3 .. 6 C4
Ilford IG3 .... 57 C1
Lombard Bsns Pk
SW19 .... 179 D1
Thornton Heath CR0 .... 204 B2
Lombard Ct EC3 ...... 252 D6
Lombard Ho 4 SE10 ... 142 A5
Lombard La EC4 ...... 241 B1
Lombard Rd N11 .... 31 B5
SW11 .... 136 B3
SW19 .... 179 D1
Lombard Rdbt CR0 .... 204 B2
Lombard St EC3 .95 B1 242 D1
Lombard Trad Est SE7 . 121 B2
Lombard Wall SE7 ..... 121 B2
Lombardy Pl W2 ...... 245 D5
Lombardy Ret Pk UB3 . 106 B6
Lomley Ho 10 SW2 .... 160 C5
Lomond Cl N15 .... 51 C4
Wembley HA0 .... 66 B1
Lomond Ct HA3 .... 42 D6
Lomond Gdns CR2 .... 223 A1
Lomond Gr SE5 .... 139 B5
Lomond Ho 10 SE5 .... 139 B4
Loncroft Rd SE5 ...... 139 C6
Londale Ct SE10 ...... 142 A4
Londesborough Ho 1
N16 .... 73 C4
Londesborough Rd N16 . 73 C4
London Acad The SW4 . 137 C2
London Aquarium★
SE1 .... 250 C1
London Arena E14 .... 119 D3
London Bridge
EC4,SE1 ...... 117 B6 252 D5
London Bridge City Pier
SE1 .... 117 C5 253 A4
London Bridge Hospl
SE1 .... 117 B5 252 D4
London Bridge St
SE1 .... 117 B5 252 D3
London Bridge Sta
SE1 .... 117 B5 252 D3
London Business Sch
NW1 .... 92 D3 237 C6
London Butterfly House
TW8 .... 131 B4
London Canal Mus
N1 .... 94 A5 233 B4
London Central Mosque★
NW8 .... 92 C4 230 B1
London Chest Hospl E2 . 96 C5
London City Airport
E16 .... 122 B5
London Clinic
NW1 .... 93 A3 238 B5
London Coll of Fashion
EC2 .... 95 C3 243 B6
London Coll of Fashion The
W1 .... 238 B1
London Coll of Printing
SE11 .... 116 D3 261 D5
London Ct 3 SW18 .... 157 C6
London Docklands Visitor Ctr
E14 .... 120 A4
London Dungeon The★
SE1 .... 117 B5 252 D4
London Eye (Millennium
Wheel)★ SE1 .116 B4 250 C2
London Fields East Side
E8 .... 74 B1
London Fields JMI Sch
E8 .... 96 B6
London Fields Sta E8 ... 74 B1
London Fields West Side
E8 .... 74 A1
London Foot Hospl
W1 .... 93 C3 239 A5
London Gas Mus The E3,
E16 .... 98 B3
London Group Bsns Pk
NW2 .... 46 A1
London Guildhall Univ
E1 .... 95 D1 243 C1
E14 .... 97 C1
EC2 .... 95 B2 242 C3
EC3 .... 95 D1 243 D2
London Guildhall Univ (Coll
of Tech & Design) E1 .. 96 A1
London Ho NW8 .... 230 B4
Edgware HA8 .... 26 A6
London Hospital Dental Inst
E1 .... 96 B2
London Hospital Medical
Coll E1 .... 96 B2
London Hospl (Mile End) The
E2 .... 96 D4
London Hospl (St Clements)
The E3 .... 97 B4
London Ind Pk The E6 . 100 C2
London Independent Hospl
The E1 .... 96 D2
London Inst The
EC1 .... 94 C3 241 B5
EC1 .... 94 D2 241 C4
EC1 .... 95 A3 242 A5
SW17 .... 181 B5
W1 .... 238 C1
London La E8 .... 74 B1
Bromley BR1 .... 186 D3
London Mews W2 ..... 236 D2
London Nautical Sch The
SE1 .... 116 C5 251 B4
London Oratory Sch The
SW6 .... 135 C5 265 B4
London Peace Pagoda★
SW3 .... 267 D4
London Rd E13 .... 99 A5
SE1 .... 116 D3 261 D6
SE22,SE23 .... 162 C3
Ashford TW15,TW18,
TW19,TW14 .... 148 B2
Barking IG11 .... 79 A1
Brentford TW7,TW8 .... 131 B4
Bromley BR1 .... 186 D3
Enfield EN2 .... 5 B1
Ewell KT17 .... 216 B3
Hackbridge SM6,CR4 .. 219 B6
Harrow HA1 .... 64 C6
Hounslow TW3,TW7,TW1,
TW8 .... 130 B3
Kingston u T KT1,KT2 .. 176 B1
Mitcham CR4 .... 202 D6
Mitcham CR4 .... 180 D2
Morden SM4 .... 201 C5
North Cheam KT4,SM3,
SM4 .... 216 B3
Romford RM7,RM8 ...... 59 C3
Stanmore HA7 .... 25 D6
Stoneleigh KT17,KT4,SM3 216 B3
Thornton Heath CR0,CR7,
SW16 .... 204 C3
Twickenham TW1 ...... 153 A4
Wembley HA9 .... 66 A2
CR4 .... 203 A2
London Road Rdbt
TW1 .... 153 A5
London Sch of Economics &
Political Science
WC2 .... 94 B1 240 D1
London St EC3 .... 253 B6
W2 .... 92 B1 236 C1
London Stile 5 W4 .... 110 C1
London Terr 1 E2 .... 96 A5
London Theological
Seminary at Kensit
Memorial Coll N3 ..... 29 A1
London Toy & Model Mus
W2 .... 114 A6 246 A6
London Transport Mus★
WC2 .... 250 B6
London Wall EC2 95 B2 242 D3
London Wharf 4 E2 .... 96 B6
London Zoo★
NW1 .... 93 A5 231 A4
Lonesome Prim Sch
CR4 .... 181 B1
Lonesome Way CR4 ... 181 C2
Long Acre WC2 . 94 A1 240 B1
Long Acre Ct W13 ...... 87 A2
Long Deacon Rd E4 .... 20 C3
Long Ditton Cty Inf Sch
KT6 .... 197 C1
Long Dr W3 .... 89 C1
Greenford UB6 .... 85 D6
Ruislip HA4 .... 62 D4
Long Elmes HA3 .... 24 A2
Long Field NW9 .... 27 C2
Long La EC1 .... 94 D2 241 D4
N2 .... 48 B6
N3 .... 29 D2
SE1 .... 117 B4 252 D1
Croydon CR0 .... 206 C3
Erith DA7 .... 147 B4
Hillingdon UB10 .... 60 D1
Stanwell TW15,TW19 .... 148 B3
Long Leys E4 .... 36 A4
Long Mark Rd 5 E16 ... 99 D2
Long Mead NW9 .... 27 D2
Long Meadow 20 N7 .... 71 D3
Long Meadow Cl BR3,
BR4 .... 208 A2
Long Pond Rd SE3 .... 142 C4
Long Rd SW4 .... 137 C1
Long Reach Rd IG11 .. 101 D3
Long Ridges N2 .... 49 A6
Long St E2 .... 95 D4
Long Wlk SE1 .... 263 B6
SE18 .... 144 D6
Kingston u T KT3 ...... 199 A6
Long Yd WC1 ... 94 B3 240 C5
Longacre Pl SM5 ...... 219 A2
Longacre Rd E17 .... 36 B2
Longbeach Rd SW11 .. 136 D2
Longberrys NW2 .... 69 B5
Longboat Row UB1 .... 85 B1
Longbow Ho 29 N1 ..... 95 C6
Longbridge Ho RM8 .... 80 B4
Longbridge Rd
Barking IG11 .... 79 C3
Dagenham RM8 .... 80 B4
Longbridge Way SE13 . 164 A6
Longbury Dr BR5 ..... 190 B1
Longcliffe Ho SW18 ... 157 D6
Longcroft SE9 .... 166 C1
Longcrofte Rd HA8 ..... 25 D3
Longdale Sq N1 .... 234 B6
Longdon Wood BR2 ... 226 A4
Longdown Rd SE6 .... 185 C6
Longfellow Rd E17 ..... 53 B3
Worcester Park KT4 .... 200 B1
Longfellow Way SE1 .. 263 D3
Longfield
3 Bromley BR1 .... 186 D2
Loughton IG10 .... 21 C6
Longfield Ave E17 ...... 53 A5
NW7 .... 28 A3
W5 .... 109 C6
Carshalton SM6 .... 203 A1
Enfield EN3 .... 6 C5

Longfield Ave *continued*
Wembley HA9 .44 A1
Longfield Cres SE23, SE26 .162 C1
Longfield Ct 4 N2 .48 A6
Longfield Dr SW14 .154 D6
SW19 .180 C2
Longfield Est SE1 .263 D3
Longfield Fst & Mid Schs HA2 .41 C3
Longfield Ho E17 .53 B4
W5 .109 C6
Longfield Rd W5 .87 C1
Longfield St SW18 .157 C4
Longford Ave
Feltham TW14 .149 D5
Southall UB1 .107 D6
Stanwell TW19 .148 A3
Longford Cl
Hampton TW12 .173 C6
Hayes UB4 .106 D6
Longford Ct 2 E5 .74 D4
6 NW4 .46 C5
1 W12 .111 C4
Southall UB1 .107 C5
West Ewell KT19 .215 A4
Longford Gdns
Hayes UB4 .106 D6
Sutton SM1 .218 A6
Longford Ho 7 E1 .96 C1
1 Catford BR1 .186 B5
Hampton TW12 .173 C6
Longford Ind Est TW12 173 D4
Longford Rd TW2 .151 D3
Longford Sch TW14 .149 D4
Longford St NW1 93 B3 238 D6
Longford Way TW19 .148 A3
Longford Wlk 9 SW2 .160 C4
Longhayes Ave RM6 .58 D5
Longhayes Ct RM6 .58 D5
Longheath Gdns CR0 .206 C4
Longhedge Ho SE26 .184 A6
Longhedge Lane Ind Est N18 .33 D4
Longhill Rd SE6 .164 B1
Longhook Gdns UB5 .84 B4
Longhope Cl SE15 .139 D6
Longhurst Ho 8 W9 .91 B4
Longhurst Rd SE13 .164 C6
Croydon CR0 .206 B3
Longland Ct E9 .75 A3
SE1 .118 A1
Longland Dr N20 .13 D2
Longlands Ct E17 .35 A2
W11 .244 D6
Mitcham CR4 .181 A2
Sidcup DA15 .167 D1
Longlands Park Cres DA15 .167 C2
Longlands Prim Sch DA15 .167 C1
Longlands Rd DA15 .167 D1
Longleat Ho SW1 .259 C2
Longleat Rd EN1 .17 C6
Longleat Villas 3 DA6 .147 A1
Longleat Way TW14 .149 B4
Longleigh Ho 8 SE5 .139 C4
Longleigh La SE2 .146 C6
Longlents Ho 3 NW10 .89 B6
Longley Ave HA0 .88 B6
Longley Ho 5 N19 .71 C4
Longley Rd SW17 .180 D4
Harrow HA1 .42 B5
Thornton Heath CR0 .204 D2
Longley St SE1 .118 A2
Longley Way NW2 .68 C5
Longman Ho 9 E2 .96 D5
10 E8 .95 D6
Longmead BR7 .188 C1
Longmead Dr DA14 .168 D2
Longmead Ho SE27 .183 A5
Longmead Prim Sch UB7 .104 A2
Longmead Rd SW17 .180 D5
Hayes UB3 .105 D6
Thames Ditton KT7 .196 D2
Longmeadow Rd DA15 .167 C3
Longmoor Point 14 SW15 .156 B3
Longmore Ave EN4,EN5 .14 B5
Longmore St SW1 .115 C2 259 A3
Longnor Rd E1 .96 D4
Longreach Ct IG11 .101 B5
Longridge Ho SE1 .262 B5
Longridge La UB1 .85 D1
Longridge Rd SW5 .113 C2 255 B3
Longs Ct 2 TW9 .132 B1
Long's Ct W1 .249 D5
Longshaw Prim Sch E4 .20 B1
Longshaw Rd E4 .20 B1
Longshore SE8 .119 B2
Longstaff Cres SW18 .157 C4
Longstaff Rd SW18 .157 C5
Longstone Ave NW10 .89 D6
Longstone Rd SW17 .181 B5
Longthorne Ho 20 E3 .97 B4
Longthornton Rd SW16 181 D1
Longton Ave SE26 .184 A6
Longton Gr SE26 .184 B6
Longville Rd SE11 .261 D4
Longwalk Rd UB11 .104 D5
Longwood Dr SW15 .156 A5
Longwood Gdns IG2,IG6, IG5 .56 C6
Longwood Par IG6 .56 D6
Longworth Cl SE28 .102 D1
Loning The NW9 .45 D5
Enfield EN3 .6 C5
Lonsdale Ave E6 .100 A3
Wembley HA9 .66 A3
Lonsdale Cl E6 .100 A3
SE12 .165 D1
Edgware HA8 .26 B5
Hatch End HA5 .23 A2
Hayes UB8 .83 A2
Lonsdale Cres IG2 .56 D3
Lonsdale Dr EN2 .16 A6
Lonsdale Dr N EN2 .4 A1
Lonsdale Gdns CR7, SW16 .204 B5
Lonsdale Ho 6 N4 .51 A2
SW6 .135 C2
Lonsdale Mews W11 .91 B1
4 Richmond TW9 .132 C4
Lonsdale Pl N1 .72 C1
Lonsdale Rd E11 .54 D2
NW6 .91 B6
SE25 .206 B5
SW13 .133 D5
W4 .111 D2
W11 .91 B1
Bexley DA7 .147 B3
Southall UB2 .106 D3
Lonsdell Ho 9 SW2 .160 C5
Loobert Rd N15 .51 C6
Looe Gdns IG6 .56 D6
Loop Rd BR7 .189 A4
Lopen Rd N18 .33 C6
Lopen Works N18 .33 C6
Lopez Ho 4 SW9 .138 A2
Lorac Ct 18 SM2 .217 C1
Loraine Cl EN3 .18 C6
Loraine Ct BR7 .188 D5
Loraine Ho 1 SM5 .219 B4
Loraine Rd N7 .72 B4
W4 .132 D6
Lord Ave IG5 .56 B6
Lord Chancellor Wlk KT2 .177 A2
Lord David Pitt Ho 8 SE24 .138 C1
Lord Gdns IG5 .56 B5
Lord Holland La 5 SW9 .138 C3
Lord Knyvetts Ct 3 TW19 .148 A5
Lord Napier Pl W6 .112 A1
Lord North St SW1 .260 A5
Lord Roberts Mews SW6 .265 C3
Lord Roberts Terr SE18 122 C1
Lord St E16 .122 A5
Lord Warwick St SE18 .122 B3
Lordell Pl SW19 .178 C4
Lord's (Middlesex Cty Cricket Gd)* NW8 .92 B4 229 D2
Lords Cl SE21 .161 A2
Feltham TW13 .151 A2
Lord's Cricket Mus NW8 .92 B4 229 D1
Lords Ct 3 HA8 .27 A3
Lord's Ct NW8 .229 D1
Lord's View NW8 .229 D1
Lordship Gr N16 .73 B6
Lordship Ho 3 N16 .73 B6
Lordship La N22 .33 B2
SE22 .161 D5
Lordship Lane Jun & Inf Schs N22 .33 A2
Lordship Park Mews N16 .73 A6
Lordship Pk N16 .73 B6
Lordship Pl SW3 .267 A5
Lordship Rd N16 .73 B6
Northolt UB5 .63 A1
Lordship Terr N16 .73 B6
Lordsmead Rd N17 .33 C1
Loreburn Ho 2 N7 .72 B4
Lorenzo St N1,WC1 .233 C2
Loretto Gdns HA3 .44 A5
Lorian Cl N12 .29 D6
Loring Rd N20 .14 C2
Isleworth TW7 .130 D3
Loris Rd W6 .112 C3
Lorn Ct SW9 .138 C3
Lorn Rd SW9 .138 C3
Lorne Ave CR0 .206 D2
Lorne Cl NW8 .92 C4 230 B1
Lorne Ct SW15 .156 D5
Lorne Gdns E11 .55 C5
5 W11 .112 D4
Croydon CR0 .206 D2
Lorne Ho 7 E1 .97 A2
3 N11 .31 B5
Lorne Rd E7 .77 C4
E17 .53 C4
N4 .50 B1
Harrow HA3 .24 D1
2 Richmond TW10 .154 B6
Lorraine Ct 10 NW1 .71 B1
Beckenham BR3 .186 A2
Lorraine Pk HA3 .24 C3
Lorrimore Rd SE17 .138 D6
Lorrimore Sq SE17 .138 D6
Lorton Ho 9 NW6 .91 C6
Loseberry Rd KT10 .212 B3
Lostock Ho 10 SW8 .137 D3
Lothair Rd W5 .109 D4
Lothair Rd N N4 .50 D3
Lothair Rd S N4 .50 D2
Lothbury EC2 .95 B1 242 C2
Lothian Ave UB4 .84 B2
Lothian Cl HA0 .65 A5
Lothian Rd SW9 .138 D4
Lothrop St W10 .91 A4
Lots Rd SW10 .136 A5 266 B3
Loubet St SW17 .180 D4
Loudoun Ave IG6 .56 D4
Loudoun Rd NW8 92 A6 229 B5
Loudwater Cl TW16 .194 A5
Loudwater Rd TW16 .194 A5
Lough Rd N7 .72 B2
Loughborough Ct 7 SW9 .138 D2
Loughborough Jun & Inf Schs SW9 .138 D3
Loughborough Junction Sta SW9 .138 D2
Loughborough Pk SW9 138 D1
Loughborough Rd SE5, SW9 .138 D3
Loughborough St SE11 .116 B1 260 D1
Loughton Way IG9 .21 D3
Louis Ct 3 RM10 .81 D2
Louis Mews N10 .31 B2
Louisa Ct TW2 .152 C2
Louisa Gdns E1 .96 D3
Louisa Ho SW15 .133 D1
Louisa St E1 .96 D3
Louise Bennett Cl 9 SE24 .138 D1
Louise Ct 4 E11 .55 B4
N22 .32 C2
Louise De Marillac Ho 18 E1 .96 C2
Louise Graham Ho 5 IG11 .101 B6
Louise Rd E15 .76 C2
Louise White Ho 1 N19 49 D1
Louisville Rd SW17 .159 A1
Lousada Lo N14 .15 C5
Louvaine Rd SW11 .136 B1
Lovage App E6 .100 A2
Lovat Cl NW2 .67 D5
Lovat La EC3 .253 A5
Lovat Wlk TW5 .129 A5
Lovatt Cl HA8 .26 D4
Lovatt Ct SW12 .159 B3
Lovatt Dr HA4 .39 D4
Love La EC2 .95 A1 242 B2
N17 .33 D3
SE18 .122 D2
SE25 .206 B6
Bexleyheath DA5 .169 C5
Cheam SM3 .217 A2
Long Ditton KT6 .213 D6
Mitcham CR4 .202 C6
Morden SM4 .201 D2
Pinner HA5 .41 A6
Love Wlk SE5 .139 B3
Loveday Ho 2 SW2 .160 C3
Loveday Rd W13 .109 B5
Lovegrove St SE1 .140 A6
Lovegrove Wlk E14 .120 A5
Lovekyn Cl KT2 .176 B1
Lovel Ave DA16 .146 A3
Lovelace Ave BR2 .210 C3
Lovelace Gdns
Barking IG11 .80 A4
Surbiton KT6 .197 D2
Lovelace Gn SE9 .144 B2
Lovelace Ho 12 E8 .95 D6
Lovelace Prim Sch KT9 213 C3
Lovelace Rd SE21 .161 A3
Barnet EN4 .14 C4
Surbiton KT6 .197 D2
Loveland Mans 6 IG11 .79 D1
Lovelinch Cl SE15 .140 C6
Lovell Ho E8 .96 A6
4 SW19 .180 A2
Lovell Pl SE16 .119 A3
Lovell Rd
Richmond TW10 .153 C1
Southall UB1 .85 D1
Loveridge Mews NW6 .69 B2
Loveridge Rd NW6 .69 B2
Lover's Wlk W1 115 A5 248 A3
Lovett Dr SM5 .202 B2
Lovett Way NW10 .67 A3
Lovette Ho 3 E3 .97 C4
Lovibonds Ave
Hillingdon UB7 .82 B1
Orpington BR6 .226 D5
Low Cross Wood La SE21 .161 D1
Low Hall Cl E4 .19 D4
Low Hall La E17 .53 A3
Low Ho IG11 .102 A5
Lowbrook Rd IG1 .78 D4
Lowdell Cl UB7 .82 A1
Lowden Rd N9 .18 B3
SE24 .139 A1
Southall UB1 .107 A6
Lowder Ho 6 E1 .118 B5
Lowe Ave E16 .99 A2
Lowell Ho 10 SE5 .139 A5
Lowell St E14 .97 A1
Lower Addiscombe Rd CR0 .205 C1
Lower Addison Gdns W14 .113 A4 244 A1
Lower Belgrave St SW1 .115 B3 258 C5
Lower Boston Rd W7 .108 C4
Lower Broad St RM10 .103 C6
Lower Camden BR7 .188 B2
Lower Church St CR0 .220 D6
Lower Clapton Rd E5 .74 C4
Lower Comm S SW15 .134 B2
Lower Coombe St CR0 .221 A4
Lower Downs Rd SW20 178 D2
Lower Fosters NW4 .46 C4
Lower George St 13 TW10 .153 D6
Lower Gn W CR4 .202 C6
Lower Gravel Rd BR2 .210 B1
Lower Green Rd KT10 .212 A6
Lower Grosvenor Pl SW1 .115 B3 258 D6
Lower Grove Rd TW10 .154 B6
Lower Hall La E4 .35 A6
Lower Ham Rd KT2 .175 D4
Lower Hampton Rd TW12,TW16 .172 D1
Lower James St W1 .249 B6
Lower John St W1 .249 B6
Lower Kenwood Ave EN2 .16 A6
Lower Lea Crossing E14,E16 .120 C6
Lower Maidstone Rd N11 .31 C4
Lower Mall W6 .112 B1
Lower Marsh SE1 .116 C4 251 A1
Lower Marsh La KT1, KT5 .198 C5
Lower Merton Rise NW3 70 C1
Lower Morden La SM4 .201 A3
Lower Mortlake Rd TW9 .132 B2
Lower Park Rd N11 .31 C5
Belvedere DA17 .125 C2
Loughton IG10 .21 D6
Lower Pk 5 SW15 .156 D6
Lower Place Bsns Ctr NW10 .89 A5
Lower Queen's Rd IG9 .21 D2
Lower Rd N2 .30 B3
SE16 .118 C4
Belvedere DA17 .125 D3
Harrow HA2 .42 B1
Sutton SM1 .218 A4
Lower Richmond Rd SW14,TW9 .132 D2
SW15 .134 C2
Lower Robert St WC2 .250 B5
Lower Sloane St SW1 .115 A1 258 A2
Lower Strand NW9 .27 D1
Lower Sunbury Rd TW12 .173 C1
Lower Sydenham Sta SE26 .185 B5
Lower Teddington Rd KT1 .175 D2
Lower Terr NW3 .70 A5
Lower Thames St EC3 .117 C6 253 A5
Lower Tub WD2 .8 B4
Lower Wood Rd KT10 .213 B2
Lowerwood Ct W11 .91 A1
Lowestoft Cl 5 E5 .74 C6
Loweswater Cl HA9 .65 D6
Loweswater Ho E3 .97 B3
Lowfield Rd NW6 .69 C1
W3 .89 A1
Lowick Rd HA1 .42 C4
Lowland Gdns RM7 .59 D3
Lowlands NW3 .70 C2
Lowlands Rd Harrow HA1 .42 B2
Pinner HA5 .40 C3
Lowman Rd N7 .72 B4
Lowndes Cl SW1 .258 B5
Lowndes Ct SW1 .257 D6
Lowndes Lo EN5 .1 D2
Lowndes Pl SW1 .115 A3 258 A5
Lowndes Sq SW1 .114 D4 247 D1
Lowndes St SW1 .115 A3 258 A6
Lownds Ct BR1 .187 A1
Lowood Ct SE19 .183 D5
Lowood Ho 11 E1 .118 C6
Lowood St E1 .118 B6
Lowry Cres CR4 .180 C1
Lowry Ct 3 SE16 .118 B1
Lowry Ho N17 .33 D2
Lowry Lo 2 HA0 .65 D3
Lowry Rd RM8 .80 B3
Lowth Rd SE5 .139 A3
Lowther Cl WD6 .10 B6
Lowther Dr EN2 .4 A1
Lowther Hill SE23 .163 A4
Lowther Ho 11 E8 .95 D6
SW1 .259 B1
Lowther Jun & Inf Sch SW13 .134 A6
Lowther Rd E17 .35 A1
N7 .72 C3
SW13 .133 D4
Kingston u T KT2 .176 B2
Stanmore HA7 .44 B6
Loxdon Ct RM6 .58 B3
Loxford Ave E6 .99 D5
Loxford Ho SW1 .258 B3
Loxford La IG1 .79 B3
Loxford Rd IG11 .78 D2
Loxford Sch of Science & Tech IG1 .79 B3
Loxham Rd E4 .35 D3
Loxham St WC1 .233 B1
Loxley Cl SE26 .184 D5
Loxley Rd SW18 .158 B3
Loxley Rd *continued*
Hampton TW12 .173 B6
Loxton Rd SE23 .163 A3
Loxwood Cl TW14 .149 C3
Loxwood Rd N17 .51 C6
Loyola Prep Sch IG9 .21 C3
Lubavitch House Gram Sch N2 .48 A4
Lubbock Ct BR7 .188 B3
Lubbock Ho 18 E14 .119 D6
Lubbock Rd BR7 .188 B3
Lubbock St SE14 .140 C5
Lucan Ho N1 .235 D5
Lucan Pl SW3 .114 C2 257 B3
Lucan Rd EN5 .1 A2
Lucas Ave E13 .99 B6
Harrow HA2 .63 C6
Lucas Ct SE26 .185 A5
SW11 .268 B1
Lucas Ho 2 SW8 .137 C3
Lucas Rd SE20 .184 C4
Lucas Sq NW11 .47 C3
Lucas St SE4,SE8 .141 C4
Lucas Vale Prim Sch SE8 .141 C4
Lucerne Cl N14 .16 A1
Lucerne Ct
8 Beckenham BR3 .185 C3
5 Erith DA18 .125 A3
Lucerne Gr E17 .54 B5
Lucerne Mews W8 .245 B4
Lucerne Rd N5 .72 D4
Orpington BR6 .211 D1
Thornton Heath CR7 .205 A5
Lucey Rd SE16 .118 A3
Lucey Way SE16 .118 A2
Lucie Ave TW15 .170 D4
Lucien Rd SW17 .181 A6
SW18 .157 D2
Lucille Ho SE26 .184 B4
Lucknow St SE18 .145 C5
Lucorn Cl SE12 .164 D5
Lucraft Ho 12 SW2 .160 A4
Luctons Ave IG9 .21 C3
Lucy Ashe Ho SE17 .261 D3
Lucy Brown Ho SE1 .252 B3
Lucy Gdns RM8 .81 A5
Luddesdon Rd DA8 .147 C5
Ludford Cl NW9 .27 C1
Croydon CR0 .220 D4
Ludgate Broadway EC4 241 D1
Ludgate Cir EC4 .94 D1 241 C1
Ludgate Hill EC4 94 D1 241 D1
Ludgate Sq EC4 .241 D1
Ludham NW5 .70 D3
Ludham Cl SE28 .102 C1
Ludlow Cl Bromley BR2 .209 A6
Harrow HA2 .63 B4
Ludlow Ct W3 .111 A4
Ludlow Rd W5 .87 C3
Feltham TW13 .172 A6
Ludlow St EC1 .242 A6
Ludlow Way N2 .48 A5
Ludovick Wlk SW15 .133 C1
Ludwick Mews SE14 .141 A5
Luffield Rd SE2 .124 B3
Luffman Rd SE12 .165 B1
Lugard Ho W12 .112 B5
Lugard Rd SE15 .140 B4
Lugg App E12 .78 C5
Luke Ho 31 E1 .96 B1
Luke St EC2 .95 C3 243 A6
Lukes Ct N3 .47 C6
Lukin Cres E4 .20 B1
Lukin St E1 .96 C1
Lullingstone Cl BR5 .190 B3
Lullingstone Cres BR5 .190 B3
Lullingstone Ho 20 SE15 .140 C6
Lullingstone La SE13 .164 B5
Lullingstone Rd 3 DA17 .147 B6
Lullington Garth N12 .29 B5
Borehamwood WD6 .10 D6
Bromley BR1 .186 C3
Lullington Rd SE20 .184 A3
Dagenham RM9 .81 A1
Lulot Gdns N19 .71 B6
Lulworth NW1 .71 D1
SE17 .262 C2
Lulworth Ave
Hounslow TW5,TW7 .130 A5
Wembley HA9 .43 C2
Lulworth Cl HA2 .63 B5
Lulworth Cres CR4 .180 C1
Lulworth Ct N14 .16 A1
Lulworth Dr HA5 .41 A2
Lulworth Gdns HA2 .63 B6
Lulworth Ho SW8 .270 C3
Lulworth Rd SE9 .166 A2
SE15 .140 B3
Bexley DA16 .145 D3
Lulworth Waye UB4 .84 B1
Lumley Cl DA17 .125 C1
Lumley Ct WC2 .250 B5
Lumley Flats SW1 .258 A2
Lumley Gdns SM3 .217 A3
Lumley Ho KT3 .199 B1
Lumley Rd SM1,SM3 .217 A3
Lumley St W1 .238 B1
Lumsdon NW8 .91 D6
Luna Rd CR7 .205 A6
Lunan Ho 12 E3 .97 B5
Lund Point E15 .98 A6
Lundin Wlk WD1 .22 D6
Lundy Dr UB3 .105 C2
Lunham Rd SE19 .183 C4
Lupin Cl SW2 .160 D2
Lupin Cl *continued*
Croydon CR0 .206 D1
Lupin Point SE1 .253 D1
Lupin Cres IG11 .78 D2
Lupton Cl SE12 .187 B6
Lupton St NW5 .71 C4
Lupus Ct SE19 .183 B2
Lupus St SW1 .115 C1 259 B1
Luralda Gdns E14 .120 B1
Lurgan Ave W6 .134 D6
Lurline Gdns SW11 .137 A4 268 B2
Luscombe Ct BR2 .186 C1
Luscombe Ho SW18 .157 B6
Luscombe Way SW8 .138 A5 270 A4
Lusher Ho SW15 .156 D5
Lushington Ho KT12 .194 C3
Lushington Rd NW10 .90 B5
SE6 .185 D5
Lushington Terr 11 E8 .74 A3
Lutea Ho SM2 .218 A1
Luther Cl HA8 .11 A2
Luther King Cl E17 .53 A3
Luther Rd TW11 .174 D5
Luton Pl SE10 .142 A5
Luton Rd E13 .99 A3
E17 .53 B6
Sidcup DA14 .168 C1
Luton St NW8 .92 B3 236 D5
Luttrell Ave SW15 .156 B6
Lutwyche Rd SE6 .163 B2
Lutyens Ho SW1 .259 A1
Luxborough Ho W1 .238 A4
Luxborough St W1 .93 A2 238 A4
Luxborough Twr W1 .238 A4
Luxemburg Gdns W6 .112 D2
Luxfield Rd SE9 .166 A3
Luxford St SE16 .118 D2
Luxmore St SE4 .141 B4
Luxor St SE5 .139 A2
Lyal Rd E3 .97 A5
Lyall Ave SE21 .183 D6
Lyall Mews SW1 .115 A3 258 A5
Lyall Mews W SW1 .258 A5
Lyall St SW1 .115 A3 258 A5
LyceÈ Francais Charles de Gaulle (French Univ Coll) SW7 .114 B2 256 C4
LyceÈ The SE11 116 C1 261 B1
Lycett Ho 10 SW2 .160 A4
Lycett Pl 3 W12 .112 A4
Lych Gate Wlk UB3 .105 D6
Lychgate Manor HA1 .42 C2
Lyconby Gdns CR0 .207 A2
Lydd Cl DA15 .167 C1
Lydd Rd DA7 .147 B5
Lydden Ct SE9 .167 C5
Lydden Gr SW18 .157 D4
Lydden Rd SW18 .157 D4
Lydeard Rd E6 .78 B1
Lydford NW1 .232 B5
Lydford Cl 22 N16 .73 C3
Lydford Rd N15 .51 B4
NW2 .68 D2
W9 .91 B3
Lydgate Ho 8 N16 .73 C3
Lydhurst Ave SW2 .160 B2
Lydia Lo HA1 .64 C4
Lydney Cl SE15 .139 C5
SW19 .157 A2
Lydon Rd SW4 .137 C2
Lydstep Rd BR7 .188 C6
Lydwell Ho 29 SW8 .137 D3
Lyford Rd SW18 .158 C3
Lyford St SE7 .122 A2
Lygoe Ho 18 N6 .49 D2
Lygoe Rd N2 .30 C2
Lygon Ho 1 E2 .96 A4
Lygon Pl SW1 .258 C5
Lyham Cl SW2 .160 A5
Lyham Rd SW2 .160 A5
Lyle Cl CR4 .203 A2
Lyly Ho SE1 .262 D5
Lyme Farm Rd SE12 .143 B1
Lyme Gr E9 .74 C1
Lyme Grove Ho 2 E9 .74 C1
Lyme Rd DA16 .146 B4
Lyme St NW1 .71 C1 232 A6
Lymer Ave SE19 .183 D5
Lymescote Gdns SM1 .217 C6
Lyminge Cl DA14 .189 D6
Lyminge Gdns SW17, SW18 .158 C3
Lymington Ave N22 .32 D1
Lymington Cl 2 E6 .100 B2
SW16 .181 D1
Lymington Ct SM1 .218 A5
Lymington Dr HA4 .61 B6
Lymington Gdns KT19 .215 D3
Lymington Lo E14 .120 B3
Lymington Mans NW6 .69 D2
Lymington Rd NW6 .69 D2
Dagenham RM8 .58 D1
Lympne N17 .33 B1
Lympstone Gdns SE15 .140 A5
Lynbridge Gdns N13 .32 D6
Lynbrook Cl SE15 .139 C5
Lynch Cl SE3 .142 D3
Lynch Wlk 2 SE8 .141 B6
Lynchen Cl TW5 .128 B4
Lyncott Cres SW4 .137 B1
Lyncourt SE3 .142 B3
Lyncroft Ave HA5 .41 A4
Lyncroft Gdns NW6 .69 C3
W13 .109 C5

Lyncroft Gdns continued
Isleworth TW3 152 A6
Lyncroft Mans 4 NW6 69 C3
Lyndale NW2 69 B5
Lyndale Ave NW2 69 B5
Lyndale Cl SE3 142 D6
Lynde Ho 2 SW4 137 D2
Walton-on-T KT12 194 C3
Lyndean Ind Est SE2 124 C3
Lynden Gate SW15 156 B4
Lynden Hyrst CR0 221 D6
Lyndhurst BR7 188 D4
Lyndhurst Ave N12 30 D4
NW7 27 C4
SW16 181 D1
Northwood HA5 22 B2
Southall UB1 107 D5
Sunbury TW16 194 A6
Tolworth KT5 198 D1
Twickenham TW2,TW4 151 C3
Lyndhurst Cl NW10 67 B5
Bexleyheath DA7 147 D2
Orpington BR6 226 D4
South Croydon CR0 221 D5
Lyndhurst Ct 11 E18 37 A2
7 Belmont SM2 217 C1
Lyndhurst Dr E10 54 A2
New Malden KT3 199 D2
Lyndhurst Gdns N3 29 A2
NW3 70 B3
Barking IG11 79 C2
Enfield EN1 5 C1
Ilford IG2 57 B3
Northwood HA5 22 B2
Lyndhurst Gr SE5,SE15 139 D3
Lyndhurst Ho 2 SW15 156 A4
Lyndhurst Jun & Inf Sch
SE5 139 B3
Lyndhurst Lo 3 E14 120 B2
Lyndhurst Rd E4 36 A3
N18 34 A6
N22 32 C4
NW3 70 B3
Bexleyheath DA7 147 D2
Greenford UB6 85 D3
Thornton Heath CR7 204 C5
Lyndhurst Sq SE15 139 D4
Lyndhurst Terr NW3 70 B3
Lyndhurst Way SE15 139 D3
Belmont SM2 217 C1
Lyndon Ave Bexley DA15 167 D6
Hackbridge SM6 219 A5
Hatch End HA5 23 A4
Lyndon Rd DA17 125 C2
Lyndon Yd SW17 179 D6
Lyndum Ct N22 32 C5
Lyne Cres E17 35 B2
Lyne Ct NW9 45 B2
Lynegrove Ave TW15 171 A5
Lyneham Wlk E5 75 A3
Pinner HA5 39 D6
Lynette Ave SW4 159 C5
Lynfield Ct SE23 162 D4
Lynford Cl HA8 27 A2
Lynford French Ho
SE17 262 A2
Lynford Gdns
Edgware HA8 10 D1
Ilford IG3 79 D6
Lynford Terr N9 17 D3
Lynhurst Cres UB10 61 B1
Lynhurst Rd UB10 61 A1
Lynmere Rd DA16 146 B3
Lynmouth Ave
Enfield EN1 17 D5
West Barnes SM4 200 D2
Lynmouth Dr HA4 62 B5
Lynmouth Gdns
Heston TW5 128 D4
Wembley UB6 65 B1
Lynmouth Rd E17 53 A4
N2 48 D5
N16 51 D1
Wembley UB6 87 B6
Lynn Cl Ashford TW15 171 B5
Harrow HA3 24 B1
Lynn Ct SW16 181 D5
Lynn Ho SE15 140 A6
Lynn Rd E11 76 C5
SW12 159 B4
Ilford IG2 57 B2
Lynn St EN2 5 B4
Lynne Cl 7 BR6 227 D2
Lynne Ct NW6 69 D1
SE23 163 B4
SW20 178 B2
South Croydon CR2 221 C4
Lynne Way NW10 67 C2
Northolt UB5 84 D5
Lynne Wlk KT10 212 A3
Lynnett Ct E9 75 A2
Lynnett Rd RM8 58 D1
Lynstead Cl BR1 187 C1
Lynsted Cl DA6 169 D6
Lynsted Ct 4 BR3 185 A1
Lynsted Gdns SE9 143 D2
Lynton KT7 197 A2
Lynton Ave N12 30 B6
NW9 45 D5
W13 87 A1
Lynton Cl NW10 67 D3
Chessington KT9 214 A4
Isleworth TW7 130 D1
Lynton Cres IG2 56 D3
Lynton Ct N13 32 A5
SE20 184 B2
9 W3 89 A1
Sutton SM2 218 A2
Lynton Est SE1 118 A2
Lynton Gdns N11 31 D4
Enfield EN1 17 C4
Lynton Grange N2 48 D6
Lynton Ho 15 W2 91 D1
Lynton Lo N5 72 D3
Lynton Mans SE1 261 A6
Lynton Mead N20 13 D2
Lynton Rd E4 35 D5
N8 50 A4
NW6 91 B5
SE1 118 D3 263
W3 110 D6
Harrow HA2 63 A6
New Malden KT3 199 B4
Thornton Heath CR0 204 C3
Lynton Terr 4 W3 89 A1
Lynton Wlk UB4 83 C4
Lynwood Cl E18 37 C2
Harrow HA2 63 A5
Lynwood Dr KT4 216 A6
Lynwood Gdns
Croydon CR0 220 B4
Southall UB1 85 B1
Lynwood Gr N21 16 C3
Orpington BR6 211 C1
Lynwood Rd SW17 180 D6
W5 88 A3
Thames Ditton KT7 196 D1
Lyon Bsns Est IG11 101 C5
Lyon Ct HA4 39 D1
Lyon Ho NW8 237 A5
Lyon Meade HA7 25 C2
Lyon Park Ave HA0 66 B2
Lyon Park Jun & Inf Schs
HA0 66 B1
Lyon Rd SW19 180 A2
Harrow HA1 42 D3
Lyon St N1 72 B1
Lyon Way UB6 86 C6
Lyons Pl NW8 92 B3 236 C5
Lyons Wlk W14 254 A4
Lyonsdown Ave EN5 14 A5
Lyonsdown Ct EN5 14 A6
Lyonsdown Rd EN5 14 A6
Lyonsdown Sch EN5 14 A6
Lyoth Rd BR5 227 A6
Lyric Dr UB6 85 D3
Lyric Mews SE26 184 C6
Lyric Rd SW13 133 D4
Lysander 20 NW9 27 D2
Lysander Gdns KT5 198 B3
Lysander Gr N19 49 D1
Lysander Ho 10 E2 96 B5
Lysander Rd Ruislip HA4 61 B6
Wallington CR0 220 B2
Lysander Way BR6 227 A5
Lysia Ct SW6 134 D5
Lysia St SW6 134 D5
Lysias Rd SW12 159 B5
Lysons Wlk SW15 156 A6
Lytchet Rd BR1 187 B3
Lytchet Way EN3 6 C4
Lytchgate Cl CR2 221 C1
Lytcott Dr KT8 195 B6
Lytcott Gr SE22 161 D6
Lytham Ave WD1 22 D5
Lytham Ct 5 UB1 85 D1
Lytham Gr W5 88 B4
Lytham St SE17 117 B1 262 C1
Lyttelton Ct N2 48 A4
Lyttelton Rd E10 76 A5
N2 48 A4
Lytten Ct 6 W12 112 A4
Lyttleton Cl NW3 70 C1
Lyttleton Ct UB4 84 C3
Lyttleton Ho 10 E9 74 C1
Lyttleton Rd N8 50 C6
Lytton Ave N13 16 C2
Enfield EN3 7 A5
Lytton Cl N2 48 B4
Northolt UB5 63 B1
Lytton Ct WC1 240 B3
Lytton Gdns SM6 219 D4
Lytton Gr SW15 157 A5
Lytton Ho 3 TW12 173 D4
Lytton Rd E11 54 C2
Hatch End HA5 23 A3
New Barnet EN5 2 A1
Lytton Strachy Path 8
SE28 124 B6
Lyveden Rd SE3 143 B5
SW17,SW19 180 D4

M

Mabbett Ho 2 SE18 144 C6
Mabel Evetts Ct UB3 106 B6
Mabel Thornton Ho 12
N16 73 B4
Maberley Cres SE19 184 A3
Maberley Ct SE19 184 A3
Maberley Rd SE19 182 C2
Mabledon Pl NW1,WC1 232 D1
Mablethorpe Rd SW6 264 A3
Mabley St E9 75 A3
Macallister Ho 8 SE18 144 D6
Macaret Cl N20 14 A4
Macarthur Cl E7 77 A2
MacArthur Ho 4 SW2 160 A4
Macaulay Ave KT10 212 C6
Macaulay CE Prim Sch
SW4 137 B1
Macaulay Ct SW4 137 B2
Macaulay Ho 10 N16 73 C5
2 W10 91 A2
Macaulay Rd E6 99 D5
Macaulay Rd continued
SW4 137 B2
Macaulay Sq SW4 137 B1
Macaulay Way 2 SE28 124 B5
Macbean St SE18 122 D3
Macbeth Ho 4 N1 95 C5
Macbeth St W6 112 B1
Macclesfield Rd
EC1 95 A4 235 A2
SE25 206 C4
Macclesfield St W1 249 D6
Macdonald Ave RM10 81 D5
Macdonald Ct TW3 130 A1
Macdonald Ho 2
SW11 137 A3
Macdonald Rd E7 77 A4
E17 36 A1
N11 30 D5
N19 71 C6
Macduff Rd
SW11 137 A4 268 B2
Mace Cl E1 118 B5
Mace Gateway E16 121 B6
Mace Ho 2 E17 53 D6
Mace St E2 96 D5
Macey Ho 9 SE10 142 A6
SW11 267 A1
Macfarlane La TW7 131 A6
Macfarlane Rd W12 112 C5
Macfarren Ho 9 W10 91 A4
MacFarren Pl NW1 238 B5
MacGregor Ho 2
SW12 159 D3
Macgregor Rd E16 99 C2
Machell Rd SE15 140 C2
Mackay Ho 33 W12 112 B6
Mackay Rd SW4 137 B2
Mackennal St
NW8 92 C5 230 B4
Mackenzie Cl 7 W12 112 B6
Mackenzie Ct 1 N8 50 A5
Mackenzie Ho 5 NW2 68 A5
Mackenzie Rd N7 72 B2
Penge BR3 184 D1
Mackenzie Wlk E14 119 C5
Mackeson Rd NW3 70 D4
Mackie Ho SW2 160 C4
Mackie Rd 18 SW2 160 C4
Mackintosh La E9 74 D3
Macklin Ho SE23 162 B2
Macklin St WC2 94 A1 240 B2
Mackonochie Ho EC1 241 A4
Mackrow Wlk 11 E14 120 A6
Macks Rd SE16 118 A2
Mackworth Ho NW1 232 A2
Mackworth St NW1 232 A2
Maclean Ho 9 SE18 122 B2
Maclean Rd SE23 163 A5
Macleod Ho 4 SE18 144 A4
Macleod Rd N21 16 A6
Macleod St
SE17 117 A1 262 B1
Maclise Rd
W14 113 A3 254 A5
Macmillan Ct HA2 41 C1
Macmillan Ho NW4 68 B4
Macnamara Ho SW10 266 C4
Macoma Rd SE18 145 B6
Macoma Terr SE18 145 B6
Maconochies Rd E14 119 D1
Macquarie Way E14 119 D2
Macready Ho W1 237 B3
Macready Pl 2 N7 72 A4
Macroom Ho W9 91 B4
Macroom Rd W9 91 B4
Mac's Pl EC4 241 B2
Mada Rd BR6 226 D5
Madame Tussaud's*
NW1 93 A3 238 A5
Maddams St E3 97 D3
Maddison Cl TW11 174 D4
Maddock Way SE17 138 D6
Maddocks Cl DA14 191 A5
Maddocks Ho 3 E1 118 B6
Maddox Ct 1 E4 20 B3
Maddox St W1 248 D6
Madeira Ave BR1 186 C3
Madeira Gr IG8 37 C4
Madeira Rd E11 54 C1
N13 16 D1
SW16 182 A5
Mitcham CR4 202 D5
Madeley Ct W5 88 A1
Madeley Rd W5 88 A1
Madeline Gr IG1 79 B3
Madeline Rd SE20 184 A3
Madge Gill Way 4 E6 100 A6
Madge Hill W7 108 C6
Madinah Rd E8 74 A3
Madingley 11 KT1 176 C1
Madingley Ct TW1 153 C6
Madison Cl 45 E3 97 D4
Madison Cres DA7 146 C5
Madison Gdns
Beckenham BR2 208 D6
Bexley DA7 146 C5
Madison Ho E3 98 A4
Madras Ho IG1 78 D4
Madras Pl N7 72 C2
Madras Rd IG1 78 D4
Madrid Rd SW13 134 A5
Madron St SE17 117 C1 263 B2
Mafeking Ave E6 100 A5
Brentford TW8 132 A6
Ilford IG2 57 B2
Mafeking Rd E16 98 D3
N17 34 A1
Enfield EN1 5 D2
Magdala Ave N19 71 C6
Magdala Rd
Isleworth TW7 131 A2
South Croydon CR2 221 B1
Magdalen Ct SE25 206 A4
Magdalen Pas E1 253 D6
Magdalen Rd SW18 158 B3
Magdalen St SE1 253 A3
Magdalene Cl 7 SE15 140 B3
Magdalene Gdns E6 100 C3
Magdalene Ho 7
SW15 156 D5
Magdalene Rd TW17 192 B6
Magee St SE11 138 C6
Magellan Ct 9 NW10 67 B1
Magellan Ho 16 E1 96 D3
Magellan Pl 10 E14 119 C2
Magnaville Rd WD2 8 D4
Magnin Cl 5 E8 96 A6
Magnolia Cl KT2 176 D4
E10 75 C6
Magnolia Ct 2 N12 29 D5
SE26 184 C5
SW11 158 D5
3 Belmont SM2 217 D1
Harrow HA3 44 B2
Hillingdon UB10 60 D2
Northolt UB5 85 A3
Richmond TW9 132 D4
Magnolia Ho 13 SE8 141 B6
Magnolia Lo E4 19 D1
Magnolia Pl SW4 160 A6
W5 87 D2
Magnolia Rd W4 132 D6
Magnolia Way KT19 215 A3
Magnolia Wharf W4 132 D6
Magpie Alley EC4 241 B1
Magpie Cl E7 76 D3
NW9 27 C1
Enfield EN1 6 A4
Magpie Hall Cl BR2 210 A3
Magpie Hall La BR2 210 B3
Magpie Hall Rd WD2 8 C2
Magpie Pl SE14 141 A6
Maguire Dr TW10 175 C6
Maguire St SE1 117 D4 253 D2
Mahatma Ganhi Ind Est 1
SE24 138 D1
Mahlon Ave HA4 62 B2
Mahogany Cl SE16 119 A5
Mahon Cl EN1 5 D4
Mahoney Ho SE14 141 B4
Maida Ave E4 19 D4
W2 92 A3 236 B5
Maida Rd DA17 125 C3
Maida Vale W9 92 A4 229 A1
Maida Vale Psychiatric Hospl
W9 92 A3 236 B6
Maida Vale Sta W9 91 D4
Maida Way E4 19 D4
Maiden Erlegh Ave
DA5 169 A3
Maiden La NW1 71 D1
SE1 117 A5 252 B4
WC2 116 A6 250 B6
Maiden Rd E15 76 C1
Maidenstone Hill SE10 142 A4
Maids of Honour Row 4
TW9 153 D6
Maidstone Bldgs SE1 252 C3
Maidstone Ho 4 E14 97 D1
Maidstone Rd N11 31 D4
Sidcup DA14 191 C3
Mail Coach Yd 24 E2 95 C4
Main Ave EN1 17 D6
Main Rd
Sidcup DA14,DA15 167 C1
St Paul's Cray BR5 190 C1
Main St TW13 172 D5
Mainridge Rd BR7,SE9 188 C6
Mainwaring Ct 3 CR4 181 A1
Mais Ho SE26 162 B2
Maismore St SE15 140 A6
Maison Alfort HA3 24 C2
Maisonettes The SM1 217 B3
Maitland Cl 5 SE10 141 D5
Hounslow TW4 129 B2
Maitland Ct W2 246 C6
Maitland Ho 17 E2 96 C5
SW1 269 A6
Maitland Park Rd NW3 70 D2
Maitland Park Villas
NW3 70 D2
Maitland Pl E5 74 C4
Maitland Rd E15 76 D2
SE26 184 D4
Majendie Rd SE18 123 B1
Majestic Ct N4 50 D1
Majestic Way CR4 180 D1
Major Rd E15 76 B3
22 SE16 118 A3
Makepeace Ave N6 71 A6
Makepeace Mans N6 71 A6
Makepeace Rd E11 55 A5
Northolt UB5 85 A6
Makinen Ho IG9 21 C3
Makins St SW3 257 B3
Malabar Ct 20 W12 112 B6
Malabar St E14 119 C4
Malacca Ho E1 97 A2
Malam Ct SE11 261 A3
Malam Gdns 3 E14 119 D6
Malatia CR2 221 A2
Malay Ho 2 E1 118 C5
Malbrook Rd SW15 134 B1
Malcolm Cl SE20 184 C3
Malcolm Cres NW4 46 A3
Malcolm Ct E7 76 D2
Malcolm Ct continued
NW4 46 A3
W5 88 B3
Stanmore HA7 25 C5
Malcolm Dr KT6 198 A1
Malcolm Ho 18 N1 95 C5
Malcolm Pl E2 96 C3
Malcolm Prim Sch
SE20 184 C3
Malcolm Rd E1 96 C3
SE20 184 C3
SE25 206 A3
SW19 179 A4
Ickenham UB10 60 B4
Malcolm Way E11 55 A5
Malcolms Way N14 15 C6
Malcolmson Ho SW1 259 D1
Malden Ave SE25 206 B6
Northolt UB6 64 C2
Malden Cres NW1 71 A2
Malden Ct N4 51 A3
West Barnes KT3 200 B6
Malden Green Ave KT4 200 A1
Malden Hill KT3 199 D6
Malden Hill Gdns KT3 199 D6
Malden Junc KT3 199 D4
Malden Manor Prim Sch
KT3 199 C2
Malden Manor Sta KT3 199 C2
Malden Parochial CE Prim
Sch KT4 199 C1
Malden Pk KT3 199 D3
Malden Pl NW5 71 A3
Malden Rd NW5 71 A2
Cheam KT4,SM3 216 D4
New Malden KT3,KT4 199 D2
Malden Way KT3 200 A5
Malden Way (Kingston By
Pass) KT3,KT5 199 C4
Maldon Cl E15 76 B3
N1 235 B6
SE5 139 C2
Maldon Ct E6 100 C6
Wallington SM6 219 C3
Maldon Rd N9 17 D1
W3 111 A6
Wallington SM6 219 B3
Maldon Wlk IG8 37 C4
Malet Pl WC1 239 C5
Malet St WC1 93 D2 239 D4
Maley Ave SE27 160 D2
Malford Ct E18 37 A1
Malford Gr E18 54 D6
Malfort Rd SE5 139 C2
Malham Rd SE23 162 D3
Malham Road Ind Est
SE23 162 D3
Malins Cl EN5 12 C6
Mall Ct W5 110 A6
Mall Rd W6 112 B1
Mall Studios 9 NW3 70 D3
Mall The N14 16 A1
SW1 115 D5 249 C3
SW14 155 A6
W5 110 A6
6 Bexleyheath DA6 147 C1
Brentford TW8 131 D6
4 Bromley BR1 209 A6
Harrow HA3 44 B3
Kingston u T KT6 197 D4
Mall The (Prep Sch)
TW2 152 B1
Mallams Mews 1 SW9 138 D2
Mallard Cl E9 75 B2
NW6 91 C6
W7 108 C4
New Barnet EN5 14 B5
Twickenham TW4 151 C4
Mallard Ct E4 20 B4
E12 78 B3
E17 54 B6
NW9 45 A2
Ilford IG1 79 A6
15 Richmond TW10 153 D5
Mallard Ho NW8 230 A3
7 SE15 139 D4
Mallard Path SE28 123 B3
Mallard Pl TW1 153 A1
Mallard Point 5 E3 97 C4
Mallard Way NW9 45 A2
Mallard Wlk
Beckenham BR3 206 D4
Foots Cray DA14 190 C4
Mallards E11 55 A2
Mallards Rd IG8 37 B3
Mallet Dr UB5 63 B3
Mallet Ho 11 SW15 156 A6
Mallet Rd SE13 164 B5
Malling SE13 163 D6
Malling Cl CR0 206 C3
Malling Gdns SM4 202 A3
Malling Ho 9 BR3 185 C3
Malling Way BR2 208 D2
Mallinson Ct 2 E11 76 C6
Mallinson Rd SW11 158 D6
Wallington SM6 219 D5
Mallon Gdns E1 243 D3
Mallord St SW3 136 B6 266 D6
Mallory Bldgs EC1 241 C5
Mallory Cl SE4 141 A1
Mallory Gdns EN4 15 A4
Mallory Ho E14 98 A2
Mallory St NW8 92 C3 237 B6
Mallow Cl CR0 206 D1
Mallow Mead NW7 29 A3
Mallow St EC1 242 C6
Mallows The UB10 60 D5
Malmains Cl BR3 208 B5
Malmains Way BR3 208 B5
Malmesbury 31 E2 96 C5
Malmesbury Cl HA5 40 A5
Malmesbury Fst Sch
SM4 202 A2
Malmesbury Inf Sch E3 97 B4
Malmesbury Mid Sch
SM4 202 A3
Malmesbury Rd E3 97 B5
E16 98 C2
E18 36 D2
Morden SM4 202 A3
Malmesbury Terr E16 98 D2
Malmsey Ho SE11 260 D2
Malmsmead Ho E9 75 A3
Malorees Jun & Inf Schs
NW6 68 D1
Malory Sec Sch BR1 187 A6
Malpas Dr HA5 40 D4
Malpas Rd E8 74 B2
SE4 141 B3
Dagenham RM9 80 D2
Malt Mill SE1 253 C3
Malt St SE1 140 A6
Malta Rd E10 53 C2
Malta St EC1 241 D6
Maltby Dr EN1 6 B5
Maltby Rd KT9 214 C2
Maltby St SE1 117 D3 263 C6
Maltham Terr N18 34 B4
Malthouse Dr W4 133 D6
Feltham TW13 172 D5
Malthouse Pas SW13 133 C3
Malthus Path 7 SE28 124 C5
Malting Ho E14 119 B6
Malting Way TW7 130 D2
Maltings W4 110 C1
Maltings Cl SW13 133 C3
Maltings Lo W4 133 C5
Maltings Pl SW6 265 D1
Maltings The BR6 211 D1
Malton Ho SE25 205 C5
Malton Mews SE18 145 C6
1 W10 91 A1
Malton Rd W10 91 A1
Malton St SE18 145 C6
Maltravers St WC2 251 A6
Malva Cl SW18 157 D6
Malvern Ave E4 36 B3
Bexley DA7 147 A5
Harrow HA2 63 B5
Malvern Cl SE20 184 A1
W10 91 B2
Ickenham UB10 60 C6
Mitcham CR4 203 C6
Surbiton KT6 198 A1
Malvern Court SW7 256 D4
Malvern Ct Belmont SM2 217 C1
3 Surbiton KT6 198 A1
Malvern Dr
Feltham TW13 172 D5
Ilford IG3 79 D4
Woodford IG8 37 C6
Malvern Gdns NW2 69 A6
Harrow HA3 44 A5
Malvern Ho N16 51 D1
Malvern Lo N12 30 B6
Malvern Mews NW6 91 C4
Malvern Pl NW6 91 B4
Malvern Rd E6 100 A6
E8 74 A1
E11 76 D6
N8 50 C6
N17 52 A6
N19 49 D1
NW6 91 C4
Enfield EN3 7 A6
Hampton TW12 173 C3
Harlington UB3 127 C5
Surbiton KT6 198 A1
Thornton Heath CR7 204 C5
Malvern Terr N1 234 A6
N9 17 D3
Malvern Way W13 87 B2
Malwood Rd SW12 159 B5
Malyons Rd SE13 163 D6
Malyons Terr SE13 163 D6
Malyons The TW17 193 B3
Managers St E14 120 A5
Manatee Pl SM6 219 D5
Manaton Cl SE15 140 B2
Manaton Cres UB1 85 C1
Manbey Gr E15 76 C2
Manbey Park Rd E15 76 C2
Manbey Rd E15 76 C2
Manbey St E15 76 C2
Manbre Rd W6 134 C6
Manbrough Ave E6 100 C4
Manchester Dr W10 91 A3
Manchester Gr E14 120 A1
Manchester Ho SE17 262 B2
Manchester Mans N19 49 D2
Manchester Mews W1 238 A3
Manchester Rd E14 120 A3
N15 51 B3
South Norwood CR7 205 A6
Manchester Sq
W1 93 A1 238 B2
Manchester St
W1 93 A2 238 A3
Manchester Way RM10 81 D4
Manchuria Rd SW11 159 A5
Manciple St
SE1 117 B3 262 D6
Mandalay Ho 6 N16 73 B4

Mandalay Rd SW4 ... 159 C6
Mandarin Ct NW10 ... 67 B2
6 SE8 ... 141 C6
Mandarin Way UB4 ... 84 D1
Mandela Cl NW10 ... 67 A1
36 W12 ... 112 B6
Mandela Ho 18 E2 ... 95 D4
Mandela Rd E16 ... 99 A1
Mandela St NW1 93 C6 232 B6
SW9 ... 138 C5
Mandela Way
SE1 ... 117 C2 263 B4
Manderville Ho SE1 ... 263 D2
Mandeville Cl 5 SE3 ... 142 D5
SW19 ... 179 A2
Mandeville Ct NW3 ... 69 D3
Mandeville Ctyd SW11 ... 268 A1
Mandeville Dr KT6 ... 197 D1
Mandeville Ho 8 SW4 ... 159 C6
Mandeville JMI Sch E5 ... 75 A5
Mandeville Pl W1 ... 238 B2
Mandeville Rd N14 ... 15 C2
Enfield EN3 ... 7 A6
Isleworth TW7 ... 131 A3
Littleton TW17 ... 192 C4
Northolt UB5 ... 63 C1
Mandeville Sch UB5 ... 63 B2
Mandeville St E5 ... 75 A5
Mandrake Rd SW17 ... 158 D1
Mandrake Way 2 E15 ... 76 C1
Mandrell Rd SW2 ... 160 A6
Manesty Ct N14 ... 15 D4
Manette St W1 ... 239 D1
Manfred Ct 6 SW15 ... 157 B6
Manfred Rd SW15 ... 157 B6
Manger Rd N7 ... 72 A2
Mangold Way 4 DA18 ... 125 A3
Manilla St E14 ... 119 C4
Manister Rd SE2 ... 124 A3
Manitoba Ct 23 SE16 ... 118 C4
Manitoba Gdns 6 BR6 227 D2
Manley Ct N16 ... 73 D5
Manley Ho SE11 ... 261 A2
Manley St NW1 ... 231 A6
Manly Dixon Dr EN3 ... 7 A6
Mann Cl 1 CR0 ... 221 A5
Mannebury Prior N1 ... 233 D3
Manneby Ho 17 E9 ... 96 C6
Mannering Ho 16 SW2 ... 160 B6
Mannin Rd RM6 ... 58 B2
Manning Ct 3 SE28 ... 124 B5
Manning Gdns HA3 ... 43 D2
Manning Ho 6 E17 ... 54 A6
3 W11 ... 91 A1
Manning Pl TW10 ... 154 B5
Manning Rd E17 ... 53 A4
Dagenham RM10 ... 81 C1
Manningford Cl EC1 ... 234 C2
Manningtree Cl SW19 ... 157 A3
Manningtree Rd HA4 ... 62 B4
Manningtree St 1 E1 ... 96 A1
Mannock Rd N22 ... 50 D6
Mann's Cl TW7 ... 152 D6
Manns Rd HA8 ... 26 C4
Manny Shinwell Ho
SW6 ... 264 D5
Manoel Rd TW2 ... 152 A2
Manor Ave SE4 ... 141 B3
Hounslow TW4 ... 128 D3
Northolt UB5 ... 63 B1
Manor Circus TW9 ... 132 C2
Manor Cl E17 ... 35 A1
NW7 ... 27 B5
NW9 ... 44 D4
SE28 ... 102 C1
Chipping Barnet EN5 ... 1 A1
New Malden KT4 ... 199 C1
Ruislip HA4 ... 39 D1
Manor Cottages App N2 30 A1
Manor Cotts N2 ... 30 A1
Manor Court Rd W7 ... 108 C6
Manor Cres KT5 ... 198 C3
Manor Ct E4 ... 20 C3
E10 ... 53 D1
N2 ... 48 D4
N14 ... 15 D2
N20 ... 14 D1
SE15 ... 139 D4
7 SW2 ... 160 B6
SW6 ... 265 D1
SW16 ... 160 A1
W3 ... 110 C2
3 Barking IG11 ... 79 D1
Harrow HA1 ... 42 D3
Kingston u T KT2 ... 176 C2
Tolworth KT5 ... 198 C3
Twickenham TW2 ... 152 A2
5 Wembley HA9 ... 66 A3
Manor Dr N14 ... 15 B3
N20 ... 14 D1
NW7 ... 27 B5
Feltham TW13 ... 172 D5
Hinchley Wood KT10 ... 213 A5
Sunbury TW16 ... 172 A1
Surbiton KT5 ... 198 C3
Wembley HA9 ... 66 B4
West Ewell KT19 ... 215 C2
Manor Dr N KT3,KT4 ... 199 B2
Manor Dr The KT4 ... 199 C1
Manor Farm Ave TW17 192 D3
Manor Farm Cl KT4 ... 199 C1
Manor Farm Ct E6 ... 100 B4
Manor Farm Dr E4 ... 20 C1
Manor Farm Rd
South Norwood CR7,
SW16 ... 182 C1
Wembley HA0 ... 87 D5
Manor Gate UB5 ... 63 A1
Manor Gdns N7 ... 72 A5
SW4 ... 137 C3
SW20 ... 179 B1
W3 ... 110 C2
8 W4 ... 111 C1
Hampton TW12 ... 174 A3
Richmond TW10,TW9 ... 132 B1
Ruislip HA4 ... 62 C3
South Croydon CR2 ... 221 D2
Sunbury TW16 ... 172 A1
Manor Gr SE15 ... 140 C6
Beckenham BR3 ... 185 D1
Richmond TW9 ... 132 C2
Manor Gt SW15 ... 157 A6
Manor Hall Ave NW4 ... 28 D1
Manor Hall Dr NW4 ... 28 D1
Manor Hall Gdns E10 ... 53 C1
Manor Ho E12 ... 77 D4
N14 ... 15 D3
NW1 ... 237 B4
Brentford TW8 ... 109 C1
Wallington SM6 ... 219 B3
Manor House Ct W9 ... 236 A5
Manor House Dr NW6 ... 68 D1
Manor House Hospl
NW11 ... 47 D1
Manor House Sch W7 ... 108 C6
Manor House Way TW7 131 B2
Manor Inf Sch IG11 ... 79 D2
Manor Jun Sch (Mix)
IG11 ... 79 D2
Manor La SE12 ... 164 C5
Feltham TW13 ... 150 A2
Harlington UB3 ... 127 B6
Sunbury TW16 ... 172 B1
Sutton SM1 ... 218 A3
Manor Lane Terr SE13 ... 164 C6
Manor Mans N7 ... 72 A5
7 NW3 ... 70 C2
Manor Mews NW6 ... 91 C5
SE4 ... 141 B3
Manor Mount SE23 ... 162 C3
Manor Oak Mans SE22 ... 162 B5
Manor Par N16 ... 73 D6
Harrow HA1 ... 42 D3
Manor Park Cl BR4 ... 207 D1
Manor Park Cres HA8 ... 26 C4
Manor Park Dr HA2 ... 41 D6
Manor Park Gdns HA8 ... 26 C4
Manor Park Prim Sch
SM1 ... 218 A3
Manor Park Rd E12 ... 77 D4
N2 ... 48 B6
NW10 ... 89 D6
Chislehurst BR7 ... 189 B2
Sutton SM1 ... 218 A3
West Wickham BR4 ... 207 D1
Manor Park Sta E12 ... 77 D4
Manor Pk SE13 ... 164 C6
Chislehurst BR7 ... 189 B2
Richmond TW9 ... 132 B1
Manor Pl SE17 ... 117 A1 262 A2
Chislehurst BR7 ... 189 B1
East Bedfont TW14 ... 150 A3
Mitcham CR4 ... 203 C6
Sutton SM1 ... 217 D4
Manor Prim Sch E15 ... 98 C5
Manor Rd E10 ... 53 C2
E15,E16 ... 98 C4
E17 ... 35 A1
N16 ... 51 C1
N17 ... 34 B2
N22 ... 32 A4
SE25 ... 206 A6
SW20 ... 179 B1
W13 ... 109 A6
Ashford TW15 ... 170 C5
Barking IG11 ... 79 D2
Beckenham BR3 ... 185 D1
Belmont SM2 ... 217 B1
Chipping Barnet EN5 ... 1 A1
East Molesey KT8 ... 196 B5
Enfield EN2 ... 5 B3
Harrow HA1 ... 43 A3
Hayes UB3 ... 84 A1
Ilford RM6 ... 58 D3
Loughton IG10 ... 21 B5
Mitcham CR4 ... 203 C6
Old Bexley DA5 ... 169 D3
Richmond TW10,TW9 ... 132 B1
Ruislip HA4 ... 39 B1
Sidcup DA15 ... 168 A1
Teddington TW11 ... 175 B5
Twickenham TW2 ... 152 B2
Wallington SM5,SM6 ... 219 B3
Walton-on-T KT12 ... 193 D2
West Wickham BR4 ... 223 D6
Manor Rd N
Hackbridge SM5,SM6 ... 219 B4
Hinchley Wood KT7 ... 213 A6
Manor Rd S KT10 ... 212 C4
Manor Sch NW6 ... 69 A1
NW10 ... 90 C6
Manor Sq RM8 ... 80 C6
Manor Street Est SW3 ... 267 B6
Manor The W1 ... 248 C5
Manor Vale TW8 ... 109 C1
Manor View N3 ... 29 D1
Manor Way E4 ... 36 B6
NW9 ... 45 C5
SE3 ... 143 A1
W3 ... 110 C2
Beckenham BR3 ... 207 C6
Manor Way *continued*
Bromley BR2 ... 210 A3
Harrow HA2 ... 41 D5
Mitcham CR4 ... 203 C6
New Malden KT4 ... 199 D1
Old Bexley DA5 ... 169 C3
Petts Wood BR5 ... 211 A5
Ruislip HA4 ... 39 D1
South Croydon CR2 ... 221 D2
Southall UB2 ... 106 D2
Manor Way The SM6 ... 219 B4
Manor Waye UB8 ... 82 A6
Manorbrook SE12,SE3 ... 143 A1
Manordene Cl KT7 ... 197 A1
Manordene Rd SE28 ... 102 D1
Manorfield Cl 3 N19 ... 71 C4
Manorfield JMI Sch E14 97 D2
Manorfields Cl BR7 ... 211 D6
Manorgate Rd KT2 ... 176 C2
Manorside EN5 ... 1 A1
Manorside Cl SE2 ... 124 D2
Manorside Prim Sch N3 30 A2
Manorway Enfield EN1 ... 17 C4
Woodford IG8 ... 37 C5
Manprest Ct E12 ... 78 B3
Manresa Rd
SW3 ... 114 C1 257 A1
Mansard Beeches
SW17 ... 181 A5
Mansard Cl HA5 ... 40 D6
Mansard Manor 4
SM2 ... 218 A1
Manse Cl UB3 ... 127 B6
Manse Ct DA14 ... 190 C5
Manse Rd N16 ... 73 D5
Mansel Ct SW11 ... 267 B1
Mansel Gr E17 ... 35 C2
Mansel Rd SW19 ... 179 B4
Mansell Ho SW8 ... 269 B2
Mansell Rd W3 ... 111 B4
Southall UB6 ... 85 D2
Mansell St E1 ... 95 D1 243 D1
Mansergh Cl SE18 ... 144 A5
Mansfield Ave N15 ... 51 B5
East Barnet EN4 ... 15 A5
Ruislip HA4 ... 40 B1
Mansfield Cl N9 ... 18 A5
Mansfield Ct 27 E2 ... 95 D6
Mansfield Dr UB4 ... 83 C3
Mansfield Hill E4 ... 19 D3
Mansfield Ho SW15 ... 156 D5
Mansfield Hts N2 ... 48 D4
Mansfield Mews W1 ... 238 C3
Mansfield Pl 11 NW3 ... 70 A4
Mansfield Rd E11 ... 55 B3
E17 ... 53 B5
NW3 ... 70 D4
W3 ... 88 D3
Chessington KT9 ... 213 D3
Ilford IG1 ... 78 C6
South Croydon CR2 ... 221 B2
Mansfield St W1 93 B2 238 C3
Mansford St E2 ... 96 A5
Manship Rd CR4 ... 181 A2
Mansion Cl SW9 ... 138 C4
Mansion Gdns NW3 ... 69 D5
Mansion House* EC4 ... 242 C1
Mansion House Pl EC3,
EC4 ... 242 C1
Mansion House St EC2 242 C1
Mansion House Sta
EC4 ... 117 A6 252 B6
Mansions The NW6 ... 69 B3
Manson Mews
SW7 ... 114 B2 256 C3
Manson Pl SW7 114 B2 256 C3
Manstead Gdns RM6 ... 58 C2
Manston N17 ... 33 B1
NW1 ... 71 C1
Manston Ave UB2 ... 107 C2
Manston Cl SE20 ... 184 C2
Manston Gr KT2 ... 175 D5
Manstone Rd NW2 ... 69 A3
Mantell Ho SW4 ... 159 C6
Manthorpe Rd SE18 ... 123 A1
Mantilla Rd SW17 ... 181 A6
Mantle Rd SE4 ... 141 A2
Mantle Way E15 ... 76 C1
Mantlet Cl SW16 ... 181 C3
Manton Ave W7 ... 109 A4
Manton Cl UB3 ... 105 C6
Manton Ho N16 ... 73 B5
Manton Rd SE2 ... 124 A2
Enfield EN3 ... 7 C5
Mantua St 28 SW11 ... 136 B2
Mantus Cl E1 ... 96 C3
Mantus Rd E1 ... 96 C3
Manus Way N20 ... 14 A3
Manville Gdns SW17 ... 159 B1
Manville Rd SW17 ... 159 B1
Manwood Rd SE4 ... 163 B5
Manwood St E16 ... 122 B5
Many Gates SW12 ... 159 B2
Manygate La TW17 ... 193 A3
Mape St E2 ... 96 B3
Mapes Ho 5 NW6 ... 69 A1
Mapesbury Ct NW2 ... 69 A3
Mapesbury Rd NW2 ... 69 A2
Mapeshill Pl NW2 ... 68 C2
Maple Ave E4 ... 35 B4
W3 ... 111 C5
Harrow HA2 ... 63 D6
Yiewsley UB7 ... 104 B6
Maple Cl N3 ... 29 C4
N16 ... 52 A3
SW4 ... 159 D5
Buckhurst Hill IG9 ... 21 D1
Hampton TW12 ... 173 B4
Maple Cl *continued*
Hayes UB4 ... 84 D4
Mitcham CR4 ... 181 B2
Petts Wood BR5 ... 211 B4
Ruislip HA4 ... 40 B3
Maple Cres DA15 ... 168 A5
Maple Ct E6 ... 100 C2
NW2 ... 68 D4
SE6 ... 163 D3
11 SW16 ... 182 C5
2 Croydon CR0 ... 221 A4
7 Dagenham RM8 ... 58 D2
Kingston u T KT3 ... 199 B6
4 Pinner Green HA5 ... 22 C1
Maple Gdns
Burnt Oak HA8 ... 27 C3
Stanwell TW19 ... 148 A2
Maple Gr NW9 ... 45 A2
W5 ... 109 D3
Brentford TW8 ... 131 B5
Southall UB1 ... 85 B2
Maple Gr Bsns Ctr TW4 128 C1
Maple Ho 13 E17 ... 53 D6
11 NW3 ... 70 D2
5 SE8 ... 141 B5
2 Kingston u T KT6 ... 198 A4
Maple Ind Est TW13 ... 150 A1
Maple Inf Sch KT6 ... 197 D4
Maple Leaf Dr DA15 ... 167 D3
Maple Leaf Sq 27 SE16 118 D4
Maple Lo NW9 ... 67 B6
SW15 ... 157 A5
Maple Mews NW6 ... 91 D5
SW16 ... 182 B5
Maple Pl W1 ... 239 B5
Yiewsley UB7 ... 104 B6
Maple Rd E11 ... 54 C3
SE20 ... 184 C2
Hayes UB4 ... 84 D4
Kingston u T KT6 ... 197 D4
Maple St W1 ... 93 C3 239 B5
Maple Way TW13 ... 150 B1
Maple Wlk W10 ... 90 D3
Maplecroft Cl E6 ... 100 A1
Mapledale Ave CR0 ... 222 A5
Mapledene BR7 ... 189 A5
Mapledene Est E8 ... 74 A1
Mapledene Rd E8 ... 74 A1
Mapledown Sch NW2 ... 46 C2
Maplehurst 2 BR2 ... 186 C1
Maplehurst Cl KT1 ... 198 A5
Mapleleafe Gdns IG6 ... 56 D6
Maples Pl E1 ... 96 B2
Maples The KT8 ... 175 C3
Maplestead Rd SW2 ... 160 B4
Dagenham RM9 ... 102 B6
Maplethorpe Rd CR7 ... 204 D5
Mapleton Cl BR2 ... 209 A3
Mapleton Cres SW18 ... 157 D5
Enfield EN3 ... 6 C5
Mapleton Rd E4 ... 20 A1
SW18 ... 157 D5
Enfield EN1 ... 6 B3
Maplin Cl N21 ... 16 B5
Maplin Ho 9 SE2 ... 124 D4
Maplin Rd E16 ... 99 B1
Maplin St E3 ... 97 B4
Mapperley Cl 3 E11 ... 55 A3
Mapperley Dr IG8 ... 36 C3
Mar Ho 4 SE7 ... 143 C6
Marada Ho NW6 ... 69 A1
Marais W4 ... 133 A5
Maran Way DA18 ... 124 D3
Marban Rd W9 ... 91 B4
Marble Arch*
W1 ... 114 D6 247 D6
Marble Arch Sta
W1 ... 92 D1 237 D1
Marble Cl W3 ... 110 D5
Marble Dr NW2 ... 46 D2
Marble Hill* TW1 ... 153 C4
Marble Hill Cl TW1 ... 153 B4
Marble Hill Gdns TW1 ... 153 B4
Marble Ho SE18 ... 123 D1
W9 ... 91 B3
Marbleford Ct 4 N6 ... 49 D2
Marbrook Ct SE12 ... 165 C1
Marcellina Way BR6 ... 227 D5
March 23 NW9 ... 27 D2
March Ct SW15 ... 134 B1
March Rd 5 TW1 ... 153 A4
Marchant Ct SE1 ... 263 D2
Marchant Ho 13 SW2 ... 160 B6
Marchant Rd E11 ... 76 B6
Marchbank Rd
W14 ... 135 B6 264 D6
Marchmont Ho 10
SW16 ... 181 C5
Marchmont Rd
Richmond TW10 ... 154 B6
Wallington SM6 ... 219 C1
Marchmont St
WC1 ... 94 A3 240 A6
Marchside Cl TW5 ... 128 D4
Marchwood Cl 17 SE5 ... 139 C5
Marchwood Cres W5 ... 87 D1
Marcia Rd SE1 ... 117 C2 263 B3
Marcilly Rd SW18 ... 158 B6
Marco Rd W6 ... 112 C3
Marcon Ct 29 E8 ... 74 B3
Marcon Pl E8 ... 74 B3
Marconi Rd E10 ... 53 C1
Marconi Way UB1 ... 85 D1
Marcourt Lawns W5 ... 88 A3
Marcus Ct E15 ... 98 C6
Brentford TW8 ... 132 A5
Marcus Garvey Mews
SE22 ... 162 B6
Marcus Garvey Way 9
SE24 ... 138 C1
Marcus Ho 13 SE15 ... 139 D4
Marcus St E15 ... 98 D6
SW18 ... 157 D5
Marcus Terr SW18 ... 157 D5
Mardale Ct NW7 ... 28 A3
Mardale Dr NW9 ... 45 B4
Mardell Rd CR0 ... 206 D4
Marden Ave BR2 ... 209 A3
Marden Cres CR0 ... 204 B3
Marden Ho 6 E8 ... 74 B3
Marden Rd N17 ... 33 C1
Thornton Heath CR0 ... 204 B3
Marden Sq SE16 ... 118 B3
Mardon Rd W13 ... 109 A4
Mardyke Ho SE17 ... 262 D4
Mare St E8 ... 74 B2
E8,E2 ... 96 B6
Marechal Niel Ave
DA15 ... 167 B1
Marechal Niel Par
DA15 ... 167 B1
Maresby Ho E4 ... 19 D2
Maresfield CR0 ... 221 C5
Maresfield Gdns NW3 ... 70 A2
Marfleet Cl SM5 ... 218 C6
Margaret Ave E4 ... 19 D5
Margaret Bondfield Ave
IG11 ... 80 A1
Margaret Bondfield Ho
4 E3 ... 97 A5
22 N7 ... 71 D3
Margaret Ct W1 ... 239 A2
New Barnet EN4 ... 2 B1
Margaret Gardner Dr
SE9 ... 166 B2
Margaret Herbison Ho
SW6 ... 264 D5
Margaret Hill Ho N8 ... 50 A4
Margaret Ho 16 W6 ... 112 C1
Margaret Ingram Cl
SW6 ... 264 C5
Margaret Lockwood Cl
KT5 ... 198 B5
Margaret Mcmillan Ho 10
N19 ... 49 D2
Margaret Rd N16 ... 51 D1
Barnet EN4 ... 2 B1
Bexley DA5 ... 168 D5
Margaret St W1 ... 93 C1 239 A2
Margaret Way IG4 ... 56 A3
Margarets Ct HA8 ... 26 D5
Margaret's Ct E11 ... 54 B2
SE1 ... 252 C3
Margaretta Terr
SW3 ... 136 C6 267 B6
Margaretting Rd E12 ... 55 C1
Margate Rd SW2 ... 160 A6
Margery Fry Ct N7 ... 72 A5
Margery Park Rd E7 ... 77 A2
Margery Rd RM8 ... 80 D5
Margery St WC1 ... 94 C4 234 A1
Margetson Ho N16 ... 51 D3
Margin Dr SW19 ... 178 D6
Margravine Gdns W6 ... 112 D1
W14 ... 254 A2
Margravine Rd
W6 ... 112 D1 264 A6
Marham Gdns
SW17,SW18 ... 158 C3
Morden SM4 ... 202 A3
Maria Cl 10 SE1 ... 118 A2
Maria Fidelis Convent Sch
NW1 ... 93 C4 232 B1
NW1 ... 93 D4 232 C2
Maria Ho 13 SW9 ... 138 C4
Maria Terr E1 ... 96 D3
Maria Theresa Cl KT3 ... 199 B4
Marian Cl UB4 ... 84 D3
Marian Ct E9 ... 74 C3
Sutton SM1 ... 217 D3
Marian Lo 5 SW20 ... 178 D3
Marian Pl E2 ... 96 B5
Marian Rd SW16 ... 181 C2
Marian Sq E2 ... 96 B5
Marian St 2 E2 ... 96 B5
Marian Vian Prim Sch
BR3 ... 207 A4
Marian Way NW10 ... 67 D1
Maribor 13 SE10 ... 142 A5
Maricas Ave HA3 ... 24 B2
Marie Curie SE5 ... 139 C4
Marie Lloyd Ct 13 SW9 ... 138 B1
Marie Lloyd Gdns 1
N19 ... 50 A2
Marie Lloyd Ho N1 ... 235 C3
Marien Ct E4 ... 36 B5
Marigold Cl UB1 ... 107 A6
Marigold Rd N17 ... 34 C3
Marigold St SE16 ... 118 B4
Marigold Way CR0 ... 206 D1
Marilea Ct W5 ... 109 D4
Marina App UB4 ... 85 A2
Marina Ave KT3 ... 200 B4
Marina Cl 1 BR2 ... 209 A6
Marina Ct 11 E3 ... 97 C4
Marina Dr DA16 ... 145 C3
Marina Gdns RM7 ... 59 D4
Marina Way TW11 ... 175 D3
Marine Dr 5 SE18 ... 122 B2
Marine St SE16 ... 118 A3
Marine Twr 29 SE8 ... 141 B6
Marinefield Rd SW6 ... 135 D3
Marinel Ho 25 SE5 ... 139 A5
Mariner Gdns TW10 ... 153 C1
Mariner Rd E12 ... 78 C4
Mariners Mews E14 ... 120 B2
Marion Ave TW17 ... 192 D4
Marion Ct 4 SW17 ... 180 C5
Marion Gr IG8 ... 36 C6
Marion Rd NW7 ... 28 A5
Thornton Heath CR0 ... 205 B4
Marion Richardson JMI Sch
E1 ... 96 D1
Marischal Rd SE13 ... 142 B2
Maritime Ho 5 SW4 ... 137 C2
Maritime Ind Est SE7 ... 121 B2
Maritime St E3 ... 97 B3
Marius Mans 3 SW17 ... 159 A2
Marius Rd SW17 ... 159 A2
Marjorie Gr SW11 ... 136 D1
Marjorie McClure Sch
BR7 ... 189 A2
Marjory Kinnon Sch
TW14 ... 149 C6
Mark Ave E4 ... 19 D5
Mark Cl Bexley DA7 ... 147 A4
Keston BR2 ... 226 A4
Southall UB1 ... 107 D5
Mark Ho 3 E2 ... 96 D5
Mark La EC3 ... 117 C6 253 B6
Mark Lo 9 EN4 ... 2 C1
Mark Mans W12 ... 112 A4
Mark Rd N22 ... 32 D1
Mark Sq EC2 ... 243 A6
Mark St E15 ... 76 C1
EC2 ... 243 A6
Markab Rd HA6 ... 22 A5
Markeston Gn WD1 ... 22 D6
Market Ct W1 ... 239 A2
Market Ctr The UB2 ... 106 B2
Market La HA8 ... 27 A2
Market Mews
W1 ... 115 B5 248 C3
Market Par E10 ... 53 D3
E17 ... 53 B6
1 N9 ... 18 A2
SE25 ... 206 A5
Feltham TW13 ... 151 A2
Market Pl N2 ... 48 C6
1 SE16 ... 118 B2
W1 ... 239 A2
3 W3 ... 111 A5
2 Bexleyheath DA7 ... 147 C1
Brentford TW8 ... 131 C5
Kingston u T KT1 ... 175 D1
Market Pl The NW11 ... 47 D5
Market Rd N7 ... 72 A2
Mortlake TW9 ... 132 C2
Market Sq E14 ... 97 D1
Bromley BR1 ... 187 A1
Market Sq The N9 ... 18 B2
Market St E6 ... 100 C5
SE18 ... 122 C2
Market The SM1,SM5 ... 202 A1
Market Way E14 ... 97 D1
1 Wembley HA0 ... 66 A3
Markfield Gdns E4 ... 19 D4
Markfield Ho N15 ... 52 A5
Markfield Rd N15 ... 52 A4
Markham Ho 9 SE21 ... 183 C6
1 Dagenham RM10 ... 81 C5
Markham Pl SW3 ... 257 C2
Markham Sq
SW3 ... 114 D1 257 C2
Markham St
SW3 ... 114 C1 257 B2
Markhole Cl TW12 ... 173 B3
Markhouse Ave E17 ... 53 A3
Markhouse Pas E17 ... 53 B3
Markhouse Rd E17 ... 53 B3
Markland Ho W10 ... 112 D6
Markmanor Ave E17 ... 53 B2
Marks Gate Jun & Inf Schs
RM6 ... 59 A6
Marksbury Ave TW9 ... 132 C2
Markstone Ho SE1 ... 251 C1
Markway The TW16 ... 172 C1
Markwell Cl SE26 ... 184 B6
Markyate Ho W10 ... 90 C3
Markyate Rd RM8 ... 80 B3
Marl Rd SW18 ... 136 A1
Marland Ho SW1 ... 257 D6
Marlands Rd IG5 ... 56 B6
Marlang Ct BR3 ... 186 B2
Marlborogh Rd TW7,
TW8 ... 131 B5
Marlborough 11 SW19 ... 156 D3
W9 ... 229 A2
Marlborough Ave 3 E8 ... 96 A6
N14 ... 15 C1
Edgware HA8 ... 10 D1
Ruislip HA4 ... 39 B3
Marlborough Cl N20 ... 14 D1
SE17 ... 261 D3
SW19 ... 180 C4
Broom Hill BR6 ... 211 D3
Marlborough Cres W4 ... 111 C3
Marlborough Ct W8 ... 255 A4
7 Buckhurst Hill IG9 ... 21 C2
Harrow HA1 ... 42 B5
Wallington SM6 ... 219 C1
Marlborough Day Hospl
NW8 ... 92 A5 229 A4
Marlborough Dr IG5 ... 56 A6
Marlborough Flats
SW3 ... 257 B4
Marlborough Gdns N20 ... 14 D1
Surbiton KT6 ... 197 D2
Marlborough Gr SE1 ... 118 A1
Marlborough Hill
NW8 ... 92 A6 229 B5
Harrow HA1 ... 42 C5
Marlborough Ho N4 ... 51 A1
NW8 ... 229 A3

Marlborough Ho continued
SW19 156 D1
Richmond TW10 154 C6
Marlborough House SW1 249 B3
Marlborough Jun & Inf Sch
Harrow HA1 42 C5
Isleworth TW7 131 A4
Marlborough La SE7 143 C5
Marlborough Mans 5 NW6 69 C3
Marlborough Par 1 UB10 82 D3
Marlborough Park Ave DA15 168 A3
Marlborough Pl NW8 92 A5 229 B4
Marlborough Prim Sch SW3 114 C2 257 B3
Marlborough Rd E4 35 D4
E7 77 C1
E15 76 C4
E18 55 A6
N9 18 A3
N19 72 A6
N22 32 B4
SE18 123 A3
SW1 115 C5 249 B3
SW19 180 C4
W4 111 A1
W5 109 D4
Ashford TW15 170 A5
Bexley DA16 146 D2
Bromley BR2 209 C5
Dagenham RM8 80 C4
Feltham TW13 150 D2
Hampton TW12 173 C4
Hillingdon UB10 82 D4
Richmond TW10 154 B5
Romford RM7 59 D5
South Croydon CR2 221 A1
Southall UB2 106 C3
Sutton SM1 217 C6
Marlborough Sch DA15 168 A4
Marlborough St SW3 114 C2 257 B3
Marlborough Trad Est TW9 132 D4
Marlborough Yd N19 71 D6
Marlbury NW8 91 D6
Marler Rd SE23 163 B3
Marlesford Ct SM6 219 C4
Marley Ave DA7 146 D6
Marley Cl N15 50 D5
Greenford UB6 85 C4
Marley Ho 14 W11 112 D6
Marley Wlk NW2 68 C3
Marlfield Ct KT3 199 D2
Marlin Cl TW16 171 C4
Marlin Ho SW15 157 A6
Marling Ct TW12 173 B4
Marlingdene Cl TW12 173 C4
Marlings Cl BR7 211 C5
Marlings Park Ave BR7 211 C6
Marlins Cl 3 SM1 218 A3
Marloes Cl HA0 65 D4
Marloes Rd W8 113 D3 255 C5
Marlow Cl SE20 206 B6
Marlow Cres TW1 152 D5
Marlow Ct N14 15 C4
NW6 68 D1
NW9 45 D6
1 W7 108 C5
Marlow Dr SM3 216 D5
Marlow Gdns UB3 105 B3
Marlow Ho 44 E2 95 D4
SE1 263 C6
14 W2 91 D1
Teddington TW11 175 A6
Marlow Rd E6 100 B4
SE20 184 B1
Southall UB2 107 B3
Marlow Studio Workshops 43 E2 95 D4
Marlow Way SE16 118 D4
Marlowe Bsns Ctr 2 SE14 141 A5
Marlowe Cl BR7 189 B4
Marlowe Ct SE19 183 D5
SW3 257 B3
6 Kingston u T KT2 175 D6
Marlowe Gdns SE9 166 C5
Marlowe Ho 15 N16 73 C4
SE8 119 B1
Kingston u T KT1 197 D5
Marlowe Lo CR0 223 A6
Marlowe Rd E17 54 A5
Marlowe Sq CR4 203 C5
Marlowe Way CR0 220 A6
Marlowes The NW8 92 B6 229 C6
Marlston NW1 231 D1
Marlton St SE10 120 D1
Marlwood Cl DA15 167 C2
Marmadon Rd SE18,SE2 123 D2
Marmion App E4 35 C6
Marmion Ave E4 35 B6
Marmion Cl E4 35 B6
Marmion Ho 13 SW12 159 B4
Marmion Mews 4 SW11 137 A2
Marmion Rd SW11 137 A1
Marmont Rd SE15 140 A5
Marmora Ho E1 97 A2
Marmora Rd SE22 162 C5
Marmot Rd TW4 128 D2
Marne Ave N11 31 B6
Bexley DA16 146 A2
Marne St W10 91 A4
Marnell Way TW4 128 D2
Marner Prim Sch E3 97 D3
Marney Rd SW11 137 A1
Marnfield Cres SW2 160 B3
Marnham Ave NW2 69 A4
Marnham Cres UB6 85 D5
Marnham Ct HA0 65 C3
Marnock Ho SE17 262 C2
Marnock Rd SE4 163 B6
Maroon Ho 15 E14 97 A2
Maroon St E14 97 A2
Maroons Way SE6 185 C5
Marqueen Twrs SW16 182 B3
Marquess Rd N1 73 B2
Marquess Rd N N1 73 B2
Marquess Rd S 17 N1 73 A2
Marquis Cl HA0 66 B1
Marquis Ct N4 50 B1
Barking IG11 79 C3
1 Kingston u T KT1 198 A5
Marquis Rd N4 50 C1
N22 32 B4
NW1 71 D2
Marrabon Cl DA15 168 A3
Marrayat Sq SW6 264 A2
Marrick Cl SW15 134 A1
Marrick Ho 17 NW6 91 D6
Marrilyne Ave EN3 7 B5
Marriner Ct UB3 105 C6
Marriot Rd N10 30 D2
Marriott Cl TW14 149 B5
Marriott Ho 8 SE6 186 A6
Marriott Rd E15 98 C6
N4 50 B1
Marriotts Cl NW9 45 D3
Marryat Ct 12 W6 112 B2
Marryat Ho SW1 259 A1
Marryat Pl SW19 179 A6
Marryat Rd SW19 179 A6
Marryatt Ct W5 88 B1
Marsala Rd SE13 141 D1
Marsalis Ho 2 E3 97 C4
Marsden Rd N9 18 B2
SE15 139 D2
Marsden St NW5 71 A2
Marsden Way 2 BR6 227 D4
Marsh Ave CR4 181 A1
Marsh Cl NW7 11 D1
Marsh Ct E8 74 A2
3 SW19 180 A2
Marsh Dr NW9 45 D3
Marsh Farm Rd TW2 152 D3
Marsh Green Prim Sch RM10 103 C5
Marsh Green Rd RM10 103 C6
Marsh Hall HA9 66 B5
Marsh Hill E9 75 A3
Marsh Ho SW1 259 D1
SW8 269 B2
Marsh La E10 75 C6
N17 34 B2
NW7 11 C1
Stanmore HA7 25 C4
Marsh Rd Pinner HA5 41 A5
Wembley HA0 87 D5
Marsh St E14 119 D2
Marsh Wall E14 119 D4
Marshall Cl N11 15 B1
SW18 158 A5
Harrow HA1 42 B2
Hounslow TW4 151 B6
Marshall Ct SW4 270 B1
Marshall Dr UB4 83 D2
Marshall Ho N1 235 D4
NW6 91 B5
SE17 262 C2
4 New Malden KT3 199 C5
Marshall Path 10 SE28 124 B6
Marshall Rd E10 75 D5
N17 33 B2
Marshall St W1 93 C1 239 B1
Marshalls Gr SE18 122 A2
Marshall's Pl SE16 263 D5
Marshall's Rd SM1 217 D4
Marshalsea Rd SE1 117 A4 252 B2
Marsham Cl BR7 188 D5
Marsham Ct SW1 259 D4
19 SW19 156 D3
Marsham St SW1 115 D2 259 D4
Marshbrook Cl SE3 143 D2
Marshfield St E14 120 A3
Marshgate Bsns Ctr E15 98 A5
Marshgate La E15 75 D1
Marshside Cl N9 18 C3
Marshwood Ho 10 NW6 91 C6
Marsland Cl SE17 261 D1
Marsom Ho N1 235 C3
Marston SE17 262 B4
Marston Ave
Chessington KT9 214 A2
Dagenham RM10 81 C5
Marston Cl NW6 70 A1
Dagenham RM10 81 C5
Marston Ct Sidcup DA14 189 D6
Walton-on-T KT12 194 C1
Marston Ho SW9 138 C3
Marston Rd TW11 175 B5
Marston Way SE19 183 A3
Marsworth Ave HA5 22 D2
Marsworth Cl UB4 85 A2
Marsworth Ho 8 E2 96 A6
Martaban Rd N16 73 D6
Martel Pl E8 73 D2
Martell Rd SE21 161 B1
Martello St E8 74 B1
Martello Terr E8 74 B1
Marten Rd E17 35 C1
Martens Ave DA7 147 D1
Martha Rd E15 76 C2
Martha St E1 96 C1
Martham Cl SE28 124 D6
Marthorne Cres HA3 24 B1
Martin Bowes Rd SE9 144 B2
Martin Cl N9 18 D3
Uxbridge UB10 82 A5
Martin Cres CR0 204 C1
Martin Ct 10 E14 120 A4
SW19 179 C3
Southall UB2 107 B4
Martin Dene DA6 169 B6
Martin Dr UB5 63 B3
Martin Gdns RM8 80 D4
Martin Gr SM4 201 C6
Martin Ho SE1 262 B5
SW8 270 A4
6 New Malden KT3 199 C5
Martin La EC4 252 D6
Martin Prim Sch N2 30 C1
Martin Rd RM8 80 D4
Martin Rise DA6 169 B6
Martin Way SW19,SW20, SM4 201 B6
Martinbridge Trad Est EN1 18 B6
Martindale SW14 155 A6
Martindale Ave 2 E16 121 A6
Martindale Ho 20 E14 119 D6
Martindale Rd SW12 159 B4
Hounslow TW4 129 A2
Martineau Cl KT10 212 B4
Martineau Ho SW1 259 A1
Martineau Mews N5 72 D4
Martineau Rd N5 72 D4
Martingale Cl TW16 194 A5
Martingales Cl TW10 153 D1
Martini Dr EN3 7 C6
Martins Cl BR4 224 B6
Martins Mount EN5 1 D1
Martin's Rd BR2 186 D1
Martins The SE26 184 B5
Wembley HA9 66 B5
Martins Wlk N10 31 A2
Martlesham N17 33 C1
Martlet Gr 5 UB5 84 D4
Martlett Ct WC2 240 B1
Martlett Lo NW3 69 D4
Martley Dr IG2 56 D4
Martley Ho SW8 269 B2
Martock Cl HA3 43 A5
Martock Ct 10 SE15 140 B4
Martock Gdns N11 31 A5
Marton Cl SE6 163 C1
Marton Rd 2 N16 73 C5
Martyn Ct HA8 26 B6
Martyn Ho SE2 146 D6
Martynside 22 NW9 27 D2
Marvel Ho 5 SE5 139 B5
Marvell Ave UB4 84 A2
Marvels Cl SE12 165 B2
Marvels La SE12 165 C1
Marvels Lane Prim Sch SE12 187 D6
Marville Ho SW18 158 B5
Marville Rd SW6 135 B5 264 C3
Marvin Ho 9 SE18 144 D6
Marvin St 3 E8 74 B2
Marwell Cl BR4 224 D6
Marwood Cl DA16 146 B2
Mary Adelaide Cl SW15 155 C1
SW15 177 C6
Mary Ann Bldgs SE8 141 C6
Mary Cl HA7 44 B5
Mary Datchelor Cl SE5 139 B4
Mary Dine Ct SW8 270 D3
Mary Gn NW8 91 D6
Mary Ho 6 SW9 138 B3
6 W6 112 C1
Mary James Ho 29 E2 96 A5
Mary Jones Ho 13 E14 119 C6
Mary Lawrenson Pl 1 SE3 143 A5
Mary Macarthur Ho
5 E2 96 D4
3 Belvedere DA17 125 C3
1 Dagenham RM10 81 C5
W14 264 A6
Mary McArthur Ho 12 N19 49 D2
Mary Peters Dr UB6 64 B3
Mary Pl W11 113 A6 244 A5
Mary Rose Cl TW12 173 C2
Mary Rose Mall E6 100 B2
Mary Secole Cl 21 E8 95 D6
Mary St 5 E16 98 D2
N1 95 A6 235 B5
Mary Terr NW1 232 A5
Mary Wharrie Ho 4 NW3 70 D1
Maryatt Ave HA2 63 D6
Marybank SE18 122 B2
Marygold Ho TW3 130 A4
Maryland Ct KT1 176 D1
Maryland Pk E15 76 C3
Maryland Point E15 76 C2
Maryland Prim Sch E15 76 C3
Maryland Rd E15 76 B3
N22 32 C4
W9 91 C3
South Norwood CR7 182 D2
Maryland Sq E15 76 C3
Maryland St E15 76 C3
Maryland Sta E15 76 C2
Maryland Way TW16 172 A1
Maryland Wlk N1 235 A6
Marylands Rd W9 91 D3
Marylebone Flyover NW1 92 C2 237 A3
Marylebone High St W1 93 A2 238 B4
Marylebone La W1 93 A1 238 B2
Marylebone Mews W1 238 C3
Marylebone Pas W1 239 B2
Marylebone Rd NW1 92 D2 237 D4
Marylebone St W1 93 A2 238 B3
Marylebone Sta NW1 92 D3 237 C5
Marylee Way SE11 116 B2 260 D3
Marymount International Sch KT2 177 A3
Maryon Gr SE7 122 A2
Maryon Mews NW3 70 C4
Maryon Rd SE7 122 A2
Maryrose Way N20 14 B3
Mary's Terr TW1 153 A4
Maryville DA16 145 D3
Masbro' Rd W14 112 D3
Mascalls Ct 13 SE7 143 C6
Mascalls Rd SE7 143 C6
Mascotte Rd 2 SW15 134 D1
Mascotts Cl NW2 68 B5
Masefield Ave
Borehamwood WD6 10 D6
Harrow HA7 24 D5
Southall UB1 107 C6
Masefield Cres N14 15 C5
Masefield Ct N5 73 B3
New Barnet EN5 2 A1
10 Surbiton KT6 197 D2
Masefield Gdns E6 100 C3
Masefield Ho 1 NW6 91 C4
Masefield La UB4 84 C3
Masefield Rd TW13 173 B6
Masefield View BR6 227 A5
Masefield Way TW19 148 B3
Masham Ho 6 DA18 124 D4
Mashie Rd W3 89 C1
Maskall Cl SW2 160 C3
Maskani Wlk SW16 181 C3
Maskell Rd SW17 158 A1
Maskelyne Cl SW11 136 C4 267 B2
Mason Bradbear Ct 5 N1 73 B2
Mason Cl E16 121 A6
SE16 118 A1
SW20 178 D2
Bexleyheath DA7 147 D2
Hampton TW12 173 B2
Mason Ct 4 SE19 183 D3
Wembley HA9 66 C6
Mason Ho 16 E9 74 C1
8 N11 31 C5
13 SE1 118 A2
Mason Rd Sutton SM1 217 D3
Woodford IG8 36 C6
Mason St SE17 117 B2 262 D4
Mason's Arms Mews W1 248 D6
Masons Ave HA3 42 D5
Mason's Ave EC2 242 C2
Croydon CR0 221 A5
Masons Hill SE18 122 D2
Bromley BR2 209 B5
Mason's Pl EC1 235 A2
Mitcham CR4 180 D2
Mason's Yd SW1 249 B4
Massey Cl N11 31 B5
Massey Ct 7 E6 99 C6
Massie Rd E8 74 A2
Massingberd Way SW17 181 B6
Massinger St SE1,SE17 263 A3
Massingham St E1 96 D3
Masson Ave HA4 62 C2
Mast Ct 17 SE16 119 A2
Mast House Terr E14 119 C2
Master Gunner's Pl 1 SE18 144 A4
Masterman Ho 1 SE5 139 B5
Masterman Rd E6 100 A4
Masters Ct HA4 61 C6
Masters Dr SE16 118 B1
Masters Lo 22 E1 96 C1
Master's St 14 E1 96 D2
Mastin Ho SW18 157 C3
Mastmaker Rd E14 119 C4
Maswell Park Cres TW3 152 A6
Maswell Park Rd TW3 130 A1
Matcham Rd E11 76 D5
Matching Ct 13 E3 97 C4
Matchless Dr SE18 144 C5
Matfield Cl BR2 209 A4
Matfield Rd DA17 147 C6
Matham Gr SE22 139 D1
Matham Rd KT8 196 B4
Mathart Ct E4 36 B4
Matheson Lang Ho SE1 251 A1
Matheson Rd W14 113 B2 254 C3
Mathews Ave E6 100 C5
Mathews Park Ave E15 76 D2
Mathieson Ct SE1 251 D1
Mathieson Ho 10 E4 20 C4
Matilda Cl SE19 183 B3
Matilda Ho E1 118 A5
Matilda St N1 94 B6 233 D6
Matlock Cl SE24 139 A1
Matlock Cres SM3 217 A4
Matlock Ct NW8 229 A4
7 SE5 139 B1
Matlock Gdns SM1,SM3 217 A4
Matlock Pl SM1,SM3 217 A4
Matlock Rd E10 54 A3
Matlock St E14 97 A1
Matlock Way KT3 177 B2
Maton Ho SW6 264 C4
Matson Ct IG8 36 C3
Matson Ho 16 E9 74 D2
9 SE16 118 B3
Matthew Cl W10 90 D3
Matthew Ct 4 E17 54 A6
Mitcham CR4 203 D4
Matthew Parker St SW1 249 D1
Matthews Ct N5 73 A4
Matthews Ho 3 E14 97 C2
Matthews Rd UB6 64 B3
Matthews St SW11 136 D3
Matthias Ct 12 TW10 154 A5
Matthias Ho 2 N16 73 C3
Matthias Rd N16 73 C3
Mattingly Way 4 SE15 139 D5
Mattison Rd N4 50 D3
Mattock La W5,W13 109 C5
Maud Cashmore Way SE18 122 B3
Maud Gdns E13 98 D5
Barking IG11 101 D5
Maud Rd E10 76 A5
E13 98 D5
Maud St E16 98 D2
Maude Ho 3 E2 96 A5
Maude Rd E17 53 A4
SE5 139 C4
Maude Terr E17 53 A5
Maudesville Cotts W7 108 C5
Maudlins Gn E1 118 A5
Maudslay Rd SE9 144 B2
Maudsley Ho TW8 110 A1
Maudsley Hospl The SE5 139 B3
Maugham Ct 5 W3 111 A3
Mauleverer Rd SW2 160 A6
Maundeby Wlk NW10 67 C2
Maunder Rd 4 W7 108 D5
Maunsel St SW1 115 D2 259 C4
Mauretania Bldg 11 E1 118 D6
Maurice Ave N22 32 D1
Maurice Browne Cl NW7 28 D4
Maurice Ct 3 TW8 131 D5
Maurice Ho 1 SW9 138 B3
Maurice St W12 90 B1
Maurice Wlk NW11 48 A5
Maurier Cl UB5 84 C6
Mauritius Rd SE10 120 C2
Maury Rd N16 74 A5
Mavelstone Cl BR1 188 A2
Mavelstone Rd BR1 188 A2
Maverton Rd E3 97 C6
Mavery Ct 4 BR1 186 D3
Mavis Ave KT19 215 C3
Mavis Cl KT19 215 C3
Mavis Ct 33 NW9 27 D1
Mavis Wlk 9 E6 100 A2
Mavor Ho N1 233 D5
Mawbey Ho SE1 263 D1
Mawbey Pl SE1 117 D1 263 D1
Mawbey Rd SE1 263 D1
Mawbey St SW8 270 A3
Mawdley Ho SE1 251 B1
Mawney Cl RM7 59 D6
Mawney Rd RM7 59 D6
Mawson Cl SW20 179 A1
Mawson Ho EC1 241 A4
Mawson La W4 133 D6
Maxden Ct SE15 140 A2
Maxey Gdns RM9 81 A4
Maxey Rd SE18 123 A2
Dagenham RM9 81 A4
Maxfield Cl N20 14 A4
Maxim Rd N21 16 C5
Maxted Pk HA1 42 C2
Maxted Rd SE15 139 D2
Maxwell Cl CR0 204 A1
Maxwell Ct SE21 162 A3
Maxwell Gdns BR6 227 D5
Maxwell Ho N22 32 B4
12 SE18 144 D6
Chislehurst BR7 188 D3
Maxwell Rd SW6 135 D5 265 D3
Ashford TW15 171 A4
Bexley DA16 146 A2
West Drayton UB7 104 B2
Maxwelton Ave NW7 27 B5
Maxwelton Cl NW7 27 B5
May Bate Ave KT2 175 D2
May Cl KT9 214 B2
May Ct 2 SW19 180 A2
May Gdns Elstree WD6 9 D5
Wembley HA0 87 C4
May Rd E4 35 C4
E13 99 A5
Twickenham TW2 152 C3
May St W14 254 C1
W14 254 D1
May Terr IG1 78 D4
May Tree Ho SE4 141 B2
May Wynne Ho E16 99 B1
Maya Rd N2 48 A5
Mayall Rd SE24 160 D6
Maybank Ave E18 37 B1
Maybank Ave continued
Wembley HA0 65 A3
Maybank Gdns HA5 40 A4
Maybank Rd E18 37 C2
Maybells Commercial Est IG11 102 D5
Mayberry Pl KT5 198 B2
Maybourne Cl SE26 184 B5
Maybourne Grange CR0 221 C6
Maybury Cl Enfield EN1 6 B5
Petts Wood BR5 210 D4
Maybury Ct W1 238 B3
Harrow HA1 42 B3
Penge BR3 185 B3
Maybury Gdns NW10 68 B2
Maybury Mews N6 49 C2
Maybury Rd E13 99 C3
Barking IG11 102 A5
Maybury St SW17 180 C5
Maychurch Cl HA7 25 D3
Maycroft
2 Coney Hall BR2 208 D1
Pinner Green HA5 22 B1
Maycross Ave SM4 201 C5
Mayday Gdns SE3 144 A3
Mayday Hospl CR7 204 D3
Mayday Rd CR0,CR7 204 D3
Maydeb Ct RM6 59 B3
Maydew Ho SE16 118 C2
Maydwell Ho 6 E14 97 C2
Mayefield Rd CR7 204 B4
Mayerne Rd SE9 165 D6
Mayesbrook Rd
Barking IG11 101 D6
Dagenham RM8,IG3 80 B5
Mayesford Rd RM6 58 C2
Mayespark Prim Sch IG3 80 A5
Mayeswood Rd SE12 187 C6
Mayfair Ave
Bexley DA16 146 D4
Dagenham RM6 58 D3
Ilford IG1 56 C1
New Malden KT4 200 A1
Twickenham TW2 152 A4
Mayfair Cl
Beckenham BR3 185 D2
Surbiton KT6 198 A1
Mayfair Ct 1 SW19 179 A3
1 Beckenham BR3 185 D2
7 South Croydon CR0 221 D6
Mayfair Gdns N17 33 B4
Woodford IG8 37 A3
Mayfair Pl W1 248 D4
Mayfair Terr N14 15 D4
Mayfield DA7 147 B2
Mayfield Ave N12 30 B6
N14 15 D2
W4 111 C2
W13 109 B4
Broom Hill BR6 211 D2
Harrow HA3 43 B4
Woodford IG8 37 A4
Mayfield Cl E8 73 D2
SE20 184 B2
SW4 159 D6
Ashford TW15 170 D4
Hillingdon UB10 82 D4
Hinchley Wood KT7 197 B1
Mayfield Cres N9 18 B5
Thornton Heath CR7 204 B5
Mayfield Ct SM2 218 A1
Mayfield Dr HA5 41 B5
Mayfield Gdns NW4 46 D3
W7 86 C2
Mayfield High Sch RM8 58 C1
Mayfield Ho 30 E2 96 B5
N16 51 C2
Mayfield Mans SW15 157 B6
Mayfield Prim Sch W7 86 B1
Mayfield Rd E4 20 B2
E8 73 D1
E13 98 D3
E17 35 A1
N8 50 B3
SW19 179 B2
W3 110 D6
W12 111 C4
Bromley BR1 210 A4
Dagenham RM8 58 C1
Enfield EN3 6 D3
South Croydon CR2 221 B1
Sutton SM2 218 B2
Mayfield Villas DA14 190 C4
Mayfields HA9 66 C6
Mayfields Cl HA9 66 C6
Mayflower Cl SE16 118 D2
Ruislip HA4 39 A3
Mayflower Ho 2 IG11 101 B6
Mayflower JMI Sch E14 97 D1
Mayflower Lo N3 47 B6
N10 31 A2
Mayflower Rd SW9 138 A2
Mayflower St 1 SE16 118 C4
Mayfly Cl HA5 40 C2
Mayfly Gdns 12 UB5 84 D4
Mayford NW1 232 B4
Mayford Cl SW12 158 D4
Penge BR3 206 D6
Mayford Rd SW12 159 A4
Maygood Ho N1 234 A4
Maygood St N1 94 C5 234 A4
Maygrove Rd NW6 69 B2
Mayhew Cl E4 19 C1

Mayhew Ct 2 SE5 139 B1
Mayhill Rd SE7 143 B6
Barnet EN5 13 A5
Mayland Mans 4 IG11 78 D1
Maylands Dr DA14 168 D1
Maylands Ho SW3 257 B3
Maylands Rd WD1 22 C6
Maynard Cl N15 51 C4
SW6 135 D5 265 D3
Maynard Ct EN3 7 C5
Maynard Ho E1 97 A4
SE18 123 A2
Maynard Rd E17 54 A4
Maynards Quay E1 118 C6
Maynooth Gdns CR4 202 D2
Mayo Ct W13 109 B3
Mayo Rd NW10 67 C2
Thornton Heath CR0 205 B4
Walton-on-T KT12 194 A2
Mayola Rd E5 74 C4
Mayow Rd SE23,SE26 184 D6
Mayplace Cl DA7 147 D2
Mayplace La SE18 144 D6
Mayplace Rd W DA7 147 C1
Mayroyd Ave KT6 214 C6
May's Buildings Mews
SE10 142 B5
Mays Ct WC2 250 A5
May's Ct SE10 142 B5
May's Hill Rd BR2 208 C6
Mays La EN5 12 C5
Mays Rd TW11,TW12 174 B5
Maysoule Rd SW11 136 B1
Mayston Mews 3 SE10 121 A1
Maythorne Cotts SE13 164 B5
Mayton St N7 72 B5
Maytree Cl HA8 11 A1
Maytree Ct Mitcham CR4 203 A6
Northolt UB5 85 A4
Maytree La HA7 24 D3
Maytree Wlk SW2 160 C2
Mayville Jun & Inf Schs
E11 76 C6
Mayville Rd E11 76 C6
Ilford IG1 78 D3
Mayward Ho 7 SE5 139 C4
Maywood Cl BR3 185 D3
Maze Hill SE10,SE3 142 C6
Maze Hill Ho 8 SE10 142 B6
Maze Hill Sch SE10 142 C6
Maze Hill Specl Sch
SE10 142 A5
Maze Hill Sta SE10 142 C6
Maze Rd TW9 132 C5
Mazenod Ave NW6 69 C1
Mc Call Cres SE7 122 A1
Mcadam Dr EN2 4 D3
McAuley Cl SE1 116 C3 261 A6
SE9 166 C6
McBride Ho 5 E3 97 B5
McCall Cl SW4 138 A3
McCall Ho N7 72 A4
Mccarthy Ct SW11 267 B1
McCarthy Rd TW13 172 D5
McCoid Way SE1 252 A1
Mcconnell Ho SW8 269 C1
McCormick Ho 9 SW2 160 C3
McCrone Mews 3 NW3 70 B2
McCullum Rd E3 97 B6
McDermott Cl SW11 136 C2
McDermott Rd SE15 140 A2
McDonald Ho 1 KT2 176 B3
McDonough Cl KT9 214 A4
McDougall Ct TW9 132 C3
McDowall Cl E16 98 D2
McDowall Rd SE5 139 A4
McEntee Ave E17 35 A2
McEntee Sch The E17 35 B2
McEwan Way E15 98 B6
McGlashon Ho 10 E1 96 A3
McGrath Rd E15 76 D2
McGregor Ct 8 N1 95 C4
McGregor Rd W11 91 B2
Mcguffie Ct E17 53 B6
McIndoe Ct N1 235 C6
McIntosh Cl SM6 220 A1
McIntosh Ho 11 SE16 118 C2
McIntyre Ct 19 SW4 138 A3
McKay Rd SW20 178 C4
McKay Trad Est W10 91 A3
McKellar Cl WD2 8 A2
McKenna Ho 3 E3 97 B5
McKerrell Rd SE15 140 A4
McKiernan Ct 2 SW11 136 C3
McKinlay Ct BR3 185 B1
McKinnon Wood Ho 23
E2 96 A4
Mcleod Ct SE21 162 A3
McLeod Ho 3 SE23 162 C2
McLeod Rd SE2 124 B2
McLeod's Mews
SW7 113 D2 255 D4
McManus Ho 3 SW11 136 B2
McMillan Ct 2 SE6 154 D3
Mcmillan Ho SE4 141 A2
McMillan St SE8 141 C6
Mcmorran Ho N7 72 A4
McNair Rd UB2 107 D3
Mcneil Rd SE5 139 C3
McNicol Dr NW10 89 A5
McRae La CR4 202 D2
Mead Cl 3 NW1 71 A1
Harrow HA3 24 B2
Mead Cres E4 36 A6
Carshalton SM1 218 C4
Mead Ct NW9 45 B4
Mead Cty Inf Sch The
KT19 215 D4
Mead Field HA2 63 B5
Mead Gr RM6 58 D6
Mead Ho W11 244 C4
Mead House La UB4 83 B3
Mead Lo W4 111 B4
Mead Path SW17 180 B4
Mead Pl E9 74 C2
Thornton Heath CR0 205 A1
Mead Plat NW10 67 A2
Mead Rd
Chislehurst West BR7 189 A4
Edgware HA8 26 C4
Richmond TW10 153 C1
Mead Road Inf Sch
BR7 189 A4
Mead Row SE1 116 C3 261 A6
Mead The N2 30 A1
W13 87 B2
Beckenham BR3 186 A2
Ickenham UB10 60 C6
Wallington SM6 219 D2
West Wickham BR4 208 B1
Mead Way Croydon CR0 223 A6
Hayes BR2 209 A3
Hayes BR2,BR4 208 D3
Ilford IG3 79 C4
Ruislip HA4 39 B3
Meadcroft Ho 4 KT3 199 C2
Meadcroft Rd SE17 138 D6
Meade Cl W4 132 C6
Meader Ct SE14 140 D5
Meadfield HA8 10 D2
Meadfield Gn HA8 10 D2
Meadfoot Rd SW16 181 C2
Meadhurst Pk TW16 171 C4
Meadlands Dr TW10 153 D2
Meadlands Prim Sch
TW10 175 C6
Meadow Ave CR0 206 D3
Meadow Bank 7 SW15 157 B6
Meadow Cl E4 19 D3
E9 75 B3
SE6 185 C5
SW20 200 C5
Barnet EN5 13 B5
Bexley DA6 169 B6
Chislehurst West BR7 188 D5
Enfield EN3 7 A5
High Barnet EN5 1 C1
Hinchley Wood KT10 212 D5
Northolt UB5 85 C5
Richmond TW10 154 A3
Ruislip HA4 39 D3
Sutton SM1 218 A6
TW4 151 C5
Meadow Croft BR1 210 B6
Meadow Dr N10 49 B6
NW4 28 C1
Meadow Garth NW10 67 B2
Meadow Gdns HA8 27 A4
Meadow Hill KT3 199 C3
Meadow Mews SW8 270 C5
Meadow Pl
SW8 138 A5 270 B4
W4 133 C5
Meadow Rd
SW8 138 B5 270 C4
SW19 180 A3
Ashford TW15 171 B5
Barking IG11 80 A1
Bromley BR2 186 C1
Carshalton SM1 218 C3
Claygate KT10 212 C2
Dagenham RM9 81 B2
Feltham TW13 151 A2
Loughton IG10 21 D6
Pinner HA5 41 A5
Southall UB1 107 B6
Meadow Row SE1 262 A5
Meadow Specl Sch UB8 82 A2
Meadow Stile CR0 221 A5
Meadow The BR7 189 A4
Meadow View
Harrow HA1 42 C1
Sidcup DA15 168 B4
Meadow View Rd
Hayes UB4 83 B3
Thornton Heath CR7 204 D4
Meadow Way NW9 45 B4
Chessington KT9 214 A3
Locksbottom BR6 226 C5
Ruislip HA4 40 B3
Wembley HA9 65 D4
Meadow Way The HA3 24 C2
Meadow Waye TW5 129 A5
Meadow Wlk E18 55 A5
Dagenham RM9 81 B2
Ewell KT17 215 D1
Hackbridge SM6 219 B5
West Ewell KT17,KT19 215 D1
Meadow Wood Sch WD2 8 A6
Meadowbank N21 16 B5
NW3 70 D1
SE3 142 D2
Surbiton KT5 198 B3
Meadowbank Cl SW6 134 C5
Meadowbank Gdns
TW5 128 B4
Meadowbank Rd NW9 45 B2
Meadowbanks EN5 12 A6
Meadowcourt Rd SE3 142 D1
Meadowcroft 9 W4 110 C1
Meadowcroft Rd N13 16 C2
Meadowgate Sch SE4 141 A2
Meadows Cl E10 75 C6
Meadows Ct DA14 190 B4
Meadows End TW16 172 A2
Meadowside SE9 143 C1
Twickenham TW1 153 D4
Meadowsweet Cl 3 E16 99 D2
West Barnes KT3 200 C5
Meadowview TW17 193 A2
Meadowview Rd SE6 185 C5
Bexley DA5 169 B5
West Ewell KT19 215 C1
Meads Ct E15 76 D2
Meads La IG3 57 D2
Meads Rd N22 32 D1
Enfield EN3 7 A4
Meads The Burnt Oak HA8 27 B4
Cheam SM3 217 A5
Uxbridge UB8 82 A3
Meadside Cl BR3 185 A2
Meadvale Rd W5 87 C3
Croydon CR0 206 A3
Meadway N14 16 A2
NW11 47 D3
SW20 200 C5
Ashford TW15 170 C6
Barnet EN5 1 C1
Beckenham BR3 186 A2
Enfield EN3 6 D6
Tolworth KT5 199 A1
Twickenham TW2 152 B3
Woodford IG8 37 C5
KT10 212 A1
Meadway Cl NW11 47 D3
Harrow HA5 23 D4
Meadway Ct NW11 47 D3
W5 88 B2
Dagenham RM8 81 B6
Meadway Gate NW11 47 C3
Meadway Gdns HA4 39 B3
Meadway The SE3 142 B3
Buckhurst Hill IG9 21 D3
Meaford Way SE20 184 B3
Meakin Est SE1 263 A6
Meakin Ho N7 72 B3
Meanley Rd E12 78 A3
Meard St W1 239 C1
Meath Ho SE24 160 D5
Meath Rd E15 98 D5
Ilford IG1 79 A5
Meath St SW11 137 B4 268 C2
Mecklenburgh Pl WC1 240 C6
Mecklenburgh Sq
WC1 94 B3 240 C6
Medburn St NW1 232 C4
Medcalf Rd EN3 7 B6
Medcroft Gdns SW14 133 A1
Mede Ho BR1 187 B5
Medebourne Cl SE3 143 A2
Medesenge Way N13 32 D4
Medfield St SW15 156 B4
Medhurst Cl 17 E3 97 A5
Median Rd E5 74 C3
Medical Coll of St
Bartholomew's Hospl The
EC1 94 D3 241 D5
Medina Ave KT10 212 C5
Medina Ct N7 72 C5
Medina Gr N7 72 C5
Medina Ho SE15 140 C1
Medina Rd N7 72 C5
Medland Cl CR4 203 A1
Medlar Cl 1 UB5 84 D5
Medlar Ho 3 DA15 168 A1
Medlar St SE5 139 A4
Medley Rd NW6 69 C2
Medora Rd SW2 160 B4
Medresco Ho NW3 70 B3
Medusa Rd SE6,SE13 163 D5
Medway Bldgs E3 97 A5
Medway Cl Croydon CR0 206 C3
Ilford IG1 79 A3
Medway Ct SE25 205 C4
WC1 233 A1
Medway Dr UB6 86 D5
Medway Gdns HA0 65 A4
Medway Ho N16 73 B4
NW8 237 A4
SE1 252 D1
6 Kingston u T KT2 175 D2
Medway Par 1 UB6 86 D5
Medway Rd E3 97 A5
Medway St
SW1 115 D3 259 D5
Medwin St SW4 138 B1
Meecham Ct 1 SW11 136 C3
Meerbrook Rd SE3,SE9 143 C2
Meeson Rd E15 76 D1
Meeson St E5 75 A4
Meeting House Alley 7
E1 118 B5
Meeting House La SE15 140 B5
Mehetabel Rd E9 74 C3
Meister Cl IG1 57 B1
Melanda Cl BR7 188 B5
Melanie Cl DA7 147 A4
Melaris Mews 1 NW6 69 C3
Melba Ct E8 73 D1
Melbourne Ave N13 32 B4
W13 109 A5
Harrow HA2,HA5 41 D6
Melbourne Cl
Broom Hill BR6 211 C2
Ickenham UB10 60 C4
Wallington SM6 219 C3
Melbourne Ct E5 75 A4
N10 31 B3
SE20 184 A3
W9 236 B6
Twickenham TW2 152 B3
Melbourne Gdns RM6 59 A4
Melbourne Gr SE22 139 D1
Melbourne Ho W8 245 A3
Hayes UB4 84 C3
Melbourne Mews SE6 164 A4
SW9 138 C4
Melbourne Pl WC2 240 D1
Melbourne Rd E6 100 B5
E10 53 D2
E17 53 A5
SW19 179 C2
Ilford IG1 56 D1
Teddington TW11 175 C4
Wallington SM6 219 C3
Melbourne Sq 21 SW9 138 C4
Melbourne Way EN1 17 D5
Melbrook Ho 11 SE22 139 C2
Melbury Ave UB2 107 D3
Melbury Cl
Chislehurst West BR7 188 B4
Claygate KT10 213 B2
Melbury Ct W8 113 B3 254 D6
Melbury Dr SE5 139 C5
Melbury Gdns SW20 178 B2
Melbury Ho SW8 270 C4
Twickenham TW2 152 B2
Melbury Rd
W14 113 B3 254 D6
Harrow HA3 44 B4
Melchester 3 W11 91 B1
Melchester Ho 1 N19 71 D5
Melcombe Ct NW1 237 C4
Melcombe Gdns HA3 44 B3
Melcombe Ho SW8 270 C3
Melcombe Pl NW1 237 C4
Melcombe Prim Sch
W6 134 D6
Melcombe St
NW1 92 D3 237 D5
Meldex Cl NW7 28 C4
Meldon Cl SW6 265 D2
Meldone KT3 199 B1
Meldone Cl KT5 198 D3
Meldrum Rd IG3 80 A6
Melfield Gdns SE6 186 A5
Melfont Ave CR7 204 D6
Melford Ave IG11 79 D2
Melford Cl KT9 214 B3
Melford Ct E5 74 B5
SE22 162 A4
2 Sutton SM2 218 A1
Melford Rd E6 100 B4
E11 76 C6
E17 53 B5
SE21,SE22 162 A3
Ilford IG1 79 B6
Melfort Rd CR7 204 D6
Melgund Rd N5 72 C3
Melina Cl UB3 83 B2
Melina Ct NW8 229 C1
SW15 134 A2
Melina Pl NW8 92 B4 229 C1
Melina Rd W12 112 B4
Melior Ct N6 49 C3
Melior Pl SE1 253 A2
Melior St SE1 117 C4 253 A2
Meliot Rd SE6 164 B2
Melisa Ct N6 49 D2
Mell St 6 SE10 120 C1
Meller Cl SM6 220 A5
Melling Dr EN1 6 A4
Melling St SE18 145 C6
Mellington Ct 2 N16 74 A5
Mellish Cl IG11 101 D6
Mellish Ct KT6 198 A3
Mellish Flats E10 53 C2
Mellish Gdns IG8 37 A5
Mellish Ho 12 E1 96 B1
Mellish Ind Est E16 121 D3
Mellish St E14 119 C3
Mellison Rd SW17 180 C5
Mellitus St W12 89 D1
Mellor Cl KT12 195 B2
Mellor Ct 2 SW19 180 A3
Mellor Ho 2 SE21 183 C6
Mellow La E UB4 83 A3
Mellow La W UB10 83 A4
Mellow Lane Sch UB4 83 A3
Mellows Rd
Redbridge IG5 56 B6
Wallington SM6 219 D3
Mells Cres SE9 188 B6
Melody Rd SW18 158 A6
Melon Pl W8 245 B2
Melon Rd E11 76 C5
SE15 140 A4
Melrose Ave N22 32 D2
NW2 68 C3
SW16 204 C6
SW19 157 C1
Borehamwood WD6 10 D6
Greenford UB6 85 D5
Mitcham CR4 181 B3
Twickenham TW2 151 D4
Melrose Cl SE12 165 B3
Greenford UB6 85 D5
Hayes UB4 84 A2
Melrose Cres BR6 227 B3
Melrose Ct SW18 157 B5
5 W13 109 A5
Melrose Dr UB1 107 C5
Melrose Gdns W6 112 C3
Edgware HA8 26 D1
Kingston u T KT3 199 B6
Melrose Ho NW6 91 C4
SW1 258 D2
Melrose Rd 1 SW13 133 D3
SW18 157 B5
Melrose Rd *continued*
SW19 179 C2
Pinner HA5 41 B5
Melrose Sch CR4 202 C6
Melrose Terr W6 112 C3
Melrose Tudor SM6 220 A3
Melsa Rd SM4 202 A3
Melthorne Dr HA4 62 C5
Melthorpe Gdns SE3 144 A4
Melton Cl HA4 40 C1
Melton Ct SW7 256 D3
11 Croydon CR0 221 D6
Sutton SM2 218 A1
1 Twickenham TW1 153 B4
Melton Ho E5 74 A6
Melton St NW1 93 D4 232 C1
Melville Ave SW20 178 A3
Greenford UB6 64 D3
South Croydon CR2 221 D3
Melville Cl UB10 61 B5
Melville Court Flats
W12 112 B4
Melville Ct SE8 119 A2
4 W4 110 C1
Melville Gdns N13 32 D5
Melville Ho SE10 142 A4
New Barnet EN5 14 B5
Melville Pl 4 N1 73 A1
Melville Rd E17 53 B6
NW10 67 B1
SW13 134 A4
Sidcup DA14 168 C2
Melville Villas Rd W3 111 B5
Melvin Ct 11 TW9 132 C4
Melvin Rd SE20 184 C2
Melwood Ho 22 E1 96 B1
Melyn Cl N7 71 C4
Memel Ct EC1 242 A5
Memel St EC1 242 A5
Memess Path 4 SE18 144 C6
Memorial Ave E15 98 C4
Memorial Cl TW5 129 B6
Memorial Hospl SE18 144 C3
Mendham Ho SE1 263 A6
Mendip Cl SE26 184 C6
Harlington UB3 127 B5
North Cheam KT4 216 C6
Mendip Ct SE14 140 C6
12 SW11 136 A2
Mendip Dr NW2,NW11 69 A6
Mendip Ho 2 N4 51 B2
Mendip Hos 12 E2 96 C4
Mendip Rd SW11 136 A2
Bushey WD2 8 A5
Ilford IG2 57 C4
Mendora Rd
SW6 135 B5 264 C4
Menelik Rd NW2 69 B4
Menlo Gdns SE19 183 B3
Mennie Ho 5 SE18 144 B4
Menora Prim Sch HA8 27 A3
Menorah Foundation Sch
NW2 69 A5
Menorah Gram Sch
NW11 47 A2
Menorah Prim Sch
NW11 47 A2
Menotti St 5 E2 96 A3
Menteath Ho 5 E14 97 C1
Mentmore Cl HA3 43 C3
Mentmore Terr E8 74 B1
Mentone Ct SW8 270 B2
Meon Ct TW7 130 C3
Meon Rd W3 111 A4
Meopham Rd CR4,SW16 181 C2
Mepham Cres HA3 24 A3
Mepham Gdns HA3 24 A3
Mepham St SE1 116 C5 251 A3
Mera Dr DA7 147 D1
Merantum Way SW19 180 A2
Merbury Cl SE13 164 B6
Merbury Rd SE28 123 C4
Merbury St SE18 122 D3
Mercator Pl E14 119 C1
Mercator Rd SE13 142 B1
Mercer Cl KT7 196 D2
Mercer Pl HA5 22 C1
Mercer St WC2 94 A1 240 A1
Merceron Ho 3 E2 96 C4
Merceron St E1 96 B3
Mercers Cl SE10 120 D2
Mercer's Cotts 10 E3 97 A1
Mercers Pl W6 112 D2
Mercers Rd N19 71 D5
Merchant St E3 97 B4
Merchant Taylors'
Almshouses SE13 142 C1
Merchant Taylors Hall
EC3 242 D1
Merchants Lo 5 E17 53 C5
Merchiston Rd SE6 164 B2
Merchland Rd SE9 167 A3
Merchon Ho N7 71 C4
Mercia Gr SE13 142 A1
Mercia Ho 9 SE5 139 A3
Mercier Rd SW15 157 A6
Mercury 23 NW9 27 D2
Mercury Ct 3 E14 119 C2
8 SW9 138 C4
Mercury Ctr TW14 150 B6
Mercury Ho TW8 109 D1
Mercury Rd TW8 109 C1
Mercury Way SE14 140 D6
Mercy Terr SE13 163 D6
Mere Cl SW15,SW19 156 D4
Orpington BR6 226 D6
Mere End CR0 206 D2
Mere Rd TW17 192 D3
Merebank La CR0,SM6 220 B3
Meredith Ave NW2 68 C3
Meredith Cl HA5 22 D3
Meredith Ho 17 N16 73 C3
Meredith Mews SE4 141 B1
Meredith St E13 99 A4
EC1 234 C1
Meredyth Rd SW13 134 A3
Mereside BR6 226 C6
Meretone Cl SE4 141 A1
Meretune Ct SM4 201 B6
Merevale Cres SM4 202 A3
Mereway Industry TW2 152 C3
Mereway Rd TW2 152 C3
Merewood Cl 1 BR1 188 C1
Mereworth Cl BR2 208 D4
Mereworth Dr SE18 145 A5
Mereworth Ho 3 SE15 140 C6
Merganser Ct 17 SE8 141 B6
Meridan Ct SE13 142 B1
Meriden Cl BR1 187 D3
Meriden Ct SW3 257 A1
Meriden Ho 26 N1 95 C6
3 Chipping Barnet EN5 1 A1
Meridian Building SE10 142 B5
Meridian Ct 4 SE6 164 D3
Croydon CR0 220 C4
Meridian Ho SE10 120 C2
Meridian Pl E14 120 A4
Meridian Prim Sch
SE10 142 B6
Meridian Rd SE7 143 D5
Meridian Trad Est SE7 121 B2
Meridian Way N9,N18 18 D1
Enfield EN3 19 A5
Meridian Wlk N17 33 C4
Merifield Rd SE9 143 C1
Merino Cl E11 55 C5
Merino Pl DA15 168 A6
Merioneth Ct 7 W7 86 D2
Merivale Rd SW15 135 A1
Harrow HA1 42 A2
Merlewood Dr BR7 188 B2
Merley Ct NW9 45 A1
Merlin 26 NW9 27 D2
Merlin Cl Mitcham CR4 202 C6
4 Northolt UB5 84 C4
South Croydon CR0 221 C4
Wallington SM6 220 B2
Merlin Cres HA8 26 B2
Merlin Ct N22 32 C2
Beckenham BR2 208 D5
Ruislip HA4 61 B6
Merlin Gdns BR1 165 A1
Merlin Gr BR3 207 C4
Merlin Ho NW3 69 D4
7 W4 111 B1
Enfield EN3 18 D6
Merlin Prim Sch BR1 165 A1
Merlin Rd E12 77 D6
Bexley DA16 146 A1
Merlin Rd N DA16 146 A1
Merlin St EC1 94 C4 234 A1
Merling Cl KT9 213 D3
Merlins Ave HA2 63 B5
Mermaid Ct N4 50 C3
SE1 117 B4 252 C2
SE16 119 B5
Mermaid Ho 8 E14 120 A6
Mermaid Twr 22 SE8 141 B6
Meroe Ct N16 73 C6
Merredene St SW2 160 B5
Merriam Cl E4 36 A5
Merrick Rd UB2 107 B4
Merrick Sq SE1 117 B3 262 C6
Merricks Ct 5 SW14 132 D1
Merridale SE12 164 D6
Merridene N21 16 D5
Merrielands Cres RM9 103 B5
Merrielands Ret Pk
RM9 103 B5
Merrilands Rd KT4 200 C1
Merrilees Rd DA15 167 C4
Merrilyn Cl KT10 213 A2
Merriman Rd SE3 143 C4
Merrington Rd SW6 265 B6
Merrion Ave HA7 25 D5
Merritt Gdns KT9 213 C2
Merritt Rd SE4 163 B6
Merrivale N14 15 D6
NW1 232 B5
Merrivale Ave IG4 55 D5
Merrow Ct CR4 180 B1
Merrow St SE17 117 B1 262 C1
Merrow Way CR0 224 A2
Merrow Wlk SE17 262 D2
Merry Fiddlers RM8 81 B6
Merry Hill Rd WD2 8 A3
Merry Hill Sch WD2 8 A4
Merrydown Way BR7 188 B2
Merryfield SE3 142 D3
Merryfield Gdns HA7 25 C5
Merryfield Ho SE12 165 C1
Merryhill Cl E4 19 D4
Merryhills Ct N14 15 C6
Merryhills Dr EN2 4 A1
Merryhills Prim Sch EN2 4 B1
Merryweather Ct 1
KT3 199 C4
Mersea Ho IG11 78 D2
Mersey Ct 10 KT2 175 D2
Mersey Ho 10 N7 72 C3
Mersey Rd E17 53 B6
Mersey Wlk UB5 85 C5
Mersham Dr NW9 44 D4
Mersham Pl SE20 184 B2
South Norwood CR7 183 B1
Mersham Rd CR7 183 B1

Merstone Ho SW18 ....157 D5
Merten Rd RM6 ....59 A2
Merthyr Terr SW13 ....134 B6
Merton Abbey Mills
SW18 ....157 D3
SW19 ....180 A2
Merton Abbey Prim Sch
SW19 ....179 D2
Merton Ave W4 ....111 D2
Hillingdon UB10 ....60 D1
Northolt UB5 ....64 A3
Merton Court Sch
DA14 ....190 C6
Merton Ct DA16 ....146 B3
Merton Gdns BR5 ....210 D4
Merton Hall Gdns
SW20 ....179 A2
Merton Hall Rd SW19 ..179 A2
Merton High St SW19 .180 A3
Merton Ho SW18 ....157 C3
Merton Ind Pk SW19 ..180 A2
Merton La N6 ....70 D6
Merton Lo EN5 ....14 A6
Merton Mans SW20 ..178 D1
Merton Park Fst Sch
SW19 ....179 C1
Merton Park Par SW19 179 B2
Merton Park Sta SW19 179 C2
Merton Pl 9 SW19 ....180 A3
Merton Rd E17 ....54 A3
SE25 ....206 A4
SW18 ....157 C4
SW19 ....179 D3
Barking IG11 ....79 D1
Enfield EN2 ....5 B5
Harrow HA2 ....42 A1
Ilford IG3 ....57 D2
Merton Rise NW3 ....70 C1
Merton Road Ind Est
SW18 ....157 C4
Merton Tech Coll SM4 .201 B4
Merton Tech Coll (Annexe)
SW19 ....179 C2
Merton Way
East Molesey KT8 ....196 A6
Hillingdon UB10 ....60 D1
Merttins Rd SE15 ....162 D6
Meru Cl NW5 ....71 A3
Mervan Rd SW2 ....138 C1
Mervyn Ave BR7,SE9 ...167 A2
Mervyn Rd W13 ....109 A3
Lower Halliford TW17 ...193 A2
Mervyn Stockwood Ho 1
SE9 ....167 A2
Messaline Ave W3 ....89 A1
Messent Rd SE9 ....165 D6
Messeter Pl SE9 ....166 C5
Messina Ave NW6 ....69 C1
Messiter Ho N1 ....233 D5
Metcalf Rd TW15 ....170 D5
Metcalfe Ho 28 SW8 ...137 D3
Metcalfe Wlk 2 TW13 173 A6
Meteor St SW11 ....137 A1
Meteor Way SM6 ....220 A1
Metford Cres EN3 ....7 C5
Metherell Ho N21 ....17 B5
Methering Way NW9 ....27 C2
Methley Ho 8 N7 ....72 B6
Methley St SE11 116 C1 261 B1
Methodist Central Hall
SW1 ....115 D4 249 D1
Methuen Cl HA8 ....26 C3
Methuen Pk N10 ....49 B6
Methuen Rd
Belvedere DA17 ....125 D2
Bexley DA6 ....147 B1
Edgware HA8 ....26 C3
Methwold Rd W10 ....90 D2
Metro Bsns Ctr The
SE26 ....185 B5
Metro Ctr Hayes UB4 ...106 C6
West Barnes SM4 ....200 D2
Metro Ind Ctr TW7 ....130 C3
Metropolitan Benefit
Societies Almshouses 3
N1 ....73 C2
Metropoliton Police Cadet
Training Sch NW9 ....45 C6
Meudon Ct KT6 ....197 D4
Mews Pl IG8 ....37 A6
Mews St E1 ....118 A5
Mews The N8 ....50 C5
SW16 ....182 B2
Beckenham BR3 ....185 C2
Redbridge IG4 ....55 D4
Mexborough NW1 ....232 A5
Mexfield Rd SW15 ....157 B6
Meyer Gn EN1 ....6 A5
Meyer Ho 1 SW12 ....159 B4
Meymott St SE1 116 D5 251 C3
Meynell Cres E9 ....74 D1
Meynell Gdns E9 ....74 D1
Meynell Rd E9 ....74 D1
Meyrick Ho 8 E14 ....97 C2
Meyrick Rd NW10 ....68 A2
SW11 ....136 C2
Miah Terr 10 E1 ....118 A5
Miall Wlk SE26 ....185 A6
Micawber Ave UB8 ....82 C3
Micawber Ct N1 ....235 B2
Micawber Ho 24 SE16 ...118 A4
Micawber St N1 .95 A4 235 B2
Michael Cliffe Ho EC1 .234 B1
Michael Faraday Ho
SE17 ....262 D1
Michael Faraday Prim Sch
SE17 ....117 B1 262 D1
Michael Gaynor Cl W7 108 D5
Michael Marshall Ho 2
SE9 ....167 A2
Michael Rd E11 ....54 D1
SE25 ....205 C6
SW6 ....135 D4 265 D2
Michaelmas Cl SW20 ..200 C6
Michaels Cl SE13 ....142 C1
Michaelson Ho 4 SE21 183 C6
Michelangelo Ct 14
SE16 ....118 B1
Micheldever Rd SE12 ..164 D5
Michelham Gdns TW1 .152 D1
Michelle Ct N12 ....30 A5
W3 ....111 B6
Michels Almshouses 11
TW10 ....154 A6
Michel's Row 2 TW9 ..132 A1
Michelsdale Dr 3 TW9 132 A1
Michelson Ho SE11 ....260 D3
Michigan Ave E12 ....78 B4
Michigan Ho E14 ....119 C3
Michleham Down N12 ..29 B6
Mickledore NW1 ....232 B3
Mickleham Cl BR5 ....190 A1
Mickleham Gdns SM3 .217 A2
Mickleham Rd BR5 ....190 A1
Mickleham Way CR0 ...224 B1
Micklethwaite Rd
SW6 ....135 C6 265 B5
Mickleton Ho 30 W2 ....91 C2
Midas Bsns Ctr RM10 ...81 D4
Midcroft HA4 ....39 C1
Middle Dene NW7 ....11 B1
Middle Green Cl 3 KT5 198 B3
Middle La N8 ....50 A4
Teddington TW11 ....174 D4
Middle Lane Mews N8 ..50 A4
Middle Mill KT5 ....198 B6
Middle Park Ave SE9 ..165 D4
Middle Park Prim Sch
SE9 ....165 D4
Middle Rd 12 E13 ....99 A5
N10 ....30 C2
SW16 ....181 D1
East Barnet EN4 ....14 C5
Harrow HA2 ....42 B1
Middle Row W10 ....91 A3
Middle Row Prim Sch
W10 ....91 A3
Middle St EC1 ....242 A4
Croydon CR0 ....221 A5
Middle Temple
EC4 ....116 C6 251 A6
Middle Temple La
EC4 ....116 C6 251 A6
Middle Way SW16 ....181 D1
Hayes UB4 ....84 C3
Middle Way The HA3 ....24 D1
Middlefield NW8 92 B6 229 C6
Middlefield Gdns IG2 ...56 D3
Middlefielde W13 ....87 B2
Middleham Gdns N18 ...34 A4
Middleham Rd N18 ....34 A4
Middlesborough Rd N18 34 A4
Middlesex Bsns Ctr
UB2 ....107 B4
Middlesex Ct 5 W4 ...111 D2
Harrow HA1 ....42 D4
Middlesex Cty Cricket Sch
N3 ....29 D1
Middlesex Ho 6 SE20 .184 C3
Middlesex Hospl
W1 ....93 C2 239 B3
Middlesex Hospl Annexe
W1 ....239 B4
Middlesex Pas EC1 ....241 D3
Middlesex Pl 13 E9 ....74 C2
Middlesex Rd CR4 ....204 A4
Middlesex St E1 .95 D2 243 C2
Middlesex Univ N17 ....33 D4
NW4 ....46 B5
Middlesex Univ (Bounds
Green) N11 ....31 C4
Middlesex Univ (Cat Hill)
EN4 ....15 A6
Middlesex Univ (Enfield
Campus) EN3 ....18 C6
Middlesex Univ Trent Park
EN4 ....3 C3
Middleton Ave E4 ....19 B1
Foots Cray DA14 ....190 C5
Greenford UB5 ....86 B5
Middleton Bldgs W1 ..239 A3
Middleton Cl E4 ....19 B1
Middleton Ct BR1 ....187 B3
Middleton Dr SE16 ....118 D4
Pinner HA5 ....40 A6
Middleton Gdns IG2 ....56 D3
Middleton Gr N7 ....72 A3
Middleton Ho E8 ....73 D1
SE1 ....262 C5
Middleton Mews N7 ....72 A3
N22 ....32 A3
Middleton Rd E8 ....73 D1
NW11 ....47 C2
Carshalton CR4,SM5 ...202 B2
Hayes UB3 ....83 B2
Middleton St E2 ....96 B4
Middleton Way SE13 ...142 B1
Middleway NW11 ....47 D4
Midfield Prim Sch BR5 190 A3
Midfield Way BR5 ....190 B2
Midford Ho 1 NW4 ....46 D5
Midford Pl W1 ....239 B5
Midholm NW11 ....47 D5
Wembley HA9 ....44 C1
Midholm Cl NW11 ....47 D5
Midholm Rd CR0 ....223 A6
Midhope Ho WC1 ....233 B1
Midhope St WC1 ....233 B1
Midhurst SE26 ....184 C4
Midhurst Ave N10 ....49 A6
Thornton Heath CR0 ....204 C2
Midhurst Ct N8 ....50 A2
Midhurst Gdns UB10 ....61 A1
Midhurst Hill DA6 ....169 C6
Midhurst Ho 6 E14 ....97 B1
Midhurst Par N10 ....49 A6
Midhurst Rd W13 ....109 A3
Midland Pl E14 ....120 A1
Midland Rd E10 ....54 A2
NW1 ....94 A5 233 A3
Midland Terr NW2 ....68 D5
NW10 ....89 C3
Midleton Rd KT3 ....177 A1
Midlothian Rd E3 ....97 B3
Midmoor Rd SW12 ....159 C3
SW19 ....179 A2
Midship Cl SE16 ....118 D5
Midship Point E14 ....119 C4
Midstrath Rd NW10 ....67 C4
Midsummer Ave TW4 ..129 B1
Midsummer Ct SE12 ...143 A1
Midway SM3 ....201 B2
Midway Ho EC1 ....234 D2
Midwinter Cl 3 DA16 .146 A2
Midwood Cl NW2 ....68 B5
Mighell Ave IG4 ....55 D4
Milan Ct N11 ....31 D5
Milan Rd UB1 ....107 B4
Milborne Gr SW10 ....256 B1
Milborne Ho 11 E9 ....74 C2
Milborne St E9 ....74 C2
Milborough Cres SE12 .164 C5
Milbourne La KT10 ....212 A3
Milbourne Lodge Jun Sch
KT10 ....212 B2
Milbrook KT10 ....212 A2
Milburn Dr 1 UB7 ....104 A6
Milburn Ho SW20 ....178 B1
Milcote St SE1 ....251 D1
Mildenhall Rd E5 ....74 C5
Mildmay Ave N1 ....73 B2
Mildmay Ct N1 ....73 B3
Mildmay Gr N1 ....73 B3
Mildmay Ho 6 SW15 ...156 C6
Mildmay Mission Hospl
E2 ....95 D4
Mildmay Pk N1 ....73 B3
Mildmay Rd N1 ....73 C3
Ilford IG1 ....78 D5
Mildmay St N1 ....73 B2
Mildon Ho EN3 ....6 C3
Mildred Ave Hayes UB3 .105 B3
Northolt UB5 ....63 D3
Mildura Ct N8 ....50 B5
Mile End Pl E1 ....96 D3
Mile End Rd E1,E3 ....96 D3
Mile End Sta E3 ....97 B4
Mile End The E17 ....34 D2
Mile Rd Carshalton SM6 .203 A1
Wallington CR0,SM6 ...203 C1
Miles Bldgs NW1 ....237 A4
Miles Coverdale Prim Sch
W12 ....112 C4
Miles Ct E1 ....96 B1
Croydon CR0 ....220 D6
Miles Dr SE28 ....123 C5
Miles Ho 5 SE10 ....120 C1
Miles Lo E15 ....76 B3
Harrow HA1 ....42 B4
Miles Pl NW8 ....236 D4
Miles Rd N8 ....50 A6
Mitcham CR4 ....202 C6
Miles St SW8 ..138 A6 270 B5
Miles Way N20 ....14 C2
Milespit Hill NW7 ....28 C5
Milestone Cl N9 ....18 A2
Sutton SM2 ....218 B1
Milestone Ct TW7 ....131 A4
Milestone Green SW14 133 B1
Milestone Ho KT1 ....197 D5
Milestone Rd SE19 ....183 D4
Milfoil St W12 ....112 A6
Milford Cl SE2 ....147 A6
Milford Ct 3 N16 ....51 C1
Southall UB1 ....107 C5
Milford Gdns
Croydon CR0 ....206 D4
Edgware HA8 ....26 C3
Wembley HA0 ....65 D3
Milford Gr SM1 ....218 A4
Milford La WC2 116 C6 251 A6
Milford Mews SW16 ....160 B1
Milford Rd W13 ....109 B5
Southall UB1 ....107 C6
Milk St E16 ....122 D5
EC2 ....95 A1 242 B2
Plaistow BR1 ....187 B4
Milk Yd E1 ....118 C6
Milkwell Gdns IG8 ....37 B3
Milkwell Yd SE5 ....139 A4
Milkwood Rd SE24 ....138 D1
Mill Bridge EN5 ....13 B5
Mill Cl SM5 ....219 A6
Mill Cnr EN5 ....1 B4
Mill Ct E10 ....76 A5
NW7 ....29 A2
14 SE28 ....124 B6
Mill Farm Ave TW16 ...171 C3
Mill Farm Cl HA5 ....22 C1
Mill Farm Cres TW4 ...151 A3
Mill Gdns SE26 ....162 B1
Mill Gn CR4 ....203 A2
Mill Green Bsns Pk
CR4 ....203 A2
Mill Green Rd CR4 ....203 A2
Mill Hill SW13 ....134 A2
Mill Hill Broadway Sta
NW7 ....27 C4
Mill Hill Circus NW7 ...27 D5
Mill Hill Cty High Sch
NW7 ....11 C2
Mill Hill East Sta NW7 ..29 A3
Mill Hill Ind Est NW7 ...27 D4
Mill Hill Rd SW13 ....134 A3
W3 ....110 D4
Mill Hill Sch NW7 ....28 B6
Mill Hill Terr 9 W3 ....110 D5
Mill Ho IG8 ....36 D5
Mill La E4 ....7 D2
NW6 ....69 B3
SE18 ....122 C1
Carshalton SM5 ....219 A5
Croydon CR0 ....220 C5
Dagenham RM6 ....59 A3
Woodford IG8 ....36 D5
Mill Lane Trad Est CR0 .220 B5
Mill Mead Rd N17 ....52 B6
Mill Pl E14 ....97 A1
Chislehurst BR7 ....188 D2
Kingston u T KT1 ....198 B6
Mill Plat TW7 ....131 A3
Mill Plat Ave TW7 ....131 A3
Mill Rd E16 ....121 B5
SW19 ....180 A3
Ilford IG1 ....78 C5
Twickenham TW2 ....152 A2
Mill Ridge HA8 ....26 C5
Mill River Trad Est EN3 ...7 A1
Mill Row N1 ....95 C6
Mill St SE1 ....117 D4 253 D2
W1 ....249 A6
Kingston u T KT1 ....198 A6
Mill Trad Est The NW10 .89 A4
Mill Vale BR2 ....186 D1
Mill View Cl KT17 ....215 D1
Mill View Gdns CR0 ...222 D5
Mill Way NW7 ....27 C5
Feltham TW14 ....150 B6
Mill Yd E1 ....118 A6
Millais Ave E12 ....78 C3
Millais Ct 10 UB5 ....84 D5
Millais Gdns HA8 ....26 C1
Millais Rd E11 ....76 B4
Enfield EN1 ....17 D6
New Malden KT3 ....199 C2
Millais Way KT19 ....215 A4
Milland Ho 11 SW15 ....156 A3
Millard Cl 21 N16 ....73 C3
Millard Ho SE8 ....119 B1
Millard Terr RM10 ....81 C2
Millbank SW1 ..116 A2 260 A3
Wallington SM6 ....219 D3
Millbank Ho KT6 ....198 B2
Millbank Prim Sch
SW1 ....115 D2 259 D3
Millbank Way SE12 ....165 A6
Millbourne Rd TW13 ...173 A6
Millbrook 1 E18 ....55 A6
Millbrook Ave DA16 ...145 B1
Millbrook Gdns RM6 ...59 A3
Millbrook Ho 4 SE15 ..140 A6
Millbrook Rd N9 ....18 B3
SW9 ....138 D2
Millbrooke Ct 7 SW15 157 A6
Millcroft Ho SE6 ....185 D6
Millender Wlk SE16 ...118 C2
Millennium Bridge*
SE1,EC4 ....252 A5
Millennium Dome*
SE10 ....120 C5
Millennium Dr E14 ....120 B2
Millennium Pl 27 E2 ....96 B5
Millennium Sq SE1 ....253 D2
Miller Cl HA5 ....22 C1
Miller Ct 8 NW9 ....46 A5
Bexleyheath DA7 ....147 D2
Miller Ho N15 ....50 D5
9 SW2 ....160 A4
Miller Rd SW19 ....180 B4
Thornton Heath CR0 ....204 C1
Miller St NW1 ....232 A4
Miller Wlk SE1 ....251 B3
Millercl CR4 ....202 D2
Miller's Ave E8,N16 ....73 D3
Millers Cl NW7 ....28 A6
Millers Ct 3 HA0 ....88 A5
Miller's Ct 1 W4 ....111 D1
Millers Green Cl EN2 ....4 D2
Millers Mead Ct SW19 .180 B3
Miller's Terr 1 E8 ....73 D3
Miller's Way W6 ....112 C4
Millers Wharf Ho E1 ..118 A5
Millers Yd N3 ....29 D3
Millet Rd UB6 ....85 D5
Millfarm Bsns Pk TW4 .151 A4
Millfield N4 ....72 C6
Charlton TW16 ....171 B2
Kingston u T KT1 ....198 B6
Millfield Ave E17 ....35 B2
Millfield La N6 ....70 D6
Millfield Pl N6 ....71 A6
Millfield Rd
Burnt Oak HA8 ....27 A1
Twickenham TW4 ....151 B3
Millfields JMI Sch E5 ..74 C4
Millfields Rd E5 ....74 C5
Millgrove St 6 SW11 ...137 A3
Millharbour E14 ....119 D4
Millhaven Cl RM6 ....58 B3
Millhouse Pl SE27 ....182 D6
Millicent Fawcett Ct
N17 ....33 D2
Millicent Preston Ho 4
IG11 ....101 B6
Millicent Rd E10 ....53 B1
Milligan St E14 ....119 B6
Milling Rd HA8 ....27 B3
Millington Ho N16 ....73 B5
Millington Rd UB3 ....105 C3
Millman Ct SE3 ....143 B5
WC1 ....240 C5
Millman Mews WC1 ...240 C5
Millman Pl WC1 ....240 D5
Millman St WC1 .94 B3 240 C5
Millmark Gr SE14 ....141 A3
Millmarsh La EN3 ....7 B3
Millmead Bsns Ctr N17 .52 B6
Millmead Ind Ctr N17 ..52 B6
Millner Ct SE4 ....141 B3
Millpond Est SE16 ....118 B4
Mills Cl UB10 ....82 C5
Mills Ct 7 E11 ....76 C5
Mills Gr E14 ....98 A1
NW4 ....46 D6
Mills Ho E17 ....54 B6
SW8 ....269 B2
Mills Row W4 ....111 B2
Millshot Cl SW6 ....134 C4
Millside SM5 ....218 D6
Millside Pl TW7 ....131 B3
Millson Cl N20 ....14 B2
Millstream Cl N13 ....32 C5
Millstream Rd
SE1 ....117 D4 253 C1
Millwall Dock Rd E14 ..119 C3
Millward Wlk 14 SE18 .144 C6
Millway Gdns UB5 ....63 B2
Millwood Rd TW3,TW7 .152 A6
Millwood St 10 W10 ....91 A2
Milman Cl HA5 ....40 D6
Milman Rd NW6 ....91 A5
Milman's Ho SW10 ....266 C5
Milman's St
SW10 ....136 B6 266 C5
Milne Ct 4 E18 ....37 A2
Milne Field HA5 ....23 C3
Milne Gdns SE9 ....166 A6
Milne Ho 15 SE18 ....122 B2
Milner Dr TW2 ....152 B4
Milner Ho 2 SW11 ....136 B2
Hayes UB4 ....84 B4
Milner Pl N1 ....94 C6 234 B6
Milner Rd E15 ....98 C4
SW19 ....179 D2
Dagenham RM8 ....80 C6
Kingston u T KT1 ....197 D6
Morden SM4 ....202 B4
South Norwood CR7 ....205 B6
Milner Sq N1 ....72 D1
Milner St SW3 .114 D2 257 C4
Milner Wlk DA15 ....167 B3
Milnthorpe Rd W4 ....133 B6
Milo Rd SE22 ....161 D5
Milrood Ho 4 E1 ....96 D2
Milroy Wlk SE1 ....251 C4
Milson Rd W14 112 D3 254 A6
Milsted Ho 23 E5 ....74 B3
Milton Ave E6 ....78 A1
N6 ....49 C2
NW9 ....45 A6
NW10 ....89 B6
Barnet EN5 ....13 B6
Carshalton SM1 ....218 C4
Croydon CR0 ....205 B2
Milton Cl N2 ....48 A3
SE1 ....117 D2 263 C3
Carshalton SM1 ....218 B5
Hayes UB4 ....84 A1
Milton Court Rd SE14 .141 A6
Milton Cres IG2 ....57 A3
Milton Ct EC2 ....242 C4
NW11 ....47 A3
SE14 ....141 A6
SW6 ....135 A2
9 SW18 ....157 C6
Dagenham RM6 ....58 C2
Kingston u T KT2 ....176 A6
Twickenham TW2 ....152 C1
Uxbridge UB10 ....60 D5
Milton Dr
Borehamwood WD6 ....10 D6
Littleton TW17 ....192 A5
Milton Gdns TW19 ....148 B3
Milton Gr N11 ....31 D5
N16 ....73 C4
Milton Ho 19 E2 ....96 C4
2 SE5 ....139 B5
12 Beckenham BR3 ....185 C3
5 Kingston u T KT2 ....176 D4
Sutton SM1 ....217 C5
Milton House Mans E8 .73 D4
Milton Lo N21 ....16 D3
3 Sidcup DA14 ....190 A6
Twickenham TW1 ....152 D4
Milton Pk N6 ....49 C2
Milton Pl 3 N7 ....72 C3
Milton Rd E17 ....53 C5
N6 ....49 C2
N15 ....50 D6
NW7 ....28 A5
1 NW9 ....46 A2
SE24 ....160 D6
SW14 ....133 B2
SW19 ....180 A4
W3 ....111 B5
W7 ....108 D6
Belvedere DA17 ....125 C2
Bexley DA16 ....145 D4
Croydon CR0 ....205 B2
Harrow HA1 ....42 C5
Milton Rd *continued*
Mitcham CR4 ....181 A3
Sutton SM1 ....217 C4
Uxbridge UB10 ....60 D4
Wallington SM6 ....219 D2
TW12 ....173 C3
Milton St EC1,EC2 95 B2 242 C4
Milton Way UB7 ....104 B2
Milverton NW5 ....71 A3
Milverton Dr UB10 ....61 A4
Milverton Gdns IG3 ....79 D6
Milverton Ho SE23 ....163 A1
Milverton Rd NW6 ....68 C1
Milverton St
SE11 ....116 C1 261 B1
Milverton Way SE9 ...188 C6
Milward St E1 ....96 B2
Mimosa N15 ....51 B4
Mimosa Ct SW4 ....270 B1
Mimosa Ho UB4 ....84 C2
Mimosa Rd UB4 ....84 C2
Mimosa St SW6 135 B4 264 D1
Mina Rd SE17 ..117 C1 263 B2
SW19 ....179 C2
Minard Rd SE6 ....164 C3
Minchenden Cres N14 ..15 D1
Minchenden Ct N14 ....15 D2
Minchin Ho 6 E14 ....97 C1
Mincing La EC3 117 C6 253 A6
Minden Rd SE20 ....184 B2
Cheam SM3 ....217 B6
Minehead Ct HA2 ....63 C6
Minehead Rd SW16 ...182 B5
Harrow HA2 ....63 C5
Minera Mews SW1 ....258 B4
Mineral St SE18 ....123 C2
Minerva Cl SW9 ....138 C5
Sidcup DA14 ....189 C6
Minerva Rd E4 ....35 D3
NW10 ....89 B4
Kingston u T KT1 ....176 B1
Minerva St E2 ....96 B5
Minet Ave NW10 ....89 C5
Minet Dr UB3 ....106 A5
Minet Gdns NW10 ....89 C5
Hayes UB3 ....106 B5
Minet Jun & Inf Schs
UB3 ....106 B5
Minet Rd SE5,SW9 ....138 D3
Minford Gdns W14 ....112 D4
Ming St E14 ....119 C6
Mingard Wlk N7 ....72 B5
Minimax Cl TW14 ....150 A5
Ministry Way SE9 ....166 B2
Mink Ct TW4 ....128 C3
Minniedale KT5 ....198 B4
Minnow Wlk SE17 ....263 B3
Minories EC3 ..117 D6 253 C6
Minshaw Ct
Sidcup DA14 ....189 D6
1 Sidcup DA14 ....190 A6
Minshull Pl 23 BR3 ....185 C3
Minshull St SW8 ....269 C1
Minson Rd E9 ....96 D6
Minstead Gdns SW15 ..155 D4
Minstead Way KT3 ....199 C3
Minster Ave SM1 ....217 C6
Minster Dr CR0 ....221 C4
Minster Gdns KT8 ....195 B5
Minster Rd NW2 ....69 A3
Bromley BR1 ....187 B3
Minster Wlk N8 ....50 A5
Minsterley Ave TW16,
TW17 ....193 C5
Minstrel Ct HA3 ....24 C1
Minstrel Gdns KT5 ....198 B5
Mint Bsns Pk 12 E16 ....99 A2
Mint Cl UB10 ....82 D4
Mint Rd SM5,SM6 ....219 B4
Mint St SE1 ....252 B2
Mint Wlk CR0 ....221 A5
Mintern Cl N13 ....16 D1
Mintern St N1 ...95 B5 235 D4
Minterne Ave UB2 ....107 C2
Minterne Rd HA3 ....44 B4
Minterne Waye UB4 ....84 C1
Minton Ho SE11 ....261 A4
Minton Mews 3 NW6 ..69 D2
Mirabel Rd
SW6 ....135 B5 264 D4
Miranda Cl 16 E1 ....96 C2
Miranda Ct W3 ....88 B1
Miranda Ho 17 N1 ....95 C5
6 Belvedere DA17 ....125 C1
Miranda Rd N19 ....49 C1
Mirfield Ct SE20 ....184 A1
Mirfield St SE7 ....121 D3
Miriam Ct DA14 ....190 B6
Miriam Rd SE18 ....123 C1
Mirravale Trad Est RM6 .59 A2
Mirren Cl HA2 ....63 B5
Mirror Path SE12 ....165 C1
Misbourne Rd UB10 ....82 C6
Missenden SE17 ....262 D1
Missenden Cl TW14 ....149 D3
Missenden Gdns SM4 ..202 A3
Missenden Ho NW8 ....237 A6
Mission Gr E17 ....53 A4
Mission Grove Prim Sch
E17 ....53 B5
Mission Pl SE15 ....140 A4
Mission Sq 13 TW8 ....132 A6
Misterton Ct SW11 ....266 D2
Mistletoe Cl CR0 ....206 D1
Mistley Thorn IG1 ....56 C2

Mistral SE5 139 C4
Mistral Ct E4 19 D1
Mistys Field KT12 194 C1
Mitali Pas 13 E1 96 A1
Mitcham Garden Village
CR4 203 A4
Mitcham Ho 9 SE5 139 A4
Mitcham Ind Est CR4 181 A2
Mitcham Junction Sta
CR4 203 A4
Mitcham La SW16 181 C5
Mitcham Pk CR4 202 D5
Mitcham Rd E6 100 A4
SW17 180 D5
Ilford IG3 57 D2
Mitcham Sta CR4 202 C5
Mitcheldean Ct SE15 139 C5
Mitchell 19 NW9 27 D2
Mitchell Brook Prim Sch
NW10 67 C2
Mitchell Cl SE2 124 C2
Belvedere DA17 125 D3
Mitchell Ct 20 E10 53 D2
Mitchell Ho W4 110 D1
31 W12 112 B6
Mitchell Rd N13 33 A5
Orpington BR6 227 D4
Plaistow BR1 187 A2
Mitchell St EC1 95 A3 242 B6
Mitchell Way NW10 67 A2
Mitchell Wlk E6 100 B2
Mitchellbrook Way
NW10 67 B2
Mitchison Rd N1 73 B2
Mitchley Rd N17 52 A6
Mitford Cl KT9 213 C2
Mitford Rd N19 72 A6
Mitre Bridge Ind Pk W10 90 B3
Mitre Cl
Shepperton TW17 193 B3
Sutton SM2 218 B1
Mitre Ct 9 E18 37 A2
EC2 242 B2
Belvedere DA17 125 C1
1 Dagenham RM6 58 B2
Mitre Ho RM7 59 D5
Mitre Rd E15 98 C5
SE1 116 C4 251 B2
Mitre Sq EC3 243 B1
Mitre St EC3 95 C1 243 B1
Mitre The 9 E14 119 B6
Mitre Way W10 90 B2
Moat Cl BR6 227 D2
Moat Cres N3 47 D6
Moat Croft DA16 146 C2
Moat Ct SE9 166 B5
Sidcup DA15 167 D1
9 Sidcup DA15 168 A1
Moat Dr 4 E13 99 C5
Harrow HA1 42 B5
Ruislip HA4 39 C2
Moat Farm Rd UB5 63 B1
Moat Lo The HA1 64 C6
Moat Pl SW9 138 B2
W3 88 D1
Moat Side Enfield EN3 6 D1
Feltham TW13 172 C6
Moat The KT3 177 C2
Moatbridge Sch SE9 165 D5
Moatfield NW6 69 A1
Moberly Rd SW4 159 D4
Mobey Ct SW4 270 A1
Moblin Lo IG9 21 C3
Moby Dick RM6 59 B5
Mocatta Ho 9 E1 96 B3
Modbury Gdns NW5 71 A2
Modder Pl SW15 134 D1
Model Cotts SW14 133 A2
Model Farm Cl SE9 166 A1
Modling Ho 8 E2 96 D5
Moelwyn Hughes Ct N7 71 D3
Moelyn Mews HA1 43 A4
Moffat Ct SW17 180 C6
SW19 179 C5
Moffat Ho 24 SE5 139 A5
Moffat Rd N13 32 A4
SW17 180 D6
South Norwood CR7 183 B1
Mogden La TW7 152 D6
Mohawk Ho 31 E3 97 A5
Mohmmad Khan Rd E11 54 D1
Mohr Ct N22 32 B3
Moiety Rd E14 119 C4
Moineau 18 NW9 27 D2
Moira Cl N17 33 C1
Moira Ct SW17 159 A2
Moira Rd SE9 144 B1
Moland Mead SE16 118 D1
Molasses Ho 1 SW11 136 A2
Molasses Row 2 SW11 136 A2
Mole Abbey Gdns KT8 195 D6
Mole Ct 2 W12 111 C4
West Ewell KT19 215 A4
Mole Ho NW8 236 D5
Molember Ct KT7 196 C5
Molember Rd KT8 196 C4
Molescroft SE9 167 A1
Molesey Ave KT12,KT8 195 B4
Molesey Dr SM3 217 A5
Molesey Ho E2 243 C6
Molesey Hospl KT8 195 C4
Molesey Park Ave KT8 195 D4
Molesey Park Cl KT8 196 A4
Molesey Park Rd KT8 196 A4
Molesey Rd KT12 195 A2
Molesford Rd SW6 265 A1
Molesham Cl KT8 195 D6
Molesham Way KT8 195 D6
Molesworth Ho 9
SE17 138 D6
Molesworth St SE13 142 A2
Moliner Ct 4 BR3 185 C3
Mollie Davis Ct SE19 183 D4
Mollison Ave EN3 7 B5
Mollison Dr SM6 220 A1
Mollison Way HA8 26 C1
Molly Huggins Cl SW12 159 C4
Molton Ho N1 233 D5
Molyneux Dr SW17 181 B6
Molyneux St W1 92 C2 237 B3
Mona Rd SE15 140 C3
Mona St E16 98 D2
Monarch Cl
Coney Hall BR4 224 D4
East Bedfont TW14 149 C4
Monarch Ct N2 48 A4
W5 87 C2
Monarch Dr E16 99 D2
Monarch Mews SW16 182 C5
Monarch Par CR4 180 D1
Monarch Pl IG9 21 C2
Monarch Rd DA17 125 C3
Monarch's Way HA4 39 C1
Monastery Gdns EN2 5 B3
Monaveen Gdns KT8 195 D6
Monck St SW1 115 D3 259 D5
Monck's Row SW18 157 B5
Monclar Rd SE5 139 B1
Moncorvo Cl
SW7 114 C4 247 A1
Moncrieff Cl 4 E6 100 A1
Moncrieff St SE15 140 A3
Mondial Way UB7 127 A5
Mondragon Ho SW8 270 B2
Monega Prim Sch E12 77 D2
Monega Rd E7,E12 77 D2
Monet Ct 15 SE16 118 B1
Moneyer Ho N1 235 C2
Monica James Ho 12
DA14 168 A1
Monica Shaw Ct NW1 232 D3
Monier Rd E3 75 C1
Monivea Rd BR3 185 B3
Monk Ct W12 112 A5
Monk Dr E16 121 A6
Monk St SE18 122 C2
Monken Hadley CE Prim Sch
EN6 1 C4
Monkfrith Ave N14 15 B5
Monkfrith Cl N14 15 B4
Monkfrith Prim Sch N14 15 A4
Monkfrith Way N14 15 B4
Monkham's Ave IG8 37 B5
Monkham's Dr IG8 37 B5
Monkham's La IG8,IG9 37 B6
Monkleigh Rd SM4,
SW20 201 A5
Monkridge 3 N8 49 D2
Monks Ave
East Molesey KT8 195 B4
New Barnet EN5 14 A5
Monks Cl SE2 124 D2
Enfield EN2 5 A3
Harrow HA2 63 D6
Ruislip HA4 62 D4
Monks Cres KT12 194 B1
Monks Dr W3 88 C1
Monks Orchard Rd BR3,
CR0 207 C2
Monks Orchard Sch
CR0 206 D4
Monks Park Gdns HA9 66 D1
Monks Pk HA9 67 A2
Monks Rd EN2 5 A3
Monks Way NW11 47 B5
Beckenham BR3 207 C3
Harmondsworth UB7 126 A6
Orpington BR5 211 B1
Monksdene Gdns SM1 217 D5
Monksfield N4 72 C6
Monkswell Ct N10 31 A2
Monkswood Gdns
Borehamwood WD6 11 B6
Ilford IG5 56 C6
Monkton Ct W14 254 C6
Monkton Ho 22 E5 74 B3
32 SE16 118 D4
Monkton Rd DA16 145 D3
Monkton St
SE11 116 C2 261 B4
Monkville Ave NW11 47 B5
Monkville Par 1 NW11 47 B5
Monkwell Sq EC2 242 B3
Monmouth Ave E18 55 B6
Teddington KT1 175 C3
Monmouth Cl W4 111 B3
Bexley DA16 146 A1
Mitcham CR4,SW16 204 A5
Monmouth Ct 9 W7 86 D2
Monmouth Gr TW8 110 A2
Monmouth Ho 5 NW5 71 B2
SW18 157 C5
Monmouth Pl W2 91 D1
Monmouth Rd E6 100 B4
N9 18 C2
W2 91 C1
Dagenham RM9 81 B3
Hayes UB3 105 D2
Monmouth St
WC2 94 A1 240 A1
Monnery Rd N19 71 C5
Monnow Rd SE1 118 A2
Mono La TW13 150 B2
Monoux Almshouses
E17 53 D5
Monoux Gr E17 35 C2
Monro Gdns HA3 24 C3
Monro Ho 21 NW3 70 A4
SW15 156 B6
Monroe Cres EN1 6 B4
Monroe Dr SW14 154 D6
Monroe Ho 16 N19 49 D2
Mons Way BR2 210 A3
Monsal Ct E5 75 A4
Monsell Rd N4,N5 72 D5
Monson Prim Sch SE14 140 D5
Monson Rd NW10 90 B5
SE14 140 D5
Montacute Rd SE6 163 B4
Bushey WD2 8 C4
Morden SM4 202 B3
Montagu Cres N18 34 B6
Montagu Ct W1 237 D3
Montagu Gdns N18 34 B6
Wallington SM6 219 C4
Montagu Ind Est N18 34 C6
Montagu Mans
W1 92 D2 237 D3
Montagu Mews N W1 237 D3
Montagu Mews S W1 237 D2
Montagu Mews W W1 237 D2
Montagu Pl W1 92 D2 237 D3
Montagu Rd N9,N18 18 C1
NW4 46 A3
Montagu Row W1 237 D3
Montagu Sq W1 92 D1 237 D2
Montagu St W1 92 D1 237 D2
Montague Ave SE4 141 C1
W7 108 D5
Montague Cl SE1 252 C4
Walton-on-T KT12 194 A2
Montague Fell HA0 65 A4
Montague Gdns W3 110 C6
Montague Pl
WC1 93 D2 239 D4
Montague Rd E8 74 A3
E11 76 D6
N8 50 B4
N15 52 A5
SW19 179 D3
W7 108 D4
W13 87 B1
Hounslow TW3 129 D2
Richmond TW10 154 A5
Southall UB2 107 A2
Thornton Heath CR0 204 D1
Uxbridge UB8 60 A1
Montague Sq SE15 140 C5
Montague St
WC1 94 A2 240 A4
Montague Street EC1 242 A3
Montague Terr 1 BR2 209 A5
Montague Way UB2 107 A3
Montalt Ho IG8 36 D6
Montalt Rd IG8 36 D5
Montana Gdns SE26 185 B5
5 Sutton SM1 218 A3
Montana Rd SW17 159 A1
SW20 178 C2
Montbelle Prim Sch
SE9 166 D1
Montbelle Rd SE9 166 D1
Montcalm Cl Hayes BR2 209 A3
Hayes UB4 84 B4
Montcalm Ho E14 119 C3
Montcalm Rd SE7 143 D5
Montclare St E2 95 D3 243 C6
Monteagle Ave IG11 79 A2
Monteagle Ct 27 N1 95 C5
Monteagle Prim Sch
RM9 102 B6
Monteagle Way E5 74 A5
SE15 140 B2
Montefiore Ct 2 N16 51 D1
Montefiore St 2 SW8 137 B3
Montem Prim Sch N7 72 B5
Montem Rd SE23 163 B4
New Malden KT3 199 C5
Montem St N4 50 B1
Montenotte Rd N8 49 C4
Montesole Ct 5 HA5 22 C1
Montesquieu Terr 3
E16 98 D1
Montford Pl
SE11 116 C1 261 A1
Montford Rd TW16 194 A5
Montfort Ho 4 E2 96 C4
E14 120 A3
Montfort Pl SW19 156 D3
Montgo Cl 10 SW2 138 C1
Montgolfier Wlk UB5 85 A4
Montgomery Ave KT10 212 C6
Montgomery Cl
Bexley DA15 167 D5
Mitcham CR4 204 A5
Montgomery Ct W4 133 A6
Montgomery Ho 5
SW14 133 B2
Montgomery Lo 34 E1 96 C3
Montgomery Rd W4 111 A2
Edgware HA8 26 B4
Montholme Rd SW11 158 D5
Monthorpe Rd 16 E1 96 A2
Montolieu Gdns SW15 156 B6
Montpelier Ave W5 87 C2
Bexley DA5 168 D4
Montpelier Cl UB10 82 C6
Montpelier Ct W5 87 D2
5 Beckenham BR2 208 D5
Montpelier Gdns E6 99 D4
Dagenham RM6 58 C2
Montpelier Gr NW5 71 C3
Montpelier Mews SW7 257 B6
Montpelier Pl 21 E1 96 C1
SW7 257 B6
Montpelier Prim Sch
W5 87 D2
Montpelier Rd N3 30 A2
SE15 140 B4
W5 87 D2
Sutton SM1 218 A4
Montpelier Rise NW11 47 A2
Wembley HA9 43 D1
Montpelier Row SE3 142 D3
Twickenham TW1 153 C4
Montpelier Sq
SW7 114 C4 247 B1
Montpelier St
SW7 114 C3 257 B6
Montpelier Terr SW7 247 B1
Montpelier Vale SE3 142 D3
Montpelier Way NW11 47 A2
Montpelier Wlk
SW7 114 C3 257 B6
Montrave Rd SE20 184 C3
Montreal Ho UB4 84 B4
Montreal Pl WC2 250 C6
Montreal Rd IG1 57 A2
Montrell Rd SW2 160 A3
Montrose Ave NW6 91 A5
Bexley DA16 145 C2
Burnt Oak HA8 27 B2
Sidcup DA15 168 A4
Twickenham TW2 151 D4
Montrose Cl
Ashford TW15 171 A5
Bexley DA16 145 D2
Woodford IG8 37 A6
Montrose Cres N12 30 A4
1 Wembley HA0 66 A2
Montrose Ct NW9 27 A1
NW11 47 B5
2 SE6 164 D2
SW7 114 B4 246 D1
Montrose Gdns
Mitcham CR4 180 D1
Sutton SM1 217 D6
Montrose Ho E14 119 C3
SW1 248 B1
Montrose Pl
SW1 115 A4 248 B1
Montrose Rd
East Bedfont TW14 149 B5
Harrow HA3 24 D1
Montrose Villas W6 112 A1
Montrose Way SE23 162 D3
Montserrat Ave IG8 36 B3
Montserrat Cl SE19 183 B5
Montserrat Rd SW15 135 A1
Monument Gdns SE13 164 A6
Monument St
EC3 117 B6 252 D6
Monument Sta
EC3 117 B6 252 D6
Monument The* EC3 252 D6
Monument Way N17 51 D6
Monza St E1 118 C6
Moodkee St SE16 118 C3
Moody St E1 96 D4
Moon Ct SE12 143 A1
Moon La EN5 1 B2
Moon St N1 94 D6 234 C6
Moor La EC2 95 B2 242 C3
Chessington KT9 214 A3
Moor Lane Jun Sch
KT9 214 B3
Moor Mead Rd TW1 153 A5
Moor Park Gdns KT2 177 C3
Moor Pl EC2 242 C3
Moor St W1 239 D1
Moorcroft HA8 26 D2
Moorcroft Gdns BR1 210 A4
Moorcroft La UB8 82 C2
Moorcroft Rd SW16 160 A1
Moorcroft Sch UB8 82 D2
Moorcroft Way HA5 41 A4
Moordown SE18 144 D4
Moore Cl SW14 133 A2
Mitcham CR4 181 B1
Wallington SM6 220 A1
Moore Cres RM9 102 B6
Moore Ho 6 E1 118 C6
16 E2 96 C4
N8 50 A5
5 SE10 120 D1
1 SE27 183 A6
SW17 158 B1
Moore Park Ct SW6 265 D4
Moore Park Rd
SW6 135 D5 265 C3
Moore Rd SE19 183 A4
Moore St SW3 114 D2 257 C4
Moore Wlk E7 77 A4
Moorefield Rd N17 33 D1
Mooreland Rd BR1 187 A2
Moorey Cl 2 E15 98 D6
Moorfield Ave W5 87 D3
Moorfield Rd
Chessington KT9 214 A3
Enfield EN3 6 C4
Moorfields EC2 95 B2 242 C3
Moorfields Ct 6 SW16 181 C6
Moorfields Eye Hospl
EC1 95 B4 235 C1
Moorfields Highwalk
EC2 242 C3
Moorfields Prim Sch
EC1 95 B3 242 C6
Moorgate EC2 95 B2 242 C3
Moorgate Pl EC2 242 C2
Moorgate Sta
EC2 95 B2 242 C3
Moorgreen Ho EC1 234 C2
Moorhead Way SE3 143 B2
Moorhen Ct 35 SE8 141 B6
Moorhouse 17 NW9 27 D2
Moorhouse Rd W2 91 C1
Harrow HA3 43 D6
Moorings The E16 99 C2
Moorland Cl TW4 151 C4
Moorland Rd SW9 138 D1
Moorlands UB5 85 A6
Moorlands Ave NW7 28 B4
Moormead Dr KT19 215 C3
Moorside Rd BR1 186 D6
Moortown Rd WD1 22 C6
Moot Ct NW9 44 C4
Mora Prim Sch NW2 68 C4
Mora Rd NW2 68 C4
Mora St EC1 95 A4 235 B1
Morant Ho SW9 138 B3
Morant Pl N22 32 B2
Morant St E14 119 C6
Morat St SW9 138 B4 270 D2
Moravian Cl SW3 266 D5
Moravian Pl
SW10 136 B6 266 D5
Moravian St 10 E2 96 C4
Moray Ave UB3 105 D5
Moray Cl HA8 10 D2
Moray Ho 8 E1 97 A3
11 Kingston u T KT6 198 A4
Moray Mews N4,N7 72 B6
Moray Rd N4,N7 72 B6
Mordaunt Gdns RM9 81 A1
Mordaunt Ho 4 NW10 89 B6
34 SW8 137 D3
Mordaunt Rd NW10 89 B6
Mordaunt St SW9 138 B2
Morden Court Par SM4 201 D5
Morden Ct SM4 201 D5
Morden Farm Mid Sch
SM4 201 A2
Morden Fst Sch SM4 201 C4
Morden Gdns
Greenford UB6 64 D3
Mitcham CR4 202 B5
Morden Hall SW19 201 D6
Morden Hall Rd SM4 202 A5
Morden Hill SE13 142 A3
Morden Ho SM4 201 C5
Morden La SE13 142 A4
Morden Lo BR2 186 B1
Morden Mount Prim Sch
SE13 141 D3
Morden Park Sch Sports Ctr
SM4 201 B4
Morden Rd SE3 143 A3
SW19 179 D1
Dagenham RM6 59 A2
Mitcham CR4,SM4 202 B5
Morden Road Mews
SE3 143 A3
Morden Road Sta
SW19 179 D1
Morden South Sta SM4 201 C4
Morden St SE13 141 D4
Morden Sta SW19 201 D6
Morden Way SM3 201 C2
Morden Wharf Rd SE10 120 C3
Mordern Ho NW1 237 B5
Mordon Rd IG3 57 D2
Mordred Rd SE6 164 C2
More Cl E16 98 D1
W14 113 A2 254 A3
More House Sch
SW1 114 D3 257 D5
Morecambe Cl 2 E1 96 D2
Morecambe Gdns HA7 25 D6
Morecambe St
SE17 117 B2 262 B2
Morecambe Terr N18 33 B6
Morecoombe Cl KT2 176 D3
Moredown Ho 3 E8 74 A3
Moree Way N18 34 A6
Moreland Ct 3 NW2 69 C5
Moreland Prim Sch
EC1 94 D4 234 D1
Moreland St EC1 94 D4 234 D2
Moreland Way E4 20 A1
Morell Ho 5 SW9 138 B3
Morella Rd SW11,SW12 158 D4
Morello Ave UB8 82 D2
Morello Ct HA9 66 B5
Moremead Rd SE6 185 C6
Morena St SE6 163 D4
More's Gdn SW3 266 D5
Moresby Ave KT5 198 D2
Moresby Rd E5 52 B1
Moresby Wlk 6 SW8 137 B3
Moreton Ave TW7 130 C4
Moreton Cl E5 52 C1
N15 51 B3
NW7 28 C4
Moreton Green Fst Sch
SM4 202 B4
Moreton Ho SE16 118 B3
SW17 180 B6
Moreton Pl
SW1 115 C1 259 B2
Moreton Rd N15 51 B3
North Cheam KT4 216 B6
South Croydon CR2 221 B3
Moreton St
SW1 115 D1 259 C2
Moreton Terr
SW1 115 C1 259 B2
Moreton Terr Mews N
SW1 259 B2
Moreton Terr Mews S
SW1 259 B2
Moreton Twr 3 W3 110 D5
Morford Cl HA4 40 B2
Morford Way HA4 40 B2
Morgan Ave E17 54 B5
Morgan Cl RM10 81 C1
Morgan Ct 5 SW11 136 B3
Ashford TW15 170 D5
Morgan Ho SW1 259 B3
SW8 269 B2
Morgan Rd N7 72 C3
W10 91 B2
Plaistow BR1 187 A3
Teddington TW11 174 C4
Morgan St E3 97 A4
E16 98 D2
Morgan Terr RM6 58 C4
Morgans La
SE1 117 C5 253 A3
Morgan's La UB3 83 B2
Morgan's Wlk SW11 267 A3
Moriatry Cl N7 72 A4
Morie St SW18 157 D6
Morieux Rd E10 53 B1
Moring Rd SW17 181 A6
Moriss Ho 5 E5 74 B6
Morkyns Wlk SE21 161 C1
Morland Ave CR0 205 C1
Morland Cl NW11 47 D1
Hampton TW12 173 B5
Mitcham CR4 202 C6
Morland Ct W12 112 B4
Morland Est E8 74 A1
Morland Gdns NW10 67 B1
Southall UB1 107 D5
Morland Ho NW1 232 B3
NW6 91 C6
SW1 260 A4
W11 91 A1
Morland Mews N1 72 C1
Morland Rd E17 52 D4
SE20 184 D4
Croydon CR0 205 D2
Dagenham RM10 81 C1
Harrow HA3 44 A5
Ilford IG1 78 D6
Sutton SM1 218 A3
Morland Road Day Hospl
RM10 103 C6
Morley Ave E4 36 B3
N18 34 A6
N22 32 D1
Morley Cl BR6 226 D6
Morley Coll SE1 116 C3 261 B6
Morley Cres Edgware HA8 11 A2
Ruislip HA4 62 C6
Morley Cres E HA7 43 D6
Morley Cres W HA7 43 C6
Morley Ct E4 35 B5
Beckenham BR2 208 D5
Beckenham BR3 186 B2
Morley Hill EN2 5 B5
Morley Ho N16 74 A6
SW2 160 A4
Morley Rd E10 54 A1
E15 98 D5
SE13 142 A1
Barking IG11 101 B6
Cheam SM3 201 B1
Chislehurst BR7 189 A2
Dagenham RM6 59 A4
Twickenham TW1 153 D5
Morley St SE1 116 C4 251 B1
Morna Rd SE5 139 A3
Morning La E9 74 C2
Morningside JMI Sch E9 74 C2
Morningside Rd KT4 216 C6
Mornington Ave
W14 113 B2 254 C3
Bromley BR1 209 D6
Ilford IG1 56 C2
Mornington Avenue Mans
W14 254 C3
Mornington Cl IG8 37 A6
Mornington Cres
NW1 93 C5 232 A4
Cranford TW5 128 B4
Mornington Crescent Sta
NW1 93 C5 232 A4
Mornington Ct NW1 232 A4
Mornington Gr E3 97 C4
Mornington Mews 2
SE5 139 A4
Mornington Pl NW1 232 A4
4 SE8 141 B5
Mornington Rd E4 20 B4
E11 54 D1
SE14,SE8 141 B5
Ashford TW15 171 A5
Southall UB6 85 D3
Woodford IG8 36 D6
Mornington St
NW1 93 B5 231 D4
Mornington Terr
NW1 93 B5 231 D4
Mornington Wlk TW10 175 C6
Morocco St SE1 117 C4 253 A1
Morpeth Gr E9 96 D6
Morpeth Rd E9 96 D6
Morpeth Sec Sch E2 96 C4
Morpeth St E2 96 D4
Morpeth Terr
SW1 115 C3 259 A4
Morpeth Wlk N17 34 B3
Morrab Gdns IG3 79 D5

Morrel Cl EN5 2 A2
Morrel Ct 10 E2 96 A5
Morris Ave E12 78 B3
Morris Blitz Ct 2 N16 73 D4
Morris Cl Croydon CR0 207 A4
Orpington BR6 227 C5
Morris Ct E4 19 D1
3 SE5 139 B1
Morris Gdns SW18 157 C4
Morris Ho 17 E2 96 C4
10 N19 71 C4
NW8 237 A5
1 SW4 138 A1
Morris Pl N4 72 C6
Morris Rd E15 76 C4
Dagenham RM8 81 B6
Isleworth TW7 130 D2
Morris St E1 96 B1
E14 97 D2
Morrish Rd SW2 160 A4
Morrison Ave N17 51 C6
Morrison Bldgs 3 E1 96 A1
Morrison Ct N12 30 C3
5 Chipping Barnet EN5 1 A1
Morrison Ho SW2 160 C3
Morrison Rd
Barking IG11 103 A5
Hayes UB4 84 B4
Morrison St SW11 137 A2
Morrison Yd N17 33 D1
Morriss Ho 7 SE16 118 B4
Morriston Cl WD1 22 C5
Morritt Ho 3 HA0 65 D3
Morse Cl E13 99 A4
Morshead Mans W9 91 C4
Morshead Rd W9 91 C4
Morson Rd EN3 19 A5
Morstan Gdns SE9 188 B6
Mortain Ho 9 SE16 118 B2
Morten Cl SW4 159 D5
Morteyne Rd N17 33 B2
Mortham St E15 98 C6
Mortimer Cl 1 NW2 69 B5
SW16 159 D2
Mortimer Cres NW6 91 D6
Worcester Pk KT4 215 B5
Mortimer Ct NW8 229 B3
Mortimer Dr EN1 17 C6
Mortimer Est NW6 91 D6
Mortimer Ho 6 W11 112 D5
W14 254 B3
Mortimer Lo 11 SW19 157 A3
Mortimer Market WC1 239 B5
Mortimer Pl NW6 91 D6
Mortimer Rd E6 100 B4
N1 73 C1
NW10 90 C4
W13 87 C1
Mitcham CR4 180 D2
Mortimer Sch SW16 159 D2
Mortimer Sq W11 112 D6
Mortimer St W1 93 C2 239 B3
Mortimer Terr NW5 71 B4
Mortlake Cl CR0 220 A5
Mortlake Dr CR4 180 C2
Mortlake High St SW14 133 B2
Mortlake Rd E16 99 B1
SW14,TW9 132 C4
Ilford IG1 79 B4
Mortlake Sta SW14 133 A2
Mortlock Cl SE15 140 B4
Mortlock Ct E12 77 D4
Morton Cres N14 31 D6
Morton Ct UB5 64 A3
Morton Gdns SM6 219 C3
Morton Ho SE17 138 D6
SE27 183 B5
Morton Mews SW5 255 C3
Morton Pl SE1 261 A5
Morton Rd E15 76 D1
N1 73 A1
Morden SM4 202 B4
Morton Way N14 31 D6
Morval Rd SW2 160 C6
Morvale Cl DA17 125 B2
Morven Rd SW17 158 D1
Morville St E3 97 C5
Morwell St WC1 239 D3
Moscow Pl W2 245 C6
Moscow Rd W2 113 D6 245 C6
Mosedale NW1 231 D1
Moselle Ave N22 32 C1
Moselle Cl N8 50 B6
Moselle Ho 2 N17 33 D3
Moselle Pl N17 33 D3
Moselle Sch N17 33 C1
Moselle St N17 33 D3
Moselle Upper Sch N17 51 A6
Moss Cl E1 96 A2
Hatch End HA5 23 A1
Moss Gdns CR2 222 D1
Moss Hall Cres N12 30 A4
Moss Hall Ct N12 29 D4
Moss Hall Gr N12 29 D4
Moss Hall Jun & Inf Schs
N12 29 D4
Moss La HA5 23 A1
Moss Rd RM10 81 C1
Mossborough Cl N12 29 D4
Mossbury Rd SW11 136 C2
Mossdown Cl DA17 125 C2
Mossford Ct IG6 56 D6
Mossford Gn IG6 57 A6
Mossford St E3 97 B3
Mossington Gdns SE16 118 C2
Mosslea Rd SE20 184 C4
Bromley BR2 209 D4
Orpington BR6 227 A5
Mossop St SW3 114 C2 257 B4
Mossville Gdns SM4 201 B5
Mosswell Ho 4 N10 31 A3
Moston Cl UB3 105 D1
Mostyn Ave HA9 66 B3
Mostyn Gardens Prim Sch
SW9 138 C4
Mostyn Gdns NW10 90 D5
Mostyn Gr E3 97 C5
Mostyn Lo N5 73 A4
Mostyn Rd SW9 138 C4
SW19 179 B1
Burnt Oak HA8 27 C3
Bushey WD2 8 A6
Mosul Way BR2 210 A3
Motcomb St
SW1 115 A3 258 A6
Mothers Sq The 13 E5 74 B4
Motley Ave EC2 243 A6
Motley St SW8 137 C3
Motspur Park Sta KT3 200 B4
Motspur Pk KT3 200 A3
Mottingham Ct SE9 166 B3
Mottingham Gdns SE9 165 D3
Mottingham La SE9,
SE12 165 C3
Mottingham Prim Sch
SE9 166 B1
Mottingham Rd N9 18 D4
SE9 166 B1
Mottingham Sta SE9 166 B3
Mottisfont Rd SE2 124 B2
Moules Ct SE5 139 A5
Moulins Rd E9 74 D1
Moulsford Ho 5 N7 72 A3
32 W2 91 C2
Moulton Ave TW3,TW5 129 B3
Mound The SE9 166 C1
Moundfield Rd N16 52 A3
Mounsey Ho 10 W10 91 A4
Mount Adon Pk SE21,
SE22 162 A4
Mount Angelus Rd
SW15 155 D4
Mount Ararat Rd TW10 154 A6
Mount Arlington 3
BR2 186 C1
Mount Ash Rd SE26 162 B1
Mount Ave E4 19 D1
W5 87 D2
Southall UB1 85 C1
Mount Carmel RC Sec Sch
N7 72 B3
N19 49 D1
Mount Cl W5 87 C2
Bromley BR1 188 A2
Cockfosters EN4 3 A1
Mount Ct
6 Kingston u T KT2 176 D3
West Wickham BR4 224 C6
Mount Culver Ave
DA14 190 D4
Mount Dr Bexley DA6 169 A6
Harrow HA2,HA5 41 B4
Wembley HA9 67 A6
Mount Eaton Ct W5 87 C2
Mount Echo Ave E4 19 D3
Mount Echo Dr E4 19 D3
Mount Ephraim La
SW16 159 D1
Mount Ephraim Rd
SW16 159 D1
Mount Felix KT12 193 D1
Mount Gdns SE26 162 B1
Mount Gr HA8 27 B6
Mount House (St Martha's
Senior Sch) The EN6 1 C4
Mount Lo N6 49 C3
Mount Mews TW12 173 D2
Mount Mills EC1 234 D1
Mount Nod Rd SW16,
SW2 160 B1
Mount Olive Ct W7 108 C4
Mount Park Ave HA1 64 C6
Mount Park Cres W5 87 D1
Mount Park Rd W5 87 D1
Harrow HA1 64 B5
Pinner HA5 40 A4
Mount Pk SM5 219 A1
Mount Pl 7 W3 110 D5
Mount Pleasant N14 15 D4
SE27 183 A6
WC1 94 C3 241 A5
Cockfosters EN4 2 D1
Ilford IG1 79 A3
Ruislip HA4 62 D6
Wembley HA0 88 B6
Mount Pleasant Cres N4 50 B2
Mount Pleasant Hill E5 74 C6
Mount Pleasant La E5 52 B1
Mount Pleasant Rd E17 35 A1
N17 33 C1
NW10 90 C6
SE13 164 A5
W5 87 C3
Kingston u T KT3 199 A6
Mount Pleasant Villas
N4 50 B2
Mount Prim Sch The
KT3 199 A6
Mount Rd NW2 68 C5
NW4 46 A3
SE19 183 B4
SW18,SW19 157 D2
Barnet EN4 14 C6
Bexley DA6 169 A6
Chessington KT9 214 B3
Dagenham RM8 59 B1
Mount Rd *continued*
Feltham TW13 151 A1
Hayes UB3 106 A4
Kingston u T KT3 199 B6
Mitcham CR4 180 C1
Mount Row W1 115 B6 248 C5
Mount Sch NW7 28 C5
Mount Sq The NW3 70 A5
Mount St W1 115 A6 248 B5
Mount Stewart Ave HA3 43 D2
Mount Stewart Jun & Inf
Schs HA3 43 D2
Mount Terr E1 96 B2
Mount The E5 74 B6
N2 30 C1
N20 14 A2
NW3 70 A5
W8 245 A3
Bexleyheath DA6 169 D6
Croydon CR2 221 A3
New Malden KT3 199 D6
North Cheam KT4 216 B4
Wembley HA9 67 A6
Mount Tyndal NW3 48 B1
Mount Vernon NW3 70 A4
Mount View W5 87 D3
Enfield EN2 4 B5
Southall UB2 106 D2
HA6 22 A4
Mount View Rd E4 20 B4
N4 50 B3
NW9 45 B4
Claygate KT10 213 B1
Mount Villas SE27 160 D1
Mountacre Cl SE26 183 D6
Mountague Pl 2 E14 120 A6
Mountain Ho SE11 260 C2
Mountaire Ct NW9 45 B4
Mountbatten Cl SE18 145 C6
6 SE19 183 C5
Mountbatten Ct IG9 21 D2
Mountbatten Gdns BR3 207 A5
Mountbatten Ho N6 49 A2
Mountbatten Mews
SW18 158 A3
Mountbel Rd HA7 25 A1
Mountcombe Cl KT6 198 A2
Mountearl Gdns SW16,
SW2 160 B1
Mountfield NW2 69 B6
Mountfield Cl SE6 164 B3
Mountfield Ct SE13 164 B5
Mountfield Rd E6 100 C4
N3 47 C6
W5 88 A1
Mountford Ho EN2 4 D1
Mountford St 4 E1 96 A1
Mountfort Cres N1 72 C1
Mountfort Terr 1 N1 72 C1
Mountgrove Rd N5 73 A5
Mounthurst Rd BR2 208 D2
Mountington Park Cl
HA3 43 D3
Mountjoy Cl SE2 124 B4
Mountjoy Ho EC2 242 A3
Mounts Pond Rd SE3,
SE13 142 B3
Mountside HA7 25 A2
Mountview NW7 11 B1
5 SW16 160 B1
Mountview Ct N8 50 D5
Mountview Theatre Sch
N8 50 A3
Mountwood KT8 195 D6
Mountwood Ho W5 87 D3
Mourne Ho NW3 70 A2
Movers La IG11 101 C6
Mowat Ct 3 KT4 215 D6
Mowatt Cl N19 49 D1
Mowbray Ct N22 32 C2
SE19 183 D2
Mowbray Gdns UB5 85 C6
Mowbray Ho 5 N2 30 B1
Mowbray Rd NW6 69 A1
SE19 183 D2
Edgware HA8 26 C6
New Barnet EN5 14 A6
Richmond TW10 153 C1
Mowlem JMI Sch E2 96 C5
Mowlem St E2 96 B5
Mowlem Trad Est N17 34 C3
Mowll St SW9 138 C5
Moxon Cl E13 98 D5
Moxon St W1 93 A2 238 A3
Hadley EN5 1 B2
Moye Cl 9 E2 96 A5
Moyers Rd E10 54 A2
Moylan Rd W6 135 A6 264 B5
Moyle Ho SW1 269 B6
Moyne Ho 16 SW9 138 D1
Moyne Pl NW10 88 C5
Moynihan Dr N21 16 A6
Moys Cl CR0 204 A3
Moyser Rd SW16 181 B5
Mozart St W10 91 B4
Mt Carmel RC Prim Sch
W5 109 C3
Muchelney Rd SM4 202 A3
Mudchute Sta E14 119 D2
Mudie Ho 8 SW2 160 A4
Muggeridge Cl CR2 221 B3
Muggeridge Rd RM10 81 D4
Muir Rd E5 74 A5
Muir St E16 122 A5
Muirdown Ave SW14 133 B1
Muirfield W3 89 C1
Muirfield Cl 23 SE16 118 B1
South Oxhey WD1 22 C6
Muirfield Cres E14 119 D3
Muirfield Gn WD1 22 C6
Muirfield Rd WD1 22 C6
Muirkirk Rd SE6 164 A3
Mulbarton Ct BR7 189 B4
Mulberry Ave TW19 148 A3
Mulberry Bsns Ctr
SE16 118 D4
Mulberry Cl E4 19 C2
N8 50 A4
NW3 70 B4
NW4 46 C6
SE7 143 D6
SE22 162 A5
SW3 266 D5
SW16 181 C6
Barnet EN4 2 B1
Northolt UB5 85 A5
Mulberry Cres
Brentford TW8 131 C5
West Drayton UB7 104 C4
Mulberry Ct 1 E11 76 B4
EC1 234 D1
N5 72 D3
NW10 67 B2
10 W9 91 B4
Barking IG11 79 D1
4 Surbiton KT6 197 D2
Twickenham TW1 152 D1
Mulberry Ho 1 E2 96 C4
8 SE8 141 B6
Mulberry La CR0 205 D1
Mulberry Mews SE14 141 B4
2 Wallington SM6 219 C2
Mulberry Par UB7 104 C4
Mulberry Pl W6 112 A1
Mulberry Rd E8 73 D1
Mulberry Sch for Girls
E1 118 B6
Mulberry Sec Sch E1 96 B1
Mulberry St 5 E1 96 A1
Mulberry Trees TW17 193 B2
Mulberry Way E18 37 B1
Ilford IG6 57 A5
Mulberry Wlk
SW3 136 B6 266 D6
Mulgrave Chambers
SM2 217 D2
Mulgrave Hall SM2 217 D2
Mulgrave Ho 20 SE18 122 B2
Mulgrave Manor SM2 217 D2
Mulgrave Prim Sch
SE18 122 C2
Mulgrave Rd NW10 67 D4
W5 87 D3
W14 264 C6
Belmont SM2 217 C2
Croydon CR0 221 B5
Harrow HA1 65 A6
Mulholland Cl CR4 181 B1
Mulkern Rd N19 49 D1
Mull Ho 13 E3 97 B5
Mull Wlk N1 73 B2
Mullard Ho WC1 239 C4
Mullards Cl CR4 202 D1
Mullen Twr EC1 241 A5
Mullens Ho 7 SW15 156 C6
Muller Ho SE18 122 C1
Mullet Gdns 5 E2 96 A4
Mulletsfield WC1 233 B1
Mullins Path SW14 133 B2
Mullion Cl HA3 23 D2
Mullion Wlk WD1 22 D6
Mulready St NW8 237 A5
Multi Way W3 111 C4
Multon Ho E9 74 C1
Multon Rd SW18 158 B4
Mulvaney Way SE1 252 D1
Mumford Ct EC2 242 B2
Mumford Rd SE24 160 D6
Muncaster Cl TW15 170 C6
Muncaster Rd SW11 159 A6
Ashford TW15 170 D5
Muncies Mews SE6 164 A2
Mund St W14 113 B1 254 D1
Mundania Ct SE22 162 B5
Mundania Rd SE22 162 C5
Munday Ho SE1 262 C5
Munday Rd E16 121 A6
Munden Ho 5 E3 97 D4
Munden St W14 113 A2 254 A4
Mundesley Cl WD1 22 C6
Mundford Rd E5 74 C6
Mundon Gdns IG1 57 B1
Mundy Ho 8 W10 91 A4
Mundy St N1 95 C4
Mungo-Park Cl WD2 8 A2
Munnery Way BR6 226 D6
Munnings Gdns TW7 152 B6
Munro Ho SE1 252 D1
SE1 251 A1
Munro Mews W10 91 A2
Munro Rd WD2 8 A6
Munslow Gdns SM1 218 B4
Munstead Ct 12 SM2 218 A1
Munster Ave TW4 151 A6
Munster Ct SW6 135 B3
Teddington TW11 175 C4
Munster Gdns N13 33 A6
Munster Rd
SW6 135 A4 264 B2
Teddington TW11 175 C4
Munster Residences
SW6 264 B2
Munster Sq NW1 93 B3 238 D6
Munton Rd SE1,
SE17 117 A2 262 B4
Murchison Ave DA5 169 A3
Murchison Ho 1 W10 91 A2
Murchison Rd E10 76 A6
Murdoch Ho 4 SE16 118 C3
Murdock Cl E16 98 D1
Murdock St SE15 140 B6
Murfett Cl SW19 157 A2
Muriel Ct 17 E10 53 D2
Muriel St N1 94 B6 233 D4
Murillo Rd SE13 142 C1
Murley Ct N21 17 A4
Murphy Ho SE1 261 D6
Murphy St SE1 116 C4 251 A1
Murray Ave Bromley BR1 187 B1
Isleworth TW3 151 D6
Murray Cres HA5 22 D2
Murray Ct 5 HA1 42 D3
Murray Gr N1 95 B5 235 C3
Murray Ho 21 SE18 122 B2
Murray Mews NW1 71 D1
Murray Rd SW19 178 D4
W5 109 C2
Richmond TW10 153 C2
Murray Sq E16 121 B6
Murray St NW1 71 D1
Murray Terr NW3 70 B4
Mus of Garden History
SE1 260 C5
Mus of London*
EC2 95 A2 242 A3
Mus of Mankind
W1 115 C6 249 A5
Mus of Richmond
TW10 153 D6
Mus of the Great Eastern
Railway E16 122 C4
Mus of the Moving Image
SE1 250 D4
Musard Rd W6 135 A6 264 B6
Musbury St E1 96 C1
Muscal W6 264 A6
Muscatel Pl SE5 139 C4
Muschamp Inf Sch
SM5 218 C6
Muschamp Jun Sch
SM5 218 C6
Muschamp Rd SE15 139 D2
Carshalton SM1,SM5 218 C6
Muscott Ho 15 E2 96 A6
Muscovy Ho DA18 125 A4
Muscovy St EC3 253 B6
Museum Ho 7 E2 96 C4
Museum St WC1 94 A1 240 A2
Musgrave Cl EN4 2 A4
Musgrave Cres
SW6 135 C4 265 B2
Musgrave Ct SW11 267 A2
Musgrave Rd TW7 130 D4
Musgrove Ho 1 E9 74 D2
Musgrove Rd SE14 141 A4
Musical Mus The TW8 132 A6
Musjid Rd 7 SW11 136 B3
Musquash Way TW4 128 C3
Muston Rd E5 74 B6
Mustow Pl 2 SW6 135 B3
Muswell Ave N10 31 B1
Muswell Hill N10 49 C6
Muswell Hill Bdwy N10 49 B6
Muswell Hill Jun & Inf Schs
N10 49 B6
Muswell Hill Pl N10 49 B5
Muswell Hill Rd N10 49 A4
Muswell Mews N10 49 B6
Muswell Rd N10 31 B1
Mutrix Rd NW6 91 C6
Mutton Pl NW1 71 A2
Muybridge Rd KT3 177 A1
Myatt Ct SE4 141 B3
Myatt Garden Prim Sch
SE4 141 B3
Myatt Ho SE5 138 D3
Myatt Rd SW9 138 D4
Myatts Field Ct SE5 139 A4
Mycenae Rd SE3 143 A6
Mychell Ho 8 SW19 180 A3
Myddelton Ave EN1 5 C5
Myddelton Cl EN1 5 D4
Myddelton Gdns N21 17 A4
Myddelton Ho N8 50 A6
Myddelton Pas
EC1 94 C4 234 B2
Myddelton Pk N20 14 B2
Myddelton Rd N8 50 A5
Myddelton Sq
EC1 94 C4 234 B2
Myddelton St
EC1 94 C4 234 B1
Myddleton Ave N4 73 A6
Myddleton Rd N22 32 B3
Myers Ho 5 SE5 139 A5
Myers La SE14 140 D6
Mylis Cl SE26 184 B6
Mylius Cl SE14 140 C4
Mylne Cl W6 112 A1
Mylne Ho N21 17 B5
Mylne St EC1 234 A3
Mynterne Ct 16 SW19 156 D3
Myra St SE2 124 A2
Myrdle Ct 8 E1 96 A1
Myrdle St E1 96 A1
Myrna Cl SW19 180 C3
Myron Pl SE13 142 A2
Myrtle Alley SE18 122 C3
Myrtle Ave Hatton TW14 149 C6
Ruislip HA4 40 B2
Myrtle Cl East Barnet EN4 14 D3
Hillingdon UB8 82 B2
West Drayton UB7 104 B3
Myrtle Gdns W7 108 C5
Myrtle Gr Enfield EN2 5 B5
Kingston u T KT3 177 A1
Myrtle Ho SE14 140 D4
Myrtle Rd E6 100 A6
E17 53 A3
N13 17 B1
W3 111 A5
Croydon CR0 223 C5
Hampton TW12 174 A4
Hounslow TW3 130 A3
Ilford IG1 78 D6
Sutton SM1 218 A3
Myrtle Wlk 20 N1 95 C5
Myrtledene Rd SE2 124 A1
Mysore Rd SW11 136 D1
Myton Rd SE21 161 B1
Mytton Ho SW8 270 C3

N

Nadine St SE7 121 C1
Nadir Ct E11 55 A2
Naffenton Rise IG10 21 D6
Nagle Cl E17 36 B1
Nags Head N7 72 B4
Nags Head Ct EC1 242 B5
Nag's Head La DA16 146 B2
Nags Head Rd EN3 6 D1
Nailsworth Ct 3 SE15 139 C6
Nainby Ho SE11 261 A3
Nairn Ct SW19 179 D4
3 Wallington SM6 219 C2
Nairn Rd HA4 62 C2
Nairn St E14 98 A2
Nairne Gr SE5,SE24 139 B1
Naish Ct N1 233 B6
Nallhead Rd TW13 172 C5
Nalton Ho 4 NW6 70 A1
Namba Roy Cl SW16 182 B6
Namton Dr CR7,SW16 204 B5
Nan Clark's La NW7 11 D2
Nankin St E14 97 C1
Nansen Ct 1 E11 76 C6
Nansen Ho 7 NW10 67 B1
Nansen Rd SW11 137 A2
Nansen Village 5 N12 29 D6
Nant Ct NW2 69 B6
Nant Rd NW2 69 B6
Nant St E2 96 B4
Nantes Cl SW18 136 A1
Naoroji St WC1 234 A1
Napier 15 NW9 27 D2
Napier Ave E14 119 C1
SW6 135 B2
Napier Cl SE14,SE8 141 B5
W14 254 C6
West Drayton UB7 104 B3
Napier Ct N1 235 C4
SE12 165 B1
SW6 135 B2
13 Croydon CR0 221 D6
Hayes UB4 84 C3
1 Surbiton KT6 197 D2
Napier Gr N1 95 A5 235 B4
Napier Lo TW15 171 B4
Napier Pl W14 113 B3 254 C5
Napier Rd E6 100 C5
E11 76 C5
E15 98 C5
N17 51 C6
NW10 90 B4
SE25 206 B5
W14 113 B3 254 C5
Ashford TW15 171 B3
Bromley BR2 209 B5
Enfield EN3 18 D6
Erith DA17 125 B2
Isleworth TW7 131 A1
South Croydon CR2 221 B1
Wembley HA0 65 D2
Napier Terr N1 72 D1
Napier Wlk TW15 171 B3
Napoleon Rd E5 74 B5
Twickenham TW1 153 B4
Napton Cl UB4 85 A3
Narbonne Ave SW4 159 C6
Narborough Cl UB10 61 A6
Narborough St SW6 135 D3
Narcissus Rd NW6 69 C3
Nardini 12 NW9 27 D2
Narford Rd E5 74 A6
Narrow St E14 119 A6
6 W3 110 D5
Narrow Way BR2 210 A3
Nascot St W12 90 C1
Naseby Cl NW6 70 A1
Hounslow TW7 130 C4
Naseby Ct DA14 189 D6
Naseby Rd SE19 183 B4
Dagenham RM10 81 C5
Naseby Twr SE14 141 A5
Nash Cl SM1 218 B5
Nash Ct HA3 43 B3
Nash Gn BR1 187 A4
Nash Ho 1 E17 53 D5
SW1 258 D1
Nash La BR2 225 A2
Nash Rd N9 18 C2
SE4 163 A6
Ilford RM6 58 D5
Nash Street NW1 231 D2
Nash Way HA3 43 B3
Nashe Ho SE1 262 C5
Nasmyth St W6 112 B3

Nassau Path 6 SE28 ..124 C5
Nassau Rd SW13 ......133 D4
Nassau St W1 ....239 A3
Nassington Rd NW3 ....70 D4
Nat West Twr★ EC2 ....243 A2
Natal Rd N11 ....32 A4
SW16 ....181 D4
Ilford IG1 ....78 D4
South Norwood CR7 .....205 B6
Natalie Cl TW14 ....149 B4
Natalie Mews TW2 ....152 B1
Nathan Ct N9 ....18 C4
Nathan Ho SE11 ....261 B3
Nathan Way SE28,SE18 .123 D3
Nathaniel Cl E1 ......243 D3
Nathaniel Ct E17 ....53 A3
Nathans Rd HA0 ....65 C6
Nation Way E4 ....20 A3
National Army Mus★
SW3 ....136 D6 267 D6
National Fan Mus SE10 142 A5
National Film Theatre
SE1 ....250 D4
National Gallery★
W1 ....115 D6 249 D5
National Hospital for Neurology & Neurosurgery
N2 ....48 C5
National Hospl The
WC1 ....94 A3 240 B5
National Maritime Mus★
SE10 ....142 B6
National Physical Laboratory
TW11 ....174 C4
National Portrait Gallery★
W1 ....115 D6 249 D5
National Portrait Gallery (Annexe)★
SW1 ....115 D5 249 D4
National Postal Mus
EC1 ....95 A1 242 A2
National Theatre
SE1 ....116 B5 250 D4
National Wks TW4 .....129 B2
Natural History Mus★
SW7 ....114 B3 256 C5
Naval Row E14 ....120 A6
Navarino Gr E8 ....74 A2
Navarino Mans E8 ......74 A2
Navarino Rd E8 ....74 A2
Navarre Rd E6 ....100 A5
Navarre St E2 ....243 C6
Navenby Wlk 13 E3 .....97 C3
Navestock Cl E4 ....20 A1
Navestock Cres IG8 ....37 C2
Navestock Ho IG11 ...102 B5
Navestock Terr IG8 .....37 C3
Navigator Dr UB2 .....108 A4
Navy St SW4 ....137 D2
Nayland Ho SE6 ....186 A6
Naylor Gr EN3 ....18 D6
Naylor Ho SE17 ....262 D2
13 SW8 ....137 D3
5 W10 ....91 B4
Naylor Rd N20 ....14 A2
SE15 ....140 B5
Nazareth Cl SE15 ......140 B3
Neal Ave UB1 ....85 B3
Neal Cl HA6 ....22 A2
Neal St WC2 ....94 A1 240 A1
Neald Ct HA9 ....66 C3
Neald Par HA9 ....66 B3
Nealden St SW9 ....138 B2
Neale Cl N2 ....48 A6
Neale Ct N10 ....31 B3
Neal's Yd WC2 ....240 A1
Near Acre NW9 ....27 D2
Neasden Cl NW10 .....67 C3
Neasden Junc NW10 ....67 C4
Neasden La NW10 ......67 C3
NW10 ....67 B5
Neasden La N NW10 ....67 C5
Neasden Sta NW10 .....67 C3
Neasham Rd RM8 ....80 B3
Neate St SE5 ....139 C6
SE5 ....139 D6
Neath Gdns SM4 ......202 A3
Neathouse Pl SW1 ....259 A4
Neats Acre HA4 ....39 B2
Neatscourt Rd E16 .....99 D2
Nebraska St
SE1 ....117 B4 252 C1
Neckinger SE16 117 D3 263 D6
Neckinger Est SE16 ..263 D6
Neckinger St SE1 ....263 D6
Nectarine Way SE13 ..141 D3
Nedahall Ct 4 NW11 ...47 B2
Needham Ho SE11 ....261 A3
Needham Rd W11 ......91 C1
Needham Terr NW2 .....68 D5
Needleman St SE16 ...118 D4
Needwood Ho N4 ....51 A1
Neela Cl UB10 ....60 D4
Neeld Cres NW4 ....46 B4
Wembley HA9 ....66 C3
Neil Cl TW15 ....171 A5
Neil Wates Cres 18
SW2 ....160 C3
Neilson-Terry Ct 9
SW9 ....138 B1
Nelgarde Rd SE6 ......163 C4
Nell Gwynn Ave TW17 .193 B3
Nell Gwynn Ho SW3 ...257 B3
Nella Rd W6 ....134 D6
Nelland Ct SE6 ....163 B2
Nelldale Rd SE16 ......118 C2
Nellgrove Rd UB10 .....82 D3
Nello James Gdns SE27 183 B6
Nelson Cl
East Bedfont TW14 .....149 D3
Hillingdon UB10 ....82 D4
Thornton Heath CR0 ....204 D1
Walton-on-T KT12 ......194 B1
Nelson Ct SE16 ....119 B5
Carshalton SM5 ....218 D5
Nelson Gdns E2 ....96 A4
Twickenham TW3,TW4 ...151 C5
Nelson Grove Rd SW19 180 A2
Nelson Ho 1 W5 ....88 A4
Nelson Hospl SW20 ....179 B1
Nelson La UB10 ....82 D4
Nelson Mandela Cl N10 .31 A1
Nelson Mandela Rd
SE3 ....143 C2
Nelson Pas EC1 ....235 B2
Nelson Pl N1 ....234 D3
Sidcup DA14 ....190 A6
Nelson Prim Sch E6 ...100 C5
Twickenham TW2 ....151 D5
Nelson Rd E4 ....35 D4
E11 ....55 B5
N8 ....50 B3
N9 ....18 B2
N15 ....51 C5
SE10 ....142 A6
SW19 ....180 A3
Ashford TW15 ....170 A5
Bromley BR2 ....209 C5
Enfield EN3 ....18 D5
Erith DA17 ....125 B1
Harmondsworth TW6 ....126 B4
Harrow HA1 ....42 C1
Hillingdon UB10 ....82 D4
New Malden KT3 ....199 B4
Sidcup DA14 ....190 A6
Stanmore HA7 ....25 C4
Twickenham TW2,TW4 ...151 C5
Nelson Sq SE1 .116 D4 251 C2
Nelson St E1 ....96 B1
E6 ....100 B5
E6 ....100 C6
E16 ....120 D6
Nelson Terr N1 ....234 D3
Nelson Trad Est SW19 .179 D2
Nelson's Monument★
WC2 ....250 A4
Nelsons Row SW4 .....137 D1
Nemoure Rd W3 ....111 A6
Nene Gdns TW13 ......151 B2
Nene Rd TW6,UB7 .....126 D4
Nene Road Rdbt TW6 .126 D4
Nepaul Rd 17 SW11 ...136 C2
Nepean St SW15 ......156 A4
Neptune Ct 5 E14 .....119 C2
Neptune Ho 14 N16 .....73 C3
2 SE16 ....118 C3
Neptune Rd
Harlington TW6 ....127 A4
Harrow HA1 ....42 B3
Neptune St SE16 ......118 C3
Nero Ct 6 TW8 ....131 D5
Nesbit Cl SE3 ....142 C2
Nesbit Rd SE9 ....143 D1
Nesbitt Ho DA6 ....169 D6
Nesbitt Sq SE19 ....183 C3
Nesham Ho 14 N1 ......95 C6
Nesham St E1 ....118 A5
Ness St 9 SE16 ....118 A3
Nesta Rd IG8 ....36 D4
Nestle's Ave UB3 ......105 D3
Nestor Ave N21 ....16 D5
Nestor Ho 18 E2 ....96 B5
Nether Cl N3 ....29 C3
Nether St N3 ....29 D4
N12 ....30 A5
Netheravon Rd W4 ....111 D1
W7 ....108 D5
Netheravon Rd S W4 ..111 D1
Netherbury Rd W5 ....109 D3
Netherby Gdns EN2 ......4 A1
Netherby Ho 23 SW8 ..137 D3
Netherby Rd SE23 .....162 C4
Nethercombe Ho 1
SE3 ....143 A6
Nethercott Ho 27 E3 ....97 D4
Nethercourt Ave N3 .....29 C4
Netherfield Gdns IG11 ..79 B1
Netherfield Rd N12 .....29 D5
SW17 ....159 A1
Netherford Rd SW4 ...137 C3
Netherhall Gdns NW3 ...70 A3
Netherhall Way NW3 ....70 A3
Netherlands Rd EN5 .....14 B5
Netherleigh Cl N6 ....49 B1
Netherton Gr
SW10 ....136 A6 266 B5
Netherton Rd N15 ....51 B3
Isleworth TW1 ....153 B6
Netherwood 19 N2 ......30 B1
Netherwood Rd W14 ...112 D4
Netherwood St NW6 ....69 C2
Nethewode Ct DA17 ...125 D3
Netley 18 SE5 ....139 C4
Netley Cl Cheam SM3 ..216 D3
New Addington CR0 ....224 A1
Netley Ct IG2 ....57 B4
Netley Dr KT12 ....195 B2
Netley Gdns SM4 ......202 A2
Netley Prim Sch
NW1 ....93 C4 232 A1
Netley Rd E17 ....53 B4
Brentford TW8 ....132 A6
Ilford IG2 ....57 B4
Netley Rd *continued*
Morden SM4 ....202 A2
Netley Rd (W) TW6 ....127 B4
Netley St NW1 ...93 C4 232 A1
Nettlecombe NW1 ....71 D1
Nettleden Ave HA9 .....66 C2
Nettleden Ho SW3 .....257 B3
Nettlefold Pl SE27 .....160 D1
Nettlestead Cl 16 BR3 .185 C3
Nettleton Rd SE14 .....140 D4
Harlington TW6 ....126 D4
Ickenham UB10 ....60 B4
Nettlewood Rd SW16 ..181 D3
Neuchatel Rd SE6 .....163 B2
Nevada Cl KT3 ....199 A5
Nevada St SE10 ....142 A6
Nevena Ct 3 SW2 .....160 C6
Nevern Mans SW5 .....255 A2
Nevern Pl SW5 .113 C2 255 B3
Nevern Rd SW5 ....255 A3
Nevern Sq SW5 113 C2 255 B3
Nevil Ho 7 SW9 ....138 D3
Nevil Ct SW10 ....266 A4
Nevil Rd N16 ....73 C5
Neville Ave KT3 ....177 B2
Neville Cl E11 ....76 D5
NW1 ....232 D3
NW6 ....91 B5
SE15 ....140 A4
17 SE15 ....140 A5
W3 ....111 A4
Hounslow TW3 ....129 D3
Sidcup DA15 ....189 D6
Neville Ct NW8 ....229 C3
10 SW12 ....159 C4
Neville Dr N2 ....48 A3
Neville Gdns RM8 ....80 D5
Neville Gill Cl SW18 ...157 D5
Neville Ho N11 ....31 A6
Neville Pl N22 ....32 B2
Neville Rd E7 ....77 B1
NW6 ....91 B5
W5 ....87 D3
Croydon CR0 ....205 B2
Dagenham RM8 ....80 D5
Kingston u T KT1 ....176 C1
Richmond TW10 ....153 C2
Neville St SW7 .114 B1 256 C2
Neville Terr SW7 ....256 C2
Neville Wlk SM5 ......202 C2
Neville's Ct NW2 ....68 A5
Nevin Dr E4 ....19 D3
Nevin Ho UB3 ....105 A3
Nevinson Cl SW18 ....158 B5
Nevis Rd SW17 ....159 A2
Nevitt Ho N1 ....235 D3
New Ash Cl N2 ....48 B6
New Barn Cl SM6 .....220 B2
New Barn St E13 ....99 B3
New Barnet Sta EN5 ....14 B6
New Barns Ave CR4 ...203 D5
New Beckenham Sta
BR3 ....185 B3
New Belmont Ho 4
SE23 ....162 C3
New Bentham Ct 11 N1 .73 A1
New Bond St
W1 ....115 B6 248 D6
New Brent St NW4 ......46 C4
New Bridge St
EC4 ....94 D1 241 C1
New Broad St
EC2 ....95 C2 243 A3
New Broadway W5 .....109 D6
7 Hillingdon UB10 ......82 D3
New Bsns Ctr The NW10 89 D4
New Burlington Mews
W1 ....249 A6
New Burlington Pl W1 .249 A6
New Burlington St W1 249 A6
New Butt La SE8 ......141 C5
New Caledonian Wharf
SE16 ....119 B3
New Campden Ct 7
NW3 ....70 A4
New Cavendish St
W1 ....93 B2 238 C3
New Change EC4 95 A1 242 A1
New Chapel Sq TW13 ..150 B3
New Charles St EC1 ...234 D2
New Church Ct 3 SE19 184 A3
New Church Rd SE5 ...139 B6
32 SE5 ....139 A5
New City Prim Sch E13 .99 C4
New City Rd E13 ....99 C4
New Cl SW19 ....202 A6
Feltham TW13 ....173 A5
New Colebrooke Ct
SM5 ....219 A1
New College Ct 6 NW3 .70 A2
New College Par 1
NW3 ....70 B1
New Compton St
WC2 ....94 A1 240 A1
New Concordia Wharf
SE1 ....253 D2
New Covent Garden Flower Market SW8 ..138 A6 270 A5
New Covent Garden Fruit & Vegetable Market
SW8 ....137 D5 269 C3
New Cross SE14 ....141 B5
New Cross Gate SE14 .140 D4
New Cross Gate Sta
SE14 ....141 A5
New Cross Hospl SE14 .140 C5
New Cross Rd SE14 ....141 A4
New Cross Sta SE14 ...141 B5
New Ct EC4 ....241 A1
N16 ....51 B1
13 NW3 ....70 A4
Northolt UB5 ....63 D3
New Den The(Millwall FC)
SE16 ....118 C1
New Eltham Sta SE9 ...166 D3
New End NW3 ....70 A5
New End Prim Sch NW3 70 A4
New End Sq NW3 ....70 B4
New England Est IG11 .101 A5
New Farm Ave BR2 ....209 A5
New Fetter La
EC4 ....94 C1 241 B2
New Furness Prim Sch The
NW10 ....90 A5
New Garden Dr UB7 ...104 A4
New Globe Wlk SE1 ...252 A4
New Goulston St E1 ...243 C2
New Green Pl SE19 ...183 C4
New Heston Rd TW5 ...129 B5
New Inn Broadway EC2 243 B6
New Inn Pas WC2 ......240 D1
New Inn Sq EC2 ....243 B6
New Inn St EC2 ....243 B6
New Inn Yd EC2 .95 C3 243 B6
New James Ct SE15 ....140 B2
New Jubilee Ct 1 IG8 ..37 A3
New Kelvin Ave TW11 .174 C4
New Kent Rd
SE1 ....117 A2 262 B4
New King St SE8 ......141 C6
New Kings Rd SW6 ....135 C3
New King's Rd
SW6 ....135 C3 265 B1
New Kings Sch SW6 ...135 B3
New London St EC3 ...253 B6
New Lydenburg Commercial Est E16 ....121 C3
New Lydenburg St SE7 121 C3
New Malden Sta KT3 ..199 C6
New Mill Rd BR5 ......190 C2
New Mount St E15 ......76 B1
New North Pl EC2 .....243 A6
New North Rd
N1 ....95 B6 235 C5
New North St
WC1 ....94 B2 240 C4
New Oak Rd N2 ....30 A1
New Oxford St
WC1 ....94 A1 240 A2
New Palace Yd
SW1 ....116 A4 250 A1
New Par Ashford TW15 ..170 B6
Yiewsley UB7 ....104 A5
New Park Ave N13 ......17 B1
New Park Cl UB5 ....63 A2
New Park Ct 26 SW2 ..160 A4
New Park Est N18 ......34 C5
New Park Ho N13 ....32 B6
New Park Par 14 SW2 .160 A4
New Park Rd SW2 .....160 A4
Ashford TW15 ....171 A5
New Pl CR0 ....223 C2
New Place Sq SE16 ...118 B3
New Plaistow Rd E15 ...98 C6
New Pond Par HA4 .....62 A5
New Priory Ct 9 NW6 ..69 C1
New Quebec St W1 ...237 D1
New Rd E1 ....96 B2
E4 ....36 A6
N8 ....50 A4
N9 ....18 A2
N10 ....30 C2
N22 ....33 A2
NW7 ....29 A3
SE2 ....124 D1
Bexley DA16 ....146 B3
Brentford TW8 ....109 D1
Carshalton CR4 ....203 A1
Dagenham RM10 ....103 D5
East Bedfont TW14 ....149 B5
East Molesey KT8 .....195 C6
Elstree WD6 ....9 D5
Esher KT10 ....212 A4
Feltham TW13 ....173 A5
Feltham TW14 ....150 B3
Harlington TW6,UB7 ...127 A5
Harrow HA1 ....64 D4
Hillingdon UB8 ....83 A2
Hounslow TW3 ....129 D1
Ilford IG3 ....79 C6
Kingston u T KT2 ....176 C3
Littleton TW17 ....192 D6
Richmond TW10 ......175 C6
New Rd Units TW3 ....129 D1
New River Cres N13 ....32 D6
New River Ct N5 ....73 B4
New River Sports & Recreation Ctr N22 ....32 D3
New River Way N4 ......51 B2
New Row WC2 .116 A6 250 A6
New Royal Horticultural Society SW1 ....259 C5
New Scotland Yard★
SW1 ....115 D3 259 C6
New Southgate Ind Est 10
N11 ....31 C5
New Southgate Sta N11 .31 B5
New Spring Gdns Wlk
SE11 ....260 B1
New Sq WC2 ...94 B1 240 D2
East Bedfont TW14 ....149 A3
New Sq Pas WC2 ......241 A2
New St EC2 .....95 C2 243 B3
New St Sq EC4 ..94 C1 241 B2
New Street Hill BR1 ...187 C5
New Tower Bldgs 21
E1 ....118 B5
New Trinity Rd 1 N2 ....30 B1
New Union Cl E14 .....120 A3
New Union St EC2 .....242 C3
New Victoria Hospl
KT3 ....177 C2
New Wanstead E11 .....55 A3
New Way Rd NW9 ......45 C5
New Wharf Rd
N1 ....94 A5 233 B4
New Woodlands Sch
BR1 ....186 C6
New Zealand Ave KT12 193 D1
Newall Ho SE1 ....262 B6
Newall Rd TW6 ....127 A4
Newark Cres NW10 .....89 B4
Newark Ct KT12 ......194 C1
Newark Ho 3 SW9 ....138 D3
Newark Knok E6 ......100 C2
Newark Par NW4 ....46 A6
Newark Rd CR2 ....221 B2
Newark St E1 ....96 B2
Newark Way NW4 ......46 A6
Newbery Ho N1 ....73 A1
Newbiggin Path WD1 ...22 C6
Newbold Cotts 4 E1 ...96 C1
Newbolt Ave SM3 .....216 D3
Newbolt Ho SE17 .....262 C2
Newbolt Rd HA7 ....24 D5
Newborough Gn KT3 ..199 B5
Newborough Ho SW19 .180 B3
Newbridge Ct SW17 ..180 A6
Newbridge Point 3
SE23 ....162 D1
Newburgh Rd W3 .....111 A5
Newburgh St W1 ......239 B1
Newburn Ho SE11 .....260 D2
Newburn St
SE11 ....116 B1 260 D2
Newbury Ave EN3 ....7 B6
Newbury Cl UB5 ....63 B2
Newbury Cotts 4 IG2 ..57 A3
Newbury Ct E5 ....75 A3
7 E11 ....55 A5
Sidcup DA14 ....189 D6
Newbury Gdns KT19 ..215 D4
Newbury Ho N22 ....32 A2
SW9 ....138 D3
13 W2 ....91 D1
Newbury Mews NW5 ....71 A2
Newbury Park Prim Sch
IG2 ....57 B3
Newbury Park Sta IG2 ..57 B3
Newbury Rd E4 ....36 A4
Bromley BR2 ....209 A6
Harmondsworth TW6 ...126 B4
Ilford IG2 ....57 C3
Newbury St EC1 ......242 A4
Newbury Way UB5 .....63 B2
Newby NW1 ....232 A2
Newby Cl EN1 ....5 C3
Newby Pl E14 ....120 A6
Newby St SW8 ....137 B2
Newcastle Cl EC4 ......241 C2
Newcastle Ct EC4 .....252 B6
Newcastle Ho W1 .....238 A4
Newcastle Pl W2 92 B2 236 D4
Newcastle Row EC1 ...241 B5
Newcombe Ho N5 ......73 A3
Newcombe Pk NW7 ....27 C5
Wembley HA0 ....88 B6
Newcombe Rise UB7 ...82 A1
Newcombe St W8 .....245 B4
Newcome Gdns SW16 .182 A6
Newcome Ho E5 ....74 B5
Newcomen Ho 5 NW5 ..71 B4
Newcomen Rd E11 .....76 D5
SW11 ....136 B2
Newcomen St
SE1 ....117 B4 252 C2
Newcourt Ho 26 E2 ....96 B4
Newcourt St
NW8 ....92 C5 230 A3
Newcroft Cl UB8 ....82 B2
Newdales Cl N9 ....18 A2
Newdene Ave UB5 ......84 D5
Newdigate Ho 5 E14 ...97 B1
1 Kingston u T KT2 ....176 D4
Newell St E14 ....97 B1
Newent Cl SE15 ....139 C5
Carshalton SM5 ....202 D1
Newfield Cl TW12 .....173 C2
Newfield Prim Sch
NW10 ....67 D1
Newfield Rise NW2 .....68 B5
Newgale Gdns HA8 .....26 B2
Newgate CR0 ....205 A1
Newgate Cl TW13 .....151 A1
Newgate St E4 ....20 C1
EC1 ....94 D1 241 D2
Newham Acad of Music
E6 ....100 A6
Newham Coll of F Ed (Royal Docks Campus) E16 ..123 A5
Newham Coll of F Ed (Stratford Campus)
E15 ....76 C1
Newham Com Coll E6 .100 B5
Newham General Hospl
E13 ....99 C3
Newham Gn N22 ....32 C2
Newham Ho IG10 ....21 D5
Newham Sch of Nursing
E3 ....97 D3
Newham Sixth Form Coll
E13 ....99 B3
Newham Way E6 ......100 B3
Newham Way *continued*
E13 ....99 B2
Newham's Row SE1 ...253 B1
Newhaven Cl UB3 .....105 D2
Newhaven Cres TW15 .171 B5
Newhaven Gdns SE9 ..143 D1
Newhaven La 3 E16 ....99 A2
Newhaven Rd SE25 ....205 B4
Newhouse 5 KT3 ......199 C2
Newhouse Ave RM6 ....58 D6
Newhouse Cl KT3 .....199 C2
Newhouse Wlk SM4 ...202 A2
Newick Cl DA5 ....169 D5
Newick Rd E5 ....74 C5
Newing Gn BR1 ....187 D3
Newington Barrow Way
N7 ....72 B5
Newington Butts
SE1,SE11 ....116 D2 261 D3
Newington Cswy
SE1 ....117 A3 262 A6
Newington Green Mans
N16 ....73 B3
Newington Green Prim Sch
N16 ....73 B3
Newington Green Rd N1 73 B3
Newington Ind Est
SE17 ....262 A3
Newland Cl HA5 ....23 B4
Newland Ct EC1 ....242 C6
Wembley HA9 ....66 C6
Newland Dr EN1 ....6 B4
Newland Gdns W13 ...109 A4
Newland Ho N8 ....50 A6
17 SE14 ....140 D6
Newland House Sch
TW1 ....174 D6
Newland House Sch Annex
TW1 ....174 D6
Newland Rd N8 ....50 A6
Newland St E16 ....122 B5
Newlands NW1 ....232 A2
Newlands Ave KT7 ....196 C1
Newlands Cl
Edgware HA8 ....10 A1
Southall UB2 ....107 A1
Wembley HA0 ....65 C2
Newlands Croft SE20 ..184 D4
Newlands Ct 8 SE9 ...166 C5
SW16 ....182 A5
Newlands Pk SE26 ....184 D5
Newlands Pl EN5 ....12 D6
Newlands Quay E1 ....118 C6
Newlands Rd SW16 ...182 A1
Woodford IG8 ....20 D2
Newlands The SM6 ...219 D1
Newlands Way KT9 ...213 C3
Newling Cl E6 ....100 B1
Newlyn NW1 ....232 B5
Newlyn Cl UB8 ....82 C2
Newlyn Gdns HA2 ......41 B2
Newlyn Rd N17 ....33 D2
Bexley DA16 ....145 D3
Chipping Barnet EN5 .....1 B1
Newman Pas W1 ......239 B3
Newman Rd E13 ....99 B4
E17 ....52 D4
Hayes UB3 ....106 B6
Plaistow BR1 ....187 A2
Thornton Heath CR0 ...204 B1
Newman St W1 .93 C2 239 B3
Newman's Ct EC3 .....242 D1
Newman's Row WC2 ..240 D3
Newman's Way EN4 .....2 A4
Newmarket Ave UB5 ...63 D3
Newmarket Gn SE9 ...165 D4
Newmill Ho E3 ....98 A3
Newminster Rd SM4 ...202 A3
Newmount NW3 ....70 B3
Newnes Path SW15 ...134 B1
Newnham Ave HA4 .....40 C1
Newnham Cl
Loughton IG10 ....21 D5
Northolt UB5 ....64 A2
South Norwood CR7 ...183 A1
Newnham Gdns UB5 ...64 A2
Newnham Ho SE6 .....164 A1
9 SW15 ....156 D5
Newnham Jun & Inf Schs
HA4 ....40 C1
Newnham Lo 10 DA17 .125 C1
Newnham Rd N22 ......32 C2
Newnham Terr SE1 ....261 A6
Newnham Way HA3 ....44 A4
Newnhams Cl BR1 .....210 B6
Newnton Cl N4 ....51 B2
Newport Ave E13 ....99 B3
E14 ....120 B6
Newport Cl EN3 ....7 A6
Newport Ct WC2 ......249 D6
Newport Ho E3 ....97 A4
Newport Jun & Inf Schs
E10,E11 ....76 A6
Newport Lo 2 EN1 .....17 C6
Newport Mead WD1 ....22 D6
Newport Pl WC2 ......249 D6
Newport Rd E10 ....76 B6
E17 ....53 A5
SW13 ....134 A4
Harmondsworth TW6 ...126 C4
Hayes UB4 ....83 B2
Newport St
SE11 ....116 B2 260 D4
Newquay Cres HA2 ....63 A6
Newquay Ho SE11 ....261 A2
Newquay Rd SE6 .....164 A2
Newry Rd TW1 ....153 A6
Newsam Ave N15 ......51 B4

Newsholme Dr N21 16 B6
Newstead Ave BR6 227 C6
Newstead Cl N12 30 C4
Newstead Ct UB5 85 A4
Newstead Rd SE12 164 D4
Newstead Way SW19 178 D6
Newstead Wlk SM5 202 A2
Newstead Wood Sch for Girls
BR6 227 B5
Newton Ave N10 31 B2
W3 111 A4
Newton Cl E17 53 A3
Harrow HA2 63 C6
Newton Farm Fst & Mid Schs
HA2 63 B6
Newton Gr W4 111 C2
Newton Ho 1 E1 118 B6
10 E17 54 A6
NW8 91 D6
22 SW8 137 D3
Newton Point 1 E16 98 D1
Newton Prep Sch
SW8 137 B4 268 D2
Newton Rd E15 76 B3
N15 52 A4
NW2 68 C5
SW19 179 A3
W2 91 D1
Bexley DA16 146 A2
Harrow HA3 24 C1
Isleworth TW7 130 D3
Wembley HA0 66 B1
Newton St WC2 94 A1 240 B2
Newton Terr BR2 209 D3
Newton Way N18 33 A5
Newton Wlk HA8 26 D2
Newton's Yd 14 SW18 157 C6
Newtown Ct SW4 159 B6
SW11 268 C1
Newtown St
SW11 137 B4 268 C2
Newyears Green La UB9 38 B3
Niagara Ave W5 109 C2
Niagara Cl N1 235 B4
Niagara Ct 6 SE16 118 C3
Niagara Ho W5 109 C2
Nibthwaite Rd HA1 42 C4
Nichol Cl N14 15 D3
Nichol La BR1 187 A3
Nicholas Cl UB6 85 D5
Nicholas Ct SE12 165 A3
W4 133 C5
Nicholas Gdns W5 109 D4
Nicholas Ho SE26 184 B4
2 SW15 156 A6
W13 87 C1
Nicholas La EC2,EC4 252 D6
Nicholas Pas EC3 252 D6
Nicholas Rd E1 96 C3
Dagenham RM8 81 B5
Deacons Hill WD6 10 B6
Wallington CR0 220 A4
Nicholas Stacey Ho 3
SE7 121 B1
Nicholay Rd N19 49 D1
Nicholes Rd TW3 129 C1
Nicholl Ho N4 51 A1
Nicholl St E2 96 A6
Nicholls Ave UB8 82 C3
Nicholls Point E15 99 A6
Nichols Cl N4 50 C1
Chessington KT9 213 C2
Nichols Gn W5 88 A2
Nicholson Ho SE17 262 C2
2 SE18 144 A4
Nicholson Rd CR0 205 D1
Nicholson St SE1 251 C3
Nickelby Cl SE28 102 C1
Nickleby Cl UB8 82 D1
Nickleby Ho 15 SE1 118 A4
7 W11 112 D5
Nicol Cl 6 TW1 153 B5
Nicola Cl Croydon CR2 221 A2
Harrow HA3 24 B1
Nicola Terr DA7 147 A4
Nicole Ho SE25 206 A6
Nicoll Ct N10 31 B3
NW10 89 C6
Nicoll Pl NW4 46 B2
Nicoll Rd NW10 89 C6
Nicoll Way WD6 11 B6
Nicolson 14 NW9 27 D2
Nicolson Dr WD2 8 A2
Nicosia Rd SW18 158 C4
Niederwald Rd SE26 185 A6
Nield Rd UB3 105 D4
Nigel Cl UB5 85 A6
Nigel Ct N3 29 D3
Nigel Fisher Way KT9 213 D1
Nigel Ho EC1 241 A4
Nigel Mews IG1 78 D4
Nigel Playfair Ave W6 112 B1
Nigel Rd E7 77 C3
SE15 140 A2
Nigeria Rd SE7 143 D5
Nighthawk 16 NW9 27 D2
Nightingale Ave E4 36 C5
Nightingale Cl E4 36 C6
W4 133 A6
Carshalton SM5 219 A6
Pinner HA5 40 C4
Nightingale Ct 1 E11 55 B4
12 E14 120 A3
N4 72 B6
SE19 183 D4
SW6 265 D1
1 Harrow HA1 42 D3
Nightingale Dr KT19 214 D2
Nightingale Gr SE13 164 B6
Nightingale Ho 21 E1 95 C6
7 E1 118 A5
SE18 122 C1
W12 90 C1
Hayes UB3 105 D2
Nightingale La E11 55 B4
N8 50 A6
SW11,SW12 159 A5
Bromley BR1 187 D1
Richmond TW10 154 A4
Nightingale Lo 5 W9 91 C2
Nightingale Pl SE18 144 D6
Nightingale Prim Sch
E18 55 C5
N22 32 B2
SE18 122 D1
Nightingale Rd E5 74 B5
N9 18 C4
N22 32 B3
NW10 89 D5
W7 108 D5
Carshalton SM5 219 A6
East Molesey KT8 195 D4
Hampton TW12 173 C4
Petts Wood BR5 211 A3
Walton-on-T KT12 194 B2
Nightingale Sq SW12 159 A4
Nightingale Vale SE18 144 C6
Nightingale Way E6 100 A2
Nightingale Wlk SW18,
SW4 159 B5
Nightingales The TW19 148 B3
Nile Cl N16 73 D5
Nile Ho N1 235 C2
Nile Path 6 SE18 144 C6
Nile Rd E13 99 C5
Nile St N1 95 B4 235 C2
Nile Terr SE1,
SE15 117 D1 263 D1
Nimegen Way 9 SE22 161 C6
Nimmo Dr WD2 8 B4
Nimrod 9 NW9 27 C2
Nimrod Cl UB5 84 D4
Nimrod Pas 4 N1 73 C2
Nimrod Rd SW16 181 B5
Nine Acres Cl E12 78 A3
Nine Acres Sch SE18 123 B1
Nine Elms Cl TW14 149 D3
Nine Elms La
SW8 137 D6 269 C5
Nineteenth Rd CR4 204 A5
Ninhams Wood BR6 226 C4
Ninth Ave UB3 106 A6
Nisbet 10 NW9 27 C2
Nisbet Ho E9 74 D3
Nita Ct SE12 165 A3
Nithdale Rd SE18 145 A5
Nithsdale Gr UB10 61 A5
Niton Cl EN5 12 D5
Niton Rd TW9 132 C2
Niton St SW6 134 D5
No 1 Mag Rd SE28 123 D5
No 1 St SE18 122 D3
No 2 St SE18 122 D3
Nobel Dr TW6 127 C5
Nobel Ho 8 SE5 139 A3
Nobel Rd N18 34 C6
Noble Cnr TW5 129 C4
Noble Ct E1 118 B6
Mitcham CR4 180 B1
Noble Ho 12 E1 118 A6
Noble St EC2 95 A1 242 A2
Noblefield Hts N2 48 D4
Noel 13 NW9 27 D2
Noel Baker Ct 4 E11 76 C6
Noel Coward Ho SW1 259 B3
Noel Ct TW4 129 B2
Noel Dene W5 109 C1
Noel Ho 3 NW3 70 B1
Noel Park Jun & Inf Schs
N22 32 C1
Noel Park Rd N22 32 C1
Noel Rd E6 100 A3
N1 94 D5 234 D4
W3 88 D1
Noel Sq RM8 80 C4
Noel St W1 93 C1 239 B1
Noel Terr SE23 162 C2
Nolan Way E5 74 A4
Noll Ho N7 72 B6
Nolton Pl HA8 26 B2
Nonsuch Ct SM3 217 A2
Nonsuch High Sch for Girls
SM3 216 D1
Nonsuch Prim Sch
KT17 216 B3
Nora Gdns NW4 46 D5
Norbiton Ave KT1,KT2 176 C1
Norbiton Common Rd
KT1,KT3 198 D6
Norbiton Hall KT2 176 B1
Norbiton Rd E14 97 B1
Norbiton Sta KT1 176 C1
Norbroke St W12 111 D6
Norbrook Gdns NW10 88 B4
Norburn St W10 91 A2
Norbury Ave
Isleworth TW3 130 B1
South Norwood CR7,
SW16 182 C1
Norbury Cl SW16 182 D2
Norbury Court Rd
SW16 182 A1
Norbury Cres SW16 182 C1
Norbury Cross SW16 204 A6
Norbury Fst & Mid Sch
HA1 42 C4
Norbury Gdns RM6 58 D4
Norbury Gr NW7 11 C1
Norbury Hill SW16 182 D3
Norbury Manor Girls High
Sch CR7 182 C2
Norbury Manor Prim Sch
SW16 182 A2
Norbury Rd E4 35 C5
South Norwood CR7 205 A6
Norbury Rise SW16 204 A6
Norbury Sta SW16 182 B2
Norbury Trad Est SW16 182 B1
Norcombe Gdns HA3 43 C4
Norcombe Ho 2 N19 71 D5
Norcott Cl UB4 84 C3
Norcott Rd N16 74 A5
Norcroft Gdns SE22 162 A4
Norcutt Rd TW2 152 C3
Norden Ho 25 E2 96 B4
Norden Point NW2 46 C1
Nore Ct NW10 68 A1
Norfolk Ave N13 32 D4
N15 51 D3
Norfolk Cl N2 48 C6
N13 32 D4
Cockfosters EN4 3 A1
5 Twickenham TW1 153 B5
Norfolk Cres W2 92 C1 237 B2
Sidcup DA15 167 C4
Norfolk Ct
4 Chipping Barnet EN5 1 A1
Surbiton KT5 198 B3
Wembley HA0 65 C2
Norfolk Gdns DA7 147 B4
Norfolk Ho E8 73 D4
EC4 252 A6
SE3 142 C6
SE8 141 C4
SE20 184 C2
SW1 259 D4
4 SW15 156 C4
11 SW19 180 A3
13 W3 88 C1
2 Croydon CR0 221 B6
Richmond TW10 154 C6
3 Stanmore HA7 25 C5
Norfolk House Prep Sch
N10 31 B1
Norfolk House Rd
SW16 160 A1
Norfolk Mans SW11 267 D1
10 SW18 157 C6
Norfolk Pl W2 92 B1 236 D2
Bexley DA16 146 A3
Norfolk Rd E6 100 B6
E17 34 D1
NW8 92 B6 229 D5
NW10 67 C1
SW19 180 C4
Barking IG11 79 C1
Barnet EN5 1 C2
Claygate KT10 212 C3
Dagenham RM10 81 D3
Enfield EN3 18 B6
Feltham TW13 150 C3
Harrow HA1 41 D4
Ilford IG3 57 C2
South Norwood CR7 205 A6
Norfolk Row
SE1,SE11 116 B2 260 C4
Norfolk Sq W2 92 B1 236 D2
Norfolk Sq Mews W2 236 D1
Norfolk St E7 77 A3
Norgrove St SW12 159 A4
Norhyrst Ave SE25 205 D6
Norland Ho 13 W11 112 D5
Norland Pl W11 113 A5 244 B3
Norland Place Sch
W11 113 A5 244 A3
Norland Rd W11 112 D5
Norland Sq
W11 113 A5 244 B3
Norlands Cres BR7 188 D2
Norley Vale SW15 156 A3
Norlington Boys Sch E10 54 B1
Norlington Rd E10,E11 54 B1
Norman Ave N22 33 A2
Feltham TW13 151 B2
Southall UB1 107 A6
Twickenham TW1 153 C4
Norman Butler Ho 10
W10 91 A3
Norman Cl N22 33 A2
Orpington BR6 227 A5
Norman Cres
Heston TW5 128 D5
Northwood HA5 22 C2
Norman Ct N4 50 C2
NW10 68 A1
SE22 162 A4
SW16 182 C5
7 Hampton TW12 173 C2
Ilford IG2 57 B3
Woodford IG8 37 B5
Norman Gr E3 97 A5
Norman Ho 6 E11 76 C6
SW8 270 A4
Feltham TW13 151 B2
Lower Halliford TW17 192 C2
Norman Par DA14 168 D2
Norman Rd E6 100 B3
E11 76 C6
N15 51 D4
SE10 141 D5
SW19 180 A3
Ashford TW15 171 B4
Belvedere DA17 125 D3
Belvedere DA17 125 D5
Norman Rd *continued*
Ilford IG1 78 D3
Sutton SM1 217 C3
Thornton Heath CR7 204 D4
Norman St EC1 95 A4 235 B1
Norman Way N14 16 A2
W3 88 D1
Normanby Cl SW15 157 B6
Normanby Rd NW10 67 D4
Normand Mews W14 264 B6
Normand Park Prim Sch
W14 135 B6 264 D6
Normand Rd
W14 135 B6 264 C6
Normandy Ave EN5 1 B1
Normandy Cl SE26 163 A1
Normandy Dr UB3 83 A1
Normandy Ho 4 NW4 28 D1
Normandy Rd SW9 138 C4
Normandy Terr E16 99 B1
Normanhurst TW15 170 C5
Normanhurst Ave DA16 146 D4
Normanhurst Dr TW1 153 B6
Normanhurst Rd SW2 160 B2
St Paul's Cray BR5 190 B1
Walton-on-T KT12 194 D1
Normanhurst Sch E4 20 B4
Normans Cl NW10 67 B2
Hillingdon UB8 82 A2
Normans Mead NW10 67 B2
Normansfield Ave KT1,
KT8 175 C3
Normansfield Hospl
KT8 175 C3
Normanshire Dr E4 35 D6
Normanton Ave SW18,
SW19 157 C2
Normanton Ct CR2 221 C3
Normanton Ho 6 SW4 159 C5
Normanton Pk E4 20 C2
Normanton Rd CR2 221 C2
Normanton St SE23 162 D2
Normington Cl SW16 182 C5
Norrice Lea N2 48 B4
Norris 11 NW9 27 D2
Norris Ho 22 E9 96 C6
12 N1 95 C6
Norris St SW1 249 C5
Norroy Rd SW15 134 D1
Norrys Cl EN4 2 D1
Norrys Rd EN4 2 D1
Norse Ho 13 SE5 139 A3
Norseman Cl 3 IG3 58 B1
Norseman Way UB6 85 D6
Norstead Pl SW15 156 A2
North Access Rd E17 52 D3
North Acre NW9 27 C2
North Acton Rd NW10 89 B4
North Acton Sta W3 89 B2
North Audley St
W1 115 A6 248 A6
North Ave N18 34 A6
W13 87 B2
Harrow HA2 41 D3
Hayes UB3 106 A6
8 Richmond TW9 132 C4
Southall UB1 107 B6
Wallington SM5 219 A1
North Bank NW8 92 C4 230 A1
North Beckton Prim Sch
E6 100 B2
North Birkbeck Rd E11 76 B5
North Block 18 E1 118 C6
North Branch Ave NW10 90 C4
North Carriage Dr
W2 114 C6 247 B6
North Church Ho 19 E2 96 A6
North Circular Rd E17 35 D2
E18 37 C1
N2 30 B2
N3,NW2,NW4 47 A4
N13 32 C5
NW10 67 C3
Ilford IG1,E12 78 C4
Wanstead IG1,IG8,E18 55 D4
North Cl Bexley DA6 146 D1
Dagenham RM10 103 C6
Ducks Island EN5 12 C6
East Bedfont TW14 149 B5
Merton SM4 201 A5
North Colonnade E14 119 C5
North Common Rd W5 110 A6
Uxbridge UB8 60 A3
North Countess Rd E17 35 B2
North Cray Prim Sch
DA14 191 A4
North Cray Rd DA14 191 A5
North Cres E16 98 B3
N3 29 B1
WC1 239 C4
North Crofts SE21 162 B3
North Cross Rd SE22 162 A6
Ilford IG6 57 A5
North Ct SW1 260 A5
North Dene NW7 11 B1
Hounslow TW5 129 D4
North Dr SW16 181 C6
Beckenham BR3 207 D5
Hounslow TW3,TW7 130 A3
Orpington BR6 227 C4
Ruislip HA4 39 C2
North Dulwich Sta
SE21 161 B6
North Ealing Prim Sch
W5 87 B3
North Ealing Sta W3 88 B1
North End NW3 70 A6
Buckhurst Hill IG9 21 C4
North End *continued*
Croydon CR0 221 A6
North End Ave NW3 70 A6
North End Cres
W14 113 B2 254 C3
North End Ho
W14 113 A2 254 B3
North End La BR6 226 D1
North End Par W14 254 B3
North End Rd NW11 47 D1
W14 113 B1 254 D1
Wembley HA9 66 D5
North End Way NW3 70 A6
North Eyot Gdns 5 W6 111 D1
North Farm IG10 21 C5
North Feltham Trad Est
TW14 128 B1
North Flower Wlk
W2 114 B6 246 C5
North Gate NW8 92 C5 230 A3
North Gates N12 30 B2
North Gdns SW19 180 B3
North Glade DA5 169 B3
North Gn NW9 27 C3
North Gower St
NW1 93 C4 232 B1
North Gr N6 49 A2
N15 51 B4
North Greenwich Sta
SE10 120 C4
North Haringay Jun & Inf Sch
N8 50 C5
North Harrow Sta HA2 41 D4
North Hill N6 49 A3
North Hill Ave N6 48 D3
North Hill Ct N6 49 A2
North Ho 3 SE8 119 B1
North Hyde Gdns UB3 106 A2
North Hyde La UB2 107 A1
North Hyde Rd UB3 105 D3
North La TW11 174 D4
North Lo N22 31 D1
New Barnet EN5 14 A6
North Lodge Cl SW15 156 D6
North London Boys Sch
N16 52 A1
North London Collegiate Sch
The HA7,HA8 26 A5
North London Nuffield Hospl
EN2 4 C3
North Mall N9 18 B2
North Mews
WC1 94 B3 240 D5
North Middlesex Hospl
N18 33 C5
North Mount N20 14 A2
North Par
Chessington KT9 214 B3
Edgware HA8 26 C1
Southall UB1 85 C1
North Pas SW18 157 C6
North Pk SE9 166 C5
North Pl SW19 180 D3
Teddington TW11 174 D4
North Pole La BR2 225 A2
North Pole Rd W10 90 C2
North Prim Sch UB1 107 B6
North Rd N2 30 C2
N6 49 A2
N7 72 A2
N9 18 B3
SE18 123 C2
SW19 180 A4
W5 109 D3
Belvedere DA17 125 D4
Brentford TW8 132 A6
Bromley BR1 187 B2
Dagenham RM6 59 A4
East Bedfont TW14 149 B5
Edgware HA8 26 D2
Hayes UB3 83 B2
Heston TW5 128 C6
Ilford IG3 79 C6
Kingston u T KT6 197 D3
Richmond TW9 132 C3
Southall UB1 107 C6
West Drayton UB7 104 B3
1 West Wickham BR4 207 D1
North Residence IG3 58 B4
North Ride W2 114 C6 247 A5
North Rise W2 237 B1
North Row W1 115 A6 248 A6
North Sheen Sta TW10 132 C1
North Side Wandsworth
Comm SW18 158 B6
North Sq N9 18 B2
NW11 47 C4
North St E13 99 B5
NW4 46 C4
SW4 137 C2
Barking IG11 79 A1
Bexleyheath DA7 147 C1
Carshalton SM5 218 D4
Isleworth TW7 131 A2
Plaistow BR1 187 A2
North Tenter St E1 243 D1
North Terr SW3 257 A5
North Verbena Gdns
W6 112 A1
North View SW19 178 C5
W5 87 C3
Pinner HA5 40 C2
North View Rd N8 49 D6
North Villas NW1 71 D2
North Way N9 18 D2
N11 31 C4
NW9 44 D6
Pinner HA5 40 D5
North Way *continued*
Uxbridge UB10 60 A1
North Weald La KT2 175 D5
North Wembley Sta HA0,
HA9 65 D5
North Western Ave WD6 9 B4
North Westminster Com Sch
NW1 92 C2 237 A4
W9 91 C3
North Westminster Com Sch
(Upper) W2 92 B2 236 C3
North Wharf Rd
W2 92 B2 236 C3
North Wlk W2 114 A6 246 A5
New Addington CR0 224 A3
North Wood Lo NW3 69 D4
North Woolwich Rd
E16 121 B5
North Woolwich Rdbt
E16 121 D5
North Woolwich Sta
E16 122 C4
North Worple Way
SW14 133 B2
Northampton Gr N1 73 B3
Northampton Pk N1 73 B2
Northampton Rd
EC1 94 C3 241 B6
Croydon CR0 222 A6
Enfield EN3 7 A1
Northampton Sq
EC1 94 D4 234 C1
Northampton St N1 73 A1
Northanger Rd SW16 182 A4
Northaw Ho W10 90 C3
Northbank Rd E17 36 A1
Northborough Rd
SW16 182 A1
Northbourne BR2 209 A2
Northbourne Ho 21 E5 74 B3
N14 15 D4
Northbourne Rd SW4 159 D6
Northbrook CE Sec Sch
SE12 164 D6
Northbrook Rd N22 32 A3
SE13 164 C6
Barnet EN5 13 A5
Ilford IG1 78 C6
Thornton Heath CR0 205 B4
Northburgh St
EC1 94 D3 241 D6
Northbury Prim Sch
IG11 79 A2
Northchurch SE17 262 D2
Northchurch Rd N1 73 B1
Wembley HA9 66 C2
Northchurch Terr N1 73 C1
Northcliffe Cl KT4 215 C5
Northcliffe Dr N20 13 B3
Northcote 1 HA5 22 C1
Northcote Ave W5 110 A6
Isleworth TW7 153 A6
Southall UB1 107 A6
Tolworth KT5 198 D2
Northcote Ho UB4 84 D2
Northcote Rd E17 53 A5
NW10 67 C1
SW11 158 D6
Isleworth TW7 153 A6
Kingston u T KT3 199 B6
Sidcup DA14 189 C6
Thornton Heath CR0 205 B3
Northcott Ave N22 32 A2
Northcourt W1 239 B4
Northcroft Ct 8 W12 112 A4
Northcroft Rd W13 109 B3
West Ewell KT19 215 C1
Northdene Gdns N15 51 D3
Northdown Cl HA4 61 D5
Northdown Gdns IG2 57 C4
Northdown Rd DA16 146 C3
Northdown St
N1 94 B5 233 C3
Northern Ave N9 17 D2
Northern Hts N8 49 D2
Northern Perimeter Rd
TW6 127 C4
Northern Perimeter Road
(W) TW6 126 B4
Northern Rd E13 99 B5
Northern Relief Rd IG11 79 A2
Northernhay Wlk SM4 201 A5
Northesk Ho 6 E1 96 B3
Northey St E14 119 A6
Northfield IG10 21 D6
Northfield Ave W13,W5 109 B4
Pinner HA5 40 D5
Northfield Cl
Bromley BR1 188 A2
Hayes UB3 105 D3
Northfield Cres SM3 217 A4
Northfield Gdns RM9 81 B4
Northfield Hall N6 49 A2
Northfield Ho 3 SE15 140 A6
Northfield Ind Est HA0 88 C6
Northfield Par UB3 105 D3
Northfield Path RM9 81 B4
Northfield Pk UB3 105 D3
Northfield Rd E6 78 B1
N16 51 C2
W13 109 B4
Cockfosters EN4 2 C2
Dagenham RM9 81 B4
Enfield EN3 18 B6
Heston TW5 128 D5

Northfields SW18 135 C1
Northfields Prospect
SW18 135 C1
Northfields Rd W3 89 A2
Northfields Sta W5 109 C3
Northfleet Ho SE1 252 C2
Northgate Bsns Ctr EN1 6 B1
Northgate Ct 15 SW9 138 C2
Northgate Dr NW9 45 C3
Northiam N12 29 C6
WC1 233 B1
Northiam St E9 96 B6
Northington St
WC1 94 B3 240 D5
Northlands Ave BR6 227 C4
Northlands St SE5 139 A3
Northleach Ct 2 SE15 139 C6
Northleigh Ho 36 E3 97 D4
Northmoor 4 SE23 162 D1
Northolm HA8 27 B6
Northolme Gdns HA8 26 C2
Northolme Rd N5 73 A4
Northolme Rise BR6 227 C6
Northolt N17 33 C1
Northolt Ave HA4 62 B3
Northolt Gdns UB6 64 D3
Northolt High Sch UB5 63 B2
Northolt Park Inf Sch
UB5 63 D3
Northolt Park Sta HA2 63 D4
Northolt Prim Sch UB5 63 A1
Northolt Rd
Harmondsworth TW6 126 A4
Harrow HA2 64 A5
Northolt Sta UB5 63 C2
Northover BR1 164 D1
Northport St N1 235 D5
Northrop Rd TW6 127 C4
Northside Prim Sch N12 30 A5
Northside Rd BR1 187 A2
Northspur Rd SM1 217 C5
Northstead Rd SW2 160 C2
Northumberland Alley
EC3 243 B1
Northumberland Ave
E12 55 C1
WC2 116 A5 250 A4
Bexley DA16 145 C2
Enfield EN1 6 B4
Hounslow TW7 130 D4
Northumberland Cl
TW19 148 A5
Northumberland Cres
TW14 149 C5
Northumberland Ct
3 Hounslow TW3 129 D1
South Croydon CR2 221 C3
Northumberland Gdns
N9 17 D1
Bromley BR1 210 C5
Hounslow TW7 131 A5
Mitcham CR4 203 D4
Northumberland Gr N17 34 B3
Northumberland Heath Prim Sch DA8 147 D5
Northumberland Ho
NW5 71 C2
Northumberland Mans
E5 74 C4
Northumberland Park Com Sch N17 34 A3
Northumberland Park Ind Est
N17 34 B3
Northumberland Park Sports Ctr N17 34 A3
Northumberland Park Sta
N17 34 B3
Northumberland Pk N17 34 A3
Erith DA8 147 D5
Northumberland Pl W2 91 C1
26 Richmond TW10 153 D6
Northumberland Rd E6 100 A1
E17 53 C2
Harrow HA2 41 C4
New Barnet EN5 14 A4
Northumberland St
WC2 250 A4
Northumbria St E14 97 C1
Northview 1 N7 72 A5
Northview Cres NW10 67 D4
Northview Dr IG8 37 D1
Northview Prim Sch
NW10 67 D3
Northway NW11 47 D4
Merton SM4 201 A5
Wallington SM6 219 C4
Northway Cir NW7 27 B6
Northway Cres NW7 27 C6
Northway Ct NW11 47 D4
NW7 27 B6
Northway Rd SE5 139 A2
Croydon CR0 205 D2
Northway Sch NW7 11 B1
Northways Par 2 NW3 70 B1
Northwest Pl N1 234 B4
Northwick Ave HA3 43 D3
Northwick Circ HA3 43 C3
Northwick Cl
NW8 92 B3 236 C6
Northwick Ho NW8 236 B6
Northwick Park Hospl
HA1 43 A2
Northwick Park Rd HA1 42 D3
Northwick Park Sta HA3 43 B2
Northwick Rd
South Oxhey WD1 22 C6
Wembley HA0 87 D6
Northwick Terr
NW8 92 B3 236 C6
Northwold Dr HA5 40 C6
Northwold JMI Sch E5 74 A6
Northwold Rd E5,N16 74 A6
Northwood Comp Sch
HA6 22 B2
Northwood Gdns N12 30 B5
Greenford UB6 64 D3
Ilford IG5 56 C5
Northwood Hills Cir HA6 22 A2
Northwood Hills Sta
HA6 22 A1
Northwood Pinner & District Cottage Hospl HA6 22 A2
Northwood Pl DA18 125 B3
Northwood Prim Sch
DA18 125 B3
Northwood Rd N6 49 B2
SE23 163 B3
South Norwood CR7 183 A1
Wallington SM5 219 A2
Northwood Twr 1 E17 54 A5
Northwood Way
1 SE19 183 C4
Northwood HA6 22 A3
Norton Ave KT5 198 D2
Norton Cl E4 35 C5
Enfield EN1 6 B3
Norton Ct
Beckenham BR3 185 B2
Ilford IG2 57 B3
Norton Folgate E1 243 B4
Norton Gdns SW16 182 A1
Norton Ho 33 E1 96 B1
14 E2 96 D5
8 SE18 122 C2
16 SW9 138 B3
5 New Malden KT3 199 C5
Norton Rd E10 53 B1
Wembley HA0 65 D2
Norval Gn 1 SW9 138 C3
Norval Rd HA0 43 B1
Norvic Ho 5 SE5 139 A3
Norway Gate SE16 119 A3
Norway Pl E14 97 B1
Norway St SE10 141 D6
Norwegian Sch SW19 178 C3
Norwich Ho 6 E14 97 D1
Norwich Mews IG3 58 A1
Norwich Pl 7 DA6 147 C1
Norwich Rd E7 77 A3
Greenford UB6 85 D6
Northwood HA6 39 D6
South Norwood CR7 205 A6
Norwich St EC4 94 C1 241 A2
Norwich Wlk HA8 27 A3
Norwood Ave HA0 88 B5
Norwood Cl
Southall UB2 107 C2
Twickenham TW2 152 B2
Norwood Cres TW6 127 A4
Norwood Dr HA2 41 C3
Norwood Gdns
Hayes UB4 84 C3
Southall UB2 107 B2
Norwood Green Inf Sch
UB2 107 B1
Norwood Green Jun Sch
UB2 107 A1
Norwood Green Rd
UB2 107 C2
Norwood Heights Sh Ctr 13
SE19 183 C4
Norwood High St SE27 183 A6
Norwood Ho 22 E14 119 D6
Norwood Hospl SE19 183 B4
Norwood Junction Sta
SE25 206 A5
Norwood Park Rd SE27 183 A5
Norwood Rd SE24,SE27 160 D3
Southall UB2 107 C2
Norwood Sch SE27 183 A6
Norwood Terr UB2 107 D2
Notley St SE5 139 B5
Notre Dame RC Prim Sch
SE18 144 D6
Notre Dame RC Sec Sch
SE1 116 D3 261 C6
Notson Rd SE25 206 B5
Notting Barn Rd W10 90 D3
Notting Hill & Ealing High Sch W13 87 B2
Notting Hill Gate
W11 113 C5 245 A4
Notting Hill Gate Sta
W11 113 C5 245 A4
Nottingdale Sq W11 244 A4
Nottingham Ave E16 99 C1
Nottingham Ct WC2 240 A1
Nottingham Ho N4 51 A1
34 SE5 139 A3
Nottingham Pl
W1 93 A2 238 A4
Nottingham Rd E10 54 A3
SW17 158 D3
Croydon CR2 221 A3
Isleworth TW7 130 D3
Nottingham St W1 238 A4
Nottingham Terr NW1 238 A5
Nottingwood Ho W11 244 A6
Nova Mews SM4 201 A2
Nova Rd CR0 205 A2
Novar Cl BR6 211 D2
Novar Rd SE9 167 A3
Novello Ho 6 W10 91 B4
Novello St SW6 135 C4 265 A2
Nowell Rd SW13 134 A6
Nower Ct HA5 41 B5
Nower Hill HA5 41 B5
Nower Hill High Sch
HA5 41 C5
Noyna Rd SW17 158 D1
Nuding Cl SE13 141 C2
Nuffield Ct TW5 129 B5
Nuffield Lo 14 W9 91 C2
Nugent Ct SW16 181 C6
Nugent Rd N19 50 A1
SE25 205 D6
Nugent Terr
NW8 92 A5 229 B3
Nugents Ct HA5 23 A2
Nugent's Pk HA5 23 B2
Numa Ct TW8 131 D5
Nun Ct EC2 242 C2
Nuneaton Rd RM9 81 A1
Nuneham SW16 181 D6
Nunhead Cres SE15 140 B2
Nunhead Gr SE15 140 C2
Nunhead La SE15 140 B2
Nunhead Sta SE15 140 C3
Nunnington Cl SE9 166 A1
Nunn's Rd EN2 5 A3
Nupton Dr EN5 12 C5
Nursery Ave N3 30 A1
Bexley DA7 147 B2
Croydon CR0 222 D6
Nursery Cl SE4 141 B3
SW15 134 D1
Broom Hill BR6 211 D2
Croydon CR0 222 D6
Enfield EN3 6 D4
Feltham TW14 150 B4
Ilford RM6 58 D3
Woodford IG8 37 B5
Nursery Ct 7 N17 33 D3
W13 87 A2
Nursery Gdns
Chislehurst West BR7 188 D4
Enfield EN3 6 D4
Hounslow TW4 151 B6
Sunbury TW16 171 D1
Nursery La E2 95 D6
E7 77 A2
W10 90 C2
Nursery Rd E9 74 C2
N2 30 B2
N14 15 C4
SW9 138 B1
SW19 179 D1
SW19 179 A3
Loughton IG10 21 C6
Mitcham CR4 202 C6
Pinner HA5 40 C6
South Norwood CR7 205 B5
Sunbury TW16 171 D1
Sutton SM1 218 A4
Nursery St N17 33 D3
Nursery Walk Ct NW4 46 B6
Nursery Wlk NW4 46 C6
Nurserymans Rd N11 15 A2
Nurstead Rd DA8 147 C5
Nutborn Ho SW19 178 D4
Nutbourne St W10 91 A4
Nutbrook St SE15 140 A2
Nutbrowne Rd RM9 103 B6
Nutcroft Rd SE15 140 B5
Nutfield Cl N18 34 A4
Carshalton SM5 218 C5
Nutfield Gdns Ilford IG3 80 A6
Northolt UB5 84 C5
Nutfield Rd E15 76 A4
NW2 68 A5
SE22 139 D1
Thornton Heath CR7 204 D5
Nutfield Way BR6 226 D6
Nutford Pl W1 92 D1 237 C2
Nuthatch Cl TW19 148 B3
Nuthatch Gdns SE28 123 B4
Nuthurst Ave SW2 160 B2
Nutkin Wlk UB8 60 A1
Nutley Terr NW3 70 B2
Nutmeg Cl E16 98 C3
Nutmeg La E14 98 B1
Nutt Gr HA8 9 D2
Nutt St SE15 139 D5
Nuttall St N1 95 C5
Nutter La E11 55 C4
Nutty La TW17 193 A6
Nutwell St SW17 180 C5
Nuxley Rd DA17 125 C1
NW London Jewish Day Prim Sch NW6 69 A1
Nyanza St SE18 145 B6
Nye Bevan Est E5 74 D5
Nye Bevan Ho SW6 264 C4
Nye's Wharf SE15 140 A6
Nylands Ave TW9 132 C3
Nymans Gdns SW20 200 B6
Nynehead St SE14 141 A5
Nyon Gr SE6 163 B2
Nyton Cl N19 50 A1

O

Oak Apple Ct SE12 165 A3
Oak Ave N8 50 A5
N10 31 B3
N17 33 C3
Croydon CR0 223 D6
Enfield EN2 4 B5
Hampton TW12,TW13 173 A4
Oak Ave *continued*
Heston TW5 129 A5
Uxbridge UB10 60 D6
West Drayton UB7 104 C3
Oak Bank CR0 224 A2
Oak Cl N14 15 B4
Sutton SM1 218 A6
Oak Cottage Cl 11 SE6 164 D3
Oak Cotts W7 108 C4
Oak Cres E16 98 C2
Oak Ct E4 35 D4
Bromley BR1 188 B1
Oak Dene W13 87 B2
Oak Farm WD6 11 A6
Oak Farm Jun & Inf Schs
UB10 82 D6
Oak Gdns Burnt Oak HA8 27 A1
Croydon CR0 223 C6
Oak Gr NW2 69 A4
Ruislip HA4 40 B1
Sunbury TW16 172 B3
West Wickham BR4 208 A1
Oak Grove Rd SE20 184 C1
Oak Hall Rd E11 55 B3
Oak Hill Chingford IG8 36 C3
Surbiton KT6 198 A2
Oak Hill Cl IG8 36 B3
Oak Hill Coll N14 15 A5
Oak Hill Cres
Chingford IG8 36 C3
Surbiton KT6 198 A2
Oak Hill Ct IG8 36 C3
Oak Hill Gr KT6 198 A3
Oak Hill Lo NW3 69 D4
Oak Hill Park Mews
NW3 70 A4
Oak Hill Pk NW3 69 D4
Oak Hill Prim Sch IG8 36 C4
Oak Hill Rd KT6 198 A3
Oak Hill Way NW3 70 A4
Oak Ho 8 E14 120 A4
11 N2 30 B1
N16 73 B6
N22 32 A3
8 NW3 70 D2
SE20 184 B1
13 Sidcup DA15 168 A1
Oak La E14 119 B6
N2 30 B1
N11 31 D4
Isleworth TW7 130 C1
Twickenham TW1 153 A4
Woodford IG8 36 D6
Oak Lo E11 55 A2
N21 16 B5
4 Ashford TW16 171 D3
Oak Lodge Cl HA7 25 C5
Oak Lodge Dr BR4 207 D2
Oak Lodge Prim Sch
BR4 207 D2
Oak Lodge Sch N2 48 A5
SW12 159 A4
Oak Park Gdns SW19 156 D3
Oak Park Mews N16 73 D5
Oak Rd W5 109 D6
Kingston u T KT3 177 B1
Oak Rise IG9 21 D1
Oak Row CR4 181 C1
Oak Tree Ave N2 47 D6
Oak Tree Cl W5 87 C1
Stanmore HA7 25 C3
Oak Tree Ct W3 110 D6
Elstree WD6 9 D5
Oak Tree Dell NW9 45 B4
Oak Tree Dr N20 13 D3
Oak Tree Gdns BR1 187 B5
Oak Tree Ho W9 91 D3
Oak Tree Rd
NW8 92 C4 230 A1
Oak Village NW5 71 A4
Oak Way N14 15 B4
W3 111 C5
Croydon CR0 206 D3
East Bedfont TW14 149 C3
Oakbank Ave KT12 195 B2
Oakbank Gr SE24 139 A1
Oakbrook 3 BR3 185 D1
Oakbrook Cl BR1 187 B6
Oakbury Rd SW6 135 D3
Oakcombe Cl KT3 177 C2
Oakcourt 16 SE15 139 D5
Oakcroft SE12 165 B1
Oakcroft Bsns Ctr KT9 214 B4
Oakcroft Cl HA5 22 B1
Oakcroft Ho 3 KT3 199 C2
Oakcroft Rd SE13 142 B3
Chessington KT9 214 B4
Oakcroft Villas KT9 214 B4
Oakdale N14 15 B3
Beckenham BR3 186 A1
Oakdale Ave Harrow HA3 44 A4
Northwood Hills HA6 22 A1
Oakdale Cl WD1 22 C6
Oakdale Ct N19 72 A6
Oakdale Gdns E4 36 A5
Oakdale Inf Sch E18 37 B1
Oakdale Jun Sch E18 37 B1
Oakdale Lo NW4 29 A2
Oakdale Rd E7 77 B1
E11 76 B6
E18 37 B1
N4 51 B3
SE15 140 C2
SW16 182 A5
South Oxhey WD1 22 C6
Oakdale Way CR4 203 A2
Oakden St SE11 116 C2 261 B4
Oakdene 3 SE15 140 B4
Oakdene *continued*
1 SE19 183 C5
Oakdene Ave
Chislehurst West BR7 188 C5
Thames Ditton KT7 197 A1
Oakdene Cl HA5 23 B3
Oakdene Dr KT5 199 A1
Oakdene Ho N16 51 C1
Enfield EN2 4 D2
Oakdene Lo SE20 184 B3
Oakdene Mews SM3 201 B1
Oakdene Pk N3 29 B3
Oakdene Rd
Broom Hill BR5 211 D4
Hillingdon UB10 82 D5
Oake Ct SW15 157 A6
Oaken Dr KT10 212 D2
Oaken La KT10 212 C5
Oakend Ho 10 N4 51 B2
Oakenholt Ho 1 SE2 124 D4
Oakenshaw Cl KT6 198 A2
Oakes Cl E6 100 B1
Oakeshott Ave N6 71 A6
Oakey La SE1 261 A6
Oakfield E4 35 D5
Oakfield Ave HA3 43 B6
Oakfield Cl
New Malden KT3 199 D4
Ruislip HA4 39 D3
Oakfield Ct N3 29 D2
N8 50 A2
NW2 46 D2
SW4 160 A5
2 W5 110 C5
Croydon CR2 221 A2
Oakfield Gdns N18 33 C6
3 SE19 183 C5
Beckenham BR3 207 C4
Carshalton SM5 202 D1
Greenford UB6 86 B4
Oakfield Ho 2 IG1 78 D5
Oakfield La BR2 225 C4
Oakfield Lo 8 IG1 78 D5
Oakfield Rd E6 100 A6
E17 35 A1
N3 29 D2
N4 50 C2
N14 16 A2
SE20 184 B3
SW19 156 D1
Ashford TW15 170 D5
Ilford IG1 78 D5
Thornton Heath CR0 205 A1
Oakfield Sch SE21 161 B3
Oakfield St
SW10 136 A6 266 A6
Oakfields KT12 194 A1
Oakfields Rd NW11 47 A3
Oakford Rd NW5 71 C4
Oakhall Ct E11 55 B3
Ashford TW16 171 D5
Oakhall Dr TW16 171 D5
Oakham Cl SE6 163 B2
Oakham Dr BR2 208 D5
Oakham Ho W10 90 C3
Oakhampton Rd NW7 28 D3
Oakhill KT10 213 A2
Oakhill Ave NW3 69 D4
Hatch End HA5 23 A1
Oakhill Ct SE23 162 C5
SW15 157 B6
SW19 178 D3
8 Surbiton KT6 198 A3
Oakhill Ho BR5 190 A2
Oakhill Pl SW15 157 C6
Oakhill Rd SW15 157 B6
SW16 182 B2
Beckenham BR3 186 A1
Orpington BR6 227 D6
Sutton SM1 218 A5
Oakhouse Rd DA6 169 C6
Oakhurst Ave
Bexley DA7 147 A5
East Barnet EN4 14 C4
Oakhurst Cl E17 54 C5
Bromley BR7 188 B2
4 Teddington TW11 174 C5
Oakhurst Ct E17 54 C5
Oakhurst Gdns E4 20 D3
E11,E17 54 C5
Bexley DA7 147 A5
Oakhurst Gr SE22 140 A1
Oakhurst Rd KT19 215 B2
Oakington 14 KT1 176 C1
Oakington Ave
Harrow HA2 41 C2
Hayes UB3 105 B2
Wembley HA9 66 B5
Oakington Dr TW16 172 C1
Oakington Manor Dr
HA9 66 C3
Oakington Manor Prim Sch
HA9 66 D3
Oakington Rd W9 91 C3
Oakington Way N8 50 A2
Oakland Pl IG9 21 A2
Oakland Rd E15 76 C4
Oakland Way KT19 215 C2
Oaklands N21 16 B2
W13 87 A2
Chislehurst BR7 189 B4
Croydon CR0 220 D3
Twickenham TW2 152 A4
Oaklands Ave N9 18 B5
Hounslow TW7 130 D6
Sidcup DA15 167 D4
Thames Ditton KT10 196 B1
Thornton Heath CR7 204 C5
Oaklands Ave *continued*
West Wickham BR4 223 D5
Oaklands Cl Bexley DA6 169 B6
Chessington KT9 213 C4
Orpington BR5 211 C3
Wembley HA0 65 D3
Oaklands Ct NW10 89 C6
1 Wembley HA0 65 D3
Oaklands Gr W12 112 A5
Oaklands Ho SE4 141 B2
Oaklands Mews NW2 68 D4
Oaklands Park Ave IG1 79 A6
Oaklands Pas NW2 68 D4
Oaklands Pl 8 SW4 137 D1
Oaklands Prim Sch W7 108 D4
Oaklands Rd N20 13 B4
NW2 68 D4
SW14 133 B2
W7,W13 109 A4
Bexley DA6 169 B6
Bromley BR1 186 C3
Oaklands Sch
Isleworth TW3 130 B2
Loughton IG10 21 C6
Oaklands Sec Sch E2 96 B4
Oaklands Way SM6 219 D1
Oaklea Pas KT1 197 D6
Oakleafe Gdns IG6 56 D6
Oakleigh Ave N20 14 C3
Edgware HA8 26 D2
Tolworth KT6 214 D6
Oakleigh Cl N20 14 D1
Oakleigh Cres N20 14 C1
Oakleigh Ct SE20 184 B3
Burnt Oak HA8 27 A1
East Barnet EN4 14 C5
Southall UB1 107 B5
Surbiton KT6 214 B6
Oakleigh Gdns N20 14 B3
Edgware HA8 26 B5
Orpington BR6 227 C4
Oakleigh Lo IG3 80 A5
Oakleigh Mews N20 14 A2
Oakleigh Park Ave BR7 188 C2
Oakleigh Park Sta EN4 14 C4
Oakleigh Pk N N20 14 B3
Oakleigh Pk S N20 14 C3
Oakleigh Rd
Hatch End HA5 23 B4
Hillingdon UB10 61 A1
Oakleigh Rd N N20 14 C2
Oakleigh Rd S N11 31 A6
Oakleigh Sch N20 14 D1
Oakleigh Way
Mitcham CR4 181 B2
1 Tolworth KT6 198 D1
Oakley Ave W5 110 C6
Barking IG11 79 D1
Wallington CR0 220 A4
Oakley Cl E4 20 A1
7 E6 100 A1
W7 108 C6
Hounslow TW7 130 B4
Oakley Cres EC1 234 D3
Oakley Ct CR4 203 A2
Oakley Dr SE13 164 B5
Keston Mark BR2 226 A5
New Eltham DA15 167 B3
Oakley Gdns N8 50 B4
SW3 136 C6 267 B6
Oakley Ho SW1 257 D4
W5 110 C6
Oakley Pk DA14,DA15 168 C4
Oakley Pl SE1 117 D1 263 C1
Oakley Rd N1 73 B1
SE25 206 B4
Harrow HA1 42 C3
Oakley Sq NW1 93 C5 232 B4
Oakley St SW3 136 C6 267 A6
Oakley Wlk W6 134 D6
Oaklodge Way NW7 27 D4
Oakman Ho 29 SW19 156 D3
Oakmead Ave BR2 209 A3
Oakmead Ct HA7 25 C6
Oakmead Gdns HA8 27 B6
Oakmead Pl CR4 180 C2
Oakmead Rd SW12 159 B3
Wallington CR0 203 D3
Oakmeade HA5 23 C4
Oakmere Rd SE2 146 A6
Oakmont Pl 6 BR6 211 B1
Oakridge Dr N2 48 B6
Oakridge La BR1 186 B5
Oakridge Rd BR1 186 C6
Oaks Ave SE19 183 C5
Feltham TW13 151 A2
North Cheam KT4 216 B4
Oaks Gr E4 20 C2
Oaks La Ilford IG2 57 C5
South Croydon CR0 222 C5
Oaks Rd CR0 222 C4
Oaks Sh Ctr The W3 111 A5
Oaks The N12 29 D6
NW6 68 D1
NW10 68 B1
SE18 123 A1
SW19 179 A4
Bromley BR2 210 C3
Chingford IG8 36 C3
Enfield EN2 4 D2
Hayes UB4 83 A5
Long Ditton KT6 213 C5
Ruislip HA4 39 C2
Oaks Way
Long Ditton KT6 197 D1
Wallington SM5 218 D1
Oaksford Ave SE26 162 B1
Oakshade Rd BR1 186 B6

Oakshaw Rd SW18 ...157 D4
Oakshott Ct NW1 ...232 C3
Oakthorpe Ct N13 ...33 A5
Oakthorpe Prim Sch
N13 ...33 A5
Oakthorpe Rd N13 ...32 C5
Oaktree Ave N13 ...16 D1
Oaktree Gr IG1 ...79 B3
Oaktree Sch EN4 ...15 A5
Oakview Gdns N2 ...48 B5
Oakview Gr CR0 ...207 A1
Oakview Lo NW11 ...47 B2
Oakview Rd SE6 ...185 D5
Oakway SW20 ...200 C5
Beckenham BR2 ...186 B1
Oakway Cl DA5 ...169 A5
Oakways SE9 ...166 D5
Oakwell Ho 24 SW8 ...137 D3
Oakwood Ave N14 ...15 D4
Beckenham BR2,BR3 ...186 A1
Bromley BR2 ...209 B6
Mitcham CR4 ...180 B1
Southall UB1 ...107 C6
Oakwood Cl N14 ...15 C5
Chislehurst West BR7 ...188 C4
Oakwood Cres N21 ...16 B5
Wembley UB6 ...65 B2
Oakwood Ct 6 E4 ...20 C4
1 E6 ...100 A6
W14 ...113 B3 254 C6
Beckenham BR3 ...186 A1
Oakwood Dr SE19 ...183 C4
Burnt Oak HA8 ...27 A4
Oakwood Gdns Ilford IG3 79 D6
Orpington BR6 ...227 A6
Sutton SM1 ...217 C6
Oakwood La
W14 ...113 B3 254 C6
Oakwood Park Rd N14 ...16 A5
Oakwood Pl CR0 ...204 C3
Oakwood Rd NW11 ...47 D4
SW20 ...178 A2
Orpington BR6 ...227 A6
Pinner Green HA5 ...22 B1
Thornton Heath CR0 ...204 C3
Oakwood Sta N14 ...15 C6
Oakwood View N14 ...15 D4
Oakworth Rd W10 ...90 D2
Oarsman Pl KT8 ...196 C5
Oasis The 4 BR1 ...187 C1
Oast Ct 8 E14 ...119 B6
Oast Lo W4 ...133 C5
Oat La EC2 ...95 A1 242 B2
Oates Cl BR2 ...208 B6
Oatfield Ho 1 N15 ...51 C3
Oatfield Rd BR6 ...211 D1
Oatland Rise E17 ...35 A1
Oatlands Ct 3 SW19 ...156 D3
Oatlands Dr KT13 ...193 C1
Oatlands Rd EN3 ...6 C4
Oatwell Ho SW3 ...257 B3
Oban Cl E13 ...99 C3
Oban Ho E14 ...98 B1
Barking IG11 ...101 B5
Oban Rd E13 ...99 C4
SE25 ...205 B5
Oban St E14 ...98 B1
Oberon Ho 5 N1 ...95 C5
Oberon Way TW17 ...192 A6
Oberstein Rd 15 SW11 ...136 B1
Oborne Cl SE24 ...160 D6
O'Brian Ho 10 E1 ...96 D4
Observatory Gdns W8 ...245 B2
Observatory Rd SW14 ...133 A1
Occupation La SE18 ...144 D4
W5 ...109 D2
Occupation Rd
SE17 ...117 A1 262 A2
W13 ...109 B4
Ocean St E1 ...96 D2
Ockbrook 3 E1 ...96 C2
Ockendon Rd N1 ...73 B2
Ockham Dr BR5 ...190 A3
Ockley Ct SM1 ...218 A4
Ockley Ho 8 KT2 ...176 D4
Ockley Rd SW16 ...160 A1
Thornton Heath CR0 ...204 B2
Octagon Arc EC2 ...243 A3
Octagon The NW3 ...69 C4
Octavia Cl CR4 ...202 C4
Octavia Ho W10 ...91 A3
Octavia Rd TW7 ...130 D2
Octavia St
SW11 ...136 C4 267 B1
Octavia Way 12 SE28 ...124 B6
Octavius St SE8 ...141 C5
October Ct BR2 ...208 D6
October Pl NW4 ...46 D6
Odard Rd KT8 ...195 C5
Odeon Ct 1 E16 ...99 A2
NW10 ...89 C6
Odeon Par SE9 ...144 A1
Wembley UB6 ...65 B2
Odessa Inf Sch E7 ...77 A3
Odessa Rd E7 ...76 D4
NW10 ...90 A5
Odessa St SE16 ...119 B3
Odette Ct N20 ...14 A1
Odette Duval Ho 24 E1 ...96 C2
Odette Ho 6 SE27 ...183 B6
Odger St SW11 ...136 D3
Odhams Wlk WC2 ...240 B1
Odin Ho 6 SE5 ...139 A3
O'Donnell Ct WC1 ...240 B6
O'Driscoll Ho W12 ...90 B1
Odyssey Bsns Pk HA4 ...62 B3
Offa's Mead E9 ...75 A4
Offenbach Ho 12 E2 ...96 D5
Offenham Rd BR7,SE9 ...188 B6
Offers Ct KT1 ...198 B6
Offerton Rd SW4 ...137 C2
Offham Ho SE17 ...263 A3
Offham Slope N12 ...29 B5
Offley Ho 10 E9 ...74 D2
Offley Rd SW9 ...138 C5
Offord Cl N17 ...34 A4
Offord Rd N1 ...72 B1
Offord St N1 ...72 B1
Ogden Ho TW13 ...173 A6
Ogilby St SE18 ...122 B2
Ogilvie Ho 11 E1 ...96 D1
Oglander Rd SE15 ...139 D2
Ogle St W1 ...93 C2 239 A4
Oglethorpe Rd RM10 ...81 C5
O'Gorman Ho SW10 ...266 B4
O'Grady Ho 17 E17 ...53 D6
Ohio Rd E13 ...98 D3
Oil Mill La W6 ...112 A1
Okeburn Rd SW17 ...181 A5
Okehampton Cl N12 ...30 B5
Okehampton Cres
DA16 ...146 C4
Okehampton Rd NW10 ...90 D6
Okeover Manor SW4 ...137 B1
Olaf Palme Ho TW13 ...150 B1
Olaf St W11 ...112 D6
Old Bailey EC4 ...94 D1 241 D1
Old Barn Cl SM2 ...217 A1
Old Barrack Yd SW1 ...248 A1
Old Bellgate Wharf E14 119 C3
Old Bethnal Green Rd
E2 ...96 B4
Old Bexley CE Prim Sch
DA5 ...169 B3
Old Bldgs WC2 ...241 A2
Old Bond St
W1 ...115 C6 249 A5
Old Borrowfield 7 E15 ...98 C6
Old Brewery Mews NW3 70 B4
Old Bridge Cl UB5 ...85 C5
Old Bridge St KT1 ...175 D1
Old Broad St EC2 95 B1 242 D2
Old Bromley Rd BR1 ...186 B5
Old Brompton Rd
SW5,SW7 ...114 A1 256 B3
Old Burlington St
W1 ...115 C6 249 A5
Old Castle St E1 95 D1 243 D2
Old Cavendish St W1 ...238 C1
Old Change Ct EC4 ...242 A1
Old Chapel Pl 2 N10 ...49 B6
Old Charlton Rd TW17 ...193 A4
Old Church Ct N11 ...31 B5
Old Church La NW9 ...67 B6
Ealing UB6 ...87 A4
Stanmore HA7 ...25 C4
Old Church Path KT10 ...212 A4
Old Church Rd E1 ...96 D1
E4 ...19 C1
Old Church St SW3 ...256 D1
Old Claygate La KT10 ...213 A3
Old Clem Sq 12 SE18 ...144 C6
Old Compton St
W1 ...93 D1 239 C1
Old Cote Dr TW5 ...129 C6
Old County Hall SE1 ...250 C2
Old Court (Mus & Liby)
HA0 ...65 C3
Old Court Ho W8 ...245 C1
Old Court Pl
W8 ...113 D4 245 C1
Old Covent Garden
WC2 ...250 B6
Old Ctyd The BR1 ...187 B2
Old Dairy Mews 4 NW5 71 B2
Old Deer Park Gdns
TW9 ...132 A2
Old Devonshire Rd
SW12 ...159 B4
Old Dock Cl TW9 ...132 C6
Old Dover Rd SE3 ...143 B5
Old Farm Ave N14 ...15 C4
Sidcup DA15 ...167 C2
Old Farm Cl TW4 ...129 B1
Old Farm Ct UB2 ...107 D2
Old Farm Rd N2 ...30 B2
TW12 ...173 C4
Old Farm Rd E DA15 ...168 A2
Old Farm Rd W DA15 ...167 D2
Old Fish St Hill EC4 ...252 A6
Old Fleet La EC4 ...241 C2
Old Fold Cl EN5 ...1 B4
Old Fold La EN5 ...1 B4
Old Ford Ho CR0 ...220 A5
Old Ford Inf Sch E3 ...97 B5
Old Ford Jun Sch E3 ...97 B5
Old Ford Rd E2,E3 ...96 D5
Old Ford Trad Ctr E3 ...97 C6
Old Forge Cl HA7 ...25 A6
Old Forge Cres TW17 ...192 D3
Old Forge Mews W12 ...112 B4
Old Forge Rd EN1 ...5 D5
Old Forge Way DA14 ...190 B6
Old Gloucester St
WC1 ...94 A2 240 B4
Old Hall Cl HA5 ...23 A2
Old Hall Dr HA5 ...23 A2
Old Hatch Manor HA4 ...40 A2
Old Hill
Chislehurst West BR7 ...188 C2
Orpington BR6 ...227 C2
Old Homesdale Rd BR2 209 C5
Old Hospital Cl SW12,
SW17 ...158 D3
Old House Cl SW19 ...179 A5
Old House Gdns 9
TW1 ...153 C5
Old Howlett's La HA4 ...39 B3
Old Jamaica Rd SE16 ...118 A3
Old James St SE15 ...140 B2
Old Jewry EC2 ...95 B1 242 C1
Old Kent Rd
SE1 ...117 C1 263 B2
SE1,SE15 ...140 B6
Old Kenton La NW9 ...44 D4
Old Kingston Rd KT4 ...215 A5
Old Laundry The 14
SW18 ...136 B1
Old Lodge Pl 7 TW1 ...153 B5
Old Lodge Way HA7 ...25 A5
Old Maidstone Rd BR8,
DA14 ...191 B3
Old Malden La KT4 ...215 C6
Old Manor Dr TW7 ...152 A5
Old Manor Way BR7,
SE9 ...188 B5
Old Manor Yd SW5 ...255 C3
Old Market Sq 11 E2 ...95 D4
Old Marylebone Rd
NW1 ...92 C2 237 B3
Old Mill Ct E18 ...55 C6
Old Mill Rd SE18 ...145 B6
Old Mitre Ct EC4 ...241 B1
Old Montague St E1 ...96 A2
Old Nichol St E2 95 D3 243 C6
Old North St WC1 ...240 C4
Old Nursery Pl TW15 ...170 D5
Old Oak Common La
NW10 ...89 C3
Old Oak La NW10 ...89 D4
Old Oak Prim Sch W12 ...89 D1
Old Oak Rd W3 ...111 D6
Old Orch TW16 ...172 C1
Old Orch The NW3 ...70 D4
Old Orchard Cl Barnet EN4 2 B5
Hillingdon UB8 ...82 C1
Old Palace JMI Sch E3 ...97 D4
Old Palace La TW9 ...153 C6
Old Palace Rd CR0 ...221 A5
Old Palace Sch CR0 ...220 D5
Old Palace Terr 8
TW9 ...153 D6
Old Palace Yd 2 TW9 ...153 D6
Old Paradise St
SE11 ...116 B2 260 C4
Old Park Ave SW12 ...159 A5
Enfield EN2 ...5 A1
Old Park Gr EN2 ...5 A1
Old Park Ho N13 ...32 B6
Old Park La W1 115 B5 248 C3
Old Park Mews TW5 ...129 B5
Old Park Rd N13 ...32 B6
SE2 ...124 A1
Enfield EN2 ...4 D2
Old Park Rd S EN2 ...4 D1
Old Park Ridings N21 ...17 A6
Old Park View EN2 ...4 D2
Old Perry St BR7 ...189 C3
Old Pound Cl TW7 ...131 A4
Old Priory UB9 ...38 D2
Old Pye St SW1 ...259 C6
Old Pye Street Est SW1 259 C5
Old Quebec St W1 ...237 D1
Old Queen St
SW1 ...115 D4 249 D1
Old Rd SE13 ...142 C1
Enfield EN3 ...6 C4
Old Rectory Gdns HA8 ...26 C4
Old Redding HA3 ...24 A6
Old Royal Free Pl N1 ...234 B5
Old Royal Free Sq
N1 ...94 C6 234 B5
Old Royal Horticultural
Society SW1 ...259 C4
Old Royal Observatory
Greenwich (National
Maritime Mus Annexe)★
SE10 ...142 B5
Old Ruislip Rd UB5 ...84 C5
Old School Cl SW19 ...179 C1
3 Penge BR3 ...185 A1
Old School Cres E7 ...77 A2
Old School Ho The EN2 ...4 D2
Old School Sq KT7 ...196 D3
Old Seacoal La EC4 ...241 C1
Old South Lambeth Rd
SW8 ...138 A5 270 B4
Old Sq WC2 ...241 A2
Old St E13 ...99 B5
EC1 ...95 B3 242 B6
Old St Andrews Mans
NW9 ...67 B6
Old Stable Mews N5 ...73 A5
Old Station Rd UB3 ...105 D3
Old Street Sta
EC1 ...95 B3 242 D6
Old Sun Wharf E14 ...119 A6
Old Swan Wharf SW11 266 D2
Old Swan Yd SM5 ...218 D4
Old Theatre Ct SE1 ...252 B4
Old Town SW4 ...137 C2
Croydon CR0 ...220 D5
Old Tramyard SE18 ...123 C2
Old Woolwich Rd SE10 ...120 B1
Old York Rd SW18 ...157 D6
Oldberry Rd HA8 ...27 B4
Oldborough Rd HA0 ...65 C5
Oldbury Ct E9 ...75 A3
Oldbury Pl W1 ...93 A2 238 B4
Oldbury Rd EN1 ...6 A3
Oldegate Ho 1 E6 ...99 D6
Oldfield Cl Bromley BR1 ...210 B5
Northolt UB6 ...64 C2
Oldfield Cl *continued*
Stanmore HA7 ...25 A5
Oldfield Farm Gdns UB6 86 B6
Oldfield Gr SE16 ...118 D2
Oldfield Ho SW16 ...181 B6
14 W4 ...111 C1
Oldfield House Sch
TW12 ...173 B2
Oldfield La N UB6 ...64 B1
Oldfield La S UB6 ...86 A4
Oldfield Mews N6 ...49 C2
Oldfield Prim Sch UB6 ...86 B5
Oldfield Rd N16 ...73 C5
NW10 ...67 D1
SW19 ...179 A4
W3,W12 ...111 D4
Bexleyheath DA7 ...147 A3
Bromley BR1 ...210 B5
Hampton TW12 ...173 B2
Oldfields Cir UB5 ...64 A2
Oldfields Rd SM1,SM3 ...217 C6
Oldfields Trad Est SM1 ...217 C5
Oldham Ho 10 SE21 ...183 C6
Oldham Terr W3 ...111 A5
Oldhill St N16 ...52 A1
Olding Ho 6 SW12 ...159 C4
Oldmead Ho 8 RM10 ...81 D2
Oldridge Rd SW12 ...159 B4
Oldstead Rd BR1 ...186 B6
Oleander Cl BR6 ...227 B3
O'Leary Sq E1 ...96 C2
Olga JMI Sch E3 ...97 A5
Olga St 18 E3 ...97 A5
Olinda Rd N16 ...51 D3
Oliphant St W10 ...91 A4
Olive Blythe Ho 14 W10 ...91 A3
Olive Rd E13 ...99 C4
NW2 ...68 C4
3 SW19 ...179 D3
W5 ...109 D3
Olive Tree Ho N4 ...50 C3
7 SE15 ...140 C6
Olive Waite Ho NW6 ...69 D1
Oliver Ave SE25 ...205 D6
Oliver Cl W4 ...132 D6
Oliver Ct SE18 ...123 A2
Isleworth TW7 ...130 D2
Oliver Gdns E6 ...100 A2
Oliver Goldsmith Prim Sch
NW9 ...45 B4
Oliver Goldsmith Prim Schs
SE5 ...139 D4
Oliver Gr SE25 ...205 D5
Oliver Ho 19 SE16 ...118 A4
SW8 ...270 A4
Oliver Rd E10 ...75 D5
E17 ...54 A4
Kingston u T KT3 ...177 A1
Sutton SM1 ...218 B4
Oliver's Yd EC1 ...242 D6
Olivette St 1 SW15 ...134 D1
Ollard's Gr IG10 ...21 D6
Ollerton Gn E3 ...97 B6
Ollerton Rd N11 ...31 D5
Olley Cl SM6 ...220 A2
Ollgar Cl W12 ...111 D5
Olliffe St E14 ...120 A3
Olmar St SE1 ...140 A6
Olmar Wharf SE1 ...140 A6
Olney Ho NW8 ...237 B6
Olney Rd SE17 ...139 A6
Olron Cres DA6 ...169 A6
Olven Rd SE18 ...145 A6
Olveston Wlk SM5 ...202 B3
Olwen Mews HA5 ...22 D1
Olyffe Ave DA16 ...146 A3
Olyffe Dr BR3 ...186 A2
Olympia Ex Hall
W14 ...113 A3 254 B5
Olympia Way
W14 ...113 A3 254 B5
Olympia Yd W2 ...245 D5
Olympian Ct 1 E14 ...119 C2
Olympic Ho W10 ...90 C1
Olympic Way
Greenford UB6 ...85 D6
Wembley HA9 ...66 C4
Olympic Way Ind Est
HA9 ...66 D4
Olympic Way Ret Pk
HA9 ...66 C4
Olympus Sq E5 ...74 A5
Oman Ave NW2 ...68 C4
Oman Ct NW4 ...68 B4
Ombersley Ho N4 ...51 A2
Omeara St SE1 ...252 B3
Omega Cl E14 ...119 D3
Omega Ho SW10 ...266 B4
Omega Pl N1 ...233 B3
Omega St SE14 ...141 C4
Ommaney Rd SE14 ...141 A4
Omnibus Way E17 ...35 C1
Ondine Rd SE15 ...139 D1
One Tree Cl SE23 ...162 C5
Onega Gate SE16 ...119 A3
O'Neill Ho NW8 ...229 D3
O'Neill Path 11 SE18 ...144 C6
Ongar Cl RM6 ...58 C4
Ongar Ho 15 N1 ...73 B2
Ongar Rd SW6 ...135 C6 265 B6
Onra Rd E17 ...53 C2
Onslow Ave TW10 ...154 A6
Onslow Avenue Mans 10
TW10 ...154 A6
Onslow Cl E4 ...20 B2
Thames Ditton KT7 ...196 C1
Onslow Cres BR7 ...188 D2
Onslow Ct SW10 ...256 B1
Onslow Dr DA14 ...168 D2
Onslow Gdns E18 ...55 C6
N10 ...49 B4
N21 ...16 C6
SW7 ...114 B1 256 C2
Thames Ditton KT7 ...196 C1
Wallington SM6 ...219 C1
Onslow Ho 1 W10 ...91 A4
1 Kingston u T KT2 ...176 B2
Onslow Mews E SW7 ...256 C3
Onslow Mews W SW7 ...256 C3
Onslow Par N14 ...15 B3
Onslow Rd
New Malden KT3 ...200 A5
Richmond TW10 ...154 A5
Thornton Heath CR0 ...204 C1
Onslow Sq SW7 114 B2 256 D3
Onslow St EC1 ...241 B5
Onslow Way KT7 ...196 C1
Ontario St SE1 ...116 D3 261 D6
Ontario Way E14 ...119 C6
Onyx Ho KT4 ...199 B1
Opal Cl E16 ...99 D1
Opal Ho KT4 ...199 B1
Opal Mews 2 IG1 ...78 D6
Opal St SE11 ...116 D1 261 C2
Open Air Theatre, Regent's
Park (30) NW1 ...231 A1
Openshaw Rd SE2 ...124 B2
Openview SW17,SW18 ...158 B2
Operating Theatre Mus &
Herb Garret
SE1 ...117 B5 252 D3
Ophelia Gdns NW2 ...69 A5
Ophir Terr SE15 ...140 A4
Opie Ho NW8 ...230 B4
Opossum Dr TW4 ...128 C2
Oppenheim Rd SE13 ...142 A3
Oppidans Rd NW3 ...70 D1
Orange Gr E11 ...76 C5
4 E11 ...76 C5
Orange Hill Rd HA8 ...27 A3
Orange Pl SE16 ...118 C3
Orange St WC2 115 D6 249 D5
Orange Yd WC2 ...239 D1
Orangery La SE9 ...166 B6
Orangery The TW10 ...153 C2
Oratory La SW3 ...256 D2
Oratory RC Prim Sch
SW3 ...114 C1 257 A2
Oratory The★
SW7 ...114 C3 257 A5
Orb St SE17 ...117 B2 262 C3
Orbain Rd SW6 135 A5 264 B3
Orbel St SW11 ...136 C4 267 A1
Orchard Ave N3 ...47 C6
N14 ...15 C4
N20 ...14 B2
Ashford TW15 ...171 A4
Carshalton CR4 ...203 A1
Croydon CR0 ...207 A1
Erith DA17 ...147 B6
Hatton TW14 ...149 B6
Heston TW5 ...129 A5
Hinchley Wood KT7 ...213 A6
Kingston u T KT3 ...199 C6
Southall UB1 ...107 B5
Orchard Bsns Ctr SE26 ...185 B5
Orchard Cl E4 ...35 C6
E11 ...55 B5
N1 ...73 A1
NW2 ...68 A5
SE23 ...162 C5
SW20 ...200 C5
W10 ...91 A2
Ashford TW15 ...171 A4
Bexley DA7 ...147 A4
Bushey WD2 ...8 B3
Edgware HA8 ...26 A4
Ruislip HA4 ...39 A2
Walton-on-T KT12 ...194 B2
Wembley HA0 ...88 A6
West Ewell KT19 ...214 D2
Orchard Cotts UB3 ...105 C4
Orchard Cres
Edgware HA8 ...27 A5
Enfield EN1 ...5 D4
Orchard Ct E10 ...53 D1
N14 ...15 C5
N22 ...32 A3
SW13 ...133 D2
W1 ...238 A2
Croydon BR3 ...207 C1
Edgware HA8 ...26 B5
Hounslow TW7 ...130 B5
New Malden KT4 ...200 A1
Wallington SM6 ...219 B3
Walton-on-T KT12 ...193 D1
Orchard Cty Fst Sch The
KT8 ...196 B5
Orchard Dr SE3 ...142 C3
Edgware HA8 ...26 B5
Sunbury TW17 ...193 C6
Orchard Gate NW9 ...45 C5
Thames Ditton KT10 ...196 B1
Wembley UB6 ...65 B2
Orchard Gdns
Chessington KT9 ...214 A4
Sutton SM1 ...217 C3
Orchard Gn BR6 ...227 C6
Orchard Gr SE20 ...184 A3
Croydon CR0 ...207 A2
Edgware HA8 ...26 D2
Harrow HA3 ...44 B4
Orpington BR6 ...211 D1
BR6 ...227 D6
Orchard Hill SE13 ...141 D4
Orchard Ho SE5 ...139 A4
Orchard Ho *continued*
11 SE16 ...118 C3
W12 ...112 A5
Orchard JMI Sch E9 ...74 C1
Orchard Jun & Inf Sch The
TW3 ...151 C6
Orchard La SW20 ...178 B2
Thames Ditton KT8 ...196 B3
Woodford IG8 ...37 C6
Orchard Lo N12 ...14 A1
Orchard Mead NW11 ...69 C6
Orchard Mews N1 ...73 B1
Orchard Pl E14 ...120 C6
N17 ...33 D3
Orchard Rd N6 ...49 B2
Belvedere DA17 ...125 C2
Bexley DA16 ...146 B2
Brentford TW8 ...131 C6
Bromley BR1 ...187 C2
Chessington KT9 ...214 A4
Chipping Barnet EN5 ...1 B1
Dagenham RM10 ...103 C6
Enfield EN3 ...18 C6
Hampton TW12 ...173 B3
Hayes UB3 ...106 A6
Hounslow TW4 ...151 C6
Kingston u T KT1 ...176 A1
Mortlake TW9 ...132 C2
Orpington BR6 ...226 D3
Sidcup DA14 ...189 C6
Sunbury TW16 ...172 B3
Sutton SM1 ...217 C4
Twickenham TW1 ...153 B6
Orchard Rise
Croydon CR0 ...207 B1
Kingston u T KT2 ...177 A2
Mortlake TW10 ...132 D1
Pinner HA5 ...39 D6
Orchard Rise E DA15 ...167 D6
Orchard Rise W DA15 ...167 C6
Orchard School Sports Ctr
SE20 ...184 A2
Orchard Sq W14 ...254 C1
Orchard St E17 ...53 A5
W1 ...238 B2
Thames Ditton KT7 ...197 B2
Orchard Terr EN1 ...18 A5
Orchard The N14 ...15 B6
N21 ...17 B5
NW11 ...47 C4
SE3 ...142 B3
W4 ...111 B2
W5 ...87 D2
Ewell KT17 ...215 D1
Hounslow TW3 ...130 A3
Orchard Way
Ashford TW15 ...148 B2
Carshalton SM1 ...218 B4
Croydon BR3,CR0 ...207 A3
Enfield EN1 ...5 C2
Esher KT10 ...212 A2
Orchard Way Prim Sch
CR0 ...207 A2
Orchardleigh Ave EN3 ...6 C3
Orchardmede N21 ...17 B5
Orchards The TW15 ...171 B5
Orchardson Ho NW8 ...236 D5
Orchardson St
NW8 ...92 B3 236 D5
Orchid Cl 1 E6 ...100 A2
Southall UB1 ...85 A1
Orchid Ct HA9 ...66 A6
Orchid Grange N14 ...15 C4
Orchid Lo N14 ...15 C4
Orchid Rd N14 ...15 C4
Orchid St W12 ...112 A6
Orde 6 NW9 ...27 D2
Orde Hall St WC1 94 B2 240 C4
Orde Ho 10 N16 ...73 B4
Ordell Ct 30 E3 ...97 B5
Ordell Rd E3 ...97 B5
Ordnance Cl TW13 ...150 A2
Ordnance Cres SE10 ...120 C4
Ordnance Hill
NW8 ...92 B6 229 D5
Ordnance Mews NW8 ...229 D4
Ordnance Rd E16 ...98 D2
SE18 ...144 C6
Enfield EN3 ...7 B6
Oregano Cl UB7 ...104 B6
Oregano Dr E14 ...98 B1
Oregon Ave E12 ...78 B4
Oregon Cl KT3 ...199 A5
Oregon Sq BR6 ...211 B1
Orestes Ct 8 E18 ...55 A6
Orford Ct SE27 ...160 D2
Stanmore HA7 ...25 C4
Wallington SM6 ...219 C3
Orford Gdns TW1 ...152 D2
Orford Rd E17 ...53 D4
E18 ...55 B6
SE6 ...163 D1
Organ Crossroads KT17 216 A1
Oriana Ho 3 E14 ...119 B6
Oriel Cl CR4 ...203 D6
Oriel Ct NW3 ...70 A4
6 Croydon CR0 ...205 B1
Oriel Dr SW13 ...134 C6
Oriel Gdns IG5 ...56 B6
Oriel Jun & Inf Sch
TW13 ...151 A1
Oriel Rd E9 ...74 D2
Oriel Way UB5 ...63 D1
Orient Ind Pk E10 ...75 C6
Orient St SE11 ...116 D2 261 C4

Orient Way E5 ....74 D5
Oriental City NW9 ....45 B6
Oriental Rd E16 ....121 D5
Oriole Way SE28 ....124 B6
Orion Bsns Ctr SE14 ...118 D1
Orion Ctr The CR0 ....220 A6
Orion Ho 20 E1 ....96 B3
Orion Rd N11 ....31 A4
Orion Way HA6 ....22 A6
Orissa Rd SE18 ....123 C1
Orkney Ho N1 ....233 C6
Orkney St SW11 ....137 A3
Orlando Rd SW4 ....137 C2
Orleans Cl KT10 ....212 B6
Orleans Ct 9 TW1 ....153 B4
Orleans Inf Sch TW1 ....153 B4
Orleans Park Sec Sch
TW1 ....153 B4
Orleans Rd SE19 ....183 B4
Twickenham TW1 ....153 C4
Orleston Mews N7 ....72 C2
Orleston Rd N7 ....72 C2
Orley Farm Rd HA1 ....64 C5
Orley Farm Sch HA1 ....64 B5
Orlop St SE10 ....120 C1
Ormanton Rd SE26 ....184 A6
Orme Ct W2 ...113 D6 245 C5
Orme Ct Mews W2 ....245 D5
Orme Ho 8 E8 ....95 D6
Orme La W2 ...113 D6 245 C5
Orme Rd
Kingston u T KT1,KT3 ....176 D1
Sutton SM1 ....217 D2
Orme Sq W2 ....245 C5
Ormeley Rd SW12 ....159 B3
Ormerod Gdns CR4 ....181 A2
Ormesby Cl SE28 ....124 D6
Ormesby Way HA3 ....44 B4
Ormiston Gr W12 ....112 B5
Ormiston Rd SE10 ....121 A1
Ormond Ave
Hampton TW12 ....173 D2
Orpington BR6 ....227 A6
22 Richmond TW10 ....153 D6
Ormond Cl WC1 ....240 B4
Ormond Cres TW12 ....173 D2
Ormond Dr TW12 ....173 D3
Ormond Ho 7 N16 ....73 B6
Ormond Mews WC1 ....240 B5
Ormond Rd N4,N19 ....50 A1
Richmond TW10 ....153 D6
Ormond Yd SW1 ....249 B4
Ormonde Ct SW15 ....134 C1
Ormonde Gate
SW3 ....114 D1 257 D1
Ormonde Pl SW1 ....258 B3
Ormonde Rd SW14 ....133 A2
Ormonde Rise IG9 ....21 C3
Ormonde Terr
NW8 ....92 D6 230 C5
Ormrod Ct W11 ....91 B1
Ormsby SM2 ....217 D1
Ormsby Gdns UB6 ....86 A5
Ormsby Lo 7 W4 ....111 C3
Ormsby Pl N16 ....73 D5
Ormsby Point 6 SE18 ....122 D2
Ormsby St E2 ....95 D5
Ormside St SE15 ....140 C6
Ormskirk Rd WD1 ....22 D5
Ornan Rd NW3 ....70 C3
Oronsay Wlk 18 N1 ....73 A2
Orpheus Ho 25 N19 ....49 D2
Orpheus St SE5 ....139 B4
Orpheus Twr 6 SE14 ....141 A5
Orpington Gdns N18 ....17 C1
Orpington Hospl BR6 ....227 D4
Orpington Mans N21 ....16 C3
Orpington Rd N21 ....16 D3
St Paul's Cray BR7 ....211 C6
Orpington Sta BR6 ....227 C6
Orpwood Cl TW12 ....173 B4
Orsett Mews W2 91 D1 236 A2
Orsett St SE11 .116 B1 260 D2
Orsett Terr W2 ..92 A1 236 A2
Woodford IG8 ....37 C3
Orsman Rd N1 ....95 C6
Orton St E1 ....118 A5
Orville Rd SW11 ....136 B3
Orwell Cl UB3 ....105 C6
Orwell Ct E8 ....96 A6
N5 ....73 A4
Orwell Ho W12 ....112 A6
Orwell Lo 2 E18 ....55 A5
Orwell Rd E13 ....99 C6
Osbaldeston Rd N16 ....52 A1
Osbert St SW1 ....259 C3
Osberton Rd SE12 ....165 A6
Osborn Cl E8 ....96 A6
Osborn La SE23 ....163 A4
Osborn St E1 ...95 D2 243 D3
20 E1 ....96 A2
Osborn Terr SE3 ....142 D1
Osborne Ave TW19 ....148 B3
Osborne Cl
Beckenham BR3 ....207 A5
Cockfosters EN4 ....2 D2
Feltham TW13 ....172 D5
Osborne Ct 16 E10 ....53 D2
W5 ....88 A2
10 Surbiton KT6 ....198 A3
Osborne Gdns NW7 ....28 D3
South Norwood CR7 ....183 A1
Osborne Gr E17 ....53 B5
Osborne Mews E17 ....53 B5
Osborne Pl SM1 ....218 B3
Osborne Rd E7 ....77 B3
E9 ....75 B2
E10 ....75 D6
N4 ....50 C1
N13 ....16 C1
NW2 ....68 B2
W3 ....110 D4
Buckhurst Hill IG9 ....21 B3
Dagenham RM9 ....81 B3
Enfield EN3 ....7 A3
Erith DA17 ....147 B6
Hounslow TW3,TW4 ....129 B2
Kingston u T KT2 ....176 A3
South Norwood CR7 ....183 A1
Southall UB1 ....86 A1
Walton-on-T KT12 ....194 A1
Osborne Sq RM9 ....81 B4
Osbourne Ct HA2 ....41 D5
Osbourne Ho TW10 ....154 C6
Osbourne Terr 1
SW17 ....181 A5
Oscar Faber Pl 8 N1 ....73 C1
Oscar St SE8 ....141 C4
Oseney Cres NW5 ....71 D2
Osgood Ave BR6 ....227 D3
Osgood Gdns 1 BR6 ....227 D3
O'Shea Gr E3 ....97 B6
Osidge JMI Sch N14 ....15 C3
Osidge La N14 ....15 B3
Osier Ct E1 ....96 D3
Osier Mews W4 ....133 D6
Osier St E1 ....96 C3
Osier Way E10 ....75 D5
Mitcham CR4 ....202 D4
Osiers Ct 3 KT1 ....175 D2
Osiers Rd SW18 ....135 C1
Oslac Rd SE6 ....185 D5
Oslo Ct NW8 ....230 A3
SW19 ....180 B3
Oslo Ho 2 SE5 ....139 A3
Oslo Sq SE16 ....119 A3
Osman Cl N15 ....51 B3
Osman Rd N9 ....18 A1
W6 ....112 C3
Osmani JMI Sch E1 ....96 A2
Osmington Ho SW8 ....270 D3
Osmond Cl HA2 ....64 A6
Osmond Gdns SM6 ....219 C3
Osmund St W12 ....89 D2
Osnaburgh St
NW1 ....93 B3 238 D6
Osnaburgh Terr NW1 ....238 D6
Osney Ho 4 SE2 ....124 D4
Osney Wlk SM5 ....202 B3
Osprey 7 NW9 ....27 D2
Osprey Cl E6 ....100 A2
E11 ....55 A5
E17 ....35 A3
Cheam SM1 ....217 B3
West Drayton UB7 ....104 A4
Osprey Ct NW3 ....69 D3
Osprey Ho E4 ....35 B4
3 E14 ....119 A6
SE15 ....139 D4
Osprey Mews EN3 ....18 B6
Ospringe Cl 9 SE20 ....184 C3
Ospringe Ct SE9 ....167 B5
Ospringe Ho SE1 ....251 B3
Ospringe Rd NW5 ....71 C4
Osram Ct W6 ....112 C3
Osric Path 8 N1 ....95 C5
Ossian Rd N4 ....50 B2
Ossie Garvin Rdbt UB4 106 C6
Ossington Bldgs W1 ....238 A3
Ossington Cl W2 ....245 B5
Ossington St
W2 ....113 D6 245 C5
Ossory Rd SE1 ....140 A6
Ossulston St
NW1 ....93 D4 232 D2
Ossultan Pl N2 ....48 A6
Ossulton Way N2 ....48 A5
Ostade Rd SW2 ....160 B4
Osten Mews
SW7 ....113 D3 255 D5
Oster Terr E17 ....52 D4
Osterley Ave TW7 ....130 B5
Osterley Cl BR5 ....190 A2
Osterley Cres TW7 ....130 D4
Osterley Ct
Hounslow TW7 ....130 B4
7 Northolt UB5 ....84 C4
Osterley Gdns UB2 ....108 A4
Osterley Ho 5 E14 ....97 D1
Osterley La
Isleworth TW7 ....108 C1
Southall UB2,TW7 ....107 D1
Osterley Lo 1 TW7 ....130 C4
Osterley Park* TW7 ....108 B1
Osterley Park Rd UB2 ....107 B3
Osterley Park View Rd
W7 ....108 C4
Osterley Rd N16 ....73 C4
Hounslow TW7 ....130 C4
Osterley Sta TW7 ....130 B5
Osterley Views UB2 ....108 B4
Osterly Gdns CR7 ....183 A1
Ostliffe Rd N13 ....33 A5
Oswald Rd UB1 ....107 A5
Oswald St E5 ....74 D5
Oswald Terr NW2 ....68 C5
Oswald's Mead E9 ....75 A4
Osward Pl N9 ....18 B2
Osward Rd SW12,SW17 ....158 D2
Oswell Ho 9 E1 ....118 B5
Oswin St SE11 .116 D2 261 D4
Oswyth Rd SE5 ....139 C3
Otford Cl SE20 ....184 C2
Otford Cl *continued*
Bromley BR1 ....210 C6
Old Bexley DA5 ....169 D5
Otford Cres SE4 ....163 B5
Otford Ho SE1 ....252 D1
6 SE15 ....140 C6
Otha Ho 18 SW9 ....138 A3
Othello Cl SE11 ....261 C2
Otho Ct 5 TW8 ....131 D5
Otis St E3 ....98 A4
Otley App IG2 ....56 D3
Otley Dr IG2 ....56 D3
Otley Ho N5 ....72 D5
Otley Rd E16 ....99 C1
Otley Terr E5 ....74 C5
Ottawa Ho 4 HA4 ....40 C1
Ottaway Ct E5 ....74 A5
Ottaway St E5 ....74 A5
Otter Rd UB6 ....86 A3
Otterbourne Rd E4 ....20 B1
1 Croydon CR0 ....221 A6
Otterburn Gdns TW7 ....131 A5
Otterburn Ho 12 SE5 ....139 A5
Otterburn St SW17 ....180 D4
Otterden Cl BR6 ....227 C4
Otterden St SE6 ....185 C5
Otterfield Rd UB7 ....104 A5
Ottershaw Ho
Mitcham CR4 ....180 B1
St Paul's Cray BR5 ....190 B2
Otto St SE17 ....138 D6
Otway Ct N4 ....50 B3
Otway Gdns WD2 ....8 C4
Oulton Cl E5 ....74 C6
Oulton Cres IG11 ....79 D3
Oulton Rd N15 ....51 B4
Oulton Way WD1 ....23 B6
Oundle Ave WD2 ....8 A5
Our Lady & St John's RC Jun & Inf Sch TW8 ....109 C1
Our Lady & St Joseph RC JMI Sch N1 ....73 C2
Our Lady & St Philip Neri RC Prim Sch SE26 ....185 A6
Our Lady & St Philip Neri RC Sch
SE23 ....162 D1
SE26 ....185 A6
Our Lady of Dolours RC Prim Sch W2 ....91 D2
Our Lady of Grace Inf Sch NW2 ....68 C6
Our Lady of Grace Jun Sch NW2 ....68 B5
Our Lady of Grace Sch SE7 ....143 B6
Our Lady of Lourdes Prim Sch NW10 ....89 A6
Our Lady of Lourdes RC Prim Sch
N11 ....31 C5
N12 ....30 A2
SE13 ....142 B2
Our Lady of Lourds RC Prim Sch E11 ....55 A3
Our Lady of Muswell Prim Sch N10 ....49 A6
Our Lady of Muswell RC Prim Sch N10 ....31 A1
Our Lady of the Assumption RC Inf Sch E2 ....96 C5
Our Lady of the Rosary RC Prim Sch DA15 ....167 C5
Our Lady of the Sacred Heart RC Prim Sch (Annexe) N7 ....72 B2
Our Lady of the Sacred Heart RC Sch N7 ....72 B3
Our Lady of the Visitation RC Prim Sch UB6 ....86 A3
Our Lady of Victories RC Prim Sch
SW7 ....114 A2 256 B3
SW15 ....134 D1
Our Lady Queen of Heaven RC Prim Sch SW19 ....156 D4
Our Lady RC JMI Sch E14 ....97 B1
Our Lady's Convent High Sch N15 N16 ....51 C2
Ouseley Rd SW12 ....158 D3
Outer Circ NW8 .92 C4 230 B3
Outgate Rd NW10 ....67 D1
Outram Pl N1 ...94 A6 233 B6
Outram Rd E6 ....100 A6
N22 ....31 D2
Croydon CR0 ....221 D6
Outwich St EC3 ....243 B2
Outwood Ho 3 SW2 ....160 B4
Oval Ct HA8 ....27 A3
Oval Mans SE11 ....270 D6
Oval Pl SW8 ...138 B5 270 D4
Oval Prim Sch CR0 ....205 C1
Oval Rd NW1 ...93 B6 231 C6
Croydon CR0 ....205 C1
Oval Rd N RM10 ....103 D6
Oval Rd S RM10 ....103 D5
Oval Sta SE11 ....138 C6
Oval The E2 ....96 B5
Sidcup DA15 ....168 A4
Oval The (Surrey Cnty Crkt Gd) SE11 ....138 C6
Oval Way SE11 .116 B1 260 D1
Overbrae BR3 ....185 C5
Overbrook Wlk HA8 ....26 C3
Overbury Ave BR3 ....208 A6
Overbury Ct 1 BR3 ....208 A6
Overbury Ho 3 E5 ....74 D4
Overbury Rd N4,N15 ....51 B3
Overbury St E5 ....74 D4
Overcliff Rd SE13 ....141 C2
Overcourt Cl DA15 ....168 B5
Overdale Ave KT3 ....177 B1
Overdale Rd W5 ....109 C3
Overdown Rd SE6 ....185 D6
Overhill Rd SE21,SE22 ....162 A4
Overhill Way BR3 ....208 B4
Overlea Rd E5 ....52 A2
Overmead SE9 ....167 B4
Oversley Ho 17 W2 ....91 C2
Overstand Cl BR3 ....207 C4
Overstone Gdns CR0 ....207 B2
Overstone Ho 17 E14 ....97 C1
Overstone Rd W6 ....112 C2
Overstrand Mans SW11 268 A1
Overton Cl NW10 ....67 A2
Hounslow TW7 ....130 D4
Overton Ct E11 ....55 A2
Overton Dr E11 ....55 B2
Dagenham RM6 ....58 C2
Overton Grange Sch
SM2 ....217 D1
Overton Ho SW15 ....155 D4
Overton Rd E10 ....53 A1
N14 ....16 A6
SE2 ....124 D3
SW9 ....138 C3
Belmont SM2 ....217 C1
Overton's Yd CR0 ....221 A5
Overy Ho SE1 ....251 C1
Ovesdon Ave HA2 ....41 B1
Ovett Cl SE19 ....183 C4
Ovex Cl E14 ....120 A4
Ovington Ct SW3 ....257 B5
Ovington Gdns SW3 ....257 B5
Ovington Mews SW3 ....257 B5
Ovington Sq
SW3 ....114 C3 257 B5
Ovington St
SW3 ....114 C2 257 B4
Owen Cl SE28 ....124 C5
Hayes UB4 ....84 B4
Thornton Heath CR0 ....205 B3
Owen Ct UB4 ....84 B4
Owen Ho 11 N19 ....71 C4
Feltham TW14 ....150 A4
5 Twickenham TW1 ....153 B4
Owen Rd N13 ....33 A5
Hayes UB4 ....84 B4
Owen St EC1 ....234 C3
Owen Way NW10 ....67 A3
Owen Wlk 7 SE20 ....184 A3
Owenite St SE2 ....124 B2
Owen's Ct EC1 ....234 C2
Owen's Row EC1 ....234 C2
Owens Way SE23 ....163 A4
Owgan Cl SE5 ....139 B5
Oxberry Ave SW6 ....135 A3
Oxbridge Ct 4 W4 ....110 D1
Oxendon St
SW1,W1 ....115 D6 249 C5
Oxenford St SE15 ....139 D2
Oxenham Ho 13 SE8 ....141 C6
Oxenholme NW1 ....232 B3
Oxenpark Ave HA9 ....44 A2
Oxestalls Rd SE8 ....119 A1
Oxford & Cambridge Mans
NW1 ....237 B3
Oxford Ave NW10 ....90 C4
SW20 ....179 A1
Harlington TW6 ....127 D5
Hounslow TW5 ....107 C1
Oxford Cir W1 ..93 C1 239 A1
Oxford Circus Ave W1 ....239 A1
Oxford Circus Sta
W1 ....93 C1 239 A1
Oxford Cl N9 ....18 B2
Littleton TW15,TW17 ....171 A3
Mitcham CR4 ....203 C6
Oxford Cres KT3 ....199 B3
Oxford Ct EC4 ....252 C6
16 W3 ....88 C1
W4 ....110 D1
8 W7 ....86 D2
17 Kingston u T KT6 ....198 A4
Oxford Dr HA4 ....62 C6
Oxford Gardens Prim Sch
W10 ....90 D1
Oxford Gate W6 ....112 D2
Oxford Gdns N20 ....14 B3
N21 ....17 A4
W4 ....132 C6
W10 ....90 D1
Oxford Mews DA5 ....169 C4
Oxford Rd E15 ....76 B2
N4 ....50 C1
N9 ....18 B2
NW6 ....91 C5
SE19 ....183 B4
SW15 ....135 A1
W5 ....109 D6
Carshalton SM2,SM5 ....218 C3
Enfield EN3 ....18 B6
Harrow HA1 ....42 A3
Harrow HA3 ....42 D6
Ilford IG1 ....79 A3
Sidcup DA14 ....190 B5
Teddington TW11,TW12 ....174 B5
Wallington SM6 ....219 C3
Woodford IG8 ....37 D5
Oxford Rd N W4 ....110 D1
Oxford Rd S W4 ....110 D1
Oxford Sq W2 ...92 C1 237 B1
Oxford St W1 ...93 B1 238 D1
Oxford Way TW13 ....172 D6
Oxford Wlk UB1 ....107 B5
Oxgate Ct Par NW2 ....68 A6
Oxgate Ctr NW2 ....68 B6
Oxgate Gdns NW2 ....68 B6
Oxhawth Cres BR2 ....210 D3
Oxhey Dr HA6,WD1 ....22 B6
Oxhey La HA5 ....23 C5
Oxhey Ridge Cl HA6 ....22 B5
Oxhey Wood JMI Schs
WD1 ....22 C6
Oxleas E6 ....100 D1
Oxleas Cl DA16 ....145 B3
Oxleay Rd HA2 ....41 C1
Oxleigh Cl KT3 ....199 C4
Oxley Cl SE1 ....118 A1
Oxleys Rd NW2 ....68 B5
Oxlip Cl 2 CR0 ....206 D1
Oxlow La RM10 ....81 C4
Oxo Tower SE1 ....251 B5
Oxo Tower Wharf SE1 ....251 B5
Oxonian St SE22 ....139 D1
Oxted Cl CR4 ....202 B6
Oxted Ct N16 ....51 C1
Oxtoby Way SW16 ....181 D2
Oyster Catcher Terr IG5 .56 C6
Oyster Catchers Cl E16 .99 B1
Oyster Row E1 ....96 C1
Ozolins Way E16 ....99 A1

P

Pablo Neruda Cl 4
SE24 ....138 D1
Pace Pl E1 ....96 B1
Pacific Cl TW14 ....149 D3
Pacific Ho 15 E1 ....96 D3
Pacific Rd E16 ....99 A1
Packenham Ho 21 E2 ....95 D4
24 N19 ....49 D2
Packham Ct KT4 ....216 C5
Packington Ho 22 SW9 138 A3
Packington Sq
N1 ....95 A6 235 A6
Packington St
N1 ....94 D6 234 D5
Packmores Rd SE9 ....167 B6
Padbury SE17 ....263 B1
Padbury Cl TW14 ....149 B3
Padbury Ct E2 ....95 D4
Padbury Ho NW8 ....237 B6
Paddenswick Ct W6 ....112 B3
Paddenswick Rd W6 ....112 A3
Paddington Cl UB4 ....84 D3
Paddington Com Hospl
W9 ....91 C2
Paddington Ct 10 W7 ....86 D2
Paddington Gn
W2 ....92 B2 236 C4
Paddington Green Prim Sch
NW8 ....92 B3 236 C5
Paddington St W1 ....238 A4
Paddington Sta
W2 ....92 B1 236 C2
Paddock Cl SE3 ....143 A3
SE26 ....184 D6
New Malden KT4 ....199 C1
Northolt UB5 ....85 C5
Orpington BR6 ....226 D4
Paddock Ct SW20 ....200 C5
Paddock Gdns SE19 ....183 C4
Paddock Lo 13 EN1 ....17 C6
Paddock Rd NW2 ....68 A6
Bexleyheath DA6 ....147 A1
Ruislip HA4 ....62 D5
Paddock Sch SW15 ....133 D1
Paddock The UB10 ....60 D4
Paddock Way BR7 ....189 B3
Paddocks Cl HA2 ....63 D4
Paddocks Gn NW9 ....44 D1
Paddocks The
Addington CR0 ....223 C2
Cockfosters EN4 ....2 D2
Wembley HA9 ....66 D6
Padfield Rd SE5 ....139 A2
Padnall Ct RM6 ....58 D6
Padnall Rd RM6 ....58 D5
Padstow Ho 12 E14 ....119 B6
Padstow Rd EN2 ....4 D4
Padstow Wlk TW14 ....149 D3
Padua Rd SE20 ....184 C2
Pagden St SW8 ....268 D2
Page Cl Dagenham RM9 ....81 A3
Hampton TW12 ....173 A4
Harrow HA3 ....44 B3
Page Cres CR0 ....220 D3
Page Ct NW7 ....28 A3
Page Green Rd N15 ....52 A4
Page Green Terr N15 ....51 D4
Page Heath La BR1 ....209 D6
Page Heath Villas BR1 ....209 D6
Page High N22 ....50 C6
Page Ho SE10 ....142 A6
Page Mdw NW7 ....28 A3
Page Rd TW14 ....149 B5
Page St NW7 ....28 A3
SW1 ....115 D2 259 D4
Pageant Ave NW9 ....27 C2
Pageant Cres SE16 ....119 B5
Pageant Wlk CR0 ....221 C5
Pageantmaster Ct EC4 ....241 C1
Pagehurst Rd CR0 ....206 B2
Page's Ct N10 ....31 A1
Page's Hill N10 ....31 A1
Page's La N10 ....31 A1
Page's Wlk SE1 117 C3 263 B5
Page's Yd W4 ....133 C6
Paget Ave SM1 ....218 B5
Paget Cl TW12 ....174 B6
Paget Ct UB7 ....104 A4
Paget Gdns BR7 ....188 D2
Paget Ho 15 E2 ....96 C5
Paget La TW7 ....130 C2
Paget Pl
Kingston u T KT2 ....177 A4
Thames Ditton KT7 ....196 D1
Paget Rd N16 ....51 B1
Hillingdon UB10 ....83 A3
Ilford IG1 ....78 D4
Paget Rise SE18 ....144 C5
Paget St EC1 ....234 C2
Paget Terr SE18 ....144 D6
Pagham Ho W10 ....90 C3
Pagin Ho N15 ....51 C4
Pagitts Gr EN4 ....1 D4
Pagnell St SE14 ....141 B5
Pagoda Ave TW9 ....132 B2
Pagoda Gdns SE3 ....142 B3
Paignton Rd N15 ....51 C3
Ruislip HA4 ....62 A5
Paine Ct SE3 ....142 D6
Paines Cl HA5 ....41 A6
Paine's La HA5 ....23 A1
Pain's Cl CR4 ....181 B1
Painsthorpe Rd 3 N16 .73 C5
Painswick Ct 1 SE15 ....139 D5
Painters Rd IG2,RM6 ....58 A6
Paisley Rd N22 ....32 D2
Carshalton SM5 ....202 B1
Pakeman Ho SE1 ....251 D2
Pakeman Prim Sch N7 ....72 B5
Pakeman St N7 ....72 B5
Pakenham Cl SW12 ....159 A3
Pakenham St
WC1 ....94 B3 240 D6
Palace Ave W8 113 D4 245 D2
Palace Court Gdns N10 .49 C6
Palace Ct NW3 ....69 D3
SE9 ....166 B5
SW2 ....160 C2
W2 ....113 D6 245 C5
Harrow HA3 ....44 A3
South Norwood CR7 ....205 B5
Palace Garden Mews
W8 ....245 B4
Palace Gardens Terr
W8 ....113 D5 245 C3
Palace Gate
W8 ....114 A4 246 A1
Palace Gates Rd N22 ....31 D2
Palace Gdns
Buckhurst Hill IG9 ....21 D3
Enfield EN2 ....5 B1
Palace Gdns Mews
W8 ....113 D5 245 D3
Palace Gn W8 .113 D5 245 C3
Croydon CR0 ....223 B1
Palace Gr SE19 ....183 D3
Bromley BR1 ....187 B2
Palace Mans W14 ....254 B4
Palace Mews E17 ....53 B5
SW1 ....258 B3
SW6 ....264 D4
Palace of Ind HA9 ....66 C4
Palace Par E17 ....53 C5
Palace Pl SW1 ....259 A6
Palace Rd N8 ....49 D4
N11 ....32 A3
SE19 ....183 D3
SE27,SW16,SW2 ....160 C2
Bromley BR1 ....187 B2
East Molesey KT8 ....196 B6
Kingston u T KT1 ....197 D5
Ruislip HA4 ....63 A4
Palace Sq SE19 ....183 D3
Palace St SW1 .115 C3 259 A6
Palace View SE12 ....165 A2
Bromley BR1 ....209 B6
Croydon CR0 ....223 B4
Palace View Rd E4 ....35 D5
Palamon Ct SE1 ....263 D2
Palamos Rd E10 ....53 C1
Palatine Ave N16 ....73 C4
Palatine Rd N16 ....73 C4
Palermo Rd NW10 ....90 A5
Palestine Gr SW19 ....180 B2
Palewell Cl BR5 ....190 B1
Palewell Common Dr
SW14 ....155 B6
Palewell Pk SW14 ....133 B1
Palfrey Pl SW8 .138 B5 270 D4
Palgrave Ave UB1 ....107 C6
Palgrave Ho 4 NW3 ....70 D3
7 SE5 ....139 A5
Twickenham TW2 ....152 A4
Palgrave Rd W12 ....111 D3
Palissy St 35 E2 ....95 D4
Pall Mall SW1 .115 D5 249 C3
Pall Mall E
SW1 ....115 D5 249 D4
Pall Mall Pl SW1 ....249 B3
Pallant Ho SE1 ....262 D5
Pallant Way BR6 ....226 C5
Pallet Way SE18 ....144 A4
Palliser Ct W14 ....254 A1
Palliser Ho 21 E1 ....96 D3
3 SE10 ....142 B6
Palliser Rd W14 113 A1 254 A1
Palm Ave DA14 ....190 D4
Palm Cl E10 ....75 D5
Palm Ct N16 ....73 B6
N22 ....32 B3
17 SE15 ....139 D5
Beckenham BR3 ....207 B6
Palm Gr W5 ....110 A3
Palm Tree Ct 3 N17 ....33 D1
Palm Tree Ho 2 SE14 .140 D5

Palmar Cres DA7 ... 147 C3
Palmar Rd DA7 ... 147 C3
Palmeira Rd DA16 ... 146 D2
Palmer Ave KT4,SM3 ... 216 C4
Palmer Cl Heston TW5 ... 129 C4
West Wickham BR4 ... 224 B6
Palmer Cres KT1 ... 198 A6
Palmer Ct NW10 ... 89 B6
Palmer Gdns EN5 ... 12 D6
Palmer Ho 5 N19 ... 71 C5
8 NW5 ... 71 C4
6 SE14 ... 140 D5
Palmer Pl N7 ... 72 C3
Palmer Rd E13 ... 99 B3
Dagenham RM8 ... 58 D1
Palmer St SW1 ... 259 C6
Palmer's Ct 11 N11 ... 31 C5
Palmers Gr KT8 ... 195 C5
Palmers Green High Sch
N21 ... 16 C2
Palmers Green Sta N13 ... 32 B6
Palmers La EN3 ... 6 C4
Palmers Rd E2 ... 96 D5
SW14 ... 133 A2
SW16 ... 182 B1
Palmer's Rd N11 ... 31 C5
Palmerston Cres N13 ... 32 B5
SE18 ... 145 A6
Palmerston Ct 22 E3 ... 96 D5
E17 ... 53 B5
2 Buckhurst Hill IG9 ... 21 C2
9 Surbiton KT6 ... 197 D2
Palmerston Ctr HA3 ... 42 D6
Palmerston Gr 4
SW19 ... 179 C3
Palmerston Ho SW11 ... 268 B1
W8 ... 245 A3
Palmerston Rd E7 ... 77 B2
E17 ... 53 B5
N22 ... 32 B4
NW6 ... 69 B1
NW6 ... 69 C1
SW14 ... 133 A1
SW19 ... 179 C3
W3 ... 111 A3
Buckhurst Hill IG9 ... 21 C3
Carshalton SM5 ... 219 A4
Farnborough BR6 ... 227 A3
Harrow HA3 ... 42 D6
Hounslow TW3 ... 130 A4
Sutton SM1 ... 218 A3
Thornton Heath CR0 ... 205 B4
Twickenham TW2 ... 152 C5
Palmerston Way SW8 ... 268 D3
Pamela Ct N12 ... 29 D4
NW10 ... 68 A1
Pamela Gdns HA5 ... 40 B4
Pamela Ho 14 E8 ... 95 D6
Pamlion Ct N4 ... 50 A2
Pampisford Rd CR2 ... 220 D1
Pams Way KT19 ... 215 B3
Panama Ho 5 E1 ... 96 D2
Panbro Ho 7 SE18 ... 144 B4
Pancras La EC2 ... 242 C1
Pancras Rd NW1 ... 93 D5 232 D4
Pandora Ct 4 KT6 ... 198 A3
Pandora Rd NW6 ... 69 C2
Panfield Mews IG2 ... 56 C3
Panfield Rd SE2 ... 124 A3
Pangbourne NW1 ... 232 A1
Pangbourne Ave W10 ... 90 C2
Pangbourne Ct N20 ... 14 A4
SW17 ... 180 A6
Pangbourne Dr HA7 ... 26 A5
Pangbourne Ho 4 N7 ... 72 A3
Panhard Pl UB1 ... 107 D6
Pank Ave EN5 ... 14 A6
Pankhurst Cl 7 SE14 ... 140 D5
Isleworth TW7 ... 130 D2
Pankhurst Rd KT12 ... 194 C2
Panmuir Rd SW20 ... 178 B2
Panmure Cl N5 ... 72 D4
Panmure Ct 11 UB1 ... 86 A1
Panmure Rd SE26 ... 162 B1
Panorama Ct N6 ... 49 C3
Pansy Gdns W12 ... 112 A6
Panther Dr NW10 ... 67 B3
Pantiles Cl N13 ... 32 D5
Pantiles The NW11 ... 47 B4
Bromley BR1 ... 210 A6
Bushey WD2 ... 8 B3
Erith DA7 ... 147 B5
Panton St SW1 ... 249 C5
Panyer Alley EC2 ... 242 A2
Panyer Alley Steps EC4 ... 242 A2
Paper Mill Wharf E14 ... 119 A6
Papermill Cl SM5 ... 219 A4
Papillons Wlk SE3 ... 143 A2
Papworth Gdns N7 ... 72 B3
Papworth Way SW2 ... 160 C4
Parade Mans 2 NW4 ... 46 B4
10 SE5 ... 139 A3
Parade Mews SE27,SW2 ... 160 D2
Parade The
SW11 ... 136 D5 267 D4
Ashford TW16 ... 171 D3
Claygate KT10 ... 212 C2
Greenford UB6 ... 65 B3
2 Kingston u T KT2 ... 176 A1
Wallington CR0 ... 220 B3
Paradise Pas N7 ... 72 C3
Paradise Pl 15 SE7 ... 122 A2
Paradise Rd SW4 ... 138 A3
Richmond TW10 ... 154 A6
Paradise Row E2 ... 96 B4
Paradise St SE16 ... 118 B4
Paradise Wlk
SW3 ... 136 D6 267 D6
Paragon Cl E16 ... 99 A1
Paragon Ct NW4 ... 29 A2
Paragon Gr KT5 ... 198 B3
Paragon Mews SE1 ... 262 D4
Paragon Pl SE3 ... 142 D3
Paragon Rd E9 ... 74 C2
Paragon The SE3 ... 143 A3
Paramount Bldg EC1 ... 241 C6
Paramount Ct WC1 ... 239 B5
Paramount Ho 8 E11 ... 76 C5
Parbury Rd SE23 ... 163 A5
Parbury Rise KT9 ... 214 A2
Parchmore Rd CR7 ... 205 A6
Parchmore Way CR7 ... 182 D1
Pardes House & Beis Yaakov Sch (Boys) N3 ... 29 B1
Pardon St EC1 ... 241 D6
Pardoner St
SE1 ... 117 B3 262 D6
Parfett St E1 ... 96 A1
Parfew Ct 2 SE22 ... 162 B2
Parfrey St W6 ... 134 C6
Pargraves Ct HA9 ... 66 C6
Parham Dr IG2 ... 56 D4
Paris Gdn SE1 ... 116 D5 251 C4
Paris Ho 12 E2 ... 96 B5
Parish CE Prim Sch
BR1 ... 187 A3
Parish Church CE Inf & Jun Schs CR0 ... 220 D5
Parish Ct KT6 ... 198 A3
Parish Gate Dr DA15 ... 167 C5
Parish La SE20 ... 184 D3
Parish Wharf 6 SE7 ... 122 A2
Park App DA16 ... 146 B1
Park Ave E6 ... 100 C5
N3 ... 29 D2
N13 ... 16 C1
N18 ... 34 A6
N22 ... 32 B2
NW2 ... 68 C2
NW10 ... 88 B4
NW10 ... 88 B5
NW11 ... 47 D1
SW14 ... 133 B1
Barking IG11 ... 79 A2
Enfield EN1 ... 17 C5
Ilford IG1 ... 56 C1
Isleworth TW3 ... 151 D5
Mitcham CR4 ... 181 B3
Orpington BR6 ... 226 C6
Plaistow BR1 ... 187 A4
Ruislip HA4 ... 39 C3
Southall UB1 ... 107 C5
Upper Halliford TW17 ... 193 C6
Wallington SM5 ... 219 A2
West Wickham BR4 ... 224 A6
Woodford IG8 ... 37 B5
Park Ave E KT17 ... 216 A2
Park Ave N N8 ... 49 D5
NW10 ... 68 B3
Park Ave S N8 ... 49 D5
Park Ave W KT17 ... 216 A2
Park Avenue Mews
CR4 ... 181 B3
Park Avenue Rd N17 ... 34 B3
Park Bsns Ctr 4 NW6 ... 91 C4
Park Chase HA9 ... 66 B4
Park Cl 20 E9 ... 96 C6
N12 ... 30 B6
NW2 ... 68 B5
NW10 ... 88 B4
SW1 ... 247 C1
W14 ... 113 B3 254 D6
Hampton TW12 ... 174 A2
Harrow HA3 ... 24 C2
Isleworth TW3,TW7 ... 152 A6
Kingston u T KT2 ... 176 C2
Wallington SM5 ... 218 D2
Park Cotts 10 TW1 ... 153 B5
Park Cres N3 ... 30 A3
W1 ... 93 B3 238 C5
Enfield EN2 ... 5 B1
Harrow HA3 ... 24 C2
Twickenham TW2 ... 152 B3
Park Cres Mews E W1 ... 238 D5
Park Cres Mews W W1 ... 238 C5
Park Croft HA8 ... 27 A2
Park Ct 2 E4 ... 20 A2
E17 ... 53 D4
N11 ... 31 D3
N12 ... 30 B5
SE21 ... 161 B1
SW4 ... 159 D6
SW11 ... 268 C2
SW12 ... 159 A3
2 Beckenham BR3 ... 207 D6
London EN5 ... 14 B4
New Malden KT3 ... 199 B5
Teddington KT1 ... 175 C2
Wallington SM6 ... 220 A3
Wembley HA9 ... 66 A3
Park Dr N21 ... 17 A5
NW11 ... 47 D1
SE7 ... 144 A6
SW14 ... 133 B1
W3 ... 110 C3
Harrow HA2 ... 41 C2
Harrow Weald HA3 ... 24 C4
Park Dwellings 7 NW3 ... 70 D3
Park End NW3 ... 70 C4
Bromley BR1 ... 186 D2
Park Farm Cl N2 ... 48 A6
Pinner HA5 ... 40 B4
Park Farm Ct UB3 ... 105 C6
Park Farm Rd
Bromley BR1 ... 187 D2
Kingston u T KT2 ... 176 A3
Park Flats N6 ... 48 C2
Park Gate N2 ... 48 B6
N21 ... 16 B4
W5 ... 87 D2
Park Gate Ct TW12 ... 174 A5
Park Gate Mans N2 ... 48 B6
Park Gates HA2 ... 63 C4
Park Gdns NW9 ... 44 D6
Kingston u T KT2 ... 176 B5
Park Gr E15 ... 99 A6
N11 ... 31 D3
Bromley BR1 ... 187 B2
Edgware HA8 ... 26 B5
Park Grove Rd E11 ... 76 C6
Park Hall Rd N2 ... 48 C5
SE21 ... 161 B1
Park Hall Road Trad Est
SE21 ... 161 B1
Park High Sch HA7 ... 25 D1
Park Hill SE23 ... 162 C3
SW4 ... 159 D6
W5 ... 87 D2
Bromley BR1 ... 210 B5
Loughton IG10 ... 21 D6
Richmond TW10 ... 154 B5
Wallington SM5 ... 218 D2
Park Hill Cl SM5 ... 218 C3
Park Hill Ct SW17 ... 158 D1
W5 ... 87 D2
Croydon CR0 ... 221 C6
Park Hill Inf Sch CR0 ... 221 C5
Park Hill Jun Sch CR0 ... 221 C5
Park Hill Rd
Beckenham BR2 ... 186 C1
South Croydon CR0 ... 221 C5
Wallington SM6 ... 219 B1
Park Hill Rise CR0 ... 221 D5
Park Hill Sch KT2 ... 176 C3
Park Hill Wlk 10 NW3 ... 70 D3
Park Ho 35 E9 ... 74 C1
N4 ... 72 D6
N21 ... 16 B4
8 SE5 ... 139 B4
SE26 ... 184 A5
Sidcup DA14 ... 190 A5
Park House Gdns TW1 ... 153 C6
Park House Mid Sch
SW19 ... 179 B6
Park La E15 ... 98 B6
N9 ... 17 D1
N17 ... 34 A3
W1 ... 115 A6 248 A5
Cheam SM3 ... 217 A2
Cranford TW5 ... 128 A5
Croydon CR0 ... 221 B5
Harrow HA2 ... 63 D5
Hayes UB4 ... 83 C3
Ilford RM6 ... 58 D3
Richmond TW9 ... 131 D1
Stanmore HA7 ... 9 A1
Teddington TW11 ... 174 D4
Wallington SM5,SM6 ... 219 A3
Wembley HA9 ... 66 A4
Park Lane Cl N17 ... 34 A3
Park Lane Prim Sch HA9 ... 66 A3
Park Lawn CR7 ... 183 A1
Park Lea Ct N16 ... 51 C2
Park Lo 10 E1 ... 118 B5
N12 ... 30 A5
NW2 ... 68 C4
11 NW8 ... 70 B1
3 W5 ... 87 B3
Park Lorne NW8 ... 230 B1
Park Mans 5 NW4 ... 46 B4
NW8 ... 230 A3
SE26 ... 162 C1
SW1 ... 247 C1
SW6 ... 264 B1
SW8 ... 270 B6
SW11 ... 267 C1
W6 ... 111 D3
Park Mead Bexley DA15 ... 168 B5
Harrow HA2 ... 63 D5
Park Mews W10 ... 91 A5
Chislehurst West BR7 ... 188 D4
Stanwell TW19 ... 148 B4
Park Nook Gdns EN2 ... 5 B6
Park Par NW9 ... 45 B6
NW10 ... 89 D5
W3 ... 110 C3
Hayes UB3 ... 83 C1
Park Pl E14 ... 119 C5
SW1 ... 115 C5 249 A4
W3 ... 110 C2
W5 ... 109 D5
Hampton TW12 ... 174 A4
Wembley HA9 ... 66 B4
Park Place Dr W3 ... 110 C3
Park Place Villas W2 ... 236 B4
Park Prim Sch E15 ... 76 D1
Park Rd E6 ... 99 C6
E10 ... 53 C1
E12 ... 77 B6
E15 ... 99 A6
E17 ... 53 B4
N2 ... 48 B6
N8 ... 49 D4
N8,N15 ... 50 D5
N11 ... 31 D3
N14 ... 15 D4
N18 ... 34 A6
NW1,NW8 ... 92 C3 237 B6
NW4 ... 46 B3
NW9 ... 45 B2
NW10 ... 89 C6
SE25 ... 205 C5
SW19 ... 180 C4
W4 ... 133 B6
Park Rd *continued*
W7 ... 108 D6
Ashford TW15 ... 170 D5
Barnet EN4 ... 2 C1
Beckenham BR3 ... 185 C3
Bromley BR1 ... 187 B2
Cheam SM3 ... 217 A2
Chipping Barnet EN5 ... 1 B1
Chislehurst West BR7 ... 188 D4
East Molesey KT8 ... 196 A5
Feltham TW13 ... 172 D6
Hackbridge SM6 ... 219 B6
Hampton TW12 ... 174 A5
Hayes UB4 ... 83 C2
Ilford IG1 ... 79 B5
Isleworth TW3,TW7 ... 152 A6
Isleworth TW7 ... 131 B3
Kingston u T KT2,TW10 ... 176 C3
Lower Halliford TW17 ... 192 C1
New Malden KT3 ... 199 B5
Richmond TW10 ... 154 B5
Sunbury TW16 ... 172 B3
Surbiton KT5 ... 175 C2
Teddington KT1 ... 175 C2
Teddington TW11 ... 174 D4
Twickenham TW1 ... 153 C5
Uxbridge UB8 ... 60 A2
Wallington SM6 ... 219 B3
Wembley HA0 ... 66 A2
Park Rd E W3 ... 111 A4
Uxbridge UB10 ... 82 A5
Park Rd N W3 ... 110 D4
W4 ... 111 B1
Park Ridings N8 ... 50 C6
Park Rise SE23 ... 163 A3
Harrow HA3 ... 24 C2
Park Rise Rd SE23 ... 163 A3
Park Road Ho 3 KT2 ... 176 C3
Park Row SE10 ... 142 B6
Park Royal NW10 ... 88 D6
Park Royal Bsns Ctr
NW10 ... 89 A3
Park Royal Metro Ctr
NW10 ... 88 D3
Park Royal Rd NW10,W3 ... 89 A3
Park Royal Sta W5 ... 88 C3
Park S SW11 ... 268 A1
Park Sch IG1 ... 56 D1
Park Sheen 3 SW14 ... 132 D1
Park Side NW2 ... 68 B4
Chigwell IG9 ... 21 B2
Park Sq E NW1 ... 93 B3 238 D6
Park Sq Mews NW1 ... 238 C5
Park Sq W NW1 ... 93 B3 238 C5
Park St SE1 ... 117 A5 252 B4
W1 ... 115 A6 248 A5
Croydon CR0 ... 221 A6
Teddington TW11 ... 174 C4
Park St James NW8 ... 230 C5
Park Steps W2 ... 247 B6
Park Terr
Carshalton SM5 ... 218 C5
Enfield EN3 ... 7 A5
New Malden KT4 ... 200 A1
Park The N6 ... 49 A3
NW11 ... 47 D1
SE23 ... 162 C3
W5 ... 109 D5
Sidcup DA14 ... 190 A5
Wallington SM5 ... 218 D3
Park Twrs W1 ... 248 C3
Park View N5 ... 73 A4
N21 ... 16 B4
NW2 ... 68 C4
W3 ... 89 A2
Hatch End HA5 ... 23 B2
Morden SM4 ... 202 B4
New Malden KT3 ... 199 D6
Wembley HA9 ... 66 D3
Yiewsley UB7 ... 104 A6
Park View Cres N11 ... 31 B6
Park View Ct N12 ... 30 C6
NW9 ... 45 A5
SW18 ... 157 C5
Park View Dr CR4 ... 180 B1
Park View Gdns N22 ... 32 C2
NW4 ... 46 D4
Barking IG11 ... 101 C5
Redbridge IG4 ... 56 B5
Park View Ho SE24 ... 160 D5
Park View Rd N3 ... 29 D2
N17 ... 34 A1
NW10 ... 67 D4
SE9 ... 166 D2
W5 ... 88 A2
Bexley DA16 ... 146 D2
Hillingdon UB8 ... 82 C1
Northwood HA5 ... 22 B3
Southall UB1 ... 107 C5
Park Village E
NW1 ... 93 B5 231 D3
Park Village W
NW1 ... 93 B5 231 C4
Park Villas RM6 ... 58 D3
Park Vista SE10 ... 142 B6
Park Walk Prim Sch
SW10 ... 136 B6 266 C5
Park Way N20 ... 30 D6
NW11 ... 47 A4
W3 ... 110 C2
East Molesey KT8 ... 195 D6
Edgware HA8 ... 26 D2
Enfield EN2 ... 4 C3
Feltham TW14 ... 150 B4
Ruislip HA4 ... 40 A1
Park Way Ct HA4 ... 39 D1
Park West W2 ... 92 C1 237 B1
Park West Pl W1,
W2 ... 92 C1 237 B2
Park Wlk SW10 ... 136 B6 266 C6
Parkcroft Rd SE12 ... 164 D4
Parkdale N11 ... 31 D4
Parkdale Cres KT4 ... 215 B5
Parkdale Rd SE18 ... 123 C1
Parke Rd SW13 ... 134 A4
Sunbury TW16 ... 194 A5
Parker Cl E16 ... 122 A5
Parker Ct N1 ... 235 B6
SW4 ... 270 A1
SW19 ... 179 A3
Parker Ho 4 SE18 ... 122 D1
Parker Mews WC2 ... 240 B2
Parker Rd CR0 ... 221 A4
Parker St E16 ... 122 A5
WC2 ... 94 A1 240 B2
Parkers Rd N10 ... 30 C2
Parkers Row 12 SE16 ... 118 A4
Parker's Row SE1 ... 253 D1
Parkfield 3 TW7 ... 130 C4
Parkfield Ave SW14 ... 133 C1
Feltham TW13 ... 150 A1
Harrow HA2 ... 24 A1
Hillingdon UB10 ... 82 D4
Northolt UB5 ... 84 D5
Parkfield Cl Edgware HA8 ... 26 D4
Northolt UB5 ... 85 A5
Parkfield Cres
Feltham TW13 ... 150 A1
Harrow HA2 ... 24 A1
Ruislip HA4 ... 63 A5
Parkfield Dr UB5 ... 84 D5
Parkfield Gdns HA2 ... 41 D6
Parkfield Ho HA2 ... 23 D2
Parkfield Ind Est SW11 ... 137 A3
Parkfield Par TW13 ... 150 A1
Parkfield Prim Sch NW4 ... 46 B2
Parkfield Rd NW10 ... 68 B1
SE14 ... 141 B4
Feltham TW13 ... 150 A1
Harrow HA2 ... 64 A5
Northolt UB5 ... 85 A5
Uxbridge UB10 ... 60 D6
Parkfield St N1 ... 94 C5 234 B4
Parkfield Way BR2 ... 210 B4
Parkfields SW15 ... 134 C1
Croydon CR0 ... 207 B1
Parkfields Ave NW9 ... 45 B1
SW20 ... 178 B1
Parkfields Cl SM5 ... 219 A4
Parkfields Rd TW10 ... 176 B5
Parkgate SE3 ... 142 D2
Parkgate Ave EN4 ... 2 A4
Parkgate Cl KT2 ... 176 D4
Parkgate Cres EN4 ... 2 A4
Parkgate Gdns SW14 ... 155 B6
Parkgate Mews N6 ... 49 C2
Parkgate Rd
SW11 ... 136 C5 267 B3
Wallington SM5,SM6 ... 219 B3
Parkham Ct BR2 ... 186 C1
Parkham St
SW11 ... 136 C4 267 A1
Parkham Way N10 ... 31 C1
Parkhill Inf Sch IG5 ... 56 C6
Parkhill Jun Sch IG5 ... 56 C6
Parkhill Prim Sch IG5 ... 56 B6
Parkhill Rd E4 ... 20 A4
NW3 ... 70 D3
Sidcup DA5 ... 169 B4
Sidcup DA15 ... 167 C1
Parkholme Rd E8 ... 74 A2
Parkhouse St SE5 ... 139 B5
Parkhurst Ct N7 ... 72 A4
Parkhurst Gdns 2 DA5 ... 169 C4
Parkhurst Inf Sch N17 ... 34 A1
Parkhurst Rd E12 ... 78 C4
E17 ... 53 A5
N7 ... 72 A4
N11 ... 31 A5
N17 ... 34 A1
N22 ... 32 B4
Carshalton SM1 ... 218 B4
Old Bexley DA5 ... 169 C4
Parkin Ho SE20 ... 184 D3
Parkinson Ct EC1 ... 235 D2
N1 ... 235 C1
Parkinson Ho 6 E9 ... 74 C1
Parkland Ct E15 ... 76 C3
W14 ... 244 A2
Parkland Gdns 12
SW19 ... 156 D3
Parkland Gr
Ashford TW15 ... 170 C6
Hounslow TW7 ... 130 D4
Parkland Rd N22 ... 32 B1
Ashford TW15 ... 170 C6
Woodford IG8 ... 37 B3
Parkland Wlk N4,N8 ... 50 B2
Parklands N6 ... 49 B2
SE22 ... 162 B6
Bushey WD2 ... 8 A5
Kingston u T KT5 ... 198 B4
Parklands Cl SW14 ... 155 A6
Barnet EN4 ... 2 B5
Parklands Ct TW5 ... 128 D3
Parklands Dr N3 ... 47 A6
Parklands Par TW5 ... 128 D3
Parklands Rd SW16 ... 181 B5
Parklands Way KT4 ... 215 C6
Parklea Cl NW9 ... 27 C2
Parkleigh Ct SW19 ... 179 D1
Parkleigh Rd SW19 ... 179 D1
Parkleys
Richmond KT2,TW10 ... 175 D6
Richmond TW10 ... 176 A6
Parkmead SW15 ... 156 B5
Parkmead Gdns NW7 ... 27 D4
Parkmore Cl IG8 ... 37 A6
Parkshot TW9 ... 132 A1
Parkside N3 ... 29 D3
NW7 ... 28 A4
SE3 ... 142 D5
SW19 ... 178 D6
W3 ... 111 C5
W5 ... 110 A6
1 Beckenham BR3 ... 185 D1
Cheam SM3 ... 217 A2
Hayes UB3 ... 105 C6
Sidcup DA14 ... 168 B2
Teddington TW12 ... 174 A5
Parkside Ave SW19 ... 178 D5
Bromley BR1 ... 210 A5
Parkside Cl SE20 ... 184 C3
Parkside Cres N7 ... 72 C5
Tolworth KT5 ... 199 A3
Parkside Ct 2 E11 ... 55 A3
N22 ... 32 B4
NW2 ... 68 D2
Parkside Dr HA8 ... 10 C1
Parkside Est E9 ... 96 D6
Parkside Gdns SW19 ... 178 D6
East Barnet EN4 ... 15 A4
Parkside Lo DA17 ... 125 D1
Parkside Rd
Belvedere DA17 ... 125 D2
Hounslow TW3 ... 151 D6
Parkside St SW11 ... 268 A1
Parkside Terr N18 ... 33 B6
Parkside Way HA2 ... 42 A5
Parkstead Rd SW15 ... 156 B6
Parkstone Ave N18 ... 33 D5
Parkstone Rd E17 ... 54 A6
3 SE15 ... 140 A3
Parkthorne Cl HA2 ... 41 D3
Parkthorne Dr HA2 ... 41 D3
Parkthorne Rd SW12 ... 159 D4
Parkview UB6 ... 87 A4
Parkview Ct SE20 ... 184 B2
SW6 ... 135 A3
Parkview Lo BR3 ... 207 D6
Parkview Rd CR0 ... 206 A1
Parkville Rd
SW6 ... 135 B5 264 C3
Parkway N14 ... 16 A2
NW1 ... 93 B6 231 C5
SW20 ... 200 D5
Erith DA18 ... 125 A3
Hillingdon UB10 ... 60 D1
Ilford IG3 ... 79 D5
Woodford IG8 ... 37 C5
Parkway Prim Sch
DA18 ... 125 A3
Parkway The
Cranford TW5 ... 128 B5
Hayes UB2,UB3,UB4,TW5 ... 106 B3
Hayes UB4 ... 84 D2
Parkway Trad Est TW5 ... 128 C6
Parkwood N20 ... 14 D2
NW8 ... 230 C5
Beckenham BR3 ... 185 C3
Parkwood Ave KT10 ... 196 A1
Parkwood Gr TW16 ... 194 A6
Parkwood Mews N6 ... 49 B3
Parkwood Prim Sch N4 ... 72 D6
Parkwood Rd SW19 ... 179 B5
Hounslow TW7 ... 130 D4
Sidcup DA5 ... 169 B4
Parliament Ct NW3 ... 70 C4
Parliament Hill NW3 ... 70 C4
Parliament Hill Mans
NW5 ... 71 A4
Parliament Hill Sch
NW5 ... 71 A4
Parliament Mews
SW14 ... 133 A3
Parliament Sq
SW1 ... 116 A4 250 A1
Parliament St
SW1 ... 116 A4 250 A2
Parma Cres SW11 ... 136 D1
Parminter Ind Est 23 E2 ... 96 B5
Parmiter St E2 ... 96 B5
Parmoor Ct EC1 ... 242 A6
Parnall Ho 11 SE19 ... 183 C6
Parnell Cl W12 ... 112 B3
Edgware HA8 ... 27 A6
Parnell Rd E3 ... 97 B6
Parnham St E14 ... 97 A1
Parolles Rd N19 ... 49 C1
Paroma Rd DA17 ... 125 C3
Parr Cl N9 ... 34 B6
Parr Ct N1 ... 235 C4
Feltham TW13 ... 172 C6
Parr Rd E6 ... 99 D6
Stanmore HA7 ... 26 A2
Parr St N1 ... 95 B5 235 C4
Parrington Ho 1 SW4 ... 159 D5
Parr's Pl TW12 ... 173 C3
Parry Ave E6 ... 100 B1
Parry Cl KT17 ... 216 A1
Parry Ho 32 E1 ... 118 B5
Parry Pl SE18 ... 122 D2
Parry Rd SE25 ... 205 C6
W10 ... 91 A4
Parry St SW8 ... 138 A6 270 B6
Parsifal Coll NW3 ... 69 C4
Parsifal Ho NW3 ... 69 C4
Parsifal Rd NW6 ... 69 C3
Parsley Gdns CR0 ... 206 D1
Parsloes Ave RM9 ... 81 A3

Parsloes Prim Sch RM9 ..81 B2
Parson Ct SE13 ....141 D1
Parson St NW4 ....46 C6
Parsonage Cl UB3 .....83 D1
Parsonage Gdns EN2 .....5 A1
Parsonage La Enfield EN2 ..5 B3
  Sidcup DA14 ....191 B6
Parsonage Manorway
  DA8,DA17 ....147 C6
Parsonage St E14 ....120 A2
Parsons Gn
  SW6 ....135 C3 265 A1
Parsons Gr HA8 ....10 C1
Parsons Green La
  SW6 ....135 C4 265 A2
Parsons Green Sta
  SW6 ....135 C4 265 A1
Parsons Ho 21 SW2 ...160 A4
  W2 ....236 C5
Parsons Lo NW6 ......69 D1
Parsons Mead KT8 ....196 A6
Parson's Mead CR0 ...204 D1
  Deacons Hill HA8 ......10 C1
Parsons Rd E13 ......99 C5
Parthenia Rd
  SW6 ....135 C4 265 B1
Partingdale La NW7 ...28 D5
Partington Cl N19 ....49 D1
Partridge Cl 1 E16 ...99 D2
  Bushey WD2 ....8 A3
  Ducks Island EN5 ......12 C5
  Stanmore HA7 ....26 A6
Partridge Ct EC1 .....241 C6
Partridge Dr BR6 .....227 A4
Partridge Gn SE9 ....166 C1
Partridge Ho 20 E3 ...97 B5
Partridge Rd
  8 Hampton TW12 ...173 C4
  Sidcup DA14 ....189 C6
Partridge Sq 3 E6 ....100 A2
Partridge Way N22 ...32 A2
Pasadena Cl UB3 .....106 B4
Pascal St SW8 ..137 D5 269 D4
Pascall Ho SE17 ....139 A6
Pascoe Rd SE13 ......164 B6
Pasley Cl SE17 ....262 A1
Pasquier Rd E17 .....53 A6
Passey Pl SE9 ......166 B5
Passfield Dr E14 .....97 D2
Passfield Ho SE16 ...118 A5
Passfield Path 13 SE28 .124 B6
Passfields SE6 ....164 A1
  W14 ....254 C1
Passing Alley EC1 ....241 D5
Passingham Ho TW5 ..129 C6
Passmore Gdns N11 ...31 D4
Passmore Ho 12 N9 ...18 A1
Passmore St
  SW1 ....115 A1 258 A1
Passmores Edwards Ho
  N11 ....31 D3
Pasteur Cl NW9 ......45 C1
Pasteur Gdns N18 ....33 A5
Paston Cres SE12 ....165 B4
Pastor Ct N6 ....49 C3
Pastor St SE1,
  SE11 ....116 D2 261 D4
Pasture Cl Bushey WD2 ..8 A4
  Wembley HA0 ....65 B5
Pasture Rd SE6 ......164 D3
  Dagenham RM9 ......81 B3
  Wembley HA0 ....65 B5
Pastures Mead UB10 ..60 C2
Pastures The N20 ....13 B3
Pat Shaw Ho 2 E1 ...96 D3
Patch Cl UB10 ....60 A2
Patcham Terr SW8 ...268 A2
Patching Way UB4 ....85 A2
Patchway Ct 4 SE15 .139 C6
Patent Ho E14 ....97 D2
Pater St W8 ...113 C3 255 A5
Paternoster Row
  EC2,EC4 ....95 A1 242 A1
Paternoster Sq
  EC4 ....94 D1 241 D2
Pates Manor Dr TW14 ..149 B4
Path The SW19 ......179 D2
Pathfield Rd SW16 ...181 D4
Patience Rd SW11 ....136 C3
Patio Cl SW4 ....159 D6
Patmore Ho 9 N16 ...73 C3
Patmore St
  SW8 ....137 C4 269 B2
Paton Cl E3 ....97 C4
Paton Ho 3 SW9 ....138 B3
Paton St EC1 ....235 A1
Patricia Ct SE2 ......146 B5
  Chislehurst BR7 ......189 B2
Patricia Villas N17 ...34 B2
Patrick Coman Ho EC1 234 C1
Patrick Connolly Gdns 41
  E3 ....97 D4
Patrick Rd E13 ......99 C4
Patriot Sq E2 ....96 B5
Patrol Pl SE6 ....163 D5
Patshull Ho SE21 ....161 A3
Patshull Rd NW5 ....71 C2
Patson Cl E5 ....74 D5
Patten Ho N4 ......51 A1
Patten Rd SW18 ....158 C4
Pattenden Rd SE6 ...163 B3
Patterdale NW1 ......231 D1
Patterdale Cl BR1 ....186 C4
Patterdale Rd SE15 ..140 C5
Patterson Ct SE19 ...183 D4

Patterson Rd SE19 ....183 D4
Pattina Wlk SE16 .....119 A5
Pattison Point 10 E16 ..99 A2
Pattison Ho 1 E1 .....96 D1
  SE1 ....252 B2
Pattison Rd NW2 .....69 C5
Pattison Wlk SE18 ....123 A1
Paul Byrne Ho 3 N2 ..48 A6
Paul Cl E15 ....76 C1
Paul Ct N3 ....29 A1
  7 N18 ....34 A6
Paul Gdns CR0 ......221 D6
Paul Ho 18 W10 .....91 A3
Paul Julius Cl E14 ...120 B6
Paul Robeson Cl E6 ..100 C4
Paul St E15 ....98 C6
  EC2 ....95 C3 243 A6
Paulet Rd SE5 ......138 D4
Paulhan Rd HA3 ....43 D5
Paulin Dr N21 ......16 C4
Pauline Cres TW2 ...152 A3
Pauline Ho 19 E1 ....96 A2
Paulinus Cl BR5 ....190 C1
Paul's Ho E3 ....97 B2
Paulson Ho 7 IG11 ..78 D1
Paultons Ho SW3 ...266 D6
Paultons Sq
  SW3 ....136 B6 266 D6
Pauntley Ho 6 N19 ..49 C1
Pauntley St 4 N19 ...49 C1
Pavan Ct 29 E2 .....96 C4
Paved Ct 8 TW9 ....153 D6
Paveley Dr
  SW11 .....136 C5 267 A3
Paveley Ho 18 E9 ...96 C6
  N1 ....233 C3
Paveley St NW8 ..92 C3 237 B6
Pavement Mews 1 RM6 58 D2
Pavement Sq CR0 ...206 A1
Pavement The E11 ...54 A1
  11 SE27 ....183 A6
  SW4 ....137 C1
  W5 ....110 A3
Pavet Cl RM10 ......81 D2
Pavilion Ct NW3 ....70 B3
  5 NW3 ....70 A4
  3 SW19 ....179 A3
Pavilion L Ctr The BR1 .187 A1
Pavilion Lo 2 SE17 ...261 A2
Pavilion Mans 10 SW9 .138 B1
Pavilion Mews N3 ....29 C1
Pavilion Rd
  SW1 ....114 D3 257 D5
  Redbridge IG1 ....56 B2
Pavilion St SW1 ....257 D5
Pavilion Terr W12 ...90 C1
  Kingston u T KT1 .....197 A4
Pavilion Way
  Burnt Oak HA8 ....27 A3
  Ruislip HA4 ....62 C6
Pawleyne Cl SE20 ....184 C3
Pawsey Cl E13 ......99 A6
Pawson's Rd CR0 ...205 A4
Paxford Rd HA0 ....65 B6
  Walton-on-T KT12 ...194 C2
Paxton Cl 1 SE26 ...185 A6
  Mitcham CR4 ....180 D1
Paxton Ho SE17 .....262 D2
Paxton Pl SE27 .....183 C6
Paxton Prim Sch SE19 .183 C4
Paxton Rd N17 .....34 A3
  SE23 ....163 A1
  Plaistow BR1 ....187 A3
Paxton Terr SW1 ...268 D2
Payens Wlk W6 135 A6 264 A5
Paymal Ho 28 E1 ...96 C2
Payne Ho N1 ......233 D5
Payne Rd E3 ....97 D5
Payne St SE8 ......141 B6
Paynell Ct SE3 .....142 C2
Paynesfield Ave SW14 .133 B2
Paynesfield Rd WD2 ..8 D4
Payzes Gdns IG8 ....36 D5
Peabody Ave
  SW1 ....115 B1 258 D1
Peabody Bldgs 6 SE5 .139 A4
  SE17 ....262 C3
Peabody Cl SW1 ....268 D6
  CR0 ....206 C1
Peabody Cotts N17 ...33 C2
Peabody Ct EC1 ....242 B5
  9 SE5 ....139 B4
Peabody Est E1 .....118 A6
  4 E1 ....118 D2
  18 E2 ....96 B5
  EC1 ....241 D5
  EC1 ....242 B5
  SE1 ....252 A3
  SE1 ....251 B3
  SE24 ....161 A4
  SW1 ....259 A4
  SW6 ....135 B6 264 D6
  17 W6 ....112 C1
  W10 ....90 C2
  WC2 ....240 C1
Peabody Hill SE21 ...161 A3
Peabody Sq SE1 ....251 C4
Peabody Twr EC1 ...242 B5
Peabody Yd N1 .....235 A6
Peace Ct 10 NW9 ...46 A5
Peace Gr HA9 ......66 D6
Peace St SE18 ......144 C6
Peach Rd W10 .....91 A4

Peaches Cl SM2 .....217 A1
Peachum Rd SE3 ....142 C6
Peacock Ave TW14 ..149 B3
Peacock Est N17 ....33 D3
Peacock St
  SE17 ....116 D2 261 D3
Peacock Wlk E16 ....99 B1
Peacock Yd SE17 ...261 D3
Peak Hill SE26 .....184 C6
Peak Hill Ave SE26 ..184 C6
Peak Hill Gdns SE26 .184 C6
Peak Ho N4 ....51 A4
Peak The SE26 .....162 C1
Peaketon Ave IG4 ...55 D4
Peal Gdns W13 .....87 A3
Peall Rd CR0 ......204 B3
Pear Ave TW17 ....193 C6
Pear Cl NW9 ......45 B5
  SE14 ....141 A5
Pear Pl SE1 ....251 A2
Pear Rd 20 SE15 ...139 D5
Pear Tree Ave UB7 ..82 B1
Pear Tree Cl 22 E2 ..95 D6
  Mitcham CR4 ......180 C1
Pear Tree Ct EC1 ...241 B5
  SW15 ....134 B1
Pear Tree Ho SE4 ...141 B1
Hanes UB8 ....83 A1
Pear Tree Rd TW15 ..171 A5
Pearce Cl 2 CR4 ...181 A1
Pearce Ho N19 .....71 C5
  7 SW2 ....160 A4
Peacefield Ave 5
  SE23 ....162 C3
Peacroft Rd E11 ....76 B6
Peardon St SW8 ....137 B3
Peaseswood Ave HA7 .25 D2
Peafield Ho 1 N5 ....73 A3
Peafield Rd SE23 ...161 C5
Pearl Cl E6 ....100 C1
  NW2 ....46 D2
Pearl Ct 18 NW9 ...46 A5
Pearl Rd E17 ......53 C6
Pearl St E1 ....118 B5
Pearlstones Ct RM10 .103 C6
Pearmain Cl SW15 ..134 B1
Pearman St SE1 116 C4 251 B1
Pears Rd TW3 .....130 A2
Pearscroft Ct
  SW5 ....135 D4 265 D1
Pearscroft Rd
  SW5 ....135 D4 265 D1
Pearson Cl SW15 ...134 C3
Pearson St E2 ....95 B5
Pearson's Ave SE8,SE14 141 C4
Pearson Ho SW15 ...134 D3
Peartree Ave SW17 .158 A1
Peartree Cl RM8 ....80 B4
Peartree La E1 ....118 C6
Peartree Rd EN1 ...95 B3 242 A6
Peary Ho 3 NW10 ...67 B1
Peary Pl E2 ....96 C4
Peas Mead Terr E4 ..36 A6
Peatfield Cl DA15 ...167 C1
Pebworth Lo SE25 ..205 D5
Pebworth Rd HA1 ..65 A6
Peckarmans Wood
  SE21,SE26 ....162 A1
Peckett Sq 3 N5 ...72 C4
Peckford Pl SW9 ...138 C3
Peckham High St SE15 140 A4
Peckham Hill St SE15 .140 A5
Peckham Park Prim Schs
  SE15 ....140 A5
Peckham Park Rd SE15 140 A5
Peckham Rd SE5 ...139 C4
Peckham Rye SE15,SE22 140 B1
  SE22 ....140 A1
Peckham Rye Jun & Inf Sch
  SE15 ....140 A1
Peckham Rye Sta SE15 140 A3
Peckwater St NW5 ...71 C3
Pedlars Wlk N7 .....72 A3
Pedley Rd RM8 ....58 C1
Pedley St E1 .....95 D3 243 D5
Pedro St E5 ....74 D4
Pedworth Gdns 4
  SE16 ....118 C2
Peebles Ct UB1 ....86 A1
Peek Cres SW19 ....178 D5
Peel Centre (Metropoliton
  Police Training
  Establishment) NW9 ..45 D6
Peel Cl E4 ....19 C2
  N9 ....18 A1
Peel Ct UB6 ......86 A4
  Redt ridge IG5 ....56 A6
Peel Dr NW9 ......45 D6
Peel Gr E2 ....96 C5
Peel Pass W8 .....245 A5
Peel Pl IG5 ....37 D1
Peel Prec NW6 ...91 C5
Peel Rd E18 ....36 D2
  NW6 ....91 B4
  Farnborough BR6 ....227 A3
  Harrow HA3 ....42 D6
  Wembley HA9,HA0 ...65 D5
Peel St W8 ...113 C5 245 A4
Peel Way UB8 .....82 A2
Peel Yates Ho SE2 ..122 A2
Peerglow Est EN3 ...18 C6
Peerless St EC1 ..95 B4 235 C1
Pegamoid Rd N18 ...34 C6
Pegasus Ct NW10 ...90 B4
  Brentford TW8 ....117 B1
  Kingston u T KT1 .....197 D6

Pegasus Ho 9 E1 ....96 D3
Pegasus Pl 2 SW8 ..138 C6
  SE11 ....261 C2
Pegasus Rd CR0,CR9 ..220 C2
Pegasus Way N11 ...31 B4
Pegg Rd TW5 ......128 B3
Peggotty Way UB8 ..82 D1
Peggy Quirke Ct 2 E11 66 A2
Pegley Gdns SE12 ..165 A2
Pegwell Ho 19 E5 ...75 A2
Pegwell St SE18 ....145 C5
Pekin St E14 ....97 C1
Pekoe SE1 ....253 D3
Peldon Ct TW10 ....154 B6
Peldon Pas 2 TW10 .154 B6
Pele Ct N17 ....33 B3
Pelham Ave IG11 ...101 D6
Pelham Cl SE5 .....139 C2
Pelham Cotts DA5 ..169 D3
Pelham Cres SW7 ..257 A3
Pelham Ct SW3 ....257 A3
Pelham Ho W14 ...254 C3
Pelham Pl SW7 ....257 A3
Pelham Prim Sch
  SW19 ....179 C3
  Bexleyheath DA7 ....147 C3
Pelham Rd E18 ....55 B6
  N15 ....51 D5
  N22 ....32 C1
  SW19 ....179 C3
  Bexleyheath DA7 ....147 C2
  Ilford IG1 ....79 B6
Penge BR3,SE20 ...184 C1
Pelham St SW7 114 B2 256 D4
Pelican Ho 7 SE8 ...119 B2
Pelican Wlk SW9 ...138 D1
Pelier St SE17 .....139 A6
Pelinore Rd SE6 ...164 C2
Pella Ho SE11 ......260 D2
Pellant Rd SW6 135 A6 264 B4
Pellatt Gr N22 .....32 C2
Pellatt Rd SE22 ....161 D6
Pellerin Rd N16 ....73 C3
Pellew Ho 3 E1 ....96 B3
Pelling St E14 .....97 C1
Pellipar Cl N13 ....16 C1
Pellipar Gdns SE18 ..122 B1
Pellipar Rd SE18 ...122 B1
Pelly Ct 4 E17 .....54 A5
Pelly Rd E13 ......99 A5
Pelter St E2 ....95 D4
Pelton Ct CR2 ....221 D4
Pelton Rd SE10 ...120 C1
Pembar Ave E17 ...53 A6
Pember Rd NW10 ...90 D4
Pemberley Chase KT19 214 A3
Pemberley Cl KT19 ..214 A3
Pemberley Ho KT19 .214 D3
  Dagenham RM6 .....59 A4
Pemberton Ct 18 E1 ..96 C4
Pemberton Gdns N19 ..71 C5
  Esher KT10 ....212 A5
Pemberton Pl 2 E8 ..74 B1
Pemberton Rd N4 ...50 D4
  East Molesey KT8 ...196 A5
Pemberton Row E4 ...241 B2
Pemberton Terr N19 ..71 C5
Pembridge Ave TW4 ..151 B3
Pembridge Cres
  W11 ....113 C6 245 A6
Pembridge Gdns
  W2 ....113 C6 245 A5
Pembridge Mews
  W11 ....113 C6 245 A6
Pembridge Pl 1 SW15 157 C6
  W2 ....113 C6 245 A6
Pembridge Rd
  W11 ....113 C6 245 A6
Pembridge Sq
  W2 ....113 C6 245 A6
Pembridge Villas
  W11 ....113 C6 245 A6
Pembroke Ave Enfield EN1 ..6 B4
  Harrow HA3 ....43 B6
  Surbiton KT5 ....198 D4
Pembroke Bldgs NW10 90 A4
Pembroke Cl SW1 ...248 B1
Pembroke Ct 11 W7 ..86 D2
Pembroke Gdns
  W8 ....113 C3 254 D4
  Dagenham RM10 ...81 D5
Pembroke Gdns Cl W8 255 A5
  Harrow HA3 ....43 C5
Pembroke Hall NW4 ..46 C6
Pembroke Ho SW15 ..156 A6
  16 W2 ....91 B1
  W3 ....111 A4
Pembroke Mews N10 ..31 A5
  W8 ....255 A5
Pembroke Pl W8 ...255 A5
  Edgware HA8 ....26 C3
  Hounslow TW7 ......130 C3
Pembroke Rd E6 ...100 C2
  E17 ....53 C6
  N8 ....50 A6
  N10 ....31 A5
  N13 ....17 A1
  N15 ....51 D5
  SE25 ....205 C5
  W8 ....113 C2 255 A4
  Bromley BR1 ....187 D1
  Greenford UB6 ....85 D5
  Ilford IG3 ....57 D2
  Mitcham CR4 ....181 A1
  Ruislip HA4 ....39 D1
  Wembley HA9 ....65 D5
Pembroke Sq
  W8 ....113 C3 255 A5
Pembroke St N1 72 A1 233 B6
Pembroke Studios W8 254 D5

Pennington Ct continued
  SE16 ....119 A5
Pennington Dr N21 ...16 A6
Pennington Lo 18 KT5 .198 A4
Pennington St E1 ...118 A6
Penniston Cl N17 ...33 A1
Penny Ct SW10 ....266 B6
Penny La TW17 ....193 C2
Penny Mews SW12 ..159 B4
Penny Rd NW10 ....88 D4
Penny Royal SM6 ..219 D2
Penny Sangam Day Hospl
  UB2 ....107 B3
Pennyfields E14 ...119 C6
Pennyford Ct NW8 ..236 C6
Pennymore Wk W9 ...91 B3
Pennyroyal Ave E6 ..100 C1
Penpoll Rd E8 .....74 B2
Penrhyn Ave E17 ...35 C2
  SW4 ....133 A1
Penrhyn Cres E17 ..35 C2
Penrhyn Gdns KT1 ..197 D5
Penrhyn Gr E17 ...35 C2
Penrhyn Rd KT1 ...198 A6
Penrith Cl SW15 ...157 A6
  Beckenham BR3 .....185 D2
Penrith Pl SE27 ....160 D2
Penrith Rd N15 ....51 B4
  New Malden KT3 ....199 B5
  South Norwood CR7 ..204 D3
Penrith St SW16 ...181 C4
Penrose Gr
  SE17 ....117 A1 262 A1
Penrose Ho N21 ....16 B6
  SE17 ....262 A1
Penrose St
  SE17 ....117 A1 262 A1
Penry St SE1 ......263 B3
Penryn Ho SE11 ...261 C2
Penryn St NW1 ..93 D5 232 C4
Pensbury Pl SW8 ...137 C3
Pensbury St SW8 ...137 C3
Pensford Ave TW9 ..132 C3
Penshurst 3 NW5 ...71 A2
Penshurst Ave DA15 ..168 A5
Penshurst Gdns HA8 ..26 D5
Penshurst Gn BR2 ..208 D4
Penshurst Ho 1 SE15 .140 C6
Penshurst Rd E9 ...74 D1
  N17 ....33 D3
  Erith DA7 ....147 B4
  Thornton Heath CR7 ..204 D3
Penshurst Way SM2 ..217 C1
Penshurst Wlk 4 BR2 .208 D4
Pensilver Cl EN4 ....2 C1
Penstemon Cl N3 ...29 C4
Pentelow Gdns TW14 .150 A5
Pentire Rd E17 .....36 B2
Pentland Ave
  Edgware HA8 ....10 D2
  Littleton TW17 ....192 C4
Pentland Cl NW11 ..69 A6
Pentland Ho 7 N16 ..51 D1
  17 NW5 ....71 A2
Pentland Pl UB5 ....85 A6
Pentland Rd WD2 ....8 A5
Pentland St SW18 ..158 A5
Pentland Way UB10 ..61 A5
Pentlands Cl CR4 ...203 B6
Pentlands BR3 .....186 A2
Pentlow St SW15 ..134 C2
Pentney Rd 5 E4 ...20 B3
  SW12 ....159 C3
  SW19,SW20 ....179 A2
Penton Gr N1 .....234 A3
Penton Ho N1 ....234 A3
  3 SE2 ....124 D4
  Sutton SM2 ....218 A1
Penton Pl SE17 116 D1 262 D2
Penton Rise WC1 94 B4 233 D2
Penton St N1 ...94 C5 234 A3
Pentonville Rd
  N1 ....94 B5 233 C3
Pentrich Ave EN1 ...6 A5
Pentridge St SE15 ..139 D5
Pentyre Ave N18 ...33 B5
Penwerris Ave TW5,
  TW7 ....130 A5
Penwerris Ct TW7 ..130 A5
Penwith Rd SW18 ..157 D2
Penwood Ho 4 SW15 155 D5
Penwortham Ct 1 N22 32 C1
Penwortham Prim Sch
  SW17 ....181 B4
Penwortham Rd SW16 181 C4
Penylan Pl HA8 ....26 C3
Penywern Rd
  SW5 ....113 C1 255 B2
Penzance Ho SE11 ..261 B2
Penzance Pl
  W11 ....113 A5 244 B4
Penzance St
  W11 ....113 A5 244 A4
Peony Ct IG8 ......36 C3
Peony Gdns W12 ...112 A6
Peperfield WC1 ....233 C1
Pepler Ho 17 W10 ..91 A3
Peploe Rd NW6 ....90 D5
Pepper Cl E6 ......100 B2
Pepper St E14 .....119 D3
  SE1 ....252 A2
Peppermead Sq SE13 163 C6
Peppermint Cl CR0 ..204 A2
Peppermint Pl 5 E11 ..76 C2
Peppie Cl N16 .....73 C6
Pepsi Trocadero W1 ..249 C5

Pepys Cl UB10 ... 60 D4
Pepys Cres 2 E16 ... 121 A5
Ducks Island EN5 ... 12 C6
Pepys Ct SW20 ... 178 C1
Pepys Ho 14 E2 ... 96 C4
SW4 ... 159 D6
Pepys Rd SE14 ... 140 D3
SW20 ... 178 C2
Pepys Rise BR6 ... 211 D1
Pepys St EC3 ... 117 C6 253 B6
Perak Ct KT5 ... 199 A2
Perceval Ave NW3 ... 70 C3
Perceval Ct UB5 ... 63 C3
Perch St E8 ... 73 D4
Percheron Cl TW7 ... 130 D2
Percheron Rd WD6 ... 11 B5
Percival Ct N17 ... 33 D3
Percival Gdns RM6 ... 58 C3
Percival Rd SW14 ... 133 A1
Enfield EN1 ... 5 D1
Feltham TW13 ... 149 D2
Orpington BR6 ... 226 D6
Percival St EC1 ... 94 D4 234 D1
Percival Way KT19 ... 215 B4
Percy Ave TW15 ... 170 C5
Percy Bilton Ct TW5 ... 129 D4
Percy Bryant Rd TW16 ... 171 C3
Percy Bush Rd UB7 ... 104 B3
Percy Cir WC1 ... 94 B4 233 D2
Percy Ct 1 KT5 ... 198 B3
Percy Gdns Enfield EN3 ... 18 D6
Hayes UB4 ... 83 C4
3 Isleworth TW7 ... 131 A2
New Malden KT4 ... 199 C1
Percy Ho 4 SW16 ... 181 C6
Percy Mews W1 ... 239 C3
Percy Pas W1 ... 239 C3
Percy Rd E11 ... 54 C2
E16 ... 98 C2
N12 ... 30 A5
N21 ... 17 A4
SE20 ... 184 D2
SE25 ... 206 A4
W12 ... 112 A4
Bexleyheath DA7 ... 147 A3
Carshalton CR4 ... 203 A2
Hampton TW12 ... 173 C3
Ilford IG3 ... 58 A2
Isleworth TW7 ... 131 A1
Romford RM7 ... 59 D6
Twickenham TW2 ... 152 A3
Percy St W1 ... 93 D2 239 C3
Percy Way TW2 ... 152 A3
Peregrine Cl NW10 ... 67 B3
Peregrine Ct 7 SE8 ... 141 C6
Bexley DA16 ... 145 D4
Peregrine Gdns CR0 ... 223 A6
Peregrine Ho EC1 ... 234 D2
6 SW11 ... 136 C2
Peregrine Rd TW16 ... 171 D1
Peregrine Way SW19,
SW20 ... 178 C3
Performing Arts & Tech Sch
SE25 ... 205 B3
Perham Rd W14 113 B1 254 B1
Peridot St E6 ... 100 A2
Perifield SE21 ... 161 A3
Perimeade Rd UB6 ... 87 C5
Periton Rd SE9 ... 143 D1
Perivale UB6 ... 86 D5
Perivale Gdns W13 ... 87 B3
Perivale Grange UB6 ... 87 A4
Perivale Ind Pk UB6 ... 87 B5
Perivale La UB6 ... 87 A4
Perivale Lo UB6 ... 87 A4
Perivale New Bsns Ctr
UB6 ... 87 C5
Perivale Prim Sch UB6 ... 87 C5
Perivale Sta UB6 ... 87 A5
Perkin Cl HA0 ... 65 B3
Perkins Ct TW15 ... 170 B5
Perkins Ho 13 E14 ... 97 B2
Perkins Rd IG2 ... 57 B4
Perkins Rents SW1 ... 259 C5
Perkins Sq SE1 ... 252 B4
Perks Cl SE3 ... 142 C2
Perley Ho 10 E3 ... 97 B2
Perotti Ho SW6 ... 135 D2
Perpins Rd SE9 ... 167 C5
Perran Rd SE24,SW2 ... 160 D2
Perran Wlk TW8 ... 110 A1
Perren St NW5 ... 71 B2
Perrers Rd W6 ... 112 B2
Perrin Cl TW15 ... 170 B5
Perrin Grange HA9 ... 66 B6
Perrin Rd HA0 ... 65 B4
Perring Est E3 ... 97 C2
Perrin's Ct 17 NW3 ... 70 A4
Perrin's La NW3 ... 70 A4
Perrin's Wlk NW3 ... 70 A4
Perronet Ho SE1 ... 261 D5
Perry Ave W3 ... 89 B1
Perry Cl UB8 ... 82 D1
Perry Ct 2 N15 ... 51 C3
Perry Garth UB5 ... 84 C6
Perry Gdns N9 ... 17 C1
Perry Hall Prim Sch
BR6 ... 211 D3
Perry Hill SE6 ... 163 B1
Perry Ho 24 SW2 ... 160 A4
Perry How KT4 ... 199 D1
Perry Mead Bushey WD2 ... 8 A5
Enfield EN2 ... 4 D3
Perry Rise SE23 ... 163 A1
Perry St BR7 ... 189 C4
Perry Street Gdns BR7 ... 189 C4
Perry Vale SE23 ... 162 D2
Perryfield Way NW9 ... 45 D3
Perryfield Way *continued*
Richmond TW10 ... 153 B2
Perryman Ho IG11 ... 101 A6
Perrymans Farm Rd IG2 57 B4
Perrymead St
SW6 ... 135 D3 265 C1
Perrymount Prim Sch
SE23 ... 162 D2
Perryn Ct 1 TW1 ... 153 A4
Perryn Ho W3 ... 111 C6
Perryn Rd 1 SE16 ... 118 B3
W3 ... 111 B6
Perry's Pl W1 ... 239 C2
Perrywood Ho 17 E5 ... 74 B3
Persant Rd SE6 ... 164 C2
Perserverance Pl SW9 ... 138 C5
Perseverance Works 18
E2 ... 95 C4
Pershore Cl IG2 ... 56 D4
Pershore Gr SM5 ... 202 B3
Pert Cl N10 ... 31 B4
Perth Ave NW9 ... 45 B2
Hayes UB4 ... 84 C3
Perth Cl SW20 ... 178 A1
Perth Ct 5 SE5 ... 139 B1
Perth Ho N1 ... 72 B1
12 W3 ... 88 C1
Perth Rd E10 ... 53 B1
E13 ... 99 B5
N4 ... 50 C1
N22 ... 32 D2
Barking IG11 ... 101 B6
Beckenham BR3 ... 186 A1
Ilford IG2 ... 56 D3
Perth Terr IG2 ... 57 A2
Perwell Ave HA2 ... 41 B1
Perystreete SE23 ... 162 C2
Petavel Rd TW11 ... 174 C4
Peter Ave NW10 ... 68 B1
Peter Best Ho 6 E1 ... 96 B1
Peter Bradley Ct RM9 ... 81 B1
Peter Butler Ho 6 SE1 118 A4
Peter Hills Ho 6 SE16 ... 118 A2
Peter Hills with St Mary's &
St Paul's CE Prim Sch
SE16 ... 118 D5
Peter Ho SW8 ... 270 A4
Peter James Bsns Ctr
UB3 ... 106 A4
Peter Kennedy Ct CR0 ... 207 B3
Peter St W1 ... 115 D6 249 C6
Peterboat Cl SE10 ... 120 C2
Peterborough Ct EC4 ... 241 B1
Peterborough Gdns IG1 56 A2
Peterborough Mews
SW6 ... 135 C3
Peterborough Prim Sch
SW6 ... 135 C3
Peterborough Rd E10 ... 54 B3
SW6 ... 135 C2
Carshalton SM5 ... 202 C3
Harrow HA1 ... 42 D2
Peterborough Villas
SW6 ... 265 C2
Peterchurch Ho SE15 ... 140 B6
Petergate SW11 ... 136 A1
Peterhead Ct 12 UB1 ... 86 A1
Peterley Bsns Ctr 21 E2 ... 96 B5
Peters Cl Bexley DA16 ... 145 C3
Dagenham RM8 ... 58 D1
Stanmore HA7 ... 25 D4
Peters Ct 9 W2 ... 91 D1
Peter's Ct SW4 ... 160 A5
Peter's La EC1 ... 241 D4
Peter's Lo HA8 ... 26 B4
Peter's Path SE26 ... 184 B6
Petersfield Cl N18 ... 33 A5
Petersfield Rd W3 ... 111 A4
Petersfield Rise SW15 ... 156 B3
Petersham Cl
Cheam SM1 ... 217 C3
Richmond TW10 ... 153 D2
Petersham Dr BR5 ... 190 A1
Petersham Gdns BR5 ... 189 D1
Petersham Ho SW7 ... 256 C4
Petersham La SW7 ... 256 A6
Petersham Mews
SW7 ... 114 A3 256 B5
Petersham Pl
SW7 ... 114 A3 256 B6
Petersham Rd TW10 ... 154 A3
Petersham Terr CR0 ... 220 A5
Peterstone Rd SE2 ... 124 B4
Peterstow Cl SW19 ... 157 A2
Peterwood Pk CR9 ... 220 B6
Peterwood Way CR0 ... 220 B6
Petherton Ct NW10 ... 90 D6
10 Harrow HA1 ... 42 D3
Petherton Ho N4 ... 51 A1
Petherton Rd N5 ... 73 A3
Petiver Cl 26 E9 ... 74 C1
Petley Rd W6 ... 134 D5
Peto Pl NW1 ... 238 D6
Peto St N E16 ... 98 D1
Petrel Ct 7 SE21 ... 161 B2
Petrie Cl NW2 ... 69 A2
Petrie Ho 3 SE18 ... 144 C6
Petros Gdns 1 NW3 ... 70 A2
Pett St SE7 ... 122 A2
Petticoat Lane Mkt*
EC2 ... 95 D2 243 C3
Petticoat Sq E1 ... 243 C2
Petticoat Twr E1 ... 243 C2
Pettit's Pl RM10 ... 81 C3
Pettit's Rd RM10 ... 81 C3
Pettiward Cl SW15 ... 134 C1
Pettman Cres SE18,SE28 123 B3
Pett's Hill UB5 ... 63 D3
Petts La TW17 ... 192 C5
Petts Wood Rd BR5 ... 211 B4
Petts Wood Sta BR5 ... 211 A4
Pettsgrove Ave HA0 ... 65 C3
Petty France
SW1 ... 115 C3 259 C6
Petworth Cl UB5 ... 63 B1
Petworth Gdns SW20 ... 200 B6
Hillingdon UB10 ... 83 A6
Petworth Ho 16 SE22 ... 139 C2
Petworth Rd N12 ... 30 C5
Bexleyheath DA6 ... 169 C6
Petworth St
SW11 ... 136 C4 267 B2
Petyt Pl SW3 ... 136 C6 267 A5
Petyward SW3 ... 114 C2 257 B3
Pevensey Ave N11 ... 31 D5
Enfield EN1 ... 5 C3
Pevensey Cl TW7 ... 130 A5
Pevensey Ct 10 E18 ... 37 A2
SW16 ... 160 C1
4 W3 ... 110 D4
Pevensey Ho 5 E1 ... 97 A2
Pevensey Rd E7 ... 77 A4
SW17 ... 180 B6
Feltham TW13 ... 151 A3
Peverel E6 ... 100 C1
Peverel Ho RM10 ... 81 C6
Peverett Cl N11 ... 31 B5
Peveril Dr TW11 ... 174 B5
Peveril Ho SE1 ... 262 D5
Pewsey Cl E4 ... 35 C5
Pewsham Ho N4 ... 51 A1
Pewterers Ct N3 ... 29 B2
Peyton Ho N11 ... 31 A6
Peyton Pl SE10 ... 142 A5
Pharamond NW2 ... 68 D2
Pharaoh Cl CR4 ... 202 D2
Pheasant Cl E16 ... 99 B1
Phelp St SE17 ... 139 B6
Phelps Ho SW15 ... 134 D2
Phelps Way UB3 ... 105 D2
Phene St SW3 ... 136 C6 267 B6
Phil Brown Pl 3 SW8 ... 137 B2
Philadelphia Ct SW10 ... 266 B3
Philbeach Gdns
SW5 ... 113 C1 255 A2
Philchurch Pl 25 E1 ... 96 A1
Phildor Ct NW11 ... 47 A3
Philia Ho 2 NW1 ... 71 C1
Philimore Cl SE18 ... 123 C1
Philip Ct W2 ... 236 C4
Enfield EN2 ... 5 B4
Philip Gdns CR0 ... 223 B6
Philip Ho N20 ... 14 D2
10 NW6 ... 91 D6
Philip La N15 ... 51 C6
Philip Rd SE15 ... 140 A2
Philip St E13 ... 99 A3
Philip Turner Est 28 E9 ... 74 C1
Philip Wlk SE15 ... 140 B2
Philipot Almshouse
SE9 ... 166 B5
Philipot Path SE9 ... 166 B5
Philippa Gdns SE9 ... 165 D6
Phillimore Ct W8 ... 245 B1
Phillimore Gardens Cl
W8 ... 113 C3 255 A6
Phillimore Gdns NW10 ... 90 C6
W8 ... 113 C4 245 A1
Phillimore Pl
W8 ... 113 C4 245 A1
Phillimore Terr W8 ... 255 B6
Phillimore Wlk
W8 ... 113 C3 255 B6
Phillip Ho E1 ... 243 D3
Phillipp St N1 ... 95 C6
Phillips Cl SM5 ... 203 A1
Phillips Ct Edgware HA8 ... 26 C4
Hayes UB4 ... 84 B4
Philpot La EC3 ... 253 A6
Philpot Sq SW6 ... 135 D2
Philpot St E1 ... 96 B1
Phineas Pett Rd SE9 ... 144 A2
Phipp St EC2 ... 95 C3 243 A6
Phipp's Bridge Rd CR4,
SW19 ... 202 B6
Phipps Bridge Sta CR4 ... 202 B6
Phipps Hatch La EN2 ... 5 A5
Phipps Ho 1 SE7 ... 121 B1
16 W12 ... 112 B6
Phoebeth Rd SE4 ... 163 C6
Phoenix Cl 18 E8 ... 95 D6
West Wickham BR4 ... 224 C6
Phoenix Coll SM4 ... 202 A4
Phoenix Ct E4 ... 19 D1
E14 ... 119 C2
2 SE14 ... 141 A6
SE25 ... 206 A4
4 Brentford TW8 ... 110 A1
Enfield EN3 ... 6 C5
Phoenix Dr BR2 ... 225 D5
Phoenix High Sch W12 112 A6
Phoenix Ind Est HA1 ... 42 D5
Phoenix Lodge Mans 1
W6 ... 112 C2
Phoenix Pl WC1 ... 94 B3 240 D6
Phoenix Rd NW1 93 D4 232 C2
SE20 ... 184 C4
Phoenix Sch E3 ... 97 B4
Phoenix St WC2 ... 239 D1
Phoenix Trad Est UB6 ... 87 D6
Phoenix Trad Pk TW8 ... 109 D1
Phoenix Way TW5 ... 128 D6
Phoenix Wharf Rd SE1 253 D1
Phyllis Ave KT3 ... 200 B4
Phyllis Ho CR0 ... 220 D4
Physic Pl SW3 ... 136 D6 267 C6
Picador Ho 1 RM10 ... 81 D2
Picardy Manorway
DA17 ... 125 D4
Picardy Rd DA17 ... 125 C2
Picardy St DA17 ... 125 C3
Piccadilly W1 ... 115 C5 249 A4
Piccadilly Arc SW1 ... 249 A4
Piccadilly Cir*
W1 ... 115 D6 249 C5
Piccadilly Circus Sta
SW1 ... 115 D6 249 C5
Piccadilly Pl W1 ... 249 B5
Pickard St EC1 ... 234 D2
Pickering Ave E6 ... 100 C4
Pickering Gdns N11 ... 31 A4
SE25 ... 205 D3
Pickering Ho N4 ... 51 B2
4 SE18 ... 122 C2
17 W2 ... 91 D1
W5 ... 109 C2
Pickering Mews W2 ... 91 D1
Pickering Pl SW1 ... 249 B3
Pickering St N1 ... 234 D6
Pickets Cl WD2 ... 8 C3
Pickets St SW12 ... 159 B4
Pickett Croft HA7 ... 25 D2
Pickett's Lock La N9 ... 18 D2
Pickford Cl DA7 ... 147 A3
Pickford La DA7 ... 147 A3
Pickford Rd DA7 ... 147 A2
Pickfords Wharf N1 ... 235 A3
Pickhurst Gn BR2 ... 208 D2
Pickhurst Inf Sch BR2 ... 208 D3
Pickhurst Jun Sch BR2 208 D3
Pickhurst La BR2,BR3,
BR4 ... 208 C2
Pickhurst Mead BR2 ... 208 D2
Pickhurst Pk BR2 ... 208 D4
Pickhurst Rise BR4 ... 208 B1
Pickwick Cl TW4 ... 151 A6
Pickwick Ct SE9 ... 166 B3
Pickwick Ho 18 SE16 ... 118 A4
3 W11 ... 112 D5
Pickwick Mews N18 ... 33 C5
Pickwick Pl HA1 ... 42 C2
Pickwick Rd SE21 ... 161 C4
Pickwick St SE1 ... 252 A1
Pickwick Way BR7 ... 189 A4
Pickworth Cl SW8 ... 270 B3
Picton Ho 1 SW4 ... 160 A4
Picton Pl W1 ... 238 B1
Picton St SE5 ... 139 B5
Pied Bull Ct WC1 ... 240 B3
Pied Bull Yd WC1 ... 240 B3
Piedmont Rd SE18 ... 123 B1
Pield Heath Ave UB8 ... 82 C3
Pield Heath Rd UB8 ... 82 B3
Pier Ho SW3 ... 267 B5
Pier Par 3 E16 ... 122 C5
Pier Rd E16 ... 122 C4
Feltham TW14 ... 150 B6
Pier St E14 ... 120 A2
Pier Terr SW18 ... 136 A1
Pier Way SE18 ... 123 B3
Pierhead Wharf 37 E1 ... 118 B5
Piermont Pl BR1 ... 188 A1
Piermont Rd SE22 ... 162 B6
Pierrepoint SE25 ... 205 C6
Pierrepoint Rd W3 ... 110 D6
Pierson Ho 12 SE19 ... 183 C6
Pigeon Ct E4 ... 36 A4
Pigeon La TW12 ... 173 C6
Piggott Ho 2 E2 ... 96 D5
Pigott St E14 ... 97 C1
Pike Cl Hillingdon UB10 ... 82 B6
Plaistow BR1 ... 187 B5
Pike Rd NW7 ... 27 B6
Pike's End HA5 ... 40 B5
Pikestone Cl UB4 ... 85 A3
Pikethorne SE23 ... 162 D2
Pilgrim Cl SM4 ... 201 D2
Pilgrim Hill SE27 ... 183 A6
Pilgrim Ho SE1 ... 262 D5
Pilgrim St EC4 ... 241 C1
Pilgrimage St
SE1 ... 117 B4 252 C1
Pilgrims Cl N13 ... 32 B6
Northolt UB5 ... 64 A3
Pilgrims Cloisters 18
SE5 ... 139 C5
Pilgrims Ct SE3 ... 143 A4
Enfield EN1 ... 5 B3
Pilgrim's La NW3 ... 70 B4
Pilgrims Mews E14 ... 120 B6
Pilgrim's Rise EN4 ... 14 C6
Pilgrims Way 5 E6 ... 100 A6
N19 ... 49 D1
Wembley HA9 ... 44 D1
Pilgrim's Way CR2 ... 221 D3
Pilgrims Way Prim Sch
SE15 ... 140 C6
Pilkington Ct 1 NW9 ... 46 A5
Pilkington Rd 4 SE15 ... 140 B3
Orpington BR6 ... 227 A6
Pillar of Fire Society Church
& Bible Sch NW4 ... 46 D4
Pillions La UB4 ... 83 B3
Pilot Ind Ctr NW10 ... 89 C3
Pilsden Cl SW19 ... 156 D3
Piltdown Rd WD1 ... 22 D6
Pilton Est The CR0 ... 220 D6
Pilton Pl SE17 ... 262 B2
Pimento Ct W5 ... 109 D3
Pimlico Sta
SW1 ... 115 D1 259 C2
Pimlico Rd SW1 115 A1 258 B2
Pimlico Sch
SW1 ... 115 C1 259 B1
Pimlico Wlk 1 N1 ... 95 C4
Pinchbeck Rd BR6 ... 227 D2
Pinchin St E1 ... 118 A6
Pincombe Ho SE17 ... 262 C2
Pincott Pl SE4 ... 140 D2
Pincott Rd SW19 ... 180 A2
8 Bexleyheath DA6 ... 147 C1
Pindar St EC2 ... 95 C2 243 A4
Pindock Mews W9 ... 91 D3
Pine Apple Ct SW1 ... 259 A6
Pine Ave E15 ... 76 B3
West Wickham BR4 ... 207 D1
Pine Cl N14 ... 15 C4
8 N19 ... 71 C6
3 SE20 ... 184 C2
Stanmore HA7 ... 25 B6
Pine Coombe CR0 ... 222 D4
Pine Ct E8 ... 73 D1
Northolt UB5 ... 85 A4
Pine Gdns Ruislip HA4 ... 62 B6
Surbiton KT5 ... 198 C3
Pine Glade BR6 ... 226 B4
Pine Gr N4,N19 ... 72 B6
N20 ... 13 C3
SW19 ... 179 B5
Pine Ho 15 SE16 ... 118 C4
Pine Lo SW15 ... 157 A5
Pine Pl UB4 ... 83 D3
Pine Rd N11 ... 15 A2
NW2 ... 68 D4
Pine Ridge SM5 ... 219 A1
Pine St EC1 ... 94 C3 241 A6
Pine Tree Cl TW5 ... 128 B4
Pine Tree Ho SE14 ... 140 D5
Pine Tree Lo BR2 ... 208 D5
Pine Trees Dr UB10 ... 60 A4
Pine Wlk KT5 ... 198 C3
Pine Wood TW16 ... 172 A2
Pinecrest Gdns BR6 ... 226 D4
Pinecroft
East Wickham DA16 ... 146 A5
Harrow HA3 ... 44 B4
Pinecroft Cres EN5 ... 1 A1
Pinedene 2 SE15 ... 140 B4
Pinefield Cl E14 ... 119 C6
Pinehurst BR7 ... 188 D4
Pinehurst Ct 5 W11 ... 91 B1
Pinehurst Wlk 4 BR6 ... 211 B1
Pinelands Cl 7 SE3 ... 142 D5
Pinemartin Cl NW2 ... 68 C5
Pines Ct 14 SW19 ... 156 D3
Pines Rd BR1 ... 188 A1
Pines The N14 ... 15 C6
SE19 ... 182 D4
Sunbury TW16 ... 194 A6
Woodford IG8 ... 21 A1
Pineview Ct 5 E4 ... 20 A3
Pinewood BR7 ... 188 C4
Pinewood Ave
Harrow HA5 ... 23 D4
Hillingdon UB8 ... 82 B1
Sidcup DA15 ... 167 C3
Pinewood Cl Harrow HA5 23 D4
Orpington BR6 ... 211 B1
South Croydon CR0 ... 223 A5
Pinewood Ct SW4 ... 159 D5
Enfield EN2 ... 4 D2
Pinewood Dr BR6 ... 227 C3
Pinewood Gr W5 ... 87 C1
Pinewood Pl KT19 ... 215 B4
Pinewood Rd SE2 ... 146 D6
Bromley BR2 ... 209 A5
Feltham TW13 ... 150 B1
Pinfold Rd SW16 ... 182 A6
Pinglestone Cl UB7 ... 126 A5
Pinkcoat Cl TW13 ... 150 B1
Pinkerton Ct KT2 ... 176 D1
Pinkerton Pl SW16 ... 181 D6
Pinkham Mans W4 ... 110 C1
Pinkham Way (North
Circular Rd)
N10 ... 31 A3
N12 ... 30 D3
Pinkwell Ave UB3 ... 105 B2
Pinkwell Jun & Inf Schs
UB3 ... 105 A2
Pinkwell La UB3 ... 105 B2
Pinley Gdns RM9 ... 102 B6
Pinn Way HA4 ... 39 C2
Pinnacle Hill DA7 ... 147 D1
Pinnacle Hill N DA7 ... 147 D1
Pinnacle Ho E14 ... 120 A3
Pinnell Rd SE9 ... 143 D1
Pinner Ct HA5 ... 41 C5
Pinner Gn HA5 ... 22 C1
Pinner Gr HA5 ... 41 A4
Pinner Hill HA5 ... 22 B3
Pinner Hill Rd HA5 ... 22 C1
Pinner Ho 31 SE5 ... 139 A3
Pinner Park Ave HA2 ... 24 A1
Pinner Park Cty Fst & Mid
Schs HA5 ... 41 D6
Pinner Park Gdns HA2 ... 24 A1
Pinner Rd
Harrow HA1,HA2 ... 42 A3
Northwood HA6 ... 22 A1
Pinner HA2,HA5 ... 41 C5
Pinner Sta HA5 ... 41 A5
Pinner View HA1,HA2 ... 42 A4
Pinner Wood Fst & Mid Schs
HA5 ... 22 C2
Pintail Cl E6 ... 100 A2
Pintail Ct 40 SE8 ... 141 B6
Pintail Rd IG8 ... 37 B3
Pintail Way UB4 ... 84 D2
Pinter Ho 30 SW9 ... 138 A3
Pinto Cl WD6 ... 11 B5
Pinto Way SE3 ... 143 B1
Pioneer Cl W12 ... 90 B1
Pioneer St SE15 ... 140 A4
Pioneer Way W12 ... 90 C1
Pioneers Ind Pk CR0 ... 204 A1
Piper Cl N7 ... 72 B2
Piper Rd KT1 ... 198 C6
Pipers Gdns CR0 ... 207 A2
Pipers Gn NW9 ... 45 A4
Pipers Green La HA8 ... 10 A1
Pipewell Rd SM5 ... 202 C3
Pippenhall SE9 ... 166 D5
Pippin Cl NW2 ... 68 B5
Croydon CR0 ... 207 B1
Pippin Ct 5 EN4 ... 2 C1
Pippins Ct SW8 ... 270 C6
Ashford TW15 ... 170 D4
Piquet Rd SE20 ... 184 C1
Pirbright Cres CR0 ... 224 A2
Pirbright Ho 11 KT2 ... 176 D4
Pirbright Rd SW18 ... 157 C3
Pirie St 6 E16 ... 121 B5
Pit Ho NW10 ... 67 B5
Pitcairn Cl RM7 ... 59 C5
Pitcairn Ho 1 E9 ... 74 C1
Pitcairn Rd CR4 ... 180 D3
Pitchford St E15 ... 76 C1
Pitfield Cres SE28 ... 124 A5
Pitfield Ho N5 ... 73 A3
Pitfield St N1 ... 95 C5
Pitfield Way NW10 ... 67 A2
Enfield EN3 ... 6 C4
Pitfold Rd SE12 ... 165 A4
Pitlake CR0 ... 220 D6
Pitman Ho N21 ... 16 B6
4 SE8 ... 141 C4
Pitman St SE5 ... 139 A5
Pitmans Coll HA0 ... 65 D2
Pitmaston Ho 2 SE13 ... 142 A3
Pitsea Pl E1 ... 96 D1
Pitsea St E1 ... 96 D1
Pitshanger Ct 2 W5 ... 87 C3
Pitshanger La W5 ... 87 C3
Pitshanger Manor Mus & Art
Gallery W5 ... 109 D5
Pitt Cres SW19 ... 179 D6
Pitt Ho 4 SW11 ... 136 B1
Pitt Rd Harrow HA2 ... 64 A6
Orpington BR6 ... 227 A4
Thornton Heath CR0,CR7 ... 205 A4
Pitt St W8 ... 113 C4 245 B2
Pittman Gdns IG1 ... 79 A3
Pitt's Head Mews W1 ... 248 B3
Pittsmead Ave BR2 ... 209 A2
Pittville Gdns SE25 ... 206 A6
Pixfield Ct BR2 ... 186 D1
Pixley St E14 ... 97 B1
Pixton 11 NW9 ... 27 C2
Pixton Way CR2 ... 223 B1
Place Farm Ave BR5,
BR6 ... 211 B1
Plains The 7 E4 ... 20 C4
Plaistow Gr E15 ... 98 D6
Bromley BR1 ... 187 B3
Plaistow Hospl E13 ... 99 C5
Plaistow La BR1 ... 187 C2
Plaistow Park Rd E13 ... 99 B5
Plaistow Rd E13,E15 ... 98 D5
Plaistow Sta E13 ... 98 D5
Plane St SE26 ... 162 B1
Plane Tree Cres TW13 ... 150 B1
Plane Tree Ho SE7 ... 121 D1
SE8 ... 141 A6
Plane Tree Wlk 4
SE19 ... 183 C4
Planetarium The*
NW1 ... 93 A3 238 A5
Planetree Ct W6 ... 112 D2
Plantagenet Cl KT19 ... 215 B4
Plantagenet Gdns RM6 ... 58 D2
Plantagenet Ho SE18 ... 122 B3
Plantagenet Pl RM6 ... 58 D2
Plantagenet Rd EN5 ... 2 A1
Plantain Pl SE1 ... 252 C2
Plantation The SE3 ... 143 A3
Plasel Ct E13 ... 99 B6
Plashet Gr E6 ... 77 D1
Plashet Rd E7 ... 77 B1
Plashet Sch E6 ... 78 A1
Plassy Rd SE6 ... 163 D4
Platina St EC2 ... 242 D6
Plato Pl 1 SW6 ... 135 B3
Plato Rd SW2 ... 138 A1
Platt Halls (a) 35 NW9 ... 27 D1
Platt Halls (b) 37 NW9 ... 27 D1
Platt Halls (c) 38 NW9 ... 27 D1
Platt St NW1 ... 232 C4
Platt's Eyot TW12 ... 173 C1
Platt's La NW3 ... 69 C5
Platts Rd EN3 ... 6 C4
Plaxdale Ho SE17 ... 263 A3
Plaxtol Cl BR1 ... 187 C2
Plaxtol Rd DA8 ... 147 C5
Plaxton Ct E11 ... 76 D5
Playfair St W6 ... 112 C1
Playfield Cres SE22 ... 161 D6
Playfield Rd HA8 ... 27 A1
Playford Rd N4 ... 72 B6
N4 ... 72 C6
Playgreen Way SE6 ... 185 C6
Playground Cl BR3 ... 184 D1
Playhouse Yd EC4 ... 241 C1
Pleasance Rd SW15 ... 156 B6
St Paul's Cray BR5 ... 190 B1
Pleasance The SW15 ... 134 B1
Pleasant Gr CR0 ... 223 B5

Pleasant Pl N1 72 D1
Pleasant Row NW1 231 D5
Pleasant View Pl BR6 227 A3
Pleasant Way HA0 87 C5
Pleasaunce Ct SE9 144 B1
Plender Ct NW1 232 B5
Plender St NW1 93 C6 232 B5
Pleshey Rd N7 71 D4
Plevna Cres N15 51 C3
Plevna Ho 1 N9 18 A1
Plevna Rd N9 18 B1
Hampton TW12 173 D2
Plevna St E14 120 A3
Pleydell Ave SE19 183 D3
W6 111 D2
Pleydell Ct EC4 241 B1
Pleydell Gdns SE19 183 D4
Pleydell St EC4 241 B1
Plimsoll Cl E14 97 D1
Plimsoll Rd N4 72 D5
Plough Ct EC3 252 D6
Plough Farm Cl HA4 39 B3
Plough La SE22 161 D5
SW17,SW19 180 A6
Wallington CR0,SM6 220 A3
Plough Lane Cl CR0, SM6 220 A3
Plough Pl EC4 241 B2
Plough Rd SW11 136 B1
West Ewell KT19 215 B1
Plough St 10 E1 96 A1
Plough Terr SW11 136 B1
Plough Way SE16 119 A2
Plough Yd EC2 243 B5
Ploughmans Cl NW1 232 C6
Ploughmans End TW7 152 B6
Plover Ct 37 SE8 141 B6
Plover Ho 4 SW9 138 C5
Plover Way SE16 119 A3
Hayes UB4 84 D2
Plowman Cl N18 33 B5
Plowman Ho SW19 156 D2
Plowman Way RM8 58 C1
Plum Garth TW8 109 D2
Plum La SE18 145 A5
Plumbers Row E1 96 A1
Plumbridge St 7 SE10 142 A4
Plumcroft Prim Sch SE18 145 A6
Plume Ho SE10 141 D6
Plummer Ct SE13 163 D5
Plummer La CR4 180 D1
Plummer Rd SW4 159 D4
Plumpton Cl UB5 63 C2
Plumpton Way SM5 218 C5
Plumstead Common Rd SE18 145 A6
Plumstead High St SE18,SE2 123 C2
Plumstead Manor Sch SE18 145 B6
Plumstead Rd SE18, SE28 123 A2
Plumstead Sta SE18 123 B2
Plumtree Cl
Dagenham RM10 81 D2
Wallington SM6 219 D1
Plumtree Ct EC4 241 C2
Plymouth Ho 10 IG11 80 A1
Plymouth Rd E16 99 A2
Bromley BR1 187 B2
Plymouth Wharf E14 120 B2
Plympton Ave NW6 69 B1
Plympton Cl 8 DA17 125 A3
Plympton Pl NW1 237 A5
Plympton Rd NW6 69 B1
Plympton St NW8 237 A5
Plymstock Rd DA16 146 C5
Pocklington Cl NW9 27 C1
Pocklington Ct SW15 156 A3
Pocock Ave UB7 104 B3
Pocock St SE1 116 D4 251 D2
Podmore Rd SW18 136 A1
Poets Corner SW1 260 A6
Poet's Rd N5 73 B3
Poets Way HA1 42 C5
Point Cl SE10 142 A4
Point Hill SE10 142 A4
Point Pl HA9 66 D1
Point Pleasant SW18 135 C1
Point Terr E7 77 B3
Pointalls Cl N3 30 A1
Pointer Cl SE28 102 D1
Pointer Sch The SE3 143 A5
Pointers Cl E14 119 D1
Poland St W1 93 C1 239 B1
Pole Hill Rd E4 20 A4
Hayes UB4 83 A4
Polebrook Rd SE3 143 C2
Polecroft La SE6 163 B2
Polesden Gdns SW20 178 B1
Polesworth Ho 16 W2 91 C2
Polesworth Rd RM9 80 D1
Polish War Meml HA4 62 C2
Pollard Cl E16 121 A6
N7 72 B4
Pollard Ho N1 233 C3
North Cheam KT4 216 C4
Pollard Rd N20 14 C2
Morden SM4 202 B4
Pollard Row E2 96 A4
Pollard St E2 96 A4
Pollard Wlk DA14 190 C4
Pollards Cl IG10 21 C6
Pollards Cres SW16 204 A6
Pollards Hill E SW16 204 B6
Pollards Hill N SW16 204 B6
Pollards Hill S SW16 204 B6
Pollards Hill W SW16 204 B6
Pollards Wood Rd SW16 204 A6
Pollen St W1 238 D1
Pollitt Dr NW8 92 B3 236 D6
Pollock Ho W10 91 A3
Polperro Cl BR6 211 D3
Polperro Mans 3 NW6 69 C3
Polsted Rd SE6 163 B4
Polthorne Gr SE18 123 B2
Polworth Rd SW16 182 A5
Polygon Rd NW1 93 D5 232 C3
Polygon The NW8 229 D6
1 SW4 137 C1
Polytechnic St SE18 122 C2
Pomell Way E1 243 D2
Pomeroy Ct W11 91 A1
Pomeroy Ho 5 E2 96 D5
Pomeroy St SE14 140 C4
Pomfret Rd SE5 138 D2
Pomoja La N19 72 A6
Pomona Ho 10 SE8 119 A2
Pond Cl N12 30 C4
SE3 143 A3
Pond Cottage La BR3, BR4 207 C1
Pond Cotts SE21 161 C3
Pond Farm Est E5 74 C5
Pond Gn HA4 61 C6
Pond Hill Gdns SM3 217 A2
Pond Ho SW3 257 A3
Pond Mead SE21 161 B5
Pond Path BR7 188 D4
Pond Pl SW3 114 C2 257 A3
Pond Rd E15 98 C5
SE3 142 D3
Pond Sq N6 49 A1
Pond St NW3 70 C3
Pond Way TW11 175 C4
Ponder St 5 N7 72 B1
Ponders End Ind Est EN3 7 B1
Ponders End Sta EN3 19 A6
Pondfield End IG10 21 C4
Pondfield Ho 4 N5 73 A3
SE27 183 A5
Pondfield Rd
Dagenham RM10 81 D3
Orpington BR6 226 D5
West Wickham BR2 208 C1
Pondside Cl UB3 127 B6
Pondwood Rise BR6 211 C2
Ponler St E1 96 B1
Ponsard Rd NW10 90 B4
Ponsford St E9 74 C2
Ponsonby Ho 13 E2 96 C5
16 E2 96 C5
Ponsonby Pl SW1 115 D1 259 D2
Ponsonby Rd SW15 156 B4
Ponsonby Terr SW1 259 D2
Pont St SW1 114 D3 257 D5
Pont St Mews SW1 257 C5
Pontefract Ct UB5 63 D3
Pontefract Rd BR1 186 D5
Ponton Ho SW2 160 C3
Ponton Rd SW8 137 D6 269 D5
Pontypool Pl SE1 251 C2
Pool Cl BR3 185 C5
Pool Ct SE6 163 C2
Pool End Cl TW17 192 C4
Pool Ho NW8 236 D4
Pool Rd KT12,KT8 195 B4
Poole Cl HA4 61 C6
Poole Court Rd TW5 129 A3
Poole Ct N1 73 C1
Hounslow TW5 129 A3
Poole Ho SE11 260 D5
Poole Rd E9 74 D2
Harrow HA1 42 B2
West Ewell KT19 215 B2
Poole St N1 95 B6 235 C5
Poole Way UB4 83 C4
Pooles Bldgs EC1 241 A5
Pooles Ct IG3 80 A5
Pooles La SW10 266 A3
Dagenham RM9 103 A5
Pooles Park Prim Sch N4 72 B6
Pooles Pk N4 72 C6
Poolmans St SE16 118 D4
Poolsford Rd NW9 45 C5
Poonah St E1 96 C1
Pope Cl SW17,SW19 180 B4
East Bedfont TW14 149 D3
Pope Ct 10 KT2 175 D6
Pope Ho 3 SE5 139 B5
7 SE16 118 B2
Pope John RC Prim Sch W12 112 B6
Pope Rd BR2 209 D4
Pope St SE1 253 B1
Pope Street Ct SE9 166 B3
Pope's Ave TW2 152 C2
Popes Dr N3 29 C2
Popes Gr CR0 223 B5
Pope's Gr TW1,TW2 152 D2
Pope's Head Alley EC3 242 D1
Pope's La W5 110 A3
Pope's Rd SW9 138 C2
Popham Cl TW13 151 B1
Popham Ct N16 73 C5
Popham Gdns TW9 132 D2
Popham Rd N1 95 A6 235 A6
Popham St N1 234 D6
N1 95 A6 235 A6
Poplar Ave Mitcham CR4 180 D2
Orpington BR6 226 D6
Southall UB2 107 D3
Yiewsley UB7 104 B6
Poplar Bath St 10 E14 119 D6
Poplar Bsns Pk E14 120 A6
Poplar Cl E9 75 B3
Pinner Green HA5 22 D2
Poplar Cres KT19 215 A2
Poplar Ct E4 35 D4
4 SW16 160 B1
SW19 179 C5
Northolt UB5 84 C5
13 Twickenham TW1 153 C5
Poplar Farm Cl KT19 215 A2
Poplar Fst Sch SW19 201 C6
Poplar Gdns KT3 177 B1
Poplar Gr N11 31 A4
W6 112 C4
Kingston u T KT3 199 B6
Wembley HA9 67 A5
Poplar High St E14 119 D6
Poplar Ho SE4 141 B1
19 SE16 118 D4
Poplar La BR3 207 D4
Poplar Mews W12 112 C5
Poplar Mount DA17 125 D2
Poplar Pl SE28 124 C6
W2 113 D6 245 D6
Hayes UB3 106 A6
Poplar Rd SE24 139 A1
SW19 179 C1
Ashford TW15 171 A5
Cheam SM3 201 B1
Poplar Rd S SW19 201 C6
Poplar Sta E14 119 D6
Poplar Way
Feltham TW13 150 B1
Ilford IG6 57 A5
Poplar Wlk SE24 139 A1
Thornton Heath CR0 205 A1
Poplars Cl HA4 39 C1
Poplars Ho 14 E17 53 D6
Poplars Rd E17 53 D3
Poplars The N14 15 B6
NW5 71 C3
Poppins Ct EC4 241 C1
Poppleton Rd E11 54 C3
Poppy Cl SM6 203 A1
Poppy La CR0 206 C1
Porch Way N20 14 D1
Porchester Ct W2 245 D6
Porchester Gate W2 246 A5
Porchester Gdn Mews W2 91 D1
Porchester Gdns W2 113 D6 245 D6
Porchester Mead BR3 185 D4
Porchester Mews W2 91 D1
Porchester Pl W2 237 B1
Porchester Rd W2 91 D1
Kingston u T KT1 176 D1
Porchester Sq W2 91 D1
Porchester Terr W2 114 A6 246 A6
Porchester Terr N W2 91 D1
Porcupine Cl SE9 166 A2
Porden Rd SW2 138 B1
Porlock Ave HA1,HA2 42 A1
Porlock Ho 5 SE26 162 A1
Porlock Rd EN1 17 D4
Porlock St SE1 117 B4 252 D2
Porrington Cl BR7 188 C2
Port Cres E13 99 B3
Port Ho 6 SW11 136 A2
Port Royal Pl 3 N16 73 C3
Portal Cl SE27 160 C1
Hillingdon UB10 60 B1
Ruislip HA4 62 B4
Portbury Cl 16 SE15 140 A4
Portchester Cl SE24 139 B1
Portchester Ct W2 91 D1
Porte 10 NW9 27 D2
Portelet Ct 1 N1 95 C6
Portelet Rd E1 96 D4
Porten Hos W14 254 A5
Porten Rd W14 254 A5
Porter Rd E6 100 B1
Porter Sq N19 50 A1
Porter St SE1 117 A5 252 B4
W1 237 D4
Porters & Walters Almshouses N22 32 B3
Porters Ave RM8,RM9 80 C3
Porters Way UB7 104 B4
Porteus Rd W2 236 B4
Portgate Cl W9 91 B3
Porthcawe Rd SE26 185 B6
Porthkerry Ave DA16 146 A1
Portia Ct 12 IG11 80 A1
Portia Way E3 97 B3
Porticos The SW3 266 C5
Portinscale Rd SW15 157 B6
Portishead Ho 29 W2 91 C2
Portland Ave N16 51 D2
New Malden KT3 199 D2
Sidcup DA15 168 A5
Portland Cl RM6 59 A4
Portland Commercial Est IG11 102 C5
Portland Cotts CR0 203 D2
Portland Cres 1 SE9 166 A2
Feltham TW13 171 B6
Southall UB6 86 A2
Stanmore HA7 25 D1
Portland Cres W HA7 43 D6
Portland Ct 7 N1 73 C1
1 SE14 141 A6
Portland Dr EN2 5 C5
Portland Gdns N4 50 D3
Dagenham RM6 58 D4
Portland Gr SW8 138 B4 270 C2
Portland Ho 20 SW2 160 C3
Portland Hospl for Women & Children The W1 238 D5
Portland Mans SE25 206 B4
Portland Mews W1 239 B1
Portland Pl SE25 206 A5
W1 93 B2 238 D3
Portland Rd N15 51 D5
SE9 166 A2
SE25 206 B4
W11 113 A5 244 B4
W11 113 A6 244 A5
Ashford TW15 148 A1
Bromley BR1 187 C5
Hayes UB4 83 C4
Kingston u T KT1 198 B6
Mitcham CR4 180 C1
Southall UB2 107 B3
Portland Rise N4 51 A1
Portland Sq 4 E1 118 B5
Portland St SE17 117 B1 262 C1
Portland Terr TW9 131 D1
Portland Village W6 112 C3
Portman Ave SW14 133 B2
Portman Cl W1 93 A1 238 A2
Bexleyheath DA7 147 A2
Portman Dr IG8 37 D1
Portman Gate NW1 237 B5
Portman Gdns NW9 27 B1
Hillingdon UB10 60 C1
Portman Hts 1 NW3 69 C5
Portman Lo N21 16 D6
Portman Mews S W1 238 A1
Portman Pl E2 96 C4
Portman Rd KT1 176 B1
Portman Sq W1 93 A1 238 A2
Portman St W1 93 A1 238 A1
Portman The NW11 47 C2
Portman Twrs W1 237 D2
Portmeadow Wlk SE2 124 D4
Portmeers Cl E17 53 C3
Portnall Rd W9 91 B4
Portobello Ct Est W11 91 B1
Portobello Ho 6 SW27 182 D5
Portobello Mews W11 245 A5
Portobello Rd W10 91 A2
W11 113 B6 244 D6
Portobello Road Mkt* W10 91 A2
Porton Ct KT6 197 C3
Portpool La EC1 94 C2 241 A4
Portree Cl N22 32 B3
Portree St E14 98 B1
Portrush Ct 9 UB1 86 A1
Portsdown HA8 26 C5
Portsdown Ave NW11 47 B3
Portsdown Mews NW11 47 B3
Portsea Hall W2 237 B1
Portsea Ho 6 SW15 156 B3
Portsea Mews W2 237 B1
Portsea Pl W2 237 B1
Portslade Rd SW8 137 C3
Portsmouth Ave KT7 197 A2
Portsmouth Rd SW15 156 C4
Esher KT10 212 A5
Kingston u T KT1,KT6 197 C3
Thames Ditton KT6,KT7 197 C3
Portsmouth St WC2 240 D1
Portsoken St E1,EC3 253 C6
Portswood Pl 10 SW15 155 D5
Portugal Gdns TW2 152 A2
Portugal St WC2 94 B1 240 D1
Portway E15 98 D6
Portway Gdns SE18 143 D5
Portway Sch E13 98 D6
Poseidon Ct 4 E14 119 C2
Post La TW2 152 B3
Post Office App E7 77 B3
Post Office Way SW8 137 D5 269 C4
Post Rd UB2 107 D3
Postern Gn EN2 4 C2
Postern The EC2 242 B3
Postmill Cl CR0 222 D5
Postway Mews 1 IG1 78 D5
Potier St SE1 262 D5
Pott St E2 96 B4
Potter Cl CR4 181 B1
Potter St HA5 22 B2
Potter Street Hill HA5 22 B3
Potterhill Ct TW11 175 B3
Potteries The EN5 13 C6
Potterne Cl 5 SW19 156 D4
Potters Cl CR0 207 A1
Potters Fields SE1 117 C5 253 B3
Potters Gr KT3 199 A5
Potters Heights Cl HA5 22 B3
Potter's La SW16 181 D4
High Barnet EN5 1 C1
Potters Lo E14 120 A1
Potters Mews 4 WD6 9 D5
Potters Rd SW6 136 A3
Potter's Rd EN5 1 D1
Pottersfield EN1 5 C1
Pottery La W11 113 A5 244 B4
Pottery Rd TW8 132 A6
Pottery St SE16 118 B4
Poulett Gdns TW1 153 A3
Poulett Rd E6 100 B5
Poullett Ho SW2 160 D3
Poulters Wood BR2 225 D3
Poulton Ave SM1,SM5 218 B5
Poulton Cl E8 74 B2
Poultry EC2 95 B1 242 C1
Pound Cl
Long Ditton KT6 197 C1
Orpington BR6 227 B6
Pound Court Dr BR6 227 B6
Pound Green Ct 4 DA5 169 C4
Pound La NW10 68 A2
Pound Park Rd SE7 121 D2
Pound Pl SE9 166 C5
Pound St SM5 218 D3
Pountney Rd SW11 137 A2
Poverest Rd BR5 211 D4
Povey Ho SE17 263 A3
SW2 160 C5
Powder Mill La TW2, TW4 151 C3
Powell Cl
Chessington KT9 213 D3
Edgware HA8 26 B4
Wallington SM6 220 A1
Powell Ct 19 E17 53 D6
Croydon CR2 221 A4
Powell Gdns RM10 81 C4
Powell Rd E5 74 B5
Buckhurst Hill IG9 21 C4
Powell's Wlk W4 133 D6
Power Ho 12 TW9 132 C4
Power Ho The W4 111 D2
Power Rd W4 110 C2
Powers Ct TW1 153 D4
Powerscroft Rd E5 74 C4
Foots Cray DA14 190 C4
Powis Ct Bushey WD2 8 B3
Edgware HA8 26 B6
Powis Gdns NW11 47 B2
W11 91 B1
Powis Ho WC2 240 B2
Powis Mews W11 91 B1
Powis Pl WC1 94 A3 240 B5
Powis Rd E3 97 D4
Powis Sq W11 91 B1
Powis St SE18 122 D2
Powis Terr W11 91 B1
Powle Terr IG1 79 B3
Powlett Ho NW1 71 B2
Powlett Pl NW1 71 B1
Pownall Gdns TW3 129 D1
Pownall Rd E8 96 A6
Hounslow TW3 129 D1
Pownsett Terr IG1 79 A3
Powrie Ho 4 SW11 136 B3
Powster Rd BR1 187 B5
Powys Cl DA7 146 D6
Powys Ct N11 32 A5
Powys La N13 32 A5
N14 32 A6
Poynder Ct 3 N7 72 A3
Poynder Lo TW7 131 A4
Poynders Ct 9 SW4 159 C5
Poynders Gdns SW12 159 C4
Poynders Rd SW12,SW4 159 D4
Poynings Rd N19 71 C5
Poynings Way N12 29 C5
Poyntell Cres BR7 189 B2
Poynter Ct 12 UB5 84 D5
Poynter Ho NW8 236 C6
10 W11 112 D5
Poynter Rd EN1 18 A6
Poynton Rd N17 34 A1
Poyntz Rd SW11 136 D3
Poyser St E2 96 B5
Praed Mews W2 236 D2
Praed St W2 92 B1 236 D2
Pragel St E13 99 C5
Pragnell Rd SE12 165 B2
Prague Pl SW2 160 A6
Prah Rd N4 72 C6
Prairie St SW8 137 B3
Pratt Mews NW1 232 A5
Pratt St NW1 93 C6 232 A6
Pratt Wlk SE1, SE11 116 B2 260 D4
Prayle Gr NW2 46 D1
Prebend Gdns W4,W6 111 D2
Prebend Mans 4 W4 111 D2
Prebend St N1 95 A6 235 A6
Precinct Rd UB3 106 A6
Precinct The N1 235 A5
N5 72 D3
East Molesey KT8 195 D6
Precincts The SM4 201 C3
Preedy Ho N1 233 D4
Premier Ct EN3 6 D5
Premier Lo N3 29 C2
Premier Park Rd NW10 88 D5
Premier Pl E14 119 C6
Prendergast Ho 7 SW4 159 D4
Prendergast Rd SE3 142 C2
Prendergast Sch SE4 141 C1
Prentice Ct 2 SW19 179 B5
Prentis Rd SW16 181 D6
Prentiss Ct SE7 121 D2
Presburg Rd KT3 199 C4
Prescelly Pl HA8 26 B2
Prescot St E1 117 D6 253 D6
Prescott Ave BR5 210 D3
Prescott Ho 13 SE17 138 D6
Prescott Pl SW4 137 D1
Presentation Mews SW2 160 B3
President Dr E1 118 B5
President Ho EC1 234 D1
President St EC1 235 A2
Press Ho NW10 67 B5
Press Rd NW10 67 B5
Prestage Way E14 120 A6
Prestbury Rd E7 77 C1
Prestbury Sq SE9 188 B6
Prested Rd SW11 136 C1
Preston Ave E4 36 B4
Preston Cl SE1 263 A4
Twickenham TW2 152 C1
Preston Ct Sidcup DA14 189 D6
Walton-on-T KT12 194 C1
Preston Dr E11 55 C4
Bexley DA16 146 D4
West Ewell KT19 215 D2
Preston Gdns NW10 67 C2
Enfield EN3 7 A6
Redbridge IG1 56 A3
Preston Hill HA3 44 B3
Preston Ho SE1 263 C6
SE1 263 A4
1 SE18 122 C2
3 Dagenham RM10 81 C5
Preston Manor High Sch HA9 66 B6
Preston Park Prim Sch HA9 43 D1
Preston Pl NW2 68 A2
Richmond TW10 154 A6
Preston Rd E11 54 C3
SE19 182 D4
SW20 177 D3
Littleton TW17 192 C4
Wembley HA3,HA9 66 A6
Preston Road Sta HA3 44 A1
Preston Waye HA3 44 A1
Prestons Rd BR2 225 A6
Preston's Rd E14 120 A5
Prestwich Terr SW4 159 D6
Prestwick Cl UB2 107 A1
Prestwick Ct UB1 108 A6
Prestwick Rd WD1 22 D6
Prestwood Ave HA3 43 B5
Prestwood Cl SE18 146 A6
Harrow HA3 43 B5
Prestwood Gdns CR0 205 A2
Prestwood Ho 3 SE16 118 B3
Prestwood St N1 235 B3
Pretoria Ave E17 53 A5
Pretoria Cres E4 20 A3
Pretoria Ho 3 HA4 40 C1
Pretoria Rd E4 20 B3
E11 54 B1
E16 98 D3
N17 33 D4
SW16 181 C5
Ilford IG1 78 D3
Pretoria Rd N N18 33 D4
Pretty Cnr HA6 22 A5
Prevost Rd N11 15 A2
Priam Ho 17 E2 96 B5
Price Cl NW7 29 A4
SW17 158 D1
Price Ct HA1 43 A4
Price Ho N1 235 A5
Price Rd CR0 220 D3
Price Way TW12 173 A4
Price's St SE1 251 D4
Price's Yd N1 233 D5
Prichard Ct N7 72 B3
SW11 266 D1
Pricklers Hill EN5 13 D5
Prickley Wood BR2 208 D1
Priddy's Yd 4 CR0 221 A6
Prideaux Ho WC1 233 D2
Prideaux Pl W3 111 B6
WC1 94 B4 233 D2
Prideaux Rd SW9 138 A2
Pridham Rd CR7 205 B5
Priest Park Ave HA2 63 C6
Priestfield Rd SE23 163 A1
Priestlands Park Rd DA15 167 D1
Priestley Cl N16 51 D2
Priestley Gdns RM6 58 B3
Priestley Ho EC1 242 B6
2 NW5 71 B2
6 Wembley HA9 67 A5
Priestley Rd CR4 181 A1
Priestley Way E17 52 D6
NW2 46 A1
Priestman Point 25 E3 97 D4
Priestmead Fst & Mid Schs HA3 43 B6
Priests Bridge SW14 133 C2
Priest's Ct EC2 242 A2
Prim Sch of Our Lady Immaculate KT6 198 D1
Prima Rd SW9 138 C5
Primrose Ave Enfield EN2 5 C4
Ilford RM6 58 B2
Primrose Cl SE6 186 A5
Carshalton SM6 203 B1
Harrow HA2 63 B5
Primrose Ct 11 SW12 159 D4
New Malden KT4 200 A2
Primrose Gdns NW3 70 C2
Ruislip HA4 62 C3
Primrose Hill EC4 241 B1
Primrose Hill Ct NW3 70 D1
Primrose Hill Prim Sch NW1 93 A6 231 B6
Primrose Hill Rd NW1,NW3 70 D1 230 C6
Primrose Hill Sta NW1 71 A1
Primrose Hill Studios NW1 231 A6
Primrose Ho 7 SE15 140 A4
1 Richmond TW9 132 B4
Primrose La CR0 206 D1

Primrose Mans SW11 268 A2
Primrose Mews 9 NW1 70 D1
Primrose Rd E10 53 D1
E18 37 B1
Primrose Sq E9 96 C6
Primrose St EC2 95 C2 243 B4
Primrose Way HA0 87 D5
Primrose Wlk KT17 215 D1
Primula St W12 90 A1
Prince Albert Ct NW8 230 C5
Prince Albert Rd
NW8 92 D5 230 C5
Prince Arthur Ct 19 NW3 70 A4
Prince Arthur Mews 20
NW3 70 A4
Prince Arthur Rd NW3 70 A3
Prince Charles Dr NW2 46 C2
Prince Charles Rd SE3 142 D4
Prince Charles Way
SM6 219 B5
Prince Consort Dr BR7 189 B2
Prince Consort Rd
SW7 114 B3 256 C6
Prince Edward Mans
W2 245 B6
Prince Edward Rd E9 75 B2
Prince George Ave N14 15 D6
Prince George Rd N16 73 C4
Prince George's Ave
SW20 178 C1
Prince Georges Rd
SW19 180 B2
Prince Henry Rd SE7 143 D5
Prince Imperial Rd
SE18 144 B4
Chislehurst West BR7 188 D3
Prince John Rd SE9 166 A6
Prince of Orange La 3
SE10 142 A5
Prince Of Wales Cl NW4 46 B5
Prince of Wales Dr
SW11 137 A4 268 A2
Prince Of Wales Mans
SW4 159 B6
SW11 268 B2
Prince of Wales Pas
NW1 232 A1
Prince Of Wales Rd E16 99 C1
NW5 71 A2
SE3 142 D4
Prince Of Wales' Rd
SM1 218 B6
Prince of Wales Sch EN3 7 B6
Prince Of Wales Terr
W4 111 C1
W8 245 D1
Prince Rd SE25 205 C4
Prince Regent E16 99 C2
Prince Regent Ct SE16 119 A5
Prince Regent La E13 99 C3
Prince Regent Mews
NW1 232 A1
Prince Regent Rd TW3 130 A2
Prince Regent Sta E16 121 C6
Prince Rupert Rd SE9 144 B1
Prince St SE8 141 B6
Prince William Ct
TW15 170 B5
Princedale Rd
W11 113 A5 244 B4
Princelet St E1 95 D2 243 D4
Princes Arc SW1 249 B4
Princes Ave N3 29 D2
N10 49 B6
N13 32 C5
N22 31 D2
NW9 44 D5
W3 110 C3
Petts Wood BR5 211 C4
Tolworth KT6 214 C6
Wallington SM5 218 D1
Woodford IG8 37 C6
Prince's Ave UB1 85 D1
Princes Cir WC2 94 A1 240 A2
Princes Cl N4 50 D1
NW9 44 C5
Edgware HA8 26 C5
Sidcup DA14 168 D1
Prince's Cl TW11,TW12 174 B6
Princes Ct E1 118 B6
NW2 69 A3
NW3 70 B4
New Malden KT3 199 D6
Wembley HA9 66 A3
Prince's Ct SE16 119 B3
Princes Dr HA1 42 C6
Princes Gate
SW7 114 C4 246 D1
Prince's Gate
SW7 114 C4 247 A1
Princes Gate Ct SW7 246 D1
Princes Gate Mews
SW7 114 B3 256 D6
Princes Gdns
SW7 114 B3 256 D6
W3 88 C2
W5 87 C3
Princes Ho W11 245 A5
Princes La N10 49 B6
Princes Mews TW3 129 C1
Prince's Mews
W2 113 D6 245 C6
W6 112 B1
Princes Par NW11 47 A3
Princes Park Ave NW11 47 A4
Hayes UB3 105 B6
Princes Park Circ UB3 105 B6
Princes Park Cl UB3 105 B6
Princes Park La UB3 105 B6
Princes Park Par UB3 105 B6
Princes Pl SW1 249 B4
W11 113 A5 244 A4
Prince's Plain BR2 210 A1
Prince's Plain Prim Sch
BR2 210 A2
Princes Rd N18 34 C6
SE20 184 D4
W13 109 B5
Ashford TW15 170 B5
Buckhurst Hill IG9 21 C2
Feltham TW13 149 D1
Ilford IG6 57 B5
Kingston u T KT2 176 C3
Richmond TW9 132 B4
Richmond TW10 154 B6
Prince's Rd SW14 133 B2
SW19 179 C4
Teddington TW11,TW12 174 B6
Princes Rise SE13 142 A3
Princes Riverside Rd 7
SE16 118 D5
Prince's Sq W2 113 D6 245 C6
Princes St N17 33 C4
W1 238 D1
Bexley DA7 147 B2
Sutton SM1 218 B4
Prince's St EC2 95 B1 242 C1
Richmond TW10,TW9 154 A6
Prince's Terr E13 99 B6
Princes Way
SW15,SW19 157 A3
W3 110 C3
Buckhurst Hill IG9 21 C2
Coney Hall BR4 224 D5
Croydon CR0 220 B3
Ruislip HA4 63 A4
Princes Yd W11 244 B3
Princess Alexandra School of
Nursing The E1 96 B2
Princess Alice Ho W10 90 C3
Princess Alice Way
SE28 123 B4
Princess Ave HA9 66 A6
Princess Beatrice Ho
SW10 255 C1
Princess Christian Coll
WC1 94 A2 240 B4
Princess Cres N4 72 D6
Princess Ct NW6 69 D1
11 SW19 178 D3
W1 237 C3
W2 245 D6
3 Croydon CR0 221 D6
Princess Frederica CE Prim
Sch NW10 90 C5
Princess Grace Hospl The
W1 93 A3 238 A5
Princess La HA4 39 C1
Princess Louise Hospl
W10 90 C2
Princess Mary Ho SW1 259 D3
Princess May JMI Sch
N16 73 D4
Princess May Rd N16 73 C4
Princess Mews NW3 70 B2
Kingston u T KT1 198 B6
Princess Par
Dagenham RM10 103 C5
Locksbottom BR6 226 C5
Princess Park Manor
N11 31 A5
Princess Rd NW1 93 A6 231 B6
NW6 91 C5
Thornton Heath CR0 205 A3
Princess St SE1 261 D5
Princessa Ct EN2 17 B6
Princethorpe Ho W2 91 D2
Princethorpe Rd SE26 184 D6
Princeton Ct SW15 134 D2
Princeton Mans WC1 240 C3
Princeton Mews 3
KT2 176 C2
Princeton St
WC1 94 B2 240 C4
Pringle Gdns SW16 181 C6
Print Village Ind Est
SE15 139 D3
Printer St EC4 241 B2
Printing House Yd 17 E2 95 C4
Printinghouse La UB3 105 C4
Printon Ho 12 E3 97 B2
Priolo Rd SE7 121 C1
Prior Ave SM2,SM5 218 C1
Prior Bolton St N1 72 D2
Prior Rd IG1 78 C5
Prior St SE10 142 A5
Prior Weston Prim Sch
EC1 95 A3 242 B5
Prioress Ho 2 E3 97 D4
Prioress Rd SE27 160 D1
Prioress St SE1 262 D5
Priors Croft E17 35 B1
Priors Field UB5 63 A2
Priors Gdns HA4 62 C3
Priors Lo 4 TW10 154 A5
Priors Mead EN1 5 C4
Priorty Ct SE15 140 C1
Priory Ave E4 19 C1
E17 53 C4
N8 49 D5
W4 111 C3
Cheam SM3 216 D4
Orpington BR5 211 B3
Wembley HA0 64 D4
Priory CE Mid Sch
SW19 179 D5
Priory Cl E4 19 B1
E18 37 A2
N3 29 B2
N14 15 B6
N20 13 B4
3 SW19 179 D2
Beckenham BR3 207 A6
Bromley BR7 188 B2
Bushey HA7 8 D1
Hampton TW12 173 B2
Hayes UB3 106 B6
Ruislip HA4 39 D1
Sunbury TW16 172 A3
Wembley HA0 64 D4
Priory Cres SE19 183 A3
Cheam SM3 216 D4
Wembley HA0 65 A5
Priory Ct E6 99 D6
E9 74 D3
E17 53 B6
EC4 241 D1
SW8 137 D4 269 D2
SW15 133 D1
Bushey WD2 8 A3
Cheam SM1 217 B3
Cheam SM3 217 A4
Hounslow TW3 129 D2
Ilford RM6 58 B3
4 Wembley HA0 88 A5
Priory Dr SE2 124 D1
Bushey HA7 8 D1
Priory Field Dr HA8 26 D6
Priory Gdns N6 49 B3
SE25 205 D5
SW13 133 D2
6 W4 111 C2
W5 88 A4
Hampton TW12 173 B2
Wembley HA0 65 A4
Priory Gn N1 233 C4
Priory Gr SW8 138 A4 270 A1
Priory Grange N2 48 D6
Priory Hill HA0 65 A4
Priory Ho E1 243 C4
EC1 241 C6
3 SE7 143 C6
SW1 259 C2
Priory Hospl The SW15 133 D1
Priory House Sch SE6 163 D3
Priory La SW15 155 D6
East Molesey KT8 195 D5
Priory Leas SE9 166 A3
Priory Lo 7 W4 110 C1
W5 87 C1
Coney Hall BR4 224 C5
Priory Mans 17 NW3 70 D2
SW10 256 B1
Priory Park Rd NW6 91 B6
Wembley HA0 65 A4
Priory Pk SE3 142 D2
Priory Rd E6 99 D5
N8 49 D5
NW6 69 D1
SW19 180 B3
W4 111 B3
Barking IG11 79 B1
Cheam SM3 216 D4
Chessington KT9 214 A5
Hampton TW12 173 C3
Isleworth TW3 152 A6
Richmond TW9 132 C5
Thornton Heath CR0 204 C2
Priory Sch SE25 205 D5
Priory St 16 E3 97 D4
Priory Terr NW6 91 D6
Priory The N8 49 D5
SE1 251 C1
SE3 142 D1
Croydon CR0 220 C5
21 Kingston u T KT6 198 A4
Priory View WD2 8 C4
Priory Villas N11 30 D5
Priory Way
Harmondsworth UB7 126 A6
Harrow HA2 41 D5
Southall UB2 106 D3
Priory Wlk
SW10 114 A1 256 B1
Priscilla Ho 8 TW16 171 D3
Pritchard Ho 34 E2 96 A5
Pritchard's Rd E2 96 A5
Priter Rd SE16 118 A3
Priter Road Hostel 14
SE16 118 A3
Private Rd EN1 17 C6
Probert Rd SW2 160 C6
Probyn Ho SW1 259 D4
Probyn Rd SW2 160 D2
Procter Ho 12 SE5 139 B5
Procter St WC1 94 B2 240 C3
Proctor Cl CR4 181 A2
Proctor Ho 5 SE1 118 A1
Proctors Cl TW14 150 A3
Prodger 8 NW9 27 D2
Progress Bsns Pk CR9 220 B6
Progress Way N22 32 C2
Croydon CR0 220 B6
Enfield EN1 18 A6
Prome Ho 3 N16 73 B4
Promenade Approach Rd
W4 133 C5
Promenade Mans HA8 26 C5
Promenade The W4 133 C4
Pronto Trad Est UB4 83 C2
Prospect Cl SE26 184 B6
Belvedere DA17 125 C2
Hounslow TW5 129 B4
Ruislip HA4 40 D2
Prospect Cotts SW18 135 C1
Prospect Cres TW2 152 A5
Prospect Hill E17 53 D5
Prospect Ho 1 E8 73 D2
9 E17 54 A6
N1 234 A3
SE1 261 D5
14 W10 90 D1
Prospect Pl E1 118 C5
N2 48 B5
N17 33 C3
4 NW2 69 B5
6 SE8 141 B6
SW20 178 B3
2 W4 111 B1
Bromley BR2 209 B6
Prospect Rd NW2 69 C5
Barnet EN5 1 D1
Thames Ditton KT6 197 C3
Woodford IG8 37 C5
Prospect Ring N2 48 B6
Prospect St SE16 118 B4
Prospect Vale SE7,SE18 122 A2
Prospect Wharf E1 118 C6
Prospero Ho 7 DA17 125 C1
Prospero Rd N19 49 D1
Prothero Gdns NW4 46 B4
Prothero Ho NW10 67 B1
Prothero Rd
SW6 135 B5 264 C4
Protheroe Ho 4 N17 51 D6
Prout Gr NW10 67 D4
Prout Rd E5 74 B5
Provence St N1 235 A4
Providence Ct W1 248 B6
Providence Ho E9 96 D6
Providence La UB3 127 B5
Providence Pl N1 234 C5
Providence Rd UB7 104 B5
Providence Row N1 233 C3
Providence Sq 4 SE1 118 A4
Providence Twr 1
SE16 118 A4
Provincial Terr 2 SE20 184 D3
Provost Ct NW3 70 D2
Provost Rd NW3 70 D1
Provost St N1 95 B4 235 C2
Prowse Ave WD2 8 A2
Prowse Pl NW1 71 C1
Pruden Cl N14 15 C2
Prudent Pas EC2 242 B1
Prusom St E1 118 B5
Prusom's Island 8 E1 118 C5
Pryors The NW3 70 B5
Public Record Office
EC4,WC2 94 C1 241 A2
Richmond TW9 132 D5
Public Record Office Mus
EC4,WC2 241 A2
Pudding La EC3 252 D6
Pudding Mill La E15 97 D6
Puddle Dock
EC4 116 D6 251 D6
Puffin Cl BR3 206 D4
Puffin Terr IG5 56 C6
Pugin Ct N1 72 C1
Pulborough Rd SW18 157 B4
Pulborough Way TW4 128 C1
Pulford Rd N15 51 B3
Pulham Ave N2 48 B5
Pulham Ho SW8 270 C3
Puller Rd EN5 1 A3
Pulleyns Ave E6 100 A4
Pullman Ct SW2 160 B3
Pullman Gdns SW15 156 C5
Pullman Pl SE9 166 A6
Pulross Rd SW9 138 B2
Pulteney Cl 13 E3 97 B6
Pulteney Gdns 9 E18 55 B6
Pulteney Rd E18 55 B6
Pulteney Terr N1 94 B6 233 D6
Pulton Ho SE4 141 A1
Pulton Pl SW6 135 C5 265 A3
Puma Ct E1 243 C4
Pump Alley 8 TW8 131 D5
Pump Cl UB5 85 C5
Pump Ct EC4 241 A1
Pump La SE14 140 C5
Hayes UB3 106 A4
Pump Lane Ind Est UB3 106 A4
Pump Pail N CR0 221 A5
Pump Pail S CR0 221 A5
Pumping Station Rd
W4 133 C6
Punderson's Gdns E2 96 B4
Purbeck Ave KT3 199 D3
Purbeck Dr NW2 68 D6
Purbeck Ho SW8 270 C3
Purbrook Est SE1 253 B1
Purbrook Ho 2 SW15 156 B3
Purbrook St SE1 263 B6
Purcell Cres
SW6 135 A5 264 A4
Purcell Ho SW10 266 C5
Southall UB1 85 C1
Twickenham TW2 152 B5
Purcell Mews NW10 67 C1
Purcell Rd UB6 85 D2
Purcell St N1 95 C5
Purcells Ave HA8 26 C5
Purchese St
NW1 93 D5 232 D3
Purday Ho 4 W10 91 B4
Purdey Ct 3 KT4 200 A1
Purdon Ho 10 SE15 140 A4
Purdy St E3 97 D3
Purland Cl RM8 59 B1
Purland Rd SE28,SE18 123 D4
Purley Ave NW2 69 A6
Purley Oaks Prim Sch
CR2 221 B1
Purley Pl N1 72 D1
Purley Rd N9 17 C1
South Croydon CR2 221 B1
Purley View Terr CR2 221 B1
Purley Way
Croydon CR0,CR9 220 C3
Thornton Heath CR0 204 B1
Purley Way Cres CR0 204 B2
Purneys Rd SE9 143 D1
Purrett Rd SE18 123 D1
Purser Ho 3 SW2 160 C5
Pursers Cross Rd
SW6 135 B4 264 D2
Pursewardens Cl W13 109 C5
Pursley Rd NW7 28 B3
Purves Rd NW10 90 C5
Purvis Ho CR0 205 B2
Pusey Ho 16 E14 97 C1
Puteaux Ho 6 E2 96 D5
Putney Bridge App
SW6 135 A2
Putney Bridge Rd
SW15 135 B1
Putney Bridge Sta SW6 135 B2
Putney Comm SW15 134 C2
Putney Gdns RM6 58 B4
Putney Heath SW15 156 C5
Putney Heath La SW15 156 D5
Putney High Sch SW15 156 D6
Putney High St SW15 135 A1
Putney Hill SW15 156 D6
Putney Hospl SW15 134 C2
Putney Park Ave SW15 134 A1
Putney Park La SW15 156 B6
Putney School of Art &
Design SW15 135 A1
Putney Sta SW15 135 A1
Pycombe Cnr N12 29 B6
Pycroft Way N9 34 A6
Pylbrook Rd SM1 217 D5
Pylon Trad Est E16 98 B3
Pylon Way CR0 204 A1
Pym Cl EN4 14 B6
Pym Ho SW9 138 C3
Pymers Mead SE21 161 A3
Pymmes Brook Ho 3
N10 31 A3
Pymmes Cl N13 32 B5
N17 34 B2
Pymmes Gdns N N9 17 D1
Pymmes Gdns S N9 17 D1
Pymmes Green Rd N11 15 C1
Pymmes Rd N13 32 A5
Pymms Brook Dr EN4 2 C1
Pynchester Cl UB10 60 C6
Pyne Rd KT6 198 C1
Pynfolds SE16 118 B4
Pynham Cl SE2 124 B3
Pynnacles Cl HA7 25 B5
Pynnersmead SE24 161 A6
Pyramid Ho N12 30 A6
Pyrford Ho 12 SW9 138 D1
Pyrland Rd N5 73 B3
Richmond TW10 154 B5
Pyrmont Gr SE27 160 D1
Pyrmont Rd W4 132 C6
Pytchley Cres SE19 183 A4
Pytchley Rd SE22 139 C2

Q

Quadrangle Cl SE1 263 A4
Quadrangle Lo SW19 179 C4
Quadrangle The E17 35 B1
SE24 161 A6
SW6 264 A3
SW10 266 B2
W2 237 A2
W12 90 C1
Stanmore HA7 25 C3
Quadrant Arc W1 249 B5
Quadrant Cl NW4 46 B4
Quadrant Gr NW5 70 D3
Quadrant Ho E15 98 C4
Quadrant Rd
Richmond TW9 131 D1
Thornton Heath CR7 204 D5
Quadrant The SW20 179 A2
4 W10 90 D4
Bexley DA7 146 D5
Richmond TW9 132 A1
Sutton SM2 218 A2
Quaggy Wlk SE3 143 A1
Quainton Hall Sch HA1 42 C4
Quainton St NW10 67 B5
Quaker Ct EC1 242 B6
Quaker La UB2 107 C3
Quaker St E1 95 D3 243 C5
Quakers Course NW9 27 D2
Quakers Pl E7 77 D3
Quakers Wlk N21 17 B5
Quality Ct WC2 241 A2
Quantock Cl UB3 127 B5
Quantock Ct UB6 64 C3
Quantock Dr KT4 216 C6
Quantock Gdns NW2 68 D6
Quantock Ho N16 51 D1
Quarley Way 6 SE15 139 D5
Quarr Rd SM5 202 C3
Quarrendon St SW6 135 C3
Quarry Park Rd SM1 217 B2
Quarry Rd SW18 158 A5
Quarry Rise SM1 217 B2
Quarterdeck The E14 119 C4
Quartermain Ho SM4 202 A4
Quartermile La E10,E15 75 D4
Quay West TW11 175 B5
Quayside Ct 6 SE16 118 D5
Quebec & Crown Wharves
E14 97 B1
Quebec Mews W1 237 D1
Quebec Rd Hayes UB4 84 C1
Ilford IG1 56 D2
Quebec Way SE16 119 A4
Quebeck Ind Est SE16 119 A3
Quedgeley Ct 3 SE15 139 D6
Queen Adelaide Ct
SE20 184 C4
Queen Adelaide Rd
SE20 184 C3
Queen Alexandra Mans
WC1 233 A1
Queen Alexandra's Ct 5
SW19 179 B5
Queen Anne Ave BR2 208 D6
Queen Anne Dr KT10 212 C1
Queen Anne Gate DA7 146 D2
Queen Anne Mews W1 238 D3
Queen Anne Rd E9 74 D2
Queen Anne St
W1 93 B2 238 C3
Queen Annes Cl TW2 152 B1
Queen Anne's Gate
SW1 115 D4 249 C1
Queen Anne's Gdns W4 111 C3
W5 110 A4
Enfield EN1 17 C5
Mitcham CR4 202 D6
Queen Anne's Gr W4 111 C3
W5 110 A4
Enfield EN1 17 C5
Queen Anne's Pl EN1 17 C5
Queen Borough Gdns
BR7 189 B4
Queen Caroline St W6 112 C1
Queen Charlotte's Maternity
Hospl W6 112 A2
Queen Elizabeth Ct EN5 1 B1
Queen Elizabeth Gdns
SM4 201 C5
Queen Elizabeth Hall &
Purcell Room SE1 250 D4
Queen Elizabeth Hospital for
Children The E2 96 A5
Queen Elizabeth Hospl
SE7 144 A5
Queen Elizabeth II Con Ctr
SW1 249 D1
Queen Elizabeth II Sch
W9 91 B3
Queen Elizabeth Rd E17 53 A6
Kingston u T KT2 176 B1
Queen Elizabeth St
SE1 117 D4 253 C2
Queen Elizabeth Wlk
SW13 134 B4
Queen Elizabeth's Cl
N16 73 B6
Queen Elizabeth's Coll
SE10 142 A5
Queen Elizabeth's Dr
N14 16 A3
Queen Elizabeth's Girls Sch
EN5 1 B1
Queen Elizabeth's Hunting
Lodge Mus E4 20 D4
Queen Elizabeth's Wlk
N16 73 B6
Wallington SM6 219 D4
Queen Margaret Flats 22
E2 96 B4
Queen Margarets Ct N1 73 C3
Queen Margaret's Gr N1 73 C3
Queen Mary Ave SM4 200 D4
Queen Mary Cl KT9 214 C5
Queen Mary Rd SE19 182 D4
Charlton TW17 171 A1
Queen Mary's Ave SM5 218 D1
Queen Mary's Gdns
NW1 231 A1
Queen Mary's Hospl
NW3 70 A5
Sidcup DA14 190 A4
Queen Mary's Univ Hospl
SW15 156 A5
Queen of Denmark Ct
SE16 119 B3
Queen Sq WC1 94 A2 240 B4
Queen Sq Pl WC1 240 B5
Queen St EC4 117 A6 252 B6
N17 33 C4
W1 115 B5 248 C4
Bexley DA7 147 B2
Croydon CR0 221 A4
Queen St Pl EC4 252 B6
Queen Terr Cotts W7 108 C4
Queen Victoria Ave HA0 65 D1
Queen Victoria Mon
SW1 249 A2
Queen Victoria St
EC4 117 A6 252 A6
Queenborough Gdns
IG2 56 C5
Queenhithe EC4 252 B6
Queens Acre SM3 217 A1
Queens Ave N10 49 B6
N20 14 B2
Feltham TW13 172 C6
Stanmore HA7 25 C1

Queen's Ave N3 .....30 A2
N21 .....16 D3
Southall UB1 .....86 A1
Woodford IG8 .....37 B5
Queen's CE Jun Mix Sch The
TW9 .....132 C5
Queen's CE Jun Sch The
TW9 .....132 C5
Queen's Cir
SW11 .....137 B5 268 C3
Queen's Cl Edgware HA8 .26 C5
Wallington SM6 .....219 B3
Queen's Club Gdns
W14 .....135 A6 264 B6
Queen's Club The
W14 .....113 A1 254 B1
Queen's Coll W1 93 B2 238 C3
Queens Cres TW10 .....154 B6
Queen's Cres NW5 .....71 A2
Queens Ct 4 E14 .....119 B6
E17 .....53 C4
8 NW11 .....47 B4
SE5 .....139 C3
SW11 .....268 C2
Beckenham BR3 .....185 D3
5 Buckhurst Hill IG9 .....21 C2
Stanmore HA7 .....25 B1
Queen's Ct E11 .....54 C2
NW8 .....229 C4
NW11 .....47 C4
SW13 .....134 A2
W2 .....245 D5
8 W5 .....87 C2
Beckenham BR3 .....185 C2
Croydon CR2 .....221 A3
1 Kingston u T KT2 .....176 C3
3 Richmond TW10 .....154 B5
Thornton Heath CR7 .....204 C4
Queens Down Rd E5 .....74 B4
Queens Dr E10 .....53 C2
Tolworth KT5 .....198 C3
Queen's Dr N4 .....72 D6
W3 .....88 C1
Thames Ditton KT7 .....197 A3
Queen's Elm Sq SW3 ..256 D1
Queen's Gallery The★
SW1 .....115 B4 248 D1
Queens Gate IG4 .....56 B5
Queen's Gate
SW7 .....114 A3 256 B5
Queens Gate Gdns BR7 189 B2
Queen's Gate Gdns
SW7 .....114 A3 256 B5
Queen's Gate Mews
SW7 .....114 A3 256 B6
Queen's Gate Pl
SW7 .....114 A3 256 B5
Queen's Gate Pl Mews
SW7 .....114 A3 256 B5
Queen's Gate Terr
SW7 .....114 A3 256 B6
Queens Gdns NW4 .....46 C4
Queen's Gdns
W2 .....114 A6 246 A6
W5 .....87 C3
Heston TW5 .....129 A4
Queen's Gr NW8 .92 B6 229 D5
Queen's Grove Rd E4 ...20 B3
Queen's Head St
N1 .....94 D6 234 D5
Queen's Head Yd SE1 ..252 C3
Queens Ho 1 SE17 .....139 B6
Queen's Ho TW11 .....174 D4
Queen's Hospl CR0 .....205 A3
Queen's House The
SE10 .....142 B6
Queens Keep 10 TW1 ..153 C5
Queens La N10 .....49 B6
Queens Manor Prim Sch
SW6 .....134 D5
Queens Mans NW4 .....46 B4
NW6 .....69 D3
Queen's Mans W6 .....112 D2
Queen's Mead Rd BR2 .186 D1
Queen's Mews
W2 .....113 D6 245 C6
Queen's Mkt 1 E13 .....99 C6
Queens Par NW2 .....68 C2
7 NW4 .....46 B4
W5 .....88 B1
Queen's Par N11 .....32 A3
3 N11 .....30 D5
Queens Parade Cl N11 ..30 D5
Queens Park Com Sch
NW6 .....90 D6
Queens Park Ct 5 W10 .90 D4
Queens Park Gdns
TW13 .....149 D1
Queen's Park Prim Sch
W10 .....91 A3
Queen's Park Sta NW6 ..91 B5
Queen's Pas BR7 .....188 D4
Queen's Pl SM4 .....201 C5
Queen's Quay EC4 .....252 B6
Queens Rd Hayes UB3 ...83 C1
Morden SM4 .....201 C5
Twickenham TW1 .....153 A3
West Drayton UB7 .....104 B4
Queen's Rd E11 .....54 C2
E13 .....99 C6
E17 .....53 C3
N3 .....30 A2
N9 .....18 B2
N11 .....32 A4
NW4 .....46 C4
Queen's Rd *continued*
SE14,SE15 .....140 C4
SW14 .....133 B2
SW19 .....179 C4
W5 .....88 A1
Barking IG11 .....79 A2
Beckenham BR3 .....185 A1
Bexley DA16 .....146 B3
Bromley BR1 .....187 A1
Buckhurst Hill IG9 .....21 C2
Chislehurst West BR7 ...188 D4
Enfield EN1 .....5 C1
Feltham TW13 .....150 B3
Hampton TW12 .....173 D6
Hounslow TW3 .....129 D2
Kingston u T KT2 .....176 C3
Mitcham CR4 .....202 B6
New Malden KT3 .....199 D4
Richmond KT2,TW10 .....176 C5
Richmond TW10 .....154 B5
Southall UB2 .....107 A4
Teddington TW11 .....174 D4
Thames Ditton KT7 .....196 D4
Thornton Heath CR0 .....205 A3
Wallington SM6 .....219 B3
Queen's Rd W E13 .....99 B5
Queens Reach KT8 .....196 C5
Queen's Ride SW13 .....134 B2
Queen's Rise TW10 .....154 B5
Queen's Road Sta SE15 140 C4
Queen's Row SE17 .....139 B6
Queens Terr E13 .....99 B6
NW8 .....92 B5 229 C4
Queen's Terr TW7 .....131 A1
Queens Walk Ho W5 ....87 C2
Queens Way NW4 .....46 C4
Croydon CR0 .....220 B3
Feltham TW13 .....172 C6
Queens Well Ave N20 ...30 C6
Queens Wlk E4 .....20 B3
NW9 .....67 A6
Ashford TW15 .....170 A6
Harrow HA1 .....42 C5
Ruislip HA4 .....62 C5
Queen's Wlk
SW1 .....115 C5 249 A3
W5 .....87 C2
Queen's Wood Rd N6 ...49 B3
Queens Yd E9 .....75 C2
Queen's Yd W1 .....239 B5
Queensberry Ho 6
TW9 .....153 D6
Queensberry Mews W
SW7 .....256 C4
Queensberry Pl
SW7 .....114 B2 256 C4
Queensberry Way SW7 256 C4
Queensborough Ct N3 ..47 B5
Queensborough Mews
W2 .....246 A6
Queensborough Pas
W2 .....246 A6
Queensborough Terr
W2 .....113 D6 245 D6
Queensbridge Ct 1 E2 .95 D5
Queensbridge Inf Sch
E8 .....73 D1
Queensbridge Pk TW7 .152 C6
Queensbridge Rd E2,E8 .95 D6
E8 .....73 D1
Queensbury IG9 .....21 B3
Queensbury Circ Par
HA3 .....44 A6
Queensbury Ct CR7 ....183 A1
Queensbury Rd NW9 ....45 B2
Wembley HA0 .....88 B5
Queensbury St N1 .....73 A1
Queensbury Sta HA7,HA8 44 B6
Queensbury Station Par
HA8 .....44 B6
Queenscourt HA9 .....66 A4
Queenscroft Rd SE9 ...165 D5
Queensdale Cres W11 .112 D5
Queensdale Pl W11 ...244 A3
Queensdale Rd
W11 .....113 A5 244 A3
Queensdale Wlk W11 ..244 A3
Queensferry Wlk N17 ...52 B5
Queensfield Ct SM3 ...216 C4
Queensgate Ct N12 .....29 D5
Queensgate Gdns
SW15 .....134 B1
Queensgate Pl 10 NW6 .69 C1
Queensland Ave N18 ....33 A4
SW19 .....179 D2
Queensland Ct N10 .....31 B3
Queensland Ho 2 E16 .122 C5
Queensland Pl N7 .....72 C4
Queensland Rd N7 .....72 C4
Queensmead
NW8 .....92 B6 229 D6
Queensmead Sec Sch
HA4 .....62 D4
Queensmere (Southlands Coll) SW19 .....156 D2
Queensmere Cl SW19 .156 D2
Queensmere Ct SW13 .134 A6
Queensmere Rd SW19 .156 D2
Queensmill Rd SW6 ...134 D5
Queensmill Sch SW6 ..135 C3
Queensthorpe Rd SE26 184 D6
Queenstown Rd
SW8 .....137 B5 268 C4
Queenstown Road Sta
SW8 .....137 B4 268 D2
Queensville Rd SW12,
SW4 .....159 D4
Queensway W2 113 D6 245 D6
Queensway *continued*
Coney Hall BR4 .....224 D4
Enfield EN3 .....6 C1
Petts Wood BR5 .....211 A3
Sunbury TW16 .....172 B1
Queensway Sta
W2 .....113 D6 245 D5
Queenswell Jun & Inf Schs
N20 .....14 B2
Queenswood Ave E17 ...36 A2
Hampton TW12 .....173 D4
Hounslow TW3,TW5 .....129 B3
Thornton Heath CR7 ....204 C4
Wallington CR0,SM6 ....219 D4
Queenswood Ct
11 SE27 .....183 B6
5 SW4 .....160 A6
Queenswood Gdns E11 .55 B1
Queenswood Pk N3 ....29 A2
Queenswood Rd SE23 .163 A1
Sidcup DA15 .....167 D5
Quelch Ho 2 N19 .....71 D3
Quemerford Rd N7 .....72 B3
Quendon Ho W10 .....90 C3
Quenington Ct 5 SE15 139 D6
Quennel Ho 7 SW12 ..159 C4
Quentin Pl SE13 .....142 C2
Quentin Rd SE13 .....142 C2
Quentington Mans
SW6 .....264 C2
Quernmore Cl BR1 ....187 A4
Quernmore Rd N4 .....50 C3
Plaistow BR1 .....187 A4
Querrin St SW6 .....136 A3
Quested Ct 27 E8 .....74 B3
Quex Mews NW6 .....91 C6
Quex Rd NW6 .....91 C6
Quick Rd W4 .....111 C1
Quick St N1 .....94 D5 234 D3
Quicks Rd SW19 .....179 D3
Quickswood NW3 .....70 C1
Quiet Nook BR2 .....225 D5
Quill La SW15 .....134 D1
Quill St N4 .....72 C5
W5 .....88 A5
Quilp St SE1 .....252 A2
Quilter Ho 11 W9 .....91 B4
Quilter St E2 .....96 A4
SE18 .....123 D1
Quilting Ct 23 SE16 ....118 D4
Quinta Dr EN5 .....12 C6
Quintin Ave SW20 .....179 B2
Quintin Ct W4 .....133 A5
Quintock Ho 2 TW9 ...132 C4
Quinton Cl
Beckenham BR3 .....208 A6
Hackbridge SM6 .....219 B4
Heston TW5 .....128 B5
Quinton Ho SW8 .....270 A4
Quinton Kynaston Sch
NW8 .....92 B6 229 C5
Quinton Rd KT7 .....197 A1
Quinton St SW18 .....158 A2
Quixley St E14 .....120 B6
Quorn Rd SE22 .....139 C2

R

Rabbit Row W8 .....245 B4
Rabbits Rd E12 .....78 A4
Rabbs Farm Prim Sch
UB7 .....104 A6
Rabournmead Dr UB5 ..63 A3
Raby Rd KT3 .....199 B5
Raby St E14 .....97 A1
Raccoon Way TW4 ....128 C3
Rachel Ct SM2 .....218 B1
Rachel McMillon Coll (Annexe) SE1 .117 A3 262 B5
Rachel Point E5 .....74 A4
Racine 15 SE5 .....139 C4
Rackham Cl DA16 .....146 B3
Rackham Mews SW16 .181 C4
Racton Rd SW6 135 C6 265 A5
Radbourne Ave W5 ....109 C2
Radbourne Cl E5 .....74 D4
Radbourne Cres E17 ....36 B1
Radbourne Ct HA3 .....43 B3
Radbourne Rd SW12 ..159 D3
Radcliff Ho EC1 .....241 A4
Radcliff Mews TW12 ...174 A5
Radcliffe Ave NW10 .....90 A5
Enfield EN2 .....5 A4
Radcliffe Gdns SM5 ...218 C1
Radcliffe Ho 10 SE16 ..118 B2
Radcliffe Path 5 SW8 .137 B3
Radcliffe Rd N21 .....16 D3
SE1 .....263 B6
Harrow HA3 .....25 A1
South Croydon CR0 .....221 D5
Radcliffe Sq SW15 .....156 D5
Radcliffe Way UB5 .....84 D4
Radcot Point 2 SE23 ..162 D1
Radcot St SE11 .....261 B1
Raddington Rd W10 ....91 A2
Radfield Way SE9 .....167 B4
Radford Ho 8 E14 .....97 D2
N7 .....72 B3
Radford Rd SE13 .....164 A5
Radford Way IG11 .....101 D4
Radipole Rd
SW6 .....135 B4 264 C2
Radius Pk TW6 .....127 D1
Radland Rd E16 .....99 A1
Radlet Ave SE23 .....162 B2
Radlett Cl E7 .....76 D2
Radlett Pl NW8 ..92 C6 230 A6
Radley Ave IG3 .....80 A4
Radley Cl TW14 .....149 D3
Radley Ct 25 SE16 .....118 D4
3 Catford BR1 .....186 A6
Radley Gdns HA3 .....44 A5
Radley Ho NW1 .....237 C6
13 SE2 .....124 D4
Radley Lo 30 SW19 ....156 D3
Radley Mews W8 .....255 B5
Radley Rd N17 .....33 C1
Radley Sq E5 .....74 C6
Radley Terr 1 E16 .....98 D2
Radley's La E18 .....37 A1
Radleys Mead RM10 ....81 D2
Radlix Rd E10 .....53 C1
Radnor Ave Bexley DA16 168 B6
Harrow HA1 .....42 C4
Radnor Cl
Chislehurst BR7 .....189 C4
Mitcham CR4 .....204 A5
Radnor Cres SE18 .....146 A5
Redbridge IG4 .....56 B4
Radnor Ct 6 SE23 .....162 D1
W7 .....86 D1
Harrow HA3 .....24 D2
Radnor Gdns Enfield EN1 ..5 C4
Twickenham TW1 .....152 D2
Radnor Gr UB10 .....82 C5
Radnor Lo W2 .....236 D1
Radnor Mews
W2 .....92 B1 236 D1
Radnor Pl W2 ...92 C1 237 A1
Radnor Rd NW6 .....91 A6
SE15 .....140 A5
Harrow HA1 .....42 C4
Twickenham TW1 .....152 D2
Radnor St EC1 ...95 A4 235 B1
Radnor Terr
W14 .....113 B2 254 C4
Radnor Way NW10 .....88 D3
Radnor Wlk 14 E14 ....119 C2
SW3 .....114 D1 257 C1
Croydon CR0 .....207 A3
Radstock Ave HA3 .....43 B6
Radstock Cl N11 .....31 A4
Radstock St SW11 .....267 A3
Radwell Ho SW2 .....160 C6
Raebarn Ct 6 SW16 ...160 A1
Raebarn Gdns EN5 .....12 B6
Raeburn Ave
Surbiton KT3 .....198 D3
Tolworth KT5,KT6 .....198 D3
Raeburn Cl NW11 .....48 A3
Teddington KT1 .....175 D3
Raeburn Ho 7 UB5 .....84 D5
Raeburn Rd Edgware HA8 26 C2
Hayes UB4 .....83 B5
Sidcup DA15 .....167 C5
Raeburn St SW2 .....138 A1
RAF Mus★ NW9 .....28 A1
Raffles Ct NW4 .....46 B5
Edgware HA8 .....26 B6
Rafford Way BR1 .....209 B6
Ragate Ho E5 .....74 A5
Ragged School Mus The
E3 .....97 A2
Raggleswood BR7 .....188 C2
Raglan Cl TW4 .....151 B6
Raglan Ct SE12 .....165 A6
SW9 .....138 C2
Croydon CR0,CR2 .....220 D3
Wembley HA9 .....66 C5
Raglan Jun & Inf Schs
EN1 .....17 C4
Raglan Prim Sch BR2 ..209 D5
Raglan Rd E17 .....54 B4
SE18 .....123 A1
Bromley BR2 .....209 C5
Enfield EN1 .....17 D4
Erith DA17 .....125 B2
Raglan St NW5 .....71 B2
Raglan Terr HA2 .....63 D4
Raglan Way UB5 .....64 A2
Ragley Cl W3 .....111 A4
Ragwort Ct 1 SE26 ....184 B5
Rahere Ho EC1 .....235 A2
Railey Mews NW5 .....71 C3
Railshead Rd TW1,TW7 .131 B1
Railton Rd SE24 .....160 D6
Railway App N4 .....50 C3
SE1 .....252 D4
Harrow HA1,HA3 .....42 D5
9 Twickenham TW1 ....153 A4
Wallington SM6 .....219 B3
Railway Ave SE16 .....118 C4
Railway Cotts W6 .....112 C4
Railway Gr SE14 .....141 B5
Railway Pl DA17 .....125 C3
Railway Rd TW11 .....174 D6
Railway Rise SE22 .....139 C1
Railway Side SW13 ....133 C2
Railway St N1 .....233 B3
Dagenham RM6 .....58 C2
Railway Terr E17 .....36 A2
SE13 .....163 D6
East Bedfont TW13,TW14 150 A3
Rainborough Cl NW10 ..67 A2
Rainbow Ave E14 .....119 D1
Rainbow Ct 3 SE14 ...141 A6
Rainbow Ind Est SW20 .178 B1
Rainbow Quay SE16 ...119 A3
Rainbow St SE5 .....139 C5
Rainbow Works N15 ....52 A4
Raine St E1 .....118 B5
Raine's Foundation Sch
E2 .....96 B4
Raine's Foundation Sec Sch
E2 .....96 C5
Rainford Ho 9 N7 .....72 B6
Rainham Cl SE9 .....167 C5
SW11 .....158 C5
Rainham Ho NW1 .....232 B5
Rainham Rd NW10 .....90 C4
Rainham Rd N RM10 ....81 D6
Rainham Rd S RM10 ....81 D4
Rainhill Way E3 .....97 C4
Rainsborough Ave SE8 119 A2
Rainsford Cl HA7 .....25 C5
Rainsford Ct NW10 .....88 D5
Rainsford Ho 14 SW2 ..160 B6
Rainsford Rd NW10 .....88 D5
Rainsford St W2 .....237 A2
Rainstar Est N18 .....34 C6
Rainton Rd SE7 .....121 A1
Rainville Rd W6 .....134 C6
Raisins Hill HA5 .....40 C6
Raith Ave N14 .....15 D1
Raleigh Ave Hayes UB4 ..84 B2
Wallington SM6 .....219 D4
Raleigh Cl NW4 .....46 C4
Pinner HA5 .....40 D2
Ruislip HA4 .....61 D6
Raleigh Ct 2 SE16 ....118 D5
SE19 .....183 D5
W13 .....87 B2
Beckenham BR3 .....185 D2
Wallington SM6 .....219 B2
Raleigh Dr N20 .....14 C1
Esher KT10 .....212 B3
Tolworth KT5 .....199 A1
Raleigh Gdns SW2 .....160 B5
Mitcham CR4 .....202 D6
Raleigh Ho 30 SW8 ....137 D3
1 Thames Ditton KT7 ...197 A2
Raleigh Mews N1 .....234 D5
6 Orpington BR6 .....227 D3
Raleigh Rd N8 .....50 C5
SE20 .....184 D3
Enfield EN2 .....5 B1
Feltham TW13,TW14 ....149 D2
Richmond TW9 .....132 B2
Southall UB2 .....107 A1
Raleigh St N1 ...94 D6 234 D5
Raleigh Way N14 .....16 A3
Feltham TW13 .....172 C5
Ralph Ct 8 W2 .....91 D1
Ralph Perring Ct BR3 ..207 C5
Ralston St SW3 .....257 C1
Ram St SW18 .....157 D6
Rama Cl SW16 .....182 A3
Rama Ct HA1 .....64 C6
Ramac Ind Est SE7 ....121 B1
Ramac Way SE7 .....121 B1
Ramar Ho 11 E1 .....96 A2
Rambler Cl SW16 .....181 C6
Rambler Ct 11 NW9 .....46 A5
Rame Cl SW17 .....181 A5
Ramilles Cl SW2 .....160 A5
Ramillies Pl W1 .93 C1 239 A1
Ramillies Rd NW7 .....11 C2
W4 .....111 B3
Bexley DA15 .....168 B5
Ramillies St W1 .....239 A1
Ramney Dr EN3 .....7 A6
Rampart St E1 .....96 B1
Rampayne St SW1 .....259 C2
Rampton Cl E4 .....19 C1
Ram's Episcopal Prim Sch
E9 .....74 C3
Rams Gr RM6 .....59 A5
Ramsay Ho NW8 .....230 A4
Ramsay Rd E7 .....76 D4
W3 .....111 A4
Ramscroft Cl N9 .....17 C4
Ramsdale Rd SW17 ....181 A5
Ramsdean Ho 1 SW15 156 B3
Ramsden Rd N11 .....30 D5
SW12 .....159 A4
Ramsey Cl NW9 .....45 D3
Greenford UB6 .....64 B3
Ramsey Ct N8 .....49 D4
Croydon CR0 .....220 D6
Ramsey Ho 14 SW9 ....138 C5
7 SW19 .....179 D2
Ramsey Rd CR7 .....204 B3
Ramsey St E2 .....96 A3
Ramsey Way N14 .....15 C4
Ramsey Wlk 6 N1 .....73 B2
Ramsfort Ho 4 SE16 ..118 B2
Ramsgate Cl 8 E16 ...121 B5
Ramsgate St E8 .....73 D2
Ramsgill App IG2 .....57 D5
Ramsgill Dr IG2 .....57 D5
Ramulis Dr UB4 .....84 D3
Ramus Wood Ave BR6 .227 C3
Rance Ho 12 SE7 .....122 A2
Rancliffe Gdns SE9 ....144 A1
Rancliffe Rd E6 .....100 A5
Randal Cremer JMI Sch
E2 .....95 D5
Randall 9 NW9 .....27 D2
Randall Ave NW2 .....67 D5
Randall Cl
SW11 .....136 C4 267 A2
Randall Ct NW7 .....28 A3
Randall Pl SE10 .....142 A5
Randall Rd
SE11 .....116 B2 260 C3
Randall Row SE11 .....260 C3
Randell's Rd N1 .94 A6 233 B6
Randisbourne Gdns
SE6 .....163 D1
Randle Rd TW10 .....175 C6
Randlesdown Rd SE6 ..163 D1
Randmore Ct 6 BR3 ..185 C3
Randolph App E16 .....99 C1
Randolph Ave
W9 .....92 A4 229 A1
Randolph Cl KT2 .....177 A5
Randolph Cres
W9 .....92 A3 236 A6
Randolph Ct HA5 .....23 C3
Randolph Gdns NW6 ....91 D5
Randolph Gr RM6 .....58 C4
Randolph Mews
W9 .....92 A3 236 B5
Randolph Rd E17 .....53 D4
W9 .....92 A3 236 B5
Keston Mark BR2 .....210 B1
Southall UB1 .....107 B4
Randolph St NW1 .....71 C1
Randon Cl HA2 .....23 D1
Ranelagh Ave SW6 ....135 B2
SW13 .....134 A3
Ranelagh Cl HA8 .....26 C6
Ranelagh Dr
Edgware HA8 .....26 C6
Isleworth TW1 .....153 C6
Ranelagh Gardens (site of Chelsea Flower Show)
SW1 .....115 A1 258 B1
Ranelagh Gardens Mans
SW6 .....135 A2
Ranelagh Gdns E11 .....55 C4
SW6 .....135 B2
W4 .....133 A5
3 W6 .....111 D3
Ilford IG1 .....56 C1
Ranelagh Gr
SW1 .....115 A1 258 B2
Ranelagh Ho SW3 .....257 C2
Ranelagh Mans 4 SW6 135 B3
Ranelagh Pl KT3 .....199 C4
Ranelagh Prim Sch E15 .98 C5
Ranelagh Rd E6 .....100 C5
E11 .....76 C4
E15 .....98 C5
N17 .....51 C6
N22 .....32 B2
NW10 .....89 D5
SW1 .....115 C1 259 B1
W5 .....109 D4
Southall UB1 .....106 D5
Wembley HA0 .....65 D2
Ranfurly Rd SM1 .....217 C6
Rangdon St EC3 .....243 C1
Range Villas TW17 .....192 A2
Range Way TW17 .....192 C2
Rangefield Prim Sch
BR1 .....186 C5
Rangefield Rd BR1 ....186 D5
Rangemoor Rd N15 .....51 D4
Ranger's Rd E4 .....20 D4
Buckhurst Hill IG9,IG10 ...21 A4
Rangers Sq SE10 .....142 B4
Rangeworth Pl DA15 ..167 D1
Rangoon Ho 5 N16 .....73 B4
Rankin Cl NW9 .....45 C6
Rankine Ho SE1 .....262 A5
Ranleigh Gdns DA7 ....147 B5
Ranmere St SW12 .....159 B3
Ranmoor Cl HA1 .....42 B5
Ranmoor Gdns HA1 .....42 C5
Ranmore Ave CR0 .....221 D5
Ranmore Ct 3 SW20 ..178 D2
Kingston u T KT6 .....197 D4
Rann House 1 SW14 ..133 B2
Rannoch Cl HA8 .....10 D2
Rannoch Ct 9 KT6 ....198 A4
Rannoch Rd W6 .....134 D6
Rannock Ave NW9 .....45 C2
Ransford Ho 16 SE21 ..183 C6
Ransom Rd 1 SE7 ....121 C1
Ranston St NW1 .....237 A4
Ranulf Rd NW2 .....69 B4
Ranwell Cl 11 E3 .....97 B6
Ranwell Ho 10 E3 .....97 B6
Ranworth Rd N9 .....18 C2
Ranyard Cl KT9 .....214 B5
Raphael Ct 9 SE16 ....118 B1
Raphael Dr KT7 .....196 D2
Raphael St SW7 .....247 C1
Rapide 12 NW9 .....27 C2
Rapley Ho 19 E2 .....96 A4
Rashleigh Ct 8 SW8 ..137 B2
Rashleigh Ho WC1 ....233 A1
Rasper Rd N20 .....14 A2
Rastell Ave SW12 .....159 D3
Ratcliff Rd E7 .....77 C3
Ratcliffe Cl SE12 .....165 A4
Ratcliffe Cross St E1 ...96 D1
Ratcliffe Ho 12 E14 .....97 A1
Ratcliffe La 18 E14 .....97 A1
Ratcliffe Orch 9 E1 ...118 D6
Rathbone Ho 5 E16 ....98 D1
NW6 .....91 C6
10 SW19 .....178 D3
Rathbone Mkt 2 E16 ...98 D2
Rathbone Pl W1 93 D1 239 C2
Rathbone Point E5 .....74 A4
Rathbone St E16 .....98 D1
W1 .....93 C2 239 B3
Rathcoole Ave N8 .....50 B4
Rathcoole Gdns N8 .....50 B4
Rathfern Prim Sch
SE23 .....163 B3
Rathfern Rd SE6 .....163 B3
Rathgar Ave W13 .....109 C5
Rathgar Cl N3 .....29 B1
Rathgar Rd SW9 .....138 D2
Rathmell Dr SW4 .....159 D5
Rathmore Rd SE7 .....121 B1
Ratier 13 NW9 .....27 C2
Rattray Ct 3 SE6 .....164 D2

Rattray Rd SW2 160 C6
Raul Rd SE15 140 A4
Rav Pinter Cl N16 51 C2
Raveley St NW5 71 C4
Raven Ho 10 SE16 118 D2
Raven Rd E18 37 C1
Raven Row E1 96 B2
Ravendale Rd TW16 171 D1
Ravenet Ct SW4 159 B6
SW11 268 C1
Ravenet St
SW11 137 B4 268 C1
Ravenfield Rd SW17 158 D1
Ravenhill Rd E13 99 C5
Ravenings Par IG3 58 A1
Ravenna Rd SW15 156 D6
Ravenor Ct UB6 85 D3
Ravenor Park Rd UB6 86 A4
Ravenor Prim Sch UB6 85 C4
Ravens Cl NW9 27 C1
Bromley BR2 186 D1
Enfield EN1 5 C3
Ravens Way SE3,SE12 165 A6
Ravens Wood Boys Sch
BR2 225 D5
Ravensbourne 3 TW1 153 C5
Ravensbourne Ave
Bromley BR2,BR3 186 C2
Catford BR2 186 B3
Stanwell TW19 148 A3
Ravensbourne Coll of Design & Communication
BR7 188 B5
Ravensbourne Ct SE6 163 C4
Ravensbourne Gdns
W13 87 B2
Ravensbourne Ho NW8 237 A4
10 Catford BR1 186 B5
Ravensbourne Park Cres
SE6 163 B4
Ravensbourne Pk SE6 163 C4
Ravensbourne Pl SE13 141 D3
Ravensbourne Rd SE23 163 B3
Bromley BR1,BR2 209 A6
Twickenham TW1 153 C5
Ravensbourne Sch The
BR2 209 B4
Ravensbourne Sta BR3 186 B3
Ravensbury Ave SM4 202 A4
Ravensbury Ct CR4 202 B5
Ravensbury Gr CR4 202 B5
Ravensbury La CR4 202 B5
Ravensbury Rd SW18 157 D2
St Paul's Cray BR5 211 D5
Ravensbury Terr SW18 157 D2
Ravenscar NW1 232 A5
Ravenscar Lo 13 SW19 178 D3
Ravenscar Rd
Catford BR1 186 C6
Surbiton KT6 214 B6
Ravenscourt 1 N16 74 A5
Sunbury TW16 171 D2
Ravenscourt Ave W6 112 A2
Ravenscourt Cl HA4 39 A2
Ravenscourt Gdns W6 112 A2
Ravenscourt Park Mans
W6 112 B3
Ravenscourt Park Prep Sch
W6 112 A2
Ravenscourt Park Sta
W6 112 B2
Ravenscourt Pk W6 112 A2
Ravenscourt Pl W6 112 B2
Ravenscourt Rd W6 112 B2
St Paul's Cray BR5 190 B1
Ravenscourt Sq W6 112 A3
Ravenscraig Rd N11 31 C6
Ravenscroft Ave NW11 47 B2
Wembley HA9 44 B2
Ravenscroft Cl 4 E16 99 A2
Ravenscroft Cotts
Barnet EN5 1 C1
Barnet EN5 13 C5
Ravenscroft Cres SE9 166 B1
Ravenscroft Ct NW11 47 B2
Ravenscroft Prim Sch
E16 99 A3
Ravenscroft Rd E16 99 A2
W4 111 A2
Penge BR3 184 D1
Ravenscroft Sch N20 13 B4
Ravenscroft St E2 95 D4
Ravensdale Ave N12 30 B6
Ravensdale Com Est
N16 52 A3
Ravensdale Gdns SE19 183 B3
Ravensdale Mans N8 50 A3
Ravensdale Rd N16 51 D3
Hounslow TW4 129 A2
Ravensdon St
SE11 116 C1 261 B1
Ravensfield RM9 80 D4
Ravensfield Gdns KT19 215 C4
Ravenshaw St NW6 69 B3
Ravenshill BR7 188 D2
Ravenshurst Ave NW4 46 C5
Ravenside KT6 197 D4
Ravenside Cl N18 34 D5
Ravenslea Rd SW11,
SW12 158 D4
Ravensleigh Gdns BR1 187 B5
Ravensmead Rd BR2 186 B3
Ravensmede Way W4 111 D2
Ravensroost SE19 183 B2
Ravenstone
SE17 117 C1 263 B1
Ravenstone Jun & Inf Schs
SW12 159 A2
Ravenstone Rd N8 50 C6
NW9 45 D3
Ravenstone St SW12 159 A3
Ravensview Ct KT6 197 D4
Ravenswood DA5 169 A3
Ravenswood Ave
Tolworth KT6 214 C6
West Wickham BR4 208 A1
Ravenswood Cres
Harrow HA2 63 B6
West Wickham BR4 208 A1
Ravenswood Gdns TW7 130 C4
Ravenswood Pk HA6 22 A4
Ravenswood Rd E17 54 A5
SW12 159 B4
Croydon CR0 220 D5
Ravenswood Road Ind Est 5
E17 54 A5
Ravensworth Ct SW6 265 A3
Ravensworth Rd NW10 90 B4
SE9 188 B6
Ravent Rd SE11 116 B2 260 D4
Ravey St EC2 95 C3 243 A6
Ravine Gr SE18 145 C6
Rawlings Cl 3 BR6 227 D3
Rawlings St
SW3 114 D2 257 C4
Rawlins Cl N3 47 A6
South Croydon CR2 223 B1
Rawlinson Ct NW2 46 C2
Rawlinson Ho SE13 142 B1
Rawlinson Point 8 E16 98 D2
Rawnsley Ave CR4 202 C4
Rawreth Wlk N1 235 B6
Rawson Ct SW11 268 B1
Rawson St
SW11 137 B4 268 C1
Rawsthorne Cl E16 122 B5
Rawstone Wlk 5 E13 99 A5
Rawstorne Pl EC1 234 C2
Rawstorne St
EC1 94 D4 234 C2
Ray Cl KT9 213 C2
Ray Ct W13 109 B5
Woodford IG8 37 D4
Ray Gdns Barking IG11 102 A5
Stanmore HA7 25 B5
Ray Ho 7 W10 90 D1
Ray Lodge Prim Sch IG8 37 D4
Ray Lodge Rd IG8 37 D4
Ray Massey Way 3 E6 100 A6
Ray Rd KT8 195 D4
Ray St EC1 241 B5
Ray Wlk N7 72 B6
Raybell Ct TW7 130 D3
Rayburne Ct W14 254 A6
Buckhurst Hill IG9 21 C3
Raydean Rd EN5 13 D6
Raydon St N19 71 B6
Raydons Gdns RM9 81 A3
Rayfield Cl BR2 210 A3
Rayford Ave SE12 164 D4
Rayleas Cl SE18 144 D4
Rayleigh Ave TW11 174 C4
Rayleigh Cl N13 17 B1
Rayleigh Ct N22 33 A2
2 Kingston u T KT1 176 B1
Rayleigh Rd 5 E16 121 B5
N10 30 C2
N13 17 B1
SW19 179 B2
Woodford IG8 37 C3
Rayleigh Rise CR2 221 C2
Raymead Ave CR7 204 C4
Raymede Twr W10 90 D2
Raymere Gdns SE18 145 C5
Raymond Ave E18 36 D1
W13 109 A3
Raymond Cl SE26 184 C5
Raymond Ct N10 31 A3
Raymond Postgate Ct 5
SE28 124 B6
Raymond Rd E13 99 C6
SW19 179 A4
Beckenham BR3 207 A5
Ilford IG2 57 B2
Raymond Way KT10 213 A2
Raymouth Rd SE16 118 B2
Raynald Ho 15 SW16 160 A1
Rayne Ct E18 54 D5
SE1 253 C2
Rayne Ho 1 SW12 159 A5
W9 91 D3
Rayner Ct 10 W12 112 C4
Rayner Twrs E10 53 C2
Rayners Cl HA0 65 D3
Rayners Gdns UB5 84 B4
Rayners La Harrow HA2 63 D6
Pinner HA5 41 B3
Rayners Lane Sta HA5 41 B2
Rayner's Rd SW15 157 A6
Raynes Ave E11 55 C2
Raynes Ct NW2 69 A4
Raynes Park High Sch
KT3 200 B6
Raynes Park Sta SW20 178 C1
Raynesfield SW20 200 C6
Raynham W2 237 A2
Raynham Ave N18 34 A5
Raynham Ho 1 E1 96 D3
Raynham Prim Sch N18 34 A5
Raynham Rd N18 34 A5
W6 112 B2
Raynham Terr N18 34 A5
Raynor Cl UB1 107 B5
Raynor Pl N1 235 B6
Raynton Cl Harrow HA2 41 A2
Hayes UB4 83 D3
Raynton Dr Hayes UB4 83 C5
Hayes UB4 83 D3
Raynton Rd EN3 6 D6
Rays Ave N18 34 C6
Rays Rd N18 34 C6
West Wickham BR4 208 A2
Raywood Cl UB7 127 A5
Re Sassoon Ho SE15 140 C4
Reachview Cl 14 NW1 71 C1
Read Cl KT7 197 A2
Read Ct E17 53 D3
Read Ho N11 30 D6
4 SE11 138 C6
Reade Ct 6 W3 111 A3
Reade Ho 7 SE10 142 B6
Reade Wlk NW10 67 C1
Reading Ho SE15 140 A6
W2 236 A1
Reading La E8 74 B2
Reading Rd Northolt UB5 64 A3
Sutton SM1 218 A3
Reading Way NW7 29 A5
Readman Ct 8 SE20 184 B2
Reads Cl IG1 78 D5
Reapers Cl NW1 232 C6
Reapers Way TW7 152 B6
Reardon Ho 5 E1 118 B5
Reardon Path 31 E1 118 B5
Reardon St E1 118 B5
Reaston St SE14 140 D5
Reay Prim Sch
SW9 138 B5 270 D3
Rebecca Ct
Beckenham BR3 185 C2
Sidcup DA14 190 B6
Rebecca Ho 10 N12 29 D6
Reckitt Rd W4 111 C1
Record St SE16 140 C6
Recovery St SW17 180 C5
Recreation Rd SE26 184 D6
Bromley BR2 186 D1
Southall UB2 107 A2
Recreation Way CR4,
SW16 204 A6
Rector St N1 95 A6 235 A5
Rectory Bsns Ctr 5
DA14 190 B6
Rectory Cl E4 19 C1
N3 29 B2
SW20 200 C6
Littleton TW17 192 C6
Long Ditton KT6 197 C1
Sidcup DA14 190 B6
Stanmore HA7 25 B5
Rectory Cres E11 55 C3
Rectory Ct E11 76 D5
E18 36 D2
Cranford TW5 128 C3
Feltham TW13 172 C6
Wallington SM6 219 C4
Rectory Field Cres SE7 143 C5
Rectory Gdns N8 50 A5
SW4 137 C2
Beckenham BR3 185 C2
Northolt UB5 85 B6
Rectory Gn BR3 185 B2
Rectory Gr SW4 137 C2
Croydon CR0 220 D6
Hampton TW12,TW13 173 B6
Rectory La SW17 181 A5
Edgware HA8 26 C4
Long Ditton KT6 197 C1
Sidcup DA14 190 C6
Wallington SM6 219 C4
Rectory Orch SW19 179 A6
Rectory Paddock Sch
BR5 190 C1
Rectory Park Ave UB5 85 B4
Rectory Pl SE18 122 C2
Rectory Rd E12 78 B3
E17 53 D5
N16 73 D5
SW13 134 A3
Beckenham BR3 185 C2
Cranford TW5 128 C3
Dagenham RM10 81 D1
Hayes UB3 84 A1
Keston BR2 225 D1
Southall UB2 107 B3
Sutton SM1 217 D5
1 W3 111 A5
Rectory Road Sta N16 73 D5
Rectory Sch TW12 173 C5
Rectory Sq E1 96 D2
Rectory Way UB10 60 D5
Reculver Ho 2 SE15 140 C6
Reculver Mews N18 34 A6
Reculver Rd SE16 118 D1
Red Anchor Cl SW3 267 A5
Red Barracks Rd 4
SE18 122 B2
Red Cedars Rd BR6 211 C2
Red Hill BR7 188 D5
Red Hill Prim Sch BR7 188 D5
Red House La DA6 147 A1
Red House Rd CR0 203 D3
Red La KT10 213 A2
Red Leys UB8 60 A1
Red Lion Bsns Ctr KT6 214 B5
Red Lion Cl 9 SE17 139 B6
Red Lion Ct EC4 241 B1
Red Lion Hill N2 30 B1
Red Lion La SE18 144 C4
Red Lion Pl SE18 144 C4
Red Lion Rd KT6 214 C6
Red Lion Row SE17 139 A6
Red Lion Sq WC1 94 B2 240 C3
Red Lion St WC1 94 B2 240 C3
Red Lion St *continued*
Richmond TW10 153 D6
Red Lion Yd W1 248 B4
Red Lo BR4 208 A2
Red Lodge Rd BR3,BR4 208 B2
Red Oak Cl BR6 226 D6
Red Pl W1 248 A6
Red Post Hill SE21,SE24 161 B6
Red Post Ho E6 77 D1
Red Rover SW13 134 A2
Redan Pl W2 91 D1
Redan St W14 112 D3
Redan Terr SE5 138 D3
Redberry Gr SE23,SE26 162 C1
Redbourn Ho W10 90 C3
Redbourne Ave N3 29 C2
Redbourne Ho 7 E14 97 B1
N3 29 C2
Redbridge Coll RM6 58 B4
Redbridge Ent Ctr IG1 79 A6
Redbridge Gdns SE5 139 C5
Redbridge Inf Sch IG4 56 A4
Redbridge Jun Sch IG4 56 A4
Redbridge La E IG4 56 A4
Redbridge La W E11 55 C3
Redbridge Rdbt IG4 55 D3
Redbridge Sta IG4 55 D3
Redburn St
SW3 136 D6 267 C6
Redburn Trad Est EN3 18 D5
Redcar Cl UB5 63 D2
Redcar Ho SE26 184 B4
Redcar St SE5 139 A5
Redcastle Cl E1 118 C6
Redchurch St E2 95 D3 243 C6
Redcliffe Cl SW5 255 C1
Redcliffe Gdns
SW10 135 D6 265 D6
Ilford IG1 56 C1
Redcliffe Mews SW10 255 D1
Redcliffe Missionary
Training Coll W4 132 D5
Redcliffe Pl SW10 266 A5
Redcliffe Rd
SW10 136 A6 266 B6
Redcliffe Sq
SW10 113 D1 255 D1
Redcliffe St SW10 265 D6
Redcliffe Wlk
Wembley HA9 66 D5
5 Wembley HA9 67 A5
Redclose Ave SM4 201 C4
Redclyf Ho 12 E1 96 C3
Redclyffe Rd E6 99 C6
Redclyffe Terr 2 SM2 217 C1
Redcroft 5 NW6 69 C2
Redcroft Rd UB1 86 A1
Redcross Way
SE1 117 A5 252 B3
Redding Ho SE18 122 A3
Reddings Ave WD2 8 A6
Reddings Cl NW7 27 D6
Reddings The NW7 11 D1
Reddins Rd SE15 140 A6
Reddons Rd BR3 185 A3
Rede Ho 2 E12 78 C3
Rede Pl W2 113 C6 245 B6
Redesdale Gdns TW7 131 A5
Redesdale St SW3 267 C6
Redfern Ave TW2,TW4 151 C4
Redfern Ho 6 E13 98 D6
Redfern Rd NW10 67 C1
SE6 164 A4
Redfield La
SW5 113 D2 255 C4
Redfield Mews SW5 255 B4
Rediff Est SE16 119 B3
Redford Ave
Thornton Heath CR7 204 B5
Wallington SM6 220 A2
Redford Cl TW13 149 D2
Redford Wlk N1 235 A6
Redgate Dr BR2 225 B6
Redgate Terr SW15 156 D5
Redgrave Cl SE25 205 D3
Redgrave Rd SW15 134 D2
Redhill Ct SW2 160 C2
Redhill Dr HA8 27 A1
Redhill St NW1 93 B4 231 D2
Redif Ho RM10 81 D4
Redington Gdns NW3 69 D4
Redington Ho N1 233 D4
Redington Rd NW3 69 D4
Redknap Ho TW10 153 C1
Redland Gdns KT8 195 B5
Redlands N15 51 B5
Teddington TW11 175 A4
Redlands Ct BR1 186 D3
Redlands JMI Sch E1 96 C2
Redlands Rd EN3 7 A4
Redlands The 5 BR3 185 D1
Redlands Way SW2 160 B4
Redleaf Cl DA17 147 C6
Redleaves Ave TW15 170 D4
Redlees Cl TW7 131 A1
Redlynch Ct
W14 113 A4 244 B1
Redlynch Ho 27 SW9 138 C4
Redman Cl UB5 84 C5
Redman Ho EC1 241 A4
SE1 252 B1
Redman's Rd E1 96 C2
Redmayne Ho 15 SW9 138 B3
Redmead La E1 118 A5
Redmead Rd UB3 105 C2
Redmill Ho 24 E1 96 B3
Redmond Ho N1 233 D5
Redmore Rd W6 112 B2
Redpoll Way DA18 124 D3
Redriff Prim Sch SE16 119 A4
Redriff Rd SE16 119 A3
Redriffe Rd E13 98 D6
Redroofs Cl BR3 185 D2
Redrose Trad Ctr 1 EN4 14 B6
Redrup Ho 21 SE14 140 D6
Redruth Cl N22 32 B3
Redruth Ho SM2 217 D1
Redruth Rd E9 96 C6
Redstart Cl E6 100 A2
SE14 141 A5
Redston Rd N8 49 D5
Redvers Rd N22 32 C1
Redvers St E2 95 C4
Redway Dr TW2 152 A4
Redwing Path SE28 123 B4
Redwing Rd SM6 220 B2
Redwood Cl N14 15 D4
SE16 119 A5
Hillingdon UB10 82 D5
Sidcup DA15 168 A3
South Oxhey WD1 22 D6
Woodford IG9 21 B2
Redwood Ct N19 49 D2
NW6 69 A1
Northolt UB5 85 A4
10 Surbiton KT6 197 D2
Redwood Est TW5 128 B6
Redwood Gdns E4 19 D5
Redwood Mews 2
SW4 137 B2
Redwood Twr E11 76 B5
Redwood Way EN5 12 D6
Redwood Wlk KT6 197 D1
Redwoods SW15 156 A3
Reece Mews SW7 256 C4
Reed Ave BR6 227 C5
Reed Cl E16 99 A2
SE12 165 A6
Reed Ho SW15 156 A5
Reed Mans 6 E11 55 A3
Reed Place Bsns Park
TW17 192 B1
Reed Rd N17 33 D1
Reede Gdns RM10 81 D3
Reede Rd RM10 81 D2
Reede Way RM10 81 D2
Reedham Cl N17 52 B5
Reedham St SE15 140 A2
Reedholm Villas N16 73 B4
Reed's Pl NW1 71 C1
Reedsfield Cl TW15 148 D1
Reedsfield Rd TW15 170 D6
Reedworth St
SE11 116 C2 261 B3
Reef Ho E14 120 A3
Reenglass Rd HA7 25 D6
Rees Dr HA7 26 A6
Rees Gdns CR0 205 D3
Rees Ho 6 N17 33 D3
Rees St N1 95 A6 235 B5
Reesland Cl E12 78 C2
Reets Farm Cl NW9 45 C3
Reeves Ave NW9 45 B2
Reeves Cnr CR0 220 D6
Reeves Cnr Sta CR0 220 D6
Reeves Ho SE1 251 A1
W1 248 A5
Reeves Mews
W1 115 A6 248 B5
Reeves Rd E3 97 D3
SE18 144 D6
Reform Row N17 33 D1
Reform St SW11 136 D3
Regal Cl E1 96 A2
W5 87 D2
Regal Cres SM6 219 B5
Regal Ct N18 33 D5
2 Mitcham CR4 202 D6
Wembley HA0 65 D4
Regal Dr N11 31 B5
Regal La NW1 231 B5
Regal Pl 8 E3 97 B4
SW6 265 D3
Regal Way HA3 44 A3
Regan Ho 1 N18 33 D4
Regan Way N1 95 C5
Regatta Ho TW11 175 A6
Regency Cl W5 88 A1
Hampton TW12 173 B5
Regency Cres 3 NW4 28 D1
Regency Ct 21 E9 96 C6
4 SE19 184 A3
Enfield EN1 17 B6
4 Surbiton KT5 198 B4
Sutton SM1 217 D4
Regency Dr HA4 39 C1
Regency Gdns KT12 194 C1
Regency Ho N3 29 B1
Regency Lo NW3 70 B1
1 Buckhurst Hill IG9 21 D2
Regency Mews 1 NW10 68 A2
Beckenham BR3 186 A2
Isleworth TW7 152 C6
Regency St
SW1 115 D2 259 D3
Regency Way DA7 147 A2
Regency Wlk
Croydon CR0 207 B3
8 Richmond TW10 154 A6
Regent Ave UB10 60 D1
Regent Bsns Ctr UB3 106 A4
Regent Cl N12 30 A5
Cranford TW4 128 B4
Harrow HA3 44 A3
Regent Ct N3 29 D3
1 N16 51 D2
Regent Ct *continued*
NW8 230 A1
Regent Gdns IG3 58 A2
Regent Ho W14 254 A4
Regent Lo 9 SW2 160 B3
Regent Pl SW19 180 A5
W1 249 B6
Croydon CR0 205 D1
Regent Rd SE24 160 D6
Kingston u T KT5 198 C4
Regent Sq 23 E3 97 D4
WC1 94 A4 233 B1
Belvedere DA17 125 D2
Regent St W1 115 C6 249 A6
W4 110 C1
Regents Ave N13 32 C5
Regents Bridge Gdns
SW8 270 B4
Regents Canal Ho 21
E14 97 A1
Regents Cl Hayes UB4 83 C2
South Croydon CR2 221 C2
Regent's Coll
NW1 93 A3 238 A6
Regents Ct E8 96 A6
22 Beckenham BR3 185 C3
Bromley BR1 186 D3
Stanmore HA8 26 A6
Regents Dr BR2 225 D3
Regents Mews
NW8 92 A5 229 B4
Regent's Park
NW1 93 A4 231 A3
Regent's Park Barracks
NW1 231 D3
Regent's Park Rd N3 47 B6
NW1 93 A6 231 A6
Regent's Park Sta
NW1 93 B3 238 C5
Regent's Park Terr
NW1 231 C6
Regents Pl
1 Kingston u T KT2 176 A2
Loughton IG10 21 D4
Regent's Pl SE3 143 A3
Regents Plaza 2 NW6 91 D5
Regent's Row E8 96 A6
Regents Wharf 3 E2 96 B6
Regina Coeli RC Prim Sch
CR2 220 D1
Regina Point SE16 118 C3
Regina Rd N4 50 B1
SE25 206 A6
W13 109 A5
Southall UB2 107 A2
Regina Terr W13 109 B5
Reginald Ct BR3 186 A2
Reginald Pl 6 SE8 141 C5
Reginald Rd E7 77 A2
SE8 141 C5
Reginald Sorenson Ct
E11 54 B2
Reginald Sq SE8 141 C5
Regis Ct N8 50 B5
NW1 237 C4
SW19 180 C2
East Bedfont TW14 149 B5
Regis Rd NW5 71 B3
Regnart Bldgs NW1 232 B1
Regnolruf Ct KT12 194 A2
Reid Cl HA5 40 A5
Reid Ct SW14 133 A3
Reidhaven Rd SE18 123 C2
Reigate Ave SM3,SM4 201 D1
Reigate Rd Catford BR1 164 D1
Grove Pk BR1,SE12 165 A2
Ilford IG3 79 D6
Reigate Way SM6 220 A3
Reighton Rd E5 74 A6
Relay Rd W12 112 C5
Relf Rd SE15 140 A2
Relko Gdns SM1 218 B3
Relton Mews SW7 257 B6
Rembrandt Cl E14 120 B3
Rembrandt Ct 10 SE16 118 B1
West Ewell KT19 215 D2
Rembrandt Rd SE13 142 C1
Edgware HA8 26 C1
Remembrance Ave N2 47 D6
Remington Rd E6 100 A1
N15 51 B3
Remington St
N1 94 D5 234 D3
Remnant St WC2 240 C2
Remount Rd SE28 123 D5
Remsted Ho 5 NW6 91 D6
Remus Rd E3 75 C1
Renbold Ho 5 SE10 142 A4
Rendle Cl CR0 206 A4
Rendlebury Ho 17 SE18 122 B2
Rendlesham Ho 3 E5,
N16 74 A5
Rendlesham Rd E5 74 A5
Enfield EN2 4 D4
Renforth St SE16 118 C4
Renfree Way TW17 192 C2
Renfrew Cl E6 122 C6
Renfrew Ct TW5 129 A3
Renfrew Ho NW6 91 D5
Renfrew Rd
SE11 116 D2 261 C3
Hounslow TW5 129 A3
Kingston u T KT2 177 A3
Renmuir St SW17 180 D4
Rennell Ho 18 E9 74 D2

Rennell St SE13 ... 142 A2
Renness Rd E17 ... 53 A6
Rennets Cl SE9 ... 167 C6
Rennets Wood Rd SE9 ... 167 B6
Rennie Cotts 24 E1 ... 96 C3
Rennie Ct SE1 ... 251 C4
Enfield EN3 ... 7 C5
Rennie Ho SE1 ... 262 A5
Rennie St SE1 ... 116 D5 251 C4
Renoir Ct 7 SE16 ... 118 B1
Renown Cl CR0 ... 204 D1
Rensburg Rd E17 ... 52 D3
Rensburg Villas E17 ... 52 D4
Renshaw Cl 7 DA17 ... 147 B6
Renshaw Ct SW19 ... 179 A6
Renshaw Ho 11 SW27 ... 182 D5
Renters Ave NW4 ... 46 C3
Renton Cl SW2 ... 160 B5
Renwick Rd IG11 ... 102 B4
Repens Way UB4 ... 84 D3
Rephidim St SE1 ... 263 A5
Replingham Rd SW18 ... 157 C3
Reporton Rd
SW6 ... 135 A5 264 B3
Repository Rd SE7,SE18 122 B1
Repton Ave Hayes UB3 ... 105 B2
Wembley HA0 ... 65 C4
Repton Cl SM1,SM5 ... 218 C3
Repton Ct BR3 ... 185 D2
Repton Ho 2 E14 ... 97 A1
SW1 ... 259 B3
Repton Rd Harrow HA3 ... 44 B5
Orpington BR6 ... 227 D5
Repton St E14 ... 97 A1
Reservoir Rd N14 ... 15 C6
SE4 ... 141 A3
Ruislip HA4 ... 39 B5
Resolution Wlk SE18 ... 122 B3
Restell Cl SE3 ... 142 C6
Restmor Way SM5,SM6 ... 219 A6
Reston Pl SW7 ... 246 A1
Restons Cres DA15,SE9 ... 167 C5
Restormel Cl TW3 ... 151 C6
Retcar Pl N19 ... 71 B6
Retford St E2 ... 95 C5
Retingham Way E4 ... 19 D2
Retreat Cl HA3 ... 43 C4
Retreat Ho 5 E9 ... 74 C2
Retreat Pl E9 ... 74 C2
Retreat Rd TW9 ... 153 D6
Retreat The NW9 ... 45 B4
SW14 ... 133 C2
Harrow HA2 ... 41 C2
North Cheam KT4 ... 216 B6
South Norwood CR7 ... 205 B5
Surbiton KT5 ... 198 B3
Reunion Row E1 ... 118 B6
Reveley Sq SE16 ... 119 A4
Revell Rd Cheam SM1 ... 217 B2
Kingston u T KT1 ... 176 D2
Revell Rise SE18 ... 145 D6
Revelon Rd SE4 ... 141 A2
Revelstoke Rd SW18,
SW19 ... 157 C2
Reventlow Rd SE9 ... 167 A3
Reverdy Rd SE1 ... 118 A2
Reverend Cl HA2 ... 63 D5
Revesby Rd SM5 ... 202 C3
Review Rd NW2 ... 67 D6
Dagenham RM10 ... 103 D6
Rewell St SW6 ... 136 A5 266 A3
Rewley Rd SM4 ... 202 B3
Rex Ave TW15 ... 170 C5
Rex Ho TW13 ... 151 A1
Rex Par 2 IG8 ... 37 C4
Rex Pl W1 ... 115 A5 248 B4
Reydon Ave E11 ... 55 C3
Reygate Ct N4 ... 51 A3
Reynard Cl SE4 ... 141 A2
Bromley BR1 ... 210 C6
Reynard Dr SE19 ... 183 D3
Reynard Mills Trad Est
TW8 ... 109 C1
Reynard Pl SE14 ... 141 A6
Reynardson Rd N17 ... 33 A3
Reynardson's Ct 3 N17 ... 51 D6
Reynolds Ave E12 ... 78 C3
Chessington KT9 ... 214 A1
Dagenham RM6 ... 58 C2
Reynolds Cl NW11 ... 47 D2
SW19 ... 180 B2
Carshalton SM5 ... 202 D1
Reynolds Ct E11 ... 76 D5
Ilford RM6 ... 58 D6
Reynolds Dr HA8 ... 44 B6
Reynolds Ho 19 E2 ... 96 C5
N4 ... 50 A1
NW8 ... 229 D3
SW1 ... 259 D3
Enfield EN1 ... 18 A6
Reynolds Pl SE3 ... 143 B5
12 Richmond TW10 ... 154 B5
Reynolds Rd SE15 ... 140 C1
W4 ... 111 A3
Hayes UB4 ... 84 C3
New Malden KT3 ... 199 B2
Reynolds Way CR0 ... 221 C4
Rheidol Mews N1 ... 235 A4
Rheidol Terr N1 ... 95 A6 235 A5
Rhein Ho N8 ... 50 A6
Rheola Cl N17 ... 33 D2
Rhoda St E2 ... 95 D3 243 D6
Rhodes Ave N22 ... 31 C2
Rhodes Avenue Prim Sch
N22 ... 31 C2
Rhodes Ho N1 ... 235 C2
W12 ... 112 B5
Rhodes St N7 ... 72 B3
Rhodesia Rd E11 ... 76 B6
SW9 ... 138 A3
Rhodes-Moorhouse Ct
SM4 ... 201 C3
Rhodeswell Rd E14 ... 97 A2
Rhodrons Ave KT9 ... 214 A3
Rhondda Gr E3 ... 97 B4
Rhyl Prim Sch NW5 ... 71 A2
Rhyl Rd UB6 ... 86 D5
Rhyl St NW5 ... 71 A2
Rhys Ave N11 ... 31 D3
Rialto Rd CR4 ... 181 A1
Ribble Cl IG8 ... 37 C4
Ribblesdale Ave N11 ... 31 A4
Northolt UB5 ... 63 D2
Ribblesdale Ho 11 NW6 ... 91 C6
Ribblesdale Rd N8 ... 50 B5
SW16 ... 181 B5
Ribbon Dance Mews
SE5 ... 139 B4
Ribchester Ave UB6 ... 86 D4
Ribston Cl BR2 ... 210 B1
Ribstone Ho 12 E9 ... 74 D2
Ricardo Path 5 SE28 ... 124 C5
Ricardo St E14 ... 97 D1
Ricards Lodge High Sch
SW19 ... 179 B5
Ricards Rd SW19 ... 179 B5
Riccal Ct 2 NW9 ... 27 C2
Riceyman Ho WC1 ... 234 A1
Rich La SW5 ... 255 C2
Rich St E14 ... 119 B6
Richard Alibon Prim Sch
RM10 ... 81 C3
Richard Anderson Ct 1
SE14 ... 140 D5
Richard Atkins Prim Sch
SW2 ... 160 A4
Richard Burton Ct 4
IG9 ... 21 C2
Richard Challoner Sch
KT3 ... 199 B2
Richard Cl SE18 ... 122 A2
Richard Cloudesley Sch
EC1 ... 95 A3 242 A5
Richard Cobden Prim Sch
NW1 ... 93 C6 232 B5
Richard Ct EN5 ... 1 A2
Richard Fell Ho 2 E12 ... 78 C4
Richard Fox Ho N4 ... 73 A5
Richard Ho 8 SE16 ... 118 C2
Richard House Dr E16 ... 100 A1
E16 ... 99 D1
Richard Knight Ho SW6 265 B2
Richard Neale Ho 2
E1 ... 118 B6
Richard Pk IG10 ... 21 D4
Richard St 10 E1 ... 96 B1
Richard Thornton Ho
SW19 ... 179 C1
Richards Cl Bushey WD2 ... 8 B4
Harlington UB3 ... 127 B6
Harrow HA1 ... 43 A4
Hillingdon UB10 ... 82 C6
Richards Ct BR3 ... 184 D2
Richards Pl E17 ... 53 C6
Richard's Pl SW3 ... 257 B4
Richardson Cl 19 E8 ... 95 D6
Richardson Ct 20 SW4 ... 138 A3
Richardson Ho TW7 ... 130 D2
Richardson Rd E15 ... 98 C5
Richardson's Mews W1 239 A5
Richbell Pl WC1 ... 240 C4
Richborne Terr
SW8 ... 138 B5 270 D4
Richborough Ho 14 E5 ... 74 B4
10 SE15 ... 140 C6
Richborough Rd NW2 ... 69 A4
Richens Cl TW3 ... 130 B3
Riches Rd IG1 ... 79 A6
Richfield Ct 4 BR3 ... 185 B2
Richfield Rd WD2 ... 8 A4
Richford Gate W6 ... 112 C3
Richford Rd E15 ... 98 D6
Richford St W6 ... 112 C3
Richings Ho BR5 ... 190 A2
Richland Ho 4 SE15 ... 140 A4
Richlands Ave KT17 ... 216 A4
Richman Ho 10 SE8 ... 119 B1
Richmond Adult Coll
TW9 ... 131 D1
Richmond Ave E4 ... 36 B5
N1 ... 94 B6 233 D6
NW10 ... 68 C2
SW20 ... 179 A2
Feltham TW14 ... 149 C5
Hillingdon UB10 ... 60 D2
Richmond Bldgs W1 ... 239 C1
Richmond Bridge TW1 153 D5
Richmond Bridge Mans 1
TW1 ... 153 D5
Richmond Circus TW9 ... 132 A1
Richmond Cl E17 ... 53 B3
Richmond Coll
W8 ... 113 D3 255 D6
Richmond TW10 ... 154 A4
Richmond Cres E4 ... 36 B5
N1 ... 94 C6 234 A6
N9 ... 18 A3
Richmond Ct SW1 ... 247 D1
SW20 ... 178 B1
Bromley BR1 ... 187 B3
12 Kingston u T KT2 ... 176 C3
Mitcham CR4 ... 202 B6
Wembley HA9 ... 66 B6
Richmond Dr TW17 ... 193 B3
Richmond Gdns NW4 ... 46 A4
Harrow HA3 ... 24 D3
Richmond Gn CR0 ... 220 A5
Richmond Gr N1 ... 72 D1
Surbiton KT5 ... 198 B3
Richmond Hill TW10 ... 154 A5
Richmond Hill Ct 5
TW10 ... 154 A5
Richmond Ho NW1 ... 231 D3
SE17 ... 262 C2
12 SE26 ... 162 A1
Richmond Ho(Annexe of
Rectory Sch) TW12 ... 173 B5
Richmond Mans SW5 ... 255 C2
SW15 ... 135 A2
14 Twickenham TW1 ... 153 D5
Richmond Mews W1 ... 239 C1
Richmond Park TW10 ... 155 A3
Richmond Park Rd
SW14 ... 133 B1
Kingston u T KT2 ... 176 A3
Richmond Pl SE18 ... 123 A2
Richmond Rd E4 ... 20 B3
E7 ... 77 B3
E8 ... 74 A1
E11 ... 76 B6
N2 ... 30 A1
N11 ... 32 A4
N15 ... 51 C3
SW20 ... 178 B2
W5 ... 110 A4
Ilford IG1 ... 79 A5
Isleworth TW7 ... 131 A2
Kingston u T KT2 ... 176 A4
New Barnet EN5 ... 14 A6
Thornton Heath CR7 ... 204 D5
Twickenham TW1 ... 153 C4
Wallington CR0 ... 220 A5
Richmond St E13 ... 99 A5
Richmond Sta TW9 ... 132 A1
Richmond Terr
SW1 ... 116 A4 250 A2
Richmond upon Thames Coll
TW2 ... 152 C4
Richmond Way E11 ... 77 A6
W12,W14 ... 112 D4
Richmount Gdns SE3 ... 143 A2
Rickard Cl NW4 ... 46 A5
SW2 ... 160 C3
Rickards Cl KT6 ... 214 A6
Rickett St SW6 ... 265 B6
Rickman Ho 26 E2 ... 96 C3
Rickman St 25 E1 ... 96 C3
Rickmansworth Rd HA5 ... 22 C1
Rickthorne Rd 6 N19 ... 72 A6
Rickyard Path SE9 ... 144 A1
Riddell Ct SE1 ... 263 C2
Ridding La UB6 ... 64 D3
Riddons Rd SE12 ... 187 C6
Ride The Brentford TW8 ... 109 C1
Enfield EN3 ... 6 D2
Rideout St SE18 ... 122 B2
Rider Cl DA15 ... 167 C5
Ridgdale St E3 ... 97 D5
Ridge Ave N21 ... 17 B4
Ridge Cl NW4 ... 28 D1
NW9 ... 45 B5
SE28 ... 123 B4
Ridge Crest EN2 ... 4 B4
Ridge Hill NW11 ... 47 A1
Ridge Ho 4 KT2 ... 176 D3
Ridge Prim Sch SM3 ... 201 A1
Ridge Rd N8 ... 50 B3
N21 ... 17 B3
NW2 ... 69 B5
Cheam SM3 ... 201 B1
Mitcham CR4 ... 181 B3
Ridge Terr N21 ... 17 A4
Ridge The Barnet EN5 ... 13 B6
Orpington BR6 ... 227 B6
Sidcup DA5 ... 169 B4
Surbiton KT5 ... 198 C4
Twickenham TW2 ... 152 B4
Ridge Way TW13 ... 151 A1
Ridgebrook Rd SE3,SE9 143 D2
Ridgemont Gdns HA8 ... 27 A6
Ridgemount Ave CR0 ... 222 D6
Ridgemount Cl SE20 ... 184 B3
Ridgemount Gdns EN2 ... 4 D3
Ridgeon Ct N22 ... 32 B4
Ridges The E4 ... 35 C6
Ridgeview Cl EN5 ... 12 D5
Ridgeview Rd N20 ... 14 A1
Ridgeway 7 SE19 ... 183 C4
SW19,SW20 ... 178 D2
Hayes BR2 ... 225 A6
11 Richmond TW10 ... 154 A5
Walton-on-T KT12 ... 193 D1
Woodford IG8 ... 37 C6
Ridgeway Ave EN4 ... 14 D5
Ridgeway Cres BR6 ... 227 C5
Ridgeway Crescent Gdns
BR6 ... 227 C5
Ridgeway Ct HA5 ... 23 C3
Ridgeway Dr W3 ... 110 C3
Plaistow BR1 ... 187 B6
Ridgeway E DA15 ... 167 D6
Ridgeway Gdns N6 ... 49 C2
Redbridge IG4 ... 56 A4
Ridgeway Rd TW7 ... 130 C4
Ridgeway Rd N TW7 ... 130 C5
Ridgeway The E4 ... 20 A3
N3 ... 29 D3
N11 ... 30 D6
N14 ... 16 A2
NW7 ... 28 B6
NW9 ... 45 B5
Ridgeway The *continued*
NW11 ... 47 B1
W3 ... 110 C3
Croydon CR0 ... 220 B5
Enfield EN2 ... 4 B5
Harrow HA2 ... 41 D3
Kenton HA3 ... 43 C3
Pinner HA2 ... 41 B4
Ruislip HA4 ... 40 A2
Stanmore HA7 ... 25 C4
Ridgeway W DA15 ... 167 C6
Ridgeway Wlk UB5 ... 63 A2
Ridgewell Cl N1 ... 235 B6
SE26 ... 185 B6
Dagenham RM10 ... 103 D6
Ridgmount Gdns
WC1 ... 93 D2 239 C4
Ridgmount Pl WC1 ... 239 C4
Ridgmount Rd SW18 ... 157 D6
Ridgmount St
WC1 ... 93 D2 239 C4
Ridgway Ct SW19 ... 178 D4
Ridgway Gdns SW19 ... 178 D3
Ridgway Pl SW19 ... 179 A4
Ridgway Rd SW9 ... 138 D2
Ridgway The SM2 ... 218 B1
Ridgwell Rd E16 ... 99 C2
Riding House St
W1 ... 93 C2 239 A3
Riding The NW11 ... 47 B2
Ridings Ave N21 ... 17 A6
Ridings Cl N6 ... 49 C2
Ridings The W5 ... 88 B3
London EN4 ... 14 B4
Sunbury TW16 ... 172 A2
Surbiton KT5 ... 198 C4
Ridler Rd EN1 ... 5 C5
Ridley Ave W13 ... 109 B3
Ridley Ct SW16 ... 182 A4
Ridley Ho 14 SW11 ... 136 C2
Ridley Rd E7 ... 77 C4
E8 ... 73 D3
NW10 ... 90 A5
SW19 ... 179 D3
Bexley DA16 ... 146 B4
Bromley BR2 ... 208 D6
Ridley Road Mkt E8 ... 73 D3
Ridsdale Rd SE20 ... 184 B2
Riefield Rd SE9 ... 167 A6
Riesco Dr CR0 ... 222 C2
Riffel Rd NW2 ... 68 C3
Rifle Ct SE11 ... 138 C6
Rifle Pl W11 ... 112 D5
Rifle Range La HA1 ... 42 D1
Rifle St E14 ... 97 D2
Rigault Rd SW6 ... 135 A3
Rigby Cl CR0 ... 220 C5
Rigby La UB3 ... 105 A4
Rigby Mews IG1 ... 78 C6
Rigby Pl EN3 ... 7 C6
Rigden St E14 ... 97 D1
Rigeley Rd NW10 ... 90 A4
Rigg App E10 ... 53 A1
Rigg Ho 2 SW4 ... 160 A4
Rigge Pl SW4 ... 137 D1
Riggindale Rd SW16 ... 181 D6
Rignold Ho 6 SE5 ... 139 C3
Rigo Ho 9 E1 ... 96 D2
Riley Ho 9 E3 ... 97 C3
1 SW4 ... 159 D4
SW10 ... 266 C5
Riley Rd SE1 ... 117 D3 263 C6
Enfield EN3 ... 6 C5
Riley St SW10 ... 136 B5 266 C4
Rill Ho 24 SE5 ... 139 C5
Rinaldo Rd SW12 ... 159 B4
Ring Cl BR1 ... 187 B3
Ring Cross Prim Sch N7 72 B3
Ring Ho 14 E1 ... 118 C6
Ring Way N11 ... 31 C4
Ringcroft St N7 ... 72 C3
Ringer's Rd BR1 ... 209 A6
Ringford Ho SW18 ... 157 B6
Ringford Rd SW18 ... 157 C5
Ringlet Cl E16 ... 99 B2
Ringlewell Cl EN1 ... 6 B3
Ringmer Ave
SW6 ... 135 A4 264 B1
Ringmer Gdns 2 N19 ... 72 A6
Ringmer Ho 15 SE22 ... 139 C2
Ringmer Pl N21 ... 17 B6
Ringmer Way BR1 ... 210 B4
Ringmore Rise SE23 ... 162 B4
Ringsfield Ho SE17 ... 262 B1
Ringslade Rd N22 ... 32 B1
Ringstead Ct SM1 ... 218 B3
Ringstead Rd SE6 ... 163 D4
Carshalton SM1 ... 218 B3
Ringway UB2 ... 107 A1
Ringwold Cl BR3 ... 185 A3
Ringwood Ave N2 ... 48 D6
Croydon CR0 ... 204 A2
Ringwood Cl HA5 ... 40 C6
Ringwood Gdns 18 E14 119 C2
SW15 ... 156 A3
Ringwood Rd E17 ... 53 B3
Ringwood Way N21 ... 16 D4
Hampton TW12 ... 173 C6
Ripley Cl Bromley BR1 ... 210 B4
New Addington CR0 ... 224 A2
Ripley Ct 1 CR4 ... 180 B1
Ripley Gdns SW14 ... 133 B2
Sutton SM1 ... 218 A4
Ripley Ho 5 SE26 ... 184 B5
SW1 ... 269 A6
13 Kingston u T KT2 ... 176 D4
Ripley House SW14 ... 133 C2
Ripley Mews E11 ... 54 C3
Ripley Rd E16 ... 99 C1
Belvedere DA17 ... 125 C2
Enfield EN2 ... 5 A4
Hampton TW12 ... 173 C3
Ilford IG3 ... 79 D6
Riplington Ct SW15 ... 156 B4
Ripon Cl UB5 ... 63 C2
Ripon Gdns
Chessington KT9 ... 213 D3
Redbridge IG1 ... 56 A2
Ripon Rd N9 ... 18 B4
N17 ... 51 B6
SE18 ... 144 D6
Ripon Way WD6 ... 11 B6
Rippersley Rd DA16 ... 146 A4
Ripple Ct 10 IG11 ... 101 B6
Ripple Jun Sch IG11 ... 101 C6
Ripple Prim Sch IG11 ... 79 C1
Ripple Rd Barking IG11 ... 101 C6
Barking RM9 ... 102 A6
Rippleside Commercial Est
IG11 ... 102 C6
Ripplevale Gr N1 ... 72 B1
Rippolson Rd SE18 ... 123 D1
Ripston Rd TW15 ... 171 B5
Risborough SE17 ... 262 A4
Risborough Cl 4 N10 ... 49 B6
Risborough Dr KT4 ... 200 A2
Risborough Ho NW8 ... 237 B6
Risborough St SE1 ... 251 D2
Risdon Ho 20 SE16 ... 118 C4
Risdon St 21 SE16 ... 118 C4
Rise The E4 ... 20 C3
E11 ... 55 A4
N13 ... 32 C6
NW7 ... 27 D4
NW10 ... 67 B5
Buckhurst Hill IG9 ... 21 D4
Deacons Hill WD6 ... 10 B6
Edgware HA8 ... 26 D5
Greenford HA0,UB6 ... 65 A3
Hillingdon UB10 ... 82 B5
Sidcup DA5 ... 168 C4
Risedale Rd DA7 ... 147 D2
Riseholme Ho 14 SE22 ... 139 C2
Riseldine Rd SE23 ... 163 A5
Rising Sun Ct EC1 ... 241 D3
Risinghill St N1 ... 234 A4
Risingholme Cl HA3 ... 24 C2
Risingholme Rd HA3 ... 24 C1
Risings The E17 ... 54 B5
Risley Ave N17 ... 33 B2
Risley Avenue Jun & Inf Schs
N17 ... 33 C2
Risley Ho 7 E9 ... 74 D2
Rita Rd SW8 ... 138 B5 270 C4
Ritches Rd N15 ... 51 A4
Ritchie Ho 11 E14 ... 98 B1
N19 ... 49 D2
8 SE16 ... 118 C3
Ritchie Rd CR0 ... 206 B3
Ritchie St N1 ... 94 C5 234 B4
Ritchings Ave E17 ... 53 A5
Ritherdon Rd SW17 ... 159 B2
Ritson Ho N1 ... 233 C5
Ritson Rd E8 ... 74 A2
Ritter St SE18 ... 144 C6
Ritz Par W5 ... 88 B3
Rivaz Pl E9 ... 74 C2
Riven Ct 10 W2 ... 91 D1
Rivenhall Gdns E11,E18 ... 54 D5
River Ave N13 ... 16 D2
Thames Ditton KT7 ... 197 A2
River Bank N21 ... 17 A4
Thames Ditton KT7 ... 196 D4
River Barge Cl E14 ... 120 A4
River Brent Bsns Pk
W7 ... 108 C3
River Cl E11 ... 55 C3
Ruislip HA4 ... 39 D3
Southall UB2 ... 108 A4
River Cotts BR5 ... 190 C1
River Crane Way TW13 151 B2
River Ct E11 ... 55 C3
SE1 ... 251 C5
Kingston u T KT6 ... 197 D4
River Front EN1 ... 5 C2
River Gdns
Carshalton SM5 ... 219 A5
Feltham TW14 ... 150 B6
River Gdns Bsns Ctr
TW14 ... 128 B1
River Grove Pk BR3 ... 185 B2
River Ho 1 SE26 ... 162 B1
SW13 ... 133 C3
River La TW10 ... 153 D3
River Meads Ave TW13,
TW2 ... 151 D1
River Mount KT12 ... 193 D2
River Park Rd N22 ... 32 B1
River Pl N1 ... 73 A1
River Rd Barking IG11 ... 101 D3
Buckhurst Hill IG9 ... 21 D3
River Reach TW11 ... 175 C5
River Road Bsns Pk
IG11 ... 101 D4
River St EC1 ... 94 C4 234 A2
River Terr W6 ... 112 C1
River View EN2 ... 5 A2
River View Gdns TW1 ... 152 D2
River Way SE10 ... 120 D3
Twickenham TW13,TW2 ... 151 D2
West Ewell KT19 ... 215 C3
River Wlk KT12 ... 194 A3
Riverains The SW11 ... 266 C1
Riverbank KT8 ... 196 C5
Riverbank Rd BR1 ... 165 A1
Riverbank Way TW8 ... 131 C6
Rivercourt Rd W6 ... 112 B1
Riverdale Dr SW18 ... 157 D3
Riverdale Gdns TW1 ... 153 C6
Riverdale Rd SE18 ... 123 D1
Bexley DA5 ... 169 B5
Erith DA8 ... 125 D1
Feltham TW13 ... 173 B6
Twickenham TW1 ... 153 C5
Riverdene HA8 ... 11 A1
Riverdene Rd IG1 ... 78 D5
Riverfleet WC1 ... 233 B2
Riverford Ho 28 W2 ... 91 C2
Riverhead Cl E17 ... 34 D1
Riverholme KT8 ... 196 C6
Riverine Ct HA7 ... 25 A5
Rivermead
East Molesey KT8 ... 196 A6
Kingston u T KT6 ... 197 D4
Rivermead Cl TW11 ... 175 B5
Rivermead Ct SW6 ... 135 B2
Ealing UB6 ... 87 A4
Rivermead Ho E9 ... 75 A3
Sunbury TW16 ... 194 C6
Rivernook Cl KT12 ... 194 C4
Riverpark Gdns BR2 ... 186 B3
Riversdale Gdns N22 ... 32 C2
Riversdale Prim Sch
SW18 ... 157 C3
Riversdale Rd N5 ... 73 A5
Thames Ditton KT7 ... 197 A3
Riversdene N5 ... 73 A5
Riversfield Rd EN1 ... 5 C2
Riverside NW4 ... 46 B2
SE6 ... 185 B6
SE7 ... 121 B3
SW11 ... 267 B4
WC1 ... 233 B2
Oatlands Pk TW17 ... 193 C2
Sunbury TW16 ... 172 D1
Twickenham TW1 ... 153 B3
Riverside Apartments
N13 ... 32 B5
Riverside Ave KT8 ... 196 B4
Riverside Bsns Ctr
SW18 ... 157 D3
Riverside Bsns Pk
SW19 ... 180 A2
Riverside Cl E5 ... 74 C6
W7 ... 86 C3
Hackbridge SM6 ... 219 B5
Kingston u T KT1 ... 197 D5
St Paul's Cray BR5 ... 190 C1
Riverside Cotts IG11 ... 101 B5
Riverside Ct E4 ... 19 D5
SE12 ... 142 D1
SW8 ... 269 D6
Richmond TW11 ... 175 C5
Riverside Dr NW11 ... 47 A3
W4 ... 133 C4
Mitcham CR4 ... 202 C4
Richmond TW10 ... 153 B1
Riverside Est EN3 ... 19 A5
Riverside Gdns N3 ... 47 A6
W6 ... 112 B1
Enfield EN2 ... 5 A3
Wembley HA0 ... 88 A5
Riverside Ho N12 ... 29 D6
SW19 ... 202 A5
Riverside Ind Est SE10 ... 120 D3
Barking IG11 ... 102 A4
Riverside Mans 4 E1 ... 118 C5
Riverside Pl N11 ... 15 C1
Stanwell TW19 ... 148 A5
Riverside Prim Sch
SE16 ... 118 A4
Riverside Rd E15 ... 98 A5
N15 ... 52 A3
SW17,SW19 ... 158 A1
Sidcup DA14 ... 169 A2
Stanwell TW19 ... 148 A5
Riverside The KT8 ... 196 B6
Riverside Wlk
Isleworth TW7 ... 130 C2
3 West Wickham BR4 ... 207 D1
Riverside Works IG11 ... 78 D1
Riverside Workshops
SE1 ... 252 B4
Riverston Sch SE12 ... 165 A6
Riverstone Ct KT2 ... 176 B2
Riverton Cl W9 ... 91 B4
Riverview TW17 ... 193 B2
Riverview Ct 14 DA17 ... 125 C1
Riverview Gdns SW13 ... 134 B6
Riverview Gr W4 ... 132 D6
Riverview Hts SE18 ... 144 D5
Riverview Lo NW9 ... 67 B6
Riverview Pk SE6 ... 163 C2
Riverview Prim Sch
KT19 ... 215 B4
Riverview Rd W4 ... 132 D6
Worcester Pk KT19 ... 215 B4
Riverway N13 ... 32 C6
Riverwood La BR7 ... 189 B2
Rivet Ho SE1 ... 263 D2
Rivington Ave IG8 ... 37 D1
Rivington Cres NW7 ... 27 D3
Rivington Ct NW10 ... 90 A6
Rivington Pl EC2 ... 95 C4
Rivington St EC2 ... 95 C4
Rivington Wlk 4 E8 ... 96 A6
Rivulet Rd N17 ... 33 A3
Rixon Ho SE18 ... 144 D6
Rixon St N7 ... 72 C5
Rixsen Rd E12 ... 78 A3
Roach Rd E3 ... 75 C1
Roach Works E3 ... 75 C1
Roads Pl N19 ... 72 A6
Roan Ind Est CR4 ... 180 D2

Roan St SE10 ....142 A6
Robarts Cl HA5 ....40 B4
Robb Rd HA7 ....25 A4
Robbins Hall EN3 ....18 D5
Robert Adam St W1 ....238 A2
Robert Bell Ho 2 SE16 118 A2
Robert Blair Prim Sch
N7 ....72 A2
Robert Browning Prim Sch
SE17 ....117 B1 262 C2
Robert Burns Ho N17 ...34 B3
Robert Cl W9 ....236 B5
Robert Clack Lower Sch
RM8 ....81 B6
Robert Clack Upper Sch
RM8 ....59 C1
Robert Dashwood Way
SE17 ....262 A3
Robert Gentry Ho W14 254 B1
Robert Gerard Ho 7
SE27 ....183 B6
Robert Jones Ho 3
SE16 ....118 A2
Robert Keen Cl 17 SE15 140 A4
Robert Lowe Cl SE14 ..140 D5
Robert Owen Ho 8 E2 .95 D4
SW6 ....134 D4
Robert Owen Lo 5 E5 ..74 B4
Robert St E16 ....122 D5
NW1 ....93 B4 231 D1
SE18 ....123 B2
WC2 ....250 B5
Croydon CR0 ....221 A5
Robert Sutton Ho 20 E1 .96 C2
Roberta St E2 ....96 A4
Roberton Dr BR1 ....187 C2
Roberts Cl SE9 ....167 B3
Cheam SM3 ....216 D1
Yiewsley UB7 ....104 A5
Roberts Ct NW10 ....67 C2
SE20 ....184 C2
W5 ....88 A1
Roberts Ho 2 N11 ....31 B5
10 SE18 ....144 A4
5 SE27 ....160 D1
Roberts Mews SW1 ...258 A5
Robert's Pl EC1 ....241 B6
Roberts Rd E17 ....35 D2
NW7 ....29 A4
Belvedere DA17 ....125 C1
Robertsbridge Rd SM5 .202 B4
Robertson Ho 11 SE10 .142 A4
4 SE18 ....144 B4
1 SW17 ....180 C5
Robertson Rd E15 ....98 A6
Robertson St SW8 ....137 B3
Robeson St 8 E3 ....97 B2
Robin Cl NW7 ....11 C1
Hampton TW12 ....173 A5
Robin Cres E16 ....99 D2
Robin Ct 13 E14 ....120 A3
Wallington SM6 ....219 C2
Robin Gr N6 ....71 A6
Brentford TW8 ....131 C6
Harrow HA3 ....44 B3
Robin Hill Dr BR7 ....188 A4
Robin Ho NW8 ....230 A3
Robin Hood SW15 ....155 C1
Robin Hood Ct SM1 ....217 D3
Robin Hood Dr HA3 ....24 D3
Robin Hood Gdns 12
E14 ....120 A6
Robin Hood Inf Sch
SM1 ....217 C3
Robin Hood Jun Sch
SM1 ....217 D3
Robin Hood La E14 ....120 A6
SW15 ....177 C6
Bexley DA6 ....169 A6
Sutton SM1 ....217 D3
Robin Hood Prim Sch
SW15 ....177 C5
Robin Hood Way UB6 ...64 D2
Robin Hood Way (Kingston By Pass) KT2,SW15,
SW20 ....177 C5
Robina Cl Bexley DA6 ...146 D1
HA6 ....22 A2
Robinhood Cl CR4 ....203 C6
Robinhood La CR4 ....203 C6
Robinia Cres E10 ....75 D6
Robins Ct SE12 ....165 C1
Richmond TW10 ....154 A5
Robin's Ct SW4 ....160 A5
Beckenham BR3 ....186 B1
Robins Gr BR4 ....225 A5
Robinscroft Mews
SE10 ....141 D4
Robinsfield Inf Sch
NW8 ....92 C5 230 A4
Robinson Cres WD2 ....8 A3
Robinson Ct N1 ....234 D6
4 Richmond TW9 ....132 B1
Robinson Ho 11 E14 ....97 C2
4 W10 ....90 D1
Robinson Rd E2 ....96 C5
SW19 ....180 C4
Dagenham RM10 ....81 C4
Robinson St SW3 ....267 C6
Robinson's Cl W13 ....87 A2
Robinwood Pl SW15 ....177 B6
Robsart St SW9 ....138 C3
Robson Ave NW10 ....68 A1
Robson Cl E6 ....100 A1
Enfield EN2 ....4 D3
Robson Ct N12 ....30 A5
Robson Rd SE21,SE27 ..161 A1
Roby Ho EC1 ....242 A6
Roch Ave HA8 ....26 B1
Rochdale 8 SE19 ....183 C4
Rochdale Rd SE2 ....124 B2
Rochdale Way 4 SE8 ..141 C5
Roche Ho 15 E14 ....119 B6
Roche Rd SW16 ....182 B2
Roche Wlk SM5 ....202 B3
Rochelle Cl SW11 ....136 B1
Rochelle Ct 14 E1 ....96 C1
Beckenham BR3 ....185 D3
Rochelle St 31 E2 ....95 D4
Rochemont Wlk 2 E8 ..96 A6
Rochester Ave E13 ....99 C6
Bromley BR1 ....187 B1
Feltham TW13 ....149 D2
Rochester Cl SW16 ....182 A3
1 Bexley DA15 ....168 B5
Enfield EN1 ....5 C4
Rochester Ct 1 E2 ....96 B3
7 NW1 ....71 C1
NW9 ....45 B4
SE25 ....184 A1
Rochester Dr
Bexleyheath DA5 ....169 C5
Pinner HA5 ....40 D4
Rochester Gdns
Redbridge IG1 ....56 B2
South Croydon CR0 ....221 C5
Rochester Ho SE1 ....252 D1
18 SE15 ....140 C6
Rochester Mews NW1 ..71 C1
Rochester Par TW13 ....150 A1
Rochester Pl NW1 ....71 C1
Rochester Rd NW1 ....71 C2
Carshalton SM5 ....218 D4
Northwood HA6 ....39 D6
Rochester Row
SW1 ....115 C2 259 B4
Rochester Sq NW1 ....71 C1
Rochester St SW1 ....259 C5
Rochester Terr NW1 ....71 C2
Rochester Way SE3,SE9 143 D2
SE9 ....144 C2
Rochester Wlk SE1 ....252 C4
Rochford N17 ....33 C1
Rochford Ave RM6 ....58 C4
Rochford Cl 2 E6 ....99 D5
Rochford Way CR0 ....204 A3
Rochford Wlk 3 E8 ....74 A1
Rochfort Ho 4 SE8 ....119 B1
Rock Ave 13 SW14 ....133 B2
Rock Cl CR4 ....180 B1
Rock Gdns RM10 ....81 D3
Rock Grove Way SE16 .118 A2
Rock Hill SE19 ....183 D6
Rock St N4 ....72 C6
Rockbourne Rd SE23 ..162 D3
Rockell's Pl SE22 ....162 B5
Rockfield Ho 2 NW4 ...46 D5
SE10 ....142 A6
Rockford Ave UB6 ....87 B5
Rockhall Rd NW2 ....68 D4
Rockhampton Cl 4
SE27 ....182 C6
Rockhampton Rd
SE27,SW16 ....182 C6
South Croydon CR2 ....221 C2
Rockingham Cl SW15 ..133 D1
Rockingham Ct 19 BR3 185 C3
Rockingham St
SE1 ....117 A3 262 A5
Rockland Rd SW15 ....135 A1
Rocklands N3 ....29 B3
Rocklands Dr HA7 ....25 C1
Rockley Ct 9 W14 ....112 D4
Rockley Rd W14 ....112 D4
Rockliffe Manor Prim Sch
SE18 ....145 D6
Rockmount JMI Lower Schs
SE19 ....183 B4
Rockmount JMI Upper Schs
SE19 ....183 B4
Rockmount Rd
SE18,SE2 ....123 D1
SE19 ....183 B4
Rocks La SW13 ....134 A2
Rockstraw Ho 5 NW3 ..70 D1
Rockware Ave UB6 ....86 C6
Rockways EN5 ....11 D5
Rockwell Gdns SE19 ...183 C6
Rockwell Rd RM10 ....81 D3
Rockwood Ct N16 ....52 A2
Rocliffe St N1 ...94 D5 234 D3
Rocombe Cres SE23 ...162 C4
Rocque Ho SW6 ....264 C4
Rocque La SE3 ....142 D2
Rodborough Rd NW11 ..47 C1
Rodd Est TW17 ....193 B4
Roden Gdns CR0 ....205 C3
Roden St N7 ....72 B5
Ilford IG1 ....78 C5
Rodenhurst Ct SW4 ...159 D6
Rodenhurst Rd SW4 ...159 D5
Roderick Ho 3 SE16 ...118 C2
Roderick Rd NW3 ....70 D4
Rodgers Cl WD6 ....9 D5
Rodgers Ho 4 SW4 ...159 D4
Roding Ct 6 W12 ....111 C4
Roding Ho N1 ....234 A5
Roding Hospl IG4 ....55 D6
Roding La IG9 ....21 D3
Roding La N IG8 ....37 D1
Roding La S IG4 ....55 D5
Roding Lo IG1 ....55 D3
Roding Mews E1 ....118 A5
Roding Prim Sch RM8 ..80 C3
Roding Rd E5 ....75 A3
E6 ....100 D2
Roding Valley Sta IG9 ...37 D6
Roding View IG9 ....21 D3
Rodings Ct E4 ....36 B5
Rodings The
Chipping Barnet EN5 ....1 A1
4 Woodford IG8 ....37 C4
Rodmarton St
W1 ....92 D2 237 D3
Rodmell WC1 ....233 B1
Rodmell Cl UB4 ....85 A3
Rodmell Slope N12 ....29 B5
Rodmere St SE10 ....120 C1
Rodmill La SW2 ....160 A4
Rodney Cl
New Malden KT3 ....199 C4
Pinner HA5 ....41 A2
Thornton Heath CR0 ....204 D1
Walton-on-T KT12 ....194 C1
Rodney Ct NW8 ....236 B6
Rodney Gdns Hayes BR4 225 A4
Pinner HA5 ....40 C4
Rodney Ho 4 E14 ....119 D2
N1 ....233 D3
W11 ....245 A6
Rodney Pl E17 ....35 B1
SE17 ....117 A2 262 B4
SW19 ....180 A2
Rodney Rd E11 ....55 B5
SE17 ....117 B2 262 C3
Mitcham CR4 ....202 C6
New Malden KT3 ....199 C4
Twickenham TW4 ....151 C4
Walton-on-T KT12 ....194 C1
Rodney St N1 ...94 B5 233 D3
Rodway Rd SW15 ....156 A4
Bromley BR1 ....187 B2
Rodwell Cl 2 HA4 ....40 C1
Rodwell Rd SE22 ....161 D5
Roe 5 NW9 ....27 D2
Roe End NW9 ....45 A5
Roe Gn NW9 ....45 A4
Roe Green Jun & Inf Schs
NW9 ....44 D5
Roe La NW9 ....45 A5
Roe Way SM6 ....220 A2
Roebourne Way E16 ...122 C4
Roebuck Cl N17 ....33 D4
Feltham TW13 ....172 B6
Roebuck Ct E4 ....36 A3
2 New Malden KT3 ....199 C4
Roebuck Ho SW1 ....259 A6
Roebuck La IG9 ....21 C3
Roebuck Rd KT9 ....214 C3
Roedean Ave EN3 ....6 C5
Roedean Cl EN3 ....6 C4
Roedean Cres SW15 ...155 C6
Roehampton CE Prim Sch
SW15 ....156 B4
Roehampton Cl SW15 .134 A1
Roehampton Ct SW13 .134 A2
Roehampton Dr BR7 ...189 A4
Roehampton Gate
SW15 ....155 C5
Roehampton Gate Cty Prim
Sch SW15 ....155 C5
Roehampton High St
SW15 ....156 A4
Roehampton La SW15 .156 A5
Roehampton Lane
SW15 ....156 B3
Roehampton Vale
SW15 ....155 D2
Roffey Ct 9 NW9 ....46 A5
Roffey St E14 ....120 A4
Roger Ascham Prim Schs
E17 ....35 B2
Roger Dowley Ct 8 E2 .96 C5
Roger St WC1 ...94 B3 240 D5
Roger Stone Ct NW10 ...67 B6
Roger's Almshouses 2
SW9 ....138 B1
Rogers Est 28 E2 ....96 C4
Rogers Gdns RM10 ....81 C3
Rogers Ho SW1 ....259 D4
9 Dagenham RM10 ....81 C5
Rogers Rd E16 ....98 D1
SW17 ....180 C6
Dagenham RM10 ....81 C3
Rogers Wlk N12 ....13 D1
Rojack Rd SE23 ....162 D3
Rokeby Gdns IG8 ....37 A2
Rokeby Ho 9 SW12 ....159 B4
WC1 ....240 C5
Rokeby Pl SW20 ....178 B3
Rokeby Rd SE4 ....141 B3
Rokeby Sch E15 ....76 B1
Kingston u T KT2 ....177 A3
Rokeby St E15 ....98 C6
Rokeland Ho SE4 ....141 A1
Rokell Ho BR3 ....185 D5
Roker Park Ave UB10 ...60 A4
Rokesby Cl DA16 ....145 B3
Rokesby Pl HA0 ....65 D3
Rokesly Ave N8 ....50 A4
Rokesly Jun & Inf Schs
N8 ....50 A4
Roland Ct SE19 ....183 D2
Roland Gdns
SW7 ....114 A1 256 B2
Roland Mews 1 E1 ....96 D2
Roland Rd E17 ....54 B5
Roland Way SE17 ....262 D1
SW7 ....114 A1 256 B2
Worcester Pk KT4 ....215 D6
Roles Gr RM6 ....59 A5
Rolfe Cl EN4 ....2 C1
Rolfe Ho N11 ....30 D6
Rolinsden Way BR2 ...225 D4
Roll Gdns IG2 ....56 C4
Rolland Ho W7 ....86 C2
Rollesby Rd KT19,KT9 ..214 C2
Rollesby Way SE28 ....102 C1
Rolleston Ave BR5 ....210 D3
Rolleston Cl BR5 ....210 D2
Rolleston Rd CR2 ....221 B1
Rollins St SE15 ....140 C6
Rollit Cres TW3 ....151 C6
Rollit Ho N7 ....72 C3
Rollit St N7 ....72 C3
Rollo Ct SW11 ....268 C1
Rolls Bldgs EC4 ....241 B2
Rolls Park Ave E4 ....35 D5
Rolls Park Rd E4 ....35 D5
Rolls Pas EC4 ....241 A2
Rolls Rd SE1 ...118 A1 263 D2
Rollscourt Ave SE24 ...161 A6
Rolt St SE8 ....141 A6
Rolvenden Gdns BR1 ...187 D3
Rolvenden Pl N17 ....34 A2
Roma Rd E17 ....53 A6
Roma Read Cl SW15 ...156 B4
Roman Cl W3 ....110 D4
Feltham TW14 ....150 C6
Roman Ind Est CR0 ....205 C2
Roman Rd E2,E3 ....96 D5
E3 ....97 B6
E6 ....100 A3
N10 ....31 B3
N12 ....30 C2
W4 ....111 D2
Ilford IG1 ....78 D2
Roman Rise SE19 ....183 B4
Roman Road Prim Sch
E6 ....99 D3
Roman Sq SE28 ....124 A5
Roman Square Mkt 1
E3 ....97 B5
Roman Way N7 ....72 B2
4 SE15 ....140 C5
Croydon CR0 ....220 D6
Enfield EN1 ....17 D6
Romanfield Rd SW2 ...160 B4
Romanhurst Ave BR2 ..208 C5
Romanhurst Gdns BR2,
BR3 ....208 C5
Romany Gdns E17 ....35 A2
Cheam SM3 ....201 C2
Romany Ho 3 N9 ....18 A1
Romany Prospect SE19 183 B4
Romany Rise BR5 ....211 A1
Romayne Ho SW4 ....137 D2
Romberg Rd SW17 ....159 A1
Romborough Gdns
SE13 ....164 A6
Romborough Way SE13 164 A6
Romeland WD6 ....9 D5
Romer Ho 9 SW2 ....160 B6
12 W10 ....91 B4
Romero Cl SW9 ....138 B2
Romero Sq SE9 ....143 C1
Romey Mews W1 ....238 A4
Romeyn Rd SW16 ....160 B1
Romford Ho 17 N1 ....73 B2
Romford Rd E12,E7 ....77 C3
E15 ....76 D2
Romford St E1 ....96 B2
Romilly Dr WD1 ....23 A6
Romilly Rd N4 ....72 D6
Romilly St W1 ....249 D6
Romily Ct SW6 ....135 A3
Rommany Ct SE27 ....183 B6
Rommany Rd SE27 ....183 B6
Romney Cl N17 ....34 B2
NW11 ....48 A1
7 SE14 ....140 C5
Ashford TW15 ....171 A5
Chessington KT9 ....214 A4
Harrow HA2 ....41 C2
Romney Ct 9 NW3 ....70 C2
9 W12 ....112 C4
16 Northolt UB5 ....84 D5
Romney Dr Bromley BR1 187 D3
Harrow HA2 ....41 C2
Romney Gdns DA7 ....147 B4
Romney Ho EN1 ....18 A6
Romney Par UB4 ....83 B5
Romney Rd SE10 ....142 B6
SE18 ....123 A3
Hayes UB4 ....83 B5
New Malden KT3 ....199 B3
Romney Row NW2 ....68 D6
Romney St SW1 116 A3 260 A5
Romola Rd SE24,SW2 ..160 D3
Romsey Cl ER6 ....227 A4
Romsey Gdns RM9 ....102 D6
Romsey Ho 5 SW11 ....136 B1
Romsey Rd W13 ....109 A6
Dagenham RM9 ....102 D6
Romulus Ct 7 TW8 ....131 D5
Ron Leighton Way E6 .100 A6
Rona Rd NW3 ....71 A4
Rona Wlk 7 N1 ....73 B2
Ronald Ave E15 ....98 C4
Ronald Cl BR3 ....207 B4
Ronald Ho SE9 ....143 C1
Ronald Ross Prim Sch
SW19 ....157 A4
Ronald St E1 ....96 C1
Ronalds Rd N5 ....72 C3
Plaistow BR1 ....187 A2
Ronaldshay N4 ....50 C1
Ronaldstone Rd DA15 .167 C5
Ronart St HA3 ....42 D6
Rondu Rd NW2 ....69 A3
Ronelean Rd KT6 ....214 B5
Ronver Lo E4 ....20 C1
Ronver Rd SE12 ....164 D3
Rood La EC3 ...117 C6 253 A6
Rook Lo IG1 ....55 D3
Rook Wlk E6 ....100 A1
Rookby Ct N21 ....16 D2
Rooke Way SE10 ....120 D1
Rookeries Cl TW13 ....150 C1
Rookery Cl NW9 ....45 D4
Rookery Cotts EN4 ....3 B2
Rookery Cres RM10 ....81 D1
Rookery Dr BR7 ....188 C2
Rookery La BR2 ....209 D3
Rookery Rd SW4 ....137 C1
Rookery Way NW9 ....45 D4
Rookes Heath High Sch
HA2 ....63 C5
Rookfield Ave N10 ....49 C5
Rookfield Cl N10 ....49 C5
Rooks Terr UB7 ....104 A4
Rooksmead Rd TW16 ...172 A1
Rookstone Rd SW17 ...180 D5
Rookwood Ave
Wallington SM6 ....219 D4
West Barnes KT3 ....200 A5
Rookwood Gdns E4 ....20 D2
Rookwood Ho IG11 ....101 B5
Rookwood Rd N16 ....52 A2
Rootes Dr W10 ....90 D2
Rope St SE16 ....119 A3
Rope Yard Rails SE18 ..122 D3
Ropemaker Rd SE16 ...119 A3
Ropemaker St
EC2 ....95 B2 242 C4
Ropemaker's Fields 7
E14 ....119 B6
Roper Ho 13 SE21 ....183 C6
Roper La SE1 ...117 C4 253 B1
Roper St 1 SE9 ....166 C5
Roper Way CR4 ....181 A1
Ropers Ave E4 ....36 A5
Roper's Orchard SW3 ..267 A5
Ropers Wlk 13 SE24 ...160 C4
Ropery Bsns Est SE7 ..121 C2
Ropery St E3 ....97 B3
Ropewalk Gdns 16 E1 ...96 A1
Ropley St 6 E2 ....96 A5
Rosa Alba Mews N5 ....73 A4
Rosa Ave TW15 ....170 C6
Rosa Parks Ho 8 SW9 .138 B3
Rosalind Ct 6 IG11 ....80 A1
Rosalind Ho 25 N1 ....95 C5
Rosaline Rd
SW6 ....135 A5 264 B3
Rosaline Terr SW6 ....264 B3
Rosamond St SE26 ....162 B1
Rosamun St UB2 ....107 A2
Rosamund Cl CR2 ....221 B4
Rosary Cl TW3,TW5 ....129 A3
Rosary Gdns
SW7 ....114 A2 256 B3
Ashford TW15 ....170 D6
Bushey WD2 ....8 C4
Rosary RC Inf Sch TW5 129 C6
Rosary RC Jun Sch
TW5 ....129 C6
Rosary RC Prim Sch
NW3 ....70 C3
Rosaville Rd
SW6 ....135 B5 264 C3
Rosbury SW15 ....157 A5
Roscoe St EC1 ...95 A3 242 B5
Roscoff Cl HA8 ....27 A2
Roscommon Ho 2 NW3 70 B3
Rose & Crown Ct EC2 ..242 A2
Rose & Crown Yd SW1 249 B3
Rose Alley EC2 ....243 B3
SE1 ....252 B4
Rose Ave E18 ....37 B1
Mitcham CR4 ....180 D2
Morden SM4 ....202 A4
Rose Bank Cl N12 ....30 C5
Rose Bates Dr NW9 ....44 C5
Rose Bruford Coll SE8 .141 C6
Rose Bruford Coll of Speech
& Drama DA15 ....168 B3
Rose Bush Ct NW3 ....70 D3
Rose Cotts KT10 ....212 B3
Rose Croft Gdns NW2 ..68 A5
Rose Ct E1 ....243 D3
10 SW19 ....179 B5
Harrow HA2 ....64 A6
Ilford IG1 ....78 D2
7 Wembley HA0 ....88 A5
Rose Dale BR6 ....226 D6
Rose End KT4 ....200 D1
Rose Garden Cl HA8 ....26 A4
Rose Gdns W5 ....109 D3
Feltham TW13 ....150 A2
Southall UB1 ....85 C3
Rose Glen NW9 ....45 B5
Rose Hill
Morden SM4,SM5 ....202 A2
Sutton SM1 ....201 D1
Rose Hill Park W SM1 .218 A6
Rose La RM6 ....59 A5
Rose Lawn WD2 ....8 A3
Rose St WC2 ...116 A6 250 A6
Rose Way SE12 ....165 A6
Rose Wlk Surbiton KT5 .198 D4
West Wickham BR4 ....224 B6
Roseacre Cl W13 ....87 B2
Littleton TW17 ....192 C4
Roseacre Lo EN3 ....6 C1
Roseacre Rd DA16 ....146 B2
Rosebank SE20 ....184 B3
SW6 ....134 C5
2 W3 ....89 B1
Rosebank Ave HA0 ....64 D4
Rosebank Cl TW11 ....175 A4
Rosebank Gdns E3 ....97 B5
1 W3 ....89 B1
Rosebank Gr E17 ....53 B6
Rosebank Rd E17 ....53 D3
W7 ....108 C4
Rosebank Villas E17 ....53 C5
Rosebank Way W3 ....89 B1
Rosebank Wlk NW1 ....71 D1
14 SE7 ....122 A2
Roseberry Gdns N4 ....50 D3
Orpington BR6 ....227 C5
Roseberry Pl E8 ....73 D2
Roseberry St SE16 ....118 B2
Rosebery Ave E12 ....78 B2
EC1 ....94 C4 234 B1
N17 ....34 A1
Harrow HA2 ....63 B4
Kingston u T KT3 ....199 D6
Sidcup DA15 ....167 C4
South Norwood CR7 ....183 A1
Rosebery Cl SM4 ....200 D3
Rosebery Ct EC1 ....241 A6
W1 ....248 C4
Chessington KT9 ....214 B3
Rosebery Gdns N8 ....50 A4
W13 ....87 A1
Sutton SM1 ....217 D4
Rosebery Ho 22 E2 ....96 C5
Rosebery Ind Pk N17 ....34 B1
Rosebery Mews N10 ....31 C1
Rosebery Rd N9 ....18 A2
N10 ....31 C1
SW2 ....160 A5
Cheam SM1,SM2 ....217 B2
Isleworth TW3,TW7 ....152 A6
Kingston u T KT1 ....176 D1
Rosebery Sq EC1 ....241 A5
Kingston u T KT1 ....176 D1
Rosebine Ave TW2 ....152 B4
Rosebriars KT10 ....212 A3
Rosebury Rd SW6 ....135 D3
Rosebury Vale HA4 ....62 A6
Rosecourt Rd CR0 ....204 B3
Rosecroft N22 ....32 B2
Rosecroft Ave NW3 ....69 C5
Rosecroft Gdns TW2 ....152 B3
Rosecroft Rd UB1 ....85 C3
Rosecroft Wlk
Pinner HA5 ....40 D4
Wembley HA0 ....65 D3
Rosedale Ave UB3 ....83 B2
Rosedale Cl SE2 ....124 B3
W7 ....108 D4
Stanmore HA7 ....25 B4
Rosedale Ct N5 ....72 D4
Rosedale Gdns RM9 ....80 B1
Rosedale Ho N16 ....51 B1
Rosedale Lo N14 ....15 B4
Rosedale Rd E7 ....77 C3
Dagenham RM9 ....80 B1
Ewell KT17 ....216 A3
Richmond TW9 ....132 A1
Rosedale Terr W6 ....112 B3
Rosedene NW6 ....90 D6
Rosedene Ave SW16 ...160 B1
Greenford UB6 ....85 C4
Morden SM4 ....201 C4
Thornton Heath CR0 ....204 A2
Rosedene Gdns IG2 ....56 C5
Rosedene Terr E10 ....75 D6
Rosedew Rd W6 ....134 D6
Rosefield Cl SM5 ....218 C3
Rosefield Ct EN4 ....2 D1
Rosefield Gdns E14 ....119 C6
Rosehart Mews 8 W11 .91 C1
Rosehatch Ave RM6 ....58 D6
Roseheath Rd TW4 ....151 B6
Rosehill Claygate KT10 ..213 A2
Hampton TW12 ....173 C2
Rosehill Ave SM1,SM5 ..202 A1
Rosehill Ct SM4 ....202 A2
Rosehill Gdns
Greenford UB6 ....64 D3
Sutton SM1 ....218 A6
Rosehill Rd SW18 ....158 A6
Roseland Cl N17 ....33 B3
Roseland Ho SW6 ....135 A2
Roseleigh Ave N5 ....72 D4
Roseleigh Cl 12 TW1 ..153 D5
Roselle Ct W5 ....88 A1
Rosemary Ave N3 ....29 D1
N9 ....18 B3
NW2 ....47 D5
East Molesey KT8 ....195 C5
Enfield EN2 ....5 C4
Hounslow TW4 ....128 D3
Rosemary Cl
Hillingdon UB8 ....82 C2
Thornton Heath CR0 ....204 A3
Rosemary Cotts 3
SW19 ....178 C3
Rosemary Dr 15 E14 ....98 B1
Redbridge IG4 ....55 D4
Rosemary Gdns SW14 .133 A2
Chessington KT9 ....214 A4
Dagenham RM8 ....59 B1
Rosemary Ho N1 ....235 D5
Rosemary La SW14 ....133 A2
Rosemary Mews N1 ....235 D6
Rosemary Rd SE15 ....139 D5
SW17 ....158 A1
Bexley DA16 ....145 D4
Rosemary Sch
EC1 ....94 D3 241 C6

Rosemary Sch *continued*
N1 95 A6 235 B6
Rosemead NW9 46 A2
Rosemead Ave
Feltham TW13 149 D2
Mitcham CR4 181 C1
Wembley HA9 66 A3
Rosemead Sch SE27 161 A2
Rosemont Ave N12 30 A4
Rosemont Mans 11 NW3 69 D2
Rosemont Rd NW3 70 A2
W3 110 D6
Kingston u T KT3 199 A6
Richmond TW10 154 A5
Wembley HA0 88 A6
Rosemoor St
SW3 114 D2 257 C3
Rosemount 5 SM6 219 C2
Rosemount Ct 2 W3 110 D5
Burnt Oak HA8 27 A3
Rosemount Dr BR1 210 B5
Rosemount Lo W3 110 D6
Rosemount Point 10
SE23 162 D1
Rosemount Rd W13 87 A1
Rosenau Cres SW11 267 C1
Rosenau Rd
SW11 136 D4 267 C2
Rosendale Inf Sch
SE21 161 A4
Rosendale Jun Sch
SE21 161 A4
Rosendale Rd SE21,
SE24 161 A3
Roseneath Ave N21 16 D3
Roseneath Rd SW11 159 A5
Roseneath Wlk EN1 5 C1
Rosens Wlk HA8 10 D1
Rosenthal Rd SE6 164 A5
Rosenthorpe Rd SE15 162 D6
Roserton St E14 120 A4
Rosery The CR0 206 D3
Roses The IG8 36 D3
Rosethorn Cl SW12 159 D4
Rosetta Cl SW8 270 B3
Rosetta Ct SE19 183 C3
Rosetta Prim Sch E16 99 B2
Rosetti Terr RM8 80 B4
Roseveare Rd SE12 187 C6
Roseville N21 16 C3
Roseville Ave TW3,TW4 151 C6
Roseville Rd UB3 106 A2
Rosevine Rd SW20 178 C2
Roseway SE21 161 B5
Edgware HA8 27 A6
Rosewell Cl SE20 184 B3
Rosewood Ave UB6 65 A2
Rosewood Cl DA14 168 C1
Rosewood Ct 2 E11 76 B4
Bromley BR1 187 D2
Ilford RM6 58 C4
Kingston u T KT2 176 C3
Rosewood Dr TW17 192 B4
Rosewood Gr SM1 218 A6
Rosewood Ho 9 NW3 69 D2
Rosewood Sq W12 90 A1
Rosher Cl E15 76 B1
Roshni Ho SW17 180 C4
Rosina Ct SW17 180 C5
Rosina St E9 74 D2
Roskeen Ct 1 SW19 178 C3
Roskell Rd SW15 134 D2
Roskild Ct HA9 66 B4
Roslin Ho 2 E1 118 D6
Roslin Rd W3 110 D3
Roslin Way BR1 187 A5
Roslyn Cl CR4 180 B1
Roslyn Rd N15 51 C4
Rosmead Rd
W11 113 A6 244 B6
Rosoman Pl EC1 241 B6
Ross Ave NW7 29 A5
Dagenham RM8 59 B1
Ross Cl Harrow HA3 24 A3
Hayes UB3 105 B2
Ross Ct NW9 45 C6
4 SW15 156 D4
W13 87 B2
Chislehurst West BR7 188 B3
Croydon CR2 221 A2
Ross Ho 18 E1 118 B5
6 SE18 144 A4
Twickenham TW2 151 D2
Ross Par SM6 219 B2
Ross Rd SE25 205 C6
Twickenham TW2 152 A3
Wallington SM6 219 C3
Ross Way SE9 144 A2
Rossal Ct SE20 184 B3
Rossall Cres NW10 88 B4
Rossanne Ho N3 29 D3
Rossdale SM1 218 C3
Rossdale Dr N9 18 C5
NW9 45 A1
Rossdale Rd SW15 134 C1
Rosse Mews SE3 143 B4
Rossendale Ho 7 E5 74 B6
Rossendale St E5 74 B6
Rossendale Way
NW1 93 C6 232 B6
Rossendon Ct 1 SM6 219 C2
Rossetti Gdns Mans
SW3 267 C6
Rossetti Ho SW1 259 D3
Rossetti Mews NW8 229 D5
Rossetti Rd SE16 118 B1
Rossignol Gdns SM5 219 A6
Rossindel Rd TW3 151 C6
Rossington Cl EN1 6 B5
Rossington St E5 74 A5
Rossiter Fields EN5 13 B5
Rossiter Rd SW12 159 B3
Rossland Cl DA6 169 D6
Rosslyn Ave E4 20 D2
SW13 133 D2
Dagenham RM8 59 C2
East Barnet EN4 14 C5
Feltham TW14 150 A5
Rosslyn Cl Ashford TW16 171 C4
Coney Hall BR4 224 D5
Hayes UB3 83 B2
Rosslyn Cres Harrow HA1 42 D5
Wembley HA9 66 A4
Rosslyn Ct NW3 70 C3
Rosslyn Hill NW3 70 B3
Rosslyn Ho 8 TW9 132 B4
Rosslyn Mans NW6 70 A2
Rosslyn Park Mews NW3 70 B3
Rosslyn Rd E17 54 A5
Barking IG11 79 B1
Twickenham TW1 153 C5
Rossmore Ct NW1 237 C6
Rossmore Rd
NW1 92 C3 237 B6
Rossway Dr WD2 8 B6
Rosswood Gdns SM6 219 C2
Rosswood Lo CR0 222 D6
Rostella Rd SW17 180 B6
Rostrever Gdns UB3 105 C5
Rostrevor Ave N15 51 D3
Rostrevor Gdns UB2 107 A1
Rostrevor Mans SW6 264 C2
Rostrevor Rd
SW6 135 B4 264 C2
SW19 179 C5
Rotary St SE1 261 D6
Roth Wlk N7 72 B6
Rothay NW1 231 D2
Rothbury Gdns TW7 131 A5
Rothbury Rd E9 75 C1
Rothbury Wlk N17 34 A3
Rother Ho SE15 140 B1
Rotherfield Ct
N1 73 B1 235 C6
Rotherfield Prim Sch
N1 95 A6 235 B6
Rotherfield Rd Enfield EN3 6 D6
Wallington SM5 219 A3
Rotherfield St
N1 73 A1 235 B6
Rotherham Wlk SE1 251 C3
Rotherhill Ave SW16 181 D4
Rotherhithe SE16 119 B5
Rotherhithe Holiday Inn
(River Bus) SE16 119 B5
Rotherhithe New Rd
SE16 118 B1
Rotherhithe Old Rd
SE16 118 D2
Rotherhithe Prim Sch
SE16 118 D2
Rotherhithe St SE16 118 C4
10 SE16 118 B4
Rotherhithe Sta SE16 118 C4
Rotherhithe Tunnel
SE16 118 D5
Rothermere Rd CR0 220 B3
Rotherwick Hill W5 88 B3
Rotherwick Rd NW11 47 C2
Rotherwood Cl SW20 179 A2
Rotherwood Rd SW15 134 D2
Rothery St N1 234 D6
Rothesay Ave
SW14,TW10 132 D1
SW20 179 A1
Northolt UB6 64 B2
Rothesay Ct 4 SE6 164 D2
13 SE11 138 C6
SE12 165 B1
Rothesay Rd SE25 205 C5
Rothley Ct NW8 236 C6
Rothsay Rd E7 77 C2
Rothsay St SE1 117 C3 263 A5
Rothsay Wlk 16 E14 119 C2
Rothschild Rd W4 111 A3
Rothschild St SE27 182 D6
Rothwell Ct HA1 42 D4
Rothwell Gdns RM9 102 C6
Rothwell Ho TW5 129 C6
Rothwell Rd RM9 102 C6
Rothwell St NW1 230 D6
10 NW1 70 D1
Rotten Row
SW1 114 D4 247 C2
Rotterdam Dr E14 120 A3
Rotunda Mus SE18 122 B1
Rouel Rd SE16 118 A2
SE16 118 A3
Rougemont Ave SM4 201 C3
Round Gr CR0 206 D2
Round Hill SE23 162 C1
Roundabout Ho HA6 22 A2
Roundacre SW19 156 D2
Roundel Cl SE4 141 B1
Roundell Ho 14 SE21 183 C6
Rounders Ct 7 RM10 81 D2
Roundhay Cl SE23 162 D2
Roundhedge Way EN2 4 B5
Roundhill Dr EN2 4 B1
Roundshaw Ctr SM6 220 A1
Roundtable Rd BR1 164 D1
Roundtree Rd HA0 65 B3
Roundway The N17 33 B2
Roundway The *continued*
Claygate KT10 212 D2
Roundways HA4 61 D5
Roundwood BR7 188 C1
Roundwood Ave UB11 105 A5
Roundwood Cl HA4 39 B2
Roundwood Rd NW10 67 C1
Rounton Rd E3 97 C3
Roupell Ho 7 KT2 176 B3
Roupell Rd SW2 160 B3
Roupell St SE1 116 C5 251 B3
Rousden St NW1 71 C1
Rouse Gdns SE21 183 C6
Routemaster Cl E13 99 B4
Routh Ct TW14 149 B3
Routh Rd SW18 158 C4
Routh St E6 100 B2
Rover Ho 27 N1 95 C6
Rowallan Ct 3 SE6 164 D3
Rowallan Rd
SW6 135 A5 264 A3
Rowallen Par RM8 58 C1
Rowan N10 31 B1
Rowan Ave E4 35 B4
Rowan Cl SW16 181 C2
W5 110 A4
Harrow HA7 24 D4
Kingston u T KT3 177 C1
Wembley HA0 65 A5
Rowan Cres SW16 181 C2
Rowan Ct 18 SE15 139 D5
SE26 184 C6
SW11 158 D5
SW20 178 B1
11 Kingston u T KT2 176 C3
Rowan Dr NW9 46 A6
Rowan Gdns CR0 221 D5
Rowan High Sch SW16 181 C1
Rowan Ho 5 NW3 70 D2
NW10 89 C3
East Bedfont TW14 149 B5
Sidcup DA14 167 D1
Rowan Pl UB3 105 D6
Rowan Prep Sch
Claygate KT10 212 C1
Claygate KT10 212 D1
Rowan Rd SW16 181 C1
W6 112 D2
Bexleyheath DA7 147 A2
Brentford TW8 131 B5
West Drayton UB7 104 A2
Rowan Way RM6 58 C6
Rowan Wlk N2 48 A4
N19 71 C6
W10 91 A3
Keston Mark BR2 226 B5
1 New Barnet EN5 13 D6
Rowans The N13 17 A1
Ashford TW16 171 D5
Rowantree Cl N21 17 B3
Rowantree Rd N21 17 B3
Enfield EN2 4 D3
Rowanwood Ave DA15 168 A3
Rowben Cl N20 13 D3
Rowberry Cl SW6 134 C5
Rowcross St
SE1 117 D1 263 D2
Rowdell Rd UB5 85 C6
Rowden Par E4 35 C4
Rowden Park Gdns E4 35 C4
Rowden Rd E4 35 D4
Penge BR3 185 B2
West Ewell KT19 215 A4
Rowditch La SW11 137 A3
Rowdon Ave NW10 68 B1
Rowdowns Rd RM9 81 B1
Rowe Gdns IG11 102 A5
Rowe La E9 74 C3
Rowe Wlk HA2 63 C5
Rowena Cres SW11 136 C3
Rowfant Rd SW12,SW17 159 A2
Rowhill Mans 11 E5 74 B4
Rowhill Rd E5 74 B4
Rowington Cl W2 91 D2
Rowland Ave HA3 43 C6
Rowland Ct E16 98 D3
Rowland Gr SE26 162 B1
Rowland Hill Almshouses
TW15 170 C5
Rowland Hill Ave N17 33 B4
Rowland Hill Ho SE1 251 C2
Rowland Hill St NW3 70 C3
Rowland Way SW19 179 D2
Ashford TW15 171 B3
Rowlands Ave HA5 23 D4
Rowlands Cl N6 49 A3
NW7 28 A3
Rowlands Rd RM8 81 B6
Rowley Ave DA15 168 B4
Rowley Cl HA0 66 B1
Rowley Gdns N4 51 A2
Rowley Green Rd EN5 12 A6
Rowley Ho SE8 141 C6
Rowley Ind Pk W3 110 D3
Rowley La
Borehamwood EN5 11 D6
EN5 11 D6
Rowley Rd N15 51 A4
Rowley Way
NW8 92 A6 229 A6
NW8 92 A6 229 B6
Rowlheys Pl UB7 104 A3
Rowlls Rd KT1 198 B6
Rowney Gdns RM9 80 C2
Rowney Rd RM9 80 B2
Rowntree Cl NW6 69 C2
Rowntree Clifford Cl 7
E13 99 B4
Rowntree Path 1 SE28 124 B5
Rowntree Rd TW2 152 C3
Rowse Cl E15 98 A6
Rowsham Ct HA1 64 C5
Rowsley Ave NW4 46 C6
Rowstock 1 NW5 71 D2
Rowstock Gdns N7 71 D3
Rowton Rd SE18 145 A5
Roxborough Ave
Harrow HA1 42 C2
Hounslow TW7 130 D5
Roxborough Pk HA1 42 C2
Roxbourne Cl UB5 62 D2
Roxbourne Fst & Mid Schs
HA2 63 A6
Roxburgh Rd SE27 182 D5
Roxburn Way HA4 61 D5
Roxby Pl SW6 135 C6 265 B6
Roxeth Ct TW15 170 C5
Roxeth Fst & Mid Sch
HA2 64 B6
Roxeth Gr HA2 63 D4
Roxeth Green Ave HA2 63 D6
Roxeth Hill HA2 64 C6
Roxeth Manor Fst & Mid
Schs HA2 63 C5
Roxford Cl TW17 193 C4
Roxford Ho 2 E3 97 D3
Roxley Rd SE13 163 D5
Roxton Gdns CR0 223 C3
Roxwell 10 NW1 71 B2
Roxwell Rd W12 112 A4
Barking IG11 102 A5
Roxwell Trad Pk E10 53 A2
Roxwell Way IG8 37 C3
Roxy Ave RM6 58 C2
Roy Gdns IG2 57 D4
Roy Gr TW12 173 D4
Roy Ho N1 235 D5
Roy Ridley Ho 6 SW4 137 D2
Roy Sq E14 119 A6
Royal Acad of Arts★
W1 115 C6 249 A5
Royal Acad of Dancing The
SW11 266 D1
Royal Acad of Music
NW1 238 B5
Royal Albert Hall★
SW7 114 B4 246 C1
Royal Albert Sta E16 122 A6
Royal Albert Way E16 122 B6
Royal Arc W1 249 A5
Royal Army Medical Coll
SW1 116 A1 260 A2
Royal Ave SW3 114 D1 257 C2
Worcester Pk KT4 215 C6
Royal Avenue Ho SW3 257 C2
Royal Ballet Sch
W14 113 A1 254 A2
Royal Brompton & Nat Heart
Hospl The
SW3 114 C1 257 A2
Royal Cir SE27 160 D1
Royal Cl N16 51 C1
Hillingdon UB7 82 B1
Ilford IG3 58 A2
Worcester Pk KT4 215 C6
Royal Coll of Art
SW7 114 B3 256 D5
SW7 114 B4 246 C1
Royal Coll of Art Sculpture
Sch SW11 136 C5 267 A3
Royal Coll of Midwives
W1 93 B2 238 C3
Royal Coll of Music
SW7 114 B3 256 C6
Royal Coll of Obstetricians &
Gynaecologists
NW1 92 D3 237 C6
Royal Coll of Organists
SW7 114 B4 246 C1
Royal Coll of Physicians
NW1 93 B3 238 D6
Royal Coll of Science
SW7 114 B3 256 C6
Royal Coll of Surgeons
WC2 94 B1 240 D2
Royal College St
NW1 93 C6 232 B6
Royal Courts of Justice
WC2 94 C1 241 A1
Royal Cres W11 113 A5 244 A3
Ruislip HA4 63 A5
Royal Crescent Mews
W11 112 D5
Royal Ct SE9 166 B3
SE16 119 B3
Enfield EN1 17 C5
9 Kingston u T KT2 176 D3
Royal Docks Rd E6 100 D2
Royal Duchess Mews
SW12 159 B4
Royal Ear Hospl
WC1 93 D3 239 C5
Royal Exchange★ EC3 242 D1
Royal Exchange Ave
EC3 242 D1
Royal Exchange Bldgs
EC3 242 D1
Royal Festival Hall★
SE1 116 B5 250 D3
Royal Free Hospl NW3 70 C3
Royal Gdns W7 109 A3
Royal Geographical Society
SW7 114 B4 246 D1
Royal Hill SE10 142 A5
Royal Hospital (Army
Pensioners)
SW1 115 A1 258 A1
Royal Hospital Rd
SW3 114 D1 257 D1
Royal Hospl SW15 157 A5
Royal La Hillingdon UB7 82 B1
Hillingdon UB8 82 B3
Royal Langford 3 NW6 91 D5
Royal London Est N17 34 B4
Royal London Est The
NW10 89 B5
Royal London Homeopathic
Hospl The WC1 94 A2 240 B4
Royal London Hospl
(Whitechapel) The E1 96 B2
Royal Marsden Hospl
SW3 114 B1 256 D2
Royal Masonic Hospl
W6 112 A2
Royal Mews KT8 196 C6
Royal Mews The
SW1 115 B3 258 D6
Royal Military Sch of Music
(Kneller Hall) TW2 152 B5
Royal Mint Pl 5 E1 118 A6
Royal Mint St
E1 117 D6 253 D6
Royal Nat TN&E Hospl The
W5 87 C2
Royal National Orthopaedic
Hospl
W1 93 B3 238 D5
Stanmore HA7 9 C2
Royal National TNE Hospl
The WC1 94 B4 233 C2
Royal Naval Coll SE10 142 B6
Royal Naval Pl SE14 141 B5
Royal Oak Ct 9 N1 95 C4
Royal Oak Pl SE22 162 B5
Royal Oak Rd 5 E8 74 B2
Bexleyheath DA6 147 C1
Royal Oak Sta W2 91 D2
Royal Opera Arc SW1 249 C4
Royal Orchard Cl SW18 157 A4
Royal Par SE3 142 D3
SW6 264 A4
W5 88 A4
Chislehurst BR7 189 A3
11 RM10 81 D2
Royal Parade Mews
BR7 189 A3
Royal Park Prim Sch
DA14 169 A1
Royal Pl 11 SE10 142 A5
Royal Rd E16 99 D1
SE17 138 D6
Sidcup DA14 168 D1
Teddington TW11 174 B5
Royal Route HA9 66 B4
Royal Russell Sch (Ballards)
CR0 222 B3
Royal Sch The NW3 70 B4
Royal St SE1 116 B3 260 D6
Royal United Services Mus
SW1 250 A3
Royal Veterinary Coll
NW1 93 D6 232 C5
Royal Victor Pl E3 96 D5
Royal Victoria Pl E16 121 B5
Royal Victoria Sta E16 121 A6
Royal Wlk SM6 219 B5
Royalty Mews W1 239 C1
Royalty Studios W11 91 A1
Roycraft Ave IG11 101 D5
Roycroft Cl E18 37 B2
SW2 160 C3
Roydene Rd SE18 123 C1
Roydon Cl 7 SW11 136 D3
Royle Cres W13 87 A3
Roymount Ct TW2 152 C1
Royston Ave E4 35 D5
Carshalton SM1 218 B5
Wallington SM6 219 D4
Royston Cl Cranford TW5 128 B4
Walton-on-T KT12 194 A1
Royston Ct 1 E13 99 A6
Hinchley Wood KT10 212 D6
Redbridge IG1 55 D3
3 Richmond TW9 132 B4
Tolworth KT6 214 C6
Royston Gdns IG1 55 D3
Royston Gr HA5 23 C4
Royston Ho N11 31 A6
14 SE15 140 A6
Royston Par IG1 55 D3
Royston Park Rd HA5 23 C5
Royston Prim Sch SE20 184 D2
Royston Rd SE20 184 D2
Richmond TW10 154 A6
Royston St 25 E2 96 C5
Roystons The KT5 198 D4
Rozel Ct 3 N1 95 C6
Rozel Rd SW4 137 C2
Rubastic Rd UB2 106 C3
Rubens Rd UB5 84 D5
Rubens St SE6 163 B2
Ruby Rd E17 53 C6
Ruby St SE15 140 B6
Ruby Triangle SE15 140 B6
Ruckholt Cl E10 75 D5
Ruckholt Rd E10 75 D5
Ruckledge Ave NW10 90 A5
Rudall Cres NW3 70 B4
Rudbeck Ho 10 SE15 140 A5
Ruddington Cl E5 75 A4
Ruddock Cl HA8 27 A3
Ruddstreet Cl SE18 123 A2
Rudge Ho 1 SE16 118 A3
Rudgwick Terr
NW8 92 C6 230 B5
Rudhall Ho 4 SW2 160 C5
Rudland Rd DA7 147 D2
Rudloe Rd SW12 159 C4
Rudolf Pl SW8 270 B5
Rudolph Ct SE22 162 B4
Rudolph Rd E13 98 D5
NW6 91 C5
Rudstone Ho 10 E3 97 D4
Rudyard Ct SE1 252 D1
Rudyard Gr NW7 27 A4
Ruegg Ho 5 SE18 144 C6
Ruffetts Cl CR2 222 B1
Ruffetts The CR2 222 B1
Rufford Cl HA3 43 A3
Rufford St N1 94 A6 233 B6
Rufford Twr 5 W3 110 D5
Rufforth Ct 1 NW9 27 C2
Rufus Bsns Ctr SW18 157 D2
Rufus Cl HA4 63 A5
Rufus Ho SE1 263 D6
Rufus St N1 95 C4
Rugby Ave N9 17 D3
Northolt UB6 64 B2
Wembley HA0 65 C4
Rugby Cl HA1 42 C5
Rugby Gdns RM9 80 C2
Rugby Mans W14 254 B4
Rugby Rd NW9 44 D5
W4 111 C4
Dagenham RM9 80 C2
Twickenham TW1,TW2,
TW7 152 C5
Rugby St WC1 94 B3 240 C5
Rugg St E14 119 C6
Rugless Ho 2 E14 120 A4
Rugmere 4 NW1 71 A1
Ruislip Cl UB6 85 D3
Ruislip Ct HA4 61 D6
Ruislip Gardens Prim Sch
HA4 61 D4
Ruislip Gardens Sta HA4 62 A4
Ruislip Lido HA4,HA5 39 B5
Ruislip Lido Railway
HA4 39 B5
Ruislip Manor Sta HA4 40 A1
Ruislip Rd UB6,UB5 85 C4
Ruislip Rd E
Ealing UB6,W7 86 D3
Greenford UB6 86 B3
Ruislip St SW17 180 D6
Ruislip Sta HA4 39 D1
Rum Cl E1 118 C6
Rumball Ho 22 SE5 139 C5
Rumbold Rd
SW6 135 D5 265 D3
Rumford Ho SE1 262 A5
Rumsey Cl TW12 173 B4
Rumsey Rd SW9 138 B2
Runacres Ct SE17 262 A1
Runbury Circ NW9 67 B6
Runcorn Cl N17 52 B5
Runcorn Pl W11 244 A6
Rundell Cres NW4 46 B4
Rundell Twr SW8 270 C2
Runes Cl CR4 202 C5
Runnelfield HA1 64 C5
Running Horse Yd 12
TW8 132 A6
Runnymead Ho TW10 154 C6
Runnymede SW19 180 B2
Runnymede Cl TW2 151 D4
Runnymede Cres SW16 182 A2
Runnymede Ct 1 SM6 219 B2
Runnymede Gdns
Greenford UB6 86 C5
Twickenham TW2 151 D4
Runnymede Ho E9 75 A4
Runnymede Rd TW2 151 D5
Runway The HA4 62 C3
Rupack St 3 SE16 118 C4
Rupert Ave 6 HA9 66 A3
Rupert Ct W1 249 C6
Rupert Gdns SW9 138 D3
Rupert Ho SE11 261 B3
Rupert Rd N19 71 D6
NW6 91 B5
W4 111 C3
Rupert St W1 115 D6 249 C6
Rural Way SW16 181 B3
Ruscoe Ho 12 SW27 182 D5
Ruscoe Rd E16 98 D1
Ruscombe Way TW14 149 D4
Rush Croft Sch E4 35 D3
Rush Green Rd RM7,RM8,
RM10 59 D1
Rush Hill Mews 3
SW11 137 A2
Rush Hill Rd SW11 137 A2
Rusham Rd SW12 158 D4
Rushbrook Cres E17 35 B2
Rushbrook Ho 20 SW8 137 D3
Rushbrook Rd SE9 167 A2
Rushbury Ct 4 TW12 173 C2
Rushby Ct SW4 270 A1
Rushcroft Rd E4 35 D3
SW2,SW9 138 C1
Rushcutters Ct 18 SE16 119 A2
Rushden Cl SE19 183 B3
Rushden Gdns NW7 28 C4
Ilford IG5 56 C6
Rushdene SE2 124 D3
Rushdene Ave EN4 14 C4
Rushdene Cl UB5 84 C5
Rushdene Cres UB5 84 C4

Rushdene Rd HA5 40 D3
Rushen Wlk SM5 202 B1
Rushet Rd BR5 190 A1
Rushett Cl KT7 197 B1
Rushett Rd KT7 197 B2
Rushey Cl KT3 199 B5
Rushey Gn SE6 163 D4
Rushey Green Prim Sch SE6 163 D3
Rushey Hill EN2 4 B1
Rushey Mead SE4 163 C6
Rushford Rd SE4 163 B5
Rushgrove Ave NW9 45 D5
Rushgrove Ct NW9 45 C4
Rushgrove St SE18 122 B2
Rushlake Ho 3 SW11 137 A3
Rushley Cl BR2 226 A4
Rushman Villas KT3 199 D5
Rushmead 5 E2 96 B4
Richmond TW10 153 B1
Rushmead Cl CR0 221 D4
Rushmere Ct KT4 216 A6
Rushmere Ho 2 SW15 156 A3
Rushmere Pl SW19 178 D5
Rushmon Pl SM3 217 A2
Rushmoor Cl HA5 40 B5
Rushmore Cl BR1 210 A6
Rushmore Cres 9 E5 74 D4
Rushmore Ho 9 N7 71 D3
Rushmore JMI Sch E5 74 D4
Rushmore Rd E5 74 D4
E5 75 A4
Rusholme Ave RM10 81 C5
Rusholme Gr SE19 183 C5
Rusholme Rd SW15 157 A5
Rushout Ave HA3 43 B3
Rushton Ho 26 SW8 137 D3
Rushton St N1 95 B5 235 D4
Rushworth St SE1 116 D4 251 D1
Rushy Meadow La SM5 218 C5
Rushy Meadow Prim Sch SM5 218 C5
Ruskin Ave E12 78 A2
Bexley DA16 146 A3
Feltham TW14 149 D5
Richmond TW9 132 C5
Ruskin Cl NW11 47 D3
Ruskin Ct N21 16 B4
SE5 139 B2
SE9 166 B5
Ruskin Dr Bexley DA16 146 A2
North Cheam KT4 216 C6
Orpington BR6 227 C5
Ruskin Gdns W5 87 D3
Harrow HA3 44 B5
Ruskin Gr DA16 146 A3
Ruskin Ho SW1 259 D3
Ruskin Par CR0 221 B3
Ruskin Park Ho SE5 139 B2
Ruskin Rd N17 33 D2
Belvedere DA17 125 C2
Croydon CR0 220 D6
Isleworth TW7 130 D2
Southall UB1 107 A6
Wallington SM5 219 A3
Ruskin Way SW19 180 B2
Ruskin Wlk N9 18 A2
SE24 161 A6
Bromley BR2 210 B3
Rusland Ave BR6 227 B5
Rusland Hts HA1 42 C5
Rusland Park Rd HA1 42 C5
Rusper Cl NW2 68 C5
Stanmore HA7 25 C6
Rusper Ct SW9 138 A3
Rusper Rd N17,N22 51 A6
Dagenham RM9 80 C2
Russel Cl BR3 208 A6
Russel Ct N14 15 D6
Russell Ave N22 32 D1
Russell Cl NW10 67 A1
SE7 143 C5
W4 133 D6
Bexleyheath DA7 147 C1
Ruislip HA4 62 C6
Russell Ct 4 E10 53 D2
5 SE15 140 B3
SW1 249 B3
SW11 268 B1
SW16 182 B5
Bromley BR1 186 D3
New Barnet EN5 2 A1
Surbiton KT6 198 A2
Wallington SM6 219 C3
Wembley HA0 66 A1
Russell Gdns N20 14 C2
NW11 47 A3
W14 113 A3 254 A6
Ilford IG2 57 B2
Richmond TW10 153 C2
West Drayton UB7 104 C1
Russell Gdns Mews W14 113 A3 254 A6
Russell Gr NW7 27 C6
33 SW9 138 C4
Russell Ho 15 E14 97 C1
SW1 259 A2
Russell Kerr Cl W4 133 A5
Russell La N20 14 D2
Russell Lo 5 E4 20 A2
Russell Par NW11 47 A3
Russell Pickering Ho 2 SW4 138 A2
Russell Pl NW3 70 C3
SE16 119 A3
Russell Prim Sch The TW10 153 D3
Russell Rd E4 35 B6
E10 53 D3
E16 99 B1
E17 53 B6
N8 49 D3
N13 32 B4
N15 51 C4
N20 14 C2
NW9 45 D3
SW19 179 C3
W14 113 A3 254 B5
Buckhurst Hill IG9 21 C3
Enfield EN1 5 D5
Lower Halliford TW17 193 A2
Mitcham CR4 202 C6
Northolt UB5 64 A3
Twickenham TW1,TW2 152 D5
Walton-on-T KT12 194 A3
Russell Sch The TW10 153 D2
Russell Sq WC1 94 A3 240 A5
Russell Square Sta WC1 94 A3 240 A5
Russell St WC2 116 A6 250 B6
Russell Way SM1 217 D3
Russell Wlk 4 TW10 154 B5
Russet Ave TW16,TW17 193 C6
Russet Cl UB10 83 A3
Russet Cres N7 72 B3
Russet Ct NW2 68 B5
6 Barnet EN4 2 C1
Russet Dr CR0 207 A1
Russet Ho TW3 129 B1
Russet House Sch EN1 6 B4
Russet Way SE13 141 D3
Russets Cl E4 36 B6
Russia Ct EC2 242 B2
Russia Dock Rd SE16 119 A5
Russia La E2 96 C5
Russia Row EC2 242 B1
Russian Submarine SE18 121 D3
Russington Rd TW17 193 B3
Rust Sq SE5 139 B5
Rusthall Ave W4 111 B3
Rusthall Cl CR0 206 C3
Rusthall Mans W4 111 B2
Rustic Ave SW16 181 B3
Rustic Pl HA0 65 D4
Rustic Wlk E16 99 B1
Rustington Wlk SM4 201 B2
Ruston Ave KT5 198 D2
Ruston Gdns N14 15 A5
Ruston Mews W11 91 A1
Ruston Rd SE18 122 A3
Ruston St E3 97 B6
Rutford Rd SW16 182 A5
Ruth Cl HA7 44 B5
Ruth Ct 14 E3 97 A5
Ruth Ho W10 91 A3
Rutherford Cl SM2 218 B2
Rutherford Ho 12 E1 96 B3
Teddington TW11 174 D5
7 Wembley HA9 67 A5
Rutherford St SW1 115 D2 259 C4
Rutherford Twr 10 UB1 85 D1
Rutherford Way Bushey WD2 8 C3
Wembley HA9 66 C4
Rutherglen Rd SE2 146 A6
Rutherwyke Cl KT17 216 A2
Ruthin Cl NW9 45 C3
Ruthin Rd SE3 143 A6
Ruthven St E9 96 D6
Rutland Ave DA15 168 A4
Rutland Cl SW14 133 A2
SW19 180 C3
Sidcup DA5 168 D3
Rutland Ct SE5 139 B1
SW7 247 B1
15 W3 88 C1
Chislehurst BR7 188 C2
Enfield EN3 18 B6
Sidcup BR7 167 A2
Rutland Dr Morden SM4 201 C2
Richmond TW10 154 A3
Rutland Gate SW7 114 C4 247 B1
Belvedere DA17 125 D1
Hayes BR2 208 D5
Rutland Gate Mews SW7 247 A1
Rutland Gdns N4 51 A3
SW7 114 C4 247 B1
W13 87 A2
Dagenham RM8 80 C3
South Croydon CR0 221 C4
Rutland Gdns Mews SW7 247 B1
Rutland Gr W6 112 B1
Rutland Ho 18 SE18 122 B2
2 SE20 184 C2
10 SW15 156 C4
W8 255 C5
6 Northolt UB5 63 C2
Tolworth KT6 198 C1
Rutland Lo SE6 163 B2
Rutland Mews E SW7 257 B6
Rutland Mews S SW7 257 A6
Rutland Mews W SW7 257 A6
Rutland Park Gdns NW2 68 C2
Rutland Park Mans NW2 68 C2
Rutland Pk NW2 68 C2
SE6 163 B2
Rutland Pl EC1 241 D4
Bushey WD2 8 B3
Rutland Rd E7 77 D1
E9 96 D6
Rutland Rd *continued*
E11 55 B4
E17 53 C3
SW19 180 C3
Harrow HA1 42 A3
Hayes UB3 105 B2
Ilford IG1 78 D5
Southall UB1 85 C2
Twickenham TW2 152 B2
Rutland St SW7 257 B6
Rutland Studios NW10 90 A4
Rutland Wlk SE6 163 B2
Rutley Cl SE11 138 D6
Rutlish Rd SW19 179 C2
Rutlish Sch (Boys) SW20 179 B1
Rutter Gdns CR4 202 B5
Rutters Cl UB7 104 C4
Rutt's Terr SE14 140 D4
Rutts The WD2 8 B3
Ruvigny Gdns SW15 134 D2
Ruvigny Mans SW15 134 D2
Ruxbury Ct TW15 148 A1
Ruxley Cl Ruxley DA14 191 A4
West Ewell KT19 214 D3
Ruxley Cnr DA14 191 A4
Ruxley Corner Ind Est DA14 190 D4
Ruxley Cres KT10 213 B1
Ruxley Ct KT19 215 A3
Ruxley La KT19 215 B3
Ruxley Manor Prim Sch SE9 188 C6
Ruxley Mews KT19 214 D3
Ruxley Ridge KT10 213 A1
Ryall's Ct N20 14 D1
Ryan Cl SE9 143 C1
Ruislip HA4 40 B1
Ryan Ct SW16 182 A3
Ryan Dr TW8 131 A6
Ryarsh Cres BR6 227 C4
Rycott Path SE22 162 A4
Rycroft Way N17 51 D6
Ryculff Sq SE3 142 D3
Rydal Cl NW4 29 A2
Rydal Cres UB6 87 C5
Rydal Ct Edgware HA8 26 B5
Wembley HA9 44 A2
Rydal Dr Erith DA7 147 C4
West Wickham BR4 224 C6
Rydal Gdns NW9 45 C4
SW15 177 C5
Twickenham TW2,TW3 151 D5
Wembley HA9 43 C1
Rydal Ho 25 SW8 137 D3
Rydal Lo N17 34 A3
Rydal Rd SW16 181 D6
Rydal Water NW1 232 A1
Rydal Way Enfield EN3 18 C5
Ruislip HA4 62 C4
Ryde Ho 1 NW6 91 C6
Ryde Pl TW1 153 D5
Ryde Vale Rd SW12 159 C2
Ryders Ho SE9 165 C1
Ryders Rd KT12 194 D1
Ryder Cl BR1 187 B5
Ryder Ct E10 75 D6
SW1 249 B4
Ryder Dr SE16 118 B1
Ryder Ho 14 E1 96 C3
5 SW19 179 D2
Ryder St SW1 249 B4
Ryder Yd SW1 249 B4
Ryder's Terr NW8 92 A5 229 A4
Rydon Mews SW19 178 C3
Rydon St N1 235 B6
Rydons Cl SE9 144 A2
Rydston Cl 2 N7 72 B1
Rye Cl DA5 169 D5
Rye Ct BR3 185 B2
Rye Hill Pk SE15 140 C1
Rye Ho 10 SE16 118 C4
Rye La SE15 140 A3
Rye Rd SE15 140 D1
Rye The N14 15 C4
Rye Way HA8 26 B4
Rye Wlk SW15 156 D6
Ryecotes Mead SE21 161 C3
Ryecroft Ave TW2 151 D3
Ryecroft Cres EN5 12 B6
Ryecroft Rd SE13 164 A6
SW16 182 C4
Orpington BR5 211 B3
Ryecroft St SW6 135 D4 265 C1
Ryedale SE22 162 B5
Ryedale Ct 6 TW12 173 C2
Ryefield Ave UB10 60 D1
Ryefield Cres HA5,HA6 22 A1
Ryefield Ct HA6 22 A1
Ryefield Path 7 SW15 156 A3
Ryefield Prim Sch UB10 83 B6
Ryefield Rd SE19 183 A4
Ryegates 2 SE15 140 B3
Ryehill Ct KT3 199 D2
Ryeland Cl UB7 82 A1
Ryelands Cres SE12 165 C5
Ryelands Inf Sch SE25 206 B4
Ryfold Rd SW19 157 C1
Ryhope Rd N11 31 B6
Ryland Cl TW13 171 D6
Ryland Ct EN2 5 B1
Ryland Ho 11 SW16 181 C5
Ryland Rd NW5 71 B2
Rylandes Rd NW2 68 A5
Rylett Cres W12 111 D3
Rylett Rd W12 111 D3
Rylston Rd N13 17 B1
SW6 135 B6 264 C5
Rylton Ho KT12 194 A1
Rymer Rd CR0 205 C2
Rymer St SE24 160 D5
Rymill St E16 122 C5
Rysbrack St SW1 257 C6
Rythe Ct KT7 197 A2
Rythe Ho 7 BR1 186 B5
Rythe Rd KT10 212 C3

S

Sabah Ct TW15 170 C6
Sabella Ct E3 97 B5
Sabine Rd SW11 137 A2
Sable Cl TW4 128 C2
Sable Ct 3 KT3 199 C4
Sable St N1 72 D1
Sach Rd E5 74 B6
Sacketts Ho 24 SW9 138 C4
Sackville Ave BR2 209 A1
Sackville Cl HA2 64 B5
Sackville Gdns IG1 56 B1
Sackville Ho N8 50 A5
16 SW16 160 A1
Sackville Rd SM2 217 C1
Sackville St W1 115 C6 249 B5
Sacred Heart Catholic Prim Sch KT3 200 A5
Sacred Heart High Sch W6 112 C2
Harrow HA3 24 C1
Sacred Heart Jun Sch W6 112 D2
Sacred Heart Prim Sch SW15 156 A6
Sacred Heart RC Jun & Inf Schs SW11 136 C3
Sacred Heart RC Prim Sch N20 14 C2
Ruislip HA4 61 C6
Teddington TW11 175 B3
Sacred Heart RC Sch The SE5 139 A4
Saddlebrook Pk TW16 171 C3
Saddlers Cl Arkley EN5 12 B6
Borehamwood WD6 11 B5
Hatch End HA5 23 C5
Saddlers Mews SW8 270 B2
Teddington KT1 175 C2
Wembley HA0 64 D4
Saddlers Path WD6 11 B6
Saddlescombe Way N12 29 C5
Sadler Cl CR4 180 D1
Sadler Ho 17 E3 97 D4
EC1 234 C2
Sadlers Ride KT8 174 A1
Saffron Ave E14 120 B6
Saffron Cl NW11 47 B3
Croydon CR0 204 A3
Saffron Ct E15 76 C3
10 N1 73 B2
Saffron Hill EC1 94 C2 241 B4
Saffron St EC1 241 B4
Saffron Way KT6 197 D1
Saffron Wharf SE1 253 D2
Sage Cl 7 E6 100 B2
Sage St E1 118 C6
Sage Way WC1 233 C1
Sage Yd KT6 198 B1
Sahara Ct UB1 107 A6
Saigasso Cl E16 99 D1
Sail St SE11 116 C3 260 D4
Sailmakers Ct SW6 136 A2
Saimet 3 NW9 27 D2
Sainfoin Rd SW17 159 A2
Sainsbury Rd SE19 183 C5
St Agatha's Dr KT2 176 B4
St Agatha's Gr SM5 202 D1
St Agatha's RC Prim Sch KT2 176 B4
St Agatha's RC Sch KT2 176 B3
St Agnes Cl E9 96 C6
St Agnes Pl SE11 138 D6
St Agnes' RC JMI Sch E3 97 D4
St Agnes RC Prim Sch NW2 69 A5
St Aidans Ct IG11 102 B5
St Aidan's Prim Sch N4 50 C2
St Aidan's RC Prim Sch IG1 57 B1
St Aidan's Rd SE22 162 B6
W13 109 B4
St Albans Ave W4 111 B3
Feltham TW13 172 D5
St Alban's Ave E6 100 C4
St Alban's CE Prim Sch EC1 94 C2 241 A4
St Alban's Cl NW11 47 C1
St Albans Cres N22 32 C2
St Alban's Cres IG8 37 A2
St Alban's Gdns TW11 175 A5
St Alban's Gr W8 113 D3 255 D6
Carshalton SM5 202 C2
St Albans Ho 2 SW16 182 C6
St Albans La NW11 47 C1
St Albans Mans W8 255 D6
St Alban's Pl N1 94 D6 234 C5
St Alban's RC Prim Sch SE15 139 D4
East Molesey KT8 196 A4
St Albans Rd Cheam SM1 217 B4
Ilford IG3 57 D2
St Albans Rd *continued*
Kingston u T KT2 176 A4
Monken Hadley EN5 1 A3
St Alban's Rd NW5 71 B5
NW10 89 C6
Woodford IG8 37 A3
St Alban's St SW1 249 C5
St Albans Studios W8 255 D6
St Albans Terr W6 264 A6
St Alban's Villas NW5 71 A5
St Alfege Pas SE10 142 A6
St Alfege Rd SE7 143 D6
St Alfege with St Peter's CE Prim Sch SE10 142 A6
St Aloysius' RC Coll N6 49 C1
St Aloysius' RC Jun & Inf Sch NW1 232 C2
St Alphage Ct NW9 45 B6
St Alphage Gdn EC2 242 B3
St Alphage Highwalk EC2 242 B3
St Alphage Wlk HA8 27 A1
St Alphege Rd N9 18 C4
St Alphonsus Rd SW4 137 D1
St Amunds Cl SE6 185 C6
St Andrew & St Francis CE Prim Sch NW2 68 A2
St Andrew St EC4 241 B3
St Andrew's & St Mark's Sch KT6 197 D4
St Andrews Ave HA0 65 A4
St Andrew's CE Prim Sch N1 94 B6 233 D6
N14 15 D3
SW9 138 A3
Enfield EN1 5 C3
St Andrew's CE Sch N20 13 B2
St Andrews Cl 25 SE16 118 B1
Ruislip HA4 62 D6
Stanmore HA7 25 C1
St Andrew's Cl N12 30 A6
NW2 68 B5
2 Hounslow TW7 130 C4
Upper Halliford TW17 193 B5
St Andrews Ct W4 133 A4
St Andrew's Ct E17 35 A1
SW18 158 A2
New Malden KT3 199 D6
St Andrews Dr HA7 25 C2
St Andrew's Gr N16 51 B1
St Andrew's Greek Sch NW1 71 C2
St Andrew's High Sch CR0 220 D4
St Andrew's Hill EC4 94 D1 241 D1
St Andrew's Hospl E3 97 D3
St Andrew's Mans W1 238 A3
St Andrews Mews SE3 143 A5
St Andrew's Mews N16 51 C1
St Andrew's Pl NW1 238 D6
St Andrews RC Prim Sch SW16 182 A5
St Andrews Rd E17 35 A1
N9 18 C4
NW9 45 B1
Carshalton SM5 218 C5
Sidcup DA14 168 D1
St Andrew's Rd E11 54 C3
E13 99 B4
NW2 68 B2
NW11 47 B3
W3 89 C1
W7 108 C4
W14 264 B6
3 Croydon CR0 221 A4
Enfield EN1 5 B2
Hillingdon UB10 82 B6
Kingston u T KT6 197 D3
Redbridge IG1 56 B2
St Andrew's Sq W11 91 A1
Kingston u T KT6 197 D3
St Andrews Terr WD1 22 C5
St Andrew's Twr UB1 108 A6
St Andrews Way E3 97 D3
St Andrew's Wharf SE1 253 D2
St Angela's RC Sch E7 77 B2
St Anna Rd EN5 12 D6
St Anne St E14 97 B1
St Annes Catholic High Sch for Girls (Upper) N13 32 C6
St Anne's CE Prim Sch SW18 157 D6
St Annes Cl WD1 22 C6
St Anne's Cl N6 71 A5
St Anne's Ct NW6 91 A6
W1 239 C1
St Anne's Flats NW1 232 C2
St Annes Gdns NW10 88 B4
St Anne's Pas E14 97 B1
St Anne's Prim Sch TW19 148 A4
St Anne's RC High Sch for Girls EN2 5 B1
St Anne's RC JMI Sch E1 96 A3
St Anne's RC Prim Sch SE11 138 B6 270 C6
St Anne's Rd E11 76 B6
Wembley HA0 65 D3
St Anne's Row E14 97 B1
St Anne's Trad Est E14 97 B1
St Ann's IG11 101 A6
St Ann's CE Prim Sch N15 51 B4
St Ann's Cres SW18 158 A5
St Ann's Ct NW4 46 B6
St Ann's Ctr HA1 42 C3
St Ann's Gdns NW5 71 A2
St Ann's General Hospl N4,N15 51 A4
St Ann's Hill SW18 158 A5
St Ann's Ho WC1 234 A1
St Ann's La SW1 259 D5
St Ann's Park Rd SW18 158 A5
St Anns Rd SW13 133 D4
St Ann's Rd N9 17 D3
N15 51 B4
W11 112 D6
2 Barking IG11 101 A6
Harrow HA1 42 C3
St Ann's Sch W7 108 C5
Morden SM4 201 D4
St Ann's St SW1 115 D3 259 D6
St Ann's Terr NW8 92 B5 229 D4
St Ann's Villas W11 112 D5 244 A3
St Ann's Way CR2 220 D2
St Anselm's Ct SW16 182 A5
St Anselm's Pl W1 248 C6
St Anselm's RC Fst & Mid Sch HA1 42 C2
St Anselm's RC Prim Sch SW17 159 A1
Southall UB2 107 B3
St Anselms Rd UB3 105 D4
St Anthony's Ave IG8 37 C3
St Anthonys Cl SW17 158 C2
St Anthony's Cl 8 E1 118 A5
St Anthony's Ct 2 SW12 159 A5
SW17 159 A2
Orpington BR6 226 D6
St Anthony's Flats NW1 232 C3
St Anthony's Hospl KT4 200 D1
St Anthony's RC Prim Sch SE22 162 A5
St Anthony's RC Prim Schs E7 77 B1
St Anthony's Way TW14 127 D1
St Antony's RC Prim Sch SE20 184 B2
St Antony's RC Sch NW7 27 B5
Woodford IG8 37 A6
St Antony's Rd E7 77 B1
St Arvans Cl CR0 221 C5
St Asaph Ct SE4 140 D2
St Asaph Rd SE4 140 D2
St Aubins Ct N1 235 D6
St Aubyns E18 54 D5
St Aubyn's Ave SW19 179 B5
Hounslow TW3,TW4 151 C6
St Aubyns Cl BR6 227 D5
St Aubyn's Ct SW19 179 A4
St Aubyns Gdns BR6 227 D6
St Aubyn's Prep Sch IG8 36 D3
St Aubyn's Rd SE19 183 D4
St Audrey Ave DA7 147 C3
St Augustine's Ave W5 88 A4
Bromley BR1,BR2 210 A4
South Croydon CR2 221 A1
Wembley HA9 66 A5
St Augustine's CE Prim & Sec Schs NW6 91 C5
St Augustines Ct BR3 185 A1
St Augustine's Ct E11 54 D1
St Augustine's Prim Sch DA17 125 B2
St Augustine's RC Prim Sch W6 135 A6 264 B5
Ilford IG2 56 D4
St Augustine's Rd NW1 71 D1
Erith DA17 125 B2
St Augustines's RC Prim Sch SE6 186 A5
St Austell Cl HA8 26 B1
St Austell Rd SE13 142 B3
St Awdry's Rd IG11 79 B1
St Barnabas & St Philip CE Prim Sch W8 113 C3 255 A5
St Barnabas CE Prim Sch SW1 115 A1 258 B2
St Barnabas Cl BR3 186 A1
St Barnabas Ct HA3 24 A2
St Barnabas' Gdns KT8 195 C4
St Barnabas Rd E17 53 C3
Mitcham CR4 181 A3
Sutton SM1 218 B3
Woodford IG8 37 C3
St Barnabas St SW1 258 B2
St Barnabas Terr E9 74 D3
St Barnabas Villas SW8 138 A4 270 B2
St Bartholomew's Cl SE26 184 C6
St Bartholomew's Hospl EC1 94 D2 241 D3
St Bartholomew's Prim Sch SE26 184 C6
St Bartholomew's Rd E6 100 B5
St Bede's RC Inf Sch SW12 159 D3
St Bede's RC Prim Sch RM6 58 C4
St Benedict's Cl SW17 181 A5
St Benedict's Sch W5 87 D2
St Benets Cl SW17 158 C2
St Benet's Gr SM5 202 A2
St Benet's Pl EC3 252 D6
St Bernadette RC Jun Mix Sch SW12 159 C4

St Bernadette's RC Fst & Mid Sch HA3 ....44 B5
St Bernadette's RC Prim Sch UB10 ....82 D6
St Bernard Ho 6 E14 ..120 A3
St Bernards CR0 ......221 C5
St Bernards Cl 8 SE27 183 B6
St Bernards Ho 1 KT6 214 A6
St Bernard's Rd E6 ....99 D6
St Blaise Ave BR1 ....187 B1
St Bonaventure's RC Sec Sch E7 ....77 A1
St Boniface Catholic Prim Sch SW17 ....180 D5
St Botolph St E1, EC3 ....95 D1 243 C2
St Brelades Ct N1 ....235 D6
St Briavel's Ct 4 SE15 .139 C5
St Bride St EC4 .94 D1 241 C2
St Bride's Ave EC4 ....241 C1
Edgware HA8 ....26 B2
St Brides Cl DA18 ....124 D4
St Bride's Pas EC4 ....241 C1
St Catherines Cl SW17 .158 C2
St Catherine's Convent Girls Prep & Senior Schs TW1 ....153 A2
St Catherines Ct TW13 .150 A3
St Catherine's Ct 8 W4 ....111 C3
St Catherine's Dr SE14 .140 D3
St Catherines Farm Ct HA4 ....39 A3
St Catherines Mews SW3 ....257 C4
St Catherine's RC Mid Sch SW20 ....200 C4
St Catherine's RC Prim Sch EN5 ....1 C1
St Catherine's RC Sch for Girls DA6 ....169 D6
St Catherines Rd E4 ....19 C2
Ruislip HA4 ....39 B3
St Cecilia's RC Prim Sch SM3 ....216 D6
St Chads Cl KT6 ....197 C2
St Chad's Gdns RM6 ....59 A2
St Chad's Pl WC1 ....233 C2
St Chad's RC Prim Sch SE25 ....205 C4
St Chad's Rd RM6 ....59 A2
St Chad's St WC1 ....233 B2
St Charles' Hospl W10 ..90 D2
St Charles Pl W10 ....91 A2
St Charles RC Prim Sch W10 ....90 D2
St Charles RC Sixth Form Coll W10 ....90 D2
St Charles Sq W10 ....90 D2
St Christina's RC Sch NW8 ....92 C5 230 B4
St Christopher's Cl TW7 ....130 C4
St Christophers Dr UB3 106 B6
St Christophers Gdns CR7 ....204 C6
St Christopher's Ho NW1 ....232 C3
St Christopher's Hospice SE26 ....184 C5
St Christopher's Mews SM6 ....219 C3
St Christopher's Pl W1 238 B2
St Christopher's Sch NW3 ....70 B3
Beckenham BR3 ....186 A1
St Clair Dr KT4 ....216 B4
St Clair Ho 14 E3 ....97 B4
St Clair Rd E13 ....99 B5
St Clair's Rd CR0 ....221 C6
St Clare Bsns Pk TW12 174 A4
St Clare St EC3 ....243 C1
St Clement Danes CE Prim Sch WC2 ....94 B1 240 C1
St Clements & St James CE Prim Sch W11 113 A5 244 A4
St Clements Ct N7 ....72 B2
7 SE14 ....140 D6
8 W11 ....112 D6
St Clement's Ct EC3 ....252 D6
St Clements Ho KT12 ..194 A2
St Clement's Hts SE26 .184 A6
St Clement's La WC2 ..240 D1
St Clements Mans 3 SW6 ....134 D6
St Clements St N7 ....72 C1
St Cloud Rd SE27 ....183 B6
St Columba's Ct E15 ....76 C4
St Columbas Ho 2 E17 .53 D5
St Columba's RC Sch for Boys DA6 ....169 D6
St Columb's Ho 11 W10 ..91 A2
St Crispins Cl NW3 ....70 C4
St Crispin's Cl UB1 ....85 B1
St Cross St EC1 ..94 C2 241 B4
St Cuthbert with St Matthias Prim Sch SW5 113 D1 255 C2
St Cuthberts Gdns 1 HA5 ....23 B3
St Cuthberts Rd N13 ...32 C4
St Cuthbert's Rd NW2 ..69 B2
St Cyprian's St SW17 ..180 D6
St Davids Cl 27 SE16 ...118 B1
Wembley HA9 ....67 A5
St David's Cl BR4 ....207 D2
St David's Coll BR4 ....207 D2
St Davids Ct 5 E11 ....55 B4
St David's Ct 1 E17 ....54 A6
8 Southall UB1 ....86 A1
St David's Dr HA8 ....26 B2
St David's Jun Sch TW15 ....148 B1
St David's Pl NW4 ....46 B2
St David's Sq E14 ....119 D1
St Denis Rd SE27 ....183 B6
St Dionis Rd SW6 ....135 B3
St Domingo Ho SE18 ..122 B3
St Dominic's RC JMI Schs E9 ....75 A2
St Dominic's RC Prim Sch NW5 ....70 D3
St Dominic's Sixth Form Coll (RC) HA1 ....64 C6
St Donatt's Rd SE14 ....141 B4
St Dunstans SM1 ....217 B2
St Dunstan's Alley EC3 .253 A5
St Dunstan's Ave W3 ..111 B6
St Dunstan's CE Prim Sch SM3 ....217 A1
St Dunstans Cl UB3 ....105 D2
St Dunstan's Coll SE6 ..163 C3
St Dunstan's Ct EC4 ....241 B1
St Dunstan's Gdns W3 .111 B6
St Dunstan's Hill EC3 ..253 A5
Cheam SM1,SM3 ....217 A3
St Dunstan's La EC3 ....253 A5
Beckenham BR3 ....208 A4
St Dunstans Rd E7 ....77 C2
St Dunstan's Rd SE25 ..205 D5
W6 ....112 D1
W7 ....108 C4
Cranford TW5 ....128 B3
Feltham TW13 ....149 D1
St Edmunds Ave HA4 ...39 B3
St Edmund's Catholic Prim Sch TW2 ....151 D4
St Edmunds Cl SW17 ..158 C2
Erith DA18 ....124 D4
St Edmund's Cl NW8 ...230 C5
St Edmund's Ct NW8 ....230 C5
St Edmunds Dr HA7 ....25 A2
St Edmund's La TW2 ..151 D4
St Edmund's RC JMI Sch E14 ....119 C2
St Edmund's RC Prim Sch N9 ....18 B3
St Edmunds Rd N9 ....18 A4
St Edmund's Rd IG1 ....56 B3
St Edmund's Terr NW8 ....92 D6 230 C5
St Edward's CE Comp Sch RM7 ....59 C3
St Edward's Cl NW11 ...47 C3
St Edward's Coll N20 ...12 B3
St Edward's Ct NW11 ....47 C3
St Edwards Ct 3 E10 ...54 A2
St Edward's RC Prim Sch E6 ....99 D5
NW1 ....92 C3 237 B5
St Egberts Way E4 ....20 A3
St Elizabeth Ct 8 E10 ...53 D2
N12 ....30 A6
St Elizabeth's RC Prim Sch TW10 ....154 B5
St Elmo Rd W12 ....111 D4
St Elmos Rd SE16 ....119 A4
St Elphege's RC Prim Sch SM6 ....220 A2
St Erkenwald Mews IG11 ....101 B6
St Erkenwald Rd IG11 .101 B6
St Ermin's Hill SW1 ....259 C6
St Ervan's Rd W10 ....91 B2
St Eugene of Mazenod RC Prim Sch NW6 ....91 C6
St Faith's CE Prim Sch SW18 ....158 A6
St Faith's Cl EN2 ....5 A4
St Faith's Rd SE24 ....160 D3
St Fillans Rd SE6 ....164 A4
St Francesca Cabrini Prim Sch SE23 ....162 C5
St Francis Cl BR6 ....211 C3
St Francis de Sales RC Prim Sch N17 ....33 D3
St Francis' Ho NW1 ....232 C3
St Francis Lo HA0 ....64 D5
St Francis RC Jun & Inf Sch SE15 ....140 A5
St Francis RC Jun & Inf Schs E15 ....76 C3
St Francis RC Prim Sch W11 ....112 D6
St Francis Rd SE22 ....139 C1
St Francis Way IG1 ....79 B4
St Francis Xavier Sixth Form Coll SW12 ....159 B5
St Gables Ct N11 ....31 D3
St Gabriel's CE Prim Sch SW1 ....115 C1 259 A1
St Gabriel's Cl E11 ....55 B1
St Gabriel's Rd NW2 ....68 D3
St George Ho SW11 ....268 B1
St George St W1 ....115 B6 248 D6
St George the Martyr CE Prim Sch WC1 .94 B3 240 D5
St George's Ave E7 ....77 B1
N7 ....71 D4
NW9 ....45 B5
W5 ....109 D4
Southall UB1 ....107 B6
St George's Battersea CE Prim Sch SW8 137 C5 269 B3
St George's Bickley CE Prim Sch BR1 ....187 D1
St George's Cath NW1 .231 D2
St George's Cath RC Jun & Inf Sch SE1 ..116 D3 261 C6
St George's CE Jun & Inf Sch SE5 ....139 C5
St George's Circ SE1 ....116 D3 261 C6
St Georges Cl HA0 ....65 A5
St George's Cl NW11 ....47 B3
St Georges Ct E6 ....100 B3
E17 ....54 B4
SE20 ....184 B2
SW15 ....135 B1
Harrow HA3 ....43 A3
St George's Ct SE1 ....261 C5
SW3 ....257 A4
SW7 ....256 A5
St George's Dr SW1 ....115 C1 259 A2
Ickenham UB10 ....60 B6
South Oxhey WD1 ....23 A6
St George's Field W2 ....92 C1 237 B1
St George's Gdns KT6 .214 D6
St George's Gr SW17 ...158 B1
St Georges Hanover Sq Sch W1 ....115 A6 248 B5
St George's Ho NW1 ....232 B3
St George's Hospl SW17 ....180 B5
St Georges Ind Est N22 .32 D3
St George's Ind Est KT2 175 D5
St George's La EC3 ....253 A6
St Georges Lo N10 ....49 C5
St George's Mews NW1 .70 D1
SE1 ....261 B6
St George's RC Cath SE1 ....116 C3 261 B6
St George's RC Fst & Mid Sch HA1 ....64 D5
St George's RC Prim Sch EN2 ....5 B3
St George's RC Sec Sch W9 ....91 D5
St Georges Rd W4 ....111 B4
Bromley BR1 ....210 B6
Dagenham RM9 ....81 A4
Orpington BR5 ....211 B3
St George's Rd E7 ....77 B2
E10 ....76 A5
N9 ....18 A1
N13 ....16 B2
NW11 ....47 B3
SE1 ....116 D3 261 C5
SW19 ....179 B4
W7 ....108 D5
Beckenham BR3 ....185 D2
Enfield EN1 ....5 D5
Feltham TW13 ....172 D6
Isleworth TW1 ....153 B6
2 Kingston u T KT2 ....176 C3
Mitcham CR4 ....203 B6
Redbridge IG1 ....56 B2
Richmond TW9 ....132 B2
Ruxley DA14 ....190 D4
Wallington SM6 ....219 B3
St Georges Rd W BR1 .188 A1
St George's Residences 4 SW2 ....160 C6
St Georges Sh & L Ctr HA1 ....42 C3
St Georges Sq 1 E14 ..119 A6
St George's Sq E7 ....77 B1
SW1 ....115 D1 259 C1
Kingston u T KT3 ....199 C6
St George's Square Mews SW1 ....259 C1
St George's Way SE15 .139 C6
St George's Wlk CR0 ...221 A5
St Georges's Ct EC4 ....241 C2
St Gerards Cl SW4 ....159 C6
St German's Pl SE3 ....143 A4
St German's Rd SE23 ..163 A3
St Gildas' RC Jun Sch N8 ....50 A3
St Giles Ave Dagenham RM10 ....81 D1
Uxbridge UB10 ....61 A4
St Giles Cir WC1 93 D1 239 D2
St Giles Cl Dagenham RM10 ....81 D1
Orpington BR6 ....227 B3
St Giles Colls WC1 ....94 A2 240 B4
St Giles Ct W13 ....109 C5
WC2 ....240 A2
St Giles High St WC2 ....93 D1 239 D2
St Giles Hospl SE5 ....139 C4
St Giles Pas WC2 ....239 D1
St Giles Rd SE5 ....139 C4
St Giles' Sch CR2 ....220 D2
St Giles Twr 3 SE5 ....139 C4
St Gilles Ho 15 E2 ....96 D5
St Gothard Rd SE21, SE27 ....183 B6
St Gregory Cl HA4 ....62 C4
St Gregory's RC High Sch HA3 ....43 D4
St Gregory's RC Prim Sch W5 ....87 D2
St Helena Ho WC1 ....234 A1
St Helena Rd SE16 ....118 D2
St Helena St WC1 ....234 A1
St Helena Terr 23 TW9 .153 D6
St Helens KT7 ....196 D2
St Helen's Cres SW16 ..182 B2
St Helen's Gdns W10 ....90 D1
St Helen's Pl EC3 ....243 A2
St Helen's RC Inf Sch E17 ....54 A4
St Helen's RC Prim Sch E13 ....99 A3
SW9 ....138 C2
St Helen's RC Prim Sch (Annexe) SW9 ....138 B3
St Helens Rd 7 DA18 .124 D4
St Helen's Rd SW16 ...182 B2
W13 ....109 C5
Redbridge IG1 ....56 B3
St Helens Sch UB10 ....60 C1
St Helier Ave SM4 ....202 A3
St Helier Ct 4 N1 ....95 C6
St Helier Hospl SM5 ...202 A1
St Helier Sta SM4 ....201 C3
St Heliers Ave TW3, TW4 ....151 C6
St Helier's Rd E10 ....54 A3
St Hilda's Ave TW15 ...170 A5
St Hildas Cl SW17 ....158 C2
St Hilda's Cl NW6 ....68 D1
St Hilda's Rd SW13 ....134 B6
St Hildas Wharf E1 ....118 C5
St Hubert's Ho 1 E14 .119 C3
St Hughes Cl SW17 ....158 C2
St Hugh's Rd SE20 ....184 B3
St Ignatius Coll Upper Sch EN1 ....6 B6
St Ignatius RC Fst & Mid Sch TW16 ....172 A2
St Ignatius' RC Prim Sch N15 ....51 D3
St Ivian Ct 3 N10 ....31 B1
St James' & St Michaels CE Sch W2 ....114 A6 246 B6
St James Apartments 2 E17 ....53 A4
St James Ave N20 ....14 C1
Cheam SM1 ....217 C3
St James' Ave W13 ....109 A5
St James CE Jun Sch E7 77 A3
St James CE Prim Sch EN3 ....6 C3
St James Cl N20 ....14 C1
New Barnet EN4 ....2 B1
St James' Cl New Malden KT3 ....199 D4
Ruislip HA4 ....62 C6
St James Ct 11 E2 ....96 A4
E12 ....77 C6
SE3 ....143 B4
10 W4 ....110 C1
Thornton Heath CR0 ....204 D2
St James' Ct SW1 ....259 B6
W4 ....111 B3
7 Kingston u T KT1 ....198 A6
St James Gate IG9 ....21 B3
St James' Gdns HA0 ....66 A1
St James Hatcham CE Prim Sch SE14 ....141 A4
St James Ind Mews SE1 ....118 A1
St James' Mans NW6 ...69 C1
St James Mews E14 ...120 A3
St James RC Prim Sch BR5 ....210 D4
St James Rd Carshalton SM5 ....218 C5
Sutton SM1,SM2 ....217 C3
St James' Rd E15 ....76 D3
N9 ....18 B2
Kingston u T KT6 ....197 D3
Mitcham CR4 ....181 A3
St James School Flats 5 N7 ....72 C3
St James St W6 ....112 C1
St James Street Sta E17 53 A4
St James The Great RC (Aided) Sch CR7 ....182 D1
St James the Less Prim Sch SW1 ....115 D1 259 C2
St James Way DA14 ...191 A5
St James's SE14 ....141 A4
St James's App EC2 ....243 A5
St James's Ave E2 ....96 C5
Beckenham BR3 ....207 A6
Hampton TW12 ....174 A5
St James's CE Jun & Inf Sch SE16 ....118 A3
St James's CE Prim Sch N10 ....49 A5
St James's Cl NW8 ....230 C5
SE18 ....123 A1
SW17 ....158 D2
St James's Cloisters 2 SE22 ....139 D1
St James's Cotts 14 TW10 ....153 D6
St James's Cres SW9 ..138 C2
St James's Ct 8 N18 ....34 A5
St James's Dr SW12,SW17 ....158 D4
SW17 ....158 D3
St James's Gdns W11 ....113 A5 244 A4
St James's Gr SW11 ...136 D3
St James's La N10 ....49 B5
St James's Lo 4 CR0 ..205 C1
St James's Market SW1 249 C5
St James's Mews E17 ...53 A4
St James's Palace SW1 ....115 C5 249 B3
St James's Park SW1 ..249 C2
St James's Park Sta SW1 ....115 D3 259 C6
St James's Pas EC3 ....243 B1
St James's Pk CR0 ....205 A2
St James's Pl SW1 ....115 C5 249 A3
St James's RC High Sch NW9 ....27 D2
St James's Rd SE1,SE16 118 A2
Croydon CR0 ....205 B2
Hampton TW12 ....173 D5
Kingston u T KT1 ....175 D1
St James's Sch TW2 ...152 C1
St James's Sq SW1 ....115 C5 249 B4
St James's St E17 ....53 A4
SW1 ....115 C5 249 A4
St James's Terr NW8 ...230 C4
2 SW12 ....159 A3
St James's Terrace Mews NW8 ....230 C5
St James's Wlk EC1 ...241 C6
St Jerome's Gr UB3 ....83 A1
St Joachim's RC Prim Sch E16 ....99 C1
St Joan of Arc RC Prim Sch N5 ....73 A4
St Joan's Rd N9 ....17 D2
St John & St James CE Prim Sch N18 ....33 D5
St John Angell Town CE Prim Sch SW9 ....138 C3
St John Baptist CE Prim Sch BR1 ....186 A6
St John CE Prim Sch SE17 ....117 A2 262 B3
St John Cl SW6 ....265 A4
St John Evangelist RC Prim Sch N1 ....94 D5 234 C4
St John Fisher RC Fst & Mid Sch HA5 ....41 C5
St John Fisher RC Prim Sch SW20 ....200 D4
Erith DA18 ....125 A3
Wembley UB6 ....87 C4
St John of Jerusalem CE JMI Sch E9 ....74 C1
St John Rigby RC Coll BR4 ....224 B4
St John St EC1 ..94 D3 241 C6
St John the Baptist CE Jun Sch KT1 ....175 D3
St John the Baptist JMI Sch N1 ....95 C5
St John the Baptist RC Jun Sch E2 ....96 C5
St John the Divine CE Prim Sch SE5 ....138 D5
St John Vianney RC Prim Sch N8 ....50 D5
St John's & St Clements CE Prim Sch SE15 ....140 A2
St John's (Highbury Vale) CE Prim Sch N5 ....72 D5
St John's (Shirley) CE Prim Sch CR0 ....222 D5
St John's (Upper Holloway) Prim Sch N19 ....71 D6
St John's Ave N11 ....30 D5
NW10 ....89 D6
SW15 ....156 D6
St Johns CE Fst Sch HA7 25 B6
St John's CE Inf Sch NW4 ....46 B4
St John's CE JMI Sch E2 96 C5
St Johns CE Mid Sch HA7 ....25 A6
St John's CE Prim Sch N11 ....30 D6
N20 ....14 A2
SE20 ....184 C3
Buckhurst Hill IG9 ....21 B3
Kingston u T KT1 ....198 A6
St John's Church Rd E9 .74 C3
St Johns Cl N14 ....15 C5
St John's Cl N20 ....14 A1
Wembley HA9 ....66 A3
St Johns Concert Hall SW1 ....260 A5
St John's Cotts 2 SE20 184 C3
St John's Cres SW9 ...138 C2
St John's Ct E11 ....54 D1
IG9 ....21 B3
N4 ....72 D6
N5 ....72 D4
5 NW3 ....70 A2
SE13 ....142 A3
W6 ....112 B2
2 Harrow HA1 ....42 D3
Isleworth TW7 ....130 D3
Kingston u T KT1 ....198 A5
St Johns Dr KT12 ....194 C1
St John's Dr SW18 ....157 D3
St John's Est SE1 ....253 C1
St John's Gdns W11 ....113 B6 244 C5
St John's Gr N19 ....71 C6
3 SW13 ....133 D3
1 Richmond TW9 ....132 A1
St John's Hill SW11 ....136 B1
St John's Hill Gr SW11 .136 B1
St Johns Ho 5 SE17 ...139 B6
St John's La EC1 94 D2 241 D4
St John's Mans E5 ....74 C3
St John's Par W13 ....109 B5
3 Sidcup DA14 ....190 B6
St John's Park Mans N19 ....71 C5
St John's Path EC1 ....241 C5
St John's Pk SE3 ....143 A5
St John's Pl EC1 ....241 C5
St John's Prim Sch W13 ....109 A6
St John's RC Jun & Inf Sch SE16 ....119 A4
St Johns Rd Ilford IG2 ...57 C2
Kingston u T KT3 ....199 A6
St John's Rd E4 ....35 D6
E6 ....100 A6
E16 ....99 A1
E17 ....36 A1
N15 ....51 C3
NW11 ....47 B3
SE20 ....184 C4
SW11 ....136 C1
SW19 ....179 A4
Barking IG11 ....101 C6
Bexley DA16 ....146 B2
Carshalton SM5 ....218 C5
Croydon CR0 ....220 D5
East Molesey KT8 ....196 B5
Feltham TW13 ....173 B6
Harrow HA1 ....42 D3
Isleworth TW7 ....130 D3
Orpington BR5,BR6 ....211 C3
Richmond TW9 ....132 A1
Sidcup DA14 ....190 B6
Southall UB2 ....107 A3
Sutton SM1 ....217 D6
Teddington KT1 ....175 C1
Wembley HA9 ....66 A3
St John's Sch SW6 ....135 A4 264 B2
St John's Sq EC1 94 D3 241 C5
St John's Sta SE8 ....141 C3
St John's Terr E7 ....77 B2
SE18 ....145 B6
W10 ....90 D3
Enfield EN2 ....5 B6
St John's Vale SE8 ....141 C3
St John's Village 4 N11 30 D5
St John's Villas N19 ....71 D6
W8 ....255 D5
St John's Way N19 ....49 D1
St John's Wood Ct NW8 ....229 D1
St John's Wood High St NW8 ....92 C5 230 A3
St John's Wood Jun Prep Sch NW8 ....92 C4 230 A2
St John's Wood Park NW8 ....92 B6 229 C6
St John's Wood Rd NW8 ....92 B4 229 D1
St John's Wood Sta NW8 ....92 B5 229 C4
St John's Wood Terr NW8 ....92 C5 230 A4
St Johnstone Ho 15 N12 29 D6
St Joseph's Acad SE3 ..142 C2
St Josephs Cl BR6 ....227 D4
St Joseph's Cl W10 ....91 A2
St Joseph's Coll Mill Hill Missionaries NW7 ....27 D6
St Joseph's Convent Prep Sch KT8 ....196 A4
St Joseph's Convent Prim Sch NW4 ....46 B5
St Joseph's Convent Sch E11 ....55 A3
St Josephs Ct 19 E10 ...53 D2
St Joseph's Ct E4 ....20 B4
St Joseph's Dr UB1 ...107 B5
St Joseph's Flats NW1 .232 C2
St Josephs Gr NW4 ....46 B5
St Joseph's Ho W6 ....112 D2
St Joseph's Hospice E9, E8 ....96 B6
St Joseph's Prim Sch W7 ....108 C5
St Joseph's RC Coll SW16 ....182 D4
St Josephs RC Fst & Mid Sch HA3 ....25 A1
St Joseph's RC Inf Sch E10 ....75 C6
SE19 ....183 A4
St Joseph's RC Jun & Inf Sch SE1 ....117 A4 252 B2
SE5 ....139 A5
SE16 ....118 A4
SE16 ....118 C3
St Joseph's RC Jun & Inf Schs NW10 ....67 C1
Wembley HA9 ....66 B3
St Joseph's RC Jun Sch E10 ....53 D1
SE19 ....183 A4
St Josephs RC Prim Sch SW18 ....157 C6
Barking IG11 ....101 A6
St Joseph's RC Prim Sch N19 ....49 B1
SE8 ....141 C5
SE10 ....120 C1
SW3 ....114 D2 257 C3
W9 ....92 A4 229 A1
WC2 ....94 A1 240 B2
Dagenham RM9 ....81 B4
Kingston u T KT1 ....176 B1
St Joseph's RC Sch BR1 ....187 B3
St Joseph's Rd N9 ....18 C3

St Joseph's St SW8 268 D2
St Joseph's Vale SE3 142 B2
St Jude St N16 73 C3
St Jude's & St Paul's Prim Sch N1 73 C2
St Jude's CE Prim Sch SE24 160 D6
St Jude's Prim Sch SE1 116 D3 261 C5
St Jude's Rd E2 96 B5
St Julian's Cl SW16 182 C6
St Julian's Farm Rd SE27,SW16 182 D6
St Julian's Rd NW6 91 C6
St Katharine Dock* E1 117 D5 253 D4
St Katharine Pier E1 117 D5 253 D4
St Katharine's Ho N1 234 A4
St Katharine's Way E1 117 D5 253 D4
St Katherine's Prec NW1 231 C4
St Katherines Rd DA18 124 D4
St Katherine's Row EC3 243 B1
St Keverne Rd SE9 188 A6
St Kilda Rd W13 109 A4
Orpington BR6 211 D1
St Kilda's Rd N16 51 C1
Harrow HA1 42 C3
St Kitts Terr SE19 183 C5
St Laurence's Cl NW6 90 D6
St Lawrence CE Mid Sch KT8 196 B5
St Lawrence Cl HA8 26 B3
St Lawrence Ct N1 235 D6
St Lawrence Dr HA5 40 B4
St Lawrence Ho SE1 263 B6
St Lawrence RC Sch TW13 150 B2
St Lawrence St E14 120 A5
St Lawrence Terr W10 91 A2
St Lawrence Way SW9 138 C3
St Leonards Ave HA3 43 C4
St Leonard's Ave E4 36 B4
St Leonards CE Prim Sch SW16 181 D5
St Leonards Cl 4 DA16 146 A2
St Leonards Ct SW14 133 A2
St Leonard's Ct N1 235 D2
St Leonards Gdns IG1 79 A3
St Leonard's Gdns TW5 129 A4
St Leonard's Hospl N1 95 C5
St Leonards Rd SW14 133 A2
St Leonard's Rd E14 98 A2
NW10 89 B3
W13 109 C6
Claygate KT10 212 D2
Croydon CR0 220 D5
Kingston u T KT6 197 D4
Thames Ditton KT7 197 A2
St Leonards Rise BR6 227 C4
St Leonard's Sq NW5 71 A2
Kingston u T KT6 197 D4
St Leonard's St E3 97 D4
St Leonard's Terr SW3 114 D1 257 D1
St Leonard's Wlk SW16 182 B3
St Loo Ave SW3 136 C6 267 B6
St Loo Ct SW3 267 C6
St Louis Rd SE27 183 B6
St Loy's Rd N17 51 D6
St Lucia Dr E15 98 D6
St Luke Ct 5 E10 53 D2
St Luke's Ave SW4 137 D1
Enfield EN2 5 B5
Ilford IG1 78 D3
St Luke's CE JMI Sch E14 120 B2
St Luke's CE Prim Sch E16 98 D1
SE27 183 A5
W9 91 B4
Kingston u T KT2 176 B2
Richmond TW9 132 C4
St Luke's Cl EC1 95 A3 242 B6
SE25 206 B3
St Luke's Ct W11 91 B1
St Luke's Hospl W1 93 C3 239 A5
St Luke's Mews W11 91 B1
St Luke's Path 1 IG1 78 D3
St Luke's Prim Sch EC1 95 A4 235 B1
St Luke's Rd W11 91 B2
Uxbridge UB10 60 A1
St Luke's Sq E16 98 D1
St Luke's St SW3 257 B2
St Luke's Woodside Hospl N10 49 A5
St Malo Ave N9 18 C1
St Margaret Clitherow RC Prim Sch NW10 67 A4
St Margaret Clitherow RC Sch SE28 124 B5
St Margaret St SW1 250 A1
St Margarets IG11 101 B6
St Margarets Ave N20 14 A3
Ashford TW15 170 D5
Hillingdon UB8 82 C3
Longlands DA15 167 B1
St Margaret's Ave N8,N15 50 D5
Cheam SM3 217 A5
Harrow HA2 64 A5
St Margarets Bsns Ctr 11 TW1 153 B5
St Margaret's CE Prim Sch SE18 123 A1
St Margaret's Cres SW15 156 B6
St Margaret's Ct E15 76 C4
SW15 134 B1
9 Twickenham TW1 153 B5
St Margaret's Dr TW1 153 B6
St Margaret's Gr E11 76 D5
SE18 145 A6
Twickenham TW1 153 A5
St Margaret's La W8 113 D3 255 C5
St Margarets Lo W3 110 D4
St Margarets Rd Edgware HA8 26 D5
Ruislip HA4 39 B3
St Margaret's Rd E12 77 C6
N17 51 C6
NW10 90 C4
SE4 141 B1
W7 108 C4
Isleworth TW1 153 B6
St Margarets Rdbt TW1 153 B6
St Margaret's Sch NW3 69 D4
St Margaret's Sta TW1 153 B5
St Margaret's Terr SE18 123 A1
St Mark St E1 95 D1 243 D1
St Mark's CE Prim Sch SE11 138 B6 270 D6
SE25 206 A5
Bromley BR2 209 A6
St Marks Cl 5 SE10 142 A5
St Mark's Cl EN5 1 D2
St Mark's Cres NW1 93 A6 231 B6
St Mark's Ct 7 E10 53 D2
W7 108 C4
St Mark's Fst Sch CR4 180 D1
St Marks Gate E9 75 B1
St Mark's Gr SW10 135 D5 265 D4
St Mark's Hill KT6 198 A3
St Marks Ho 6 SE17 139 B6
St Mark's Ho 8 E17 54 A5
St Mark's Hospl EC1 94 D4 234 D2
St Marks Ind Est E16 121 D5
St Mark's Pl SW19 179 B4
W11 91 A1
St Mark's Prim Sch N19 72 A6
W7 108 C4
St Mark's RC Sch TW3 129 C2
St Mark's Rd SE25 206 A5
W5 110 A5
W7 108 C4
W10 90 D2
W11 91 A1
Bromley BR2 209 B6
Enfield EN1 17 D6
Mitcham CR4 181 A1
Teddington TW11 175 B3
St Mark's Rise E8 73 D3
St Mark's Sq NW1 231 A5
St Martha's Convent Jun Sch for Girls EN5 1 A1
St Martin of Porres RC Prim Sch N11 31 C4
St Martin-in-the-Fields High Sch SW2 160 C3
St Martin's Almshos NW1 232 A6
St Martin's App HA4 39 C2
St Martin's Ave E6 99 D5
St Martins Cl Erith DA18 124 D4
South Oxhey WD1 22 C6
St Martin's Cl NW1 232 A6
Enfield EN1 6 B4
St Martins Ct N1 95 C6
St Martin's Ct SE27 160 D2
WC2 250 A6
St Martin's La WC2 116 A6 250 A5
St Martin's Le Grand EC1 242 A2
St Martin's Pl WC2 250 A5
St Martin's Rd N2 30 B3
N9 18 B2
SW9 138 B3
St Martin's St WC2 249 D5
St Martin's Way SW17 158 A1
St Mary & St Joseph's Sch DA14 190 A5
St Mary & St Michael Jun & Inf Sch E1 96 C1
St Mary & St Pancras CE Prim Sch NW1 93 D5 232 C3
St Mary Abbots CE Prim Sch W8 113 D4 245 C1
St Mary Abbot's Ct W14 254 C5
St Mary Abbot's Pl W8 254 D5
St Mary Abbots Terr W14 254 D5
St Mary at Hill EC3 117 C6 253 A5
St Mary Ave SM6 219 B5
St Mary Axe EC3 95 C1 243 B2
St Mary Graces Ct E1 253 D5
St Mary le Bow Church* EC2 242 B1
St Mary- le-Park Ct SW11 267 B3
St Mary Magdalene CE Prim Sch N7 72 C2
St Mary Magdalene CE Sec Sch TW10 154 C6
St Mary Magdalene Prim Sch SE15 140 B3
St Mary Magdalene's CE Prim Sch W2 91 D2
St Mary Magdalens RC Prim Sch SE4 141 A1
St Mary Magdelen's RC Jun Sch NW2 68 B2
St Mary Newington Cl SE17 263 B2
St Mary of the Angels Cath Prim Sch W2 91 C1
St Mary Rd E17 53 D5
St Mary St SE18 122 C2
St Marychurch St SE16 118 C4
St Marylebone CE Sch W1 93 A2 238 B4
St Marys IG11 101 B6
St Mary's & St Peter's Prim Sch TW11 174 D5
St Mary's App E12 78 B3
St Marys Ave UB2 107 D2
St Mary's Ave E11 55 B2
N3 29 B1
Beckenham BR2 208 C6
Teddington TW11 174 D4
St Mary's Bryanston Square CE Sch W1 92 D2 237 C4
St Mary's CE High Sch (Lower & Upper) NW4 46 C6
St Mary's CE High Sch (Middle) NW4 46 C6
St Mary's CE Inf Sch N8 50 B5
St Mary's CE JMI Sch SE18 122 C2
St Mary's CE Jun Sch N8 50 A5
NW4 46 B4
St Mary's CE Prim Sch E17 53 D5
N1 94 D6 234 D6
N3 29 B3
NW10 67 C2
SE13 163 D6
SW15 134 D2
Chessington KT9 214 B2
East Barnet EN4 14 C5
Long Ditton KT7 197 B1
St Mary's CE Sch TW19 148 A4
St Mary's Church Sch TW1 153 A4
St Mary's Cl N17 34 A2
Chessington KT9 214 B1
Ewell KT17 215 D1
St Paul's Cray BR5 190 B1
Sunbury TW16 194 A5
St Mary's Cottage Hospl TW12 173 B2
St Mary's Cres NW4 46 B6
Hayes UB3 105 D6
Hounslow TW7 130 C5
St Marys Ct E6 100 B3
SE7 143 D5
St Mary's Ct E11 54 D1
N12 30 A3
W5 109 D4
W6 111 D3
Kingston u T KT3 199 C6
Wallington SM6 219 C4
St Mary's Dr TW14 149 A4
St Mary's Est 2 SE16 118 C4
St Mary's Flats NW1 232 C2
St Mary's Gate W8 255 C5
St Mary's Gdns SE11 261 B4
St Mary's Gn 1 N2 48 A6
St Mary's Gr N1 72 D2
SW13 134 B2
W4 132 D6
Richmond TW10,TW9 132 B1
St Mary's High Sch CR0 205 A1
St Mary's Ho N1 234 D6
W5 109 D3
St Mary's Hospl W2 92 B1 236 D2
St Mary's Inf Sch E17 53 D5
St Mary's Kilburn CE Prim Sch NW6 91 C6
St Mary's Lo E11 55 B3
St Mary's Mans NW10 89 C6
W2 92 B2 236 C4
St Mary's Medical Sch W2 92 B1 236 D2
St Mary's Mews NW6 69 D1
St Mary's Path N1 234 D6
St Mary's Pl SE9 166 C5
W5 109 D4
W8 113 D3 255 C5
St Mary's RC Inf Sch CR0 205 B1
St Mary's RC Jun & Inf Schs N15 51 B4
St Mary's RC Jun Sch E17 54 A6
Carshalton SM5 218 D3
Croydon CR0 205 B1
St Mary's RC Prim Sch E4 20 B3
NW6 91 C5
SE9 166 C6
SW4 159 C6
SW8 137 B4 268 D2
SW19 179 C3
W4 133 C6
W10 91 A3
W14 112 D3
Beckenham BR3 186 A3
Enfield EN3 6 D1
Isleworth TW7 131 A2
St Mary's RC Sch TW7 131 A2
St Marys Rd IG1 79 B6
St Mary's Rd E10 76 A6
E13 99 B5
N2 30 B3
N8 50 A5
N9 18 C3
NW10 89 C6
NW11 47 A2
SE15 140 C3
SE25 205 C6
SW19 179 B5
W5 109 D5
East Barnet EN4 14 D4
East Molesey KT8 196 B4
Hayes UB3 105 D6
Kingston u T KT6 197 D3
Surbiton KT6 197 C1
Worcester Pk KT4 215 C6
St Mary's Roman Catholic Inf Sch SM5 218 D4
St Mary's Sch Hampstead NW3 70 B3
St Mary's Sq W2 236 C4
W5 109 D4
St Mary's Stoke Newington CE JMI Sch N16 73 C6
St Mary's Terr W2 236 C4
St Mary's Twr EC1 242 B5
St Mary's Univ Coll TW1 152 D1
St Marys View HA3 43 C4
St Mary's Wlk SE11 261 B4
Hayes UB3 105 D6
St Matthew St SW1 259 C5
St Matthew's Ave KT6 198 B1
St Matthew's CE Fst Sch SW20 178 A2
St Matthews CE Prim Sch SW1 115 D3 259 D6
St Matthew's CE Prim Sch Surbiton KT6 198 A2
Yiewsley UB7 104 A5
St Matthew's CE Sch EN3 18 C6
St Matthews Ct 6 E10 53 D2
E15 76 D1
N10 31 A1
SE1 262 A5
St Matthew's Ct TW15 170 C5
St Matthews Dr BR1 210 B6
St Matthew's Ho 8 SE17 139 B6
St Matthew's Lo NW1 232 B4
St Matthew's Rd SW2 160 B6
W5 110 A5
St Matthew's Row E2 96 A3
St Matthias CE Sch E2 95 D3 243 D6
St Matthias Cl NW9 45 D4
St Matthias's CE Prim Sch N16 73 C4
St Maur Rd SW6 135 B4 264 D1
St Merryn Cl SE18 145 B5
St Merryn Ct BR3 185 C3
St Michael Twr E17 53 B4
St Michael-at-Bowes CE Jun Sch N13 32 C4
St Michael's & St Martin's RC Prim Sch TW4 129 B2
St Michael's Alley EC3 242 D1
St Michaels Ave N9 18 C4
St Michael's Ave HA9 66 C2
St Michaels Camden Town CE Prim Sch & Our Lady's RC Prim Sch NW1 93 C6 232 A6
St Michael's CE Prim Sch N6 49 A2
N22 32 B2
Enfield EN2 5 A4
St Michaels Cl 4 E16 99 D2
Bromley BR1 210 A6
Worcester Pk KT4 215 D6
St Michael's Cl N3 29 B1
N12 30 C5
Erith DA18 124 D4
St Michael's Ct N11 15 A1
NW11 47 B2
St Michael's East Wickham CE Sch DA16 146 C4
St Michael's Flats NW1 232 C3
St Michael's Gdns W10 91 A2
St Michael's Hospl EN2 5 B4
St Michael's Prim Sch SE26 185 A6
SW18 157 B4
St Michael's RC Gram Sch N12 30 A5
St Michael's RC Prim Sch E6 100 B5
Ashford TW15 170 C5
St Michael's RC Sec Sch SE16 118 A4
St Michaels Rd TW15 170 C5
St Michael's Rd NW2 68 C4
SW9 138 B3
Bexley DA16 146 B2
Croydon CR0 205 A1
Wallington SM6 219 C2
St Michael's Rise DA16 146 B4
St Michael's St W2 92 C1 237 A2
St Michael's Terr N22 32 A2
St Mildred's Ct EC2 242 C1
St Mildreds Rd SE12, SE6 164 D4
St Mirren Ct EN5 14 A6
St Monica's JMI Sch N1 95 C4
St Monica's RC Prim Sch N14 16 A1
St Nicholas CE JMI Sch WD6 9 D5
St Nicholas CE Prim Sch TW17 192 D3
St Nicholas Cl WD6 9 D5
St Nicholas Ct SE18 123 D1
St Nicholas Ctr SM1 217 D3
St Nicholas Dr TW17 192 C2
St Nicholas' Flats NW1 232 C3
St Nicholas Glebe SW17 181 A4
St Nicholas Ho SE8 141 C6
St Nicholas Prep Sch NW9 67 A6
St Nicholas Rd SE18 123 D2
Sutton SM1 217 D3
Thames Ditton KT7 196 D3
St Nicholas Sch CR9 220 C4
St Nicholas St SE8 141 C4
St Nicholas Way SM1 217 D3
St Nicolas La BR7 188 A2
St Ninian's Ct N20 14 D1
St Norbert Gn SE4 141 A1
St Norbert Rd SE4 141 A1
St Olaf's Rd SW6 135 A5 264 B3
St Olaves Ct W2 245 C5
St Olave's Ct EC2 242 C1
St Olave's Est SE1 253 B2
St Olave's Gdns SE11 261 A4
St Olave's Mans SE11 261 A4
St Olaves Prep Sch SE9 166 D2
St Olave's Rd E6 100 C6
St Olave's Wlk SW16 181 D1
St Osmund's RC Prim Sch SW13 133 D4
St Oswald's Pl SE11 116 B1 260 C1
St Oswald's Rd SW16 182 D2
St Oswulf St SW1 259 D3
St Owen Ho SE1 263 B6
St Pancras Almshouses 13 NW5 70 D3
St Pancras Commercial Ctr NW1 232 B6
St Pancras Ct N2 30 B1
St Pancras Hospl NW1 93 D6 232 C5
St Pancras Sta WC1 94 A4 233 A2
St Pancras Way NW1 93 C6 232 C6
St Patrick's RC Inf Sch E1 118 B5
St Patrick's RC Jun Sch E1 118 B5
St Patrick's RC Prim Sch NW5 71 B3
St Patrick's RC Sch E17 53 A5
SE18 123 B2
St Paul St N1 235 B5
St Paul's & All Hallows CE Jun & Inf Sch N17 34 A3
St Paul's Ave NW2 68 C2
SE16 118 D5
Harrow HA3 44 B5
St Paul's Cath* EC4 95 A1 242 A1
St Paul's Cath Sch EC4 95 A1 242 A1
St Paul's Catholic Sch TW16 172 A2
St Paul's CE JMI Sch E1 118 A6
St Paul's CE Jun & Inf Sch SE17 117 A1 262 A1
St Paul's CE Jun Sch KT2 176 C3
St Pauls CE Prim Sch TW8 131 D6
St Paul's CE Prim Sch N11 31 B5
N21 16 D4
NW3 70 D1
W6 112 C1
Chessington KT9 214 A4
St Paul's CE Sch NW7 28 B6
St Paul's Church Yd EC4 95 A1 242 A1
St Pauls Cl W5 110 B4
Hayes UB3 105 B1
St Paul's Cl SE7 121 D1
Ashford TW15 171 A5
Carshalton SM5 202 C1
Chessington KT9 213 D4
Hounslow TW3,TW4 129 A3
St Paul's Cray Rd BR7 189 B2
St Pauls Cres NW1 71 D1
St Paul's Ct 5 N19 72 A6
Hounslow TW4 129 A2
St Paul's Dr E15 76 B3
St Paul's Girls' Sch W6 112 D2
St Pauls Mews NW1 71 D1
St Paul's Pl N1 73 B2
St Paul's RC Prim Sch N22 32 B1
Thames Ditton KT7 196 C2
St Paul's RC Sec Sch SE2 146 A6
St Pauls Rd Barking IG11 101 A6
St Pauls Rd *continued*
Richmond TW9 132 B2
St Paul's Rd N1 73 A2
N17 34 A2
Brentford TW8 131 D6
South Norwood CR7 205 A6
St Pauls Rise N13 32 D4
St Paul's Sch SW13 112 A1
St Paul's Sq BR2 187 A1
St Paul's Sta EC2 95 A1 242 A2
St Paul's Terr SE17 138 D6
St Paul's Twr 13 E10 53 D2
St Pauls View WC1 234 A1
St Paul's Way E3 97 C2
N3 29 D3
St Paul's Way Sec Sch E3 97 C2
St Paul's with Lukes JMI Sch E3 97 B2
St Pauls with St Michaels Haggerston CE JMI Sch E8 96 A6
St Paul's Wood Hill BR5,BR7 189 D1
St Peter Chanel RC Prim Sch DA14 190 C5
St Peter in Chains RC Inf Sch N8 50 A3
St Peters & St Pauls RC Prim Sch EC1 94 D3 241 D6
St Peter's Alley EC3 242 D1
St Peters Ave N12 30 C3
St Peter's Ave N18 34 A6
St Peter's CE Prim Sch W6 112 A1
W9 91 C3
St Peters Cl SW17 158 C2
Chislehurst BR7 189 B3
Ilford IG2 57 D5
St Peter's Cl E2 96 A5
Arkley EN5 12 B6
Bushey WD2 8 B3
Ruislip HA4 62 D6
St Peters Ct SE4 141 B3
SE12 164 D6
East Molesey KT8 195 C5
St Peter's Ct NW4 46 C4
St Peter's Eaton Square CE Sch SW1 115 B3 258 D5
St Peter's Gdns SE27 160 C1
St Peter's Gr W6 112 A2
St Peters Ho N15 52 A5
WC1 233 B1
St Peter's Ho N16 51 C2
4 SE17 139 B6
St Peter's Path E17 54 C5
St Peter's Pl W9 91 D3
St Peter's Prim Sch SE17 117 B1 262 C1
South Croydon CR2 221 C2
St Peter's RC Prim Sch SE18 122 D2
Dagenham RM9 103 B6
St Peters Rd KT1 176 C1
St Peter's Rd N9 18 B3
W6 112 A1
Croydon CR0 221 B4
East Molesey KT8 195 C5
Isleworth TW1 153 B6
Southall UB1 85 C2
St Peter's Sch E1 118 C5
St Peter's Sq E2 96 A5
W6 111 D1
St Peter's St N1 94 D6 234 D5
Croydon CR2 221 B3
St Peter's Street Mews N1 234 D4
St Peter's Terr SW6 264 B3
St Peter's Villas 5 W6 112 A2
St Peters Way UB3 105 B1
St Peter's Way N1 73 C1
W5 87 D2
St Petersburgh Mews W2 245 C6
St Petersburgh Pl W2 113 D6 245 C5
St Philip Ho WC1 234 A1
St Philip Sq 1 SW8 137 B3
St Philip St SW8 137 B3
St Philip's Ave KT4 216 B6
St Philip's Rd E8 74 A2
Kingston u T KT6 197 D3
St Philips Sch KT9 213 D2
St Philip's Way N1 235 B5
St Philomena's Sch SM5 218 C3
St Quentin Ho SW18 158 B5
St Quentin Rd DA16 145 D2
St Quintin Ave W10 90 D2
St Quintin Gdns W10 90 C2
St Quintin Rd E13 99 B5
St Raphael's RC Prim Sch UB5 84 B5
St Raphael's Way NW10 67 A3
St Regis Cl N10 31 B1
St Regis Hts NW3 69 D5
St Richard of Chichester RC Sec Sch NW1 71 C1
St Richards Ct TW10 153 B1
St Richard's with St Andrew's CE Prim Sch TW10 153 B1
St Robert Southwell RC Prim Sch NW9 45 A3
St Ronan's 2 N3 29 C2
St Ronans Cl EN4 2 B5

St Ronans Cres IG8 ....37 A3
St Rule St SW8 ....137 C3
St Savior's CE Inf Sch
W5 ....109 D6
St Saviours SW4 ....137 B1
St Saviours & St Olaves CE Sch SE1 ....117 B3 262 D5
St Saviour's CE JMI Sch
E14 ....97 D2
St Saviour's CE Prim Sch
E17 ....53 B2
SE24 ....139 A2
W9 ....91 D3
St Saviour's Coll SE27 .183 B6
St Saviours Ct N22 ....31 D1
Harrow HA1 ....42 C4
St Saviour's RC Prim Sch
SE13 ....142 A1
St Saviour's Rd SW2 ..160 B6
Thornton Heath CR0 ....205 A3
St Saviour's Wharf SE1 253 D2
St Scholastica's RC JMI Sch
E5 ....74 A5
St Silas Pl NW5 ....71 A2
St Simon's Ave SW15 ..156 C6
St Stephen CE Prim Sch
W12 ....112 C4
St Stephen's Ave E17 ...54 A4
W12 ....112 B4
W13 ....87 B1
St Stephen's CE Jun Sch
Twickenham TW1 ....153 B5
Twickenham TW1 ....153 B5
St Stephen's CE Prim Sch
SE8 ....141 C3
SW8 ....138 B5 270 C4
W2 ....91 C2
St Stephen's Cl E17 ....53 D4
NW5 ....70 D3
NW8 ....230 B5
Southall UB1 ....85 C2
St Stephen's Cres W2 ...91 C1
Thornton Heath CR7 ....204 C6
St Stephens Ct N8 ....50 B3
W13 ....87 B1
St Stephen's Gdns
3 SW15 ....157 B6
W2 ....91 C1
Twickenham TW1 ....153 C5
St Stephen's Gr SE13 ..142 A2
St Stephens Ho 7
SE17 ....139 B6
St Stephen's Mews 34
W2 ....91 C2
St Stephens Par E6 ....77 C1
St Stephen's RC Prim Sch
DA16 ....146 A3
St Stephens Rd E6 ....77 C1
Ducks Island EN5 ....12 D6
St Stephen's Rd E3 ....97 B5
E17 ....53 D4
W13 ....87 C1
Enfield EN3 ....6 D6
Hounslow TW3,TW4 ....151 C6
Yiewsley UB7 ....104 A5
St Stephen's Row EC4 .242 C1
St Stephen's Terr SW8 .270 C3
St Swithin's La
EC4 ....117 B6 252 C6
St Swithun Wells RC Prim Sch HA4 ....62 D5
St Swithun's Rd SE13 ..164 B6
St Teresa RC Prim Sch
RM8 ....80 C4
St Teresa's RC Fst & Mid Sch
HA3 ....24 A2
St Teresa's RC Prim Sch
SM4 ....202 B3
St Theresa Ct E4 ....20 B4
St Theresa's RC Prim Sch
N3 ....47 D6
St Theresa's Rd TW14 ..127 D1
St Thomas a'Becket Prim Sch
SE2 ....124 A3
St Thomas' CE JMI Sch
N16 ....52 A1
St Thomas' Cl KT6 ....198 B1
St Thomas Ct 10 E10 ....53 D2
Old Bexley DA5 ....169 C4
St Thomas' Dr
Hatch End HA5 ....23 A2
Orpington BR5 ....211 A1
St Thomas Gdns IG1 ....79 A2
St Thomas' Gdns NW5 ..71 A2
St Thomas Ho 2 E1 ....96 D1
St Thomas More RC Prim Sch
SE9 ....144 A2
Bexley DA7 ....147 B3
St Thomas More RC Sch
KT8 ....196 A4
St Thomas More RC Sec Sch
SE9 ....166 C5
St Thomas More Sch
N22 ....32 C3
St Thomas of Canterbury RC Mid Sch CR4 ....203 A6
St Thomas of Canterbury RC Prim Sch SW6 135 B5 264 C4
St Thomas Rd E16 ....99 A1
N14 ....15 D4
St Thomas' Rd W4 ....133 A6
St Thomas St
SE1 ....117 B5 252 D3
St Thomas the Apostle Coll The SE15 ....140 C4
St Thomas's CE Prim Sch
W10 ....91 A3
St Thomas's Hospl
SE1 ....116 B3 260 C6
St Thomas's Hospl Medical Sch SE1 ....116 B3 260 C5
St Thomas's Pas 20 E9 ..74 C1
St Thomas's Rd N4,N5 ..72 C5
NW10 ....89 C6
St Thomas's Sq E9 ....74 C1
St Thomas's Way
SW6 ....135 B5 264 D4
St Timothy's Mews 3
BR1 ....187 B2
St Ursula Gr HA5 ....41 A4
St Ursula Rd UB1 ....85 C1
St Ursula's Convent Sch
SE10 ....142 B5
St Vincent Cl SE27 ....182 D5
St Vincent De Paul Ho 20
E1 ....96 C2
St Vincent De Paul Prim Sch
SW1 ....115 C3 259 A5
St Vincent Ho SE1 ....263 C6
St Vincent Rd TW2 ....152 A5
St Vincent St W1 ....238 B3
St Vincent's Hospl HA5 ..39 D6
St Vincents RC Prim Sch
SE9 ....188 A6
St Vincent's RC Prim Sch
NW7 ....28 C5
W1 ....93 A2 238 B3
W3 ....110 D6
St Vincent's RC Sch RM8 80 C6
St Wilfrid's Cl EN4 ....14 C6
St Wilfrid's Rd EN4 ....14 C6
St William of York RC Prim Sch SE23 ....163 A3
St William of York RC Sec Boys Sch (Upper) N1 ..72 A1
St Winefride's Ave E12 ..78 B3
St Winefride's RC Prim Sch
E12 ....78 B3
St Winifred's RC Inf Sch
SE12 ....164 C6
St Winifred's RC Jun Sch
SE12 ....164 D4
St Winifred's Rd TW11 .175 B4
Saints Cl SE27 ....182 D6
Saints Dr E7 ....77 D3
SS Peter & Paul RC Prim Sch
BR5 ....189 C1
SS Peter & Paul's Prim Sch
IG1 ....79 B5
SS Peter & Paul's RC Prim Sch CR4 ....202 D5
Sala Ho SE3 ....143 B1
Salamanca Pl SE1 ....260 C3
Salamanca St
SE1,SE11 ....116 B2 260 C3
Salamander Cl KT2 ....175 C5
Salamander Quay KT1 .175 D2
Salcombe Dr
Dagenham RM6 ....59 B3
West Barnes SM4 ....200 D1
Salcombe Gdns NW7 ...28 C4
SW4 ....137 B1
Salcombe Ho 6 SE23 .162 C2
Salcombe Lo NW5 ....71 A4
Salcombe Pk IG10 ....21 D6
Salcombe Prep Sch N14 15 B4
Salcombe Rd E17 ....53 B2
23 N16 ....73 C3
Ashford TW15 ....148 A1
Salcombe Way
Hayes UB4 ....83 C4
Ruislip HA4 ....62 A6
Salcot N4 ....72 B6
Salcott Rd SW11 ....158 D6
Croydon CR0 ....220 B4
Sale Pl W2 ....92 C1 237 A2
Sale St E2 ....96 A3
Salehurst Cl HA3 ....44 A4
Salehurst Rd SE4 ....163 B5
Salem Ho 13 E9 ....74 D2
Salem Pl CR0 ....221 A5
Salem Rd W2 ..113 D6 245 D6
Salesian Coll
SW11 ....136 C4 267 A1
Salford Ho 4 E14 ....120 A2
Salford Rd SW12,SW2 ..159 D3
Salisbury Ave N3 ....47 B6
Barking IG11 ....79 C1
Cheam SM1,SM2 ....217 B2
Salisbury Cl SE17 ....262 C4
Worcester Pk KT4 ....215 D5
Salisbury Ct E9 ....75 A3
EC4 ....241 C1
N3 ....29 B1
15 SE16 ....118 A3
W4 ....111 C2
Edgware HA8 ....26 B6
Enfield EN2 ....5 B1
UB5 ....63 D3
Salisbury Gdns SW19 ..179 A3
Buckhurst Hill IG9 ....21 D2
Salisbury Hall Gdns E4 .35 C4
Salisbury Ho 3 E14 ....97 D1
N1 ....234 C6
SW1 ....259 D2
SW19 ....156 D1
1 Ruislip HA4 ....40 C1
Stanmore HA7 ....25 A4
Salisbury Lower Sch N9 18 C4
Salisbury Mans N4,N15 ..50 D4
Salisbury Mews SW6 ..264 C3
Salisbury Mews *continued*
Bromley BR2 ....210 A4
Salisbury Pl SW9 ....138 D5
W1 ....237 C4
Salisbury Prim Sch E12 .78 A3
Salisbury Rd E4 ....19 C1
E7 ....77 A2
E10 ....76 A6
E12 ....77 D3
E17 ....54 A4
N4 ....50 D4
N9 ....18 A1
N22 ....32 D1
SE25 ....206 A3
SW19 ....179 A3
W13 ....109 B4
Bromley BR2 ....210 A4
Dagenham RM10 ....81 D2
Enfield EN3 ....7 B6
Feltham TW13 ....150 C3
Harlington TW6 ....149 A5
Harrow HA1 ....42 B4
High Barnet EN5 ....1 A2
Hounslow TW4 ....128 C2
Ilford IG3 ....79 C6
Kingston u T KT3 ....199 B6
Old Bexley DA5 ....169 C3
Pinner HA5 ....40 A5
Richmond TW9 ....132 A1
Southall UB2 ....107 A2
Wallington SM5 ....218 D2
Worcester Pk KT4 ....215 C5
Salisbury Sq EC4 ....241 B1
Salisbury St NW8 ....237 A5
10 W3 ....111 A4
Salisbury Terr SE15 ....140 C2
Salisbury Upper Sch N9 18 C4
Salisbury Wlk N19 ....71 C6
Salix Cl TW16 ....172 B3
Salix Ct N3 ....29 C4
Salliesfield TW2 ....152 B5
Salmen Rd E13 ....98 D5
Salmon La E14 ....97 A1
Salmon Rd DA17 ....125 C1
Salmon St NW9 ....45 A2
Salmond Cl HA7 ....25 A4
Salmons Rd N9 ....18 A3
Chessington KT9 ....214 A2
Salomons Rd E13 ....99 C2
Salop Rd E17 ....52 D3
Salt Hill Cl UB8 ....60 A3
Saltash Cl SM1 ....217 B4
Saltash Ho SE11 ....261 C2
Saltash Rd DA16 ....146 C4
Saltcoats Rd W4 ....111 C4
Saltcroft Cl HA9 ....44 D1
Saltdene N4 ....50 B1
Salter Cl HA2 ....63 B4
Salter Ho 8 SW16 ....181 C6
Salter Rd SE16 ....119 A5
Salter St 10 E14 ....119 C6
NW10 ....90 A4
Salterford Rd SW17 ....181 A4
Salters' Hall Ct EC4 ....252 C6
Salter's Hill SE19 ....183 B5
Salters Rd E17 ....54 B5
W10 ....90 D3
Salterton Rd N7 ....72 B5
Saltley Cl E6 ....100 A1
Saltoun Rd SW2,SW9 ..138 C1
Saltram Cl N15 ....51 D5
Saltram Cres W9 ....91 C4
Saltwell St E14 ....119 C6
Saltwood Gr SE17 ....262 C1
Salusbury Prim Sch
NW6 ....91 B6
Salusbury Rd NW6 ....91 A6
Salvador SW17 ....180 D5
Salvatarian RC Coll HA3 24 C1
Salvia Gdns UB6 ....87 A5
Salvin Rd SW15 ....134 D2
Salway Cl IG8 ....37 A3
Salway Ho E10 ....75 D6
SW8 ....270 B2
Salway Pl E15 ....76 C2
Salway Rd E15 ....76 B2
Salween Ho 2 N16 ....73 B4
Sam Bartram Cl SE7 ..121 C1
Sam Manners Ho 7
SE10 ....120 C1
Sam March Ho 5 E14 ..98 B1
Samantha Cl E17 ....53 B2
Samantha Ct E11 ....54 C2
Samaritan Hospl for Women
NW1 ....237 C4
Sambrook Ho 19 E1 ....96 C2
Sambrook Mews SE6 .163 D3
Sambrooke Ct EN1 ....17 D6
Samels Ct W6 ....112 A1
Samford Ho N1 ....234 A5
Samford St NW8 92 C3 237 A5
Samos Rd SE20 ....184 B1
Sampson Ave EN5 ....12 D6
Sampson Cl DA17 ....125 A3
Sampson Ct TW17 ....193 A4
Sampson St E1 ....118 A5
Samson Ho SE18 ....123 A2
Samson St E13 ....99 C5
Samuel Cl E8 ....95 D6
E17 ....53 C3
SE14 ....140 D6
SE18 ....122 A2
Samuel Ct BR3 ....207 D6
Samuel Ho 15 E8 ....95 D6
Samuel Johnson Cl
SW16 ....182 B6
Samuel Jones Ind Est 15
SE15 ....139 C5
Samuel Lewis Bldgs N1 .72 C2
Samuel Lewis Trust Dwellings
E8 ....74 A4
6 SE5 ....139 A4
SW3 ....257 A3
SW6 ....135 C5 265 B4
W14 ....254 B4
Samuel Lewis Trust Est
N15 ....51 C3
Samuel Rhodes Sch
N1 ....94 C6 234 A6
Samuel Richardson Ho
W14 ....254 C3
Samuel St SE18 ....122 B2
Samuel's Cl 2 W6 ....112 C2
Sancroft Cl NW2 ....68 B5
Sancroft Ct SW11 ....267 B2
Sancroft Rd HA3 ....25 A1
Sancroft St
SE11 ....116 C1 260 D2
Sanctuary Rd TW19, TW6 ....148 C5
Sanctuary St SE1 ....252 B2
Sanctuary The 35 E1 ....118 B5
SW1 ....115 D3 259 D6
Bexley DA5 ....168 D5
Morden SM4 ....201 C3
Sandal Rd N18 ....34 A5
New Malden KT3 ....199 C5
Sandal St E15 ....98 C6
Sandale Cl N16 ....73 B5
Sandall Cl W5 ....88 A3
Sandall Ho 6 E3 ....97 A5
Sandall Rd NW5 ....71 C2
W5 ....88 A3
Sandalwood Cl 10 E1 ...97 A3
Sandalwood Dr HA4 ....39 A2
Sandalwood Ho 6 NW3 69 D2
Sidcup DA15 ....167 D1
Sandalwood Rd TW13 .150 B1
Sandbach Pl SE18 ....123 A1
Sandbourne 12 NW8 ....91 D6
4 W11 ....91 C1
Sandbourne Ave SW19 179 D1
Sandbourne Rd SE4 ....141 A3
Sandbrook Cl NW7 ....27 B4
Sandbrook Rd N16 ....73 C5
Sandby Ct BR3 ....185 B2
Sandby Gn SE9 ....144 A2
Sandby Ho 6 NW6 ....91 C6
11 SE5 ....139 C4
Sandcroft Cl N13 ....32 D4
Sandcroft Ho SE11 ....260 D2
Sandell St SE1 ....251 A2
Sandells Ave TW15 ....171 A6
Sanderling Ct 20 SE8 ..141 B6
SE28 ....124 C6
Sanders Cl TW12 ....174 A5
Sanders Ho SW16 ....182 A4
WC1 ....234 A2
Sanders La NW7 ....28 C3
Sanders Way 3 N19 ....49 D1
Sanderson Cl NW5 ....71 B4
Sanderson Ho 7 SE8 ..119 B1
Sanderstead Ave NW2 ..69 A6
Sanderstead Cl SW12 ..159 C4
Sanderstead Rd E10 ....53 A1
South Croydon CR2 ....221 B1
Sandfield WC1 ....233 B1
Sandfield Gdns CR7 ..204 D6
Sandfield Pl CR7 ....205 A6
Sandfield Rd CR7 ....204 D6
Sandford Ave N22 ....33 A2
Sandford Cl E6 ....100 B3
Sandford Ct N16 ....51 C1
Barnet EN5 ....1 D2
Sandford Rd E6 ....100 B4
Bexleyheath DA6,DA7 ....147 A2
Bromley BR2 ....209 A5
Sandford Row SE17 ....262 D2
Sandford St SW6 ....265 D3
Sandford Wlk 4 N16 ...73 D6
SE14 ....141 A6
Sandgate Ho 15 E5 ....74 B4
W5 ....87 C2
14 Beckenham BR3 ....185 C3
Sandgate La SW17, SW18 ....158 C3
Sandgate Rd DA16 ....146 C5
Sandgate St SE15 ....140 B6
Sandgate Trad Est
SE15 ....140 B6
Sandham Ct SW4 ....270 B1
Sandham Point 10
SE18 ....122 D2
Sandhills CR0,SM6 ....219 D4
Sandhills Mdw TW17 ..193 A2
Sandhills The SW10 ....266 B6
Sandhurst Ave
Harrow HA2 ....41 D3
Tolworth KT5 ....198 D2
Sandhurst Cl NW9 ....44 C6
South Croydon CR2 ....221 C1
Sandhurst Ct SW2 ....138 A1
Sandhurst Dr IG3 ....79 D4
Sandhurst Ho 10 E1 ....96 C2
Sandhurst Mkt SE6 ....164 A3
Sandhurst Prim Sch
SE6 ....164 C3
Sandhurst Rd N9 ....18 D5
SE6 ....164 B3
Bexley DA5 ....168 D6
London HA8,NW9 ....44 C6
Sidcup DA15 ....168 A1
Sandhurst Way CR2 ..221 C1
Sandiford Rd SM3 ....217 B6
Sandiland Cres BR2 ..224 D6
Sandilands CR0 ....222 A5
Sandilands Rd
SW6 ....135 D4 265 C1
Sandilands Sta CR0 ..221 D6
Sandison St SE15 ....140 A2
Sandland St WC1 ....240 D3
Sandling Rise SE9 ....166 C1
Sandlings Cl SE15 ....140 B3
Sandlings The N22 ....50 D6
5 N22 ....32 C1
Sandmere Rd SW4 ....138 A1
Sandon Cl KT10 ....196 B1
Sandon Ct IG3 ....80 A5
Sandon Ho 5 SW2 ....160 A4
Sandow Cres UB3 ....105 D3
Sandown Ave KT10 ....212 A3
Sandown Cl TW5 ....128 A4
Sandown Ct 2 SM2 ..217 D1
Sandown Gate KT10 ....212 B5
Sandown Ho SE26 ....184 B4
2 W4 ....111 A1
Sandown Park KT10 ..212 A6
Sandown Rd SE25 ....206 B4
Esher KT10 ....212 A4
Sandown Way UB5 ....63 B3
Sandpiper Cl E17 ....34 D3
SE16 ....119 B4
Sandpiper Ct 11 E14 ..120 A3
1 SE8 ....141 C5
Sandpiper Rd SM1 ....217 B3
Sandpiper Terr IG5 ....56 D6
Sandpit Pl SE7 ....122 A1
Sandpit Rd BR1 ....186 C5
Sandpits Rd
Richmond TW10 ....153 D2
South Croydon CR0 ....222 D4
Sandra Cl N17 ....33 A2
Isleworth TW3 ....151 D6
Sandra Ho KT8 ....196 B4
Sandridge Cl HA1 ....42 C5
Sandridge Ct N4 ....73 A6
Sandridge St 2 N19 ....71 C6
Sandringham Ave
SW20 ....179 A1
Sandringham Cl
1 SW19 ....156 D3
Enfield EN1 ....5 C3
Ilford IG6 ....57 A6
Sandringham Cres HA2 .63 D6
Sandringham Ct
18 SE16 ....118 D5
SW15 ....156 D5
W1 ....239 B1
W9 ....229 B1
3 Beckenham BR3 ....186 A2
Hillingdon UB10 ....83 A3
Sandringham Dr
Ashford TW15 ....170 A6
Bexley DA16 ....145 C3
Sandringham Flats
WC2 ....249 D6
Sandringham Gdns N8 ..50 A3
N12 ....30 B4
Cranford TW5 ....128 A4
Ilford IG6 ....57 A6
Sandringham Ho W14 .254 A4
Richmond TW10 ....154 C6
Sandringham Prim Sch
E7 ....77 C3
Sandringham Rd E7 ....77 C3
E8 ....73 D3
E10 ....54 B3
N22 ....33 A1
NW2 ....68 B2
NW11 ....47 A2
Barking IG11 ....79 D2
North Cheam KT4 ....216 A5
Northolt UB5 ....63 C1
Plaistow BR1 ....187 A5
Stanwell TW19,TW6 ....148 A6
Thornton Heath CR0 ....205 A4
Sandrock Pl CR0 ....222 D4
Sandrock Rd SE13 ....141 C2
Sands End La
SW6 ....135 D4 265 D2
Sandstone TW9 ....132 C5
Sandstone Pl N19 ....71 B6
Sandstone Rd SE12 ....165 B2
Sandtoft Rd SE7 ....143 B6
Sandways 6 TW9 ....132 C4
Sandwell Cres 2 NW6 .69 C2
Sandwell Mans 3 NW6 .69 C2
Sandwich Ho 9 SE16 ..118 C4
WC1 ....233 A1
Sandwich St
WC1 ....94 A4 233 A1
Sandwick Cl NW7 ....28 A3
Sandy Bury BR6 ....227 B5
Sandy Dr TW14 ....149 C3
Sandy Hill Ave SE18 ..122 D1
Sandy Hill La SE18 ....122 D2
Sandy Hill Rd SE18 ....122 D1
Sandy La Belmont SM2 .217 A1
Eastbury HA6 ....22 A6
Harrow HA3 ....44 C3
Mitcham CR4 ....181 A2
Richmond TW10 ....153 D2
St Paul's Cray BR5 ....190 D2
Teddington KT8,TW11 ....175 B3
Walton-on-T KT12 ....194 C3
Sandy La N SM6 ....219 D3
Sandy La S SM6 ....219 C1
Sandy Lo N6 ....49 C2
Sandy Rd NW3 ....69 D6
Sandy Ridge BR7 ....188 C4
Sandy Way Croydon CR0 223 B5
Walton-on-T KT12 ....193 D1
Sandycombe Rd
East Bedfont TW14 ....150 A3
Richmond TW9 ....132 C3
Sandycoombe Rd TW1 153 C5
Sandycroft SE2 ....146 A6
Sandyhill Rd IG1 ....78 D4
Sandymount Ave HA7 ..25 D5
Sandy's Row E1 ....243 B3
Sanford La 3 N16 ....73 D6
Sanford St SE14,SE8 ..141 A6
Sanford Terr N16 ....73 D5
Sanger Ave KT9 ....214 B4
Sangley Rd SE6 ....164 A3
SE25 ....205 C5
Sangora Rd 17 SW11 ..136 B1
Sankey Ho 23 E2 ....96 C5
Sans Wlk EC1 ...94 D3 241 C6
Sansom Rd E11 ....76 D5
Sansom St SE5 ....139 B4
20 SE5 ....139 B5
Santana Ho SE18 ....144 D5
Santley Ho SE1 ....251 B1
Santley St SW4 ....138 B1
Santos Rd SW18 ....157 C5
Sapcote Trad Ctr NW10 .67 D2
Saperton Wlk SE11 ....260 D4
Saphora Cl BR6 ....227 B3
Sapperton Ct EC1 ....242 A5
Sapphire Cl E6 ....100 C1
Dagenham RM8 ....58 C1
Sapphire Ct 8 E1 ....118 A5
Sapphire Rd SE8 ....119 A2
Sara Lane Ct 31 N1 ....95 C5
Sara Turnbull Ho 2
SE18 ....122 B2
Saracen Cl CR0 ....205 B3
Saracen St E14 ....97 C1
Sarah Bonnell Sch E15 .76 C2
Sarah Ct UB5 ....85 B5
Sarah Ho 11 E1 ....96 B1
Sarah House SW15 ....133 D1
Sarah Swift Ho SE1 ....252 D2
Saratoga Rd E5 ....74 C4
Sardeson Ho 13 SW27 .182 D5
Sardinia St WC2 ....240 C2
Sargents Hill N2 ....30 C2
Sarjant Path SW19 ....156 D2
Sark Cl TW5 ....129 C5
Sark Ho 5 N1 ....73 A2
Enfield EN3 ....6 D5
Sark Wlk E16 ....99 B1
Sarnersfield Ho SE15 ..140 B5
Sarnes Ct 4 N11 ....31 B5
Sarnesfield Rd EN2 ....5 B2
Sarratt Ho W10 ....90 C2
Sarre Rd NW2 ....69 B3
Sarsden Bldgs W1 ....238 B1
Sarsen Ave TW3 ....129 C3
Sarsfeld Rd SW12,SW17 158 D3
Sarsfield Rd UB6 ....87 C5
Sartor Rd SE15 ....140 D1
Sarum Hall Sch NW3 ...70 C1
Sarum Ho W11 ....244 D5
Sassoon 4 NW9 ....27 D2
Satanita Cl E16 ....99 D1
Satchell Mead NW9 ....27 D2
Satchwell Rd 24 E2 ....96 A4
Saul Ct 4 SE15 ....139 D6
Sauls Gn E11 ....76 C5
Saunders Cl 14 E14 ....119 B6
Saunders Ho 11 SW2 ..160 C3
5 W11 ....112 D5
Saunders Ness Rd E14 .120 B2
Saunders Rd SE18 ....123 D1
Hillingdon UB10 ....82 B6
Saunders St SE11 ....261 A4
Saunders Way SE28 ....124 B6
Saunderton Rd HA0 ....65 B3
Saunton Ave UB3 ....127 D5
Saunton Ct UB1 ....108 A6
Savage Gdns E6 ....100 B1
EC3 ....253 B6
Savana N16 ....73 C6
Savernake Ct HA7 ....25 B4
Savernake Ho N4 ....51 B2
Savernake Rd N9 ....18 A5
NW3 ....70 D4
Savery Dr KT6 ....197 C2
Savile Cl
New Malden KT3 ....199 C4
Thames Ditton KT7 ....197 A1
Savile Gdns CR0 ....221 D6
Savill Gdns SW20 ....200 A6
Savill Ho E16 ....122 D5
2 SW4 ....159 D5
Savill Row IG8 ....36 D4
Saville Cres TW15 ....171 B4
Saville Rd E16 ....122 A5
W4 ....111 B3
Dagenham RM6 ....59 B2
Twickenham TW1 ....152 D3
Saville Row W1 115 C6 249 A6
Coney Hall BR2 ....208 D1
Enfield EN3 ....6 D3
Savin Lo 7 SM2 ....218 A1
Savona Cl 15 SW19 ....178 D3
Savona Ct SW20 ....178 D2
Savona St SW8 137 C5 269 A3
Savoy Ave UB3 ....105 C1
Savoy Bldgs W12 ....111 D6
Savoy Circus W3 ....111 D6
Savoy Cl E15 ....98 C6
Edgware HA8 ....26 C5
Savoy Ct SW5 ....255 B4
WC2 ....250 B5
Savoy Hill WC2 ....250 C5
Savoy Par EN1 ....5 C2
Savoy Pl WC2 ..116 B6 250 C5

Savoy Row WC2 ... 250 C6
Savoy St WC2 ... 116 B6 250 C5
Savoy Steps WC2 ... 250 C5
Savoy Way WC2 ... 250 C5
Sawbill Cl UB4 ... 84 D2
Sawkins Cl SW19 ... 157 A2
Sawley Rd W12 ... 112 A5
Sawtry Cl SM5 ... 202 C2
Sawyer Cl N9 ... 18 A2
Sawyer Ho 15 SE21 ... 183 C6
Sawyer St SE1 ... 117 A4 252 A2
Sawyer's Hill TW10 ... 154 B4
Sawyers Lawn W13 ... 87 A1
Saxby Rd SW2 ... 160 A4
Saxham Rd IG11 ... 101 D5
Saxlingham Rd E4 ... 20 B1
Saxon Ave TW13 ... 151 B2
Saxon Bsns Ctr SW19 ... 180 A2
Saxon Cl E17 ... 53 C2
Hillingdon UB8 ... 82 A2
Surbiton KT6 ... 197 D3
Saxon Cty Jun Sch
TW17 ... 192 C4
Saxon Dr W3 ... 88 D2
Saxon Gdns UB1 ... 107 A6
Saxon Hall W2 ... 245 C5
Saxon Ho 4 SW4 ... 137 D1
Feltham TW13 ... 151 B2
Saxon Rd E3 ... 97 B5
E6 ... 100 B3
N22 ... 32 D2
SE25 ... 205 B4
Ashford TW15 ... 171 B4
Bromley BR1 ... 186 D3
Ilford IG1 ... 78 D3
Southall UB1 ... 107 A6
Wembley HA9 ... 67 A5
Saxon Way N14 ... 15 D5
Saxon Wlk DA14 ... 190 C4
Saxonbury Ave TW16 ... 172 B1
Saxonbury Cl CR4 ... 202 B6
Saxonbury Ct 16 N7 ... 71 D3
2 N7 ... 72 A3
Saxonbury Gdns KT6 ... 197 C1
Saxonfield Cl SW2 ... 160 B4
Saxony Par UB3 ... 83 A2
Saxton Cl SE13 ... 142 B2
Saxville Rd BR5 ... 190 B1
Sayer Ho SE4 ... 141 A1
Sayers Ho 4 N2 ... 30 B1
Sayer's Wlk TW10 ... 154 B4
Sayes Court St SE8 ... 141 B6
Sayes Ct SE8 ... 141 B6
Sayesbury La N18 ... 34 A5
Scadbury Gdns BR5 ... 190 A1
Scadbury Park Nature
Reserve BR7 ... 189 D4
Scads Hill Cl BR5,BR6 ... 211 D3
Scafell NW1 ... 232 A2
Scala St W1 ... 239 B4
Scales Rd N17 ... 52 A6
Scampston Mews 5
W10 ... 90 D1
Scampton Rd TW6 ... 148 B5
Scandrett St 38 E1 ... 118 B5
Scarba Wlk N1 ... 73 B2
Scarborough Rd E11 ... 54 B1
N4 ... 50 C1
N9 ... 18 C4
Harlington TW6 ... 149 A5
Scarborough St E1 ... 243 D1
Scarbrook Rd CR0 ... 221 A5
Scardale Ho 12 E5 ... 74 B6
Scarle Rd HA0 ... 65 D2
Scarlet Rd SE6 ... 164 C1
Scarlette Manor Wlk 10
SE24 ... 160 C4
Scarsbrook Ho 2 SW2 160 C5
Scarsbrook Rd SE3 ... 143 D2
Scarsdale Pl W8 ... 255 C6
Scarsdale Rd HA2 ... 64 A5
Scarsdale Villas
W8 ... 113 C3 255 B5
Scarth Rd SW13 ... 133 D2
Scawen Cl SM5 ... 219 A4
Scawen Rd SE8 ... 119 A1
Scawfell St E2 ... 95 D5
Scaynes Link N12 ... 29 C6
Sceptre Ho 9 E1 ... 96 C3
Sceptre Rd E2 ... 96 C4
Sch of Nursing
W1 ... 93 C2 239 A4
Sch of Pharmacy
WC1 ... 94 A3 240 B6
Sch of the Douay Martyrs
UB10 ... 60 D4
Schiller International Univ
BR4 ... 224 B4
Schofield Wlk SE3 ... 143 A5
Scholars Ho 6 E4 ... 20 B3
Scholars Rd E4 ... 20 B3
SW12 ... 159 C3
Scholefield Rd N19 ... 71 D6
Scholey Ho SW11 ... 136 C2
Schomberg Ho SW1 ... 259 D4
Schonfeld Sq N16 ... 51 B1
School App 22 E2 ... 95 C4
School Bell Cloisters 15
E3 ... 97 A5
School Cotts DA14 ... 190 C5
School Flats SW8 ... 270 A1
School Ho SE1 ... 263 A4
School House La TW11 175 C3
School La Bexley DA16 ... 146 B2
Lower Halliford TW17 ... 192 D2
Pinner HA5 ... 41 A5
Surbiton KT6 ... 198 B1
Teddington KT1 ... 175 C2
School of Finance &
Management N7 ... 72 B2
School of St David & St
Katharine The N8 ... 50 A5
School Pas
3 Kingston u T KT1 ... 176 B1
Southall UB1 ... 107 B6
School Rd E12 ... 78 B4
NW10 ... 89 B3
Ashford TW15 ... 170 D4
Chislehurst BR7 ... 189 A3
Dagenham RM10 ... 103 D6
East Molesey KT8 ... 196 B5
Hampton TW12 ... 174 A4
Hounslow TW3 ... 130 A2
Littleton TW15 ... 170 D3
Teddington KT1 ... 175 C2
School Road Ave TW12 174 A4
School Way RM8 ... 80 C5
School Wlk TW16 ... 193 D6
Schoolbell Mews 16 E3 ... 97 A5
Schoolhouse La E1 ... 118 D6
Schoolway N12 ... 30 B4
Schooner Cl E14 ... 120 B3
1 SE16 ... 118 D4
Schubert Rd SW15 ... 157 B6
Elstree WD6 ... 9 D5
Science Mus*
SW7 ... 114 B3 256 C5
Scilly Isles KT10 ... 212 C6
Sclater St E1 ... 243 D6
Scoles Cres SW2 ... 160 C3
Scoresby St SE1 ... 251 C3
Scoresdale SE19 ... 183 C2
Scorton Ave UB6 ... 87 A5
Scorton Ho 2 N1 ... 95 C5
Scot Gr HA5 ... 22 D3
Scotch Comm W13 ... 87 B2
Scotch Ho SW1 114 D4 247 C1
Scoter Cl IG8 ... 37 B3
Scoter Ct 23 SE8 ... 141 B6
Scotia Bldg 10 E1 ... 118 D6
Scotia Ct 3 SE16 ... 118 C3
Scotia Rd 24 SW2 ... 160 C4
Scotland Gn N17 ... 33 D1
Scotland Green Rd EN3 ... 18 D6
Scotland Green Rd N EN3 7 A1
Scotland Pl SW1 ... 250 A3
Scotland Rd IG9 ... 21 C3
Scotney Ho E9 ... 74 C2
Scots Cl TW19 ... 148 A3
Scotsdale Cl
Cheam SM3 ... 217 A1
St Paul's Cray BR5,BR7 ... 211 C5
Scotsdale Rd SE12 ... 165 B6
Scotson Ho SE11 ... 261 A3
Scotswood St
EC1 ... 94 C3 241 B6
Scotswood Wlk N17 ... 34 A3
Scott Cl SW16 ... 182 B2
West Drayton UB7 ... 104 B2
West Ewell KT19 ... 215 A3
Scott Cres HA2 ... 63 D6
Scott Ct 17 N16 ... 73 C5
4 SW11 ... 137 B3
W4 ... 111 B4
Scott Ellis Gdns
NW8 ... 92 B4 229 C1
Scott Farm Cl KT7 ... 197 B1
Scott Gdns TW5 ... 128 D5
Scott Ho 6 E13 ... 99 A5
N1 ... 235 C6
N7 ... 72 B2
3 N18 ... 34 A5
NW8 ... 237 A5
2 NW10 ... 67 B1
4 Erith DA17 ... 125 B1
Richmond TW10 ... 153 C2
Scott Lidgett Cres SE16 118 A4
Scott St E1 ... 96 B3
Scott Trimmer Way
TW3 ... 129 A3
Scott Wilkie Prim Sch
E16 ... 99 C1
Scottes La RM8 ... 58 D1
Scott's Ave
Ashford TW16 ... 171 C3
Beckenham BR2 ... 186 B1
Scotts Ct 6 W12 ... 112 B4
Scotts Dr TW12 ... 173 D3
Scotts Farm Rd KT19 ... 215 A2
Scott's La BR2,BR3 ... 186 B1
Scotts Park Prim Sch
BR1 ... 187 C2
Scotts Rd Plaistow BR1 ... 187 A3
Southall UB2 ... 106 D3
Scott's Rd E10 ... 54 A1
W12 ... 112 B4
Scott's Sufferance Wharf
SE1 ... 253 D1
Scott's Way TW16 ... 171 C3
Scott's Yd EC4 ... 252 C6
Scottwell Dr NW9 ... 45 D4
Scoulding Ho 6 E14 ... 119 C3
Scoulding Rd E16 ... 99 A1
Scouler St E14 ... 120 B6
Scout App NW10 ... 67 C4
Scout Way NW7 ... 27 B6
Scovell Cres SE1 ... 252 A1
Scovell Rd SE1 ... 252 A1
Scrattons Terr IG11 ... 103 A5
Scriven Ct 2 E8 ... 95 D6
Scriven St E8 ... 95 D6
Scrooby St SE6 ... 163 D5
Scrope Ho EC1 ... 241 A4
Scrubs La NW10,W10,W12 90 B3
Scrutton Cl SW12 ... 159 D4
Scrutton St EC2 ... 95 C3 243 A5
Scudamore La NW9 ... 45 A5
Scutari Rd SE22 ... 162 C6
Scylla Cres TW6&TW14 ... 148 D4
Scylla Rd SE15 ... 140 B2
East Bedfont TW14,TW6 ... 148 D5
Seabright St 27 E2 ... 96 B4
Seabrook Dr BR4 ... 224 C6
Seabrook Gdns RM7 ... 59 C2
Seabrook Rd RM8 ... 80 D5
Seacole Cl W3 ... 89 B2
Seacole Ct N15 ... 51 D4
Seacole Lo N21 ... 16 B6
Seacourt Rd SE2 ... 124 D4
Seacroft Gdns WD1 ... 22 D6
Seafield Rd N11 ... 31 D6
Seaford Cl HA4 ... 61 B6
Seaford Ho 8 SE16 ... 118 C4
Seaford Rd E17 ... 53 D6
N15 ... 51 C4
W13 ... 109 B5
Enfield EN1 ... 5 C1
Seaford St WC1 ... 233 B1
Seaforth Ave KT3 ... 200 B5
Seaforth Cres N5 ... 73 A3
Seaforth Gdns N21 ... 16 C3
Woodford IG8 ... 37 C5
Worcester Pk KT19 ... 215 D3
Seaforth Lo 2 SW13 ... 133 D3
Seaforth Pl SW1 ... 259 B6
Seager Pl E3 ... 97 B2
Seagrave Lo SW6 ... 265 B6
Seagrave Rd
SW6 ... 135 C6 265 B6
Seagrave Cl E1 ... 96 D2
Seagry Rd E11 ... 55 B2
Seal Ho SE1 ... 262 D6
Seal St E8 ... 73 D4
Sealand Rd TW6 ... 148 C5
Sealand Wlk UB5 ... 85 A4
Searle Ct N4 ... 50 B1
2 Mitcham CR4 ... 180 C2
Searle Ho 15 E1 ... 96 D2
Searles Cl
SW11 ... 136 C5 267 B3
Searles Rd SE1 ... 262 D4
Sears St SE5 ... 139 B5
Searson Ho SE17 ... 261 D3
Seasalter Ho 10 SW9 ... 138 C4
Seasprite Cl 10 UB5 ... 84 D4
Seath Ho 4 SE26 ... 184 B5
Seaton Ave IG3 ... 79 D3
Seaton Cl 6 E13 ... 99 A3
SE11 ... 261 C2
SW15 ... 156 B4
Twickenham TW2 ... 152 B5
Seaton Dr TW15 ... 148 A2
Seaton Gdns HA4 ... 62 A6
Seaton Point E5 ... 74 A4
Seaton Rd Bexley DA16 ... 146 C5
Hayes UB3 ... 105 B5
Mitcham CR4 ... 180 C1
Twickenham TW2 ... 152 A5
Wembley HA0 ... 88 A5
Seaton St N18 ... 34 A5
Seavington Ho 3 SE5 ... 139 C2
Sebastian Ct 10 IG11 ... 79 D1
Sebastian Ho 22 N1 ... 95 C5
Sebastian St EC1 94 D4 234 D1
Sebastopol Rd N9 ... 34 A6
Sebbon St N1 ... 72 D1
Sebergham Gr NW7 ... 28 A3
Sebert Rd E7 ... 77 B4
Sebright Ho 21 E2 ... 96 A5
Sebright JMI Sch E2 ... 96 A5
Sebright Rd EN5 ... 1 A2
Secker Cres HA3 ... 24 A2
Secker Ho SW9 ... 138 D3
Secker St SE1 ... 251 A3
Second Ave E12 ... 78 A3
E13 ... 99 A4
E17 ... 53 C4
N18 ... 34 C6
NW4 ... 46 D5
SW14 ... 133 C2
W3 ... 111 D5
W10 ... 91 A3
Dagenham RM10 ... 103 D5
Enfield EN1 ... 17 D6
Hayes UB3 ... 105 D5
Ilford RM6 ... 58 C4
Walton-on-T KT12 ... 194 B3
Wembley HA9 ... 65 D6
Second Cl KT8 ... 196 A5
Second Cross Rd TW2 ... 152 C2
Second Way HA9 ... 66 D4
Sedan Way
SE17 ... 117 C1 263 A2
Sedcombe Cl DA14 ... 190 C6
Sedcote Rd EN3 ... 18 D6
Sedding St SW1 ... 258 A4
Seddon Ho EC2 ... 242 A4
Seddon Rd SM4 ... 202 B4
Seddon St WC1 ... 94 B4 233 D1
Sedge Rd N17 ... 34 C3
Sedgebrook Rd SE3 ... 143 D2
Sedgecombe Ave HA3 ... 43 C4
Sedgefield Ct UB5 ... 63 D3
Sedgeford Rd W12 ... 111 D5
Sedgehill Rd SE6 ... 185 D5
Sedgehill Sch SE6 ... 185 D5
Sedgemere Ave N2 ... 48 A6
Sedgemere Rd SE2 ... 124 C3
Sedgemoor Dr RM10 ... 81 C4
Sedgeway SE6 ... 164 D3
Sedgewick Ho SW19 ... 156 D2
Sedgewood Cl BR2 ... 208 D2
Sedgley Ho N4 ... 72 B6
Sedgmoor Pl SE5 ... 139 C5
Sedgwick Ave UB10 ... 60 D1
Sedgwick Rd E10 ... 76 A6
Sedgwick St E9 ... 74 D3
Sedleigh Rd SW18 ... 157 B5
Sedlescombe Rd
SW6 ... 135 C6 265 A6
Sedley Cl EN1 ... 6 B5
Sedley Ct SE26 ... 162 B2
Sedley Ho SE11 ... 260 D2
Sedley Pl W1 ... 238 C1
Sedum Cl NW9 ... 44 D4
Seeley Dr SE21 ... 183 C6
Seelig Ave NW9 ... 46 A2
Seely Rd SW17 ... 181 A4
Seething La
EC3 ... 117 C6 253 B6
Seething Wells Halls of
Residence KT6 ... 197 C3
Seething Wells La KT6 ... 197 C3
Sefton Ave NW7 ... 27 B5
Harrow HA3 ... 24 B2
Sefton Cl BR5 ... 211 D5
Sefton Ct TW5 ... 129 D4
Sefton Lo 2 TW1 ... 153 C5
Sefton Rd Croydon CR0 ... 206 A1
St Paul's Cray BR5 ... 211 D5
Sefton St SW15 ... 134 C2
Segal Cl SE23 ... 163 A4
Sekforde St EC1 ... 94 D3 241 C6
Sekhon Terr TW13 ... 151 C1
Selan Gdns UB4 ... 84 B2
Selbie Ave NW10 ... 67 D3
Selborne 2 SW11 ... 137 A2
Selborne Ave E12 ... 78 C4
E17 ... 53 B5
Sidcup DA5 ... 169 A3
Selborne Gdns NW4 ... 46 A5
Wembley UB6 ... 87 A5
Selborne Ho SE1 ... 252 C1
Selborne Prim Sch UB6 ... 86 D5
Selborne Rd E17 ... 53 C4
N14 ... 16 A1
N22 ... 32 B2
1 SE5 ... 139 B3
Ilford IG1 ... 78 C6
Kingston u T KT3 ... 177 C1
Sidcup DA14 ... 190 B6
South Croydon CR0 ... 221 D5
Selborne Wlk E17 ... 53 B5
Selbourne Ave KT6 ... 214 C5
Selby Chase HA4 ... 62 B6
Selby Cl 14 E6 ... 100 A2
Chessington KT9 ... 214 A1
Chislehurst West BR7 ... 188 C4
Selby Ct TW2 ... 152 B2
Selby Gdns UB1 ... 85 C3
Selby Gn SM5 ... 202 C2
Selby Ho 10 SW4 ... 159 C5
6 W10 ... 91 A4
Selby Rd E11 ... 76 C5
E13 ... 99 B2
N17 ... 33 C4
SE20 ... 184 A1
W5 ... 87 C3
Ashford TW15 ... 171 A4
Carshalton SM5 ... 202 C2
Selby St E1 ... 96 A3
Selden Ho 2 SE15 ... 140 C3
Selden Rd SE15 ... 140 C3
Selden Wlk N7 ... 72 B6
Seldon Ho SW1 ... 259 A1
SW8 ... 269 A3
Selena Ct N20 ... 14 D1
Selfridges W1 ... 238 B1
Selhurst Cl SW19 ... 156 D3
Selhurst New Ct SE25 ... 205 C3
Selhurst New Rd SE25 ... 205 C3
Selhurst Park (Crystal Palace
FC) SE25 ... 205 C5
Selhurst Pl SE25 ... 205 C3
Selhurst Rd N9 ... 17 C1
SE25 ... 205 C4
Selhurst Sta SE25 ... 205 C4
Selina Ho NW8 ... 236 D6
Selinas La RM8 ... 59 B2
Selkirk Ct N17 ... 33 C1
Selkirk Ho N1 ... 233 C6
4 N16 ... 73 C5
Selkirk Rd SW17 ... 180 C6
Twickenham TW2 ... 152 A3
Sellers Hall Cl N3 ... 29 C3
Sellincourt Inf Sch
SW17 ... 180 C4
Sellincourt Jun Sch
SW17 ... 180 C4
Sellincourt Rd SW17 ... 180 C4
Sellindge Cl BR3 ... 185 B3
Sellons Ave NW10 ... 89 D6
Sellwood Dr EN5 ... 12 D6
Selma Ho W12 ... 90 B1
Selman Ho 3 E9 ... 75 A2
Selsdon Ave CR2 ... 221 B2
Selsdon Cl KT6 ... 198 A4
Selsdon Ct 4 UB1 ... 85 D1
Selsdon High Sch CR2 ... 222 D1
Selsdon Park Rd CR0,
CR2 ... 223 B1
Selsdon Rd E11 ... 55 A2
E13 ... 99 C5
NW2 ... 67 D6
SE27 ... 182 D6
South Croydon CR2 ... 221 B2
Selsdon Road Ind Est
CR2 ... 221 B2
Selsdon Way E14 ... 119 D3
Selsea Pl N16 ... 73 C3
Selsey Cres DA16 ... 146 D4
Selsey St E14 ... 97 C2
Selvage La NW7 ... 27 B6
Selway Cl HA5 ... 40 B6
Selwood Ho 1 N4 ... 51 B2
Selwood Pl
SW7 ... 114 B1 256 C2
Selwood Rd Cheam SM3 201 B1
Chessington KT9 ... 213 D4
Croydon CR0 ... 206 B1
Selwood Terr SW7 ... 256 C2
Selworthy Cl E11 ... 55 A4
Selworthy Ho SW11 ... 266 D2
Selworthy Rd SE6 ... 163 B1
Selwyn Ave E4 ... 36 A4
Ilford IG3 ... 57 D3
Richmond TW9 ... 132 B2
Selwyn Cl TW4 ... 129 A1
Selwyn Cres DA16 ... 146 B1
Selwyn Ct E17 ... 53 C4
SE3 ... 142 D2
Edgware HA8 ... 26 D3
8 Richmond TW10 ... 154 B6
Selwyn Ho 3 SW15 ... 156 D5
Selwyn Inf Sch E4 ... 36 A4
Selwyn Jun Sch E4 ... 36 A4
Selwyn Prim Sch E13 ... 99 A6
Selwyn Rd E3 ... 97 B5
E13 ... 99 B6
NW10 ... 67 C1
New Malden KT3 ... 199 B4
Semley Ho SW1 ... 258 C3
Semley Pl SW1 ... 115 B2 258 C3
Semley Rd SW16 ... 182 A1
Senate St SE15 ... 140 C3
Senator Wlk SE28 ... 123 B3
Senators Lo 20 E3 ... 97 A5
Sencler Ho SE2 ... 146 D6
Sendall Ct 13 SW11 ... 136 B2
Seneca Rd CR7 ... 205 A5
Senga Rd SM6 ... 203 A1
Senhouse Rd SM3 ... 216 D5
Senior St W2 ... 91 D2
Senlac Rd SE12 ... 165 B3
Sennen Rd EN1 ... 17 D4
Sennen Wlk SE9 ... 166 A1
Senrab St E1 ... 96 D1
Sentinel Cl UB5 ... 85 A3
Sentinel Ho NW4 ... 46 C5
SentinelSq NW4 ... 46 C5
September Ct UB1 ... 107 D5
September Way HA7 ... 25 B4
Sequoia Cl WD2 ... 8 B3
Sequoia Gdns BR6 ... 211 D2
Sequoia Pk HA5 ... 23 D4
Seraph Ct EC1 ... 95 A4 235 A2
Serbin Cl E10 ... 54 A2
Sergeant Ind Est The
SW18 ... 157 D5
Serica Ct 14 SE10 ... 142 A5
Serjeants' Inn EC4 ... 241 B1
Serlby Ct W14 ... 254 C6
Serle St WC2 ... 94 B1 240 D2
Sermon La EC4 ... 242 A1
Serpentine Ct 10 SE16 ... 118 D4
Serpentine Gallery*
W2 ... 114 B4 246 D2
Serpentine Rd
W2 ... 114 D5 247 C3
Serpentine The*
W2 ... 114 C5 247 B3
Service Route No 1 E15 ... 76 B1
Service Route No 2 E15 ... 76 B1
Service Route No 3 E15 ... 76 B1
Serviden Dr BR1 ... 187 D2
Servite Ho N14 ... 15 B6
SE13 ... 141 D4
SE26 ... 184 C4
Beckenham BR3 ... 185 B2
Worcester Pk KT4 ... 215 D6
Servite RC Prim Sch
SW10 ... 136 A6 266 A6
Servius Ct 2 TW8 ... 131 D5
Setchell Rd SE1 117 D2 263 C4
Setchell Way SE1 ... 263 C4
Seth St 18 SE16 ... 118 C4
Seton Ct 3 NW9 ... 46 A5
Seton Gdns RM9 ... 80 C1
Settle Point 11 E13 ... 99 A5
Settles St E1 ... 96 A1
Settrington Rd SW6 ... 135 D3
Seven Acres
Carshalton SM5 ... 218 C6
Northwood HA6 ... 22 A4
Seven Dials WC2 94 A1 240 A1
Seven Kings High Sch
IG2 ... 57 B2
Seven Kings Rd IG3 ... 79 D6
Seven Kings Sta IG3 ... 57 C1
Seven Mills JMI Sch
E14 ... 119 C4
Seven Sisters N15 ... 51 D4
Seven Sisters Inf Sch
N15 ... 51 B4
Seven Sisters Rd N4,N7,
N15 ... 51 A2
Seven Sisters Sta N15 ... 51 C4
Seven Stars Cnr W12 ... 112 A3
Seven Ways Par IG2 ... 56 C4
Sevenoaks Rd SE4 ... 163 B5
Orpington BR6 ... 227 D4
Sevenoaks Way BR5 ... 190 C1
Seventh Ave E12 ... 78 B4
Hayes UB3 ... 106 A5
Severn Ct 11 KT2 ... 175 D2
Severn Dr Enfield EN1 ... 6 A5
Hinchley Wood KT10 ... 213 A6
Severn Ho 7 W10 ... 91 A4
Severn Way NW10 ... 67 D3
Severnake Cl E14 ... 119 C2
Severus Rd SW11 ... 136 C1
Seville Ho 11 E1 ... 118 A5
Seville Mews N1 ... 73 C1
Seville St SW1 ... 247 D1
Sevington Rd NW4 ... 46 B3
Sevington St W9 ... 91 D3
Seward Rd W7 ... 109 A4
Penge BR3 ... 184 D1
Seward St EC1 ... 95 A4 235 A1
Sewardstone Gdns E4 ... 19 D6
Sewardstone Rd E2 ... 96 C5
E4 ... 19 D6
Sewdley St E5 ... 74 D5
Sewell Ho 7 N16 ... 73 C3
Sewell Rd SE28 ... 124 B4
Sewell St E13 ... 99 A4
Sextant Ave E14 ... 120 B2
Sexton's Ho 4 SE13 ... 142 A6
Seychelle Ct BR3 ... 185 D3
Seymour Ave N17 ... 34 A1
West Barnes SM4 ... 200 D2
Seymour Cl
East Molesey KT8 ... 196 A4
Hatch End HA5 ... 23 B2
Seymour Ct E4 ... 20 D2
N10 ... 31 A1
N16 ... 52 A1
N21 ... 16 B5
NW2 ... 68 B6
SW15 ... 134 B1
Seymour Dr BR2 ... 210 B1
Seymour Gdns SE4 ... 141 A2
Feltham TW13 ... 172 C6
Kingston u T KT5 ... 198 B4
Redbridge IG1 ... 56 B1
Ruislip HA4 ... 40 D1
Twickenham TW1 ... 153 B4
Seymour Ho NW1 ... 232 D1
1 SW8 ... 137 C3
WC1 ... 240 A6
Seymour Mews W1 ... 238 A2
Seymour Pl SE25 ... 206 B5
W1 ... 92 D1 237 C2
Seymour Rd E4 ... 19 D3
E6 ... 99 D6
E10 ... 53 B1
N3 ... 29 D3
N8 ... 50 D4
N9 ... 18 B2
SW18 ... 157 B5
SW19 ... 156 D1
W4 ... 111 A2
Carshalton CR4 ... 203 A2
East Molesey KT8 ... 196 A4
Hampton TW12 ... 174 A5
Teddington KT1 ... 175 D2
Wallington SM5 ... 219 A3
Seymour St SE18 ... 123 A3
W1 ... 92 D1 237 D1
Seymour Terr SE20 ... 184 B2
Seymour Villas SE20 ... 184 A2
Seymour Way TW16 ... 171 C3
Seymour Wlk
SW10 ... 136 A6 266 A6
Seyssel St E14 ... 120 A2
Shaa Rd W3 ... 111 B6
Shacklegate La TW11 ... 174 C6
Shackleton Cl SE23 ... 162 B2
Shackleton Ct 2 SE21 ... 161 B2
4 W12 ... 112 B4
7 Stanwell TW19 ... 148 A5
Shackleton Ho 5 E1 ... 118 C5
4 NW10 ... 67 B1
Shackleton Rd UB1 ... 107 B6
Shacklewell Ho 3 E8 ... 73 D4
Shacklewell JMI Sch E8 73 D4
Shacklewell La E8 ... 73 D3
Shacklewell Rd N16 ... 73 D4
Shacklewell Row E8 ... 73 D4
Shacklewell St 30 E2 ... 95 D4
Shad Thames
SE1 ... 117 D4 253 D2
Shadbolt Cl KT4 ... 215 D6
Shadwell Ct UB5 ... 85 B5
Shadwell Dr UB5 ... 85 B4
Shadwell Gdns E1 ... 118 C6
Shadwell Pierhead E1 ... 118 C6
Shadwell Sta E1 ... 118 B6
Shady Bush Cl WD2 ... 8 A4
Shaef Way TW11 ... 175 A3
Shafter Rd RM10 ... 81 D2
Shaftesbury Ave
W1 ... 115 D6 249 D6
Enfield EN3 ... 6 D3
Feltham TW14 ... 150 A5
Harrow HA1,HA2 ... 42 A1
Kenton HA3 ... 44 A3
New Barnet EN5 ... 2 A1
Southall UB2 ... 107 C3
Shaftesbury Circ HA2 ... 42 A1
Shaftesbury Ct N1 ... 235 C3
1 SE5 ... 139 B1
3 SE28 ... 124 C5
Dagenham RM6 ... 58 C2
Shaftesbury Gdns NW10 89 C3
Shaftesbury Ho 18 N16 ... 73 C5
SE25 ... 206 A3
W2 ... 245 D6
Shaftesbury Lo 9 E14 ... 97 D1
Shaftesbury Mews W8 ... 255 B5
Shaftesbury Park Chambers
1 SW11 ... 137 A2
Shaftesbury Prim Sch
E7 ... 77 C1
Shaftesbury Rd E4 ... 20 B3

Shaftesbury Rd *continued*
E7 77 C1
E10 53 C1
E17 53 D3
N4,N19 50 A1
N18 33 D4
Beckenham BR3 185 B1
Carshalton SM5 202 C2
Richmond TW9 132 A2
Shaftesbury Sch HA3 23 D2
Shaftesbury St N1 235 C3
Shaftesbury Way TW2 152 B1
Shaftesbury Waye UB4 84 C1
Shaftesburys The IG11 101 A5
Shafteswood Ct SW17 158 D1
Shafto Mews SW1 257 D5
Shafton Rd E9 96 D6
Shafts Ct EC3 243 A1
Shaftsbury Ct E6 100 C1
SW6 265 D1
Shaftsbury Mews 2
SW4 159 C6
Shaftsbury Park Prim Sch
SW11 137 A3
Shahjalal Ho 18 E2 96 A5
Shakespeare Ave N11 31 C5
NW10 89 B6
Feltham TW14 150 A5
Hayes UB4 84 B2
Shakespeare Cres E12 78 B2
NW10 89 B6
Shakespeare Dr HA3 44 B3
Shakespeare Gdns N2 48 D5
Shakespeare Ho 3 E9 74 C1
N14 15 D2
1 Erith DA17 125 B1
Shakespeare Rd E17 34 D1
N3 29 C2
NW7 28 A6
SE24 138 D1
W3 111 A5
W7 108 D6
Bexley DA7 147 A4
Shakespeare Twr EC2 242 B4
Shakespeare Way
TW13 172 C6
Shakespeares Globe Theatre
(site of) SE1 252 B4
Shakspeare Mews 7
N16 73 C4
Shakspeare Wlk N16 73 C4
Shalcomb St
SW10 136 A6 266 B5
Shalden Ho 6 SW15 155 D5
Shaldon Dr Merton SM4 201 A4
Ruislip HA4 62 C5
Shaldon Rd HA8 26 B1
Shalfleet Dr W10 112 D6
Shalford NW10 90 A6
3 Woodford IG8 37 C4
Shalford Cl BR6 227 A4
Shalford Ct N1 234 C4
Shalford Ho SE1 262 D6
Shalimar Gdns W3 111 A6
Shalimar Lo W3 111 A6
Shalimar Rd W3 111 A6
Shallons Rd SE9 188 D6
Shalston Villas KT5,KT6 198 B3
Shalstone Rd SW14,
TW9 132 D2
Shamrock Ho SE26 184 A6
Shamrock Rd CR0 204 B3
Shamrock St SW4 137 D2
Shamrock Way N14 15 B3
Shand St SE1 117 C4 253 B2
Shandon Rd SW4 159 C5
Shandy St E1 96 D3
Shanklin Gdns WD1 22 C6
Shanklin Rd N8 49 D4
N15 52 A5
Shannon Cl NW2 68 D5
Southall UB2 106 D1
Shannon Cnr KT3 200 A5
Shannon Commercial Ctr
KT3 200 A5
Shannon Ct N16 73 C5
NW10 68 A2
9 SE15 139 D5
Thornton Heath CR0 205 A1
Shannon Gr SW9 138 B1
Shannon Pl NW8 92 C5 230 B4
Shannon Way BR3 185 D4
Shanti Ct SW18 157 C3
Shap Cres SM5 202 D1
Shapla JMI Sch E1 118 A6
Shapland Way N13 32 B5
Shapwick Cl N11 30 D5
Shardcroft Ave SE24 160 D6
Shardeloes Rd SE14 141 B3
Shard's Sq SE15 140 A6
Sharebourne Ho SW2 160 C6
Sharland Cl CR7 204 C3
Sharman Ct DA14 190 A6
Sharnbrook Ho W6 265 A6
Sharnbrooke Cl DA16 146 C2
Sharon Cl KT6 197 C1
Sharon Gdns E9 96 C6
Sharon Rd W4 111 B1
Enfield EN3 7 A3
Sharp Ho SW8 137 B2
Sharpe Cl W7 86 D2
Sharples Hall St 8 NW1 70 D1
Sharpness Cl UB4 85 A2
Sharpness Ct 2 SE15 139 D5
Sharps La HA4 39 B2
Sharratt St SE15 140 C6
Sharstead St
SE17 116 D1 261 C1
Sharvel La UB5 84 B6
Sharwell Ho SW18 157 D5
Sharwood WC1 233 D3
Shaver's Pl SW1 249 C5
Shaw Ave IG11 103 A5
Shaw Cl SE28 124 B5
Bushey WD2 8 C2
Shaw Ct N19 72 A6
12 SW11 136 B2
8 W3 111 A3
Shaw Dr KT12 194 C2
Shaw Gdns IG11 103 A5
Shaw Ho 6 E14 97 A1
5 E16 122 C5
6 Erith DA17 125 B1
Shaw Path BR1 164 D1
Shaw Rd SE22 139 C1
Catford BR1 164 D1
Enfield EN3 6 D4
Shaw Sq E17 35 A2
Shaw Way SM6 220 A1
Shawbrooke Rd SE9 143 D1
Shawbury Ct SE22 161 D6
Shawbury Rd SE22 161 D6
Shawfield Ct UB7 104 A3
Shawfield Pk BR1 187 D1
Shawfield St
SW3 114 C1 257 B1
Shawford Ct 8 SW15 156 A4
Shawford Rd KT19 215 B2
Shaws Wood Cotts EN4 3 C3
Shearing Dr SM4 202 A2
Shearling Way N7 72 A2
Shearman Rd SE3 142 D2
Shears Ct TW16 171 C3
Shears The TW16 171 C3
Shearsmith Ho 14 E1 118 A6
Shearwater Ct 24 SE8 141 B6
Shearwater Rd SM1 217 B3
Shearwater Way UB4 84 D1
Sheaveshill Ave NW9 45 C5
Sheaveshill Ct NW9 45 C5
Sheaveshill Par NW9 45 C5
Sheen Common Dr
SW14,TW10 154 C6
Sheen Court Rd TW10 132 C1
Sheen Ct TW10 132 C1
Sheen Gate Gdns SW14 133 A1
Sheen Gr N1 94 C6 234 A6
Sheen La SW14 133 A1
Sheen Mount JMI Sch
SW14 154 D6
Sheen Pk TW10,TW9 132 A1
Sheen Rd
Richmond TW10,TW9 132 B1
St Paul's Cray BR5 211 D5
Sheen Way SM6 220 B3
Sheen Wood SW14 155 A6
Sheendale Rd TW9 132 B1
Sheenewood SE26 184 B6
Sheep La E8 96 B6
Sheep Walk Mews 7
SW19 179 A4
Sheepcote Cl TW5 128 A5
Sheepcote La SW11 136 D3
Sheepcote Rd HA1 42 D3
Sheepcotes Rd RM6 59 A5
Sheephouse Way KT3 199 C2
Sheepwalk TW17 192 B3
Sheerwater Rd E16 99 D2
Sheffield Ho 14 SE15 139 D4
Sheffield Rd TW14,TW6 149 A6
Sheffield Sq 2 E3 97 B4
Sheffield St WC2 240 C1
Sheffield Terr
W8 113 C5 245 B3
Sheffield Way TW14,
TW6 149 B6
Shefton Rise HA6 22 A3
Shelbey Ct BR1 186 D2
Shelbourne Cl HA5 41 B6
Shelbourne Ho 20 N19 49 D2
Shelbourne Rd N17 34 B2
Shelburne Ct SW15 156 D6
Shelburne Ho 9 SW16 181 C5
Shelburne Rd N7 72 B4
Shelbury Cl DA14 168 A1
Shelbury Rd SE22 162 B6
Sheldon Ave N6 48 D3
Sheldon Cl SE12 165 B6
SE20 184 B2
Sheldon Ct SW8 270 A3
Barnet EN5 1 D1
Sheldon Ho E4 36 C4
9 E9 74 D2
Teddington TW11 175 A4
Sheldon Rd N18 33 C6
NW2 68 D4
Dagenham RM9 81 A1
Erith DA7 147 B4
Sheldon St CR0 221 A5
Sheldrake Cl E16 122 B5
Sheldrake Ho 15 SE16 118 D2
Sheldrake Pl
W8 113 C4 245 A2
Sheldrick Cl CR4 180 B1
Shelduck Cl E15 76 D3
Shelduck Ct 36 SE8 141 B6
Sheldwich Terr BR2 210 A3
Shelford 20 KT1 176 C1
Shelford Ct 7 E5 52 B1
Shelford Pl N16 73 B5
Shelford Rd EN5 12 C5
Shelford Rise SE19 183 D3
Shelgate Rd SW11 158 D6
Shelgrove Rd N16 73 C3
Shell Cl BR2 210 A3
Shell Ctr SE1 250 D3
Shell Rd SE13 141 D2
Shelley N8 50 A6
Shelley Ave E12 78 A2
Greenford UB6 86 B4
Shelley Cl SE15 140 B3
Edgware HA8 26 C6
Greenford UB6 86 B4
Hayes UB4 84 A2
Orpington BR6 227 C5
Shelley Cres
Heston TW5 128 D4
Southall UB1 85 B1
Shelley Ct 12 E10 53 D2
8 E11 55 A5
N4 50 B1
SW3 267 D6
9 Kingston u T KT2 175 D6
Wembley HA0 65 C4
West Barnes KT3 200 A4
Shelley Dr DA16 145 C4
Shelley Gdns HA0 65 C6
Shelley Ho 21 E2 96 C4
9 N16 73 C4
SE17 262 B2
SW1 269 A6
Shelley Sch
SE11 116 C2 261 B3
Shelley Way SW17 180 B4
Shellness Rd E5 74 B3
Shellwood Rd SW11 136 D3
Shelly Lo EN2 5 B4
Shelmerdine Cl E3 97 C2
Shelson Ave TW13 171 D6
Shelton Rd SW19 179 C2
Shelton St WC2 94 A1 240 A1
Shene Ho EC1 241 A4
Shene Sec Sch SW14 133 C1
Shenfield Ho 3 SE18 143 D5
Shenfield Rd IG8 37 B3
Shenfield St N1 95 C5
Shenley Ave HA4 39 D1
Shenley Rd SE5 139 C4
Heston TW5 129 A4
Shenstone W13 109 C5
Shenstone Gdns IG2 57 D4
Shenstone Ho SW16 181 C5
Shepherd Cl W1 248 A6
Shepherd Ho 10 E14 97 D1
N7 72 A2
Shepherd Mkt W1 248 C3
Shepherd St
W1 115 B5 248 C3
Shepherdess Pl N1 235 B2
Shepherdess Wlk
N1 95 A5 235 B3
Shepherd's Bush Gn
W12 112 C4
Shepherd's Bush Market
W12 112 C4
Shepherd's Bush Pl
W12 112 D4
Shepherd's Bush Rd
W6 112 C3
Shepherd's Bush Sta
W12 112 D4
Shepherds Cl Ilford RM6 58 D5
Orpington BR6 227 D5
Shepperton TW17 192 D3
Shepherd's Cl N6 49 B3
Shepherds Ct 8 W12 112 D4
Shepherds Gn BR7 189 B3
Shepherd's Hill N6 49 C3
Shepherd's La E9 74 D2
Shepherds Leas SE9 145 B1
Shepherds Path UB5 63 A2
Shepherds Pl W1 248 A6
Shepherds Way CR2 222 D1
Shepherds Wlk NW2 68 A6
Bushey WD2 8 B2
Shepherd's Wlk NW3 70 B4
Shepiston La UB3 105 A1
Shepley Cl SM5 219 A5
Shepley Ct SW16 181 C6
Shepley Mews EN3 7 C6
Sheppard Cl Enfield EN1 6 B5
Kingston u T KT6 198 A5
Sheppard Dr SE16 118 B1
Sheppard Ho 28 E2 96 A5
8 SW2 160 C3
18 SW11 136 B2
Sheppard St E16 98 D3
Sheppard's Ct
Harrow HA1 42 C2
Wembley UB6 64 D2
Shepperton Bsns Park
TW17 193 A4
Shepperton Court Dr
TW17 192 D4
Shepperton Ct TW17 192 D3
Shepperton Rd
N1 95 B6 235 C6
Littleton TW17,TW18 192 A5
Petts Wood BR5 211 A3
Shepperton Sta TW17 193 A4
Shepperton Studios
TW17 192 B6
Sheppey Gdns RM9 80 C1
Sheppey Ho 18 E5 74 B4
Sheppey Rd RM9 80 C1
Sheppey Wlk N1 73 A1
Shepton Ct SW11 266 D2
Shepton Hos 11 E2 96 C4
Sherard Ct N19 72 A5
Sherard Ho 24 E9 74 C1
Sherard Rd SE9 166 A6
Sheraton Bsns Ctr UB6 87 C5
Sheraton Cl WD6 10 B6
Sheraton Ho SW1 268 D6
Sheraton Lo HA3 42 C6
Sheraton St W1 239 C1
Sheraton The 22 KT6 198 A4
Sherborne Ave Enfield EN3 6 C3
Southall UB2 107 C2
Sherborne Cl UB4 84 C1
Sherborne Cres SM5 202 C2
Sherborne Ct SE20 184 C1
Sherborne Gdns NW9 44 C6
W13 87 B2
Sherborne Ho SW1 258 D2
SW8 270 C3
Sherborne La EC4 252 D6
Sherborne Rd
Broom Hill BR5 211 D4
Cheam SM3 201 C1
Chessington KT9 214 A3
East Bedfont TW14 149 B3
Sherborne St N1 95 B6 235 C6
Sherboro Rd 1 N15 51 D3
Sherbourne Ct 1
TW12 173 C2
Sherbourne Gdns
TW17 193 C2
Sherbourne Pl HA7 25 A4
Sherbrook Gdns N21 16 D4
Sherbrooke Cl DA7 147 C1
Sherbrooke Ho 9 E2 96 C5
Sherbrooke Rd
SW6 135 A5 264 B3
Sherbrooke Terr SW6 264 B3
Shere Cl KT9 213 D3
Shere Ho SE1 262 C6
Shere Rd IG2 56 C4
Sheredan Rd E4 36 C5
Sherfield Gdns SW15 155 D5
Sheridan N8 50 C5
Sheridan Bldgs WC2 240 B1
Sheridan Cl UB10 83 A3
Sheridan Cres BR7 188 D1
Sheridan Ct NW6 70 A1
W7 108 D6
Harrow HA1 42 B3
Hounslow TW4 151 A6
Sheridan Gdns HA3 43 D3
Sheridan Ho 16 E1 96 C1
7 N16 73 C5
SE11 261 B3
Sheridan Lo EN5 1 D1
Sheridan Pl SW13 133 D2
Hampton TW12 174 A2
Harrow HA1 42 C2
Sheridan Rd E7 76 D5
E12 78 B3
SW19 179 B2
Belvedere DA17 125 C2
Bexleyheath DA7 147 A2
Richmond TW10 153 C1
Sheridan St 28 E1 96 B1
Sheridan Terr UB5 63 D3
Sheridan Way 5 BR3 185 B2
Sheridan Wlk NW11 47 C3
Sheridon Ct SW5 255 C3
Sheringdale Prim Sch
SW18 157 B3
Sheringham NW8 229 D6
Sheringham Ave E12 78 B3
N14 15 D5
Twickenham TW2 151 C3
Sheringham Dr IG11 80 A3
Sheringham Ho NW1 237 B4
Sheringham Jun Sch
E12 78 B4
Sheringham Rd N7 72 C2
SE20 206 C6
Sheringham Twr UB1 107 D6
Sherington Ave HA5 23 C3
Sherington Prim Sch
SE7 143 B6
Sherington Rd SE7 143 B6
Sherland Rd TW1 152 D3
Sherleys Ct HA4 61 C6
Sherlies Ave BR6 227 C6
Sherlock Ct NW8 229 C6
Sherlock Holmes Mus
NW1 92 D3 237 D5
Sherlock Mews W1 238 A4
Sherman Rd BR1 187 A2
Shernhall St E17 54 A4
E17 54 A5
Shernwood Ho 1 E18 55 A5
Sherrard Rd E7,E12 77 D2
Sherrards Way EN5 13 D5
Sherrick Green Rd
NW10 68 B3
Sherriff Ct NW6 69 C2
Sherriff Rd NW6 69 C2
Sherrin Rd E10 75 D4
Sherringham Ave N17 34 A1
Feltham TW13 150 A1
Sherringham Ct 1 N3 29 C2
Sherrock Gdns NW4 46 A5
Sherry Mews IG11 79 B1
Sherston Ct SE1 261 D4
WC1 234 A1
Sherwin Ho 1 SE11 138 C6
Sherwin Rd SE14 140 D4
Sherwood NW6 69 A1
Long Ditton KT6 213 D6
Sherwood Ave E18 55 B6
SW16 181 D2
Greenford UB6 64 C3
Hayes UB4 84 B3
Ruislip HA4 39 C3
Sherwood Cl SW13 134 B2
Sherwood Cl *continued*
W13 109 B5
Bexley DA5 168 C5
Sherwood Ct SE13 141 D3
11 SW11 136 A2
W1 237 C3
5 West Wickham BR4 207 D1
Sherwood Gdns E14 119 C2
SE16 118 B1
Barking IG11 79 B1
Sherwood Hall 7 N2 48 A6
Sherwood Ho N4 51 A2
Sherwood Park Ave
DA15 168 B5
Sherwood Park Rd
Mitcham CR4 203 D5
Sutton SM1 217 C3
Sherwood Park Sch
SM6 219 D5
Sherwood Prim Sch
CR4 203 C5
Sherwood Rd NW4 46 C6
SW19 179 B3
Bexley DA16 145 C2
Croydon CR0 206 B1
Hampton TW12 174 A5
Harrow HA2 64 A6
Ilford IG6 57 B5
Sherwood St N20 14 B1
W1 249 B6
Sherwood Terr N20 14 B1
Sherwood Way BR4 224 A6
Shetland Cl WD6 11 B5
Shetland Rd E3 97 B5
Shield Dr TW8 131 A6
Shield Rd TW15 171 B6
Shieldhall St SE2 124 C2
Shifford Path SE23 162 D1
Shillaker Ct W3 111 D5
Shillibeer Pl W1 237 B3
Shillingford Ho 40 E3 97 D4
Shillingford St 22 N1 72 D1
Shinfield St W12 90 C1
Shinglewell Rd DA8 147 C5
Shinners Cl SE25 206 A4
Ship & Mermaid Row
SE1 253 A2
Ship La SW14 133 A3
Ship St SE8 141 C4
Ship Tavern Pas EC3 253 A6
Shipka Rd SW12 159 B3
Shiplake Ct SW17 180 B6
Shiplake Ho 45 E2 95 D4
Shipley Ct SE20 184 A1
Shipley Ho 32 SW8 137 D3
Shipman Par SE23 163 A2
Shipman Rd E16 99 C1
SE23 162 D2
Shipton Cl RM8 80 D5
Shipton Ho 14 E2 95 D5
7 NW5 71 A2
Shipton Rd UB8 60 B4
Shipton St E2 95 D4
Shipwright Rd SE16 119 A4
Shipwright Yd SE1 253 A3
Shirburn Cl SE23 162 C4
Shirbutt St E14 119 D6
Shire Ct Erith DA18 124 D3
Ewell KT17 215 D1
Shire Ho E11 76 D5
Shire Horse Way TW7 130 D2
Shire La
Farthing Street BR6,BR2 227 B2
Orpington BR6 227 C3
Shire Pl SW18 158 A4
Shirebrook Rd SE3 143 D2
Shirehall Cl NW4 46 D3
Shirehall Gdns NW4 46 D3
Shirehall La NW4 46 D3
Shirehall Pk NW4 46 D3
Shiremeade WD6 10 B6
Shires The TW10 176 A6
Shirland Mews W9 91 B4
Shirland Rd W9 91 C3
Shirley Ave
Carshalton SM1 218 C4
Croydon CR0 206 D1
Sidcup DA5 168 D3
Shirley Church Rd CR0 223 A5
Shirley Cl TW3 152 A6
Shirley Cres BR3 207 A5
Shirley Ct NW9 45 B4
SW16 204 B6
8 W13 109 A5
Ilford IG2 57 B4
Shirley Dr TW3 152 A6
Shirley Gdns W7 108 D5
Barking IG11 79 C2
Shirley Gr N9 18 D4
SW11 137 A2
Shirley High Sch CR0 222 D5
Shirley Hills Rd CR0 222 D3
Shirley Ho 18 SE5 139 B5
Shirley House Dr SE7 143 C5
Shirley Lo 4 SE26 185 A6
Shirley Oaks Hospl CR0 206 C2
Shirley Oaks Rd CR0 222 D6
Shirley Park Rd CR0 206 C1
Shirley Rd E15 76 C1
W4 111 B4
Croydon CR0 206 B1
Enfield EN2 5 A2
Sidcup DA15 167 C1
Shirley St E16 98 D1
Shirley Way CR0 223 B5
Shirleys Cl E17 53 D4
Shirlock Rd NW3 70 D4
Shobden Rd N17 33 B2
Shobroke Cl NW2 68 C5
Shoe La EC4 94 C1 241 B2
Shoebury Rd E6 78 B1
Shoelands Ct NW9 45 B6
Sholto Rd TW6 148 C6
Shooters Ave HA3 43 C5
Shooters Hill SE18 144 C4
Shooters Hill Rd
SE3,SE10 142 C4
SE18,SE3,SE7 143 C5
Shooters Rd EN2 4 D4
Shoot-Up Hill NW2 69 A2
Shore Bsns Ctr 31 E9 74 C1
Shore Cl Feltham TW14 150 A4
Hampton TW12 173 A5
Shore Gr TW13 151 C2
Shore Ho SW8 137 B2
Shore Mews 30 E9 74 C1
Shore Pl E9 74 C1
Shore Rd E9 74 C1
Shorediche Cl UB10 60 B5
Shoreditch Ct 2 E8 73 D1
Shoreditch High St
E2 95 C3 243 B6
Shoreditch Sta
E1 95 D3 243 D5
Shoreham Cl SW18 157 D6
Croydon CR0 206 C3
Sidcup DA5 168 D3
Shoreham Rd BR5 190 B1
Shoreham Rd (E) TW6 148 A6
Shoreham Rd (W) TW6 148 A6
Shoreham Way BR2 209 A3
Shorncliffe Rd
SE1 117 D1 263 C2
Shorndean St SE6 164 A3
Shorne Cl 3 DA15 168 B5
Shornefield Cl BR1 210 C6
Shorrolds Rd
SW6 135 B5 264 D4
Short La TW15,TW19 148 B3
Short Rd E11 76 C6
E15 98 B6
W4 133 C6
Stanwell TW19 148 A5
Short St SE1 251 B2
Short Way N12 30 C4
Twickenham TW2 152 A4
Shortcroft Mead Ct
NW10 68 A3
Shortcroft Rd KT17 215 D1
Shortcrofts Rd RM9 81 B2
Shorter St EC3 117 D6 253 D6
Shortgate N12 29 B6
Shortlands W6 112 D2
Harlington UB3 127 B6
Shortlands Cl N18 17 B1
Erith DA17 125 B3
Shortlands Gdns BR2 186 C1
Shortlands Gr BR2 208 B6
Shortlands Rd E10 53 D2
Beckenham BR2,BR3 208 C6
Kingston u T KT2 176 B3
Shortlands Sta BR2 186 C1
Shorts Croft NW9 44 D5
Shorts Gdns
WC2 94 A1 240 A1
Shorts Rd SM5 218 C3
Shortway SE9 144 A2
Shotfield SM6 219 B2
Shott Cl SM1 218 A3
Shottendane Rd
SW6 135 C4 265 A2
Shottery Cl SE9 166 A1
Shottfield Ave SW14 133 C1
Shottsford 1 W11 91 C1
Shoulder of Mutton Alley 10
E14 119 A6
Shouldham St
W1 92 C2 237 B3
Showers Way UB3 106 A5
Shrapnel Cl SE18 144 A5
Shrapnel Rd SE9 144 B2
Shreveport Ho 23 N19 49 D2
Shrewsbury Ave SW14 133 B1
Harrow HA3 44 A5
Shrewsbury Cl KT6 214 A6
Shrewsbury Cres NW10 89 B6
Shrewsbury Ho SE11 270 D5
SW3 267 A5
Shrewsbury House Sch
KT6 214 A6
Shrewsbury La SE18 144 D4
Shrewsbury Mews 33
W2 91 C2
Shrewsbury Rd E7 77 D2
N11 31 D4
W2 91 C1
Beckenham BR3 207 A6
Carshalton SM5 202 C2
Harlington TW14,TW6 149 B5
Shrewsbury St W10 90 C3
Shrewsbury Wlk 7
TW7 131 A2
Shrewton Rd SW17 180 D3
Shroffold Rd BR1 164 D1
Shropshire Cl CR4 204 A5
Shropshire Ct W7 86 D1
Shropshire Pl WC1 239 B5
Shropshire Rd N22 32 B3
Shroton St NW1 92 C2 237 B4
Shrubberies The E18 37 A1
Ilford IG2 57 D4
Shrubbery Gdns N21 16 D4
Shrubbery Rd N9 18 A1
SW16 182 A6
Southall UB1 107 C5
Shrubbery The 7 E11 55 B4

Shrubbery The *continued*
2 Surbiton KT6 198 A1
Shrubland Gr KT4 216 C5
Shrubland Rd E8 96 A6
E10 53 C2
E10 53 C4
Shrublands Ave CR0 223 C4
Shrublands Cl N20 14 B2
SE26 162 C1
Shrubs Ho SW1 259 D3
Shrubsall Cl SE9 166 A3
Shubbery Cl N1 235 B5
Shurland Ave EN4 14 B5
Shurland Gdns SE15 139 D5
Shurlock Dr BR6 227 A4
Shuters Sq W14 254 C1
Shuttle Cl DA15 167 D4
Shuttle St E1 96 A3
Shuttlemead DA5 169 B4
Shuttleworth Rd SW11 136 C3
Sibella Rd SW4 137 D3
Sibley Cl DA6 169 A6
Sibley Ct UB8 83 A2
Sibley Gr E12 78 A1
Sibthorp Rd 2 CR4 180 D1
Sibthorpe Rd SE12 165 C4
Sibton Rd SM5 202 C2
Sicilian Ave WC1 240 B3
Sidbury St SW6 135 A4 264 A2
Sidcup By Pass Rd
Sidcup DA14 189 C6
St Paul's Cray BR5,BR7 190 B3
Sidcup Hill DA14 190 B5
Sidcup Hill Gdns DA14 190 C5
Sidcup Hill Prim Sch
DA14 190 B5
Sidcup Pl DA14 190 A5
Sidcup Rd SE9 166 A3
Sidcup Sta DA14,DA15 168 A2
Sidcup Tech Ctr DA14 190 D4
Siddeley Dr TW4 129 A3
Siddons Ct WC2 240 C1
Siddons Ho 8 NW3 70 D3
W2 236 D3
Siddons La NW1 92 D3 237 D5
Siddons Rd N17 34 A2
SE23 163 A2
Croydon CR0 220 D5
Side Rd E17 53 B4
Sidewood Rd DA15,SE9 167 B3
Sidford Ho SE1 260 D5
Sidford Pl SE1 116 B3 260 D5
Sidgwick Ho 26 SW9 138 A3
Sidings Mews N7 72 C4
Sidings The E11 54 A1
Sidlaw Ho N16 51 D1
Sidmouth Ave TW7 130 C3
Sidmouth Dr HA4 62 A5
Sidmouth Ho 18 SE15 140 A5
W1 237 B2
Sidmouth Par NW2 68 C1
Sidmouth Rd E10 76 A5
NW2 68 C1
Bexley DA16 146 C5
Sidmouth St
WC1 94 B4 233 C1
Sidney Ave N13 32 B5
Sidney Boyd Ct NW6 69 C1
Sidney Elson Way E6 100 C5
Sidney Gdns TW8 131 D6
Sidney Godley (VC) Ho 31
E2 96 C4
Sidney Gr EC1 234 C3
Sidney Ho 4 E2 96 D5
3 SE18 144 B4
Sidney Miller Ct 8 W3 110 D5
Sidney Rd E7 77 A5
N22 32 B3
SE25 206 A4
SW9 138 B3
Harrow HA2 42 A6
Penge BR3 185 A1
Twickenham TW1 153 B5
Walton-on-T KT12 194 B1
Sidney Sq E1 96 C2
Sidney St E1 96 C2
Sidworth St 6 E8 74 B1
Siebert Rd SE3 143 A6
Siedle Ho 9 SE18 144 C6
Siege Ho 21 E1 96 B1
Siemens Rd SE18 121 D3
Sierra Dr RM9 103 D5
Sigdon Rd E8 74 A3
Sigers The HA5 40 B3
Signmakers Yd NW1 231 D5
Sigrist Sq 4 KT2 176 A2
Silbury Ave CR4 180 C2
Silbury Ho 9 SE26 162 A1
Silbury St N1 235 C2
Silchester Ct
Ashford TW15 148 A2
Thornton Heath CR7 204 C5
Silchester Rd W10 90 D1
Silecroft Rd DA7 147 C4
Silesia Bldgs E8 74 B1
Silex St SE1 116 D4 251 D1
Silicone Bsns Ctr UB6 87 C5
Silk Cl SE12 165 A5
Silk Ho NW9 45 B6
Silk Mills Path SE13 142 A2
Silk Mills Sq E9 75 B2
Silk St EC2 95 A2 242 B4
Silkfield Rd NW9 45 C4
Silks Ct E11 54 C1
Silkstream Par HA8 27 A2
Silkstream Rd HA8 27 A2
Sillitoe Ho N1 235 D5
Silsoe Ho NW1 231 D3
Silsoe Rd N22 50 B6
Silver Birch Ave E4 35 B4
Silver Birch Cl N11 31 A4
Ickenham UB10 60 A4
Silver Birch Ct EN3 18 D6
Silver Birch Gdns E6 100 B3
Silver Birch Rd SE28 124 A5
Silver Cl SE14 141 A5
Harrow HA3 24 B3
Silver Cres W4 110 D2
Silver Ct N19 71 C5
Silver Ind Est N17 33 D1
Silver Jubilee Way
TW4 128 B3
Silver La BR4 224 B6
Silver Pl W1 249 B6
Silver Rd W12 112 D6
Silver Spring Cl DA8 147 D6
Silver St N18 33 C6
Enfield EN1 5 B2
Silver Street Sta N18 33 D5
Silver Way
Hillingdon UB10 82 D5
Romford RM7 59 D6
Silver Wlk SE16 119 B5
Silverbirch Ct E8 73 D1
Silverbirch Wlk 1 NW3 71 A2
Silverburn Ho 4 SW9 138 D4
Silvercliffe Gdns EN4 2 C1
Silverdale NW1 232 A2
SE26 184 C6
Enfield EN2 4 A1
Silverdale Ave IG3 57 D4
Silverdale Cl 1 W7 108 D5
Cheam SM1 217 B4
Northolt UB5 63 B3
Silverdale Dr SE9 166 A2
Sunbury TW16 172 B1
Silverdale Factory Ctr
UB3 106 A4
Silverdale Gdns UB3 106 A4
Silverdale Par IG3 57 D4
Silverdale Rd E4 36 B4
Bexleyheath DA7 147 D3
Hayes UB3 106 A4
Orpington BR5 211 A5
Silverhall St TW7 131 A2
Silverholme Cl HA3 44 A2
Silverland St E16 122 B5
Silverleigh Rd
Thornton Heath CR7 204 C4
CR7 204 B4
Silvermead 7 E18 37 A2
Silvermere Rd SE6 163 D5
Silvers IG9 21 C3
Silverston Way HA7 25 C4
Silverstone Ct 6 BR1 187 C1
Silverthorn 15 NW6 91 D6
Silverthorn Gdns E4 19 C2
Silverthorne Rd SW8 137 B3
Silverton Lo SE19 183 C3
Silverton Rd W6 134 D6
Silvertown Sta E16 122 A5
Silvertown Way E16 121 A5
Silvertree La UB6 86 B4
Silverwood Cl BR3 185 C3
Silvester Ho 17 E1 96 B1
27 E2 96 C4
2 W11 91 B1
Silvester Rd SE22 161 D6
Silvester St SE1 252 C1
Silwood St SE16 118 C1
Simba Ct TW1 152 D3
Simla Cl SE14 141 A6
Simla Ho SE1 252 D1
Simmil Rd KT10 212 C3
Simmons Cl N20 14 C3
Chessington KT9 213 C2
Simmons Ho 16 E2 96 A4
N7 72 B6
Simmons La E4 20 B2
Simmons Rd SE18 122 D1
Simmons' Way N20 14 C2
Simms Cl SM5 218 C6
Simms Rd SE1 118 A2
Simnel Rd SE12 165 B4
Simon Cl W11 113 B6 244 D6
Simon Ct 5 SE28 124 B5
W9 91 C4
Simon Gray Gdns KT2 175 D2
Simon Lo 31 SW19 156 D3
Simon Marks (Jewish) JMI
Sch N16 73 D6
Simon Peter Ct EN2 4 D3
Simonds Rd E10 75 C6
Simone Cl BR1 187 D2
Simons Wlk E15 76 B3
Simpson Cl N21 16 B6
Simpson Dr W3 89 B1
Simpson Ho NW8 230 A1
SE11 260 C1
Wembley HA9 65 D6
Simpson Rd
Richmond TW10 175 C6
Twickenham TW4 151 B5
Simpson St SW11 136 C3
Simpson Way KT6 197 C3
Simpson's Cotts BR2 225 C5
Simpson's Rd E14 119 D6
Bromley BR2 209 A6
Sim's Cotts KT10 212 D2
Sims Wlk SE3 142 D1
Sinai Sch HA3 44 C3
Sinclair Ct N5 73 A2
21 Beckenham BR3 185 C3
5 Croydon CR0 221 D6
Sinclair Gdns W14 112 D4
Sinclair Gr NW11 46 D3
Sinclair Ho 1 SW12 159 D3
Sinclair Mans 13 W12 112 D4
Sinclair Rd E4 35 B5
W14 113 A3 254 A6
Sinclairs Ho 14 E3 97 B5
Sinclare Cl EN1 5 D4
Singapore Rd W13 109 A5
Singer St EC2 235 D1
Singlegate Prim Sch
SW19 180 B3
Singleton Cl
SW17,SW19 180 D3
Thornton Heath CR0 205 A2
Singleton Rd RM9 81 B3
Singleton Scarp N12 29 C5
Sinnott Rd E17 34 D2
Sion Ct TW1 153 B3
Sion Rd TW1 153 B3
Sion-Manning Sch for Girls
W10 90 D2
Sion-Manning Sec Sch
W10 91 A2
Sippetts Ct IG1 57 B1
Sipson Cl UB7 126 C6
Sipson La UB3,UB7 126 D6
Sipson Rd
Harlington UB7 126 C6
West Drayton UB7 104 B2
Sipson Way UB7 126 C5
Sir Abraham Dawes Cotts
SW15 135 A1
Sir Alexander Cl W3 111 D5
Sir Alexander Rd W3 111 D5
Sir Cyril Black Way 2
SW19 179 C3
Sir Francis Drake Prim Sch
SE8 119 A1
Sir George Monoux Sixth
Form Coll E17 35 D1
Sir Henry Floyd Ct HA7 9 B2
Sir James Barrie Prim Sch
SW8 137 C4 269 B1
Sir John Cass's Foundation &
Redcoat CE Sec Sch
E1 96 D2
Sir John Cass's Foundation
CE Prim Sch
EC3 95 C1 243 B1
Sir John Lillie Prim Sch
SW6 135 A6 264 B5
Sir Martin Bowes Ho 15
SE18 122 C2
Sir Oswald Stoll Foundation
The SW6 265 C4
Sir Thomas Abney JMI Sch
N16 51 B1
Sir Thomas More Est
SW3 136 B6 266 D5
Sir William Burrough JMI
Sch E14 97 A1
Sir William Powell's Almshos
SW6 135 A2
Sirdar Rd N22 33 A1
W11 113 A6 244 A5
Mitcham CR4 181 A4
Sirinham Point SW8 270 D5
Sirita Cl HA3 24 B1
Sirius Bldg 13 E1 118 D6
Sirus Rd HA6 22 A5
Sise La EC4 242 C1
Siskin Ho 14 SE16 118 D2
Sisley Rd IG11 101 D6
Sispara Gdns SW18 157 B5
Sissinghurst Ho 17
SE15 140 C6
Sissinghurst Rd CR0 206 A2
Sissulu Ct 9 E6 99 C6
Sister Mabel's Way 14
SE15 140 A5
Sisters Ave SW11 136 D1
Sistova Rd SW12 159 B3
Sisulu Pl SW9 138 C2
Site of Changing of the
Guard SW1 249 A1
Sittingbourne Ave EN1 17 B5
Sitwell Gr HA7 24 D5
Siverst Cl UB5 63 D2
Sivill Ho 9 E2 95 D4
Siviter Way RM10 81 D1
Siward Rd N17 33 B2
SW17 158 A1
Bromley BR2 209 C6
Six Bridges Ind Est SE1 118 A1
Sixth Ave E12 78 B4
W10 91 A4
Hayes UB3 105 D5
Sixth Cross Rd TW2 152 A1
Skardu Rd NW2 69 A3
Skeena Hill SW18,SW19 157 A4
Skeffington Rd E6 100 B6
Skeffington St SE18 123 A3
Skeggs Ho 5 E14 120 A3
Skegness Ho 3 N7 72 B1
Skelbrook St SW18 158 A2
Skelgill Rd SW15 135 B1
Skelley Rd E15 76 D1
Skelton Cl 7 E8 73 D2
Skelton Ho N16 73 C3
Skelton Rd E7 77 A2
Skelton's La E10 53 D2
Skelwith Rd W6 134 C6
Skenfrith Ho SE15 140 B6
Skerne Rd KT2 175 D2
Sketchley Gdns SE16 118 D1
Sketty Rd EN1 5 D2
Skiers St E15 98 C6
Skiffington Cl SW2 160 C3
Skinner Ct E17 53 C4
Skinner Pl SW1 258 A3
Skinner St EC1 94 C3 241 B6
Skinners Almshouses
N13 16 C1
Skinners Company Sch
(Upper) N16 51 D2
Skinner's Company's Lower
Sch E5 52 B1
Skinners La EC4 252 B6
Hounslow TW5 129 D4
Skipsea Ho SW18 158 B5
Skipsey Ave E6 100 B4
Skipton Cl N11 31 A4
Skipton Dr UB3 105 A3
Skipton Ho SE4 141 A1
Skipwith Ho EC1 241 A4
Skipworth Rd E9 96 C6
Skomer Wlk N1 73 A1
Skua Ct 42 SE8 141 B6
Sky Peals Rd IG8 36 B3
Skylines E14 120 A4
Slade Ct NW2 69 A3
Barnet EN5 1 D2
Slade Ho TW4 151 B5
Slade The SE18 145 C6
Slade Twr E10 75 C6
Slade Wlk SE17 139 A6
Sladebrook Rd SE3 143 D2
Sladedale Rd SE18 123 C1
Sladen Pl 12 E5 74 B4
Slades Cl EN2 4 C2
Slades Dr BR7 189 A6
Slades Gdns EN2 4 C2
Slades Hill EN2 4 C2
Slades Rise EN2 4 C2
Slagrove Pl SE13 163 D6
Slaidburn St
SW10 136 A6 266 B5
Slaithwaite Rd SE13 142 A1
Slaney Ct NW10 68 C1
Slater Ho 4 N16 51 D3
Slatter 1 NW9 27 D2
Slattery Rd TW13 150 C3
Sleaford Ho 16 E3 97 C3
Sleaford Ind Est
SW8 137 C5 269 B3
Sleaford St
SW8 137 C5 269 B3
Sleat Ho 9 E3 97 B5
Sledmere Ct TW14 149 C3
Slievemore Cl 8 SW4 137 D2
Sligo Ho 8 E1 96 D3
Slingsby Pl WC2 250 A6
Slippers Pl SE16 118 B3
Sloane Ave
SW3 114 C2 257 B3
Sloane Avenue Mans
SW3 257 C3
Sloane Ct E SW3 258 A2
Sloane Ct W SW3 258 A2
Sloane Gate Mans SW1 258 A4
Sloane Gdns
SW1 115 A2 258 A3
Orpington BR6 227 A5
Sloane Ho 7 E9 74 C1
Sloane Hospl BR3 186 B2
Sloane Sq SW1 257 D3
Sloane Square Sta
SW1 115 A2 258 A3
Sloane St SW1 114 D3 257 D5
Sloane Terr SW1 258 A4
Sloane Terr Mans SW1 258 A4
Sloane Wlk CR0 207 B3
Slocum Cl SE28 124 C6
Slomon Ho 2 W10 91 A4
Slough La NW9 45 A3
Sly St 7 E1 96 B1
Smaldon Cl UB7 104 C3
Smallberry Ave TW7 130 D3
Smallberry Green Prim Sch
TW7 131 A4
Smallbrook Mews W2 236 C1
Smalley Cl N16 73 D5
Smallwood Jun & Inf Schs
SW17 180 B6
Smallwood Rd SW17 180 B6
Smarden Cl DA17 125 C1
Smarden Gr SE9 188 B6
Smart St E2 96 D4
Smart's Pl N18 34 A5
WC1,WC2 240 B2
Smeaton Cl KT9 213 D2
Smeaton Ct SE1 262 A5
Smeaton Rd SW18 157 C4
Holdbrook EN3 7 C6
Smeaton St E1 118 B5
Smedley St SW4 137 D3
Smeed Rd E3 75 C1
Smetheton Ho 12 E9 96 C6
Smiles Pl SE13 142 A3
Smith Cl SE16 118 D5
Smith Sq SW1 116 A3 260 A5
Smith St SW3 114 D1 257 C1
Surbiton KT5 198 B3
Smith Terr SW3 114 D1 257 C1
Smithers Ho 3 SE20 184 D3
Smithfield Mkt EC1 241 D3
Smithfield St
EC1 94 D2 241 C3
Smithies Ct E15 76 A3
Smithies Rd SE2 124 B2
Smith's Ct W1 249 C6
Smiths Point E13 99 A6
Smith's Yd SW18 158 A2
Smithson Rd N17 33 B2
Smithwood Cl SW19 157 A2
Smithy JMI Sch E1 96 C2
Smithy St E1 96 C2
Smock Wlk CR0 205 A3
Smoothfield TW3 129 C1
Smugglers Way SW18 135 D1
Smyrk's Rd
SE17 117 C1 263 B1
Smyrna Mans 8 NW6 69 C1
Smyrna Rd NW6 69 C1
Smythe St E14 119 D6
Snakes La EN4,N14 3 C1
Snakes La E IG8 37 C4
Snakes La W IG8 37 B4
Snaresbrook Dr HA7 26 A6
Snaresbrook Hall 11 E18 55 A6
Snaresbrook Ho E18 54 D5
Snaresbrook Prim Sch
E18 55 A5
Snaresbrook Rd E11 54 D5
Snaresbrook Sta E11 55 A4
Snarsgate St W10 90 C2
Sneath Ave NW11 47 B2
Snell's Pk N18 33 D4
Sneyd Rd NW2 68 C4
Snipe Ct 5 SE8 141 A6
Snow Hill EC1 94 D2 241 C3
Snow Ho SE27 160 D1
Snowberry Cl E11 76 B4
Snowbury Rd 6 SW6 135 D3
Snowden Ave UB10 82 D5
Snowden Dr NW9 45 C3
Snowden St EC2 95 C3 243 A5
Snowdon Cres UB3 105 A3
Snowdon Rd TW6 149 A5
Snowdown Cl SE20 184 D2
Snowdrop Cl 2 TW12 173 C4
Snowman Ho NW6 91 D6
Snowsfield Prim Sch
SE1 117 C4 253 A2
Snowsfields
SE1 117 B4 252 D2
Snowshill Rd E12 78 A3
Snowy Fielder Waye
TW7 131 B3
Soames St SE15 139 D2
Soames Wlk KT3 177 C2
Soane Ct 8 NW1 71 C1
Soane Ho SE17 262 D1
Soane Mus WC2 94 B1 240 C2
Soham Rd EN3 7 B6
Soho* W1 93 D1 239 C2
Soho Mills SM6 203 B1
Soho Parish CE Prim Sch
W1 115 D6 249 C6
Soho Sq W1 93 D1 239 C2
Soho St W1 239 C2
Sojourner-Truth Cl 11
E8 74 B2
Solander Gdns E1 118 B6
12 E1 118 C6
Solar Ct N3 29 D3
Soldene Ct N7 72 B2
Solebay St E1 97 A3
Solent Ho 6 E1 97 A2
Solent Rd NW6 69 C3
West Bedfont TW6 148 B5
Solent Rise E13 99 A4
Soley Mews WC1 234 A2
Solna Ave SW15 156 C6
Solna Rd N21 17 B4
Solomon Ave N9 34 A6
Solomon's Pas SE15 140 B1
Solon New Rd SW4 138 A1
Solon Rd SW2 138 A1
Solway Cl TW4 129 A2
Solway Ho 12 E1 96 D3
Solway Lo 4 IG8 37 A3
Solway Rd N22 32 D2
SE22 140 A1
Somaford Gr EN4 14 B5
Somali Rd NW2 69 B3
Somborne Ho SW15 156 A4
Sombrook Ho SE11 261 A3
Somer Ct SW6 265 A5
Somerby Rd IG11 79 B1
Somercoates Cl EN4 2 C2
Somerfield Ho SE16 118 D1
Somerfield Rd N4 72 D6
Somerford Cl HA5 40 A5
Somerford Gr N16 73 D4
N17 34 A3
Somerford Grove Est
N16 73 D4
Somerford St E1 96 B3
Somerford Way SE16 119 A4
Somerhill Ave DA15 168 B4
Somerhill Rd DA16 146 B3
Somerleyton Rd SW9 138 C1
Somers Cl NW1 232 C4
Somers Cres W2 237 A1
Somers Pl SW2 160 B4
Somers Rd E17 53 B5
SW2 160 B5
Somers Town Est
NW1 93 C5 232 B3
Somers Way WD2 8 A4
Somersby Est SE20 184 C3
Somersby Gdns IG4 56 B4
Somerset Ave SW20 178 B1
Bexley DA16 145 D1
Chessington KT9 213 D4
Somerset Cl N17 33 B1
New Malden KT3 199 C3
Woodford IG8 37 A2
Somerset Ct W7 86 D1
2 Hampton TW12 173 C2
Somerset Gdns N6 49 A2
N17 33 C3
SE13 141 D3
SW16 204 B6
Somerset Gdns *continued*
Teddington TW11 174 C5
Somerset Hall N17 33 C3
Somerset Ho SW19 157 A1
WC2 116 B6 250 D6
Somerset Lo SW15 134 B1
9 Brentford TW8 131 D6
Somerset Rd E17 53 C3
N17 51 D6
N18 33 D5
NW4 46 C5
SW19 157 A1
W4 111 B3
W13 109 C5
Brentford TW8 131 C6
Enfield EN3 7 C5
Harrow HA1 42 A4
Kingston u T KT1 176 B1
New Barnet EN5 14 A6
Southall UB1 85 C2
Teddington TW11 174 C5
Somerset Sq
W14 113 B4 244 C1
Somerset Waye TW5 129 A5
Somersham Rd DA7 147 A3
Somerton Ave TW9 132 D2
Somerton Rd NW2 69 A5
SE15 140 B1
Somertrees Ave SE12 165 B2
Somervell Rd HA2 63 C3
Somerville Ct SW16 181 D4
Somerville Ho 10 SW15 156 D5
Somerville Rd SE20 184 D3
Ilford RM6 58 C4
Sonderburg Rd 13 N7 72 B6
Sondes St SE17 139 B6
Sonia Ct N12 30 A6
Edgware HA8 26 B3
Sonia Gdns N12 30 A6
NW10 67 D4
Heston TW5 129 C5
Sonning Ct CR0 222 A6
Sonning Gdns TW12 173 A4
Sonning Ho 32 E2 95 D4
Sonning Rd CR0 206 A3
Soper Cl E4 35 B5
Soper Mews EN3 7 C5
Sophia Cl N7 72 B2
Sophia Ho N15 51 D5
10 W6 112 C1
Sophia Rd E10 53 D1
E13 99 B2
Sophia Sq 14 SE16 119 A6
Sopwith 2 NW9 27 D2
Sopwith Ave KT9 214 A3
Sopwith Cl TW10 176 B5
Sopwith Rd TW5 128 C5
Sopwith Way SW11 268 C4
Kingston u T KT2 176 A2
Sorbus Ct EN2 4 D3
Sorenson Ct 2 E10 75 D6
Sorrel Cl SE28 124 A5
Sorrel Gdns E6 100 A2
Sorrel Ho TW3 130 A4
Sorrel La 16 E14 98 B1
Sorrell Cl SE14 141 A5
7 SW9 138 C3
Sorrento Rd SM1 217 D5
Sotheby Rd N5 73 A4
Sotheran Cl E8 96 A6
Sotheron Pl SW6 265 D3
Soudan Rd
SW11 136 D4 267 C1
Souldern Rd 10 W14 112 D3
South Access Rd E17 53 A3
South Acre NW9 27 D1
South Acton Sta W3,
W4 111 A3
South Africa Rd W12 112 B6
South Audley St
W1 115 A5 248 B4
South Ave E4 20 A4
NW11 47 D5
Richmond TW9 132 C3
Southall UB1 107 B6
Wallington SM5 219 A1
South Avenue Gdns
UB1 107 B6
South Bank KT6 198 A3
South Bank Bsns Ctr
SW8 137 D6 269 D5
South Bank Lo 2 KT6 198 A3
South Bank Terr KT6 198 A3
South Bank Univ
SW8 137 D4 269 D2
SE1 116 D3 261 D6
South Bermondsey Sta
SE16 118 C1
South Birkbeck Rd E11 76 B5
South Black Lion La
W6 112 A1
South Block 19 E1 118 C6
South Bolton Gdns
SW10 255 D2
South Building SE10 142 B5
South Camden Com Sch
NW1 93 D5 232 C3
South Carriage Dr
SW1,SW7 114 D4 247 C2
South Church Ct E6 100 B5
South Cl N6 49 B3
Bexley DA6 146 D1
Dagenham RM10 103 C6
Hadley EN5 1 B2
Morden SM4 201 C3

South Cl *continued*
Pinner HA5 ....41 B2
Pinner Green HA5 ....22 D2
Twickenham TW2 ....151 C1
West Drayton UB7 ....104 C3
South Colonnade E14 .119 C5
South Common Rd UB8 .60 A2
South Countess Rd E17 .35 B1
South Cres E16 ....98 B3
WC1 ....239 C3
South Cross Rd IG6 ....57 A4
South Croxted Rd SE21 183 B6
South Croydon Sta CR2 221 B3
South Ct 17 SW15 ....156 D5
South Dene NW7 ....11 B1
South Dr
Beckenham BR3 ....208 A4
Orpington BR6 ....227 C3
Ruislip HA4 ....39 C1
South Ealing Cemy W5 109 D2
South Ealing Rd W5 ...109 D3
South Ealing Sta W5 ..109 D3
South Eastern Ave N9 ..17 D1
South Eaton Pl
SW1 ....115 A2 258 B4
South Eden Park Rd
BR3 ....207 D4
South Edwardes Sq
W8 ....255 A5
South End W8 .113 D3 255 D6
Croydon CR0 ....221 A4
South End Cl NW3 ....70 C4
South End Gn NW3 ....70 C4
South End Rd NW3 ....70 C4
South End Row
W8 ....113 D3 255 D6
South Esk Rd E7 ....77 C2
South Gate Ave TW13 ..171 B6
South Gdns SW19 ....180 B3
Wembley HA9 ....66 C6
South Gipsy Rd DA16 ..146 D2
South Glade DA5 ....169 B3
South Gr E17 ....53 B4
N6 ....49 A1
N15 ....51 B4
South Greenford Sta
UB6 ....86 C4
South Grove Ho N6 ....49 A1
South Grove Prim Sch
E17 ....53 B3
South Hampstead High Sch (Jun Dept) NW3 ....70 A2
South Hampstead High Sch for Girls NW3 ....70 B2
South Hampstead Sta
NW8 ....70 A1
South Harringay Jun & Inf Schs N4 ....50 D4
South Harrow Sta HA2 ..64 A5
South Hill BR7 ....188 B4
South Hill Ave HA1,HA2 ..64 B5
South Hill Gr HA1 ....64 C4
South Hill Pk NW3 ....70 C4
South Hill Pk Gdns NW3 70 C4
South Hill Rd BR2 ....208 C5
South Island Pl SW9 ...138 C5
South Kensington Sta
SW7 ....114 B2 256 D4
South Kenton Sta HA9 ..43 C1
South La
Kingston u T KT1 ....197 D6
New Malden KT3 ....199 B3
South La W KT3 ....199 B5
South Lambeth Pl SW8 270 B6
South Lambeth Rd
SW8 ....138 A5 270 B4
South Lo NW8 ....229 C2
6 New Barnet EN5 ....13 D6
Twickenham TW2 ....152 A5
South Lodge Ave CR4, CR7,SW16 ....204 A5
South Lodge Cres EN2 ...3 D1
South Lodge Dr N14 ...15 D6
South London Coll
SE27 ....182 D6
South London Montessori Sch The SW11 136 C4 267 A1
South Mall N9 ....18 A1
South Mead NW9 ....27 D2
West Ewell KT19 ....215 D1
South Merton Sta
SW20 ....201 B6
South Molton La
W1 ....93 B1 238 C1
South Molton Rd E16 ...99 A1
South Molton St
W1 ....93 B1 238 C1
South Mount N20 ....14 A2
South Norwood Ctry Pk
SE25 ....206 C5
South Norwood High Sch
SE25 ....206 B4
South Norwood Hill
SE19,SE25 ....183 D1
South Norwood Prim Sch
SE25 ....206 A5
South Oak Rd SW16 ...182 B6
South Ordnance Rd EN3 .7 C5
South Par W4 ....111 B2
Edgware HA8 ....26 C1
South Parade
SW3 ....114 B1 256 D2
South Park Cres SE6 ..164 D3
Ilford IG1 ....79 C5
South Park Ct 24 BR3 ..185 C3
South Park Dr
Barking IG11 ....79 C4
Ilford IG3 ....79 C5
South Park Gr KT3 ....199 A5
South Park Hill Rd CR2 221 B4
South Park Inf Sch IG3 .79 C5
South Park Jun Sch IG1 79 C5
South Park Mews SW6 135 D2
South Park Rd SW19 ..179 D4
Ilford IG1 ....79 B5
South Park Terr IG1 ....79 C5
South Park Villas IG3 ...79 C4
South Park Way HA4 ....62 C3
South Pl EC2 ....95 B2 242 D3
Enfield EN3 ....18 C6
Surbiton KT5 ....198 B2
South Pl Mews EC2 ...242 D3
South Quay Plaza E14 .119 D4
South Quay Sta E14 ...119 D4
South Rd N9 ....18 A3
SE23 ....162 D2
SW19 ....180 B4
W5 ....109 D2
Dagenham RM6 ....59 A3
Edgware HA8 ....26 D2
Feltham TW13 ....172 D5
Hampton TW12 ....173 B4
Ilford RM6 ....58 C4
Southall UB1 ....107 B5
Twickenham TW2 ....152 B1
West Drayton UB7 ....104 C3
South Residence IG3 ...58 B4
South Rise W2 ....247 B6
South Rise Prim Sch
SE18 ....123 B1
South Rise Way SE18 ..123 B2
South Row SE3 ....142 D3
South Ruislip Sta HA4 ..62 C3
South Sea St SE16 ....119 B3
South Side W6 ....111 D3
South Sq NW11 ....47 D3
WC1 ....241 A3
South St W1 ...115 A5 248 B4
Bromley BR1 ....187 A1
Enfield EN3 ....18 D6
Isleworth TW7 ....131 A2
South Tenter St
E1 ....95 D1 243 D1
South Terr N22 ....31 D1
SW7 ....114 C2 257 A4
Surbiton KT6 ....198 A3
South Thames Coll
SW15 ....156 D6
SW18 ....157 D6
South Thames Coll (Roehampton Centre)
SW15 ....156 A5
South Tottenham Sta
N15 ....51 D4
South Vale SE19 ....183 C4
Harrow HA1 ....64 C4
South View SW19 ....178 D4
Bromley BR1 ....187 C1
South View Cl DA5 ....169 B5
South View Cres IG2 ....56 D3
South View Ct SE19 ...183 A3
8 SE23 ....162 C3
South View Rd N8 ....50 A6
Northwood HA5 ....22 B4
South Villas NW1 ....71 D2
South Way N9 ....18 C2
N11 ....31 C4
Croydon CR0 ....223 A5
Harrow HA2 ....41 C5
Wembley HA9 ....66 C3
South West London Coll
SW16 ....159 D1
South Western Hospl
SW9 ....138 B2
South Western Rd TW1 153 B5
South Wharf Rd
W2 ....92 B1 236 D2
South Wimbledon Sta
SW19 ....179 D3
South Wlk
Coney Hall BR4 ....224 C5
Hayes UB3 ....83 B2
South Woodford Sta E18 37 B1
South Worple Way
SW14 ....133 B2
South Yd EC1 ....242 C4
Southacre Way HA5 ....22 C2
Southall Ct UB1 ....107 B6
Southall Ent Ctr UB2 ..107 C4
Southall La TW5 ....106 B1
Southall Pl SE1 ....252 C1
Southall Sta UB1 ....107 B4
Southam Ho 9 W10 ....91 A3
Southam St W10 ....91 A3
Southampton Bldgs
WC2 ....241 A3
Southampton Gdns
CR4 ....204 A4
Southampton Pl WC1 ..240 B3
Southampton Rd NW5 ..70 D3
Stanwell TW19,TW6 ....148 B5
Southampton Row
WC1 ....94 A2 240 B4
Southampton St WC2 ..250 B6
Southampton Way SE5 139 C5
Southbank KT7 ....197 B2
Southborough Cl KT6 .197 D1
Southborough Ho SE17 263 B2
Southborough La BR1, BR2 ....210 B4
Southborough Prim Sch
BR2 ....210 C4
Southborough Rd E9 ...96 D6
Southborough Rd *continued*
Bromley BR1,BR2 ....210 A5
Surbiton KT6 ....198 A1
Southborough Rd (The Lane)
KT6 ....198 A1
Southborough Sch KT6 214 A5
Southbourne BR2 ....209 A2
Southbourne Ave NW9 ..27 B1
Southbourne Cl HA5 ...41 A2
Southbourne Cres NW4 .47 A5
Southbourne Ct NW9 ...27 A1
Southbourne Gdns
SE12 ....165 B6
Ilford IG1 ....79 A3
Ruislip HA4 ....40 B1
Southbridge Pl CR0 ...221 A4
Southbridge Rd CR0 ...221 A4
Southbridge Way UB2 .107 A4
Southbrook Mews
SE12 ....164 D5
Southbrook Rd SE12 ..164 D5
SW16 ....182 A2
Southbury NW8 ....229 B6
Southbury Ave EN1 ....6 A1
Southbury Prim Sch EN3 .6 C1
Southbury Rd Enfield EN1 .5 D1
Enfield EN1,EN3 ....6 B1
Southbury Sta EN3 ....6 B1
Southchurch Rd E6 ....100 B5
Southcombe St W14 ..254 A4
Southcote Ave
Feltham TW13 ....150 A2
Tolworth KT5 ....198 D2
Southcote Rd E17 ....53 A4
N19 ....71 C4
SE25 ....206 B3
Southcote Rise HA4 ....39 B2
Southcott Ho 31 E3 ....97 D4
W9 ....236 B5
Southcroft Ave
Bexley DA16 ....145 C2
West Wickham BR4 ....224 A6
Southcroft Rd SW17 ...181 A4
Orpington BR6 ....227 C5
Southdean Gdns SW19 157 B2
Southdene Ct N11 ....15 C1
Southdown N7 ....72 A2
Southdown Ave W7 ...109 A3
Southdown Cres
Harrow HA2 ....42 A1
Ilford IG2 ....57 C4
Southdown Dr SW20 ..178 D3
Southdown Rd SW20 ..178 D2
Southend Cl SE9 ....166 D5
Southend Cres SE9 ...166 D5
Southend La SE6 ....185 C6
Southend Rd E6 ....78 B1
Beckenham BR3 ....185 C2
Woodford IG8 ....37 D1
Southend Road (North Circular Rd) E17,E18 ...36 C2
Southern Ave SE25 ...205 D6
East Bedfont TW14 ....150 A3
Southern Gr E3 ....97 B3
Southern Perimeter Rd
East Bedfont TW6 ....148 C5
Feltham TW14,TW6 ....149 B6
Stanwell TW19,TW6 ....148 C5
Southern Rd E13 ....99 B5
N2 ....48 D5
Southern Road Inf Sch
E13 ....99 B5
Southern Road Jun Sch
E13 ....99 B5
Southern Row W10 ....91 A3
Southern St N1 ....233 C4
Southern Way RM7 ....59 C3
Southerngate Way
SE14 ....141 A5
Southernhay IG10 ....21 D6
Southerton Rd W6 ...112 C2
Southey Ho SE17 ....262 B2
Southey Rd N15 ....51 C4
SW9 ....138 C4
SW19 ....179 C3
Southey St SE20 ....184 D3
Southfield EN5 ....12 D5
Southfield Cl UB8 ....82 C4
Southfield Cotts W7 ...108 D4
Southfield Gdns TW1, TW2 ....174 D6
Southfield Pk HA2 ....41 D5
Southfield Prim Sch
W4 ....111 C4
Southfield Rd W4 ....111 B4
Enfield EN3 ....18 C5
Orpington BR7 ....211 D6
Southfields NW4 ....46 B6
Thames Ditton KT8 ....196 C3
Southfields Ave TW15 .170 D4
Southfields Ct SM3 ...217 C6
Southfields Rd SW18 ..157 C5
Southfields Sch SW18 .157 C3
Southfields Sta SW18 ..157 B3
Southfleet Rd BR6 ....227 C4
Southgate Cir 3 N14 ...15 D3
Southgate Coll N14 ...15 D2
Southgate Ct N1 ....73 B1
Southgate Gr N1 ....73 B1
Southgate Ho 7 E17 ...54 A6
Southgate Rd N1 73 B1 235 D6
Southgate Sch EN4 ....15 B6
Southgate Sta N14 ....15 D3
Southgate Way N2 ....30 C2
Southholme Cl SE19 ..183 C2
Southill La HA5 ....40 B5
Southill Rd BR7 ....188 B3
Southill St E14 ....97 D1
Southlake Prim Sch
SE2 ....124 D4
Southland Rd SE18 ...145 D5
Southland Way TW7 ...152 B6
Southlands Ave BR6 ..227 C3
Southlands Coll SW15 .156 A6
Southlands Dr SW19 ..156 D2
Southlands Gr BR1 ....210 A6
Southlands Rd BR1,BR2 209 D5
Southmead Jun & Inf Sch
SW19 ....157 A3
Southmead Rd SW19 ..157 A3
Southmont Rd KT10 ..212 C5
Southmoor Way E9 ....75 B3
Southold Rise SE9 ....166 B1
Southolm St
SW11 ....137 B4 268 D1
Southover N12 ....29 C6
Plaistow BR1 ....187 A5
Southport Rd SE18 ....123 B2
Southridge Pl SW20 ...178 D3
Southsea Rd KT1 ....198 A5
Southside N7 ....71 D4
Southside Comm SW19 178 D4
Southside Ind Est SW8 269 A2
Southside Quarter 4
SW11 ....136 D3
Southspring SE9 ....167 B4
Southvale Rd SE3 ....142 C3
Southview Ave NW10 ...67 D3
Southview Cl SW17 ...181 A5
Southview Dr E18 ....55 B6
Southview Gdns SM6 ..219 C1
Southview Rd BR1 ....186 B6
Southville SW8 137 D4 269 D1
Southville Cl
East Bedfont TW14 ....149 C3
West Ewell KT19 ....215 B1
Southville Cres TW14 ..149 C3
Southville Jun & Inf Schs
TW14 ....149 D3
Southville Rd
East Bedfont TW14 ....149 C4
Thames Ditton KT7 ....197 B2
Southwark Bridge
SE1,EC4 ....117 A6 252 B5
Southwark Bridge Office Village SE1 ....252 B3
Southwark Bridge Rd
SE1 ....117 A5 252 B3
Southwark Cath*
SE1 ....117 B5 252 C4
Southwark Coll
SE1 ....116 D4 251 C2
SE15 ....140 B5
SE15 ....140 C4
Southwark Coll (Blackfriars Ctr) SE1 ....251 C3
Southwark Coll (Camberwell Centre) SE5 ....139 C5
Southwark Coll (Grange Ctr)
SE1 ....263 B5
Southwark Coll (Surrey Docks Ctr) SE16 ....118 B3
Southwark Park Est 11
SE16 ....118 B2
Southwark Park Prim Sch
SE16 ....118 B3
Southwark Park Rd
SE16 ....118 A2 263 D4
Southwark Pl BR1 ....210 B6
Southwark St
SE1 ....117 A5 252 A3
Southwater Cl 8 E14 ...97 B1
Beckenham BR3 ....185 D3
Southway N20 ....13 C2
NW11 ....47 D4
SW20 ....200 D5
Hayes BR2 ....209 A2
Wallington SM6 ....219 C4
Southwell Ave UB5 ....63 C2
Southwell Gdns SW7 ..256 A3
Southwell Grove Rd E11 76 C6
Southwell Ho 13 N16 ...73 C3
8 SE16 ....118 B2
Southwell Rd SE5 ....139 A2
Kenton HA3 ....43 D3
Thornton Heath CR0 ....204 C3
Southwest Rd E11 ....54 B1
Southwick Mews W2 ..236 D2
Southwick Pl W2 ....237 A1
Southwick St W2 92 C1 237 A2
Southwick Yd W2 ....237 A1
Southwold Dr IG11 ....80 A3
Southwold JMI Sch E5 ..74 B6
Southwold Mans W9 ...91 C4
Southwold Rd E5 ....74 C6
Old Bexley DA5 ....169 D5
Southwood Ave N6 ....49 B2
Kingston u T KT2,KT3 ....177 A2
Southwood Cl
Bromley BR1 ....210 B5
North Cheam KT4 ....200 D1
Southwood Ct EC1 ....234 C1
NW11 ....47 D4
Southwood Dr KT5 ....199 A1
Southwood Gdns
Hinchley Wood KT10 ....213 A5
Ilford IG2 ....56 D5
Southwood Hall N6 ....49 B3
Southwood Ho SE9 ....166 D2
W11 ....244 A6
Southwood Hospl (Geriatric)
N6 ....49 A2
Southwood Hts N6 ....49 B2
Southwood Inf Sch RM9 81 A4
Southwood La N6 ....49 A2
Southwood Lawn Rd N6 49 B2
Southwood Mans N6 ...49 B3
Southwood Park N6 ....49 A2
Southwood Rd SE9 ....166 D2
SE28 ....124 B5
Southwood Smith Ho 4
E2 ....96 B4
Southwood Smith St
N1 ....234 C5
Southwyck Ho SW9 ....138 C1
Sovereign Bsns Ctr EN3 ..7 B2
Sovereign Cl E1 ....118 B6
W5 ....87 C2
Ruislip HA4 ....39 C1
Sovereign Cres SE16 ..119 A6
Sovereign Ct E1 ....118 B6
Bromley BR2 ....210 B3
East Molesey KT8 ....195 B5
Harlington UB7 ....126 D5
3 Richmond TW9 ....132 B1
Sovereign Gr HA0 ....65 D5
Sovereign Ho 23 E1 ....96 B3
NW7 ....27 B6
SE18 ....122 B3
3 SW19 ....179 A4
Ashford TW15 ....170 A6
Sovereign Mews 6 E2 .95 D5
Sovereign Pk NW10 ....88 D3
Sovereign Rd IG11 ....102 C4
Sowerby Cl SE9 ....166 B6
Spa Cl SE19 ....183 C2
Spa Ct 12 SE16 ....118 A3
Spa Hill CR7,SE19 ....183 B2
Spa Rd SE16 ...117 D3 263 D5
Spa Sch SE1 ....118 A2
Spa View 6 SW16 ....160 B1
Space Waye TW14 ....150 B6
Spade Wlk NW3 ....69 D3
Spafield St EC1 ....241 A6
Spalding Cl HA8 ....27 C3
Spalding Ct HA8 ....26 B6
Spalding Ho SE4 ....163 A6
Spalding Rd NW4 ....46 C3
SW17 ....181 B5
Spanby Rd E3 ....97 C3
Spangate SE3 ....142 D2
Spaniards Cl NW11 ....48 B1
Spaniards End NW3 ....48 B1
Spaniards Rd NW3 ....70 A6
Spanish Bilingual Sch
W10 ....91 A2
Spanish Pl W1 ....238 B2
Spanish Rd SW18 ....158 A6
Sparkbridge Rd HA1 ...42 C5
Sparke Terr 2 E16 ....98 D1
Sparkford Gdns N11 ....31 A5
Sparkford Ho SW11 ...266 D2
Sparks Cl W3 ....89 B1
Dagenham RM8 ....80 D6
Hampton TW12 ....173 A4
Sparrow Cl TW12 ....173 A4
Sparrow Dr BR5 ....211 B1
Sparrow Farm Dr
TW14 ....150 D4
Sparrow Farm Inf Sch
TW14 ....150 C4
Sparrow Farm Jun Sch
TW14 ....150 C4
Sparrow Farm Rd KT17, KT4 ....216 B4
Sparrow Gn RM10 ....81 D5
Sparrow's Farm L Ctr
SE9 ....167 A4
Sparrows Herne WD2 ....8 A4
Sparrows La SE9 ....167 A3
Sparrows Way WD2 ....8 A4
Sparsholt Rd N19 ....50 B1
Barking IG11 ....101 C6
Sparta St SE10 ....142 A4
Speakers' Corner*
W1 ....114 D6 247 D6
Speaker's Ct 3 CR0 ...205 B1
Speakman Ho SE4 ....141 A2
Spear Mews
SW5 ....113 C2 255 B3
Spearman St 8 SE18 ..144 C6
Spearpoint Gdns IG2 ...57 D5
Spears Rd N19 ....50 A1
Speart La TW5 ....129 A5
Spectrum Ho NW5 ....71 A4
Spedan Cl NW3 ....70 A5
Speed Ho EC2 ....242 B4
Speedwell Ct 7 N12 ...29 D6
Speedwell Ho 9 N12 ...29 D6
Speedwell St 5 SE8 ...141 C5
Speedy Pl WC1 ....233 A1
Speer Rd KT7 ....196 D3
Speirs Cl KT3 ....199 D3
Speke Rd CR7 ....183 B1
Spekehill SE9 ....166 B1
Speldhurst Cl 2 BR2 ..208 D4
Speldhurst Rd E9 ....74 D1
W4 ....111 B3
Spellbrook Wlk N1 ...235 B6
Spelman Ho 14 E1 ....96 A2
Spelman St E1 ....96 A2
Spelthorne Coll TW15 .170 B6
Spelthorne Cty Inf Sch
TW15 ....171 B4
Spelthorne Gr TW16 ...171 D3
Spelthorne La TW15, TW17 ....171 A2
Spence Cl SE16 ....119 B4
Spencer Ave N13 ....32 B4
Hayes UB4 ....84 A2
Spencer Cl N3 ....29 C1
NW10 ....88 B4
Orpington BR6 ....227 D6
Woodford IG8 ....37 C5
Spencer Ct SW20 ....178 B2
5 Farnborough BR6 ....227 A3
Spencer Dr N2 ....48 A3
Spencer Gdns SW14 ...155 A6
Spencer Hill SW19 ....179 A3
Spencer Hill Rd SW19 .179 A3
Spencer Ho NW3 ....70 B5
NW4 ....46 B4
31 SW8 ....137 D3
SW19 ....156 D1
24 SW19 ....156 D3
Spencer Mews SE21 ...161 B3
W6 ....264 A6
Spencer Park Ct SW18 .158 B6
Spencer Pk SW18 ....158 B6
Spencer Pl 16 N1 ....72 D1
SW1 ....259 B5
Thornton Heath CR0 ....205 B2
Spencer Rd E6 ....99 D6
N8 ....50 B4
N11 ....31 B6
N17 ....34 A2
SW18 ....158 B6
SW20 ....178 B2
W3 ....111 A5
W4 ....133 A5
Bromley BR1 ....186 D3
East Molesey KT8 ....196 A4
Harrow HA3 ....24 C1
Hounslow TW3,TW5,TW7 130 A4
Ilford IG3 ....57 D1
Mitcham CR4 ....203 A6
South Croydon CR2 ....221 C3
Sutton CR4 ....203 A2
Twickenham TW2 ....152 C2
Wembley HA0 ....65 C6
Spencer Rise NW5 ....71 B5
Spencer St EC1 .94 D4 234 C1
Southall UB2 ....106 D4
Spencer Wlk 15 NW3 ...70 A4
SW15 ....134 D1
Spenlow Ho 2 SE16 ...118 A3
Spens Ho WC1 ....240 C5
Spenser Ct 5 TW10 ...175 D6
Spenser Gr N16 ....73 C4
Spenser Rd SE24 ....160 D6
Spenser St SW1 ....259 B6
Spensley Wlk N16 ....73 B5
Speranza St SE18 ....123 D1
Sperling Rd N17 ....33 C1
Spert St E14 ....119 A6
Spey St E14 ....98 A2
Speyside N14 ....15 C5
Spezia Rd NW10 ....90 A5
Spice Ct 2 E1 ....118 A5
10 SW11 ....136 A2
Spicer Cl SE5,SW9 ....138 D3
Walton-on-T KT12 ....194 C3
Spicer Ct EN1 ....5 C2
Spices Yd CR0 ....221 A4
Spigurnell Rd N17 ....33 B2
Spikes Bridge Rd UB1 .107 A6
Spilsby Cl NW9 ....27 C1
Spindle Cl SE18 ....122 A3
Spindle Ho 8 DA15 ...168 A1
Spindlewood Gdns CR0 221 C4
Spindrift Ave E14 ....119 D2
Spinel Cl SE18 ....123 D1
Spinnaker Ct 2 KT1 ...175 D2
Spinnaker Ho E14 ....119 C4
Spinnells Rd HA2 ....41 B1
Spinney Cl
New Malden KT3 ....199 C4
Worcester Pk KT4 ....215 D6
Yiewsley UB7 ....104 A6
Spinney Dr TW14 ....149 A4
Spinney Gdns SE19 ...183 D5
Dagenham RM9 ....81 A3
Spinney Oak BR1 ....188 A1
Spinney The N21 ....16 C4
SW13 ....134 B6
SW16 ....159 D1
Barnet EN5 ....1 D3
Cheam SM3 ....216 C4
Ruxley DA14 ....191 A5
Stanmore HA7 ....26 A6
Sunbury TW16 ....172 A2
Wembley HA0 ....65 A5
Spinneys The BR1 ....188 B1
Spire Ct 10 TW10 ....154 A5
Spire Ho W2 ....246 B6
Spires The EN5 ....1 A2
Spirit Quay E1 ....118 B5
Spital Sq E1 ....95 C2 243 B4
Spital St E1 ....96 A2
Spital Yd E1 ....243 B4
Spitalfields Mkt
E1 ....95 D2 243 C4
Spitfire Est The TW5 ...106 C1
Spitfire Way TW5 ....106 C1
Splendour Wlk SE16 ..118 C1
Spode Ho SE11 ....261 A5
Spondon Rd N15 ....52 A5
Spoonbill Cl UB4 ....84 D2
Spooner 8 NW9 ....27 D3
Spooner Ho TW5 ....129 C6
Spooner Wlk SM6 ....219 D3
Sporle Ct 6 SW11 ....136 B2
Sportsbank St SE6 ....164 A4
Spottons Gr N17 ....33 A2
Spout Hill CR0 ....223 C3
Spratt Hall Rd E11 ....55 A3
Spray St SE18 ....122 D2
Spreighton Rd KT8 ....195 D5
Sprewell SW15 ....157 A5
Spriggs Ho 14 N1 ....72 D1
Sprimont Pl
SW3 ....114 D2 257 C2

Spring Bridge Rd W5 ..109 D6
Spring Cl Dagenham RM8 .58 D1
Ducks Island EN5 ..12 D6
Spring Cnr TW13 ..149 D1
Spring Cott 10 W12 ..112 A4
Spring Cotts KT6 ..197 D4
Spring Court Rd EN2 ..4 C5
Spring Ct 10 E18 ..55 B6
W7 ..108 B6
Spring Dr HA5 ..40 A3
Spring Gdns N5 ..73 A3
SW1 ..116 A5 250 A4
East Molesey KT8 ..196 A5
Wallington SM6 ..219 C3
Woodford IG8 ..37 C3
Spring Gr W4 ..132 C6
Hampton TW12 ..173 D2
Loughton IG10 ..21 D5
Mitcham CR4 ..181 A2
Spring Grove Cres TW3, TW5 ..130 A4
Spring Grove Jun & Inf Sch TW7 ..130 B3
Spring Grove Rd
Hounslow TW3,TW5,TW7 130 A4
Richmond TW10 ..154 B6
Spring Hill E5 ..52 A2
SE26 ..184 C6
Spring Ho SW19 ..179 B2
WC1 ..234 A1
Spring La E5 ..52 B1
N10 ..49 A6
SE25 ..206 B3
Spring Lake HA7 ..25 B6
Spring Mews W1 ..237 D4
Spring Park Ave CR0 ..222 D6
Spring Park Jun & Inf Schs CR0 ..223 C5
Spring Park Rd CR0 ..222 D6
Spring Pl N3 ..47 C6
NW5 ..71 B3
Spring Rd TW13 ..149 D1
Spring Shaw Rd BR5 ..190 A2
Spring St W2 ..92 B1 236 C1
Spring Terr TW10 ..154 A6
Spring Vale DA7 ..147 D1
Spring Villa Rd HA8 ..26 C3
Spring Wlk E1 ..96 A2
Springall St 9 SE15 ..140 B5
Springalls Wharf 2 SE16 ..118 A4
Springbank N21 ..16 B5
Springbank Rd SE13 ..164 C5
Springbank Wlk NW1 ..71 D1
Springbourne Ct BR3 ..186 A2
Springclose La SM3 ..217 A2
Springcroft Ave N2 ..48 D5
Springdale Rd N16 ..73 B4
Springett Ho 15 SW2 ..160 B6
Springfield E5 ..52 B1
SE25 ..206 A6
Bushey WD2 ..8 B3
Springfield Ave N10 ..49 C6
SW20 ..201 B6
Hampton TW12 ..173 D4
Springfield Cl N12 ..29 D5
Stanmore HA7 ..9 A1
Springfield Ct E5 ..52 B1
NW3 ..70 C1
7 W3 ..89 A1
2 Ilford IG1 ..78 D3
9 Kingston u T KT1 ..198 A6
Wallington SM6 ..219 B3
Springfield Cty Prim Schs TW16 ..171 D1
Springfield Dr IG2 ..57 A3
Springfield Gdns E5 ..52 B1
NW9 ..45 B4
Bromley BR1 ..210 B5
Ruislip HA4 ..40 B1
West Wickham BR4 ..223 D6
Woodford IG8 ..37 C3
Springfield Gr SE7 ..143 C6
Sunbury TW16 ..172 A2
Springfield Ho 1 SE5 ..139 C3
W3 ..111 A5
Springfield Hospl SW17 ..158 C1
Springfield La NW6 ..91 D6
Springfield Mount NW9 .45 C4
Springfield Pl KT3 ..199 A5
Springfield Rd E4 ..20 C4
E6 ..78 B1
E15 ..98 C4
E17 ..53 B3
N11 ..31 C5
N15 ..52 A5
NW8 ..92 A6 229 B5
SE26 ..184 B5
SW19 ..179 B5
W7 ..108 C5
Ashford TW15 ..170 B5
Bexley DA16 ..146 B2
Bexleyheath DA7 ..147 D1
Bromley BR1 ..210 B5
Harrow HA1 ..42 C3
Hayes UB4 ..106 C5
Kingston u T KT1 ..198 A6
South Norwood CR7 ..183 A2
6 Teddington TW11 ..175 A5
Twickenham TW2 ..151 C3
Wallington SM6 ..219 B3
Springfield Rise SE26 ..162 B1
Springfield Wlk NW6 ..91 D6
3 Orpington BR6 ..211 B1
Springfields 9 EN5 ..13 D6
Springhallow Sch W13 .87 A1
Springhill Cl SE5 ..139 B2
Springhurst Cl CR0 ..223 B4
Springpark Dr N4 ..51 A1
Beckenham BR3 ..208 A6
Springpond Rd RM9 ..81 A3
Springrice Rd SE13 ..164 B5
Springvale Ave TW8 ..110 A1
Springvale Ct SE12 ..143 A1
Springvale Terr 5 W14 ..112 D3
Springwater WC1 ..240 C4
Springwater Cl SE18 ..144 C4
Springway HA1 ..42 B2
Springwell Ave NW10 ..89 D6
Springwell Cl SW16 ..182 B6
Springwell Ct TW5 ..128 D3
Springwell Jun & Inf Schs TW5 ..129 A5
Springwell Rd SW16 ..182 C5
Heston TW5 ..128 D4
Springwood Cres HA8 ..11 A2
Springwood Ct CR2 ..221 C4
Sprowston Mews E7 ..77 A3
Sprowston Rd E7 ..77 A3
Spruce Ct E4 ..35 B4
W5 ..110 A3
Spruce Hills Rd E17 ..36 A1
Spruce Ho 15 SE16 ..118 D4
Spruce Pk BR2 ..208 D5
Sprucedale Gdns CR0 .222 D4
Sprules Rd SE4 ..141 A3
Spur Rd N15 ..51 B5
SE1 ..116 C4 251 A2
Brentford TW7 ..131 B5
Edgware HA8 ..26 A6
Feltham TW14 ..128 B1
Wallend IG11 ..101 A4
Spurfield KT8 ..195 D6
Spurgeon Ave SE19 ..183 B2
Spurgeon Rd SE19 ..183 B3
Spurgeon St SE1 ..117 B3 262 C6
Spurgeon's Coll SE25 ..183 C1
Spurling Rd SE22 ..139 D1
Dagenham RM9 ..81 B2
Spurstowe Rd E8 ..74 B2
Spurstowe Terr E8 ..74 B3
Spurway Par 2 IG2 ..56 B4
Square Rigger Row 7 SW11 ..136 A2
Square The SW6 ..265 A1
W6 ..112 C1
Hayes UB11 ..105 B5
Ilford IG1 ..56 C2
12 Richmond TW10 ..153 D6
Wallington SM5 ..219 A3
Woodford IG8 ..37 A5
Squarey St SW17 ..158 A1
Squire Ct 2 CR0 ..205 C1
Squire Gdns NW8 ..229 C1
Squire's Almshouses 7 E17 ..53 D5
Squires Bridge Rd KT17 ..192 B5
Squires Ct N3 ..30 A2
SW4 ..270 B1
SW19 ..179 C6
Squires Ho 3 SE18 ..144 D6
Squires La N3 ..30 A2
Squire's Mount NW3 ..70 B5
Squire's Rd TW17 ..192 C5
Squires The RM7 ..59 D3
Squires Wlk TW15 ..171 B3
Squires Wood Dr BR7 ..188 B3
Squirrel Cl TW4 ..128 C2
Squirrel Mews W13 ..109 A6
Squirrels Cl N12 ..30 A6
Hillingdon UB10 ..60 C1
Orpington BR6 ..211 C1
Squirrels Ct 4 KT4 ..215 D6
Squirrels Gn KT4 ..216 A6
Squirrel's La IG9 ..21 D1
Squirrels The SE13 ..142 B2
Bushey WD2 ..8 B5
Pinner HA5 ..41 B6
Squirrels Trad Est UB3 .105 D3
Squirries St E2 ..96 A4
Stable Cl UB5 ..85 C5
Stable Mews SE27 ..183 A5
Stable Way W10 ..90 C1
Stable Wlk N2 ..30 B2
Stable Yard Rd SW1 ..115 C4 249 B2
Stables End BR6 ..227 A5
Stables The IG9 ..21 C4
Stables Way SE11 ..116 C1 261 A2
Staburn Ct HA8 ..27 A1
Stacey Ave N18 ..34 C6
Stacey Cl E10 ..54 B4
Stacey St N7 ..72 C5
WC2 ..93 D1 239 D1
Stack Ho SW1 ..258 B3
Stackhouse St SW1 ..257 C6
Stacy Path 21 SE5 ..139 C5
Staddon Ct BR3 ..207 A5
Stadium Bsns Ctr HA9 ..66 D5
Stadium Rd SE7,SE18 ..144 B6
Stadium St SW10 ..136 A5 266 B3
Stadium Way HA9 ..66 C4
Staffa Rd E10 ..53 A1
Stafford Cl E17 ..53 B3
N14 ..15 C6
NW6 ..91 C4
Cheam SM3 ..217 A2
Stafford Cripps Ho 30 E2 ..96 C4
SW6 ..264 D5
Stafford Cross CR0 ..220 B3
Stafford Ct SW8 ..270 A2
W7 ..86 D1
W8 ..255 B6
Stafford Gdns CR0 ..220 B3
Stafford Ho SE1 ..263 D2
Stafford Mans SW11 ..267 C3
13 W14 ..112 D3
Stafford Morris Ho 9 E15 ..98 C6
Stafford Pl SW1 115 C3 259 A6
Richmond TW10 ..154 B4
Stafford Rd E3 ..97 B5
E7 ..77 D2
NW6 ..91 C4
Croydon CR0 ..220 C4
Harrow HA3 ..24 A3
Kingston u T KT3 ..199 A6
Ruislip HA4 ..61 D4
Sidcup DA14 ..189 C6
Wallington CR0,SM6 ..220 A3
Stafford St W1 ..249 A4
Stafford Terr W8 ..113 C3 255 A6
Staffordshire St SE15 ..140 A4
Stag Cl HA8 ..27 A1
Stag La SW15 ..155 D2
Buckhurst Hill IG9 ..21 B2
Edgware HA8,NW9 ..45 A6
Stag Lane Fst & Mid Schs HA8 ..26 C1
Stag Pl SW1 ..115 C3 259 A6
Stagg Hill EN4 ..2 C6
Stags Ct KT7 ..197 A2
Stags Way TW7 ..130 D6
Stagshaw Ho 17 SE22 ..139 C2
Stainbank Rd CR4 ..203 B6
Stainby Cl UB7 ..104 A3
Stainby Rd N15 ..51 D5
Stainer Ho SE9 ..143 C1
Stainer St SE1 ..252 D3
Staines Ave SM3 ..216 D6
Staines By-Pass TW15 .170 A4
Staines Rd
East Bedfont TW14 ..149 B4
Feltham TW14,TW3 ..150 C6
Hounslow TW4,TW3 ..129 C1
Ilford IG1 ..79 B4
Twickenham TW13,TW2 .151 D1
Hounslow TW3 ..129 C1
Twickenham TW2 ..152 A1
Staines Rd E TW12, TW16 ..172 C2
Staines Rd W TW15 ..171 B3
Staines Wlk DA14 ..190 C4
Stainford Cl TW15 ..171 B5
Stainforth Rd E17 ..53 C5
Ilford IG2 ..57 B2
Staining La EC2 ..242 B2
Stainmore Cl BR7 ..189 B2
Stainsbury St 26 E2 ..96 C5
Stainsby Pl E14 ..97 C1
Stainsby Rd E14 ..97 C1
Stainton Rd SE13 ..164 B4
Enfield EN3 ..6 C4
Stalbridge Ho NW1 ..232 A3
Stalbridge St NW1 ..237 B4
Stalham St SE16 ..118 B3
Stambourne Ho SW8 ..270 B2
Stambourne Way SE19 183 D3
West Wickham BR4 ..224 A5
Stamford Bridge Stadium (Chelsea FC) SW6 ..135 D5 265 C4
Stamford Brook Ave W6 ..111 D3
Stamford Brook Gdns 1 W6 ..111 D3
Stamford Brook Mans 2 W6 ..111 D2
Stamford Brook Rd W6 111 D3
Stamford Brook Sta W6 ..111 D2
Stamford Cl N15 ..52 A5
Harrow Weald HA3 ..24 C3
Southall UB1 ..107 C6
Stamford Ct W6 ..112 A2
Edgware HA8 ..26 B6
Stamford Dr BR2 ..208 D5
Stamford Gdns RM9 ..80 C1
Stamford Grove E 1 N16 ..52 A1
Stamford Grove W 4 N16 ..52 A1
Stamford Hill N16 ..51 D1
Stamford Hill Mans 1 N16 ..51 D1
Stamford Hill Prim Sch N15 ..51 B3
Stamford Hill Sta N16 ..51 C2
Stamford Ho N15 ..52 A5
Stamford Lo 2 N16 ..51 D2
Stamford Mans 2 N16 ..52 A1
Stamford Rd E6 ..100 A6
N1 ..73 C2
N15 ..52 A4
Dagenham RM9 ..80 C1
Stamford St SE1 ..116 C5 251 B4
Stamp Pl E2 ..95 D4
Stanard Cl N16 ..51 C2
Stanborough Cl TW12 .173 B4
Stanborough Ho 4 E3 ..97 D3
Stanborough Pas E8 ..73 D2
Stanborough Rd TW3, TW7 ..130 B2
Stanbridge Mans SW15 134 C2
Stanbridge Pl N21 ..16 D2
Stanbridge Rd SW15 ..134 C2
Stanbrook Ct W1 ..249 A4
Stanbrook Rd SE2 ..124 B4
Stanburn Fst & Mid Schs HA7 ..25 C3
Stanbury Ct 16 NW3 ..70 D2
Stanbury Rd SE15 ..140 B3
SE15 ..140 C3
Stancroft NW9 ..45 C4
Standale Gr HA4 ..39 A4
Standard Ind Est E16 ..122 B4
Standard Pl 14 EC2 ..95 C4
Standard Rd NW10 ..89 B3
Belvedere DA17 ..125 C1
Bexleyheath DA6 ..147 A1
Enfield EN3 ..7 A6
Hounslow TW4 ..129 A2
Standen Rd SW18 ..157 C4
Standfield Rd RM10 ..81 C3
Standish Ho SE9 ..143 B1
6 W6 ..112 A2
Standish Rd W6 ..112 A2
Standlake Point 1 SE23 ..162 D1
Stane Cl SW19 ..179 D3
Stane Way SE18 ..144 A5
Stanedge Ct SW16 ..182 A5
Stanesgate Ho 20 SE15 140 A5
Stanetto Ct 3 RM6 ..58 B2
Stanfield Ho NW8 ..236 D6
9 Northolt UB5 ..84 D5
Stanfield Rd 13 E3 ..97 A5
Stanford Cl
Hampton TW12 ..173 B4
Romford RM7 ..59 D3
Ruislip HA4 ..39 A3
Stanford Ct N11 ..31 A5
SW6 ..265 D1
W8 ..255 D5
Stanford Ho IG11 ..102 B5
Stanford Mid Sch SW16 ..181 D2
Stanford Pl SE1 117 C2 263 A3
Stanford Rd N11 ..30 D5
SW16 ..182 A1
W8 ..113 D3 255 D6
Stanford St SW1 ..259 C3
Stanford Way SW16 ..181 D1
Stangate Cres WD6 ..11 C6
Stangate Gdns HA7 ..25 B6
Stangate Lo N21 ..16 B4
Stangate Mansi TW1 ..152 D1
Stanger Rd SE25 ..206 A5
Stanhope Ave N3 ..47 B6
Harrow HA3 ..24 B2
Hayes BR2 ..209 A1
Stanhope Cl 28 SE16 ..118 D4
Stanhope Ct N3 ..29 B1
Stanhope Gate W1 ..248 B4
Stanhope Gdns N4 ..51 A3
N6 ..49 C3
NW7 ..27 D5
SW7 ..114 A2 256 B4
Dagenham RM8 ..81 B5
Redbridge IG1 ..56 B1
Stanhope Gr BR3 ..207 B5
Stanhope Ho N6 ..49 C3
5 N11 ..31 B6
SE8 ..141 B5
4 SW15 ..156 C6
Stanhope Mews E SW7 ..114 A2 256 B4
Stanhope Mews S SW7 256 B3
Stanhope Mews W SW7 ..114 A2 256 B4
Stanhope Park Rd UB6 .86 A3
Stanhope Pl W2 ..237 C1
Stanhope Prim Sch UB6 86 A3
Stanhope Rd E17 ..53 D4
N6 ..49 C2
N12 ..30 A5
Bexleyheath DA7 ..147 A3
Dagenham RM8 ..81 B5
Ducks Island EN5 ..12 D5
Sidcup DA15 ..190 A6
South Croydon CR0 ..221 C5
Southall UB6 ..86 A2
Wallington SM5 ..219 A1
Stanhope Row W1 ..248 C3
Stanhope St NW1 ..93 C4 232 A1
Stanhope Terr W2 ..114 B6 246 D6
Stanier Cl SW5 ..254 D1
Stanlake Rd W12 ..112 C5
Stanlake Villas W12 ..112 C5
Stanley Ave
Barking IG11 ..101 D5
Beckenham BR2,BR3 ..208 A6
Dagenham RM8 ..59 B2
Greenford UB6 ..86 A6
Wembley HA0 ..66 A1
West Barnes KT3 ..200 A4
Stanley Bldgs NW1 ..233 A3
Stanley Cl SW8 ..270 C5
Wembley HA0 ..66 A1
Stanley Cres W11 ..113 B6 244 C6
Stanley Ct SW19 ..179 C4
11 W5 ..87 C2
Belmont SM2 ..217 D1
Wallington SM5 ..219 A1
Stanley Cty Inf Sch TW2 ..174 C6
Stanley Cty Jun Sch TW2 ..174 C6
Stanley Gardens Rd TW11 ..174 C5
Stanley Gdns NW2 ..68 C3
W3 ..111 C4
W11 ..244 C6
Mitcham CR4 ..181 A4
Wallington SM6 ..219 C2
Stanley Gr SW11 ..137 A3
Thornton Heath CR0 ..204 C3
Stanley Ho E11 ..54 C3
18 E14 ..97 C1
35 SW8 ..137 D3
Stanley Horstead Twr E10 ..75 D6
Stanley Mans SW10 ..266 B6
SW17 ..158 D2
Stanley Park Dr HA0 ..88 B6
Stanley Park High Sch SM5 ..219 A2
Stanley Park Inf Sch SM5 ..218 D1
Stanley Park Jun Sch SM5 ..218 D1
Stanley Park Rd SM5, SM6 ..219 A1
Stanley Pas NW1 ..233 A3
Stanley Rd E4 ..20 B3
E10 ..53 D3
E12 ..78 A3
E15 ..98 B6
E17 ..36 D2
N2 ..48 B6
N9 ..17 D2
N10 ..31 B3
N11 ..31 D5
N15 ..50 D5
2 NW9 ..46 A2
SW14 ..132 D1
SW19 ..179 C4
W3 ..111 A3
Ashford TW15 ..170 A5
Bromley BR2 ..209 C5
Enfield EN1 ..5 C2
Harrow HA2 ..64 A6
Hounslow TW3 ..130 A1
Ilford IG1 ..79 B6
Mitcham CR4 ..181 A3
Morden SM4 ..201 C5
Northwood HA6 ..22 A2
Orpington BR6 ..211 D1
Sidcup DA14 ..168 A1
Southall UB1 ..107 A6
Sutton SM2 ..217 D1
Teddington TW11,TW2 ..174 C5
Thornton Heath CR0 ..204 C3
Twickenham TW2 ..152 B1
Wallington SM5 ..219 A1
Wembley HA9 ..66 B2
Stanley St SE14,SE8 ..141 B5
Stanley Studios SW10 .266 B6
Stanley Tech High Sch SE25 ..205 D6
Stanley Terr 7 N19 ..72 A6
Stanleycroft Cl TW7 ..130 C4
Stanmer St SW11 ..136 C3
Stanmore Gdns
Richmond TW9 ..132 B2
Sutton SM1 ..218 A5
Stanmore Hill HA7 ..25 B6
Stanmore Ho 21 SW8 ..137 D3
Stanmore Lo HA7 ..25 B6
Stanmore Pl NW1 ..231 D6
Stanmore Rd E11 ..54 D1
N15 ..50 D5
Richmond TW9 ..132 B2
Stanmore Sixth Form Ctr HA7 ..25 C4
Stanmore St N1 .94 B6 233 C6
Stanmore Sta HA7 ..25 D6
Stanmore Terr 3 BR3 .185 C1
Stannard Cotts 23 E1 ..96 C3
Stannard Mews E8 ..74 A2
Stannard Rd E8 ..74 A2
Stannary Pl SE11 ..261 B1
Stannary St SE11 ..116 C1 261 B1
Stannet Way SM6 ..219 C4
Stansbury Ho 3 W10 ..91 A4
Stansfeld Ho SE1 ..263 D3
Stansfeld Rd E6 ..99 D1
Stansfield Rd RM10 ..81 C2
Stansfield Rd SW9 ..138 B2
Cranford TW4,TW5 ..128 B3
Stansgate Rd RM10 ..81 C5
Stanstead Cl BR2 ..208 D3
Stanstead Gr SE23 ..163 B3
Stanstead Ho E3 ..98 A3
Stanstead Manor SM1 .217 C2
Stanstead Rd E11 ..55 B4
SE23,SE6 ..163 A3
Stansted Cres DA5 ..168 D3
Stansted Rd TW6 ..148 B5
Stanswood Gdns SE5 ..139 C5
Stanthorpe Cl SW16 ..182 A5
Stanthorpe Rd SW16 ..182 A5
Stanton Ave TW11 ..174 C4
Stanton Cl
North Cheam KT4 ..200 D1
West Ewell KT19 ..214 D3
Stanton Ct N3 ..29 C2
N16 ..51 B2
5 Sidcup DA15 ..168 A1
Stanton Ho 8 SE10 ..142 A6
Stanton Rd SW13 ..133 D3
SW20 ..178 D2
Thornton Heath CR0 ..205 A2
Stanton Sq SE26 ..185 B6
Stanton Way SE26 ..185 B6
Stanway Ct 23 N1 ..95 C5
Stanway Gdns W3 ..110 C5
Stanway Gdns *continued*
Edgware HA8 ..27 A5
Stanway St N1 ..95 C5
Stanwell Rd
Ashford TW15 ..170 A6
East Bedfont TW14,TW19, TW6 ..148 D4
TW15 ..148 A1
Stanwick Rd W14 ..113 B2 254 C3
Stanworth Ct TW5 ..129 C5
Stanworth St SE1 ..253 D1
Stanyhurst SE23 ..163 A3
Stapelhurst Ho 18 E5 ..74 B3
Stapenhill Rd HA0 ..65 B5
Staple Inn WC2 ..241 A3
Staple Inn Bldgs WC2 .241 A3
Staple St SE1 ..117 B4 252 D1
Staplefield Cl 3 SW2 .160 A3
Hatch End HA5 ..23 A3
Stapleford N17 ..33 C1
Stapleford Ave IG2 ..57 C4
Stapleford Cl E4 ..20 A1
SW19 ..157 A4
Kingston u T KT1 ..198 C6
Stapleford Rd HA0 ..65 D1
Stapleford Way IG11 ..102 B4
Staplehurst Ct SW11 ..158 D5
Staplehurst Rd SE13 ..164 C6
Sutton SM5 ..218 C1
Staples Cl SE16 ..119 A5
Staples Corner (East) NW2 ..46 B1
Staples Corner (West) NW2 ..46 B1
Staples Corner Bsns Pk NW2 ..46 B1
Stapleton Gdns CR0 ..220 C3
Stapleton Hall N4 ..50 B2
Stapleton Hall Rd N4 ..50 B2
Stapleton Ho 10 E2 ..96 B4
Stapleton Rd SW17 ..159 A1
Erith DA7 ..147 B6
Orpington BR6 ..227 D5
Stapley Rd DA17 ..125 C1
Staplyton Rd EN5 ..1 A2
Star & Garter Hill TW10 ..154 A4
Star & Garter Mans SW15 ..134 D2
Star Alley EC3 ..253 B6
Star Ct UB10 ..83 A3
Star La E16 ..98 C3
Star Path UB5 ..85 C5
Star Prim Sch E16 ..98 C3
Star Rd W14 ..113 B1 254 C1
Hillingdon UB10 ..83 A3
Hounslow TW7 ..130 B3
Star St W2 ..92 C1 237 A2
Star Works NW10 ..90 A4
Star Yd WC2 ..94 C1 241 A2
Starboard Way E14 ..119 C3
Starcross St NW1 ..93 C4 232 B1
Starfield Rd W12 ..112 A4
Starliner Ct N7 ..72 C2
Starling Cl
Buckhurst Hill IG9 ..21 A3
Pinner HA5 ..40 C6
Starling Ho NW8 ..230 A4
Starling Wlk TW12 ..173 A5
Starmans Cl RM9 ..103 A6
Starts Cl BR6 ..226 C5
Starts Hill Ave BR6 ..226 D4
Starts Hill Rd BR6 ..226 D4
Starveall Cl UB7 ..104 B3
State Farm Ave BR6 ..227 A4
Staten Gdns TW1 ..152 D3
Statham Gr N16 ..73 B5
N18 ..33 C5
Statham Ho SW8 ..269 A2
Stathard Ho 18 E1 ..96 C3
Station App E11 ..55 A4
E17 ..53 C4
2 E18 ..37 B1
N11 ..31 B5
N12 ..29 D6
NW10 ..89 D4
SE3 ..143 B2
SE9 ..166 B3
SE26 ..185 B5
SW6 ..135 A2
SW16 ..181 D5
Ashford TW15 ..170 B6
5 Beckenham BR3 ..185 C2
Belmont SM2 ..217 A1
Bexley DA16 ..146 A3
Bexleyheath DA7 ..147 A3
Chislehurst BR7 ..188 C1
Chislehurst BR7 ..188 A4
3 Croydon CR0 ..221 B6
Greenford UB6 ..64 B1
Hampton TW12 ..173 C2
Hayes BR2 ..209 A1
Hayes UB3 ..105 D3
Hinchley Wood KT10 ..212 D5
4 Kingston u T KT1,KT2 .176 C2
New Barnet EN5 ..2 A1
6 New Malden KT4 ..200 A1
Orpington BR6 ..227 D6
Pinner HA5 ..41 A6
Richmond TW9 ..132 C4
Ruislip HA4 ..39 D1
Shepperton TW17 ..193 A4
South Ruislip HA4 ..62 B3

Station App *continued*
Sunbury TW16 .172 A2
1 Surbiton KT6 .198 A3
Wembley HA0 .65 B2
Woodford IG9 .37 D6
Worcester Pk KT19 .216 A3
Yiewsley UB7 .104 A5
Station Approach Rd
W4 .133 A5
Station Ave 5 SW9 .138 D2
Kingston u T KT3 .199 C6
West Ewell KT19 .215 D1
Station Bldgs SW20 .178 C1
Station Blgs W5 .110 B5
Station Cl N3 .29 C2
Hampton TW12 .173 D2
Station Cres N15 .51 B5
SE3 .121 A1
Ashford TW15 .170 A6
Wembley HA0 .65 B2
Station Ct 1 E10 .53 D2
5 SE15 .140 C3
Station Est 1 E18 .37 B1
Beckenham BR3 .206 D5
Station Estate Rd TW14 150 B3
Station Gdns W4 .133 A5
Station Gr Wembley HA0 .66 A2
2 Wembley HA0 .66 A3
Station Hill BR2 .225 A6
Station House Mews N9 34 A6
Station Par 2 E11 .55 A4
4 N14 .15 D3
NW2 .68 C2
4 SW12 .159 A3
W3 .88 C1
W5 .110 B5
Ashford TW15 .170 B6
Barking IG11 .79 A1
Cockfosters EN4 .3 A1
Dagenham RM10 .81 C2
Edgware HA8 .26 A3
Feltham TW14 .150 B4
Harrow HA2 .63 D4
Harrow HA3 .25 A1
Northolt UB5 .63 C1
Richmond TW9 .132 C4
Ruislip HA4 .61 B6
South Harrow UB5 .63 D4
Woodford IG9 .37 D6
Station Pas E18 .37 B1
SE15 .140 C4
Station Pl N4 .72 C6
Station Rd E4 .20 B3
E7 .77 A4
E10 .76 A5
E12 .78 A4
E17 .53 A4
N3 .29 C1
N11 .31 B5
N17 .52 A6
N19 .71 C5
N21 .16 D3
N22 .32 B1
NW4 .46 A4
NW7 .27 C4
NW10 .89 D5
SE13 .142 A2
SE20 .184 C4
SE25 .205 D5
SW13 .133 D3
SW19 .180 A2
W5 .88 B1
W7 .108 C5
Ashford TW15 .170 B6
Belvedere DA17 .125 C3
Bexleyheath DA7 .147 A2
Bromley BR2 .186 C1
Carshalton SM5 .218 D4
Chessington KT9 .214 A3
Claygate KT10 .212 C3
Croydon CR0 .205 A1
Edgware HA8 .26 C4
Esher KT10 .212 B6
Hampton TW12 .173 D2
Harrow HA1 .42 D4
Harrow HA1,HA2 .41 D4
Hayes UB3 .105 C2
Hounslow TW3 .129 D1
Ilford IG1 .78 D5
Ilford IG6 .57 B6
Kingston u T KT2 .176 C2
New Barnet EN5 .13 D6
Orpington BR6 .227 D6
Plaistow BR1 .187 A2
Romford RM6 .58 D2
Shepperton TW17 .193 A4
Sidcup DA14,DA15 .168 A1
Sunbury TW16 .172 A3
Teddington KT1 .175 D2
Teddington TW11 .175 A4
Thames Ditton KT7 .196 D2
Twickenham TW1 .152 D4
West Barnes KT3 .200 B4
West Drayton UB7 .104 A4
West Wickham BR4 .208 A1
Station Rd N DA17 .125 D3
Station Rise SE27 .160 D2
Station Sq BR5 .211 A4
Station St E15 .76 B1
E16 .122 D5
Station Terr NW10 .90 D5
SE5 .139 A4
Station View UB6 .86 B6
Station Way
Buckhurst Hill IG9 .37 D6
Station Way *continued*
Cheam SM2,SM3 .217 A1
Station Yd TW1 .153 A4
Stationers Hall Ct EC4 .241 D1
Staunton Ho SE17 .263 A3
Staunton Rd KT2 .176 B3
Staunton St SE8 .141 B6
Stave Yard Rd SE16 .119 A5
Staveley NW1 .232 A2
Staveley Cl E9 .74 C3
N7 .72 A4
SE15 .140 C4
8 SE15 .140 B4
Staveley Ct 4 E11 .55 A4
Staveley Gdns W4 .133 B4
Staveley Rd W4 .133 B5
Ashford TW15 .171 B4
Staverdale Lo W14 .254 D6
Stavers Ho 18 E3 .97 B5
Staverton Rd NW2 .68 C1
Stavordale Rd N5 .72 D4
Carshalton SM5 .202 A2
Stayner's Rd E1 .96 D3
Stayton Rd SM1 .217 C5
Stead St SE17 .117 B2 262 C3
Steadfast Rd KT1 .175 D2
Steadman Ct EC1 .242 B6
Steadman Ho 4 RM10 .81 C5
Steam Farm La TW14 .127 D1
Stean St E8 .95 D6
Stebbing Ho 8 W11 .112 D5
Stebbing Way IG11 .102 A5
Stebon JMI Sch E14 .97 C2
Stebondale St E14 .120 A2
Stedham Pl WC1 .240 A2
Stedman Cl UB10 .60 C5
Steedman St
SE17 .117 A2 262 A3
Steeds Rd N10 .30 D2
Steele Ho E15 .98 C5
Steele Rd E11 .76 C4
N17 .51 C6
NW10 .89 A5
W4 .111 A3
Isleworth TW7 .131 A1
Steele Wlk DA8 .147 D5
Steele's Mews N NW3 .70 D2
Steele's Mews S NW3 .70 D2
Steele's Rd NW3 .70 D2
Steel's La 23 E1 .96 C1
Steen Way 7 SE22 .161 C6
Steep Cl BR6 .227 D2
Steep Hill SW16 .159 D1
South Croydon CR0 .221 C4
Steeple Cl SW6 .135 A3
SW19 .179 A6
Steeple Ct 19 E1 .96 B3
Steeple Wlk N1 .235 B6
Steeplestone Cl N18 .33 A5
Steerforth St SW18 .158 A2
Steers Mead CR4 .180 D2
Steers Way SE16 .119 A4
Steetley Ct 14 SM2 .218 A1
Steinman Ct TW7 .130 D2
Stelfax Ho WC1 .233 D2
Stella Rd SW17 .180 D4
Stellar Ho 4 N17 .33 D4
Stellman Cl E5 .74 A5
Stembridge Rd SE20 .184 B1
Sten Cl EN3 .7 C6
Stephan Cl E8 .96 A6
Stephen Cl BR6 .227 D5
Stephen Ct 18 SW19 .156 D3
Stephen Fox Ho 7 W4 111 C1
Stephen Hawking Sch
E14 .97 A1
Stephen Mews W1 .239 C3
Stephen Pl SW4 .137 C2
Stephen Saunders Ct
SW11 .158 C6
Stephen St W1 .239 C3
Stephendale Rd SW6 .136 A3
Stephens Ct E16 .98 D3
SE4 .141 A2
Stephen's Rd E15 .98 C6
Stephenson Ct SM2 .217 B1
Stephenson Ho 6 NW3 .70 D3
2 NW5 .71 B4
SE1 .262 A6
SE2 .124 D1
Stephenson Rd E17 .53 A4
W7 .86 D1
Twickenham TW4 .151 C4
Stephenson St E16 .98 C2
NW10 .89 D4
Stephenson Way
NW1 .93 C3 239 B6
Stepney Cswy E1 .96 D1
Stepney Day Hospl E1 .96 C1
Stepney Gn E1 .96 D2
Stepney Green Boys Sec Sch
E1 .96 D2
Stepney Green Ct 3 E1 .96 D2
Stepney Green Sta E1 .96 D3
Stepney Greencoat CE JMI
Sch E14 .97 B1
Stepney High St E1 .96 D2
Stepney Way E1 .96 C2
Sterling Ave Edgware HA8 26 B6
Upper Halliford TW17 .193 C6
Sterling Cl NW10 .68 A1
Sterling Gdns SE14 .141 A6
Sterling Ho SE9 .143 B1
Sterling Ind Est RM10 .81 D4
Sterling Pl W5 .110 A2
Sterling Rd EN2 .5 B5
Sterling St SW7 .257 B6
Sterling Way (North Circular
Rd) N18 .33 C5
Stern Cl IG11 .102 C5
Sterndale Rd W14 .112 D3
Sterne St W12 .112 D4
Sternhall La SE15 .140 A2
Sternhold Ave SW12,
SW2 .159 D2
Sterry Cres RM10 .81 C3
Sterry Dr
Thames Ditton KT7 .196 C3
Worcester Pk KT19 .215 C4
Sterry Gdns RM10 .81 C2
Sterry Rd Barking IG11 .101 D6
Dagenham RM10 .81 C3
Sterry St SE1 .252 C1
Steucers La SE23 .163 A3
Stevanne Ct 1 DA17 .125 C1
Steve Biko Ct W10 .90 D3
Steve Biko La SE6 .185 C6
Steve Biko Rd N7 .72 C5
Steve Biko Way TW3 .129 C2
Stevedale Rd DA16 .146 C3
Stevedore St 3 E1 .118 B5
Stevenage Rd E6 .78 C2
SW6 .134 D4
Stevens Ave E9 .74 C2
Stevens Cl
Beckenham BR3 .185 C4
Hampton TW12 .173 B4
Pinner HA5 .40 C4
Stevens Ct BR3 .185 C4
Stevens Gn WD2 .8 A3
Stevens' La KT10 .213 A2
Stevens Rd RM8 .80 C5
Stevens St SE1 .263 B6
Stevenson Cl EN5 .14 B5
Stevenson Cres SE16 .118 B1
Stevenson Ho NW8 .229 A6
1 SW11 .136 D3
Wembley HA9 .65 D6
Steventon Rd W12 .111 D6
Stew La EC4 .252 A6
Steward St E1 .95 C2 243 B4
Stewards Holte Wlk 3
N11 .31 B6
Stewart Ave TW17 .192 C5
Stewart Cl NW9 .45 A3
Chislehurst West BR7 .188 D6
Hampton TW12 .173 A4
Stewart Fleming Prim Sch
SE20 .206 C6
Stewart Headlam JMI Sch
E1 .96 B3
Stewart Ho SE1 .263 A5
Stewart Quay UB3 .105 C4
Stewart Rainbird Ho 1
E12 .78 C3
Stewart Rd E15 .76 B4
Stewart St E14 .120 A4
Stewart's Gr
SW3 .114 C1 257 A2
Stewart's Rd
SW8 .137 C4 269 A2
Stewartsby Cl N18 .33 A5
Steyne Rd W3 .110 D5
Steyning Gr SE9 .188 B6
Steyning Way TW4 .128 C1
Steynings Way N12 .29 C5
Steynton Ave DA5 .168 D2
Sthrathbrook Rd SW16 182 B3
Stickland Rd DA17 .125 C2
Stickleton Cl UB6 .85 D4
Stifford Ho E1 .96 C2
Stile Hall Gdns W4 .110 C1
Stile Hall Par 6 W4 .110 C1
Stile Path TW16 .194 A5
Stilecroft Gdns HA0 .65 B5
Stileman Ho 4 E3 .97 B2
Stiles Cl Bromley BR2 .210 B3
Erith DA8 .125 D1
Stillingfleet Rd SW13 .134 A6
Stillington St
SW1 .115 C2 259 B4
Stillness Prim Sch
SE23 .163 A5
Stillness Rd SE23 .163 B5
Stilton Cres NW10 .67 A1
Stilwell Rdbt UB8 .104 D6
Stipularis Dr UB4 .84 D3
Stirling Cl SW16 .181 C2
Stirling Cnr EN5,WD6 .11 B5
Stirling Ct W13 .109 B6
WC2 .240 C1
Stirling Gr TW3 .130 A3
Stirling Ho 5 SE18 .122 D1
Stirling Mans NW6 .70 A2
Stirling Rd E13 .99 B5
E17 .53 A6
N17 .34 A2
N22 .32 D2
SW9 .138 A3
W3 .110 D3
Harrow HA3 .42 D6
Hayes UB3 .106 B6
Stanwell TW19,TW6 .148 B5
Twickenham TW2 .151 D4
Stirling Way
Borehamwood WD6 .11 B6
Croydon CR0 .204 A2
Stiven Cres HA2 .63 B5
Stoatley Ho 10 SW15 .156 A3
Stock Exchange EC2 .242 D1
Stock Orchard Cres N7 .72 B3
Stock Orchard St N7 .72 B3
Stock St E13 .99 A5
Stockbeck NW1 .232 B3
Stockbridge Ho EN2 .4 D3
Stockbury Rd CR0 .206 C3
Stockdale Rd RM8 .81 B6
Stockdove Way UB6 .86 D4
Stocker Gdns RM9 .80 C1
Stockfield Rd SW16 .160 B1
Claygate KT10 .212 C3
Stockholm Ho E1 .118 A6
Stockholm Rd SE16 .118 C1
Stockholm Way 9 E1 .118 A5
Stockhurst Cl SW15 .134 D3
Stockingswater La EN3 .7 B2
Stockleigh Hall NW8 .230 B4
Stockley Cl UB7 .104 D4
Stockley Ctry Pk UB7 .104 C6
Stockley Farm Rd UB7 .104 D3
Stockley Park Bsns Pk
UB11 .105 A5
Stockley Rd UB7 .104 D4
Stockport Rd SW16 .181 D2
Stocks Ct 5 E1 .96 D3
Stocks Pl 16 E14 .119 B6
Stocksfield Rd E17 .54 A6
Stockton Gdns N17 .33 A3
NW7 .11 C1
Stockton Ho 16 E2 .96 B4
HA2 .41 C1
Stockton Rd N17 .33 A3
N18 .34 B4
Stockwell Ave SW9 .138 B2
Stockwell Cl BR1 .187 B1
Stockwell Gdns
SW9 .138 B4 270 C1
Stockwell Gn SW9 .138 B3
Stockwell Jun & Inf Sch
SW9 .138 B2
Stockwell La SW9 .138 B3
Stockwell Park Cres
SW9 .138 B3
Stockwell Park Rd
SW9 .138 B4 270 D1
Stockwell Park Sch
SW9 .138 B4 270 C1
Stockwell Park Wlk
SW9 .138 C2
Stockwell St SE10 .142 A6
Stockwell Sta SW4 .138 A3
Stockwell Terr SW9 .270 C1
Stodart Rd SE20 .184 C2
Stoddart Ho SW8 .270 D5
Stodmarsh Ho 28 SW9 .138 C4
Stofield Gdns SE9 .165 D1
Stoford Cl SW19 .157 A4
Stoke Newington Church St
N16 .73 C6
Stoke Newington Comm
N16 .73 D6
Stoke Newington High St
N16 .73 D5
Stoke Newington Rd
N16 .73 D4
Stoke Newington Sch
N16 .73 B5
Stoke Newington Sta
N16 .73 D6
Stoke Pl NW10 .89 D4
Stoke Rd KT2 .177 A3
Stokenchurch St
SW6 .135 D4 265 C1
Stokes Ct N2 .48 C5
Stokes Rd E6 .100 A3
Croydon CR0 .206 D3
Stokesby Rd KT9 .214 B2
Stokesley St W12 .89 D1
Stokley Ct N8 .50 A5
Stoll Cl NW2 .68 C5
Stoms Path SE6 .185 C5
Stonard Rd N13 .16 C1
Barking RM8 .80 B4
Stondon Pk SE23 .163 A5
Stondon Wlk E6 .100 A5
4 E6 .99 D5
Stone Bldgs WC2 94 B2 240 D3
Stone Cl SW4 .137 C3
Dagenham RM8 .81 B6
Yiewsley UB7 .104 B5
Stone Cres TW14 .149 D4
Stone Gate 8 NW5 .71 A2
Stone Gr HA8 .26 B5
Stone Grove Ct HA8 .26 B5
Stone Hall Rd N21 .16 C4
Stone Lake Ret Pk SE7 121 C2
Stone Park Ave BR3 .207 D5
Stone Pl KT4 .216 A6
Stone Rd BR2 .208 D4
Stone St CR0,CR9 .220 C3
Stonebanks KT12 .194 A2
Stonebridge Ct 8 NW10 67 B1
Stonebridge Ctr The
N15 .52 A4
Stonebridge Park HA9 .66 D1
Stonebridge Park Sta
NW10 .66 D1
Stonebridge Pk NW10 .67 B1
Stonebridge Prim Sch The
NW10 .89 B6
Stonebridge Rd N15 .51 D4
Stonebridge Way HA9 .66 D2
Stonechat Sq 6 E6 .100 A2
Stonecot Cl SM3 .201 A1
Stonecot Hill SM4 .201 A1
Stonecroft Way CR0 .204 A2
Stonecutter St EC4 .241 C2
Stonefield N4 .72 B6
Stonefield Cl
Bexleyheath DA7 .147 C2
Ruislip HA4 .63 A3
Stonefield Mans N1 .234 A5
Stonefield St N1 94 C6 234 B6
Stonefield Way SE7 .143 D5
Ruislip HA4 .63 A3
Stonegrove Gdns HA8 .26 A5
Stonehall Ave IG1 .56 A3
Stoneham Rd N11 .31 C5
Stonehaven BR3 .185 D1
Stonehill Cl SW14 .155 B6
Stonehill Ct E4 .19 D4
Stonehill Rd SW14 .155 B6
W4 .110 C1
Stonehills Ct SE21 .161 C1
Stonehill's Mans 3
SW16 .160 A2
Stonehorse Rd EN3 .18 C6
Stonehouse NW1 .232 B5
Stonehouse Ct EC2 .243 B2
Stonehouse Ho 27 W2 .91 C2
Stoneleigh Ave Enfield EN1 6 B4
North Cheam KT17,KT4 .216 A5
Stoneleigh Broadway
KT17 .216 A3
Stoneleigh Cres KT19 .215 D3
Stoneleigh Ct 4 N17 .33 D1
Redbridge IG5 .56 A6
Stoneleigh Fst Grant Maintd
Sch KT4 .216 B4
Stoneleigh Lo 13 TW9 .132 B4
Stoneleigh Park Ave
CR0 .206 D3
Stoneleigh Park Rd
KT19,KT4 .216 A3
Stoneleigh Pl W11 .112 D6
Stoneleigh Rd N17 .33 D1
Carshalton SM5 .202 C2
Redbridge IG5 .56 B6
Stoneleigh St W11 .112 D6
Stoneleigh Sta KT19 .216 A3
Stoneleigh Terr N19 .71 B6
Stonemasons Cl N15 .51 B5
Stonenest St N4 .50 B1
Stones End St SE1 .252 A1
Stonewall E6 .100 C2
Stoneworth Ct SE25 .206 A3
Stoney Alley SE18 .144 C3
Stoney Deep TW11 .175 A6
Stoney La E1 .243 B2
SE19 .183 D4
Stoney St SE1 .117 B5 252 C4
Stoneyard La E14 .119 D6
Stoneycroft Cl SE12 .164 D4
Stoneydown E17 .53 A5
Stoneydown Ave E17 .53 A5
Stoneydown Ho 2 E17 .53 A5
Stoneydown Park Prim Sch
E17 .53 A5
Stoneyfields Gdns HA8 .27 A6
Stoneyfields La HA8 .27 A6
Stonhouse St SW4 .137 D1
Stonnell's Rd SW11 .158 D6
Stonor Rd W14 .113 B2 254 C3
Stonycroft Cl EN3 .7 A3
Stopes St SE15 .139 D5
Stopford Rd E13 .99 A6
SE17 .261 D1
Stopher Ho SE1 .251 D1
Storace Ho 6 SW4 .138 A1
Store Rd E16 .122 C4
Store St E15 .76 B3
WC1 .93 D2 239 C4
Storers Quay E14 .120 B2
Storey Ct NW8 .229 C1
Storey Ho 12 E14 .119 D6
Storey Prim Sch E16 .122 D5
Storey Rd E17 .53 B5
N6 .48 D3
Storey St E16 .122 C4
Storey's Gate
SW1 .115 D4 249 D1
Stories Rd SE5 .139 C2
Stork Rd E7 .77 A2
Storks Rd SE16 .118 A3
Storksmead Rd HA8 .27 C3
Stormont House Sch E5 74 B4
Stormont Rd N6 .48 D2
SW11 .137 A1
Stormont Way KT9 .213 C3
Stormount Dr UB3 .105 A4
Storrington WC1 .233 B1
Storrington Rd CR0 .205 D1
Story St N1 .72 B1
Stothard Pl E1 .243 B4
Stothard St 11 E1 .96 C3
Stoughton Ave SM3 .217 A3
Stoughton Cl SE11 .260 D3
SW15 .156 A3
Stour Ave UB2 .107 C3
Stour Cl BR2 .225 C4
Stour Rd E3 .75 C1
Dagenham RM10 .81 C6
Stourcliffe Cl W1 .237 C2
Stourcliffe St W1 .237 C1
Stourhead Cl 6 SW19 .156 D4
Stourhead Gdns SW20 .200 A6
Stourton Ave TW13 .173 B6
Stow Cres E17 .35 A3
Stowage SE8 .141 D6
Stowe Cres HA4 .39 A3
Stowe Gdns N9 .17 D3
Stowe Ho 11 N16 .73 C5
NW11 .48 A3
Stowe Pl N15 .51 C6
Stowe Rd W12 .112 B4
Stowell Ho 2 N8 .50 A5
Stowford Coll SM2 .218 A1
Stowting Rd BR6 .227 C4
Stox Mead HA3 .24 B2
Stracey Rd E7 .77 A4
NW10 .89 B6
Strachan Pl SW19,SW20 178 C4
Stradbroke Gr
Buckhurst Hill IG9 .21 D3
Redbridge IG5 .56 B6
Stradbroke Rd N5 .73 A4
Stradbrook Cl HA2 .63 B5
Stradella Rd SE24 .161 A5
Straffan Lo 8 NW3 .70 C2
Strafford Ho 9 SE8 .119 B1
Strafford Rd W3 .111 A4
High Barnet EN5 .1 A2
Hounslow TW3 .129 B2
Twickenham TW1 .153 A4
Strafford St E14 .119 C4
Strahan Rd E3 .97 A4
Straight The UB2 .107 A4
Straightsmouth SE10 .142 A5
Strait Rd E6 .122 B6
Straker's Rd SE15 .140 B1
Strale Ho 17 N1 .95 C6
Strand WC2 .116 B6 250 C6
Strand La WC2 .250 D6
Strand on the Green Inf Sch
W4 .132 C6
Strand on the Green Jun Sch
W4 .132 C6
Strand Pl N18 .33 C6
Strandfield Cl SE18 .123 C1
Strand-on-the-Green
W4 .132 C6
Strang Ho N1 .235 A5
Strangways Terr W14 .254 C5
Stranraer Way N1 .72 A1
1 West Bedfont TW6 .148 A5
Strasburg Rd
SW11 .137 A4 268 B1
Stratfield Ho SE12 .165 A2
Stratfield Park Cl N21 .16 D4
Stratford Ave UB10 .82 B5
Stratford Bus Sta E15 .76 B1
Stratford Cl IG11 .80 A1
Stratford Ct KT3 .199 B5
Stratford Ctr E15 .76 B1
Stratford Gr SW15 .134 D1
Stratford House Ave
BR1 .210 A6
Stratford Office Village The
1 E15 .76 C1
Stratford Pl W1 .238 C1
Stratford Rd E13 .99 A6
W8 .113 C3 255 B5
Harlington TW6 .149 A6
Hayes UB4 .84 B3
Southall UB2 .107 A2
Thornton Heath CR7 .204 D6
Stratford Sch E7 .77 A1
E7 .77 B2
Stratford Sta E15 .76 B1
Stratford Studios W8 .255 C5
Stratford Villas NW1 .71 D1
Strath Terr SW11 .136 C1
Strathan Cl SW18 .157 A5
Strathaven Rd SE12 .165 B5
Strathblaine Rd SW11 .136 B1
Strathcona Rd HA9 .65 D6
Strathdale SW16 .182 B5
Strathdon Dr SW17 .158 B1
Strathearn Ave
Harlington UB3 .127 D5
Twickenham TW2 .152 A3
Strathearn House W2 .247 A6
Strathearn Pl
W2 .114 C6 247 A6
Strathearn Rd SW19 .179 C6
Cheam SM1 .217 C3
Stratheden Par SE3 .143 A5
Stratheden Rd SE3 .143 A5
Strathfield Gdns IG11 .79 B2
Strathleven Rd SW2 .160 A6
Strathmore Ct NW8 .230 A2
Strathmore Gdns N3 .29 D2
W8 .245 B4
Edgware HA8 .26 D1
Strathmore Rd SW19 .157 C1
Teddington TW11,TW2 .174 C6
Thornton Heath CR0 .205 B2
Strathmore Sch TW10 .153 D2
Strathnairn St SE1 .118 A2
Strathray Gdns NW3 .70 C2
Strathville Rd SW18 .157 D2
Strathyre Ave SW16 .204 C6
Stratton Ave EN2 .5 B6
Stratton Cl SW19 .179 C1
Bexleyheath DA7 .147 A2
Edgware HA8 .26 B4
Heston TW5 .129 C4
Walton-on-T KT12 .194 C1
Stratton Ct 4 N1 .73 C1
10 Kingston u T KT6 .198 A4
Stratton Dr IG11 .79 D2
Stratton Gdns UB1 .85 C1
Stratton Ho HA8 .26 B6
Stratton Rd SW19 .179 C1
Bexleyheath DA7 .147 A2
Sunbury TW16 .171 D1
Stratton St W1 .115 B5 248 D4
Strattondale St E14 .120 A3
Strauss Rd W4 .111 B4
Strawberry Hill Cl TW1 152 D1
Strawberry Hill Rd
TW1 .152 D1
Strawberry Hill Sta
TW2 .152 D1
Strawberry La SM5 .219 A5
Strawberry Terr N10 .30 D2
Strawberry Vale N2 .30 B2
Twickenham TW1 .153 A1
Strayfield Rd EN2 .4 D6

Streakes Field Rd NW2 68 A6
Stream Way DA17 147 C6
Streamdale SE2 146 B6
Streamside Cl N9 17 D3
Bromley BR2 209 A5
Streatfeild Ave E6 100 B6
Streatfield Rd HA3,HA7 43 D6
Streatham & Tooting Adult Inst SW16 160 B2
Streatham Cl SW16 160 A2
Streatham Comm N SW16 182 B5
Streatham Comm S SW16 182 B4
Streatham Common Sta SW16 181 D3
Streatham Ct SW16 160 A1
Streatham High Rd SW16,SW2 182 A5
Streatham Hill SW2 160 A3
Streatham Hill & Clapham High Sch SW2 160 B3
Streatham Hill Sta SW2 160 A2
Streatham Pl SW2 160 A4
Streatham Rd CR4 181 A2
Streatham St WC1 240 A2
Streatham Sta SW16 181 D5
Streatham Vale SW16 181 D3
Streathbourne Rd SW17 159 A1
Streathem Wells Prim Sch SW2 160 C2
Streatleigh Par 4 SW16 160 A2
Streatley Pl NW3 70 B4
12 NW3 70 A4
Streatley Rd NW6 69 B1
Streeters La SM6 219 D5
Streetfield Mews SE3 143 A2
Streimer Rd E15 98 A5
Strelley Way W3 111 C6
Stretton Lo W13 109 B6
Stretton Rd Croydon CR0 205 C2
Richmond TW10 153 C2
Strickland Ct SE15 140 A2
Strickland Ho 26 E2 95 D4
Strickland Row SW18 158 B4
Strickland St SE8 141 C4
Strickland Way 4 BR6 227 D4
Stride Rd E13 98 D5
Stringer Hos 19 N1 95 C6
Strode Cl N10 31 A3
Strode Ho 3 SW2 160 C3
Strode Rd E7 77 A4
N17 33 C1
NW10 68 A2
SW6 135 A5 264 A4
Strome Ho NW6 91 D5
Strone Rd E7,E12 77 D2
Strone Way UB4 85 A3
Strongbow Cres SE9 166 B6
Strongbow Rd SE9 166 B6
Strongbridge Cl HA2 41 C1
Stronsa Rd W12 111 D4
Strood Ho SE1 252 D1
12 SE20 184 C3
Stroud Cres SW15 156 A1
Stroud Field UB5 63 A2
Stroud Gate HA2 63 D4
Stroud Green Gdns CR0 206 C2
Stroud Green Prim Sch N4 50 C1
Stroud Green Rd N4 50 C1
Stroud Green Way CR0 206 C3
Stroud Rd SE25 206 A3
SW19 157 C1
Stroud Way TW15 171 A4
Stroudes Cl KT4 199 D2
Stroudley Ho SW8 269 B2
Stroudley Wlk E3 97 D4
Strouds Cl RM6 58 B4
Strout's Pl 2 E2 95 D4
Struan Ho 11 E11 55 A4
Strudwick Ct SW4 270 B1
Strutton Ground SW1 115 D3 259 C5
Strype St E1 243 C3
Stuart Ave NW9 46 A2
W5 110 B4
Harrow HA2 63 B5
Hayes BR2 209 A1
Walton-on-T KT12 194 B1
Stuart Cl UB10 60 C2
Stuart Cres N22 32 B2
Croydon CR0 223 B5
Hayes UB3 83 A1
Stuart Ct E4 20 D2
2 Elstree WD6 9 D5
Stuart Evans Cl DA16 146 C2
Stuart Gr TW11 174 C5
Stuart Ho 1 E9 74 D1
5 SW4 138 A1
W14 254 A4
Stuart Lo SE25 183 C1
Stuart Mill Ho N1 233 C3
Stuart Pl CR4 180 D2
Stuart Rd NW6 91 C4
SE15 140 C1
SW19 157 C1
W3 111 A5
Barking IG11 101 D6
Bexley DA16 146 B4
East Barnet EN4 14 D4
Harrow HA3 42 D6
Richmond TW10 153 B1
South Norwood CR7 205 A5
Stubbs Dr SE16 118 B1
Stubbs Ho 1 E2 96 D4
N4 50 B1
Stubbs Mews RM8 80 B4
Stubbs Point E13 99 B3
Stubbs Way SW19 180 B2
Stucley Pl 18 NW1 71 B1
Stucley Rd TW5,TW7 130 A5
Studd St N1 94 D6 234 C6
Studdridge St SW6 135 C3
Studholme Ct NW3 69 C4
Studholme St SE15 140 B5
Studio Pl SW1 247 D1
Studios Rd TW17 192 B6
Studios The 4 SW4 137 C1
SW8 269 D1
Studland SE17 262 C2
Studland Cl DA15 167 D1
Studland Ho E14 97 A1
Studland Rd SE26 184 D5
W7 86 C1
Kingston u T KT2 176 A4
Studland St W6 112 B2
Studley Ave E4 36 B3
Studley Cl E5 75 A3
Studley Ct Redbridge IG4 55 D3
Sidcup DA14 190 B5
Studley Dr IG4 55 D3
Studley Grange Rd W7 108 D4
Studley Rd E7 77 B2
SW4 138 A3
Dagenham RM9 80 D1
Study Prep Sch The SW19 178 C5
Stukeley Rd E7 77 B1
Stukeley St WC2 94 A1 240 B2
Stumps Hill La BR3 185 C4
Stunnell Ho 23 SE14 140 D6
Sturdee Ho 2 E2 96 A5
Sturdy Ho 26 E3 97 A5
Sturdy Rd SE15 140 B3
Sturge Ave E17 35 D1
Sturge St SE1 117 A4 252 A2
Sturgeon Rd SE17 117 A1 262 A1
Sturges Field BR7 189 B4
Sturgess Ave NW4 46 B2
Sturmer Way N7 72 B3
Sturminster Cl UB4 84 C1
Sturminster Ho SW8 270 D3
Sturrock Cl N15 51 B5
Sturry St E14 97 D1
Sturt St N1 235 B3
Stutfield St E1 96 A1
Stuttle Ho 9 E1 96 A3
Styles Gdns SW9 138 D2
Styles Ho SE1 251 C3
Styles Way BR3 208 A5
Sudbourne Prim Sch SW2 160 B6
Sudbourne Rd SW2 160 B6
Sudbrook Gdns TW10 154 A1
Sudbrook La TW10 154 A2
Sudbrooke Rd SW12 159 A5
Sudbury E6 100 C1
Sudbury & Harrow Road Sta HA0 65 B3
Sudbury Ave HA0 65 D4
Sudbury Court Dr HA1 65 A5
Sudbury Court Rd HA1 65 A5
Sudbury Cres Plaistow BR1 187 A5
Wembley HA0 65 B3
Sudbury Croft HA0 64 D4
Sudbury Ct E5 75 A4
SW8 269 D2
Sudbury Gdns CR0 221 C4
Sudbury Heights Ave UB6 65 A3
Sudbury Hill HA1 64 C5
Sudbury Hill Cl HA0 64 D5
Sudbury Hill Sta HA1 64 C4
Sudbury Ho SW18 157 D6
Sudbury Jun & Inf Schs HA0 65 B4
Sudbury Rd IG11 79 D3
Sudbury Town Sta UB6 65 B2
Sudeley St N1 94 D5 234 D3
Sudlow Rd SW18 157 C6
Sudrey St SE1 252 A1
Suez Ave UB6 86 D5
Suez Rd EN3 7 A2
Suffield Ho SE17 261 D2
Suffield Rd E4 35 D6
2 N15 51 D4
SE20 184 C1
Suffolk Cl WD6 11 B6
Suffolk Ct 3 SW16 182 C6
Ilford IG3 57 C3
Suffolk Ho SE20 184 C2
11 W3 88 C1
4 Croydon CR0 221 B6
Suffolk La EC4 252 C6
Suffolk Park Rd E17 53 A5
Suffolk Pl SW1 249 D4
Suffolk Rd 4 E13 99 A4
N15 51 B3
NW10 67 C1
SE25 205 D5
SW13 134 A5
Barking IG11 79 B1
Dagenham RM10 81 D3
Enfield EN3 18 B6
Foots Cray DA14 190 C4
Harrow HA2 41 B4
Ilford IG3 57 C3
Worcester Pk KT4 215 D6
Suffolk St E7 77 A4
Suffolk St *continued*
SW1 115 D5 249 D4
Suffolks Prim Sch EN1 6 B3
Sugar House La E15 98 A5
Sugar Loaf Wlk 6 E2 96 C4
Sugden Ho SE11 260 D4
Sugden Rd SW11 137 A1
Hinchley Wood KT7 197 B1
Sugden Way IG11 101 D5
Sulby Ho SE4 141 A1
Sulgrave Gdns 11 W6 112 C4
Sulgrave Rd W6 112 C3
Sulina Rd SW2 160 A4
Sulivan Ct SW6 135 C3
Sulivan Ent Ctr SW6 135 C2
Sulivan Prim Sch SW6 135 C3
Sulivan Rd SW6 135 C2
Sulkin Ho 11 E2 96 D4
Sullivan Ave E16 99 D2
Sullivan Cl SW11 136 C2
East Molesey KT8 195 D6
Sullivan Ct N16 51 D1
SW5 255 B4
4 Croydon CR0 206 A1
Sullivan Ho SE11 260 D3
SW1 268 D6
Twickenham TW2 152 B5
Sullivan Rd SE11 116 C2 261 B4
Sullivan Way WD6 9 C5
Sullivans Reach KT12 193 D2
Sultan Rd E11 55 B5
Sultan St SE5 139 A5
Penge BR3 184 D1
Sumatra Rd NW6 69 C2
Sumburgh Rd SW12 159 A5
Summer Ave KT8 196 C4
Summer Gdns KT8 196 C4
Summer Gr WD6 9 D5
Summer Hill Bickley BR7 188 C1
Deacons Hill WD6 10 C6
Summer Ho SE13 142 B1
Summer Rd East Molesey KT8 196 B4
Thames Ditton KT7,KT8 196 D4
Summer Trees TW16 172 B2
Summercourt Rd E1 96 C1
Summerene Cl SW16 181 C3
Summerfield 6 BR1 187 B2
Summerfield Ave N12 30 C4
NW6 91 A5
Summerfield La KT6 213 D6
Summerfield Rd W5 87 B3
Loughton IG10 21 D5
Summerfield St SE12 164 D4
Summerhill Cl BR6 227 C5
Summerhill Gr EN1 17 C5
Summerhill Rd N15 51 B5
Summerhill Way CR4 181 A2
Summerhouse Ave TW5 129 A4
Summerhouse Rd N16 73 C6
Summerland Gdns N10 49 B6
Summerland Grange N10 49 B6
Summerlands Ave W3 111 A6
Summerlands Lo BR6 226 C4
Summerlee Ave N2 48 D5
Summerlee Gdns N2 48 D5
Summerley St SW18 157 D2
Summers Cl Belmont SM2 217 C1
Wembley HA9 44 D1
Summers La N12 30 B3
Summers Row N12 30 C4
Summers St EC1 241 A5
Summersby Rd N6 49 B3
Summersell Ho SE27 183 B5
Summerside Prim Sch N12 30 B4
Summerstown SW17 180 A6
Summerton Way SE28 102 D1
Summerville Gdns SM1 217 B2
Summerwood Rd TW1, TW7 152 D5
Summit Ave NW9 45 B4
Summit Cl N14 15 C2
NW9 45 B5
Edgware HA8 26 C3
Summit Ct NW2 69 A3
Summit Dr IG8 37 D1
Summit Est N16 52 A2
Summit Rd E17 53 D5
Northolt UB5 63 C1
Summit The TW16 172 A3
Summit Way N14 15 B2
SE19 183 C3
Sumner Ave SE15 139 D4
Sumner Bldgs SE1 252 A4
Sumner Cl BR6 227 A4
Sumner Ct SW8 270 A2
Sumner Gdns CR0 204 C1
Sumner Ho 1 E3 97 D2
Sumner Pl SW7 114 B2 256 D3
Sumner Place Mews SW7 256 D3
Sumner Rd SE15 139 D5
Harrow HA1 42 A2
Thornton Heath CR0 204 D1
Sumner Rd S CR0 204 C1
Sumner St SE1 117 A5 252 A4
Sumpter Cl NW3 70 A2
Sun Alley 6 TW9 132 A1
Sun Ct EC3 242 D1
Sun in the Sands SE3 143 B5
Sun La SE3 143 B5
Sun Life Trad Est TW14 128 A2
Sun Pas 8 SE16 118 A3
Sun Rd W14 113 B1 254 C1
Sun St EC2 95 B2 242 D4
Sun St Pas EC2 95 C2 243 A3
Sunbeam Cres W10 90 C3
Sunbeam Rd NW10 89 B3
Sunbury Ave NW7 27 B6
SW14 133 B1
Sunbury Court Island TW16 194 D6
Sunbury Court Rd TW16 172 C1
Sunbury Cres TW13 171 D6
Sunbury Cross TW16 172 A3
Sunbury Cross Ctr 9 TW16 171 D3
Sunbury Ct 3 SE14 140 D6
2 Chipping Barnet EN5 1 A1
Sunbury TW16 172 D1
Sunbury Ct (Con Ctr) TW16 172 D1
Sunbury Gdns NW7 27 B5
Sunbury Ho 33 E2 95 D4
Sunbury Int Bsns Ctr TW16 171 C2
Sunbury La SW11 136 B4 266 D2
Walton-on-T KT12 194 A3
Sunbury Manor Sch TW16 171 D2
Sunbury Rd Cheam SM3 217 A5
Feltham TW13 171 D6
Sunbury St SE18 122 B3
Sunbury Sta TW16 172 A2
Sunbury Way TW13 172 C5
Sunbury Workshops 39 E2 95 D4
Suncroft Pl SE26 162 C1
Sunderland Ct SE22 162 A4
12 Stanwell TW19 148 A5
Sunderland Ho 26 W2 91 C2
Sunderland Mount SE23 162 D2
Sunderland Rd SE23 162 D2
W5 109 D3
Sunderland Terr W2 91 D1
Sunderland Way E12 77 D6
Sundew Ave W12 112 A6
Sundew Ct 9 HA0 88 A5
Sundial Ave SE25 205 D6
Sundial Ct KT5 214 D6
Sundorne Rd SE7 121 C1
Sundown Rd TW15 171 A5
Sundridge Ave Bexley DA16 145 B2
Bromley BR1,BR7 188 A3
Sundridge Ho 4 E9 74 D1
Sundridge Par BR1 187 B3
Sundridge Park Sta BR1 187 B3
Sundridge Rd CR0 206 A1
Sunfields Pl SE3 143 B5
Sunland Ave DA6 147 A1
Sunleigh Ct HA0 88 A6
Sunleigh Rd HA0 88 A6
Sunley Gdns UB6 87 A6
Sunlight Cl SW19 180 A4
Sunmead Rd TW16 194 A6
Sunna Gdns TW16 172 B1
Sunniholme Ct CR2 221 A3
Sunningdale N14 31 D5
W13 87 B2
Sunningdale Ave W3 111 C6
Barking IG11 79 B1
Feltham TW13 151 A2
Ruislip HA4 40 C1
Sunningdale Cl E6 100 B4
22 SE16 118 B1
SE28 103 A1
Stanmore HA7 25 A3
3 Surbiton KT6 214 A6
Sunningdale Ct
13 Kingston u T KT2 176 C3
15 Southall UB1 86 A1
Sunningdale Gdns NW9 45 A4
W8 255 B5
Sunningdale Rd Bromley BR1,BR2 210 A4
Cheam SM1 217 B4
Sunningfields Cres NW4 28 B1
Sunningfields Rd NW4 46 B6
Sunninghill Ct 9 W3 111 A4
Sunninghill Gdns IG2 57 D4
Sunninghill Rd SE13 141 D3
Sunny Bank SE25 206 A6
Sunny Cres NW10 67 A1
Sunny Gardens Rd NW4 46 C6
Sunny Hill NW4 46 B6
Sunny Hill Ct NW4 28 B1
Sunny Nook Gdns CR2 221 B2
Sunny Pl NW4 46 C5
Sunny Rd The EN3 6 D4
Sunny View NW9 45 B4
Sunny Way N12 30 C3
Sunnycroft Rd SE25 206 A6
Hounslow TW3 129 D3
Southall UB1 85 C2
Sunnydale BR6 226 C6
Sunnydale Gdns NW7 27 C4
Sunnydale Rd SE12 165 B6
Sunnydene Ave HA4 62 A6
Sunnydene Gdns HA0 65 C2
Sunnydene St SE26 185 A6
Sunnyfield NW7 27 D6
Sunnyfields Prim Sch NW4 46 B6
Sunnyhill Cl E5 75 A4
Sunnyhill Prim Sch SW16 182 B6
Sunnyhill Rd SW16 182 A6
Sunnyhurst Cl SM1 217 C5
Sunnymead Ave CR4 203 D6
Sunnymead Ct W5 109 D6
Sunnymead Rd NW9 45 B2
SW15 156 B6
Sunnymede Ave KT19 215 C1
Sunnymede Dr IG6 56 D5
Sunnyside 3 NW2 69 B5
SW19 179 A4
Walton-on-T KT12 194 C4
Sunnyside Dr E4 20 A4
Sunnyside Ho 2 NW2 69 B5
Sunnyside Pl SW19 179 A4
Sunnyside Rd E10 53 C1
N19 49 D2
W5 109 D5
Ilford IG1 79 B5
Teddington TW11 174 B6
Sunnyside Rd E N9 18 A1
Sunnyside Rd N N9 18 A1
Sunnyside Rd S N9 18 A1
Sunray Ave SE5,SE24 139 B1
Bromley BR2 210 B3
Tolworth KT5 214 D6
Sunrise Cl TW13 151 B1
Sunrise View NW7 27 D4
Sunset Ave E4 19 D3
Woodford IG8 36 D6
Sunset Ct 4 IG8 37 C3
Sunset Gdns SE25 183 D1
Sunset Rd SE5 139 B1
SE28 124 A5
SW19 178 B5
Sunset View EN5 1 A3
Sunshine Way CR4 180 D1
Sunwell Cl SE15 140 B4
Superior Dr 4 BR6 227 D2
Surbiton Cres KT1,KT6 198 A5
Surbiton Ct KT6 197 D3
Surbiton Hall Cl KT1 198 A5
Surbiton High Sch KT1 198 A5
Surbiton High Sch Jun Sch for Girls KT1 198 A5
Surbiton Hill Pk KT5 198 C4
Surbiton Hill Rd KT6 198 A4
Surbiton Hospl KT6 198 A3
Surbiton Prep Sch KT6 198 A4
Surbiton Rd KT1 198 A5
Surbiton Sta KT6 198 A3
Surcot Ho 2 SW4 137 D3
Surlingham Cl SE28 124 D6
Surma Cl E1 96 A3
Surr St N7 72 A3
Surrendale Pl W9 91 C3
Surrey Canal Rd SE14, SE16,SE8 140 D6
Surrey Commercial Wharf SE16 118 D5
Surrey Cres 1 W4 110 C1
Surrey Ct N3 47 A6
Surrey Gdns N4 51 A3
Surrey Gr SE17 263 A1
Carshalton SM1 218 B5
Surrey Ho 8 SE16 118 D5
Surrey La SW11 136 C4 267 B1
Surrey Lo SW20 178 C1
Surrey Mews SE27 183 C6
Surrey Mount SE23 162 B3
Surrey Quays Rd SE16 118 D4
Surrey Quays Sh Ctr SE16 118 D3
Surrey Quays Sta SE16 118 D2
Surrey Rd SE15 162 D6
Barking IG11 79 C1
Dagenham RM10 81 D3
Harrow HA1 42 A4
West Wickham BR4 207 D1
Surrey Row SE1 116 D4 251 D2
Surrey Sq SE17 117 C1 263 B2
Surrey Square Inf Sch SE17 117 C1 263 A2
Surrey Square Jun Sch SE17 117 C1 263 A2
Surrey St 4 E13 99 B4
WC2 116 B6 250 D6
Croydon CR0 221 A5
Surrey Terr SE17 263 B2
Surrey Twr 5 SE20 184 C3
Surrey Water Rd SE16 118 D5
Surrey Wharf SE1 140 A6
Surridge Ct 15 SW9 138 A3
Surridge Gdns SE19 183 B4
Susan Lawrence Ho 3 E12 78 C4
Susan Lawrence Jun & Inf Schs E14 97 D1
Susan Rd SE3 143 B3
Susan Wood BR7 188 C2
Susannah St E14 98 A1
Sussex Ave TW7 130 C2
Sussex Cl N19 72 A6
New Malden KT3 199 C5
Redbridge IG4 56 B4
4 Twickenham TW1 153 B5
Sussex Cres UB5 63 C2
Sussex Ct SE10 142 A6
4 SW13 133 D3
W2 236 C1
Mitcham CR4 204 A4
Sussex Gate N6 48 D4
Sussex Gdns N4 51 A4
N6 48 D4
W2 92 B1 236 D1
Chessington KT9 213 D2
Sussex Ho NW3 70 C2
Richmond TW9 132 B3
Sussex Lo W2 236 D1
Sussex Mans SW7 256 C3
WC2 250 B6
Sussex Mews E W2 236 D1
Sussex Mews W W2 246 D6
Sussex Pl NW1 92 D3 237 C6
W2 92 B1 236 D1
New Malden KT3 199 C5
Sussex Rd E6 100 C6
Erith DA8 147 D5
Harrow HA1 42 A4
Mitcham CR4 204 A4
New Malden KT3 199 C5
Sidcup DA14 190 B5
South Croydon CR2 221 B2
Southall UB2 106 D3
Uxbridge UB10 61 A3
Wallington SM5 218 D2
2 West Wickham BR4 207 D1
Sussex Ring N12 29 C5
Sussex Sq W2 114 B6 246 D6
Sussex St E13 99 B4
SW1 258 D2
Sussex Way N7,N19 72 A6
N19 49 D1
Cockfosters EN4 15 B6
Sussex Wlk 18 SW9 138 D1
Sutcliffe Cl NW11 47 D4
Sutcliffe Ho UB3 84 A1
Sutcliffe Rd SE18 145 C6
Bexley DA16 146 C3
Sutherland Ave W9 92 A3 236 A6
W13 87 B1
Bexley DA16 145 C1
Broom Hill BR5 211 D4
Hayes UB3 106 A2
Sunbury TW16 171 D1
Sutherland Cl EN5 1 A1
Sutherland Ct N16 73 B5
NW9 44 D4
2 W9 91 C3
Sutherland Dr SW19 180 B2
Sutherland Gdns SW14 133 C2
North Cheam KT4 200 B1
Sunbury TW16 171 D1
Sutherland Gr SW18,SW19 157 B4
Teddington TW11 174 C5
Sutherland Ho 8 SE18 144 B4
7 SW15 156 C4
W8 255 C5
W13 109 A6
Richmond TW10 153 C2
Sutherland Pl W2 91 C1
Sutherland Point 1 E5 74 B4
Sutherland Rd E3 97 B5
E17 53 A6
N9 18 B3
N17 34 A2
W4 133 C6
W13 87 A1
Belvedere DA17 125 C3
Enfield EN3 18 D6
Southall UB1 85 B1
Thornton Heath CR0 204 C2
Sutherland Row SW1 258 D2
Sutherland Sq SE17 117 A1 262 A1
Sutherland St SW1 115 B1 258 D2
Sutherland Wlk SE17 262 B1
Sutlej Rd SE7 143 C5
Sutterton St N7 72 B2
Sutton Arc SM1 217 D3
Sutton Cl Beckenham BR3 185 D2
Pinner HA5 40 A4
Sutton Common Rd Cheam SM3 201 C1
Sutton SM1,SM3 217 D6
Sutton Common Sta SM1 217 D6
Sutton Court Rd E13 99 C4
W4 133 A6
Hillingdon UB10 82 D6
Sutton SM1,SM2 218 A2
Sutton Courtenay Ho SW17 180 B6
Sutton Cres EN5 12 D6
Sutton Ct 9 E5 74 B4
SE19 183 D3
W4 133 A6
W5 110 A5
East Molesey KT8 195 B4
Sutton SM2 218 A2
Sutton Dene TW3 129 D4
Sutton Est SW3 114 C1 257 B2
Sutton Est The W10 90 C2
Sutton Gdns Barking IG11 101 C5
Croydon CR0 205 D4
Sutton Gn IG11 101 C6
Sutton Gr SM1 218 B3
Sutton Gram Sch For Boys SM1 218 A3
Sutton Hall Rd TW5 129 C5
Sutton High Sch For Girls SM1 217 D2
Sutton Ho N21 16 B6
Sutton La TW3,TW4,TW5 129 B3
Sutton La N W4 111 A1
Sutton La S W4 133 A6
Sutton Par NW4 46 C5

Sutton Park Rd SM1, SM2 217 D2
Sutton Pl E9 74 C3
Sutton Rd E13 98 D3
E17 34 D2
N10 31 A2
Barking IG11 101 C6
Heston TW5 129 C4
Sutton Row W1 239 D2
Sutton Sq E9 74 C3
Hounslow TW5 129 B4
Sutton St E1 96 C1
Sutton Sta SM2 218 A2
Sutton Way W10 90 C2
Hounslow TW5 129 B4
Suttons Way EC1 242 B5
Swaby Rd SW17,SW18 158 A2
Swaffield Prim Sch SW18 158 A4
Swaffield Rd SW18 158 A4
Swain Cl SW16 181 B4
Swain Rd CR7 205 A4
Swains Cl UB7 104 A4
Swain's La N6 71 B6
Swains Rd CR4,SW17, SW19 180 D3
Swainson Ho N7 72 C4
Swainson Rd W3 111 D4
Swakeleys Dr UB10 60 C3
Swakeleys Rd UB10 60 C5
Swakeleys Rdbt UB8, UB10 60 A4
Swakeleys Sch UB10 82 D5
Swaledale Cl N11 31 A4
Swallands Rd SE6 163 C1
Swallow Cl SE14 140 D4
Bushey WD2 8 A3
Swallow Ct 1 SE12 165 A4
4 W9 91 C2
Chingford IG8 36 B3
Ilford IG2 56 D4
5 Ruislip HA4 40 C1
Swallow Dr NW10 67 B2
Northolt UB5 85 C5
Swallow Gdns SW16 181 D5
Swallow Ho N8 50 B6
NW8 230 A4
Swallow Pk KT6 214 B5
Swallow Pl W1 238 D1
Swallow St E6 100 A2
W1 115 C6 249 B5
Swallowbrook Bsns Ctr UB4 106 D5
Swallowfield NW1 231 D1
Swallowfield Rd SE7 121 B1
Swallowfield Way UB3 105 B4
Swallows Ct 5 SE20 184 D3
Swaminarayan Sch The NW10 67 B2
Swan & Pike Rd Enfield EN3 7 C5
Enfield EN3 7 C5
Swan App E6 100 A2
Swan Cl E17 35 A3
Croydon CR0 205 C2
Feltham TW13 173 A6
Swan Ct E14 97 B1
N20 14 A2
SW3 257 B1
SW6 265 A3
Swan Ctr SW17 158 A1
Swan Dr NW9 27 C1
Swan Ho N1 73 B1
Enfield EN3 18 C6
Swan La EC4 117 B6 252 D5
N20 14 A1
Loughton IG10 21 C4
Swan Mead SE1 117 C3 263 A5
Swan Mews SW9 138 B3
Swan Pas 4 E1 118 A6
Swan Pl SW13 133 D3
Swan Rd SE16 118 C4
SE18 121 D3
Feltham TW13 173 A6
Southall UB1 85 D1
West Drayton UB7 104 A4
Swan St SE1 117 A4 252 B1
Isleworth TW7 131 B2
Swan The BR4 224 A6
Swan Way EN3 6 D3
Swan Wlk SW3 136 D6 267 C6
Oatlands Pk TW17 193 C2
Swan Yd N1 72 D2
Swanage Ct 5 N1 73 C1
Swanage Ho SW8 270 C3
Swanage Rd E4 36 A3
SW18 158 A5
Swanage Waye UB4 84 C1
Swanbourne SE17 262 A3
Swanbourne Ho NW8 237 A6
Swanbridge Rd DA7 147 C4
Swandon Way SW18 135 D1
Swanfield St E2 95 D4
Swanlea Sec Sch E1 96 B3
Swanley Ho SE17 263 B2
Swanley Rd DA16 146 C4
Swanmore Ct SW18 158 A5
Swann Ct 6 TW7 131 A2
Swanne Ho 12 SE10 142 A5
Swanscombe Ho
11 W11 112 D5
1 St Paul's Cray BR5 190 B1
Swanscombe Point 7 E16 98 D2
Swanscombe Rd 5 W4 111 C1
W11 112 D5
Swansea Rd Enfield EN3 6 C1
Harlington TW14,TW6 149 B5
Swansland Gdns E17 35 A2
Swansmere Sch KT12 194 C1
Swanton Gdns SW19 156 D3
Swanton Rd DA8 147 D5
Swanwick Cl SW15 155 D4
Swaton Rd E3 97 C3
Swaylands Rd DA17 147 C6
Swaythling Cl N18 34 B6
Swaythling Ho 2 SW15 155 D5
Sweden Gate SE16 119 A2
Swedenborg Gdns E1 118 B6
Swedish Sch SW13 133 D6
Sweeney Cres SE1 253 D1
Sweet Briar Gn N9 17 D1
Sweet Briar Gr N9 17 D1
Sweet Briar Wlk N18 33 D6
Sweetcroft La UB10 60 C1
Sweetmans Ave HA5 40 D6
Sweets Way N20 14 B2
Swell Ct E17 53 D3
Swete St E13 99 A5
Swetenham Wlk SE18 123 A1
Sweyn Pl SE3 143 A3
Swift Cl E17 35 A3
Harrow HA2 63 D6
Hayes UB3 83 D1
Swift Ct SM2 217 D1
Swift Ho 8 E18 55 B6
15 N16 73 C5
1 SW9 138 C5
Swift Rd Feltham TW13 173 A6
Southall UB2 107 B3
Swift St SW6 135 B4 264 C2
Swiftsden Way BR1 186 C4
Swinbrook Rd W10 91 A2
Swinburne Cres CR0 206 C3
Swinburne Ct 4 SE5 139 B1
Swinburne Ho 15 E2 96 C4
Swinburne Rd SW15 134 A1
Swinderby Rd HA0 66 A2
Swindon Cl IG3 57 C1
Swindon Rd TW6 149 A6
Swindon St W12 112 C5
Swinfield Cl TW13 173 A6
Swinford Gdns SW9 138 D2
Swingate La SE18 145 C5
Swingfield Ho 5 E9 96 C6
Swinley Ho NW1 231 D2
Swinnerton St E9 75 A3
Swinton Cl HA9 44 D1
Swinton Ho 17 E2 96 A4
Swinton Pl WC1 233 C2
Swinton St WC1 94 B4 233 C2
Swires Shaw BR2 225 D4
Swiss Cottage NW3 70 B1
Swiss Cottage Sch NW8 92 B6 229 D6
Swiss Cottage Sta NW3 70 B1
Swiss Terr 7 NW3 70 B1
Swithland Gdns SE9 188 C6
Swyncombe Ave W5 109 B2
Swynford Gdns 7 NW4 46 A5
Sybil Mews N4 50 D3
Sybil Phoenix Cl SE8 118 D1
Sybil Thorndike Casson Ho SW5 255 B1
Sybil Thorndike Ho 7 N1 73 A2
Sybourn Inf Sch Annexe E10 53 A1
Sybourn Jun & Inf Schs E17 53 B2
Sybourn St E17 53 B2
Sycamore Ave N3 47 D6
W5 109 D3
Bexley DA15 167 D5
Hayes UB3 105 C6
Sycamore Cl E16 98 C3
N9 34 A6
SE9 166 A2
W3 111 C5
Carshalton SM5 218 D4
Feltham TW13 150 A1
New Barnet EN4 14 B5
Northolt UB5 85 A6
Yiewsley UB7 104 B6
Sycamore Ct E7 77 A2
N12 14 A1
N19 71 D5
NW6 91 C6
4 SE5 139 A4
SE12 164 D5
SE26 184 C6
10 SW16 182 C5
Hillingdon UB8 82 C3
Hounslow TW4 129 A1
Surbiton KT6 198 A2
Sycamore Gdns W6,W12 112 B3
Mitcham CR4 180 B1
Sycamore Gr NW9 45 A2
SE6 164 A5
SE20 184 A2
Kingston u T KT3 199 C6
Sycamore Hill N11 31 A4
Sycamore Ho 18 N2 30 B1
2 N16 73 B6
10 NW3 70 D2
17 SE16 118 D4
SE20 184 D4
3 W6 112 B4
4 Buckhurst Hill IG9 21 D2
Sycamore Lo SW15 134 B2
7 Ashford TW16 171 D3
Sycamore Mews 4 SW4 137 C2
Sycamore Rd SW19, SW20 178 C4
Sycamore St EC1 242 A5
Sycamore Way TW11 175 C4
Sycamore Wlk 1 W10 91 A3
Ilford IG6 57 A5
Sydenham Ave N21 16 B6
SE26 184 B5
Sydenham High Sch For Girls SE26 184 B6
Sydenham Hill SE21, SE22,SE23,SE26,SE19 162 A1
Sydenham Hill Sta SE21 161 D1
Sydenham Ho 16 KT6 197 D2
Sydenham Ind Est SE26 185 B5
Sydenham Park Mans 2 SE26 162 C1
Sydenham Park Rd SE23,SE26 162 C1
Sydenham Pk SE26 162 C1
Sydenham Rd SE26 184 D5
Thornton Heath CR0 205 B2
Sydenham Rise SE23 162 B2
Sydenham Sec Sch SE26 162 B1
Sydenham Sta SE26 184 C6
Sydenham Station App SE26 184 C6
Sydmons Ct SE23 162 C4
Sydner Mews N16 73 D4
Sydner Rd N16 73 D4
Sydney Cl SW3 256 D3
Sydney Cotts KT10 212 D2
Sydney Cres TW15 170 D4
Sydney Ct Hayes UB4 84 C3
Surbiton KT6 214 A6
Sydney Gr NW4 46 C4
Sydney Ho 4 W4 111 C2
Sydney Mews SW3 256 D3
Sydney Pl SW7 257 A3
Sydney Rd E11 55 B3
N8 50 C5
N10 31 B3
SE2 124 D3
SW20 178 D1
W13 109 A4
Bexley DA6 146 D1
East Bedfont TW14 150 A3
Enfield EN2 5 B1
Richmond TW10,TW9 132 A1
Sidcup DA14 189 C6
Sutton SM1 217 C4
Teddington TW11 174 D5
Woodford IG8 37 A6
Sydney Russell Sch RM9 80 D3
Sydney St SE18 123 A3
SW3 114 C1 257 A2
Sydney Terr KT10 212 D2
Sylva Ct 3 SW15 156 D4
Sylvan Ave N3 29 C1
N22 32 C3
NW7 27 D4
Dagenham RM6 59 B3
Sylvan Ct N12 29 D6
Croydon CR2 221 A2
Sylvan Gdns KT6 197 D2
Sylvan Gr NW2 68 D4
SE15 140 B6
Sylvan Hill SE19 183 C2
Sylvan Ho N21 16 B6
Sylvan Rd E7 77 B2
E11 55 A4
E17 53 C4
SE19 183 D2
Ilford IG1 79 A6
Sylvan Way Coney Hall BR4 224 C4
Dagenham RM8 80 B5
Sylvan Wlk BR1 210 B6
Sylvana Cl UB10 82 B6
Sylverdale Rd CR0 220 D5
Sylvester Ave BR7 188 B4
Sylvester Ho 7 E8 74 B2
Sylvester Path 8 E8 74 B2
Sylvester Rd E8 74 B2
E17 53 B2
N2 30 B1
Wembley HA0 65 C3
Sylvia Ave HA5 23 B4
Sylvia Cotts 3 SE8 141 C4
Sylvia Ct N1 235 C3
Wembley HA9 66 D1
Sylvia Gdns HA9 66 D1
Sylvia Pankhurst Ho
12 E2 96 D4
16 Dagenham RM10 81 C5
Symes Mews NW1 232 A4
Symington Ho SE1 262 C5
Symons St SW3 114 D2 257 D3
Syon Gate Way Brentford TW8 131 B5
Hounslow TW7,TW8 131 A5
Syon House TW8 131 C4
Syon La Brentford TW7 130 D6
Brentford TW7,TW8 131 B5
Syon Lane Sta TW7 131 A5
Syon Lo 6 SE12 165 A4
Syon Park Cotts TW8 131 C4
Syon Park Gdns TW7 130 D5
Syringa Ho SE4 141 B2

T

Tabard Ct 3 E14 98 A1
Tabard Ho SE1 262 D6
Teddington KT1 175 C2
Tabard St SE1 117 B3 262 C6
Tabernacle Ave 7 E13 99 A3
Tabernacle St EC2 95 B3 242 D6
Tableer Ave SW4 159 D6
Tabley Rd N7 72 A4
Tabor Ct 3 SM3 217 A2
Tabor Gdns SM2,SM3 217 B1
Tabor Gr SW19 179 B3
Tabor Rd W6 112 B3
Tachbrook Est SW1 115 D1 259 D1
Tachbrook Mews SW1 259 A4
Tachbrook Rd East Bedfont TW14 149 D4
Southall UB2 106 D2
Tachbrook St SW1 115 C2 259 B3
Tack Mews SE4 141 C2
Tadbourne Ct 1 HA8 27 A3
Tadema Ho NW8 236 D5
Tadema Rd SW10 136 A5 266 B3
Tadlow KT1 198 C6
Tadmor Cl TW16 193 D5
Tadmor St W12 112 D5
Tadworth Ave KT3 199 D4
Tadworth Ho SE1 251 C1
Tadworth Rd NW2 68 A6
Taeping St E14 119 D2
Taffy's How CR4 202 C6
Taft Way 41 E3 97 D4
Tailworth St 15 E1 96 A2
Tait 7 NW9 27 D3
Tait Ct 9 E3 97 B6
SW8 269 D2
Tait Ho 2 N19 71 C4
SE1 251 B3
Tait Rd CR0 205 C2
Talacre Rd NW5 71 A2
Talbot Ave N2 48 B6
Talbot Cl N15 51 D5
Talbot Cres NW4 46 A4
Talbot Ct EC3 252 D6
NW9 67 B5
Talbot Gdns IG3 80 A6
Talbot Grove Ho 9 W11 91 A1
Talbot Ho E14 97 D1
N7 72 C5
Talbot Pl SE3 142 C3
Talbot Rd E6 100 C5
E7 77 A4
N6 49 A3
N15 51 D5
N22 31 C2
SE22 139 C1
W2 91 C1
W11 91 B1
W13 109 A5
Ashford TW15 170 A5
Dagenham RM9 81 B1
Harrow HA3 24 D1
Isleworth TW1,TW7 131 A1
South Norwood CR7 205 B5
Southall UB2 107 A2
Twickenham TW2 152 D3
Wallington SM5 219 A3
Wembley HA0 65 D2
Talbot Sq W2 92 B1 236 C1
Talbot Wlk NW10 67 C2
W11 91 A1
Talbot Yd SE1 252 C3
Talcott Path 12 SW2 160 C3
Talfourd Pl SE15 139 D4
Talfourd Rd SE15 139 D4
Talgarth Rd W6 112 D1
W14 113 A1 254 B2
Talgarth Wlk NW9 45 C4
Talia Ho E14 120 A3
Talina Ctr SW6 266 A1
Talisman Cl 2 IG3 58 B1
Talisman Sq SE26 184 A6
Talisman Way HA9 66 B5
Tall Elms Cl BR2 208 D4
Tall Trees SW16 204 B6
Tallack Cl HA3 24 C3
Tallack Rd E10 53 B1
Talleyrand Ho SE5 139 A3
Tallis Cl E16 99 B1
Tallis Gr SE7 143 B6
Tallis St EC4 251 B6
Tallis View NW10 67 B2
Talma Gdns TW2 152 C4
Talma Rd SW2 138 C1
Talmage Cl SE23 162 C4
Talman Gr HA7 25 D4
Talmud Torah Sch N16 51 D2
Talmudical Coll N16 51 B2
Talwin St E3 97 D4
Tamar Cl E3 97 B6
Tamar Ho SE11 261 B2
Tamar Sq IG8 37 B4
Tamar St SE7 122 A2
Tamar Way N17 52 A6
Tamarind Ct 8 W3 89 A1
Tamarind Ho 4 SE15 140 A5
Tamarind Yd 5 E1 118 A5
Tamarisk Sq W12 111 D6
Tamesa Ho TW17 192 C2
Tamesis Gdns KT4 215 C6
Tamian Ind Est TW4 128 C1
Tamian Way TW4 128 C1
Tamworth N7 72 A2
Tamworth Ave IG8 36 C4
Tamworth La CR4 203 B6
Tamworth Manor High Sch CR4 203 D6
Tamworth Pk CR4 203 B6
Tamworth Pl 3 CR0 221 A6
Tamworth Rd CR0 221 A6
Tamworth St SW6 135 C6 265 A5
Tan Yard La DA5 169 C4
Tancred Rd N4 50 D3
Tandem Ctr SW19 180 B2
Tandridge Ct SM2 217 D2
Tandridge Dr BR5,BR6 211 B1
Tandridge Pl 2 BR6 211 B1
Tanfield Ave NW2 67 D5
Tanfield Rd CR0 221 A4
Tangier Rd TW10 132 D2
Tangle Tree Cl N3 29 D1
Tangleberry Cl BR1 210 B5
Tanglewood Cl Bushey HA7 8 C2
Hillingdon UB10 82 C3
South Croydon CR0 222 C5
Tanglewood Way TW13 150 B1
Tangley Gr SW15 155 D4
Tangley Park Rd TW12 173 B4
Tanglyn Ave TW17 192 D4
Tangmere N17 33 B1
WC1 233 C1
Tangmere Gdns UB5 84 C5
Tangmere Gr KT2 175 D5
Tangmere Way NW9 27 C1
Tanhurst Ho 27 SW2 160 A4
Tankerton Rd KT6 214 B6
Tankerton St WC1 233 B1
Tankerton Terr CR0 204 B3
Tankerville Rd SW16 182 A3
Tankridge Rd NW2 68 B6
Tanner Ho SE1 253 B1
1 SW19 180 A2
Tanner Point E13 99 A6
Tanner St SE1 117 C4 253 B1
Barking IG11 79 A2
Tanners Cl KT12 194 B3
Tanners End La N18 33 C5
Tanner's Hill SE8 141 C4
Tanners La IG6 57 A6
Tannery Cl Beckenham BR3,CR0 206 D4
Dagenham RM10 81 D5
Tannington Terr N5 72 C5
Tannsfeld Rd SE26 184 D5
Tansley Cl N7 71 D3
Tanswell St SE1 251 A1
Tansy Cl E6 100 C1
Tant Ave E16 98 D1
Tantallon Rd SW12 159 A3
Tantony Gr RM6 58 D6
Tanworth Gdns HA5 22 C1
Tanza Rd NW3 70 D4
Tapestry Cl SM2 217 D1
Tapley Ho 11 SE1 118 A4
Taplow NW3 70 B1
Taplow Ct CR4 202 C5
Taplow Ho 36 E2 95 D4
Taplow Rd N13 33 A6
Taplow St N1 95 A5 235 B3
Tapp St E1 96 B3
Tappesfield Rd SE15 140 C2
Tapping Cl 5 KT2 176 C3
Tapster St EN5 1 B2
Tara Ct 4 Beckenham BR3 185 D1
9 Buckhurst Hill IG9 21 C2
Taranto Ho 11 E1 96 D2
Tarbert Rd SE22 161 C6
Tarbert Wlk E1 118 C6
Target Cl TW14 149 C5
Target Ho W13 109 B5
Target Rdbt UB5 85 B6
Tariff Rd N17 34 A4
Tarleton Ct 2 N22 32 C1
Tarleton Gdns SE23 162 B3
Tarling Cl DA14 168 B1
Tarling Ho 27 E1 96 B1
Tarling Rd E16 98 D1
N2 30 A1
Tarling St E1 96 C1
Tarn St SE1 117 A3 262 A5
Tarnbank EN2 16 A6
Tarnbrook Ct SW1 258 A3
Tarns The NW1 232 A2
Tarnwood Pk SE9 166 B3
Tarplett Ho 22 SE14 140 D6
Tarquin Ho SE26 184 A6
Tarragon Cl SE14 141 A5
Tarragon Gr SE26 184 D4
Tarranbrae NW6 69 A1
Tarrant Ho E2 96 C4
Tarrant Pl W1 237 C3
Tarriff Cres SE8 119 B2
Tarrington Cl SW16 159 D1
Tartan Ho 8 E14 98 A1
Tarver Rd SE17 116 D1 261 D2
Tarves Way SE10 141 D5
Tash Pl N11 31 B5
Tasker Cl UB7 127 A5
Tasker Ho 18 E14 97 B2
Barking IG11 101 B5
Tasker Rd NW3 70 D3
Tasman Ct TW16 171 C3
Tasman Ho 17 E1 118 B5
Tasman Rd SW9 138 A2
Tasman Wlk E16 99 D1
Tasmania Terr N18 33 A4
Tasso Rd W6 135 A6 264 A6
Tasso Yd W6 264 A5
Tatchbury Ho 3 SW15 155 D5
Tate Gallery (Britain)The★ SW1 116 A2 260 A3
Tate Gallery of Modern Art★ SE1 116 D6 251 D4
Tate Gdns WD2 8 C4
Tate Ho 18 E2 96 D5
Tate Rd E16 122 B5
Cheam SM1 217 C3
Tatnell Rd SE23 163 A5
Tattersall Cl SE9 166 A6
Tatton Cres E5,N16 51 D2
Tatum Rd NW10 67 B1
Tatum St SE17 117 C2 262 D3
Tauheed Cl N4 73 A6
Taunton Ave SW20 178 B1
Hounslow TW3 130 A3
Taunton Cl SM3 201 C1
Taunton Dr N2 30 A1
Enfield EN2 4 C2
Taunton Ho W2 236 A1
Taunton Mews NW1 237 C5
Taunton Pl NW1 92 D3 237 C6
Taunton Rd SE12 164 D6
Greenford UB6 85 D6
Taunton Way HA7 26 A1
Tavern Cl SM5 202 C2
Tavern La SW9 138 C3
Taverner Ho N16 73 B5
Taverner Sq 4 N5 73 A4
Taverners Cl W11 244 A3
Taverners Way E4 20 C3
Tavistock Ave E17 53 A6
Wembley UB6 87 A5
Tavistock Cl N16 73 C3
Tavistock Cres W11 91 B2
Mitcham CR4 204 A5
Tavistock Ct WC1 239 D6
1 Croydon CR0 205 B1
Tavistock Gdns IG3 79 C4
Tavistock Gr CR0 205 B2
Tavistock Ho 2 W11 91 B2
Tavistock Mews 1 W11 91 B1
Tavistock Pl N14 15 B5
WC1 94 A3 240 A6
Tavistock Rd E7 76 D4
E15 76 D2
E18 55 A6
N4,N15 51 B3
NW10 89 D5
W11 91 B2
4 Beckenham BR2 208 D5
Bexley DA16 146 C4
Carshalton SM5 202 B1
Croydon CR0 205 B1
Edgware HA8 26 C2
Uxbridge UB10 61 A3
Tavistock Sq WC1 93 D3 239 D6
Tavistock St WC2 116 A6 250 B6
Tavistock Terr N19 71 D5
Tavistock Twr SE16 119 A3
Tavistock Wlk SM5 202 B1
Taviton St WC1 93 D3 239 C6
Tavy Bridge SE2 124 C4
Tavy Cl SE11 261 B2
Tawney Rd SE28 124 B6
Tawny Cl W13 109 B5
Feltham TW13 150 A1
Tawny Way SE16 118 D2
Tay Ho 8 E3 97 B5
Tayben Ave TW2 152 C5
Taybridge Rd SW11 137 A1
Tayburn Cl E14 98 A1
Tayfield Cl UB10 61 A5
Tayler Ct NW8 229 C6
Taylor Ave TW9 132 D3
Taylor Cl N17 34 A3
Hampton TW12 174 A5
Hounslow TW3 130 A4
3 Orpington BR6 227 D4
Taylor Ct E15 76 A3
SE20 184 C1
W13 109 C5
Taylor Ho 10 SW2 160 C3
Taylor Rd Mitcham CR4 180 C3
Wallington SM6 219 B3
Taylor's Bldgs SE18 122 D2
Taylors Cl DA14 167 D1
Taylors Ct TW13 150 A2
Taylor's Gn W3 89 C1
Taylor's La NW10 67 C1
SE26 184 B6
Hadley EN5 1 B4
Taylorsmead NW7 28 A5
Taymount Grange 2 SE23 162 C2
Taymount Rise SE23 162 C2
Tayport Cl N1 72 A1
Tayside Ct 6 SE5 139 B1
Tayside Dr HA8 10 D2
Taywood Rd UB5 85 B4
Teak Cl SE16 119 A5
Teal Cl E16 99 D2
Teal Ct NW10 67 B2
30 SE8 141 B6
Wallington SM6 219 C3
Teal Pl SM1 217 B3
Tealby Ct N7 72 B2
Teale St E2 96 A5
Tealing Dr KT19 215 B4
Teasel Cl CR0 206 D1
Teasel Way E15 98 C4
Teather St 20 SE5 139 C5
Tebbs Ho 14 SW2 160 C4
Tebworth Rd N17 33 D3

Teck Cl TW7 131 A3
Ted Hennem Ho RM10 81 D5
Ted Roberts Ho 24 E2 96 B5
Ted Williams Ct 6
SE18 122 B2
Tedder 5 NW9 27 D3
Tedder Cl
Chessington KT9 213 C3
Hillingdon UB10 60 B1
Tedder Rd CR2 222 D1
Teddington Memorial Hospl
TW11 174 C4
Teddington Park Rd
TW11 174 D6
Teddington Pk TW11 174 D5
Teddington Sch TW11 175 C4
Teddington Sta TW11 175 A4
Tedworth Gdns SW3 257 C1
Tedworth Sq
SW3 114 D1 257 C1
Tee The W3 89 C1
Tees Ave UB6 86 D5
Tees Ct W7 86 B1
Teesdale Ave TW7 131 A4
Teesdale Cl E2 96 B5
Teesdale Gdns SE25 183 C1
Isleworth TW7 131 A4
Teesdale Rd E11 54 D2
Teesdale St E2 96 B5
Teeswater Ct DA18 124 D3
Teevan Cl CR0 206 A2
Teevan Rd CR0 206 A2
Teignmouth Cl 6 SW4 137 D1
Edgware HA8 26 B1
Teignmouth Gdns UB6 87 A4
Teignmouth Rd NW2 68 D2
Bexley DA16 146 C3
Telcote Way HA4 40 C2
Telegraph Hill NW3 69 D5
Telegraph La KT10 212 D3
Telegraph Mews IG3 58 A1
Telegraph Pl E14 119 D2
Telegraph Rd SW15 156 C4
Telegraph St EC2 242 C2
Telemann Sq SE3 143 B2
Telfer Cl 4 W3 111 A4
Telfer Ho EC1 234 D1
8 SE21 183 C6
Telferscot JMI Sch
SW12 159 D3
Telferscot Rd SW12 159 D3
Telford Ave SW12,SW2 160 A3
Telford Avenue Mans 7
SW2 160 A3
Telford Cl E17 53 A2
SE19 183 D4
Telford Dr KT12 194 C2
Telford Ho SE1 262 A6
8 W10 91 A2
2 Belvedere DA17 125 C3
Telford Parade Mans 8
SW2 160 A3
Telford Rd 2 NW9 46 A3
W10 91 A2
New Eltham BR7,DA15 167 B2
Southall UB1 85 D1
Twickenham TW4 151 C4
Telford Rd (North Circular
Rd) N11 31 C5
Telford Terr SW1 269 A6
Telford Way W3 89 C2
Hayes UB4 85 A2
Telham Rd E6 100 C5
Tell Gr SE22 139 D1
Tellson Ave SE18 144 A4
Telscombe Cl BR6 227 C6
Telscombe Ho SW11 268 A1
Temair Ho 1 SE10 142 A5
Temeraire St SE16 118 C4
Tempelhof Ave NW2 46 C2
Temperley Rd SW12 159 A4
Templar Ct RM7 59 D5
Templar Dr SE28 102 D1
Templar Ho 9 E5 74 C6
NW2 69 B2
Templar Pl TW12 173 C3
Templar St SE5 138 D3
Templars Ave NW11 47 B3
Templars Cres N3 29 C1
Templars Dr HA3 24 B4
Templars Ho E15 75 D3
Temple Ave
EC4 116 C6 251 B6
N20 14 B4
Croydon CR0 223 B5
Dagenham RM8 59 C1
Temple Cl E11 54 C2
N3 29 B1
SE18 123 A3
Temple Ct SW8 270 A3
Temple Dwellings 7 E2 96 B5
Temple Fortune Ct 9
NW11 47 B4
Temple Fortune Hill
NW11 47 C4
Temple Fortune Ho 3
NW11 47 B4
Temple Fortune La
NW11 47 C3
Temple Fortune Par 5
NW11 47 B4
Temple Gdns N21 16 D2
NW11 47 B3
Dagenham RM8 80 D5
Temple Gr NW11 47 C3
Enfield EN2 4 D2
Temple Hall Ct 1 E4 20 B2
Temple Ho 11 E17 53 D6
Temple Ho *continued*
4 N7 71 C5
13 SW11 136 C2
Temple La EC4 94 C1 241 B1
Temple Lo EN5 14 B4
Temple Mead Cl HA7 25 B4
Temple Mills La E10,E15 76 A4
Temple Mills Rd E9 75 C4
Temple Par EN5 14 B4
Temple Pk UB8 82 C4
Temple Pl WC2 116 B6 250 D6
Temple Rd E6 100 A6
N8 50 B5
NW2 68 C5
W4 111 A3
W5 109 D3
Croydon CR0 221 B4
Hounslow TW3 130 A1
Richmond TW9 132 B2
Temple Sheen SW14 155 A6
Temple Sheen Rd
SW14 133 A1
Temple St E2 96 B5
Temple Sta
WC2 116 C6 251 A6
Temple Terr N22 32 C1
Temple Way SM1 218 B5
Temple West Mews
SE11 261 C5
Templecombe Rd E9 96 C6
Templecombe Way
SM4 201 A4
Templecroft TW15 171 B4
Templedene BR2 186 B1
Templeman Rd W7 86 D2
Templemead Cl W3 89 C1
Templemead Ho E9 75 A4
Templemore DA14 190 B5
Templeton Ave E4 35 D6
Templeton Cl 25 N16 73 C3
SE19 183 B2
Templeton Ct E10 53 D1
Templeton Pl
SW5 113 C2 255 B3
Templeton Rd N4,N15 51 B3
Templewood W13 87 B2
Templewood Ave NW3 69 D5
Templewood Gdns NW3 69 D5
Templewood Point NW2 69 B6
Tempsford Cl EN2 5 A2
Tempsford Ct HA1 42 D3
Temsford Cl HA2 24 A1
Tenbury Cl E7 77 D3
Tenbury Ct SW12 159 D3
Tenby Ave HA3 25 B1
Tenby Cl N15 51 D5
Dagenham RM6 59 A3
Tenby Ct E17 53 A4
Tenby Gdns UB5 63 C2
Tenby Ho N7 72 B2
W2 236 A1
Hayes UB3 105 A3
Tenby Rd E17 53 A4
Bexley DA16 146 D4
Dagenham RM6 59 A3
Edgware HA8 26 B1
Enfield EN3 6 C1
Tench St E1 118 B5
Tenda Rd SE16 118 B2
Tendring Ho SW2 160 C5
Tendring Way RM6 58 C4
Tenham Ave SW2 159 D2
Tenison Ct W1 249 A6
Tenison Way SE1 251 A3
Tenniel Cl W2 245 D6
Tennis St SE1 117 B4 252 C2
Tennison Ave WD6 10 D6
Tennison Rd SE25 205 D4
Tenniswood Rd EN1 5 C4
Tennyson Ave E11 55 A2
E12 78 A1
NW9 45 A6
Twickenham TW1 152 D3
West Barnes KT3 200 B4
Tennyson Cl
Bexley DA16 145 D4
Enfield EN3 18 D6
Feltham TW14 150 A5
Tennyson Ct SW6 265 D1
3 Richmond TW10 175 D6
Tennyson Ho 2 DA17 125 B1
Tennyson Rd E10 75 D6
E15 76 C1
E17 53 B3
NW6 91 B6
NW7 28 A5
SE20 184 D3
SW19 180 A4
W7 108 D6
Ashford TW15 170 A5
Hounslow TW3 130 A3
Tennyson St SW8 137 B3
Tensing Ct TW19 148 A3
Tensing Ho N1 72 D2
Tensing Rd UB2 107 C3
Tent St E1 96 B3
Tentelow La UB2 107 D3
Tenter Ground E1 243 C3
Tenterden Cl NW4 46 D6
SE9 188 B6
Tenterden Dr NW4 46 D6
Tenterden Gdns NW4 46 D6
Croydon CR0 206 A2
Tenterden Gr NW4 46 D6
Tenterden Ho SE17 263 B2
Tenterden Rd N17 33 D3
Croydon CR0 206 A2
Dagenham RM8 81 B6
Tenterden St W1 238 D1
Tenzing Ct 4 SE9 166 A2
Terborch Way 6 SE22 161 C6
Terence Ct 6 DA17 147 B6
Terence Messenger Twr
E10 75 D6
Teresa Mews E17 53 C5
Teresa Wlk N10 49 B4
Terling Cl E11 76 D5
Terling Ho W10 90 C2
Terling Rd RM8 81 C6
Terling Wlk N1 235 A6
Terminus Pl SW1 258 D5
Tern Ho 8 SE15 139 D4
Terrace Ave NW10 90 C4
Terrace Gdns SW13 133 D3
Terrace La TW10 154 A5
Terrace Rd E9 74 C1
E13 99 B6
Walton-on-T KT12 194 B3
Terrace The E4 20 C1
EC4 241 B1
N2 49 A5
NW6 91 C6
9 SE8 119 B2
SW13,SW14 133 C3
1 Woodford IG8 37 A4
Terrace Wlk RM9 81 A3
Terraces The 6 SW20 178 D3
Terrapin Ct SW17 159 B1
Terrapin Rd SW17 159 B1
Terrapins KT6 197 D2
Terrick Rd N22 32 A2
Terrick St W12 90 B1
Terrilands HA5 41 B6
Territorial Ho SE11 261 B3
Terront Rd N15 51 A5
Terry Ho SW2 160 C3
Tessa Sanderson Pl 6
SW8 137 B2
Tessa Sanderson Way
UB6 64 B3
Testerton Wlk 3 W11 112 D6
Testwood Ct W7 108 C6
Tetcott Rd
SW10 136 A5 266 A3
Tetherdown N10 49 A6
Tetherdown Prim Sch
N10 49 A5
Tetty Way BR1,BR2 187 A1
Teversham La
SW8 138 A4 270 B2
Teviot Cl DA16 146 B4
Teviot St E14 98 A2
Tewkesbury Ave SE23 162 B4
Pinner HA5 41 A4
Tewkesbury Cl N15 51 B3
Tewkesbury Gdns NW9 44 D6
Tewkesbury Rd N15 51 B3
W13 109 A6
Carshalton SM5 202 B1
Tewkesbury Terr N11 31 D4
Tewson Rd SE18 123 C1
Teyham Ct SW11 158 D5
Teynham Ave EN1 17 B5
Teynham Gn BR2 209 A4
Teynham Ho SE9 167 B5
Teynton Terr N17 33 A2
Thackeray Ave N17 34 A1
Thackeray Cl SW19 178 D3
Harrow HA2 41 C1
Hayes UB8 82 D1
Isleworth TW7 131 A3
Thackeray Ct SW3 257 C2
W5 88 B1
W14 254 A5
Thackeray Dr RM6 58 B2
Thackeray Ho WC1 240 A6
Thackeray Manor SM1 218 A3
Thackeray Mews E8 74 A2
Thackeray Rd E6 99 D5
SW8 137 B3
Thackeray St W8 255 D6
Thackery Lo TW14 149 B5
Thackrah Cl N2 30 A1
Thakeham Cl SE26 184 B5
Thalia Cl SE10 142 B6
Thame Rd SE16 118 D4
Thames Ave
SW10 136 A4 266 B2
Dagenham RM9,RM13 103 D3
Wembley UB6 86 D5
Thames Bank SW14 133 A3
Thames Barrier Visitor Ctr★
SE18 121 D3
Thames Circ E14 119 C2
Thames Cl TW12 173 D1
Thames Cres W4 133 C5
Thames Ct 10 SE15 139 D5
Hampton KT8 173 D1
Thames Ditton Cty Fst Sch
KT7 196 D3
Thames Ditton Island
KT7 197 A4
Thames Ditton Jun Sch
KT7 196 D2
Thames Ditton Sta KT7 196 D2
Thames Eyot 7 TW1 153 A3
Thames Haven KT6 197 D4
Thames Hts SE1 253 C2
Thames Link Ho 7
TW9 132 A1
Thames Mead KT12 194 A2
Thames Meadow
East Molesey KT8 195 C6
Lower Halliford TW17 193 C1
Thames Pl SW15 134 D2
Thames Quay E14 119 D4
SW10 266 B1
Thames Rd E16 121 D5
W4 132 D6
Barking IG11 102 A4
Thames Reach W6 134 C6
Thames Road Ind Est
E16 121 D4
Thames Side
Kingston u T KT1 175 D2
Thames Ditton KT7 197 B3
Thames St SE10 141 D6
East Molesey TW12 173 D1
Kingston u T KT1,KT2 175 D1
Sunbury TW16 194 B6
Walton-on-T KT12 193 D2
Thames Valley Univ
W5 109 D5
Thames View Ho TW12 194 A3
Thames View Inf Sch
IG11 102 A5
Thames View Jun Sch
IG11 101 D5
Thames Village W4 133 A4
Thames Wlk
SW11 136 C5 267 A4
Thamesbank Pl SE28 102 C1
Thamesfield Ct TW17 193 A2
Thamesgate Cl TW10 175 B6
Thameside TW11 175 D3
Thameside Ctr TW8 132 B6
Thameside Ind Est E16 121 D4
Thamesmead Com Coll
DA18 125 A4
Thamesmead Sch
TW17 193 B3
Thamesmead Sh Ctr
SE28 124 A6
Thamesmere Dr SE28 124 A6
Thamespoint TW11 175 D3
Thamesvale Cl TW3 129 C3
Thane Mans N7 72 B5
Thane Villas N7 72 B5
Thane Works N7 72 B5
Thanescroft Gdns CR0 221 C5
Thanet Ct 14 W3 88 C1
Thanet Dr BR2 225 D5
Thanet Ho 1 SE27 160 D1
WC1 233 A1
Thanet Lo NW2 69 A2
Thanet Pl CR0 221 A4
Thanet Rd DA5 169 C4
Thanet St WC1 94 A4 233 A1
Thanington Ct DA15 167 C5
Thant Cl E10 75 D5
Tharp Rd SM6 219 D3
Thatcham Ct N20 14 A4
Thatcham Gdns N20 14 A4
Thatcher Cl UB7 104 A4
Thatchers Way TW7 152 B6
Thatches Gr RM6 59 A5
Thavie's Inn EC4 241 B2
Thaxted Ct N1 235 D3
Thaxted Ho SE16 118 C2
Dagenham RM10 81 D1
Thaxted Lo 3 E18 55 B6
Thaxted Pl 9 SW20 178 D3
Thaxted Rd SE9 167 A2
Buckhurst Hill IG9 21 D4
Thaxton Rd
W14 135 B6 264 D6
Thayer St W1 93 A2 238 B2
Thayers Farm Rd BR3 185 A2
Theatre Mus WC2 250 B6
Theatre St SW11 136 D2
Theberton St N1 94 D6 234 C6
Theed St SE1 116 C5 251 B3
Thelbridge Ho 28 E3 97 D4
Thelma Gdns SE3 144 A4
Thelma Gr TW11 175 A4
Theobald Cres HA3 24 A2
Theobald Rd E17 53 C2
Croydon CR0 220 D6
Theobald St SE1 262 C5
Theobalds Ct N4 73 A6
Theobalds Park Rd EN2 4 D6
Theobald's Rd
WC1 94 B2 240 C4
Theodora Way HA5 39 D6
Theodore Ho 1 SW15 156 A6
Theodore Rd SE13 164 B5
Therapia La
Croydon CR0 204 A3
Wallington CR0 203 D2
Wallington CR0 204 A2
Therapia Lane Sta CR0 204 A2
Therapia Rd SE22 162 C5
Theresa Rd W6 112 A2
Therfield Ct N4 73 A6
Thermopylae Gate E14 119 D2
Theseus Wlk N1 234 D3
Thesiger Rd SE20 184 D3
Thessaly Ho SW8 269 A3
Thessaly Rd
SW8 137 C4 269 B2
Thesus Ho 2 E14 98 B1
Thetford Cl N13 32 D4
Thetford Ct 3 SE21 162 B2
New Malden KT3 199 C4
Thetford Gdns RM9 103 A6
Thetford Ho SE1 263 C6
Thetford Rd
Ashford TW15 148 A1
Dagenham RM9 80 D1
New Malden KT3 199 C4
Thetis Terr TW9 132 C6
Theydon Gr IG8 37 C4
Theydon Rd E5 74 C6
Theydon St E17 53 B2
Thicket Cres SM1 218 A4
Thicket Gr SE20 184 A3
Dagenham RM9 80 C2
Thicket Rd SE20 184 B3
Sutton SM1 218 A4
Thicket The UB7 82 A1
Third Ave E12 78 B3
3 E13 99 A4
E17 53 C4
W3 111 D5
W10 91 A4
Dagenham RM10 103 D5
Enfield EN1 17 D6
Hayes UB3 105 D5
Ilford RM6 58 C3
Wembley HA9 65 D6
Third Cl KT8 196 A5
Third Cross Rd TW2 152 B2
Third Way HA9 66 D4
Thirleby Rd
SW1 115 C3 259 B5
Burnt Oak HA8 27 B2
Thirlestone Ct N10 31 A1
Thirlmere NW1 231 D2
Thirlmere Ave UB6 87 C4
Thirlmere Gdns HA9 43 D1
Thirlmere Ho 20 N16 73 B4
Twickenham TW1 152 D6
Thirlmere Rd N10 31 B2
SW16 181 D6
Thirlmere Rise BR1 186 D4
Thirsk Cl UB5 63 C2
Thirsk Rd SE25 205 B5
SW11 137 A1
Mitcham CR4 181 A3
Thistle Ct N17 52 B5
Thistle Gr SW7 256 B1
Thistle Ho 6 E14 98 A1
Thistlebrook SE2 124 C4
Thistlecroft Gdns HA7 25 D1
Thistledene KT7 196 C3
Thistledene Ave HA2 63 A5
Thistlemead BR7 188 D1
Thistlewaite Rd E5 74 B5
Thistlewood Cl 3 N7 72 B6
Thistleworth Cl TW7 130 B5
Thistley Cl N12 30 C4
Thomas a' Beckett Cl
HA0 64 D4
Thomas Arnold Prim Sch
RM9 81 B1
Thomas Baines Rd
SW11 136 B2
Thomas Becket JMI Sch
SE25 206 A3
Thomas Burt Ho 9 E2 96 B4
Thomas Buxton Jun & Inf
Sch E1 96 A3
Thomas Ct E17 53 D4
W7 86 C1
Dagenham RM8 80 C6
Thomas Dean Rd SE26 185 B6
Thomas Dinwiddy Rd
SE12 165 B2
Thomas Doyle St SE1 261 D6
Thomas Fairchild JMI Sch
N1 95 A5 235 B4
Thomas Gamuel Prim Sch
E17 53 C3
Thomas Hardy Ho N22 32 B2
Thomas Hewlett Ho HA1 64 C4
Thomas Ho 3 E9 74 C2
4 SW4 138 A1
Thomas Hollywood Ho 3
E2 96 C5
Thomas Jones Prim Sch
W11 91 A1
Thomas' La SE6 163 C4
Thomas More Ho EC2 242 A3
Thomas More Sq E1 118 A6
Thomas More St E1 118 A5
Thomas More Way N2 48 A6
Thomas North Terr 3
E16 98 D2
Thomas Pl W8 255 C5
Thomas Pooley Ct KT6 198 A2
Thomas Rd E14 97 C2
Thomas Road Ind Est
E14 97 C1
Thomas St SE18 122 D2
Thomas Tallis Sch SE3 143 B2
Thomas Wall Cl SM1 217 D3
Thomas Watson Cottage
Homes The EN5 13 A6
Thomas's Prep Sch
SW11 158 D6
SW11 136 B4 266 D1
Thompson Ave TW9 132 C2
Thompson Ct IG1 79 A6
Thompson Ho SE14 140 D6
11 W10 91 A3
Thompson Rd SE22 161 D5
Dagenham RM9 81 B5
Uxbridge UB10 60 A1
Thompson's Ave 6 SE5 139 A5
Thomson Cres CR0 204 C1
Thomson Ho SE17 263 A3
SW1 259 D1
Southall UB1 107 A6
Thomson Rd HA3 42 C6
Thorburn Ho SW1 248 A1
Thorburn Sq SE1 118 A2
Thorburn Way SW19 180 B2
Thoresby Ho N16 73 B5
Thoresby St N1 95 A4 235 B2
Thorkhill Gdns KT7 197 B1
Thorkhill Rd KT7 197 B2
Thorn Ave WD2 8 A3
Thorn Cl Bromley BR2 210 C3
Northolt UB5 85 B4
Thorn Ham Ho SE1 262 D6
Thornaby Gdns N18 34 B5
Thornaby Ho 15 E2 96 B4
Thornbill Ho 1 SE15 140 A5
Thornbury 3 NW4 46 C5
Thornbury Ave TW7 130 B5
Thornbury Cl N16 73 C3
Thornbury Ct W11 245 A6
Croydon CR2 221 B3
Hounslow TW7 130 C5
Thornbury Ho N6 49 C1
Thornbury Rd SW2 160 A5
Hounslow TW7 130 B4
Thornbury Sq N6 49 C1
Thornby Rd E5 74 C5
Thorncliffe Ct SW2 160 A5
Thorncliffe Rd SW2 160 A5
Southall UB2 107 B1
Thorncombe Rd SE22 161 C6
Thorncroft Rd SM1 217 D4
Thorncroft St
SW8 138 A5 270 A3
Thorndale Ho N16 51 C1
Thorndean St SW18 158 A2
Thorndene Ave N11 15 A3
Thorndike Ave UB5 84 D6
Thorndike Cl
SW10 136 A5 266 A4
Thorndike Ho SW1 259 C2
Thorndike St
SW1 115 D2 259 C3
Thorndon Cl BR5 189 D1
Thorndon Gdns KT19 215 C4
Thorndon Rd BR5 189 D1
Thorndyke Ct HA5 23 B3
Thorne Cl E11 76 C4
E16 99 A1
Erith DA8 147 D6
Littleton TW15 171 A3
Thorne Ho 34 E2 96 C4
4 E14 120 A3
Thorne Pas 7 SW13 133 D3
Thorne Rd SW8 138 A5 270 B3
Thorne St SW13,SW14 133 C2
Thorneloe Gdns CR0,
CR9 220 D3
Thorne's Cl BR3 208 A6
Thorness Ct SW18 158 A5
Thornet Wood Rd BR1 210 C6
Thornewill Ho 7 E1 118 C6
Thorney Cres
SW11 136 B5 266 D3
Thorney Ct W8 246 A1
Thorney Hedge Rd W4 110 D2
Thorney St
SW1 116 A2 260 A4
Thorneycroft Cl KT12 194 C3
Thorneycroft Dr EN3 7 C6
Thorneycroft Ho 11 W4 111 C1
Thornfield Ave NW7 29 A2
Thornfield Ct NW7 29 A2
Thornfield Ho 4 E14 119 C6
Thornfield Par NW7 29 A3
Thornfield Rd W12 112 B4
Thornford Rd SE13 164 A6
Thorngate Rd W9 91 C3
Thorngrove Rd E13 99 B6
Thornham Gr E15 76 B3
Thornham St SE10 141 D6
Thornhaugh St WC1 239 D5
Thornhill Ave SE18 145 C5
Surbiton KT6 214 A6
Thornhill Bridge Wharf
N1 233 C5
Thornhill Cres N1 72 B1
Thornhill Ct N8 49 D3
Thornhill Gdns E10 75 D6
Barking IG11 79 C1
Thornhill Gr N1 72 C1
Thornhill Ho N1 72 C1
12 W4 111 C1
Thornhill Prim Sch N1 72 C1
Thornhill Rd E10 75 D6
N1 72 C1 234 A6
Ickenham UB10 60 C4
Surbiton KT6 214 B6
Thornton Heath CR0 205 A2
Thornhill Sq N1 72 B1
Thornhill Way TW17 192 C4
Thornicroft Ho 12 SW9 138 B3
Thornlaw Rd SE27 182 D6
Thornley Cl N17 34 A3
Thornley Dr HA2 63 D6
Thornley Pl 2 SE10 120 C1
Thornsbeach Rd SE6 164 A2
Thornsett Pl SE20 184 B1
Thornsett Rd SE20 184 B1
SW18 157 D3
Thornsett Terr SE20 184 B1
Thornton Ave SW2 159 D3
W4 111 C2
Thornton Heath CR0 204 B3
West Drayton UB7 104 B3
Thornton Cl UB7 104 B3
Thornton Ct N7 72 A3
SW20 200 D4
Thornton Dene BR3 185 C1
Thornton Gdns SW12 159 D3
Thornton Gr HA5 23 C4
Thornton Heath Pond
CR7 204 C4

Thornton Heath Sta CR7 205 A5
Thornton Hill SW19 179 A3
Thornton Ho 7 E11 55 A3
SE17 263 A3
Thornton Lo CR7 205 A6
Thornton Pl W1 237 D4
Thornton Rd E11 76 B6
N18 18 C1
SW12,SW2 159 D3
SW14 133 B2
SW19 178 D3
Belvedere DA17 125 D2
Carshalton SM5 202 B1
High Barnet EN5 1 A2
Ilford IG1 78 D4
Plaistow BR1 187 A5
Thornton Heath CR0,CR7 204 B3
Thornton Rd E SW19 178 D4
Thornton Row CR7 204 C4
Thornton St SW9 138 C3
Thornton Way NW11 47 D3
Thorntree Ct W5 88 A2
Thorntree Rd SE7 121 D1
Thorntree Sch SE7 121 B1
Thornville Gr CR4 180 B1
Thornville St SE8 141 C4
Thornwell Ct W7 108 C4
Thornwood Cl E18 37 B1
Thornwood Rd SE13 164 C6
Thornycroft Ct TW9 132 B3
Thorogood Gdns E15 76 C3
Thorold Ho SE1 252 A2
6 SW2 160 A4
Thorold Rd N22 32 A3
Ilford IG1 57 A1
Thorparch Rd SW8 137 D5 269 D3
Thorpe Cl SE26 184 D6
W10 91 A1
Orpington BR6 227 C6
Thorpe Coombe Hospl E17 54 A6
Thorpe Cres E17 35 B1
Thorpe Ct EN2 4 D2
Thorpe Hall W5 87 D2
Thorpe Hall Prim Sch E17 36 A2
Thorpe Hall Rd E17 36 A2
Thorpe Ho N1 233 D5
Thorpe Rd E6 100 B6
E7 76 D4
E17 36 A1
N15 51 C3
Barking IG11 79 B1
Kingston u T KT2 176 A3
Thorpebank Rd W12 112 A5
Thorpedale Gdns IG6 56 D5
Thorpedale Rd N4 50 B1
Thorpewood Ave SE23, SE26 162 B2
Thorpland Ave UB10 61 A5
Thorsden Way 2 SE19 183 C5
Thorverton Rd NW2 69 A5
Thoydon Rd E3 97 A5
Thrale Almhouses SW16 182 A5
Thrale Rd SW16 181 C5
Thrale St SE1 252 B3
Thrasher Cl 20 E8 95 D6
Thrawl St E1 95 D2 243 D3
Thrayle Ho 2 SW9 138 B2
Threadgold Ho 8 N1 73 B2
Threadneedle St EC2,EC3 95 B1 242 D1
Three Bridges Bsns Ctr UB2 108 A4
Three Bridges Prim Sch UB2 107 D3
Three Colt St E14 119 B6
Three Colts La E2 96 B3
Three Corners DA7 147 D3
Three Cups Yd WC1 240 D3
Three Kings Yd W1 248 C6
Three Mill La E3 98 A4
Three Nun Ct EC2 242 B2
Three Oak La SE1 253 C2
Three Oaks Cl UB10 60 B5
Threshers Pl W11 244 A6
Thriffwood SE23,SE26 162 D1
Thrigby Rd KT9 214 B2
Thring Ho 2 SW9 138 B3
Throckmorten Rd E16 99 B1
Throgmorton Ave EC2 95 B1 242 D2
Throgmorton St EC2 95 B1 242 D2
Throwley Cl SE2 124 C3
Throwley Rd SM1 217 D3
Throwley Way SM1 217 D3
Thrupp Cl CR4 181 B1
Thrush Gn HA2 41 C5
Thrush St SE17 262 A2
Thunder Rd RM9 103 B3
Thunderer Rd RM9 103 B2
Thurbarn Rd SE6 185 D5
Thurland Ho 3 SE16 118 B2
Thurland Rd SE16 118 A3
Thurlby Cl HA1 43 A3
Thurlby Croft NW4 46 C6
Thurlby Rd SE27 182 C6
Wembley HA0 65 D2
Thurleigh Ave SW12 159 A5
Thurleigh Ct SW12 159 A5
Thurleigh Rd SW12 159 A5
Thurleston Ave SM4 201 A4
Thurlestone Ave N12 30 D4
Ilford IG3 79 D4
Thurlestone Cl TW17 193 A3
Thurlestone Ct 1 UB1 85 D1
Thurlestone Par TW17 193 A3
Thurlestone Rd SE27 182 C6
Thurloe Cl SW7 257 A4
Thurloe Ct SW3 257 A3
Thurloe Pl SW7 114 B2 256 D4
Thurloe Place Mews SW7 256 D4
Thurloe Sq SW7 114 C2 257 A4
Thurloe St SW7 114 B2 256 D4
Thurlow Cl E4 35 D4
Thurlow Ct 6 E11 55 A4
Thurlow Gdns HA0 65 D3
Thurlow Hill SE21 161 A2
Thurlow Ho 17 SW16 160 A1
Thurlow Park Rd SE21, SE24 161 A2
Thurlow Park Sch SE27 160 D2
Thurlow Rd NW3 70 B3
W7 109 A4
Thurlow St SE17 117 C1 263 A1
Thurlow Terr NW5 71 A3
Thurlow Twrs SE27 160 C1
Thurlston Rd HA4 62 A5
Thurnby Ct TW2 152 C1
Thurnscoe NW1 232 A5
Thursland Rd DA14 191 A5
Thursley Cres CR0 224 B1
Thursley Gdns SW19 156 D2
Thursley Ho 10 SW2 160 B4
3 Kingston u T KT2 176 D3
Thursley Rd SE9 166 B1
Thurso Ho NW6 91 D5
Thurso St SW17 180 B6
Thurstan Rd SW20 178 B3
Thurston Ho 4 BR3 185 D4
Thurston Ind Est SE13 141 D2
Thurston Rd SE8,SE13 141 D3
Southall UB1 85 B1
Thurtle Rd E2 95 D5
Thurza Ct TW7 130 D3
Thyer Cl BR6 227 A4
Thyra Gr N12 29 D4
Tibbatt's Rd E3 97 D3
Tibbenham Wlk E13 98 D5
Tibbets Cl SW19 156 D3
Tibbet's Corner SW19 156 D4
Tibbet's Ride SW19 156 D4
Tiber Gdns N1 233 B5
Ticehurst Cl BR5 190 A3
Ticehurst Rd SE23 163 A2
Tickford Cl SE2 124 C4
Tickford Ho NW8 230 A1
Tidal Basin Rd E16 120 D6
Tidbury Ct SW8 269 A3
Tidemill Prim Sch SE8 141 C5
Tidenham Gdns CR0 221 C5
Tideswell 10 NW5 71 B4
Tideswell Rd SW15 134 C1
Croydon CR0 223 C5
Tideway Cl TW10 175 C6
Tideway Ct 9 SE16 118 D5
Tideway Ho E14 119 C4
Tideway Ind Est SW8 137 C6 269 B5
Tideway Wharf SW13 133 C3
Tideway Yd SW13 133 C3
Tidey St E3 97 C2
Tidford Rd DA16 145 D3
Tidworth Ho 13 SE22 139 C2
Tidworth Rd E3 97 C3
Tiepigs La BR2,BR4 208 D1
Tierney Ct 4 CR0 221 D6
Tierney Rd SW2 160 A3
Tierney Terr SW2 160 A3
Tiffin Girls' Sch KT2 176 A4
Tiffin Sch KT2 176 B1
Tiger La BR2 209 B5
Tiger Way E5 74 B4
Tilbrook Rd SE3,SE9 143 C2
Tilbury Cl 13 SE15 139 D5
St Paul's Cray BR5 190 B1
Tilbury Ho 4 SE14 140 D6
Tilbury Rd E6 100 B5
E10 54 A2
Tildesley Rd SW15 156 C5
Tile Farm Rd BR6 227 B5
Tile Kiln La N6 49 C1
N13 33 A5
Ruislip UB9 38 D2
Tilehurst NW1 231 D1
Tilehurst Point 2 SE2 124 C4
Tilehurst Rd SW17,SW18 158 B3
Cheam SM3 217 A3
Tileyard Rd N7 72 A1
Tilford Ave CR0 224 A1
Tilford Gdns SW19 156 D3
Tilford Ho 8 SW2 160 B4
Tilia Rd E5 74 B4
Tilleard Ho 4 W10 91 A4
Tiller Ho 30 N1 95 C6
Tiller Rd E14 119 C3
Tillet Sq SE16 119 A4
Tillet Way 4 E2 96 A4
Tillett Cl NW10 67 A2
Tilling Ho 1 SE15 140 B2
Tilling Rd NW2 46 C2
Tillingbourne Gdns N3 47 B6
Tillingbourne Way N3 47 B5
Tillingham Way N12 29 D6
Tillman Ho 8 SW2 160 B3
Tillman St E1 96 B1
Tillotson Ct SW8 269 D3
Tillotson Rd N9 17 D2
Harrow HA3 23 D3
Ilford IG1 56 C2
Tilney Ct EC1 242 B6
Kingston u T KT6 197 D4
Woodford IG9 21 A2
Tilney Dr IG9 21 A2
Tilney Gdns 12 N1 73 B2
Tilney Rd
Buckhurst Hill IG9 21 B2
Dagenham RM9 81 B2
Southall UB2 106 C2
Tilney St W1 248 B4
Tilson Gdns SW2,SW4 160 A4
Tilson Ho SW2 160 A4
Tilson Rd N17 34 A2
Tilston Cl E11 76 D5
Tilt Yard App SE9 166 B5
Tilton St SW6 264 B5
Tiltwood The W3 111 A6
Timber Cl BR7 188 C1
Timber Mill Way SW4 137 D2
Timber Pond Rd SE16 118 D4
Timber St EC1 242 A6
Timbercroft KT19 215 C4
Timbercroft Inf Sch SE18 145 C5
Timbercroft La SE18 145 C5
Timberdene NW4 28 D1
Timberland Cl 15 SE15 140 A5
Timberland Rd E1 96 B1
Timberwharf Rd N16 52 A3
Time Sq E8 73 D3
Times Sq SM1 217 D3
Timothy Cl 1 SW4 159 C6
Bexley DA6 169 A6
Timothy Ho DA18 125 A4
Timothy Rd E3 97 B2
Timsbury Wlk 5 SW15 156 A3
Tina Ct SW16 160 C1
Tincal St SW9 138 D4
Tinniswood Cl N5 72 C3
Tinsley Rd E1 96 C2
Tintagel Cres SE22 139 D1
Tintagel Dr HA7 25 D6
Tintagel Ho SE20 184 A3
Tintern Ave NW9 44 D6
Tintern Cl SW15 157 A6
SW19 180 A4
Tintern Ct W13 109 A6
Tintern Gdns N14 16 A4
Tintern Ho NW1 231 D3
SW1 258 C3
Tintern Rd N22 33 A2
Carshalton SM5 202 B1
Tintern St SW4 138 A1
Tintern Way HA2 41 D1
Tinto Rd E16 99 A3
Tinwell Mews WD6 11 B6
Tinworth St SE11 116 A1 260 B2
Tippett Ct E6 100 B5
Tippetts Cl EN2 5 A4
Tipthorpe Rd SW11 137 A2
Tipton Dr CR0 221 C4
Tiptree 7 NW1 71 B1
Tiptree Cl E4 20 A1
Tiptree Cres IG5 56 C6
Tiptree Ct EN2 5 B1
Tiptree Dr EN2 5 B1
Tiptree Rd HA4 62 B4
Tirlemont Rd CR2 221 A1
Tirrell Rd CR0 205 A3
Tisbury Ct W1 249 C6
Tisbury Rd SW16 182 A1
Tisdall Pl SE17 117 B2 262 D3
Tissington Ct 4 SE16 118 D2
Titan Bsns Est 3 SE8 141 C5
Titan Ct TW8 110 B1
Titchborne Row W2 237 B1
Titchfield Rd NW8 92 D6 230 C4
Carshalton SM5 202 B1
Enfield EN3 7 A6
Titchfield Wlk SM5 202 B2
Titchwell Rd SW18 158 B3
Tite St SW3 136 D6 267 C6
Tithe Barn Cl KT2 176 B2
Tithe Barn Way UB5 84 B5
Tithe Cl NW7 28 A2
Hayes UB4 83 D2
Tithe Ct NW4 28 A2
Tithe Farm Ave HA2 63 C5
Tithe Farm Cl HA2 63 C5
Tithe Wlk NW7 28 A2
Titian Ave WD2 8 C4
Titley Cl E4 35 C5
Titmus Cl UB8 83 A1
Titmuss Ave SE28 124 B6
Titmuss St W12 112 C4
Tivendale N8 50 A6
Tiverton Ave IG5 56 C6
Tiverton Dr SE9 167 A3
Tiverton Prim Sch N15 51 B3
Tiverton Rd N4,N15 51 B3
N18 33 C5
NW6,NW10 90 D6
Edgware HA8 26 B1
Hounslow TW3 130 A3
Ruislip HA4 62 A5
Wembley HA0 88 A5
Tiverton St SE1 117 A3 262 A6
Tiverton Way KT9 213 D3
Tivoli Ct SE16 119 B5
Tivoli Gdns 11 SE7 122 A2
Tivoli Rd N8 49 D4
Tivoli Rd *continued*
SE27 183 A5
Hounslow TW4 129 A1
Tobago St E14 119 C4
Tobin Cl NW3 70 C1
Toby Ct N9 18 C4
Toby La E1 97 A3
Toby Way KT5,KT6 214 D6
Todd Ho 3 N2 30 B1
Todds Wlk N7 72 B6
Tokenhouse Yd EC2 242 C2
Tokyngton Ave HA9 66 C2
Toland Sq SW15 156 A6
Tolcairn Ct 2 DA17 125 C1
Tolcarne Dr HA5 40 B6
Tolchurch 2 W11 91 C1
Toley Ave HA3,HA9 44 A2
Tolhurst Ho 5 W10 91 A4
Tollbridge Cl W10 91 A3
Tollesbury Gdns IG6 57 B6
Tollet St E1 96 D3
Tollgate Dr SE21 161 C2
Hayes UB4 106 D6
Tollgate Ho 1 NW6 91 D5
Tollgate Jun Mix & Inf Sch CR0 206 C3
Tollgate Prim Sch E13 99 C3
Tollgate Rd E6 100 A2
Tollhouse Way N19 71 C6
Tollington Ct N4 72 B6
Tollington Pk N4 72 B6
Tollington Pl N4 72 B6
Tollington Rd N7 72 B4
Tollington Way N7 72 A5
Tolmers Sq NW1 93 C3 239 B6
Tolpaide Ho SE11 261 A3
Tolpuddle Ave 2 E13 99 C6
Tolpuddle St N1 94 C5 234 A4
Tolsford Rd E5 74 B3
Tolson Ho 2 TW7 131 A2
Tolson Rd TW7 131 A2
Tolverne Rd SW20 178 C2
Tolworth Cl KT6 198 D1
Tolworth Gdns RM6 58 D4
Tolworth Girls' Sch KT6 214 B5
Tolworth Hospl KT6 214 C6
Tolworth Inf Sch KT6 198 B1
Tolworth Jun Sch KT6 198 B1
Tolworth Junc KT6 214 D6
Tolworth Par RM6 59 A4
Tolworth Park Rd KT6 214 B6
Tolworth Rd KT6 214 A6
Tolworth Rise N KT5 198 D1
Tolworth Rise S KT5 198 D1
Tolworth Sta KT5 214 D6
Tolworth Underpass KT5,KT6 214 D6
Tom Coombs Cl SE9 144 A1
Tom Cribb Rd SE18, SE28 123 B3
Tom Groves Cl E15 76 B3
Tom Hood Cl E15 76 B3
Tom Hood Sec Sch E11 76 D5
Tom Jenkinson Rd 5 E16 121 A5
Tom Mann Cl IG11 101 C6
Tom Nolan Cl E15 98 C5
Tom Smith Cl SE10 142 C6
Tom Smith Ho 3 E17 54 A4
Tom Williams Ho SW6 264 C5
Tomahawk Gdns 4 UB5 84 D4
Tomkyns Ho SE11 261 A3
Tomline Ho SE1 252 A3
Tomlin's Gr E3 97 C4
Tomlins Orch IG11 101 A6
Tomlin's Terr E14 97 A1
Tomlins Wlk 4 N7 72 B6
Tomlinson Cl E2 95 D4
5 W4 110 D1
Tompion Ho EC1 241 D6
Tompion St EC1 234 D1
Tomson Ho SE1 263 C6
Tonbridge Cres HA3 44 A5
Tonbridge Hos WC1 233 A1
Tonbridge Rd KT12,KT8 195 B5
Tonbridge St WC1 94 A4 233 A1
Toneborough 14 NW8 91 D6
Tonfield Rd SM3 201 B1
Tonge Cl BR3 207 C4
Tonsley Hill SW18 157 D6
Tonsley Pl SW18 157 D6
Tonsley Rd SW18 157 D6
Tonsley St SW18 157 D6
Tonstall Rd CR4 181 A1
Tooke Cl HA5 23 A2
Took's Ct EC4 241 A2
Tooley St SE1 117 C5 253 A3
Toorack Rd HA3 24 B1
Tooting Bec SW17 159 A1
Tooting Bec Gdns SW16 181 D6
Tooting Bec Rd SW16 181 C5
SW17 181 B6
Tooting Bec Sta SW17 159 A1
Tooting Broadway SW17 180 D5
Tooting Broadway Sta SW17 180 C5
Tooting Gr SW17 180 C5
Tooting High St SW17, SW19 180 C5
Tooting Sta SW17 180 D4
Tootswood Rd BR2,BR3 208 C5
Top House Rise E4 20 A4
Top Pk BR3 208 C4
Topaz Ho KT4 199 B1
Topcliffe Dr BR6 227 B4
Topham Ho 8 SE10 142 A5
Topham Sq N17 33 A2
Topham St EC1 241 A6
Topiary Sq TW9 132 B2
Topley St SE9 143 D1
Topmast Point E14 119 C4
Topsfield Cl N8 49 D4
Topsfield Par N8 50 A3
Topsfield Rd N8 50 A4
Topsham Rd SW17 181 A6
Tor Ct W8 245 B2
Tor Gdns W8 113 C4 245 A2
Tor Ho N6 49 B3
Tor Rd DA16 146 C4
Torbay Ct 13 NW1 71 B1
Torbay Mans NW6 91 B6
Torbay Rd NW6 69 B1
Harrow HA2 63 A6
Torbay St 15 NW1 71 B1
Torbitt Way IG2 57 D4
Torbridge Cl HA8 26 A3
Torbrook Cl DA5 169 A5
Torcross Dr SE23 162 C2
Torcross Rd HA4 62 C5
Torfell 5 E18 36 D1
Tormead Cl SM1 217 C2
Tormount Rd SE18 145 C6
Tornay Ho E9 74 C1
N1 233 C4
Toronto Ave E12 78 B4
Toronto Rd E11 76 B4
Ilford IG1 57 A1
Torquay Gdns IG4 55 D5
Torquay St W2 91 D2
Torr Rd SE20 184 D3
Torre Wlk SM5 202 C1
Torrens Ct SE5 139 B2
Torrens Rd E15 76 D2
SW2 160 B6
Torrens Sq E15 76 D2
Torrens St EC1 94 D5 234 C3
Torres Sq E14 119 C1
Torriano Ave NW5 71 D3
Torriano Cotts NW5 71 C3
Torriano Jun & Inf Schs NW5 71 D3
Torridge Gdns SE15 140 C1
Torridge Rd CR7 204 D4
Torridon Ho NW6 91 D5
Torridon Inf Sch SE6 164 B2
Torridon Jun Sch SE6 164 B2
Torridon Rd SE13,SE6 164 B3
Torrington Ave N12 30 B5
Torrington Cl N12 30 B6
Claygate KT10 212 C2
Torrington Ct N12 30 B6
SE26 184 A5
Harrow HA2 63 D5
Torrington Dr HA2 63 D5
Torrington Gdns N11 31 C4
Wembley UB6 65 C1
Torrington Gr N12 30 C5
Torrington Pk N12 30 B6
Torrington Pl E1 118 A5
WC1 93 D2 239 C4
Torrington Rd E18 55 A6
Claygate KT10 212 C2
Dagenham RM8 59 B1
Ruislip HA4 62 A5
Wembley UB6 87 C6
Torrington Sq WC1 93 D3 239 D5
Thornton Heath CR0 205 B2
Torrington Way SM4 201 C3
Tortington Ho 1 SE15 140 B5
Torver Rd HA1 42 C5
Torver Way BR6 227 B5
Torwood Rd SW15 156 A6
Totham Lo SW20 178 B2
Tothill Ho SW1 259 D4
Tothill St SW1 115 D4 249 D1
Totland Ho SW18 157 D5
Totnes Rd DA16 146 C5
Totnes Villas N11 31 C5
Totnes Wlk N2 48 B5
Tottan Terr E1 96 D1
Tottenhall 5 NW1 71 A1
Tottenhall Inf Sch N13 32 C4
Tottenhall Rd N13 32 D4
Tottenham Court Rd W1 93 C2 239 B4
Tottenham Court Road Sta W1 93 D1 239 D2
Tottenham Gn E 2 N15 51 D5
Tottenham Gn E South Side 3 N15 51 D5
Tottenham Hale N15 52 A5
Tottenham Hale Ret Pk N15 52 A5
Tottenham Hale Sta N17 52 B6
Tottenham La N8 50 B4
Tottenham Mews W1 239 B4
Tottenham Rd N1 73 C2
Tottenham St W1 93 C2 239 B4
Totterdown St SW17 180 D5
Totteridge & Whetstone Sta N20 14 A2
Totteridge Comm N20 12 C3
Totteridge Ho SW11 136 B3
Totteridge La N20 13 D3
Totteridge Rd EN3 6 D6
Totteridge Village N20 13 B3
Totternhoe Cl HA3 43 C4
Totton Rd CR7 204 C6
Touchard Ho N1 235 D1
Toulmin St SE1 117 A4 252 A1
Toulon St SE5 139 A5
Toulouse Ct 2 SE16 118 B1
Tournay Rd SW6 135 B5 264 D4
Toussaint Wlk 18 SE16 118 A3
Tovil Cl SE20 184 B1
Tovy Ho 6 SE1 118 A1
Towcester Rd E3 98 A3
Tower Bldgs 22 E1 118 B5
Tower Br App E1,EC3 253 C5
Tower Bridge* E1,EC3,SE1 117 D5 253 C4
Tower Bridge Bsns Complex SE16 118 B3
Tower Bridge Bsns Sq SE16 118 B2
Tower Bridge Piazza SE1 253 C3
Tower Bridge Prim Sch SE1 117 D4 253 C2
Tower Bridge Rd EC3,SE1 117 D5 253 C3
Tower Bridge Sq SE1 253 C2
Tower Cl SE20 184 B3
Orpington BR6 227 D5
Tower Ct E5 51 D2
NW8 230 B4
WC2 240 A1
Tower Gardens Rd N17 33 B2
Tower Gateway Sta EC3 117 D6 253 C6
Tower Gdns KT10 213 A1
Tower Gr KT13 193 C1
Tower Hamlets Coll E1 96 C2
E1 96 D1
E14 97 D1
E14 119 D6
Tower Hamlets Rd E7 76 D3
E17 53 C6
Tower Hill EC3 117 D6 253 C5
Tower Hill Sta EC3 117 D6 253 C6
Tower Hill Terr EC3 253 B5
Tower Mans SE1 263 C5
Tower Mews E5 75 A3
E17 53 C5
Tower Pier EC3 117 C5 253 B4
Tower Pl EC3 253 B5
Tower Rd NW10 68 A1
Bexleyheath DA7 147 D1
Orpington BR6 227 D5
Twickenham TW1,TW2 152 D1
Tower Rise TW9 132 A2
Tower Royal EC4 252 C6
Tower St WC2 240 A1
Tower Terr N22 32 B1
Tower The* EC3 117 D6 253 C5
Tower View CR0 207 A2
Tower Wharf SE1 253 C2
Tower Wlk SE1 263 A4
Towergate SE1 263 A4
Towers Ave UB10 83 A4
Towers Ct UB10 83 A4
Towers Pl TW10 154 A6
Towers Rd Hatch End HA5 23 A4
Southall UB1 85 C3
Towers The NW5 71 B5
1 Richmond TW9 132 B1
Towfield Ct TW13 151 B2
Towfield Rd TW13 151 B2
Town Field Way TW7 131 A3
Town Hall Approach Rd N15 51 D5
Town Hall Rd SW11 136 D2
Town La TW19 148 A2
Town Meadow TW8 131 D5
Town Quay IG11 100 D6
Town Quay Wharf IG11 100 D6
Town Rd N9 18 B2
Town The EN2 5 B2
Town Tree Rd TW15 170 C5
Towncourt Cres BR5 211 B5
Towncourt La BR5 211 B2
Towncourt Path N4 51 A1
Townend Ct 6 BR1 186 D2
Towney Mead UB5 85 B5
Towney Mead Ct UB5 85 B5
Townfield Rd UB3 105 D5
Townfield Sq UB3 105 D6
Towngate Bsns Pk IG11 102 A4
Townhall Ave 3 W4 111 B1
Townholm Cres W7 108 D3
Townley Ct E15 76 D2
Townley Gram Sch for Girls DA5 169 B5
Townley Rd SE22 161 C6
Bexley DA6 169 B6
Townley St SE17 117 B1 262 C2
Townmead Bsns Ctr SW6 136 A2
Townmead Rd SW6 136 A3
Richmond TW9 132 D3
Towns Ho 4 SW4 137 D2
Townsend Ave N14 31 D6
Townsend Ho 12 SE1 118 A2
Townsend Ind Est NW10 89 A5
Townsend La NW9 45 B3
Townsend Prim Sch SE17 117 C2 263 A4
Townsend Rd N15 51 D4
SE18 122 D3
Ashford TW15 170 A5
Southall UB1 107 A5
Townsend St SE1,SE17 117 C2 263 A4
Townsend Way HA6 22 A3

Townsend Yd N6 49 B1
Townshend Cl DA14 190 C4
Townshend Ct NW8 230 B4
Townshend Est
NW8 92 C5 230 A4
Townshend Ho 19 SE18 122 B2
Townshend Rd
NW8 92 C6 230 A5
Chislehurst West BR7 188 D5
Richmond TW9 132 B1
Townshend Terr TW9 132 B1
Townson Ave UB5 84 B5
Townson Way UB5 84 A5
Towpath TW17 192 B1
Towpath Way CR0 205 D4
Towton Rd SE27 161 A2
Toxteth Ho N4 51 A2
Toynbec Cl BR7 188 D6
Toynbee Rd SW19,SW20 179 A2
Toynbee St E1 95 D2 243 C3
Toyne Way N6 48 D3
Tracey Ave NW2 68 C3
Tracy Ct HA7 25 C3
Tracy Ho 12 E3 97 B4
Trade Cl N13 32 C6
Trade Twr 8 SW11 136 A2
Trade Winds Ct 1 E1 118 A5
Trader Rd E6 100 D1
Tradescant Ho 15 E9 74 C1
Tradescant Rd
SW8 138 A5 270 B3
Trading Estate Rd NW10 89 A3
Traemore Ct SW16 160 C1
Trafalgar Ave N17 33 C4
SE15 139 D6
North Cheam KT4,SM3,
SM4 200 D1
Trafalgar Bsns Ctr
IG11 101 D3
Trafalgar Cl 1 SE16 119 A2
Trafalgar Ct E6 100 C6
Hounslow TW3 129 B2
West Barnes KT3 200 B6
Trafalgar Gdns E1 96 D2
W8 255 D6
Trafalgar Gr SE10 142 B6
Trafalgar Ho SE17 262 B2
Trafalgar Inf Sch TW2 152 B2
Trafalgar Jun Sch TW2 152 B2
Trafalgar Pl E11 55 A5
N18 34 A5
Trafalgar Rd SE10 120 C1
SW19 180 A3
Twickenham TW2 152 B2
Trafalgar Sq*
SW1 115 D5 249 D4
Trafalgar St
SE17 117 B1 262 D2
Trafalgar Terr HA1 42 C1
Trafalgar Trad Est EN3 7 A1
Trafalgar Way E14 120 A5
Croydon CR0 220 C6
Trafford Cl E15 75 D3
Trafford Ho N1 235 D4
Trafford Rd CR7 204 B4
Tragail SW15 157 A6
Traherne Lo 3 TW11 174 D5
Traitors Gate
EC3 117 D5 253 C4
Tralee Ct 31 SE16 118 B1
Tramway Ave E15 76 B1
N9 18 C4
Tramway Path CR4 202 C5
Trance Way W3 110 C3
Tranmere Ct 5 SM2 218 A1
Tranmere Ho 7 N7 72 C3
Tranmere Rd N9 17 D4
SW17,SW18 158 A2
Twickenham TW2 151 D4
Tranquil Pass SE3 142 D3
Tranquil Vale SE3 142 C3
Transept St NW1 237 B3
Transmere Cl BR5 211 A3
Transmere Rd BR5 211 A3
Transom Cl SE16 119 A2
Transom Sq E14 119 D1
Transport Ave TW8 131 B6
Tranton Rd SE16 118 B3
Trappes Ho 2 SE16 118 B2
Traps La KT2,KT3 177 C2
Travel Clinic, Hospl for
Tropical Diseases
WC1 93 C3 239 B5
Travellers Way TW5 128 C3
Travers Cl E17 34 D2
Travers Ho 6 SE10 142 B6
Travers Rd N7 72 C5
Travis Ho SE10 142 A4
Treacy Cl WD2 8 A2
Treadgold Ho 7 W11 112 D6
Treadgold St W11 112 D6
Treadway St E2 96 B5
Treasury Buildings
SW1 250 A2
Treaty Ctr TW3 129 D2
Treaty St N1 94 B6 233 C5
Trebeck St W1 248 C3
Treborough Ho W1 238 A4
Trebovir Rd
SW5 113 C2 255 B3
Treby St E3 97 B3
Trecastle Way 3 N7 71 D4
Tredegar Rd E3 97 B5
N11 31 D3
Tredegar Sq E3 97 B4
Tredegar Terr E3 97 B4
Trederwen Rd E8 96 A6
Tredown Rd SE26 184 C5
Tredwell Cl BR2 210 A5
Tredwell Rd SE27 182 D6
Tree Cl TW10 153 D3
Tree Ct WD6 9 D5
Tree Rd E16 99 C1
Tree Tops 1 IG8 37 A6
Tree Tops View IG10 21 D4
Tree View Cl SE19 183 C2
Treen Ave SW13 133 D2
Trees The N16 51 B2
Treetops Cl SE2 125 A1
Treetops Ct CR7 205 A4
Treewall Gdns BR1 187 B6
Trefgarne Rd RM10 81 C6
Trefil Wlk N7 72 A4
Trefoil Ho DA18 125 A4
Trefoil Rd SW18 158 A6
Trefusis Ct TW5 128 B4
Tregaron Ave N8 50 A3
Tregaron Gdns KT3 199 C5
Tregarvon Rd SW11 137 A1
Tregenna Ave HA2 63 C4
Tregenna Cl 1 N14 15 C6
Tregenna Ct HA2 63 C4
Trego Rd E9 75 C1
Tregony Rd BR6 227 D4
Tregothnan Rd SW9 138 A2
Treguntar Rd
SW10 114 A1 256 A1
Trehern Rd 12 SW14 133 B2
Treherne Ct SW9 138 D4
SW17 181 A6
Trehurst St E5 75 A3
Trelawn Rd E10 76 A5
SW2 160 C6
Trelawney Est E9 74 C2
Trelawney Ho SE1 252 A2
Trelawny Cl E17 53 D5
Trellis Ho SW19 180 A3
Trellis Sq 1 E3 97 B4
Treloar Gdns SE19 183 B4
Tremadoc Rd SW4 137 D1
Tremaine Cl SE4 141 C3
Tremaine Rd SE20 184 B1
Trematon Ho SE11 261 B2
Trematon Pl TW11 175 C3
Tremlett Gr N19 71 C5
Tremlett Mews N19 71 C5
Trenance Gdns IG3 80 A5
Trenchard Ave HA4 62 B4
Trenchard Cl NW9 27 C2
Stanmore HA7 25 B4
Trenchard Ct SM4 201 C3
Trenchard St SE10 120 B1
Trenchold St
SW8 138 A6 270 A5
Trend Ct W13 109 B5
Trendell Ho 4 E14 97 C1
Trenholme Cl SE20 184 B3
Trenholme Rd SE20 184 B3
Trenholme Terr SE20 184 B3
Trenmar Gdns NW10 90 B4
Trenmar Lo NW10 90 B4
Trent Ave W5 109 C3
Trent CE Prim Sch EN4 2 D1
Trent Ct E11 55 A4
Trent Ctry Pk EN4 3 A3
Trent Gdns N14 15 B5
Trent Ho SE15 140 C1
4 Kingston u T KT2 175 D2
Trent Rd SW2 160 B6
Buckhurst Hill IG9 21 B3
Trent Way Hayes UB4 83 C4
North Cheam KT4 216 C5
Trentham Lo 8 EN1 17 C6
Trentham St SW18 157 C3
Trentwood Side EN2 4 B2
Treport St SW18 157 D4
Tresco Cl BR1 186 C4
Tresco Gdns IG3 80 A6
Tresco Ho SE11 261 A2
Tresco Rd SE15 140 B1
Trescoe Gdns HA2 41 A2
Tresham Cres
NW8 92 C3 237 A6
Tresham Rd IG11 79 D1
Tresham Wlk E9 74 C3
Tresidder Ho 10 SW4 159 D4
Tresilian Ave N21 16 B6
Tressel Cl 20 N1 72 D1
Tressillian Cres SE4 141 C2
Tressillian Rd SE4 141 C2
Trestis Cl UB4 84 D2
Treswell Rd RM9 103 A6
Tretawn Gdns NW7 11 C1
Tretawn Pk NW7 27 C6
Trevallyn Lo 1 KT2 176 D2
Trevanion Rd W14 254 B2
Treve Ave HA1 42 B2
Trevelayan Rd SW17 180 D4
Trevelyan Ave E12 78 B4
Trevelyan Cres HA3 43 D2
Trevelyan Ct KT3 199 D2
Trevelyan Gdns NW10 90 C6
Trevelyan Ho 16 E2 96 D4
SE5 138 D5
6 Twickenham TW1 153 C5
Trevelyan Rd E15 76 D4
Trevenna Ho 13 SE23 162 D1
Treveris St SE1 251 D3
Treversh Ct 7 BR1 186 D2
Treverton St W10 90 D3
Treverton Twr W10 90 D2
Treves Cl N21 16 B6
Treves Ho E1 96 A3
Treville St SW15 156 B4
Treviso Rd SE23 163 A2
Trevithick Cl TW14 149 D3
Trevithick Ho 3 NW5 71 B4
13 SE16 118 B2
SW8 269 C2
Trevithick St SE8 141 C6
Trevone Gdns HA5 41 A3
Trevor Cl Harrow HA3 24 D3
Hayes BR2 209 A2
Isleworth TW7 152 D6
New Barnet EN4 14 B5
Northolt UB5 84 C5
Trevor Cres HA4 61 D4
Trevor Gdns
Burnt Oak HA8 27 B2
Northolt UB5 84 C5
Trevor Pl SW7 114 C4 247 B1
Trevor Rd SW19 179 A3
Burnt Oak HA8 27 B2
Hayes UB3 105 C4
Woodford IG8 37 A3
Trevor Sq SW7 114 C4 247 B1
Trevor St SW7 114 C4 247 B1
Trevose Ho SE11 260 D2
Trevose Rd E17 36 B2
Trewenna Dr KT9 213 D3
Trewince Rd SW20 178 C2
Trewint St SW18 158 A2
Trewsbury House 2
SE2 124 D4
Trewsbury Rd SE26 184 D5
Triandra Way UB4 84 D2
Triangle Ct E16 99 C2
Triangle Ctr UB1 108 B5
Triangle Pl SW4 137 D1
Triangle Rd 7 E8 96 B6
Triangle The E8 96 B6
EC1 241 D6
N19 49 D2
Barking IG11 79 A2
Kingston u T KT3 177 A1
Tribune Ct 16 NW9 46 A5
Trident Gdns 6 UB5 84 D4
Trident Ho 9 E14 98 A1
Trident St SE16 118 D2
Trident Way UB2 106 B3
Trigon Rd SW8 138 B5 270 D4
Trilby Rd SE23 162 D2
Trillo Ct IG1 57 C2
Trim St SE8 141 B6
Trimdon NW1 232 B5
Trimmer Ct TW7 130 D2
Trimmer Wlk 11 TW8 132 A6
Trinder Rd N4,N19 50 A1
Ducks Island EN5 12 C6
Tring Ave W5 110 B5
Southall UB1 85 B1
Wembley HA9 66 C2
Tring Cl IG2 57 B4
Tring Ct TW1 175 A6
Trinidad Ho 17 E14 119 B6
Trinidad St E14 119 B6
Trinity Ave N2 48 B6
Enfield EN1 17 D5
Trinity Church Rd
SW13 134 B6
Trinity Church Sq
SE1 117 A3 262 B6
Trinity Cl E11 76 C6
SE13 142 B1
3 SW4 137 C1
Hounslow TW4 129 A1
Keston Mark BR2 210 A1
Trinity Coll of Music
W1 93 A1 238 B2
Trinity Cotts TW9 132 B2
Trinity Cres SW17 159 A2
Trinity Ct 8 E4 20 A2
2 N1 95 C6
N21 16 D3
SE9 166 D5
SE16 119 A4
SE23 162 C1
SE25 205 C3
WC1 240 C6
Twickenham TW2 152 C2
Trinity Gdns E16 98 D2
11 E18 55 B6
SW2,SW9 138 B1
Trinity Gn E1 96 C2
Trinity Gr 8 SE10 142 A4
Trinity Ho 5 E17 53 D6
SE1 262 B6
Trinity Homes 14 SW2 138 B1
Trinity Mews SE20 184 B2
Trinity Par TW3 129 D2
Trinity Pl EC3 253 C5
Bexley DA6 147 B1
Trinity RC High Sch (Lower)
IG8 37 A6
Trinity RC High Sch (Upper
Sch) IG8 36 D6
Trinity RC High Sch (Upper)
IG8 37 A6
Trinity Rd N2 48 B6
N22 32 A3
N22 32 B2
SW17,SW18 158 C4
SW19 179 C4
Ilford IG6 57 A6
Richmond TW9 132 B2
Southall UB1 107 A5
Trinity Rise SE24,SW2 160 D4
Trinity Sch Croydon CR0 222 C6
Dagenham RM10 81 C4
Trinity Sq EC3 117 C6 253 B6
Trinity St 9 E16 99 A2
SE1 117 B3 262 C6
Enfield EN2 5 A3
Trinity St Mary's CE Prim Sch
SW12 159 A3
Trinity Terr IG9 21 B4
Trinity Way E4 35 B4
W3 111 D6
Trinity Wharf Bsns Ctr
SE16 119 B4
Trio Pl SE1 117 A4 252 B1
Triscott Ho UB3 106 A5
Tristan Ct 41 SE8 141 B6
Tristan Sq SE3 142 C2
Tristram Cl E17 54 B6
Tristram Rd BR1 186 D6
Triton Ct EC2 242 D5
Triton Ho 2 E14 119 D2
Triton Sq NW1 239 A6
Tritton Ave CR0 220 A4
Tritton Ho N21 17 B5
Tritton Rd SE21,SE27 161 B1
Triumph Cl UB7 127 A4
Triumph Ho IG11 102 A4
Triumph Rd E6 100 B1
Triumph Trad Est N17 34 A4
Trocette Mans SE1 263 B6
Trojan Ct NW6 69 A1
9 W7 109 A5
Trojan Ind Est NW10 67 D2
Trojan Way CR0 220 B5
Troon Cl 34 SE16 118 B1
Troon Ho 11 E14 97 A1
Troon St E1 97 A1
Tropical Ct 2 W10 90 D4
Trosley Rd DA17 147 C6
Trossachs Rd SE22 161 C6
Trothy Rd SE1 118 A2
Trotman Ho SE14 140 C4
Trott Rd N10 31 A3
Trott St SW11 136 C4 267 A1
Trotwood Ho 3 SE16 118 B4
Troughton Rd SE7 121 B1
Troutbeck NW1 231 D1
Troutbeck Rd SE14 141 A4
Trouville Rd SW4 159 C5
Trowbridge Rd E9 75 B2
Trower Ho 5 E9 75 A2
Trowlock Ave TW11 175 C4
Trowlock Way TW11 175 D4
Troy Ct 5 SE18 122 D2
W8 255 A6
Troy Rd SE19 183 B4
Troy Town SE15 140 A2
Troy Town Flats SE15 140 A2
Troyes Ho NW3 70 D3
Trubshaw Rd UB2 107 D3
Trulock Ct N17 34 A3
Trulock Rd N17 34 A3
Truman Cl 2 HA8 27 A3
Truman's Rd 24 N16 73 C3
Trump St EC2 242 B1
Trumpers Way W7 108 D3
Trumpeters Inn TW9 153 C6
Trumpington Rd E7 76 D4
Trundle St SE1 252 A2
Trundlers Way WD2 8 C3
Trundleys Rd SE8 141 A6
Trundley's Rd SE8 118 D1
Trundley's Terr SE8 118 D2
Truro Gdns IG1 56 A2
Truro Ho 25 W2 91 C2
Truro Rd E17 53 B5
N22 32 B3
Truro St NW5 71 A2
Truro Way UB4 83 C4
Trusedale Rd E6 100 B1
Truslove Rd SE27 182 D5
Trussley Rd W6 112 C3
Trust Wlk SE21 160 D3
Tryfan Cl IG4 55 D4
Tryon St SW3 114 D1 257 C2
Trystings Cl KT10 213 A2
Tuam Rd SE18 145 B6
Tubbenden Cl BR6 227 C5
Tubbenden Dr BR6 227 B4
Tubbenden Jun & Inf Schs
BR6 227 B4
Tubbenden La BR6 227 C5
Tubbenden La S BR6 227 B3
Tubbs Rd NW10 89 D5
Tudor Ave
Hampton TW12 173 C3
North Cheam KT4 216 B4
Tudor Cl N6 49 C2
NW3 70 C2
NW7 28 A4
NW9 67 A6
SW2 160 B5
Ashford TW15 170 A6
Bromley BR7 188 B2
Cheam SM3 217 A2
Chessington KT9 214 A3
Hampton TW12 174 A5
Pinner HA5 40 A4
Wallington SM6 219 C1
Woodford IG8 37 B5
Tudor Cres EN2 5 A4
Tudor Ct E17 53 B2
N1 73 C2
5 SE16 118 D5
W5 110 C4
Feltham TW13 172 C6
Sidcup DA14 168 A1
4 Stanwell TW19 148 A5
Teddington TW11 174 D4
3 W13 87 C1
Tudor Ct S HA9 66 C3
Tudor Dr
Kingston u T KT2 176 A5
Walton-on-T KT12 194 D1
Tudor Dr *continued*
West Barnes SM4 201 A3
Tudor Ent Pk HA3 42 B6
Tudor Est NW10 88 D5
Tudor Gables NW7 27 D6
Tudor Gdns NW9 67 A6
SW14 133 C2
W3 88 C1
Twickenham TW1 152 D3
West Wickham BR4 224 A5
Tudor Gr E9 74 C1
Tudor Ho 34 E9 74 C1
W14 112 D2
Tolworth KT6 198 C1
Tudor Mews 2 NW10 68 A2
Tudor Par SE9 144 A1
Romford RM6 58 D2
Tudor Pl SW19 180 C3
Tudor Prim Sch N3 30 A2
Southall UB1 107 A6
West Barnes SM4 200 D2
Tudor Rd E4 35 D4
E6 99 C6
E9 96 B6
N9 18 C4
SE19 183 D3
SE25 206 B4
Ashford TW15 171 B4
Barking IG11 79 D1
Barnet EN5 1 D2
Beckenham BR3 208 A6
Hampton TW12 173 C3
Harrow HA3 24 B1
Hayes UB3 83 B1
Isleworth TW3 130 B1
Kingston u T KT2 176 C3
Pinner Green HA5 22 C1
Southall UB1 107 A6
Tudor Sq UB3 83 B2
Tudor St EC4 116 C6 251 B6
Tudor Way N14 15 D3
W3 110 C4
Hillingdon UB10 60 C2
Orpington BR5 211 B3
Tudor Well Cl HA7 25 B5
Tudor Wlk DA5 169 A5
Tudors The 2 BR3 185 D1
Tudway Rd SE3,SE9 143 C1
Tuffield Ho 9 SE18 122 C2
Tufnell Ct 12 E3 97 B6
Tufnell Park Mans 2
N7 72 A5
Tufnell Park Prim Sch
N7 71 D4
Tufnell Park Rd N19,N7 71 D4
Tufnell Park Sta N19 71 C4
Tufton Ct SW1 260 A5
Tufton Gdns KT8 173 D1
Tufton Rd E4 35 C6
Tufton St SW1 116 A3 260 A5
Tugboat St SE28 123 C4
Tugela Rd CR0 205 B3
Tugela St SE6 163 B2
Tugmutton Cl BR6 226 D4
Tuke Sch SE15 140 B4
Tulip Cl 5 E6 100 B2
Croydon CR0 206 D1
Hampton TW12 173 B4
Southall UB2 108 A4
Tulip Gdns E4 20 B1
Ilford IG1 78 D2
Tull St CR4 202 D2
Tullis Ho 12 E9 74 C1
Tulse Cl BR3 208 A6
Tulse Hill SW2 160 D2
SW2,SE24 160 C4
Tulse Hill Sta SE27 160 D2
Tulse Ho SW2 160 C5
Tulsemere Rd SE21,
SE27 161 A2
Tumbling Bay KT12 194 A3
Tummons Gdns SE25 183 C1
Tunbridge Ct 1 SE26 162 A1
Tunbridge Ho EC1 234 C2
Tuncombe Rd N18 33 C6
Tunis Ho E1 97 A2
Tunis Rd W12 112 B5
Tunley Gn 16 E14 97 B2
Tunley Rd NW10 89 C6
SW12,SW17 159 A2
Tunmarsh La E13 99 C4
Tunnan Leys E6 100 C1
Tunnel Ave SE10 120 B4
SE10 120 D2
Tunnel Avenue Trad Est
SE10 120 B4
Tunnel Gdns N11 31 C3
Tunnel Link Rd TW6 148 C6
Tunnel Rd SE16 118 C4
Tunnel Rd E TW6 126 D4
Tunnel Rd W TW6 126 D4
Tunstall Cl BR6 227 C4
Tunstall Ct 14 TW9 132 B4
Tunstall Rd SW9 138 B1
Croydon CR0 205 C1
Tunstall Wlk 10 TW8 132 A6
Tunstock Way DA17 125 A3
Tunworth Cl NW9 45 A3
Tunworth Cres SW15 155 D5
Tupelo Rd E10 75 D6
Tupman Ho 21 SE16 118 A4
Turberville Ho 1 SW9 138 B2
Turene Cl SW18 136 A1
Turin Rd N9 18 C4
Turin St E2 96 A4
Turkey Oak Cl SE19 183 C2
Turkey St EN3 6 B6
Turkey Street Sta EN3 6 C6
Turks Cl UB8 82 C4
Turk's Head Yd EC1 241 C4
Turks Row SW3 114 D1 257 D2
Turle Rd N4 72 B6
SW16 182 A1
Turlewray Cl N4 50 B1
Turley Cl E15 98 C6
Turnagain La EC4 241 C2
Turnage Rd RM8 59 A1
Turnant Rd N17 33 A2
Turnberry Cl 24 SE16 118 B1
Turnberry Way BR6 211 B1
Turnbull Ho N1 234 D6
Turnbury Cl SE28 102 D1
Turnchapel Mews 1
SW4 137 B2
Turner Ave N15 51 C5
Mitcham CR4 180 D2
Twickenham TW2 152 A1
Turner Cl NW11 47 D3
7 SW9 138 D4
Hayes UB4 83 A4
Turner Ct 9 SE5 139 B1
19 SE16 118 C4
Turner Dr NW11 47 D3
Turner Ho N4 50 B1
NW8 230 A4
SW1 259 D3
WC2 250 B5
6 Twickenham TW1 153 D5
Turner Lo 10 SW19 156 D3
Turner Rd E17 54 A6
Edgware HA8 26 B1
New Malden KT3 199 B2
Turner St E1 96 B2
E16 98 D1
Turners Meadow Way
BR3 185 B2
Turner's Rd E3 97 B2
Turners Way CR0 220 C6
Turneville Rd
W14 135 B6 264 C6
Turney Rd SE21 161 B4
Turney Sch SE21 161 A4
Turnham Green Sta
W4 111 C2
Turnham Green Terr
W4 111 C2
Turnham Ho SE4 141 A1
Turnham Prim Sch SE4 141 A1
Turnham Rd SE4 141 A1
Turnmill Ho 8 SW2 160 C6
Turnmill St EC1 94 D2 241 C4
Turnour Ho 32 E1 96 B1
Turnpike Cl SE8 141 B5
Turnpike Ct DA6 146 D1
Turnpike Ho EC1 234 D1
Turnpike La N8 50 C6
Sutton SM1 218 A3
Uxbridge UB10 82 A5
Turnpike Lane Sta N15 50 D6
Turnpike Link CR0 221 C6
Turnpike Way TW7 131 A4
Turnpin La 2 SE10 142 A6
Turnstone Cl E13 99 A4
NW9 27 C1
Uxbridge UB10 60 D3
Turnstone Ct 32 SE8 141 B6
Turpentine La
SW1 115 B1 258 D1
Turpin Cl EN3 7 C6
Turpin Ho SW11 268 C2
Turpin Rd TW14 149 D5
Turpin Way N19 49 D1
Wallington SM6 219 B1
Turpington Cl BR2 210 A2
Turpington La BR2 210 A3
Turquand St SE17 262 B3
Turret Gr SW4 137 C2
Turret Ho KT2 176 A4
Turton Ho 5 SE18 144 D6
Turton Rd HA0 66 A3
Turville Ho NW8 237 A6
Turville St E2 243 C6
Tuscan Ho 36 E2 96 C4
Tuscan Rd SE18 123 B1
Tuskar St SE10 120 C1
Tutshill Ct 5 SE15 139 C5
Tuttle Ho SW1 259 D1
Tuttlebee La IG9 21 A2
Tweed Ct W7 86 C1
Tweed Ho E14 98 A3
Tweedale Ct E15 76 A3
Tweeddale Gr UB10 61 A5
Tweeddale Jun & Inf Schs
SM5 202 B2
Tweeddale Rd SM5 202 B1
Tweedmouth Rd E13 99 B5
Tweedy Cl EN1 17 D6
Tweedy Rd BR1 187 A2
Tweezer's Alley WC2 251 A6
Twelve Acre Ho 5 E12 78 C5
Twelvetrees Cres E3 98 A3
Twentyman Cl IG8 37 A5
Twickenham Bridge
TW9 153 C6
Twickenham Cl CR0 220 B5
Twickenham Gdns
Greenford UB6 65 A3
Harrow Weald HA3 24 C3
Twickenham Rd E11 76 B6
Feltham TW13 151 B1
Isleworth TW1,TW7 131 A2
Richmond TW1,TW9 131 C1
Teddington TW11 175 A6

Twickenham Rugby Football Union Ground TW2 152 C5
Twickenham Sta TW1 153 A4
Twickenham Trad Ctr TW1 152 D5
Twig Folly Cl E2 96 D5
Twilley St SW18 157 D4
Twine Cl IG11 102 B4
Twine Ct E1 118 C6
Twineham Gn N12 29 C6
Twining Ave TW2 152 B1
Twinn Rd NW7 29 A4
Twisden Rd NW5 71 B4
Twiss Ho 6 SE18 122 D1
Twybridge Way NW10 67 A1
Twyford Abbey Rd NW10 88 B4
Twyford Ave N2 48 D6
W3 110 C6
Twyford CE High Sch W3 110 D5
Twyford Cres W3 110 C5
Twyford Ct N10 49 A6
W3 110 C6
6 Wembley HA0 88 A5
Twyford Ho N5 72 D5
6 N15 51 C3
Twyford Par KT6 198 C1
Twyford Pl WC2 240 C2
Twyford Rd
Carshalton SM5 202 B1
Harrow HA2 41 D2
Ilford IG1 79 A3
Twyford St N1 94 B6 233 C6
Twynholm Mans SW6 264 A4
Tyas Rd E16 98 D3
Tybenham Rd SW19 201 C6
Tyberry Rd EN3 6 C2
Tyburn La HA1 42 D2
Tyburn RC Inf Sch NW8 92 B3 236 D6
Tyburn Tree (site of) W2 247 C6
Tyburn Way W1 247 D6
Tye La BR6 227 A3
Tyer's Est SE1 253 A2
Tyers Gate SE1 117 C4 253 A1
Tyers Ho 1 SW16 181 C5
Tyers St SE11 116 B1 260 C2
Tyers Terr SE11 116 B1 260 D1
Tyeshurst Cl SE2 125 A1
Tylecroft Rd SW16 182 A1
Tylehurst Gdns IG1 79 A3
Tyler Cl E2 95 D5
Tyler St SE10 120 C1
Tylers Ct 4 E17 53 C5
5 Wembley HA0 88 A5
Tylers Gate HA3 44 A3
Tylers Path SM5 218 D4
Tylers Way WD2 8 C6
Tylney Ave SE19 183 D5
Tylney Ho 19 E1 96 B1
Tylney Rd E7 77 C4
Bromley BR1 187 D1
Tymperley Ct SW19 157 A3
Tynamara KT1 197 D5
Tynan Cl TW14 150 A3
Tyndale La N1 72 D1
Tyndale Mans N1 72 D1
Tyndale Terr 13 N1 72 D1
Tyndall Gdns E10 76 A6
Tyndall Rd E10 76 A6
Bexley DA16 145 D2
Tyne Ct W7 86 C1
Tyne Ho 8 KT2 175 D2
Tyne St E1 243 D2
Tynedale Ct E14 119 D1
Tyneham Cl 10 SW11 137 A2
Tyneham Rd SW11 137 A2
Tynemouth Cl E6 100 D1
Tynemouth Dr EN1 6 A5
Tynemouth Rd N15 51 D5
SE18 123 C1
Mitcham CR4 181 A3
Tynemouth St SW6 136 A3
Tynemouth Terr 8 N15 51 D5
Tynte Ct E9 75 A3
Tynwald Ho 14 SE26 162 A1
Type St E2 96 D5
Tyrawley Rd SW6 265 C2
Tyrell Cl HA1 64 C4
Tyrell Ct SM5 218 D4
Tyrols Rd SE23 162 D3
Tyron Way DA14 189 D5
Tyrone Rd E6 100 B4
Tyrrel Way NW9 46 A2
Tyrrell Ave DA16 168 B6
Tyrrell Ho SW1 269 B6
Catford BR3 185 D5
Tyrrell Rd SE22 140 A1
Tyrrell Sq CR4 180 C2
Tyrwhitt Rd SE4 141 C2
Tysoe Ave EN3 7 B6
Tysoe St EC1 234 B1
Tyson Rd SE23 162 C4
Tyssen JMI Sch N16 52 A1
Tyssen Rd N16 73 D5
Tyssen St E8 73 D2
N1 95 C5
Tythe Cl KT12 194 B3
Tytherton 30 E2 96 C5
Tytherton Rd N19 71 D5

U

Uamvar St E14 97 D2
Uckfield Rd Enfield EN3 6 D6
Mitcham CR4 181 A2
Udall St SW1 259 B3
Udimore Ho W10 90 C2
Udney Park Rd TW11 175 A4
Uffington Rd NW10 90 B6
SE27 182 C6
Ufford Cl HA3 23 D3
Ufford Rd HA3 23 D3
Ufford St SE1 116 C4 251 B2
Ufton Ct UB5 84 D4
Ufton Gr N1 73 B1
Ufton Rd N1 73 C1
Uhura Sq 19 N16 73 C5
Ujima Ct N19 50 A1
SW16 182 A6
Ujima Ho SW16 182 A6
Uk Cotts UB3 105 B4
Ullathorne Rd SW16 181 C6
Ulleswater Rd N14 16 B1
Ullin St E14 98 A2
Ullswater SW15 156 D5
Ullswater Cl
Bromley BR1 186 C3
Hayes UB4 83 C5
Kingston u T KT2,SW15 177 B6
Ullswater Cres SW15 177 B6
Ullswater Ct 2 E18 37 A1
HA2 41 C2
Ullswater Ho SE15 140 C6
Ullswater Rd
SE27,SW16 160 D2
SW13 134 A5
Ulster Ct KT2 175 D4
Ulster Gdns N13 33 A6
Ulster Pl NW1 238 C5
Ulundi Rd SE3 142 C6
Ulva Rd SW15 134 D1
Ulverscroft Rd SE22 162 A6
Ulverston Rd E17 36 B1
Ulverstone Rd SE27 160 D2
Ulysses Rd NW6 69 B3
Umberston St E1 96 B1
Umbria St SW15 156 A5
Umfreville Rd N4 50 D3
Una Ho 7 NW5 71 B2
Under Cliff SE10 142 A4
Undercliff Rd SE13 141 D2
Underhill EN5 13 C6
Underhill Ct EN5 13 C6
Underhill Ho 7 E14 97 C2
Underhill Jun & Inf Schs EN5 13 A6
Underhill Pas NW1 231 D6
Underhill Rd SE21,SE22 162 B4
Underhill St NW1 231 D5
Underne Ave N14 15 B2
Undershaft EC3 95 C1 243 A1
Undershaw Rd BR1 164 D1
Underwood CR0 224 A3
Underwood Ct 3 E10 53 D1
Underwood Ho W6 112 B3
Underwood Rd E1 96 A3
E4 35 D5
Woodford IG8 37 D3
Underwood Row N1 235 B2
Underwood St N1 95 A4 235 B2
Underwood The SE9 166 B2
Undine Rd E14 119 D2
Undine St SW17 180 D5
Uneeda Dr UB6 86 B6
Unicorn Bldg 14 E1 118 D6
Unicorn Sch TW9 132 B4
Unicorn Works N17 34 C3
Union Ct SW4 138 A3
2 Richmond TW10 154 A6
Union Dr E1 97 A3
Union Gr SW8 137 D3
Union Mews SW9 138 A3
Union Rd N11 31 D4
SW8 137 D3
Bromley BR2 209 D4
Northolt UB5 85 C5
Thornton Heath CR0 205 A2
Wembley HA0 66 A2
Union Sq N1 95 A6 235 B5
Union St E15 98 A6
SE1 117 A5 252 A3
High Barnet EN5 1 A2
Kingston u T KT1 175 D1
Union Wlk E2 95 D4
Union Yd W1 238 D1
Unity Cl NW10 68 A2
SE19 183 A5
Unity Mews NW1 232 C4
Unity Rd EN3 6 C6
Unity Way SE18 121 D3
Univ Coll Jun Sch NW3 70 A4
Univ Coll London
W1 93 C2 239 B4
WC1 93 D3 239 C6
Univ College Hospl (Annexe) W1 93 A2 238 B4
Univ College London WC1 94 A3 240 B6
Univ of East London E15 76 C2
E15 98 B6
Dagenham RM8 80 A4
Univ of East London (Holbrook Centre) E15 98 D5
Univ of Greenwich (Rachel Mcmillan Campus) SE8 141 C6
Univ of Greenwich (Riverside Ho Annexe) SE18 122 C3
Univ of Greenwich Avery Hill Campus Mansion Site SE9 167 A5
Univ of Greenwich Avery Hill Campus Southwood Site SE9 167 B4
Univ of Greenwich The SW15 156 A4
Univ of Greenwich Woolwich Campus SE18 122 C2
Univ of London WC1 94 A4 233 A1
Univ of London (King's Coll Hall) SE5 139 B2
Univ of London (Queen Mary & Westfield Coll) E1 97 A3
Univ of London (Raymont Hall) SE4 141 B2
Univ of London Goldsmith's Coll SE14 141 A4
Univ of London Observatory NW7 27 D4
Univ of North London N7 72 C3
Univ of North London (Carleton Grange Hall) 2 N7 71 D4
Univ of Westminster
NW1 93 C3 239 A6
NW8 92 C3 237 A5
W1 93 C2 239 A3
W1 93 C2 239 A4
W1 93 C2 239 B3
W1 93 A2 238 A4
W1 93 B1 238 D2
Univ of Westminster (Harrow Campus) HA1 43 A2
University Cl NW7 27 D3
University Coll Hospl WC1 93 C3 239 B5
University College Sch NW3 70 A3
University Gdns DA5 169 B4
University Mans SW15 134 D2
University of North London (Tufnel Park Hall) N7 71 C5
University Pl DA8 147 D5
University Rd SW19 180 B4
University St WC1 93 C3 239 B5
Unwin Ave TW14 149 B6
Unwin Cl SE15 140 A6
Unwin Rd SW7 114 B3 256 D6
Isleworth TW7 130 C2
Upbrook Mews W2 92 A1 236 B1
Upcerne Rd SW10 136 A5 266 B3
Upchurch Cl SE20 184 B3
Upcott Ho 33 E3 97 D4
4 E9 74 C1
Upcroft Ave HA8 27 A6
Updale Rd DA14 189 D6
Upfield CR0 222 B5
Upfield Rd W7 86 D2
Upgrove Manor Way 12 SE24 160 C4
Uphall Prim Sch IG1 78 D3
Uphall Rd IG1 78 D3
Upham Park Rd W4 111 C2
Uphill Dr NW7 27 C5
NW9 45 A4
Uphill Gr NW7 27 C6
Uphill Rd NW7 27 C6
Upland Ct SE23 162 C2
Upland Inf Sch DA7 147 B2
Upland Jun Sch DA7 147 B2
Upland Rd 8 E13 99 A3
SE22 162 A5
Bexley DA7 147 B2
Croydon CR2 221 B3
Sutton SM2 218 B1
Uplands BR3 185 C1
Uplands Ave E17 34 D1
Uplands Bsns Pk E17 52 D6
Uplands Cl SW14 154 D6
Uplands Ct N21 16 C4
Uplands Park Rd EN2 4 C3
Uplands Rd N8 50 B4
East Barnet EN4 15 A3
Ilford RM6 58 D6
Woodford IG8 37 D3
Uplands The HA4 40 A1
Uplands Way N21 16 C6
Upnall Ho 16 SE15 140 C6
Upney La IG11 79 D1
Upney Sta IG11 79 D1
Upnor Way SE17 263 B2
Uppark Dr IG2 57 A3
Upper Abbey Rd DA17 125 C2
Upper Addison Gdns W14 113 A4 244 A2
Upper Belgrave St SW1 115 A3 258 B6
Upper Berkeley St W1 92 D1 237 D1
Upper Beulah Hill SE19 183 C2
Upper Brighton Rd KT6 198 A2
Upper Brockley Rd SE4 141 B3
Upper Brook St W1 115 A6 248 A6
Upper Butts TW8 131 C6
Upper Caldy Wlk 14 N1 73 A2
Upper Cheyne Row SW3 136 C6 267 A6
Upper Clapton Rd E5 74 B6
Upper Dengie Wlk N1 235 A6
Upper Elmers End Rd BR3 207 A4
Upper Farm Rd KT8 195 B5
Upper Fosters NW4 46 C5
Upper Gn E CR4 203 A6
Upper Gn W CR4 180 D1
Upper Gr SE25 205 D5
Upper Grosvenor St W1 115 A6 248 A5
Upper Grotto Rd TW1 152 D2
Upper Ground SE1 116 C5 251 A4
Upper Grove Rd DA17 147 B6
Upper Gulland Wlk 19 N1 73 A2
Upper Halliford Rd TW17 193 C6
Upper Halliford Sta TW16 171 C1
Upper Ham Rd KT2, TW10 175 D6
Upper Harley St NW1 238 B5
Upper Hawkwell Wlk N1 235 B6
Upper Holloway Sta N19 71 D6
Upper Holly Hill Rd DA17 125 D1
Upper James St W1 249 B6
Upper John St W1 249 B6
Upper Lodge Mews TW12 174 A4
Upper Mall W6 112 B1
Upper Marsh SE1 116 B4 260 D6
Upper Montague St W1 92 D2 237 C3
Upper Mulgrave Rd SM2 217 A1
Upper North St E3,E14 97 C2
Upper Park Rd N11 31 C5
NW3 70 D3
Belvedere DA17 125 D2
Bromley BR1 187 C2
Kingston u T KT2 176 C4
Upper Phillimore Gdns W8 113 C4 245 A1
Upper Pk IG10 21 D6
Upper Rawreth Wlk N1 235 B6
Upper Rd E13 99 A4
N2 30 C2
Wallington SM6 219 D3
Upper Richmond Rd SW15 134 C1
Upper Richmond Rd W TW10,SW14,SW15 133 A1
Upper Selsdon Rd CR2 221 D1
Upper Sheridan Rd DA17 125 C2
Upper Shirley Rd CR0 222 D5
Upper Sq TW7 131 A2
Upper St N1 94 D6 234 C5
Upper St Martin's La WC2 250 A6
Upper Sunbury Rd TW12 173 C2
Upper Sutton La TW5 129 C4
Upper Tachbrook St SW1 259 B4
Upper Teddington Rd KT1,KT8 175 C2
Upper Terr NW3 70 A5
Upper Thames St EC4 117 A6 252 B6
Upper Tollington Pk N4 50 C1
Upper Tooting Independent High Sch SW17 158 D2
Upper Tooting Park Mans 1 SW17 159 A2
Upper Tooting Pk SW17 158 D2
Upper Tooting Rd SW17 158 D1
Upper Town Rd UB6 85 D3
Upper Tulse Hill SW2 160 B3
Upper Vernon Rd SM1 218 B3
Upper Walthamstow Rd E17 54 B6
Upper Wickham La DA16 146 B4
Upper Wimpole St W1 93 A2 238 B4
Upper Woburn Pl NW1,WC1 93 D4 232 D1
Upperton Rd DA14 189 D5
Upperton Rd E E13 99 C4
Upperton Rd W E13 99 C4
Uppingham Ave HA7 25 C1
Upsdell Ave N13 32 C4
Upshire Ho E17 35 B1
Upstall St SE5 138 D4
Upton Ave E7 77 A1
Upton Cl DA5 169 B5
Upton Cross E13 99 A6
Upton Cross Prim Sch E13 99 B6
Upton Ct SE20 184 C3
4 SW19 178 D3
Southall UB1 107 D5
Upton Day Hospl DA6 147 A1
Upton Dene SM2 217 D1
Upton Gdns HA3 43 C3
Upton La E7 77 A1
Upton Lodge Cl WD23 8 A4
Upton Park Rd E7 77 B1
Upton Park Sta E13 99 C6
Upton Prim Sch DA5 169 B6
Upton Rd N18 34 A5
Upton Rd *continued*
SE18 145 A6
Bexley DA6 169 A6
Hounslow TW3 129 C2
South Norwood CR7 183 B1
Upton Rd S DA5 169 B5
Upton Villas 4 DA6 147 A1
Upway N12 30 C4
Upwood Rd SE12 165 A5
SW16 182 A2
Urlwin St SE5 139 A6
Urlwin Wlk SW9 138 D4
Urmston Dr SW19 157 A3
Urmston Ho 8 E14 120 A2
Urquhart Ct BR3 185 B3
Ursula Lo DA14 190 B5
Ursula Mews N4 51 A1
Ursula St SW11 136 C4 267 A1
Ursuline Convent Sch SW20 178 D2
Urswick Gdns RM9 81 A1
Urswick Rd E5,E9 74 C3
Dagenham RM9 81 A1
Usborne Mews SW8 270 D4
Usher Rd E3 97 B5
Usk Rd SW11 136 A1
Usk St E2 96 D4
Utopia Village NW1 71 A1 231 A6
Uvedale Rd
Dagenham RM10 81 C5
Enfield EN2 17 B6
Uverdale Rd SW10 136 A5 266 B3
Uxbridge Coll
Hayes UB3 106 A6
Uxbridge UB8 60 A2
Uxbridge High Sch UB8 82 A5
Uxbridge Rd W3,W5 110 C5
W12 112 B5
W13 109 C6
Feltham TW13 150 D2
Hampton TW12,TW13 173 D5
Hayes UB4 106 C6
Hillingdon UB10,UB4 83 C2
Kingston u T KT1,KT6 197 D4
Southall UB1,UB2,W5,W7 108 B5
Uxbridge Rd (Stanmore) HA7 25 A5
Uxbridge Road (Harrow Weald) HA3 24 B3
Uxbridge Road (Hatch End) HA5 23 B3
Uxbridge St W8 113 C5 245 A4
Uxendon Cres HA3,HA9 44 A1
Uxendon Hill HA9 44 B2
Uxendon Manor Prim Sch HA3 44 A4

V

Vaine Ho 4 E9 75 A2
Valan Leas BR2 208 C6
Valance Ave E4 20 D3
Vale Ave WD6 10 D6
Vale Cl N2 48 D6
W9 92 A4 229 A1
Locksbottom BR6 226 C4
Twickenham TW1 153 A1
Vale Cres SW15 177 C6
Vale Croft Claygate KT10 212 D1
Pinner HA5 41 A4
Vale Ct W3 111 D5
W9 92 A4 229 A1
Barnet EN5 1 D1
Wembley HA0 65 C5
Vale Dr EN5 13 C6
Vale End SE22 139 D1
Vale Est The W3 111 C5
Vale Farm Sports Ctr HA0 65 B4
Vale Gr N4 51 A2
W3 111 B5
Vale La W3 88 C2
Vale Lo SE23 162 C2
Vale of Health NW3 70 B5
Vale Rd E7 77 B2
N4 51 A2
Bickley BR1 188 C1
Claygate KT10 212 D1
Mitcham CR4 203 D5
Sutton SM1 217 D4
Worcester Pk KT19,KT4 215 D5
Vale Rd N KT6 214 A6
Vale Rise NW11 47 B1
Vale Road S KT6 214 A6
Vale Row N5 72 D5
Vale Royal N7 72 A1
Vale Sch The N4 51 B3
Vale Terr N4 51 A3
Vale The N10 31 A2
N14 16 A4
NW11 69 A6
SW3 136 B6 266 D6
W3 111 C5
Ashford TW16 172 A4
Croydon CR0 222 D6
Feltham TW14 150 B5
Heston TW5 129 A6
Ruislip HA4 62 C4
Woodford IG8 37 A3
Valence Ave RM8 80 D6
Valence Cir RM8 81 A5
Valence Jun & Inf Schs RM8 80 D6
Valence Wood Rd RM8 81 A5
Valencia Rd HA7 25 C6
Valens Ho 1 SW2 160 C3
Valentia Pl SW9 138 C1
Valentine Ave DA5 169 A3
Valentine Ct SE23 162 D2
Valentine Ho 11 SW4 159 C5
Valentine Pl SE1 116 D4 251 C2
Valentine Rd E9 74 D2
Harrow HA2 64 A5
Valentine Row SE1 251 C1
Valentines High Sch (Lower) IG2 56 D4
Valentines High Sch (Upper) IG2 56 C3
Valentines Rd IG1 56 D1
Valerian Way E15 98 C4
Valerie Ct Bushey WD2 8 A4
Sutton SM2 217 D1
Valeswood Rd BR1 186 D5
Valetta Gr E13 99 A5
Valetta Rd W3 111 D4
Valette Ct N10 49 B5
Valette Ho E9 74 C2
Valette St E8 74 B2
Valiant Cl 13 UB5 84 D4
Valiant Ho 5 SE7 121 C1
SW11 266 D1
Valiant Way E6 100 B2
Vallance Rd E1 96 A3
N22 31 C1
Vallentin Rd E17 54 A5
Valley (Charlton Athletic FC) The SE7 121 C1
Valley Ave N12 30 B6
Valley Cl HA5 22 B1
Valley Ct IG8 37 B3
Valley Dr NW9 44 D3
Valley Fields Cres EN2 4 C3
Valley Gdns SW19 180 B3
Wembley HA0 66 B1
Valley Gr SE7 121 C1
Valley Ho E5 52 C1
4 N9 18 A1
Valley L Ctr SE9 167 A4
Valley Mews TW1 153 A2
Valley Pl KT6 198 A3
Valley Prim Sch BR2 186 D1
Valley Prospect 3 SE19 183 C4
Valley Rd SW16 182 B6
Beckenham BR2 186 C1
St Paul's Cray BR5 190 B2
Uxbridge UB10 82 A5
Valley Side E4 19 C3
Valley Side Par E4 19 C2
Valley View EN5 13 A5
Valley Wlk CR0 222 C6
Valleyfield Rd SW16 182 B5
Valleylink Est EN3 19 A5
Valleyside SE7 121 D1
Valliere Rd NW10 90 A4
Valliers Wood Rd DA15 167 C3
Vallis Way W13 87 A2
Chessington KT9 213 D4
Valmar Rd SE5 139 A4
Valmar Trad Est 7 SE5 139 A4
Valnay St SW17 180 D5
Valognes Ave E17 35 A2
Valois Ho SE1 263 C6
Valonia Gdns SW18 157 B5
Vambery Rd SE18 145 A6
Van Dyck Ave KT3 199 B2
Van Gogh Ct E14 120 B3
Vanbern Ho NW5 71 A2
Vanborough Ct 4 SM2 218 A2
Vanbrough Cres UB5 84 C6
Vanbrugh Ct SE11 261 B3
Vanbrugh Dr KT12 194 C3
Vanbrugh Fields SE3 142 D5
Vanbrugh Hill SE10,SE3 142 D6
Vanbrugh Ho 8 E9 74 C1
Vanbrugh Mews KT12 194 C2
Vanbrugh Park Rd SE3 142 D5
Vanbrugh Park Rd W SE3 142 D5
Vanbrugh Pk SE3 142 D5
Vanbrugh Rd W4 111 B3
Vanbrugh Terr SE3 142 D4
Vanburgh Cl 2 E16 99 D2
Orpington BR6 211 C1
Vanburgh Ho E1 243 C4
Vancouver Rd SE23 163 B2
Edgware HA8 26 D2
Hayes UB4 84 B3
Richmond TW10 175 C6
Vancover Ho 33 E1 118 B5
Vanderbilt Rd SW18 158 A3
Vanderbilt Villas 1 W12 112 D4
Vandome Cl E16 99 B1
Vandon Ct SW1 259 B6
Vandon Pas SW1 259 B6
Vandon St SW1 259 B6
Vandy St EC2 243 A5
Vandyke Cl SW15 156 D5
Vandyke Cross SE9 166 A6
Vane Cl NW3 70 B4
Harrow HA3 44 B3
Vane Ho 15 N2 30 B1
Vane St SW1 259 B4
Vanessa Cl DA17 125 C1
Vanfame Ct KT3 199 D6
Vange Ho W10 90 C2
Vanguard Cl E16 99 B2
Thornton Heath CR0 204 D1
Vanguard Ho 7 SW19 180 A3
6 Stanwell TW19 148 A5
Vanguard St SE8 141 C4

Vanguard Way SM6 220 A1
Vanneck Sq SW15 156 A6
Vanoc Gdns BR1 187 A6
Vansittart Rd E7 77 A4
Vansittart St 7 SE14 141 A5
Vanston Pl SW6 135 C5 265 B4
Vant Rd SW17 180 D5
Vantage Mews E14 120 A5
Vantrey Ho SE11 261 A3
Varcoe Rd SE16 118 C1
Varden St E1 96 B1
Vardens Rd SW11 136 B1
Vardon Cl W3 89 B1
Vardon Ho SE10 142 A4
Varey Ho E1 97 A4
Varley Ho 5 NW6 91 C6
Varley Par NW9 45 C5
Varley Rd E16 99 B1
Varley Way CR4 180 B1
Varna Rd SW6 135 B5 264 C3
Hampton TW12 173 D2
Varndell St NW1 93 C4 232 A2
Varsity Dr TW1,TW7 152 D5
Varsity Row SW14 133 A3
Vartry Rd N15 51 C3
Vassal Ho E3 97 A4
Vassall Rd SW9 138 C5
Vat Ho SW8 270 B4
Vauban Est SE16 263 D5
Vauban St SE16 117 D3 263 D5
Vaudeville Ct N4 72 C6
Vaughan Almshouses
TW15 170 D5
Vaughan Ave NW4 46 A4
W6 111 D2
Vaughan Est 3 E2 95 D4
Vaughan Fst & Mid Sch
HA1 42 A3
Vaughan Gdns IG1 56 B2
Vaughan Ho SE1 251 C2
Vaughan Rd E15 76 D2
SE5 139 A2
Bexley DA16 145 D3
Harrow HA1 42 B3
Thames Ditton KT7 197 B2
Vaughan St SE16 119 B4
Vaughan Way E1 118 A5
Vaughan Williams Cl
SE8 141 C5
Vauxhall Bridge Rd
SW1 115 C2 259 B3
Vauxhall Cross
SE1,SW8 116 A1 260 B1
Vauxhall Gdns CR2 221 A2
Vauxhall Gr
SW8 138 B6 270 C6
Vauxhall Prim Sch
SE11 116 B1 260 D2
Vauxhall St
SE11 116 B1 260 D2
Vauxhall Sta
SE11 116 A1 260 B1
Vauxhall Wlk SE11 260 C2
Vawdrey Cl E1 96 C3
Vaynor Ho N7 72 A4
Veals Mead CR4 180 C2
Vectis Ct SW18 157 D5
Vectis Gdns SW17 181 B4
Vectis Rd SW17 181 B4
Veda Rd SE13 141 C1
Vega Cres HA6 22 A5
Vega Rd WD2 8 A4
Velde Way 1 SE22 161 C6
Veldene Way HA2 63 B5
Vellacott Ho W12 90 B1
Velletri Ho 17 E2 96 D5
Vellum Dr SM5 219 A5
Venables Cl RM10 81 D4
Venables St NW8 92 B2 236 D4
Vencourt Pl W6 112 A2
Venetia Rd N4 50 D3
W5 109 D4
Venetian Rd SE5 139 A3
Venice Ct 14 SE5 139 A5
Venita Manor SE27 182 C5
Venmead Ct DA17 125 C2
Venn Ho N1 233 D5
Venn St SW4 137 C1
Venner Rd SE26 184 C5
Ventnor Ave HA7 25 B1
Ventnor Dr N20 13 D2
Ventnor Gdns IG11 79 C2
Ventnor Mans IG11 79 C2
Ventnor Rd SE14 140 D5
Sutton SM2 217 D1
Ventnor Terr N15 52 A5
Venture Cl DA5 169 A4
Venture Ct 3 SE12 165 A4
Venue St E14 98 A2
Venus Rd SE18 122 B3
Vera Ave N21 16 C6
Vera Ct 1 W2 91 D1
Vera Lynn Cl 5 E7 77 A4
Vera Rd SW6 135 A4 264 B2
Verbena Cl E16 98 D3
Verbena Gdns W6 112 A1
Verdant Ct 3 SE6 164 C4
Verdant La SE6 164 C3
Verdayne Ave CR0 222 D6
Verdi Ho 2 NW6 91 A5
Verdun Rd SE18,SE2 146 A6
SW13 134 A5
Vere Bank SW19 157 B3
Vere St W1 93 B1 238 C1
Vereker Dr TW16 194 A6
Vereker Rd W14 254 B1
Verity Cl W11 91 A1
Verity Ct N9 18 D3
Verity Ho 15 E3 97 B4
Vermeer Ct E14 120 B3
Vermont Cl EN2 4 D1
Vermont Ho E17 35 B1
Vermont Rd SE19 183 C4
SW18 157 D5
Sutton SM1 217 D5
Verne Ct 9 W3 111 A3
Verney Gdns RM9 81 A4
Verney Ho NW8 237 A6
Hounslow TW3 130 A1
Verney Rd SE16 118 B1
Dagenham RM9 81 A4
Verney St NW10 67 B5
Verney Way SE16 118 B1
Vernham Rd SE18 145 A6
Vernon Ave E12 78 B4
SW20 178 D1
Woodford IG8 37 B3
Vernon Cl KT19 215 A2
Vernon Cres EN4 15 A5
Vernon Ct NW2 69 B5
W5 109 C6
Stanmore HA7 25 B2
Vernon Dr HA7 25 A2
Vernon Ho NW9 45 D4
SE11 260 D1
Vernon House Sch
NW10 67 B3
Vernon Mews W14 254 B3
Vernon Pl WC1 240 B3
Vernon Rd E3 97 B5
E11 54 C1
E15 76 C1
E17 53 B4
N8 50 C6
SW14 133 B2
Feltham TW13 149 D2
Ilford IG3 57 D1
Sutton SM1 218 B3
Vernon Rise WC1 233 D2
Greenford UB6 64 B3
Vernon Sq WC1 233 D2
Vernon St W14 113 A2 254 B3
Vernon Yd W11 113 B6 244 C6
Veroan Rd DA7 147 A3
Verona Ct 10 SE14 140 D6
Verona Dr KT6 214 A6
Verona Rd E7 77 A1
Veronica Gdns CR4,
SW16 181 C2
Veronica Ho SE4 141 B2
Veronica Rd SW17 159 B2
Veronique Gdns IG6 57 A4
Verran Rd SW12 159 B4
Versailles Rd SE20 184 A3
Verulam Ave E17 53 B2
Verulam Ct NW9 46 A2
4 Southall UB1 86 A1
Verulam Ho 1 W6 112 C4
Verulam Rd UB6 85 C3
Verulam St EC1 94 C2 241 A4
Vervain Ho 2 SE15 140 A5
Verwood Dr EN4 2 D2
Verwood Ho SW8 270 D3
Verwood Lo 1 E14 120 B2
Verwood Rd HA2 24 A1
Veryan Ct 2 N8 49 D4
Vesage Ct EC1 241 B3
Vesey Gdns RM10 81 C5
Vesey Path 15 E14 97 D1
Vespan Rd W12 112 A4
Vesta Rd SE4,SE14 141 A3
Vestris Rd SE23 162 D2
Vestry House (Mus) E17 53 D5
Vestry Mews 12 SE5 139 C4
Vestry Rd E17 53 D5
SE5 139 C4
Vestry St N1 95 B4 235 C2
Vevey St SE23,SE6 163 B2
Vi & John Rubens Ho
IG2 56 C3
Viaduct Pl 23 E2 96 B4
Viaduct Rd N2 30 C1
Viaduct St E2 96 B4
Viaduct The E18 37 B1
Harrow HA2 64 A5
Wembley HA0 88 A6
Vian St SE13 141 D2
Viant Ho 11 NW10 67 B1
Vibart Gdns SW2 160 B4
Vibart Wlk N1 233 B6
Vic Johnson Ho 14 E3 97 B6
Vicarage Ave SE3 143 A5
Vicarage Cl
New Malden KT4 199 C1
Northolt UB5 63 B1
Ruislip HA4 39 B2
Vicarage Cres
SW11 136 B4 266 C1
Vicarage Ct N12 29 D5
7 SW15 156 A4
W8 245 C2
Beckenham BR3 207 A6
East Bedfont TW14 149 A4
Vicarage Dr SW14 155 B6
Barking IG11 79 A1
Beckenham BR3 185 C2
Vicarage Farm Ct TW5 129 B5
Vicarage Farm Rd TW3,
TW4,TW5 129 A4
Vicarage Fields KT12 194 C3
Vicarage Fields Sh Ctr The
IG11 79 A1
Vicarage Gate
W8 113 D5 245 C3
Vicarage Gdns SW14 155 B6
W8 245 B3
Vicarage Gdns *continued*
Mitcham CR4 202 C6
Vicarage Gr SE5 139 B4
Vicarage Ho 1 KT1 176 B1
Vicarage La E6 100 C4
E15 76 D1
Ilford IG1 57 B1
Vicarage Pk SE18 123 A1
Vicarage Prim Sch E6 100 B4
Vicarage Rd E10 53 D1
E15 76 D1
N17 34 A2
NW4 46 A3
SE18 123 A1
SW14 155 B6
Ashford TW16 171 D4
Croydon CR0 220 C5
Dagenham RM10 81 D1
Kingston u T KT1,KT2 175 D1
Old Bexley DA5 169 D3
Strawberry Hill TW2 152 C2
Sutton SM1 217 D5
Teddington KT1,KT8 175 C2
Teddington TW11 175 A5
Twickenham TW2 152 A5
Vicarage Way NW10 67 B5
Harrow HA2 41 C2
Vicarage Wlk
SW11 136 B4 266 D2
Vicars Bridge Cl HA0 88 A5
Vicar's Cl E9 96 C6
E15 99 A6
Enfield EN1 5 C3
Vicar's Green Cty Prim Sch
HA0 87 C5
Vicars Hill SE13 141 D1
Vicar's Moor La N21 16 D4
Vicars Oak Rd SE19 183 C4
Vicar's Rd NW5 71 A3
Vicar's Wlk RM8 80 B5
Viceroy Cl N2 48 C6
Viceroy Ct NW8 230 B4
5 Croydon CR0 205 B1
Viceroy Lo 6 KT6 198 A4
Viceroy Par N2 48 C6
Viceroy Rd SW8 138 A4 270 A2
Vickers Ct 10 TW19 148 A5
Vickery Ct EC1 242 B6
Victor Cazalet Ho N1 234 C6
Victor Gr HA0 66 A1
Victor Ho N20 14 D1
Victor Mills Cotts BR8 191 C3
Victor Rd NW10 90 B4
SE20 184 D3
Harrow HA2 42 A6
Teddington TW11 174 C6
Victor Seymour Inf Sch
SM5 218 D4
Victor Villas N9 17 B1
Victoria & Albert Mus★
SW7 114 B3 256 D5
Victoria Arc SW1 258 D5
Victoria Ave E6 99 D6
EC2 243 B3
N3 29 B2
Barnet EN4 2 B1
East Molesey KT8 195 D6
Hackbridge SM5,SM6 219 A5
Hillingdon UB10 60 D1
Hounslow TW3,TW4 151 C6
Kingston u T KT6 197 D3
Wembley HA9 66 D2
Victoria Bglws DA14 191 B3
Victoria Bldgs 18 E8 96 B6
Victoria Bsns Ctr DA16 146 B3
Victoria Cl Barnet EN4 2 B1
East Molesey KT8 195 C6
Harrow HA1 42 D3
Hayes UB3 83 B1
Victoria Coach Sta
SW1 115 B2 258 C3
Victoria Cotts N10 31 A1
Ilford IG6 57 A4
7 Richmond TW9 132 C4
3 E1 96 A2
Victoria Cres N15 51 C4
SE19 183 C4
SW19 179 B3
Victoria Ct 3 E1 118 A6
1 E18 55 B6
SE26 184 C4
5 SW4 159 D5
W3 110 C4
Wembley HA9 66 C2
Victoria Dock Rd E16 121 B6
Victoria Dr SW19 156 D3
Victoria Emb
WC2 116 C6 251 A5
Victoria Gdns
W11 113 C5 245 A4
Heston TW5 129 A4
Victoria Gr N12 30 B5
W8 114 A3 256 A6
Victoria Gr Mews W2 245 C5
Victoria Ho SW1 258 C2
6 SW4 159 D5
2 W12 112 A4
Edgware HA8 26 D4
Victoria Ind Est W3 89 C2
Victoria Jun Sch The
TW13 150 B3
Victoria La
Chipping Barnet EN5 1 B1
Hayes UB3 105 B1
Victoria Lo 4 SW19 178 C3
Victoria Mans 8 N7 72 C3
NW10 68 B1
Victoria Mews NW6 91 C6
Victoria Mews *continued*
SW18 158 A3
Victoria Park Ct 11 E9 74 C1
Victoria Park Ind Ctr E3 75 B1
Victoria Park Rd E9 74 D1
Victoria Park Sq E2 96 C4
Victoria Pas NW8 236 C6
Victoria Pl 16 TW10 153 D6
Victoria Point 10 E13 99 A5
Victoria Rd E4 20 C3
E11 76 C4
E13 99 A5
E17 36 A1
E18 55 B6
N4 50 B1
N9 17 D1
N15 52 A5
N18 33 D6
N22 31 D2
NW4 46 D5
NW6 91 B6
NW7 27 D5
NW10 89 C3
SW14 133 B2
W5 87 B2
W8 114 A3 256 A6
Barking IG11 78 D2
Bexleyheath DA6 147 C1
Bromley BR2 209 D4
Buckhurst Hill IG9 21 D2
Chislehurst West BR7 188 C5
Dagenham RM10 81 D3
Feltham TW13 150 B3
Kingston u T KT1 176 B1
Kingston u T KT6 197 D3
Mitcham CR4 180 D3
New Barnet EN4 2 B1
Ruislip HA4 62 B4
Sidcup DA15 168 A1
Southall UB2 107 B3
Sutton SM1 218 B3
Teddington TW11 175 A4
Twickenham TW1 153 B4
Victoria Ret Pk HA4 62 D3
Victoria Rise SW4 137 B2
Victoria Sq SW1 258 D6
Victoria St E15 76 C1
SW1 115 C3 259 B5
Erith DA17 125 B1
Victoria Sta
SW1 115 B2 258 D4
Victoria Terr N4 50 C1
NW10 89 C3
Harrow HA1 42 C1
Victoria Villas TW9 132 B1
Victoria Way SE7 143 C6
Victorian Gr N16 73 C5
Victorian Rd N16 73 D5
Victors Dr TW12 173 A4
Victors Way EN5 1 B2
Victory Ave SM4 202 A4
Victory Bsns Ctr The
TW7 130 D1
Victory Pl 6 E14 119 A6
SE17 117 B2 262 C4
SE19 183 C4
Victory Prim Sch
SE17 117 A2 262 B4
Victory Rd E11 55 B5
SW19 180 A3
Victory Road Mews 5
SW19 180 A3
Victory Way SE16 119 A4
Heston TW5 106 C1
Victory Wharf E14 119 A6
Victory Wlk SE8 141 C4
Video Ct N4 50 A2
Vidler Cl KT9 213 C2
Vienna Cl IG5 37 D1
View Cl N6 48 D2
Harrow HA1 42 B5
View Cres N8 49 D4
View Point SE3 142 D2
View Rd N6 48 D3
View The SE2 125 A1
Viewfield Cl HA3 44 A2
Viewfield Rd SW18 157 B5
Bexley DA5 168 C3
Viewland Rd SE18 123 D1
Viewside Lo N6 49 C3
Viga Rd N21 16 C5
Vigilant Cl SE26 184 A6
Vignoles Rd RM7 59 C2
Vigo St W1 115 C6 249 A5
Viking Cl 12 E3 97 A5
Viking Ct TW12 173 D2
Viking Gdns E6 100 A3
Viking Ho 3 SE5 139 A3
3 SE7 122 A2
Viking Pl E10 53 B1
Viking Prim Sch UB5 84 D4
Viking Rd UB1 107 A6
Villa Rd SW9 138 C2
Villa St SE17 117 B1 262 D1
Villacourt Rd SE18,SE2 146 A6
Village Arc The 2 E4 20 B3
Village Cl E4 36 A5
NW3 70 B3
Village Ct E17 53 D4
SE3 142 C2
Village Gate TW17 192 D4
Village Home The IG6 57 A6
Village Hts IG8 36 D5
Village Inf Sch RM10 81 C1
Village Mount 18 NW3 70 A4
Village Park Cl EN1 17 C5
Village Rd N3 29 A1
Enfield EN1 17 C6
Village Row SM2 217 C1
Village Sch The NW3 70 D2
Village The SE7 143 D6
SW11 136 D2
Village Way NW10 67 B4
SE21 161 B5
Ashford TW15 170 C6
Beckenham BR3 207 C6
Pinner HA5 41 B2
Village Way E HA2 41 C2
Villas Rd SE18 123 A2
Villiers Ave
Kingston u T KT5 198 B5
Twickenham TW2 151 B3
Villiers Cl E10 75 C6
Kingston u T KT5 198 B5
Villiers Ct N20 14 A4
SW11 267 B2
Villiers High Sch UB1 107 B5
Villiers Ho 15 E9 96 C6
W5 109 D6
Villiers Rd NW2 68 A2
Hounslow TW7 130 C3
Kingston u T KT1 198 B6
Penge BR3 184 D1
Southall UB1 107 B5
Villiers St WC2 250 B4
Vincam Cl TW2 151 C4
Vince Ct N1 235 D1
Vince St EC1 95 B4 235 D1
Vincent Ave KT5 215 A6
Vincent Cl Barnet EN5 1 D2
Bromley BR2 209 B5
Harmondsworth UB7 126 C6
Sidcup DA15 167 C3
Vincent Ct N4 50 A1
NW4 46 D5
SW9 270 D1
W1 237 C2
Vincent Dr
Hillingdon UB10 82 B6
Upper Halliford TW17 193 C6
Vincent Gdns NW2 67 D5
Vincent Ho KT3 199 D5
Vincent Rd E4 36 B4
N15 51 A5
N22 32 C1
SE18 122 D2
W3 111 A3
Croydon CR0 205 C2
Dagenham RM9 81 A1
Hounslow TW4 128 D2
Hounslow TW7 130 B4
Kingston u T KT1 198 C6
Wembley HA0 66 B1
Vincent Row TW12 174 A5
Vincent Sq N22 32 C1
SW1 115 D2 259 C4
Vincent St E16 98 D2
SW1 115 D2 259 D4
Vincent Terr N1 94 D5 234 D4
Vincents Cl SE16 119 A4
Vincents Path UB5 63 A2
Vine Cl Surbiton KT5 198 B3
Sutton SM1 218 A5
West Drayton UB7 104 C2
Vine Cotts 3 W7 108 C5
Southall UB2 107 D2
Vine Ct E1 96 A2
Harrow HA3 44 A3
Vine Gdns IG1 79 A3
Vine Gr UB10 60 C1
Vine Hill EC1 241 A5
Vine La SE1 117 C5 253 B3
Hillingdon UB10 82 B6
Vine Lo N12 30 A4
Vine Pl W5 110 A5
Hounslow TW3 129 D1
Vine Rd SW13 133 D2
East Molesey KT8 196 A5
Green St Gn BR6 227 D2
Vine Sq W14 254 D1
Vine St EC3 95 D1 243 C1
W1 249 B5
Vine St Bridge EC1 241 B5
Vine Yd SE1 252 B2
Vinegar St E1 118 B5
Vinegar Yd SE1 253 A2
Vineries Bank NW7 28 B5
Vineries Cl
Dagenham RM9 81 B2
Harmondsworth UB7 126 C6
Vineries The N14 15 C5
Enfield EN1 5 C2
Viners Cl KT12 194 C3
Vines Ave N3 29 D2
Vines Prim Sch The
SW11 137 A1
Vinewood Ct E17 54 B4
Viney Ct 9 SW4 159 D5
Viney Rd SE13 141 D2
Vineyard Ave NW7 29 A3
Vineyard Cl SE6 163 C3
Kingston u T KT1 198 B6
Vineyard Gr N3 29 D2
Vineyard Hill Rd SW19 179 C6
Vineyard Path SW14 133 B2
Vineyard Rd TW13 150 A1
Vineyard Row KT1,KT8 175 C2
Vineyard Sch The
TW10 154 A5
Vineyard The TW10 154 A6
Vineyard Wlk EC1 241 A6
Vineyards The TW13 150 A1
Vining St SW2,SW9 138 C1
Vinlake Ave UB10 60 C5
Vinson Ho N1 235 D3
Vinter Ct TW17 192 C4
Vintners Ct EC4 252 B6
Vintry Mews 3 E17 53 C5
Viola Ave SE2 124 B1
Feltham TW14 150 C5
Stanwell TW19 148 A3
Viola Sq W12 111 D6
Violet Ave Enfield EN2 5 B5
Hillingdon UB8 82 B2
Violet Cl SM6 203 A1
Violet Gdns CR0 220 D3
Violet Hill NW8 92 A5 229 A3
Violet Hill Ho NW8 229 A3
Violet La CR0 220 D3
Violet Rd E3 97 D3
E17 53 C3
E18 37 B1
Violet St E2 96 B3
Violet Terr UB8 82 C2
Violette Szabo Ho 4
SE27 183 B6
VIP Trad Est SE7 121 C2
Virgil Pl W1 237 C3
Virgil St SE1 116 B3 260 D6
Virginia Cl KT3 199 A5
Virginia Ct 7 SE16 118 D4
Virginia Ho 3 E14 120 A6
Teddington TW11 175 A5
Virginia JMI Sch E2 95 D4
Virginia Rd 19 E2 95 D4
South Norwood CR7 182 D2
Virginia St E1 118 A6
Virginia Wlk SW2 160 B5
Viscount Cl N11 31 B5
Viscount Ct 9 W11 91 C1
Viscount Dr E6 100 B2
Viscount Gr 3 UB5 84 D4
Viscount Point 7
SW19 179 C3
Viscount Rd TW19 148 A3
Viscount St EC1 242 A4
Viscount Way TW6 127 C1
Vista Ave EN3 6 D3
Vista Dr IG4 55 D4
Vista The SE9 165 D4
Vista Way HA3 44 A3
Vita Et Pax Sch N14 15 B6
Vittoria Ho N1 233 D5
Vittoria Prim Sch
N1 94 C5 234 A4
Viveash Cl UB3 105 D3
Vivian Ave NW4 46 B4
Wembley HA9 66 C2
Vivian Ct N12 29 D5
Vivian Gdns HA9 66 C3
Vivian Ho N4 51 B2
Vivian Mans 1 NW4 46 B4
Vivian Rd E3 97 A5
Vivian Sq SE15 140 B2
Vivian Way N2 48 B4
Vivien Cl KT9 214 A1
Vivienne Cl TW1 153 D5
Voce Rd SE18 145 B5
Voewood Cl KT3 199 D3
Vogans Mill SE1 253 D2
Vogler Ho 6 E1 118 C6
Vollasky Ho 5 E1 96 A2
Volta Way CR0 204 B1
Voltaire 2 SE5 139 D4
15 Richmond TW9 132 B4
Voltaire Ct 12 SW11 137 A3
Voltaire Rd SW4 137 D2
Voltaire Way UB3 105 C6
Voluntary Pl E11 55 A3
Vorley Rd N19 71 C6
Voss Ct SW16 182 A4
Voss St E2 96 A4
Voyager Bsns Est 10
SE16 118 A3
Vulcan Cl SM6 220 B1
Vulcan Gate EN2 4 C3
Vulcan Rd SE4 141 B3
Vulcan Sq E14 119 C2
Vulcan Terr SE4 141 B3
Vulcan Way N7 72 B2
Vyne The DA7 147 D2
Vyner Ct E5 74 A6
Vyner Rd W3 111 B6
Vyner St E2 96 B6
Vyners Sch UB10 60 B4
Vyners Way UB10 60 C3
Vyvyan Ho SE18 144 C4

W

Wadding St
SE17 117 B2 262 C3
Waddington Cl EN1 5 C1
Waddington Rd E15 76 B2
Waddington St E15 76 B2
Waddington Way SE19 183 B2
Waddon Cl CR0 220 C5
Waddon Court Rd CR0 220 C5
Waddon Inf Sch CR9 220 C3
Waddon Marsh Sta
CR0 220 C6
Waddon Marsh Way
CR0 204 B1
Waddon New Rd CR0 220 D6
Waddon Park Ave CR0 220 C5
Waddon Rd CR0 220 D5
Waddon Sta CR0 220 C4
Waddon Way CR0,CR2,
CR9 220 D2
Wade Ct N10 31 B3

Wade Ct *continued*
Wembley HA0 ....65 D5
Wade Ho 13 SE1 ....118 A4
1 Enfield EN1 ....17 C6
Wade's Gr N21 ....16 C4
Wade's Hill N21 ....16 C4
Wade's La TW11 ......175 A5
Wade's Pl E14 ....119 D6
Wadeson St E2 ....96 B5
Wadeville Ave RM6 .....59 B2
Wadeville Cl DA17 ......125 C1
Wadham Ave E17 ....35 D3
Wadham Cl TW17 ......193 A2
Wadham Gdns
NW3 ....70 C1 230 A6
Northolt UB6 ....64 B2
Wadham Rd E17 ....35 D2
SW15 ....135 A1
Wadhurst Cl SE20 .....184 B1
Wadhurst Ct E6 ....100 C5
Wadhurst Rd W4 ....111 B3
Wadley Rd E11 ....54 C2
Wadsworth Bsns Ctr
UB6 ....87 C5
Wadsworth Cl
Enfield EN3 ....18 D6
Wembley UB6 ....87 C5
Wadsworth Rd UB6 .....87 C5
Wager St E3 ....97 B3
Waggoners Rdbt TW5 .128 B4
Waghorn Rd E13 ....99 C6
Harrow HA3 ....43 D6
Waghorn St SE15 ......140 A2
Wagner St SE15 ....140 C5
Wagon Rd EN6,EN5 ....1 D6
Wagstaff Gdns RM9 .....80 C1
Waights Ct KT2 ....176 A2
Waikato Lo IG9 ....21 C3
Wainford Cl SW19 .....156 D3
Wainwright Gr TW7 ...130 B1
Wainwright Ho 3 E1 ...118 C5
SW8 ....269 C1
Waite Davies Rd SE12 .164 D4
Waite St SE15 ....139 D6
Waitelands Ho KT3 ....199 B5
Waithman St EC4 ......241 C1
Wakefield Gdns SE19 ..183 C3
Redbridge IG1 ....56 A3
Wakefield Ho 6 SE15 .140 A4
SE22 ....162 B3
Wakefield Mews WC1 ..233 B1
Wakefield Rd N11 ......31 D5
N15 ....51 D4
19 Richmond TW10 ....153 D6
Wakefield St E6 ....100 A6
N18 ....34 A5
WC1 ....94 A4 233 B1
Wakeham St 9 N1 ......73 B2
Wakehams Hill HA5 .....41 B6
Wakehurst Rd SW11 ...158 D6
Wakelin Ho 19 N1 .....72 D1
SE23 ....163 A4
Wakelin Rd E15 ....98 C5
Wakeling Ho 8 SE27 ..160 D1
Wakeling Rd W7 ....86 D2
Wakeling St 13 E14 ....97 A1
Wakelyn Ho 14 E9 ......96 C6
Wakeman Ho HA8 ....26 A6
Wakeman Rd NW10 .....90 D4
Wakemans Hill Ave NW9 45 B4
Wakering Rd IG11 ......79 A1
Wakerings The IG11 ....79 A2
Wakerly Cl 6 E6 ......100 B1
Wakley St EC1 ..94 D4 234 C2
Walberswick St SW8 ..270 B3
Walbrook 9 E18 ....55 A6
EC4 ....252 C6
Walburgh St E1 ....96 B1
Walcorde Ave SE17 ....262 B3
Walcot Ct CR0 ....222 A6
Walcot Gdns SE11 .....261 A4
Walcot Ho 9 SE22 .....139 C2
Walcot Rd EN3 ....7 B3
Walcot Sq SE11 116 C2 261 B4
Walcott St SW1 ....259 B4
Waldair Ct E16 ....122 D4
Waldeck Gr SE27 ......160 D1
Waldeck Rd N15 ....50 D6
SW14 ....133 A2
W4 ....132 C6
W13 ....87 B1
Waldeck Terr SW14 ....133 A2
Waldegrave Ct
11 Barking IG11 ....101 B6
1 Teddington TW11 ....174 D5
Waldegrave Gdns TW1 152 D1
Waldegrave Ho 5
SW15 ....156 C6
Waldegrave Pk TW1 ...174 D6
Waldegrave Rd N8 .....50 C6
SE19 ....183 D3
W5 ....110 B6
Bromley BR1 ....210 B5
Dagenham RM8 ....80 C6
Teddington TW11 ......174 D6
Waldegrave Sch for Girls
TW2 ....152 B1
Waldegrove CR0 ....221 D5
Waldemar Ave SW6 ...135 A3
W13 ....109 C5
Waldemar Avenue Mans
SW6 ....264 A1
Waldemar Rd SW19 ...179 C5
Walden Ave N13 ....33 A6
Chislehurst West BR7 ...188 B6
Walden Cl DA17 ....125 B1
Walden Ct SW8 ....269 D2
Walden Gdns CR7,SW16 204 B5
Walden Ho SW1 ....258 B3
8 SW11 ....137 A3
Barnet EN4 ....2 C1
Walden Rd N17 ....33 B2
Chislehurst West BR7 ...188 B4
Walden St E1 ....96 B1
Walden Way NW7 ....28 D4
Waldenshaw Rd SE23 ..162 C3
Waldo Cl SW4 ....159 C6
Waldo Ind Est BR1 ....209 D6
Waldo Pl SW19 ....180 C3
Waldo Rd NW10 ....90 B4
Bromley BR1 ....209 D6
Waldorf Cl CR2 ....220 D1
Waldram Cres SE23 ...162 C3
Waldram Park Rd SE23 162 D3
Waldram Pl 6 SE23 ...162 C3
Waldrist Way DA18 ...125 B4
Waldron Gdns BR2 ....208 B6
Waldron Ho 17 SW2 ...160 B6
Waldron Mews SW3 ...266 D6
Waldron Rd SW18 .....158 A1
Harrow HA1,HA2 ....42 C1
Waldronhyrst CR0,CR2 .220 D4
Waldrons The CR0 .....221 A4
Waldron's Yd HA2 ......64 B6
Waldstock Rd SE28 ...124 A6
Waleran Cl HA7 ....24 D4
Waleran Flats SE1 .....263 A4
Walerand Rd SE13 .....142 A3
Wales Ave SM5 ....218 C3
Wales Farm Rd W3 .....89 B2
Waleton Acres SM6 ...219 C2
Waley St 1 E1 ....97 A2
Walfield Ave N20 ....13 D4
Walford Ct SE1 ....263 B6
Walford High Sch UB5 ..85 A6
Walford Ho 4 E1 ....96 B1
Walford Rd N16 ....73 C4
Walfrey Gdns RM9 ......81 A1
Walham Ct 15 NW3 .....70 D2
Walham Gr
SW6 ....135 C5 265 A4
Walham Green Arc
SW6 ....265 B4
Walham Rise 1 SW19 .179 A4
Walham Yd SW6 ....265 A4
Walk The N13 ....16 C1
Ashford TW16 ....171 D3
Walkden Hall (Hall of
Residence) KT2 ....177 B6
Walkden Rd BR7 ......188 C5
Walker Cl N11 ....31 C6
SE18 ....123 A2
W7 ....108 C5
East Bedfont TW14 ....149 D4
Hampton TW12 ....173 B4
Walker Ho NW1 ....232 C3
Walker Prim Sch N14 ..15 D2
Walker's Ct W1 ....249 C6
Walker's Pl SW15 .....135 A1
Walkerscroft Mead
SE21 ....161 A3
Walkinshaw Ct 14 N1 ...73 A1
Walks The N2 ....48 B6
Walkynscroft 1 SE15 ..140 B3
Wall Ct N4 ....50 B1
Wall End Ct E6 ....100 C6
Wall End Rd E6 ....78 C1
Wall St N1 ....73 B2
Wallace Cl SE28 ......124 D6
Upper Halliford TW17 ..193 B5
Uxbridge UB10 ....82 A5
Wallace Collection*
W1 ....238 A2
Wallace Cres SM5 ....218 D3
Wallace Ho N7 ....72 B2
Wallace Rd N1,N5 ....73 A2
Wallasey Cres UB10 ....60 C5
Wallbrook Bsns Ctr
TW4 ....128 B2
Wallbrook Ho N9 ....18 C2
Wallbutton Rd SE4 ....141 A3
Wallcote Ave NW2 ......46 D1
Walled Gdn The TW16 .194 B6
Waller Dr HA6 ....22 A2
Waller Rd SE14 ....140 D3
Wallers Cl RM9 ....103 B6
Wallett Ct 9 NW1 ......71 C1
Wallflower St W12 .....111 D6
Wallgrave Rd SW5 ....255 C3
Wallingford Ave W10 ...90 D1
Wallington Cl HA4 ......39 A3
Wallington Ct 10 SM6 ..219 B2
Wallington Green SM6 .219 B4
Wallington High Sch for
Boys SM6 ....219 B5
Wallington Rd IG3 ......57 D2
Wallington Sq 4 SM6 .219 C2
Wallington Sta SM6 ...219 B2
Wallis Alley SE1 ....252 B2
Wallis Cl SW11 ....136 B2
Wallis Rd E9 ....75 C2
Southall UB1 ....85 D1
Wallorton Gdns SW14 .133 B1
Wallside EC2 ....242 B3
Wallwood Rd E11 ....54 B2
Wallwood St E14 ....97 B2
Walm La NW2 ....68 C2
Walmar Cl EN4 ....2 B4
Walmer Cl E4 ....19 D2
Orpington BR6 ....227 B4
Walmer Gdns W13 ....109 A4
Walmer Ho 11 SE20 ...184 C3
8 W10 ....90 D1
Walmer Pl W1 ....237 C4
Walmer Rd W10 ....90 C1
W11 ....113 A6 244 A5
Walmer St NW1 ....237 C4
Walmer Terr SE18 .....123 B2
Walmgate Rd UB6 ......87 B6
Walmington Fold N12 ..29 C4
Walmsley Ho 1 SW16 .181 C6
Walnut Ave UB7 ....104 C3
Walnut Cl SE8 ....141 B6
Carshalton SM5 ....218 D3
Hayes UB3 ....105 C6
Ilford IG6 ....57 A5
Walnut Ct 2 E17 ....54 A5
Walnut Gdns E15 ......76 C3
Walnut Gr EN1 ....17 B6
Walnut Mews SM2 .....218 A1
Walnut Rd E10 ....75 D6
Walnut Tree Ave CR4 ..202 C6
Walnut Tree Cl SW13 .133 D4
Chislehurst BR7 ....189 A2
Walnut Tree Cotts
SW19 ....179 A5
Walnut Tree Ho SW10 ..265 D6
Walnut Tree Rd SE10 ..120 C1
Brentford TW8 ....132 A6
Charlton TW17 ....171 A1
Dagenham RM8 ....81 A6
Heston TW5 ....129 B6
Walnut Tree Walk Prim Sch
SE11 ....116 C2 261 A4
Walnut Tree Wlk
SE11 ....116 C2 261 A4
Walnut Way
Buckhurst Hill IG9 ......21 D1
Ruislip HA4 ....62 C2
Walpole Ave TW9 .....132 B3
Walpole Cl W13 ....109 C4
Hatch End HA5 ....23 C4
Walpole Cres 7 TW11 .174 D5
Walpole Ct NW6 ....70 A1
W5 ....109 D5
7 W14 ....112 D3
Twickenham TW2 ......152 C2
Walpole Gdns W4 .....111 A1
Twickenham TW2 ......152 C1
Walpole Lo W13 ....109 C5
Walpole Mews NW8 ...229 C5
Walpole Pl 3 SE18 ...122 D2
6 Teddington TW11 ....174 D5
Walpole Rd E6 ....77 C1
E17 ....53 A5
E18 ....36 D2
N17 ....33 A1
N17 ....51 A6
SW19 ....180 B4
Bromley BR2 ....209 D4
Croydon CR0 ....221 B6
Surbiton KT6 ....198 A3
Teddington TW11 ......174 D5
Twickenham TW2 ......152 C2
Walpole St
SW3 ....114 D1 257 D2
Walrond Ave HA9 ....66 A3
Walsham Cl N16 ....52 A1
SE28 ....124 D6
Walsham Ho SE14 ....140 D3
SE17 ....262 C2
Walsham Rd SE14 .....140 D3
Feltham TW14 ....150 B4
Walsingham NW8 .....229 D6
Walsingham Gdns
KT19 ....215 D3
Walsingham Ho E4 .....20 B4
Walsingham Lo SW13 .134 A4
Walsingham Mans
SW6 ....265 D4
Walsingham Pk BR7 ...189 B1
Walsingham Pl SW4,
SW11 ....159 A5
Walsingham Rd E5 .....74 A5
W13 ....109 A5
Enfield EN2 ....17 B6
Mitcham CR4 ....202 D4
St Paul's Cray BR5 ....190 B2
Walsingham Wlk DA17 .147 C6
Walt Whitman Cl 6
SE24 ....138 D1
Walter Besant Ho 20 E1 96 D4
Walter Ct 3 W3 ....89 A1
Walter Green Ho SE15 .140 C4
Walter Ho SW10 ......266 C4
Walter Hurford Par 4
E12 ....78 C4
Walter Northcott Ho 2
NW6 ....69 C3
Walter Savill Twr E17 ...53 C3
Walter St E2 ....96 D4
2 Kingston u T KT2 ....176 A2
Walter Terr E1 ....96 D1
Walter Wlk HA8 ....27 A4
Walters Cl SE17 ....262 B3
Walters Ho 3 SE5 .....139 C3
10 SE17 ....138 D6
Walters Rd EN3 ....6 C1
Walter's Rd SE25 ......205 C5
Walters Way SE23 .....162 D5
Walters Yd BR1 ....187 A1
Walterton Rd W9 ....91 C3
Waltham Ave NW9 .....44 C3
Hayes UB3 ....105 B3
Waltham Ct E17 ....36 A2
Waltham Dr HA8 ....44 C6
Waltham Forest Coll
E17 ....35 D1
Waltham Forest Tech Coll
(Chingford Annexe) E4 35 C5
Waltham Gdns EN3 ......6 C6
Waltham Green Ct
SW6 ....265 C3
Waltham Ho NW8 .....229 A6
10 SW9 ....138 B3
Waltham Park Way E17 .35 C3
Waltham Pk E17 ....35 C2
Waltham Rd
Carshalton SM5 ....202 C1
Southall UB2 ....107 A3
Waltham Way E4 ....19 C2
Walthamstow Ave E4 ...35 C3
Walthamstow Ave (North
Circular Rd) E4 ....35 B4
Walthamstow Bsns Ctr
E17 ....36 A1
Walthamstow Central Sta
E17 ....53 C4
Walthamstow Queen's Road
Sta E17 ....53 C4
Walthamstow Sch for Girls
E17 ....53 D5
Waltheof Ave N17 ....33 B2
Waltheof Gdns N17 .....33 B2
Walton Ave Cheam SM3 .217 B5
Harrow HA2 ....63 B4
New Malden KT3 ......199 D5
Walton Bridge Rd KT12,
TW17 ....193 C2
Walton Cl E5 ....74 D5
NW2 ....68 B6
SW8 ....138 A5 270 B4
Harrow HA1 ....42 B5
Walton Croft HA1 ....64 C4
Walton Ct EN5 ....14 A6
Walton Dr NW10 ....67 B2
Harrow HA1 ....42 B5
Walton Gdns W3 ....88 D2
Feltham TW13 ....171 D6
Wembley HA9 ....66 A6
Walton Gn CR0 ....224 A1
Walton Ho E2 ....243 D6
10 E17 ....53 D6
N7 ....72 B5
1 N9 ....34 A6
SW18 ....157 C5
Kingston u T KT2 ....176 A3
Walton La
Lower Halliford TW17 ...193 B2
Oatlands Pk KT13,TW17 .193 B1
Walton Pl SW3 ....257 C6
Walton Rd E12 ....78 C4
E13 ....99 C5
N15 ....51 D5
East Molesey KT8,KT12 ..195 C5
Harrow HA1 ....42 B5
Sidcup DA14 ....168 C1
Walton-on-T KT12&KT8 .194 D4
Walton St SW3 .114 C3 257 B5
Enfield EN2 ....5 B4
Walton Way W3 ....88 D2
Mitcham CR4 ....203 C5
Walworth Lower Sch
SE17 ....117 B1 262 D2
Walworth Pl
SE17 ....117 A1 262 B1
Walworth Rd
SE17 ....117 A1 262 B2
Walworth Sch
SE17 ....117 C1 263 B1
Walworth Upper Sch
SE1 ....117 C1 263 B1
Walwyn Ave BR1 ......209 D6
Wanborough Dr SW15 .156 B3
Wanderer Dr IG11 ....102 C4
Wandle Bank SW19 ...180 B3
Wallington CR0 ....220 A5
Wandle Court Gdns
CR0 ....220 A5
Wandle Ct 4 W12 .....111 C4
Wallington CR0 ....220 A5
West Ewell KT19 ......215 A4
Wandle Ho NW8 ....237 A4
SW18 ....157 D4
6 Catford BR1 ....186 B5
Wandle Lo CR0 ....220 A5
Wandle Pk Sta CR0 ...220 C6
Wandle Prim Sch
SW18 ....157 D3
Wandle Rd SW17 ......158 C2
Croydon CR0 ....221 A5
Hackbridge SM6 ....219 B6
Morden SM4 ....202 B4
Wallington CR0 ....220 A5
Wandle Side
Croydon CR0 ....220 B5
Hackbridge SM6 ....219 B5
Wandle Tech Pk CR4 ..202 D2
Wandle Trad Est CR4 ..202 D2
Wandle Valley Sch
SM5 ....202 C2
Wandle Way SW18 ....157 D3
Mitcham CR4 ....202 D4
Wandon Rd
SW6 ....135 D5 265 D3
Wandsworth Bridge Rd
SW6 ....135 D2 265 C1
Wandsworth Common Sta
SW12 ....158 D4
Wandsworth Common West
Side SW18 ....158 A6
Wandsworth Gyratory
SW18 ....157 D6
Wandsworth High St
SW18 ....157 D6
Wandsworth Mus
SW15 ....135 A1
Wandsworth Plain
SW18 ....157 D6
Wandsworth Rd
SW8 ....138 A5 270 A3
Wandsworth Road Sta
SW4 ....137 C3
Wandsworth Town Sta
SW18 ....135 D1
Wangey Rd RM6 ....58 D2
Wangford Ho 13 SW9 ..138 D1
Wanless Rd SE24 .....139 A2
Wanley Rd SE5 ....139 B1
Wanlip Rd E13 ....99 B3
Wansbeck Ct EN2 ....4 D2
Wansbeck Rd E3,E9 ....75 B1
Wansdown Pl
SW6 ....135 D5 265 C4
Wansey St SE17 117 A2 262 B3
Wansford Rd IG8 ....37 C2
Wanstead CE Prim Sch
E11 ....55 A4
Wanstead Cl BR1 .....187 C1
Wanstead High Sch E11 55 C3
Wanstead Hospl E11 ....55 B5
Wanstead La IG1 ....56 A3
Wanstead Park Ave E12 .77 D6
Wanstead Park Rd IG1 ..56 A1
Wanstead Park Sta E7 ..77 B4
Wanstead Pl E11 ....55 A4
Wanstead Rd BR1 .....187 C1
Wanstead Sta E11 ......55 B3
Wantage Rd SE12 .....164 D6
Wantz Rd RM10 ....81 D3
Wapping Dock St 19 E1 118 B5
Wapping High St E1 ..118 B5
Wapping La E1 ....118 B5
Wapping Sta E1 ....118 C5
Wapping Wall E1 .....118 C5
War Memorial Homes
W4 ....133 B5
Warbank La KT2 ....177 D3
Warbeck Rd W12 ......112 B4
Warberry Rd N22 ....32 B1
Warboys App KT2 .....176 D4
Warboys Cres E4 ....36 A5
Warboys Rd KT2 ......176 D4
Warburton Cl HA3 ......24 B4
Warburton Ct SE15 ....140 A2
Ruislip HA4 ....62 A6
Warburton Ho 5 E8 ....96 B6
Warburton Rd 8 E8 ....96 B6
Twickenham TW2 ......151 D3
Warburton St 6 E8 .....96 B6
Warburton Terr E17 ....35 D1
Ward Point SE11 ......261 A3
Ward Rd E15 ....98 B6
N19 ....71 C5
Wardalls Ho 12 SE8 ...141 B6
Wardell Cl NW7 ....27 C3
Wardell Ct N2 ....48 B6
Wardell Ho 6 SE10 ...142 A6
Warden Ave HA2 ....41 B1
Warden Rd NW5 ....71 A2
Wardens Field Cl 2
BR6 ....227 D2
Wardens Gr SE1 ......252 A3
Wardle St E9 ....74 D3
Wardley Lo E11 ....54 D3
Wardley St SW18 .....157 D4
Wardlow 8 NW5 ....71 B4
Wardo Ave
SW6 ....135 A4 264 A2
Wardour Mews W1 ....239 B1
Wardour St W1 .93 D1 239 C1
Wardrobe Pl EC4 .....241 D1
Wardrobe Terr EC4 ...251 D6
Wardrobe The 3 TW9 .153 D6
Wards Rd IG2 ....57 B2
Ware Ct Cheam SM1 ...217 B4
Edgware HA8 ....26 A6
Wareham Cl TW3 .....129 D1
Wareham Ct 2 N1 ......73 C1
Wareham Ho SW8 .....270 C4
Waremead Rd IG2 ......56 D4
Warepoint Dr SE28 ...123 B4
Warfield Rd NW10 ......90 D4
East Bedfont TW14 ....149 C4
Hampton TW12 ....173 D2
Warfield Yd 6 NW10 ...90 D4
Wargrave Ave N15 ......51 D3
Wargrave Ho 46 E2 ....95 D4
Wargrave Rd HA2 ......64 A5
Warham Rd N4 ....50 D4
Croydon CR2 ....221 A3
Harrow HA3 ....24 D1
Warham St SE5 ....138 D5
Waring Cl BR6 ....227 D2
Waring Dr BR6 ....227 D2
Waring Ho 10 E2 ....96 A4
Waring Rd DA14 ......190 C4
Waring St SE27 ....183 A6
Warkworth Gdns TW7 .131 A5
Warkworth Rd N17 .....33 B3
Warland Rd SE18 .....145 C5
Warley Ave
Dagenham RM8 ....59 B2
Hayes UB4 ....84 A1
Warley Cl E10 ....53 B1
Warley Ho N1 ....73 B2
Warley Rd N9 ....18 C2
Hayes UB4 ....84 A2
Woodford IG8 ....37 B3
Warley St E2 ....96 D4
Warlingham Rd CR7 ..204 D5
Warlock Rd W9 ....91 C3
Warlters Cl N7 ....72 A4
Warlters Rd N7 ....72 A4
Warltersville Mans N19 .50 A2
Warltersville Rd N4,N8,
N19 ....50 A2
Warming Cl E5 ....74 D5
Warmington Rd SE24 ..161 A5
Warmington St 3 E13 ..99 A3
Warminster Gdns SE25 184 A1
Warminster Rd SE25 ...184 A1
Warminster Sq SE25 ...184 A1
Warminster Way CR4 ..181 B1
Warmley Ct 5 SE15 ...139 C6
Warmsworth NW1 ....232 A6
Warncliffe Ho 3 SW15 156 C6
Warndon St SE16 .....118 C2
Warne Pl 4 DA15 .....168 B5
Warneford Rd HA3 .....44 A6
Warneford St E9 ....96 B6
Warner Ave SM3 ....217 A6
Warner Cl E15 ....76 C3
NW9 ....46 A2
Harlington UB3 ....127 B5
Warner Ct SM3 ....217 A6
Warner Ho 4 E9 ....74 D2
NW8 ....229 A2
SE13 ....141 D3
1 Beckenham BR3 .....185 D4
Warner Pl E2 ....96 A4
Warner Rd E17 ....53 A5
N8 ....49 D5
SE5 ....139 A4
Bromley BR1 ....186 D3
Warner St EC1 ..94 C3 241 A5
Warner Yd EC1 ....241 A5
Warners Cl IG8 ....37 A5
Warnford Ho SW15 ...155 C5
Warnford Ind Est UB3 .105 C4
Warnford Rd BR6 .....227 D3
Warnham WC1 ....233 C1
Warnham Court Rd
SM5 ....218 D1
Warnham Ho 6 SW2 ..160 B4
Warnham Rd N12 ....30 C5
Warple Mews W3 ......111 C4
Warple Way W3,W12 ..111 C4
Warren Ave E11 ....76 B5
SW14,TW10 ....132 D1
Bromley BR1 ....186 C3
Orpington BR6 ....227 D3
South Croydon CR2 ...222 D1
Warren Cl N9 ....18 D4
SE21 ....161 A4
Bexleyheath DA6 ......169 C6
Hayes UB4 ....84 C2
Wembley HA9 ....65 D6
KT10 ....212 A4
Warren Comp Sch RM6 .59 B4
Warren Cres N9 ....17 D4
Warren Ct N1 ....234 A4
N17 ....52 A6
6 W5 ....87 C2
17 Beckenham BR3 ....185 C3
6 Croydon CR0 ....205 C1
Warren Cutting KT2 ...177 B3
Warren Dr Ruislip HA4 ..40 D2
Southall UB6 ....86 A3
Warren Dr N KT5,KT6 .198 D1
Warren Dr S KT5 ......199 A1
Warren Dr The E11 .....55 C2
Warren Fields HA7 .....25 C6
Warren Gdns E15 ....76 B3
Warren Hill IG10 ....21 C6
Warren Ho 21 E3 ....97 D4
Warren La SE18 ....122 D3
Stanmore HA7 ....9 A2
Warren Mews W1 .....239 A5
Warren Park Rd SM1,
SM2 ....218 C2
Warren Pk KT2 ....177 A4
Warren Pond Rd E4 ....20 D4
Warren Rd E4 ....20 A2
E10 ....76 A5
E11 ....55 C2
NW2 ....67 D6
SW19 ....180 C4
Ashford TW15 ....171 C3
Bexleyheath DA6 ......169 C6
Bushey WD2 ....8 B3
Croydon CR0 ....205 D1
Hayes BR2 ....225 A6
Ickenham UB10 ....60 B4
Ilford IG6 ....57 B4
Kingston u T KT2 ......177 A4
Sidcup DA14 ....168 C1
Twickenham TW2 ......152 B5
Warren Rise KT3 .....177 B2
Warren Road Prim Sch
BR6 ....227 D4
Warren St W1 ...93 C3 239 A5
Warren Street Sta
NW1 ....93 C3 239 B6
Warren Terr RM6 ....58 D5
Warren The E12 ....78 A4
Hayes UB4 ....84 A1
Heston TW5 ....129 B5
Worcester Pk KT19 ....215 B5
Warren Way NW7 ....29 A4
Warren Wlk 1 SE7 ....143 C6
Warren Wood Cl BR2 ..225 A6
Warrender Prim Sch
HA4 ....39 D2
Warrender Rd N19 ......71 C4
Warrender Way HA4 ...40 A2
Warrens Shawe La HA8 .10 D2
Warriner Dr N9 ....18 A1
Warriner Gdns
SW11 ....137 A4 268 A1
Warrington Cres
W9 ....92 A3 236 A6
Warrington Gdns W9 ..236 A5
Warrington Pl E14 ....120 A5

Warrington Rd
Croydon CR0 220 D5
Dagenham RM8 81 A6
Harrow HA1 42 C4
21 Richmond TW10 153 D6
Warrington Sq RM8 80 D6
Warrior Sq E12 78 C4
Warsaw Cl HA4 62 B2
Warspite Ho 3 E14 119 D2
Warspite Rd SE18 122 A3
Warton Rd E15 98 A6
Warwall E6 100 D1
Warwick W14 113 B2 254 D3
Warwick Ave W9 92 A3 236 A5
Edgware HA8 11 A1
Harrow HA2 63 B4
Warwick Avenue Sta
W9 92 A3 236 A5
Warwick Boys Sch E17 54 A5
Warwick Chambers
W8 255 A6
Warwick Cl Bushey WD2 8 C4
Hampton TW12 174 A3
New Barnet EN4 14 B6
Sidcup DA5 169 B4
Warwick Cres
W2 92 A2 236 A4
Hayes UB4 83 D3
Warwick Ct 3 E5 74 B6
5 N2 48 A6
N11 31 D4
NW2 69 A3
W7 86 D1
WC1 240 D3
1 Beckenham BR2 186 C1
Harrow HA1 42 C6
Northolt UB5 63 C3
Surbiton KT6 214 A6
Warwick Dene W5 110 A5
Warwick Dr SW15 134 B2
Warwick Gdns N4 51 A4
W14 113 B2 254 D4
Ilford IG1 56 D1
Thames Ditton KT7 196 D4
Thornton Heath CR7 204 C5
Warwick Gr E5 52 B1
Surbiton KT5 198 B2
Warwick Ho 10 E5 74 C6
N4 51 A1
11 SW9 138 C3
6 SW15 156 C4
9 W3 88 C1
6 Kingston u T KT2 176 A2
Warwick House St
SW1 249 D4
Warwick La EC4 94 D1 241 D1
Warwick Lo Cheam SM1 217 B4
Twickenham TW2 151 D1
Warwick Mans SW5 255 A4
Warwick Park Sch
SE15 139 D4
Warwick Pas EC4 241 D2
Warwick Pl W5 109 D4
W9 92 A2 236 A4
Warwick Pl N SW1 259 A3
Warwick Rd E4 35 C5
E11 55 B4
E12 78 A3
E15 76 D2
E17 35 B1
N11 31 D4
N18 33 D6
SE20 206 B6
W5 110 A5
W14,SW5 113 B2 254 D4
Ashford TW15 170 A5
Barnet EN5 1 D1
Bexley DA16 146 C2
Enfield EN3 7 B6
Hounslow TW4 128 B2
Kingston u T KT3 199 A6
Sidcup DA14 190 B5
Southall UB2 107 B3
Sutton SM1 218 A3
Teddington KT1 175 C2
Thames Ditton KT7 196 D4
Thornton Heath CR7 204 C6
Twickenham TW2 152 C3
Yiewsley UB7 104 A5
Warwick Row
SW1 115 B3 258 D6
Warwick Sq EC4 241 D2
SW1 115 C1 259 A2
Warwick Sq Mews
SW1 259 A3
Warwick St W1 115 C6 249 B6
Warwick Terr E17 54 B4
SE18 145 B6
Warwick Way
SW1 115 B2 258 D2
Warwick Yd EC1 242 B5
Warwickshire Path SE8 141 B5
Warwickshire Rd N16 73 C4
Wasdale NW1 231 D1
Washbrook Ho SW2 160 C5
Washington Ave E12 78 B4
Washington Ct SW17 180 D4
Washington Ho E17 35 B1
SW1 247 C1
Washington Rd E6 77 C1
2 E18 36 D1
SW13 134 A5
Kingston u T KT1 176 C1
North Cheam KT4 200 B1
Wastdale Rd SE23 162 D3
Wat Tyler Ho N8 50 A6
Wat Tyler Rd SE10 142 B4
Watchfield Ct 7 W4 111 A1
Watcombe Cotts TW9 132 C6
Watcombe Rd SE25 206 B4
Water Brook La NW4 46 C4
Water Gdns HA7 25 B4
Water Gdns The
W2 92 C1 237 B2
Water La E15 76 C2
N9 18 B4
SE14 140 C5
Ilford IG3 79 D5
Kingston u T KT1 175 D2
Richmond TW10,TW9 153 D6
Sidcup DA14 169 B2
Twickenham TW1 153 A3
Water Lily Cl UB2 108 A4
Water Mews SE15 140 C1
Water Mill Way TW13 151 C2
Water Rd HA0 88 B6
Water St WC2 251 A6
Water Tower Cl UB8 60 A3
Water Tower Hill CR0 221 B4
Water Tower Ho W8 245 A3
Water Tower Pl N1 234 C5
Waterbank Rd SE6 186 A6
Waterbeach Rd RM9 80 C2
Watercress Pl N1 73 C1
Waterdale Rd SE2 146 A6
Waterden Rd E15 75 C2
Waterer Ho 7 SE6 186 A6
Waterer Rise SM6 219 D2
Waterfall Cl N14 15 C1
Waterfall Cotts SW19 180 B4
Waterfall Rd N11,N14 15 C1
SW19 180 B4
Waterfall Terr SW17 180 C4
Waterfield Cl SE28 124 B5
Belvedere DA17 125 C3
Waterfield Gdns SE25 205 C4
Waterfield Sch SE28 124 A5
Waterford Ho W11 244 D6
Waterford Rd
SW6 135 D5 265 C3
Watergardens The KT2 177 A4
Watergate EC4 251 C6
Watergate Ho 5 SE18 122 C2
Watergate Sch SE13 141 D1
Watergate St SE8 141 C6
Watergate Wlk WC2 250 B4
Waterglade Ctr The
W5 109 D6
Waterhall Ave E4 36 C6
Waterhall Cl E17 34 D2
Waterhead NW1 232 A2
Waterhedge Mews EN1 17 D6
Waterhouse Cl E16 99 D2
NW3 70 B3
W6 112 D1
Waterhouse Ct 5
TW11 174 D5
Wateridge Cl E14 119 C3
Wateringbury Cl BR5 190 B1
Waterloo Bridge
SE1,WC2 116 B6 250 D5
Waterloo Cl E9 74 C3
East Bedfont TW14 149 D3
Waterloo East Sta
SE1 116 C5 251 B3
Waterloo Gdns E2 96 C5
Waterloo Int Sta
SE1 116 B4 250 D2
Waterloo Pl
SW1 115 D5 249 C4
Richmond TW9 132 C6
Waterloo Rd E6 77 C1
E7 76 D3
E10 53 C2
NW2 68 A6
SE1 116 C4 251 B2
Carshalton SM1 218 B3
Waterloo Sta
SE1 116 C4 251 A2
Waterloo Terr N1 72 D1
Waterlow Ct NW11 47 D2
Waterlow Rd N19 49 C1
Waterman St SW15 134 D2
Waterman Way E1 118 B5
Watermans Ct 12 TW8 131 D6
Watermans Mews 1
W5 110 A6
Watermead TW14 149 C3
Watermead Ho E9 75 B3
Watermead La CR4 202 D2
Watermead Rd SE6 186 A6
Watermead Way N17 34 B1
Watermeadow La SW6 136 A3
Watermeads High Sch
SM4 202 B3
Watermen's Sq 1 SE20 184 C3
Watermill Bsns Ctr EN3 7 B3
Watermill Cl TW10 153 C1
Watermill La N18 33 C5
Watermill Way SW19 180 A2
Watermint Quay N16 52 A2
Waters Gdns RM10 81 C3
Waters Pl SW15 134 C3
Waters Rd SE6 164 C1
Kingston u T KT1 176 D1
Waters Sq KT1 198 D6
Watersedge KT19 215 A4
Watersfield Way HA8 26 A3
Watership Down Ho E11 54 D2
Waterside E17 52 C3
4 Beckenham BR3 185 C2
Waterside Cl E3 97 B6
28 SE16 118 A4
Barking IG11 80 A4
Northolt UB5 85 B4
Surbiton KT6 214 A6
Waterside Dr KT12 194 B4
Waterside Pl NW1 231 B6
Waterside Point SW11 267 B4
Waterside Rd UB2 107 C3
Waterside Trad Ctr W7 108 C3
Waterside Way SW17 180 A5
Watersmeet Way SE28 102 D1
Waterson St E2 95 D4
Watersplash Cl KT1 198 A6
Watersplash La
Hayes UB3 106 A2
Southall TW5 106 B1
Watersplash Rd TW17 192 C5
Waterview Ho E14 97 A2
Waterworks Cnr E17 36 C1
Waterworks La E5 74 D6
Waterworks Rd SW2 160 B5
Watery La SW19,SW20 179 B1
Hayes UB3 105 B1
Northolt UB5 84 C5
Sidcup DA14 190 B4
Wates Way CR4 202 D3
Wateville Rd N17 33 A2
Watford By-Pass WD6 9 C4
Watford Cl SW11 267 B2
Watford Rd E16 99 A2
Elstree WD6 9 C5
Harrow HA1 43 A1
Northwood HA6 22 A4
Wembley HA0,HA1 65 A5
Watford Way NW4 46 A5
Watford Way (Barnet
By-Pass) NW9 27 D3
Watkin Ho N16 51 D2
Watkin Rd HA9 66 D5
Watkinson Rd N7 72 B2
Watling Ave HA8 27 B2
Watling Ct EC4 242 B1
1 Elstree WD6 9 D5
Watling Gate NW9 45 C5
Watling Gdns NW2 69 A2
Watling Ho 10 SE18 144 C6
Watling St EC4 95 A1 242 B1
Bexleyheath DA6,DA7 147 D1
Watlings Cl CR0 207 A3
Watlington Gr SE26 185 A5
Watney Cotts SW14 133 A2
Watney Mkt E1 96 B1
Watney Rd SW14 133 A2
Watney St E1 96 B1
Watneys Rd CR4 203 D4
Watson Ave E6 78 C1
Cheam SM3 217 A6
Watson Cl N16 73 B3
SW19 180 C3
Watson Ho 3 SW2 160 A4
Watson St E13 99 B5
Watsons Lo 4 RM10 81 D2
Watson's Mews W1 237 B3
Watsons Rd N22 32 B2
Watson's St SE8 141 C5
Wattisfield Rd E5 74 C5
Watts Cl N15 51 C4
Watts Gr E3 97 D2
Watts Ho 6 W10 91 A2
Watt's La
Chislehurst BR7 189 A2
Teddington TW11 175 A5
Watts Point E13 99 A6
Watts Rd KT7 197 A2
Watts St E1 118 B5
Wauthier Cl N13 32 D5
Wavel Ct 7 E1 118 C5
7 SW16 160 A1
Wavel Mews N8 49 D5
NW6 69 D1
Wavel Pl SE26 183 D6
Wavell Dr DA15 167 C5
Wavell Ho N6 49 A3
Wavendon Ave W4 111 B1
Waveney Ave SE15 140 B1
Waveney Cl E1 118 A5
Waveney Ho SE15 140 B1
Waverley Ave E4 35 B6
E17 54 B6
Sutton SM1 217 D6
Tolworth KT5 199 A3
Twickenham TW2,TW4 151 C3
Wembley HA9 66 B3
Waverley Cl E18 37 C1
Bromley BR2 209 D4
East Molesey KT8 195 C4
Hayes UB3 105 B2
Waverley Cres SE18 123 B1
Waverley Ct 3 NW6 69 A1
W1 238 B4
Enfield EN2 5 A2
Waverley Gdns E6 100 A2
NW10 88 B5
Barking IG11 101 C5
Ilford IG6 57 B6
Northwood HA6 22 A2
Waverley Gr N3 47 A6
Waverley Ind Pk HA1 42 B6
Waverley Pl N4 50 D1
NW8 92 B5 229 C4
Waverley Rd E17 54 A6
E18 37 C2
N8 50 A2
N17 34 B3
SE18 123 B1
SE25 206 B6
Enfield EN2 4 D2
Harrow HA2 41 A1
Southall UB1 107 C6
Stoneleigh KT17,KT4 216 B3
Waverley Sch EN3 6 C1
Waverley Sch (Upper)
SE15 162 C6
Waverley Way SM2,SM5 218 C2
Waverly Ct NW3 70 D2
Waverton Ho 2 E3 97 B6
Waverton Rd SW18 158 A4
Waverton St
W1 115 B5 248 C4
Wavertree Ct 9 SW2 160 A3
Wavertree Rd E18 37 A1
SW2 160 B3
Waxham NW5 70 D3
Waxlow Cres UB1 85 C1
Waxlow Ho UB4 84 C2
Waxlow Rd NW10 89 B5
Waxwell Cl HA5 22 D1
Waxwell La HA5 22 D1
Wayborne Gr HA4 39 A3
Waye Ave TW5 128 A4
Wayfarer Rd UB5 85 A4
Wayfield Link SE9 167 B5
Wayford St SW11 136 C3
Wayland Ave E8 74 A3
Wayland Ho 13 SW9 138 C3
Waylands UB3 83 B2
Waylands Ct IG1 79 B4
Waylands Mead BR3 185 D2
Waylett Ho SE11 261 A1
Waylett Pl SE27 160 D1
Wembley HA0 65 D4
Wayman Ct E8 74 B2
Wayne Cl BR6 227 D5
Waynflete Ave CR0 220 D5
Waynflete Sq 18 W10 90 D1
Waynflete St SW18 158 A2
Wayside NW11 47 A1
SW14 155 A6
New Addington CR0 223 D2
Wayside Ave WD2 8 B5
Wayside Cl N14 15 C5
Wayside Commercial Est
IG11 102 A5
Wayside Ct
Hounslow TW7 130 C3
Twickenham TW1 153 C5
Wembley HA9 66 C5
Wayside Gdns RM10 81 C3
Wayside Gr BR7,SE9 188 B6
Wayside Mews IG2 56 C4
Weald Cl 16 SE16 118 B1
Keston Mark BR2 226 A6
Weald Fst & Mid Sch
HA3 24 D3
Weald La HA3 24 B2
Weald Rd UB10 82 C5
Weald Rise HA3 24 D2
Weald Sq E5 74 B6
Weald The BR7 188 B4
Weald Way Hayes UB4 83 C4
Romford RM7 59 D3
Wealdstone Rd SM3 217 B6
Wealdwood Gdns HA5 23 D4
Weale Rd E4 20 B1
Weall Ct HA5 41 A5
Wear Pl 13 E2 96 B4
Weardale Ct EN5 12 C6
Weardale Gdns EN2 5 B4
Weardale Ho N4 51 A2
Weardale Rd SE13 142 B1
Wearmouth Ho 1 E3 97 B2
Wearside Rd SE13 141 D1
Weatherbury 6 W2 91 C1
Weatherbury Ho 3 N19 71 D5
Weatherill Ct SE25 206 B3
Weatherley Cl E3 97 B2
Weathersfield Ct SE9 166 B5
Weaver Cl E16 122 D6
Weaver Ct 2 E2 96 B3
Weaver Ho 13 E1 96 A3
Weaver St E1 96 A3
Weaver Wlk SE27 182 D6
Weavers Cl TW7 130 C1
Weaver's Field Sch E2 96 B3
Weavers Ho 4 E11 55 A3
Weaver's La
SE1 117 C5 253 B3
Weavers Way NW1 232 C6
6 NW1 71 D1
Webb Ct 6 SE28 124 B6
W3 110 D4
Webb Est E5 52 A2
Webb Gdns 1 E13 99 A3
Webb Ho SW8 269 D3
2 Dagenham RM10 81 C5
Feltham TW13 151 A1
Webb Pl NW10 89 D4
Webb Rd SE3 142 D6
Webb St SE1 117 C3 263 A5
Webber Cl WD6 9 D5
Webber Ho 6 IG11 78 D1
Webber Row
SE1 116 D4 251 C1
Webber St SE1 116 D4 251 C1
Webbs Rd UB4 84 B4
Webb's Rd SW11 158 D6
Webbscroft Rd RM10 81 D4
Webheath 6 NW6 69 B1
Webster Gdns W5 109 D5
Webster Ho 16 N16 73 C3
Webster Rd E11 76 A5
SE16 118 A3
Weddell Ho 23 E1 96 D3
Wedderburn Rd NW3 70 B3
Barking IG11 101 C6
Wedgewood Ct
1 Beckenham BR2 208 D5
Sidcup DA5 169 B4
Wedgewood Ho SW1 259 A1
Wedgewood Mews W1 239 D1
Wedgwood Ho 17 E2 96 D4
SE11 261 A5
Wedgwood Way SE19 183 A3
Wedlake St W10 91 A3
Wedmore Gdns N19 71 D6
Wedmore Rd UB6 86 B4
Wedmore St N19 71 D5
Weech Rd NW6 69 C4
Weedington Rd NW5 71 A3
Weedon Ho W12 90 A1
Weekley Sq SW11 136 B2
Weeks Ho TW10 175 C6
Weigall Rd SE12,SE3 143 A1
Weighhouse St W1 238 B1
Weighton Rd SE20 184 B1
Harrow HA3 24 B2
Weihurst Ct SM1 218 C3
Weihurst Gdns SM1 218 B3
Weimar St SW15 135 A2
Weir Hall Ave N18 33 B4
Weir Hall Gdns N18 33 B5
Weir Hall Rd N18 33 B4
Weir Ho 8 SW12 159 C4
Weir Rd SW12 159 C4
SW18,SW19 157 D1
Old Bexley DA5 169 D4
Walton-on-T KT12 194 A3
Weirdale Ave N20 14 D2
Weir's Pas NW1 232 D2
Weiss Rd SW15 134 D2
Welbeck Ave Hayes UB4 84 B3
Plaistow BR1 187 B6
Sidcup DA15 168 A3
Welbeck Cl N12 30 B5
Ewell KT17 216 A1
New Malden KT3 199 D4
Welbeck Ct W14 254 C4
Hayes UB4 84 B3
Welbeck Mans 10 NW6 69 C3
Welbeck Rd E6 99 D4
Carshalton SM1,SM5 218 B6
East Barnet EN4 14 C5
Harrow HA2 41 D1
SM5 202 C1
Welbeck St W1 93 B1 238 C2
Welbeck Villas N21 17 A3
Welbeck Way W1 238 C2
Welbeck Wlk SM5 202 B1
Welbourne Prim Sch
N17 52 A6
Welby Ho N19 49 D2
Welby St SE5 138 D4
Welch Pl HA5 22 C2
Weld Pl N11 31 B5
Weldon Cl HA4 62 B2
Weldon Ct N21 16 B6
Thornton Heath CR7 204 D4
Weldon Dr KT8 195 B5
Welfare Rd E15 76 C1
Welford Cl E5 74 D5
Welford Ct 12 NW1 71 B1
7 SW8 137 C3
Welford Pl SW19 179 A6
Welham Rd SW16,SW17 181 B4
Welhouse Rd SM5 202 C1
Well App EN5 12 C6
Well Cl SW16 182 B6
Ruislip HA4 63 A5
Well Cottage Cl E11 55 C2
Well Ct EC4 242 B1
Well Gr N20 14 B3
Well Hall Par SE9 144 B1
Well Hall Pleasaunce
SE9 144 A1
Well Hall Rd SE9 144 B1
Well Ho 11 N9 18 A1
Well La SW14 155 A6
Well Rd NW3 70 B5
Ducks Island EN5 12 C6
Well St E9 74 C1
E15 76 C2
Well Wlk NW3 70 B5
Wellacre Rd HA3 43 B3
Wellan Cl DA15,DA16 168 B6
Welland Gdns UB6 86 D5
Welland Ho SE15 140 C1
Welland Mews E1 118 A5
Welland St SE10 142 A6
Wellands Cl BR1 188 B1
Wellbrook Rd BR6 226 C4
Wellby Ct 1 E13 99 C5
Wellclose Sq E1 118 A6
Wellclose St 11 E1 118 A6
Wellday Ho 2 E9 75 A2
Welldon Cres HA1 42 C3
Welldon Park Fst Sch
HA2 64 A4
Welldon Park Mid Sch
HA2 64 A4
Weller Ho 20 SE16 118 A4
Weller St SE1 252 A2
Wellers Ct NW1 233 A3
Wellesley Ave W6 112 B3
Wellesley Cl 8 SE7 121 C1
Wellesley Court Rd 1
CR0 221 B6
Wellesley Cres TW2 152 C1
Wellesley Ct W9 92 A4 229 A2
Cheam SM3 201 A1
Twickenham TW2 152 C1
Wellesley Gr CR0 221 B6
Wellesley Ho NW1 232 C1
Wellesley Park Mews EN2 4 D3
Wellesley Pl NW1 232 C1
Wellesley Rd E11 55 A4
E17 53 C3
N22 32 C1
Wellesley Rd *continued*
NW5 71 A3
W4 110 D1
Croydon CR0 205 A1
Harrow HA1 42 C4
Ilford IG1 57 A1
Sutton SM2 218 A2
Twickenham TW2 152 C1
Wellesley Road Sta
CR0 221 B6
Wellesley St E1 96 D2
Wellesley Terr
N1 95 A4 235 B2
Wellfield Ave N10 49 B6
Wellfield Rd SW16 182 B6
Wellfit St 6 SE24 138 D2
Wellgarth UB6 65 B2
Wellgarth Rd NW11 47 D1
Wellhouse Rd BR3 207 C5
Welling High St DA16 146 B2
Welling Sch DA16 146 B4
Welling Sta DA16 146 A3
Welling Way DA16 145 B2
Wellingfield Ct 1
DA16 146 A2
Wellings Ho UB3 106 B5
Wellington N8 50 A5
1 NW9 27 D3
Wellington Arch SW1 248 B2
Wellington Ave E4 19 D2
N9 18 B1
N15 52 A3
SE18 123 A3
Hatch End HA5 23 B2
Hounslow TW3,TW4 151 C6
North Cheam KT4 216 C5
Sidcup DA15 168 A5
Wellington Bldgs 14 E3 97 C4
SW1 258 B1
Wellington Cl SE14 140 D4
W11 91 C1
Walton-on-T KT12 193 D1
Wellington Cres KT3 199 A6
Wellington Ct NW8 229 D3
SW1 247 C1
SW6 265 D1
SW18 158 C6
WC2 250 A6
Stanwell TW19 148 A4
5 Surbiton KT6 198 A3
Teddington TW12 174 B5
Wellington Gdns SE7 121 C1
Hampton TW12,TW2 174 B6
Wellington Gr SE10 142 B5
Wellington Ho 18 NW3 70 D2
4 W5 88 A4
Northolt UB5 63 C1
Stanmore HA7 9 A1
Wellington Hospl (North)
NW8 92 B5 229 D3
Wellington Hospl (South)
NW8 92 B5 229 D3
Wellington JMI Sch E3 97 C4
Wellington Mans 1 E10 53 C1
N16 73 D4
Wellington Mews SE22 140 A1
Wellington Mus (Apsley
House) SW1 115 A4 248 B2
Wellington Par DA15 168 A6
Wellington Park Est
NW2 68 A6
Wellington Pl N2 48 C4
NW8 92 B4 229 D2
Wellington Prim Sch E4 19 D2
Hounslow TW3 129 B3
Wellington Rd E6 100 B5
E7 76 D4
E10 53 A1
E11 55 A4
E17 53 A5
NW8 92 B5 229 D3
NW10 90 D4
SW19 157 C2
W5 109 C3
Ashford TW15 170 A5
Bexley DA5 168 D6
Bromley BR2 209 C5
Enfield EN1 17 C5
Erith DA17 125 B1
Harrow HA3 42 C6
Hatch End HA5 23 B2
Hatton TW14 149 C6
Teddington TW12,TW2 174 B6
Thornton Heath CR0 204 D2
Wellington Rd N TW4 129 B2
Wellington Rd S TW4 151 B6
Wellington Row E2 96 A4
Wellington Sq
SW3 114 D1 257 C2
Wellington St SE18 122 C2
WC2 116 B6 250 C6
1 Barking IG11 101 A6
Wellington Terr 2 E1 118 B5
Harrow HA1 42 B1
Wellington Way E3 97 C4
Wellmead IG3 58 A2
Wellmeadow Rd
SE13,SE6 164 C3
W7 109 A2
Wellow Wlk SM5 202 B1
Wells Cl 2 UB5 84 C4
Wells Ct N1 73 C3
16 NW3 70 A4
1 NW6 91 C5
Wells Dr NW9 45 B1

374 Wel – Wes

Wells Gdns
Dagenham RM10 81 D3
Redbridge IG1 56 A2
Wells Ho EC1 234 C2
9 SE16 118 C3
W5 109 D6
12 W10 91 A3
4 Barking IG11 80 A1
Plaistow BR1 187 B5
Wells Ho The NW3 70 B4
Wells House Rd NW10 89 C2
Wells Mews W1 239 B2
Wells Park Ct SE26 184 B6
Wells Park Rd SE26 184 B6
Wells Prim Sch IG8 37 A6
Wells Rd W12 112 C4
Bromley BR1 188 B1
Wells Rise NW8 92 D6 230 C5
Wells Sq WC1 233 D1
Wells St W1 93 C1 239 B2
Wells Terr N4 72 C6
Wells The N14 15 D4
Wells Way SE5 139 C6
SW7 114 B3 256 C6
Wells Yd 2 N7 72 C3
Wellside Gdns SW14 155 A6
Wellsmoor Gdns BR1 210 C6
Wellsprings Cres HA9 66 D5
Wellstead Ave N9 18 D4
Wellstead Rd E6 100 C5
Wellwood Ct SW15 134 C1
Wellwood Rd IG3 58 A2
Welsby Ct W5 87 C2
Welsford St SE1 118 A2
Welsh Cl E13 99 A4
Welsh Harp Field Centre NW9 45 B1
Welsh Ho 14 E1 118 B5
Welshpool Ho 22 E8 96 A6
Welshpool St 1 E8 96 B6
Welshside NW9 45 C3
Welstead Ho 5 E1 96 B1
Welstead Way W4 111 D2
Weltje Rd W6 112 A1
Welton Ho E1 96 D2
SE5 139 C4
Welton Rd SE18 145 C5
Welwyn Ave TW14 149 D5
Welwyn St E2 96 C4
Welwyn Way UB4 83 C3
Wembley HA0 65 D2
Wembley Arena HA9 66 C4
Wembley Bsns Ctr HA9 66 D5
Wembley Central Sta HA9 66 A3
Wembley Commercial Ctr HA9 65 D6
Wembley Conference Ctr HA9 66 C4
Wembley Exhibition Halls HA9 66 C4
Wembley High Sch HA0 65 C5
Wembley Hill Rd HA9 66 B4
Wembley Hospl HA0 65 D2
Wembley Manor Jun & Inf Sch HA9 66 A5
Wembley Park Dr HA9 66 B5
Wembley Park Sta HA9 66 C5
Wembley Rd TW12 173 C2
Wembley Stadium HA9 66 C3
Wembley Stadium Ind Est
Wembley HA9 66 C5
Wembley HA9 66 D4
Wembley Stadium Sta HA9 66 B3
Wembley Way HA9 66 D2
Wemborough Rd HA7 25 C3
Wembury Rd N6 49 B2
Wemyss Rd SE3 142 D3
Wendela Ct HA1 64 C6
Wendell Park Prim Sch W12 111 D4
Wendell Rd W12 111 D4
Wenderholme CR2 221 B3
Wendle Ct SW8 270 A5
Wendling NW5 70 D3
Wendling Rd SM1,SM5 218 B6
Wendon St E3 97 B6
Wendover NW9 45 D3
SE17 117 C1 263 A1
Wendover Cl UB4 85 A3
Wendover Ct 4 NW2 69 C5
W1 238 A3
W3 89 A3
Bromley BR2 209 B6
Wendover Dr KT3 199 D3
Wendover Ho W1 238 A3
Wendover Rd NW10 89 D5
SE9 143 D2
Bromley BR1,BR2 209 B6
Wendover Way
Bexley DA16 146 A1
Bushey WD2 8 A5
Wendy Cl EN1 17 D5
Wendy Ho N12 30 B5
Wendy Way HA0 88 A6
Wengham Ho W12 112 A6
Wenham Ho SW8 269 A3
Wenlake Ho EC1 242 A6
Wenlock Ct N1 235 D3
Wenlock Gdns 13 NW4 46 A5
Wenlock Rd N1 95 A5 235 B3
Burnt Oak HA8 27 A4
Wenlock St N1 95 B5 235 C3
Wennington Rd E3 96 D5
Wensdale Ho E5 74 A6
Wensley Ave IG8 37 A3
Wensley Cl SE9 166 B5
Wensley Rd N18 34 B4
Wensleydale Gdns TW12 173 D3
Wensleydale Ho 8 N4 51 A2
Wensleydale Rd TW12 173 D3
Wentland Cl SE6 164 B2
Wentland Rd SE6 164 B2
Wentway Ct W13 87 A3
Wentwood Ho 1 E5 74 B6
Wentworth Ave N3 29 C3
Deacons Hill WD6 10 B6
Wentworth Cl N3 29 D3
SE28 102 D1
Ashford TW15 170 D6
Hayes BR2 225 A6
Long Ditton KT6 213 D6
Morden SM4 201 C2
Orpington BR6 227 C3
Wentworth Cres SE15 140 A5
Hayes UB3 105 B3
Wentworth Ct SW18 157 D5
W6 264 A5
High Barnet EN5 1 A2
20 Kingston u T KT6 198 A4
Southall UB2 106 C2
2 Surbiton KT6 214 A6
Twickenham TW2 152 C1
Wentworth Dr HA5 40 A4
Wentworth Dwellings E1 243 C2
Wentworth Gdns N13 16 D1
Wentworth Hall NW7 28 C5
Wentworth Hill HA9 44 C1
Wentworth Lo N3 29 D3
Wentworth Mews E3 97 B4
Wentworth Pk N3 29 D3
Wentworth Pl HA7 25 B4
Wentworth Rd E12 77 D4
NW11 47 B3
Southall UB2 106 D2
Thornton Heath CR0 204 C2
Wentworth St E1 95 D2 243 D3
Wentworth Way HA5 41 A5
Wenvoe Ave DA7 147 D3
Wernbrook St SE18 145 A6
Werndee Rd SE25 206 A5
Werneth Hall Rd IG5 56 C6
Werrington St NW1 93 C5 232 B3
Werter Rd SW15 135 A1
Wescott Cl 2 N15 51 D3
Wesley Ave E16 121 B5
NW10 89 B4
Hounslow TW3 129 B3
Wesley Cl N7 72 B6
SE17 261 D3
Harrow HA2 64 A6
Wesley Ho SE24 161 B5
Wesley Rd E10 54 A2
N10 30 C2
NW10 89 A6
Hayes UB3 84 A1
Wesley Sq W11 91 A1
Wesley St W1 238 B3
Wesleyan Pl NW5 71 B4
Wessex Ave SW19 201 C6
Wessex Cl Ilford IG3 57 C3
Kingston u T KT1,KT2 176 D2
Wessex Ct SW15 156 D6
5 Stanwell TW19 148 A5
Wessex Dr HA5 23 A3
Wessex Gardens Prim Sch NW11 47 A1
Wessex Gdns NW11 47 A1
Wessex Ho 4 N19 71 D5
SE1 263 D1
Wessex La UB6 86 B5
Wessex Rd TW6 126 A2
Wessex St E2 96 C4
Wessex Way NW11 47 A1
Wesson Ho 3 CR0 206 A1
West Acton Prim Sch W3 88 D1
West Acton Sta W3 88 C1
West App BR5 211 A4
West Arbour St E1 96 D1
West Ave E17 53 D4
N2 47 D6
N3 29 C4
NW4 46 D4
Hayes UB3 105 D6
Pinner HA5 41 B2
Southall UB1 107 B6
Wallington SM6 220 A3
West Avenue Rd E17 53 D5
West Bank N16 51 C2
Barking IG11 100 D6
Enfield EN2 5 A3
West Barnes La KT3, SW20 200 B6
West Block 17 E1 118 C6
West Brompton Sta SW5 113 C1 255 B1
West Brow BR7 188 D5
West Carriage Dr W2 114 C5 247 A4
West Central Ave NW10 90 B4
West Central St WC1 240 A2
West Chantry HA3 23 D2
West Cl N9 17 D1
Arkley EN5 12 B6
Ashford TW15 170 A6
Cockfosters EN4 3 A1
Greenford UB6 86 A5
West Cl *continued*
Wembley HA9 44 B1
West Common Rd BR2 225 B5
West Cotts NW6 69 C3
West Cromwell Rd W14 113 B1 254 D2
West Cross Ctr TW8 131 B6
West Cross Route W10, W11 112 D6
West Cross Way TW8 131 B6
West Croydon Sta CR9 205 A1
West Ct E17 53 D5
Hounslow TW7 130 A5
Wembley HA0 65 C6
West Dr SW16 181 C6
Harrow HA3 24 B4
West Drayton Park Ave UB7 104 A3
West Drayton Prim Sch UB7 104 A4
West Drayton Rd UB8 82 D1
West Drayton Sta UB7 104 A5
West Drive Gdns HA3 24 B4
West Dulwich Sta SE21 161 B3
West Ealing Bsns Ctr W13 109 A6
West Ealing Sta W13 109 B6
West Eaton Pl SW1 258 A4
West Eaton Pl Mews SW1 258 A4
West Ella Rd NW10 67 C1
West End Ave E10 54 B4
Pinner HA5 40 D5
West End Ct NW6 69 D1
Pinner HA5 40 D5
West End Gdns UB5 84 C5
West End La NW6 69 D2
Harlington UB7 127 A5
Pinner HA5 40 D5
West End Rd
Ruislip HA4,UB5 62 A4
Ruislip UB5 62 C1
Southall UB1 107 A5
West Ewell Cty Inf Sch KT19 215 B3
West Ewell Cty Jun Sch KT19 215 B3
West Finchley Sta N3 29 D4
West Garden Pl W2 237 B1
West Gate W5 88 A4
West Gdns E1 118 B6
SW19 180 C4
West Gr SE10 142 B4
Woodford IG8 37 C5
West Green Pl UB6 86 B6
West Green Prim Sch N15 51 A5
West Green Rd N15 51 B5
West Halkin St SW1 115 A3 258 A6
West Hall Rd TW9 132 D4
West Hallowes SE9 166 A3
West Ham Church Prim Sch E15 98 D6
West Ham La E15 76 C1
West Ham Sta E15 98 C4
West Hampstead Mews NW6 69 D2
West Hampstead Sta NW6 69 C2
West Hampstead Thameslink Sta NW6 69 C2
West Harding St EC4 241 B2
West Harrow Sta HA1 42 A3
West Hatch Manor HA4 39 D2
West Heath Ave NW11 47 C1
West Heath Cl NW3 69 C5
West Heath Ct NW11 47 C1
West Heath Dr NW11 47 C1
West Heath Gdns NW3 69 C5
West Heath Rd NW3 69 D5
SE2 146 D6
West Hill N6 49 A1
SW15 157 A5
Harrow HA2 64 C6
South Croydon CR2 221 C1
Wembley HA9 44 B1
West Hill Ct N6 71 A5
West Hill Hall HA2 64 C6
West Hill Prim Sch SW18 157 C6
West Hill Rd SW18 157 B5
West Hill Way N20 13 D3
West Ho 4 SE20 184 D3
5 SW12 159 C4
Barking IG11 78 D2
West House Cl SW19 157 A3
West India Ave E14 119 C5
West India Dock Rd E14 119 C6
West India Ho 1 E14 119 C6
West India Quay Sta E14 119 C6
West Kensington Ct W14 254 C2
West Kensington Mans W14 254 C1
West Kensington Sta W14 113 B1 254 C2
West La SE16 118 B4
West Lea Sch N9 17 C1
West Links HA0 87 D4
West Lodge Ave W3 110 C5
West Lodge Ct W3 110 C5
West Lodge Fst & Mid Schs HA5 40 D5
West Lodge Prep Sch DA14 168 A1
West London Shooting Grounds UB5 84 B5
West London Stad The W12 90 B2
West Mall W11 245 B4
West Mead Ruislip HA4 62 C4
West Ewell KT19 215 C2
West Mersea Cl 9 E16 121 B5
West Mews SW1 259 A3
West Middlesex Univ Hosp TW7 131 A3
West Norwood Sta SE27 160 D1
West Oak BR3 186 B2
West Park Ave TW9 132 D4
West Park Cl
Dagenham RM6 58 D4
Heston TW5 129 B6
West Park Rd
Richmond TW9 132 C4
Southall UB2 108 B5
West Pk SE9 166 A3
West Pl SW19 178 C5
West Point 2 SE1 118 A1
West Poultry Ave EC1 241 C3
West Quarters W12 90 A1
West Quay Dr UB4 85 A2
West Ramp TW6 126 C4
West Rd E15 98 D6
N2 30 B2
N17 34 B4
SW3 136 D6 267 D6
SW4 159 D6
W5 88 A2
Dagenham RM6 59 A3
East Barnet EN4 15 A3
East Bedfont TW14 149 B4
Kingston u T KT2,KT3 177 A2
West Drayton UB7 104 B3
West Ridge Gdns UB6 86 A5
West Row W10 91 A3
West Ruislip Elementary Sch UB10 61 A5
West Ruislip Sta HA4 61 A6
West Sheen Vale TW9 132 B1
West Side Comm SW19 178 C5
West Smithfield EC1 94 D2 241 D3
West Sq SE11 116 D3 261 C5
West St 26 E2 96 B5
E11 76 C5
E17 53 D4
WC2 93 D1 239 D1
Bexley DA7 147 B2
Bromley BR1 187 A1
Carshalton SM5 218 D4
Croydon CR0 221 A4
Harrow HA1 42 C1
Sutton SM1 217 D3
West Street La SM5 218 D4
West Street Pl 1 CR0 221 A4
West Surrey Ests TW15 171 A2
West Sutton Sta SM1 217 C4
West Temple Sheen SW14 154 D6
West Tenter St E1 95 D1 243 D1
West Terr DA15 167 C3
West Thames Coll TW7 130 C4
West Thornton Prim Sch CR0 204 B3
West Towers HA5 40 D3
West Twyford Prim Sch NW10 88 C5
West View
East Bedfont TW14 149 A4
Ilford RM6 58 C4
West View Gdns WD6 9 D5
West Warwick Pl SW1 259 A3
West Way N18 33 B6
NW10 67 B5
Burnt Oak HA8 27 A4
Croydon CR0 223 A5
Heston TW5 129 B4
Petts Wood BR5 211 B4
Pinner HA5 40 D5
Ruislip HA4 39 D1
Shepperton TW17 193 B3
West Wickham BR4 208 C3
West Way Gdns CR0 222 D6
West Ways HA6 22 A1
West Wickham Sta BR3 208 A2
West Wlk East Barnet EN4 15 A3
Hayes UB3 106 A5
West Woodside DA5 169 A3
Westacott UB4 83 C2
Westacott Cl N19 49 D1
Westbank Rd TW12 174 A4
Westbeech Rd N22 50 C6
Westbere Dr HA7 25 D5
Westbere Rd NW2 69 A3
Westbourne Ave W3 89 B1
Cheam SM3 217 A6
Westbourne Cl UB4 84 C3
Westbourne Cres W2 246 C6
Westbourne Ct W2 236 A2
Westbourne Dr SE23 162 D2
Westbourne Gdns W2 91 D1
Westbourne Gr W2,W11 91 C1
Westbourne Gr Mews 7 W11 91 C1
Westbourne Gr Terr W2 91 D1
Westbourne Grove W11 113 B6 244 D6
Westbourne Ho SW1 258 C2
Heston TW5 129 C6
8 Twickenham TW1 153 B4
Westbourne Par 4 UB10 82 D3
Westbourne Park Rd W2 91 C1
W11 91 B1
Westbourne Park Sta W11 91 B2
Westbourne Park Villas W2 91 C2
Westbourne Pl N9 18 B1
Westbourne Prim Sch SM1 217 C5
Westbourne Rd N7 72 B2
SE26 184 D4
Bexley DA7 147 A5
Croydon CR0 205 D3
Feltham TW13 149 D1
Hillingdon UB8 82 D3
Westbourne St W2 114 B6 246 C6
Westbourne Terr W2 92 A1 236 B2
Westbourne Terr Mews W2 236 A2
Westbourne Terr Rd W2 92 A2 236 A3
Westbridge Cl W12 112 A5
Westbridge Rd SW11 136 C4 267 A2
Westbrook Ave TW12 173 B3
Westbrook Cl EN4 2 B2
Westbrook Cres EN4 2 B2
Westbrook Ct SE3 143 B4
Westbrook Ho 5 E2 96 C4
5 SW4 159 C6
Westbrook Rd SE3 143 B4
Heston TW5 129 B5
South Norwood CR7 183 B1
Westbrook Sq EN4 2 B2
Westbrooke Cres DA16 146 C2
Westbrooke Rd
Bexley DA16 146 C2
New Eltham DA15 167 B2
Westbrooke Sch DA16 146 D2
Westbury Ave N22 32 D1
Claygate KT10 212 D2
Southall UB1 85 C3
Wembley HA0 66 A1
Westbury Cl Ruislip HA4 40 A2
Shepperton TW17 192 D3
Westbury Ct N22 33 A1
SW4 159 B5
3 Barking IG11 101 B6
Beckenham BR3 185 D2
1 Buckhurst Hill IG9 21 C2
Westbury Gr N12 29 C4
Westbury Ho 1 E17 53 C5
Westbury House Sch KT3 199 B4
Westbury La IG9 21 C2
Westbury Lodge Cl HA5 40 D6
Westbury Pl 2 TW8 131 D6
Westbury Rd E7 77 B2
E17 53 C5
N11 32 A4
N12 29 D5
SE20 184 D2
W5 88 A1
Barking IG11 101 B6
Beckenham BR3 207 A6
Bromley BR1 187 D2
Buckhurst Hill IG9 21 C3
Feltham TW13 150 D3
Ilford IG1 78 C6
New Malden KT3 199 B4
Thornton Heath CR0 205 B3
Wembley HA0 66 A1
Westbury Terr E7 77 B2
Westbush Ct 1 W12 112 B4
Westchester Ct NW4 46 D6
Westchester Dr NW4 46 D6
Westchester Ho W2 237 C1
Westcliff Ho 13 N1 73 B2
Westcombe Ave CR0 204 B2
Westcombe Ct 1 SE3 142 D5
Westcombe Dr EN5 13 C6
Westcombe Hill SE3, SE10 143 A6
Westcombe Park Lo UB4 83 B2
Westcombe Park Rd SE3 142 D5
Westcombe Park Sta SE3 121 A1
Westcoombe Ave SW20 177 D2
Westcote Rd SW16 181 C5
Westcote Rise HA4 39 A2
Westcott Cl BR1 210 A4
Westcott Cres W7 86 C2
Westcott Ho 1 E14 119 D6
Westcott Rd SE17 138 D6
Westcroft Cl NW2 69 A4
Enfield EN3 6 C5
Westcroft Ct NW9 44 D4
3 W6 112 A2
Westcroft Gdns SM4 201 B5
Westcroft Rd SM5,SM6 219 A4
Westcroft Sq W6 112 A2
Westcroft Way NW2 69 A4
Westdale Rd SE18 144 D6
Westdean Ave SE12 165 C3
Westdean Cl SW18 157 D5
Westdown Rd E15 76 A4
SE6 163 C4
Westerdale Ct N5 72 D4
Westerdale Rd 2 SE10 121 A1
Westerfield Rd 1 N15 51 D4
Westergate W5 88 A2
Westergate Rd SE2 147 A6
Westerham NW1 232 A5
13 Kingston u T KT6 198 A4
Westerham Ave N9 17 C1
Westerham Dr DA15 168 B5
Westerham Ho SE1 262 D6
Westerham Lo 10 BR3 185 C3
Westerham Rd E10 53 D2
Keston BR2 225 D2
Westerland BR7 189 A4
Westerley Cres SE26 185 B5
Western Ave NW11 46 D3
W3 89 B1
Ealing UB6 87 C4
Hillingdon HA4,UB4,UB5, UB10 61 C1
Northolt UB5 85 C6
Ruislip UB8,UB9,UB10 60 B3
Western Ct N3 29 C4
4 W3 89 B1
3 W9 91 B5
Southall UB2 107 A3
Western Dr TW17 193 B3
Western Eye Hospl The NW1 92 D2 237 C4
Western Gdns W5 110 C6
Western International Market UB2 106 B2
Western La SW12 159 A4
Western Mews W9 91 B3
Western Par EN5 13 D6
Western Pl 13 SE16 118 C4
Western Rd E13 99 C5
E17 54 A4
N2 48 D5
N22 32 B1
NW10 89 A3
SW9 138 C2
W5 109 D6
Mitcham CR4,SW19 180 C1
Southall UB2 106 D2
Sutton SM1 217 C3
Western Terr W6 112 A1
Western View UB3 105 D4
Western Way SE28 123 C4
New Barnet EN5 13 D5
Western Wharf 2 SE15 140 A6
Westernville Gdns IG2 57 A2
Westferry Cir E14 119 C5
Westferry Rd E14 119 C3
Westferry Sta E14 119 C6
Westfield
1 Farnborough BR6 227 A3
Loughton IG10 21 C6
Westfield Cl NW9 45 A6
SW10 266 A3
Cheam SM1 217 B4
Enfield EN3 7 A2
Westfield Ct 1 W10 90 D4
Kingston u T KT6 197 D4
Westfield Dr HA3 43 D5
Westfield Gdns HA3 43 D5
Westfield Ho 6 SE16 118 D2
Westfield La HA3 43 D5
Westfield Pk HA5 23 B3
Westfield Rd NW7 11 C1
W13 109 A5
Beckenham BR3 185 B1
Cheam SM1 217 B4
Dagenham RM9 81 B4
Kingston u T KT6 197 D4
Mitcham CR4 180 D1
Thornton Heath CR0 220 D6
Walton-on-T KT12 195 A2
Westfield St SE18 121 D3
Westfield Way E1 97 A3
Ruislip HA4 61 D5
Westfields SW13 133 D2
Westfields Ave SW13 133 C2
Westfields Rd W3 88 D2
Westfields Sch SW13 133 D2
Westgate Bsns Ctr W10 90 D3
2 W10 91 A3
Westgate Ct SE12 165 A3
16 SW9 138 C2
Westgate Rd SE25 206 B5
Beckenham BR3 186 A2
Westgate St E8 96 B6
Westgate Terr SW10 135 D6 265 D6
Westglade Ct HA3 43 D4
Westgrove La SE10 142 A4
Westhay Gdns SW14 154 D6
Westhill Ct W11 244 D6
Westhill Pk N6 71 A6
Westholm NW11 47 D5
Westholme BR6 211 D2
Westholme Gdns HA4 40 A1
Westhope Ho 18 E2 96 A4
Westhorne Ave SE9 165 C5
Westhorpe Rd SW15 134 C2
Westhurst Dr BR7 188 D5
Westlake 10 SE16 118 C2
Westlake Cl N13 16 C1
Hayes UB4 85 A3
Westland Cl TW19 148 A5
Westland Ct 9 UB5 84 D4
Westland Dr BR2,BR4 224 D6
Westland Ho 1 E16 122 C5
Westland Lo 1 BR1 187 C1
Westland Pl N1 235 C2
Westlands Cl UB3 106 A2
Westlands Ct KT8 196 C5
Westlands Terr 3 SW12 159 C5
Westlea Rd W7 109 A3
Westleigh Ave SW15 156 C6
Westleigh Ct 12 E11 55 A4

Westleigh Ct *continued*
N12 29 D4
Westleigh Dr BR1 188 A2
Westleigh Gdns HA8 26 C1
Westlinton Cl NW7 29 A4
Westly Ct NW2 68 D2
Westmacott Dr TW14 149 D3
Westmacott Ho NW8 236 D5
Westmark Point 13 SW15 156 B3
Westmead SW15 156 B5
Westmead Cnr SM5 218 C4
Westmead Rd SM1 218 B4
Westmeath Ho NW2 68 A5
Westmere Dr NW7 11 B1
Westmill Ct N4 73 A6
Westminster Abbey* SW1 116 A3 260 A6
Westminster Abbey Choir Sch SW1 115 D3 259 D6
Westminster Ave CR7 182 D1
Westminster Bridge SE1,SW1 116 A4 250 B1
Westminster Bridge Rd SE1 116 B4 250 C1
Westminster Cath* SW1 115 C3 259 A5
Westminster Cath Choir Sch SW1 115 C2 259 B4
Westminster Cath RC Prim Sch SW1 115 D1 259 D2
Westminster City CE Sch SW1 115 C3 259 B6
Westminster City Hall SW1 259 B6
Westminster Cl
East Bedfont TW14 150 A3
Teddington TW11 175 A5
Westminster Coll
SW1 115 C3 259 B6
SW1 115 D2 259 C4
SW11 137 A4 268 B2
W1 115 D6 249 C6
Westminster Ct E11 55 B3
22 SE16 118 D5
5 SW18 157 C6
South Norwood CR7 183 A1
Westminster Dr N13 32 A5
Westminster Gdns E4 20 C3
SW1 260 A4
Barking IG11 101 C5
Westminster Ind Est E16 121 D3
Westminster Pier SE1, SW1 250 B1
Westminster Rd N9 18 B3
W7 108 C5
Carshalton SM1,SM5 218 B6
Westminster Sch SW1 116 A3 260 A6
Westminster Sta SW1 116 A4 250 B1
Westmoat Cl BR3 186 A3
Westmont Rd KT10 212 C6
Westmoor Gdns EN3 6 D3
Westmoor Rd EN3 6 D3
Westmoor St SE7 121 D3
Westmore Ct SW15 157 A6
Westmoreland Ave DA16 145 C1
Westmoreland Ho NW10 90 A4
Westmoreland Pl SW1 258 D1
W5 87 D2
5 Bromley BR1 209 A6
Westmoreland Rd SE17 139 B6
SW13 134 A4
Beckenham BR2,BR3 208 D5
Bromley BR2 209 A5
London HA3,NW9 44 B5
Westmoreland St W1 238 B3
Westmoreland Terr SE20 184 B3
SW1 115 B1 258 D1
Westmorland Cl E12 77 D6
3 Twickenham TW1 153 B5
Westmorland Ct 12 KT6 197 D2
Westmorland Dr SM2 217 D1
Westmorland Rd E17 53 C3
Bromley BR2 209 A5
Harrow HA1 41 D4
Westmorland Sq CR4 204 A4
Westmorland Way CR4 203 D4
Westmount Ct W5 88 B2
Westmount Rd SE9 144 C1
Westoe Rd N9 18 B2
Weston Ave
East Molesey KT8 195 B5
Thames Ditton KT10,KT7 196 C2
Weston Ct N4 73 A5
N20 14 A4
3 Kingston u T KT1 198 A6
Weston Dr HA7 25 B2
Weston Ed Ctr The SE5 139 A3
Weston Gdns TW7 130 C4
Weston Gn
Dagenham RM9 81 B4
Thames Ditton KT7 196 C1
Weston Gr 1 BR1 186 D2
Weston Green Prep Sch KT7 196 C1
Weston Green Rd KT7 196 C2
Weston Ho 9 E9 96 C6
4 NW6 69 A1
Weston Park Cl KT7 196 C1
Weston Park Prim Sch N8 50 B4
Weston Pk N8 50 B3
Weston Pk *continued*
Kingston u T KT1 176 A1
Thames Ditton KT10,KT7 196 C1
Weston Rd W4 111 A3
Bromley BR1 186 D3
Dagenham RM9 81 A4
Enfield EN2 5 B3
Ruislip HA4 61 D1
Thames Ditton KT7 196 C1
Weston Rise N1, WC1 94 B4 233 D2
Weston St SE1 117 B4 252 D2
Weston Wlk 3 E8,E9 74 B1
Westonbirt Ct 6 SE15 139 D6
Westone Mans 5 IG11 79 D1
Westover Hill NW3 69 C6
Westover Rd SW18 158 A5
Westow Hill SE19 183 D4
Westow St SE19 183 C4
Westpark W5 87 D1
Westpoint SW15 156 D5
Beckenham BR2 208 B6
Westpoint Trad Est W3 88 D2
Westpole Ave EN4 3 B1
Westport Ct UB4 84 C3
Westport Rd E13 99 B3
Westport St E1 96 D1
Westrow SW15 156 C5
Westrow Dr IG11 80 A2
Westrow Gdns IG3 79 D5
Westside N2 48 D6
NW4 28 B1
Westside Ct 1 W9 91 C3
Westthorpe Gdns NW4 46 C6
Westview W7 86 C1
Westview Cl NW10 67 D3
W10 90 C1
Westview Cres N9 17 C4
Westview Ct 3 WD6 9 D5
Westview Dr IG8 37 D1
Westville Rd W12 112 A4
Thames Ditton KT7 197 A2
Westward Rd E4 35 B5
Westward Way HA3 44 A3
Westway SW20 200 C5
W10,W12 112 A6
Westway (Elevated Rd) W10 91 B2
Westway Cl SW20 200 B6
Westway Cross Sh Pk UB6 86 C6
Westway Ct UB5 85 C6
Westways KT19 215 D4
Westwell 4 NW5 71 A2
Westwell Rd SW16 182 A4
Westwell Road App SW16 182 A4
Westwick 7 KT1 176 C1
Westwick Gdns W14 112 D4
Cranford TW4,TW5 128 B3
Westwood Ave SE19 183 A2
Harrow HA2 63 D4
Westwood Cl
Bromley BR1 209 D6
Esher KT10 212 A5
Ruislip HA4 38 D3
Westwood Ct 3 SE23 162 C3
7 SW19 179 B5
Enfield EN1 17 C5
Westwood Gdns SW13 133 D2
Westwood Hill SE26 184 B6
Westwood Ho 5 N4 51 B2
W12 112 C5
Westwood Inf Sch DA16 145 C1
Westwood Jun Sch DA16 145 C1
Westwood La DA16 145 D1
Westwood Pk SE23 162 B4
Westwood Rd 12 E16 121 B5
SW13 133 D2
Ilford IG3 58 A2
Westwood Sch SE19 183 B3
Westwood Tech Coll DA16 145 C1
Wetheral Ct SW17 180 B6
Wetheral Dr HA7 25 C1
Wetherby Cl UB5 63 D2
Wetherby Ct SE25 183 C1
Wetherby Gdns SW5 114 A2 256 A3
Wetherby Mans SW5 255 C2
Wetherby Mews SW5 255 D2
Wetherby Pl SW7 114 A2 256 B3
Wetherby Rd EN2 5 A4
Wetherby Way KT9 214 A1
Wetherden St E17 53 B2
Wetherell Rd E9 96 D6
Wetherill Rd N10 31 A2
Wetland Centre The SW13 134 B5
Wevco Wharf SE15 140 B6
Wexford Ho 9 E1 96 C2
Wexford Rd SW12 158 D4
Wey Ct KT19 215 A4
Wey Ho NW8 236 D5
Weybourne St SW18 158 A2
Weybridge Ct 19 SE16 118 B1
Weybridge Ho N4 51 A2
Weybridge Point 11 SW11 136 D3
Weybridge Rd CR7 204 C5
Weydown Cl SW19 157 A3
Weyhill Ho 27 SE5 139 A3
Weyhill Rd 6 E1 96 A1
Weylond Rd RM8 81 B5
Weyman Rd SE3 143 C4
Weymarks The N17 33 B4
Weymouth Ave NW7 27 C5
W5 109 C3
Weymouth Cl 1 E6 100 D1
Weymouth Ct 5 E2 95 D5
15 SW2 160 B4
Belmont SM2 217 C1
Weymouth Ho SW8 270 C3
Weymouth Mews W1 93 B2 238 C4
Weymouth Rd UB4 83 C4
Weymouth St W1 93 B2 238 C4
Weymouth Terr E2 95 D5
Weymouth Wlk HA7 25 A4
Whadcoat St N4 72 C6
Whadden Ho 10 SE5 139 C2
Whaddon Ho SW1 247 D1
Whalebone Ave RM6 59 B3
Whalebone Gr RM6 59 B3
Whalebone La N RM6 59 A6
Whalebone La S RM6, RM8 59 B2
Whales Yd E15 76 C1
Wharf Bridge Rd TW7 131 B2
Wharf La TW1 153 A3
Wharf Pl E2 96 B6
Wharf Rd E15 98 B6
N1 95 A5 235 A3
NW1 93 D6 232 D5
Enfield EN3 19 A5
Wharf St E16 98 C2
Wharfdale Cl N11 31 A4
Wharfdale Rd N1 94 A5 233 B4
Wharfedale Ct 5 E5 74 D4
Wharfedale Gdns CR7, SW16 204 B6
Wharfedale St SW10 255 C1
Wharfside Rd E16 98 C1
Wharncliffe Dr UB1 108 B5
Wharncliffe Gdns SE25 183 C1
Wharncliffe Rd SE25 183 C1
Wharton Cl NW10 67 C2
Wharton Ho SE1 263 C6
Wharton Rd BR1 187 B2
Wharton St WC1 94 B4 233 D1
Whateley Rd SE20 184 D3
SE22 161 D6
Whatley Ave SW20 201 A6
Whatman Rd SE23 162 D4
Wheat Sheaf Cl E14 119 D2
Wheatfield Way KT1 176 A1
Wheatfields E6 100 D1
Enfield EN3 7 A3
Wheathill Ho SE20 184 B1
Wheathill Rd SE20 206 B6
Wheatland Ho 7 SE22 139 C2
Wheatlands TW5 129 C6
Wheatlands Rd SW17 159 A1
Wheatley Cl NW4 28 A1
Wheatley Gdns N9 17 C2
Wheatley Ho NW5 71 B4
3 SW15 156 A4
Wheatley Mans 8 IG11 80 A1
Wheatley Rd TW7 130 D2
Wheatley St W1 238 B3
Wheatley's Ait TW16 194 A4
Wheatly Cres UB3 106 A6
Wheatsheaf Cl UB5 63 A3
Wheatsheaf La SW6 134 C5
SW8 270 B4
Wheatsheaf Par 6 BR4 207 D1
Wheatsheaf Terr SW6 264 D3
Wheatstone Cl SW19 180 C2
Wheatstone Ho 7 W10 91 A2
Wheatstone Rd W10 91 A2
Wheeler 2 NW9 27 D3
Wheeler Ct 5 SW11 136 B2
Wheeler Gdns N1 233 B6
Wheeler La E1 243 C4
Wheelers Cross IG11 101 B5
Wheelers Dr HA4 39 A3
Wheeler's St SM1 217 C5
Wheelwright St N7 72 B1
Whelan Way SM6 219 D5
Wheldon Ct SE1 253 C2
Wheler Ho E1 243 C5
Wheler St E1 95 D3 243 C5
Whellock Rd W4 111 C3
Whernside Cl SE28 124 C6
Whetstone Cl N20 14 B2
Whetstone Park WC2 94 B1 240 C2
Whetstone Rd SE3 143 D4
Whewell Rd N19 72 A6
Whichcote St SE1 251 A3
Whidborne Bldgs WC1 233 A1
Whidborne Cl SE8 141 C3
Whidborne St WC1 233 B1
Whimbrel Cl SE28 124 C6
Whimbrel Way UB4 84 D2
Whinchat Rd SE18,SE28 123 B3
Whinfell Cl SW16 181 D5
Whinyates Rd SE9 144 A2
Whippendell Cl BR5 190 B2
Whippendell Way BR5 190 B1
Whippingham Ho 17 E3 97 B4
Whipps Cross E17 54 B4
Whipps Cross Ho E17 54 B4
Whipps Cross Hospl E10, E11 54 B3
Whipps Cross Rd E11 54 C3
Whiskin St EC1 94 D4 234 C1
Whisperwood Cl HA3 24 C3
Whistler Gdns HA8 26 B1
Whistler St N5 72 D3
Whistler Twr SW10 266 A3
Whistler Wlk SW10 266 B4
Whistlers Ave SW11 136 B5 266 D3
Whiston Ho 18 N1 72 D1
Whiston Rd E2 96 A6
Whitakers Lo EN2 5 B4
Whitbread Cl N17 34 A2
Whitbread Ctr EC1 242 C5
Whitbread Rd SE4 141 B1
Whitburn Rd SE13 142 A1
Whitby Ave NW10 88 D4
Whitby Ct N7 72 A4
Whitby Gdns NW9 44 C6
Carshalton SM1,SM5 218 B6
Whitby Ho NW8 229 A5
Whitby Rd SE18 122 B2
Carshalton SM1,SM5 218 B6
Harrow HA2 64 A5
Ruislip HA4 62 C6
Whitby St E1 243 C6
Whitcher Cl SE14 141 A6
Whitcher Pl NW1 71 C2
Whitchurch Ave HA8 26 B3
Whitchurch Cl HA8 26 B4
Whitchurch Ct SW17 180 B6
Whitchurch Fst & Mid Sch HA7 25 D3
Whitchurch Gdns HA8 26 B4
Whitchurch Ho SE6 164 A1
16 W10 90 D1
Whitchurch La HA8 26 B3
Whitchurch Par HA8 26 C3
Whitchurch Rd W11 112 D6
Whitcomb Ct W1 249 D5
Whitcomb St WC2 115 D6 249 D5
White Acre NW9 27 D1
White Bear Pl NW3 70 B4
White Bear Yd EC1 241 A5
White Bridge Ave CR4 202 B6
White Bridge Cl TW14 149 D5
White Butts Rd HA4 62 D5
White City W10 90 C1
White City Cl W12 112 C6
White City Rd W12 112 C6
White City Sta W12 112 C6
White Conduit St N1 234 B4
White Craig Cl HA5 23 C5
White Gate Gdns HA3 24 D3
White Hart Ct EC2 243 A3
White Hart La N17 33 A3
N17 33 C3
NW10 67 D2
SW13 133 C2
White Hart Lane (Tottenham Hotspur FC) N17 34 A3
White Hart Lane Sch N22 32 D3
White Hart Lane Sta N17 33 D3
White Hart Rd SE18 123 C2
White Hart Rdbt UB5 84 D5
White Hart St SE11 116 C1 261 B2
White Hart Terr N17 33 D3
White Hart Yd SE1 252 C3
White Heart Ave UB8 83 A2
White Heron Mews TW11 174 D4
White Ho N9 18 C2
3 SW4 159 D4
2 SW11 136 B3
White Ho The N17 51 C6
NW1 238 D6
White Horse Hill BR7, SE9 188 C6
White Horse La E1 96 D2
White Horse Rd E1 97 A1
E6 100 B4
White Horse St W1 115 B5 248 D3
White Horse Yd EC2 242 C2
White House Ct N14 15 D2
1 Beckenham BR3 186 A2
White House Dr HA7 25 C6
White House La EN2 5 A4
White Kennett St E1 243 B2
White Ledges W13 87 C1
White Lion Ct EC3 243 A1
White Lion Hill EC4 116 D6 251 D6
White Lion St N1 94 C5 234 B3
White Lion Yd W1 248 C6
White Lo SE19 182 D3
7 W5 87 C2
White Lodge Cl N2 48 B3
Sutton SM2 218 A1
White Lodge The Royal Ballet Sch TW10 155 B3
White Oak Dr BR3 186 A1
White Oak Gdns DA15 167 D4
White Orchards N20 13 B3
Stanmore HA7 25 A5
White Post La E9 75 C2
White Post St SE14, SE15 140 C5
White Rd E15 76 C1
White St UB2 106 D4
Whiteadder Way E14 119 D2
Whitear Wlk E15 76 B2
Whitebarn La RM10 103 C6
Whitebeam Ave BR2 210 C3
Whitebeam Cl SW9 270 D3
Whitebeam Ho 3 NW3 70 D2
Whitechapel High St E1 95 D1 243 D2
Whitechapel Rd E1 96 B2
Whitechapel Sta E1 96 B2
Whitechurch La 2 E1 96 A1
Whitecliff Ho SW18 157 D5
Whitecote Rd UB1 86 A1
Whitecroft Cl BR3 208 B5
Whitecroft Way BR3 208 B5
Whitecross Pl EC2 242 D4
Whitecross St EC1 95 A3 242 B5
Whitefield Ave NW2 46 C1
Whitefield Cl SW15 157 A5
Whitefield Sch E17 36 A1
Whitefield Sec Sch NW11 46 D2
Whitefoot La BR1 164 B1
Whitefoot Terr BR1 164 D1
Whitefriars Ave HA3 24 C1
Whitefriars Centre Coll HA3 42 C6
Whitefriars Ct N12 30 B5
Whitefriars Dr HA3 24 C1
Whitefriars Fst & Mid Sch HA3 24 C1
Whitefriars St EC4 94 C1 241 B1
Whitefriars Trad Est HA3 24 B1
Whitegates 4 EN5 13 D6
Whitehall SW1 250 A2
Whitehall Cres KT9 213 D3
Whitehall Ct SW1 116 A5 250 B3
Whitehall Gdns E4 20 C3
SW1 250 A3
W3 110 C5
W4 132 D6
Whitehall La IG9 21 A2
Whitehall Lo N10 49 A6
Woodford IG8 21 A1
Whitehall Mans 3 N19 49 C1
Whitehall Park Rd W4 132 D6
Whitehall Pk N19 49 C1
Whitehall Pl WC2,SW1 116 A5 250 A3
Wallington SM5 219 B4
Whitehall Prim Sch E4 20 C2
Whitehall Rd E4 20 C2
W7 109 A4
Bromley BR2 209 D5
Harrow HA1 42 C2
Thornton Heath CR7 204 C4
Woodford IG8 21 A1
Whitehall St N17 33 D3
Whitehaven Cl BR2 209 A5
Whitehaven St NW8 237 A5
Whitehead Cl N18 33 B5
SW18 158 A4
Whitehead Ct N10 31 A2
Whitehead Ho 8 SW15 156 D6
Whitehead's Gr SW3 114 C2 257 B3
Whiteheath Ave HA4 39 A2
Whiteheath Inf Sch HA4 39 A3
Whiteheath Jun Sch HA4 39 A2
Whitehorn Ho 6 E1 118 C5
Whitehorse La SE25 205 C5
Whitehorse Manor Inf Sch CR7 205 B5
Whitehorse Manor Jun Sch CR7 205 B5
Whitehorse Mews SE1 261 C6
Whitehorse Rd E1 97 A2
Thornton Heath CR0,CR7 205 B3
Whitehouse Est E10 54 A3
Whitehouse Way N14 15 B1
Whitelands Coll, Roehampton Inst SW18 157 A4
Whitelands Ho SW3 257 D2
Whitelegg Rd E13 98 D5
Whiteley Ho 9 SW4 159 D4
Whiteley Rd SE19 183 B5
Whiteleys Ctr W2 91 D1
Whiteleys Ho TW13 151 C1
Whiteleys Par 5 UB10 82 D3
Whiteleys Way TW13 151 C1
Whitelock Ho 21 E9 74 D2
Whiteness Ho 18 SW9 138 C4
Whiteoak Ho SE19 183 A3
Whiteoaks La UB6 86 B5
Whites Ave IG2 57 C3
Whites Dr BR2 208 D2
White's Grounds SE1 117 C4 253 B2
White's Grounds Est SE1 253 B2
White's Mdw BR1 210 C5
White's Row E1 95 D2 243 C3
White's Sq SW4 137 D1
Whitestile Rd TW8 109 D1
Whitestone La NW3 70 A5
Whitestone Wlk NW3 70 A5
Whitethorn Ave UB7 104 B6
Whitethorn Gdns
Croydon CR0 222 B6
Enfield EN2 17 B6
Whitethorn Pl UB7 104 B5
Whitethorn St E3 97 C2
Whiteways NW4 46 D5
Whitewebbs Way BR5 189 D2
Whitfield Ct 3 SE21 183 C6
SW4 270 A1
Redbridge IG1 56 B2
Whitfield Gdns W1 239 B4
Whitfield Ho NW8 237 A5
Whitfield Pl W1 239 B5
Whitfield Rd E6 77 C1
SE10,SE13 142 B4
Whitfield Rd *continued*
Erith DA7 147 B5
Whitfield St W1 93 C2 239 B4
Whitford Gdns CR4 202 D6
Whitgift Ave CR2 221 A3
Whitgift Ct CR2 221 A3
Whitgift Ctr CR0 221 A6
Whitgift Ho SE11 260 C4
SW11 267 A2
Croydon CR2 221 A3
Whitgift Sch CR2 221 A3
Whitgift St SE11 116 B2 260 C4
Croydon CR0 221 A5
Whiting Ave IG11 78 D1
Whitings Hill JMI Sch EN5 12 C6
Whitings Rd EN5 12 C6
Whitings The IG2 57 C4
Whitings Way E6 100 C2
Whitington Ave EC3 243 A1
Whitland Rd SM5 202 B1
Whitley Cl TW19 148 A5
Whitley Ho SW1 269 B6
Whitley Rd N17 33 C1
Whitlock Dr SW19 157 A3
Whitman Ho 20 E2 96 C4
Whitman Rd E3 97 A3
Whitmead Cl CR2 221 C2
Whitmore Cl N11 31 B5
Whitmore Gdns NW10 90 C5
Whitmore High Sch HA1, HA2 42 A1
Whitmore Ho 20 E1 95 C6
N11 30 D6
Whitmore Jun & Inf Sch N1 95 B6 235 D5
Whitmore Rd N1 95 C6
Beckenham BR3 207 B6
Harrow HA1 42 A2
Whitnell Ct 7 SW15 156 D6
Whitnell Way SW15 156 D6
Whitney Ave IG4 55 D5
Whitney Ho 6 SE22 139 C2
Whitney Rd E10 53 D2
Whitney Wlk DA14 191 A4
Whitstable Cl
Beckenham BR3 185 B2
Ruislip HA4 61 C6
Whitstable Ho 11 W10 90 D1
Whitstable Pl 9 CR0 221 A4
Whitsters Ho SE1 253 C2
Whitta Rd E12 77 D4
Whittaker 3 NW9 27 D3
Whittaker Ave TW10, TW9 153 D6
Whittaker Ct SW4 270 B1
Whittaker Pl 24 TW10 153 D6
Whittaker Rd E6 77 D1
Cheam SM3 217 B5
Whittaker St SW1 258 A3
Whittam Ho SE27 183 A5
Whittell Gdns SE26 162 C1
Whitten Lo N12 30 C6
Whittingham 6 N17 34 B3
Whittingham Ct W4 133 C5
Whittingstall Mans SW6 264 D1
Whittingstall Rd SW6 135 B4 264 D1
Whittington Ave UB4 83 D2
Whittington Ct N2 48 D4
SE20 184 B1
Whittington Hospl The N19 71 C6
Whittington Mews N12 30 A6
Whittington Rd N22 32 A3
Whittington Way HA5 41 A4
Whittle 4 NW9 27 D3
Whittle Cl E17 53 A2
Southall UB1 85 D1
Whittle Rd Heston TW5 128 C5
Southall UB2 107 D4
Whittlebury Cl SM5 218 D1
Whittlebury Ho N4 51 A2
Whittlesea Cl HA3 24 A3
Whittlesea Path HA3 24 A2
Whittlesea Rd HA3 24 A2
Whittlesea Sch HA3 24 A3
Whittlesey St SE1 116 C5 251 B3
Whitton NW3 70 D1
Whitton Ave E UB6 65 A2
Whitton Ave W UB5,UB6 64 B3
Whitton Cl UB6 65 B2
Whitton Dene
Isleworth TW2,TW3,TW7 152 B6
Twickenham TW2,TW7 152 B5
Whitton Dr UB6 65 A2
Whitton Manor Rd TW7 152 A5
Whitton Rd
Hounslow TW3 151 D6
Twickenham TW1 153 A4
Whitton Road Rdbt TW1 152 D5
Whitton Sch TW2 151 D2
Whitton Sta TW2 152 A4
Whitton Waye TW2, TW3 151 C5
Whitton Wlk E3 97 C4
Whitwell Ho 11 E5 74 B6
Whitwell Rd E13 99 A4
Whitworth Ho SE1 262 B5
Whitworth Rd SE18 144 C5

Whitworth Rd *continued*
SE25 205 D5
Whitworth St SE10 120 C1
Whorlton Rd SE15 140 B2
Whychcote Point NW2 46 C2
Whymark Ave N22 50 D6
Whytecroft TW5 128 D5
Whyteville Ho E7 77 B2
Whyteville Rd E7 77 B2
Whytlaw Ho 11 E3 97 B2
Wick Ho 1 KT1 175 D2
Wick La E3 75 B1
E3 97 C6
Wick Mews 1 E9 75 A2
Wick Rd E9 75 A2
Teddington TW11 175 C3
Wick Sq E9 75 B2
Wicker St 2 E1 96 B1
Wickers Oake SE19 183 D6
Wickersley Rd 9 SW11 137 A2
Wicket Rd UB6 87 A4
Wicket The CR0 223 C3
Wickets The TW15 170 A6
Wickfield Ho 29 SE16 118 A4
Wickford Ho 4 E1 96 C3
Wickford St E1 96 C3
Wickford Way E17 52 D5
Wickham Ave
Cheam KT4,SM3 216 C3
Croydon CR0 207 A1
Wickham Chase BR4 208 C2
Wickham Cl Enfield EN3 6 C2
New Malden KT3 199 D4
Wickham Common Prim Sch
BR4 225 A4
Wickham Court Rd BR4 224 A6
Wickham Cres BR4 224 A6
Wickham Ct DA16 145 C3
Wickham Gdns SE4 141 B2
Wickham Ho E1 96 C2
SW15 156 D5
Wickham La SE2,SE18 146 A6
Wickham Mews SE4 141 B3
Wickham Rd E4 36 A3
SE4 141 B2
Beckenham BR3 207 D6
Croydon CR0 207 B1
Harrow HA3 24 B1
Wickham St
SE11 116 B1 260 C2
Bexley DA16 146 A4
Wickham Way BR3 208 A4
Wickliffe Ave N3 29 A1
Wickliffe Gdns HA9 66 D6
Wicklow Ct SE26 184 C5
Wicklow Ho N16 51 D1
Wicklow St WC1 94 B4 233 C2
Wicks Cl SE12 187 D6
Wickstead Ho TW8 110 B1
Wicksteed Ho SE1 262 B5
Wickway Ct 7 SE15 139 D6
Wickwood St SE5 138 D3
Widdenham Rd N7 72 B4
Widdicombe Ave HA2 63 A6
Widdin St E15 76 C1
Wide Way CR4 203 D6
Widecombe Ct N2 48 B4
Widecombe Gdns IG4 56 A5
Widecombe Ho 33 SE5 139 A3
Widecombe Rd SE9 166 A1
Widecombe Way N2 48 B5
Widegate St E1 243 B3
Widenham Cl HA5 40 C4
Widford 8 NW1 71 B2
Widford Ho N1 234 C3
Widgeon Cl E16 99 B1
Widgeon Path SE28 123 B3
Widley Rd W9 91 C3
Widmer Ct TW5 129 A3
Widmore Lodge Rd
BR1 187 D1
Widmore Rd
Bromley BR1 187 C1
Hillingdon UB8 82 D3
Widnes Ho 6 N7 72 C3
Wieland Rd HA6 22 A3
Wigan Ho E5 52 B1
Wigeon Way UB4 84 D1
Wiggins Mead NW9 27 D3
Wigginton Ave HA9 66 D2
Wightman Rd N4,N8 50 C4
Wighton Mews TW7 130 C3
Wigley Rd TW13 150 D3
Wigmore Ct 4 W13 109 A5
Wigmore Hall W1 238 C2
Wigmore Pl W1 93 B1 238 C2
Wigmore Rd SM5 202 C1
Wigmore St W1 93 A1 238 B2
Wigmore Wlk SM5 218 B6
Wigram Ct SW11 267 A2
Wigram Ho 6 E14 119 D6
Wigram Rd E11 55 C3
Wigram Sq E17 54 A6
Wigston Cl N18 33 C5
Wigston Rd E13 99 B3
Wigton Gdns HA7 26 A2
Wigton Pl SE11 261 B1
Wigton Rd E17 35 B2
Wilberforce Ct 2 SE28 124 C5
Edgware HA8 26 B6
Wilberforce Ho 4
SW11 136 B2
Wilberforce Prim Sch
W10 91 A4
Wilberforce Rd N4 72 D6
Wilberforce Rd *continued*
N4,N5 73 A5
NW9 46 A3
Wilberforce Way SW19 178 D4
Wilbraham Ho SW8 270 A3
Wilbraham Pl SW1 258 A4
Wilbury Prim Sch N18 33 B5
Wilbury Way N18 33 B5
Wilby Mews
W11 113 B5 244 D4
Wilcox Cl SW8 270 B4
Wilcox Gdns TW17 192 B6
Wilcox Ho 6 E3 97 B2
Wilcox Pl SW1 259 B5
Wilcox Rd SW8 138 A5 270 A4
Sutton SM1 217 D4
Teddington TW11 174 B6
Wild Ct WC2 94 B1 240 C2
Wild Goose Dr SE14 140 C4
Wild Hatch NW11 47 C3
Wild March Ct EN3 7 A6
Wild St WC2 94 B1 240 C1
Wildcroft Gdns HA8 25 D4
Wildcroft Manor SW15 156 C4
Wildcroft Rd SW15 156 C4
Wilde Cl E8 96 A6
Wilde Pl N13 32 D4
SW18 158 B4
Wilde Rd DA8 147 D5
Wilder Cl HA4 40 B1
Wilderness Rd BR7 188 D3
Wilderness The
East Molesey KT8 196 A4
Hampton TW12 173 D6
Wilderton Rd N16 51 C2
Wildfell Rd SE6 163 D4
Wilding Ho 17 E9 74 D2
Wild's Rents
SE1 117 C3 263 A6
Wildwood Cl SE12 164 D4
Wildwood Gr NW3 48 A1
Wildwood Rd NW11 48 A2
Wildwood Rise NW11 48 A1
Wilford Cl EN2 5 B2
Wilford Ho 3 SE18 122 D1
Wilford Rd CR0 205 A2
Wilfred Fienburgh Ho
N7 71 D4
Wilfred Owen Cl SW19 180 A4
Wilfred St SW1 115 C3 259 A6
Wilfrid Gdns W3 89 A2
Wilkes Rd 3 TW8 132 A6
Wilkes St E1 95 D2 243 D4
Wilkie Ho SW1 259 D2
Wilkin St NW5 71 B2
Wilkins Cl Hayes UB3 105 D1
Mitcham CR4 180 C2
Wilkins Ho SW1 269 A6
Wilkinson Ct SW17 180 B6
Wilkinson Ho 17 E14 97 A2
N1 235 D3
Isleworth TW7 130 D2
Wilkinson Rd E16 99 C1
Wilkinson St
SW8 138 B5 270 C3
Wilkinson Way W4 111 B4
Wilks Gdns CR0 207 A1
Wilks Pl N1 95 C5
Will Crooks Gdns SE9 143 D1
Will Miles Ct 6 SW19 180 A3
Will Thorne Pav The
E16 100 A1
Willan Rd N17 33 C1
Willan Wall E16 120 D6
Willard St SW8 137 B2
Willbury Ho 4 N7 71 D3
Willcocks Cl KT9 214 A5
Willcott Rd W3 110 D5
Willenfield Rd NW10 89 A5
Willenhall Ave EN5 14 A5
Willenhall Ct EN5 14 A5
Willenhall Dr UB3 105 C6
Willenhall Rd SE18 122 D1
Willersley Ave
Orpington BR6 227 B5
Sidcup DA15 167 D4
Willersley Cl DA15 167 D3
Willes Rd NW5 71 B2
Willesden Community Hospl
The NW10 68 A1
Willesden Green Sta
NW2 68 C2
Willesden High Sch
NW10 90 B6
Willesden Junction Sta
NW10 89 D4
Willesden La NW2,NW6 68 D1
Willet Cl 3 UB5 84 C4
Willett Cl BR5 211 C3
Willett Ho 7 E13 99 A5
SW9 138 A2
Willett Pl CR7 204 C4
Willett Rd CR7 204 C4
Willett Way BR5,BR6 211 C3
William Allen Ho HA8 26 B3
William Atkinson Ho
N17 33 C3
William Banfield Ho 10
SW6 135 B3
William Barefoot Dr
SE9 166 C1
William Bellamy Jun & Inf
Schs RM10 81 C6
William Booth Meml
Training Coll SE5 139 B3
William Booth Rd SE20 184 A2
William Brown Ct SE27 160 D2
William Byrd Sch UB3 127 A6
William C Harvey Sch
N17 33 B1
William Carey Way HA1 42 C3
William Caslon Ho 28 E2 96 B5
William Channing Ho 6
E2 96 B4
William Cl SE13 142 A2
Southall UB2 108 A4
William Covell Cl EN2 4 B5
William Ct 4 W5 87 C2
Ilford IG6 57 B5
William Davies Prim Sch
E7 77 D2
William Davis Prim Sch
E2 96 A3
William Dromey Ct NW6 69 B1
William Dunbar Ho NW6 91 B5
William Ellis Sch NW5 71 A5
William Ellis Way 16
SE16 118 A3
William Evans Ho 9
SE8 118 D2
William Ford CE Jun Sch The
RM10 81 C1
William Gdns SW15 156 B6
William Guy Gdns 47 E3 97 D4
William Harvey Ho 1
SW19 157 A3
William Ho N13 32 D4
NW2 68 C5
William IV St
WC2 116 A6 250 A5
William Margrie Cl 1
SE15 140 A3
William Mews
SW1 114 D4 247 D1
William Morley Cl E6 99 D6
William Morris Acad
W6 112 D1
William Morris Cl E17 53 B6
William Morris Ho W6 134 D6
William Morris Mid Sch
CR4 203 D6
William Morris Sch E17 35 A2
William Morris Way
SW6 136 A3
William Patten JMI Sch
N16 73 D6
William Rainbird Ho 8
N17 33 D3
William Rathbone Ho 3
E2 96 B4
William Rd NW1 93 C4 232 A1
SW19 179 A3
Sutton SM1 218 A3
William Rushbrooke Ho 4
SE16 118 A2
William Saville Ho 2
NW6 91 B5
William Smith Ho 10
DA17 125 C3
William Sq 15 SE16 119 A6
William St E10 53 D3
N17 33 D3
SW1 114 D4 247 D1
Barking IG11 79 A1
Carshalton SM5 218 D5
William Torbitt Inf Sch
IG2 57 D4
William Torbitt Jun Sch
IG2 57 D4
William Tyndale Prim Sch
N1 72 D1
William Wood Ho 3
SE26 162 C1
Williams Ave E17 35 B2
William's Bldgs 1 E2 96 C3
Williams Cl N8 49 D3
Williams Gr N22 32 C2
Kingston u T KT6 197 C3
Williams Ho 9 E3 97 C4
9 E9 96 B6
7 E14 97 A1
14 SW2 160 C3
Williams La SW14 133 A3
Morden SM4 202 A4
Williams Rd UB2 107 A2
William's Rd W13 109 A5
Williams Terr CR0 220 C2
Williamson Cl SE10 120 D1
Williamson Ct SE17 262 A1
Williamson Rd N4 50 D3
Williamson St N7 72 A4
Williamson Way NW7 29 A4
Willifield Way NW11 47 C4
Willingale Cl IG8 37 C4
Willingdon Rd N22 32 D1
Willingham Cl 4 NW5 71 C3
Willingham Terr NW5 71 C3
Willingham Way KT1 176 C1
Willington Ct E5 75 A5
Willington Prep Sch
SW19 179 B5
Willington Rd SW9 138 A2
Willis Ave SM2 218 C2
Willis Ho 2 E12 78 C5
7 E14 119 D6
Willis Rd E15 98 D5
Thornton Heath CR0 205 A2
Willis St E14 97 D1
Willows The CR0 223 A6
Willmore End SW19 179 D1
Willoughby Ave CR0 220 B4
Willoughby Gr N17 34 B3
Willoughby Ho 34 E1 118 B5
EC2 242 C3
Willoughby La N17 34 B3
Willoughby Mews N17 34 B3
Willoughby Park Rd N17 34 B3
Willoughby Rd N8 50 C5
NW3 70 B4
Kingston u T KT2 176 B2
Twickenham TW1 153 D6
Willoughby St WC1 240 A3
Willoughby Way SE7 121 B2
Willoughbys The SW14 133 C1
Willow Ave SW13 133 D3
Sidcup DA15 168 A5
Yiewsley UB7 104 B6
Willow Bridge Rd N1 73 A2
Willow Cl 12 SE6 164 D3
Bexley DA5 169 B5
Brentford TW8 131 C6
Bromley BR2 210 B4
Buckhurst Hill IG9 21 D1
Willow Cotts
Carshalton CR4 202 D2
Richmond TW9 132 C6
Willow Ct EC2 243 A6
N7 72 B3
SW9 138 C4
3 SW16 160 B1
W4 133 C5
Barking IG1 79 A3
Charlton TW16 171 C3
8 Dagenham RM8 58 D2
Harrow HA3 24 D2
Kingston u T KT3 198 D6
Thornton Heath CR7 205 B4
7 E11 76 C6
Willow Ctr The CR4 202 D3
Willow Dean HA5 22 D1
Willow Dene WD2 8 C4
Willow Dr EN5 1 A1
Willow End N20 13 C2
Northwood HA6 22 A4
Surbiton KT6 198 A1
Willow Farm La SW15 134 B2
Willow Gdns
Hounslow TW5 129 C4
Ruislip HA4 61 D6
Willow Gn NW9 27 C2
Borehamwood WD6 11 B6
Willow Gr E13 99 A5
Chislehurst West BR7 188 D4
Ruislip HA4 39 D1
Willow Hall NW3 70 B4
Willow Ho 14 N2 30 B1
9 NW3 70 D2
W10 90 D3
Feltham TW14 150 B6
Willow La CR4 202 D3
Willow Lo SW6 134 D4
SW15 134 B2
6 Charlton TW16 171 D3
New Barnet EN5 14 A6
Willow Manor SM1 217 B4
Willow Mount CR0 221 C5
Willow Pl SW1 115 C2 259 B4
Willow Rd NW3 70 B4
W5 110 A4
Dagenham RM6 59 A3
Enfield EN1 5 C3
Kingston u T KT3 199 A5
Wallington SM6 219 B1
Willow St E4 20 B4
EC2 95 C3 243 A6
Willow Tree Cl E3 97 B6
SW18 157 D3
Hayes UB4 84 C3
Willow Tree Ct DA14 189 D5
Willow Tree La UB4 84 C3
Willow Tree Prim Sch
UB5 63 A2
Willow Tree Wlk BR1 187 B2
Willow Vale W12 112 A5
Chislehurst West BR7 188 D4
Willow View SW19 180 B2
Willow Way N3 29 D3
SE26 162 C1
9 W11 112 D6
Sunbury TW16 194 A5
Twickenham TW2 151 D2
Wembley HA0 65 A5
West Ewell KT19 215 B2
Willow Wlk E17 53 B4
12 N2 30 B1
N15 50 D5
N21 16 B5
SE1 117 D2 263 C4
Cheam SM1,SM3 217 B5
Orpington BR6 226 D5
Willow Wood Cres
SE25 205 C3
Willowbank SW6 135 A2
Willowbank Rd SE15 139 D6
Willowbrook Rd
Southall UB2 107 C3
Stanwell TW19 148 A2
Willowcourt Ave HA3 43 B4
Willowdene N6 48 D2
1 SE15 140 B4
5 SE15 140 B5
Willowdene Cl TW2 152 A4
Willowdene Ct N20 14 A4
Willowfield Sec Sch E17 52 D6
Willowhayne Dr KT12 194 B2
Willowhayne Gdns KT4 216 C4
Willowmead Cl W5 87 D2
Willowmere KT10 212 A4
Willows Ave SM4 201 D4
Willows Cl HA5 22 C1
Willows Specl Sch The
UB4 84 D3
Willows Terr NW10 89 D5
Willows The E12 78 C1
Willows The *continued*
N20 14 A1
Beckenham BR3 185 C2
Claygate KT10 212 C2
IG10 21 D6
Willowtree Cl UB10 61 A5
Willowtree Way SW16 182 C2
Willrose Cres SE2 124 B1
Wills Cres TW3 151 D5
Wills Gr NW7 28 B5
Willsbridge Ct 1 SE15 139 D6
Willshaw St SE14 141 C4
Wilman Gr E8 74 A1
Wilmar Cl UB4 83 B3
Wilmar Gdns BR4 207 D1
Wilmcote Ho W2 91 D2
Wilmer Cl TW10 176 B5
Wilmer Cres KT2,TW10 176 B5
Wilmer Gdns N1 95 C6
Wilmer Ho 5 E3 97 A5
Wilmer Lea Cl E15 76 B1
Wilmer Pl N16 73 D6
Wilmer Way N14 31 D5
Wilmers Ct 5 NW10 89 B6
Wilmington Ave W4 133 B5
Wilmington Ct SW16 182 A3
Wilmington Gdns IG11 79 C1
Wilmington Sq
WC1 94 C4 234 A1
Wilmington St WC1 234 A1
Wilmot Cl N2 30 A1
SE15 140 A5
Wilmot Pl NW1 71 C1
W7 108 C5
Wilmot Rd E10 75 D6
N17 51 B6
Carshalton SM5 218 D3
Wilmot St E2 96 B3
Wilmount St SE18 122 D2
Wilna Rd SW18 158 A4
Wilnett Ct 4 RM6 58 B2
Wilnett Villas 5 RM6 58 B2
Wilsham St
W11 113 A5 244 A4
Wilshaw Ho 10 SE8 141 C5
Wilsmere Dr
Harrow Weald HA3 24 C3
Northolt UB5 63 A3
Wilson Ave CR4 180 C2
Wilson Cl Croydon CR2 221 B3
Wembley HA9 44 B2
Wilson Dr HA9 44 B2
Wilson Gdns HA1 42 A2
Wilson Gr SE16 118 B4
Wilson Ho NW6 70 A1
2 SE7 143 C6
39 SW8 137 D3
Wilson Rd E6 99 D4
SE5 139 C4
Chessington KT9 214 B2
Redbridge IG1 56 B2
Wilson St E17 54 A4
EC2 95 B2 242 D4
N21 16 C4
Wilson's Ave 2 N17 33 D1
Wilson's Pl E14 97 B1
Wilson's Rd W6 112 D1
Wilson's Sch SM6 220 A2
Wilstone Cl UB4 85 A3
Wiltern Ct NW2 69 A2
Wilthorne Gdns RM10 81 D1
Wilton Ave W4 111 C1
Wilton Cres
SW1 115 A4 248 A1
SW19 179 B2
Wilton Ct 16 E1 96 B1
N10 31 A1
4 Richmond TW10 154 A6
7 Woodford IG8 37 A4
Wilton Est E8 74 A2
Wilton Gdns
East Molesey KT8 195 C6
Walton-on-T KT12 194 D1
Wilton Gr SW19 179 B2
New Malden KT3 199 D3
Wilton Ho 8 SE22 139 C2
Wilton Mews
SW1 115 B3 258 B6
Wilton Par TW13 150 B2
Wilton Pl SW1 115 A4 248 A1
2 Beckenham BR3 208 A6
4 Harrow HA1 42 D3
Wilton Rd N10 31 A1
SE2 124 C2
SW1 115 C2 259 A4
SW19 180 C3
Cockfosters EN4 2 D1
Hounslow TW4 128 D2
Wilton Row SW1 248 A1
Wilton Sq N1 95 B6 235 C6
Wilton St SW1 115 B3 258 C6
Wilton Terr SW1 258 A6
Wilton Villas N1 235 C5
Wilton Way E8 74 A2
Wilton Wlk TW13 150 B3
Wiltshire Cl NW7 27 D5
SW3 257 C3
Wiltshire Ct 2 N4 50 B1
Barking IG11 79 A2
Wiltshire Gdns N4 51 A3
Twickenham TW2 152 A3
Wiltshire La HA5 40 A5
Wiltshire Rd SW9 138 C2
Thornton Heath CR7 204 C6
Wiltshire Row
N1 95 B6 235 D5
Wilverley Cres KT3 199 C3
Wimbart Rd SW2 160 B4
Wimbledon Bridge
SW19 179 B4
Wimbledon Chase Mid Sch
SW20 179 A2
Wimbledon Chase Sta
SW20 179 A1
Wimbledon Cl 2 SW20 178 D3
Wimbledon Coll SW19 178 D3
Wimbledon Common
SW19 178 B6
Wimbledon Common Prep
Sch SW19 178 D3
Wimbledon High Sch
SW19 179 A4
Wimbledon Hill Rd
SW19 179 B4
Wimbledon House Sch
SW19 179 C2
Wimbledon Lawn Tennis Mus
SW19 157 A1
Wimbledon Park Ct
SW19 157 B3
Wimbledon Park Prim Sch
SW19 157 D2
Wimbledon Park Rd
SW18,SW19 157 B3
Wimbledon Park Side
SW19 156 D3
Wimbledon Park Sta
SW19 157 C1
Wimbledon Rd SW17 180 A6
Wimbledon Sch of Art
SW19 179 A2
Wimbledon Sch of Art
Annexe SW19 179 C3
Wimbledon Sta SW19 179 B4
Wimbledon Stadium
SW17 180 A6
Wimbledon Stadium Bsns Ctr
SW17 157 D1
Wimbledon Windmill Mus
SW19 156 C1
Wimbolt St E2 96 A4
Wimborne 2 DA14 190 B6
Wimborne Ave
Hayes UB4 84 B1
Southall UB2 107 C2
St Paul's Cray BR5,BR7 211 D5
Wimborne Cl SE12 164 D6
Buckhurst Hill IG9 21 C2
North Cheam KT4 200 C1
Wimborne Ct 1 UB5 63 C2
Wimborne Dr
London HA8,NW9 44 C6
Pinner HA5 41 A2
Wimborne Gdns W13 87 B2
Wimborne Ho NW1 237 B5
SW8 270 D3
SW12 159 C1
Croydon CR0 206 C4
Wimborne Rd N9 18 A2
N17 33 C1
Wimborne Way BR3 207 A5
Wimbourne Ct N1 235 C4
SW19 180 B3
South Croydon CR2 221 C2
Wimbourne St
N1 95 B5 235 C4
Wimpole Cl
Bromley BR2 209 C5
1 Kingston u T KT1 176 C1
Wimpole Mews
W1 93 B2 238 C3
Wimpole St W1 93 B1 238 C2
Wimshurst Cl CR0 204 A1
Winans Wlk SW9 138 C3
Winant Ho 17 E14 119 D6
Wincanton Cres UB5 63 C3
Wincanton Gdns IG6 56 D6
Wincanton Rd SW18 157 B4
Winch Ho SW10 266 B4
Winchcomb Gdns SE9 143 D2
Winchcombe Ct 6
SE15 139 C6
Winchcombe Rd SM5 202 C1
Winchelsea Ave DA7 147 B5
Winchelsea Cl SW15 156 D6
Winchelsea Ho 11 SE16 118 C4
Winchelsea Rd E7 77 A4
N17 51 C6
NW10 89 B6
Winchelsey Rise CR2 221 D2
Winchendon Rd
SW6 135 B4 264 D2
Teddington TW11,TW12 174 B6
Winchester Ave NW6 69 A1
NW9 44 C6
Heston TW5 129 B6
Winchester Cl 11 E6 100 B1
SE17 261 D3
Beckenham BR2 208 D6
Enfield EN1 17 C6
Kingston u T KT2 176 D3
Winchester Ct W8 245 C2
Winchester Dr HA5 40 D4
Winchester Ho 18 E3 97 B4
1 SE18 143 D5
SW3 266 D5
W2 236 A1
5 Barking IG11 80 A1
Winchester Pk BR2 208 D6
Winchester Pl 6 E8 73 D3
N6 49 B1
Winchester Rd E4 36 A3
N6 49 B1
N9 18 A3
NW3 70 B1
Beckenham BR2 208 D6

Winchester Rd *continued*
Bexley DA16 146 D3
Feltham TW13 151 B1
Harlington UB3 127 C5
Harrow HA3 44 A5
Ilford IG1 79 B5
Northwood HA6 40 A6
Twickenham TW1 153 B5
Walton-on-T KT12 194 A1
Winchester Sq SE1 252 C4
Winchester St
SW1 115 B1 258 D2
W3 111 A4
Winchester Wlk SE1 252 C4
Winchet Wlk CR0 206 C3
Winchfield Cl HA3 43 C3
Winchfield Ho SW15 155 D5
Winchfield Rd SE26 185 A5
Winchilsea Cres KT8 174 A1
Winchilsea Ho NW8 229 D1
Winchmore Hill Rd N14, N21 16 A4
Winchmore Hill Sta N21 16 D4
Winchmore Sch N21 17 A2
Winchmore Villas N21 16 B4
Winchstone Cl TW17 192 B5
Winckley Cl HA3 44 B4
Wincott St SE11 116 C2 261 B3
Wincrofts Dr SE9 145 B1
Windall Cl SE20 184 A2
Windborough Rd SM5 219 A1
Windcott Ct HA3 43 C2
Windermere NW1 231 D2
12 SW15 156 D5
Windermere Ave N3 47 C6
NW6 91 A6
SW19 201 D6
Ruislip HA4 40 D2
Wembley HA9 43 C1
Windermere Cl
East Bedfont TW14 149 D3
Orpington BR6 226 D5
TW19 148 A2
Windermere Ct SW13 133 D6
Barnet EN5 1 D1
Wembley HA9 43 C2
Windermere Gdns IG4 56 A4
Windermere Gr HA9 43 C1
Windermere Hall HA8 26 B5
Windermere Ho E3 97 B3
Twickenham TW1 152 D6
Windermere Point 3
SE15 140 C5
Windermere Rd N10 31 B2
N19 71 C6
SW15 177 C5
SW16 181 D1
W5 109 C3
Croydon CR0 205 D1
Southall UB1 85 B2
West Wickham BR4 224 C6
Windermere Way UB7 104 B5
Winders Rd SW11 136 C3
Windfield Cl SE26 184 D6
Windham Rd TW9 132 B2
Winding Way RM8 80 C5
Windlass Pl SE8 119 A2
Windlesham Gr SW19 156 D3
Windley Cl SE23 162 C2
Windmill WC1 240 C4
Windmill Alley 7 W4 111 C2
Windmill Bridge Ho 1
CR0 205 C1
Windmill Bsns Ctr UB2 108 A5
Windmill Bsns Village
TW16 171 C2
Windmill Cl 11 SE1 118 A2
3 SE13 142 A3
Charlton TW16 171 C3
Long Ditton KT6 197 C2
Windmill Ct NW2 69 A2
W5 109 C2
Windmill Dr SW4 159 B6
Keston BR2 225 C4
Windmill Gdns EN2 4 C2
Windmill Gr CR0 205 A3
Windmill Hill NW3 70 A5
1 NW3 70 A4
Enfield EN2 5 A2
Ruislip HA4 39 D1
Windmill Ho SE1 251 B3
Windmill La E15 76 B2
Borehamwood EN5 11 D5
Bushey WD2 8 C3
Isleworth TW7,UB2,W7 108 C2
Southall UB2 108 A4
Southall UB6 86 A2
Thames Ditton KT7 197 B2
Windmill Lo TW16 171 C2
Windmill Pas 10 W4 111 C2
Windmill Rd N18 33 B6
SW18 158 B5
SW19 156 B1
W4 111 C2
Brentford TW8,W5 109 C1
Charlton TW16 171 C2
Hampton TW12 174 A5
Mitcham CR4 203 C5
Thornton Heath CR0 205 A2
Windmill Rd W TW16 171 C1
Windmill Rise KT2 176 D3
Windmill Row SE11 261 A1
Windmill Sch SW2 160 A6
Windmill St W1 93 D2 239 C3
Bushey WD2 8 C3
Windmill Terr TW17 193 C2
Windmill Trad Est
TW16 171 C2
Windmill Way HA4 39 D1
Windmill Wlk SE1 251 B2
Windrose Cl SE16 118 D4
Windrush Cl SW11 136 B1
W4 133 A5
Ickenham UB10 60 B4
Windrush Ho NW8 236 D4
Windrush La SE23 162 D1
Windrush Prim Sch
SE28 124 B5
Windsock Cl 1 SE16 119 B2
Windsor Ave E17 35 A1
SW19 180 A2
Cheam SM3 217 A5
East Molesey KT8 195 C6
Edgware HA8 10 D1
Hillingdon UB10 60 D1
New Malden KT3 199 A4
Windsor Cl N3 29 A1
SE27 183 A6
Chislehurst West BR7 188 D5
Harrow HA2 63 C5
Northwood Hills HA6 22 A1
Windsor Cres
Harrow HA2 63 C5
Wembley HA9 66 D5
Windsor Ct E17 53 B6
N11 30 D5
N14 15 C4
NW3 69 C4
NW11 47 A3
20 SE16 118 D5
SE19 183 C2
SW3 257 B2
2 SW4 137 C1
SW6 135 A2
SW11 136 B3
4 SW18 157 C6
W2 245 C6
Ashford TW16 172 A3
Bromley BR1 210 A6
Bushey WD2 8 A4
Windsor Ctr The SE27 183 A6
Windsor Dr EN4 14 D5
Windsor Gdns W9 91 C3
Hayes UB3 105 B3
Wallington CR0 220 A5
Windsor Gr SE27 183 A6
Windsor Ho 4 E2 96 D4
N1 235 B4
N4 51 A1
NW1 231 D2
NW2 69 A2
2 NW4 28 D1
4 W4 111 A1
7 Northolt UB5 63 C2
Windsor Mews SE6 164 A3
SE23 163 A3
Windsor Park Rd UB3 127 D5
Windsor Pk SW19 180 A2
Windsor Pl SW1 259 B4
Windsor Rd E4 35 D6
E7 77 C3
E10 75 D6
E11 77 A6
N3 29 A1
N7 72 A5
N13 16 C1
N17 34 A1
NW2 68 B2
W5 110 A6
Ashford TW16 172 A4
Bexleyheath DA6 147 A1
Cranford TW4,TW5 128 C3
Dagenham RM8 81 A5
Ducks Island EN5 12 D5
Harrow HA3 24 B2
Ilford IG1 79 A4
Kingston u T KT2 176 A3
Richmond TW9 132 B3
South Norwood CR7 182 D1
Southall UB2 107 B3
Teddington TW11 174 B5
Worcester Pk KT4 216 A6
Windsor St N1 94 D6 234 D6
Windsor Terr N1 95 A4 235 B2
Windsor Way
W14 113 A2 254 A4
Windsor Wharf E9 75 B3
Windsor Wlk SE5 139 B3
Walton-on-T KT12 194 D1
Windspoint Dr SE15 140 B6
Windus Rd N16 51 D1
Windus Wlk N16 51 D1
Windy Ridge BR1 188 A2
Windy Ridge Cl SW19 178 D5
Wine Cl E1 118 C6
Wine Office Ct EC4 241 B2
Winery La KT1 198 B6
Winfield Ho SW11 136 B3
Winford Ct 15 SE15 140 A4
Winford Ho E3 75 B1
Winford Par 9 UB1 85 D1
Winforton St SE10 142 A4
Winfrith Rd SW18 158 A3
Wingate Cres CR0 204 A3
Wingate Ho 26 E3 97 D4
8 N16 73 B4
Wingate Rd W6 112 B3
Foots Cray DA14 190 C4
Ilford IG1 78 D3
Wingate Trad Est N17 33 D3
Wingfield Ho 16 E2 95 D4
NW6 91 D5
Wingfield Mews SE15 140 A2
Wingfield Prim Sch
SE3 143 B2
Wingfield Rd E15 76 C4
Wingfield Rd *continued*
E17 53 D4
Kingston u T KT2 176 C4
Wingfield St SE15 140 A2
Wingfield Way HA4 62 B2
Wingford Rd SW2 160 A5
Wingham 3 NW5 71 A2
Wingham Ho 3 SE26 184 B5
Wingmore Rd SE24 139 A2
Wingrad Ho 14 E1 96 C2
Wingrave SE17 262 C3
Wingrave Ho NW8 237 B6
Wingrave Rd W6 134 C6
Wingreen 13 NW8 91 D6
Wingrove Rd SE6 164 C2
Wings Cl SM1 217 C4
Winifred House Hospl
EN5 11 D5
Winifred Pl N12 30 A5
Winifred Rd SW19 179 C2
Dagenham RM8 59 A1
Hampton TW12 173 C6
Winifred St E16 122 B5
Winifred Terr EN1 17 D4
Winifrede Paul Ho 7
NW5 71 B4
Winkfield Rd E13 99 B5
N22 32 C2
Winkley Ct N10 49 B5
Harrow HA2 63 C5
Winkley St 6 E2 96 B5
Winkworth Cotts 13 E1 96 C3
Winlaton Rd BR1 186 B6
Winmill Rd RM8 81 B5
Winn Bridge Cl IG8 37 D2
Winn Common Rd
SE18 145 C6
Winn Rd SE12 165 B3
Winnett St W1 249 C6
Winningales Ct IG5 56 A6
Winnings Wlk UB5 63 A2
Winnington Cl N2 48 B3
Winnington Ho 8 SE5 139 A5
Winnington Rd N2 48 B3
Enfield EN3 6 C6
Winnipeg Dr 3 BR6 227 D2
Winnipeg Ho UB4 84 B3
Winns Ave E17 53 B6
Winns Mews N15 51 C5
Winns Prim Sch The E17 35 B1
Winns Terr E17 53 C6
Winsbeach E17 36 B1
Winscombe Cres W5 87 D3
Winscombe Ct W5 87 D3
Winscombe St N19 71 B6
Winscombe Way HA7 25 A5
Winsford Rd SE6 163 B1
Winsford Terr N18 33 B5
Winsham Gr SW11 159 A6
Winsham Ho NW1 232 D2
Winslade Ho 4 E5 74 B6
Winslade Rd SW2 160 A6
Winslade Way SE6 163 D4
Winsland Mews W2 236 C2
Winsland St W2 92 B1 236 C2
Winsley St W1 239 B2
Winslow SE17 263 A1
Winslow Cl 2 NW10 67 C5
Pinner HA5 40 B3
Winslow Gr E4 20 C2
Winslow Rd W6 134 C6
Winslow Way TW13 151 A1
Winsmoor Ct EN2 4 D2
Winsor Prim Sch E6 100 C1
Winsor Terr E6 100 C2
Winstanley Rd SW11 136 B2
Winston Ave NW9 45 C2
Winston Cl Harrow HA3 24 D4
Romford RM7 59 D5
Winston Ct
7 Bromley BR1 187 B2
Harrow HA3 23 D3
Winston Rd N16 73 B4
Winston Way IG1 79 A5
Winston Wlk W4 111 B2
Winter Ave E6 100 A6
Winter Box Wlk TW10 154 B6
Winter Lo 19 SE16 118 A1
Winterborne Ave BR6 227 B5
Winterbourne Ho W11 244 A5
Winterbourne Jun & Inf Schs
CR7 204 C5
Winterbourne Rd SE6 163 B3
Dagenham RM8 80 C6
Thornton Heath CR7 204 C5
Winterbrook Rd SE24 161 A5
Winterburn Cl N11 31 A4
Winterfold Cl SW19 157 A2
Wintergreen Cl 7 E6 100 A2
Winterleys 7 NW6 91 B5
Winter's Ct E4 19 D1
Winters Rd KT7 197 B2
Winterslow Ho 20 SE5 139 A3
Winterstoke Gdns NW7 28 A5
Winterstoke Rd SE6 163 B3
Winterton Ct KT1 175 D2
Winterton Ho 15 E1 96 C1
Winterton Pl SW10 266 B6
Winterwell Rd SW2 160 A6
Winthorpe Rd SW15 135 A1
Winthrop Ho 10 W12 112 B6
Winthrop St E1 96 B2
Winthrop Wlk HA9 66 A5
Winton Ave N11 31 C3
Winton Cl N9 18 D4
Winton Ct 15 KT6 197 D2
Winton Gdns HA8 26 B3
Winton House Sch CR0 221 D6
Winton Prim Sch
N1 94 B5 233 C3
Winton Rd BR6 226 D4
Winton Way SW16 182 C5
Wintour Ho HA9 65 D6
Wirral Wood Cl BR7 188 C4
Wirrall Ho 15 SE26 162 A1
Wisbeach Rd CR0 205 B4
Wisden Ho SW8 270 D5
Wisdom Ct 5 TW7 131 A2
Wisdons Cl RM7,RM10 59 D1
Wise La NW7 28 A4
Wise Rd E15 98 B6
Wiseman Ct 12 SE19 183 C5
Wiseman Rd E10 75 C6
Wiseton Rd SW17 158 D3
Wishart Rd SE3 143 D3
Wisley Ho SW1 259 C2
Wisley Rd SW11 159 A6
St Paul's Cray BR5 190 B3
Wistaria Cl BR6 226 D6
Wisteria Cl NW7 27 D4
Ilford IG1 78 D3
Wisteria Rd SE13 142 B1
Wistow Ho 14 E2 96 A6
Witan St E2 96 B4
Witanhurst La N6 49 A1
Witchwood Ho 11 SW9 138 C2
Witcombe Point 13
SE15 140 A4
Witham Ct E10 75 D5
Witham Ho 35 SE5 139 A3
Witham Rd SE20 206 C6
W13 109 B5
Dagenham RM10 81 C3
Hounslow TW7 130 B4
Witherby Cl CR0 221 C4
Witherington Rd N5 72 C3
Withers Cl KT9 213 C2
Withers Mead NW9 27 D2
Withers Pl EC1 242 B6
Witherston Way SE9 166 C1
Withington Rd N2 30 C2
Withy Ho 4 E1 96 D3
Withy La HA4 39 A4
Withy Mead E4 20 B1
Witley Cres CR0 224 A2
Witley Ct UB2 107 B2
Witley Gdns UB2 107 B2
Witley Ho 2 SW2 160 B4
Witley Ind Est UB2 107 B2
Witley Point 8 SW15 156 B3
Witley Rd N19 71 C6
Witney Cl Hatch End HA5 23 B4
Ickenham UB10 60 B4
Witney Path SE23 162 D1
Witten Ho KT3 199 B1
Wittenham Way E4 20 B1
Wittering Cl KT2 175 D5
Wittering Ho 9 SW11 136 D3
Wittersham Rd BR1 186 D5
Wittingham Com Prim Sch
E17 35 A2
Witts Ho KT2 198 B6
Wivenhoe Cl SE15 140 B2
Wivenhoe Ct TW4 129 B1
Wivenhoe Rd IG11 102 B5
Wiverton Rd SE26 184 C5
Wix Prim Sch SW4 137 B1
Wix Rd RM9 102 D6
Wixom Ho SE9 143 C1
Wix's La SW4 137 B1
Woburn W13 87 B2
Woburn Cl SE28 102 D1
SW19 180 A4
Bushey WD2 8 A5
Woburn Ct 4 E18 37 A1
32 SE16 118 B1
Croydon CR0 205 A1
Richmond TW9 132 B2
1 DA6 147 A1
Woburn Pl WC1 94 A3 240 A5
Woburn Rd
Carshalton SM5 202 C1
Croydon CR0 205 A1
Woburn Sq WC1 93 D3 239 D5
Woburn Twr 14 UB5 84 D4
Woburn Wlk WC1 232 D1
Wodehouse Ave SE15 139 D4
Wodehouse Ct 10 W3 111 A3
Woffington Cl KT1,KT8 175 C2
Woking Cl SW15 133 D1
Wolcot Ho NW1 232 B3
Woldham Pl BR2 209 C5
Woldham Rd BR2 209 C5
Wolds Dr BR6 226 C4
Wolf Fields Prim Sch
UB2 107 B2
Wolfe Cl Hayes BR2 209 A3
Hayes UB4 84 B4
Wolfe Cres SE7 121 D1
34 SE16 118 D4
Wolfe Ho 19 W12 112 B6
Wolferton Rd E12 78 B4
Wolfington Rd SE27 182 D6
Wolfram Cl SE13 164 C6
Wolfson Ct NW11 47 A2
SE1 253 D2
Wolfson Hillel Prim Sch
N14 15 D5
Wolftencroft Cl SW11 136 B2
Wollaston Cl SE1 262 A4
Wolmer Gdns HA8 10 C1
Wolmer Rd HA8 26 D6
Wolseley Ave SW18,
SW19 157 C2
Wolseley Gdns W4 132 D6
Wolseley Rd E7 77 B1
Wolseley Rd *continued*
N8 49 D4
N22 32 B2
W4 111 A2
Carshalton CR4 203 A2
Harrow HA3 42 C6
Wolseley St
SE1 117 D4 253 D1
Wolsey Ave E6 100 C4
E17 53 B6
Wolsey Cl SW20 178 B3
Isleworth TW3 130 A1
Kingston u T KT2 176 D2
Southall UB2 108 A3
Worcester Pk KT19,KT4 216 A4
Wolsey Cres SM4 201 B2
Wolsey Ct NW6 70 A1
SE9 166 B5
Bromley BR1 186 D3
Wolsey Dr
Kingston u T KT2 176 A4
Walton-on-T KT12 194 D1
Wolsey Gr HA8 27 B3
Wolsey Ho 2 TW12 173 D4
Wolsey Jun & Inf Schs
CR0 224 A1
Wolsey Mews NW5 71 C2
Orpington BR6 227 D3
Wolsey Rd N1 73 B3
Ashford TW15 170 B6
Ashford TW16 171 D4
East Molesey KT8 196 B5
Enfield EN1 6 B3
Hampton TW12 174 A4
Wolsey St E1 96 C2
Wolsey Way KT9 214 C3
Wolstenholme HA7 25 B5
Wolstonbury N12 29 C5
Wolvercote Rd SE2 124 D4
Wolverley St E2 96 B4
Wolverton SE17 263 A2
Wolverton Ave KT2 176 C2
Wolverton Gdns W5 110 B6
W6 112 D2
Wolverton Mans W5 110 B5
Wolverton Rd HA7 25 B3
Wolverton Way N14 15 C6
Wolves La N22 32 C4
Womersley Rd N4,N8 50 B3
Wonford Cl KT2,KT3 177 C2
Wontner Cl 5 N1 73 A1
Wontner Rd SW12,
SW17 158 D2
Wooburn Cl UB8 82 D3
Wood Cl E2 96 A3
NW9 45 B2
Harrow HA1 42 B2
Wood Dene 6 SE15 140 B4
Wood Dr BR7 188 A4
Wood End UB3 83 C1
Wood End Ave HA2 64 A4
Wood End Cl UB5 64 B3
Wood End Gdns UB5 64 A3
Wood End Green Rd
UB3 83 C1
Wood End Inf Sch UB5 64 B3
Wood End Jun Sch UB6 64 B3
Wood End La UB5 63 D3
Wood End Park Prim Sch
UB3 105 A6
Wood End Rd HA1,UB5 64 B4
Wood End Way UB5 64 A3
Wood Field NW3 70 D3
Wood Green Sta N22 32 C1
Wood Ho 6 NW6 91 B5
4 SW4 137 D3
Wood La N6 49 C4
N6 49 B3
NW9 45 B2
W12 112 C6
Dagenham RM10 81 A5
Hounslow TW7 130 D5
Ruislip HA4 61 C6
Stanmore HA7 9 B2
Woodford IG8 36 D5
Wood Lane Sch W12 90 B1
Wood Lodge Gdns BR1 188 A3
Wood Lodge La BR4 224 A5
Wood Mead N17 34 A4
Wood Point 8 E16 99 A2
Wood Rd TW17 192 C5
Wood Ride Barnet EN4 2 B4
St Paul's Cray BR5 211 C5
Wood Rise HA5 40 A4
Wood Side Sch DA17 125 D2
Wood St E16 121 B6
E17 54 B5
EC2 95 A1 242 B2
W4 111 C1
Carshalton CR4 203 A2
Chipping Barnet EN5 1 A1
Kingston u T KT1 175 D1
Kingston u T KT2 176 A2
Wood Street Sta E17 54 B5
Wood Vale N10 49 C4
SE22 162 B4
Wood Way BR6 226 C6
Wood Wharf SE10 142 A6
Woodall Ho TW7 130 D2
Woodall Rd EN3 18 D5
Woodbank Rd BR1 164 D1
Woodbastwick Rd SE26 185 A5
Woodberry Ave N21 16 D2
Harrow HA2 42 A5
Woodberry Cl TW16 172 A4
Woodberry Cres N10 49 B6
Woodberry Down N4 51 A2
Woodberry Down JMI Schs
N4 51 A2
Woodberry Gdns N12 30 A4
Woodberry Gr N4 51 A2
N12 30 A4
Woodberry Way E4 20 A4
N12 30 A4
Woodbine Cl TW2 152 B2
Woodbine Gr SE20 184 B3
Enfield EN2 5 B5
Woodbine La KT4 216 C5
Woodbine Pl E11 55 A3
Woodbine Rd DA15 167 C3
Woodbine Terr E9 74 C2
Woodbines Ave KT1 197 D6
Woodborough Rd
SW15 134 B1
Woodbourne Ave
SW16 159 D1
Woodbourne Cl SW16 160 A1
Woodbourne Dr KT10 212 D2
Woodbourne Gdns
SM6 219 B1
Woodbridge Cl 10 N7 72 B6
4 NW2 68 A5
Woodbridge Ct N16 73 B5
Woodbridge High Sch
IG8 37 B3
Woodbridge Ho E11 54 D1
Woodbridge Rd IG11 79 D3
Woodbridge St
EC1 94 D3 241 C6
Woodbrook Rd SE2 146 B6
Woodbrook Sch BR3 185 B2
Woodburn Cl NW4 46 D4
Woodbury Cl E11 55 B5
Croydon CR0 221 D6
Woodbury Ct 1 W13 87 B3
Woodbury Ho 4 SE26 162 B1
Woodbury Park Rd W13 87 B3
Woodbury Rd E17 53 D5
Woodbury St SW17 180 C5
Woodchester Sq W2 91 D2
Woodchurch Cl DA14 167 B1
Woodchurch Dr BR1 187 D3
Woodchurch Ho 15
SW9 138 C4
Woodchurch Rd NW6 69 D1
Woodclyffe Dr BR7 188 C1
Woodcock Ct HA3 44 A2
Woodcock Dell Ave HA3 43 D2
Woodcock Hill HA3 43 C3
Woodcock Ho 4 E14 97 C2
Woodcocks E16 99 D2
Woodcombe Cres SE23 162 C3
Woodcot Cl EN3 18 C5
Woodcote Ave NW7 28 C4
Thornton Heath CR7 204 D5
Wallington SM6 219 B1
Woodcote Cl KT2 176 B5
Woodcote Dr BR6 211 B2
Woodcote Ho 4 SE8 141 B6
Woodcote Mews
Loughton IG10 21 D4
Wallington SM6 219 B2
Woodcote Pl 1 SE27 182 D5
Woodcote Rd E11 55 A2
Wallington SM6 219 C1
Woodcott Ho 1 SW15 156 A4
Woodcroft N21 16 C3
SE9 166 B1
South Croydon CR0 221 C5
Wembley UB6 65 A2
Woodcroft Ave NW7 27 C4
Stanmore HA7 25 A2
Woodcroft Cres UB10 82 D6
Woodcroft Jun & Inf Schs
HA3 27 C3
Woodcroft Mews SE8 119 A2
Woodcroft Rd CR7 204 D3
Woodedge Cl E4 20 D3
Woodend SE19 183 A4
Sutton SM1 218 A6
Thames Ditton KT10 212 A6
Woodend Gdns EN2 4 A1
Woodend Rd E17 36 A1
Wooder Gdns E7 77 A4
Wooderson Cl SE25 205 C5
Woodfall Ave EN5 13 B6
Woodfall Rd N4 72 C6
Woodfall St SW3 257 C1
Woodfarrs SE5 139 B1
Woodfield Ave NW9 45 C5
SW16 159 D1
W5 87 C3
Wallington SM5 219 A1
Wembley HA0 65 C5
Woodfield Cl SE19 183 A3
1 Enfield EN1 5 C1
Woodfield Cres W5 87 D3
Woodfield Dr EN4 15 A3
Woodfield Gdns KT3 199 D4
Woodfield Gr SW16 159 D1
Woodfield Ho 6 E5 74 B6
11 SE23 162 D1
New Malden KT3 199 D4
Woodfield Pl W9 91 B3
Woodfield Rd W5 87 C3
W9 91 B2
Cranford TW4,TW5 128 B3
Hinchley Wood KT10,KT7 212 D6
Woodfield Rise WD2 8 B4
Woodfield Sch NW9 45 C1
Woodfield Way N11 31 D3
Woodfields Ct SM1 218 A5

Woodford Ave IG2,IG4,
IG5,IG8 56 B5
Woodford Bridge Rd
IG4 56 A5
Woodford Cres HA5 22 B1
Woodford Cty High Sch for
Girls IG8 36 D4
Woodford Green Prep Sch
IG8 37 A4
Woodford Green Prim Sch
IG8 37 A5
Woodford Ho 5 E18 55 A5
13 SE18 144 D6
Woodford New Rd E17 54 C6
E18 36 D3
Woodford Pl HA9 44 A1
Woodford Rd E7 77 B4
E18 55 A6
Woodford Sta IG8 37 B4
Woodford Trad Est IG8 37 D1
Woodforde Ct UB3 105 B1
Woodgate Ave KT9 213 D3
Woodgate Cres HA6 22 A4
Woodgate Dr SW16 181 D3
Woodger Rd W12 112 C4
Woodget Cl E6 100 A1
Woodgrange Ave N12 30 B4
W5 110 C5
Enfield EN1 18 A5
Harrow HA3 43 D4
Woodgrange Cl HA3 43 D4
Woodgrange Ct 1 BR2 208 D1
Woodgrange Gdns EN1 18 A5
Woodgrange Inf Sch E7 77 B4
Woodgrange Mans HA3 43 C4
Woodgrange Park Sta
E12 77 D3
Woodgrange Rd E7 77 A3
Woodgrange Terr EN1 18 A5
Woodhall NW1 232 A1
Woodhall Ave SE21 161 D1
Hatch End HA5 23 A2
Woodhall Dr SE21 161 D1
Hatch End HA5 23 A2
Woodhall Gate HA5 22 D3
Woodhall Ho SW18 158 B5
Woodhall La WD1 23 A6
Woodhall Sch WD1 23 A6
Woodham Ct E11 54 D5
Woodham Rd SE6 164 A1
Woodhatch Cl 16 E6 100 A2
Woodhaven Gdns IG6 57 A5
Woodhayes BR7 188 D4
Woodhayes Rd SW19,
SW20 178 C4
Woodhead Dr BR6 227 C6
Woodheyes Rd NW10 67 C3
Woodhill SE7,SE18 122 A2
Woodhill Cres HA3 43 D3
Woodhill Prim Sch
SE18 122 A2
Woodhouse Ave UB6 86 D5
Woodhouse Cl
Hayes UB3 105 C3
Wembley UB6 86 D5
Woodhouse Eaves HA6 22 A5
Woodhouse Gr E12 78 A2
Woodhouse Rd E11 76 D5
N12 30 C4
Woodhouse Sixth Form Coll
N12 30 B4
Woodhurst Ave BR5 211 A3
Woodhurst Rd SE2 124 A2
W3 111 A6
Woodington Cl SE9 166 C5
Woodison St E3 97 A3
Woodknoll Dr BR7 188 B2
Woodland App UB6 65 A2
Woodland Cl NW9 45 A3
SE19 183 C4
Ickenham UB10 60 D6
West Ewell KT19 215 C2
Woodford IG8 21 B1
Woodland Cres SE10 142 C6
18 SE16 118 D4
Woodland Ct 10 E11 55 A4
NW4 47 A4
Cheam SM1 217 C2
Woodland Gdns E17 54 C5
N10 49 B4
Isleworth TW7 130 C2
Woodland Hill SE19 183 C4
Woodland Rd E4 20 A3
N11 31 B5
SE19 183 D4
Thornton Heath CR7 204 C5
Woodland Rise N10 49 B5
Wembley UB6 65 A2
Woodland St 2 E8 73 D2
Woodland Terr SE7 122 A2
Woodland Way N21 16 C2
NW7 27 D4
SE2 124 D2
Croydon CR0 207 A1
Merton SM4 201 B5
Mitcham CR4 181 A3
Petts Wood BR5 211 A4
Tolworth KT5 214 D6
West Wickham BR4 224 A5
Woodford IG8 21 B1
Woodland Wlk NW3 70 C3
9 SE10 120 C1
West Ewell KT19 214 C2
Woodlands N12 30 A4
NW11 47 A4

Woodlands *continued*
SW4 137 B1
SW20 200 D5
Beckenham BR3 185 D3
Harrow HA2 41 C5
Woodlands Ave E11 55 B1
N3 30 A2
W3 110 D5
Dagenham RM6 59 A2
Kingston u T KT3 177 B2
Ruislip HA4 40 D2
Sidcup DA15 167 C3
Worcester Pk KT4 216 A6
Woodlands Cl NW11 47 A4
Bromley BR1 188 B1
Claygate KT10 212 D1
Woodlands Ct NW10 90 D6
SE22 162 B4
9 Bromley BR1 186 D2
Southall UB1 107 C6
Woodlands Dr
Harrow HA7 24 D4
Sunbury TW16 172 C1
Woodlands Gr SE10 120 C1
Hounslow TW7 130 C3
Woodlands Gt SW15 157 B6
Woodlands Inf Sch IG1 79 B3
Woodlands Jun Sch IG1 79 B3
Woodlands Par TW15 171 A4
Woodlands Park Jun & Inf
Schs N15 51 A4
Woodlands Park Rd N15 51 A4
SE10 142 C6
Woodlands Rd E11 76 C6
E17 54 A6
N9 18 C3
SW13 133 D2
Bexleyheath DA7 147 A2
Bromley BR1 188 B1
Enfield EN2 5 B4
Harrow HA1 42 D4
Ilford IG1 79 A5
Isleworth TW7 130 C3
Southall UB1 106 D5
Surbiton KT6 197 D2
Woodlands St SE13 164 B4
Woodlands The N5 73 A4
N14 15 B3
SE13 164 B4
SE19 183 A3
Isleworth TW7 130 D3
Mitcham CR4 203 A6
Stanmore HA7 25 B5
Thames Ditton KT10 212 A6
Woodlands Way SW15 157 B6
Woodlawn Cl SW15 157 B6
Woodlawn Cres TW2 151 D2
Woodlawn Dr TW13 150 D2
Woodlawn Rd SW6 134 D4
Woodlea Dr BR2 208 C4
Woodlea Lo EN1 17 C5
Woodlea Rd N16 73 C5
Woodleigh 3 E18 37 A2
1 Kingston u T KT5 198 B4
Woodleigh Ave N12 30 C4
Woodleigh Ct N22 32 B2
Woodleigh Gdns SW16 160 A1
Woodley Cl SW17 180 D3
Woodley La SM1,SM5 218 C5
Woodlodge 4 SW19 179 B5
Woodman La E4 20 C6
Woodman Par 4 E16 122 C5
Woodman St E16 122 C5
E16 122 D5
Woodmans Gr NW10 67 D3
Woodmans Mews W12 90 B2
Woodmansterne Prim Sch
SW16 181 D2
Woodmansterne Rd
SW16 181 D2
Sutton SM5 218 C1
Woodmere SE9 166 B3
Woodmere Ave CR0 206 D2
Woodmere Cl CR0 206 D2
Woodmere Ct N14 15 B4
Woodmere Gdns CR0 206 D2
Woodmere Way BR3 208 B4
Woodnook Rd SW16 181 B5
Woodpecker Cl N9 18 B5
Bushey WD2 8 A3
Harrow HA3 24 D2
Woodpecker Rd SE28 124 C6
Woodquest Ave SE24 161 A6
Woodridge Cl EN2 4 C4
Woodridge Prim Sch
N12 13 C1
Woodridings Ave HA5 23 B2
Woodridings Cl HA5 23 B3
Woodridings Ct N22 31 D2
Woodriffe Rd E11 54 B2
Woodrow SE18 122 B2
Woodrow Ave UB4 83 D3
Woodrow Cl UB6 65 B1
Woodrow Ct 3 N17 34 B3
Woodruff Ho SW2 160 C5
Woodrush Cl 4 SE14 141 A5
Woodrush Way RM6 58 D5
Woods Ho SW8 269 A2
Wood's Mews
W1 115 A6 248 A6
Wood's Pl SE1 263 B5
Wood's Rd SE15 140 B4
Woods The Eastbury HA6 22 A5
Uxbridge UB10 60 D4
Woodseer St E1 95 D2 243 D4
Woodsford SE17 262 C1
Woodsford Sq
W14 113 A4 244 B2

Woodshire Rd RM10 81 D5
Woodside N10 49 A6
N13 16 C1
NW11 47 C4
SW19 179 B5
Buckhurst Hill IG9 21 C2
Walton-on-T KT12 194 A1
Woodside Ave N6 48 D5
N12 30 A6
SE25 206 B4
Chislehurst West BR7 189 A5
Thames Ditton KT10 196 C2
Wembley HA0 88 A6
Woodside Cl Ruislip HA4 39 B3
Stanmore HA7 25 B5
Tolworth KT5 199 A2
Wembley HA0 88 A6
Woodside Com Sch E13 99 C3
Woodside Court Rd
CR0 206 A2
Woodside Cres DA15 167 C1
Woodside Ct 8 N12 29 D6
W5 110 A5
Enfield EN2 4 D4
Woodside End HA0 88 A6
Woodside Gdns E4 35 D4
N17 33 D1
Woodside Gn SE25 206 A3
Woodside Gr N12 14 A1
Woodside Grange Rd
N12 29 D6
Woodside Ho SW19 179 B4
Woodside Jun & Inf Sch
CR0 206 A2
Woodside Jun & Inf Schs
E17 54 A6
Woodside La N12 14 A1
Bexley DA5 168 D5
Woodside Park Ave E17 54 B5
Woodside Park Rd N12 30 A6
Woodside Park Sch N11 30 D5
N12 14 A1
N12 29 D6
Woodside Pk SE25 206 B3
Woodside Pl HA0 88 A6
Woodside Rd E13 99 C3
N22 32 C3
SE25 206 B3
Bromley BR1 210 A4
Kingston u T KT2 176 A3
Kingston u T KT3 177 C1
Northwood HA6 22 A3
Sidcup DA15 167 C1
Sutton SM1 218 A5
Woodford IG8 37 A6
Woodside Sta SE25 206 B3
Woodside Way
Croydon CR0 206 C3
Streatham CR4 181 C2
Woodsome Rd NW5 71 B5
Woodspring Rd SW19 157 A2
Woodstar Ho 3 SE15 140 A5
Woodstead Gr HA8 26 A4
Woodstock Ave NW11 47 A2
W13 109 A3
Cheam SM3 201 B2
Isleworth TW7 153 A6
Southall UB1 85 B4
Woodstock Cl
Sidcup DA5 169 B3
Stanmore HA7 26 A1
Woodstock Cres N9 18 B5
Woodstock Ct SE11 260 D2
SE12 165 A5
Kingston u T KT2 176 D1
Woodstock Dr UB10 60 B4
Woodstock Gdns
Hayes UB4 83 D2
Ilford IG3 80 A6
Woodstock Gr W12 112 D4
Woodstock Ho 2 N5 73 A4
Hayes UB3 83 B2
Woodstock La N KT6 213 C6
Woodstock La S KT10,
KT6 213 C4
Woodstock Mews W1 238 B3
Woodstock Rd E7 77 C1
E17 36 B1
N4 50 C1
NW11 47 B1
W4 111 C3
Bushey WD2 8 D4
Croydon CR0 221 B5
Wallington SM5,SM6 219 A3
Wembley HA0 66 B1
Woodstock Rise SM3 201 B2
Woodstock St W1 238 C1
Woodstock Terr E14 119 D6
Woodstock The SM3 201 B2
Woodstock Way CR4 181 C1
Woodstone Ave KT17,
KT4 216 A3
Woodsyre SE26 183 D6
Woodthorpe Rd SW15 134 B1
Ashford TW15 170 A6
Woodtree Cl NW4 28 C1
Woodvale Ave SE25 183 D1
Woodvale Ct SE25 205 D6
Bromley BR1 187 B1
Woodvale Way NW11 68 D5
Woodvale Wlk SE27 183 A5
Woodview Cl N4 50 D2
SW15 177 B6
Orpington BR6 227 A6
Woodville SE3 143 B4
Woodville Cl SE12 165 A6
Teddington TW11 175 A6
Woodville Ct 3 SE10 142 A4

Woodville Gdns NW11 46 D2
W5 88 A1
Ilford IG6 56 D5
Ruislip HA4 39 A2
Surbiton KT6 197 D2
Woodville Gr 2 DA16 146 A2
Woodville Ho SE1 263 C6
Woodville Rd E11 54 D1
E17 53 B5
E18 37 B1
N16 73 C3
NW6 91 B5
NW11 47 A2
W5 87 D1
Merton SM4 201 C5
New Barnet EN5 1 D2
Richmond TW10 153 C1
South Norwood CR7 205 B6
Woodville St 16 SE7 122 A2
Woodville The W5 87 D1
Woodward Ave NW4 46 A4
Woodward Cl KT10 212 D2
Woodward Gdns
Dagenham RM9 80 C1
Harrow HA7 24 D3
Woodward Rd RM9 80 C1
Woodwarde Rd SE22 161 C5
Woodway Cres HA1 43 A3
Woodwell St SW18 158 A6
Woodyard Cl NW5 71 A3
Woodyard La SE21 161 C4
Woodyates Rd SE12 165 B4
Wool Rd SW20 178 B3
Woolacombe Rd SE3 143 C3
Woolacombe Way UB3 105 C2
Woolcombes Ct 4
SE16 118 D5
Woolden Ho 2 E4 20 C4
Wooler St SE17 117 B1 262 D2
Woolf Cl SE28 124 B5
Woolf Ct 7 W3 111 A3
Woolf Mews WC1 240 A6
Woollaston Rd N4 50 D3
Woolley Ho SW9 138 D2
Woollon Ho 1 E1 96 C1
Woolmead Ave NW9 46 A2
Woolmer Gdns N18 34 A5
Woolmer Ho 2 E5 74 B6
Woolmer Rd N18 34 A5
Woolmore JMI Sch
E14 120 A6
Woolmore St E14 120 A6
Woolneigh St SW6 135 D3
Woolpack Ho 1 E9 74 C2
Woolridge Way E9 74 C1
Woolstaplers Way SE16 118 A2
Woolston Cl E17 34 D1
Woolstone Ho 7 E2 96 A6
Woolstone Rd SE23 163 A2
Woolven Ho SE3 142 D6
Woolwich & Greenwich Com
Coll SE18 123 A2
Woolwich Arsenal Sta
SE18 122 D2
Woolwich Church St
SE7,SE18 122 A3
SE18 122 C3
Woolwich Coll (Charlton Ctr)
SE7 121 D2
Woolwich Comm SE18 144 C6
Woolwich Dockyard Ind Est
SE18 122 A3
Woolwich Dockyard Sta
SE18 122 B2
Woolwich High St SE18 122 C3
Woolwich Manor Way
E6 100 C1
E16 122 D5
Woolwich Manorway
E16 122 D4
Woolwich Poly Lower Sch
SE18 122 D3
Woolwich Poly Upper Sch
SE18 122 D1
Woolwich Rd SE2 125 B1
SE7,SE10 121 C2
Belvedere DA17 125 C1
Bexleyheath DA7 147 C2
Wooster Gdns E14 98 B1
Wootton Gr N3 29 C2
Wootton Ho SE9 167 B5
Wootton St SE1 116 C5 251 B3
Worbeck Rd SE20 184 C1
Worcester Ave N17 34 A3
Worcester Cl
Croydon CR0 223 C6
Mitcham CR4 181 A1
Worcester Cres NW7 11 C1
Woodford IG8 37 C6
Worcester Ct N12 29 D5
W7 86 D1
Ashford TW15 170 D5
Harrow HA1 42 C6
Walton-on-T KT12 194 C1
Worcester Pk KT4 215 C5
Worcester Dr W4 111 C4
Ashford TW15 170 D5
Worcester Gdns SW11 158 D6
Northolt UB6 64 B2
Redbridge IG1 56 A2
Worcester Pk KT4 215 C5
Worcester Ho SE11 261 A5
9 SW15 156 C4
W2 236 A1
Worcester Mews 2
NW6 69 D2
Worcester Park Rd KT5 215 B5

Worcester Park Sta
KT4 200 A1
Worcester Rd E12 78 B4
E17 34 D1
11 SW19 179 B5
Belmont SM2 217 C1
Worcesters Ave EN1 6 A5
Worcesters Prim Sch EN1 5 D5
Wordsworth N8 50 C5
Wordsworth Ave E12 78 A1
E18 54 D6
Greenford UB6 86 B5
Wordsworth Ct HA1 42 B2
Wordsworth Dr KT4,
SM3 216 C4
Wordsworth Ho NW6 91 C4
15 SE18 144 C6
Wordsworth Par 1 N15 50 D5
Wordsworth Pl 11 NW5 70 D3
Wordsworth Rd N16 73 C4
SE1 263 D3
SE20 184 D3
Bexley DA16 145 C4
Hampton TW12,TW13 173 B6
Wallington SM6 219 D2
Wordsworth Way UB7 104 B2
Wordsworth Wlk NW11 47 C5
Worfield St
SW11 136 C5 267 B3
Worgan St SE11 116 B1 260 C2
SE16 118 D2
Working Men's Coll
NW1 93 C5 232 B4
Worland Rd E15 76 C1
World Bsns Ctr TW6 127 A4
Worlds End La BR6 227 D1
World's End La EN2 4 B1
World's End Pas SW10 266 C4
World's End Pl SW10 266 B4
Worlidge St W6 112 C1
Worlingham Rd SE22 139 D1
Wormholt Park Prim Sch
W12 112 A6
Wormholt Rd W12 112 A5
Wormwood St EC2 243 A2
Wornington Rd W10 91 A2
Wornum Ho 3 NW6 91 A5
Woronzow Rd
NW8 92 C6 230 A5
Worple Ave SW19 178 D3
Isleworth TW7 153 A6
Worple Cl HA2 41 B1
Worple Ct SW19 179 A4
Worple Prim Sch TW7 131 A1
Worple Rd SW19,SW20 178 D2
Isleworth TW7 131 A1
Worple Road Mews
SW19 179 B4
Worple St SW14 133 B2
Worple Way Harrow HA2 41 B1
Richmond TW10 132 A1
Worship St EC2 95 C3 243 A5
Worslade Rd SW17 180 B6
Worsley Bridge Jun Sch
BR3 185 C3
Worsley Bridge Rd BR3,
SE6 185 C5
Worsley Ct N3 29 D4
Worsley Ho 9 SE23 162 B2
Worsley Rd E11 76 C4
Worsopp Dr SW4 159 C6
Worth Cl BR6 227 C4
Worth Gr SE17 262 C1
Worthfield Cl KT19 215 B1
Worthing Cl 5 E15 98 C6
Worthing Rd TW5 129 B6
Worthington Cl CR4 203 B6
Worthington Ho EC1 234 B2
16 SW2 160 C4
Worthington Rd KT6 198 B1
Wortley Rd E6 77 D1
Thornton Heath CR0 204 C2
Worton Ct TW7 130 C1
Worton Gdns TW7 130 B3
Worton Hall Est TW7 130 C1
Worton Rd TW7 130 C2
Worton Way TW3,TW7 130 B3
Wotton Rd NW2 68 C5
18 SE8 141 B6
Wouldham Rd E16 98 D1
Wragby Rd E11 76 C5
Wrampling Pl N9 18 A3
Wray Ave IG5 56 C6
Wray Cres N4 72 B6
Wray Ct N4 72 B6
Wray Ho 11 SW2 160 A3
Wrayburn Ho 25 SE16 118 A4
Wrayfield Rd SM3 216 D5
Wrays Way UB4 83 C3
Wraysbury Cl TW4 151 A6
Wrekin Rd SE18 145 A5
Wren Ave NW2 68 C4
Southall UB2 107 B2
Wren Cl E16 98 D1
N9 18 D3
Wren Cres WD2 8 A3
Wren Ct CR0 221 B4
Wren Gdns RM9 80 D3
Wren Ho 27 E3 97 A5
SW1 259 C1
4 Hampton TW12 173 D4
Wren Landing E14 119 C5
Wren Path SE28 123 B4
Wren Rd SE5 139 B4
Dagenham RM9 80 D3
Sidcup DA14 168 C1
Wren St WC1 94 B3 240 D6
Wren View N6 49 C1

Wrens Ave TW15 171 A6
Wren's Park Ho E5 74 B6
Wrentham Ave NW10 90 D5
Wrenthorpe Rd BR1 186 C6
Wrenwood Way HA5 40 B5
Wrestlers Ct EC3 243 A2
Wrexham Rd E3 97 C5
Wricklemarsh Rd SE3 143 D4
Wrigglesworth St SE14 140 D5
Wright Cl SE13 142 B1
Wright Gdns TW17 192 C4
Wright Ho SW15 156 B6
Wright Rd TW5 128 C5
Wrighton Ct SM1 217 B2
Wrights Cl RM10 81 D4
Wright's Gn SW4 137 D1
Wright's La W8 113 D3 255 C6
Wrights Pl NW10 67 A2
Wrights Rd SE25 205 C6
Wright's Rd E3 97 B5
Wright's Row SM5 219 B4
Writtle Ho 36 NW9 27 D1
Wrotham Ho SE1 262 D6
Beckenham BR3 185 B3
Wrotham Rd 11 NW1 71 C1
W13 109 C5
Bexley DA16 146 C4
Monken Hadley EN5 1 A3
Wrottesley Rd NW10 90 A5
SE18 145 A6
Wroughton Rd SW11 158 D5
Wroughton Terr NW4 46 B5
Wroxall Rd RM9 80 C2
Wroxham Gdns N11 31 D3
Wroxham Rd SE28 124 D6
Wroxton Rd SE15 140 C3
Wrythe Gn SM5 218 D5
Wrythe Green Rd SM5 218 D5
Wrythe La SM1,SM5,SM4 218 C5
Wulfstan St W12 89 D1
Wyatt Cl SE16 119 B4
Bushey WD2 8 C4
Feltham TW13 150 D3
Hayes UB4 84 A2
Wyatt Ct HA0 66 A1
Wyatt Dr SW13 134 B5
Wyatt Ho NW8 236 D5
SE3 142 D3
Wyatt Park Mans 1
SW2 160 A2
Wyatt Park Rd SW2 160 B2
Wyatt Rd E7 77 A2
N5 73 A5
Wyatt's La E17 54 A6
Wybert St NW1 239 A6
Wyborne Ho NW10 67 A1
Wyborne Prim Sch SE9 166 D3
Wyborne Way NW10 67 A1
Wyburn Ave EN5 1 B2
Wyche Gr CR2 221 A1
Wycherley Cl SE3 142 D5
Wycherley Cres EN5 13 D5
Wychwood Ave
Edgware HA8 25 D4
South Norwood CR7 205 A6
Wychwood Cl
Ashford TW16 172 A4
Edgware HA8 25 D4
Wychwood End N6 49 C2
Wychwood Gdns IG5 56 C5
Wychwood Ho N4 51 A2
Wychwood Way SE19 183 B4
Wyclif Ct EC1 234 C1
Wyclif St EC1 234 C1
Wycliffe Cl DA16 145 D4
Wycliffe Ho 18 N16 73 C4
Wycliffe Rd SW11 137 A3
7 SW11 137 A2
SW19 179 D4
Wycombe Ct SE3 143 A5
Wycombe Gdns NW11 69 C6
Wycombe Ho NW8 237 A6
Wycombe Pl SW18 158 A5
Wycombe Rd N17 34 A2
Redbridge IG2 56 B4
Wembley HA0 88 C6
Wydell Cl SM4 200 D3
Wydenhurst Rd CR0 206 B2
Wydeville Manor Rd
SE12 187 B6
Wye Cl Ashford TW15 170 D6
Broom Hill BR6 211 D2
Ruislip HA4 39 A3
Wye Ct W13 87 B2
Wye St SW11 136 B3
Wyemead Cres E4 20 C2
Wyersdale Ho N4 51 A2
Wyevale Cl HA5 40 A6
Wyfold Ho 10 SE2 124 D4
Wyfold Rd SW6 135 A5 264 A3
Wyke Cl TW7 130 D6
Wyke Gdns W7 109 A3
Wyke Rd E3 75 C1
SW20 178 C1
Wykeham Ave RM9 80 C2
Wykeham Cl UB7 126 C6
Wykeham Ct NW4 46 C4
Wykeham Gn RM9 80 C2
Wykeham Hill HA9 44 B1
Wykeham Ho SW19 179 C2
Wykeham Prim Sch
NW9 67 C5
Wykeham Rd NW4 46 C4
Harrow HA3 43 B5
Wykeham Rise N20 13 A3
Wylchin Cl HA5 39 D6
Wyld Way HA9 66 D2
Wyldes Cl NW11 48 A1

Wyldfield Gdns N9 .....17 D2
Wyleu St SE23 ....163 A4
Wylie Rd UB2 ....107 C3
Wyllen Cl E1 ....96 C3
Wylo Dr EN5 ....12 A5
Wymering Mans 6 W9 .91 C4
Wymering Rd W9 ....91 C4
Wymond St SW15 .....134 C2
Wymondham Ct NW8 ..229 D6
Wynan Rd E14 ....119 D1
Wynard Terr SE11 .....260 D2
Wynash Gdns SM5 .....218 C3
Wynaud Ct N22 ....32 B4
Wynbourne Ct SE20 ...184 B1
Wyncham Ave DA15 ...167 C3
Wynchgate N14 ....16 A4
Harrow Weald HA3 ......24 C3
Wyncroft Cl BR1 ....210 B6
Wyndale Ave NW9 ......44 C3
Wyndcliff Rd SE7 ......143 B6
Wyndcroft Cl EN2 ....4 D2
Wyndham Cl
Belmont SM2 ....217 C1
Orpington BR6 ....211 A1
Wyndham Cres N19 .....71 C5
Twickenham TW4 ....151 C5
Wyndham Ct W7 ......109 A2
Wyndham Deedes Ho 27
E2 ....96 A5
Wyndham Ho SW1 ....258 A3
Wyndham Mews W1 ..237 C3
Wyndham Pl W1 ......237 C3
Wyndham Rd E6 ....77 D1
SE5 ....139 A5
W13 ....109 B3
East Barnet EN4 ....14 D3
Kingston u T KT2 ....176 B3
Wyndham St W1 92 D2 237 C4
Wyndham Yd W1 ......237 C3
Wyneham Rd SE24 ....161 B6
Wynell Rd SE23 ....162 D1
Wynford Ho N1 ....233 D4
Wynford Pl DA17 ......147 C6
Wynford Rd N1 ..94 B5 233 D4
Wynford Way SE9 .....166 B1
Wynlie Gdns HA5 ....22 B1
Wynndale Rd E18 ....37 B2
Wynne Ct 4 TW7 ......131 A2
Wynne Ho SE14 ....140 D4
Wynne Rd SW9 ....138 C3
Wynn's Ave DA15 ......168 A6
Wynnstay Gdns
W8 ....113 C3 255 B6
Wynter Ho 20 SW9 ....138 B3
Wynter St SW11 ....136 A1
Wynton Gdns SE25 ....205 D4
Wynton Pl W3 ....88 D1
Wynyard Ho SE11 .....260 D2
Wynyatt St EC1 ..94 D4 234 C2
Wyre Gr Edgware HA8 ....10 D1
Hayes UB3 ....106 A2
Wyresdale Cres UB6 ....86 D4
Wyteleaf Cl HA4 ....39 A3
Wytham Ho NW8 ......236 D5
Wythburn Ct W1 ......237 C2
Wythburn Pl W1 ......237 C2
Wythens Wlk SE9 .....166 D5
Wythenshawe Rd RM10 .81 C5
Wythes Cl BR1 ....188 B1
Wythes Rd E16 ....122 A5
Wythfield Rd SE9 ......166 B5
Wyvenhoe Rd HA2 ......64 A5
Wyvern Est The KT3 ...200 A5
Wyvil Prim Sch
SW8 ....138 A5 270 B4
Wyvil Rd SW8 ..138 A5 270 A4
Wyvis St E14 ....97 D2

Y

Yabsley St E14 ....120 A5
Yaldam Ho SE1 ....263 A3
Yalding Ho 20 E5 ....74 B3
Yalding Rd SE16 ....118 A2
Yale Cl TW4 ....151 B6
Yale Ct NW6 ....69 D3
Yarborough Rd SW19 ..180 B2
Yardley Cl E4 ....19 D6
Yardley Ct SM3 ....216 D4
Yardley La E4 ....19 D6
Yardley Prim Sch E4 ....20 A5
Yardley St WC1 ....234 A1
Yarmouth Cres N17 .....52 B4
Yarmouth Pl W1 ....248 C3
Yarnfield Sq 14 SE15 ...140 A4
Yarnton Way DA17,DA18 125 B3
Yarrow Cres E6 ....100 A2
Yarrow Ho 10 E14 .....120 A3
W10 ....90 C2
Yateley St SE18 ....121 D3
Yates Ct NW2 ....68 D2
Yates Ho 15 E2 ....96 A4
Yatesbury Ct E5 ....75 A3
Yatton Ho W10 ....90 C2
Ye Market CR0 ....221 B3
Yeading Ave HA2 ....41 A1
Yeading Ct UB4 ....84 C3
Yeading Fork UB4 ......84 C3
Yeading Gdns UB4 ......84 B2
Yeading Ho UB4 ....84 D2
Yeading Jun & Inf Schs
UB4 ....84 C2
Yeading La Hayes UB4 ...84 B2
Northolt UB4,UB5 ....84 C4
Yeadon Ho W10 ....90 C2
Yeames Cl W13 ....87 A1
Yearby Ho W10 ....90 C3
Yeate St N1 ....73 B1
Yeatman Rd N6 ....48 D3
Yeats Cl NW10 ....67 C2
Yeend Cl KT8 ....195 C5
Yeldham Ho W6 ......112 D1
Yeldham Rd W6 ....112 D1
Yellowhammer Ct NW9 .27 C1
Yelverton Lo TW1 .....153 C4
Yelverton Rd SW11 ....136 B3
Yenston Cl SM4 ....201 C3
Yeo St E3 ....97 D2
Yeoman Cl SE27 ....160 D1
Yeoman Ct TW5 ....129 B5
Yeoman Ho SE1 ....263 D2
Yeoman Rd UB5 ....63 A1
Yeoman St SE8 ....119 A2
Yeomans Acre HA4 .....40 A3
Yeomans Mews TW7 ...152 B6
Yeomans Row
SW3 ....114 C3 257 B5
Yeomans Way EN3 ....6 C3
Yeomans Yd E1 ....253 D6
Yeovil Cl BR6 ....227 C6
Yeovil Ho N7 ....72 B6
W10 ....90 C3
Yeovilton Pl KT2 ....175 C5
Yerbury Prim Sch N19 ..71 D5
Yerbury Rd N19 ....71 D5
Yesodey Hatorah Gram Sch
N16 ....51 D2
Yester Dr BR7 ....188 A3
Yester Pk BR7 ....188 B4
Yester Rd BR7 ....188 B3
Yew Ave UB7 ....104 A6
Yew Cl IG9 ....21 D2
Yew Ct E4 ....35 B4
Yew Gr NW2 ....68 D4
Yew Ho SE14 ....141 B3
Yew Tree Ave N2 ....47 D6
Yew Tree Cl N21 ....16 C4
Bexley DA16 ....146 A4
New Malden KT4 ....199 C1
Yew Tree Cotts KT10 ...212 B6
Yew Tree Ct 4 NW11 ....47 B4
8 Sutton SM2 ....218 A1
Yew Tree Gdns RM6 .....59 A4
Yew Tree Grange 2
W5 ....109 C6
Yew Tree Ho KT4 ......199 C1
Yew Tree Rd W12 ......111 D6
Hillingdon UB10 ....82 B6
Yew Tree Wlk TW4 .....151 B6
Yew Trees TW17 ....192 B5
Yew Wlk HA1 ....42 C1
Yewdale Cl BR1 ....186 C4
Yewfield Rd NW10 ......67 D2
Yews The TW15 ....170 D6
Yewtree Cl N22 ....31 C2
Harrow HA2 ....41 D5
Yewtree Rd BR3 ....207 B6
Yiewsley Ct UB7 ....104 A5
Yoakley Rd N16 ....73 C6
Yoke Cl N7 ....72 A2
Yolande Gdns SE9 .....166 A6
Yonge Pk N4,N7 ....72 C5
York Ave SE17 ....262 B2
SW14 ....155 A6
W7 ....108 C5
Hayes UB3 ....83 A1
Sidcup DA15 ....167 D2
Stanmore HA7 ....25 B1
York Bldgs WC2 116 A6 250 B5
York Bridge
NW1 ....93 A3 238 A6
York Cl E6 ....100 B1
17 SE5 ....139 A3
W7 ....108 C5
Morden SM4 ....201 D5
York Ct Beckenham BR3 .186 B2
Kingston u T KT2 ....175 D4
Wallington SM6 ....219 C3
York Gate N14 ....16 A4
NW1 ....238 B5
York Gr SE15 ....140 C4
York Hill SE27,SW16 ....160 D1
York Ho E4 ....35 C6
N1 ....233 C3
N5 ....72 C3
3 N7 ....71 D2
1 NW4 ....28 D1
SE1 ....116 B3 260 D5
SE25 ....205 C5
SE26 ....184 C5
SW3 ....257 D2
W1 ....237 C4
W3 ....111 A6
10 W3 ....88 C1
W8 ....245 C2
Enfield EN2 ....5 B4
1 Ilford IG1 ....78 D6
4 Kingston u T KT2 .....176 B3
York Ho *continued*
Richmond TW9 ....132 C4
Richmond TW10 ....154 C6
York House Pl
W8 ....113 D4 245 C2
York Mans 1 NW9 .....46 A3
SW11 ....268 B2
W1 ....238 A4
York Mews NW5 ....71 B3
Ilford IG1 ....78 C5
York Par NW9 ....46 A3
Brentford TW8 ....109 D1
York Pl SW11 ....136 B2
WC2 ....250 B5
Ilford IG1 ....78 C6
York Place Mans NW1 .237 D4
York Rd E4 ....35 C5
E7 ....77 A2
E10 ....76 A5
E17 ....52 D4
N11 ....31 D4
N18 ....34 B5
N21 ....17 B4
SE1 ....116 B4 250 D2
SW11,SW18 ....136 B2
SW19 ....180 A4
W3 ....89 B1
W5 ....109 C3
Belmont SM1,SM2 ......217 C1
Brentford TW8 ....109 D1
Hounslow TW3 ....129 D2
Ilford IG1 ....78 C6
Kingston u T KT2 ....176 B3
New Barnet EN5 ....14 B6
Northwood Hills HA6 .....22 A1
4 Richmond TW10 .....154 B6
Teddington TW11 ....174 C6
Thornton Heath CR0 ....204 C2
York Rise NW5 ....71 B5
Orpington BR6 ....227 C6
York Road Bsns Ctr
SW11 ....136 B3
York Sq 14 E14 ....97 A1
York St W1 .....92 D2 237 D4
Barking IG11 ....101 A6
Carshalton CR4 ....203 A2
Twickenham TW1 ....153 A3
York St Chambers W1 .237 C4
York Terr EN2 ....5 A5
York Terr E NW1 .93 A3 238 B5
York Terr W
NW1 ....93 A3 238 A5
York Way N1 ....233 B5
N1,N7,NW1 ....72 A1
N20 ....14 D1
York Way *continued*
Chessington KT9 ....214 A1
Feltham TW13 ....151 B1
York Way Ct N1 ....233 B5
Yorkland Ave DA16 ....145 D1
Yorkley Ho W10 ....90 C3
Yorkshire Cl N16 ....73 C5
Yorkshire Gdns N18 .....34 B5
Yorkshire Grey SE9 ....165 D6
Yorkshire Grey Yd WC1 240 C3
Yorkshire Rd E14 ....97 A1
Mitcham CR4 ....204 A5
Yorkton St E2 ....96 A5
Young Rd E16 ....99 C1
Young St W8 ..113 D4 245 C1
Youngmans Cl EN2 ....5 A4
Young's Bldgs EC1 .....242 B6
Youngs Ct SW11 ....268 B1
Youngs Rd IG2 ....57 B4
Yoxall Ho W10 ....90 C3
Yoxley App IG2 ....57 A3
Yoxley Dr IG2 ....57 A3
Yukon Rd SW12 ....159 B4
Yuletide Cl NW10 ....67 C2
Yunus Khan Cl E17 .....53 C4

Z

Zampa Rd SE16 ....118 C1
Zander Ct E2 ....96 A4
Zangwill Ho NW6 ....91 B5
Zangwill Rd SE18,SE3 ..143 D4
Zealand Ave UB7 ......126 A5
Zealand Ho 11 SE5 ....139 A3
4 SE7 ....122 A2
Zealand Rd E3 ....97 A5
Zennor Rd SW12 ......159 C3
Zenoria St SE22 ....139 D1
Zermatt Rd CR7 ....205 A5
Zetland Ho W8 ....255 C6
Zetland St E14 ....98 A2
Zion Ho 6 E1 ....96 C1
Zion Pl CR7 ....205 B5
Zion Rd CR7 ....205 B5
Zoar St SE1 ....117 A5 252 A4
Zodiac Ct CR0 ....204 D1
Zodiac Ho 3 E3 ....97 C3
Zoffany St N19 ....71 D6

List of numbered locations

This atlas shows thousands more place names than any other London street atlas. In some busy areas it is impossible to fit the name of every place.

Where not all names will fit, some smaller places are shown by a number. If you wish to find out the name associated with a number, use this listing.

The places in this list are also listed normally in the Index.

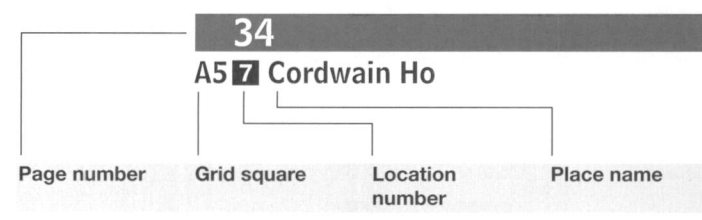

34

A5 7 Cordwain Ho

Page number | Grid square | Location number | Place name

1
A1 **1** Hertswood Ct
2 Sunbury Ct
3 Meriden Ho
4 Norfolk Ct
5 Morrison Ct
6 Kingshill Ct
7 Baronsmere Ct
8 Chartwell Ct

2
C1 **1** Braeburn Ct
2 Bramley Ct
3 Cox Ct
4 Golden Ct
5 Pippin Ct
6 Russet Ct
7 High Birch Ct
8 Joystone Ct
9 Mark Lo
10 Edgeworth Ct

5
C1 **1** Woodfield Cl
2 Fielders Cl

9
D5 **1** Watling Ct
2 Stuart Ct
3 Westview Ct
4 Potters Mews

13
D6 **1** Rowan Wlk
2 Ford Ho
3 Glenwood Ho
4 Whitegates
5 Lisa Lo
6 South Lo
7 Hockington Ct
8 Eysham Ct
9 Springfields
10 Bure Ct
11 Coleridge Ct
12 Chaucer Ct

14
B6 **1** Redrose Trad Ctr
2 Lancaster Road Ind Est
C5 **1** Feline Ct
2 Brookhill Ct
3 Littlegrove Ct
4 Desmond Ho

15
C6 **1** Tregenna Cl
2 Catherine Ct
3 Conisbee Ct
4 Ashmead
D3 **1** Dennis Par
2 Broadway The
3 Southgate Cir
4 Station Par
5 Bourneside
6 Bourneside Cres

17
C6 **1** Wade Ho
2 Newport Lo
3 Halcyon
4 Lerwick Ct
5 Anchor Ct
6 Grassmere Ct
7 Datchworth Ct
8 Trentham Lo
9 Austin Ct
10 Cedar Grange
11 Brookview Ct
12 Chestbrook Ct
13 Paddock Lo
14 Hamlet Lo
15 Haven Lo

18
A1 **1** Plevna Ct
2 Lea Ho
3 Brook Ho
4 Valley Ho

5 Chiltern Ho
6 Blenheim Ho
7 Penn Ho
8 Romany Ho
9 Gilpin Ho
10 Anvil Ho
11 Well Ho
12 Passmore Ho
13 Durbin Ho
A2 **1** Market Par
2 Beechwood Mews
3 Keats Par
4 Cedars Rd
5 Cross Keys Cl
6 Dorman Pl
7 Concourse The

20
A2 **1** Lea Ct
2 Park Ct
3 Conference Cl
4 Berrybank Cl
5 Russell Lo
6 Brunswick Lo
7 Kenilworth Ct
8 Trinity Ct
9 Kingsmead Lo
10 Fairlawns
A3 **1** Knight Ct
2 Grant Ct
3 Chantry The
4 Bowyer Ct
5 Pineview Ct
6 Ellen Ct
7 Leaview Ct
8 Chelsea Ct
9 Bramley Ct
10 Garenne Ct
11 Kendal Ct
B2 **1** Temple Hall Ct
2 Larkshall Bsns Ctr
3 Endlebury Ct
4 James Ct
5 Holmes Ct
B3 **1** Maddox Ct
2 Village Arc The
3 Cambridge Rd
4 Crown Bldgs
5 Pentney Rd
6 Scholars Ho
7 Cranworth Cres
C4 **1** Connaught Ct
2 Woolden Ho
3 Fairmead Ct
4 Lockhart Lo
5 Cavendish Ct
6 Oakwood Ct
7 Plains The
8 Hadleigh Ct
9 Forest Ho
10 Mathieson Ho

21
C2 **1** Westbury Ct
2 Palmerston Ct
3 Ibrox Ct
4 Richard Burton Ct
5 Queens Ct
6 Gunnels Ct & Hastingwood Ct
7 Marlborough Ct
8 Avenue The
9 Tara Ct
D2 **1** Regency Lo
2 Kings Ct
3 Beech Ct
4 Sycamore Ho

22
C1 **1** Northcote
2 Edwin Ware Ct
3 Chalfont Wlk
4 Maple Ct
5 Montesole Ct

23
B3 **1** St Cuthberts Gdns
2 Cherry Croft Gdns
3 Cornwall Cl
4 Dunsford Ct

25
C5 **1** Belgrave Gdns
2 Heywood Ct
3 Norfolk Ho
4 Garden Ct
5 Chatsworth Ct
6 Chartridge Ct
7 Hardwick Ct
8 Cheltenham Ct
9 Cargrey Ho
10 Holbein Ho
C6 **1** Bickley Ct
2 Kelmscott Ct
3 Elstree Ho
4 Brompton Ct
5 Kenmare Ct

27
A1 **1** Colesworth Ho
2 Crokesley Ho
3 Curtlington Ho
4 Clare Ho
5 Kedyngton Ho
A3 **1** Tadbourne Ct
2 Truman Cl
3 Lords Ct
4 Hutton Row
5 Compton Cl
6 Botham Cl
7 Bradman Row
C2 **1** Rufforth Ct
2 Temple Hall Ct
3 Riccal Ct
4 Lindholme Ct
5 Driffield Ct
6 Jack Ashley Ct
7 Folkingham La
8 Leander Ct
9 Daniel Ct
10 Nimrod
11 Nisbet
12 Pixton
13 Rapide
14 Ratier
D1 **1** Gauntlet
2 Guilfoyle
3 Grebe
4 Gates
5 Galy
6 Folland
7 Firefly
8 Halifax
9 Debussy
10 Crosbie
11 Grant Ct
12 Ham Ct
13 Deal Ct
14 Ember Ct
15 Canterbury Ct
16 Beaumont Ct
17 Cirrus
18 Defiant
19 Dessouter
20 Douglas
21 Cobham
22 Clayton
23 Camm
24 Bradon
25 Boarhound
26 Bodmin
27 Bleriot
28 Blackburn
29 Audax
30 Anson
31 Albatross
32 Arran Ct
33 Mavis Ct
34 Goosander Ct
35 Platt Halls (a)
36 Writtle Ho
37 Platt Halls (b)
38 Platt Halls (c)

D2 **1** Slatter
2 Sopwith
3 Saimet
4 Sassoon
5 Roe
6 Orde
7 Osprey
8 Prodger
9 Randall
10 Porte
11 Norris
12 Nardini
13 Noel
14 Nicolson
15 Napier
16 Nighthawk
17 Moorhouse
18 Moineau
19 Mitchell
20 Lysander
21 Lillywhite
22 Martynside
23 March
24 Kemp
25 Mercury
26 Merlin
27 Hudson
28 Hawker
29 Hawfinch
30 Heracles
31 Hector
D3 **1** Wellington
2 Wheeler
3 Whittaker
4 Whittle
5 Tedder
6 Cranwell Ct
7 Tait
8 Spooner

28
D1 **1** York Ho
2 Windsor Ho
3 Regency Cres
4 Normandy Ho

29
C2 **1** Sherringham Ct
2 St Ronan's
3 Crescent Rise
4 Elm Ct
D6 **1** Brookfield Ct
2 Magnolia Ct
3 Dunbar Ct
4 Haughmond
5 Nansen Village
6 Beechcroft Ct
7 Speedwell Ct
8 Woodside Ct
9 Speedwell Ho
10 Rebecca Ho
11 Ashbourne Ct
12 Forest Ct
13 Beecholme
14 Greville Lo
15 St Johnstone Ho

30
B1 **1** New Trinity Rd
2 Garden Ho
3 Todd Ho
4 Sayers Ho
5 Mowbray Ho
6 Bouchier Ho
7 Cleveland Ho
8 Goodyear Ho
9 Lochleven Ho
10 Berwick Ho
11 Oak Ho
12 Willow Wlk
13 Craven Ho
14 Willow Ho
15 Vane Ho
16 Foskett Ho
17 Elmfield Ho
18 Sycamore Ho
19 Netherwood
D5 **1** Halliwick Ct

2 Halliwick Court Par
3 Queen's Par
4 St John's Village
5 Hartland Ct
6 Kennard Mans
7 Bensley Cl

31
A3 **1** Campe Ho
2 Betstyle Ho
3 Pymmes Brook Ho
4 Mosswell Ho
5 Hampden Ct
6 Crown Ct
B1 **1** Cedar Ct
2 Carisbrook
3 St Ivian Ct
4 Barrington Ct
5 Essex Lo
B5 **1** Caradoc Evans Ct
2 Roberts Ho
3 Lorne Ho
B6 **1** Grovefield
2 Lapworth
3 Stewards Holte Wlk
4 Sarnes Ct
5 Stanhope Ho
6 Holmsdale Ho
C5 **1** Barbara Martin Ho
2 Jerome Ct
3 Limes Cl
4 Arnos Grove Ct
5 Cedar Ct
6 Betspath Ho
7 Curtis Ho
8 Mason Ho
9 Danford Ho
10 New Southgate Ind Est
11 Palmer's Ho

32
A4 **1** Brownlow Ct
2 Latham Ct
3 Fairlawns
4 Beaumaris
C1 **1** Penwortham Ct
2 Tarleton Ct
3 Holmeswood Ct
4 Kwesi Johnson Ct
5 Sandlings The

33
D1 **1** Honeysett Rd
2 Wilson's Ave
3 Palm Tree Ct
4 Stoneleigh Ct
5 Brook St
D3 **1** Charles Ho
2 Moselle Ho
3 Ermine Ho
4 Kathleen Ferrier Ct
5 Concord Ho
6 Rees Ho
7 Nursery Ct
8 William Rainbird Ho
D4 **1** Regan Ho
2 Isis Ho
3 Boundary Ct
4 Stellar Ho
5 Cooperage Cl

34
A5 **1** Angel Pl
2 Cross St
3 Scott Ho
4 Beck Ho
5 Booker Rd
6 Bridport Ho
7 Cordwain Ho
8 St James's Ct
9 Highmead

A6 **1** Walton Ho
2 Alma Ho
3 Brompton Ho
4 Field Ho
5 Bradwell Mews
6 Angel Corner Par
7 Paul Ct
8 Cuthbert Rd
B3 **1** Kenneth Robbins Ho
2 Charles Bradlaugh Ho
3 Woodrow Ct
4 Cheviot
5 Corbridge
6 Whittingham
7 Eastwood Cl
8 Alnwick
9 Bamburgh
10 Bellingham
11 Briars Cl

36
B5 **1** Hedgemoor Ct
2 Hewitt Ho
3 Castle Ho
4 Bailey Ct
5 Harcourt Ho
6 Gerboa Ct
D1 **1** Chatham Rd
2 Washington Rd
3 Cherry Tree Ct
4 Grosvenor Lo
5 Torfell
D2 **1** Hillboro Ct
2 Dorchester Ct

37
A1 **1** Chiltons The
2 Ullswater Ct
3 Leigh Ct
4 Woburn Ct
A2 **1** Lindal Ct
2 Hockley Ct
3 Woodleigh
4 Milne Ct
5 Cedar Ct
6 Elizabeth Ct
7 Silvermead
8 Laurel Mead Ct
9 Mitre Ct
10 Pevensey Ct
11 Lyndhurst Ct
A3 **1** New Jubilee Ct
2 Chartwell Ct
3 Greenwood
4 Solway Lo
A4 **1** Terrace The
2 Broomhill Ct
3 Clifton Ct
4 Fairstead Lo
5 Hadleigh Lo
6 Broadmead Ct
7 Wilton Ct
8 Fairfield Ct
9 Higham Ct
A6 **1** Tree Tops
2 Cranfield Ct
B1 **1** Station Est
2 Station App
3 James Ct
C3 **1** Liston Way
2 Elizabeth Ct
3 Coopersole Cl
4 Sunset Ct
5 Lambourne Ct
C4 **1** Hope Cl
2 Rex Par
3 Shalford
4 Rodings The

40
C1 **1** Salisbury Ho
2 Rodwell Cl
3 Pretoria Ho
4 Ottawa Ho
5 Swallow Ct

42
D3 **1** Nightingale Ct
2 St John's Ct
3 Gayton Ct
4 Wilton Pl
5 Murray Ct
6 Cymbeline Ct
7 Knowles Ct
8 Charville Ct
9 Lime Ct
10 Petherton Ct

46
A2 **1** Milton Rd
2 Stanley Rd
A3 **1** York Mans
2 Telford Rd
A5 **1** Pilkington Ct
2 Cousins Ct
3 Seton Ct
4 Frensham Ct
5 Chatton Ct
6 Geraldine Ct
7 Swynford Gdns
8 Miller Ct
9 Roffey Ct
10 Peace Ct
11 Rambler Ct
12 Lion Ct
13 Wenlock Gdns
14 Dogrose Ct
15 Harry Ct
16 Tribune Ct
17 Bonville Gdns
18 Pearl Ct
B4 **1** Vivian Mans
2 Parade Mans
3 Georgian Ct
4 Florence Mans
5 Park Mans
6 Cheyne Cl
7 Queens Par
8 Central Mans
C5 **1** Courtney Ho
2 Golderton
3 Thornbury
4 Brampton La
5 Ashwood Ho
6 Longford Ct
D5 **1** Midford Ho
2 Rockfield Ho
3 Lisselton Ho
4 Acrefield Ho

47
B2 **1** Berkeley Ct
2 Exchange Mans
3 Beechcroft Ct
4 Nedahall Ct
B3 **1** Charlton Lo
2 Clifton Gdns
B4 **1** Hallswelle Par
2 Belmont Par
3 Temple Fortune Ho
4 Yew Tree Ct
5 Temple Fortune Par
6 Courtleigh
7 Arcade Ho
8 Queens Ct
9 Temple Fortune Ct
B5 **1** Monkville Par
2 Ashbourne Par

48
A6 **1** St Mary's Gn
2 Dunstan Ct
3 Paul Byrne Ho
4 Longfield Ct
5 Warwick Ct
6 Branksome Ct
7 Sherwood Hall

49
B6 **1** Dorchester Ct
2 Old Chapel Pl
3 Athenaeum Pl

4 Risborough Cl
C1 1 Calvert Ct
2 Academy The
3 Whitehall Mans
4 Pauntley St
5 Archway Hts
6 Pauntley Ho
D1 1 Louise White Ho
2 Levison Way
3 Sanders Way
D2 1 Eleanor Rathbone Ho
2 Christopher Lo
3 Monkridge
4 Marbleford Ct
5 High London
6 Garton Ho
7 Hilltop Ho
8 Caroline Martyn Ho
9 Arthur Henderson Ho
10 Margaret Mcmillan Ho
11 Enid Stacy Ho
12 Mary McArthur Ho
13 Bruce Glasier Ho
14 John Wheatley Ho
15 Keir Hardie Ho
16 Monroe Ho
17 Iberia Ho
18 Lygoe Ho
19 Lambert Ho
20 Shelbourne Ho
21 Arkansas Ho
22 Lafitte Ho
23 Shreveport Ho
24 Packenham Ho
25 Orpheus Ho
26 Fayetville Ho
27 Bayon Ho
D4 1 Kelland Cl
2 Veryan Ct
3 Coulsdon Ct

50

A1 1 Beeches The
2 Lambton Ct
A2 1 Marie Lloyd Gdns
2 Jessie Blythe La
3 Leyden Mans
4 Brambledown
5 Lochbie
A5 1 Mackenzie Ct
2 Stowell Ho
3 Campsbourne Ho
B1 1 Lawson Ct
2 Wiltshire Ct
3 Hutton Ct
D5 1 Wordsworth Par

51

A2 1 Finmere Ho
2 Keynsham Ho
3 Kilpeck Ho
4 Knaresborough Ho
5 Leighfield Ho
6 Lonsdale Ho
7 Groveley Ho
8 Wensleydale Ho
9 Badminton Ct
B2 1 Selwood Ho
2 Mendip Ho
3 Ennerdale Ho
4 Delamere Ho
5 Westwood Ho
6 Bernwood Ho
7 Allerdale Ho
8 Chattenden Ho
9 Farningham Ho
10 Oakend Ho
C1 1 Godstone Ct
2 Farnham Ct
3 Milford Ct
4 Cranleigh Ct
5 Haslemere Ct
6 Belmont Ct
7 Hockworth Ho
8 Garratt Ho
9 Fairburn Ho
C3 1 Oatfield Ho
2 Perry Ct
3 Henrietta Ho
4 Bournes Ho
5 Chisley Rd
6 Twyford Ho
7 Langford Cl
8 Hatchfield Ho
D1 1 Stamford Hill Mans
2 Montefiore Ct
3 Berwyn Ho
4 Clent Ho
5 Chiltern Ho
6 Laindon Ho
7 Pentland Ho
D2 1 Regent Ct
2 Stamford Lo
3 Holmwood Ct
D3 1 Sherboro Rd
2 Wescott Ct
3 Cadoxton Ave
4 Slater Ho
D4 1 Westerfield Rd
2 Suffield Rd
D5 1 Greenway Cl
2 Tottenham Gn E
3 Tottenham Gn E South Side
4 Deaconess Ct
5 Elliot Ct
6 Bushmead Cl
7 Beaufort Ho
8 Tynemouth Terr
D6 1 Holcombe Rd
2 Chaplin Rd
3 Reynardson's Ct
4 Protheroe Ho

52

A1 1 Stamford Grove E
2 Stamford Mans
3 Grove Mans
4 Stamford Grove W
B1 1 Hawkwood Mount
2 Holmbury View
3 High Hill Ferry
4 Leaside Ho
5 Courtlands
6 Ivy Ho
7 Shelford Ct

53

A4 1 Hammond Ct
2 St James Apartments
3 Grange The
A5 1 Bristol Park Rd
2 Stoneydown Ho
3 Callonfield
4 Hardyng Ho
C1 1 Wellington Mans
2 Clewer Ct
3 Cochrane Ct
C5 1 Westbury Ho
2 Hatherley Ho
3 Vintry Mews
4 Tylers Ct
5 Merchants Lo
6 Gillards Mews
7 Blacksmiths Ho
8 Central Par
D1 1 Fitzgerald Ct
2 Bechervaise Ct
3 Underwood Ct
D2 1 Station Ct
2 Howell Ct
3 Atkinson Ct
4 Russell Ct
5 St Luke Ct
6 St Matthews Ct
7 St Mark's Ct
8 St Elizabeth Ct
9 Emmanuel Ct
10 StThomas Ct
11 Beaumont Ho
12 Shelley Ct
13 St Paul's Twr
14 Flack Ct
15 King Ct
16 Osborne Ct
17 Muriel Ct
18 All Saints Twr
19 St Josephs Ct
20 Mitchell Ct
21 Cornwell Ct
D5 1 Nash Ho
2 St Columbas Ho
3 Attlee Terr
4 Astins Ho
5 Lindens The
6 Kevan Ct
7 Squire's Almshouses
8 Berry Field Cl
9 Holmcroft Ho
10 Connaught Ct
D6 1 Hollingbury Ct
2 Mace Ho
3 Gaitskell Ho
4 Hancocke Ho
5 Trinity Ho
6 Fanshaw Ho
7 Hilltop
8 Batten Ho
9 Bradwell Ho
10 Walton Ho
11 Temple Ho
12 Gower Ho
13 Maple Ho
14 Poplars Ho
15 Cedars Ho
16 Kimm Ho
17 O'Grady Ho
18 Latham Ho
19 Powell Ct
20 Crosbie Ho

54

A2 1 Ayerst Ct
2 Dare Ct
3 St Edwards Ct
A4 1 Jane Sabina Colard's Almshouses
2 Ellen Miller Ho
3 Tom Smith Ho
A5 1 Northwood Twr
2 Walnut Ct
3 Albert Whicher Ho
4 Pelly Ct
5 Ravenswood Road Ind Est
6 Holland Ct
7 Emberson Ho
8 St Mark's Ho
9 Alfred Villas
A6 1 St David's Ct
2 Golden Par
3 Chestnuts Ct
4 Matthew Ct
5 Gilbert Ho
6 Manning Ho
7 Southgate Ho
8 Boyden Ho
9 Prospect Ho
10 Newton Ho

55

A3 1 Aldham Hall
2 Parkside Ct
3 Mapperley Cl
4 Weavers Ho
5 Cyns Ct
6 Reed Mans
7 Thornton Ho
8 Hardwick Ct
A4 1 Kingsley Grange
2 Station Par
3 Gwynne Ho
4 Staveley Ct
5 Devon Ho
6 Thurlow Ct
7 Hollies The
8 Little Holt
9 Dudley Ct
10 Woodland Ct
11 Struan Ho
12 Westleigh Ct
A5 1 Shernwood Ho
2 Orwell Lo
3 Hermitage Ct
4 Gowan Lea
5 Woodford Ho
6 Eagle Ct
7 Newbury Ct
8 Shelley Ct
9 Hardy Ct
10 Dickens Ct
11 Byron Ct
A6 1 Millbrook
2 Elmbrook
3 Grange The
4 Glenavon Lo
5 Glenwood Ct
6 Ferndown
7 Embassy Ct
8 Orestes Ct
9 Walbrook
10 Helmsley
11 Snaresbrook Hall
B4 1 Nightingale Ct
2 Chelston Ct
3 Grosvenor Ct
4 Louise Ct
5 St Davids Ct
6 Cedar Ct
7 Shrubbery The
B6 1 Victoria Ct
2 Kenwood Gdns
3 Thaxted Lo
4 Albert Rd
5 Albert Ho
6 Falcon Ct
7 Deborah Ct
8 Swift Ho
9 Pulteney Gdns
10 Spring Ct
11 Trinity Gdns

56

B4 1 High View Par
2 Spurway Par

57

A3 1 Catherine Ct
2 Lincoln Ct
3 Ivy Terr
4 Newbury Cotts

58

B1 1 Caledonian Cl
2 Talisman Cl
3 Norseman Cl
4 Frank Slater Ho
5 Brooks Mans
6 Brooks Par
B2 1 Mitre Ct
2 Coppins The
3 Stanetto Ct
4 Wilnett Ct
5 Wilnett Villas
D2 1 Pavement Mews
2 Chadview Ct
3 Granary Ct
4 Bedwell Ct
5 Chapel La
6 Faulkner Cl
7 Maple Ct
8 Willow Ct
9 Cedar Terr

63

C2 1 Wimborne Ct
2 Haydock Green Flats
3 Brighton Dr
4 Blaycon Ct
5 Fakenham Cl
6 Rutland Ho
7 Windsor Ho

65

D3 1 Oaklands Ct
2 Lowry Lo
3 Morritt Ho
4 Lancelot Par

66

A2 1 Montrose Cres
2 Peggy Quirke Ct
3 Copland Mews
4 Coronet Par
5 Charlotte Ct
A3 1 Market Way
2 Station Gr
3 Lodge Ct
4 Central Sq
5 Manor Ct
6 Rupert Ave

67

A5 1 Curie Ho
2 Darwin Ho
3 Goldbeaters Wlk
4 Greenrig Wlk
5 Redcliffe Wlk
6 Priestley Ho
7 Rutherford Ho
8 Fleming Ho
9 Lister Ho
10 Edison Ho
B1 1 Kingthorpe Terr
2 Scott Ho
3 Peary Ho
4 Shackleton Ho
5 Amundsen Ho
6 Brentfield Ho
7 Nansen Ho
8 Stonebridge Ct
9 Magellan Ct
10 Leadbetter Ct
11 Viant Ho
12 Jefferies Ho
C5 1 Hazelwood Ct
2 Winslow Cl

68

A2 1 Regency Mews
2 Tudor Mews
A5 1 Bergen Ho
2 Carton Ho
3 Woodbridge Cl
4 Mackenzie Ho
5 Banting Ho

69

A1 1 Fountain Ho
2 Kingston Ho
3 Waverley Ct
4 Weston Ho
5 Mapes Ho
6 Athelstan Gdns
7 Leff Ho
B1 1 Alma Birk Ho
2 Brooklands Ct
3 Brooklands Court Apartments
4 Cleveland Mans
5 Buckley Ct
6 Webheath
B5 1 Mortimer Cl
2 Sunnyside Ho
3 Sunnyside
4 Prospect Pl
C1 1 Linstead St
2 Embassy Ho
3 Acol Ct
4 Kings Wood Ct
5 Douglas Ct
6 King's Gdns
7 Carlton Mans
8 Smyrna Mans
9 New Priory Ct
10 Queensgate Pl
11 Brondesbury Mews
C2 1 Dene Mans
2 Sandwell Cres
3 Sandwell Mans
4 Hampstead West
5 Redcroft
C3 1 Melaris Mews
2 Walter Northcott Ho
3 Polperro Mans
4 Lyncroft Mans
5 Marlborough Mans
6 Alexandra Mans
7 Cumberland Mans
8 Cavendish Mans
9 Ambassador Ct
10 Welbeck Mans
11 Inglewood Mans
C5 1 Portman Hts
2 Hermitage Ct
3 Moreland Ct
4 Wendover Ct
D2 1 Beswick Mews
2 Worcester Mews
3 Minton Mews
4 Doulton Mews
5 Laurel Ho
6 Sandalwood Ho
7 Iroko Ho
8 Banyan Ho
9 Rosewood Ho
10 Ebony Ho
11 Rosemont Mans

70

A1 1 Harrold Ho
2 Glover Ho
3 Byron Ct
4 Nalton Ho
A2 1 Petros Gdns
2 Heath Ct
3 Imperial Twrs
4 Fairhurst
5 St John's Ct
6 New College Ct
A4 1 Windmill Hill
2 Highgrove Point
3 Gainsborough Ho
4 Heath Mans
5 Pavilion Ct
6 Holly Berry La
7 New Campden Ct
8 Benham's Pl
9 Holly Bush Vale
10 Gardnor Mans
11 Mansfield Pl
12 Streatley Pl
13 New Ct
14 Bird In Hand Yd
15 Spencer Wlk
16 Wells Ct
17 Perrin's Ct
18 Village Mount
19 Prince Arthur Ct
20 Prince Arthur Mews
21 Monro Ho
B1 1 New College Par
2 Northways Par
3 Noel Ho
4 Campden Ho
5 Centre Hts
6 Hickes Ho
7 Swiss Terr
8 Leitch Ho
9 Jevons Ho
10 Langhorne Ct
11 Park Lo
12 Avenue Lo
B2 1 Belsize Park Mews
2 Baynes Mews
3 McCrone Mews
B3 1 Belsize Court Garages
2 Roscommon Ho
3 Akenside Ct
C2 1 Banff Ho
2 Glenloch Ct
3 Havercourt
4 Holmfield Ct
5 Gilling Ct
6 Howitt Cl
7 Manor Mans
8 Straffan Lo
9 Romney Ct
10 Lancaster Stables
11 Eton Garages
D1 1 Hancock Nunn Ho
2 Higginson Ho
3 Duncan Ho
4 Mary Wharrie Ho
5 Rockstraw Ho
6 Cleaver Ho
7 Chamberlain St
8 Sharples Hall St
9 Primrose Mews
10 Rothwell St
D2 1 Alder Ho
2 Hornbeam Ho
3 Whitebeam Ho
4 Aspen Ho
5 Rowan Ho
6 Beech Ho
7 Chestnut Ho
8 Oak Ho
9 Willow Ho
10 Sycamore Ho
11 Maple Ho
12 Hazel Ho
13 Elaine Ct
14 Faircourt
15 Walham Ct
16 Stanbury Ct
17 Priory Mans
18 Wellington Ho
19 Grange The
D3 1 Cayford Ho
2 Du Maurier Ho
3 Isokon Flats
4 Palgrave Ho
5 Garnett Ho
6 Stephenson Ho
7 Park Dwellings
8 Siddons Ho
9 Mall Studios
10 Park Hill Wlk
11 Wordsworth Pl
12 Fraser Regnart Ct
13 St Pancras Almshouses

71

A1 1 Bridge Ho
2 Hardington
3 Mead Cl
4 Rugmere
5 Tottenhall
6 Beauvale
7 Broomfield
A2 1 Silverbirch Wlk
2 Penshurst
3 Wingham
4 Westwell
5 Chislet
6 Burmarsh
7 Shipton Ho
8 Stone Gate
9 Leysdown
10 Headcorn
11 Lenham
12 Halstow
13 Fordcombe
14 Cannington
15 Langridge
16 Athlone Ho
17 Pentland Ho
18 Beckington
19 Hawkridge
20 Edington
B1 1 Ferdinand Ho
2 Harmood Ho
3 Hawley Rd
4 Hawley Mews
5 Leybourne St
6 Barling
7 Tiptree
8 Havering
9 Candida Ct
10 Lorraine Ct
11 Donnington Ct
12 Welford Ct
13 Torbay Ct
14 Bradfield Ct
15 Torbay St
16 Leybourne Rd
17 Haven St
18 Stucley Pl
B2 1 Ashington
2 Priestley Ho
3 Leonard Day Ho
4 Old Dairy Mews
5 Monmouth Ho
6 Alpha Ct
7 Una Ho
8 Widford
9 Hey Bridge
10 Roxwell
B4 1 Denyer Ho
2 Stephenson Ho
3 Trevithick Ho
4 Brunel Ho
5 Newcomen Ho
6 Faraday Ho
7 Winifrede Paul Ho
8 Wardlow
9 Fletcher Ct
10 Tideswell
11 Grangemill
12 Hambrook Ct
13 Calver
C1 1 Durdans Ho
2 Philia Ho
3 Bernard Shaw Ct
4 Foster Ct
5 Bessemer Ct
6 Hogarth Ct
7 Rochester Ct
8 Soane Ct
9 Wallett Ct
10 Inwood Ct
11 Wrotham Rd
12 Caulfield Ct
13 Bruges Pl
14 Reachview Cl
15 Highstone Mans
C3 1 Eleanor Ho
2 Falkland Pl
3 Kensington Ho
4 Willingham Cl
5 Kenbrook Ho
6 Aborfield
7 Great Field
8 Appleford
9 Forties The
C4 1 Benson Ct
2 Tait Ho
3 Manorfield Cl
4 Greatfield Cl
5 Longley Ho
6 Lampson Ho
7 Davidson Ho
8 Palmer Ho
9 Lambourn Cl
10 Morris Ho
11 Owen Ho
C5 1 Hunter Ho
2 Fisher Ho
3 Lang Ho
4 Temple Ho
5 Palmer Ho
C6 1 Flowers Mews
2 Sandridge St
3 Bovingdon Cl
4 Laurel Cl
5 Forest Way
6 Larch Cl
7 Pine Cl
9 Alder Mews
10 Aspen Cl
D1 1 Hillier Ho
2 Gairloch Ho
3 Cobham Mews
4 Bergholt Mews
5 Blakeney Cl
6 Weavers Way
7 Allensbury Pl
D2 1 Rowstock
2 Carters Cl
3 York Ho
4 Hungerford Rd
5 Cliff Ct
6 Camelot Ho
D3 1 Blake Ho
2 Quelch Ho
3 Lee Ho
4 Willbury Ho
5 Howell Ho
6 Holmsbury Ho
7 Leith Ho
8 Betchworth Ho
9 Rushmore Ho
10 Dugdale Ho
11 Horsendon Ho
12 Colley Ho
13 Coombe Ho
14 Ivinghoe Ho
15 Buckhurst Ho
16 Saxonbury Ct
17 Charlton Ct
18 Apollo Studios
19 Barn Cl
20 Long Meadow
21 Landleys Field
22 Margaret Bondfield Ho
23 Haywood Lo
D4 1 Fairlie Ct
2 Univ of North London (Carleton Grange Hall)
3 Trecastle Way
4 Hilldrop Est
5 Hyndman Ho
6 Carpenter Ho
7 Graham Ho
D5 1 Melchester Ho
2 Norcombe Ho
3 Weatherbury Ho
4 Wessex Ho
5 Archway Bsns Ctr
D6 1 Bowerman Ct
2 Hargrave Mans
3 Church Garth
4 John King Ct

72

A3 1 Kimble Ho
2 Saxonbury Ct
3 Poynder Ct
4 Pangbourne Ho
5 Moulsford Ho
A4 1 Arcade The
2 Macready Pl
A5 1 Northview
2 Tufnell Park Mans
A6 1 Christie Ct
2 Ringmer Gdns
3 Kingsdown Rd
4 Cottenham Ho
5 St Paul's Ct
6 Rickthorne Rd
7 Stanley Terr
B1 1 Kerwick Cl
2 Rydston Cl
3 Skegness Ho
4 Frederica St
5 Ponder St
6 Kings Ct
7 Freeling St
B4 1 Buckmaster Ho
2 Loreburn Ho
3 Cairns Ho
4 Halsbury Ho
5 Chelmsford Ho
6 Cranworth Ho
B6 1 Berkeley Wlk
2 Lazar Wlk
3 Thistlewood Cl
4 Tomlins Wlk
5 Andover Ho
6 Barmouth Ho
7 Chard Ho
8 Methley Ho
9 Rainford Ho
10 Woodbridge Cl
11 Allerton Wlk
12 Falconer Wlk
13 Sonderburg Rd
C1 1 Mountfort Terr
2 Davey Lo
3 Carfree Cl
C3 1 Blaney Pl
2 Wells Yd
3 Milton Pl
4 Hartnoll Ho
5 St James School Flats
6 Widnes Ho
7 Tranmere Ho
8 Victoria Mans
9 Formby Ct

A2
1 Murchison Ho
2 Macaulay Ho
3 Chesterton Ho
4 Chiltern Ho
5 Lionel Ho
6 Watts Ho
7 Wheatstone Ho
8 Telford Ho
9 Golborne Mews
10 Millwood St
11 St Columb's Ho

A3
1 Sycamore Wlk
2 Westgate Bsns Ctr
3 Buspace Studios
4 Bosworth Ho
5 Golborne Gdns
6 Appleford Ho
7 Adair Twr
8 Gadsden Ho
9 Southam Ho
10 Norman Butler Ho
11 Thompson Ho
12 Wells Ho
13 Paul Ho
14 Olive Blythe Ho
15 Katherine Ho
16 Breakwell Ct
17 Pepler Ho
18 Edward Kennedy Ho

A4
1 Onslow Ho
2 Slomon Ho
3 Stansbury Ho
4 Tilleard Ho
5 Tolhurst Ho
6 Selby Ho
7 Severn Ho
8 Mundy Ho
9 Macfarren Ho
10 Mounsey Ho
11 Courtville Ho
12 Croft Ho
13 Batten Ho
14 Bantock Ho
15 Banister Ho

A5
1 Lancefield Ct
2 Verdi Ho
3 Wornum Ho

B1
1 Tavistock Mews
2 Silvester Ho
3 Melchester
4 Clydesdale Ho
5 Pinehurst Ct
6 Colville Sq Mews
7 Denbigh Ho

B2
1 Blagrove Rd
2 Tavistock Ho
3 Leamington Ho

B4
1 Boyce Ho
2 Farnaby Ho
3 Danby Ho
4 Purday Ho
5 Naylor Ho
6 Novello Ho
7 Leeve Ho
8 Longhurst Ho
9 Harrington Ct
10 Mulberry Ct
11 Quilter Ho
12 Romer Ho
13 Kilburn Ho

B5
1 Claremont Ct
2 William Saville Ho
3 Western Ct
4 Bond Ho
5 Crone Ct
6 Wood Ho
7 Winterleys
8 Carlton Ho
9 Fiona Ct

C1
1 Shottsford
2 Tolchurch
3 Casterbridge
4 Sandbourne
5 Anglebury
6 Weatherbury
7 Westbourne Gr Mews
8 Rosehart Mews
9 Viscount Ct
10 Hereford Mans
11 Hereford Mews

C2
1 Ascot Ho
2 Ashgrove Ct
3 Lockbridge Ct
4 Swallow Ct
5 Nightingale Lo
6 Hammond Lo
7 Penfield Lo
8 Harvey Lo
9 Hunter Lo
10 Barnard Lo
11 Falcon Lo
12 Johnson Lo
13 Livingstone Lo
14 Nuffield Lo
15 Finch Lo
16 Polesworth Ho
17 Oversley Ho
18 Derrycombe Ho
19 Buckshead Ho
20 Combe Ho
21 Culham Ho
22 Dainton Ho
23 Devonport Ho
24 Hanwell Ho
25 Truro Ho
26 Sunderland Ho
27 Stonehouse Ho
28 Riverford Ho
29 Portishead Ho
30 Mickleton Ho
31 Keyham Ho
32 Moulsford Ho
33 Shrewsbury Mews
34 St Stephen's Mews

C3
1 Westside Ct

C4
1 Sutherland Ct
2 Austen Ho
3 Fielding Ho
4 Park Bsns Ctr
5 John Ratcliffe Ho
6 Wymering Mans

C5
1 Wells Ct
2 Cambridge Ct
3 Durham Ct

C6
1 Ryde Ho
2 Glengall Pass
3 Leith Yd
4 Daynor Ho
5 Varley Ho
6 Sandby Ho
7 Colas Mews
8 Bishopsdale Ho
9 Lorton Ho
10 Marshwood Ho
11 Ribblesdale Ho
12 Holmesdale Ho
13 Kilburn Vale Est
14 Kilburn Bridge

D1
1 Vera Ct
2 Alexander Mews
3 Gurney Ho
4 Burdett Mews
5 Greville Lo
6 Hatherley Ct
7 Bridge Field Ho
8 Ralph Ct
9 Peters Ct
10 Riven Ct
11 Cervantes Ct
12 Bishops Ct
13 Newbury Ho
14 Marlow Ho
15 Lynton Ho
16 Pembroke Ho
17 Pickering Ho

D3
1 Ellwood Ct

D5
1 Tollgate Ho
2 Regents Plaza
3 Royal Langford

D6
1 Farndale Ct
2 Birchington Ct
3 Greville Mews
4 Goldsmith's Pl
5 Remsted Ho
6 Bradwell Ho
7 Cheshunt Ho
8 Haliwell Ho
9 Braddock Ho
10 Philip Ho
11 Hillsborough Ct
12 Sandbourne
13 Wingreen
14 Toneborough
15 Silverthorn
16 Kington Ho
17 Marrick Ho
18 Broadoak Ho
19 Boadoak Ho

95

C4
1 Pimlico Wlk
2 Aske Ho
3 Hathaway Ho
4 Haberdasher Pl
5 Fairchild Ho
6 Burtt Ho
7 Enfield Cloisters
8 McGregor Ct
9 Royal Oak Ct
10 Hoxton Mkt
11 Bath Pl
12 Chapel Ct
13 Chapel Pl
14 Standard Pl
15 Cleeve Workshops
16 Cleeve Ho
17 Printing House Yd
18 Perseverance Works
19 Crooked Billet Yd
20 Drysdale Ho
21 Castlefrank Ho
22 School App
23 Basing House Yd
24 Mail Coach Yd

C5
1 Bracer Ho
2 Scorton Ho
3 Fern Cl
4 Macbeth Ho
5 Oberon Ho
6 Buckland Ct
7 Crondall Ct
8 Osric Path
9 Caliban Twr
10 Celia Ho
11 Juliet Ho
12 Bacchus Wlk
13 Malcolm Ho
14 Homefield St
15 Crondall Pl
16 Blanca Ho
17 Miranda Ho
18 Falstaff Ho
19 Charmian Ho
20 Myrtle Wlk
21 Arden Ho
22 Sebastian Ho
23 Stanway Ct
24 Jerrold St
25 Rosalind Ho
26 Cordelia Ho
27 Monteagle Ct
28 John Parry Ct
29 James Anderson Ct
30 Ben Jonson Ct
31 Sara Lane Ct

C6
1 Portelet Ct
2 Trinity Ct
3 Rozel Ct
4 St Helier Ct
5 Corbiere Ho
6 Kenning Ho
7 Higgins Ho
8 Cavell Ho
9 Girling Ho
10 Fulcher Ho
11 Francis Ho
12 Norris Ho
13 Kempton Ho
14 Nesham Ho
15 Crossbow Ho
16 Catherine Ho
17 Strale Ho
18 Horner Hos
19 Stringer Hos
20 Whitmore Ho
21 Nightingale Ho
22 Fletcher Ho
23 Arrow Ho
24 Archer Ho
25 Meriden Ho
26 Rover Ho
27 Bowyer Ho
28 Longbow Ho
29 Tiller Ho
31 Canalside Studios
32 Bishopgate
33 Holburn
34 Fenchurch

D4
1 Gorsuch Pl
2 Strout's Pl
3 Vaughan Est
4 George Loveless Ho
5 Baroness Rd
6 James Brine Ho
7 Arthur Wade Ho
8 Robert Owen Ho
9 Sivill Ho
10 Georgina Gdns
11 Old Market Sq
12 Cuff Point
13 Bakers Rents
14 Leopold Bldgs
15 Dunmore Point
16 Wingfield Ho
17 Gascoigne Pl
18 Mandela Ho
19 Virginia Rd
20 Briggs Ho
21 Packenham Ho
22 Gowan Ho
23 Kirton Gdns
24 Chambord Ho
25 Ducal St
26 Strickland Ho
27 Alliston Ho
28 Gibraltar Wlk
29 Equity Sq
30 Shacklewell St
31 Rochelle St
32 Sonning Ho
33 Culham Ho
34 Hurley Ho
35 Palissy St
36 Taplow Ho
37 Chertsey Ho
38 Sunbury Ho
39 Sunbury Workshops
40 Datchet Ho
41 Hocker St
42 Coll Sharp Ct
43 Marlow Studio Workshops
44 Marlow Ho
45 Shiplake Ho
46 Wargrave Ho
47 Iffley Ho

D5
1 Queensbridge Ct
2 Godwin Ho
3 Kent Ct
4 Brunswick Ho
5 Weymouth Ct
6 Sovereign Mews
7 Dunloe Ct
8 Cremer Bsns Ctr
9 James Hammett Ho
10 Allgood St
11 Horatio St
12 Cadell Ho
13 Horatio Ho
14 Shipton St

D6
1 Hilborough Ct
2 Scriven Ct
3 Livermere Ct
4 Angrave Ct
5 Angrave Pas
6 Benfleet Ct
7 Belford Ho
8 Orme Ho
9 Clemson Ho
10 Longman Ho
11 Lowther Ho
12 Lovelace Ho
13 Harlowe Ho
14 Pamela Ho
15 Samuel Ho
16 Acton Ho
17 Loanda Ct
18 Phoenix Cl
19 Richardson Cl
20 Thrasher Ct
21 Mary Secole Cl
22 Canal Path
23 Pear Tree Cl
24 Hebden Ct
25 Charlton Ct
26 Laburnum Ct
27 Mansfield Ct

96

A1
1 Manningtree St
2 Whitechurch La
3 Morrison Bldgs
4 Mountford St
5 Mulberry St
6 Weyhill Rd
7 Fordham St
8 Myrtle Ct
9 Buckle St
10 Plough St
11 Goodman's Stile
12 Mitali Pas
13 Basil Ho
14 Hogarth Ct
15 Ropewalk Gdns
16 Golding Terr
17 Delafield Ho
18 Drewett Ho
19 Harkness Ho
20 Batson Ho
21 Danvers Ho
22 Bicknell Ho
23 Everard Ho
24 Philchurch Pl
25 Hadfield Ho
26 Kindersley Ho
27 Langmore Ho
28 Halliday Ho

A2
1 Arthur Deakin Ho
2 Albert Cotts
3 Victoria Cotts
4 Boden Ho
5 Vollasky Ho
6 Daplyn St
7 Hobsons Pl
8 Hanbury Ho
9 Links Yd
10 Casson Ho
11 Ramar Ho
12 Greatorex Ho
13 Chicksand Ho
14 Spelman Ho
15 Tailworth St
16 Monthorpe Rd
17 Bloomfield Ho
18 Davenant Ho
19 Pauline Ho
20 Osborn St
21 Green Dragon Yd
22 King's Arms Ct
23 Fieldgate Mans

A3
1 Bentworth Ct
2 Kerbela St
3 Fuller Cl
4 Kinsham Ho
5 Menotti St
6 Barwell Ho
7 Grimsby St
8 Eckersley St
9 Stuttle Ho
10 McGlashon Ho
11 Fleet Street Hill
12 Bratley St
13 Weaver Ho
14 John Pritchard Ho

A4
1 Lygon Ho
2 Brabner Ho
3 Delta St
4 Tillet Way
5 Mullet Gdns
6 Elver Gdns
7 Cobden Ho
8 Lampern Sq
9 Jeremy Bentham Ho
10 Waring Ho
11 St James Ct
12 Hague St
13 Westhope Ho
14 Johnson Ho
15 Yates Ho
16 Simmons Ho
17 Swinton Ho
18 Eversley Ho
19 Rapley Ho
20 Dence Ho
21 Dickinson Ho
22 Hutton Ho
23 McKinnon Wood Ho
24 Satchwell Rd

A5
1 London Terr
2 Sturdee Ho
3 Maude Ho
4 Haig Ho
5 Jellicoe Ho
6 Ropley St
7 Guinness Trust Bldgs
8 Ion Sq
9 Moye Cl
10 Morrel Ct
11 Courtauld Ho
12 Drummond Ho
13 Atkinson Ho
14 Gurney Ho
15 Halley Ho
16 Goldsmith's Sq
17 Ken Wilson Ho
18 Shahjalal Ho
19 Crofts Ho
20 April Ct
21 Sebright Ho
22 Beechwood Ho
23 Gillman Ho
24 Cheverell Ho
25 Besford Ho
26 Dinmont Ho
27 Wyndham Deedes Ho
28 Sheppard Ho
29 Mary James Ho
30 Hadrian Est
31 Blythendale Ho
32 George Vale Ho
33 Lion Mills
34 Pritchard Ho

A6
1 Broke Wlk
2 Rochemont Wlk
3 Marlborough Ave
4 Rivington Wlk
5 Magnin Cl
6 Gloucester Sq
7 Woolstone Ho
8 Marsworth Ho
9 Cheddington Ho
10 Linslade Ho
11 Cosgrove Ho
12 Blisworth Ho
13 Eleanor Ct
14 Wistow Ho
15 Muscott Ho
16 Boxmoor Ho
17 Linford Ho
18 Pendley Ho
19 North Church Ho
20 Debdale Ho
21 Broadway Market Mews
22 Welshpool Ho
23 Ada Ho

B1
1 Jacob Mans
2 Wicker St
3 Langdale St
4 Walford Ho
5 Welstead Ho
6 Peter Best Ho
7 Sly St
8 Barnett St
9 Kinder St
10 Richard St
11 Sarah Ho
12 Mellish Ho
13 Dickson Ho
14 Joscoyne Ho
15 Bridgen Ho
16 Wilton Ct
17 Silvester Ho
18 Greenwich Ct
19 Tylney Ho
20 Damien Ct
21 Siege Ho
22 Melwood Ho
23 Colstead Ho
24 Hungerford St
25 Burwell Cl
26 Chapman Ho
27 Tarling Ho
28 Sheridan St
29 Brinsley St
30 Dunch St
31 Luke Ho
32 Turnour Ho
33 Norton Ho

B3
1 Rochester Ct
2 Weaver Ct
3 Greenheath Bsns Ctr
4 Glass St
5 Herald St
6 Northesk Ho
7 Codrington Ho
8 Heathpool Ct
9 Mocatta Ho
10 Harvey Ho
11 Blackwood Ho
12 Rutherford Ho
13 Bullen Ho
14 Fremantle Ho
15 Pellew Ho
16 Ashington Ho
17 Dinnington Ho
18 Bartholomew Sq
19 Steeple Ct
20 Orion Ho
21 Fellbrigg St
22 Eagle Ho
23 Sovereign Ho
24 Redmill Ho
25 Berry Ho
26 Grindall Ho

B4
1 Charles Dickens Ho
2 Adrian Bolt Ho
3 William Rathbone Ho
4 Southwood Smith Ho
5 Rushmead
6 William Channing Ho
7 John Cartwright Ho
8 Charles Darwin Ho
9 Thomas Burt Ho
10 John Fielden Ho
11 Gwilym Maries Ho
12 Joseph Priestley Ho
13 Wear Pl
14 John Nettleford Ho
15 Thornaby Ho
16 Stockton Ho
17 Barnard Ho
18 Gainford Ho
19 Stapleton Ho
20 James Middleton Ho
21 Kedleston Wlk
22 Queen Margaret Flats
23 Hollybush Ho
24 Horwood Ho
25 Norden Ho
26 Newcourt Ho
27 Seabright St
28 Viaduct Pl

B5
1 Dinmont St
2 Marian St
3 Claredale Ho
4 Bradley Ho
5 Connett Ho
6 Winkley St
7 Temple Dwellings
8 Argos Ho
9 Helen Ho
10 Lysander Ho
11 Antenor Ho
12 Paris Ho
13 Nestor Ho
14 Hector Ho
15 Ajax Ho
16 Achilles Ho
17 Priam Ho
18 Peabody Est
19 Felix St
20 Cambridge Cres
21 Peterley Bsns Ctr
22 Beckwith Ho
23 Parminter Ind Est
24 Ted Roberts Ho
25 Cambridge Ct
26 West St
27 Millennium Pl
28 William Caslon Ho
29 Hugh Platt Ho
30 Mayfield Ho
31 Apollo Ho

B6
1 Welshpool St
2 Broadway Ho
3 Regents Wharf
4 London Wharf
5 Warburton Ho
6 Warburton St
7 Triangle Rd
8 Warburton Rd
9 Williams Ho
10 Booth Cl
11 Albert Cl
12 King Edward Mans
13 Victoria Bldgs

C1
1 Woollon Ho
2 Dundalk Ho
3 Anne Goodman Ho
4 Newbold Cotts
5 Kerry Ho
6 Zion Ho
7 Longford Ho
8 Bromehead St
9 Athlone Ho
10 Jubilee Mans
11 Harriott Ho
12 Brayford Sq
13 Clearbrook Way
14 Rochelle Ho
15 Winterton Ho
16 Sheridan Ho
17 Brinsley Ho
18 Dean Ho
19 Foley Ho
20 Robert Sutton Ho
21 Montpelier Pl
22 Masters Lo
23 Steel's La

C2
1 Fulneck
2 Gracehill
3 Ockbrook
4 Fairfield
5 Dunstan Hos
6 Cressy Ct
7 Cressy Hos
8 Callahan Cotts
9 Wexford Ho
10 Sandhurst Ho
11 Colverson Ho
12 Beckett Ho
13 Jarman Ho
14 Wingrad Ho
15 Armsby Ho
16 Miranda Cl
17 Drake Ho
18 Louise De Marillac Ho
19 Sambrook Ho
20 St Vincent De Paul Ho
21 Jean Pardies Ho
22 Clichy Ho
23 Le Moal Ho
24 Odette Duval Ho
25 Dagobert Ho
26 Charles Auffray Ho
27 Boisseau Ho
28 Paymal Ho
29 Ewhurst Ho

C3
1 William's Bldgs
2 Donegal Ho
3 Frederick Charrington Ho
4 Wickford Ho
5 Braintree Ho
6 Doveton Ho
7 Doveton St
8 Cephas Ho
9 Sceptre Ho
10 Bancroft Ho
11 Stothard St
12 Redclyf Ho
13 Winkworth Cotts
14 Ryder Ho
15 Hadleigh Ho
16 Hadleigh Cl
17 Amiel St
18 Stathard Ho
19 Barbanel Ho
20 Colebert Ho
21 Kenton Ho
22 Ibbott St
23 Stannard Cotts
24 Rennie Cotts
25 Rickman St
26 Rickman Ho
27 Pemell Cl
28 Pemell Ho
29 Leatherdale St
30 Goldman Ho
31 Lamplighter Cl
32 Hamilton Lo
33 Cleveland Gr
34 Montgomery Lo
35 Bardsey Pl
36 Cromwell Lo
37 Colin Winter Ho
38 Hayfield Ho

C4
1 Mulberry Ho
2 Gretton Ho
3 Merceron Ho
4 Montfort Ho
5 Westbrook Ho
6 Sugar Loaf Wlk
7 Museum Ho
8 Burnham Est
9 Globe Terr
10 Moravian St
11 Shepton Hos
12 Mendip Hos
13 Academy Ct
14 Pepys Ho
15 Swinburne Ho
16 Moore Ho
17 Morris Ho
18 Burns Ho
19 Milton Ho
20 Whitman Ho
21 Shelley Ho
22 Keats Ho
23 Dawson Ho
24 Bradbeer Ho
25 Forber Ho
26 Hughes Ho
27 Silvester Ho
28 Rogers Est
29 Pavan Ct
30 Stafford Cripps Ho
31 Sidney Godley (VC) Ho
32 Butler Ho
33 Butler St
34 Thorne Ho
35 Bevin Ho
36 Tuscan Ho

C5
1 Evesham Ho
2 James Campbell Ho
3 Thomas Hollywood Ho

96 C6
4 James Docherty Ho
5 Ebenezer Mussel Ho
6 Jameson Ct
7 Edinburgh Cl
8 Roger Dowley Ct
9 Sherbrooke Ho
10 Calcraft Ho
11 Burrard Ho
12 Dundas Ho
13 Ponsonby Ho
14 Barnes Ho
15 Paget Ho
16 Ponsonby Ho
17 Maitland Ho
18 Chesil Ct
19 Reynolds Ho
20 Cleland Ho
21 Goodrich Ho
22 Rosebery Ho
23 Sankey Ho
24 Cyprus Pl
25 Royston St
26 Stainsbury St
27 Hunslett St
28 Baildon
29 Brockweir
30 Tytherton
31 Malmesbury
32 Kingswood
C6 1 Halkett Ho
2 Colville Ho
3 Fane Ho
4 Christ Church Sq
5 Swingfield Ho
6 Greenham Ho
7 Dinmore Ho
8 Anstey Ho
9 Weston Ho
10 Carbroke Ho
11 Layton Ho
12 Smetheton Ho
13 Dawnay Ho
14 Wakelyn Ho
15 Villiers Ho
16 Paveley Ho
17 Manneby Ho
18 Kidron Way
19 Georgian Ct
20 Park Cl
21 Regency Ct
22 Norris Ho
D1 1 Pattison Ho
2 St Thomas Ho
3 Arbour Ho
4 Bladen Ho
5 Antill Terr
6 Billing Ho
7 Dowson Ho
8 Lipton Rd
9 Chalkwell Ho
10 Corringham Ho
11 Ogilvie Ho
12 Edward Mann Cl
13 Lighterman Mews
D2 1 Roland Mews
2 Morecambe Cl
3 Stepney Green Ct
4 Milrood Ho
5 Panama Ho
6 Galway Ho
7 Caspian Ho
8 Darien Ho
9 Rigo Ho
10 Flores Ho
11 Taranto Ho
12 Aden Ho
13 Frances Grey Ho
14 Master's St
15 Searle Ho
16 Diggon St
D3 1 Raynham Ho
2 Pat Shaw Ho
3 Colmar Cl
4 Withy Ho
5 Stocks Ct
6 Downey Ho
7 Bay Ct
8 Sligo Ho
9 Pegasus Ho
10 Barents Ho
11 Biscay Ho
12 Solway Ho
13 Bantry Ho
14 Aral Ho
15 Pacific Ho
16 Magellan Ho
17 Levant Ho
18 Adriatic Ho
19 Genoa Ho
20 Hawke Ho
21 Palliser Ho
22 Ionian Ho
23 Weddell Ho
D4 1 Stubbs Ho
2 Holman Ho
3 Clynes Ho
4 Windsor Ho
5 Gilbert Ho
6 Chater Ho
7 Ellen Wilkinson Ho
8 George Belt Ho
9 Ayrton Gould Ho
10 O'Brian Ho
11 Sulkin Ho
12 Jenkinson Ho
13 Bullards Pl
14 Sylvia Pankhurst Ho
15 Mary Macarthur Ho
16 Trevelyan Ho
17 Wedgwood Ho
18 Pemberton Ct
20 Walter Besant Ho
21 Barber Beaumont Ho
22 Brancaster Ho
23 Litcham Ho
D5 1 Kemp Ho
2 Piggott Ho
3 Mark Ho
4 Sidney Ho
5 Pomeroy Ho
6 Puteaux Ho
7 Doric Ho
8 Modling Ho
9 Longman Ho
10 Ames Ho
11 Alzette Ho
12 Offenbach Ho
13 Tate Ho
14 Norton Ho
15 St Gilles Ho
16 Harold Ho
17 Velletri Ho
18 Bridge Wharf
19 Gathorne St
20 Bow Brook The
22 Palmerston Ct
23 Lakeview

97
A1 1 Coltman Ho
2 Repton Ho
3 Causton Cotts
4 Delmane Ho
5 Culpepper Ho
6 Shaw Ho
7 Williams Ho
8 Jerome Ho
9 Darnley Ho
10 Mercer's Cotts
11 Troon Ho
12 Ratcliffe Ho
13 Wakeling St
14 York Sq
15 Anglia Ho
16 Cambria Ho
17 Caledonia Ho
18 Ratcliffe La
19 Bekesbourne St
20 John Scurr Ho
21 Regents Canal Ho
A2 1 Waley St
2 Edith Ramsay Ho
3 Andaman Ho
4 Atlantic Ho
5 Pevensey Ho
6 Solent Ho
7 Lorne Ho
8 Cromarty Ho
9 Hearnshaw Ho
10 Hawksmoor Ho
11 Hemlington Ho
12 Greaves Cotts
13 Donaghue Cotts
14 Ames Cotts
15 Maroon Ho
16 Blount Ho
17 Wilkinson Ho
18 Aylward Ho
A3 1 Formosa Ho
2 Galveston Ho
3 Arabian Ho
4 Greenland Ho
5 Coral Ho
6 Anson Ho
7 Lindop Ho
8 Moray Ho
9 Azov Ho
10 Sandalwood Cl
11 Broadford Ho
A5 1 Bunsen Ho
2 Bunsen St
3 Beatrice Webb Ho
4 Margaret Bondfield Ho
5 Wilmer Ho
6 Sandall Ho
7 Butley Ct
8 Josseline Ct
9 Dalton Ho
10 Brine Ho
11 Ford Cl
12 Viking Cl
13 Stanfield Rd
14 Ruth Ct
15 School Bell Cloisters
16 Schoolbell Mews
17 Medhurst Cl
18 Olga St
19 Conyer St
20 Diamond Ho
21 Daring Ho
22 Crane Ho
23 Exmoor Ho
24 Grenville Ho
25 Hyperion Ho
26 Sturdy Ho
27 Wren Ho
28 Ardent Ho
29 Senators Lo
30 Hooke Ho
31 Mohawk Ho
32 Ivanhoe Ho
B1 1 Dora Ho
2 Flansham Ho
3 Gatwick Ho
4 Ashpark Ho
5 Newdigate Ho
6 Midhurst Ho
7 Redbourne Ho
8 Southwater Cl
9 Aithan Ho
10 Britley Ho
11 Cheadle Ho
12 Elland Ho
13 Butler Ho
14 Fitzroy Ho
15 Leybourne Ho
B2 1 Wearmouth Ho
2 Elmslie Point
3 Grindley Ho
4 Stileman Ho
5 Baythorne St
6 Wilcox Ho
8 Robeson St
9 Couzens Ho
10 Perley Ho
11 Whytlaw Ho
12 Printon Ho
13 Perkins Ho
14 Bowry Ho
15 Booker Cl
16 Tunley Gn
17 Callingham Cl
18 Tasker Ho
B4 1 Trellis Sq
2 Sheffield Sq
3 Howcroft Ho
4 Astra Ho
6 Byas Ho
7 George Lansbury Ho
8 Regal Pl
9 Coburn Mews
10 Cavendish Terr
11 Buttermere Ho
12 Tracy Ho
13 Coniston Ho
14 St Clair Ho
15 Verity Ho
16 Icarus Ho
17 Whippingham Ho
18 Winchester Ho
19 Hamilton Ho
20 Longthorne Ho
B5 1 Roman Square Mkt
2 John Bond Ho
3 McKenna Ho
4 Dennis Ho
5 McBride Ho
6 Libra Rd
7 Dave Adams Ho
8 Tay Ho
9 Sleat Ho
10 Ewart Pl
11 Brodick Ho
12 Lunan Ho
13 Mull Ho
14 Sinclairs Ho
15 Driftway Ho
16 Clayhall Ct
17 Berebinder Ho
18 Stavers Ho
19 Barford Ho
20 Partridge Ho
21 Gosford Ho
22 Gullane Ho
23 Cruden Ho
24 Anglo Rd
25 Dornoch Ho
26 Dunnet Ho
27 Enard Ho
28 Fraserburgh Ho
29 Forth Ho
30 Ordell Ct
B6 1 Hampstead Wlk
2 Waverton Ho
3 Elton Ho
4 Locton Gn
5 Birtwhistle Ho
6 Clare Ho
7 Cavan Ho
8 Antrim Ho
9 Tait Ct
10 Ranwell Ho
11 Ranwell Cl
12 Tufnell Ct
13 Pulteney Cl
14 Vic Johnson Ho
C1 1 Landin Ho
2 Charlesworth Ho
3 Gurdon Ho
4 Trendell Ho
5 Menteath Ho
6 Minchin Ho
7 Donne Ho
8 Denison Ho
9 Anglesey Ho
10 Gough Wlk
11 Baring Ho
12 Hopkins Ho
13 Granville Ho
14 Gladstone Ho
15 Russell Ho
16 Pusey Ho
17 Overstone Ho
18 Stanley Ho
C2 1 Bredel Ho
2 Linton Ho
3 Matthews Ho
4 Woodcock Ho
5 Limborough Ho
6 Maydwell Ho
7 Underhill Ho
8 Meyrick Ho
9 Ambrose Ho
10 Carpenter Ho
11 Robinson Ho
12 Bramble Ho
13 Bilberry Ho
14 Bracken Ho
15 Berberis Ho
16 Busbridge Ho
C3 1 Fairmont Ho
2 Healey Ho
3 Zodiac Ho
4 Buick Ho
5 Consul Ho
6 Bentley Ho
7 Cresta Ho
8 Daimler Ho
9 Riley Ho
10 Jensen Ho
11 Lagonda Ho
12 Ireton St
13 Navenby Wlk
14 Burwell Wlk
15 Leadenham Ct
16 Sleaford Ho
C4 1 Jarret Ho
2 Marsalis Ho
3 Lovette Ho
4 Drapers Almhouses
5 Mallard Point
6 Creswick Wlk
7 Bevin Ho
8 Huggins Ho
9 Williams Ho
10 Harris Ho
11 Marina Ct
12 Electric Ho
13 Matching Ct
14 Wellington Bldgs
15 Grafton Ho
16 Columbia Ho
17 Berkeley Ho
D1 1 Colebrook Ho
2 Essex Ho
3 Salisbury Ho
4 Maidstone Ho
5 Osterley Ho
6 Norwich Ho
7 Clarissa Ho
8 Elgin Ho
9 Shaftesbury Lo
10 Shepherd Ho
11 Jeremiah St
12 Elizabeth Cl
13 Chilcot Cl
14 Fitzgerald Ho
15 Vesey Path
16 Ennis Ho
17 Kilmore Ho
D2 1 Sumner Ho
2 Irvine Ho
3 David Ho
4 Brushwood Ho
5 Limehouse Cut
6 Colmans Wharf
7 Foundary Ho
8 Radford Ho
D3 1 Broxbourne Ho
2 Roxford Ho
3 Biscott Ho
4 Stanborough Ho
5 Hillstone Ct
D4 1 Bradley Ho
2 Prioress Ho
3 Alton Ho
4 Foxley Ho
5 Munden Ho
6 Canterbury Ho
7 Corbin Ho
8 Barton Ho
9 Jolles Ho
10 Rudstone Ho
11 Baxter Ho
12 Baker Ho
13 Insley Ho
14 Hardwicke Ho
15 Glebe Terr
16 Priory St
17 Sadler Ho
18 Ballinger Point
19 Henshall Point
20 Dorrington Point
21 Warren Ho
22 Fairlie Ct
23 Regent Sq
24 Hackworth Point
25 Priestman Point
26 Wingate Ho
27 Nethercott Ho
28 Thelbridge Ho
29 Bowden Ho
30 Kerscott Ho
31 Southcott Ho
32 Birchdown Ho
33 Upcott Ho
34 Langmead Ho
35 Limscott Ho
36 Northleigh Ho
37 Huntshaw Ho
38 Chagford Ho
39 Ashcombe Ho
40 Shillingford Ho
41 Patrick Connolly Gdns
42 Lester Ct
43 Franklin St
44 Taft Way
45 Madison Cl
46 Elizabeth Ho
47 William Guy Gdns
48 Denbury Ho
49 Holsworthy Ho

98
A1 1 Langdon Ho
2 Balfron Twr
3 Tabard Ct
4 Delta Bldg
5 Kilbrennan Ho
6 Thistle Ho
7 Heather Ho
8 Tartan Ho
9 Trident Ho
B1 1 Lansbury Gdns
2 Thesus Ho
3 Adams Ho
4 Jones Ho
5 Sam March Ho
6 Arapiles Ho
7 Athenia Ho
8 Jervis Bay Ho
9 Helen Mackay Ho
10 Gaze Ho
11 Ritchie Ho
12 Circle Ho
13 Dunkeld Ho
14 Braithwaite Ho
15 Rosemary Dr
16 Sorrel La
17 East India Dock Road Tunnel
C6 1 Barnby Sq
2 Barnby St
3 Brassett Point
4 David Lee Point
5 Worthing Cl
6 Bexhill Wlk
7 Old Borrowfield
8 Elmgreen Cl
9 Stafford Morris Ho
D1 1 Newton Point
2 Sparke Terr
3 Montesquieu Terr
4 Crawford Point
5 Rathbone Ho
6 George St
7 Emily St
8 Fendt Cl
D2 1 Radley Terr
2 Rathbone Mkt
3 Thomas North Terr
4 Bernard Cassidy St
5 Mary St
6 Hughes Terr
7 Swanscombe Point
8 Rawlinson Point
9 Kennedy Cox Ho
10 Cooper St
D6 1 Harris Cotts
2 Moorey Cl
3 Euro Bsns Ctr
4 Ladywell St
5 Caistor Ho
6 Redfern Ho

99
A2 1 Odeon Ct
2 Edward Ct
3 Newhaven La
4 Ravenscroft Cl
5 Douglas Rd
6 Ferrier Point
7 Harvey Point
8 Wood Point
9 Trinity St
10 Pattinson Point
11 Clinch Ct
12 Mint Bsns Pk
A3 1 Webb Gdns
2 Eric Shipman Terr
3 Warmington St
4 Jellicoe Rd
5 Frank St
6 Seaton Cl
7 Tabernacle Ave
8 Upland Rd
9 Clove St
10 Edward St
A4 1 Bob Anker Cl
2 Lea Ct
3 Third Ave
4 Suffolk Rd
A5 1 Lettsom Wlk
2 Ashburton Terr
3 Grasmere Rd
4 Dimsdale Wlk
5 Rawstone Wlk
6 Scott Ho
7 Willett Ho
8 James Cl
9 Cordwainers Wlk
10 Victoria Point
11 Settle Point
12 Middle Rd
A6 1 Royston Ct
B4 1 Barbers Alley
2 Grengate Lo
3 Augurs La
4 Surrey St
5 Dongola Rd W
6 Bemersyde Point
7 Rowntree Clifford Cl
C5 1 Wellby Ct
2 Bishop Wilfred Wood Ct
3 Castle Point
4 Moat Dr
C6 1 Queen's Mkt
2 Tolpuddle Ave
3 Crown Mews
4 Lilac Ct
5 Hamara Ghar
6 Greenleaf Rd
7 Massey Ct
8 Florence Rd
9 Sissulu Ct
10 Austin Ct
D2 1 Partridge Cl
2 Vanburgh Cl
3 Meadowsweet Cl
4 St Michaels Cl
5 Long Mark Rd
6 Congreve Wlk
D5 1 Foxcombe Cl
2 Rochford Cl
3 Kylemore Cl
4 Stondon Wlk
5 Imperial Mews
6 Dominica Cl
D6 1 Oldegate Ho
2 Gaitskell Ho
3 Cabot Way

100
A1 1 Hadleigh Wlk
2 Hawksmoor Cl
3 Fraser Cl
4 Moncrieff Cl
5 Burlington Cl
6 Dundonald Cl
7 Oakley Cl
8 Ashwell Cl
A2 1 Orchid Cl
2 Bellflower Cl
3 Partridge Sq
4 Larkspur Cl
5 Lobelia Cl
6 Stonechat Sq
7 Wintergreen Cl
8 Garnet Wlk
9 Mavis Wlk
10 Beacons Wlk
11 Abbess Cl
12 Elmley Cl
13 Chetwood Wlk
14 Selby Cl
15 Denny Cl
16 Woodhatch Cl
A6 1 Oakwood Ct
2 Harrow Rd
3 Ray Massey Way
4 Madge Gill Way
5 Pilgrims Way
B1 1 Bowers Wlk
2 Barton Cl
3 Clayton Cl
4 Dixon Cl
5 Gautrey Sq
6 Wakerly Cl
7 Canterbury Cl
8 Goose Sq
9 Coventry Cl
10 Butterfield Sq
11 Winchester Cl
B2 1 Fleetwood Ct
2 Lymington Cl
3 Holyhead Cl
4 Bondfield Rd
5 Tulip Cl
6 Ambrose Cl
7 Sage Cl
8 Lindwood Cl
D1 1 Weymouth Ct
2 Founder Cl
3 Admirals Ct

101
A6 1 Wellington St
2 St Ann's Rd
3 Curfew Ho
4 Ardleigh Ho
5 Bamber Ho
6 Gateway Ho
B6 1 Jarvis Ct
2 Mayflower Ho
3 Westbury Ct
4 Millicent Preston Ho
5 Louise Graham Ho
6 Grange Ho
7 Basing Ho
8 Barnes Ho
9 Lexham Ho
10 Ripple Ct
11 Waldegrave Ct
12 Howard Ct

104
A6 1 Milburn Dr
2 Cousins Cl
3 Leacroft Cl

108
C5 1 Marlow Ct
2 Andrews Ct
3 Vine Cotts
4 Benjamin Ct
5 Broadway Bldgs
D5 1 Silverdale Cl
2 Burdett Cl
3 Hopefield
4 Maunder Rd

109
A5 1 Glastonbury Ct
2 Evesham Ct
3 Lacock Ct
4 Wigmore Ct
5 Melrose Ct
6 Brownlow Rd
7 Chignell Pl
8 Shirley Ct
9 Trojan Ct
10 Hatfield Rd
C6 1 Abbey Lo
2 Yew Tree Grange
3 Abinger Ct

110
A1 1 Burford Ho
2 Hope Cl
3 Centaur Ct
4 Phoenix Ct
A6 1 Watermans Mews
2 Hills Mews
3 Grosvenor Ct
4 Elton Lo
5 Hambledon Ct
C1 1 Surrey Cres
2 Forbes Ho
3 Haining Cl
4 Melville Ct
5 London Stile
6 Stile Hall Par
7 Priory Lo
8 Kew Bridge Ct
9 Meadowcroft
10 St James Ct
C5 1 Grosvenor Par
2 Oakfield Ct
3 Hart Grove Ct
4 Grosvenor Ct
D1 1 Churchdale Ct
2 Cromwell Cl
3 Cambridge Rd S
4 Oxbridge Ct
5 Tomlinson Cl
6 Gunnersbury Mews
7 Grange The
8 Gunnersbury Cl
D4 1 Cheltenham Pl
2 Beaumaris Twr
3 Arundel Ho
4 Pevensey Ct
5 Jerome Twr
6 Anstey Ct
7 Bennett Ct
8 Gunnersbury Ct
D5 1 Lantry Ct
2 Rosemount Ct
3 Moreton Twr
4 Acton Central Ind Est
5 Rufford Twr
6 Narrow St
7 Mount Pl
8 Sidney Miller Ct
9 Mill Hill Terr

111
A1 1 Arlington Park Mans
2 Sandown Ho
3 Goodwood Ho
4 Windsor Ho
5 Lingfield Ho
6 Ascot Ho
7 Watchfield Ct
8 Belgrave Ct
9 Beverley Ct
10 Beaumont Ct
11 Harvard Rd
A2 1 Church Green Ho
2 Bell Ind Est
3 Fairlawn Ct
4 Dukes Gate
5 Dewsbury Ct
6 Chiswick Terr
A3 1 Blackmore Twr
2 Bollo Ct
3 Kipling Twr
4 Lawrence Ct
5 Maugham Ct
6 Reade Ct
7 Woolf Ct
8 Shaw Ct
9 Verne Ct
10 Wodehouse Ct
11 Greenock Rd

12 Garden Ct
13 Barons Gate
14 Cleveland Rd
15 Chapter Cl
16 Beauchamp Cl
17 Holmes Ct
A4 1 Belgrave Cl
2 Buckland Wlk
3 Frampton Ct
4 Telfer Cl
5 Harlech Twr
6 Corfe Twr
7 Barwick Ho
8 Charles Hocking Ho
9 Sunninghill Ct
10 Salisbury St
A5 1 Rectory Rd
2 Derwentwater Mans
3 Market Pl
4 Hooper's Mews
5 Cromwell Pl
6 Locarno Rd
7 Edgecote Cl
8 Harleyford Manor
B1 1 Chatsworth Lo
2 Prospect Pl
3 Townhall Ave
4 Devonhurst Pl
5 Heathfield Ct
6 Horticultural Pl
7 Merlin Ho
8 Garth Rd
C1 1 Glebe Cl
2 Devonshire Mews
3 Binns Terr
4 Ingress St
5 Swanscombe Rd
6 Brackley Terr
7 Stephen Fox Ho
8 Manor Gdns
9 Coram Ho
10 Flaxman Ho
11 Thorneycroft Ho
12 Thornhill Ho
13 Kent Ho
14 Oldfield Ho
C2 1 Chestnut Ho
2 Bedford Ho
3 Bedford Cnr
4 Sydney Ho
5 Bedford Park Cnr
6 Priory Gdns
7 Windmill Alley
8 Castle Pl
9 Jonathan Ct
10 Windmill Pas
11 Chardin Rd
12 Gable Ho
C3 1 Fleet Ct
2 Ember Ct
3 Emlyn Gdns
4 Clone Ct
5 Brent Ct
6 Abbey Ct
7 Ormsby Lo
8 St Catherine's Ct
C4 1 Longford Ct
2 Mole Ct
3 Lea Ct
4 Wandle Ct
5 Beverley Ct
6 Roding Ct
7 Crane Ct
D1 1 Miller's Ct
2 British Grove Pas
3 British Grove S
4 Berestede Rd
5 North Eyot Gdns
D2 1 Flanders Mans
2 Stamford Brook Mans
3 Linkenholt Mans
4 Prebend Mans
5 Middlesex Ct
D3 1 Stamford Brook Gdns
2 Hauteville Court Gdns
3 Ranelagh Gdns

112

A2 1 Hamlet Ct
2 Derwent Ct
3 Westcroft Ct
4 Black Lion Mews
5 St Peter's Villas
6 Standish Ho
7 Chambon Pl
8 Court Mans
A4 1 Becklow Gdns
2 Victoria Ho
3 Lycett Pl
4 Kylemore Ct
5 Alexandra Ct
6 Lytten Ct
7 Becklow Mews
8 Northcroft Ct
9 Bailey Ct
10 Spring Cott
11 Landor Wlk
12 Laurence Mews
13 Hadyn Park Ct
14 Askew Mans
B2 1 Albion Gdns
2 Flora Gdns
3 Lamington St
4 Felgate Mews
5 Galena Ho
6 Albion Mews
7 Albion Ct
8 King Street Cloisters
9 Dimes Pl
10 Clarence Ct
11 Hampshire Hog La
12 Marryat Ct
B4 1 Westbush Ct
2 Goldhawk Mews
3 Sycamore Ho
4 Shackleton Ct
5 Drake Ct
6 Scotts Ct
B6 1 Abercrombie Ho
2 Bathurst Ho
3 Brisbane Ho
4 Bentinck Ho
5 Ellenborough Ho
6 Lawrence Cl
7 Mackenzie Cl
8 Carteret Ho
9 Calvert Ho
10 Winthrop Ho
11 Auckland Ho
12 Blaxland Ho
13 Havelock Cl
14 Hargraves Ho
15 Hudson Cl
16 Phipps Ho
17 Lawson Ho
18 Hastings Ho
19 Wolfe Ho
20 Malabar Ct
21 Commonwealth Ave
22 Charnock Ho
23 Canning Ho
24 Cornwallis Ho
26 Champlain Ho
27 Grey Ho
28 Durban Ho
29 Baird Ho
30 Campbell Ho
31 Mitchell Ho
32 Denham Ho
33 Mackay Ho
34 Evans Ho
35 Daws Ho
36 Mandela Cl
C1 1 Bridge Avenue Mans
2 Bridgeview
3 College Ct
4 Beatrice Ho
5 Amelia Ho
6 Edith Ho
7 Joanna Ho
8 Mary Ho
9 Adela Ho
10 Sophia Ho
11 Henrietta Ho
12 Charlotte Ho
13 Alexandra Ho
14 Bath Pl
15 Elizabeth Ho
16 Margaret Ho
17 Peabody Est
18 Eleanor Ho
19 Isabella Ho
20 Caroline Ho
21 Chancellors Wharf
C2 1 Phoenix Lodge Mans
2 Samuel's Cl
3 Broadway Arc
4 Brook Ho
5 Hammersmith Broadway
C4 1 Verulam Ho
2 Grove Mans
3 Frobisher Ct
4 Library Mans
5 Pennard Mans
6 Lanark Mans
7 Kerrington Ct
8 Granville Mans
9 Romney Ct
10 Rayner Ct
11 Sulgrave Gdns
12 Bamborough Gdns
D3 1 Grosvenor Residences
2 Blythe Mews
3 Burnand Ho
4 Bradford Ho
5 Springvale Terr
6 Ceylon Rd
7 Walpole Ct
8 Bronte Ct
9 Boswell Ct
10 Souldern Rd
11 Brook Green Flats
12 Haarlem Rd
13 Stafford Mans
14 Lionel Mans
D4 1 Vanderbilt Villas
2 Bodington Ct
3 Kingham Cl
4 Clearwater Terr
5 Lorne Gdns
6 Cameret Ct
7 Bush Ct
8 Shepherds Ct
9 Rockley Ct
10 Grampians The
11 Charcroft Ct
12 Addison Park Mans
13 Sinclair Mans
D5 1 Katherine's Wlk
2 Dorrit Ho
3 Pickwick Ho
4 Dombey Ho
5 Saunders Ho
6 Mortimer Ho
7 Nickleby Ho
8 Stebbing Ho
9 Boxmoor Ho
10 Poynter Ho
11 Swanscombe Ho
12 Darnley Terr
13 Norland Ho
14 Hume Ho
D6 1 Frinstead Ho
2 Hurstway Wlk
3 Testerton Wlk
4 Grenfell Wlk
5 Grenfell Twr
6 Barandon Wlk
7 Treadgold Ho
8 St Clements Ct
9 Willow Way
10 Florence Ho
11 Dora Ho
12 Carton Ho
13 Agnes Ho
14 Marley Ho

118

A1 1 Alison Ct
2 West Point
3 Centre Point
4 East Point
5 Proctor Ho
6 Tovy Ho
7 Brettinghurst
8 Colechurch Ho
9 Harman Cl
10 Avondale Ho
11 Lanark Ho
12 George Elliston Ho
13 Eric Wilkins Ho
14 Archers Lo
15 Culloden Cl
16 Fallow Ct
17 Fern Wlk
18 Ivy Ct
19 Winter Lo
A2 1 Cadbury Way
2 Robert Bell Ho
3 Robert Jones Ho
4 William Rushbrooke Ho
5 Helen Taylor Ho
6 Peter Hills Ho
7 Charles Mackenzie Ho
8 Drappers Way
9 Abbey Gdns
10 Maria Cl
11 Windmill Cl
12 Townsend Ho
13 Mason Ho
14 Langdon Way
15 Hannah Mary Way
A3 1 Rudge Ho
2 Spenlow Ho
3 Darnay Ho
4 Carton Ho
5 Giles Ho
6 Bowley Ho
7 Casby Ho
8 Sun Pas
9 Ness St
10 Voyager Bsns Est
11 Dockley Road Ind Est
12 Spa Ct
13 Discovery Bsns Pk
14 Priter Road Hostel
15 Salisbury Ct
16 William Ellis Way
17 John McKenna Wlk
18 Toussaint Wlk
19 Gillison Wlk
20 Bromfield Ct
21 Ben Smith Way
22 Major Rd
A4 1 Providence Twr
2 Springalls Wharf
3 Flockton St
4 Providence Sq
5 Farthing Alley
6 Peter Butler Ho
7 Brownlow Ho
8 Fleming Ho
9 Dombey Ho
10 Copperfield Ho
11 Tapley Ho
12 Parkers Row
13 Wade Ho
14 Bardell Ho
15 Nickleby Ho
16 John Felton Rd
17 Flockton St
18 Pickwick Ho
19 Oliver Ho
20 Weller Ho
21 Tupman Ho
22 Haredale Ho
23 Havisham Ho
24 Micawber Ho
25 Wrayburn Ho
26 Dartle Ct
27 Burnaby Ct
28 Waterside Cl
29 Wickfield Ho
30 Fountain Ho
31 Fountain Green Sq
A5 1 Trade Winds Ct
2 Spice Ct
3 Leeward Ct
4 Bridgeport Pl
5 Tamarind Yd
6 Cope Yd
7 Nightingale Ho
8 St Anthony's Cl
9 Stockholm Way
10 Miah Terr
11 Seville Ho
12 Douthwaite Sq
13 Codling Cl
14 Hermitage Ct
15 Capital Wharf
A6 1 Conant Mews
2 Hanson Ho
3 Victoria Ct
4 Swan Pas
5 Royal Mint Pl
6 Flank St
7 Ensign Ind Ctr
8 Sapphire Ct
9 George Leybourne Ho
10 Fletcher St
11 Wellclose St
12 Noble Ho
13 Hatton Ho
14 Shearsmith Ho
15 Breezer's Ct
16 Pennington Ct
B1 1 Hockney Ct
2 Toulouse Ct
3 Lowry Ct
4 Barry Ho
5 Lewis Ct
6 Gainsborough Ct
7 Renoir Ct
8 Blake Ct
9 Raphael Ct
10 Rembrandt Ct
11 Constable Ct
12 Da Vinci Ct
13 Gaugin Ct
14 Michelangelo Ct
15 Monet Ct
16 Weald Cl
17 Jasmin Lo
18 Birchmere Lo
19 Weybridge Ct
20 Florence Ho
21 Gleneagles Cl
22 Sunningdale Cl
23 Muirfield Cl
24 Turnberry Cl
25 St Andrews Cl
26 Kingsdown Cl
27 St Davids Cl
28 Galway Cl
29 Edenbridge Cl
30 Birkdale Cl
31 Tralee Ct
32 Woburn Ct
33 Belfry Cl
34 Troon Cl
35 Holywell Cl
B2 1 Market Pl
2 Trappes Ho
3 Thurland Ho
4 Ramsfort Ho
5 Hambley Ho
6 Holford Ho
7 Pope Ho
8 Southwell Ho
9 Mortain Ho
10 Radcliffe Ho
11 Southwark Park Est
12 Galleywall Road Trad Est
13 Trevithick Ho
14 Barlow Ho
15 Donkin Ho
16 Landmann Ho
17 Fitzmaurice Ho
18 Dodd Ho
B3 1 Perryn Rd
2 Chalfont Ho
3 Prestwood Ho
4 Farmer Ho
5 Gataker Ho
6 Gataker St
7 Cornick Ho
8 Glebe Ho
9 Matson Ho
10 Hickling Ho
B4 1 Butterfield Cl
2 Janeway Pl
3 Trotwood Ho
4 Cranbourn Ho
5 Cherry Garden Ho
6 Burton Ho
7 Morriss Ho
8 King Edward The Third Mews
9 Cathay St
10 Rotherhithe St
B5 1 China Ct
2 Wellington Terr
3 Stevedore St
4 Portland Sq
5 Reardon Ho
6 Lowder Ho
7 Meeting House Alley
8 Farthing Fields
9 Oswell Ho
10 Park Lo
11 Doughty Ct
12 Inglefield Sq
13 Chopin's Ct
14 Welsh Ho
15 Hilliard Ho
16 Clegg St
17 Tasman Ho
18 Ross Ho
19 Wapping Dock St
20 Bridewell Pl
21 New Tower Bldgs
22 Tower Bldgs
23 Chimney Ct
24 Jackman Ho
25 Fenner Ho
26 Franklin Ho
27 Frobisher Ho
28 Flinders Ho
29 Chancellor Ho
30 Beechey Ho
31 Reardon Path
32 Parry Ho
33 Vancover Ho
34 Willoughby Ho
35 Sanctuary The
36 Dundee Ct
37 Pierhead Wharf
38 Scandrett St
B6 1 Newton Ho
2 Richard Neale Ho
3 Maddocks Ho
4 Cornwall St
5 Brockmer Ho
6 Dellow Ho
7 Bewley Ho
8 Artichoke Hill
C2 1 Damory Ho
2 Antony Ho
3 Roderick Ho
4 Pedworth Gdns
5 Beamish Ho
6 Gillam Ho
7 George Walter Ho
8 Richard Ho
9 Adron Ho
10 Westlake
11 McIntosh Ho
C3 1 Blick Ho
2 Neptune Ho
3 Scotia Ct
4 Murdoch Ho
5 Edmonton Ct
6 Niagara Ct
7 Columbia Point
8 Ritchie Ho
9 Wells Ho
10 Helen Peele Cotts
11 Orchard Ho
12 Dock Offices
13 Landale Ho
14 Courthope Ho
C4 1 Mayflower St
2 St Mary's Est
3 Rupack St
4 Frank Whymark Ho
5 Adams Gardens Est
6 Hatteraick St
7 Hythe Ho
8 Seaford Ho
9 Sandwich Ho
10 Rye Ho
11 Winchelsea Ho
12 Kenning St
13 Western Pl
14 Ainsty St
15 Pine Ho
16 Beech Ho
17 Larch Ho
18 Seth St
19 Turner Ct
20 Risdon Ho
21 Risdon St
22 Aylton Est
23 Manitoba Ct
24 Calgary Ct
25 Irwell Est
26 City Bsns Ctr
C5 1 John Rennie Wlk
2 Malay Ho
3 Wainwright Ho
4 Riverside Mans
5 Shackleton Ho
6 Whitehorn Ho
7 Wavel Ct
8 Prusom's Island
C6 1 Gosling Ho
2 Vogler Ho
3 Donovan Ho
4 Knowlden Ho
5 Chamberlain Ho
6 Moore Ho
7 Thornewill Ho
8 Fisher Ho
9 All Saints Ct
10 Coburg Dwellings
11 Lowood Ho
12 Solander Gdns
13 Chancery Bldgs
14 Ring Ho
15 Juniper St
16 Gordon Ho
17 West Block
18 North Block
19 South Block
D2 1 John Kennedy Ho
2 Brydale Ho
3 Balman Ho
4 Tissington Ct
5 Harbord Ho
6 Westfield Ho
7 Albert Starr Ho
8 John Brent Ho
9 William Evans Ho
10 Raven Ho
11 Egret Ho
12 Fulmar Ho
13 Dunlin Ho
14 Siskin Ho
15 Sheldrake Ho
16 Buchanan Ct
17 Burrage Ct
18 Biddenham Ho
19 Ayston Ho
20 Empingham Ho
21 Deanshanger Ho
22 Codicote Ho
D4 1 Schooner Cl
2 Dolphin Cl
3 Clipper Cl
4 Deauville Ct
5 Colette Ct
6 Coniston Ct
7 Virginia Ct
8 Derwent Ct
9 Grantham Ct
10 Serpentine Ct
11 Career Ct
12 Lacine Ct
13 Fairway Ct
14 Harold Ct
15 Spruce Ho
16 Cedar Ho
17 Sycamore Ho
18 Woodland Cres
19 Poplar Ho
20 Adelphi Ct
21 Basque Ct
22 Aberdale Ct
23 Quilting Ct
24 Chargrove Cl
25 Radley Ct
26 Greenacre Sq
27 Maple Leaf Sq
28 Stanhope Cl
29 Hawke Pl
30 Drake Cl
31 Brass Talley Alley
32 Monkton Ho
33 James Ho
34 Wolfe Cres
D5 1 Clarence Mews
2 Raleigh Ct
3 Katherine Cl
4 Woolcombes Ct
5 Tudor Ct
6 Quayside Ct
7 Princes Riverside Rd
8 Surrey Ho
9 Tideway Ct
10 Edinburgh Ct
11 Falkirk Ct
12 Byelands Cl
13 Gwent Ct
14 Lavender Ho
15 Abbotshade Rd
16 Bellamy's Ct
17 Blenheim Ct
18 Sandringham Ct
19 Hampton Ct
20 Windsor Ct
21 Balmoral Ct
22 Westminster Ct
D6 1 Barnardo Gdns
2 Roslin Ho
3 Glamis Est
4 Peabody Est
5 East Block
6 Highway Trad Ctr The
7 Highway Bsns Pk The
8 Cranford Cotts
9 Ratcliffe Orch
10 Scotia Bldg
11 Mauretania Bldg
12 Compania Bldg
13 Sirius Bldg
14 Unicorn Bldg

119

A2 1 Trafalgar Cl
2 Hornblower Cl
3 Cunard Wlk
4 Caronia Ct
5 Carinthia Ct
6 Freswick Ho
7 Graveley Ho
8 Husbourne Ho
9 Crofters Ct
10 Pomona Ho
11 Hazelwood Ho
12 Cannon Wharf Bsns Ctr
13 Bence Ho
14 Clement Ho
15 Pendennis Ho
16 Lighter Cl
17 Mast Ct
18 Rushcutters Ct
19 Boat Lifter Way
A6 1 St Georges Sq
2 Drake Ho
3 Osprey Ho
4 Fleet Ho
5 Gainsborough Ho
6 Victory Pl
7 Challenger Ho
8 Conrad Ho
9 Lock View Ct
10 Shoulder of Mutton Alley
11 Frederick Sq
12 Helena Sq
13 Elizabeth Sq
14 Sophia Sq
15 William Sq
B1 1 Gransden Ho
2 Daubeney Twr
3 North Ho
4 Rochfort Ho
5 Keppel Ho
6 Camden Ho
7 Sanderson Ho
8 Berkeley Ho
9 Strafford Ho
10 Richman Ho
11 Hurleston Ho
12 Grafton Ho
13 Fulcher Ho
14 Citrus Ho
B2 1 Windsock Cl
2 Linberry Wlk
3 Lanyard Ho
4 Golden Hind Pl
5 James Lind Ho
6 Harmon Ho
7 Pelican Ho
8 Bembridge Ho
9 Terrace The
10 George Beard Rd
B6 1 Hamilton Ho
2 Imperial Ho
3 Oriana Ho
4 Queens Ct
5 Brightlingsea Pl
6 Faraday Ho
7 Ropemaker's Fields
8 Oast Ct
9 Mitre The
10 Bate St
11 Joseph Irwin Ho
12 Padstow Ho
13 Bethlehem Ho
14 Saunders Cl
15 Roche Ho
16 Stocks Pl
17 Trinidad Ho
18 Grenada Ho
C2 1 Olympian Ct
2 Aphrodite Ct
3 Mercury Ct
4 Poseidon Ct
5 Neptune Ct
6 Artemis Ct
7 Hera Ct
8 Ares Ct
9 Cyclops Mews
10 Magellan Pl
11 Britannia Rd
12 Deptford Ferry Rd
13 Ironmonger's Pl
14 Radnor Wlk
15 Ashdown Wlk
16 Rothsay Wlk
17 Dartmoor Wlk
18 Ringwood Gdns
19 Dockers Tanner Rd
C3 1 St Hubert's Ho
2 John Tucker Ho
3 Clare Grant Ho
4 Gilbertson Ho
5 Bowsprit Point
6 Scoulding Ho
7 Cord Way
8 Cressall Ho
9 Alexander Ho
10 Kedge Ho
C6 1 West India Ho
2 Birchfield Ho
3 Elderfield Ho
4 Thornfield Ho
5 Gorsefield Ho
6 Arborfield Ho

119 (cont.)
7 Colborne Ho
8 East India Bldgs
9 Compass Point
10 Salter St
11 Kelly Ct
12 Flynn Ct
13 Mary Jones Ho
D2 1 Brassey Ho
2 Triton Ho
3 Warspite Ho
4 Rodney Ho
5 Conway Ho
6 Exmouth Ho
7 Akbar Ho
8 Arethusa Ho
D6 1 Westcott Ho
2 Corry Ho
3 Malam Gdns
4 Devitt Ho
5 Leyland Ho
6 Wigram Ho
7 Willis Ho
8 Balsam Ho
9 Finch's Ct
10 Poplar Bath St
11 Lawless St
12 Storey Ho
13 Abbot Ho
14 Landon Wlk
15 Goodhope Ho
16 Goodfaith Ho
17 Winant Ho
18 Lubbock Ho
19 Goodwill Ho
20 Martindale Ho
21 Holmsdale Ho
22 Norwood Ho
23 Constant Ho

120
A2 1 Betty May Gray Ho
2 Castleton Ho
3 Urmston Ho
4 Salford Ho
5 Capstan Ho
6 Frigate Ho
7 Galleon Ho
8 Barons Lo
A3 1 Cardale St
2 Hickin St
3 John McDonald Ho
4 Thorne Ho
5 Skeggs Ho
6 St Bernard Ho
7 Kimberley Ho
8 Kingdon Ho
9 Lingard Ho
10 Yarrow Ho
11 Sandpiper Ct
12 Nightingale Ct
13 Robin Ct
14 Heron Ct
A4 1 Llandovery Ho
2 Rugless Ho
3 Ash Ho
4 Elm Ho
5 Cedar Ho
6 Castalia Sq
7 Alice Shepherd Ho
8 Oak Ho
9 Ballin Ct
10 Martin Ct
11 Grebe Ct
12 Kingfisher Ct
A6 1 Discovery Ho
2 Mountague Pl
3 Virginia Ho
4 Collins Ho
5 Lawless Ho
6 Carmichael Ho
7 Commodore Ho
8 Mermaid Ho
9 Bullivant St
10 Anderson Ho
11 Mackrow Wlk
12 Robin Hood Gdns
B2 1 Verwood Lo
2 Fawley Lo
3 Lyndhurst Lo
4 Blyth Cl
5 Farnworth Ho
6 Francis Cl
C1 1 Bellot Gdns
2 Thornley Pl
3 King William La
4 Bolton Ho
5 Miles Ho
6 Mell St
7 Sam Manners Ho
8 Hatcliffe Almshouses
9 Woodland Wlk
10 Earlswood Cl
D1 1 Baldrey Ho
2 Christie Ho
3 Dyson Ho
4 Cliffe Ho
5 Moore Ho
6 Collins Ho
7 Lockyer Ho
8 Halley Ho
9 Kepler Ho

121
A1 1 Layfield Ho
2 Westerdale Rd
3 Mayston Mews
A5 1 Capulet Mews
2 Pepys Cres
3 De Quincey Mews
4 Hardy Ave
5 Tom Jenkinson Rd
6 Hanameel St
7 Kennacraig Cl
8 Charles Flemmell Mews
9 Gatcombe Rd
10 Badminton Mews
11 Holyrood Mews
12 Britannia Gate
13 Dalemain Mews
A6 1 Clements Ave
2 Martindale Ave
B1 1 Phipps Ho
2 Hartwell Ho
3 Nicholas Stacey Ho
4 Frank Burton Ct
B5 1 Beaulieu Ave
2 Charles Winchup Rd
3 Audley Dr
4 Julie Garfield Mews
5 Rayleigh Rd
6 Pirie St
7 Hanameel St
8 Ramsgate Cl
9 West Mersea Cl
10 Dunlop Point
11 Cranbrook Point
12 Westwood Rd
C1 1 Ransom Rd
2 Linton Cl
3 Cedar Pl
4 Gooding Ho
5 Valiant Ho
6 Chaffey Ho
7 Benn Ho
8 Wellesley Cl
9 Gollogly Terr

122
A2 1 Harden Ct
2 Albion Ct
3 Viking Ho
4 Zealand Ho
5 Glenalvon Way
6 Parish Wharf
7 Elsinore Ho
8 Lelland Ho
9 Denmark Ho
10 Jutland Ho
11 Tivoli Gdns
12 Rance Ho
13 Peel Yates Ho
14 Rosebank Wlk
15 Paradise Pl
16 Woodville St
B2 1 Bowling Green Row
2 Sara Turnbull Ho
3 Brewhouse Rd
4 Red Barracks Rd
5 Marine Dr
6 Ted Williams Ct
7 Hereford Ho
8 Katie Rance Ct
9 Maclean Ho
10 Lloyd Ho
11 Hastings Ho
12 Cambridge Barracks Rd
13 Len Clifton Ho
14 Granby Ho
15 Milne Ho
16 Harding Ho
17 Rendlebury Ho
18 Rutland Ho
19 Townshend Ho
20 Mulgrave Ho
21 Murray Ho
22 Chatham Ho
23 Biddulph Ho
24 Carew Ho
25 Eleanor Wlk
C2 1 Preston Ho
2 Lindsay Ho
3 Fraser Ho
4 Pickering Ho
5 Watergate Ho
6 Grinling Ho
7 Glebe Ho
8 Norton Ho
9 Tuffield Ho
10 Edmundson Ho
11 Drummond Ho
12 Farrington Ho
13 Fisher Ho
14 Elliston Ho
15 Sir Martin Bowes Ho
16 Jim Bradley Cl
17 Bathway
18 Limavady Ho
C5 1 Westland Ho
2 Queensland Ho
3 Pier Par
4 Woodman Par
5 Shaw Ho
6 Glen Ho
7 Brocklebank Ho
D1 1 Branham Ho
2 Ford Ho
3 Wilford Ho
4 Parker Ho
5 Stirling Ho
6 Twiss Ho
7 Hewett Ho
D2 1 Beresford Square Market Pl
2 Central Ct
3 Walpole Ho
4 Anglesea Ave
5 Troy Ct
6 Ormsby Point
7 Haven Lo
8 Green Lawns
9 Eardley Point
10 Sandham Point
11 Bingham Point

123
A1 1 Glenmount Path
2 Claymill Ho
3 George Akass Ho
B1 1 Bert Reilly Ho
C1 1 Fox Hollow Cl
2 Goldsmid St

124
B5 1 Rowntree Path
2 Macaulay Way
3 Manning Ct
4 Chadwick Ct
5 Simon Ct
B6 1 Beveridge Ct
2 Hammond Way
3 Leonard Robbins Path
4 Lansbury Ct
5 Raymond Postgate Ct
6 Webb Ct
7 Curtis Way
8 Lytton Strachy Path
9 Keynes Ct
10 Marshall Path
11 Cross Ct
12 Octavia Way
13 Passfield Path
14 Mill Ct
15 Besant Ct
C4 1 Binsey Wlk
2 Tilehurst Point
3 Blewbury Ho
4 Coralline Wlk
5 Evenlode Ho
C5 1 Kingsley Ct
2 Wilberforce Ct
3 Shaftesbury Ct
4 Hazlitt Ct
5 Ricardo Path
6 Nassau Path
7 Malthus Path
8 Bright Ct
9 Cobden Ct
D4 1 Oakenholt Ho
2 Trewsbury House
3 Penton Ho
4 Osney Ho
5 Jacob Ho
6 Masham Ho
7 St Helens Rd
8 Clewer Ho
9 Maplin Ho
10 Wyfold Ho
11 Hibernia Point
12 Duxford Ho
13 Radley Ho

125
A3 1 Harlequin Ho
2 Dexter Ho
3 Argall Ho
4 Mangold Way
5 Lucerne Ho
6 Holstein Way
7 Abbotswood Cl
8 Plympton Cl
9 Benedict Cl
B1 1 Shakespeare Ho
2 Tennyson Ho
3 Dickens Ho
4 Chestnuts The
5 Scott Ho
6 Lansbury Ho
7 Shaw Ho
C1 1 Stevanne Ho
2 Tolcairn Ct
3 Chalfont Ct
4 Alonso Ct
5 Ariel Ct
6 Miranda Ho
7 Prospero Ho
8 Laurels The
9 Camden Ct
10 Newnham Lo
11 Court Lo
12 Flaxman Ct
13 Hertford Wlk
14 Riverview Ct
C3 1 Cressingham Ct
2 Telford Ho
3 Kelvin Ho
4 Faraday Ho
5 Jenner Ho
6 Keir Hardy Ho
7 Lennox Ho
8 Mary Macarthur Ho
9 Elizabeth Garrett Anderson Ho
10 William Smith Ho
11 Baden Powell Ho
12 Baird Ho
13 Boyle Ho

129
D1 1 Heathwood Ct
2 Aldermead
3 Northumberland Ct

130
C4 1 Osterley Lo
2 St Andrew's Cl
3 Parkfield
4 Fairways
5 Granwood Ct
6 Grovewood Ct

131
A2 1 Brewery Mews Bsns Ctr
2 Tolson Ho
3 Percy Gdns
4 Wynne Ct
5 Wisdom Ct
6 Swann Ct
7 Shrewsbury Wlk
8 King's Terr
D5 1 Galba Ct
2 Servius Ct
3 Maurice Ct
4 Leo Ct
5 Otho Ct
6 Nero Ct
7 Romulus Ct
8 Pump Alley
D6 1 Brockshot Cl
2 Westbury Pl
3 Brook La N
4 Braemar Ct
5 Brook Ct
6 Clifden Ho
7 Cedar Ct
8 Cranbrook Ct
9 Somerset Lo
10 Alexandra Rd
11 Berkeley Ho
12 Watermans Ct

132
A1 1 St Johns Gr
2 Michel's Row
3 Michelsdale Dr
4 Blue Anchor Alley
5 Clarence St
6 Sun Alley
7 Thames Link Ho
A6 1 Ferry Sq
2 Wilkes Rd
3 Albany Par
4 Charlton Ho
5 Albany Ho
6 Alma Ho
7 Griffin Ho
8 Cressage Ho
9 Tunstall Wlk
10 Trimmer Wlk
11 Running Horse Yd
12 Mission Sq
13 Distillery Wlk
B1 1 Towers The
2 Longs Ct
3 Sovereign Ct
4 Robinson Ct
5 Calvert Ct
6 Bedford Ct
7 Hickey's Almshouses
8 Church Almshouses
B4 1 Primrose Ho
2 Lawman Ct
3 Royston Ct
4 Garden Ct
5 Capel Lo
6 Devonshire Ct
7 Celia Ct
8 Rosslyn Ho
9 Branstone Ct
10 Lamerton Lo
11 Kew Lo
12 Dunraven Ho
13 Stoneleigh Lo
14 Tunstall Ct
15 Voltaire
C4 1 Clarendon Ct
2 Quintock Ho
3 Broome Ct
4 Lonsdale Mews
5 Elizabeth Cotts
6 Sandways
7 Victoria Cotts
8 North Ave
9 Grovewood
10 Hamilton Ho
11 Melvin Ct
12 Power Ho
D1 1 Hershell Ct
2 Deanhill Ct
3 Park Sheen
4 Furness Lo
5 Merricks Ct

133
B2 1 Rann House
2 Craven Ho
3 John Dee Ho
4 Kindell Ho
5 Montgomery Ho
6 Avondale Ho
7 Addington Ct
8 Dovecote Gdns
9 Firmston Ho
10 Glendower Gdns
11 Chestnut Ave
12 Trehern Rd
13 Rock Ave
D3 1 Melrose Rd
2 Seaforth Lo
3 St John's Gr
4 Sussex Ct
5 Carmichael Ct
6 Hampshire Ct
7 Thorne Pas
8 Brunel Ct
9 Beverley Path

134
D1 1 Olivette St
2 Langmore Rd
3 Glegg Pl
4 Crown Ct
5 Charlwood Terr
D6 1 Cobb's Hall
2 Dorset Mans
3 St Clements Mans
4 Bothwell St
5 Hawksmoor St

135
B3 1 Plato Pl
2 Mustow Pl
3 Laurel Bank Gdns
4 Ranelagh Mans
5 Churchfield Mans
6 Bear Croft Ho
7 Elysium Gate
8 Ethel Rankin Ct
9 Arthur Henderson Ho
10 William Banfield Ho
D3 1 Brightwells
2 Broughton Road App
3 Bulow Ct
4 Langford Rd
5 Elizabeth Barnes Ct
6 Snowbury Rd

136
A2 1 Molasses Ho
2 Molasses Row
3 Cinnamon Row
4 Calico Ho
5 Calico Row
6 Port Ho
7 Square Rigger Row
8 Trade Twr
9 Ivory Ho
10 Spice Ct
11 Sherwood Ct
12 Mendip Ct
13 Chalmers Ho
B1 1 Burke Ho
2 Fox Ho
3 Buxton Ho
4 Pitt Ho
5 Romsey Ho
6 Beverley Cl
7 Florence Ho
8 Linden Ct
9 Dorcas Ct
10 Johnson Ct
11 Agnes Ct
12 Hilltop Ct
13 Courtyard The
14 Old Laundry The
15 Oberstein Rd
16 Fineran Ct
17 Sangora Rd
18 Harvard Mans
B2 1 Benham Ct
2 Milner Ho
3 McManus Ho
4 Wilberforce Ho
5 Wheeler Ct
6 Sporle Ct
7 Holliday Sq
8 John Parker Sq
9 Carmichael Cl
10 Fenner Sq
11 Clark Lawrence Ct
12 Shaw Ct
13 Sendall Ct
14 Livingstone Rd
15 Farrant Ho
16 Jackson Ho
17 Darien Ho
18 Sheppard Ho
19 Ganley Ct
20 Arthur Newton Ho
21 Chesterton Ho
22 John Kirk Ho
23 Mantua St
24 Heaver Rd
B3 1 Archer Ho
2 White Ho
3 Powrie Ho
4 Morgan Ct
5 Fairchild Cl
6 Battersea High St
7 Musjid Rd
C2 1 Kiloh Ct
2 Lanner Ho
3 Grifton Ho
4 Kestrel Ho
5 Kite Ho
6 Peregrine Ho
7 Hawk Ho
8 Inkster Ho
9 Harrier Ho
10 Eagle Hts
11 Kingfisher Ct
12 Lavender Terr
13 Temple Ho
14 Ridley Ho
15 Eden Ho
16 Hertford Ct
17 Nepaul Rd
C3 1 Meecham Ct
2 McKiernan Ct
3 Banbury St
4 Colestown St
5 Crombie Mews
6 Frere St
D3 1 Stevenson Ho
2 Ambrose Mews
3 Harling Ct
4 Southside Quarter
5 Latchmere St
6 Dovedale Cotts
7 Roydon Cl
8 Castlemaine
9 Wittering Ho
10 Berry Ho
11 Weybridge Point

137
A2 1 Shaftesbury Park Chambers
2 Selborne
3 Rush Hill Mews
4 Marmion Mews
5 Crosland Pl
6 Craven Mews
7 Wycliffe Rd
8 Basnett Rd
9 Wickersley Rd
10 Tyneham Cl
A3 1 Hopkinson Ho
2 Macdonald Ho
3 Rushlake Ho
4 Bishopstone Ho
5 Dresden Ho
6 Millgrove St
7 Farnhurst Ho
8 Walden Ho
9 Kennard St
10 Langhurst Ho
11 Kennard Ho
12 Voltaire Ct
13 Barloch Ho
B2 1 Turnchapel Mews
2 Redwood Mews
3 Phil Brown Pl
4 Bev Callender Cl
5 Keith Connor Cl
6 Tessa Sanderson Pl
7 Daley Thompson Way
8 Rashleigh Ct
B3 1 St Philip Sq
2 Montefiore St
3 Gambetta St
4 Scott Ct
5 Radcliffe Path
6 Moresby Wlk
C1 1 Polygon The
2 Windsor Ct
3 Trinity Cl
4 Studios The
5 Bourne Ho
C2 1 Clapham Manor Ct
2 Clarke Ho
3 Gables The
4 Sycamore Mews
5 Maritime Ho
C3 1 Seymour Ho
2 Lucas Ho
3 Durrington Twr
4 Amesbury Twr
5 Fovant Ct
6 Allington Ct
7 Welford Ct
8 Ilsley Ct
D1 1 Kendoa Rd
2 Felmersham Cl
3 Abbeville Mews
4 Saxon Ho
5 Gifford Ho
6 Teignmouth Cl
7 Holwood Pl
8 Oaklands Pl
D2 1 Chelsham Rd
2 Lynde Ho
3 Greener Ho
4 Towns Ho
5 Hugh Morgan Ho
6 Roy Ridley Ho
7 Lendal Terr
8 Slievemore Cl
D3 1 Haltone Ho
2 Surcot Ho
3 Kingsley Ho
4 Wood Ho
5 Dalemain Ho
6 Fallodon Ho
7 Dartington Ho
8 Esher Ho
9 Kneller Ho
10 Lostock Ho
11 Croxteth Ho
12 Donnington Ho
13 Farnley Ho
14 Hardwick Ho
15 Bradfield Ho
16 Brocket Ho
17 Colchester Ho
18 Clive Ho
19 Chessington Ho
20 Rushbrook Ho
21 Stanmore Ho
22 Newton Ho
23 Netherby Ho
24 Oakwell Ho
25 Rydal Ho
26 Rushton Ho
27 Harcourt Ho
28 Metcalfe Ho
29 Lydwell Ho
30 Raleigh Ho
31 Spencer Ho
32 Shipley Ho
33 Naylor Ho
34 Mordaunt Ho
35 Stanley Ho
36 Alderley Ho
37 Effingham Ho
38 Grant Ho
39 Wilson Ho
40 Fraser Ho

138
A1 1 Morris Ho
2 Gye Ho
3 Clowes Ho
4 Thomas Ho
5 Stuart Ho
6 Storace Ho
7 Bedford Ho
8 Ascot Ct
9 Ascot Par
10 Ashmere Ho
11 Ashmere Gr
A2 1 Callingham Ho
2 Russell Pickering Ho
3 Lopez Ho
A3 1 Barling Ct
2 Jeffrey's Ct
3 Brooks Ct
4 Dalmeny Ct
5 Fender Ct
6 Fishlock Ct
7 Bedser Ct
8 Gover Ct
9 Clarence Wlk
10 Barton Ct
11 Allom Ct
12 Garden Ho
13 Otha Ho
14 Hayward Ct
15 Surridge Ct
16 Knox Ct
17 Jephson Ho
18 Holmes Ct
19 McIntyre Ct
20 Richardson Ct
21 Cassell Ho
22 Packington Ho
23 Bain Ho
24 Enfield Ho
25 Fawcett Ho
26 Sidgwick Ho
27 Jowett Ho
28 Beckett Ho
29 Arden Ho
30 Pinter Ho
B1 1 Freemens Hos
2 Roger's Almshouses
3 Gresham Almshouses
4 Exbury Ho
5 Glasbury Ho
6 Dalbury Ho
7 Fosbury Ho
8 Chalbury Ho
9 Neilson-Terry Ct
10 Pavilion Mans
11 Daisy Dormer Ct
12 George Lashwood Ct
13 Marie Lloyd Ct
14 Trinity Homes
B2 1 Turberville Ho
2 Thrayle Ho
B3 1 Maurice Ho
2 Thring Ho
3 Paton Ho
4 Huxley Ho
5 Morell Ho

143
A5 1 Mary Lawrenson Pl
2 Bradbury Ct
3 Dunstable Ct
A6 1 Nethercombe Ho
2 Holywell Cl
C6 1 Warren Wlk
2 Wilson Ho
3 Priory Ho
4 Mar Ho
5 Langhorne Ho
6 Games Ho
7 Erskine Ho
8 Ducie Ho
9 Downe Ho
10 Bayeux Ho
11 Elliscombe Mount
12 Harold Gibbons Ct
13 Mascalls Ct
14 Leila Parnell Pl
15 East Mascalls
16 Birch Tree Ho
17 Cherry Tree Ct
18 Elm Tree Ct
19 Cedar Ct
D5 1 Winchester Ho
2 Brentwood Ho
3 Shenfield Ho
4 Chesterford Ho

144
A4 1 Master Gunner's Pl
2 Nicholson Ho
3 Borgard Ho
4 Macleod Ho
5 Brome Ho
6 Ross Ho
7 Horne Ho
8 Pendlebury Ho
9 Dickson Ho
10 Roberts Ho
A5 1 Leyburn Ho
2 Alanbrooke Ho
3 Gardiner Ho
B4 1 Galton Ho
2 Florence Ho
3 Sidney Ho
4 Robertson Ho
5 Mennie Ho
6 Godwin Ho
7 Panbro Ho
8 Sutherland Ho
C6 1 Lawson Ho
2 Mabbett Ho
3 Petrie Ho
4 Memess Path
5 Ruegg Ho
6 Nile Path
7 Leslie Smith Sq
8 Spearman St
9 Siedle Ho
10 Watling Ho
11 O'Neill Path
12 Old Clem Sq
13 Jefferson Wlk
14 Millwall Wlk
15 Wordsworth Ho
16 Fenwick Cl
D6 1 Acworth Ho
2 Griffiths Ho
3 Squires Ho
4 Cowen Ho
5 Turton Ho
6 Alford Ho
7 Boxshall Ho
8 Macallister Ho
9 Marvin Ho
10 Kelham Ho
11 Kimber Ho
12 Maxwell Ho
13 Woodford Ho
14 Penfold Ho

146
A2 1 Wellingfield Ct
2 Woodville Gr
3 Midwinter Ct
4 St Leonards Cl

147
A1 1 Woburn Ct
2 Arundel Ct
3 Longleat Villas
4 Upton Villas
B6 1 Bevercote Wlk
2 Boevey Path
3 Lullingstone Rd
4 Benjamin Ct
5 Charton Ct
6 Terence Ct
7 Renshaw Ct
8 Grove Rd
C1 1 Friswell Pl
2 Market Pl
3 Geddes Pl
4 Janet Ct
5 Broadway Sh Ctr
6 Mall The
7 Norwich Pl
8 Pincott Rd

148
A5 1 Stranraer Way
2 Deri Dene Cl
3 Lord Knyvetts Ct
4 Tudor Ct
5 Wessex Ct
6 Vanguard Ho
7 Shackleton Ct
8 Fleetwood Ct
9 Clifton Ct
10 Vickers Ct
11 Bristol Ct
12 Sunderland Ct

153
A3 1 Katharine Rd
2 Garfield Rd
3 Arragon Rd
4 Flood La
5 John Wesley Ct
6 King Street Par
7 Thames Eyot
A4 1 Perryn Ct
2 Ivybridge Cl
3 Brook Ho
4 Latham Ct
5 March Rd
6 Berkley Ct
7 Cole Court Lo
8 Cheltenham Ave
9 Railway App
A5 1 Greenways The
2 Cole Park View
B4 1 Melton Ct
2 Amyand Park Gdns
3 Crown Ct
4 Burrell Ho
5 Owen Ho
6 Brentford v
7 Leeson Ho
8 Westbourne Ho
9 Orleans Ct
10 Lebanon Ct
B5 1 Grove The
2 Cumberland Cl
3 Westmorland Cl
4 Sussex Ct
5 Norfolk Cl
6 Nicol Cl
7 Old Lodge Pl
8 Kelvin Ct
9 St Margaret's Ct
10 Park Cotts
11 St Margarets Bsns Ctr
12 Amyand Cotts
C5 1 Howmic Ct
2 Sefton Lo
3 Ravensbourne
4 Arlington Ct
5 Georgina Ct
6 Trevelyan Ho
7 Caradon Ct
8 Green Hedges
9 Old House Gdns
10 Queens Keep
11 Beresford Ct
12 Langham Ct
13 Poplar Ct
D5 1 Richmond Bridge Mans
2 Heatherdene Mans
3 Kenton Ct
4 Arosa Rd
5 Darling Ho
6 Turner Ho
7 Blanchard Ho
8 Ashe Ho
9 Bevan Ct
10 Lawley Ho
11 Leicester Ct
12 Roseleigh Cl
13 Beaulieu Cl
14 Richmond Mans
15 Mallard Ct
D6 1 Garrick Cl
2 Old Palace Yd
3 Wardrobe The
4 Maids of Honour Row
5 Hunters Ct
6 Queensberry Ho
7 Green The
8 Old Palace Terr
9 Paved Ct
10 Golden Ct
11 Brewers La
12 Square The
13 Lower George St
14 St James's Cotts
15 Church Wlk
16 Victoria Pl
17 Castle Yd
18 Lewis Rd
19 Wakefield Rd
20 Church Terr
21 Warrington Rd
22 Ormond Ave
23 St Helena Terr
24 Whittaker Pl
25 Heron Sq
26 Northumberland Pl

154
A5 1 Lancaster Cotts
2 Lancaster Mews
3 Bromwich Ho
4 Priors Lo
5 Richmond Hill Ct
6 Glenmore Ho
7 Hillbrow
8 Heathshot
9 Friars Stile Pl
10 Spire Ct
11 Ridgeway
12 Matthias Ct
A6 1 Lichfield Terr
2 Union Ct
3 Carrington Lo
4 Wilton Ct
5 Egerton Ct
6 Beverley Lo
7 Bishop Duppa's Almshouses
8 Regency Wlk
9 Clearwater Ho
10 Onslow Avenue Mans
11 Michels Almshouses
B5 1 Chester Cl
2 Grosvenor Ct
3 Queen's Ct
4 Russell Wlk
5 Charlotte Sq
6 Jones Wlk
7 Hilditch Ho
8 Isabella Ct
9 Damer Ho
10 Eliot Ho
11 Fitzherbert Ho
12 Reynolds Pl
13 Chisholm Rd
B6 1 Alberta Ct
2 Beatrice Rd
3 Lorne Rd
4 York Rd
5 Connaught Rd
6 Albany Terr
7 Kingswood Ct
8 Selwyn Ct
9 Broadhurst Cl

155
D5 1 Allenford Ho
2 Swaythling Ho
3 Tatchbury Ho
4 Penwood Ho
5 Bramley Ho
6 Shalden Ho
7 Dunbridge Ho
8 Denmead Ho
9 Charcot Ho
10 Portswood Pl
11 Brockbridge Ho
12 Hurstbourne Ho

156
A3 1 Farnborough Ho
2 Rushmere Ho
3 Horndean Cl
4 Highcross Way
5 Timsbury Wlk
6 Foxcombe Rd
7 Ryefield Path
8 Greatham Wlk
9 Gosport Ho
10 Stoatley Ho
11 Milland Ho
12 Clanfield Ho
13 Fareham Ho
14 Grayswood Point
A4 1 Woodcott Ho
2 Lyndhurst Ho
3 Wheatley Ho
4 Allbrook Ho
5 Bordon Wlk
6 Chilcombe Ho
7 Vicarage Ct
8 Shawford Ct
9 Eastleigh Wlk
10 Kings Ct
A6 1 Theodore Ho
2 Nicholas Ho
3 Bonner Ho
4 Downing Ho
5 Johsen Ho
6 Fairfax Ho
7 Devereux Ho
8 David Ho
9 Leigh Ho
10 Clipstone Ho
11 Mallet Ho
12 Arton Wilson Ho
B3 1 Ramsdean Ho
2 Purbrook Ho
3 Portsea Ho
4 Blendworth Point
5 Eashing Point
6 Hindhead Point
7 Hilsea Point
8 Witley Point
9 Buriton Ho
10 Grately Ho
11 Hascombe Ho
12 Dunhill Point
13 Westmark Point
14 Longmoor Point
15 Cadnam Point
C4 1 Cumberland Ho
2 Devonshire Ho
3 Cornwall Ho
4 Norfolk Ho
5 Leicester Ho
6 Warwick Ho
7 Sutherland Ho
8 Carmarthen Ho
9 Worcester Ho
10 Rutland Ho
C6 1 Inglis Ho
2 Ducie Ho
3 Warncliffe Ho
4 Stanhope Ho
5 Waldegrave Ho
6 Mildmay Ho
7 Mullens Ho
D3 1 Sandringham Cl
2 Eastwick Ct
3 Oatlands Ct
4 Banning Ho
5 Grantley Ho
6 Caryl Ho
7 Duncombe Ho
8 Chilworth Ho
9 Kent Lo
10 Turner Lo
11 Marlborough
12 Parkland Gdns
13 Lewesdon Cl
14 Pines Ct
15 Ashtead Ct
16 Mynterne Ct
17 Arden
18 Stephen Ct
19 Marsham Ct
20 Doradus Ct
21 Acorns The
22 Heritage Ho
23 Conifer Ct
24 Chartwell
25 Chartwell
26 Blenheim
27 Chivelston
28 Greenfield Ho
29 Oakman Rd
30 Radley Lo
31 Simon Lo
32 Admirals Ct
D4 1 Brett Ho
2 Brett House Cl
3 Sylva Ct
4 Ross Ct
5 Potterne Ct
6 Stourhead Lo
7 Fleur Gates
8 Greenwood
D5 1 Balmoral Cl
2 Glenalmond Ho
3 Selwyn Ho
4 Keble Ho
5 Bede Ho
6 Gonville Ho
7 Magdalene Ho
8 Armstrong Ho
9 Newnham Ho
10 Somerville Ho
11 Balliol Ho
12 Windermere
13 Little Combe Cl
14 Classinghall Ho
15 Chalford Ct
16 Garden Royal
17 South Ct
18 Anne Kerr Ct
19 Ewhurst
D6 1 Geneva Ct
2 Laurel Ct
3 Cambalt Ho
4 Langham Ct
5 Lower Pk
6 King's Keep
7 Whitnell Ct
8 Whitehead Ho
9 Halford Ho
10 Humphry Ho
11 Jellicoe Ho

157
A3 1 William Harvey Ho
2 Highview Ct
3 Cameron Ct
4 Galgate Cl
5 Green Ho The
6 King Charles Wlk
7 Florys Ct
8 Ingle Ho
9 Augustus Ct
10 Albert Ct
11 Hertford Lo
12 Mortimer Lo
13 Allenswood
14 Ambleside
A6 1 Claremont
2 Downside
3 Cavendish Cl
4 Ashcombe Ct
5 Carltons The
6 Draldo Ho
7 Millbrooke Ct
8 Coysh Ct
9 Keswick Hts
10 Lincoln Ho
11 Avon Ct
B6 1 Burlington Mews
2 Cumbria Ho
3 St Stephen's Gdns
4 Atlantic Ho
5 Burton Lo
6 Manfred Ct
7 Meadow Bank
8 Hooper Ho
C6 1 Pembridge Pl
2 Adelaide Rd
3 London Ct
4 Windsor Ct
5 Westminster Ct
6 Fullers Ho
7 Bridge Pk
8 Lambeth Ct
9 Milton Ct
10 Norfolk Mans
11 Francis Snary Lo
12 Bush Cotts
13 Downbury Mews
14 Newton's Yd
D6 1 Fairfield Ct
2 Blackmore Ho
3 Lancaster Mews
4 Cricketers Mews

159
A2 1 Upper Tooting Park Mans
2 Cecil Mans
3 Marius Mans
4 Boulevard The
5 Elmfield Mans
6 Holdernesse Rd
A3 1 Heslop Ct
2 St James's Terr
3 Boundaries Mans
4 Station Par
A4 1 Hollies Way
2 Endlesham Ct
A5 1 Rayne Ho
2 Earlsthorpe Mews
B3 1 Holbeach Mews
2 Hildreth Street Mews
3 Coalbrook Mans
B4 1 Meyer Ho
2 Faraday Ho
3 Hales Ho
4 Frankland Ho
5 Graham Ho
6 Gibbs Ho
7 Dalton Ho
8 Anslie Wlk
9 Rokeby Ho
10 Caister Ho
11 Ivanhoe Ho
12 Catherine Baird Ct
13 Marmion Ho
14 Devonshire Ho
C4 1 Limerick Ct
2 Homewoods
3 Jewell Ho
4 Glanville Ho
5 Dan Bryant Ho
6 Olding Ho
7 Quennel Ho
8 Weir Ho
9 West Ho
10 Neville Ho
C5 1 Joseph Powell Cl
2 Cavendish Mans
3 Westlands Terr
4 Cubitt Ho
5 Hawkesworth Ho
6 Normanton Ho
7 Eastman Ho
8 Couchman Ho
9 Poynders Ct
10 Selby Ho
11 Valentine Ho
12 Gorham Ho
13 Deauville Mans
14 Deauville Ct
C6 1 Timothy Cl
2 Shaftsbury Mews
3 Brook Ho
4 Grover Ho
5 Westbrook Ho
6 Hewer Ho
7 Batten Ho
8 Mandeville Ho
9 George Beare Lo
D3 1 Sinclair Ho
2 MacGregor Ho
3 Ingle Ho
D4 1 Riley Ho
2 Bennett Ho
3 White Ho
4 Rodgers Ho
5 Dumphreys Ho
6 Homan Ho
7 Prendergast Ho
8 Hutchins Ho
9 Whiteley Ho
10 Tresidder Ho
11 Primrose Ct
12 Angus Ho
13 Currie Ho
D5 1 Parrington Ho
2 Savill Ho
3 Blackwell Ho
4 Bruce Ho
5 Victoria Ho
6 Victoria Ho
7 Belvedere Ct
8 Ingram Lo
9 Viney Ho
10 Bloomsbury Ho
11 Belgravia Ho
12 Barnsbury Ho

160
A1 1 De Montfort Par
2 Leigham Hall Par
3 Leigham Hall
4 Endsleigh Mans
5 John Kirk Ho
6 Raeburn Ct
7 Wavel Ct
8 Homeleigh Ct
9 Howland Ho
10 Beauclerk Ho
11 Bertrand Ho
12 Drew Ho
13 Dowes Ho
14 Dunton Ho
15 Raynald Ho
16 Sackville Ho
17 Thurlow Ho
18 Astoria Mans
A2 1 Wyatt Park Mans
2 Broadlands Mans
3 Stonehill's Mans
4 Streatleigh Par
5 Dorchester Ct
A3 1 Beaumont Ho
2 Christchurch Ho
3 Staplefield Cl
4 Chipstead Ho
5 Coulsdon Ho
6 Conway Ho
7 Telford Avenue Mans
8 Telford Parade Mans
9 Wavertree Ct
10 Hartswood Ho
11 Wray Ho
A4 1 Picton Ho
2 Rigg Ho
3 Watson Ho
4 MacArthur Ho
5 Sandon Ho
6 Thorold Ho
7 Pearce Ho
8 Mudie Ho
9 Miller Ho
10 Lycett Ho
11 Lafone Ho
12 Lucraft Ho
13 Freeman Ho
14 New Park Par
15 Argyll Ct
16 Dumbarton Ct
17 Kintyre Ct
18 Cotton Ho
19 Crossman Hos
20 Cameford Ct
21 Parsons Ho
22 Brindley Ho
23 Arkwright Ho
24 Perry Ho
25 Brunel Ho
26 New Park Ct
27 Tanhurst Ho
A6 1 King's Mews
2 Clapham Court Terr
3 Clapham Ct
4 Clapham Park Terr
5 Queenswood Ct
B1 1 Carisbrook Ct
2 Pembrook Lo
3 Willow Ct
4 Poplar Ct
5 Mountview
6 Spa View
B3 1 Charlwood Ho
2 Earlswood Ho
3 Balcombe Ho
4 Claremont Cl
5 Holbrook Ho
6 Gwynne Ho
7 Kynaston Ho
8 Tillman Ho
9 Regent Lo
10 Hazelmere Ct
11 Dykes Ct
B4 1 Archbishop's Pl
2 Witley Ho
3 Outwood Ho
4 Dunsfold Ho
5 Deepdene Lo
6 Warnham Ho
7 Albury Lo
8 Tilford Ho
9 Elstead Ho
10 Thursley Ho
11 Brockham Ho
12 Capel Lo
13 Leith Ho
14 Fairview Ho
15 Weymouth Ct
16 Ascalon Ct
B6 1 Beatrice Ho
2 Florence Ho
3 Evelyn Ho
4 Diana Ho
5 Brixton Hill Ct
6 Austin Ho
7 Manor Ct
8 Camsey Ho
9 Romer Ho
10 Gale Ho
11 Byrne Ho
12 Farnfield Ho
13 Marchant Ho
14 Rainsford Ho
15 Springett Ho
16 Mannering Ho
17 Waldron Ho
C3 1 Valens Ho
2 Loveday Ho
3 Strode Ho
4 Ethelworth Ct
5 Harbin Ho
6 Brooks Ho
7 Godolphin Ho
8 Sheppard Ho
9 McCormick Ho
10 Taylor Ho
11 Saunders Ho
12 Talcott Path
13 Derrick Ho
14 Williams Ho
15 Baldwin Ho
16 Berkeley Ct
17 Churston Cl
18 Neil Wates Cres
19 Burnell Ho
20 Portland Ho
C4 1 Ellacombe Ho
2 Booth Ho
3 Hathersley Ho
4 Brereton Ho
5 Holdsworth Ho
6 Dearmer Ho
7 Cherry Cl
8 Greenleaf Cl
9 Longford Wlk
10 Scarlette Manor Wlk
11 Chandlers Way
12 Upgrove Manor Way
13 Ropers Wlk
14 Tebbs Ho
15 Bell Ho
16 Worthington Ho
17 Courier Ho
18 Mackie Rd
19 Hamers Ho
20 Kelway Ho
21 Harriet Tubman Cl
22 Estoria Cl
23 Leckhampton Pl
24 Scotia Rd
C5 1 Eccleston Ho
2 Scarsbrook Ho
3 Purser Ho
4 Rudhall Ho
5 Hardham Ho
6 Heywood Ho
7 Haworth Ho
8 Birch Ho
9 Lonsdell Ho
10 Lomley Ho
11 Laughton Ho
C6 1 Crownstone Ct
2 Brockwell Ct
3 Nevena Ct
4 St George's Residences
5 Hanover Mans
6 Fleet Ho
7 Langbourne Ho
8 Turnmill Ho
D1 1 Thanet Ho
2 Chapman Ho
3 Beaufoy Ho
4 Easton Ho
5 Roberts Ho
6 Lloyd Ct
7 Kershaw Ho
8 Wakeling Ho
9 Edridge Ho
10 Jeston Ho
11 Lansdowne Wood Cl

161
B2 1 Coppedhall
2 Shackleton Ct
3 Bullfinch Ct
4 Gannet Ct
5 Fulmar Ct
6 Heron Ct
7 Petrel Ct
8 Falcon Ct
9 Eagle Ct
10 Dunnock Ct
11 Dunlin Ct
12 Cormorant Ct
C6 1 Velde Way
2 Delft Way
3 Arnhem Way
4 Isel Way
5 Kempis Way
6 Terborah Way
7 Steen Way
8 Deventer Cres
9 Nimegen Way
10 Hilversum Cres

162
A1 1 Tunbridge Ct
2 Harrogate Ct
3 Bath Ct
4 Leamington Ct
5 Porlock Ho
6 Cissbury Ho

7 Eddisbury Ho
8 Dundry Ho
9 Silbury Ho
10 Homildon Ho
11 Highgate Ho
12 Richmond Ho
13 Pendle Ho
14 Tynwald Ho
15 Wirrall Ho
16 Greyfriars
A6 1 Dorothy Charrington Ho
2 Keswick Ct
3 Kendall Ct
4 Halliwell Ct
B1 1 River Ho
2 Fordington Ho
3 Arbury Terr
4 Woodbury Ho
5 Gainsborough Mews
6 Forest Hill Ct
B2 1 Bromleigh Ct
2 Parfew Ct
3 Thetford Ct
4 Attleborough Ct
5 Dunton Ct
6 Frobisher Ct
7 Julian Taylor Path
8 Grizedale Terr
9 Worsley Ho
C1 1 Forest Lo
2 Sydenham Park Mans
3 William Wood Ho
C2 1 Fitzwilliam Hts
2 Taymount Grange
3 McLeod Ho
4 Featherstone Ave
5 Kingswear Ho
6 Salcombe Ho
C3 1 Harlech Ct
2 Angela Ct
3 Westwood Ct
4 New Belmont Ho
5 Pearcefield Ave
6 Waldram Pl
7 Horniman Grange
8 South View Ct
9 Heron Ct
10 Katherine Ct
D1 1 Standlake Point
2 Radcot Point
3 Newbridge Point
4 Northmoor
5 Kelmscott
6 Radnor Ct
7 Heathwood Point
8 Ashleigh Point
9 Deepdene Point
10 Rosemount Point
11 Woodfield Ho
12 Clairville Point
13 Trevenna Ho
14 Hyndewood

164
C4 1 Beaumont Terr
2 Littlebourne
3 Verdant Ct
D2 1 Kinross Ct
2 Montrose Ct
3 Rattray Ct
4 Rothesay Ct
D3 1 Edinburgh Ct
2 McMillan Ct
3 Rowallan Ct
4 Meridian Ct
5 Braemar Ct
6 Barrow Ct
7 Blair Ct
8 Darlington Ct
9 Hamilton Ct
10 Inverness Ct
11 Oak Cottage Cl
12 Willow Cl
13 Keswick Ct

165
A4 1 Swallow Ct
2 Honeysuckle Ct
3 Venture Ct
4 Cheriton Ct
5 Askham Lo
6 Syon Lo

166
A2 1 Portland Cres
2 Bourdillon Ct
3 Hillary Ct
4 Tenzing Ct
5 John Hunt Ct
6 Everest Ct
A6 1 Horsfeld Gdns
2 Foxhole Rd
C5 1 Roper St
2 Arcade The
3 Elm Terr
4 Imber Ct
5 Ashcroft Ct
6 Fairlands Ct
7 Brecon Ct
8 Newlands Ct
9 Harvard Ct
10 Garden Ct
11 Chiltern Ct
12 Fairway Ct

167
A2 1 Mervyn Stockwood Ho
2 Michael Marshall Ho
3 Keith Sutton Ho

168
A1 1 Ham Shades Cl
2 Aspen Ho
3 Medlar Ho
4 Cornel Ho
5 Stanton Ct
6 Hornbeam Ho
7 Beech Ho
8 Spindle Ho
9 Moat Ct
10 Hunters Lo
11 Edam Ct
12 Monica James Ho
13 Oak Ho
14 Crescent Ct
B5 1 Rochester Cl
2 Cobham Cl
3 Shorne Cl
4 Warne Pl

169
C4 1 Close The
2 Parkhurst Gdns
3 Chichester Ct
4 Pound Green Ct

171
D3 1 Bishops Ct
2 Ash Lo
3 Lime Lo
4 Oak Lo
5 Elm Ct
6 Willow Lo
7 Sycamore Lo
8 Priscilla Ho
9 Sunbury Cross Ctr
10 Isobel Ho

173
A6 1 Gabriel Cl
2 Metcalfe Wlk
3 Dunmow Cl
4 Burgess Cl
5 Chamberlain Wlk
C2 1 Sherbourne Ct
2 Somerset Ct
3 Jubilee Ho
4 Rushbury Ct
5 Hemming Cl
6 Ryedale Ct
7 Norman Ct
C4 1 Begonia Pl
2 Snowdrop Cl
3 Hyacinth Cl
4 Cyclamen Cl
5 Jonquil Gdns
6 Gladioli Cl
7 Daffodil Cl
8 Partridge Rd
D4 1 Acorn Cl
2 Wolsey Ho
3 Lytton Ho
4 Wren Ho
5 Faraday Ho

174
C5 1 Knaggs Ho
2 Keeling Ho
3 Elizabeth Ct
4 Oakhurst Cl
5 Charles Ct
D5 1 Waldegrave Ct
2 Gresham Ho
3 Traherne Lo
4 Fishers Ct
5 Waterhouse Ct
6 Walpole Pl
7 Walpole Cres
8 Alice Mews
9 Bychurch End

175
A5 1 Cherrywood Ct
2 Cambridge Ho
3 Gleneagles Ct
4 Christchurch Ave
5 Hales Ct
6 Springfield Rd
D2 1 Wick Ho
2 Spinnaker Ct
3 Osiers Ct
4 Trent Ho
5 Arun Ho
6 Medway Ho
7 Avon Ho
8 Tyne Ho
9 Clyde Ho
10 Mersey Ct
11 Severn Ct
12 John William Cl
D6 1 Byron Ct
2 Coleridge Ct
3 Tennyson Ct
4 Herrick Ct
5 Spenser Ct
6 Marlowe Ct
7 Brooke Ct
8 Gray Ct
9 Shelley Ct
10 Pope Ct
11 Dryden Ct

176
A1 1 Cleave's Almshos
2 Parade The
3 Drovers Ct
4 Gough Ho
5 Eden Wlk
6 Alderman Judge Mall
7 Lady Booth Rd
8 Caversham Ho
9 Littlefield Cl
10 Bentall Sh Ctr The
11 Adams Wlk
12 Kingfisher Sports Ctr The
A2 1 Regents Pl
2 Walter St
3 Canbury Bsns Pk
4 Sigrist Sq
5 Ashway Ctr
6 Warwick Ho
B1 1 Vicarage Ho
2 Rayleigh Ct
3 School Pas
4 Chippenham
5 Camm Gdns
B2 1 Onslow Ho
2 Dowler Ct
B3 1 McDonald Ho
2 Elm Ho
3 Dale Ct
4 York Ho
5 Florence Ho
6 Florence Rd
7 Roupell Ho
8 Delft Ho
C1 1 Wimpole Cl
2 Burwell
3 Caldecote
4 Fordham
5 Connington
6 Chesterton Terr
7 Westwick
8 Eureka Rd
9 Fulbourn
10 Comberton
11 Madingley
12 Grantchester
13 Cambridge Grove Rd
14 Oakington
15 Harston
16 Graveley
17 Croxton
18 Brinkley
19 Impington
20 Shelford
21 Duxford
C2 1 Farthings The
2 Brae Ct
3 Princeton Mews
4 Station App
C3 1 Queen's Ct
2 St George's Rd
3 Park Road Ho
4 Dagmar Rd
5 Tapping Cl
6 Arthur Rd
7 Borough Rd
8 Belvedere Ct
9 Braywick Ct
10 Dean Ct
11 Rowan Ct
12 Richmond Ct
13 Sunningdale Ct
14 Hawker Ct
15 Cromwell Ct
16 Kings Ct
D2 1 Trevallyn Lo
2 Chichester Ho
3 Beechcroft
4 Cedars The
5 Liddlesdale Ho W
6 Liddlesdale Ho E
7 Deerhurst
8 Brockworth
9 Alderton
D3 1 Bramley Ho
2 Abinger Ho
3 Thursley Ho
4 Ridge Ho
5 Clone The
6 Mount Ct
7 Hillside Ct
8 Hill Ct
9 Royal Ct
10 Lakeside
11 High Ashton
D4 1 Godstone Ho
2 Hambledon Ho
3 Kingswood Ho
4 Leigh Ho
5 Milton Ho
6 Newdigate Ho
7 Farleigh Ho
8 Ockley Ho
9 Effingham Ho
10 Dunsfold Ho
11 Pirbright Ho
12 Clandon Ho
13 Ripley Ho

178
C3 1 Roskeen Ct
2 Chimneys Ct
3 Rosemary Cotts
4 Victoria Lo
D2 1 Beaufort Ho
2 Kinnear Ct
3 Ranmore Ct
4 Lantern Ct
D3 1 Kingsdown
2 Wimbledon Cl
3 Beryl Harding Ho
4 Upton Ct
5 Marian Lo
6 Terraces The
7 Lanherne Ho
8 Cumberland Cl
9 Thaxted Pl
10 Rathbone Ho
11 Princess Ct
12 Downs Ct
13 Ravenscar Lo
14 Haverley
15 Savona Cl
D5 1 Lancaster Pl
2 Haygarth Pl
3 Allington Cl

179
A3 1 Mayfair Ct
2 Brunswick Ct
3 Pavilion Ct
A4 1 Walham Rise
2 Grosvenor Ct
3 Sovereign Ho
4 Holly Lo
5 Florence Ct
6 Linden Cotts
7 Sheep Walk Mews
B5 1 Lawns The
2 Prentice Ct
3 Catherine Ct
4 Woodlodge
5 Queen Alexandra's Ct
6 Lake Cl
7 Westwood Ct
8 Brambles The
9 Lismore
10 Rose Ct
11 Worcester Rd
C3 1 Ashbourne Terr
2 Sir Cyril Black Way
3 Downing Ho
4 Palmerston Gr
5 Gladstone Ct
6 Harefield Ct
7 Viscount Point
D2 1 Gilbert Cl
2 Becket Cl
3 Priory Cl
4 Hudson Ct
5 Ryder Ho
6 Eleanor Ho
7 Ramsey Ho
D3 1 Hamilton Road Mews
2 Dowman Cl

180
A2 1 Tanner Ho
2 May Ct
3 Marsh Ct
4 Lovell Ho
A3 1 Fiske Ct
2 Mellor Ct
3 Olive Rd
4 Allerton Ho
5 Victory Road Mews
6 Will Miles Ct
7 Vanguard Ho
8 Mychell Ho
9 Merton Pl
10 De Burgh Ho
11 Norfolk Ho
12 Hotham Road Mews
B1 1 Ripley Ct
2 Brooklands Ct
3 Horner La
C2 1 Linford Ct
2 Searle Ct
3 Gunnell Ct
C5 1 Robertson Ho
2 Dewar Ho
3 Jean Ho
4 Marion Ct
5 Gravenel Gdns
D1 1 Elms Cotts
2 Sibthorp Rd
3 Armfield Cotts

181
A1 1 Kennedy Cl
2 Pearce Cl
3 Mainwaring Ct
4 Coningsby Ct
5 Laburnum Ct
6 Beaumont Ct
7 Penfold Ct
8 Fitch Ct
A5 1 Osbourne Terr
2 Limetree Wlk
C5 1 Tyers Ho
2 Boothby Ho
3 Adams Ho
4 Burney Ho
5 Boswell Ho
6 Chesterfield Ho
7 Garrick Ho
8 Levett Ho
9 Shelburne Ho
10 Marchmont Ho
11 Ryland Ho
C6 1 Walmsley Ho
2 Chambers Ho
3 Fordyce Ho
4 Percy Ho
5 Langton Ho
6 Moorfields Ct
7 Hidaburn Ct
8 Salter Ho

182
C5 1 Belltrees Gr
2 Ash Ct
3 Alder Ct
4 Beech Ct
5 Acacia Ct
6 Blackthorn Ct
7 Cypress Ct
8 Hawthorn Ct
9 Hazel Ct
10 Sycamore Ct
11 Maple Ct
12 Laburnam Ct
13 Fern Lo
C6 1 James Boswell Cl
2 St Albans Ho
3 Suffolk Ct
4 Rockhampton Cl
5 Delphian Ct
D5 1 Woodcote Pl
2 Joe Hunte Ct
3 Cork Tree Ho
4 Lake Ho
5 Cedars Ho
6 Portobello Ho
7 Cooper Ho
8 Farnsworth Ho
9 Hook Ho
10 Crest The
11 Renshaw Ho
12 Ruscoe Ho
13 Sardeson Ho

183
A6 1 Moore Ho
2 Chaucer Ho
3 Bushell Ho
4 Bligh Ho
5 Hobbs Rd
6 Hogarth Ho
7 Goodbehere Ho
8 Astley Ho
9 Elder Gdns
10 Elderberry Gr
11 Pavement The
12 Dunkirk St
B6 1 Josef Perrin Ho
2 Jean Humbert Ho
3 Charles Staunton Ho
4 Violette Szabo Ho
5 Lilian Rolfe Ho
6 Odette Ho
7 Robert Gerard Ho
8 St Bernards Cl
9 Champness Cl
10 Pennington Cl
11 Queenswood Ct
C4 1 Norwood Way
2 High Limes
3 Valley Prospect
4 Plane Tree Wlk
5 City Prospect
6 Bankside Way
7 Ridgeway
8 Rochdale
9 Barrington Wlk
10 Gatestone Ct
11 Childs La
12 Carberry Rd
13 Norwood Heights Sh Ctr
C5 1 Oakdene
2 Thorsden Way
3 Oakfield Gdns
4 Georgetown Cl
5 Bridgetown Cl
6 Mountbatten Cl
7 Brabourne Cl
8 Alexandra Wlk
9 Compton Ct
10 Battenberg Wlk
11 Burma Terr
12 Wiseman Ct
C6 1 Linley Ct
2 Mellor Ho
3 Whitfield Ct
4 Michaelson Ho
5 Holberry Ho
6 Hovenden Ho
7 Huntley Ho
8 Telfer Ho
9 Markham Ho
10 Oldham Ho
11 Parnall Ho
12 Pierson Ho
13 Roper Ho
14 Roundell Ho
15 Sawyer Ho
16 Ransford Ho
17 Carmichael Ho
18 Bonne Marche Terr Mews
D3 1 Hetley Gdns
2 Clayborne Mews
3 Highland Lo
4 Mason Ct
5 Kendall Ct
6 High View

184
A3 1 Hanover Ct
2 Brunswick Ct
3 New Church Ct
4 Regency Ct
7 Owen Wlk
8 Bargrove Cl
9 Beaver Cl
B2 1 Dorset Ho
2 Collingwood Cl
3 Chartwell Way
4 Essex Twr
5 Appletree Cl
6 Ditton Pl
7 Kelvin Ct
8 Readman Ct
9 Glen Ct
10 Kingsbridge Ho
11 Carlton Ct
12 Benhurst Ct
13 Carole Ho
14 Dover Ho
15 Bettswood Ct
B5 1 Ragwort Ct
2 Firs The
3 Wingham Ho
4 Seath Ho
5 Ripley Ho
6 Lathwood Ho
7 Hurst Ho
8 George Ho
9 Browne Ho
10 Beacon Ho
11 Bailey Ho
12 Agate Ho
C2 1 Challin St
2 Rutland Ho
3 Pine Cl
C3 1 Watermen's Sq
2 St John's Cotts
3 Gladstone Mews
4 Birling Ho
5 Surrey Twr
6 Middlesex Ho
7 Adisham Ho
8 Bethesda Ct
9 Ospringe Cl
10 Goudhurst Ho
11 Walmer Ho
12 Strood Ho
13 Greatstone Ho
14 John Baird Ho
D3 1 Groombridge Ho
2 Provincial Terr
3 Smithers Ho
4 West Ho
5 Swallows Ct

185
A1 1 Clock House Ct
2 Blandford Ave
3 Old School Cl
4 Lynsted Ct
5 Florence Rd
A6 1 Paxton Ct
2 Kenton Ct
3 Grove Ct
4 Shirley Lo
B2 1 Ashton Ct
2 Coombe Ct
3 Fontaine Ct
4 Richfield Ct
5 Sheridan Way
C1 1 Christ Church Rd
2 Lea Rd
3 Stanmore Terr
C2 1 Erindale Ct
2 Bearsted Terr
3 Beck River Pk
4 Waterside
5 Station App
C3 1 Gardenia Ct
2 Brackendale Ct
3 Daniel Ct
4 Moliner Ct
5 Chartwell Lo
6 Randmore Ct
7 Dover Ho
8 Lucerne Ct
9 Malling Ho
10 Westerham Lo
11 Brasted Lo
12 Milton Ho
13 Bradsole Ho
14 Sandgate Ho
15 Adelaide Ct
16 Nettlestead Cl
17 Warren Ct
18 Alton Ct
19 Rockingham Ct
20 Camellia Ct
21 Sinclair Ct
22 Regents Ct
23 Minshull Pl
24 South Park Ct
D1 1 Parkside
2 Tudors The
3 Oakbrook
4 Tara Ct
5 Redlands The
6 Cambria
7 Hillworth
8 Kelsey Gate
9 Burrells
10 Lincoln Lo
11 Courtlands
12 Fairleas
13 Ashdown Cl
D2 1 Mayfair Ct
2 Clifton Ct
3 Fire Station Mews
D4 1 Warner Ho
2 Clifford Ho
3 Lloyd Ho
4 Thurston Ho
5 Byron Ho
6 Blake Ho
7 Keats Ho

186
A2 1 White House Ct
2 Hunters The
3 Sandringham Ct
4 Glenhurst
5 Copperfields
A6 1 Dedham Ho
2 Flatford Ho
3 Radley Ct
4 Langthorne Ct
5 Hoover Ho
6 Brunner Ho
7 Waterer Ho
8 Marriott Ho
9 Bourbon Ho
B5 1 Longford Ho
2 Ingrebourne Ho
3 Brent Ho
4 Darent Ho
5 Beverley Ho
6 Wandle Ho
7 Rythe Ho
8 Ember Ho
9 Crane Ho
10 Ravensbourne Ho
C1 1 Warwick Ct
2 Maplehurst
3 Mount Arlington
4 Arundel Ct
D2 1 Weston Gr
2 Gibbs Ho
3 Longfield
4 Hammelton Ct
5 Bracken Hill Cl
6 Townend Ct
7 Treversh Ct
8 Cameron Ho
9 Woodlands Ct
10 Blythwood Pk
11 Bromley Pk
D3 1 Homecoppice Ho
2 Kimberley Gate
3 Inglewood Ct
4 Mavery Ct
5 Glen Ct
6 Cawston Ct
7 Blendon Path

187
B2 1 Hansom Terr
2 Dainton Cl
3 St Timothy's Mews
4 Andringham Lo
5 Kendall Lo
6 Summerfield
7 Winston Ct
8 Laurels The
C1 1 Westland Lo
2 Dairsie Ct
3 Beechfield Cotts
4 Oasis The
5 Cromarty Ct
6 Silverstone Ct

188
A6 1 Beaconsfield Par
2 Cranley Par
3 Kimmeridge Gdns
4 King & Queen Cl
C1 1 Merewood Cl
2 Alpine Copse
C2 1 Ivybridge Ct
2 Greenbank Lo

190
A6 1 Minshaw Ct
2 Cyril Lo
3 Milton Lo
4 Glenwood Ct
5 Culverton Ct
6 Holmbury Manor
B1 1 Swanscombe Ho
2 Haverstock Ct
3 Arrandene Ho
4 Broomfield Ho
5 Headley Ho
6 Kenley Ho
7 Ladywell Ho
B6 1 Chudleigh

390 | **197 A2**
2 Wimborne
3 St John's Par
4 Holly Ct
5 Rectory Bsns Ctr

197
A2 1 Raleigh Ho
2 Leicester Ho
3 Gresham Ho
D2 1 Napier Ct
2 Darlington Ho
3 Charminster Ct
4 Mulberry Ct
5 Leander Ct
6 Clinton Ho
7 Hollingworth Ct
8 Gloucester Ct
9 Palmerston Ct
10 Redwood Ct
11 Hursley Ct
12 Westmorland Ct
13 Lawson Ct
14 Alexander Ct
15 Winton Ct
16 Sydenham Ho
17 Caroline Ct
18 Ellswood Ct
19 Masefield Ct

198
A1 1 Ash Tree Cl
2 Shrubbery The
3 Malvern Ct
4 Gate Ho
A3 1 Station App
2 South Bank Lo
3 Bramshott Ct
4 Pandora Ct
5 Wellington Ct
6 Glenbuck Ct
7 Leighton Ho
8 Oakhill Ct
9 Downs View Lo
10 Osborne Ct
A4 1 Effingham Lo
2 Maple Ho
3 Channon Ct
4 Falconhurst
5 Ferndown
6 Viceroy Lo
7 Frensham Ct
8 Kingsley Ho
9 Rannoch Ct
10 Stratton Ct

11 Moray Ho
12 Dulverton Ct
13 Westerham
14 Hill Ct
15 Assheton-Bennett Ho
16 Hatfield Ho
17 Oxford Ct
18 Pennington Lo
19 Austin Ho
20 Wentworth Ct
21 Priory The
22 Sheraton The
A5 1 Marquis Ct
2 Garrick Ho
A6 1 College Rdbt
2 Edinburgh Ct
3 Weston Ct
4 Grebe Terr
5 Heron Ct
6 Agar Ho
7 St James' Ct
8 Grove Ct
9 Springfield Ct
10 College Wlk
B3 1 Percy Ct
2 Holmwood
3 Middle Green Cl
B4 1 Woodleigh
2 Highcroft
3 Caernarvon Ct
4 Regency Ct
D1 1 Oakleigh Way
2 Chandler Ct

199
C2 1 Goodland Ho
2 Furzeland Ho
3 Oakcroft Ho
4 Meadcroft Ho
5 Newhouse
C4 1 Merryweather Ct
2 Roebuck Ho
3 Sable Ct
C5 1 Acacia Ho
2 Kingston Lo
3 Fairholme Ho
4 Marshall Ho
5 Norton Ho
6 Martin Ho

200
A1 1 Brookside Cres
2 Beverley Gdns
3 Purdey Ct
4 Avenue The
5 Briarwood Ct

6 Station App
202
D6 1 Fair Green Ct
2 Regal Ct
3 Lewes Ct
4 Esher Mews

205
B1 1 Tavistock Ct
2 Chartwell Cl
3 Speaker's Ct
4 Cumberland Ct
5 Viceroy Ct
6 Oriel Ct
7 Cherry Orchard Gdns
C1 1 Windm ll Bridge Ho
2 Squire Ct
3 Houston Ct
4 St James's Lo
5 Kendal Ho
6 Warren Ct
7 Kendal Ct
D1 1 Hastings Pl
2 Grant Pl
3 Clive Ho
4 Havelock Ho
5 Bellmore Ct
6 Hereford Ct
7 Chequers Ct
8 Havelock Hall

206
A1 1 Farleycroft
2 Edgecumbe Ct
3 Wesson Ho
4 Sullivan Ct
5 Kenley Ho
6 Christopher Ct
7 Jayson Ct
D1 1 Cottongrass Cl
2 Oxlip Cl
3 Eyebright Cl

207
D1 1 North Rd
2 Sussex Rd
3 Riverside Wlk
4 Christie Ho
5 Sherwood Ct
6 Wheatsheaf Par
D6 1 Linden Ct
2 Park Ct
3 Chilchester Ct
4 Iveagh Ct

208
A6 1 Overbury Ct
2 Wilton Pl
D1 1 Woodgrange Ct
2 Maycroft
3 Farnborough Cres
D4 1 Knowlton Gn
2 Speldhurst Cl
3 Bidborough Cl
4 Penshurst Wlk
D5 1 Wedgewood Ct
2 Birches The
3 Eccleshill
4 Tavistock Rd
5 Montpelier Ct

209
A5 1 Montague Terr
2 Chatsworth Ho
A6 1 Marina Cl
2 Cheveney Wlk
3 Bromley Manor Mans
4 Mall The
5 Westmoreland Pl

211
B1 1 Gleneagles Gn
2 Tandridge Pl
3 Springfield Wlk
4 Pinehurst Wlk
5 Cromer Pl
6 Oakmont Pl

214
A6 1 St Bernards Ho
2 Wentworth Ct
3 Sunningdale Cl
4 Arklow Mews
5 Edward Pinner Ct

215
D6 1 Kingsley Dr
2 Kingsley Ct
3 Mowat Ct
4 Squirrels Ct

216
A6 1 Lansdowne Copse
2 Lansdowne Ct

217
A2 1 Cheam Court Flats

2 Farnham Ct
3 Tabor Ct
C1 1 Lancaster Ct
2 Redclyffe Terr
3 Kenilworth Terr
4 Lincoln Terr
5 Garden Ct
6 Ashwood Pk
7 Lyndhurst Ct
8 Banbury Ct
9 Holly Ct
10 Castle Ho
11 Balmoral Ct
12 Hereford Ct
13 Lorac Ct
14 Camilla Ct
D1 1 Hadrian Ct
2 Sandown Ct
3 Magnolia Ct
4 Larchvale Ct
5 Alford Ct
6 Brockham Ct
7 Berrylands Ct
8 Camberley Ct
9 Dunsfold Ct
10 Courtlands
11 Leith Towers
12 Kingslee Ct

218
A1 1 Beauclere Ho
2 Melford Ct
3 Elmhurst Lo
4 Mansard Manor
5 Tranmere Ct
6 Beechcroft Lo
7 Savin Lo
8 Yew Tree Ct
9 Avondale Ct
10 Devonshire Ho
11 Hidcote Ho
12 Munstead Ct
13 Lodden Lo
14 Steetley Ct
A2 1 Grosvenor Ct
2 Forest Dene Ct
3 Cedar Ct
4 Vanborough Ct
A3 1 Goossens Cl
2 Cliffe Wlk
3 Marlins Cl
4 Clowser Ct
5 Montana Gdns

219
B2 1 Runnymede Ct
2 Dolphin Ct

3 Kings Ct
4 Cheyne Ct
5 Hendfield Ct
6 Ellerslie Ct
7 Embassy Ct
8 Chandler Ct
9 Hambledon Ct
10 Wallington Ct
11 Jasmine Ct
B4 1 Loraine Ho
2 Harcourt Lo
3 Coniston Ct
4 Alcester Ct
5 Friars Ct
6 Campbell Ho
7 Brodie Ho
8 Lesley Ct
9 Birch Ct
10 Airborne Ho
C2 1 Rossendon Ct
2 Mulberry Mews
3 Nairn Ct
4 Wallington Sq
5 Rosemount
6 Connell Ho
7 Ashby Grange

221
A4 1 West Street Pl
2 Maple Ct
3 St Andrew's Rd
4 Albury Ct
5 Chestnut Ct
6 Elgin Ct
7 Beechfield Ct
8 Barham Ct
9 Whitstable Pl
10 Ledbury Pl
A5 1 Mann Cl
2 Halstead Cl
3 Fellmongers Yd
A6 1 Otterbourne Rd
2 Charrington Rd
3 Tamworth Pl
4 Priddy's Yd
5 Hospital of the Holy Trinity (Almshouses)
6 Bellhill
B4 1 Holmlea Ct
2 Garlands Ct
3 Coombe Ct
4 Deepdale Ct
5 Galloway Path
B6 1 Wellesley Court Rd
2 Norfolk Ho

3 Station App
4 Suffolk Ho
5 Cherry Orchard Gdns
6 Harrington Ct
D6 1 Cheyne Ct
2 Fourways
3 Princess Ct
4 Tierney Ct
5 Sinclair Ct
6 Guinness Ct
7 Mayfair Ct
8 Bishopscourt
9 Gloucester Lo
10 Beverley Hyrst
11 Melton Ct
12 Cecil Ct
13 Napier Ct

227
A3 1 Westfield
2 Farnborough Ct
3 Fern Hill Pl
4 Churchill Ct
5 Spencer Ct
6 Ladycroft Gdns
7 Crabbs Croft Cl
8 Clifton Cl
D2 1 Brittenden Cl
2 Wardens Field Cl
3 Winnipeg Dr
4 Superior Dr
5 Huron Cl
6 Manitoba Gdns
7 Lynne Cl
8 Flint Cl
9 Bakers Mews
D3 1 Osgood Gdns
2 Amberley Cl
3 Rawlings Cl
4 Beblets Cl
5 Fir Tree Cl
6 Raleigh Mews
7 King Henry Mews
D4 1 Healy Dr
2 Marsden Way
3 Taylor Cl
4 Strickland Way
5 Dryland Ave
6 Adcot Wlk
7 Lichdale Cl

Hospitals

Hospitals with accident and emergency departments are highlighted in green

A

Acton Hospl W3 .....110 C4
Ashford Hospital
Stanmore Road, Ashford, Middlesex TW15 3AA ..148 A2
020 01784 884488
Athlone House (The Middlesex Hospl) N6 48 D1
Atkinson Morley's Hospl SW20 ....178 B3

B

Barking Hospl IG11 ...79 D1
Barnes Hospl SW14 ..133 C2
Beckenham Hospl BR3 ....185 B1
Bethlem Royal Hospl The BR3 ....207 C2
Blackheath Hospl SE3 ....142 C2
Bolingbroke Hospl The SW11 ....158 C6
Bowden House Hospl (Private) HA1 ....64 C6
British Home & Hospl for Incurables SE27 ....182 D5
Bromley Hospital
Cromwell Avenue, Bromley, Kent BR2 9AJ 209 B5
020 8289 7000
Brompton Hospl SW3 ....114 B1 256 D2
BUPA Bushey Hospl WD2 ....8 D3

C

Carshalton, Beddington & Wallington War Memorial Hospl SM5 ....218 D2
Cassel Hospl TW10 ..175 D6
Castlewood Day Hospl SE18 ....144 C4
Central Middlesex Hospital
Acton Lane, Park Royal, London, NW10 7NS ..89 A4
020 8965 5733
Central Public Health Laboratories NW9 ...45 C6
Chadwell Heath Hospl RM6 ....58 B4
Charing Cross Hospital
Fulham Palace Road, London, W6 8RF (A&E entrance off St Dunstan's Road) ..112 D1
020 8846 1234
Charter Nightingale Hospl The NW1 .....92 C2 237 B4
Chase Farm Hospital
The Ridgeway, Enfield, Middlesex, EN2 8JL 4 C5
020 8366 6600
Chelsea Hospl for Women SW3 ....114 C1 257 A2
Chelsea and Westminster Hospital
369 Fulham Road, Chelsea, SW10 9NH ..136 A6 266 B5
020 8746 8000
Chingford Hospl E4 ...20 A1
Chiswick Maternity Hospl W4 ....111 D1
Claypонds Hospl & Day Treatment Ctr TW8 .110 A2
Clementine Churchill Hospl The HA1 ......64 D5
Colindale Hospl NW9 .45 C6
Connaught Day Hospl E11 ....54 C3
Coppetts Wood Hospl N10 ....30 D2
Cromwell Hospl SW5 ....113 D2 255 C4
Croydon General Hospl CR0 ....205 A1

D

Devonshire Hospl W1 ....93 A2 238 B4
Dulwich Hospl SE22 .139 C1

E

Ealing Hospital
Uxbridge Road, Southall, Middlesex UB1 3HW ..108 B4
020 8574 2444
East Ham Meml Hospl E7 ....77 D1
Eastman Dental Hospl WC1 ....94 B4 240 C6
Edgware General Hospl HA8 ....26 D3
Elizabeth Garrett Anderson Hospl NW1 ..93 D4 232 D1

F

Farnborough Hospl BR6 ....226 C4
Finchley Memorial Hospl N12 ....30 A3
Fitzroy Nuffield Hospl W1 ....92 D1 237 C2

G

Garden Hospl The NW4 ....46 C6
Goldie Leigh Hospl SE2 ....146 C6
Goodmayes Hospl IG3 58 A4
Gordon Hospl The SW1 ....115 D2 259 C3
Great Ormond St Hospl for Children WC1 94 B3 240 C5
Greenwich District Hospital
Vanbrugh Hill, Greenwich, London, SE10 9HE ..120 D1
020 8858 8141
Grovelands Priory (Private Hospl) N14 .16 A3
Guy's Hospl SE1 ....117 B5 252 D2

H

Hackney Hospl E9 ....75 A3
Hamlet (Day) Hospl The TW9 ....132 A2
Hammersmith Hospital
Du Cane Road, London, W12 0HS 90 B1
020 8743 2030
Harrow Hospl HA2 ....64 C6
Hillingdon Hospital
Field Heath Road, Uxbridge, Middlesex UB8 3NN ..82 B2
01895 238282
Hither Green Hospl SE13 ....164 B5
Homerton Hospital
Homerton Row, E9 6SR ..74 D3
020 8510 5555
Hornsey Central Hospl N8 ....49 D4
Hospl for Tropical Diseases NW1 ......232 C5
Hospl of St John & St Elizabeth NW8 ....92 B5 229 C3

I

Inverforth House Hospl NW3 ....70 A6

J

Jewish Home & Hospl at Tottenham The N15 ..51 D5

K

King George Hospital
Barley Lane, Goodmayes, Ilford, Essex IG3 8YB ..58 A4
020 8983 8000
King's College Hospital
Denmark Hill, London SE5 9RS (A&E in Ruskin Wing) 139 B3
020 7737 4000
Kings Oak Hospl (Private) The EN2 ....4 C5
Kingsbury Hospl NW9 .44 C5
Kingston Hospital
Galsworthy Road, Kingston-upon-Thames, Surrey KT2 7QB 176 D2
020 8546 7711

L

Langthorne Hospl E11 76 B5
Lewisham Hospital
High Street, Lewisham, London SE13 6JH ...163 D6
020 8333 3000
Lister Hospl SW1 ....115 B1 258 C1
London Bridge Hospl SE1 ....117 B5 252 D4
London Chest Hospl E2 ....96 C5
London Clinic NW1 ....93 A3 238 B5
London Foot Hospl W1 ....93 C3 239 A5
London Hospl (Mile End) The E2 ....96 D4
London Hospl (St Clements) The E3 ...97 B4
London Independent Hospl The E1 ....96 D2

M

Maida Vale Psychiatric Hospl W9 ....92 A3 236 B6
Manor House Hospl NW11 ....47 D1
Marlborough Day Hospl NW8 ....92 A5 229 A4
Maudsley Hospl The SE5 ....139 B3
Mayday Hospital
Mayday Road, Thornton Heath CR7 7YE 204 D3
020 8401 3000
Memorial Hospl SE18 144 C3
Middlesex Hospl W1 ....93 C2 239 B3
Middlesex Hospl Annexe W1 ....239 B4
Mildmay Mission Hospl E2 ....95 D4
Molesey Hospl KT8 ..195 C4
Moorfields Eye Hospl EC1 ....95 B4 235 C1
Morland Road Day Hospl RM10 ....103 C6

N

National Hospital for Neurology & Neurosurgery N2 ....48 C5
National Hospl The WC1 ....94 A3 240 B5
National Physical Laboratory TW11 ...174 C4
Nelson Hospl SW20 ..179 B1
New Cross Hospl SE14 ....140 C5
New Victoria Hospl KT3 ....177 C2
Newham General Hospital
Glen Road, Plaistow, London E13 8SL 99 C3
020 7476 4000
Normansfield Hospl KT8 ....175 C3
North London Nuffield Hospl EN2 ....4 C3
North Middlesex Hospital
Sterling Way, Edmonton, London, N18 1QX 33 C5
020 8887 2000
Northwick Park Hospital
Watford Road, Harrow, Middlesex HA1 3UJ ..43 A2
020 8864 3232
Northwood Pinner & District Cottage Hospl HA6 ....22 A2
Norwood Hospl SE19 183 B4

O

Orpington Hospl BR6 227 D4

P

Paddington Com Hospl W9 ....91 C2
Penny Sangam Day Hospl UB2 ....107 B3
Plaistow Hospl E13 ...99 C5
Portland Hospl for Women & Children The W1 ....93 B3 238 D5
Princess Grace Hospl The W1 ....93 A3 238 A5
Princess Louise Hospl W10 ....90 C2
Priory Hospl The SW15 ....133 D1
Putney Hospl SW15 ..134 C2

Q

Queen Charlotte's Maternity Hospl W6 112 A2
Queen Elizabeth Hospital for Children The E2 ..96 A5
Queen Elizabeth Hospl SE7 ....144 A5
Queen Mary's Hospital
Frognal Avenue, Sidcup, Kent DA14 6LT 190 A4
020 8302 2678
Queen Mary's Hospl NW3 ....70 A5
Queen Mary's Univ Hospl SW15 ....156 A5
Queen's Hospl CR0 ..205 A3

R

Roding Hospl IG4 ....55 D6
Royal Brompton & Nat Heart Hospl The SW3 ....114 C1 257 A2
Royal Ear Hospl WC1 ....93 D3 239 C5
Royal Free Hospital
Pond Street, London NW3 2QG 70 C3
020 7794 0500
Royal Hospl SW15 ...157 A5
Royal London Homeopathic Hospl The WC1 ....94 A2 240 B4
Royal London Hospital (Whitechapel)
Whitechapel Road, London E1 1BB 96 B2
020 7377 7000
Royal Marsden Hospl SW3 ....114 B1 256 D2
Royal Masonic Hospl W6 ....112 A2
Royal Nat TN&E Hospl The W5 ....87 C2
Royal National Orthopaedic Hospl HA7 ....9 C2 W1 ....93 B3 238 D5
Royal National TNE Hospl The WC1 .....94 B4 233 C2

S

St Andrew's Hospl E3 .97 D3
St Ann's General Hospl N4,N15 ....51 A4
St Anthony's Hospl KT4 ....200 D1
St Bartholomew's Hospl EC1 ....94 D2 241 D3
St Charles' Hospl W10 ....90 D2
St Christopher's Hospice SE26 ....184 C5
St George's Hospital
Blackshaw Road, London SW17 ....180 B5
020 8672 1255
St Giles Hospl SE5 ...139 C4
St Helier Hospital
Wrythe Lane, Carshalton, Surrey SM5 1AA 202 A1
020 8296 2000
St Joseph's Hospice E9,E8 ....96 B6
St Leonard's Hospl N1 ....95 C5
St Luke's Hospl W1 ....93 C3 239 A5
St Luke's Woodside Hospl N10 ....49 A5
St Mark's Hospl EC1 ....94 D4 234 D2
St Mary's Cottage Hospl TW12 ....173 B2
St Mary's Hospital
Praed Street, Paddington, London, W2 1NY 92 B1 236 D2
020 7725 6666
St Michael's Hospl EN2 5 B4
St Pancras Hospl NW1 ....93 D6 232 C5
St Thomas's Hospital
Lambeth Palace Road, London SE1 7EH 116 B3 260 C6
020 7928 9292
St Vincent's Hospl HA5 ....39 D6
Samaritan Hospl for Women NW1 ....237 C4
Shirley Oaks Hospl CR0 ....206 C2
Sloane Hospl BR3 ...186 B2
South Western Hospl SW9 ....138 B2
Southwood Hospl (Geriatric) N6 ....49 A2
Springfield Hospl SW17 ....158 C1
Stepney Day Hospl E1 96 C1
Surbiton Hospl KT6 ..198 A3

T

Teddington Memorial Hospl TW11 ....174 C4
Thorpe Coombe Hospl E17 ....54 A6
Tolworth Hospl KT6 .214 C6
Travel Clinic, Hospl for Tropical Diseases WC1 ....93 C3 239 B5

U

University College Hospital
Grafton Way, London, WC1E 3BG (A&E at Cecil Fleming House, Grafton Way) .93 C3 239 B5
020 7387 9300
Upton Day Hospl DA6 147 A1

W

Wanstead Hospl E11 ..55 B5
Wellington Hospl (North) NW8 ....92 B5 229 D3
Wellington Hospl (South) NW8 ....92 B5 229 D3
Wembley Hospl HA0 ..65 D2
West Middlesex University Hospital
Twickenham Road, Isleworth, Middlesex TW7 6AF ..131 A3
020 8560 2121
Western Eye Hospl The NW1 ....92 D2 237 C4
Whipps Cross Hospital
Whipps Cross Road, Leytonstone, London, E11 1NR 54 B3
020 8539 5522
Whittington Hospital
Highgate Hill, London, N19 5NF 71 C6
020 7272 3070
Willesden Community Hospl The NW10 .....68 A1
Winifred House Hospl EN5 ....11 D5

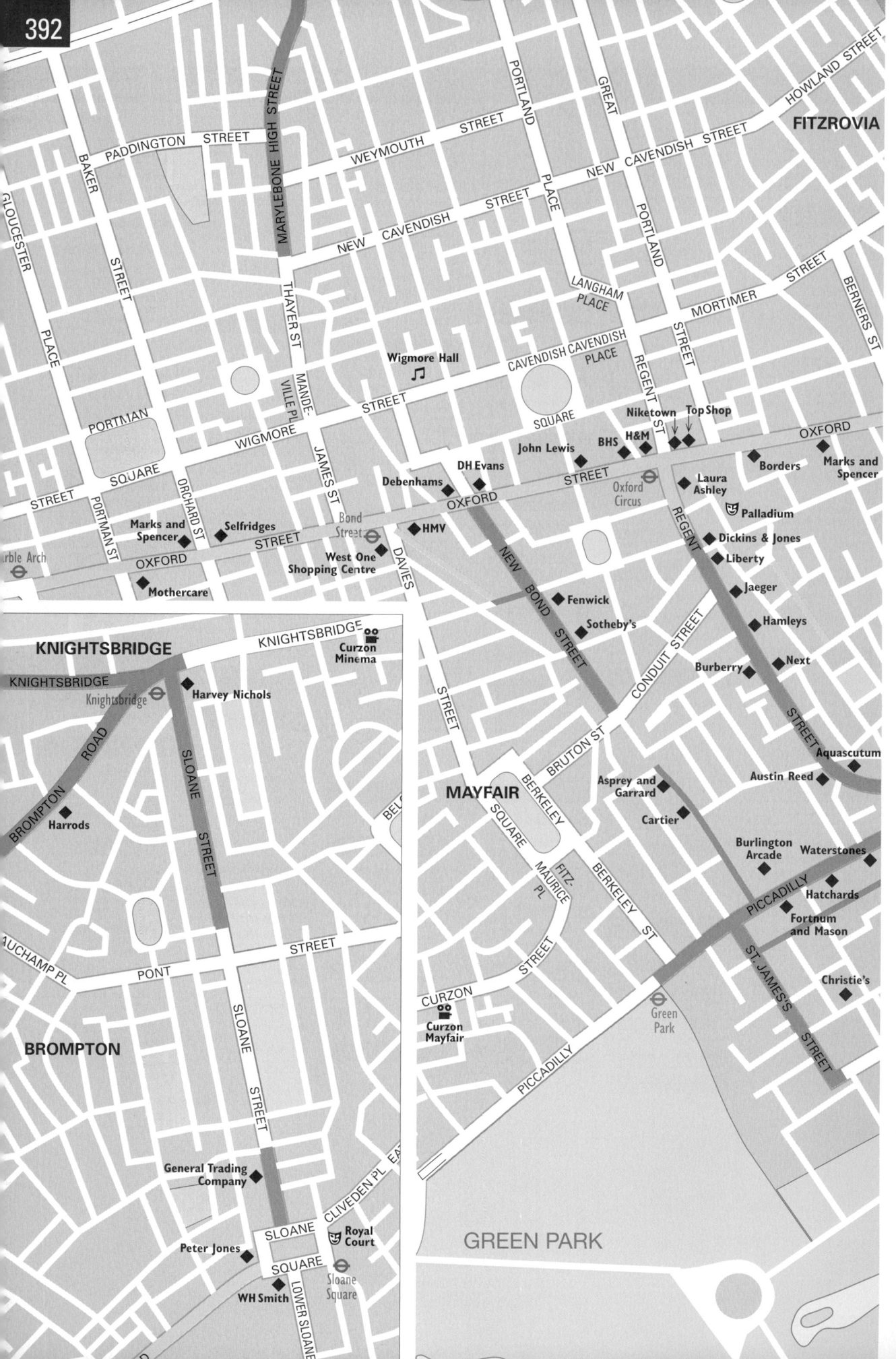

FITZROVIA

PADDINGTON STREET

BAKER STREET

GLOUCESTER PLACE

WEYMOUTH STREET

MARYLEBONE HIGH STREET

PORTLAND STREET

GREAT PORTLAND STREET

NEW CAVENDISH STREET

HOWLAND STREET

THAYER ST

MANDEVILLE PL

NEW CAVENDISH STREET

PORTLAND PLACE

LANGHAM PLACE

MORTIMER STREET

PORTLAND STREET

BERNERS ST

Wigmore Hall ♫

WIGMORE STREET

CAVENDISH SQUARE

CAVENDISH PLACE

REGENT STREET

Niketown   Top Shop

OXFORD

PORTMAN SQUARE

JAMES ST

DH Evans

John Lewis   BHS   H&M

OXFORD STREET

Borders

Marks and Spencer

STREET

ORCHARD ST

Debenhams

OXFORD

Oxford Circus

Laura Ashley

🎭 Palladium

PORTMAN ST

Marks and Spencer

Selfridges

STREET

DAVIES

HMV

Dickins & Jones

Liberty

REGENT STREET

Marble Arch

OXFORD

West One Shopping Centre

Bond Street

NEW BOND STREET

Jaeger

Hamleys

Mothercare

Fenwick

Sotheby's

Burberry

Next

KNIGHTSBRIDGE

KNIGHTSBRIDGE

Curzon Minema 🎥

CONDUIT STREET

KNIGHTSBRIDGE

Knightsbridge

Harvey Nichols

STREET

Aquascutum

BROMPTON ROAD

SLOANE STREET

BRUTON ST

Asprey and Garrard

Austin Reed

Harrods

BERKELEY STREET

MAYFAIR

Cartier

Burlington Arcade

Waterstones

BEAUCHAMP PL

SLOANE STREET

STREET

BERKELEY SQUARE

FITZ-MAURICE PL

BERKELEY ST

PICCADILLY

Hatchards

Fortnum and Mason

PONT

STREET

ST JAMES'S STREET

Christie's

BROMPTON

SLOANE STREET

CURZON STREET

Curzon Mayfair 🎥

Green Park

General Trading Company

CLIVEDEN PL EAST

PICCADILLY

Peter Jones

SLOANE

Royal Court

GREEN PARK

WH Smith

SQUARE

Sloane Square

LOWER SLOANE

BLOOMSBURY

Cinemas, theatres and shopping streets

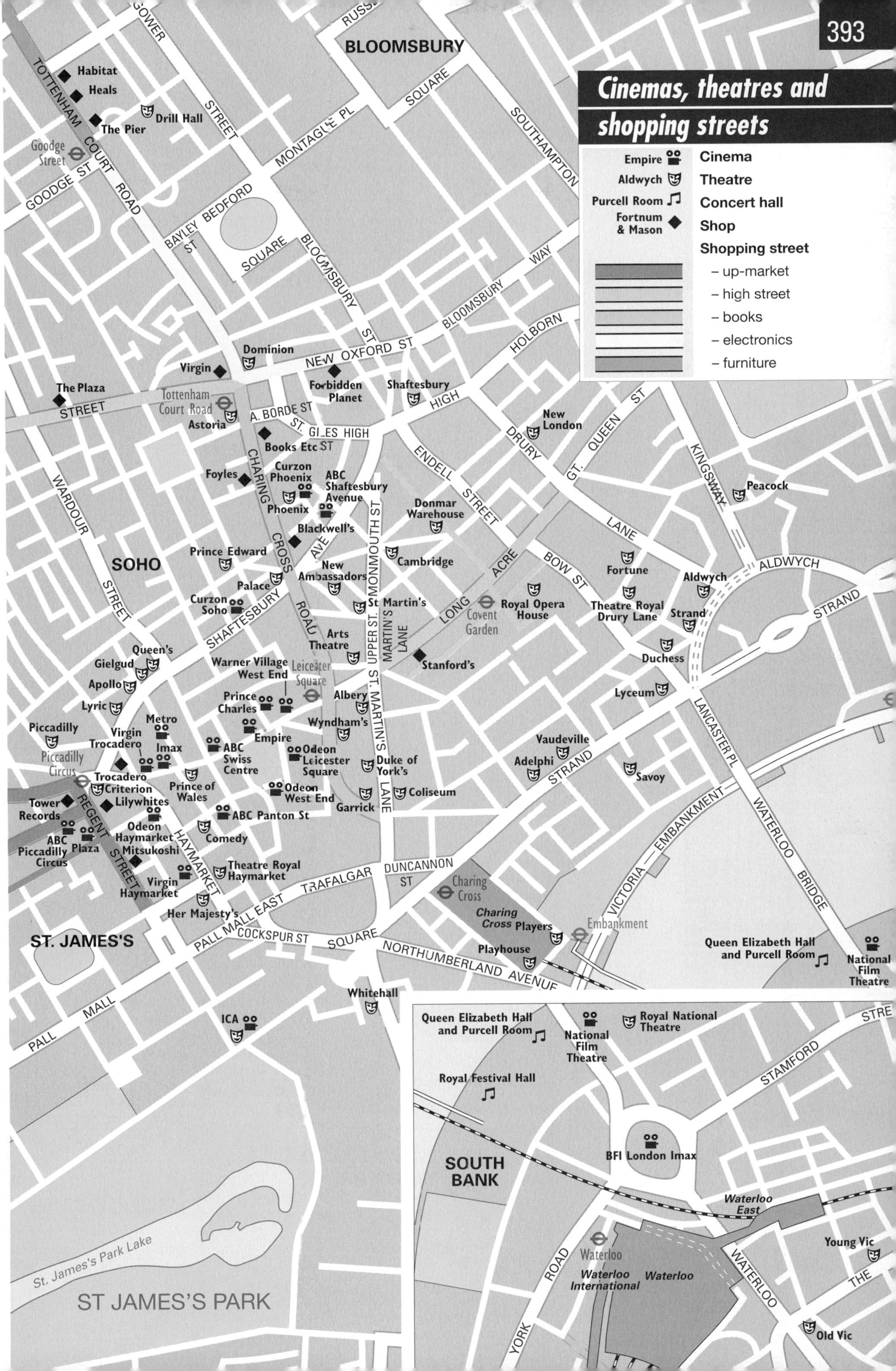

Empire	🎦	Cinema
Aldwych	🎭	Theatre
Purcell Room	♫	Concert hall
Fortnum & Mason	◆	Shop
		Shopping street
		– up-market
		– high street
		– books
		– electronics
		– furniture

Habitat
Heals
Drill Hall
The Pier
Goodge Street
GOODGE ST
TOTTENHAM COURT ROAD
BAYLEY ST
BEDFORD SQUARE
MONTAGUE PL
SQUARE
BLOOMSBURY
SOUTHAMPTON
WAY
HOLBORN

The Plaza
STREET
Virgin
Dominion
NEW OXFORD ST
Forbidden Planet
Shaftesbury
Tottenham Court Road
Astoria
A. BORDE ST
ST. GILES HIGH
ST
SHAFTESBURY
HIGH
New London
DRURY
GT. QUEEN ST
KINGSWAY
Peacock

Books Etc
Foyles
CHARING
Curzon Phoenix
ABC Shaftesbury Avenue
Phoenix
Blackwell's
Donmar Warehouse
ENDELL STREET
LANE
ALDWYCH
STRAND

WARDOUR
SOHO
Prince Edward
Palace
New Ambassadors
St Martin's
Cambridge
UPPER ST. MONMOUTH ST
ST. MARTIN'S LANE
BOW ST
ACRE
Fortune
Aldwych
Strand
STRAND

STREET
Curzon Soho
SHAFTESBURY
AVE
CROSS
Arts Theatre
LONG
Covent Garden
Royal Opera House
Theatre Royal Drury Lane
Duchess
Lyceum

Queen's
Gielgud
Apollo
Lyric
Warner Village West End
Leicester Square
ROAD
Albery
Wyndham's
Stanford's
Vaudeville
Adelphi
STRAND
Savoy

Piccadilly
Piccadilly Circus
Metro
Virgin
Trocadero
Imax
Prince Charles
Empire
ABC Swiss Centre
Odeon Leicester Square
Odeon West End
Duke of York's
Coliseum
LANCASTER PL
WATERLOO BRIDGE

Tower Records
Trocadero
Criterion
Lilywhites
Prince of Wales
Garrick
ABC Panton St

ABC
Piccadilly Circus
Plaza
REGENT
Odeon Haymarket
Mitsukoshi
Comedy

St. JAMES'S
Odeon Haymarket
HAYMARKET
Virgin Haymarket
Theatre Royal Haymarket
Her Majesty's
TRAFALGAR
DUNCANNON ST
Charing Cross
VICTORIA EMBANKMENT
Queen Elizabeth Hall and Purcell Room
National Film Theatre

PALL MALL EAST
COCKSPUR ST
SQUARE
NORTHUMBERLAND AVENUE
Charing Cross Players
Playhouse
Embankment

PALL MALL
Whitehall
ICA

SOUTH BANK
Queen Elizabeth Hall and Purcell Room
National Film Theatre
Royal National Theatre
STRE
STAMFORD

Royal Festival Hall

BFI London Imax

Waterloo East
Young Vic

St. James's Park Lake
Waterloo
Waterloo International
Waterloo
WATERLOO
THE
Old Vic

ST JAMES'S PARK

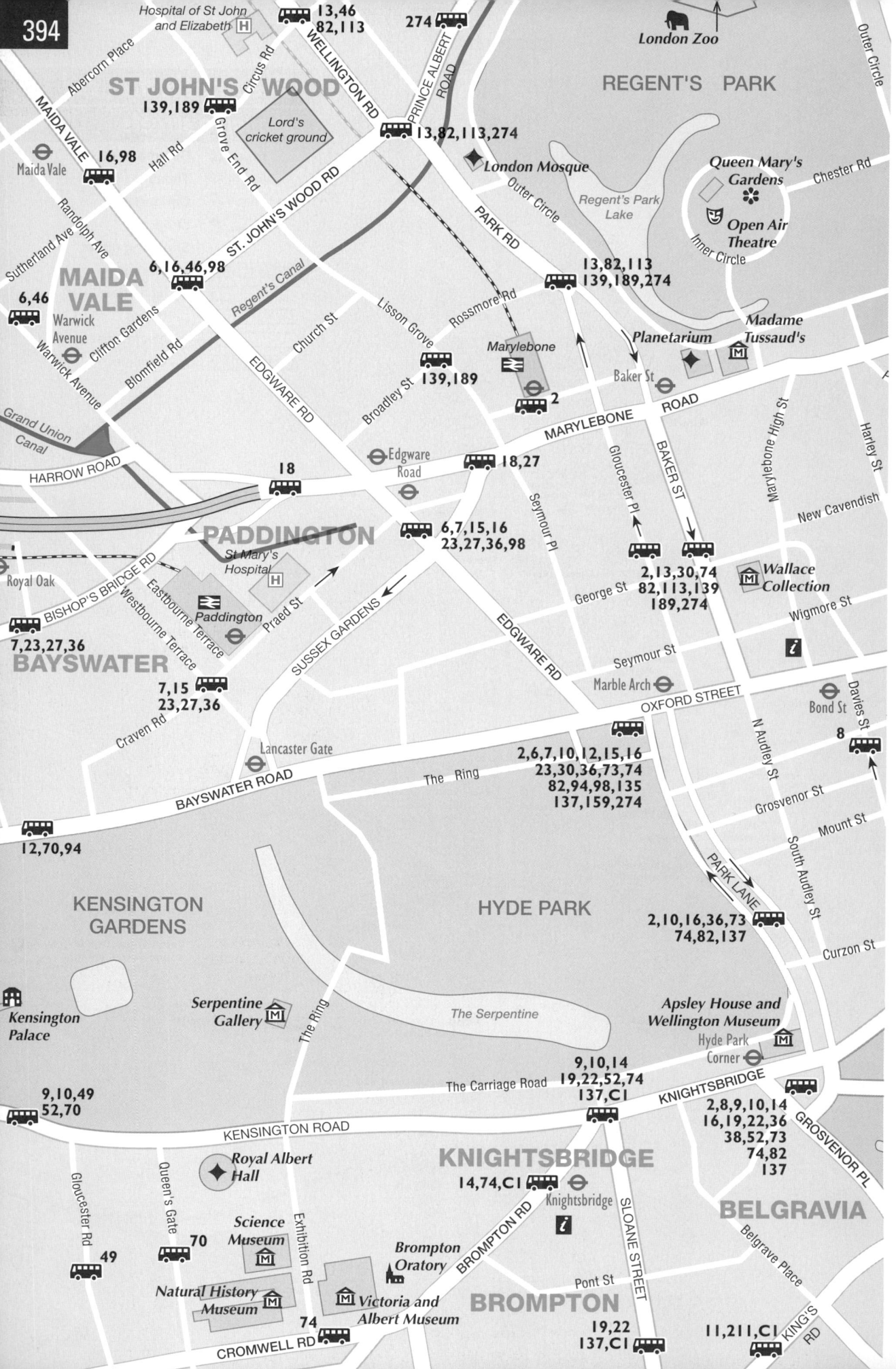

Hospital of St John
and Elizabeth **H**

13,46
82,113

274

London Zoo

ST JOHN'S WOOD

REGENT'S PARK

Abercorn Place

Circus Rd

WELLINGTON RD

PRINCE ALBERT ROAD

139,189

Lord's
cricket ground

Outer Circle

Chester Rd

MAIDA VALE

Hall Rd

Grove End Rd

13,82,113,274

London Mosque

Queen Mary's
Gardens

16,98
Maida Vale

Regent's Park
Lake

ST. JOHN'S WOOD RD

Open Air
Theatre

Randolph Ave

Sutherland Ave

6,16,46,98

PARK RD

Outer Circle

Inner Circle

MAIDA
VALE

Regent's Canal

13,82,113
139,189,274

6,46
Warwick
Avenue

Clifton Gardens

Church St

Lisson Grove

Rossmore Rd

Planetarium

Madame
Tussaud's

Blomfield Rd

EDGWARE RD

Broadley St

Marylebone

Baker St

Warwick Avenue

Grand Union
Canal

139,189

2

Marylebone High St

Harley St

HARROW ROAD

Edgware
Road

MARYLEBONE ROAD

Gloucester Pl

BAKER ST

New Cavendish

18

18,27

PADDINGTON

Seymour Pl

6,7,15,16
23,27,36,98

Wallace
Collection

St Mary's
Hospital **H**

2,13,30,74
82,113,139
189,274

Royal Oak

BISHOP'S BRIDGE RD

Eastbourne Terrace

Praed St

George St

Wigmore St

Paddington

EDGWARE RD

7,23,27,36

Westbourne Terrace

SUSSEX GARDENS

Seymour St

BAYSWATER

7,15
23,27,36

Craven Rd

Marble Arch

Bond St

8

Lancaster Gate

OXFORD STREET

Davies St

BAYSWATER ROAD

The Ring

2,6,7,10,12,15,16
23,30,36,73,74
82,94,98,135
137,159,274

N Audley St

Grosvenor St

Mount St

12,70,94

KENSINGTON
GARDENS

HYDE PARK

PARK LANE

South Audley St

2,10,16,36,73
74,82,137

Curzon St

Serpentine
Gallery

The Ring

The Serpentine

Apsley House and
Wellington Museum

Kensington
Palace

Hyde Park
Corner

9,10,14
19,22,52,74
137,C1

KNIGHTSBRIDGE

9,10,49
52,70

The Carriage Road

2,8,9,10,14
16,19,22,36
38,52,73
74,82
137

KENSINGTON ROAD

KNIGHTSBRIDGE

GROSVENOR PL

Royal Albert
Hall

14,74,C1

BELGRAVIA

Gloucester Rd

Queen's Gate

Knightsbridge

Belgrave Place

49

70

Science
Museum

Exhibition Rd

BROMPTON RD

SLOANE STREET

Pont St

Natural History
Museum

Victoria and
Albert Museum

Brompton
Oratory

BROMPTON

19,22
137,C1

11,211,C1

KING'S RD

74

CROMWELL RD

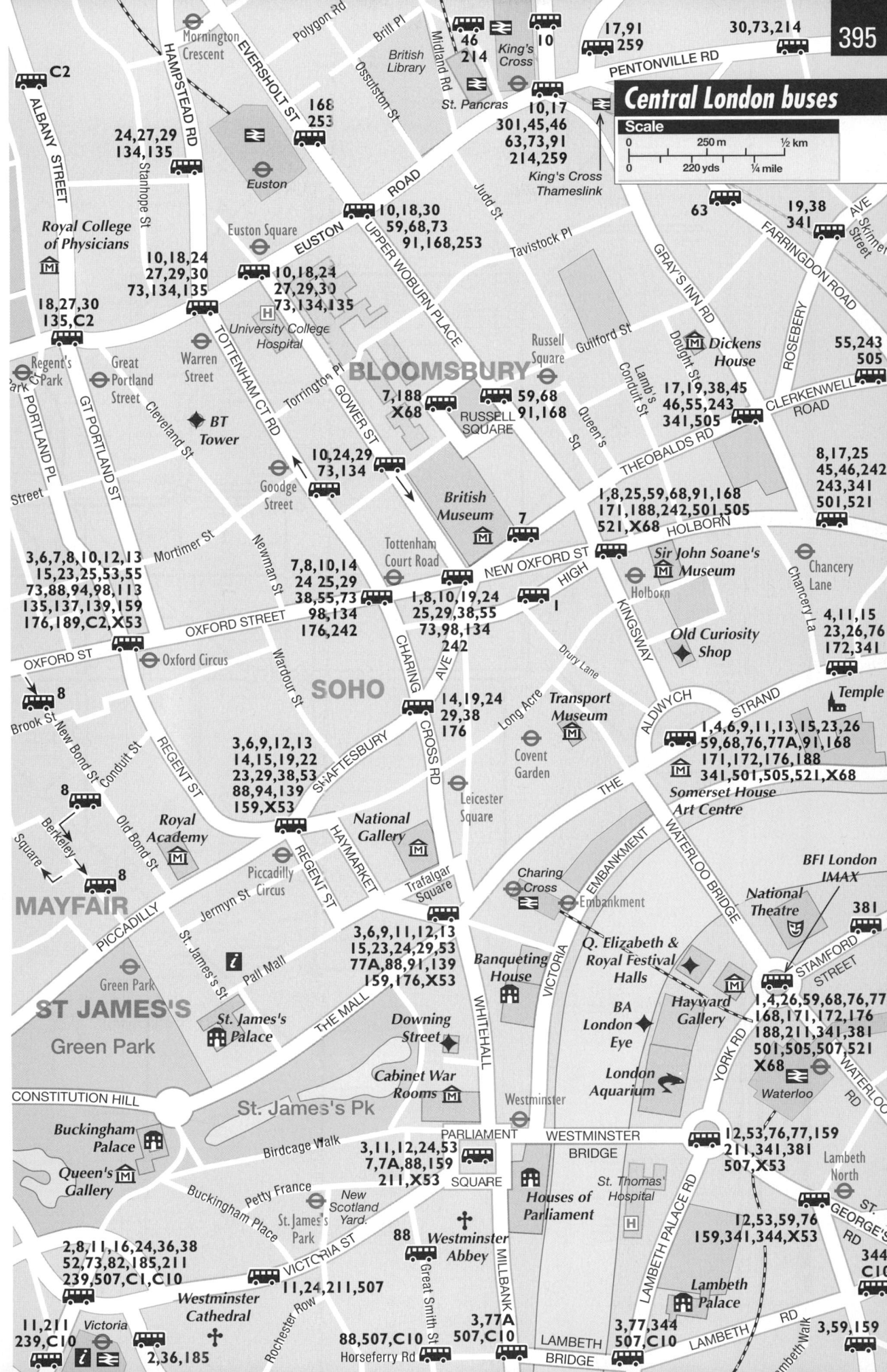

Central London buses

Scale

0 — 250 m — ½ km
0 — 220 yds — ¼ mile

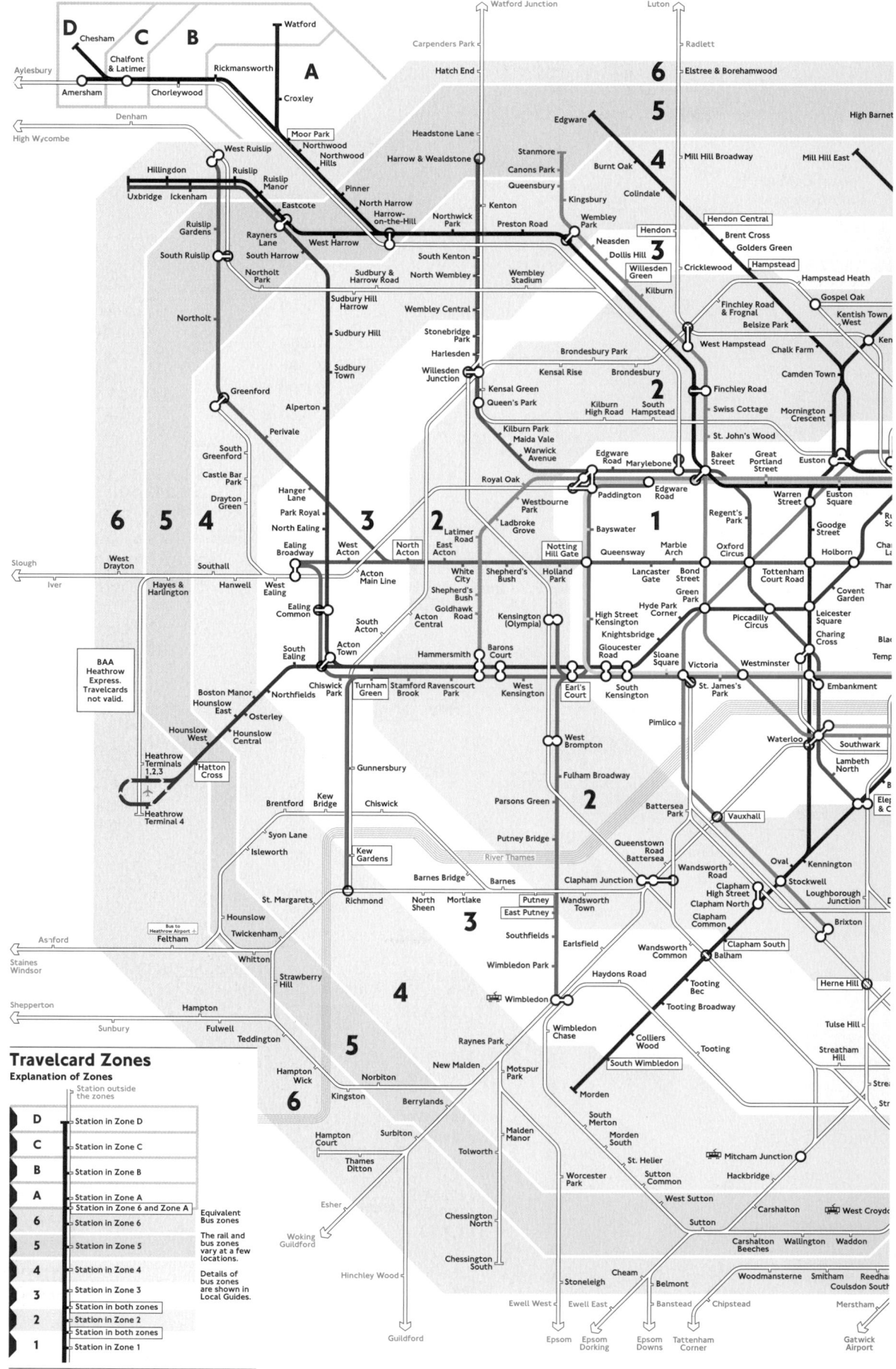

Travelcard Zones
Explanation of Zones

Station outside the zones

D	Station in Zone D
C	Station in Zone C
B	Station in Zone B
A	Station in Zone A
	Station in Zone 6 and Zone A
6	Station in Zone 6
5	Station in Zone 5
4	Station in Zone 4
3	Station in Zone 3
2	Station in both zones
2	Station in Zone 2
	Station in both zones
1	Station in Zone 1

Equivalent Bus zones

The rail and bus zones vary at a few locations.

Details of bus zones are shown in Local Guides.

Some stations and lines have restricted opening times.

London Travel Information
020 7222 1234
24 hours

The National Rail routes shown on this map are a guide to weekday, off-peak services but do not guarantee direct trains between the stations shown.

National Rail Enquiries
08457 48 49 50
24 hours

Key to lines

	Station	Interchange Station
Bakerloo		
Central		
Circle		
District		
East London *Peak hours and Sunday mornings*		
Hammersmith & City		
Jubilee		
Metropolitan		
Northern		
Piccadilly		
Victoria		
Waterloo & City		
Docklands Light Railway		
National Rail		
Connections with Tramlink		

Reg. user No. 00/3316

Places of interest

Central

City

Apple Market WC2 ....**250** B6
Bank of England EC2 ...**242** C1
Barbican EC2 ...95 A2 **242** B3
Barbican Arts & Conference
  Centre EC2 ...95 A2 **242** B4
British Library
  WC1 ....93 D4 **232** D2
British Museum
  WC1 ....94 A2 **240** A3
Central Criminal Court (Old
  Bailey) EC4 ....94 D1 **241** D2
Cleopatra's Needle
  WC2 ....116 B5 **250** C5
Courtauld Galleries
  WC2 ....**250** C6
Covent Garden
  WC2 ......116 A6 **250** B6
Custom House
  EC3 ....117 C6 **253** A5
Dickens House Museum
  WC1 ....94 B3 **240** D5
Dr Johnson's House
  EC4 ....**241** B1
Gray's Inn WC1 ..94 B2 **240** D4
Guildhall EC2 ...95 A1 **242** B2
Inner Temple EC4 ....**251** A6
John Wesley's House &
  Museum EC1 ....**242** D6
Jubilee Market WC2 .....**250** B6
Leicester Square
  WC2 ....115 D6 **249** D5
Lincoln's Inn
  WC2 ....94 B1 **240** D2
Lloyd's Building
  EC3 ....95 C1 **243** A1
London Transport Museum
  WC2 ....**250** B6
Mansion House EC4 ..**242** C1
Merchant Taylors Hall
  EC3 ....**242** D1
Middle Temple
  EC4 ....116 C6 **251** A6
Monument, The EC3 ..**252** D6
Museum of London
  EC2 ....95 A2 **242** A3
Nat West Tower EC2 ....**243** A2
National Postal Museum
  EC1 ....95 A1 **242** A2
Nelson's Monument
  WC2 ....**250** A4
Old Covent Garden
  WC2 ....**250** B6
Petticoat Lane Market
  EC2 ....95 D2 **243** C3
Public Record Office
  Museum EC4,WC2 ......**241** A2
Royal Exchange EC3 ..**242** D1
St Katharine Dock
  E1 ....117 D5 **253** D4
St Mary le Bow Church
  EC2 ....**242** B1
St Paul's Cathedral
  EC4 ....95 A1 **242** A1
Sir John Soane's Museum
  WC2 ....94 B1 **240** C2
Stock Exchange EC2 ..**242** D1
Theatre Museum WC2 **250** B6
Tower Bridge
  E1,EC3,SE1 ...117 D5 **253** C4

Tower of London
  EC3 ....117 D6 **253** C5
Traitors Gate
  EC3 ....117 D5 **253** C4

West End

Admiralty Arch SW1 ...**249** D4
Banqueting House
  SW1 ....**250** A3
Big Ben SW1 ....**250** B1
BT Tower W1 ...93 C2 **239** A4
Buckingham Palace
  SW1 ....115 C4 **249** A1
Cabinet War Rooms
  SW1 ....115 A4 **250** D2
Carlyle's House SW3 ..**267** A5
Carnaby Street
  W1 ....93 C1 **239** A1
Cenotaph SW1 ....**250** A2
Changing of the Guard (site
  of) SW1 ....**249** A1
Chelsea Barracks
  SW1 ....115 A1 **258** B1
Chelsea Physic Garden
  SW1 ....115 A1 **267** C6
Clarence House
  SW1 ....115 C5 **249** B3
Downing Street
  SW1 ....116 A4 **250** A1
Eros (Shaftesbury
  Memorial)
  W1 ....115 D6 **249** C5
Green Park
  SW1,W1 ...115 B4 **248** D2
Guards Museum
  SW1 ....115 C4 **249** B1
Holocaust Memorial Garden
  W2 ....114 D4 **247** D2
Horse Guards Parade
  SW1 ....115 D5 **249** D3
Houses of Parliament
  SW1 ....116 A3 **260** B6
Hyde Park W2 ...114 D5 **247** C3
Kensington Gardens
  W2 ....114 A5 **246** D3
Kensington Palace
  W8 ....113 D5 **245** D3
London Peace Pagoda
  SW3 ....**267** D4
London Toy & Model
  Museum W2 ..114 A6 **246** A6
Marble Arch
  W1 ....114 D6 **247** D6
Methodist Central Hall
  SW1 ....115 D4 **249** D1
National Army Museum
  SW3 ....136 D4 **267** D6
National Gallery
  SW1 ....115 D6 **249** D5
National Portrait Gallery
  SW1 ....115 D6 **249** D5
New Scotland Yard
  SW1 ....115 D3 **259** C6
Parliament Square
  SW1 ....116 A4 **250** A1
Pepsi Trocadero W1 ..**249** C5
Piccadilly Circus
  W1 ....115 D6 **249** C5
Queen Victoria Monument
  SW1 ....**249** A2
Queen's Gallery
  SW1 ....115 B4 **248** D1

Ranelagh Gardens (site of
  Chelsea Flower Show)
  SW1 ....115 A1 **258** B1
Rotten Row
  SW1 ....114 D4 **247** C2
Royal Academy of Arts
  W1 ....115 C6 **249** A5
Royal Hospital (Army
  Pensioners)
  SW1 ....115 A1 **258** A1
Royal Mews
  SW1 ....115 B3 **258** D6
Royal United Services
  Museum SW1 ....**250** A3
St James's Palace
  SW1 ....115 C5 **249** B3
St James's Park SW1 ..**249** C2
Serpentine W2 114 C5 **247** B3
Serpentine Gallery
  W2 ....114 B4 **246** D2
Soho W1 ...93 D1 **239** C2
Speakers' Corner
  W1 ....114 D6 **247** D6
Tate Gallery (Britain)
  SW1 ....116 A2 **260** A3
Trafalgar Square
  SW1 ....115 D5 **249** D4
Tyburn Tree (site of)
  W2 ....**247** C6
Wallace Collection
  W1 ....**238** A2
Wellington Arch SW1 ..**248** B2
Wellington Museum (Apsley
  House) SW1 ..115 A4 **248** B2
Westminster Abbey
  SW1 ....116 A3 **260** A6
Westminster Cathedral
  SW1 ....115 C3 **259** A5

Northern

Camden Market
  NW1 ....93 B6 **231** D6
London Central Mosque
  NW8 ....92 C4 **230** B1
London Zoo
  NW1 ....93 A5 **231** A4
Lord's Cricket Ground
  NW8 ....92 B4 **229** D2
Lord's Cricket Museum
  NW8 ....92 B4 **229** D1
Madame Tussaud's
  NW1 ....93 A3 **238** A5
Open Air Theatre, Regent's
  Park NW1 ....**231** A1
Planetarium
  NW1 ....93 A3 **238** A5
Queen Mary's Gardens
  NW1 ....**231** A1
Regent's Park
  NW1 ....93 A4 **231** A3
St George's Cathedral
  NW1 ....**231** D2
Sherlock Holmes Museum
  NW1 ....92 D3 **237** D5

Southern

Bear Gardens Museum
  SE1 ....117 A5 **252** A4
Bermondsey Market
  SE1 ....117 C3 **263** B8

Borough Market SE1 ..**252** C3
Design Museum
  SE1 ....117 D4 **253** D2
Florence Nightingale
  Museum SE1 ....**250** D1
Globe Theatre SE1 ...**252** A5
Hay's Galleria SE1 ...**253** A4
Hayward Gallery
  SE1 ....116 B5 **250** D4
HMS Belfast SE1 .....**253** B4
Imperial War Museum
  SE1,SE11 ...116 C3 **261** B5
Lambeth Palace
  SE1 ....116 B3 **260** C5
London Aquarium SE1 **250** C1
London Dungeon
  SE1 ....117 B5 **252** D4
London Eye (Millennium
  Wheel) SE1 ..116 B4 **250** C2
Millennium Bridge
  SE1,EC4 ....**252** A5
Museum of Garden History
  SE1 ....**260** C5
National Film Theatre
  SE1 ....**250** D4
National Theatre
  SE1 ....116 B5 **250** D4
Old County Hall SE1 ..**250** C2
Operating Theatre Museum
  & Herb Garret
  SE1 ....117 B5 **252** D4
Oxo Tower SE1 ....**251** B5
Royal Festival Hall
  SE1 ....116 B5 **250** D3
St George's RC Cathedral
  SE1 ....116 C3 **261** B6
Shakespeare's Globe
  Theatre (site of) SE1 .**252** B4
Southwark Cathedral
  SE1 ....117 B5 **252** C4
Tate Gallery of Modern Art
  SE1 ....116 D6 **251** D4

North

Abney Park Cemetery
  N16 ....**73** C6
Alexandra Palace N22 ...**31** D1
Barnet Museum EN5 ....1 A1
Battle of Britain Museum
  NW9 ....**27** D1
Bruce Castle Museum
  N17 ....**33** C2
Business Design Centre
  N1 ....94 C6 **234** B5
Church Farm House
  Museum NW4 ....**46** B6
Coppetts Centre N12 ...**30** D3
Forty Hall EN2 ....5 D6
Freud Museum NW3 ....**70** A2
Grange Museum of
  Community History
  NW10 ....**67**
Hampstead Heath NW3 .**70** B6
Highgate Cemetery N19 **71** B6
Kensal Green Cemetery (All
  Souls) NW10 ....**90** C4
Kenwood House NW3 ..**48** C1
London Canal Museum
  N1 ....94 A5 **233** B4
RAF Museum NW9 ....**28** A1

East

Bethnal Green Museum of
  Childhood E2 ....**96** C4
Canary Wharf E14 ....**119** D5
Epping Forest IG10 ....**21** B6
Geffrye Museum E2 ....**95** D5
London Docklands Visitor
  Centre E14 ....**120** A4
London Gas Museum
  E3,E16 ....**98** B3
Museum of the Great
  Eastern Railway E16 .**122** A4
Queen Elizabeth's Hunting
  Lodge Museum E4 ....**20** D4
Ragged School Museum
  E3 ....**97** A2
Vestry House (Museum)
  E17 ....**53** D5

South east

Blackheath SE3 ....**142** C4
Brockwell Park SE24 ..**160** D5
Cutty Sark SE10 ....**142** A6
Docklands Heritage Museum
  SE16 ....**119** B5
Dulwich Picture Gallery
  SE21 ....**161** C4
Eltham Palace SE9 ...**166** A4
Flamsteed House SE10 **142** B5
Gipsy Moth IV SE10 ...**142** A6
Greenwich Park SE10 .**142** C5
Horniman Museum &
  Gardens SE23 ....**162** B3
Livesey Museum SE15 **140** B6
Meridian Building
  SE10 ....**142** B5
Millennium Dome
  SE10 ....**120** C5
National Fan Museum
  SE10 ....**142** A5
National Maritime Museum
  SE10 ....**142** B6
Old Royal Observatory
  Greenwich SE10 .....**142** B5
Queen's House SE10 ..**142** B6
Rotunda Museum SE18 **122** B1
Russian Submarine
  SE18 ....**121** D3
Scadbury Park Nature
  Reserve BR7 ....**189** D4
South Norwood Country
  Park SE25 ....**206** C5
Thames Barrier Visitor
  Centre SE18 ....**121** D3
Well Hall Pleasaunce
  SE9 ....**144** A1

South west

Albert Memorial
  SW7 ....114 B4 **246** C1
Barnes Common SW13 134 A2
Battersea Park
  SW11 ....137 A5 **268** A3
Battersea Power Station
  SW8 ....137 B6 **268** D6

Clapham Common
  SW4 ....**137** C1
Fulham Palace SW6 ..**135** A3
Geological Museum
  SW7 ....114 B3 **256** D5
Hampton Court Palace
  KT8 ....**196** D6
Kingston Museum KT1 **176** A1
Lindsey House SW10 ..**266** D4
Natural History Museum
  SW7 ....114 B3 **256** C5
Oratory, The
  SW7 ....114 C3 **257** A5
Royal Albert Hall
  SW7 ....114 B4 **246** C1
Science Museum
  SW7 ....114 B3 **256** C5
Victoria & Albert Museum
  SW7 ....114 B3 **256** C5
Wandsworth Museum
  SW15 ....**135** A1
Wetland Centre SW13 .**134** B5
Wimbledon Common
  SW19 ....**178** B6
Wimbledon Lawn Tennis
  Museum SW19 ....**157** A1
Wimbledon Windmill
  Museum SW19 .....**156** C1

West

Chiswick House W4 ...**133** B6
Eel Pie Island TW1 ...**153** A3
Gunnersbury Park Museum
  W3 ....**110** C3
Ham House TW10 .....**153** C2
Kew Bridge Steam Museum
  TW8 ....**110** B1
Kew Gardens (Royal Botanic
  Gardens) TW9 ....**132** A4
Kew Observatory TW9 **131** C2
Kew Palace TW9 .....**132** A5
Leighton House (Art Gallery
  & Museum) W14 .....**254** D6
Little Venice W9 92 A2 **236** A4
London Butterfly House
  TW8 ....**131** B4
Marble Hill TW1 .....**153** C4
Museum of Richmond
  TW10 ....**153** D6
Musical Museum
  TW8 ....**132** A6
Osterley Park TW7 ...**108** B1
Pitshanger Manor Museum
  & Art Gallery W5 ....**109** D5
Portobello Road Market
  W10 ....**91** A2
Richmond Park TW10 .**155** A3
Syon House TW8 .....**131** C4
Walled Garden TW16 .**194** B6

North west

Harrow Museum & Heritage
  Centre HA2 ....**42** A6
Old Court (Museum &
  Library) HA0 ....**65** C3
Ruislip Lido HA4,HA5 ...**39** B5
Ruislip Lido Railway
  HA4 ....**39** B5